WEBSTER'S

SPANISH-
ENGLISH

ENGLISH-
SPANISH

DICTIONARY

WEBSTER'S
SPANISH-
ENGLISH
ENGLISH-
SPANISH
DICTIONARY

By

EDWIN B. WILLIAMS,

Professor of Romance Languages, University of Pennsylvania

GRAMERCY BOOKS
NEW YORK

Reprint edition of The Bantam New College Spanish & English Dictionary

Publicado anteriormente bajo *The Bantam New College Spanish & English Dictionary*

Reconocimiento especial a Paúl·Lloyd, catedrático de Lenguajes Romances de la Universidad de Pennsylvania, por haber suministrado asistencia en las revisiones de la sección de gramática castellana.

Esta edición del año 2004 es publicada por Gramercy Books, una división de Random House Value Publishing, una división de Random House, Inc., New York, por disposición de The Bantam Dell Publishing Group, una división de Random House, Inc.

Gramercy y el logotipo son marcas registradas de Random House, Inc.

Random House
Nueva York • Toronto • Londres
Sydney • Auckland
www.randomhouse.com

Imprenta y encuadernación
en los Estados Unidos

Reprint edition of *The Bantam New College Spanish & English Dictionary*

Grateful acknowledgement to Paul M. Lloyd, Professor of Romance Languages, University of Pennsylvania, for providing assistance with revisions to the Spanish grammar section.

This 2004 edition is published by Gramercy Books, an imprint of Random House Value Publishing, a division of Random House, Inc., New York, by arrangement with The Bantam Dell Publishing Group, a division of Random House, Inc.

Gramercy is a registered trademark and the colophon is a trademark of Random House, Inc.

Random House
New York • Toronto • London
Sydney • Auckland
www.randomhouse.com

Printed and bound in the United States

Library of Congress Cataloging-in-Publication Data

Williams, Edwin Bucher, 1891-1975.
   Webster's Spanish-English/English-Spanish dictionary / Edwin B. Williams.
       p. cm.
   Originally published: New York : Bantam, 1968.
   ISBN 0-517-22455-0
     1. Spanish language—Dictionaries—English. 2. English language—Dictionaries—Spanish.
I. Title: Spanish-English/English-Spanish dictionary. II. Williams, Edwin Bucher, 1891-1975.
Bantam new college Spanish & English dictionary. III. Title.

PC4640. W53 2004b
463'.21—dc22
                                                                    2004047413

10 9 8 7 6 5

CONTENTS

Preface vi

Prólogo vii

Labels and Grammatical Abbreviations x

Calificativos y abreviaturas gramaticales x

SPANISH-ENGLISH / ESPAÑOL-INGLÉS 1

Spanish Irregular Verbs 343

ENGLISH-SPANISH / INGLÉS- ESPAÑOL 351

Spanish Grammar 710

Spanish Pronunciation 721

La pronunciación del inglés 723

After you read an entry in one section of the dictionary, read the entry in the other section to find more information on that particular word's meaning, i.e. force and fuerza.

Luego de leer una entrada, vea la otra sección del diccionario para encontrar más información sobre el significado de las palabras. Véase, p.ej., fuerza y force.

PREFACE TO THE FIRST EDITION

This book is based on primary spoken and written sources. It is designed for speakers of either language who wish to find words or the meanings of words in the foreign language. Its purpose is, therefore, fourfold. It gives to the English-speaking users (1) the Spanish words they need to express their thoughts in Spanish and (2) the English meanings of Spanish words they need to understand Spanish, and to the Spanish-speaking users (3) the English words they need to express their thoughts in English and (4) the Spanish meanings of English words they need to understand English.

To accomplish the purpose of (1) and (3), discriminations are provided in the source language except that, because of the special facility with which the subject of the verb can be shown in Spanish and because of the convenience of showing the object with personal **a,** discriminations in the form of subject and/or object are given in Spanish on the English-Spanish side as well as on the Spanish-English side. For the purpose of (2) and (4) discriminations are not needed and are not given because the user will always have the context of what he hears or reads to guide him. However, some glosses whose purpose is not to show discrimination but rather to elaborate on the meaning of what may be judged to be an unfamiliar or obscure word or expression in the user's native language are provided in that language.

All words are treated in a fixed order according to the parts of speech and the functions of verbs; and meanings with subject, usage, and regional labels come after more general meanings.

In order to facilitate the finding of the meaning and use sought for, changes within a vocabulary entry in part of speech and function of verb, in irregular inflection, in the gender of Spanish nouns, and in the pronunciation of English words are marked with parallels instead of the usual semicolons.

Periods are omitted after labels and grammatical abbreviations and at the end of vocabulary entries.

The feminine form of a Spanish adjective used as a noun (or a Spanish feminine noun having identical spelling with the feminine form of an adjective) that falls alphabetically in a separate position from the adjective is treated in that position and is listed again as a cross reference under the adjective.

The gender of Spanish nouns is shown on both sides of the Dictionary except that the gender of masculine nouns ending in **-o,** feminine nouns ending in **-a, -dad, -tad, -tud, -ión,** and **-umbre,** masculine nouns modified by an adjective ending in **-o,** and feminine nouns modified by an adjective ending in **-a** is not shown on the English-Spanish side.

Numbers referring to the conjugations of irregular Spanish verbs are placed before the abbreviations indicating the part of speech. The list at the end of the Spanish-English part of the Dictionary includes models of all verbs that show a combination of two types of irregularity, e.g., **esforzar, seguir, teñir.**

Proper nouns and abbreviations are listed in their alphabetical position in the main body of the Dictionary. Thus **España** and **español** do not have to be looked up in two different parts of the book. And all subentries are listed in strictly alphabetical order.

The centered period is used in vocabulary entries of irregularly inflected words to mark off the final syllable that has to be detached before the syllable showing the inflection is added, e.g., **lá·piz** *m* (*pl* **-pices**) and **falsi·fy** [ˈfɔlsɪˌfaɪ] *v* (*pret & pp* **-fied**).

The pronunciation of all English simple words is shown in a new adaptation of the symbols of the International Phonetic Alphabet and in brackets. The pronunciation of English compound words is not shown provided the pronunciation of the components is shown where they appear as independent vocabulary entries.

Since vocabulary entries are not determined on the basis of etymology, homographs are included in a single entry. When the pronunciation of an English homograph changes, this is shown in the proper place after parallels.

PRÓLOGO DE LA PRIMERA EDICIÓN

Hemos basado este libro en fuentes originales del lenguaje hablado y escrito. Está destinado a los hablantes de uno u otro idioma que buscan palabras o significados de palabras en el idioma extranjero. Tiene, por lo tanto, los cuatro siguientes propósitos: al usuario de habla inglesa le suministra (1) las palabras españolas que necesita para expresar su pensamiento en español y (2) los significados ingleses de las palabras españolas que necesita para comprender el español; y al usuario de habla española le suministra (3) las palabras inglesas que necesita para expresar su pensamiento en inglés y (4) los significados españoles de las palabras inglesas que necesita para comprender el inglés.

Para lograr los propósitos indicados bajo los números (1) y (3), se suministran diferenciaciones (es decir, distinciones entre dos o más significados de una palabra) en la lengua-fuente; pero, dada la facilidad con que el sujeto del verbo puede indicarse en español y dada la conveniencia de destacar el objeto del verbo con la preposición **a**, las diferenciaciones consistentes en el sujeto o el objeto, o ambos, se dan en español tanto en la parte de inglés-español como en la parte de español-inglés. Para los propósitos indicados bajo los números (2) y (4) no se necesitan diferenciaciones y no se dan, porque el usuario siempre tendrá como guía el contexto de lo que oye o lee. Con todo, algunas glosas que no tienen por objeto indicar diferenciaciones sino más bien dilucidar el sentido de lo que parece ser una palabra o expresión raras u obscuras en la lengua nativa del usuario, se indican en esta lengua.

Los vocablos se tratan consecutivamente de acuerdo con las partes de la oración y las funciones verbales; y los significados marcados con calificativos de tema, uso y país van después de los significados más generales.

Para facilitar la búsqueda del significado y el uso deseados, los cambios en la parte de la oración y función verbal, en la flexión, en el género de los nombres españoles y en la pronunciación de las palabras inglesas van señalados con doble raya vertical, en vez del punto y coma de costumbre.

Se han omitido los puntos después de los calificativos y abreviaturas gramaticales y al fin de los artículos.

La forma femenina de un adjetivo español usado como sustantivo (o de un sustantivo femenino que se escribe lo mismo que la forma femenina de un adjetivo), que cae alfabéticamente en lugar apartado del adjetivo, se trata en este lugar y se consigna otra vez bajo el adjetivo con una referencia a la palabra traducida anteriormente.

El género de los nombres españoles aparece en ambas partes del Diccionario; pero no aparece en la parte de inglés-español el género de los nombres masculinos que terminan en **-o**, los nombres femeninos que terminan en **-a, -dad, -tad, -tud, -ión,** y **-umbre,** los nombres masculinos modificados por un adjetivo que termina en **-o** ni los nombres femeninos modificados por un adjetivo que termina en **-a**.

Los números que se refieren a los modelos de conjugación de los verbos españoles van antes de las abreviaturas que indican la parte de la oración. La lista completa de los modelos de conjugación incluye muchos que muestran una combinación de dos irregularidades, p.ej., **esforzar, seguir, teñir.**

Los nombres propios y las abreviaturas se consignan en su propio lugar alfabético en el texto del Diccionario. No hay, pues, que buscar **España** y **español** en dos partes distintas del libro. Y todos los artículos secundarios van colocados en riguroso orden alfabético.

Se usa el punto divisorio en los artículos de palabras de flexión irregular para señalar la sílaba final que debe separarse antes de agregar la sílaba que denota la flexión, p.ej., **lá•piz** (*pl* **-pices**) y **falsi•fy** [ˈfɔlsɪˌfaɪ] *v* (*pret & pp* **-fied**).

La pronunciación de todas las palabras inglesas simples se muestra por medio de una nueva adaptación de los símbolos del Alfabeto fonético internacional y entre corchetes. No se muestra la pronunciación de las palabras inglesas compuestas cuando la pronunciación de los componentes consta en los lugares donde aparecen como artículos independientes.

The author wishes to express his gratitude to many persons who have worked with him in lexicographical research and development and who helped him directly in the compilation of this book and particularly to the following: Paul Aguilar, William Beigel, Henry H. Carter, Eugenio Chang-Rodríguez, R. Thomas Douglass, David Louis Gold, Allison Gronberg, James E. Iannucci, Christopher Stavrou, Roger J. Steiner, John C. Traupman, and José Vidal.

EDWIN B. WILLIAMS

PREFACE TO THE REVISED EDITION

The main objective of this revision has been to add about 3,200 recent words and meanings, primarily from the fields of science and technology (especially computers, medicine, and genetics), communication, environment, and economics and from colloquial speech. To accommodate the new text, we have omitted (1) the repetition of the infinitive particle **(to)** and (2) many alternative pronunciations, especially of British English.

The label (Am) has been deleted in most instances because this Dictionary focuses, in its entirety, on the Spanish of the Americas. The 22 regional labels have been retained.

Credit for work on this revision is due Mario Bernal, Gerald J. Mac Donald, Liliana Montano, Roger J. Steiner, Sol Steinmetz, Carlos Vega, Lawrence Weisburg, and Diane S. Aronson.

WALTER D. GLANZE

Como la constitución de los artículos no se ha determinado a base de su etimología, se incluyen bajo un mismo artículo todos los homógrafos de una palabra. Cuando varía la pronunciación de un homógrafo inglés, se indica en su propio lugar después de la doble raya vertical.

EDWIN B. WILLIAMS

PRÓLOGO DE LA EDICIÓN AUMENTADA

El objetivo major de esta revisión ha sido agregar aproximadamente 3,200 palabras y significados recientes, principalmente de las áreas de ciencia y tecnología (especialmente computadores, medicina y genética), comunicaciones, medio ambiente y economía, y del idioma de uso común. Para adaptar el texto nuevo, hemos omitido (1) la repetición del signo de infinitivo **(to)** y (2) muchas pronunciaciones alternativas, especialmento del inglés británico.

El calificativo (Am) ha sido omitido generalmente, porque este Diccionario se concentra en el español de las Américas. Los 22 calificativos regionales han sido retenidos.

Por el trabajo rendido en esta revisión, crédito es debido a Mario Bernal, Gerald J. Mac Donald, Liliana Montano, Roger J. Steiner, Sol Steinmentzo, Carlos Vega, Lawrence Weisburg y Diane S. Aronson.

WALTER D. GLANZE

LABELS AND GRAMMATICAL ABBREVIATIONS
CALIFICATIVOS Y ABREVIATURAS GRAMATICALES

abbr abbreviation—abreviatura
(acronym) acrónimo—a word formed from the initial letters or syllables of a series of words—palabra formada de las letras o sílabas iniciales de una serie de palabras
adj adjective—adjetivo
adv adverb—adverbio
(aer) aeronautics—aeronáutica
(agr) agriculture—agricultura
(alg) algebra—álgebra
(Am) Spanish American—hispano-americano
(anat) anatomy—anatomía
(archaic) arcaico
(archeol) archeology—arqueología
(archit) architecture—arquitectura
(Arg) Argentine—argentino
(arith) arithmetic—aritmética
art article—artículo
(arti) artillery—artillería
(astr) astronomy—astronomía
(aut) automobiles—automóviles
(bact) bacteriology—bacteriología
(baseball) beisbol
(bb) bookbinding—encuadernación
(Bib) Biblical—bíblico
(billiards) billar
(biochem) biochemistry—bioquímica
(biol) biology—biología
(Bol) Bolivian—boliviano
(bowling) bolos
(bot) botany—botánica
(box) boxing—boxeo
(Brit) British—británico
(CAm) Central American—centroamericano
(cards) naipes
(carp) carpentry—carpintería
(chem) chemistry—química
(chess) ajedrez
(Chile) Chilean—chileno
(Col) Colombian—colombiano
(coll) colloquial—familiar
(com) commercial—comercial
comp comparative—comparativo
cond conditional—condicional
conj conjunction—conjunción
(C-R) Costa Rican—costarriqueño
(Cuba) Cuban—cubano
(culin) cooking—cocina
def definite—definido
dem demonstrative—demostrativo
(dent) dentistry—odontología
(dial) dialectal—dialectal
(eccl) ecclesiastical—eclesiástico
(econ) economics—economía
(Ecuad) Ecuadorian—ecuatoriano
(educ) education—educación
(elec) electricity—electricidad

(electron) electronics—electrónica
(El Salv) El Salvador
(ent) entomology—entomología
f feminine noun—nombre femenino
(fa) fine arts—bellas artes
fem feminine—femenino
(fencing) esgrima
(feud) feudalism—feudalismo
(fig) figurative—figurado
fpl feminine noun plural—nombre femenino plural
fsg feminine noun singular—nombre femenino singular
fut future—futuro
(geog) geography—geografía
(geol) geology—geología
(geom) geometry—geometría
ger gerund—gerundio
(gram) grammar—gramática
(Guat) Guatemalan—guatemalteco
(heral) heraldry—heráldica
(hist) history—historia
(Hond) Honduran—hondureño
(hort) horticulture—horticultura
(hum) humorous—jocoso
(hunt) hunting—caza
(ichth) ichthyology—ictiología
imperf imperfect—imperfecto
impers impersonal—impersonal
impv imperative—imperativo
ind indicative—indicativo
indecl indeclinable—indeclinable
indef indefinite—indefinido
inf infinitive—infinitivo
(ins) insurance—seguros
interj interjection—interjección
interr interrogative—interrogativo
intr intransitive verb—verbo intransitivo
invar invariable—invariable
(iron) ironical—irónico
(Lat) Latin—latín
(law) derecho
(letterword) a word in the form of an abbreviation which is pronounced by sounding the names of its letters in succession and which functions as a part of speech—palabra en forma de abreviatura la cual se pronuncia haciendo sonar el nombre de cada letra consecutivamente y que funciona como parte del discurso
(log) logic—lógica
m masculine noun—nombre masculino
(mach) machinery—maquinaria
(mas) masonry—albañilería
masc masculine—masculino
(math) mathematics—matemática
(mech) mechanics—mecánica
(med) medicine—medicina
(metal) metallurgy—metalurgia
(meteor) meteorology—meteorología

(Mex) Mexican—mejicano
mf masculine or feminine noun according to sex—nombre masculino o nombre femenino según el sexo
(mil) military—militar
(min) mining—minería
(mineral) mineralogy—mineralogía
(mountaineering) alpinismo
(mov) moving pictures—cine
mpl masculine noun plural—nombre masculino plural
msg masculine noun singular—nombre masculino singular
(mus) music—música
(myth) mythology—mitología
m & f masculine and feminine noun without regard to sex—nombre masculino y femenino sin tener en cuenta el sexo
(naut) nautical—náutico
(nav) naval—naval militar
neut neuter—neutro
(obs) obsolete—desusado
(obstet) obstetrics—obstetricia
(opt) optics—óptica
(orn) ornithology—ornitología
(paint) painting—pintura
(Pan) Panamanian—panameño
(Para) Paraguayan—paraguayo
(pathol) pathology—patología
pers personal—personal
(Peru) Peruvian—peruano
(pharm) pharmacy—farmacia
(philol) philology—filología
(philos) philosophy—filosofía
(phonet) phonetics—fonética
(phot) photography—fotografía
(phys) physics—física
(physiol) physiology—fisiología
pl plural—plural
(poet) poetical—poético
(pol) politics—política
poss possessive—posesivo
pp past participle—participio pasado
(P-R) Puerto Rican—puertorriqueño
prep preposition—preposición
pres present—presente

pret preterit—pretérito
pron pronoun—pronombre
(psychoanalysis) sicoanálisis
(psychol) psychology—sicología
(rad) radio—radio
ref reflexive verb—verbo reflexivo
reflex reflexive—reflexivo
rel relative—relativo
(rhet) rhetoric—retórica
(rr) railway—ferrocarril
s substantive—substantivo
(SAm) South American—sudamericano
(scornful) despreciativo
(sculp) sculpture—escultura
(S-D) Santo Domingo—República Dominicana
(sew) sewing—costura
sg singular—singular
(slang) jerga
spl substantive plural—substantivo plural
(sport) deporte
ssg substantive singular—substantivo singular
subj subjunctive—subjuntivo
super superlative—superlativo
(surg) surgery—cirugía
(surv) surveying—agrimensura
(taur) bullfighting—tauromaquia
(telg) telegraphy—telegrafía
(telp) telephony—telefonía
(telv) television—televisión
(tennis) tenis
(theat) theater—teatro
(theol) theology—teología
tr transitive verb—verbo transitivo
(typ) printing—imprenta
(Urug) Uruguayan—uruguayo
v verb—verbo
var variant—variante
v aux auxiliary verb—verbo auxiliar
(Ven) Venezuelan—venezolano
(vet) veterinary medicine—veterinaria
(vulg) vulgar—grosero
(W-I) West Indian—antillano
(zool) zoology—zoología

SPANISH-
ENGLISH

ESPAÑOL-
INGLÉS

A

A, a (a) *f* first letter of the Spanish alphabet
a *prep* at; for, to; on, upon; in, into; by; from; **a decir verdad** to tell the truth; **a la española** in the Spanish manner; **a lo que parece** as it seems; **a no ser por** if it weren't for; **a saberlo yo** if I had known it; **oler a** to smell of
abacería *f* grocery store
abace•ro -ra *mf* grocer
abad *m* abbot
abadejo *m* codfish; (orn) kinglet; (ent) Spanish fly
abadesa *f* abbess
abadía *f* abbacy; abbey
abajar *ref* to lower oneself
abaje•ño -ña *adj* (Mex) coastal, lowland ‖ *mf* (Mex) lowlander
abaje•ro -ra *adj* (Arg) lower, under ‖ *f* (Arg) bellyband, bellystrap; (Arg) saddlecloth
abaji•no -na *adj* (Col, Chile) northern ‖ *mf* (Col, Chile) northerner
abajo *adv* down, underneath; downwards; downstairs; **abajo de** down; **más abajo** lower down; **río abajo** downstream ‖ *interj* down with. . . !
abalanzar §60 *tr* to hurl ‖ *ref* to rush; venture; (*un caballo*) rear
abalear *tr* (SAm) to shoot
abalizar §60 *tr* to mark with buoys ‖ *ref* (naut) to take bearings
abalorio *m* glass bead
abaluartar *tr* to bulwark
abanar *tr* to fan
abanderado *m* colorbearer
abanderar *tr* (*un buque*) to register
abanderizar §60 *tr* to organize into bands ‖ *ref* to band together; (Chile, Peru) to join up
abandona•do -da *adj* lonely
abandonar *tr* to abandon, forsake ‖ *intr* to give up ‖ *ref* to abandon oneself; give up
abandonismo *m* defeatism
abandonista *adj & mf* defeatist
abandono *m* abandon, abandonment; neglect; forlornness; yielding
abanicar §73 *tr* to fan
abanico *m* fan; fanlight; sword; **abanico de chimenea** fire screen
abaniquear *tr* to fan
abaniqueo *m* fanning; gesticulations
abanto *adj* skittish (*bull*)
abaratamiento *m* cheapening

abaratar *tr* to cheapen; (*precios*) lower ‖ *intr & ref* to get cheap
abarca *f* sandal
abarcar §73 *tr* to embrace; encompass; surround; corner, monopolize
abarloar *tr* (naut) to bring alongside ‖ *ref* to snuggle up
abarquillar *tr & ref* to curl up
abarraganamiento *m* illicit cohabitation
abarrancar *ref* to get into a difficult situation
abarrota•do -da *adj* overcrowded
abarrotar *tr* to bar; bind, fasten; jam, pack, stuff; overstock ‖ *ref* to become a glut on the market
abarrote *m* (naut) packing; **abarrotes** groceries; hardware
abarrotería *f* (Guat) grocery store; (CAm) hardware store
abarrote•ro -ra *mf* grocer
abastecer §22 *tr* to supply, provide
abastecimiento *m* supplying; supplies, provisions
abasto *m* supply; abundance; **dar abasto** to be sufficient
abatanar *tr* to full
abatí *m* (Arg, Para) corn; corn whiskey
abatible *adj* collapsible, folding
abati•do -da *adj* downcast; abject, contemptible ‖ *f* abatis
abatimiento *m* discouragement; descent
abatir *tr* to lower; knock down; shoot down; take apart; humble; discourage ‖ *intr* (aer) to drift; (naut) to have leeway ‖ *ref* to be discouraged; be humbled; drop, fall; swoop down
abdicar §73 *tr & intr* to abdicate
abdomen *m* abdomen
abecé *m* A B C
abecedario *m* A B C's
abedul *m* birch
abeja *f* bee; **abeja maestra** or **abeja reina** queen bee
abejar *m* apiary, beehive
abeje•ro -ra *mf* beekeeper
abejorro *m* bumblebee
abejarrón *m* bumblebee
aberración *f* aberration; deviation
abertura *f* aperture; opening, crack, slit; cove; openness, frankness
abeto *m* fir tree; hemlock; **abeto del Norte, abeto falso** spruce tree
abier•to -ta *adj* open; frank
abigarra•do -da *adj* motley, variegated

abigeo *m* horse thief, cattle thief

abijar *tr* (Col) to sic

abiselar *tr* to bevel

abisma•do -da *adj* absorbed, lost in thought; mysterious

abismar *tr* to cast down; humble; spoil, ruin ‖ *ref* to sink; cave in; be humbled; give in; lose oneself; be surprised

abismo *m* abyss, chasm

abjurar *tr* to abjure; renounce

ablandabre•vas *m* (*pl* **-vas**) or **ablandahi•gos** *m* (*pl* **-gos**) good-for-nothing

ablandar *tr* to soften; soften up; soothe; loosen ‖ *intr* (*el tiempo*) to moderate ‖ *ref* to soften; relent; (*el tiempo*) moderate

ablativo *m* ablative

abnegación *f* abnegation; self-denial

abnega•do -da *adj* self-denying

abnegar *ref* to deny oneself; sacrifice oneself

aboba•do -da *adj* stupid, stupid-looking

abobar *tr* to make stupid ‖ *ref* to grow stupid

aboca•do -da *adj* (*vino*) mild, smooth; vulnerable; **abocado a** verging on

abocar §73 *tr* to bite; pour; bring near ‖ *intr* to enter ‖ *ref* to approach; have an interview

abocinar *tr* to give a flare to ‖ *intr* to fall on the face ‖ *ref* to flare

abochornar *tr* to overheat; make blush ‖ *ref* to blush; wilt

abofa•do -da *adj* (Cuba, Mex) swollen

abofetear *tr* to slap in the face

abogacía *f* law, legal profession

abogaderas *fpl* (CAm) specious arguments

abogado *m* lawyer; **abogado criminalista** criminal lawyer; **abogado de secano** quack lawyer; **abogado firmón** lawyer who will sign anything; **abogado trampista** shyster

abogar §44 *intr* to plead; **abogar por** to advocate, back

abolengo *m* ancestry, descent; inheritance

abolición *f* abolition

abolir §1 *tr* to revoke, repeal

abolorio *m* ancestry

abolladura *f* dent; bump, bruise; embossing

abollar *tr* to bump, bruise; dent; stun; emboss ‖ *ref* to get bumped, get bruised; dent, be dented

abollonar *tr* to emboss

abombar *tr* to make convex; stun, confound ‖ *ref* to rot, decompose

abominable *adj* abominable, very bad

abominación *f* abomination

abominar *tr* to detest, abominate ‖ *intr* — **abominar de** to abominate

abona•do -da *adj* trustworthy; apt, likely ‖ *mf* subscriber; (*al gas, electricidad, etc.*) consumer; (*a una localidad en el teatro*) season-ticket holder; (*al ferrocarril*) commuter

abonanzar §60 *intr* (*el tiempo*) to clear up; (*el viento*) abate

abonar *tr* to vouch for; certify; improve; fertilize; **abonar en cuenta a** to credit to the account of ‖ *intr* (*el tiempo*) to clear up ‖ *ref* to subscribe

abonaré *m* promissory note

abono *m* subscription; credit; installment; voucher; fertilizer, manure

abordar *tr* to approach; accost; undertake, plan; (naut) to board; (naut) to run afoul of; (naut) to dock ‖ *intr* to run afoul; (naut) to put into port

aborigen *adj invar* aboriginal, native; **aborígenes** *mpl* aborigines, natives

aborrascar §73 *ref* to get stormy

aborrecer §22 *tr* to abhor, detest, hate; bore ‖ *ref* to get bored

aborrecible *adj* abhorrent, hateful

aborrega•do -da *adj* (*nubes*) fleecy; (*cielo*) mackerel

aborregar *ref* (SAm) to become stupid

abortar *tr & intr* to abort

abortista *mf* abortionist

aborto *m* abortion; miscarriage; **aborto despenalizado** legalized abortion

abotagar §44 *ref* to become bloated, swell up

abotonador *m* buttonhook

abotonar *tr* to button ‖ *intr* to bud

abovedar *tr* to arch, vault

abozalar *tr* to muzzle

abra *f* cove; vale; fissure; (Mex) clearing

abrasa•dor -dora *adj* burning, hot

abrasar *tr* to set fire to, burn; parch; nip; squander; shame ‖ *intr* to burn ‖ *ref* to burn; become parched; (fig) to be burning up

abrasi•vo -va *adj & m* abrasive

abrazadera *f* clasp, clip, clamp; (typ) bracket

abrazar §60 *tr* to embrace, clasp; include; take in ‖ *ref* (*dos personas*) to embrace

abrazo *m* embrace, hug

abrebo•cas *m* (*pl* **-cas**) mouth prop, mouth gag

abrebote•llas *m* (*pl* **-llas**) bottle opener

abrecar•tas *m* (*pl* **-tas**) knife, letter opener

abreco•ches *m* (*pl* **-ches**) doorman

abrela•tas *m* (*pl* **-tas**) can opener

abreos•tras *m* (*pl* **-tras**) oyster knife

abrevadero *m* watering place, drinking trough

abrevar *tr* to water; wet, soak; irrigate; size ‖ *ref* to drink

abreviación *f* abridgment, abbreviation, shortening; hastening

abreviar *tr* to abridge; abbreviate; shorten; hasten ‖ *intr* to be quick; **abreviar con** to make short work of

abreviatura *f* abbreviation; **en abreviatura** in a hurry

abridero *m* (Mex, P-R) dive, joint

abridor *m* opener; grafting knife; **abridor de guantes** glove stretcher

abridura *f* (act of) opening

abrigadero *m* windbreak

abrigar §44 *tr* to shelter; protect; (*esperanzas, sospechas*) harbor ‖ *ref* to take shelter; wrap oneself up

abrigo *m* shelter; aid, support; cover, wrap; overcoat; (naut) harbor; **abrigo antiaéreo** air-raid shelter; **abrigo de entretiempo** topcoat, spring-and-fall coat; **al abrigo de** sheltered from, protected from; sheltered by, protected by; (*ropa*) **de mucho abrigo** heavy

abril *m* April

abrillantar *tr* to polish; glaze

abrir *m* opening; **en un abrir y cerrar de ojos** in the twinkling of an eye ‖ §83 *tr* to open; unlock, unfasten; (*el apetito*) whet; (*el bosque*) clear ‖ *intr* to open ‖ *ref* to open; **abrirse a** or **con** to unbosom oneself to

abrochador *m* buttonhook

abrochar *tr* to button, hook, fasten

abrogación *f* repeal; abrogation

abrogar *tr* to repeal; abrogate; annul

abrojo *m* thistle, thorn; **abrojos** reef, hidden rocks

abrótano *m* southernwood

abruma•do -da *adj* hazy; foggy

abruma•dor -dora *adj* crushing, oppressing; overwhelming

abrumar *tr* to crush, oppress; overwhelm; annoy ‖ *ref* to become foggy

abrup•to -ta *adj* abrupt, steep; rough, rugged

absceso *m* abscess

absenta *f* absinth

ábsida *f* or **ábside** *m* apse

absolución *f* absolution; acquittal

absoluta *f* dogmatic statement; (mil) discharge

absolutamente *adv* absolutely; by no means

absolu•to -ta *adj* absolute; arbitrary ‖ *m* absolute; **en absoluto** absolutely not ‖ *f* see **absoluta**

absolvederas *fpl* — **tener buenas absolvederas** to be an indulgent confessor

absolver §47 & §83 *tr* to absolve; to solve, to answer

absorbente *adj* absorbent; (*interesante*) absorbing

absorber *tr* to absorb; use up; attract

absorción *f* absorption

absor•to -ta *adj* absorbed; entranced

abste•mio -mia *adj* abstemious

abstener §71 *ref* to abstain

abstensionismo *m* nonparticipation

abstinente *adj* abstinent

abstracción *f* abstraction; absorption, deep thought; **hacer abstracción de** to leave out, disregard

abstrac•to -ta *adj* abstract

abstraer §75 *tr* to abstract ‖ *intr* — **abstraer de** to do without, leave aside ‖ *ref* to be abstracted or absorbed; **abstraerse de** to do without, leave aside

abstraí•do -da *adj* absorbed in thought; withdrawn

abstru•so -sa *adj* abstruse

absurdidad *f* absurdity

absur•do -da *adj* absurd ‖ *m* absurdity

abuchear *tr* & *intr* to boo, hoot

abuela *f* grandmother; **cuénteselo a su abuela** tell that to the marines

abuelo *m* grandparent; grandfather; **abuelos** grandparents; ancestors

abulta•do -da *adj* bulky, massive

abultar *tr* to enlarge; exaggerate ‖ *intr* to be bulky

abundamiento *m* abundance; **a mayor abundamiento** with greater reason

abundancia *f* abundance, plenty

abundante *adj* abundant

abundar *intr* to abound

abur *interj* good-bye!, so long!

aburguesa•do -da *adj* middle-class, bourgeois

aburguesar *ref* to become middle-class, become bourgeois

aburri•do -da *adj* bored; tiresome

aburrimiento *m* weariness, fatigue; dullness

aburrir *tr* to bore, tire ‖ *ref* to become bored

abusar *intr* to go too far; **abusar de** to abuse; impose on; overindulge in

abusión *f* superstition

abusi•vo -va *adj* abusive

abuso *m* abuse; imposition

abyec•to -ta *adj* abject

A.C. *abbr* **año de Cristo**

acá *adv* here, around here; **acá y allá** here and there; **de ayer acá** since yesterday; **¿de cuándo acá?** since when?; **desde entonces acá** since then; **más acá** here closer; **muy acá** right here

acaba•do -da *adj* complete, perfect; worn-out, exhausted ‖ *m* finish

acabamiento *m* end; completion; death; decline

acabar *tr* to end, finish, complete ‖ *intr* to end; die; **acabar con** to put an end to; end in; **acabar de** to finish; have just, e.g., **acaba de salir** he has just left; **acababa de salir** he had just left; **acabar por** to end in; end by; **no acabar de decidirse** to be unable to make up one's mind ‖ *ref* to end; be exhausted; be all over; run out of, e.g., **se me acabó el café** I have run out of coffee

acabóse *m* limit, last straw

acacia *f* acacia; **acacia falsa** locust tree

academia *f* academy

académi•co -ca *adj* academic ‖ *mf* academician

acaecer §22 *intr* to happen, occur

acaecimiento *m* happening, occurrence

acalenturar *ref* to get a fever

acalora•do -da *adj* heated; warm; fiery, excited

acaloramiento *m* ardor; passion

acalorar *tr* to heat, warm; incite, encourage; stir up ‖ *ref* to become heated; warm up

acallar *tr* to quiet, silence; pacify

acampada *f* camp

acamar *tr* (*las mieses la lluvia o el viento*) to beat down, blow over

acampamento *m* camp, encampment

acampana•do -da *adj* bell-shaped

acampar *tr*, *intr* & *ref* to encamp

acanalar *tr* to groove; flute; channel; corrugate

acantila•do -da *adj* rocky; steep, precipitous ‖ *m* cliff, bluff

acantonamiento *m* cantonment

acantonar *tr* to canton, quarter ‖ *ref* to be quartered; **acantonarse en** to limit one's activities to

acaparar *tr* to corner; monopolize; hoard

acaramela•do -da *adj* candied; smooth, honey-tongued

acarar *tr* to bring face to face

acarear *tr* to bring face to face; face, brave

acariciar *tr* to caress; (*una ilusión*) cherish

acarraladura *f* (Chile, Peru) run (*in stockings*)

acarreadi•zo -za *adj* transportable

acarrear *tr* to cart, transport, carry along; cause, occasion ‖ *ref* to incur, bring upon oneself

acarreo *m* cartage, drayage; conveyance

acartonar *ref* to shrivel up, become wizened

acasera•do -da *adj* (Chile, Peru) home-loving; (*parroquiano*) (Chile, Peru) regular ‖ *mf* (Chile, Peru) stay-at-home, home-body; (Chile, Peru) regular customer

acaso *m* chance, accident; **al acaso** at random ‖ *adv* maybe, perhaps; **por si acaso** in case of need, just in case

acatamiento *m* homage; respect

acatar *tr* to respect, hold in awe; observe

acatarrar *tr* to chill, give a cold to; (Chile, Mex) to bother, annoy ‖ *ref* to catch cold; get tipsy

acaudala•do -da *adj* rich, well-to-do

acaudalar *tr* to acquire, accumulate

acaudillar *tr* to lead, command; direct

acceder *intr* to accede; agree

accesible *adj* accessible

accesión *f* accession; acquiescence; access, entry

accésit *m* second prize, honorable mention

acceso *m* access, approach; attack, fit, spell; **acceso prohibido** no admittance

acceso•rio -ria *adj* accessory ‖ *m* accessory, fixture, attachment; **accesorios** (theat) properties

accidenta•do -da *adj* agitated; restless; rough, uneven ‖ *mf* victim, casualty

accidental *adj* accidental; acting, pro-tempore, temporary

accidentar *tr* to injure, hurt ‖ *ref* to faint

accidente *m* accident; (*del terreno*) rough-ness, unevenness; fainting spell

acción *f* action; gesture; (*parte del capital de una sociedad*) share; stock certificate; **ac-ción crecedera** growth stock; **acción de gracias** thanksgiving; **acción liberada** stock dividend; **poner en acción** to set in motion

accionar *tr* to drive ‖ *intr* to gesticulate

accionista *mf* shareholder, stockholder

acebo *m* holly tree

acebuche *m* wild olive

acecinar *tr* to dry-cure, dry-salt; (*el salmón o el arenque*) kipper ‖ *ref* to shrivel up

acechar *tr* to watch, to spy on

acecho *m* watching, spying; **al acecho** or **en acecho** on the watch, spying

acedar *tr* to turn sour; embitter ‖ *ref* to turn sour; wither

acedía *f* sourness; crabbedness; heartburn

ace•do -da *adj* sour, tart; crabbed

aceitar *tr* to oil; grease

aceite *m* oil; olive oil; **aceite de hígado de bacalao** cod-liver oil; **aceite de linaza** linseed oil; **aceite de pie de buey** neat's-foot oil; **aceite de ricino** castor oil; **aceite mineral** coal oil

aceite•ro -ra *adj* oil ‖ *mf* oiler; oil dealer ‖ *f* oilcan; oil cup; **aceiteras** cruet stand

aceito•so -sa *adj* oily, greasy

aceituna *f* olive

aceituno *m* olive tree

aceleración *f* acceleration

acelerador *m* accelerator

acelerar *tr* & *ref* to accelerate; hasten, hurry

acelga *f* Swiss chard

acémila *f* beast of burden, pack animal; dolt; drudge

acendra•do -da *adj* refined; stainless, spot-less

acendrar *tr* to refine; purify, make stainless

acento *m* accent; **acento de altura** pitch accent; **acento ortográfico** written accent, accent mark; **acento prosódico** stress ac-cent, tonic accent

acentuar §21 *tr* to accent; accentuate, em-phasize

aceña *f* water-driven flour mill

acepción *f* meaning

acepillar *tr* to plane; brush; smooth

aceptable *adj* acceptable

aceptación *f* acceptance; **aceptación de per-sonas** discrimination; partiality

aceptar *tr* to accept

acequia *f* irrigation ditch; (Bol, Col, Peru) stream, rivulet

acera *f* sidewalk

acera•do -da *adj* steel, steely; (fig) cutting, biting, sharp

acerar *tr* to steel, harden; line with a side-walk ‖ *ref* to harden; steel oneself

acer•bo -ba *adj* sour, bitter; harsh

acerca *adv* — **acerca de** about, with regard to

acercamiento *m* approach, rapprochement

acercar §73 *tr* to bring near or nearer ‖ *ref* to approach, come near or nearer

acería *f* steel mill

acerico *m* small cushion; pincushion

acero *m* steel; sword; courage, spirit

acérri•mo -ma *adj* all-out; (*enemigo*) bitter

acerrojar *tr* to bolt

acerta•do -da *adj* fit, right; skillful, sure; well-aimed

acertante *mf* winner

acertar §2 *tr* to hit; hit upon; figure out correctly; find; do right ‖ *intr* to be right; succeed; guess right; **acertar a** to happen to; succeed in; **acertar con** to come upon; find

acertijo *m* conundrum, riddle

acervo *m* heap; assets, estate; shoal; store, fund, hoard

acetato *m* acetate

acéti•co -ca *adj* acetic

acetificar §73 *tr* & *ref* to acetify

acetileno *m* acetylene

acetona *f* acetone

acia•go -ga *adj* unlucky, ill-fated, evil

acial *m* (CAm, Ecuad) whip

acíbar *m* aloes; bitterness, sorrow

acicalar *tr* to polish, burnish; dress, dress up ‖ *ref* to get all dressed up

acicate *m* long-pointed spur; incentive, stimulus

acicatear *tr* to spur, urge

acidez *f* acidity

acidificar §73 *tr & ref* to acidify

áci•do -da *adj* acid, tart, sour ‖ *m* acid

acierto *m* lucky hit, good shot; good guess; tact, prudence; ability, skill; accuracy; success

aci•mut *m* (*pl* **-muts**) azimut

aclamación *f* acclaim, applause

aclamar *tr & intr* to acclaim, to hail, to cheer

aclarar *tr* to brighten, clear; rinse; explain ‖ *intr* to get bright; clear up; dawn

aclarato•rio -ria *adj* explanatory

aclimatar *tr & ref* to acclimate

acne *f* acne

acobardar *tr* to cow, intimidate ‖ *ref* to be frightened

acocear *tr* to kick; trample upon, ill-treat

acocil *m* Mexican crayfish; **estar como un acocil** (Mex) to blush, be abashed

acoda•do -da *adj* elbow-shaped

acodar *tr* (*el brazo*) to lean; prop; (hort) to layer ‖ *ref* to lean

acodillar *tr* to bend at an angle ‖ *ref* to double up; to bend, to crumple

acogencia *f* (CAm) acceptance; reception

acoger §17 *tr* to receive, welcome; accept ‖ *ref* to take refuge; resort

acogida *f* reception, welcome; meeting place, confluence; refuge, shelter; **dar acogida a** (com) to honor

acolada *f* accolade

acolchar *tr* to quilt, pad

acolchí *m* (Mex) red-winged blackbird

acólito *m* acolyte; altar boy

acollador *m* (naut) lanyard

acomedi•do -da *adj* obliging

acometer *tr* to attack; undertake; (*el sueño, la enfermedad, el deseo a una persona*) overcome

acometida *f* attack; (*p.ej., de una línea eléctrica*) house connection

acomodación *f* accommodation

acomodadi•zo -za *adj* accommodating, obliging

acomoda•do -da *adj* convenient, suitable; comfort-loving; well-to-do

acomoda•dor -dora *adj* accommodating, obliging ‖ *mf* usher

acomodar *tr* to accommodate; usher; reconcile; suit; furnish, supply ‖ *intr* to be suitable, be convenient ‖ *ref* to comply; come to terms; hire out; make oneself comfortable

acomodo *m* arrangement, adjustment; lodgings; job, position; (Chile) neatness, tidiness

acompañador *m* companion; accompanist

acompañamiento *m* accompaniment; escort, retinue; (theat) extras, supernumeraries

acompañanta *f* female companion or escort; accompanist

acompañante *m* companion; accompanist

acompañar *tr* to accompany; escort; enclose; sympathize with

acompaño *m* (CAm) meeting; encounter

acompasa•do -da *adj* rhythmic; slow; easy-going; cautious

acompleja•do -da *adj* full of complexes

aconchar *tr* to push to safety; (naut) to beach, run aground ‖ *ref* to take shelter; (naut) to run aground; (Chile) to form a deposit

acondiciona•do -da *adj* conditioned; **bien acondicionado** well-disposed; in good condition; **mal acondicionado** ill-disposed; in bad condition

acondicionador *m* conditioner; **acondicionador de aire** air conditioner

acondicionamiento *m* conditioning; **acondicionamiento del aire** air conditioning

acondicionar *tr* to condition; put in condition; repair; season ‖ *ref* to qualify; find a job

acongojar *tr* to grieve, afflict ‖ *ref* to grieve

aconsejable *adj* advisable

aconsejar *tr* to advise, counsel, warn ‖ *ref* to seek advice, get advice

acontecer §22 *intr* to happen, occur

acontecimiento *m* happening, event

acopiar *tr* to gather together

acopio *m* gathering; stock; abundance

acoplado *m* (Arg, Chile, Urug) trailer trolley car

acoplamiento *m* coupling; joint; connection; linkup (in space)

acoplar *tr* to couple; join; connect; hitch; reconcile ‖ *ref* to be reconciled; mate; be intimate

acoquinar *tr* to intimidate

acoraza•do -da *adj* armored, armor-plated; contrary ‖ *m* battleship

acorazar §60 *tr* to armor-plate

acorchar *tr* to line with cork; turn into cork ‖ *ref* to get spongy; wither, shrivel; become corky or pithy; get numb

acorchetar *tr* to bracket

acordar §61 *tr* to agree upon; authorize; reconcile; make level or flush; remind of; tune ‖ *intr* to agree; blend ‖ *ref* to be agreed, come to an agreement; remember; **acordarse de** to remember

acorde *adj* agreed, in accord; in tune ‖ *m* accord; (mus) chord

acordeón *m* accordion

acordonar *tr* to cord, lace; (*monedas*) knurl, mill; rope off

acornar §61 *tr* to gore; butt

acornear *tr* to gore; butt

acorralar *tr* to corral, corner; intimidate

acortar *tr* to shorten; reduce; slow down; check, stop ‖ *ref* to become shorter; hold back; be timid; slow down; shrink

acosar *tr* to harass; pester

acosijar *tr* (Mex) to pursue, press, track down

acostar §61 *tr* to lay down; put to bed; (naut) to bring alongside ‖ *ref* to lie down; go to bed; (CAm, Mex) to give birth

acostumbra•do -da *adj* accustomed; customary, usual

acostumbrar *tr* to accustom ‖ *intr* to be accustomed ‖ *ref* to accustom oneself; become accustomed

acotación *f* boundary mark; marginal note; elevation mark

acotamiento *m* boundary mark; marginal note; elevation mark; stage direction

acotar *tr* to mark off, map; annotate; admit, accept; check; vouch for; select; mark elevations on

acotillo *m* sledge hammer

acre *adj* acrid; austere; biting, mordant

acrecentamiento *m* increase, growth; promotion

acrecentar §2 *tr* to increase; promote ‖ *ref* to increase; bud, blossom

acreditar *tr* to accredit; credit; get a reputation for ‖ *ref* to get a reputation, prove oneself

acree•dor -dora *adj* accrediting; deserving ‖ *mf* creditor; **acreedor hipotecario** mortgagee

acribar *tr* to sift; riddle

acribillar *tr* to riddle; harass, plague, pester

acriminar *tr* to incriminate; exaggerate

acrimonio•so -sa *adj* acrid; acrimonious

acriollar *ref* to acquire Spanish American ways

acrisolar *tr* to purify, refine; reveal, bring out

acrobacia *f* acrobatics

acróbata *mf* acrobat

acrobatismo *m* acrobatics

acrónimo *m* acronym

acrópo•lis *adj* (*pl* **-lis**) acropolis

acróstico *m* acrostic

acta *f* minutes; certificate; **acta notarial** affidavit; **actas** proceedings, transactions; **levantar acta** to write up the minutes

actitud *f* attitude; **en actitud de** getting ready to

activar *tr* to activate; hasten, expedite

actividad *f* activity

activista *mf* activist

acti•vo -va *adj* active ‖ *m* (com) assets; (com) credit side

acto *m* act; ceremony; function; commencement; thesis; **acto carnal** sexual intercourse; **acto continuo** right afterward; **acto seguido** right afterward; **acto seguido de** right after; **en acto de servicio** in the line of duty; **hacer acto de presencia** to honor with one's presence

actor *m* actor; agent; **primer actor** leading man

ac•triz *f* (*pl* **-trices**) actress; **primera actriz** leading lady

actuación *f* acting, performance; action; operation; behavior; **actuación en directo** live performance; **actuaciones** legal proceedings

actual *adj* present, present-day; up-to-date ‖ *m* current month

actualidad *f* present time; timeliness; **actualidades** current events; newsreel; **actuali-**

dad escénica theater news; **actualidad gráfica** news in pictures

actualizar §60 *tr* to bring up to date

actualmente *adv* at present, at the present time

actuante *mf* participant

actuar §21 *tr* to actuate ‖ *intr* to act; perform

actua•rio -ria *mf* actuary

acuaplano *m* aquaplane

acuarela *f* water color

acuario *m* aquarium; **Acuario** *m* (astr) Aquarius

acuartelar *tr* to billet, quarter

acuáti•co -ca *adj* aquatic

acuatizaje *m* (aer) alighting on water; (*de nave espacial*) splashdown

acuatizar §60 *intr* (aer) to alight on water

acucia *f* zeal, diligence; yearning

acuciar *tr* to goad, prod; harass; yearn for

acuclillar *ref* to squat, crouch

acuchilla•do -da *adj* knife-shaped; schooled by experience; (*vestido*) slashed

acuchillar *tr* to stab; stab to death; slash

acudir *intr* to come up, respond; apply; hang around; come to the rescue; **acudir a las urnas** to vote

acueducto *m* aqueduct

acuerdo *m* accord; agreement; memory; **de acuerdo con** in accord with; **de común acuerdo** with one accord; **estar en su acuerdo** to be in one's right mind; **ponerse de acuerdo** to come to an agreement; **recobrar su acuerdo** to come to; **tomar un acuerdo** to make a decision; **volver en su acuerdo** to come to; to change one's mind

acuitar *tr* & *ref* to grieve

acullá *adv* yonder, over there

acumulador *m* storage battery

acumular *tr* to accumulate, gather; store up ‖ *intr* & *ref* to accumulate, gather

acunar *tr* to rock; cradle

acuñación *f* coining, minting; wedging

acuñar *tr* to coin, mint; wedge; key, lock; (typ) to quoin

acuo•so -sa *adj* watery; juicy

acupuntura *f* acupuncture

acurrucar §73 *ref* to squat, crouch; huddle

acusación *f* accusation

acusa•do -da marked ‖ *mf* accused

acusar *tr* to accuse; show; (*recibo de una carta*) acknowledge ‖ *ref* to confess

acusati•vo -va *adj* & *m* accusative

acuse *m* acknowledgment

acústi•co -ca *adj* acoustic ‖ *f* acoustics

achacar §73 *tr* to impute, attribute

achaco•so -sa *adj* ailing, sickly

achaparra•do -da *adj* stocky; stubby; chubby

achaparrar *ref* to become stunted

achaque *m* sickliness, indisposition; excuse, pretext; matter, subject; weakness; (coll) monthlies

achatar *tr* to flatten ‖ *ref* (Mex) to become frightened, afraid

achica•do -da *adj* childish; abashed, disconcerted

achicador *m* scoop

achicar §73 *tr* to make smaller; humble; bail, to bail out

achicoria *f* chicory

achicharrar *tr* to scorch; bedevil ‖ *ref* to get scorched

achicharronar *tr* to squash

achín *m* (CAm) peddler; door-to-door salesman

achiquitar *ref* to lose heart, cower

achispa•do -da *adj* tipsy

achispar *tr* to make tipsy ‖ *ref* to get tipsy

achuchar *tr* to incite; crumple, crush; jostle ‖ *ref* (Arg, Urug) to shiver, have a chill

adagio *m* adage

adalid *m* chief; guide, leader; champion

adama•do -da *adj* womanish; chic, stylish

adamar *ref* to become effeminate

adán *m* dirty, ragged fellow; lazy, careless fellow ‖ **Adán** *m* Adam

adaptación *f* adaptation

adaptar *tr* to adapt

adarga *f* oval or heart-shaped leather shield

adarvar *tr* to bewilder, stun

A. de C. *abbr* **año de Cristo**

adecentar *tr* to clean up, tidy up ‖ *ref* to put on a clean shirt, dress up

adecua•do -da *adj* fitting, suitable

adecuar *tr* to fit, adapt

adefesio *m* nonsense; outlandish outfit; queer-looking fellow

adehala *f* gratuity, extra

adehesar *tr* to convert into pasture

adelanta•do -da *adj* precocious; bold, forward; (*reloj*) fast; **por adelantado** in advance ‖ *m* provincial governor

adelantamiento *m* anticipation; advancement, promotion, progress

adelantar *tr* to move forward; outstrip, get ahead of; advance; promote; improve ‖ *intr* to advance; improve; be fast ‖ *ref* to move forward; gain, be fast

adelante *adv* ahead; forward; **más adelante** farther on; later ‖ *interj* go ahead!; come in!

adelanto *m* advance, progress, improvement; advancement; payment in advance

adelfa *f* oleander

adelgazar §60 *tr* to make thin; taper; purify; argue subtly about; weaken, lessen ‖ *intr* & *ref* to get thin; taper

ademán *m* attitude; gesture; **ademanes** manners; **en ademán de** getting ready to; **hacer ademán de** to make a move to

además *adv* moreover, besides; **además de** in addition to, besides

adentellar *tr* to sink one's teeth into

adentrar *intr* & *ref* to go in; **adentrarse en el mar** to go farther out to sea

adentro *adv* inside; **mar adentro** out at sea; **ser muy de adentro** to be like a member of the family; **tierra adentro** inland ‖ **adentros** *mpl* inmost being, inmost thoughts; **en** or **para sus adentros** to oneself, to himself, etc.

adep•to -ta *adj* initiated ‖ *mf* follower

aderezar §60 *tr* to dress, adorn; cook; (*una tela*) starch; season; repair; lead; (*bebidas*)

mix; (*vinos*) blend ‖ *ref* to dress, get ready

aderezo *m* dressing; seasoning, condiment; starch; finery; equipment; set of jewelry

adestrar §2 *tr* & *ref* var of **adiestrar**

adeuda•do -da *adj* indebted, in debt

adeudar *tr* to owe; to be liable for; charge ‖ *intr* to become related by marriage ‖ *ref* to run into debt

adeudo *m* debt, indebtedness; customs duty; charge, debit

adherencia *f* adhesion; **tener adherencias** to have connections

adherente *adj* adherent ‖ *m* adherent; **adherentes** accessories

adherir §68 *intr* & *ref* to adhere; stick

adhesión *f* adherence, adhesion

adhesi•vo -va *adj* adhesive

adición *f* addition; (*en un café o restaurante*) check

adicionar *tr* to add; add to

adic•to -ta *adj* devoted; supporting ‖ *mf* supporter, follower

adiestramiento *m* training; breaking in

adiestrar *tr* to train; teach; lead, guide ‖ *ref* to train, practice

adietar *tr* to put on a diet

adinera•do -da *adj* wealthy, well-to-do

adiós *m* adieu, good-bye ‖ *interj* adieu!, good-bye!

aditamento *m* addition; accessory

aditi•vo -va *adj* & *m* additive

adivinación *f* prophecy; guessing, divination; **adivinación del pensamiento** mind reading

adivina•dor -dora *mf* guesser; good guesser; **adivinador del pensamiento** mind reader

adivinaja *f* riddle, puzzle

adivinanza *f* riddle; guess

adivinar *tr* to prophesy; guess, divine; (*un enigma*) solve; (*el pensamiento ajeno*) read

adivi•no -na *mf* fortuneteller; guesser

adjetivo *m* adjective

adjudicar §73 *tr* to adjudge, award ‖ *ref* to appropriate

adjuntar *tr* to join, connect; add; enclose

adjun•to -ta *adj* added, attached; enclosed ‖ *mf* associate ‖ *m* adjunct; adjective

adminículo *m* aid, auxiliary; gadget; meddler; **adminículos** emergency equipment

administración *f* administration, management; headquarters

administra•dor -dora *mf* administrator, manager; **administrador de correos** postmaster

administrar *tr* to administer, manage

admiración *f* admiration; wonder; exclamation mark

admira•dor -dora *mf* admirer

admirar *tr* to admire; surprise ‖ *ref* to wonder; **admirarse de** to wonder at

admisible *adj* admissible

admisión *f* admission; (mach) intake

admitir *tr* to admit; allow; accept, recognize; agree to

adobar *tr* to repair, restore; dress, prepare; cook, stew; (*carne, pescado*) pickle; (*pieles*) tan

adobe *m* adobe

adobera *f* (SAm) brick-shaped cheese; mold for brick-shaped cheese

adobo *m* repairing; dressing; cooking; pickling; tanning; pickled meat or fish

adocena•do -da common, ordinary

adoctrinar *tr* to indoctrinate, teach, instruct

adolecer §22 *intr* to fall sick; **adolecer de** to suffer from ‖ *ref* — **adolecerse de** (archaic) to sympathize with, feel sorry for

adolescencia *f* adolescence

adolescente *adj* & *mf* adolescent

adonde *conj* where, whither

adónde *adv* where, whither

adopción *f* adoption

adoptar *tr* to adopt

adoquín *m* paving stone, paving block; (coll) blockhead

adoquina•do -da *adj* paved with cobblestones ‖ *m* cobblestone paving

adorable *adj* adorable

adoración *f* adoration, worship; **Adoración de los Reyes** Epiphany

adora•dor -dora *mf* adorer, worshiper ‖ *m* suitor

adorar *tr* & *intr* to adore, worship

adormecer §22 *tr* to put to sleep ‖ *ref* to go to sleep; get sleepy

adormeci•do -da *adj* sleepy, drowsy; numb; calm

adormidera *f* opium poppy

adormilar *ref* to doze, drowse

adornar *tr* to adorn; (*un cuento*) embroider

adornista *mf* decorator

adorno *m* adornment, decoration; **adorno de escaparate** window dressing

adosar *tr* to lean; push close

adquirir §40 *tr* to acquire; **adquirir en propiedad** to buy, purchase

adquisición *f* acquisition

adrede *adv* on purpose

Adriáti•co -ca *adj* & *m* Adriatic

adscribir §83 *tr* to attribute; assign

adscripción *f* attribution; assignment

aduana *f* customhouse; **aduana seca** inland customhouse; **exento de aduana** duty-free; **sujeto de aduana** dutiable

aduane•ro -ra *adj* customhouse; customs ‖ *m* customhouse officer, customs inspector

aduar *m* Arab settlement; gipsy camp; Indian ranch

adueñar *ref* to take possession

adujar *tr* (naut) to coil ‖ *ref* (naut) to curl up

adular *tr* to flatter, fawn on

adu•lón -lona *adj* fawning, groveling ‖ *mf* fawner

adúltera *f* adulteress

adulterar *tr* to adulterate ‖ *intr* to commit adultery ‖ *ref* to become adulterated, to spoil

adulterio *m* adultery

adúlte•ro -ra *adj* adulterous ‖ *m* adulterer ‖ *f* see **adúltera**

adultez *f* adulthood

adul•to -ta *adj* & *mf* adult

adulzar §60 *tr* to sweeten; (*metales*) soften

adunar *tr* to join, bring together

adundar *ref* (CAm) to become stupid

adus•to -ta *adj* grim, stern, gloomy; scorching hot

advenedi•zo -za *adj* strange; foreign ‖ *mf* stranger; foreigner; outsider; parvenu, upstart; nouveau riche

advenimiento *m* advent, coming; accession; **esperar el santo advenimiento** to wait in vain

advenir §79 *intr* to come, arrive; happen

adverbio *m* adverb

adversa•rio -ria *mf* adversary

adversidad *f* adversity

advertencia *f* observation; notice, remark; warning; preface

adverti•do -da *adj* capable, clever, wide-awake

advertir §68 *tr* to notice, observe; notify, warn; point out ‖ *ref* to become aware

Adviento *m* (eccl) Advent

adyacente *adj* adjacent

aeración *f* aeration; ventilation; air conditioning

aére•o -a *adj* air, aerial; overhead, elevated; airy, light, fanciful

aerodinámi•co -ca *adj* aerodynamic ‖ *f* aerodynamics

aeródromo *m* aerodrome, airdrome; **aeródromo de urgencia** emergency-landing field

aerofluyente *adj* streamlined

aeroespacial *adj* aerospace

aerofumigación *f* crop dusting

aeromedicina *f* aviation medicine

aeromodelismo *m* model-airplane building

aeromodelista *mf* model-airplane builder

aeromodelo *m* model airplane

aeromotor *m* windmill; airplane motor

aeromoza *f* air hostess, stewardess

aeronáuti•co -ca *adj* aeronautic ‖ *f* aeronautics

aeronave *f* airship; **aeronave cohete** rocket ship

aeropista *f* landing strip

aeroplano *m* aeroplane

aeroposta *f* air mail

aeropostal *adj* air-mail

aeropropulsor *m* airplane engine; **aeropropulsor por reacción** jet engine

aeropuerto *m* airport

aeroscala *f* transit point

aerosol *m* aerosol

aeroste•ro -ra *adj* aviation ‖ *m* flyer; airman

aerotaxi *m* air taxi

aeroterrestre *adj* air-ground

aerovía *f* airway

afable *adj* affable, friendly, agreeable

afama•do -da *adj* noted, famous

afamar *tr* to make famous ‖ *ref* to become famous

afán *m* hard work; eagerness, zeal; task; worry

afanar *tr* to press, hurry ‖ *intr* to strive, toil ‖ *ref* to strive, toil; busy oneself

afano•so -sa *adj* hard, laborious; hard-working

afarolar *ref* to make a fuss, get excited

afear *tr* to deface, disfigure; blame
afeblecer §22 *intr* to grow feeble, get thin
afección *f* affection, fondness; (med) affection
afectación *f* affectation
afecta•do -da *adj* affected; **estar afectado de** (*p.ej., los riñones*) to have (*e.g., kidney*) trouble
afectar *tr* to affect; hurt, injure ‖ *ref* to be moved, be stirred
afecti•vo -va *adj* emotional
afec•to -ta *adj* fond; kind; affected; **afecto a** fond of; (*un empleo, un servicio, etc.*) attached to; **afecto de** suffering from ‖ *m* affection, fondness; emotion
afectuo•so -sa *adj* affectionate; kind
afeitado *m* shave; **afeitado a ras** close shave
afeitar *tr* to shave; adorn; ‖ *ref* to shave; paint
afeite *m* cosmetics, rouge, make-up
afeminación *f* effeminacy
afemina•do -da *adj* effeminate
afeminar *tr* to effeminate ‖ *ref* to become effeminate
aferra•do -da *adj* stubborn, obstinate
aferrar *tr* to seize; catch; hook; (naut) to moor; (naut) to furl ‖ *ref* to interlock, hook together; cling; insist
Afganistán, el Afghanistan
afga•no -na *adj & mf* Afghan
afianzar §60 *tr* to guarantee, vouch for; bail; fasten; prop up; grasp; support ‖ *ref* to hold fast, steady oneself
afición *f* fondness, liking, taste; ardor, zeal; fans, public
aficiona•do -da *adj* fond; amateur; **aficionado a** fond of ‖ *mf* amateur; fan, follower
aficionar *tr* to win, win the attachment of ‖ *ref* — **aficionarse a** or **de** to become fond of; become a follower of, become a fan of
afiebra•do -da *adj* feverish
afiebrar *ref* (SAm) to get a fever
afi•jo -ja *adj* affixed ‖ *m* affix
afila•do -da *adj* sharp; tapering; pointed; peaked
afilador *m* grinder, sharpener; razor strop
afilalápi•ces *m* (*pl* -ces) pencil sharpener
afilar *tr* to grind, sharpen; (*una navaja de afeitar*) strop; (Arg & Urug) to flirt with ‖ *ref* to sharpen, get sharp; taper, get thin
afiliar §77 & **regular** *tr* to affiliate, take in ‖ *ref* — **afiliarse a** to join
afiligranar *tr* to filigree; adorn, embellish
afilón *m* knife sharpener; razor strop
afín *adj* near, bordering; like, similar; related ‖ *mf* relative by marriage
afinador *m* tuner; tuning hammer, tuning key
afinar *tr* to purify, refine, perfect; trim; tune
afincar §73 *intr & ref* to buy up real estate
afinidad *f* affinity; **por afinidad** by marriage
afirmar *tr* to strengthen, secure, fasten; assert ‖ *ref* to hold fast; steady oneself
afirmati•vo -va *adj & f* affirmative
aflicción *f* affliction; sorrow, grief
afligir §27 *tr* to afflict, grieve; (Mex) to beat, whip ‖ *ref* to grieve
aflojar *tr* to slacken, let go; loosen ‖ *intr* to slacken, slow up; abate, lessen ‖ *ref* to come loose; slacken
aflora•do -da *adj* flour; fine, elegant
aflorar *tr* to sift ‖ *intr* to crop out
afluencia *f* flowing; affluence, abundance; crowd, jam, rush; fluency; **horas de afluencia** rush hour
afluente *adj* flowing; abundant; fluent ‖ *m* tributary
afluir §20 *intr* to flow; pour, flock
afmo. *abbr* **afectísimo**
afofar *tr* to make fluffy, make spongy
afonizar §60 *tr & ref* to unvoice
aforar *tr* to gauge, measure; appraise
aforismo *m* aphorism
afortuna•do -da *adj* fortunate; happy
afrancesa•do -da *adj & mf* Francophile
afrecho *m* bran
afrenta *f* affront
afrentar *tr* to affront ‖ *ref* to be ashamed
afrento•so -sa *adj* outrageous, disgraceful
Africa *f* Africa
africa•no -na *adj & mf* African
afrodísía•co -ca *adj & m* aphrodisiac
afrontamiento *m* confrontation
afrontar *tr* to bring face to face; defy ‖ *ref* — **afrontarse con** to confront, meet face to face
afuera *adv* outside ‖ *interj* clear the way!, look out! ‖ **afueras** *fpl* outskirts, environs
afuetada *f* or **afuetadura** *f* (SAm) beating
agachadiza *f* snipe; **hacer la agachadiza** to duck
agachar *tr* to lower, bend down ‖ *ref* to crouch, squat; cower; (SAm) to give in, yield
agalla *f* gallnut; (*de pez*) gill; (*de ave*) ear lobe; **agallas** courage, guts
ágape *m* banquet, love feast
agarradera *f* hold, grip; handle; **tener agarraderas** to have connections
agarrada *f* brawl, fight, scrap
agarra•do -da *adj* stingy, tight ‖ *f* see **agarrada**
agarrar *tr* to grab, grasp; take hold of; get, obtain ‖ *intr* to take hold; take root; stick ‖ *ref* to grapple; have a good hold; worry; **agarrarse a** to take hold of, cling to
agarro *m* clench, clutch, grip
agarrochar *tr* to jab with a goad
agarrón *m* brawl, fight; grip, tug
agarrotar *tr* to garrote; bind, tie up ‖ *ref* to become numb
agasajar *tr* to regale, lionize, make a fuss over
agasajo *m* kindness, attention; lionization; favor, gift; treat; party
agavillar *tr* to bind or tie in sheaves ‖ *ref* to band together
agazapar *tr* to grab, to nab ‖ *ref* to crouch; to hide
agencia *f* agency; bureau; (Chile) pawn shop; **agencia de noticias** news agency; **agencia matrimonial** marriage broker
agenciar *tr* to manage to bring about; promote ‖ *ref* to manage
agenda *f* notebook

agente *m* agent; policeman; **agente de policía** policeman; **agente viajero** traveling salesman, commercial traveler

agigantar *tr* to make huge ‖ *ref* to become huge

ágil *adj* agile; flexible, light

agilitar *tr* & *ref* to limber up

agita•do -da *adj* agitated, excited, exalted; (*mar*) rough

agitar *tr* to agitate; shake; wave; stir ‖ *intr* to agitate ‖ *ref* to be agitated; shake; wave; get excited; (*el mar*) get rough

aglomeración *f* agglomeration; crowd; built-up area

aglomerado *m* briquet, coal briquet

aglutinar *tr* to stick together ‖ *ref* to cake

agnósti•co -ca *adj* & *mf* agnostic

agobiar *tr* to overburden; exhaust, oppress

agolpar *ref* to flock, throng

agonía *f* agony, throes of death; agony, anguish; yearning; craving

agonizar §60 *tr* (*al moribundo*) to assist, attend; harass ‖ *intr* to be in the throes of death

agorar §3 *tr* to augur, foretell

agore•ro -ra *adj* fortunetelling; ill-omened; superstitious ‖ *mf* fortuneteller

agostar *tr* to burn up, to parch ‖ *ref* to dry up; (*la esperanza, la felicidad*) fade away

agostero *m* harvest helper

agosto *m* August; harvest; harvest time; **hacer su agosto** to make hay while the sun shines

agota•do -da *adj* exhausted; sold out; out of print

agotar *tr* to exhaust, wear out, use up ‖ *ref* to become exhausted, be used up; go out of print; run out

agracia•do -da *adj* charming, graceful; nice, pretty ‖ *mf* winner

agradable *adj* agreeable; pleasant

agradar *tr* to please ‖ *intr* to be pleasing ‖ *ref* to be pleased

agradecer §22 *tr* to thank; **agradecerle a uno una cosa** to thank someone for something

agradeci•do -da *adj* thankful, grateful; rewarding

agradecimiento *m* thanks, gratitude

agrado *m* agreeableness, graciousness; pleasure, liking

agrandar *tr* to enlarge ‖ *ref* to grow larger

agranelar *tr* (*cuero*) to grain, pebble

agrapar *tr* to clamp

agrariense *adj* & *mf* agrarian

agra•rio -ria *adj* agrarian

agravar *tr* to weigh down; aggravate; exaggerate; oppress ‖ *ref* to get worse

agraviar *tr* to wrong, offend ‖ *ref* to take offense

agravio *m* wrong, offense; **agravios de hecho** assault and battery

agravio•so -sa *adj* offensive, insulting

agraz *m* (*pl* **agraces**) sour grape; sour-grape juice; bitterness, displeasure; **en agraz** prematurely

agredir §1 *tr* to attack, assault

agregado *m* aggregate; concrete block; attaché; (Arg) tenant farmer

agregar §44 *tr* to add; attach; appoint ‖ *ref* to join

agremiado *m* union member

agremiar *tr* to unionize

agresión *f* aggression

agresi•vo -va *adj* aggressive

agre•sor -sora *adj* aggressive ‖ *mf* aggressor

agreste *adj* country, rustic; wild, rough; uncouth

agriar §77 & *regular tr* to make sour; exasperate ‖ *ref* to turn sour; become exasperated

agrícola *adj* agricultural ‖ *mf* farmer

agricultura *f* agriculture

agridulce *adj* bittersweet

agriera *f* (Chile) heartburn; **agrieras** (Col) cruet stand

agrietar *tr* & *ref* to crack

agrimensor *m* surveyor

agrimensura *f* surveying

agringar §44 *ref* to act like a gringo

a•grio -gria *adj* sour, acrid; uneven, rough; brittle ‖ **agrios** *mpl* citrus fruit

agronomía *f* agronomy

agropecua•rio -ria *adj* land-and-cattle, farm

agrumar *tr* & *ref* to curd, clot

agrupar *tr* & *ref* to group, cluster

agrura *f* sourness; unpleasantness; **agruras** citrus fruit

agua *f* water; (*de un tejado*) slope; **agua abajo** downstream; **agua arriba** upstream; **agua bendita** holy water; **agua corriente** running water; **agua de Colonia** eau de Cologne; **agua de marea** tidewater; **agua gaseosa** carbonated water; **agua oxigenada** hydrogen peroxide; **aguas** mineral springs; (*de sedas; de piedras preciosas*) water, sparkle; **aguas mayores** equinoctial tide; feces; **aguas menores** ordinary tide; urination; **cubrir aguas** to have under roof; **entre dos aguas** under water, under the surface of the water; (coll) undecided

aguacate *m* avocado, alligator pear; pear-shaped emerald

aguacero *m* shower

aguada *f* source of water; water color; watering station

aguade•ro -ra *adj* water ‖ *m* watering place

agua•do -da *adj* watery; thin, watered; weak, washed out, limp; dull, insipid ‖ *f* see **aguada**

agua•dor -dora *mf* water carrier ‖ *m* paddle, bucket

aguafies•tas *mf* (*pl* **-tas**) kill-joy, wet blanket, crapehanger

aguafortista *mf* etcher

aguafuerte *f* etching; **grabar al aguafuerte** to etch

aguaitar *intr* to spy, watch ‖ *tr* to watch, wait for

aguaje *m* watering place; tidal wave; strong current; (*de buque*) wake

aguamala *f* jellyfish

aguamanil *m* ewer, wash pitcher; washstand

aguama•nos *m* (*pl* **-nos**) water for washing hands; washstand

aguamarina *f* aquamarine

aguanie•ves *f* (*pl* **-ves**) wagtail

aguano•so -sa *adj* watery, soaked

aguantada *f* patience, forbearance

aguantar *tr* to hold up, sustain; bear, endure, tolerate; hold back, control ‖ *intr* to last, hold out ‖ *ref* to restrain oneself; keep quiet; **aguantarse las lágrimas** to swallow one's tears

aguante *m* patience, endurance; strength, vigor

aguar §10 *tr* to water; spoil, mar ‖ *ref* to become watery; fill up with water; be spoiled

aguardar *tr* to await, wait for; grant time to ‖ *intr* to wait; **aguardar a que** to wait until

aguardentera *f* liquor bottle, brandy flask

aguardentería *f* liquor store

aguardento•so -sa *adj* brandy; (*voz*) whiskey

aguardiente *m* brandy; spirituous liquor; **aguardiente de caña** rum; **aguardiente de manzana** applejack

aguardo *m* hunter's blind

aguarrás *m* turpentine, oil of turpentine

aguasar *ref* (Arg & Chile) to become countrified

aguazal *m* swamp, pool

agudeza *f* acuteness, acuity; sharpness; witticism; **agudeza visual** visual acuity

agu•do -da *adj* acute; sharp; keen; witty

agüero *m* augury; omen; forecast

aguerri•do -da *adj* inured, hardened

aguijada *f* goad, spur; prod

aguijar *tr* to goad, spur, prod ‖ *intr* to hurry along

aguijón *m* goad, spur; sting; thorn; stimulus; **dar coces contra el aguijón** to kick against the pricks

aguijonear to goad, incite; sting

águila *f* eagle; **¿águila o sol?** (Mex) heads or tails?; **ser un águila** to be wide-awake, be a wizard

aguile•ño -ña *adj* aquiline; sharp-featured

aguilón *m* (*de grúa*) boom, jib; (*del tejado*) gable

aguinaldo *m* Christmas gift, Epiphany gift; Christmas carol

aguja *f* needle; hatpin; steeple, spire; (*del reloj*) hand; **aguja de gancho** crochet needle; **aguja de hacer media** knitting needle; **aguja de zurcir** darning needle; **agujas** (rr) switch; **buscar una aguja en un pajar** to look for a needle in a haystack

agujerear *tr* to make a hole in, pierce, perforate

agujero *m* hole; pincushion; **agujero negro** black hole

agujeta *f* (*de la jeringa*) needle; shoestring; **agujetas** stitches, twinges

agusanar *ref* to get wormy; become worm-eaten

aguzanie•ves *f* (*pl* **-ves**) wagtail

aguzar §60 *tr* to sharpen; incite, stir up; stare at; (*las orejas*) prick up

ah-chís *interj* kerchoo!

aherrojar *tr* to fetter, shackle; oppress

aherrumbrar *tr* & *ref* to rust

ahí *adv* there; **de ahí que** hence; **por ahí** that way

ahija•do -da *mf* godchild; protégé ‖ *m* godson ‖ *f* goddaughter

ahilar *ref* to faint from hunger; waste away; grow poorly; turn sour

ahincar §73 *tr* to urge, press; importune ‖ *ref* to hasten

ahinco *m* earnestness, zeal, eagerness

ahitar *tr* to cloy, surfeit, stuff

ahi•to -ta *adj* surfeited, stuffed; fed up, disgusted ‖ *m* surfeit; indigestion

ahoga•do -da *adj* drowned; smothered; sunk; close, unventilated; **mate ahogado** stalemate; **perecer ahogado** to drown; **verse ahogado** to be swamped

ahogar §44 *tr* to drown; suffocate, smother; (*cal*) slake; (*plantas*) soak; oppress; extinguish; stalemate ‖ *ref* to drown; suffocate; drown oneself

ahogo *m* shortness of breath; great sorrow; stringency

ahondar *tr* to make deeper; go deep into ‖ *intr* to go deep, go deeper

ahora *adv* now; presently; **ahora bien** now then, so then; **ahora mismo** right now; **por ahora** for the present

ahorcajar *ref* to sit astride

ahorcar §73 *tr* to hang ‖ *ref* to hang, be hanged; hang oneself

ahorra•do -da *adj* saving, thrifty

ahorrar *tr* to save; spare ‖ *ref* to save or spare oneself

ahorrati•vo -va *adj* saving, thrifty; stingy ‖ *f* economy

ahorro *m* economy; **ahorros** savings

ahuchar *tr* to hoard

ahuecar §73 *tr* to hollow, hollow out; loosen, fluff up; **ahuecar la voz** to speak in deep and solemn tones ‖ *ref* to be puffed up

ahula•do -da *adj* waterproof, impermeable *m* overshoe

ahumar *tr* to smoke ‖ *intr* to be smoky ‖ *ref* to get smoked up; look or taste smoky; get drunk

ahusar *tr* & *ref* to taper

ahuyentar *tr* to put to flight; scare away ‖ *ref* to flee, run away

aira•do -da *adj* angry; wild; depraved

airar §4 *tr* to anger ‖ *ref* to get angry

aire *m* air; **al aire libre** in the open air; **darse aires** to put on airs

airear *tr* to air, aerate, ventilate ‖ *ref* to get aired; catch cold

airón *m* aigrette, panache; gray heron

airo•so -sa *adj* airy; drafty; graceful, light; resplendent; successful

aislación *f* insulation

aislacionista *adj* & *mf* isolationist

aislador *m* insulator

aislamiento *m* isolation; (elec) insulation

aislar §4 *tr* to isolate; detach, separate; (elec) to insulate ‖ *ref* to live in seclusion

ajar *m* garlic field ‖ *tr* to crumple, muss; (*marchitar*) wither; tamper with; abuse, ill-treat ‖ *ref* to get mussed; wither

ajedrea *f* (bot) savory

ajedrecista *mf* chess player

ajedrez *m* chess; chess set

ajenjo *m* (*Artemisia*) wormwood; (*licor*) absinthe; (*sinsabores y penas*) (fig) wormwood, bitterness; **ajenjo del campo** or **ajenjo mayor** (*Artemisia absinthium*) wormwood

aje•no -na *adj* another's; extraneous, foreign; different; contrary; free; insane; uninformed; **lo ajeno** what belongs to someone else

ajetrear *tr* to drive, harass ‖ *ref* to bustle about; fidget

ajetreo *m* bustle, fuss

ají *m* (*pl* **ajíes**) chili; chili sauce; **ponerse como un ají** (Chile) to turn red as a tomato

aji•mez *m* (*pl* **-meces**) mullioned window

ajo *m* garlic; garlic clove; garlic sauce

ajorca *f* bracelet, anklet

ajornalar *tr* to hire by the day ‖ *ref* to hire out by the day

ajuar *m* housefurnishings; trousseau

ajuiciar *tr* to bring to one's senses ‖ *ref* to come to one's senses

ajustable *adj* adjustable

ajusta•do -da *adj* just, right; tight, close-fitting

ajustar *tr* to adapt, fit, adjust; hire; arrange; reconcile; fasten; settle ‖ *intr* to fit ‖ *ref* to fit; hire out; be hired; come to an agreement

ajuste *m* fit; fitting, adjustment; hiring; arrangement; reconciliation; settlement; agreement

ajusticiar *tr* to execute, put to death

ala *f* wing; (*del sombrero*) brim; (*de puerta, mesa, etc.*) leaf; (*de pez*) fin; (*de hélice*) blade; (football) end; **ahuecar el ala** to beat it; **ala en flecha** (aer) sweptback wing; **alas** boldness, courage; **volar con sus propias alas** to stand on one's own feet

Alá *m* Allah

alabanza *f* praise

alabar *tr* to praise ‖ *ref* to boast

alabarda *f* halberd

alabardero *m* halberdier; hired applauder, claqueur

alabastro *m* alabaster

álabe *m* drooping branch; bucket, paddle; cog

alabear *tr* & *ref* to warp

alacena *f* cupboard, wall closet; (naut) locker; (Mex) booth, stall

alacrán *m* scorpion

ala•do -da *adj* winged

alamar *m* frog (*button and loop on a garment*)

alambica•do -da *adj* precious, oversubtle, fine-spun; begrudged

alambicar §73 *tr* to distill; refine to excess

alambique *m* still, alembic; (*de laboratorio*) retort; **por alambique** sparingly

alambrada *f* chicken wire; wire mesh; (mil) barbed wire; (elec) wiring

alambrado *m* chicken wire; wire mesh; wire fence; (elec) wiring; (mil) wire entanglement

alambraje *m* (elec) wiring

alambrar *tr* to fence with wire; string with wire; wire

alambre *m* wire; **alambre cargado** live wire; **alambre de púas** barbed wire; **alambre sin aislar** bare wire

alambrera *f* wire screen; wire cover

alameda *f* poplar grove; mall, shaded walk

álamo *m* poplar; **álamo de Italia** Lombardy poplar; **álamo negro** black poplar; **álamo temblón** aspen

alampar *ref* to have a craving

alancear *tr* to lance, spear

alano *m* mastiff, great Dane

alarde *m* display, ostentation; (mil) review; **hacer alarde de** to make a show of; boast of

alardear *intr* to boast, brag, show off

alardo•so -sa *adj* showy, ostentatious

alargar §44 *tr* to extend, lengthen, stretch; hand; to increase; let out ‖ *ref* to go away, withdraw; grow longer; be long-winded

alarido *m* howl, shout, yell, whoop

alarma *f* alarm; (aer) alert; **alarma aérea** air-raid warning; **alarma de incendios** fire alarm; **alarma de ladrones** burglar alarm

alarmar *tr* to alarm; alert ‖ *ref* to become alarmed

alarmista *mf* alarmist

alastrar *tr* (*las orejas*) to throw back; (naut) to ballast ‖ *ref* to lie flat, cower

ala•zán -zana *adj* sorrel, reddish-brown ‖ *mf* sorrel horse

alba *f* dawn, daybreak

albacea *m* executor ‖ *f* executrix

albahaquero *m* flowerpot

alba•nés -nesa *adj* & *mf* Albanian

albañal *m* sewer, drain

albañil *m* mason, bricklayer

albañilería *f* masonry

albarán *m* rent sign; bulletin; (com) check list

albarca *f* sandal

albarda *f* packsaddle

albardilla *f* (*tejadillo sobre los muros*) coping; shoulder pad

albaricoque *m* apricot

albaricoquero *m* apricot tree

alba•tros *m* (*pl* **-tros**) albatross

albayalde *m* white lead

albear *intr* to turn white; (Arg) to get up at dawn

albedrío *m* free will; fancy, caprice, pleasure; **libre albedrío** free will

albéitar *m* veterinarian

alberca *f* pond, pool; tank, reservoir; **en alberca** roofless

albérchigo *m* clingstone peach

albergar §44 *tr* to shelter, harbor; house ‖ *intr* & *ref* to take shelter; take lodgings

albergue *m* shelter, refuge; lodging; den, lair

albero *m* dishcloth, dishrag; white earth

al•bo -ba *adj* (poet) white ‖ *f* see **alba**
albóndiga *f* meat ball, fish ball
albor *m* whiteness; dawn
alborada *f* dawn; morning serenade; reveille
alborear *intr* to dawn
albor•noz *m* (*pl* **-noces**) terry cloth; burnoose; cardigan; beach robe
alborota•do -da *adj* hasty, rash; noisy; rough
alborota•dor -dora *mf* agitator, rioter
alborotapue•blos *mf* (*pl* **-blos**) (coll) rabble rouser
alborotar *tr* to agitate, arouse, stir up ‖ *intr* to make a racket ‖ *ref* to get excited; riot; (*la mar*) get rough
alboroto *m* agitation, disturbance; noise, riot; **alborotos** (CAm) candied popcorn; **armar un alboroto** to raise a racket
alborozar §60 *tr* to gladden, cheer, overjoy, elate
alborozo *m* joy, merriment, elation
albricias *fpl* reward for good news; reward given on the occasion of some happy event; **en albricias de** as a token of ‖ *interj* good news!, congratulations!
albufera *f* saltwater lagoon
ál•bum *m* (*pl* **-bumes**) album; **álbum de recortes** scrapbook
albumen *m* albumen
albúmina *f* albumin
albuminar *tr* (phot) to emulsify
albur *m* risk, chance
alcachofa *f* artichoke
alcahue•te -ta *mf* bawd, procurer, go-between; screen, fence; schemer; gossip
alcahuetear *tr* to procure; harbor ‖ *intr* to pander
alcaide *m* governor, warden, jailer
alcalde *m* mayor, chief burgess; **alcalde de monterilla** small-town mayor; **tener el padre alcalde** to have a friend at court
alcaldesa *f* mayoress
álcali *m* alkali
alcali•no -na *adj* alkaline
alcallería *f* pottery
alcana *f* henna
alcance *m* reach, scope, extent; range; pursuit; capacity; late news; import; coverage; brains, intelligence; **al alcance de** within reach of, within range of; **alcance de la vista** eyesight, eyeshot; **alcance del oído** earshot; **dar alcance a** to catch up with
alcancía *f* child's bank; bin, hopper
alcanfor *m* camphor
alcantarilla *f* sewer; culvert
alcantarillar *tr* to sewer
alcanza•do -da *adj* needy, hard up
alcanzar §60 *tr* to reach; overtake, catch up to; grasp; obtain; understand; live through ‖ *intr* to succeed; (*un arma de fuego*) carry; manage; suffice
alcaparrosa *f* vitriol
alcaravea *f* caraway
alcatraz *m* gannet, pelican
alcázar *m* fortress; castle, royal palace; quarterdeck
alce *m* elk, moose
alcista *adj* bullish ‖ *mf* (fig) bull

alcoba *f* bedroom; **alcoba de respeto** master bedroom
alcohol *m* alcohol
alcohóli•co -ca *adj* & *mf* alcoholic
alconafta *f* gasohol
alcor *m* hill, elevation, eminence
alcornoque *m* cork oak; blockhead
alcorque *m* cork-soled shoe; trench for water around a tree
alcorza *f* sugar paste, sugar icing; **ser una alcorza** (Arg) to be highly emotional
alcurnia *f* ancestry, lineage
alcuza *f* olive-oil can
aldaba *f* knocker, door knocker; bolt, crossbar; latch; hitching ring; **aldaba dormida** deadlatch; **tener buenas aldabas** to have pull
aldabonazo *m* knock on the door
aldea *f* village, hamlet
aldea•no -na *adj* village; rustic ‖ *mf* villager
aleación *f* alloy
alear *tr* to alloy ‖ *intr* to flap the wings; to flap one's arms; to convalesce
aleccionar *tr* to teach, instruct; to train, to coach
aleda•ño -ña *adj* bordering ‖ *m* border, boundary
alega•dor -dora *adj* quarrelsome; litigious
alegar §44 *tr* to allege; to declare, assert ‖ *intr* (Col, Hond) to quarrel
alegoría *f* allegory
alegóri•co -ca *adj* allegoric(al)
alegrar *tr* to cheer, gladden; (*un fuego*) to stir ‖ *ref* to be glad, to rejoice; to get tipsy
alegre *adj* glad; bright; cheerful, light-hearted; careless; fast, spicy; **alegre de cascos** scatterbrained
alegría *f* cheer, joy, gladness; brightness, gaiety
aleja•do -da *adj* distant, remote
alejandri•no -na *adj* & *mf* Alexandrine
alejar *tr* & *ref* to move aside, move away
alelar *tr* to make stupid ‖ *ref* to grow stupid
aleluya *m* & *f* hallelujah ‖ *m* Easter time ‖ *f* doggerel; daub; **aleluya navideña** Christmas card ‖ *interj* hallelujah!
ale•mán -mana *adj* & *mf* German
Alemania *f* Germany
alenta•do -da *adj* brave, spirited; proud, haughty; well, healthy ‖ *f* deep breath
alentar §2 *tr* to encourage, cheer up ‖ *intr* to breathe ‖ *ref* to take heart; get well, recover
alerce *m* larch
alergia *f* allergy
alero *m* eaves
alerón *m* aileron
alerta *adv* on the alert ‖ *interj* watch out!, look out! ‖ *m* (mil) alert; (mil) watchword
alertar *tr* to alert
aler•to -ta *adj* alert, watchful, vigilant
alesaje *m* bore
alesna *f* awl
aleta *f* small wing; (*de pez*) fin; (*de hélice*) blade; **aletas** (*natación*) flippers
aletargar §44 *tr* to benumb; put to sleep ‖ *ref* to get drowsy, fall asleep

aletear *intr* to flap the wings; flap, flip, flutter

aleve *adj* treacherous, perfidious

alevosía *f* treachery, perfidy

alevo•so -sa *adj* treacherous, perfidious

alfabetizar §60 *tr* to alphabetize; teach reading and writing to

alfabeto *m* alphabet

alfaneque *m* buzzard

alfanje *m* cutlass

alfarería *f* pottery

alfarero *m* potter

alféizar *m* splay; embrasure

alfeñicar §73 *tr* to candy, ice ‖ *ref* to grow thin; be affected, finical

alfeñique *m* almond-flavored sugar paste; affectation, prudery; thin, delicate person; weakling

alfé•rez *m* (*pl* -**reces**) (mil) second lieutenant; (mil) subaltern (Brit); **alférez de fragata** (nav) ensign; **alférez de navío** (nav) lieutenant (j.g.)

alfil *m* bishop

alfiler *m* pin; **alfiler de corbata** stickpin, scarfpin; **alfiler de madera** clothespin; **alfiler de seguridad** safety pin; **alfileres** pin money

alfilerar *tr* to pin, pin up

alfiletero *m* pincase, needlecase

alfombra *f* carpet; rug

alfombrar *tr* to carpet

alforfón *m* buckwheat

alforja *f* shoulder bag; traveling supplies; **pasarse a la otra alforja** to go too far, take too much liberty

alforza *f* pleat, tuck

al•foz *m* (*pl* -**foces**) outskirts; dependence; mountain pass

alga *f* alga; **alga marina** seaweed; **algas** algae

algaida *f* brush, thicket; sandbank

algalia *f* civet; catheter

algarabía *f* Arabic; (coll) gibberish, jabber; (coll) hubbub, uproar

algarada *f* outcry; uproar

algarroba *f* carob bean

algarrobo *m* carob

algazara *f* Moorish battle cry; din, uproar

álgebra *f* algebra

algebrai•co -ca *adj* algebraic

álgi•do -da *adj* cold, icy, frigid

algo *pron indef* something; anything; **algo por el estilo** something of the sort ‖ *adv* somewhat, a little, rather

algodón *m* cotton; **algodón pólvora** guncotton; **estar criado entre algodones** to be brought up in comfort

algodoncillo *m* milkweed

algodono•so -sa *adj* cottony

alguacil *m* bailiff; mounted police officer at the head of the processional entrance of the bullfighters

alguien *pron indef* somebody, someone

algún *adj indef* apocopated form of **alguno**, used only before masculine singular nouns and adjectives

algu•no -na *adj indef* some, any; not any; **alguna vez** sometimes; ever ‖ *pron indef* someone; **algunos** some

alhaja *f* jewel, gem; **buena alhaja** a bad egg, a sly fellow

alhajera *f* or **alhajero** *m* jewelry box

alharaca *f* fuss, ado, ballyhoo; **hacer alharacas** to make a fuss

alharaquien•to -ta *adj* fussy, noisy

alhe•lí *m* (*pl* -**líes**) gillyflower (*Matthiola incana*); wallflower (*Cheiranthus*)

alheña *f* henna; blight, mildew

alheñar *tr* to henna; blight, mildew ‖ *ref* (*el pelo*) to henna

alhucema *f* lavender

alhumajo *m* pine needles

alia•do -da *adj* allied ‖ *mf* ally

aliaga *f* furze, gorse

alianza *f* alliance; wedding ring; (Bib) covenant

aliar §77 *tr* to ally ‖ *ref* to ally, become allied; form an alliance

alias *adj* & *m* alias

alicaí•do -da *adj* failing, weak; crestfallen, discouraged

alicates *mpl* pliers

aliciente *m* inducement, incentive

alienar *tr* to alienate; enrapture

aliento *m* breath, breathing; courage, spirit; **dar aliento a** to encourage; **de mucho aliento** arduous, difficult, endless; **nuevo aliento** second wind; **sin aliento** out of breath

alifafe *m* complaint, indisposition

aligerar *tr* to lighten; alleviate, ease; hasten; shorten

aligustre *m* privet

alijador *m* lighter; lighterman; sander

alijar *tr* to unload, lighten; sandpaper

aligeramiento *m* easing; alleviation; **aligeramiento de impuestos** tax relief

alimaña *f* varmint, small predacious animal

alimentante *mf* person obliged to provide child support

alimentar *tr* to feed, nourish; (*p.ej., esperanzas*) to cherish, foster ‖ *ref* to feed, nourish oneself

alimenti•cio -cia *adj* alimentary, nourishing

alimento *m* food, nourishment; encouragement; **alimentos** foodstuffs; allowance; alimony

alindar *tr* to mark off; embellish, prettify ‖ *intr* to border, be contiguous

alinea•do -da *adj* lined up, aligned; **no alineado** nonaligned, Third World

alinear *tr* & *ref* to align, line up

aliñar *tr* to dress, season

aliño *m* dressing, seasoning

aliquebra•do -da *adj* crestfallen

alisar *tr* to smooth; polish, sleek; iron lightly

aliso *m* alder tree

alistar *tr* to list; enlist, enroll; stripe ‖ *ref* to enlist, enroll; get ready

aliteración *f* alliteration

aliviar *tr* to alleviate, relieve, soothe; remedy; lighten; hasten ‖ *ref* to get better, recover

alivio *m* alleviation, relief; remedy
aljaba *f* quiver
aljama *f* mosque; synagogue; Moorish quarter; ghetto
aljamía *f* Spanish of Moors and Jews; Spanish written in Arabic characters
aljez *m* gypsum
aljibe *m* water tender, tank barge; oil tanker; cistern
aljófar *m* imperfect pearl; (fig) dewdrops
aljofifa *f* floor mop
aljofifar *tr* to mop
alma *f* soul, heart, spirit; (*persona*) living soul; crux, heart; sweetheart; (*de carril*) web; (*de cañón*) bore; (*de escalera*) newel; **dar el alma, entregar el alma, rendir el alma** to give up the ghost
almacén *m* warehouse; store, department store; storehouse; (phot) magazine
almacenaje *m* storage; **almacenaje de datos** (*ordenador*) data storage, memory
almacenamiento *m* storage; (*ordenador*) data storage, memory
almacenar *tr* to store; store up, hoard; to store (electronic) data
almacenista *mf* storekeeper ‖ *m* warehouseman
almáciga *f* seedbed, tree nursery
almádana *f* spalling hammer
almagre *m* red ocher
almajara *f* (hort) hotbed
almanaque *m* almanac; calendar
almeja *f* clam
almena *f* merlon
almenaje *m* battlement
almendra *f* almond; (*de cualquier fruto drupáceo*) kernel; **almendra amarga** bitter almond; **almendra de Málaga** Jordan almond; **almendra tostada** burnt almond
almendrado *m* macaroon
almendro *m* almond tree
almiar *m* haystack, hayrick
almíbar *m* simple syrup; fruit juice; **estar hecho un almíbar** to be as sweet as pie
almibarar *tr* to preserve in syrup; (*sus palabras*) honey ‖ *intr* to candy
almidón *m* starch; paste; **almidón de maíz** cornstarch
almidona•do -da *adj* starched; spruce, dapper; stiff, prim
almidonar *tr* to starch
alminar *m* minaret
almiranta *f* admiral's wife; flagship
almirante *m* admiral
almi•rez *m* (*pl* **-reces**) brass mortar
almizcle *m* musk
almizclera *f* muskrat
almizclero *m* musk deer
almohada *f* pillow; **consultar con la almohada** to sleep it over
almohadilla *f* cushion; pad; (Chile) pincushion
almohaza *f* currycomb
almohazar §60 *tr* to currycomb
almoneda *f* auction; clearance sale
almonedar *tr* to auction
almorranas *fpl* piles, hemorrhoids

almorta *f* grass pea
almorzada *f* double handful, heavy breakfast
almorzar §35 *tr* to lunch on ‖ *intr* to lunch, have lunch
almuecín *m* or **almuédano** *m* muezzin
almuerzo *m* lunch
alna•do -da *mf* stepchild
aloca•do -da *adj* mad, wild, reckless ‖ *mf* madcap
alocar §73 *tr* to drive crazy
alocución *f* address, speech
áloe *m* or **aloe** *m* aloe; aloes
alojar *tr* to lodge; quarter, billet ‖ *intr & ref* to lodge; be quartered or billeted
alojo *m* accommodations, lodging
alondra *f* lark
aloquecer §22 *ref* to go crazy, lose one's mind
alosa *f* shad
alpaca *f* alpaca; alpaca wool; alpaca cloth; German silver
alpargata *f* hemp sandal, espadrille
alpende *m* tool shed; lean-to, penthouse
Alpes *mpl* Alps
alpestre *adj* alpine
alpinismo *m* mountain climbing
alpi•no -na *adj* alpine
alpiste *m* canary seed, birdseed; **quedarse alpiste** to be disappointed
alquería *f* farmhouse
alquibla *f* kiblah
alquiladi•zo -za *adj & mf* hireling
alquilar *tr* to rent, let, hire ‖ *ref* to hire out; be for rent
alquiler *m* rent, rental, hire; **alquiler de coches** car-rental service; **alquiler sin chófer** drive-yourself service; **de alquiler** for rent, for hire
alquilona *f* cleaning woman, charwoman
alquimia *f* alchemy
alquitarar *tr* to distill
alquitrán *m* tar; **alquitrán de hulla** coal tar
alquitranado *m* tarpaulin
alquitranar *tr* to tar
alrededor *adv* around; **alrededor de** around; about, approximately ‖ **alrededores** *mpl* environs, surroundings, outskirts
Alsacia *f* Alsace
alsacia•no -na *adj & mf* Alsatian
alta *f* discharge from hospital; (mil) certificate of induction into active service; **dar de alta** to discharge from the hospital; **darse de alta** to join, be admitted; (mil) to report for duty
altane•ro -ra *adj* towering; arrogant, haughty
altar *m* altar; **altar mayor** high altar; **conducir al altar** to lead to the altar
alta•voz *m* (*pl* **-voces**) loudspeaker
altea *f* (bot) marshmallow
alteración *f* alteration; disturbance; uneven pulse; altercation, quarrel
alterar *tr* to alter; disturb; agitate, upset; falsify; lessen ‖ *ref* to alter; be disturbed; be agitated; lessen; (*el pulso*) flutter
altercación *f* or **altercado** *m* argument, wrangle, bickering
altercar §73 *intr* to argue, bicker, wrangle

alternar *tr & intr* to alternate; **alternar con** to go around with

alternati•vo -va *adj* alternating, alternative; *f* choice, option; admission as a matador; **no tener alternativa** to have no choice

alter•no -na *adj* alternate

alteza *f* sublimity ‖ **Alteza** *f* (*tratamiento*) Highness

altibajo *m* downward thrust; **altibajos** uneven ground; ups and downs

altillo *m* hillock; (*oficina en una tienda o taller*) balcony; (Arg, Ecuad) attic, garret

altimetría *f* altimetry

altiplanicie *f* tableland

altitud *f* altitude; height

altivez *f* or **altiveza** *f* arrogance, haughtiness, pride

alti•vo -va *adj* haughty, proud; high, lofty

al•to -ta *adj* high; upper; top; loud; (*horas*) late; **ponerse tan alto** to take offense, be hoity-toity ‖ *m* height, altitude; story, floor; stop, halt; **de alto a bajo** from top to bottom; **hacer alto** to stop; **pasar por alto** to overlook, disregard ‖ *f* see **alta** ‖ **alto** *adv* high up; loud; aloud ‖ **alto** *interj* halt!

altoparlante *m* loudspeaker

altozanero *m* (Col) public errand boy

altozano *m* hill, knoll; upper part of town; (CAm, Col, Ven) parvis

altruísta *adj* altruistic ‖ *mf* altruist

altura *f* height, altitude; high seas; juncture, point, stage; (mus) pitch; (naut) latitude; **a estas alturas** at this juncture; **a la altura de** (naut) off; **estar a la altura de** to be up to, be equal to; be abreast of; **por estas alturas** around here

alucinación *f* hallucination

alucinante *adj* hallucinogenic

alud *m* avalanche

aludi•do -da *adj* above-mentioned

aludir *intr* to allude

alumbra•do -da *adj* lighted; enlightened; tipsy ‖ *m* lighting; lighting system

alumbramiento *m* lighting; childbirth, accouchement

alumbrar *tr* to light, illuminate; (*a los ciegos*) give sight to; enlighten; (*aguas subterráneas*) discover and bring to the surface ‖ *intr* to have a child ‖ *ref* to get tipsy

alumbre *m* alum

aluminio *m* aluminum

alumnado *m* student body

alum•no -na *mf* (*niño criado como si fuera hijo*) foster child; (*discípulo*) pupil, student; **alumno mimado** teacher's pet

alunizaje *m* lunar landing

alunizar §60 *intr* to land on the moon

alusión *f* allusion

álveo *m* bed of a stream, river bed

alvéolo *m* alveolus; (*de diente*) socket; (*de rueda de agua*) bucket

alza *f* rise, advance. increase; **jugar al alza** to bull the market

alzada *f* height (*e.g., of a horse*)

alza•do -da *adj* (SAm) insolent; rebellious; *m* lump sum, cash settlement; front elevation; (bb) quire, gathering

alzapaño *m* curtain holder; tieback

alzapié *m* snare, trap

alzaprima *f* crowbar, lever; (*de instrumento de arco*) (mus) bridge

alzaprimar *tr* to pry, pry up; arouse, stir up

alzapuer•tas *m* (*pl* -**tas**) (archaic) dumb player, supernumerary

alzar §60 *tr* to raise, lift, hoist; pick up; (*la hostia*) elevate; hide, lock up; (*naipes*) cut; (bb) to gather ‖ *ref* to rise, get up; revolt; **alzarse con** to abscond with

alzaválvu•las *m* (*pl* -**las**) tappet

alzo *m* (CAm) theft

allá *adv* there, over there; back there; **allá en** over in; back in; **el más allá** the beyond; **más allá** farther on, farther away; **más allá de** beyond; **por allá** thereabouts; that way

allanar *tr* to level, smooth, flatten; (*una dificultad*) iron out, overcome, get around; (*una casa*) break into; to subdue ‖ *intr* to level off ‖ *ref* to tumble down; yield; submit; humble oneself

allega•do -da *adj* near, close; related; partisan ‖ *mf* relative; partisan

allegar §44 *tr* to collect, gather; reap ‖ *intr* to approach ‖ *ref* to approach; be attached, be a follower, agree

allende *adv* beyond; **allende de** besides, in addition to ‖ *prep* beyond

allí *adv* there; **allí dentro** in there; **por allí** that way; around there

ama *f* housekeeper; housewife, lady of the house; landlady, proprietress; **ama de casa** housewife; **ama de cría** or **de leche** wet nurse; **ama de llaves** housekeeper; **ama seca** dry nurse

amable *adj* amiable, kind, obliging; (*digno de ser amado*) lovable

amachinar *ref* to cohabit; get intimate

ama•do -da *adj & mf* beloved

ama•dor -dora *adj* fond, loving ‖ *mf* lover

amadrigar §44 *tr* to welcome, receive with open arms ‖ *ref* to burrow; go into seclusion

amaestrar *tr* to teach, coach; (*a los animales*) train

amagar §44 *tr* to show signs of, threaten; feint ‖ *intr* to look threatening

amago *m* threat, menace; sign, indication; feint

amainar *tr* to lessen; (naut) to lower, shorten ‖ *intr* to subside, die down; lessen; yield ‖ *ref* to lessen; yield

amalgama *f* amalgam

amalgamar *tr & ref* to amalgamate

amamantar *tr* to nurse, to suckle

amancebamiento *m* cohabitation, concubinage, liaison

amancebar *ref* to cohabit, live in concubinage

amancillar *tr* to stain, spot; sully, tarnish

amanecer *m* dawn, daybreak ‖ *v* §22 *intr* to dawn, begin to get light; begin to appear; get awake, start the day

amanecida *f* dawn, daybreak
amanera•do -da *adj* mannered, affected
amansar *tr* (*animal*) to tame; (*caballo*) break; soothe, appease
amante *adj* fond, loving ‖ *mf* lover
amaño *m* skill, cleverness, dexterity; trick; **amaños** tools, implements
amapola *f* poppy
amar *tr* to love
amaraje *m* alighting on water
amarar *intr* to alight on water
amargar §44 *tr* to make bitter; embitter; (*una tertulia, una velada*) spoil ‖ *intr & ref* to become bitter; become embittered
amar•go -ga *adj* bitter; sour; distressing ‖ **amargos** *mpl* bitters
amargura *f* bitterness; sorrow, grief
amarillear *intr* to turn yellow, show yellow
amarillecer §22 *intr* to become yellow
amarillen•to -ta *adj* yellowish
amarillez *f* yellowness
amari•llo -lla *adj & m* yellow
amarra *f* mooring cable; **amarras** support, protection; **soltar las amarras** (naut) to cast off
amarrar *tr* to moor; lash, tie up; (*las cartas*) stack
amartelar *tr* to make love to; make jealous ‖ *ref* to fall in love; become jealous
amartillar *tr* to hammer; (*un arma de fuego*) to cock
amasar *tr* to knead; mix; massage; (*dinero*) amass; concoct
amatista *f* amethyst
Amazonas *m* Amazon
ambages *mpl* ambiguity, quibbling; **sin ambages** straight to the point
ámbar *m* amber
Amberes *f* Antwerp
ambición *f* ambition
ambicionar *tr* to strive for, be eager for
ambicio•so -sa *adj* ambitious; eager; **ambicioso de figurar** social climber
ambiental *adj* environmental
ambiente *m* atmosphere; **medio ambiente** environment; situation
ambi•gú *m* (*pl* **-gúes**) buffet supper; bar, refreshment bar
ambigüedad *f* ambiguity
ambi•guo -gua *adj* ambiguous; (*género*) (gram) common
ámbito *m* boundary, limit; compass, scope
ambladura *f* amble
amblar *intr* to amble
am•bos -bas *adj & pron indef* both; **ambos a dos** both, both together
ambrosía *f* ragweed
ambulancia *f* ambulance; **ambulancia de correos** mail car, railway post office
ambulante *adj* itinerant, traveling ‖ *m* railway mail clerk
ambulato•rio -ria *adj* ambulatory ‖ *m* welfare center, public clinic; ambulance
amedrentar *tr* to frighten, scare
amelona•do -da *adj* melon-shaped; mentally retarded; lovesick

amén *interj* amen! ‖ *m* amen ‖ *adv* — **amén de** aside from; in addition to
amenaza *f* threat, menace
amenazar §60 *tr* to threaten, menace
amenguar §10 *tr* to lessen, diminish; belittle; dishonor
amenidad *f* amenity
amenizar §60 *tr* to make pleasant, brighten, cheer
ame•no -na *adj* agreeable, pleasant
amento *m* catkin
América *f* America; **la América Central** Central America; **la América del Norte** North America; **la América del Sur** South America; **la América Latina** Latin America
americana *f* sack coat, jacket
americanizar §60 *tr* to Americanize
america•no -na *adj & mf* American; Spanish American ‖ *f* see **americana**
amerizar §60 *intr* to alight on water
ametralladora *f* machine gun
ametrallar *tr* to machine-gun
amiba *f* amoeba
amiga *f* friend; mistress; schoolmistress; girls' school
amigable *adj* amicable, friendly
amigacho *m* chum, crony, pal
amígdala *f* tonsil
amigdalitis *f* tonsillitis
ami•go -ga *adj* friendly; fond ‖ *mf* friend; sweetheart; **amigo del alma** bosom friend ‖ *f* see **amiga**
amigote *m* chum, crony, pal
amilanar *tr* to terrify, intimidate
aminorar *tr* to lessen, diminish
amistad *f* friendship; liaison; **hacer las amistades** to make up; **romper las amistades** to fall out, become enemies
amistar *tr* to bring together ‖ *ref* to become friends
amisto•so -sa *adj* friendly
amniocentesis *f* amniocentesis
amnistía *f* amnesty
amnistiar §77 *tr* to amnesty, grant amnesty to
amo *m* head of family; landlord, proprietor; boss; **ser el amo del cotarro** to rule the roost
amoblar §61 *tr* to furnish
amodorrar *ref* to get drowsy; fall asleep; grow numb
amohinar *tr* to annoy, irritate, vex
amojonar *tr* to mark off with landmarks
amoladera *f* grindstone, whetstone
amolar §61 *tr* to grind, sharpen; bore, annoy
amoldar *tr* to mold; model, pattern, fashion; adjust, adapt
amonestación *f* admonition; marriage banns
amonestar *tr* to admonish, warn; publish the banns of
amoníaco *m* ammonia
amontonar *tr* to heap, pile; accumulate; hoard ‖ *ref* to collect, gather; crowd; get angry; (Mex) to gang up
amor *m* love; **al amor del agua** with the current; obligingly; **al amor de la lumbre**

by the fire, in the warmth of the fire; **amores** love affair; **amor propio** amourpropre; conceit; **por amor de** for the sake of

amorata•do -da adj livid, black-and-blue

amordazar §60 tr to muzzle; gag

amorío m love-making; love affair

amoro•so -sa adj loving, affectionate, amorous

amortajar tr to shroud; (carp) to mortise

amortecer §22 tr to deaden, muffle ‖ ref to die away, become faint

amortiguador m shock absorber; door check; (de automóvil) bumper; **amortiguador de luz** dimmer; **amortiguador de ruido** muffler

amortiguar §10 tr to deaden, muffle; soften, tone down; dim; damp; (un golpe) cushion; (ondas electromagnéticas) damp

amortizar §60 tr to amortize; (una deuda) pay off

amoscar §73 ref to get peeved; (Mex) to blush, be embarrassed

amotina•do -da adj mutinous, rebellious ‖ mf mutineer, rebel, rioter

amotinar tr to stir up; incite to mutiny ‖ ref to rise up, mutiny, rebel

amover §47 tr to discharge, dismiss

amovible adj removable, detachable

amparar tr to shelter, protect ‖ ref to seek shelter; protect oneself

amparo m shelter, protection, refuge; stall; aid, favor

amperio m ampere

amperio-hora m (pl **amperios-hora**) amperehour

ampliación f amplification; (phot) enlargement

ampliar §77 tr to amplify, enlarge; widen; (phot) to enlarge

amplificador m amplifier

amplificar §73 tr to amplify; expand, enlarge; magnify

am•plio -plia adj ample; spacious, roomy

amplitud f amplitude; roominess

ampo m dazzling white; snowflake

ampolla f blister; bubble; cruet; bulb, light bulb

ampollar tr & ref to blister

ampolleta f vial; sandglass, hourglass; bulb, light bulb; cruet

ampulosidad f bombast, pomposity

ampulo•so -sa adj bombastic, pompous

amputar tr to amputate

amueblar tr to furnish

amujera•do -da adj effeminate

amuleto m amulet, charm

amurallar tr to wall, wall in

amurcar §73 tr to gore

amusgar §44 tr (las orejas el toro, el caballo) to throw back

anacardo m cashew; cashew nut

anacróni•co -ca adj anachronistic

anacronismo m anachronism

ánade mf duck

anadear intr to waddle

anadeo m waddle, waddling

anales mpl annals

analfabetismo m illiteracy

analfabe•to -ta adj & mf illiterate

analgési•co -ca adj analgesic ‖ m painkiller, analgesic

análi•sis m & f (pl **-sis**) analysis; **análisis costobeneficio** cost-benefit analysis; **análisis de sistemas** systems analysis; **análisis gramatical** parsing; **análisis ocupacional** job analysis

analista mf analyst; annalist

analíti•co -ca adj analytic(al)

analizar §60 tr to analyze; **analizar gramaticalmente** to parse

analogía f analogy; similarity

análo•go -ga adj analogous; similar

ana•ná m (pl **-naes**) pineapple

ananás m pineapple

anaquel m shelf

anaranja•do -da adj & m (color) orange

anarquía f anarchy

anárqui•co -ca adj anarchic(al)

anarquista mf anarch, anarchist

anatema m & f anathema; curse

anatomía f anatomy

anatómi•co -ca adj anatomic(al) ‖ mf anatomist

anatomista mf anatomist

anca f croup, haunch; buttock, rump; **a ancas** or **a las ancas** mounted behind another person; **anca de rana** frog's leg; **dar ancas vueltas** (Mex) to give odds

ancianidad f old age

ancia•no -na adj old, aged ‖ m old man; (eccl) elder ‖ f old woman

ancla f anchor; **echar anclas** to cast anchor; **levar anclas** to weigh anchor

anclar intr to anchor

anclote m kedge, kedge anchor

ancón m bay, cove

áncora f anchor

ancorar intr to anchor

ancheta f (Arg) foolishness; ridiculous act

an•cho -cha adj wide, broad; full, ample; loose, loose-fitting ‖ m width, breadth

anchoa f anchovy

anchura f width, breadth; fullness, ampleness; looseness; comfort, ease

anchuro•so -sa adj wide, broad; spacious, roomy

andada f thin, hard-baked cracker; **andadas** (de conejos y otros animales) tracks; **volver a las andadas** to revert to one's old tricks

andaderas fpl gocart, walker

anda•do -da adj gone by, elapsed; frequented, trodden; worn, used; ordinary ‖ m gait ‖ f see **andada**

andadores mpl leading strings

andadura f pace, gait; amble; (Mex) mount

Andalucía f Andalusia

anda•luz -luza adj & mf Andalusian

andaluzada f tall story, exaggeration, fish story

andamiaje m scaffolding

andamio m scaffold; platform

andanada *f* (naut) broadside; (taur) covered upper section; (coll) scolding; (fig) fusillade

andante *adj* walking; errant, wandering

andanza *f* wandering, rambling; fate, fortune

andar *m* gait, pace, walk ‖ §5 *tr* (*p.ej., dos millas*) to go; (*un camino*) go down or up ‖ *intr* to go, walk; run; travel; act, behave; (*p.ej., un reloj*) go, run, work; be, feel; go by, pass, elapse; go (*to bear up, to last*), e.g., **anduve diez horas sin comer** I went ten hours without eating ‖ *ref* to go by, to pass, to elapse; to go away; **andarse sin** to go without

andarie·go -ga *adj* wandering, roving; swift, fleet

andas *fpl* litter; stretcher; bier

andén *m* railway platform; quay; footpath

Andes *mpl* Andes

andinismo *m* mountain climbing in the Andes

andi·no -na *adj* Andean

andraje·ro -ra *mf* ragpicker

andrajo *m* rag, tatter; ragamuffin, scalawag

andrajo·so -sa *adj* ragged, raggedy, in tatters

andurriales *mpl* byways, out-òf-the-way place

anea *f* cattail, bulrush

aneblar §2 *tr* to cloud; becloud ‖ *ref* to become clouded; get dark

anécdota *f* anecdote

anegar §44 *tr* to flood; drown ‖ *ref* to become flooded; drown

ane·jo -ja *adj* annexed; accessory ‖ *m* annex; dependency; supplement

anemia *f* anaemia

anémi·co -ca *adj* anaemic

anestesia *f* anaesthesia

anestesiar *tr* anaesthetize

anestési·co -ca *adj & m* anaesthetic

aneurisma *m & f* aneurysm

anexar *tr* to annex

ane·xo -xa *adj* annexed; accessory ‖ *m* annex; dependency

anfi·bio -bia *adj* amphibious

anfiteatro *m* amphitheater

anfitrión *m* host

anfitriona *f* hostess

ánfora *f* voting urn, ballot box

anfractuo·so -sa *adj* winding, tortuous

angarillas *fpl* handbarrow; panniers; cruet stand

ángel *m* angel; **ángel custodio** or **de la guarda** guardian angel; **ángel patudo** wolf in sheep's clothing; **tener ángel** to have great charm

angelical or **angéli·co -ca** *adj* angelic(al)

angina *f* angina; **angina de pecho** angina pectoris

angloparlante *adj* English-speaking ‖ *mf* speaker of English

anglosa·jón -jona *adj & mf* Anglo-Saxon

angos·to -ta *adj* narrow

anguila *f* eel; **anguilas** (*para botar un barco al agua*) ways; **escurrirse como una anguila** to be as slippery as an eel

angular *adj* angular

ángulo *m* angle; corner

angulo·so -sa *adj* (*facciones*) angular

angurria *f* (SAm) raging hunger; greed

angustia *f* anguish, distress, grief

angustia·do -da *adj* distressed, grieved

angustiar *tr* to distress, afflict, grieve

angustio·so -sa *adj* distressed, grieved; worrisome

anhelar *tr* to crave, want badly ‖ *intr* to pant; yearn; **anhelar por** to long for

anhélito *m* hard breathing

anhelo *m* craving; yearning, longing

anhelo·so -sa *adj* eager, yearning; breathless, panting

anhí·dro -dra *adj* anhydrous

Aníbal *m* Hannibal

anidar *tr* to harbor, shelter ‖ *intr & ref* to nestle, make a nest; live

anilina *f* aniline

anilla *f* curtain ring; (*en la gimnasia*) ring; hoop

anillo *m* ring; cigar band; **anillo de compromiso** or **de pedida** engagement ring; **anillo sigilar** signet ring

ánima *f* soul; (*de arma de fuego*) bore

animación *f* animation; liveliness; bustle, movement

anima·do -da *adj* animated, lively

animador *m* (*de un café-cantante*) master of ceremonies

animal *adj & m* animal

animar *tr* to enliven; encourage; strengthen; drive ‖ *ref* to take heart, feel encouraged

ánimo *m* mind, spirit; courage, valor, energy; attention, thought

animosidad *f* animosity, ill will

animo·so -sa *adj* brave, courageous; spirited; ready, disposed

aniña·do -da *adj* babyish, childish

anión *m* anion

aniquilar *tr* to annihilate, destroy ‖ *ref* to be annihilated; decline, waste away; be humbled

anís *m* anise; anise-flavored brandy

aniversa·rio -ria *adj & m* anniversary

anoche *adv* last night

anochecer *m* nightfall, dusk ‖ *v* §22 *intr* to grow dark; arrive or happen at nightfall; end the day; go to sleep ‖ *ref* to get dark; get cloudy; slip away

anochecida *f* nightfall, dusk

anodi·no -na *adj* innocuous, ineffective, harmless

ánodo *m* anode

anomalía *f* anomaly

anóma·lo -la *adj* anomalous

anonadar *tr* to annihilate, destroy; overwhelm; humble

anóni·mo -ma *adj* anonymous ‖ *m* anonymity; **guardar** or **conservar el anónimo** to preserve one's anonymity

anorexia *f* anorexia

anormal *adj* abnormal

anotar *tr* to annotate; note, jot down; point out

anquilosa·do -da *adj* stiff-jointed; old-fashioned

ánsar *m* goose; wild goose

am
an

ansia *f* anxiety, anguish; eagerness; **ansias** (Ven) nausea

ansiar §77 & *regular tr* to long for, yearn for ‖ *intr* to be madly in love

ansiedad *f* anxiety, worry; pain

ansio·so -sa *adj* anxious; anguished; longing; covetous

ant. *abbr* **anticuado**

anta *f* elk

antagonismo *m* antagonism

antaño *adv* last year; of yore, long ago

antárti·co -ca *adj* antarctic

ante *prep* before, in the presence of; in front of; at, with ‖ *m* elk; buff

antea·do -da *adj* buff; (Mex) damaged, shopworn

anteanoche *adv* the night before last

anteayer *adv* the day before yesterday

antebrazo *m* forearm

antecámara *f* antechamber, anteroom

antecedente *adj* antecedent ‖ *m* antecedent; **antecedentes** antecedents

anteceder *tr* to precede, go before

antece·sor -sora *mf* predecessor; ancestor

antedatar *tr* to antedate

antedi·cho -cha *adj* aforesaid, abovementioned

antelación *f* previousness, anticipation

antemano — **de antemano** in advance, beforehand

antena *f* (ent) antenna; (rad) antenna, aerial; **antena de conejo** rabbit ears; **en antena** on the air; **antena interior incorporada** built-in antenna; **llevar a las antenas** to put on the air

antenombre *m* title, honorific

anteojera *f* spectacle case; blinker, blinder

anteojo *m* eyeglass; spyglass; **anteojos** eyeglasses, spectacles; binoculars; blinkers

antepasa·do -da *adj* before last ‖ **antepasados** *mpl* ancestors

antepecho *m* railing, guardrail; parapet; window sill

antepenúltima *f* antepenult

anteponer §54 *tr* to place in front; prefer

anteportada *f* half title, bastard title

anteportal *m* porch, vestibule

antepuer·ta *f* portière

antepuerto *m* entrance to a mountain pass; (naut) outer harbor

anterior *adj* front; previous; earlier

antes *adv* before; sooner, soonest; rather; previously; **antes bien** rather; on the contrary; **antes de** before; **antes (de) que** before; **cuanto antes** as soon as possible

antesala *f* antechamber; (*p.ej., de médico*) waiting room; **hacer antesala** to dance attendance

antiaére·o -a *adj* antiaircraft

antiartísti·co -ca *adj* inartistic

antibéli·co -ca *adj* antiwar

anticartel *adj* antitrust

anticientífi·co -ca *adj* unscientific

anticipación *f* preparation, anticipation; **con anticipación** in advance

anticipa·do -da *adj* future; advance; **por anticipado** in advance

anticipar *tr* to anticipate, hasten; to move ahead ‖ *ref* to happen early; **anticiparse a** to anticipate, to get ahead of

anticipo *m* anticipation; advance payment, down payment; retaining fee

anticoncepti·vo -va *adj & m* contraceptive

anticongelante *m* antifreeze

anticonstitucional *adj* unconstitutional

anticua·do -da *adj* antiquated; old-fashioned; obsolete

anticua·rio -ria *adj* antiquarian ‖ *mf* antiquarian, antiquary; antique dealer

anticuerpo *m* antibody

antideporti·vo -va *adj* unsportsmanlike

antiderrapante or **antideslizante** *adj* nonskid

antideslumbrante *adj* antiglare

antidetonante *adj & m* antiknock

antídoto *m* antidote

antieconómi·co -ca *adj* uneconomic(al)

antier *adv* the day before yesterday

antiesclavista *adj* antislavery ‖ *mf* abolitionist

anti·faz *m* (*pl* **-faces**) veil, mask

antífona *f* anthem

antigás *adj invar* gas (*e.g., mask, shelter*)

antigramatical *adj* ungrammatical

antigravedad *f* weightlessness

antigualla *f* antique; relic, antique; has-been

antiguar §10 *intr & ref* to attain seniority

antigüedad *f* antiquity; seniority; (*mueble u otro objeto de arte antiguos*) antique; **antigüedades** antiquities; antiques

anti·guo -gua *adj* old; ancient; antique; former ‖ *mf* veteran; senior

antihigiéni·co -ca *adj* unsanitary

antílope *m* antelope

antilla·no -na *adj & mf* West Indian

Antillas *fpl* Antilles

antimateria *f* antimatter

antimonio *m* antimony

antiobre·ro -ra *adj* antilabor

antiparras *spl* spectacles

antipatía *f* dislike, antipathy

antipáti·co -ca *adj* disagreeable, uncongenial

antipatrióti·co -ca *adj* unpatriotic

antiproyectil *adj* antimissile

antirreflejo *adj invar* nonreflecting

antirresbaladi·zo -za *adj* nonskid

antirrobo *adj invar* theft-proof, burglar-proof

antisemíti·co -ca *adj* anti-Semitic

antisépti·co -ca *adj & m* antiseptic

antisono·ro -ra *adj* soundproof

antisoviéti·co -ca *adj* anti-Soviet

antitanque *adj* antitank

antiterrorista *adj invar & mf* antiterrorist

antíte·sis *f* (*pl* **-sis**) antithesis

antitóxi·co -ca *adj* antitoxic

antitoxina *f* antitoxin

antojadi·zo -za *adj* capricious, whimsical

antojar *ref* to seem; fancy; seem likely; have a notion to + *inf*; take a fancy to + *inf*

antojo *m* caprice, fancy, whim; snap judgment; birthmark; **antojos** moles, warts; **a su antojo** as one pleases

antología *f* anthology

antónimo *m* antonym

antorcha f torch; **antorcha a soplete** blowtorch

antracita f anthracite

ántrax m anthrax

antro m cave, cavern; (fig) den

antropología f anthropology

antruejo m carnival

anual adj annual

anualidad f annuity; year's pay; annual occurrence

anuario m yearbook; directory; bulletin, catalogue; **anuario telefónico** telephone directory

anublar tr to cloud; dim, darken; blight, wither || ref to become cloudy; be withered; (las esperanzas de uno) fade away

anudar tr to tie, fasten, knot; unite; resume || ref to get knotted; be united; fade away, wilt, fail

anuente adj consenting

anular tr to annul; nullify; remove, discharge || ref to be passed over

anunciar tr to announce; advertise || intr to advertise

anunciante mf advertiser

anuncio m announcement; advertisement

anverso m obverse

anzuelo m fishhook; **picar en el anzuelo** or **tragar el anzuelo** to swallow the bait, swallow the hook

añadi•do -da adj additional || m false hair, switch

añadidura f addition; extra weight, extra measure; **de añadidura** extra, in the bargain; **por añadidura** besides

añadir tr to add; increase

añafil m straight Moorish trumpet

añagaza f bird call; decoy, lure; trap, trick

añe•jo -ja adj aged; stale; musty, rancid

añicos mpl bits, pieces; **hacer añicos** to tear to pieces, break to pieces; **hacerse añicos** to wear oneself out

añil m indigo; bluing

añilar tr to dye with indigo; (la ropa blanca) to blue

año m year; **año bisiesto** leap year; **año económico** fiscal year; **año lectivo** school year; **año luz** (pl años luz) light-year; **años** birthday; **cumplir ... años** to be . . . years old

añoranza f longing, sorrow

añorar tr to long for, sorrow for; grieve over || intr to yearn; sorrow, grieve

año•so -sa adj aged, old

aojada f (Col) skylight; (Col) transom

aojar tr to cast the evil eye on, jinx

aojo m evil eye, jinx

aovar intr to lay eggs

ap. abbr **aparte, apóstol**

apabilar tr to trim

apabullar tr to mash, crush; squelch

apacentar §2 tr & ref to pasture, graze; feed

apacible adj gentle, mild; calm

apaciguamiento m pacification, appeasement

apaciguar §10 tr to pacify, appease || ref to calm down

apachurrar tr to crush, squash, mash

apadrinar tr to sponsor; act as godfather for; back, support; second

apagabron•cas m (pl -cas) bouncer

apagador m extinguisher; (de piano) damper

apagaincen•dios m (pl -dios) fire extinguisher

apagar §44 tr to extinguish, put out; (la luz, la radio) turn off; (la cal) slake; (el sonido) damp, muffle; (el fuego del enemigo) silence; (la sed) quench; (el dolor) deaden || ref to go out; subside, calm down, fade away

apagón m blackout

apalabrar tr to bespeak; consider || ref to agree

apalabrear intr (SAm) to make an appointment

apalancar §73 tr to raise with a lever or crowbar

apalear tr to shovel; beat; pile up

apandar tr to steal

apantallar tr to dazzle, amaze; (elec) to shield, screen

apañar tr to grasp; pick up; steal; repair, mend; wrap up || ref to be handy

apañuscar §73 tr to crumple, rumple; steal; (CAm, Col, Ven) to jam, crowd

aparador m sideboard, buffet; showcase; workshop; (Mex) show window, store window

aparar tr to prepare; adorn; block; (las manos, la falda, el pañuelo, la capa) hold out

aparato m apparatus; ostentation, show; exaggeration; radio set; television set; telephone; airplane; camera; bandage, application; (theat) scenery, properties; **aparato auditivo** hearing aid; **aparato de relojería** clockwork; **aparatos sanitarios** bathroom fixtures; **ponerse al aparato** to go or to come to the phone

aparato•so -sa adj showy, pompous, ostentatious

aparcamiento m parking; parking space; **aparcamiento subterraneo** underground garage

aparcar §44 tr & intr to park

aparcería f partnership, sharecropping

aparce•ro -ra mf partner, sharecropper; (Arg) customer

aparear tr to pair, match; mate || ref to pair; mate

aparecer §22 intr & ref to appear; show up

aparecido m ghost, specter

aparejador m builder

aparejar tr to prepare; prime, size; harness

aparejo m preparation; harness; set, kit; priming, sizing; (mas) bond; **aparejos** tools, implements, equipment

aparentar tr to feign, pretend; look, look to be

aparente adj apparent, seeming; evident; right, proper

aparición f apparition

apariencia f appearance, aspect; sign, indication; **salvar las apariencias** to save face

aparqueamiento m parking

aparquear *tr & intr* to park

aparqueo *m* parking

aparragar §44 *ref* to crouch, squat; (CAm) to loll, sprawl

apartadero *m* siding, side track; turnout

aparta•do -da *adj* distant, remote; aloof; (*camino*) side, back; different ‖ *m* side room; post-office box; vocabulary entry; section

apartamento *m* apartment, apartment house

apartar *tr* to take aside; separate; push away; shunt; (*el ganado*) sort ‖ *ref* to separate; move away, keep away, stand aside; withdraw; get divorced; give up

aparte *adv* apart, aside; **aparte de** apart from ‖ *prep* apart from ‖ *m* (theat) aside

apasiona•do -da *adj* passionate; devoted, tender, loving; sore

apasionar *tr* to impassion, appeal deeply to; afflict ‖ *ref* to become impassioned; be stirred up; fall madly in love

apatía *f* apathy

apáti•co -ca *adj* apathetic

apatusco *m* ornament, finery

apdo. *abbr* **apartado**

apeadero *m* horse block; flag stop, wayside station; platform; temporary quarters

apear *tr* to help dismount, help down; bring down; remove; overcome; prop up ‖ *ref* to dismount, get off; back down; stop, put up

apechugar §44 *intr* to push with the chest; **apechugar con** to make the best of

apedazar §60 *tr* to mend, patch; cut or tear to pieces

apedrear *tr* to stone; stone to death; pit; speckle ‖ *intr* to hail ‖ *ref* to be damaged by hail; be pitted

apegar §44 *ref* to become attached, grow fond

apego *m* attachment, fondness

apelación *f* medical consultation; remedy, help; (law) appeal

apelante *adj* appellate

apelar *intr* to appeal, make an appeal; have recourse; refer

apelativo *m* (CAm) surname, family name

apeldar *tr* — **apeldarlas** (coll) to flee, run away

apelmazar §60 *tr* to squeeze, compress ‖ *ref* to cake

apelotonar *tr* to form into a ball ‖ *ref* to form a ball; curl up

apellidar *tr* to call, name; proclaim

apellido *m* name; surname, last name, family name; **apellido de soltera** maiden name

apenar *tr & ref* to grieve

apenas *adv* hardly, scarcely; **apenas si** hardly, scarcely ‖ *conj* no sooner, as soon as

apéndice *m* appendage; (anat) appendix

apendicitis *f* appendicitis

apercancar §73 *ref* (Chile) to get moldy, mildew

apercibir *tr* to prepare; provide; warn; perceive; collect ‖ *ref* to get ready; be provided; **apercibirse de** to notice

apergaminar *ref* to dry up, become yellow and wrinkled

aperitivo *m* appetizer

aperla•do -da *adj* pearly

apero *m* tools, equipment, outfit; riding gear

aperrear *tr* to set the dogs on; harass, plague, pester

apersogar §44 *tr* to tether

apersona•do -da *adj* — **bien apersonado** presentable; **mal apersonado** unpresentable

apersonar *ref* to appear in person; have an interview

apertura *f* opening

apesadumbrar or **apesarar** *tr & ref* to grieve

apestar *tr* to infect with the plague; corrupt; sicken, nauseate; infest ‖ *intr* to stink ‖ *ref* to be infected with the plague

apesto•so -sa *adj* stinking, foul-smelling; pestilent; sickening

apetecer §22 *tr* to hunger for, thirst for, crave

apetecible *adj* desirable, tempting

apetencia *f* hunger, appetite, craving

apetito *m* appetite

apetito•so -sa *adj* tasty; tempting; gourmand

ápex *m* apex

apiadar *tr* to move to pity; take pity on ‖ *ref* to have pity

ápice *m* apex; bit, whit; crux; **estar en los ápices de** to be up in

apilar *tr & ref* to pile, pile up

apimpollar *ref* to sprout, put forth shoots

apiñar *tr & ref* to crowd, jam

apio *m* celery

apisonadora *f* road roller

apisonar *tr* to tamp; roll

aplacar §73 *tr* to placate, appease, pacify; (*la sed*) to quench

aplanacalles *m* (SAm) idler; lazy person

aplanar *tr* to smooth, make even; to astonish; **aplanar las calles** to loaf, bum around ‖ *ref* to collapse; become discouraged

aplanchar *tr* to iron

aplanetizar §60 *intr* to land on another planet

aplastar *tr* to flatten, crush, smash; dumbfound

aplaudida *f* applause

aplaudir *tr & intr* to applaud

aplauso *m* applause; **aplausos** applause

aplazada *f* or **aplazamiento** *m* delay; procrastination

aplazar §60 *tr* to postpone; convene; summon

aplicación *f* appliance, application; diligence

aplica•do -da *adj* industrious, studious; applied

aplicar §73 *tr* to apply; attribute ‖ *ref* to apply; apply oneself

aplomar *tr* to plumb; make straight or vertical ‖ *intr* to be vertical ‖ *ref* to collapse; (Chile) to be embarrassed; (Mex) to be slow, be backward

aplomo *m* aplomb, poise, self-possession; gravity

apoca•do -da *adj* diffident, timid, irresolute; humble, lowly

apocar §73 *tr* to cramp, contract; narrow; humble, belittle

apodar *tr* to nickname; make fun of

apodera•do -da *adj* empowered, authorized ‖ *m* proxy; attorney

apoderamiento *m* authorization; power of attorney

apoderar *tr* to empower, authorize ‖ *ref* — **apoderarse de** to seize, grasp; take possession of

apodo *m* nickname

apofanía *f* ablaut

apogeo *m* apogee; (fig) height, apogee

apolilla•do -da *adj* moth-eaten, mothy

apolilladura *f* moth hole

apolillar *tr* (*la polilla, p.ej., las ropas*) to eat ‖ *ref* to become moth-eaten

apoliti•co -ca *adj* apolitical, nonpolitical

apología *f* eulogy

apoltronar *ref* to loaf around; loll, sprawl

apontizaje *m* deck-landing

apontizar §60 *intr* to deck-land

apoplejía *f* apoplexy

apopléti•co -ca *adj* & *mf* apoplectic

aporcar §73 *tr* (*las hortalizas*) to hill

aporrear *tr* to beat, club, cudgel; annoy ‖ *ref* to drudge, slave

aportación *f* contribution; dowry

aportar *tr* to contribute; bring; lead; (*como dote*) bring ‖ *intr* to show up; reach port

aporte *m* contribution

aposentar *tr* to put up, lodge ‖ *ref* to take lodging

aposento *m* lodging; room; inn

apostadero *m* stand, post; naval station

apostar *tr* to post, station ‖ §61 *tr* to bet, wager ‖ *intr* to bet; compete

apostilla *f* note, comment

apóstol *m* apostle

apóstrofe *m* & *f* apostrophe (*words addressed to absent person*)

apóstrofo *m* apostrophe (*written sign*)

apostura *f* neatness, spruceness; bearing, carriage

apoyabra•zos *m* (*pl* **-zos**) armrest

apoyali•bros *m* (*pl* **-bros**) book end

apoyar *tr* to support, hold up; lean, rest; abet, back ‖ *intr* & *ref* to lean, rest, be supported

apoyatura *f* (mus) grace note

apoyo *m* support, prop; backing, approval

apreciable *adj* appreciable; estimable

apreciación *f* appraisal

apreciar *tr* to appreciate; appraise; esteem

aprecio *m* appreciation, esteem

aprehender *tr* to apprehend, catch; think, conceive

aprehensión *f* apprehension

aprehensi•vo -va *adj* apprehensive

aprehensor *m* captor

apremiar *tr* to press, urge; compel, force; hurry; harass; (*a un deudor*) dun ‖ *intr* to be urgent

apremio *m* pressure; urgency; compulsion; oppression; surtax for late payment; (*demanda de pago*) dun

aprender *tr* & *intr* to learn; **aprender haciendo** to learn by doing

apren•diz -diza *mf* apprentice; **aprendiz de imprenta** printer's devil

aprendizaje *m* apprenticeship; **pagar el aprendizaje** to pay for one's inexperience

aprensar *tr* to press; oppress

aprensión *f* apprehension; misgiving, prejudice

aprensi•vo -va *adj* apprehensive

apresar *tr* to grasp, seize; capture

aprestador *m* primer

aprestar *tr* to prepare; (*tejidos*) process; prime; size ‖ *ref* to get ready

apresto *m* preparation; equipment; priming; sizing

apresurar *tr* & *ref* to hurry, hasten

apretadera *f* strap, rope; **apretaderas** pressure

apreta•do -da *adj* compact, tight; close, intimate; dense, thick; difficult, dangerous; mean, stingy; **estar muy apretado** to be in a bad way

apretar §2 *tr* to tighten; squeeze; pinch; hug; harass, importune; afflict, beset; (*un botón*) press; (*los puños*) clench; (*los dientes*) grit; (*la mano*) shake ‖ *intr* to pinch; insist; get worse; push hard, press forward; **apretar a correr** to start running; **apretar con** to close in on ‖ *ref* to grieve, be distressed; crowd

apretón *m* pressure, squeeze; struggle; dash, run; **apretón de manos** handshake

apretura *f* crush, jam; tightness; fix, trouble; need, want

aprietarropa *m* clothespin

¡aprieta! *interj* (coll) baloney!

aprieto *m* crush, jam; fix

aprisa *adv* fast, quickly

aprisco *m* sheepfold

aprisionar *tr* to imprison; bind, tie; shackle

aprobación *f* approbation, approval; pass, passing grade

aproba•do -da *adj* excellent ‖ *m* pass

aprobar §61 *tr* & *intr* to approve; pass

aprontar *tr* to hand over without delay; expedite

apropia•do -da *adj* appropriate, fitting, proper

apropiar *tr* to hand over; fit, adapt ‖ *ref* to appropriate; preëmpt

aprovechable *adj* available, usable

aprovecha•do -da *adj* thrifty; stingy; diligent; well-spent ‖ *mf* opportunist

aprovechar *tr* to make good use of, take advantage of; (*una caída de agua*) harness ‖ *intr* to be useful; progress, improve ‖ *ref* — **aprovecharse de** to avail oneself of, take advantage of

aprovisionar *tr* to provision, supply, furnish

aproxima•do -da *adj* approximate, rough

aproximar *tr* to bring near; approximate ‖ *ref* to come near; approximate

aptitud *f* aptitude; suitability

ap•to -ta *adj* apt; suitable

apuesta *f* bet, wager

apues•to -ta *adj* neat, spruce, elegant ‖ *f* see **apuesta**

apulgarar *ref* to become mildewed

apuntador *m* (theat) prompter

apuntalar *tr* to prop up, underpin

apuntar *tr* to point; point at; aim; aim at; take note of; sharpen; stitch, darn, patch; correct; prompt; stake, to put up; (theat) to prompt || *intr* to begin to appear; dawn || *ref* (*el vino*) to begin to turn sour; register; get tipsy

apunte *m* note; rough sketch; stake; rogue, rascal; (theat) cue

apuñalar *tr & intr* to stab

apuñear *tr* to punch

apura•do -da *adj* needy, hard up; difficult, dangerous; hurried, rushed

apurar *tr* to purify, refine; clear up, verify; finish; drain, use up, exhaust; hurry, press; annoy || *ref* to worry, grieve; exert oneself, strive

apuro *m* need, want; grief, sorrow; haste, urgency; **apuros** financial embarrassment

aquejar *tr* to grieve, afflict

aquel, aquella *adj dem* (*pl* **aquellos, aquellas**) that, that . . . yonder

aquél, aquélla *pron dem* (*pl* **aquéllos, aquéllas**) that; that one, that one yonder; the one; the former || *m* charm, appeal

aquelarre *m* witches' Sabbath

aquello *pron dem* that; that thing, that matter

aquende *adv* on this side || *prep* on this side of

aquerenciar *ref* to become fond or attached

aquí *adv* here; **aquí dentro** in here; **de aquí en adelante** from now on; **por aquí** this way

aquiescencia *f* acquiescence

aquietar *tr* to quiet, calm

aquilatar *tr* to assay; check; refine

Aquiles *m* Achilles

aquilón *m* north wind

ara *f* altar; altar slab; **en aras de** for the sake of

árabe *adj* Arab, Arabian; (archit) Moresque || *mf* Arab, Arabian || *m* (*idioma*) Arabic

Arabia, la Arabia

arábi•go -ga *adj* Arabian, Arabic || *m* (*idioma*) Arabic; **estar en arábigo** (coll) to be Greek

arabismo *m* (*estudio, voz, rasgo*) Arabism

aracanga *f* macaw

arado *m* plow

Aragón *m* Aragon

arago•nés -nesa *adj & mf* Aragonese

arancel *m* tariff

arancelar *tr* (CAm) to pay

arancela•rio -ria *adj* tariff, customs

arándano *m* whortleberry; **arándano agrio** cranberry

arandela *f* bobèche; (mach) washer

araña *f* spider; chandelier

arañar *tr* to scratch; scrape; scrape together

arañazo *m* scratch

araño *m* scratching

aráquida *f* peanut

arar *tr* to plow

arbitraje *m* arbitration

arbitrar *tr & intr* to arbitrate; referee; umpire

arbitra•rio -ria *adj* arbitrary

arbitrio *m* free will; means, ways; **arbitrios** excise taxes

arbitrista *mf* wild-eyed dreamer

árbi•tro -tra *mf* arbiter; referee || *m* umpire

árbol *m* tree; axle, shaft; **árbol del caucho** rubber plant; **árbol de levas** camshaft; **árbol de mando** drive shaft; **árbol de Navidad** Christmas tree; **árbol motor** drive shaft

arbola•do -da *adj* wooded; (*mar*) high || *m* woodland

arboleda *f* grove

arbollón *m* sewer, drain

arbotante *m* flying buttress

arbusto *m* shrub

arca *f* chest, coffer; tank; ark; **arca de agua** water tower; **arca de la alianza** ark of the covenant; **arca de Noé** ark, Noah's ark

arcada *f* arcade; archway; stroke of bow; **arcadas** retching

arcai•co -ca *adj* archaic

arcaísmo *m* archaism

arcaizante *adj* obsolescent

arcángel *m* archangel

arca•no -na *adj & m* secret

arcar §73 *tr* to arch

arce *m* maple tree

arcilla *f* clay; **arcilla figulina** potter's clay

arco *m* arch; (*de cuna o mecedor*) rocker; (elec, geom) arc; (mus) bow; **arco iris** rainbow; **arco triunfal** triumphal arch; memorial arch

arcón *m* large chest; bin, bunker

archiduque *m* archduke

archienemigo *m* archenemy

archipiélago *m* archipelago; (coll) maze, entanglement || **Archipiélago** *m* Aegean Sea

archiva•dor -dora *mf* file clerk || *m* filing cabinet; letter file

archivar *tr* to file; file away; hide away

archivero *m* city clerk

archivo *m* archives; files; filing; (Col) office

ardentía *f* heartburn; (*en las olas de la mar*) phosphorescence

arder *tr* to burn || *intr* to burn; blaze; **estar que arde** to be coming to a head || *ref* to burn up

ardid *m* artifice, trick, wile

ardi•do -da *adj* burnt-up; bold, intrepid; angry

ardiendo *adj invar* burning

ardiente *adj* ardent; fiery, passionate; burning, hot

ardilla *f* squirrel; **ardilla de tierra** gopher; **ardilla ladradora** prairie dog; **ardilla listada** chipmunk

ardillón *m* gopher

ardite *m* old Spanish coin of little value; **no me importa un ardite** (coll) I don't care a hang; **no valer un ardite** to be not worth a straw

ardor *m* ardor; eagerness, fervor, zeal; vehemence; courage, dash

ardoro•so -sa *adj* fiery, enthusiastic; balky, restive

ar•duo -dua *adj* arduous, difficult

área f area; small plot; **área de descansar** rest area; **área de servicio** service area

arena f sand; grit; arena; **arena movediza** quicksand; **arenas** arena; (pathol) stones

arenal m sandy place; quicksand

arenga f harangue

arengar tr & intr to harangue

arenis•co -ca adj sandy, gritty; sand ‖ f sandstone

areno•so -sa adj sandy

arenque m herring

areómetro m hydrometer

arepa f corn griddle cake

arete m eardrop, earring

arfada f (naut) pitching

arfar intr (naut) to pitch

argadijo m or **argadillo** m bobbin, reel; restless fellow

argado m prank, trick, artifice

argamasa f mortar

argamasar tr to mortar, plaster; (los materiales de construcción) mix

árgana f (mach) crane; **árganas** panniers

Argel f Algiers

Argelia f Algeria

argeli•no -na adj & mf Algerian

argentar tr to silver

argenti•no -na adj & mf Argentine, Argentinean ‖ **la Argentina** Argentina, the Argentine

argolla f large iron ring; (que se pone en la nariz a un animal) ring; engagement ring

argonauta m Argonaut

argucia f subtlety; trick

argüir §6 tr to argue, argue for; prove; accuse ‖ ref to argue, dispute

argumenta•dor -dora adj argumentative ‖ mf arguer

argumentar tr to argue for; prove ‖ intr & ref to argue, dispute

argumento m argument

aria f (mus) aria

aridez f aridity, dryness

ári•do -da adj arid; (aburrido, falto de interés) dry

Aries m Aries

ariete m battering ram; **ariete hidráulico** hydraulic ram

arimez m projection

a•rio -ria adj & mf Aryan ‖ f see **aria**

aris•co -ca adj churlish, surly, evasive; (caballo) vicious

arista f edge; (intersección de dos planos) ridge; (del grano de trigo) beard; **arista de encuentro** (archit) groin

aristocracia f aristocracy

aristócrata mf aristocrat

aristocráti•co -ca adj aristocratic

Aristóteles m Aristotle

aristotéli•co -ca adj & mf Aristotelian

aritméti•co -ca adj arithmetical ‖ mf arithmetician ‖ f arithmetic

arlequín m harlequin

arma f arm, weapon; **alzarse en armas** to rise up, rebel; **arma blanca** steel blade; **arma corta** pistol; **arma de fuego** firearm;

jugar a las armas to fence; **sobre las armas** under arms

armada f fleet, armada; navy

armadía f raft, float

armadijo m trap, snare

arma•do -da adj armed; (hormigón) reinforced ‖ f see **armada**

arma•dor -dora mf assembler ‖ m recruiter of fishermen and whalers

armadura f armor; framework; skeleton; (elec) armature; (de imán) keeper

armamentismo m military preparedness

armamentis•to -ta adj militarist, arms ‖ mf arms dealer

armamento m armament

armar tr to arm; (un arma) load; (una bayoneta) fix; mount, assemble; build; equip; (el hormigón) reinforce; (una nave) fit out; (caballero) dub; start, stir up; **armarla** to start a row ‖ ref to arm oneself; get ready; balk

armario m closet, wardrobe; **armario botiquín** medicine cabinet; **armario de luna** wardrobe with mirror; **armario frigorífico** refrigerator

armatoste m hulk

armazón f frame; assemblage; skeleton

armella f screw eye, eyebolt

arme•nio -nia adj & mf Armenian ‖ **Armenia** f Armenia

armería f arms shop; arms museum; arms

armero m gunsmith; (para las armas) rack

armiño m ermine

armisticio m armistice

armonía f harmony

armóni•co -ca adj & m harmonic ‖ f harmonica; **armónica de boca** mouth organ

armonio•so -sa adj harmonious

armonizar §60 tr & intr to harmonize

arnés m armor, coat of mail; harness; **arneses** harness, trappings; outfit, equipment; accessories

aro m hoop; rim; **aro de émbolo** piston ring

aroma m aroma, fragrance

aromáti•co -ca adj aromatic

arpa f harp

arpar tr to claw, scratch; tear, rend

arpegio m arpeggio

arpeo m grappling iron

arpía f harpy; shrew, jade

arpillera f burlap, sackcloth

arpista mf harpist

arpón m harpoon

arponear tr & intr to harpoon

arqueada f (mus) bow

arquear tr to arch; (la lana) beat; (una nave) gauge; to audit ‖ intr to retch ‖ ref to bow

arqueología f archeology

arquería f arcade

arquero m archer, bowman; goalkeeper, goalie

arquitecto m architect

arquitectóni•co -ca adj architectural

arquitectura f architecture

arrabal m suburb; **arrabales** outskirts

arracada f earring with pendant

arracimar ref to cluster, bunch

arraiga•do -da *adj* deep-rooted; property-owning, landed

arraigar §44 *tr* to establish, strengthen ‖ *intr* to take root ‖ *ref* to take root; become settled

arraigo *m* taking root; stability; property, real estate

arramblar *tr* to cover with sand or gravel; sweep away

arrancadero *m* starting point

arrancar §73 *tr* to root up, pull out, pull up; snatch, wrest; (*lágrimas*) draw forth ‖ *intr* to start; set sail; leave; originate

arranque *m* pull; fit, impulse; jerk, sudden start; sally, outburst; (aut) start, starter; **arranque a mano** (aut) hand cranking; **arranque automático** (aut) self-starter

arrapiezo *m* rag, tatter; whippersnapper

arras *fpl* earnest money, pledge; dowry

arrasar *tr* to level; wreck, demolish; fill to the brim ‖ *intr* to clear up ‖ *ref* to clear up; fill up

arrastra•do -da *adj* mean, crooked ‖ *mf* wretch, crook

arrastrar *tr* to drag, drag along; drag down; impel ‖ *intr* to drag, trail; crawl, creep ‖ *ref* to drag, trail; crawl, creep; drag on; cringe

arrastre *m* drag; crawl; washout; influence; haulage; (*influencia política y social*) (Cuba, Mex) drag

arrayán *m* myrtle

arre *interj* gee!, get up!

arreador *m* muleteer; (SAm) whip

arrear *tr* to drive ‖ *intr* to hurry ‖ *ref* to lose all one's money

arrebata•do -da *adj* rash, reckless; (*color del rostro*) flushed, ruddy

arrebatar *tr* to snatch; carry away; attract; move, stir ‖ *ref* to be carried away, be overcome

arrebatiña *f* scuffle, scramble; **andar a la arrebatiña** to scramble

arrebato *m* rage, fury; ecstasy, rapture

arrebol *m* (*de las nubes*) red; (*de las mejillas*) rosiness; (*afeite*) rouge; **arreboles** red clouds

arrebozar §60 *tr* to muffle ‖ *ref* to muffle one's face

arrebujar *tr* to jumble together; wrap ‖ *ref* to wrap oneself up

arreciar *intr* & *ref* to grow worse; become more violent; grow stronger

arrecife *m* stone-paved road; dike; reef; **arrecife de coral** coral reef

arredrar *tr* to drive back; frighten ‖ *ref* to draw back; shrink; be frightened

arregazar §60 *tr* to tuck up

arreglar *tr* to adjust, regulate, settle; arrange; fix, repair ‖ *ref* to adjust, settle; arrange; conform; **arreglárselas** to manage, make out

arreglo *m* adjustment, regulation; settlement; arrangement; order, rule; agreement; **con arreglo a** in accordance with

arregostar *ref* to take a liking

arregosto *m* liking, taste

arrellanar *ref* to loll, sprawl; like one's work

arremangar §44 *tr* (*las mangas*) to turn up; (*la ropa*) to tuck up ‖ *ref* to turn up one's sleeves; tuck up one's dress; take a firm stand

arremeter *tr* to attack, assail; (*un caballo*) to spur ‖ *intr* to attack; be offensive to look at; **arremeter contra** to light into, sail into

arremetida *f* attack; (*de un caballo*) sudden start; push; short, wild run

arremolinar *ref* to crowd, mill around; whirl

arrendajo *m* (orn) jay; mimic

arrendar §2 *tr* to rent; (*una caballería*) tie ‖ *ref* to rent, be rented

arreo *m* adornment; (SAm) drove; **arreos** harness, trappings

arrepenti•do -da *adj* repentant ‖ *mf* penitent

arrepentimiento *m* repentance

arrepentir §68 *ref* to repent, be repentant; **arrepentirse de** (*p.ej., un pecado*) to repent

arrequives *mpl* finery; attendant circumstances

arresta•do -da *adj* bold, daring

arrestar *tr* to arrest ‖ *ref* to rush boldly

arresto *m* arrest; boldness, daring; **bajo arresto** under arrest

arrezagar §44 *tr* to tuck up

arriada *f* flood

arriar §77 *tr* to flood; (naut) to lower, strike; slacken ‖ *ref* to be flooded

arriba *adv* up, upward; above; upstairs; uptown; on top; **arriba de** up; **de arriba abajo** from top to bottom; from beginning to end; superciliously; **más arriba** farther up; **río arriba** upstream ‖ *interj* up with . . . !

arribada *f* arrival (*by sea*); **de arribada** (naut) emergency

arribar *intr* to put into port; arrive; to recover, make a comeback; (naut) to fall off to leeward

arribista *adj* & *mf* parvenu, upstart

arribo *m* arrival

arricete *m* shoal, bar

arriendo *m* rent, rental; lease

arriero *m* muleteer

arriesga•do -da *adj* dangerous, risky; bold, daring

arriesgar §44 *tr* to risk, jeopardize ‖ *ref* to take a risk

arriesgo *m* (SAm) risk; hazard

arrimadillo *m* wainscot

arrimar *tr* to bring close, move up; (*un golpe*) give; abandon, neglect; give up; get rid of ‖ *ref* to come close, move up; snuggle up; lean; depend

arrinconar *tr* to corner; put aside; abandon, neglect; get rid of ‖ *ref* to live in seclusion

arrisca•do -da *adj* enterprising; brisk, spirited; craggy

arriscar §73 *tr* to risk ‖ *ref* to take a risk; (*las reses*) plunge over a cliff

arrisco *m* risk

arritmia *f* arrhythmia

arrivista *adj* & *mf* parvenu, upstart

arrizar §60 *tr* to reef

arroba *f* Spanish weight of about 25 pounds
arrobar *tr* to entrance, enrapture ‖ *ref* to be enraptured
arrobo *m* ecstasy, rapture
arroce•ro -ra *adj* rice ‖ *mf* rice grower; rice merchant
arrocinar *tr* to bestialize ‖ *ref* to become bestialized; fall madly in love
arrodajar *ref* (CAm) to squat down with one's legs crossed
arrodillar *ref* to kneel, kneel down
arrogancia *f* arrogance
arrogante *adj* arrogant
arrogar §44 *tr* to adopt ‖ *ref* to arrogate to oneself
arrojadi•zo -za *adj* for throwing, projectile
arroja•do -da *adj* bold, fearless, rash
arrojalla•mas *m* (*pl* -mas) flame thrower
arrojar *tr* to throw, hurl; emit; bring forth; yield ‖ *ref* to rush, rush forward
arrojo *m* boldness, fearlessness, rashness
arrollado *m* (elec) coil
arrolla•dor -dora *adj* sweeping, devastating
arrollamiento *m* winding
arrollar *tr* to roll; roll up; wind, coil; (*al enemigo*) rout; dumbfound; knock down, run over
arropar *tr* to wrap, wrap up ‖ *ref* to bundle up
arrope *m* grape syrup; honey syrup
arropía *f* taffy
arrostrar *tr* to face; to like ‖ *intr* —**arrostrar con** or **por** to face, resist ‖ *ref* to rush into the fight
arroyada *f* gully; flood, freshet
arroyo *m* stream, brook; gutter; street; (*de lágrimas, sangre, etc.*) stream
arroz *m* rice
arrufar *tr* to sic, incite
arruga *f* wrinkle; crease, rumple
arrugar §44 *tr* to wrinkle; crease, rumple; (*la frente*) to knit; (Cuba, Mex) to bother, annoy ‖ *ref* to wrinkle; crease, rumple; shrink, shrivel; (Cuba, Mex) to lose courage, lose heart
arruinar *tr* to ruin ‖ *ref* to go to ruin
arrullar *tr* to sing to sleep, lull to sleep; to court, woo ‖ *intr* to coo ‖ *ref* to coo; (*las palomas*) to bill
arrullo *m* billing and cooing; lullaby
arrumaje *m* stowage; ballast
arrumar *tr* to stow ‖ *ref* to become overcast
arrumbar *tr* to cast aside, neglect; silence; (*una costa*) determine the lay of ‖ *intr* (naut) to take bearings ‖ *ref* to get seasick; (naut) to take bearings
arsenal *m* arsenal, armory; dockyard, shipyard
arsénico *m* arsenic
art. *abbr* **artículo**
arte *m* & *f* art; trick; knack; fishing gear; **artes y oficios** arts and crafts; **bellas artes** fine arts; **no tener arte ni parte en** to have nothing to do with
artefacto *m* artifact; appliance, device, contrivance; **artefactos de alumbrado** lighting fixtures; **artefactos sanitarios** bathroom fixtures
artemisa *f* sagebrush
arteria *f* artery
artería *f* craftiness, cunning
arte•ro -ra *adj* crafty, cunning, sly
artesa *f* trough; Indian canoe
artesanía *f* craftsmanship
artesa•no -na *mf* artisan, craftsman ‖ *f* craftswoman
artesón *m* kitchen tub; coffer, caisson (*in ceiling*)
árti•co -ca *adj* arctic
articulación *f* articulation; (*de huesos*) joint; **articulación universal** universal joint
articular *tr* to articulate
articulista *mf* feature writer
artículo *m* article; item; joint; (*en un diccionario*) entry; **artículo de fondo** leader, editorial; **artículos de consumo** consumers' goods; **artículos de deporte** sporting goods; **artículos de primera necesidad** basic commodities; **artículos para caballeros** men's furnishings
artífice *mf* artificer; craftsman
artificial *adj* artificial
artificio *m* artifice; workmanship; appliance, device; cunning; trick, ruse
artificio•so -sa *adj* ingenious, skillful; cunning, scheming, deceptive
artilugio *m* contraption, jigger
artillería *f* artillery
artillero *m* artilleryman, gunner
artimaña *f* trap; trick, cunning
artista *mf* artist
artísti•co -ca *adj* artistic
artolas *fpl* mule chair, cacolet
artríti•co -ca *adj* & *mf* arthritic
artritis *f* arthritis
arúspice *m* diviner, soothsayer
arveja *f* vetch, tare; (Chile) pea
arzobispo *m* archbishop
arzón *m* saddletree; **arzón delantero** saddlebow; **arzón trasero** cantle
as *m* ace; **as de fútbol** football star; **as de la pantalla** movie star; **as del volante** speed king
asa *f* handle; juice; **en asas** with arms akimbo
asa•do -da *adj* roasted; **bien asado** well done; **poco asado** rare ‖ *m* roast
asador *m* spit
asadura *f* entrails
asalaria•do -da *mf* wage earner
asaltar *tr* to assail, assault, storm; overtake, overcome
asalto *m* assault, attack; (box) round; (mil) storm; **tomar por asalto** to take by storm
asamblea *f* assembly
asar *tr* to roast ‖ *ref* to be burning up
asbesto *m* asbestos
ascendencia *f* ancestry
ascendente *adj* ascending; up
ascender §51 *tr* to promote ‖ *intr* to ascend, go up; be promoted; **ascender a** to amount to
ascendiente *adj* ascending; up ‖ *mf* ancestor ‖ *m* ascendancy, upper hand

ascensión *f* ascension, ascent
ascenso *m* ascent; promotion
ascensor *m* elevator; freight elevator
ascensorista *mf* elevator operator
asceta *mf* ascetic
ascéti•co -ca *adj* ascetic
asco *m* disgust, nausea, loathing; **dar asco** to turn the stomach; **estar hecho un asco** to be filthy; **hacer ascos de** to turn one's nose up at; **ser un asco** to be contemptible; be worthless
ascua *f* ember, live coal; **estar sobre ascuas** to be on needles and pins ‖ **ascuas** *interj* ouch!
asea•do -da *adj* clean, neat, tidy
asear *tr & ref* to clean up, tidy up; make one's toilet
asechamiento *m* or **asechanza** *f* snare, trap
asechar *tr* to set a trap for
asediar *tr* to besiege; harass
asedio *m* siege
asegundar *tr* to repeat right away
asegurable *adj* insurable
aseguración *f* insurance policy
asegura•dor -dora *mf* insurer, underwriter
asegurar *tr* to fasten, secure; assure; assert; seize; imprison; (*garantizar por un precio contra determinado accidente o pérdida*) insure ‖ *ref* to make sure; take out insurance
asemejar *tr* to make like; compare; resemble ‖ *ref* to be similar
asenso *m* assent; **dar asenso a** to believe
asentada *f* sitting; **de una asentada** at one sitting
asentaderas *fpl* (coll) buttocks
asentadillas — a asentadillas sidesaddle
asenta•do -da *adj* sedate; stable ‖ *f* see **asentada**
asentador *m* strap, razor strop
asentar §2 *tr* to seat; place; establish; tamp down, level; hone, sharpen; note down; (*un golpe*) impart; (*en la mente de uno*) impress; affirm; suppose ‖ *intr* to be becoming ‖ *ref* to sit down; be established, establish oneself; settle
asentimiento *m* assent
asentir §68 *intr* to assent
aseo *m* cleanliness, neatness, tidiness; care; toilet
asépti•co -ca *adj* aseptic
aseptizar §60 *tr* to purify, make aseptic
asequible *adj* accessible, obtainable
aserción *f* assertion
aserradero *m* sawmill
aserra•dor -dora *mf* sawyer; (coll) fiddler ‖ *f* power saw
aserraduras *fpl* sawdust
aserrar §2 *tr* to saw
aserrín *m* sawdust
aserruchar *tr* (SAm) to saw
aserto *m* assertion
asesinar *tr* to assassinate, murder
asesinato *m* assassination, murder
asesi•no -na *adj* murderous ‖ *mf* assassin, murderer

asesorar *tr* to advise ‖ *ref* to seek advice; get advice
asestar *tr* to aim; shoot; (*un golpe*) deal
aseveración *f* assertion, declaration
aseverar *tr* to assert, declare
asfaltar *tr* to asphalt
asfalto *m* asphalt
asfixia *f* asphyxiation
asfixiar *tr* to asphyxiate
así *adv* so, thus; **así . . . como** both . . . and; **así como** as soon as; as well as; **así que** as soon as; with the result that; **así y todo** even so, anyhow; **por decirlo así** so to speak; **y así sucesivamente** and so on
Asia *f* Asia; **el Asia Menor** Asia Minor
asiáti•co -ca *adj & mf* Asian, Asiatic
asidero *m* handle; occasion, pretext
así•duo -dua *adj* assiduous; frequent, persistent
asiento *m* seat; site; (*de un edificio*) settling; (*de una botella, una silla, etc.*) bottom; sediment; list, roll; wisdom, maturity; **asiento abatible** reclining seat; **asiento de rejilla** cane seat; **asiento lanzable** (aer) ejection seat; **asientos** buttocks; **planchar el asiento** to be a wallflower; **tome Vd. asiento** have a seat
asignación *f* assignment; salary; allowance
asignar *tr* to assign
asignatorio *m* heir, inheritor
asignatura *f* course, subject
asila•do -da *mf* inmate
asilar *tr* to shelter; place in an asylum; silo ‖ *ref* to take refuge; be placed in an asylum
asilo *m* asylum; shelter, refuge; (*para menesterosos*) home; **asilo de huérfanos** orphan asylum; **asilo de locos** insane asylum; **asilo de pobres** poorhouse
asilla *f* fastener; collarbone; **asillas** shoulder pole
asimetría *f* asymmetry
asimilar *tr* to compare; take in ‖ *intr* to be alike ‖ *ref* to assimilate; **asimilarse a** to resemble
asimismo *adv* also, likewise
asir §7 *tr* to grasp, seize ‖ *intr* to take root ‖ *ref* to take hold; fight, grapple; **asirse a** or **de** to cling to
Asiria *f* Assyria
asi•rio -ria *adj & mf* Assyrian
asistencia *f* attendance; assistance; reward; audience, persons present; welfare, social work; (Mex) sitting room, parlor; **asistencias** allowance, support
asistenta *f* charwoman, cleaning woman
asistente *adj* attendant; present ‖ *m* assistant, helper; bystander, spectator, person present; (mil) orderly
asistir *tr* to assist, help; attend; serve, wait on ‖ *intr* to be present; **asistir a** to be present at, attend
asma *f* asthma
asna *f* she-ass, jenny ass; **asnas** rafters
asnal *adj* donkey; brutish
asno *m* ass, donkey, jackass
asociación *f* association

asocia•do -da *adj* associated; associate ‖ *mf* associate, partner

asociar *tr* to associate; take as partner ‖ *ref* to become associated; become a partner; become partners

asolamiento *m* razing, destruction

asolar *tr* to parch, burn ‖ *ref* to become parched ‖ §61 *tr* to raze, destroy

asoleada *f* or **asoleadura** *f* (SAm) sunstroke

asolear *tr* to sun ‖ *ref* to bask; get sunburned

asomar *tr* (*p.ej., la cabeza*) to show, stick out ‖ *intr* to begin to show or appear; show ‖ *ref* to show, appear; stick out; get tipsy

asombradi•zo -za *adj* timid, shy

asombrar *tr* to shade; (*un color*) darken; frighten, astonish, amaze ‖ *ref* to be frightened; be astonished, amazed

asombro *m* fright; astonishment

asombro•so -sa *adj* astonishing, amazing

asomo *m* mark, token, sign; appearance; **ni por asomo** nothing of the kind, not by a long shot

asordar *tr* to deafen

aspa *f* X-shaped figure; reel; (*de molino de viento*) wheel, vane; propeller blade

aspar *tr* to reel; crucify; annoy, harass ‖ *ref* to writhe; take great pains

aspaviento *m* fuss, excitement

aspecto *m* aspect

aspereza *f* harshness; roughness; bitterness, sourness; gruffness

asperjar *tr* to sprinkle; sprinkle with holy water

áspe•ro -ra *adj* harsh; rough; bitter; gruff

áspid *m* asp

aspirador *m* vacuum cleaner; **aspirador de gasolina** (aut) vacuum tank

aspirante *m* applicant, candidate; **aspirante a cabo** private first class; **aspirante de marina** midshipman

aspirar *tr* to suck in, draw in; inhale ‖ *intr* to aspire; inhale, breathe in

aspirina *f* aspirin

asquear *tr* to loathe ‖ *ref* to be nauseated

asquero•so -sa *adj* disgusting, loathsome; nauseating; squeamish

asta *f* spear; shaft; flagpole, staff, mast; antler; (*de toro*) horn; **a media asta** at half-mast; **dejar en las astas del toro** to leave high and dry

asta•do -da *adj* horned ‖ *m* bull

ástato *m* astatine

aster *m* aster

asterisco *m* asterisk

astil *m* handle; shaft

astilla *f* chip, splinter

astillar *tr* & *ref* to chip, splinter

Astillejos *mpl* (astr) Castor and Pollux

astillero *m* dockyard, shipyard

astro *m* star, heavenly body; (fig) star, leading light

astrofísica *f* astrophysics

astrología *f* astrology

astronauta *m* astronaut

astronáuti•co -ca *adj* astronautic ‖ *f* astronautics

astronave *f* spaceship; **astronave tripulada** manned spaceship

astronavegación *f* space travel

astronomía *f* astronomy

astronómi•co -ca *adj* astronomic(al)

astróno•mo -ma *mf* astronomer

astro•so -sa *adj* ill-fated; vile, contemptible; ragged, shabby

astucia *f* cunning, craftiness; trick

asturia•no -na *adj* & *mf* Asturian

astu•to -ta *adj* astute, cunning; tricky

asueto *m* day off; leisure

asumir *tr* to assume, take on

asunción *f* assumption

asunto *m* subject, matter; affair, business; theme; **asuntos internacionales** world affairs

asurar *tr* to burn; parch; harass, worry

asurcar §73 *tr* to furrow, plow

asustadi•zo -za *adj* scary, skittish

asustar *tr* to scare, frighten

atabal *m* kettledrum; timbrel

ataca•do -da *adj* irresolute, undecided; mean, stingy

atacar §73 *tr* to attack; attach, fasten; pack, jam; (*un barreno*) tamp; corner, contradict ‖ *intr* to attack

ata•do -da *adj* timid, shy; weak, irresolute; insignificant; cramped ‖ *m* pack, bundle, roll

ataguía *f* cofferdam

atajar *tr* to stop, intercept, interrupt; to partition off ‖ *intr* to take a short cut ‖ *ref* to be abashed

atajo *m* short cut; (*en un escrito*) cut

atalaya *m* guard, lookout ‖ *f* watchtower; elevation

atalayar *tr* to watch from a watchtower; spy on

atanquía *f* depilatory ointment

atañer §70 *tr* to concern

ataque *m* attack; **ataque por sorpresa** surprise attack

atar *tr* to tie, fasten

ataracea *f* marquetry, inlaid work

atarantar *tr* to stun, daze

atardecer *m* late afternoon ‖ *v* §22 *intr* to draw toward evening; happen in the late afternoon

atarea•do -da *adj* busy

atarear *tr* to give an assignment to; overload with work ‖ *ref* to toil, work hard, keep busy

atarjea *f* sewer

atarugar §44 *tr* to peg, wedge; plug; stuff, fill; silence, shut up ‖ *ref* to become confused

atasajar *tr* to slash, hack; (*carne*) jerk

atascadero *m* mudhole; (fig) pitfall

atascar §73 *tr* to stop, stop up, clog, obstruct ‖ *ref* to get stuck; stuff oneself; clog, get clogged

atasco *m* sticking, clogging; obstruction

ataúd *m* casket, coffin

ataujía *f* damascene work

ataujiar §77 *tr* to damascene

ataviar §77 *tr* to dress, adorn, deck out

atávi•co -ca adj atavistic

atavío m dress, adornment; **atavíos** finery, frippery, chiffons

atediar tr to tire, bore

ateísmo m atheism

ateísta mf atheist

atelaje m harness

atemorizar §60 tr to frighten

atemperar tr to soften, moderate, temper; adjust, adapt

Atenas f Athens

atención f attention; **en atención a** in view of

atender §51 tr to attend to; heed, pay attention to; take care of; (a los parroquianos) wait on

atener §71 ref— **atenerse a** to abide by, rely on

ateniense adj & mf Athenian

atenta•do -da adj moderate, prudent; cautious ‖ m attempt, assault

atentar tr to attempt, try to commit ‖ intr — **atentar a** or **contra** (p.ej., la vida de una persona) to attempt ‖ §2 ref to grope

aten•to -ta adj attentive; courteous, polite ‖ f favor (letter)

atenuar §21 tr to extenuate

ate•o -a adj & mf atheist

aterciopela•do -da adj velvety

ateri•do -da adj stiff, numb with cold

aterrada f landfall

aterrajar tr to thread, tap

aterraje m landing

aterrar tr to terrify ‖ §2 tr to destroy, demolish; cover with earth ‖ intr to land ‖ ref to stand inshore

aterrizaje m landing; **aterrizaje a ciegas** blind landing; **aterrizaje aplastado** or **en desplome** pancake landing; **aterrizaje forzoso** emergency landing; **aterrizaje sin choque** soft landing

aterrizar §60 intr to land

aterronar tr to make lumpy ‖ ref to cake, lump

aterrorizar §60 tr to terrify

atesorar tr to treasure; hoard; (virtudes, perfecciones) possess

atesta•do -da adj stuffed, jammed; obstinate, stubborn ‖ m certificate

atestar tr (law) to attest ‖ §2 & **regular** tr to jam, pack, stuff, cram; stuff

atestiguar §10 tr to attest, testify, depose

atezar §60 tr to tan; blacken ‖ ref to become tanned, become sunburned

atiborrar tr to stuff ‖ ref to stuff, stuff oneself

atiesar tr to stiffen; tighten ‖ ref to become stiff; become tight

atildar tr to mark with a tilde, dash, or accent mark; point out; find fault with; tidy up, trim, adorn

atina•do -da adj careful, keen, wise

atinar tr to find, come upon ‖ intr to guess, guess right; be right; manage

atirantar tr (Mex) to make taut; brace ‖ ref (Mex) to die, pass away

atisbadero m peephole

atisbar tr to watch, spy on

atisbo m glimpse, look, peek

atizar §60 tr to stir, poke; snuff; rouse; (p.ej., un puntapié) let go

Atlánti•co -ca adj & m Atlantic

at•las m (pl **-las**) atlas

atleta mf athlete

atleticismo m athletics

atléti•co -ca adj athletic ‖ f athletics

atmósfera f atmosphere

atmosféri•co -ca adj atmospheric

atoar tr (naut) to tow

atocinar tr (un cerdo) to cut up; make into bacon; (coll) to murder ‖ ref to get angry; fall madly in love

atocha f esparto

atolondra•do -da adj confused; scatterbrained

atolondrar tr to confuse, bewilder

atolladero m mudhole; obstacle, difficulty

atollar intr & ref to get stuck, get stuck in the mud

atómi•co -ca adj atomic

átomo m atom

atóni•to -ta adj astounded, aghast

atontar tr to stun; to confuse, bewilder

atorar tr to clog, obstruct ‖ intr & ref to stick, get stuck; choke

atormentar tr to torment; torture

atornillar tr to screw, screw on

atortillar tr (SAm) to squash, flatten

atortolar tr to rattle, scare, intimidate

atosigar §44 tr to poison; harass ‖ ref to be in a hurry

atrabanca•do -da adj overworked; (Mex) hasty, rash; (Ven) deep in debt

atrabancar §73 tr & intr to rush through

atrabilia•rio -ria adj irascible, grouchy

atracada f quarrel, row

atracador m hold-up man

atracar §73 tr to hold up; bring up; stuff; (naut) to bring alongside, dock ‖ intr (naut) to come alongside, dock ‖ ref to stuff; quarrel

atracción f attraction; amusement

atraco m holdup

atracón m stuffing, gluttony; fight; push, shove

atracti•vo -va adj attractive ‖ m attraction; attractiveness

atraer §75 tr to attract

atragantar tr to choke down ‖ ref to choke; **atragantarse con** to choke on

atraillar §4 tr to leash; master, subdue

atrampar ref to fall into a trap; be stopped up; stick; get stuck

atrancar §73 tr to bar; obstruct ‖ intr to stride; read falteringly ‖ ref to get stuck; (una ventana) stick; (Mex) to stick to one's opinion

atrapamos•cas m (pl **-cas**) flytrap; (bot) Venus's-flytrap

atrapar tr to trap, catch; get, land, net

atrás adv back, backward; behind; before; previously; **atrás de** back of, behind; **hacerse atrás** to back up, move back; **hacia atrás** backwards; the other way

atrasa•do -da *adj* late; (*reloj*) slow; needy; back; retarded; in arrears; **atrasado de medios** short of funds; **atrasado de noticias** behind the times

atrasar *tr* to slow down; retard; set back, turn back; delay; leave behind; postdate ‖ *intr* to be slow ‖ *ref* to be slow; lose time; lag, stay behind; be late; be in debt

atraso *m* delay, slowness; backwardness; lag; **atrasos** arrears, delinquency

atravesada *f* (SAm) crossing

atravesar §2 *tr* to cross, go across; pierce; pass through, go through; put crosswise; stake, wager ‖ *ref* to butt in; fight, wrangle; get stuck

atrayente *adj* attractive

atreguar §10 *tr* to give a truce to; grant an extension to ‖ *ref* to agree to a truce

atrever *ref* to dare; **atreverse con** or **contra** to be impudent toward

atrevi•do -da *adj* bold, daring; impudent

atrevimiento *m* boldness, daring; impudence

atribuir §20 *tr* to attribute, ascribe ‖ *ref* to assume

atribular *tr* & *ref* to grieve

atributo *m* attribute

atril *m* lectern; music stand

atrincherar *tr* to entrench ‖ *ref* to dig in

atrio *m* hall, vestibule; court, courtyard; parvis

atri•to -ta *adj* contrite

atrocidad *f* atrocity; enormity

atrofia *f* atrophy

atrofiar *tr* & *ref* to atrophy

atrojar *tr* (*granos*) to garner; (Mex) to befuddle

atrona•do -da *adj* reckless, thoughtless

atronar §61 *tr* to deafen; stun ‖ *intr* to thunder

atropella•do -da *adj* brusk, violent; hasty; tumultuous

atropellar *tr* to trample; knock down; run over; disregard; do hurriedly ‖ *intr* & *ref* to act hastily or recklessly

atropello *m* trampling; knocking down; running over; abuse, insult; outrage

a•troz *adj* (*pl* **-troces**) atrocious; huge, enormous

atto. *abbr* atento

atufar *tr* to anger, irritate ‖ *ref* to get angry; (*el vino*) turn sour

atún *m* tuna

aturdi•do -da *adj* reckless, harebrained

aturdir *tr* to stun; perplex, bewilder

atusar *tr* to trim; smooth ‖ *ref* to dress fancily; (*el bigote*) twist

audacia *f* audacity

au•daz *adj* (*pl* **-daces**) audacious

audición *f* audition; hearing; concert; listening

audiencia *f* audience, hearing; audience chamber; royal tribunal; provincial high court

audífono *m* hearing aid; earphone

audiofrecuencia *f* audio frequency

audiómetro *m* audiometer

auditor *m* judge advocate; **auditor de guerra** judge advocate (*in army*); **auditor de marina** judge advocate (*in navy*)

auditorio *m* (*concurso de oyentes*) audience; (*local*) auditorium

auge *m* height, acme; boom; vogue; **estar en auge** to be booming

augur *m* augur

augurar *tr* to augur; wish ‖ *intr* to augur

augurio *m* augury; wish

augus•to -ta *adj* august

aula *f* classroom, lecture room; **aula magna** assembly hall

aulaga *f* gorse, furze

aullar §8 *intr* to howl

aullido *m* howl, howling

aúllo *m* howl

aumentar *tr* to augment, increase, enlarge; promote; exaggerate ‖ *intr* & *ref* to augment, increase

aumento *m* augmentation, increase, enlargement; promotion; (Guat, Mex) postscript, addition; **ir en aumento** to be on the increase

aun *adv* even; **aun cuando** although

aún *adv* still, yet

aunar §8 *tr* & *ref* to join, unite; combine, mix

aunque *conj* although, though

aúpa *interj* up!; **de aúpa** swanky; **los de aúpa** (taur) the picadors

aupar §8 *tr* to help up; extol

aura *f* gentle breeze; breath; popularity; turkey vulture

áure•o -a *adj* gold, golden

aureola *f* halo, aureole

auricular *m* earpiece, receiver; **auricular de casco** headpiece

auriga *m* (poet) coachman, charioteer

aurora *f* aurora, dawn; roseate hue

ausencia *f* absence

ausentar *tr* to send away ‖ *ref* to absent oneself

ausente *adj* absent; absent-minded ‖ *mf* absentee

auspiciar *tr* to sponsor, foster, back

auspicio *m* auspice; **bajo los auspicios de** under the auspices of

auste•ro -ra *adj* austere; harsh; honest; penitent

Australia *f* Australia

australia•no -na *adj* & *mf* Australian

Austria *f* Austria

austría•co -ca *adj* & *mf* Austrian

austro *m* south wind

auténtica *f* certificate; certification

autenticar §73 *tr* to authenticate

auténti•co -ca *adj* authentic; real ‖ *f* see **auténtica**

autillo *m* tawny owl

autísti•co -ca *adj* autistic

auto *m* edict; short Biblical play; miracle play; auto; **auto de prisión** commitment, warrant for arrest; **auto sacramental** play in honor of the Sacrament

autoabastecimiento *m* self-sufficiency

autoadhesi•vo -va *adj* self-adhesive

at
au

autoamortizable *adj* self-liquidating
autobanco *m* drive-in bank
autobiografía *f* autobiography
autobombo *m* self-glorification
autobús *m* autobus, bus
autocamión *m* motor truck
autocasa *f* motor home; mobile home; trailer
autocine *m* (Chile, Cuba) drive-in theater
autocinema *f* (Mex) drive-in theater
autocráti•co -ca *adj* autocratic(al)
autócto•no -na *adj* native, indigenous
autodefensa *f* self-defense
autodestrucción *f* self-destruction
autodeterminación *f* self-determination
autodidac•to -ta *adj* self-taught
autodisciplina *f* self-discipline
autodominio *m* self-control
autódromo *m* automobile race track
auto-escuela *f* driving school
autógena *f* welding
autogestión *f* self-administration; independence
autogobierno *m* self-government
autografiar §77 *tr* to autograph
autógra•fo -fa *adj & m* autograph
autoguia•do -da *adj* self-guided, homing
autolimpiador or **autolimpiante** *adj invar* self-cleaning
automación *f* automation
autómata *m* automaton
automáti•co -ca *adj* automatic
automatización *f* automation
automóvil *m* automobile
automovilista *mf* motorist
autonomía *f* autonomy; cruising radius
autóno•mo -ma *adj* autonomous, independent
autopega•do -da *adj* self-sealing
autopiano *m* player piano
autopista *f* turnpike, automobile road
autopsia *f* autopsy
au•tor -tora *mf* author; (*de un crimen*) perpetrator || *f* authoress
autoreactor *m* ramjet (engine)
autoridad *f* authority; pomp, display
autorita•rio -ria *adj & mf* authoritarian
autoriza•do -da *adj* authoritative
autorizar §60 *tr* to authorize; legalize; exalt
autorretrato *m* self-portrait
autoservicio *m* self-service
autostop *m* hitchhiking; **viajar en autostop** to hitchhike
autostopista *mf* hitchhiker
auto-teatro *m* drive-in movie theater
autovía *m* railway motor coach || *f* turnpike, automobile road
auxiliar *adj* auxiliary || *mf* auxiliary; aid, helper; substitute teacher || *v* §77 & **regular** *tr* to aid, help, assist; (*a un moribundo*) attend
auxilio *m* aid, help, assistance; **acudir en auxilio a** or **de** to come to the aid of; **auxilio en carretera** road service; **primeros auxilios** first aid
avahar *tr* to steam; breathe warmth on || *intr* to steam, give off vapor || *ref* to steam,

give off vapor; warm one's hands with one's breath
aval *m* indorsement; countersignature
avalancha *f* avalanche
avalorar *tr* to estimate; encourage
avaluación *f* appraisal, valuation
avaluar §21 *tr* to appraise, estimate
avalúo *m* appraisal, valuation
avance *m* advance; advance payment; (com) balance; (com) estimate; (mov) preview; **avance rápido** (mach, mov) fast forward
avante *adv* (naut) fore
avanza•do -da *adj* advanced; **avanzado de edad** advanced in years || *f* outpost, advance guard
avanzar §60 *tr* to advance, extend; propose || *intr & ref* to advance; approach
avanzo *m* balance sheet; estimate
avaricia *f* avarice
avaricio•so -sa *adj* avaricious
avarien•to -ta *adj* avaricious || *mf* miser
ava•ro -ra *adj* miserly || *mf* miser
avasallar *tr* to subject, subjugate, enslave || *ref* to submit
ave *f* bird; fowl; **ave canora** songbird; **ave de corral** barnyard fowl; **ave de mal agüero** Jonah, jinx; **ave de paso** bird of passage; **ave de rapiña** bird of prey; **ave fría** lapwing; **ave zancuda** wading bird
avecinar *tr* to bring near || *ref* to approach; take up residence
avecindar *tr* to domicile || *ref* to become a resident
avejentar *tr & ref* to age prematurely
avejigar §44 *tr, intr & ref* to blister
avellana *f* hazelnut
avellanar *tr* to countersink || *ref* to ̄shrivel, shrivel up
avellano *m* hazel, hazel tree
avemaría *f* Hail Mary, Ave Maria; **al avemaría** at sunset; **en un avemaría** in a jiffy; **saber como el avemaría** to have a thorough knowledge of
avena *f* oats
avenar *tr* to drain
avenate *m* gruel, oatmeal gruel
avenencia *f* agreement; deal, bargain
avenida *f* avenue; allée; flood, freshet; gathering, assemblage
aveni•do -da *adj* — **bien avenido** in agreement; **mal avenido** in disagreement || *f* see **avenida**
avenimiento *m* agreement; reconciliation
avenir §79 *tr* to reconcile, bring together || *ref* to be reconciled, agree; compromise; correspond
aventa•dor -dora *mf* winnower || *m* fan
aventaja•do -da *adj* excellent, outstanding; advantageous
aventajar *tr* to advance; put ahead; excel || *ref* to advance, win an advantage; excel
aventar §2 *tr* to fan; winnow; scatter to the winds; blow; drive away || *ref* to swell up; flee, run away
aventón *m* (Guat, Mex, Peru) push, shove; (*llevada gratuita*) (Mex) free ride; **pedir aventón** (Mex) to hitchhike

aventura f adventure; danger, risk
aventura•do -da adj hazardous, venturesome
aventurar tr to adventure, venture, hazard ‖ ref to adventure, take a risk; venture, to risk
aventure•ro -ra adj adventuresome, adventurous ‖ m adventurer, soldier of fortune ‖ f adventuress
avergonzar §9 tr to shame; embarrass ‖ ref to be ashamed; be embarrassed
avería f aviary; breakdown, failure; (com) damage; (naut) average
averiar §77 tr to damage ‖ ref to suffer damage; break down
averiguable adj ascertainable
averiguar §10 tr to ascertain, find out
aversión f aversion, dislike; **cobrar aversión a** to take a dislike for
aves•truz m (pl -truces) ostrich
avezar §60 tr to accustom ‖ ref to become accustomed
aviación f aviation
avia•dor -dora mf aviator, flyer ‖ m aviator, airman; (mil) airman; **aviador postal** air-mail pilot ‖ f aviatrix, airwoman
aviar §77 tr to make ready, prepare; equip, provide; **estar, encontrarse** or **quedar aviado** to be in a mess, be in a jam ‖ ref to hurry; (aer) to take off
avia•triz (pl -trices) aviatrix
avidez f avidity, greediness
ávi•do -da adj avid, greedy, eager
aviejar tr & ref to age prematurely
aviento m winnowing fork, pitchfork
avie•so -sa adj crooked, distorted; evil-minded, perverse
avilantar ref to be insolent
avilantez f insolence; meanness
avillana•do -da adj rustic, boorish
avillanar tr to debase, make boorish ‖ ref to become boorish
avinagra•do -da adj vinegarish, sour, crabbed
avinagrar tr to sour ‖ ref to become sour; turn into vinegar
avío m provision; arrangement; load; **¡al avío!** let's go!; **avíos** equipment, tools, outfit; **avíos de pescar** fishing tackle
avión m airplane; (orn) martin; **avión bi-rreactor** twin-jet plane; **avión de caza** pursuit plane; **avión a chorro, avión de propulsión a chorro** or **a reacción** jet plane; **avión de travesía** airliner; **avión supersónico** supersonic aircraft
avión-correo m mailplane
avioneta f small plane; **avioneta de alquiler** taxiplane
avisa•ches m (pl -ches) car caller
avisa•do -da adj prudent, wise; **mal avisado** rash, thoughtless
avisa•dor -dora adj warning ‖ mf informer; adviser ‖ m electric bell; **avisador de incendio** fire alarm
avisar tr to advise, inform; warn; report on
aviso m advice, information; warning; care, prudence; dispatch boat; advertisement; **sobre aviso** on the lookout

avispa f wasp
avispa•do -da adj brisk, wide-awake; (SAm) startled, scared
avispar tr to spur; to stir up ‖ ref to fret, worry
avispón m hornet
avistar tr to descry ‖ ref to meet, have an interview
avitaminosis f vitamin deficiency
avituallar tr to supply, provision ‖ ref to take in supplies
avivar tr to brighten, enlive, revive ‖ intr & ref to brighten, revive
avizor adj watchful, alert ‖ m watcher; **avizores** (slang) eyes
avizorar tr to watch, spy on ‖ ref to hide and watch, spy
ax interj ouch!, ow!
axioma m axiom
axiomáti•co -ca adj axiomatic
ay interj ay!, alas! **¡ay de mí!** woe is me! ‖ m sigh
aya f nurse, governess
ayer adj & m yesterday
ayo m tutor
ayuda m valet; **ayuda de cámera** valet de chambre ‖ f help, aid; enema
ayudanta f assistant; **ayudanta de cocina** kitchenmaid
ayudante m aid, assistant; adjutant; **ayudante de campo** aide-de-camp
ayudantía f (universidad) assistantship
ayudar tr to aid, help, assist
ayunar intr to fast
ayu•no -na adj fasting; uninformed; **en ayunas** or **en ayuno** fasting; before breakfast; uninformed; missing the point ‖ m fast, fasting
ayuntamiento m town or city council; town or city hall; sexual intercourse
azabacha•do -da adj jet, jet-black
azabache m jet; **azabaches** jet trinkets
aza•cán -cana adj menial ‖ mf drudge ‖ m water carrier
azada f hoe
azadón m hoe; grub hoe; **azadón de peto** or **de pico** mattock
azadonar tr to hoe
azafata f air hostess, stewardess; lady of the queen's wardrobe
azafate m wicker tray
azafrán m saffron
azafrana•do -da adj saffron
azafranar tr to saffron
azahar m orange or lemon blossom
azar m chance, hazard; accident, misfortune; fate, destiny; losing card; losing throw; (persona o cosa que traen mala suerte) Jonah
azarar ref to go awry; get rattled
azaro•so -sa adj hazardous, risky; unlucky
ázi•mo -ma adj unleavened
azófar m brass
azoga•do da adj fidgety, restless ‖ m quicksilver foil; **temblar como un azogado** to shake like a leaf

azogar §44 *tr* (*un espejo*) to silver ‖ *ref* to have mercury poisoning; shake, become agitated

azogue *m* quicksilver; market place; (coll) mirror

azonza•do -da *adj* stupid, dumb

azor *m* goshawk

azorar *tr* to abash; excite, stir up

Azores *fpl* Azores

azotar *tr* to whip, scourge; beat; flail; beat down upon

azote *m* whip; lash; (fig) scourge; **azotes y galeras** tiresome fare

azotea *f* flat roof, roof terrace

azteca *adj & mf* Aztec

azúcar *m* sugar; **azúcar de caña** cane sugar; **azúcar de remolacha** beet sugar

azucarar *tr* to sugar, sugarcoat; sugar over

azucare•ro -ra *adj* sugar ‖ *m* sugar bowl

azucena *f* Madonna lily, white lily

azufrar *tr* to sulfur

azufre *m* sulfur; brimstone

azul *adj & m* blue; **azul marino** navy blue

azular *tr* to color blue, dye blue

azulear *intr* to turn blue

azulejar *tr* to tile, cover with tiles

azulejo *m* glazed colored tile (orn) roller; (orn) indigo bunting; (orn) bee eater

azulones *mpl* blue jeans

azuzar §60 *tr* to sic; tease, incite

B

B, b (be) *f* second letter of the Spanish alphabet

B. *abbr* **Beato, Bueno**

baba *f* drivel, spittle, slobber; (*de culebras, peces, etc.*) slime

babear *intr* to slobber; froth

babel *m & f* (coll) bedlam, confusion; **estar en babel** to be daydreaming

babero *m* bib

Babia *f* — **estar en Babia** to be daydreaming

babieca *adj* silly, simple ‖ *mf* simpleton

Babilonia *f* (*imperio*) Babylonia; (*ciudad*) Babylon

babilóni•co -ca *adj* Babylonian

babilo•nio -nia *adj & mf* Babylonian ‖ *f* see **Babilonia**

bable *m* Asturian dialect; patois

babor *m* (naut) port

babosa *f* slug

babosada *f* (CAm, Mex) stupidity; foolish act

babosear *tr* to slobber over ‖ *intr* to slobber

babo•so -sa *adj* slobbery; (*con las damas*) (coll) mushy ‖ *m* (CAm) scoundrel ‖ *f* see **babosa**

babucha *f* slipper, mule

babuino *m* baboon

bacalao or **bacallao** *m* codfish

baceta *f* (cards) widow

bacía *f* basin, vessel; shaving dish

bacilo *m* bacillus

bacín *m* chamber pot

Baco *m* Bacchus

bacteria *f* bacterium

bacteria•no -na *adj* bacterial

bacteriología *f* bacteriology

bacteriólo•go -ga *mf* bacteriologist

báculo *m* staff; crook; (fig) staff, comfort; **báculo pastoral** crozier

bacha *f* (Mex) (cigarette) butt

bache *m* hole, rut; blip; **bache aéreo** air pocket

bachi•ller -llera *adj* garrulous ‖ *mf* garrulous person ‖ **bachiller** *mf* bachelor

bachillerar *tr* to confer the bachelor's degree on ‖ *ref* to receive the bachelor's degree

bachillerato *m* baccalaureate, bachelor's degree

bachillerear *intr* to babble, prattle

bachillería *f* babble, prattle; gossip

badajo *m* clapper

badana *f* (dressed) sheepskin; **zurrarle a uno la badana** to tan someone's hide

badén *m* gully, gutter

badil *m* fire shovel

badulaque *m* nincompoop

bagaje *m* beast of burden; (mil) baggage

bagatela *f* trinket; triviality; (Chile, Peru) pinball

bagazo *m* waste pulp, bagasse

bagre *adj* (Bol, Col) showy, gaudy; (CAm) sly, slick; (SAm) coarse, ill-bred; (Mex) stupid ‖ *m* catfish

bahareque *m* (CAm, Col, Ven) small hut

bahía *f* bay

bahorrina *f* slop; riffraff

bailable *adj* for dancing ‖ *m* ballet

bailadero *m* dance floor, dance hall

baila•dor -dora *mf* dancer

bailar *tr* (*p.ej., un vals*) to dance; (*un trompo*) spin ‖ *intr* to dance; spin; wobble

baila•rín -rina *mf* dancer ‖ *f* ballerina; **bailarina ombliguista** belly dancer

baile *m* dance; ball; ballet; **baile de etiqueta** dress ball, formal dance; **baile de los globos** bubble dance; **baile de máscaras** masked ball, masquerade ball; **baile de San Vito** (pathol) Saint Vitus's dance; **baile de trajes** costume ball, fancy-dress ball

baja *f* (*de los precios*) fall, drop; (*en la guerra*) casualty; **dar baja** to go down, decline; **dar de baja** to drop; (mil) to mark absent; **darse de baja** to drop out; **jugar a la baja** to bear the market

bajaca *f* (Ecuad) hair ribbon
bajada *f* descent; slope; downspout; (rad) lead-in wire
bajagua *f* (Mex) cheap tobacco
bajamar *f* low tide
bajar *tr* to lower, take down; bring down; (*la escalera*) go down, descend; humble ‖ *intr* to come down, go down; get off ‖ *ref* to bend down; get off; humble oneself
bajel *m* ship, vessel
bajeza *f* humbleness, lowliness; meanness, baseness
bajío *m* shoal, sandbank; pitfall; lowland
bajista *adj* bearish ‖ *mf* (fig) bear
ba•jo -ja *adj* low, under, lower; short; mean, base; lowly, humble; (mus) bass ‖ *m* shoal, sandbank; (mus) bass ‖ *f* see **baja** ‖ **bajo** *adv* down; low, in a low voice ‖ **bajo** *prep* under
bajón *m* bassoon; (*en el caudal, la salud, etc.*) decline, loss
bajonista *mf* bassoon player
bajorrelieve *m* bas-relief
bala *f* bullet; bale; **bala fría** spent bullet; **bala perdida** stray bullet; **ni a bala** (SAm) under no circumstances
balaca *f* boasting, show
balaceo *m* or **balacera** *f* (SAm) shooting; shootout
balada *f* ballad; (mus) ballade
bala•dí *adj* (*pl* -**díes**) trivial, paltry, cheap
baladro *m* scream, shout, outcry
baladronada *f* boast, boasting
baladronear *intr* to boast, brag
bálago *m* chaff
balance *m* balance, balance sheet; rocking, swinging; hesitation, doubt; (*de una nave*) rolling
balancear *tr* to balance ‖ *intr* & *ref* to rock, swing; hesitate, waver; (*la nave*) roll
balancín *m* balance beam; singletree; rocker arm; seesaw
balandra *f* sloop
balandrán *m* cassock
balanza *f* scales, balance; comparison, judgment; **balanza de pagos** balance of payments
balar *intr* to bleat; (coll) to pine
balastar *tr* to ballast
balasto *m* ballast
balaustre *m* baluster, banister
balay *m* wicker basket
balazo *m* shot; bullet wound
balbucear *tr* to stammer ‖ *intr* to stammer, stutter; to babble, to prattle
balbucir §1 *tr* & *intr* var of **balbucear**
Balcanes, los the Balkans
balcarrotas *fpl* (SAm) sideburns; (Mex) locks falling over sides of face
balcón *m* balcony
baldar *tr* to cripple; incapacitate; inconvenience; trump
balde *m* bucket, pail; **de balde** free, gratis; over, in excess; **en balde** in vain
baldear *tr* to wash with pails of water; (*una excavación*) bail out
baldí•o -a *adj* uncultivated; idle, lazy; care-

less; useless, vain; unfounded ‖ *m* untilled land
baldón *m* insult; blot, disgrace
baldonar *tr* to insult; stain, disgrace
baldosa *f* floor tile, paving tile; flagstone
baldra•gas *m* (*pl* -**gas**) jellyfish
balduque *s* red tape, wrapping tape
balear *tr* to shoot at, shoot, shoot to death
baleo *m* (SAm) shooting
balido *m* bleat, bleating
balísti•co -ca *adj* ballistic
baliza *f* buoy, beacon; danger signal
balizaje *m* (aer) airway lighting; (naut) buoys
balizar §60 *tr* to mark with buoys; mark off
balnea•rio -ria *adj* bathing ‖ *m* watering place, spa
balompié *m* football, soccer
balón *m* football; bale; balloon
baloncesto *m* basketball
balota *f* ballot
balotar *intr* to ballot
balsa *f* pool, puddle; raft; float; corkwood; **balsa salvavidas** life float
bálsamo *m* balsam, balm
balsear *tr* to cross by raft; ferry across
balsero *m* ferryman
bálti•co -ca *adj* Baltic
baluarte *m* bulwark
balumba *f* confusion; row
ballena *f* whale; whalebone; (*de corsé*) stay
ballesta *f* crossbow; spring, auto spring
ba•llet *m* (*pl* -**llets**) ballet
bambalinas *fpl* (theat) flies, borders
bambolear *intr* to sway, reel, wobble
bambolla *f* hulk; show, sham; show-off
bam•bú *m* (*pl* -**búes**) bamboo
banana *f* banana; (rad) plug
banane•ro -ra *adj* banana ‖ *m* banana tree
banano *m* banana tree
banas *fpl* (Mex) banns
banasta *f* hamper, large basket
banca *f* bench; banking; stand, fruit stand; (*en el juego*) bank; **banca de hielo** iceberg; **hacer saltar la banca** to break the bank
banca•rio -ria *adj* banking, bank
bancarrota *f* bankruptcy; **hacer bancarrota** to go bankrupt
bancarrote•ro -ra *adj* & *mf* bankrupt
banco *m* bench; bank; (*de peces*) school; **banco de ahorros** savings bank; **banco de datos** (*ordenador*) data bank; memory; **banco de hielo** iceberg; **banco de liquidación** clearing house
banda *f* band; ribbon; faction, party; flock; border, edge; bank, shore; (*de la mesa de billar*) cushion; **banda ciudadana** citizens band, CB; **banda de rodamiento** (aut) tread; **banda de tambores** drum corps; **irse a la banda** (naut) to list
bandada *f* flock, covey; (*de gente*) (coll) flock
bandaje *m* tire
bandazo *m* swerving; (naut) lurch
bandear *tr* to go through, pierce; to pursue; to make love to ‖ *ref* to manage
bandeja *f* tray; dish, platter

bandera *f* flag, banner; **con banderas desplegadas** with flying colors
banderilla *f* (taur) banderilla; **poner una banderilla a** to taunt; hit for a loan
banderín *m* (mil) color corporal; recruiting post
banderola *f* streamer, pennant; transom
bandido *m* bandit
bando *m* proclamation; faction, side
bandolera *f* bandoleer; female bandit; **en bandolera** across the shoulders
bandolero *m* highwayman, brigand
bandurria *f* Spanish lute
banquero *m* banker
banqueta stool, footstool; (Guat, Mex) sidewalk
banquete *m* banquet
banquetear *tr, intr & ref* to banquet
banquisa *f* floe, iceberg
bañadera *f* bathtub
bañado *m* chamber pot; marshland
baña•dor -dora *adj* bathing ‖ *mf* bather ‖ *m* bathing suit
bañar *tr* to bathe; dip; coat by dipping ‖ *ref* to bathe
bañera *f* bathtub
bañista *mf* bather; frequenter of a spa or seaside resort
baño *m* bath; bathing; bathroom; bathtub; **baño de asiento** sitz bath; **baño de ducha** shower bath; **baños** bathing place; spa
bao *m* (naut) beam
baptista *adj & mf* Baptist
baptisterio *m* baptistery
baque *m* thud, thump; bump, bruise
baquelita *f* bakelite
ba•quet *m* (*pl* **-quets**) bucket seat
baqueta *f* ramrod; drumstick; **correr baquetas** or **pasar por baquetas** to run the gauntlet
baquía *f* knowledge of the road, paths, rivers, etc. of a region; manual skill
baquia•no -na *adj* skillful, expert ‖ *mf* scout, pathfinder, guide
báqui•co -ca *adj* Bacchic
bar *m* bar; cocktail bar
barahunda *f* uproar, tumult
baraja *f* (*de naipes*) deck, pack; gang, mob; confusion, mix-up
barajadura *f* shuffling; dispute, quarrel
barajar *tr* (*naipes*) to shuffle; jumble, to mix ‖ *intr* to shuffle; fight, quarrel ‖ *ref* to get jumbled or mixed
baranda *f* railing; (*de la mesa de billar*) cushion
barandilla *f* balustrade, railing
barata *f* cheapness; barter; (Mex) bargain sale; (Chile, Peru) cockroach; (Col, Mex) junk store
baratero *m* shopkeeper
baratía *f* (SAm) cheapness
baratija *f* trinket
baratillo *m* second-hand goods; second-hand shop; bargain counter
baratío *m* (CAm) junk store
bara•to -ta *adj* cheap ‖ *m* bargain sale; **dar de barato** to admit for the sake of argu-

ment; **de barato** gratis, free ‖ *f* see **barata** ‖ **barato** *adv* cheap
báratro *m* (poet) hell
baratura *f* cheapness
baraúnda *f* uproar, tumult
barba *f* (*parte de la cara*) chin; (*pelo en ella*) beard; (*del papel*) deckle edge; (*de ave*) gill, wattle; **barba española** Spanish moss; **barbas** whiskers; **hacer la barba a** to shave; to bore, annoy; (Mex) to fawn on; **llevar por la barba** to lead by the nose; **mentir por la barba** (coll) to tell fish stories ‖ *m* (theat) old man
barbacoa *f* barbecue; (Col) kitchen cupboard; (Peru) attic
barbada *f* lower jaw of horse; bridle curb ‖ **la Barbada** Barbados
barbar *intr* to grow a beard; strike root
barbaridad *f* barbarism; outrage; piece of folly; large amount; **¡qué barbaridad!** how awful!, what nonsense!
barbarie *f* barbarity, barbarism
barbarismo *m* illiteracy; outrage; (gram) barbarism
bárba•ro -ra *adj* barbaric; barbarous ‖ *mf* barbarian
barbear *tr* to reach with the chin; be as high as ‖ *intr* to reach the same height; **barbear con** to be as high as
barbechar *tr* to plow for seeding; fallow
barbecho *m* fallow; **firmar como en un barbecho** to sign with one's eyes closed
barbería *f* barber shop
barberil *adj* barber
barbe•ro -ra *mf* barber; (Mex) flatterer
barbilampi•ño -ña *adj* smooth-faced, beardless; beginning, green
barbilla *f* tip of chin; (*de pluma*) barb; (*de pez*) wattle
bar•bón -bona *adj* bearded ‖ *m* graybeard; solemn old fellow; billy goat
barboquejo *m* chin strap
barbotar *tr & intr* to mutter, mumble
barbuchas *adj* beardless
barbu•do -da *adj* bearded, long-bearded, heavy-bearded ‖ *m* shoot, sucker
barbullar *tr & intr* to blabber
barca *f* small boat; bark; **barca perforador** offshore (oil) rig
barcia *f* chaff
barco *m* boat, ship; **barco cisternas** or **barco tanque** tanker; **barco de carga** cargo boat; **barco náufrago** shipwreck
barchi•lón -lona *mf* (Ecuad, Peru) nurse, orderly; (Arg, Bol, Peru) quack
barda *f* thatch; bard, horse armor
bardana *f* burdock
bardar *tr* to thatch; (*caballo*) bard
bardo *m* bard
baremo *m* (*escala*) scale; rate table
bargueño *m* carved inlaid secretary
bario *m* barium
barjuleta *f* haversack
barloventear *intr* to wander around; turn to windward
barlovento *m* windward
barman *m* bartender

bar·niz *m* (*pl* **-nices**) varnish; (*de la loza, la porcelana, etc.*) glaze; gloss, polish; (*conocimientos superficiales*) smattering; (aer) dope

barnizar §60 *tr* to varnish

barómetro *m* barometer; **barómetro aneroide** aneroid barometer

barón *m* baron

baronesa *f* baroness

barquero *m* boatman

barquilla *f* (naut) log; (naut) log chip; (aer) nacelle

barquillero *m* waffle iron; harbor boatman

barquillo *m* cone; waffle

barquín *m* bellows

barra *f* bar; (*de dinamita*) stick; (*en el tribunal*) bar, railing; **barra colectora** (elec) bus bar; **barra de labios** or **para los labios** lipstick; **barra imantada** bar magnet; **barras paralelas** (sport) parallel bars

barrabasada *f* fiendish prank, mean trick

barraca *f* cabin, hut; cottage; storage shed

barracón *m* barracks; fair booth

barragana *f* concubine

barranca *f* gorge, ravine, gully

barranco *m* gorge, ravine, gully; difficulty, obstruction; cliff, precipice

barrar *tr* to daub, smear

barrear *tr* to barricade; bar shut

barredera *f* street sweeper

barre·dor -dora *mf* sweeper; **barredora de alfombras** carpet sweeper; **barredora de nieve** snowplow

barredura *f* sweeping; **barreduras** sweepings

barremi·nas *m* (*pl* **-nas**) mine sweeper

barrena *f* auger, drill, gimlet; (*espiga para taladrar*) bit; (aer) spin; **barrena picada** (aer) tail spin; **entrar en barrena** (aer) to go into a spin

barrenar *tr* to drill; (*un buque*) to scuttle; blast; upset, frustrate; violate

barrende·ro -ra *mf* sweeper

barreno *m* large drill; drill hole; blast hole; pride, vanity; (Chile) mania, pet idea; **dar barreno a** (*un buque*) to scuttle

barreño *m* earthen dishpan

barrer *tr* to sweep, sweep away; graze ‖ *intr* to sweep; **barrer hacia dentro** to look out for oneself

barrera *f* barrier; barricade; (mil) barrage; crockery cupboard; tollgate; (rr) crossing gate; (taur) fence around inside of ring; (taur) first row of seats; **barrera de arrecifes** barrier reef; **barrera de paso a nivel** (rr) crossing gate; **barrera de sonido** or **barrera sónica** sound barrier

barriada *f* district, quarter

barrial *m* (SAm) mudhole; muddy ground

barrica *f* cask, barrel

barriga *f* belly; (*de una vasija, una pared, etc.*) bulge

barri·gón -gona or **barrigu·do -da** *adj* big-bellied

barril *m* barrel

barrilero *m* cooper, barrel maker

barrio *m* ward, quarter; suburb; **barrio bajo** slums; **barrio comercial** shopping district, business district; **el otro barrio** the other world; **estar vestido de barrio** to be dressed in house clothes

barro *m* mud; clay; earthenware; pimple; (coll) money; (Arg, Urug) blunder

barro·co -ca *adj* & *m* baroque

barro·so -sa *adj* muddy; pimply

barrote *m* heavy bar; bolt; cross brace

barruntar *tr* to guess; to sense

barrunto *m* guess, conjecture; sign, token, foreboding

bartola *f* belly; **a la bartola** lazily

bartolina *f* (CAm, W-I) jail, dungeon

bártulos *mpl* household tools; **liar los bártulos** to pack up one's belongings

barullo *m* confusion, tumult

basar *tr* to base; build ‖ *ref* — **basarse en** to base one's judgment on, rely on

basca *f* nausea, squeamishness; fit of temper, tantrum

basco·so -sa *adj* nauseated, squeamish

báscula *f* scales; platform scale

base *f* base; basis; **a base de** on the basis of

bási·co -ca *adj* basic

Basilea *f* Basle, Basel

basílica *f* basilica

basilisco *m* basilisk; **estar hecho un basilisco** to be in a rage

basquear *intr* to be nauseated

basquetbol *m* basketball

bastante *adj* enough ‖ *adv* enough; fairly, rather ‖ *m* enough

bastar *intr* to be enough, suffice; abound, be more than enough ‖ *ref* to be self-sufficient

bastardilla *f* italics

bastar·do -da *adj* & *mf* bastard

bastedad *f* coarseness; roughness; (CAm) abundance; excess

bastidor *m* frame; stretcher; (theat) wing; **entre bastidores** behind the scenes

bastilla *f* hem

bastillar *tr* to hem

bas·to -ta *adj* coarse, rough; uncouth ‖ *m* packsaddle; (naipe) club; **el basto** the ace of clubs

bastón *m* stick, staff; cane, walking stick; baton; **bastón de esquiar** ski pole or stick

bastoncillo *m* small stick; (*de la retina*) rod

bastonear *tr* to cane, beat

basura *f* sweepings; rubbish, litter, refuse; horse manure

basural *m* (SAm) dump; trash pile

basurero *m* trash can; rubbish dump; rubbish collector

basurita *f* trifle

bata *f* smock; dressing gown, wrapper; **bata de baño** bathrobe

batacazo *m* thud, bump

bataclán *m* (Cuba) burlesque show

bataclana *f* (Cuba) showgirl, stripteaser

batahola *f* racket, hubbub

batalla *f* battle; (*de un vehículo*) wheel base; (*de la silla de montar*) seat; (paint) battle piece; **batalla campal** pitched battle; **librar batalla** to do battle

batallar *intr* to battle, fight; hesitate, waver

ba
ba

bata·llón -llona adj (cuestión) controversial, moot ‖ m battalion
batata f sweet potato; (Arg) timidity
bate m baseball bat
batea f tray; flat-bottomed boat; (rr) flatcar
bateador m batter
batear tr & intr to bat
batel m small boat
batelero m boatman
batería f battery; footlights; **batería de cocina** kitchen utensils
baterista mf drummer
batiboleo m (Cuba, Mex) noise; confusion
bati·do -da adj (camino) beaten; (tejido) moiré ‖ m batter; milk shake; (rad) beat ‖ f battue; combing, search
batidor m beater; scout, ranger; **batidor de huevos** egg beater; **batidor de oro** goldbeater
batidora • beater, mixer
batiente m jamb; (hoja de puerta) leaf, door; (de piano) damper; wash, place where surf breaks
batihoja m goldbeater; sheet-metal worker
batimiento m beating; (phys) beat
batín m smoking jacket
batintín m Chinese gong
batir tr to beat; batter, beat down; (las alas) flap; (manos) clap; (las olas) ply; **batir tiendas** (mil) to strike camp
batiscafo m bathyscaphe
bato m simpleton, rustic
batuque m (Arg) uproar, rumpus, jamboree; **armar un batuque** (Arg) to raise a rumpus
baturrillo m hodgepodge
batuta f (mus) baton; **llevar la batuta** to boss the show
baúl m trunk; **baúl mundo** large trunk; **baúl ropero** wardrobe trunk
bauprés m bowsprit
bautismo m baptism; **bautismo de aire** first flight
bautista adj Baptist ‖ mf Baptist; baptizer; **el Bautista** John the Baptist
bautisterio m baptistery
bautizar §60 tr to baptize; (el vino) water
bautizo m baptism; christening party
báva·ro -ra adj & mf Bavarian
Baviera f Bavaria
baya f berry
bayeta f baize
ba·yo -ya adj bay ‖ m bay horse ‖ f see baya
bayoneta f bayonet
bayonetear tr to bayonet
bayunca f or **bayuna** f (CAm) bar; tavern
baza f trick; **meter baza en** to butt into
bazar m bazaar
ba·zo -za adj yellowish-brown ‖ m yellowish brown; spleen ‖ f see baza
bazofia f refuse, offal, garbage
bazuca f bazooka
bazucar §73 tr to stir, shake; tamper with
be m baa
beata f lay sister
beatería f cant, hypocrisy
beatificar §73 tr to beatify
beatísi·mo -ma adj most holy

bea·to -ta adj blessed; pious, devout; bigoted, prudish ‖ mf beatified person; devout person; bigot; churchgoer ‖ f see beata
bebé m baby; doll
bebede·ro -ra adj (archaic) drinkable ‖ m watering place; (Col, Ecuad, Mex) watering trough
bebedi·zo -za adj drinkable ‖ m potion, philter
bebe·dor -dora adj drinking ‖ mf drinker; hard drinker
beber m drink, drinking ‖ tr & intr to drink; **beber de** or **en** to drink out of ‖ ref to drink, drink up; (p.ej., un libro) to drink in
bebestible adj drinkable ‖ m drink
bebezón f (Col) drunk, spree
bebible adj drinkable
bebi·do -da adj tipsy, unsteady ‖ f drink
bebistrajo m dose, mixture
beborrotear intr to tipple
beca f scholarship, fellowship; (de los colegiales) sash
becacín m snipe, whole snipe
becacina f snipe, great snipe
becada f woodcock
beca·rio -ria mf scholar, fellow
becerra f snapdragon
becerrillo m calfskin
bece·rro -rra mf yearling calf ‖ m calfskin ‖ f see becerra
becuadro m (mus) natural sign
bedel m beadle
befa f jeer, flout, scoff
befar tr to jeer at, to scoff at ‖ intr (un caballo) to move the lips
be·fo -fa adj blobber-lipped; knock-kneed ‖ m (de animal) lip ‖ f see befa
beisbol m baseball
beisbolero m or **beisbolista** m baseball player
bejuco m cane, liana
beldad f beauty
beldar §2 tr to winnow
belén m crèche; bedlam, confusion; madhouse; gossip ‖ **Belén** Bethlehem
bel·fo -fa adj (labio) blobber; blobber-lipped ‖ m (de animal) lip; blobber lip
belga adj & mf Belgian
Bélgica f Belgium
bélgi·co -ca adj Belgian ‖ f see Bélgica
belicista mf warmonger
béli·co -ca adj warlike
belico·so -sa adj bellicose
beligerante adj & mf belligerent
belitre adj low, mean ‖ m scoundrel
bella·co -ca adj cunning, sly; wicked ‖ mf scoundrel
bellaquear intr to cheat, be crooked; (SAm) to be stubborn; rear
bellaquería f cunning, slyness; wickedness
belleza f beauty; **belleza exótica** glamour girl
be·llo -lla adj beautiful, fair
bellota f acorn; carnation bud
bem·bo -ba adj thick-lipped; (Mex) simple, silly ‖ mf (persona) thicklips
bemol adj & m (mus) flat; **tener bemoles** to be a tough job

bencedrina *f* benzedrine
bencina *f* benzine
bendecir §11 *tr* to bless; consecrate; **bendecir la mesa** to say grace
bendición *f* benediction, blessing; godsend; (*en la mesa*) grace; **bendiciones** wedding ceremony; **echar la bendicióna** to have nothing more to do with
bendi•to -ta *adj* blessed, saintly; simple, silly; happy; (*agua*) holy; **como el pan bendito** as easy as pie ‖ *m* simple-minded soul
benedícite *m* grace; **rezar el benedícite** to say grace
benedicti•no -na *adj* & *mf* Benedictine ‖ *m* benedictine
beneficencia *f* beneficence; charity, welfare; social service
beneficia•do -da *mf* person or charity receiving the proceeds of a benefit performance
beneficiar *tr* to benefit; (*la tierra*) cultivate; (*una mina*) work, exploit; (*minerales*) process, reduce; (*una región del país*) serve; season; slaughter ‖ *ref* — **beneficiarse de** to take advantage of
beneficia•rio -ria *mf* beneficiary
beneficio *m* benefit; profit, gain, yield; (*de una mina*) exploitation; smelting, ore reduction; benefit performance; **a beneficio de** for the benefit of; on the strength of; **beneficios sociales** fringe benefits
benefici•so -sa *adj* beneficial, profitable
benéfi•co -ca *adj* charitable, benevolent
beneméri•to -ta *adj* & *mf* worthy; **benemérito de la patria** national hero
beneplácito *m* approval, consent
benevolencia *f* benevolence
benévo•lo -la *adj* benevolent, kind-hearted
bengala *f* Bengal light; (aer) flare
benignidad *f* benignity, mildness, kindness; (*del tiempo*) mildness
benig•no -na *adj* benign, mild, kind; (*tiempo*) clement, mild
benjamín *m* baby (*the youngest child*)
beodez *f* drunkenness
beo•do -da *adj* & *mf* drunk
bequista *mf* (CAm, Cuba) scholarship holder; grant winner
berbi•quí *m* (*pl* -**quíes**) brace; **berbiquí y barrena** brace and bit
berenjena *f* eggplant
berenjenal *m* eggplant patch; (coll) predicament, jam, fix
bergante *m* scoundrel, rascal
bergantín *m* (naut) brig; **bergantín goleta** (naut) brigantine
berilio *m* beryllium
berkelio *m* berkelium
berli•nés -nesa *adj* Berlin ‖ *mf* Berliner
bermejear *intr* to turn bright red; look bright red
berme•jo -ja *adj* vermilion, bright-red
berme•jón -jona *adj* red, reddish
bermellón *m* vermilion
berrear *intr* to bellow, low; bawl, yowl
berrenchín *m* rage, tantrum
berrido *m* bellow; scream, yowl

berrín *m* touchy person, cross child
berrinche *m* tantrum, conniption
berro *m* water cress
berza *f* cabbage
berzal *m* cabbage patch
berzas *m* or **berzotas** *m* dunderhead, flop
besalamano *m* (obs) announcement, written in the third person and marked B.L.M. (*kisses your hand*)
besamanos *m* levee, reception at court; throwing kisses
besar *tr* to kiss; to graze ‖ *ref* to bump heads together
beso *m* kiss; **beso sonado** buss
bestia *adj* stupid ‖ *mf* dunce ‖ *f* beast; **bestia de carga** beast of burden
bestial *adj* beastly; (coll) terrific
besucar §73 *tr* & *intr* to keep on kissing
besu•cón -cona *adj* kissing ‖ *mf* kisser
besuquear *tr* & *intr* to keep on kissing
betabel *m* (Mex) beet
betún *m* bitumen, pitch; shoe polish
bezo *m* blubber lip; proud flesh
bezu•do -da *adj* thick-lipped
biberón *m* nursing bottle
Biblia *f* Bible
bíbli•co -ca *adj* Biblical
bibliófi•lo -la *mf* bibliophile
bibliografía *f* bibliography
bibliógra•fo -fa *mf* bibliographer
biblioteca *f* library; **biblioteca de consulta** reference library; **biblioteca de préstamo** lending library
biblioteca•rio -ria *mf* librarian
bibliotecnia *f* bookmaking; library science
biblioteconomía *f* library science
bicameral *adj* bicameral
bicarbonato *m* bicarbonate
bicicleta *f* bicycle
bicherío *m* (SAm) vermin
bichero *m* boat hook
bicho *m* bug, insect; vermin; animal; fighting bull; simpleton; brat; **bicho viviente** living soul; **mal bicho** scoundrel; ferocious bull
bidón *m* (*bote, lata*) can; (*tonel de metal*) drum
biela *f* connecting rod
bielda *f* winnowing rack; winnowing
bieldar *tr* to winnow
bieldo *m* winnowing pitch rake
bien *adv* well; readily; very; indeed; **ahora bien** now then; **bien como** just as; **bien que** although; **más bien** rather; somewhat; **no bien** as soon as; scarcely ‖ *s* welfare; property; darling; **bienes** wealth, riches, possessions; **bienes de fortuna** worldly possessions; **bienes dotales** dower; **bienes inmuebles** real estate; **bienes muebles** personal property; **bienes raíces** real estate; **bienes relictos** estate; **bienes semovientes** livestock; **bien público** commonweal; **en bien de** for the sake of
bienal *adj* biennial
bienama•do -da *adj* dearly beloved
bienandanza *f* happiness, prosperity
bienaventura•do -da *adj* happy, blissful; blessed; simple

bienaventuranza *f* happiness, bliss; blessedness

bienestar *m* well-being, welfare

bienhabla•do -da *adj* well-spoken

bienhada•do -da *adj* fortunate, lucky

bienhe•chor -chora *adj* beneficent ‖ *m* benefactor ‖ *f* benefactress

bienintenciona•do -da *adj* well-meaning

bienio *m* biennium

bienquerencia *f* affection, fondness

bienquistar *tr* to bring together, reconcile

bienvenida *f* safe arrival; welcome; **dar la bienvenida a** to welcome

bienveni•do -da *adj* welcome ‖ *f* see **bienvenida**

bienvivir *intr* to live in comfort; live decently, properly

bif•tec *m* (*pl* **-tecs**) beefsteak

bifurcar §73 *ref* to branch, fork

bigamia *f* bigamy

bíga•mo -ma *adj* bigamous ‖ *mf* bigamist

bigornia *f* two-horn anvil

bigote *m* mustache; **bigotes** (*del gato*) whiskers; **tener bigotes** to have a mind of one's own

bigudí *m* hair curler

bikini *m* bikini (swimsuit)

bilingüe *adj* bilingual

bilis *f* bile; **descargar la bilis** to vent one's spleen

bilma *f* (med) compress

billar *m* billiards; billiard table; billiard room; **billar romano** pinball

billete *m* ticket; note, bill; **billete de abono** season ticket; commutation ticket; **billete de banco** bank note; **billete de ida y vuelta** round-trip ticket; **billete kilométrico** mileage ticket; **medio billete** half fare

billetero *m* billfold; ticket agent

billón *m* (U.S.A.) trillion; (Brit) billion

bimba *f* top hat; (Mex) drinking spree

bimotor *adj* twin-motor ‖ *m* twin-motor plane

biodegradable *adj* biodegradable

biofísi•co -ca *adj* biophysical ‖ *f* biophysics

biografía *f* biography

biógra•fo -fa *mf* biographer

biología *f* biology

biólo•go -ga *mf* biologist

biombo *m* folding screen

bioplasma *f* bioplasm

biopsia *f* biopsy

bióxido *m* dioxide

bioquími•co -ca *adj* biochemical ‖ *mf* biochemist ‖ *f* biochemistry

bipartición *f* fission, splitting

bípe•do -da *adj* & *mf* biped; human

biplano *m* biplane

biplaza *m* (aer) two-seater

birimbao *m* jews'-harp

birlar *tr* to knock down, shoot down; outwit; **birlar algo a alguien** to snitch something from someone

birlocha *f* kite

Birmania *f* Burma

birma•no -na *adj* & *mf* Burmese

biro *m* or **birome** *f* (Arg) ball-point pen

birreta *f* biretta, red biretta

birrete *m* mortarboard, academic cap

bis *interj* encore! ‖ *m* encore

bisabue•lo -la *mf* great-grandparent ‖ *m* great-grandfather ‖ *f* great-grandmother

bisagra *f* hinge

bisar *tr* to repeat

bisbisar *tr* to mutter, mumble

bisecar §73 *tr* to bisect

bisel *m* bevel edge

biselar *tr* to bevel

bisies•to -ta *adj* leap

bismuto *m* bismuth

bisnie•to -ta *mf* great-grandchild ‖ *m* great-grandson ‖ *f* great-granddaughter

biso•jo -ja *adj* squint-eyed, cross-eyed

bisonte *m* bison; buffalo

biso•ño -ña *adj* green, inexperienced ‖ *mf* greenhorn, rookie

bisté *m* or **bistec** *m* beefsteak

bisun•to -ta *adj* dirty, greasy

bisutería *f* costume jewelry

bitácora *f* binnacle

bitoque *m* bung; (CAm) sewer; (Mex) spigot

Bizancio Byzantium

bizanti•no -na *adj* & *mf* Byzantine

bizarría *f* gallantry, bravery; magnanimity

biza•rro -rra *adj* gallant, brave; magnanimous

bizcar §73 *tr* to wink ‖ *intr* to squint

biz•co -ca *adj* squint-eyed, cross-eyed

bizcocho *m* biscuit; cake, sponge cake; hardtack; bisque

bizma *f* poultice

bizmar *tr* to poultice

biznie•to -ta *mf* var of **bisnieto**

bizquear *intr* to squint

bizquera *f* squint

blanca *f* steel blade; **sin blanca** penniless

blanca•zo -za *adj* whitish

blan•co -ca *adj* white; (*tez*) fair; (*fuerza*) water; (*arma*) steel; (*cobarde*) yellow; blank ‖ *mf* (*persona*) white; coward ‖ *m* (*color*) white; blank; target; aim, object; interval; white heat; blank form; **dar en el blanco** to hit the mark; **en blanco** (*hoja*) blank; **hacer blanco** to hit the mark; **quedarse en blanco** to not get the point; to be disappointed ‖ *f* see **blanca**

blancor *m* whiteness

blancura *f* whiteness; purity

blancuz•co -ca *adj* whitish; dirty-white

blandear *tr* to persuade; brandish ‖ *intr* & *ref* to yield, give in

blandengue *adj* soft, colorless

blandir §1 *tr*, *intr* & *ref* to brandish

blan•do -da *adj* bland, soft; indulgent; flabby; sensual; cowardly; (*ojos*) tender

blandón *m* wax candle; candlestick

blandura *f* blandness, softness; tolerance; flabbiness, sensuality; flattery; mild weather; cowardice

blanqueadura *f* whitening; bleaching; whitewash

blanquear *tr* to whiten, bleach; blanch; whitewash; tin ‖ *intr* to turn white

blanqueci•no -na *adj* whitish

blanqui•llo -lla *adj* white, whitish ‖ *m* (Guat, Mex) egg; (Chile, Peru) white peach
blasfemar *tr* to blaspheme, curse
blasfemia *f* blasphemy
blasfe•mo -ma *adj* blasphemous ‖ *mf* blasphemer
blasón *m* (*ciencia de los escudos de armas; escudo de armas*) heraldry; (heral) charge; (fig) glory, honor
blasonar *tr* to emblazon; (fig) to emblazon, extol ‖ *intr* to boast; **blasonar de** to boast of being
bledo *m* straw; **no me importa un bledo** or **no se me da un bledo de ello** that doesn't matter a rap to me
blindaje *m* armor; (elec) shield
blindar *tr* to armor, armor-plate; (elec) to shield
B.L.M. *abbr* besalamano
bloc *m* (*pl* **bloques**) pad
blof *m* bluff
blofear *intr* to bluff
blon•do -da *adj* blond, fair, flaxen, light; (Arg) curly ‖ *f* blond lace
bloque *m* block; (*de papel*) pad; **bloque de hormigón** concrete block
bloquear *tr* to blockade; (*un coche, un tren*) brake; (*créditos*) freeze
bloqueo *m* blockade; (*de crédito*) freezing; **bloqueo vertical** (telv) vertical hold
b.l.p. *abbr* besa los pies
blujins *mpl* blue jeans
blusa *f* blouse, smock; (*de mujer*) shirtwaist; (Col) jacket
boardilla *f* dormer window; garret
boato *m* show, pomp
bobada *f* folly, piece of folly
bobalías *mf* simpleton, dunce
bobali•cón -cona *adj* simple, silly ‖ *mf* simpleton, nitwit
bobear *intr* to talk nonsense; to dawdle, loiter around
bobería *f* folly, nonsense
bóbilis—de bóbilis free, for nothing; without effort
bobina *f* bobbin; (elec) coil; **bobina de chispas** spark coil; **bobina de encendido** ignition coil, spark coil; **bobina de sintonía** tuning coil
bobinar *tr* to wind
bo•bo -ba *adj* simple, foolish, stupid ‖ *mf* simpleton, fool ‖ *m* (archaic) clown, jester
boca *f* mouth; speech; taste, flavor; (*del estómago*) pit; **a boca de jarro** immoderately; at close range; **boca de agua** hydrant; **boca de dragón** (bot) snapdragon; **boca de riego** hydrant; **buscarle a uno la boca** to draw someone out; **decir con la boca chica** to offer as a mere formality; **no decir esta boca es mía** to not say a word
bocacalle *f* street entrance; intersection
boca•caz *m* (*pl* **-caces**) spillway
bocadillo *m* tape, ribbon; snack, bite; farmer's snack in the field; sandwich
bocadito *m* little bit; (Cuba) cigarillo (*cigaret wrapped in tobacco*)

bocado *m* bite, morsel; bit; **bocado de Adán** Adam's apple; **no tener para un bocado** to not have a cent
bocal *m* narrow-mouthed pitcher; (*de un puerto*) narrows
bocallave *f* keyhole
bocamanga *f* cuff, wristband
bocanada *f* (*de líquido*) swallow; (*de humo*) puff; (*de viento*) gust; boasting
bocartear *tr* to crush, stamp
bocaza *f* loudmouth; gossip
bocera *f* smear on lips
boceto *m* sketch, outline; wax model, clay model
bocina *f* horn, trumpet; auto horn; phonograph horn; ear trumpet
bocio *m* goiter
bocoy *m* large barrel
bocha *f* bowling ball
bochar *tr* (Mex, Ven) to turn down; (Mex, Ven) insult
boche *m* small hole in ground for boys' game; (Ven) slight, snub
bochinche *m* uproar, tumult, row
bochorno *m* sultry weather; blush, embarrassment, shame
bochorno•so -sa *adj* sultry, stuffy; embarrassing, shameful
boda *f* marriage, wedding; **bodas de Camacho** banquet, lavish feast
bodega *f* wine cellar; dock warehouse; granary; grocery store; (*de nave*) hold; cellar; (*hombre que bebe mucho*) tank
bodegón *m* hash house, beanery; saloon; still life
bodegue•ro -ra *mf* cellarer; grocer
bodijo *m* unequal match; simple wedding
bodoque *m* lump; dunce, dolt; (Mex) bump, lump
bodoquera *f* peashooter
bóer *mf* Boer
bofe *adj invar* (CAm) unpleasant, disgusting ‖ *m* (coll) lung; (P-R) cinch, snap; **echar el bofe** or **los bofes** to drudge, to grind; **bofes** lights (*of sheep, etc.*)
bofetada *f* slap in the face
boga *mf* rower ‖ *f* vogue, fashion; rowing
bogar §44 *intr* to row
bogavante *m* lobster
bohardilla *f* dormer window; garret
bohe•mio -mia *adj* & *mf* Bohemian
bohío *m* hut, shack
boicotear *tr* to boycott
boicoteo *m* boycott, boycotting
boina *f* beret
boj *m* boxwood
boja *f* southernwood
bojar *tr* to measure the perimeter of; (*el cuero*) scrape clean ‖ *intr* to measure
bola *f* ball; marble; bowling; shoe polish; shoeshine; (cards) slam; lie, deceit; (Mex) brawl, riot; **bola de alcanfor** moth ball; **bola de cristal** crystal ball; **bola de nieve** snowball; **bola rompedora** wrecking ball; **bolas** Gaucho lasso tipped with balls; **dejar que ruede la bola** to let things take

their course; **raspar la bola** (Chile) to clear out, beat it

bolada *f* (*de una bola*) throw; luck, opportunity; (Arg) billiard stroke; (Chile) dainty, tidbit; (Guat, Mex) lie, fib

bolado *m* (CAm) rumor

bolazo *m* hit with a ball; **de bolazo** (coll) hurriedly, right away; (Mex) at random

bolchevique *adj & mf* Bolshevik

bolchevismo *m* Bolshevism

boleada *f* (Arg) hunting with bolas; (Mex) shoeshine; (Peru) flunking

bolear *tr* to throw; (Arg) to catch with bolas; (*zapatos*) (Mex) to shine; (SAm) to kick out, flunk ‖ *intr* to play for fun; lie; boast ‖ *ref* (Arg, Urug) to rear and fall backwards; upset; blush

bole•ro -ra *mf* bolero dancer ‖ *m* bolero (*dance; music; jacket*); (Mex) bootblack ‖ *f* bowling alley; **bolera encespada** bowling green

boleta *f* pass, permit, admission ticket; (mil) billet; ballot

boletería *f* ticket office

boletín *m* bulletin; ticket; form; press release

boleto *m* ticket

boliche *m* bowling; bowling alley; (SAm) hash house

bólido *m* fireball, bolide

bolígrafo *m* ball-point pen

bolilápiz *m* (Mex) ball-point pen

bolillo *m* bobbin for making lace; frame for stiffening lace cuffs

Bolivia *f* Bolivia

bolivia•no -na *adj & mf* Bolivian

bo•lo -la *adj* (CAm, Mex) drunk; *m* ninepin, tenpin; dunce, blockhead; (*de escalera*) newel; (cards) slam; **bolos** bowling, ninepins, tenpins; **jugar a los bolos** to bowl

Bolonia *f* Bologna

bolsa *f* purse, pocketbook; pouch; stock exchange, stock market; (*en el vestido*) bag, pucker; grant, award; **bolsa de agua caliente** hotwater bottle; **bolsa de aire** (aut) air bag; **bolsa de hielo** ice bag; **bolsa de trabajo** employment bureau; **bolsa isotérmica** Thermos bottle; **hacer bolsa** (*un vestido*) to bag; **jugar a la bolsa** to play the market

bolsear *tr* to pick the pocket of; (Arg, Bol, Urug) to jilt; (Chile) to sponge on

bolsero *m* (SAm) sponger; (Mex) pickpocket

bolsicalculadora *f* pocket calculator

bolsillo *m* pocket; purse, pocketbook

bolsista *m* broker, stockbroker; (CAm, Mex) pickpocket

bolso *m* purse, pocketbook; **bolso de mano** handbag

bollo *m* bun, roll; bump, lump; dent; (*en un vestido*) puff; (*en adorno de tapicería*) tuft; **bollo de crema** cream puff

bomba *f* pump; bomb; fire engine; lamp globe; high hat; firecracker; soap bubble; bombshell; **a prueba de bombas** bombproof; **bomba atómica** atomic bomb; **bomba coche** car bomb; **bomba cohete** rocket bomb; **bomba de engrase** grease

gun; **bomba de hidrógeno** hydrogen bomb; **bomba de incendios** fire engine; **bomba de profundidad** depth bomb; **bomba de sentina** bilge pump; **bomba estomacal** stomach pump; **bomba neutrónica** neutron bomb; **bomba rompedora** blockbuster; **bomba volante** buzz bomb; **caer como una bomba** to fall like a bombshell; to burst in unexpectedly

bombachas *fpl* loose-fitting baggy trousers

bombardear *tr & intr* to bomb; bombard; **bombardear en picado** to dive-bomb

bombardeo *m* bombing; bombarding; **bombardeo en picado** dive bombing

bombardero *m* bomber; bombardier

bomba-reloj *f* time bomb

bombazo *m* bomb explosion; bomb hit; bomb damage

bombear *tr* to bomb; ballyhoo, puff up; pump; (SAm) to reconnoiter; (Col) to fire, dismiss ‖ *ref* to camber, bulge

bombero *m* fireman; pumpman

bombilla *f* bulb, light bulb; lamp chimney; tube for sucking up maté; **bombilla de destello** flash bulb

bombillo *m* trap, stench trap; (naut) pump

bombista *m* lamp maker; (*el que da bombos*) booster

bom•bo -ba *adj* astounded, stunned; (W-I) lukewarm ‖ *m* bass drum; ballyhoo; (naut) barge, lighter; **dar bombo a** to ballyhoo, puff up; **irse al bombo** (Arg) to fail ‖ *f* see **bomba**

bombón *m* bonbon, candy

bombona *f* carboy

bombonera *f* candy box

bona•chón -chona *adj* goodnatured, kind, simple

bonancible *adj* (*tiempo*) fair; (*mar*) calm; (*viento*) moderate

bonanza *f* fair weather, calm seas; prosperity, boom; rich ore pocket

bona•zo -za *adj* kind-hearted

bondad *f* kindness; favor; **tener la bondad de** to have the kindness to

bondado•so -sa *adj* kind, generous

bonete *m* cap, hat; candy bowl

bonetería *f* hat shop; notion store

bongo *m* (SAm) barge; canoe

boniato *m* sweet potato

bonificar §73 *tr* to improve; give a discount on

boni•to -ta *adj* pretty, nice; pretty good

bono *m* bond; food voucher

boñiga *f* manure, cow dung

boom *m* (*mercado, bolsa*) boom

boqueada *f* gasp of death

boquear *tr* to pronounce, utter ‖ *intr* to gasp

boquerel *m* nozzle

boquete *m* gap, breach, opening

boquiabier•to -ta *adj* open-mouthed

boquian•cho -cha *adj* wide-mouthed

boquiangos•to -ta *adj* narrow-mouthed

boquihundi•do -da *adj* hollow-mouthed

boquilla *f* (*de instrumento de viento*) mouthpiece; (*de pipa*) stem; (*de cigarro*) tip; (*de aparato de alumbrado*) burner; cigar holder, cigarette holder; (*de manguera*) nozzle; opening in irrigation canal; opening at bottom of trouser leg

boquirro•to -ta *adj* garrulous

boquiverde *adj* obscene, smutty

bórax *m* borax

borbollar or **borbollear** *intr* to bubble up

borbollón *m* bubbling; **a borbollones** impetuously

borborigmos *mpl* rumbling of the bowels

borbotar *intr* to bubble up, bubble over

borce•guí *m* (*pl* **-guíes**) high shoe

borda *f* hut; (naut) gunwale; **arrojar, echar** or **tirar por la borda** to throw overboard

bordada *f* (naut) tack; **dar bordadas** (naut) to tack; pace to and fro

bordado *m* embroidery

bordadura *f* embroidery

bordar *tr* to embroider

borde *m* border, edge; fringe; rim; **borde de la acera** curb; **borde del mar** seaside

bordear *tr* to border ‖ *intr* to go on the edge; (naut) to tack

bordo *m* (naut) board; (naut) side; (naut) tack; (Guat, Mex) dam, dike; **a bordo** (naut) on board; **al bordo** (naut) alongside; **de alto bordo** seagoing; distinguished, important

bordón *m* (*de tambor*) snare; pilgrim's staff; pet word; burden, refrain

bordonear *intr* to grope along with a stick; to go around begging

borgoña *m* Burgundy (*wine*) ‖ **la Borgoña** Burgundy

borgo•ñón -ñona *adj & mf* Burgundian

boricua or **borinque•ño -ña** *adj & mf* Puerto Rican

borla *f* tassel; powder puff; **tomar la borla** to take a higher degree, take the doctor's degree

borne *m* binding post; (*de la lanza*) tip

bornear *tr* to bend, twist; (*sillares pesados*) set in place ‖ *intr* to swing at anchor ‖ *ref* to warp

borra *f* fuzz, nap, lint

borrachera *f* drunkenness; spree, binge; great exaltation; (coll) piece of folly; **pegarse una borrachera** to go on a binge

borrachería *f* (Mex) bar, tavern

borrachín *m* drunkard

borra•cho -cha *adj* drunk; (*habitualmente*) drinking ‖ *mf* drunkard

borrador *m* blotter, day book; rough draft; eraser

borradura *f* striking out, scratching out

borraj *m* borax

borrajear *tr & intr* to scribble; doodle

borrar *tr* to scratch out, cross out; erase, rub out; darken, obscure; blot, smear

borrasca *f* storm, tempest; upset, setback

borrasco•so -sa *adj* stormy

borregos *mpl* fleecy clouds

borrica *f* she-ass; stupid woman

borrico *m* ass, donkey; sawhorse; stupid fellow, ass

borricón *m* or **borricote** *m* drudge

borrón *m* blot; rough draft; blemish; (fig) blot, stain

borronear *tr* to scribble

borro•so -sa *adj* blurred, smudgy, fuzzy; muddy, thick

boruca *f* noise, clamor, uproar

borujo *m* lump, clump

boscaje *m* woodland; (paint) woodland scene

bosque *m* forest, woodland; **bosque maderable** timberland

bosquejar *tr* to sketch, outline; make a rough model of

bosquejo *m* sketch, outline; rough model

bostezar §60 *intr* to yawn, gape

bostezo *m* yawn, yawning

bota *f* shoe, boot; leather wine bag; liquid measure (*125 gallons or 516 liters*); **bota de agua** gum boot; **bota de montar** riding boot; **ponerse las botas** (coll) to hit the jack pot, come out on top

botador *m* boat pole; punch, nailset

botadura *f* launching

botafuego *m* hothead, firebrand

botalón *m* (naut) boom; **botalón de foque** (naut) jib boom

botáni•co -ca *adj* botanical ‖ *mf* botanist ‖ *f* botany

botanista *mf* botanist

botar *tr* to throw, hurl; throw away, throw out; (*un buque*) launch; (*el timón*) shift; fire, dismiss; squander ‖ *intr* to jump; bounce ‖ *ref* (*un caballo*) to buck

botarate *m* madcap, wild man; spendthrift

bote *m* boat, small boat; can, jar, pot; bounce; blow, thrust; (Mex) jug, jail; **bote de paso** ferryboat; **bote de porcelana** apothecary's jar; **bote de remos** rowboat; **bote de salvamento** or **bote salvavidas** lifeboat; **de bote en bote** crowded, jammed; **de bote y voleo** thoughtlessly

botella *f* bottle

botica *f* drug store; medicine

botica•rio -ria *mf* druggist, apothecary

botija *f* earthenware jug with short narrow neck; (CAm, Ven) hidden treasure; (SAm) belly; **decirle a uno botija verde** (Cuba) to let someone have it, tell someone off; **estar hecho una botija** (*un niño*) to be cross and scream; (*una persona*) be fat, be pudgy

botijo *m* earthenware jar with spout and handle

botín *m* booty, plunder, spoils; spat, legging; (Chile) sock

botina *f* shoe, high shoe

botiquín *m* medicine kit, first-aid kit; medicine chest; first-aid station; (Ven) saloon

bo•to -ta *adj* (*sin filo o punta*) blunt, dull; (fig) dull, slow ‖ *m* leather bag ‖ *f* see **bota**

botón *m* button; (*de mueble o puerta*) knob; (*de reloj de bolsillo*) stem; (bot) bud; (elec) push button; **botón de oro** buttercup; **botón de puerta** doorknob; **botones** *msg* bellboy, bellhop

bou *m* fishing with a dragnet between two boats

bóveda f dome, vault; crypt; (aut) cowl; **bóveda celeste** canopy of heaven

boxeador m boxer; (Mex) brass knuckles

boxear intr to box

boxeo m boxing

bóxer m brass knuckles

boxibalón m punching bag

boya f buoy; **boya salvavidas** life buoy

boyante adj buoyant; lucky, successful; (que no cala lo que debe calar) (naut) light

boyera f or **boyeriza** f ox stable

boyerizo m or **boyero** m ox driver

bozal adj simple, stupid ‖ m muzzle; head-harness bells; headstall

bozo m down on upper lip; lips, mouth; headstall

B.p. abbr **Bendición papal**

Br. abbr **bachiller**

bracear intr to swing the arms; swim with overhead strokes; struggle

brace•ro -ra adj arm, hand; thrown with the hand ‖ m man who offers his arm to a lady; day laborer; migrant worker; **de bracero** arm in arm

bra•co -ca adj pug-nosed

braga f diaper, clout; hoisting rope; **bragas** panties, step-ins; breeches; **calzarse las bragas** to wear the pants

bragadura f crotch

braga•zas m (pl -zas) easy mark, henpecked fellow

braguero m (para hernias) truss; (entre-piernas) crotch

bragueta f fly

bragui•llas m (pl -llas) brat

brama f rut, mating, mating time

bramante adj bellowing, roaring ‖ m pack-thread, twine

bramar intr to bellow, roar; (el viento) howl; rage, storm

bramido m bellow, roar; howling; raging

brasa f live coal, red-hot coal

brasero m brazier; (Col) bonfire; (Mex) hearth, fireplace

Brasil, el Brazil

brasile•ño -ña adj & mf Brazilian

bravata f bravado, bragging; **echar bravatas** to talk big

bravatear intr to brag, boast

bravear intr to talk big, four-flush

braveza f bravery; ferocity; (de los elementos) fury, violence

braví•o -a adj ferocious; wild, untamed, un-cultivated; crude, unpolished; (mar) rough, wild; (terreno) rough, rugged

bra•vo -va adj (valiente) brave; fine, excel-lent; fierce, savage, wild; (mar) rough; magnificent; angry, mad; (perro) vicious; (toro) game; boasting; (chili) strong ‖ interj bravo!

bravu•cón -cona adj four-flushing ‖ mf four-flusher

bravura f bravery; fierceness; gameness; bra-vado, boasting

braza f fathom

brazada f stroke, pull (with the arm); **bra-zada de pecho** breast stroke

brazado m armful, armload

brazal m arm band; **brazal de luto** mourning band

brazalete m bracelet

brazo m arm; (de animal) foreleg; **a brazo partido** hand to hand (i.e., without weap-ons); **asidos del brazo** arm in arm; **brazo derecho** right-hand man; **brazos** hands, workmen; backers; **hecho un brazo de mar** dressed to kill

brea f tar, wood tar; calking substance; pack-ing canvas; **brea seca** rosin

brear tr to annoy, mistreat, beat; tar

brebaje m beverage, drink

brécol m or **brécoles** mpl broccoli

brecha f opening; (en un muro) breach; breakthrough

brega f fight, struggle, quarrel; trickery; drudgery

bregar §44 intr to strive, struggle, toil

breña f or **breñal** m or **breñar** m rocky thicket

breque m brake

brequear tr & intr to brake

bresca f honeycomb

Bretaña f Brittany; **la Gran Bretaña** Great Britain

brete m fetters, shackles; tight squeeze, fix

bretones mpl Brussels sprouts

breva f early fig; cinch, snap

breval m early-fig tree

breve adj brief, short; **en breve** shortly, soon

brevedad f brevity, shortness; **a la mayor brevedad** as soon as possible

brevete m note, mark

brezal m heath, moor

brezo m heath, heather

briba f loafing; **andar a la briba** to loaf around

bri•bón -bona adj loafing, crooked ‖ mf loafer, crook

bribonada f loafing, crookedness

bribonear intr to loaf around, be crooked

brida f bridle

brigada f brigade; gang, squad; warrant of-ficer

brillante adj bright, brilliant, shining ‖ m diamond, gem

brillantez f brilliance

brillantina f brilliantine; metal polish

brillar intr to shine; sparkle

brillazón f (Arg, Bol, Urug) pampa mirage

brillo m brightness, brilliance; sparkle; **sacar brillo a** to shine

brillo•so -sa adj (que brilla por el mucho uso) shiny; shining, brilliant

brin m canvas

brincar §73 tr to bounce up and down; skip; skip over ‖ intr to jump, leap; be touchy, get angry easily

brinco m bounce; jump, leap; **en dos brincos** or **en un brinco** in an instant

brindador m toaster

brindar tr to invite; offer; **brindar a uno con una cosa** to offer someone something ‖ intr — **brindar a** or **por** to drink to, toast ‖ ref — **brindarse a** to offer to

brin•dis *m* (*pl* **-dis**) invitation, treat; toast

brío *m* spirit, enterprise; elegance; **cortar los bríos a** to cut the wings of

brio•so -sa *adj* spirited, lively, enterprising; elegant

brisa *f* breeze; residue of pressed grapes

brisera *f* or **brisero** *m* glass lamp shade (*for candles*)

británi•co -ca *adj* British, Britannic

brita•no -na *adj* British ‖ *mf* Briton, Britisher

brizna *f* chip, particle; (Ven) drizzle

brl. *abbr* **barril**

broca *f* reel, spindle; drill, bit

brocado *m* brocade

brocal *m* (*de pozo*) curbstone; (*de bota*) mouthpiece; (*de banqueta*) (Mex) curb

brocamantón *m* diamond brooch

bróculi *m* broccoli

brocha *f* brush; loaded dice; **de brocha gorda** house (*painter*); (coll) crude, heavy-handed

brochada *f* stroke with a brush; rough sketch

brochazo *m* stroke with a brush

broche *m* clasp, clip, fastener; (*conjunto de dos piezas*) hook and eye; (Chile) paper clip; **broche de oro** punch line; **broche de presión** snap, catch; **broches** (Ecuad) cuff buttons

brocheta *f* skewer

broma *f* joke, jest; fun; shipworm; **bromas aparte** joking aside; **en broma** in fun, jokingly; **gastar una broma a** to play a joke on

bromear *intr & ref* to joke, jest; have a good time

bromhídri•co -ca *adj* hydrobromic

bromista *adj* joking ‖ *mf* joker

bromo *m* bromine

bromuro *m* bromide

bronca *f* row, quarrel; rough joke, poor joke; **armar una bronca** to start a row

bronce *m* bronze; **bronce de cañón** gun metal

broncea•do -da *adj* bronze; tanned, sunburned ‖ *m* bronzing; bronze finish; tan, sunburn

bronceador *m* suntan lotion

broncear *tr, intr & ref* to bronze; tan, sunburn

bron•co -ca *adj* coarse, rough; gruff, crude; (*voz*) harsh, hoarse ‖ *f* see **bronca**

bronquitis *f* bronchitis

broquel *m* buckler, shield; (fig) shield

broqueta *f* skewer

brota *f* bud, shoot

brotadura *f* budding, sprouting; gushing; (*de la piel*) eruption, rash

brotar *tr* to bring forth, produce ‖ *intr* to bud, sprout; gush; (*la piel*) break out

brote *m* bud, shoot; outbreak; (*de petróleo*) gush, spurt

broza *f* (*maleza*) underbrush; (*hojas, ramas, cortezas*) brushwood; (*desperdicio*) trash, rubbish; printer's brush

bruces — **dar** or **caer de bruces** to fall on one's face

bruja *f* witch, sorceress; barn owl; (*mujer fea*) hag; (*mujer de mala vida*) prostitute; (W-I) spook

brujear *tr* (*bestias salvajes*) (Ven) to hunt ‖ *intr* to practice witchcraft

brujería *f* witchcraft, sorcery, magic

brujo *m* sorcerer, wizard

brújula *f* (*flechilla*) magnetic needle; (*instrumento*) compass; (*agujero para la puntería*) sight; **perder la brújula** to lose one's touch

brujulear *tr* (*las cartas*) to uncover gradually; suspect

brulote *m* fire ship; (Arg, Chile, Bol) vulgarity, insult

bruma *f* fog, mist

brumo•so -sa *adj* foggy, misty

bruñido *m* burnish, polish; burnishing

bruñir §12 *tr* to burnish, polish; put rouge on; (CAm) to annoy

brus•co -ca *adj* brusque, gruff; sudden; (*curva*) sharp

bruselas *fpl* tweezers ‖ **Bruselas** Brussels

brusquedad *f* brusqueness, gruffness; suddenness; (*de una curva*) sharpness

brutal *adj* brutal; sudden; huge, terrific; stunning

brutalidad *f* brutality; stupidity; tremendous amount

bruteza *f* brutality; (archaic) roughness

bru•to -ta *adj* brute; rough, coarse; stupid; gross ‖ *mf* (*persona*) brute; blockhead ‖ *m* (*animal*) brute

bu *m* (*pl* **búes**) bugaboo; **hacer el bu a** to scare, frighten

buceador *m* or **buceadora** *f* diver

bucear *intr* to dive, be a diver; delve, search

buceo *m* diving

bucle *m* curl, lock

buche *m* (*de ave*) craw, crop, maw; (*de líquido*) mouthful; (*del vestido*) bag, pucker; (*para secretos*) bosom; belly; (Ecuad) high hat; (Guat, Mex) goiter; **sacar el buche a** to make (*someone*) open up

budín *m* pudding

buen *adj* var of **bueno,** used before masculine singular nouns

buenamente *adv* with ease; gladly, willingly; conveniently

buenaventura *f* fortune, good luck; (*adivinación*) fortune; **decirle a uno la buenaventura** to tell someone his fortune

bue•no -na *adj* good; kind; (*sano*) well; (*tiempo*) good, fine; **a buenas** willingly; **¡buena es ésa** (or **ésta)!** that's a good one; **de buenas a primeras** all of a sudden; from the start; **¿de dónde bueno?** where have you been?, what's new?

buey *m* ox, bullock, steer

búfa•lo -la *mf* buffalo

bufanda *f* muffler, scarf

bufar *intr* to snort

bufete *m* writing desk; law office; (*de un abogado*) clients; law practice; refreshment; (Col) bedpan; **abrir bufete** to open a law office

bufido *m* snort

bu•fo -fa *adj* comic; (Ven) spongy ‖ *mf* buffoon

bu•fón -fona *adj* clownish ‖ *m* clown, buffoon; jester; peddler

bufonada *f* buffoonery; sarcasm

bufonería *f* buffoonery; peddling

bufones•co -ca *adj* clownish; coarse, crude

bugui-bugui *m* boogie-woogie

buharda *f* dormer; dormer window; garret

buhardilla *f* dormer window; garret

buho *m* eagle owl; shy fellow

buhonería *f* peddler's kit; peddler's wares

buhonero *m* peddler, hawker

buitre *m* vulture

buje *m* axle box, bushing

bujería *f* gewgaw, trinket

bujía *f* candle; candlestick; candle power; (*de motor de explosión*) spark plug

bulbo *m* bulb

bulevar *m* boulevard

bulevardero *m* boulevardier, man about town

Bulgaria *f* Bulgaria

búlga•ro -ra *adj* & *mf* Bulgarian

bulimia *f* bulimia

bulto *m* bulk, volume; bust, statue; parcel, piece of baggage; bump, swelling; pillowcase; form, mass; **a bulto** broadly, by guess; **buscar el bulto a** to keep after; **de bulto** evident; **escurrir** or **huir el bulto** to duck

bulla *f* noise; crowd; loud argument

bullaje *m* crush, mob (*of people*)

bullanga *f* racket, disturbance

bullebulle *mf* busybody, bustler

bulle•ro -ra *adj* noisy; inflammatory

bullicio *m* brawl, riot, uprising; (*rumor que hace mucha gente*) rumble

bullicio•so -sa *adj* brawling, riotous; rumbling ‖ *mf* rioter

bullir §13 *tr* to move ‖ *intr* to boil; abound; bustle, hustle; swarm; move, stir; be restless ‖ *ref* to move, stir

buniato *m* sweet potato

buñuelo *m* cruller, fritter, bun; botch, bungle

buque *m* ship, vessel; (*de una nave*) hull; (*de cualquier cosa*) capacity; (C-R) doorframe; **buque almirante** admiral; **buque cisterna** tanker; **buque de guerra** warship; **buque de vapor** steamer, steamship; **buque de vela** sailboat; **buque escucha** vedette; **buque escuela** training ship; **buque fanal** or **buque faro** lightship; **buque mercante** merchantman, merchant vessel; **buque portaminas** mine layer; **buque tanque** tanker; **buque velero** sailing vessel

burbuja *f* bubble

burbujear *intr* to bubble

burdégano *m* hinny

burdel *m* brothel, disorderly house

Burdeos Bordeaux

bur•do -da *adj* coarse, rough

burear *tr* (Col) to fool ‖ *intr* to have fun

burga *f* hot springs

bur•gués -guesa *adj* middle-class, bourgeois; (*antiartístico*) bourgeois ‖ *m* middle-class man ‖ *f* middle-class woman

burguesía *f* middle class, bourgeoisie; **alta burguesía** upper middle class; **pequeña burguesía** lower middle class

burla *f* hoax, trick; joke; ridicule; **burlas aparte** joking aside; **de burlas** in fun, for fun

burladero *m* safety island, safety zone; (*en las plazas de toros*) covert; (*en los túneles*) safety niche; hiding place

burla•dor -dora *adj* joking; deceptive ‖ *mf* wag, prankster, practical joker ‖ *m* seducer, libertine

burlar *tr* to make fun of; deceive; disappoint; outwit, frustrate; (*a una mujer*) seduce ‖ *intr* to scoff ‖ *ref* to joke; **burlarse de** to make fun of

burlería *f* derision, mockery; deception, trick; scorn, derision; fish story

burles•co -ca *adj* funny, comic, burlesque

burlete *m* weather stripping

bur•lón -lona *adj* joking ‖ *mf* joker ‖ *m* mockingbird

bu•ró *m* (*pl* **-rós**) writing desk; (Mex) night table

burócrata *mf* jobholder, bureaucrat

burra *f* she-ass; stupid woman; drudge (*woman*)

burrajear *tr* & *intr* to scribble; doodle

burra•jo -ja *adj* (Mex) coarse, stupid ‖ *m* dung (*used as fuel*)

bu•rro -rra *adj* stupid, asinine ‖ *m* donkey, jackass; sawbuck, sawhorse; (Mex) stepladder; **burro cargado de letras** learned jackass; **burro de carga** drudge ‖ *f* see **burra**

bursátil *adj* stock-market

busca *f* search; **en busca de** in search of

buscani•guas *m* (*pl* **-guas**) (Col) snake

buscapié *m* (*para dar a entender algo*) hint; (*para averiguar algo*) feeler ‖ **busca•piés** *m* (*pl* **-piés**) snake

buscaplei•tos *mf* (*pl* **-tos**) troublemaker

buscar §73 *tr* to seek, hunt, look for; (Mex) to provoke; **buscar tres pies al gato** to be looking for trouble ‖ *ref* to take care of oneself; **buscársela** to manage to get along; to ask for it

buscareta *f* wren

buscarrui•dos *mf* (*pl* **-dos**) troublemaker

buscavi•das *mf* (*pl* **-das**) snoop, busybody; go-getter

bus•cón -cona *adj* searching; cheating ‖ *mf* seeker; thief, cheat; (min) prospector ‖ *f* loose woman

busi•lis *m* (*pl* **-lis**) trouble; **ahí está el busilis** that's the trouble; **dar en el busilis** to hit the nail on the head

búsqueda *f* search, hunt

busto *m* bust

butaca *f* armchair, easy chair; orchestra seat

butifarra *f* Catalonian sausage; loose sock, loose stocking; (Peru) ham and salad sandwich

bution•do -da *adj* lewd, lustful

buz *m* (*pl* **buces**) kiss of gratitude and reverence; lip; **hacer el buz** (archaic) to bow and scrape

buzo *m* diver

buzón *m* plug, stopper; mailbox, letter box; (*agujero para echar las cartas*) slot, letter drop; **buzón de alcance** special-delivery box; late-collection slot

C

C, c (ce) *f* third letter of the Spanish alphabet

c. *abbr* **capítulo, compañía, corriente, cuenta**

c *abbr* **caja, cargo, contra, corriente**

cabal *adj* exact; full, complete, perfect; **no estar en sus cabales** to be not in one's right mind ‖ *adv* exactly; completely ‖ *interj* right!

cábala *f* intrigue; divination

cabalgada *f* raid on horseback; gathering of riders

cabalgador *m* rider, horseman

cabalgadura *f* mount, horse; beast of burden

cabalgar §44 *intr* to go horseback riding

cabalgata *f* cavalcade

caballa *f* mackerel

caballada *f* drove of horses; nonsense, stupidity

caballaje *m* stud service

caballazo *m* collision of two horses, trampling by a horse; (Chile, Peru) bitter attack

caballerango *m* (Mex) stableman

caballeres·co -ca *adj* chivalric, knightly; gentlemanly

caballerete *m* (coll) dude

caballería *f* mount, horse, mule; cavalry; chivalry, knighthood; **andarse en caballerías** to fall all over oneself in compliments; **caballería andante** knight-errantry; **caballería mayor** horse, mule; **cabellería menor** ass, donkey

caballeriza *f* stable; stable hands

caballerizo *m* groom, stableman

caballe·ro -ra *adj* riding, mounted; stubborn ‖ *m* knight, nobleman; gentleman; mister; horseman, cavalier, rider; **armar caballero** to knight; **caballero andante** knight errant; **caballero de industria** crook, adventurer, sharper; **Caballero de la triste figura** Knight of the Rueful Countenance (*Don Quijote*); **ir caballero en** to ride

caballerosidad *f* chivalry, gentlemanliness

caballerote *m* boorish fellow, cad

caballete *m* (*bastidor para sostener un cuadro o pizarra*) easel; (*de tejado*) ridge, hip; (*lomo de tierra*) ridge; (*artificio usado como soporte*) trestle, sawbuck, horse; (*de la nariz*) bridge; chimney cap; (*del ave*) breastbone; little horse

caballista *m* horseman; mounted smuggler ‖ *f* horsewoman

caballito *m* little horse; merry-go-round; **caballito del diablo** dragonfly

caballo *m* horse; (*en ajedrez*) knight; playing card (*figure on horseback equivalent to* queen); (slang) heroin; **a caballo** on horseback; **a caballo de** astride; **a caballo regalado no se le mira el diente** never look a gift horse in the mouth; **caballo blanco** (*persona que da dinero para una empresa dudosa*) angel; **caballo de batalla** battle horse; (*de una controversia*) gist, main point; (*aquello en que uno sobresale*) forte, strong point; **caballo de carreras** race horse; **caballo de fuerza** French horsepower, metric horsepower; **caballo de tiro** draft horse; **caballo de Troya** Trojan horse; **caballo de vapor** French horsepower, metric horsepower; **caballo de vapor inglés** horsepower; **caballo mecedor** rocking horse, hobbyhorse; **caballo padre** stallion; **caballo semental** stallion

caballu·no -na *adj* horse, horselike

cabaña *f* cabin, hut; drove, flock; livestock; pastoral scene; (Arg) cattlebreeding ranch

cabañuelas *fpl* (Arg, Bol) first summer rains; (Mex) winter rains

caba·ret *m* (*pl* -**rets**) cabaret

cabecear *tr* (*un libro*) to put a headband on; (*el vino*) head; (*una media*) put a new foot on ‖ *intr* to nod; bob the head; (*en señal de negación*) shake the head; (*los caballos*) toss the head; (*la caja de un carruaje*) lurch; (*un buque*) pitch

cabeceo *m* (*de la cabeza*) nod, bob, shake; (*de la caja del carruaje*) lurching; (*del buque*) pitch, pitching

cabecera *f* (*de cama, mesa, etc.*) head; bedside; headboard; headwaters; (*de una casa, un campo*) end; (*del capítulo de un libro*) heading; (*de periódico*) headline; capital, county seat; bolster, pillow; (typ) headpiece, vignette; **cabecera de cartel** top billing; **cabecera de puente** (mil) bridgehead

cabecilla *mf* scalawag ‖ *m* ringleader ‖ *f* **cabecilla de alfiler** pinhead

cabellar *intr* to grow hair; to put on false hair ‖ *ref* to put on false hair

cabellera *f* head of hair; foliage; (*del cometa*) coma; (bot) mistletoe

cabello *m* hair; **cabello de Venus** maidenhair; **cabellos de ángel** cotton candy; **en cabello** with the hair down; **en cabellos** bareheaded; **traído por los cabellos** farfetched

cabellu·do -da *adj* hairy

caber §14 *intr* to fit, go; have enough room; be possible; happen, befall; **no cabe duda** there is no doubt; **no cabe más** that's the limit; **no caber de** to be bursting with; **no caber en sí** to be beside oneself; be puffed up with pride; **todo cabe en** anything can be expected of

cabestrar *tr* to put a halter on

cabestrillo *m* sling

cabestro *m* halter; **llevar** or **traer del cabestro** to lead by the halter; (fig) to lead by the nose

cabeza *f* head; chief city, capital; **cabeza de chorlito** scatterbrains; (Arg) forgetful person; **cabeza de motín** ringleader; **cabeza de playa** beachhead; **cabeza de puente** bridgehead; **cabeza de turco** butt, scapegoat; **cabeza mayor** head of cattle; **cabeza menor** head of sheep, goats, etc.; **de cabeza** headfirst; on end; on one's own; by heart; **ir cabeza abajo** to go downhill; **irse de la cabeza** to go out of one's mind; **mala cabeza** headstrong person; **por su cabeza** on one's own; **romperse la cabeza** to rack one's brains

cabezada *f* butt with the head; blow on the head; (*de buque*) pitch, pitching; (*de bota*) instep; (*de libro*) headband; **dar cabezadas** to nod; (*un buque*) to pitch

cabezal *m* pillow, cushion; bolster

cabezo *m* hillock; summit, peak; reef

cabe•zón -zona *adj* big-headed; stubborn; (*licor*) (Chile) strong ‖ *m* (*en la ropa*) hole for the head; tax register

cabezonada *f* stubbornness

cabezu•do -da *adj* big-headed; headstrong; (*vino*) heady

cabezuela *f* little head; (*harina gruesa del trigo*) middling; cornflower

cabida *f* room, space, capacity; influence, pull; **tener cabida en** to be included in

cabildear *intr* to lobby

cabildeo *m* lobbying

cabildero *m* lobbyist

cabildo *m* chapter (*of a cathedral*); chapter meeting; town hall

cabina *f* cabin; (*locutorio del teléfono*) booth; bathhouse, dressing room

cabio *m* rafter; joist

cabizba•jo -ja *adj* crestfallen, downcast

cable *m* cable; rope, hawser; **cable de remolque** towline; **cable de retén** guy wire

cablegrafiar §77 *tr & intr* to cable

cablegráfi•co -ca *adj* cable

cablegrama *m* cablegram

cabo *m* end, tip; (*punta de tierra que penetra en el mar*) cape; (*mango*) handle; small bundle; small piece; boss, foreman; cord, rope, cable; (mil) corporal; **al cabo** finally, at last; **al cabo de** at the end of; **atar cabos** (coll) to put two and two together; **Cabo de Buena Esperanza** Cape of Good Hope; **Cabo de Hornos** Cape Horn; **cabos** (*de caballo*) paws, nose, and mane; eyes, eyebrows, and hair; clothing; **cabo suelto** loose end; **estar al cabo de** to be well informed about; **llevar a cabo** to carry out, to accomplish

cabotaje *m* coasting trade

cabra *f* goat; nanny goat; (Chile) light two-wheel carriage; (Chile) sawbuck; (Col, Cuba, Ven) trick, gyp, loaded dice; **cabras** light clouds

cabrahigo wild fig

cabrería *f* goat stable; goat-milk dairy

cabre•ro -ra *mf* goatherd

cabrestante *m* capstan

cabrilla *f* sawbuck, sawhorse; (ichth) grouper; **cabrillas** skipping stones; (*olas blancas en el mar*) whitecaps

cabrillear *intr* (*el mar*) to be covered with whitecaps; shimmer

cabrio *m* rafter; joist

cabrí•o -a *adj* goat; goatish ‖ *m* herd of goats

cabriola *f* caper; somersault; **dar cabriolas** to cut capers

cabriolear *intr* to caper, frisk, prance

cabritilla *f* kid, kidskin

cabrito *m* kid; **cabritos** (Chile) popcorn

cabrón *m* buck, billy goat; complaisant cuckold; (Chile) pimp

cabronada *f* shamelessness; shameless forbearance

cabru•no -na *adj* goat

cacahuate *adj* (Mex) pocked ‖ *m* peanut

cacahuete *m* peanut

cacahuete•ro -ra *mf* peanut vendor

cacalote *m* (Mex) raven; (CAm, Mex) candied popcorn; (Cuba) break, blunder

cacao *m* chocolate tree; cocoa, chocolate; **pedir cacao** to call quits; **tener mucho cacao** (Guat) to have a lot of pep

cacaraña *f* pit, pock

cacarear *tr* to crow over, boast of ‖ *intr* (*la gallina*) to cackle; (*el gallo*) crow

cacareo *m* (*de la gallina*) cackling; (*del gallo*) crowing; (*de una persona*) (coll) crowing, boasting

cacatúa *f* cockatoo

cacea *f* trolling; **pescar a la cacea** to troll

cacear *tr* to stir with a dipper or ladle ‖ *intr* to troll

cacería *f* hunting; hunting party; (*animales cobrados en la caza*) bag; hunting scene

cacerola *f* casserole, saucepan

cacique *m* Indian chief; bossy fellow; (*en asuntos políticos*) (coll) boss; (Chile) lazy lummox; **cacique veranero** Baltimore oriole, hangbird

caciquismo *m* bossism

cacle *m* (Mex) sandal

caco *m* thief, pickpocket; coward

cacto *m* cactus

cacumen *m* summit; acumen, keen insight

cacha•co -ca *adj* (SAm) sporty ‖ *m* (SAm) sport, dude

cachada *f* thrust or wound made with the horns

cachalote *m* sperm whale

cachar *tr* to break to pieces; (*la madera*) slit, split; to butt with the horns; (Arg, Ecuad, Urug) to make fun of; (Chile) to grasp, understand

cacharpari *m* (Arg, Bol, Peru) send-off party

cacharro *m* crock, earthen pot; piece of crockery; piece of junk; (CAm, W-I) jail; (Col) trinket

cachaza *f* sloth, phlegm; rum; first froth on cane juice when boiled

cachazu•do -da *adj* slothful, phlegmatic ‖ *mf* sluggard

cachear *tr* to frisk

cacheo *m* frisking

cachetada *f* box on the ear

cachete *m* slap in the face; cheek, swollen cheek; dagger

cachetear *tr* to box on the ear

cachetero *m* dagger; dagger man

cachetina *f* brawl, fistfight

cachicuer•no -na *adj* horn-handled

cachillada *f* brood, litter

cachimba *f* (*para fumar*) pipe; (Arg, Urug) well, spring; (Chile) revolver

cachimbo *m* (*para fumar*) pipe; (Cuba) sugar mill; **chupar cachimbo** (Ven) to smoke a pipe; (*un niño*) (Ven) to suck its finger

cachiporra *f* billy, bludgeon

cachivache *m* good-for-nothing; **cachivaches** broken pottery; pots and pans; junk, trash

cacho *m* slice, piece; (*mercadería que no se vende*) (Chile) drug on the market

cachón *m* (*ola de agua*) breaker; splash of water; **cachones** surf

cachon•do -da *adj* (*perra*) in rut; sexy

cacho•rro -rra *mf* cub, whelp, pup ‖ *m* little pistol

cachucha *f* rowboat; cap; Andalusian dance

cachuela *f* gizzard; fricassee of pork

cachu•pín -pina *mf* (CAm, Mex) Spanish settler in Latin America

cada *adj* each; every; **cada vez más** more and more; **cada vez que** whenever

cadalso *m* stand, platform; (*para la ejecución de un reo*) scaffold

cadarzo *m* floss, floss silk

cadáver *m* corpse, cadaver

cadavéri•co -ca *adj* cadaverous

cadena *f* chain; (telv) network; **cadena anti-rresbaladiza** (aut) skid chain; **cadena de presidiarios** chain gang; **cadena perpetua** life imprisonment

cadencia *f* cadence, rhythm

cadencio•so -sa *adj* rhythmical

cadenero *m* (surv) lineman

cadera *f* hip

cadete *m* (mil) cadet; (Arg, Bol) apprentice (*without pay*), errand boy

cadillo *m* burdock

cadmio *m* cadmium

caducar §73 *intr* to be in one's dotage; be worn out; lapse, expire

caducidad *f* feebleness; expiration

caedi•zo -za *adj* tottery, ready to fall over ‖ *m* lean-to

caer §15 *intr* to fall; droop; fall due; be, be found; fade; (*el sol, el día, el viento*) decline; happen; **caer a** to face, overlook; **caer bien** to fit; be becoming; make a hit; **caer de plano** to fall flat; **caer en** (*cierto día*) to come on, fall on, happen on; (*cierta página*) be found on; **caer en cama** to fall

ill; **caer en favor** to be in favor; **caer en la cuenta** to catch on, get the point; **caer en que** to realize that; **caer mal** to fit badly; be unbecoming; fall flat; **no caigo** (coll) I don't get it ‖ *ref* to fall, fall down; be, be found; **caerse de su peso, caerse de suyo** to be self-evident; **caerse muerto de** (*p.ej., alegría, miedo, risa*) to be overcome with

café *adj* tan ‖ *m* coffee; coffee tree; coffee house; café; (Arg) reprimand; (Mex) tantrum; **café cantante** night club; **café de maquinilla** drip coffee; **café solo** black coffee

cafetal *m* coffee plantation

cafetalero *m* (SAm) coffee planter; coffee dealer

cafetear *intr* to drink coffee

cafetera *f* coffee pot; (Arg) jalopy; **cafetera eléctrica** electric percolator

cafetería *f* cafeteria

cafete•ro -ra *adj* coffee ‖ *mf* coffee dealer; coffee-bean picker ‖ *f* see **cafetera**

cafeto *m* coffee tree

cagar §44 *tr* to spot, stain, spoil ‖ *intr* to defecate ‖ *ref* to defecate; be scared

cagatin•ta *m* or **cagatin•tas** *m* (*pl* -tas) office drudge, penpusher

ca•gón -gona *adj* cowardly ‖ *mf* coward

caída *f* fall; spill, tumble; drop; failure; blunder, slip; (*de una cortina*) hang; **a la caída de la noche** at nightfall; **a la caída del sol** at sunset; **caída de agua** waterfall; **caída radiactiva** fallout; **caídas** coarse wool; witticisms

caí•do -da *adj* fallen; (*cuello*) turndown; (*párpado, hombro*) drooping; dejected, crestfallen; **caído en desuso** obsolete ‖ **caídos** *mpl* interest due; **los caídos** (*en la guerra*) the fallen ‖ *f* see **caída**

caimán *m* alligator; schemer

Caín *m* Cain; **pasar las de Caín** (coll) to have a frightful time

Cairo, El Cairo

caja *f* box; case, chest, coffer; (*de caudales*) safe, strongbox; (*para dinero contante*) cashbox; (*dinero contante*) cash; (*ataúd*) casket, coffin; (*de reloj de bolsillo*) case; (*donde se pagan las cuentas en los hoteles*) desk; cashier's desk; (*del aparato de radio o televisión*) cabinet; (*de coche*) body; (*tambor*) drum; (*de fusil*) stock; (*de ascensor, de escalera*) shaft, well; (mach) housing; (typ) case; **caja alta** upper case; **caja baja** lower case; **caja clara** snare drum; **caja de ahorros** savings bank; **caja de cambio de marchas** transmission-gear box; **caja de caudales** safe; **caja de cigüeñal** crankcase; **caja de colores** paintbox; **caja de embalaje** packing box or case; **caja de enchufe** (elec) outlet; **caja de engranajes** gear case; **caja de fuego** firebox; **caja de fusibles** fuse box; **caja de ingletes** miter box; **caja de menores** petty cash; **caja de registro** manhole; **caja de reloj** watchcase; **caja de seguridad** safe; safe-deposit box; **caja de sorpresa** jack-in-the-box; **caja de velocidades** transmission-gear box; **caja fuerte** safe, bank vault; **caja postal de ahorros** postal savings bank; **caja registradora** cash register; **despedir** or **echar con cajas destempladas** to send packing, give the gate

caje•ro -ra *mf* boxmaker; (*en un banco*) cashier, teller; (*en un hotel*) desk clerk

cajeta *f* little box; tobacco box; **de cajeta** (CAm, Mex) fine

cajetilla *f* pack (*of cigarettes*)

cajetín *m* rubber stamp; (typ) box

cajista *mf* compositor

cajón *m* large box, bin; (*caja movible de un mueble*) drawer; (*que se cierra con llave*) locker; (*que sirve de tienda*) booth, stall; (Chile) long gully; (Mex) dry-goods store; (SAm) coffin; **cajón de aire comprimido** caisson; **cajón de sastre** (coll) odds and ends; muddlehead; **ser de cajón** to be in vogue, be the thing

cal *f* lime; **cal apagada** slaked lime; **cal viva** quicklime; **de cal y canto** strong, tough

cala *f* calla lily; cove, inlet; (*de fruta*) sample slice; (*de buque*) hold; suppository

calabacear *tr* (*a un alumno*) to flunk; (*una mujer a un pretendiente*) to jilt

calabacera *f* calabash, pumpkin, squash

calabaza *f* calabash, gourd, pumpkin, squash; dolt; **dar calabaza** a (*un alumno*) to flunk; (*un pretendiente*) to jilt

calabo•bos *m* (*pl* **-bos**) steady drizzle

calabocero *m* jailer, warden

calabozo *m* dungeon; cell, prison cell

calada *f* soaking; (*del ave de rapiña*) swoop; scolding

calado *m* openwork, drawn work; fretwork; (*del agua*) depth; (naut) draught

calafatear *tr* to calk

calafateo *m* calking

calamar *m* squid

calambre *m* cramp

calamidad *f* calamity

calamita *f* magnetic needle

calamito•so -sa *adj* calamitous

cálamo *m* reed, stalk; (poet) pen; (poet) flute, reed

calamoca•no -na *adj* (*algo embriagado*) tipsy; (*chocho*) doddering

calaña *f* nature, kind; pattern; fan

calar *tr* to pierce; soak; wedge; cut open work in; (*un melón*) cut a plug in; (*la bayoneta*) fix; (*un puente levadizo*) lower; (*las redes de pesca*) lower in the water; (*un buque cierta profundidad*) draw; (*a una persona o las intenciones de una persona*) size up, see through; (Arg) to stare at ‖ *ref* to get soaked, get drenched; (*introducirse*) slip in; (*el ave de rapiña*) swoop down; miss fire; (*el sombrero*) pull down tight; (*las gafas*) stick on; **calarse hasta los huesos** to get soaked to the skin

cala•to -ta *adj* (Peru) naked; (Peru) penniless

calavera *m* daredevil; libertine ‖ *f* skull; (*imitación de la calavera*) death's-head; (Mex) tail light

calaverada *f* recklessness, daredeviltry; escapade

calaverear *tr* to spoil, make ugly ‖ *intr* to act recklessly; go on a spree

calcado *m* tracing

calcañal *m* or **calcañar** *m* heel

calcar §73 *tr* to trace; copy, imitate; tread on

calce *m* wedge; iron tire; iron tip; (*de un documento*) (CAm, Mex, P-R) bottom, foot

calceta *f* stocking; fetter, shackle; **hacer calceta** to knit

calcetería *f* hosiery; hosiery shop

calcete•ro -ra *mf* hosier; stocking mender

calcetín *m* sock

calcificar §73 *tr* & *ref* to calcify

calcio *m* calcium

calco *m* tracing; copy, imitation

calcula•dor -dora *adj* calculating; (*egoísta, interesado*) (fig) calculating ‖ *mf* calculator ‖ *f* calculating machine; **calculadora de bolsillo** pocket calculator

calcular *tr* & *intr* to calculate; (*suponer*) (fig) calculate

cálculo *m* calculation; (math, pathol) calculus; **cálculo biliar** gallstone; **cálculo renal** kidney stone

calchona *f* (Chile) goblin, bogey; (Chile) witch, old hag

calda *f* heating, warming; **caldas** hot springs

caldeamiento *m* heating

caldear *tr* to heat; weld ‖ *ref* to get hot; get overheated

caldeo *m* heating; welding

caldera *f* boiler; pot, kettle; (Arg) coffee pot, teapot

calderero *m* boilermaker

calderilla *f* holy-water vessel; copper coin; small change; mountain currant

caldero *m* kettle, pot; (*reloj de bolsillo*) (Arg) turnip

calderón *m* caldron; (*signo*) (mus) pause, hold

caldillo *m* light broth; sauce for fricassee; (Mex) meat bits in broth

caldo *m* broth; sauce, gravy, dressing; salad dressing; (Mex) syrup; (Mex) sugar-cane juice; **caldo de la reina** eggnog; **caldos** wet goods

calefacción *f* heating; **calefacción por agua caliente** hot-water heat; **calefacción por aire caliente** hot-air heat

calefactor *m* heater man; (electron) heater, heater element

calefón *m* (Arg) hot-water heater

calendar *tr* to date

calendario *m* calendar; **hacer calendarios** to meditate; to make wild predictions

calenta•dor -dora *adj* heating ‖ *m* heater; warming pan; (*reloj de bolsillo*) turnip; **calentador a gas** gas heater; **calentador de agua** water heater

calentamiento *m* heating

calentar §2 *tr* to heat; warm; beat; (Chile) to bore, annoy; **calentar la silla** (*detenerse demasiado*) to warm a chair ‖ *ref* to heat up, run hot; warm oneself; warm up; (*estar en celo las bestias*) be in heat; (Chile, Ven) to become annoyed, get angry

calentón m warm-up; **darse un calentón** to stop and warm up

calentura f fever, temperature

calenturien•to -ta adj feverish; exalted; (Chile) consumptive

calenturón m high fever

calenturo•so -sa adj feverish

calera f limekiln; limestone quarry

calesa f chaise

caleta f cove, inlet

caletre m judgment, acumen

calibrador m calipers; **calibrador de alambre** wire gauge

calibrar tr to calibrate; to gauge

calibre m caliber; gauge; bore, diameter

calicanto m rubble masonry

cali•có m (pl **-cós**) calico

calidad f quality; condition, term; rank, nobility; importance; **a calidad de que** provided that; **calidad de vida** quality of life; **en calidad de** in the capacity of

cáli•do -da adj warm, hot

calidoscopio m kaleidoscope

calientaca•mas m (pl **-mas**) bed warmer

calienta•piés m (pl **-piés**) foot warmer

caliente adj hot; fiery, vehement; (en celo) hot; **caliente de cascos** hotheaded; **en caliente** while hot; at once

califa m caliph

califato m caliphate

calificación f qualification; (nota en un examen) grade, mark; rating, standing

calificar §73 tr to qualify; certify; ennoble; (un examen) mark; (en los registros electorales) (Chile) to register || ref (archaic) to prove one's noble birth; (en los registros electorales) (Chile) to register

calificati•vo -va adj qualifying || m (nota en la escuela) grade, mark; (en un diccionario) usage label

California f California; **la Baja California** Lower California

caligrafía f penmanship

calina f haze

calino•so -sa adj hazy

Calíope f Calliope

calipso m calypso || **Calipso** f Calypso

calistenia f calisthenics

calisténi•co -ca adj calisthenic

cá•liz m (pl **-lices**) chalice; **cáliz de dolor** cup of sorrow

cali•zo -za adj lime, limestone || f limestone

calma f calm; calm weather; quiet, tranquility; slowness; (cesación) letup, suspension; **calma chicha** dead calm; **calmas ecuatoriales** doldrums; **en calma** in suspension; (mercado) steady; (mar) calm, smooth

calmante adj soothing; pain-relieving || m sedative

calmar tr to calm, soothe || intr to grow calm; abate || ref to calm down

calmazo m dead calm

cal•mo -ma adj barren, treeless; fallow, uncultivated || f see **calma**

calmo•so -sa adj calm; slow, lazy

calmu•do -da adj calm; (viento) (naut) light; (tiempo) (naut) mild

caló m gypsy slang, underworld slang

calofriar §77 ref to become chilled

calofrío m chill

calor m heat; warmth; (fig) warmth, enthusiasm; **hace calor** it is hot, it is warm; **tener calor** (una persona) to be hot, be warm

calorífe•ro -ra adj heat || m heater, furnace; heating system; foot warmer

calorífu•go -ga adj heatproof; fireproof

caloro•so -sa adj warm, hot; (fig) warm, enthusiastic, hearty

calotear tr (Arg) to gyp, cheat

calpul m (Guat) gathering, meeting; (Hond) Indian mound

caluma f (Peru) gorge in the Andes; (Peru) Indian hamlet

calumnia f calumny, slander

calumniar tr to slander

calumnio•so -sa adj slanderous

caluro•so -sa adj warm, hot; (fig) warm, enthusiastic, hearty

calva f bald spot; bare spot, clearing; (en un tejido) worn spot

calvario m (sufrimiento moral) cross; series of misfortunes; string of debts || **Calvario** m Calvary; Stations of the Cross

calvero m clearing; clay pit

calvez f or **calvicie** f baldness

cal•vo -va adj bald; barren, bare || f see **calva**

calza f wedge; stocking; **calzas** hose, breeches, tights; **en calzas prietas** in a tight fix

calzada f highway, causeway; (S-D) sidewalk

calzado m footwear, shoes

calzador m shoehorn

calzar §60 tr to shoe, put shoes on; provide with shoes; (cierto tamaño de zapatos, guantes, etc.) wear, take; (un zapato a una persona) fit; wedge; (una rueda) block, scotch; (la pata de una mesa) block up; tip or trim with iron; (plantas) (hort) to hill || intr (Arg) to get the place sought; **calzar bien** to wear good footwear; **calzar mal** to wear poor footwear || ref to get; (zapatos, guantes) put on, wear; put one's shoes on; (a una persona) dominate, manage

calzo m wedge; chock, skid

calzón m trousers, pants; **calzones** trousers, breeches; **calzarse los calzones** to wear the pants

calzonarias fpl (Col) suspenders

calzona•zos m (pl **-zos**) jellyfish; henpecked husband

calzoncillos mpl underdrawers

callada f (naut) abatement, lull; **a las calladas** or **de callada** on the quiet; **dar la callada por respuesta** to give no answer

calla•do -da adj silent; mysterious, secret || f see **callada**

callampa f (Chile) felt hat; (Chile) large ear; (Chile) mushroom

callana f (SAm) Indian baking bowl; (reloj de bolsillo) (Chile) turnip; (Chile) behind; (Chile, Peru) flowerpot

callao m pebble

callar *tr* to silence; not mention; (*un secreto*) keep; calm, quiet ‖ *intr* & *ref* to become silent, keep silent; keep quiet, keep still; **callarse la boca** (coll) to shut up, clam up

calle *f* street; **calle de travesía** cross street; **calle mayor** main street; **dejar en la calle** to deprive of one's livelihood

calleja *f* side street, alley; subterfuge, pretext

callejear *intr* to walk around the streets, to ramble around

calleje•ro -ra *adj* street; gadabout ‖ *m* street guide; list of addresses of newspaper subscribers

callejón *m* alley, lane; **callejón sin salida** blind alley

callejuela *f* side street, alley; subterfuge, pretext

callicida *m* corn cure

callo *m* callus; (*en el pie*) corn; **callos** tripe

callo•so -sa *adj* callous

cama *f* bed; (*para las bestias*) bedding, litter; **cama imperial** four-poster; **cama turca** day bed; **guardar cama** to be sick in bed

camachuelo *m* (orn) bullfinch

camada *f* brood, litter; layer, stratum; (*de ladrones*) den

camafeo *m* cameo

camaleón *m* chameleon

cámara *f* chamber; hall; (*cuerpo legislador*) house, chamber; (*aparato fotográfico*) camera; (*tubo de goma del neumático*) inner tube; (*del arma de fuego*) chamber, breech; (*para cartuchos*) magazine; board, council; (*mueble donde se conservan los alimentos*) icebox; (*evacuación*) bowels; (aer) cockpit; **cámara agrícola** grange; **cámara ardiente** funeral chamber; **cámara cinematografica** movie camera; **cámara de combustión** (aut) combustion chamber; **cámara de compensación** clearing house; **cámara de fuelle** folding camera; **cámara de las máquinas** (naut) engine room; **Cámara de los Comunes** House of Commons; **Cámara de los Lores** House of Lords; **cámara de oxígeno** oxygen tent; **Cámara de Representantes** House of Representatives; **cámara frigorífica** cold-storage room; **cámara indiscreta** candid camera; **cámaras** loose bowels

camarada *m* comrade

camarera *f* waitress; chambermaid, maid; (*en los barcos*) stewardess; (*que sirve a una reina o princesa*) lady in waiting

camarero *m* waiter; valet; (*en un barco o avión*) steward

camarilla *f* clique, coterie, cabal; palace coterie

camarín *m* boudoir; (theat) dressing room

cámaro *m* var of **camarón**

camarógrafo *m* cameraman

camarón *m* shrimp, prawn; (CAm, Col) tip, gratuity; (Ven) nap; **ponerse como un camarón** to blush

camarote *m* stateroom, cabin

camasquin•ce *mf* (*pl* **-ce**) meddlesome person, kibitzer

cambalachar *tr* & *intr* var of **cambalachear**

cambalache *m* exchange, swap; (Arg) second-hand shop

cambalachear *tr* to swap, exchange, trade off ‖ *intr* to swap, exchange

cambiadis•cos *m* (*pl* **-cos**) record changer

cambiante *adj* changing; fickle; iridescent ‖ **cambiantes** *mpl* iridescence

cambiar *tr* to change; exchange ‖ *intr* to change; **cambiar de** (*p.ej., sombreros, ropa, trenes*) change; **cambiar de marcha** to shift gears ‖ *ref* to change

cambiavía *m* switch; switchman

cambio *m* change; exchange; rate of exchange; (aut) shift; (rr) switch; **cambio de marchas, cambio de velocidades** gearshift; **en cambio** on the other hand

cambista *mf* moneychanger; banker ‖ *m* (Arg) switchman

cambullón *m* (Mex, Col, Ven) barter, exchange; (Chile) subversion; (Peru) scheming, trickery

camelar *tr* to flirt with; cajole, tease

camelo *m* flirtation; joke; false rumor

camellero *m* camel driver

camello *m* camel

camellón *m* drinking trough; flower bed

came•ro -ra *adj* bed ‖ *mf* maker of bedding ‖ *m* (Col) highway

camilla *f* stretcher; couch; round table with heater underneath; (Mex) clothing store

camillero *m* stretcher-bearer

caminante *mf* walker; traveler on foot ‖ *m* groom attending his master's horse

caminar *tr* (*cierta distancia*) to walk ‖ *intr* to walk; go; travel, journey; behave

caminata *f* long walk, hike; outing, jaunt

camine•ro -ra *adj* road, highway

camino *m* road, way; (*viaje*) journey; (*tira larga que se pone en mesas o pisos*) (SAm) runner; **a medio camino (entre)** halfway (between); **camino de** on the way to; **camino de herradura** bridle path; **camino de hierro** railway; **camino de ruedas** wagon road; **Camino de Santiago** Way of St. James (*Milky Way*); **camino de sirga** towpath; **camino de tierra** dirt road; **camino real** highroad; **camino trillado** beaten path; **echar camino adelante** to strike out

camión *m* truck, motor truck; (Mex) bus; **camión volquete** dump truck

camionaje *m* trucking

camione•ro -ra *adj* truck ‖ *m* trucker, teamster

camioneta *f* light truck; station wagon

camionetilla *f* (Guat) station wagon

camión-grua *m* tow truck

camionista *m* trucker, teamster

camisa *f* (*de hombre*) shirt; (*de mujer*) chemise; (*de la culebra*) slough; (*de un libro*) jacket; (*para papeles*) folder; (*de una pieza mecánica*) jacket, casing; (*de un horno de fundición*) lining; **camisa de agua** water jacket; **camisa de dormir** nightshirt; **camisa de fuerza** strait jacket; **cambiarse la camisa** to become a turncoat

camisería *f* haberdashery; shirt factory

camise•ro -ra *mf* haberdasher; shirt maker
camiseta *f* undershirt; (*de traje de baño*) top
camisola *f* stiff shirt
camisolín *m* dickey, shirt front
camón *m* bay window; **camón de vidrios** glass partition
camorra *f* quarrel, row; **armar camorra** to raise Cain, raise a row; **buscar camorra** to be looking for trouble
camorrista *adj* quarrelsome ‖ *mf* quarrelsome person
camote *m* onion; (Mex) sweet potato; (Chile) lie, fib; (Chile, Peru) sweetheart; (Arg, Ecuad) blockhead; (Mex) churl; (El Salv) black-and-blue mark; **tomar un camote** to become infatuated
camotear *tr* (Arg) to filch, snitch; (Guat) to bother ‖ *intr* (Mex) to wander around aimlessly
campal *adj* pitched (*battle*)
campamento *m* camp; encampment
campana *f* bell; (*para la protección de plantas*) bell glass, bell jar; (*de las guarniciones de alumbrado eléctrico*) canopy; **campana de buzo** diving bell; **por campana de vacante** (Mex) rarely, seldom
campanada *f* stroke of a bell, ring of a bell; scandal
campanario *m* belfry, steeple
campanear *tr* (*las campanas*) to ring ‖ *intr* to ring the bells ‖ *ref* to strut
campanero *m* bell ringer; bell founder
campanil *adj* bell ‖ *m* belfry, bell tower
campanilla *f* hand bell; door bell; bubble; (anat) uvula; **de (muchas) campanillas** of great importance
campano *m* cowbell
campante *adj* proud, satisfied; outstanding
campanu•do -da *adj* bell-shaped; pompous, high-sounding
campaña *f* campaign; cruise; countryside
campar *intr* to camp; to excel, stand out
campear *intr* to go to pasture; (*las sementeras*) turn green; stand out, excel; reconnoiter; ride through the fields to check the cattle
campecha•no -na *adj* frank, good-natured, cheerful ‖ *f* (Mex) mixed drink; (Ven) hammock
campeche *m* logwood
campeón *m* champion; **campeón de venta** best seller
campeona *f* championess
campeonato *m* championship
campe•ro -ra *adj* unsheltered, in the open
campesi•no -na *adj* country, rural, peasant ‖ *mf* peasant, farmer ‖ *m* countryman ‖ *f* countrywoman
campestre *adj* country, rural
campiña *f* countryside, open country
campo *m* (*terreno sembradío; sitio o foco de varias actividades*) field; (*en oposición a la ciudad*) country; ground, background; (*campamento*) (mil) camp; **a campo traviesa** across country; **campo de batalla** battlefield; **campo de ensayos** proving ground; **campo de juego** playground;

campo de pruebas testing ground; **campo de tiro** range, shooting range; **campo magnético** magnetic field; **campo santo** cemetery; **levantar el campo** (mil) to break camp; **quedar en el campo** to fall in battle
camposanto *m* cemetery
camuesa *f* pippin (*apple*)
camueso *m* pippin (*tree*)
camuflaje *m* camouflage
camuflar *tr* to camouflage
can *m* dog; (*de arma de fuego*) trigger
cana *f* gray hair; **echar una cana al aire** to cut loose, step out; **peinar canas** to be getting old
Canadá, el Canada
canadiense *adj & mf* Canadian
canal *m* (*cauce artificial*) canal; (*estrecho en el mar*) channel; (*anat*) duct, canal; (telv) channel; **Canal de la Mancha** English Channel; **Canal de Panamá** Panama Canal; **Canal de Suez** Suez Canal; **canal alimenticio** alimentary canal ‖ *f* channel; (*conducto del tejado*) gutter; (*estría*) flute, groove; pipe; (*de un libro*) fore edge
canalización *f* (*de agua o gas*) mains, pipes; ductwork; (elec) wiring; **canalización de consumo** (elec) house current
canalizar §60 to channel; pipe; (elec) to wire
canalizo *m* (naut) waterway, fairway
canalón *m* rain-water spout; shovel hat; **canalones** ravioli
canalla *m* churl, scoundrel ‖ *f* riffraff, canaille
canallada *f* dirty trick, meanness
canana *f* cartridge belt
canapé *m* sofa, couch
Canarias *fpl* Canaries
cana•rio -ria *adj & mf* Canarian ‖ *m* canary, canary bird ‖ *fpl* see **Canarias**
canasta *f* basket, hamper
canastilla *f* basket; (*ropa para el niño que ha de nacer*) layette; (*equipo de novia*) (dial) trousseau
canastillo *m* basket-weave tray
canasto *m* hamper ‖ **canastos** *interj* confound it!
cáncamo *m* eyebolt; **cáncamo de argolla** ringbolt
cancanear *intr* to loaf around; stammer
cancel *m* storm door; folding screen
cancela *f* door of ironwork
cancelar *tr* to cancel; (*una deuda*) pay off
cáncer *m* cancer; **Cáncer** (astr) Cancer; **cáncer pulmonar** lung cancer
cancerología *f* cancer research; oncology
cancero•so -sa *adj* cancerous
cancilla *f* lattice gate
canciller *m* chancellor
cancillería *f* chancellery
canción *f* song; poem, lyric poem; **canción de amor** love song; **canción de cuna** cradlesong, lullaby; **canción típica** folk song; **volver a la misma canción** to sing the same old song
cancionero *m* songbook; anthology
cancionista *mf* popular singer

ca
ca

canco *m* (Chile) flowerpot; (Chile) earthen jug; (Chile) chamber pot; (Bol) buttock; **cancos** (Chile) woman's broad hips

cancón *m* bugaboo; **hacer un cancón a** (Mex) to try to bluff

cancha *f* field, ground; race track; golf links; tennis court; cockpit; (Urug) path, way; **estar en su cancha** (Arg, Chile, Urug) to be in one's element; **tener cancha** (Arg) to have pull ‖ *interj* gangway!

canche *adj* (Col) tasteless, poorly seasoned; (CAm) blond

candado *m* padlock

candar *tr* to lock, padlock

candela *f* candle; candlestick; fire, light; **con la candela en la mano** at death's door

candelabro *m* candelabrum

candelecho *m* elevated hut for watching the vineyard

candelero *m* candlestick; brass olive-oil lamp; fishing torch

candelilla *f* catkin; (Arg, Chile) will-o'-the-wisp; glowworm

candida•to -ta *mf* candidate

candidatura *f* candidacy; list of candidates; voting paper

candidez *f* whiteness; innocence

cándi•do -da white; simple, innocent

candil *m* open olive-oil lamp

candilejas *fpl* footlights

candon•go -ga *adj* fawning, slick; loafing, shirking ‖ *mf* fawner, flatterer; loafer, shirker ‖ *f* fawning; teasing

candonguear *tr* to kid, tease ‖ *intr* to scheme to get out of work

candor *m* innocence, ingenuousness

caneca *f* glazed earthen bottle

cane•co -ca *adj* (Arg, Bol) tipsy ‖ *f* see **caneca**

canela *f* cinnamon; (*cosa fina*) (coll) peach

canela•do -da *adj* cinnamon-colored

cane•lo -la *adj* cinnamon ‖ *m* (*árbol*) cinnamon ‖ *f* see **canela**

canelón *m* rain-water spout; large icicle; cinnamon candy

cane•sú *m* (*pl* -**súes**) (*prenda*) guimpe; (*pieza de una prenda*) yoke

cangilón *m* jug, jar, bucket; (*de draga*) bucket, scoop; rut, track

cangrejo *m* crab

cangrena *f* gangrene

cangrenar *ref* to have gangrene

canguro *m* kangaroo

caníbal *adj* & *mf* cannibal

canica *f* (*bolita*) marble; (*juego*) marbles

canicie *f* whiteness (*of hair*)

canícula *f* dog days ‖ **Canícula** *f* Dog Star

caniculares *mpl* dog days

cani•jo -ja *adj* (coll) weak, sickly ‖ *mf* (coll) weakling

canilla *f* shank (*of leg*); (*espita, grifo*) tap; bobbin, spool; (Mex) strength

cani•no -na *adj* canine ‖ *m* canine, canine tooth ‖ *f* excrement of dogs

canje *m* exchange

canjear *tr* to exchange

ca•no -na *adj* gray; gray-haired; hoary, old ‖ *f* see **cana**

canoa *f* canoe; launch

canoe•ro -ra *mf* canoeist

canon *m* canon

canóni•co -ca *adj* canonical ‖ *f* rules of canonical life

canóniga *f* nap before eating; drunk

canónigo *m* canon

canonizar §60 *tr* to canonize; approve

canonjía *f* sinecure

cano•ro -ra *adj* (*voz*) melodious; (*ave*) song, sweet-singing

cano•so -sa *adj* gray-haired

canotié *m* straw hat, skimmer

cansa•do -da *adj* tired, weary; exhausted, worn-out; tiresome

cansancio *m* tiredness, fatigue

cansar *tr* to tire, weary; bore ‖ *intr* be tiresome ‖ *ref* to tire, get tired

cantable *adj* tuneful, singable ‖ *m* (*del libreto de una zarzuela*) lyric; (*de una zarzuela*) musical passage

canta•dor -dora *mf* singer of popular songs

cantaletear *tr* to say over and over again; make fun of

cantalupo *m* cantaloupe

cantante *adj* singing ‖ *mf* singer

cantar *m* song, singing; chant; **Cantar de los Cantares** Song of Songs ‖ *tr* to sing; chant; sing of; **cantarlas claras** to speak out ‖ *intr* to sing; chant; creak, squeak; squeal, peach; **cantar de plano** to make a full confession

cántara *f* jug, pitcher

cantárida *f* Spanish fly

canta•rín -rina *adj* (*voz*) melodious; fond of singing ‖ *mf* singer ‖ *m* professional singer

cántaro *m* jug, pitcher; jugful; ballot box; **llover a cántaros** to rain pitchforks

canta•triz *f* (*pl* -**trices**) singer

cantautor *m* song writer

cantera *f* quarry; talent, genius

cántico *m* canticle

cantidad *f* quantity; amount; sum; **cantidad de movimiento** (mech) momentum

cantiga *f* poem of the troubadours

cantilena *f* ballad, song; **salir con la misma cantilena** to sing the same old song

cantimplora *f* siphon; carafe, decanter; (*frasco para llevar bebida*) canteen; (Col) powder flask; (Guat) mumps

cantina *f* cantine; lunchroom, station restaurant; barroom

cantinera *f* camp follower

cantinero *m* bartender

canto *m* song; singing; (*división del poema épico*) canto; (*de notas iguales y uniformes*) chant; (*extremidad*) edge; (*esquina*) corner; (*de cuchillo*) back; (*de pan*) crust; stone, pebble; **canto de corte** cutting edge; **canto del cisne** swan song

cantonera *f* corner reinforcement; corner table, corner shelf; streetwalker

cantonero *m* corner loafer

can•tor -tora *adj* singing; (*pájaro*) song ‖ *mf* singer ‖ *m* chanter; minstrel; poet, bard

canto•so -sa *adj* rocky, stony
canturrear *tr & intr* to hum
canturreo *m* hum, humming
canzonetista *mf* popular singer
caña *f* cane; reed; stalk, stem; (*del brazo o la pierna*) long bone; (*de bota o media*) leg; wineglass; **caña de azúcar** sugar cane; **caña de pescar** fishing rod
cañada *f* glen, ravine, gully; cattle path; brook
cañamazo *m* canvas, burlap; embroidered canvas
cañamiel *f* sugar cane
cáñamo *m* hemp
cañamones *mpl* birdseed
cañaveral *m* canebrake; sugar-cane plantation
cañería *f* pipe; pipe line; piping; **cañería maestra** gas main, water main
cañero *m* pipe fitter, plumber; sugar-cane dealer; (SAm) cheat; (SAm) bluffer
cañista *m* pipe fitter, plumber
caño *m* pipe, tube; gutter, sewer; ditch; (*chorro*) spurt, jet; (*canal angosto*) channel; organ pipe; (*río pequeño*) (Col) stream
cañón *m* (*pieza de artillería*) cannon; (*valle estrecho*) canyon; (*de arma de fuego; de pluma*) barrel; (*pluma de ave*) quill; (*de escalera*) well; (*de columna; de ascensor*) shaft; organ pipe; (Col) trunk of tree; **cañón de campaña** fieldpiece; **cañón de chimenea** flue, chimney flue; **cañón obús** howitzer
cañonear *tr* to cannonade, to shell
cañutazo *m* gossip
caoba *f* mahogany
caos *m* chaos
caóti•co -ca *adj* chaotic
cap. *abbr* **capitán, capítulo**
capa *f* cloak, cape, mantle; (*de pintura*) coat; (*lo que cubre*) bed, layer; (*apariencia, pretexto*) (fig) cloak, mask; **capa del cielo** canopy of heaven; **capa de ozono** ozone layer; **andar de capa caída** to be on the decline, be in a bad way; (*comedia*) **de capa y espada** cloak-and-sword; (*intriga, espionaje*) **de capa y espada** cloak-and-dagger; **so capa de** under the guise of
capacidad *f* capacity; **capacidad competitiva** competitiveness
capacitar *tr* to enable, qualify; to empower ‖ *ref* to become qualified
capacha *f* fruit basket; (SAm) jail
capacho *m* fruit basket; hamper; (*de albañil*) hod
capar *tr* to geld, castrate; curtail
caparazón *m* caparison; horse blanket; nose bag; (*de crustáceo*) shell
caparrosa *f* vitriol
capa•taz *m* (*pl* **-taces**) overseer, foreman, boss
ca•paz *adj* (*pl* **-paces**) (*grande*) capacious, spacious; (*que tiene cierta aptitud; diestro, instruído*) capable; **capaz de** capable of; with a capacity of; **capaz para** competent in; qualified for; with room for
capcio•so -sa *adj* crafty, deceptive

capea *f* amateur free-for-all bullfight
capear *tr* (*al toro*) to challenge; (*el mal tiempo*) weather; deceive, take in ‖ *intr* (naut) to lay to; (Guat) to play hooky
capellán *m* chaplain
capeo *m* capework (*of bullfighter*)
caperucita *f* little pointed hood; **Caperucita Roja** Little Red Ridinghood
caperuza *f* pointed hood; chimney cap
capilla *f* (*parte de una iglesia con altar*) chapel; (*de los reos de muerte*) death house; (*pliego suelto*) proof sheet; cowl, hood, cape; **estar en capilla** to be in the death house; to be on pins and needles; **estar expuesto en capilla ardiente** to be on view, to lie in state
capiller *m* churchwarden, sexton
capillo *m* baby cap; baptismal cap; hood; cocoon; (*del cigarro*) filler
capirotazo *m* fillip
capirote *m* hood; doctor's cap and hood; cardboard or paper cone (*worn on head*); fillip
capitación *f* poll tax
capital *adj* capital; main, principal; paramount; (*enemigo*) mortal ‖ *m* (*dinero que produce renta*) capital; (*dinero que se presta para producir renta*) principal; **capital de inversión** investment capital ‖ *f* capital
capitalismo *m* capitalism
capitalista *adj* capitalistic ‖ *mf* capitalist; shareholder, investor
capitalizar §60 *tr* to capitalize; (*los intereses devengados*) compound
capitán *m* captain; leader; **capitán de bandera** flag captain; **capitán de corbeta** (nav) lieutenant commander; **capitán del puerto** harbor master
capitana *f* flagship
capitanear *tr* to captain; lead, command
capitanía *f* captaincy; (mil) company
capitel *m* (*de una iglesia*) spire; (*de una columna*) capital
capitolio *m* capitol
capitoste *m* big shot
capítula *f* chapter (*of Scriptures*)
capitular *tr* to accuse; agree on ‖ *intr* to capitulate
capitulear *intr* (Arg, Chile, Peru) to lobby
capituleo *m* (Arg, Chile, Peru) lobbying
capitulero *m* (Arg, Chile, Peru) political henchman, lobbyist
capítulo *m* chapter; chapter house; subject, matter; errand; main point; **ganar capítulo** (coll) to win one's point; **llamar a capítulo** to take to task, call to account; **perder capítulo** to lose one's point
ca•pó *m* (*pl* **-pós**) hood (*of auto*)
capolar *tr* to cut to pieces, chop up
ca•pón -pona *adj* castrated ‖ *m* eunuch; (*pollo*) capon; bundle of firewood; (*golpe*) fillip ‖ *f* shoulder strap
caponera *f* coop for fattening capons; place of welcome; (*cárcel*) coop, jail
caporal *m* chief, leader; foreman (*on cattle ranch*)

capota *f* bonnet; (aer) cowling; (aut) top

capotaje *m* (aer) nosing over

capotar *intr* to upset; (aer) to nose over

capote *m* cape, cloak; (coll) frown, scowl; (Chile, Mex) beating; **capote de monte** poncho; **de capote** (Mex) on the sly; **dar capote a** to flabbergast; (*un rezagado*) to leave hungry; **decir para su capote** to say to oneself; **echar un capote** to turn the conversation

capotear *tr* (*al toro*) to challenge; (*dificultades*) evade, duck; beguile, take in; (*una obra teatral*) cut, make cuts in

Capricornio *m* Capricorn

capricho *m* caprice, whim, fancy

capricho•so -sa *adj* capricious, whimsical; willful

caprichu•do -da *adj* capricious, whimsical

cápsula *f* capsule; (*de botella*) cap

capsular *tr* to cap

captación *f* capture; (*de las aguas de un río*) harnessing; (rad) tuning in, picking up

captar *tr* to catch; (*la confianza de una persona*) win; (*las aguas de un río*) harness; (*las ondas radiofónicas*) tune in, pick up; (*lo que uno dice*) get, grasp ‖ *ref* to attract, win

captura *f* capture, catch

capturar *tr* to capture, catch

capucha *f* cowl, hood; circumflex accent

capuchina *f* garden nasturtium, Indian cress; Capuchin nun; confection of egg yolks

capucho *m* cowl, hood

capuchón *m* lady's cloak and hood; (*de una plumafuente*) cap; (aut) valve cap

capullo *m* cocoon; coarse spun silk; bud; **capullo de rosa** rosebud

capuzar §60 *tr* to throw in headfirst; (*un buque*) overload at the bow

caqui *adj* khaki ‖ *m* khaki; Japanese persimmon

caquinos *mpl* (Mex) guffaw, outburst of laughter

cara *f* face; look, countenance; façade, front; (*de disco de fonógrafo*) side; **a cara descubierta** openly; **a cara o cruz** heads or tails; **cara a** facing; **cara al público** with an audience; **cara de acelga** sallow face; **cara de ajo** vinegar face; **cara de hereje** (*persona de feo aspecto*) fright, baboon; **cara de vinagre** vinegar face; **dar la cara** to take the consequences; **de cara** in the face; facing; **echar a cara o cruz** to flip a coin; **hacer cara a** to stand up to; **tener buena cara** to look well, to look good; **tener mala cara** to look ill, to look bad

cárabe *m* amber

carabina *f* carbine; chaperon

caracol *m* snail; snail shell; (*de pelo*) curl; (*trazado en espiral*) spiral; (*del oído*) cochlea

carácter *m* (*pl* **caracteres**) character; (*marca que se pone a las reses*) brand

característi•co -ca *adj* characteristic ‖ *m* (theat) old man ‖ *f* characteristic; (theat) old woman

caracteriza•do -da *adj* distinguished

caracterizar §60 *tr* to characterize; to confer a distinction on; (*un personaje en la escena*) to interpret ‖ *ref* to dress and make up for a role

caradu•ro -ra *adj* brazen; shameless ‖ *f* scoundrel

caramba *interj* confound it!; upon my word!

carámbano *m* icicle

carambola *f* carom; double shot; trick, cheating

carambolear *intr* to carom ‖ *ref* to get tipsy

caramelo *m* caramel; drop, lozenge

carantamaula *f* ugly false face; (*persona*) ugly mug

carantoña *f* ugly false face; **carantoñas** adulation, fawning

carátula *f* mask; (*profesión de actor*) stage, theater; title page; (*de reloj*) (Mex, Guat) face

caravana *f* caravan; (*casa rodante*) trailer

caravanera *f* caravansary

caray *m* var of **carey**

carbohielo *m* dry ice

carbóli•co -ca *adj* carbolic

carbón *m* (*de leña*) charcoal; (*de piedra*) coal; (*electrodo de carbono de la lámpara de arco o la pila*) carbon; black crayon; (*honguillo parásito*) smut; **carbón de bujía** cannel coal, jet coal; **carbón tal como sale** run-of-mine coal

carboncillo *m* charcoal, charcoal pencil

carbonera *f* bunker, coal bunker; coalbin; (Col) coal mine

carbonería *f* coalyard

carbone•ro -ra *adj* coal, charcoal; coaling ‖ *mf* coaldealer; charcoal burner ‖ *f* see **carbonera**

carbonilla *f* fine coal; (*en los cilindros*) carbon

carbonizar §60 *tr* to char

carbono *m* carbon

carbunclo *m* (*piedra*) carbuncle; (pathol) carbuncle

carbunco *m* (pathol) carbuncle

carbúnculo *m* (*piedra*) carbuncle

carburador *m* carburetor

carburo *m* carbide

carcacha *f* (Mex) jalopy

carcaj *m* quiver

carcajada *f* outburst of laughter

cárcel *f* jail, prison; (*para oprimir dos piezas de madera encoladas*) clamp

carcele•ro -ra *adj* jail ‖ *m* jailer, warden

carcinóge•no -na *adj* carcinogenic; cancer-causing ‖ *m* carcinogen

carcinoma *f* carcinoma

carcoma *f* woodworm, borer; anxiety, worry; spendthrift

carcomer *tr* to bore, gnaw away at; undermine, harass ‖ *ref* to become worm-eaten

cardán *m* universal joint

cardenal *m* cardinal; cardinal bird; black-and-blue mark

cardenillo *m* verdigris

cárde•no -na *adj* purple; dapple-gray; (*agua*) opaline

cardía•co -ca *adj* cardiac ‖ *mf* (*persona que padece del corazón*) cardiac ‖ *m* (*remedio*) cardiac

cardinal *adj* cardinal

cardo *m* thistle

cardume *m* school (*of fish*)

carear *tr* to bring face to face; compare ‖ *intr* — **carear a** to overlook ‖ *ref* to meet face to face

carecer §22 *intr* — **carecer de** to lack, need, be in want of

carecimiento *m* lack, need, want

carencia *f* lack, need, want

carente *adj* — **carente de** lacking

careo *m* meeting; confrontation

care•ro -ra *adj* dear, expensive

carestía *f* scarcity, want, dearth; high prices; **carestía de la vida** high cost of living

careta *f* mask; **careta antigás** gas mask

carey *m* hawksbill turtle; tortoise shell

carga *f* load, loading; (*mercancías que se transportan*) freight, cargo; (*peso u obligación que pesan sobre una persona*) burden; (*de substancia explosiva, de electricidad, de soldados contra el enemigo*) charge; charge, responsibility, obligation; **carga de familia** dependent; **carga de punta** (elec) peak load; **carga por eje** axle load; **carga útil** pay load; **echar la carga a** to put the blame on; **volver a la carga** to keep at it

cargaderas *fpl* (Col) suspenders

cargadero *m* loading platform; freight station

carga•do -da *adj* loaded; (*cielo*) overcast, cloudy; (*atmósfera, tiempo*) close, sultry; (*alambre eléctrico*) hot, charged; (*café, té*) strong; (*rato, hora*) busy; **cargado de años** along in years; **cargado de espaldas** round-shouldered, stoop-shouldered

cargador *m* loader, stevedore; carrier, porter; (*de acumulador*) charger

cargamento *m* load; (naut) loading; (naut) cargo, shipment

cargante *adj* boring, annoying, tiresome

cargar §44 *tr* (*un peso, mercancías; un carro, un mulo, un barco; un horno; un arma de fuego; a una persona*) to load; (*una persona con un peso u obligación*) burden; (*un acumulador; al enemigo*) charge; (*a una persona*) charge with; entrust with; annoy, bore, weary; **cargar en cuenta a** (*una persona*) to charge to the account of; **cargar** (*a una persona*) **de** to charge with; burden with ‖ *intr* to load; (*el viento*) turn; crowd; incline, tip; (*el acento*) fall; eat too much, drink too much; **cargar con** to pick up; walk away with; (*un fusil*) shoulder; take on; **cargar sobre** to rest on; bother, pester; devolve on ‖ *ref* (*el cielo*) to become overcast; (*el viento*) turn; become annoyed, be bored; **cargarse de** to have a lot of; (*lágrimas*) be bathed in

cargaréme *m* receipt, voucher

cargazón *f* loading; (*en el estómago, la cabeza, etc.*) heaviness; mass of heavy clouds; (Arg) clumsy job; (Chile) good

crop; **cargazón alta** (coll) high office; high official

cargo *m* job, position; duty, responsibility; burden, weight; management; (*falta que se atribuye a uno; cantidad que uno debe y la acción de anotarla*) charge; **a cargo de** in charge of; **cargo de conciencia** sense of guilt; **girar a cargo de** to draw on; **hacerse cargo de** to take charge of; to realize, become aware of; to look into; **librar a cargo de** to draw on; **vestir el cargo** to look the part

cargosear *tr* (Arg, Chile) to pester

cargo•so -sa *adj* annoying, bothersome; onerous, costly

carguero *m* (naut) freighter; (Arg, Urug) beast of burden

cariaconteci•do -da *adj* downcast, woebegone

cariar §77 *tr* & *intr* to decay

cariátide *f* caryatid

Caribdis *f* Charybdis

caribe *adj* Caribbean ‖ *m* savage, brute

caricatura *f* (*descripción o figura grotescas; retrato festivo*) caricature; (*retrato festivo*) cartoon

caricaturista *mf* caricaturist; cartoonist

caricaturizar §60 *tr* to caricature; cartoon

caricia *f* caress; endearment

caridad *f* charity; **la caridad bien ordenada empieza por uno mismo** charity begins at home

caries *f* decay, tooth decay; caries

carilla *f* (*de colmenero*) mask; (*de libro*) page

carille•no -na *adj* full-faced

carillón *m* carillon

carine•gro -gra *adj* swarthy

cariño *m* love, affection; loved one; (Chile) gift, present; **cariños** caresses, endearments; (Arg) greetings

cariño•so -sa *adj* loving, affectionate

caripare•jo -ja *adj* stone-faced, impassive

carirraí•do -da *adj* brazen-faced, shameless

carisma *f* charisma

carismáti•co -ca *adj* charismatic

carita *f* little face; **dar** or **hacer carita** (*una mujer coqueta*) (Mex) to smile back

caritati•vo -va *adj* charitable

cariz *m* (*de la atmósfera, el tiempo*) appearance, look; (*de un asunto*) look, outlook; (*de la cara de uno*) look; **mal cariz** angry look, scowl

carlinga *f* (aer) cockpit

Carlomagno *m* Charlemagne

Carlos *m* Charles

carlota *f* pudding; **carlota rusa** charlotte russe ‖ **Carlota** *f* Charlotte

carmelita *f* (Hond) station wagon

carmen *m* song, poem; house and garden (*in Granada*)

carmesí (*pl* -síes) *adj* & *m* crimson

carnada *f* bait; (coll) bait, trap

carnal; *adj* carnal; (*hermano*) full; (*primo*) first

carnaval *m* carnival

carne *f* (*parte blanda del cuerpo humano y del animal*) flesh; (*la comestible del ani-*

mal) meat; **carne de cañón** cannon fodder; **carne de cerdo asada** roast pork; **carne de cordero** lamb; **carne de gallina** goose flesh; **carne de horca** gallows bird; **carne de res** beef; **carne de ternera** veal; **carne de vaca asada** roast of beef; **carne de venado** venison; **carne fiambre** cold meat; **carne sin hueso** cinch, snap; **carne y sangre** flesh and blood; **cobrar carnes** to put on flesh; **echar carnes** (Mex) to swear, curse; **en carnes** naked; **en vivas carnes** stark-naked

carnear *tr* (Arg, Chile, Urug) to butcher, slaughter; (Arg, Urug) to stab; (Chile) to take in, swindle

carnero *m* sheep; (*carne de este animal*) mutton; (*osario*) charnel house; family vault; (*persona que no tiene voluntad propia*) (Arg, Chile) sheep; **cantar para el carnero** (Arg, Bol, Urug) to die; **no hay tales carneros** there's no truth to it

car•net *m* (*pl* -**nets**) notebook; membership card; (Arg) dance card; **carnet de chófer** driver's license; **carnet de identidad** identification card

carnicería *f* butcher shop, meat market; (fig) carnage, massacre

carnice•ro -ra *adj* carnivorous; bloodthirsty ‖ *mf* butcher

carnosidad *f* fleshiness, corpulence; (*excrecencia carnosa anormal*) proud flesh

carno•so -sa *adj* fleshy; meaty, fat

ca•ro -ra *adj* (*de subido precio; amado, querido*) dear ‖ *f* see **cara** ‖ **caro** *adv* dear

carpa *f* carp; awning, tent; stand at a fair; **carpa dorada** goldfish

carpanta *f* raging hunger

carpeta *f* (*cubierta para mesas*) table cover; (*par de cubiertas para documentos*) letter file, portfolio; (*factura*) invoice; (Col) accounting department; (Peru) writing desk

carpintería *f* carpentry; carpenter shop; **carpintería de taller** millwork

carpintero *m* carpenter; woodpecker; **carpintero de carreta** wheelwright

carra•co -ca *adj* old, decrepit ‖ *f* (*barco viejo*) tub, hulk; (*instrumento de madera para producir un ruido desapacible*) rattle; (*berbiquí*) ratchet drill ‖ **la Carraca** Cádiz navy yard

carraspear *intr* to be hoarse

carraspera *f* hoarseness

carrera *f* (*paso del que corre*) run; (*lucha de velocidad*) race; (*sitio para correr*) race track; (*espacio recorrido corriendo*) course, stretch; (*curso de la vida, profesión*) career; (*calle*) avenue, boulevard; (*raya, crencha*) part (*in hair*); (*en las medias*) run; (*hilera*) row, line; (*viga*) rafter, girder; (*movimiento del émbolo del motor*) stroke; **a carrera abierta** at full speed; **carrera a pie** foot race; **carrera armamentista** or **de armamentos** arms race; **carrera ascendente** upstroke; **carrera de baquetas** gauntlet; **carrera de caballos** horse race; **carrera de campanario** steeplechase; **carrera de obstáculos** obstacle

race; steeplechase; **carrera de relevos** relay race; **carrera descendente** downstroke; **carrera de vallas** hurdle race; **carreras** horse racing, turf

carrerista *adj* horsy ‖ *mf* racegoer; auto racer; bicycle racer ‖ *m* outrider ‖ *f* (slang) streetwalker

carreta *f* cart; **carreta de bueyes** oxcart

carrete *m* reel, spool; fishing reel; (elec) coil

carretear *tr* to cart, haul; (*un carro, una carreta*) drive; (aer) to taxi ‖ *intr* (aer) to taxi

carretera *f* highway, road; **carretera de peaje** turnpike; **carretera de vía libre** expressway, limited-access highway

carretería *f* carts; wagon work; carting business; wagon shop

carrete•ro -ra *adj* wagon, carriage ‖ *m* wheelwright; teamster; charioteer; **jurar como un carretero** to swear like a trooper ‖ *f* see **carretera**

carretilla *f* wheelbarrow; baggage truck; (*para enseñar a los niños a andar*) gocart; (*buscapiés*) snake, serpent; (Arg, Chile, Urug) jaw; **carretilla de mano** handcart; **carretilla elevadora** lift truck; **de carretilla** offhand

carretón *m* cart, wagon, dray; gocart; (rr) truck; covered wagon

carricoche *m* covered wagon

carricuba *f* street sprinkler

carril *m* (*barra de acero en el ferrocarril*) rail, track; (*huella*) track, rut; (*hecho por el arado*) furrow; lane, path; (Chile) train; (Chile, P-R) railroad; **carril de toma** third rail

carrilera *f* track, rut

carrilero *m* (Peru) railroader

carrillera *f* jaw; chin strap

carrillo *m* cheek, jowl; pulley; **comer a dos carrillos** to eat like a glutton; have two sources of income; play both sides

carrizo *m* ditch reed

carro *m* cart, wagon; car, auto; (mach) carriage; **carro alegórico** float; **carro blindado** armored car; **carro correo** mail car; **carro de asalto** tank; **carro de combate** combat car, tank; **carro de equipajes** baggage car; **carro de mudanza** moving van; **carro de riego** street sprinkler; **carro frigorífero** refrigerator car; **carro fúnebre** hearse; **Carro mayor** Big Dipper; **Carro menor** Little Dipper; **carro romano** chariot; **pare Vd. el carro** hold your horses

ca•rró *m* (*pl* -**rrós**) diamond

carrocería *f* (*de automóvil*) body

carrocha *f* eggs (*of insect*)

carromato *m* covered wagon

carro•ño -ña *adj* & *f* carrion

carro-patrulla *f* (SAm) patrol car; police car

carroza *f* coach, carriage; **carroza alegórica** float; **carroza fúnebre** hearse

carruaje *m* carriage

carta *f* (*comunicación escrita*) letter; (*constitución escrita de un país*) charter; (*naipe*) card, playing card; map; **carta aérea** airmail letter; **carta blanca** carte blanche;

carta calumniosa poison-pen letter; **carta certificada** registered letter; **carta de marear** (naut) chart; **carta de naturaleza** naturalization papers; **carta general** form letter; **carta por avión** air-mail letter; **poner las cartas boca arriba** to put one's cards on the table

cartabón m carpenter's square

cartagi•nés -nesa adj & mf Carthaginian

Cartago f Carthage

cartapacio m notebook; schoolboy's satchel; writing book; (papeles contenidos en una carpeta) file, dossier

cartear intr to play low cards (in order to see how the game stands) ‖ ref to write to each other

cartel m show bill, poster, placard; cartel, trust; (pasquín) lampoon; (de toreros) bill, line-up; (del torero) fame, reputation; **cartel de teatro** bill, show bill; **dar cartel a** to headline; **se prohíbe fijar carteles** post no bills; **tener cartel** to be the rage

cartela f card; bracket

cartelera f billboard; (en los periódicos) amusement page, theater section

cartelero m billposter

cartelón m show bill

carteo m finessing; exchange of letters

cárter m (mach) housing; **cárter de engranajes** gearcase; **cárter del cigüeñal** crankcase

cartera f portfolio; pocket flap; **cartera de bolsillo** billfold, wallet

cartería f sorting room

carterista m pickpocket, purse snatcher

cartero m letter carrier, postman

cartilagino•so -sa adj gristly

cartílago m gristle

cartilla f primer, speller, reader; notebook; (de la caja de ahorros) deposit book; **cartilla de racionamiento** ration book

cartivana f (bb) hinge, joint

cartón m cardboard, pasteboard; cardboard box; **cartón de yeso y fieltro** plasterboard; **cartón picado** stencil; **cartón tabla** wallboard

cartoné — **en cartoné** (bb) in boards, bound in boards

cartucho m cartridge

cartulina f fine cardboard

casa f (edificio para habitar) house; (hogar, domicilio) home; (establecimiento comercial o industrial) firm, concern; (familia) household; (escaque) square; **a casa** home, homeward; **casa consistorial** town hall, city hall; **casa de azotea** penthouse; **casa de campo** country house; **casa de caridad** poorhouse; **casa de citas** house of assignation; **casa de correos** post office; **casa de empeños** pawnshop; **casa de expósitos** foundling home; **casa de fieras** menagerie; **casa de huéspedes** boarding house; **casa de juego** gambling house; **casa de locos** madhouse; **casa de modas** dress shop; **casa de moneda** mint; **casa de préstamos** pawnshop; **casa de salud** private hospital; **casa de socorro** first-aid station; **casa de**

vecindad or **de vecinos** apartment house, tenement house; **casa editorial** publishing house; **casa matriz** main office; **casa pública** brothel; **casa real** royal palace; royal family; **casas baratas** low-cost housing; **casa solar** or **solariega** ancestral mansion; manor house; **casa y comida** board and lodging; **¡convida la casa!** the drinks are on the house!; **en casa** home, at home; **ir a buscar casa** to go house hunting; **poner casa** to set up housekeeping

casabe m var of **cazabe**

casaca f dress coat; marriage contract; (Guat, Hond) lively whispered conversation; **volver la casaca** to become a turncoat

casade•ro -ra adj marriageable

casa•do -da adj married ‖ mf married person; **(los) no casados** (coll) singles

casal m country place; (Arg) pair, couple

casamente•ro -ra adj matchmaking ‖ mf matchmaker

casamiento m marriage; wedding

casapuerta f entrance hall, vestibule

casaquilla f jacket

casar tr to marry; marry off; match; harmonize; (law) to annul, repeal ‖ intr to marry, get married ‖ ref to marry, get married; **no casarse con nadie** to get tied up with nobody

casatienda f store and home combined

cascabel m sleigh bell, jingle bell; rattlesnake; **ponerle cascabel al gato** to bell the cat

cascabelear intr to jingle; to act tactlessly

cascabeleo m jingle

cascabele•ro -ra adj tactless, thoughtless ‖ mf featherbrain ‖ m baby's rattle

cascabillo m jingle bell; chaff, husk; cup of acorn

cascada f cascade, waterfall

cascajo m pebble; gravel, rubble; broken jar; piece of junk; **estar hecho un cascajo** to be old and worn-out, be a wreck

cascanue•ces m (pl -ces) nutcracker

cascar §73 tr to crack, break, split; beat, strike, hit ‖ ref to crack, break, split

cáscara f hull, peel, rind, shell; bark, crust; **cáscara rueda** (Arg) ring-around-a-rosy; **ser de la cáscara amarga** to be wild and flighty; hold advanced views; (Mex) to be determined

cascarón m eggshell

cascarra•bias mf (pl -bias) crab, grouch

casco m (pieza que sirve para proteger la cabeza del soldado, el bombero, etc.) helmet; (uña de las caballerías) hoof; (pedazo de vasija rota) potsherd; (capa de la cebolla) coat, shell; (del sombrero) crown; (cuerpo de la nave) hull; (de un barco inservible) hulk; (barril, pipa) barrel, tank, cask, vat; (pieza del teléfono) headset, headpiece; bottle; (mach) shell, casing; (gajo de la naranja) (Arg, Col, Chile) slice; (Peru) chest, breast; **casco de población** or **casco urbano** city limits; **romperse los cascos** to rack one's brain

casera f landlady; housekeeper

casería f country place; customers

caserío *m* country house; small settlement, hamlet

case•ro -ra *adj* homemade; homeloving; (*remedio*) household; house, home; (*sencillo*) homely ‖ *mf* owner, proprietor; renter; caretaker; janitor; huckster; vendor ‖ *m* landlord ‖ *f* see **casera**

caseta *f* (*casa sin piso alto*) cottage; (*de una feria*) stall, booth; bathhouse

casete *m* cassette

casi *adv* almost, nearly; **casi nada** next to nothing; **casi nunca** hardly ever

casilla *f* hut, shack, shed; cabin, lodge; stall, booth; (*escaque*) square; (*compartimiento en un mueble*) pigeonhole; (*división del papel rayado*) column, square; (*taquilla*) ticket office; (*de locomotora o camión*) cab; (Bol, Chile, Peru, Urug) post-office box; (Ecuad) water closet; (Cuba) bird trap; **sacarle a uno de sus casillas** to jolt someone out of his old habits; drive someone crazy

casille•ro -ra *mf* (rr) crossing guard ‖ *m* filing cabinet, set of pigeonholes

casino *m* casino; club; clubhouse

caso *m* case; chance; event; **caso de conformidad** in case you agree; **caso que** in case; **de caso pensado** deliberately, on purpose; **en todo caso** at all events; **hacer al caso** to be to the purpose; **hacer caso de** to take into account, pay attention to; **hacer caso omiso de** to pass over in silence, not mention; **no venir al caso** to be beside the point; **poner por caso** to take as an example; **venir al caso** to be just the thing

casorio *m* hasty marriage, unwise marriage

caspa *f* dandruff, scurf

cáspita *interj* well well!, upon my word!

caspo•so -sa *adj* full of dandruff

casquete *m* (*cubierta que se ajusta al casco de la cabeza*) skullcap; skull, cranium; (*pieza de la armadura que cubre el casco de la cabeza*) helmet; (*pieza del teléfono*) headset

casquillo *m* butt, cap, tip; bushing, sleeve; ferrule; horseshoe

casquiva•no -na *adj* scatterbrained

casta *f* caste; kind, quality; breed, race

castaña *f* chestnut; (*moño*) knot, chignon; demijohn; **castaña de Indias** horse chestnut; **castaña de Pará** Brazil nut

castañeta *f* castanet; snapping of the fingers

castañetear *tr* (*los dedos*) to snap, click; (*p.ej., una seguidilla*) click off with the castanets ‖ *intr* to click; (*los dientes*) chatter

casta•ño -ña *adj* chestnut, chestnut-colored; (*p.ej., pelo*) brown; (*p.ej., ojos*) hazel ‖ *m* chestnut tree; **castaño de Indias** horse chestnut ‖ *f* see **castaña**

castañuela *f* castanet; **estar como unas castañuelas** to be bubbling over with joy

castella•no -na *adj & mf* Castilian ‖ *m* Castilian, Spanish (*language*) ‖ *f* chatelaine

casticidad *f* purity, correctness (*in language*)

casticismo *m* purism

castidad *f* chastity

castiga•dor -dora *mf* punisher ‖ *m* seducer, Don Juan

castigar §44 *tr* to punish, chastise; (*la carne*) mortify; (*los gastos*) cut down, curtail; (*obras, escritos*) correct, emend; (*un tornillo*) (Mex) tighten

castigo *m* punishment, chastisement

Castilla *f* Castile; **Castilla la Nueva** New Castile; **Castilla la Vieja** Old Castile

castillete *m* (min) derrick; tower

castillo *m* castle; (*montura sobre un elefante*) howdah; **castillo en el aire** castle in Spain, castle in the air; **castillo de naipes** house of cards; **castillo de proa** forecastle

casti•zo -za *adj* chaste, pure, correct; pure-blooded; real, regular

cas•to -ta *adj* chaste, pure ‖ *f* see **casta**

castor *m* beaver

castrar *tr* to castrate; (*una planta*) prune, cut back; weaken

casual *adj* casual, accidental, chance

casualidad *f* accident, chance; chance event; **por casualidad** by chance

casuca or **casucha** *f* shack, shanty

casulla *f* chasuble

cata *f* tasting; taste, sample

catacal•dos *mf* (*pl* **-dos**) rolling stone; busybody

catacumba *f* catacomb

catafoto *m* (rear) reflector

cata•lán -lana *adj & mf* Catalan, Catalonian

catalejo *m* spyglass

catalogar §44 *tr* to catalogue

catálogo *m* catalogue

Cataluña *f* Catalonia

cataplasma *f* poultice; **cataplasma de mostaza** mustard plaster

catapulta *f* catapult

catapultar *tr* to catapult

catar *tr* to taste, sample; check, examine; be on the lookout for

catarata *f* cataract, waterfall; (pathol) cataract

catarro *m* (*inflamación de las membranas mucosas*) catarrh; (*resfriado*) head cold

catástrofe *f* catastrophe

catavino *m* cup for tasting wine

catavi•nos *m* (*pl* **-nos**) winetaster; (*borracho*) rounder

catear *tr* to hunt, look for; (*a un alumno*) to flunk; to explore; (*una casa*) to search

catecismo *m* catechism

cátedra *f* chair, professorship; academic subject; teacher's desk; classroom; **poner cátedra** to hold forth

catedral *f* cathedral

catedrático *m* university professor

categoría *f* category; status, standing; class, kind; condition, quality; **de categoría** prominent

caterva *f* throng, crowd

catéter *m* catheter

cateterizar §60 *tr* to catheterize

cátodo *m* cathode

católi•co -ca *adj* catholic; Catholic; **no estar muy católico** to be under the weather ‖ *mf*

Catholic; **católico romano** Roman Catholic

catorce *adj & pron* fourteen ‖ *m* fourteen; (*en las fechas*) fourteenth

catorcea•vo -va *adj & m* fourteenth

catorza•vo -va *adj & m* fourteenth

catre *m* cot; **catre de tijera** folding cot

catrecillo *m* campstool, folding canvas chair

ca•trín -trina *adj* (CAm, Mex) sporty, swell ‖ *mf* (CAm, Mex) sport, dude

caucasia•no -na or **caucási•co -ca** *adj & mf* Caucasian

Cáucaso *m* Caucasus

cauce *m* river bed; channel, ditch, trench

caución *f* precaution; (law) bail, security

caucionar *tr* to guard against; (law) to give bail for

cauchal *m* rubber plantation

caucho *m* rubber; rubber plant; (Col) rubber raincoat; **caucho esponjoso** foam rubber; **cauchos** (*chanclos*) rubbers

caudal *adj* of great volume ‖ *m* (*de agua*) volume; abundance; wealth

caudalo•so -sa *adj* of great volume; abundant; rich, wealthy

caudillo *m* chief, leader; military leader; caudillo, head of state

causa *f* cause; (law) suit, trial; (Chile) bite, snack; (Peru) potato salad; **a** or **por causa de** on account of, because of

causa•dor -dora *adj* causing ‖ *mf* (*persona*) cause

causante *mf* (*persona*) cause; (law) principal, constituent; (Mex) taxpayer

causar *tr* to cause

causear *tr* (Chile) to get the best of ‖ *intr* (Chile) to have a bite

causeo *m* (Chile) bite, snack

cáusti•co -ca *adj* caustic

cautela *f* caution

cautelo•so -sa *adj* cautious, guarded

cauterizar §60 *tr* to cauterize

cautín *m* soldering iron

cautivar *tr* to take prisoner; attract, win over; (*encantar*) captivate

cautiverio *m* or **cautividad** *f* captivity

cauti•vo -va *adj & mf* captive

cau•to -ta *adj* cautious

cavar *tr* to dig, dig up ‖ *intr* (*una herida*) to go deep; (*el caballo*) to paw; **cavar en** to study thoroughly, to delve into

caverna *f* cavern, cave

cavidad *f* cavity

cavilar *tr* to brood over ‖ *intr* to worry, fret

cavilo•so -sa *adj* suspicious, mistrustful; (CAm) gossipy; (Col) touchy

cayado *m* (*de pastor*) crook; (*de obispo*) crozier

cayo *m* key, reef; **Cayo Hueso** Key West; **Cayos de la Florida** Florida Keys

caz *m* (*pl* **caces**) flume, millrace

caza *m* pursuit plane, fighter; **caza de reacción** jet fighter ‖ *f* chase, hunt; hunting; (*animales que se cazan*) game; **a caza de** on the hunt for; **caza al hombre** man hunt; **caza de grillos** fool's errand, wild-goose chase; **ir de caza** to go hunting

cazaautógra•fos *mf* (*pl* **-fos**) autograph seeker

cazabe *m* cassava, manioc; cassava bread

caza•dor -dora *adj* hunting ‖ *m* hunter; huntsman; **cazador de alforja** trapper; **cazador de cabezas** head-hunter; **cazador de dotes** fortune hunter; **cazador furtivo** poacher ‖ *f* huntress; hunting jacket; jacket

cazanoti•cias (*pl* **-cias**) *m* newshawk ‖ *f* newshen

cazasubmarinos *m* sub(marine) chaser

cazar §60 *tr* to chase; hunt; catch; (*en un descuido o error*) catch up; (*un descuido o error*) catch; (*adquirir con maña*) wangle; (*con halagos o engaños*) take in ‖ *intr* to hunt

cazarreactor *m* jet fighter

cazcalear *intr* to buzz around

cazo *m* dipper, ladle; glue pot; (*de cuchillo*) back

cazuela *f* earthen casserole; stew; (archaic) gallery for women; (SAm) chicken stew

cazu•rro -rra *adj* sullen, surly

cazuz *m* ivy

C. de J. *abbr* **Compañía de Jesús**

cebada *f* barley

cebadera *f* nose bag

cebador *m* (mach) primer

cebar *tr* (*a un animal*) to fatten; (*un horno*) feed; (*un arma de fuego, una bomba, un carburador*) prime; (*una pasión, la esperanza*) nourish; (*atraer*) lure; (*un clavo, un tornillo*) make catch, make take hold; (*un anzuelo*) bait ‖ *intr* (*un clavo, un tornillo*) to catch, take hold ‖ *ref* (*una enfermedad, una epidemia*) to rage; **cebarse en** to be absorbed in; vent one's fury on

cebo *m* fattening; feed; bait; lure; (*carga de un arma de fuego*) primer; priming

cebolla *f* onion; bulb; (*del velón*) oil receptacle

cebra *f* zebra

ce•bú *m* (*pl* **-búes**) zebu

ceca *f* mint; **de Ceca en Meca** or **de la Ceca a la Meca** hither and thither, from pillar to post

cecear *intr* to lisp

ceceo *m* lisp, lisping

cecina *f* dried beef

cedazo *m* sieve

ceder *tr* to yield, cede, give up ‖ *intr* to yield, give way, give in; slacken, relax; go down, decline

cedro *m* cedar; **cedro de Virginia** juniper, red cedar

cédula *f* (*de papel*) slip; form, blank; rent sign; certificate, document; **cédula de vecindad** or **cédula personal** identification papers

cedulón *m* proclamation, public notice; (*pasquín*) lampoon

céfiro *m* zephyr

cegar §66 *tr* to blind; (*un agujero*) plug, stop up; (*una puerta, una ventana*) wall up ‖ *intr* to go blind; be blinded ‖ *ref* to be blinded

cega•to -ta *adj* dim-sighted, weak-eyed

ceguedad *f* blindness

ca
ce

ceguera *f* blindness; blackout
Ceilán Ceylon
ceila•nés -nesa *adj & mf* Ceylonese
ceja *f (pelo sobre la cuenca del ojo)* eyebrow; edge, rim; cloud cap; clearing for a road; **arquear las cejas** to raise one's eyebrows; **fruncir las cejas** to knit one's brow; **quemarse las cejas** to burn the midnight oil
cejar *intr* to back up; turn back; slacken
cejijun•to -ta or **ceju•do -da** *adj* beetle-browed; scowling
celada *f* ambush; trap, trick
celador *m* guard *(e.g., in a museum)*; (elec) lineman; (Urug) policeman
celaje *m* cloud effect; skylight, transom; ghost
celar *tr* to see to; watch over, keep an eye on; hide; carve
celda *f* cell; **celda de castigo** solitary confinement
celdilla *f* cell; niche
celebración *f* celebration; applause; *(de una reunión)* holding
celebrante *m (sacerdote)* celebrant
celebrar *tr* to celebrate; *(una reunión)* hold; *(aprobar)* welcome; *(un matrimonio)* perform; *(misa)* say ‖ *intr (decir misa)* to celebrate; be glad ‖ *ref* to take place, be held; be celebrated
célebre *adj* celebrated, famous; funny, witty; pretty
celebridad *f (fama; persona)* celebrity
celeridad *f* speed, swiftness
celeste *adj* celestial; sky-blue
celestial *adj* celestial, heavenly; stupid, silly
celestina *f* procuress, bawd
celestinaje *m* procuring, pandering
celibato *m* celibacy; bachelor
célibe *adj* celibate, single, unmarried ‖ *mf* celibate, single person ‖ *m* bachelor ‖ *f* unmarried woman
celinda *f* mock orange
celo *m* zeal; envy; *(impulso reproductivo en las bestias)* heat, rut; **celos** jealousy
celofán *m* or **celofana** *f* cellophane
celosía *f (celotipia)* jealousy; *(enrejado de listoncillos)* lattice window, jalousie
celo•so -sa *adj (que tiene celo)* zealous; *(que tiene celos)* jealous; fearful, distrustful; (naut) unsteady
celotipia *f* jealousy
celta *adj* Celtic ‖ *mf* Celt ‖ *m (idioma)* Celtic
célti•co -ca *adj* Celtic
célula *f* cell
celuloide *m* celluloid; **llevar al celuloide** to put on the screen
cellisca *f* sleet, sleet storm
cellisquear *intr* to sleet
cementerio *m* cemetery
cemento *m* cement; concrete; **cemento armado** reinforced concrete
cena *f* supper; dinner ‖ **la Cena** the Last Supper
cena•dor -dora *mf* diner-out ‖ *m* arbor, bower, summerhouse
cenaduría *f* (Mex) supper club
cenagal *m* quagmire
cenago•so -sa *adj* muddy, miry

cenaoscu•ras *mf (pl* **-ras)** recluse; skinflint
cenar *tr* to have for supper, have for dinner ‖ *intr* to have supper, have dinner
cencerrada *f* tin-pan serenade
cencerrear *intr* to keep jingling; rattle, jangle; play out of tune
cencerro *m* cowbell; **a cencerros tapados** cautiously
cendal *m* gauze, sendal
cenefa *f* edging, trimming, border
cenicero *m* ash tray
cenicien•to -ta *adj* ashen, ash-gray ‖ **la Cenicienta** Cinderella
cenit *m* zenith
ceniza *f* ash; ashes; **cenizas** ashes; **huir de las cenizas y caer en las brasas** to jump from the frying pan into the fire
ceni•zo -za *adj* ashen, ash-gray ‖ *f* see **ceniza**
cenojil *m* garter
cenote *m* (Mex) deep underground water reservoir
censo *m* census; **levantar el censo** to take the census
censor *m* censor; **censor jurado de cuentas** certified public accountant
censura *f* censure; censoring; gossip; **censura de cuentas** auditing
censurar *tr (criticar, reprobar)* to censure; *(formar juicio de)* censor
centauro *m* centaur
centa•vo -va *adj* hundredth ‖ *m* hundredth; cent
centella *f* flash of lightning; flash of light; spark; *(de ingenio, de ira)* (fig) spark, flash
centellar or **centellear** *intr* to flash, spark; glimmer, gleam, twinkle
centenar *m* hundred; **a centenares** by the hundreds
centena•rio -ria *adj* centennial ‖ *mf* centenarian ‖ *m* centennial
cente•no -na *adj* hundredth ‖ *m* rye
centési•mo -ma *adj & m* hundredth
centígra•do -da *adj* centigrade
centímetro *m* centimeter
cénti•mo -ma *adj* hundredth ‖ *m* hundredth; centime
centinela *mf (persona)* watch, guard ‖ *m & f (soldado)* sentinel, sentry; **hacer de centinela** to stand sentinel
centípedo *m* centipede
central *adj* central ‖ *m* sugar mill, sugar refinery ‖ *f* headquarters, main office; powerhouse; (telp) exchange, central; **central de correos** main post office; **central de teléfonos** telephone exchange
centralista *mf* telephone operator
centralizar §60 *tr & ref* to centralize
centrar *tr* to center; hit the center ‖ *ref* to concentrate; stress
céntri•co -ca *adj* center, central; *(próximo al centro de la ciudad)* downtown
centrifugadora *f* centrifuge; spin-dryer
centro *m* center; middle; business district, downtown; club; object, goal, purpose; **centro de mesa** centerpiece; **centro docente** educational institution; **pegar centro** (CAm) to hit the bull's-eye

Centro América f Central America
centroamerica•no -na adj & mf Central American
cénts. abbr **céntimos**
ceñi•do -da adj tight, tight-fitting; lithe, svelte; thrifty
ceñidor m belt, girdle, sash
ceñir §72 tr to gird; girdle; fasten around the waist; fasten, tie; abridge, shorten; surround; (la espada) gird on; (mil) to besiege ‖ ref (reducirse en los gastos) to tighten one's belt; (a pocas palabras) restrict oneself; adapt oneself; **ceñirse a** (p.ej., un muro) to hug, keep close to
ceño m frown; (del cielo, las nubes, el mar) threatening look; (cerco, aro) hoop, ring, band; **arrugar el ceño** to knit one's brow; **mirar con ceño** to frown at
ceño•so -sa or **ceñu•do -da** adj beetlebrowed; frowning, grim, gruff
cepa f (de árbol) stump; (de la cola del animal) stub; (de la vid) vinestalk; (de una famila o linaje) strain; **de buena cepa** of well-known quality
cepillar tr to plane; brush; smooth; (SAm) to flatter
cepillo m (instrumento para alisar la madera) plane; (utensilio para limpieza) brush; (cepo para limosnas) charity box, poor box; (CAm, Mex) flatterer; **cepillo de cabeza** hairbrush; **cepillo de dientes** toothbrush; **cepillo de ropa** clothesbrush; **cepillo de uñas** nail brush
cepo m (de limosnas) poor box; (rama de árbol) bough, branch; (trampa) snare, trap; (del yunque) stock; (para devanar la seda) reel; clamp, vise; (para asegurar a un reo) stocks, pillory; **¡cepos quedos!** quiet!, stop it!
cera f wax; **cera de abejas** beeswax; **cera de los oídos** earwax; **cera de lustrar** polishing wax; **cera de pisos** floor wax; **ceras honeycomb**; **ser como una cera** to be wax in one's hands
cerámi•co -ca adj ceramic
cerbatana f peashooter; ear trumpet; spokesperson, go-between
cerca m close-up; **tener buen cerca** to look good at close quarters ‖ f fence, wall; **cerca viva** hedge ‖ adv near; **cerca de** near, close to; about; to, at the court of; **de cerca** closely; at close range
cercado m fence, wall; walled-in garden or field
cercanía f nearness, proximity; **cercanías** neighborhood, vicinity
cerca•no -na adj close, near; adjoining, neighboring; (que debe acontecer en breve) early
cercar §73 tr to fence in, wall in; encircle, surround; crowd around; (mil) to besiege
cercenar tr to clip, trim; curtail; cut out
cerciorar tr to inform, assure ‖ ref to find out; **cerciorarse de** to ascertain, find out about
cerco m (aro, anillo) hoop, ring; (marco de puerta o ventana) casing, frame; (círculo que aparece alrededor del sol o la luna) halo; (reunión de personas) circle, group; fence, wall; (mil) siege; **poner cerco a** (mil) to lay siege to
cerda f bristle, horsehair; (hembra del cerdo) sow
cerdear intr to be weak in the forelegs; (las cuerdas de un instrumento) rasp, grate; hold back, look for excuses
Cerdeña f Sardinia
cerdo m hog; (persona sucia) pig, swine; (hombre sin cortesía) cad, ill-bred fellow; **cerdo de muerte** pig to be slaughtered; **cerdo de vida** pig not old enough to be slaughtered; **cerdo marino** porpoise
cerdo•so -sa adj bristly
cereal adj & m cereal
cerebro m brain; (seso, inteligencia) brain, brains
ceremonia f ceremony; formality; **de ceremonia** formal; **hacer ceremonias** to stand on ceremony; **por ceremonia** as a matter of form
ceremonio•so -sa adj ceremonious, punctilious; (que gusta de ceremonias) formal
cereza f cherry
cerezo m cherry tree
cerilla f wax taper; wax match
cerillera f or **cerillero** m match box
cerneja f fetlock
cerner §51 tr to sift; (el horizonte) scan ‖ intr to bud, blossom; drizzle ‖ ref to waddle; (el ave) soar, hover; (un mal) threaten; **cernerse sobre** (amenazar) to hang over
cerní•calo m (orn) sparrow hawk; ignoramus; jag, drunk
cernir §28 tr to sift
cero m zero; **empezar de cero** to start from scratch; **ser un cero a la izquierda** to not count, be a nobody
cerote m shoemaker's wax; fear
cerotear tr (el hilo) to wax ‖ intr (Chile) to drip
cerra•do -da adj closed; close; incomprehensible; (cielo) cloudy, overcast; (barba) thick; (curva) sharp; quiet, reserved, secretive; dense, stupid
cerradura f lock; closing, locking; **cerradura embutida** mortise lock
cerrajería f locksmith business; hardware; hardware store
cerrajero m locksmith; hardware dealer; (el que trabaja el hierro frío) ironworker
cerrar §2 tr to close, shut; lock; bolt; (el puño) clench; enclose; (la radio) turn off; **cerrar con llave** to lock ‖ intr to close, shut; (la noche) fall; **cerrar con** (el enemigo) to close in on; **cerrar en falso** (una puerta, cerradura, etc.) to not catch ‖ ref to close, to shut; lock; **cerrarse en falso** to not heal right
cerrazón f gathering storm clouds; (Arg) heavy fog
cerre•ro -ra adj free, loose; untamed; haughty; (Mex) rough, unpolished; (café) (Ven) bitter

cerril *adj* rough, uneven; wild, untamed; boorish, rough

cerrillar *tr* to knurl, mill

cerro *m* hill, hillock; (*entre dos surcos*) ridge; (*espinazo*) backbone; (*del animal*) neck; **en cerro** bareback; **echar por los cerros de Úbeda** to talk nonsense; **por los cerros de Úbeda** off the beaten path

cerrojo *m* bolt; **cerrojo dormido** dead bolt

certamen *m* literary competition; contest, match

certe•ro -ra *adj* certain, sure, accurate; well-informed; (*tiro*) well-aimed; (*tirador*) good, crack

certeza *f* certainty

certidumbre *f* certainty; sureness

certificación *f* certification; certificate

certifica•do -da *adj* registered ‖ *m* registered letter, registered package; certificate; **certificado de estudios** transcript

certificar §73 *tr* to certify; (*una carta*) register

certitud *f* certainty

cerval *adj* deer; (*miedo*) intense

cervato *m* fawn

cervecería *f* brewery; beer saloon

cervece•ro -ra *adj* beer ‖ *mf* brewer

cerveza *f* beer; **cerveza a presión** draught beer; **cerveza de marzo** bock beer

cer•viz *f* (*pl* **-vices**) cervix; nape of the neck; **bajar** or **doblar la cerviz** to humble oneself; **levantar la cerviz** to raise one's head, become proud; **ser de dura cerviz** to be ungovernable

cesación *f* cessation, suspension

cesante *adj* retired, out of office ‖ *mf* pensioner

cesantía *f* retirement; dismissal (*of a public official*)

cesar *intr* to stop, cease

César *m* Caesar

cese *m* ceasing; notice of retirement; **cese de alarma** all-clear; **cese de fuego** ceasefire

césped *m* lawn, sward; sod, turf

cesta *f* basket; (*para jugar a la pelota*) wicker scoop; **cesta de costura** sewing basket; **cesta para compras** market basket

cesto *m* basket; washbasket; **cesto de la colada** clothesbasket, washbasket; **estar hecho un cesto** to be overcome with sleep; **ser un cesto** to be crude and ignorant

cetrería *f* falconry

cetrero *m* falconer

cetri•no -na *adj* (*tez*) sallow; jaundiced, melancholy

cetro *m* scepter; (*para aves*) perch, roost; (*eccl*) verge; **cetro de bufón** bauble; **cetro de locura** fool's scepter; **empuñar el cetro** to ascend the throne

cf. *abbr* **confesor**

cg. *abbr* **centigramo**

C.I. *abbr* **cociente intelectual**

cía. *abbr* **compañía**

cía *f* hipbone

cianamida *f* cyanamide

cianuro *m* cyanide

ciar §77 *intr* to back up; back water; ease up

cibernética *f* cybernetics

ciborio *m* ciborium

cicatear *intr* to be stingy

cicate•ro -ra *adj* stingy ‖ *mf* miser, niggard

cica•triz *f* (*pl* **-trices**) scar

cicatrizar §60 *tr* to heal; (*una impresión dolorosa*) (Arg) to heal ‖ *ref* to heal; to scar

Cicerón *m* Cicero

ciclamor *m* Judas tree; **ciclamor del Canadá** redbud

cícli•co -ca *adj* cyclic(al)

ciclismo *m* bicycle racing

ciclista *mf* bicyclist; bicycle racer

ciclo *m* cycle; series (of lectures); (*en las escuelas*) (Arg, Urug) term

ciclón *m* cyclone

cicuta *f* hemlock

cidra *f* citron (*fruit*)

cidrada *f* citron (*candied rind*)

cidro *m* citron (*tree or shrub*)

cie•go -ga *adj* blind; blocked, stopped up; **más ciego que un topo** blind as a bat ‖ *mf* blind person ‖ *m* blind man ‖ *f* blind woman; **a ciegas** blindly; thoughtlessly; without looking

cielo *m* sky, heavens; (*clima, tiempo*) skies, climate, weather; (*de una cama*) canopy; (*mansión de los bienaventurados*) Heaven; **a cielo abierto** in the open air, outdoors; **a cielo descubierto** openly; **a cielo raso** in the open air, outdoors; in the country; **cielo de la boca** roof of the mouth; **cielo máximo** (aer) ceiling; **cielo raso** ceiling; **llovido del cielo** heaven-sent, manna from heaven

cielorraso *m* ceiling

ciem•piés *m* (*pl* **-piés**) centipede

cien *adj* hundred, a hundred, one hundred

ciénaga *f* swamp, marsh, mudhole

ciencia *f* science; knowledge; learning; **a ciencia cierta** with certainty

ciencia-ficción *f* science fiction

cieno *m* mud, mire, silt

cieno•so -sa *adj* muddy, miry, silty

ciento *adj* & *m* hundred, a hundred, one hundred; **por ciento** per cent

cierne *m* budding, blossoming; **en cierne** in blossom; only beginning

cierrarrenglón *m* marginal stop

cierre *m* closing; shutting; snap, clasp, fastener; latch, lock; (*de una tienda, de la Bolsa*) close; (*paro de trabajo*) shutdown; **cierre cremallera** zipper; **cierre de portada** metal shutter (*of store front*); **cierre de puerta** door check; **cierre hermético** weather stripping; **cierre relámpago** zipper

cierro *m* closing; shutting; (Chile) fence, wall; (Chile) envelope

cier•to -ta *adj* certain; a certain; (*acertado, verdadero*) true; (*seguro*) sure; **por cierto** for sure ‖ **cierto** *adv* surely, certainly

cierva *f* hind

ciervo *m* deer, stag, hart

cierzo *m* cold north wind

cifra *f* (*número*) cipher; (*escritura secreta*) code; (*enlace de dos o más letras empleado en sellos*) device, monogram, emblem; abbreviation; amount, sum; **en cifra** in code; in brief; mysteriously

cifrar *tr* to cipher, code; abridge; calculate; **cifrar la dicha en** to base one's happiness in; **cifrar la esperanza en** to place one's hope in ‖ *ref* to be abridged; **cifrarse en** to be based on

cifrario *m* (com) code

cigarra *f* harvest fly, locust

cigarrera *f* cigar case; cigar girl

cigarrería *f* cigar store, tobacco store

cigarre·ro -ra *mf* cigar maker; cigar dealer ‖ *f* see **cigarrera**

cigarrillo *m* cigarette; **cigarrillo con filtro** filter cigarette

cigarro *m* cigar; **cigarro de papel** cigarette; **cigarro puro** cigar

cigoñal *m* well sweep; (*del motor de explosión*) crankshaft

cigüeña *f* stork; crank, winch

cigüeñal *m* var of **cigoñal**

cilampa *f* (CAm) drizzle

cilicio *m* haircloth, hair shirt

cilindrada *f* piston displacement

cilindrar *tr* to roll

cilíndri·co -ca *adj* cylindrical

cilindro *m* cylinder; roll, roller; (Mex) barrel organ, hand organ

cima *f* (*de árbol*) top; (*de montaña*) top, summit; **dar cima a** to complete, to carry out; **por cima** (coll) at the very top

cimarra *f* — **hacer cimarra** (Arg, Chile) to play hooky

cima·rrón -rrona *adj* (*animal*) wild, untamed; (*planta*) wild; (*esclavo*) fugitive; (*marinero*) lazy; (*maté*) (Arg, Urug) black, bitter

cimarronear *intr* (Arg, Urug) to drink black maté ‖ *ref* (*el esclavo*) to flee, run away

címbalo *m* cymbal

cimbel *m* decoy pigeon, stool pigeon

cimborio or **cimborrio** *m* dome

cimbrar or **cimbrear** *tr* to brandish; swing, sway; bend; thrash, beat ‖ *ref* to swing, sway; shake

cimbre·ño -ña *adj* flexible, pliant; lithe, willowy

cimentar §2 *tr* to found, establish; lay the foundations of

cime·ro -ra *adj* top, uppermost

cimiento *m* foundation, groundwork; basis, source

cimitarra *f* scimitar

cinabrio *m* cinnabar

cinanquia *f* quinsy

cinc *m* (*pl* **cinces**) zinc

cincel *m* chisel, graver

cincelar *tr* to chisel, engrave

cinco *adj* & *pron* five; **las cinco** five o'clock ‖ *m* five; (*en las fechas*) fifth; **¡choque Vd.** *esos cinco!* or **¡vengan esos cinco!** put it here!, shake!; **decirle a uno cuántas son cinco** to tell someone what's what

cincograbado *m* zinc etching

cincuenta *adj, pron* & *m* fifty

cincuenta·vo -va *adj* & *m* fiftieth

cincha *f* cinch; **a revienta cinchas** at breakneck speed; reluctantly

cinchar *tr* to cinch; band, hoop

cincho *m* girdle, sash; iron hoop; iron tire

cine *m* movie; **cine en colores** color movies; **cine hablado** talkie; **cine mudo** silent movie; **cine parlante** talkie; **cine sonoro** sound movie

cineasta *mf* motion-picture producer; movie fan ‖ *m* movie actor ‖ *f* movie actress

cinedrama *m* screenplay

cinelandia *f* (coll) movieland

cinema *m* var of **cine**

cinemateca *f* film library

cinematografiar §77 *tr* & *intr* to cinematograph, film

cinematógrafo *m* cinematograph; motion picture; motion-picture projector; motion-picture theater

cinematurgo *m* scriptwriter

cinescopio (telv) *m* kinescope

cineteatro *m* movie house

cinéti·co -ca *adj* kinetic ‖ *f* kinetics

cínga·ro -ra *adj* & *mf* gypsy

cíni·co -ca *adj* cynical; impudent; slovenly, untidy ‖ *mf* cynic ‖ *m* Cynic

cinismo *m* cynicism; impudence

cinta *f* ribbon; (*tira de papel, celuloide, etc.*) tape; film; measuring tape; (*borde de la acera*) curb; fillet, scroll; **cinta aislante** electric tape, friction tape; **cinta de medir** tape measure; **cinta de teleimpresor** ticker tape; **cinta grabada de televisión** video tape; **cinta perforada** punched tape

cintillo *m* hatband; fancy hat cord; ring set with a gem; (*borde de la acera*) (P-R) curb; hair ribbon

cinto *m* belt, girdle; waist

cintura *f* (*parte estrecha del cuerpo humano sobre las caderas*) waist; waistline; (*de una chimenea*) throat; **meter en cintura** to bring to reason

cinturón *m* belt, sash; sword belt; **cinturón de asiento** seat belt; **cinturón de seguridad** safety belt; **cinturón retráctil** retractable safety belt; **cinturón salvavidas** safety belt

cíper *m* (Mex) zipper

cipo *m* milestone; signpost; memorial pillar

cipote *adj* (Col, Ven) stupid; (Guat) chubby ‖ *mf* (Hond, El Salv, Ven) brat

ciprés *m* cypress

circo *m* circus

circón *m* zircon

circonio *m* zirconium

circuito *m* circuit; (*de carreteras, ferrocarriles, etc.*) network; race track; **corto circuito** (elec) short circuit

circulación *f* circulation; traffic; **circulación rodada** vehicular traffic

circular *adj* circular ‖ *f* circular, circular letter; **circular noticiera** newsletter ‖ *tr* & *intr* to circulate

círculo *m* circle; club; clubhouse

circuncidar *tr* to circumcise; clip, curtail

circundante *adj* surrounding

circundar *tr* to surround, go around

circunferencia *f* circumference

circunfle•jo -ja *adj* circumflex

circunlocución *f* or **circunloquio** *m* circumlocution

circunnavegación *f* circumnavigation

circunnavegar §44 *tr* to circumnavigate

circunscribir §83 *tr* to circumscribe ‖ *ref* to hold oneself down; be held down

circunscripción *f* circumscription; district, subdivision

circunspec•to -ta *adj* circumspect

circunstancia *f* circumstance

circunstancia•do -da *adj* circumstantial, detailed

circunstancial *adj* circumstantial

circunstanciar *tr* to circumstantiate, to describe in detail

circunstante *adj* surrounding; present ‖ *mf* bystander, onlooker

circunveci•no -na *adj* neighboring

circunvolar §61 *tr* to fly around

cirial *m* (eccl) processional candlestick

ciriga•llo -lla *mf* gadabout

ciríli•co -ca *adj* Cyrillic

cirio *m* wax candle

Ciro *m* Cyrus

ciruela *f* plum; **ciruela claudia** greengage; **ciruela pasa** prune

ciruelo *m* plum, plum tree; stupid fellow

cirugía *f* surgery; **cirugía cosmética, decorativa** or **estética** face lifting

ciruja•no -na *mf* surgeon

ciscar §73 *tr* to soil, dirty; (Cuba, Mex) to shame; annoy ‖ *ref* to soil one's clothes, have an accident

cisco *m* culm; row, disturbance

cisma *m* schism; discord, disagreement; (Arg) worry, concern; (Col) gossip; (Col) fastidiousness

cismáti•co -ca *adj* schismatic; dissident; (Col) gossipy; (Col) fastidious ‖ *mf* schismatic; dissident

cisne *m* swan; (Arg) powder puff

cisterna *f* cistern; reservoir; toilet tank

cita *f* date, appointment, engagement; (*mención, pasaje textual*) citation, quotation; **cita a ciegas** blind date; **cita previa** by appointment; **darse cita** to make a date

citación *f* citation, quotation; (*ante un juez*) citation, summons

citar *tr* to make a date with, have an appointment with; cite, quote; (*ante un juez*) cite, summon; (*al toro*) incite, provoke ‖ *ref* to make a date, have an appointment

cítara *f* (mus) zither

ciudad *f* city; city council; **la ciudad Condal** Barcelona; **la ciudad del Apóstol** Santiago de Compostela; **la ciudad del Betis** Seville; **la ciudad del Cabo** Capetown or Cape Town; **la ciudad de los Califas** Cordova; **la ciudad de los Reyes** Lima, Peru; **la ciudad de María Santísima** Seville; **la ciudad Imperial** or **Imperial ciudad** Toledo

ciudadanía *f* citizenship

ciudada•no -na *adj* city; citizen; civic ‖ *mf* citizen; urbanite

ciudadela *f* citadel; (Cuba) tenement house

cívi•co -ca *adj* civic; city; domestic; public-spirited

civil *adj* civil; civilian ‖ *mf* civilian ‖ *m* guard, policeman

civilidad *f* civility

civilista *adj* civil-law ‖ *mf* authority on civil law; (Chile) antimilitarist

civilización *f* civilization

civilizar §60 *tr* to civilize

civismo *m* good citizenship

cizalla *f* shears; metal shaving, metal clipping; **cizalla de guillotina** gate shears, guillotine shears; **cizallas** shears

cizallar *tr* to shear

cizaña *f* darnel; contamination, corruption; discord; **sembrar cizaña** to sow discord

clac *m* (*pl* **claques**) opera hat, claque, crush hat; (*sombrero de tres picos*) cocked hat

clamar *tr* to cry out for ‖ *intr* to cry out; **clamar contra** to cry out against; **clamar por** to cry out for

clamor *m* clamor, outcry; (*toque de difuntos*) knell, toll; fame

clamorear *tr* to clamor for ‖ *intr* to clamor; (*tocar a muerto*) toll

clamoreo *m* clamoring; tolling

clamoro•so -sa *adj* clamorous; loud, noisy

clan *m* clan

clandestinista *mf* (Guat) bootlegger

clandesti•no -na *adj* clandestine

claque *f* claque, hired clappers

clara *f* white of egg; bald spot; (*de un trozo de tela*) thin spot; (*en el tiempo lluvioso*) break, let-up

claraboya *f* (*ventana en el techo*) skylight; (*en la parte alta de la pared*) transom; (*esp. en las iglesias la parte superior de la nave que tiene una serie de ventanas*) clerestory

clarear *tr* to brighten, light up ‖ *intr* (*empezar a amanecer*) to get light, dawn; (*el mal tiempo*) clear up ‖ *ref* (*una tela*) to show through; show one's hand

clarecer §22 *ref* to dawn

clarete *m* claret

claridad *f* clarity; clearness; brightness; fame, glory; blunt remark; **claridades** plain language

clarido•so -sa *adj* (CAm, Mex) blunt, rude, plain-spoken

clarificar §73 *tr* to clarify; brighten, light up; (*lo que estaba turbio*) clear

clarín *m* clarion; fine cambric; (Chile) sweet pea

clarinada *f* clarion call; uncalled-for remark

clarinete *m* clarinet

clarión *m* chalk

clarividencia *f* clairvoyance; clear-sightedness

clarividente *adj* clairvoyant; clear-sighted ‖ *mf* clairvoyant

cla•ro -ra *adj* clear; (*de color*) light; (*pelo*) thin, sparse; (*té*) weak; famous, illustrious; (*cerveza*) light; **a las claras** publicly, openly, frankly || *m* gap; (*en el bosque*) glade, clearing; space, interval; (*ventana u otra abertura*) light; (*claraboya*) skylight; (*en las nubes*) break; **claro de luna** brief moonlight; **de claro en claro** evidently; from one end to the other; **pasar la noche de claro en claro** to not sleep all night; **poner** or **sacar en claro** to explain, clear up; (*un borrador*) to copy || *f* see **clara** || **claro** *adv* clearly || **claro** *interj* sure!, of course!; **¡claro está!**, **¡claro que sí!** sure!, of course!

claror *m* brightness; **claror de luna** moonlight, moonglow

claru•cho -cha *adj* watery, thin

clase *f* class; classroom; **clase alta** upper class; **clase baja** lower class; **clase media** middle class; **clase obrera** working class; **clases** noncommissioned officers, warrant officers; **clases pasivas** pensioners

clasicista *mf* classicist

clási•co -ca *adj* classical || *mf* classicist || *m* classic

clasificador *m* filing cabinet

clasificar §73 *tr* to classify; class; sort; file || *ref* to class

clasismo *m* segregation

clasista *mf* segregationist

claudicar §73 *intr* (*cojear*) to limp; (*obrar defectuosamente*) bungle; back down

claustral *adj* cloistral

claustro *m* cloister; (*junta de la universidad*) faculty

cláusula *f* (*de un contrato u otro documento*) clause; (*gram*) sentence

clausula•do -da *adj* (*estilo*) choppy || *m* series of clauses

clausular *tr* to close, finish, conclude

clausura *f* confinement; seclusion; enclosure; adjournment

clausurar *tr* (*una asamblea, un tribunal, etc.*) to close, adjourn; (*un comercio por orden gubernativa*) suspend, close up

clava *f* club

clavadista *mf* (Mex) diver

clava•do -da *adj* studded with nails; exact, precise; (*reloj*) stopped; sharp, e.g., **a las siete clavadas** at seven o'clock sharp || *m* (Mex) dive

clavar *tr* to nail; (*un clavo*) drive; (*una daga, un punzón*) stick; (*una piedra preciosa*) set; (*los ojos, la atención*) fix; (*a un caballo al herrarlo*) prick; cheat || *ref* to prick oneself; get cheated; (Mex) to dive; **clavárselas** (CAm) to get drunk

clave *m* harpsichord || *f* (*de un enigma, código, etc.*) key; (*piedra con que se cierra el arco*) (archit) keystone; (mus) clef

clavel *m* carnation, pink; **clavel de ramillete** sweet william; **clavel reventón** double-flowered carnation

clavelón *m* marigold

clavellina *f* carnation, pink

clave•ro -ra *mf* keeper of the keys || *m* clove tree || *f* nail hole

claveta *f* peg, wooden peg

clavetear *tr* to stud; tip, put a tip on; wind up, settle

clavicordio *m* clavichord

clavícula *f* clavicle, collarbone

clavija *f* pin, peg, dowel; (elec) plug; (mus) peg; **apretarle a uno las clavijas** to put the screws on someone

clavillo *m* or **clavito** *m* brad, tack; (*que sujeta las hojas de unas tijeras*) pin, rivet; clove

clavo *m* nail; (*capullo seco de la flor del clavero*) clove; migraine; keen sorrow; (*artículo que no se vende*) (Arg, Bol, Chile) drug on the market; (Col) bad deal; (Hond, Mex) rich vein of ore; (Ven) heartburn; **clavo de alambre** wire nail; **clavo de especia** (*flor*) clove; **clavo de herrar** horseshoe nail; **dar en el clavo** to hit the nail on the head

clemátide *f* clematis

clemencia *f* clemency

clemente *adj* clement, merciful

cleptóma•no -na *mf* kleptomaniac

clerecía *f* clergy

clerical *adj* & *m* clerical

clericato *m* or **clericatura** *f* priesthood

clerigalla *f* (contemptuous) priests

clérigo *m* cleric, priest; **clérigo de misa y olla** priestlet

clerizonte *m* shabby-looking priest; fake priest

clero *m* clergy

cleró•fo•bo -ba *adj* priest-hating || *mf* priest hater

cliché *m* (*lugar común*) cliché

cliente *mf* (*parroquiano de una tienda*) customer; (*de un abogado*) client; (*de un médico*) patient; (*de un hotel*) guest

clientela *f* customers; clientele; patronage, protection; practice

clima *m* climate; country, region; **clima artificial** air conditioning

climatización *f* air conditioning

climatizar §60 *tr* to air-condition

clíni•co -ca *adj* clinical || *mf* clinician || *f* clinic; private hospital; **clínica de reposo** nursing home, convalescent home

clip *m* paper clip

cliqueteo *m* clicking

clisar *tr* (typ) to plate

clisé *m* (*plancha clisada*) cliché, plate; (phot) plate; (*lugar común*) cliché

clo *m* cluck; **decir clo** (Chile) to kick the bucket; **hacer clo clo** (*la gallina clueca*) to cluck

cloaca *f* sewer

clocar §81 *intr* to cluck

cloquear *intr* to cluck

cloqueo *m* cluck, clucking

clorhídri•co -ca *adj* hydrochloric

cloro *m* chlorine

clorofila *f* chlorophyll

cloroformizar §60 *tr* to chloroform

cloroformo *m* chloroform

cloruro *m* chloride

ci
cl

clóset *m* (SAm) (wall) closet
club *m* (*pl* **clubs**) club; **club náutico** yacht club
clubista *mf* club member
clue•co -ca *adj* broody; decrepit
c.m.b., C.M.B. *abbr* **cuyas manos beso**
coa *f* (Mex) hoe; (Chile) thieves' jargon
coacción *f* coercion, compulsion
coaccionar *tr* to coerce, compel
coacervar *tr* to pile up
coactar *tr* to coerce, compel
coadunar *tr* & *ref* to mix together
coadyuvar *tr* & *intr* to help, aid, assist
coagular *tr* & *ref* (*la sangre*) to coagulate; (*la leche*) curdle
coágulo *m* clot
coalición *f* coalition
coalla *f* woodcock
coartada *f* alibi
coartar *tr* to limit, restrict
coba *f* hoax; flattery
cobalto *m* cobalt
cobarde *adj* cowardly; timid; (*vista*) dim, weak ‖ *mf* coward
cobardear *intr* to act cowardly; be timid
cobardía *f* cowardice; timidity
cobayo *m* guinea pig
cobertera *f* lid; bawd, procuress
cobertizo *m* shed; (*tejado saledizo*) covered balcony, penthouse
cobertor *m* bedcover, bedspread; lid
cobertura *f* cover; covering; (*garantía metálica*) coverage
cobija *f* curved tile; top, lid; short mantilla; (W-I) guano roof; **cobijas** bedclothes
cobijar *tr* to cover; shelter, protect
cobijo *m* covering; shelter, protection; (*hospedaje sin manutención*) lodging
cobra *f* team of mares used in threshing; (hunt) retrieval
cobra•dor -dora *adj* (*perro*) retrieving ‖ *mf* collector; trolley conductor
cobranza *f* collecting; (hunt) retrieval
cobrar *tr* (*lo perdido*) to recover; (*lo que otro le debe*) collect; (*un cheque*) cash; (*cierto precio*) charge; acquire, get; (*una cuerda*) pull in; (*pedir, reclamar*) dun; (hunt) to retrieve; **cobrar afición a** to take a liking for; **cobrar al número llamado** (telp) to reverse the charges; **cobrar ánimo** to take courage; **cobrar carnes** to put on flesh; **cobrar fuerzas** to gain strength ‖ *intr* to get hit ‖ *ref* to recover, come to
cobre *m* copper; copper or brass kitchen utensils; **batir el cobre** to hustle, work with a will; **cobres** (mus) brasses
cobre•ño -ña *adj* copper
cobrero *m* coppersmith
cobri•zo -za *adj* coppery
cobro *m* collection; recovery; **cobro contra entrega** collect on delivery; **en cobro** in a safe place
coca *f* (*en una cuerda*) kink; (coll) head; (slang) cocaine; **de coca** (Mex) free; (Mex) in vain
cocaína *f* cocaine

cocción *f* cooking, baking; (*de objetos cerámicos*) baking, burning
cocear *intr* to kick; (*resistir*) balk, rebel
cocer §16 *tr* to cook; boil; (*pan; ladrillos*) bake; digest ‖ *intr* to cook; boil; ferment ‖ *ref* to suffer a long time
coci•do -da *adj* cooked ‖ *m* Spanish stew
cociente *m* quotient; **cociente intelectual** intelligence quotient
cocina *f* (*pieza*) kitchen; (*arte*) cooking, cuisine; (*aparato*) stove; **cocina de presión** pressure cooker; **cocina económica** kitchen range
cocinar *tr* to cook ‖ *intr* to meddle
cocine•ro -ra *mf* cook
cocinilla *m* meddler ‖ *f* kitchenette; chafing dish; **cocinilla sin fuego** fireless cooker
coco *m* cocoanut; (*moño*) topknot, chignon; (*duende*) bogeyman; (*gesto, mueca*) face, grimace; (*sombrero hongo*) (Col, Ecuad) derby hat; **hacer cocos** to make a face; (*los enamorados*) to make eyes
cocodrilo *m* crocodile
cócora *adj* boring, tiresome ‖ *mf* bore, pest
coco•so -sa *adj* worm-eaten
cocotero *m* cocoanut palm or tree
coctel *m* or **cóctel** *m* cocktail; cocktail party
coctelera *f* cocktail shaker
cocuma *f* (Peru) roast corn on the cob
cochambre *m* dirty, stinking thing, pigsty
cochambro•so -sa *adj* dirty, stinking
coche *m* carriage; coach; car; taxi; (*puerco*) hog; **caminar en el coche de San Francisco** to go or to ride on shank's mare; **coche bar** (rr) club car; **coche bomba** fire engine; (coll) car bomb; **coche celular** Black Maria, prison van; **coche de alquiler** cab, hack; **coche de carreras** racing car; **coche de correos** mail car; **coche de plaza** or **de punto** cab, hack; **coche de reparto** (delivery) van; **coche de serie** (aut) stock car; **coche fúnebre** hearse; **coche rural** station wagon
coche-cama *m* (*pl* **coches-camas**) sleeping car
cochecillo *m* baby carriage; **cochecillo para inválidos** wheelchair; **cochecillo para niños** baby carriage
coche-comedor *m* (*pl* **coches-comedores**) (rr) diner, dining car
coche-correo *m* (*pl* **coches-correo**) (rr) mail car
coche-fumador *m* (*pl* **coches-fumadores**) (rr) smoker, smoking car
coche-habitación *m* (*pl* **coches-habitación**) trailer
cochera *f* coach house; livery stable; carbarn; garage
cochería *f* (Arg, Chile) livery stable
coche•ro -ra *adj* easy to cook ‖ *m* coachman, driver; **cochero de punto** cabby, hackman ‖ *f* see **cochera**
cocherón *m* coach house; (*depósito de locomotoras*) roundhouse
coche-salón *m* (*pl* **coches-salón**) (rr) parlor car
cochevira *f* lard

cochina *f* sow; (*mujer sucia y desaliñada*) trollop

cochinada *f* piggishness, filthiness; dirty trick

cochinillo *m* sucking pig

cochi•no -na *adj* piggish, filthy; (*tacaño*) stingy; (Ven) cowardly ‖ *mf* hog; (*persona muy sucia*) (coll) pig, dirty person ‖ *f* see **cochina**

cochite hervite *adj, adv & m* helter-skelter

cochitril *m* pigsty; den, hovel

cochura *f* batch of dough

codadura *f* (hort) layer

codal *adj* elbow ‖ *m* prop, shoring

codazo *m* poke, nudge; **dar codazo a** (Mex) to tip off

codear *tr* (SAm) to sponge on ‖ *intr* to elbow, elbow one's way ‖ *ref* to hobnob, rub elbows

codelincuencia *f* complicity

codelincuente *mf* accomplice

codera *f* elbow patch; elbow itch

códice *m* codex

codicia *f* covetousness, greed, cupidity

codiciar *tr* to covet

codicilo *m* codicil

codicio•so -sa *adj* covetous, greedy; (*laborioso*) hard-working

codificar §73 *tr* to codify

código *m* code; **código penal** criminal code; **código universal de producto** universal product code (UPC)

codillo *m* (*de animal*) knee; (*estribo*) stirrup; (*de un tubo*) elbow; (*de la rama cortada*) stump

codo *m* elbow; (Guat, Mex) miser, tightwad; **dar de codo a** to nudge; to spurn; **empinar el codo** to crook the elbow; **hablar por los codos** to talk too much

codor•niz *f* (*pl* **-nices**) quail

coeducación *f* coeducation

coeficiente *adj & m* coefficient

coetáne•o -a *adj & mf* contemporary

coexistencia *f* coexistence

coexistir *intr* to coexist

cofa *f* (naut) top; **cofa de vigía** (naut) crow's-nest

cofrade *mf* member, fellow member ‖ *m* brother ‖ *f* sister

cofradía *f* brotherhood, sisterhood; association, fraternity

cofre *m* coffer, chest, trunk

cogedor *m* dustpan; coal shovel, ash shovel

coger §17 *tr* to catch, seize, take hold of: collect, gather, pick; overtake; surprise; hold ‖ *intr* to be, be located; fit ‖ *ref* to get caught; cling; get involved

cogida *f* collecting, gathering, picking; (taur) hook

cogollo *m* (*de la lechuga*) heart; (*de la berza*) head; (*de una planta*) shoot; (*del árbol*) top; (*lo mejor*) cream, pick

cogote *m* back of the neck

cogotera *f* havelock

cogotu•do -da *adj* thick-necked; (coll) proud, stiff-necked; (SAm) moneyed

cogulla *f* cowl, frock; **cogulla de fraile** (bot) monkshood

cohabitar *intr* to live together; (*el hombre y la mujer*) cohabit

cohechar *tr* to bribe; plow just before sowing ‖ *intr* to take a bribe

cohecho *m* bribe

cohered•ero -ra *mf* coheir ‖ *f* coheiress

coherente *adj* coherent

cohesión *f* cohesion

cohete *m* (*fuego artificial*) rocket, skyrocket; (*motor a reacción*) rocket; (coll) fidgety person; **cohete de señales** (aer) flare; **cohete intermedio** or **cohete de alcance medio** intermediate-range missile; **cohete lanzador** booster rocket

cohetería *f* missilery

cohibente *adj* (elec) nonconducting

cohibi•do -da *adj* timid, self-conscious

cohibir *tr* to check, restrain, inhibit; (Mex) to oblige

cohombro *m* cucumber

cohonestar *tr* to gloss over, rationalize

coima *f* rake-off paid to operator of a gambling table; concubine; (SAm) bribe

coincidencia *f* coincidence

coincidir *intr* to coincide; happen at the same time; be at the same time (*at a given place*); agree

coito *m* coition, coitus

coja *f* lame woman; lewd woman

cojear *intr* to limp; (*una mesa, una silla*) wobble; (*adolecer de algún vicio*) slip, lapse, have a weakness

cojera *f* (*anormalidad del que cojea*) lameness; (*movimiento del que cojea*) limp

cojijo *m* bug, insect; peeve

cojijo•so -sa *adj* peevish

cojín *m* cushion

cojincillo *m* pad

cojinete *m* cushion; sewing cushion; (mach) bearing; **cojinete de bolas** ball bearing; **cojinete de rodillos** roller bearing

co•jo -ja *adj* lame, crippled; (*mesa, silla*) wobbly; (*pierna*) game ‖ *mf* lame person, cripple ‖ *f* see **coja**

cojón *m* testicle

cok *m* var of **coque**

col. *abbr* **colonia, columna**

col *f* cabbage; **col de Bruselas** Brussels sprouts

cola *f* (*de animal, de ave, de cometa*) tail; (*de un vestido*) train, trail; (*de personas que esperan turno*) queue; (*extremidad posterior*) tail end, rear end; (*de una clase de alumnos*) bottom; (*pasta fuerte*) glue; **cola del pan** bread line; **cola de milano** or de **pato** dovetail; **cola de pescado** isinglass; **cola de retazo** size, sizing; **hacer cola** to queue, to stand in line

colaboración *f* collaboration; (*en un periódico, coloquio, etc.*) contribution

colaboracionista *mf* collaborationist

colabora•dor -dora *adj* collaborating ‖ *mf* collaborator; contributor

colaborar *intr* to collaborate; (*en un periódico, coloquio, etc.*) contribute

colación *f* (*cotejo; refacción ligera*) collation; (*de un grado de universidad*) conferring;

parish land; **sacar a colación** to mention, bring up; **traer a colación** to bring up; adduce as proof; bring up irrelevantly

colacionar tr to collate; compare; (*un beneficio*) confer

colactánea f foster sister

colactáneo m foster brother

colada f washing powder; wash; (*garganta entre montañas*) gulch; cattle run; **todo saldrá en la colada** it will all come out in the wash; the day of reckoning will come

coladera f strainer; (Mex) sewer

coladero m strainer; cattle run; narrow pass

colador m strainer, colander

colapez f or **colapiscis** f isinglass

colapso m breakdown, collapse; **colapso nervioso** nervous breakdown

colar tr (*un grado universitario*) to confer ‖ §61 tr (*un líquido*) to strain; bleach in hot lye, buck; (*metales*) cast; (*una moneda falsa*) pass off; **colar el hueso por** (coll) to squeeze through ‖ intr to run, ooze; squeeze through; come in, slip in; drink wine; **colar a fondo** to sink; **no colar** (*una cosa*) to not be believed ‖ ref to seep, seep through; slip in, slip through; make a slip; lie; **colarse de gorra** to crash the gate

colateral adj collateral ‖ mf (*pariente*) collateral ‖ m (com) collateral

colcrén m cold cream

colcha f quilt, counterpane, bedspread

colchón m mattress; **colchón de aire** air mattress; **colchón de muelles** bedspring, spring mattress; **colchón de plumas** feather bed

coleada f wag (*of the tail*); (Mex, Ven) throwing the bull by twisting its tail

colear tr (taur) to grab by the tail; (*la res*) (Mex, Ven) to throw by twisting the tail; (Col, Ven) to nag, harass; (Guat) to trail after; (*reprobar en un examen*) (Chile) to flunk ‖ intr to wag the tail; stay alive, keep going; (*los últimos vagones de un tren*) sway; (aer) to fishtail; **colear en** (*cierta edad*) (CAm, W-I) to border on, be close to; **todavía colea** it's not over yet

colección f collection

coleccionar tr to collect

coleccionista mf collector

colecta f collection for charity; (eccl) collect

colectar tr to collect; (*obras antes sueltas*) collect in one volume

colecti•cio -cia adj new, untrained, green; (*tomo*) omnibus

colecti•vo -va adj collective

colector m collector; catch basin; (elec) commutator; (aut) manifold

colega mf colleague ‖ m confrere

colegial m schoolboy; (Mex) greenhorn, beginner

colegiala f schoolgirl

colegiatura f scholarship; (Mex) tuition

colegio m school, academy; (*sociedad de hombres de una misma profesión*) college (*e.g., of cardinals, electors*)

colegir §57 tr to gather, collect; conclude, infer

cólera m cholera‖ f anger, wrath; (*bilis*) bile; **montar en cólera** to fly into a rage

coléri•co -ca adj choleric, irascible

colesterol m cholesterol

coleta f pigtail; (*del torero*) cue, queue; (coll) postscript; **cortarse la coleta** to quit the bull ring; to quit, retire; **tener** or **traer coleta** to have serious consequences

coletero m wren

coleto m buff jacket; (coll) body, one's body, oneself; **decir para su coleto** (coll) to say to oneself; **echarse al coleto** to eat up, drink up; read from cover to cover

colgadero m hanger, hook; clothes rack

colgadizo m lean-to, penthouse; projection over a door, canopy

colga•do -da adj pending, unsettled; **dejar colgado** to disappoint, frustrate; **quedarse colgado** to be disappointed, frustrated

colgador m clothes hanger, coat hanger

colgajo m rag, tatter

colgante adj hanging, dangling; (*puente*) suspension ‖ m drop, pendant; (archit) festoon; (P-R) watch fob

colgar §63 tr to hang; impute, attribute; (*a un alumno*) flunk; (*a un reo*) hang ‖ intr to hang, hang down, dangle; droop; (telp) to hang up; **colgar de** to hang from, hang on; depend on

coli•brí m (pl -bríes) humming bird

cóli•co -ca adj & m colic ‖ f upset stomach

coliche m (coll) at-home, open house

coliflor f cauliflower

coligar §44 ref to join forces, make common cause

colilla f butt, stump, stub

co•lín -lina adj (*caballo o yegua*) bobtailed ‖ m bobwhite; **colín de Virginia** bobwhite ‖ f see **colina**

colina f hill, knoll

colindante adj adjacent, contiguous

colindar intr to be adjacent

colino•so -sa adj hilly

colirio m eyewash

coliseo m coliseum

colisión f collision; bruise, bump

colista mf person standing in line

colitis f colitis

colma•do -da adj abundant, plentiful ‖ m food store, grocery store; seafood restaurant

colmar tr to fill up; (*las esperanzas de uno*) fulfill; overwhelm; **colmar de** to shower with, overwhelm with

colmena f beehive

colmenar m apiary

colmene•ro -ra mf beekeeper

colmillo m eyetooth, canine tooth; (*del elefante*) tusk; **tener el colmillo retorcido** to cut one's eyeteeth

col•mo -ma adj brimful, overflowing ‖ m overflow; thatch, thatch roof; (*de un sorbete*) topping; **eso es el colmo** (coll) that's the limit; **para colmo de** to top off

colocación f (*acción de poner una persona o cosa en un lugar*) location; (*disposición de una cosa respecto del lugar que ocupa*) placement; (*inversión de dinero*) investment; (*empleo*) position, employment, job

colocar §73 *tr* to place, put; (*una trampa*) set ‖ *ref* to get placed, find a job; (*venderse*) sell

colodra *f* milk bucket; drinking horn; (*bebedor de vino*) (coll) toper

colofón *m* colophon

colofonia *f* rosin

coloide *adj* & *m* colloid

colon *m* colon; (gram) main clause

Colón *m* Columbus

colonia *f* colony; cologne; silk ribbon; housing development; (W-I) sugar plantation ‖ **Colonia** *f* Cologne; **la Colonia del Cabo** Cape Colony

colonial *adj* colonial; overseas ‖ **coloniales** *mpl* imported foods

colonizar §60 *tr* & *intr* to colonize

colono *m* colonist, settler; tenant farmer; (W-I) owner of sugar plantation

coloquial *adj* colloquial

coloquialismo *m* colloquialism

coloquio *m* colloquy, talk, conference

color *m* color; (*substancia para pintar*) paint; (*para pintarse el rostro*) rouge; **colores** (*bandera*) colors; (*persona*) **de color** of color, colored; (*zapatos*) tan; **sacar los colores a** to make blush; **so color de** under color of, under pretext of; **verlo todo de color de rosa** to see everything through rose-colored glasses

colora•do -da *adj* red, reddish; (*libre, obsceno*) off-color; (*aparentemente justo y razonable*) specious; **ponerse colorado** to blush

colorado•te -ta *adj* ruddy, sanguine

colorante *adj* & *m* coloring

colorar *tr* to color; dye; stain

colorear *tr* to color; (fig) to color, excuse, palliate ‖ *ref* (*la cereza, el tomate, etc.*) to redden, turn red

colorete *m* rouge; **ponerse colorete** to put on rouge

colorir §1 *tr* to color; (fig) to color, palliate ‖ *intr* to take on color

colosal *adj* colossal

coloso *m* colossus

columbrar *tr* to discern, descry, glimpse; to guess

columna *f* column; **columna de dirección** steering column; **quinta columna** fifth column

columnata *f* colonnade

columnista *mf* columnist

columpiar *tr* to swing ‖ *ref* to swing; to seesaw; (coll) to swing, swagger

columpio *m* swing; **columpio de tabla** seesaw

colusión *f* collusion

collada *f* mountain pass; (naut) steady blow

collado *m* hill, height

collar *m* necklace; dog collar, horse collar; (*aro de hierro asegurado al cuello del malhechor*) collar, band; (*plumas del cuello de ciertas aves*) frill, ring; (*cadena que* *rodea el cuello como insignia*) cord, chain; (mach) collar

collera *f* horse collar; chain gang; **colleras** (Arg, Chile) cuff links

co•llón -llona *adj* cowardly ‖ *mf* coward

coma *m* (pathol) coma ‖ *f* comma; (*en inglés se emplea el punto en aritmética para separar los enteros de las fracciones decimales*) decimal point

comadre *f* mother or godmother (*with respect to each other*); gossip (*woman*); friend, neighbor (*woman*)

comadrear *intr* to gossip, go around gossiping

comadreja *f* weasel

comadrería *f* gossip, idle gossip

comadre•ro -ra *adj* gossipy ‖ *mf* gossip

comadrón *m* accoucheur

comadrona *f* midwife

comandancia *f* command; commander's headquarters; (mil) majority

comandante *m* commander, commandant; (mil) major

comandar *tr* (mil, nav) to command

comando *m* (mil) command; **comando a distancia** remote control

comarca *f* district, region, country

comarcar §73 *tr* to plant in a line at regular intervals ‖ *intr* to border, be contiguous

comato•so -sa *adj* comatose

comba *f* bend, curve; warp, bulge; skipping rope; **saltar a la comba** to jump rope, skip rope

combar *tr* to bend, curve ‖ *ref* to bend, curve; warp, bulge; sag

combate *m* combat, fight; **combate revancha** (box) return bout; **fuera de combate** hors de combat; (box) knockout

combatiente *adj* & *m* combatant

combatir *tr* to combat, fight; beat, beat upon ‖ *intr* & *ref* to combat, fight, struggle

combinación *f* combination; (*de trenes*) connection

combinar *tr* & *ref* to combine

com•bo -ba *adj* bent, curved, crooked; warped ‖ *m* trunk or rock to stand wine casks on ‖ *f* see **comba**

combustible *adj* combustible ‖ *m* (*substancia que arde con facilidad*) combustible; (*substancia que sirve para calentar, cocinar, etc.*) fuel; **combustible alternativo** alternate fuel

combustión *f* combustion

comede•ro -ra *adj* eatable ‖ *m* manger, feed trough; (Mex) haunt, hangout; **limpiarle a uno el comedero** to deprive someone of his bread and butter

comedia *f* drama, play; theater; comedy; (fig) farce; **comedia cómica** (*drama de desenlace festivo*) comedy; **hacer la comedia** to pretend, make believe

comedian•te -ta *mf* hypocrite ‖ *m* actor, comedian ‖ *f* actress. comedienne

comedi•do -da *adj* courteous, polite; moderate; obliging, accommodating

comedimiento *m* courtesy, politeness; moderation

comediógra•fo -fa *mf* playwright
comedir §50 *ref* to be courteous; restrain oneself, be moderate; be obliging; **comedirse a** to offer to, volunteer to
comedón *m* blackhead
come•dor -dora *adj* heavy-eating ‖ *m* dining room; restaurant, eating place; dining-room suite; **comedor de beneficencia** soup kitchen
comején *m* termite
comendador *m* prelate, prior; knight commander; (*de una orden militar*) commander
comensal *mf* dependent, servant; table companion
comentar *tr* to comment on ‖ *intr* to comment; to gossip
comentario *m* comment, commentary; **comentarios** talk, gossip
comentarista *mf* commentator
comento *m* comment, commentary; deceit, falsehood
comenzar §18 *tr & intr* to commence, begin, start
comer *m* eating, food ‖ *tr* to eat; to feed on; to gnaw away; to consume; (*alguna renta*) to enjoy; to itch; (*una pieza en el juego de damas*) to take; **comer vivo** to have it in for; **sin comerlo ni beberlo** (coll) without having anything to do with it; **tener qué comer** to have enough to live on ‖ *intr* to eat; to dine, to have dinner; to itch ‖ *ref* to eat up; (*las uñas*) to bite; (*el dinero*) (coll) to consume, eat up; (*omitir*) to skip, skip over; **comerse unos a otros** to be at loggerheads
comerciable *adj* marketable; sociable
comercial *adj* commercial, business
comerciante *mf* merchant, trader, dealer; **comerciante al por mayor** wholesaler; **comerciante al por menor** retailer
comerciar *intr* to trade, deal
comercio *m* commerce, trade, business; store, shop; business center; commerce, intercourse; **comercio de artículos de regalo** gift shop; **comercio exterior** foreign trade
comestible *adj* eatable ‖ *m* food, foodstuff
cometa *m* comet ‖ *f* kite
cometer *tr* (*un crimen, una falta*) to commit; (*un negocio a una persona*) commit, entrust; (*figuras retóricas*) employ
cometido *m* assignment, duty; commitment
comezón *f* itch
comicastro *m* ham, ham actor
comicios *mpl* polls; **acudir a los comicios** to go to the polls
cómi•co -ca *adj* comic, comical; dramatic ‖ *mf* actor; comedian; **cómico de la legua** strolling player, barnstormer ‖ *f* actress; comedienne
comida *f* (*alimento*) food; (*el que se toma a horas señaladas*) meal; (*el principal de cada día*) dinner; **comida corrida** (Mex) table d'hôte
comidilla *f* hobby; **la comidilla del pueblo** the talk of the town

comienzo *m* beginning, start; **a comienzos de** around the beginning of
comilitona *f* spread, feast
comi•lón -lona *adj* heavy-eating ‖ *mf* hearty eater ‖ *f* hearty meal, spread
comilias *fpl* quotation marks
cominear *intr* (*el hombre*) to fuss around like a woman
comiquear *intr* to put on amateur plays
comiquillo *m* ham, ham actor
comisar *tr* to seize, confiscate
comisario *m* commissary; commissioner; **comisario de a bordo** purser
comisión *f* commission; committee; (*recado*) errand
comisiona•do -da *mf* commissioner ‖ *m* committeeman
comisionar *tr* to commission
comiso *m* seizure, confiscation; confiscated goods
comisura *f* corner (*e.g., of lips*)
comité *m* committee; **comité planeador** steering committee
comitente *mf* constituent
comitiva *f* retinue, suite; procession
como *adv* as, like; so to speak, as it were ‖ *conj* as; when; if; so that; as soon as; as long as; inasmuch as; **así como** as well as; **como no** unless; **como que** because, inasmuch as; **como quien dice** so to speak; **tan luego como** as soon as
cómo *adv* how; why; what; **¿a cómo es. . .?** how much is. . .?; **¿cómo no?** why not?
cómoda *f* bureau, commode, chest
comodidad *f* comfort; convenience; advantage, interest
comodín *m* joker, wild card; gadget, jigger; excuse, alibi
cómo•do -da *adj* handy, convenient; comfortable ‖ *f* see **cómoda**
como•dón -dona *adj* comfort-loving, self-indulgent, easy-going
compac•to -ta *adj* compact
compadecer §22 *tr* to pity, feel sorry for ‖ *ref* to harmonize; **compadecerse con** to harmonize with; **compadecerse de** to pity, feel sorry for
compadraje *m* clique, cabal
compadrar *intr* to become a godfather; become friends
compadre *m* father or godfather (*with respect to each other*); friend, companion
compadrear *intr* to be close friends; (Arg, Urug) to brag, show off
compadrería *f* close companionship
compadrito *m* (Arg) bully
compaginar *tr* to arrange, put in order ‖ *ref* to fit, agree; blend
companage *m* snacks, cold cuts
compañerismo *m* companionship
compañe•ro -ra *mf* companion; partner; mate; **compañero de cama** bedfellow; **compañero de candidatura** (pol) running mate; **compañero de cuarto** roommate; **compañero de juego** playmate; **compañero de viaje** fellow traveler ‖ *f* (*esposa*) helpmeet

compañía f company; society; **compañía de desembarco** (nav) landing force; **compañía matriz** parent company; **hacerle compañía a una persona** to keep someone company

compañón m testicle; **compañón de perro** orchid

comparación f comparison

comparar tr to compare

comparati•vo -va adj comparative

comparecencia f (law) appearance

comparecer §22 intr (law) to appear

comparendo m (law) summons

comparsa mf (theat) supernumerary, extra ‖ f supernumeraries, extras

compartimiento m distribution, division; compartment; **compartimiento estanco** watertight compartment

compartir tr to distribute, divide; share

compás m (brújula) compass; (instrumento para trazar curvas) compass or compasses; rule, measure; (mus) time, measure; (mus) bar, measure; (mus) beat; **a compás** (mus) in time; **compás de calibres** calipers; **compás de división** dividers; **llevar el compás** (mus) to keep time

compasible adj compassionate; pitiful

compasión f compassion; **¡por compasión!** for pity's sake!

compasi•vo -va adj compassionate

compatri•cio -cia mf or **compatriota** mf fellow countryman, compatriot

compeler tr to compel

compendiar tr to condense, summarize

compendio m compendium; **en compendio** in a word

compendio•so -sa adj compendious

compensación f compensation; (com) clearing, clearance

compensar tr to compensate; compensate for ‖ intr to compensate ‖ ref to be compensated for

competencia f (aptitud) competence; (rivalidad) competition; dispute; area, field; **de la competencia de** in the domain of; **sin competencia** unmatched (prices)

competente adj competent; reliable

competer intr to be incumbent

competición f competition

competi•dor -dora adj competing ‖ mf competitor

competir §50 intr to compete; **poder competir** to be competitive

compilación f compilation

compilar tr to compile

compinche mf chum, crony, pal

complacencia f complacency

complacer §22 tr to please, humor ‖ ref to be pleased, take pleasure

complaciente adj obliging; indulgent

comple•jo -ja adj & m complex; **complejo de inferioridad** inferiority complex

complementar tr to complement

complemento m complement; completion; perfection; accessory; **complemento directo** (gram) direct object

completar tr to complete; perfect

comple•to -ta adj complete; (autobús, tranvía) full

complexión f constitution

complexiona•do -da adj — **bien complexionado** strong, robust; **mal complexionado** weak, frail

comple•xo -xa adj complex

complica•do -da adj complicated, complex

complicar §73 tr to complicate; involve ‖ ref to become complicated; become involved

cómplice mf accomplice, accessory

complicidad f complicity

com•plot m (pl -plots) plot, intrigue

compone•dor -dora mf composer, compositor; typesetter; arbitrator; repairer ‖ m stick, composing stick; **amigable componedor** mediator, umpire

componenda f compromise, settlement, reconciliation

componente adj component, constituent ‖ m component, constituent; member ‖ f (mech) component

componer §54 tr to compose; compound; mend, repair; pacify, reconcile; arrange; put in order; restore, strengthen; (huesos dislocados) (Am) to set; (Col) to bewitch ‖ ref to compose oneself; get dressed; make up, become friends again; (pintarse el rostro) make up; **componérselas** to make out, manage

comportable adj bearable, tolerable

comportamentismo m behaviorism

comportamiento m behavior, conduct

comportar tr to support; bring about, entail ‖ ref to act, behave

comporte m behavior; carriage, bearing

composición f composition; agreement; (circunspección) composure, restraint; **hacer una composición de lugar** to lay one's plans carefully

compositi•vo -va adj (gram) combining

composi•tor -tora mf composer ‖ m (Arg, Urug) horse trainer, trainer of fighting cocks

compostura f composition; agreement; (circunspección) composure, restraint; repair, repairing, mending; (aseo) neatness; adulteration; (Arg, Urug) training

compota f compote, preserves; **compota de frutas** stewed fruit; **compota de manzanas** applesauce

compotera f (vasija) compote

compra f purchase, buy; shopping; **compra al contado** cash purchase; **compra a plazos** installment buying; **hacer compras, ir de compras** to go shopping

compra•dor -dora mf purchaser, buyer; shopper

comprar tr to purchase, buy; (sobornar) buy off ‖ intr to shop

compraventa f dealing, business, bargain, trading; resale

comprender tr (entender) to understand; (entender; abrazar) comprehend; (contener, incluir) comprise

comprensible adj comprehensible, understandable

CO
CO

comprensión f understanding, comprehension; inclusion

comprensi•vo -va adj understanding; comprehensive; **comprensivo de** inclusive of

compresa f (med) compress; **compresa higiénica** sanitary napkin

compresión f compression

comprimido m tablet

comprimir tr to compress; restrain, repress; flatten

comprobación f checking, verification; proof

comprobante adj proving ‖ m certificate, voucher, warrant; proof; claim check

comprobar §61 tr to check, verify; prove

comprometer tr to compromise; endanger, jeopardize; force, oblige; (un negocio a un tercero) entrust ‖ ref to promise; commit oneself; become engaged

comprometi•do -da adj awkward, embarrassing; engaged to be married

comprometimiento m commitment, promise; predicament, awkward situation; compromise

compromiso m commitment, promise; appointment, engagement; predicament, awkward situation; betrothal

compuerta f hatch, half door; floodgate, sluice

compues•to -ta adj & m composite, compound

compulsar tr to collate; make an authentic copy of

compungi•do -da adj remorseful

compungir §27 tr to make remorseful ‖ ref to feel remorse

compurgar §44 tr (el reo la pena) (Mex) to finish serving

computar tr & intr to compute

cómputo m computation, calculation

comulgante mf (eccl) communicant

comulgar §44 tr to administer communion to ‖ intr to take communion

comulgatorio m communion rail, altar rail

común adj common ‖ m community; water closet; toilet; **el común de las gentes** the general run of people; **por lo común** commonly

comunal adj common; community ‖ m community

comune•ro -ra adj popular ‖ m shareholder

comunicación f communication; connection

comunicado m communiqué; letter to the editor, official announcement

comunica•dor -dora adj communicating

comunicante mf communicant, informant

comunicar §73 tr to communicate; notify, inform; connect, put into communication ‖ intr to communicate ‖ ref to communicate; communicate with each other

comunicati•vo -va adj communicative

comunidad f community

comunión f communion; political party; sect

comunismo m communism

comunista mf communist

comunistizar §60 tr to convert to communism ‖ ref to become communistic

comunizar §60 tr to communize

con prep with; to, towards; in spite of; **con que** and so; whereupon; **con tal (de) que** provided that; **con todo** however, nevertheless

conato m effort, endeavor; (delito que no llegó a consumarse) attempt

cónca•vo -va adj concave

concebible adj conceivable

concebir §50 tr & intr to conceive

conceder tr to concede, admit; grant

concejal m alderman, councilman; **concejales** city fathers

concejo m town council; town hall; council meeting; (expósito) foundling

concentrar tr & ref to concentrate

concéntri•co -ca adj concentric

concepción f conception

concepto m concept; opinion, judgment; (dicho ingenioso) conceit, witticism; point of view; **en concepto de** under the head of; **tener buen concepto de** or **tener en buen concepto** to have a high opinion of, to hold in high esteem

conceptuar §21 tr to deem, judge, regard

conceptuo•so -sa adj witty, epigrammatic

concerniente adj relative

concernir §28 tr to concern

concertar §2 tr to concert; mend, repair; (un casamiento; la paz) arrange; (huesos dislocados) set; (poner de acuerdo) reconcile; (un pacto) conclude; harmonize ‖ intr to concert; agree ‖ ref to come to terms, become reconciled; agree

concertino m concertmaster

concertista mf (mus) manager; (mus) performer, soloist

concesión f concession, admission; grant

concesionario m licensee; (comerciante) dealer

concesi•vo -va adj concessive

conciencia f (conocimiento que uno tiene de su propia existencia) consciousness; (sentimiento del bien y del mal) conscience; (conocimiento) awareness; **cobrar conciencia de** to become aware of; **en conciencia** in all conscience

concienciación f consciousness raising

concienzu•do -da adj conscientious; thorough

concierto m concert, harmony; (función de música) concert; (composición de música) concerto

concilia•dor -dora adj conciliatory

conciliar tr to conciliate, reconcile ‖ ref (el respeto, la estima, etc.) to conciliate, win

concilio m (eccl) council

conci•so -sa adj concise

concitar tr to stir up, incite, agitate

conciudada•no -na mf fellow citizen

concluir §20 tr to conclude; convince ‖ intr & ref to conclude, end

conclusión f conclusion

concluyente adj conclusive, convincing

concomitar tr to accompany, go with

concordancia f concordance; (gram, mus) concord

concordar §61 *tr* to harmonize; reconcile; make agree ‖ *intr* to agree

concordia *f* concord; **de concordia** by common consent

concre·to -ta *adj* concrete

concubina *f* concubine

concubio *m* (archaic) bedtime

concuñada *f* sister-in-law

concuñado *m* brother-in-law

concurrencia *f* (*acaecimiento de varios sucesos en un mismo tiempo*) concurrence; (*competencia comercial*) competition; (*ayuda*) assistance, crowd, gathering, attendance

concurrente *adj* concurrent; competing ‖ *mf* competitor, contender, entrant

concurri·do -da *adj* crowded, full of people; well-attended

concurrir *intr* to concur; gather, meet, come together; compete, contend; coincide; **concurrir con** (*p.ej., dinero*) to contribute

concursante *mf* contender

concursar *tr* to declare insolvent ‖ *intr* to contend, compete

concurso *m* contest, competition; (*de gente*) concourse, crowd, throng; backing, coöperation; show, exhibition; **concurso de acreedores** meeting of creditors; **concurso de belleza** beauty contest; **concurso hípico** horse show

concusión *f* concussion; extortion, shakedown

concha *f* (*de molusco o crustáceo*) shell; (*cada una de las dos partes del caparazón de los moluscos bivalvos*) half shell; (*en que se sirve el pescado*) scallop; (*carey*) tortoise shell; oyster; shellfish; horseshoe bay; (theat) prompter's box; **concha de peregrino** scallop shell; (zool) scallop; (*ostras*) **en su concha** on the half shell; **tener muchas conchas** to be sly, cunning

conchabanza *f* comfort; collusion, cabal

conchabar *tr* to join, unite; hire ‖ *ref* to gang up; hire out

conchabero *m* (Col) pieceworker

condado *m* county; earldom

conde *m* count, earl; gypsy chief

condecoración *f* decoration

condecorar *tr* to decorate

condena *f* sentence; penalty, jail term; **condena judicial** conviction

condenación *f* condemnation; (*la eterna*) damnation

condena·do -da *adj* condemned; damned; (Chile) shrewd, clever ‖ *mf* sentenced person; **los condenados** the damned

condenar *tr* to condemn; convict; (*a la pena eterna*) damn; (*p.ej., una ventana*) shut off, block up; (*una habitación*) padlock ‖ *ref* to condemn oneself, confess one's guilt; (*a la pena eterna*) be damned

condensar *tr* to condense ‖ *ref* to condense, be condensed

condesa *f* countess

condescendencia *f* acquiescence, compliance

condescender §51 *intr* to acquiesce, comply; **condescender a** to accede to

condescendiente *adj* acquiescent, obliging

condición *f* condition, state; position, situation; standing; nature, character, temperament; **a condición (de) que** on condition that; **en buenas condiciones** in good condition, in good shape; **tener condición** to have a bad temper

condicional *adj* conditional

condimentar *tr* to season

condimento *m* condiment, seasoning

condiscípulo *m* fellow student

condolencia *f* condolence

condoler §47 *ref* to condole; **condolerse de** to sympathize with, feel sorry for, commiserate with

condominio *m* condominium

condonar *tr* to condone, overlook

cóndor *m* condor; (Chile, Ecuad) gold coin

conducción *f* conveyance, transportation; guiding, leading; (aut) drive, driving; **conducción a la derecha** right-hand drive; **conducción a la izquierda** left-hand drive; **conducción interior** closed car

conducente *adj* conducive

conducir §19 *tr* to conduct; manage, direct; guide, lead; convey, transport; drive; employ, hire ‖ *intr* to lead; conduce ‖ *ref* to conduct oneself, behave

conducta *f* conduct; management, direction; guidance; conveyance; conduct, behavior

conducto *m* pipe; conduit; (anat) duct, canal; agency, intermediary, channel; **por conducto de** through

conduc·tor -tora *adj* conducting ‖ *mf* driver, motorist; (*cobrador en un vehículo público*) conductor ‖ *m & f* (elec & phys) conductor; **buen conductor, buena conductora** good conductor; **mal conductor, mala conductora** bad or poor conductor ‖ *m* (rr) engineman, engine driver

conectar *tr* to connect

conecti·vo -va *adj* connective

conejera *f* burrow, warren; (coll) joint, dive

conejillo *m* young rabbit; **conejillo de Indias** guinea pig

conejo *m* rabbit

conexión *f* connection

conexionar *tr* to connect; put in touch ‖ *ref* to connect; make contacts

confabulación *f* collusion, connivance

confabular *ref* to connive, scheme, plot

confección *f* making, preparation, confection; tailoring; ready-made suit; **confección a medida** suit made to order; **de confección** ready-made

confeccionar *tr* (*ropa*) to make; (*una receta*) make up, concoct

confeccionista *mf* ready-made clothier

confederación *f* confederacy; alliance

confedera·do -da *adj & mf* confederate

confederar *tr & ref* to confederate

conferencia *f* (*reunión para tratar asuntos internacionales, etc.*) conference; (*plática para tratar de algún negocio*) interview; (*disertación en público o en la universidad*) lecture; **conferencia telefónica** (telp) long-distance call

conferenciante *mf* conferee; lecturer
conferenciar *intr* .to confer, hold an interview
conferencista *mf* (Arg) lecturer
conferir §68 *tr* to confer, award, bestow; discuss; compare ‖ *intr* to confer
confesante *mf* confessor
confesar §2 *tr, intr & ref* to confess
confesión *f* confession; denomination, faith, religion
confe•so -sa *adj* confessed; (*judío*) converted ‖ *mf* converted Jew ‖ *m* lay brother
confesonario *m* confessional
confesor *m* confessor
confiable *adj* reliable, dependable
confia•do -da *adj* unsuspecting; haughty, self-confident
confianza *f* confidence; self-confidence, self-assurance; familiarity; secret deal; **de confianza** reliable
confianzu•do -da *adj* overconfident; overfamiliar
confiar §77 *tr* to confide, entrust; strengthen the confidence of ‖ *intr & ref* to confide, trust; **confiar** or **confiarse de** or **en** to confide in, trust in; rely on
confidencia *f* confidence; secret; **de mayor confidencia** top secret
confidencial *adj* confidential
confiden•te -ta *adj* trustworthy, faithful ‖ *mf* confident ‖ *m* spy; informer; secret agent; love seat
configurar *tr* to shape, form
confín *m* confine, border, boundary; **los confines** the confines
confina•do -da *adj* exiled ‖ *m* prisoner
confinamiento *m* confinement; abutment
confinar *tr* to exile; confine ‖ *intr* to border
confirmar *tr* to confirm
confiscar §73 *tr* to confiscate
confita•do -da *adj* hopeful, confident; (*bañado de azúcar*) candied
confitar *tr* (*frutas*) to candy; (*en almíbar*) preserve; (*endulzar*) sweeten
confite *m* candy, bonbon, confection; **confites** confectionery
confitera *f* candy box; candy jar
confitería *f* confectionery; confectionery store
confite•ro -ra *mf* confectioner ‖ *f* see **confitera**
confitura *f* preserves, confiture; **confituras** confectionery
conflagración *f* conflagration
conflagrar *tr* to set fire to
conflicti•vo -va *adj* conflicting; anguished
conflicto *m* conflict; (*apuro*) fix, jam
confluencia *f* confluence
confluir §20 *intr* to flow together; crowd, gather
conformador *m* hat block
conformar *tr* to shape; (*un sombrero*) to block ‖ *intr & ref* to conform, comply, yield, agree
conforme *adj* in agreement ‖ *adv* depending on circumstances; fine, O.K.; **conforme a** according to ‖ *conj* as, in proportion as; as soon as ‖ *m* approval

conformidad *f* conformance, conformity; resignation
confort *m* comfort
confortable *adj* comfortable; comforting
confortante *adj* comforting; tonic ‖ *mf* comforter ‖ *m* tonic
confr. *abbr* **confesor**
confricar §73 *tr* to rub
confrontar *tr* (*poner en presencia; cotejar*) to confront ‖ *intr* to border; to agree ‖ *ref* to get along, agree; **confrontarse con** (*hacer frente a*) to confront
confundir *tr* to confuse; (*turbar, dejar desarmado*) confound ‖ *ref* to become confused; (*en la muchedumbre*) get lost
confusión *f* confusion
confutar *tr* to confute
congal *m* (Mex) brothel, whorehouse
congelador *m* freezer
congelar *tr* to congeal, freeze; (*créditos*) (fig) to freeze ‖ *ref* to congeal, freeze
congenial *adj* congenial (*having the same nature*)
congeniar *intr* to be congenial, get along well
congéni•to -ta *adj* congenital
congestión *f* congestion
congestionar *tr* to congest ‖ *ref* to congest, become congested
conglobar *tr* to lump together
congoja *f* anguish, grief
congojo•so -sa *adj* distressing; distressed
congosto *m* narrow mountain pass
congraciar *tr* to win over ‖ *ref* to ingratiate oneself; **congraciarse con** to get into the good graces of
congratulación *f* congratulation
congratular *tr* to congratulate ‖ *ref* to congratulate oneself, rejoice
congregación *f* congregation; **la Congregación de los fieles** the Roman Catholic Church
congregar §44 *tr* to bring together ‖ *ref* to congregate, come together
congresal *m* (Arg, Chile) congressman
congresista *mf* delegate; member of congress ‖ *m* congressman ‖ *f* congresswoman
congreso *m* (*asamblea legislativa*) congress; (*reunión para deliberar sobre intereses comunes*) meeting, convention
congrio *m* conger eel
cóni•co -ca *adj* conical
conjetura *f* conjecture, guess
conjeturar *tr & intr* to conjecture, guess
conjugación *f* conjugation
conjugar §44 *tr* to conjugate; combine
conjunción *f* conjunction; combination
conjuntamente *adv* together
conjuntista *m* chorus man ‖ *f* chorus girl
conjunti•vo -va *adj* conjunctive; subjunctive
conjun•to -ta *adj* joined, combined, united ‖ *m* whole, entirety, ensemble; unit; group; (theat) chorus; **de conjunto** general; **en conjunto** as a whole; **en su conjunto** in its entirety
conjura or **conjuración** *f* conspiracy, plot

conjuramentar *tr* to swear in ‖ *ref* to take an oath

conjurar *tr* to swear in; conjure, entreat; conjure away, exorcise ‖ *intr* to conspire, plot ‖ *ref* to conspire, join in a conspiracy

conjuro *m* (*invocación supersticiosa*) conjuration; adjuration, entreaty

conllevar *tr* (*los trabajos*) to share in bearing; (*a una persona*) tolerate, stand for; (*las adversidades*) suffer

conmemorar *tr* to commemorate, memorialize

conmigo *pron* with me, with myself

conmilitón *m* fellow soldier

conminar *tr* to threaten

conmoción *f* commotion; concussion, shock

conmove•dor -dora *adj* touching, moving, stirring

conmover §47 *tr* to touch, move, affect; stir, stir up; shake, upset ‖ *ref* to be touched, be moved

conmutación *f* commutation

conmutador *m* (elec) change-over switch; (SAm) telephone exchange

conmutar *tr* to commute

connivencia *f* connivance; **estar en connivencia** to connive

cono *m* cone; **cono de proa** nose cone; **cono de viento** (aer) wind cone, wind sock

conoce•dor -dora *adj* knowledgeable ‖ *mf* expert, connoisseur

conocer §22 *tr* to know; meet, get to know; tell, distinguish; (law) to try ‖ *intr* to know; **conocer de** or **en** to know, have knowledge of ‖ *ref* to know oneself; know each other; meet, meet each other

conoci•do -da *adj* known, well-known, familiar; distinguished, prominent ‖ *mf* acquaintance

conocimiento *m* knowledge; understanding; acquaintance; consciousness; (com) bill of lading; **con conocimiento de causa** knowingly, with full knowledge; **conocimiento de embarque** (com) bill of lading; **conocimientos** knowledge; **hablar con pleno conocimiento de causa** to know what one is talking about; **perder el conocimiento** to lose consciousness; **por su real conocimiento** (Arg) for real money; **recobrar el conocimiento** to regain consciousness; **venir en conocimiento de** to come to know

conque *adv* and so ‖ *m* condition, terms

conquista *f* conquest

conquista•dor -dora *adj* conquering ‖ *m* conqueror; (*ladrón de corazones*) ladykiller

conquistar *tr* to conquer; (*ganar la voluntad de*) win over

consabi•do -da *adj* well-known; abovementioned

consagrar *tr* to consecrate; devote; dedicate; (*una nueva palabra*) authorize ‖ *ref* to devote oneself; make a name for oneself

consciente *adj* conscious

conscripción *f* conscription

conscripto *m* conscript, draftee

consecución *f* obtaining, getting

consecuencia *f* (*correspondencia lógica entre sus elementos*) consistency; (*acontecimiento que resulta necesariamente de otro*) consequence; **en consecuencia** accordingly; **guardar consecuencia** to remain consistent; **traer a consecuencia** to bring in

consecuente *adj* (*que tiene proporción consigo mismo*) consistent; (*que sigue en orden a otra cosa*) consecutive

consecuti•vo -va *adj* consecutive

conseguir §67 *tr* to get, obtain; **conseguir + inf** to succeed in + *ger*

conseja *f* story, fairy tale; cabal

conseje•ro -ra *adj* advisory ‖ *mf* advisor, counselor; councilor

consejo *m* advice, counsel; board; council; **consejos** advice; **un consejo** a piece of advice

consenso *m* consensus

consenti•do -da *adj* spoiled, pampered; (*marido*) indulgent

consenti•dor -dora *adj* acquiescent; pampering ‖ *mf* acquiescent person; (*de niños*) pamperer ‖ *m* cuckold

consentimiento *m* consent

consentir §68 *tr* to allow; admit; pamper, spoil ‖ *intr* to consent; come loose; **consentir + inf** to think that + *ind*; **consentir con** to be indulgent toward; **consentir en** to consent to ‖ *ref* to begin to crack up; (Arg) to be proud

conserje *m* janitor, concierge

conserva *f* preserves; preserved food; pickles; (naut) convoy; **conservas alimenticias** canned goods; **llevar en su conserva** (naut) to convoy; **navegar en (la) conserva** (naut) to sail in a convoy

conservación *f* conservation; preservation; self-preservation; maintenance, upkeep

conserva•dor -dora *adj* preservative; (pol) conservative ‖ *mf* conservative ‖ *m* curator

conservar *tr* to conserve, keep, maintain; preserve ‖ *ref* to take good care of oneself; keep

conservati•vo -va *adj* conservative, preservative

conservatorio *m* (*p.ej., de música*) conservatory; (Arg) private school; (Chile) hothouse, greenhouse

conservera *f* cannery; (Mex) preserve dish

conservería *f* canning

conserve•ro -ra *adj* canning ‖ *mf* canner ‖ *f* see **conservera**

considerable *adj* considerable; large, great, important

consideración *f* consideration; **ser de consideración** to be of importance, be of concern; **someter a consideración** to take under advisement

considera•do -da *adj* (*que guarda consideración a los demás*) considerate; (*digno de respeto*) respected, esteemed; (*que obra con reflexión*) cautious, prudent

considerando *conj & m* whereas

considerar *tr* to consider; treat with consideration

consigna f slogan; watchword; (mil) orders; (rr) checkroom

consignación f consignment

consignar tr to consign; assign; state in writing, set forth

consignatario m consignee

consigo pron with him, with her, with them, with you; with himself, with herself, with themselves, with yourself or yourselves

consiguiente adj consequential; **ir** or **proceder consiguiente** to act consistently ‖ m consequence; **por consiguiente** consequently, therefore

consilia•rio -ria mf advisor, counselor

consistencia f consistence, consistency

consistente adj consistent

consistir intr to consist; **consistir en** (estar compuesto de) to consist of; (residir en) consist in

consistorio m consistory; town council; town hall

conso•cio -cia mf copartner; companion, fellow member

consola f console, console table; bracket

consolación f consolation

consolar §61 tr to console

consolidar tr to fund, refund; strengthen; repair

consommé m consommé

consonancia f consonance; rhyme

consonante adj consonantal; rhyming ‖ m rhyme ‖ f consonant

consonar §61 intr to be in harmony; rhyme

cónsone adj harmonious ‖ m (mus) chord

consorcio m consortium; partnership; fellowship

consorte mf consort, mate, spouse; partner, companion; **consortes** (law) colitigants; (law) accomplices

conspi•cuo -cua adj outstanding, prominent

conspiración f conspiracy

conspirar intr to conspire

constancia f constancy; certainty, proof

constante adj constant; steady, regular; sure, certain ‖ f constant

constar intr to be clear, be certain; be on record; have the right rhythm; **constar de** to consist of; **hacer constar** to state, make known; **y para que conste** in witness whereof

constatación f proof

constatar tr to prove, establish, show

constelación f constellation; climate, weather; epidemic

consternar tr to depress, dismay

constipación f or **constipado** m cold, cold in the head

constipar tr (los poros) to stop up ‖ ref to catch cold

constitución f constitution

constituir §20 tr to constitute; establish, found; **constituir en** to force into ‖ ref — **constituirse en** to set oneself up as

constituti•vo -va adj & m constituent

constituyente adj (para dictar o reformar la constitución) constituent

constreñir §72 tr to constrain, force, compel; constrict, compress

construcción f construction; building, structure; **construcción de buques** shipbuilding

construc•tor -tora adj construction ‖ mf builder, constructor; **constructor de buques** shipbuilder

construir §20 tr to build, construct

consuegro m fellow father-in-law (with respect to the father of one's son-in-law or daughter-in-law), father-in-law of one's child

consuelda f comfrey; **consuelda real** field larkspur; **consuelda sarracena** goldenrod

consuelo m consolation; joy, delight; **sin consuelo** inconsolably; to excess

consueta m (theat) prompter

consuetudina•rio -ria adj customary, usual

cónsul m consul

consulado m consulate, consulship; (casa u oficina) consulate

consular adj consular

consulta f consultation; opinion; reference

consultación f consultation

consultar tr to consult; take up, discuss; advise ‖ intr to consult, confer

consulti•vo -va adj advisory

consul•tor -tora mf consultant

consultorio m dispensary

consuma•do -da adj consummate ‖ m consommé

consumar tr to consummate; fulfill, carry out

consumerismo m consumerism

consumición f consumption; drink (in bar or restaurant)

consumi•do -da adj thin, weak, emaciated; fretful

consumi•dor -dora mf consumer; customer (in bar or restaurant)

consumir tr to consume; exhaust; harass, wear down ‖ ref to consume, waste away; long, yearn

consumo m consumption; drink (in bar or restaurant); customers; **consumos** octroi

consunción f consumption; (pathol) consumption

consuno adv — **de consuno** together, in accord

consunti•vo -va adj consumptive; (crédito) consumer

contabilidad f accounting, bookkeeping

contabilista mf accountant, bookkeeper

contabilizadora f computer

contabilizar §60 tr to enter in the ledger

contable adj countable ‖ mf accountant, bookkeeper

contactar intr to contact, be in contact

contacto m contact; **ponerse en contacto con** to get in touch with

conta•do -da adj scarce, rare; **al contado** cash, for cash; **contados** a few; **de contado** right away; **por de contado** of course

contador m counter; accountant; (que mide el agua, gas, electricidad) meter; (law) receiver; **contador de abonado** house meter; **contador de Geiger** Geiger counter; **contador kilométrico** speedometer; **contador**

público titulado certified public accountant

contaduría f accountancy; accountant's office; box office for advanced sales

contagiar tr to infect; corrupt

contagio m contagion

contagio·so -sa adj contagious

contaminación f contamination; **contaminación ambiental** environmental pollution

contaminante m pollutant

contaminar tr to contaminate; (un texto) corrupt; (la ley de Dios) break

contante adj (dinero) ready

contar §61 tr to count; regard, consider; tell, relate; **contar . . . años** to be . . . years old; **dejarse contar diez** (box) to take the count; **tiene sus horas contadas** his days are numbered ‖ intr to count; **a contar desde** beginning with; **contar con** to count on, rely on; reckon with; expect to

contemplación f contemplation; leniency, condescension

contemplar tr to contemplate; be lenient to ‖ intr to contemplate

contemporáne·o -a adj contemporaneous, contemporary ‖ mf contemporary

contemporizar §60 intr to temporize

contención f containment; contention, strife; (law) suit, litigation

contencio·so -sa adj contentious

contender §51 intr to contend

contendiente mf contender, contestant

contenedor m container

contener §71 tr to contain ‖ ref to contain oneself

conteni·do -da adj moderate, restrained ‖ m content, contents

contenta f gift or treat; indorsement; (mil) certificate of good conduct; (law) release

contentadi·zo -za adj easy to please

contentamiento m contentment

contentar tr to content; reconcile; (com) to indorse

conten·to -ta adj content, contented, glad ‖ m content, contentment; **a contento** to one's satisfaction; **no caber de contento** (coll) to be beside oneself with joy ‖ f see **contenta**

conteo m calculation, estimate, count

contera f tip, metal tip

contesta f answer; (Mex) chat

contestación f answer; argument, debate; **mala contestación** back talk

contestar tr to answer ‖ intr to answer; agree

contesto m (Mex) reply

contexto m interweaving; context

conticinio m dead of night

contienda f contest, dispute, fight

contigo pron with thee, with you

conti·guo -gua adj contiguous, adjoining

continencia f continence

continental adj continental

continente adj continent ‖ m (cosa que contiene en sí a otra) container; (aire del semblante, compostura del cuerpo) mien, bearing; (gran extensión de tierra rodeada por los océanos) continent

contingencia f contingency

contingente adj contingent ‖ m contingent; share, quota

continuar §21 tr & intr to continue; **continuará** to be continued

continuidad f continuity

conti·nuo -nua adj continuous, continual; (mach) endless ‖ **continuo** adv continuously

contonear ref to strut, swagger

contoneo m strut, swagger

contorcer §74 ref to writhe

contorno m contour, outline; **contornos** environs, neighborhood

contorsión f contortion

contra prep against; toward, facing ‖ m (concepto opuesto) con ‖ f trouble, inconvenience; (al comprador) (Cuba) gift, extra; (Chile) antidote; **llevar la contra a** to disagree with

contraalmirante m rear admiral

contraatacar §73 tr & intr to counterattack

contraataque m counterattack

contrabajo m contrabass, double bass

contrabajón m double bassoon

contrabalancear tr to counterbalance

contrabalanza f counterbalance

contrabandear intr to smuggle

contrabandista adj smuggling; contraband ‖ mf smuggler, contrabandist

contrabando m smuggling, contraband; **meter de contrabando** to smuggle, smuggle in

contrabarrera f second row of seats (in bull ring)

contracalle f parallel side street

contracarril m (rr) guardrail

contracción f contraction; (reducción del ritmo normal de los negocios) recession; (al estudio) (Chile, Peru) concentration

contracepti·vo -va adj & m contraceptive

contracorriente f countercurrent, crosscurrent; (entre aguas) undertow

contracultura f counterculture

contrachapado m plywood

contradecir §24 (impv sg -dice) tr to contradict

contradicción f contradiction

contradic·tor -tora adj contradictory ‖ mf contradicter

contradicto·rio -ria adj contradictory

contraer §75 tr to contract; (deudas) incur; (el discurso o idea) condense ‖ ref to contract; shrink; (Chile, Peru) to concentrate, apply oneself

contraescalón m riser (of stairway)

contraespía mf counterspy

contraespionaje m counterespionage

contrafallar tr & intr to overtrump

contrafallo m overtrump

contrafigura f counterpart

contrafuero m infringement, violation

contrafuerte m abutment, buttress

contragolpe m counterstroke; kickback; (box) counter

contrahace·dor -dora adj counterfeiting; fake ‖ mf counterfeiter; fake; impersonator

contrahacer §39 *tr* to counterfeit, copy, imitate; fake; impersonate; (*un libro*) pirate ‖ *ref* to pretend to be

contra·haz *f* (*pl* **-haces**) wrong side

contrahe·cho -cha *adj* counterfeit, fake; deformed

contrahechura *f* counterfeit, fake

contrahuella *f* riser (*of stairway*)

contralor *m* comptroller

contralto *mf* contralto (*person*) ‖ *m* contralto (*voice*)

contraluz *f* view against the light; **a contraluz** against the light

contramaestre *m* foreman; (naut) boatswain; **segundo contramaestre** boatswain's mate

contramandar *tr* to countermand

contramandato *m* countermand

contramano *adv* — **a contramano** in the wrong direction, the wrong way

contramarcha *f* countermarch; reverse

contramarchar *intr* to countermarch; to go in reverse

contraofensiva *f* counteroffensive

contraorden *f* cancellation

contraparte *f* counterpart

contrapasar *intr* to go over to the other side

contrapelo *adv* — **a contrapelo** against the hair, against the grain; the wrong way; **a contrapelo de** against, counter to

contrapesar *tr* to offset, counterbalance

contrapeso *m* counterweight; counterbalance; (*para completar el peso de carne, etc.*) makeweight

contraponer §54 *tr* to set opposite; oppose; compare

contraportada *f* (*del disco*) flip side

contraprestación *f* return favor

contraproducente *adj* self-defeating, unproductive

contraprueba *f* second proof

contrapuerta *f* storm door; vestibule door

contrapuntear *tr* to sing in counterpoint; taunt, be sarcastic to ‖ *ref* to taunt each other

contrapunto *m* counterpoint

contrapunzón *m* nailset, punch

contrariar §77 *tr* to counteract, oppose; annoy, provoke

contrariedad *f* opposition; interference; annoyance, bother

contra·rio -ria *adj* opposite, contrary; harmful ‖ *mf* enemy, opponent, rival ‖ *m* opposite, contrary; **al contrario** on the contrary; **de lo contrario** otherwise

contrarreferencia *f* cross reference

Contrarreforma *f* Counter Reformation

contrarregistro *m* (*para comprobar si algún género ha pasado por la frontera*) double check; (*de una experiencia científica*) control

contrarréplica *f* (law) rejoinder

contrarrestar *tr* to resist, counteract; (*la pelota*) return

contrarrevolución *f* counterrevolution

contrasentido *m* misinterpretation; mistranslation; nonsense

contraseña *f* countersign; baggage check; **contraseña de salida** (mov, theat) check

contrastar *tr* to resist; (*las pesas y medidas*) check ‖ *intr* to resist; contrast

contraste *m* resistance; contrast; assayer; assayer's office; (naut) sudden shift in the wind

contratar *tr* to contract for; hire, engage

contratiempo *m* misfortune, disappointment, setback

contratista *mf* contractor

contrato *m* contract

contratreta *f* counterplot

contratuerca *f* lock nut, jam nut

contravalidación *f* (*documento*) validation

contravalidar *tr* to validate; confirm

contraveneno *m* counterpoison, antidote

contravenir §79 *intr* to act contrary; **contravenir a** to contravene, act counter to

contraventana *f* window shutter

contravidriera *f* storm sash

contrayente *mf* contracting party (*to a marriage*)

contribución *f* contribution; tax; **contribución de sangre** military service; **contribución industrial** excise tax; **contribución territorial** land tax

contribui·dor -dora *mf* contributor; taxpayer

contribuir §20 *tr* & *intr* to contribute

contribuyente *mf* contributor; taxpayer

contrición *f* contrition

contrincante *m* competitor, rival; fellow candidate

contristar *tr* to sadden

contri·to -ta *adj* contrite

control *m* control, check; **control de la natalidad** or **de los nacimientos** birth control; **control remoto** remote control

controlador *m* controller; **controlador aéreo** air-traffic controller

controlar *tr* to control, check

controversia *f* controversy

controvertible *adj* controversial, controvertible

controvertir §68 *tr* to controvert

contubernio *m* cohabitation; evil alliance

contumacia *f* contumacy; (law) contempt

contu·maz *adj* (*pl* **-maces**) contumacious; germ-bearing; (law) guilty of contempt of court

contumelia *f* contumely

contundente *adj* bruising; impressive, convincing

contundir *tr* to bruise

conturbar *tr* to trouble, worry, upset

contusión *f* contusion

contusionar *tr* (Chile) to bruise

convalecencia *f* convalescence

convalecer §22 *intr* to convalesce, recover

convaleciente *adj* & *mf* convalescent

convalidar *tr* to confirm

conveci·no -na *adj* neighboring ‖ *mf* neighbor

convencer §78 *tr* to convince

convencimiento *m* conviction

convención *f* (*acuerdo; conformidad; asamblea*) convention; political convention

convencional *adj* conventional

convenible *adj* docile, compliant; (*precio*) fair, reasonable

conveniencia *f* (*comodidad*) convenience; (*acuerdo, convenio*) agreement; fitness, suitability; (*formas sociales*) propriety; domestic employment; **conveniencias** income, property

conveniencie•ro -ra *adj* comfort-loving

conveniente *adj* (*cómodo*) convenient; fit, suitable; advantageous; proper

convenio *m* pact, covenant, treaty

convenir §79 *intr* to agree; (*concurrir, juntarse*) convene; be suitable, be becoming; be important, be necessary; **conviene a saber** to wit, namely ‖ *ref* to agree, come to an agreement

conventillo *m* (SAm) tenement house

convento *m* convent, monastery; **convento de religiosas** convent

converger §17 or **convergir** §27 *intr* to converge; concur

conversa *f* chat, conversation

conversación *f* conversation

conversacional *adj* conversational

conversar *intr* to converse; live, dwell

conversión *f* conversion

conver•so -sa *adj* converted ‖ *mf* convert ‖ *m* lay brother ‖ *f* see **conversa**

convertible *adj* convertible ‖ *m* (aut) convertible

convertir §68 *tr* to convert; turn ‖ *ref* to convert; be converted; **convertirse en** to turn into, become

conve•xo -xa *adj* convex

convic•to -ta *adj* convicted, found guilty

convida•do -da *mf* guest ‖ *f* treat

convidar *tr* to invite; treat; move, incite; **convidarle a uno con alguna cosa** to treat someone to something ‖ *ref* to offer one's services

convincente *adj* convincing

convite *m* invitation; treat, banquet, party; **convite a escote** Dutch treat

convivir *intr* to live together

convocar §73 *tr* to convoke, call together; (*p.ej., una huelga*) call; acclaim

convoy *m* convoy; escort; cruet stand; (rr) train

convoyar *tr* to convoy

convulsionar *tr* to convulse

conyugal *adj* conjugal

cónyuge *mf* spouse, consort ‖ **cónyuges** *mpl* couple, husband and wife

co•ñac *m* (*pl* **-ñacs** or **-ñaques**) cognac

cooperación *f* coöperation

cooperar *intr* to coöperate

cooperati•vo -va *adj* coöperative

cooptar *tr* to coöpt

coordena•do -da *adj* coördinate ‖ *f* (math) coördinate

coordinante *adj* (gram) coördinating

coordinar *tr* & *intr* to coördinate

copa *f* goblet, wineglass; (*del sombrero*) crown; brazier; vase; drink; sundae; playing card, representing a bowl, equivalent to heart; (*del dolor*) (fig) cup; (sport) cup

copar *tr* (*la puesta equivalente a todo el dinero de la banca*) to cover; (*todos los puestos en una elección*) sweep; (mil) to cut off and capture

copartícipe *mf* copartner, joint partner

copear *intr* to sell wine or liquor by the glass; (coll) to tipple

copero *m* cabinet for wineglasses

copete *m* (*cabello levantado sobre la frente*) pompadour; (*de plumas; de una montaña*) crest; (*de un caballo*) forelock; (*de lana, cabello, plumas, etc.*) tuft; (*de un mueble*) top, finial; (*de un sorbete*) topping; **de alto copete** aristocratic, important; **tener mucho copete** to be high-hat

copetu•do -da *adj* tufted; high, lofty; high-hat

copia *f* plenty, abundance; copy; **copia al carbón** carbon copy; **copia fiel** true copy

copiador *m* or **copiadora** *f* copy(ing) machine; duplicator

copiante *mf* copier, copyist

copiar *tr* to copy, copy down

copiloto *m* copilot

copio•so -sa *adj* copious, abundant

copista *mf* copier, copyist

copla *f* couplet; ballad, popular song; **coplas** verse, poetry; **coplas de ciego** doggerel

comple•ro -ra *mf* vendor of ballads; poetaster

coplista *mf* poetaster

copo *m* bundle of cotton, flax, hemp, etc. to be spun; **copo de nieve** snowflake; **copos de jabón** soap flakes

copón *m* ciborium, pyx

copo•so -sa *adj* bushy; flaky, woolly

copu•do -da *adj* bushy, thick

copular *ref* to copulate

coque *m* coke

coqueluche *f* whooping cough

coqueta *adj* coquettish ‖ *f* coquette, flirt; (W-I) dressing table

coquetear *intr* to coquette, flirt; try to please everybody

coquetería *f* coquetry, flirting; affectation

coque•tón -tona *adj* coquettish, kittenish ‖ *m* flirt, lady-killer

coracha *f* leather bag

coraje *m* anger; mettle, spirit

coraju•do -da *adj* ill-tempered; (Arg) brave, courageous

coral *adj* (mus) choral ‖ *m* (mus) chorale; (*zoófito; esqueleto calizo del zoófito; color*) coral; **corales** coral beads

corambre *f* hides, skins

Corán *m* Koran

coranvo•bis *m* (*pl* **-bis**) fat solemn look

coraza *f* armor; cuirass; (sport) guard

corazón *m* heart; (*centro de una cosa*) core; **de corazón** heartily; **hacer de tripas corazón** to pluck up courage

corazonada *f* impulsiveness; hunch, presentiment; entrails

corbata *f* necktie, cravat; scarf; **corbata de mariposa, corbata de lazo** bow tie; **corbata de nudo corredizo** four-in-hand tie

corbatín *m* bow tie

corbeta *f* corvette

Córcega f Corsica
corcel m steed, charger
corcova f hump, hunch
corcova•do -da adj humpbacked, hunchbacked ‖ mf humpback, hunchback
corcovar tr to bend
corcovear intr to buck; grumble; (Mex) to be afraid
corcha f cork bark; cork bucket (for cooling wine)
corchea f (mus) quaver, eighth note
corche•ro -ra adj cork ‖ f cork bucket (for cooling wine)
corcheta f eye (of hook and eye)
corchete m snap; hook and eye; hook (of hook and eye); (signo) bracket; **corchete de presión** snap fastener
corcho m cork; cork, cork stopper; cork wine cooler; cork box; cork mat; **corcho bornizo, corcho virgen** virgin cork
cordada f (mountaineering) party of two or three men roped together
cordaje m cordage; (naut) rigging
cordal adj wisdom (tooth) ‖ m (mus) tailpiece
cordel m cord, string; (distance of) five steps; cattle run; **a cordel** in a straight line
cordelejo m string; **dar cordelejo a** to make fun of; (Mex) to keep putting off
cordera f ewe lamb; (mujer dócil y humilde) (fig) lamb
cordería f cordage
corderillo m lambskin
corderi•no -na adj lamb ‖ f lambskin
cordero m lamb; lambskin; (hombre dócil y humilde) (fig) lamb
corderuna f lambskin
cordial adj cordial; (dedo) middle ‖ m cordial
cordialidad f cordiality
cordillera f chain of mountains
cordobana f — **andar a la cordobana** to go naked
cordón m lace; (de cuerda o alambre) strand; cordon; milled edge of coin; (de monje) rope belt; **cordón umbilical** umbilical cord
cordoncillo m rib, ridge; braid; (de monedas) milling
cordura f prudence, wisdom
Corea f Korea; **la Corea del Norte** North Korea; **la Corea del Sur** South Korea
corea•no -na adj & mf Korean
corear tr to compose for a chorus; accompany with a chorus; join in singing; agree obsequiously with
coreografía f choreography
coriáce•o -a adj leathery
Corinto f Corinth
corista m choir priest; (theat) chorus man ‖ f chorus girl, chorine
cori•to -ta adj naked; bashful, timid
cormorán m cormorant
cor•nac m (pl -nacs) or **cornaca** m mahout
cornada f hook with horns; goring; (en la esgrima) upward thrust
cornadura f or **cornamenta** f (del toro, la vaca, etc.) horns; (del ciervo) antlers

cornamusa f bagpipe
córnea f cornea
cornear tr to butt; to gore
corneja f daw, crow
cornejo m dogwood
córne•o -a adj horn, horny ‖ f see **córnea**
corneta f bugle; swineherd's horn; **corneta acústica** ear trumpet; **corneta de llaves** cornet, cornet-à-pistons; **corneta de monte** hunting-horn
cornisa f cornice
cornisamento m (archit) entablature
corno m horn; dogwood; **corno inglés** (mus) English horn
Cornualles Cornwall
cornucopia f cornucopia; sconce with mirror
cornu•do -da adj horned, antlered; cuckold ‖ m cuckold
coro m chorus; choir; choir loft; **a coros** alternately; **de coro** by heart; **hacer coro a** to echo
corolario m corollary
corona f (cerco de metal; moneda; dignidad real; parte visible de una muela) crown; (cerco de flores) garland, wreath; (aureola) halo; (de eclesiástico) tonsure; (la que corresponde a un título nobiliario) coronet; **corona nupcial** bridal wreath
coronación f coronation
coronamento m or **coronamiento** m coronation; completion, termination; (archit) coping; (naut) taffrail
coronar tr to crown; complete, finish; top, surmount; (checkers) to crown
coronel m colonel
coronelía f colonelcy
coronilla f (de la cabeza) crown; **andar** or **bailar de coronilla** to be hard at it; **estar hasta la coronilla** to be fed up
corotos mpl belongings; utensils
corpiño m bodice, waist; (Arg) brassiere
corporación f corporation
corporal adj corporal, bodily
corpu•do -da adj corpulent
corpulen•to -ta adj corpulent
corpúsculo m corpuscle; particle
corral m corral, stockyard; barnyard; fishpond; theater; **corral de madera** lumberyard; **corral de vacas** pigpen; **hacer corrales** to play hooky
correa f strap, thong; (aer, mach) belt; **besar la correa** to eat humble pie; **correa de seguridad** (aer, aut) safety belt
corrección f (acción de corregir; reprensión) correction; (calidad de correcto) correctness
correcti•vo -va adj & m corrective
correc•to -ta adj correct
correc•tor -tora mf corrector; **corrector de pruebas** proofreader
corredera f track, slide; slide valve; (del trombón) slide; (naut) log; (naut) log line; (puerta) **de corredera** sliding
corredi•zo -za adj slide; sliding; (nudo) slip
corre•dor -dora adj running ‖ mf runner ‖ m corridor; porch, gallery; (el que interviene en compras y ventas de efectos comer-

ciales, etc.) broker; (mil) scout; **corredor de apuestas** bookmaker

corregidor *m* Spanish magistrate; chief magistrate of Spanish town

corregir §57 *tr* to correct; temper, moderate ‖ *intr* (W-I) to have a bowel movement ‖ *ref* to mend one's ways

correlación *f* correlation

correlacionar *tr & intr* to correlate

correlati•vo -va *adj & m* correlative

corre•lón -lona *adj* (SAm) fast, swift; (Col, Mex) cowardly

correncia *f* bashfulness; looseness of the bowels

correnti•o -a *adj* running; free, easy ‖ *f* looseness of the bowels

corren•tón -tona *adj* jolly, full of fun

corrento•so -sa *adj* swift, rapid

correo *m* mail; post office; mail train; postman; courier; **correo aéreo** air mail; **correo urgente** special delivery; **echar al correo** to mail, to post

correo•so -sa *adj* leathery, tough

correr *tr* (*un caballo*) to run, race; (*un riesgo*) run; travel over; overrun; (*una cortina*) draw; (*un toro*) fight; chase, pursue; auction; confuse; throw out; **correrla** to run around all night ‖ *intr* to run; race; pass, elapse; circulate, be common talk; be current; **a todo correr** at full speed; **correr a** to sell for; **correr a cargo de** or **por cuenta de** to be the business of; **correr con** to be on good terms with; be in charge of; (*mes*) **que corre** current ‖ *ref* (*a derecha o a izquierda*) to turn; be confused; be embarrassed, be ashamed; slide, glide; (*una bujía, un color*) run; go too far

correría *f* short trip, excursion; foray, raid

correspondencia *f* correspondence; contact, communication; agreement, harmony; (*en el metro*) connection; (*en una carretera*) interchange

corresponder *intr* to correspond; (*dos habitaciones*) communicate; **corresponder a** (*un beneficio, el afecto de una persona*) to return, reciprocate; concern; be up to ‖ *ref* (*comunicarse por escrito*) to correspond; (*dos cosas*) correspond with each other; be in agreement; be attached to each other

correspondiente *adj* corresponding; correspondent; respective ‖ *mf* correspondent

corresponsal *mf* correspondent

corretaje *m* brokerage

corretear *tr* to harass, pursue; (CAm) to drive away; (Chile) to speed up ‖ *intr* to race around

correveidi•le *mf* (*pl* **-le**) gossip; go-between

corrida *f* run; bullfight; (*carrera de entrenamiento de un caballo*) trial run; **corrida de banco** run on the bank; **corrida de toros** bullfight

corri•do -da *adj* (*peso, medida*) in excess; (*letra*) cursive, continued, unbroken; abashed, ashamed; wordly-wise, sophisticated ‖ *m* overhang; street ballad ‖ *f* see **corrida**

corriente *adj* (*agua*) running; (*actual*) current; common, ordinary; regular; well-known; fluent ‖ *adv* all right, O.K. ‖ *m* current month; **al corriente** on time; informed, aware, posted ‖ *f* current, stream; (elec) current; **corriente de aire** draft; **Corriente del Golfo** Gulf Stream; **ir contra la corriente** to go against the tide

corrillo *m* circle, clique

corrimiento *m* running; sliding; watery discharge; embarrassment, shyness; landslide; rheumatism

corro *m* (*cerco de gente; espacio circular*) ring; (*juego de niñas*) ring-around-a-rosy; **corro de brujas** fairy ring; **hacer corro** to make room

corroborar *tr* to corroborate; strengthen

corroer §62 *tr & ref* to corrode

corromper *tr* to corrupt; spoil; rot; seduce; bribe; annoy ‖ *intr* to smell bad ‖ *ref* to become corrupted; spoil; rot

corrosión *f* corrosion

corrosi•vo -va *adj & m* corrosive

corrugar §44 *tr* to shrink; wrinkle

corrupción *f* corruption; seduction; bribery; stench

corruptela *f* corruption

corruptible *adj* corruptible; (*p.ej., frutas*) perishable

corrusco *m* crust of bread

corsa *f* (naut) day's run

corsario *m* corsair

corsé *m* corset

cor•so -sa *adj & mf* Corsican ‖ *m* (naut) privateering; (SAm) drive, promenade ‖ *f* see **corsa**

corta *f* clearing, cutting, felling

cortaalam•bres *m* (*pl* **-bres**) wire cutter

cortabol•sas *m* (*pl* **-sas**) pick-pocket

cortacésped *m* lawn mower

cortaciga•rros *m* (*pl* **-rros**) cigar cutter

cortacircui•tos *m* (*pl* **-tos**) (elec) fuse

cortacorriente *m* (elec) change-over switch

cortada *f* cut, cutting

cortadillo *m* drinking cup

corta•do -da *adj* (*estilo*) choppy; (SAm) hard up ‖ *f* see **cortada**

corta•dor -dora *adj* cutting ‖ *mf* cutter ‖ *m* butcher ‖ *f* cutting machine

cortafrío *m* cold chisel

cortafuego *s* fire wall

cortahie•los *m* (*pl* **-los**) icebreaker

cortalápi•ces *m* (*pl* **-ces**) pencil sharpener

cortante *adj* cutting, sharp ‖ *m* butcher; butcher knife

cortapape•les *m* (*pl* **-les**) paper cutter

cortapi•cos *m* (*pl* **-cos**) (ent) earwig; **cortapicos y callares** little children should be seen and not heard

cortaplu•mas *m* (*pl* **-mas**) penknife

cortapu•ros *m* (*pl* **-ros**) cigar cutter

cortar *tr* to cut; trim; chop; cut off; cut out; omit; cut short; cut up; carve; (*la corriente; la ignición*) cut off ‖ *intr* to cut; (*el viento, el frío*) be cutting; **cortar de vestir** to cut cloth; gossip ‖ *ref* to become speechless;

(*la leche*) curdle, turn sour; (*la piel*) chap, crack

cortarrenglón *m* marginal stop

cortaú•ñas *m* (*pl* **-ñas**) nail clipper

cortavi•drios *m* (*pl* **-drios**) glass cutter

cortaviento *m* windshield

corte *m* cut; cutting; (*filo de un arma, cuchillo, etc.; borde de un libro*) edge; cross section; (*de un vestido*) cut, fit; piece of material; harvest; **corte de pelo** haircut; **corte de pelo a cepillo** crew cut; **corte de traje** suiting ‖ *f* (*de un rey*) court; (*corral*) yard; stable, fold; (*tribunal de justicia*) court; **Cortes** Parliament; **darse cortes** (SAm) to put on airs; **hacer la corte a** to pay court to; **la Corte** the Capital (*Madrid*)

cortedad *f* shortness; smallness; lack; bashfulness

cortejar *tr* to escort, attend, court; court, woo

cortejo *m* courting; courtship; (*séquito*) cortege; gift, treat; (coll) beau

cortera *f* (Chile) streetwalker

cortero *m* (Chile) day laborer

cortés *adj* courteous, polite, courtly

cortesana *f* courtesan

cortesana•zo -za *adj* overpolite, obsequious

cortesanía *f* courtliness

cortesa•no -na *adj* courtly, courteous ‖ *m* courtier ‖ *f* see **cortesana**

cortesía *f* courtesy, politeness, courtliness; gift, favor; (*inclinación de la cabeza o el cuerpo en señal de respeto*) curtsy; (*de una carta*) conclusion; **hacer una cortesía to** make a bow; curtsy

corteza *f* bark; peel, rind, skin; (*de pan*) crust; coarseness; (*envoltura exterior de un órgano*) cortex; **corteza cerebral** cortex

cortijo *m* farm, farmhouse

cortil *m* barnyard

cortina *f* curtain; **correr la cortina** to pull the curtain aside; **cortina de hierro** iron curtain; **cortina de humo** smoke screen

cortinal *m* fenced-in field

cortinilla *f* shade, window shade

cortisona *f* cortisone

cor•to -ta *adj* short; dull; bashful, shy; speechless; **a la corta o a la larga** sooner or later; **desde muy corta edad** from earliest childhood ‖ *f* see **corta**

cortocircuitar *tr & ref* (elec) to short-circuit

cortocircuito *m* (elec) short circuit

cortometraje *m* (mov) short

corva *f* ham, back of knee; (vet) curb

corvejón *m* gambrel, hock; (orn) cormorant

cor•vo -va *adj* arched, bent, curved ‖ *m* hook ‖ *f* see **corva**

cor•zo -za *mf* roe deer

cosa *f* thing; **cosa de** a matter of; **cosa de cajón** a matter of course; **cosa de mieles** something fine; **cosa de nunca acabar** endless bore; **cosa de oír** something worth hearing; **cosa de risa** something to laugh at; **cosa de ver** something worth seeing; **cosa nunca vista** something unheard-of; **cosa que** so that; **cosa rara** strange to say; **como si tal cosa** as if nothing had happened; **en cosa de** in a matter of; **no . . . gran cosa** not much; **no haber tal cosa** to be not so; **otra cosa** something else; **¿qué cosa?** what's new?

cosa•co -ca *adj & mf* Cossack ‖ *m* Cossack (*horseman*)

coscolina *f* (Mex) loose woman

cos•cón -cona *adj* sly, crafty

cosecha *f* crop, harvest; harvest time; **cosecha de vino** vintage; **de su cosecha** (coll) out of one's own head

cosechar *tr* to harvest, reap ‖ *intr* to harvest

coseche•ro -ra *mf* harvester, reaper; vintner

cose-pape•les *m* (*pl* **-les**) stapler

coser *tr* to sew; join, unite closely; **coser a preguntas** to riddle with questions; **coser a puñaladas** to cut to pieces ‖ *intr* to sew; **ser coser y cantar** to be a cinch ‖ *ref—* **coserse con** or **contra** to be closely attached to

cosméti•co -ca *adj & m* cosmetic

cósmi•co -ca *adj* cosmic

cosmonauta *mf* cosmonaut

cosmonave *f* spacecraft

cosmonavegación *f* space travel

cosmopolita *adj & mf* cosmopolitan

cosmos *m* cosmos; (bot) cosmos

coso *m* enclosure for bullfighting

cosquillas *fpl* tickling, ticklishness; **buscarle a uno las cosquillas** to try to irritate a person; **no sufrir cosquillas** or **tener malas cosquillas** to be touchy

cosquillear *tr* to tickle; tease, taunt; stir up the curiosity of; scare ‖ *intr* to tickle ‖ *ref* to be curious; enjoy oneself

cosquilleo *m* tickling, tickling sensation

cosquillo•so -sa *adj* ticklish; (*que se ofende fácilmente*) touchy

costa *f* coast, shore; cost, price; **a toda costa** at all costs; **Costa Brava** Mediterranean coast in province of Gerona, Spain; **Costa Firme** Spanish Main; **costa marítima** seacoast; **costas** (law) costs

costado *m* side; (*del ejército*) flank; (Mex) station platform; **costados** ancestors, stock

costal *m* bag, sack; **costal de los pecados** human body (*full of sin*); **estar hecho un costal de huesos** to be nothing but skin and bones

costanera *f* slope; **costaneras** rafters

costane•ro -ra *adj* sloping; coastal ‖ *f* see **costanera**

costanilla *f* short steep street

costar §61 *intr* to cost; **cueste lo que cueste** cost what it may

costarricense or **costarrique•ño -ña** *adj & mf* Costa Rican

coste *m* cost; **a coste y costas** at cost

costear *tr* to pay for, defray the cost of; sail along the coast of ‖ *intr* to sail along the coast ‖ *ref* to pay; pay one's way

coste•ño -ña *adj* sloping; coastal

coste•ro -ra *adj* coastal

costilla *f* rib; wealth; **costillas** back, shoulders

costillu•do -da *adj* heavy-set, broad-shouldered

costo *m* cost; **costo de la vida** cost of living; **costo, seguro y flete** cost, insurance, and freight

costo•so -sa *adj* costly, expensive; grievous

costra *f* scab, scale; (*moco de una vela*) snuff

costro•so -sa *adj* scabby, scaly

costumbre *f* custom, habit; **de costumbre** usual; usually; **tener por costumbre** to be in the habit of

costumbrista *mf* critic of manners and customs

costura *f* sewing, needlework; dressmaking; (*unión de dos piezas cosidas*) seam; **alta costura** fashion designing, haute couture

costurar or **costurear** *tr* (CAm, Mex) to sew

costurera *f* seamstress, dressmaker

costurero *m* sewing table

cota *f* coat of arms; coat of mail

cotarrera *f* gossipy woman

cotarro *m* night shelter (*for beggars and tramps*); **alborotar el cotarro** to raise a row

cotejar *tr* to compare, collate

cotejo *m* comparison, collation

cotidia•no -na *adj* daily, everyday

cotilla *f* gossip, tattletale

cotín *m* (sport) backstroke

cotización *f* quotation; dues

cotizante *adj* dues-paying

cotizar §60 *tr* to quote; prorate || *intr* to collect dues; pay dues

coto *m* price; fixed price; term, limit

cotón *m* printed cotton

cotona *f* work shirt

cotonía *f* dimity

cotorra *f* parrot; parakeet; magpie; chatterbox; (Mex) night shelter

cotorrear *intr* to gossip, gabble

cotufa *f* Jerusalem artichoke; delicacy, tidbit; **hacer cotufas** (Bol) to be fastidious; **pedir cotufas en el golfo** to ask for the moon

coturno *m* buskin

covacha *f* cave; cubbyhole; shanty; doghouse

covachuelista *m* clerk, government clerk

coxcojita *f* hopscotch; **a coxcojita** hippety-hop

coy *m* (naut) hammock

coyunda *f* strap for yoking oxen; sandal string; marriage; tyranny

coyuntura *f* joint, articulation; (*sazón, oportunidad*) juncture

coz *f* (*pl* **coces**) kick; big end; ebb; (coll) insult; **dar coces contra el aguijón** to kick against the pricks

c.p.b., C.P.B. *abbr* **cuyos pies beso**

cps. *abbr* **compañeros**

crabrón *m* hornet

crac *m* (*ruido seco*) crack; crash; **hacer crac** to crash, fail

cráneo *m* cranium, skull

crápula *f* drunkenness, debauchery; riffraff

crapulo•so -sa *adj* drunken; vicious; evil

crascitar *intr* to crow, croak

cra•so -sa *adj* fat, greasy, thick; (*ignorancia*) crass, gross

cráter *m* crater

creación *f* creation

crea•dor -dora *adj* creative || *mf* creator

crear *tr* to create; appoint; found || *ref* to make for oneself, build up; trump up

creati•vo -va *adj* creative

crecede•ro -ra *adj* growth; large enough to allow for growth

crecepelo *m* hair restorer

crecer §22 *intr* to grow; increase; (*el río*) rise, swell; (*la luna*) wax || *ref* to grow; take on more authority; get bolder

creces *fpl* growth, increase; excess, extra; **con creces** amply, in abundance

crecida *f* freshet, flood

creciente *adj* growing, increasing || *f* —**creciente de la luna** waxing of the moon, crescent; **creciente del mar** high tide, flood tide

crecimiento *m* growth, increase; **crecimiento cero** zero growth

credenciales *fpl* credentials

crédito *m* credit

credo *m* creed; credo; **con el credo en la boca** with one's heart in one's mouth; **en un credo** in a trice

crédu•lo -la *adj* credulous

creederas *fpl* — **tener buenas creederas** to be gullible

creencia *f* belief; (*crédito que se presta a un hecho*) credence; (*secta*) creed

creer §43 *tr & intr* to believe; **¡ya lo creo!** I should say so! || *ref* to believe; believe oneself to be

creíble *adj* believable, credible

creí•do -da *adj* credulous; gullible

crema *f* cream; cold cream; shoe polish; (gram) diaeresis; **crema de menta** creme de menthe; **crema dental** or **crema dentífrica** toothpaste; **crema desvanecedora** vanishing cream

cremación *f* cremation

cremallera *f* rack; zipper

cremato•rio -ria *adj & m* crematory

crémor *m* cream of tartar

cremo•so -sa *adj* creamy

crencha *f* part (*in hair*); hair on each side of part

crepitar *intr* to crackle

crepuscular *adj* twilight

crepúsculo *m* twilight

cresa *f* maggot

crespar *tr & ref* to curl

cres•po -pa *adj* curly; curled; angry, irritated; stylish, conceited; (*estilo*) turgid || *m* curl

crespón *m* crape; **crespón fúnebre** crape; mourning band

cresta *f* crest; **cresta de gallo** cockscomb; (bot) cockscomb

creta *f* chalk || **Creta** *f* Crete

cretense *adj & mf* Cretan

cretona *f* cretonne

creyente *adj* believing || *mf* believer

creyón *m* crayon

cría *f* brood, litter; breeding; raising, rearing; nursing

criada *f* female servant, maid; **criada de casa, criada de servir** housemaid

co
cr

criadero *m* nursery, tree nursery; fish hatchery; oyster bed

criadilla *f* testicle; potato

cria·do -da *adj* — **bien criado** well-bred; **mal criado** ill-bred ‖ *mf* servant ‖ *f* see **criada**

cria·dor -dora *mf* breeder ‖ *f* wet nurse

criamiento *m* care, upkeep

crianza *f* raising, rearing; nursing; (*urbanidad*) breeding, manners; **buena crianza** good breeding; **mala crianza** bad breeding

criar §77 *tr* to raise, rear, bring up; breed; grow; nurse, nourish; fatten; create; foster

criatura *f* (*toda cosa creada; persona que debe su cargo o situación a otra*) creature; little child, little creature

criba *f* screen, sieve

cribar *tr* to screen, sieve

cribo *m* screen, sieve

cric *m* (*pl* **crics**) jack

crimen *m* crime; **crimen de lesa majestad** lese majesty; **crímenes de oficinistas** white-collar crime

criminal *adj* & *mf* criminal

criminar *tr* to accuse, incriminate

criminología *f* criminology

crimino·so -sa *adj* & *mf* criminal

crines *fpl* mane

crío *m* (coll) baby, infant

crio·llo -lla *adj* & *mf* Creole

cripta *f* crypt

crisálida *f* chrysalis

crisantemo *m* chrysanthemum

cri·sis *f* (*pl* **-sis**) crisis; (*pánico económico*) depression, slump; mature judgment; **crisis del servicio doméstico** servant problem; **crisis de llanto** crying fit; **crisis de vivienda** housing shortage; **crisis energética** energy crisis; **crisis ministerial** cabinet crisis; **crisis nerviosa** fit of nerves

crisma *f* (coll) head, bean

crisol *m* crucible

crispar *tr* to cause to twitch ‖ *ref* to twitch

crispatura *f* twitch, twitching

crispir *tr* to grain, to marble

cristal *m* crystal; glass; pane of glass; mirror, looking glass; **cristal cilindrado** plate glass; **cristal de reloj** watch crystal; **cristal de roca** rock crystal; **cristal hilado** glass wool, spun glass; **cristal laminado** laminated glass, safety glass; **cristal tallado** cut glass

cristalera *f* China closet; sideboard; glass door

cristalería *f* glassworks, glass store; glassware; glass cabinet

cristali·no -na *adj* crystalline ‖ *m* lens, crystalline lens

cristalizar §60 *tr* & *ref* to crystallize

cristianar *tr* to baptize, christen

cristiandad *f* Christendom

cristianismo *m* Christianity

cristianizar §60 *tr* to Christianize

cristia·no -na *adj* & *mf* Christian ‖ *m* soul, person; Spanish; watered wine

Cristo *m* Christ; crucifix; **donde Cristo dió las tres voces** in the middle of nowhere

Cristóbal *m* Christopher

criterio *m* criterion

crítica *f* (*jucio sobre una obra literaria, etc.; censura de la conducta de alguno*) criticism; (*arte de juzgar una obra literaria, etc.*) critique; gossip

criticar §73 *tr* & *intr* to criticize

críti·co -ca *adj* critical; (*criticón*) critical (*faultfinding*) ‖ *mf* critic ‖ *f* see **crítica**

criti·cón -cona *adj* critical, faultfinding ‖ *mf* critic, faultfinder

critiquizar §60 *tr* to overcriticize

crizneja *f* braid of hair

croar *intr* to croak

croata *adj* & *mf* Croatian

crocante *m* almond brittle, peanut brittle

crocitar *intr* to crow, croak

croco *m* crocus

croché *m* crochet

crochet *m* (box) hook

croma·do -da *adj* chrome ‖ *m* chromium plating

cromar *tr* to chrome

cromo *m* chromium

cromosoma *m* chromosome

crónica *f* chronicle; news chronicle, feature story

cróni·co -ca *adj* chronic; longstanding; (*vicio*) inveterate ‖ *f* see **crónica**

cronista *mf* chronicler; reporter, feature writer; **cronista de radio** newscaster

cronología *f* chronology

cronometra·dor -dora *mf* (sport) timekeeper

cronometraje *m* (sport) clocking, timing

cronómetro *m* chronometer; stop watch

croqueta *f* croquette

cro·quis *m* (*pl* **-quis**) sketch

croscitar *intr* to crow, croak

crótalo *m* rattlesnake; castanet

cruce *m* crossing; crossroads, intersection; exchange (*e.g., of letters*); (*avería*) (elec) crossed wires, short circuit; **cruce a nivel** grade crossing; **cruce en trébol** cloverleaf intersection

crucero *m* crossroads; railroad crossing; (archit) transept; (aer, naut) cruise, cruising; (nav) cruiser; **crucero a nivel** grade crossing

crucial *adj* crucial

crucificar §73 *tr* to crucify

crucifijo *m* crucifix

crucifixión *f* crucifixion

crucigrama *m* crossword puzzle

cruda *f* (Mex) hangover

crudeza *f* crudeness, rawness; (*del agua*) hardness, harshness, roughness; blustering; **crudezas** undigested food

cru·do -da *adj* crude, raw; (*agua*) hard; harsh, rough; (*tiempo*) raw; (*lienzo*) unbleached; **estar crudo** (P-R) to be rusty; (Mex) to have a hangover ‖ *f* see **cruda**

cruel *adj* cruel

crueldad *f* cruelty

cruen·to -ta *adj* bloody

crujía *f* corridor, hall; hospital ward; block of houses; (naut) midship gangway; **crujía de**

piezas suite of rooms; **sufrir una crujía** (coll) to have a hard time of it

crujido m creak; crackle; clatter; chatter; rustle

crujir intr to creak; crackle; clatter; chatter; rustle; crunch

crup m croup

crustáce•o -a adj crustaceous ‖ m crustacean

cruz f (pl **cruces**) cross; (de una moneda) tails; (typ) dagger; **Cruz del Sur** Southern Cross; **¡cruz y raya!** (coll) that's enough!; **de la cruz a la fecha** from beginning to end

cruza f (SAm) intersection; crossbreeding

cruzada f (expedición contra los infieles; propaganda contra un vicio) crusade; crossroads, intersection

cruza•do -da adj crossed; (de raza mixta) cross; double-breasted ‖ m (el que toma parte en una cruzada) crusader; (caballero de una orden militar) knight; twill ‖ f see **cruzada**

cruzar §60 tr to cross; (la tela) twill; (cartas) exchange; crossbreed; (naut) to cruise, cruise over ‖ intr to cross; cruise ‖ ref to cross each other, cross one another's path; (alistarse para una cruzada) take the cross; **cruzarse con** (otro automóvil) to pass; **cruzarse de brazos** (estar ocioso) to cross one's arms

cs. abbr **céntimos, cuartos**

cte. abbr **corriente**

c/u abbr **cada uno**

cuad. abbr **cuadrado**

cuaderna f (naut) frame

cuaderno m notebook; folder; **cuaderno de bitácora** (naut) logbook; **cuaderno de hojas cambiables** or **sueltas** loose-leaf notebook

cuadra f hall, large room; stable; dormitory, ward; croup, rump; block

cuadra•do -da adj square; square-shouldered; perfect ‖ m square; (regla) ruler; (en las medias) clock; **de cuadrado** perfectly; (que se mira frente a frente) full-faced

cuadragési•mo -ma adj & m fortieth

cuadrangular adj quadrangular ‖ m home run

cuadrángu•lo -la adj quadrangular ‖ m quadrangle

cuadrante m quadrant; (de reloj) face, dial; **cuadrante solar** sundial

cuadrar tr to square; please; (al toro) (taur) to square off, line up ‖ ref to square; stand at attention; take on a serious air

cuadrilla f group, party; crew, gang

cuadrillazo m (SAm) surprise attack

cuadrillo m (saeta) bolt (arrow)

cuadrimotor m four-motor plane

cua•dro -dra adj square ‖ m square; (lienzo, pintura) painting, picture; (marco de pintura, ventana, etc.) frame; (de jardín) patch, flower bed; staff, personnel; (mil) cadre; (sport) team; (theat) scene; (coll) sight, mess; **a cuadros** checked; **cuadro de costumbres** sketch of manners and customs; **cuadro de distribución** switchboard;

cuadro de mando instrument panel; (aut) dashboard; **cuadro indicador** score board; **cuadro vivo** tableau; **en cuadro** square, e.g., **ocho pulgadas en cuadro** eight inches square; topsy-turvy; **quedarse en cuadro** to be all alone in the world; (mil) to be skeletonized ‖ f see **cuadra**

cuadrúpe•do -da adj & m quadruped

cuádruple adj & m quadruple

cuadruplicar §73 tr & ref to quadruple

cuajada f curd

cuajado m mincemeat

cuajar tr to curd, curdle, thicken, jelly; please, suit ‖ intr to take hold, catch on, jell, take shape; (Mex) to chatter, prattle ‖ ref to curd, curdle, thicken, jelly; sleep sound; become crowded

cuajo m curd; (Mex) chatter, prattle; (en la escuela) (Mex) recess

cual adj rel & pron rel such as; **el cual** which; who; **lo cual** which; **por lo cual** for which reason ‖ adv as ‖ prep like

cuál adj interr & pron interr which, what; which one

cualidad f quality, characteristic, trait

cualquier adj indef (pl **cualesquier**) apocopated form of **cualquiera**, used only before masculine nouns and adjectives

cualquiera (pl **cualesquiera**) pron indef anyone; **cualquiera que** whichever; whoever ‖ adj indef any ‖ adj rel whichever ‖ m (persona poco importante) nobody

cuan adv as

cuán adv how, how much

cuando conj when; although; in case; since; **aun cuando** even if, even though; **cuando más** at most; **cuando menos** at least; **cuando mucho** at most; **cuando quiera** whenever; **de cuando en cuando** from time to time ‖ prep (coll) at the time of

cuándo adv when; **cuándo . . . cuándo** sometimes . . . sometimes; **¿de cuándo acá?** since when?; how come?

cuantía f quantity; importance; **delito de mayor cuantía** felony; **delito de menor cuantía** misdemeanor; **de mayor cuantía** first-rate; **de menor cuantía** second-rate, of little importance

cuantiar §77 tr to estimate, appraise

cuánti•co -ca adj quantum

cuantio•so -sa adj large, substantial

cuan•to -ta adj rel & pron rel as much as, whatever, all that which; **cuantos** as many as, all those who, everybody who; **unos cuantos** some few ‖ **cuanto** adv as soon as; as long as; **cuanto antes** as soon as possible; **cuanto más . . . tanto más** the more . . . the more; **cuanto más que** all the more because; **en cuanto** as soon as; while; insofar as; **en cuanto a** as to, as for; **por cuanto** inasmuch as; **por cuanto . . . por tanto** inasmuch as . . . therefore ‖ **cuan•to** m (pl **-ta**) quantum

cuán•to -ta adj interr & pron interr how much; **cuántos** how many ‖ **cuánto** adv how, how much; how long; how long ago; **cada cuánto** how often

cuáque•ro -ra *adj & mf* Quaker

cuarenta *adj, pron & m* forty

cuarenta•vo -va *adj & m* fortieth

cuarentena *f* forty; quarantine; forty days, forty months, forty years; **poner en cuarentena** to quarantine; withhold one's credence in

cuaresma *f* Lent

cuaresmal *adj* Lenten

cuarta *f* fourth, fourth part; (*de la mano*) span; (CAm, W-I) horse whip

cuartago *m* nag, pony

cuartear *tr* to divide in four parts; divide; (*la aguja*) (naut) to box; (CAm, W-I) to whip ‖ *ref* to crack, split; (taur) to step aside, dodge

cuartel *m* quarter; (*de una ciudad*) section, ward; (*terreno*) lot; flower bed; (mil) barracks; (*buen trato*) (mil) quarter; (*armazón de tablas para cerrar la escotilla*) (naut) hatch; (coll) house, home; **cuartel de bomberos** engine house, firehouse; **cuarteles** (mil) quarters; **cuartel general** (mil) headquarters

cuartelada *f* mutiny, military uprising

cuartelazo *m* (mil) coup, putsch; (mil) takeover

cuarte•rón -rona *mf* quadroon ‖ *m* quarter; (*de puerta*) panel; (*de ventana*) shutter

cuarteto *m* quartet

cuartilla *f* sheet of paper

cuar•to -ta *adj* fourth; quarter ‖ *m* fourth; quarter; room, bedroom; quarter-hour; **cuarto creciente** (*de la luna*) first quarter; **cuarto de aseo** lavatory; **cuarto de baño** bathroom; **cuarto de dormir** bedroom; **cuarto de estar** living room; **cuarto delantero** (*de la res*) forequarter; **cuarto de los niños** nursery; **cuarto de luna** quarter; **cuarto menguante** (*de la luna*) last quarter; **cuarto obscuro** (phot) darkroom; **cuartos** money, cash; **cuarto trasero** (*p.ej., de vaca*) rump ‖ *f see* **cuarta**

cuarzo *m* quartz

cuate *adj* (Mex) twin; (Mex) like ‖ *mf* (Mex) twin; (Mex) pal

cuatrilli•zo -za *mf* quadruplet

cuatrinca *f* foursome

cuatro *adj & pron* four; (Mex) deceit, swindle; **las cuatro** four o'clock ‖ *m* four; (*en las fechas*) fourth; (*de voces*) quartet; **más de cuatro** (coll) quite a number

cuatrocien•tos -tas *adj & pron* four hundred ‖ **cuatrocientos** *m* four hundred

cuba *f* cask, barrel; tub, vat; (*persona de mucho vientre*) (coll) tub; (*persona que bebe mucho*) (coll) toper; **cuba de riego** street sprinkler

cuba•no -na *adj & mf* Cuban

cubertería *f* silverware, cutlery

cubeta *f* keg, cask; pail; bowl, toilet bowl; (*del termómetro*) cup; (chem, phot) tray; (Mex) high hat

cubicaje *m* piston displacement, cylinder capacity

cubicar *tr* (*elevar al cubo*) to cube; measure the volume of; have a piston displacement of

cúbi•co -ca *adj* cubic; (*raíz*) cube

cubierta *f* cover; envelope; roof; (*de un libro*) paper cover; (*de un neumático*) casing, shoe; (*del motor de un coche*) hood; (naut) deck; **bajo cubierta separada** under separate cover; **cubierta de aterrizaje** (nav) flight deck; **cubierta de cama** bedcover; **cubierta de mesa** table cover; **cubierta de paseo** (naut) promenade deck; **cubierta de vuelo** (nav) flight deck; **cubierta principal** (naut) main deck; **entre cubiertas** (naut) between decks

cubiertamente *adv* secretly

cubier•to -ta *adj* covered; (*cielo*) overcast ‖ *m* cover, roof, shelter; (*servicio de mesa para una persona*) cover; knife, fork, and spoon; table d'hôte, prix fixe; **a cubierto de** under cover of; protected from; **bajo cubierto** under cover, indoors ‖ *f see* **cubierta**

cubil *m* (*de fieras*) lair, den; (*de arroyo*) bed

cubilete *m* (*de cocinero*) copper mold; dicebox; mince pie; high hat; (SAm) scheming, wirepulling

cubo *m* bucket; (*de rueda*) hub; (*de un candelero; de una llave de caja*) socket; cube; (mach) barrel, drum; (math) cube; (Arg) finger bowl

cubreasiento *m* seat cover

cubrecama *f* counterpane, bedcover

cubrecorsé *m* corset cover

cubrefuego *m* curfew

cubrelibro *m* jacket

cubrenuca *f* havelock

cubrerrueda *f* mudguard

cubresexo *m* G-string

cubretablero *m* (aut) cowl

cubretetera *f* cozy, tea cozy

cubrir §83 *tr* to cover, cover over, cover up ‖ *ref* to cover oneself; be covered; put one's hat on; (*el cielo*) become overcast; (*satisfacer una deuda*) cover

cucaña *f* greased pole to be climbed as a game; (coll) cinch

cucañe•ro -ra *mf* loafer, parasite

cucar §73 *tr* to wink; to make fun of; (*la caza*) to sight; to incite, stir up ‖ *intr* (*el ganado*) to go off on a run (*when bitten by flies*)

cucaracha *f* roach, cockroach

cucarache•ro -ra *adj* (W-I) sly, tricky; (W-I) amorous, lecherous

cucarda *f* cockade

cuclillas — **en cuclillas** squatting, crouching

cuclillo *m* cuckoo; (coll) cuckold

cu•co -ca *adj* sly, tricky; cute ‖ *mf* sly person ‖ *m* bogeyman; cuckoo; **hacer cuco a** to poke fun at

cu•cú *m* (*pl* **-cúes**) cuckoo (*call*)

cuculla *f* cowl, hood

cucurucho *m* paper cone, ice-cream cone; **hacer cucurucho a** (Chile) to deceive, take in

cuchara f spoon; (*cazo*) dipper, ladle; (*para áridos; para achicar el agua en los botes*) scoop; (*de albañil*) trowel; (Mex) pickpocket; **cuchara de sopa** tablespoon; **media cuchara** (Mex) mason's helper; ordinary fellow; fellow with heavy accent; **meter su cuchara** to butt in

cucharada f spoonful; ladleful; scoop

cucharear *tr* to spoon, ladle out

cucharetear *intr* to stir the pot, stir with a spoon; to meddle

cucharilla f teaspoon; (*de soldador*) ladle

cucharón m large spoon; soup ladle, dipper; scoop; **despacharse con el cucharón** to look out for number one

cuchichear *intr* to whisper

cuchilla f knife; (*hoja de arma blanca de corte*) blade; (*de patín de hielo*) runner; (*cerro escarpado*) hogback; (*de interruptor*) (elec) blade; (poet) sword; **cuchilla de carnicero** butcher knife, cleaver

cuchillada f slash, gash, hack; **cuchilladas** fight, quarrel; **dar cuchillada** (*un actor o un teatro*) to be the hit of the town

cuchillería f cutlery; cutler's shop

cuchillero m cutler

cuchillo m knife; (*en un vestido*) gore; (naut) triangular sail; **cuchillo de trinchar** carving knife; **cuchillo de vidriero** putty knife; **pasar a cuchillo** to put to the sword

cuchitril m hovel, den

cuchufleta f joke, fun, wisecrack

cuchufletear *intr* to joke, make fun, wisecrack

cuelga f fruit hung up for keeping; birthday present

cuelgaca•pas m (*pl* **-pas**) cloak hanger

cuello m (*del cuerpo*) neck; (*de una prenda*) collar; shirt collar; **cuello almidonado** stiff collar; **cuello de camisa** shirtband; **cuello de cisne** gooseneck; **cuello de pajarita** or **doblado** wing collar; **levantar el cuello** to get back on one's feet again

cuenca f wooden bowl; (*del ojo*) socket; basin, river basin; **cuenca de polvo** dust bowl

cuenco m earthen bowl; hollow

cuenta f count, calculation; account; (*factura*) bill; (*en un restaurante*) check; (*del rosario*) bead; **abonar en cuenta a** to credit to the account of; **a cuenta** or **a buena cuenta** on account; **adeudar en cuenta a** to charge to the account of; **a fin de cuentas** after all; **caer en la cuenta** to get the point; **cargar en cuenta a** to charge to the account of; **correr por cuenta de** to be the responsibility of, to be under the administration of; **cuenta atrás** countdown; **cuenta corriente** current account; **cuenta de gastos** expense account; **cuenta de la vieja** counting on one's fingers; **cuentas del gran capitán** overdrawn account; **cuentas galanas** illusions; **darse cuenta de** to realize, become aware of; **de cuenta** of importance; **más de la cuenta** too long; too much; **pedir cuentas a** to bring to account; **por la cuenta** apparently;

por mi cuenta to my way of thinking; **tomar por su cuenta** to take upon oneself; **vamos a cuentas** (coll) let's settle this

cuentacorrentista mf depositor

cuentago•tas m (*pl* **-tas**) dropper, medicine dropper

cuentakilóme•tros m (*pl* **-tros**) odometer

cuente•ro -ra adj (coll) gossipy ‖ mf (coll) gossip

cuentista adj (coll) gossipy ‖ mf story teller; short-story writer; (coll) gossip

cuento m story, tale; short story; prop, support; tip, point; (*cómputo*) count; (coll) gossip, evil talk; (coll) disagreement; **cuento de hadas** fairy tale; **cuento del tío** (SAm) gyp, swindle; **cuento de nunca acabar** (coll) endless affair; **cuento de penas** (coll) hard-luck story; **cuento de viejas** old wives' tale; **Cuentos de Calleja** collection of nursery stories; **dejarse de cuentos** (coll) to come to the point; **estar en el cuento** to be well-informed; **¡puro cuento!** pure fiction!; **sin cuento** countless; **traer a cuento** to bring up; **venir a cuento** (coll) to be opportune; **vivir del cuento** to live by one's wits

cuerda f cord, rope; watch spring; winding a watch or clock; (*acción de ahorcar*) hanging; fishing line; (aer, anat, geom) chord; (mus) string; **acabarse la cuerda** to run down, e.g., **se acabó la cuerda** the watch ran down; **bajo cuerda** secretly, underhandedly; **cuerda de presos** chain gang; **cuerda de remolcar** tow rope; **cuerda de tripa** (mus) catgut; **cuerda tirante** tight rope; **dar cuerda a** to give free rein to; (*un reloj*) to wind; **estar en su cuerda** to be in one's element; **sin cuerda** unwound, run-down

cuer•do -da adj wise, prudent; sane ‖ f see **cuerda**

cuerna f antler; horns

cuerno m horn; (mus) horn; **cuerno de caza** huntinghorn; **cuerno inglés** (mus) English horn

cuero m (*pellejo de buey*) hide; (*después de curtido*) leather; wineskin; **cuero cabelludo** scalp; **cuero en verde** rawhide; **en cueros** stark-naked

cuerpear *intr* (Arg) to duck, dodge

cuerpo m body; (*parte del vestido hasta la cintura*) waist; (*talle, aspecto*) build; (*de escritos, leyes, etc.*) corpus; corps, staff; (mil) corps; **cuerpo a cuerpo** hand to hand; **cuerpo celeste** heavenly body; **cuerpo compuesto** (chem) compound; **cuerpo de aviación** air corps; **cuerpo de baile** corps de ballet; **cuerpo de bomberos** fire brigade, fire company; **cuerpo de ejército** army corps; **Cuerpo de Paz** Peace Corps; **cuerpo de redacción** editorial staff; **cuerpo simple** (chem) simple substance; **dar con el cuerpo en tierra** (coll) to fall flat on the ground; **de cuerpo entero** fulllength; **de medio cuerpo** half-length; **descubrir el cuerpo** to drop one's guard; **en cuerpo** or **en cuerpo de camisa** in shirt sleeves; **estar de cuerpo presente** to be on view, to lie in state; **hacer del cuerpo** (coll) to have a movement of the bowels

cueru·do -da *adj* thick-skinned; annoying, boring; bold, shameless

cuervo *m* raven; **cuervo marino** cormorant; **cuervo merendero** rook

cuesco *m* (*de la fruta*) stone; (*del molino de aceite*) millstone; windiness

cuesta *f* hill, slope, grade; charity drive; **cuesta abajo** downhill; **cuesta arriba** uphill; **llevar a cuestas** to be burdened with

cuestión *f* question; dispute, quarrel; matter; **cuestión batallona** much-debated question; **cuestión palpitante** burning question; **en cuestión de** in a matter of

cuestionable *adj* questionable

cuestionar *tr* to question ‖ *intr* (Arg) to argue

cuestionario *m* questionnaire

cuestua·rio -ria or **cuestuo·so -sa** *adj* profitable, lucrative

cuetear *ref* (Col) to blow up, explode; (Col) to die, kick the bucket; (Mex) to get drunk

cueva *f* cave; cellar; (*de ladrones, fieras, etc.*) den

cufi·fo -fa *adj* (Chile) tipsy

cugulla *f* cowl

cui·co -ca *adj* foreign, outside ‖ *m* (Mex) cop, policeman

cuidado *m* care, concern, worry; **¡cuidado con . . .!** beware of . . .!, look out for!; **de cuidado** dangerously; **estar de cuidado** to be dangerously ill; **pierda Vd. cuidado** don't worry; **salir de su cuidado** (*una mujer*) to be delivered; **tener cuidado** to beware, be careful

cuidadora *f* (Mex) governess, chaperon

cuidado·so -sa *adj* careful, concerned, worried; watchful

cuidar *tr* to take care of, watch over ‖ *intr* — **cuidar de** to take care of, care for; care to ‖ *ref* to take care of oneself; **cuidarse de** to care about; be careful to

cuita *f* trouble, worry; longing, yearning

cuja *f* bedstead

culata *f* buttock, haunch; (*de la escopeta*) butt; (*de imán*) keeper, yoke; **culata de cilindro** cylinder head

culatazo *m* kick, recoil

culebra *f* snake; (*del alambique*) coil; **culebra de anteojos** cobra; **culebra de cascabel** rattlesnake; **saber más que las culebras** to be crafty

culebrear *intr* to wriggle; wind, meander; zigzag

culebrón *m* foxy fellow; (Mex) poor farce

cule·co -ca *adj* self-satisfied; madly in love

cu·lí *m* (*pl* **-líes**) coolie

culina·rio -ria *adj* culinary

culipandear *intr* & *ref* (CAm, W-I) to welsh, be evasive

culminar *intr* to culminate

culo *m* seat, behind, backside; (*de animal*) buttocks; (*de un vaso*) bottom; **culo de mal asiento** fidgety person; **volver el culo** to run away

culote *m* base

culpa *f* blame, guilt, fault; **echar la culpa a** to put the blame on; **tener la culpa** to be wrong, be to blame

culpable *adj* blamable, guilty, culpable

culpa·do -da *adj* guilty ‖ *mf* culprit

culpar *tr* to blame, censure, accuse ‖ *ref* to take the blame

cultedad *f* fustian, affectation

culteranismo *m* euphuism, Gongorism

cultiparlar *intr* to speak in a euphuistic manner

cultismo *m* learned word; cultism, Gongorism

cultivar *tr* to cultivate; till

cultivo *m* cultivation; **cultivo de secano** dry farming

cul·to -ta *adj* cultivated, cultured; (*vocablo*) learned ‖ *m* worship; cult; **culto a la personalidad** personality cult

cultura *f* culture, cultivation

culturar *tr* to cultivate, till

cumbre *adj* top, greatest ‖ *f* summit; acme, pinnacle; **conferencia en la cumbre** summit meeting

cúmel *m* kümmel

cumiche *m* (CAm) baby (*youngest member of family*)

cumpa *m* (SAm) pal, buddy; comrade

cúmplase *m* approval, O.K.

cumplea·ños *m* (*pl* **-ños**) birthday

cumpli·do -da *adj* full; perfect; (*en muestras de urbanidad*) correct ‖ *m* correctness; courtesy; present

cumplimentar *tr* to compliment; to pay a complimentary visit to; to carry out, execute; (*un cuestionario*) to fill out

cumplimente·ro -ra *adj* effusive, obsequious

cumplimiento *m* (*muestra de urbanidad*) compliment; (*conducta decorosa*) correctness; fulfillment; perfection; **por cumplimiento** as a matter of pure formality

cumplir *tr* to fulfill, perform, execute; **cumplir años** to have a birthday; **cumplir . . . años** to be . . . years old ‖ *intr* to fall due; to expire; to keep one's promise; to finish one's service in the army; **cumplir con** to fulfill; to fulfill one's obligation to; **cumplir por** to act on behalf of; to pay the respects of ‖ *ref* to be fulfilled, to come true; to fall due; **cúmplase** approved

cumquibus *m* wherewithal

cúmulo *m* heap, pile, lot

cuna *f* cradle

cundido *m* olive, vinegar, and salt for shepherds; olive oil, cheese, and honey to make children eat

cundir *intr* to spread; swell, puff up; increase

cunear *tr* to cradle, rock in a cradle ‖ *intr* to rock, swing, sway

cune·co -ca *mf* (Ven) baby (*youngest member of family*)

cuneta *f* gutter, ditch

cuña *f* wedge; (typ) quoin; **ser buena cuña** to take up a lot of room

cuñada *f* sister-in-law

cuñado *m* brother-in-law

cuñete *m* keg

cuño *m* die; stamp; mark

cuota *f* quota, share; fee, dues; tuition fee

cupé *m* coupé

cupo *m* quota, share; (Mex) capacity

cupón *m* coupon; **cupón de racionamiento** ration coupon

cúpula *f* cupola; dome

cuquillo *m* cuckoo

cura *m* curate; (coll) priest; **este cura** (*yo*) (coll) yours truly (*I*) ‖ *f* cure; care, treatment; **cura de aguas** water cure; **cura de almas** care of souls; **cura de hambre** starvation diet; **cura de reposo** rest cure; **cura de urgencia** first aid; **no tener cura** to be hopeless, be incorrigible

curaca *m* (SAm) boss, chief ‖ *f* (Bol, Peru) priest's housekeeper

curación *f* cure, treatment

curade•ro -ra *mf* caretaker ‖ *m* (law) guardian

curande•ro -ra *mf* quack, healer

curar *tr* (*a un enfermo*) to treat; (*sanar*) cure, heal; (*curtir*) cure; (*la madera*) season; (*una herida*) dress ‖ *intr* to cure; recover; **curar de** to take care of; recover from; mind, pay attention to ‖ *ref* to cure; cure oneself; get well, recover; get drunk; **curarse de** to recover from, get over; **curarse en salud** to be forewarned

curati•vo -va *adj & f* curative

curda *f* jag, drunk

cureña *f* gun carriage

curia *f* (hist) curia; (*de rey*) court; (*conjunto de abogados*) bar

curiales•co -ca *adj* hairsplitting, legalistic

curiosear *tr* to pry into ‖ *intr* to snoop; browse around

curiosidad *f* curiosity; (*objeto de arte raro y curioso*) curio; neatness, tidiness; care, carefulness

curio•so -sa *adj* curious; neat, tidy; careful ‖ *mf* busybody ‖ *m* (Ven) healer, medical man

currinche *m* cub reporter; hit playwright

cu•rro -rra *adj* flashy, sporty ‖ *m* sport, dandy

curruca *f* (orn) whitethroat; **curruca de cabeza negra** blackcap, warbler

curruta•co -ca *adj* dudish, sporty; chubby ‖ *m* dude, sport ‖ *f* chic dame

cursa•do -da *adj* skilled, experienced; (*asignatura*) taken

cursante *mf* student

cursar *tr* (*una materia, estudios*) to take, study; (*conferencias*) attend; (*una carta*) forward; (*un paraje*) frequent, to haunt ‖ *intr* to study; be current

cursear *intr* to have diarrhea

cursería *f* cheapness, flashiness, vulgarity; flashy lot of people

cursi *adj* cheap, flashy, vulgar, loud ‖ *m* sporty guy ‖ *f* flashy dame

cursien•to -ta *adj* diarrheic

cursilería *f* cheapness, flashiness, vulgarity; flashy lot of people

cursillo *m* refresher course; short course of lectures

cursi•vo -va *adj* cursive; italic ‖ *f* cursive; italics

curso *m* course; academic year, school year; price, quotation, current rate; **curso académico** academic year; **curso legal** legal tender; **cursos** loose bowels; **dar curso a** to give way to; to forward

cursor *m* slide; sliding contact; **cursor de procesiones** marshal

curtiduría *f* tannery

curtiembre *f* tannery

curtir *tr* (*las pieles*) to tan; (*el cutis de una persona*) tan, sunburn; harden, inure; **estar curtido en** to be skilled in, be expert in ‖ *ref* to become tanned, sunburned; become hardened; be weather-beaten

curva *f* curve; bend

curvadura *f* painful exhaustion

cur•vo -va *adj* curved, bent ‖ *f* see **curva**

cusca *f* (Col) jag, drunk; (Mex) prostitute, slut

cúspide *f* (*de montaña*) peak; (*de diente*) cusp; apex, tip, top

custodia *f* custody, care; (*de un preso*) guard; (eccl) monstrance

custodiar *tr* to guard, watch over

custodio *m* custodian; guard

cususa *f* (CAm) rum

cu•tí *m* (*pl* -**tíes**) bedtick, ticking

cutícula *f* cuticle

cutio *m* work, labor

cu•tis *m* (*& f*) (*pl* -**tis**) skin, complexion; **cutis anserina** goose flesh

cu•yo -ya *adj rel* whose

c/v *abbr* **cuenta de venta**

Ch

Ch, ch (che) *f* fourth letter of the Spanish alphabet

chabacanada or **chabacanería** *f* crudeness, coarseness, vulgarity

chabaca•no -na *adj* crude, coarse, vulgar ‖ *m* (Mex) apricot tree

chabola *f* shack, shanty; (mil) foxhole

chacal *m* jackal

chacanear *tr* (Chile) to spur, goad on; (Chile) to annoy, bother

chacare•ro -ra *mf* (SAm) farm laborer, field worker; (Col) quack doctor; (Urug) gossip

chacarrachaca *f* row, racket

chacolotear *intr* to clatter

chacota *f* laughter, racket; **hacer chacota de** to make fun of

chacotear *intr* to laugh and make a racket

chacra *f* farm house; small farm; sown field

chacua•co -ca *adj* ugly, crude, boorish ‖ *m* (CAm) cigar butt; (CAm) cheap cigar

cháchara *f* chatter, idle talk; **chácharas** trinkets, junk

chacharear *intr* to chatter

chafallar *tr* to botch

chafandín *m* conceited ass

chafar *tr* to rumple, muss; flatten; cut short; (Chile) to dismiss, send off

chafarrinar *tr* to blot, stain

chafarrinón *m* blot, stain; **echar un chafarrinón a** to insult, throw mud at

chaflán *m* chamfer

chaflanar *tr* to chamfer

chal *m* shawl

cha•lán -lana *adj* horse-dealing ‖ *mf* horse dealer; horse trader ‖ *m* broncobuster, horsebreaker ‖ *f* scow, flatboat

chalanear *tr* (*un negocio*) to pull off shrewdly; (*un caballo*) break; (Arg) to take advantage of ‖ *intr* to horse-trade

chalanería *f* horse trading

chalanes•co -ca *adj* horse-trading

chaleco *m* vest, waistcoat; **al chaleco** (Mex) by force; (Mex) for nothing; **chaleco salvavidas** life jacket

chalecón *m* (Mex) crook

chalupa *f* small two-master; launch, lifeboat; (Mex) corncake

chama•co -ca *mf* (Mex) youngster, urchin

chamago•so -sa *adj* (Mex) dirty, filthy; (Mex) botched

chamarasca *f* brushwood; brush fire

chamarille•ro -ra *mf* junk dealer, secondhand dealer ‖ *m* gambler

chamari•llón -llona *mf* poor card player

chamarra *f* sheepskin jacket

chamarreta *f* loose jacket; square poncho

chamba *f* fluke, scratch; (Mex) work

chambelán *m* chamberlain; (Mex) atomizer, spray

chambergo *m* (orn) bobolink; (Arg) soft hat

chambe•rí *adj* (*pl* **-ríes**) (Peru) showy, flashy

cham•bón -bona *adj* awkward, clumsy; lucky

chambonada *f* awkwardness, clumsiness; stroke of luck

chambonear *intr* to foozle

chambra *f* blouse; (Ven) din, uproar

chambrana *f* trim (*around a door*)

chamburgo *m* (Col) stagnant water, puddle

chamico *m* jimson weed; **dar chamico a** (SAm) to bewitch

chamorrar *tr* to shear

champán *m* sampan; (coll) champagne

champaña *f* champagne

cham•pú *m* (*pl* **-púes**) shampoo

chamuchina *f* rabble; populace

chamuscar §73 *tr* to singe, scorch; (Mex) to undersell

chamusco *m* singe, scorch

chamusquina *f* singeing; fight, row, quarrel; **oler a chamusquina** to look like a fight; smack of heresy

chancar §73 *tr* to crush; beat, beat up; botch

chance *m* (SAm) opportunity, chance

chancear *intr* & *ref* to joke, jest

chance•ro -ra *adj* joking, jesting

chanciller *m* chancellor

chancla *f* old shoe; house slipper

chancleta *mf* good-for-nothing ‖ *f* slipper; (Ven) accelerator

chanclo *m* overshoe, rubber

chancha *f* cheat, lie; (Chile) slut; **hacer la chancha** (Bol, Col, Chile) to play hooky

chanche•ro -ra *mf* (Arg, Chile) pork butcher

chan•cho -cha *adj* dirty, filthy ‖ *m* pig ‖ *f* see **chancha**

chanchulle•ro -ra *mf* crook

chandal *m* or **chándal** *m* jump suit, gym suit

changador *m* (SAm) errand boy

changarro *m* (Mex) small shop

chan•go -ga *adj* (Chile) dull, stupid; (Mex) sly, crafty ‖ *mf* (Mex) monkey ‖ *m* (Arg) house boy

chan•guí *m* (*pl* **-guíes**) trick, deception

chantaje *m* blackmail

chantajista *mf* blackmailer

chantar *tr* to put on; (SAm) to throw hard; (Urug) to keep waiting ‖ *ref* (*p.ej., el sombrero*) to clap on

chantre *m* cantor, precentor

chanza *f* joke, jest

chao *interj* (coll) good-by

chapa *f* sheet, plate; (*hoja fina de madera*) veneer; (*en las mejillas*) flush; (coll) good sense, judgment; (Chile) lock, bolt; **chapa de circulación** (aut) license plate; **chapas** flipping coins

chapa•do -da *adj* plated; veneered; **chapado a la antigua** old-fashioned

chapalear *intr* (*el agua; las manos y los pies en el agua*) to splash; (*la herradura floja*) clatter

chapar *tr* to cover or line with sheets of metal; veneer

chaparrear *intr* to pour

chapa•rro -rra *mf* (Mex) child, little one; (Mex) runt ‖ *m* scrub oak

chaparrón *m* downpour

chapea•do -da *adj* lined with sheets of metal; veneered ‖ *m* plywood; veneer

chapear *tr* to cover or line with sheets of metal; veneer

chapista *m* tinsmith, tinman

chapitel *m* (*remate de torre*) spire; (*capitel de columna*) capital

chapodar *tr* to trim, clear of branches; to curtail

chapotear *tr* to sponge, moisten ‖ *intr* to splash

chapucear *tr* & *intr* to botch, bungle

chapuce•ro -ra *adj* crude, rough; clumsy, bungling ‖ *mf* bungler; amateur ‖ *m* blacksmith; junk dealer

chapurrar *tr* & *intr* to jabber

chapurreo *m* jabber

cha•puz *m* (*pl* **-puces**) duck, ducking

chapuzar §60 *tr*, *intr* & *ref* to duck

chaqué *m* cutaway coat, morning coat

chaqueta *f* jacket

chaquetilla *f* short jacket; (Ecuad) lady's vest

chaquetón *m* reefer, pea jacket

charamusca *f* brushwood, firewood; (Mex) candy twist

charanga *f* (mil) brass band

charangue•ro -ra *adj* crude, rough; bungling, clumsy ‖ *mf* bungler

charca *f* pool

charco *m* puddle

charla *f* talk, chat; talk, lecture; chatter, prattle

charla•dor -dora *adj* garrulous; gossipy ‖ *mf* chatterbox; gossip

charlar *intr* to talk, chat; chatter, prattle

charla•tán -tana *adj* garrulous; gossipy ‖ *mf* chatterbox; gossip; charlatan

charlatanería *f* garrulity, loquacity

charlatanismo *m* charlatanism; garrulity, loquacity

charnela *f* (*de puerta; de molusco*) hinge; (mach) knuckle

charol *m* varnish; patent leather; lacquered tray; **calzarse las de charol** (Arg, Urug) to hit the jackpot; **darse charol** to blow one's own horn

charola•do -da *adj* shiny

charolar *tr* to varnish, lacquer

charpa *f* pistol belt; (*cabestrillo*) sling

charquear *tr* (*carne de vaca*) to jerk; slash, cut to pieces

charqui *m* jerked beef

charrada *f* country dance; boorishness; tawdry ornamentation

charretera *f* epaulet; garter; (*del aguador*) shoulder pad

charriada *f* (Mex) rodeo

cha•rro -rra *adj* coarse, ill-bred; flashy, loud, showy; Salamanca ‖ *mf* peasant; Salamanca peasant ‖ *m* broad-brimmed hat; Mexican cowboy

chasca *f* brushwood

chascar §73 *tr* (*la lengua*) to click; (*algún manjar*) crunch; (*engullir*) swallow ‖ *intr* to crack, crackle

chascarrillo *m* funny story

chas•co -ca *adj* (Arg, Bol) crinkly, crinkly-haired ‖ *m* joke, trick; disappointment; **dar un chasco a** to play a trick on; **llevar** or **llevarse (un) chasco** to be disappointed

chas•cón -cona *adj* (Bol, Chile) disheveled; (Bol, Chile) bushy-haired; (Bol, Chile) clumsy, unskilled

cha•sis *m* (*pl* **-sis**) chassis

chasquear *tr* (*un látigo*) to crack; play a trick on; disappoint ‖ *intr* to crack ‖ *ref* to be disappointed

chasqui *m* (SAm) messenger, courier

chasquido *m* crack; crackle

chata *f* barge, scow; flatcar; bedpan; (Mex) dear, darling

chatarra *f* iron slag; junk, scrap iron

chatarrería *f* junk yard

chatarre•ro -ra *mf* junk dealer, scrapiron dealer

cha•to -ta *adj* flat; flat-nosed; blunt; commonplace; disappointed ‖ *m* wineglass ‖ *f* see **chata**

chatre *adj* (Chile, Ecuad) all dressed up

chauvinismo *m* chauvinism

cha•val -vala *adj* (coll) young ‖ *m* lad ‖ *f* lass

chaveta *f* cotter pin; **perder la chaveta** to go out of one's head

chayote *m* chayote, vegetable pear; dunce, fool

chazar §60 *tr* (*la pelota*) to stop; (*el sitio donde paró la pelota*) to mark

che *interj* (SAm) say!, hey!

checar *tr* (Mex) to check

che•co -ca *adj* & *mf* Czech

checoeslova•co -ca *adj* & *mf* Czecho-Slovak

Checoeslovaquia *f* Czecho-Slovakia

checoslova•co -ca *adj* & *mf* Czecho-Slovak

Checoslovaquia *f* Czecho-Slovakia

chechén *m* (Mex) poison ivy

chécheres *mpl* trinkets, junk

chelín *m* shilling

cheque *m* check; **cheque de viajeros** traveler's check

chequear *tr* (CAm, W-I) to check

chequeo *m* control; checkup

chequera *f* checkbook

chévere *adj* *invar* terrific, fabulous; **¡que chévere!** terrific!

chica *f* lass, little girl; girl; my dear; **chica de cita** call girl; **chica de la vida alegre** party girl

chicalote *m* Mexican poppy

chicle *m* chewing gum

chiclear *intr* (Mex) to chew gum

chi•co -ca *adj* small, little; young ‖ *mf* child, youngster ‖ *m* lad, little boy; young fellow; old man; hand, turn ‖ *f* see **chica**

chicolear *intr* to pay compliments, to flirt ‖ *ref* (Arg, Peru) to enjoy oneself

chico•te -ta *mf* husky youngster ‖ *m* cigar; cigar stub; whip

chicotear *tr* to beat up; kill

chicue•lo -la *adj* small, little ‖ *m* little boy ‖ *f* little girl

chicha *f* corn liquor; **no ser ni chicha ni limonada** to be good for nothing

chícharo *m* pea; (Col) poor cigar; (Mex) apprentice

chicharra *f* harvest fly; chatterbox; **cantar la chicharra** (coll) to be hot and sultry

chicharrón *m* residue of hog's fat; burnt meat; sunburned person; wrinkled person

chiche *adj* *invar* nice, pretty

chichear *tr* & *intr* to hiss

chi•chón -chona *adj* (CAm) easy; (SAm) joking; (Guat) large-breasted ‖ *m* lump, bump on the head

chifla *f* hissing, whistling; paring knife; **estar de chifla** (Mex) to be in a bad humor

chifla•do -da *adj* (coll) daffy, nutty ‖ *mf* crackbrain, nut

chifladura *f* daffiness, nuttiness; whim, wild idea

chiflar *tr* (*a un actor*) to hiss; (*vino o licor*) to gulp down; (*el cuero*) to pare ‖ *intr* to whistle; (*las aves*) (Guat, Mex) to sing ‖ *ref* to go crazy

chifle *m* whistle; (*para cazar aves*) bird call; powder flask

chiflido *m* whistle, hiss

ch
ch

chiflón *m* (SAm) cold blast of air; rapids; slide of loose stone

chilaba *f* jelab, jellaba

Chile *m* Chile

chile•no -na *adj & mf* Chilean

chilote *m* (CAm) ear of corn

chilla *f* fox call, hare call; clapboard; (Chile) small fox; (Mex) top gallery

chillar *intr* to shriek; to squeak; to hiss, sizzle; (*los colores*) to scream || *ref* to take offense

chillido *m* shriek, scream

chi•llón -llona *adj* shrill, high-pitched; screaming; (*color*) loud

chimenea *f* chimney, smokestack; fireplace, hearth; stovepipe hat; (naut) funnel

chimpancé *m* chimpanzee

china *f* Chinese woman; china, porcelain; pebble; nursemaid; (Col) spinning top || **China** *f* China

chinche *mf* bore, tiresome person || *m* (*clavito de cabeza chata*) thumbtack || *f* (*insecto*) bedbug; **caer** or **morir como chinches** to die like flies

chinchorre•ro -ra *adj* gossipy, mischievous

chincho•so -sa *adj* boring, tiresome

chinero *m* china closet

chines•co -ca *adj* Chinese || **chinescos** *mpl* (mus) bell tree

chingar §44 *tr* to tipple; (CAm) to bob, dock; (CAm, Mex) to bother, annoy || *ref* to tipple; fail

chin•go -ga *adj* (CAm) short; (CAm) dull, blunt; (CAm) naked

chinguirito *m* cheap rum; swig of liquor

chi•no -na *adj & mf* Chinese || *m* (*idioma*) Chinese; (Col) boy, newsboy; (Mex) curl || *f* see **china**

chipichipi *m* drizzle, mist

Chipre *f* Cyprus

chiquero *m* pigsty; bull pen

chiquillada *f* childish prank

chiqui•to -ta *adj* small, little || *mf* little one || *m* (*de vino*) snifter; (Arg) moment, instant || *f* five cents; **no andarse con** or **en chiquitas** to talk right off the shoulder

chiquitura *f* trifle, small matter

chiribita *f* spark; daisy; **chiribitas** spots before the eyes

chiribitil *m* garret; cubbyhole

chirimbolos *mpl* utensils, vessels

chirimía *f* hornpipe

chiripa *f* (billiards) fluke, scratch; stroke of luck

chirivía *f* parsnip

chirle *adj* insipid, tasteless

chirlo *m* slash or scar on the face

chirlota *f* (Mex) meadow lark

chirona *f* jail, jug

chirriar §77 *intr* to creak, squeak; shriek; hiss, sizzle; sing or play out of tune || *ref* (Col) to go on a spree; (Col) to shiver

chirrido *m* creak, squeak; shriek; hiss, sizzle

chirrión *m* squeaky cart; (SAm) whip

chis *interj* sh-sh!; ¡chis, chis! pst!

chischás *m* clash of swords

chisguete *m* swig of wine; squirt

chisme *m* piece of gossip; trinket; **chisme de vecindad** idle talker; **chismes** gossip; articles; **chismes de aseo** toilet articles

chismear *intr* to gossip

chismo•so -sa *adj* gossipy, catty || *mf* gossip

chispa *f* spark; (*pequeña cantidad*) drop; lightning; (fig) sparkle, wit; (coll) drunk, spree; (Col) rumor; **coger una chispa** to go on a drunk; **chispa de entrehierro** (elec) jump spark; **chispas** sprinkle (*of rain*); **dar chispa** (Guat, Mex) to work, to click; **echar chispas** to blow up, hit the ceiling

chispeante *adj* sparkling

chispar *tr* to throw (someone) out

chispear *intr* to spark; sparkle; drizzle, sprinkle

chis•po -pa *adj* tipsy || *m* swallow, drink || *f* see **chispa**

chisporrotear *intr* to spark, sputter

chispo•so -sa *adj* sputtering, sparking

chisquero *m* pocket lighter

chistar *intr* to speak, say something; **no chistar** to not say a word

chiste *m* joke; witticism; **caer en el chiste** to get the point; **dar en el chiste** to hit the nail on the head

chistera *f* fish basket; (coll) top hat

chisto•so -sa *adj* funny; witty || *mf* funny person; wit

chita *f* anklebone; quoits; **a la chita callando** quietly, secretly; **dar en la chita** to hit the nail on the head

chiticalla *mf* (*persona que no revela lo que sabe*) (coll) clam || *f* (coll) secret

chito *interj* hush!, sh-sh!

chivato *m* kid, young goat; (*soplón*) squealer; (Bol) apprentice, helper; (Chile) cheap rum

chi•vo -va *mf* kid || *m* billy goat; (Mex) day's wage; (Col, Ecuad, Ven) fit of rage || *f* nanny goat

chocante *adj* shocking; coarse, crude; (Col) annoying; (Mex) disagreeable

chocar §73 *tr* to shock, annoy, irritate; surprise; (*vasos*) clink; please; ¡choque Vd. esos cinco! shake! || *intr* to shock; collide; clash, fight

chocarre•ro -ra *adj* coarse, crude || *mf* crude joker

choclo *m* wooden overshoe; (Mex) low shoe; (SAm) tender ear of corn

chocolate *m* chocolate

chocha *f* woodcock

chochear *intr* to be in one's dotage; dote, be infatuated

chochera *f* dotage; (Arg, Peru) favorite

cho•chez *f* (*pl* -checes) dotage; doting act or remark

cho•cho -cha *adj* doting; doddering || *m* stick of cinnamon candy; **chochos** candy to quiet a child || *f* see **chocha**

chófer *m* chauffeur

chofeta *f* fire pan (*for lighting cigars*)

cho•lo -la *adj* half-breed (*Indian and white*) || *mf* Indian; half-breed; (Chile) coward; (SAm) darling

cholla *f* (coll) noodle, head; (coll) ability, brains

chomite *m* (Mex) coarse wool; (Mex) woolen skirt

chontal *m* uneducated person

chopo *m* black poplar; gun, rifle; **chopo de Italia** Lombardy poplar; **chopo del Canadá** or **de Virginia** cottonwood; **chopo lombardo** Lombardy poplar

choque *m* shock; collision, impact; clash, conflict, skirmish; (elec) choke, choke coil; **choque en cadena** (aut) pileup, mass collision

choricería *f* sausage shop

chorizo *m* smoked pork sausage

chorlito *m* plover, golden plover; scatterbrains

chorrea•do -da *adj* dirty; spotty

chorrear *intr* to gush, spurt, spout; drip; trickle

chorrera spout, channel; cut, gulley; rapids; lace front, jabot; (Arg) string, stream

chorrillo *m* constant stream; **irse por el chorrillo** to follow the current; **tomar el chorrillo de** to get the habit of

chorro *m* jet, spurt; stream, flow; **a chorros** in abundance; **chorro de arena** sandblast

chotaca•bras *m* (*pl* **-bras**) goatsucker

chotear *tr* to make fun of; (Guat) to keep an eye on

choteo *m* jeering, mocking

choza *f* hut, cabin, lodge

chubasco *m* squall, shower; (fig) temporary setback; **chubasco de agua** rainstorm; **chubasco de nieve** blizzard

chubasco•so -sa *adj* stormy, threatening

chucruta *f* sauerkraut

chucha *f* female dog, bitch; drunk, jag; (Col) opossum; (Col) body odor

chuchaque *m* (Ecuad) hangover

chuchear *tr* (*caza menor*) to trap ‖ *intr* to whisper

chuchería *f* knickknack, trinket; delicacy, tidbit

chu•cho -cha *adj* (CAm) mean, stingy; (*fruto*) (Col) watery; (Col) wrinkled ‖ *m* (coll) dog ‖ *f* see **chucha**

chue•co -ca *adj* (Mex) twisted, bent; (SAm) bow-legged; (Mex) crippled ‖ *m* (Mex) dealing in stolen goods ‖ *f* stump; hockey; hockey ball

chufa *f* groundnut

chufletear *intr* to joke, jest

chula *f* flashy dame (*in lower classes of Madrid*)

chulada *f* light-hearted remark; vulgarity

chul•co -ca *mf* (Bol) baby (*youngest child*)

chulear *tr* to tease; (Mex) to flirt with

chuleta *f* chop, cutlet; slap, smack; (*de los estudiantes*) (coll) crib, pony; **chuleta de cerdo** pork chop; **chuleta de ternera** veal chop; **chuletas** sideburns, side whiskers

chu•lo -la *adj* flashy, sporty; foxy, slick; (Guat, Mex) pretty, cute ‖ *m* sporty fellow (*in lower classes of Madrid*); pimp, procurer; gigolo; butcher's helper; (taur) attendant on foot ‖ *f* see **chula**

chumbera *f* prickly pear

chume•ro -ra *mf* (CAm) apprentice

chunches *mpl* (CAm) junk, stuff

chunga *f* jest, fun

chunguear *ref* to jest, joke

chupa *f* frock, coat; (Arg) drunk, jag; (Arg) tobacco pouch

chupa•do -da *adj* thin, skinny; drunk; (*falda*) tight ‖ *f* suck; pull (*on a cigar*)

chupador *m* teething ring, pacifier

chupaflor *m* (Mex, Ven) hummingbird

chupalla *f* straw hat

chupamirto *m* (Mex) hummingbird

chupar *tr* to suck; (*la hacienda ajena*) milk, sap; absorb ‖ *intr* to suck ‖ *ref* to get thin, lose strength; (*los labios*) smack

chupatin•tas *mf* (*pl* **-tas**) (coll) office drudge

chupete *m* (*para un niño*) pacifier; lollipop; **de chupete** fine, splendid

chu•pón -pona *mf* swindler ‖ *m* (bot) sucker, shoot; (mach) plunger; baby bottle; pacifier

chupópte•ro -ra *mf* sponge

chuquisa *f* (Chile, Peru) prostitute

churrasco *m* barbecue

churrasquear *tr* to barbecue

churre *m* filth, dirt, grease

churrete *m* dirty spot (*on hands or face*)

churrigueres•co -ca *adj* churrigueresque; loud, flashy, tawdry

chu•rro -rra *adj* (*lana*) coarse; (*carnero*) coarse-wooled ‖ *m* coarse-wooled sheep; fritter; botch

churrulle•ro -ra *adj* gossipy, loquacious ‖ *mf* gossip, chatterbox

churrusco *m* burnt piece of bread

churumbela *f* hornpipe, flageolet; maté cup; (Col) worry, anxiety; (Col, Ecuad) pipe

churumo *m* (coll) substance (*money, brains, etc.*)

chus *interj* here! (*to call a dog*); **no decir chus ni mus** to not say boo

chus•co -ca *adj* droll, funny; (Peru) ill-mannered; (*perro*) (Peru) mongrel

chusma *f* galley slaves; mob, rabble

chuza *f* (Mex) strike (*in bowling*)

D

D, d (de) *f* fifth letter of the Spanish alphabet

D. *abbr* **don**

D.ᵃ *abbr* **doña**

daca give me, hand over; **andar al daca y toma** to be at cross purposes

dactilógra•fo -fa *mf* typist ‖ *m* typewriter

dactilograma *m* fingerprint

dádiva *f* gift, present

dadivo•so -sa *adj* liberal, generous

da•do -da *adj* given; **dado que** provided, as

ch
da

long as ‖ *m* die; **cargar los dados** to load the dice; **dados** dice; **el dado está tirado** the die is cast

daga *f* dagger

dalia *f* dahlia

dama *f* lady, dame; maid-in-waiting; (*en el juego de damas*) king; (*en el ajedrez y los naipes*) queen; (theat) leading lady; concubine, mistress; **dama joven** (theat) young lead; **damas** checkers; **señalar dama** (*en el juego de damas*) to crown a man

damajuana *f* demijohn

damasquina•do -da *adj & m* damascene

damasquinar *tr* to damascene

damasqui•no -na *adj* damascene

damero *m* checkerboard

damisela *f* young lady; courtesan

damnación *f* damnation

damnificar §73 *tr* to damage, hurt

da•nés -nesa *adj* Danish ‖ *mf* Dane ‖ *m* (*idioma*) Danish

dáni•co -ca *adj* Danish

Danubio *m* Danube

danza *f* dance; dancing; dance team; **danza de cintas** Maypole dance; **danza de figuras** square dance; **meter en la danza** to drag in, involve

danza•dor -dora *mf* dancer

danzar §60 *tr* to dance ‖ *intr* to dance; butt in

danza•rín -rina *mf* dancer; meddler; scatterbrain

dañable *adj* harmful; reprehensible

daña•do -da *adj* bad, wicked; spoiled

dañar *tr* to hurt, damage, injure; spoil ‖ *ref* to be damaged; spoil

dañi•no -na *adj* harmful, destructive, noxious; wicked

daño *m* damage, harm; (Arg) witchcraft; **a daño de** on the responsibility of; **daños y perjuicios** (law) damages; **en daño de** to the detriment of; **hacer daño** to be harmful; **hacer daño a** to hurt; **hacerse daño** to hurt oneself; to get hurt

daño•so -sa *adj* harmful, injurious

dar §23 *tr* to give; cause; hit, strike; (*el reloj la hora*) strike; (*cartas*) deal; (*un paseo*) take; (*los buenos días*) wish; (*un film*) show; (*una capa de pintura*) put on, apply; **dar a conocer** to make known; **dar a luz** to bring out, publish; **dar cuerda a** (*un reloj*) to wind; **dar curso a** to circulate; **dar de beber a** to give something to drink to; **dar de comer a** to give something to eat to; **dar la razón a** to admit that (*someone*) is right; **dar prestado** to lend; **dar palmadas** to clap the hands; **dar por** to consider as; **dar que hablar** to cause talk; to stir up criticism; **dar que hacer** to cause annoyance or trouble; **dar que pensar** to give food for thought; to give rise to suspicion ‖ *intr* to take place; to hit, strike; (*el reloj; dos, tres, etc. horas*) to strike; to tell, intimate; **dar a** to overlook; **dar con** to run into; **dar contra** to run against, strike against; **dar de sí** to stretch, to give; **dar en** to overlook; to hit; to run into; to fall into; to be bent on; (*un chiste*)

to catch on to; **dar sobre** to overlook; **dar tras** to pursue hotly ‖ *ref* to give oneself up; to give in, yield; to occur, be found; **darse a** to devote oneself to; **darse a conocer** to make a name for oneself, make oneself known; to get to know each other; **darse cuenta de** to realize, become aware of; **darse la mano** to shake hands; **dárselas de** to pose as; **darse por aludido** to take the hint; **darse por entendido** to show an understanding; to show appreciation; **darse por ofendido** to take offense; **darse por vencido** to give up, to acknowledge defeat

dardo *m* dart; cutting remark

dares y tomares *mpl* quarrels, disputes

dársena *f* basin, marina, inner harbor

darvinia•no -na *adj & mf* Darwinian, Darwinist

darvinismo *m* Darwinism

data *f* date; (*en una cuenta*) item; **de larga data** of long standing; **estar de mala data** to be in a bad humor

datar *tr & intr* to date; **datar de** to date from

dátil *m* date

datilera *f* date, date palm

dati•vo -va *adj & m* dative

dato *m* datum; basis, foundation

de *prep* of; from; about; **acompañado de** accompanied by; **cubierto de** covered with; **de noche** in the nighttime; **de no llegar nosotros a la hora** if we do not arrive on time; **más de** more than; **tratar de** to try to

deán *m* (eccl) dean

deanato *m* or **deanazgo** *m* deanship

debajo *adv* below, underneath; **debajo de** below, under

debate *m* debate; altercation, argument

debatir *tr & intr* to debate; fight, argue ‖ *ref* to struggle

debe *m* debit

debelar *tr* to conquer, vanquish

deber *m* duty; (*deuda*) debt; homework, school work; **últimos deberes** last rites ‖ *tr* to owe ‖ *v aux* to have to, ought to, must, should; **deber de** must, most likely ‖ *ref* to be committed; **deberse a** to be due to

debidamente *adv* duly

debi•do -da *adj* due, owed; proper, right; **debido a** due to

débil *adj* weak

debilidad *f* weakness, debility

debilitar *tr & ref* to weaken

débito *m* debt, debit; responsibility

debutante *mf* debutant(e), beginner

debutar *intr* to make one's start, appear for the first time

década *f* decade

decadencia *f* decadence

decadente *adj & mf* decadent

decaer §15 *intr* to decay, decline, fail, weaken; (naut) to drift from the course

decampar *intr* (mil) to decamp

decanato *m* deanship

decano *m* dean

decanta•do -da *adj* puffed-up, overrated

decapitar *tr* to decapitate

decelerar *tr, intr, & ref* to decelerate
decencia *f* decency
decenio *m* decade
dece•no -na *adj & m* tenth
decentar §2 *tr* to cut the first slice of; begin to damage ‖ *ref* to get bedsores
decente *adj* decent, proper; decent-looking
decepción *f* disappointment
decepcionar *tr* to disappoint
decidi•do -da *adj* decided, determined
decidir *tr* to decide; persuade ‖ *intr & ref* to decide
deci•dor -dora *adj* facile, fluent, witty
decimal *adj & m* decimal
déci•mo -ma *adj & m* tenth
decimocta•vo -va *adj* eighteenth
decimocuar•to -ta *adj* fourteenth
decimono•no -na *adj* nineteenth
decimonove•no -na *adj* nineteenth
decimoquin•to -ta *adj* fifteenth
decimosépti•mo -ma *adj* seventeenth
decimosex•to -ta *adj* sixteenth
decimoterce•ro -ra *adj* thirteenth
decimoter•cio -cia *adj* thirteenth
decir *m* say-so; **al decir de** according to ‖ §24 *tr* to say; tell; (*disparates*) talk; **como si dijéramos** so to speak, in a manner of speaking; **decir entre sí** to say to oneself; **decirle a uno cuántas son cinco** to tell a person what's what; **decir para sí** to say to oneself; **decir por decir** to talk for talk's sake; **decir que no** to say no; **decir que sí** to say yes; **decírselo a una persona deletreado** to spell it out to a person; **es decir** that is to say; **mejor dicho** rather; **¡por algo te lo dije!** I told you so!; **por decirlo así** so to speak ‖ *intr* to suit, fit; **¡diga!** (*al contestar el teléfono*) hello! ‖ *ref* to be said; be called; **se dice** it is said, they say
decisión *f* decision
decisi•vo -va *adj* decisive
declamar *tr & intr* to declaim
declaración *f* declaration; (*en bridge*) bid; **declaración de renta** tax return
declarante *mf* declarant, deponent; (*en el juego de bridge*) bidder
declarar *tr* to declare; (*en bridge*) bid; (*law*) to depose ‖ *ref* to declare oneself; break out, take place
declarati•vo -va *adj* declarative
declinación *f* declination; fall, drop; decline; (gram) declension
declinar *tr & intr* to decline
declive *m* descent, declivity, slope
declividad *f* declivity
decodificador *m* (telv) decoder
decollaje *m* (aer) take-off
decollar *intr* (aer) to take off
decomisar *tr* to seize, confiscate
decomiso *m* seizure, confiscation
decoración *f* decoration; memorizing; (theat) set, scenery; **decoraciones** (theat) scenery; **decoración interior** interior decoration
decorado *m* decoration; (theat) décor, scenery; memorizing
decora•dor -dora *mf* decorator
decorar *tr* to decorate; memorize

decoro *m* decorum; honor, respect; decency, propriety
decoro•so -sa *adj* decorous; respectful; decent
decrecer §22 *intr* to decrease, grow smaller, grow shorter
decrepitar *intr* to crackle
decrépi•to -ta *adj* decrepit
decretar *tr* to decree
decreto *m* decree
decurso *m* course; **en el decurso de** in the course of
dechado *m* sample, model, example; (*labor de las niñas*) sampler
dedada *f* touch, spot; **dar una dedada de miel a** to feed the hopes of
dedal *m* thimble
dedalera *f* foxglove
dedeo *m* (mus) finger dexterity
dedicación *f* dedication; (*aplicación*) diligence
dedicar §73 *tr* to dedicate; devote; autograph ‖ *ref* to devote oneself
dedicatoria *f* dedication
dedil *m* fingerstall
dedillo *m* little finger; **saber** or **tener al dedillo** to have at one's finger tips, have a thorough knowledge of
dedo *m* finger; toe; bit; **alzar el dedo** (*en señal de dar palabra*) to raise one's hand; **cogerse los dedos** to burn one's fingers; **dedo auricular** little finger; **dedo cordial, de en medio,** or **del•corazón** middle finger; **dedo gordo** thumb; big toe; **dedo índice** index finger, forefinger; **dedo meñique** little finger; **dedo mostrador** forefinger; **dedo pulgar** thumb; big toe; **estar a dos dedos de** to be within an ace of; **irse de entre los dedos** (coll) to slip between the fingers; **tener en la punta de los dedos** to have at one's fingertips
deducción *f* deduction; drawing off
deducir §19 *tr* (*concluir*) to deduce; (*rebajar*) deduct; (law) to allege
defecar §73 *intr* to defecate
defección *f* defection
defeccionar *intr & ref* (Chile) to defect
defecti•vo -va *adj* defective
defecto *m* defect; shortage, lack; **en defecto de** for lack of
defectuo•so -sa *adj* defective; lacking
defender §51 *tr* to defend; protect; delay, interfere with
defensa *f* defense; fender, guard; (*del toro*) horn; (*del elefante*) tusk; (*del automóvil*) bumper; **defensa marítima** (Arg) sea wall; **defensa propia** self-defense
defensi•vo -va *adj & f* defensive
defen•sor -sora *adj* defending ‖ *mf* defender; (law) counsel for the defense
deferencia *f* deference
deferente *adj* deferential
deferir §68 *tr* to delegate ‖ *intr* to defer
deficiencia *f* deficiency
deficiente *adj* deficient
défi•cit *m* (*pl* **-cits**) deficit
deficita•rio -ria *adj* deficit

da
de

definición *f* definition; decision, verdict
defini•do -da *adj* definite; sharp, defined
definir *tr* to define; settle, determine
definiti•vo -va *adj* definitive; **en definitiva** after all, in short
deflación *f* deflation
deflector *m* baffle
deformación *f* deformation; (rad) distortion
deformar *tr* to deform; disfigure; distort
deforme *adj* deformed
deformidad *f* deformity; gross error
defraudar *tr* to defraud, cheat; (*las esperanzas de una persona*) defeat; (*la claridad del día*) cut off
defuera *adv* outside; **por defuera** on the outside
defunción *f* decease, demise
degeneración *f* (*acción y efecto de degenerar*) degeneration; (*estado de degenerado; depravación*) degeneracy
degenera•do -da *adj & mf* degenerate
degenerar *intr* to degenerate
deglutir *tr & intr* to swallow
degollar §3 *tr* to cut the throat of; kill, massacre; (*un vestido*) cut low in the neck; (*el actor una obra dramática*) butcher, murder; become obnoxious to
degradante *adj* degrading
degradar *tr* to degrade; (mil) to break
degüello *m* throat-cutting; massacre; (*de un arma*) neck; **tirar a degüello** to try to harm
degustar *tr* (*probar*) to taste; (*percibir con deleite el sabor de*) to savor
dehesa *f* pasture land, meadow; (taur) range
deidad *f* deity
deificar §73 *tr* to deify
dejación *f* abandonment; (CAm, Chile, Col) negligence
dejadez *f* laziness; negligence; slovenliness; low spirits
deja•do -da *adj* lazy; negligent; slovenly; dejected
dejamiento *m* laziness; negligence; indolence, languor, indifference
dejar *tr* to leave; abandon; let, allow, permit; **dejar caer** to drop, let fall; **dejar feo** to slight; **dejar fresco** to leave in the lurch; **dejar por** + *inf* or **que** + *inf* to leave (*something*) to be + *pp*, e.g., **hemos dejado dos manuscritos por corregir** or **que corregir** we left two manuscripts to be corrected ‖ *intr* to stop; **dejar de** to stop, cease; fail to ‖ *ref* to be slovenly, neglect oneself; (*una barba*) grow; **dejarse de** (*disparates*) to cut out; (*preguntas*) stop asking; (*dudas*) put aside; **dejarse ver** to show up; be evident
dejillo *m* (*gusto que deja alguna comida*) aftertaste; (*acento regional*) local accent
dejo *m* (*gusto que deja alguna comida*) aftertaste; abandonment; slovenliness, neglect; local accent; (*placer o disgusto que queda después de hecha una cosa*) (fig) aftertaste
delación *f* accusation, denunciation
delantal *m* apron

delante *adv* before, ahead, in front; **delante de** before, ahead of, in front of
delantera *f* front; front row; advantage, lead; cowcatcher; **coger** or **tomar la delantera a** to get ahead of; get a start on; **delanteras** overalls
delante•ro -ra *adj* front, foremost, first ‖ *m* — **delantero centro** (*fútbol*) center forward ‖ *f* see **delantera**
delatar *tr* to accuse, denounce
delega•do -da *mf* delegate
delegar §44 *tr* to delegate
deleitable *adj* delectable, enjoyable
deleitar *tr & ref* to delight
deleite *m* delight
deleito•so -sa *adj* delightful
deletrear *tr & intr* to spell; decipher
deletreo *m* spelling
deleznable *adj* (*poco durable*) perishable; (*que se rompe fácilmente*) crumbly, fragile; (*que se desliza con facilidad*) slippery
delfín *m* (*primogénito del rey de Francia*) dauphin; (*mamífero cetáceo*) dolphin
delgadez *f* thinness, leanness; delicateness, lightness; perspicacity
delga•do -da *adj* thin, lean; delicate, light; sharp, perspicacious; (*terreno*) poor, exhausted ‖ *adv* — **hilar delgado** to hew close to the line; split hairs
delgadu•cho -cha *adj* skinny; slight
deliberar *tr & intr* to deliberate
delicadeza *f* delicacy, delicateness; scrupulousness
delica•do -da *adj* delicate; scrupulous
delicia *f* delight
delicio•so -sa *adj* delicious, delightful
delicti•vo -va *adj* punishable; criminal
delincuencia *f* guilt, criminality
delincuente *adj* guilty, criminal ‖ *mf* criminal
delineante *mf* designer ‖ *m* draughtsman
delinquir §25 *intr* to transgress, be guilty
deliquio *m* faint, swoon; weakening
delirante *adj* delirious
delirar *intr* to be delirious, rant, rave; talk nonsense
delirio *m* delirium; nonsense
delito *m* crime; **delito de incendio** arson; **delito de lesa majestad** lese majesty; **delito de mayor cuantía** (law) felony; **delito de menor cuantía** (law) misdemeanor
deludir *tr* to delude
demacra•do -da *adj* emaciated, wasted, thin
demago•go -ga *mf* demagogue
demanda *f* demand, petition; charity box; lawsuit; undertaking; (*del Santo Grial*) quest; **demanda maxima** (elec) peak load; **en demanda de** in search of; **tener demanda** to be in demand
demanda•do -da *mf* (law) defendant
demandante *mf* (law) complainant, plaintiff
demandar *tr* to ask for, request; (law) to sue ‖ *intr* (law) to sue, bring suit
demarcar §73 *tr* to demarcate
demás *adj* — **el demás ...** the other... , the rest of the ...; **estar demás** to be useless, to be in the way; **lo demás** the

rest; **por lo demás** furthermore, besides ‖ *pron* others; **los demás** the others, the rest ‖ *adv* besides; **por demás** in vain; too, too much

demasía *f* excess, surplus; daring, boldness; evil, guilt, wrong; insolence; **en demasía** excessively, too much

demasia•do -da *adj & pron* too much; **demasia•dos -das** too many ‖ **demasiado** *adv* too, too much, too hard

demasiar §77 *intr* to go too far

demediar *tr* to divide in half; use up half of; reach the middle of ‖ *intr* to be divided in half

dementa•do -da *adj* insane; demented

demente *adj* insane ‖ *mf* lunatic

democracia *f* democracy

demócrata *mf* democrat

demócrati•co -ca *adj* democratic

demoler §47 *tr* to demolish

demolición *f* demolition

demonía•co -ca *adj* demoniacal

demonio *m* demon, devil; **estudiar con el demonio** to be full of devilishness

demora *f* delay

demorar *tr & ref* to delay

demostración *f* demonstration

demostra•dor -dora *mf* demonstrator ‖ *m* hand (*of clock*)

demostrar §61 *tr* to demonstrate

demostrati•vo -va *adj* demonstrative

demudar *tr* to change, alter; disguise, cloak ‖ *ref* to change countenance, color

denegación *f* denial, refusal

denegar §66 *tr* to deny, refuse

denegrecer §22 *tr* to blacken ‖ *ref* to turn black

dengo•so -sa *adj* affected, finicky, overnice; (Col) strutting

dengue *m* affectation, finickiness, overniceness; (Col) strut, swagger

denguear *ref* (Col) to strut, swagger

denigrar *tr* to defame, revile; insult

denominación *f* denomination

denoda•do -da *adj* bold, daring

denostar §61 *tr* to abuse, insult, mistreat

denotar *tr* to denote

densidad *f* density; darkness, confusion

den•so -sa *adj* dense; dark, confused; crowded; thick, close

denta•do -da *adj* toothed; (*sello de correo*) perforated ‖ *m* gear; teeth

dentadura *f* set of teeth; **dentadura artificial** or **postiza** denture

dental *adj & f* dental

dentellada *f* bite; tooth mark

dentellar *intr* (*los dientes*) to chatter

dentellear *tr* to nibble, nibble at

dentera *f* envy; eagerness; **dar dentera** to set the teeth on edge; make the mouth water

dentición *f* teething

dentífri•co -ca *adj* (*pasta, polvos*) tooth ‖ *m* dentifrice

dentista *mf* dentist

dentistería *f* dentistry

dentística *f* (Chile) dentistry

dentro *adv* inside, within; **dentro de** inside, within; **dentro de poco** shortly; **por dentro** on the inside

denuedo *m* bravery, courage, daring

denuesto *m* abuse, insult, mistreatment

denuncia *f* denunciation; report; proclamation

denunciar *tr* to denounce; report; (*la guerra*) proclaim

deparar *tr* to furnish, provide; offer, present

departamento *m* department; (rr) compartment; (*piso*) apartment; naval district (*in Spain*)

departir *intr* to chat, converse

depauperación *f* impoverishment; exhaustion, weakening

depauperar *tr* to impoverish; exhaust, weaken

dependencia *f* dependence, dependency; branch, branch office; relationship, friendship; accessory; personnel

depender *intr* to depend; **depender de** to depend on; be attached to, belong to

dependienta *f* female employee, clerk

dèpendiente *adj* dependent; branch ‖ *mf* employee, clerk

deplorable *adj* deplorable

deplorar *tr* to deplore

deponer §54 *tr* to depose; set aside, remove; (*las armas*) lay down ‖ *intr* to depose; (*evacuar el vientre*) have a movement; (CAm, Mex) to vomit

deportación *f* deportation

deporta•do -da *mf* deportee

deportar *tr* to deport

deporte *m* sport; outdoor recreation

deportista *mf* sport fan ‖ *m* sportsman ‖ *f* sportswoman

deporti•vo -va *adj* sport, sports

depositante *mf* depositor

depositar *tr* to deposit; (*la esperanza, la confianza*) put, place; (*el equipaje*) check; (*a una persona en seguro*) commit; store ‖ *ref* to deposit, settle

deposita•rio -ria *mf* trustee; (*de un secreto*) repository ‖ *m* public treasurer

depósito *m* deposit; depot, warehouse; tank, reservoir; (*de libros en una biblioteca*) stack; (mil) depot; **depósito comercial** bonded warehouse; **depósito de agua** reservoir; **depósito de cadáveres** morgue; **depósito de cereales** grain elevator; **depósito de equipajes** (rr) checkroom; **depósito de gasolina** (aut) gas tank; **depósito de locomotoras** roundhouse; **depósito de municiones** munition dump

depravación *f* depravity, depravation

deprava•do -da *adj* depraved

depravar *tr* to deprave ‖ *ref* to become depraved

deprecar §73 *tr* to entreat, implore

depreciación *f* depreciation

depreciar *tr & ref* to depreciate

depresión *f* depression; drop, dip; (*en un muro*) recess

deprimir *tr* to depress; press down; push in; belittle; humiliate ‖ *ref* to be depressed; (*la frente de una persona*) recede

de
de

depurar *tr* to purify, cleanse; purge

derecha *f* right hand; right-hand side; (pol) right; **a la derecha** on the right, to the right

derechamente *adv* rightly; straight, direct; properly; wisely

derechazo *m* blow with the right; (box) right

dereche·ro -ra *adj* right, just

derechista *adj* rightist ǁ *mf* rightist, right-winger

dere·cho -cha *adj* right; right-hand; right-handed; straight; upright, standing; (CAm) lucky ǁ *m* right; law; exemption, privilege; road, path; (*de tela, papel, tabla*) right side; **derecho consuetudinario** common law; **derecho de gentes** law of nations, international law; **derecho de subscripción** (*a una nueva emisión de acciones*) (com) right; **derecho de tránsito** or **paso** right of way; **derecho internacional** international law; **derecho penal** criminal law; **derechos** dues, fees, taxes; (*de aduana*) duties; **derechos de almacenaje** storage, cost of storage; **derechos de autor** royalty; **derechos del hombre** rights of man; **derechos de propiedad literaria** or **derechos reservados** copyright; **derechos humanos** human rights; **según derecho** by right, by rights ǁ *f* see **derecha** ǁ **derecho** *adv* straight, direct; rightly

deriva (aer, naut) drift; **ir a la deriva** (naut) to drift, be adrift

derivado *m* by-product

derivar *tr* to derive ǁ *intr & ref* to derive, be derived; (aer, naut) to drift

dermatitis *f* dermatitis

derogar §44 *tr* to abolish, destroy, repeal

derrabar *tr* to dock, cut off the tail of

derrama·do -da *adj* extravagant, lavish

derramamiento *m* pouring, spilling; shedding; spreading; lavishing, wasting

derramar *tr* to pour, spill; (*sangre*) shed; spread, publish abroad; (*dinero*) lavish, waste ǁ *ref* to run over, overflow; spread, scatter; (*una corriente, un río*) open, empty; (*la plumafuente*) leak

derrame *m* pouring, spilling; (*de sangre*) shed, shedding; spread, scattering; lavishing, wasting; overflow; leakage; slope; chamfering; (pathol) discharge, effusion

derrapada *f* or **derrapaje** *f* (aut) skidding

derredor *m* circumference; **al** or **en derredor** around, round about

derrelícto *m* (naut) derelict

derrelínquir §25 *tr* to abandon, forsake

derrenga·do -da *adj* crooked, out of shape; crippled, lame

derrengar §44 or §66 *tr* to bend, make crooked; cripple

derreniego *m* curse

derreti·do -da *adj* madly in love; (*mantequilla*) drawn ǁ *m* concrete

derretimiento *m* thawing, melting; intense love, passion

derretir §50 *tr* to thaw, melt; (*la mantequilla*) draw; (*la hacienda*) squander ǁ *ref* to thaw, melt; fall madly in love; be quite susceptible; be worried, be impatient

derribar *tr* to destroy, tear down, knock down; wreck; (*un árbol*) fell; bring down, shoot down; overthrow; humiliate ǁ *ref* to fall down, tumble down; throw oneself on the ground

derribo *m* demolition, wrecking; (*de un árbol*) felling; overthrow; (*de un avión enemigo*) bringing down; **derribos** debris, rubble

derrocadero *m* rocky precipice

derrocar §73 or §81 *tr* to throw or hurl from a height; ruin, wreck, tear down; bring down, humble, overthrow

derrocha·dor -dora *mf* wastrel, squanderer

derrochar *tr* to waste, squander

derroche *m* wasting, squandering, extravagance

derrota *f* defeat, rout; road, route, way; (*de embarcación*) course

derrotadamente *adv* shabbily, poorly

derrotar *tr* to rout, put to flight; wear out; ruin ǁ *ref* (naut) to drift from the course

derrotero *m* course, route; ship's course

derrotismo *m* defeatism

derrotista *adj & mf* defeatist

derrubiar *tr & ref* to wash away, wear away

derrubio *m* washout

derruir §20 *tr* to tear down, demolish

derrumbadero *m* crag, precipice; hazard, risky business

derrumbamiento *m* headlong plunge; cave-in, collapse; **derrumbamiento de tierra** landslide

derrumbar *tr* to throw headlong ǁ *ref* to plunge headlong; collapse, cave in, crumble

derrumbe *m* precipice; landslide; cave-in

derviche *m* dervish

desabonar *ref* to drop one's subscription

desabono *m* cancellation of subscription; discredit, disparagement

desabor *m* insipidity, tastelessness

desabotonar *tr* to unbutton ǁ *intr* to blossom, bloom

desabri·do -da *adj* insipid, tasteless; gruff, surly; (*tiempo*) unsettled

desabrigar §44 *tr* to uncover, bare ǁ *ref* to bare oneself; undress

desabrir *tr* to give a bad taste to; displease, embitter

desabrochar *tr* to unclasp, unbutton, unfasten ǁ *ref* to unbosom oneself

desacalorar *ref* to cool off

desacatamiento *m* incivility, disrespect

desacatar *tr* to treat disrespectfully

desacato *m* incivility, disrespect, contempt; (*para con las cosas sagradas*) profanation

desacelerar *tr & ref* to decelerate

desacerta·do -da *adj* mistaken, wrong

desacertar §2 *intr* to be mistaken, be wrong

desacierto *m* error, mistake, blunder

desacomoda·do -da *adj* inconvenient; out of work; in straightened circumstances

desacomodar *tr* to inconvenience; discharge, dismiss

desacomodi·do -da *adj* (SAm) rude; impolite

desacomodo *m* discharge, dismissal

desaconseja•do -da *adj* ill-advised
desaconsejar *tr* to dissuade
desacordar §61 *tr* to put out of tune ‖ *ref* to get out of tune; become forgetful
desacorde *adj* out of tune; incongruous
desacostumbra•do -do -da *adj* unusual
desacostumbrar *tr* to break of a habit
desacreditar *tr* to discredit; disparage
desacuerdo *m* discord, disagreement; error, mistake; unconsciousness; forgetfulness
desadaptación *f* maladjustment
desadeudar *tr* to free of debt ‖ *ref* to get out of debt
desadormecer §22 *tr* to awaken; free of numbness ‖ *ref* to get awake; shake off the numbness
desadorna•do -da *adj* unadorned, plain; bare, uncovered
desadverti•do -da *adj* unnoticed; inattentive
desadvertimiento *m* inadvertence
desafección *f* dislike
desafec•to -ta *adj* adverse, hostile; opposed ‖ *m* dislike
desaferrar *tr* to unfasten, loosen; make (*a person*) change his mind; (*las áncoras*) weigh
desafiar §77 *tr* to challenge, defy, dare; rival, compete with
desafición *f* dislike
desaficionar *tr* to cause to dislike
desafilar *tr* to make dull ‖ *ref* to become dull
desafina•do -da *adj* flat, out of tune
desafío *m* challenge, dare; rivalry, competition
desafora•do -da *adj* colossal, huge; disorderly, outrageous
desafortuna•do -da *adj* unfortunate
desafuero *m* excess, outrage
desagracia•do -da *adj* ungraceful, graceless
desagradable *adj* disagreeable
desagradar *tr & intr* to displease ‖ *ref* to be displeased
desagradeci•do -da *adj* ungrateful
desagradecimiento *m* ungratefulness
desagrado *m* displeasure
desagraviar *tr* to make amends to, indemnify
desagravio *m* amends, indemnification
desagregación *f* disintegration
desagregar §44 *ref* to disintegrate
desaguadero *m* drain, outlet; (*ocasión de continuo gasto*) (fig) drain
desaguar §10 *tr* to drain, empty; squander, waste ‖ *intr* to flow, empty ‖ *ref* to drain, be drained
desagüe *m* drainage, sewerage; drain, outlet
desaguisa•do -da *adj* illegal ‖ *m* offense, outrage, wrong
desahijar *tr* (*las crías del ganado*) to wean ‖ *ref* (*las abejas*) to swarm
desahogadamente *adv* freely; comfortably, easily; impudently
desahoga•do -da *adj* brazen, forward; roomy; in comfortable circumstances
desahogar §44 *tr* to relieve, comfort; (*deseos, pasiones*) give free rein to ‖ *ref* to take it easy, get comfortable; unbosom oneself, open up one's heart; get out of

debt; **desahogarse en** (*denuestos*) to burst forth in
desahogo *m* brazenness; ample room; comfort; outlet, relief; comfortable circumstances
desahuciar *tr* to deprive of hope; evict, oust, dispossess ‖ *ref* to lose all hope
desahucio *m* eviction, ousting, dispossession
desaira•do -da *adj* unattractive, unprepossessing; unsuccessful
desairar *tr* to slight, snub, disregard
desaire *m* slight, snub, disregard; unattractiveness, lack of charm
desajustar *tr* to put out of order ‖ *ref* to get out of order; disagree
desalabanza *f* belittling, disparagement
desalabar *tr* to belittle, disparage
desala•do -da *adj* eager, in a hurry
desalar *tr* to desalt; clip the wings of ‖ *ref* to hasten, rush; **desalarse por** to be eager to
desalentar §2 *tr* to put out of breath; discourage ‖ *ref* to become discouraged
desalforjar *ref* to loosen one's clothing
desaliento *m* discouragement
desalinización *f* desalinization
desaliña•do -da *adj* slovenly, untidy; careless, slipshod
desaliño *m* slovenliness, untidiness; carelessness, neglect
desalma•do -da *adj* cruel, inhuman
desalojar *tr* to oust, evict; (*al enemigo*) to dislodge; (*el camino*) to clear ‖ *intr* to leave, move away, move out
desalquila•do -da *adj* vacant, unrented
desalterar *tr* to calm, quiet
desalumbra•do -da *adj* dazzled, blinded; confused, unsure of oneself
desamable *adj* unlikeable, unlovable
desamar *tr* to dislike, hate, detest
desamarrar *tr* to untie, unfasten; (naut) to unmoor
desamistar *ref* to fall out, become estranged
desamor *m* dislike, coldness; hatred
desamorrar *tr* to make (*a person*) talk
desamparar *tr* to abandon, forsake; give up
desamparo *m* abandonment, desertion; helplessness
desamuebla•do -da *adj* unfurnished
desandar §5 *tr* to retrace, go back over
desandraja•do -da *adj* ragged, in tatters
desangrar *tr* to bleed; drain; (fig) to bleed, impoverish ‖ *ref* to lose a lot of blood
desanimación *f* discouragement, downheartedness
desanima•do -da *adj* discouraged, downhearted; (*reunión*) lifeless, dull
desanimar *tr* to discourage, dishearten ‖ *ref* to become discouraged
desánimo *m* discouragement
desanublar *tr & ref* to clear up, brighten up
desanudar *tr* to untie; disentangle
desapacible *adj* unpleasant, disagreeable
desapadrinar *tr* to disavow; disapprove
desaparecer §22 *intr & ref* to disappear
desapareci•do -da *adj* missing; extinct ‖ **desaparecidos** *mpl* missing persons
desaparecimiento *m* disappearance

desaparejar *tr* to unharness, unhitch; (naut) to unrig

desaparición *f* disappearance; (Ven) death

desapasiona·do -da *adj* dispassionate, impartial

desapego *m* dislike, coolness, indifference

desapercibi·do -da *adj* unprepared; wanting; unnoticed

desapiada·do -da *adj* merciless, pitiless

desaplica·do -da *adj* idle, lazy

desapodera·do -da *adj* headlong, impetuous; violent, wild; excessive

desapoderar *tr* to dispossess; deprive of power ‖ *ref* — **desapoderarse de** to lose possession of, give up possession of

desapolillar *tr* to free of moths ‖ *ref* to expose oneself to the weather

desapreciar *tr* to depreciate

desaprecio *m* depreciation

desaprender *tr* to unlearn

desaprensión *f* composure, nonchalance

desapretar §2 *tr* to slacken, loosen; (typ) to unlock

desaprobación *f* disapproval

desaprobar §61 *tr & intr* to disapprove

desapropiar *tr* to divest ‖ *ref* — **desapropiarse de** to divest oneself of

desaprovecha·do -da *adj* unproductive; indifferent, lackadaisical

desaprovechar *tr* to not take advantage of ‖ *intr* to slip back

desarmable *adj* dismountable

desarmador *m* hammer (*of gun*); (Mex) screwdriver

desarmamiento *m* disarmament; arms reduction

desarmar *tr* to disarm; dismount, dismantle, take apart; (*la cólera*) temper, calm ‖ *intr & ref* to disarm

desarme *m* disarmament; dismantling, dismounting

desarraigar §44 *tr* to uproot, dig up; expel, drive out

desarregla·do -da *adj* out of order; slovenly, disorderly; intemperate

desarrimo *m* lack of support; stand-offishness

desarrollar *tr & intr* to develop, unroll, unfold ‖ *ref* to develop; unroll, unfold; take place

desarrollo *m* development; unrolling, unfolding; **ayuda al desarrollo** developmental aid

desarropar *tr & ref* to undress

desarrugar §44 *tr & ref* to unwrinkle

desarzonar *tr* to unsaddle, unhorse

desasea·do -da *adj* dirty, unclean, slovenly

desasentar §2 *tr* to remove; displease ‖ *ref* to stand up

desaseo *m* dirtiness, uncleanliness, slovenliness

desasir §7 *tr* to let go, let go of ‖ *ref* to come loose; let go; **desasirse de** to let go of; give up, get free of

desasosegar §66 *tr* to disquiet, worry, disturb

desasosiego *m* disquiet, worry

desastra·do -da *adj* disastrous; unfortunate, wretched; ragged, shabby

desastre *m* disaster; **ir al desastre** to go to rack and ruin

desastro·so -sa *adj* disastrous

desatacar §73 *tr* to unbuckle, untie

desatar *tr* to untie, undo, unfasten; solve, unravel ‖ *ref* to come loose; free oneself; (*la tempestad*) break loose; forget oneself, go too far; **desatarse en** (*denuestos*) to burst forth in

desatascar §73 *tr* to pull out of the mud; (*un conducto obstruído*) unclog; (*a una persona de un apuro*) extricate

desataviar §77 *tr* to disarray, undress

desatavío *m* disarray, undress, slovenliness

desate *m* (*de palabras*) flood; **desate del vientre** loose bowels

desatención *f* inattention; discourtesy, disrespect

desatender §51 *tr* to slight, disregard, pay no attention to

desatenta·do -da *adj* wild, disorderly, extreme

desaten·to -ta *adj* inattentive; discourteous, disrespectful

desatina·do -da *adj* wild, disorderly; foolish, nonsensical ‖ *mf* fool

desatinar *tr* to bewilder, confuse ‖ *intr* to talk nonsense, act foolishly; lose one's bearings

desatino *m* folly, nonsense; awkwardness, loss of touch

desatolondrar *tr* to bring to ‖ *ref* to come to one's senses

desatollar *tr* to pull out of the mud

desatornillador *m* screwdriver

desatornillar *tr* to unscrew

desatraillar §4 *tr* to unleash

desatrampar *tr* to unclog

desatrancar §73 *tr* to unbar, unbolt; unclog

desatufar *ref* to get out of the close air; cool off, quiet down

desautoriza·do -da *adj* unauthorized

desavenencia *f* disagreement, discord

desavenir §79 *tr* to cause disagreement among ‖ *ref* to disagree; **desavenirse con** to differ with, disagree with

desaventura *f* misfortune

desaviar §77 *tr* to mislead, lead astray

desavisa·do -da *adj* unadvised; ill-advised; thoughtless, careless

desayuna·do -da *adj* — **estar desayunado** to have had breakfast

desayunar *intr* to breakfast ‖ *ref* to breakfast; **desayunarse con** to have breakfast on; **desayunarse de** to get the first news of

desayuno *m* breakfast

desazón *f* insipidity, tastelessness; annoyance, displeasure; discomfort

desazonar *tr* to make tasteless; annoy, displease ‖ *ref* to feel ill

desbancar §73 *tr* to win the bank from; cut out, to supplant

desbandada *f* — **a la desbandada** helter-skelter, in confusion

desbandar *ref* to run away; disband; desert

desbarajustar *tr* to put out of order ‖ *ref* to get out of order, break down

desbarata·do -da *adj* debauched, corrupt ‖ *mf* libertine

desbaratar *tr* to destroy, spoil, ruin; squander, waste; (mil) to rout, throw into confusion ‖ *intr* to talk nonsense ‖ *ref* to be unbalanced

desbarrancadero *m* precipice

desbastar *tr* to smooth off; waste, weaken; (*a una persona inculta*) polish ‖ *ref* to become polished

desbautizar §60 *ref* to lose one's temper

desbeber *intr* (coll) to urinate

desbloquear *tr* to relieve the blockade of; (*crédito*) to unfreeze

desboca·do -da *adj* (*pieza de artillería*) wide-mouthed; (*herramienta*) nicked; (*caballo*) runaway; (*persona*) foul-mouthed

desbocar §73 *tr* to break the mouth of, break the spout of ‖ *intr* (*un río*) to empty; (*una calle*) run, open, end ‖ *ref* (*un caballo*) to run away, break loose; curse, swear

desbordamiento *m* overflow

desbordar *tr* to overwhelm ‖ *intr* & *ref* to overflow

desbozalar *tr* to unmuzzle

desbravar *tr* to tame, break in ‖ *intr* & *ref* to abate, moderate; cool off, calm down

desbrozar §60 *tr* to clear of underbrush, clear of rubbish

desbulla *f* oyster shell

desbulla·dor -dora *mf* oyster opener ‖ *m* oyster fork

desbullar *tr* (*la ostra*) to open

descabal *adj* incomplete, imperfect

descabalgar §44 *intr* to dismount, alight from a horse

descabella·do -da *adj* disheveled; rash, wild

descabellar *tr* to muss, dishevel

descabeza·do -da *adj* crazy, rash, wild

descabezar §60 *tr* to behead; (*un árbol*) top; (*una dificultad*) get the best off; **descabezar el sueño** to doze, snooze ‖ *intr* to border ‖ *ref* to rack one's brains

descabullir §13 *ref* to sneak out, slip away; refuse to face the facts

descachalandra·do -da *adj* untidy; tattered

descacharra·do -da *adj* (CAm) dirty, slovenly, ragged

descaecer §22 *intr* to decline, lose ground

descaecimiento *m* weakness; depression, despondency

descalabazar §60 *ref* to rack one's brain

descalabra·do -da *adj* banged on the head; **salir descalabrado** to come out the loser, be worsted

descalabrar *tr* to bang on the head; knock down ‖ *ref* to bang one's head

descalabro *m* misfortune, setback, loss

descalcificar §73 *tr* to decalcify

descalificar §73 *tr* to disqualify

descalzar §60 *tr* (*las botas, los guantes*) to take off; (*a una persona*) take the shoes or stockings off; undermine ‖ *ref* to take one's shoes or stockings off; take one's gloves

off; (*las botas, los guantes*) take off; (*el caballo*) lose a shoe

descal·zo -za *adj* barefooted; seedy, down at the heel

descamar *ref* to scale, scale off

descaminadamente *adv* off the road, on the wrong track

descaminar *tr* to mislead, lead astray ‖ *ref* to get lost; run off the road

descamino *m* going astray; leading astray; nonsense; contraband, smuggled goods

descamisa·do -da *adj* shirtless, ragged ‖ *m* wretch, ragamuffin

descampa·do -da *adj* free, open ‖ *m* open country

descansadero *m* resting place, stopping place

descansa·do -da *adj* rested, refreshed; calm, restful

descansar *tr* to rest, relieve; (*la cabeza, el brazo*) rest, lean ‖ *intr* to rest; lean; not worry; (*yacer en el sepulcro*) rest; **descansar en** to trust in

descanso *m* rest; peace, quiet; (*de la escalera*) landing; (theat) intermission; (Chile) toilet

descantillar *tr* to chip off; deduct

descañonar *tr* to pluck; shave against the grain; gyp

descapiruzar §60 *tr* (Col) to muss, rumple, crumple

descapotable *adj* & *m* (aut) convertible

descara·do -da *adj* barefaced, brazen, saucy

descarar *ref* to be impudent; **descararse a** to have the nerve to

descarga *f* unloading; (*de un arma de fuego*) discharge; (com) discount; (elec) discharge; **descarga de aduana** customhouse clearance

descargar §44 *tr* to unload; (*de una deuda u obligación*) free; (*un arma de fuego*) discharge; (*un golpe*) strike, deal; (elec) to discharge ‖ *intr* to unload; (*un río*) empty; (*una calle, paseo*) open; (*una nube en lluvia*) burst ‖ *ref* to unburden oneself; resign; **descargarse con** or **en uno de algo** to unload something on someone; **descargarse de** to get rid of; resign from; (*una imputación, un cargo*) clear oneself of

descargo *m* unloading; (*de una obligación*) discharge; (*del cargo que se hace a uno*) release, acquittal; receipt

descargue *m* unloading

descariño *m* coolness, indifference

descarnadamente *adv* right off the shoulder, bluntly

descarnar *tr* to remove the flesh from; chip; wear away; detach from earthly matters ‖ *ref* to lose flesh

descaro *m* brazenness, effrontery

descarriar §77 *tr* to mislead, lead astray ‖ *ref* to go wrong, go astray

descarrilamiento *m* derailment

descarrilar *intr* to jump the track; wander from the point ‖ *ref* to jump the track

descartable *adj* disposable

descartar *tr* to cast aside, reject; discard ‖ *ref* to shirk, evade; **descartarse de** (*un compromiso*) to shirk, evade

descarte *m* casting aside, rejection; discarding; (*cartas desechadas*) discard; shirking, evasion

descasar *tr* to divorce; disturb, disarrange

descascar §73 *tr* to husk, shell, peel ‖ *ref* to break to pieces; jabber, talk too much

descascarar *tr* to shell, peel ‖ *ref* to shell off, peel off

descascarillar *tr* & *ref* to shell, peel

descasta•do -da *adj* ungrateful, ungrateful to one's family

descaudala•do -da *adj* ruined, penniless

descendencia *f* descent

descendente *adj* descendent, descending; (*tren*) down

descender §51 *tr* to bring down, lower; (*la escalera*) descend, go down ‖ *intr* to descend, go down; flow, run; decline

descendiente *mf* descendant

descenso *m* descent; (*de temperatura*) drop; decline

descentralizar §60 *tr* to decentralize

desceñi•do -da *adj* loose-fitting, loose

descepar *tr* to pull up by the roots; extirpate, exterminate

descerebrar *tr* to brain

descerraja•do -da *adj* corrupt, evil, wicked

desciframiento *m* deciphering, decoding; resolving

descifrar *tr* to decipher, decode, figure out

desclasificar §73 *tr* to disqualify

descocer §16 *tr* to digest

descoco *m* impudence, insolence

descocholla•do -da *adj* (Chile) ragged

descolar *tr* to dock, crop; (*a un empleado*) (CAm) to discharge, fire; (Mex) to slight, snub

descolgar §63 *tr* to unhook; take down, lower; (*el auricular*) pick up ‖ *ref* to come down, come off; to show up suddenly; **descolgarse con** to blurt out

descolón *m* (Mex) slight, snub

descolorar *tr* & *ref* to discolor, fade

descolori•do -da *adj* faded, off color

descollante *adj* prominent, outstanding; chief, main

descollar §61 *intr* to tower, stand out; (fig) to excel, stand out

descomedi•do -da *adj* immoderate, excessive; rude, discourteous

descomedir §50 *ref* to be rude, be discourteous

descomer *intr* to have a bowel movement

descómo•do -da *adj* inconvenient

descompasa•do -da *adj* extreme, excessive

descompletar *tr* to break (*a set or series*)

descomponer §54 *tr* to decompose; disturb, disorganize; put out of order; set at odds ‖ *ref* to decompose; (*una persona, la salud de una persona*) fall to pieces; (*el tiempo*) change for the worse; (*el rostro*) become distorted; (*un aparato*) get out of order; to lose one's temper; **descomponerse con** to get angry with

descomposición *f* decomposition; disorder, disorganization; discord

descompostura *f* decomposition; disorder, untidiness; brazenness

descompresión *f* decompression

descompues•to -ta *adj* out of order; brazen, discourteous; irritated; drunk

descomulgar §44 *tr* to excommunicate

descomunal *adj* huge, colossal, enormous, extraordinary; (coll) humongous

desconcerta•do -da *adj* out of order; disconcerted, baffled, bewildered; slovenly; unbridled

desconcertar §2 *tr* to put out of order; disturb, upset; (*un hueso*) dislocate; disconcert, bewilder

desconcierto *m* disrepair; disorder; mismanagement; confusion; discomfiture; disagreement; lack of restraint; loose bowels

desconchabar *tr* to dislocate ‖ *ref* to become dislocated; disagree, fall out

desconchado *m* scaly part of wall; (*en la porcelana*) chip

desconchar *tr* & *ref* to chip, chip off; scale off

desconectar *tr* to detach; disconnect

desconfia•do -da *adj* distrustful, suspicious

desconfianza *f* distrust

desconfiar §77 *intr* to lose confidence; **desconfiar de** to lose confidence in, to distrust

desconformar *intr* to dissent, disagree ‖ *ref* to not go well together

descongelación *f* thaw, thawing out

descongelador *m* defroster

descongelar *tr* to melt; defrost; (com) to unfreeze

descongestión *f* decongestion; freeing up

descongestionar *tr* to decongest; free up

desconocer §22 *tr* to not know; disavow, disown; not recognize; slight, ignore; not see ‖ *ref* to be unknown; be quite changed, be unrecognizable

desconocidamente *adv* unknowingly

desconoci•do -da *adj* unknown; strange, unfamiliar; ungrateful ‖ *mf* unknown, unknown person

desconsentir §68 *tr* to not consent to

desconsidera•do -da *adj* ill-considered; inconsiderate

desconsola•do -da *adj* disconsolate, downhearted; (*estómago*) weak

desconsuelo *m* disconsolateness, grief; upset stomach

descontaminación *f* decontamination; **descontaminación de radiactividad** radioactive decontamination

descontar §61 *tr* to discount; deduct; take for granted; **dar por descontado que** to take for granted that

descontentadi•zo -za *adj* hard to please

desconten•to -ta *adj* & *m* discontent

descontinuar §21 *tr* to discontinue

descontrola•do -da *adj* uncontrolled; deregulated

descontrolar *tr* (com) deregulate; decontrol

desconvenar *tr* to call off

desconvenir §79 *intr* to disagree; not go together, not match; not be suitable ‖ *ref* to disagree

desconvidar *tr* to cancel an invitation to; (*lo prometido*) take back

descopar *tr* to top (*a tree*)

descorazonar *tr* to discourage

descorchar *tr* to remove the bark from; (*una botella*) uncork; break into

descornar §61 *tr* to dehorn ‖ *ref* to rack one's brains

descorrer *tr* to run back over; (*una cortina, un cerrojo*) draw ‖ *intr & ref* to flow, run off

descortés *adj* discourteous, impolite

descortesía *f* discourtesy, impoliteness

descortezar §60 *tr* to strip the bark from; take the crust off; polish ‖ *ref* to become polished

descoser *tr* to unstitch, rip ‖ *ref* to loose one's tongue; (coll) to break wind

descosi•do -da *adj* disorderly, wild; indiscreet; desultory ‖ *m* wild man; rip, open seam

descote *m* low neck

descoyuntar *tr* to dislocate; bore, annoy ‖ *ref* (*p.ej., el brazo*) to throw out of joint

descrédito *m* discredit

descreer §43 *tr* to disbelieve; discredit ‖ *intr* to disbelieve

descreí•do -da *adj* disbelieving, unbelieving ‖ *mf* disbeliever, unbeliever

descriar §77 *ref* to spoil; waste away

describir §83 to describe

descripción *f* description

descripti•vo -va *adj* descriptive

descto. *abbr* **descuento**

descuadrar *intr* to disagree; **descuadrar con** (Mex) to displease

descuajar *tr* to liquefy, dissolve; uproot; discourage ‖ *ref* to liquefy; drudge

descuartizar §60 *tr* to tear to pieces; quarter

descubierta *f* open pie; inspection; reconnoitering; (naut) scanning the horizon; **a la descubierta** openly; in the open; reconnoitering

descubiertamente *adv* clearly, openly

descubier•to -ta *adj* bareheaded; (*campo*) bare, barren; (*expuesto a reconvenciones*) under fire ‖ *m* deficiency, shortage; exposition of the Holy Sacrament; **al descubierto** in the open; unprotected; (*sin tener disponibles las acciones que se venden*) short, e.g., **vender al descubierto** to sell short ‖ *f* see **descubierta**

descubri•dor -dora *mf* discoverer ‖ *m* (mil) scout

descubrimiento *m* discovery

descubrir §83 *tr* to discover; uncover, lay open, reveal; invent; (*p.ej., una estatua*) unveil ‖ *ref* to take off one's hat, uncover; be discovered; open one's heart

descuello *m* excellence, superiority; great height; haughtiness

descuento *m* discount; deduction, rebate

descuerar *tr* (Chile) to skin, flay; (Chile) to discredit, flay

descuerno *m* slight, snub

descuida•do -da *adj* careless, negligent; slovenly, dirty; off guard

descuidar *tr* to overlook, neglect; divert, distract, relieve ‖ *ref* to be careless, not bother; be diverted

descuide•ro -ra *mf* sneak thief

descuido *m* carelessness, negligence, neglect; slip, mistake, blunder; oversight; **al descuido** with studied carelessness; **en un descuido** when least expected

descuita•do -da *adj* carefree

deschavetar *intr* to get rattled; go mad; flip one's lid

desde *prep* since, from; after; **desde ahora** from now on; **desde entonces** since then, ever since; **desde hace** for, e.g., **estoy aquí desde hace cinco días** I've been here for five days; **desde luego** at once; of course; **desde que** since

desdecir §24 (*impv sg* **-dice**) *intr* to slip back; be out of harmony ‖ *ref* — **desdecirse de** to take back, retract

desdén *m* scorn, disdain; **al desdén** with studied neglect

desdenta•do -da *adj* toothless

desdeñar *tr* to scorn, disdain ‖ *ref* to be disdainful; **desdeñarse de** to loathe, despise; not deign to

desdeño•so -sa *adj* scornful, disdainful

desdicha *f* misfortune; indigence

desdicha•do -da *adj* unfortunate, unlucky; poor, wretched; backward, timid

desdinerar *tr* to impoverish

desdoblar *tr & intr* to unfold, spread open; split, divide

desdorar *tr* to remove the gold or gilt from; tarnish, sully; disparage

desdoro *m* tarnish, blemish, blot; disparagement

deseable *adj* desirable

desear *tr* to desire, wish

desecar §73 *tr & ref* to dry; drain

desechable *adj* disposable

desechar *tr* to discard, throw out, cast aside; underrate; blame, censure; (*la llave de una puerta*) turn

desecho *m* remainder; offal, rubbish; castoff; scorn, contempt; short cut; **desecho de hierro** scrap iron

desegregación *f* desegregation

desellar *tr* to unseal

desembalaje *m* unpacking

desembalar *tr* to unpack

desembarazar §60 *tr* to free, clear, empty, open ‖ *ref* to free oneself; be cleared, emptied; **desembarazarse de** to get rid of

desembarazo *m* naturalness, lack of restraint; delivery, childbirth; **con desembarazo** naturally, readily

desembaracadero *m* wharf, pier, landing

desembarcar §73 *tr* to unload, debark, disembark ‖ *intr* to land, debark, disembark; (*de un carruaje*) get out, alight; (*la escalera al plano bajo*) end ‖ *ref* to land, debark, disembark

de
de

desembarco m landing, debarkation, disembarkation; (*de la escalera*) landing

desembarque m unloading, debarkation, disembarkation

desembocadura f (*de una calle*) opening, outlet; (*de un río*) mouth

desembocar §73 intr (*una calle*) open, to end; (*un río*) flow, empty

desembolsar tr to disburse, pay out

desembolso m disbursement, payment

desembragar §44 tr (*el motor*) to disengage ‖ intr to throw the clutch out

desembrague m disengagement, clutch release

desembravecer §22 tr to tame; calm, quiet, pacify

desembriagar §44 tr & ref to sober up

desembrollar tr to untangle, unravel

desemejante adj — **desemejante de** dissimilar from or to, unlike; **desemejantes** dissimilar, unlike

desemejar tr to change, disfigure ‖ intr to be different, not look alike

desempacar §73 tr to unpack, unwrap ‖ ref to cool off, calm down

desempalagar §44 tr to rid of nausea ‖ ref to get rid of nausea

desempañar tr (*el vidrio*) to wipe the steam or smear from; take the diaper off

desempapelar tr to unwrap; (*una pared, una habitación*) scrape the wallpaper from

desempaquetar tr to unpack; unwrap

desempatar tr to break the tie between; (*los votos*) break the tie in

desempate m breaking a tie

desempedrar §2 tr to remove the paving stones from; (*un sitio empedrado*) pound; **ir desempedrando la calle** to dash down the street

desempeñar tr (*un papel*) to play (*a rôle*); (*un cargo*) fill, perform; (*a uno de un empeño*) disengage; (*un deber*) discharge; free of debt; take out of hock ‖ ref to get out of a jam; get out of debt

desempeño m acting, performance; disengagement; (*de un deber*) discharge; payment of a debt; taking out of hock

desempernar tr to unbolt

desemplea•do -da adj & mf unemployed

desempleo m unemployment; **desempleo en masa** mass unemployment

desempolvar tr to dust; renew, take up again ‖ ref to brush up

desempolvorar tr to dust, dust off

desenamorar tr to alienate; ref to grow apart; **desenamorarse de** to get fed up with

desencadenar tr to unchain, unleash ‖ ref to break loose

desencajar tr to dislocate; disconnect ‖ ref to get out of joint; (*el rostro*) be contorted

desencaminar tr to lead astray, mislead

desencantamiento m disenchantment, disillusion

desencantar tr to disenchant, disillusion

desencantarar tr (*nombres o números*) to draw; (*un nombre o nombres*) exclude from balloting

desencanto m disenchantment, disillusion

desencarecer §22 tr to lower the price of ‖ intr & ref to come down in price

desencerrar §2 tr to release, set free; disclose, reveal

desencoger §17 tr to unfold, spread out ‖ ref to relax, shake off one's timidity

desencolar tr to unglue ‖ ref to become unglued

desenconar tr to take the soreness out of; calm down

desenchufar tr to unplug, disconnect

desendiosar tr to bring down a peg

desenfadaderas fpl — **tener buenas desenfadaderas** to be resourceful

desenfada•do -da adj free, easy, unconstrained

desenfado m ease, naturalness; relaxation, calmness

desenfoca•do -da adj out of focus

desenfrena•do -da adj unbridled, wanton, licentious

desenfrenar tr to unbridle ‖ ref to yield to temptation; fly into a passion; (*la tempestad, el viento*) break loose

desenfreno m unruliness, wantonness, licentiousness

desenfundar tr to take out of its sheath, bag, pillowcase, etc.

desenganchar tr to unhook, uncouple, unfasten, disengage; to unhitch

desenganche m unhooking, disengaging; unhitching

desengañar tr to disabuse, undeceive; disillusion; disappoint

desengaño m disabusing; disillusionment; disappointment; plain fact, plain truth

desengrana•do -da adj out of gear

desengranar tr to unmesh; disengage, throw out of gear

desengraso m (Chile) dessert

desenlace m outcome, result; (*de un drama, novela, etc.*) dénouement

desenlazar §60 tr to untie; solve; (*el nudo de un drama*) unravel

desenmarañar tr to disentangle; (*una cosa obscura*) unravel

desenmascarar tr to unmask ‖ ref to take one's mask off

desenojar tr to appease, free of anger ‖ ref to calm down; be amused

desenredar tr to disentangle; clear up ‖ ref to extricate oneself

desenredo m disentanglement; (*de un drama, novela, etc.*) dénouement

desenrollar tr to unroll, unwind, unreel

desensartar tr to unstring, unthread

desensillar tr to unsaddle (*a horse*)

desentablar tr to disrupt; break off (*a bargain, friendship, etc.*)

desentender §51 ref — **desentenderse de** to take no part in, not participate in; affect ignorance of, pretend to be unaware of

desenterrar §2 tr to dig up; disinter; (fig) to unearth, dig up; (fig) to recall to mind

desentona•do -da adj out of tune, flat

desentonar *tr* to humble, bring down a peg ‖ *intr* to be out of tune; be out of harmony ‖ *ref* to talk loud and disrespectfully

desentono *m* dissonance, false note; loud tone of voice

desentornillar *tr* to unscrew

desentrampar *ref* to get out of debt

desentrañar *tr* to disembowel; figure out, unravel ‖ *ref* to give away all that one has

desentrena•do -da *adj* out of training

desentronizar §60 *tr* to dethrone; strip of influence

desentumecer §22 *tr* to relieve of numbness ‖ *ref* to be relieved of numbness

desenvainar *tr* to unsheathe; (*las uñas el animal*) show, stretch out; bare, uncover

desenvoltura *f* naturalness, ease of manner, offhandedness; fluency; lewdness, boldness (*chiefly in women*)

desenvolver §47 & §83 *tr* to unfold, unroll, unwrap; unwind; unravel, clear up; develop ‖ *ref* to unroll; unwind; develop, evolve; extricate oneself; be forward

desenvuel•to -ta *adj* free and easy, offhand; fluent; brazen, bold, lewd

deseo *m* desire, wish

deseo•so -sa *adj* desirous, anxious

desequilibra•do -da *adj* unbalanced

desequilibrar *tr* to unbalance ‖ *ref* to become unbalanced

desequilibrio *m* disequilibrium, imbalance; derangement, mental instability

deserción *f* desertion

desertar *tr* & *intr* to desert

desertor *m* deserter

deservicio *m* disservice

desesperación *f* despair; **ser una desesperación** to be unbearable

desespera•do -da *adj* despairing, desperate ‖ *mf* desperate person

desesperanza *f* hopelessness

desesperanza•do -da *adj* hopeless

desesperanzar §60 *tr* to discourage ‖ *ref* to lose hope

desesperar *tr* to drive to despair; exasperate ‖ *intr* to lose hope; be exasperated ‖ *ref* to be desperate, lose all hope

desestancar §73 *tr* to open up, unclog; make free of duty; open the market to

desestimar *tr* to hold in low regard; refuse, reject

deséxito *m* failure

desfachata•do -da *adj* brazen, impudent

desfachatez *f* brazenness, impudence

desfalcar §73 *tr* & *intr* to embezzle

desfalco *m* embezzlement

desfallecer §22 *tr* to weaken ‖ *intr* to grow weak; faint, faint away; lose courage

desfalleci•do -da *adj* weak; faint

desfallecimiento *m* weakness; fainting; discouragement

desfavorable *adj* unfavorable

desfigurar *tr* to disfigure; distort, misrepresent; disguise; change, alter ‖ *ref* to look different

desfiladero *m* defile, pass

desfilar *intr* to defile, parade, file by

desfile *m* review, parade

desflorar *tr* to deflower; mention in passing

desfogar §44 *tr* (*un horno*) to vent; (*la cal*) slake; (*una pasión*) give free rein to ‖ *intr* (*una tempestad*) to break into rain and wind ‖ *ref* to give vent to one's anger

desfondar *tr* to stave in; (*una nave*) bilge; (*agr*) to trench-plow

desforestar *tr* to deforest

desgaire *m* slovenliness; disdain, scorn; **al desgaire** scornfully; carelessly, with affected carelessness

desgajar *tr* to tear off; split off ‖ *ref* to come off, come loose; arise, originate; separate, break away

desgana *f* lack of appetite; indifference; boredom; **a desgana** unwillingly, reluctantly

desgarba•do -da *adj* ungainly, uncouth

desgarrar *tr* to tear, rend; (*la flema*) cough up ‖ *ref* to tear oneself away

desgarro *m* tear, rent; brazenness, effrontery; boasting, bragging; (Chile, Col) phlegm, mucus

desgasta•do -da *adj* worn (out); eroded; (*llanta*) treadless; (*tela*) threadbare

desgastar *tr* to wear away, wear down; to weaken, spoil ‖ *ref* to wear away; grow weak, decline

desgaste *m* wear, wearing away

desgoberna•do -da *adj* ungovernable, uncontrollable

desgobernar §2 *tr* to misgovern; (*un hueso*) dislocate ‖ *intr* (naut) to steer poorly ‖ *ref* to twist and turn in dancing

desgobierno *m* misgovernment; dislocation

desgonzar §60 *tr* to unhinge; disconnect

desgracia *f* misfortune; (*acontecimiento adverso*) mishap; (*pérdida de favor*) disfavor, disgrace; (*aspereza en el trato*) gruffness; (*falta de gracia*) lack of charm; **correr con desgracia** to have no luck; **por desgracia** unfortunately

desgracia•do -da *adj* unfortunate; unattractive, unpleasant; disagreeable ‖ *mf* wretch, unfortunate

desgraciar *tr* to displease; spoil ‖ *ref* to spoil; fail; fall out, disagree

desgranar *tr* (*el maíz*) to shell; (*un racimo*) to pick the grapes from ‖ *ref* (*piezas ensartadas*) to come loose

desgreñar *tr* to dishevel ‖ *ref* to get disheveled; pull each other's hair

deshabita•do -da *adj* unoccupied

deshabituar §21 *tr* to break of a habit

deshacer §39 *tr* to undo; untie; take apart; wear away, consume, destroy; melt; put to flight, rout; (*un tratado o negocio*) violate ‖ *ref* to get out of order; vanish, disappear; **deshacerse de** to get rid of; **deshacerse en** (*cumplidos*) to lavish; (*lágrimas*) burst into; **deshacerse por** to strive hard to

desharrapa•do -da *adj* ragged, in rags

deshebillar *tr* to unbuckle

deshebrar *tr* to unravel, unthread

deshecha *f* sham, pretense; dismissal; **hacer la deshecha** to feign, pretend; (Mex) to pretend lack of interest

de
de

deshelar §2 *tr* to thaw, melt; defrost; (aer) to deice ‖ *intr* to thaw, melt

deshereda•do -da *adj* disinherited; underprivileged

desheredar *tr* to disinherit ‖ *ref* to be a disgrace to one's family

desherrar §2 *tr* to unchain, unshackle; (*a una caballería*) unshoe

desherrumbrar *tr* to remove the rust from

deshidratar *tr* to dehydrate

deshielo *m* thaw; defrosting; détente

deshilachar *ref* to fray

deshila•do -da *adj* in a file; **a la deshilada** in single file; secretly ‖ *m* openwork, drawn work

deshilar *tr* to unweave; (*reducir a hilos*) shred ‖ *ref* to fray; get thin

deshilvana•do -da *adj* disconnected, desultory

deshincar §73 *tr* to pull up, pull out

deshinchar *tr* to deflate; (*la cólera*) give vent to ‖ *ref* (*un tumor*) to go down; (*una persona orgullosa*) become deflated

deshojar *tr* to strip of leaves; tear the pages out of ‖ *ref* to lose the leaves

deshollejar *tr* (*la uva*) to peel, skin; (*las habichuelas*) shell

deshollina•dor -dora *mf* chimney sweep; curious observer ‖ *m* long-handled brush or broom

deshones•to -ta *adj* immodest, indecent; improper

deshonor *m* dishonor; disgrace

deshonrar *tr* to dishonor; degrade; disfigure

deshonra *f* dishonor; disrespect; **tener a deshonra** to consider improper

deshonrabue•nos *mf* (*pl* **-nos**) slanderer; (coll) black sheep

deshonrar *tr* to disgrace; (*a una mujer*) seduce; insult

deshonro•so -sa *adj* disgraceful, improper, discreditable

deshora *f* wrong time; **a deshora** at the wrong time, inopportunely; suddenly, unexpectedly

deshuesar *tr* (*la carne de un animal*) to bone; (*la fruta*) stone, take the pits out of

deshumedecer §22 *tr* to dehumidify

desidia *f* laziness, indolence

desidio•so -sa *adj* lazy, indolent ‖ *mf* lazy person

desier•to -ta *adj* desert; deserted ‖ *m* desert; wilderness

designar *tr* to designate; (*un trabajo*) plan

designio *m* design, plan, scheme

desigual *adj* unequal; unlike; rough, uneven; difficult; inconstant

desigualar *tr* to make unequal ‖ *ref* to become unequal; (*aventajarse*) get ahead

desigualdad *f* inequality; roughness, unevenness

desilusión *f* disillusionment; disappointment

desilusionar *tr* to disillusion; disappoint ‖ *ref* to become disillusioned; be disappointed

desimanar or **desimantar** *tr* to demagnetize

desimpresionar *tr* to undeceive

desinclina•do -da *adj* disinclined

desinencia *f* (gram) termination, ending

desinfectante *adj & m* disinfectant

desinfectar or **desinficionar** *tr* to disinfect

desinflación *f* deflation

desinflamar *tr* to take the soreness out of

desinflar *tr* to deflate; let the air out of; (*a una persona*) deflate

desinhibición *f* loss of inhibitions

desinsectación *f* insect control

desinsectar *intr* to exterminate insects

desintegración *f* disintegration

desintegrar *tr & ref* to disintegrate

desinterés *m* disinterestedness

desinteresa•do -da *adj* (*imparcial*) disinterested; (*poco interesado*) uninterested

desinteresar *ref* to lose interest

desintonizar §60 *tr* (rad) to tune out; (rad) to put out of tune

desintoxicación *f* detoxification; sobering (up)

desintoxicar *tr* to detoxify; sober up

desistir *intr* to desist

desjarretar *tr* to hamstring; bleed to excess

desjuicia•do -da *adj* lacking judgment, senseless

desjuntar *tr* to disjoin, separate

deslabonar *tr* to unlink; disconnect ‖ *ref* to come loose; withdraw

deslastrar *tr* to unballast

deslava•do -da *adj* faded, colorless; barefaced ‖ *mf* barefaced person

deslavar *tr* to wash superficially; fade, take the life out of

desleal *adj* disloyal; unfair

deslealtad *f* disloyalty

deslechar *tr* (Col) to milk

desleír §58 *tr* to dissolve; dilute; (*los colores, la pintura*) thin; (*sus pensamientos*) express too diffusely ‖ *ref* to dissolve; become diluted

deslengua•do -da *adj* foul-mouthed, shameless

desliar §77 *tr* to untie, undo; unravel ‖ *ref* to come untied

desligar §44 *tr* to untie, unbind; disentangle; excuse ‖ *ref* to come untied, come loose

deslindar *tr* to mark the boundaries of; distinguish; define, explain

des•liz *m* (*pl* **-lices**) sliding; (*superficie lisa*) slide; slip, blunder; peccadillo, indiscretion

deslizade•ro -ra *adj* slippery ‖ *m* slippery place; launching way

deslizadi•zo -za *adj* slippery

deslizador *m* (aer) glider

deslizar §60 *tr* to slide; (*decir por descuido*) let slip ‖ *intr* to slide; slip; glide ‖ *ref* to slide; slip; glide; slip away, sneak away; (*un reparo*) slip out; (*caer en una flaqueza*) slide back, backslide

deslomar *tr* to break or strain the back of ‖ *ref* to break or strain one's back; **no deslomarse** to not strain oneself

desluci•do -da *adj* quiet, lackluster; dull, undistinguished

deslucir §45 *tr* to tarnish; deprive of charm, deprive of distinction; discredit

deslumbramiento m dazzle, glare; bewilderment, confusion

deslumbrante adj dazzling; bewildering, confusing

deslumbrar tr to dazzle; bewilder, confuse

deslustra•do -da adj dull, flat, dingy; (vidrio) ground, frosted

deslustrar tr to tarnish; dull, dim; (el vidrio) frost; discredit ‖ ref to tarnish

deslustre m tarnishing; dulling, dimming; discredit; (del vidrio) frosting

deslustro•so -sa adj ugly, unbecoming

desmadejar tr to enervate, weaken

desmagnetizar §60 tr to demagnetize

desmán m excess, misconduct; misfortune, mishap

desmanchar tr (Chile) to clean of spots

desmanda•do -da adj disobedient, unruly

desmandar tr to cancel, countermand ‖ ref to misbehave; go away, keep apart; get out of control

desmanear tr to unfetter, unshackle

desmantela•do -da adj dilapidated

desmantelar tr to dismantle; (naut) to unmast; (naut) to unrig

desmaña f awkwardness, clumsiness

desmaña•do -da adj awkward, clumsy

desmaquillar tr & ref to take makeup off

desmaya•do -da adj faint, languid, weak; unconscious; (color) dull

desmayar tr to depress, discourage ‖ intr to lose heart, be discouraged; falter ‖ ref to faint

desmayo m depression, discouragement; faint, fainting fit; weeping willow

desmedi•do -da adj excessive; boundless, limitless

desmedir §50 ref to go too far, be impudent

desmedra•do -da adj weak, run-down

desmedrar tr to impair ‖ intr & ref to decline, deteriorate

desmejorar tr to impair, spoil ‖ intr & ref to decline, go into a decline

desmelenar tr to muss, dishevel, rumple

desmembrar §2 tr to dismember

desmemoria f forgetfulness

desmemoria•do -da adj forgetful

desmemoriar ref to become forgetful

desmentida f contradiction; **dar una desmentida a** to give the lie to

desmentir §68 tr to belie, give the lie to; conceal ‖ intr to be out of line ‖ ref to contradict oneself

desmenudear tr & intr (Col) to sell at retail

desmenuzar §60 tr to crumble; chop up; examine in detail; criticize harshly ‖ ref to crumb, crumble

desmerece•dor -dora adj unworthy

desmerecer §22 tr to be unworthy of ‖ intr to decline in value; **desmerecer de** to compare unfavorably with

desmesura f excess, lack of restraint

desmesura•do -da adj excessive, disproportionate; insolent ‖ mf insolent person

desmigajar tr & ref to crumble, break up

desmigar §44 tr & ref to crumble, crumb

desmilitarizar §60 tr to demilitarize; **zona desmilitarizada** demilitarized zone

desmirria•do -da adj exhausted, emaciated, run-down

desmochar tr (un árbol) to top; (al toro) dehorn; (una obra artística) cut

desmodular tr to demodulate

desmola•do -da adj toothless

desmontable adj demountable

desmontar tr (un terreno) to level; (un bosque) clear; dismantle, dismount, take apart, knock down; (las piezas de artillería del enemigo) knock out; (al jinete el caballo) unhorse, to throw; (un arma de fuego) uncock ‖ ref to dismount, alight

desmoralizar §60 tr to demoralize

desmorona•di•zo -za adj crumbly

desmoronar tr to wear away ‖ ref to wear away; crumble, decline

desmotadera f burler; **desmotadera de algodón** cotton gin

desmotar tr (la lana) to burl; (el algodón) gin

desmovilizar §60 tr to demobilize

desmurador m mouser

desnatadora f cream separator

desnatar tr to skim; remove the slag from; take the choicest part of

desnaturalizar §60 tr to denaturalize; (el alcohol) denature; alter, pervert

desnivel m unevenness; difference of level

desnivelar tr to make uneven ‖ ref to become uneven

desnudar tr to undress; strip, lay bare; (la espada) draw ‖ ref to undress, get undressed; become evident; **desnudarse de** to get rid of

desnudez f nakedness; bareness

desnu•do -da adj naked, nude; bare; destitute, penniless ‖ **el desnudo** the nude

desnutrición f undernourishment, malnutrition

desnutri•do -da adj undernourished

desobedecer tr & intr to disobey

desobediencia f disobedience

desobediente adj disobedient

desocupación f unemployment; idleness, leisure

desocupa•do -da adj unemployed; idle; free, unoccupied, vacant, empty ‖ mf unemployed person

desocupar tr to empty, vacate ‖ intr (una mujer) to be delivered ‖ ref to become empty, vacated; become unemployed, become idle

desodorante adj & m deodorant

desodorizar §60 tr to deodorize

desoír §48 tr to not hear, pretend not to hear

desolación f desolation

desola•do -da adj desolate, disconsolate

desolar §61 tr to desolate, lay waste ‖ ref to be desolate, be disconsolate

desoldar §61 tr to unsolder ‖ ref to come unsoldered

desolla•do -da adj brazen, impudent

desollar §61 tr to skin, flay; harm, hurt; **desollar vivo** (hacer pagar mucho más de *lo justo)* fleece, skin alive; (*murmurar acerbamente de)* (coll) to flay

desopilar *ref* to roar with laughter

desopinar *tr* to defame, discredit

desorbita•do -da *adj* popeyed; crazy

desorbitar *tr* to pop wide-open

desorden *m* disorder

desordena•do -da *adj* disorderly, unruly

desordenar *tr* to put out of order ‖ *ref* to get out of order; be unruly; go too far

desoreja•do -da *adj* infamous, degraded; (*que canta mal)* (Peru) off tune; (Cuba) shameless; (Cuba) spendthrift, prodigal; (Guat) stupid; (Chile) without handles

desorganizar §60 *tr* to disorganize

desorientación *f* disorientation; confusedness; going astray

desorientar *tr* to lead astray; confuse

desovar *intr* to spawn

desove *m* spawning; spawning season

desovillar *tr* to unravel, disentangle; encourage

desoxidar *tr* to deoxidize; clean of rust

despabiladeras *fpl* snuffers

despabila•do -da *adj* wide-awake

despabilar *tr (una candela)* to snuff, trim; (*la hacienda)* dissipate; (*una comida)* dispatch; (*robar)* snitch; (*matar)* dispatch ‖ *ref* to brighten up; wake up; leave, disappear

despacio *adv* slow, slowly; at leisure; (Arg, Chile) in a low voice

despacio•so -sa *adj* slow, easy-going

despachaderas *fpl* surly reply; resourcefulness

despacha•do -da *adj* brazen, impudent; quick, resourceful

despachante *m* (Arg) clerk; **despachante te de aduana** (Arg) customhouse broker

despachar *tr* to send, ship; dispatch, expedite; discharge, dismiss; decide, settle; sell; *(a los parroquianos)* wait on; *(la corre spondencia)* attend to; hurry; *(matar)* dispatch, kill ‖ *intr* to hurry; make up one's mind; work, be employed ‖ *ref* to hurry; *(una mujer)* be delivered; speak out

despacho *m* shipping; dispatch, expedition; discharge, dismissal; *(tienda)* store, shop; *(aposento para el estudio)* study; *(aposento para los negocios)* office; *(comunicación por telégrafo o teléfono)* dispatch; (Chile) attic; **despacho de billetes** ticket office; **despacho de localidades** box office; **estar al despacho** to be pending; **tener buen despacho** to be expeditious

despachurrar *tr* to crush, smash, squash; *(dejar sin tener que replicar)* squelch; *(lo que uno trata de decir)* butcher, murder

despampanante *adj* stunning, terrific

despampanar *tr (las vides)* to prune, trim; astound ‖ *intr* to give vent to one's feelings ‖ *ref* to fall and hurt oneself

despancar §73 *tr* to husk *(corn)*

desparejar *tr (dos cosas que forman pareja)* to break, separate *(a pair)*

desparpajar *tr* to tear apart ‖ *intr* to rant, rave ‖ *ref* to rant, rave; (CAm, Mex, W-I) to wake up

desparramar *tr* to scatter, spread; *(el agua)* to spill; *(la hacienda)* squander ‖ *ref* to scatter, spread; make merry

despartir *tr* to divide, part, separate; to reconcile

despatarrada *f* split (*in dancing)*; **hacer la despatarrada** to stretch out on the floor pretending to be ill or injured

despatarrar *tr* to dumbfound ‖ *ref* to open one's legs wide, fall down with legs outspread; lie motionless; be dumbfounded

despavori•do -da *adj* terrified

despea•do -da *adj* footsore

despear *ref* to get sore feet

despecti•vo -va *adj* contemptuous; (gram) pejorative

despecha•do -da *adj* spiteful, enraged

despechar *tr* to spite, enrage; *(destetar)* to wean ‖ *ref* to be enraged; despair, lose hope

despecho *m* spite; despair; weaning; **a despecho de** despite, in spite of; **por despecho** out of spite

despechugar §44 *tr* to carve the breast of ‖ *ref* (coll) to go with bare breast, bare one's breast

despedazar §60 *tr* to break to pieces; *(la honra de uno)* to ruin; *(el alma de una persona)* break ‖ *ref* to break to pieces; **despedazarse de risa** to split one's sides laughing

despedida *f* farewell, leave-taking; *(de una carta)* close, conclusion; *(copla final)* envoi

despedir §50 *tr* to throw; emit, send forth; discharge, dismiss; *(al que sale de la casa)* see off; *(un mal pensamiento)* banish; **despedir en la puerta** to see to the door ‖ *ref* to take leave, say good-by; give up one's job; **despedirse a la francesa** to take French leave; **despedirse de** to take leave of, say good-by to

despega•do -da *adj* gruff, surly

despegar §44 *tr* to loosen, unglue, unseal; open; separate, detach ‖ *intr* (aer) to take off ‖ *ref* to come off; **despegarse con** to be unbecoming to

despego *m* dislike, indifference

despegue *m* (aer) take-off; **despegue vertical** vertical take-off

despeina•do -da *adj* unkempt

despeja•do -da *adj (frente)* wide; *(día, cielo)* clear, cloudless; bright, sprightly; *(en el trato)* unconstrained

despejar *tr* to clarify, explain; free; *(una incógnita)* (math) to find ‖ *ref* to brighten up, cheer up; *(el cielo, el tiempo; una situación dificultosa)* clear up; *(un borracho)* sober up

despejo *m* ease, naturalness; talent, intelligence, understanding

despelotar *ref* to disrobe

despeluzar §60 *tr* to muss the hair of; make the hair of *(a person)* stand on end ‖ *ref (el pelo)* to stand on end

despeluznante *adj* hair-raising, horrifying

despellejar *tr* to skin, flay; slander, malign

despenalización *f* legalization

despenalizar §60 *tr* to legalize; condone

despenar *tr* to console; (coll) to kill; (Chile) to deprive of hope

despender *tr* to spend, squander; (*el tiempo*) to waste

despensa *f* pantry; food supplies; day's marketing; stewardship; (naut) storeroom

despensero *m* butler, steward; (naut) storekeeper

despeñadamente *adv* hastily; boldly

despeñade•ro -ra *adj* precipitous ‖ *m* precipice; danger, risk

despeñadi•zo -za *adj* precipitous

despeñar *tr* to hurl, throw, push ‖ *ref* to hurl oneself, jump; fall headlong; (*en vicios, pecados, pasiones*) plunge downward

despeño *m* plunge; headlong fall; ruin, failure, collapse; (coll) loose bowels

despepitar *tr* to seed, remove the seeds from ‖ *ref* to rush around madly, go around screaming; **despepitarse por** to be mad about

desperdicia•do -da *adj* wasteful, prodigal ‖ *mf* spendthrift, prodigal

desperdiciar *tr* to waste, squander; (*la ocasión de aprovechar una cosa*) miss, lose

desperdicio *m* waste, squandering; **desperdicios** waste; waste products; by-products; rubbish; **no tener desperdicio** to be excellent, be useful

desperdigar §44 *tr* to separate, scatter

desperecer §22 *ref* to long eagerly

desperezar §60 *ref* to stretch, stretch one's arms and legs

desperfecto *m* blemish, flaw, imperfection

desperna•do -da *adj* footsore, weary

desperta•dor -dora *mf* awakener ‖ *m* alarm clock; warning

despertar §2 *tr* to awaken; arouse, stir ‖ *intr* & *ref* to awaken, wake up

despestañar *tr* to pluck the eyelashes of ‖ *ref* to look hard, strain one's eyes

despiada•do -da *adj* cruel, pitiless

despichar *tr* to squeeze dry; (Col, Chile) to crush, flatten ‖ *intr* (coll) to croak, die

despidiente *m* stick placed between a hanging scaffold and wall; **despidiente de agua** flashing

despido *m* layoff, discharge

despier•to -ta *adj* wide-awake, alert; **soñar despierto** to daydream

despilfarra•do -da *adj* wasteful; ragged ‖ *mf* prodigal; raggedy person

despilfarrar *tr* to squander, waste ‖ *ref* to spend recklessly

despilfarro *m* squandering, waste, extravagance; slovenliness

despintar *tr* to remove the paint from; disfigure, distort, spoil; **no despintarle a uno los ojos** to not take one's eyes from a person ‖ *intr* to decline, slip back; **despintar de** to be unworthy of ‖ *ref* to fade, wash off; **no despintársele a uno** to not fade from one's memory

despiojar *tr* to delouse; (coll) to free from poverty

despique *m* revenge

despistar *tr* to outwit, throw off the track ‖ *ref* to run off the track, run off the road

desplacer *m* displeasure ‖ §22 *tr* to displease

desplantar *tr* to uproot; throw out of plumb ‖ *ref* to get out of plumb; lose one's upright posture

desplaya•do -da *adj* broad, open, wide ‖ *m* (Arg) wide sandy beach

desplayar *tr* to widen, spread out ‖ *ref* (*el mar*) to recede from the beach

desplaza•do -da *adj* displaced ‖ *mf* displaced person

desplazar §60 *tr* (*cierto peso de agua*) to displace; move, transport ‖ *ref* to move

desplegar §66 *tr* to unfold, spread; display; explain; (mil) to deploy ‖ *ref* to unfold, spread out; (mil) to deploy

despliegue *m* unfolding, spreading out; display; (mil) deployment

desplomar *tr* to throw out of plumb ‖ *ref* to get out of plumb; collapse, tumble; fall down in a faint; (*un trono*) crumble; (aer) to pancake

desplome *m* leaning; collapse, tumbling; falling in a faint; downfall; (aer) pancaking

desplumar *tr* to pluck; (*dejar sin dinero*) fleece ‖ *ref* to molt

despoblado *m* wilderness, deserted spot

despoblar §61 *tr* to depopulate; lay waste; clear, lay bare

despojar *tr* to strip, despoil, divest; dispossess ‖ *ref* to undress; **despojarse de** to divest oneself of; (*ropa*) take off

despojo *m* dispoilment; dispossession; booty, plunder, spoils; prey, victim; **despojos** scraps, leavings; mortal remains; secondhand building materials

despolarizar §60 *tr* to depolarize

despolvar *tr* to dust

despolvorear *tr* to dust, dust off; scatter

desportillar *tr* to chip, nick ‖ *ref* to chip, chip off

desposa•do -da *adj* handcuffed; newly married ‖ *mf* newlywed

desposar *tr* to marry ‖ *ref* to be betrothed, get engaged; get married

desposeer §43 *tr* to dispossess ‖ *ref* —**desposeerse de** to divest oneself of

desposorios *mpl* betrothal, engagement; marriage, nuptials

despostar *tr* to cut up, carve; butcher

déspota *m* despot

despóti•co -ca *adj* despotic

despotismo *m* despotism

despotricar §73 *intr* & *ref* to rave, rant

despreciable *adj* contemptible, despicable

despreciar *tr* to scorn, despise; slight, snub; overlook, forgive; reject ‖ *ref* —**despreciarse de** to not deign to

despreciati•vo -va *adj* contemptuous, scornful

desprecio *m* scorn, contempt; slight, snub

desprender *tr* to loosen, unfasten, detach; emit, give off; (chem) to liberate ‖ *ref* to come loose, come off; issue, come forth;

desprenderse de to give up, part with; be deduced from

desprendi•do -da *adj* generous, disinterested

desprendimiento *m* loosening, detachment; emission, liberation; generosity, disinterestedness; landslide; (chem) liberation

despreocupación *f* relaxation; impartiality; indifference

despreocupa•do -da *adj* relaxed, unconcerned; impartial; indifferent

despreocupante *adj* relaxing

despreocupar *ref* to relax; **despreocuparse de** to forget about, be unconcerned about

desprestigiar *tr* to disparage, run down ‖ *ref* to lose caste, lose one's standing, lose face

desprestigio *m* disparagement; loss of standing, discredit

despreveni•do -da *adj* off one's guard; **coger a uno desprevenido** to catch someone unawares

desproporciona•do -da *adj* disproportionate

despropósito *m* absurdity, nonsense; malapropism

desproveer §43 & §83 *tr* to deprive

desprovis•to -ta *adj* destitute; **desprovisto de** lacking, devoid of

después *adv* after, afterwards; **después de** after; **después (de) que** after

despuli•do -da *adj* ground (*glass*)

despumar *tr* to skim

despuntar *tr* to dull, blunt; (*un cabo o punta*) (naut) to double, round ‖ *intr* to begin to sprout; (*empezar a amanecer*) dawn; stand out ‖ *ref* to get dull

desquiciar *tr* to unhinge; shake loose, upset; unsettle, perturb; overthrow, undermine

desquitar *tr* to recover, retrieve; compensate ‖ *ref* to retrieve a loss; get revenge, get even

desquite *m* recovery, retrieval; retaliation, revenge; (sport) return match

desrazonable *adj* unreasonable

desrielar *intr* to jump the track

destaca•do -da *adj* outstanding, distinguished

destacamiento *m* (mil) detachment; (mil) detail

destacar §73 *tr* to highlight, point up; emphasize; make stand out; (mil) to detach; (mil) to detail ‖ *intr* to stand out, be conspicuous ‖ *ref* to stand out, project; (fig) to stand out

destajar *tr* to arrange for, establish the terms for; (*la baraja*) cut; carve up

destaje•ro -ra or **destajista** *mf* pieceworker, jobber; free lance

destajo *m* piecework; job, contract; **a destajo** by the piece, by the job; freelancing; **hablar a destajo** to talk too much

destapar *tr* to open, uncover, take the lid off; uncock, unplug; reveal ‖ *ref* to get uncovered; throw off the covers; unbosom oneself

destaponar *tr* to uncock, unplug; (*una botella; las fosas nasales*) unstop

destartala•do -da *adj* tumble-down, ramshackle

destazar §60 *tr* to carve up

destechar *tr* to unroof

destejar *tr* to remove the tiles from; leave unprotected

destejer *tr* to unbraid, unknit, unweave; upset, disturb

destellar *tr* & *intr* to flash

destello *m* flash, beam, sparkle

destempla•do -da *adj* disagreeable, unpleasant; inharmonious, out of tune; indisposed; (*clima; pulso*) irregular

destemplanza *f* unpleasantness; discord; indisposition; (*del pulso*) irregularity; (*del tiempo*) inclemency; excess

destemple *m* dissonance; indisposition; disorder, disturbance

desteñir §72 *tr* to discolor ‖ *intr* & *ref* to fade

desternillante *adj* sidesplitting

desternillar *ref* — **desternillarse de risa** to split one's sides with laughter

desterra•do -da *adj* exiled ‖ *mf* exile

desterrar §2 *tr* to exile, banish; (fig) to banish

destetar *tr* to wean ‖ *ref* — **destetarse con** to have known since childhood

destete *m* weaning

destiempo *m* — **a destiempo** untimely

destiento *m* surprise, shock

destierro *m* exile; backwoods

destilación *f* distillation

destiladera *f* still; scheme, stratagem

destilar *tr* to distill; filter; exude ‖ *intr* to drip

destilatorio *m* distillery; (*alambique*) still

destilería *f* distillery

destinación *f* destination

destinar *tr* to destine; assign, designate

destinata•rio -ria *mf* addressee; consignee; (*de homenaje, aplausos*) recipient

destino *m* (*lugar a donde va una persona o una remesa*) destination; (*suerte, encadenamiento fatal de los sucesos*) fate, destiny; employment; place of employment; **con destino a** bound for

destituir §20 *tr* to deprive; dismiss, discharge

destorcer §74 *tr* to untwist, straighten ‖ *ref* to become untwisted; (naut) to drift

destornilla•do -da *adj* rash, reckless, out of one's head

destornillador *m* screwdriver

destornillar *tr* to unscrew ‖ *ref* to lose one's head, go berserk

destoser *ref* to cough (*artificially, to attract attention*)

destrabar *tr* to loosen, untie, detach

destraillar §4 *tr* unleash

destral *m* hatchet

destreza *f* skill, dexterity

destripacuen•tos *m* (*pl* -tos) (coll) butter-in

destripar *tr* to disembowel, gut; crush, mangle; spoil (*a story by telling its outcome*)

destripaterro•nes *m* (*pl* -nes) (coll) clodhopper

destriunfar *tr* to force to play trump

destrocar §81 *tr* to swap back again

destronar *tr* to dethrone; overthrow

destroncar §73 *tr* to chop down; chop off; ruin; exhaust, wear out

destrozar §60 *tr* to shatter, break to pieces; destroy; squander; (*al ejército enemigo*) wipe out

destrozo *m* havoc, destruction; rout, annihilation, defeat

destrucción *f* destruction

destructi•vo -va *adj* destructive

destructor *m* (nav) destroyer

destruir §20 *tr* to destroy ‖ *ref* (alg) to cancel each other

desuellaca•ras *m* (*pl* -ras) sloppy barber; scoundrel

desuello *m* skinning, flaying; shamelessness; (*precio excesivo*) (coll) highway robbery

desuncir §36 *tr* to unyoke

desunir *tr* to disunite; take apart ‖ *ref* to disunite; come apart

desusa•do -da *adj* obsolete, out of use; uncommon, unusual; estar desusado (*perder la práctica*) to be rusty

desuso *m* disuse; caído en desuso obsolete

desvaí•do -da *adj* lank, ungainly; (*color*) dull

desvainar *tr* to shell

desvali•do -da *adj* helpless, destitute

desvalijar *tr* (*una valija, baúl, etc.*) to rifle; rob, wipe out

desvalorar *tr* to devalue

desvalorizar §60 *tr* to devalue

desván *m* garret, loft

desvanecedor *m* (phot) mask

desvanecer §22 *tr* to dispel, dissipate; (*una conspiración*) break up; (*la sospecha*) banish; (phot) to mask ‖ *ref* to disappear, vanish, evanesce; evaporate; faint, faint away, swoon; (rad) to fade

desvanecimiento *m* disappearance, evanescence; dissipation; pride, vanity; faintness, fainting spell; (phot) masking; (rad) fading, fadeout

desvaria•do -da *adj* delirious, raving

desvariar §77 *intr* to be delirious, rave, rant

desvarío *m* delirium, raving; absurdity, nonsense, extravagance; whim, caprice; inconstancy

desvela•do -da *adj* wakeful, sleepless; watchful, vigilant; anxious, worried

desvelar *tr* to keep awake, not let sleep ‖ *ref* to keep awake, go without sleep; be watchful, be vigilant; desvelarse por to be anxious about, be worried about

desvelo *m* wakefulness, sleeplessness; watchfulness, vigilance; anxiety, worry, concern

desvenar *tr* to strip (*tobacco*)

desvencija•do -da *adj* rickety, ramshackle

desvencijar *tr* to break, tear apart ‖ *ref* to go to rack and ruin

desvendar *tr* to unbandage, undress

desventaja *f* disadvantage

desventaja•do -da *adj* disadvantaged; deprived

desventajo•so -sa *adj* disadvantageous

desventura *f* misfortune

desventura•do -da *adj* unfortunate; fainthearted; stingy

desvergonza•do -da *adj* shameless, impudent

desvergüenza *f* shamelessness, impudence

desvestir §50 *tr* & *ref* to undress

desviación *f* deviation, deflection; detour; (rad, telv) drift

desviacionismo *m* deviationism

desviacionista *mf* deviationist

desviadero *m* (rr) siding, turnout

desvia•do -da *adj* devious; (gone) astray; off track; lost

desviar §77 *tr* to deviate, deflect; turn aside; dissuade; parry, ward off; (rr) to switch ‖ *ref* to deviate, deflect; turn aside; branch off; be dissuaded

desvío *m* deviation, deflection; coldness, indifference; detour; (rr) siding, sidetrack

desvirgar §44 *tr* to deflower, ravish

desvirtuar §21 *tr* to weaken, spoil, impair

desvivir *ref*—desvivirse por to be crazy about; desvivirse por + *inf* to be eager to + *inf*, to do one's best to + *inf*

desvolvedor *m* wrench

desvolver §47 & §83 *tr* to alter, change; (*la tierra*) turn up; (*una tuerca o tornillo*) loosen, unscrew

detall *m* — al detall at retail

detalladamente *adv* in detail

detallar *tr* to detail, tell in detail; retail, sell at retail

detalle *m* detail; retail; ahí está el detalle that's the point

detallista *mf* retailer; person fond of details

detección *f* detection

detectar *tr* to detect

detective *m* detective

detector *m* detector; detector de mentiras lie detector

detención *f* detention, detainment; delay; care, thoroughness

detener §71 *tr* to detain; stop; arrest; keep, retain; (*el aliento*) hold ‖ *ref* to stop; linger, tarry

detenidamente *adv* carefully, thoroughly

deteni•do -da *adj* careful, thorough; hesitant, timid; stingy, mean ‖ *mf* person held in custody

detenimiento *m* var of detención

detergente *adj* & *m* detergent

deteriorar *tr* & *ref* to deteriorate

deterioro *m* deterioration

determinación *f* determination; decision

determina•do -da *adj* determined, resolute; (*artículo*) (gram) definite

determinar *tr* to determine; cause, bring about ‖ *ref* to decide

detestar *tr* to detest; curse; detestar + *inf* to hate to + *inf*

detonar *intr* to detonate

detraer §75 *tr* to withdraw, take away, detract; defame, vilify

detrás *adv* behind; detrás de behind, back of; por detrás behind; behind one's back; por detrás de behind the back of

detrimento *m* harm, detriment

deuda *f* debt; indebtedness

deu•do -da *mf* relative ‖ *m* kinship ‖ *f* see deuda

deu•dor -dora *adj* indebted ‖ *mf* debtor; deudor hipotecario mortgagor; deudor moroso delinquent (*in payment*)

de
de

devalar *intr* (naut) to drift from the course

devaluación *f* devaluation

devanar *tr* to wind, roll; (*un cuento*) to unfold ‖ *ref* (CAm, Mex, W-I) to roll with laughter; (CAm, Mex, W-I) to writhe in pain

devanear *intr* to talk nonsense; loaf around

devaneo *m* nonsense; loafing; flirtation

devastación *f* devastation

devastar *tr* to devastate

develar *tr* to reveal; (*p.ej., una estatua*) unveil

devengar §44 *tr* (*salarios*) to earn; (*intereses*) draw, earn

devoción *f* devotion

devolución *f* return, restitution

devolver §47 & §83 *tr* to return, give back, send back; pay back; (coll) to vomit ‖ *ref* to return, come back

devorar *tr* to devour

devo•to -ta *adj* devout; devoted; devotional ‖ *mf* devotee; devout person; **devoto del volante** car enthusiast ‖ *m* object of worship

D.F. *abbr* **Distrito Federal**

d/f *abbr* **días fecha**

dho. *abbr* **dicho**

día *m* day; daytime; daylight; **al día** per day; up to date; **al otro día** on the following day; **buenos días** good morning; **dar los días a** to wish (*someone*) many happy returns of the day; **de día** in the daytime, in the daylight; **día de años** birthday; **día de ayuno** fast day; **día de carne** meat day; **día de engañabobos** December 28th, day when practical jokes are played on unsuspecting people; **día de inauguración** (fa) private view; **día de la raza** Columbus Day; **día del juicio** judgment day; **día de los caídos** Memorial Day; **día de los difuntos** All Souls' Day; **día de ramos** Palm Sunday; **día de Reyes** Epiphany; **día de todos los santos** All Saints' Day; **día de trabajo** workday; weekday; **día de vigilia** fast day; **día festivo** holiday; **día inhábil** day off; holiday; **día laborable** workday, weekday; **día lectivo** school day; **día puente** day off between two holidays; **el día de Año Nuevo** New Year's Day; **el día menos pensado** when least expected; **el mejor día** some fine day; **en cuatro días** in a few days; **en pleno día** in broad daylight; **en su día** in due time; **ocho días** a week; **poner al día** to bring up to date; **quince días** two weeks, a fortnight; **tener sus días** to be up in years; **un día sí y otro no** every other day; **vivir al día** to live from hand to mouth

diabetes *f* diabetes

diabéti•co -ca *adj* & *mf* diabetic

diablillo *m* imp

diablo *m* devil; (Chile) ox-drawn log drag; **ahí será el diablo** (coll) there will be the devil to pay; **diablo cojuelo** tricky devil; **diablos azules** delirium tremens

diablura *f* devilment, deviltry, mischief

diabóli•co -ca *adj* devilish, diabolical

diaconisa *f* deaconess

diácono *m* deacon

diacríti•co -ca *adj* diacritical

diadema *f* diadem; (*adorno femenino*) tiara

diáfa•no -na *adj* diaphanous

diafragma *m* diaphragm

diagno•sis *f* (*pl* -**sis**) diagnosis

diagnosticar §73 *tr* to diagnose

diagonal *adj* diagonal ‖ *f* diagonal, bias

diagrama *m* diagram

dialecto *m* dialect

dialogar *intr* to talk

diálogo *m* dialogue

diamante *m* diamond

diametral or **diamétri•co -ca** *adj* diametrical

diámetro *m* diameter

diana *f* bull's-eye; (mil) reveille; **hacer diana** to hit the bull's-eye

diantre *m* devil ‖ *interj* the devil!, the deuce!

diapasón *m* tuning fork; pitch pipe; (*p.ej., del violín*) finger board; **bajar el diapasón** to lower one's voice, to change one's tune

diapositiva *f* slide, lantern slide

dia•rio -ria *adj* daily ‖ *m* diary; daily, daily paper; **diario hablado** newscast

diarismo *m* journalism

diarrea *f* diarrhea

diástole *f* diastole

diatermia *f* diathermy

dibujante *mf* sketcher, illustrator ‖ *m* draftsman

dibujar *tr* to draw, sketch, design; outline ‖ *ref* to be outlined; appear, show

dibujo *m* drawing, sketch, design; outline; **dibujo al carbón** charcoal drawing; **dibujo animado** animated cartoon; **no meterse en dibujos** to attend to one's business

di•caz *adj* (*pl* -**caces**) sarcastic, witty

dicción *f* diction; word

diccionario *m* dictionary

díceres *mpl* sayings; rumor(s)

diciembre *m* December

dicloruro *m* dichloride

dicotomía *f* dichotomy; (*entre médicos*) split fee

dictado *m* dictation; **escribir al dictado** to take dictation; (*lo que otro dicta*) to take down

dictador *m* dictator

dictadura *f* dictatorship

dictáfono *m* dictaphone

dictamen *m* dictum, judgment, opinion

dictar *tr* to dictate; (*una ley*) promulgate; inspire, suggest; (*una conferencia*) give, deliver (*a lecture*)

dicterio *m* taunt, insult

dicha *f* happiness; luck; **por dicha** by chance

dicharache•ro -ra *adj* obscene, vulgar

dicharacho *m* obscenity, vulgarity; wisecrack

di•cho -cha *adj* said; **dicho y hecho** no sooner said than done; **mejor dicho** rather; **tener por dicho** to consider settled ‖ *m* saying; promise of marriage, one's word; witticism; insult; **dicho de las gentes** talk, hearsay, gossip ‖ *f* see **dicha**

dicho•so -sa *adj* happy; lucky, fortunate; annoying, tiresome
didácti•co -ca *adj* didactic
diecinueve *adj & pron* nineteen ‖ *m* nineteen; (*en las fechas*) nineteenth
diecinuevea•vo -va *adj & m* nineteenth
dieciocha•vo -va *adj m* eighteenth
dieciocho *adj & pron* eighteen ‖ *m* eighteen; (*en las fechas*) eighteenth
dieciséis *adj & pron* sixteen ‖ *m* sixteen; (*en las fechas*) sixteenth
dieciseisa•vo -va *adj & m* sixteenth
diecisiete *adj & pron* seventeen ‖ *m* seventeen; (*en las fechas*) seventeenth
diecisietea•vo -va *adj & m* seventeenth
diente *m* tooth; (*de elefante y otros animales*) tusk, fang; (*de peine, sierra, rastrillo*) tooth; (*de rueda dentada*) cog; **dar diente con diente** to shake all over; **decir entre dientes** to mutter, to mumble; **diente canino** eyetooth, canine tooth; **diente de león** dandelion; **estar a diente** to be famished; **tener buen diente** to be a hearty eater; **traer entre dientes** to have a grudge against; to talk about
diére•sis *f* (*pl* **-sis**) diaeresis; (*señal que indica la metafonía*) umlaut
diesel *m* diesel motor
dieseléctri•co -ca *adj* diesel-electric
dies•tro -tra *adj* right; handy, skillful; shrewd, sly; favorable; **a diestro y siniestro** wildly, right and left ‖ *m* expert fencer; bullfighter on foot; matador; halter, bridle ‖ *f* right hand; **juntar diestra con diestra** to join forces
dieta *f* diet; **dietas** per diem; **estar a dieta** to diet, be on a diet
dietario *m* family budget
dietista *mf* dietitian
diez *adj & pron* ten; **las diez** ten o'clock ‖ *m* ten; (*en las fechas*) tenth
diezmar *tr* (*causar gran mortandad en*) to decimate; (*pagar el diezmo de*) tithe
diezmo *m* tithe
difamación *f* defamation, vilification
difamar *tr* to defame, vilify
diferencia *f* difference; **a diferencia de** unlike; **partir la diferencia** to split the difference
diferenciar *tr* to differentiate ‖ *intr* (*discordar*) to differ, dissent ‖ *ref* (*distinguirse una cosa de otra*) to differ, be different
diferente *adj* different
diferir §68 *tr* to defer, postpone, put off ‖ *intr* to differ, be different
difícil *adj* difficult, hard; hard to please
difícilmente *adv* with difficulty
dificultad *f* difficulty; (*reparo que se opone a una opinión*) objection
dificultar *tr* to make difficult; consider difficult ‖ *intr* to raise objections ‖ *ref* to become difficult
dificulto•so -sa *adj* difficult, troublesome; objecting; (coll) ugly, homely
difidencia *f* distrust
difidente *adj* distrustful
difteria *f* diphtheria

difundir *tr* to diffuse; spread, disseminate; divulge, publish; broadcast ‖ *ref* to diffuse; spread
difun•to -ta *adj & mf* deceased; **difunto de taberna** dead-drunk ‖ *m* corpse
difu•so -sa *adj* diffuse; extended; wordy
digerible *adj* digestible
digerir §68 *tr* to digest; **no digerir** to not bear, not stand ‖ *intr* to digest
digestible *adj* digestible
digestión *f* digestion
digesti•vo -va *adj & m* digestive
digesto *m* (law) digest
dígito *m* digit
dignación *f* condescension
dignar *ref* to deign, condescend
dignatario *m* dignitary, official
dignidad *f* dignity; bishop, archbishop
dignificar §73 *tr* to dignify
dig•no -na *adj* worthy; fitting, suitable; (*grave, decoroso*) dignified
digresión *f* digression
dije *m* amulet, charm, trinket; (*persona de excelentes cualidades*) jewel; person all dressed-up; handy person
dilacerar *tr* to tear to pieces; (*la honra, el orgullo*) damage
dilación *f* delay
dilapidación *f* waste; squandering
dilapidar *tr* to squander
dilatación *f* expansion; serenity
dilatar *tr* to dilate, expand; defer, postpone; (*p.ej., la fama*) spread ‖ *ref* to dilate, expand; spread; be wordy; delay
dilección *f* true love
dilec•to -ta *adj* dearly beloved
dilema *m* dilemma
diletante *adj & mf* dilettante
diletantismo *m* dilettantism
diligencia *f* diligence; step, démarche; errand; dispatch, speed; stagecoach; **hacer una diligencia** to do an errand; to have a bowel movement
diligente *adj* diligent; quick, ready
dilucidación *f* explanation; enlightenment
dilucidar *tr* to elucidate, explain
dilución *f* dilution
diluí•do -da *adj* dilute
diluir §20 *tr* to dilute; thin ‖ *ref* to dilute; melt; dissolve
diluviar *intr* to rain hard, pour
diluvio *m* deluge
dimanar *intr* to spring up; **dimanar de** to spring from, originate in
dimensión *f* dimension
dimes *mpl* — **andar en dimes y diretes con** to bicker with
diminuti•vo -va *adj & m* (gram) diminutive
diminu•to -ta *adj* tiny, diminutive; defective
dimisión *f* resignation
dimisorias *fpl* — **dar dimisorias a** to discharge, fire
dimitir *tr* to resign, resign from ‖ *intr* to resign
din *m* (coll) dough, money
Dinamarca *f* Denmark

de
di

dinamar•qués -quesa *adj* Danish ‖ *mf* Dane ‖ *m* Danish (*language*)
dinámi•co -ca *adj* dynamic
dinamita *f* dynamite
dinamitar *tr* to dynamite
dínamo *f* dynamo
dinasta *m* dynast
dinastía f dynasty
dindán *m* ding-dong
dinerada *f* or **dineral** *m* large sum of money
dinero *m* money; currency; wealth; **dinero contante** cash; **dinero contante y sonante** ready cash, spot cash, **dinero de bolsillo** pocket money
dinero•so -sa *adj* moneyed, wealthy
dintel *m* lintel, doorhead
dióce•si *f* or **dióce•sis** *f* (*pl* -**sis**) diocese
diodo *m* diode
dios *m* god; **Dios mediante** God willing; **¡por Dios!** goodness!, for heaven's sake; **¡válgame Dios!** bless me!; **¡vaya con Dios!** off with you!
diosa *f* goddess
diploma *m* diploma
diplomacia *f* diplomacy
diploma•do -da *adj* & *mf* graduate
diplomar *tr* & *ref* to graduate
diplomáti•co -ca *adj* diplomatic ‖ *mf* diplomat
diptongar §44 *tr* & *ref* to diphthongize
diptongo *m* diphthong
diputación *f* congress; commission
diputa•do -da *mf* deputy, representative
diputar *tr* to commission, delegate; designate
dique *m* dike, jetty; dry dock; check, stop; **dique seco** dry dock
dirección *f* direction; (*señas en una carta*) address; administration, management; directorship; (aut) steering; **de dirección única** one-way; **dirección a la derecha** right-hand drive; **dirección a la izquierda** left-hand drive; **perder la dirección** to lose control of the car
directi•vo -va *adj* managing ‖ *mf* director, manager ‖ *f* management
direc•to -ta *adj* direct; straight
direc•tor -tora *adj* directing, guiding; managing, governing ‖ *mf* director, manager; (*de un periódico*) editor; (*de una escuela*) principal; (*de una orquesta*) conductor; **director de escena** stage manager; **director de funeraria** funeral director; **director gerente** managing director
directorio *m* directorship; directory
dirigente *mf* leader, head, executive
dirigible *adj* & *m* dirigible
dirigir §27 *tr* to direct; manage; (*un automóvil*) steer; (*una carta; la palabra*) address; (*una obra*) dedicate ‖ *ref* to go, betake oneself; turn; **dirigirse a** to address; apply to
dirimir *tr* to dissolve, annul; (*una dificultad*) solve; (*una controversia*) settle, mediate
discar §73 *tr* & *intr* to dial
disceptar *intr* to discuss, debate
discerniente *adj* discerning
discernir §28 *tr* to discern; distinguish

disciplina *f* discipline; **disiplinas** scourge, whip
disciplina•do -da *adj* disciplined; (*flores*) many-colored
disciplinar *tr* to discipline; teach; scourge, whip
discípu•lo -la *mf* disciple; pupil
disco *m* disk; (*del gramófono*) record, disk; (sport) discus; **disco de cola** (rr) taillight; **disco de goma** (*para un grifo*) washer (*for a spigot*); **disco de identificación** identification tag; **disco de larga duración** long-playing record; **disco de señales** (rr) semaphore; **disco selector** (telp) dial; **disco vertebral** spinal disk; **siempre el mismo disco** the same old song
discóbolo *m* discus thrower
discófi•lo -la *mf* record lover, discophile
disco•lo -la *adj* ungovernable, wayward
disconforme *adj* disagreeing
discontinuar §21 *tr* to discontinue
discordancia *f* discordance
discordar §61 *intr* to be out of tune; disagree
discorde *adj* discordant, disagreeing; (mus) discordant, out of tune
discordia *f* discord
discoteca *f* discothèque, disco; record cabinet; record library
discreción *f* discretion; wit; witticism; **a discreción** at discretion; (mil) unconditionally
discrepancia *f* discrepancy; dissent
discrepar *intr* to differ, disagree
discretear *intr* to try to be clever, try to sparkle
discre•to -ta *adj* (*juicioso*) discreet; (*discontinuo*) discrete; witty
discrimen *m* risk, hazard; difference
discriminación *f* discrimination
discriminar *tr* to discriminate against ‖ *intr* to discriminate
discriminato•rio -ria *adj* discriminatory
disculpa *f* excuse, apology
disculpar *tr* to excuse; pardon, overlook ‖ *ref* to apologize; **disculparse con** to apologize to; **disculparse de** to apologize for
discurrir *tr* to contrive, invent; guess, conjecture ‖ *intr* to ramble, roam; occur, take place; discourse; reason; pass, elapse
discursi•s•to -ta *adj* long-winded; (coll) windy; *mf* windbag; big talker
discursi•vo -va *adj* meditative
discurso *m* discourse, speech; (*paso del tiempo*) course; **discurso de sobremesa** after-dinner speech
discusión *f* discussion
discutible *adj* debatable
discutir *tr* to discuss ‖ *intr* to discuss; argue
disecar §73 *tr* to dissect; (*un animal muerto*) stuff; (*una planta*) mount
diseminar *tr* to disseminate; scatter ‖ *ref* to scatter
disensión *f* (*oposición*) dissent; (*contienda*) dissension
disentería *f* dysentery
disentir §68 *intr* to dissent
diseñar *tr* to draw, sketch; design, outline

diseño m drawing, sketch; design, outline
disertar intr to discourse, discuss
diser•to -ta adj fluent, eloquent
disfavor m disfavor
disforme adj formless; monstrous, ugly
disforzar §35 ref (Peru) to be prudish, be finical
dis•fraz m (pl **-fraces**) disguise; (traje de máscara) costume, fancy dress
disfrazar §60 tr to disguise ‖ ref to disguise oneself; wear fancy dress, masquerade, dress in costume
disfrutar tr to enjoy, to use ‖ intr —**disfrutar de** to enjoy, use; **disfrutar con** to enjoy, take enjoyment in
disfrute m enjoyment, use
disfunción f dysfunction
disgregar §44 tr & intr to disintegrate, break up
disgusta•do -da adj tasteless, insipid; sad, sorrowful; disagreeable; (Mex) hard to please
disgustar tr to displease ‖ ref to be displeased; fall out, become estranged
disgusto m displeasure; annoyance, unpleasantness; grief, sorrow; difference, quarrel; **a disgusto** against one's will
disidencia f dissidence; (de una doctrina) dissent
disidente adj dissident ‖ mf dissident, dissenter
disidir intr to dissent
disíla•bo -ba adj dissyllabic ‖ m dissyllable
disímil adj dissimilar
disimilar tr & ref to dissimilate
disimula•do -da adj sly, underhanded; **a lo disimulado** or **a la disimulada** underhandedly; **hacer la disimulada** to feign ignorance
disimular tr to dissemble, dissimulate, hide, conceal; overlook, pardon ‖ intr to dissemble, dissimulate
disimulo m dissembling, dissimulation; indulgence
disipación f dissipation
disipa•do -da adj dissipated; spendthrift ‖ mf debauchee; spendthrift
disipar tr to dissipate ‖ ref to be dissipated; disappear, evanesce
dislate m nonsense
dislocar §73 tr to dislocate ‖ ref to dislocate; be dislocated
disloque m tops, top notch
disminución f diminution; decrease; **disminución física** handicap, disability
disminuir §20 tr, intr & ref to diminish
disociar tr to dissociate
disolución f dissolution; disbandment; (relajación de costumbres) dissoluteness, dissipation
disolu•to -ta adj dissolute ‖ mf debauchee
disolver §47 & §83 tr to dissolve; disband; destroy, ruin ‖ intr & ref to dissolve
disonancia f dissonance
disonar §61 intr to be dissonant, lack harmony, disagree; cause surprise; sound bad

dispar adj unlike, different; (que no hace juego) odd
disparada f sudden flight; **a la disparada** like a shot, in mad haste; **de una disparada** (Arg) right away; **tomar la disparada** (Arg) to take to one's heels
disparadero m trigger
disparador m trigger; (de reloj) escapement; **poner en el disparador** to drive mad
disparar tr to throw, hurl; shoot, fire ‖ intr to rant, talk nonsense ‖ ref to dash away, rush away; (un caballo) run away; (una escopeta) to go off; be beside oneself
disparata•do -da adj absurd, nonsensical; frightful
disparatar intr to talk nonsense; act foolishly
disparate m folly, nonsense; blunder, mistake; outrage
dispare•jo -ja adj unequal, different, uneven, disparate; rough, broken
disparidad f disparity
disparo m shot, discharge; nonsense; (mach) release, trip; **cambiar disparos** to exchange shots
dispendio m waste, extravagance
dispendio•so -sa adj expensive
dispensar tr to excuse, pardon; exempt; dispense; dispense with
dispensario m dispensary; **dispensario de alimentos** soup kitchen
dispepsia f dyspepsia
dispersar tr & ref to disperse
displicente adj disagreeable; cross, fretful; peevish
disponer §54 tr to dispose, arrange; direct, order ‖ intr to dispose; **disponer de** to dispose of, have at one's disposal ‖ ref to prepare, get ready; get ready to die, make one's will
disponible adj available, disposable
disposición f disposition, arrangement, layout; inclination; preparation; disposal; predisposition; state of health; elegance; **estar a la disposición de** to be at the disposal of, be at the service of; **última disposición** last will and testament
dispositivo m appliance, device
dispues•to -ta adj ready, prepared; comely, graceful; clever, skillful; **bien dispuesto** well-disposed; well, in good health; **mal dispuesto** ill-disposed, unfavorable; ill, indisposed
disputa f dispute; fight, struggle; **sin disputa** beyond dispute
disputar tr to dispute, question; argue over; fight for ‖ intr to dispute; debate, argue; fight
disquería f record shop
disque•ro -ra mf record dealer
distancia f distance; **a distancia** at a distance; **a larga distancia** long-distance; **tomar distancia** to stand aside, stand off
distante adj distant
distar intr to be distant, be far; be different
distender §51 tr to distend; (p.ej., las piernas) stretch ‖ ref to distend; relax; (un reloj) run down

di
di

distensión *f* distension; relaxation of tension
distinción *f* (*honor, prerrogativa*) distinction; (*diferencia*) distinctness; **a distinción de** unlike
distingui•do -da *adj* distinguished; refined, urbane, smooth
distinguir §29 *tr* to distinguish; give distinction to; make out
distinti•vo -va *adj* distinctive ‖ *m* badge, insignia; distinction; distinctive mark
distin•to -ta *adj* distinct; different; **distintos** various, several
distorsión *f* distortion
distorsionar *tr* to distort, twist, bend
distracción *f* distraction; (*licencia en las costumbres*) dissipation; (*substracción de fondos*) embezzlement
distraer §75 *tr* to distract; amuse, divert, entertain; seduce; embezzle
distraí•do -da *adj* absent-minded, distracted; licentious, dissolute; (Chile, Mex) untidy, careless
distribución *f* distribution; electric supply system; timing gears, valve gears
distribui•dor -dora *adj* distributing ‖ *mf* distributor ‖ *m* (aut) distributor; slide valve; **distribuidor automático** vending machine
distribuir §20 *tr* to distribute
distrito *m* district; (rr) section; **distrito electoral** precinct; **distrito postal** zone, postal zone
disturbar *tr* to disturb
disturbio *m* disturbance
disuadir *tr* to dissuade
disyunti•vo -va *adj* disjunctive ‖ *f* dilemma
disyuntor *m* circuit breaker
dita *f* bond, surety
diuca *m* (Arg, Chile) teacher's pet ‖ *f* (Arg, Chile) finch (*Fringilla diuca*)
diuréti•co -ca *adj* & *m* diuretic
diur•no -na *adj* day, daytime
diva *f* goddess; (mus) diva
divagación *f* digression; wandering
divagar §44 *intr* to digress; ramble, wander
diván *m* divan; **diván cama** day bed
divergir §27 *intr* to diverge
diversidad *f* diversity; abundance
diversificación *f* diversification
diversificar §73 *tr* & *ref* to diversify
diversión *f* diversion
diver•so -sa *adj* diverse, different; **diversos** several, various, divers
diverti•do -da *adj* amusing, funny; (Am) tipsy
divertimiento *m* diversion, amusement
divertir §68 *tr* to divert; amuse ‖ *ref* to enjoy oneself, have a good time
dividendo *m* dividend
dividir *tr* to divide ‖ *ref* to divide, be divided; separate
divieso *m* boil
divinidad *f* divinity; (*persona dotada de gran belleza*) beauty
divinizar §60 *tr* to deify; exalt, extol
divi•no -na *adj* divine
divisa *f* badge; emblem; motto; goal, ideal; currency, foreign exchange

divisar *tr* to descry, espy
división *f* division; (*deportes*) class, category; league
divisor *m* (math) divisor; **máximo común divisor** greatest common divisor; **divisor de voltaje** (rad) voltage divider
divisoria *f* dividing line; (geog) divide
di•vo -va *adj* godlike, divine ‖ *m* god; (mus) opera star ‖ *f* see **diva**
divorciar *tr* to divorce ‖ *ref* to divorce, get divorced
divorcio *m* divorce; divergency (*in opinion*); (Col) jail for women
divulgación *f* divulging, disclosure; popularization
divulgar §44 *tr* to divulge, disclose; popularize
D.ⁿ *abbr* don
dobladillar *tr* to hem
dobladillo *m* hem
dobla•do -da *adj* rough, uneven; stocky, thickset; double-dealing ‖ *m* (mov) dubbing
doblaje *m* (mov) dubbing
doblar *tr* to double; fold, crease; bend; (*una esquina*) turn, round; (*un promontorio*) double; (*una película, generalmente en otro idioma*) dub; (bridge) to double; (Mex) to shoot down ‖ *intr* to turn; (*tocar a muerto*) toll; (mov, theat) to double, stand in; (bridge) to double ‖ *ref* to double; fold, crease; bend; bow, stoop; give in, yield
doble *adj* double; heavy, thick; stocky, thickset; deceitful, two-faced ‖ *adv* double, doubly ‖ *mf* (mov, theat) double, stand-in ‖ *m* double; fold, crease; (*toque de difuntos*) toll, knell; (*suma que se paga por la prórroga de una operación a plazos en la bolsa*) margin; **al doble** doubly
doblegar §44 *tr* to fold; bend; (*una espada*) brandish, flourish; sway, dominate ‖ *ref* to fold; bend; give in, yield
doblete *adj* medium ‖ *m* (*piedra falsa; cada una de dos palabras que poseen un mismo origen*) doublet; (bridge) doubleton
do•blez *m* (*pl* **-bleces**) fold, crease; (*del pantalón*) cuff; duplicity, double-dealing
doce *adj* & *pron* twelve; **las doce** twelve o'clock ‖ *m* twelve; (*en las fechas*) twelfth
docea•vo -va *adj* & *m* twelfth
docena *f* dozen; **docena del fraile** baker's dozen
docencia *f* (Arg) teaching; (Arg) teaching staff
docente *adj* educational, teaching
dócil *adj* docile; soft, ductile
doc•to -ta *adj* learned ‖ *mf* scholar
doc•tor -tora *mf* doctor ‖ *f* (coll) bluestocking
doctorado *m* doctorate
doctoran•do -da *mf* candidate for the doctor's degree
doctorar *tr* to grant the doctor's degree to ‖ *ref* to get the doctor's degree
doctrina *f* doctrine; teaching, instruction; learning; catechism; preaching the Gospel
doctrinar *tr* to teach, instruct

doctrino *m* orphan (*in orphanage*); **parecer un doctrino** to look scared

documentación *f* documentation; **documentación del buque** ship's papers

documental *adj* documentary ‖ *m* (mov) documentary

documentar *tr* to document

documento *m* document; **documento de prueba** (law) exhibit

dogal *m* (*para atar las caballerías*) halter; (*para ahorcar a un reo*) noose, halter, hangman's rope; **estar con el dogal a la garganta** or **al cuello** to be in a tight spot

dogmáti·co -ca *adj* dogmatic

do·go -ga *mf* bulldog

dolamas *fpl* or **dolames** *mpl* hidden defects of a horse; complaints, aches and pains

dolar §61 *tr* to hew

dólar *m* dollar

dolencia *f* ailment, complaint

doler §47 *tr* to ache, pain; grieve, distress; **dolerle a uno el dinero** to hate to spend money ‖ *intr* to ache, hurt, pain ‖ *ref* to complain; feel sorry; repent

doliente *adj* sick, ill; aching, suffering; sad, sorrowful ‖ *mf* sufferer, patient ‖ *m* mourner

dolo *m* deceit, fraud, guile

dolor *m* ache, pain; grief, sorrow; regret, repentance; **dolor de cabeza** headache; **dolor de muelas** toothache; **dolor de oído** earache; **dolor de yegua** (CAm) lumbago; **estar con dolores** to be in labor

dolori·do -da *adj* sore, painful; grieving, disconsolate

doloro·so -sa *adj* painful; sorrowful, sad

dolo·so -sa *adj* deceitful, guileful

domador *m* horsebreaker; animal tamer

domar *tr* to tame, break; master

domeñar *tr* to master, subdue

domesticar §73 *tr* to domesticate; tame

domésti·co -ca *adj* domestic, household ‖ *mf* domestic, servant

domiciliar *tr* to domicile, settle; (*una carta*) (Mex) to address ‖ *ref* to be domiciled, take up one's residence

domicilio *m* domicile, home; dwelling, house; **domicilio social** home office, company office

dominación *f* domination; (mil) eminence, high ground

dominante *adj* dominant; (*mandón*) domineering ‖ *f* (mus) dominant

dominar *tr* to dominate; check, restrain, subdue; (*una ciencia, un idioma*) master ‖ *intr* to dominate; (*mandar imperiosamente*) domineer ‖ *ref* to restrain oneself

dómine *m* schoolmaster, Latin teacher; pedant

domingo *m* Sunday; **domingo de ramos** Palm Sunday; **domingo de resurrección** Easter Sunday; **guardar el domingo** to keep the Sabbath

dominguillo *m* tumbler

dominica·no -na *adj* & *mf* Dominican

dominio *m* dominion; domain; (*de una ciencia, de un idioma*) mastery; (*del aire*) supremacy

domi·nó *m* (*pl* **-nós**) (*traje*) domino; (*juego*) dominoes; (*fichas*) set of dominoes

dom.° *abbr* **domingo**

domo *m* dome

dompedro *m* four-o'clock

don *m* gift, present; talent, natural gift; Don (*Spanish title used before masculine Christian names*); **don de acierto** knack for doing the right thing; **don de errar** knack for doing the wrong thing; **don de gentes** charm, social grace; **don de lenguas** linguistic facility; **don de mando** ability to lead, generalship

dona *f* gift, present; **donas** wedding presents from the bridegroom to the bride

donación *f* gift, bequest; endowment

donada *f* lay sister

donado *m* lay brother

dona·dor -dora *mf* donor

donaire *m* charm, grace; witticism; cleverness

donairo·so -sa *adj* charming, graceful; witty; clever

donar *tr* to donate, give

doncel *adj* mild, mellow ‖ *m* (*joven noble aun no armado caballero*) bachelor; (*hombre virgen*) virgin

doncella *f* maiden, virgin; housemaid; lady's maid; maid of honor; (Col, Ven) felon, whitlow

doncellez *f* maidenhood, virginity

doncellona *f* or **doncellueca** *f* unmarried woman, maiden lady

donde *conj* where; wherever; in which; **donde no** otherwise; **por donde quiera** anywhere, everywhere ‖ *prep* at or to the house, office, or store of

dónde *adv* where; **a dónde** where, whither; **de dónde** from where, whence; **por dónde** which way; for what cause, for what reason

dondequiera *adv* anywhere; **dondequiera que** wherever

dondiego *m* four-o'clock; **dondiego de día** morning-glory; **dondiego de noche** four-o'clock

donillero *m* sharper, smoothy

donjuán *m* four-o'clock

donosidad *f* charm, grace, wit

dono·so -sa *adj* charming, graceful, witty

donostiarra *adj* San Sebastian ‖ *mf* native or inhabitant of San Sebastian

donosura *f* charm, grace, wit

doña *f* Doña (*Spanish title used before feminine Christian names*)

doñear *intr* (coll) to hang around women

doquier or **doquiera** *conj* wherever; **por doquier** everywhere

dorada *f* (ichth) gilthead

doradillo *m* fine brass wire

dora·do -da *adj* golden; gilt ‖ *m* gilt, gilding; **dorados** bronze trimmings (*on furniture*) ‖ *f* see **dorada**

di
do

dorar *tr* to gold-plate; gild; (*tostar ligeramente*) brown; (*paliar*) sugar-coat ‖ *ref* to turn golden; turn brown
dormi•lón -lona *adj* sleepy ‖ *mf* sleepyhead ‖ *f* reclining armchair; mimosa; (Mex) headrest; (Ven) sleeping gown; **dormilonas** pearl earrings
dormir §30 *tr* to put to sleep; (*p.ej., una borrachera*) sleep off ‖ *intr* to sleep; spend the night ‖ *ref* to sleep; fall asleep; (*entorpecerse, p.ej., el pie*) go to sleep
dormirlas *m* hide-and-seek
dormitar *intr* to doze, nap
dormitorio *m* bedroom; (*muebles propios de esta habitación*) bedroom suit
dorsal *m* (sport) number (*worn on shirt*)
dorso *m* back
dos *adj & pron* two; **las dos** two o'clock ‖ *m* two; (*en las fechas*) second
dosal•bo -ba *adj* (*horse*) with two white feet
doscien•tos -tas *adj & pron* two hundred ‖ **doscientos** *m* two hundred
dosel *m* canopy, dais
doselera *f* valance, drapery
dosificación *f* dosage
dosificar §73 *tr* (*un medicamento*) to dose, give in doses
do•sis *f* (*pl* **-sis**) dose
dos-pie•zas *m* (*pl* **-zas**) two-piece bathing suit
dotación *f* (*de una mujer; de una fundación*) endowment; (nav) complement; (aer) crew; (*de remeros*) (sport) crew; staff, personnel
dotar *tr* to give a dowry to; endow; (*un buque*) staff, man; (*una oficina*) staff; equip; fix the wages for
dote *m & f* dowry, marriage portion ‖ *m* (*en el juego de naipes*) stack of chips ‖ *f* endowment, talent, gift; **dotes de mando** leadership
dovela *f* voussoir
doza•vo -va *adj & m* twelfth
d/p *abbr* **días plazo**
dracma *f* (*moneda griega*) drachma; (*peso farmacéutico*) dram
draga *f* dredge; (*barco*) dredger
dragado *m* dredging
dragami•nas *m* (*pl* **-nas**) mine sweeper
dragar §44 *tr* to dredge
dragón *m* dragon; (*planta*) snapdragon; (*soldado*) dragoon
dragonear *intr* to flirt; boast; **dragonear de** to boast of being; pretend to be, pass oneself off as
drama *m* drama
dramáti•co -ca *adj* dramatic ‖ *mf* (*autor*) dramatist; actor ‖ *f* (*arte y género*) drama
dramatizar §60 *tr* to dramatize
dramaturgo *m* dramatist
drásti•co -ca *adj* drastic
dren *m* drain
drenaje *m* drainage
drenar *tr* to drain
driblar *tr & intr* to dribble
dril *m* drill; duck; **dril de algodón** denim
driza *f* (naut) halyard
dro. *abbr* **derecho**

droga *f* drug; annoyance, bother; deceit, trick; (Chile, Mex, Peru) bad debt; (Cuba) drug on the market; **drogas milagrosas** wonder drugs
drogadic•to -ta *adj* drug-addicted ‖ *mf* drug addict
drogado *m* doping
drogar §44 *tr* to dope
droguería *f* drug store; drug business; (*comercio de substancias usadas en química, industria, medicina, bellas artes*) drysaltery (Brit)
drogue•ro -ra *mf* druggist; drysalter (Brit)
droguista *mf* druggist; (coll) crook, cheat; (Arg) toper, drunk
droláti•co -ca *adj* droll, snappy
dromedario *m* dromedary; big heavy animal; brute (*person*)
druida *m* druid
dúa *f* (min) gang of workmen
dual *adj & m* dual
dualidad *f* duality; (Chile) tie vote
ducado *m* duchy, dukedom; (*moneda antigua*) ducat; **gran ducado** grand duchy
dúctil *adj* ductile; easy to handle
ducha *f* (*chorro de agua en una cavidad del cuerpo*) douche; (*chorro de agua sobre el cuerpo entero*) shower bath; (*lista en los tejidos*) stripe; **ducha en alfileres** needle bath
duchar *tr* to douche; give a shower bath to ‖ *ref* to douche; take a shower bath
du•cho -cha *adj* experienced, expert, skillful ‖ *f* see **ducha**
duda *f* doubt; **sin duda** doubtless, no doubt, without doubt
dudable *adj* doubtful
dudar *tr* to doubt; question ‖ *intr* to hesitate; **dudar de** to doubt
dudo•so -sa *adj* doubtful; dubious
duela *f* stave (*of barrel*)
duelista *m* duelist
duelo *m* (*combate entre dos*) duel; grief, sorrow; bereavement, mourning; (*los que asisten a los funerales*) mourners; **batirse en duelo** to duel, to fight a duel; **duelos** hardships; **sin duelo** in abundance
duende *m* elf, goblin; gold cloth, silver cloth; (coll) restless daemon; **tener duende** to be burning within
due•ño -ña *mf* owner, proprietor; **dueño de sí mismo** one's own master; **ser dueño de** to be master of; be at liberty to, be free to ‖ *m* master, landlord ‖ *f* mistress, landlady, housekeeper; duenna; matron; **dueña de casa** housewife
duermevela *f* doze, light sleep; (*sueño fatigoso e interrumpido*) fitful sleep
dula *f* common pasture land; land irrigated from common ditch
dulce *adj* sweet; (*agua*) fresh; (*metal*) soft, ductile; gentle, mild, pleasant; (*manjar*) tasteless, insipid ‖ *m* candy; piece of candy; preserves; **dulce de almíbar** preserved fruit; **dulces** candy
dulcera *f* candy dish, preserve dish
dulcería *f* candy store, confectionery store

dulce•ro -ra *adj* sweet-toothed ‖ *mf* confectioner ‖ *f* see **dulcera**

dulcificar §73 *tr* to sweeten; appease, mollify ‖ *ref* to sweeten, turn sweet

dulcinea *f* sweetheart; ideal

dulzaina *f* flageolet

dulza•rrón -rrona *adj* cloying, sickening

dulzo•so -sa *adj* sweetish

dulzura *f* sweetness; pleasantness, kindliness; (*del clima*) mildness; endearment, sweet word

duna *f* dune

dun•do -da *adj* (CAm, Col) simple, stupid ‖ *mf* (CAm, Col) simpleton

dúo *m* duet, duo

duodéci•mo -ma *adj & m* twelfth

duodeno *m* duodenum

duplica•do -da *adj & m* duplicate; **por duplicado** in duplicate

duplicar §73 *tr* to duplicate; double; repeat

duplicata *f* duplicate

duplicidad *f* (*falsedad*) duplicity; (*calidad de doble*) doubleness

du•plo -pla *adj & m* double

duque *m* duke; **gran duque** grand duke

duquesa *f* duchess; **gran duquesa** grand duchess

dura *f* durability; **de dura** or **de mucha dura** strong, durable

durable *adj* durable, lasting

duración *f* duration, endurance; (*espacio de tiempo del uso de una cosa*) life

durade•ro -ra *adj* durable, lasting

durante *prep* during, for

durar *intr* to last; remain; (*la ropa*) last, wear, wear well

durazno *m* peach; peach tree

dureza *f* hardness; harshness, roughness; **dureza de corazón** hardheartedness; **dureza de oído** hardness of hearing; **dureza de vientre** constipation

durmiente *adj* sleeping; **la Bella Durmiente** Sleeping Beauty ‖ *mf* sleeper ‖ *m* girder, sleeper, stringer; tie, railroad tie; (Ven) steel bar

du•ro -ra *adj* hard; (*huevo*) hard-boiled; harsh, rough; cruel; stubborn, obstinate; unbearable; strong, tough; stingy; (*tiempo*) stormy; **duro de corazón** hard-hearted; **duro de oído** hard of hearing; **duro de película** movie hero; **estar muy duro con** to be hard on; **ser duro de pelar** to be hard to put across; be hard to deal with ‖ *m* dollar (*Spanish coin worth five pesetas*) ‖ *f* see **dura** ‖ **duro** *adv* hard

dux *m* (*pl* **dux**) doge

d/v *abbr* días vista

do
ec

E

E, e (e) *f* sixth letter of the Spanish alphabet

e *conj* (used before words beginning with *i* or *hi* not followed by a vowel) and

ea *interj* hey!

ebanista *m* cabinetmaker, woodworker

ebanistería *f* cabinetmaking, woodwork; cabinetmaker's shop

ébano *m* ebony

ebriedad *f* drunkenness

e•brio -bria *adj* drunk; (*p.ej., de ira*) blind ‖ *mf* drunk

ebrio•so -sa *adj* drinking ‖ *mf* drinker

ebullición *f* boiling

eclécti•co -ca *adj & mf* eclectic

eclesiásti•co -ca *adj & m* ecclesiastic

eclipsar *tr* to eclipse; (fig) to outshine ‖ *ref* to be in eclipse; (fig) to disappear

eclipse *m* eclipse

eclip•sis *f* (*pl* **-sis**) var of **elipsis**

eclisa *f* (rr) fishplate

eco *m* echo; (*del tambor*) rumbling; **hacer eco** to echo; attract attention; **tener eco** to be well received, catch on

ecología *f* ecology

ecológi•co -ca *adj* ecologic(al)

ecologista *mf* or **ecólogo** *m* ecologist

economato *m* stewardship; commissary, company store, coöperative store

economía *f* economy; want, poverty; **economía política** economics; **economías** savings

económi•co -ca *adj* economic; (*que gasta poco; poco costoso*) economical; cheap; miserly, niggardly

economista *mf* economist

economizar §60 *tr* to economize, save; avoid ‖ *intr* to economize, save; skimp

ecónomo *m* steward, trustee; supply priest

ecuación *f* equation

ecuador *m* equator ‖ **el Ecuador** Ecuador

ecuánime *adj* calm, composed; impartial

ecuanimidad *f* equanimity; impartiality

ecuatoria•no -na *adj & mf* Ecuadoran, Ecuadorian

ecuestre *adj* equestrian

eculcorante *adj* sweetening ‖ *m* sweetener

ecuméni•co -ca *adj* ecumenic(al)

eczema *m & f* eczema

echacan•tos *m* (*pl* **-tos**) good-for-nothing

echacuer•vos *m* (*pl* **-vos**) pimp, procurer; cheat

echada *f* cast, throw; man's length; (Arg, Mex) boast, hoax

echadero *m* place to stretch out

echadi•zo -za *adj* discarded, waste; spying ‖ *mf* foundling ‖ *m* spy

echa•do -da *adj* stretched out; (C-R) lazy, indolent; **estar echado** (CAm, Mex, P-R) to have an easy job (or easy life) ‖ *f see* **echada**

echar *tr* to throw, throw away, throw out; issue, emit; publish; discharge, dismiss; swallow; (*p.ej., agua*) pour; (*p.ej., un cigarrillo*) smoke; (*la baraja*) deal; (*una partida de cartas*) play; (*una llave*) turn; (*un discurso*) deliver; (*un drama*) put on; (*maldiciones*) utter; (*pelo, dientes, renuevos*) grow, put forth; (*impuestos*) impose, levy; (*la buenaventura*) tell; (*precio, distancia, edad, etc.*) ascribe, attribute; (*una mirada*) cast; (*sangre*) shed; (*la culpa*) lay; (*una mano*) lend; **echar abajo** to demolish, destroy; overthrow; **echar a pasear** to dismiss unceremoniously; **echar a perder** to spoil, ruin; **echar a pique** to sink; **echar de menos** to miss; **echarla de** to claim to be, boast of being; **echarlo todo a rodar** to upset everything; hit the ceiling ‖ *intr* — **echar a** to begin to; burst out (*e.g., crying*); **echar a perder** to spoil, ruin; **echar de ver** to notice, happen to see; **echar por** (*un empleo, un oficio*) to go into, take up; (*la derecha, la izquierda*) turn toward; (*un camino*) go down ‖ *ref* to throw oneself; lie down, stretch out; (*el viento*) fall; (*un abrigo*) throw on; (*una gallina*) set; **echarse a** to begin to; **echarse a morir** to give up in despair; **echarse a perder** to spoil, be ruined; **echarse atrás** to back out; **echarse de ver** to be easy to see; **echárselas de** to claim to be, boast of being; **echarse sobre** to rush at, fall upon

echazón *f* jettison, jetsam

echiquier *m* Exchequer

edad *f* age; **edad crítica** change of life; **edad de quintas** draft age; **edad escolar** school age; **Edad Media** Middle Ages; **edad viril** prime of life; **mayor edad** majority; **menor edad** minority

edecán *m* aide-de-camp

edema *f* edema

edición *f* edition; publication; **la segunda edición de** the spit and image of

edicto *m* edict

edificación *f* construction, building; buildings; (*inspiración con el buen ejemplo*) edification, uplift

edificante *adj* edifying

edificar §73 *tr* to construct, build; (*dar buen ejemplo a*) edify, uplift

edificio *m* edifice, building

editar *tr* to publish

edi•tor -tora *adj* publishing ‖ *mf* publisher

editorial *adj* publishing; editorial ‖ *m* editorial ‖ *f* publishing house

editorialista *mf* editorial writer

editorializar §60 *intr* (Urug) to editorialize

edredón *m* eider down

educación *f* education

educacional *adj* educational

educa•dor -dora *mf* educator

educan•do -da *mf* pupil, student

educar §73 *tr* to educate; (*los sentidos*) train; (*al niño o el adolescente*) rear, bring up

educati•vo -va *adj* educational

EE.UU. *abbr* **Estados Unidos**

efectismo *m* sensationalism

efectista *adj* sensational, theatrical ‖ *mf* sensationalist

efectivamente *adv* actually, really; as a matter of fact

efecti•vo -va *adj* actual, real; (*empleo, cargo*) regular, permanent; (*vigente*) effective; **hacer efectivo** to carry out; (*un cheque*) to cash; **hacerse efectivo** to become effective ‖ *m* cash; **efectivo en caja** cash on hand

efecto *m* effect; end, purpose; article; (*en el juego de billar*) English; **a ese efecto** for that purpose; **al efecto** for the purpose; **con efecto** or **en efecto** indeed, as a matter of fact; **efecto útil** efficiency, output; **llevar a efecto** or **poner en efecto** to put into effect, carry out; **surtir efecto** to work, have the desired effect

efectuar §21 *tr* to carry out, effect, effectuate ‖ *ref* to take place

efervescencia *f* effervescence

efervescente *adj* effervescent

eficacia *f* efficacy

efi•caz *adj* (*pl* **-caces**) efficacious, effectual; efficient

eficiencia *f* efficiency

eficiente *adj* efficient

efigie *f* effigy

efíme•ro -ra *adj* ephemeral

efugio *m* evasion, subterfuge

efusión *f* effusion; (*manifestación de afectos muy viva*) warmth, effusiveness; **efusión de sangre** bloodshed

efusi•vo -va *adj* effusive

égida *f* aegis

egip•cio -cia *adj & mf* Egyptian

Egipto *m* Egypt

eglantina *f* sweetbriar

eglefino *m* haddock

égloga *f* eclogue

egoísmo *m* egoism

egoísta *adj* egoistic ‖ *mf* egoist

egolatría *f* self-worship, self-glorification

egotismo *m* egotism

egotista *adj* egotistic(al) ‖ *mf* egotist

egre•gio -gia *adj* distinguished, eminent

egresar *intr* to graduate

egreso *m* departure; graduation

eje *m* (*pieza alrededor de la cual gira un cuerpo*) axle, shaft; (*línea que divide en dos mitades; línea recta alrededor de la cual se supone que gira un cuerpo*) axis; (fig) core, crux; **eje de balancín** rocker, rockershaft; **eje de carretón** axletree; **eje motor** drive shaft; **eje tándem** dual axle; dual rear

ejecución *f* execution

ejecutante *mf* performer

ejecutar *tr* to execute; perform

ejecutivamente *adv* expeditiously

ejecuti•vo -va *adj* urgent, pressing; insistent; executive ‖ *m* executive

ejecu•tor -tora *adj* executive ‖ *mf* executor;

ejecutor de la justicia executioner; **ejecutor testamentario** executor (*of a will*) ‖ *f* — **ejecutora testamentaria** executrix

ejemplar *adj* exemplary ‖ *m* pattern, model; (*de una obra impresa*) copy; precedent; (*caso que sirve de escarmiento*) example; **ejemplar de cortesía** complimentary copy; **ejemplar muestra** sample copy; **sin ejemplar** unprecedented; as a special case

ejemplarizar §60 *tr* to set an example to; exemplify

ejemplificar §73 *tr* to exemplify

ejemplo *m* example, instance; **por ejemplo** for example, for instance; **sin ejemplo** unexampled

ejercer §78 *tr* (*la medicina*) to practice; (*la caridad*) show, exercise; (*una fuerza*) exert ‖ *intr* to practice; **ejercer de** to practice as, work as

ejercicio *m* exercise; drill, practice; (*de un cargo u oficio*) tenure; (*uso constante*) exertion; (*año económico*) fiscal year; **hacer ejercicio** to take exercise; (mil) to drill

ejercitar *tr* to exercise; practice; drill, train ‖ *ref* to exercise; practice

ejército *m* army; **ejército permanente** standing army; **los tres ejércitos** the three arms of the service

ejido *m* commons

ejote *m* (CAm, Mex) string bean

el, la (*pl* **los, las**) *art def* the ‖ *pron dem* that, the one; **el que** who, which, that; he who, the one that

él *pron pers masc* he, it; him, it

elabora•do -da *adj* elaborate; finished

elaborar *tr* to elaborate; (*una teoría*) work out; (*el metal, la madera*) fashion, to work

elación *f* magnanimity, nobility; (*de estilo y lenguaje*) pomposity

elástica *f* knit undershirt; **elásticas** (Ven) suspenders

elasticidad *f* elasticity

elásti•co -ca *adj* elastic ‖ *m* elastic; bedspring ‖ *f* see **elástica**

eléboro *m* hellebore

elección *f* election; choice

electi•vo -va *adj* elective

elec•to -ta *adj* elect

electorado *m* electorate

electorero *m* henchman, heeler

electricidad *f* electricity

electricista *mf* electrician

eléctrico -ca *adj* electric(al)

electrificar §73 *tr* to electrify

electrizar §60 *tr* to electrify

electro *m* electromagnet

electroafeitadora *f* electric shaver

electrocutar *tr* to electrocute

electrodo *m* electrode

electrodomésti•co -ca *adj* electric-appliance ‖ *m* electric appliance

electróge•no -na *adj* generating electricity ‖ *m* electric generator

electroimán *m* electromagnet

electrólisis *f* electrolysis

electrólito *m* electrolyte

electromagnéti•co -ca *adj* electromagnetic

electromo•tor -tora or **-triz** *adj* (*pl* **-tores -toras -trices**) electromotive

electrón *m* electron

electróni•co -ca *adj* electronic ‖ *f* electronics

electrostáti•co -ca *adj* electrostatic

electrotecnia *f* electrical engineering

electrotipar *tr* to electrotype

electrotipo *m* electrotype

elefante *m* elephant; **elefante blanco** (fig) (SAm) white elephant

elegancia *f* elegance; style, stylishness

elegante *adj* elegant; stylish ‖ *mf* fashion plate

eleganto•so -sa *adj* elegant

elegía *f* elegy

elegía•co -ca *adj* elegiac

elegible *adj* eligible

elegir §57 *tr* to elect; choose, select

elemental *adj* (*primordial; simple, no compuesto*) elemental; (*que se refiere a los principios de una ciencia o arte; de fácil comprensión*) elementary

elemento *m* element; (*de una pila o batería*) cell; **elemento de compuestos** (gram) combining form; **elemento en rastro** trace element; **estar en su elemento** to be in one's element

elenco *m* catalogue, list, table; (theat) cast

elepé *adj* (*disco*) long-playing; LP ‖ *m* long-playing record

elevación *f* elevation; **elevación a potencias** (math) involution

eleva•do -da *adj* elevated, high; lofty, sublime

elevador *m* elevator; **elevador de granos** grain elevator

elevar *tr* to elevate, lift; (math) to raise ‖ *ref* to ascend, rise; be exalted; become conceited

elfo *m* elf

elidir *tr* to eliminate; (*una vocal*) elide

eliminar *tr* to eliminate; strike out ‖ *ref* (Mex) to go away, leave

elipse *f* (geom) ellipse

elip•sis *f* (*pl* **-sis**) (gram) ellipsis

elípti•co -ca *adj* (geom & gram) elliptic(al)

elisión *f* elision

elitista *adj* & *mf* elitist

elocución *f* public speaking, elocution

elocuencia *f* eloquence

elocuente *adj* eloquent

elogiable *adj* praiseworthy

elogiar *tr* to praise, eulogize

elogio *m* praise, eulogy

elogio•so -sa *adj* laudatory, glowing

elote *m* (Mex, Guat) ear of corn; **coger asando elotes** (CAm) to catch in the act; **pagar los elotes** (CAm) to be the goat

elucidar *tr* to elucidate

eludir *tr* to elude, evade, avoid

elusi•vo -va *adj* evasive; elusive

ella *pron pers fem* she, it; her, it; (coll) the trouble

ello *pron pers neut* it; (coll) the trouble; **ello es que** the fact is that ‖ *m* (psychoanalysis) id

ec
el

E.M. *abbr* **Estado Mayor**

emancipar *tr* to emancipate

embadurnamiento *m* daub, daubing

embadurnar *tr* to daub

embaír §1 *tr* to deceive, take in, hoax

embajada *f* embassy; ambassadorship; (iron) fine proposition

embajador *m* ambassador; **embajadores** ambassador and wife

embajadora *f* ambassadress

embalaje *m* packing; package; (sport) sprint

embalar *tr* to pack ‖ *intr* (sport) to sprint ‖ *ref* (*el motor*) to race; (sport) to sprint

embaldosado *m* tile paving

embaldosar *tr* to pave with tile

embalsamar *tr* to embalm; perfume

embalsar *tr* to dam, dam up

embalse *m* dam; damming; backwater

embanastar *tr* to put in a basket; pack, jam, overcrowd

embanquetar *tr* (Mex) to line with sidewalks

embarazada *adj fem* pregnant ‖ *f* pregnant woman

embarazar §60 *tr* (*estorbar*) to embarrass; obstruct; make pregnant ‖ *ref* to be embarrassed, be encumbered; become pregnant

embarazo *m* embarrassment; obstruction; awkwardness; pregnancy

embarazo•so -sa *adj* embarrassing, troublesome

embarbillar *tr* to rabbet

embarcación *f* boat, ship; embarkation (*of passengers*)

embarcadero *m* pier, wharf; (rr) platform; **embarcadero de ganado** (Arg) loading chute; **embarcadero flotante** landing stage

embarcador *m* shipper

embarcar §73 *tr* to ship ‖ *intr* to entrain ‖ *ref* to embark, ship; get involved

embarco *m* embarkation (*of passengers*)

embargar §44 *tr* to embargo; paralyze; (law) to seize, attach

embargo *m* embargo; indigestion; (law) seizure, attachment; **sin embargo** however, nevertheless

embarnizar §60 *tr* to varnish

embarque *m* shipment, embarkation (*of freight*)

embarrada *f* blunder

embarrancar §73 *tr, intr & ref* to run into a ditch; (*una nave*) run aground

embarrar *tr* to splash with mud; smear, stain; (CAm, Mex) to involve in a shady deal; **embarrarla** (Arg) to spoil the whole thing

embarrilar *tr* to barrel, put in barrels

embarullar *tr* to muddle, make a mess of; bungle, botch

embastar *tr* to baste, stitch

embate *m* blow, attack; (*del mar*) beating, dashing; (*de viento*) gust; **embates de la fortuna** hard knocks

embauca•dor -dora *mf* trickster; impostor; con man

embaucar §73 *tr* to trick, bamboozle, swindle

embaula•do -da *adj* crowded, packed, jammed

embaular §8 *tr* to put in a trunk; jam, pack in

embayar *ref* (Ecuad) to fly into a rage

embazar §60 *tr* to dye brown; hinder, obstruct; astound, dumbfound ‖ *ref* to get bored; be upset, get sick at the stomach

embebecer §22 *tr* to entertain, amuse, fascinate, enchant

embeber *tr* to absorb, soak up; soak; contain, include; embed; contract, shrink ‖ *intr* to contract, shrink ‖ *ref* to be enchanted, be enraptured; become absorbed or immersed; become well versed

embebi•do -da *adj* (*vocal*) elided; (*columna*) engaged

embelecar §73 *tr* to cheat, dupe, bamboozle

embeleco *m* cheating, fraud; bore; **embelecos** cuteness

embeleñar *tr* to dope, stupefy; enchant, bewitch

embelequería *f* (Col, Mex, W-I) fraud, swindle

embelesar *tr* to charm, enrapture, fascinate

embeleso *m* charm, fascination, delight

embellece•dor -dora *adj* embellishing, beautifying ‖ *m* (aut) hubcap ‖ *f* beautician

embellecer §22 *tr* to embellish, beautify

embellecimiento *m* embellishment, beautification

embermejecer §22 *tr* to dye red; make blush ‖ *ref* to blush

emberrinchar *ref* to fly into a rage

embestida *f* attack, assault; (*detención intempestiva*) buttonholing

embesti•dor -dora *mf* beat, sponger

embestir §50 *tr* to attack, assail; to strike; buttonhole, waylay ‖ *intr* to attack, charge, rush

embetunar *tr* to blacken; cover with tar

embicar §73 *tr* (Mex) to turn upside down, tilt ‖ *intr* (Arg, Chile) to run aground

emblandecer §22 *tr* to soften; placate, mollify ‖ *ref* to soften, yield

emblanquecer §22 *tr* to whiten; bleach ‖ *ref* to turn white

emblema *m* emblem

emblemáti•co -ca *adj* emblematic(al)

embobar *tr* to amaze, fascinate ‖ *ref* to stand gaping

embocadero *m* mouth, outlet

embocadura *f* nozzle; (*de río*) mouth; (*del freno; de instrumento de viento*) mouthpiece; (*de cigarrillo*) tip; (*del vino*) taste; stage entrance

embocar §73 *tr* to catch in the mouth; put in the mouth; take on, undertake; gulp down; try to put over ‖ *intr & ref* to enter, pass

embolada *f* stroke

embolado *m* bull with wooden balls on horns; (theat) minor role; (coll) trick, hoax

embolar *tr* (*los cuernos del toro*) to put wooden balls on; (*ei calzado*) to shine ‖ *ref* (CAm, Mex) to get drunk

embolia *f* embolism

émbolo *m* (mach) piston; **émbolo buzo** (mach) plunger

embolsar *tr* to pocket, take in

embonar *tr* to fertilize; suit, be becoming to

emboquillar *tr (los cigarrillos)* to put tips on; *(una galería o túnel)* cut an entrance in; *(las junturas entre los ladrillos)* (Chile) to point, chink

emborrachar *tr* to intoxicate ‖ *ref* to get drunk; *(los colores de una tela)* run

emborrar *tr* to stuff, pad, wad; gulp down

emborrascar §73 *tr* to stir up, irritate ‖ *ref* to get stormy; *(un negocio)* fail; *(la veta de una mina)* (Arg, CAm, Mex) to peter out

emborronar *tr* to blot; scribble

emboscada *f* ambush, ambuscade

emboscado *m* draft dodger

emboscar §73 *tr (tropas para sorprender al enemigo)* to ambush ‖ *ref* to ambush, lie in ambush; shirk, take an easy way out

embota•do -da *adj* blunt, dull; (Chile) black-pawed

embotadura *f* bluntness, dullness

embotar *tr* to blunt, dull; dull, weaken; *(el tabaco)* put in a jar

embotella•do -da *adj (discurso)* prepared ‖ *m* bottling; *(del tráfico)* bottleneck

embotellamiento *m* bottling; traffic jam

embotellar *tr* to bottle; *(un negocio)* tie up; (nav) to bottle up

embotijar *tr (un suelo)* to underlay with jugs ‖ *ref* to swell up with anger

embovedar *tr* to vault, vault over; put in a vault

emboza•do -da *adj* muffled up ‖ *mf* person muffled up to eyes

embozar §60 *tr* to muffle up to the eyes; *(p.ej., a un perro)* muzzle; disguise ‖ *ref* to muffle oneself up to the eyes

embozo *m* muffler, cloak held over the face; fold back *(of bed sheet)*; cunning, dissimulation; **quitarse el embozo** to drop one's mask

embragar §44 *tr (el motor)* to engage ‖ *intr* to throw the clutch in

embrague *m* clutch; engagement

embravecer §22 *tr* to enrage, make angry ‖ *ref* to get angry; *(el mar)* get rough

embraveci•do -da *adj* angry; rough, wild

embrear *tr* to tar, cover with tar; calk with tar

embregar §44 *ref* to wrangle

embriagar §44 *tr* to intoxicate, make drunk; enrapture ‖ *ref* to get drunk

embriaguez *f* drunkenness; rapture

embridar *tr* to bridle; check, restrain

embriología *f* embryology

embrión *m* embryo

embroca *f* poultice

embrocar §73 *tr* to empty; *(el toro al torero)* to catch between the horns ‖ *ref* (C-R) to fall on one's face; (Mex) to put on over the head

embrollar *tr* to tangle, muddle, embroil

embrollo *m* entanglement, muddle, embroilment; deception, trick

embromar *tr* to joke with, play jokes on; bore, annoy ‖ *ref* to be bored, be annoyed

embrujar *tr* to bewitch

embrutecer §22 *tr* to brutify, stupefy

embrutecimiento *m* brutalization; coarsening

embuchado *m* pork sausage; subterfuge; *(de la urna electoral)* stuffing (of ballot box)

embudar *tr* to put a funnel in; trick, trap

embudista *adj* tricky, scheming ‖ *mf* schemer

embudo *m* funnel; trick; (mil) shell hole; **embudo de bomba** (mil) bomb crater

embullar *tr* to stir up, excite, key up ‖ *ref* to become excited, keyed up

emburujar *tr* to jumble, pile up ‖ *ref* to wrap oneself up

embuste *m* lie, falsehood, trick; **embustes** baubles, trinkets; *(del niño)* cuteness

embuste•ro -ra *adj* lying, false, tricky ‖ *mf* liar, cheat

embuti•do -da *adj* inlaid, flush ‖ *m* inlay, marquetry; pork sausage; lace insertion

embutir *tr* to stuff, pack tight; insert; inlay; set flush; *(una hoja de metal)* fashion, hammer into shape ‖ *ref* to squeeze in; stuff oneself

emergencia *f* emergence; incident

emerger §17 *intr* to emerge; *(un submarino)* surface

emersión *f* emersion; *(de un submarino)* surfacing

eméti•co -ca *adj & m* emetic

emigración *f* emigration; migration

emigra•do -da *mf* émigré

emigrante *adj & mf* emigrant

emigrar *intr* to emigrate; migrate

eminencia *f* eminence

eminente *adj* eminent

emisa•rio -ria *mf* emissary ‖ *m* outlet

emisión *f (acción de exhalar; acción de lanzar ondas luminosas, etc.)* emission; *(títulos creados de una vez)* (com) issue; *(acción de emitir títulos nuevos)* (com) issuance; (rad) broadcast; **emisión seriada** (rad) serial

emi•sor -sora *adj* emitting; broadcasting ‖ *m* (rad) transmitter ‖ *f* broadcasting station

emitir *tr* to emit, send forth; issue, give out; *(p.ej., opiniones)* utter, express; (com) to issue; (rad) to broadcast

emoción *f* emotion

emocional *adj* emotional

emocionante *adj* moving, touching; thrilling, exciting

emocionar *tr* to move, stir; thrill

emoti•vo -va *adj* emotional

empacadi•zo -za *adj* (Arg) touchy

empaca•do -da *adj* (Arg) gruff, grim

empacar §73 *tr* to pack, crate ‖ *ref* to be stubborn; *(un animal)* balk, get balky

empa•cón -cona *adj* stubborn; balky

empacha•do -da *adj* backward, fumbling

empachar *tr* to hinder, embarrass; disguise; surfeit, upset the stomach of ‖ *ref* blush, be embarrassed; be upset, have indigestion

empacho *m* hindrance; embarrassment, bashfulness; indigestion

empacho•so -sa *adj* sickening; shameful

empadronar *tr* to register, take the census of ‖ *ref* to register, be registered in the census

em
em

empalagar §44 *tr* to cloy, pall, surfeit; bore, weary

empalago•so -sa *adj* cloying, sickening, mawkish; boring, annoying; fawning

empalar *tr* impale

empalizada *f* palisade, stockade, fence

empalizar §60 *tr* to fence in

empalmar *tr* to splice, connect, join, couple; combine ‖ *intr* to connect, make connections; **empalmar con** to connect with; follow, succeed

empalme *m* splice, connection, joint, coupling; combination; (elec) joint; (rr) connection, junction

empanada *f* pie; fraud

empanadilla *f* pie

empana•do -da *adj* unlighted, unventilated ‖ *f* see **empanada**

empanar *tr* to crumb, bread; (*las tierras*) sow with wheat

empantanar *tr* to flood; obstruct

empaña•do -da *adj* dim, misty; blurred, fogged; (*voz*) flat

empañar *tr* (*a las criaturas*) to swaddle; blur, fog, dim, dull; tarnish, sully ‖ *ref* to blur, fog, dim, dull

empañetar *tr* to plaster

empapar *tr* to soak; soak up, absorb; drench ‖ *ref* to soak; be soaked; to become imbued; be surfeited

empapelado *m* papering, paper hanging; wallpaper; paper lining

empapela•dor -dora *mf* paper hanger

empapelar *tr* to wrap in paper; paper, line with paper; wallpaper; bring a criminal charge against

empaque *m* packing; look, appearance, mien; stiffness, stuffiness; brazenness

empaquetadura *f* gasket

empaquetar *tr* to pack; jam, stuff ‖ *ref* to pack; pack in; dress up

empareda•do -da *mf* recluse ‖ *m* sandwich

emparedar *tr* to wall in, confine

emparejar *tr* to pair, match; smooth, make level; even, make even; (*una puerta*) close flush ‖ *intr* to come up, come abreast; **emparejar con** to catch up with ‖ *ref* to pair, match

emparentar §2 *intr* to become related by marriage; **emparentar con** (*buena gente*) to marry into the family of; (*una familia rica*) marry into

emparrado *m* arbor, bower

emparrillar *tr* to grill

empasta•dor -dora *mf* bookbinder

empastadura *f* binding

empastar *tr* (*un diente*) to fill; (*un libro*) bind with stiff covers; convert into pasture land ‖ *ref* (Chile) to be overgrown with weeds

empaste *m* (*de diente*) filling; stiff binding

empastelar *tr* (typ) to pie

empatar *tr* (*en la votación y los juegos*) to tie; join, connect; tie, fasten ‖ *intr* to tie ‖ *ref* to tie; **empatársela a una persona** to be a match for someone; **empatárselo a una persona** (Guat, Hond) to put it over on someone

empate *m* tie, draw; (Col) penholder; (Ven) waste of time

empatía *f* empathy

empavar *tr* (Ecuad) to annoy; (Peru) to kid, razz

empavesado *m* (naut) dressing, bunting

empavesar *tr* to bedeck with flags and bunting; (*un buque*) dress; (*un monumento*) veil ‖ *ref* to become overcast

empavonar *tr* to blue; grease, spread grease over ‖ *ref* (CAm) to dress up

empecina•do -da *adj* stubborn

empecinamiento *m* stubbornness; determination

empecinar *tr* to tar; dip in pitch ‖ *ref* to be stubborn; persist

empederni•do -da *adj* hardened, inveterate; hard-hearted

empedra•do -da *adj* cloud-flecked; pockmarked; (*caballo*) dark-spotted ‖ *m* stone paving

empedrar §2 *tr* to pave with stones; bespatter

empegado *m* tarpaulin

empegar §44 *tr* to coat with pitch, dip in pitch; (*el ganado lanar*) mark with pitch

empeine *m* instep; (*de la bota*) vamp; (*enfermedad cutánea*) tetter; (*región central del hipogastrio*) pubes

empelotar *ref* to get all tangled up; get into a row; take all one's clothes off; (Mex, W-I) to fall madly in love

empella *f* vamp

empellar *tr* to push, shove

empeller §31 *tr* to push, shove

empellón *m* push, shove; **a empellones** pushing, roughly

empenachar *tr* to adorn with plumes

empeña•do -da *adj* (*disputa*) bitter, heated; **no empeñado** noncommitted

empeñar *tr* (*dar en prenda*) to pawn; (*una lucha*) launch, begin; (*prendar, hipotecar*) pledge; (*la palabra*) pledge; force, compel ‖ *ref* to commit oneself, bind oneself; go into debt; (*una lucha, una disputa*) begin, start; **empeñarse en** to engage in; persist in, insist on

empeñe•ro -ra *mf* (Mex) pawnbroker

empeño *m* pledge, engagement, commitment; (*prenda*) pawn; pawnshop; persistence, insistence; eagerness, perseverance; effort, endeavor; pledge, backer, patron; favor, protection; **con empeño** eagerly

empeño•so -sa *adj* eager, persistent

empeorar *tr* to impair, make worse ‖ *intr* & *ref* to get worse, deteriorate

empequeñecer §22 *tr* (*hacer más pequeño*) to make smaller, dwarf; (*amenguar la importancia de*) belittle ‖ *ref* to get smaller, dwarf

emperador *m* emperor; **los emperadores** the emperor and empress

empera•triz *f* (*pl* **-trices**) empress

emperchar *tr* to hang on a clothes rack

emperejilar *tr* & *ref* to dress up, spruce up

emperezar §60 *tr* to delay, put off ‖ *intr* & *ref* to get lazy

empericar §73 *ref* (Col, Ecuad) to get drunk; (Mex) to blush

emperifollar *tr & ref* to dress up gaudily

empernar *tr* to bolt

empero *conj* but, however, yet

emperrar *ref* to get stubborn

empezar §18 *tr & intr* to begin

empicar §73 *ref* to become infatuated

empicotar *tr* to pillory

empiema *m* empyema

empina·do -da *adj* high, lofty; steep; stiff, stuck-up ‖ *f* (aer) zoom, zooming; **irse a la empinada** (*un caballo*) to rear

empinar *tr* to raise, lift; tip over; (*el codo*) crook; (aer) to zoom ‖ *intr* to be a toper ‖ *ref* to stand on tiptoe; (*un caballo*) rear; tower, rise high; (aer) to zoom

empingorota·do -da *adj* influential; proud, haughty

empingorotar *tr* to put on top ‖ *ref* to climb up, get up; be stuck-up

empíre·o -a *adj & m* empyrean

empíri·co -ca *adj* empiric(al) ‖ *mf* empiricist

empizarrado *m* slate roof

empizarrar *tr* to roof with slate

emplastar *tr* to put a plaster on; put make-up on; (*un negocio*) tie up, obstruct ‖ *ref* to put make-up on; smear oneself up

emplásti·co -ca *adj* sticky

emplasto *m* plaster, poultice

emplazamiento *m* emplacement, location; (law) summons

emplazar §60 *tr* to place, locate; summon, summons

emplea·do -da *mf* employee; (*de oficina, de tienda*) clerk; **empleado público** civil servant

emplear *tr* to employ; use; (*el dinero*) invest; **estarle a uno bien empleado** to serve someone right ‖ *ref* to be employed; busy oneself; **empleárselo mal** to act up, misbehave

empleo *m* employ, employment; use; job, position, occupation

empleomanía *f* eagerness to hold public office

empleóma·no -na *mf* public officeholder, bureaucrat

emplomar *tr* to lead; line with lead; (*un techo*) cover with lead; put a lead seal on; (*un diente*) (Arg) to fill

emplumar *tr* to put a feather on; adorn with feathers; tar and feather; (Hond) to thrash; **emplumarlas** (Col) to beat it ‖ *intr* to fledge, grow feathers

emplumecer §22 *intr* to fledge, grow feathers

empobrecer §22 *tr* to impoverish ‖ *intr & ref* to become poor

empodrecer §22 *intr & ref* to rot

empolva·do -da *adj* (Mex) dusty

empolvar *tr* to cover with dust; (*el rostro*) powder ‖ *ref* to get dusty; (*el rostro*) powder; (Mex) to get rusty

empolla·do -da *adj* primed for an examination

empollar *tr* (*huevos*) to brood, hatch; (*estudiar con mucha detención*) bone up on ‖ *intr* to grind, be a grind; **empollar sobre** to bone up on ‖ *ref* to hatch; bone up on

empo·llón -llona *mf* (coll) grind

emponcha·do -da *adj* (SAm) poncho-wearing; (SAm) crafty, hypocritical; (SAm) suspicious-looking

emponzoñar *tr* to poison; corrupt

emporcar §81 *tr* to soil, dirty

emporra·do -da *adj* (*drogas*) high

empotra·do -da *adj* built-in; recessed

empotrar *tr* to embed, recess, fasten in a wall ‖ *intr & ref* to fit, interlock

emprende·dor -dora *adj* enterprising

emprender *tr* to undertake; **emprenderla con** to squabble with, have it out with; **emprenderla para** to set out for

empreñar *tr* to make pregnant ‖ *ref* to become pregnant

empresa *f* enterprise, undertaking; company, concern, firm; device, motto; (*la parte patronal*) management; **empresa anunciadora** advertising agency; **empresa de tranvías** traction company; **pequeña empresa** small business

empresarial *adj* managerial

empresa·rio -ria *mf* contractor; business leader, industrialist; manager; promoter; theatrical manager; **empresario de circo** showman; **empresario de pompas fúnebres** undertaker; **empresario de publicidad** advertising man; **empresario de teatro** impresario, theater manager

emprestar *tr* to borrow

empréstito *m* loan, government loan

empujar *tr* to push, shove; replace ‖ *intr* to push, shove

empujatierra *f* bulldozer

empuje *m* push; (*fuerza o presión ejercidas por una cosa sobre otra*) thrust; (*espíritu emprendedor*) enterprise, push

empujón *m* hard push, shove; **tratar a empujones** to push around

empuñadura *f* (*de la espada*) hilt; first words of a story; (*de bastón o paraguas*) handle

empuñar *tr* to seize, grasp, clutch; (*un empleo o puesto*) obtain; (*la mano*) (Chile) to clench; (Bol) to punch; **empuñar el bastón** (fig) to seize the reins

emular *tr & intr* to emulate; **emular con** to emulate, vie with

ému·lo -la *adj* emulous ‖ *mf* rival

emulsión *f* emulsion

emulsionar *tr* to emulsify

en *prep* at; in; into; by; on; of, e.g., **pensar en** to think of

enaceitar *tr* to oil ‖ *ref* to get oily, get rancid

enagua *f* petticoat; skirt; **enaguas** petticoat

enagüillas *fpl* kilt, short skirt

enajenación *f* alienation; estrangement; rapture; (*distracción*) absent-mindedness; **enajenación mental** mental derangement

enajenar *tr* (*la propiedad, el dominio; a un amigo*) to alienate, estrange; enrapture, transport ‖ *ref* to be enraptured, be transported; **enajenarse de** to dispossess oneself of; (*un amigo*) become alienated from

enaltecer §22 *tr* to exalt, extol

enamoradi•zo -za *adj* susceptible

enamora•do -da *adj* lovesick; (*propenso a enamorarse*) susceptible ‖ *mf* sweetheart ‖ *m* lover

enamorar *tr* to make love to; enamor, captivate ‖ *ref* to fall in love

enamoricar §73 *ref* to trifle in love

enangostar *tr* & *ref* to narrow

ena•no -na *adj* dwarfish ‖ *mf* dwarf

enarbolar *tr* to hoist, hang out; (*una espada*) brandish ‖ *ref* to get angry; (*el caballo*) rear

enarcar §73 *tr* to arch; (*los toneles*) hoop ‖ *ref* to become confused, be bashful; (*el caballo*) (Mex) to rear

enardecer §22 *tr* to inflame, excite ‖ *ref* to get excited; (*una parte del cuerpo*) become inflamed, get sore

enarenar *tr* to throw sand on ‖ *ref* (naut) to run aground

enastar *tr* (*una herramienta*) to put a handle on; (*una bandera*) put a shaft on

encabalgamiento *m* gun carriage; trestlework; (*en el verso*) enjambment

encabalgar §44 *tr* to provide with horses ‖ *intr* to lean, rest

encaballar *tr* to overlap; (typ) to pie

encabezamiento *m* heading; (*fórmula con que comienza un documento*) opening words; tax list; tax rate; **encabezamiento de factura** billhead

encabezar §60 *tr* (*un escrito*) to put a heading or title on; head; register; (*vinos*) fortify

encabritar *ref* (*un caballo*) to rear; (*un buque*) shoot up, pitch up; (*un avión*) nose up

encadenar *tr* to chain, put in chains; brace, buttress; bind, tie together; tie down

encajar *tr* to fit, fit in, make fit; insert, put in; (*un golpe*) give, let go; (*dinero*) put away; (*un chiste*) tell at the wrong time; to palm off; throw, hurl; **encajar una cosa a uno** to foist something on someone, palm something off on someone ‖ *intr* to fit; (*una puerta*) close right ‖ *ref* to squeeze one's way; (*una prenda de vestir*) put on; butt in, intrude

encaje *m* (*tejido de mallas*) lace; (*labor de taracea*) inlay, mosaic; recess, groove; fitting, matching; insertion; appearance, look

encaje•ro -ra *mf* lacemaker; lace dealer

encajonado *m* cofferdam

encajonar *tr* to box, crate, case; squeeze in ‖ *ref* (*un río*) to narrow, narrow down; squeeze in, squeeze through

encalambrar *ref* to get cramps

encalar *tr* (*espolvorear con cal*) to lime, sprinkle with lime; (*blanquear con cal*) whitewash

encalma•do -da *adj* (*mercado de valores*) dull, quiet; (*mar, viento*) becalmed

encalvecer §22 *intr* to get bald

encalladero *m* sand bank, shoal

encallar *intr* to run aground; fail, get stuck

encallecer §22 *intr* (*la piel*) to become callous ‖ *ref* to become callous; (fig) to become callous, become hardened

encamar *tr* to spread out on the ground ‖ *ref* to take to bed; (*el grano*) droop, bend over

encaminar *tr* to direct, show the way to; (*sus esfuerzos, su atención*) direct ‖ *ref* to set out

encanalar *tr* to channel, pipe

encandecer §22 *tr* to make white-hot

encandila•do -da *adj* (*sombrero*) cocked; stiff, erect

encandilar *tr* to daze, befuddle; (*un fuego*) to stir ‖ *ref* (*los ojos*) to flash

encanecer §22 *intr* & *ref* to turn gray; get old; become moldy

encanta•do -da *adj* absent-minded, distracted; (*casa*) rambling

encanta•dor -dora *adj* charming, enchanting ‖ *mf* charmer ‖ *f* enchantress

encantamiento *m* charm, enchantment

encantar *tr* to charm, enchant, bewitch

encante *m* auction sale; auction house

encanto *m* charm, enchantment, spell

encantusar *tr* to coax, wheedle

encañada *f* gorge, ravine

encañar *tr* (*el agua*) to pipe; (*las tierras*) drain; (*las plantas*) prop up; wind on a spool

encañizada *f* reed fence; weir

encañonar *tr* to pipe; wind on a spool; (*un pliego*) (typ) to tip in

encaperuzar §60 *tr* to put a hood on ‖ *ref* to put on one's hood

encapotar *tr* to cloak ‖ *ref* to frown; cloud over, become overcast

encaprichar *ref* to insist on getting one's way; become infatuated

encaracolado *m* spiral ornament, spiral work

encara•do -da *adj* — **bien encarado** well-featured; **mal encarado** ill-featured

encaramar *tr* to raise up, lift up; praise, extol; elevate, exalt ‖ *ref* to climb, get on top; rise, tower; blush

encarar *tr* to aim, point; (*una dificultad*) face ‖ *intr* & *ref* to come face to face

encarcelar *tr* to incarcerate, imprison, jail; (*piezas de madera recién encoladas*) clamp; plaster in ‖ *ref* to stay indoors

encarecer §22 *tr* (*el precio*) to raise; raise the price of; extol; urge; overrate ‖ *intr* & *ref* to rise, rise in price

encarecidamente *adv* earnestly, insistently, eagerly

encarga•do -da *mf* agent, representative; **encargado de negocios** chargé d'affaires

encargamiento *m* duty; obligation; charge

encargar §44 *tr* (*mercancías*) to order; (*confiar*) entrust; urge, warn ‖ *ref* to take charge, be in charge

encargo *m* assignment, job, charge; (*pedido*) order; warning; **como de encargo** or **ni de encargo** just the thing, as if made to order

encariñamiento *m* endearment

encariñar *tr* to awaken love in ‖ *ref* — **encariñarse con** to become fond of, become attached to

encarnación *f* incarnation, embodiment

encarna•do -da *adj* red; Caucasian-skin-("flesh")-colored; (*de forma humana*) incarnate

encarnar *tr* to incarnate, embody; (*el anzuelo*) bait ‖ *intr* to become incarnate; (*una herida*) heal over

encarnecer §22 *intr* to put on flesh

encarniza•do -da *adj* bloodshot; bloody, fierce, bitter, hard-fought

encarnizar §60 *tr* to anger, provoke ‖ *ref* to get angry; become fierce; **encarnizarse con** or **en** to be merciless to

encaro *m* aim; stare; blunderbuss

encarrilar *tr* to put back on the rails; set right, put on the right track; guide, direct

encarruja•do -da *adj* wrinkled; (*pelo*) kinky; (*terreno*) (Mex) rough

encartar *tr* to enroll, register; outlaw; (*un naipe*) slip in ‖ *ref* to be unable to discard

encartonar *tr* to cover with cardboard; (*libros*) bind in boards

encasar *tr* (*un hueso dislocado*) to set (*a broken bone*)

encasillado *m* set of pigeonholes; (*lista de candidatos apoyados por el gobierno*) government slate; (SAm) checkerwork

encasillar *tr* to pigeonhole; sort out, classify; (*el gobierno a un candidato*) slate

encasquetar *tr* (*un sombrero*) to stick on the head; (*una idea*) drive in; force on

encasquillar *tr* to put a tip on; (*un caballo*) shoe ‖ *ref* to stick, get stuck

encastilla•do -da *adj* haughty, proud

encastillar *tr* to fortify with castles; pile up ‖ *ref* to stick, get stuck; take to the hills; stick to one's opinion

encastrar *tr* to engage, mesh

encastre *m* engaging, meshing; groove, socket; insert

encauchar *tr* to cover with rubber, line with rubber

encausar *tr* to prosecute, sue, bring to trial

encausticar §73 *tr* to wax

encáustico *m* floor wax, furniture polish

encauzar §60 *tr* (*una corriente*) to channel; guide, direct

encavar *ref* to hide, burrow

encebollado *m* beef stew with onions

encelar *tr* to make jealous ‖ *ref* to get jealous; be in rut

encella *f* cheese mold

encenagar §44 *ref* to get covered with mud; wallow in vice

encencerrar *tr* (*al ganado*) to put a bell on

encendajas *fpl* kindling, brush

encendedor *m* lighter; **encendedor de bolsillo** pocket lighter

encender §51 *tr* to light, kindle; ignite, fire to; (*la luz, la radio*) turn on; (*la lengua*) burn; stir up, excite ‖ *ref* to catch fire, ignite; become excited; blush

encendi•do -da *adj* bright, high-colored; red, flushed; keen, enthusiastic ‖ *m* ignition

encenizar §60 *tr* to cover with ashes ‖ *ref* to get covered with ashes

encepar *tr* to put in the stocks ‖ *intr & ref* to take deep root

encera•do -da *adj* wax, wax-colored; (*huevo*) boiled ‖ *m* oilcloth; tarpaulin; (*pizarra*) blackboard

encerar *tr* to wax ‖ *intr & ref* (*el grano*) to ripen, turn yellow

encerotar *tr* (*el hilo*) to wax

encerradero *m* sheepfold; (taur) bull pen

encerrar §2 *tr* to shut in; lock in, lock up; contain, include; encircle; imply ‖ *ref* to lock oneself in; go into seclusion; **encerrarse con** to be closeted with

encerrona *f* dilemma; tight spot; (coll) fix

encespedar *tr* to sod

encestar *tr* to put in a basket; (coll) to sink (*a basketball*)

encía *f* gum

encíclica *f* encyclical

enciclopedia *f* encyclopedia

enciclopédi•co -ca *adj* encyclopedic

encierro *m* locking up, confinement; inclusion; encirclement; lockup, prison; solitary confinement; retirement, retreat; (taur) bull pen

encima *adv* above, overhead, on top; at hand, here now; besides, in addition; **de encima** (Chile) in the bargain; **echarse encima** to take upon oneself; **encima de** on, upon; above, over; **por encima** hastily, superficially; **por encima de** above, over; in spite of; **quitarse de encima** to get rid of, shake off

encina *f* holm oak, evergreen oak

encinta *adj* pregnant; **dejar encinta** to make pregnant

encintado *m* curb

encintar *tr* to trim with ribbons; provide with curbs

enclaustrar *tr* to cloister; hide away

enclavar *tr* to nail; pierce, transfix; (*el pie del caballo*) prick; cheat

enclave *m* enclave

enclavijar *tr* to dowel; (*un instrumento*) to peg

enclenque *adj* sickly, feeble

enclíti•co -ca *adj & m* enclitic

enclocar §81 *intr & ref* to brood

encofrado *m* planking, timbering; (*para el hormigón*) form

encoger §17 *tr* to shrink, shrivel; discourage; draw in ‖ *intr* to shrink, shrivel ‖ *ref* to shrink, shrivel; be discouraged; be bashful; (*humillarse*) cringe; (*en la cama*) curl up; **encogerse de hombros** to shrug one's shoulders

encogi•do -da *adj* bashful, timid

encogimiento *m* shrinkage; crouch; bashfulness, timidity; **encogimiento de hombros** shrug

encojar *tr* to cripple, lame ‖ *ref* to become lame; feign illness

encolar *tr* to glue; (*la superficie que ha de pintarse*) size; (*el vino*) clarify; (*p.ej., una pelota*) throw out of reach

encolerizar §60 *tr* to anger ‖ *ref* to get angry

encomendar §2 *tr* to commend, entrust, commit; knight ‖ *ref* to commend oneself; send regards

encomiar *tr* to praise, extol

encomienda *f* charge, commission; commendation, praise; favor, protection; knight's cross; royal land grant (*with Indian inhabitants*); parcel post; (Mex) fruit stand

encomio *m* encomium

enconamiento *m* soreness; rancor, ill will

enconar *tr* to make sore, inflame; aggravate, irritate ‖ *ref* to get sore, become inflamed; (*una herida; el ánimo de uno*) rankle, fester

enconchar *ref* to draw back into one's shell, keep aloof

encono *m* rancor, ill will; (Col, Chile, Mex, W-I) soreness

encono•so -sa *adj* sore, sensitive; harmful; rancorous

encontra•do -da *adj* opposite, facing; contrary; hostile; **estar encontrados** to be at odds

encontrar *tr* to encounter, meet; (*hallar*) find ‖ *intr* to meet; collide ‖ *ref* to meet, meet each other; be, be situated; find oneself; **encontrarse con** to meet, run into

encontrón *m* bump, jolt, collision

encopeta•do -da *adj* aristocratic, of noble descent; conceited, boastful

encorajar *tr* to encourage ‖ *ref* to fly into a rage

encorajinar *ref* to fly into a rage; (Chile) to break up, go to ruin

encorchar *tr* (*botellas*) to cork; (*abejas*) to hive

encordar §61 *tr* (*un violín, una raqueta*) to string; wrap, wind up with rope

encordelar *tr* to string; tie with strings

encornudar *tr* to cuckold, make a cuckold of ‖ *intr* to grow horns

encorralar *tr* to corral

encortinar *tr* to curtain

encorvada *f* stoop, bending over; **hacer la encorvada** to malinger

encorvar *tr* to bend over ‖ *ref* to stoop, bend over; be partial, be biased

encovar §61 *tr* & *ref* to hide away

encrespar *tr* to curl; (*el pelo*) make stand on end; (*plumas*) ruffle; (*las olas*) stir up; irritate, anger ‖ *ref* to curl; bristle, stand on end; (*el mar, las olas*) get rough; get involved; bristle, get angry

encresta•do -da *adj* proud, haughty

encrucijada *f* crossroads, street intersection; ambush, snare, trap

encrudecer §22 *tr* to make raw; aggravate

encuadernación *f* bookbinding; (*taller*) bindery; **encuadernación a la holandesa** half binding

encuaderna•dor -dora *mf* bookbinder

encuadernar *tr* to bind; **sin encuadernar** unbound

encuadrar *tr* (*encerrar en un marco o cuadro*) to frame; (*incluir dentro de sí*) encompass; (*encajar*) insert, fit in; (Arg) to summarize

encuadre *m* film adaptation; (mov & telv) frame

encubar *tr* to put in a cask or vat; (min) to shore up

encubierta *f* fraud, deception

encubrimiento *m* concealment; (law) complicity

encubrir §83 *tr* to hide, conceal ‖ *ref* to hide; disguise oneself

encuentro *m* encounter, meeting; clash, collision; (*hallazgo*) find; (sport) game, match; **encuentro fronterizo** border clash; **llevarse de encuentro** (CAm, Mex, W-I) to knock down, run over; (CAm, Mex, W-I) to drag down to ruin; **mal encuentro** foul play; **salir al encuentro a** to go to meet; get ahead of; take a stand against

encuerar *tr* to strip of clothes; fleece ‖ *ref* to strip, get undressed

encuesta *f* inquiry; **encuesta demoscópica** opinion poll; survey

encuestador *m* pollster

encuitar *ref* to grieve

encumbra•do -da *adj* high, lofty; sublime; influential

encumbramiento *m* height, elevation; exaltation

encumbrar *tr* to raise, elevate; exalt ‖ *ref* to rise; be exalted; be proud; be flowery, use flowery speech; (*subir una cosa a mucha altura*) tower

encunar *tr* to cradle; catch between the horns

encurtido *m* pickle

encurtir *tr* to pickle

enchapado *m* veneer

enchapar *tr* to veneer

encharcar §73 *tr* to make a puddle of; (*el estómago*) upset ‖ *ref* to turn into a puddle; wallow in vice

enchavetar *tr* to key

enchichar *ref* (SAm) to get drunk; (CAm) to get angry

enchilada *f* (Guat, Mex) corn cake with tomato sauce seasoned with chili

enchilado *m* (Cuba, Mex) shellfish stew with chili sauce

enchilo•so -sa *adj* (CAm, Mex) spicy, hot

enchinar *tr* to pave with pebbles; (Mex) to curl ‖ *ref* (Mex) to get goose flesh

enchispar *tr* to make drunk ‖ *ref* to get drunk

enchivar *ref* (Col, Ecuad, CAm) to fly into a rage

enchufar *tr* (*un tubo o caño*) to fit; (*dos tubos o caños*) connect, connect together; (*dos negocios*) merge; (elec) to connect, plug in ‖ *intr* to fit ‖ *ref* to merge

enchufe *m* fitting; (*de tubo o caño*) male end; (*de dos tubos*) joint; (elec) connector; (elec) plug; (elec) receptacle; sinecure, easy job; **tener enchufe** to have pull, have a drag

enchufismo *m* spoils system; wire pulling

enchufista *m* spoilsman

ende *adv* — **por ende** therefore

endeble *adj* feeble, weak; worthless

endecha *f* dirge

endechadera *f* hired mourner

endemia *f* endemic

endémi•co -ca *adj* endemic

endemonia•do -da *adj* possessed of the devil; furious, wild; (coll) devilish

endenantes *adv* recently

endentar §2 *tr & intr* to mesh

endentecer §22 *intr* to teethe

enderezar §60 *tr* to stand up; straighten; direct; put in order; regulate ‖ *intr* to go straight ‖ *ref* to stand up, straighten up; head, make one's way; go straight; (aer) to flatten out, level off

endeuda•do -da *adj* indebted

endeudamiento *m* indebtedness

endeudar *ref* to run into debt; acknowledge one's indebtedness

endevota•do -da *adj* pious, devout; fond, devoted

endiabla•do -da *adj* devilish; deformed, ugly; mean, wicked; (Arg) difficult, complicated

endilgar §44 *tr* to send, direct; to spring, unload

endiosar *tr* to deify ‖ *ref* to get stuck-up; get absorbed

endominga•do -da *adj* Sunday; all dressed up

endomingar §44 *ref* to get dressed in one's Sunday best

endosante *mf* endorser

endosar *tr* (*un documento de crédito*) to endorse; (*una cosa poco grata*) unload

endosata•rio -ria *mf* endorsee

endoso *m* endorsement

endriago *m* fabulous monster

endri•no -na *adj* sloe-colored ‖ *m* (*arbusto*) sloe, blackthron ‖ *f* (*fruto*) sloe

endrogar §44 *ref* to run into debt

endulzar §60 *tr* to sweeten; make bearable

endura•dor -dora *adj* saving, stingy

endurar *tr* to harden; delay, put off; (*tolerar*) endure; save, spare ‖ *ref* to get hard

endurecer §22 *tr* to harden; (*robustecer, acostumbrar*) inure

endureci•do -da *adj* hard, strong; inured; hard-hearted; tenacious, obstinate

enebrina *f* juniper berry

enebro *m* juniper

enecha•do -da *adj & mf* foundling

eneldo *m* dill

enema *f* enema

enemiga *f* enmity, hatred

enemi•go -ga *adj* enemy; hostile ‖ *mf* enemy, foe; **el enemigo malo** the Evil One ‖ *f* see **enemiga**

enemistad *f* enmity

enemistar *tr* to make an enemy of; make enemies of ‖ *ref* to become enemies

energéti•co -ca *adj* energy; power

energía *f* energy; power; **energía atómica** atomic power (or energy); **energías alternas** alternate energy sources; **energía solar** solar energy

enérgi•co -ca *adj* energetic

energúme•no -na *adj* fiendish ‖ *mf* crazy person, wild person

enero *m* January

enervar *tr* to enervate; weaken

enési•mo -ma *adj* nth

enfadadi•zo -za *adj* peevish, irritable

enfadar *tr* to annoy, bother; anger

enfado *m* annoyance, bother; anger

enfado•so -sa *adj* annoying, disagreeable

enfaldar *ref* to tuck up one's skirt

enfardar *tr* to bale, pack

énfa•sis *m* (*pl* -sis) emphasis; bombast, affected speech

enfasizar §60 *tr* to emphasize

enfáti•co -ca *adj* emphatic; affected

enfermar *tr* to make sick ‖ *intr* to get sick

enfermedad *f* sickness, illness, disease

enfermera *f* nurse; **enfermera ambulante** visiting nurse

enfermería *f* infirmary

enfermero *m* male nurse

enfermi•zo -za *adj* sickly; (*clima*) unhealthy

enfer•mo -ma *adj* sick, ill; (*enfermizo*) sickly; **enfermo de amor** lovesick ‖ *mf* patient

enfermo•so -sa *adj* sickly

enfiestar *ref* to have a good time

enfilar *tr* to line up; (*p.ej., perlas*) string; aim; go down, go up; (mil) to enfilade ‖ *intr* to bear

enfisema *m* emphysema

enflaquecer §22 *tr* to make thin; weaken ‖ *intr* to get thin; flag, slacken ‖ *ref* to get thin, lose weight

enflauta•do -da *adj* pompous, inflated

enflautar *tr* to blow up, inflate; cheat

enfocar §73 *tr* to focus; (fig) to size up

enfoque *m* focus, focusing; (fig) approach (*to a problem*)

enfoscar §73 *tr* to trim with mortar; patch with mortar; darken, make dark ‖ *ref* to become sullen, become grouchy; become absorbed in business; become overcast

enfrailar *tr* to make a friar or monk of ‖ *ref* to become a friar or monk

enfranque *m* shank

enfrascar §73 *tr* to bottle ‖ *ref* to become involved, intangled; be sunk in work; have a good time

enfrenar *tr* (*un caballo*) to bridle; (*un tren*) brake; check

enfrentamiento *m* (*policía, masas*) confrontation

enfrentar *tr* to put face to face; (*p.ej., al enemigo*) face ‖ *intr* to be facing ‖ *ref* to meet face to face; **enfrentarse con** to stand up to; cope with

enfrente *adv* opposite, in front; **enfrente de** opposite, in front of; opposed to

enfriadera *f* bottle cooler, ice pail

enfriar §77 *tr* to cool, chill; kill ‖ *intr & ref* to cool off

enfundar *tr* to sheathe, put in a case; stuff; (*un tambor*) muffle

enfurecer §22 *tr* to infuriate, anger ‖ *ref* to rage

enfurruñar *ref* to sulk

engalanar *tr* to adorn, deck out, dress

engalla•do -da *adj* straight, erect; haughty

engallador *m* checkrein

enganchar *tr* to hook; (*un caballo*) hitch; (*un coche de ferrocarril*) couple; recruit; inveigle ‖ *intr* to get caught ‖ *ref* to get caught; (mil) to enlist

enganche *m* hook; hooking; hitching; coupling; inveigling; recruiting; enlisting; (rr) coupler

engañabo•bos *mf* (*pl* -bos) bamboozler

engaña•dor -dora *adj* deceptive; (*simpático*) winsome

engañar *tr* to deceive, cheat, fool; (*el tiempo*) while away; (*el sueño, el hambre*) ward off; wheedle ‖ *ref* to be mistaken

engañifa *f* deception, trick

engaño *m* deception, deceit, fraud; mistake; falsehood; **llamarse a engaño** to back out because of fraud

engaño•so -sa *adj* deceptive

engargantar *tr* (*un ave*) to stuff the throat of ‖ *intr* & *ref* to mesh, engage

engarzar §60 *tr* to link, string, wire; curl; enchase; (Col) to hook

engastar *tr* to enchase, mount, set

engaste *m* enchasing, mounting, setting

engatusar *tr* to coax, wheedle; inveigle

engendrar *tr* to beget, engender; (geom) to generate

engendro *m* foetus; botch, bungle; (*criatura informe*) runt, stunt; **mal engendro** (coll) young tough

engolfar *intr* to go far out in the ocean ‖ *ref* to go far out in the ocean; become deeply involved; be lost in thought

engoma•do -da *adj* (Chile) all dressed up ‖ *m* (CAm) hangover

engomar *tr* to gum ‖ *ref* to have a hangover

engorda *f* fattening; animals being fattened

engordar *tr* to fatten ‖ *intr* to get fat; (coll) to get fat, get rich

engorro *m* bother, nuisance, obstacle

engorro•so -sa *adj* annoying

engoznar *tr* to hinge, to hang on a hinge

engranaje *m* gear, gears, teeth; (fig) link, connection; **engranaje de distribución** (aut) timing gears; **engranaje de tornillo sin fin** worm gear

engranar *tr* to gear, mesh; throw into gear ‖ *intr* to gear, mesh

engrandecer §22 *tr* to amplify, enlarge, magnify; exalt, extol; enhance

engrane *m* gear; mesh

engranerar *tr* (*el grano*) to store

engrapa•dor -dora *mf* stapler

engrapar *tr* to clamp, cramp

engrasador *m* grease cup; **engrasador de pistón** grease gun

engrasar *tr* to grease; smear with grease

engrase *m* greasing; grease

engravar *tr* to spread gravel over

engredar *tr* to chalk, to clay

engreí•do -da *adj* conceited, vain

engreimiento *m* conceit, vanity

engreír §58 *tr* to make conceited; spoil, pamper ‖ *ref* to become conceited

engreña•do -da *adj* disheveled

engrescar §73 *tr* to incite to fight; incite to merriment ‖ *ref* to pick a fight; join in the fun

engrifar *tr* to curl, crisp ‖ *ref* to curl up; stand on end; (*un caballo*) rear

engrillar *tr* to shackle, fetter ‖ *ref* (*las patatas*) to sprout

engringar §44 *ref* to act like a foreigner

engrosar §61 *tr* to broaden; enlarge ‖ *intr* to get fat ‖ *ref* to broaden; swell, get bigger

engrudar *tr* to paste

engrudo *m* paste

engualdrapar *tr* to caparison

enguapear *ref* (Mex) to get drunk

enguirnaldar *tr* to garland, wreathe; trim, bedeck

engullir §13 *tr* to gulp down

engurrio *m* sadness, melancholy

enhebrar *tr* (*una aguja*) to thread; (*perlas*) string; (*mentiras*) rattle off

enhestar §2 *tr* to stand upright, erect; hoist, lift up

enhies•to -ta *adj* upright, straight, erect

enhilar *tr* to thread; direct; line up; (*ideas*) marshal ‖ *intr* to set out

enhorabuena *adv* safely, luckily; **enhorabuena que** thank heavens that ‖ *f* congratulations; **dar la enhorabuena a** to congratulate

enhoramala *adv* unluckily, under an unlucky star; **nacer enhoramala** to be born under an unlucky star; **vete enhoramala** go to the devil

enhornar *tr* to put into the oven

enigma *m* enigma, riddle, puzzle

enigmáti•co -ca *adj* enigmatic(al)

enjabonar *tr* to soap, lather; (*adular*) (coll) to soft-soap; (*reprender*) (coll) to upbraid

enjaezar §60 *tr* to harness, put trappings on

enjalbegado *m* whitewashing

enjalbegar §44 *tr* to whitewash; (*el rostro*) paint ‖ *ref* to paint the face

enjambrar *intr* (*las abejas*) to swarm; to multiply in great numbers

enjambre *m* swarm

enjaretado *m* grating, lattice work

enjarrar *ref* (C-R, Mex) to stand with arms akimbo

enjaular *tr* to cage; jail, lock up

enjergar §44 *tr* to launch, get started, start on a shoestring

enjoyar *tr* to adorn with jewels; set with precious stones; adorn

enjuagadien•tes *m* (*pl* -tes) mouthwash

enjuagar §44 *tr* to rinse, rinse out

enjuague *m* rinse; rinsing water; mouthwash; rinsing cup; (coll) plot

enjugador *m* drier; clotheshorse

enjugama•nos *m* (*pl* -nos) towel, hand towel

enjugaparabri•sas *m* (*pl* -sas) windshield wiper

enjugar §44 *tr* (*secar*) to dry; (*el sudor*) wipe, wipe off; (*lágrimas*) wipe away; (*deudas, un déficit*) wipe out ‖ *ref* to lose weight

enjuiciamiento *m* procedure; prosecution, suit; trial; judgment, sentence

enjuiciar *tr* to prosecute, sue; try; judge

enjundio•so -sa *adj* fatty, greasy; solid, substantial

enju•to -ta *adj* (*tiempo, clima; ojos*) dry; lean, skinny; quiet, stolid ‖ **enjutos** *mpl* brushwood; (*para excitar la gana de beber*) tidbits

enlabiar *tr* to entice, take in; press one's lips against

enlace *m* connection, linking; relationship; betrothal, engagement; marriage; (mil, phonet) liaison; (rr) connection, junction

enlaciar *tr, intr & ref* to wither, wilt, shrivel; rumple

enladrillado *m* brickwork; bricklaying; brick paving

enladrillar *tr* to pave with bricks

enlajado *m* (Ven) flagstone

enlajar *tr* (Ven) to pave with flagstones

enlardar *tr* to baste

enlatado *m* canning

enlatar *tr* to can; roof with tin, line with tin

enlazar §60 *tr* to connect, link; lace; (*un animal con el lazo*) lasso ǁ *intr* (*p.ej., dos trenes*) to connect ǁ *ref* to be connected, be linked; connect; get married; become related by marriage

enlechar *tr* to grout

enlistonado *m* lathing, lath

enlistonar *tr* to lath

enlodar *tr* to muddy, smear with mud; plaster with mud; seal with mud; (fig) to sling mud at

enloquecer §22 *tr* to drive crazy ǁ *intr* to go crazy

enloquecimiento *m* insanity, madness

enlosado *m* flagstone paving

enlosar *tr* to pave with flagstones

enlozar §60 *tr* to enamel

enlozado *m* enamelware

enlucido *m* plaster, coat (*of plaster*)

enlucir §45 *tr* (*una pared*) to plaster; (*la plata*) polish

enlutar *tr* to put in mourning, hang with crape; darken, sadden ǁ *ref* to dress in mourning

enmaderar *tr* to cover with boards; build the framework for

enmagrecer §22 *tr* to make thin ǁ *intr & ref* to get thin

enmalecer §22 *tr* to spoil ǁ *ref* to get full of weeds, be overgrown with weeds

enmarañar *tr* to entangle; confuse ǁ *ref* to become entangled; become overcast, get cloudy

enmarcar §73 *tr* to frame

enmarchitar *tr & ref* to wither

enmaridar *intr & ref* to take a husband

enmarillecer §22 *ref* to turn yellow, turn pale

enmasar *tr* (*tropas*) to mass

enmascarar *tr* to mask; camouflage ǁ *ref* to put on a mask; masquerade

enmasillar *tr* to putty

enmendación *f* emendation

enmendar §2 *tr* (*corregir*) to emend; (*reformar*) amend; (*resarcir*) make amends for ǁ *ref* to amend, mend one's ways, go straight

enmienda *f* (*corrección*) emendation; (*propuesta de variante*) amendment; (*satisfacción del daño hecho*) amends

enmohecer §22 *tr* to make moldy; rust; neglect ǁ *ref* to get moldy; rust; (*la memoria*) get rusty; fade away

enmontar *ref* (CAm, Mex, Col, Ven) to become overgrown with brush

enmudecer §22 *tr* to hush, silence ǁ *intr* to hush up, keep quiet; become dumb, lose one's voice

enmuescar §73 *tr* to notch; (carp) to mortise

ennegrecer §22 *tr* to blacken, dye black ǁ *ref* to turn black; (*el porvenir*) be black

ennoblecer §22 *tr* to ennoble; glorify, enhance

ennoblecimiento *m* ennoblement; glory, splendor; (*grandeza de alma*) nobility

enodio *m* fawn, young deer

enojada *f* (Mex) fit of anger

enojadi•zo -za *adj* irritable, ill-tempered

enojar *tr* to anger; annoy, vex ǁ *ref* to get angry; **enojarse con** or **contra** to get angry with (*a person*); **enojarse de** to get angry at (*a thing*)

enojo *m* anger; annoyance, bother

eno•jón -jona *adj* (Chile, Ecuad, Mex) irritable, ill-tempered

enojo•so -sa *adj* annoying, bothersome

enorgullecer §22 *tr* to fill with pride, make proud ǁ *ref* to be proud; **enorgullecerse de** to pride oneself on

enorme *adj* enormous, huge

enotecnia *f* wine making; oenology

enquiciar *tr* (*una puerta, una ventana*) to hang; fasten, make firm

enrabiar *tr* to enrage ǁ *intr* to have rabies ǁ *ref* to become enraged

enramar *tr* (*ramos*) to intertwine; adorn with branches ǁ *intr* to sprout branches ǁ *ref* to hide in the branches

enranciar *tr* to make rancid ǁ *ref* to get rancid

enrarecer §22 *tr* to rarefy; make scarce ǁ *intr* to become scarce ǁ *ref* to rarefy; become scarce

enrarecimiento *m* (*p.ej., del aire*) thinness; scarceness, scarcity

enrasar *tr* to make flush; grade, level ǁ *intr* to be flush

enratonar *ref* to get sick from eating mice; (Ven) to have a hangover

enredadera *adj* (*planta*) climbing ǁ *f* climbing plant, vine

enreda•dor -dora *mf* gossip, busybody

enredar *tr* to catch in a net; (*redes, una trampa*) set; tangle up; involve, entangle; (*una pelea*) start; intertwine, interweave; endanger, compromise ǁ *intr* to romp around, be frisky ǁ *ref* to get tangled up; get involved, become entangled; (coll) to have an affair

enredijo *m* entanglement

enredo *m* tangle; involvement, entanglement, complication; restlessness; friskiness; mischievous lie; (*de una novela, un drama*) plot; (*trato ilícito de hombre y mujer*) liaison

enre•dón -dona *adj* scheming ǁ *mf* schemer

enredo•so -sa *adj* entangled, complicated, difficult

enrejado *m* grating, trellis, latticework; iron railing; grill; openwork embroidery

enrejar *tr* to grate, lattice; (*una ventana*) put a grate on; fence with an iron grating; (*ladrillos, tablas*) pile alternately crosswise; (Mex) to darn

enrielar *tr* to make into ingots; lay rails on; put on the tracks; put on the right track

enriquecer §22 *tr* to enrich ‖ *intr & ref* to get rich

enrisca•do -da *adj* craggy, full of cliffs

enrizar §60 *tr & ref* to curl

enrocar §73 *tr & intr* (chess) to castle

enrodrigar §44 *tr* to prop, prop up

enrojar *tr* to redden, make red; (*el horno*) to heat up ‖ *ref* to redden, turn red

enrojecer §22 *tr* to make red; make red-hot; make blush ‖ *intr* to blush ‖ *ref* to turn red; get red-hot; flush; get sore, get inflamed

enromar *tr* to make dull, make blunt

enronquecer §22 *tr* to make hoarse ‖ *intr & ref* to get hoarse

enronquecimiento *m* hoarseness

enroque *m* (chess) castling

enroscar §73 *tr* to coil, twist, screw in ‖ *ref* to coil, twist

enrubiar *tr* to bleach, make blond ‖ *ref* to turn blond

enrubio *m* bleaching; bleaching lotion

enrular *tr & ref* (Arg) to curl

ensacar §73 *tr* to bag, put in a bag

ensaimada *f* twisted coffee cake

ensalada *f* salad; hodgepodge; fiasco, flop

ensaladera *f* salad bowl

ensalmar *tr* (*un hueso*) to set; treat or heal by incantation

ensalmo *m* incantation, spell; **como por ensalmo** as if by magic

ensalzar §60 *tr* to exalt, elevate, extol

ensamblar *tr* to assemble, join, fit together; **ensamblar a cola de milano** or **a cola de pato** to dovetail

ensanchador *m* glove stretcher

ensanchar *tr* to widen, enlarge; (*una prenda ajustada*) ease, let out; (*el corazón*) unburden ‖ *intr & ref* to be proud and haughty

ensanche *m* widening, extension; (*de una calle*) extension; suburban development; allowance (*for enlargement of garment*)

ensandecer §22 *intr* to go crazy

ensangrenta•do -da *adj* bloody, gory

ensangrentar §2 *tr* to bathe in blood; stain with blood ‖ *ref* to rage, go wild; (*p.ej., las manos*) bloody, make bloody

ensañar *tr* to anger, enrage ‖ *ref* to be cruel, be merciless; (*una enfermedad*) rage

ensartar *tr* (*una aguja*) to thread; (*cuentas*) string; stick; rattle off ‖ *ref* to squeeze in

ensayar *tr* to try, try on, try out; (*un espectáculo*) rehearse; (*minerales*) assay; teach, train; test ‖ *ref* to practice

ensaye *m* assay

ensayista *mf* essayist; (Chile) assayer

ensayo *m* trying, trial; testing, test; (*género literario*) essay; (*de minerales*) assay; exer-

cise, practice; (theat) rehearsal; **ensayo de choque** (aut) crash test; **ensayo general** dress rehearsal

ensenada *f* inlet, cove

enseña *f* standard, ensign

enseña•do -da *adj* trained, informed; (*perro de caza*) trained

enseñanza *f* teaching; education, instruction; (*ejemplo que sirve de experiencia*) lesson; **enseñanza superior** higher education

enseñar *tr* to teach; train; show, point out ‖ *intr* to teach

enseñorear *ref* to control oneself; **enseñorearse de** to take possession of

enseres *mpl* utensils, equipment, household goods

enseriar *ref* to become serious

ensillar *tr* to saddle

ensimismamiento *m* absorption in thought, deep thought

ensimismar *ref* to become absorbed in thought; (Chile, Ecuad, Peru) to be proud, be boastful

ensoberbecer §22 to make proud ‖ *ref* to become proud; (*el mar, las olas*) swell, get rough

ensoberbecimiento *m* haughtiness

ensombrecer §22 *tr* to darken ‖ *ref* to get dark; become sad and gloomy

ensoña•dor -dora *adj* dreamy ‖ *mf* dreamer

ensopar *tr* to dip, dunk; soak, drench

ensordece•dor -dora *adj* deafening

ensordecer §22 *tr* to deafen; (*una consonante sonora*) unvoice ‖ *intr* to become deaf; play deaf, not answer ‖ *ref* to unvoice

ensortijar *tr* to curl, make curly; (*la nariz de un animal*) ring, put a ring in ‖ *ref* to curl

ensuciar *tr* to dirty, soil; stain, smear; defile, sully ‖ *ref* to soil oneself; take bribes

ensueño *m* dream; daydream

entablado *m* flooring; wooden framework

entablar *tr* to board, board up; (*un hueso roto*) splint; (*una conversación*) start; (*p.ej., una batalla*) launch; (*un pleito*) bring; (*las piezas del ajedrez y de las damas*) set up ‖ *ref* (*el viento*) to settle

entable *m* boarding; (*en los juegos de ajedrez y damas*) position of men; (Col) business, undertaking

entablillar *tr* (*un hueso roto*) to splint

enta•blón -blona *adj* (Peru) blustering, bragging ‖ *mf* (Peru) bully

entalegar §44 *tr* to bag, put in a bag; (*dinero*) hoard

entalladura *f* carving, sculpture; engraving slot, groove, mortise; cut, incision (*in a tree*)

entallar *tr* to carve, sculpture; engrave; notch; groove, mortise; (*un traje*) fit, tailor ‖ *intr* to take shape; (*el vestido*) fit; go well, be fitting

entallecer §22 *intr & ref* to shoot, sprout

entapizar §60 *tr* to tapestry, hang with tapestry; cover with a fabric; overgrow, spread over

entarimado *m* parquet, inlaid floor, hardwood floor

entarimar *tr* to parquet, to put an inlaid floor on ‖ *ref* to put on airs

entarugar §44 *tr* to pave with wooden blocks ‖ *ref (el sombrero)* (Ven) to stick on

ente *m* being; (coll) guy, odd fellow

enteca•do -da or **ente•co -ca** *adj* sickly, frail

enteleri•do -da *adj* shaking with cold, shaking with fright; sickly, frail

entena *f* lateen yard

entena•do -da *mf* stepchild ‖ *m* stepson ‖ *f* stepdaughter

entendederas *fpl* (coll) brains; **tener malas entendederas** (coll) to have no brains

entende•dor -dora *adj* understanding, intelligent ‖ *mf* understanding person; **al buen entendedor, pocas palabras** a word to the wise is enough

entender *m* understanding, opinion ‖ §51 *tr* to understand; intend, mean ‖ *intr* —**entender de** to be a judge of; be experienced as; **entender de razón** to listen to reason; **entender en** to be familiar with, deal with ‖ *ref* to be understood; have a secret understanding; **entenderse con** to get along with; concern; *(una mujer)* have an affair with

entendi•do -da *adj* expert, skilled; informed; **no darse por entendido** to take no notice, pretend not to understand; **los entendidos** informed sources; **un entendido en** a well-informed person in

entendimiento *m* understanding

entenebrecer §22 *tr* to darken; confuse ‖ *ref* to get dark; become confused

entera•do -da *adj* informed, posted; (Chile) conceited; (Chile) intrusive, meddlesome ‖ *mf* insider

enterar *tr* to inform, acquaint; to pay; (Arg, Chile) to complete ‖ *intr* (Chile) to get better; (Chile) to drift along ‖ *ref* to find out; to recover; **enterarse de** to find out about, become aware of

entereza *f* entirety, completeness; wholeness; perfection; fairness; constancy, fortitude; strictness

enteri•zo -za *adj* in one piece

enternece•dor -dora *adj* moving, touching

enternecer §22 *tr* to move, touch ‖ *ref* to be moved to pity

enternecimiento *m* pity, compassion

ente•ro -ra *adj* entire, whole, complete; honest, upright; firm, energetic; sound, vigorous; *(tela)* strong, heavy ‖ *m* (arith) integer; payment; (Chile) balance; **por entero** entirely, wholly, completely

enterrador *m* gravedigger

enterramiento *m* burial, interment; *(hoyo)* grave; *(monumento)* tomb

enterrar §2 *tr* to bury, inter; outlive, survive ‖ *ref* to hide away

entesar §2 *tr* to stretch, make taut

entibar *tr* to prop up, shore up ‖ *intr* to rest, lean

entibiar *tr* to cool off; temper, moderate ‖ *ref* to cool off, cool down

entidad *f* entity; importance, consequence, moment; body, organization

entierramuer•tos *m* (*pl* **-tos**) gravedigger

entierro *m* burial, interment; *(hoyo)* grave; *(monumento)* tomb; funeral; funeral cortege; buried treasure

entintar *tr* to ink; ink in; stain with ink; dye

entoldar *tr* to cover with awnings; adorn with hangings ‖ *ref* to get cloudy, become overcast; swell with pride

entomología *f* entomology

entonación *f* intonation; blowing of bellows

entona•do -da *adj* arrogant; haughty; harmonious, in tune

entonar *tr* to intone; sing in tune; *(el órgano)* blow; *(colores)* harmonize; tone, tone up; *(alabanzas)* sound ‖ *intr* to sing in tune ‖ *ref* to be puffed up with pride

entonces *adv* then ‖ *m* — **por aquel entonces** at that time

entonelar *tr* to put in barrels, put in casks

entongar §44 *tr* (Mex, W-I) to pile up, pile in rows; (Col) to drive crazy

entono *m* intoning; arrogance, haughtiness

entontecer §22 *tr* to make foolish, make stupid ‖ *intr* & *ref* to become foolish, become stupid

entorchado *m* bullion; **ganar los entorchados** to win one's stripes

entorna•do -da *adj* ajar, half-closed

entornar *tr* to half-close; *(los ojos)* squint; *(una puerta)* leave ajar; *(volcar)* upset ‖ *ref* to upset

entornillar *tr* to twist, screw up

entorno *m* environment

entorpecer §22 *tr* to stupefy; obstruct, delay; benumb; *(una cerradura, una ventana)* make stick ‖ *ref* to stick, get stuck

entortar §61 *tr* to bend, make crooked; knock out the eye of ‖ *ref* to bend, get crooked

entrada *f* entrance, entry; admission; arrival; income, receipts; admission ticket; entrance hall; *(número de personas que asisten a un espectáculo)* house; *(producto de cada función)* gate; *(amistad en alguna casa)* entree; *(naipes que guarda un jugador)* hand; *(de una comida)* entree; *(visita breve)* short call; (Col) down payment; (Mex) attack, onslaught; (elec) input; **dar entrada a** to admit; to give an opening to; *(un buque)* to give the right of entry to; **entrada de taquilla** gate; **entrada general** top gallery; **entrada llena** full house; **mucha entrada** good house, good turnout; **se prohibe la entrada** no admittance

entra•do -da *adj* (Chile) officious, self-assertive; **entrado en años** advanced in years ‖ *f* see **entrada**

entra•dor -dora *adj* *(enamoradizo)* susceptible; (Mex) lively, energetic; (Chile) officious, self-assertive

entrama•do -da *adj* half-timbered ‖ *m* timber framework

entram•bos -bas *adj* & *pron indef* both; **entrambos a dos** both

entrampar *tr* to ensnare, trap; trick, deceive; overload with debt ‖ *ref* to get trapped; be tricked; run into debt

entrante adj entering; (p.ej., tren) inbound, incoming; (próximo, que viene) next ‖ mf entrant; **entrantes y salientes** (coll) hangers-on

entraña f internal organ; (fig) heart, center; **entrañas** entrails; (fig) heart, feeling; (fig) disposition, temper

entrañable adj close, intimate

entrañar tr to put away deep, bury deep; involve; (malos pensamientos) harbor ‖ ref to go deep into; be buried deep; be close, be intimate

entrapajar tr to wrap up, bandage

entrar tr to bring in; overrun, invade; influence ‖ intr to enter, go in, come in; (un río) empty; (el viento, la marea) rise; attack; begin; **entrar a matar** (taur) to go in for the kill; **entrar en** to enter, enter into, go into; fit into; adopt, take up; **que entra** next

entre prep (en medio de) between; (en el número de) among; (en el intervalo de) in the course of; **entre manos** at hand; **entre mí** to myself; **entre que** while; **entre tanto** meanwhile; **entre Vd. y yo** between you and me

entreabier•to -ta adj half-open; (puerta) ajar

entreabrir §83 tr to half-open; leave ajar

entreacto m entr'acte

entreca•no -na adj graying, grayish

entrecarril m (Ven) gauge

entrecejo m space between the eyebrows; frown; **fruncir el entrecejo** to frown; **mirar con entrecejo** to frown at

entrecoger §17 tr to catch, seize; press hard, hold down

entrecoro m chancel

entrecorta•do -da adj broken, intermittent

entrecortar tr to break in on, keep interrupting

entre•cruz m (pl -cruces) interweaving

entrecruzar §60 tr & ref to intercross; interweave, interlace; to interbreed

entrecubiertas fpl between-decks

entrechocar §73 ref to collide, clash

entredicho m interdiction, prohibition; (law) injunction; (Bol) alarm bell; **poner en entredicho** to cast doubt upon

entredós m (tira de encaje) insertion; (typ) long primer

entrefilete m short feature, special item

entrefi•no -na adj medium

entrega f delivery; (p.ej., de una plaza fuerte) surrender; (cuaderno de un libro que se vende suelto) fascicle; (de una revista) issue, number; **por entregas** in instalments

entregar §44 tr to deliver; hand over, surrender; fit in, insert; **entregarla** to die ‖ ref to give in, surrender; abandon oneself; to devote oneself; **entregarse de** to take possession of, take charge of

entrehierro m (elec) spark gap; (phys) air gap

entrelazar §60 tr to interlace, interweave

entremediar tr to put between

entremedias adv in between; in the meantime; **entremedias de** between; among

entremés m hors d'œuvre, side dish; short farce (inserted in an auto or performed between two acts of a comedia)

entremesear tr (una conversación) to enliven

entremeter tr to put in, insert ‖ ref to meddle, intrude, butt in

entremeti•do -da adj meddling, meddlesome ‖ mf meddler, intruder, busybody

entremezclar tr & ref to intermingle, intermix

entremorir §30 & §83 intr to flicker, die out

entrenador m (sport) coach, trainer, handler

entrenamiento m (sport) coaching, training

entrenar tr & ref (sport) to coach, train

entrepaño m (de una puerta) panel; (espacio entre dos columnas, etc.) pier; shelf

entreparecer §60 ref to show through

entrepiernas fpl crotch; patches in the crotch of trousers; (Chile) bathing trunks

entrepuentes mpl between-decks; (naut) steerage

entrerrenglón m interline; space between the lines

entrerrenglonar tr to write between the lines

entrerriel m gauge

entrerrisa f giggle

entrerrosca f (mach) nipple

entresacar §73 tr to pick, pick out, select; cull, sift; (árboles; el pelo) thin out

entresemana adv (SAm) weekdays; workdays

entresijo m secret; mystery; **tener muchos entresijos** to be mysterious, be hard to figure out

entresuelo m mezzanine, entresol

entretallar tr to carve, engrave; carve in bas-relief; do openwork in; intercept

entretanto adv meantime, meanwhile ‖ m meanwhile; **en el entretanto** in the meantime

entretecho m (Arg, Chile, Urug) attic, garret

entretejer tr to interweave

entretela f interlining

entretelar tr to interline

entretención f amusement, entertainment

entretener §71 tr to amuse, entertain; (el tiempo) while away; maintain, keep up; put off, delay; (el dolor) allay; (el hambre) stave off (by taking a bite before mealtime); try to get one's mind off ‖ ref to amuse oneself, be amused

entreteni•do -da adj amusing, entertaining; (rad) continuous, undamped ‖ f kept woman; **dar la entretenida a** or **con la entretenida a** to stall off by constant talk

entretenimiento m amusement, entertainment; upkeep, maintenance

entretiempo m in-between season; **de entretiempo** spring-and-fall (coat)

entreventana f pier

entrever §80 tr to glimpse, descry, catch a glimpse of; guess, suspect

entreverar tr to mix ‖ ref (Arg) to get all mixed together; (dos grupos de caballería) (Arg) to clash in hand-to-hand combat

entrevía f gauge

entrevista f interview

entrevistar *ref* to have an interview
entristecer §22 *tr* to sadden, make sad ‖ *ref* to sadden, become sad
entrojar *tr* to store in a granary
entrometer *tr* & *ref* var of **entremeter**
entrometi•do -da *adj* & *mf* var of **entremetido**
entronar *tr* to enthrone
entroncamiento *m* connection, relationship; (*de caminos, ferrocarriles*) junction
entroncar §73 *tr* to prove relationship between ‖ *intr* to be related; (*dos caminos, ferrocarriles, etc.*) connect
entronerar *tr* (*una bola de billar*) to pocket
entronizar §60 *tr* to enthrone; exalt; popularize ‖ *ref* to be puffed up with pride
entronque *m* connection, relationship; (*de caminos, ferrocarriles*) junction
entruchar *tr* to decoy, trick
entru•chón -chona *adj* tricky ‖ *mf* trickster
entuerto *m* wrong, harm, injustice
entumecer §22 *tr* to make numb ‖ *ref* (*un miembro*) to get numb, go to sleep; (*el mar*) swell, get rough
entupir *tr* to stop up, clog; pack tight ‖ *ref* to get stopped up, get clogged
enturbiar *tr* to stir up, make muddy; confuse, upset
entusiasmar *tr* to enthuse, make enthusiastic ‖ *ref* to enthuse, become enthusiastic
entusiasmo *m* enthusiasm; inspiration
entusiasta *adj* enthusiastic ‖ *mf* enthusiast
entusiásti•co -ca *adj* enthusiastic
enumerar *tr* to enumerate
enunciar *tr* to enunciate, enounce
enunciati•vo -va *adj* (gram) declarative
envainar *tr* to sheathe
envalentonar *tr* to embolden, make bold ‖ *ref* to pluck up, take courage
envanecer §22 *tr* to make vain ‖ *ref* to become vain, get conceited
envanecimiento *m* vanity, conceit
envaramiento *m* stiffness
envarar *tr* to make numb, to stiffen ‖ *ref* to get stiff; get numb
envasar *tr* (*p.ej., trigo*) to pack, sack; (*p.ej., vino*) bottle; (*p.ej., pescado*) can; (*una espada*) thrust, poke; (*mucho vino*) put away ‖ *intr* to tipple
envase *m* container; bottle, jar; can; packing; bottling; canning; **envase de hojalata** tin can
envedijar *ref* to get tangled; come to blows
envejecer §22 *tr* to age, make old ‖ *intr* & *ref* to age, grow old; get out of date
envejeci•do -da *adj* old, aged; experienced, tried
envenenar *tr* to poison; (*llenar de amargura*) envenom, embitter; (*las palabras o conducta de una persona*) put an evil interpretation on ‖ *ref* to take poison
enverdecer §22 *intr* to turn green
envergadura *f* (*de las alas abiertas del ave*) spread; (*ancho de una vela*) breadth; (aer) span, wingspread; (fig) compass, spread, reach

envés *m* wrong side; (*del cuerpo humano*) back
enviado *m* envoy
enviar §77 *tr* to send; (*mercancías*) ship; **enviar a buscar** to send for; **enviar a paseo** to send on his way, dismiss without ceremony; **enviar por** to send for
enviciar *tr* to corrupt, vitiate; (*mimar*) spoil ‖ *intr* to have many leaves and little fruit ‖ *ref* to become addicted; **enviciarse con** or **en** to addict oneself to, become addicted to
envidar *tr* to bid against, bet against ‖ *intr* to bid, bet
envidia *f* envy; desire
envidiable *adj* enviable
envidiar *tr* to envy, begrudge; desire, want
envidio•so -sa *adj* envious; greedy, covetous ‖ *mf* envious person
envilecer §22 *tr* to debase, vilify, revile ‖ *ref* to degrade oneself
envío *m* sending; (*de mercancías*) shipment; (*de dinero*) remittance; (*en una obra*) autograph, inscription
envirota•do -da *adj* stiff, stuck-up
envite *m* bet; bid, offer, invitation; push, shove; (*apuesta adicional a un lance o suerte*) side bet; **al primer envite** right off, at the start
enviudar *intr* (*una mujer*) to become a widow; (*un hombre*) become a widower
envoltorio *m* bundle; (*defecto en el paño*) knot
envoltura *f* cover, wrapper, envelope; swaddling clothes
envolver §47 & §83 *tr* to wrap, wrap up; (*hilo, cinta*) wind, roll up; (*al niño*) swaddle; imply, mean; involve; envelop; (*dejar cortado y sin salida en la disputa*) floor; (mil) to encircle ‖ *ref* to become involved; have an affair
enyerbar *tr* (Col, Chile, Mex) to bewitch ‖ *ref* to be covered with grass; (Mex) to fall madly in love; (Mex) to take poison
enyesar *tr* to plaster; put in a plaster cast; (*la tierra, el vino*) gypsum
enyugar §44 *tr* to yoke
enzima *f* enzyme
enzolvar *tr* (Mex) to clog, stop up
epazote *m* (CAm, Mex) Mexican tea
E.P.D. *abbr* **en paz descanse**
epénte•sis *f* (*pl* **-sis**) epenthesis
eperlano *m* smelt
épica *f* epic poetry
epice•no -na *adj* (gram) epicene, common
épi•co -ca *adj* epic ‖ *m* epic poet ‖ *f* see **épica**
epicúre•o -a *adj* epicurean ‖ *mf* epicurean, epicure
epidemia *f* epidemic
epidémi•co -ca *adj* epidemic
epidemiología *f* epidemiology
epidermis *f* epidermis; **tener la epidermis fina** or **sensible** to be touchy
Epifanía *f* Epiphany, Twelfth-day
epígrafe *m* epigraph; inscription; headline, title; device, motto
epigrama *m* epigram
epilepsia *f* epilepsy

en
ep

epilépti•co -ca *adj & mf* epileptic
epilogar §44 *tr* to sum up, summarize
episcopalista *adj & mf* Episcopalian
episodio *m* episode
epistemología *f* epistemology
epístola *f* epistle
epitafio *m* epitaph
epíteto *m* epithet
epitomar *tr* to epitomize
epítome *m* epitome
E.P.M. *abbr* **en propia mano**
época *f* epoch; **hacer época** to be epoch-making
epopeya *f* epic, epic poem
equidad *f* equity; (*templanza habitual*) equableness; (*moderación en el precio*) reasonableness
equiláte•ro -ra *adj* equilateral
equilibra•do -da *adj* balanced; (fig) sensible, even-tempered
equilibrar *tr* to balance, equilibrate; (*el presupuesto*) balance ‖ *ref* to balance, equilibrate
equilibrio *m* equilibrium, balance, equipoise; (*del presupuesto*) balancing; **equilibrio político** balance of power
equilibrista *mf* balancer, ropedancer
equinoccial *adj* equinoctial
equinoccio *m* equinox
equipaje *m* baggage; piece of baggage; equipment; (naut) crew; **equipaje de mano** hand baggage
equipar *tr* to equip
equiparar *tr* to compare
equi•pier *m* (*pl* **-piers**) teammate
equipo *m* equipment, outfit; crew, gang; (sport) team; **equipo de alta fidelidad** stereo system; hi-fi set; **equipo de novia** trousseau; **equipo de urgencia** first-aid kit
equitación *f* horsemanship, riding
equitati•vo -va *adj* fair, equitable; (*tranquilo*) equable
equivalente *adj & m* equivalent
equivaler §76 *intr* to be equal, be equivalent
equivocación *f* mistake; mistakenness
equivoca•do -da *adj* mistaken, wrong
equivocar §73 *tr* (*una cosa por otra*) to mistake, mix ‖ *ref* to be mistaken, make a mistake; be wrong; **equivocarse con** to be mistaken for; **equivocarse de** to be wrong in, take the wrong . . .
equívo•co -ca *adj* equivocal, ambiguous ‖ *m* equivocation, ambiguity; pun
equivoquista *mf* equivocator; punster
era *f* era, age; threshing floor; vegetable patch, garden bed
eral *m* two-year-old bull
erario *m* state treasury
erección *f* erection; foundation, establishment
eremita *m* hermit
ergástulo *m* dungeon, slave prison
ergio *m* erg
ergotismo *m* argumentativeness; (pathol) ergotism
ergotista *adj invar* argumentative; dogmatic; *mf* dogmatist; know-it-all

erguir §33 *tr* to raise; straighten up ‖ *ref* to straighten up; swell with pride
erial *adj* unplowed, uncultivated ‖ *m* unplowed land, uncultivated land
erigir §27 *tr* to erect, build; found, establish; (*a nueva condición*) elevate ‖ *ref* —**erigirse en** to be elevated to; set oneself up as
eriza•do -da *adj* bristling, bristly, spiny
erizar §60 *tr* to make stand on end, cause to bristle ‖ *ref* to stand on end, to bristle
erizo *m* (*mamífero*) hedgehog; (*zurrón espinoso de la castaña*) bur, thistle; (*púas de hierro que coronan lo alto de una muralla*) cheval-de-frise; (*persona de carácter áspero*) curmudgeon; **erizo de mar** (zool) sea urchin
ermita *f* hermitage
ermita•ño -ña *mf* hermit
erogación *f* (*de bienes o caudales*) distribution; expenditure; (Peru, Ven) gift, charity; (Mex) outlay
erogar §44 *tr* to distribute; (Ecuad) to contribute; (Mex) to cause
erosión *f* erosion
erosionar *tr & ref* to erode
erradicar §73 *tr* to eradicate
erra•do -da *adj* mistaken, wrong
errar §34 *tr* to miss ‖ *intr* to err, be mistaken, be wrong; wander ‖ *ref* to be mistaken, be wrong
errata *f* erratum; printer's error
erróne•o -a *adj* erroneous
error *m* error, mistake; **error de pluma** clerical error; **salvo error u omisión** barring error or omission
eructar *intr* to belch; (coll) to brag
eructo *m* belch, belching
erudición *f* erudition, learning
erudi•to -ta *adj* erudite, learned ‖ *mf* scholar, savant; **erudito a la violeta** egghead, highbrow
erugino•so -sa *adj* rusty
erumpir *intr* (*un volcán*) to erupt
erupción *f* eruption
esbel•to -ta *adj* slender, lithe, willowy
esbirro *m* bailiff, constable; (*el que ejecuta órdenes injustas*) myrmidon, henchman
esbozar §60 *tr* to sketch, outline
esbozo *m* sketch, outline
escabechar *tr* to pickle; (*el pelo, la barba*) dye; (*reprobar en un examen*) flunk; stab to death ‖ *ref* to dye one's hair; (*el pelo, la barba*) dye
escabeche *m* pickle; pickled fish; hair dye
escabel *m* stool; footstool; (*para medrar*) stepping stone
escabio•so -sa *adj* mangy
escabro•so -sa *adj* scabrous, risqué; scabrous, uneven, rough, harsh
escabuche *m* weeding hoe
escabullir §13 *ref* to slip away, sneak away; slip out, wiggle out
escafandra *f* diving suit; **escafandra espacial** space suit
escafandrista *mf* diver

escala *f* (*escalera de mano*) ladder, stepladder; (*línea graduada de instrumento*) scale; (*de buque*) call; (*de avión*) stop; (*puerto donde toca una embarcación*) port of call; (*serie de las notas musicales*) scale; **en escala de** on a scale of; **en grande escala** on a large scale; **escala móvil** (*de salarios*) sliding scale; **hacer escala** (naut) to call

escalada *f* scaling, climbing; breaking in; escalation

escalador *m* climber; (*ladrón*) burglar, housebreaker

escalación *f* escalation

escalafón *m* roster, roll, register

escalar *tr* (*subir, trepar*) to scale; break in, burglarize; (*la compuerta de la acequia*) open ‖ *intr* to climb; (naut) to call ‖ *ref* to escalate

escalato·rres *m* (*pl* **-rres**) steeplejack, human fly

escalda·do -da *adj* cautious, scared, wary; (*mujer*) lewd, loose

escaldar *tr* to scald; make red hot ‖ *ref* to get scalded; chafe

escalera *f* stairs, stairway; (*la portátil*) ladder; (*de naipes*) sequence; (*en el póker*) straight; **de escalera abajo** from below stairs, from the servants; **escalera de caracol** winding stairway; **escalera de escape** fire escape; **escalera de husillo** winding stairway; **escalera de incendios** fire escape; **escalera de mano** ladder; **escalera de salvamento** fire escape; **escalera de tijera** or **escalera doble** ladder; **escalera excusada** or **falsa** private stairs; **escalera extensible** extension ladder; **escalera hurtada** secret stairway; **escalera mecánica, móvil** or **rodante** escalator, moving stairway

escalerilla *f* low step; car step; (*en las medias*) runner; (*de naipes*) sequence; thumb index

escalfar *tr* (*huevos*) to poach; (*el pan*) bake brown

escalinata *f* stone steps, front steps

escalo *m* burglary, breaking in

escalofria·do -da *adj* chilly

escalofrío *m* chill

escalón *m* step, rung; (*grada de la escalera*) tread; (fig) step, echelon, grade; (*paso con que uno adelanta sus pretensiones*) (fig) stepping stone; (mil) echelon; (rad) stage

escalonamiento *m* ranking; gradation

escalonar *tr* to space out, spread out; (*las horas de trabajo*) stagger; (mil) to echelon

escalope *m* (*loncha delgada de carne*) scallop (*thin slice of meat*)

escalpar *tr* to scalp

escalpelo *m* scalpel

escama *f* scale; fear, suspicion

escamar *tr* (*los peces*) to scale; (coll) to frighten ‖ *ref* to be frightened

escamondar *tr* to trim, prune

escamo·so -sa *adj* scaly

escamotea·dor -dora *mf* prestidigitator; swindler

escamotear *tr* to whisk out of sight, cause to vanish; (*una carta*) palm; swipe, snitch

escampada *f* clear spell, break in rain

escampar *tr* to clear out ‖ *intr* to stop raining; ease up; ¡**ya escampa!** there you go again! ‖ *ref* — **escamparse del agua** to get in out of the rain

escampavía *f* (naut) cutter, revenue cutter

escamujar *tr* (*un árbol, esp. un olivo*) to prune; (*ramas*) clear out

escanciar *tr* (*vino*) to pour, serve, drink ‖ *intr* to drink wine

escandalizar §60 *tr* to scandalize ‖ *ref* to be scandalized; be outraged, be exasperated

escándalo *m* scandal; **causar escándalo** to make a scene

escandalo·so -sa *adj* scandalous; noisy, riotous; loud, flashy

escandallo *m* (naut) sounding lead; (*del contenido de varios envases*) testing, sampling; cost accounting

escandina·vo -va *adj* & *mf* Scandinavian

escandir *tr* (*versos*) to scan

escansión *f* scansion; (telv) scanning

escaño *m* settle, bench with a back; (*en las Cortes*) seat; park bench; (Guat) nag

escañuelo *m* footstool

escapada *f* escape, flight; short trip, quick trip

escapar *tr* to free, save; (*un caballo*) drive hard ‖ *intr* to escape; flee, run away; **escapar en una tabla** to have a narrow escape ‖ *ref* to escape; flee, run away; (*el gas, el agua*) leak; **escapársele a uno** to let slip; not notice

escaparate *m* show window; (*armario con cristales*) cabinet; wardrobe, clothes closet; **escaparete de tienda** shop window

escaparatista *mf* window dresser

escapatoria *f* escape, getaway; (*de atenciones, deberes, etc.*) (fig) escape; (*efugio, pretexto*) (coll) evasion, subterfuge

escape *m* escape; flight; (*de gas, agua*) leak; (*de reloj*) escapement; (aut) exhaust valve; (aut) exhaust, exhaust pipe; **a escape** at full speed, on the run; **escape de rejilla** (rad) grid leak; **escape libre** (aut) cutout

escápula *f* shoulder blade, scapula

escaque *m* square; chess

escarabajear *tr* to bother, worry, harass ‖ *intr* to swarm, crawl; scrawl, scribble

escarabajo *m* black beetle; (*imperfección en los tejidos*) flaw; (*persona pequeña*) runt

escaramuza *f* skirmish

escaramuzar §60 *intr* to skirmish

escarapela *f* (*divisa en forma de lazo*) cockade; dispute ending in hair pulling

escarapelar *intr* & *ref* to quarrel, wrangle

escarbadien·tes *m* (*pl* **-tes**) toothpick

escarbar *tr* (*el suelo*) to scratch, scratch up; (*la lumbre*) poke; (*los dientes, los oídos*) pick; pry into

escarcha *f* frost, hoarfrost

escarchar *tr* (*confituras*) to frost, put frosting on; (*la tierra del alfarero*) dilute with water; spangle ‖ *intr* — **escarcha** there is frost

escardar or **escardillar** *tr* to weed, weed out
escardillo *m* weeding hoe
escariar *tr* to ream
escarlata *adj* scarlet ‖ *f* scarlet fever
escarlatina *f* scarlet fever
escarmentar §2 *tr* to make an example of ‖ *intr* to learn one's lesson
escarmiento *m* example, lesson, warning; caution, wisdom; punishment
escarnecer §22 *tr* to scoff at, make fun of
escarnio *m* scoff, scoffing
escarola *f* endive
escarpa *f* scarp, escarpment; (Mex) sidewalk
escarpa•do -da *adj* steep; abrupt, craggy
escarpia *f* hooked spike
escarpín *m* pump
escasamente *adv* barely; hardly
escasear *tr* to give sparingly; cut down on, avoid; bevel ‖ *intr* to be scarce
escase•ro -ra *adj* sparing; saving, frugal; stingy ‖ *mf* sk:nflint
escasez *f* (*falta de una cosa*) scarcity; (*pobreza*) need, want; (*mezquindad*) stinginess
esca•so -sa *adj* (*poco abundante*) scarce; (*no cabal*) scant; (*muy económico*) parsimonious, frugal; (*tacaño*) stingy; (*oportunidad*) dim, slim, slight; **estar escaso de** to be short of
escatimar *tr & intr* to scrimp
escena *f* (*parte del teatro donde se representan las obras*) stage; (*subdivisión de un acto*) scene; incident, episode; **poner en escena** to stage
escenario *m* stage; (*disposición de la representación*) setting; (*guión de un cine*) scenario; (*antecedentes de una persona o cosa*) background
escenarista *mf* scenarist
escéni•co -ca *adj* scenic
escenificar §73 *tr* to adapt for the stage
escépti•co -ca *adj* sceptic(al) ‖ *mf* sceptic
Escila *f* Scylla; **entre Escila y Caribdis** between Scylla and Charybdis
Escipión *m* Scipio
escisión *f* (biol) fission; (surg) excision
esclarecer §22 *tr* to light up, brighten; explain, elucidate; ennoble ‖ *intr* to dawn
esclareci•do -da *adj* noble, illustrious
esclavitud *f* slavery
esclavización *f* enslavement
esclavizar §60 *tr* to enslave
escla•vo -va *adj & mf* slave
escla•vón -vona *adj & mf* Slav
esclerosis múltiple *f* multiple sclerosis
esclusa *f* lock; floodgate; **esclusa de aire** caisson
esclusero *m* lock tender
escoba *f* broom
escobada *f* sweep; sweeping
escobar *tr* to sweep with a broom
escobazar §60 *tr* to sprinkle with a wet broom
escobén *m* (naut) hawse
escobilla *f* brush, whisk; gold and silver sweepings; (elec) brush
escocer §16 *intr* to smart, sting ‖ *ref* to hurt; chafe, become chafed

esco•cés -cesa *adj* Scotch, Scottish ‖ *mf* Scot ‖ *m* Scotchman; (*whisky; dialecto*) Scotch; **los escoceces** the Scotch, the Scottish
Escocia *f* Scotland; **la Nueva Escocia** Nova Scotia
escofina *f* rasp
escofinar *tr* to rasp
escoger §17 *tr* to choose, pick out
escogi•do -da *adj* choice, select
escolar *adj* school ‖ *m* pupil
escolaridad *f* schooling, school attendance; curriculum
escolimo•so -sa *adj* impatient, gruff, restless
escolta *f* escort
escoltar *tr* to escort
escollar *intr* (Arg) to run aground on a reef; (Arg, Chile) to fail
escollera *f* jetty, breakwater
escollo *m* (*peñasco a flor de agua*) reef, rock; (*peligro*) pitfall; (*obstáculo*) stumbling block
escombrar *tr* to clear out
escombro *m* (pez) mackerel; **escombros** debris, rubble, rubbish
esconder *tr* to hide, conceal; harbor, contain ‖ *ref* to hide; lurk
escondi•do -da *adj* hidden; **a escondidas** secretly; **a escondidas de** without the knowledge of
escondite *m* hiding place; (*juego de muchachos*) hide-and-seek; **jugar al escondite** to play hide-and-seek
escondrijo *m* hiding place
escopeta *f* shotgun; **escopeta blanca** gentleman hunter; **escopeta de caza** fowling piece; **escopeta de dos cañones** double-barreled shotgun; **escopeta de viento** air rifle; **escopeta negra** professional hunter
escopetazo *m* gunshot; gunshot wound; bad news, blow; (SAm) sarcasm; insult
escoplear *tr* to chisel
escoplo *m* chisel
escorbuto *m* scurvy
escoria *f* dross, scoria, slag; (fig) dross, dregs
escorial *m* cinder bank, slag dump
escorpión *m* scorpion; **Escorpión** *m* (astr) Scorpio
escorzar §60 *tr* to foreshorten
escorzo *m* foreshortening
escota *f* (naut) sheet
escota•do -da *adj* low-neck ‖ *m* low neck
escotadura *f* low neck, low cut in neck
escotar *tr* to cut to fit; draw water from, drain; cut low in the neck ‖ *intr* to go Dutch
escote *m* low neck; (*encajes en el cuello de una vestidura*) tucker; **ir a escote** or **pagar a escote** to go Dutch
escotilla *f* (naut) hatchway, scuttle
escotillón *m* hatch, trap door, scuttle; (theat) trap door
escozor *m* burning, smarting, stinging; grief, sorrow
escriba *m* scribe
escribanía *f* court clerkship; desk; writing materials
escribano *m* court clerk; lawyer's clerk

escribiente *mf* clerk, office clerk; **escribiente a máquina** typist
escribir §83 *tr & intr* to write ‖ *ref* to enroll, enlist; write to each other; **no escribirse** to be impossible to describe
escriño *m* casket, jewel case; straw basket
escri•to -ta *adj* streaked ‖ *m* writing; (law) brief, writ; **poner por escrito** to write down, put in writing
escri•tor -tora *mf* writer
escritorio *m* writing desk; office; **escritorio ministro** kneehole desk, office desk; **escritorio norteamericano** rolltop desk
escritura *f* writing; script, handwriting, longhand; (law) deed, indenture; (law) sworn statement; **escritura al tacto** touch typewriting ‖ **Escritura** *f* Scripture; **Sagrada Escritura** Holy Scripture, Holy Writ
escriturar *tr* to notarize; (*p.ej., a un actor*) book ‖ *ref* (taur) to sign up for a fight
escrnía. *abbr* **escribanía**
escrno. *abbr* **escribano**
escrófula *f* scrofula
escrúpulo *m* scruple
escrupulo•so -sa *adj* scrupulous; exact
escrutar *tr* to scrutinize; (*los votos*) count
escrutinio *m* scrutiny; counting of votes
escuadra *f* (*pequeño número de personas o de soldados*) squad; (*pieza de metal para asegurar las ensambladuras*) angle iron; (*de carpintero*) square; (*de dibujante*) triangle; (nav) squadron
escuadrar *tr* (carp) to square
escuadrilla *f* (aer) squadron
escuadrón *m* (mil) squadron
escualidez *f* squalor
escuáli•do -da *adj* squalid
escualor *m* squalor
escucha *mf* listener ‖ *m* (mil) scout, vedette ‖ *f* listening; (*en un convento*) chaperon; **escuchas telefónicas** listening in on telephone conversations; wiretapping; **estar de escucha** (coll) to eavesdrop
escuchar *tr* to listen to; (*atender a*) heed; (*radiotransmisiones*) monitor ‖ *intr* to listen ‖ *ref* to like the sound of one's own voice
escudar *tr* to shield
escudero *m* esquire; nobleman; lady's page
escudete *m* escutcheon; (*refuerzo en la ropa*) gusset; (*planchuela delante de la cerradura*) escutcheon, escutcheon plate
escudilla *f* bowl
escudo *m* shield; buckler; (*delante de la cerradura*) escutcheon plate; **escudo de armas** coat of arms; **escudo térmico** (*de una cápsula espacial*) heat shield
escudriñar *tr* to scrutinize
escuela *f* school; **escuela de artes y oficios** trade school; **escuela de párvulos** kindergarten; **escuela de verano** summer school; **escuela dominical** Sunday school; **Escuela Naval Militar** Naval Academy; **escuela preparatoria** prep school; **hacer escuela** to be the leader of a school (*of thought*)
escuelante *mf* (Mex) schoolteacher ‖ *m* (Mex) schoolboy ‖ *f* (Mex) schoolgirl

escuerzo *m* toad
escue•to -ta *adj* free, unencumbered; bare, unadorned
escuintle *adj* (Mex) sickly ‖ *m* (*perro*) (Mex) mutt; (Mex) brat
esculcar §73 *tr* to frisk
esculpir *tr & intr* to sculpture, carve; engrave
escultismo *m* outdoor activities
escultista *m* outdoorsman
escultor *m* sculptor
escultora *f* sculptress
escultura *f* sculpture
escultural *adj* sculptural; statuesque
escupidera *f* cuspidor; chamber pot
escupidura *f* spit; fever blister
escupir *tr & intr* to spit
escurrepla•tos *m* (*pl* -tos) dish rack
escurridero *m* drainpipe; drainboard; slippery spot
escurridi•zo -za *adj* slippery
escurri•do -da *adj* narrow-hipped; abashed, confused
escurridor *m* colander
escurriduras *fpl* dregs, lees
escurrir *tr* (*una vasija; un líquido; la vajilla*) to drain; to wring, wring out; **escurrir el bulto** to duck ‖ *intr* to drip, ooze, trickle; slide, slip ‖ *ref* to drip, ooze, trickle; slide, slip; slip away; (*un reparo*) slip out
esdrúju•lo -la *adj* accented on the antepenult ‖ *m* word or verse accented on the antepenult
ese, esa *adj dem* (*pl* **esos, esas**) that (*near you*) ‖ **ese** *f* sound hole (*of violin*); **hacer eses** to reel, stagger
ése, ésa *pron dem* (*pl* **ésos, ésas**) that (*near you*); **ésa** your city
esencia *f* essence; **esencia de pera** banana oil; **quinta esencia** quintessence
esencial *adj & m* essential
esfera *f* sphere; (*del reloj*) dial
esféri•co -ca *adj* spherical ‖ *m* football
esfero *m* or **esferográfica** *f* (Col) ball-point pen
esfinge *f* sphinx; spiteful woman
esforza•do -da *adj* brave, vigorous, enterprising
esforzar §35 *tr* to strengthen, invigorate; encourage ‖ *ref* to exert oneself; strive
esfuerzo *m* effort, exertion, endeavor; courage, vigor, spirit
esfumar *tr* to stump ‖ *ref* to disappear, fade away
esgarrar *tr* (*la flema*) to try to cough up ‖ *intr* to clear the throat
esgrima *f* fencing
esgrimidura *f* fencing
esgrimir *tr* to wield, brandish; (*un argumento*) swing ‖ *intr* to fence
esgrimista *mf* (Arg, Chile, Peru) fencer; (Chile) swindler, panhandler
esguazar §60 *tr* to ford
esguazo *m* fording; ford
esguince *m* dodge, duck; (*gesto de disgusto*) frown; twist, sprain, wrench

eslabón *m* (*de cadena*) link; (*hierro acerado para sacar fuego de un pedernal; cilindro de acero para afilar cuchillos*) steel
eslabonar *tr* to link; link together, string together ‖ *intr* to link
eslálom *m* slalom
esla•vo -va *adj* Slav, Slavic ‖ *mf* Slav ‖ *m* (*idioma*) Slavic
esla•vón -vona *adj* & *mf* Slav
eslogan *m* (*consigna usada en fórmulas publicitarias*) slogan
eslora *f* (naut) length
eslova•co -ca *adj* & *mf* Slovak
esmaltar *tr* to enamel; embellish
esmalte *m* enamel; **esmalte para las uñas** nail polish
esmera•do -da *adj* careful, painstaking
esmeralda *f* emerald
esmerar *tr* to polish, shine; examine, check ‖ *ref* to take pains, do one's best
esmeril *m* emery
esmeriladora *f* emery wheel
esmerilar *tr* to grind or polish with emery
esmero *m* care, neatness
esmoladera *f* grindstone
esmoquin *m* tuxedo, dinner coat
esnifar *tr* & *intr* (*heroína*) to sniff
esnob *adj* snobbish ‖ *mf* (*pl* **esnobs**) snob
esnobismo *m* snobbery, snobbishness
esnobista *adj* snobbish
eso *pron dem* that; **a eso de** about; **eso es** that's it; that is; **por eso** for that reason; therefore
esófago *m* esophagus
espabila•do -da *adj* intelligent; bright
espabilar *ref* to know the ropes; be well informed
espaciador *m* space bar
espacial *adj* space, spatial
espaciar §77 (Arg, Chile) & **regular** *tr* to space; spread, scatter ‖ *ref* to expatiate; amuse oneself, relax
espacio *m* space; **espacio de chispa** spark gap; **espacio exterior** outer space; **espacio libre** (*entre dos cosas*) clearance; **espacio muerto** (*en el cilindro de un motor*) clearance; **por espacio de** in the space of
espacio•so -sa *adj* spacious, roomy; slow, deliberate
espada *m* swordsman; (taur) matador ‖ *f* sword; playing card (*representing a sword*) equivalent to spade; **entre la espada y la pared** between the devil and the deep blue sea
espadachín *m* swordsman; (*amigo de pendencias*) bully
espadaña *f* cattail, bulrush, reed mace; (*campanario*) bell gable
espadilla *f* (*remo que se usa como timón*) scull; (*aguja para sujetar el pelo*) bodkin; red insignia of Order of Santiago
espadín *m* rapier
espadón *m* (coll) brass hat
espagueti *m* spaghetti
espalar *tr* to shovel
espalda *f* back; **a espaldas de uno** behind one's back; **de espaldas a** with one's back

to; **tener buenas espaldas** to have broad shoulders; **volver las espaldas a** to turn a cold shoulder to
espaldar *m* (*de silla*) back; (*enrejado para plantas*) trellis, espalier
espaldarazo *m* slap on the back; (*ceremonia para armar caballero*) accolade; **dar el espaldarazo a** to accept, approve
espalera *f* trellis, espalier
espantada *f* (*de un animal*) sudden flight; (*desistimiento ocasionado por el miedo*) cold feet
espantadi•zo -za *adj* shy, skittish, scary
espantajo *m* scarecrow; (*persona fea*) fright
espantamos•cas *m* (*pl* **-cas**) (*para poner a los caballos*) fly net; (*aparato para asustar y alejar las moscas*) fly chaser
espantapája•ros *m* (*pl* **-ros**) scarecrow
espantar *tr* to scare, frighten; scare away ‖ *ref* to get scared; be surprised, marvel
espanto *m* fright, terror; (*amenaza*) threat; ghost
espantosidad *f* fright; frightfulness; awfulness
espanto•so -sa *adj* frightening, terrifying
España *f* Spain; **la Nueva España** New Spain (*Mexico in the early days*)
espa•ñol -ñola *adj* Spanish; **a la española** in the Spanish manner ‖ *mf* Spaniard ‖ *m* (*idioma*) Spanish; **los españoles** the Spanish ‖ *f* Spanish woman
españolería *f* Spanishness; hispanophilia
españolada *f* Spanish mannerism; Spanish remark
españolizar §60 *tr* to make Spanish, Hispanicize; translate into Spanish ‖ *ref* to become Spanish
esparadrapo *m* sticking plaster
esparaván *m* spavin
esparavel *m* mortarboard
esparcimiento *m* spreading, scattering, dissemination; diversion, relaxation; frankness, openness
esparcir §36 *tr* to spread, scatter; divert, relax ‖ *ref* to spread, scatter; disperse; take it easy, relax
espárrago *m* asparagus; (*perno*) stud bolt; awning pole
esparrancar §73 *ref* to spread one's legs wide apart
esparta•no -na *adj* & *mf* Spartan
esparto *m* esparto grass
espasmo *m* spasm
espasmódi•co -ca *adj* spasmodic
espásti•co -ca *adj* spastic
espato *m* spar; **espato flúor** fluor spar
espátula *f* spatula; putty knife
especia *f* spice
especia•do -da *adj* spicy
especial *adj* especial, special
especialidad *f* speciality; (*ramo a que se consagra una persona o negocio*) specialty
especialista *mf* specialist
especializar §60 *tr, intr* & *ref* to specialize
especiar *tr* to spice
especie *f* (*categoría de la clasificación biológica*) species; (*clase, género*) sort, kind;

(*caso, asunto*) matter; (*chisme, cuento*) news, rumor; appearance, pretext, show; remark; **en especie** in kind; **soltar una especie** to try to draw someone out

especie•ro -ra *mf* spice dealer ‖ *m* spice box

especificar §73 *tr* to specify; itemize

específi•co -ca *adj* specific ‖ *m* specific; patent medicine

espécimen *m* (*pl* **especímenes**) specimen

especio•so -sa *adj* (*engañoso*) specious; nice, neat, perfect

especiota *f* hoax, wild idea

espectáculo *m* spectacle; **dar un espectáculo** to make a scene; **espectáculo de atracciones** side show

especta•dor -dora *mf* witness; spectator

espectral *adj* ghostly

espectro *m* specter, phantom, ghost; (*phys*) spectrum

especular *tr* to check, examine; contemplate ‖ *intr* to speculate

espejear *intr* to sparkle

espejismo *m* mirage

espejo *m* mirror, looking glass; model; **espejo de cuerpo entero** full-length mirror, pier glass; **espejo de retrovisión** rear-view mirror; **espejo de vestir** full-length mirror, pier glass; **espejo retrovisor** rear-view mirror

espelunca *f* cave, cavern

espeluznante *adj* hair-raising

espera *f* wait, waiting; (*puesto para cazar*) blind, hunter's blind; composure, patience, respite; delay; (*law*) stay; **no tener espera** to be of the greatest urgency

esperanza *f* hope; **tener puesta su esperanza en** to pin one's faith on

esperanza•do -da *adj* hopeful (*having hope*)

esperanza•dor -dora *adj* hopeful (*giving hope*)

esperanzar §60 *tr* to give hope to

esperanzo•so -sa *adj* hopeful, full of hope

esperar *tr* (*aguardar*) to wait for, await; (*tener esperanza de conseguir*) expect, hope for; **ir a esperar** to go to meet ‖ *intr* to wait; hope; **esperar + inf** to hope to + inf; **esperar a** to wait until; **esperar desesperando** to hope against hope; **esperar en** to put one's hope in; **esperar que** to hope that; **esperar sentado** to have a good wait

esperinque *m* smelt

esperma *f* sperm

esperpento *m* monstrosity; freak; nonsense

espesar *m* depth, thickness (*of woods*) ‖ *tr* to thicken; (*un tejido*) weave tighter ‖ *ref* to thicken, get thick or thicker

espe•so -sa *adj* thick; dirty, greasy

espesor *m* thickness; (*de un flúido, gas, masa*) density

espesura *f* thickness; (*matorral*) thicket; (*cabellera muy espesa*) shock of hair; dirtiness, greasiness

espetar *tr* to skewer; pierce, pierce through; **espetar algo a** to spring something on ‖ *ref* to be solemn; be pompous; settle down

espetón *m* (*hurgón*) poker; (*asador*) skewer, spit; jab, poke

espía *mf* spy; squealer ‖ *f* (*naut*) warping; (*cuerda*) (naut) warp

espiar §77 *tr* to spy on ‖ *intr* to spy; (*naut*) to warp

espichar *tr* to prick; (*dinero*) (Chile) to cough up; (Chile, Peru) to tap ‖ *intr* (coll) to die ‖ *ref* (Mex, W-I) to get thin

espiche *m* (*arma o instrumento puntiagudo*) prick; (naut) peg, bung

espichón *m* stab, prick

espiga *f* (bot) ear, spike; peg, pin, tenon; (*clavo sin cabeza*) brad; (*badajo*) clapper; (*de una llave*) stem

espigar §44 *tr* to glean; tenon, dowel ‖ *intr* (*los cereales*) to form ears ‖ *ref* to grow tall, shoot up

espigón *m* sharp point, spur; (*mazorca*) ear of corn; (*cerro puntiagudo*) peak; breakwater

espina *f* thorn, spine; (*de los peces*) fishbone; doubt, uncertainty; sorrow; (anat) spine; **dar mala espina a** to worry; **espina de pescado** herringbone; **espina de pez** fishbone; **espina dorsal** spinal column; **estar en espinas** to be on pins and needles

espinaca *f* spinach; **espinacas** spinach

espinal *adj* spinal

espinapez *m* herringbone; thorny matter, difficulty

espinar *m* thorny spot; (fig) thorny matter ‖ *tr* to prick; (*árboles*) protect with thornbushes; hurt, offend

espinazo *m* backbone; (*de un arco*) keystone

espinel *m* trawl, trawl line

espineta *f* spinet

espinilla *f* (*de la pierna*) shin, shinbone; (*granillo en la piel*) blackhead

espino *m* hawthorn; **espino artificial** barbed wire; **espino negro** blackthorn

espinochar *tr* (*el maíz*) to husk

espino•so -sa or **espinu•do -da** *adj* thorny; (*pez*) bony; (*difícil*) (fig) thorny, knotty

espiocha *f* pickaxe

espión *m* spy

espionaje *m* spying, espionage

espira *f* turn

espiración *f* breathing; exhalation

espiral *adj* spiral ‖ *f* (*línea curva que da vueltas alrededor de un punto*) spiral; (*del reloj*) hairspring; (*de humo*) curl, wreath

espirar *tr* to breath; encourage ‖ *intr* to breathe; exhale, expire; (*el viento*) (poet) to blow gently

espiritismo *m* spiritualism

espirito•so -sa *adj* spirited, lively; (*licor*) spirituous

espíritu *m* spirit; (*mente*) mind; (*aparecido, fantasma*) ghost, spirit; **espíritu de equipo** teamwork; **Espíritu Santo** Holy Ghost, Holy Spirit; **dar, despedir, exhalar** or **rendir el espíritu** to give up the ghost

espiritual *adj* spiritual; sharp, witty

espiritualismo *m* spiritualism

espita *f* tap, cock; (coll) tippler

espitar *tr* to tap

esplendidez *f* splendor, magnificence

es
es

espléndi·do -da *adj* splendid, magnificent; generous, open-handed; (poet) brilliant, radiant

esplendor *m* splendor

esplendoro·so -sa *adj* resplendent

espliego *m* lavender

esplín *m* melancholy

espolada *f* prick with spur; **espolada de vino** shot of wine

espolear *tr* to spur, spur on

espoleta *f* fuse; (*hueso*) wishbone

espolón *m* (*del gallo, una montaña, un buque de guerra*) spur; dike, jetty, mole, cutwater; (*prominencia córnea de las caballerías*) fetlock; (*sabañón*) chilblain

espolvorear *tr* (*quitar el polvo de; esparcir el polvo sobre*) dust; (*el azúcar*) sprinkle

esponja *f* sponge; (*sablista*) sponge, sponger; **beber como una esponja** to drink like a fish; **tirar la esponja** to throw in (or up) the sponge

esponja·do -da *adj* proud, puffed-up; fresh, healthy

esponjar *tr* to puff up, make fluffy ‖ *ref* to puff up, become fluffy; be puffed up, be conceited; look fresh and healthy

esponjo·so -sa *adj* spongy

esponsales *mpl* betrothal, engagement

espontanear *ref* to make a clean breast of it; open one's heart

espontáne·o -a *adj* spontaneous ‖ *m* (taur) spectator who jumps into the ring to take on the bull

espora *f* spore

esporádi·co -ca *adj* sporadic

esposa *f* wife; **esposas** handcuffs, manacles

esposar *tr* to handcuff, manacle

espo·so -sa *mf* spouse ‖ *m* husband ‖ *f* see **esposa**

espuela *f* spur; **echar la espuela** (coll) to take a nightcap; **espuela de caballero** delphinium, rocket larkspur; **espuela de galán** nasturtium

espuelar *tr* (SAm) to spur, goad

espuerta *f* two-handled esparto basket

espulgar §44 *tr* to delouse; scrutinize

espuma *f* foam; (*en un vaso de cerveza; saliva parecida a la espuma*) froth; (*película de impurezas en la superficie de un líquido*) scum; **crecer como espuma** to grow like weeds; to have a meteoric rise; **espuma de caucho** foam rubber; **espuma de jabón** lather; **espuma de mar** meerschaum

espumadera *f* skimmer

espumajear *intr* to froth at the mouth

espumajo·so -sa *adj* foamy, frothy

espumante *adj* foaming; (*vino*) sparkling

espumar *tr* to skim ‖ *intr* to foam, froth; (*el jabón*) lather; (*el vino*) sparkle; increase rapidly

espumarajo *m* froth, frothing at the mouth

espumilla *f* voile; (CAm, Ecuad) meringue

espumo·so -sa *adj* foamy, frothy; (*cubierto de una película*) scummy; (*jabonoso*) lathery; (*vino*) sparkling

espu·rio -ria *adj* spurious

espurrear or **espurriar** *tr* to squirt with water from the mouth

esputar *tr & intr* to spit

esputo *m* spit, saliva

esq. *abbr* **esquina**

esqueje *m* cutting, slip

esquela *f* note; announcement; death notice; **esquela amorosa** billet-doux

esqueléti·co -ca *adj* skeleton; skeletal, thin, wasted

esqueleto *m* skeleton; (CAm, Mex) blank form; (Chile) sketch, outline

esquema *m* scheme, diagram

es·quí *m* (*pl* **-quís**) ski; skiing; **esquí acuático** water ski; water skiing; **esquí remolcado** ski-joring

esquia·dor -dora *adj* ski ‖ *mf* skier

esquiar §77 *intr* to ski

esquiciar *tr* to sketch

esquicio *m* sketch

esquifar *tr* (naut) to fit out, staff, man

esquife *m* skiff

esquiismo *m* skiing

esquila *f* sheepshearing; hand bell

esquilar *tr* to shear, fleece

esquilimo·so -sa *adj* fastidious, squeamish

esquilmar *tr* to harvest; (*las plantas el jugo de la tierra*) drain, exhaust; (*una fuente de riqueza*) drain, squander, use up; carry away, steal

esquilmo *m* harvest, farm produce; (Mex) farm scrapings

esquilmo·so -sa *adj* fastidious

esquimal *adj & mf* Eskimo

esquina *f* corner; (SAm) corner store; **a la vuelta de la esquina** around the corner; **doblar la esquina** to turn the corner; **hacer esquina** (*un edificio*) to be on the corner; **las cuatro esquinas** puss in the corner

esquina·do -da *adj* sharp-cornered; difficult, unsociable

esquinar *tr* to be on the corner of; put in the corner; alienate ‖ *intr* — **esquinar con** to be on the corner of ‖ *ref* — **esquinarse con** to fall out with

esquinazo *m* corner; (Arg, Chile) serenade; **dar esquinazo a** to give the slip to, to shake off

esquinencia *f* quinsy

esquinera *f* corner piece (*of furniture*)

esquirla *f* splinter

esquirol *m* scab, strikebreaker

esquisto *m* schist

esquite *m* (CAm, Mex) popcorn

esquivar *tr* to avoid, evade, shun; dodge ‖ *ref* to withdraw; dodge

esquivez *f* aloofness, gruffness

esqui·vo -va *adj* aloof, gruff

estable *adj* stable, permanent; full-time ‖ *mf* regular guest, permanent guest

establecer §22 *tr* to establish, institute ‖ *ref* to settle, take up residence; start a business, open an office

establecimiento *m* establishment; place of business; decree, ordinance, statute

establo *m* stable

estaca *f* stake, picket, pale; cudgel, club; (*clavo largo*) spike; (hort) cutting

estacada *f* stockade, palisade; dueling ground; **dejar en la estacada** to leave in the lurch; **quedarse en la estacada** to succumb on the field of battle, fall in a duel; fail; lose out

estacar §73 *tr* to stake, stake off; tie to a stake ‖ *ref* to stand stiff

estación *f* (*cada una de las cuatro divisiones del año*) season; (*sitio en que paran los trenes; radioemisora*) station; (*lugar en que se hace alto en un paseo, etc.*) stop; **estación balnearia** bathing resort; **estación de cabeza** (rr) terminal; **estación de carga** freight station; **estación de empalme** junction; **estación de gasolina** gas station, filling station; **estación de la seca** dry season; **estación de paso** (rr) way station; **estación depuradora** sewage-disposal plant; **estación de radiodifusión** broadcasting station; **estación de seguimiento** tracking station; **estación de servicio** service station; **estación difusora** or **emisora** broadcasting station; **estación espacial** space station; **estación gasolinera** gas station, filling station; **estación meteorológica** weather station; **estación telefónica** telephone exchange

estacional *adj* seasonal

estacionamiento *m* stationing; parking; parking lot

estacionar *tr* to station; stand, park ‖ *intr* to stand, park ‖ *ref* to station oneself; be stationary; stand, park; **se prohíbe estacionarse** no standing, no parking

estaciona•rio -ria *adj* stationary

estada *f* stay, stop

estadía *f* (*ante un pintor*) sitting; stop, stay; (com) demurrage

estadio *m* stadium; phase, stage; (*longitud*) furlong

estadista *mf* (*perito en estadística*) statistician ‖ *m* statesman

estadística *f* statistics

estadísti•co -ca *adj* statistical ‖ *m* statistician ‖ *f* see **estadística**

estadiunense *adj* American, United States ‖ *mf* American

estadi•zo -za *adj* (*aire*) heavy, stifling; (*agua*) stagnant

estado *m* state; state, condition, status; statement, report; **en estado de buena esperanza** or **en estado interesante** in the family way; **estado asistencial** welfare state; **estado civil** marital status; **estado de ánimo** state of mind; **estado de cuentas** (com) statement; **estado libre asociado** commonwealth; **estado llano** commons, common people; **estado mayor** (mil) staff; **estado mayor conjunto** joint chiefs of staff; **estado mayor general** general staff; **Estados Unidos** *msg* the United States; **estado tapón** buffer state; **estar en estado de guerra** to be under martial law; **los Estados Unidos** *mpl* the United States;

tomar estado to take a wife; to go into the church

estado-policía *m* (*pl* **estados-policías**) police state

estadounidense or **estadunidense** *adj* American, United States ‖ *mf* American

estafa *f* swindle, trick; (*estribo*) stirrup

estafar *tr* to swindle, trick; overcharge

estafeta *f* post, courier; post office; diplomatic mail

estallar *intr* to burst; explode; (*un incendio, una revolución; la guerra*) break out; (*la ira*) break forth

estallido *m* report, crash, explosion; crack; (*p.ej., de la guerra*) outbreak; **dar un estallido** to crash, explode

estambre *m* (*hebras de lana e hilo formado de ellas*) worsted; (bot) stamen; **estambre de la vida** course or thread of life

estampa *f* stamp, print, engraving; press; printing; (*footstep*) track; aspect, appearance; **dar a la estampa** to publish, bring out; **parecer la estampa de la herejía** to be a sight, be a mess; **la propia estampa de** the very image of

estampado *m* printing, stamping; printed fabric, cotton print ·

estampar *tr* to stamp, print, engrave; (*en al ánimo*) fix, engrave; (*p.ej., el pie*) leave a mark of; (bb) to tool; (*arrojar con fuerza*) (coll) to dash, slam

estampida *f* report, crash, explosion; stampede

estampido *m* report, crash, explosion; **estampido sónico** (aer) sonic boom

estampilla *f* (*sello con letrero para estampar*) stamp; (*sello con una firma en facsímile*) rubber stamp; (*sello de correos o fiscal*) stamp

estampillar *tr* to stamp; rubber-stamp

estanca•do -da *adj* stagnant; (fig) stagnant, dead

estancar §73 *tr* to stanch; stem, check; (*un negocio*) suspend, hold up; corner; monopolize ‖ *ref* to become stagnant, become choked up

estancia *f* stay, sojourn; (*aposento*) living room; day in hospital; cost of day in hospital; (*estrofa*) stanza; (mil) bivouac; (Arg, Urug, Chile) cattle ranch; (Col) small country place; (Ven) truck farm

estanciero *m* rancher, cattle raiser

estan•co -ca *adj* stanch, watertight ‖ *m* government monopoly; cigar store, government store (*for sale of tobacco, matches, postage stamps, etc.*); archives; (Ecuad) liquor store

estándar *m* standard

estandardizar §60 or **estandarizar** §60 *tr* to standardize

estandarte *m* banner, standard

estandartizar §60 *tr* to standardize

estanque *m* basin, reservoir; pond, pool

estanque•ro -ra *mf* storekeeper, tobacconist; (Ecuad) saloonkeeper ‖ *m* reservoir tender

es
es

estanquillo *m* cigar store, government store (*for sale of tobacco, matches, postage stamps, etc.*); (Col, Ecuad) bar, saloon; (Mex) booth, stand

estante *adj* located, being; settled, permanent ‖ *m* shelf; shelving; bookcase, open bookcase

estantería *f* shelves, shelving; book stack

estañar *tr* to tin; tin-plate; solder; (Ven) to hurt, injure; (Ven) to fire

estaño *m* tin

estaquilla *f* peg, dowel, pin; (*clavo pequeño sin cabeza*) brad; (*clavo largo*) spike

estaquillar *tr* to peg, dowel; nail

estar §37 *v aux* (*to form progressive form*) to be, e.g., **están aprendiendo el español** they are learning Spanish ‖ *intr* to be; be in, be home; be ready; **¿a cuántos estamos?** what day of the month is it?; **¡está bien!** O.K.!, all right!; **estar a** to cost, sell at; **estar bien** to be well; **estar bien con** to be on good terms with; **estar de** to be (*on a temporary basis*); **estar de más** to be in the way; be unnecessary; be idle; **estar de viaje** to be on a trip; **estar mal** to be sick, be ill; **estar mal con** to be on bad terms with; **estar para** to be about to; **estar por** to be for, be in favor of; to be about to; to have a mind to; to remain to be + *pp;* **estar sobre sí** to be wary, be on one's guard ‖ *ref* (*p.ej., en casa*) to stay; (*p.ej., quieto*) to keep

estarcido *m* stencil

estarcir §36 *tr* to stencil

estatal *adj* state

estáti•co -ca *adj* static; dumbfounded, speechless

estatificar §73 *tr* to nationalize

estatizar §60 *tr* to nationalize

estatorreactor *m* ramjet (engine)

estatua *f* statue; **quedarse hecho una estatua** to stand aghast

estatuir §20 *tr* to order, decree; establish, prove

estatura *f* stature

estatuta•rio -ria *adj* statutory

estatuto *m* statute

estay *m* (naut) stay; **estay mayor** (naut) mainstay

este, esta *adj dem* (*pl* **estos, estas**) this ‖ *m* east; east wind

éste, ésta *pron dem* (*pl* **éstos, éstas**) this one, this one here; the latter; **ésta** this city

estela *f* (*de un buque*) wake; (*de cohete, humo, cuerpo celeste, etc.*) trail

estenógrafo *m* (Cuba) ball-point pen

estenotipia *f* stenotypy; machine stenography

estepa *f* steppe

estera *f* mat; matting; **cargado de esteras** out of patience

esterar *tr* to cover with matting ‖ *intr* to bundle up for the cold

estercolar *m* dunghill ‖ §61 *tr* to dung, to manure

estercolero *m* manure pile, dunghill; manure collector

estereofóni•co -ca *adj* stereophonic, stereo

estereoscópi•co -ca *adj* stereoscopic, stereo

estereotipa•do -da *adj* stereotyped

estéril *adj* (*que no produce nada*) sterile; (*inútil, vano*) futile

esterilización *f* sterilization

esterilizar §60 *tr* to sterilize ‖ *ref* to become sterile

esterlina *adj fem* (*libra*) sterling (*pound*)

esternón *m* breastbone

estero *m* tideland; estuary; (Arg) swamp, marsh; (Chile) stream; (Col, Ven) pool, puddle

esterto *m* death rattle; (*ruido en ciertas enfermedades, perceptible por la auscultación*) stertor, râle; **estertor agónico** death rattle

esteta *mf* aesthete ‖ *f* beautician

estéti•co -ca *adj* aesthetic ‖ *f* aesthetics

estetoscopio *m* stethoscope

estiaje *m* low water

estiba *f* (naut) stowage

estibador *m* stevedore, longshoreman

estibar *tr* to pack, stuff; (naut) to stow

estiércol *m* dung, manure

esti•gio -gia *adj* Stygian ‖ **Estigia** *f* Styx

estigma *m* stigma

estigmatizar §60 *tr* to stigmatize

estilar *tr* (*una escritura*) to draw up in proper form; be given to ‖ *intr & ref* to be in fashion

estilete *m* (*puñal*) stiletto

estilo *m* style; **por el estilo** like that, of the kind; **por el estilo de** like; **estilo directo** (gram) direct discourse; **estilo indirecto** (gram) indirect discourse

estilográfica *f* fountain pen

estima *f* esteem; (naut) dead reckoning

estimable *adj* estimable; considerable; appreciable, computable; esteemed

estimación *f* esteem, estimation; estimate, evaluation

estimar *tr* (*tener en buen concepto*) to esteem; (*apreciar, valuar*) estimate; think, believe; appreciate, thank; be fond of, like; **estimar en poco** to hold in low esteem

estimativa *f* judgment; instinct

estimulante *adj & m* stimulant

estimular *tr* to stimulate

estímulo *m* stimulus

estío *m* summer

estipendio *m* stipend; wages

estípti•co -ca *adj* styptic; constipated; mean, stingy

estipular *tr* to stipulate

estiradamente *adv* scarcely, hardly; violently

estira•do -da *adj* conceited, stuck-up; prim, neat; tight, closefisted

estirar *tr* to stretch; (*alambre, metal*) draw; (*planchar ligeramente*) iron lightly; (*un escrito, discurso, cargo, etc.*) (fig) to stretch out; (*el dinero*) (fig) to stretch ‖ *ref* to stretch; put on airs

estirón *m* jerk, tug; **dar un estirón** to grow up in no time

estirpe *f* race, stock, lineage; (*linaje*) strain, pedigree

estitiquez *f* constipation

estival *adj* summer

esto *pron dem* that; **en esto** at this point; **por esto** for this reason

estocada *f* thrust, stab, lunge; (*herida*) stab, stab wound; (*cosa que ocasiona dolor*) blow

Estocolmo *f* Stockholm

estofa *f* brocade; quality, kind

estofado *m* stew

estoi•co -ca *adj & mf* stoic

estóli•do -da *adj* stupid, imbecile

estómago *m* stomach; **estómago de avestruz** iron digestion; **tener buen estómago** or **mucho estómago** to be thick-skinned; have an easy conscience

estopa *f* (*de lino o cáñamo*) tow; (*de calafatear*) (naut) oakum; **estopa de acero** steel wool; **estopa de algodón** cotton waste

estopilla *f* (*tela muy sutil*) lawn; (*tela ordinaria de algodón*) cheesecloth

estoque *m* rapier; sword lily, gladiola

estoquear *tr* to stab with a rapier

estor *m* blind, shade, window shade

estorbar *tr* to hinder, obstruct; inconvenience, bother, annoy ‖ *intr* to be in the way

estorbo *m* hindrance, obstruction; inconvenience, bother, annoyance

estorbo•so -sa *adj* hindering; bothersome, annoying

estornino *m* starling; **estornino de los pastores** grackle, myna

estornudar *intr* to sneeze

estornudo *m* sneeze, sneezing

estrado *m* (*tarima del trono*) dais; lecture platform; (archaic) lady's drawing room; **estrados** courtrooms, law courts; **citar para estrados** to subpoena

estrafala•rio -ria *adj* odd, eccentric; sloppy, sloppily dressed ‖ *mf* screwball

estragar §44 *tr* to spoil, damage, vitiate

estrago *m* damage, ruin, havoc

estrambote *m* tail (*of sonnet*)

estrambóti•co -ca *adj* odd, weird

estrangul *m* (mus) reed, mouthpiece

estrangular *tr & ref* to strangle, choke

estraperlear *intr* to deal in the black market

estraperlista *adj* black-market ‖ *mf* black-market dealer

estraperlo *m* black market

estrapontín *m* folding seat, jump seat

estratagema *f* stratagem; craftiness

estratega *m* strategist

estrategia *f* strategy; **alta estrategia** grand strategy

estratégi•co -ca *adj* strategic(al) ‖ *m* strategist

estratificar §73 *tr & ref* to stratify

estrato *m* stratum, layer

estratosfera *f* stratosphere

estraza *f* rag; brown paper

estrechar *tr* (*reducir a menor ancho*) narrow; (*apretar*) tighten; press, pursue; force, compel; hug, embrace; squeeze; **estrechar la mano a** to shake hands with ‖ *ref* to narrow down; contract; hug, embrace; (*reducir los gastos*) retrench; **estrecharse en**

to squeeze in; **estrecharse la mano** (*dos personas*) to shake hands

estrechez *f* narrowness; rightness; (*amistad íntima*) closeness, intimacy; austerity, strictness; poverty, want, need; trouble, jam; **estrechez de miras** narrow outlook, narrow-mindedness; **hallarse en gran estrechez** to be in dire straits

estre•cho -cha *adj* narrow; tight; close, intimate; austere, strict; stingy, tight; poor, needy; mean ‖ *m* (*paso angosto en el mar*) strait; fix, predicament

estrechura *f* narrowness; tightness; closeness, intimacy; austerity, strictness; trouble, predicament

estregar §66 *tr* to rub hard; scour

estregón *m* hard rub

estrella *f* star; (typ) asterisk, star; (mov & theat) star; (*hado, destino*) (fig) star; **estrella de los Alpes** edelweiss; **estrella de mar** starfish; **estrella de rabo** comet; **estrella filante** or **fugaz** shooting star; **estrella fulgurante** (astr) flare star; **estrella polar** pole-star; **estrella vespertina** evening star; **ver las estrellas** (fig) to see stars

estrella•do -da *adj* (*cielo*) starry; star-spangled; star-shaped; (*huevos*) fried

estrellamar *m* starfish

estrellar *adj* star ‖ *tr* to star, spangle with stars; (*huevos*) fry; shatter, dash to pieces ‖ *ref* to be spangled with stars; crash; **estrellarse con** to clash with

estrellón *m* large star; (*fuego artificial*) star; smash-up

estremecer §22 *tr* to shake; (*el aire*) rend; (fig) to shake, upset ‖ *ref* to shake, tremble, shiver, shudder

estrena *f* (*regalo que se da en señal de agradecimiento*) handsel; first use

estrenar *tr* to use for the first time, wear for the first time; (*un drama*) perform for the first time; (*un cine*) show for the first time; try out for the first time ‖ *ref* to make the day's first transaction; appear for the first time; (*un drama, un cine*) open

estrenista *mf* first-nighter

estreno *m* beginning, debut; première, first performance; first use

estre•nuo -nua *adj* strenuous, vigorous, enterprising

estreñimiento *m* constipation

estreñir §72 *tr* to constipate

estrépito *m* racket, crash; fuss, show

estrepito•so -sa *adj* loud, noisy, boisterous; notorious; shocking

estría *f* flute, groove

estriar §77 *tr* to flute, groove

estribar *intr* to lean, rest; be based, depend

estriberón *m* stepping stone

estribillo *m* (*de un poema*) burden, refrain; pet word, pet phrase

estribo *m* (*de coche*) step; (*de automóvil*) running board; (*apoyo para el pie*) footboard; (*para el pie del jinete*) stirrup; abutment, buttress; (fig) foundation, support;

es
es

perder los estribos to fly off the handle; lose one's head

estribor *m* starboard

estricnina *f* strychnine

estricote *m* (Ven) riotous living; **al estricote** hither and thither

estric•to -ta *adj* strict, severe, rigorous; proper, punctual; (*sentido de una palabra*) narrow

estrictura *f* (pathol) stricture

estrige *f* barn owl; (*Athene noctua*) little owl

estro *m* poetic inspiration; (*de animal*) rut, heat

estrofa *f* strophe

estroncio *m* strontium

estropajo *m* mop; dishcloth; **servir de estropajo** to be forced to do the dirty work; be treated with indifference

estropajo•so -sa *adj* raggedy, slovenly; (*carne*) tough, leathery; spluttering

estropear *tr* to spoil, ruin, damage; abuse, mistreat; cripple, maim ‖ *ref* to spoil, go to ruin; fail

estropicio *m* breakage; havoc, ruin; fracas, rumpus

estructura *f* structure

estruendo *m* noise, crash, boom; confusion, uproar; pomp, show; fame

estruendo•so -sa *adj* noisy, booming

estrujar *tr* to. squeeze; press, crush, mash; bruise; rumple; drain, exhaust

estuante *adj* hot, burning

estuario *m* estuary; tideland

estucar §73 *tr* to stucco

estuco *m* stucco; **estuco de París** plaster of Paris

estuche *m* case, box; (*caja y utensilios que se guardan en ella*) kit; casket, jewel case; (*para tijeras*) sheath; **estuche de afeites** compact, vanity case; **ser un estuche** to be a handy fellow

estudia•do -da *adj* affected, studied

estudiantado *m* student body

estudiante *mf* student

estudiantil *adj* student

estudiar *tr* to study; (*la lección a una persona*) to hear (*someone's lesson*) ‖ *intr* to study; **estudiar para . . .** to study to become . . .

estudio *m* study; (*aposento*) studio; (mus) étude; **altos estudios** advanced studies

estudio•so -sa *adj* studious ‖ *m* student, scholar

estufa *f* stove; steam cabinet, steam room; foot stove; (*invernáculo*) hothouse

estul•to -ta *adj* stupid, silly, foolish

estupefac•to -ta *adj* stupefied, dumbfounded

estupen•do -da *adj* stupendous; famous, distinguished

estúpi•do -da *adj* stupid ‖ *mf* dolt

estupor *m* stupor; surprise, amazement

estuprar *tr* to rape, violate

estupro *m* rape, violation

estuque *m* stucco

esturión *m* sturgeon

etapa *f* stage; **a etapas pequeñas** by easy stages

éter *m* ether

etére•o -a *adj* ethereal

eternidad *f* eternity

eternizar §60 *tr* to prolong endlessly ‖ *ref* to be endless, be interminable

eter•no -na *adj* eternal

éti•co -ca *adj* ethical ‖ *f* ethics

etileno *m* ethylene

etilo *m* ethyl

étimo *m* etymon

etimología *f* etymology; **etimología popular** folk etymology

etíope *adj & mf* Ethiopian

etiópi•co -ca *adj & m* Ethiopic

etiqueta *f* (*marbete*) tag, label; (*ceremonial que se debe observar*) etiquette; (*ceremonia en la manera de tratarse*) formality; **de etiqueta** formal, full-dress; **de etiqueta menor** semiformal; **estar de etiqueta** to have become cool toward each other

etiquetar *tr* to tag, label

etiquete•ro -ra *adj* formal, ceremonious; full of compliments

etiquez *f* (pathol) consumption

étni•co -ca *adj* ethnic(al); (gram) gentilic

etnografía *f* ethnography

etnología *f* ethnology

E.U.A. *abbr* **Estados Unidos de América**

eucalipto *m* eucalyptus

Eucaristía *f* Eucharist

eufemismo *m* euphemism

eufemísti•co -ca *adj* euphemistic

eufonía *f* euphony

eufóni•co -ca *adj* euphonic, euphonious

euforia *f* euphoria; endurance, fortitude

eufuísmo *m* euphuism

eufuísti•co -ca *adj* euphuistic

eugenesia *f* eugenics

eunuco *m* eunuch

euritmia *f* regular pulse

euro *m* east wind

Europa *f* Europe

europe•o -a *adj & mf* European

eutanasia *f* euthanasia

eutrapelia *f* moderation; lightheartedness; simple pastime

evacuación *f* evacuation; **evacuación de basuras** garbage disposal

evacuar §21 & regular *tr* to evacuate; (*un trámite*) transact; (*una visita*) pay; (*un encargo, un asunto*) do, carry out; **evacuar el vientre** to have a bowel movement ‖ *intr* to evacuate; have a bowel movement

evadi•do -da *adj* escaped ‖ *mf* escapee

evadir *tr* to avoid, evade, elude ‖ *ref* to evade; escape, flee

evaluar §21 *tr* to evaluate; value

evangéli•co -ca *adj* evangelic(al)

evangelio *m* gospel, gospel truth ‖ **Evangelio** *m* Gospel, Evangel

evangelista *m* Gospel singer or chanter; (Mex) public writer, penman ‖ **Evangelista** *m* Evangelist

evaporar *tr & ref* to evaporate

evaporizar §60 *tr, intr & ref* to vaporize

evasión *f* (*efugio, evasiva*) evasion; (*fuga*) escape

evasi•vo -va *adj* evasive ‖ *f* loophole, pretext, excuse

evento *m* chance, happening, contingency; (Col) sports event; **a todo evento** in any event

eventual *adj* contingent; (*emolumentos; gastos*) incidental

eventualidad *f* eventuality, contingency; uncertainty

evidencia *f* evidence, obviousness; (*prueba judicial*) evidence; **evidencia moral** moral certainty

evidenciar *tr* to show, make evident

evidente *adj* evident, obvious

evitable *adj* avoidable

evitación *f* avoidance; prevention

evitar *tr* to avoid, shun; (*p.ej., el polvo*) keep off; prevent; **evitar + *inf*** to avoid + *ger*; save from + *ger*, e.g., **la luz de la luna nos evitó tener que encender los faroles** the light of the moon saved us from having to light the lights

evo *m* (poet) age, aeon; (theol) eternity

evocar §73 *tr* to evoke; (*p.ej., los demonios*) invoke

evolución *f* evolution; change, development (*of one's point of view, plans, conduct, etc.*)

evolucionar *intr* to evolve; change, develop; (mil & nav) to maneuver

evolucionista *adj & mf* evolutionist; evolutionary

ex *adj* ex- (*former*), e.g., **el ex presidente** the ex-president

ex abrupto *adv* brashly ‖ *m* brash remark

exacción *f* (*de impuestos, deudas, multas, etc.*) exaction, levy; (*cobro injusto*) extortion

exacerbar *tr* to exacerbate, aggravate

exactitud *f* exactness; punctuality

exac•to -ta *adj* exact; punctual, faithful ‖ **exacto** *interj* right!

exactor *m* tax collector

exagerar *tr* to exaggerate

exalta•do -da *adj* exalted; extreme, hotheaded; wrought-up; radical

exaltar *tr* to exalt; extol ‖ *ref* to be wrought-up, get excited

examen *m* examination; **examen de ingreso** entrance examination; **sufrir un examen** to take an examination

examinar *tr* to examine; inspect ‖ *ref* to take an examination; **examinarse de ingreso** to take entrance examinations

exangüe *adj* bloodless; weak, exhausted; dead

exánime *adj* (*sin vida*) lifeless; (*desmayado*) faint, in a faint, lifeless

exasperar *tr* to exasperate

Exc.ª *abbr* **Excelencia**

excandecer §22 *tr* to incense, enrage

excarcelación *f* release

excarcelar *tr* (*a un preso*) to release

excavadora *f* power shovel

excavar *tr* to excavate; loosen soil around

excedente *adj* excess; excessive; on leave ‖ *m* excess, surplus; **excedente de ganancia** profit margin

exceder *tr* (*ser mayor que*) to exceed; (*aventajar*) excel ‖ *ref* to go too far, go to extremes; **excederse a sí mismo** to outdo oneself

excelencia *f* excellence, excellency; **por excelencia** par excellence; **Su Excelencia** Your Excellency

excelente *adj* excellent

excel•so -sa *adj* lofty, sublime ‖ **el Excelso** the Most High

excéntrica *f* eccentric

excentricidad *f* eccentricity

excéntri•co -ca *adj* eccentric; (*barrio*) outlying ‖ *mf* eccentric ‖ *f* see **excéntrica**

excepción *f* exception; **a excepción de** with the exception of

excepcional *adj* exceptional

excepto *prep* except

exceptuar §21 *tr* to except; (*eximir*) exempt

excerpta or **excerta** *adj* excerpt

excesi•vo -va *adj* excessive; excess

exceso *m* excess; **exceso de equipaje** excess baggage; **exceso de peso** excess weight; **exceso de velocidad** speeding

excitable *adj* excitable

excitación *f* excitement; excitation

excitante *adj & m* stimulant

excitar *tr* to excite, stir up, stimulate ‖ *ref* to become excited

exclamación *f* exclamation

exclamar *tr & intr* to exclaim

exclaustrar *tr* (*a un religioso*) to secularize

excluir §20 *tr* to exclude

exclusión *f* exclusion; **con exclusión de** to the exclusion of; **exclusión de contribución** tax deduction

exclusiva *f* rejection, turndown; sole right, monopoly; (*anticipación de una noticia por un periódico*) news beat

exclusive *adv* exclusively ‖ *prep* exclusive of, not counting

exclusivista *adj* exclusive, clannish ‖ *mf* snob

exclusi•vo -va *adj* exclusive ‖ *f* see **exclusiva**

Exc.ᵐᵒ *abbr* **Excelentísimo**

ex combatiente *m* ex-serviceman

excomulgar §44 *tr* to excommunicate; ostracize, banish

excomunión *f* excommunication

excoriar *tr* to skin ‖ *ref* to skin oneself; (*p.ej., el codo*) skin

excrementar *intr* to have a bowel movement

excremento *m* excrement

exculpar *tr* to exculpate, exonerate

excursión *f* excursion, outing

excursionista *mf* excursionist, tourist

excusa *f* excuse; **a excusa** secretly; **excusa es decir** it is unnecessary to say

excusabaraja *f* basket with lid

excusable *adj* excusable; avoidable

excusadamente *adv* unnecessarily

excusa•do -da *adj* exempt; unnecessary; private, set apart; (*puerta*) side ‖ *m* toilet

excusa•lí *m* (*pl* **-líes**) small apron

excusar *tr* to excuse; exempt; avoid; prevent; make unnecessary; **excusar** + *inf* to not have to + *inf* ‖ *ref* to excuse oneself; apologize; **excusarse de** + *inf* to decline to + *inf*
exención *f* exemption
exencionar *tr* to exempt
exentamente *adv* freely; frankly, simply
exentar *tr* to exempt
exen•to -ta *adj* exempt; open, unobstructed; free, disengaged
exequias *fpl* obsequies
exfolia•dor -dora *adj* tear-off
exhalación *f* exhalation; flash of lightning; shooting star; fume, vapor; **como una exhalación** like a flash of lightning
exhalar *tr* to exhale, emit; (*suspiros, quejas*) breathe forth; **exhalar el último suspiro** to breathe one's last ‖ *ref* to exhale; (*con el ejercicio violento del cuerpo*) breathe hard; hurry; crave
exhausti•vo -va *adj* exhaustive
exhaus•to -ta *adj* exhausted; wasted away
exheredar *tr* to disinherit
exhibición *f* exhibition; exhibit; **exhibición repetida** (telv) rerun
exhibición-venta *f* sales exhibit
exhibir *tr* to exhibit; (Mex) to pay ‖ *ref* to make oneself evident
exhilarante *adj* exhilarating; (*gas*) laughing
exhortar *tr* to exhort
exhumar *tr* to exhume
exigencia *f* exigency, requirement
exigente *adj* exigent, demanding
exigir §27 *tr* to exact, require, demand
exi•guo -gua *adj* meager, scanty
exila•do -da *adj & mf* exile
exi•mio -mia *adj* choice, select, superior; distinguished
eximir *tr* to exempt
existencia *f* existence; **en existencia** in stock; **existencias** (com) stock
existente *adj* existing, extant; in stock
existir *intr* to exist
exitazo *m* smash hit
exitista *adj* (Arg) me-too ‖ *mf* (Arg) me-tooer
éxito *m* (*resultado feliz*) success; (*canción, cine, etc. que ha tenido mucho éxito*) hit; (*resultado de un negocio*) outcome, result; **éxito de librería** best seller; **éxito de taquilla** box-office hit, good box office; **éxito de venta** best seller; **éxito rotundo** smash hit
exito•so -sa *adj* (Arg) successful
ex li•bris *m* (*pl* **-bris**) bookplate
exobiología *f* exobiology
éxodo *m* exodus; **éxodo de técnicos** brain drain
exonerar *tr* to exonerate, relieve; discharge, dismiss; **exonerar el vientre** to have a bowel movement
exorar *tr* to beg, entreat
exorbitante *adj* exorbitant
exorcizar §60 *tr* to exorcise
exornar *tr* to adorn, embellish
exóti•co -ca *adj* exotic; striking, stunning, glamorous

expandir *tr & ref* (Arg, Chile) to expand, extend, spread
expansión *f* expansion; (*manifestación efusiva*) expansiveness; (*difusión de una opinión*) spread; rest, recreation
expansionar *ref* to expand; open one's heart; relax, take it easy
expansi•vo -va *adj* expansive
expatria•do -da *adj & mf* expatriate
expectación *f* expectancy; **expectación de vida** life expectancy
expectativa *f* expectation; **estar en la expectativa de** to be expecting, be on the lookout for
expectorar *tr & intr* to expectorate
expediar *tr* to expedite; handle without delay; rush, speed
expedición *f* (*excursión para realizar una empresa*) expedition; (*remesa*) shipment; (*de un certificado, títulos, etc.*) issuance; (*agilidad, facilidad*) expedition
expedi•dor -dora *mf* sender, shipper
expediente *m* expedient; makeshift, apology; (*agilidad, facilidad*) expedition; (*todos los papeles correspondientes a un asunto*) dossier; (law) action, proceedings; **expediente académico** (educ) record
expedienteo *m* red tape
expedir §50 *tr* to send, ship, remit; (*títulos*) issue; (*despachar, cursar*) expedite
expeditar *tr* to expedite
expediti•vo -va *adj* expeditious
expedi•to -ta *adj* ready; clear, open, unencumbered
expeler *tr* to expel, eject
expende•dor -dora *mf* dealer, retailer; ticket agent; **expendedor de moneda falsa** distributor of counterfeit money
expendeduría *f* cigar store (*for sale of state-monopolized articles*)
expender *tr* to spend; dispense; sell at retail; (*moneda falsa*) circulate
expendio *m* shop, store; retail; (Mex) cigar store
expensar *tr* (Chile, Guat, Mex) to pay the cost of
expensas *fpl* expenses
experiencia *f* (*enseñanza que se adquiere con la práctica o con el vivir; suceso en que uno ha participado, cosa que uno ha experimentado*) experience; (*ensayo, experimento*) experiment
experimenta•do -da *adj* experienced
experimentar *tr* to experience, undergo, feel; test, try, try out ‖ *intr* to experiment
experimento *m* experiment; **experimento piloto** pilot test, pilot run
exper•to -ta *adj & m* expert
expiación *f* expiation, atonement; purification
expiar §77 *tr* to expiate, atone for; purify
expirar *intr* to expire
explanación *f* grading, leveling; explanation
explanada *f* esplanade
explanar *tr* to grade, level; explain
explayar *tr* to enlarge, extend ‖ *ref* to spread out, extend; go for an outing; expatiate,

talk at length; **explayarse con** to unbosom oneself to

explicación *f* explanation

explicar §73 *tr* to explain; (*exponer*) expound; (*exculpar*) explain away; (*una clase*) teach ‖ *intr* to explain ‖ *ref* to explain oneself; understand, make out

explicati•vo -va *adj* explanatory

explíci•to -ta *adj* explicit

exploración *f* exploration; (mil) scouting; (telv) scanning

explora•dor -dora *mf* explorer ‖ *m* boy scout; (mil) scout

explorar *tr* to explore; (mil) to scout; (telv) to scan

explosión *f* explosion; (*de gases en un motor*) combustion

explosi•vo -va *adj & m* explosive ‖ *f* (phonet) explosive

explotación *f* operation, running; exploitation; **explotación abusiva** (geol) overexploitation (of resources)

explotar *tr* to operate, run; (*una mina*) work; exploit ‖ *intr* to explode

exponente *m* exponent; (fig) interpreter, apologist

exponer §54 *tr* to expose; (*explicar*) expound; (*a un niño recién nacido*) abandon ‖ *intr* to display, show, exhibit; (eccl) to expose the Host ‖ *ref* to expose oneself; be on view

exportación *f* exportation, export; (*mercaderías que se exportan*) exports

exporta•dor -dora *mf* exporter

exportar *tr & intr* to export

exposición *f* exposition; (*a un peligro; con relación a los puntos cardinales*) exposure; (phot) exposure; (rhet) exposition; **exposición universal** world's fair

exposición-venta *f* sales exhibit

exposímetro *m* light meter

expósi•to -ta *mf* foundling

exposi•tor -tora *mf* exhibitor

exprés *m* express train; (Mex) express company

expresa•do -da *adj* above-mentioned

expresamente *adv* express, expressly

expresar *tr* to express ‖ *ref* to express oneself

expresión *f* expression; (*acción de exprimir*) squeezing; (*zumo exprimido*) juice; **expresiones** regards

expresi•vo -va *adj* expressive; kind, affectionate

expre•so -sa *adj* express ‖ *m* (*tren muy rápido; correo extraordinario*) express; express company

exprimidera *f* squeezer; **exprimidera de naranjas** orange squeezer

exprimi•do -da *adj* lean, skinny; stiff, stuck-up; affected, prim, prudish

exprimidor *m* wringer; squeezer; **exprimidor de ropa** clothes wringer

exprimir *tr* to squeeze, press; (*p.ej., la ropa blanca*) wring, wring out; (*extraer apretando*) express

ex profeso *adv* on purpose

expropiar *tr* to expropriate

expues•to -ta *adj* dangerous, hazardous

expugnar *tr* to take by storm

expulsanie•ves *m* (*pl -ves*) snowplow

expulsar *tr* to expel

expulsión *f* expulsion

expurgar §44 *tr* to expurgate

exquisi•to -ta *adj* exquisite

extasiar §77 & **regular** *ref* to go into ecstasy

éxta•sis *m* (*pl -sis*) ecstasy

extáti•co -ca *adj* ecstatic

extemporal *adj* unseasonable

extemporáne•o -a *adj* unseasonable; untimely, inopportune

extender §51 *tr* to extend, stretch out, spread out; spread; (*un documento*) draw up ‖ *ref* to extend, stretch out; spread; **extenderse a** or **hasta** to amount to

extendidamente *adv* at length, in detail

extensión *f* extension; (*vasta superficie, p.ej., del océano*) expanse; (*alcance, importancia*) extent; extending

extensi•vo -va *adj* extensive; **hacer extensivos a** to extend (*e.g., good wishes*) to

exten•so -sa *adj* extensive, extended, vast; **por extenso** at length, in detail

extenuar §21 *tr* to weaken, emaciate

exterior *adj* exterior, outer, outside; foreign ‖ *m* exterior, outside; appearance, bearing; **al exterior** or **a lo exterior** on the outside; outwardly; **del exterior** from abroad; **en el exterior** on the outside; abroad; **en exteriores** (mov) on location

exterioridad *f* externals, outward appearance; **exterioridades** pomp, show

exteriorista *adj* outgoing, outgiving ‖ *mf* extrovert

exteriorizar §60 *tr* to reveal ‖ *ref* to unbosom one's heart

exterminar *tr* to exterminate

exterminio *m* extermination

exter•no -na *adj* external ‖ *mf* day pupil

extinción *f* extinction; cancellation, elimination

extinguidor *m* (SAm) (*incendios*) fire extinguisher

extinguir §29 *tr* to extinguish, put out; wipe out, put an end to; fulfil, carry out; (*un plazo, un tiempo*) spend, serve ‖ *ref* to be extinguished, go out; come to an end

extin•to -ta *adj* (*volcán*) extinct; deceased ‖ *mf* deceased

extintor *m* fire extinguisher; **extintor de espuma** foam extinguisher; **extintor de granada** fire grenade

extirpar *tr* to extirpate, eradicate

extorno *m* premium adjustment (*based on change in policy*)

extorsión *f* extortion; harm, damage

extorsionar *tr* to harm, damage; extort

extra *adj* extra; **extra de** in addition to, besides ‖ *mf* (theat) extra ‖ *m* (*de un periódico*) extra; extra, bonus

extracción *f* extraction; (*en la lotería*) drawing numbers; **extracción de raíces** (math) evolution

extractar *tr* (*un escrito*) to abstract

ex
ex

extracto *m* (*de un escrito*) abstract; (pharm) extract
extractor *m* extractor; remover; **extractor de aire** ventilator; **extractor de humos** smoke evacuator
extracurricular *adj* extracurricular
extradición *f* extradition
extraer §75 *tr* to extract; pull; (*la raíz*) (math) to extract
extrafuerte *adj* heavy-duty
extragalácti•co -ca *adj* extragalactic
extralimitar *ref* to go too far
extramural *adj* extramural
extanjerismo *m* borrowing
extranje•ro -ra *adj* foreign, alien ‖ *mf* foreigner, alien; **extranjero enemigo** enemy alien ‖ *m* foreign country; **al extranjero** abroad; **del extranjero** from abroad; **en el extranjero** abroad
extrañar *tr* to banish, expatriate; surprise; find strange; miss ‖ *ref* to be surprised; refuse
extrañeza *f* strangeness, peculiarity; (*desavenencia*) estrangement; wonder, surprise
extra•ño -ña *adj* foreign; (*raro, singular*) strange; extraneous; **extraño a** unconnected with ‖ *mf* foreigner
extraoficial *adj* unofficial
extraordina•rio -ria *adj* extraordinary; extra, special ‖ *m* extra dish; special mail; (*de un periódico*) extra
extrapla•no -na *adj* extra-flat
extrapolar *tr & intr* to extrapolate
extrarradio *m* outer edge of town
extrasensorial *adj* extrasensory
extraterrestre *adj* extraterrestrial; otherworldly
extravagancia *f* (*singularidad, ridiculez*) extravagance, wildness, folly

extravagante *adj* (*singular, ridículo*) extravagant, wild, foolish; (*correspondencia en la casa de correos*) in transit
extravia•do -da *adj* lost, misplaced; astray, gone astray; (*lugar*) out-of-the-way
extraviar §77 *tr* to lead astray, mislead; mislay, misplace ‖ *ref* to get lost, go astray; go wrong; get out of line
extravío *m* going astray; loss; misleading; misconduct; misplacement
extrema *f* (*escasez grande*) extremity; (*de la vida*) end, last moment
extremar *tr* to carry far, carry to the limit ‖ *ref* to strive hard
extremaunción *f* extreme unction; last rites (*Roman Catholic*)
extreme•ño -ña *adj* frontier
extremidad *f* extremity; end, tip; **extremidades** (*pies y manos*) extremities; **la última extremidad** one's last moment
extremismo *m* extremism
extremista *mf* extremist
extre•mo -ma *adj* extreme; utmost; critical, desperate ‖ *m* extremity; (*de la calle*) end; (*del dedo*) tip; (*punto último*) extreme; great care; (*de una conversación, una carta*) point; winter pasture; **al extremo de** to the point of; **de extremo a extremo** from one end to the other; **hacer extremos** to be demonstrative, gush ‖ *f* see **extrema**
extremo•so -sa *adj* extreme, forthright; effusive, gushy, demonstrative
extrínse•co -ca *adj* extrinsic
extroversión *f* extroversion
extroverti•do -da *mf* extrovert
exuberante *adj* exuberant; luxuriant
exudar *tr & intr* to exude
exultante *adj* exultant
exultar *intr* to exult
exvoto *m* votive offering
eyacular *tr & intr* to ejaculate

F

F, f (efe) *f* seventh letter of the Spanish alphabet
f.a.b. *abbr* franco a bordo
fabada *f* pork-and-bean stew (*in Asturias*)
fábrica *f* factory, plant; building, masonry; (eccl) vestry
fabricación *f* manufacture; **fabricación en serie** mass production
fabricante *mf* manufacturer
fabricar §73 *tr* to manufacture; devise, invent; fabricate
fabril *adj* factory
fabriquero *m* manufacturer; charcoal burner; churchwarden
fábula *f* fable; (*p.ej., de un drama*) plot, story; rumor, gossip; (*mentira*) story, lie; (*objeto de murmuración*) talk of the town

fabulario *m* book of fables
fabulo•so -sa *adj* fabulous
facción *f* faction; feature; battle; **estar de facción** (mil) to be on duty; **facciones** features
facciona•rio -ria *adj* factional
faceta *f* facet
facetada *f* (Mex) flat joke
face•to -ta *adj* (Mex) affected; (Mex) finicky ‖ *f* see **faceta**
facial *adj* facial
fácil *adj* easy; pliant, yielding; likely; loose, wanton
facilidad *f* facility, ease, easiness; **facilidades de pago** easy payments
facilitar *tr* to facilitate, expedite; furnish, supply

facili•tón -tona *adj* bumbling, brash ‖ *mf* bumbler

facinero•so -sa *adj* wicked ‖ *mf* villain

facistol *m* choir desk

facón *m* (Arg, Urug) gaucho knife

facsimilar *tr* to facsimile; copy

facsímile *m* facsimile

factible *adj* feasible

factor *m* factor; commission merchant; baggageman; freight agent

factoría *f* trading post; (Ecuad, Peru) foundry; (Mex) factory

factura *f* invoice, bill; workmanship; **factura simulada** pro forma invoice; **según factura** as per invoice

facturación *f* invoicing, billing (*del equipaje*) checking

facturar *tr* to invoice, bill; (*el equipaje*) check

facultad *f* faculty; (*de la universidad*) school; knowledge, skill; power; **facultad de altos estudios** graduate school

facultar *tr* to empower, authorize

facultati•vo -va *adj* faculty; optional ‖ *m* doctor, physician

facundia *f* eloquence, fluency

facun•do -da *adj* eloquent, fluent

facha *mf* (*adefesio*) sight ‖ *f* look, appearance; **facha a facha** face to face

fachada *f* façade; (*de un libro*) title page; look, build, bearing; **hacer fachada con** to overlook, to look out on

facha•do -da *adj* — **bien fachado** good-looking ‖ *f* see *fachada*

fachenda *m* boaster, show-off ‖ *f* boasting

fachendear *intr* to boast, show off

fachendista or **fachen•dón -dona** or **fachendo•so -sa** *adj* boastful ‖ *mf* boaster, show-off

fachinal *m* (Arg) marshland

fada *f* fairy, witch

faena *f* work; toil; chore, task, job; (taur) windup; (taur) stunt, trick; (mil) fatigue, fatigue duty; (Guat, Mex, W-I) extra work, overtime; (Ecuad) morning work in the field; (Chile) gang of farm hands

faenero *m* (Chile) farm hand

Faetón *m* Phaëthon

fagot *m* bassoon

faisán *m* pheasant

faja *f* sash, girdle; bandage; band, strip; newspaper wrapper; (*de carretera*) lane; (*de tierra*) strip; **faja central** or **divisoria** median strip; **faja medical** supporter

fajar *tr* to wrap; bandage; swaddle; (*un periódico o revista*) put a wrapper on; beat, thrash; to attack ‖ *ref* to put on a sash

fajardo *m* meat pie

fajín *m* sash

fajina *f* bundle of sticks; fire wood; (mil) call to quarters

fajo *m* bundle; (*de papel moneda*) roll; swig; (Mex) blow; (Mex) leather belt; **fajos** swaddling clothes

falacia *f* deception; deceitfulness

falange *f* phalanx

falangia *f* daddy-longlegs

fa•laz *adj* (*pl* -**laces**) deceitful; deceptive

falba•lá *m* (*pl* -**aes**) gore; flounce, ruffle

falce *m* sickle; falchion

falda *f* skirt, dress; (*regazo*) lap; flap; fold; (*del sombrero*) brim; foothill; (*mujer*) skirt; **cosido a las faldas de** tied to the apron strings of

falde•ro -ra *adj* skirt; (*perro*) lap; lady-loving ‖ *m* lap dog

faldillas *fpl* skirts, coattails

faldón *m* coattail; shirttail; saddle flap

falible *adj* fallible

fáli•co -ca *adj* phallic

falo *m* penis, phallus

falsada *f* swoop (*of bird of prey*)

falsa•rio -ria *adj* lying ‖ *mf* falsifier, crook; liar

falsear *tr* to falsify; counterfeit; forge; (*la verdad*) distort; (*una cerradura*) pick; bevel ‖ *intr* to sag, buckle; give, give way

falsedad *f* falsity; (*mentira*) falsehood

falsete *m* falsetto; plug, tap; door (*between rooms*)

falsetista *f* falsetto

falsía *f* falsity, treachery; unsteadiness

falsificación *f* falsification; fake; counterfeit; forgery

falsificar §73 *tr* to falsify; fake; counterfeit; forge

falsilla *f* guide lines

fal•so -sa *adj* false; counterfeit; (*caballo*) vicious ‖ *m* patch; **coger en falso** (Mex) to catch in a lie; **envidar en falso** to bluff

falta *f* fault; lack, want; misdeed; absence; (*ausencia de la clase*) cut; (sport) fault; **a falta de** for want of; **echar en falta** to miss; **falta de ortografía** misspelling; **hacer falta** to be needed; be lacking; **hacerle falta a uno** to need, e.g., **le hacen falta a Juan estos libros** John needs these books; to miss, e.g., **Vd. me hace mucha falta** I miss you very much; **sin falta** without fail

faltar *intr* to be missing, be lacking, be wanting; fall short; run out; be absent; fail; die; lack, need, e.g., **me falta dinero** I lack money, I need money; **faltar a la clase** to cut class; **faltar a la verdad** to fail to tell the truth; **faltar a una cita** to fail to keep an appointment; **faltar . . . para** to be . . . to, e.g., **faltan cinco minutos para las dos** it is five minutes to two; **faltar poco para** to come near; **faltar por** to remain to be, e.g., **faltan por escribir dos cartas** two letters remain to be written

fal•to -ta *adj* short, lacking; (*peso o medida*) short; (Arg) dull, stupid; (Col) proud, vain; **falto de** short of ‖ *f* see **falta**

fal•tón -tona *adj* dilatory, remiss; (Arg) simple-minded

falto•so -sa *adj* addlebrained; (Col) quarrelsome; (CAm, Mex) disrespectful

faltriquera *f* pocket; handbag; **faltriquera de reloj** watch fob; **rascarse la faltriquera** to cough up

falúa *f* barge, tender

falucho *m* felucca

ex
fa

falla f failure, breakdown; defect; (geol) fault; (Mex) baby's bonnet

fallar tr to trump; judge, pass judgment on ‖ intr to fail, miss; misfire; sag, weaken; break down; judge, pass judgment

falleba f espagnolette

fallecer §22 intr to die; fail, expire

falleci•do -da adj deceased, late

falli•do -da adj unsuccessful; bankrupt; (deuda) uncollectible

fallir §13 intr to fail; (Ven) to go bankrupt

fa•llo -lla adj (Chile) silly, simple; **estar fallo a** to be out of (cards of a suit) ‖ m short suit; decision; judgment; verdict; **fallo humano** human error; **tener fallo a** or **de** to be out of ‖ f see **falla**

fama f fame; reputation; rumor; (Chile) bull's-eye; **correr fama** to be rumored; **es fama** it is said, it is rumored

faméli•co -ca adj famished, starving

familia f family

familiar adj familiar; family; (sin ceremonia) informal; (lenguaje, estilo) colloquial ‖ m member of the family; member of the household; acquaintance; **familiar dependiente** dependent

familiaridad f familiarity

familiarizar §60 tr to familiarize ‖ ref to become familiar; become too familiar; familiarize oneself

famo•so -sa adj famous; (excelente) famous; (formidable) some, e.g., **famoso sujeto** some guy

fámu•lo -la mf servant

fanal m beacon, lighthouse; lantern; bell glass, bell jar; lamp shade

fanáti•co -ca adj fanatic(al) ‖ mf fanatic; (sport) fan

fanatismo m fanaticism

fanega f 1.58 bu.; **fanega de tierra** 1.59 acres

fanfarria f fanfare; blustering

fanfa•rrón -rrona adj blustering, bragging; flashy ‖ mf blusterer, braggart

fanfarronada f bluster, bravado

fanfarronnear intr to bluster, brag

fanfarronería f blustering, bragging, sword rattling

fanfurriña f pet, peeve

fango m mud, mire; **llenar de fango** (fig) to sling mud at

fango•so -sa adj muddy; sticky, gooey

fanguero m (Cuba, Mex, P-R) mud, quagmire

fantasear tr to dream of ‖ intr to fancy, to daydream; **fantasear de** to boast of being

fantasía f fantasy; fancy, conceit, vanity; imagery; **con fantasía** (Arg) hard; **de fantasía** fancy, imitation; **tocar por fantasía** (Ven) to play by ear

fantasio•so -sa adj vain, conceited

fantasma m phantom, ghost; stuffed shirt; (telv) ghost; **fantasma magnético** magnetic curves ‖ f scarecrow, hobgoblin

fantas•món -mona adj (coll) conceited ‖ mf conceited person ‖ m stuffed shirt; (coll) scarecrow

fantásti•co -ca adj fantastic; fancy; conceited

fantoche m puppet, marionette; nincompoop, whippersnapper

faquín m street porter, errand boy

fara•lá m (pl -laes) ruffle, flounce; frill

faramalla mf cheat, swindler ‖ f jabber, claptrap; bluff, fake; (Chile) bragging

faramalle•ro -ra or **farama•llón -llona** adj scheming, swindling ‖ mf schemer, swindler

farándula f (baile) farandole; gossip, scheming; theater people; (de gente) (Arg) crush, milling

farandulear intr to boast, to show off

Faraón m Pharaoh

faraute m herald, messenger; interpreter; (actor) prologue; busybody

fardel m bag, bundle; sloppy person

fardo m bundle, package

farero m lighthouse keeper

farfa•lá m (pl -laes) ruffle, flounce

farfullar tr (p.ej., una lección) to sputter through; (p.ej., una tarea) stumble through ‖ intr to sputter

faringe f pharynx

fariseo m pharisee; Pharisee; lanky good-for-nothing

farmacéuti•co -ca adj pharmaceutical ‖ mf pharmacist

farmacia f pharmacy, drug store; **farmacia de guardia** drug store open all night

fármaco m drug, medicine

faro m lighthouse, beacon; floodlight; (aut) headlight; (fig) beacon; **faro piloto** (aut) spotlight; **faros de carretera** (aut) bright lights; **faros de cruce** (aut) dimmers; **faros de población** or **de situación** (aut) parking lights

farol m lamp, light; lantern; street light; (rr) headlight; (coll) conceited fellow; (Bol) bay window; **farol de tope** (naut) headlight

farola f lighthouse; street lamp, lamppost

farolear intr to boast, brag

farole•ro -ra adj boasting ‖ mf boaster ‖ m lamplighter

farolillo m heartseed; Canterbury bell; **farolillo veneciano** Chinese lantern, Japanese lantern

farota f minx, vixen

farotear intr (Col) to romp around, make a racket

faro•tón -tona adj brazen, cheeky ‖ mf cheeky person

farra f salmon trout; (SAm) revelry

fárrago m hodgepodge

farraquista m scatterbrain; muddlehead

farrear intr to celebrate; (coll) to goof off

farro m grits

farru•co -ca adj bold, fearless; ill-humored ‖ mf Galician abroad, Asturian abroad

farru•to -ta adj (Arg, Bol, Chile) sickly

farsa f farce; humbug

farsante adj & mf fake, fraud, humbug

fas — por fas o por nefas rightly or wrongly, in any event

fascinante adj fascinating

fascinar *tr* to fascinate, bewitch; cast a spell on, cast the evil eye on

fascismo *m* fascism

fascista *adj & mf* fascist

fase *f* phase

fastidiar *tr* to bore, annoy; cloy, sicken; disappoint ‖ *ref* to get bored; suffer, be a victim

fastidio *m* boredom, annoyance; distaste, nausea

fastidio•so -sa *adj* boring, annoying; cloying, sickening; annoyed, displeased

fas•to -ta *adj* happy, blessed ‖ *m* pomp, show

fastuo•so -sa *adj* vain, pompous; magnificent

fatal *adj* fatal; bad, evil; (law) unextendible

fatalidad *f* fatality; misfortune

fatalismo *m* fatalism

fatalista *mf* fatalist

fatalmente *adv* fatally; inevitably; unfortunately; badly, poorly

fatídi•co -ca *adj* ominous, fateful

fatiga *f* fatigue; hard breathing; **fatigas** hardship

fatigante *adj* tiresome; fatiguing

fatigar §44 *tr* to fatigue, tire, weary; annoy, bother ‖ *ref* to get tired

fatigo•so -sa *adj* fatiguing, tiring; trying, tedious

fa•tuo -tua *adj* fatuous; conceited ‖ *mf* simpleton

fauces *fpl* (anat) fauces; (fig) jaws, mouth

fauna *f* fauna

fauno *m* faun

faus•to -ta *adj* happy, fortunate ‖ *m* pomp, magnificence

fausto•so -sa *adj* magnificent

fau•tor -tora *mf* abettor, accomplice

favor *m* favor; **a favor de** under cover of; by means of; in favor of; **hágame Vd. el favor de** do me the favor to; **por favor** please; **vender favores** to peddle influence

favorable *adj* favorable

favorecer §22 *tr* to favor; flatter

favoritismo *m* favoritism

favori•to -ta *adj & mf* favorite

fayanca *f* unstable posture

faz *f* (*pl* **faces**) face; aspect, look; (*de monedas o medallas*) obverse; **faces** cheeks; **faz a faz** face to face

F.C. *abbr* **ferrocarril**

fe *f* faith; testimony, witness; certificate; **¡a fe mía!** upon my faith!; **dar fe de** to certify; **en fe de lo cual** in witness whereof; **fe de erratas** list of errata; **hacer fe** to be valid; **la fe del carbonero** simple faith

fealdad *f* ugliness

Febe *f* Phoebe

feble *adj* weak, sickly; (*moneda, aleación*) lacking in weight or fineness

Febo *m* Phoebus

febrero *m* February

febril *adj* feverish

fécula *f* starch

feculen•to -ta *adj* starchy; fecal

fecundar *tr* to fecundate, to fertilize

fecun•do -da *adj* fecund, fertile

fecha *f* date; **con fecha de** under date of; **de larga fecha** of long standing; **hasta la fecha** to date

fechador *m* (Chile, Mex) canceler, postmark

fechar *tr* to date

fechoría *f* misdeed, villainy

federación *f* federation

federal *adj & mf* federal

federar *tr & ref* to federate

feéri•co -ca *adj* fairy

fehaciente *adj* authentic

feldespato *m* feldspar

felicidad *f* felicity, happiness; luck

felicitar *tr* to felicitate, congratulate, wish happiness to

feli•grés -gresa *mf* parishioner, church member

feligresía *f* parish; congregation

Felipe *m* Philip

fe•liz *adj* (*pl* **-lices**) happy; lucky; (*oportuno*) felicitous

fe•lón -lona *adj* perfidious, treacherous ‖ *mf* wicked person

felonía *f* perfidy, treachery

felpa *f* plush; drubbing; severe reprimand

felpu•do -da *adj* plushy, downy ‖ *m* mat, door mat

femenil *adj* feminine, womanly

femeni•no -na *adj* feminine; (*sexo*) female ‖ *m* feminine

fementi•do -da *adj* false, treacherous

feminismo *m* feminism

fenecer §22 *tr* to finish, close ‖ *intr* to come to an end; die

Fenicia *f* Phoenicia

feni•cio -cia *adj & mf* Phoenician ‖ *f* see **Fenicia**

fé•nix *m* (*pl* **-nix** or **-nices**) phoenix

fenobarbital *m* phenobarbital

fenomenal *adj* phenomenal

fenómeno *m* phenomenon; monster, freak

fe•o -a *adj* ugly ‖ *m* slight; **hacer un feo a** to slight ‖ **feo** *adv* (Arg, Col, Mex) bad, e.g., **oler feo** to smell bad

feo•te -ta *adj* ugly, hideous

feral *adj* cruel, bloody

fe•raz *adj* (*pl* **-races**) fertile

féretro *m* bier

feria *f* weekday; market; fair; day off; (Mex) small change; (Mex) con man; (CAm, Mex) extra, tip, gratuity; **revolver la feria** to upset the applecart

ferial *adj* week (*day*); market (*day*) ‖ *m* market; fair

feriante *adj* fair-going ‖ *mf* fairgoer

feriar *tr* to buy, sell; give, present; (Mex) to give change for

feri•no -na *adj* wild, savage; (*tos*) whooping (*cough*)

fermentación *f* ferment; fermentation

fermentar *tr & intr* to ferment

fermento *m* ferment

ferocidad *f* ferocity, fierceness

ferósti•co -ca *adj* irritable; hideous

fe•roz *adj* (*pl* **-roces**) ferocious, fierce

férre•o -a *adj* iron

ferrería *f* ironworks, foundry

ferretear *tr* to trim with iron; work in iron

ferretería *f* ironworks; hardware; hardware store

ferrete•ro -ra *mf* hardware dealer

ferrocarril *m* railroad, railway; **ferrocarril de cremallera** rack railway, mountain railroad

ferrocarrile•ro -ra *adj* railroad, rail ‖ *m* railroader

ferrotipo *m* tintype

ferrovia•rio -ria *adj* railroad, rail ‖ *m* railroader

fértil *adj* fertile

fertilizar §60 *tr* to fertilize

férula *f* flexible splint; ferule; **estar bajo la férula de** to be under the thumb of

férvi•do -da *adj* fervid; (*fiebre; sed*) burning

ferviente *adj* fervent

fervor *m* fervor, zeal

fervoro•so -sa *adj* ardent, zealous

festejar *tr* to fete, honor, entertain; celebrate; court, woo; (Mex) to beat, thrash

festejo *m* feast, entertainment; celebration; courting, wooing; (Peru) revelry; **festejos** public festivities

festín *m* feast, banquet

festinar *tr* to hurry through; (CAm) to entertain

festival *m* festival, music festival

festividad *f* festivity; feast day; witticism

festi•vo -va *adj* festive, gay; witty; (*digno no de celebrarse*) solemn

festón *m* festoon

festonear *tr* to festoon

fetiche *m* fetish

féti•do -da *adj* fetid, foul

feto *m* fetus

feú•co -ca or **feú•cho -cha** *adj* hideous, repulsive

feudal *adj* feudal

feudalismo *m* feudalism

feudo *m* fief; **feudo franco** freehold

fiable *adj* trustworthy

fiado *m* — **al fiado** on credit; **en fiado** on bail

fia•dor -dora *mf* bail; **salir fiador por** to go bail for ‖ *m* fastener; catch, pawl; (Chile, Ecuad) chin strap

fiambre *adj* cold, cold-served; (*noticias*) old, stale ‖ *m* cold lunch, cold food; stale news; (Arg) dull party; **fiambres** cold cuts

fiambrera *f* dinner pail, lunch basket

fiambrería *f* (Arg) delicatessen store

fianza *f* guarantee, surety; bond; bail; **fianza carcelera** bail

fiar §77 *tr* to entrust, confide; guarantee; give credit to; sell on credit ‖ *intr* & *ref* to trust

fiasco *m* fiasco

fibra *f* fiber; (fig) fiber, strength, vigor; **fibras del corazón** heartstrings

fibro•so -sa *adj* fibrous

ficción *f* fiction

ficciona•rio -ria *adj* fictional

fice *m* (ichth) hake

ficti•cio -cia *adj* fictitious

ficha *f* chip; counter; domino; filing card; police record; (elec) plug; **ficha catalográfica** index card; **ficha perforada** punch card; **llevar ficha** to have a police record; **ser una buena ficha** to be a sly fox

ficha•dor -dora *mf* file clerk

fichar *tr* to file; play, move; black-list; (Cuba) to cheat ‖ *intr* (Col) to die

fichero *m* card index, filing cabinet

fidedig•no -na *adj* reliable, trustworthy

fideicomisa•rio -ria *mf* trustee

fideicomiso *m* trusteeship

fidelería *f* (Arg, Ecuad, Peru) vermicelli factory, noodle factory

fidelidad *f* fidelity; punctiliousness; **alta fidelidad** (rad) high fidelity

fideo *m* skinny person; (Arg) joke; (Arg) confusion, disorder; **fideos** vermicelli

Fidias *m* Phidias

fiducia•rio -ria *adj* & *mf* fiduciary

fiebre *f* fever; **fiebre del heno** hay fever; **fibre tifoidea** typhoid fever

fiel *adj* faithful; exact; punctilious; honest, trustworthy ‖ *m* inspector of weights and measures; (*en las balanzas*) pointer; (*de las tijeras*) pin; **fiel de romana** inspector of weights in a slaughterhouse; **los fieles** the faithful

fielato *m* inspector's office; octroi

fieltro *m* felt; felt hat; felt rug

fiera *f* wild animal; (*persona*) fiend; (taur) bull; **ser una fiera para** to be a fiend for

fierabrás *m* spitfire, little terror

fierecilla *f* shrew

fiereza *f* fierceness; cruelty; deformity

fie•ro -ra *adj* fierce, wild; cruel; deformed, ugly; huge, tremendous; **echar** or **hacer fieros** to bluster ‖ *f* see **fiera**

fierro *m* (SAm) branding iron

fierros *mpl* (Ecuad, Mex) tools

fiesta *f* feast, holy day; holiday; celebration, festivity; **estar de fiesta** (coll) to be in a holiday mood; **fiesta de la hispanidad** or **fiesta de la raza** Columbus Day; **fiesta de todos los santos** All Saints' Day; **fiesta onomástica** saint's day, birthday; **fiestas** holiday, vacation; **hacer fiesta** to take off (*from work*); **hacer fiestas a** to act up to, to fawn on; **la fiesta brava** bullfighting; **no estar para fiestas** to be in no mood for joking; **por fin de fiestas** to top it off; **se acabó la fiesta** let's drop it

fieste•ro -ra *adj* merry, cheerful ‖ *mf* merrymaker, party-goer

figón *m* cheap restaurant

figura *f* figure; face, countenance; (*naipe*) face card; (mus) note; (theat) character; **figura retórica** figure of speech; **hacer figura** to cut a figure

figuración *f* representation; (Arg) status, social standing

figura•do -da *adj* figurative

figurar *tr* to depict, trace, represent; feign ‖ *intr* to figure, be in the limelight ‖ *ref* to figure, imagine

figurati•vo -va *adj* figurative, representative

figurería *f* face, grimace

figurilla *mf* silly little runt ‖ *f* figurine

figurín *m* dummy, model; fashion plate

figurina *f* figurine

figurita *mf* silly little runt

figurón *m* stuffed shirt; **figurón de proa** (naut) figurehead

fija *f* hinge; trowel; (*caballo*) (Peru) sure bet; **la fija** sure thing

fijacarte•les *m* (*pl* **-les**) billposter

fijación *f* fixing, fastening; posting; **fijación de precios** price fixing

fijado *m* (phot) fixing

fija•dor -dora *adj* fixing ‖ *m* carpenter who installs doors and windows; fixing bath; sprayer; (mas) pointer; hair set, hair spray

fijamárge•nes *m* (*pl* **-nes**) margin stop

fijapeína•dos *m* (*pl* **-dos**) hair set, hair spray

fijar *tr* to fix; fasten; (*carteles*) post; (*una fecha; los cabellos; una imagen fotográfica; los precios; la atención; una hora, una cita*) fix; (*residencia*) establish; paste, glue ‖ *ref* to settle; notice; **fijarse en** to notice; pay attention to; be intent on

fijeza *f* firmness, stability; steadfastness; **mirar con fijeza** to stare at

fi•jo -ja *adj* fixed; firm, solid, secure, fast; sure, determined; **de fijo** surely ‖ *f* see **fija**

fil *m* — **estar en fil** or **en un fil** to be alike; **fil derecho** leapfrog

fila *f* row, line; file; (*línea que los soldados forman de frente*) rank; dislike, hatred; **cerrar las filas** (mil) to close ranks; **en fila** in single file; **en filas** (mil) in active service; **fila india** single file, Indian file; **llamar a filas** (mil) to call to the colors; **pasarse a las filas de** to go over to; **romper filas** (mil) to break ranks

filamento *m* filament

filantropía *f* philanthropy

filántrop•po -pa *mf* philanthropist

filar *tr* (naut) to pay out slowly

filarmónica *f* (Mex) accordion

filarmóni•co -ca *adj* philharmonic

filatelia *f* philately

filatelista *mf* philatelist

filatería *f* fast talking; wordiness

filate•ro -ra *adj* fast-talking; wordy ‖ *mf* fast talker; great talker

file•no -na *adj* cute, tiny

filete *m* (*de carne o pescado*) filet or fillet; (*asador*) spit; edge, rim; narrow hem; (*de tornillo*) thread; snaffle bit; (archit, bb) fillet; (typ) rule, fancy rule

filetear *tr* to fillet; (*un tornillo*) thread; (bb) to tool

filiación *f* filiation; description, characteristics; (mil) regimental register

filial *adj* filial ‖ *f* affiliate, branch

filiar §77 *tr* to register ‖ *ref* to enroll

filibustero *m* filibuster, buccaneer

filigrana *f* filigree; (*en el papel*) watermark

filipi•no -na *adj* Filipine, Filipino ‖ *mf* Filipino ‖ **Filipinas** *fpl* Philippines

Filipo *m* Philip (*of Macedonia*)

Filis *f* Phyllis

filiste•o -a *adj & mf* Philistine ‖ *m* tall, fat fellow

film *m* (*pl* **-films** or **filmes**) film

filmadora *f* movie camera

filmar *tr* to film, shoot

filo *m* edge; ridge; dividing line; (CAm, Mex) hunger; **al filo de** at, at about; **dar filo a** to sharpen; **filo del viento** direction of the wind; **pasar al filo de la espada** to put to the sword; **por filo** exactly

filobús *m* trolley bus, trackless trolley

filocommunista *adj & mf* procommunist

filología philology

filólo•go -ga *mf* philologist

filón *m* seam, vein; (fig) gold mine

filo•so -sa *adj* sharp

filosofía *f* philosophy

filosófi•co -ca *adj* philosophic(al)

filóso•fo -fa *mf* philosopher

filote *m* (Col) corn silk; (Col) ear of green corn

filtración *f* filtering; leak; (fig) leak, loss

filtrado *m* filtrate

filtrar *tr* to filter ‖ *intr* to leak; ooze ‖ *ref* to filter; (*el dinero*) leak away, disappear

filtro *m* filter; (*brebaje para conciliar el amor*) philter, love potion

filu•do -da *adj* (SAm) sharp-edged

filván *m* featheredge

fimo *m* dung, manure

fin *m* end; aim, purpose, end; **a fin de** to, in order to; **a fin de que** in order that, so that; **a fines de** toward the end of, late in; **al fin** finally; **al fin del mundo** far, far away; **al fin y a la postre** or **al fin y al cabo** after all, in the end; **dar fin a** to put an end to; **fin de semana** weekend; **por fin** finally, in short; **sin fin** endless; endlessly; **un sin fin de** no end of

fina•do -da *adj* deceased, late ‖ *mf* deceased

final *adj* final ‖ *m* end; (mus) finale; **por final** finally ‖ *f* (sport) finals; **final de partido** windup

finalidad *f* end, purpose

finalista *mf* finalist

finalizar §60 *tr* to end, terminate; (*una escritura*) (law) to execute ‖ *intr* to end, terminate

financiación *f* financing

financiamiento *m* (SAm) financial backing

financiar *tr* to finance

financie•ro -ra *adj* financial ‖ *mf* financier

finanzas *fpl* finances

finar *intr* to die ‖ *ref* to yearn

finca *f* property, piece of real estate; farm, ranch; **buena finca** sly fellow

fincar §73 *tr* (P-R) to cultivate, farm ‖ *intr* to buy up real estate; (Col) to reside, rest, be based ‖ *ref* to buy up real estate

fincha•do -da *adj* vain, conceited

fi•nés -nesa *adj* Finnic; Finnish ‖ *mf* Finn ‖ *m* (*idioma uraliano*) Finnic; (*idioma de Finlandia*) Finnish

fineza *f* fineness; kindness, courtesy; token of affection, favor

fingi•do -da *adj* fake, sham; false, deceitful

fingir §27 *tr & intr* to feign, pretend, fake ‖ *ref* to pretend to be

finiquitar *tr* (*una cuenta*) to settle, to close; finish, wind up

finiquito *m* settlement, closing; **dar finiquito a** to settle, close; finish, wind up

finíti•mo -ma adj bordering, neighboring
fini•to -ta adj finite
finlan•dés -desa adj Finnish ‖ mf Finn, Finlander ‖ m Finnish
Finlandia f Finland
fi•no -na adj fine; (ligero, casi transparente) sheer; (esbelto) thin, slender; (paño, papel, etc.) thin; (agua) pure; polite, courteous; shrewd, cunning
finta f feint
finura f fineness, excellence; politeness; courtesy
finústi•co -ca adj overobsequious
firma f signature; signing; firm; firm name; mail to be signed; **con mi firma** under my hand; **firma en blanco** blank check
firmamento m firmament
firmante adj signatory ‖ mf signer, signatory
firmar tr & intr to sign
firme adj firm, steady; solid, hard; staunch, unswerving ‖ adv firmly, steadily ‖ m roadbed; **de firme** hard, e.g., **llover de firme** to rain hard
firmeza f firmness; constancy, fortitude
firmón m shyster who signs anything
fiscal adj fiscal, treasury ‖ m treasurer; district attorney; busybody
fiscalizar §60 tr to control, inspect; prosecute; pry into
fisco m state treasury, exchequer
fisga f fish spear; prying, snooping; banter, raillery
fisgar §44 tr to harpoon, fish with a spear; pry into ‖ intr to pry, snoop; mock, jeer ‖ ref to mock, jeer
fis•gón -gona mf (coll) mocker, jester; (coll) snooper, busybody
físi•co -ca adj physical; (Mex, W-I) finicky, prudish ‖ mf physicist ‖ m physique ‖ f physics; **física de las partículas** particle physics; **física del estado sólido** solid state physics; **física molecular** molecular physics
fisil adj fissionable
fisiología f physiology
fisiológi•co -ca adj physiological
fisión f fission
fisionable adj fissionable
fisonomía f physiognomy
fistol m sly fellow; (Mex) necktie pin
fisura f (anat, min) fissure; **fisura del paladar** cleft palate
fla•co -ca adj thin, skinny; feeble, weak, frail; insecure, unstable ‖ m weak spot
flacu•cho -cha adj skinny
flagrante adj occurring, actual; **en flagrante** in the act
flamante adj bright, flaming; brand-new, spick-and-span
flameante adj flamboyant
flamear intr to flame; flare up (with anger); flutter, wave
flamen•co -ca adj Flemish; buxom; Andalusian gypsy; flashy, snappy, gypsyish ‖ mf Fleming ‖ m (idioma) Flemish; Andalusian gypsy dance, song, or music; (orn) flamingo

fláme•o -a adj flamelike
flamíge•ro -ra adj (poet) flaming; (archit) flamboyant
flan m custard
flanco m side, flank; **coger por el flanco** to catch off guard
Flandes f Flanders
flanquear tr to flank
flaquear intr to weaken, flag; become faint; become discouraged
flaqueza f thinness, skinniness; weakness; instability
flashback m (retrospectiva) flashback
flato m gas; gloominess, melancholy
flato•so -sa adj flatulent, windy; gloomy, melancholy
flauta f flute
flautín m piccolo
flautista mf flautist, flutist
flebitis f phlebitis
fleco m fringe; ragged edge; **flecos** bangs
flecha f arrow; (aer) sweepback
flechar tr (el arco) to draw; (a una persona) wound with an arrow, kill with an arrow; infatuate
flechero m archer, bowman
fleje m iron strap, iron hoop
flema f phlegm
flemáti•co -ca adj phlegmatic(al); (coll) cool
flemón m gumboil
flequillo m bangs
Flesinga f Flushing
fletante m shipowner; (Arg, Chile, Ecuad) conveyancer
fletar tr (una nave) to charter; (ganado) load; (bestias de carga, carros, etc.) (Arg, Chile, Ecuad, Mex) to hire ‖ ref (Arg) to sneak in, slip in; (Cuba, Mex) to beat it, clear out
flete m (naut) freight, cargo; (Arg, Bol, Col, Urug) race horse; **salir sin flete** (Col, Ven) to beat it
flexible adj flexible; (sombrero) soft ‖ m soft hat; (elec) flexible cord
flexo m gooseneck lamp
flinflanear intr to tinkle
flirt m or **flirtación** f flirting
flirtear intr to flirt
flojear intr to ease up, idle; flag, weaken
flojedad f slackness; looseness; limpness; laziness; weakness
flojel m fluff, nap; down, soft feathers
flo•jo -ja adj slack, loose; limp; languid; lazy; weak; (precios) sagging; (viento) light; lax, careless
flor f flower; (de árbol frutal) blossom; (del cuero) grain; (fig) compliment, bouquet; **a flor de** even with, flush with; **a flor de agua** at water level; **decir flores a** to flatter; to flirt with; **flor de la edad** bloom of youth; **flor de la vida** prime of life; **flor del campo** wild flower; **flor de lis** (escudo de armas de Francia) lily, fleur-de-lis; **flor de mano** paper flower, artificial flower; **la flor de la canela** the tops; **la flor y nata de** the cream of
flora f flora

floral *adj* floral

florcita *f* little flower; **andar de florcita** (Arg, Bol, Chile, Urug) to stroll around with a flower in one's buttonhole, take it easy

florear *tr* to flower, decorate with flowers; (*los naipes*) stack; (*harina*) bolt ‖ *intr* (*la punta de la espada*) to quiver; twang away on a guitar; throw bouquets

florecer §22 *intr* to flower, blossom, bloom; (*prosperar*) flourish ‖ *ref* to become moldy

floreciente *adj* flowering, florescent; flourishing

florenti•no -na *adj* & *mf* Florentine

floreo *m* idle talk; bright remark; (*de la punta de la espada*) quivering; (*de la guitarra*) twanging; (*mus*) flourish; **andarse con floreos** to beat about the bush

florera *f* flower girl

florería *f* flower shop

flore•ro -ra *adj* flattering, jesting ‖ *mf* flatterer, jester; florist ‖ *m* (*vaso para flores*) vase; (*maceta con flores*) flowerpot; flower stand, jardiniere; (*cuadro, pintura*) flower piece ‖ *f* see **florera**

florescencia *f* florescence

floresta *f* woods, woodland; grove; rural setting; anthology

florete *m* (*esgrima*) fencing; (*espadín*) foil

floretear *tr* to decorate with flowers ‖ *intr* to fence

flori•do -da *adj* flowery, full of flowers; choice, select

florilegio *m* anthology

floripondio *m* (SAm) angel's-trumpet

florista *mf* florist

floristería *f* flower shop

florón *m* large flower; finial; rosette; (*typ*) tailpiece, vignette

flota *f* fleet; **flota petrolera** tanker fleet

flotación *f* buoyancy

flotador *m* float

flotaje *m* log driving

flotante *adj* floating; (*barba*) flowing ‖ *m* (Col) braggart

flotar *intr* to float; (*una bandera*) wave

flote *m* floating; **a flote** afloat

fluctuar §21 *intr* to fluctuate; bob up and down; wave; waver; be in danger

fluente *adj* fluent, flowing; (*hemorroides*) bleeding

fluidez *f* fluidity

flúi•do -da *adj* fluid; (*estilo, lenguaje*) fluent ‖ *m* fluid

fluir §20 *intr* to flow

flujo *m* flow, flux; (*acceso de la marea*) floodtide; **flujo de risa** fit of noisy laughter; **flujo de vientre** loose bowels; **flujo y reflujo** ebb and flow

flúor *m* fluorine

fluorescencia *f* fluorescence

fluorescente *adj* fluorescent

fluorhídri•co -ca *adj* hydrofluoric

fluorización *f* fluoridation

fluorizar §60 *tr* to fluoridate

fluoroscopio *m* fluoroscope

fluoruro *m* fluoride

flux *m* (*en el póker*) flush; suit of clothes; **estar en flux** to be penniless; **hacer flux** to blow in everything without settling accounts; **tener flux** to be lucky

fluxión *f* (*acumulación morbosa de humores*) congestion; (*enrojecimiento de la cara y el cuello*) flush; (*constipado de narices*) cold in the head; **fluxión de muelas** swollen cheek; **fluxión de pecho** pneumonia

foca *f* seal

focal *adj* focal

foco *m* focus; (*de vicios*) center; (*de un absceso*) core; electric light

fodo•lí *adj* (*pl* -**líes**) meddlesome

fodon•go -ga *adj* (Mex) dirty, slovenly

fo•fo -fa *adj* soft, fluffy, spongy

fogaje *m* (*contribución*) hearth money; blush, flush; (Arg) fire, blaze; (Arg, Mex) rash, eruption

fogata *f* blaze, bonfire

fogón *m* cooking stove; (*de máquina de vapor*) firebox

fogonazo *m* powder flash

fogonero *m* fireman, stoker

fogosidad *f* fire, spirit, dash

fogo•so -sa *adj* fiery, spirited

fol. *abbr* **folio**

folgo *m* foot muff

foliar *tr* to folio

folio *m* folio; **al primer folio** right off; **de a folio** enormous; **en folio** folio

folklore *m* folklore

follaje *m* foliage; gaudy ornament; (*palabrería*) fustian

follar *tr* to shape like a leaf ‖ §61 *tr* to blow with bellows

folletín *m* newspaper serial (*printed at bottom of page*); pamphlet

folleto *m* brochure, pamphlet, tract

fo•llón -llona *adj* careless, indolent, lazy; arrogant, cowardly ‖ *mf* lazy loafer, knave ‖ *m* noiseless rocket

fomentar *tr* to foment; foster, encourage, promote; warm

fonda *f* inn, restaurant; (Chile) refreshment stand

fondeadero *m* anchorage

fondea•do -da *adj* well-heeled

fondear *tr* (*un buque*) to search; scrutinize, examine closely ‖ *intr* to cast anchor ‖ *ref* to save up for a rainy day

fondillos *mpl* seat (*of trousers*)

fondista *mf* innkeeper

fondo *m* bottom; (*de un cuarto, una tienda*) back, rear; (*del mar, de una piscina, etc.*) floor; (*de un cilindro, barril, etc.*) head; background; (*de una casa*) depth; (*de un paño*) ground; (*caudal*) fund; (*lo esencial*) bottom; **a fondo** thoroughly; **bajos fondos sociales** underworld, scum of the earth; **colar a fondo** to sink; **dar fondo** to cast anchor; **echar a fondo** to sink; **en el fondo** at bottom; **estar en fondos** to have funds available; **fondo de amortización** sinking fund; **fondos** (*caudales, dinero*) funds; **irse a fondo** to go to the bottom; (*un negocio*)

fi
fo

to fail; **tener buen fondo** to be good-natured
fonducho *m* cheap eating house
fonéti•co -ca *adj* phonetic
foniatría *f* speech correction
fónica *f* phonics
fono *m* (Chile) earphone
fonoabsorbente *adj* sound-absorbent; sound-deadening
fonocaptor *m* pickup
fonógrafo *m* phonograph; record player
fonología *f* phonology
fontanería *f* plumbing; water-supply system
fontane•ro -ra *adj* fountain ‖ *m* plumber, tinsmith
foque *m* (naut) jib; (coll) piccadilly collar
foraji•do -da *adj* fugitive ‖ *mf* fugitive, outlaw, bandit
foráne•o -a *adj* foreign, strange; offshore
foraste•ro -ra *adj* outside, strange; foreign ‖ *mf* outsider, stranger
forbante *m* freebooter
forcejar or **forcejear** *intr* to struggle, resist, contend
forceju•do -da *adj* strong, husky, robust
fór•ceps *m* (*pl* **-ceps**) forceps
forestal *adj* forest
forja *f* forge; forging; silversmith's forge; foundry, ironworks; mortar
forjar *tr* to forge; build with stone and mortar; roughcast; (*mentiras*) forge ‖ *ref* to forge; hatch, think up
forma *f* form, shape; way; (*de un libro*) format; **de forma que** so that, with the result that; **tener buenas formas** to have a good figure
formación *f* formation; **formación de palabras** word formation
formal *adj* formal, ceremonious; express, definite; reliable; sedate; serious
formalidad *f* formality; reliability; seriousness
formar *tr* to form; to shape, fashion; train, educate ‖ *intr* to form; form a line, stand in line ‖ *ref* to form; form a line, stand in line; take form, grow, develop
formato *m* format
formidable *adj* formidable
formidolo•so -sa *adj* scared, frightened; frightful, horrible
fórmula *f* formula; prescription; **por fórmula** as a matter of form
formular *tr* to formulate
formulario *m* form, blank; **formulario de pedido** order blank
fornicación *f* fornication
fornicar *intr* to fornicate; to have sex
forni•do -da *adj* husky, sturdy, robust
foro *m* forum; (*abogacía*) bar; (*del escenario*) back, rear
forrado *m* lining; padding
forraje *m* forage, fodder
forrajear *tr & intr* to forage
forrar *tr* to line; (*un vestido*) face; (*un libro, un paraguas*) cover; (*un lienzo*) stretch ‖ *ref* (Guat, Mex) to stuff oneself
forro *m* lining; cover, covering; (naut)

sheathing, planking; **forro de freno** brake lining; **ni por el forro** not by a long shot
fortalecer §22 *tr* to fortify, strengthen
fortaleza *f* fortitude; strength, vigor; fortress, stronghold
fortificación *f* fortification
fortificante *m* tonic
fortificar §73 *tr* to fortify
fortín *m* small fort; bunker
fortui•to -ta *adj* fortuitous
fortuna *f* fortune; **correr fortuna** (naut) to ride the storm; **de fortuna** makeshift; **por fortuna** fortunately; **probar fortuna** to try one's luck
fortunón *m* windfall
forza•do -da *adj* forced; (*p.ej., entrada*) forcible; (*sonrisa*) (fig) forced; (*trabajos*) hard ‖ *m* galley slave
forzar §35 *tr* to force
forzo•so -sa *adj* unavoidable; strong, husky; (*trabajos*) hard; (*aterrizaje; marcha*) forced ‖ *f* — **hacer la forzosa a** to put the squeeze on
forzu•do -da *adj* strong, husky, robust
fosa *f* grave; (aut) pit; **fosa de los leones** (Bib) lions' den
fosar *tr* to dig a ditch around
fos•co -ca *adj* dark; cross, sullen; (*tiempo*) threatening
fosfato *m* phosphate
fosforera *f* matchbox
fosforescente *adj* phosphorescent
fósforo *m* (*cuerpo simple*) phosphorus; match; **fósforo de seguridad** safety match
fósil *adj & m* fossil
foso *m* hole, pit; (*que rodea un castillo o fortaleza*) moat; (theat & aut) pit
fotingo *m* jalopy, jitney
foto *f* photo; **foto fija** still
fotocopia *f* photocopy
fotocopiador *m* or **fotocopiadora** *f* photocopier
fotocopiar *tr* to photocopy
fotodrama *m* photoplay
fotofija *m* photo-finish camera
fotogéni•co -ca *adj* photogenic
fotograbado *m* photoengraving
fotografía *f* (*arte*) photography; (*imagen, retrato*) photograph; photograph gallery; **fotografía aérea** aerial photograph(y)
fotografiar §77 *tr & intr* to photograph
fotógra•fo -fa *mf* photographer
fotómetro *m* light meter
fotoperiodismo *m* photojournalism
fotopila *f* solar battery
fotostatar *tr & intr* to photostat
fotóstato *m* photostat
fototubo *m* phototube
fra. *abbr* **factura**
frac *m* (*pl* **-fraques**) full-dress coat, tails, swallow-tailed coat
fracasar *intr* to fail; break to pieces
fracaso *m* failure; breakdown, crash
fracción *f* fraction
fraccionar *tr* to divide up; break up
fracciona•rio -ria *adj* fractional

fractura _f_ fracture; breaking open, breaking in

fracturar _tr_ to fracture; break open, break in || _ref (p.ej., un brazo)_ to fracture

fragancia _f_ fragrance; good reputation

fragante _adj_ fragrant; **en fragante** (archaic) in the act

fragata _f_ frigate; **fragata ligera** corvette

frágil _adj_ fragile; _(quebradizo; que cae fácilmente en el pecado)_ frail; (Mex) poor, needy

fragmento _m_ fragment

fragor _m_ crash, roar, thunder

fragoro•so -sa _adj_ noisy, thundering

fragosidad _f_ roughness, unevenness; _(de un bosque)_ thickness, denseness; rough road

frago•so -sa _adj_ rough, uneven; thick, dense; noisy, thundering

fragua _f_ forge

fraguar §10 _tr_ to forge; hatch, scheme; _(mentiras)_ forge || _intr_ to forge; _(la cal, el cemento)_ set

fraile _m_ friar, monk; **fraile de misa y olla** friarling; **fraile rezador** praying mantis

frambesia _f_ (pathol) yaws

frambuesa _f_ raspberry

frambueso _m_ raspberry bush

francachela _f_ feast, spread; carousal, high time; (Arg) excessive familiarity

francalete _m_ strap with buckle

fran•cés -cesa _adj_ French; **despedirse a la francesa** to take French leave || _m_ Frenchman; _(idioma)_ French || _f_ Frenchwoman

francesada _f_ French remark; French invasion of Spain in 1808

francesilla _f_ French roll; (bot) turban buttercup

Francia _f_ France

francisca•no -na _adj_ & _mf_ Franciscan

francmasón _m_ Freemason

francmasonería _f_ Freemasonry

fran•co -ca _adj_ generous, liberal; outspoken, candid, frank; _(camino)_ free, open; _(suelo)_ loamy; free, gratis; Frankish; **franco a bordo** free on board; **franco de porte** postpaid || _mf_ Frank || _m_ franc; _(idioma)_ Frankish

francolín _m_ black partridge

franco•te -ta _adj_ frank, wholehearted

francotirador _m_ sniper

franela _f_ flannel

frangente _m_ accident, mishap

frangir §27 _tr_ to break up, break to pieces

frangollar _tr_ to bungle, to botch

frangollo _m_ porridge; mash for cattle; bungle, botch

franja _f_ fringe; strip, band; (opt) fringe

franjar _tr_ to fringe

franquear _tr_ to exempt; cross, go over; grant; free, enfranchise; _(un camino)_ open, clear; _(una carta)_ frank, pay the postage for; **a franquear en destino** postage will be paid by addressee || _ref_ to yield; **franquearse con** to open one's heart to

franqueo _m_ freeing, liberation; postage; **franqueo concertado** postage permit

franqueza _f_ generosity; candidness, frankness; freedom

franquía _f_ (naut) sea room; **en franquía** (naut & fig) in the open

franquicia _f_ franchise; exemption, tax exemption; **franquicia postal** franking privilege

franquista _mf_ Francoist

frasca _f_ leaves, twigs, brush; (Guat, Mex) high jinks

frasco _m_ flask; _(p.ej., de aceitunas)_ jar

frase _f_ phrase; _(oración cabal)_ sentence; idiom; **frase hecha** saying, proverb; cliché; **gastar frases** to talk all around the subject

frasear _tr_ to phrase || _intr_ to talk all around the subject

frasquera _f_ bottle frame, liquor case

fratás _m_ plastering trowel

fraternal _adj_ brotherly, fraternal

fraternidad _f_ fraternity, brotherhood

fraternizar §60 _intr_ to fraternize

frater•no -na _adj_ brotherly, fraternal

fraude _m_ fraud; **fraude fiscal** tax evasion

fraudulen•to -ta _adj_ fraudulent

fray _m_ Fra

frecuencia _f_ frequency; **alta frecuencia** high frequency; **baja frecuencia** low frequency; **con frecuencia** frequently

frecuentar _tr_ _(ir con frecuencia a)_ to frequent; keep up, repeat

frecuente _adj_ frequent; _(usual)_ common

fregadero _m_ sink, kitchen sink

frega•do -da _adj_ annoying, bothersome; cunning; (SAm) stubborn; (P-R) brazen || _m_ scrubbing; mopping; mess

frega•dor -dora _mf_ dishwasher

fregar §66 _tr_ _(restregar)_ to rub; _(restregar para limpiar)_ scrub, scour; _(el pavimento)_ mop; _(los platos)_ wash; annoy, bother

fregasue•los _m_ (pl -los) mop, floor mop

frega•triz _f_ (pl -trices) var of **fregona**

fre•gón -gona _adj_ annoying, bothersome; brazen || _f_ _(criada que friega el pavimento)_ scrub woman; _(criada que lava la vajilla)_ dishwasher, scullery maid

freiduría _f_ fried-fish shop

freír §58 & §83 _tr_ to fry; bore to death || _intr_ to fry; **dejarle a uno freír en su aceite** to let someone stew in his own juice || _ref_ to fry; be bored to death; **freírsele a** to try to fool, scheme to deceive

fréjol _m_ kidney bean

frenar _tr_ to bridle, check, hold back; _(un automóvil, tren)_ brake

frene•sí _m_ (pl -síes) frenzy

frenéti•co -ca _adj_ frantic; mad, furious; wild

frenillo _m_ muzzle; **no tener frenillo en la lengua** to not mince one's words

freno _m_ _(parte de la brida)_ bit; _(aparato para parar el movimiento de los vehículos)_ brake; (fig) brake, check, curb; **freno de contrapedal** coaster brake; **freno de disco** disk brake; **freno de tambor** drum brake; **morder el freno** to champ the bit

frenología _f_ phrenology

frentazo _m_ (Mex) rebuff

frente _m_ & _f_ _(de un edificio)_ front || _m_ (mil)

fo
fr

front, front line; **al frente de** at the head of, in charge of ‖ *f* brow, forehead; face, front; head; **a frente** straight ahead; **arrugar la frente** to knit the brow; **de frente** straight ahead; abreast; **en frente de** in front of; against, opposed to; **frente a** in front of; compared with

freo *m* channel, strait

fresa *f* strawberry; (*de fresadora*) cutter

fresado *m* milling, millwork

fresadora *f* milling machine

fresal *m* strawberry patch

fresar *tr* to mill

fresca *f* fresh air; cool part of the day; blunt remark, piece of one's mind

fresca•chón -chona *adj* bouncing, buxom; (*viento*) brisk

fresca•les *mf* (*pl* -**les**) forward sort of person

frescamente *adv* recently; cheekily, brazenly

fres•co -ca *adj* (*acabado de hacer o suceder*) fresh; (*moderadamente frío*) cool; (*pintura*) fresh, wet; (*tela, vestido*) light; calm, unruffled; buxom, ruddy; cheeky, fresh; **estar fresco** to be in a fine pinch; **quedarse tan fresco** to show no offense, be indifferent or unconcerned ‖ *m* coolness; fresh air; fresh bacon; (*fa*) fresco; cool drink; **al fresco** in the open air; in the night air; **hace fresco** it is cool; **tomar el fresco** to go out for some fresh air ‖ *f* see **fresca**

frescor *m* freshness; cool, coolness

fresco•te -ta *adj* plump and rosy

frescura *f* freshness; cool, coolness; unconcern, offhand manner; sharp reply; cheek, impudence

fresno *m* ash tree; (*madera*) ash

fresquera *f* meat closet, food cabinet, icebox

fresquería *f* ice-cream parlor, soft-drink store

fresque•ro -ra *mf* fish dealer; (Peru) soft-drink vendor ‖ *f* see **fresquera**

freudismo *m* Freudianism

freza *f* dung; spawning; hole made by game

frialdad *f* coldness; carelessness, laxity; stupidity; (*pathol*) frigidity; (*pathol*) impotence; (*fig*) coolness, coldness

friáti•co -ca *adj* chilly; awkward, stupid; (*ropa*) cold

fricar §73 *tr* to rub

fricasé *m* fricassee

fricción *f* rubbing; massage; (*pharm*) rubbing liniment; (*phys*) friction

friccionar *tr* to rub; massage

friega *f* rubbing, massage; annoyance, bother; flogging, whipping

frigidez *f* frigidity; coldness

frígi•do -da *adj* frigid; cold

frigorífero *m* freezing chamber

frigorífi•co -ca *adj* refrigerating; cold-storage ‖ *m* refrigerator; (Arg, Urug) packing house, cold-storage plant

fríjol *m* bean, kidney bean; **fríjol de media luna** Lima bean; **¡fríjoles!** (W-I) absolutely no!

frijolear *tr* (Guat) to annoy, molest

frijolizar §60 *tr* (Peru) to bewitch

frí•o -a *adj* cold; dull, weak, colorless; (*fig*) cold, cool ‖ *m* cold; **fríos** chills and fever;

coger frío to catch cold; **hace frío** it is cold; **tener frío** (*una persona*) to be cold; **tomar frío** to catch cold

friole•ro -ra *adj* chilly ‖ *f* trifle, trinket; snack, bite

frisar *tr* to rub; to fit, fasten; (naut) to calk ‖ *intr* to agree, get along; **frisar con** or **en** to border on

friso *m* dado, wainscot; (archit) frieze

fri•són -sona *adj & mf* Frisian

fritada *f* fry

fri•to -ta *adj* fried; bored to death ‖ *m* fry; (Ven) daily bread

fritura *f* fry

frívo•lo -la *adj* frivolous; trifling

fronda *f* leaf; (*de helecho*) frond; sling-shaped bandage; **frondas** frondage, foliage

frondo•so -sa *adj* leafy; woodsy

frontalera *f* yoke pad

frontera *f* frontier, border; front, façade

fronteri•zo -za *adj* frontier, border; facing, opposite

fronte•ro -ra *adj* frontier, border; facing, opposite; front ‖ *f* see **frontera**

frontín *m* (Mex) flip, fillip

fron•tis *m* (*pl* -**tis**) front, façade

frontispicio *m* frontispiece; (coll) face

frontón *m* (*encima de puertas o ventanas*) gable, pediment; pelota court; pelota wall; handball court

frotamiento *m* rubbing; (phys) friction

frotar *tr* to rub; to chafe ‖ *ref* to rub

fro•tis *m* (*pl* -**tis**) (bact) smear

fructuo•so -sa *adj* fruitful

frugal *adj* (*en comer y beber*) temperate; (*no muy abundante*) frugal

fruición *f* enjoyment, satisfaction; (*del mal ajeno*) evil satisfaction

fruiti•vo -va *adj* enjoyable

frunce *m* shirr, shirring, gathering

frunci•do -da *adj* grim, gruff, stern; (Chile) temperate; (Chile) sad, gloomy ‖ *m* shirr, shirring, gathering

fruncir §36 *tr* to wrinkle, pucker, pleat; (*la frente*) knit; (*los labios*) curl, purse; (*la verdad*) twist, disguise; shirr, gather ‖ *ref* to affect modesty, be shocked

fruslería *f* trifle, trinket; (coll) futility, triviality

frusle•ro -ra *adj* futile, trivial, trifling ‖ *m* rolling pin

frustrar *tr* to frustrate, thwart

fruta *f* fruit; **fruta del tiempo** fruit in season; **fruta de sartén** fritter, pancake; **frutas** fruit; **frutas agrias** citrus fruit

frutal *adj* fruit ‖ *m* fruit tree

frutería *f* fruit store

frute•ro -ra *adj* fruit ‖ *mf* fruit dealer ‖ *m* fruit dish; tray of imitation fruit

frutilla *f* (*del rosario*) bead; Chilean strawberry; gumdrop

fruto *m* (bot & fig) fruit; **fruto de bendición** legitimate offspring; **frutos** produce; **sacar fruto de** to derive benefit from

fu *interj* faugh! fie!; (*del gato*) spit!; **ni fu ni fa** neither this nor that

fucilazo *m* heat lightning, sheet lightning

fuego *m* fire; (*para encender un cigarrillo*) light; (*de arma de fuego*) firing; lighthouse, beacon; hearth, home; rash, eruption; sore, fever blister; **abrir fuego** to open fire; **echar fuego** to blow up, hit the ceiling; **¡fuego!** fire!; **fuego fatuo** will-o'-the-wisp; **fuego graneado** or **nutrido** drumfire; **fuegos artificiales** fireworks; **hacer fuego** to fire, shoot; **marcar a fuego** to brand; **pegar fuego a** to set fire to, set on fire; **poner a fuego y sangre** to lay waste; **prenderse fuego** to catch on fire; **romper fuego** to open fire; stir up a row; **tocar a fuego** to sound the fire alarm

fuelle *m* fold, pucker, wrinkle; (*instrumento para soplar*) bellows; (*cubierta de coche*) folding carriage top; wind clouds; (*persona soplona*) gossip, talebearer

fuente *f* fountain, spring; public hydrant; font, baptismal font; platter, tray; (fig) source; **beber en buenas fuentes** to have good sources of information; **fuente de gasolina** gasoline pump; **fuente de sodas** soda fountain; **fuente para beber** drinking fountain; **fuentes termales** hot springs

fuer *m* — **a fuer de** as a, by way of

fuera *adv* out, outside; away, out of town; **desde fuera** from the outside; **fuera de** outside of; away from; out of; aside from; in addition to; **fuera de que** aside from the fact that; **fuera de sí** beside oneself; **por fuera** on the outside

fuera-bordo *m* outboard motor

fuere•ño -ña *mf* (Mex) hick, stranger

fuero *m* law, statute; code of laws; jurisdiction; exemption, privilege; **fuero interior** conscience, inmost heart; **fueros** pride, arrogance

fuerte *adj* strong; hard; loud; heavy; **hacerse fuerte** to stick to one's guns; (mil) to hole up, to dig in ‖ *adv* hard; loud ‖ *m* fort, fortress; forte, strong point

fuerza *f* force, strength, power; (*de un ejército*) main body; literal meaning; (phys) force; **a fuerza de** by dint of, by force of; **a la fuerza** forcibly, by force; **a viva fuerza** by main strength; **fuerza aérea** air force; **fuerza de agua** water power; **fuerza de sangre** animal power; **fuerza mayor** (law) force majeure, act of God; **fuerza motriz** motive power; **fuerza pública** police; **fuerza viva** kinetic energy; **hacer fuerza** to strain, struggle; to carry weight; **por fuerza** perforce, necessarily; **ser fuerza +** *inf* to be necessary to + *inf*

fuete *m* whip

fufar *intr* (el gato) to spit

fuga *f* flight; (*salida de un gas o líquido*) leak; ardor, vigor; (mus) fugue; **darse a la fuga** to take flight, run away; **fuga de capitales** capital flight; **poner en fuga** to put to flight

fugar §44 *ref* to flee, escape, run away

fu•gaz *adj* (*pl* **-gaces**) fleeting, passing; (*estrella*) shooting

fugiti•vo -va *adj & mf* fugitive

fugui•llas *m* (*pl* **-llas**) (coll) hustler

fula•no -na *mf* so-and-so

fulcro *m* fulcrum

fulgor *m* brilliance, radiance

fulgurar *intr* to flash

fulmicotón *m* guncotton

fulminar *tr* to strike with lightning; strike dead; (*censuras, amenazas, etc.*) thunder; (*balas o bombas*) hurl

fullería *f* trickery, cheating

fulle•ro -ra *adj* crooked, cheating ‖ *mf* crook, cheat; **fullero de naipes** cardsharp

fumada *f* puff, whiff

fumadero *m* smoking room; **fumadero de opio** opium den

fuma•dor -dora *adj* smoking ‖ *mf* smoker

fumar *tr* to smoke ‖ *intr* to smoke; **fumar en pipa** to smoke a pipe; **se prohibe fumar** no smoking ‖ *ref* to squander; stay away from; (*la clase*) cut

fumarada *f* (*de humo*) puff; (*de tabaco*) pipeful

fumigación *f* fumigation; **fumigación aérea** crop dusting

fumigar §44 *tr* to fumigate

fumista *m* stove or heater repairman; stove or heater dealer

fumistería *f* stove or heater shop

fumo•so -sa *adj* smoky

funámbu•lo -la *mf* ropewalker

función *f* function; duty, office, function; (*espectáculo teatral*) show, performance; **entrar en funciones** to take office, take up one's duties; **función benéfica** charitable performance; **función de aficionados** amateur performance; **función de títeres** puppet show; **función secundaria** side show

funcional *adj* functional

funcionariado *m* bureaucracy

funcionario *m* functionary, public official, civil servant

funcione•ro -ra *adj* officious, fussy

fund. *abbr* **fundador**

funda *f* case, sheath, envelope, slip; (*para una espada*) scabbard; (*para proteger los muebles*) slip cover; **funda de almohada** pillowcase; **funda de asientos** seat cover; **funda de gafas** spectacle case

fundación *f* foundation

fundadamente *adv* with good reason; on good authority

funda•dor -dora *adj* founding ‖ *mf* founder

fundamental *adj* fundamental

fundamentar *tr* to lay the foundations of

fundamento *m* foundation; (*razón, motivo*) grounds, reason; basis; reliability, sense; (Col) skirt

fundar *tr* to found, base ‖ *ref* — **fundarse en** to be based on; base one's opinion on

fundente *adj* molten ‖ *m* flux

fundería *f* foundry

fundible *adj* fusible

fundición *f* (*acción de fundir*) founding; (*fábrica*) foundry; (*herrería*) forge; (*hierro colado*) cast iron; (typ) font

fundi•do -da *adj* melted; (*individuo*) ruined; (elec) shorted, blown out

fundidor *m* founder, foundryman

fundillo m (Cuba, Mex) behind, buttocks

fundir tr (p.ej., metales) to found; (campanas, estatuas) cast; (derretir para purificar) smelt; (colores) mix; (un filamento eléctrico) burn out ‖ intr to smelt ‖ ref to melt; fuse; (un filamento eléctrico) burn out; fail, founder; (fig) to fuse, merge

fúnebre adj (marcha, procesión) funeral; (triste) funereal

funeral adj funeral; (triste, lúgubre) funereal ‖ m funeral; **funerales** funeral

funerala — **a la funerala** (mil) with arms inverted (as a token of mourning)

funera•rio **-ria** adj funeral ‖ m mortician, funeral director ‖ f (empresa) undertaking establishment; (local) funeral home, funeral parlor

funes•to **-ta** adj ill-fated; sad, sorrowful; (p.ej., influencia) baneful

fungir §27 intr (CAm, Mex) to act, function

fungo m (pathol) fungus

fungo•so **-sa** adj fungous

funicular adj & m funicular

funique adj awkward; dull, tiresome

furgón m wagon, truck; (rr) freight car, boxcar; (rr) caboose

furgoneta f light truck, delivery truck

furia f fury

furibun•do **-da** adj furious, frenzied

furio•so **-sa** adj furious; (muy grande) terrific, tremendous

furor m rage, furor; **causar furor** to make a splash, cause a stir; **hacer furor** to be all the rage

furti•vo **-va** adj furtive; sneaky, poaching

furúnculo m boil

fusa f (mus) demisemiquaver

fus•co **-ca** adj dark

fusela•do **-da** adj streamlined

fuselaje m fuselage

fusible adj fusible ‖ m (elec) fuse

fusil m gun, rifle

fusilar tr to shoot, execute; plagiarize

fusilazo m (tiro de fusil) gunshot, rifle shot; (relámpago sin ruido) heat lightning, sheet lightning

fusilería f rifle corps; rifles, guns; (descarga) fusillade

fusión f fusion; melting; **fusión de empresas** (com) merger

fusionar tr & ref to fuse, merge

fusta f brushwood, twigs; teamster's whip

fustán m fustian; cotton petticoat; (Ven) skirt

fuste m wood, timber; shaft, stem; (fig) importance, substance

fustigar §44 tr to whip, lash; rebuke harshly

fútbol m football; soccer, **fútbol asociación** soccer

fútil adj futile, trifling, inconsequential

futilidad f futility

futre m (SAm) dandy, dude

futu•ro **-ra** adj future ‖ m future; (gram) future; fiancé; **futuros** (com) futures ‖ f fiancée

G

G, g (ge) f eighth letter of the Spanish alphabet

G. abbr gracia

gaba•cho **-cha** adj & mf Pyrenean; (coll) Frenchy ‖ m (coll) Frenchified Spanish (language)

gabán m overcoat

gabardina f gabardine; raincoat with belt

gabarra f barge, lighter

gabarro m (en una piedra) nodule; (en un tejido) flaw, defect; mistake

gabinete m cabinet; (de médico, abogado, etc.) office; studio, study; laboratory; (Col) glassed-in balcony; **de gabinete** armchair, theoretical; **gabinete de aseo** washroom; **gabinete de lectura** reading room

gablete m gable

gacela f gazelle

gaceta f government journal; newspaper; **mentir más que la gaceta** to lie like a trooper

gacetilla f town talk, gossip column; short item

gacetillero m gossip columnist

gacetista mf newspaper reader; newsmonger

gacilla f (CAm) safety pin

gacha f watery mass; (Col, Ven) earthenware bowl; **gachas** mush, pap; porridge; mud; **gachas de avena** oatmeal; **hacerse unas gachas** to be mushy

ga•cho **-cha** adj turned down; flopping; (sombrero) slouch; **a gachas** on all fours ‖ f see **gacha**

gachumbo m (SAm) hard fruit shell

gachu•pín **-pina** mf (CAm, Mex) Spanish settler in Latin America

gaéli•co **-ca** adj Gaelic ‖ mf Gael ‖ m Gaelic (language)

gafa f clamp; (enganche de los anteojos) temple; **gafas** glasses; **gafas de sol** or **gafas para sol** sunglasses

gafe m jinx, hoodoo

ga•fo **-fa** adj claw-handed; foot-sore ‖ f see **gafa**

gaguear intr to stutter

gaita f hornpipe; hurdy-gurdy; chore, hard task; neck; **gaita gallega** bagpipe

gaite•ro **-ra** adj flashy, gaudy ‖ m piper, bagpipe player

gajes mpl wages, salary; **gajes del oficio** cares of office, occupational annoyances

gajo *m* broken branch; (*de un racimo de uvas*) small stem; (*división interior de ciertas frutas*) slice; (*de horca*) tine, prong; (*ramal de montes*) spur; curl

gala *f* fine clothes; (*lo más selecto*) choice, cream; tip, fee; **de gala** full-dress; **hacer gala de** to glory in; **llevarse la gala** to win approval

galafate *m* slick thief

galai‧co -ca *adj* Galician

galán *m* good-looking fellow; lover, gallant, ladies' man; (*el que sirve de escolta a una dama*) escort, cavalier; (theat) leading man; **galán joven** (theat) juvenile; **primer galán** (theat) leading man

galancete *m* (theat) juvenile

gala‧no -na *adj* elegant, graceful; spruce, smartly dressed; rich, tasteful

galante *adj* (*con las damas*) gallant; (*con los caballeros*) flirtatious; (*mujer*) wanton, loose

galantear *tr* to court, woo, make love to; sue, entreat

galantería *f* gallantry; charm, elegance; generosity

galanura *f* charm, elegance

galápago *m* pond tortoise; (*del arado*) moldboard; light saddle; ingot

galardón *m* reward, recompense

galardonar *tr* to reward, recompense

galaxia *f* galaxy

galbana *f* laziness; shiftlessness

galbano‧so -sa *adj* lazy; phlegmatic

gale‧no -na *adj* gentle; mild ‖ *m* (coll) physician, doctor

galeón *m* (naut) galleon

galeote *m* galley slave

galera *f* covered wagon; women's jail; (*de hospital*) ward; (naut & typ) galley

galerada *f* wagonload; (typ) galley; (typ) galley proof

galería *f* gallery; **galería de tiro** shooting gallery; **galerías** department store; **hablar para la galería** to play to the gallery

galerna *f* stormy wind from the northwest (*on the northern coast of Spain*)

Gales *f* Wales; **el país de Gales** Wales; **la Nueva Gales del Sur** New South Wales

ga‧lés -lesa *adj* Welsh ‖ *m* Welshman; Welsh (*language*) ‖ *f* Welsh woman

galguear *intr* (CAm, Mex, Arg) to be hungry

gal‧go -ga *adj* (Col) sweet-toothed ‖ *m* greyhound ‖ *f* greyhound bitch; rolling stone; mange, rash

Galia, la Gaul

gálibo *m* template, pattern; (rr) gabarit

galicismo *m* Gallicism

gáli‧co -ca *adj* Gallic ‖ *m* syphilis; syphilitic

galillo *m* uvula; gullet

galimatí‧as *m* (*pl* **-as**) gibberish, nonsense; confusion

galiparia *f* Frenchified Spanish

ga‧lo -la *adj* Gaulish ‖ *mf* Gaul ‖ *m* Gaulish (*language*)

galocha *f* clog, wooden shoe

galón *m* braid, galloon; (*medida para líquidos*) gallon; (mil) chevron, stripe

galopar *intr* to gallop

galope *m* gallop; **a galope** at a gallop; in great haste; **a galope tendido** on the run

galopea‧do -da *adj* hasty, sketchy ‖ *m* beating, punching

galopear *intr* to gallop

galopillo *m* scullion, kitchen boy

galopín *m* ragamuffin; (*hombre taimado*) wise guy; (naut) cabin boy

galpón *m* (SAm) iron shed; (Col) tile works

galvanizar §60 *tr* to electroplate; galvanize

galvanoplastia *f* electroplating

galladura *f* tread (*of egg*)

gallardete *m* streamer, pennant

gallardía *f* gallantry; elegance; nobility; generosity

gallar‧do -da *adj* gallant; elegant; noble; generous; (*temporal*) fierce

gallear *intr* to stand out, excel; shout, yell, threaten

galle‧go -ga *adj* & *mf* Galician

gallera *f* cockpit

galleta *f* hardtack, ship biscuit; cracker; little pitcher; slap

gallina *adj* chicken-hearted ‖ *mf* chicken-hearted person ‖ *f* hen; **estar como gallina en corral ajeno** to be like a fish out of water; **gallina ciega** blindman's buff; **gallina de Guinea** guinea fowl

gallinería *f* poultry shop; cowardice

galline‧ro -ra *mf* poultry dealer ‖ *m* hencoop, henhouse; poultry basket; top gallery; babel, madhouse

gallipavo *m* turkey; sour note

gallito *m* (*el que figura sobre los demás*) somebody; **gallito del lugar** cock of the walk

gallo *m* cock, rooster; false note, sour note; boss; frog in the throat; (box) bantamweight; (Col, C-R, Mex) strong man; **gallo de bosque** wood grouse; **gallo de pelea** gamecock; **tener mucho gallo** to be cocky

gallofa *f* vegetables; French roll; talk, gossip

gallofear *intr* to beg, bum, loaf around

gallofe‧ro -ra *adj* begging, loafing ‖ *mf* beggar, loafer

gama *f* doe, female fallow deer; (mus & fig) gamut

gamberrismo *m* gangsterism, rowdyism

gambe‧rro -rra *adj* & *mf* libertine ‖ *m* hoodlum, tough, rowdy

gambeta *f* crosscaper; caper, prance

gambito *m* gambit

gamo *m* buck, male fallow deer

gamón *m* asphodel

gamonal *m* field of asphodel; boss

gamuza *f* chamois

gana *f* desire; will; **darle a uno la gana de** to feel like, e.g., **le da la gana de trabajar** he feels like working; **de buena gana** willingly; **de gana** in earnest; willingly; **de mala gana** unwillingly; **tener ganas de** to feel like, to have a mind to

ganadería *f* cattle, livestock; brand, stock; cattle raising; cattle ranch

ganade‧ro -ra *adj* cattle, livestock ‖ *mf* cattle breeder; cattle dealer ‖ *m* cattleman

fu
ga

ganado *m* cattle, livestock; **ganado caballar** horses; **ganado cabrío** goats; **ganado lanar** sheep; **ganado mayor** large farm animals (*cows, bulls, horses, and mules*); **ganado menor** small farm animals (*sheep, goats, pigs*); **ganado menudo** young cattle; **ganado moreno** swine; **ganado ovejuno** sheep; **ganado porcino** swine; **ganado vacuno** cattle

gana•dor -dora *adj* winning; earning; hardworking ‖ *mf* winner; earner

ganancia *f* gain, profit; (Guat, Mex) extra, bonus; **ganancias y pérdidas** profit and loss

ganancial *adj* profit

ganancio•so -sa *adj* gainful, profitable; earning ‖ *mf* earner

ganapán *m* errand boy; boor

ganapierde *m & f* giveaway

ganar *tr* (*dinero trabajando*) to earn; (*la victoria luchando*) win; (*beneficios en los negocios*) gain; (*a una persona en una contienda*) beat, defeat; (*aventajar*) excel; (*la voluntad de una persona*) win over; (*alcanzar*) reach; **ganar algo a alguien** to win something from someone; **ganar de comer** to earn a living ‖ *intr* to earn; (*mejorar*) improve ‖ *ref* to win over; **ganarse la vida** to earn a livelihood

ganchero *m* log driver; (Chile) odd-jobber; (Ecuad) gentle mount

ganchillo *m* crochet needle; crochet, crochet work; **hacer ganchillo** to crochet

gancho *m* hook;· shepherd's crook; coaxer; procurer, pimp; hairpin; (Col, Ecuad) lady's saddle; **gancho de botalones** (naut) gooseneck; **echar el gancho a** to hook in, to land; **tener gancho** (*una mujer*) to have a way with the men

gandaya *f* (coll) bumming, loafing

gandujar *tr* to pleat, shirr

gan•dul -dula *adj* loafing, idling ‖ *mf* loafer, idler

gandulear *intr* to loaf, idle

ganfo•rro -rra *mf* scoundrel

ganga *f* bargain

ganglio *m* ganglion

gangocho *m* burlap

gango•so -sa *adj* snuffling, nasal

gangrena *f* gangrene

gangrenar *tr & ref* to gangrene

gángster *m* gunman, gangster

gangsteril *adj* gangster(like)

gangsterismo *m* gangsterism; mobsterism

ganguear *intr* to snuffle, talk through the nose

gangue•ro -ra *adj* bargain-hunting; self-seeking ‖ *mf* bargain hunter

gano•so -sa *adj* desirous; (*caballo*) (Chile) spirited, fiery

gan•so -sa *mf* dope, dullard ‖ *m* goose; gander; **ganso bravo** wild goose ‖ *f* female goose

Gante Ghent

ganzúa *f* (*garfio*) picklock, lock pick; (*persona*) picklock; pumper (*of secrets*)

gañán *m* farm hand; rough, husky fellow

gañido *m* yelp; croak

gañir §12 *intr* (*el perro*) to yelp; (*p.ej., el cuervo*) croak

garabatear *tr* to scribble ‖ *intr* to hook; beat about the bush; scribble

garabato *m* hook; pothook; scribbling; weeding hoe; (*bozal*) muzzle; (*de una mujer*) winsomeness; **garabato de carnicero** meathook; **garabatos** wiggling of hands and fingers

garabato•so -sa *adj* full of scrawls; winsome

garage *m* or **garaje** *m* garage

garagista *m* garbage man

garambaina *f* gaudy trimming; **garambainas** simpering, smirking; (coll) scribble

garante *adj* responsible ‖ *mf* guarantor, voucher

garantía *f* guarantee, guaranty; warranty; **garantia anticorrosión** antirust warranty

garantir §1 *tr* to guarantee

garantizar §60 *tr* to guarantee

garañón *m* stud jackass; stud camel; stallion

garapiña *f* icing, sugar-coating; iced pineapple drink

garapiñar *tr* to ice, sugar-coat; candy

garapiñera *f* ice-cream freezer

garbanzo *m* chickpea; **garbanzo negro** (fig) black sheep

garbeo *m* walk; promenade

garbillar *tr* to sieve, screen riddle

garbillo *s* sieve, screen; riddled ore

garbo *m* jauntiness, grace, fine bearing; generosity

garbo•so -sa *adj* jaunty, graceful, spruce, sprightly; generous

gardu•ño -ña *mf* (archaic) sneak thief ‖ *f* stone marten, beech marten

garete *m* — **al garete** (naut) adrift

garfa *f* claw

garfio *m* hook, gaff

gargajear *intr* to cough up phlegm, hawk

gargajo *m* phlegm

garganta *f* throat; (*de un río, una vasija, etc.*) neck, throat; (*del pie*) instep; (*entre montañas*) ravine, gorge; (*del arado*) sheath; (*de una polea*) groove; (archit) shaft; **tener buena garganta** to have a good voice

gargantear *intr* to warble

gargantilla *f* necklace

gárgara *f* gargling; **gárgaras** (*líquido*) gargle; **hacer gárgaras** to gargle

gargarear *intr* to gargle

gargarismo *m* gargling; (*líquido*) gargle

gargarizar §60 *intr* to gargle

gárgola *f* gargoyle

garguero *m* gullet; (*caña del pulmón*) windpipe

garita *f* sentry box; porter's lodge; (*de una fortificación*) watchtower; railroad-crossing box; privy (*with one seat*); **garita de centinela** sentry box; **garita de señales** (rr) signal tower

garito *m* gambling den

garlito *m* fish trap; trap, snare

garlopa *f* jack plane, trying plane

garnar *intr* to drizzle

garra f claw, talon; catch, hook; **caer en las garras de** to fall into the clutches of

garrafa f carafe, decanter; **garrafa corchera** demijohn

garrafal adj awful, terrible

garrafiñar tr to snatch

garrafón m carboy, demijohn

garramar tr to snitch

garranchuelo m crab grass

garrapata f cattle tick, sheep tick; (mil) disabled horse; (Chile) little runt; (Mex) slut

garrapatear intr to scrawl, scribble

garrapato m pothook, scrawl; **garrapatos** scrawl

garri•do -da adj handsome, elegant

garroba f carob bean

garrocha f goad; (sport) pole

garrotazo m blow with a club

garrote m club, cudgel; garrote (method of execution; iron collar used for such execution); (Mex) brake; **dar garrote a** to garrote

garrote•ro -ra adj (Chile) stingy ‖ m (Mex) brakeman

garrotillo m croup

garrucha f pulley, sheave

gárru•lo -la adj chirping; (hablador) garrulous; (arroyo) babbling; (viento) rustling

garúa drizzle

garuar §21 intr to drizzle

garulla f mob, rabble

garza f heron; **garza real** gray heron

gar•zo -za adj blue ‖ f see **garza**

garzón m boy, youth; suitor; woman chaser

gas m gas; **gas de alumbrado** illuminating gas; **gas exhilarante** or **hilarante** laughing gas; **gas lacrimógeno** tear gas; **gas mostaza** mustard gas

gasa f gauze, chiffon; (tira de gasa negra con que se rodea el sombrero en señal de luto) hatband

Gascuña f Gascony

gasear tr to gas

gaseo•so -sa adj gaseous ‖ f soda water, carbonated water

gasificar §73 tr to gasify; exalt, elate ‖ ref to gasify

gasista m gas fitter; (Chile) gasworker

gasoducto m gas pipe line

gasógeno m gas generator, gas producer; mixture of benzine and alcohol used for lighting and cleaning

gas-oil m diesel oil

gasolina f gasoline

gasolinera f motor boat; gas station, filling station

gasómetro m gasholder, gas tank

gastadero m waste

gasta•do -da adj worn-out; used up; spent; (chiste) crummy, corny

gasta•dor -dora adj & mf spendthrift ‖ m convict; (mil) sapper, pioneer

gastadura f worn spot

gastar tr (dinero, tiempo) to spend; (en cosas inútiles) waste; (echar a perder con el uso) wear out; (consumir) use up; (p.ej., una barba) wear; (un coche) keep; **gastarlas** to act, behave ‖ intr to spend ‖ ref to wear; wear out; become used up; waste away

gasto m cost, expense; wear; **gastos de conservación** or **de entretenimiento** upkeep; **gastos de explotación** operating expenses; **gastos menudos** petty expenses; **hacer el gasto** to do most of the talking; to be the subject of conversation; **hacer frente a los gastos** to meet expenses; **meterse en gastos con** to go to the expense of

gasto•so -sa adj wasteful, extravagant

gástri•co -ca adj gastric

gastronomía f gastronomy

gastróno•mo -ma mf gourmet

gata f she-cat; low-hanging cloud; Madrid woman; (Mex) maid, servant girl; **a gatas** on all fours, on hands and knees

gatada f catty act

gatatumba f faked attention, fake emotion, faked pain

gatazo m gyp

gatea•do -da adj catlike; grained, striped ‖ m crawling, climbing; scratching, clawing

gatear tr to scratch, claw; snitch ‖ intr to crawl, climb

gatera f cathole; (naut) hawsehole

gatería f cats; gang of toughs; fake humility

gate•ro -ra adj full of cats ‖ mf cat lover ‖ f see **gatera**

gates•co -ca adj catlike, feline

gatillo m (de arma de fuego) trigger; little pickpocket

gato m cat; tomcat; (instrumento para levantar pesos) jack, lifting jack; sly fellow; sneak thief; native of Madrid; **gato montés** wildcat; **gato rodante** dolly; **vender gato por liebre** to gyp, cheat

gatopardo m cheetah

gauchada f (SAm) sly trick; (SAm) good turn

gauchaje m (SAm) gathering of Gauchos

gauches•co -ca adj Gaucho

gau•cho -cha adj (SAm) Gaucho; (Arg, Chile) sly, crafty ‖ m (SAm) Gaucho; (SAm) good horseman ‖ m (Arg) mannish woman; (Arg) loose woman

gaultería f wintergreen

gaveta f drawer, till

gavia f ditch, drain; (ave) gull; (min) gang of basket passers; (naut) topsail

gavilán m sparrow hawk; (de la pluma) nib; (en la escritura) hair stroke; ingrowing nail

gavilla f sheaf, bundle; gang

gaviota f sea gull

gavota f gavotte

gaya f colored stripe; (ave) magpie

gayar tr to trim with colored stripes

ga•yo -ya adj cheerful, bright, showy ‖ m (orn) jay ‖ f see **gaya**

gayola f cage; jail

gayomba f Spanish broom

gazapa f lie

gazapatón m blunder, slip

gazapera f rabbit warren; gang, gang of thugs; brawl, row

gazapo *m* young rabbit; sly fellow; slip, boner, blunder; (*de actor*) fluff
gazmiar *tr* (*oliendo*) to sniff; (*comiendo*) nibble ‖ *ref* to complain
gazmoñada *f* or **gazmoñería** *f* prudishness, priggishness
gazmoñe·ro -ra or **gazmo·ño -ña** *adj* prudish, priggish, strait-laced, demure ‖ *mf* prude, prig
gaznápiro *m* gawk, boob, bumpkin
gaznate *m* gullet; (Mex) fritter
gazpacho *m* cold vegetable soup; (Hond) leftovers
gazuza *f* hunger
Gedeón *m* Gideon
gehena *m* Gehenna
géiser *m* geyser
gel *m* gel
gelatina *f* gelatine
gema *f* gem; (bot) bud
geme·lo -la *adj & mf* twin; **gemelos** twins; binoculars; cuff links; **gemelos de campo** field glasses; **gemelos de teatro** opera glasses ‖ **Gemelos** *mpl* (astr) Gemini
gemido *m* moan, groan; wail, whine; howl, roar
Géminis *m* (astr) Gemini
gemiquear *intr* (Chile) to whine
gemir §50 *intr* to moan, groan; wail, whine; howl, roar
gen *m* gene
genciana *f* gentian
gendarme *m* policeman
genealogía *f* genealogy
generación *f* generation
genera·dor -dora *adj* generating ‖ *m* generator
general *adj* general; common, usual; **en general** or **por lo general** in general ‖ *m* general; **capitán general de ejército** five-star general; **general de brigada** brigadier, brigadier general; **general de división** major general ‖ **generales** *fpl* general information, personal data
generala *f* general's wife; call to arms
generalato *m* generalship
generalidad *f* generality; majority; **la generalidad de** the general run of
generalísimo *m* generalissimo
generalizar §60 *tr & intr* to generalize ‖ *ref* to become generalized
generar *tr* to generate
genéri·co -ca *adj* generic; (*artículo*) indefinite; (*nombre*) common; showing gender
género *m* kind, sort; way, manner; cloth, material; (biol, log) genus; (gram) gender; **de género** genre; **género chico** one-act play, one-act operetta; **género de punto** knit goods, knitwear; **género humano** humankind; **género ínfimo** light vaudeville; **género novelístico** fiction; **género picaresco** burlesque; **géneros** goods, merchandise, material; **géneros de pieza** yard goods; **géneros para vestidos** dress goods
genero·so -sa *adj* generous; highborn; noble, magnanimous; (*vino*) rich, full

géne·sis *f* (*pl* **-sis**) genesis ‖ **el Génesis** (Bib) Genesis
genéti·co -ca *adj* genetic ‖ *f* genetics
genial *adj* inspired, geniuslike; pleasant, agreeable; temperamental
geniazo *m* fiery temper
genio *m* (*índole, carácter*) temperament, disposition; (*don altísimo de invención; persona que lo posee; espíritu tutelar, deidad pagana*) genius; fire, spirit
genital *adj* genital ‖ **genitales** *mpl* genitals
geniti·vo -va *adj* genitive
genitourina·rio -ria *adj* genitourinary
genocida *adj* genocidal ‖ *mf* genocide
genocidio *m* genocide
Génova *f* Genoa
geno·vés -vesa *adj & mf* Genoese
gente *f* people; (*parentela, familia*) folks; race, nation; troops; **gente baja** lower classes, rabble; **gente bien** nice people; **gente de bien** decent people; **gente de capa parda** country people; **gente de coleta** bullfighters; **gente de color** colored people; **gente de la cuchilla** butchers; **genta de la vida airada** bullies; underworld; **gente del bronce** bright, lively people; **gente del rey** convicts; **gente de mal vivir** toughs, underworld; **gente de mar** seafaring people; **gente de paz** (*palabras con las cuales se contesta al que pregunta ¿quién?*) friend; **gente de pluma** (coll) clerks; **gente de su majestad** convicts; **gente de trato** tradespeople; **gente forzada** convicts; **gente menuda** small fry; common people
gentecilla *f* mob, rabble
gentil *adj* heathen, gentile; elegant, genteel; noble ‖ *mf* heathen, pagan
gentileza *f* elegance, gentility, courtesy; gallantry; show, splendor; (*hidalguía*) nobility
gentilhombre *m* (*pl* **gentileshombres**) gentleman; messenger to the king; my good man; **gentilhombre de cámara** gentleman in waiting
gentili·cio -cia *adj* national; family; (gram) gentile
gentilidad *f* heathendom
gentío *m* crowd, mob
gentualla or **gentuza** *f* rabble, riffraff
genui·no -na *adj* genuine
geofísi·co -ca *adj* geophysical ‖ *mf* geophysicist ‖ *f* geophysics
geografía *f* geography
geográfi·co -ca *adj* geographic(al)
geógra·fo -fa *mf* geographer
geología *f* geology
geológi·co -ca *adj* geologic(al)
geólo·go -ga *mf* geologist
geómetra *mf* geometrician
geometría *f* geometry; **geometría del espacio** solid geometry
geométri·co -ca *adj* geometric(al)
geopolíti·co -ca *adj* geopolitical ‖ *f* geopolitics
geranio *m* geranium
gerencia *f* management; manager's office
gerente *m* manager, director; **gerente de**

publicidad advertising manager; **gerente de ventas** sales manager
geriatría *f* geriatry
geriatra *adj* geriatrical ‖ *mf* geriatrician
geriátri•co -ca *adj* geriatrical
germanía *f* gypsy slang, cant of thieves
germanizar §60 *tr* to Germanize
germen *m* germ; **germen plasma** germ plasm
germicida *adj* germicidal ‖ *m* germicide
germinal *adj* germ; germinal
germinar *intr* to germinate
gerontología *f* gerontology
gerundio *m* gerund; present participle; bombastic writer or speaker
gestación *f* gestation
gestear *intr* to make faces
gesticular *intr* to make a face, to make faces; (*hacer ademanes*) to gesticulate
gestión *f* step, measure; management; action, proceeding, negotiation
gestionar *tr* to promote, pursue; manage; negotiate
gesto *m* face; wry face, grimace; look, appearance; (*movimiento, ademán*) gesture
ges•tor -tora *adj* managing ‖ *m* manager
gestu•do -da *adj* cross-looking
ghetto *m* ghetto
giba *f* hump; annoyance
giga *f* jig
giganta *f* giantess
gigante *adj* giant ‖ *m* giant; (*en las procesiones*) giant figure
gigantes•co -ca *adj* gigantic
gigantez *f* giant size
gigantilla *f* large-headed masked figure; little fat woman
gigan•tón -tona *mf* huge giant ‖ *m* giant figure
gigote *m* chopped-meat stew; **hacer gigote** to chop up
gilí *adj* foolish, stupid
gimnasia *f* gymnastics; **gimnasia sueca** Swedish movements, setting-up exercises
gimnasio *m* gymnasium; secondary school, academy
gimnasta *mf* gymnast
gimnásti•co -ca *adj* gymnastic ‖ *f* gymnastics
gimotear *intr* to whine
gimoteo *m* whining
ginebra *f* gin; (*de voces*) buzz, din; confusion, disorder ‖ **Ginebra** *f* Geneva
ginebri•no -na *adj & mf* Genevan
ginecología *f* gynecology
ginecológi•co -ca *adj* gynecologic(al)
ginecólo•go -ga *mf* gynecologist
ginesta *f* Spanish broom
gira *f* var of **jira**
gira•do -da *mf* drawee
gira•dor -dora *mf* drawer
giralda *f* weathercock (*in the form of person or animal*)
girándula *f* girandole
girar *tr* (*una visita*) to pay; (com) to draw ‖ *intr* to turn; rotate, gyrate; trade; (com) to draw
girasol *m* sunflower, sycophant

girato•rio -ria *adj* revolving ‖ *f* revolving bookcase
gi•ro -ra *adj* (Guat) drunk; (Mex) cocky ‖ *m* turn; rotation; revolution; course, trend, turn; turn of phrase; boast, threat; gash, slash; line of business; trade; (com) draft; **giro a la vista** sight draft; **giro postal** money order ‖ *f* see **gira**
giroflé *m* clove
giroscopio *m* gyroscope
gis *m* (Col) slate pencil
gitana *f* gypsy woman, gypsy girl
gitanada *f* gypsy trick; fawning, flattery
gitanería *f* band of gypsies; gypsy life; fawning, flattery
gitanes•co -ca *adj* gypsyish
gita•no -na *adj* gypsy; flattering; sly, tricky ‖ *mf* gypsy ‖ *m* Gypsy (*language*) ‖ *f* see **gitana**
glaciación *f* freezing
glacial *adj* glacial; (*zona*) frigid; (fig) cold, indifferent
glaciar *m* glacier
glándula *f* gland; **glándula cerrada** ductless gland
glasé *m* glacé silk
glasea•do -da *adj* glossy, shiny
glicerina *f* glycerin
global *adj* total; global, world-wide
globo *m* globe; (*aparato que, lleno de un gas, se eleva en el aire*) balloon; (*bomba de lámpara*) globe, lamp shade; **globo de aire** (aut) air bag; **globo del ojo** eyeball; **globo sonda** trial balloon; **lanzar un globo sonda** (fig) to send up a trial balloon
glóbulo *m* globule; (physiol) corpuscle; **glóbulo rojo** red cell
gloria *f* glory; **ganar la gloria** to go to glory; **oler a gloria** to smell heavenly; **saber a gloria** to taste heavenly
gloriar §77 *tr* to glorify ‖ *intr* to recite the rosary ‖ *ref* to glory
glorieta *f* arbor, bower, summerhouse; public square; traffic circle
glorificar §73 *tr* to glorify ‖ *ref* to glory
glorio•so -sa *adj* glorious; boastful
glosa *f* gloss
glosa•dor -dora *adj* commenting ‖ *mf* commentator
glosar *tr* to gloss; audit; (Col) to scold ‖ *intr* to find fault
glosario *m* glossary
glóti•co -ca *adj* glottal
glo•tón -tona *adj* gluttonous ‖ *mf* glutton
glotonería *f* gluttony
glucosa *f* glucose
gluglú *m* (*del agua*) gurgle, glug; (*del pavo*) gobble; **hacer gluglú** to gurgle, to glug
gluglutear *intr* to gobble
gnomo *m* gnome
gob. *abbr* **gobierno**
gobernación *f* governing; government; department of the interior; (Arg) territory
gobernad•dor -dora *adj* governing ‖ *m* governor
gobernalle *m* rudder, helm

ga
go

gobernante *adj* governing ‖ *mf* ruler ‖ *m* self-appointed head

gobernar §2 *tr* to govern; guide, direct; control, rule; (*un buque*) steer ‖ *intr* to govern; steer

goberno·so -sa *adj* orderly

gobierno *m* government; governor's office, governorship; management; control, rule; guidance; (*de un buque*) navigability; **de buen gobierno** (*buque*) navigable; **gobierno de monigotes** puppet government; **gobierno doméstico** housekeeping; **gobierno exilado** government in exile; **para su gobierno** for your guidance; **servir de gobierno** to serve as a guide

goce *m* enjoyment

go·do -da *adj* Gothic ‖ *mf* Goth; Spanish noble; (Arg, Chile) Spaniard

gofio *m* roasted corn meal

gol *m* goal

gola *f* gullet

goldre *m* quiver

goleta *f* schooner

golf *m* golf

golfán *m* white water lily

golfista *mf* golfer

gol·fo -fa *mf* ragamuffin ‖ *m* gulf; open sea; **golfo de Méjico** Gulf of Mexico; **golfo de Vizcaya** Bay of Biscay

Gólgota, el (Bib) Golgotha

golilla *f* gorget, ruff; magistrate's collar; pipe flange; (*de los caños de barro*) collar, sleeve; (*del gallo*) erectile bristles

golondrina *f* swallow; **empresa golondrina** fly-by-night outfit

golosina *f* delicacy, tidbit; eagerness, appetite; trifle

golosinear *intr* to go around eating candy

golo·so -sa *adj* sweet-toothed; (*glotón*) gluttonous; (*apetitoso*) tasty

golpe *m* blow, stroke, hit; bump, bruise; heartbeat; crowd, throng, flock; (*del bolsillo*) flap; (*pestillo*) bolt, latch; (*de licor*) shot; surprise, wonder; (*infortunio*) blow; witticism; **dar golpe** to make a hit; **de golpe** all at once, suddenly; **de golpe y porrazo** slambang; **de un golpe** at one stroke; **golpe de ariete** water hammer; **golpe de calor** heatstroke; **golpe de estado** coup d'état; **golpe de fortuna** stroke of fortune; **golpe de gracia** coup de grâce; **golpe de mano** surprise attack; **golpe de mar** surge; **golpe de ojo** glance; **golpe de teatro** dramatic turn of events; **golpe de tos** fit of coughing; **golpe de vista** glance, look; view; **golpe en vago** miss, flop; **golpe mortal** deathblow; **no dar golpe** to not raise a hand, not do a stroke of work

golpear *tr* to strike, hit, beat; bump, bruise ‖ *intr* to beat, strike; (*el reloj*) tick; (*el motor de combustión interna*) knock

golpete *m* door catch, window catch

golpetear *tr & intr* to beat; rattle

golpismo *m* government by coup d'état

gollería *f* delicacy, dainty; **pedir gollerías** to ask for too much

gollete *m* throat, neck; (*de botella*) neck

goma *f* gum, rubber; (*tira de goma elástica*) rubber band; (*neumático*) tire; **goma arábiga** gum arabic; **goma de borrar** eraser, rubber; **goma de mascar** chewing gum; **goma espumosa** foam rubber; **goma laca** shellac

gomecillo *m* blind man's guide

gomia *f* bugaboo; waster; glutton

gomo·so -sa *adj* gum; gummy ‖ *m* dude, dandy

góndola *f* gondola

gondolero *m* gondolier

gongo *m* gong

gonorrea *f* gonorrhea

gordal *adj* large-size

gordia·no -na *adj* Gordian

gordi·flón -flona or **gordin·flón -flona** *adj* chubby, pudgy, fatty ‖ *mf* fatty

gor·do -da *adj* fat, plump; fatty, greasy; coarse; big, large; whopping big; (*agua*) hard ‖ *m* fat, suet; first prize (*in lottery*) ‖

gordo *adv* — **hablar gordo** to talk big

gordura *f* fatness, plumpness, stoutness, corpulence; fat, grease

gorgojo *m* grub, weevil; dwarf, runt; **gorgojo del algodón** boll weevil

gorgojo·so -sa *adj* grubby

gorgón *m* (Col) concrete

gorgonear *intr* (*el pavo*) to gobble

gorgoritear *intr* to trill

gorgorito *m* trill

gorgotear *intr* to burble, gurgle

gorgotero *m* peddler, hawker

gorigori *m* lugubrious funeral chant

gorila *f* gorilla; (coll) thug; strong-arm man

gorjear *intr* to warble, trill ‖ *ref* (*el niño*) to gurgle

gorra *f* cap; bumming, sponging; **andar de gorra** to sponge; **colarse de gorra** (coll) to crash the gate; **gorra de visera** cap; **vivir de gorra** to live on other people

gorrada *f* tipping the hat

gorrear *intr* (Ecuad) to sponge

gorretada *f* tipping the hat

gorrión *m* sparrow; **gorrión triguero** bunting

gorrista *adj* sponging ‖ *mf* sponger

gorro *m* cap, bonnet; baby's bonnet; **gorro de dormir** nightcap

go·rrón -rrona *adj* sponging ‖ *mf* sponger ‖ *m* pivot; journal, gudgeon

gota *f* drop; (pathol) gout; **gotas** touch of rum or brandy in coffee; **sudar la gota gorda** to work one's head off

gotear *intr* to drip, dribble; (*llover a gotas espaciadas*) sprinkle

gotera *f* drip, dripping; mark left by dripping; (*en el techo*) leak; (*adorno de una cama*) valance; **estar lleno de goteras** to be full of aches and pains; **es una gotera** it's a constant drain; **goteras** aches, pains; (Col) environs, outskirts

góti·co -ca *adj* Gothic; noble, illustrious ‖ *m* Gothic

goto·so -sa *adj* gouty ‖ *mf* gout sufferer

gozar §60 *tr* (*poseer*) to enjoy ‖ *intr* to enjoy oneself; **gozar de** (*poseer*) to enjoy ‖ *ref* to enjoy oneself; rejoice

gozne m hinge

gozo m joy, enjoyment; **no caber en sí de gozo** to be beside oneself with joy; **saltar de gozo** to leap with joy

gozo•so -sa adj joyful; **gozoso con** or **de** joyful over

gozque m or **gozquejo** m little yapping dog

grabación f (de disco) recording; **grabación sobre cinta** tape recording

grabado m engraving; print, cut, picture; (de disco) recording; **grabado en madera** wood engraving, woodcut; **grabado fuera de texto** inset, insert

graba•dor -dora adj recording ‖ mf engraver ‖ f recorder; **grabadora de cinta** tape recorder

grabador-reproductor m cassette recorder

grabadura f engraving

grabar tr to engrave; (un sonido, una canción, un disco, etc.) record; **grabar en** or **sobre cinta** to tape-record ‖ ref to become engraved

gracejada f (CAm, Mex) cheap comedy, clownishness

gracejar intr to be engaging, witty; joke

gracejo m lightness, winsome manner, charm; (CAm, Mex) clown

gracia f witticism, witty remark, joke; grace; gracefulness; favor; pardon; (de un chiste) point; name; **caer en gracia a** to be pleasing to; **de gracia** gratis; **decir dos gracias a** to tell someone a thing or two; **en gracia a** because of; **gracia de Dios** daily bread; air and sunshine; **gracias** thanks; **¡gracias!** thanks!; **gracias a** thanks to; **¡gracias a Dios!** thank heavens!; **hacer gracia** to be pleasing; **hacer gracia de algo a uno** to exempt or free someone from something; **hacerle a uno gracia** to strike someone as funny; **¡linda gracia!** nonsense!; **tener gracia** to be funny, be surprising

graciable adj kind, gracious; easy to grant

grácil adj thin, small, slender

gracio•so -sa adj (que tiene donaire, gracia) graceful; (afable, fino) gracious; (agudo, chistoso) funny, witty; (que se da de balde) free, gratis ‖ mf comic ‖ m gracioso (gay, comic character in Spanish comedy)

grada f step, stair; row of seats; grandstand; altar step; (agr) harrow; (plano inclinado sobre el cual se construyen los barcos) slip; **gradas** stone steps; (Chile, Peru) atrium; **gradas al aire libre** bleachers

gradar tr (agr) to harrow

gradería f stone steps; row of seats; bleachers; **gradería cubierta** grandstand

gradiente m (phys) gradient ‖ f slope, gradient

grado m step; grade; degree; (título que se da en las universidades) degree; (sección en las escuelas) grade, form, class; (mil) rank; **de buen grado** willingly; **de grado en grado** by degrees; **de grado o por fuerza** willy-nilly; **de mal grado** unwillingly; **en sumo grado** to a great extent; **mal de mi grado** unwillingly, against my wishes

graduación f graduation; (de las bebidas espirituosas) strength; (mil) rank

gradual adj gradual

graduan•do -da mf (persona próxima a graduarse en la universidad) graduate (candidate for a degree)

graduar §21 tr to graduate, grade; (un grifo, una válvula, etc.) regulate; appraise, estimate ‖ ref to graduate

grafía f graph

gráfi•co -ca adj graphic(al); printing; illustrated; picture, camera ‖ m diagram ‖ f graph

grafito m graphite

grafospasmo m writer's cramp

gragea f colored candy; sugar-coated pill

grajear intr (los cuervos) to caw; (los niños) gurgle

grajien•to -ta adj foul-smelling

gra•jo -ja mf rook, crow; chatterbox ‖ m body odor

gral. abbr **general**

gramática f grammar; **gramática parda** shrewdness, mother wit

gramatical adj grammatical

gramáti•co -ca adj grammatical ‖ mf grammarian ‖ f see **gramática**

gramil m marking gauge, gauge

gramo m gram

gramófono m gramophone

gramola f console phonograph; portable phonograph

gran adj apocopated form of **grande,** used only before nouns of both genders in the singular

grana f seed; seeding; seeding time; red; **dar en grana** to go to seed

granada f pomegranate; (proyectil explosivo) grenade; **granada de mano** hand grenade; **granada de metralla** shrapnel; **granada extintora** fire extinguisher, fire grenade

granadero m grenadier

granadilla f passionflower

granadina f grenadine

grana•do -da adj choice, select; mature, expert ‖ m pomegranate; **granado blanco** rose of Sharon ‖ f see **granada**

granalla f filings

granangular adj wide-angle

granate m adj invar & m garnet

Gran Bretaña, la Great Britain

grande adj big, large; great ‖ m grandee

grandeza f bigness, largeness; greatness; (tamaño) size; (magnificencia) grandeur; grandees; grandeeship

grandi•llón -llona adj oversize, overgrown

grandio•so -sa adj grandiose, grand

grandor m size

granea•do -da adj spattered; (fuego) heavy and continuous

granear tr to sow; (la pólvora; una piedra litográfica) grain; stipple

granel — a granel in bulk, loose; at random; lavishly

granelar tr (el cuero) to grain

granero m granary

granete m center punch

go
gr

granífu•go -ga adj hail-dispersing
granito m granite
granizada f hailstorm; (Arg, Chile) iced drink
granizar §60 tr (p.ej., golpes) to hail; sprinkle || intr to hail
granizo m hail
granja f farm, grange; dairy; country place
granjear tr to earn, gain; win, win over || ref to win, win over
granjería f husbandry; gain, profit
granje•ro -ra mf farmer; merchant, trader
grano m grain; (baya) berry; (baya de la uva) grape; (tumorcillo en la piel) pimple; (peso) grain; **grano de belleza** beauty spot; **grano de café** coffee bean; **granos** (fruto de los cereales) grain; **ir al grano** to come to the point
granuja m scoundrel; (muchacho vagabundo) waif || f loose grape; grapeseed
granujo m pimple
granular adj granular; pimply || tr & ref to granulate
gránulo m granule
grapa f clamp, clip, staple
grasa f fat, grease; (polvo) pounce; (Mex) shoe polish; **grasa de ballena** blubber; **grasas** slag
grasien•to -ta adj greasy
grasilla f pounce
gra•so -sa adj fatty, greasy || m fattiness, greasiness || f see **grasa**
grasones mpl wheat porridge
graso•so -sa adj greasy; (pathol) fatty
grata f wire brush; (carta) favor
gratificar §73 tr to gratify; reward, recompense; tip, fee
gratín m — **al gratín** au gratin
gratis adv gratis
gratisda•to -ta adj free, gratis
gratitud f gratitude
gra•to -ta adj pleasing; free; (Bol, Chile) grateful || f see **grata**
gratuidad f cost exemption; exemption from fees
gratui•to -ta adj gratuitous; free, gratis
grava f gravel; crushed stone
gravamen m burden, obligation; encumbrance, lien; assessment
gravar tr to burden, encumber; assess || ref to get worse
grave adj grave, serious, solemn; hard, difficult; (que pesa) heavy; (sonido) grave, deep, low; (música) majestic, noble; (negocio) important; (enfermedad) serious; (acento) grave; paroxytone
gravedad f gravity; seriousness; **de gravedad** seriously; gravely; **gravedad nula** weightlessness, zero gravity
gravedo•so -sa adj heavy, pompous
gravidez f pregnancy
grávi•do -da adj pregnant
gravitación f gravitation
gravitar intr to gravitate; **gravitar sobre** to weigh down on
gravo•so -sa adj burdensome, onerous, costly; boring, tiresome

graznar intr to caw, croak; cackle; (al cantar) (fig) cackle
graznido m caw, croak; cackle; (canto que disuena mucho) (fig) cackle
Grecia f Greece
grecia•no -na adj Grecian
gre•co -ca adj & mf Greek
greda f clay, fuller's earth
grega•rio -ria adj (que vive confundido con otros) gregarious; slavish, servile
gregoria•no -na adj Gregorian
gremial adj guild; trade-union, union || m guildsman; union member
gremio m guild, corporation; trade union, union; association, society
greña f confusion, entanglement; (de cabello) shock, tangled mop; **andar a la greña** to get into a hot argument; (dos mujeres) to pull each other's hair
greñu•do -da adj bushy-headed, shock-headed
gres m sandstone; stoneware
gresca f tumult, uproar; row, quarrel
grey f (de ganado menor) flock; group, party; nation, people; (de fieles) flock, congregation
grie•go -ga adj Greek || mf Greek || m (idioma) Greek; **hablar en griego** to not make sense
grieta f crack, crevice, chink; (en la piel) chap
grieta•do -da adj crackled || m crackleware
grietar ref to crack, split; (la piel) become chapped
gri•fo -fa adj (pelo) kinky, tangled; (letra) script; (W-I) colored; (Mex) drunk; (Col) conceited || mf person of color; (Mex) drunk || m faucet, spigot, tap, cock; (myth) griffin; (Peru) gas station, (Mex) marijuana || f (Mex) marijuana
grilla f female cricket; (rad) grid; (Col) fight, quarrel; (SAm) annoyance, bother; **¡ésa es grilla!** (coll) you expect me to believe that!
grillar intr (el grillo) to chirp || ref (las semillas, bulbos, etc.) to sprout
grillete m fetter, shackle
grillo m (insecto) cricket; (brote tierno) sprout, shoot; **grillos** fetters, shackles
grima f fright, horror; **dar grima** to grate on the nerves
grin•go -ga mf (disparaging) foreigner; (anglosajón) gringo || m gibberish; **hablar en gringo** to talk nonsense
griñón m (toca de monja) wimple; (melocotón) nectarine
gripe f grippe
gris adj gray; dull, gloomy || m gray; **hacer gris** (el tiempo) to be sharp, be brisk
grisáce•o -a adj grayish
gri•sú m (pl -súes) firedamp
grita f shouting; hubbub, uproar; **dar grita a** to hoot at
gritar intr to shout, cry out
gritería f shouting, outcry, uproar
grito m cry, shout; scream, shriek; **el último grito** the latest thing, all the rage; **poner el**

grito en el cielo to raise the roof, scream wildly

gro. abbr **género**

Groenlandia f Greenland

grosella f currant; **grosella silvestre** gooseberry

grosellero m currant bush; **grosellero silvestre** gooseberry bush

grosería f grossness, coarseness; churlishness, rudeness; stupidity; vulgarity

grose•ro -ra adj gross, coarse; churlish, rude; stupid; vulgar ‖ mf churl, boor

grosor m thickness, bulk

grosura f fat, suet, tallow; meat diet; coarseness, vulgarity

grotes•co -ca adj grotesque

grúa f crane, derrick; **grúa de bote** (naut) davit; **grúa de auxilio** wrecking crane; **grúa de caballete** gantry crane

grúa-remolque m tow truck

grue•so -sa adj big, thick, bulky, heavy; coarse, ordinary; stout, fat; (mar) rough, heavy; **en grueso** in gross, in bulk ‖ f (doce docenas) gross

grulla f (orn) crane

grumete m ship's boy, cabin boy

grumo m clot, curd; bunch, cluster

grumo•so -sa adj clotty, curdly

gruñido m (de cerdo) grunt; (de perro cuando amenaza) growl; (de persona) grumble; (de puerta) creak; grumble, scolding

gruñir §12 intr (el cerdo) to grunt; (el perro) growl; (una persona) grumble; (una puerta) creak

gru•ñón -ñona adj grumpy, grumbly ‖ mf crosspatch

grupa f croup, rump

grupada f squall

grupal adj group

grupo m group; (mach & elec) unit

grupúsculo m splinter group

gruta f grotto

grutes•co -ca adj & m (fa) grotesque

Gruyère m Swiss cheese

gte. abbr **gerente**

guaca f (Bol, Peru) Indian tomb; hidden treasure

guacal m crate

guacama•yo -ya adj (P-R) flashy, sporty ‖ m macaw

guachapear tr to splash with the feet; bungle, botch ‖ intr to clank, clatter

guachinan•go -ga adj flattering, sly ‖ mf (disparaging term used by Cubans) Mexican

gua•cho -cha adj (SAm) homeless, orphan; (SAm) odd, unmatched

guadal m bog, swamp; sand hill, dune

Guadalupe f Gaudeloupe

guadama•cí m (pl -cíes) embossed leather

guadaña f scythe

guadañadora f mowing machine

guadañar tr to cut with a scythe

guadarnés m harness room; harness man

guagua f trifle; (SAm) baby; (W-I) bus; (Col) paca

guagüita f (Cuba, P-R) station wagon

guajada f (Mex) nonsense, folly

guaje adj (Hond, Mex) foolish, stupid ‖ m (Hond, Mex) calabash, gourd; (CAm) piece of junk

guaji•ro -ra mf (W-I) peasant, yokel

guajolote m turkey; (Mex) simpleton

gualda f (bot) weld, dyer's rocket

gual•do -da adj yellow ‖ f see **gualda**

gualdrapa f housing, trappings; dirty rag hanging from clothes

gualdrapear tr to line up head to tail ‖ intr (las velas) to flap

Gualterio m Walter

guanaco m (SAm) dope, simpleton; (SAm) tall lanky fellow; (zool) guanaco

guanajo m turkey; (W-I) boob, dunce

guano m palm tree; bird manure

guante m glove; **arrojar el guante** to throw down the gauntlet; **echar un guante** to pass the hat; **guantes** tip, fee; **recoger el guante** to take up the gauntlet; **salvo el guante** excuse my glove

guantelete m gauntlet

guantería f glove shop

guantón m box on the ear

guapear intr to bluster, swagger; dress to kill

guape•tón -tona adj handsome; flashy, sporty; bold, fearless ‖ m bully, tough

guapeza f good looks; flashiness, sportiness; (coll) boldness, daring; bravado

gua•po -pa adj handsome, good-looking; flashy, sporty; bold, daring ‖ m (hombre pendenciero) bully; gallant, lady's man

guapura f good looks

guarache m (Mex) leather sandal; (Mex) tire patch

guarapo m sugar-cane juice; fermented juice of sugar cane

guarda mf guard, custodian ‖ m (Arg) trolley-car conductor; **guarda de la aduana** customhouse officer; **guarda forestal** forest ranger ‖ f guard, custody; (de la ley) observance; (de la espada) guard; (de la cerradura) ward; (bb) flyleaf

guardabarrera mf (rr) gatekeeper

guardaba•rros m (pl -rros) fender, mudguard, dashboard

guardabosque m gamekeeper; forest ranger; shortstop

guardabrisa m windshield; (naut) glass candle shade

guardacantón m spur stone

guardacarril m (rr) railguard

guardacar•tas m (pl -tas) letter file

guardaco•ches m (pl -ches) car watcher

guardacos•tas m (pl -tas) revenue cutter, coast guard cutter; **guardacostas** mpl (servicio) coast guard

guarda•dor -dora adj guarding, protecting; mindful, observant; stingy ‖ m guardian, keeper; observer

guardaespal•das m (pl -das) bodyguard

guardafango m fender, mudguard

guardafre•nos m (pl -nos) (rr) brakeman, flagman

guardafuego m fender, fireguard

guardagu•jas m (pl -jas) (rr) switchman

guardajo•yas *m* (*pl* **-yas**) jewel case
guardalado *m* railing, parapet
guardalmacén *m* warehouseman; (Cuba) country station master
guardamalleta *f* valance
guardameta *m* goalkeeper
guardamue•bles *m* (*pl* **-bles**) warehouse, furniture warehouse
guardanieve *m* snowshed
guardapelo *m* locket
guardapolvo *m* (*sobretodo ligero*) duster; (*resguardo para preservar del polvo*) cover, cloth; (*del reloj*) inner lid; (*sobre una puerta o ventana*) hood
guardapuerta *f* storm door
guardar *tr* to guard; watch over; protect; put away; show, observe; save, e.g., ¡**Dios guarde a la Reina!** God save the Queen ‖ *intr* to keep, save; ¡**guarda!** look out!, watch out! ‖ *ref* to be on one's guard; **guardarse de** to look out for, watch out for, guard against
guardarraya *f* (CAm, W-I) boundary line, property line
guardarropa *mf* keeper of the wardrobe ‖ *m* (*armario donde se guarda la ropa*) wardrobe; (*local destinado a la custodia de ropa en establecimientos públicos*) checkroom, cloakroom; check boy ‖ *f* check girl, hat girl
guardarropía *f* (theat) wardrobe
guardasilla *f* chair rail
guardaventana *f* storm window
guardavía *m* (rr) trackwalker, lineman
guardavida *m* lifeguard
guardavien•tos *m* (*pl* **-tos**) (*abrigo contra los vientos*) windbreak; (*mitra de chimenea*) chimney pot
guardavivo *m* bead, corner bead
guardería *f* guard, guardship; **guardería infantil** day nursery
guardesa *f* woman guard
guardia *m* guard, guardsman; **guardia civil** rural policeman; **guardia marina** midshipman, middy; **guardia urbano** policeman ‖ *f* (*cuerpo de hombres armados; manera de defenderse en la esgrima*) guard; (naut) watch; **de guardia** on duty; on guard; **guardia civil** rural police; **guardia de asalto** shock troops; **guardia de corps** (mil) bodyguard; **guardia de cuartillo** (naut) dogwatch; **guardia suiza** Swiss Guards
guar•dián -diana *mf* guardian ‖ *m* watchman
guardilla *f* attic; attic room
guardo•so -sa *adj* careful, neat, tidy; (*que ahorra mucho*) thrifty; (*mezquino*) stingy
guarecer §22 *tr* to take in, give shelter to; keep, preserve; (*a un enfermo*) treat ‖ *ref* to take refuge, take shelter
guarida *f* den, lair; shelter; haunt, hangout, hide-out
guarismo *m* cipher, figure

guarnecer §22 *tr* to trim, adorn; equip, provide; bind, edge; (*joyas*) set; stucco, plaster; (*frenos*) line; (*un cojinete*) bush; (*una plaza fuerte*) man, garrison; (culin) garnish
guarnición *f* trimming; equipping; binding, edging; (*de joyas*) setting; stuccoing, plastering; (*de la espada*) guard; (*de frenos*) lining; (*del émbolo*) packing; (*tropa que guarnece un lugar*) garrison; (culin) garnish; **guarniciones** fixtures, fittings; (*de la caballería*) harness
guarnicionar *tr* to garrison
guarnicionero *m* harness maker
guaro *m* (CAm) sugar-cane liquor
gua•rro -rra *mf* hog
guasa *f* heaviness, churlishness; joking, kidding
guasca *f* rawhide; whip; **dar guasca a** to whip, thrash
guasería *f* (SAm) coarseness, crudity; (Chile) timidity
gua•so -sa *adj* (SAm) coarse, crude, uncouth ‖ *mf* (Chile) peasant ‖ *f* see **guasa**
gua•són -sona *adj* heavy, churlish; funny, comical ‖ *mf* dullard, churl; joker, kidder
guata *f* wadding, padding; (Arg, Chile, Peru) belly, paunch; (*de una pared*) (Chile) bulging, warping; (Ecuad) boon companion; **echar guata** (Chile) to prosper
guatemalte•co -ca *adj & mf* Guatemalan
guáter *m* toilet, water closet
guau *m* (*ladrido del perro*) bowwow; (bot) woodbine, Virginia creeper; **guau guau** (*perro*) bowwow ‖ *interj* bowwow!
guay *interj* — ¡**guay de mí!** (poet) woe is me!
guayaba *f* guava, guava apple
guayabo *m* guava tree; lie, trick
guayaco *m* lignum vitae
Guayana *f* Guyana
gubernamental *adj* governmental; (*defensor*) strong-government
gubernati•vo -va *adj* governmental
gubia *f* gouge
guedeja *f* shock of hair; lion's mane
guerra *f* war, warfare; billiards; **Gran guerra** Great War; **guerra a muerte** war to the death; **guerra bacteriana** or **bacteriológica** germ warfare; **guerra de guerrillas** guerrilla warfare; **guerra de las dos Rosas** War of the Roses; **guerra de los Cien Años** Hundred Years' War; **guerra del Transvaal** Boer War; **guerra de ondas** radio jamming; **guerra de Troya** Trojan War; **guerra fría** cold war; **Guerra Mundial** World War; **guerra nuclear** nuclear war; **guerra relámpago** blitzkrieg; **hacer la guerra** to wage war
guerrea•dor -dora *adj* warring ‖ *mf* warrior
guerrear *intr* to war, wage war, fight; struggle, resist
guerre•ro -ra *adj* war, warlike; warring; mischievous ‖ *mf* fighter ‖ *m* warrior, soldier, fighting man ‖ *f* tight-fitting military jacket

guerrilla *f* band of skirmishers; guerrilla band; guerrilla warfare
guerrillear *intr* to skirmish; wage guerrilla warfare
guerrillero *m* guerrilla
guía *mf* guide, leader; adviser ‖ *m* (mil) guide ‖ *f* guide; guidance; directory; (*del viajero*) guidebook; (*caballo*) leader; (*de la bicicleta*) handle bar; (*del bigote*) turned-up end; (*de la sierra*) fence; marker; shoot, sprout; (mach) guide; (rr) timetable; **guías** reins; **guía sonora** sound track; **guía telefónica** telephone directory; **guía turística** tourist guide
guiadera *f* (mach) guide
guiar §77 *tr* to guide, lead; (*un automóvil*) steer, drive; pilot; (*una planta, una vid*) train ‖ *intr* to shoot, sprout ‖ *ref* — **guiarse por** to be guided by, go by
guija *f* pebble; grass pea
guijarro *m* cobble, cobblestone
guije•ño -ña *adj* pebbly; hard-hearted
guijo *m* gravel
guijo•so -sa *adj* gravelly; pebbly
güila *f* (Mex) prostitute
guillame *m* rabbet plane
Guillermo *m* William
guillotina *f* guillotine; paper cutter
guillotinar *tr* to guillotine
guimbalete *m* pump handle
guinche *m* or **güinche** *m* (mach) crane
guinda *f* sour cherry
guindal *m* sour cherry tree
guindaleza *f* (naut) hawser
guindar *tr* to hoist, raise; win; (*ahorcar*) hang, string up
guindilla *m* policeman, cop; Guinea pepper
guindo *m* sour cherry tree
guindola *f* (naut) boatswain's chair; (naut) life buoy
guinea *f* (*moneda*) guinea
guineo *m* small banana
guinga *f* gingham
guiña *f* (Col, Ven) bad luck
guiñada *f* wink; (naut) yaw
guiñapo *m* rag, tatter; ragamuffin
guiñar *tr* (*el ojo*) to wink ‖ *intr* to wink; (naut) to yaw ‖ *ref* to wink at each other
guiño *m* wink; **hacer guiños a** to make eyes at; **hacerse guiños a** to make faces at each other
guión *m* banner, standard; cross (*carried before prelate in procession*); (*signo ortográfico*) hyphen; (*signo ortográfico largo*)

dash; (mil) guidon; (mov & theat) scenario; (rad & telv) script; (mus) repeat sign; **guión de montaje** (mov) cutter's script; **guión de rodaje** (mov) shooting script
guionista *mf* (mov) scenarist; (mov) scriptwriter; (mov) subtitle writer
guirigay *m* gibberish; confusion, hubbub
guirindola *f* frill, jabot
guirlache *m* almond brittle, peanut brittle
guirnalda *f* garland, wreath
guisa *f* way, manner, wise; **a guisa de** in the manner of, like
guisado *m* stew, meat stew
guisante *m* pea; **guisante de olor** sweet pea
guisar *tr* to cook; stew; arrange, prepare ‖ *intr* to cook
guiso *m* dish
guisote *m* hash
guita *f* twine; (coll) dough, money
guitarra *f* guitar
guitarrista *mf* guitarist
gui•tón -tona *mf* tramp, bum
gula *f* gluttony; gorging, guzzling
gulo•so -sa *adj* gluttonous; guzzling
gumía *f* Moorish poniard
gurrumi•no -na *adj* weak, puny ‖ *m* henpecked husband ‖ *f* uxoriousness
gusanear *intr* to swarm
gusanera *f* nest of worms; ruling passion
gusanien•to -ta *adj* wormy, grubby
gusanillo *m* small worm; twist stitch; (*de la barrena*) spur; **matar el gusanillo** to take a shot of liquor before breakfast
gusano *m* worm; **gusano de luz** glowworm; **gusano de seda** silk worm; **gusano de tierra** earthworm
gusano•so -sa *adj* wormy, grubby
gusarapo *m* waterworm, vinegar worm
gustación *f* tasting; taste
gustar *tr* to taste; try, sample; please, be pleasing to; like, e.g., **me gustan estas peras** I like these pears ‖ *intr* to like e.g., **como Vd. guste** as you like; **gustar de** to like; like to
gustillo *m* slight taste, touch
gusto *m* taste; flavor; liking; caprice, whim; pleasure; **a gusto** as you like it; **con mucho gusto** with pleasure, gladly; **encontrarse a gusto** or **estar a gusto** to like it (*e.g., in the country*); **tanto gusto** so glad to meet you
gusto•so -sa *adj* tasty; agreeable, pleasant; ready, willing, glad
gutapercha *f* gutta-percha
gutural *adj* guttural

gu
ha

H

H, h (hache) *f* ninth letter of the Spanish alphabet
haba *f* bean, broad bean; (*simiente del café y*

el cacao) bean; **ser habas contadas** to be a sure thing
Habana, La Havana

haber *m* salary, wages; credit, credit side; **haberes** property, wealth ‖ *v* §38 *tr* to have; get, get hold of ‖ *v aux* to have, e.g., **lo he visto a menudo** I have seen it often; **haber de** + *inf* to be to + *inf*, e.g., **ha de llegar a mediodía** he is to arrive at noon ‖ *v impers* there to be, e.g., **ha habido tres personas allí** there were three people there; **haber que** + *inf* to be necessary to + *inf;* **no hay de qué** you're welcome, don't mention it ‖ *ref* to behave oneself; **habérselas con** to deal with; to have it out with

habichuela *f* kidney bean; **habichuela verde** string bean

hábil *adj* skillful, capable; (*día*) work

habilidad *f* skill, ability, capability; (*lo que se ejecuta con gracia*) feat; (*enredo, embuste*) scheme, trick

habilido•so -sa *adj* skillful

habilitación *f* qualification; backing, financing; equipping, outfitting; **habilitaciones** fixtures

habilitar *tr* to qualify; back, finance; equip, fit out; (*en un examen*) pass

habitabilidad *f* habitability; (aut) interior (space)

habitable *adj* inhabitable

habitación *f* habitation; (*edificio donde se habita*) house, home, dwelling; (*aposento de la casa o el hotel*) room; (*donde vive una especie vegetal o animal*) habitat

habitante *mf* (*de una casa*) dweller, occupant; (*de una población*) inhabitant

habitar *tr* to inhabit, live in; (*una casa, un piso*) occupy ‖ *intr* to live

hábito *m* garment, dress; habit, custom; **ahorcar los hábitos** to doff the cassock, to leave the priesthood; to change jobs; **el hábito no hace al monje** clothes don't make the man

habitua•do -da *mf* habitué

habitual *adj* habitual; regular, usual

habituar §21 *tr* to accustom ‖ *ref* to become accustomed

habitud *f* relationship, connection; custom, habit

habla *f* speech; **al habla** speaking

hablada *f* talk, talking

habla•dor -dora *adj* talkative; gossipy ‖ *mf* talker, chatterbox; gossip

habladuría *f* cut, sarcasm; **andar con habladurías** to go around gossiping

hablante *adj* speaking ‖ *mf* speaker

hablar *tr* (*una lengua*) to speak, talk; (*disparates*) talk ‖ *intr* to speak, talk; **es hablar por demás** it's wasted talk; **estar hablando** (*una pintura, una estatua*) to be almost alive; **hablar claro** to talk straight from the shoulder

hablilla *f* story, piece of gossip

hablista *mf* speaker, good speaker

hacede•ro -ra *adj* feasible, practicable

hacenda•do -da *adj* landed, property-owning ‖ *mf* landholder, property owner; cattle rancher; plantation owner

hacendar §2 *tr* (*el dominio de bienes raíces*) to pass on ‖ *ref* to buy property in order to settle down

hacende•ro -ra *adj* thrifty

hacendista *m* economist, fiscal expert; man of independent means

hacendo•so -sa *adj* hard-working, thrifty

hacer §39 *tr* (*crear, producir, formar*) to make; (*ejecutar, llevar a cabo*) do; (*un baúl*) pack; (*un papel*) play; (*un mandato*) give; (*un drama*) act, perform; pretend to be; (*una pregunta*) ask; **hace** ago, e.g., **hace un mes** a month ago; **hacer** + *inf* to have + *inf*, e.g., **le hice tomar un libro en la biblioteca** I had him get a book at the library; to make + *inf*, e.g., **el médico me hizo guardar cama** the doctor made me stay in bed; to have + *pp*, e.g., **hará construir una casa** he will have a house built; **hacer . . . que** to be . . . since, e.g., **hace un año que yo estuve aquí** it is a year since I was here; to be for. . . , e.g., **hace un año que estoy aquí** I have been here for a year; for expressions like **hacer frío** to be cold, see the noun ‖ *intr* to act; **hacer a** to fit; **hacer al caso** (coll) to be to the purpose; **hacer como que** + *ind* to pretend to + *inf;* **hacer de** to act as, work as; **hacer por** to try to ‖ *ref* to become, get to be, grow; **hacerse a** to become accustomed to; **hacerse a un lado** to step aside; **hacerse con** to make off with; **hacerse chiquito** to sing small; **hacérsele a uno difícil** to strike one as difficult; **hacerse viejo** to grow old; kill time

hacia *prep* toward; (*cierta hora o época*) about, near; **hacia abajo** downward; **hacia adelante** forward; **hacia arriba** upward; **hacia atrás** backward; the wrong way; **hacia dentro** inward; **hacia fuera** outward

hacienda *f* farmstead, landed estate, country property; property, possessions; ranch; (Arg) cattle, livestock; **hacienda pública** public finance, federal income; **haciendas** household chores

hacina *f* pile, heap; shock, stack

hacinar *tr* to pile, heap, stack

hacha *f* axe; (*hacha pequeña*) hatchet; torch; firebrand; four-wick wax candle; **hacha de armas** battleaxe

hachazo *m* blow with an axe

hachear *tr* & *intr* to hew, hack, or chop with an axe

hachero *m* torchbearer; (*candelero*) torch stand; (*leñador*) woodcutter

hachich *m* or **hachís** *m* hashish

hacho *m* torch; (*sitio elevado cerca de la costa*) beacon, beacon hill

hada *f* fairy; (*mujer que encanta por su belleza, gracia, etc.*) charmer; **hada madrina** fairy godmother

hadar *tr* (*determinar el hado*) to predestine, foreordain; (*pronosticar*) to foretell; (*encantar*) to charm, cast a spell on

hado *m* fate, destiny

haiga *m* (slang) flashy auto; (slang) sport

halagar §44 *tr* (*lisonjear*) to flatter; (*demostrar cariño a*) cajole, fawn on; (*agradar*) gratify, please

halago *m* flattery; cajolery; gratification; **halagos** flattery, blandishments

halagüe•ño -ña *adj* flattering; fawning; gratifying, pleasing; bright, rosy, promising

halar *tr* (naut) to haul, pull

halcón *m* falcon

halconear *intr* (*la mujer*) to chase after men

halconería *f* falconry

halconero *m* falconer

halda *f* skirt; **poner haldas en cinta** to pull up one's skirts to run; roll up one's sleeves

halieto *m* fish hawk, osprey

hálito *m* breath; vapor; (poet) gentle breeze

halitosis *f* halitosis

halo *m* halo

haló *interj* (*teléfono*) hello!

halógeno *m* halogen

halterio *m* dumbbell

halterofilia *f* weight lifting

halterofilista *mf* weight lifter

haluro *m* halide

hallar *tr* to find; (*averiguar*) find out, discover ‖ *ref* to find oneself; to be; **hallarse bien con** to be satisfied with; **hallárselo todo hecho** to never have to turn a hand; **no hallarse** to feel uncomfortable, not like it

hallazgo *m* (*cosa hallada*) find; (*acción de hallar*) finding, discovery; (*premio al que ha hallado una cosa perdida*) reward, finder's reward, e.g., **diez dólares de hallazgo** ten dollars reward

hallulla *f* bread baked on embers or hot stones; (Chile) fine bread

hamaca *f* hammock

hamamelina *f* witch hazel

hambre *f* hunger; (*escasez general de comestibles*) famine; **matar de hambre** to starve to death; **morir de hambre** to starve to death, die of starvation; **pasar hambre** to go hungry; **tener hambre** to be hungry

hambrear *tr & intr* to starve, famish

hambrien•to -ta *adj* hungry, starving

hambruna *f* (SAm) mad hunger; (Ecuad) starvation

hamburguesa *f* hamburger sandwich

hamo *m* fishhook

hampa *f* underworld life; denizens of the underworld

hampes•co -ca *adj* underworld

hampón *m* bully, tough

hangar *m* (aer) hangar

hara•gán -gana *adj* idling, loafing, lazy ‖ *mf* idler, loafer

haraganear *intr* to idle, loaf, hang around

harapien•to -ta *adj* ragged, tattered

harapo *m* rag, tatter; **andar** or **estar hecho un harapo** (coll) to go around in rags

harapo•so -sa *adj* ragged, tattered

harén *m* harem

harina *f* (*especialmente del trigo*) flour; (*de cualquier grano*) meal; **estar metido en harina** to be deeply absorbed; to be fat and heavy; **harina de avena** oatmeal; **harina**

de maíz corn meal; **ser harina de otro costal** to be a horse of another color

harine•ro -ra *adj* flour ‖ *m* flour dealer; flour bin

harino•so -sa *adj* floury, mealy

harnear *tr* (Col, Chile) to sift

harnero *m* sieve

ha•rón -rona *adj* lazy ‖ *mf* lazy loafer

harpillera *f* burlap, sackcloth

hartar *tr* to stuff, cram; satisfy, satiate; tire, bore; overwhelm, deluge ‖ *intr* to have one's fill ‖ *ref* to stuff; be satiated; tire, be bored

hartazgo *m* or **hartazón** *m* fill, bellyful; **darse un hartazgo** to eat one's fill; **darse un hartazgo de** to have or to get one's fill of

har•to -ta *adj* full, fed up; very much; **harto de** full of, fed up with, sick of ‖ **harto** *adv* enough; very, quite

hartura *f* fill, satiety; full satisfaction; abundance

hasta *adv* even ‖ *prep* until, till; to, as far as; down to, up to; as much as; **hasta ahora** up till now; **hasta aquí** so far; **hasta después** so long, good-by; **hasta la vista** or **hasta luego** so long, good-by; **hasta mañana** see you tomorrow; **hasta más no poder** to the utmost; **hasta no más** to the utmost; **hasta que** until, till

hastial *m* gable end; (*hombrón rústico*) bumpkin

hastiar §77 *tr* to surfeit, sicken, cloy; (*fastidiar*) bother, annoy, bore

hastío *m* surfeit, loathing, disgust; bother, annoyance, boredom

hataca *f* large wooden ladle; (*cilindro para extender la masa*) rolling pin

hatajo *m* small herd, small flock; (*p.ej., de disparates*) lot, flock

hato *m* (*de ganado vacuno*) herd; (*de ovejas*) flock; (*de ropa*) pack, bundle; (*de gente*) clique, ring; (*de gente malvada*) gang; everyday outfit; (*de disparates*) flock, lot; cattle ranch; **liar el hato** to pack up, pack one's baggage; **revolver el hato** to stir up trouble

haya *f* beech tree; (*madera*) beech ‖ **La Haya** The Hague

hayaca *f* (Ven) mince pie

hayo *m* (Col) coca; (Col) coca leaves (*mixed for chewing*)

hayuco *m* beechnut, mast

haz *m* (*pl* **haces**) bunch, bundle; (*de leña*) fagot; (*de mieses*) sheaf; (*de rayos*) beam, pencil; (*de soldados*) file ‖ *f* (*pl* **haces**) face; (*de la tierra*) surface; (*de paño o tela*) right side; (*de un edificio*) façade, front; **a sobre haz** on the surface; **ser de dos haces** to be two-faced

hazaña *f* feat, exploit, deed

hazañería *f* fuss

hazañe•ro -ra *adj* fussy

hazaño•so -sa *adj* gallant, courageous

hazmerreír *m* laughingstock, butt

he *adv* behold, lo and behold; **he aquí** here is, here are; **he allí** there is, there are

hebilla *f* buckle

hebra *f* thread; fiber; (*en la madera*) grain; (*del discurso*) (fig) thread; **de una hebra** (Chile) all at once; **pegar la hebra** to strike up a conversation; to keep on talking

hebre•o -a *adj & mf* Hebrew ‖ *m* (*idioma*) Hebrew

hebro•so -sa *adj* fibrous, stringy

hecatombe *f* hecatomb

hechicera *f* witch, sorceress; (*mujer que por su belleza cautiva*) enchantress

hechicería *f* witchcraft, sorcery, wizardry; (fig) fascination, charm

hechice•ro -ra *adj* bewitching, charming, enchanting; magic ‖ *mf* sorcerer, magician; charmer, enchanter ‖ *m* wizard, sorcerer ‖ *f* see **hechicera**

hechizar §60 *tr* to bewitch, cast a spell on; (fig) to bewitch, charm, enchant ‖ *intr* to practice sorcery; (fig) to be charming, enchant

hechi•zo -za *adj* fake, artificial; (*de quita y pon*) detachable; made, manufactured; (*producto*) local, home ‖ *m* spell, charm; magic, sorcery; (fig) magic, sorcery, glamour; (fig) charmer; **hechizos** (*de una mujer*) charms

he•cho -cha *adj* accustomed; finished; turned into; (*traje*) ready-made; (*llegado a la edad adulta*) full-grown ‖ *m* act, deed; fact; event; (*hazaña*) feat; **de hecho** in fact; **en hecho de verdad** as a matter of fact; **estar en el hecho de** to catch on to; **hecho consumado** fait accompli ‖ **hecho** *interj* all right!, OK!

hechura *f* form, shape, cut, build; creation, creature; workmanship; (Chile) drink, treat; **hechuras** cost of making; **no tener hechura** to be impracticable

heder §51 *tr* to bore, annoy, tire ‖ *intr* to stink, reek

hediondez *f* stench, stink

hedion•do -da *adj* stinking, smelly; annoying, boring; obscene, filthy, dirty ‖ *m* bean trefoil; skunk

hedor *m* stench, stink

helada *f* freezing; (*escarcha*) frost; **helada blanca** hoarfrost

heladera *f* refrigerator; (Chile) ice-cream tray

heladería *f* ice-cream parlor

hela•do -da *adj* cold, icy; (*pasmado por el miedo, la sorpresa, etc.*) frozen; (*esquivo, indiferente*) cold, chilly; (*cubierto de azúcar*) (Ven) iced ‖ *m* cold drink; (*manjar*) water ice; (*sorbete*) ice cream; **helado al corte** brick ice cream ‖ *f* see **helada**

hela•dor -dora *adj* freezing ‖ *f* ice-cream freezer

helar §2 *tr* to freeze; harden, congeal; dumbfound; discourage ‖ *intr* to freeze ‖ *ref* to freeze; harden, congeal, set; (*cubrirse de hielo*) to ice

helecho *m* fern

heléni•co -ca *adj* Hellenic

hele•no -na *adj* Hellenic ‖ *mf* Hellene

helero *m* glacier

hélice *f* helix; (*de un buque*) screw, propeller; (*de un avión*) propeller

helicóptero *m* helicopter

helio *m* helium

heliotropo *m* heliotrope

helipuerto *m* heliport

hematíe *m* red cell

hembra *adj invar* (*animal, planta, herramienta*) female; weak, thin, delicate ‖ *f* female; (*del corchete*) eye; (*tuerca*) nut; **hembra de terraja** (mach) die

hembraje *m* (SAm) females of a flock or herd

hembrilla *f* (mach) female part or piece; (*armella*) eyebolt

hemeroteca *f* periodical library

hemiciclo *m* (*semicírculo*) hemicycle; (*gradería semicircular*) amphitheater; (*espacio central del salón de sesiones de las Cortes*) floor

hemisferio *m* hemisphere

hemistiquio *m* hemistich

hemofilia *f* hemophilia

hemoglobina *f* hemoglobin

hemorragia *f* hemorrhage

hemorroides *fpl* hemorrhoids

hemóstato *m* hemostat

henal *m* hayloft

henar *m* hayfield

henchir §50 *tr* to fill; (*un colchón*) stuff; (*a una persona, p.ej., de favores*) heap, shower ‖ *ref* to be filled; stuff, stuff oneself

hendedura *f* crack, split, cleft

hender §51 *tr* to crack, split, cleave; (*el aire, las ondas*) cleave; make one's way through ‖ *ref* to crack, split

hendidura *f* crack, split, cleft

henil *m* hayloft, haymow

henna *f* henna

heno *m* hay

heñir §72 *tr* to knead; **hay mucho que heñir** there's still a lot of work to do

heraldía *f* heraldry

heráldi•co -ca *adj* heraldic ‖ *f* heraldry

heraldo *m* herald

herbáce•o -a *adj* herbaceous

herbajar *tr & intr* to graze

herbaje *m* herbage

herba•rio -ria *adj* herbal ‖ *m* (*libro*) herbal; (*colección*) herbarium

herbicida *m* weed killer

herbo•so -sa *adj* grassy

hercúle•o -a *adj* herculean

heredad *f* country estate

heredar *tr & intr* to inherit; **heredar a** to inherit from

herede•ro -ra *mf* heir, inheritor; owner of an estate; **heredero forzoso** heir apparent ‖ *m* heir ‖ *f* heiress

heredita•rio -ria *adj* hereditary

hereje *mf* heretic

herejía *f* heresy; insult, outrage; outrageous price

herencia f heritage, inheritance; (*transmisión de caracteres biológicos*) heredity; (*patrimonio de un difunto*) estate

heréti•co -ca adj heretic(al)

herida f injury, wound; insult, outrage; **renovar la herida** to open an old sore; **tocar en la herida** to sting to the quick

heri•do -da adj hurt, wounded; (*ofendido*) hurt ‖ mf injured person, wounded person; **los heridos** the injured, the wounded ‖ f see **herida**

herir §68 tr to injure, hurt, wound; (*ofender*) hurt; (*golpear*) strike; (*el sol sobre*) beat down upon; (*un instrumento de cuerda*) play; (*la cuerda de un instrumento*) pluck; touch, move

hermana f sister; **hermana de leche** foster sister; **hermana política** sister-in-law; **media hermana** half sister

hermanar tr to match, mate; combine, join; harmonize ‖ ref to match; become attached as brothers or sisters or brother and sister

hermanastra f stepsister

hermanastro m stepbrother

hermandad f brotherhood; sisterhood; close friendship; close relationship

herma•no -na adj (*p.ej., idioma*) sister ‖ mf companion, mate ‖ m brother; **hermano de leche** foster brother; **hermano político** brother-in-law; **hermanos** brother and sister; brothers and sisters; **hermanos siameses** Siamese twins; **medio hermano** half brother; **primo hermano** first cousin ‖ f see **hermana**

herméti•co -ca adj hermetic(al); air-tight; impenetrable; tight-lipped

hermosear tr to beautify, embellish

hermo•so -sa adj beautiful; (*caballero*) handsome

hermosura f beauty; (*mujer hermosa*) belle, beauty

hernia f hernia

héroe m hero

heroi•co -ca adj heroic; (*remedio*) desperate

heroína f heroine; (pharm) heroin

heroinómano m heroin addict

heroísmo m heroism

herrada f wooden bucket

herrador m horseshoer

herradura f horseshoe; **mostrar las herraduras** (*un caballo*) to kick, be vicious; (coll) to show one's heels

herraje m hardware, ironwork

herramental adj tool ‖ m toolbox, tool bag

herramienta f tool; set of tools; (coll) teeth; (coll) horns

herrar §2 tr (*guarnecer con hierro*) to fit with hardware; (*un caballo*) to shoe; (*marcar con hierro candente*) to brand; (*un barril*) to hoop

herrería f forge, blacksmith shop; blacksmithing; ironworks; rumpus

herrero m blacksmith; **herrero de grueso** ironworker; **herrero de obra** steelworker

herrete m tip, metal tip

herretear tr to tip, put a metal tip on

herrín m rust

herón m (*tejo de hierro horadado*) quoit; (*arandela*) washer

herrumbre f rust; (*honguillo parásito*) rust, plant rot

herrumbro•so -sa adj rusty

herventar §2 tr to boil

hervidero m boiling; bubbling spring; (*en el pecho*) rattle; (*de gente*) swarm

hervidor m boiler, cooker

hervir §68 intr to boil; (*el mar; una persona encolerizada*) boil, seethe; swarm, teem

hervor m boil, boiling; (*de la juventud*) fire, restlessness; **alzar el hervor** to begin to boil

hervoro•so -sa adj ardent, fiery, impetuous

heterócli•to -ta adj irregular; unconventional

heterodinar tr to heterodyne

heterodi•no -na adj heterodyne

heterodo•xo -xa adj heterodox

heterogeneidad f heterogeneity

heterogéne•o -a adj heterogeneous

hexámetro m hexameter

hez f (pl **heces**) (fig) scum, dregs; **heces** lees, dregs; feces, excrement

hiato m hiatus

hibisco m hibiscus

hibridación f hybridization

hibridar tr & intr to hybridize

híbri•do -da adj & m hybrid

hidal•go -ga adj noble, illustrious ‖ m nobleman ‖ f noblewoman

hidalguez f or **hidalguía** f nobility

hidra f hydra

hidratar tr & ref to hydrate

hidrato m hydrate

hidráuli•co -ca adj hydraulic ‖ f hydraulics

hidroala m (*vehículo mixto de buque y avión*) hydrofoil

hidroaleta f (*miembro alar del hidroala*) hydrofoil

hidroavión m hydroplane

hidrocarburo m hydrocarbon

hidroeléctri•co -ca adj hydroelectric

hidrófi•lo -la adj (*algodón*) absorbent (*cotton*)

hidrofobia f hydrophobia

hidrófu•go -ga adj waterproof

hidrógeno m hydrogen

hidropesía f dropsy

hidróxido m hydroxide

hiedra f ivy

hiel f bile, gall; (fig) gall, bitterness, sorrow; **echar la hiel** to strain, overwork

hielo m ice; (fig) coldness, coolness; **hielo flotante** drift ice, ice pack; **hielo seco** dry ice; **romper el hielo** (*quebrantar la reserva*) to break the ice

hiena f hyena

hienda f dung

hierba f grass; (*especialmente la que tiene propiedades medicinales*) herb; **hierba de la plata** honesty; **hierba del asno** evening primrose; **hierba de París** truelove; **hierba gatera** catnip; **hierba pastel** woad; **hierbas** grass, pasture; herb poison; years of age (*said of animals*); **mala hierba** weed; wayward young fellow

hierbabuena *f* mint
hierro *m* iron; (*marca candente que se pone a los ganados*) brand; **hierro colado** cast iron; **hierro colado en barras** pig iron; **hierro de desecho** scrap iron; **hierro de marcar** branding iron; **hierro dulce** wrought iron; **hierro fundido** cast iron; **hierro galvanizado** galvanized iron; **hierro ondulado** corrugated iron; **hierros** irons, fetters; **llevar hierro a Vizcaya** to carry coals to Newcastle
higa *f* baby's fist-shaped amulet; scorn, contempt; **dar higa** to misfire; **no dar dos higas por** to not give a rap for
hígado *m* liver; **echar los hígados** to strain, to overwork; **hígados** guts, courage; **malos hígados** hatred, grudge; **ser un hígado** to be a nuisance
higiene *f* hygiene
higiéni•co -ca *adj* hygienic
higo *m* fig; **higo chumbo** prickly pear; **higo paso** dried fig; **no valer un higo** to be not worth a continental
higuera *f* fig tree; **higuera chumba** prickly pear
hija *f* daughter; **hija política** daughter-in-law
hijas•tro -tra *mf* stepchild ‖ *m* stepson ‖ *f* stepdaughter
hi•jo -ja *mf* child; (*de un animal*) young; **hijo de bendición** legitimate child; good child; **hijo de la cuna** foundling; **hijo del amor** love child; **hijo de leche** foster child ‖ *m* son; **cada hijo de vecino** every man Jack, every mother's son; **hijo del agua** good sailor; good swimmer; **hijo de su padre** chip off the old block; **hijo de sus propias obras** self-made man; **hijo político** son-in-law; **hijos** children; descendants ‖ *f* see **hija**
hijodalgo *m* (*pl* **hijosdalgo**) nobleman
hijuela *f* little girl, little daughter; (*tira de tela*) gore; branch drain; side path
hijuelero *m* rural postman
hijuelo *m* shoot, sucker
hila *f* row, line; (*acción de hilar*) spinning; **a la hila** in single file; **hilas** (*hebras para curar heridas*) lint
hilacha *f* shred, fraying; **hilacha de acero** steel wool; **hilacha de algodón** cotton waste; **hilacha de vidrio** spun glass; **hilachas** lint; **mostrar la hilacha** (Arg) to show one's worst side
hilachen•to -ta *adj* tattered; in rags
hilachos *mpl* (Mex) rags, tatters
hilacho•so -sa *adj* frayed, raggedy
hilada *f* row, line; (mas) course
hilado *m* spinning; (*hilo*) yarn, thread
hila•dor -dora *adj* spinning ‖ *mf* spinner ‖ *f* spinning machine
hilandería *f* spinning; spinning mill
hilande•ro -ra *adj* spinning ‖ *m* spinning mill
hilar *tr & intr* to spin; **hilar delgado** to hew close to the line; **hilar largo** to drag on
hilarante *adj* laughable; (*gas*) laughing
hilaza *f* yarn, thread; lint; **descubrir la hilaza** to show one's true nature

hilera *f* row, line; fine thread, fine yarn; (*parhilera*) ridgepole; (mil) file
hilo *m* thread; (*hebras retorcidas*) yarn; (*alambre*) wire; (*de perlas*) string; (*de agua*) thin stream; (*de luz*) beam; linen, linen fabric; (*de un discurso, de la vida*) (fig) thread; **hilo bramante** twine; **hilo de la muerte** end of life; **hilo de masa** (aut) ground wire; **hilo de medianoche** midnight sharp; **hilo dental** dental floss; **hilo de tierra** (elec) ground wire; **irse al hilo** or **tras el hilo de la gente** to follow the crowd; **manejar los hilos** to pull strings; **perder el hilo de** to lose the thread of
hilván *m* basting, tacking; basting stitch; (Chile) basting thread; (Ven) hem; **hablar de hilván** to jabber along
hilvanar *tr* to baste, tack; sketch, outline; (*hacer con precipitación*) hurry; (Ven) to hem ‖ *intr* to baste, tack
himnario *m* hymnal, hymn book
himno *m* hymn; **himno nacional** national anthem
hin *m* neigh, whinny
hincadura *f* driving, thrusting, sticking
hincapié *m* stamping the foot; **hacer hincapié en** to lay great stress on, to emphasize
hincar §73 *tr* to drive, thrust, stick, sink; (*la rodilla*) go down on, fall on ‖ *ref* to kneel, kneel down; **hincarse de rodillas** to go down on one's knees
hincha *mf* (sport) fan, rooter ‖ *f* grudge, ill will
hinchable *adj* inflatable; (*goma de mascar*) bubble
hincha•do -da *adj* swollen; swollen with pride; (*estilo, lenguaje*) pompous, high-flown ‖ *m* (*de un neumático*) inflation ‖ *f* (sport) fans, rooters
hinchar *tr* to swell; inflate; (*un neumático*) pump up; exaggerate, embroider ‖ *ref* to swell; swell up, become puffed up (*with pride*)
hinchazón *f* swelling; vanity, conceit; (*del estilo, lenguaje*) bombast
hinchismo *m* (sport) fans, rooters
hin•dú -dúa (*pl* **-dúes -dúas**) *adj & mf* Hindoo, Hindu
hiniesta *f* Spanish broom
hinojo *m* fennel; **de hinojos** on one's knees
hipar *intr* to hiccup; (*los perros cuando siguen la caza*) pant, snuffle; (*gimotear*) whimper; be worn out; **hipar por** to long for; long to
hiperacidez *f* hyperacidity
hipérbola *f* (geom) hyperbola
hipérbole *f* (rhet) hyperbole
hiperbóli•co -ca *adj* (geom & rhet) hyperbolic
hipersensible *adj* (*alérgico*) hypersensitive
hipertensión *f* hypertension, high blood pressure
hípica *f* (horseback) riding; equestrianism
hípi•co -ca *adj* horse, equine
hipnosis *f* hypnosis

hipnóti•co -ca *adj* hypnotic ‖ *mf* hypnotic ‖ *m (medicamento que provoca el sueño)* hypnotic

hipnotismo *m* hypnotism

hipnotista *mf* hypnotist

hipnotizar §60 *tr* to hypnotize

hipo *m* hiccup; longing, desire; **tener hipo contra** to have a grudge against; **tener hipo por** to desire eagerly

hipocondría•co -ca *adj* & *mf* hypochondriac

hipocresía *f* hypocrisy

hipócrita *adj* hypocritical ‖ *mf* hypocrite

hipodérmi•co -ca *adj* hypodermic

hipódromo *m* hippodrome, race track

hipopótamo *m* hippopotamus

hiposulfito *m* hyposulfite

hipoteca *f* mortgage; **¡buena hipoteca!** you may believe it, if you want to!

hipotecar §73 *tr* to mortgage

hipoteca•rio -ria *adj* mortgage

hipotenusa *f* hypotenuse

hipóte•sis *f* (*pl* **-sis**) hypothesis; **hipótesis de guía** working hypothesis

hipotéti•co -ca *adj* hypothetic(al)

hiriente *adj* cutting, stinging

hirsu•to -ta *adj* hairy, bristly; (fig) brusque, gruff

hirviente *adj* boiling

hisopear *tr* to sprinkle with holy water

hisopo *m* (bot) hyssop; aspergillum, sprinkler of holy water; paint brush, shaving brush

hispalense *adj* & *mf* Sevillian

hispáni•co -ca *adj* & *mf* Hispanic

hispanista *mf* Hispanist

hispa•no -na *adj* Spanish; Spanish American ‖ *mf* Spaniard; Spanish American

hispanohablante or **hispanoparlante** *adj* Spanish-speaking ‖ *mf* speaker of Spanish

híspi•do -da *adj* bristly, spiny

histéri•co -ca *adj* hysterical

histerismo *m* hysteria

histología *f* histology

historia *f* history; story, tale; **de historia** notorious, infamous; **dejarse de historias** to come to the point; **historia de lagrimitas** (coll) sob story; **historias** gossip, meddling; **pasar a la historia** to become a thing of the past; **picar en historia** to turn out to be serious

historia•do -da *adj* richly adorned; overadorned; *(cuadro, dibujo)* storied

historial *adj* historical ‖ *m* record, dossier

historiar §77 & regular *tr* to tell the history of; tell the story of; *(un suceso histórico)* (fa) to depict

histórico -ca *adj* historic(al)

historieta *f* anecdote, brief story; **historieta gráfica** comic strip

histrión *m* actor; juggler; buffoon

histrióni•co -ca *adj* histrionic

hita *f* brad; landmark, milestone

hi•to -ta *adj* fixed, firm; *(casa, calle)* next; *(caballo)* black ‖ *m (clavo fijado en la tierra)* peg, hob; *(juego)* quoits; *(blanco)* target; *(mojón)* landmark, milestone; **dar en el hito** to hit the nail on the head; **mirar de hito en hito** to eye up and down ‖ *f* see **hita**

Hno. *abbr* **Hermano**

hoba•chón -chona *adj* lumpish

hocicar §73 *tr* to nuzzle, root; keep on kissing ‖ *intr* to nuzzle, root; run into a snag; *(la proa)* (naut) to dip

hocico *m* snout; *(de una persona)* snout; sour face; **caer de hocicos** to fall on one's face; **meter el hocico en todo** to poke one's nose into everything; **poner hocico** to make a face

hogaño *adv* this year; at the present time

hogar *m* fireplace, hearth; furnace; home; family life; *(hoguera)* bonfire

hogare•ño -ña *adj* home-loving ‖ *mf* homebody, stay-at-home

hogaza *f* large loaf of bread

hoguera *f* bonfire

hoja *f (de planta, libro, mesa, muelle, puerta plegadiza, etc.; pétalo de flor)* leaf; *(de planta acuática)* pad; *(de papel)* sheet; blank sheet; *(de cuchillo, sierra, espada, etc.)* blade; *(hojuela de metal)* foil; *(de persiana)* slat; *(del patín)* runner; **doblar la hoja** to change the subject; **hoja clínica** clinical chart; **hoja de afeitar** razor blade; **hoja de embalaje** packing slip; **hoja de encuadernador** (bb) end paper; **hoja de estaño** tin foil; **hoja de estudios** transcript; **hoja de guarda** (bb) flyleaf; **hoja del anunciante** tear sheet; **hoja de lata** tin, tin plate; **hoja de nenúfar** lily pad; **hoja de paga** pay roll; **hoja de parra** fig leaf; **hoja de pedidos** order blank; **hoja de rodaje** (mov) shooting record; **hoja de ruta** waybill; **hoja de servicios** service record; **hoja de trébol** cloverleaf *(intersection)*; **hoja maestra** master blade *(of spring)*; **hojas del autor** (typ) advance sheets; **hoja suelta** leaflet, handbill; (bb) flyleaf; **hoja volante** leaflet, handbill

hojalata *f* tin, tin plate

hojalatería *f* tinsmith's shop; tinwork

hojalatero *m* tinsmith, tinner

hojaldre *m* & *f* puff paste

hojarasca *f* dead leaves; trash, rubbish; bluff, vain show

hojear *tr* to leaf through ‖ *intr* to scale off; *(las hojas de los árboles)* flutter

hojita *f* leaflet; **hojita de afeitar** razor blade

hojo•so -sa *adj* leafy

hojuela *f (hoja de otra compuesta)* leaflet; *(fruta de sartén)* pancake; *(hoja muy delgada de metal)* foil; **hojuela de estaño** tin foil

hola *interj* hey!, hello!

Holanda *f* Holland

holan•dés -desa *adj* Dutch; **a la holandesa** *(bb)* half-bound ‖ *mf* Hollander ‖ *m* Dutchman; *(idioma)* Dutch ‖ *f* Dutch woman

holga•chón -chona *adj* lazy, idle ‖ *mf* loafer, idler

holgadero *m* hangout

holga•do -da *adj* idle, unoccupied; *(vestido)* loose, full, roomy; *(que vive con bienestar)* fairly well-off

hi
ho

holganza *f* idleness, leisure; pleasure, enjoyment

holgar §63 *intr* to idle, be idle; take it easy, rest up; not fit, be too loose; be unnecessary, be of no use; be glad ‖ *ref* to be glad; be amused

holga•zán -zana *adj* idle, lazy ‖ *mf* idler, loafer

holgazanear *intr* to idle, loaf, bum around

hol•gón -gona *adj* pleasure-loving ‖ *mf* loafer, lizard

holgorio *m* fun, merriment

holgura *f* looseness, fulness; enjoyment, merriment; comfort, easy circumstances; (mach) play

holocausto *m* holocaust

hollar §61 *tr* to tread on, to trample on

hollejo *m* hull, peel, skin

hollín *m* soot

hollinar *tr* (Chile) to cover with soot

hollinien•to -ta *adj* sooty

hombracho *m* big husky fellow

hombrada *f* manly act

hombradía *f* manliness, courage

hombre *m* man; husband, man; my boy, old chap; **buen hombre** good-natured fellow; ¡**hombre al agua!**' or ¡**hombre a la mar!** man overboard!; **hombre bueno** arbiter, referee; **hombre de bien** honorable man; **hombre de buenas prendas** man of parts; **hombre de ciencia** scientist; **hombre de dinero** man of means; **hombre de estado** statesman; **hombre de letras** man of letters; **hombre de mundo** man of the world; **hombre de suposición** man of straw; **hombre hecho** grown man ‖ *interj* man alive!, upon my word!

hombre-anuncio *m* sandwich man

hombrear *tr* (Arg) to carry on the shoulders; (Mex) to aid, back ‖ *intr* to try to be somebody; (*una mujer*) to be mannish; **hombrear con** to try to be equal

hombrecillo *m* little man; (*lúpulo*) hop

hombrera *f* (*del vestido*) shoulder; shoulder pad; epaulet

hombre-rana *m* (*pl* **hombres-ranas**) frogman

hombría *f* manliness; **hombría de bien** honor, probity

hombrillo *m* (*de la camisa*) yoke; shoulder piece

hombro *m* shoulder; **arrimar el hombro** to lend a hand, put one's shoulder to the wheel; **encoger los hombros** to let one's shoulders droop; **encogerse de hombros** to shrug one's shoulders; to crouch, to shrink with fear; to not answer; **mirar por encima del hombro** to look down upon; **salir en hombros** to be carried off on the shoulders of the crowd

hombru•no -na *adj* mannish

homenaje *m* homage; (feud) homage; (Chile) gift, favor; **homenaje de boca** lip service; **rendir homenaje a** to swear allegiance to

homeópata *mf* homeopath

homeopatía *f* homeopathy

homicida *adj* homicidal ‖ *mf* homicide

homicidio *m* homicide

homilía *f* homily

homogeneidad *f* homogeneity

homogeneizar §60 *tr* to homogenize

homogéne•o -a *adj* homogeneous

homologación *f* confirmation, ratification; (sport) validation

homologar §44 *tr* to confirm, ratify; (*un récord*) (sport) to validate

homólo•go -ga *adj* homologous ‖ *m* colleague

homóni•mo -ma *adj* homonymous; of the same name ‖ *mf* namesake ‖ *m* homonym

homosexual *adj* & *mf* homosexual; gay

homúnculo *m* guy, little runt

honda *f* sling

hondazo *m* blow with a sling

hondear *tr* (naut) to sound

hondillos *mpl* patches in the crotch of pants

hon•do -da *adj* deep; (*terreno*) low ‖ *m* bottom ‖ *f* see **honda** ‖ **hondo** *adv* deep

hondón *m* (*de la aguja*) eye; (*de un vaso*) bottom; lowland

hondonada *f* lowland, ravine

hondura *f* depth, profundity; **meterse en honduras** to go beyond one's depth

hondure•ño -ña *adj* & *mf* Honduran

honestidad *f* decency; chastity; modesty; honesty, probity; fairness, reasonableness

hones•to -ta *adj* decent; chaste, pure; modest; honest, upright; (*precio*) fair, reasonable

hongo *m* fungus, mushroom; (*sombrero*) bowler, derby

honor *m* honor; **en honor a la verdad** as a matter of fact, to tell the truth; **hacer honor a** to do honor to; (*la firma*) to honor

honorable *adj* honorable

honora•rio -ria *adj* honorary ‖ *s* fee, honorarium

honorífi•co -ca *adj* honorific

honra *f* honor; **tener a mucha honra** to be proud of

honradez *f* honesty, integrity

honra•do -da *adj* honorable

honrar *tr* to honor ‖ *ref* to feel honored

honrilla *f* — **por la negra honrilla** out of concern for what people will say

honro•so -sa *adj* honorable

hopo *m* tuft, shock (*of hair*); bushy tail; **seguir el hopo a** (coll) to keep right after

hora *f* hour; (*momento determinado para algo*) time; **a la hora** on time; **a la hora de ahora** right now; **a la hora en punto** on the hour; **a las pocas horas** within a few hours; **dar hora** to fix a time; **dar la hora** (*el reloj*) to strike; **de última hora** up-to-date; most up-to-date; (*noticias*) late; **en buen hora** or **en hora buena** safely, luckily; all right; **en mal hora** or **en hora mala** unluckily, in an evil hour; **fuera de horas** after hours; **hasta altas horas** until late into the night; **hora de acostarse** bedtime; **hora de aglomeración** rush hour; **hora de cierre** closing time; curfew; **hora de comer** mealtime; **hora de verano** daylight-saving time; **hora de verdad** (taur) kill; **hora legal** or oficial standard time; **hora punta** peak hour; rush hour; **horas de afluencia** rush hour; **horas extra** overtime; **horas de consulta** office hours (*of a doctor*); **horas de ocio** leisure hours; **horas de punta** rush hour; **horas extraordinarias de trabajo** overtime

horadar *tr* to drill, bore, pierce

hora•rio -ria *adj* hour ‖ *m* hour hand; clock; (*de ferrocarriles*) timetable; **horario escolar** roster

horca *f* (*para levantar la paja*) pitchfork; (*para ahorcar a un condenado*) gallows, gibbet; (*de ajos, cebollas, etc.*) string

horcajadas — a horcajadas astride, astraddle

horcajadillas — a horcajadillas astride, astraddle

horcajadura *f* crotch

horcajo *m* (*confluencia de dos ríos*) fork; (*para mulas*) yoke

horcón *m* pitchfork; forked prop (*for fruit trees*); upright, prop

horchata *f* orgeat

horda *f* horde

horero *m* (*reloj*) hour hand

horizontal *adj & f* horizontal

horizonte *m* horizon

horma *f* form, mold; shoe tree; hat block; **hallar la horma de su zapato** to meet one's match

hormiga *f* ant; (*enfermedad que causa comezón*) itch

hormigón *m* concrete; **hormigón armado** reinforced concrete

hormigonera *f* concrete mixer

hormigo•so -sa *adj* antlike; full of ants; anteaten; (*picante*) itchy

hormiguear *intr* (*ponerse en movimiento gente o animales*) to swarm; (*experimentar una sensación de hormigas corriendo por el cuerpo*) crawl, creep; abound, teem

hormiguero *m* anthill; (*de gente*) swarm, mob

hormillón *m* hat block

hormón *m* or **hormona** *f* hormone

hornacina *f* niche

hornada *f* (*cantidad que se cuece de una vez en un horno*) batch, bake; (*conjunto de individuos de una misma promoción*) crop

hornazo *m* Easter cake filled with hard-boiled eggs; Easter gift to Lenten preacher

horne•ro -ra *mf* baker

hornilla *f* kitchen grate; pigeonhole

hornillo *m* kitchen stove; hot plate; (*de la pipa de fumar*) bowl

horno *m* oven, furnace; (*para cocer ladrillos*) kiln; **alto horno** blast furnace; **horno de cal** limekiln; **horno de fundición** smelting furnace; **horno de ladrillero** brickkiln

horóscopo *m* horoscope; **sacar un horóscopo** to cast a horoscope

horqueta *f* pitchfork; fork, prop; (*ángulo agudo en un río*) (Arg) bend

horquilla *f* pitchfork; (*de bicicleta*) fork; (*de microteléfono*) cradle; (*alfiler para sujetar el pelo*) hairpin

horrar *tr* to save

hórreo *m* granary; (in Asturias and Galicia) crib or granary raised on pillars (*to protect grain from mice and dampness*)

horrible *adj* horrible

horripilante *adj* hair-raising, blood-curdling

horror *m* horror; **tener horror a** to have a horror of

horrorizar §60 *tr* to horrify

horroro•so -sa *adj* horrid; hideous, ugly

hortaliza *f* vegetable

hortela•no -na *adj* garden ‖ *mf* gardener

hortera *m* clerk, helper ‖ *f* wooden bowl

hortícola *adj* horticultural

horticul•tor -tora *mf* horticulturist

horticultura *f* horticulture

hos•co -ca *adj* dark, dark-skinned; sullen, grim, gloomy

hospedaje *m* lodging

hospedar *tr* to lodge ‖ *ref* to lodge, stop, put up

hospedería *f* hospice; inn, hostelry

hospede•ro -ra *mf* innkeeper

hospicio *m* hospice; poorhouse; orphan asylum

hospital *m* hospital; **estar hecho un hospital** (*una persona*) to be full of aches and pains; (*una casa*) to be turned into a hospital; **hospital de la sangre** poor relations; **hospital de primera sangre** (mil) field hospital; **hospital robado** bare house

hospitala•rio -ria *adj* hospitable

hospitalidad *f* hospitality; (*estancia del enfermo en el hospital*) hospitalization

hospitalizar §60 *tr* to hospitalize

hosquedad *f* darkness; sullenness, grimness, gloominess

hostelería *f* restaurant and hotel business

hostería *f* inn, hostelry

hostia *f* sacrificial victim; wafer; (eccl) wafer, Host

hostigar §44 *tr* to scourge; harass; to pester; cloy, surfeit

hostigo•so -sa *adj* cloying, sickening

hostil *adj* hostile

hostilidad *f* hostility

hostilizar §60 *tr* to antagonize; (*al enemigo*) harry, harass

hotel *m* (*establecimiento donde se da comida y alojamiento por dinero*) hotel; (*casa particular lujosa*) mansion

hotele•ro -ra *adj* hotel ‖ *mf* hotelkeeper

hoy *adv & s* today; **de hoy a mañana** any time now; **de hoy en adelante** from now on; **hoy día** nowadays

hoya *f* hole, pit, ditch; (*sepultura*) grave; valley; (*almáciga*) seedbed; river basin

hoyanca *f* potter's field

hoyo *m* hole; grave; pockmark

hoyo•so -sa *adj* full of holes

hoyuelo *m* dimple; (*juego de muchachos*) pitching pennies

hoz *f* (*pl* **hoces**) sickle; narrow pass, defile; **de hoz y de coz** headlong, recklessly

ho
ho

hozar §60 *tr & intr* to nuzzle, root

hta. *abbr* **hasta**

huacal *m* var of **guacal**

huachinango *m* (Mex) red snapper

hucha *f* workingman's chest; (*alcancía*) toy bank; (*dinero ahorrado*) savings, nest egg

huchear *intr* to cry, shout

hue•co -ca *adj* hollow; (*mullido*) soft, fluffy, spongy; (*voz*) deep, resounding; vain, conceited; (*estilo, lenguaje*) affected, pompous ‖ *m* hollow; interval; (*en un muro, una hilera de coches, etc.*) opening; (*empleo sin proveer*) opening; **hueco de la axila** armpit; **hueco de escalera** stair well

huélfago *m* (vet) heaves

huelga *f* (*ocio*) rest, leisure, idleness; recreation; pleasant spot; (*cesación del trabajo en señal de protesta*) strike; (mach) play; **huelga de brazos caídos** sit-down strike; **huelga de hambre** hunger strike; **huelga general** general strike; **huelga patronal** lockout; **huelga por solidaridad** sympathy strike; **huelga sentada** sit-down strike; **ir a la huelga** or **ponerse en huelga** to go on strike

huelguista *mf* striker

huella *f* track, footprint; trace, mark; rut; (*acción de hollar*) tread, treading; (*peldaño en que se asienta el pie*) tread; **huella dactilar** or **digital** fingerprint; **huella de sonido** sound track; **seguir las huellas de** to follow in the footsteps of

huérfa•no -na *adj* orphan; orphaned; alone, deserted ‖ *mf* orphan; (Chile, Peru) foundling

hue•ro -ra *adj* rotten; (fig) empty, hollow; (Guat, Mex) blond; **salir huero** (coll) to flop, turn out bad ‖ *mf* (Guat, Mex) blond

huerta *f* vegetable garden; fruit garden; irrigated region

huerte•ro -ra *mf* (Arg, Peru) gardener

huerto *m* (*de árboles frutales*) orchard; (*de verduras*) kitchen garden

huesa *f* grave

huesear *intr* to beg (alms)

huesillo *m* (Chile, Peru) sun-dried peach

hueso *m* bone; (*de ciertas frutas*) stone, pit; drudgery; **a otro perro con ese hueso** tell that to the marines; **calarse hasta los huesos** to get soaked to the skin; **hueso de la alegría** crazy bone, funny bone; **hueso de la suerte** wishbone; **hueso duro de roer** a hard nut to crack; **la sin hueso** the tongue; **no dejarle a uno un hueso sano** to beat someone up; to pick someone to pieces; **no poder con sus huesos** to be all in; **soltar la sin hueso** to talk too much; to pour forth insults; **tener los huesos molidos** to be all fagged out

hueso•so -sa *adj* bony

hués•ped -peda *mf* (*persona alojada en casa ajena*) guest; (*persona que hospeda a otra en su casa*) host; (*mesonero*) innkeeper, host

hueste *f* followers; (*ejército*) army, host

huesu•do -da *adj* bony, big-boned

hueva *f* roe, fish roe

hueve•ro -ra *mf* egg dealer ‖ *f* eggcup; oviduct

huevo *m* egg; **huevo a la plancha** fried egg; **huevo al plato** shirred egg; **huevo del té** tea ball; **huevo de zurcir** darning egg or gourd; **huevo duro** hard-boiled egg; **huevo escalfado** poached egg; **huevo estrellado** or **frito** fried egg; **huevo pasado por agua** soft-boiled egg; **huevos revueltos** scrambled eggs

huída *f* flight; (*de un líquido*) leak; (*ensanche en un agujero*) flare, splay; (*de caballo*) shying

huidi•zo -za *adj* fugitive; evasive

huincha *f* (SAm) tape; (SAm) tape measure

huipil *m* (Mex) colorful poncho worn by Indian women

huir §20 *tr* to flee, avoid, shun; (*el cuerpo*) duck ‖ *intr* to flee; (*el tiempo*) fly; (*de la memoria*) to slip ‖ *ref* to flee

hule *m* (*tela impermeable*) oilcloth; rubber; (taur) blood, goring

hulear *intr* (CAm) to gather rubber

hulla *f* coal; **hulla azul** tide power; wind power; **hulla blanca** white power; water power

hullera *f* colliery, coal mine

humanidad *f* humanity; fatness

humanista *adj & mf* humanist

humanita•rio -ria *adj & mf* humanitarian

huma•no -na *adj* (*perteneciente al hombre*) human; (*compasivo, misericordioso; civilizador*) humane

humareda *f* cloud of smoke

humeante *adj* smoking, smoky; steamy, reeking

humear *tr* (SAm) to fumigate ‖ *intr* to smoke; steam, reek; put on airs; (*reliquias de un alboroto, enemistad, etc.*) last, persist

humectador *m* humidifier

humedad *f* humidity, dampness, moisture

humedecer §22 *tr* to humidify, dampen, moisten, wet

húme•do -da *adj* humid, damp, moist

humero *m* smokestack, chimney

húmero *m* humerus

humidificador *m* air humidifier

humildad *f* humility

humilde *adj* humble

humilladero *m* calvary, road shrine; priedieu

humillante *adj* humiliating

humillar *tr* (*abatir el orgullo de*) to humble; (*avergonzar*) humiliate, (*la cabeza*) bow; (*el cuerpo, las rodillas*) bend ‖ *ref* to humble oneself; cringe, grovel

humo *m* smoke; steam, fume; **a humo de pajas** lightly, thoughtlessly; **bajar los humos a** (coll) to humble, take down a peg; **echar más humo que una chimenea** to smoke like a chimney; **humos** airs, conceit; hearths, homes; **irse todo en humo** to go up in smoke; **tragar el humo** to inhale; **vender humos** to peddle influence

humor *m* humor; **de mal humor** out of humor; **estar de humor para** to be in the humor for; **seguir el humor a** to humor
humorismo *m* humor, humorousness
humorista *mf* humorist
humorísti•co -ca *adj* humorous
humo•so -sa *adj* smoky
hundible *adj* sinkable
hundir *tr* to sink; plunge; (*abrumar*) overwhelm; confound, confute; destroy, ruin ‖ *ref* to sink; collapse; settle, cave in; come to ruin; disappear, vanish
húnga•ro -ra *adj & mf* Hungarian ‖ *m* (*idioma*) Hungarian
Hungría *f* Hungary
hupe *m* punk
huracán *m* hurricane
huranía *f* shyness, unsociability
hura•ño -ña *adj* shy, unsociable
hurgar §44 *tr* to poke; (fig) to stir up, incite; **peor es hurgallo** (i.e., **hurgarlo**) better keep hands off ‖ *intr* to poke ‖ *ref* (*la nariz*) to pick
hurgón *m* poker; thrust, stab
hurgonazo *m* (*con hurgón*) poke; jab, stab, thrust
hurgonear *tr* to poke; to jab, to stab at
hurgonero *m* poker

hu•rón -rona *adj* shy, diffident ‖ *mf* prier, snooper; shy person, diffident person ‖ *m* ferret
huronear *tr* to ferret, hunt with a ferret; to ferret out
huronera *f* ferret hole; lair, hiding place
hurtadillas — a hurtadillas by stealth, on the sly; **a hurtadillas de** unbeknown to
hurtar *tr* to steal; (*en pesos y medidas*) cheat; (*el suelo*) wear away; plagiarize; **hurtar el cuerpo** to dodge, duck ‖ *ref* to withdraw, hide
hurto *m* thieving; theft; **a hurto** stealthily, on the sly; **coger con el hurto en las manos** to catch with the goods; **hurto mayor** grand larceny
husma *f* snooping; **andar a la husma** to go around snooping
husmear *tr* to scent, smell out; pry into ‖ *intr* (*la carne*) to smell bad, become gamy
husmo *m* gaminess, high odor; **estar al husmo** to wait for a chance
huso *m* (*para hilar*) spindle; (*para devanar*) bobbin; (*cilindro del torno*) drum; **huso horario** time zone; **ser más derecho que un huso** to be as straight as a ramrod
huta *f* hunter's blind
huy *interj* ouch!
huyente *adj* (*frente*) receding; (*ojeada*) shifty

I

I, i (i) *f* tenth letter of the Spanish alphabet
ib. *abbr* **ibídem**
ibéri•co -ca *adj* Iberian
ibe•ro -ra *adj & mf* Iberian
íbice *m* ibex
ice•berg *m* (*pl* **-bergs**) iceberg
iconoclasia *f or* **iconoclasmo** *m* iconoclasm
iconoclasta *mf* iconoclast
iconoscopio *m* (telv) iconoscope
ictericia *f* jaundice
ictericia•do -da *adj* jaundiced
ictiología *f* ichthyology
ida *f* going; departure; rashness; sally; trail; **de ida y vuelta** round-trip; **idas y venidas** comings and goings
idea *f* idea; **mudar de idea** to change one's mind
ideal *adj & m* ideal
idealista *adj & mf* idealist
idealizar §60 *tr* to idealize
idear *tr* to think up, devise
idemista *adj* yes-saying ‖ *mf* yes sayer
idénti•co -ca *adj* identic(al); (*muy parecido*) very similar
identidad *f* identity, sameness
identificación *f* identification
identificar §73 *tr* to identify
ideología *f* ideology
idíli•co -ca *adj* idyllic

idilio *m* idyll
idioma *m* language; (*modo particular de hablar*) idiom, speech
idiomáti•co -ca *adj* idiomatic; language, linguistic
idiosincrasia *f* idiosyncrasy
idiota *adj* idiotic ‖ *mf* idiot
idiotez *f* idiocy
idiotismo *m* ignorance; (*idiotez*) idiocy; (gram) idiom
i•do -da *adj* wild, scatterbrained; drunk ‖ **los idos** the dead ‖ *f see* **ida**
idolatrar *tr* to idolize
idolatría *f* idolatry; (*amor excesivo a una persona*) idolization
ídolo *m* idol
idoneidad *f* fitness, suitability
idóne•o -a *adj* fit, suitable
idus *mpl* ides
iglesia *f* church; **entrar en la iglesia** to go into the church; **llevar a la iglesia** to lead to the altar
iglesie•ro -ra *adj* (Arg) church-going ‖ *mf* (Arg) church goer
igna•ro -ra *adj* ignorant
ignominio•so -sa *adj* ignominious
ignorancia *f* ignorance
ignorante *adj* ignorant ‖ *mf* ignoramus
ignorar *tr* to not know, be ignorant of

igno•to -ta *adj* unknown

igual *adj* equal; (*liso, llano*) smooth, even, level; (*no variable*) firm, constant, equable; indifferent; **me es igual** it makes no difference to me ‖ *m* equal; equal sign; **al igual de** like, after the fashion of; **al igual que** as; while, whereas; **en igual de** instead of

iguala *f* equalization; agreement

igualación *f* equalization; agreement

igualar *tr* to equal; (*alisar, allanar*) smooth, even, level; make equal, match; deem equal ‖ *intr & ref* to be equal

igualdad *f* equality; smoothness, evenness; **igualdad de ánimo** equanimity; **igualdad de oportunidades** equal opportunity

igualmente *adv* likewise; **igualmente que** the same as

ijada *f* (*de animal*) flank; (*del cuerpo humano*) loin; (*dolor en estas partes*) stitch; **tener su ijada** to have its weak side or point

ijadear *intr* to pant

ijar *m* flank; loin

ilegal *adj* illegal

ilegible *adj* illegible

ilegíti•mo -ma *adj* illegitimate

ile•so -sa *adj* unscathed, unharmed

iletra•do -da *adj* unlettered, uncultured

ilíci•to -ta *adj* illicit, unlawful

ilimita•do -da *adj* limitless

ilitera•to -ta *adj* illiterate

ilógi•co -ca *adj* illogical

ilote *m* ear of corn

iludir *tr* to elude, evade

iluminación *f* illumination

iluminador *m* lighting engineer

iluminar *tr* to illuminate, light, light up ‖ *ref* to light up, brighten

ilusión *f* illusion; (*esperanza infundada*) delusion; enthusiasm, zeal; dream; **forjarse or hacerse ilusiones** to kid oneself, indulge in wishful thinking

ilusionar *tr* to delude ‖ *ref* to have illusions, indulge in wishful thinking; be enraptured, be beguiled

ilusionista *mf* prestidigitator, magician

ilusi•vo -va *adj* illusive

ilu•so -sa *adj* deluded, misguided; (*propenso a ilusionarse*) visionary

iluso•rio -ria *adj* illusory

ilustración *f* illustration; enlightenment; illustrated magazine

ilustra•do -da *adj* illustrated; learned, informed; enlightened

ilustrar *tr* (*adornar con grabados alusivos al texto*) to illustrate; make illustrious, make famous; explain, elucidate; enlighten ‖ *ref* to become famous; be enlightened

ilustre *adj* illustrious

imagen *f* image; picture

imaginación *f* imagination

imaginar *tr, intr & ref* to imagine

imagina•rio -ria *adj* imaginary

imaginati•vo -va *adj* imaginative ‖ *f* imagination; understanding

imaginería *f* fancy colored embroidery; carving or painting of religious images

imán *m* magnet; (fig) lodestone; **imán de herradura** horseshoe magnet; **imán inductor** (elec) field magnet

imanar or imantar *tr* to magnetize

imbatible *adj* unbeatable

imbécil *adj & mf* imbecile

imbecilidad *f* imbecility

imberbe *adj* beardless

imbíbi•to -ta *adj* including; included

imbornal *m* drain hole

imborrable *adj* indelible; unforgettable

imbuir §20 *tr* to imbue

imitación *adj invar* imitation ‖ *f* imitation; **a imitación de** in imitation of; **de imitación** imitation, fake

imita•do -da *adj* imitated; mock, sham; imitation

imitar *tr* to imitate

impaciencia *f* impatience

impacientar *tr* to make impatient ‖ *ref* to get impatient

impaciente *adj* impatient

impacto *m* impact, hit; (*señal que deja el proyectil*) mark; **impacto directo** direct hit

impar *adj* odd, uneven; (*que no tiene igual*) unmatched ‖ *m* odd number

imparcial *adj* impartial; (*que no entra en ningún partido*) nonpartisan

impartir *tr* to distribute, impart; (*lecciones*) to give

impás *m* finesse

impasible *adj* impassible, impassive

impávi•do -da *adj* dauntless, fearless, intrepid

impecable *adj* impeccable

impedancia *f* impedance

impedi•do -da *adj* disabled, crippled

impedimento *m* impediment, obstacle, hindrance

impedir §50 *tr* to hinder, prevent

impeler *tr* to impel; spur, incite

impenetrable *adj* impenetrable

impenitente *adj & mf* impenitent

impensable *adj* unthinkable

impensa•do -da *adj* unexpected

imperar *intr* to rule, reign, command

imperati•vo -va *adj & m* imperative

imperceptible *adj* imperceptible

imperdible *m* safety pin

imperdonable *adj* unpardonable, unforgivable

imperece•ro -ra *adj* imperishable, undying

imperfección *f* imperfection

imperfec•to -ta *adj & m* imperfect

imperial *adj* imperial ‖ *f* imperial, roof (*of a coach or bus*)

imperialista *adj & mf* imperialist

impericia *f* unskillfulness, inexpertness

imperio *m* empire; dominion, sway

imperio•so -sa *adj* (*que manda con imperio*) imperious; (*indispensable*) imperative

imperi•to -ta *adj* unskilled, inexpert

impermeable *adj* impermeable; water-proof ‖ *m* raincoat

impersonal *adj* impersonal

impertérri•to -ta *adj* dauntless, intrepid

impertinencia *f* impertinence; irrelevance; fussiness

impertinente *adj* impertinent; (*que no viene al caso*) irrelevant; (*nimiamente suscepti-ble*) fussy ‖ **impertinentes** *mpl* lorgnette

impetrar *tr* to beg (for); obtain by entreaty

ímpetu *m* impetus; force; haste

impetuo•so -sa *adj* impetuous

impiedad *f* (*falta de religión*) impiety; (*falta de compasión*) pitilessness

impí•o -a *adj* (*irreligioso*) impious; (*falto de compasión*) pitiless

impla *f* wimple

implacable *adj* relentless

implantar *tr* to implant; introduce

implementos *mpl* implements; tools

implicar §73 *tr* (*envolver*) to implicate; (*incluir en esencia*) imply ‖ *intr* to stand in the way

implíci•to -ta *adj* implicit, implied

implorar *tr* to implore

implume *adj* featherless

imponente *adj* imposing ‖ *mf* depositor, investor

imponer §54 *tr* (*la voluntad de uno, silencio, tributos*) to impose; (*dinero a rédito*) invest; (*dinero en depósito*) deposit; instruct; impute falsely ‖ *intr* to dominate, command respect ‖ *ref* (*responsabilidades*) to assume; command attention, command respect; **imponerse a** to dominate, command the respect of; **imponerse de** to learn, to find out

imponible *adj* taxable

impopular *adj* unpopular

impopularidad *f* unpopularity

importación *f* importation; import; imports

importa•dor -dora *mf* importer

importancia *f* importance; (*extensión, tamaño*) size; **ser de la importancia de** to be the concern of

importante *adj* important; large

importar *tr* (*introducir en un país*) to import; amount to; involve, imply; concern ‖ *intr* to import; be important; matter

importe *m* amount

importunar *tr* to importune

importu•no -na *adj* (*molesto*) importunate; (*fuera de sazón*) inopportune

imposibilita•do -da *adj* paralyzed, disabled

imposibilitar *tr* to make impossible ‖ *ref* to become paralyzed, become disabled

imposible *adj* impossible

imposición *f* (*de la voluntad de uno*) imposition; burden; imposture; (*de dinero*) deposit; (*typ*) make-up

impos•tor -tora *mf* impostor; slanderer

impostura *f* imposture

impotable *adj* undrinkable

impotencia *f* impotence

impotente *adj* impotent

impracticable *adj* impracticable, impassable; impractical

impreci•so -sa *adj* imprecise; vague

impregnar *tr* to impregnate, saturate

impremedita•do -da *adj* unpremeditated

imprenta *f* printing; printing shop; (*lo que se publica impreso*) printed matter; (*máquina para imprimir o prensar; conjunto de periódicos o periodistas*) press

imprentar *tr* (*la ropa*) (Chile) to press, iron; (Ecuad) to mark

imprescindible *adj* indispensable, essential

impresentable *adj* unpresentable

impresión *f* (*efecto producido en el ánimo; señal que una cosa deja en otra por presión*) impression; (*acción de imprimir*) printing; (*los ejemplares de una edición*) edition, issue; (phot) print; **impresión dactilar** or **digital** fingerprint

impresionable *adj* impressionable

impresionante *adj* impressive

impresionar *tr* to impress; (*un disco fonográfico*) record; (phot) to expose ‖ *intr* to make an impression ‖ *ref* to be impressed

impreso *m* printed paper or book; **impreso derivado** (*ordenador*) printout; **impresos** printed matter

impre•sor -sora *mf* printer

imprevisible *adj* unforeseeable

imprevisión *f* improvidence, lack of foresight

imprevi•sor -sora *adj* improvident

imprevis•to -ta *adj* unforeseen, unexpected ‖ **imprevistos** *mpl* emergencies, unforeseen expenses

imprimar *tr* to prime

imprimir *tr* (*respeto, miedo; movimiento*) to impart ‖ §83 *tr* to stamp, imprint, impress; (*un disco fonográfico*) press; (typ) to print

improbable *adj* improbable

improbar §61 *tr* to disapprove

improbidad *f* dishonesty; hardness, arduousness

ímpro•bo -ba *adj* dishonest; (*trabajo*) arduous

improcedente *adj* wrong; unfit, untimely

improducti•vo -va *adj* unproductive; unemployed

impronunciable *adj* unpronounceable

improperar *tr* to insult, revile

improperio *m* insult, affront

impropi•cio -cia *adj* unpropitious

impro•pio -pia *adj* improper; (*ajeno*) foreign

impróspe•ro -ra *adj* unsuccessful

imprόvi•do -da *adj* unprepared

improvisación *f* improvisation; meteoric rise; (mus) impromptu

improvisadamente *adv* suddenly, unexpectedly; extempore

improvisar *tr* & *intr* to improvise

improvi•so -sa *adj* unforeseen, unexpected

imprudencia *f* imprudence; **imprudencia temeraria** criminal negligence

imprudente *adj* imprudent

impudicia *f* immodesty

impúdi•co -ca *adj* immodest

impues•to -ta *adj* informed ‖ *m* tax; **impuesto sobre el valor añadido** or **impuesto al valor agregado** value-added tax; **impuesto sobre la renta** income tax

impugnar *tr* to impugn, contest

impulsar *tr* to impel; drive

impulsión f impulse, drive
impulsi•vo -va adj impulsive
impulso m impulse
impune adj unpunished
impunidad f impunity
impureza f impurity
impu•ro -ra adj impure
imputar tr to impute; credit on account
inabordable adj unapproachable
inacabable adj endless, interminable
inaccesible adj inaccessible
inacción f inaction
inacentua•do -da adj unaccented
inactividad f inactivity
inacti•vo -va adj inactive
inadecua•do -da adj inadequate; unsuited
inadvertencia f inadvertence, oversight
inadverti•do -da adj inadvertent, unwitting; careless, thoughtless; unseen, unnoticed
inagotable adj inexhaustible
inaguantable adj unbearable
inalámbri•co -ca adj wireless
inalcanzable adj unattainable
inamisto•so -sa adj unfriendly
inamovible adj irremovable; undetachable; (incorporado) built-in
inamovilidad f irremovability; tenure, permanent tenure
inane adj inane
inanición f starvation
inanima•do -da adj inanimate, lifeless
inapelable adj unappealable; unavoidable
inapetencia f loss of appetite
inapreciable adj inappreciable; imperceptible
inarmóni•co -ca adj unharmonious
inarrugable adj wrinkle-free
inarticula•do -da adj inarticulate
inartísti•co -ca adj inartistic
inasequible adj unattainable; unobtainable
inastillable adj nonshatterable, shatter-proof
inatacable adj unattackable; **inatacable por** resistant to
inaudi•to -ta adj unheard-of; outrageous
inauguración f inauguration; (de una estatua) unveiling
inaugural adj inaugural
inaugurar tr to inaugurate; (p.ej., una estatua) unveil
inaveriguable adj unascertainable
inca mf Inca
incai•co -ca adj Inca, Incan
incalificable adj unqualifiable; (infame, atroz) unspeakable
incambiable adj unchangeable
incandescente adj incandescent
incansable adj untiring, indefatigable
incapacitar tr to incapacitate; (law) to declare incompetent
inca•paz adj (pl **-paces**) incapable, unable; not large enough; stupid; (law) incompetent; frightful, unbearable
incasable adj unmarriageable; opposed to marriage; (por su fealdad) unable to find a husband
incautar ref — **incautarse de** to hold until claimed; (law) to seize, attach

incau•to -ta adj unwary, heedless
incendajas fpl kindling
incendiar tr to set on fire ‖ ref to catch fire
incendia•rio -ria adj incendiary ‖ mf incendiary, firebug
incendio m fire; (fig) fire, passion
incensar §2 tr to incense, burn incense before; (fig) to flatter
incensario m censer, incense burner
incenti•vo -va adj & m incentive
inceremonio•so -sa adj unceremonious
incertidumbre f uncertainty, incertitude
incesante adj unceasing
incesto m incest
incestuo•so -sa adj incestuous
incidencia f incidence; **por incidencia** by chance
incidente adj incident; incidental ‖ m incident
incidir tr to make an incision in ‖ intr — **incidir en culpa** to fall into guilt; **incidir en** or **sobre** to strike, impinge on
incienso m incense; (olíbano) frankincense
incier•to -ta adj uncertain
incineración f incineration; (de cadáveres) cremation
incinerar tr to incinerate; (cadáveres) cremate
incipiente adj incipient
incisión f incision; (mordacidad en el lenguaje) incisiveness, sarcasm
incisi•vo -va adj incisive; biting, sarcastic
inci•so -sa adj (estilo del escritor) choppy ‖ m comma; clause; sentence
incitar tr to incite
incivil adj rude, impolite
inciviliza•do -da adj uncivilized
inclemencia f inclemency; **a la inclemencia** in the open, without shelter
inclemente adj inclement
inclinación f inclination; bent, leaning, propensity; nod, bow
inclinar tr, intr & ref to incline; bend, bow
íncli•to -ta adj illustrious, renowned
incluir §20 tr to include; (en una carta) inclose
inclusa f foundling home
incluse•ro -ra mf foundling
inclusión f inclusion; friendship
inclusive adv inclusive, inclusively ‖ prep including
inclusi•vo -va adj inclusive
inclu•so -sa adj inclosed ‖ f see **inclusa** ‖ **incluso** adv inclusively; (hasta, aun) even ‖ **incluso** prep including
incobrable adj uncollectible; irrecoverable
incógni•to -ta adj (no conocido) unknown; (que no se da a conocer) incognito ‖ mf (persona) incognito ‖ m (condición de no ser conocido) incognito; **de incógnito** (sin ser conocido) incognito ‖ f (math & fig) unknown quantity
incoherente adj incoherent
íncola m inhabitant
incolo•ro -ra adj colorless
incólume adj unharmed, safe

incombustible *adj* incombustible, fireproof; cold, indifferent

incomerciable *adj* unmarketable

incomible *adj* uneatable, inedible

incomodar *tr* to inconvenience, disturb

incomodidad *f* inconvenience; annoyance, discomfort

incómo•do -da *adj* inconvenient; annoying, uncomfortable ‖ *m* inconvenience; discomfort

incomparable *adj* incomparable

incompartible *adj* unsharable

incompasi•vo -va *adj* pitiless, unsympathetic

incompatible *adj* incompatible; (*acontecimientos, citas, horas de clase, etc.*) conflicting

incompetente *adj* incompetent

incompetible *adj* unmatchable

incomple•to -ta *adj* incomplete

incomponible *adj* unmendable, beyond repair

incomprable *adj* unpurchasable

incomprensible *adj* incomprehensible

incomprensión *f* incomprehension

incomunicación *f* isolation, solitary confinement

incomunica•do -da *adj* incommunicado; in solitary confinement

inconcebible *adj* inconceivable

inconclu•so -sa *adj* unfinished

inconcluyente *adj* inconclusive

inconcu•so -sa *adj* undeniable

incondicional *adj* unconditional

incone•xo -xa *adj* unconnected; (*inaplicable*) irrelevant

inconfidente *adj* distrustful

inconformidad *f* nonconformity; disagreement

inconformista *mf* nonconformist

inconfundible *adj* unmistakable

incon•gruo -grua *adj* incongruous

inconocible *adj* unknowable

inconquistable *adj* unconquerable; (*que no se deja vencer con ruegos y dádivas*) unbending, unyielding

inconsciencia *f* unconsciousness; unawareness

inconsciente *adj* unconscious; unaware; **lo inconsciente** the unconscious

inconsecuencia *f* (*falta de consecuencia o correspondencia en dichos y hechos*) inconsistency

inconsecuente *adj* inconsistent; (*que no se deduce de otra cosa*) inconsequential

inconsidera•do -da *adj* inconsiderate

inconsiguiente *adj* inconsequential, illogical

inconsistencia *f* (*falta de cohesión*) inconsistency

inconsistente *adj* inconsistent

inconsolable *adj* inconsolable

inconstante *adj* inconstant

inconstitucional *adj* unconstitutional

inconsútil *adj* seamless

incontable *adj* countless, innumerable

incontenible *adj* irrepressible

incontestable *adj* incontestable

incontinente *adj* incontinent ‖ *adv* at once, instantly

incontrastable *adj* invincible; inconvincible; (*argumento*) unanswerable

incontrovertible *adj* incontrovertible

inconveniencia *f* inconvenience; unsuitability; impoliteness; impropriety

inconveniente *adj* inconvenient; unsuitable; impolite; improper ‖ *m* drawback; disadvantage; objection

incordio *m* bore, nuisance

incorporación *f* incorporation, embodiment

incorpora•do -da *adj* (*el que estaba echado*) sitting up; (*montado en la construcción*) built-in

incorporar *tr* to incorporate, embody ‖ *ref* to incorporate; (*el que estaba echado*) sit up; **incorporarse a** to join

incorrec•to -ta *adj* incorrect

incrédu•lo -la *adj* incredulous ‖ *mf* disbeliever, doubter

increíble *adj* incredible

incremento *m* increment, increase

increpar *tr* to chide, rebuke

incriminar *tr* to incriminate; (*un delito, falta, defecto*) exaggerate the gravity of

incruen•to -ta *adj* bloodless

incrustar *tr* to incrust; (*embutir por adorno*) inlay

incubadora *f* incubator

incubar *tr & intr* to incubate ‖ *ref* (fig) to be brewing

incuestionable *adj* unquestionable

inculcar §73 *tr* to inculcate‖ *ref* to become obstinate

inculpable *adj* blameless, guiltless

inculpar *tr* to accuse, blame

incultivable *adj* untillable

incul•to -ta *adj* uncultivated, untilled; uncultured; (*estilo*) coarse, sloppy

incumbencia *f* incumbency, duty, obligation, province

incumbir *intr* — **incumbir a** to be incumbent on

incumplimiento *m* nonfulfillment

incunable *m* incunabulum

incurable *adj & mf* incurable

incuria *f* carelessness, negligence

incurio•so -sa *adj* careless, negligent

incurrir *intr* — **incurrir en** to incur

incursión *f* incursion, inroad, raid

indagación *f* investigation, research

indagatorio *m* deposition of the accused

indagar §44 *tr* to investigate

indebidamente *adv* unduly

indebi•do -da *adj* undue; wrong

indecencia *f* indecency

indecente *adj* indecent

indecible *adj* unspeakable, unutterable

indeci•so -sa *adj* undecided, indecisive; (*contorno, forma*) vague, obscure

indeclinable *adj* unavoidable; (gram) indeclinable

indecoro•so -sa *adj* improper

indefectible *adj* unfailing

indefendible *adj* indefensible

indefen•so -sa *adj* defenseless, undefended

im
in

indefinible *adj* indefinable
indefini•do -da *adj* indefinite; limitless; vague
indeleble *adj* indelible
indelibera•do -da *adj* unpremeditated
indelica•do -da *adj* indelicate
indemne *adj* unharmed, undamaged
indemnidad *f* (*seguridad contra un daño*) indemnity
indemnización *f* (*compensación*) indemnity, indemnification; **indemnización por despido** severance pay
indemnizar §60 *tr* to indemnify
independencia *f* independence
independiente *adj & mf* independent
independizar §60 *tr* to free, emancipate ‖ *ref* to become independent
indescriptible *adj* indescribable
indeseable *adj & mf* undesirable
indesea•do -da *adj* unwanted
indesmallable *adj* runproof
indestructible *adj* indestructible
indetermina•do -da *adj* indeterminate; (gram) indefinite
indevo•to -ta *adj* impious; not fond, not devoted
india *f* wealth, riches; **Indias Occidentales** West Indies; **la India** India
indiana *f* printed calico
india•no -na *adj & mf* Spanish American; East Indian; West Indian ‖ *m* man back from America with great wealth; **indiano de hilo negro** (coll) skinflint ‖ *f* see **indiana**
indicación *f* indication; **por indicación de** at the direction of
indica•do -da *adj* appropriate, advisable; **muy indicado** just the thing, just the person
indica•dor -dora *adj* indicating, pointing ‖ *m* indicator; gauge; (*de tránsito*) traffic signal
indicar §73 *tr* to indicate
indicati•vo -va *adj & m* indicative
índice *m* index; **índice de libros prohibidos** (eccl) Index; **índice de materias** table of contents; **índice en el corte** thumb index
indiciar *tr* to betoken, indicate; surmise, suspect
indicio *m* sign, token, indication; **indicios vehementes** circumstantial evidence
indiferente *adj* indifferent; (*que no importa*) immaterial
indígena *adj* indigenous ‖ *mf* native
indigente *adj* indigent
indigestar *ref* to be indigestible; be disliked, be unbearable
indigestible *adj* indigestible
indigestión *f* indigestion
indignación *f* indignation
indigna•do -da *adj* indignant
indignar *tr* to anger, provoke ‖ *ref* to become indignant
indignidad *f* (*falta de mérito*) unworthiness; (*acción reprobable*) indignity
indig•no -na *adj* unworthy
índigo *m* indigo
in•dio -dia *adj & mf* Indian ‖ *f* see **india**

indirec•to -ta *adj* indirect ‖ *f* hint, innuendo; **indirecta del padre Cobos** broad hint
indiscernible *adj* indiscernible
indiscre•to -ta *adj* indiscreet
indiscrimina•do -da *adj* indiscriminate; non-discriminating
indisculpable *adj* inexcusable
indiscutible *adj* undeniable
indisoluble *adj* indissoluble
indispensable *adj* unpardonable; indispensable
indisponer §54 *tr* (*alterar la salud de*) to indispose, upset; disturb, upset; **indisponer a uno con** to set someone against, prejudice someone against ‖ *ref* to become indisposed; **indisponerse con** to fall out with
indisponible *adj* unavailable
indispues•to -ta *adj* indisposed
indistintamente *adv* indistinctly; indiscriminately, without distinction
indistin•to -ta *adj* indistinct
individual *adj* individual; (*habitación en un hotel; partido de tenis*) single
individualidad *f* individuality
indivi•duo -dua *adj* individual; indivisible ‖ *mf* (*persona indeterminada*) (coll) individual ‖ *m* (*cada persona*) individual; (*miembro de una corporación*) member, fellow
indócil *adj* unteachable; headstrong, unruly
indocumenta•do -da *adj* unidentified; unqualified ‖ *mf* nobody (*person of no account*)
indochi•no -na *adj & mf* Indo-Chinese ‖ **la Indochina** Indochina
indoeurope•o -a *adj & m* Indo-European
índole *f* kind, class; nature, disposition, temper
indolente *adj* stolid, impassive; (*perezoso*) indolent
indolo•ro -ra *adj* painless
indoma•do -da *adj* untamed
indone•sio -sia *adj & mf* Indonesian ‖ **la Indonesia** Indonesia
inducción *f* induction
inducido *m* (*de dínamo o motor*) (elec) armature
inducir §19 *tr* to induce
inductor *m* (*de dínamo o motor*) (elec) field
indudable *adj* doubtless
indulgente *adj* indulgent
indultar *tr* to pardon; free, exempt
indulto *m* pardon; exemption
indumentaria *f* clothing, dress; historical study of clothing
indumento *m* clothing, dress
industria *f* industry; **de industria** on purpose
industrial *adj* industrial ‖ *m* industrialist
industrializar §60 *tr* to industrialize
industriar *tr* to teach, instruct, train ‖ *ref* to get along, manage
industrio•so -sa *adj* industrious
inédi•to -ta *adj* unpublished; new, novel; unknown
inefable *adj* ineffable
ineficacia *f* inefficacy

inefi•caz *adj* (*pl* **-caces**) inefficacious, ineffectual

inelegible *adj* ineligible

ineludible *adj* inescapable

inenarrable *adj* indescribable

inencogible *adj* unshrinkable

inencontrable *adj* unobtainable

inequidad *f* inequity

inequívo•co -ca *adj* unmistakable

inercia *f* inertia

inerme *adj* unarmed

inerte *adj* inert; slow, sluggish

inescrupulo•so -sa *adj* unscrupulous

inescrutable or **inescudriñable** *adj* inscrutable

inespera•do -da *adj* unexpected, unforeseen; unhoped for

inestable *adj* unstable

inevitable *adj* unavoidable, inevitable

inexactitud *f* inaccuracy, inexactness

inexac•to -ta *adj* inaccurate, inexact

inexcusable *adj* inexcusable, unpardonable; unavoidable; indispensable

inexistencia *f* nonexistence

inexorable *adj* inexorable

inexperiencia *f* inexperience

inexplicable *adj* inexplicable, unexplainable

inexplica•do -da *adj* unexplained, unaccounted for

inexplora•do -da *adj* unexplored; (*mar*) uncharted

inexpresable *adj* inexpressible

inexpues•to -ta *adj* (phot) unexposed

inexpugnable *adj* impregnable; firm, unshakable

inextinguible *adj* unextinguishable; perpetual, lasting; (*sed*) unquenchable; (*risa*) uncontrollable

inextirpable *adj* ineradicable

infalible *adj* infallible

infamación *f* defamation

infamar *tr* to defame, discredit

infame *adj* infamous; vile, frightful ‖ *mf* scoundrel

infamia *f* infamy

infancia *f* infancy

infan•do -da *adj* odious, unmentionable

infanta *f* female child; infanta (*any daughter of a king of Spain; wife of an infante*)

infante *m* male child; infante (*any son of a king of Spain who is not heir to the throne*); (mil) infantryman; **infante de coro** choirboy

infantería *f* infantry; **infantería de marina** marines, marine corps

infantil *adj* infant, infantile, childlike; innocent

infarto *m* (heart) infarct

infatigable *adj* indefatigable

infatuar §21 *tr* to make vain ‖ *ref* to become vain

infaus•to -ta *adj* fatal, unlucky

infección *f* infection

infeccionar *tr* to infect

infeccio•so -sa *adj* infectious

infectar *tr* to infect

infec•to -ta *adj* foul, corrupt; infected; fetid

infecun•do -da *adj* sterile, barren

infe•liz (*pl* **-lices**) *adj* unhappy; simple, good-hearted ‖ *m* wretch, poor soul

inferior *adj* inferior; lower; **inferior a** inferior to; lower than; less than; smaller than ‖ *m* inferior

inferioridad *f* inferiority

inferir §68 *tr* to infer; lead to, entail; (*una herida*) inflict; (*una ofensa*) cause, offer

infernáculo *m* hopscotch

infernal *adj* infernal

infernar §2 *tr* to damn; irritate, annoy

infernillo *m* chafing dish

infestar *tr* to infest ‖ *ref* to become infested

inficionar *tr* to infect ‖ *ref* to become infected

infidelidad *f* infidelity; (*conjunto de infieles*) unbelievers

infidente *adj* faithless, disloyal

infiel *adj* (*falto de fidelidad*) unfaithful; (*no exacto*) inaccurate, inexact; (*no cristiano*) infidel ‖ *mf* infidel

infierno *m* hell; **en el quinto infierno** or **en los quintos infiernos** far, far away

infijo *m* (gram) infix

infiltrar *tr* & *ref* to infiltrate

ínfi•mo -ma *adj* lowest; humblest, most abject; meanest, vilest

infinidad *f* infinity

infiniti•vo -va *adj* & *m* infinitive

infini•to -ta *adj* infinite ‖ *m* infinite; (math) infinity ‖ **infinito** *adv* greatly, very much

infirme *adj* infirm

inflación *f* inflation; (*vanidad*) conceit

inflaciona•rio -ria *adj* inflationary

inflado *m* inflation (*of a tire*)

inflamable *adj* inflammable, flammable

inflamación *f* ignition, inflammation; ardor, enthusiasm; (pathol) inflammation

inflamar *tr* to set on fire; inflame ‖ *ref* to catch fire; become inflamed

inflar *tr* to inflate; exaggerate; puff up with pride ‖ *ref* to inflate; be puffed up with pride

inflexible *adj* inflexible; unyielding, unbending

inflexión *f* inflection; **inflexión vocálica** (*metafonía*) umlaut

inflexionar *tr* to umlaut

infligir §27 *tr* to inflict

influencia *f* influence

influenciar *tr* to influence

influenza *f* influenza

influir §20 *intr* to have influence; have great weight; **influir en** or **sobre** to influence

influjo *m* influence; rising tide

influyente *adj* influential

información *f* information; (law) judicial inquiry, investigation; **informaciones** testimonial

informal *adj* (*que no se ajusta a las reglas debidas*) informal; unreliable

informar *tr* & *intr* to inform ‖ *ref* to inquire, find out

informática *f* computer science

informati•vo -va *adj* informational; (*sección de un periódico*) news

in
in

informe *adj* shapeless, formless; misshapen ‖ *m* piece of information; report; **informes** information; **informes confidenciales** inside information
infortuna•do -da *adj* unfortunate, unlucky
infortunio *m* misfortune; (*acaecimiento desgraciado*) mishap
infracción *f* infraction, infringement
infraconsumo *m* underconsumption
infrac•to -ta *adj* unperturbable
infraestructura *f* substructure; (rr) roadbed
inframundo *m* underworld
infrarro•jo -ja *adj* & *m* infrared
infrascri•to -ta *adj* undersigned; hereinafter mentioned
infrecuente *adj* infrequent
infringir §27 *tr* to infringe, break, violate
infructuo•so -sa *adj* fruitless, unfruitful
ínfulas *fpl* conceit, airs; **darse ínfulas** to put on airs
infunda•do -da *adj* unfounded, groundless, baseless
infundio *m* lie, fib
infundir *tr* to infuse, instill
infusión *f* infusion; (*acción de echar agua sobre el que se bautiza*) sprinkling; **estar en infusión para** to be all set for
ingeniar *tr* to think up ‖ *ref* to manage; **ingeniarse a** or **para** to manage to; **ingeniarse para ir viviendo** to manage to get along
ingeniería *f* engineering; **ingeniería genética** genetic engineering
ingeniero *m* engineer; **ingeniero de caminos, canales y puertos** government civil engineer
ingenio *m* talent, creative faculty; talented person; cleverness, skill, wit; (*artificio mecánico*) apparatus, device; (*del encuadernador*) paper cutter; engine of war; **afilar** or **aguzar el ingenio** to sharpen one's wits; **ingenio de azúcar** sugar refinery
ingeniosidad *f* ingenuity; wittiness
ingenio•so -sa *adj* (*dotado de ingenio; hecho con ingenio*) ingenious; (*agudo, sutil*) witty
ingéni•to -ta *adj* innate, inborn
ingente *adj* huge, enormous
ingenuidad *f* ingenuousness
inge•nuo -nua *adj* ingenuous
ingerir §68 *tr* & *ref* var of **injerir**
ingestión *f* (food) consumption; ingestion
Inglaterra *f* England
ingle *f* groin
in•glés -glesa *adj* English; **a la inglesa** in the English manner ‖ *m* Englishman; (*idioma*) English; **el inglés medio** Middle English; **los ingleses** the English ‖ *f* Englishwoman
ingramatical *adj* ungrammatical
ingratitud *f* ingratitude, ungratefulness
ingra•to -ta *adj* (*desagradecido*) ungrateful; (*desagradecido; desagradable, áspero; improductivo*) thankless ‖ *mf* ingrate
ingravidez *f* lightness, tenuousness; (*gravedad nula*) weightlessness
ingrávi•do -da *adj* light, tenuous; weightless
ingrediente *m* ingredient
ingresa•do -da *mf* new student

ingresar *tr* to deposit ‖ *intr* to enter, become a member; (*beneficios*) come in ‖ *ref* (Mex) to enlist
ingreso *m* entrance; admission; **ingresos** income, revenue
íngri•mo -ma *adj* solitary, alone
inhábil *adj* unable; unskillful; unfit, unqualified
inhabilidad *f* inability; unskillfulness; unfitness
inhabilitar *tr* to disable, to disqualify, to incapacitate
inhabita•do -da *adj* uninhabited
inhabitua•do -da *adj* unaccustomed
inherente *adj* inherent
inhibir *tr* to inhibit
inhospitala•ria -ria *adj* inhospitable
inhóspi•to -ta *adj* inhospitable
inhumanidad *f* inhumanity
inhuma•no -na *adj* inhuman, inhumane; (Chile) filthy
iniciación *f* initiation
inicial *adj* & *f* initial
iniciar *tr* to initiate ‖ *ref* to be initiated
iniciativa *f* initiative
ini•cuo -cua *adj* wicked, iniquitous
inigualable *adj* incomparable
iguala•do -da *adj* unequaled
ininteligente *adj* unintelligent
ininteligible *adj* unintelligible
ininterrumpi•do -da *adj* uninterrupted
iniquidad *f* iniquity
injerencia *f* interference, meddling
injerir §68 *tr* to insert, introduce; (*alimentos*) take in; (hort) to graft ‖ *ref* to interfere, meddle, intrude
injertar *tr* (hort & surg) to graft
injerto *m* (hort & surg) graft; transplant
injuria *f* offense, insult; abuse, wrong; damage, harm
injuriar *tr* to offend, insult; abuse, wrong; harm, damage
injurio•so -sa *adj* offensive, insulting; abusive; harmful; (*lenguaje*) profane
injusticia *f* injustice
injustifica•do -da *adj* unjustified
injus•to -ta *adj* unjust
inmacula•do -da *adj* immaculate
inmanejable *adj* unmanageable; unhandy
inmarcesible *adj* unfading
inmaterial *adj* immaterial
inmaturo -ra *adj* immature
inmediación *f* immediacy; proximity, nearness; **inmediaciones** neighborhood, outskirts
inmediatamente *adv* immediately; **inmediatamente que** as soon as
inmedia•to -ta *adj* immediate; close, adjoining, next; next above; next below; (*pago*) prompt; **venir a las inmediatas** to get into the thick of the fight
inmejorable *adj* superb, unsurpassable
inmemorial *adj* immemorial
inmen•so -sa *adj* immense
inmensurable *adj* immeasurable
inmereci•do -da *adj* undeserved
inmergir §27 *tr* to immerse

inmersión f immersion
inmigración f immigration
inmigrante mf immigrant
inmigrar intr to immigrate
inminente adj imminent
inmiscuir §20 & regular tr to mix ‖ ref to meddle, interfere
inmobilia•rio -ria adj real-estate
inmoble adj motionless; firm, constant
inmodera•do -da adj immoderate
inmodes•to -ta adj immodest
inmódi•co -ca adj excessive
inmoral adj immoral
inmortal adj immortal, deathless ‖ mf immortal
inmortalizar §60 tr to immortalize
inmotiva•do -da adj groundless; unmotivated
inmovilizar §60 tr to immobilize; (un caudal) tie up
inmueble m property, piece of real estate; inmuebles real estate
inmun•do -da adj dirty, filthy
inmune adj immune
inmunizar §60 tr to immunize
inmutar tr to change, alter; disturb, upset ‖ ref to change, alter; change countenance; sin inmutarse without batting an eye
inna•to -ta adj innate, inborn; natural
innatural adj unnatural
innavegable adj (río) unnavigable; (embarcación) unseaworthy
innecesa•rio -ria adj unnecessary
innegable adj undeniable
innoble adj ignoble
innocuidad f harmlessness
inno•cuo -cua adj harmless
innovación f innovation
innovar tr to innovate
innumerable adj innumerable
inocencia f innocence
inocentada f simpleness; blunder; (Ecuad) April Fools' joke
inocente adj & mf innocent; coger por inocente to make an April fool of
inocen•tón -tona adj simple, gullible ‖ mf gull, dupe
inoculación f inoculation
inocular tr to inoculate; contaminate, pervert
inodo•ro -ra adj odorless ‖ m deodorizer; (excusado que funciona con agua corriente) toilet
inofensi•vo -va adj inoffensive
inolvidable adj unforgettable
inope adj impecunious
inopia f indigence
inoportu•no -na adj inopportune, untimely
inorgáni•co -ca adj inorganic
inortodo•xo -xa adj unorthodox
inoxidable adj (acero) stainless; inoxidizable
inquietante adj disquieting, upsetting
inquietar tr to disquiet, worry; stir up, excite
inquie•to -ta adj anxious, worried
inquietud f disquiet, worry, concern
inquili•no -na mf tenant, renter
inquina f aversion, dislike, ill will
inquirir §40 tr to inquire, inquire into
inquisición f inquiry; inquisition

insabible adj unknowable
insaciable adj insatiable
insania f insanity
insa•no -na adj insane; imprudent
insatisfacción f dissatisfaction
insatisfe•cho -cha adj unsatisfied
inscribir §83 tr to inscribe; (law) to record ‖ ref to enroll, register
inscripción f inscription; enrollment, registration
insecticida adj & m insecticide
insecto m insect
insegu•ro -ra adj insecure, unsafe; uncertain
insensa•to -ta adj foolish, stupid
insensible adj callous, hard-hearted, unfeeling; imperceptible
inseparable adj inseparable; undetachable ‖ mf inseparable ‖ m lovebird
insepul•to -ta adj unburied
inserción f insertion
inserir §68 tr to insert; (injertar) graft, engraft
insertar tr to insert
inservible adj useless
insidia f snare, ambush; plotting
insidiar tr to ambush, waylay; trap, trick
insidio•so -sa adj insidious
insigne adj noted, famous, renowned
insignia f badge, decoration, insignia; banner, standard
insignificante adj insignificant
insince•ro -ra adj insincere
insinuación f insinuation, hint
insinuante adj engaging, slick, crafty
insinuar §21 tr to insinuate; suggest, hint at ‖ ref to creep in, slip in; ingratiate oneself; flow, run; insinuarse en to work one's way in
insípi•do -da adj insipid, vapid
insistir intr to insist
ínsi•to -ta adj inbred, innate
insociable adj unsociable
insolencia f insolence
insolentar tr to make insolent ‖ ref to become insolent
insolente adj insolent
insóli•to -ta adj unusual
insoluble adj insoluble
insolvencia f insolvency
insomne adj sleepless
insomnio m insomnia
insondable adj fathomless; inscrutable
insonorización f soundproofing
insonoriza•do -da adj soundproof
insonorizar §60 tr to soundproof
insono•ro -ra adj soundproof
insospecha•do -da adj unsuspected
insostenible adj untenable
inspección f inspection; inspectorship; inspección técnica de vehículos (I.T.V.) car inspection
inspeccionar tr to inspect
inspiración f inspiration; inhalation
inspirante adj inspiring
inspirar tr & intr to inspire; (atraer a los pulmones) inhale, breathe in ‖ ref to be inspired

in
in

instalación f plant, factory; outfit, equipment; arrangements, fittings; installment; **instalación sanitaria** plumbing

instalar tr to install ‖ ref to settle

instantáne•o -a adj instantaneous ‖ f snapshot

instante m instant, moment; **al instante** right away, immediately; **por instantes** uninterruptedly; any time

instantemente adv insistently, urgently

instar tr to press, urge ‖ intr to be pressing, be urgent

instaurar tr to restore; reestablish

instigar §44 tr to instigate

instilar tr to instill

instinti•vo -va adj instinctive

instinto m instinct

institución f institution; **instituciones** (de un Estado) constitution; (de una ciencia, arte, etc.) principles

instituir §20 tr to institute, found

instituto m institute; (de una orden religiosa) rule, constitution; **instituto de segunda enseñanza** or **de enseñanza media** high school

institu•triz f (pl **-trices**) governess

instrucción f instruction; education

instructi•vo -va adj instructive

instruc•tor -tora mf teacher, instructor ‖ m (mil) drillmaster ‖ f instructress

instruí•do -da adj well-educated; well-posted

instruir §20 tr to instruct; (un proceso o expediente) draw up

instrumentar tr to instrument

instrumentista mf instrumentalist

instrumento m instrument; (persona que se emplea para alcanzar un resultado) tool; **instrumento de cuerda** (mus) stringed instrument; **instrumento de viento** (mus) wind instrument

insubordina•do -da adj insubordinate

insubstituíble adj irreplaceable

insudar intr to drudge

insuficiente adj insufficient

insufrible adj insufferable

ínsula f island; one-horse town

insular adj insular ‖ mf islander

insulina f insulin

insulsez f tastelessness; dullness, heaviness

insul•so -sa adj tasteless; dull, heavy

insultada f insult

insultar tr to insult ‖ ref to faint, swoon

insulto m insult; fainting spell

insume adj expensive

insumergible adj unsinkable

insuperable adj insurmountable

insurgente adj & mf insurgent

insurrección f insurrection

intac•to -ta adj intact, untouched

intachable adj blameless, irreproachable

integración f integration

integridad f integrity; virginity

ínte•gro -gra adj integral, whole; honest

intelecto m intellect

intelectual adj & mf intellectual

intelectualidad f intellectuality; (conjunto de los intelectuales de un país o región) intelligentsia

inteligencia f intelligence; **estar en inteligencia con** to be in collusion with

inteligente adj intelligent; trained, skilled

inteligible adj intelligible

intemperancia f intemperance

intemperante adj intemperate

intemperie f inclement weather; **a la intemperie** in the open, unsheltered

intempesti•vo -va adj unseasonable, inopportune, untimely

intención f intention; (cautelosa advertencia) caution; (instinto dañino de un animal) viciousness; **con intención** deliberately, knowingly; **de intención** on purpose

intendencia f intendance; (SAm) mayoralty

intendente m intendant; quartermaster general; (SAm) mayor

intensar tr & ref to intensify

intensidad f intensity

intensificar §73 tr & ref to intensify

intensión f intensity

intensi•vo -va adj intensive

inten•so -sa adj intense

intentar tr to try, to attempt; intend; try out

intento m intent, purpose; **de intento** on purpose

intentona f rash attempt (to rob, escape, etc.)

interacción f interaction

interamerica•no -na adj inter-American

intercalar tr to intercalate, insert

intercambiar tr & ref to interchange

intercambio m interchange, exchange

interceder intr to intercede

interceptar tr to intercept

intercep•tor -tora mf interceptor ‖ m trap; separator; (aer) interceptor

interdecir §24 tr to interdict, forbid

interés m interest; **intereses creados** vested interests; **poner a interés** to put out at interest

interesa•do -da adj interested ‖ mf interested party

interesante adj interesting

interesar tr to interest; involve ‖ intr to be interesting ‖ ref — **interesarse en** or **por** to be interested in, take an interest in

interescolar adj interscholastic, intercollegiate

interfec•to -ta adj murdered ‖ mf victim of murder

interferencia f interference

interferir §68 tr to interfere with ‖ intr to interfere

interfono m intercom

ínterin adv meanwhile ‖ conj while, as long as ‖ m (pl **ínterines**) temporary incumbency

interinar tr to fill temporarily, fill in an acting capacity

interi•no -na adj temporary, acting, interim

interior adj interior, inner, inside; home, domestic ‖ m interior, inside; mind, soul; **interiores** entrails, insides

interioridad *f* inside; **interioridades** inside story, private matters
interjección *f* interjection
interlinear *tr* to interline; (typ) to space, lead
interlocu•tor -tora *mf* speaker, party; interviewer
intermedia•rio -ria *adj & mf* intermediary ‖ *m* (com) middleman
interme•dio -dia *adj* intermediate ‖ *m* interval, interim; (mus) intermezzo; (theat) intermission, entr'acte
intermitente *adj* intermittent ‖ *m* (aut) direction light, turning light
internacional *adj* international
internacionalizar §60 *tr* to internationalize
interna•do -da *mf* (mil) internee ‖ *m* boarding school
internamiento *m* internment
internar *tr* to send inland; intern ‖ *intr* to move inland ‖ *ref* to move inland; take refuge, hide; insinuate oneself; **internarse en** to go deeply into
internista *mf* internist
inter•no -na *adj* internal; inside ‖ *mf* boarding-school student; **interno de hospital** intern
interpelar *tr* to seek the protection or aid of; interrogate; interpellate
interpolar *tr* to interpolate; interpose; interrupt briefly
interponer §54 *tr* to interpose; appoint as mediator ‖ *ref* to intervene, intercede
interprender *tr* to take by surprise
interpresa *f* surprise action; surprise seizure
interpretar *tr* to interpret
intérprete *mf* interpreter
interrogación *f* interrogation; question mark
interrogar §44 *tr & intr* to question, interrogate
interrumpir *tr* to interrupt
interruptor *m* (elec) switch; **interruptor automático** (elec) circuit breaker; **interruptor del encendido** (aut) ignition switch; **interruptor de resorte** (elec) snap switch
intersección *f* (geom) intersection
intersticio *m* interstice; interval
intervalo *m* interval
intervención *f* intervention; inspection; (de cuentas) audit, auditing; (surg) operation; **intervención de los precios** price control; **no intervención** nonintervention
intervenir §79 *tr* to take up, work on; inspect, supervise; (cuentas) audit; (un teléfono) tap; (surg) operate on ‖ *intr* to mediate, intervene, intercede; participate; happen
interventor *m* election supervisor; (com) auditor
inter•viev *m* (pl **-vievs**) interview
intervievar *tr* to interview
intesta•do -da *adj & mf* intestate
intesti•no -na *adj* internal; domestic ‖ *m* intestine; **intestino delgado** small intestine; **intestino grueso** large intestine
intimación *f* announcement, notification
intimar *tr* to announce ‖ *intr & ref* to become well-acquainted, to become intimate

intimidad *f* intimacy; (parte íntima o personal) privacy
intimidar *tr* to intimidate
inti•mo -ma *adj* intimate; (más interno) innermost
intitular *tr* to entitle ‖ *ref* to use a title; be called
intocable *mf* untouchable
intolerante *adj & mf* intolerant
inton•so -sa *adj* unshorn; ignorant; (libro o revista) uncut ‖ *mf* ignoramus
intoxicación *f* intoxication; poisoning
intoxicar §73 *tr* to poison, intoxicate
intracruzamiento *m* inbreeding
intranquilidad *f* uneasiness, worry
intranquilizar §60 *tr* to make uneasy, worry
intranqui•lo -la *adj* uneasy, worried
intransigente *adj & mf* intransigent, die-hard
intransiti•vo -va *adj* intransitive
intrascendente *adj* unimportant; nonessential
intratable *adj* unmanageable; impassable; unsociable
intrepidez *f* intrepidity
intrépi•do -da *adj* intrepid
intriga *f* intrigue
intrigar §44 *tr* (excitar la curiosidad de) to intrigue ‖ *intr* to intrigue ‖ *ref* to be intrigued
intrinca•do -da *adj* intricate
intrincar §73 *tr* to complicate; confuse, bewilder
intríngu•lis *m* (pl **-lis**) hidden motive, mystery
intrínse•co -ca *adj* intrinsic(al)
introducción *f* introduction
introducir §19 *tr* to introduce; insert, put in ‖ *ref* to gain access; meddle, interfere, intrude
introito *m* (de un escrito o una oración) introduction; (de un poema dramático) prologue; (eccl) introit
introspecti•vo -va *adj* introspective
introverti•do -da *mf* introvert
intru•so -sa *adj* intrusive ‖ *mf* intruder, interloper
intuición *f* intuition
intuir §20 *tr* to guess, sense
intuito *m* view, glance, look; **por intuito de** in view of
inundación *f* flood, inundation
inundar *tr* to flood, inundate
inurba•no -na *adj* discourteous, unmannerly
inusita•do -da *adj* (no ordinario) unusual; obsolete, out of use
inusual *adj* unusual
inútil *adj* useless
invadir *tr* to invade
invalidar *tr* to invalidate
invalidez *f* invalidity
inváli•do -da *adj & mf* invalid
invariable *adj* invariable
invasión *f* invasion
inva•sor -sora *mf* invader
invectiva *f* invective
invectivar *tr* to inveigh against
invencible *adj* invincible

in
in

invención *f* invention; finding, discovery; deception

invendible *adj* unsalable

inventar *tr* to invent

inventariar §77 & regular *tr* to inventory

inventario *m* inventory

inventi•vo -va *adj* inventive ‖ *f* inventiveness

invento *m* invention

inven•tor -tora *adj* inventive ‖ *mf* inventor

inverecun•do -da *adj* shameless, brazen

inverisímil *adj* improbable, unlikely

invernáculo *m* greenhouse, hothouse, conservatory

invernada *f* wintertime; (SAm) pasture land; (Ven) torrential rain

invernadero *m* greenhouse, hothouse; winter resort; winter pasture

invernal *adj* winter ‖ *m* cattle shed (*in winter-pasture land*)

invernar §2 *intr* to winter; be winter

inverni•zo -za *adj* winter; wintery

inverosímil *adj* improbable, unlikely

inversión *f* inversion; (*de dinero*) investment; (gram) inverted order

inversionista *adj* investment ‖ *mf* investor

inver•so -sa *adj* inverse, opposite; **a** or **por la inversa** on the contrary

inversor *m* investor

invertebra•do -da *adj* & *m* invertebrate

inverti•do -da *adj* inverted ‖ *mf* invert

invertir §68 *tr* to invert; (*dinero*) invest; (*tiempo*) spend; reverse

investidura *f* investment, investiture; station, standing

investigación *f* investigation, research; **investigación mercológica** market research

investigar §44 *tr* to investigate ‖ *intr* to research

investir §50 *tr* — **investir con** or **de** (*poner en posesión de*) to invest with

invetera•do -da *adj* inveterate, confirmed

invic•to -ta *adj* unconquered

invidencia *f* blindness

invidente *adj* blind ‖ *mf* blind person

invierno *m* winter; rainy season

inviolabilidad *f* inviolability; undamageability

invisible *adj* invisible ‖ *m* (Mex) hair net; **en un invisible** in an instant

invitación *f* invitation

invita•do -da *mf* guest

invitar *tr* to invite

invocar §73 *tr* to invoke

involunta•rio -ria *adj* involuntary

invulnerable *adj* invulnerable

inyección *f* injection; **inyección secundaria** booster shot

inyectable *adj* injectable ‖ *m* ampule, phial

inyecta•do -da *adj* bloodshot, inflamed

inyectar *tr* to inject ‖ *ref* to become congested; become inflamed

ionizar §60 *tr* to ionize ‖ *ref* to be ionized

ionosfera *f* ionosphere

ir §41 *intr* to go; be becoming, fit, suit; be at stake; **ir a** + *inf* to be going to + *inf* (*to express futurity*); **ir a buscar** to go get, go for; **ir a parar en** to end up in; **ir con**

cuidado to be careful; **ir con miedo** to be afraid; **ir con tiento** to watch one's step; **ir de caza** to go hunting; **ir de pesca** to go fishing; **lo que va de** so far (as); **¡qué va!** of course not!; **¡vaya!** the deuce!; what a . . . ! ‖ *ref* to go away; leak; wear away; get old; break to pieces

ira *f* anger, wrath, ire

iracun•do -da *adj* angry, wrathful, irate

Irak, el Iraq

Irán, el Iran

ira•nés -nesa or **ira•nio -nia** *adj* & *mf* Iranian

ira•qués -quesa or **iraquiano -na** *adj* & *mf* Iraqi

iris *m* (*pl* **iris**) (*del ojo*) iris; rainbow

Irlanda *f* Ireland

irlan•dés -desa *adj* Irish ‖ *m* Irishman; (*idioma*) Irish; **los irlandeses** the Irish ‖ *f* Irishwoman

ironía *f* irony

iróni•co -ca *adj* ironic(al)

ironizar §60 *tr* to ridicule

irracional *adj* irrational

irradiar *tr* to radiate, irradiate; (*difundir*) broadcast ‖ *intr* to radiate

irrazonable *adj* unreasonable

irreal *adj* unreal

irrealidad *f* unreality

irrebatible *adj* irrefutable

irreconocible *adj* unrecognizable

irrecuperable *adj* irretrievable

irrecusable *adj* unimpeachable

irredimible *adj* irredeemable

irreemplazable *adj* irreplaceable

irreflexión *f* rashness, thoughtlessness

irreflexi•vo -va *adj* rash, thoughtless

irregular *adj* irregular ‖ *m* (mil) irregular

irregularidad *f* irregularity; embezzlement

irrelevante *adj* irrelevant

irreligio•so -sa *adj* irreligious

irrellenable *adj* nonrefillable

irremediable *adj* irremediable

irremisible *adj* unpardonable

irreparable *adj* irreparable

irreprimible *adj* irrepressible

irreprochable *adj* irreproachable

irresistible *adj* irresistible

irresoluble *adj* unworkable, unsolvable

irrespetuo•so -sa *adj* disrespectful

irresponsable *adj* irresponsible

irresuel•to -ta *adj* hesitant, wavering

irreverente *adj* irreverent

irrigación *f* irrigation

irrigar §44 *tr* to irrigate

irrisible *adj* laughable, absurd

irrisión *f* derision, ridicule; laughingstock

irritante *adj* & *m* irritant

irritar *tr* to irritate ‖ *ref* to become exasperated

irrompible *adj* unbreakable

irrumpir *intr* to burst in; **irrumpir en** to burst into

irrupción *f* sudden attack; invasion

isi•dro -dra *mf* hick, jake, yokel

isla *f* island; (*manzana de casas*) block; **isla de peatones** or **isla de seguridad** safety zone (for pedestrians); **islas Baleares** Balearic Islands; **islas Canarias** Canary Islands; **islas de Barlovento** Windward Islands; **islas de Sotavento** Leeward Islands; **islas Filipinas** Philippine Islands

Islam, el Islam

islan•dés -desa *adj* Icelandic || *mf* Icelander || *m* (*idioma*) Icelandic

Islandia *f* Iceland

isle•ño -ña *adj* island || *mf* islander; (Cuba) Canarian

isleta *f* isle

isométri•co -ca *adj* isometric

isométrica *f* isometrics

isósce•les *adj* (*pl* **-les**) isosceles

isótopo *m* isotope

israe•lí (*pl* **-líes**) *adj* & *mf* Israeli

israelita *adj* & *mf* Israelite

istmo *m* isthmus

Italia *f* Italy

italia•no -na *adj* & *mf* Italian

itáli•co -ca *adj* Italic; (typ) italic || *f* (typ) italics

itinera•rio -ria *adj* & *m* itinerary

izar §60 *tr* (naut) to hoist, haul up

izquierda *f* left hand; left-hand side; (pol) left; **a la izquierda** left, on the left, to the left

izquierdear *intr* to go wild, go astray, go awry

izquierdista *adj* leftist || *mf* leftist, leftwinger

izquierdizante *adj* leftish

izquier•do -da *adj* left; left-hand; left-handed; crooked; **levantarse del izquierdo** to get out of bed on the wrong side || *f* see **izquierda**

J

J, j (jota) *f* eleventh letter of the Spanish alphabet

jabalcón *m* strut, brace

jaba•lí *m* (*pl* **-líes**) wild boar

jabalina *f* javelin; wild sow

jabardillo *m* (*de insectos*) noisy swarm; noisy throng

jabeque *m* (naut) xebec; gash in the face

jabón *m* soap; cake of soap; **dar jabón a** to softsoap; **dar un jabón a** (coll) to upbraid, to reprimand; **jabón de afeitar** shaving soap; **jabón de Castilla** Castile soap; **jabón de tocador** or **de olor** toilet soap; **jabón de sastre** soapstone, French chalk; **jabón en polvo** soap powder

jabonado *m* soaping; (*ropa lavada o por lavar*) wash

jabonadura *f* soaping; **dar una jabonadura a** to lambaste, upbraid; **jabonaduras** soapy water; soapsuds

jabonar *tr* to soap; reprimand

jaboncillo *m* cake of toilet soap; **jaboncillo de sastre** soapstone, French chalk

jabone•ro -ra *adj* soap; (*toro*) yellowish, dirty-white || *mf* soapmaker; soap dealer || *f* soap dish

jabonete *m* cake of toilet soap

jabono•so -sa *adj* soapy, lathery

jaca *f* pony, jennet

jacal *m* (Guat, Mex, Ven) hut, shack

jácara *f* merry ballad; cheerful song and dance; night revelers; story, argument; fake, hoax, lie; annoyance, bother

jacarear *intr* to go serenading, go singing in the street; be disagreeable

jáca•ro -ra *adj* & *m* braggart || *f* see **jácara**

jacinto *m* hyacinth

jaco *m* nag, jade; gray parrot

jactancia *f* boasting, bragging

jactancio•so -sa *adj* boastful, bragging

jactar *ref* to boast, brag; **jactarse de** to boast of

jade *m* jade

jadeante *adj* panting

jadear *intr* to pant

jadeo *m* panting

ja•ez *m* (*pl* **-eces**) harness, piece of harness; ilk, stripe, kind; **jaeces** trappings

jaguar *m* jaguar

jagüel *m* (Arg) reservoir

jaharrar *tr* to plaster

jalar *tr* to pull; flirt with || *intr* to get out, beat it || *ref* to get drunk

jalbegar §44 *tr* to whitewash; (*el rostro*) to paint || *ref* to paint the face

jalbegue *m* whitewash; whitewashing; paint, make-up

jalda•do -da *adj* bright-yellow

jalea *f* jelly; **hacerse una jalea** to be madly in love

jalear *tr* (*a los que bailan y cantan*) to animate with clapping and shouting; (*a los perros*) to incite, urge on; (Chile) to tease, pester || *intr* to dance the jaleo || *ref* to have a noisy time; swing and sway

jaleo *m* cheering, shouting; jamboree; jaleo (*vivacious Spanish solo dance*)

jalis•co -ca *adj* (Guat, Mex) drunk || *m* (Mex) straw hat

jalma *f* small packsaddle

jalón *m* surveying rod, range pole; (Guat, Mex) swig of liquor; (CAm) beau; **jalón de mira** leveling rod

jalonar *tr* to stake out, mark out

jalonear *tr* (Mex) to pull, jerk

jalonero *m* (surv) rodman

jamaica *m* Jamaica rum || *f* (Mex) charity fair

jamaica•no -na or **jamaiqui•no -na** *adj* & *mf* Jamaican

jamar *tr* to eat

jamás *adv* never; ever

in
ja

jamba f jamb
jambaje m doorframe, window frame
jamelgo m jade, nag
jamete m samite
jamón m ham
jamona f fat middle-aged woman
jamugas fpl mule chair
jánda·lo -la adj & mf Andalusian
Jantipa f or **Jantipe** f Xanthippe
Japón, el Japan
japo·nés -nesa adj & mf Japanese ‖ m (idioma) Japanese
jaque m (lance del ajedrez) check; bully; **dar jaque a** to check; **dar jaque mate a** to checkmate; **en jaque** in check; **estar muy jaque** to be full of pep; **jaque mate** checkmate; **tener en jaque** to hold a threat over the head of ‖ interj check!
jaquear tr to check; (al enemigo) harass
jaqueca f sick headache; **dar una jaqueca a** to bore to death
jacqueco·so -sa adj boring, tiresome
jaquemar m jack (figure that strikes a clock bell)
jarabe m syrup; sweet drink; **jarabe de pico** lip service, idle promise
jarana f merrymaking; rumpus; carousal; spree; trick, deceit; jest, joke; small guitar; **ir de jarana** to go on a spree
jaranear tr (CAm, Col) to swindle, cheat ‖ intr to go on a spree; raise a rumpus; joke
jarane·ro -ra adj merrymaking; cheerful, merry ‖ mf merrymaker, reveler
jarano m sombrero
jarcia f fishing tackle; jumble, mess; **jarcias** tackle, rigging; **jarcia trozada** junk (old cable)
jardín m garden, flower garden; (baseball) field, outfield; (naut) privy, latrine; **jardín central** (baseball) center field; **jardín de la infancia** kindergarten; **jardín derecho** (baseball) right field; **jardín izquierdo** (baseball) left field
jardinera f jardiniere, flower stand; basket carriage; summer trolley car, open trolley car
jardinería f gardening
jardine·ro -ra mf gardener; **jardinero adornista** landscape gardener ‖ m (baseball) fielder, outfielder ‖ f see **jardinera**
jardinista mf landscape gardener
jarea f (Mex) hunger
jarear intr (Bol) to stop for a rest ‖ ref (Mex) to flee, run away; (Mex) to swing, sway; (Mex) to die of starvation
jareta f (sew) casing
jari·fo -fa adj showy, spruce, natty
jaro·cho -cha adj brusk, bluff ‖ m insulting fellow; Veracruz peasant
jarope m syrup; nasty potion
jarra f jug, jar, water pitcher; **de jarras** or **en jarras** with arms akimbo
jarrete m hock, gambrel
jarretera f garter
jarro m pitcher; **echar un jarro de agua (fría) a** to pour cold water on
jarrón m (vaso para adornar chimeneas,

consolas, etc.) vase; (sobre un pedestal) urn
jaspe m jasper
jaspea·do -da adj marbled, speckled ‖ m marbling, speckling
jaspear tr to marble, speckle
jateo m foxhound
ja·to -ta mf calf
Jauja f Cockaigne; ¿**estamos aquí o en Jauja?** where do you think you are?; **vivir en Jauja** to live in the lap of luxury
jaula m cage; (embalaje de listones de madera) crate; (Mex) open freight car; (Cuba, P-R) police wagon; **jaula de locos** insane asylum, madhouse
jauría f pack (of hounds)
java·nés -nesa adj & mf Javanese ‖ m (idioma) Javanese
jazmín m jasmine; **jasmín de la India** gardenia
jazz m jazz
J.C. abbr Jesucristo
jebe m alum; (SAm) rubber
jedive m khedive
jefa f female head or leader; **jefa de ruta** hostess (on a bus)
jefatura f headship, leadership; (de policía) headquarters
jefe m chief, boss, head, leader; (de una tribu) chieftain; **jefe de cocina** chef; **jefe do coro** choirmaster; **jefe de equipajes** (rr) baggage master; **jefe de estación** stationmaster; **jefe del estado** chief of state; **jefe del gobierno** chief executive; **jefe de redacción** editor in chief; **jefe de ruta** guide; **jefe de tren** (rr) conductor; **jefe de tribu** chieftain; **quedar jefe** (Chile) to gamble away everything
jején m gnat, sandfly
jenabe m or **jenable** m mustard
jengibre m ginger
Jenofonte m Xenophon
jeque m sheik
jerarca m hierarch, head
jerarquía f hierarchy; **de jerarquía** important
jeremiada f jeremiad
jeremiquear intr to moan; pour out one's troubles
jerez m sherry
jerga f coarse cloth; straw mattress; (lenguaje especial de ciertos oficios; lenguaje difícil de entender) jargon
jergón m straw mattress; ill-fitting clothes; (persona torpe y estúpida) lummox
Jericó Jericho
jerife m shereef
jerigonza f (lenguaje especial de ciertos oficios; lenguaje difícil de entender) jargon; (lenguaje vulgar, caló) slang; piece of folly
jeringa f syringe; (para inyectar materias blandas en una máquina) gun; annoyance, plague; **jeringa de engrase** or **grasa** grease gun
jeringar §44 tr to syringe; inject; give an enema to; plague
jeringazo m injection, shot; squirt

jeringuilla *f* (*jeringa pequeña*) syringe; (bot) mock orange

Jerjes *m* Xerxes

jeroglífi•co -ca *adj & m* hieroglyphic

Jerónimo *m* Jerome

jer•sey *m* (*pl* **-seis**) jersey, sweater

Jerusalén Jerusalem

Jesucristo *m* Jesus Christ

jesuíta *adj & m* Jesuit

jesuíti•co -ca *adj* Jesuitic(al)

Jesús *m* Jesus; (*imagen del niño Jesús*) bambino; **en un decir Jesús** in an instant; **¡Jesús, María y José!** my gracious!

jeta *f* hog's snout, pig face; (*rostro de una persona*) phiz, mug; **estar con tanta jeta** to make a long face; **poner jeta** to pucker one's lips

jetu•do -da *adj* thick-lipped; grim, gruff

Jhs. *abbr* **Jesús**

jíba•ro -ra *mf* (W-I) white peasant

jibia *f* cuttlefish

jícara *f* chocolate cup; (CAm, Mex, W-I) calabash cup

jícaro *m* calabash (tree)

jifia *f* swordfish

jilguero *m* linnet, goldfinch

jilote *m* (Mex) green ear of corn

jineta *f* (zool) genet

jinete *m* rider, horseman

jinetear *tr* (*caballos cerriles*) to break in ‖ *intr* to show off one's horsemanship

jinglar *intr* to swing, to rock

jingoísmo *m* jingoism

jingoísta *adj & mf* jingo

jipa•to -ta *adj* pale, wan; insipid, tasteless; (Guat) drunk

jipijapa *m* Panama hat ‖ *f* jipijapa; strip of jipijapa straw

jira *f* strip of cloth; outing, picnic; trip, tour; swing, political trip

jirón *m* rag, tatter, shred; (*de una falda*) facing; pennant; bit, drop, shred; **hacer jirones** to tear to shreds

jitomate *m* (Mex) tomato

joco•so -sa *adj* jocose, jocular

jocotal *m* (CAm, Mex) Spanish plum (*tree*)

jocote *m* (CAm, Mex) Spanish plum (*fruit*)

jocoyote *m* (Mex) baby (*youngest child*)

jofaina *f* washbowl, basin

jolgorio *m* fun, merriment

jonrón *m* (baseball) home run

Jordán *m* Jordan (*river*); **ir al Jordán** to be born again

Jordania *f* Jordan (*country*)

jorda•no -na *adj & mf* Jordanian

jorguín *m* sorcerer, wizard

jorguina *f* sorceress, witch

jorguinería *f* sorcery, witchcraft

jornada *f* journey, trip, stage; day's journey; (*horas del trabajo diario del obrero*) workday; (*tiempo que dura la vida de un hombre*) lifetime; battle; (*muerte*) passing; summer residence of diplomat or diplomatic corps; event, occasion; undertaking; (mil) expedition; (*de un drama*) (archaic) act; **a grandes** or **largas jornadas** by forced marches; **al fin de la jornada** in the end; **caminar por sus jornadas** to proceed with circumspection; **hacer mala jornada** to get nowhere; **jornada ordinaria** full time; **jornada reducida** reduced working hours

jornal *m* day's work; day's pay; **a jornal** by the day; **jornal mínimo** minimum wage

jornalero *m* day laborer

joroba *f* hump; annoyance, bother

joroba•do -da *adj* humpbacked, hunchbacked; annoyed, bothered ‖ *mf* humpback, hunchback

jorobar *tr* to annoy, pester

jorongo *m* (Mex) poncho; (Mex) woolen blanket

jota *f* (*letra del alfabeto*) J; jota (*Spanish folk dance and music*); jot, iota, tittle; vegetable soup; **sin faltar una jota** with not a whit left out

joven *adj* young; **ser joven de esperanzas** to have a bright future ‖ *mf* youth, young person; **de joven** as a youth, as a young man, as a young woman

jovial *adj* jovial

joya *f* jewel; (*brocamantón*) diamond brooch; (*agasajo*) gift, present; (*persona o cosa de mucha valía*) (fig) jewel, gem; **joya de familia** heirloom; **joyas** jewelry; trousseau; **joyas de fantasía** costume jewelry

joyante *adj* glossy

joyelero *m* jewel case, casket

joyería *f* (*conjunto de joyas*) jewelry; jewelry shop; jewelry trade

joye•ro -ra *mf* jeweler ‖ *m* jewel case, casket

Juan *m* John; **Buen Juan** sap, easy mark; **Juan Español** the Spanish people, the typical Spaniard; **San Juan Bautista** John the Baptist

Juana *f* Jane, Jean, Joan; **Juana de Arco** Joan of Arc, Jeanne d'Arc; **juanas** glove stretcher

juanete *m* bunion; high cheekbone

jubilación *f* retirement; (*renta de la persona jubilada*) pension, retirement annuity

jubila•do -da *adj* retired ‖ *mf* retired person, pensioner

jubilar *tr* to retire, pension; throw out ‖ *intr* to rejoice; retire, be pensioned ‖ *ref* to rejoice; retire, be pensioned; (Col) to decline, go to pieces; (CAm, Ven) to play hooky; (Cuba, Mex) to become a past master

jubileo *m* much coming and going, great doings; (eccl) jubilee; **por jubileo** once in a long time

júbilo *m* jubilation

jubilo•so ‣sa *adj* jubilant, joyful

jubón *m* jerkin

judaísmo *m* Judaism

judería *f* (*raza judaica*) Jewry; (*barrio de los judíos*) ghetto

judía *f* Jewess; kidney bean, string bean; **judía de careta** black-eyed bean; **judía de la peladilla** Lima bean

judicatura *f* judicature; (*cargo de juez*) judgeship

judicial *adj* judicial, judiciary

ja
ju

judí•o -a adj Jewish || mf Jew || f see **judía**
juego m (acción de jugar) play, playing; (ejercicio recreativo en el cual se gana o se pierde) game; (vicio de jugar) gambling; (lugar donde se ejecutan ciertos juegos): (bowling) alley; (tennis) court; (baseball) field; (tantos necesarios para ganar la partida) game;ِ(de muebles) suit, suite; (de café) service; (de vajilla) set; (de luces, colores, aguas) play; (mach) play; (p.ej., de diplomacia) (fig) game; **a juego** to match, e.g., **una silla a juego** a chair to match; **conocer el juego de** to see through, to have the number of; **en juego** at hand; **hacer juego** to match; **hacer juego con** to match, to go with; **juego de alcoba** bedroom suit; **juego de azar** game of chance; **juego de bolas** (mach) ball bearing; **juego de campanas** chimes; **juego de comedor** dining-room suit; **juego de envite** gambling game, game played for money; **juego de escritorio** desk set; **juego de la cuna** cat's cradle; **juego de la pulga** tiddlywinks; **juego del corro** ring-around-a-rosy; **juego del salto** leapfrog; **juego del tres en raya** tick-tack-toe played with movable counters or pebbles; **juego de manos** legerdemain, sleight of hand; roughhousing; **juego de niños** (cosa muy fácil) child's play; **juego de palabras** play on words, pun; **juego de pelota** ball game; pelota; **juego de piernas** footwork; **juego de por ver** (Chile) game played for fun; **juego de prendas** game of forfeits, forfeits; **juego de suerte** game of chance; **juego de tejo** shuffleboard; **juego de timbres** glockenspiel; **juego de vocablos** or **voces** play on words, pun; **juego limpio** fair play; **juego público** gambling house; **juegos de sociedad** parlor games; **juegos malabares** juggling; flimflam; **juego sucio** foul play; **no ser cosa de juego** to be no laughing matter; **por juego** in fun, for fun; **verle a uno el juego** to be on to someone
juerga f carousal, spree; **juerga de borrachera** drinking bout, binge; **ir de juerga** (coll) to go on a spree
juerguista mf carouser, reveler
jue•ves m (pl **-ves**) Thursday; **Jueves Santo** Maundy Thursday
juez m (pl **jueces**) judge; **juez de alzadas** appellate judge; **juez de guardia** coroner; **juez de instrucción** examining magistrate; **juez de paz** justice of the peace; **juez de salida** (sport) starter; **juez de tiempo** (sport) timekeeper
jugada f (lance) play, throw, stroke, move; **mala jugada** dirty trick
juga•dor -dora mf player; gambler; **jugador de manos** prestidigitator; **jugador de ventaja** sharper
jugar §42 tr (p.ej., un naipe, una partida de juego) to play; (una espada) wield; (arriesgar) stake, risk; (las manos, los dedos) move; **jugarle a uno las bebidas** to match someone for the drinks || intr to play; to gamble; (hacer juego dos cosas) match;

(intervenir) figure, participate; **jugar a** (p.ej., los naipes, el tenis) to play; **jugar con** (un contrario) to play; (una persona; los sentimientos de una persona) toy with; match; **jugar en** to have a hand in || ref (p.ej., la vida) to risk; to be at stake; **jugarse el todo por el todo** to stake all, shoot the works
jugarreta f bad play, poor play; mean trick, dirty trick
juglar m minstrel, jongleur; (bufón) (archaic) juggler
juglaría f minstrelsy
jugo m (p.ej., de la naranja) juice; (de la carne) gravy; (líquido orgánico) juice; (fig) gist, essence, substance; **en su jugo** (culin) au jus; **jugo de muñeca** elbow grease
jugo•so -sa adj juicy; substantial, important
juguete m toy, plaything; (burla) joke, jest; (theat) skit; **de juguete** toy, e.g., **soldado de juguete** toy soldier; **juguete de movimiento** mechanical toy; **por juguete** for fun, in fun
juguetear intr to frolic, romp, sport
juguete•ro -ra adj toy || mf toy dealer || m whatnot, étagère
juguete-sorpresa m (pl **juguetes-sorpresa**) jack-in-the-box
jugue•tón -tona adj playful, frisky
juicio m judgment; (law) trial; **estar en su cabal juicio** to be in one's right mind; **estar fuera de juicio** to be out of one's mind; **juicio de Dios** (hist) ordeal; **pedir en juicio** (law) to sue
juicio•so -sa adj judicious, wise
julepe m scolding; scare, fright
julepear tr to scold; whip; (SAm) to scare, frighten; (Mex) to weary, tire out
julio m July
julo m lead cow, lead mule
jumen•to -ta mf ass, donkey
juncal adj willowy, rushy; (fig) willowy, lissome
juncia f sedge; **vender juncia** to boast, brag
junco m (embarcación china) junk; (bot) rush, bulrush; **junco de Indias** (bot) rattan; **junco de laguna** (bot) rush, bulrush
junco•so -sa adj rushy, full of rushes
jungla f jungle
junio m June
junípero m juniper
junquera f rush, bulrush
junquillo m jonquil
junta f meeting, conference; board, council; junction, union; joint, seam; (empaquetadura) gasket; (arandela) washer; **junta de comercio** board of trade; **junta de charnela** (mach) knuckle; **junta de sanidad** board of health; **junta universal** (mach) universal joint
juntamente adv together; at the same time
juntar tr to join, unite; gather, gather together; (una puerta) half-close || ref to gather together; go along; copulate
jun•to -ta adj joined, united; **jun•tos -tas** together || f see **junta** || **junto** adv together;

at the same time; **junto a** near, close to; **junto con** along with, together with; **todo junto** at the same time, all at once

juntura *f* junction; (*p.ej., de una cañería; de un hueso*) joint; connection, coupling

jura *f* oath

jura•do -da *adj* (*enemigo*) sworn ‖ *m* (*conjunto de cuidadanos encargados de determinar la culpabilidad del acusado; conjunto de examinadores de un certamen*) jury; (*cada uno de los expresados individuous*) juror; juryman

juramentar *tr* to swear in ‖ *ref* to take an oath, be sworn in

juramento *m* oath; (*voto, reniego*) curse, swearword; **prestar juramento a** to swear to; **tomar juramento a** to swear in

jurar *tr* to swear; (*la verdad de una cosa*) swear to; swear allegiance to ‖ *intr* (*pronunciar un juramento*) to swear, take an oath; (*echar votos o reniegos*) swear, curse; **jurar** + *inf* to swear to + *inf* ‖ *ref* to swear; **jurársela** or **jurárselas a uno** to have it in for someone, swear to get even with someone

jure•ro -ra *mf* (SAm) false witness

jurídi•co -ca *adj* juridical

jurisconsulto *m* (*el que escribe sobre el derecho*) jurist; (*jurisperito*) legal expert

jurisdicción *f* jurisdiction

jurisperito *m* jurist, legal expert

jurisprudencia *f* jurisprudence

jurista *mf* jurist

juro *m* right of perpetual ownership; **de juro** inevitably, for sure

justa *f* joust, tournament

justamente *adv* just, just at that time; justly; (*ajustadamente*) tightly

justar *intr* to joust, to tilt

justicia *f* justice; (*castigo de muerte*) execution; **de justicia** justly, deservedly; **hacer justicia a** to do justice to; **ir por justicia** to go to court, to bring suit

justicie•ro -ra *adj* just, fair; stern, righteous

justificable *adj* justifiable

justifica•do -da *adj* (*hecho*) just, right; (*persona*) just, upright

justificante *m* voucher, proof

justificar §73 *tr* to justify; (typ) to justify

justillo *m* jerkin, waist

justipreciar *tr* to estimate, appraise

jus•to -ta *adj* just; right, exact; (*apretado*) tight ‖ *mf* just person ‖ *f* see **justa** ‖ **justo** *adv* just; right, in tune; tight; (*con estrechez*) in straitened circumstances

Jutlandia *f* Jutland

ju•to -ta *mf* Jute

juvenil *adj* juvenile, youthful

juventud *f* youth; young people

juzgado *m* court of law; courtroom; court of one judge

juzgar §44 *tr & intr* to judge; **a juzgar por** judging by; **juzgar de** to judge, pass judgment on

K

K, k (ka) *f* twelfth letter of the Spanish alphabet

karate *m* or **karaté** *m* karate

karateka *m* karate expert

kermesse *f* var of **quermés**

keroseno *m* kerosene, coal oil

kg. *abbr* **kilogramo**

kilate *m* var of **quilate**

kilo *m* kilo, kilogram

kilociclo *m* kilocycle

kilogramo *m* kilogram

kilometraje *m* kilometrage, distance in kilometers

kilométri•co -ca *adj* kilometric; (coll) interminable, long-drawn-out

kilómetro *m* kilometer

kilovatio *m* kilowatt

kilovatio-hora *m* (*pl* **kilovatios-hora**) kilowatt-hour

kimono *m* var of **quimono**

kinescopio *m* (telv) kinescope

kiosco *m* var of **quiosco**

kirieleisón *m* dirge; **cantar el kirieleisón** to beg mercy

km. *abbr* **kilómetro**

kph. *abbr* **kilómetros por hora**

kv. *abbr* **kilovatio**

kv-h *abbr* **kilovatio-hora**

L

L, l (ele) thirteenth letter of the Spanish alphabet

la *art def fem* of **el** ‖ *pron pers fem* her, it; you ‖ *pron dem* that, the one; **la que** who, which, that; she who, the one that

laberinto *m* labyrinth, maze

labia *f* fluency, smoothness

labial *adj & f* labial

labio *m* lip; (fig) edge, lip; **chuparse los labios** to smack one's lips; **labio leporino** harelip; **leer en los labios** to lip read

labiolectura *f* lip reading

labio•so -sa adj fluent, smooth

labor f labor, work; (*cultivo de los campos*) farming, tilling; (*obra de coser, bordar, etc.*) needlework, fancywork, embroidery; **hacer labor** to match; **labor blanca** linen work, linen embroidery; **labor de ganchillo** crocheting

laborable adj workable; arable, tillable; (*dia*) work

laborante m journeyman; political henchman

laborar tr to work ‖ intr to scheme

laboratorio m laboratory; **laboratorio de idiomas** language laboratory; **laboratorio espacial** space laboratory; Skylab

laborio•so -sa adj (*trabajador*) laborious, industrious; (*trabajoso*) laborious, arduous

laborismo m British Labour Party

laborista adj Labour ‖ mf Labourite

laborterapia f work therapy

labra f carving

labrada f fallow ground (*to be sown the following year*)

labrade•ro -ra adj arable, tillable

labra•do -da adj wrought, fashioned; carved; figured, embroidered ‖ m carving; **labrado de madera** wood carving ‖ f see **labrada**

labra•dor -dora adj work; farm ‖ mf farmer; (*campesino*) peasant ‖ m plowman; **el Labrador** Labrador

labrantí•o -a adj farm ‖ m farmland

labranza f farming; farm, farmland

labrar tr to work, fashion; (*la piedra, la madera*) carve; (*arar*) plow; (*construir o mandar construir*) build; till, cultivate; cause, bring about ‖ intr to make a lasting impression

labrie•go -ga mf peasant

laca f lacquer; shellac; **laca de uñas** nail polish; **lacas** lacquer ware

lacayo m lackey, footman

lacear tr to tie with a bow; adorn with bows; (*la caza*) drive within shot; (*la caza menor*) trap, snare

lacería f poverty, want; trouble, bother; leprosy

lacerio•so -sa adj poor, needy

lacero m lassoer; poacher; dogcatcher

la•cio -cia adj faded, withered; languid; (*cabello*) lank, straight

lacóni•co -ca adj laconic

lacra f fault, defect; (*señal dejada por una enfermedad*) mark, remains; sore; scab, scar

lacrimóge•no -na adj tear, tear-producing

lacrimo•so -sa adj lachrymose, tearful

lactar tr to suckle

lácte•o -a adj milky

lacustre adj lake

ladear tr to tip, tilt; bend, lean; (*un avión*) bank ‖ intr to tip, tilt; bend, lean; turn away, turn off; (*la aguja de brújula*) deviate ‖ ref to tip, tilt; bend, lean; be equal, be even; (Chile) to fall in love; **ladearse a** (*un dictamen, un partido*) to lean to or toward

ladeo m tipping, tilting; bending, leaning; inclination, bent

lade•ro -ra adj side, lateral ‖ f hillside

ladilla f crab louse; **pegarse como ladilla** to stick like a leech

ladi•no -na adj crafty, sly, cunning; polyglot

lado m side; direction; (*del hilo telefónico*) end; **al lado** nearby; **dejar a un lado** to leave aside; **de lado** square, e.g., **diez centímetros de lado** ten centimeters square; **de otro lado** on the other hand; **de un lado** on the one hand; **echar a un lado** to cast aside; to finish up; **hacer lado** to make room; **hacerse a un lado** to step aside; **lados** backers, advisers; **mirar de lado** or **de medio lado** to look askance at; to sneak a look at; **ponerse al lado de** to take sides with; **por el lado de** in the direction of; **tirar por su lado** to pull for oneself

ladrar tr (*p.ej., injurias*) to bark ‖ intr to bark

ladrido m bark, barking; slander, blame

ladrillador m bricklayer

ladrillal m brickyard

ladrillo m brick; (*azulejo*) tile; (*p.ej., de chocolate*) cake; **ladrillo de fuego** or **ladrillo refractario** firebrick

la•drón -drona adj thievish, thieving ‖ mf thief ‖ m sluice gate; **ladrón de corazones** heartbreaker, lady-killer

ladronera f den of thieves; thievery; (*alcancía*) child's bank

ladronería f (Arg) gang of thieves; (Arg) wave of thieving

ladronzue•lo -la mf petty thief

lagaña f var of **legaña**

lagar m wine press; olive press; (*establecimiento*) winery

lagarta f female lizard; sly woman; (ent) gypsy moth

lagartija f green lizard; wall lizard

lagarto m lizard; sly fellow; (Mex) fop, dandy; **lagarto de Indias** alligator

lago m lake

lagotear tr & intr to flatter, wheedle

lágrima f tear; (*de cualquier licor*) drop; **beberse las lágrimas** to hold back one's tears; **deshacerse en lágrimas** to weep one's eyes out; **lágrimas de cocodrilo** crocodile tears; **llorar a lágrima viva** to shed bitter tears

lagrimear intr to weep easily, be tearful; (*los ojos*) fill

lagrimo•so -sa adj tearful; (*ojos*) watery

laguna f (*lago pequeño*) lagoon; (*hueco, omisión*) lacuna, gap

laical adj lay

laicismo m secularism

laja f slab, flagstone

lama f mud, ooze, slim; pond scum

lambrija f earthworm; skinny person

lamedero m salt lick

lame•dor -dora adj licking ‖ mf licker ‖ m syrup; **dar lamedor** to lose at first in order to take in one's opponent

lamedura f lick, licking

lamentable adj lamentable

lamentación f lamentation

lamentar tr, intr & ref to lament, mourn

lamento *m* lament

lamento•so -sa *adj* lamentable; plaintive

lamer *tr* to lick; lap, lap against; (*las llamas un tejado*) to lick ‖ *ref* (*p.ej., los dedos*) to lick

lame•rón -rona *adj* (coll) sweet-toothed

lametada *f* lap, lick

lámina *f* sheet, plate, strip; (*plancha grabada*) engraving; (*pintura en cobre*) copper plate; (*figura estampada*) cut, picture, illustration

laminador *m* rolling mill

laminar *tr* to laminate; (*el hierro, el acero*) roll

lampadario *m* floor lamp

lámpara *f* lamp, light; (*mancha en la ropa*) grease spot, oil spot; (rad) vacuum tube; **atizar la lámpara** to fill up the glasses again; **lámpara de alcohol** spirit lamp; **lámpara de arco** arc lamp, arc light; **lámpara de bolsillo** flashlight; **lámpara de carretera** (aut) bright light; **lámpara de cruce** (aut) dimmer; **lámpara de pie** floor lamp; **lámpara de sobremesa** table lamp; **lámpara de socorro** trouble light; **lámpara de soldar** blowtorch; **lámpara de techo** ceiling light; (aut) dome light; **lámpara inundante** floodlight; **lámpara testigo** pilot light

lamparilla *f* rushlight; aspen

lampi•ño -ña *adj* beardless; hairless

lampista *mf* lamplighter ‖ *m* tinsmith, plumber, glazier, electrician

lana *f* wool; (CAm) common person; (CAm) swindler; **lana de acero** steel wool; **lana de ceiba** kapoc; **lana de escorias** mineral wool, rock wool; **lana de vidrio** glass wool

lance *m* cast, throw; (*en la red*) catch, haul; (*accidente en el juego*) play, move, stroke; (*ocasión crítica*) chance, pass, juncture; incident, event; (*riña*) row, quarrel; (taur) capework; **de lance** cheap; secondhand; **echar buen lance** to have a break; **lance de honor** affair of honor, duel; **tener pocos lances** to be dull and uninteresting

lancero *m* lancer, spearman, pikeman

lanceta *f* (surg) lancet; (Mex, SAm) sting

lancinante *adj* piercing

lancha *f* barge, lighter; flagstone, slab; (naut) longboat; (nav) launch; (Ecuad) mist, fog; (Ecuad) frost; **lancha automóvil** launch, motor launch; **lancha de auxilio** lifeboat (*stationed on shore*); **lancha de carreras** speedboat; **lancha de desembarco** (nav) landing craft; **lancha salvavidas** lifeboat (*on shipboard*)

lanchar *intr* (Ecuad) to get foggy; (Ecuad) to freeze

lan•dó *m* (*pl* **-dós**) landau

landre *f* swollen gland; hidden pocket

lanería *f* wool shop; **lanerías** woolens, woolen goods

langosta *f* (*insecto*) locust; (*crustáceo*) lobster, spiny lobster

langostera *f* lobster pot

langostín *m* or **langostino** *m* prawn (*Peneus*)

langostón *m* green grasshopper

languidecer §22 *intr* to languish

languidez *f* languor

lángui•do -da *adj* languid, languorous

lano•so -sa *adj* woolly

lanu•do da *adj* woolly; (Ecuad, Ven) coarse, ill-bred

lanza *f* lance, pike; (*de la manguera*) nozzle; (*palo de coche*) wagon pole

lanzabom•bas *m* (*pl* **-bas**) (aer) bomb release; (mil) trench mortar

lanzacohe•tes *m* (*pl* **-tes**) rocket launcher

lanzadera *f* shuttle; **parecer una lanzadera** to buzz around

lanza•do -da *adj* sloping; (*salida de una carrera*) (sport) running (*start*)

lanza•dor -dora *mf* thrower; **lanzador de lodo** (fig) mudslinger ‖ *m* launcher; (aer) jettison gear; (baseball) pitcher

lanzaespu•mas *m* (*pl* **-mas**) foam extinguisher

lanzalla•mas *m* (*pl* **-mas**) flame thrower

lanzamiento *m* throw, hurl, fling, launch; (*de un buque*) launching; (*de un cohete*) shot, launch; (*p.ej., de víveres*) (aer) airdrop; (*de bombas*) (aer) release; (*de paracaidistas*) (aer) jump; (law) dispossession; (naut) steeve

lanzami•nas *m* (*pl* **-nas**) (nav) mine layer

lanzapla•tos *m* (*pl* **-tos**) trap

lanzar §60 *tr* to throw, hurl, fling; (*un proyecto, un cohete, maldiciones, una ofensiva, un producto nuevo, un buque*) launch; (*una mirada*) cast; vomit, throw up; (*flores, hojas una planta*) put forth; (*una advertencia*) toss, toss out; (aer) to airdrop; (*bombas*) (aer) to release; (law) to dispossess ‖ *ref* to launch, launch forth; throw oneself; dash, rush; (aer) to jump; (sport) to sprint

lanzatorpe•dos *m* (*pl* **-dos**) (nav) torpedo tube

laña *f* clamp; rivet

lañar *tr* to clamp; (*objetos de porcelana*) rivet

lapicero *m* pencil holder; mechanical pencil; ball-point pen; **lapicero fuente** fountain pen

lápida *f* tablet, stone; **lápida supulcral** gravestone

lapidar *tr* to stone to death

lá•piz *m* (*pl* **-pices**) (*grafito*) black lead; (*barrita que sirve para escribir*) pencil, lead pencil; **lápiz de bolilla** (Para) ball-point pen; **lápiz de labios** lipstick; **lápiz de pizarra** slate pencil; **lápiz de pasta** (Chile) ball-point pen; **lápiz de plomo** graphite; **lápiz estíptico** styptic pencil; **lápiz labial** lipstick

lapizar §60 *tr* to mark or line with a pencil

la•pón -pona *adj* Lapp ‖ *mf* Lapp, Laplander ‖ *m* (*idioma*) Lapp

Laponia *f* Lapland

lapso *m* lapse

laquear *tr* to lacquer

lardo•so -sa *adj* greasy, fatty

larga *f* long billiard cue; **dar largas a** to postpone, put off

largamente *adv* at length, extensively; in comfort; generously; long, for a long time

largar §44 *tr* to let go, release; ease, slack; utter; (*un golpe*) deal, strike, give; (naut) to

la
la

unfurl; (Col) to give ‖ *ref* to move away; get away, sneak away, beat it; take to sea; (*el ancla*) to come loose

lar·go -ga *adj* long; abundant; liberal, generous; quick, ready; shrewd, cunning; (naut) loose, slack; **a la larga** in the long run, in the end; **a lo largo** lengthwise; at great length; far away; **a lo largo de** along; along with; throughout; in the course of; (*el mar*) far out in; **a lo más largo** at most; **hacerse a lo largo** to get out in the open sea; **largo de lengua** loose-tongued; **largo de uñas** light-fingered; **pasar de largo** to pass without stopping; take a quick look; miss; **ponerse de largo** to come out, make one's debut; **vestir de largo** to wear long clothes ‖ *m* length ‖ *f* see **larga** ‖ **largo** *adv* at length, at great length; abundantly ‖ **largo** *interj* get out of here!

largometraje *m* full-featured film, full-length movie

largor *m* length

larguero *m* (*palo, madero*) stringer; (*almohada larga*) bolster; (aer) longeron

largueza *f* length; liberality, generosity

larguiru·cho -cha *adj* gangling, lanky

largura *f* length

lárice *m* larch tree

laringe *f* larynx

larínge·o -a *adj* laryngeal

laringitis *f* laryngitis

laringoscopio *m* laryngoscope

larva *f* larva; mask; (*duende*) hobgoblin

lasca *f* advantage, benefit

lascar §73 *tr* (naut) to pay out, slacken; (Mex) to scratch, bruise; (*un objeto de porcelana*) (Mex) to chip

lascivia *f* lasciviousness

lasci·vo -va *adj* lascivious; playful

láser *m* laser

la·so -sa *adj* tired, exhausted; weak, wan

lástima *f* pity; (*quejido*) complaint; **contar lástimas** to tell a hard-luck story; **dar lástima** to be pitiful; **es lástima (que)** it is a pity (that); **estar hecho una lástima** to be a sorry sight; **hacer lástima** to be pitiful; **llorar lástimas** to put on a show of tears; **poner lástima** to be pitiful; **¡qué lástima!** what a pity!, what a shame!; **¡qué lástima de saliva!** what a waste of breath!

lastimar *tr* to hurt, injure; hurt, offend; bruise ‖ *ref* to hurt oneself; bruise oneself; complain

lastime·ro -ra *adj* hurtful, injurious; pitiful, sad, doleful

lastimo·so -sa *adj* pitiful

lastra *f* slab, flagstone

lastrar *tr* (aer & naut) to ballast

lastre *m* (aer & naut) ballast; (fig) wisdom, maturity; (coll) food; (rr) (Chile) ballast

lat. *abrr* **latín, latitud**

lata *f* (*hojalata*) tin, tin plate; (*envase*) tin, tin can; (*madero sin pulir*) log; (*tabla delgada*) lath; annoyance, bore; **dar la lata a** (coll) to pester; **es una lata** that's terribly boring; **estar en la lata** (Col) to be penni-

less; **¡que lata!** what a nuisance! what a curse!

latebra *f* hiding place

latebro·so -sa *adj* furtive, secretive

latente *adj* latent

lateral *adj* lateral

latido *m* (*del perro*) yelp; (*del corazón*) beat, throb; (*dolor*) pang, twinge

latifundio *m* large neglected landed estate

latigazo *m* lash; crack of whip; (*represión áspera*) lashing

látigo *m* whip, horsewhip; cinch strap

latiguear *tr* to lash, whip ‖ *intr* crack a whip

latiguillo *m* small whip; (*del actor u orador*) claptrap

latín *m* Latin; **latín de cocina** dog Latin, hog Latin; **latín rústico** or **vulgar** Vulgar Latin; **saber latín** or **mucho latín** to be very shrewd

latinajo *m* dog Latin, hog Latin; Latin word or phrase (*slipped into the vernacular*)

latinar or **latinear** *intr* to use Latin

lati·no -na *adj* Latin; (naut) lateen ‖ *mf* Latin

Latinoamérica *f* Latin America

latinoamerica·no -na *adj* Latin-American ‖ *mf* Latin American

latir *tr* (Ven) to annoy, bore, molest ‖ *intr* (*el perro*) to bark, yelp; (*el corazón*) beat, throb; **me late que** (Mex) I have a hunch that

latitud *f* latitude

la·to -ta *adj* broad ‖ *f* see **lata**

latón *m* brass; (Cuba) garbage pail

lato·so -sa *adj* annoying, boring ‖ *mf* bore

latrocinio *m* thievery; thievishness

laucha *f* (Arg, Chile) mouse

laúd *m* (mus) lute; (zool) leatherback turtle

laudable *adj* laudable

láudano *m* laudanum

laudato·rio -ria *adj* laudatory

laudo *m* (law) finding, decision

láurea *f* laurel wreath

laurea·do -da *adj* & *mf* laureate

laurean·do -da *mf* graduate, candidate for a degree

laurear *tr* to trim or adorn with laurel; crown with laurel; decorate, honor, reward

laurel *m* laurel; (*de la victoria*) laurels; **dormirse sobre sus laureles** to rest or sleep on one's laurels

láure·o -a *adj* laurel ‖ *f* see **láurea**

lauréola *f* crown of laurel, laurel wreath; (*aureola*) halo

lava *f* lava; (min) washing

lavable *adj* washable

lavabo *m* washstand; washroom, lavatory

lavaca·ras *mf* (*pl* **-ras**) fawner, flatterer, bootlicker

lavaco·ches *m* (*pl* **-ches**) car washer

lavada *f* wash(ing)

lavade·dos *m* (*pl* **-dos**) finger bowl

lavadero *m* laundry; (*tabla de lavar*) washboard; (*a orillas de un río*) washing place; (Guat, Mex, SAm) placer

lava·do -da *adj* brazen, fresh, impudent ‖ *m* wash, washing; **lavado a seco** dry cleaning; **lavado cerebral** or **de cerebro** brainwashing; **lavado químico** dry cleaning

lava•dor -dora *mf* washer ‖ *m* (phot) washer ‖ *f* washing machine; **lavadora de platos** or **de vajilla** dishwasher

lavadura *f* washing; (*agua sucia; rozadura de una cuerda*) washings

lavafru•tas *m* (*pl* **-tas**) fruit bowl, finger bowl

lavama•nos *m* (*pl* **-nos**) (*pila con caño y llave*) washstand; (*jofaina*) washbowl

lavanda *f* lavender

lavandera *f* laundress, laundrywoman, washerwoman; (orn) sandpiper

lavandero *m* launderer, laundryman

lavándula *f* lavender

lavao•jos *m* (*pl* **-jos**) eyecup

lavaparabri•sas *m* (*pl* **-sas**) windshield washer

lavapla•tos (*pl* **-tos**) *mf* (*persona*) dishwasher ‖ *m* (*aparato*) dishwasher; (Chile) kitchen sink

lavar *tr* & *ref* to wash

lavativa *f* enema; annoyance, bore

lavatorio *m* washing; washstand; toilet; washroom; (*ceremonia de lavar los pies*) maundy; (med) wash, lotion

lavavajillas *m* dishwasher

lavazas *fpl* dirty water, wash water

laxante *adj* & *m* laxative

laxar *tr* to ease, slack; (*el vientre*) loosen

la•xo -xa *adj* lax, slack; (fig) lax, loose

laya *f* spade; kind, quality

layar *tr* to spade, dig with a spade

lazada *f* bowknot

lazar §60 *tr* to lasso

lazarillo *m* blind man's guide

lazari•no -na *adj* leprous ‖ *mf* leper

lázaro *m* raggedy beggar; **estar hecho un lázaro** to be full of sores

lazo *m* bow, knot, tie; lasso, lariat; snare, trap; bond, tie; **armar lazo a** to set a trap for; **caer en el lazo** to fall into the trap; **lazo de amor** truelove knot; **lazo de unión** (fig) tie, bond

Ldo. *abbr* **Licenciado**

le *pron pers* to him, to her, to it; to you; him; you

leal *adj* loyal, faithful; reliable, trustworthy ‖ *m* loyalist

lealtad *f* loyalty; reliability, trustworthiness

le•brel -brela *mf* whippet, small greyhound

lebrillo *m* earthen washtub

lebrón *m* large hare; coward; (Mex) slicker

lección *f* lesson; (*interpretación de un pasaje*) reading; **dar la lección** to recite one's lesson; **echar** or **señalar lección** to assign the lesson; **tomar una lección a** to hear the lesson of

leccionista *mf* private tutor

lecti•vo -va *adj* school (*e.g.*, *day*)

lec•tor -tora *adj* reading ‖ *mf* reader ‖ *m* foreign-language teacher; (*empleado que anota el consumo registrado por el contador de agua, gas o electricidad*) meter reader; **lector mental** mind reader

lectura *f* reading; broad culture; public lecture; college subject; (*interpretación de un* *pasaje*) reading; (elec) playback; (typ) pica; **lectura de la mente** mind reading

lechada *f* grout; whitewash; (*para hacer papel*) pulp; (CAm, Mex, W-I) whitewash

lechar *tr* to milk; (CAm, Mex, W-I) to whitewash

leche *f* milk; (coll) sperm; **estar con la leche en los labios** to lack experience, to be young and inexperienced; **leche de manteca** buttermilk; **leche desnatada** skim milk; **leche en polvo** milk powder; **tener mala leche** to behave like a cad

lechecillas *fpl* sweetbread

lechera *f* milkmaid, dairymaid; (*vasija para guardar la leche*) milk can; (*vasija para servir la leche*) milk pitcher

lechería *f* dairy, creamery

leche•ro -ra *adj* (*que da leche*) milch; (*perteneciente a la leche*) milk; (*cicatero*) (coll) stingy ‖ *m* milkman, dairyman; (coll) lucky dog ‖ *f* see **lechera**

lecho *m* bed; (*especie de sofá*) couch; (*cauce de río*) bed; layer, stratum; **abandonar el lecho** to get up (*from illness*); **lecho de plumas** (fig) feather bed

le•chón -chona *adj* filthy, sloppy ‖ *mf* suckling pig; (*persona sucia, desaseada*) pig ‖ *m* pig ‖ *f* sow

lecho•so -sa *adj* milky ‖ *m* papaya (*tree*) ‖ *f* papaya (*fruit*)

lechuga *f* lettuce; head of lettuce; (*fuelle formado en la tela*) frill; **lechuga romana** romaine lettuce

lechugui•no -na *adj* stylish, sporty ‖ *m* dandy ‖ *f* stylish young lady

lechuza *f* barn owl, screech owl; owllike woman

lechu•zo -za *adj* owlish; (*muleto*) yearling ‖ *m* bill collector; summons server; owllike fellow ‖ *f* see **lechuza**

leer §43 *tr* to read ‖ *intr* to read; lecture; **leer en** to read (*someone's thoughts*) ‖ *ref* to read, e.g., **este libro se lee con facilidad** this book reads easily

leg. *abbr* **legal, legislatura**

lega *f* lay sister

legación *f* legation

legado *m* (*don que se hace por testamento*) legacy; (*enviado diplomático*) legate

legajo *m* file, docket, dossier

legal *adj* legal; faithful, prompt, right

legalidad *f* legality; faithfulness, promptness

legalizar §60 *tr* to legalize; authenticate

légamo *m* slime, ooze

legamo•so -sa *adj*. slimy, oozy

legaña *f* gum (*on edge of eyelids*)

legaño•so -sa *adj* gummy

legar §44 *tr* to bequeath, will

legata•rio -ria *mf* legatee

legenda•rio -ria *adj* legendary

legible *adj* legible

legión *f* legion

legislación *f* legislation

legisla•dor -dora *adj* legislating ‖ *mf* legislator

legislar *intr* to legislate

legislati•vo -va *adj* legislative

la
le

legislatura f (session of a) legislature
legista m law professor; law student
legitimar tr to legitimate; legitimize
legitimidad f legitimacy
legíti•mo -ma adj legitimate
le•go -ga adj lay; uninformed ‖ m layman; lay brother ‖ f see **lega**
legua f league; **a leguas** far, far away
leguleyo m pettifogger
legumbre f (hortaliza) vegetable; (bot) legume; (Chile) vegetable stew
leíble adj legible, readable
leída f reading
leí•do -da adj well-read; **leído y escribido** (coll) posing as learned ‖ f see **leída**
lejanía f distance, remoteness
leja•no -na adj distant, remote; (pariente) distant
lejía f lye; wash water; severe rebuke
lejiadora f washing machine
lejos adv far; **a lo lejos** in the distance; **de lejos** or **desde lejos** from a distance ‖ m glimpse; look from afar; **tener buen lejos** to look good at a distance
le•lo -la adj stupid, inane
lema m motto, slogan; theme
len adj soft, flossy
lena f spirit, vigor; breathing
lencería f linen goods, dry goods; linen closet; dry-goods store
lence•ro -ra mf linen dealer, dry-goods dealer
lendrera f fine-toothed comb
lendro•so -sa adj nitty, lousy
lene adj (suave al tacto) soft; (ligero) light; kind, agreeable
lengua f (anat) tongue; (idioma) language, tongue; (de tierra, de fuego, de zapato; badajo de campana; lengua de un animal usada como alimento) tongue; **buscar la lengua a** to pick a fight with; **dar la lengua** to chew the rag; **hacerse lenguas de** to rave about; **írsele a (uno) la lengua** to blab; **lengua madre** or **matriz** mother tongue (language from which another is derived); **lengua materna** mother tongue (language acquired by reason of nationality); **morderse la lengua** to hold one's tongue; **tener en la lengua** to have on the tip of one's tongue; **tener la lengua gorda** to talk thick; to be drunk; **tener mala lengua** to be blasphemous; to have an evil tongue; **tener mucha lengua** to be a great talker; **tirar de la lengua a** to draw out; **tomar en lenguas** to gossip about; **tomar lengua** or **lenguas** to pick up news
lenguado m sole
lenguaje m language
lengua•raz (pl **-races**) adj foul-mouthed, scurrilous; polyglot ‖ mf linguist
len•guaz adj (pl **-guaces**) garrulous
lengüeta f (de la balanza) pointer, needle; (del zapato) tongue; (anat) epiglottis; (carp) tongue; (de un instrumento de viento) (mus) reed; (Chile) paper cutter; (Mex) petticoat fringe; (SAm) chatterbox
lengüetada f licking, lapping

lengüetear intr to stick the tongue out; flicker, flutter; jabber, rant; lick
lengüilar•go -ga adj foul-mouthed, scurrilous
lengüisu•cio -cia adj (Mex, P-R) foul-mouthed, scurrilous
lenidad f lenience
lenocinio m pandering, procuring
lente m & f lens; **lente de aumento** magnifying glass; **lente de contacto** or **lente invisible** contact lens; **lentes** mpl nose glasses; **lentes de nariz** or **de pinzas** pince-nez; **lente telefotográfica** tele(photo)lens
lenteja f lentil; (del reloj) bob, pendulum bob
lentejuela f sequin, spangle
lentillas fpl contact lenses
lentitud f slowness
len•to -ta adj slow; sticky; (fuego) low
leña f firewood, kindling wood; **cargar de leña** to give a drubbing to; **llevar leña al monte** to carry coals to Newcastle
leña•dor -dora mf woodcutter ‖ m woodsman
leñame m lumber, timber; stock of firewood
leñero m wood merchant; wood purchaser; (sitio donde se guarda la leña) woodshed
leño m (madera) wood; (tronco de árbol, limpio de ramas) log; sap, blockhead; (poet) ship, vessel; **dormir como un leño** to sleep like a log
leño•so -sa adj woody
Leo m (astr) Leo
león m lion
leona f lioness
leona•do -da adj tawny, fulvous
leonera f lion cage, den of lions; dive, gambling joint; junk room, lumber room
leonero m lion keeper; keeper of a gambling joint
leontina f watch chain
leopardo m leopard
leopoldina f watch fob; (mil) Spanish shako
leotardo m leotard
lépa•ro -ra adj (CAm, Mex) indecent, improper
lepe m (Ven) flip in the ear; **saber más que Lepe** to be wide-awake
leperada f (CAm, Mex) coarseness, vulgarity
lepisma f (ent) silver fish, fish moth
lepori•no -na adj hare, harelike
lepra f leprosy
leprosería f leper house
lepro•so -sa adj leprous ‖ mf leper
lerdera f (CAm) laziness, apathy; (CAm) slowness
ler•do -da adj slow, dull; coarse, crude
lesbianismo m lesbianism
les•bio -bia adj & mf Lesbian ‖ f (mujer homosexual) Lesbian, lesbian
lesión f harm, hurt; (pathol) lesion
lesionar tr to harm, hurt, injure
lesi•vo -va adj harmful, injurious
lesna f awl
le•so -sa adj hurt, harmed, injured; wounded; offended; perverted; (SAm) simple, foolish
leste m (naut) east
letal adj lethal, deadly
letame m manure
letanía f litany; (enumeración seguida) litany

letárgi•co -ca *adj* lethargic
letargo *m* lethargy
letargo•so -sa *adj* lethargic
le•tón -tona *adj* Lettish || *mf* Lett || *m* (*idioma*) Lettish, Lett
Letonia *f* Latvia
letra *f* (*del alfabeto*) letter; (*modo de escribir propio de una persona*) hand, handwriting; (*de una canción*) words, lyric; (*com*) draft; (*typ*) type; (*sentido material*) (fig) letter; **a la letra** (*al pie de la letra*) to the letter; **a letra vista** (com) at sight; **bellas letras** belles lettres; **cuatro letras** or **dos letras** (*esquela, cartita*) a line; **en letras de molde** in print; **escribir en letra de molde** to print; **las letras y las armas** the pen and the sword; **letra a la vista** (com) sight draft; **letra de cambio** (com) bill of exchange; **letra de imprenta** (typ) type; **letra de mano** handwriting; **letra de molde** printed letter; **letra menuda** fine print; (fig) cunning; **letra muerta** dead letter; **letra negrilla** (typ) boldface; **letra redonda** or **redondilla** (typ) roman; **letras** (*literatura*) letters; (coll) a few words, a line; **primeras letras** elementary education, three R's
letra•do -da *adj* learned, lettered; pedantic || *m* lawyer
letrero *m* sign, notice; (*p.ej., en una botella*) label
letrina *f* privy, latrine; (*cloaca*) sewer; (*cosa sucia*) (fig) cesspool
letrista *mf* lyricist, writer of lyrics (*for songs*); calligrapher, engrosser
leucemia *f* leukemia
leucorrea *f* leucorrhea
leudar *tr* to leaven, ferment with yeast || *ref* (*la masa con la levadura*) to rise
leu•do -da *adj* leavened, fermented
leva *f* weighing anchor; (*mach*) cam; (*mil*) levy; (CAm, Col) trick; (CAm, Col) swindle
levada *f* (*de la espada, el florete, etc.*) flourish; (*de los astros*) rise; (*del émbolo*) stroke
levadi•zo -za *adj* (*puente*) lift
levadura *f* leaven; leavening, yeast; (*tabla*) board; **levadura comprimida** yeast cake; **levadura de cerveza** brewer's yeast; **levadura en polvo** baking powder
levantaco•ches *m* (*pl* -ches) auto jack
levantada *f* rising, getting up (*from bed or from sickbed*)
levantamiento *m* rise, elevation; insurrection, revolt, uprising; **levantamiento del cadáver** inquest; **levantamiento del censo** census taking; **levantamiento de planos** surveying
levantar *tr* to raise, lift, elevate; agitate, rouse, stir up; (*una sesión*) adjourn; (*la mesa*) clear; (*la voz*) raise; (*el campo*) break; (*gente para el ejército; un sitio; fondos*) raise; (*el ancla*) weigh; straighten up; build, construct, erect; establish, found; **levantar casa** to break up housekeeping; **levantar planos** to make a survey || *ref* to rise; (*de la cama*) get up; (*de una silla*)

stand up; straighten up; (*sublevarse*) rise up, rebel
levantaválvu•las *m* (*pl* -las) valve lifter
levantaventana *m* sash lift
levante *m* east; (*viento*) levanter; (CAm, P-R) slander, libel || **Levante** *m* (*países de la parte oriental del Mediterráneo*) Levant; northeastern Mediterranean shores of Spain, especially around Valencia, Alicante, and Murcia
levanti•no -na *adj* Levantine; of the northeastern Mediterranean shores of Spain || *mf* Levantine; native or inhabitant of the northeastern Mediterranean shores of Spain
levar *tr* (*el ancla*) to weigh || *ref* to set sail
leve *adj* (*de poco peso*) light; slight, trivial, trifling
levedad *f* lightness; trivialness
leviatán *m* (Bib & fig) leviathan
levita *m* deacon || *f* coat, frock coat
levitón *m* heavy frock coat
léxi•co -ca *adj* lexical || *m* lexicon; (*caudal de voces de un autor*) vocabulary; (*conjunto de vocablos de una lengua o dialecto*) wordstock
lexicografía *f* lexicography
lexicográfi•co -ca *adj* lexicographic(al)
lexicógra•fo -fa *mf* lexicographer
lexicología *f* lexicology
lexicón *m* lexicon
ley *f* law; loyalty, devotion; norm, standard; (*de un metal*) fineness; **a ley de caballero** on the word of a gentleman; **de buena ley** sterling, genuine; **ley de la selva** law of the jungle; **ley del menor esfuerzo** line of least resistance; **ley marcial** martial law; **ley seca** dry law; **tener** or **tomar ley a** to become devoted to; **venir contra una ley** to break a law
leyenda *f* legend
leyente *adj* reading || *mf* reader
lezna *f* awl
lía *f* plaited esparto rope; **lías** lees, dregs
lianza *f* (Chile) account, credit (*in a store*)
liar §77 *tr* to tie, bind; tie up, wrap up; (*un cigarillo*) roll; embroil, involve; **liarias** to beat it; kick the bucket || *ref* to join together, be associated; have a liaison; become embroiled, become involved; **liárselos** to roll one's own (*i.e., cigarettes*)
libación *f* libation; (*acción de beber vino u otro licor*) libation
liba•nés -nesa *adj* & *mf* Lebanese
Líbano, el Lebanon
libar *tr* to suck; taste, sip || *intr* to pour out a libation; imbibe
libelo *m* lampoon, libel; (law) petition
libélula *f* dragonfly
liberación *f* liberation; (*cancelación de la carga que grava un inmueble*) redemption; (*de una cuenta*) settlement, closing; quittance
liberal *adj* liberal; (*expedito*) quick, ready; (pol) liberal; (*de amplias miras*) (Arg) liberal-minded || *mf* (pol) liberal
liberalidad *f* liberality
liberar *tr* to free

le
li

libertad f liberty, freedom; **libertad de cátedra** academic freedom; **libertad de cultos** freedom of worship; **libertad de empresa** free enterprise; **libertad de enseñanza** academic freedom; **libertad de imprenta** freedom of the press; **libertad de los mares** freedom of the seas; **libertad de palabra** freedom of speech, free speech; **libertad de reunión** freedom of assembly; **libertad vigilada** probation; **plena libertad** free hand; **tomarse la libertad de** to take the liberty to

liberta•do -da adj bold, daring; free, brash, unrestrained

liberta•dor -dora mf liberator

libertar tr to liberate, set free; (de un peligro, la muerte, etc.) save

liberta•rio -ria adj anarchistic

libertinaje m licentiousness, profligacy; impiety, ungodliness

liberti•no -na adj & mf libertine

liber•to -ta mf (law) probationer ‖ m freedman ‖ f freedwoman

libídine f lewdness, lust; (impulso a las actividades sexuales) libido

libidino•so -sa adj libidinous

libido f libido

libra f pound; **Libra** f (astr) Libra; **libra esterlina** pound sterling

libraco m or **libracho** m trashy book

libra•do -da mf (com) drawee

libra•dor -dora mf (com) drawer

libranza f (com) draft; **libranza postal** money order

librar tr to free; save, spare; (la esperanza) place; (batalla) give, join; (com) to draw ‖ intr to be delivered, give birth; (una religiosa) receive a visitor in the locutory; (com) to draw; **librar bien** to come off well, succeed; **librar mal** to come off badly, fail ‖ ref to free oneself; escape

libre adj free; free, brash, outspoken; free, unmarried; free, loose, licentious; innocent, guiltless; **libre de culpa** (seguro, divorcio) no-fault; **libre de porte** postage prepaid

librea f livery

librecambio m free trade

librecambista mf freetrader

librepensa•dor -dora adj freethinking ‖ mf freethinker

librería f bookstore, bookshop; book business; (mueble) bookshelf; **librería de viejo** second-hand bookshop

libreril adj book

librero m bookseller; (encuadernador) bookbinder; (Cuba, Mex) bookshelf

libres•co -ca adj bookish

libreta f notebook; **libreta de banco** bankbook

libreto m (mus) libretto

librillo m earthen washtub; (de papel de fumar, de sellos, etc.) book

libro m book; **ahorcar los libros** to become a dropout; **a libro abierto** at sight; **hacer libro nuevo** to turn over a new leaf; **libro a la rústica** paperbound book; **libro de caballerías** romance of chivalry; **libro de cocina** cookbook; **libro de cheques** checkbook; **libro de chistes** joke book; **libro de lance** second-hand book; **libro de mayor venta** best seller; **libro de memoria** memo book; **libro de oro** guest book; **libro de recuerdos** scrapbook; **libro de teléfonos** telephone book; **libro de texto** textbook; **libro diario** day book; **libro en imágenes** picture book; **libro en rústica** paperbound book; **libro mayor** (com) ledger; **libro talonario** checkbook, stub book

libro-registro m (com) book

licencia f license; leave of absence; (mil) furlough; **licencia absoluta** (mil) discharge; **licencia por enfermedad** sick leave

licencia•do -da adj pedantic ‖ mf licenciate ‖ m lawyer; (mil) discharged soldier; university student (wearing the long student gown)

licenciar tr to license; allow, permit; confer the degree of licenciate or master on; (mil) to discharge ‖ ref to receive the degree of licenciate or master; become dissolute; (mil) to be discharged

licenciatura f licenciate, master's degree; graduation with a licenciate or master's degree; work leading to a licenciate or master's degree

licencio•so -sa adj licentious

liceo m (sociedad literaria, establecimiento de enseñanza popular) lyceum; (instituto de segunda enseñanza) (Chile) lycée; (Mex) primary school

licitación f bidding

licita•dor -dora mf bidder

licitar tr to bid on; (Arg) to buy at auction, to sell at auction ‖ intr to bid

líci•to -ta adj fair, just; licit, legal

licor m (bebida espiritosa; cuerpo líquido) liquor; (bebida espiritosa preparada por mezcla de azúcar y substancias aromáticas) liqueur

licorera f cellaret

licorista mf distiller; liquor dealer

licoro•so -sa adj spirituous, alcoholic; (vino) rich, generous

licuar §21 & regular tr to liquefy

lid f fight, combat; dispute, argument; **en buena lid** by fair means

líder adj leading ‖ m leader

liderar tr & intr to lead, be the leader

lidia f fight; bullfight

lidiadera f (Ecuad) quarreling, bickering

lidia•dor -dora mf fighter ‖ ref bullfighter

lidiar tr (un toro) to fight ‖ intr to fight; **lidiar con** to fight with; have to put up with

liebre f hare; (hombre cobarde) coward

liendre f nit

lien•to -ta adj damp, dank

lienza f strip of cloth

lienzo m linen (cloth); linen handkerchief; (de edificio o pared) face, front; (pintura sobre lienzo) canvas

liga *f* (*cinta elástica para asegurar las medias*) garter; (*aleación*) alloy; (*materia pegajosa para cazar pájaros*) birdlime; (*confederación, alianza*) league; (*muérdago*) mistletoe; band; **liga de goma** rubber band

ligado *m* (mus & typ) ligature

ligadura *f* tie, bond; (mus) ligature, glide; (surg) ligature

ligamento *m* ligament

ligar §44 *tr* to tie, bind; join, combine; alloy; (*bebidas*) mix; (surg) to ligate ‖ *ref* to league together; be committed; be bound or attached (*e.g., in friendship*)

ligereza *f* lightness; speed, rapidity; fickleness, inconstancy; tactlessness

ligeºro -ra *adj* light; (*té*) weak; (*tejido*) light, thin; quick; slight; **a la ligera** lightly; quickly; unceremoniously; **de ligero** thoughtlessly, rashly; **ligero de cascos** light-headed, scatter-brained; **ligero de lengua** loose-tongued; **ligero de pies** light-footed; **ligero de ropa** scantily clad ‖ **ligero** *adv* fast, rapidly

lignito *m* lignite

ligustro *m* privet

lija *f* (*pez*) dogfish; (*papel que sirve para pulir*) sandpaper; **darse lija** (W-I) to boast, brag, pat oneself on the back

lijar *tr* to sand, sandpaper

lila *adj* silly, simple ‖ *m* lilac (*color*) ‖ *f* lilac (*plant and flower*)

liºlac *f* (*pl* **-laques**) lilac

liliputiense *adj & mf* Lilliputian

lima *f* (*herramienta*) file; sweet lime; sweet-lime tree; (*del tejado*) hip; hip rafter; correcting, polishing; **lima de uñas** nail file; **lima hoya** valley (*of roof*)

limadura *f* filing; (*partecillas*) filings

limalla *f* filings

limar *tr* to file; file down; polish, touch up; smooth, smooth over; (*cercenar*) curtail

limaza *f* (*babosa*) slug; (Ven) large file

limazo *m* slime, sliminess

limbo *m* (*borde*) edge; (theol) limbo; **estar en el limbo** to be quite distraught

limen *m* (physiol, psychol & fig) threshold

limenso *m* (Chile) honeydew melon

limeºño -ña *adj & mf* Limean

limero *m* sweet-lime tree

limitaºdo -da *adj* limited; dull-witted

limitador *m* — **limitador de corriente** clock meter; slot meter

limitar *tr* to limit; cut down, reduce ‖ *intr* — **limitar con** to border on

límite *m* limit; boundary, border

limítrofe *adj* bordering

limo *m* slime, mud

limón *m* lemon; lemon tree; (*de un coche o carro*) shaft

limonada *f* lemonade

limoncillo *m* citronella

limonera *f* shaft

limonero *m* lemon tree

limosna *f* alms

limosnear *intr* to beg

limosneºro -ra *adj* almsgiving, charitable ‖ *mf* almsgiver; beggar ‖ *m* alms box

limoºso -sa *adj* slimy, muddy

limpia *f* cleaning

limpiabaºrros *m* (*pl* **-rros**) scraper, foot scraper

limpiaboºtas *m* (*pl* **-tas**) shoeshiner, bootblack; (fig) flatterer

limpiacristaºles *m* (*pl* **-les**) windshield washer

limpiachimeneºas *m* (*pl* **-as**) chimney sweep

limpiadienºtes *m* (*pl* **-tes**) toothpick

limpiaºdor -dora *adj* cleaning ‖ *mf* cleaner

limpiadura *f* cleaning; **limpiaduras** cleanings, dirt

limpiamaºnos *m* (*pl* **-nos**) (Guat, Hond) towel

limpiamente *adv* in a clean manner; with ease, skillfully; simply, sincerely; unselfishly

limpiametaºles *m* (*pl* **-les**) metal polish

limpianieve *m* snowplow

limpiaparabriºsas *m* (*pl* **-sas**) windshield wiper

limpiaºpiés *m* (*pl* **-piés**) (Mex) door mat

limpiapiºpas *m* (*pl* **-pas**) pipe cleaner

limpiapluºmas *m* (*pl* **-mas**) penwiper

limpiar *tr* to clean; (*purificar*) cleanse; (*de culpas*) exonerate; (*un árbol*) clean out, prune; (*zapatos*) shine; (*hurtar*) snitch; (*a una persona en el juego*) clean out; (*dinero en el juego*) clean up; (mil) to mop up; **limpiarle a uno de** to clean someone out of ‖ *ref* to clean, clean oneself

limpiaúºñas *m* (*pl* **-ñas**) nail cleaner, orange stick

limpiavíºas *m* (*pl* **-as**) track cleaner

limpieza *f* (*acción de limpiar*) cleaning; (*calidad de limpio*) cleanness; (*hábito del aseo*) cleanliness; neatness, tidiness, honesty; chastity; ease, skill; (*observancia de las reglas en los juegos*) fair play; **limpieza de bolsa** emptiness of the pocketbook; **limpieza de la casa** house cleaning; **limpieza en seco** dry cleaning

limºpio -pia *adj* clean; (*que tiene el hábito del aseo*) cleanly; neat, tidy; honest; chaste; clear, free; **dejar limpio** to clean out; **en limpio** (com) net; **estar limpio** to have no (criminal) record; be clean; **limpio de polvo y paja** free, for nothing; net, after deducting expenses; **poner en limpio** to make a clear or fair copy of; **quedar limpio** to be cleaned out; **sacar en limpio** to make a clear or clean copy of; deduce, understand ‖ *f* see **limpia** ‖ **limpio** *adv* fair; cleanly; **jugar limpio** to play fair

limpión *m* (*limpiadura ligera*) lick; (coll) cleaner; (Col) scolding; (Col, Ven) dustcloth; (Ecuad) dishcloth

limusina *f* limousine

lín. *abbr* **línea**

lina *f* (Chile) coarse wool

linaje *m* lineage; class, description; **linaje humano** mankind

linajuºdo -da *adj* highborn ‖ *mf* highborn person

linaza *f* flaxseed, linseed

lince *adj* keen, shrewd, discerning; (*ojos*) keen ‖ *m* lynx; (fig) keen person

lincear *tr* to see into

linchamiento *m* lynching
linchar *tr* to lynch
lindante *adj* bordering, adjoining
lindar *intr* to border, be contiguous; **lindar con** to border on
linde *m & f* limit, boundary
linde•ro -ra *adj* bordering, adjoining ‖ *m* edge; boundary stone, landmark ‖ *f* limit, boundary; (bot) spicebush
lindeza *f* prettiness, niceness; elegance; witticism, funny remark; flirting; **lindezas** insults
lin•do -da *adj* pretty, nice; fine, perfect; **de lo lindo** a lot, a great deal; wonderfully ‖ *m* dude, sissy
lindura *f* prettiness, niceness
línea *f* line; (*contorno de una figura, un vestido*) lines; figure, waistline; **conservar la línea** to keep one's figure; **leer entre líneas** to read between the lines; **línea de agua** water line; **línea de batalla** line of battle; **línea de empalme** (rr) branch line; **línea de flotación** water line; **línea de fuego** firing line; **línea de fuerza** (elec) power line; (phys) line of force; **línea del partido** party line; **línea de mira** line of sight; **línea de montaje** assembly line; **línea de puntos** dotted line; **línea de tiro** (mil) line of fire; **línea férrea** railway; **línea internacional de cambio de fecha** international date line; **línea suplementaria** (mus) added line, ledger line
lineal *adj* linear
lineamentos *mpl* lineaments
linfa *f* lymph; (poet) water
linfáti•co -ca *adj* lymphatic
lingote *m* ingot, slug; (naut) ballast bar
lingual *adj & f* lingual
lingüista *mf* linguist
lingüísti•co -ca *adj* linguistic ‖ *f* linguistics
linimento *m* liniment
lino *m* flax; (*tela*) linen; (poet) sail
linóleo *m* linoleum
linón *m* lawn
linotipia *f* linotype
linotípi•co -ca *adj* linotype
linotipista *mf* linotype operator
linotipo *m* linotype
linterna *f* lantern; **linterna eléctrica** flashlight
lío *m* bundle; (*de papeles*) batch; muddle, mess; liaison, affair; **armar un lío** to raise a row; **hacerse un lío** to get into a jam
liofilización *f* freeze-drying
liofilizar §60 *tr* to freeze-dry
lionesa — a la lionesa (culin) lyonnaise
liorna *f* hubbub, uproar ‖ **Liorna** *f* Leghorn
lio•so -sa *adj* trouble-making; knotty, troublesome
liq.ⁿ *abbr* **liquidación**
líq.° *abbr* **líquido**
liquen *m* lichen
liquidación *f* (*de una cuenta*) sale
liquidar *tr* to liquefy; (com) to liquidate ‖ *intr* (com) to liquidate ‖ *ref* to liquefy
liquidez *f* liquidity

líqui•do -da *adj & m* liquid; (com) net ‖ *f* (phonet) liquid
lira *f* (mus) lyre; (*numen de un poeta*) inspiration; poems, poetry
lírica *f* lyric poetry
líri•co -ca *adj* lyric(al); (*músico, operístico*) lyric; fantastic, utopian ‖ *m* lyric poet; (Arg, Ven) visionary ‖ *f* see **lírica**
lirio *m* (bot) iris; **lirio blanco** (*azucena*) Madonna lily; **lirio de agua** (bot) calla, calla lily; **lirio de los valles** (bot) lily of the valley
lirismo *m* lyricism; spellbinding; fancy, illusion
lirón *m* (bot) water plantain; (zool) dormouse; (coll) sleepyhead
lis *m* (bot) lily ‖ *f* (bot) iris; (heral) fleur-de-lis
Lisboa *f* Lisbon
lisia•do -da *adj* hurt, injured; crippled; (*muy deseoso*) eager ‖ *mf* cripple
lisiar *tr* to hurt, injure; cripple ‖ *ref* to become crippled
lisimaquia *f* loosestrife
li•so -sa *adj* even, smooth; (*vestido*) plain, unadorned; (*franco, sincero*) simple, plain-dealing; brash, insolent; **liso y llano** simple, easy
lisonja *f* flattery
lisonjear *tr* to flatter; please ‖ *intr* to flatter
lisonje•ro -ra *adj* flattering; pleasing ‖ *mf* flatterer
lista *f* list; (*tira*) strip; (*en un tejido*) colored stripe; (*recuento en alta voz de las personas que deben estar en un lugar*) roll call; **lista de bajas** casualty list; **lista de comidas** bill of fare; **lista de correos** general delivery; **lista de espera** waiting list; **lista de frecuencia** frequency list; **lista de pagos** pay roll; **pasar lista** to call the roll
listar *tr* to list
listero *m* roll keeper, timekeeper
listín *m* telephone directory; (S-D) newspaper
lis•to -ta *adj* ready; quick, prompt; alert, wide-awake; **estar listo** to be ready; to be finished; **listo de manos** light-fingered; **pasarse de listo** to be shrewd, be clever ‖ *f* see **lista**
listón *m* (*cinta*) ribbon, tape; (*pedazo de tabla angosta*) lath, strip of wood
listonado *m* lath, lathing
lisura *f* evenness, smoothness; plainness; candor; brashness, insolence
lit. *abbr* **literalmente**
lite *f* lawsuit
litera *f* (*vehículo llevado por hombres o por animales*) litter; (*cama fija en los camarotes*) berth; **litera alta** upper berth; **litera baja** lower berth
literal *adj* literal
litera•rio -ria *adj* literary
litera•to -ta *adj* literary ‖ *mf* literary person; **literatos** literati
literatura *f* literature; **literatura de escape** or **de evasión** escape literature
litigación *s* litigation
litigante *adj & mf* litigant

litigar §44 *tr* & *intr* to litigate
litigio *m* litigation, lawsuit; dispute
litigio•so -sa *adj* litigious
litina *s* (chem) lithia
litio *m* (chem) lithium
litisexpensas *fpl* (law) costs
litografía *f* (*arte de grabar en piedra para la reproducción en estampa*) lithography; (*estampa*) lithograph
litografiar §77 *tr* to lithograph
litógra•fo -fa *mf* lithographer
litoral *adj* coastal, littoral ‖ *m* coast, shore
litro *m* liter
liturgia *f* liturgy
litúrgi•co -ca *adj* liturgic(al)
liviandad *f* lightness; inconstancy, fickleness; lewdness
livia•no -na *adj* light; inconstant, fickle; lewd ‖ *m* leading donkey; **livianos** lights, lungs
lívi•do -da *adj* livid
liza *f* combat, fight; (*campo para lidiar*) lists; **entrar en liza** to enter the lists
lo *art def neut* (used with *masc sg* form of *adj*) the, e.g., **lo bueno** the good; what is, e.g., **lo útil** what is useful; **lo mío** what is mine; (used with *adv* or inflected *adj*) the + noun, e.g., **lo aprisa que habla** the speed with which he speaks; **lo tacaños que son** the stinginess of them; how, e.g., **Vd., no sabe lo felices que son** you do not know how happy they are; **lo más** as . . . as, e.g., **lo más temprano posible** as early as possible ‖ *pron pers masc* him, it; you; (with **estar, ser, parecer,** and the like, it stands for an adjective or noun understood and is either not translated or is translated by "so"), e.g., **Vd. está preparado pero ella no lo está** you are ready but she is not ‖ *pron dem* that; **de lo que** + *verb* than + *verb*, e.g., **ese libro ha costado más dinero de lo que vale** that book cost more money than it is worth; **lo de** the matter of, the question of, e.g., **lo de sus deudas** the matter of your debts; **lo de que** the fact that, the statement that; **lo de siempre** the same old story; **lo que** what, that which; **todo lo que** all (that), e.g., **me dió todo lo que tenía** he gave me all he had
loa *f* praise; (*del teatro antiguo*) prologue; short dramatic poem
loable *adj* laudable, praiseworthy
loar *tr* to praise
loba *f* she-wolf; ridge
lobagante *m* lobster (*Homarus*)
lobanillo *m* wen, cyst
lobato *m* wolf cub
lo•bo -ba *adj* & *mf* (Mex) half-breed ‖ *m* wolf; **coger** or **pillar un lobo** (coll) to go on a jag; **desollar** or **dormir un lobo** to sleep off a drunk; **lobo de mar** (ichth) sea wolf; (coll) old salt, sea dog; **lobo solitario** (fig) lone wolf ‖ *f* see **loba**
lóbre•go -ga *adj* dark, dismal; gloomy
lobreguez *f* darkness; gloominess
lobu•no -na *adj* wolf, wolfish
locación *f* lease
local *adj* local ‖ *m* quarters, place

localidad *f* (*lugar, sitio*) location, locality; (*plaza en un tren*) accommodations; (theat) seat
localización *f* localization; location; **localización de averías** trouble shooting
localizar §60 *tr* (*limitar a un punto determinado*) to localize; (*determinar el lugar de*) locate
locería *f* pottery
loción *f* wash; (pharm) lotion; **loción facial** after-shave lotion
lo•co -ca *adj* crazy, insane, mad; terrific, wonderful; **estar loco por** to be crazy about, to be mad about; **loco de amor** madly in love; **loco de atar** raving mad; **loco perenne** insane, demented; full of fun; **loco rematado** stark-mad; **volver loco** to drive crazy ‖ *mf* crazy person, lunatic ‖ *m* (*bufón*) fool
locomotora *f* engine, locomotive; **locomotora de maniobras** shifting engine
locro *m* (SAm) meat and vegetable stew
lo•cuaz *adj* (*pl* **-cuaces**) loquacious
locución *f* expression, locution; idiomatic phrase, idiom
locuela *f* speech, way of speaking
locue•lo -la *adj* wild, frisky ‖ *f* see **locuela**
locura *f* insanity, madness; folly, madness
locu•tor -tora *mf* announcer, commentator
locutorio *m* (*en un convento de monjas*) parlor, locutory; telephone booth
lodazal *m* mudhole
lodo *m* mud, mire; (*substancia que sirve para cerrar junturas, tapar grietas, etc.*) (chem) lute
lodo•so -sa *adj* muddy
logaritmo *m* logarithm
logia *f* (*p.ej., de francmasones*) lodge; (archit) loggia
lógi•co -ca *adj* logical ‖ *mf* logician ‖ *f* logic
logísti•co -ca *adj* logistic(al) ‖ *f* logistics
logopedía *f* speech correction
logrado -da *adj* successful
lograr *tr* to get, obtain; achieve, attain; **lograr** + *inf* to succeed in + *ger* ‖ *ref* to be successful
logrear *intr* to be a moneylender; profiteer
logre•ro -ra *adj* moneylending; profiteering ‖ *mf* moneylender; profiteer; (Chile) sponger
logro *m* attainment, success; gain, profit; usury; **dar** or **prestar a logro** to lend at usurious rates
loma *f* low hill, elevation
Lombardía *f* Lombardy
lombar•do -da *adj* & *mf* Lombard
lombriguera *f* wormhole in the ground; (bot) tansy
lom•briz *f* (*pl* **-brices**) worm, earthworm; (pathol) worm; (*persona muy alta y delgada*) beanpole; **lombriz de tierra** earthworm; **lombriz solitaria** tapeworm
lomera *f* (*de la guarnición*) backstrap; (*del tejado*) ridgepole; (bb) backing
lominhies•to -ta *adj* high-backed; conceited
lomo *m* (*de animal, libro, cuchillo*) back; (*tierra que levanta el arado*) ridge; (*carne*

li
lo

de lomo del animal) loin; (*pliegue del tejido*) crease; (bb) spine; **lomos** ribs
lona *f* canvas; sailcloth; (Mex) burlap
loncha *f* slab, flagstone; slice, strip
lonchería *f* snack bar
londinense *adj* London ‖ *mf* Londoner
Londres *m* London; **el Gran Londres** Greater London
longáni•mo -ma *adj* long-suffering
longaniza *f* pork sausage
longevidad *f* longevity
longe•vo -va *adj* long-lived
longitud *f* length; (astr & geog) longitud
lonja *f* exchange, commodity exchange; grocery store; wool warehouse; (*de carne*) slice; (*de cuero*) strip; (*a la entrada de un edificio*) elevated parvis; (Arg) rawhide
lonjeta *f* bower, summerhouse
lonjista *mf* grocer
lontananza *f* (*de una pintura*) background; **en lontananza** in the distance, on the horizon
loor *m* praise
loquear *intr* to talk nonsense, play the fool; carry on, have a high time
loquera *f* insanity
loquería *f* (Chile) madhouse, insane asylum
loque•ro -ra *mf* guard in a mental hospital ‖ *m* (Arg) confusion, pandemonium; (Arg) insane asylum
loques•co -ca *adj* crazy; funny, jolly
lorán *m* (naut) loran
lord *m* (*pl* **lores**) lord
lo•ro -ra *adj* dark-brown ‖ *m* parrot; cherry laurel; (Chile) spy; (Chile) glass bedpan; (Chile) third degree
losa *f* slab, flagstone; tomb
losange *m* lozenge; (baseball) diamond
lote *m* lot, share, portion; lottery prize; (Cuba, Mex) remnant; (Arg) dunce, simpleton; (Col) swallow, swig; (*de terreno*) (Cuba, Mex) lot
lotear *tr* (Chile) to divide up, divide into lots
lotería *f* lottery; (*juego casero*) lotto; (*cosa insegura, riesgo*) gamble
lote•ro -ra *mf* vendor of lottery tickets
lotizar §60 *tr* (Peru) to divide into lots
loto *m* lotus
loza *f* (*barro cocido y barnizado*) porcelain; crockery, earthenware; **loza fina** china, chinaware
lozanear *intr* to be luxuriant; be full of life ‖ *ref* (*deleitarse*) to luxuriate
lozanía *f* luxuriance, verdure; exuberance, vigor; pride, haughtiness
loza•no -na *adj* luxuriant, verdant; exuberant, vigorous; proud, haughty
lubricante *adj & m* lubricant
lubricar §73 *tr* to lubricate
lúbri•co -ca *adj* (*resbaladizo; lascivo*) lubricous (*slippery; lewd*)
lubrificar §73 to lubricate
lucera *f* skylight
lucerna *f* large chandelier; (*abertura, tronera*) loophole
lucero *m* bright star; (*planeta*) Venus; (*ventanillo en un muro*) light; **lucero del alba** or

de la mañana morning star; **lucero de la tarde** evening star; **luceros** (poet) eyes
luci•do -da *adj* generous, magnificent; brilliant, successful; sumptuous; (Arg) striking, dashing
lúci•do -da *adj* lucid
luciente *adj* bright, shining
luciérnaga *f* glowworm, firefly
lucifer *m* overbearing fellow ‖ **Lucifer** *m* Lucifer
lucífe•ro -ra *adj* (poet) bright, dazzling ‖ *m* morning star; (Col) match
lucimiento *m* brilliance, luster; show, dash; success; **quedar** or **salir con lucimiento** to come off with flying colors
lu•cio -cia *adj* shiny ‖ *m* salt pool; (*pez*) pike, luce
lucir §45 *tr* to light, light up; show, display; (*p.ej., un traje nuevo*) sport; help; plaster ‖ *intr* to shine ‖ *ref* to dress up; come off with great success; (*sobresalir, distinguirse*) shine; flop, e.g., **lucido me quedé** I was a flop
lucrar *tr* to get, obtain ‖ *intr & ref* to profit, make money
lucrati•vo -va *adj* lucrative
lucro *m* gain, profit; **lucros y daños** profit and loss
lucro•so -sa *adj* lucrative
luctuo•so -sa *adj* sad, mournful, gloomy
lucha *f* fight; (*disputa*) quarrel; (*actividad forzada*) struggle; (*combate cuerpo a cuerpo*) wrestling; **lucha antipolución** antipollution movement (or campaign); **lucha de la cuerda** (sport) tug of war; **lucha por la vida** struggle for existence
lucha•dor -dora *mf* fighter, wrestler
luchar *intr* (*combatir*) to fight; (*disputar*) quarrel; (*esforzarse*) struggle; (*pelear cuerpo a cuerpo*) wrestle
ludibrio *m* derision, mockery, scorn
ludir *tr, intr & ref* to rub, rub together
luego *adv* next, then; therefore; soon; once in a while; **desde luego** right away; of course; **hasta luego** good-bye, so long; **luego como** as soon as; **luego de** after, right after; **luego que** as soon as
luen•go -ga *adj* long
lúes *f* pestilence; **lúes canina** distemper; **lúes venérea** syphilis
lugano *m* (orn) siskin
lugar *m* place; site, spot; job, position; (*espacio*) room, space; (*asiento*) seat; village, hamlet; (geom) locus; **dar lugar** to make room; **dar lugar a** to give cause for; give rise to; **en lugar de** instead of, in place of; **hacer lugar** to make room; **lugar común** (*expresión trivial*) commonplace; (*retrete*) toilet, water closet; **lugar de cita** tryst; **lugares estrechos** close quarters; **lugar geométrico** locus; **lugar religioso** place of burial
lugarejo *m* hamlet
lugare•ño -ña *adj* village ‖ *mf* villager
lugarteniente *m* lieutenant
luge *m* sled
lúgubre *adj* dismal, gloomy, lugubrious

luir §20 *tr* (naut) to gall, wear; (Chile) to muss, rumple; (*vasijas de barro*) (Chile) to polish ‖ *ref* (Chile) to rub, wear away

luisa *f* (bot) lemon verbena

lujo *m* luxury; **de lujo** de luxe; **gastar mucho lujo** to live in high style; **lujo de** abundance of, excess of

lujo•so -sa *adj* luxurious

lujuria *f* lust, lechery

lujuriante *adj* (*lozano*) luxuriant, lush; (*libidinoso*) lustful

lujuriar *intr* to lust, be lustful; (*los animales*) copulate

lujurio•so -sa *adj* lustful, lecherous ‖ *mf* lecher

lu•lo -la *adj* (Chile) lank, slender ‖ *m* (Chile) bundle

lu•lú *m* (*pl* -**lúes**) spitz dog

lumbago *m* lumbago

lumbre *f* light; fire; (*para encender el cigarrillo*) light; (*hueco en un muro por donde entra la luz*) light; brightness, brilliance; knowledge, learning; **echar lumbre** to blow one's top; **lumbre del agua** surface of the water; **lumbres** tinderbox; **ni por lumbre** not for love or money; **ser la lumbre de los ojos de** to be the light of the eyes of

lumbrera *f* light, source of light; light, lamp; (*abertura por donde entran el aire y la luz*) louver; skylight; dormer window; air duct, ventilating shaft; (*persona insigne*) light, luminary; (mach) port; **lumbreras** eyes

luminar *m* luminary

luminiscente *adj* luminescent

lumino•so -sa *adj* luminous; (*idea*) bright

luminotecnia *f* lighting engineering

lun. *abbr* **lunes**

luna *f* moon; moonlight; (*tabla de cristal*) plate glass; (*espejo*) mirror; (*de los anteojos*) lens, glass; whim; **estar de buena luna** to be in a good mood; **estar de mala luna** to be in a bad mood; **luna de miel** honeymoon; **luna llena** full moon; **luna menguante** waning moon; **luna nueva** new moon; **media luna** half moon; (*figura de cuarto de luna creciente o menguante*) crescent; **quedarse a la luna de Valencia** to be disappointed

lunar *adj* lunar ‖ *m* (*mancha de la piel*) mole; (*punto en un diseño de puntos*) polka dot; (fig) stain, blot, stigma; **lunar postizo** beauty spot

lunáti•co -ca *adj & mf* lunatic

lu•nes *m* (*pl* -**nes**) Monday; **hacer San Lunes** to knock off on Monday

luneta *f* (*de los anteojos*) lens, glass; orchestra seat; (aut) rear window

lunfardo *m* (Arg) thief; underworld slang

lupa *m* magnifying glass

lupanar *m* brothel, bawdyhouse

lupia *mf* (Hond) quack, healer ‖ *f* wen, cyst; **lupias** (Col) small amount of money, small change

lúpulo *m* (*vid*) hop; (*flores desecadas de la vid*) hops

luqueta *m* slice of orange or lemon used to flavor wine; (Chile) bald spot; (*en la ropa*) (Chile) spot, hole

lu•rio -ria *adj* (Mex) mad, crazy

lusitanismo *m* Lusitanism

lusita•no -na *adj & mf* Lusitanian, Portuguese

lustrabo•tas *m* (*pl* -**tas**) shoeshiner

lustrar *tr* to shine, polish ‖ *intr* to wander, roam

lustre *m* shine, polish; luster, gloss; (*fama, gloria*) (fig) luster

lustrina *f* (Chile) shoe polish

lustro *m* five years; chandelier

lustro•so -sa *adj* shining, bright, lustrous

lutera•no -na *adj & mf* Lutheran

luto *m* (*señal exterior de duelo*) mourning; (*duelo, aflicción*) sorrow, bereavement; **estar de luto** to be in mourning; **lutos** crape; **luto riguroso** deep mourning

lutocar *m* (Chile) trash cart

luz *f* (*pl* **luces**) light; window, light; electricity; (*dinero*) money; cash; **a primera luz** at dawn; **a toda luz** or **a todas luces** everywhere; by all means; **dar a luz** to have a child; to give birth to; to bring out; to publish; **entre dos luces** at twilight; half-seas over; **luces de carretera** (aut) bright lights; **luces de cruce** (aut) dimmers; **luz de balizaje** (aer) marker light; **luz de magnesio** magnesium light; flash bulb, flashlight; **luz de matrícula** license-plate light; **luz de parada** stop light; **luz trasera** taillight; **sacar a luz** to bring to light; **salir a luz** to come to light; come out, be published; take place; **ver la luz** to see the light, see the light of day

Luzbel *m* Lucifer

lo
ll

Ll

Ll, ll (elle) *f* fourteenth letter of the Spanish alphabet

llaga *f* sore, ulcer; sorrow, grief; (*entre dos ladrillos*) (mas) seam, joint; (fig) ulcer

llagar §44 *tr* to make sore; hurt

llama *f* flame, blaze; marsh, swamp; (zool) llama; (fig) fire, passion; **saltar de las**

llamas y caer en las brasas to jump out of the frying pan into the fire

llamada *f* call; (*movimiento con que se llama la atención de uno*) sign, signal; knock, ring; reference, reference mark; (mil) call, call to arms; (Mex) cowardice; **batir** or **tocar a llamada** (mil) to sound the call to arms; **llamada a filas** (mil) call to the colors; **llamada a quintas** draft call; **llamada por cobrar** collect call

llamadera f goad

llama·do -da adj so-called ‖ f see **llamada**

llama·dor -dora mf caller ‖ m messenger; door knocker; push button

llamamiento m call; calling, vocation

llamar tr to call; (dar nombre a) name, call; summon; invoke, call upon; (la atención) attract ‖ intr to call; (golpear en la puerta) knock; (hacer sonar la campanilla) ring; (el viento) (naut) to veer ‖ ref to be called, be named; **se llama Juan** his name is John

llamarada f blaze, flare-up; (encendimiento repentino del rostro) flush; (fig) flare-up, outburst

llamarón m flare-up

llamati·vo -va adj showy, loud, flashy, gaudy; (manjar) thirst-raising

llamazar m swamp, marsh

llame m (Chile) bird net, bird trap

llamear intr to blaze, flame, flash

lla·món -mona adj (Mex) cowardly

llampo m (Chile) ore

llana f trowel, float; plain; **dar de llana** to smooth with the trowel

llanada f plain

llanero m ranger, plainsman

llaneza f plainness, simplicity; familiarity; sincerity

lla·no -na adj even, level, smooth; (parecido a un plano geométrico) plane; (sencillo) plain, simple; clear, evident; (palabras) frank; accented on the next to last syllable ‖ m plain; (de la escalera) landing ‖ f see **llana**

llanque m (Peru) rawhide sandal

llanta f (cerco exterior de la rueda) tire (of iron or rubber); (borde exterior de la rueda) rim; (pieza de hierro más ancha que gruesa) iron flat; **llanta de goma** rubber tire; **llanta de invierno** snow tire; **llanta de oruga** (de un tractor de oruga) track

llanto m weeping, crying; **en llanto** in tears

llanura f evenness, level, smoothness; (terreno extenso y llano) plain

llapan·go -ga adj (Ecuad) barefooted

llares m pothanger

llave adj key ‖ f (pieza para abrir y cerrar las cerraduras) key; (herramienta) wrench; (grifo) faucet, spigot, cock; (de arma de fuego) cock; (elec) switch; (de un instrumento de viento) (mus) key; (de un enigma, secreto, traducción, cifra; lugar estratégico más propicio) key; **bajo llave** under lock and key; **echar la llave a** to lock; **llave de caja** socket wrench; **llave de caño** pipe wrench; **llave de cubo** socket wrench; **llave de chispa** flintlock; **llave de estufa** damper; **llave de mandíbulas dentadas** alligator wrench; **llave de paso** stopcock; passkey; **llave de purga** drain cock; **llave espacial** space key; **llave inglesa** monkey wrench; **llave maestra** master key, skeleton key; **llave para tubos** pipe wrench

llave·ro -ra mf keeper of the keys; (carcelero) turnkey ‖ m key ring

llavín m latchkey

llegada f arrival

llegar §44 tr to bring up, bring close ‖ intr to arrive; happen; **llegar a** to arrive at; reach; amount to; be equal to; **llegar a** + inf to come to + inf; succeed in + ger; **llegar a ser** to become ‖ ref to come close

llena f flood

llenado m filling

llena·dor -dora adj (alimento) (Chile) filling

llenar tr to fill; (un formulario) fill out; (ciertas condiciones) fulfill; satisfy; (colmar) overwhelm ‖ intr (la luna) to be full ‖ ref to fill, fill up; stuff oneself; **llenarse a rebosar** to be filled to overflowing

llene m filling; full tank

lle·no -na adj full; **lleno a rebosar** full to overflowing; **lleno de goteras** full of aches and pains ‖ m fill, plenty; fulness, full enjoyment; completeness; full moon; (en el teatro) full house ‖ f see **llena**

lleva or **llevada** f carrying, conveying; ride; **lleva gratuita** free ride

lleva·ero -ra adj bearable, tolerable

llevar tr (transportar) to carry; (traer consigo) take; (conducir) lead; carry away, take away; (cuentas, libros; la anotación en los naipes) keep; (la correspondencia con una persona) carry on; (un drama a la pantalla) put on; (buena o mala vida) lead; (aguantar) bear, stand for; (castigo) suffer; get, obtain; win; (cierto precio) charge; (traje, vestido) wear; (armas) bear; (cierto tiempo) have been, e.g., **llevo ocho días en cama** I have been in bed for a week; (ropa) **a todo llevar** for all kinds of wear; **llevar** (cierto tiempo) **a** (uno) to be older than (someone) by (a certain age); (cierta distancia) **a** (uno) to be ahead of (someone) by (a certain distance); (cierto peso) **a** (uno) to be heavier than (someone) by (a certain weight); **llevar a las antenas** to put on the air; **llevarla hecha** to have it all figured out; **llevar puesto** to wear, to have on; **llevar** + pp to have + pp, e.g., **lleva conseguidas muchas victorias** he has won many victories ‖ ref to carry away; take, take away; carry off; win; get along; **llevarse algo a alguien** to take something away from someone

lloradue·los mf (pl -los) crybaby, sniveler

lloralásti·mas mf (pl -mas) poverty-crying skinflint

llorar tr to weep over; mourn, lament ‖ intr to weep, cry; (los ojos) water, run

llorera f crying; sobbing

lloriquear intr to whine, to whimper

lloriqueo m whining, whimpering

lloro m weeping, crying; tears

llo·rón -rona adj weeping, crying ‖ mf weeper, crybaby ‖ m weeping willow; pendulous plume ‖ f hired mourner

lloro·so -sa adj weepy; sad, tearful

llovedi·zo -za adj (agua) rain; (techo) leaky

llover §47 tr (enviar como lluvia) to rain ‖

intr to rain; **como llovido** unexpectedly; **llueva o no** rain or shine; **llueve** it is raining ‖ *ref* (*el techo*) to leak
llovido *m* stowaway
llovizna *f* drizzle
lloviznar *intr* to drizzle

llovizno•so -sa *adj* moist, damp (*from drizzle*); drizzly
lluvia *f* rain; rain water; (*copia, muchedumbre*) (fig) shower, downpour; **lluvia ácida** acid rain; **lluvia radiactiva** fallout, radioactive fallout
lluvio•so -sa *adj* rainy

M

M, m (eme) *f* fifteenth letter of the Spanish alphabet
m. *abbr* **mañana, masculino, meridiano, metro, minuto, muerto**
maca *f* flaw, blemish; bruise (*on fruit*); spot, stain; hammock
maca•co -ca *adj* ugly, misshapen ‖ *m* — **macaco de la India** rhesus
macadamizar §60 *tr* to macadamize
macadán *m* macadam
macana *f* cudgel, club; drug on the market; nonsense; (Arg) botch; (Arg) lie, trick
macanear *intr* to fib, lay it on; (Col, Ven) to manage (well)
macanu•do -da *adj* terrific, swell, grand; (Col, Ecuad) strong, husky
macarrón *m* macaroon; **macarrones** macaroni
macear *tr* to mace, hammer ‖ *intr* to pester, bore
macelo *m* slaughterhouse
macero *m* macebearer
maceta *f* stone hammer; flowerpot; flower vase; (*de herramienta*) handle; (*de cantero*) hammer; (Mex) head
macfarlán *m* inverness cape
macilen•to -ta *adj* pale, wan, gaunt
macillo *m* hammer (*of piano*)
macis *m* mace (*spice*)
macizar §60 *tr* to fill in, fill up
maci•zo -za *adj* solid; massive ‖ *m* solid; flower bed; bulk, mass; massif; wall space
macu•co -ca *adj* (Chile) sly, cunning; (Arg, Chile, Ven) important, notable; (Ecuad) old, worthless; (Arg, Chile, Peru) strong, husky ‖ *m* (Arg, Bol, Col) overgrown boy
mácula *f* spot; stain; blemish; trick, deception
macha *f* (Bol) drunkenness; (Arg) joke; (Bol) mannish woman
machaca *mf* pest, bore ‖ *f* crusher
machacar §73 *tr* to crush, mash, pound ‖ *intr* to pester, bore
macha•cón -cona *adj* boring, tiresome, importunate ‖ *mf* bore
machada *f* flock of billy goats; stupidity
machado *m* hatchet
machamartillo — **a machamartillo** solidly, firmly, lastingly
machaque•ro -ra *adj* tiresome, boring ‖ *mf* bore

machar *tr* to crush, grind, pound ‖ *ref* (Bol, Ecuad) to get drunk
machete *m* machete, cane knife
machi *mf* (Chile) quack, healer
machihembrar *tr* (*ensamblar a ranura y lengüeta*) to feather; (*ensamblar a caja y espiga*) to mortise
machina *f* derrick, crane; pile driver; (P-R) merry-go-round
machismo *m* machismo; male chauvinism
machista *m* male chauvinist
macho *adj invar* (*animal, planta, herramienta*) male; strong, robust; dull, stupid ‖ *m* sledge hammer; abutment, pillar; male; he-mule; dullard; (*del corchete*) hook; (*mach*) male piece; (coll) he-man; (C-R) blond foreigner; **macho cabrío** he-goat, billy goat; **macho de aterrajar** or **macho de terraja** (mach) tap, screw tap
machona *f* (Arg, Bol, Ecuad, Guat) mannish woman
macho•rro -rra *adj* barren, sterile ‖ *f* barren woman; (Mex) mannish woman
machucar §73 *tr* to beat, pound, bruise
machu•cho -cha *adj* sedate, judicious; elderly
madamita *m* (coll) sissy
madeja *f* hank, skein; tangle of hair; (*hombre flojo*) jellyfish; **madeja sin cuenda** hopeless tangle
madera *m* Madeira wine ‖ *f* wood; piece of wood; knack, flair; makings; **madera aserradiza** lumber; **madera contrachapada** plywood; **madera de sierra** lumber; **madera laminada** plywood; **tener madera de** to have what it takes to
maderada *f* raft, float
maderaje *m* or **maderamen** *m* woodwork
maderería *f* lumberyard
madere•ro -ra *adj* lumber ‖ *m* lumberman; carpenter; log driver
madero *m* log, beam; ship, vessel; blockhead
madrastra *f* stepmother; bother
madraza *f* doting mother
madre *adj* mother ‖ *f* mother; matron; womb; main sewer; river bed; dregs; sediment; **madre adoptiva** foster mother; **madre de leche** wet nurse; **madre patria** mother country, old country; **madre política** mother-in-law; stepmother; **sacar de madre** to annoy, to upset

‖
ma

madreperla *f* (*molusco*) pearl oyster; (*nácar*) mother-of-pearl

madreselva *f* honeysuckle

madriga•do -da *adj* twice-married; (*toro*) that has sired; worldly-wise

madriguera *f* burrow, lair, den

madrile•ño -ña *adj* Madrid ‖ *mf* native or inhabitant of Madrid

madrina *f* godmother; patroness, protectress; prop, shore, brace; joke; leading mare; **madrina de boda** bridesmaid; **madrina de guerra** war mother

madrugada *f* early morning, dawn; early rising

madruga•dor -dora *adj* early-rising ‖ *mf* early riser

madrugar §44 *intr* to get up early; be out in front

madurar *tr* to ripen; mature; think out ‖ *intr* to ripen; mature

madurez *f* ripeness; maturity

madu•ro -ra ripe; mature

maestra *f* teacher; elementary girls' school; **maestra de escuela** schoolmistress

maestranza *f* arsenal, armory; navy yard; order of equestrian knights

maestría *f* mastery; mastership

maes•tro -tra *adj* master; masterly; chief, main; (*perro*) trained ‖ *m* master; teacher; (*en la música y la pintura*) maestro; **maestro de capilla** choirmaster; **maestro de ceremonias** master of ceremonies; **maestro de equitación** riding master; **maestro de escuela** elementary schoolteacher; **maestro de esgrima** fencing master; **maestro de obras** master builder ‖ *f* see **maestra**

Magallanes *m* Magellan

magancear *intr* (Col, Chile) to loaf around

magan•to -ta *adj* dull, spiritless

magia *f* magic

magiar *adj* & *mf* Magyar; Hungarian

mági•co -ca *adj* magic ‖ *mf* magician, wizard ‖ *f* magic

magín *m* fancy, imagination

magisterio *m* teaching; teachers

magistrado *m* magistrate

magistral *adj* masterly

magnáni•mo -ma *adj* magnanimous

magnesio *m* magnesium; (phot) flashlight

magnéti•co -ca *adj* magnetic

magnetismo *m* magnetism

magnetizar §60 *tr* magnetize

magneto *m* & *f* magneto

magnetofón *m* or **magnetófono** *m* tape recorder

magnetoscopia *f* video recorder

magnificar §73 *tr* to magnify; exalt

magnífi•co -ca *adj* magnificent

magnitud *f* magnitude

mag•no -na *adj* great, e.g., **Alejandro Magno** Alexander the Great

mago *m* magician; soothsayer; (fig) wizard; expert; **Magos de Oriente** Wise Men of the East

ma•gro -gra *adj* lean, thin ‖ *m* loin of pork ‖ *f* slice of ham

maguar §10 *ref* (Ven, W-I) to be disappointed

magüeta *f* heifer

magüeto *m* young bull

maguey *m* century plant

magullar *tr* to bruise ‖ *ref* to get bruised

magullón *m* bruise; contusion

mahometa•no -na *adj* & *mf* Mohammedan

mahometismo *m* Mohammedanism

mahones *mpl* (P-R, S-D) blue jeans

mahonesa *f* mayonnaise

maído *m* meow

maitines *mpl* matins

maíz *m* maize, Indian corn; **comer maíz** to accept bribes; **maíz en la mazorca** corn on the cob

maizal *m* cornfield

maja *f* flashy dame

majada *f* sheepfold; dung, manure

majaderear *tr* to bother, annoy

majadería *f* nonsensical remark; bother, nuisance

majade•ro -ra *adj* pestiferous, stupid ‖ *mf* bore, dunce ‖ *m* pestle

majar *tr* to crush, mash, grind, pound; annoy, bother

majestad *f* majesty

majestuo•so -sa *adj* majestic

ma•jo -ja *adj* sporty; handsome, dashing; pretty, nice; all dressed up ‖ *mf* sport ‖ *m* bully ‖ *f* see **maja**

mal *adj* apocopated form of **malo**, used only before nouns in masculine singular ‖ *adv* badly, poorly; wrong; hardly, scarcely; **mal de** short of; **mal que le pese** in spite of him ‖ *m* evil; damage, harm; wrong; sickness; misfortune; **mal de altura** mountain sickness; **mal de la tierra** homesickness; **mal de mar** seasickness; **mal de piedra** (pathol) stone; **mal de rayos** radiation sickness; **mal de vuelo** airsickness; **por mal de mis pecados** to my sorrow; **tener a mal** to object to; **¡mal haya . . . !** curses on . . . !

mala *f* mail; mailbag; mailboat

malabarista *mf* juggler; sneak thief

malacate *m* whim; (*hoisting machine*) (Mex, Hond) spindle

malaconseja•do -da *adj* ill-advised

malacrianza *f* var of **malcriadez**

malagradeci•do -da *adj* ungrateful

malandante *adj* unlucky, unfortunate

malandanza *f* bad luck, misfortune

malan•drín -drina *adj* evil, wicked ‖ *mf* scoundrel, rascal

malaria *f* malaria

malaventura *f* misfortune

mala•yo -ya *adj* & *mf* Malay

mala•zo -za *adj* perverse; evil; wicked

malbaratar *tr* to undersell; squander

malcasa•do -da *adj* mismated; undutiful

malcasar *tr* to mismate ‖ *intr* & *ref* to be mismated

malcaso *m* treachery

malconten•to -ta *adj* & *mf* malcontent

malcriadez *f* rudeness; bad manners

malcria•do -da *adj* ill-bred

malcriar §77 *tr* to spoil, pamper

maldad *f* evil, wickedness

maldecir §11 *tr* to curse ‖ *intr* to curse, damn; **maldecir de** to slander, vilify

maldición *f* malediction, curse; oath, curse

maldispues•to -ta *adj* ill, indisposed; unwilling, ill-disposed

maldi•to -ta *adj* damned, accursed; wicked; (Mex) coarse, crude, indecent; **no saber maldita la cosa de** to not know a single thing about ‖ **el Maldito** the Evil One ‖ *f* (coll) tongue; **soltar la maldita** to talk too much

maleante *adj* wicked, evil ‖ *mf* crook, hoodlum, rowdy

malear *tr* to spoil; corrupt ‖ *ref* to spoil, get spoiled; be corrupted

malecón *m* levee, dike, mole, jetty

maledicencia *f* calumny, slander

maleficiar *tr* to damage, harm; to curse, bewitch, cast a spell on

maleficio *m* curse, spell; witchcraft

maléfi•co -ca *adj* evil; harmful

malentender §51 *tr* to misunderstand

malentendido *m* misunderstanding, misapprehension

malestar *m* malaise, indisposition

maleta *m* bungler; ham bullfighter ‖ *f* valise; **hacer la maleta** to pack up

maletín *m* satchel

malevolencia *f* malice, malevolence

malévo•lo -la *adj* malevolent

maleza *f* thicket, underbrush; weeds

malfuncionamiento *m* malfunction

malgasta•do -da *adj* ill-spent

malgastar *tr* to waste, squander

malgenio•so -sa *adj* ill-tempered, irritable

malhabla•do -da *adj* foul-mouthed

malhada•do -da *adj* ill-starred

malhe•cho -cha *adj* deformed ‖ *m* misdeed

malhe•chor -chora *mf* malefactor ‖ *f* malefactress

malherir §68 *tr* to injure badly

malhumora•do -da *adj* ill-humored

malicia *f* (*maldad*) evil; (*bellaquería, malevolencia*) malice; insidiousness, trickiness; suspicion

malicio•so -sa *adj* evil; malicious; insidious, tricky

malignar *tr* to corrupt, vitiate; spoil

malignidad *f* malignity

malig•no -na *adj* (*malévolo; pernicioso*) malign; (*malicioso; perjudicial*) malignant; (*pathol*) malignant

malintenciona•do -da *adj* ill-disposed, evil-minded

malmaridada *f* faithless wife

malmeter *tr* to lead astray, misguide; alienate, estrange

ma•lo -la *adj* bad, poor, evil; (*travieso*) naughty, mischievous; (*enfermo*) sick, ill; (*que no es como debiera ser*) wrong; (*inflamado, dolorido*) sore; **a la mala** (Cuba, P-R) by force; (Mex) insincere; (Mex) mean; **estar de malas** to be out of luck; **lo malo es que** the trouble is that; **malo con** or **para con** mean to; **por malas o por buenas** willingly or unwillingly; **ser malo**

de engañar to be hard to trick ‖ **el Malo** the Evil One ‖ *f* see **mala**

malogra•do -da *adj* late, ill-fated

malograr *tr* to miss ‖ *ref* to fail; come to an untimely end

malogro *m* failure, disappointment

maloliente *adj* malodorous, foul-smelling

malón *m* mean trick; (SAm) Indian incursion; (Chile) surprise party

malpara•do -da *adj* hurt; **salir malparado (de)** to fail (in), come out worsted (in)

malparar *tr* to mistreat

malparir *intr* to miscarry, have a miscarriage

malparto *m* miscarriage

malquerencia *f* dislike

malquerer §55 *tr* to dislike

malquistar *tr* to alienate, estrange ‖ *ref* to become alienated

malquis•to -ta *adj* disliked, unpopular

malrotar *tr* to squander

malsa•no -na *adj* unhealthy

malsín *m* mischief-maker

malsonante *adj* obnoxious, odious

malsufri•do -da *adj* impatient

malta *m* malt ‖ *f* asphalt, tar; dark beer; (Chile) premium beer

maltraer §75 *tr* to abuse, ill-treat; call down, scold

maltratar *tr* to abuse, ill-treat, maltreat; damage, spoil

maltre•cho -cha *adj* battered, damaged

malu•co -ca or **malu•cho -cha** *adj* sickish, upset

malva *f* mallow; **malva arbórea** hollyhock, rose mallow; **ser como una malva** to be meek and mild

malva•do -da *adj* evil, wicked ‖ *mf* evildoer

malvarrosa *f* hollyhock, rose mallow

malvavisco *m* marsh mallow

malvender *tr* to sell at a loss

malversación *f* graft, embezzlement, misappropriation

malversar *tr* & *intr* to graft, embezzle

malvezar §60 *tr* to give bad habits to ‖ *ref* to acquire bad habits

malla *f* mesh, meshing; (*de la armadura*) mail; (*traje*) tights; bathing suit

mallete *m* mallet

Mallorca *f* Majorca

mallor•quín -quina *adj* & *mf* Majorcan

mama *f* mamma

ma•má *f* (*pl* **-más**) mamma

mamada *f* suck; sucking; cinch; advantageous deal; easy profit

mama•lón -lona *adj* (Ven, W-I) loafing ‖ *mf* (Cuba) sponger

mamama *f* (Hond) granny

mamamama *f* (Peru) granny

mamar *tr* to suck; learn as a child; swallow; wangle; **mamóla** he was taken in ‖ *intr* to suck ‖ *ref* to swallow; (*obtener sin mérito*) wangle; (SAm) to get drunk; **mamarse a uno** to get the best of someone; take someone in; (Col, Chile, Peru) to do away with someone

mamarracho *m* mess, sight; (*hombre ridículo*) milksop

ma
ma

mamelón *m* knoll, mound

mamífe•ro -ra *adj* mammalian ‖ *m* mammal, mammalian

mamola *f* chuck (*under the chin*); **hacer la mamola a** to chuck under the chin; take in, make a fool of

ma•món -mona *adj* sucking; fond of sucking ‖ *mf* suckling ‖ *m* shoot, sucker; (Guat, Hond) club; (Mex) soft cake ‖ *f* chuck (*under chin*)

mamonear *tr* (Guat, Hond) to beat, cudgel; (S-D) to put off, delay; (*el tiempo*) (S-D) to waste

mamotreto *m* memo book; batch of papers; hulk, bulk

mampara *f* screen; folding screen; (Peru) glass door

mamparo *m* bulkhead

mampostería *f* rubble, rubblework; masonry, stone masonry

ma•mut *m* (*pl* **-muts**) mammoth

manada *f* (*de ganado vacuno*) herd, drove; (*de ganado lanar*) flock; (*de lobos*) pack; (*de gente*) gang, troop; (*de hierba, trigo, etc.*) handful

manade•ro -ra *adj* flowing ‖ *m* spring, source; shepherd

manantial *adj* flowing, running ‖ *m* spring, source; (fig) source

manar *tr* to run with ‖ *intr* to pour forth, run; abound

manaza *f* big hand

mancar §73 *tr* to maim, cripple ‖ *intr* (*el viento*) (naut) to abate, subside

manca•rrón -rrona *adj* (*caballería*) skinny, worn-out; (Chile) tired out, exhausted ‖ *m* old nag; (Chile, Peru) dam, dike

manceba *f* mistress, concubine

mancebía *f* bawdyhouse, brothel; wild oats; youth

mance•bo -ba *adj* youthful ‖ *m* youngster; youth, young man; (*en una farmacia, barbería, etc.*) helper ‖ *f* see **manceba**

mancerina *f* saucer with hook to hold chocolate cup

mancilla *f* spot, blemish

mancillar *tr* to spot, blemish

man•co -ca *adj* armless, one-armed; one-handed; defective, faulty ‖ *mf* cripple ‖ *m* (Chile) old nag

mancomún — **de mancomún** jointly, in common

mancomunar *tr* to unite, combine; (*fuerzas, caudales, etc.*) pool ‖ *ref* to unite, combine

mancomunidad *f* association, union; (*asociación de provincias*) commonwealth

mancornar §61 *tr* (*un novillo*) to throw and hold on the ground; (*una res vacuna*) tie a horn and front leg of; (*dos reses*) tie together by the horns; (coll) to join, bring together

mancornas or **mancuernas** *fpl* (Mex) cuff links

mancuernillas *fpl* (Guat, Hond) cuff links

mancha *f* spot, stain; (*de vegetación*) patch; speckle; (fig) stain, blot; **mancha solar** sunspot

manchar *tr* to spot, stain; speckle; (fig) to stain, disgrace ‖ *intr* to spot; ¡mancha! wet paint!

manda *f* gift, offer; bequest, legacy

mandade•ro -ra *mf* messenger ‖ *m* errand boy

mandado *m* order, command; errand; **hacer un mandado** to run an errand

manda•más *m* (*pl* **-mases**) (slang) big shot; (*jefe político*) (slang) boss

mandamiento *m* order, command; (Bib) commandment; (law) writ; **los cinco mandamientos** the five fingers of the hand

mandar *tr* to order, command; (*legar*) bequeath; (*enviar*) send; **mandar a distancia** to operate by remote control; **mandar + inf** to have + *inf*, e.g., **la mandé leer en voz alta** I had her read aloud ‖ *intr* to be in command, be the boss; **mandar llamar** to send for; **mandar por** to send for; **mande Vd.** I beg your pardon ‖ *ref* (*un enfermo*) to manage to get around; (*dos piezas*) be communicating; **mandarse con** (*otra pieza*) to communicate with; be rude to

mandarina *f* tangerine

mandatario *m* agent, proxy; chief executive

mandato *m* mandate; term (*of office*)

mandíbula *f* jaw, jawbone; **reír a mandíbula batiente** to roar with laughter

mandil *m* apron

mando *m* command; control, drive; **alto mando** (mil) high command; **mando a distancia** remote control; **mando a punta de dedo** finger-tip control; **mando de las válvulas** timing gears; **mando por botón** push-button control; **tener el mando y el palo** to be the boss, rule the roost

mandolina *f* mandolin

man•dón -dona *adj* bossy ‖ *mf* domineering person ‖ *m* (*en las minas*) boss, foreman; (*en las carreras de caballos*) (Chile) starter

mandrágora *f* mandrake

mandril *m* (mach) chuck

mandrilar *tr* to bore

manea *f* hobble

manear *tr* to hobble

manecilla *f* (*de reloj*) hand; clasp, book clasp; (bot) tendril; (typ) fist, index

manejable *adj* manageable

manejar *tr* to manage; handle, wield; (*un automóvil*) drive ‖ *ref* to behave; get around, move about

manejo *m* management; handling; intrigue, scheming; horsemanship; driving; **manejo a distancia** remote control; **manejo doméstico** housekeeping

manera *f* manner, way; **a la manera de** in the manner of; like; **de manera que** so that; **en gran manera** to a great extent; extremely; **sobre manera** exceedingly

manga *f* (*parte del vestido*) sleeve; (*tubo de caucho*) hose; waterspout; (bridge) game; **en mangas de camisa** in shirt-sleeves; **ir de manga** to be in cahoots; **manga de**

agua waterspout; cloudburst; **manga de camisa** shirt-sleeve; **manga de riego** watering hose; **manga de viento** whirlwind; **manga marina** waterspout; **mangas extras,** profits

mangana *f* lasso

manganear *tr* to lasso; (Peru) to annoy, bother

manganeso *m* manganese

mango *m* handle; **mango de escoba** broomstick; (aer) stick, control stick

mangonear *tr* to plunder ‖ *intr* to loaf around; meddle; dabble

mangosta *f* mongoose

mangote *m* sleeve protector

manguera *f* hose; (*tubo de ventilación*) funnel

mangueta *f* fountain syringe; door jamb

manguitero *m* furrier

manguito *m* muff; sleeve guard; coffee cake; (mach) sleeve

ma•ní *m* (*pl* **-níes** or **-nises**) peanut

manía *f* mania; craze, whim; grudge; **tener manía a** to dislike

maniabier•to -ta *adj* open-handed

manía•co -ca *adj* maniac(al) ‖ *mf* maniac

maníaco-depresi•vo -va *adj* manic-depressive

maniatar *tr* to tie the hands of

maniáti•co -ca *adj* stubborn; queer, eccentric; (*entusiasta*) crazy ‖ *mf* crank, eccentric

manicero *m* peanut vendor

manicomio *m* madhouse, insane asylum

manicor•to -ta *adj* closefisted, tight

manicu•ro -ra *mf* manicure, manicurist ‖ *f* manicure, manicuring

mani•do -da *adj* shabby, worn; hackneyed; (culin) high ‖ *f* haunt, hangout

manifestación *f* manifestation; (*reunión pública para dar a conocer un sentimiento u opinión*) demonstration

manifestante *mf* demonstrator

manifestar §2 *tr* to manifest; (*el Santísimo Sacramento*) expose ‖ *intr* to demonstrate ‖ *ref* to become manifest

manifies•to -ta *adj* manifest ‖ *m* manifesto; (eccl) exposition of the Host; (naut) manifest

manigua *f* (Mex, W-I) thicket, jungle; **irse a la manigua** (W-I) to revolt

manija *f* handle; clamp; crank

manilar•go -ga *adj* ready-fisted; generous

manilla *f* bracelet; handcuff, manacle

manillar *m* handle bar

maniobra *f* handling; lever; maneuver; (naut) gear, tackle

maniobrar *intr* to work with the hands; maneuver; (rr) to shift

maniota *f* hobble

manipula•dor -dora *mf* manipulator ‖ *m* (telg) key

manipular *tr* to manipulate

maniquí *m* (*pl* **-quíes**) manikin, mannequin; (*para exponer prendas de ropa*) dress form; (*de pintores y escultores*) lay figure; (fig) puppet; **ir hecho un maniquí** to be a

fashion plate ‖ *f* (*mujer joven que luce los trajes de última moda*) mannequin, model

manirro•to -ta *adj* lavish, prodigal

manivací•o -a *adj* empty-handed

manivela *f* crank; **manivela de arranque** starting crank

manjar *m* dish, food, tidbit, delicacy; lift, recreation

mano *m* first to play, e.g., **soy mano** I'm first ‖ *f* hand; (*de cuadrúpedo*) forefoot; (*de pintura*) coat; (*de papel*) quire; (*saetilla de reloj u otro instrumento*) hand; (*lance en un juego*) round, hand; (*del elefante*) trunk; pestle, masher; **a la mano** at hand, on hand; within reach; understandable; **a mano airada** violently; **asidos de la mano** hand in hand; **bajo mano** underhandedly; **caer en manos de** to fall into the hands of; **¡dame esa mano!** put it here!; **dar la mano** to lend a hand; **darse las manos** to join hands; to shake hands; **de las manos** hand in hand; **de primera mano** at first hand; first-hand; **de segunda mano** secondhand; **echar mano de** to resort to; **echar una mano** to lend a hand; to play a game; **en buena mano está** after you, you drink first; **escribir a la mano** to take dictation; **escribir a manos de** to write in care of; **estrecharse la mano** to shake hands; **ganarle a uno por la mano** to steal a march on someone; **lavarse las manos de** to wash one's hands of; **llegar a las manos** to come to blows; **malas manos** awkwardness; **mano de gato** cat's-paw; master hand, master touch; **mano de obra** labor; **mano derecha** right-hand man; **mano de santo** sure cure; **¡manos a la obra!** let's get to work!; **manos libres** outside work; **manos limpias** extras, perquisites; clean hands; **manos puercas** graft; **probar la mano** to try one's hand; **tener mano con** to have a pull with; **tener mano izquierda** to be on one's toes; **untar la mano a** to grease the palm of; **venir a las manos** to come to blows; **vivir de la mano a la boca** to live from hand to mouth

manojo *m* bunch, bundle, handful; **a manojos** in abundance

manopla *f* gauntlet; postilion's whip; (Chile) knuckles, brass knuckles

manosear *tr* to finger, paw; muss, rumple; fiddle with; pet ‖ *ref* to spoon, neck

manotada *f* slap

manotear *tr* to slap, smack; (Arg, Mex) to steal, snitch; ‖ *intr* to gesticulate

manquedad *f* lack of one or both hands or arms; disability; deficiency

mansalva — a mansalva without risk; without warning; **a mansalva de** safe from

mansarda *f* mansard, mansard roof

mansedumbre *f* gentleness, mildness, meekness; tameness

mansión *f* stay, sojourn; abode, dwelling; **hacer mansión** to stop, stay

man•so -sa *adj* gentle, mild, meek; tame ‖ *m* bellwether; farm

manta _f_ blanket; heavy shawl; (coll) beating, thrashing; (Chile, Ecuad) poncho; (Col, Mex, Ven) coarse cotton cloth; **a manta de Dios** copiously; **dar una manta a** to toss in a blanket; **manta de coche** lap robe; **manta de viaje** steamer rug; **tirar de la manta** to let the cat out of the bag

mantear _tr_ to toss in a blanket; abuse, mistreat

manteca _f_ (_grasa de los animales, esp. la del cerdo_) lard; butter; pomade; (_dinero_) (slang) dough; **como manteca** smooth as butter; **manteca de puerco** lard; **manteca de vaca** butter

mantecado _m_ custard ice cream, French ice cream

mantecón _m_ mollycoddle, milksop

mantel _m_ tablecloth; altar cloth

mantelería _f_ table linen

mantelillo _m_ embroidered centerpiece

mantelito _m_ lunch cloth

mantener §71 _tr_ to maintain; keep; keep up; sustain, defend ‖ _ref_ to keep, remain, continue

mantenida _f_ kept woman

mantenido _m_ (_hombre que vive a expensas de su mujer_) (Guat, Mex, W-I) gigolo; (Guat, Mex, W-I) sponger

mantenimiento _m_ maintenance; food, support, living

manteo _m_ mantle, cloak

mantequera _f_ churn, butter churn; butter dish

mantequería _f_ creamery; delicatessen

mantequilla _f_ butter; **mantequilla azucarada** hard sauce; **mantequilla derretida** drawn butter

mantilla _f_ mantilla (_silk or lace head scarf_); **mantillas** swaddling clothes

mantillo _m_ humus, mold

manto _m_ mantle, cloak; (_de chimenea_) mantel; (_ropa talar de algunos religiosos, catedráticos, alumnos_) robe, gown; (fig) cloak

mantón _m_ shawl, kerchief

manuable _adj_ handy

manual _adj_ (_que se hace con las manos_) hand; (_fácil de manejar_) handy; easy; easy to understand; easy-going; manual ‖ _m_ manual, handbook; notebook

manubrio _m_ handle; crank, winch

manuela _f_ open hack (_in Madrid_)

manufactura _f_ (_fábrica_) factory; (_obra fabricada_) manufacture

manufacturar _tr_ to manufacture

manuscribir §83 _tr_ to write by hand

manuscri•to -ta _adj_ & _m_ manuscript

manutención _f_ maintenance; care, upkeep; shelter, protection

manutener §71 _tr_ (law) to maintain, support

manzana _f_ apple; (_conjunto aislado de varias casas contiguas_) block, city block; (_remate en un mueble_) knob, finial; **manzana de Adán** (Chile) Adam's apple

manzanar _m_ apple orchard

manzanilla _f_ camomile; (_aceituna pequeña; vino blanco_) manzanilla (_small olive; white wine_); (_remate en un mueble_) knob, finial

manzano _m_ apple tree

maña _f_ skill, dexterity; cunning, craftiness; bad habit, vice; (_de lino, cáñamo, etc._) bunch; sister; **darse maña** to manage, contrive; **hacer maña** (Col) to fool around

mañana _adv_ tomorrow; **¡hasta mañana!** see you tomorrow!; **pasado mañana** the day after tomorrow ‖ _m_ tomorrow; (_tiempo venidero_) morrow ‖ _f_ morning; **de mañana** in the morning; **muy de mañana** very early in the morning; **por la mañana** in the morning; **tomar la mañana** to get up early; have a shot of liquor before breakfast

mañanear _intr_ to be in the habit of getting up early

mañane•ro -ra _adj_ morning; early-rising

mañanica _f_ early morning, break of day

mañanita _f_ woman's bed jacket

mañear _tr_ to manage craftily ‖ _intr_ to act with cunning

mañerear _intr_ (Arg) to dawdle, dilly-dally

mañería _f_ sterility

mañe•ro -ra _adj_ clever, shrewd; simple, easy; skittish

ma•ño -ña _mf_ (coll) Aragonese ‖ _m_ brother ‖ _f_ see **maña**

maño•so -sa _adj_ skillful, clever; crafty, tricky; vicious

mañuela _f_ craftiness, trickiness

mañue•las _mf_ (_pl_ **-las**) tricky person

mapa _m_ map; **mapa itinerario** road map ‖ _f_ — **llevarse la mapa** to take the prize

mapache _m_ coon, raccoon

mapamundi _m_ map of the world; (coll) buttocks, behind

mapurite _m_ (CAm) skunk

maque _m_ lacquer

maquear _tr_ to lacquer; (Mex) to varnish

maqueta _f_ (_en tamaño reducido_) maquette; (_en tamaño natural_) mock-up; (_de un libro_) dummy

maquillador _m_ (theat) make-up man

maquillaje _m_ (theat) make-up

maquillar _tr_ & _ref_ to make up

máquina _f_ machine; (_motor_) engine; locomotive; plan, project; (fig) machinery; (coll) heap, pile, lot; (Cuba) auto; (Chile) ganging up; **escribir a máquina** to typewrite; **máquina de afeitar** safety razor; **máquina de apostar** gambling machine; **máquina de componer** typesetter; **máquina de coser** sewing machine; **máquina de escribir** typewriter; **máquina de lavar** washing machine; **máquina de sumar** adding machine; **máquina de volar** flying machine; **máquina fotográfica** camera; **máquina sacaperras** slot machine

maquinación _f_ machination, scheming

máquina-herramienta _f_ (_pl_ **máquinas-herramientas**) machine tool

maquinal _adj_ mechanical

maquinar _tr_ to plot, scheme

maquinaria _f_ machinery; applied mechanics

maquinilla _f_ windlass, winch; clippers; **maquinilla cortapelos** clippers, hair clippers; **maquinilla de afeitar** safety razor; **maquinilla de rizar** curling iron

maquinista *mf* (*persona que fabrica máquinas*) machinist; (*persona que dirige una máquina o locomotora*) engineer; **segundo maquinista** (naut) machinist

mar *m* & *f* sea; tide, flood; **alta mar** high seas; **a mares** abundantly, copiously; **arrojarse a la mar** to plunge, take great risks; **baja mar** low tide; **correr los mares** to follow the sea; **hablar de la mar** to talk wildly, talk on and on; **hacerse a la mar** to put to sea; **la mar de** (fig) oceans of, large numbers of; **mar alta** rough sea; **mar ancha** high seas; **mar bonanza** calm sea; **mar Caribe** Caribbean Sea, Caribbean; **mar de las Antillas** Caribbean Sea; **mar de las Indias** Indian Ocean; **mar de nubes** cloud bank; **mar Latino** Mediterranean Sea; **mar llena** high tide; **meter la mar en un pozo** to attempt the impossible; **meterse mar adentro** (fig) to go beyond one's depth

maraña *f* undergrowth, thicket; silk waste; (*de hilo, pelo, etc.*) tangle; trick, scheme; puzzle

marañón *m* cashew

maraño•so -sa *adj* scheming ‖ *mf* schemer

maravilla *f* wonder, marvel; (bot) marigold, calendula; **a las maravillas** or **a las mil maravillas** magnificently; **a maravilla** wonderfully well; **por maravilla** rarely, occasionally

maravillar *tr* to astonish ‖ *ref* to wonder, marvel; **maravillarse con** or **de** to marvel at, wonder at

maravillo•so -sa *adj* wonderful, marvelous

marbete *m* label, tag; baggage check; edge, border; **marbete engomado** sticker

marca *f* mark; (*tipo de producto*) make, brand; (*de tamaño*) standard; score; record; height-measuring device; **de marca** outstanding; **marca de agua** watermark; **marca de fábrica** trademark; **marca de reconocimiento** (naut) landmark, seamark; **marca de taquilla** box-office record; **marca registrada** registered trademark

marca•do -da *adj* marked, pronounced

marcaje *m* (sport) scoring; (sport) interfering; (telp) dialing

marcapaso *m* or **marcapasos** *m* (heart) pacemaker

marcar §73 *tr* to mark; brand; embroider; (*p.ej., un pañuelo*) initial; (*la hora un reloj*) show; (*un tanto*) make, score; (*el número telefónico*) dial ‖ *ref* (*un buque*) to take bearings

marcear *tr* to shear ‖ *ref* to be Marchlike

marcial *adj* martial; gallant, noble

marcia•no -na *adj* & *mf* Martian

marco *m* frame; framework; (*de pesas y medidas*) standard

marcha *f* march; (*funcionamiento*) running, operation; (*p.ej., de los astros*) course, path; (*desenvolvimiento de un asunto*) course, march, progress; (*grado de velocidad*) rate of speed; (*de los engranajes*) (aut) speed; **cambiar de marcha** to shift gears; **en marcha** on the march; underway;

in motion; **marcha atrás** reverse; **marcha del hambre** hunger march; **marcha directa** high gear; **marcha forzada** (mil) forced march

marchamo *m* customhouse mark; (Arg, Bol) tax on slaughtered cattle

marchante *adj* commercial ‖ *m* dealer, merchant; customer

marchapié *m* running board

marchar *intr* to march; run, work, go; leave, go away; come along, proceed; **marchar en vacío** to idle ‖ *ref* to leave, go away

marchitar *tr* to wilt, wither ‖ *ref* to wilt, wither; languish

marchi•to -ta *adj* withered, faded; (fig) languid

marea *f* tide; tideland; gentle sea breeze; dew; drizzle; **marea alta** high tide; **marea baja** low tide; **marea creciente** or **entrante** flood tide; **marea menguante** ebb tide; **marea muerta** neap tide; **marea viva** spring tide; **rendir la marea** to stem the tide

marea•do -da *adj* nauseated, sick, lightheaded; seasick

mareaje *m* navigation, seamanship; (*de un buque*) course

marear *tr* to sail; annoy, pester ‖ *intr* to be annoying ‖ *ref* to get sick, get giddy; get seasick; be damaged at sea; fade

marejada *f* heavy sea; (*de desorden*) stirring, undercurrent; **marejada de fondo** ground swell

maremagno *m* or **maremágnum** *m* big mess

mareo *m* nausea, dizziness, sickness; seasickness; annoyance

marfil *m* ivory

marfile•ño -ña *adj* ivory

mar•fuz -fuza *adj* (*pl* **-fuces -fuzas**) cast aside, rejected; deceptive

marga *f* marl

margar §44 *tr* to marl

margarita *f* pearl; (bot) daisy; **margarita de los prados** English daisy; **margarita** (*impresora*) (*ordenador*) daisy wheel

margen *m* & *f* margin; border, edge; marginal note; **al margen de** aloof from; outside of; independent of; aside from; **dar margen para** to give occasion for; **dejar al margen** to leave out; **quedar al margen** to be left out of

marginal *adj* marginal

mariache *m* Mexican band and singers

marica *m* sissy, milksop ‖ *f* magpie

maricón *m* sissy

maridable *adj* marital

maridaje *m* married life; (fig) union

maridar *tr* to combine, unit ‖ *intr* to get married; to live as man and wife

marido *m* husband

mariguana *f* marihuana

mariguanza *f* (Chile) hocus-pocus; (Chile) pirouette; **mariguanzas** (Chile) clowning; (Chile) powwowing

marimacho *m* mannish woman

marimandona *f* queen bee, bossy woman

marimarica *m* sissy

marimorena f fight, row

marina f navy; (*conjunto de buques*) marine, fleet; (*cuadro o pintura*) seascape; shore, seaside; sailing, navigation; **marina de guerra** navy; **marina mercante** merchant marine

marinar tr to marinate, salt; (*un buque*) staff, man ‖ intr to be a sailor

marinera f sailor blouse; (*blusa de niño*) middy, middy blouse

marinería f sailoring; sailors

marine•ro -ra adj sea, marine; seaworthy; seafaring ‖ m mariner, seaman, sailor; **marinero de agua dulce** (*el que ha navegado poco*) landlubber (*person unacquainted with the sea*); **marinero matalote** (*hombre de mar, rudo y torpe*) landlubber (*awkward and unskilled seaman*) ‖ f see **marinera**

marines•co -ca adj sailor; sailorly

mari•no -na adj marine, sea ‖ m mariner, seaman, sailor ‖ f see **marina**

marioneta f marionette

mariposa f butterfly; butterfly valve; wing nut; rushlight; (Col) blindman's buff; **mariposa nocturna** moth

mariposear intr to flit about; be fickle

mariposón m (Cuba, Guat, Mex) fickle flirt

mariquita m sissy, milksop, popinjay ‖ f (ent) ladybird

marisabidilla f bluestocking

mariscal m blacksmith; (mil) marshal; **mariscal de campo** (mil) field marshal

marisco m shellfish; **mariscos** seafood

marisma f swamp, marsh, salt marsh

marisquería f seafood store, seafood restaurant

maríti•mo -ma adj maritime; marine, sea

maritor•nes f (pl -nes) mannish maidservant, wench

marmita f pot, boiler, kettle

marmitón m kitchen scullion

mármol m marble

marmóre•o -a adj marble

marmosete m vignette

marmota f marmot; sleepyhead; worsted cap; **marmota de Alemania** hamster; **marmota de América** ground hog, woodchuck

maroma f hemp rope, esparto rope; acrobatic stunt

maromear intr to perform acrobatic stunts, walk the tight rope; wobble, sway from side to side (*e.g., in politics*); hesitate

marome•ro -ra mf acrobat, tightrope walker; weaseler; opportunist

marqués m marquis; **los marqueses** the marquis and marchioness

marquesa f marchioness, marquise; (*sobre la puerta de un hotel*) marquee

marquesina f cover over field tent; (*sobre la puerta de un hotel*) marquee; locomotive cab

marquetería f cabinetwork, woodwork; (*taracea*) marquetry

marra•jo -ja adj sly, tricky; (*toro*) vicious

marrana f sow; slattern, slut

marranada f piggishness, filth

marranalla f rabble, riffraff

marra•no -na adj base, vile; dirty, sloppy ‖ mf hog ‖ m male hog, boar; filthy person, hog; cad, cur ‖ f see **marrana**

marrar intr to miss, fail; go astray

marras adv long ago; **hacer marras que** (Bol, Ecuad) to be a long time since

marro m game resembling quoits and played with a stone; (*juego de muchachos*) tag; (*ladeo*) dodge, duck; slip, miss

marrón adj invar maroon (*dark-red*); tan (*shoes*) ‖ m maroon; candied chestnut; stone (*used as a sort of quoit*)

marro•quí -quíes adj & mf Moroccan ‖ m morocco, morocco leather

marro•quín -quina adj & mf var of **marroquí**

marrubio m horehound

marrue•co -ca adj & mf Moroccan

Marruecos m Morocco

marrulle•ro -ra adj cajoling, wheedling ‖ mf cajoler, wheedler

Marsella f Marseille

marsopa f or **marsopla** f porpoise

mart. abbr **martes**

marta f pine marten; **marta cebellina** sable, Siberian sable; **marta del Canadá** fisher

Marte m Mars

mar•tes m (pl -tes) Tuesday; **martes de carnaval** or **carnestolendas** Shrove Tuesday

martillar tr to hammer; pester, worry ‖ intr to hammer

martillazo m blow with a hammer

martillear tr & intr var of **martillar**

martillero m (Chile) auctioneer

martillo m hammer; auction house; (*persona*) scourge; (mus) tuning hammer; (*de arma de fuego*) cock

martín m — **martín pescador** (pl **martín pescadores**) kingfisher

martinete m drop hammer; pile driver; (*del piano*) hammer

martinico m ghost, goblin

mártir mf martyr

martirio m martyrdom

márts. abbr **mártires**

marullo m surge, swell

marxista adj & mf Marxist or Marxian

marzo m March

mas conj but

más adv more; most; **a lo más** at most, at the most; **a más de** besides, in addition to; **como el que más** as the next one, as well as anybody; **cuando más** at the most; **de más** extra; too much, too many; **estar de más** to be in the way; be unnecessary; be superfluous; **los más de** most of, the majority of; **más bien** rather; **más de +** *número* more than; **más de lo que +** *verbo* more than; **más que** more than; better than; **no . . . más** no longer; **no . . . más nada** nothing more; **no . . . más que** only ‖ prep plus ‖ m more; (*signo de adición*) plus

masa f mass; (*pasta que se forma con agua y harina*) dough; (*masa aplastada*) mash;

nature, disposition; (Chile, Ecuad) puff
paste; (*p.ej., de un automóvil*) (elec)
ground; **las masas** the masses
masada *f* farm
masadero *m* farmer
masaje *m* massage; **masaje facial** facial
masajear *tr* to massage
masajista *m* masseur ‖ *f* masseuse
masar *tr* to knead; massage
mascar §73 *tr* to chew; mumble, mutter ‖ *ref*
(*un cabo*) (naut) to gall
máscara *mf* (*persona*) mask, mummer ‖ *f*
mask; (*traje, disfraz*) masquerade; **máscara antigás** gas mask
mascarada *f* masquerade
mascarilla *f* half mask; false face; death
mask
mascarón *m* false face; (*persona fea*) fright;
(archit) mask; **mascarón de proa** (naut)
figurehead
mascota *f* mascot
mascujar *tr & intr* to chew with difficulty;
mumble
masculi•no -na *adj* masculine; (*sexo*) male;
(*traje*) men's ‖ *m* masculine
mascullar *tr & intr* to mumble, mutter; to
chew with difficulty
masera *f* kneading trough
masilla *f* putty
masita *f* (mil) money withheld for clothing;
(Arg, Bol) cake
masón *m* Mason
masonería *f* Masonry
masoquis•to -ta *adj* masochistic ‖ *mf* masochist
mastelero *m* (naut) topmast
masticar §73 *tr* to chew, masticate; meditate
on; mumble
mástil *m* (*de una embarcación*) mast; (*de un
violín o guitarra*) neck; stalk; (*de pluma*)
shaft, stem; upright
mas•tín -tina *mf* mastiff; **mastín danés** Great
Dane
mastodonte *m* mastodon
mastuerzo *m* (bot) cress; dolt
masturbación *f* masturbation
masturbar *tr & ref* to masturbate
mat. *abbr* **matemática**
mata *f* bush, shrub; blade, sprig; brush,
underbrush; **mata de pelo** crop of hair,
head of hair; **mata parda** chaparro (*oak*);
saltar de la mata to come out of hiding
mataca•bras *m* (*pl* -**bras**) cold blast from the
north
matacán *m* dog poison
matacande•las *m* (*pl* -**las**) candle snuffer
matadero *m* abattoir, slaughterhouse; drudgery
mata•dor -dora *mf* killer ‖ *m* matador; **matador de mujeres** lady-killer
matadura *f* sore, gall
matafue•gos *m* (*pl* -**gos**) fire extinguisher;
(*oficial*) fireman
matalo•bos *m* (*pl* -**bos**) wolf's-bane
mata•lón -lona *mf* skinny old nag
matalotaje *m* (naut) ship stores; mess, hodgepodge

matamale•zas *m* (*pl* -**zas**) weed killer
matamari•dos *f* (*pl* -**dos**) many times a
widow
matamo•ros *m* (*pl* -**ros**) bully
matamos•cas *m* (*pl* -**cas**) fly swatter; flypaper
matanza *f* slaughter, massacre; butchering;
pork products; (CAm) butcher shop; (Ven)
slaughterhouse
matape•rros *m* (*pl* -**rros**) harum-scarum,
street urchin
matar *tr* to kill; butcher; (*el fuego, la luz*) put
out; (*la cal*) slack; (*el metal*) mat; (*un
color*) tone down; (*un naipe*) spot; play a
card higher than; (*a un caballo*) gall; bore
to death; (*el tiempo, el hambre, etc.*) (fig)
to kill ‖ *intr* to kill ‖ *ref* to kill oneself;
drudge, overwork; be disappointed; **matarse con** to quarrel with; **matarse por** to
struggle for; struggle to
matarratas *m* rat poison; (*aguardiente de
mala calidad*) rotgut
matarro•tos *m* (*pl* -**tos**) (Chile) pawnshop
matasa•nos *m* (*pl* -**nos**) quack doctor
matasellar *tr* to cancel, postmark
matase•llos *m* (*pl* -**llos**) postmark
matasie•te *m* (*pl* -**te**) bully, swashbuckler
matatí•as *m* (*pl* -**as**) moneylender, pawnbroker
matazar•zas *m* (*pl* -**zas**) weed killer
mate *adj* dull, flat ‖ *m* checkmate; (SAm)
maté; (SAm) maté gourd; **dar mate a** to
checkmate; make fun of; **dar mate ahogado a** to stalemate; **mate ahogado** stalemate
matear *tr* to plant at regular intervals; make
dull; (Chile) to checkmate ‖ *ref* (*el trigo*) to
sprout; (*un perro de caza*) hunt through the
bushes
matemáti•co -ca *adj* mathematical ‖ *mf*
mathematician ‖ *f* mathematics; **matemática** mathematics
materia *f* matter; material, stuff; **materia
colorante** dyestuff; **materia de guerra**
matériel; **materia prima** or **primera materia** raw material
material *adj* material; (*grosero*) crude ‖ *m*
material; (*conjunto de objetos necesario
para un servicio*) matériel; (typ) matter,
copy; **material de guerra** matériel; **material fijo** (rr) permanent way; **material móvil** or **rodante** (rr) rolling stock; **ser material** to be immaterial
materialismo *m* materialism
materialista *mf* materialist; (Mex) truck
driver
materializar §60 *tr* (*beneficios*) to realize
maternal *adj* maternal, mother; (*afectos, cuidados, etc.*) motherly
maternidad *f* maternity; motherhood
mater•no -na *adj* maternal, mother
matinal *adj* morning
matinée *f* matinée; dressing gown, wrapper
ma•tiz *m* (*pl* -**tices**) shade, hue, nuance
matizar §60 *tr* (*diversos colores*) to blend;
(*un color, un sonido*) shade; (*en cuanto al
color*) match
matón *m* bully, browbeater

ma
ma

matorral *m* thicket, underbrush

matraca *f* rattle, noisemaker; taunting, bantering; bore, pest; **dar matraca a** to taunt, to tease

matraquear *intr* to make a racket; to taunt, tease

ma•traz *m* (*pl* **-traces**) flask

matre•ro -ra *adj* cunning, shrewd ‖ *m* (SAm) cheat, swindler

matriarca *f* matriarch

matricida *adj* matricidal ‖ *mf* matricide

matricidio *m* matricide

matrícula *f* register, roster, roll; license; registry

matricular *tr* & *ref* to matriculate

matrimonialmente *adv* as husband and wife

matrimoniar *intr* to marry, get married

matrimonio *m* marriage, matrimony; (*marido y mujer*) married couple; **matrimonio consensual** common-law marriage

ma•triz *adj* (*pl* **-trices**) main, first, mother ‖ *f* matrix; (*de libro talonario*) stub; screw nut; first draft

matrona *f* matron; matronly lady

matronal *adj* matronly

matun•go -ga *adj* skinny, full of sores ‖ *m* old nag

maturran•go -ga *adj* (SAm) poor, clumsy ‖ *m* (SAm) stranger; (SAm) old nag ‖ *f* trickery

Matusalén *m* Methuselah; **vivir más años que Matusalén** to be as old as Methuselah

matute *m* smuggling; smuggled goods; gambling den

matutear *intr* to smuggle

matute•ro -ra *mf* smuggler

matutinal or **matuti•no -na** *adj* morning

maula *mf* lazy loafer; poor pay; tricky person, cheat ‖ *f* junk, trash; remnant; trickery

maulería *f* remnant shop; trickiness

maullar §8 *intr* to meow

maullido *m* or **maúllo** *m* meow

mausoleo *m* mausoleum

máxima *f* maxim; principle

máxime *adv* chiefly, mainly, especially

máxi•mo -ma *adj* maximum; top; superlative ‖ *m* maximum ‖ *f* see **máxima**

may. *abbr* **mayúscula**

maya *f* May queen; English daisy

mayal *m* flail

mayear *intr* to be Maylike

mayestáti•co -ca *adj* royal

mayido *m* meow

mayo *m* May; Maypole

mayonesa *f* mayonnaise

mayor *adj* greater; larger; older, elder; greatest; largest; oldest, eldest; major; elderly; (*calle*) main; (*altar; misa*) high; **hacerse mayor de edad** to come of age; **ser mayor de edad** to be of age ‖ *m* chief, head, superior; **al por mayor** wholesale; **mayor de edad** (*persona de edad legal*) major; **mayores** elders; ancestors, forefathers; **mayor general** staff officer

mayoral *m* boss, foreman; head shepherd; stagecoach driver; (Arg) streetcar conductor

mayorazgo *m* primogeniture; entailed estate descending by primogeniture; first-born son

mayordoma *f* stewardess, housekeeper

mayordomo *m* steward, butler, majordomo

mayoreo *m* wholesale

mayoría *f* (*mayor edad; el mayor número, la mayor parte*) majority; superiority; **alcanzar su mayoría de edad** to come of age; **mayoría cómoda** solid majority; **mayoría de edad** majority

mayoridad *f* majority

mayorista *adj* (Arg, Chile) wholesale ‖ *mf* (Arg, Chile) wholesaler

mayorita•rio -ria *adj* majority

mayormente *adv* chiefly, mainly, mostly

mayúscu•lo -la *adj* (*letra*) capital; awful, tremendous ‖ *f* capital, capital letter

maza *f* mace; heavy drumstick; bore, pedant; **la maza y la mona** constant companions; **maza de gimnasia** Indian club

mazacote *m* barilla; concrete, cement; botched job; tough, doughy food; (coll) bore

mazar §60 *tr* to churn

mazmorra *f* dungeon

mazo *m* mallet, maul; bunch; (*de la campana*) clapper; (*hombre fastidioso*) bore, pest

mazonería *f* stone masonry; (*obra de relieve*) relief; gold or silver embroidery

mazorca *f* ear of corn; cocoa bean; (*husada*) spindleful; (*de un balustre*) spindle; **comer maíz de** or **en la mazorca** to eat corn on the cob

mazorral *adj* coarse, crude

m/c *abbr* **mi cargo, mi cuenta, moneda corriente**

m/cta *abbr* **mi cuenta**

m/cte *abbr* **moneda corriente**

me (used as object of verb) *pron pers* me, to me ‖ *pron reflex* myself; to myself

meada *f* urination, water; urine stain

meadero *m* urinal

meados *mpl* urine

meaja *f* crumb; **meaja de huevo** tread

meandro *m* meander; wandering speech, wandering writing

mear *tr* to urinate on ‖ *intr* & *ref* to urinate

Meca, La Mecca

¡mecachis! *interj* wow!, geez!

mecáni•co -ca *adj* mechanical; low, mean ‖ *m* (*obrero perito en el arreglo de las máquinas*) mechanic; (*obrero que fabrica y compone máquinas*) machinist; workman, repairman; driver, chauffeur; **mecánicos** (CAm, Cuba, S-D) blue jeans ‖ *f* mechanics; (*aparato que da movimiento a un artefacto*) machinery, works; meanness; **mecánicas** household chores

mecánico-dentista *m* dental technician

mecanismo *m* mechanism, machinery

mecanizar §60 *tr* to mechanize; motorize

mecanógrafa *f* typist

mecanografía *f* typewriting; **mecanografía al tacto** touch typewriting

mecanografiar §77 *tr* & *intr* to typewrite

mecanógra•fo -fa *mf* typist, typewriter
mecapale•ro -ra *m* (Mex) messenger, porter
mece•dor -dora *adj* swinging, rocking ‖ *m* stirrer; (*columpio*) swing ‖ *f* rocker, rocking chair
mecer §46 *tr* (*un líquido*) to stir; (*la cuna*) rock ‖ *ref* to rock, swing
mecha *f* (*de vela o bujía*) wick; (*tubo de pólvora*) fuse; lock of hair; (*para mechar carne*) slice of bacon; bundle of thread; (Col, Ecuad, Ven) joke
mechar *tr* (*la carne*) to lard, interlard
mechera *f* shoplifter
mechero *m* (*p.ej.*, *de cigarrillos*) lighter, pocket lighter; (*de aparato de alumbrado*) burner; (*de candelero*) socket; shoplifter; **mechero encendedor** pilot, pilot light
mechón *m* cowlick; (Guat) torch
medalla *f* medal; medallion
medallón *m* medallion; (*joya en que se colocan retratos, etc.*) locket
médano *m* dune, sandbank
media *f* stocking; (math) mean; **media corta** (Arg) sock; **media media** (Arg, Ecuad, Ven) sock; **y media** half past, e.g., **las dos y media** half past two
mediación *f* mediation
media•do -da *adj* half over; half-full; **a mediados de** about the middle of; **mediada la tarde** in the middle of the afternoon
media•dor -dora *mf* mediator
mediana *f* long billiard cue
medianería *f* party wall; party fence
mediane•ro -ra *adj* middle; mediating ‖ *mf* mediator; partner; owner of a row house
medianía *f* average; (*persona que carece de dotes relevantes*) mediocrity
media•no -na *adj* middling, medium; average, fair; mediocre ‖ *f* see **mediana**
medianoche *f* midnight; small meat pie
mediante *adj* interceding ‖ *prep* by means of, by virtue of
mediar *intr* to be half over; be in the middle; intercede, mediate; elapse; take place
mediatinta *f* half-tone
medible *adj* measurable
medical *adj* medical
medicamento *m* medicine
medicamento•so -sa *adj* medicinal
medicastro *m* quack
medicina *f* medicine; **medicina general** general medicine
medicinar *tr* to treat ‖ *ref* to take medicine
medición *f* measurement; metering
médi•co -ca *adj* medical ‖ *mf* doctor, physician; **médico de cabecera** family physician; **médico de urgencia** emergency doctor; **médico general** general practitioner
medida *f* measurement; measure; caution, moderation; **a medida de** in proportion to; according to; **a medida que** in proportion as; **en la medida que** to the extent that; **hecho a la medida** custom-made; **medida para áridos** dry measure; **medida para líquidos** liquid measure; **tomarle a uno las medidas** to take someone's measure, size up someone

medidamente *adv* with moderation
medidor *m* measurer; (Mex, SAm) meter
medie•ro -ra *mf* hosier; partner
medieval *adj* medieval
medievalista *mf* medievalist
medievo *m* Middle Ages
me•dio -dia *adj* middle; medium; medieval; half; a half, e.g., **media libra** a half pound; half a, e.g., **media naranja** half an orange; average, mean; mid, in the middle of, e.g., **a media tarde** in mid afternoon, in the middle of the afternoon; **a medias** half; half-and-half; **ir a medias** (**con**) to go halves (with), go fifty-fifty (with) ‖ *m* middle; medium, environment; step, measure; means; (*en el espiritismo*) medium; (baseball) shortstop; (arith) half; (*del ruedo*) (taur) center; **a medio** half; **en medio de** in the middle of; in the midst of; **justo medio** happy medium, golden mean; **medio ambiente** environment; situation; **medio centro** (*deporte*) center half; **medios de comunicación** mass media; **por medio de** by means of; **quitarse de en medio** to get out of the way ‖ *f* see **media** ‖ **medio** *adv* half
mediocre *adj* mediocre
mediocridad *f* mediocrity
mediodía *m* noon, midday; south; **en pleno mediodía** at high noon; **hacer mediodía** to stop for the noon meal
mediquillo *m* quack
medir §50 *tr* to measure ‖ *intr* to measure ‖ *ref* to act with moderation
meditabun•do -da *adj* meditative
meditar *tr* to meditate; plan, contemplate ‖ *intr* to meditate
mediterráne•o -a *adj* inland ‖ **Mediterráne•o -na** *adj* & *m* Mediterranean
mé•dium *m* (*pl* **-dium** or **diums**) medium
medra *f* growth, prosperity
medrana *f* fear
medrar *intr* to thrive, prosper, improve
medro *m* growth, prosperity; **medros** progress
medro•so -sa *adj* fearful, scared; frightful, terrible
médula *f* or **medula** *f* marrow, medulla; (bot) pith; (fig) pith, gist, essence; **médula espinal** spinal cord
medular *adj* pithy
medusa *f* jellyfish
mefistoféli•co -ca *adj* Mephistophelian
megaciclo *m* megacycle
megáfono *m* megaphone
me•go -ga *adj* meek, gentle, mild
megohmio *m* megohm
Méj. *abbr* **Méjico**
mejica•no -na *adj* & *mf* Mexican
Méjico *m* Mexico; **Nuevo Méjico** New Mexico
meji•do -da *adj* beaten with sugar and milk
mejilla *f* cheek
mejor *adj* better; best; (*licitador*) highest; **a lo mejor** unexpectedly; worse luck; perhaps, maybe; **el mejor día** some fine day ‖ *adv* better; best; **mejor dicho** rather

ma
me

mejora *f* growth, improvement; higher bid; alteration

mejoramiento *m* improvement

mejorana *f* sweet marjoram

mejorar *tr* to improve; (*los licitadores el precio de una cosa*) raise; **mejorando lo presente** present company excepted ‖ *intr* & *ref* to improve, get better, recover; make progress; (*el tiempo*) to clear up; **¡que se mejore!** get well!

mejoría *f* improvement; (*en una enfermedad*) betterment, recovery

mejunje *m* brew, potion, mixture

mela•do -da *adj* honey-colored ‖ *m* thick cane syrup

melancolía *f* (*tristeza vaga*) melancholy; (*depresión moral*) melancholia

melancóli•co -ca *adj* melancholy

melaza *f* molasses

melcocha *f* taffy, molasses candy

melchor *m* German silver

melena *f* hair falling over the eyes; long hair, loose hair; (*del león*) mane; (*del caballo*) forelock; **andar a la melena** to pull each other's hair; to get into a fight; **estar en melena** (coll) to have one's hair down

melga *f* ridge made by plow; (Col, Chile) plot of ground to be sown; (Hond) small piece of work to be finished

melindre *m* honey fritter; (*dulce de pasta de mazapán*) ladyfinger; narrow ribbon; prudery, finickiness

melindrear *intr* to be prudish, be finicky

melindro•so -sa *adj* prudish, finicky

melocotón *m* peach tree; peach

melocotonero *m* peach tree

melodía *f* melody

melodio•so -sa *adj* melodious

melodramáti•co -ca *adj* melodramatic

melón *m* melon; (*Cucumis melo*) muskmelon; blockhead; bald head; **melón de agua** watermelon

melo•so -sa *adj* sweet, honeyed; gentle, mild, mellow

mella *f* dent, nick, notch; gap, hollow; harm, injury; **hacer mella a** to have an effect on; **hacer mella en** to harm

mellar *tr* to dent, nick, notch; harm

melli•zo -za *adj* & *mf* twin

membrana *f* membrane; (*del teléfono, micrófono*) diaphragm

membrete *m* note, memo; letterhead; heading; written invitation

membrillero *m* quince tree

membrillo *m* quince; quince tree

membru•do -da *adj* brawny, burly

memeches — **a memeches** (CAm) on horseback

memela *f* (CAm, Mex) cornmeal pancake

me•mo -ma *adj* foolish, simple ‖ *mf* fool, simpleton

memorán•dum *m* (*pl* **-dum**) memorandum book, notebook; (*sección en los periódicos*) professional services; (*papel con membrete*) letterhead

memorar *tr* & *ref* to remember

memoria *f* memory; (*exposición de ciertos hechos*) memoir; account, record; (*ordenador*) data storage, memory; **de memoria** by heart; **encomendar a la memoria** to commit to memory; **hablar de memoria** (coll) to say the first thing that comes to one's mind; **hacer memoria de** to bring up; **memorias** memoirs; regards

memorial *m* memorandum book; memorial, petition; (law) brief

memorizar §60 *tr* to memorize

mena *f* ore

menaje *m* household furniture; school supplies

mención *f* mention

mencionar *tr* to mention

men•daz *adj* (*pl* **-daces**) mendacious ‖ *mf* liar

mendicante *adj* & *mf* mendicant

mendigante *adj* begging, mendicant ‖ *mf* beggar, mendicant

mendigar §44 *tr* to beg for ‖ *intr* to beg, go begging

mendi•go -ga *mf* beggar

mendiguez *f* begging

mendo•so -sa *adj* false, wrong

mendrugo *m* crumb, crust

menear *tr* to stir, shake; wiggle; (*la cola*) wag; (*un negocio*) manage; **peor es meneallo** (i.e., **menearlo**) better keep hands off ‖ *ref* to shake; wiggle; wag; hustle, bestir oneself

meneo *m* stirring, shaking; wagging; hustling; drubbing, thrashing

menester *m* need; want, lack; job, occupation; **haber menester** to be necessary, to be need for; **menesteres** bodily needs; property; implements, tools; **ser menester** to be necessary

menestero•so -sa *adj* needy ‖ *mf* needy person

menestra *f* vegetable soup

menes•tral -trala *mf* mechanic

meng. *abbr* **menguante**

mengua *f* want, lack; poverty; decline; decrease, diminution; **en mengua de** to the discredit of

mengua•do -da *adj* timid, cowardly; simple, silly; mean, stingy; wretched, miserable; poor, needy; fatal

menguante *adj* decreasing; declining; waning ‖ *f* decrease; decline; low water; ebb tide; **menguante de la luna** wane, waning of the moon

menguar §10 *tr* to diminish, lessen; discredit ‖ *intr* to diminish, lessen; decline; decrease; (*la luna*) wane; (*la marea*) fall

mengue *m* (coll) devil

menina *f* young lady in waiting

menino *m* noble page of the royal family

menor *adj* less, lesser; smaller; younger; least; smallest; youngest; slightest; minor ‖ *m* minor; **al por menor** retail; **menor de edad** minor; **por menor** retail; in detail, minutely ‖ *f* minor premise

Menorca *f* Minorca

menoría *f* inferiority, subordination; (*tiempo de menor edad*) minority

menorista *adj* (Arg, Chile) retail ‖ *mf* (Arg, Chile) retailer

menor•quín -quina *adj & mf* Minorcan

menos *adv* less; fewer; least; fewest; **al menos** at least; **a lo menos** at least; **a menos que** unless; **echar de menos** to miss; **¡menos mal!** lucky break!; **menos mal que** it is a good thing that; **no poder menos de** + *inf* to not be able to help + *ger;* **por lo menos** at least; **tener en menos** to think little of; **venir a menos** to decline; become poor ‖ *prep* less, minus; (*al decir la hora*) of, to, e.g., **las tres menos diez** ten minutes of (or to) three ‖ *m* less; (*signo de resta o sustracción*) minus, minus sign

menoscabar *tr* to lessen, diminish, reduce; damage; discredit

menoscabo *m* lessening, reduction; damage; discredit; **con menoscabo de** to the detriment of

menoscuenta *f* part payment

menospreciable *adj* despicable, contemptible

menospreciar *tr* to underestimate, underrate; scorn, despise

menosprecio *m* underestimation; scorn

mensaje *m* message

mensajería *f* public conveyance; **mensajerías** transportation company; shipping line

mensaje•ro -ra *mf* messenger ‖ *m* harbinger

men•so -sa *adj* (Mex) foolish, stupid

menstruar §21 *intr* to menstruate

menstruo *m* menses

mensual *adj* monthly

mensualidad *f* monthly pay, monthly installment

ménsula *f* bracket; elbow rest

mensurar *tr* to measure

menta *f* mint; **menta piperita** peppermint; **menta romana** or **verde** spearmint

menta•do -da *adj* famous, renowned

mentar §2 *tr* to mention

mente *f* mind

mentecatería or **mentecatez** *f* simpleness, folly

menteca•to -ta *adj* simple, foolish ‖ *mf* simpleton, fool

mentidero *m* hangout; gossip column

mentir §68 *tr* to disappoint ‖ *intr* to lie; be misleading; (*un color*) clash; **¡miento!** my mistake!

mentira *f* lie; error, mistake; **mentira inocente** or **oficiosa** white lie; **parece mentira** it's hard to believe

mentirilla *f* fib, white lie; **de mentirillas** for fun

mentirón *m* whopper

mentiro•so -sa *adj* lying; false, deceptive; full of errors ‖ *mf* liar

men•tís *m* (*pl* **-tís**) insulting contradiction; **dar un mentís a** to give the lie to

mentón *m* chin

me•nú *m* (*pl* **-nús**) menu

menudamente *adv* in detail; at retail

menudear *tr* to make frequently; tell in detail; (Col) to sell at retail ‖ *intr* to happen frequently, be frequent; go into detail; (Arg) to grow, increase

menudencia *f* smallness; trifle; meticulousness; **menudencias** pork products; (Col, Mex) giblets

menudeo *m* constant repetition; detailed accounting; **al menudeo** at retail

menudillos *mpl* giblets

menu•do -da *adj* small, slight, minute; futile, worthless; meticulous; common, vulgar; petty ‖ *m* innards (*of fowl and other animals*); rice coal; **al menudo** at retail; **a menudo** often; **menudos** small change; **por menudo** in detail; at retail

meñique *adj* little, tiny; (*dedo*) little ‖ *m* little finger

meollo *m* marrow; pith; (*seso*) brain; brains, intelligence; gist, marrow, essence

me•ón -ona *adj* (*niño*) piddling; (*niebla*) dripping

mequetrefe *m* whippersnapper

mercachifle *m* peddler; small dealer

mercadear *intr* to deal, trade

merca•der -dera *mf* merchant; **mercader de grueso** wholesale merchant

mercadería *f* merchandise, commodity; **mercaderías** goods, merchandise

mercado *m* market; **lanzar al mercado** to put on the market; **mercado de valores** stock market; **mercado negro** black market

mercaduría *f* commodity

mercancía *f* trade, commerce; merchandise; piece of merchandise; **mercancías** goods, merchandise ‖ **mercancías** *msg* (*pl* **-as**) freight train

mercante *adj & m* merchant

mercantil *adj* mercantile

mercar §73 *tr* to buy ‖ *intr* to trade

merced *f* pay, wages; favor, grace; **a merced de** at the mercy of; **merced a** thanks to; **merced de agua** distribution of irrigating water; **vuestra merced** your grace

mercena•rio -ria *adj* mercenary ‖ *m* mercenary; day laborer, hireling

mercería *f* haberdashery, notions store; dry-goods store; hardware store

mercología *f* marketing

mercurio *m* mercury

merecer §22 *tr* to deserve, merit; (*lo que se desea*) attain; (*alabanza*) win; (*cierta suma*) be worth; **merecer la pena** to be worthwhile ‖ *intr* to be deserving; **merecer bien de** to deserve the gratitude of

mereci•do -da *adj* deserved ‖ *m* just deserts; **llevar su merecido** to get what's coming to one

mereciente *adj* deserving

merecimiento *m* desert, merit

merendar §2 *tr* to lunch on, have for lunch; keep an eye on, peep at ‖ *intr* to lunch ‖ *ref* to manage to get; (*en el juego*) (Chile) to clean out

merendero *m* lunchroom; picnic grounds

merendona *f* fine spread

merengar §44 *tr* to whip (*cream*)

merengue *m* meringue

me
me

mere•triz f (pl **-trices**) harlot

meridiana f lounge, couch; afternoon nap; meridian line; **a la meridiana** at noon

meridia•no -na adj meridian; bright, dazzling ‖ m meridian ‖ f see **meridiana**

meridional adj southern ‖ mf southerner

merienda f lunch, snack; hunchback

meri•no -na adj merino; (cabello) thick and curly ‖ mf merino ‖ m merino shepherd; merino wool

mérito m merit, desert; value, worth; **hacer mérito de** to make mention of; **hacer méritos** to try to please, put one's best foot forward

merito•rio -ria adj meritorious ‖ m volunteer worker; unpaid learner, apprentice

merluza f (pez) hake; drunk, spree

merma f decrease, reduction; leakage, shrinkage

mermar tr to decrease, reduce ‖ intr to decrease, shrink, dwindle

mermelada f marmalade

me•ro -ra adj mere, pure; (Col, Ven) alone ‖ m grouper, jewfish ‖ **mero** adv (CAm) almost, soon

merodea•dor -dora adj marauding ‖ m marauder

merodear intr to maraud

mes m month; monthly pay; menses; **caer en el mes del obispo** to come at the right time

mesa f table; (mostrador) counter; (escritorio) desk; (de arma blanca o herramienta) flat side; (de escalera) landing; (comida) fare, food; (conjunto de dirigentes) board; **alzar la mesa** to clear the table; **hacer mesa limpia** to clean up (in gambling); **levantar la mesa** to clear the table; **mesa de batalla** sorting table; **mesa de extensión** extension table; **mesa de juego** gambling table; **mesa de milanos** scanty fare; **mesa de trucos** pool table; **mesa perezosa** drop table; **poner la mesa** to set or lay the table; **tener a mesa y mantel** to feed, support; **tener mesa** to keep open house

mesana f (naut) mizzen

mesar tr (los cabellos) to tear, pull out ‖ ref — **mesarse los cabellos** to pull out one's hair; pull out each other's hair

mescolanza f jumble, hodgepodge, medley

meseguería f harvest watch

mesera f waitress

mesero m journeyman on monthly pay; waiter

meseta f plateau, tableland; (de escalera) landing

Mesías m Messiah

mesilla f mantel, mantelpiece; (de escalera) landing; window sill

mesita f stand, small table; **mesita portateléfono** telephone table

mesnada f armed retinue; band, company

mesón m inn, tavern; (Chile) bar; (Chile) counter

mesone•ro -ra adj inn, tavern ‖ mf innkeeper, tavern keeper

mester m (archaic) craft, trade; (archaic) literary genre; **mester de clerecía** clerical verse of the Middle Ages; **mester de ju-**

glaría popular minstrelsy of the Middle Ages

mesti•zo -za adj & mf half-breed; (perro) mongrel

mesura f dignity, gravity; calm, restraint; courtesy, civility

mesura•do -da adj dignified, sedate; calm, restrained; polite; moderate, temperate

mesurar tr to temper, moderate ‖ ref to act with restraint

meta f goal

metafonía f umlaut

metáfora f metaphor

metafóri•co -ca adj metaphorical

metal m metal; money; (de la voz) timbre; condition, quality; (mus) brass; **el vil metal** filthy lucre; **metal blanco** nickel silver; **metal de imprenta** type metal

metale•ro -ra adj (Bol, Chile, Peru) metal ‖ m (Bol, Chile, Peru) metalworker

metáli•co -ca adj metallic ‖ m metalworker; cash, coin

metalistería f metalwork

metalizar §60 tr to make metallic; put a metal coating on; turn into cash ‖ ref to become mercenary

metaloide m nonmetal

metalurgia f metallurgy

metamorfo•sis f (pl **-sis**) metamorphosis

metano m methane

metástasis f metastasis

metate m (CAm, Mex) flat stone on which corn is ground

metáte•sis f (pl **-sis**) metathesis

mete•dor -dora mf smuggler

metedura f disgrace, shame

meteduría f smuggling

metemuer•tos m (pl **-tos**) stagehand; busybody, meddler

meteo f weather bureau, weather report

meteóri•co -ca adj meteoric

meteoro m or **metéoro** m meteor; atmospheric phenomenon

meteorología f meteorology

meter tr to put, place; insert; (un ruido) make; (miedo) cause; (mentiras) tell; (chismes, enredos) start; (dinero en el juego) stake; to smuggle; (un golpe) strike ‖ ref to project; meddle, butt in; **meterse a** to set oneself up as; take it upon oneself to; **meterse con** to pick a quarrel with; **meterse en** to get into; to plunge into; empty into

meticulo•so -sa adj meticulous; shy, timid

meti•do -da adj close, tight; rich, abundant; meddlesome; **muy metido con** on close terms with; **muy metido en** deeply involved in ‖ m push; punch; strong lye; loose leaf; (tela) seam

metódi•co -ca adj methodic(al)

metodista adj & mf Methodist

método m method

metraje m distance or length in meters; (cine) **de corto metraje** short; (cine) **de largo metraje** full-length

metralla f scrap iron; grapeshot; shrapnel

métri•co -ca adj metric(al) ‖ f prosody

metro *m* meter; ruler; tape measure; subway; **metro plegadizo** folding rule

metrónomo *m* metronome

metrópoli *f* metropolis; mother country

metropolita•no -na *adj* metropolitan ‖ *m* subway; (eccl) metropolitan

Méx. *abbr* **México**

mexcal *m* agave liquor

mexica•no -na *adj* & *mf* Mexican

México *m* Mexico; **Nuevo México** New Mexico

mezcal *m* var of **mexcal**

mezcla *f* mixture; (*argamasa*) mortar; (*tejido*) tweed

mezclar *tr* to mix; blend ‖ *ref* to mix; (*introducirse uno entre otros*) mingle; intermarry; meddle

mezclilla *f* light tweed

mezcolanza *f* jumble, hodgepodge, medley

mezquinar *tr* to be stingy with ‖ *intr* to be stingy

mezquindad *f* meanness, stinginess; need, poverty; smallness, tininess; wretchedness

mezqui•no -na *adj* mean, stingy; needy, poor; small, tiny; wretched

mezquita *f* mosque

mi *adj poss* my

mí (used as object of a preposition) *pron pers* me ‖ *pron reflex* myself

miar §77 *intr* to meow

miau *m* meow

mica *f* mica; (Guat) flirt; **ponerse una mica** (CAm) to go on a jag

mico *m* long-tailed monkey; libertine; hoodlum; **dar mico** to not keep a date

microbio *m* microbe

microbiología *f* microbiology

microbús *m* (Chile) jitney

microfaradio *m* microfarad

microficha *f* microcard

micro•film *m* (*pl* -**films** or -**filmes**) microfilm

microfilmar *tr* to microfilm

micrófono *m* microphone

microonda *f* microwave

microordenador *m* microcomputer

micropelícula *f* microfilm

microprocesador *m* chip, microprocessor

microscópi•co -ca *adj* microscopic

microscopio *m* microscope

microsurco *adj invar* microgroove ‖ *m* microgroove

microteléfono *m* handset, French telephone

mi•cho -cha *mf* pussy cat

miedo *m* fear, dread; **miedo cerval** great fear; **por miedo de** for fear of; **por miedo (de) que** for fear that; **tener miedo (a)** to be afraid (of); **tener miedo de** to be in fear of, be afraid of; be afraid to

miedo•so -sa *adj* fearful, afraid

miel *f* honey; (*jarabe saturado*) molasses; **dejar con la miel en los labios** to spoil the fun for; **hacerse de miel** to be peaches and cream

mielga *f* lucerne

miembro *m* member; (*extremidad del hombre y los animales*) member, limb

mientes *fpl* mind, thought; wish, desire; **caer en las mientes** or **en mientes** to come to mind; **parar** or **poner mientes en** to reflect on; **venírsele a uno a las mientes** to come to one's mind

mientras *conj* while; whereas; **mientras que** while; whereas; **mientras tanto** meanwhile

miérco•les *m* (*pl* -**les**) Wednesday; **miércoles de ceniza** Ash Wednesday

mies *f* cereal, grain; harvest time; **mieses** grain fields

miga *f* (*porción pequeña*) bit; (*parte más blanda del pan*) crumb; (fig) substance; **hacer buenas migas con** to get along well with; **migas** fried crumbs

migaja *f* bit, piece; (*de inteligencia*) smattering; **migajas** crumbs; leavings

migajón *m* crumb; substance

migar §44 *tr* (*el pan*) to crumb; (*p.ej., la leche*) put crumbs in

migrato•rio -ria *adj* migratory

miguelear *tr* (CAm) to make love to

miguele•ño -ña *adj* (Hond) impolite, discourteous

mijo *m* millet

mil *adj* & *m* thousand, a thousand, one thousand; **a las mil quinientas** at an unearthly hour

milagre•ro -ra *adj* superstitious; miracle-working

milagro *m* (*hecho sobrenatural*) miracle; (*cosa rara*) wonder; votive offering; **colgar el milagro a** to put the blame on; **vivir de milagro** to have a hard time getting along; have had a narrow escape

milagrón *m* fuss, excitement

milagro•so -sa *adj* miraculous; marvelous, wonderful

milano *m* burr, down; (orn) kite

mil•deu *m* (*pl* -**deues**) mildew

milena•rio -ria *adj* millennial ‖ *m* millennium

milenio *m* millennium

milenrama *f* yarrow

milési•mo -ma *adj* & *m* thousandth

miliamperio *m* milliampere

milicia *f* militia; soldiery; warfare; military service

milicia•no -na *adj* military ‖ *m* militiaman

miligramo *m* milligram

milímetro *m* millimeter

militante *adj* militant

militar *adj* military; army ‖ *m* soldier, military man ‖ *intr* to fight, go to war; struggle; serve in the army; (*surtir efecto*) militate

militarismo *m* militarism

militarista *adj* & *mf* militarist

militarizar §60 *tr* to militarize

mílite *m* soldier

milpa *f* (CAm, Mex) cornfield

milla *f* mile

millar *m* thousand

millarada *f* about a thousand; **echar millaradas** to boast about one's wealth

millo *m* millet

millón *m* million

me
mi

millona•rio -ria *adj* of a million or more inhabitants ‖ *mf* millionaire

mimar *tr* to fondle, pet; pamper, indulge, spoil

mimbre *m* & *f* (bot) osier; wicker, withe

mimbrear *intr* & *ref* to sway

mimbre•ño -ña *adj* willowy

mimbrera *f* (bot) osier, osier willow

mimbro•so -sa *adj* osier; (*hecho de mimbre*) wicker

mimeografiar §77 *tr* to mimeograph

mimeógrafo *m* mimeograph

mímica *f* mimicry; sign language

mimo *m* (*entre los griegos y romanos*) mime; fondling, petting; pampering

mimo•so -sa *adj* delicate, tender; finicky, fussy

mina *f* mine; (*de lápiz*) lead; (fig) mine, gold mine, storehouse; underground passage; (SAm) moll; **beneficiar una mina** to work a mine; **mina de carbón** or **mina hullera** coal mine; **voló la mina** the truth is out

minado *m* mine work; (nav) mining

mina•dor -dora *adj* (nav) mine-laying ‖ *m* (mil) miner; (nav) mine layer

minar *tr* to mine; undermine; consume; plug away at ‖ *intr* to mine

minarete *m* minaret

mineraje *m* mining; **mineraje a tajo abierto** strip mining

mineral *adj* & *m* mineral

mineralogía *f* mineralogy

minería *f* mining; mine operators

mine•ro -ra *adj* mining ‖ *m* miner; mine operator; (fig) source, origin

mingitorio *m* street urinal

min•gón -gona *adj* (Ven) spoiled, pampered

miniar *tr* to paint in miniature; (*un manuscrito*) illuminate

miniatura *f* miniature

miniaturización *f* miniaturization

minifalda *f* miniskirt

míni•mo -ma *adj* minimum; tiny, small, minute; least, smallest ‖ *m* minimum ‖ *f* tiny bit

mini•no -na *mf* kitty, pussy

miniordenador *m* minicomputer

ministerial *adj* ministerial

ministerio *m* ministry, cabinet, government; **formar ministerio** to form a government; **ministerio de Hacienda** Treasury Department (U.S.A.); Treasury (Brit); **ministerio de la Gobernación** Department of the Interior (U.S.A.); Home Office (Brit); **ministerio del Ejército** Department of the Army (U.S.A.); War Office (Brit); **ministerio de Marina** Department of the Navy (U.S.A.); Board of Admiralty (Brit); **Ministerio de Relaciones Exteriores** State Department; Foreign Ministry; **ministerio radiofónico** (theol) radio ministry

ministrar *tr* to administer; furnish

ministro *m* minister; bailiff, constable; **ministro de asuntos exteriores** foreign minister; **ministro de Gobernación** Home Secretary (Brit); **ministro de Hacienda** Secretary of the Treasury (U.S.A.); Chan-

cellor of the Exchequer (Brit); **ministro de Justicia** Attorney General (U.S.A.); **primer ministro** prime minister, premier

minorar *tr* to diminish, reduce; weaken

minorati•vo -va *adj* & *m* laxative

minoría *f* minority

minoridad *f* minority

minorista *m* retailer

minorita•rio -ria *adj* minority

minucia *f* trifle; **minucias** minutiae

minucio•so -sa *adj* minute, meticulous

minué *m* or **minuete** *m* minuet

minúscu•lo -la *adj* (*letra*) small; small, tiny ‖ *f* small letter

minusvalía *f* (physical) handicap

minuta *f* first draft, rough draft; memorandum; menu, bill of fare; roll, list

minutero *m* minute hand

minu•to -ta *adj* minute ‖ *m* minute ‖ *f* see **minuta**

mí•o -a *adj poss* mine; of mine, e.g., **un amigo mío** a friend of mine ‖ *pron poss* mine

miope *adj* near-sighted ‖ *mf* near-sighted person

miopía *f* near-sightedness

mira *f* (*de arma de fuego, telescopio, etc.*) sight; aim, object, purpose; target; watchtower; **estar a la mira** to be on the lookout; **poner la mira en** to have designs on

mirada *f* glance, look; **apuñalar con la mirada** to look daggers at; **mirada de soslayo** side glance

miradero *m* (*lugar desde donde se mira*) lookout; (*persona o cosa que es objeto de la atención pública*) cynosure

mira•do -da *adj* cautious, circumspect; **bien mirado** highly regarded ‖ *f* see **mirada**

mirador *m* belvedere; bay window, oriel

miramiento *m* considerateness, courtesy, regard; look; **miramientos** fuss, bother

miranda *f* eminence, vantage point

mirar *tr* to look at, watch; consider, contemplate; **mirar bien** to look with favor on; **mirar por encima** to glance at ‖ *intr* to look, glance; ¡**mira!** look out!; **mirar a** to look at, glance at; face, overlook; aim at; aim to; **mirar por** to look after ‖ *ref* to look at oneself; look at each other; **mirarse en ello** to watch one's step; **mirarse en una persona** to be all wrapped up in a person

mirasol *m* sunflower

miríada *f* myriad

mirilla *f* peephole; (*para dirigir visuales*) target; (phot) finder

miriñaque *m* hoop skirt, crinoline; bauble, trinket; (Arg) cowcatcher

mirística *f* nutmeg tree

mirlar *ref* to try to look important

mirlo *m* blackbird; solemn look; **mirlo blanco** rare bird; **soltar el mirlo** to start to jabber

mirmidón *m* tiny fellow, nincompoop

mi•rón -rona *adj* onlooking; nosy ‖ *mf* onlooker; (*de una partida de juego*) kibitzer; busybody

mirra *f* myrrh
mirto *m* myrtle
misa *f* mass; **cantar misa** to say mass; **como en misa** in dead silence; **misa cantada** High Mass; **misa de prima** early mass; **misa mayor** High Mass; **misa rezada** Low Mass
misal *m* missal
misantropía *f* misanthropy
misántropo *m* misanthrope
misar *intr* to say mass; to hear mass
misario *m* acolyte
misceláne•o -a *adj* miscellaneous ‖ *f* miscellany
miseran•do -da *adj* pitiful
miserear *intr* to be stingy
miseria *f* misery, wretchedness; poverty; stinginess; trifle, pittance; **comerse de miseria** to live in great poverty
misericordia *f* compassion, mercy, pity
misericordio•so -sa *adj* merciful
míse•ro -ra *adj* miserable, wretched ‖ *mf* wretch
mísil *m* missile; **mísil crucero** cruise missile; **mísil dirigible** guided missile
misión *f* mission; ration for harvesters; **ir a misiones** to go away as a missionary
misional *adj* missionary
misionario *m* missionary; envoy, messenger
misionero *m* missionary
misi•vo -va *adj & f* missive
mismísi•mo -ma *adj* very same, self-same
mis•mo -ma *adj & pron indef* same; own, very; -self, e.g., **ella misma** herself; myself, e.g., **yo mismo** I myself; yourself, himself, herself, itself; **así mismo** likewise, also; **casi lo mismo** much the same; **lo mismo** just the same; **lo mismo me da** it's all the same to me; **mismo . . . que** same . . . as; **por lo mismo** for that very reason ‖ **mismo** *adv* right, e.g., **ahora mismo** right now; **aquí mismo** right here
mistela *f* flavored brandy; needled must, spiked must
misterio *m* mystery; **hablar de misterio** to talk mysteriously
misterio•so -sa *adj* mysterious
misticismo *m* mysticism
místi•co -ca *adj* mystic(al) ‖ *mf* mystic
mistificación *f* hoax, mystification
mistificar §73 *tr* to hoax, mystify
mistifori *m* hodgepodge
misturera *f* (Peru) flower girl
mita *f* mite, cheese mite; (SAm) Indian slave labor; (*turno en el trabajo*) (Arg, Chile) shift, turn
mitad *f* half; middle; **a (la) mitad de** halfway through; **cara mitad** better half; **en la mitad de** in the middle of; **la mitad de** half the; **mitad y mitad** half-and-half; **por la mitad** in half, in the middle
míti•co -ca *adj* mythical
mitigar §44 *tr* to mitigate, appease, allay
mitin *m* (*pl* **mitins** or **mítines**) meeting, rally

mito *m* myth
mitología *f* mythology
mitológi•co -ca *adj* mythological
mitón *m* mitten
mitra *f* chimney pot; (eccl) miter
mixtificación *f* hoax, mystification
mixtificar §73 *tr* to hoax, mystify
mixtifori *m* hodgepodge
mixtión *f* mixture
mix•to -ta *adj* mixed ‖ *m* compound number; sulphur match; explosive compound
mixtura *f* mixture
mixturar *tr* to mix
mixturera *f* (Peru) flower girl
miz *interj* here, pussy!, here, kitty!
mízcalo *m* edible milk mushroom
m/l *abbr* **mi letra**
m/n *abbr* **moneda nacional**
mobilia•rio -ria *adj* personal (*property*) ‖ *m* furniture, suite of furniture
moblaje *m* furniture, suite of furniture
moblar §61 *tr* to furnish
moca *m* Mocha coffee ‖ *f* (Ecuad) mudhole; (Mex) wineglass
mocador *m* handkerchief
mocar §73 *tr* to blow the nose of ‖ *ref* to blow one's nose
mocarro *m* snot
mocasín *m* moccasin
mocear *intr* to act young; sow one's wild oats
mocedad *f* youth; wild oats
mocerío *m* young people
mocero *adj masc* woman-crazy
mocetón *m* strapping young fellow
mocetona *f* buxom young woman
mocil *adj* youthful
moción *f* motion, movement; (*en junta deliberante*) motion; **hacer** or **presentar una moción** to make a motion
mocionante *mf* mover
mocionar *tr & intr* to move
moci•to -ta *adj* young ‖ *mf* youngster
moco *m* (*humor segregado por una membrana mucosa*) mucus; (*mocarro*) snot; (*extremo del pabilo de una vela*) snuff; **a moco de candil** by candle light; **llorar a moco tendido** to cry like a baby; **moco de pavo** crest of a turkey; trifle; (bot) cockscomb
moco•so -sa *adj* snotty, snively; rude, ill-bred; flip, saucy; mean, worthless ‖ *mf* brat
mochar *tr* to butt; chop off; (Arg) to rob; (Col) to fire
mochil *m* errand boy for farmers in the field
mochila *f* knapsack, haversack; tool bag; (mil) ration
mochín *m* (slang) executioner
mo•cho -cha *adj* blunt, stub, flat; (*árbol*) topped; stub-horned; mutilated; (Mex) reactionary ‖ *m* butt end
mochuelo *m* (orn) little owl; (*de una o más palabras*) omission; **cargar con el mochuelo** or **tocarle a** (*uno*) **el mochuelo** to get the worst of a deal
moda *f* fashion, mode, style; **a la moda de** after the fashion of, in the style of; **alta**

moda haute couture; **de moda** in fashion; **fuera de moda** out of fashion; **pasar de moda** to go out of fashion

modales *mpl* manners

modalidad *f* manner, way, nature, kind

modelar *tr* to model; to form, shape; to mold ‖ *ref* to model; **modelarse sobre** to pattern oneself after

modelo *adj invar* model, e.g., **ciudad modelo** model city ‖ *mf* model, mannequin, fashion model ‖ *m* model, pattern; form, blank; equal, peer; style; **modelo estrella** (aut) crest-line model

modera•do -da *adj* moderate

moderador *m* regulator; (*para retardar el efecto de los neutrones*) moderator

moderar *tr* to moderate, control, restrain ‖ *ref* to moderate, control oneself, restrain oneself

modernizar §60 *tr* to modernize

moder•no -na *adj* modern

modestia *f* modesty

modes•to -ta *adj* modest

modicidad *f* moderateness, reasonableness

módi•co -ca *adj* moderate, reasonable

modificante *adj* modifying ‖ *m* (gram) modifier

modificar §73 *tr* to modify

modismo *m* idiom

modista *f* dressmaker; **modista de sombreros** milliner

modistería *f* dressmaking; ladies' dress shop

modistilla *f* dressmaker's helper; unskilled dressmaker

modisto *m* ladies' tailor

modo *m* manner, mode, way; (gram) mood, mode; **al** or **a modo de** like, on the order of; **de buen modo** politely; **de ese modo** at that rate; **de tal modo que** with the result that; **de modo que** so that; and so; **de ningún modo** by no means; **de todos modos** anyhow, at any rate; **en cierto modo** after a fashion; **modo de empleo** usage; instructions for use; **modo de ser** nature, disposition; **por modo de** as, by way of; **sobre modo** extremely; **uno a modo de** a sort of, a kind of

modorra *f* drowsiness, heaviness

modorrar *tr* to make drowsy ‖ *ref* to get drowsy, fall asleep; (*la fruta*) get squashy

modo•rro -rra *adj* drowsy, heavy; dull, stupid; (*fruta*) squashy ‖ *f see* **modorra**

modo•so -sa *adj* quiet, well-behaved

modrego *m* boor, awkward fellow

modulación *f* modulation; **modulación de altura** or **de amplitud** amplitude modulation; **modulación de frecuencia** frequency modulation

modular *tr & intr* to modulate

módulo *m* module; **módulo lunar** lunar lander, lunar module

modulo•so -sa *adj* harmonious

mofa *f* jeering, scoffing, mockery

mofeta *f* skunk; (*gas pernicioso que se desprende de las minas*) blackdamp, firedamp

moflete *m* fat cheek, jowl

mofletu•do -da *adj* fat-cheeked

mo•gol -gola *adj & mf* Mongol, Mongolian

mogollón *m* — **comer de mogollón** (coll) to sponge

mo•gón -gona *adj* one-horned, broken-horned

mogote *m* knoll, hillock; stack of sheaves; budding antler

mohatra *f* fake sale; cheating

mohien•to -ta *adj* moldy, musty; (*hierro*) rusty

mohín *m* face, grimace

mohina *f* annoyance, displeasure

mohí•no -na *adj* sad, melancholy, moody; (*caballo, buey, vaca*) black, black-nosed ‖ *mf* hinny ‖ *m* blue magpie ‖ *f see* **mohina**

moho *m* mold; must; (*del hierro*) rust; laziness; **no dejar criar moho** to keep in constant use, to use up quickly

moho•so -sa *adj* moldy, rusty; (*hierro*) rusty; (*chiste*) stale

Moisés *m* Moses

moja•do -da *adj* wet; (*p.ej., por la lluvia*) drenched, soaked; (*húmedo*) moist; (*phonet*) liquid ‖ *m* (Mex) wetback

mojar *tr* to wet; (*la lluvia a una persona*) drench, soak; (*humedecer*) dampen, moisten; (*ensopar*) dunk; stab ‖ *intr* — **mojar en** to get mixed up in ‖ *ref* to get wet; get drenched, get soaked

mojarrilla *mf* jolly person

moje *m* or **mojete** *m* sauce, gravy

mojicón *m* muffin, bun; slap in the face

mojiganga *f* masquerade, mummery; clowning

mojigatería or **mojigatez** *f* hypocrisy; prudery, sanctimoniousness

mojiga•to -ta *adj* hypocritical; prudish, sanctimonious ‖ *mf* hypocrite; prude, sanctimonious person

mojinete *m* (*de un muro*) coping; (*de un tejado*) ridge; (Arg) gable; (Chile) gable end

mojón *m* boundary stone, landmark; (*montón sin orden*) pile, heap; (*guía en desplobado*) road mark; (*porción de excremento humano*) turd

moldar *tr* to mold; put molding on

molde *m* mold; pattern; cast, stamp, matrix; (*persona*) model, ideal; (*letra*) **de molde** printed; **venir de molde** to be just right

moldear *tr* to mold; (*vaciar*) cast; put molding on

moldura *f* molding

moldurar *tr* to put molding on

mole *adj* soft ‖ *m* (Mex) stew seasoned with chili sauce ‖ *f* bulk, mass

molécula *f* molecule

molende•ro -ra *mf* miller, grinder ‖ *m* chocolate grinder; (CAm) grinding table

moler §47 *tr* (*granos*) to grind, mill; annoy, harass, weary; tire out, fatigue; chew; **moler a palos** to beat up

molesquina *f* moleskin

molestar *tr* to disturb, molest; bother, annoy; tire, weary ‖ *ref* to bother; be annoyed; **molestarse en** to take the trouble to

molestia *f* disturbance, discomfort; annoyance, bother, nuisance
moles•to -ta *adj* bothersome, troublesome; boring, tedious; bored, tired
molesto•so -sa *adj* bothersome
moleteado *m* knurl
moletear *tr* to knurl
molibdeno *m* molybdenum
molicie *f* softness; effeminacy; voluptuous living
moli•do -da *adj* ground; exhausted, worn out
molienda *f* grinding, milling; (*cantidad que se muele de una vez*) grist; (*molino*) mill; bore, annoyance; fatigue, weariness
molimiento *m* grinding; weariness
moline•ro -ra *adj* mill || *m* miller || *f* miller's wife
molinete *m* little mill; ventilating fan; (*juguete de papel*) windmill; (*movimiento que se hace con el bastón*) twirl; (*con la espada*) flourish; (*naut*) windlass; (*rueda de cohetes*) (Mex) pinwheel
molinillo *m* hand mill; **molinillo de café** coffee grinder
molino *m* mill; **luchar con los molinos de viento** to tilt at windmills; **molino de sangre** animal-driven mill; **molino de viento** windmill; **molino harinero** gristmill, flour mill
moloc *m* (Ecuad) mashed potatoes
molondrón *m* lazy bum; (Ven) large inheritance, much money
molusco *m* mollusk
mollar *adj* soft, tender; mushy, squashy; (*carne*) lean; profitable; gullible, easily taken in
mollear *intr* to give, yield; bend
molleja *f* gizzard; **criar molleja** to get lazy; **mollejas** sweetbread
mollejón *m* grindstone; big fat loafer; good-natured fellow
mollera *f* crown (*of the head*); brains, sense; **cerrado de mollera** stupid; **duro de mollera** stubborn
mollete *m* muffin
molli•no -na *adj* drizzly || *f* drizzle
mollizna *f* drizzle
momentáne•o -a *adj* momentary
momento *m* moment; **a cada momento** constantly, all the time; **al momento** at once; **de un momento a otro** at any moment
momería *f* clowning
mome•ro -ra *adj* clowning || *mf* clown
momia *f* mummy
momificar §73 *tr* to mummify
mo•mio -mia *adj* lean, skinny || *m* extra; (*ganga*) bargain; sinecure || *f* see **momia**
momo *m* face, grimace; (coll) caress
mona *f* female monkey; Barbary ape; ape, copycat; drunkenness; (*persona*) drunk; (taur) guard for right leg; **dormir la mona** to sleep off a drunk; **pillar una mona** to go on a jag; **pintar la mona** to put on airs
monacal *adj* monachal
monacato *m* monkhood
monacillo *m* altar boy, acolyte

monada *f* monkeyshine; (*gesto*) face, grimace, monkey face; darling; cuteness; flattery; folly, childishness
monaguillo *m* altar boy, acolyte
monaquismo *m* monasticism
monarca *m* monarch
monarquía *f* monarchy
monárqui•co -ca *adj* monarchic(al) || *mf* monarchist
monasterio *m* monastery
monásti•co -ca *adj* monastic
monda *f* pruning, trimming; parings, peelings; beating, whipping
mondadien•tes *m* (*pl* -**tes**) toothpick
mondadura *f* pruning, trimming; **mondaduras** peelings
mondar *tr* to clean; prune, trim; peel, pare, hull, husk; (*quitar con engaño los bienes a*) fleece; beat, whip
mon•do -da *adj* clean; pure; **mondo y lirondo** pure, unadulterated || *f* see **monda**
mondonga *f* kitchen wench
mondongo *m* intestines, insides; (*del hombre*) guts
monear *intr* to act like a monkey; boast || *ref* (Hond) to plug away; (Hond) to punch each other
moneda *f* coin; money; **la Moneda** the government of Chile; **moneda corriente** currency; common knowledge; **moneda falsa** counterfeit; **moneda menuda** change; **moneda metálica** *or* **sonante** specie; **moneda suelta** change; **pagar en la misma moneda** to pay back in one's own coin
monedar *tr* to coin, mint
monedero *m* moneybag; **monedero falso** counterfeiter
monería *f* monkeyshine; cuteness; childishness
mones•co -ca *adj* apish
moneta•rio -ria *adj* monetary
mon•gol -gola *adj* & *mf* Mongol, Mongolian
monigote *m* lay brother; rag figure, stuffed form; botched painting, botched statue; sap, boob
monipodio *m* collusion, deal, plot
monís *m* trinket; **monises** money, dough
mónita *f* cunning, smoothness, slickness
monitor *m* monitor
monja *f* nun; **monjas** lingering sparks in burning paper
monje *m* monk
monjía *f* monkhood
monjil *adj* nunnish || *m* nun's dress
mono -na *adj* cute, nice; blond; (*cabello*) red || *m* monkey, ape; (*traje de faena*) coveralls; whippersnapper, squirt; (*drogas*) withdrawal symptom; (coll) clown; (taur) attendant of picador; (Chile) pyramid of fruit or vegetables; **estar de monos** to be on the outs; **mono de Gibraltar** Barbary ape || *f* see **mona**
monóculo *m* monocle
monogamia *f* monogamy
monografía *f* monograph
monograma *m* monogram
monolíti•co -ca *adj* monolithic

mo
mo

monologar §44 *intr* to soliloquize
monólogo *m* monologue
monomanía *f* monomania
monomio *m* monomial
mono•no -na *adj* cute, sweet
monopatín *m* scooter
monoplano *m* monoplane
monopolio *m* monopoly
monopolizar §60 *tr* to monopolize
monorriel *m* monorail
monosabio *m* (taur) attendant of picador
monosílabo *m* monosyllable
monoteísta *adj* monotheistic ‖ *mf* monotheist
monotipia *f* or **monotipo** *m* monotype
monotonía *f* monotony
monóto•no -na *adj* monotonous
monóxido *m* monoxide
monseñor *m* monseigneur; (eccl) monsignor
monserga *f* gibberish
monstruo *m* monster
monstruosidad *f* monstrosity
monstruo•so -sa *adj* monstrous
monta *f* sum, total; **de poca monta** of little account
montacar•gas *m* (*pl* **-gas**) hoist, freight elevator
montadero *m* horse block
montadura *f* mounting; (*de una caballería de silla*) harness; (*engaste*) setting, mount
montaje *m* montage; setting up; (mach) assembly; (rad) hookup
montanero *m* forest ranger
montante *m* post, upright; (*suma*) amount; (*hueco cuadrilongo sobre una puerta*) transom; (*espadón*) broadsword ‖ *f* flood tide
montaña *f* mountain; mountain country; **la Montaña** the Province of Santander, Spain; **montaña de hielo** iceberg; **montaña rusa** roller coaster
monta•ñés -ñesa *adj* mountain ‖ *mf* mountaineer, highlander
montaño•so -sa *adj* mountainous
montapla•tos *m* (*pl* **-tos**) dumbwaiter
montar *tr* to mount, get on; (*un caballo, una bicicleta, los hombros de una persona*) ride; (*un servicio*) set up, establish; (*un fusil*) cock; (*una piedra preciosa*) set, mount; (*el caballo a la yegua*) cover; (*un reloj*) wind; (elec) to hook up; (mach) to assemble, to mount; (*la guardia*) (mil) to mount; (*un cabo*) (naut) to round; (*un buque*) (naut) to command; (*importar*) amount to ‖ *intr* to mount; get on top; weigh, be important; **tanto monta** it's all the same ‖ *ref* to mount; get on top; **montarse en cólera** to fly into a rage
monta•raz *adj* (*pl* **-races**) backwoods; wild, untamed ‖ *m* forester, warden
monte *m* mountain, mount; woods, woodland; obstruction, interference; backwoods, wilds; bank, kitty; dirty head of hair; **andar al monte** to take to the woods; **monte alto** forest; **monte bajo** thicket, brushwood; **monte de piedad** pawnshop; **monte pío** pension fund for widows and orphans; mutual benefit society; **monte tallar** tree farm

montear *tr* to hunt, track down; make a working drawing of; arch, vault
montecillo *m* mound, hillock
montepío *m* pension fund for widows and orphans; mutual benefit society
montera *f* cloth cap; glass roof; wife of hunter; bullfighter's black bicorne; (Hond) drunk, jag
montería *f* hunting, big-game hunting; hunting party; (Bol, Ecuad) canoe to shoot the rapids; (Mex) lumberman's camp
monterilla *f* (naut) moonsail
montero *m* hunter, huntsman; (Mex) sawmill
montés or **montesi•no -na** *adj* wild (*e.g., goat*)
montículo *m* mound, hillock
montilla *f* montilla (*a pale dry sherry*)
monto *m* sum, total
montón *m* pile, heap; (*de gente*) crowd; lot, great deal, great many; **a, de,** or **en montón** taken together; **a montones** in abundance; **ser del montón** to be quite ordinary
montonera *f* heap, pile; band of mounted rebels
montonero *m* guerrilla
montu•no -na *adj* wooded; wild, untamed, rustic
montuo•so -sa *adj* wooded, woody; rugged, hilly
montura *f* (*cabalgadura*) mount; (*de una cabalgadura*) harness; seat, saddle; (*de una piedra preciosa, de un instrumento astronómico*) mounting; (*de gafas*) frame
monumento *m* monument
monzón *m* monsoon
moña *f* doll; mannequin; ribbon, hair ribbon; drunk, jag
moño *m* topknot; crest, top; (Col) caprice, whim; (*de caballo*) (Chile) forelock; **moños** frippery
moquear *intr* to snivel
moqueo *m* snivel, sniveling
moquero *m* handkerchief
moquete *m* punch in the nose
moquillo *m* runny nose; (vet) distemper
moquita *f* mucus, snivel
mor *m* — **por mor de** for love of; because of
mora *f* black mulberry; blackberry, brambleberry; white mulberry
morada *f* dwelling; stay, sojourn
mora•do -da *adj* purple, mulberry ‖ *f* see **morada**
moral *adj* moral ‖ *m* black mulberry tree ‖ *f* (*ciencia de la conducta; conducta*) morals; (*espíritu, confianza*) morale; (*p.ej., de una fábula*) moral
moraleja *f* moral
moralidad *f* morality; (*de una fábula*) moral
morar *intr* to live, dwell
moratoria *f* moratorium
mórbi•do -da *adj* (*perteneciente a la enfermedad*) morbid; soft, delicate, mellow
morbo *m* sickness, illness; **morbo gálico** syphilis; **morbo regio** jaundice
morbo•so -sa *adj* morbid, diseased

morcilla f blood pudding, black pudding; (*añadidura que mete un actor en su papel*) gag

mor•daz adj (pl **-daces**) mordant, mordacious, sharp, caustic

mordaza f (*pañuelo o instrumento que se pone en la boca para impedir el hablar*) gag; (*aparato que sirve para apretar*) clamp, jaw; pipe vise; **poner la mordaza a** to gag

mordedura f bite

morder §47 tr to bite; nibble at; wear away; gossip about, ridicule; (Mex, Ven, W-I) to cheat ‖ intr to bite; take hold

mordicar §73 tr & intr to bite, sting

mordida f bite; (*para eludir una multa*) (Mex) payoff

mordiente m mordant

mordiscar §73 tr to nibble at ‖ intr to nibble, gnaw away; champ

mordisco m nibble, bite; champ

more•no -na adj brown, dark-brown; dark, dark-complexioned; (*de la raza negra*) black; mulato ‖ mf black person; mulato ‖ m brunet ‖ f brunette; loaf of brown bread; rick of new-mown hay

morería f Moorish quarter; Moorish land

moretón m black-and-blue mark

morfina f morphine

morfinomanía f morphine habit, drug habit

morfinóma•no -na adj addicted to morphine, addicted to drugs ‖ mf morphine addict, drug addict

morfología f morphology

moribun•do -da adj moribund, dying ‖ mf dying person

morillo m andiron, firedog

morir §30 & §83 intr to die; (*el fuego, la luz, etc.*) die away; **morir ahogado** to drown; **morir de risa** to die laughing; **morir de viejo** to die of old age; **morir helado** to freeze to death; **morir quemado** to burn to death; **morir vestido** to die a violent death ‖ ref to die; be dying; die away, die out; (*una pierna, un brazo*) go to sleep; **morirse por** to be crazy about; be dying to

moris•co -ca adj Morisco, Moorish ‖ mf Moor converted to Christianity (*after the Reconquest*); (*descendiente de mulato y española o de mulata y español*) (Mex) Morisco

mo•ro -ra adj Moorish; (*vino*) unwatered ‖ mf Moor; **hay moros en la costa** there's trouble brewing; **moro de paz** man of peace ‖ f see **mora**

moro•cho -cha adj strong, robust; (SAm) dark

morón m mound, knoll; moron

moron•do -da adj bare, stripped

moronga f (CAm, Mex) sausage

moro•so -sa adj slow, tardy; (*retrasado en el pago de deudas*) delinquent

morra f (*de la cabeza*) top, crown; (*de gato*) purr; **andar a la morra** to come to blows

morrada f slap, punch; (*golpe dado con la cabeza*) butt

morral m nose bag; (*saco de cazador*) game bag; (*de soldado, viandante, etc.*) knapsack; boor, lout

morralla f small fish; (*gente de escaso valor*) rabble, trash; (*mezcla de cosas inútiles*) junk, trash; (Mex) change, small change

morriña f blues, melancholy; **morriña de la tierra** homesickness

morriño•so -sa adj sickly; (coll) blue, melancholy

morrión m helmet; (mil) bearskin

morro m (*cosa redonda*) knob; (*monte redondo*) knoll; (*guijarro*) pebble; (*saliente que forman los labios*) snout; **beber a morro** (slang) to drink out of the bottle; **estar de morro** or **de morros** to be on the outs; **poner morro** to make a snout; **por el morro** just like that, simply so

morrocotu•do -da adj strong, thick, heavy; (*asunto, negocio*) weighty; big, enormous; (Col) rich, wealthy; (Chile) graceless, monotonous

morsa f walrus

mortaja f shroud, winding sheet; cigarette paper; (carp) mortise

mortal adj mortal; deadly; mortally ill; deathly pale; sure, conclusive ‖ m mortal

mortalidad f mortality; death rate

mortandad f massacre, mortality, butchery

morteci•no -na adj dead; dying; failing, weak; **hacer la mortecina** to play dead, to play possum

mortero m (*vaso que sirve para machacar; argamasa*) mortar; (*en los molinos de aceite*) nether stone; (arti) mortar

mortífe•ro -ra adj deadly

mortificar §73 tr to vex, annoy, bother; mortify ‖ ref (Mex) to be mortified, be embarrassed

mortual m (CAm, Mex) inheritance

mortuo•rio -ria adj mortuary, funeral; (*casa*) of the deceased ‖ m (archaic) funeral

morueco m ram

moru•no -na adj Moorish

mosai•co -ca adj Mosaic ‖ m tile, paving tile; mosaic; **mosaico de madera** marquetry

mosca f fly; (*barba*) imperial; cash, dough; disappointment; bore, nuisance; **aflojar la mosca** to shell out, to fork out; **mosca borriquera** horsefly; **mosca de las frutas** fruit fly; **mosca del vinagre** fruit fly; **mosca muerta** hypocrite; **moscas sparks**; **moscas volantes** spots before the eyes; **papar moscas** to gape, gawk

moscareta f (orn) flycatcher

moscona f hussy, brazen woman

Moscú Moscow

mosquear tr (*moscas*) to shoo; beat, whip; answer sharply ‖ intr (Mex) to sneak a ride ‖ ref to shake off annoyances; take offense

mosquero m flytrap; fly swatter

mosquete m musket

mosquetear intr (Arg, Bol) to snoop

mosquete•ro -ra adj idle ‖ mf (Arg, Bol) bystander, snooper ‖ m musketeer ‖ f wallflower

mosquetón m snap hook

mo
mo

mosquitera *f* or **mosquitero** *m* mosquito net; fly net

mosquito *m* (*Culex pungens*) mosquito; (*insecto parecido al anterior*) gnat; (coll) tippler

mostacera *f* mustard jar

mostacho *m* mustache; spot on the face

mostachón *m* macaroon

mostaza *f* mustard; (*semilla; munición*) mustard seed; **subírsele a** (*uno*) **la mostaza a las narices** to fly into a rage

mosto *m* must; **mosto de cerveza** wort

mostrador *m* (*en las tiendas*) counter; (*en las tabernas*) bar; (*de reloj*) dial

mostrar §61 *tr* to show ‖ *ref* to show; show oneself to be

mostrear *tr* to spot, splash

mostren•co -ca *adj* ownerless, unclaimed; (*que no tiene casa ni hogar*) homeless; (*animal*) stray; slow, dull; fat, heavy ‖ *mf* dolt, dullard

mota *f* mote, speck; (*en el paño*) burl, knot; hill, rise; defect, fault; (Mex, W-I) powder puff

mote *m* device, emblem, riddle; (*apodo*) nickname; (Chile) mistake; (SAm) stewed corn

motear *tr* to speck, speckle; dapple, mottle ‖ *intr* (Peru) to eat stewed corn

motejar *tr* to call names; scoff at, make fun of; **motejar de** to brand as

motín *m* mutiny, riot

motinista *m* (Peru) rioter

motivar *tr* to explain, account for; rationalize

moti•vo -va *adj* motive ‖ *m* motive, reason; (mus) motif; **con motivo de** because of; on the occasion of; **de su motivo propio** on his own accord; **motivo conductor** (mus) leitmotif; **motivos** grounds, reasons; (Chile) finickiness, prudery

moto *m* guidepost, landmark ‖ *f* motorcycle

motobomba *f* fire truck, fire engine

motocarro *m* three-wheel delivery truck

motocicleta *f* motorcycle

motocine *m* drive-in theater

motogrúa *f* truck crane

motoli•to -ta *adj* simple, stupid; **vivir de motolito** to be a sponger, live on other people ‖ *f* (orn) wagtail; (Ven) decent woman

motón *m* (naut) block, pulley

motonáuti•co -ca *adj* motorboat ‖ *f* motorboating

motonautismo *m* (sport) motorboating

motonave *f* motor launch; motor ship

motoneta *f* motor scooter; moped; light three-wheel delivery truck

mo•tor -tora *adj* motor, motive ‖ *m* motor, engine; **motor a chorro** jet engine; **motor de arranque** (aut) starter, starting motor; **motor de cuatro tiempos** four-cycle engine; **motor de dos tiempos** two-cycle engine; **motor de explosión** internal-combustion engine; **motor de reacción** jet engine; **motor fuera de borda** outboard motor; **motor térmico** heat engine ‖ *f* small motor boat

motorista *mf* motorist; motorcyclist; motorcycle racer ‖ *m* motorcycle policeman; motorman

motorización *f* motorization

motorizar §60 *tr* to motorize

motosegadora *f* power mower

motovelero *m* (naut) motor sailer

motriz *adj fem* (*fuerza*) motive

movedi•zo -za *adj* shaky, unsteady; fickle, inconstant; (*arena*) quick, shifting

mover §47 *tr* to move; (*la cola el perro*) wag; (*discordia*) stir up ‖ *intr* to move; abort, miscarry; bud, sprout ‖ *ref* to move; be moved

movible *adj* movable; fickle, inconstant, changeable

móvil *adj* movable, mobile; fickle, changeable; moving ‖ *m* moving body; cause, motive

movilizar §60 *tr* to mobilize

movimiento *m* movement, motion; **movimiento feminista** women's liberation (movement)

moza *f* girl, lass; mistress, concubine; maid, kitchen maid; (*en algunos juegos de naipes*) last hand; wash bat; **buena moza** or **real moza** good-looking woman; **moza de fortuna** or **del partido** prostitute; **moza de taberna** barmaid

mozalbete *m* lad, young fellow

mozárabe *adj* Mozarabic ‖ *mf* Mozarab

mo•zo -za *adj* young, youthful; single, unmarried ‖ *m* youth, lad; (*camarero*) waiter; (*criado*) servant; porter; (*cuelgacapas*) cloak hanger; **buen mozo** or **real mozo** handsome fellow; **mozo de caballerías** hostler, stable boy; **mozo de café** waiter; **mozo de cámara** (naut) cabin boy; **mozo de ciego** blind man's guide; **mozo de cordel** street porter, public errand boy; **mozo de cuadra** stable boy; **mozo de cuerda** public errand boy; **mozo de espuelas** groom who walks in front of master's horse; **mozo de esquina** street porter, public errand boy; **mozo de estación** station porter; **mozo de estoques** (taur) sword handler; **mozo de hotel** porter, bellhop; **mozo de paja y cebada** hostler (*at an inn*); **mozo de restaurante** waiter ‖ *f* see **moza**

mozue•lo -la *mf* youngster ‖ *m* lad, young fellow ‖ *f* lass, young woman

m/p *abbr* **mi pagaré**

m/r *abbr* **mi remesa**

Mro. *abbr* **Maestro**

M.S. *abbr* **manuscrito**

mtd. *abbr* **mitad**

mu *m* moo ‖ *f* bye-bye; **ir a la mu** to go bye-bye

muaré *adj invar & m* moiré

muca•mo -ma *mf* (Arg, Urug) house servant ‖ *f* (Arg, Chile, Urug) servant girl

muceta *f* (*de los doctores en los actos universitarios*) hood; (eccl) mozzetta

muco•so -sa *adj* mucous ‖ *f* mucous membrane

múcura *f* (Bol, Col, Ven, W-I) water pitcher; (Col) thickhead

muchacha f girl; young woman; servant girl

muchachada f youthful prank

muchachez f boyishness, girlishness

mucha•cho -cha adj young, youthful ‖ mf youth, young person; servant ‖ m boy ‖ f see **muchacha**

muchedumbre f crowd, multitude, flock

mu•cho -cha adj much, a lot of, a great deal of; (tiempo) a long ‖ pron much, a lot, a great deal ‖ **mu•chos -chas** adj & pron many ‖ **mucho** adv much; (más de lo regular) hard; often; a long time; **con mucho** by far; **ni con mucho** or **ni mucho menos** not by a long shot; **por mucho que** however much; **sentir mucho** to be very sorry; **tener mucho de** to take after

muda f change; change of voice; change of clothes; (cambio de plumas o de piel) molt, molting; molting season; **estar de muda** to be changing one's voice; **estar en muda** (coll) to keep too quiet; **hacer la muda** to molt; **muda de ropa** change of clothing

mudable adj fickle, inconstant

mudada f change of clothing; move, change of residence

mudadi•zo -za adj fickle, inconstant

mudanza f change; (cambio de domicilio) moving; fickleness, inconstancy; (en el baile) figure

mudar tr to change ‖ intr to change; **mudar de** to change ‖ ref to change; change clothing; move; move away; have a bowel movement; **mudarse de** to change

mudez f muteness, dumbness; continued silence

mu•do -da adj dumb, mute; (phonet) voiceless, surd ‖ mf mute ‖ f see **muda**

mueblaje m furniture, suite of furniture

mueble adj movable ‖ m piece of furniture; (p.ej., de un aparato de radio) cabinet; **muebles** furniture

mueblería f furniture shop

mueblista mf furniture dealer

mueca f face, grimace

muela f grindstone; knoll, mound; back tooth, grinder; **muela cordal** wisdom tooth; **muela de esmeril** emery wheel; **muela del juicio** wisdom tooth; **muela de molino** millstone

muellaje m dockage, wharfage

muelle adj soft; voluptuous ‖ m (pieza elástica de metal) spring; (obra en la orilla del mar o de un río) dock, wharf, pier; (rr) freight platform; **muelle real** mainspring

muérdago m mistletoe

muérgano m (Col, Ven) piece of junk, drug on the market; (Col, Ecuad, Ven) boor, nobody

muermo m (vet) glanders

muerte f death; **cada muerte de obispo** once in a blue moon; **dar la muerte a** to put to death; **de mala muerte** crummy, not much of a; **estar a la muerte** to be at death's door; **muerte chiquita** nervous shudder

muer•to -ta adj dead; (apagado, marchito) flat, dull; (cal, yeso) slaked; **muerto de** dying of; **muerto por** crazy about ‖ mf corpse, dead person ‖ m (en los naipes) dummy; **hacerse el muerto** to play possum; play deaf; **tocar a muerto** to toll

muesca f nick, notch; (carp) mortise

muestra f (porción de un producto que sirve para conocer su calidad) sample; model, specimen; (rótulo sobre una tienda u hotel) sign; show, exhibition, indication; (esfera de reloj) dial, face; (parada del perro para levantar la caza) set; (ademán, porte) bearing; **dar muestras de** to show signs of

mugido m moo, low; bellow, roar

mugir §27 intr (la res vacuna) to moo, low; (con ira) bellow; (el viento, el mar) roar

mugre f dirt, filth, grime

mugrien•to -ta adj dirty, filthy, grimy

muguete m lily of the valley

mujer f woman; (esposa) wife; **mujer de gobierno** housekeeper; **mujer de su casa** good manager; **mujer fatal** vamp; **ser mujer** to be a grown woman

mujeren•go -ga adj (Arg, Urug, CAm) effeminate

mujerie•go -ga adj feminine, womanly; effeminate, womanish; fond of women; **a mujeriegas** sidesaddle ‖ m flock of women

mujeril adj womanly; womanish

mújol m mullet, striped mullet

mula f mule, she-mule; junk, trash; (Arg) ingrate, traitor; (Arg) hoax; (C-R) jag, drunk; (Guat, Hond) anger, rage; (Mex) drug on the market; (Ven) flask; **devolver la mula** (CAm) to pay back in one's own coin; **echar la mula a** (Mex) to rake over the coals; **en mula de San Francisco** on shank's mare

mulada f drove of mules

muladar m dungheap, dunghill; dump, trash heap; filth

mula•to -ta adj & mf mulatto

muleta f (palo para apoyarse al andar) crutch; muleta (cloth attached to a stick, used by matador); support, prop; snack

muletilla f cross-handle cane; pet word, pet phrase; (taur) muleta

mulo m mule

multa f fine

multar tr to fine

multicopista m copying machine

multigrafiar §77 tr to multigraph

multígrafo m multigraph

multilateral adj multilateral

multiláte•ro -ra adj multilateral

multinacionales mpl multinational corporations

múltiple adj multiple, manifold ‖ m manifold; **múltiple de admisión** intake manifold; **múltiple de escape** exhaust manifold; **múltiple de uso** multipurpose

multiplicar §73 tr, intr & ref to multiply

multiplicidad f multiplicity

múlti•plo -pla adj multiple, manifold ‖ m (math) multiple

multitud f multitude

mulli•do -da adj soft, fluffy ‖ m stuffing (for cushions, pillows, etc.) ‖ f bedding, litter (for animals)

mo
mu

mullir §13 *tr* to soften, fluff up; (*la cama*) beat up, shake up; (*la tierra*) loosen around a stalk ‖ *ref* to get fluffy

munda•no -na *adj* mundane, worldly; (*mujer*) loose

mundial *adj* world-wide, world

mundillo *m* arched clotheshorse; cushion for making lace; warming pan; guelder-rose, cranberry tree; world (*of artists, scholars, etc.*)

mundo *m* world; **así va el mundo** so it goes; **desde que el mundo es mundo** since the world began; **echar al mundo** to bring into the world; to bring forth; **el otro mundo** the other world; **gran mundo** high society; **medio mundo** (*mucha gente*) half the world; **nada del otro mundo** nothing special, no great thing; **tener mucho mundo** to know one's way around; **todo el mundo** everybody; **ver mundo** to see the world, to travel

mundonuevo *m* peep show

munición *f* munition, ammunition; **de munición** (mil) government issue; (coll) done hurriedly

municionar *tr* to supply with munition

municipal *adj* municipal ‖ *m* policeman

munícipe *m* citizen

municipio *m* municipality; town council

munidad *f* susceptibility to infection

munífi•co -ca *adj* munificent

muñeca *f* (*figurilla infantil con que juegan las niñas*) doll; (*parte del cuerpo humano en donde se articula la mano con el brazo*) wrist; manikin, dress form; tea bag; (*mujer linda; mozuela frívola*) doll; **muñeca de trapo** rag doll, rag baby; **muñeca parlante** talking doll

muñeco *m* doll (*representing a male child or animal*); dummy, manikin; fop, effeminate fellow; (fig) puppet; (coll) lad, little fellow

muñequera *f* strap for wrist watch

muñequilla *f* (mach) chuck; (Arg, Chile) young ear of corn

muñidor *m* heeler, henchman

muñir §12 *tr* to convoke, summon; (pol) to fix, rig

muñón *m* (*p.ej., de un brazo cortado*) stump; (mach) journal, gudgeon; **muñón de cola** dock

mural *adj* mural

muralla *f* wall, rampart

murar *tr* to surround with a wall

murciélago *m* bat

murga *f* tin-pan band; trouble, bother; torment

muriente *adj* dying, faint

murmujear *tr & intr* to mumble

murmullar *intr* to murmur

murmullo *m* murmur; whisper; (*de aguas corrientes*) ripple; (*del viento*) rustle

murmurar *tr* to murmur, mutter; murmur at ‖ *intr* to murmur, mutter; whisper; (*las aguas corrientes*) ripple, purl; (*el viento*) rustle; gossip

muro *m* wall; **muro del sonido** sound barrier

murria *f* (coll) blues, dejection

musa *f* muse; **las Musas** the Muses; **soplarle a uno la musa** to be inspired to write poetry; be lucky at games of chance

musaraña *f* shrew, shrewmouse; bug, worm; **mirar a las musarañas** to stare vacantly

músculo *m* muscle

musculo•so -sa *adj* muscular

muselina *f* muslin

museo *m* museum; **museo de cera** waxworks

muserola *f* noseband

mus•go -ga *adj* dark-brown ‖ *m* moss

musgo•so -sa *adj* mossy, moss-covered

música *f* music; (*músicos que tocan juntos*) band; noise, racket; **con la música a otra parte** don't bother me, get out; **música celestial** nonsense; **música de fondo** background music; **poner en música** to set to music

musical *adj* musical

musicalidad *f* musicianship

music-hall *s* vaudeville theater, burlesque show

músi•co -ca *adj* musical ‖ *mf* musician; **músico mayor** bandmaster ‖ *f* see **música**

musicología *f* musicology

musicólo•go -ga *mf* musicologist

musiquero *m* music cabinet

musitar *tr & intr* to mutter, mumble

muslime *adj & mf* Muslim

muslo *m* thigh; (*de ave cocida*) leg, drumstick

mustiar *ref* to wither

mus•tio -tia *adj* sad, gloomy; (*marchito*) withered; (Mex) hypocritical; (Mex) standoffish

musul•mán -mana *adj & mf* Muslim

mutación *f* mutation; unsettled weather, change of weather; (biol) mutation, sport; (theat) change of scene

mutila•do -da *adj* crippled ‖ *mf* cripple

mutilar *tr* to mutilate; cripple

múti•lo -la *adj* mutilated; crippled

mutis *m* (theat) exit; **hacer mutis** (theat) to exit; keep quiet

mutual *adj* mutual

mutualidad *f* mutuality; mutual benefit; mutual benefit association

mutualista *mf* member of a mutual benefit association

mu•tuo -tua *adj* mutual, reciprocal

muy *adv* very; very much; too, e.g., **es muy tarde para dar un paseo tan largo** it is too late to take such a long walk; **muy de noche** late at night; **Muy señor mío** Dear Sir

N

N, n (ene) *f* sixteenth letter of the Spanish alphabet

n/ *abbr* **nuestro**

N. *abbr* **Norte**

nabo *m* turnip; (naut) mast

Nabucodonosor *m* Nebuchadnezzar

nácar *m* mother-of-pearl

nacara•do -da *adj* mother-of-pearl

nacatamal *m* (CAm, Mex) meat-filled tamale

nacela *f* nacelle

nacencia *f* birth; growth, tumor

nacer §22 *intr* to be born; bud, take rise, originate, appear; dawn ‖ *ref* bud, shoot, sprout; (*abrirse la ropa por las costuras*) split

naci•do -da *adj* natural, innate; apt, proper, fit; **nacida** née or nee ‖ *m* human being; growth, boil

naciente *adj* incipient; resurgent; (*sol*) rising ‖ *m* east

nacimiento *m* birth; origin, beginning, fountainhead; descent, lineage; (*de agua*) spring, fountainhead; crèche

nación *f* nation

nacional *adj* national; domestic ‖ *mf* national ‖ *m* militiaman

nacionalidad *f* nationality

nacionalismo *m* nationalism

nacionalista *adj & mf* nationalist

nacionalizar §60 *tr* to nationalize ‖ *ref* to be naturalized; become a citizen

nacista *adj & mf* Nazi

naco *m* (Arg, Bol, Urug) black rolled leaf of chewing tobacco; (Arg) fear, scare; (Col) stewed corn; (Col) mashed potatoes

nada *pron indef* nothing, not . . . anything; **de nada** don't mention it, you're welcome ‖ *adv* not at all

nadaderas *fpl* water wings

nada•dor -dora *adj* swimming, floating ‖ *mf* swimmer ‖ *m* (Chile) fishnet float

nadar *intr* to swim; float; fit loosely or too loosely; **nadar en** (*riqueza*) to be rolling in; (*suspiros*) be full of; (*sangre*) be bathed in

nadear *tr* to destroy, wipe out

nadería *f* trifle

nadie *pron indef* nobody, not . . . anybody; **nadie más** nobody else; **nadie más que** nobody but ‖ *m* nobody; **un don nadie** a nonentity

nado — **a nado** swimming, floating; **echarse a nado** to dive in; **pasar a nado** to swim across

nafta *f* naphtha

nagual *m* (Guat, Hond) (*dícese de un animal*) inseparable companion; (Mex) sorcerer, wizard; (Mex) lie

nagualear *intr* (Mex) to lie; (Mex) to be out looking for trouble all night

naguas *fpl* petticoat

naipe *m* playing card; deck of cards; **naipe de figura** face card; **tener buen naipe** to be lucky

naire *m* mahout

nalgada *f* shoulder, ham; blow on or with the buttocks

nalgas *fpl* buttocks, rump

nana *f* grandma; lullaby, cradlesong; (CAm, Mex, W-I) child's nurse; (Arg, Chile, Urug) child's complaint

nao *f* ship, vessel

napoleóni•co -ca *adj* Napoleonic

Nápoles *f* Naples

napolita•no -na *adj & mf* Neapolitan

naranja *f* orange; **media naranja** (coll) sidekick, better half; **naranja cajel** Seville orange, sour orange; **¡naranjas!** nonsense!

naranjada *f* orangeade; orange juice; orange marmalade

naranjal *m* orange grove

naranjo *m* orange tree; boob, simpleton

narciso *m* narcissus; fop, dandy; **narciso trompón** daffodil ‖ **Narciso** *m* Narcissus

narcóti•co -ca *adj & m* narcotic

narcotizar §60 *tr* to dope, drug

narcotraficante *mf* drug dealer

narguile *m* hookah

narigada *f* (SAm) pinch of snuff

nari•gón -gona *adj* big-nosed ‖ *m* big nose

narigu•do -da *adj* big-nosed; nose-shaped

nariguera *f* nose ring

na•riz *f* (*pl* **-rices**) nose; nostril; sense of smell; (*del vino*) bouquet; **nariz de pico de loro** hooknose; **sonarse las narices** to blow one's nose; **tabicarse las narices** to hold one's nose; **tener agarrado por las narices** to lead by the nose

narración *f* narration

narra•dor -dora *adj* narrating ‖ *mf* narrator

narrar *tr* to narrate

narrati•vo -va *adj* narrative ‖ *f* (*relato; habilidad en narrar*) narrative

narria *f* sled, sledge, drag

nasal *adj & f* nasal

nasalizar §60 *tr* to nasalize

nata *f* cream; whipped cream; élite, choice; skim, scum

natación *f* swimming

natal *adj* natal; native ‖ *m* birth; birthday

natali•cio -cia *adj* birth ‖ *m* birthday

natalidad *f* birth rate

naterón *m* cottage cheese

natillas *fpl* custard

natividad *f* birth; Christmas; (*día; festividad; pintura*) Nativity

nati•vo -va *adj* native; natural; natural-born; innate

na•to -ta *adj* born, e.g., **criminal nato** born criminal ‖ *f* see **nata**

natural *adj* natural; native; (mus) natural ‖ *mf* native ‖ *m* temper, disposition, nature; **al natural** au naturel; rough, unfinished; live; **del natural** from life, from nature

naturaleza *f* nature; disposition, temperament; nationality; **naturaleza muerta** still life

naturalidad *f* naturalness; nationality

naturalismo *m* naturalism

naturalista *mf* naturalist

mu
na

naturalización f naturalization
naturalizar §60 tr to naturalize; acclimatize ‖ ref to become·naturalized; go native
naturalmente adv naturally; easily, readily
naturismo m nudism
naufragar §44 intr to be shipwrecked; fail
naufragio m shipwreck; failure, ruin
náufra•go -ga adj shipwrecked ‖ mf shipwrecked person ‖ m shark
náusea f nausea; **dar náuseas a** to nauseate; sicken, disgust; **tener náuseas** to be nauseated, be sick at one's stomach
nauseabun•do -do adj nauseating, nauseous, loathsome, sickening
nauta m mariner, sailor
náuti•co -ca adj nautical ‖ f sailing, navigation
nava f hollow plain between mountains
navaja f folding knife; razor; penknife; tusk of wild boar; razor clam; evil tongue; **navaja barbera** straight razor
navajada f or **navajazo** m slash, gash
navajero m razor case; razor cloth
naval adj naval; nautical; **naval militar** naval
nava•rro -rra adj & mf Navarrese ‖ **Navarra** f Navarre
navazo m garden in sandy marshland
nave f ship, vessel; (de un taller, fábrica, tienda, iglesia, etc.) aisle; commercial ground floor; hall, shed, bay, building; **nave central** or **principal** (archit) nave; **nave lateral** (archit) aisle
navegable adj navigable
navegación f navigation; sailing; sea voyage; **navegación a vela** sailing
navega•dor -dora or **navegante** adj navigating ‖ mf navigator
navegar §44 tr to sail ‖ intr to navigate, sail; move around; (Mex) to suffer, bear
navel f (pl -vels) navel orange
Navidad f Christmas; Christmas time; **¡Felices Navidades!** Merry Christmas!; **contar** or **tener muchas Navidades** to be pretty old
navidal m Christmas card
navide•ño -ña adj Christmas
navie•ro -ra adj ship, shipping ‖ m shipowner; outfitter
navío m ship, vessel; **navío de guerra** warship
náyade f naiad
nazare•no -na adj & mf Nazarene ‖ m penitent in Passion Week procession ‖ **nazarenas** fpl (SAm) large gaucho spurs
nazi adj & mf Nazi
N.B. abbr **nota bene** (Lat) note well
nébeda f catnip
neblina f fog, mist
neblino•so -sa adj foggy, misty
nebulo•so -sa adj nebulous, cloudy, misty, hazy, vague; gloomy, sullen ‖ f nebula
necedad f foolishness, stupidity; nonsense
necesa•rio -ria adj necessary ‖ f water closet, privy
neceser m toilet case; sewing kit; **neceser de belleza** vanity case; **neceser de costura** workbasket

necesidad f necessity; need, want; starvation; **de necesidad** from weakness; of necessity; **necesidad mayor** bowel movement; **necesidad menor** urination
necesita•do -da adj necessitous, poor, needy; **estar necesitado de** to be in need of ‖ mf needy person
necesitar tr to necessitate; need; **necesitar + inf** to have to, need to + inf ‖ intr to be in need; **necesitar de** to be in need of, need ‖ ref to be needed, be necessary
ne•cio -cia adj foolish, stupid; imprudent; stubborn; touchy ‖ mf fool
necrología f necrology
necromancia f necromancy
néctar m nectar
neerlan•dés -desa adj Netherlandish, Dutch ‖ mf Netherlander ‖ m Dutchman; (idiom͟., Netherlandish or Dutch ‖ f Dutchwoman
nefalista mf teetotaler
nefan•do -da adj base, infamous
nefas•to -ta adj ominous, fatal, tragic
negable adj deniable
negación f negation; denial; refusal
nega•do -da adj unfit, incompetent; dull, indifferent
negar §66 tr to deny; refuse; prohibit; disown; conceal ‖ intr to deny ‖ ref to avoid; refuse; deny oneself to callers; **negarse a** to refuse; **negarse a + inf** to refuse to + inf
negati•vo -va adj negative ‖ f negative; denial; refusal
negligencia f negligence
negligente adj negligent
negociable adj negotiable
negociación f negotiation; deal, matter
negociado m department, bureau; affair, business; (SAm) illegal dealing; (Chile) store
negociante m dealer, trader
negociar tr to negotiate ‖ intr to negotiate; deal, trade
negocio m business; affair, deal, transaction; profit; (SAm) store
negocio•so -sa adj businesslike
negrear intr to turn black; look black
negre•ro -ra adj slave-trading; (fig) slave-driving ‖ mf slave trader; (fig) slave driver
negrilla f (typ) boldface
ne•gro -gra adj black, dark; gloomy; fatal, wicked; (coll) broke ‖ mf black (person); dear, darling ‖ m black; **negro de humo** lampblack
negror m or **negrura** f blackness
negruz•co -ca adj blackish
néme•sis f (pl -sis) (justo castigo; castigador) nemesis ‖ **Némesis** Nemesis
nemoro•so -sa adj (poet) woody, sylvan
ne•ne -na mf baby; dear, darling ‖ m rascal, villain
nenúfar m white water lily
neo m neon
neocelan•dés -desa adj New Zealand ‖ mf New Zealander
neoesco•cés -cesa adj & mf Nova Scotian
neófi•to -ta mf neophyte

neologismo *m* neologism
neomejica•no -na *adj & mf* New Mexican
neomicina *f* neomycin
neón *m* neon
neoyorki•no -na *adj* New York ‖ *mf* New Yorker
Nepal, el Nepal
nepa•lés -lesa *adj & mf* Nepalese
nepente *m* nepenthe
nepote *m* relative and favorite of the Pope ‖ **Nepote** Nepos
neptunio *m* neptunium
Neptuno *m* Neptune
nereida *f* Nereid
Nerón *m* Nero
nervio *m* nerve; (*del ala del insecto*) rib; strength, vigor
nerviosidad *f* nervousness
nervio•so -sa *adj* nervous; energetic, vigorous, sinewy; (*célula; centro; tónico*) nerve; (*sistema; enfermedad; postración, colapso*) nervous
nervosidad *f* nervosity; ductility, flexibility; (*de un argumento*) force, cogency
nervo•so -sa *adj* var of **nervioso**
nervu•do -da *adj* vigorous, sinewy
nervura *f* backbone (*of book*)
nesga *f* gore
nesgar §44 *tr* to gore
ne•to -ta *adj* net
neumáti•co -ca *adj* pneumatic; air ‖ *m* tire
neumonía *f* pneumonia
neuralgia *f* neuralgia
neurología *f* neurology
neurona *f* neuron
neuro•sis *f* (*pl* -sis) neurosis; **neurosis de guerra** shell shock
neuróti•co -ca *adj & mf* neurotic
neutral *adj & mf* neutral
neutralidad *f* neutrality
neutralismo *m* neutralism
neutralista *adj & mf* neutralist
neutralizar §60 *tr* to neutralize
neu•tro -tra *adj* neuter; (*que no es de un color ni de otro*) neutral; (bot, chem, elec, phonet, zool) neutral; (*verbo*) intransitive
neutrón *m* neutron
neva•do -da *adj* snow-covered; snow-white ‖ *f* snowfall
nevar §2 *tr* to make snow-white ‖ *intr* to snow
nevasca *f* snowfall; snowstorm, blizzard
nevazón *f* (SAm) snowfall
nevera *f* icebox, refrigerator; icehouse; (P-R) jail
nevería *f* ice-cream parlor
neve•ro -ra *mf* ice-cream dealer ‖ *m* place of perpetual snow; perpetual snow ‖ *f* see **nevera**
nevisca *f* snow flurry
neviscar §73 *intr* to snow lightly
nevo *m* mole; **nevo materno** birth mark
nevo•so -sa *adj* snowy
ni *conj* neither, nor; **ni . . . ni** neither . . . nor; **ni . . . siquiera** not even
niacina *f* niacin

nicaragüense or **nicaragüe•ño -ña** *adj & mf* Nicaraguan
Nicolás *m* Nicholas
nicotina *f* nicotine
nicho *m* niche
nidada *f* (*huevos en el nido*) nestful of eggs; (*pajarillos en el nido*) nest, brood, hatch
nidal *m* (*donde la gallina pone sus huevos*) nest; nest egg; haunt; source; basis, foundation
nido *m* nest; haunt; home; source; (*de ladrones*) nest, den
niebla *f* fog, mist, haze; mildew; fog, confusion; **hay niebla** it is foggy; **niebla artificial** smoke screen
nie•to -ta *mf* grandchild ‖ *m* grandson; **nietos** grandchildren ‖ *f* granddaughter
nieve *f* snow; water ice
nigromancia *f* necromancy
nihilismo *m* nihilism
nihilista *mf* nihilist
Nilo *m* Nile; **Nilo Azul** Blue Nile
nilón *m* nylon
nimbo *m* nimbus; halo
nimiedad *f* excess; fussiness, fastidiousness; timidity
ni•mio -mia *adj* excessive; fussy, fastidious; tiny
ninfa *f* nymph; **ninfa marina** mermaid
ninfea *f* white water lily
ningún *adj indef* apocopated form of **ninguno,** used only before masculine singular nouns and adjectives
ningu•no -na *adj indef* no, not any ‖ *pron indef* none, not any; neither, neither one; **ninguno de los dos** neither one ‖ **ninguno** *pron indef* nobody, no one
niña *f* child, girl; (*del ojo*) pupil; **niña del ojo** apple of one's eye; **niña exploradora** girl scout
niñada *f* childishness
niñera *f* nursemaid
niñería *f* childishness; trifle
niñero -ra *adj* fond of children ‖ *f* see **niñera**
niñez *f* childhood; childishness; (fig) infancy
ni•ño -ña *adj* childlike, childish; young, inexperienced ‖ *mf* child; (*persona joven e inexperta*) babe; **desde niño** from childhood; **niño expósito** foundling; **niño travieso** imp ‖ *m* child, boy; **niño bonito** playboy; **niño de coro** choirboy; **niño de la bola** child Jesus; lucky fellow; **niño explorador** boy scout; **niño gótico** playboy ‖ *f* see **niña**
niño-probeta *m* test-tube baby
ni•pón -pona *adj & mf* Nipponese
níquel *m* nickel
niquelar *tr* to nickel-plate
nirvana, el nirvana
níspero *m* medlar (*tree and fruit*)
níspola *f* medlar (*fruit*)
nitidez *f* brightness, clearness; sharpness
níti•do -da *adj* bright, clear; sharp
nitrato *m* nitrate
nítri•co -ca *adj* nitric
nitro *m* niter; **nitro de Chile** saltpeter
nitrógeno *m* nitrogen

na
ni

nitroglicerina *f* nitroglycerine
nitro•so -sa *adj* nitrous
nitruro *m* nitride
nivel *m* level; **nivel de burbuja** spirit level; **nivel de vida** standard of living; **nivel sonoro** noise level
nivelar *tr* to level; even, make even, grade; survey
no *adv* not; no; ¿cómo no? why not?; of course, certainly; **creer que no** to think not, believe not; ¿no? is it not so?; **no bien** no sooner; **no más que** not more than; only; **no sea que** lest; **no . . . sino** only; **ya no** no longer
nobabia *f* (aer) dope
noble *adj* noble ‖ *m* noble, nobleman
nobleza *f* nobility
noción *f* notion, idea; rudiment
nocividad *f* harmfulness
noci•vo -va *adj* noxious, harmful
noctur•no -na *adj* nocturnal; lonely, sad, melancholy; night, nighttime
noche *f* night, nighttime; darkness; **buenas noches** good evening; good night; **de la noche a la mañana** overnight; unexpectedly, suddenly; **de noche** at night, in the nighttime; **esta noche** tonight; **hacer noche en** to spend the night in; **hacerse de noche** to grow dark; **muy de noche** late at night; **por la noche** at night, in the nighttime; **noche buena** Christmas Eve; **noche de estreno** (theat) first night; **noche de uvas** New Year's Eve; **noche vieja** New Year's Eve; watch night
nochebuena *f* Christmas Eve
nochebueno *f* Christmas cake; Yule log
nochero *m* sleepwalker
nodo *m* (astr, med, phys) node
No-Do *m* (acronym for **Noticiario y Documentales**) newsreel; newsreel theater
nodriza *f* wet nurse; vacuum tank
Noé *m* Noah
nogal *m* walnut; **nogal de la brujería** witch hazel
nómada or **nómade** *adj* & *mf* nomad
nomádi•co -ca *adj* nomadic
nombradía *f* fame, renown, reputation
nombra•do -da *adj* famous
nombramiento *m* naming; appointment
nombrar *tr* to name; appoint
nombre *m* name; fame, reputation; nickname; watchword; noun; **del mismo nombre** (elec) like; **de nombres contrarios** (elec) unlike; **nombre com. cial** firm name; **nombre de lugar** place name; **nombre de pila** first name, Christian name; **nombre de soltera** maiden name; **nombre substantivo** noun; **nombre supuesto** alias
nomeolvi•des *f* (*pl* **-des**) forget-me-not
nómina *f* list, roll; payroll
nominal *adj* nominal; noun
nominar *tr* to name; appoint
nominati•vo -va *adj* & *m* nominative
non *adj* odd, uneven ‖ *m* odd number
nonada *f* trifle, nothing

no•no -na *adj* & *m* ninth
nopal *m* prickly pear
norcorea•no -na *adj* & *mf* North Korean
nordestada *f* or **nordeste** *m* (*viento*) northeaster (*wind*)
noria *f* chain pump; (*pozo*) draw well; Ferris wheel; treadmill, drudgery
norma *f* norm, standard; rule, method; (carp) square
normal *adj* normal; standard; perpendicular
Normandía *f* Normandy
norman•do -da *adj* & *mf* Norman ‖ *m* Norseman
norte *m* north; north wind; (*guía*) (fig) polestar, lodestar
Norteamérica *f* North America; America, the United States
norteamerica•no -na *adj* & *mf* North American; (*estadunidense*) American
norte•ño -ña *adj* northern
norue•go -ga *adj* & *mf* Norwegian ‖ **Noruega** *f* Norway
nos (used as object of verb) *pron pers* us; to us ‖ *pron reflex* ourselves, to ourselves; each other, to each other
noso•tros -tras *pron pers* we; us; ourselves
nostalgia *f* nostalgia
nota *f* note; (*en la escuela*) mark, grade; (*en el restaurante*) check; (mus) note; **nota de adorno** grace note; **nota tónica** keynote
notables *mpl* notables; prominent persons; (coll) VIPs
notar *tr* to note; dictate; annotate; criticize; discredit
notario *m* notary, notary public
noticia *f* news; notice, information; notion; rudiment; knowledge; **noticias de actualidad** news of the day; **noticias de última hora** late news; **una noticia** a piece of news, a news item
noticiar *tr* to notify; give notice of
noticia•rio -ria *adj* news ‖ *m* up-to-the-minute news; newsreel; newscast; **noticiario gráfico** picture page; **noticiario teatral** theater page
noticie•ro -ra *adj* news ‖ *m* newsman, reporter; late news
noticio•so -sa *adj* informed; learned; well-informed; newsy ‖ *m* news item
notificar §73 *tr* to notify; report on
no•to -ta *adj* known, well-known ‖ *m* south wind ‖ *f* see **nota**
notoriedad *f* general knowledge; fame
noto•rio -ria *adj* manifest, well-known
nov. *abbr* noviembre
novatada *f* hazing; beginner's blunder
nova•to -ta *adj* beginning ‖ *mf* beginner; freshman
novecien•tos -tas *adj* & *pron* nine hundred ‖ **novecientos** *m* nine hundred
novedad *f* newness, novelty; news; fashion; happening; change; failing health; **sin novedad** as usual; safe; well; without anything happening
novel *adj* new, inexperienced, beginning ‖ *m* beginner

novela *f* novel; story, lie; **novela caballista** novel of western life; **novela policíaca** or **policial** detective story; **novela por entregas** serial

novele•ro -ra *adj* fond of novelty; fond of fiction; gossipy; fickle

noveles•co -ca *adj* novelistic, fictional; romantic, fantastic

novelista *mf* novelist

novelísti•co -ca *adj* fictional ‖ *f* fiction

novelizar §60 *tr* to fictionalize

nove•no -na *adj & m* ninth

noventa *adj, pron & m* ninety

noventa•vo -va *adj & m* ninetieth

novia *f* fiancée; bride; **novia de guerra** war bride

noviazgo *m* engagement, courtship

novi•cio -cia *adj & mf* novice

noviembre *m* November

novilunio *m* new moon

novilla *f* heifer

novillada *f* drove of young bulls; (taur) fight with young bulls by aspiring bullfighters

novillero *m* herdsman of young cattle; (taur) aspiring fighter, untrained fighter; truant

novillo *m* young bull; (coll) cuckold; (Mex, P-R) fiancé; **hacer novillos** to play truant

novio *m* suitor; fiancé; bridegroom; **novios** engaged couple; bride and groom, newlyweds

novocaína *f* novocaine

nro. *abbr* **nuestro**

N.S. *abbr* **Nuestro Señor**

ntro. *abbr* **nuestro**

nubada *f* local shower; abundance

nubarrón *m* storm cloud

nube *f* cloud; **andar** (*los precios*) **por las nubes** to be sky-high; **bajar de las nubes** to come back to or down to earth; **poner en or•sobre las nubes** to praise to the skies

nube-hongo *f* mushroom cloud

nubla•do -da *adj* cloudy ‖ *m* storm cloud; impending danger; abundance; **aguantar el nublado** to suffer resignedly

nublar *tr* to cloud, cloud over ‖ *ref* to become cloudy

nu•blo -bla *adj* cloudy ‖ *m* storm cloud

nublo•so -sa *adj* cloudy; adverse, unfortunate

nubosidad *f* clouding, clouds

nubo•so -sa *adj* cloudy

nuca *f* nape

nuclear *adj* nuclear

núcleo *m* nucleus; core; (*de nuez*) kernel; (*de la fruta*) stone; (*de un electroimán*) core

nudillo *m* knuckle; stocking stitch; plug (*in wall*)

nudo *m* knot; bond, tie, union; crux; tangle; plot; difficulty; (*en el drama*) crisis; center, juncture; (bot) node; (naut) knot; **cortar el**

nudo gordiano to cut the Gordian knot; **hacérsele a** (*uno*) **un nudo en la garganta** to get a lump in one's throat

nudo•so -sa *adj* knotted, knotty

nuera *f* daughter-in-law

nues•tro -tra *adj poss* our ‖ *pron poss* ours

nueva *f* news; piece of news; **nuevas** *fpl* news

Nueva York *m & f* New York; **el Gran Nueva York** Greater New York

Nueva Zelandia New Zealand

nueve *adj & pron* nine; **las nueve** nine o'clock ‖ *m* nine; (*en las fechas*) ninth

nue•vo -va *adj* new; **de nuevo** again, anew; **nuevo flamante** brand-new; **¿qué hay de nuevo?** what's new? ‖ *mf* novice; freshman ‖ *f* see **nueva**

nuevomejica•no -na *adj & mf* New Mexican

Nuevo Méjico *m* New Mexico

nuez *f* (*pl* **nueces**) nut; walnut; Adam's apple; **nuez dura** (*árbol*) hickory; hickory nut; **nuez moscada** nutmeg

nulidad *f* nullity; incapacity; nobody

nu•lo -la *adj* null, void, worthless

núm. *abbr* **número**

numen *m* deity; inspiration

numeral *adj* numeral

numerar *tr* to number; count; numerate

numerario *m* cash, coin, specie

numéri•co -ca *adj* numerical

número *m* number; (*de un periódico*) copy, issue; (*de zapatos*) size; lottery ticket; **cargar** or **cobrar al número llamado** (telp) to reverse the charges; **de número** (*dícese de los individuos de una sociedad*) regular; **mirar por el número uno** to look out for number one; **número de serie** series number; **número equivocado** (telp) wrong number

numero•so -sa *adj* numerous

nunca *adv* never; **no . . . nunca** not . . . ever, never; **nunca jamás** nevermore

nupcial *adj* nuptial

nupcialidad *f* marriage rate

nupcias *fpl* nuptials, marriage; **casarse en segundas nupcias** to marry the second time

nutria *f* otter

nutrición *f* nutrition

nutri•do -da *adj* great, intense, robust, vigorous, steady; full, abounding, rich, heavy; (*carácter, letra*) thick; (*cañoneo*) heavy, sustained

nutrimento *m* or **nutrimiento** *m* nourishment, nutriment

nutrir *tr* to nourish, feed; supply, stock; support, back up; fill to overflowing

nu•triz *f* (*pl* **-trices**) wet nurse

Ñ

Ñ, ñ (eñe) *f* seventeenth letter of the Spanish alphabet
ñadi *m* (Chile) broad, shallow swamp
ñajú *m* okra, gumbo
ñámbar *m* Jamaica rosewood
ñame *m* yam; (W-I) blockhead, dunce
ñan•dú *m* (*pl* -dúes) nandu, American ostrich
ñaño -ña *adj* close, intimate; spoiled, overindulged ‖ *m* elder brother ‖ *f* elder sister; nursemaid; dear
ñapa *f* something thrown in, lagniappe; **de ñapa** in the bargain
ñaque *m* junk, pile of junk

ña•to -ta *adj* pug-nosed; (Arg) ugly, deformed
ñeque *adj* (Am) strong, vigorous; (*dícese de los ojos*) drooping ‖ *m* slap, blow; pep
ñiqueñaque *m* (coll) trash
ñisca *f* bit, fragment; excrement
ñoclo *m* macaroon
ñolombre *m* old peasant; **¡viene ñolombre!** here comes the bogeyman
ñon•go -ga *adj* slow, lazy; foolish, stupid; tricky; suspicious
ñoñería *f* or **ñoñez** *f* timidity; inanity; dotage
ño•ño -ña *adj* timid; inane; doting

O

O, o (o) eighteenth letter of the Spanish alphabet
o *conj* or; **o . . . o** either . . . or
oa•sis *m* (*pl* -sis) oasis
ob. *abbr* obispo
obduración *f* obduracy
obedecer §22 *tr* (with personal **a**) to obey ‖ *intr* to obey; **obedecer a** to yield to, be due to, be in keeping with, arise from
obediencia *f* obedience
obediente *adj* obedient
obelisco *m* obelisk; (typ) dagger
obertura *f* (mus) overture
obesidad *f* obesity
obe•so -sa *adj* obese
obispo *m* bishop
óbito *m* decease, demise
obituario *m* obituary
objeción *f* objection
objetable *adj* objectionable (*open to objection*)
objetar *tr* to object; (*dudas*) raise; (*una razón contraria*) set up, offer, present; object to
objeti•vo -va *adj* & *m* objective
objeto *m* object; subject matter; **objetos de cotillión** favors; **objeto volante no identificado** (**ovni**) unidentified flying object (UFO)
oblea *f* wafer; pill, tablet; **hecho una oblea** nothing but skin and bones
obli•cuo -cua *adj* oblique
obligación *f* obligation, duty; bond, debenture; **obligaciones** family responsibilities
obligacionista *mf* bondholder
obliga•do -da *adj* obliged, grateful; submissive; (mus) obbligato ‖ *m* (mus) obbligato
obligar §44 *tr* to obligate; oblige
obliterar *tr* to cancel
oblon•go -ga *adj* oblong
oboe *m* oboe; oboist
oboísta *mf* oboist
óbolo *m* mite
obra *f* work; **obra de** a matter of; **obra de consulta** reference work; **obra maestra**

masterpiece; **obra pía** charity; useful effort; **obra prima** shoemaking; **obras** construction, repairs, alterations; **obra segunda** shoe repairing; **poner por obra** to undertake, set to work on
obra•dor -dora *mf* worker ‖ *m* workman; shop, workshop ‖ *f* workingwoman
obraje *m* manufacture; processing
obrajero *m* foreman; (Arg) lumberman; (Bol) artisan
obrar *tr* to build; perform; work ‖ *intr* to work; act, operate, proceed; have a movement of the bowels; **obra en mi poder** I have at hand, I have in my possession
obrera *f* workingwoman
obrerismo *m* labor; labor movement
obre•ro -ra *adj* working; labor ‖ *m* workman; **los obreros** labor ‖ *f* see **obrera**
obrero-patronal *adj* labor management
obscenidad *f* obscenity
obsce•no -na *adj* obscene
obscurecer §22 *tr* to darken; dim; discredit; cloud, confuse ‖ *intr* to grow dark ‖ *ref* to cloud over; become dimmed; fade away
obscuridad *f* obscurity; darkness
obscu•ro -ra *adj* obscure; dark; gloomy; uncertain, dangerous; **a obscuras** in the dark ‖ *m* dark; (paint) shading
obsequia•do -da *mf* recipient; guest of honor
obsequiar *tr* to fawn over, flatter; present, give; court, woo
obsequio *m* flattery; gift; attention, courtesy; **en obsequio de** in honor of
obsequio•so -sa *adj* obsequious; obliging, courteous
observación *f* observation
observa•dor -dora *adj* observant ‖ *mf* observer
observancia *f* observance; deference, respectfulness
observar *tr* to observe
observatorio *m* observatory
obsesión *f* obsession
obsesionar *tr* to obsess

obsole•to -ta *adj* obsolete
obstaculizar §60 *tr* to prevent; obstruct
obstáculo *m* obstacle
obstante *adj* standing in the way; **no obstante** however, nevertheless; in spite of
obstar *intr* to stand in the way; **obstar a** or **para** to hinder, check, oppose
obstetricia *f* obstetrics
obstétri•co -ca *adj* obstetrical ‖ *mf* obstetrician
obstinación *f* obstinacy
obstina•do -da *adj* obstinate
obstinar *ref* to be obstinate
obstrucción *f* obstruction
obstruccionar *tr* to hinder, obstruct
obstruir §20 *tr* to obstruct; block; stop up
obtención *f* obtaining
obtener §71 *tr* to obtain; keep
obtenible *adj* obtainable
obturación *f* plugging up, sealing off
obturador *m* stopper, plug; (aut) choke; (aut) throttle; (phot) shutter; **obturador de guillotina** drop shutter
obtu•so -sa *adj* obtuse
obús *m* howitzer; shell; (*de válvula de neumático*) plunger
obvención *f* extra, bonus, incidental
obvencional *adj* incidental
obviar §77 **& regular** *tr* to obviate, prevent ‖ *intr* to stand in the way
ob•vio -via *adj* obvious; unnecessary
oca *f* goose
ocasión *f* occasion; opportunity, chance; danger, risk; **aprovechar la ocasión** to improve the occasion; **aprovechar la ocasión de** to avail oneself of the opportunity to; **asir la ocasión por la melena** to take time by the forelock; **de ocasión** secondhand
ocasiona•do -da *adj* dangerous, risky; exposed, subject, liable; annoying
ocasionar *tr* to occasion, cause; stir up; endanger
ocasional *adj* occasional; causal; causing; (*causa*) responsible; accidental
ocaso *m* west; (*de un cuerpo celeste*) setting; sunset; decline; end, death
occidental *adj* western; occidental
occidente *m* occident
oceáni•co -ca *adj* oceanic
océano *m* ocean
ocio *m* idleness, leisure; distraction, pastime; spare time
ocio•so -sa *adj* idle; useless, needless
oclusión *f* occlusion
oclusi•vo -va *adj* & *f* occlusive
ocote *m* (Mex) torch pine
octava *f* octave
octavilla *f* handbill; eight-syllable verse
octavín *m* piccolo
octa•vo -va *adj* eighth ‖ *mf* octoroon ‖ *m* eighth ‖ *f* see **octava**
oct.ᵉ *abbr* **octubre**
octogési•mo -ma *adj* & *m* eightieth
octubre *m* October
ocular *adj* ocular, eye ‖ *m* eyepiece, eyeglass, ocular
oculista *mf* oculist; fawner, flatterer

ocultar *tr* & *ref* to hide
ocul•to -ta *adj* hidden, concealed; (*misterioso, sobrenatural*) occult
ocupación *f* occupation; occupancy; employment
ocupa•do -da *adj* busy; occupied; **ocupada** pregnant
ocupante *adj* occupying ‖ *mf* occupant ‖ **ocupantes** *mpl* occupying forces
ocupar *tr* to occupy; busy, keep busy; employ; bother, annoy; attract the attention of ‖ *ref* to be occupied; be busy; be preoccupied; bother
ocurrencia *f* occurrence; witticism; bright idea
ocurrente *adj* witty
ocurrir *intr* to occur, happen; come; (*venir a la mente*) occur
ocha•vo -va *adj* eighth; octagonal ‖ *m* eighth; octagon
ochenta *adj, pron* & *m* eighty
ochenta•vo -va *adj* & *m* eightieth
ocho *adj* & *pron* eight; **las ocho** eight o'clock ‖ *m* eight; (*en las fechas*) eighth
ochocien•tos -tas *adj* & *pron* eight hundred ‖ **ochocientos** *m* eight hundred
oda *f* ode
odiar *tr* to hate
odio *m* hate, hatred
odio-amor *m* love-hate
odio•so -sa *adj* odious, hateful
Odisea *f* Odyssey
Odiseo *m* Odysseus
odontología *f* odontology, dentistry
odontólo•go -ga *mf* odontologist, dentist
odre *m* goatskin wine bag; (coll) toper
OEA *f* OAS
oeste *m* west; west wind
ofender *tr* & *intr* to offend ‖ *ref* to take offense
ofensa *f* offense
ofensi•vo -va *adj* & *f* offensive
ofen•sor -sora *adj* offending ‖ *mf* offender
oferta *f* offer; gift, present; **oferta y demanda** supply and demand
oficial *adj* official ‖ *m* official, officer; skilled workman; clerk, office worker; journeyman; commissioned officer; **oficial de derrota** navigator
oficiar *tr* to announce officially in writing; (*la misa*) celebrate; officiate at ‖ *intr* to officiate; **oficiar de** to act as
oficina *f* office; shop; pharmacist's laboratory; **oficina de objetos perdidos** lost-and-found department
oficines•co -ca *adj* office, clerical; bureaucratic
oficinista *mf* clerk, office worker
oficio *m* office, occupation; function, rôle; craft, trade; memo, official note; (eccl) office, service; **de oficio** officially; professionally; **hacer oficios de** to function as; **tomar por oficio** to take to, keep at
oficio•so -sa *adj* diligent; obliging; officious, meddlesome; profitable; unofficial
ofrecer *tr* & *intr* to offer; (*una recepción*) give ‖ *ref* to offer; offer oneself; happen

ñ
of

ofrecimiento *m* offer, offering; **ofrecimiento de presentación** introductory offer

ofrenda *f* offering; gift

ofrendar *tr* to make offerings of; contribute

oftalmología *f* ophthalmology

oftalmólo•go -ga *mf* ophthalmologist

ofuscación *f* obfuscation; (mental) derangement

ofuscar §73 *tr* to obfuscate; dazzle

ogro *m* ogre

Oh *interj* O!, Oh!

ohmio *m* ohm

oíble *adj* audible

oída *f* hearing; **de** or **por oídas** by hearsay

oído *m* hearing; ear; **abrir tanto oído** to be all ears; **al oído** by listening; confidentially; **decir al oído** to whisper; **hacer** or **tener oídos de mercader** to turn a deaf ear

oír §48 *tr* to hear; listen to; (*una conferencia*) attend; **oír** + *inf* to hear + *inf*, e.g., **oí entrar a mi hermano** I heard my brother come in; hear + *ger*, e.g., **oí cantar a la muchacha** I heard the girl singing; hear + *pp*, e.g., **oí tocar la campana** I heard the bell rung; **oír decir que** to hear that; **oír hablar de** to hear about ‖ *intr* to hear; listen; **¡oíga!** say!, listen!; the idea!, the very idea!

ojada *f* (Col) skylight

ojal *m* buttonhole; eyelet; grommet

ojalá *interj* God grant . . . !, would to God . . . !; **¡ojalá que** would that . . . !, I hope that . . . !

ojeada *f* glimpse, glance; **buena ojeada** eyeful

ojear *tr* to eye, stare at; cast the evil eye on; (*la caza*) start, rouse; frighten, startle

ojera *f* eyecup, eyeglass; **ojeras** (*bajo los párpados inferiores*) rings, circles

ojeriza *f* grudge, ill will

ojero•so -sa *adj* with rings or circles under the eyes

ojete *m* eyelet, eyehole

ojienju•to -ta *adj* dry-eyed, tearless

ojituer•to -ta *adj* cross-eyed

ojiva *f* ogive, pointed arch

ojo *m* eye; (*de la escalera*) opening, well; (*del puente*) bay, span; (*de agua*) spring; **a ojos vistas** visibly, openly; **costar un ojo de la cara** to cost a mint, cost a fortune; **dar los ojos de la cara por** to give one's eyeteeth for; **hasta los ojos** up to one's ears; **mirar con ojos de carnero degollado** to make sheep's eyes at; **no pegar el ojo** to not sleep a wink; **ojo de buey** (archit, meteor, naut) bull's-eye; (bot) oxeye; **ojo de la cerradura** keyhole; **poner los ojos en blanco** to roll one's eyes; **saltar a los ojos** to be self-evident; **valer un ojo de la cara** to be worth a mint ‖ *interj* beware!; look out!; attention!; **¡mucho ojo!** be careful!, watch out!; **¡ojo con . . . !** look out for . . . !; **¡ojo, mancha!** fresh paint!

ojota *f* (SAm) sandal; (SAm) tanned llama hide

ola *f* wave; (*de gente apiñada*) surge

ole *m* or **olé** *m* bravo ‖ *interj* bravo!

oleada *f* big wave; (*de gente apiñada*) surge, swell

oleaje *m* surge, rush of waves

óleo *m* oil; holy oil; oil painting; **los santos óleos** extreme unction

oleoducto *m* pipe line

oler §49 *tr* to smell; pry into; sniff out ‖ *intr* to smell, smell fragrant, smell bad; **no oler bien** to look suspicious; **oler a** to smell of, smell like; smack of

olfatear *tr* to smell, scent, sniff; (*p.ej., un buen negocio*) scent, sniff out

olfato *m* smell, sense of smell; scent; keen insight

olíbano *m* frankincense

oliente *adj* smelling, odorous

oligarquía *f* oligarchy

Olimpíada *f* Olympiad

olímpi•co -ca *adj* Olympian; Olympic; haughty

oliscar §73 *tr* to smell, scent, sniff; investigate ‖ *intr* to smell bad

oliva *f* olive; olive tree; barn owl; olive branch, peace

olivar *m* olive grove

olivillo *m* mock privet

olivo *m* olive tree; **tomar el olivo** (taur) to duck behind the barrier; beat it

olmeda *f* or **olmedo** *m* elm grove

olmo *m* elm tree

olor *m* odor; promise, hope; trace, suspicion; **olores** (Chile, Mex) spice, condiment

oloro•so -sa *adj* odorous, fragrant

olote *m* (CAm & Mex) cob, corncob

olvidadi•zo -za *adj* forgetful; ungrateful

olvida•do -da *adj* forgetful; ungrateful

olvidar *tr* & *intr* to forget; **olvidar** + *inf* to forget to + *inf* ‖ *ref* to forget oneself; **olvidarse de** to forget; **olvidarse de** + *inf* to forget to + *inf;* **olvidársele a uno** to forget, e.g., **se me olvidó mi pasaporte** I forgot my passport; **olvidársele a uno** + *inf* to forget to + *inf*, e.g., **se me olvidó cerrar la ventana** I forgot to close the window

olvido *m* forgetfulness; oblivion

olla *f* pot, kettle; stew; eddy, whirlpool; **olla a** or **de presión** pressure cooker

ollería *f* potter's shop

ollero *m* potter

ombligo *m* navel; (*centro, punto medio*) (fig) navel

omino•so -sa *adj* ominous

omisión *f* omission; oversight, neglect

omi•so -sa *adj* neglectful, remiss

omitir *tr* to omit; overlook, neglect

ómni•bus *adj* (tren) accommodation ‖ *m* (pl -bus) bus, omnibus; **ómnibus de dos pisos** double-decker

omními•do -da *adj* all-inclusive

omnipotente *adj* omnipotent

omnisciente or **omnis•cio -cia** *adj* omniscient

omnívo•ro -ra *adj* omnivorous

omóplato *m* shoulder blade

once *adj & pron* eleven; **las once** eleven o'clock ‖ *m* eleven; (*en las fechas*) eleventh

oncea•vo -va *adj & m* eleventh

once•no -na *adj & mf* eleventh

oncología *f* oncology

onda *f* wave; flicker; (*en el pelo*) wave; **onda portadora** (rad) carrier wave; **ondas entretenidas** (rad) continuous waves

ondear *tr* (*en el pelo*) to wave ‖ *intr* to wave; ripple; flow; flicker; be wavy ‖ *ref* to wave, sway, swing

ondo•so -sa *adj* wavy

ondulación *f* undulation; wave; wave motion

ondula•do -da *adj* wavy, ripply; rolling; corrugated ‖ *m* (*en el pelo*) wave

ondular *tr* (*el pelo*) to wave ‖ *intr* to undulate; (*una bandera*) wave, flutter; (*las ondas del mar*) billow; (*una culebra*) wriggle

onero•so -sa *adj* onerous, burdensome

ónice *m* or **ónique** *m* or **ónix** *m* onyx

onomásti•co -ca *adj* of proper names ‖ *m* name day ‖ *f* study of proper names

onomatopéyi•co -ca *adj* onomatopoeic

ONU *f* UN

onza *f* ounce; (zool) snow leopard

onza•vo -va *adj & m* eleventh

opa•co -ca *adj* opaque; sad, gloomy

ópalo *m* opal

opción *f* option, choice; **opción nula** or **opción cero** zero option

ópera *f* opera; **ópera semiseria** light opera; **ópera seria** grand opera

operación *f* operation; transaction; **operaciones** (*ordenador*) software

operar *tr* to operate on ‖ *intr* to operate; work ‖ *ref* to occur, come about; be operated on

opera•rio -ria *mf* worker ‖ *m* workman ‖ *f* working woman

opereta *f* operetta

operista *mf* opera singer

operísti•co -ca *adj* operatic

opia•to -ta *adj m & f* opiate

opinable *adj* moot

opinar *intr* to opine; think; pass judgment

opinión *f* opinion, view; reputation, public image

opio *m* opium

opípa•ro -ra *adj* sumptuous, lavish

oponer §54 *tr* to oppose; (*resistencia*) to offer, put up ‖ *ref* to oppose each other; face each other; **oponerse a** to oppose, be opposed to; be against, resist; compete for

oporto *m* port, port wine

oportunidad *f* opportunity; opportuneness; **oportunidades** *fpl* witticisms

oportunista *adj* opportunistic ‖ *mf* opportunist

oportu•no -na *adj* opportune, timely; proper; witty

oposición *f* opposition; competitive examination

oposi•tor -tora *adj* rivaling, competing ‖ *mf* opponent; competitor

opresión *f* oppression

opresi•vo -va *adj* oppressive

opre•sor -sora *adj* oppressive ‖ *mf* oppressor

oprimir *tr* to oppress; squeeze, press

oprobiar *tr* to defame, revile

oprobio *m* opprobrium

oprobio•so -sa *adj* opprobrious

optar *tr* to enter; assume ‖ *intr* — **optar entre** to choose between; **optar por** to choose to

ópti•co -ca *adj* optical ‖ *mf* optician ‖ *f* optics

óptimamente *adv* to perfection

óptimismo *m* optimism

optimista *adj* optimistic ‖ *mf* optimist

ópti•mo -ma *adj* fine, excellent

optometrista *mf* optometrist

opues•to -ta *adj* opposite, contrary

opugnar *tr* to attack; lay siege to; contradict

opulen•to -ta *adj* opulent

opúsculo *m* short work, opuscule

oquedad *f* hollow; hollowness

ora *conj* — **ora . . . ora** now . . . now, now . . . then

oración *f* oration, speech; prayer; sentence; **oración dominical** Lord's prayer; **ponerse en oración** to get down on one's knees

oráculo *m* oracle

ora•dor -dora *mf* orator, speaker; **orador de plazuela** soapbox orator; **orador de sobremesa** after-dinner speaker

oraje *m* rough weather, storm

oral *adj* oral

orangután *m* orang-outang

orar *intr* to pray; make a speech

orato•rio -ria *adj* oratorical ‖ *m* oratorio; (*capilla privada*) oratory ‖ *f* (*arte de la elocuencia*) oratory

orbe *m* orb; world

órbita *f* orbit

orca *f* killer whale

Órcadas *fpl* Orkney Islands

órdago — **de órdago** (coll) swell, real

orden *m & f* order; **hasta nueva orden** until further notice; **orden** *f* **de allanamiento** search warrant; **orden** *m* **de colocación** word order; **orden de pago** money order

ordenador *m* computer; **ordenador de viaje** on-board computer

ordenancista *adj* strict, severe ‖ *mf* taskmaster, disciplinarian, martinet

ordenanza *m* errand boy; (mil) orderly ‖ *f* ordinance; order, system; command; **ser de ordenanza** to be the rule

ordenar *tr* to order; put in order; ordain ‖ *ref* to be ordained, take orders

ordeñadero *m* milk pail

ordeñar *tr* to milk

ordeño *m* milking

ordinal *adj* orderly; ordinal ‖ *m* ordinal

ordinariez *f* coarseness, crudeness

ordina•rio -ria *adj* ordinary ‖ *m* daily household expenses; delivery man

orear *tr* to air ‖ *ref* to be aired; dry in the air; take an airing

orégano *m* pot or wild marjoram, winter sweet

of
or

oreja *f* ear; (*del zapato*) flap; (*de martillo*) claw; lug, flange, **aguzar las orejas** to prick up one's ears; **con las orejas caídas** crestfallen; **con las orejas tan largas** all ears; **descubrir** or **enseñar las orejas** to give oneself away

oreja•no -na *adj* (*res*) unbranded; (*animal*) skittish; shy; cautious

orejera *f* earflap, earmuff

orejeta *f* lug

ore•jón -jona *adj* coarse, uncouth; (Mex) skinny ‖ *m* strip of dried peach; pull on the ear; (*de la hoja de un libro*) dog's-ear

oreju•do -da *adj* big-eared

oreo *m* breeze

orfanato *m* orphanage

orfandad *f* orphanage, orphanhood

orfebre *m* goldsmith; silversmith

orfelinato *m* (SAm) orphanage

Orfeo *m* Orpheus

orfeón *m* glee club, choral society

organ•dí *m* (*pl* **-díes**) organdy

orgáni•co -ca *adj* organic

organillero -ra *mf* organ-grinder

organillo *m* barrel organ, hand organ, hurdy-gurdy

organismo *m* organism; organization

organista *mf* organist

organización *f* organization; **Organización de las Naciones Unidas (ONU)** United Nations (UN); **Organización de los Estados Americanos (OEA)** Organization of American States (OAS); **Organización del Tratado del Sudeste Asiático (O.T.A.S.E.)** Southwest Asia Treaty Organization (SEATO); **Organización para el Tratado del Atlántico Norte (O.T.A.N.)** North Atlantic Treaty Organization (NATO)

organizar §60 *tr* to organize

órgano *m* organ; (*de una máquina*) part; (*medio, conducto*) organ; (mus) organ

orgasmo *m* orgasm

orgía *f* orgy

orgiásti•co -ca *adj* orgiastic

orgullo *m* haughtiness; pride

orgullo•so -sa *adj* haughty; proud

oriental *adj* eastern; oriental

orientar *tr* to orient; guide, direct; (*una vela*) trim ‖ *ref* to orient oneself; find one's bearings

oriente *m* east; source, origin; east wind; youth ‖ **Oriente** *m* Orient; **el Cercano Oriente** the Near East; **el Extremo Oriente** the Far East; **el Lejano Oriente** the Far East; **el Oriente Medio** the Middle East; **el Próximo Oriente** the Near East; **gran oriente** (*logia masónica central*) grand lodge

orificar §73 *tr* to fill with gold

orífice *m* goldsmith

orificio *m* orifice, aperture, hole

origen *m* origin; source

original *adj* original; strange, odd, quaint ‖ *m* original; character; **de buen original** on good authority; **original de imprenta** copy

originar *tr* & *ref* to originate, start

orilla *f* border, edge; margin; bank, shore; sidewalk; breeze; **orillas** (Arg, Mex) outskirts; **salir a la orilla** to manage to get through

orillar *tr* to put a border or edge on; trim ‖ *intr* to come up to the shore

orillo *m* selvage, list

orín *m* rust; **orines** urine; **tomarse de orines** to get rusty

orina *f* urine

orinal *m* chamber pot

orinar *tr* to pass, urinate ‖ *intr* & *ref* to urinate

oriun•do -da *adj* & *mf* native; **ser oriundo de** to come from, hail from

orla *f* border, edge; trimming, fringe

orlar *tr* to border, put an edge on; trim, trim with a fringe

orn. *abbr* **orden**

ornamentar *tr* to ornament, adorn

ornamento *m* ornament, adornment

ornar *tr* to adorn

ornato *m* adornment, show

oro *m* gold; playing card (*representing a gold coin*) equivalent to diamond; **de oro y azul** all dressed up; **oro batido** gold leaf; **oro de ley** standard gold; **poner de oro y azul** to rake over the coals; **ponerle colores al oro** to gild the lily

oron•do -da *adj* big-bellied; hollow, spongy, puffed up; pompous, self-satisfied

oropel *m* tinsel; **gastar mucho oropel** to put up a big front

oropéndola *f* golden oriole

orozuz *m* licorice

orquesta *f* orchestra; **orquesta típica** regional orchestra

orquestar *tr* to orchestrate

órquide *f* or **orquídea** *f* orchid

ortiga *f* nettle; **ser como unas ortigas** to be a grouch

orto *m* rise (*of sun or star*)

ortodoncia *f* orthodontics; **aparato de ortodoncia** orthodontic appliance, braces

ortodo•xo -xa *adj* orthodox

ortografía *f* orthography; spelling

ortografiar §77 *tr* & *intr* to spell

oruga *f* caterpillar

orujo *m* bagasse of grapes or olives

orzuelo *m* sty

os *pron pers* & *reflex* (used as object of verb and corresponding to **vos** and **vosotros**) you, to you; yourself, to yourself; yourselves, to yourselves; each other, to each other

osa *f* she-bear; **Osa mayor** Great Bear; **Osa menor** Little Bear

osadía *f* boldness, daring

osa•do -da *adj* bold, daring

osamenta *f* skeleton; bones

osar *intr* to dare

osario *m* ossuary, charnel house

oscilar *intr* to oscillate; fluctuate; waver, hesitate

ósculo *m* kiss

oscurecer §22 *tr, intr* & *ref* var of **obscurecer**

oscuridad *f* var of **obscuridad**
oscu•ro -ra *adj & m* var of **obscuro**
osera *f* bear's den
osificar §73 *tr & ref* to ossify
oso *m* bear; **hacer el oso** to make a fool of oneself; to make love in the open; **oso blanco** polar bear; **oso hormiguero** ant bear; anteater; **oso lavador** raccoon
ostensorio *m* (eccl) monstrance
ostentar *tr* to show; make a show of ‖ *ref* to show off; boast
ostentati•vo -va *adj* ostentatious
ostento *m* portent, prodigy
ostento•so -sa *adj* magnificent, showy
osteópata *mf* osteopath
osteopatía *f* osteopathy
ostión *m* large oyster
ostra *f* oyster; **ostras en su concha** oyster cocktail, oysters on the half shell
ostracismo *m* ostracism
ostral *m* oyster bed, oyster farm
ostrería *f* oysterhouse
ostre•ro -ra *adj* oyster ‖ *m* oysterman; oyster bed, oyster farm
osu•do -da *adj* bony
osu•no -na *adj* bearish, bearlike
O.T.A.N., la NATO
O.T.A.S.E., la SEATO
otate *m* Mexican giant grass (*Guadua amplexifolia*); otate stick
otero *m* hillock, knoll
otomán *m* ottoman
otoma•no -na *adj & mf* Ottoman ‖ *f* ottoman
otoñal *adj* autumnal
otoño *m* autumn, fall
otorgar §44 *tr* to agree to; grant, confer; (law) to execute

o•tro -tra *adj indef* other, another ‖ *pron indef* other one, another one; **como dijo el otro** as someone said
ovación *f* ovation
ovacionar *tr* to give an ovation to
oval *adj* oval
óvalo *m* oval
ovante *adj* victorious, triumphant
ovario *m* ovary
oveja *f* ewe, female sheep; **oveja negra** (fig) black sheep; **oveja perdida** (fig) lost sheep
oveje•ro -ra *adj* sheep ‖ *mf* sheep raiser
oveju•no -na *adj* sheep, of sheep
ove•ro -ra *adj* blossom-colored; egg-colored
overol *m* overall
Ovidio *m* Ovid
ovillar *tr* to wind up; sum up ‖ *intr* to form into a ball ‖ *ref* to curl up into a ball
ovillo *m* ball of yarn; ball, heap; tangled ball; **hacerse un ovillo** to cower, recoil; (*hablando*) get all tangled up
ovni *m* UFO
óvulo *m* ovule; ovum
oxear *tr & intr* to shoo
oxiacanta *f* hawthorn
oxidación *f* oxidation
oxidar *tr* to oxidize ‖ *ref* to oxidize; get rusty
óxido *m* oxide; **óxido de carbono** carbon monoxide; **óxido de mercurio** mercuric oxide
oxígeno *m* oxygen
oxíto•no -na *adj* oxytone
oxte *interj* get out!, beat it!, **sin decir oxte ni moxte** without opening one's mouth
oyente *mf* hearer; (*a la radio*) listener; (*en la escuela*) auditor
ozono *m* ozone

P

P, p (pe) *f* nineteenth letter of the Spanish alphabet
P. *abbr* **Padre, Papa, Pregunta**
pabellón *m* pavilion; bell tent; flag, banner; (*de fusiles*) stack; canopy; summerhouse; (*de instrumento de viento*) bell
pabilo or **pábilo** *m* wick
Pablo *m* Paul
pábulo *m* food; support, encouragement, fuel
pacana *f* pecan
paca•to -ta *adj* mild, gentle
pacer §22 *tr* to pasture, graze; gnaw, eat away ‖ *intr* to pasture, graze
paciencia *f* patience
paciente *adj & mf* patient
pacienzu•do -da *adj* long-suffering
pacificar §73 *tr* to pacify ‖ *intr* to sue for peace ‖ *ref* to calm down
pacífi•co -ca *adj* pacific
pacifismo *m* pacifism
pacifista *adj & mf* pacifist

pa•co -ca *adj* (Chile) bay, reddish ‖ *m* paco, alpaca; Moorish sniper; sniper ‖ **Paco** *m* Frank
pacotilla *f* trash, junk; (Chile) rabble, mob; **hacer su pacotilla** to make a cleanup; **ser de pacotilla** to be shoddy, be poorly made
pacotille•ro -ra *mf* (Chile, Ven) peddler
pactar *tr* to agree upon ‖ *intr* to come to an agreement
pacto *m* pact, covenant
pacha•cho -cha *adj* (Chile) short-legged; (Chile) lax, lazy; (Chile) chubby
pa•chón -chona *adj* (CAm) shaggy, hairy, wooly ‖ *m* (*perro*) pointer; (*hombre flemático*) sluggard
pachorra *f* sluggishness, indolence
pachotada *f* silliness
padecer §22 *tr* to suffer; be victim of ‖ *intr* to suffer
padrastro *m* stepfather; hangnail

or
pa

padre *adj* huge; (Peru) terrific ‖ *m* father; stallion, sire; **padres** parents; ancestors; **tener el padre alcalde** to have pull, have a friend at court

padrina *f* godmother

padrinazgo *m* godfathership; sponsorship, patronage

padrino *m* godfather; sponsor; (*en un desafío*) second; **padrino de boda** best man; **padrinos** godparents

padrón *m* poll, census; pattern, model; memorial column; indulgent father; stallion; (Col) stock bull

padrote *m* stock animal; (Mex) pimp, procurer

paella *f* saffron-flavored stew of chicken, seafood, and rice with vegetables

paf *interj* bang!

pág. *abbr* **página**

paga *f* pay, payment; wages; fine; **como paga y señal** on account; as down payment

paga-alquiler *f* rent, rent money

pagadero -ra *adj* payable

paga•do -da *adj* pleased, cheerful; **estamos pagados** we are quits; **pagado de sí mismo** self-satisfied, conceited

paga•dor -dora *adj* paying ‖ *mf* payer ‖ *m* paymaster

paganismo *m* paganism

paga•no -na *adj & mf* pagan ‖ *m* easy mark

pagar §44 *tr* to pay; pay for; (*una bondad, una visita*) return ‖ *intr* to pay ‖ *ref* to become fond; be flattered; boast; be satisfied

pagaré *m* promissory note, I.O.U.

página *f* page

paginar *tr* to page

pago *m* payment; (*de viñas u olivares*) district, region

pagote *m* easy mark

paila *f* large pan

pairar *intr* (naut) to lie to

país *m* country, land; landscape; **el país de Gales** Wales; **los Países Bajos** (*Bélgica, Holanda y Luxemburgo*) the Low Countries; (*Holanda*) The Netherlands; **países no alineados** nonaligned nations; Third World countries

paisaje *m* landscape

paisajista *mf* landscape painter

paisa•no -na *adj* of the same country ‖ *mf* peasant; civilian; (Mex) Spaniard ‖ *m* fellow countryman; **de paisano** in civies

paja *f* straw; chaff; trash, rubbish; **no dormirse en las pajas** to not let the grass grow under one's feet; **no levantar paja del suelo** to not lift a hand, not do a stroke of work

pájara *f* paper kite; paper rooster; bird; crafty female

pajarera *f* aviary; large bird cage

pajarería *f* flock of birds; bird store; pet shop

pajare•ro -ra *adj* bright, cheerful; bright-colored, gaudy ‖ *m* bird dealer; bird fancier ‖ *f* see **pajarera**

pajarita *f* paper kite; bow tie; wing collar; piccadilly

pájaro *m* bird; crafty fellow; expert; **pájaro bobo** penguin; motmot; **pájaro carpintero** woodpecker; **pájaro de cuenta** big shot; **pájaro mosca** hummingbird

pajarota *f* or **pajarotada** *f* hoax, canard

paje *m* page; valet; dressing table; (naut) cabin boy

pajilla *f* cornhusk cigarette; **pajilla de madera** excelsior

paji•zo -za *adj* straw; straw-colored; straw-thatched

pajuela *f* short straw; sulfur match or fuse; toothpick; (Bol) match

Pakistán, el var of **Paquistán**

pakista•ní (*pl* -níes) *adj & mf* var of **paquistaní**

pala *f* shovel; (*de remo, de la azada, etc.*) blade; (*del panadero*) peel; scoop; racket; (*del calzado*) upper; (*de excavadora*) bucket; shoulder strap; (coll) cunning, craftiness

palabra *f* word; speech; (*de una canción*) words; (*derecho para hablar en asambleas*) floor; **palabras mayores** words, angry words; **remojar la palabra** to wet one's whistle; **usar de la palabra** to speak, make a speech

palabre•ro -ra *adj* wordy, windy ‖ *mf* windbag

palabrota *f* vulgarity, obscenity

palabru•do -da *adj* talkative; chattering

palacie•go -ga *adj* palace, court ‖ *m* courtier

palacio *m* palace; mansion; **palacio municipal** city hall

palada *f* shovelful; (*de remo*) stroke

paladar *m* palate; taste; gourmet

paladear *tr* to taste, relish

paladín *m* champion, hero

palafrén *m* palfrey

palanca *f* lever; pole; crowbar; **palanca de mando** (aer) control stick; **palanca de mayúsculas** shift key

palancada *f* leverage

palangana *f* washbowl, basin

palanganear *intr* to brag, give oneself airs

palanganero *m* washstand

palangre *m* trawl, trawl line

palanqueta *f* jimmy; **palanquetas** (Arg) dumbbell

palatal *adj & f* palatal

palco *m* (theat) box

palear *tr* to beat, pound; shovel

palenque *m* paling, palisade; (SAm) hitching post; (C-R) Indian ranch; (Chile) pandemonium

paleta *f* palette; small shovel; trowel; (*de una rueda*) paddle; blade, bucket, vane; shoulder blade; (*dulce con un palito que sirve de mango*) lollipop

paletilla *f* shoulder blade

paleto *m* fallow deer; rustic, yokel

palia *f* altar cloth; (eccl) pall

paliacate *m* (Mex) bandanna

paliar §77 **& regular** *tr* to palliate

palidecer §22 *intr* to pale, to turn pale

palidez *f* paleness, pallor

páli•do -da *adj* pale, pallid

palillo *m* toothpick; drumstick; bobbin; **palillos** chopsticks; castanets; rudiments; trifles

palinodia *f* backdown; **cantar la palinodia** to eat crow, eat humble pie

palique *m* chit-chat, small talk

paliquear *intr* to chat, to gossip

paliza *f* beating, thrashing

palizada *f* fenced-in enclosure; stockade; embankment

palma *f* (*de la mano*) palm; (*árbol y hoja*) palm; **batir palmas** to clap, to applaud; **llevarse la palma** to carry off the palm

palmada *f* slap; hand, applause, clapping; **dar palmadas** to clap hands

palma•rio -ria *adj* clear, evident

palmatoria *f* candlestick

palmera *f* date palm

palmito *m* palmetto; woman's face; slender figure

palmo *m* span, palm; **dejar con un palmo de narices** to disappoint

palmotear *tr* to pat; clap, applaud ‖ *intr* to clap, applaud

palo *m* stick; pole; staff; handle; tree; (*golpe*) whack; (*madera*) wood; (*grupo de naipes de la baraja*) suit; (*naut*) mast; **dar palos de ciego** to lay about, swing wildly; **de tal palo tal astilla** like father like son; **palo de escoba** broomstick; **palo en alto** (fig) big stick; **palo mayor** (naut) mainmast; **servir del palo** to follow suit

paloma *f* pigeon, dove; prostitute; (fig) dove, meek person; **paloma mensajera** carrier pigeon; **palomas** whitecaps

palomar *m* pigeon house, dovecot

palomilla *f* doveling; small butterfly; white horse; (*del caballo*) back; pillow block, journal bearing; (CAm, Mex) rabble, scum; **palomillas** whitecaps

palomita *f* doveling; (baseball) fly; **palomitas** popcorn

palpable *adj* palpable

palpar *tr* to touch, feel; grope through ‖ *intr* to grope

palpitante *adj* throbbing; thrilling; (*cuestión*) burning

palpitar *intr* to palpitate, throb; (*un afecto*) flash, break forth

pálpito *m* (SAm) hunch

palta *f* (SAm) alligator pear, avocado (*fruit*)

palto *m* (SAm) alligator pear, avocado (*tree*)

palúdi•co -ca *adj* marshy; malarial

paludismo *m* malaria

palur•do -da *adj* rustic, boorish ‖ *mf* rustic, boor

pallador *m* (SAm) Gaucho minstrel

pampa *f* pampa; **La Pampa** the Pampas

pámpana *f* vine leaf

pámpano *m* tendril; vine leaf

pan *m* bread; loaf; loaf of bread; wheat; food; livelihood; pie dough; (*de jabón, cera, etc.*) cake; gold foil or leaf; silver foil or leaf; **como el pan bendito** as easy as pie; **de pan llevar** arable, tillable; **llamar al pan pan y al vino vino** to call a spade a spade; **panes** grain, breadstuff; **venderse**

como pan bendito to sell like hot cakes ‖ **Pan** *m* Pan

pana *f* corduroy; (aut) breakdown

panacea *f* panacea

panadería *f* bakery; baking business

panade•ro -ra *mf* baker; (Chile) flatterer

panadizo *m* felon; sickly person

panal *m* honeycomb

pana•má *m* (*pl* -maes) Panama hat

paname•ño -ña *adj* & *mf* Panamanian

panamerica•no -na *adj* Pan-American

pancarta *f* placard, poster

pancista *adj* weaseling ‖ *mf* weaseler

páncre•as *m* (*pl* -as) pancreas

pancho *m* paunch, belly

pandear *intr* & *ref* to warp, bulge, buckle, sag, bend

pandereta *f* tambourine

pandilla *f* party, faction; gang, band; picnic, excursion

pan•do -da *adj* bulging; slow-moving; slow, deliberate

pandorga *f* kite; fat, lazy woman

panecillo *m* roll, crescent

panfleto *m* pamphlet

paniaguado *m* servant, minion; protégé, favorite

páni•co -ca *adj* panic, panicky ‖ *m* panic

panizo *m* Italian millet; (Chile) gangue; (Chile) abundance

panocha *f* ear of grain; ear of corn; pancake made of corn and cheese; (Mex) panocha (*brown sugar*)

panoja *f* ear of grain; ear of corn

panorama *m* panorama

pano•so -sa *adj* mealy

panqué *m* or **panqueque** *m* pancake

pantalán *m* pier, wooden pier

pantalón *m* trousers; **calzarse los pantalones** to wear the pants; **pantalones** trousers, pants; **pantalones azules** (CAm) blue jeans; **pantalones de mezclilla** (C-R, Mex) blue jeans

pantalla *f* lamp shade; fire screen; motion-picture screen; television screen; (*persona que encubre a otra*) blind; (*cine, arte del cine*) screen; fan; **llevar a la pantalla** to put on the screen; **pantalla acústica** loudspeaker; **pantalla de plata** silver screen; **pequeña pantalla** television screen; **servir de pantalla a** to be a blind for

pantano *m* bog, marsh, swamp; dam, reservoir; trouble, obstacle

pantano•so -sa *adj* marshy, swampy; muddy; knotty, difficult

panteísmo *m* pantheism

panteón *m* pantheon; cemetery

pantera *f* panther

pantomima *f* pantomime

pantoque *m* (naut) bilge

pantorrilla *f* calf (*of leg*)

pantufla *f* or **pantuflo** *m* house slipper

panty *m* panty hose

panza *f* paunch, belly

panzu•do -da *adj* paunchy, big-bellied

pañal *m* diaper; shirttail; **pañales** swaddling clothes; infancy; early stages

pa
pa

pañe•ro -ra *adj* dry-goods, cloth ‖ *mf* dry-goods dealer, clothier

paño *m* cloth; rag; (*de agujas*) paper; (*ancho de la tela*) breadth; (*mancha en el rostro*) spot; (*en, p.ej., un espejo*) blur; sailcloth, canvas; **al paño** off-stage; **conocer el paño** to know one's business, to know the ropes; **paño de adorno** doily; **paño de cocina** washrag, dishcloth; **paño de lágrimas** helping hand, stand-by; **paño de mesa** tablecloth; **paño de tumba** crape; **paño mortuorio** pall; **paños menores** under-clothing; **paños tibios** appeasement attempts

pañuelo *m* handkerchief; shawl; **pañuelo de hierbas** bandanna

papa *m* pope ‖ *f* potato; fake, hoax; food, grub; snap, cinch; **ni papa** nothing

pa•pá *m* (*pl* **-pás**) papa, daddy

papada *f* double chin; (*de animal*) dewlap; (Guat) stupidity

papado *m* papacy

papagayo *m* parrot

papalina *f* sunbonnet; drunk

papana•tas *m* (*pl* **-tas**) simpleton, gawk

paparrucha *f* hoax; trifle

papel *m* paper; piece of paper; rôle, part; character, figure; **desempeñar** or **hacer un papel** to play a rôle; **papel alquitranado** tar paper; **papel cebolla** onionskin; **papel de empapelar** wallpaper; **papel de esmeril** emery paper; **papel de estaño** tin foil; **papel de excusado** toilet paper; **papel de fumar** cigarette paper; **papel de lija** sand-paper; **papel de oficio** foolscap; **papel de seda** tissue paper; **papel de segundón** (fig) second fiddle; **papel de tornasol** litmus paper; **papel filtrante** filter paper; **papel higiénico** toilet paper; **papel moneda** paper money; **papel pintado** wallpaper; **papel secante** blotting paper; **papel viejo** waste paper; **papel volante** handbill, printed leaflet

papelada *f* farce; ridiculous act

papeleo *m* red tape

papelera *f* paper case; writing desk; waste-basket; paper factory

papelería *f* stationery store; mess of papers, litter

papelerío *m* paper work

papele•ro -ra *adj* paper; boastful, showy ‖ *mf* stationer; paper manufacturer; (Mex) paperboy ‖ *f* see **papelera**

papeleta *f* slip of paper; card, file card; ticket; **papeleta de empeño** pawn ticket

papelista *m* paper maker, paper manufacturer; stationer; paper hanger

pape•lón -lona *adj* bluffing, four-flushing ‖ *mf* bluffer, four-flusher ‖ *m* thin cardboard

papelonear *intr* to bluff, to four-flush

papelote *m* worthless piece of paper; paper kite

papel-prensa *m* newsprint

papera *f* goiter; mumps

papilla *f* pap; guile, deceit

papiro *m* papyrus

papirote *m* fillip, flick; nincompoop

paq. *abbr* **paquete**

paquear *tr* to snipe at ‖ *intr* to snipe

paque•te -ta *adj* self-important, pompous; (Arg) chic, dolled-up ‖ *m* package, parcel, bundle, bale; sport, dandy; **darse paquete** (Guat, Mex) to put on airs; **en paquete aparte** under separate cover, in a separate package; **paquetes postales** parcel post

Paquistán, el Pakistan

paquista•ní (*pl* **-níes**) or **paquistano -na** *adj* & *mf* Pakistani

Paquita *f* Fanny

par *adj* like, similar, equal; (math) even ‖ *m* pair, couple; peer; (elec, mech) couple; (math) even number; **a pares** in twos; **de par en par** wide-open; completely; overtly; **¿pares o nones?** odd or even? ‖ *f* par; **a la par** equally; jointly; at the same time; at par; **bajo la par** below par, under par; **sobre la par** above par

para *prep* to, for; towards; compared to; (*antes de*) by; **para + inf** in order to + inf; **para con** towards; **para que** in order that, so that

parabién *m* congratulation

parábola *f* parable

parabri•sa *m* or **parabri•sas** *m* (*pl* **-sas**) windshield

paracaí•das *m* (*pl* **-das**) parachute; **lanzarse en paracaídas** to parachute; **salvarse en paracaídas** to parachute to safety

paracaidismo *m* parachute jumping; (sport) sky diving

paracaidista *mf* parachutist ‖ *m* paratrooper

parachis•pas *m* (*pl* **-pas**) spark arrester

paracho•ques *m* (*pl* **-ques**) bumper

parachutar *intr* to parachute

parada *f* stop; end; stay; shutdown; (*en el juego*) stake; dam; (*para el ganado*) stall; stud farm; (*en la esgrima*) parry; (*tiro de caballerías de reemplazo*) relay; (mil) parade, dress parade, review; **parada de taxi** taxi stand

paradero *m* end; whereabouts; stopping place; wayside station

para•do -da *adj* slow, spiritless, witless; idle, unemployed; closed; proud, stiff; **quedar bien parado** to be lucky; **quedar mal parado** to be unlucky ‖ *f* see **parada**

paradoja *f* paradox

paradóji•co -ca *adj* paradoxical

parador *m* inn, wayside inn; motel; **parador de carretera** drive-in restaurant

parafina *f* paraffin

paragol•pes *m* (*pl* **-pes**) buffer, bumper

para•guas *m* (*pl* **-guas**) umbrella

Paraguay, el Paraguay

paraguaya•no -na or **paragua•yo -ya** *adj* & *mf* Paraguayan

paragüero *m* umbrella man; umbrella stand

paraíso *m* paradise

paraje *m* place, spot; state, condition

paralela *f* parallel, parallel line; **paralelas** parallel bars

paralelizar §60 *tr* to parallel, compare

parale•lo -la *adj* parallel ‖ *m* (geog) parallel ‖ *f* see **paralela**

paráli•sis *f* (*pl* -sis) paralysis
paralíti•co -ca *adj & mf* paralytic
paralizar §60 *tr* to paralyze || *ref* to become paralyzed
parámetro *m* parameter; established boundary
páramo *m* high barren plain; bleak windy spot; (Bol, Col, Ecuad) cold drizzle
paranie•ves *m* (*pl* -ves) snow fence
paraninfo *m* assembly hall, auditorium
paranoi•co -ca *adj & mf* paranoiac
parapeto *m* parapet
paraplegia *f* paraplegia
parar *tr* to stop; check; change; prepare; put up, stake; parry; order; get, acquire; (*la atención*) fix; (*la caza*) point; (*typ*) to set || *intr* to stop; (*en un hotel*) put up; **parar en** to become; run to, run as far as || *ref* to stop; stop work; stand; turn, become; (*el perro de muestra*) point; (*el pelo*) stand on end; **pararse en** to pay attention to
pararra•yo *m* or **pararra•yos** *m* (*pl* -yos) (*barra metálica que sirve para preservar los edificios del rayo*) lightning rod; (*dispositivo que sirve para preservar una instalación eléctrica de la electricidad atmosférica o de las chispas que produce*) lightning arrester
parasíti•co -ca *adj* parasitic
parási•to -ta *adj* parasitic; (elec) stray || *m* parasite; **parásitos atmosféricos** atmospherics, static
parasol *m* parasol
parato•pes *m* (*pl* -pes) bumper
Parcas *fpl* Fates
parcela *f* particle; plot of ground
parcelar *tr* to parcel, divide into lots
parcial *adj* partial; partisan || *mf* partisan
par•co -ca *adj* frugal, sparing; moderate
parcómetro *m* parking meter
parchar *tr* to mend, patch
parche *m* plaster, sticking plaster; patch; drum; drumhead; daub, botch, splotch; **parche poroso** porous plaster
pardal *m* linnet; sly fellow
pardiez *interj* by Jove!
pardillo *m* linnet
par•do -da *adj* brown, drab; dark; cloudy; (*voz*) dull, flat; (*cerveza*) dark; mulatto || *mf* mulatto || *m* brown, drab; leopard
pardus•co -ca *adj* dark-brown, drabbish
parea•do -da *adj* rhymed || *m* couplet
parear *tr* to pair; match || *ref* to pair off
parecer *m* opinion; look, mien, countenance || *v* §22 *intr* to appear; show up; look, seem; **me parece que. . . .** I think that. . . . || *ref* to look alike, resemble each other; **parecerse a** to look like
pareci•do -da *adj* like, similar; **bien parecido** good-looking; **parecido a** like, e.g., **esta casa es parecida a la otra** this house is like the other one; **parecidos** alike, e.g., **estas casas son parecidas** these houses are alike || *m* similarity, resemblance, likeness; **tener un gran parecido** to be a good likeness

pared *f* wall; **dejar pegado a la pared** to nonplus; **paredes** house
pareja *f* pair, couple; dancing partner; **correr parejas** or **a las parejas** to be abreast, arrive together; go together, match, be equal; **correr parejas con** to keep up with, keep abreast of; **parejas** (*de naipes*) pair
pareje•ro -ra *adj* even, equal; servile, fawning; forward, overfamiliar || *m* race horse
pare•jo -ja *adj* equal, like; even, smooth || *m* (CAm) dancing partner || *f* see **pareja**
parentela *f* kinsfolk, relations
parentesco *m* relationship; bond, tie
parénte•sis *m* (*pl* -sis) parenthesis; break, interval
parhilera *f* ridgepole
paria *mf* pariah, outcast
paridad *f* par, parity; comparison
parien•te -ta *adj* related || *mf* relative; (coll) spouse
parihuela *f* handbarrow; (*camilla*) stretcher
parir *tr* to bear, give birth to, bring forth || *intr* to give birth; come forth, come to light; talk well
parisiense *adj & mf* Parisian
parking *m* parking (space)
parlamentar *intr* to talk, chat; parley
parlamento *m* parliament; parley; speech; (theat) speech
parlan•chín -china *adj* jabbering || *mf* chatterbox
parlante *m* loudspeaker
parlar *intr* to speak with facility; chatter, talk too much; (*el loro*) talk
parle•ro -ra *adj* loquacious, garrulous; gossipy; (*ave*) singing, song; (*ojos*) expressive; (*arroyo, fuente*) babbling
parlotear *intr* to prattle, jabber, chin
parloteo *m* jabber, prattle
parnaso *m* (*colección de poesías*) Parnassus; **el Parnaso** Parnassus, Mount Parnassus
paro *m* shutdown, work stoppage; lockout; titmouse; (*de dados*) (SAm) throw; **paro forzoso** layoff
parodia *f* parody, travesty
parodiar *tr* to parody, travesty, burlesque
parón *m* stop; delay
paroxíto•no -na *adj & m* paroxytone
parpadear *intr* to blink, wink; flicker
parpadeo *m* blinking, winking; flicker
párpado *m* eyelid
parque *m* park; parking; parking lot; **parque de atracciones** amusement park
parqué *m* floor, inlaid floor
parqueadero *m* (Col) parking lot
parquear *tr* to park
parquímetro *m* parking meter
parra *f* grapevine; earthen jug
párrafo *m* paragraph; chat
parral *m* grape arbor
parranda *f* spree, party; (Col) large number; **andar de parranda** to go out on a spree, go out to celebrate
parricida *mf* patricide, parricide
parricidio *m* patricide, parricide

parrilla f grill, gridiron, broiler; grate, grating; grillroom, grill; **asar a la parrilla** to broil

párroco m parish priest

parroquia f parish; parish church; customers, clientele

parroquial adj parochial

parroquia•no -na mf parishioner; customer

parte m dispatch, communiqué; **parte meteorológico** weather report ‖ f part; share; party; side; direction; (papel de un actor) role; (law) party; **de un mes a esta parte** for about a month past; **en ninguna otra parte** nowhere else; **en ninguna parte** nowhere; **ir a la parte** to go shares; **la mayor parte** most, the majority; **parte del león** lion's share; **parte de por medio** (theat) bit part, walk-on; **partes** parts, gifts, talent; faction; parts, genitals; **por otra parte** in another direction; elsewhere; on the other hand; **por todas partes** everywhere; **salva sea la parte** excuse me for not mentioning where

partea•guas m (pl -guas) divide, ridge

partear tr to deliver

parte•luz m (pl -luces) mullion, sash bar

Partenón m Parthenon

partera f midwife

partición f partition, division

participar tr to notify, inform; give notice of ‖ intr to participate; partake

participio m participle

partícula f particle

particular adj particular; peculiar; private, personal ‖ m particular; matter, subject; individual; **particular a particular** (telp) person-to-person

particularizar §60 tr to itemize ‖ ref to stand out; specialize

partida f departure; entry, item; certificate; party, group, band; band of guerrillas; game; (de cartas) hand; (de tenis) set; lot, shipment; behavior; **mala partida** mean trick; **partida de campo** picnic; **partida doble** (com) double entry; **partida sencilla** (com) single entry

partida•rio -ria or **partidista** adj & mf partisan

parti•do -da adj generous, open-handed ‖ m (pol) party; decision; profit; advantage; step, measure; deal, agreement; protection, support; (casamiento que elegir) match; district, county; (sport) team; (sport) game, match; **partido de desempate** play-off; **tomar partido** to take a stand, take sides ‖ f see **partida**

partir tr to divide; distribute; share; split, split open; break; crack; upset, disconcert ‖ intr to start, depart, leave, set out; **a partir de** beginning with ‖ ref to become divided; crack, split

partisa•no -na mf (mil) partisan

partitura f (mus) score

parto m childbirth, confinement; newborn child; offspring; **estar de parto** to be in labor, be confined; **parto del ingenio** brain child

parva f light breakfast (on fast days); heap of unthreshed grain; heap, pile

parvulario m nursery school; kindergarten

parvulista mf kindergarten teacher

párvu•lo -la adj small, tiny; simple, innocent; humble ‖ mf child, tot; (niño) kindergartner

pasa f raisin; (del pelo de los negros) kink; **pasa de Corinto** currant

pasada f passage; passing; **de pasada** in passing, hastily; **mala pasada** mean trick

pasade•ro -ra adj passable ‖ f stepping stone; walkway, catwalk

pasadizo m passage, corridor, hallway, alley; catwalk

pasa•do -da adj past; gone by; overripe; spoiled; overdone; stale; burned out; antiquated; faded ‖ m past; **pasados** ancestors ‖ f see **pasada**

pasa•dor -dora mf smuggler ‖ m door bolt; bolt, pin; hatpin; brooch; stickpin; safety pin; strainer

pasaje m passage; fare; fares; passengers; **cobrar el pasaje** to collect fares

pasaje•ro -ra adj passing, fleeting; (camino, calle) common, traveled ‖ mf passenger; hotel guest; **pasajero colgado** straphanger; **pasajero no presentado** no-show

pasamano m lace trimming; (baranda) handrail; (naut) gangway

pasamonta•ña m or **pasamonta•ñas** m (pl -ñas) ski mask, storm hood

pasaporte m passport

pasapuré m potato masher

pasar m livelihood ‖ tr to pass; cross; take across; send, transfer, transm't; (contrabando) slip in; spend; swallow; excel; overlook, stand for; undergo, suffer; (un libro) go through; (una película) show; dry in the sun; tutor; study with or under; **pasarlo** to get along; live; (dícese de la salud) be; **pasar por alto** to disregard; omit, leave out, skip ‖ intr to pass; go; pass away; pass over; happen; last; spread; get along; yield; come in, e.g., **pase Vd.** come in; **pasar de** to go beyond, exceed; to go above; be more than; **pasar por** to pass by, down, through, over, etc.; pass as, pass for; stop or call at; **pasar sin** to do without ‖ ref to pass; go; excel; pass over; get along; pass away; take an examination; leak; go too far; become overripe, become overcooked; rot; melt; burn out; (una llave, un tornillo) not fit, be loose; forget; **pasarse por** to stop or call at; **pasarse sin** to do without

pasarela f footbridge; catwalk, gangplank

pasatiempo m pastime

pascua f Passover; Easter; Twelfth-night; Pentecost; Christmas; **dar las pascuas** to wish a Happy New Year; **estar como una pascua** or **unas pascuas** (coll) to be bubbling over with joy; **¡Felices Pascuas!** Merry Christmas!; **Pascua de flores** Easter; **Pascua del Espíritu Santo** Pentecost; **Pascua de Navidad** Christmas; **Pascua de Resurrección** or **Pascua florida** Easter; **Pascuas navideñas** Christmas

pase *m* (*permiso; billete gratuito; movimiento de las manos del mesmerista, el torero*) pass; (*en la esgrima*) feint; **pase de cortesía** complimentary ticket

paseante *adj* strolling ‖ *mf* stroller

pasear *tr* to walk; promenade, show off ‖ *intr* to take a walk; go for a ride ‖ *ref* to take a walk; go for a ride; wander, ramble; take it easy

pasefllo *m* processional entrance of bullfighters

paseo *m* walk, stroll, promenade; ride; drive; avenue; **dar un paseo** to take a walk; take a ride; **enviar a paseo** to send on his way, dismiss without ceremony; **paseo de caballos** bridle path; **paseo de la cuadrilla** processional entrance of the bullfighters

pasillo *m* short step; passage, corridor; (theat) short piece, sketch

pasión *f* passion

pasi•vo -va *adj* passive; (*pensión*) retirement ‖ *m* liabilities; debit side

pasmar *tr* to chill; frostbite; stun, benumb; dumbfound, astound ‖ *ref* to chill; become frostbitten; be astounded; get lockjaw; (*los colores*) become dull or flat

pasmo *m* cold; lockjaw, tetanus; astonishment; wonder, prodigy

pasmo•so -sa *adj* astounding; awesome

paso *m* step; pace; (*de la escalera*) step; gait; walk; passing; passage; step, measure, démarche; pass, permit; strait; footstep, footprint; incident, happening; (*de hélice, tornillo*) pitch; (elec) pitch; (rad) stage; (theat) short piece, sketch, skit; **al paso** in passing, on the way; **al paso que** at the rate that; (*a la vez que, mientras*) while, whereas; **ceder el paso** to make way; to keep clear; **de paso** in passing; at the same time; **paso a nivel** grade crossing; **paso de ganado** cattle crossing; **paso de ganso** goose step

paspa *f* (SAm) crack in the lips

pasquín *m* lampoon

pasquinar *tr* to lampoon

pasta *f* paste, dough, pie crust, soup paste; mash; (*para hacer papel*) pulp; cardboard; board binding; (*de un diente*) filling; (*dinero*) (coll) dough; **pasta dentrífica** toothpaste; **pasta española** marbled leather binding, tree calf; **pastas** noodles, macaroni, spaghetti, etc.; **pasta seca** cookie

pastar *tr & intr* to graze

pastel *m* pie; pastry roll; pastel; settlement, pacification; cheat, trick; (typ) pi; (typ) smear; (coll) plot, deal; **pastel de cumpleaños** birthday cake

pastelería *f* pastry; pastry shop

pastele•ro -ra *mf* pastry cook

pastelillo *m* tart, cake; (*de mantequilla*) pat

pasterizar §60 *tr* to pasteurize

pastilla *f* tablet, lozenge, drop; (*pequeña masa pastosa*) dab; (*de jabón, chocolate, etc.*) cake

pasto *m* pasture; grass; food, nourishment; **a pasto** to excess; in abundance; **a todo pasto** freely, without restriction; **de pasto** ordinary, everyday

pastor *m* shepherd; pastor

pastora *f* shepherdess

pastoral *adj & f* pastoral

pastorear *tr* (*a las ovejas o los fieles*) to shepherd; lie in ambush for; spoil, pamper; (Arg, Urug) to court

pasto•so -sa *adj* pasty, doughy; (*voz*) mellow; (Arg, Chile) grassy

pastura *f* pasture; fodder

pasu•do -da *adj* kinky

pata *f* paw, foot, leg; (*de un mueble*) leg; duck; **a cuatro patas** on all fours; **estirar la pata** to kick the bucket; **meter la pata** to butt in, to put one's foot in it; **pata de gallo** crow's-foot; blunder; piece of nonsense; **pata de palo** peg leg, wooden leg; **pata galana** game leg; lame person; **patas arriba** on one's back, upside down; topsy-turvy

patada *f* kick; stamp, stamping; step; footstep, track; **en dos patadas** in a jiffy

patalear *intr* to kick; stamp the feet

pataleta *f* fit; feigned fit or convulsion; (dial) tantrum

patán *m* churl, boor, lout; peasant

pataplún *interj* kerplunk!

patata *f* potato

patear *tr* to kick; trample on ‖ *intr* to stamp one's foot; bustle around; kick

patentar *tr* to patent

patente *adj* patent, clear, evident ‖ *f* grant, privilege, warrant; patent; **de patente** (Chile) excellent, first-class; **patente de circulación** owner's license; **patente de invención** patent; **patente de sanidad** bill of health

paternal *adj* paternal, fatherly

paternidad *f* paternity, fatherhood; **paternidad literaria** authorship

pater•no -na *adj* paternal

pateta *m* (coll) the devil; cripple

patéti•co -ca *adj* pathetic

patetismo *m* pathos

patibula•rio -ria *adj* hair-raising

patíbulo *m* scaffold

patiesteva•do -da *adj* bowlegged

patilla *f* small paw or foot; pocket flap; watermelon; (naut) compass; **patillas** sideburns, side whiskers

patín *m* small patio; skate; skid, slide, runner; (*ave marina*) petrel; **patín de cuchilla** or **de hielo** ice skate; **patín de ruedas** roller skate

patinada *f* (SAm) (aut) skidding

patinadero *m* skating rink

patina•dor -dora *mf* skater

patinaje *m* skating; skidding; **patinaje artístico** figure skating; **patinaje de fantasía** fancy skating; **patinaje de figura** figure skating

patinar *intr* to skate; skid; slip

patinazo *m* skid; slip; slip, blunder

patinete *m* scooter

patio *m* patio, court, yard; campus; (rr) yard, switchyard; **patio de recreo** playground

patituer•to -ta *adj* crooked-legged; crooked, lopsided

patizam•bo -ba *adj* knock-kneed

pato *m* duck, drake; **pagar el pato** to be the goat; **pato de flojel** eider duck

patochada *f* blunder, stupidity

patojo *m* (CAm) street urchin

patología *f* pathology

patota *f* (Arg, Urug) teen-age gang

patraña *f* fake, humbug, hoax

patria *f* country; mother country, fatherland, native land; birthplace; (*p.ej., de las artes*) home; **patria chica** native heath

patriarca *m* patriarch

patri•cio -cia *adj & mf* patrician

patrimonio *m* patrimony

pa•trio -tria *adj* native, home; paternal ‖ *f* see **patria**

patriota *mf* patriot

patrióti•co -ca *adj* patriotic

patriotismo *m* patriotism

patrocinar *tr* to sponsor, patronize

patrocinio *m* sponsorship

patrón *m* sponsor, protector; patron saint; patron; landlord; owner, master; boss, foreman; host; (*de un barco*) skipper; pattern; standard; **patrón oro** gold standard; **patrón picado** stencil

patrona *f* patroness; landlady; owner, mistress; hostess

patronal *adj* management, employers

patronato *m* employers' association; foundation; board of trustees; patronage

patronear *tr* to skipper

patro•no -na *mf* sponsor, protector; employer ‖ *m* patron; landlord; boss, foreman; lord of the manor; **los patronos** the management ‖ *f* see **patrona**

patrulla *f* patrol; gang, band

patrullar *tr & intr* to patrol

paulati•no -na *adj* slow, gradual

pausa *f* pause; slowness, delay; (mus) rest

pausa•do -da *adj* slow, calm, deliberate ‖ **pausado** *adv* slowly, calmly

pausar *tr & intr* to slow down

pauta *f* ruler; guide lines; guideline, rule, guide, standard, model

pava *f* turkey hen; **pelar la pava** to make love at a window

pavesa *f* ember, cinder, spark

pavimentar *tr* to pave

pavimento *m* pavement

pa•vo -va *adj* (coll) silly, stupid ‖ *m* turkey; turkey cock; **comer pavo** to be a wallflower; **pavo real** peacock

pavón *m* bluing; peacock

pavonar *tr* to blue

pavonear *intr & ref* to strut, swagger

pavor *m* fear, terror, dread

pavoro•so -sa *adj* frightful, dreadful

payador *m* (SAm) gaucho minstrel

payasada *f* clownishness, clownish remark

payaso *m* clown; laughingstock

paz *f* (*pl* **paces**) peace; peacefulness; **dejar en paz** to leave alone, stop pestering; **estar en paz** to be even; to be quits; **hacer las paces con** to make peace with, to come to terms with; **salir en paz** to break even

pazgua•to -ta *adj* simple, doltish ‖ *mf* simpleton, dolt

pazpuerca *f* slut, slattern

P.D. *abbr* **posdata**

peaje *m* toll

peatón *m* pedestrian; rural postman

pebete *m* punk, joss stick; fuse; (*cosa hedionda*) (coll) stinker

peca *f* freckle

pecado *m* sin

peca•dor -dora *adj* sinning, sinful ‖ *mf* sinner

pecamino•so -sa *adj* sinful

pecar §73 *intr* to sin; **pecar de** to be too, e.g., **pecar de confiado** to be too trusting

pecera *f* fish globe, fish bowl

pecino•so -sa *adj* slimy

pecio *m* flotsam

pecíolo *m* leafstalk

pécora *f* head of sheep; **buena pécora** or **mala pécora** schemer, scheming woman

peco•so -sa *adj* freckly, freckle-faced

peculado *m* embezzlement, peculation

peculiar *adj* peculiar

pecunia•rio -ria *adj* pecuniary

pechada *f* bump or push with the chest; tossing an animal (*with a bump of horse's chest*); bumping contest between two horsemen

pechar *tr* to pay as a tax; fulfill; take on; drive one's horse against; bump with the chest; strike for a loan ‖ *ref* (*dos jinetes*) to vie in a bumping contest

pechera *f* shirt front, shirt bosom; chest protector; (*del delantal*) bib; breast strap; (coll) bosom; **pechera postiza** dickey

pecho *m* chest; breast, bosom; heart, courage; **dar el pecho** to nurse, suckle; face it out; **de dos pechos** double-breasted; **de un solo pecho** single-breasted; **echar el pecho al agua** to put one's shoulder to the wheel; (coll) to speak out; **en pechos de camisa** in shirt sleeves; **tomar a pecho** to take to heart; **¡pecho al agua!** take heart!, put your shoulder to the wheel!

pechuga *f* (*del ave*) breast; slope, hill; brass, cheek; treachery, perfidy; (coll) bosom, breast

pechu•gón -gona *adj* big-chested; brazen ‖ *mf* sponger ‖ *m* slap or blow on the chest; fall on the chest

pedagogía *f* pedagogy

pedal *mf* pedal, treadle

pedalear *intr* to pedal

pedante *adj* pedantic ‖ *mf* pedant

pedantería *f* pedantry

pedantes•co -ca *adj* pedantic

pedantismo *m* pedantry

pedazo *m* piece; **hacer pedazos** to break to pieces; **hacerse pedazos** (coll) to fall to pieces; to strain, to wear oneself out; **pedazo de alcornoque, de animal** or **de bruto** dolt, imbecile, good-for-nothing; **pedazo del alma, de las entrañas** or **del corazón** (*niño*) darling, apple of one's eye; **pedazo de pan** (*pequeña cantidad*) crumb; (*precio bajo*) song

pederastia *f* pederasty
pedernal *m* flint; flintiness; flint-hearted person
pedestal *m* pedestal
pedestre *adj* pedestrian
pedestrismo *m* pedestrianism; walking; foot racing; cross-country racing
pedíatra *mf* pediatrician
pediatría *f* pediatrics
pedido *m* request; (*encargo de mercancías*) order
pedigüe•ño -ña *adj* insistent, demanding, bothersome
pedir §50 *tr* to ask, ask for; request; demand, require; need; ask for the hand of; (*mercancías*) order; (gram) to govern; **pedir prestado a** to borrow from ‖ *intr* to ask; beg; bring suit; **a pedir de boca** opportunely; as desired
pedorre•ro -ra *adj* flatulent ‖ *f* flatulence; (orn) tody; **pedorreras** tights
pedrada *f* stoning; hit or blow with a stone; hint, taunt
pedregal *m* rocky ground; pile of rocks
pedrego•so -sa *adj* stony, rocky; suffering from gallstones ‖ *mf* sufferer from gallstones
pedrejón *m* boulder
pedrera *f* quarry, stone quarry
pedrería *f* precious stones, jewelry
pedrusco *m* boulder
pedúnculo *m* stem, stalk
peer §43 *intr* & *ref* to break wind
pega *f* sticking; pitch varnish; drubbing; (*en un examen*) catch question; trick, joke; (W-I) work, jobs; **de pega** (coll) fake
pegadi•zo -za *adj* sticky; catching, contagious; sponging; fake, imitation
pegajo•so -sa *adj* sticky; contagious; tempting; soft, gentle; mushy
pegapega *f* glue
pegar §44 *tr* to stick, paste; fasten, attach, tie; (*carteles*) post; (*fuego*) set; (*una enfermedad*) transmit; (*un botón*) sew on; (*un grito*) let out; (*un salto*) take; (*un golpe, una bofetada*) let go; beat; **no pegar el ojo** to not sleep a wink ‖ *intr* to stick, catch; take root, take hold; cling; join; fit, match; be fitting; pass, be accepted; beat; knock ‖ *ref* to stick, catch; take root, take hold; hang on, stick around; (*una enfermedad*) be catching; **pegársela a uno** to make a fool of someone
pegatina *f* sticker (or tag)
pegotear *intr* to hang around, sponge
peina•do -da *adj* groomed; effeminate ‖ *m* hairdo, coiffure; (*manera de componer el pelo*) hairstyle; (*policía, soldados*) search; **peinado al agua** finger wave
peina•dor -dora *mf* hairdresser ‖ *m* wrapper, dressing gown; dressing table
peinar *tr* to comb; (*policía, soldados*) search ‖ *ref* to comb oneself, comb one's hair
peine *m* comb; sly fellow
peineta *f* back comb
pelada *f* pelt, sheepskin
peladero *m* wasteland

peladilla *f* sugar almond; small pebble
peladillo *m* clingstone peach
pela•do -da *adj* bare; bald; barren; penniless; (*decena, centena, etc.*) even ‖ *m* raggedy fellow; (W-I) haircut ‖ *f* see **pelada**
pelafus•tán -tana *mf* derelict, good-for-nothing
pelaga•tos *m* (*pl* **-tos**) wretch, ragamuffin
pelaje *m* coat, fur; (*especie, calidad*) sort, stripe
pelar *tr* (*pelo*) to cut; (*pelo, plumas*) pluck, pull out; peel, skin, husk, hull, shell; (*los dientes*) show; (*en el juego*) clean out; beat, thrash ‖ *ref* to peel off; lose one's hair; get a haircut; clear out, make a getaway; **pelárselas por** to crave; crave to
pelazón *f* poverty; misery
peldaño *m* step
pelea *f* fight; quarrel; struggle; **pelea de gallos** cockfight
pelear *intr* to fight; quarrel; struggle ‖ *ref* to fight, fight each other
pele•ón -ona *adj* pugnacious, quarrelsome; (*vino*) cheap, ordinary ‖ *mf* quarrelsome person ‖ *m* cheap wine ‖ *f* row, scuffle, fracas
peletería *f* furriery; fur shop; (Cuba) shoe store
pelete•ro -ra *mf* furrier; (Cuba) shoe dealer
peliagu•do -da *adj* furry, long-haired; arduous, ticklish
película *f* film; motion picture; **película de dibujos** animated cartoon; **película del Oeste** western; **película de terror** or **película horripilante** horror movie; **película sonora** sound film
pelicule•ro -ra *adj* moving-picture ‖ *mf* scenario writer ‖ *m* movie actor ‖ *f* movie actress
peligrar *intr* to be in danger
peligro *m* danger, peril, risk; **ponerse en peligro de paz** to be alerted for war
peligro•so -sa *adj* dangerous
pelillo *m* trifle; **echar pelillos a la mar** to bury the hatchet; **no pararse en pelillos** to not bother about trifles, pay no attention to small matters; **no tener pelillos en la lengua** to speak right out
pelirro•jo -ja *adj* red-haired, redheaded ‖ *mf* redhead
pelo *m* hair; (*en las frutas y el cuerpo humano*) down; (*del paño*) nap; (*de la madera*) grain; (*de un animal*) coat; (*en las piedras preciosas*) flaw; (*del caballo*) color; (*en el billar*) kiss; (*del reloj*) hairspring; hair trigger; fiber, filament; raw silk; **al pelo** with the hair, with the nap; perfectly, to the point; **con todos sus pelos y señales** chapter and verse; **en pelo** bareback; **escapar por un pelo** to escape by a hairbreadth, have a narrow escape; **no tener pelos en la lengua** to be outspoken, not mince words; **ponerle a uno los pelos de punta** to make one's hair stand on end; **tomar el pelo a** to make fun of, make a foo! of; **venir a pelo** to come in handy

pa
pe

pe•lón -lona *adj* bald, hairless; dull, stupid; penniless

Pélope *m* Pelops

peloponense *adj* & *mf* Peloponnesian

Peloponeso *m* Peloponnesus

pelo•so -sa *adj* hairy

pelota *f* ball; ball game; handball; **en pelota** stripped; stark-naked; **pelota acuática** water polo; **pelota rodada** (baseball) grounder; **pelota vasca** pelota, jai alai

pelotari *mf* pelota player

pelotear *intr* to knock a ball around; wrangle, argue

pelotera *f* row, brawl

pelotón *m* large ball; gang, crowd; platoon; **pelotón de fusilamiento** firing squad; **pelotón de los torpes** awkward squad

peltre *m* pewter

peluca *f* wig

peluche *m* plush, pile

pelu•do -da *adj* hairy, furry; bushy

peluquear *tr* (Col, Ven) to cut the hair of ‖ *intr* (Col, Ven) to get a haircut

peluquería *f* hairdresser's, barbershop

peluque•ro -ra *mf* hairdresser; barber; wigmaker

peluquín *m* hairpiece; toupee

pelusa *f* down; lint, fuzz; nap; jealousy, envy

pellejo *m* skin; pelt, rawhide; peel, rind; wineskin; (*la vida de uno*) (coll) hide, skin; (coll) sot, drunkard; **dar, dejar** or **perder el pellejo** to die

pellizcar §73 to pinch; nip; take a pinch of ‖ *ref* to long, pine

pellizco *m* pinch; nip; bit, pinch

pena *f* punishment; penalty; pain, hardship, toil; sorrow, grief; effort, trouble; **a duras penas** hardly, with great difficulty; **de pena** of a broken heart; **pena privativa de libertad** imprisonment; **¡qué pena!** what a pity!; **so pena de** on pain of, under penalty of; **valer la pena** to be worthwhile (to)

penacho *m* crest; tuft, plume; arrogance; (bot) tassel

pena•do -da *adj* afflicted, grieved; difficult ‖ *mf* convict

penalidad *f* trouble, hardship; (law) penalty

penalizar §60 *tr* to punish; penalize

penar *tr* to penalize; punish ‖ *intr* to suffer; linger; **penar por** to pine for, long for ‖ *ref* to grieve

penca *f* pulpy leaf; cowhide; **coger una penca** to get a jag on

penco *m* nag, jade; boor

pendejo *m* pubes; pubic hair; (coll) coward

pendencia *f* dispute, quarrel, fight; pending litigation

pendencie•ro -ra *adj* quarrelsome ‖ *mf* wrangler

pender *intr* to hang, dangle; depend; be pending

pendiente *adj* pendent, hanging, dangling; pending; under way; expecting; **estar pendiente de** (*las palabras de una persona*) to hang on; depend on; be in the process of ‖ *m* earring, pendant; watch chain ‖ *f* slope, grade; dip, pitch

péndola *f* feather; pendulum; clock; pen, quill; queen post

pendolón *m* king post

pendón *m* banner, standard, pennon

péndulo *m* pendulum; clock

pene *m* penis

penetrar *tr* to penetrate; pierce; grasp, fathom ‖ *intr* to penetrate ‖ *ref* to grasp, fathom; realize; become convinced

penicilina *f* penicillin

península *f* peninsula

peninsular *adj* & *mf* peninsular; (*ibero*) Peninsular

penique *m* penny

penitencia *f* penitence; penance; **hacer penitencia** to do penance; eat sparingly; take potluck

penitente *adj* & *mf* penitent

penol *m* (naut) yardarm

peno•so -sa *adj* arduous, difficult; suffering; conceited; shy

pensa•dor -dora *adj* thinking ‖ *mf* thinker

pensamiento *m* thought; (*planta y flor*) pansy

pensar §2 *tr* to think; think over; (*un naipe, un número, etc.*) think of; intend to; **pensar de** to think of, e.g., **¿qué piensa Vd. de este libro?** what do you think of this book? ‖ *intr* to think; **pensar en** (*dirigir sus pensamientos a*) to think of (*to turn one's thoughts to*)

pensati•vo -va *adj* pensive, thoughtful

pensión *f* pension; annuity; allowance; boardinghouse; (*para ampliar estudios*) fellowship; **pensión completa** board and lodging

pensionar *tr* to pension

pensionista *mf* pensioner; boarder; boarding-school pupil; **medio pensionista** day boarder

pentagrama *m* staff, musical staff

Pentecostés, el Pentecost

penúlti•mo -ma *adj* penultimate; next to last ‖ *f* penult

penumbra *f* penumbra; semidarkness, half-light

penuria *f* shortage

peña *f* rock, boulder; cliff; club, group, circle

peñasco *m* pinnacle; crag

peñasco•so -sa *adj* rocky, craggy

peñón *m* rock, spire; **peñón de Gibraltar** rock of Gibraltar

peón *m* laborer; pedestrian; foot soldier; farm hand; (*en el ajedrez*) pawn; (*en las damas*) man; top, peg top; spindle, axle; (taur) attendant; **peón de albañil** or **de mano** hod carrier

peor *adj* & *adv* worse; worst

pepa *f* (*de la manzana*) (Col) seed; (*del durazno*) (Arg) stone; (*canica*) (Arg) marble; (Col) lie, cheat, trick

pepe *mf* foundling ‖ *m* bib; **Pepe** Joe

pepinillo *m* gherkin

pepino *m* cucumber; **me importa un pepino** I couldn't care less

pepita *f* seed, pip; nugget; (vet) pip

peque *m* tot

pequén *m* (Chile) burrowing owl

peque•ñez f (pl **-ñeces**) smallness; infancy; trifle

peque•ño -ña adj little, small; young; low, humble

pequeño-burgués adj petit bourgeois

Pequín m Peking

pequi•nés -nesa adj & mf Pekinese

pera f pear; goatee; cinch, sinecure; pear-shaped bulb; pear-shaped switch

peral m pear tree

perca f (ichth) perch

percance m mischance, misfortune; **percances** perquisites

percatar ref — **percatarse de** to be aware of; beware of, guard against

percebe m barnacle; fool, sap

percepción f perception; collection

percibir tr to perceive; collect

percudir tr to tarnish, dull; spread through

percha f perch, pole, roost; clothes tree; coat hanger; coat hook; barber pole

perchero m rack, clothes rack, clothes hanger

perde•dor -dora adj losing || mf loser

perder §51 tr to lose; waste, squander; (un tren, una ocasión) miss; (una asignatura) flunk; ruin; spoil || intr to lose; fade || ref to get lost; miscarry; sink; become ruined; spoil; go to the dogs

perdición f perdition; loss; outrage; ruination

pérdida f loss; waste; ruination; **no tener pérdida** to be easy to find; **pérdida de reclamable** tax loss

perdi•do -da adj (bala) stray, wild; (manga) wide, loose; fruitless; (horas) off, spare, idle; distracted; inveterate; madly in love || m profligate, rake

perdido•so -sa adj unlucky; easily lost

perdigón m young partridge; profligate; heavy loser; (alumno) failure; **perdigones** (granos de plomo) shot; **perdigón zorrero** buckshot

per•diz f (pl **-dices**) partridge

perdón m pardon, forgiveness; **con perdón** by your leave

perdonable adj pardonable

perdonar tr to pardon, forgive, excuse; **no perdonar** to not miss, not omit

perdula•rio -ria adj careless, sloppy; incorrigible, vicious || mf good-for-nothing, profligate

perdurable adj long-lasting; everlasting

perdurar intr to last, last a long time, survive

perecede•ro -ra adj perishable; mortal || m extreme want

perecer §22 intr to perish; suffer; be in great want || ref to pine; **perecerse por** to be dying for; (una mujer) be mad about

peregrinación f peregrination; pilgrimage

peregri•no -na adj wandering, traveling; foreign; rare, strange; beautiful; mortal; (ave) migratory || mf pilgrim

perejil m parsley; (coll) frippery

perenne adj perennial

pereza f laziness; slowness

perezo•so -sa adj lazy; slow, dull, heavy || mf lazybones; sleepyhead || m (zool) sloth

perfección f perfection

perfeccionar tr to perfect, improve

perfec•to -ta adj & m perfect

perfidia f perfidy

pérfi•do -da adj perfidious

perfil m profile; side view; cross section; thin stroke; outline, sketch; **perfil aerodinámico** streamlining; **perfiles** finishing touches; courtesies

perfila•do -da adj (cara) long and thin; (nariz) well-formed; (facciones) delicate; streamlined

perfilar tr to profile, outline; perfect, polish, finish || ref to be outlined; show one's profile, stand sidewise; stand out; dress up

perforación f perforation; drilling; puncture; keypunching

perfora•dor -dora adj perforating; drilling || f pneumatic drill, rock drill

perforar tr to perforate; drill, bore; puncture; (una tarjeta) punch

perforista mf keypuncher

perfumar tr to perfume

perfume m perfume

pergamino m parchment

pergenio m rascal

pericia f skill, expertness

periclitar intr to be in jeopardy, be shaky

perico m (pelo postizo) periwig; parakeet; (slang) chamber pot; (CAm) compliment; **perico entre ellas** lady's man

periferia f periphery; surroundings

perifollos mpl finery, frippery, chiffons

perilla f pear-shaped ornament; goatee; knob, doorknob; (del arzón) pommel; (de la oreja) lobe; **de perilla** apropos, to the point

periodísti•co -ca adj newspaper, journalistic

periódi•co -ca adj periodic || m newspaper; periodical

periodismo m journalism

periodista mf journalist || m newspaperman || f newspaperwoman

período m period; compound sentence; (phys) cycle; **período lectivo** (en la escuela) term

peripues•to -ta adj dudish, all spruced up, sporty

periquete m jiffy; **en un periquete** in a jiffy

periquito m parakeet; **periquito de Australia** budgerigar

periscopio m periscope

peri•to -ta adj skilled, skillful; expert || m expert

perjudicar §73 tr to damage, impair, hurt, prejudice

perjudicial adj harmful, injurious, detrimental, prejudicial

perjuicio m harm, injury, damage, prejudice; **en perjuicio de** to the detriment of

perjurar intr to commit perjury; swear, be profane || ref to commit perjury; perjure oneself

perjurio m perjury

perla f pearl; **de perlas** perfectly

perlesía f palsy

permanecer §22 intr to stay, remain

permanencia f permanence; stay, sojourn

pe
pe

permanente *adj* permanent ‖ *f* permanent wave
permiso *m* permission; permit; time off; (*en el monedaje*) tolerance; leave; **con permiso** excuse me; **permiso de circulación** owner's license; **permiso de conducir** driver's license
permitir *tr* to permit, allow ‖ *ref* to be permitted; **no se permite fumar** no smoking
permutar *tr* to interchange; barter; to permute
pernear *intr* to kick; hustle; fuss, fret
pernera *f* trouser leg
pernicio•so -sa *adj* pernicious
pernil *m* trouser leg; (*anca y muslo*) ham
perno *m* bolt; **perno con anillo** ringbolt; **perno roscado** screw bolt
pernoctar *intr* to spend the night
pero *conj* but, yet ‖ *m* but; fault, defect; **poner pero a** to find fault with
perogrullada *f* platitude, inanity
peroración *f* peroration; harangue
perorar *intr* to perorate; orate
peróxido *m* peroxide; **peróxido de hidrógeno** hydrogen peroxide
perpendicular *adj & f* perpendicular
perpetrar *tr* to perpetrate
perpetuar §21 *tr* to perpetuate
perpe•tuo -tua *adj* perpetual; life
perplejidad *f* perplexity; worry, anxiety
perple•jo -ja *adj* perplexed; worried, anxious; baffling, perplexing
perra *f* bitch; tantrum; drunkenness
perrada *f* pack of dogs; dirty trick
perrera *f* kennel, doghouse; tantrum; toil, drudgery
perro *m* dog; **el perro del hortelano** dog in the manger; **perro caliente** (slang) hot dog; **perro cobrador** retriever; **perro de aguas** spaniel; **perro de lanas** poodle; **perro de muestra** pointer; **perro faldero** lap dog; **perro marino** dogfish, shark; **perro raposero** foxhound; **perro viejo** (coll) wise old owl
perro-lazarillo *m* (*pl* **perros-lazarillos**) Seeing Eye dog
persa *adj & mf* Persian
persecución *f* persecution; pursuit; annoyance, harassment
perseguir §67 *tr* to persecute; pursue; annoy, harass
perseverar *intr* to persevere
persiana *f* slatted shutter; flowered silk; louver; Venetian blind; **persiana del radiador** (aut) louver
persistir *intr* to persist
persona *f* person; personage; **persona desplazada** displaced person; **personas** people; **por persona** per capita
personaje *m* personage; (theat) character; person of importance
personal *adj* personal ‖ *m* personnel, staff, force
personalidad *f* personality
personificar §73 *tr* to personify

perspectiva *f* perspective; outlook, prospect; appearance
perspi•caz *adj* (*pl* **-caces**) perspicacious, discerning; keen-sighted
persuadir *tr* to persuade
persuasión *f* persuasion
pertenecer §22 *intr* to belong; pertain ‖ *ref* to be independent, be free
perteneciente *adj* pertaining
pértiga *f* pole, rod, staff
perti•naz *adj* (*pl* **-naces**) pertinacious; (*dolor de cabeza*) persistent
pertinente *adj* pertinent, relevant
pertrechos *mpl* supplies, provisions, equipment; tools; **pertrechos de guerra** ordnance
perturbar *tr* to perturb; disturb; upset, disconcert; confuse, interrupt
Perú, el Perú
perua•no -na *adj & mf* Peruvian
perversidad *f* perversity
perversión *f* perversion
perver•so -sa *adj* perverse; wicked, depraved ‖ *mf* profligate
perverti•do -da *mf* pervert
pervertir §68 *tr* to pervert ‖ *ref* to become perverted; go to the bad
pesa *f* weight; (CAm, Col, Ven) butcher shop
pesacar•tas *m* (*pl* **-tas**) letter scales
pesadez *f* heaviness; slowness; tiresomeness; harshness; (phys) gravity
pesadilla *f* nightmare
pesa•do -da *adj* heavy; slow; tiresome; harsh; boring
pesadumbre *f* sorrow, grief; trouble; weight, heaviness
pesaje *m* weighing; (sport) weigh-in
pésame *m* condolence; **dar el pésame a** to extend one's sympathy to
pesantez *f* (phys) gravity
pesar *m* sorrow, regret; **a pesar de** in spite of ‖ *tr* to weigh; make sorry ‖ *intr* to weigh; be heavy; cause regret, cause sorrow
pesaro•so -sa *adj* sorrowful, regretful
pesca *f* fishing; catch; **ir de pesca** to go fishing; **pesca de bajura** off-shore fishing; **pesca de gran altura** deep-sea fishing
pescadería *f* fish market; fish store; fish stand
pescade•ro -ra *mf* fish dealer, fishmonger
pescado *m* fish (*that has been caught*)
pesca•dor -dora *adj* fishing ‖ *m* fisherman ‖ *f* fisherwoman, fishwife
pescante *m* coach box; (*de una grúa*) jib; (aut) front seat; (naut) davit; (theat) trap door
pescar §73 *tr* to fish; fish for; fish out; (*peces*) catch; (coll) to manage to get ‖ *intr* to fish
pescozón *m* slap on the neck or head
pescuezo *m* neck
pesebre *m* crib, rack, manger; crèche
pesero *m* (CAm, Col, Ven) butcher; (Mex) shared taxi
pesimismo *m* pessimism
pesimista *adj* pessimistic ‖ *mf* pessimist
pési•mo -ma *adj* very bad, abominable

peso *m* weight; scale, balance; burden, load; judgment, good sense; (*unidad monetaria*) peso; **caerse de su peso** to be self-evident; **llevar el peso de la batalla** to bear the brunt of the battle; **peso atómico** atomic weight; **peso molecular** molecular weight

pespuntar *tr & intr* to backstitch

pespunte *m* backstitch

pesquera *f* fishery; fishing grounds; (*presa para detener los peces*) weir

pesquería *f* fishing; fishery

pesque•ro -ra *adj* fishing ‖ *m* fishing boat ‖ *f* see **pesquera**

pesquis *m* acumen, keenness

pesquisa *m* (Arg) detective ‖ *f* inquiry, investigation

pesquisar *tr* to investigate, inquire into

pestaña *f* eyelash; flange; fringe, edging; index tab

pestañear *intr* to wink, blink; **sin pestañear** without batting an eye

peste *f* pest, plague; epidemic; stink, stench; abundance; (Col, Peru) head cold; (Chile) smallpox; **pestes** insults

pesticida *m* pesticide

pestífe•ro -ra *adj* pestiferous; stinking

pestilencia *f* pestilence

pestillo *m* bolt; doorlatch

petaca *f* cigar case; cigarette case; tobacco pouch; leather-covered hamper

pétalo *m* petal

petardear *tr* to swindle ‖ *intr* (aut) to backfire

petardeo *m* swindling; (aut) backfire

petardo *m* petard; bomb; swindle, cheat

petate *m* sleeping bag; bedding; luggage; cheat; poor soul; **liar el petate** to pack up and get out; to kick the bucket

petición *f* petition; request; plea; (law) claim, bill; **a petición de** at the request of; **petición de mano** formal betrothal

petimetre *m* dude, sport, dandy

petirrojo *m* redbreast, robin

Petrarca *m* Petrarch

petrificar §73 *tr & ref* to petrify

petróleo *m* petroleum; **petróleo combustible** fuel oil

petrole•ro -ra *adj* oil, petroleum ‖ *mf* oil dealer ‖ *m* oil tanker

petroquími•co -ca *adj* petrochemical

petulancia *f* flippancy, pertness

petulante *adj* flippant, pert

pez *m* (*pl* **peces**) fish; reward, just desert; **como un pez en el agua** snug as a bug in a rug; **pez de plata** (ent) silverfish; **salga pez o salga rana** blindly, hit or miss ‖ *f* pitch, tar

pezón *m* stem; nipple, teat

pezonera *f* linchpin

pezuña *f* hoof

piado•so -sa *adj* merciful; pitiful; pious

piafar *intr* (*el caballo*) to paw, to stamp

piano *m* piano; **piano de cola** grand piano; **piano de media cola** baby grand

piar §77 *intr* to peep, chirp

pica *f* pike; pikeman; picador's goad; (Col) pique, resentment

picada *f* peck; bite; (Bol) knock at the door; (Arg, Bol, Urug) narrow ford; (SAm) path, trail

picadillo *m* (*carne, verduras, ajos, etc. reducidos a pequeños trozos*) hash; (*carne picada*) mincemeat

pica•do -da *adj* perforated; pitted; (*tabaco*) cut; (*hielo*) cracked; (*mar*) choppy; piqued ‖ *m* mincemeat; (aer) dive; **picado con motor** (aer) power dive ‖ *f* see **picada**

picador *m* horsebreaker; (*torero de a caballo*) picador (*mounted bullfighter*); chopping block; meat grinder

picadura *f* bite, prick, sting; nick; puncture; cut tobacco; (*en un diente*) cavity

picaflor *m* hummingbird

picahie•los *m* (*pl* **-los**) ice pick

picamade•ros *m* (*pl* **-ros**) green woodpecker

picante *adj* biting, pricking, stinging; piquant, juicy, racy; (SAm) highly seasoned ‖ *m* mordancy; piquancy

pícap *m* (Bol, Chile, Col) var of **pick-up**

picapedrero *m* stonecutter

picaplei•tos *m* (*pl* **-tos**) troublemaker; shyster, pettifogger

picaporte *m* latch; latchkey; door knocker

picar §73 *tr* to prick, pierce, puncture; sting; bite; burn; peck; nibble; pit, pock; mince, chop up, cut up; stick, poke; spur; goad; perforate; (*hielo*) crack; harass, pursue; tame; pique, annoy ‖ *intr* to itch; (*el sol*) burn; nibble; have a smattering; be catching; (*los negocios*) pick up; (aer) to dive; (*caer en el lazo*) (coll) to bite; **picar en** to nibble at; dabble in; **picar muy alto** aim high, expect too much ‖ *ref* to rot; (*la ropa*) be moth-eaten; (*el vino*) turn sour; (*un diente*) be decayed; (*el mar*) get rough; be offended; get drunk; (*drogas*) get a fix, shoot up; **picarse de** to boast of being

picardía *f* roguishness, knavery; crudeness, coarseness; mischief

picares•co -ca *adj* roguish, rascally; picaresque; rough, coarse, crude; witty, humorous

píca•ro -ra *adj* roguish; scheming, tricky; low, vile; mischievous ‖ *mf* rogue; schemer

picaza *f* magpie

picazón *f* itch, itching; annoyance

pícea *f* spruce tree

pick-up *m* pickup; phonograph

pico *m* beak, bill; (*de jarra*) spout; (*del yunque*) beak; (*del pañuelo*) corner; nib, tip; (*de la pluma de escribir*) point; peak; (*herramienta*) pick; (*de dinero*) pile, lot; talkativeness; (elec) peak; (naut) bow, prow; **callar el pico** to shut up; **darse el pico** (*las palomas*) to bill; **pico de oro** silver-tongue; **tener mucho pico** to talk too much; **y pico** odd, e.g., **trescientos y pico** three hundred odd; a little after, e.g., **a las tres y pico** a little after three o'clock

picor *m* (*del paladar*) smarting; itch, itching, burning

pico•so -sa *adj* pock-marked

picota *f* pillory; peak, point, spire

picotazo *m* peck

pe
pi

picotear *tr* to peck ‖ *intr* (*el caballo*) to toss the head; chatter, jabber, gab; (*las mujeres*) wrangle
pichel *m* pewter tankard
pichón -chona *mf* darling ‖ *m* young pigeon; **pichón de barro** clay pigeon
pie *m* foot; footing; foothold; base, stand; (*de copa*) stem; (*de la cama*) footboard; cause, origin, reason; (*de la página*) foot, bottom; (theat) cue; (Chile) down payment; **a cuatro pies** on all fours; **al pie de fábrica** at the factory; **al pie de la letra** literally; **al pie de la obra** (com) delivered; **a pie** on foot, walking; **buscar cinco** (or **tres**) **pies al gato** to be looking for trouble; **de pie** standing; up and about; firm, steady; firmly, steadily; **en pie de guerra** on a war footing; **ir a pie** to go on foot, to walk; **morir al pie del cañón** to die in the harness, to die with one's boots on; **nacer de pie** or **de pies** to be born with a silver spoon in one's mouth; **pie de atleta** athlete's foot; **pie de cabra** crowbar; **pie de imprenta** imprint, printer's mark; **pie derecho** upright, stanchion; **pie marino** sea legs; **pie plano** flatfoot; **pie quebrado** (*de verso*) short line; **vestirse por los pies** to be a man
piedad *f* (*devoción a las cosas santas*) piety; (*misericordia*) pity, mercy
piedra *f* stone; rock; (*pedernal*) flint; heavy hailstone; (pathol) stone; **piedra angular** cornerstone; (fig) cornerstone, keystone; **piedra arenisca** sandstone; **piedra azul** (chem) bluestone; **piedra de albardilla** copestone; **piedra de amolar** grindstone; **piedra de chispa** flint; **piedra de pipas** meerschaum; **piedra imán** loadstone; **piedra miliar** or **miliaria** milestone; **piedra movediza** rolling stone; **piedra pómez** pumice, pumice stone
piel *f* skin; hide, pelt; fur; leather; (*de las frutas*) peel, skin; **piel de cabra** goatskin; **piel de foca** sealskin; **piel de gallina** goose flesh ‖ *m* — **piel roja** (*pl* **pieles rojas**) (*indio norteamericano*) redskin
pienso *m* feed, feeding; **ni por pienso** by no means, don't think of it
pierna *f* leg; post, upright; **dormir a pierna suelta** or **tendida** to sleep like a log; **estirar la pierna** to lie down on the job; kick the bucket; **estirar** or **extender las piernas** to stretch one's legs, go for a walk; **ser buena pierna** (Arg, Urug) to be a good-natured fellow
pieza *f* (*órgano de una máquina o artefacto; obra dramática; composición suelta de múscia; cañón; figura que sirve para jugar a las damas, al ajedrez, etc.; moneda*) piece; (*objeto; mueble; porción de tela*) piece or article; (*habitación, cuarto*) room; **buena pieza** hussy; sly fox; **pieza de recambio** or **de repuesto** spare part; **quedarse en una pieza** or **hecho una pieza** to be dumbfounded, stand motionless
pífano *m* fife; fifer
pifia *f* (billiards) miscue; (coll) miscue, slip

pifiar *intr* to miscue
pigmentar *tr* & *ref* to pigment
pigmento *m* pigment
pigme•o -a *adj* & *mf* pygmy
pijama *f* pajamas
pila *f* basin; trough; sink; font; pile, heap; (elec) battery, cell; (elec & phys) pile; **pila de linterna** flashlight battery
pilar *m* (*de una fuente*) basin, bowl; pillar; stone post, milestone; (*persona*) (fig) pillar ‖ *tr* (*el grano*) to crush, pound
Pilatos *m* Pilate
píldora *f* pill; bad news; **píldora para dormir** sleeping pill
pileta *f* sink; basin; bowl; font; swimming pool
pilón *m* pylon; drinking trough; loaf of sugar; counterpoise; drop hammer; (Mex, Ven) tip, gratuity; **de pilón** in addition, on top of it
pilotar *tr* to pilot
pilote *m* pile
piloto *m* pilot; first mate; (Chile) hail fellow well met
pillar *tr* to pillage, plunder; catch
pi•llo -lla *adj* roguish, rascally; sly, crafty ‖ *m* rogue, rascal; crafty fellow
pilluelo *m* scamp, little scamp
pimentero *m* pepper, black pepper; pepperbox
pimentón *m* cayenne pepper, red pepper; (*condimento preparado moliendo pimientos encarnados secos*) paprika
pimienta *f* pepper, black pepper; allspice, pimento; allspice tree
pimiento *m* (*planta*) pepper, black pepper; Guinea pepper
pimpante *adj* smart, spruce
pimpollo *m* sucker, shoot, sprout; rosebud; (*árbol nuevo*) sapling; handsome child; handsome young person
pina *f* fellow
pinacoteca *f* picture gallery
pináculo *m* pinnacle
pincel *m* brush; painter; painting; (*de luz*) pencil, beam
pincelada *f* brush stroke; touch, finish, flourish
pincelar *tr* to paint; picture; (med) to pencil
pincia•no -na *adj* Valladolid ‖ *mf* native or inhabitant of Valladolid
pincha *f* kitchenmaid
pinchar *tr* to prick, jab, pierce, puncture; stir up, prod, provoke ‖ *intr* to have a puncture; **no pinchar ni cortar** to have no say ‖ *ref* (*drogas*) to get a fix, shoot up
pinchazo *m* prick, jab, puncture; provocation; **a prueba de pinchazos** punctureproof
pinche *m* scullion, kitchen boy; helper
pincho *m* thorn, prick; snack; spike
Píndaro *m* Pindar
pingajo *m* rag, tatter
pingo *m* rag, tatter; ragamuffin; horse; **andar** or **ir de pingo** (*una mujer*) to gad about
pingüe *adj* oily, greasy, fat; abundant, rich; fertile; profitable

pingüino *m* penguin

pinito *m* first step, little step; **hacer pinitos** to begin to walk; (fig) to take the first steps

pino *m* pine tree; first step; **hacer pinos** to begin to walk; (fig) to take the first steps

pinocha *f* pine needle

pinta *m* scoundrel ‖ *f* spot, mark, sign; dot; pint

pintacilgo *m* goldfinch

pintada *f* Guinea hen

pinta•do -da *adj* spotted, mottled; tipsy; accented; **el más pintado** the aptest one; the shrewdest one; the best one; **venir como pintado** to be just the thing ‖ *m* (*acto de pintar*) painting ‖ *f* see **pintada**

pintar *tr* to paint; (*una letra, un acento, etc.*) draw; picture, depict; put an accent mark on; **pintarla** to put it on, put on airs ‖ *intr* to paint; begin to turn red, begin to ripen; show, turn out ‖ *ref* to paint, put on make-up; begin to turn red, begin to ripen

pintarrajear *tr* to daub, smear

pin•to -ta *adj* speckled, spotted ‖ *f* see **pinta**

pin•tor -tora *mf* painter; **pintor de brocha gorda** painter, house painter; dauber

pintores•co -ca *adj* picturesque

pintura *f* (*color preparado para pintar*) paint; (*arte; obra pintada*) painting; **hacer pinturas** to prance; **no poder ver ni en pintura** to not be able to stand the sight of

pinture•ro -ra *adj* showy, conceited ‖ *mf* show-off

pinza *f* clothespin; (*de langosta, cangrejo, etc.*) claw; **pinzas** pliers; pincers; tweezers; forceps

pinzón *m* pump handle; (orn) finch

piña *f* fir cone, pine cone; knob; plug; cluster, knot; pineapple

piñonear *intr* (*un arma de fuego*) to click; reach the age of puberty; (coll) to be an old goat

piñoneo *m* click (*of a firearm*)

pí•o -a *adj* pious; merciful, compassionate; (*caballo*) pied, dappled ‖ *m* peeping, chirping; keen desire

piocha *f* jeweled head adornment; artificial flower made of feathers; pick

piojo *m* louse

piojo•so -sa *adj* lousy; mean, stingy

piola *f* string, cord

pione•ro -ra *adj* & *mf* pioneer

pipa *f* (*para fumar tabaco*) pipe; (*medida para vinos*) butt; wine cask; (*simiente*) pip; (mus) pipe, reed; (coll) handgun; **pipa de espuma de mar** meerschaum pipe; **pipa de riego** watering cart; **pipa de tierra** clay pipe

pipí *m* (coll) pee, urine; **hacer pipí** to pee, urinate

pipiolo *m* (CAm, Mex) child

pique *m* pique, resentment; eagerness; (*insecto*) chigger; (*naipe*) spade; **a pique** steep; **a pique de** in danger of; on the verge of; **echar a pique** to sink; ruin; **irse a pique** to sink; go to ruin, be ruined

piquera *f* bung, bunghole; (Mex) dive, joint

piquete *m* sharp jab; small hole; stake, picket; (*de soldados, de huelguistas*) picket; **piquete de ejecución** firing squad; **piquete de salvas** firing squad

pira *f* pyre

piragua *f* pirogue; (sport) single shell

piragüismo *m* canoeing

piragüista *m* (sport) crewman

pirámide *f* pyramid

pirata *m* pirate; **pirata aéreo** hijacker

piratear *intr* to pirate, be a pirate

piratería *f* piracy; **piratería aérea** hijacking, skyjacking, air piracy

pirca *f* (SAm) dry stone wall

pirco *m* (Chile) succotash

Pireo, el Piraeus

pirine•o -a *adj* Pyrenean ‖ **Pirineos** *mpl* Pyrenees

pirita *f* pyrites

piró•fa•go -ga *adj* fire-eating ‖ *mf* fire-eater

piropear *tr* to flatter, flirt with

piropo *m* garnet, carbuncle; flattery, compliment, flirtatious remark

piróscafo *m* steamship

pirotecnia *f* pyrotechnics

pirotécni•co -ca *adj* pyrotechnical ‖ *m* powder maker, fireworks manufacturer

pirueta *f* pirouette; somersault; caper

piruetear *intr* to pirouette

pisada *f* tread; footstep; footprint; trampling

pisapape•les *m* (*pl* **-les**) paperweight

pisar *tr* to trample, tread on, step on; tamp, pack down; (*p.ej., uvas*) tread; cover part of; ram; (*una tecla*) strike; (mus) to pluck; (coll) to abuse, tread all over; **pisar algo a alguien** to snitch something from someone ‖ *intr* to be right above; step ‖ *ref* (Arg) to guess wrong, come out wrong

pisaverde *m* fop, dandy

piscina *f* swimming pool; fishpond

Piscis *m* (astr) Pisces

pisco *m* Peruvian brandy

pisicorre *f* (W-I) station wagon

piso *m* tread; floor; flooring; (*de una carretera*) surface; flat, apartment; **buscar piso** to be looking for a place to live; **piso alto** top floor; **piso bajo** street floor, ground floor; **piso principal** main floor, second floor

pisón *m* ram, tamper

pisotear *tr* to trample, tread on, tread under foot; abuse, tread all over

pisotón *m* stamp, tread

pista *f* track; trace, trail; clew; race track; (*de bolera*) alley; (*de cabaret*) floor; (aer) runway; **pista de esquí** ski run; **pista de patinar** skating rink

pisto *m* (*para los enfermos*) chicken broth; vegetable cutlet; jumbled speech or writing; mess; (CAm, Mex) money

pistola *f* pistol; sprayer; rock drill; **pistola de arzón** horse pistol; **pistola engrasadora** grease gun

pistolera *f* holster

pistolerismo *m* gangsterism

pistolero *m* gangster, gunman

pistón *m* piston

pistonear *intr* to knock
pistoneo *m* knock
pistonu•do -da *adj* stunning, swank
pita *f* century plant; hiss, hissing; glass marble; string, thread
pitar *tr* to pay, pay off; (*a un torero*) whistle disapproval of ‖ *intr* to blow a whistle, whistle; blow the horn, honk; talk nonsense; **no pitar** to not be popular; **salir pitando** to run away, dash away
pitazo *m* blast, toot, honk, whistle (sound)
pitear *intr* to whistle
pitillera *f* cigarette maker; cigarette case
pitillo *m* cigarette
pito *m* whistle; horn; fife; fifer; cigarette; jackstone; (*insecto*) tick; woodpecker; (coll) continental, straw, tinker's damn
pitón *m* lump, sprig; tenderling; (*del cuerno*) tip; nozzle, spout; python
pitonisa *f* witch, siren; pythoness
pitu•so -sa *adj* tiny, cute ‖ *mf* tot
piular *intr* to peep, chirp
pivotar *intr* to pivot
pivote *m* pivot; **pivote de dirección** (aut) kingpin
píxide *f* pyx
pizarra *f* slate; blackboard
pizarrero *m* roofer, slater
pizarrín *m* slate pencil
pizca *f* mite, whit, jot
placa *f* plaque, tablet; badge; plate; slab, sheet; scab; (anat, elec, electron, phot, zool) plate; **placa de matrícula** license plate; **placa giratoria** (*de ferrocarril; de gramófono*) turntable
placaminero *m* persimmon
placebo *m* placebo
pláceme *m* congratulation
placente•ro -ra *adj* pleasant, agreeable
placer *m* pleasure; sandbank, reef; **a placer** at one's convenience ‖ *v* §52 *tr* to please
place•ro -ra *adj* public ‖ *mf* market vendor; loafer, town gossip
pláci•do -da *adj* placid; pleasing
plaga *f* plague; pest; scourge; abundance; sore; clime, region
plagar §44 *tr* to plague, infest; (*de minas*) sow
plagiar *tr* to plagiarize
plagio *m* plagiarism; abduction, kidnaping
plan *m* plan; level, height; **plan de estudios** or **plan escolar** curriculum
plana *f* plain, flat country; trowel; cooper's plane; page
plancha *f* plate, sheet; iron, flatiron; gangplank; (coll) blunder; **a la plancha** grilled; (*huevo*) fried; **plancha de blindaje** armor plate
planchado *m* ironing; pressing
planchar *tr* (*la ropa interior blanca*) to iron; (*un traje de hombre*) to press ‖ *intr* to be a wallflower
planchear *tr* to plate
planear *tr* to plan, outline; (*una tabla*) plane ‖ *intr* to hover; (aer) to volplane, glide
planeta *m* planet
planicie *f* plain

planificar §73 *tr* to plan
planilla *f* list, roll, schedule; (*de candidatos para un puesto público*) (Mex) panel; (Mex) ballot; (Mex) commutation ticket
pla•no -na *adj* plane; level, smooth, even; flat ‖ *m* plan; map; (*superficie*) plane; (aer) plane; **de plano** clearly, plainly, flatly; flat; **levantar un plano** to make a survey; **primer plano** foreground ‖ *f* see **plana**
planta *f* (*del pie*) sole; foot; plan; project; floor plan; (*del personal de una oficina*) roster; plant, factory; (bot) plant; (sport) stance; **de planta** from the ground up; **echar plantas** to swagger, bully; **planta baja** ground floor; **planta del sortilegio** (bot) witch hazel; **tener buena planta** to make a fine appearance
plantar *tr* to plant; establish, found; (*un golpe*) plant; jilt; (*en la calle, en la cárcel*) throw ‖ *ref* to take a stand; gang together; (*un animal*) balk; land, arrive
plantear *tr* to plan, outline; establish, execute, carry out; state, set up, expound, pose
plantel *m* nursery garden; educational establishment
plantificar §73 *tr* to plan, outline; (*un golpe*) plant; (*en la calle, la cárcel*) throw ‖ *ref* to land, arrive
plantilla *f* plantlet, young plant; insole; reinforced sole; model, pattern, template; (*de empleados*) staff; (*del personal de una oficina*) roster; plan, design; (*bizcocho*) ladyfinger
plantío *m* planting; garden patch; tree nursery
plantón *m* (*que ha de ser transplantado*) shoot; graft; guard, watchman; waiting, standing around
plañide•ro -ra *adj* mournful, plaintive ‖ *f* hired mourner
plañir §12 *tr* to lament, grieve over ‖ *intr* to lament, grieve, bewail
plasma *m* plasma
plasmar *tr* to mold, shape
plasta *f* paste, soft mass; flattened object; poor job, bungle
plástica *f* (*arte de plasmar*) plastic; plastic arts
plásti•co -ca *adj* plastic ‖ *m* (*substancia*) plastic ‖ *f* see **plástica**
plata *f* silver; (*moneda o monedas*) silver; wealth; money; **en plata** briefly, to the point; plainly; **plata de ley** sterling silver
plataforma *f* platform; platform car; (*del ferrocarril*) roadbed; (*programa político*) platform; (*de lanzamiento de cohete*) pad; **plataforma giratoria** (rr) turntable
platal *m* piles of money, fortune
platanal *m* or **platanar** *m* banana plantation
plátano *m* banana; banana tree; plane tree; **plátano de occidente** buttonwood tree
platea *f* (theat) orchestra, parquet
platea•do -da *adj* silvered; silver-plated; (coll) well-to-do
platear *tr* to silver, coat or plate with silver
platero *m* silversmith; jeweler

plática f talk, chat; talk, informal lecture; sermon

platicar §73 tr to talk over, discuss ‖ intr to talk, chat; discuss; preach

platillo m plate; saucer; (de la balanza) pan; (mus) cymbal; **platillo volador** or **volante** flying saucer

platino m platinum

plato m dish; plate; (de una comida) course; daily fare; **plato fuerte** main course; **plato giratorio** (del gramófono) turntable

pla•tó m (pl -tós) (mov) set

Platón m Plato

platu•do -da adj rich

plausible adj praiseworthy; acceptable

playa f beach, shore, strand; **playa infantil** sand pile

playera f fishwoman; beach shoe

plaza f plaza, square; market place; town, city; fortified town; space, room; yard; office, employment; character, reputation; seat; **sentar plaza** to enlist; **plaza de armas** parade ground; public square; **plaza de gallos** cockpit; **plaza de toros** bullring; **plaza mayor** main square

plazo m term; time; time limit; date of payment; instalment; **a plazo** on credit, on time; **en plazos** in installments

pleamar f high tide, high water

plebe f common people

plebe•yo -ya adj & mf plebeian

plegadi•zo -za adj folding; pliable

plegar §66 tr to fold; crease; pleat ‖ ref to yield, give in

plegaria f prayer; noon call to prayer

pleito m litigation, lawsuit; dispute, quarrel; fight; **pleito de acreedores** bankruptcy proceedings; **pleito homenaje** (feud) homage; **pleito viciado** mistrial

plenilunio m full moon

plenitud f fullness, abundance

ple•no -na adj full; **en plena marcha** in full swing; **en pleno rostro** right in the face

pleuresía f pleurisy

pliego m (de papel) sheet; folder; cover, envelope; bid, specification; sealed letter; printer's proof

pliegue m fold, crease, pleat; **pliegue de tabla** box pleat

plisar tr to pleat

plomada f carpenter's lead pencil; plummet; plumb bob; sinker, sinkers; scourge tipped with lead balls

plomar tr to seal with lead

plomazo m (Guat, Mex, W-I) gunshot

plomería f lead roofing; leadwork, plumbing

plomero m lead worker; plumber

plomi•zo -za adj lead, leaden

plomo m lead; (pedazo de plomo; bala) lead; (elec) fuse; (coll) bore; **a plomo** plumb, perpendicularly; straight down; just right

pluma f feather; quill; plume; pen; faucet; (CAm) hoax; (Chile) crane, derrick; **pluma esferográfica** ball-point pen; **pluma estilográfica** or **pluma fuente** fountain pen

plumaje m plumage

plúmbe•o -a adj lead

plumero m (caja o vaso para las plumas) penholder; feather duster

plumífe•ro -ra adj (escritor) hack, secondrate; (poet) feathered ‖ m padded or quilted jacket, ski jacket; hack writer; newshound

plumilla f small feather; (de la pluma fuente) point, tip; (Ven) ball-point pen

plumón m down; feather bed; (Mex) felt-tipped pen

plumo•so -sa adj downy, feathery

plural adj & m plural

pluriempleo m moonlighting

plus m extra, bonus

plusmarca f (sport) record

plusmarquista mf (sport) record breaker

plusvalía f appreciation (in value)

Plutarco m Plutarch

plutonio m plutonium

población f population; village, town, city

poblada f (SAm) riot, mob

pobla•do -da adj thick, bushy ‖ m town, community ‖ f see **poblada**

poblar §61 tr to people, populate; found, settle, colonize; (un estanque, una colmena) stock; (con árboles) plant ‖ intr to settle, colonize; multiply, be prolific ‖ ref to become full, covered, or crowded

pobre adj poor ‖ mf pauper; beggar

pobreza f poverty, want; poorness

pocilga f pigpen

poción f potion, dose

po•co -ca adj & pron (comp & super **menos**) little; few, e.g., **poca gente** few people; **pocos** few; **unos pocos** a few ‖ **poco** adv little; **a poco** shortly afterwards; **a poco de** shortly after; **dentro de poco** shortly; **por poco** almost, nearly; **tener en poco** to hold in low esteem, think little of; **un poco (de)** a little

po•cho -cha adj faded, discolored; overripe; rotten; (Chile) chubby

podar tr to prune, to trim

podenco m hound

poder m power; power of attorney, proxy; **el cuarto poder** the fourth estate; **obra en mi poder** I have at hand, I have in my possession; **poder adquisitivo** purchasing power ‖ v §53 intr to be possible; be able, have power or strength; **a más no poder** as hard as possible; **no poder con** to not be able to stand, not be able to manage; **no poder más** to be exhausted, be all in; **no poder menos de** to not be able to keep from, not be able to help ‖ v aux to be able to, may, can, might, could; **no poder ver** to not be able to stand

poderhabiente mf attorney, proxy

poderío m power, might; wealth, riches; sway, dominion

podero•so -sa adj powerful, mighty; wealthy, rich

podio m podium

podre f pus

podredumbre f corruption, putrefaction; pus; deep grief

poema m poem

pi
po

poesía *f* poetry; poem; **bella poesía** (fig) fairy tale
poeta *m* poet
poéti•co -ca *adj* poetic(al) ‖ *f* poetics
poetisa *f* poetess
pola•co -ca *adj* Polish ‖ *mf* Pole ‖ *m* (*idioma*) Polish
polaina *f* legging
polar *adj* pole; polar ‖ *f* polestar
polarizar §60 *tr* to polarize
polea *f* pulley
poleame *m* (naut) tackle
polen *m* pollen
policía *m* policeman ‖ *f* police; policing; politeness; cleanliness; neatness; **policía urbana** street cleaning
policía•co -ca or policial *adj* police; (*novela*) detective
polifacéti•co -ca *adj* many-sided
políga•mo -ma *adj* polygamous ‖ *mf* polygamist
poliglo•to -ta *adj* polyglot ‖ *mf* polyglot, linguist
polígono *m* polygon
polígrafo *m* prolific writer; copying machine; ball-point pen; lie detector
polilla *f* moth
Polimnia *f* Polyhymnia
polinizar §60 *tr* to pollinate
polinomio *m* polynomial
polio *f* (path) polio
pólipo *m* polyp
polisón *m* bustle
polista *mf* poloist, polo player
politeísta *adj* polytheistic ‖ *mf* polytheist
política *f* politics; policy; manners, politeness, courtesy; **política de café** parlor politics; **política del buen vecino** Good Neighbor Policy
políti•co -ca *adj* political; politic, tactful; polite, courteous; -in-law; e.g., **padre político** father-in-law ‖ *mf* politician ‖ *f* see **política**
polivalente *adj* manifold; (chem, bact) polyvalent
póliza *f* policy, contract; draft, check; customhouse permit; **póliza de seguro** insurance policy
polizón *m* bum, tramp; stowaway
polizonte *m* cop, policeman
polo *m* pole; popsicle; (*juego*) polo; **polo de agua** water polo; **polo de atracción popular** drawing card
pololear *tr* to bother, annoy; (Chile) to flirt with
polo•lo -la *adj* (Chile) youngster ‖ *m* (Chile) flirt; side job
Polonia *f* Poland
pol•trón -trona *adj* idle, lazy, comfort-loving ‖ *f* easy chair
polución *f* (*del ambiente*) pollution
polvareda *f* cloud of dust; rumpus
polvera *f* compact, powder case
polvo *m* dust; powder; pinch of snuff; **polvo dentífrico** tooth powder; **polvos de la madre Celestina**

hocus-pocus; **polvos de talco** talcum powder
pólvora *f* powder, gunpowder; fireworks; (*persona avispada*) live wire; **correr como pólvera en reguero** to spread like wildfire
polvorear *tr* to dust, sprinkle with dust or powder
polvorien•to -ta *adj* dusty; powdery
polvorín *m* powder magazine; powder flask; (*insecto*) tick; (Chile) spitfire
polvoro•so -sa *adj* dusty; **poner pies en polvorosa** to take to one's heels
polla *f* pullet; (*puesta en juegos de naipes*) stake, kitty; (coll) lassie
pollera *f* poultry woman; chicken coop; poultry yard; go-cart; (Arg, Chile) skirt
pollero *m* poulterer; poultry yard
polli•no -na *mf* donkey, ass
polli•to -ta *mf* chick; (*persona joven*) chick, chicken
pollo *m* chicken; (*persona joven*) chicken
pomada *f* pomade
pómez *f* pumice stone
pomo *m* pome; (*de la guarnición de la espada*) pommel; (*bola aromática*) pomander; (*frasco para perfume*) flacon; **pomo de puerta** doorknob
pompa *f* pomp; soap bubble; swell, bulge; (*de la ropa*) billowing, ballooning; (*de las alas del pavo real*) spread; (naut) pump; **pompa fúnebre** funeral
pompis *m* behind, butt, rear end
pompo•so -sa *adj* pompous; high-flown, highfalutin
pómulo *m* cheekbone
ponche *m* (*bebida*) punch; **ponche de huevo** eggnog
ponchera *f* punch bowl
pon•cho -cha *adj* lazy, careless, easy-going; (Col) chubby ‖ *m* poncho; greatcoat
ponderar *tr* to weigh; ponder, ponder over; exaggerate; praise to the skies; balance; weight
ponencia *f* paper, report
poner §54 *tr* to put, place, lay, set; arrange, dispose; (*una observación*) put in; (*una pieza dramática*) put on; (*la mesa*) set; assume, suppose; (*una ley, un impuesto*) impose; wager, stake; (*huevos*) lay; (*por escrito*) set down, put down; (*tiempo*) take; (*p.ej., miedo*) cause; make, turn; (*la luz, la radio*) turn on; (*marcha directa*) (aut) to go in; **poner en acción** to set in motion; **poner en limpio** to make a clean copy of; **poner por encima** to prefer, put ahead ‖ *ref* to put or place oneself; become, get, turn; (*el sol, los astros*) set; (*sombrero, saco, etc.*) put on; dress, dress up; get spotted; get, reach, arrive; **ponerse a** to set out to, begin to; **ponerse tan alto** to take offense, become hoity-toity
poniente *m* west; west wind
ponqué *m* poundcake
pontífice *m* pontiff
pontón *m* pontoon; pontoon bridge; (*buque viejo*) hulk
ponzoña *f* poison

ponzoño•so -sa *adj* poisonous
popa *f* poop, stern
popote *m* (Mex) straw for brooms; (*para tomar refrescos*) (Mex) straw
populache•ro -ra *adj* popular; cheap, vulgar; rabble-rousing ‖ *mf* rabble-rouser
populacho *m* populace, mob, rabble
popular *adj* popular
popularizar §60 *tr* to popularize
populo•so -sa *adj* populous
popu•rrí *m* (*pl* **-rríes**) medley
poquedad *f* paucity, scantiness; scarcity; timidity; trifle
poqui•to -ta *adj* very little; timid, shy, backward
por *prep* by; through, over; via, by way of; in, e.g., **por la mañana** in the morning; for; because of; for the sake of; on account of; in exchange for; in order to; as; about, e.g., **por Navidad** about Christmastime; out of, e.g., **por ignorancia** out of ignorance; times, e.g., **tres por cuatro** four times three; **estar por** to be on the point of, be ready to be still to be, e.g., **la carta está por escribir** the letter is still to be written; **ir por** to go for, to go after; to follow; **por ciento** per cent; **por entre** among, between; **por que** because; in order that; **por qué** why; **por + adj or adv + que** however
porcelana *f* porcelain, chinaware; (*usado por los plateros*) enamel; (Mex) washbowl
porcentaje *m* percentage
porción *f* portion
porche *m* porch, portico
pordiosear *intr* to beg, go begging
pordiose•ro -ra *mf* beggar
porfía *f* persistence, stubbornness, obstinacy; **a porfía** in emulation; insistently
porfia•do -da *adj* persistent, stubborn, obstinate; opinionated
porfiar §77 *intr* to persist; argue stubbornly
pórfido *m* porphyry
pormenor *m* detail, particular
pormenorizar §60 *tr* to detail, tell in detail; to itemize
poro *m* pore
poro•so -sa *adj* porous
poroto *m* (SAm) bean, string bean; (Chile) little runt
porque *conj* because; in order that
porqué *m* why; quantity, share; wherewithal, money
porquería *f* dirt, filth; trifle; crudity; (*alimento dañoso a la salud*) junk
porra *f* club, bludgeon; bore, nuisance; boasting; (*pelos enredados*) (Arg, Bol) knot, tangle; (Mex) claque
porrazo *m* clubbing; blow, bump, thump
porro *m* (*mariguana*) joint
porta *f* porthole
portaavio•nes *m* (*pl* **-nes**) aircraft carrier, flattop
portacandado *m* hasp
portada *f* front, façade; portal; title page; (*de una revista*) cover; **falsa portada** half title

portadis•cos *m* (*pl* **-cos**) turntable
porta•dor -dora *adj* (*onda*) (rad) carrier ‖ *mf* bearer; carrier ‖ *m* waiter's tray
portaequipaje *m* (aut) trunk
portaequipa•jes *m* (*pl* **-jes**) baggage rack
portaguan•tes *m* (*pl* **-tes**) (aut) glove compartment
portal *m* vestibule, entrance hall; porch, portico; arcade; city gate; (*de un túnel*) portal *m;* crèche
portalámpa•ras *m* (*pl* **-ras**) (elec) socket
portalón *m* gate, portal; (*en el costado del buque*) gangway
portamira *m* (surv) rodman
portamone•das *m* (*pl* **-das**) pocketbook
portanue•vas *mf* (*pl* **-vas**) newsmonger
portañuela *f* (*de los pantalones*) fly; (Col, Mex) carriage door
portapape•les *m* (*pl* **-les**) brief case
portaplu•mas *m* (*pl* **-mas**) penholder
portar *tr* to carry, bear; (hunt) to retrieve ‖ *ref* to behave, conduct oneself
portase•nos *m* (*pl* **-nos**) brassiere
portátil *adj* portable
portatinte•ro *m* inkstand
portavian•das *m* (*pl* **-das**) dinner pail
porta•voz *m* (*pl* **-voces**) megaphone; mouthpiece, spokesperson
portazgo *m* toll, road toll
portazo *m* bang, slam
porte *m* portage; carrying charge, freight; postage; behavior, conduct; dress, bearing; size, capacity; (Chile) birthday present; **porte concertado** mailing permit; **porte pagado** postage prepaid, freight prepaid
portear *tr* to carry, transport ‖ *intr* to slam ‖ *ref* (*las aves*) to migrate
portento *m* prodigy, wonder
portento•so -sa *adj* portentous, extraordinary
porte•ño -ña *adj* Buenos Aires; Valparaiso; pertaining to any large South American city with a port ‖ *mf* native or inhabitant of Buenos Aires, Valparaiso or any large South American city with a port
porte•ro -ra *mf* doorkeeper; gatekeeper; (sport) goalkeeper ‖ *m* porter, janitor; doorman; **portero electrónico** automatic door opener ‖ *f* portress, janitress
portezuela *f* small door; (*de un coche o automóvil*) door; pocket flap
pórtico *m* portico, porch; little gate
portilla *f* porthole; private cart road, private cattle pass
portillo *m* gap, opening; nick, notch; (*puerta chica en otra mayor*) wicket; gate; narrow pass; side entrance
portorrique•ño -ña *adj & mf* Puerto Rican
portua•rio -ria *adj* port, harbor, dock ‖ *m* dock hand, dock worker
Portugal *m* Portugal
portu•gués -guesa *adj & mf* Portuguese
porvenir *m* future
pos — **en pos de** after, behind; in pursuit of
posa *f* knell, toll
posada *f* inn, wayside inn; lodging; boardinghouse; home, dwelling; camp; **posadas** (Mex) pre-Christmas celebration

po
po

posade•ro -ra *mf* innkeeper; **posaderas** buttocks

posar *tr* to put down ‖ *intr* to put up, lodge; alight, perch; pose ‖ *ref* to alight, perch; settle; rest

posbéli•co -ca *adj* postwar

posdata *f* postscript

pose *f* pose; (phot) exposure

poseer §43 *tr* to own, possess, hold; have a mastery of ‖ *ref* to control oneself

posesión *f* possession; **tomar posesión** (*un cargo*) to take up

posesionar *tr* to give possession to ‖ *ref* to take possession

posesor *m* owner

poseta *f* (Ven) toilet, washroom

posfecha *f* postdate

posguerra *f* postwar period

posible *adj* possible; **hacer todo lo posible** to do one's best ‖ **posibles** *mpl* means, income, property

posición *f* position; standing

positi•vo -va *adj* positive ‖ *f* (phot) print, positive

poso *m* sediment, dregs; grounds; rest, quiet; **poso del café** coffee grounds

posponer §54 *tr* to subordinate; think less of

posta *f* (*de caballos*) relay; posthouse; stage; stake, wager; slice; **a posta** on purpose; **por la posta** posthaste; **postas** buckshot

postal *adj* postal ‖ *f* post card; **postal ilustrada** picture post card

poste *m* post, pillar, pole; **poste de alumbrado** or **de farol** lamppost; **poste de telégrafo** telegraph pole; (*persona muy alta y delgada*) beanpole; **poste indicador** road sign

póster *m* poster

postergar §44 *tr* to delay, postpone; pass over

posteridad *f* posterity; posthumous fame

posterior *adj* back, rear; later, subsequent

postigo *m* (*puerta chica en otra mayor*) wicket; (*puertecilla en una ventana*) peep window; (*puerta excusada*) postern; shutter

posti•zo -za *adj* false, artificial; (*cuello*) detachable ‖ *m* switch, false hair, rat

postóni•co -ca *adj* posttonic

postor *m* bidder; **el mejor postor** the highest bidder

postración *f* prostration

postrar *tr* to prostrate; weaken, exhaust ‖ *ref* to collapse, be prostrated; prostrate oneself

postre *adj* last, final; **a la postre** at last; afterwards ‖ *m* dessert; **postres** dessert

postulación *f* postulation; nomination

postulante *mf* applicant, candidate

póstu•mo -ma *adj* posthumous

postura *f* posture; attitude, stand; stake, wager; agreement, pact; egg, eggs; (*de huevos*) laying; **postura del sol** sunset

potabilizar §60 *tr* to make drinkable

potable *adj* drinkable

potaje *m* pottage; jumble; (*bebida*) mixture; scheme; **potajes** vegetables

potasa *f* potash

potasio *m* potassium

pote *m* pot, jug; flowerpot; **a pote** in abundance

potencia *f* potency; power; **potencia de choque** striking power

potenciación *f* (math) involution

potencial *adj* & *m* potential

potenciar *tr* (*las aguas de un río; el entusiasmo de una persona*) to harness; (*elevar a una potencia*) (math) to raise

potentado *m* potentate

potente *adj* powerful; big, huge

potestad *f* power

potista *mf* toper, soak

potosí *m* great wealth, gold mine

potra *f* filly; hernia, rupture

potranca *f* young mare

potro *m* colt; pest, annoyance

pozal *m* bucket, pail

pozo *m* well; pit; whirlpool; (min) shaft; (naut) hold; (Chile, Col) pool, puddle; (Ecuad) spring, fountain; **pozo de ciencia** fountain of knowledge; **pozo de lanzamiento** launching silo; **pozo de lobo** (mil) foxhole; **pozo negro** cesspool

P.P. *abbr* **porte pagado, por poder**

p.p.ᵈᵒ *abbr* **próximo pasado**

práctica *f* practice; method; skill; **prácticas** studies, training

prácticamente *adv* through practice, by experience

practicar §73 *tr* to practice; bring about; (*un agujero*) make, cut

prácti•co -ca *adj* practical; skillful, practiced; practicing ‖ *m* medical practitioner; (naut) pilot ‖ *f* see **práctica**

pradera *f* meadowland; prairie

prado *m* meadow, pasture; promenade

Praga *f* Prague

pral. *abbr* **principal**

pralte. *abbr* **principalmente**

prángana — estar en la prángana (Mex, W-I) to be broke; (P-R) to be naked

preámbulo *m* preamble; evasion; **no andarse en preámbulos** to come to the point

prebéli•co -ca *adj* prewar

prebenda *f* prebend; sinecure

preca•rio -ria *adj* precarious

precaución *f* precaution

precaver *tr* to stave off, head off ‖ *intr* & *ref* to be on one's guard; **precaverse contra** or **de** to guard against

precavido -da *adj* cautious

precedente *adj* preceding ‖ *m* precedent

preceder *tr* & *intr* to precede

precepto *m* precept; order, injunction; **los preceptos** the Ten Commandments

preces *fpl* devotions; supplications

precia•do -da *adj* esteemed, valued; precious, valuable; boastful, proud

preciar *tr* to appraise, estimate ‖ *ref* to boast

precintar *tr* to bind, strap; seal

precio *m* price; value, worth; esteem, credit; **a precio de quemazón** at a giveaway price; **precios de cierre** closing prices; **precio tope** ceiling price

preciosidad *f* preciousness; beauty, gem, jewel

precio•so -sa *adj* precious; valuable; witty; beautiful

preciosura *f* beauty; pretty woman

precipicio *m* precipice; destruction

precipitación *f* precipitation; **precipitación acuosa** rainfall; **precipitación radiactiva** fallout

precipitar *tr* to precipitate; rush, hurl, throw headlong ‖ *ref* to rush, throw oneself headlong

precipito•so -sa *adj* precipitous, rash, reckless; risky, dangerous

precisar *tr* to state precisely, specify; fix; need; oblige, force; determine ‖ *intr* to be necessary; be important; be urgent; **precisar de** to need

precisión *f* precision; necessity, obligation; (Chile) haste; **precisiones** data

preci•so -sa *adj* necessary; precise; (Ven) haughty

precita•do -da *adj* above-mentioned

precla•ro -ra *adj* illustrious, famous

preconizar §60 *tr* to proclaim, commend publicly

pre•coz *adj* (*pl* **-coces**) precocious

predato•rio -ria *adj* predatory

predecir §24 *tr* to predict, foretell

prédica *f* Protestant sermon; harangue

predicar §73 *tr* to preach; praise to the skies; scold, preach to

predicción *f* prediction; **predicción del tiempo** weather forecasting

predilec•to -ta *adj* favorite, preferred

predio *m* property, estate

predisponer §54 *tr* to predispose

predominante *adj* predominant

preeminente *adj* preëminent

preestreno *m* (mov) preview

prefabricar §73 *tr* to prefabricate

prefacio *m* preface

preferencia *f* preference; **de preferencia** preferably

preferente *adj* preferable; favored; (*acciones*) preferred

preferible *adj* preferable

preferir §68 *tr* to prefer

prefigurar *tr* to foreshadow

prefijar *tr* to prefix; prearrange

prefijo *m* prefix

pregón *m* proclamation, public announcement (*by town crier*)

pregonar *tr* to proclaim, announce publicly; hawk; reveal; outlaw; praise openly

pregonero *m* auctioneer; town crier

preguerra *f* prewar period

pregunta *f* question; **hacer una pregunta** to ask a question

preguntar *tr* to ask; to question ‖ *intr* to ask, inquire; **preguntar por** to ask after or for ‖ *ref* to ask oneself; wonder

pregun•tón -tona *adj* inquisitive ‖ *mf* inquisitive person

prejudicio *m* or **prejuicio** *m* prejudgment; prejudice

prelado *m* prelate

preliminar *adj* & *m* preliminary; **preliminares** (*de un libro*) front matter

preludio *m* prelude

premeditar *tr* to premeditate

premiar *tr* to reward; give an award to

premio *m* reward, prize; premium; **a premio** at a premium; **premio de enganche** (mil) bounty; **premio gordo** first prize

premio•so -sa *adj* tight, close; bothersome; strict, rigid; slow, dull

premisa *f* premise; mark, token, clue

premura *f* pressure, haste, urgency

premuro•so -sa *adj* pressing, urgent

prenda *f* pledge; security; pawn; jewel, household article; garment, article of clothing; gift, talent; darling, loved one; **en prenda** in pawn; **en prenda de** as a pledge of; **prenda perdida** forfeit; **prendas** (*juego*) forfeits; **prendas interiores** underwear

prendar *tr* to pawn; pledge; charm, captivate ‖ *ref* — **prendarse de** to take a liking for, fall in love with

prendedero *m* or **prendedor** *m* fillet, brooch; stickpin

prender *tr* to seize, grasp; catch; imprison; dress up; pin; fasten ‖ *intr* to catch; catch fire; take root; turn out well ‖ *ref* to dress up; be fastened; catch hold

prendería *f* second-hand shop

prende•ro -ra *mf* second-hand dealer

prenombra•do -da *adj* above-mentioned; foregoing

prensa *f* press; printing press; vise; press, newspapers; press, frame; **entrar en prensa** to go to press; **meter en prensa** to put the squeeze on; **prensa amarilla** yellow press; **prensa taladradora** drill press

prensado *m* pressing; (*lustre de los tejidos prensados*) sheen

prensador *m* (CAm) paper clip

prensar *tr* to press; squeeze

preña•do -da *adj* pregnant; sagging, bulging; full, charged

preñez *f* pregnancy; fullness; impending danger; inherent confusion

preocupación *f* (*posesión anticipada; cuidado, desvelo*) preoccupation; (*posesión anticipada*) preoccupancy; bias, prejudice

preocupar *tr* to preoccupy, worry ‖ *ref* to become preoccupied, be worried

preparación *f* preparation

prepara•do -da *adj* ready, prepared ‖ *m* (pharm) preparation

preparar *tr* to prepare ‖ *ref* to prepare, get ready

preparati•vo -va *adj* preparatory ‖ *m* preparation, readiness

preponderante *adj* preponderant

preposición *f* preposition

prepóste•ro -ra *adj* reversed, upset, out of order, inopportune

prerrogativa *f* prerogative

presa *f* capture, seizure; catch, prey; booty, spoils; dam; trench, ditch, flume; bit, morsel; fang, tusk, claw; fishweir; (sport) hold; **hacer presa** to seize; **ser presa de** to be a victim of; be prey to

presagiar *tr* to presage, forebode

po
pr

presagio *m* presage, omen, token

présbita or **présbite** *adj* far-sighted ‖ *mf* far-sighted person

presbiteria•no -na *adj & mf* Presbyterian

prescindir *intr* — **prescindir de** to leave aside, leave out, disregard; do without, dispense with; avoid

prescribir §83 *tr & intr* to prescribe

presencia *f* presence; show, display; **presencia de ánimo** presence of mind

presenciar *tr* to witness, be present at

presentación *f* presentation; *(de una persona en el trato de otra u otras)* introduction; *(de un nuevo automóvil, libro, etc.)* appearance

presentador *m* or **presentadora** *f* (telv) moderator

presentar *tr* to present; introduce ‖ *ref* to present oneself; appear, show up; introduce oneself

presente *adj* present; **hacer presente** to notify of, remind of; **tener presente** to bear or keep in mind ‖ *interj* here!, present! ‖ *m* present, gift; person present

presentimiento *m* presentiment, premonition

presentir §68 *tr* to have a presentiment of

preservar *tr* to preserve, protect

preservati•vo -va *adj & m* preventive; preservative

presidencia *f* presidency; chairmanship

presidente *m* president; chairman; presiding judge

presidiario *m* convict

presidio *m* garrison; fortress; citadel; penitentiary; imprisonment; hard labor; aid, help

presidir *tr* to preside over; dominate ‖ *intr* to preside

presilla *f* loop, fastener; clip; paper clip; shoulder strap

presión *f* pressure; *(cerveza)* **a presión** on draught; **presión de inflado** tire pressure

presionar *tr* to press; put pressure on ‖ *intr* to press; **presionar sobre** to put pressure on

pre•so -sa *adj* seized; imprisoned ‖ *mf* prisoner; convict; **preso preventivo** pretrial prisoner; *f* see **presa**

presta•do -da *adj* lent, loaned; **dar prestado** to lend; **pedir** or **tomar prestado** to borrow

prestamista *mf* moneylender; pawnbroker

préstamo *m* loan; **préstamo lingüístico** loan word, borrowing

prestar *tr* to lend, loan; *(oído; ayuda; noticias)* give; *(atención)* pay; *(un favor)* do; *(un servicio)* render; *(juramento)* take; *(silencio)* keep; *(paciencia)* show ‖ *intr* to give ‖ *ref (un paño, la ropa)* give, yield; be useful ‖ *ref* to lend oneself, lend itself

prestata•rio -ria *mf* borrower

presteza *f* speed, promptness, readiness

prestidigitación *f* sleight of hand

prestidigita•dor -dora *adj* captivating ‖ *mf* magician; faker, impostor

prestigio *m* prestige; good standing; spell; illusion

prestigio•so -sa *adj* captivating, spellbinding; famous, renowned; illusory

pres•to -ta *adj* quick, prompt, ready; nimble ‖ **presto** *adv* right away

presumi•do -da *adj* conceited, vain ‖ *mf* would-be

presumir *tr* to presume ‖ *intr* to boast, be conceited

presunción *f* presumption; conceit

presuntuo•so -sa *adj* conceited, vain

presuponer §54 *tr* to presuppose; budget

presupuestar *tr* to budget; *(el coste de una obra)* estimate

presupuesto *m* budget; reason, motive; supposition; estimate

presuro•so -sa *adj* speedy, quick, hasty; zealous, persistent

pretencio•so -sa *adj* pretentious, showy; conceited, vain

pretender *tr* to claim, pretend to; try for, try to do; be a suitor for ‖ *intr* to insist; **pretender** + *inf* to try to + *inf*

pretendiente *mf* pretender, claimant; office seeker ‖ *m* suitor

pretensión *f* pretension; claim; pretense; presumption; effort, pursuit

pretéri•to -ta *adj & m* past

pretil *m* parapet, railing; walk along a parapet

pretina *f* girdle, belt; waistband

pretóni•co -ca *adj* pretonic

prevalecer §22 *intr* to prevail; take root; thrive

prevaler §76 *ref* — **prevalerse de** to avail oneself of, take advantage of

prevaricar §73 *intr* to collude, connive; play false; transgress; rave, be delirious

prevención *f* preparation; prevention; foresight; warning; prejudice; stock, supply; jail, lockup; guardhouse; **a** or **de prevención** spare, emergency

preveni•do -da *adj* prepared, ready; foresighted, forewarned; stocked, full

prevenir §79 *tr* to prepare, make ready; forestall, prevent, anticipate; overcome; warn; prejudice ‖ *intr (una tempestad)* to come up ‖ *ref* to get ready; come to mind

prever §80 *tr* to foresee

pre•vio -via *adj* previous; preliminary; after, with previous, subject to, e.g., **previo acuerdo** subject to agreement; **cita previa** by appointment

previsión *f* prevision, foresight; foresightedness; forecast; **previsión del tiempo** weather forecasting

prie•to -ta *adj* dark, blackish; stingy; mean; tight, compact; dark-complexioned ‖ *mf* (W-I) darling

prima *f* early morning; bonus, bounty; (ins) premium; (mil) first quarter of the night; *(cuerda)* (mus) treble

pri•mal -mala *adj & mf* yearling

prima•rio -ria *adj* primary ‖ *m* (elec) primary

primavera *f* spring, springtime; cowslip, primrose; robin

primer *adj* apocopated form of **primero**, used only before masculine singular nouns and adjectives

prime•ro -ra *adj* first; former; early; primary; prime; (*materia*) raw ‖ *m* first; **a primeros de** around the beginning of ‖ **primero** *adv* first

primicia *f* first fruits

primige•nio -nia *adj* original, primitive

primiti•vo -va *adj* primitive

pri•mo -ma *adj* first; prime, excellent; skillful; (*materia*) raw ‖ *mf* cousin; sucker, dupe; **primo carnal** or **primo hermano** first cousin, cousin-german ‖ *f* see **prima** ‖ **primo** *adv* in the first place

primogéni•to -ta *adj & mf* first-born

primor *m* care, skill, elegance; beauty

primoro•so -sa *adj* careful, skillful, elegant; fine, exquisite

princesa *f* princess; **princesa viuda** dowager princess

principal *adj* principal, main, chief; first, foremost; essential, important; famous, illustrious; (*piso*) second ‖ *m* principal, head, chief

príncipe *m* prince; **portarse como un príncipe** to live like a prince; **príncipe de Asturias** heir apparent of the King of Spain; **príncipe de Gales** prince of Wales; **príncipes** prince and princess

principiante *adj* beginning ‖ *mf* beginner, apprentice, novice

principiar *tr, intr & ref* to begin

principio *m* start, beginning; principle; origin, source; (culin) entree; **a principios de** around the beginning of; **en un principio** at the beginning; **principio de admiración** inverted exclamation point; **principio de interrogación** inverted question mark

pringar §44 *tr* to dip or soak in grease or fat; spot or stain with grease; make bleed; slander, run down; splash ‖ *intr* to meddle; (CAm, Mex) to drizzle ‖ *ref* to peculate

pringo•so -sa *adj* greasy, fatty

prioridad *f* priority; **de máxima prioridad** of the highest priority

prisa *f* hurry, haste; urgency; crush, crowd; **darse prisa** to hurry, make haste; **estar de prisa** or **tener prisa** to be in a hurry

prisión *f* seizure, capture; imprisonment; prison; **prisión celular** cell house; **prisiones** shackles, fetters

prisione•ro -ra *mf* prisoner; (*cautivo de una pasión o afecto*) captive ‖ *m* setscrew; studbolt

prisma *m* prism

prismáticos *mpl* binoculars

priva•do -da *adj* private ‖ *m* (*de un alto personaje*) favorite ‖ *f* cesspool

privar *tr* to deprive; forbid, prohibit ‖ *intr* to be in vogue; prevail; be in favor ‖ *ref* to deprive oneself; **privarse de** to give up

privilegiar *tr* to grant a privilege to

privilegio *m* privilege

pro *m & f* profit, advantage; **¡buena pro!** good appetite!; **de pro** of note, of worth; **el pro y el contra** the pros and the cons; **en pro de** on behalf of

proa *f* (aer) nose; (naut) prow

probable *adj* probable, likely

probador *m* fitting room

probar §61 *tr* to prove; test; try; (*clothing*) try on; try out; sample; fit; suit; (*vino*) touch ‖ *intr* to taste; **probar de** to take a taste of ‖ *ref* to try on

probidad *f* probity, integrity, honesty

problema *m* problem

pro•caz *adj* (*pl* -**caces**) impudent, insolent, bold

procedencia *f* origin, source; point of departure

procedente *adj* coming, originating; proper

proceder *m* conduct, behavior ‖ *intr* to proceed; originate; behave; be proper

procedimiento *m* procedure; proceeding; process

procelo•so -sa *adj* tempestuous, stormy

prócer *adj* high, lofty ‖ *m* hero, leader

procesamiento *m* (data) processing

procesar *tr* to sue, prosecute; indict; try; (*ordenador*) to process, data-process

procesión *f* procession; origin, emergence

proceso *m* process; progress; suit, lawsuit; **proceso verbal** minutes

proclama *f* proclamation; marriage banns

proclamar *tr* to proclaim; acclaim

proclíti•co -ca *adj & m* proclitic

procurador *m* attorney, solicitor; proxy

procurar *tr* to strive for; manage as attorney; yield, produce; try to

prodigar §44 *tr* to lavish; squander; waste ‖ *ref* to be a show-off

prodigio *m* prodigy

prodigio•so -sa *adj* prodigious, marvelous; fine, excellent

pródigo -ga *adj* prodigal; lavish ‖ *mf* prodigal

producción *f* production; crop, yield, produce; **producción en masa** or **en serie** mass production

producir §19 *tr* to produce; yield, bear; cause, bring about ‖ *ref* to explain oneself; come about; take place

producto *m* product; produce; proceeds

proeza *f* prowess; feat, stunt

prof. *abbr* profeta

profanar *tr* to profane

profa•no -na *adj* profane; indecent, immodest; worldly; lay ‖ *mf* profane; worldly person; layman

profecía *f* prophecy ‖ **las Profecías** (Bib) the Prophets

proferir §68 *tr* to utter

profesar *tr & intr* to profess

profesión *f* profession; **profesión de fe** confession of faith

profe•sor -sora *mf* teacher; professor

profeta *m* prophet

profetisa *f* prophetess

profetizar §60 *tr* to prophesy

profilácti•co -ca *adj & m* prophylactic; preventive ‖ *f* hygiene

prófu•go -ga *adj & mf* fugitive ‖ *m* slacker, draft dodger

profundidad *f* profundity; depth

profundizar §60 *tr* to deepen; fathom, get to the bottom of

profun•do -da *adj* profound; deep

progenie *f* descent, lineage, parentage

progno•sis *f* (*pl* -sis) prognosis; (*del tiempo*) forecast

programa *m* program; **programa continuo** (mov) continuous showing; **programa de estudios** curriculum; **programa (para ordenador)** program(me), software

programación *f* (*ordenador*) program(m)ing; (telv) scheduling

programador *m* or **programadora** *f* (*ordenador*) program(m)er

programar *tr* to program; (*ordenador*) program(me)

progresar *intr* to progress

progresista *adj* & *mf* (pol) progressive

progreso *m* progress; **hacer progresos** to make progress

prohibir *tr* to prohibit, forbid ‖ *ref* **se prohibe fijar carteles** post no bills

prohijar *tr* to adopt

prohombre *m* (*en los gremios de los artesanos*) master; leader, head; (coll) big shot

prójimo *m* fellow man, fellow creature, neighbor; fellow

pról. *abbr* **prólogo**

prole *f* progeny, offspring

proletariado *m* proletariat

proleta•rio -ria *adj* & *m* proletarian

proliferar *intr* to proliferate

prolífi•co -ca *adj* prolific

proli•jo -ja *adj* tedious, too long; fussy, fastidious; long-winded; tiresome

prologar §44 *tr* to preface, write a preface for

prólogo *m* prologue; preface

prolongar §44 *tr* to prolong, extend; (geom) to produce

promediar *tr* to divide into two equal parts; average ‖ *intr* to mediate; be half over

promedio *m* average, mean; middle

promesa *f* promise

promete•dor -dora *adj* promising

prometer *tr* & *intr* to promise ‖ *ref* to become engaged

prometi•do -da *adj* engaged, betrothed ‖ *m* promise; fiancé ‖ *f* fiancée

prominente *adj* prominent

promiso•rio -ria *adj* promissory

promoción *f* promotion; advancement; (*conjunto de individuos que obtienen un grado en un mismo año*) class, year, crop

promontorio *m* promontory, headland; unwieldy thing

promover §47 *tr* to promote; advance, further

promulgar §44 *tr* to promulgate

pronombre *m* pronoun

pronosticar §73 *tr* to prognosticate, foretell

pronóstico *m* prognostic, forecast; almanac; (med) prognosis

pron•to -ta *adj* quick, speedy; prompt; ready ‖ *m* jerk; sudden impulse, fit of anger ‖ **pronto** *adv* right away, soon; early; promptly; **lo más pronto posible** as soon as possible; **tan pronto como** as soon as

pronunciación *f* pronunciation

pronuncia•do -da *adj* marked; (*curva*) sharp; (*pendiente*) steep; bulky

pronunciamiento *m* insurrection, uprising; (*golpe de estado militar*) pronunciamento; (law) decree

pronunciar *tr* to pronounce; utter; (*un discurso*) make, deliver; decide on ‖ *ref* to rebel; declare oneself

propaganda *f* propaganda; advertising

propagar §44 *tr* to propagate; spread; broadcast

propalar *tr* to divulge, spread

proparoxíto•no -na *adj* & *m* proparoxytone

propasar *ref* to go too far, take undue liberty

propender *intr* to tend, incline, be inclined

propensión *f* propensity; predisposition

propen•so -sa *adj* inclined, disposed, prone

propiciar *tr* to propitiate; support, favor, sponsor

propi•cio -cia *adj* propitious, favorable

propiedad *f* property; ownership; naturalness, likeness; **es propiedad** copyrighted; **propiedad horizontal** one-floor ownership in an apartment house; **propiedad literaria** copyright

propieta•rio -ria *mf* owner ‖ *m* proprietor ‖ *f* proprietress

propina *f* tip, fee, gratuity

propinar *tr* (*algo a beber*) to offer; (*medicamentos*) prescribe or administer; (*palos, golpes, etc.*) give ‖ *ref* (*una bebida*) to treat oneself to

propin•cuo -cua *adj* near, close at hand

pro•pio -pia *adj* proper, suitable; peculiar, characteristic; natural; same; himself, herself, etc.; own ‖ *m* messenger; native; **propios** public lands

proponer §54 *tr* to propose; propound; (*a una persona para un empleo*) name, present ‖ *ref* to plan; propose

proporción *f* proportion; opportunity

proporciona•do -da *adj* proportionate; fit, suitable

proporcionar *tr* to furnish, provide, supply, give; proportion; adapt, adjust

proposición *f* proposition; **proposición dominante** main clause

propósito *m* aim, purpose, intention; subject matter; **a propósito** by the way; apropos, fitting; in place; **a propósito de** apropos of; **de propósito** on purpose; **fuera de propósito** irrelevant, beside the point

propuesta *f* proposal, proposition

propulsar *tr* to propel, drive

propulsión *f* propulsion; **propulsión a chorro** jet propulsion; **propulsión a cohete** rocket propulsion

pror. *abbr* **procurador**

prorratear *tr* to prorate

prórroga *f* extension, renewal

prorrogar §44 *tr* to defer, postpone, extend

prorrumpir *intr* to spurt, shoot forth; break forth, burst out

prosa *f* prose; chatter, idle talk

prosai•co -ca *adj* prose; prosaic, dull

proscribir §83 *tr* to outlaw, proscribe

proscrip•to -ta *mf* exile, outlaw

prosecución *f* continuation, prosecution; pursuit

proseguir §67 *tr* to continue, carry on ‖ *intr* to continue

prosélito *m* proselyte

prosista *mf* prose writer; chatterbox

prosódi•co -ca *adj* (*acento*) stress

prospectar *tr* & *intr* to prospect

prosperar *tr* to make prosper ‖ *intr* to prosper, thrive

prosperidad prosperity

próspe•ro -ra *adj* prosperous, thriving, successful

prosternar *ref* to prostrate oneself

prostituir §20 *tr* to prostitute ‖ *ref* to prostitute oneself; become a prostitute

prostituta *f* prostitute

prosu•do -da *adj* (Chile, Ecuad, Peru) pompous, solemn

protagonista *mf* protagonist

protagonizar §60 *tr* to play the leading rôle of

protección *f* protection; **protección aduanera** protective tariff; **protección a la infancia** child welfare

proteger §17 *tr* to protect

protegida *f* protégée

protegido *m* protégé

proteína *f* protein

proter•vo -va *adj* perverse

protesta *f* protest; pledge, promise

protestante *adj* & *mf* protestant; Protestant

protestar *tr* to protest, asseverate; (*la fe*) profess ‖ *intr* to protest; **protestar de** (*aseverar con ahinco*) to protest (*to state positively*); **protestar contra** (*negar la validez de*) to protest (*to deny forcibly*)

protocolo *m* protocol

protoplasma *m* protoplasm

prototipo *m* prototype

protozoario *m* or **protozoo** *m* protozoön

provec•to -ta *adj* old, ripe

provecho *m* advantage, benefit; profit, gain; advance, progress; **¡buen provecho!** good luck!; good appetite!; **de provecho** useful; **provechos** perquisites

provecho•so -sa *adj* advantageous, beneficial; profitable; useful

proveedor -dora *mf* supplier, provider, purveyor; steward

proveer §43 & §83 *tr* to provide, furnish; supply; resolve, settle ‖ *intr* to provide; **proveer a** to provide for ‖ *ref* to supply oneself; have a bowel movement

provenir §79 *intr* to come, arise

Provenza, la Provence

provenzal *adj* & *mf* Provençal

proverbio *m* proverb

providencia *f* providence, foresight; step, measure

providencial *adj* providential

provincia *f* province

provisión *f* provision; supply, stock; **provisiones de boca** foodstuffs

proviso•rio -ria *adj* provisory, provisional

provocar §73 *tr* to provoke; promote, bring about; incite, tempt, move ‖ *intr* to provoke; vomit

proxeneta *mf* go-between

proximidad *f* proximity; **proximidades** neighborhood

próxi•mo -ma *adj* next; near; neighboring, close; early; **próximo pasado** last

proyección *f* projection; influence

proyectar *tr* to project; cast; design ‖ *ref* to project, stick out; (*una sombra*) be projected, fall

proyectil *m* projectile; **proyectil buscador del blanco** homing missile; **proyectil dirigido** or **teleguiado** guided missile

proyecto *m* project; **proyecto de ley** bill

proyector *m* projector, searchlight; projection machine

prudencia *f* prudence

prudente *adj* prudent

prueba *f* proof; trial, test; examination; (*de un traje*) fitting; (*de un alimento o una bebida*) sample, sampling; evidence; acrobatics; sleight of hand; (sport) event; **a prueba** on approval, on trial; **a prueba de** proof against, -proof, e.g., **a prueba de escaladores** burglarproof; **a prueba de incendio** fireproof; **prueba de alcohol** alcohol-level test; **pruebas de planas** page proof; **pruebas de primeras** first proof (*for proofreader*); **pruebas de segundas** galley proof (*for author*)

pruebista *mf* acrobat

prurito *m* itching; eagerness, itch

psicoanálisis *m* psychoanalysis

psicoanalizar §60 *tr* to psychoanalyze

psicodéli•co -ca *adj* psychedelic

psicología *f* psychology

psicológi•co -ca *adj* psychologic(al)

psicólo•go -ga *mf* psychologist

psicópata *mf* psychopath

psico•sis *f* (*pl* **-sis**) psychosis; **psicosis de guerra** war psychosis, war scare

psicoterapia *f* psychotherapy; **psicoterapia de grupo** group therapy

psicóti•co -ca *adj* & *mf* psychotic

psique *f* cheval glass ‖ **Psique** *f* Psyche

psiquiatra *mf* psychiatrist

psiquiatría *f* psychiatry

psíqui•co -ca *adj* psychic

P.S.M. *abbr* **por su mandato**

pte. *abbr* **parte, presente**

púa *f* point; prick, barb; tine, prong; (*del fonógrafo*) needle; (*del peine*) tooth; thorn; (*del puerco espín*) spine, quill; sting; graft; plectrum; tricky person

pubertad *f* puberty

publicación *f* publication

publicar §73 *tr* to publish; publicize

publicidad *f* publicity; advertising; **publicidad de lanzamiento** advance publicity

publicita•rio -ria *adj* publicity; advertising

públi•co -ca *adj* & *m* public

pucha *f* (W-I) small bouquet; (Mex) crescent roll

púcher *m* (*drogas*) pusher

pr
pu

puchero *m* pot, kettle; stew; daily bread; pouting; **hacer pucheros** to pout, screw up one's face

pucho *m* fag end, remnant; (*de cigarro*) stump; trifle, trinket; (*el hijo menor*) baby

puden•do -da *adj* ugly, shameful; obscene; (*partes*) private

pudiente *adj* powerful; well-off, well-to-do

pudín *m* pudding

pudor *m* modesty, shyness; chastity

pudoro•so -sa *adj* modest, shy; chaste

pudrición *f* rot, rotting

pudrir §83 *tr* to rot; worry ‖ *intr* to be dead and buried ‖ *ref* to rot; be worried; (*en la cárcel*) languish

pueblo *m* people; common people; town, village; **puebla de Dios** or **de Israel** children of Israel

puente *m* bridge; (dent, mus) bridge; (aut) axle, rear axle; **hacer puente** to take the intervening day off; **puente aéreo** airlift, air bridge; **puente colgante** suspension bridge; **puente de engrase** grease lift; **puente levadizo** drawbridge, lift bridge

puer•co -ca *adj* piggish, hoggish; dirty, filthy; slovenly; coarse, mean; lewd ‖ *m* hog; **puerco espín** or **espino** porcupine ‖ *f* sow; slattern, slut

puericia *f* childhood

puericultura *f* child rearing, infant care

pueril *adj* puerile, childish

puerilidad *f* puerility, childishness

puerro *m* leek; (*mariguana, hachich*) joint

puerta *f* door, doorway; gate, gateway; **a puerta cerrada** or **a puertas cerradas** behind closed doors

puerto *m* harbor, port; haven; mountain pass; **puerto aéreo** airport; **puerto brigantino** Corunna; **puerto de arribada** port of call; **puerto de mar** seaport; **puerto franco** free port; **puerto marítimo** dock, port; **puerto seco** frontier customhouse

puertorrique•ño -ña *adj & mf* Puerto Rican

pues *adv* then, well; yes, certainly; why; anyhow; **pues bien** well then; **pues que** since ‖ *conj* for, since, because, inasmuch as ‖ *interj* well!, then!

puesta *f* setting; laying; putting; (*dinero apostado*) stake; **a puesta del sol** or **a puestas del sol** at sunset; **puesta a punto** adjustment; carrying out, completion; **puesta a tierra** (elec) grounding; **puesta de largo** coming out, social debut

pues•to -ta *adj* dressed; **puesto que** since, inasmuch as ‖ *m* place; booth, stand; office; station; barracks; (*para cazadores*) blind; **puesto a punto** (aut) tuning; **puesto de socorros** first-aid station ‖ *f* see **puesta**

púgil *m* pugilist

pugilato *m* boxing; fist fight

pugilismo *m* pugilism

pugna *f* fight, battle; struggle, conflict; **en pugna con** at issue; **en pugna con** at odds with

pugnar *intr* to fight, struggle; strive, persist

pug•naz *adj* (*pl* **-naces**) pugnacious

pujante *adj* powerful, mighty, vigorous

pujar *tr* (*un proyecto*) to push; (*un precio*) raise, bid up ‖ *intr* to struggle, strain; falter; (*por decir una cosa*) grope; snivel; **pujar para adentro** (CAm, W-I) to keep silent, say nothing

pul•cro -cra *adj* neat, tidy, trim; circumspect

pulga *f* flea; **de malas pulgas** peppery, hot-tempered; **hacer de una pulga un camello** or **un elefante** to make a mountain out of a molehill; **no aguantar pulgas** to stand for no nonsense

pulgada *f* inch

pulgar *m* thumb

puli•do -da *adj* pretty; neat; polished; clean, spotless

pulimentar *tr* to polish

pulimento *m* polish

pulir *tr* to polish; finish; give a polish to

pulmón *m* lung; **pulmón de acero** or **de hierro** iron lung

pulmonía *f* pneumonia

púlpito *m* pulpit

pulpo *m* octopus

pulque *m* (Mex) agave brandy

pulsación *f* pulsation, throb, beat; strike, striking; (*del pianista, el mecanógrafo*) touch

pulsar *tr* (*un botón*) to push; (*un piano, arpa, guitarra*) play; (*una tecla*) strike; feel or take the pulse of; sound out, examine ‖ *intr* to pulsate, throb, beat

pulsear *intr* to hand-wrestle

pulsera *f* bracelet; wristlet, watch strap; **pulsera de pedida** engagement bracelet

pulso *m* pulse; steadiness, steady hand; tact, care, caution; bracelet; wrist watch; **a pulso** with hand and wrist; by main strength; (*dibujo*) freehand; **sacar a pulso** to carry out against odds; **tomar el pulso a** to take the pulse of

pulular *intr* to swarm; bud, sprout

pulverizar §60 *tr* to pulverize; atomize; spray

pulla *f* dig, cutting remark; filthy remark; witticism

pum *interj* bang!

puma *m* cougar

puna *f* (SAm) bleak tableland in the Andes; (SAm) mountain sickness

pundonor *m* point of honor; face

pundonoro•so sa *adj* punctilious, scrupulous; haughty, dignified

pungir §27 *tr* to prick; sting

punta *f* (*extremo agudo*) point; tip, end; (*del cigarro*) butt; nail; point, cape, headland; (*del toro*) horn; (*del asta del ciervo*) tine, prong; style, graver; touch, tinge, trace; (*del vino*) souring; (elec) point; **de punta** on end; on tiptoe; **de punta en blanco** in full armor; in full regalia; **estar de punta (con)** to be at odds (with); **punta de combate** (*del torpedo*) warhead; **punta de lanza** spearhead; **punta de París** wire nail; **sacar punta a** to put a point on, to sharpen; **tener en la punta de la lengua** to have on the tip of one's tongue

puntabola *f* (Bol) ball-point pen

puntada *f* hint; (sew) stitch; (*dolor agudo*) stitch, sharp pain

puntal *m* prop, support; stay, stanchion; backing, support; bite, snack; (naut) depth of hold

puntapié *m* kick; **echar a puntapiés** to kick out

puntear *tr* to dot, mark with dots; (*guitarra*) pluck; stipple; stitch ‖ *intr* (naut) to tack

puntera *f* toe, toe patch; leather tip; (coll) kick

puntería *f* aim, aiming; marksmanship

puntero *m* pointer; (*del reloj*) hand; stonecutter's chisel; punch; leading animal

puntiagu•do -da *adj* sharp-pointed

puntilla *f* brad; narrow lace edging; (*de la pluma fuente*) point; (carp) tracing point; dagger; **de puntillas** on tiptoe; **puntilla francesa** finishing nail

puntillero *m* bullfighter who delivers coup de grace with dagger

puntillo•so -sa *adj* punctilious

punto *m* (*señal de dimensiones poco perceptibles*) point, dot; stitch, loop; mesh; (*rotura en un tejido de punto*) break; jot; cabstand, hackstand; (gram) period; (math, typ, sport, fig) point; **a buen punto** opportunely; **al punto** at once; **a punto de** on the point of; **a punto fijo** for certain; **de punto** knitted; **dos puntos** (gram) colon; **en punto** sharp, on the dot; **poner punto final a** to wind up, to bring to an end; **punto de admiración** exclamation mark or point; **punto de aguja** knitting; **punto de Hungría** herringbone; **punto de media** knitwork; **punto de mira** aim; center of attraction; **¡punto en boca!** mum's the word!; **punto interrogante** question mark; **punto menos** almost; **punto muerto** dead center; (aut) neuter; **puntos y rayas** dots and dashes; **punto y coma** *msg* semicolon

puntuación *f* punctuation; mark, grade; scoring

puntual *adj* punctual; certain, sure; exact, accurate

puntualizar §60 *tr* to fix in the memory; give a detailed account of; finish; draw up

puntuar §21 *tr & intr* to punctuate; score

puntura *f* puncture, prick

punzada *f* prick; shooting pain; (*del remordimiento*) pang

punzante *adj* sharp, pricking; barbed, biting, caustic

punzar §60 *tr* to prick, puncture, punch; to sting; to grieve ‖ *intr* to sting

punzón *m* punch; pick; burin, graver; budding horn, tenderling; **punzón de marcar** center punch

puñada *f* punch

puñado *m* handful, bunch

puñal *m* dagger, poniard

puñalada *f* stab; blow, sudden sorrow; **puñalada de misericordia** coup de grâce; **puñalada trapera** stab in the back

puñetazo *m* punch; bang with the fist

puño *m* fist; cuff; wristband; grasp; fistful, handful; hilt; (*p.ej., del paraguas*) handle; (*del bastón*) head; punch; **como un puño** whopping big; tiny, microscopic; closefisted; **de su propio puño** or **de su puño y letra** in his own hand, in his own writing; **puño de herro** brass knuckles

pupa *f* pimple; fever blister

pupila *f* (*del ojo*) pupil

pupi•lo -la *mf* boarder; orphan, ward; pupil ‖ *f* see **pupila**

pupitre *m* writing desk

puquio *m* (SAm) spring or pool of fresh, clear water

puré *m* purée; **puré de patatas** mashed potatoes; **puré de tomates** stewed tomatoes

purera *f* cigar case

pureza *f* purity

purga *f* purge; purgative; drain valve

purgante *adj & m* purgative

purgar §44 *tr* to purge; physic; drain; purify, refine; expiate; (*pasiones*) control, check; (*sospechas*) clear away ‖ *ref* to take a physic; unburden oneself

puridad *f* purity

purificar §73 *tr* to purify

purita•no -na *adj & mf* puritan; Puritan

pu•ro -ra *adj* pure; sheer; (*cielo*) clear; out-and-out, outright; **de puro** completely, totally; because of being ‖ *m* cigar

púrpura *f* purple

purpura•do -da *adj* purple ‖ *m* (eccl) cardinal

purpúre•o -a *adj* purple

pusilánime *adj* pusillanimous

pústula *f* pustule

puta *f* whore

putañear or **putear** *intr* to whore around, chase after lewd women

putati•vo -va *adj* spurious

putrefac•to -ta *adj* rotten, putrid

pútri•do -da *adj* putrid, rotten

puya *f* steel point; (*del gallo*) spur

Q

Q, q (cu) *f* twentieth letter of the Spanish alphabet

q.b.s.m. *abbr* que besa su mano

q.e.p.d. *abbr* que en paz descanse

q.e.s.m. *abbr* que estrecha su mano

quántum *m* (*pl* **quanta**) quantum

que *pron rel* that, which; who, whom; **el que** he who; which, the one which; who, the one who ‖ *adv* than ‖ *conj* that; for, because; let, e.g., **que entre** let him come in; **a que** I'll bet that

qué *adj & pron interr* what, which; **¿qué tal?**

how?; hello, how's everything? ‖ *interj* what!; what a!; how!

quebrada *f* gorge, ravine, gap; brook; failure, bankruptcy

quebradi•zo -za *adj* brittle, fragile; frail

quebra•do -da *adj* weakened; bankrupt; ruptured; rough; winding ‖ *m* (math) fraction ‖ *f* see **quebrada**

quebrantable *adj* breakable

quebrantar *tr* to break; break open; break out of; grind, crush; soften, mollify; (*un contrato; la ley; un hábito; un testamento; el corazón de una persona*) break ‖ *ref* to break; become broken

quebrantaterro•nes *m* (*pl* **-nes**) clodhopper

quebranto *m* break, breaking; heavy loss; great sorrow; discouragement

quebrar §2 *tr* to break; bend, twist; crush; overcome; temper, soften ‖ *intr* to break; fail; weaken, give in ‖ *ref* to break; weaken; become ruptured

queda *f* curfew

quedar *intr* to remain; stay; be left; be left over; stop, leave off; turn out; be; be found, be located; **quedar en** to agree on; agree to; **quedar por** + *inf* or **sin** + *inf* to remain to be + *pp* ‖ *ref* to remain; stay; stop; be; be left; put up; **quedarse con** to keep, to take; **quedarse tan fresco** to show no offense

que•do -da *adj* quiet, still; gentle ‖ *f* see **queda** ‖ **quedo** *adv* softly, in a low voice; gropingly

quehacer *m* work, task, chore

queja *f* complaint, lament; whine, moan

quejar *ref* to complain; lament; whine, moan

quejido *m* complaint, whine, moan

quejumbre *f* complaining, whine, moan

quejumbro•so -sa *adj* complaining; whining, whiny

quema *f* fire; burning; **a quema ropa** point-blank; **de quema** distilled; **hacer quema** (Arg, Bol) to hit the mark

quemada *f* burnt brush; (Mex) fire

quemadero *m* incinerator; (*poste destinado para quemar a los condenados a la pena de fuego*) stake

quema•do -da *adj* burned; burnt out; angry ‖ *m* burnt brush; **oler a quemado** to smell of fire; **saber a quemado** to taste burned ‖ *f* see **quemada**

quema•dor -dora *adj* burning; incendiary ‖ *m* burner

quemadura *f* burn; (agr) smut

quemar *tr* to burn; scald; set on fire; scorch; frostbite; sell too cheap; (CAm, Mex) to betray; inform against ‖ *intr* to burn, be hot ‖ *ref* to burn; be burning up; fret; (*estar cercano a lo que se busca*) be warm, be hot; **quemarse las cejas** to burn the midnight oil

quemarropa — a quemarropa point-blank

quemazón *f* burn; burning; intense heat; (*de un fusible*) blowout; itch; cutting remark; pique, anger; (hum) bargain sale; (Arg, Bol, Chile) mirage on the pampas

que•pis *m* (*pl* **-pis**) kepi

queque *m* cake

querella *f* complaint; dispute, quarrel

querellar *ref* to complain; whine

querencia *f* liking, affection; attraction; love of home; (*de animales*) haunt; favorite spot

querencio•so -sa *adj* homing; (*sitio*) favorite

querer *m* love, affection; liking, fondness ‖ *v* §55 *tr* to wish, want, desire; like; love; **como quiera** anyhow; anyway; **como quiera que** whereas; inasmuch as; no matter how; **cuando quiera** any time; **donde quiera** anywhere; **querer bien** to love; **sin querer** unwillingly; unintentionally ‖ *v aux* to wish to, want to, desire to; will; be about to, be trying to, e.g., **quiere llover** it is trying to rain; **querer decir** to mean; **querer más** to prefer to, would rather

queri•do -da *adj* dear ‖ *mf* lover; paramour; dearie ‖ *f* mistress

quermés *f* or **quermese** *f* bazaar; village or country fair

queroseno *m* var of **keroseno**

querubín *m* cherub

quesadilla *f* cheesecake; sweet pastry

quese•ro -ra *adj* cheesy ‖ *mf* cheesemonger; cheesemaker ‖ *f* cheese board; cheese mold; cheese dish

queso *m* cheese; **queso de cerdo** headcheese; **queso helado** brick ice cream; **queso para extender** cheese spread

quevedos *mpl* nose glasses

quiá *interj* oh, no!

quicio *m* pivot hole (*of hinge*); **fuera de quicio** out of order; **sacar de quicio** to put out of order; unhinge

quiebra *f* crack; damage, loss; bankruptcy

quien *pron rel* who, whom; he who, she who; someone who, anyone who

quién *pron interr* who, whom

quienquiera *pron indef* anyone, anybody; **quienquiera que** whoever; **a quienquiera que** whomever

quie•to -ta *adj* quiet, calm; virtuous

quietud *f* quiet, calm, stillness

quijada *f* jaw, jawbone

quijotes•co -ca *adj* quixotic

quilate *m* carat

quilo *m* kilogram; **sudar el quilo** to slave, be a drudge

quilla *f* keel; (*de ave*) breastbone; **dar de quilla** (naut) to keel over

quimera *f* chimera; dispute, quarrel

química *f* chemistry

quími•co -ca *adj* chemical ‖ *mf* chemist ‖ *f* see **química**

quimicultura *f* tank farming

quimono *m* kimono

quimioterapia *f* chemotherapy

quina *f* cinchona, Peruvian bark

quincalla *f* hardware

quincallería *f* hardware store; hardware business; hardware factory

quincalle•ro -ra *mf* hardware merchant

quince *adj* & *pron* fifteen ‖ *m* fifteen; (*en las fechas*) fifteenth

quincea•vo -va *adj* & *m* fifteenth

quince•no -na *adj & m* fifteenth ‖ *f* fortnight, two weeks; two weeks' pay

quincuagési•mo -ma *adj & m* fiftieth

quiniela *f* pelota game of five; soccer lottery; daily double; (Arg, Urug) numbers game

quinien•tos -tas *adj & pron* five hundred ‖ **quinientos** *m* five hundred

quinina *f* quinine

quinqué *m* student lamp, oil lamp

quinquenal *adj* five-year

quinta *f* villa, country house; draft, induction; **ir a quintas** to be drafted; **redimirse de las quintas** to be exempted from the draft

quintacolumnista *mf* fifth columnist

quintal *m* quintal, hundredweight

quintar *tr* to draft

quinteto *m* quintet

quintilla *f* five-line stanza of eight syllables and two rhymes; any five-line stanza with two rhymes

quintilli•zo -za *mf* quint, quintuplet

Quintín — **armar la de San Quintín** to raise a rumpus, raise a row

quin•to -ta *adj* fifth ‖ *m* fifth; lot; pasture; draftee ‖ *f* see **quinta**

quinza•vo -va *adj & m* fifteenth

quiosco *m* kiosk, summerhouse; stand; **quiosco de música** bandstand; **quiosco de necesidad** comfort station; **quiosco de periódicos** newsstand

quiquiri•quí *m* (*pl* **-quíes**) cock-a-doodle-doo; cock of the walk

quirófano *m* operating room

quiromancia *f* or **quiromancía** *f* palmistry

quiropodista *mf* chiropodist

quiroprácti•co -ca *adj* chiropractic ‖ *mf* chiropractor

quirúrgi•co -ca *adj* surgical

quirurgo *m* surgeon

quiscal *m* grackle

quisicosa *f* puzzler

quisqui•do -da *adj* (Arg) constipated

quisquilla *f* trifle, triviality; **pararse en quisquillas** to bicker, make a fuss over trifles; **quisquillas** hairsplitting, quibbling

quisquillo•so -sa *adj* trifling; touchy; fastidious; hairsplitting

quiste *m* cyst

quis•to -ta *adj* — **bien quisto** well-liked, welcome; **mal quisto** disliked, unwelcome

quitaesmalte *m* nail-polish remover

quitaman•chas *mf* (*pl* **-chas**) (*persona*) clothes cleaner, spot remover ‖ *m* (*substancia*) clothes cleaner, spot remover

quitamo•tas *mf* (*pl* **-tas**) bootlicker, apple polisher

quitanie•ve *m* or **quitanie•ves** *m* (*pl* **-ves**) snowplow

quitapie•dras *m* (*pl* **-dras**) cowcatcher

quitapintura *m* paint remover

quitapón *m* pompon for draft mules; **de quitapón** detachable, removable

quitar *tr* to remove; take away; (*la mesa*) clear; (*esfuerzo, trabajo*) save; (*tiempo*) take; free; parry; **quitar algo a algo** to take something off something, remove something from something; **quitar algo a uno** to remove something from someone; take something away from someone ‖ *intr* — **de quita y pon** detachable, removable ‖ *ref* (*el sombrero, una prenda de vestir*) to take off; (*el sombrero en señal de cortesía*) tip; (*una mancha*) come out, come off; (*un vicio*) give up; withdraw

quitasol *m* parasol

quite *m* removal; hindrance; dodge; (*en la esgrima*) parry; (taur) passes made with the cape to draw the bull away from the man in danger

quizá or **quizás** *adv* maybe, perhaps

quó•rum *m* (*pl* **-rum**) quorum

R

R, r (ere) *f* twenty-first letter of the Spanish alphabet

R. *abbr* **respuesta, Reverencia, Reverendo**

rabada *f* hind quarter, rump

rabadilla *f* base of the spine

rábano *m* radish; **rábano picante** or **rusticano** horseradish; **tomar el rábano por las hojas** to be on the wrong track

ra•bí *m* (*pl* **-bíes**) rabbi

rabia *f* anger, rage; (*hidrofobia*) rabies; **tener rabia a** to have a grudge against

rabiar *intr* to rage, rave; get mad; go mad, have rabies; **que rabia** like the deuce; **rabiar por** to be dying for; be dying to

rabieta *f* tantrum

rabillo *m* leafstalk; flower stalk; (*en los cereales*) mildew spot; (*del ojo*) corner

rabio•so -sa *adj* mad, rabid

rabo *m* tail; (*del ojo*) corner; (fig) tail, train; **rabo verde** (CAm) old rake

ra•bón -bona *adj* bobtail; (Chile) bare, naked; (Mex) mean, wretched ‖ *f* camp follower; **hacer rabona** to play hooky

rabotada *f* swish of the tail; coarse remark

rabu•do -da *adj* long-tailed

racial *adj* racial

racimar *ref* to cluster, gather together

racimo *m* bunch; cluster; (*de perlas*) string

raciocinio *m* reasoning

ración *f* ration; allowance; **ración de hambre** starvation wages

racional *adj* rational

racionar *tr* to ration

racismo *m* racism

qu
ra

racista adj & mf racist
racha f split, crack; chip; squall, gust of wind; streak of luck
rada f (naut) road, roadstead
radar m radar
radiación f radiation
radicti•vo -va adj radioactive
radia•dor -dora adj radiating ‖ m radiator
radiante adj radiant; (alegre, sonriente) radiant
radiar tr to radiate; radio; broadcast; cross out, erase ‖ intr to radiate
radicación f taking root; (math) evolution
radical adj & m radical
radicar §73 intr to take root; be located ‖ ref to take root; settle; (un negocio) be based
radio m edge, outskirts; (de una rueda) spoke, rung; (de acción) radius; (chem) radium; (math) radius ‖ m & f radio
radioaficiona•do -da mf radio amateur, radio fan
radiodifundir tr & intr to broadcast
radiodifusión f broadcasting
radioemisora f broadcasting station
radioescucha mf radio listener; radio monitor
radiofrecuencia f radio frequency
radiografiar §77 tr to X-ray; radio
radiograma m X-ray (photograph)
radiola f record player
radioperturbación f jamming
radioteléfono m radio(tele)phone
radioterapia f radiotherapy
radioyente mf radio listener
raer §56 tr to scrape, scrape off; smooth, level; wipe ‖ ref to become frayed, wear away
ráfaga f gust, puff; gust of wind; flash of light; (de ametralladora) burst; **ráfaga violenta** (aer) wind shear
raí•do -da adj threadbare; barefaced
ra•íz f (pl -íces) root; **a raíz de** close to the root of; even with; right after, hard upon; **de raíz** by the root; completely; **echar raíces** to take root
raja f crack, split; splinter, chip; slice
rajar tr to crack, split; splinter, chip; slice ‖ intr to boast; chatter ‖ ref to crack, split; splinter, chip; (Mex, CAm, W-I) to back down, break one's promise
rajatabla — **a rajatabla** desperately, ruthlessly
ralea f kind, quality; breed, ilk
ralear intr to thin out; be true to form
ralentí m slow motion
ra•lo -la adj sparse, thin
rallador m grater
rallar tr to grate; grate on, annoy
rallo m grater; scraper; rasp; (de la regadera) spout, nozzle; unglazed porous jug (for cooling water by evaporation)
rama f branch, bough; **andarse por las ramas** to beat about the bush; **en rama** raw; unbound, in sheets; in the grain
ramaje m branches, foliage
ramal m (de una cuerda) strand; halter; branch; (rr) branch line

ramalazo m lash; (señal en el cutis por un golpe o enfermedad) spot, pock; sharp pain; blow, sudden sorrow
rambla f dry ravine; avenue, boulevard
ramera f whore, harlot
ramificar §73 tr & ref to ramify
ramillete m bouquet; centerpiece, epergne; (bot) cluster
ramo m branch, limb; bouquet, cluster; (de géneros, negocios, etc.) line; (p.ej., de una ciencia) branch; (de una enfermedad) touch, slight attack
ramojo m brushwood, dead wood
ramonear intr to trim twigs; browse
rampa f ramp; cramp; (aer) apron; (Bol) litter, stretcher; **rampa de lanzamiento** launching pad
ram•plón -plona adj (zapato) heavy, coarse; common, vulgar
ramplonería f coarseness, vulgarity
rana f frog; **no ser rana** to be a past master; **rana toro** bullfrog
ran•cio -cia adj rank, rancid, stale; (vino) old; old, ancient; old, old-fashioned
ranchar ref (Col, Ven) to balk
ranchear tr to sack, pillage ‖ intr & ref to build huts, form a settlement
ranchera f (Ven) station wagon
ranchero m messman; rancher, ranchman
rancho m mess; meeting, gathering; camp; thatched hut; ranch; (naut) stock of provisions; (Arg) straw hat; **hacer rancho** to make room; **hacer rancho aparte** to be a lone wolf, go one's own way
randa m pickpocket ‖ f lace trimming
rango m rank; class, nature; pomp, splendor; (elevada condición social) status, standing
ranura f groove; slot
rapagón m stripling
rapar tr to shave; crop; scrape; snatch, filch ‖ ref to shave; (una vida regalada) lead
ra•paz (pl -paces) adj thievish; rapacious ‖ m young boy, lad
rapaza f young woman, lass
rapé m snuff
rápi•do -da adj rapid ‖ m (rr) express; **rápidos** (de un río) rapids
raposa f fox; female fox; (persona) (coll) fox
raposo m male fox; foxy fellow; slipshod fellow
raptar tr to abduct; kidnap
rapto m abduction; kidnaping; rapture; faint, swoon
raque m beachcombing; **andar al raque** to go beachcombing
raquear intr to beachcomb
raquero m priate; beachcomber
raqueta f racket; battledore; badminton; snowshoe; **raqueta y volante** battledore and shuttlecock
raquíti•co -ca adj (que padece raquitis) rickety; flimsy, weak, miserable
raquitis f rickets
raramente adv rarely, seldom; oddly
rareza f rareness; rarity; oddness, strangeness; peculiarity

ra•ro -ra *adj* rare; odd, strange; thin, sparse

ras *m* evenness; **a ras** close, even, flush; **a ras de** even with, flush with; **ras con ras** flush, at the same level; grazing

rasar *tr* to graze, skim ‖ *ref* to clear up

rascacie•los *m* (*pl -los*) skyscraper

rascamoño *m* fancy hairpin; (bot) zinnia

rascar §73 *tr* to scrape; scuff; scratch; scrape clean ‖ *ref* (*una cicatriz, un grano*) to pick; get drunk

rasete *m* satinet

rasga•do -da *adj* (*boca; ventana*) wide-open; (*ojos*) large; outspoken; (Col) generous ‖ *m* tear, rip, rent

rasgar §44 *tr* to tear, rip ‖ *ref* to become torn

rasgo *m* (*de una pluma de escribir*) flourish, stroke; trait, characteristic; feat, deed; flash of wit, bright remark; **a grandes rasgos** in bold strokes; **rasgos** (*de la cara*) features

rasguear *tr* to thrum on ‖ *intr* to make a flourish

rasgón *m* tear, rip, rent

rasguñar *tr* to scratch; sketch, outline

rasguño *m* scratch; sketch, outline

ra•so -sa *adj* smooth, flat, level, even; common, plain; clear, cloudless; (coll) brazen, shameless ‖ *m* flat country; satin; **al raso** in the open

raspa *f* stalk, stem; (*de mazorca de maíz*) beard; (*de pez*) spine, backbone; shell, rind; (CAm, Mex) dirty trick, nasty joke

raspadura *f* scraping; erasure; pan sugar

raspar *tr* to scrape, scrape off; scratch, scratch out; graze; (*el vino*) bite; take, steal; (W-I) to dismiss, fire; (W-I) to scold ‖ *intr* (Ven) to go away; (Ven) to die

raspear *tr* (SAm) to scold ‖ *intr* (*una pluma*) to scratch

rastra *f* rake; harrow; drag; track, trail; (*p.ej., de cebollas*) string; (naut) drag; **pescar a la rastra** to trawl

rastracuero *m* show-off; upstart; sharper, adventurer

rastreador *m* dredge; (nav) mine sweeper

rastrear *tr* to trail, track, trace; drag; dredge; check into ‖ *intr* to rake; skim the ground, fly low

rastre•ro -ra *adj* dragging, trailing; creeping; low-flying; groveling, cringing; low, vile

rastrillar *tr* to rake; (*cáñamo, lino*) hatchel, comb; (Arg, Col) to shoot, to fire; (*un fósforo*) (Arg, Col) to strike (*a match*)

rastrillo *m* rake; hackle, hatchel, flax comb; (*de cerradura o llave*) ward; grating, iron grate; (rr) cowcatcher

rastro *m* rake; harrow; track, trail; scent; trace, vestige; slaughterhouse; wholesale meat market; rag fair; **rastro de condensación** (aer) contrail

rastrojo *m* stubble

rasura *f* shaving; scraping

rasurar *tr* & *ref* to shave

rata *f* rat; female rat; **rata del trigo** hamster

ratear *tr* to apportion; snitch

ratería *f* baseness, meanness, vileness; petty thievery; petty theft

rate•ro -ra *adj* thievish; trailing, dragging; base, vile ‖ *mf* sneak thief

raticida *f* rat poison

ratificar §73 *tr* to ratify

rato *m* time, while, little while; **a ratos** from time to time; **a ratos perdidos** in spare time, in one's leisure hours; **buen rato** pleasant time; large amount; **pasar el rato** to waste one's time; **un rato** awhile

ratón *m* mouse; (Ven) hangover; **ratón de biblioteca** bookworm

ratonera *f* (*trampa*) mousetrap; (*agujero*) mousehole; nest of mice; hut, shop

rau•do -da *adj* rapid, swift, impetuous

raya *f* stripe; (*línea fina; pez*) ray; (*en la imprenta, la escritura y la telegrafía*) dash; (*de los pantalones*) crease; (*en los cabellos*) part; boundary line, limit; (*para impedir la comunicación del incendio en los campos*) firebreak; (*del espectro*) (phys) line; (Mex) pay, wages; **a rayas** striped; **hacerse la raya** to part one's hair; **pasar de la raya** to go too far; **tener a raya** to keep within bounds

raya•no -na *adj* bordering; borderline

rayar *tr* (*papel*) to rule, line; stripe; scratch; score, mark; cross out; underscore ‖ *intr* to border; stand out; (*el alba, el día, la luz, el sol*) begin, arise, come forth; **rayar en** to verge on, border on ‖ *ref* (Col) to get rich

rayo *m* (*de luz*) ray; (*de rueda*) spoke; lightning, flash of lightning, stroke of lightning, thunderbolt; (*persona*) (fig) live wire; **echar rayos** to blow up, hit the ceiling; **rayo mortífero** death ray; **rayos X** X rays

rayón *m* rayon

raza *f* race; breed, stock; crack, slit; quality; ray of light (*coming through a crack*)

razón *f* reason; right, justice; account, story; (*cantidad o grado medidos por otra cosa tomada como unidad*) rate; (math) ratio; **a razón de** at the rate of; **con razón o sin ella** right or wrong; **hacer la razón** to return a toast; join at table; **meterse en razón** to listen to reason; **no tener razón** to be wrong; **razón social** firm name, trade name; **tener razón** to be right; be in the right

razonable *adj* reasonable

razonar *tr* to reason, reason out; itemize ‖ *intr* to reason

reabrir §83 *tr* & *ref* to reopen

reacción *f* reaction; **reacción en cadena** chain reaction

reaccionar *intr* to react

reacciona•rio -ria *adj* & *mf* reactionary

rea•cio -cia *adj* stubborn, obstinate

reactivo *m* reagent

real *adj* real; royal; fine, splendid ‖ *m* army camp; fairground; real (*old Spanish coin; Spanish money of account equal to a quarter of a peseta*)

realce *m* embossment, raised work; enhancement, lustre; emphasis; **bordar de realce** to embroider in relief; (fig) to embroider, to exaggerate

ra
re

realeza *f* royalty

realidad *f* reality; truth; **hecho realidad come true**, e.g., **un sueño hecho realidad** a dream come true

realismo *m* realism

realista *mf* (*persona que tiende a ver las cosas como son*) realist; (*partidario de la monarquía*) royalist

realización *f* realization, fulfillment; achievement; sale; **realización de beneficios** profit taking

realizar §60 *tr* to fulfill; carry out; turn into cash ‖ *ref* to become fulfilled; be carried out

realquilar *tr* to sublet

realzar §60 *tr* to raise, elevate; emboss; enhance, set off; emphasize

reanimar *tr* to revive, restore; cheer, encourage ‖ *ref* to revive, recover one's spirits

reanudar *tr* to renew, resume

reaparecer §22 *intr* to reappear

reata *f* rope to keep animals in single file; single file; **de reata** in single file; in blind submission; next, following

rebaba *f* burr, fin

rebaja *f* rebate; diminution

rebajar *tr* to lower; diminish, reduce; rebate; (*precios*) mark down; (*a una persona*) deflate; (carp) to rabbet ‖ *ref* to stoop; humble oneself

rebajo *m* rabbet, groove; offset, recess

rebalsar *tr* to dam ‖ *ref* to become dammed up; be checked; pile up, accumulate

rebanada *f* slice

rebanar *tr* to slice; cut through

rebañadera *f* grapnel

rebaño *m* flock

rebarbati•vo -va *adj* crabbed, surly

rebasar *tr* to exceed; overflow; sail past

rebatiña *f* grabbing, scramble; **andar a la rebatiña** to scramble

rebatir *tr* to repel, drive back; check; resist; strengthen; rebut, refute; deduct, rebate; beat hard

rebato *m* alarm, call to arms; alarm, excitement; (mil) surprise attack

rebeca *f* cardigan

rebelar *ref* to revolt, rebel; resist; break away

rebelde *adj* rebellious; stubborn ‖ *mf* rebel

rebeldía *f* rebelliousness; defiance, stubbornness

rebelión *f* rebellion, revolt

rebe•lón -lona *adj* balky, restive

rebobinar *tr* to rewind; unwind

reborde *m* flange, rim, collar

rebosar *tr* to cause overflow ‖ *intr* to overflow, run over; be in abundance; **rebosar de** or **en** to overflow with, burst with; be rich in; have an abundance of ‖ *ref* to overflow, run over

rebotar *tr* to bend back; repel; annoy, worry ‖ *intr* to bounce; bounce back, rebound ‖ *ref* to become annoyed, become worried

rebote *m* bounce; rebound

rebozar §60 *tr* (*la cara*) to muffle up; cover with batter ‖ *ref* to muffle up, muffle oneself up

rebozo *m* muffling; muffler; shawl; **de rebozo** secretly; **sin rebozo** frankly, openly

rebulta•do -da *adj* bulky, massive

rebullicio *m* hubbub, loud uproar

rebullir §13 *intr* to stir, begin to move; give signs of life ‖ *ref* to stir, begin to move

rebusca *f* seeking, searching; gleaning; leavings, refuse

rebusca•do -da *adj* affected, unnatural, recherché

rebuscar §73 *tr* to seek after; search into; to glean

rebuznar *intr* to bray; talk nonsense

rebuzno *m* braying; nonsense

recade•ro -ra *mf* messenger ‖ *m* errand boy

recado *m* errand; message; gift, present; daily marketing; compliments; regards; safety, security; equipment, outfit; **mandar recado** to send word; **recado de escribir** writing materials

recaer §15 *intr* to fall again; fall back; relapse; backslide; **recaer en** to fall to; **recaer sobre** to fall upon, devolve upon

recaída *f* relapse; backsliding

recalar *tr* to soak, saturate ‖ *intr* to sight land

recalcar §73 *tr* to press, squeeze; cram, pack, stuff; (*sus palabras*) stress ‖ *intr* (naut) to list, heel; **recalcar en** to lay stress on ‖ *ref* to harp on the same string; sprawl; (*p.ej., la muñeca*) sprain

recalentar §2 *tr* to overheat; (*la comida*) to warm over

recalmón *m* (naut) lull

recamado *m* embroidery

recamar *tr* to embroider

recámara *f* dressing room; (*de un arma de fuego*) breech, chamber; reserve, caution; (Mex) bedroom

recamarera *f* (Mex) chambermaid

recambio *m* spare part; (*parte, rueda, etc.*) **de recambio** spare

recapacitar *tr* to run over in one's mind ‖ *intr* to refresh one's memory; reflect

recargable *adj* rechargeable

recargar §44 *tr* to reload; overload; recharge; overcharge; overadorn; (*una cuota de impuesto*) increase; (elec) to recharge ‖ *ref* to become more feverish

recargo *m* new burden; extra charge; new charge; (*que paga el contribuyente moroso*) penalty; (pathol) rise in temperature; **recargo de tarifa** extra fare

recata•do -da *adj* cautious, circumspect; modest; shy

recatar *tr* to hide, conceal ‖ *ref* to hide; be afraid to take a stand

recato *m* caution, reserve; modesty

recauchutaje *m* recapping, retreading

recauchutar *tr* to recap, retread

recaudar *tr* (*impuestos, tributos*) to gather, collect; guard, watch over

recaudo *m* tax collecting; care, precaution; bail, surety; **a buen recaudo** under guard, in safety

recelar *tr* to fear, distrust ‖ *intr* & *ref* to fear, be afraid

recelo *m* fear, distrust

recelo•so -sa *adj* fearful, distrustful
recensión *f* review, book review
recepción *f* reception; reception desk
recepcionista *m* room clerk ‖ *f* receptionist
receptáculo *m* receptacle; shelter, refuge
receptador *m* (coll) fence, holder of stolen goods
receptar *tr* to receive, welcome; (*delincuentes*) hide, conceal; (*cosas robadas*) receive
recepti•vo -va *adj* receptive; susceptible
receptor *m* receiver; **receptor de cabeza** headpiece; **receptor telefónico** receiver
receta *f* recipe; (pharm) prescription
recetar *tr* (*un medicamento*) to prescribe; request
recibí *m* receipt; received payment
recibida *f* reception; admission
recibi•dor -dora *mf* receiver; receiving teller; ticket collector ‖ *m* reception room
recibimiento *m* reception; welcome; reception room; (*visita en que una persona recibe a sus amistades*) at-home
recibir *tr* to receive; (*visitas*) entertain ‖ *intr* to receive; entertain ‖ *ref* to be received, be admitted; **recibirse de** to be admitted to practice as; be graduated as
recibo *m* reception; receipt; hall; parlor; at-home; **acusar recibo de** to acknowledge receipt of; **estar de recibo** to be at home; **ser de recibo** to be acceptable
reciclable *adj* recyclable
reciclado *m* or **reciclaje** *m* recycling
reciclar *tr* to recycle
recién *adv* (used before past participles) recently, just, newly, e.g., **recién llegado** newly arrived; just now, recently
reciente *adv* recently
recinto *m* area, inclosure, place
re•cio -cia *adj* strong; thick, coarse, heavy; harsh; hard, bitter, arduous; (*tiempo*) severe; swift, impetuous ‖ **recio** *adv* strongly; swiftly; hard; loud
reciprocidad *f* reciprocity
recípro•co -ca *adj* reciprocal
recital *m* (*de música o poesía*) recital
recitar *tr* to recite; (*un discurso*) deliver
reclamación *f* claim, demand; objection; protest, complaint
reclamar *tr* to claim, demand; (*un ave*) decoy, lure ‖ *intr* to cry out, protest, complain
réclame *m & f* advertising
reclamo *m* bird call; decoy bird; (*para aves*) lure; allurement, attraction; advertisement; blurb, puff; reference; (typ) catchword; (SAm) complaint
reclinar *tr* (*p.ej., la cabeza*) to lean, bend ‖ *ref* to recline
reclinatorio *m* prie-dieu; couch, lounge
recluir §20 *tr* to seclude, shut in; imprison ‖ *ref* to go into seclusion
reclusión *f* seclusion; imprisonment
reclu•so -sa *adj* secluded; imprisoned ‖ *mf* prisoner; inmate
recluta *m* recruit ‖ *f* recruiting; (*del ganado disperso*) (Arg) roundup

reclutar *tr* to recruit; (Arg) to round up
recobrar *tr* to recover ‖ *ref* to recover; come to
recobro *m* recovery; (*de un motor*) pickup
recodar *intr* to lean; bend, twist, turn, wind
recodo *m* bend, twist, turn
recoger §17 *tr* to pick up; gather, collect; harvest; shorten, draw in; keep; welcome; lock up ‖ *ref* to take shelter, take refuge; withdraw; (*echarse en la cama*) retire; go home; cut down expenses
recogida *f* collection; withdrawal; suspension; **recogida de basuras** garbage collection
recogimiento *m* gathering, collecting; harvesting; seclusion, retreat; concentration; self-communion
recolectar *tr* to gather, gather in; (*el algodón*) pick
recombina•do -da *adj* (*genética*) recombinant
recomendable *adj* commendable
recomendar §2 *tr* to recommend; commend
recompensa *f* recompense, reward
recompensar *tr* to recompense, reward
recompostura *f* repair
recomprar *tr* to buy back, repurchase
reconcentrar *tr* to bring together; (*un sentimiento o afecto*) conceal, disguise ‖ *ref* to come together; be absorbed in thought
reconciliar *tr* to reconcile ‖ *ref* to become reconciled
recóndi•to -ta *adj* hidden, concealed
reconfortar *tr* to comfort, cheer
reconocer §22 *tr* to recognize; admit, acknowledge; examine; (mil) to reconnoiter ‖ *intr* (mil) to reconnoiter ‖ *ref* to be clear
reconoci•do -da *adj* grateful
reconocimiento *m* recognition; admission; acknowledgment; gratitude; reconnaissance; **reconocimiento médico** inquest
reconquista *f* reconquest
reconsiderar *tr* to reconsider
reconstruir §20 *tr* to reconstruct, rebuild, recast
recontar §61 *tr* (*volver a contar; narrar*) to recount (*to count again; narrate*)
reconvenir §79 *tr* to expostulate with, to remonstrate with
reconversión *f* reconversion
recopilar *tr* to compile
record *m* (*pl* **records**) (sport) record; **batir un record** to break a record; **establecer un récord** to make a record
recordar §61 *tr* to remember; remind ‖ *intr* to remember; get awake; come to; **si mal no recuerdo** if I remember correctly
recordati•vo -va *adj* reminding, reminiscent ‖ *m* reminder
recordatorio *m* reminder; memento
record•man (*pl* **-men**) record holder
recorrer *tr* to go over, go through; look over, look through; (*un libro*) run through; overhaul
recorrido *m* trip, run, route; (*del émbolo*) stroke; repair
recortado *m* cutout

re
re

recortar *tr* to trim, cut off; (*figuras en una tela, en un papel*) cut out; outline ‖ *ref* to stand out

recorte *m* cutting; (*de un periódico*) clipping; dodge, duck; **recortes** cuttings, trimmings

recostar §61 *tr* to lean ‖ *ref* to lean, lean back, sit back

recova *f* poultry business; poultry stand; (Arg) portico; (SAm) food market

recoveco *m* bend, turn, twist; subterfuge, trick

recreación *f* recreation

recreo *m* recreation; place of amusement

recrudecer §22 *intr & ref* to flare up, get worse

rectángu•lo -la *adj* right-angled ‖ *m* rectangle

rectificar §73 *tr* to rectify; (*un cilindro de motor*) rebore

rec•to -ta *adj* straight; (*ángulo*) right; right, just, righteous ‖ *m* rectum

rec•tor -tora *adj* governing, managing ‖ *mf* principal, superior ‖ *m* rector; (*de una universidad*) rector, president

recua *f* drove; (*de personas o cosas*) string, line

recuadro *m* panel, square; (*sección de un impreso encerrada dentro de un marco*) box

recubrir §83 *tr* to cover, cap, coat

recuento *m* count; recount; inventory

recuerdo *m* memory, remembrance; keepsake, souvenir

recuero *m* muleteer

recular *intr* to back up; (*un arma de fuego*) recoil; back down

reculón *m* backing; **a reculones** backing away, recoiling

recuperar *tr & ref* to recuperate, recover

recurrir *intr* to resort, have recourse; revert

recurso *m* recourse; resource; resort; appeal, petition

recusar *tr* to refuse, reject; (law) to challenge

rechazar §60 *tr* to refuse, reject; repel, drive back

rechazo *m* rejection; rebound, recoil

rechifla *f* catcall

rechiflar *tr & intr* to catcall, hiss ‖ *ref* to make fun

rechinar *intr* to creak, grate, squeak; act with bad grace; (Mex) to rage

rechistar *intr* to stir, say a word; **sin rechistar** without protest

rechon•cho -cha *adj* chubby, tubby, plump

rechupete — de rechupete fine, wonderful

red *f* net; netting; network, system; baggage netting; (fig) net, snare, trap; **a red barredera** with a clean sweep; **red barredera** dragnet

redacción *f* writing; editing; editorial staff; newspaper office, city room

redactar *tr* to write up; edit

redac•tor -tora *mf* writer; editor, newspaper editor; **redactor publicitario** copy writer

redada *f* (*de peces*) catch, netful; (*p.ej., de criminales*) haul, roundup

redecilla *f* hair net

rededor *m* surroundings; **al rededor (de)** around

redención *f* redemption; help, recourse

reden•tor -tora *mf* redeemer

redición *f* constant repetition

redi•cho -cha *adj* overprecise

redil *m* sheepfold

redimir *tr* to redeem; ransom; buy back

rédito *m* income, revenue, yield

redituar §21 *tr* to yield, produce

redobla•do -da *adj* stocky, heavy-built; heavy, strong; (mil) double-quick

redoblar *tr* to double; clinch; repeat ‖ *intr* (*un tambor*) to roll

redoble *m* doubling; clinching; repeating; roll of a drum

redoma *f* phial, flask

redoma•do -da *adj* sly, crafty

redonda *f* district, neighborhood; (mus) semibreve; **a la redonda** around, roundabout

redondear *tr* to round, make round; round off; round out ‖ *ref* to be well-off; be out of debt

redondel *m* circle; round cloak; (*espacio destinado a la lidia*) (taur) ring

redondilla *f* eight-syllable quatrain with rhyme abba or abab

redon•do -da *adj* round; straightforward; (*terreno*) pasture; honest; stupid ‖ *m* ring, circle; cash ‖ *f* see **redonda**

redopelo *m* row, scuffle; **al redopelo** against the grain, the wrong way; roughly, violently

reducir §19 *tr & ref* to reduce; **reducirse a** to come to, amount to; be obliged to

reducto *m* (fort) redoubt

redundante *adj* redundant

redundar *intr* to redound; overflow; **redundar en** to redound to

reduplicación *f* doubling

reelección *f* reëlection

reembarcar §73 *tr, intr & ref* to reship, reëmbark

reembarco *m* reshipment (*of persons*), reëmbarkation

reembarque *m* reshipment (*of goods*)

reembolsar *tr* to reimburse; refund ‖ *ref* to collect a debt, be reimbursed

reembolso *m* reimbursement; refund; **contra reembolso** collect on delivery; cash on delivery

reemplazar §60 *tr* to replace

reemplazo *m* replacement; (mil) replacements; (*hombre que sirve en lugar de otro*) (mil) replacement

reencuadernar *tr* (bb) to rebind

reencuentro *m* collision; (*de tropas*) clash

reenganchar *tr & ref* to reënlist

reentrada *f* reëntry

reestrenar *tr* (theat) to revive

reestreno *m* (theat) revival

reexamen *m* or **reexaminación** *f* reëxamination

reexpedición *f* forwarding, reshipment

reexpedir §50 *tr* to forward, reship

refacción *f* refreshment; allowance; repair, repairs; extra, bonus; spare part

refaccionar *tr* to finance; (SAm) to repair, renovate

refajo *m* underskirt, slip

referencia *f* reference; account, report

referi•do -da *adj* above-mentioned

referir §68 *tr* to refer; tell, report ‖ *ref* to refer

refinamiento *m* refinement

refinar *tr* to refine; polish, perfect

refinería *f* refinery

reflejar *tr* to reflect; reflect on; show, reveal ‖ *intr* to reflect

reflejo *m* glare; reflection; reflex; **reflejo acondicionado** conditioned reflex; **reflejo patelar** or **rotuliano** knee jerk

reflexión *f* reflection

reflexionar *tr* to reflect on or upon ‖ *intr* to reflect

reflugo *m* ebb

refocilar *tr* to cheer; strengthen ‖ *intr* (Arg, Urug) to lighten ‖ *ref* to be cheered; take it easy

reforma *f* reform; reformation; alteration, renovation ‖ **la Reforma** the Reformation

reformación *f* reformation

reformar *tr* to reform; mend, repair; alter, renovate; revise; reorganize ‖ *ref* to reform; hold oneself in check

reforzar §35 *tr* to reinforce; strengthen; encourage

refracción *f* refraction

refracta•rio -ria *adj* rebellious, unruly, stubborn

refrán *m* proverb, saying

refregar §66 *tr* to rub; upbraid

refrenar *tr* to curb, rein; check, restrain

refrendar *tr* to countersign; authenticate; visé; repeat

refrescar §73 *tr* to refresh; cool, refrigerate ‖ *intr* & *ref* to refresh; refresh oneself; cool off; go out for fresh air; (*el viento*) (naut) to blow up

refresco *m* refreshment; cold drink, soft drink

refriega *f* fray, scuffle

refrigerador *m* refrigerator; ice bucket

refrigerio *m* coolness; relief; pick-me-up, light lunch

refuerzo *m* reinforcement

refugia•do -da *mf* refugee

refugiar *tr* to shelter ‖ *ref* to take refuge

refugio *m* refuge; hospice; shelter; haunt; (*para peatones en medio de la calle*) safety zone; **refugio antiaéreo** air-raid shelter; **refugio antiatómico** fallout shelter

refundición *f* recast; revision; (*de una pieza dramática*) adaptation

refundir *tr* to recast; revise; (*una pieza dramática*) adapt ‖ *intr* to redound

refunfuñar *intr* to grumble, growl

refutar *tr* to refute

regadera *f* watering can; street sprinkler

regadí•o -a or **regadi•zo -za** *adj* irrigable ‖ *m* irrigated land

regala *f* gunwale

regala•do -da *adj* dainty, delicate; pleasing, pleasant; (*vida*) of ease

regalar *tr* to give; regale, entertain; treat; caress, fondle; indulge

regalía *f* privilege, perquisite; bonus; royalty; (Arg, Chile) muff

regaliz *m* licorice

regalo *m* gift, present; treat; joy, pleasure; **regalos de fiesta** favors

rega•lón -lona *adj* comfort-loving, pampered; (*vida*) soft, easy

regañar *tr* to scold ‖ *intr* to growl, snarl; grumble; quarrel; scold

regaño *m* scolding; growl, snarl; grumble

regar §66 *tr* to water, sprinkle; irrigate; spread, sprinkle, strew

regate *m* dodge, duck; (fig) dodge, subterfuge

regatear *tr* to haggle over; sell at retail; avoid, shun ‖ *intr* to haggle, bargain; duck, dodge; (naut) to race

regazo *m* lap

regenerar *tr* & *ref* to regenerate

regente *m* director, manager; registered pharmacist; (typ) foreman

regicida *mf* regicide

regicidio *m* regicide

regi•dor -dora *adj* ruling, governing ‖ *m* alderman, councilman

régimen *m* (*pl* **regímenes**) regime; diet; rate; management; (gram) government; **régimen de hambre** starvation diet; **régimen de justicia** rule of law

regimental *adj* regimental

regimentar §2 *tr* to regiment

regimiento *m* regiment; rule, government; city council

re•gio -gia *adj* regal, royal; magnificent

región *f* region

regir §57 *tr* to rule, govern; control, manage; guide, steer; (gram) to govern ‖ *intr* to prevail, be in force

registra•dor -dora *adj* registering; recording ‖ *m* registrar, recorder; inspector ‖ *f* cash register

registrar *tr* to register; record; examine, inspect ‖ *ref* to register; be recorded; take place

registro *m* registration, registry; recording; examination, inspection; entry, record; bookmark; manhole; (*de chimenea*) damper; (*de reloj*) regulator; (*de órgano*) (mus) stop; (*de piano*) (mus) pedal

regla *f* rule; (*para trazar líneas*) ruler; measure, moderation; order; menstruation; **regla de cálculo** slide rule; **reglas** monthlies, menses

reglamenta•rio -ria *adj* prescribed, statutory

reglamento *m* rules, regulations

reglar *tr* to regulate; (*papel*) rule ‖ *ref* to guide oneself, be guided

regleta *f* (typ) lead

regletear *tr* (typ) to lead, space

regocijar *tr* to cheer, delight ‖ *ref* to rejoice

regocijo *m* cheer, delight, rejoicing

regoldar §3 *intr* to belch

regolfar *intr* & *ref* to surge back, flow back, back up

regorde•te -ta *adj* dumpy, plump

re
re

regresar *intr* to return
regreso *m* return; **estar de regreso** to be back
regüeldo *m* belch, belching
reguero *m* drip, trickle; (*señal que deja una cosa que se va vertiendo*) track; irrigating ditch; **ser un reguero de pólvora** to spread like wildfire
regulador *m* regulator; (*de locomotora*) throttle; (mach) governor
regular *adj* regular; fair, moderate, medium; **por lo regular** as a rule ‖ *tr* to regulate; put in order; throttle
rehabilitación *f* rehabilitation
rehacer §39 *tr* to remake, make over, do over; mend, repair, renovate ‖ *ref* to recover, rally
rehén *m* hostage; **llevarse en rehenes** to carry off as a hostage; **toma de rehenes** hostage taking
rehilandera *f* pinwheel
rehilar *intr* to quiver; whiz by
rehilete *m* shuttlecock; (*que se lanza por diversión*) dart; dig, cutting remark; (taur) banderilla
rehuir §20 *tr* to avoid, shun; shrink from; refuse; dislike ‖ *intr & ref* to flee
rehusar *tr* to refuse, turn down
reimpresión *f* reprint
reimprimir §83 *tr* to reprint
reina *f* queen; **reina Margarita** aster, China aster; **reina viuda** queen dowager
reinado *m* reign
reinar *intr* to reign; prevail
reincidir *intr* to backslide; repeat an offense
reingreso *m* reëntry
reino *m* kingdom; **Reino Unido** United Kingdom
reinstalar *tr* to reinstate, reinstall
reintegrar *tr* to refund, pay back
reintegro *m* refund, payment
reír §58 *tr* to laugh at ‖ *intr & ref* to laugh; **reír de** or **reírse de** to laugh at
reja *f* grate, grating, grille; plowshare, colter; **entre rejas** behind bars
rejilla *f* screen; grating; lattice, latticework; cane, cane upholstery; foot brasier; fire grate; (electron) grid; (*de acumulador*) (elec) grid; (rr) baggage rack
rejón *m* spear; dagger; (taur) lance
rejonear *tr* (*el jinete al toro*) (taur) to jab with a lance made to break off in the bull's neck
rejuvenecimiento *m* rejuvenation
relación *f* relation; account, list; (*en un drama*) speech; **relación de ciego** blind man's ballad; **relaciones** betrothal, engagement; **relaciones públicas** public relations
relacionar *tr* to relate ‖ *ref* to be related
relai *m* or **relais** *m* (elec) relay
relajación *f* or **relajamiento** *m* relaxation; slackening; laxity; rupture, hernia
relajar *tr* to relax; slacken; debauch ‖ *intr* to relax ‖ *ref* to relax, become relaxed; become debauched; be ruptured
relamer *ref* to lick one's lips; gloat; to relish; boast; slick oneself up
relami•do -da *adj* prim, overnice

relámpago *m* flash of lightning; flash of wit; **relámpago fotogénico** flash bulb, flashlight; **relámpagos** lightning
relampaguear *intr* to lighten; flash
relatar *tr* to relate, report
relati•vo -va *adj* relative
relato *m* story; statement, report
relé *m* (elec) relay; **relé de televisión** television relay system
releer §43 *tr* to reread
relegar §44 *tr* to relegate; banish, exile; shelve, lay aside
relente *m* night dew, light drizzle
relevador *m* (elec) relay
relevancia *f* relevance; significance
relevante *adj* outstanding
relevar *tr* to emboss; make stand out; relieve; release; absolve; replace ‖ *intr* to stand out in relief
relevo *m* (elec) relay; (mil) relief; **relevos** (sport) relay race
relicario *m* shrine; (*medallón*) locket
relieve *m* relief; merit, distinction; **en relieve** in relief; **poner de relieve** to point out; to make stand out; **relieves** scraps, leftovers
religión *f* religion
religio•so -sa *adj* religious
relinchar *intr* to neigh
relincho *m* neigh, neighing; cry of joy
reliquia *f* relic; trace, vestige; **reliquia de familia** heirloom
reloj *m* watch; clock; meter; **como un reloj** like clockwork; **conocer el reloj** to know how to tell time; **reloj de caja** grandfather's clock; **reloj de carillón** chime clock; **reloj de cuarzo** quartz watch; **reloj de cuclillo** cuckoo clock; **reloj de ocho días cuerda** eight-day clock; **reloj de pulsera** wrist watch; **reloj de sol** sundial; **reloj despertador** alarm clock; **reloj registrador** time clock; **reloj registrador de tarjetas** punch clock
relojera *f* watch case; watch pocket
relojería *f* watchmaking, clockmaking; watchmaker's shop
reloje•ro -ra *mf* watchmaker, clockmaker ‖ *f* see **relojera**
reluciente *adj* shining, brilliant, flashing
relucir §45 *intr* to shine
relumbrar *intr* to shine, dazzle, glare
relumbre *m* beam, sparkle; flash; dazzle, glare
relumbrón *m* flash, glare; tinsel; **de relumbrón** showy, tawdry
rellano *m* (*en la pendiente de un terreno*) level stretch; (*de escalera*) landing
rellenar *tr* to refill; fill up; stuff; pad; fill out; cram, stuff ‖ *ref* to fill up; cram, stuff oneself
relle•no -na *adj* full, packed; stuffed ‖ *m* refill; filling, stuffing; padding, wadding; (*en un escrito*) filler
remachar *tr* (*un clavo ya clavado*) to clinch; (*un roblón*) rivet; stress, emphasize ‖ *ref* (Col) to maintain strict silence
remache *m* clinching; riveting; rivet
remanso *m* dead water, backwater

remar *intr* to row; toil, struggle
remata•do -da *adj* hopeless; **loco rematado** raving mad
rematador *m* auctioneer
rematar *tr* to finish, put an end to; finish off, kill off; (*en una subasta*) knock down ‖ *intr* to end ‖ *ref* to come to ruin
remate *m* end; crest, top, finial; closing; highest bid; (*en una subasta*) sale; **de remate** hopelessly
rembolsar *tr* to reimburse; repay; redeem
rembolso *m* reimbursement; **contra rembolso** C.O.D. (cash on delivery)
remecer §46 *tr & ref* to shake, swing, rock
remedar *tr* to copy, imitate; ape, mimic; mock
remediar *tr* to remedy; help; prevent; (*del peligro*) free, save
remediava•gos *m* (*pl* **-gos**) short cut
remedio *m* remedy; help; recourse; **no hay remedio** or **no hay más remedio** it can't be helped; **no tener remedio** to be unavoidable
remedión *m* (theat) substitute performance
remedo *m* copy, imitation; poor imitation
remendar §2 *tr* to patch, mend, repair; darn; emend, correct; touch up
remen•dón -dona *mf* mender, repairer; shoe mender; tailor (*who does mending*)
reme•ro -ra *mf* rower ‖ *m* oarsman
remesa *f* remittance; shipment
remesar *tr* to remit; ship
remezón *m* hard shake; tremor
remiendo *m* patch; mending, repair; retouching; emendation, correction; job printing, job work; **a remiendos** piecemeal
remilga•do -da *adj* prim and finicky; affected, smirking
remilgar §44 *intr* to be prim and finicky; smirk
remilgo *m* primness, affectation
remira•do -da *adj* circumspect, discreet
remisión *f* remission; reference
remitente *mf* sender, shipper
remitido *m* (*noticia de un particular a un periódico*) personal; letter to the editor
remitir *tr* to remit; forward, send, ship; refer; defer, postpone; pardon, forgive ‖ *intr* to remit, let up; refer ‖ *ref* to remit, let up; defer, yield
remo *m* oar; leg, arm, wing; toil, labor; (sport) rowing; **aguantar los remos** to lie or rest on one's oars
remoción *f* discharge, dismissal; removal
remodelación *f* remodeling
remodelar *tr* to remodel
remojar *tr* to soak, steep, dip; celebrate with a drink; **remojar la palabra** to wet one's whistle
remojo *m* soaking, steeping; **poner en remojo** to put off to a more suitable time
remolacha *f* beet; **remolacha azucarera** sugar beet
remolcador *m* tug, tugboat; towboat; tow car
remolcar §73 *tr* to tow; take in tow
remoler §47 *tr* to grind up; bore
remolinear *tr, intr & ref* to eddy, whirl about

remolino *m* eddy, whirlpool; swirl, whirl; disturbance, commotion; throng, crowd; cowlick
remo•lón -lona *adj* lazy, indolent ‖ *mf* shirker, quitter
remolonear *intr* to refuse to budge
remolque *m* tow; towing; trailer; **a remolque** in tow
remontar *tr* to mend, repair; frighten away; elevate, raise up; (*p.ej., un río*) go up ‖ *intr* (*en el tiempo*) go back ‖ *ref* to rise, rise up; soar; (*en el tiempo*) go back
remontuar *m* stem-winder
remoquete *m* punch; nickname; sarcasm; flirting
rémora *f* hindrance, obstacle
remordimiento *m* remorse
remo•to -ta *adj* remote; unlikely; **estar remoto** to be rusty
remover §47 *tr* to remove; shake; stir; disturb, upset; dismiss, discharge ‖ *ref* to move away
remozar §60 *tr* to rejuvenate ‖ *ref* to become rejuvenated
rempujar *tr* to push, jostle
rempujón *m* push, jostle
remuda *f* change, replacement; change of clothes
remudar *tr* to change, replace; move around
remuneración *f* remuneration; **remuneración por rendimiento** piece wage
renacer §22 *intr* to be reborn, be born again; recover
renacimiento *m* rebirth; renaissance
renacuajo *m* tadpole; (coll) shrimp, little squirt
Renania *f* Rhineland
ren•co -ca *adj* lame
rencor *m* rancor; **guardar rencor** to bear malice
rendición *f* surrender; submission; fatigue, exhaustion; yield
rendi•do -da *adj* tired, worn-out; submissive
rendija *f* crack, split, slit
rendimiento *m* submission; exhaustion; yield; output; (mech) efficiency
rendir §50 *tr* to conquer; subdue; surrender; exhaust, wear out; return, give back; yield, produce; (*gracias, obsequios, homenaje*) render ‖ *intr* to yield ‖ *ref* to surrender; yield, give in; be exhausted, be worn out
renegar §66 *tr* to deny vigorously; abhor, detest ‖ *intr* to curse; be insulting; **renegar de** to deny; curse; abhor, detest
renegociación *f* renegotiation
Renfe, la acronym for **la Red Nacional de los Ferrocarriles Españoles** the Spanish National Railroad System
renglón *m* line; **a renglón sequido** right below; **leer entre renglones** to read between the lines
reniego *m* curse
reno *m* reindeer
renombra•do -da *adj* renowned, famous
renombre *m* renown, fame
renovar §61 *tr* to renew; renovate; transform, restore; remodel

re
re

renquear *intr* to limp

renta *f* income; private income; annuity; public debt; rent; **renta nacional** gross national product

rentar *tr* to produce, yield

rentista *mf* bondholder; financier; person of independent means

renuente *adj* reluctant, unwilling

renuevo *m* sprout, shoot; renewal

renuncia *f* renunciation; resignation; (law) waiver

renunciar *tr* to renounce; resign ‖ *intr* to renounce; (*no servir al palo que se juega*) renege; **renunciar a** to give up, renounce, waive

renuncio *m* slip, mistake; (*en juegos de naipes*) renege; lie

reñi•do -da *adj* on bad terms; bitter, hard-fought

reñir §72 *tr* (*regañar*) to scold; (*una batalla, un desafío*) fight ‖ *intr* to fight; be at odds, fall out

re•o -a *adj* guilty, criminal ‖ **reo** *mf* offender, criminal; (law) defendant

reojo — **de reojo** askance, out of the corner of one's eye; hostilely

reorganizar §60 *tr & ref* to reorganize

reorientación *f* reorientation

reóstato *m* rheostat

repanchigar or **repantigar** §44 *ref* to sprawl, loll

reparar *tr* to repair, mend; make amends for; notice, observe; (*un golpe*) parry ‖ *intr* to stop; **reparar en** to notice, pay attention to ‖ *ref* to stop; refrain

reparo *m* repairing, repairs; notice, observation; doubt, objection; shelter; bashfulness

repa•rón -rona *adj* faultfinding ‖ *mf* faultfinder

repartida *f* distribution; issuing

repartir *tr* to distribute; (*naipes*) deal

reparto *m* distribution; (*de naipes*) deal; (theat) cast; **reparto de acciones gratis** stock dividend

repasar *tr* to repass; retrace; review; revise; (*la ropa*) mend

repasata *f* scolding, reprimand

repaso *m* revision; (*de una lección*) review; mending; reprimand

repatriar §77 *tr* to repatriate; send home ‖ *intr & ref* to be repatriated; go or come home

repeler *tr* to repel, repulse

repente *m* start, sudden movement; **de repente** suddenly

repenti•no -na *adj* sudden, unexpected

repentista *mf* (mus) improviser; (mus) sight reader

repentizar §60 *intr* to improvise; (mus) to sight-read, perform at sight

repercutir *intr* to rebound; reëcho, reverberate

repertorio *m* repertory

repetición *f* repetition; (mus) repeat

repetir §50 *tr & intr* to repeat

repicar §73 *tr* to mince, chop up; ring, sound; sting again ‖ *intr* peal, ring out, resound ‖ *ref* to boast, be conceited

repique *m* chopping, mincing; peal, ringing; squabble, quarrel

repiqueteo *m* pealing, ringing; beating, rapping

repisa *f* shelf, ledge; bracket; **repisa de chimenea** mantelpiece; **repisa de ventana** window sill

replantear *tr* to lay out again; reaffirm, reimplement

replegar §66 *tr* to fold over and over ‖ *ref* to fold, fold up; (mil) to fall back

reple•to -ta *adj* replete, full, loaded; fat, chubby

réplica *f* answer, retort; replica

replicar §73 *tr* to argue against ‖ *intr* to answer back, retort

repli•cón -cona *adj* saucy, flip

repliegue *m* fold, crease; (mil) falling back

repollo *m* cabbage; (*p.ej., de lechuga, col*) head

reponer §54 *tr* to replace, put back; restore; (*una pieza dramática*) revive; **repuso** he replied ‖ *ref* to recover; calm down

reportaje *m* reporting; news coverage; report

reportar *tr* to check, restrain; get, obtain; bring, carry; report ‖ *ref* to restrain or control oneself

reporte *m* report, news report; gossip

repórter *m* reporter

reporte•ro -ra *mf* reporter

reposa cabezas *f* (aut) head rest

reposar *intr & ref* to rest, repose; take a nap; (*en la sepultura*) lie, be at rest; (*poso, sedimento*) settle

reposición *f* replacement; (*de la salud*) recovery; (theat) revival

reposo *m* rest, repose

repostar *tr, intr & ref* to stock up; refuel

repostería *f* pastry shop, confectionery; pantry

reposte•ro -ra *mf* pastry cook, confectioner

repregunta *f* (law) cross-examination

repreguntar *tr* (law) to cross-examine

reprender *tr* to reprehend, scold

represa *f* dam; damming; repression, check; (*de un buque*) recapture

represalia *f* reprisal; retaliation

represar *tr* to dam; repress, check; (*de un buque*) to recapture

representación *f* representation; dignity, standing; performance; **en representación de** representing; **representación exclusiva** sole dealership

representante *adj* representing ‖ *mf* representative; actor, player; (com) agent, representative

representar *tr* to represent; show, express; state, declare; act, perform, play; (*determinada edad*) appear to be ‖ *ref* to imagine

representati•vo -va *adj* representative

reprimenda *f* reprimand

reprimir *tr* to repress

reprobación *f* reproof; flunk, failure

reprobar §61 *tr* to reprove; flunk, fail

reprochar *tr* to reproach

reproche *m* reproach
reproducción *f* reproduction; breeding
reproducir §19 *tr* & *ref* to reproduce
repro•pio -pia *adj* balky
reptar *intr* to crawl; to cringe
reptil *m* reptile
república *f* republic
republica•no -na *adj* & *mf* republican ‖ *m* patriot
repudiar *tr* to repudiate, disown, disavow
repues•to -ta *adj* secluded; spare, extra ‖ *m* stock, supply; serving table; pantry; **de repuesto** spare, extra
repugnante *adj* repugnant, disgusting
repugnar *tr* to conflict with; contradict; object to, avoid; revolt, be repugnant to ‖ *intr* to be repugnant
repujar *tr* to emboss
repulgar §44 *tr* to hem, border
repulgo *m* hem, border
repuli•do -da *adj* highly polished; all dolled up
repulsar *tr* to reject, refuse
repulsi•vo -va *adj* repulsive
repuntar *tr* (*animales dispersos*) (Arg, Chile, Urug) to round up ‖ *intr* to begin to appear; (naut) to begin to rise; (naut) to begin to ebb ‖ *ref* to begin to turn sour; fall out
repuso see **reponer**
reputación *f* reputation, repute
reputar *tr* to repute; esteem
requebra•dor -dora *adj* flirtatious ‖ *mf* flirt
requebrar §2 *tr* to break into smaller pieces; flatter, flirt with
requemar *tr* to burn again; parch; overcook; inflame; bite, sting ‖ *ref* to become tanned or sunburned; smolder, burn within
requerir §68 *tr* to notify; summon; request; urge; check, examine; require; seek, look for; reach for; court, make love to
requesón *m* cottage cheese
requiebro *m* fine crushing; flattery, flattering remarks, flirtation
requisi•to -ta *adj* requisite ‖ *m* requisite, requirement; accomplishment; **requisito previo** prerequisite
res *f* head of cattle; beast; **reses** cattle
resabio *m* unpleasant aftertaste; bad habit, vice
resabio•so -sa *adj* sly, crafty; (*caballo*) vicious
resaca *f* surge, surf; undertow; (com) redraft; (slang) hangover
resalir §65 *intr* to jut out, project
resaltar *tr* to emphasize ‖ *intr* to bounce, rebound; jut out, project; stand out
resanar *tr* to retouch, patch, repair
resarcir §36 *tr* to indemnify, make amends to; (*un daño, un agravio*) repay; (*una pérdida*) make good; to mend, repair ‖ *ref* — **resarcirse de** to make up for
resbaladi•zo -za *adj* slippery; skiddy; risky; (*memoria*) shaky
resbalar *intr* to slide; skid; slip ‖ *ref* to slide; slip; (fig) to slip, to misstep

rescatar *tr* to ransom, redeem; rescue; (*el tiempo perdido*) make up for; relieve; atone for; (Mex) to resell
rescate *m* ransom, redemption; rescue; salvage; ransom money
rescindir *tr* to rescind
rescoldera *f* heartburn
rescoldo *m* embers; smoldering; doubt, scruple; **arder en rescoldo** to smolder
resenti•do -da *adj* resentful
resentimiento *m* resentment; sorrow, disappointment
resentir §68 *ref* to be resentful; **resentirse de** to feel the bad effects of; resent; suffer from
reseña *f* outline; book review; newspaper account; (mil) review
reseñador *m* reviewer; critic
reseñar *tr* to outline; (*un libro*) review; (mil) to review
reserva *f* reserve; reservation; **con** or **bajo la mayor reserva** in strictest confidence; **reserva de caza** game preserve
reservar *tr* to reserve; put aside; postpone; exempt; keep secret ‖ *ref* to save oneself, bide one's time; beware, be distrustful
resfriado *m* cold
resfriar §77 *tr* to cool, chill ‖ *intr* to turn cold ‖ *ref* to catch cold; cool off, grow cold
resguardar *tr* to defend; protect, shield ‖ *ref* to take shelter; protect oneself
resguardo *m* defense; protection; check, voucher; collateral; (naut) wide berth, sea room
residencia *f* residence; impeachment; **residencia de ancianos** nursing home; home for the aged
residenciar *tr* to call to account; impeach
residir *intr* to reside
residuo *m* residue, remains; remainder; **residuos radiactivos** radioactive waste
resignación *f* resignation
resignar *tr* to resign ‖ *ref* to resign, become resigned; **resignarse con** (*p.ej., su suerte*) to be resigned to
resina *f* resin
resistencia *f* resistance; strength; **resistencia de rejilla** (electron) grid leak
resistente *adj* resistant; strong; (hort) hardy; **resistente al rayado** scratch-resistant
resistir *tr* to bear, stand; (*la tentación*) resist ‖ *intr* to resist; hold out; **resistir a** (*la violencia; la risa*) resist; refuse to ‖ *ref* to resist; struggle; **resistirse a** to refuse to
resma *f* ream
resobrina *f* grandniece, greatniece
resobrino *m* grandnephew, greatnephew
resolución *f* resolution; **en resolución** in brief, in a word
resolver §47 & §83 *tr* to resolve; solve; decide on; dissolve ‖ *ref* to resolve; make up one's mind
resollar §61 *intr.* to breathe; breathe hard, pant; stop for a rest
resonar §61 *intr* to resound, echo
resoplar *intr* to puff; snort
resoplido *m* puffing; snort

re
re

resorte *m* spring; springiness; means; province, scope; rubber band; **resorte espiral** coil spring; **tocar resortes** to pull wires, pull strings

respailar *intr* — **ir respailando** to scurry along

respaldar *m* back; ‖ *tr* to back; indorse ‖ *ref* to lean back; sprawl

respaldo *m* back; backing; indorsement

respectar *tr* (with personal **a**) to concern; **por lo que respecta a . . .** as far as . . . is concerned

respecti•vo -va *adj* respective

respecto *m* respect, reference, relation; **al respecto** in the matter; **respecto a** or **de** with respect to, in or with regard to

respetable *adj* respectable

respetar *tr* to respect

respeto *m* respect; consideration; **campar por sus respetos** to be inconsiderate, go one's (his, her, etc.) own way; **de respeto** spare, extra

respetuo•so -sa *adj* respectful; awesome, impressive; humble, obedient

respigón *m* hangnail

respingar §44 *intr* to balk, shy; (*elevarse el borde, p.ej., de la falda*) curl up; give in unwillingly

respin•gón -gona *adj* (*nariz*) snubby, upturned; surly, churlish

respirar *tr* to breathe ‖ *intr* to breathe; breathe freely; breathe a sigh of relief; catch one's breath, stop for a rest; **no respirar** to not breathe a word; **sin respirar** without respite, without letup

respiro *m* breathing; respite, breather, breathing spell; (*para el pago de una deuda*) extension of time

resplandecer §22 *intr* to shine; flash, glitter

resplandeciente *adj* brilliant; resplendent

resplandor *m* brilliance, radiance; resplendence; glare

responder *tr* to answer ‖ *intr* to answer, respond; correspond; answer back; **responder de** (*una cosa*) to answer for; **responder por** (*una persona*) to answer for

respon•dón -dona *adj* (coll) saucy

responsable *adj* responsible; **responsable de** responsible for

responsabilizar *tr* to put in charge; hold responsible ‖ *ref* to assume responsibility

respuesta *f* answer, response

resquebrajar *tr & ref* to crack, split

resquemar *tr & intr* to bite, sting ‖ *ref* to be parched; (*resentirse sin manifestarlo*) smolder

resquemo *m* bite, sting

resquicio *m* crack, chink; chance, opportunity

restablecer §22 *tr* to reëstablish, restore ‖ *ref* to recover

restañar *tr* to retin; (*sangre*) stanch, stop the flow of

restar *tr* to deduct; reduce; take away; (*una pelota*) return; subtract ‖ *intr* to remain, be left

restaurante *m* restaurant; **restaurante automático** automat

restaurar *tr* to restore; to recover

restitución *f* restitution, return

restituir §20 *tr* to return, give back; restore ‖ *ref* to return, come back

resto *m* rest, remainder, residue; (*en juegos de naipes*) stakes; (*de una pelota*) return; **a resto abierto** without limit; **echar el resto** to stake all, shoot the works; **restos** remains, mortal remains; **restos de serie** remnants

restregar §66 *tr* to rub hard; scrub hard

restringir §27 *tr* to restrict; constrict, to contract

resucitar *tr & intr* to resuscitate; resurrect; revive

resuel•to -ta *adj* resolute, resolved, determined; prompt, quick

resuello *m* breathing; hard breathing, panting

resulta *f* result; outcome; vacancy; **de resultas de** as a result of

resultado *m* result

resultar *intr* to result; prove to be, turn out to be; be, become

resumen *m* summary, résumé; **en resumen** in brief, in a word

resumir *tr* to summarize, sum up ‖ *ref* to be reduced, be transformed

resurrección *f* resurrection

retaguardia *f* rearguard

retal *m* piece, remnant

retama *f* Spanish broom; **retama de escoba** furze

retar *tr* to challenge, dare; blame, find fault with

retardación *f* retardation

retardar *tr* to retard, slow down

retardo *m* retard, delay

retazo *m* piece, remnant; scrap, fragment

retén *m* store, stock, reserve; catch, pawl; (mil) reserve

retener §71 *tr* to retain, keep, withhold; detain, arrest; (*el pago de un haber*) stop

retentiva *f* memory; recall

reticente *adj* deceptive, misleading; noncommittal

retintín *m* jingle, tinkling; (*en el oído*) ringing; tone of reproach, sarcasm, mockery

retiñir §12 *intr* to jingle, tinkle (*los oídos*) ring

retirada *f* retirement, withdrawal; place of refuge; (mil) retreat, retirement; (*toque*) (mil) retreat; **batirse en retirada** to beat a retreat

retirar *tr* to retire, withdraw; take away; pull back ‖ *ref* to retire, withdraw; (mil) to retire

reto *m* challenge, dare; threat

retocar §73 *tr* to retouch; touch up; (*un disco de fonógrafo*) play back

retoño *m* sprout, shoot, sucker

retorcer §74 *tr* to twist; twist together; (*las manos*) wring; (fig) to twist, misconstrue ‖ *ref* to twist; writhe

retóri•co -ca *adj* rhetorical ‖ *f* rhetoric

retornar *tr* to return, give back; back, back up ‖ *intr & ref* to return, go back

retorno *m* return; barter, exchange; reward, requital; **retorno terrestre** (elec) ground

retorta *f* (chem) retort

retozar §60 *intr* to frolic, gambol, romp

retozo *m* frolic, gambol, romping; **retozo de la risa** giggle, titter

reto•zón -zona *adj* frolicsome, frisky

retracción *f* retraction; (pathol) atrophy

retractar *tr & ref* to retract

retráctil *adj* retractable

retraer §75 *tr* to bring again, bring back; dissuade ‖ *ref* to withdraw, retire; take refuge

retraí•do -da *adj* solitary; reserved, shy

retransmisión *f* rebroadcasting

retransmitir *tr* to rebroadcast

retrasa•do -da *adj* (mentally) retarded

retrasar *tr* to delay, retard; put off; (*un reloj*) set or turn back ‖ *intr* to be too slow; (*en los estudios*) be or fall behind ‖ *ref* to delay, be late, be slow, be behind time; (*un reloj*) go or be slow

retraso *m* delay; **tener retraso** to be late

retratar *tr* to portray; photograph; imitate ‖ *ref* to sit for a portrait; have one's picture taken

retrato *m* portrait; photograph; copy, imitation; description; **el vivo retrato de** the living image of

retrepar *ref* to lean back, lean back in the chair

retreta *f* (mil) retreat, tattoo; outdoor band concert

retrete *m* toilet, lavatory

retribuir §20 *tr* to repay, pay back

retroacti•vo -va *adj* retroactive

retroalimentación *f* feedback

retroceder *intr* to retrogress; back away; back down, back out

retroceso *m* retrogression; (*de un arma de fuego*) recoil; (*de una enfermedad*) flare-up; (mach, mov) rewind(ing)

retrocohete *m* retrorocket

retrodisparo *m* retrofiring

retropropulsión *f* (aer) jet propulsion

retrospecti•vo -va *adj* retrospective ‖ *f* (mov) flashback

retrovisor *m* rear-view mirror

retrucar §73 *intr* to answer, reply; (billiards) kiss

retruco *m* (billiards) kiss

retruécano *m* pun

retumbar *intr* to resound, rumble

retumbo *m* resounding, rumble, echo

reumáti•co -ca *adj & mf* rheumatic

reumatismo *m* rheumatism

reunificación *f* reunification

reunión *f* reunion, gathering, meeting; assemblage

reunir §59 *tr* to join, unite; assemble, gather together, bring together; reunite; (*dinero*) raise ‖ *ref* to unite; assemble, gather together, come together, meet; reunite

reválida *f* final examination (*for a higher degree*)

revalorar *tr* to revaluate

revalorizar §60 *tr* to revaluate

revejecer §22 *intr & ref* to grow old before one's time

revelación *f* revelation

revelado *m* (phot) development

revelador *m* (phot) developer

revelar *tr* to reveal; (phot) to develop

revender *tr* to resell; retail

reventa *f* resale

reventar §2 *tr* to smash, crush; burst, blow out, explode; ruin; annoy, bore; (*a una persona*) work to death; (*a un caballo*) run to death ‖ *intr* to burst, blow out, explode; (*las olas*) break; (*morir*) croak; (*de ira*) blow up, hit the ceiling; **reventar por** to be dying to ‖ *ref* to burst, blow out, explode; be worked to death; (*un caballo*) be run to death

reventón *m* burst; (aut) blowout

rever §80 *tr* to revise, review; (*un caso legal*) retry

reverberar *intr* to reverberate

reverbero *m* reflector; street lamp; chafing dish

reverencia *f* reverence; bow, curtsy

reverenciar *tr* to revere, reverence ‖ *intr* to bow, curtsy

reveren•do -da *adj & m* reverend

reverso *m* back; wrong side; reverse

revertir §68 *intr* to revert

revés *m* back, reverse; wrong side; backhand; (*desgracia, contratiempo*) reverse, setback; **al revés** wrong side out; inside out; upside down; backwards

revestir §50 *tr* to put on, don; cover, coat, face, line, surface; assume, take on; disguise; (*un cuento*) adorn; invest ‖ *ref* to put on vestments; be haughty; gird oneself

revirar *tr* to turn, twist; turn over

revisada *f* examination; revision

revisar *tr* to revise, review, check; audit

revisión *f* revision, review, check

revisionismo *m* revisionism

revisionista *adj & mf* revisionist

revisor *m* inspector, examiner; (rr) conductor, ticket collector

revista *f* review; (mil) review; (theat) review, revue; (law) new trial

revistar *tr* (mil) to review

revivir *tr & intr* to revive

revocar §73 *tr* to revoke; dissuade; drive back, drive away; plaster, stucco

revocatoria *f* (SAm) recall; repeal; cancellation

revolar §61 *intr & ref* to flutter, flutter around

revolcar §81 *tr* to knock down; (*a un adversario*) floor; (*a un alumno en un examen*) flunk, fail ‖ *ref* to wallow, roll around; be stubborn

revolotear *tr* to fling up ‖ *intr* to flutter, flutter around, flit

revoltijo *m* or **revoltillo** *m* mess, jumble; stew

re
re

revolto•so -sa *adj* rebellious, riotous; (*niño*) unruly, mischievous; complicated; winding ‖ *mf* troublemaker, rioter

revolución *f* revolution

revoluciona•rio -ria *adj* & *mf* revolutionary

revolver §47 & §83 *tr* to shake; stir; turn around; turn upside down; wrap up; mess up; disturb; (*sus pasos*) retrace; alienate, estrange ‖ *intr* to retrace one's steps ‖ *ref* to retrace one's steps; turn around; toss and turn; (*un astro en su órbita*) revolve; (*el mar*) get rough

revólver *m* revolver

revuelco *m* upset, tumble; wallowing

revuelo *m* whirl, flying around; stir, commotion

revuelta *f* revolution, revolt; disturbance; turning point; fight, row

rey *m* king; swineherd; **los Reyes Católicos** Ferdinand and Isabella; **los Reyes Magos** the Three Wise Men; **ni rey ni roque** nobody; **rey de zarza** wren; **reyes** king and queen; **Reyes** Twelfth-night

reyerta *f* quarrel, wrangle

reyezuelo *m* (orn) kinglet; **reyezuelo moñudo** goldcrest

rezaga•do -da *mf* straggler, laggard

rezagar §44 *tr* to outstrip, leave behind; postpone ‖ *ref* to fall behind

rezar §60 *tr* (*una oración*) to pray; (*una oración; la misa*) say; (coll) to say, to read; (*anunciar*) (coll) to call for ‖ *intr* to pray; grumble; (coll) to say, to read; **rezar con** to concern

rezo *m* prayer; devotions

rezón *m* grapnel

rezongar §44 *tr* (CAm) to scold ‖ *intr* to grumble, growl

rezumar *intr* to ooze, seep ‖ *ref* to ooze, seep; to leak; (*una especie*) leak out

ría *f* estuary, fiord

riachuelo *m* rivulet, streamlet

riada *f* flood, freshet

ribazo *m* slope, embarkment

ribera *f* bank, shore; riverside

ribere•ño -ña *adj* riverside

ribero *m* levee, dike

ribete *m* edge, trimming, border; (*a un cuento*) embellishment

ribetear *tr* to edge, trim, border, bind

ri•co -ca *adj* rich; dear, darling

ridiculizar §60 *tr* to ridicule

ridícu•lo -la *adj* ridiculous; touchy ‖ *m* ridiculous situation; **poner en ridículo** to ridicule, expose to ridicule

riego *m* irrigation; watering

riel *m* ingot; curtain rod; rail

rielar *intr* to shimmer, gleam; (poet) to twinkle

rienda *f* rein; **a rienda suelta** swiftly, violently; with free rein

riente *adj* laughing; bright, cheerful

riesgo *m* risk, danger; **correr riesgo** to run or take a risk

riesgo•so -sa *adj* risky; dangerous

rifa *f* raffle; fight, quarrel

rifar *tr* to raffle, raffle off ‖ *intr* to raffle; fight, quarrel

rígi•do -da *adj* rigid, stiff; strict, severe

riguro•so -sa *adj* rigorous; severe

rima *f* rhyme; **rimas** poems, poetry

rimar *tr* & *ref* to rhyme

rimbombante *adj* resounding; flashy

rímel *m* mascara

rimero *m* heap, pile

Rin *m* Rhine

rincón *m* corner; nook; piece of land; (coll) home

rinconera *f* corner piece of furniture; corner table; corner cupboard

ringla *f*, **ringle** *m* or **ringlera** *f* row, tier

ringorrango *m* curlicue; frill, frippery

rinoceronte *m* rhinoceros

riña *f* fight, scuffle

riñón *m* kidney; (fig) heart, center, interior; **tener bien cubierto el riñón** to be well-heeled

río *m* river; **pescar en río revuelto** to fish in troubled waters

riostra *f* brace, stay; guy wire

riostrar *tr* to brace, stay

ripia *f* shingle

ripio *m* debris; rubble; (*palabras inútiles empleadas para completar el verso*) padding; **no perder ripio** to not miss a trick

riqueza *f* riches, wealth; richness; **riquezas del subsuelo** mineral resources

risa *f* laugh, laughter

risco *m* cliff, crag; honey fritter

risible *adj* laughable

risotada *f* guffaw, horse laugh

ristra *f* string of onions, string of garlic; (coll) string, row, file

ristre *m* lance rest

risue•ño -ña *adj* smiling

rítmi•co -ca *adj* rhythmic(al)

ritmo *m* rhythm; **a gran ritmo** at great speed

rito *m* rite

rival *mf* rival

rivalidad *f* rivalry; enmity

rivalizar §60 *intr* to vie, compete; **rivalizar con** to rival

riza•do -da *adj* curly; ripply ‖ *m* curl, curling; rippling

rizador *m* curling iron, hair curler

rizar §60 *tr* & *ref* to curl; (*la superficie del agua*) ripple

ri•zo -za *adj* curly ‖ *m* curl, ringlet; ripple; (aer) loop; **rizar el rizo** (aer) to loop the loop

ro *interj* — **¡ro ro!** hushaby!, bye-bye!

roba•dor -dora *mf* robber, thief

róbalo or **robalo** *m* (*Labrax lupus*) bass; (*Centropomus undecimalis*) snook

robar *tr* to rob, steal; (*un naipe o ficha de dominó*) draw ‖ *intr* & *ref* to steal

robinete *m* faucet, spigot, cock

roblar *tr* to clinch, rivet

roble *m* oak; (*Quercus robur*) British oak tree; husky fellow

roblón *m* rivet

robo m robbery, theft; (*naipe tomado del monte*) draw; **robo con escalamiento** burglary

ro•bot m (pl **-bots**) robot

robótica f robotics

robotización f use of robots; robotization

robus•to -ta adj robust

roca f rock

rocalla f pebbles; stone chips; large glass bead

rocallo•so -sa adj stony, pebbly

roce m rubbing; close contact

rociada f sprinkling; dew; (*de balas, piedras, etc.*) shower; (*de invectivas*) volley

rociadera f sprinkling can

rociar §77 tr to sprinkle; spray; bedew; scatter ‖ intr to drizzle; **rocía** there is dew

rocín m hack, nag; work horse, draft horse; riding horse; rough guy

rocío m dew; drizzle; sprinkling

rocke•ro -ra mf rock singer

roco•so -sa adj rocky

rodada f rut, track

roda•do -da adj (*fácil, flúido*) rounded, fluent; (*tránsito*) vehicular ‖ f see **rodada**

rodadura f rolling; rut; (*de neumático*) tread

rodaja f disk, caster; round slice

rodaje m wheels; (*de una película cinematográfica*) shooting, filming; **en rodaje** (aut) being run in; (mov) being filmed

rodamiento m bearing; (*de un neumático*) tread; **rodamientos** running gear

Ródano m Rhone

rodante adj rolling; on wheels; (Chile) wandering

rodapié m baseboard, washboard

rodar §61 tr to roll; (*una película cinematográfica*) shoot, film, take; screen, project; drag along; (*una llave*) turn; (*la escalera*) roll down; (*un nuevo coche*) run in; (*válvulas de un motor*) grind ‖ intr to roll, roll along; roll down; rotate, revolve; tumble; roam, wander about; (*por medio de ruedas*) run; prowl

Rodas f Rhodes

rodear tr to surround; round up ‖ intr to go around; go by a roundabout way; beat about the bush ‖ ref to turn, twist, toss about

rodela f buckler, target; padded ring

rodeo m detour, roundabout way; dodge, duck; rodeo, roundup; **andar con rodeos** to beat about the bush; **dar un rodeo** to go a roundabout way

rodilla f knee; floor rag, mop; padded ring; **de rodillas** kneeling, on one's knees

rodillera f kneepad; baggy knee; (*de prenda de vestir*) knee; (*del órgano*) (mus) knee swell

rodillo m roller; rolling pin; road roller; inking roller; (*de la máquina de escribir*) platen

rodrigar §44 tr to prop, prop up, stake

rodrigón m prop, stake

roer §62 tr to gnaw, gnaw away at; (*un hueso*) pick; wear down

rogar §63 tr & intr to beg; pray; **hacerse de rogar** to like to be coaxed

roí•do -da adj miserly, stingy

ro•jo -ja adj red; ruddy; red-haired; Red ‖ mf (*comunista*) Red ‖ m red; **al rojo** to a red heat

rollar tr to roll, roll up

rolli•zo -za adj round, cylindrical; plump, stocky ‖ m round log

rollo m roll, coil; roller, rolling pin; round log; yoke pad; rôle; (*de tela*) bolt

romadizo m cold in the head

romance adj (*neolatino*) Romance ‖ m Romance language; Spanish language; romance of chivalry; octosyllabic verse with alternate lines in assonance; narrative poem in octosyllabic verse; ballad; **romance heroico** hendecasyllabic verse with alternate lines in assonance

romancero m collection of Old Spanish romances

romancillo m verse of less than eight syllables with alternate lines in assonance

románi•co -ca adj (*neolatino*) Romance, Romanic; (*arquitectura*) Romanesque ‖ m Romanesque

roma•no -na adj & mf Roman

romanticismo m romanticism

románti•co -ca adj romantic

romanza f (mus) romance, romanza

romería f pilgrimage; crowd, gathering

rome•ro -ra mf pilgrim ‖ m rosemary

ro•mo -ma adj blunt, dull; flat-nosed

rompeáto•mos m (pl **-mos**) atom smasher

rompecabe•zas m (pl **-zas**) riddle, puzzle; (*figura que ha sido cortada en trozos menudos y que hay que recomponer*) jigsaw puzzle

rompehie•los m (pl **-los**) iceboat, icebreaker

rompehuel•gas m (pl **-gas**) strikebreaker

rompeo•las m (pl **-las**) mole, breakwater

romper §83 tr to break; break through; break up; tear ‖ intr to break; (*las flores*) break open, burst open; break down; **romper a** to start to, burst out

rompiente m reef, shoal; (*oleaje que choca contra las rocas*) breaker

rompope m eggnog

ron m rum; **ron de laurel** or **de malagueta** bay rum

ronca f (*época del celo*) rut; cry of buck in rutting season; bullying

roncar §73 intr to snore; (*el viento, el mar*) roar; cry in rutting season; bully

ronce•ro -ra adj slow, poky; grouchy

ron•co -ca adj hoarse; harsh ‖ f see **ronca**

roncha f weal, welt; black-and-blue mark

ronchar tr to crunch

ronda f (*de un policía; de visitas; de cigarros o bebidas*) round; (*juego del corro*) (Chile) ring-around-a-rosy; **ronda negociadora** round of negotiations

rondar tr to go around; fly around; patrol; hang around; court ‖ intr to patrol by night; gad about at nighttime; go serenading; prowl; (mil) to make the rounds

ronquedad f hoarseness; harshness

re
ro

ronquera f hoarseness
ronquido m snore; rasping sound
ronronear intr to purr
ronroneo m purr, purring
ronzal m halter
ronzar §60 tr to crunch, munch
roña f scab, mange; sticky dirt; pine bark; stinginess; spite, ill will; (Col) malingering; **jugar a roña** (Peru) to play for fun
roño•so -sa adj scabby, mangy; dirty, filthy; stingy; spiteful
ropa f clothing, clothes; dry goods; **a quema ropa** point-blank; **ropa blanca** linen; **ropa de cama** bed linen; bed-clothes; **ropa dominguera** Sunday best; **ropa hecha** ready-made clothes; **ropa interior** underwear; **ropa sucia** laundry
ropaje m clothes, clothing; gown, robe; drapery
ropaveje•ro -ra mf old-clothes dealer
rope•ro -ra mf ready-made clothier; wardrobe keeper ‖ m wardrobe, clothes closet
roque m rook, castle
roque•ño -ña adj rocky; hard, flinty
rorro m baby; (Mex) doll
rosa f rose; **rosa de los vientos** or **rosa náutica** (naut) compass card; **rosas** popcorn; **verlo todo de color de rosa** to see everything through rose-colored glasses
rosa•do -da adj rose-colored, rosy; pink; flushed ‖ f frost
rosaleda or **rosalera** f rose garden
rosario m rosary; (de sucesos) string; chain pump
ros•bif m (pl **-bifs**) roast beef
rosca f coil, spiral; (de una espiral) turn; twisted roll; (de un tornillo) thread; (Chile) padded ring
roscar §73 tr to thread
roseta f sprinkling spout or nozzle; red spot on cheek; **rosetas** popcorn
rosetón m rose window
rosita f little rose; (Chile) earring; **rositas** popcorn
rosquilla f coffeecake, doughnut, cruller
rostro m face; snout; beak; (retrato) **de rostro entero** full-faced
rostropáli•do -da mf paleface
rota f rout, defeat; (naut) route, course
rotisería f fast-food restaurant; delicatessen
rotograbado m rotogravure
rótula f lozenge; kneecap; knuckle
rotulador m felt pen
rotular tr to label, title, letter
rótulo m label, title; poster, show bill
rotun•do -da adj round; rotund, sonorous, full; peremptory
rotura f break, breaking; breach, opening; tear, tearing
roturación f (agr) reclamation
roya f (agr) blight, rust
rozamiento m rubbing; friction; (desavenencia) (fig) friction
rozar §60 tr to graze; scrape; border on; grub, stub; (las tierras) clear; (la hierba) nibble; (leña menuda) cut and gather ‖ intr to graze by ‖ ref to be on close terms, rub elbows, hobnob; falter, stammer; be alike
roznar tr to crunch ‖ intr to bray
roznido m crunch, crunching noise; bray, braying
Rte. abbr **Remite**
ru•bí m (pl **-bíes**) ruby; (de un reloj) ruby, jewel
rubia f blonde; station wagon; peseta; **rubia oxigenada** peroxide blonde; **rubia platino** platinum blonde
rubia•les mf (pl **-les**) goldilocks
ru•bio -bia adj blond, fair; golden ‖ m blond ‖ f see **rubia**
rublo m ruble
rubor m bright red; blush, flush; bashfulness
ruborizar §60 tr to make blush ‖ ref to blush
rúbrica f title, heading; (rasgo después de la firma de uno) flourish
rubricación f listing; itemization
ru•bro -bra adj red ‖ m title, heading; (Chile) (com) entry
rudimento m rudiment
ru•do -da adj coarse, rough; rude, crude; dull, stupid; hard, severe
rueca f distaff
rueda f wheel; caster, roller; (de gente) ring, circle; round slice; pinwheel; (de la cola del pavo) spread; sunfish; **hacer la rueda** (el pavo) to spread its tail; **hacer la rueda a** to play up to; **rueda de andar** treadmill; **rueda de cadena** sprocket, sprocket wheel; **rueda de escape** escapement wheel; **rueda de fuego** pinwheel; **rueda dentada** gearwheel; **rueda de paletas** paddle wheel; **rueda de prensa** press conference; **rueda de presos** line-up; **rueda de recambio** spare wheel; **rueda de tornillo sin fin** worm wheel; **rueda motriz** drive wheel
ruedo m turn, rotation; round mat; selvage; hemline; (taur) ring; **a todo ruedo** at all events
ruego m request, entreaty; prayer
ru•fián -fiana mf bawd, go-between ‖ m cur, cad
ru•fo -fa adj sandy, sandy-haired; curly-haired
rugido m roar; (de las tripas) rumble
rugir §27 intr to roar; rumble
rugo•so -sa adj rugged, wrinkled
ruibarbo m rhubarb
ruido m noise; rumor; row, rumpus
ruido•so -sa adj noisy; loud; sensational
ruin adj base, mean, vile; stingy; (animal) vicious
ruina f ruin
ruindad f baseness, meanness, vileness; stinginess; viciousness
ruino•so -sa adj tottery, run-down
ruiseñor m nightingale
ruleta f roulette; (CAm, Arg) tape measure
ruletero m (Mex) cruising taxi driver (in search of fares)
rulo m roll; rolling pin; (hair) curler
ruma•no -na adj & mf Rumanian

rumbo *m* bearing, course, direction; pomp, show; generosity; (CAm) noisy celebration; **por aquellos rumbos** in those parts; **rumbo a** bound for

rumbo•so -sa *adj* pompous, magnificent; generous

rumiar *tr & intr* to ruminate

rumor *m* rumor; (*de voces*) murmur, buzz; rumble

rumorear *tr* to rumor, circulate by a rumor ‖ *intr* to murmur, buzz, rumble ‖ *ref* to be rumored; **se rumorea que** it is rumored that

rumoro•so -sa *adj* noisy, loud, rumbling

runfla *f* or **runflada** *f* string, row; (*en los naipes*) sequence

ruptor *m* (elec) contact breaker

ruptura *f* rupture, break; crack, split; (*cesación de relaciones*) rupture

Rusia *f* Russia; **la Rusia Soviética** Soviet Russia

ru•so -sa *adj & mf* Russian

rúst. *abbr* **rústica**

rústi•co -ca *adj* rustic; coarse, crude, clumsy; (*latín*) Vulgar; **en rústica** paper-bound ‖ *m* rustic, peasant

ruta *f* route; **ruta aérea** air lane

rutilante *adj* shining, sparkling

rutina *f* routine

rutina•rio -ria *adj* routine

S

S, s (*ese*) *f* twenty-second letter of the Spanish alphabet

S. *abbr* **San, Santo, sobresaliente, sur**

sábado *m* (*de los cristianos*) Saturday; (*de los judíos*) Sabbath

sábalo *m* shad

sabana *f* savanna, pampa; **ponerse en la sabana** (Ven) to get rich overnight

sábana *f* sheet; altar cloth

sabandija *f* insect, bug, worm; (*persona*) vermin; **sabandijas** (*animales o personas*) vermin

sabanilla *f* kerchief; altar cloth

sabañón *m* chilblain

sabe•dor -dora *adj* aware, informed

sabelotodo *m* (*pl* **sabelotodo**) know-it-all, wise guy

saber *m* knowledge, learning ‖ *v* §64 *tr & intr* to know; to find out; to taste; **a saber** namely, to wit; **me sabe mal** I'm sorry, I regret; **no saber dónde meterse** to not know which way to turn; **que yo sepa** as far as I know; **saber a** to taste of; smack of; **saber a poco** to be just a taste, taste like more; **saber de** to be aware of; hear from ‖ *ref* to know; be or become known

sabidi•llo -lla *adj & mf* know-it-all

sabi•do -da *adj* well-informed; learned; **de sabido** certainly, surely

sabiduría *f* wisdom; knowledge, learning

sabiendas — **a sabiendas** knowingly, consciously; **a sabiendas de que** knowing that, aware that

sabihon•do -da *adj & mf* know-it-all

sa•bio -bia *adj* wise; learned; (*animal*) trained ‖ *mf* wise person, scholar, scientist ‖ *m* wise man, sage

sablazo *m* stroke with a saber, wound made by a saber; sponging; **dar un sablazo a** to hit for a loan

sable *m* saber, cutlass; (coll) sponging

sablear *tr* to hit for a loan, sponge on ‖ *intr* to go around sponging

sablista *mf* sponger

sabor *m* taste, flavor

saborcillo *m* slight taste, touch

saborear *tr* to flavor; taste; savor; entice; ‖ *ref* to smack one's lips; **saborearse de** to taste; to savor

sabotaje *m* sabotage

sabotear *tr & intr* to sabotage

sabro•so -sa *adj* tasty, savory, delicious

sabueso *m* bloodhound; sleuth

saburro•so -sa *adj* (*boca*) foul; (*lengua*) coated

sacaboca•do *m* or **sacaboca•dos** *m* (*pl* **-dos**) ticket punch; sure thing

sacabotas *m* (*pl* **-tas**) bootjack

sacacor•chos *m* (*pl* **-chos**) corkscrew

sacaman•chas *mf* (*pl* **-chas**) clothes cleaner, spot remover; dry cleaner; dyer

sacamue•las *m* (*pl* **-las**) tooth puller; quack, cheat

sacamuer•tos *m* (*pl* **-tos**) stagehand

sacapintura *m* paint remover

sacapun•tas *m* (*pl* **-tas**) pencil sharpener

sacar §73 *tr* (*un clavo, una espada, agua, una conclusión*) to draw; pull out; pull up; take out; extract, remove; show; bring out, publish; find out, solve; (*un secreto*) elicit, draw out; copy; (*una fotografía*) take; except, exclude; get, obtain; produce, invent, imitate; (*un premio*) win; (*una pelota*) serve; (*el pecho*) stick out; **sacar a bailar** to drag in; **sacar a relucir** to bring up unexpectedly; **sacar en claro** or **en limpio** to recopy clearly; deduce, clear up ‖ *ref* (Mex) to make off

sacarina *f* saccharin

sacasi•llas *m* (*pl* **-llas**) stagehand

sacerdocio *m* priesthood

sacerdote *m* priest

saciar *tr* to satiate

ro
sa

saco *m* bag, sack; coat, jacket; sack, plunder, pillage; (*de mentiras*) pack; **saco de dormir** sleeping bag; **saco de noche** overnight bag

sacramento *m* sacrament

sacrificar §73 *tr* to sacrifice; slaughter ‖ *intr* to sacrifice ‖ *ref* to sacrifice; sacrifice oneself

sacrificio *m* sacrifice; **sacrificio del altar** Sacrifice of the Mass

sacrilegio *m* sacrilege

sacríle·go -ga *adj* sacrilegious

sacristán *m* sacristan; sexton; **sacristán de amén** yes man

sacristía *f* sacristy, vestry

sa·cro -cra *adj* sacred

sacudida *f* shake, jar, jolt, jerk, bump; (elec) shock

sacudi·do -da *adj* intractable; determined ‖ *f* see **sacudida**

sacudir *tr* to shake; beat; jar, jolt; rock; shake off ‖ *ref* to shake, to shake oneself; rock; **sacudirse bien** to wangle one's way out

sádi·co -ca *adj* sadistic ‖ *mf* sadist

saeta *f* arrow, dart; (*del reloj*) hand; magnetic needle

saetilla *f* small arrow; (*del reloj*) hand; magnetic needle; (bot) arrowhead

saetín *m* flume, millrace

sa·gaz *adj* (*pl* **-gaces**) sagacious; keen-scented

Sagitario *m* (astr) Sagittarius

sagra·do -da *adj* sacred ‖ *m* asylum, haven, sanctuary; **acogerse a sagrado** to take sanctuary

sagrario *m* sanctuary, shrine; ciborium

sahariana *f* tight-fitting military jacket

sahornar *ref* to skin oneself

sahumar *tr* to perfume with smoke or incense; (Chile) to gold-plate, silver-plate

sainete *m* one-act farce; flavor, relish, spice, zest; sauce, seasoning; tidbit

sa·jón -jona *adj & mf* Saxon

sal *f* salt; grace, charm; wit; (CAm) misfortune; **sal de sosa** washing soda; **sales aromáticas** smelling salts; **sal gema** rock salt

sala *f* hall; drawing room, living room, sitting room; **sala de batalla** sorting room; **sala de calderas** boiler room; **sala de enfermos** infirmary; **sala de espera** waiting room; **sala de estar** living room, sitting room; **sala de fiestas** night club; **sala del cine** moving-picture house; **sala de máquinas** engine room

saladillo *m* salted peanut

Salamina *f* Salamis

salar *tr* to salt; spoil, ruin; bring bad luck to

salario *m* wages, pay; **salario de hambre** starvation wages

salcochar *tr* to boil in salt water

salcocho *m* food boiled in salt water

salchicha *f* sausage

salchiche·ro -ra *mf* pork butcher

saldar *tr* to settle, liquidate; sell out

saldo *m* settlement; balance; remnant; bargain; **saldo de mercancías** job lot; **saldo deudor** debit balance

salero *m* saltshaker, saltcellar; salt lick; grace, charm, wit

salero·so -sa *adj* charming, winsome, lively; salty, witty

salgar §44 *tr* (*el ganado*) to salt

salida *f* start; departure; exit; outcome, result; subterfuge; pretext; outlay, expenditure; projection; outlying fields; (elec) output; (sport) start; (mil) sally, sortie; (coll) witticism, sally; **salida de baño** bathrobe; **salida del sol** sunrise; **salida de teatro** evening wrap; **salida de teatros** after-theater party; **salida de tono** irrelevancy, impropriety; **salida lanzada** (sport) running start; **tener salida** to sell well; (*una muchacha*) to be popular with the boys

saliente *adj* projecting; (*p.ej., tren*) outbound; (*sol*) rising ‖ *m* east ‖ *f* projection; (*de la carretera*) shoulder

salir §65 *intr* to go out, come out; leave, go away, depart; sail; run out, come to an end; appear, show up; (*una mancha*) come out, come off; (*p.ej., el sol*) rise; shoot, spring, come up; project, stick out; make the first move; result, turn out; be elected; **salga lo que saliere** come what may; **salir a** to amount to; open into; resemble, look like; **salir al, encuentro a** to go to meet; take a stand against; get ahead of; **salir bien en un examen** to pass an examination; **salir con bien** to be successful; **salir de** depart from; cease being; get rid of; (*p.ej., su juicio, sentido*) lose; **salir disparado** to start like a shot; **salir pitando** to start off on a mad run; blow up, hit the ceiling; **salir reprobado** (*en un examen*) to fail ‖ *ref* to slip out, escape; slip off, run off; leak; boil over; **salirse con la suya** to have one's own way; carry one's point

salitre *m* saltpeter

saliva *f* saliva; **gastar saliva** to rattle along; to waste one's breath

salmo *m* psalm

salmón *m* salmon

salmuera *f* brine, pickle; salty food or drink

salobre *adj* brackish, saltish

salón *m* salon, drawing room; (*de un buque*) saloon; meeting room; **salón de actos** auditorium; **salón de baile** ballroom; **salón de belleza** beauty parlor; **salón del automóvil** automobile show; **salón de refrescos** ice-cream parlor; **salón de tertulia** or **salón social** lounge

saloncillo *m* (*p.ej., de un teatro*) rest room

salpicadero *m* control panel; (aut) dashboard

salpicar §73 *tr* to splash; sprinkle

salpimentar §2 *tr* to salt and pepper, season with salt and pepper; (fig) to sweeten

salpullido *m* rash, eruption

salpullir §13 *tr* to cause a rash on; splotch ‖ *ref* to break out

salsa *f* sauce, dressing, gravy; **salsa de ají** chili sauce; **salsa de tomate** catsup, ketchup; **salsa inglesa** Worcestershire sauce

salsera *f* gravy dish; small saucer (*to mix paints*)

saltaban·co *m* or **saltaban·cos** *m* (*pl* **-cos**) quack, mountebank; prestidigitator; nuisance

saltamon·tes *m* (*pl* **-tes**) grasshopper

saltar *tr* to jump, jump over; skip, skip over ‖ *intr* to jump, leap, hop, skip; bounce; shoot up, spurt; come loose, come off; crack, break, burst; chip; project, stick out; **saltar a la vista** or **los ojos** to be self-evident; **saltar por** to jump over, jump out of ‖ *ref* to skip; come off

saltatum·bas *m* (*pl* **-bas**) burying parson

salteador *m* highwayman, holdup man

saltear *tr* to attack, hold up, waylay; take by surprise

saltimbanco *m* var of **saltabanco**

salto *m* jump, leap, bound; skip; dive; fall, waterfall; leapfrog; **salto de altura** high jump; **salto de ángel** swan dive; **salto de cama** morning wrap, dressing gown; **salto de carpa** jackknife; **salto de esquí** ski jump; **salto de viento** (naut) sudden shift in the wind; **salto mortal** somersault; **salto ornamental** fancy dive

salubre *adj* healthful, salubrious

salud *f* health; welfare; salvation; greeting; **gastar, vender** or **verter salud** to radiate health ‖ *interj* greetings!; **¡salud y pesetas!** health and wealth!

saludar *tr* to greet, salute, hail, bow to; give regards to ‖ *intr* to salute; bow

saludo *m* greeting, salute, bow; salutation; **saludo final** conclusion

salutación *f* salutation, greeting, bow

salva *f* greeting, welcome; salvo; oath; tray; (*de aplausos; de una batería de artillería*) round

salvado *m* bran

salva·dor -dora *mf* savior, saver, rescuer ‖ **el Salvador** the Saviour; (*país de la América Central*) El Salvador

salvadore·ño -ña *adj* & *mf* Salvadoran

salvaguardar *tr* to safeguard

salvaguardia *m* bodyguard, escort ‖ *f* safeguard, safe-conduct; protection, shelter

salvaje *adj* wild, uncultivated; savage; stupid ‖ *mf* savage; dolt

salvaji·no -na *adj* wild; (*de la carne de los animales monteses*) gamy ‖ *f* wild animal; wild animals

salvamante·les *m* (*pl* **-les**) coaster

salvamento *m* salvation; lifesaving; rescue; salvage; place of safety

salvar *tr* to save, rescue; to salvage; (*una dificultad*) avoid, overcome; (*un obstáculo*) clear, get around; (*una distancia*) cover, get over; rise above; jump over; make an exception of; **salvar apariencias** to save face ‖ *ref* to save oneself, escape danger; be saved; **sálvese el que pueda** every man for himself

salvavi·das *m* (*pl* **-das**) life preserver; lifeboat; (*empleado de una estación de salvamento*) lifeguard

salvedad *f* reservation, exception

salvia *f* (bot) sage

sal·vo -va *adj* safe; omitted; **a salvo** safe, out

of danger; **a salvo de** safe from ‖ **salvo** *prep* save, except for; **salvo error u omisión (s.e.u.o.)** barring error or omission; **salvo que** *f* unless ‖ *f* see **salva**

salvoconducto *m* safe-conduct

sámara *f* (bot) key, key fruit

san *adj* apocopated and unstressed form of **santo**

sanaloto·do *m* (*pl* **-do**) cure-all

sanar *tr* to cure, heal ‖ *intr* to heal; recover

sanción *f* (*aprobación*) sanction; (*castigo, pena*) penalty

sancionar *tr* (*aprobar*) to sanction; (*imponer pena a*) penalize

sancochar *tr* to parboil

sandalia *f* sandal

sándalo *m* (yellow) sandalwood

san·dez *f* (*pl* **-deces**) folly, nonsense; piece of folly

sandía *f* watermelon

san·dio -dia *adj* foolish, nonsensical

saneamiento *m* sanitation, drainage; guarantee

sanear *tr* to guarantee; indemnify; make sanitary, drain, dry up

sangrar *tr* to bleed; drain; tap; (typ) to indent; (coll) to rob ‖ *intr* to bleed; **estar sangrando** to be new or recent; be plain or obvious ‖ *ref* to have oneself bled; (*los colores*) run

sangre *f* blood; **a sangre** by horsepower; **a sangre fría** in cold blood; **pura sangre** *m* thoroughbred; **sangre torera** bullfighting in the blood

sangría *f* bleeding; outlet, draining; ditch, trench; (*bebida*) sangaree; tap; tapping; (typ) indentation

sangrien·to -ta *adj* bloody; bleeding; cruel, sanguinary

sangrigor·do -da *adj* unpleasant

sangrilige·ro -ra *adj* nice, pleasant

sangripesa·do -da *adj* unpleasant

sangüesa *f* raspberry

sangüeso *m* raspberry bush

sanguijuela *f* leech

sanguina·rio -ria *adj* sanguinary, blood-thirsty

sanidad *f* healthiness; healthfulness; health; sanitation; **sanidad pública** health department

sanita·rio -ria *adj* sanitary

sa·no -na *adj* hale, healthy; healthful; sound; sane, earnest, sincere; safe, sure; whole, untouched, unharmed; **sano y salvo** safe and sound

santiague·ro -ra *adj* Santiago de Cuba ‖ *mf* native or inhabitant of Santiago de Cuba

santia·gués -guesa *adj* Santiago de Compostela ‖ *mf* native or inhabitant of Santiago de Compostela

santiagui·no -na *adj* Santiago de Chile ‖ *mf* native or inhabitant of Santiago de Chile

santiamén *m* jiffy; **en un santiamén** in the twinkling of an eye

santidad *f* holiness, sanctity, saintliness; **su Santidad** his Holiness

sa
sa

santificar §73 *tr* to sanctify, hallow, consecrate; (*las fiestas*) keep; excuse, justify

santiguar §10 *tr* to bless, make the sign of the cross over; punish, slap, abuse ‖ *ref* to cross oneself, make the sign of the cross

san·to -ta *adj* holy, saintly, blessed; (*día*) live-long; artless, simple; **santo y bueno** well and good ‖ *mf* saint ‖ *m* name day; image of a saint; **a santo de** because of; **desnudar a un santo para vestir a otro** to rob Peter to pay Paul; **írsele a uno el santo al cielo** to forget what one was up to; **santo y seña** password, watchword

Santo Domingo Hispaniola

santuario *m* sanctuary, shrine; (Col) buried treasure; (Col, Ven) Indian idol

santu·rrón -rrona *adj* sanctimonious ‖ *mf* sanctimonious person

saña *f* fury, rage; cruelty

sañu·do -da *adj* furious, enraged; cruel

sapiente *adj* wise, intelligent

sapo *m* toad; (coll) stuffed shirt; (Chile) little runt

saque *m* (*en el tenis*) serve, service; server; service line; (Col) distillery; **tener buen saque** to be a heavy eater and drinker

saquear *tr* to sack, plunder, pillage, loot

sarampión *m* measles

sarao *m* soirée, evening party

sarape *m* (Guat, Mex) bright-colored woolen poncho

sarcasmo *m* sarcasm

sarcásti·co -ca *adj* sarcastic

sardina *f* sardine; **como sardinas en banasta** or **en lata** packed in like sardines

sar·do -da *adj & mf* Sardinian

sarga *f* serge

sargento *m* sergeant

sarmiento *m* vine shoot, running stem

sarna *f* itch, mange

sarno·so -sa *adj* itchy, mangy

sarrace·no -na *adj & mf* Saracen

sarracina *f* scuffle, free fight; bloody brawl

sarro *m* crust; (*p.ej., en la lengua*) fur; (*en los dientes*) tartar

sarta *f* string; line, fine, series

sartén *f* frying pan; **saltar de la sartén y dar en las brasas** to jump from the frying pan into the fire

sastre *m* tailor

satélite *m* satellite; **satélite de comunicaciones** communications satellite; **satélite espía** spy satellite

satelizar §60 *tr* to put into orbit; (pol) to make a satellite of ‖ *ref* to go into orbit

satén *m* sateen

satíri·co -ca *adj* satiric(al) ‖ *mf* satirist

satirizar §60 *tr & intr* to satirize

satisfacción *f* satisfaction

satisfacer §39 *tr & intr* to satisfy ‖ *ref* to satisfy oneself, be satisfied, take satisfaction

satisfacto·rio -ria *adj* satisfactory

saturar *tr* to saturate, satiate

sauce *m* willow tree; **sauce de Babilonia** or **sauce llorón** weeping willow

saúco *m* elder, elderberry

savia *f* sap

saxofón *m* or **saxófono** *m* saxophone

saya *f* skirt; petticoat

sayo *m* smock frock, tunic; garment

sazón *f* ripeness; season; time, occasion; taste, seasoning; **a la sazón** at that time; **en sazón** in season, ripe; on time, opportunely

sazonar *tr* to ripen; season ‖ *ref* to ripen, mature

s/c *abbr* **su cuenta**

S.E. *abbr* **Su Excelencia**

se *pron reflex* himself, to himself; herself, to herself; itself, to itself; themselves, to themselves; yourself, to yourself; yourselves, to yourselves; oneself, to oneself; each other, to each other ‖ *pron pers* (used before the pronouns **lo, la, le,** etc.) to him, to her, to it, to them, to you

sebo *m* tallow; fat, suet

seca *f* drought; dry season

secador *m* drier, hair drier

secadora *f* clothes drier

secafir·mas *m* (*pl* **-mas**) blotter

secano *m* dry land, unwatered land

secansa *f* sequence

secante *m* blotting paper

secar §73 *tr* to dry, wipe dry; annoy, bore ‖ *ref* to dry, get dry; dry oneself; wither; be dry, be thirsty; (*un pozo*) run dry

secarropa *f* clothes dryer; **secarropa de travesaños** clotheshorse

sección *f* section; cross section; **sección de fondo** editorial section

secesión *f* secession

se·co -ca *adj* dry; dried up, withered; lank, lean; harsh, sharp; (*bebida*) straight, indifferent; plain, unadorned ‖ *f* see **seca**

secreta·rio -ria *adj* confidential, trusted ‖ *mf* secretary

secreter *m* secretary (*writing desk*)

secre·to -ta *adj* secret ‖ *m* secret; secrecy; hiding place, secret drawer; (*mecanismo oculto para abrir una cerradura*) key; **en el secreto de las cosas** on the inside

secta *f* sect

secta·rio -ria *adj & mf* sectarian

sector *m* sector; **sector de distribución** house current, power line

se·cuaz *adj* (*pl* **-cuaces**) partisan ‖ *mf* partisan, follower

secuela *f* sequel, result

secuencia *f* sequence

secuestrar *tr* to kidnap; (*un avión*) to hijack; (law) to sequester

secular *adj* secular

secundar *tr* to second, back

secunda·rio -ria *adj* secondary ‖ *m* (elec) secondary

sed *f* thirst; drought; **tener sed** to be thirsty

seda *f* silk; **como una seda** smooth as silk; easy as pie; sweet-natured; **seda encerada** dental floss

sedal *m* fish line

sedán *m* sedan; **sedán de reparto** delivery truck

sede *f* (*p.ej., del gobierno*) seat; (eccl) see; **Santa Sede** Holy See

sedenta•rio -ria *adj* sedentary
sede•ño -ña *adj* silk, silken
sedición *f* sedition
sedicio•so -sa *adj* seditious
sedien•to -ta *adj* thirsty; (*terreno*) dry; anxious, eager
sedimento *m* sediment
sedo•so -sa *adj* silky
seducción *f* seduction; charm, captivation
seducir §19 *tr* to seduce; tempt, lead astray; charm, captivate
seducti•vo -va *adj* seductive; tempting; charming, captivating
seduc•tor -tora *adj* seductive; tempting; charming ‖ *mf* seducer; tempter; charmer
sefar•dí (*pl* **-díes**) *adj* Sephardic ‖ *mf* Sephardi
sega•dor -dora *adj* harvesting ‖ *m* harvestman ‖ *f* harvester; mowing machine; **segadora de césped** lawn mower; **segadora trilladora** combine
segar §66 *tr* to reap, harvest, mow; mow down ‖ *intr* to reap, harvest, mow
segazón *f* harvest; harvest time
seglar *adj* secular, lay ‖ *m* layman ‖ *f* laywoman
segmento *m* segment; **segmento de émbolo** piston ring
segregacionista *mf* segregationist
segregar §44 *tr* to segregate
seguida *f* series, succession; **de seguida** without interruption, continuously; at once; in a row; **en seguida** at once, immediately
seguidilla *f* Spanish stanza made up of a quatrain and a tercet; **seguidillas** seguidilla (*Spanish dance and music*)
segui•do -da *adj* continued, successive; straight, direct; running, in a row; **todo seguido** straight ahead ‖ *f* see **seguida**
seguimiento *m* chase, hunt, pursuit; continuation; (*de vehículos espaciales*) tracking
seguir §67 *tr* to follow; pursue; continue; dog, hound ‖ *intr* to go on, continue; still be, be now; keep + *ger* ‖ *ref* to follow, ensue; issue, spring
según *prep* according to, as per; **según que** according as ‖ *conj* as, according as
segunda *f* double meaning; (aut & mus) second
segundero *m* second hand; **segundero central** sweep-second, center-second
segun•do -da *adj* second ‖ *m* second; **ser sin segundo** to be second to none ‖ *f* see **segunda**
segur *f* axe; sickle
segurador *s* security, bondsman
seguridad *f* security; safety; surety; certainty; assurance; confidence
segu•ro -ra *adj* sure, certain; secure, safe; reliable; constant; steady, unfailing ‖ *m* assurance, certainty; safety; confidence; insurance; **a buen seguro** surely, truly; **seguro contra accidentes** accident insurance; **seguro de desempleo** or **desocupación** unemployment insurance; **seguro de enfermedad** health insurance; **seguro de incendios** fire insurance; **seguro**

sobre la vida life insurance; **sobre seguro** without risk ‖ **seguro** *adv* surely
seis *adj & pron* six; **las seis** six o'clock ‖ *m* six; (*en las fechas*) sixth
seiscien•tos -tas *adj & pron* six hundred ‖ **seiscientos** *m* six hundred
selección *f* selection
seleccionar *tr* to select, choose
selec•to -ta *adj* select, choice
selva *f* forest, woods; jungle
selváti•co -ca *adj* woodsy; rustic, wild
sellar *tr* to seal; stamp; close; finish up
sello *m* seal; stamp; signet; wafer; **sello aéreo** air-mail stamp; **sello de correo** postage stamp; **sello de urgencia** special-delivery stamp; **sello fiscal** revenue stamp
semáforo *m* semaphore; traffic light
semana *f* week; week's pay; **semana inglesa** working week of five and a half days
semanal *adj* weekly
semanalmente *adv* weekly
semana•rio -ria *adj & m* weekly
semánti•co -ca *adj* semantic ‖ *f* semantics
semblante *m* face, mien, countenance; appearance, expression, look
semblanza *f* biographical sketch, portrait
sembrado *m* sown ground, grain field
sembrar §2 *tr* to seed, sow; scatter, spread; sprinkle
semejante *adj* like, similar; such; **semejante a** like; **semejantes** alike, e.g., **estas sillas son semejantes** these chairs are alike ‖ *m* resemblance, likeness; fellow, fellow man
semejanza *f* similarity, resemblance; simile; **a semejanza de** like
semejar *tr* to resemble, be like ‖ *intr & ref* to be alike; **semejar a** or **semejarse a** to resemble, be like
semen *m* semen
semental *adj* (*animal*) stud, breeding ‖ *m* sire; stallion; stock bull
semestral *adj* semester
semestre *m* semester
semibola *f* little slam
semibreve *f* (mus) whole note
semiconductor *m* semiconductor
semiconsciente *adj* semiconscious
semicul•to -ta *adj* semilearned
semidifun•to -ta *adj* half-dead
semidormi•do -da *adj* half-asleep
semifinal *adj & f* (sport) semifinal
semilla *f* seed; **semilla de césped** grass seed
semillero *m* seedbed
seminario *m* seminary; seminar; nursery
semi-remolque *m* semitrailer
semita *mf* Semite ‖ *m* (*idioma*) Semitic
semíti•co -ca *adj* Semitic
semivi•vo -va *adj* half-alive
semovientes *mpl* stock, livestock
sempiter•no -na *adj* everlasting
Sena *m* Seine
senado *m* senate
senador *m* senator
senaduría *f* senatorship
sencillez *f* simplicity, plainness, candor
senci•llo -lla *adj* simple, plain, candid; single ‖ *m* change, loose change

senda *f* path, footpath
sendero *m* path, footpath, byway
sen•dos -das *adj pl* one each, one to each, e.g., **les dio sendos libros** he gave one book to each of them, he gave each of them a book
senectud *f* age, old age
senil *adj* senile
senilidad *f* senility
senilismo *m* (pathol) senility
seno *m* bosom, breast; lap; heart; womb; bay, gulf; cavity, hollow, recess; asylum, refuge
sensación *f* sensation
sensatez *f* good sense
sensa•to -ta *adj* sensible
sensibilizar §60 *tr* to sensitize
sensible *adj* appreciable, perceptible, noticeable, sensible; considerable; sensitive; deplorable, regrettable
sensiblería *f* mawkishness
sensible•ro -ra *adj* mawkish
sensiti•vo -va *adj* (*de los sentidos*) sense, sensitive; sentient; stimulating
senso•rio -ria *adj* sensory
sensual *adj* sensual, sensuous
sentada *f* sitting; **de una sentada** at one sitting
senta•do -da *adj* seated; settled; stable, permanent; sedate; **dar por sentado** to take for granted ‖ *f* see **sentada**
sentar §2 *tr* to seat; settle; fit, suit; agree with ‖ *ref* to sit, sit down; settle, settle down
sentencia *f* maxim; (law) sentence
sentenciar *tr* to sentence; (*una cuestión*) to decide; (*p.ej.*, *un libro a la hoguera*) to consign
senti•do -da *adj* felt; deep-felt; sensitive; eloquent; **darse por sentido** to take offense ‖ *m* sense, meaning; direction; consciousness; **sentido común** common sense
sentimiento *m* sentiment; feeling; sorrow, regret
sentir *m* feeling; opinion; judgment ‖ §68 *tr* to feel; hear; be or feel sorry for; sense ‖ *intr* to feel; be sorry, feel sorry ‖ *ref* to feel; feel oneself to be; be resentful; crack, be cracked; **sentirse de** to feel; have a pain in; resent
seña *f* sign, mark, token; password, watchword; **por las señas** to all appearances; **por más señas** or **por señas** as a greater proof; **seña de tráfico** traffic sign; **señas** address; description
señal *f* sign, mark, token; landmark; bookmark; trace, vestige; scar; signal; traffic light; representation; reminder; pledge; brand; down payment; **señal de ocupado** (telp) busy signal; **señal de tramo** (rr) block signal; **señal de vídeo** video signal; **señal digital** fingerprint; **señal para marcar** (telp) dial tone
señala *f* (Chile) earmark (*on livestock*)
señala•do -da *adj* noted, distinguished
señalar *tr* to mark; show, indicate; point at, point out; signal; brand; determine, fix;

appoint; sign and seal; scar; threaten ‖ *ref* to distinguish oneself, excel
señalizar §60 *tr* to signal
señor *m* sir, mister; lord, master, owner; **muy señor mío** Dear Sir; **señores** Mr. and Mrs.; ladies and gentlemen
señora *f* madam, missus; mistress, owner; wife; **muy señora mía** Dear Madam; **Nuestra Señora** our Lady; **señora de compañía** chaperon
señorear *tr* to dominate, rule; master, control; seize, take control of; tower over; excel ‖ *intr* to strut, swagger ‖ *ref* to strut, swagger; control oneself; **señorearse de** to seize, take control of
señoría *f* lordship; ladyship; rule, sway
señoril *adj* lordly; haughty; majestic
señorío *m* dominion, sway, rule; mastery; arrogance, lordliness, majesty; gentry, nobility
señorita *f* young lady; miss
señorito *m* master; young gentleman; playboy
señuelo *m* decoy, lure; bait; enticement
separación *f* separation; **separación de poderes** (pol) separation of powers
separa•do -da *adj* separate; separated; apart; **por separado** separately; under separate cover
separar *tr* to separate; dismiss, discharge ‖ *ref* to separate; resign
separata *f* reprint, offprint
sept.ᵉ *abbr* **septiembre**
septeto *m* septet
sépti•co -ca *adj* septic
septiembre *m* September
sépti•mo -ma *adj* & *m* seventh
sepulcro *m* sepulcher, tomb, grave; **santo sepulcro** Holy Sepulcher
sepultar *tr* to bury; hide away
sepultura *f* burial; grave; **estar con un pie en la sepultura** to have one foot in the grave
sepulturero *m* gravedigger
sequedad *f* dryness, drought; gruffness, surliness
sequía *f* drought
séquito *m* retinue, suite; following, popularity
ser *m* being; essence; life ‖ *v* §69 *v aux* (to form passive voice) to be, e.g., **el discurso fue aplaudido por todos** the speech was applauded by everybody ‖ *intr* to be; **a no ser por** if it were not for; **a no ser que** unless; **érase que se era** once upon a time there was; **es decir** that is to say; **sea lo que fuere** be that as it may; **ser de** to belong to; become of; be, e.g., **el reloj es de oro** the watch is gold; **ser de ver** to be worth seeing; **soy yo** it is me, it is I
serafín *m* seraph; great beauty (*person*)
serena *f* night love song; night dew, night air
serenar *tr* to calm; pacify; cool; settle
serenata *f* serenade
serenidad *f* serenity; **serenidad del espíritu** peace of mind

sere•no -na *adj* serene, calm; clear, cloudless ‖ *m* night watchman; night dew, night air ‖ *f* see **serena**

serial *adj* serial ‖ *m* (telv) serial; **serial lacrimógeno** soap opera; **serial radiado** (rad) serial

serie *f* series; **de serie** serial; stock, e.g., **coche de serie** stock car; **en serie** mass; **fuera de serie** custom-built, special; outsize

seriedad *f* seriousness; reliability; sternness, severity; solemnity

se•rio -ria *adj* serious; reliable; stern; solemn

sermón *m* sermon

sermonear *tr & intr* to sermonize

serpear or **serpentear** *intr* to wind, meander; wriggle, squirm

serpentín *m* coil

serpiente *f* serpent, snake; **serpiente de cascabel** rattlesnake

serranía *f* range of mountains, mountainous country

serra•no -na *adj* highland, mountain ‖ *mf* highlander, mountaineer

serrar §2 *tr* to saw

serrería *f* sawmill

serrín *m* sawdust

serrucho *m* handsaw

Servia *f* Serbia

servicial *adj* accommodating, obliging

servicio *m* service; (tennis) service, serve; (Am) toilet; **en acto de servicio** in the line of duty; **fuera de servicio** out of service; inoperative; (coll) down; **libre servicio** self-service; **servicio de grúa** (aut) towing service; **servicio postventa** customer service; **servicio telegráfico y telefónico** wire service

servi•dor -dora *mf* servant; humble servant; (tennis) server; **servidor de Vd.** your servant, at your service ‖ *m* waiter; suitor ‖ *f* waitress

servidumbre *f* servitude; servants, help; compulsion; (law) easement; **servidumbre de la gleba** serfdom; **servidumbre de paso** (law) right of way; **servidumbre de vía** (rr) right of way

servil *adj* servile

servilleta *f* napkin

servilletero *m* napkin ring

ser•vio -via *adj & mf* Serbian ‖ *f* see **Servia**

servir §50 *tr* to serve; help, wait on; (*un pedido*) fill; (tennis) serve; **para servir a Vd.** at your service ‖ *intr* to serve; (*en los naipes*) follow suit; **servir de** to serve as; be used as; **servir para** to be good for, be used for ‖ *ref* to help oneself, serve oneself; have the kindness to, deign to; **servirse de** to use, make use of; **sírvase** please

serv.º *abbr* **servicio**

servocroata *adj & mf* Serbo-Croatian

servodirección *f* (aut) power steering

servoembrague *m* (aut) automatic clutch

servofreno *m* power brake

sésamo *m* sesame; **sésamo ábrete** open sesame

sesenta *adj, pron & m* sixty

sesenta•vo -va *adj & m* sixtieth

sesgar §44 *tr* (*el paño*) to cut on the bias; bevel, slant, slope

ses•go -ga *adj* beveled, slanting, sloped; oblique; stern; calm ‖ *m* bevel; bias; slant, slope; turn; compromise; **al sesgo** obliquely; on the bias

sesión *f* session; sitting; meeting; (*cada representación de un drama o película*) show; **sesión continua** (mov) continuous showing; **sesión de espiritistas** séance, spiritualistic séance

sesionar *intr* to be in session

seso *m* brain; brains, intelligence; **calentarse** or **devanarse los sesos** to rack one's brain

sestear *intr* to take a siesta; (*el ganado*) rest in the shade

sesu•do -da *adj* brainy; (Chile) stubborn

seta *f* bristle; toadstool

setecien•tos -tas *adj & m* seven hundred ‖ **setecientos** *m* seven hundred

setenta *adj, pron & m* seventy

setenta•vo -va *adj & m* seventieth

seto *m* fence; **seto vivo** hedge, quickset; **seto vivo** fence; **seto vivo** hedge, quickset

seudónimo *m* pseudonym, pen name

s.e.u.o. *abbr* **salvo error u omisión**

seve•ro -ra *adj* severe; stern; strict

sevicia *f* ferocity, cruelty

sexo *m* sex; **el bello sexo** the fair sex; **el sexo feo** the sterner sex

sextante *m* sextant

sex•to -ta *adj & m* sixth

sexual *adj* sexual, sex

si *conj* if; whether; I wonder if; **por si acaso** just in case; **si acaso** if by chance; **si no** otherwise

sí *adv* yes; indeed; (gives emphasis to verb and is often equivalent to English auxiliary verb) **él sí habla español** he does speak Spanish ‖ *pron reflex* himself, herself, itself, themselves; yourself, yourselves; oneself; each other ‖ *m* (*pl* -**síes**) yes; **dar el sí** to say yes

sia•més -mesa *adj & mf* Siamese

siberia•no -na *adj & mf* Siberian

sibila *f* sibyl

sicalipsis *f* spiciness, suggestiveness

sicalípti•co -ca *adj* spicy, suggestive, sexy

Sicilia *f* Sicily

sicilia•no -na *adj & mf* Sicilian

sico. . . var of **psico. . .**

sicofanta *m* or **sicofante** *m* informer, spy; slanderer

sico•sis *f* (*pl* -**sis**) psychosis; (*afección de la piel*) sycosis

SIDA *abbr* **síndrome de inmunidad deficiente adquirida**

sideral or **sidére•o -a** *adj* sidereal

siderurgia *f* iron and steel industry

sidra *f* cider; **sidra achampañada** hard cider

siega *f* reaping, mowing; harvest; crop

siembra *f* sowing; seeding; seedtime; sown field

siempre *adv* always; **de siempre** usual; **para siempre** or **por siempre** forever; **por siempre jamás** forever and ever; **siempre que** whenever; provided

siempreviva *f* everlasting flower

sien *f* temple (*of head*)

sierpe *f* serpent, snake

sierra *f* saw; sierra, mountain range; **sierra circular** buzz saw; **sierra continua** band saw; **sierra de armero** hacksaw; **sierra de bastidor** bucksaw; **sierra de hilar** ripsaw; **sierra de vaivén** jig saw; **sierra sin fin** band saw

sier•vo -va *mf* slave; servant; **siervo de la gleba** serf

sieso *m* anus

siesta *f* siesta; hot time of day; **siesta del carnero** nap before lunch

siete *adj & pron* seven; **las siete** seven o'clock ‖ *m* seven; (*en las fechas*) seventh; (coll) V-shaped tear or rip

sífilis *f* syphilis

sifón *m* siphon; siphon bottle; (*tubo doblemente acodado*) trap

sig.[e] *abbr* **siguiente**

sigilar *tr* to seal, stamp; conceal, keep silent

sigilo *m* seal; concealment, reserve; **sigilo sacramental** inviolable secrecy of the confessional

sigilo•so -sa *adj* tight-lipped; reserved

sigla *f* initial; abbreviation, symbol

siglo *m* (*cien años*) century; (*comercio de los hombres*) world; (*largo tiempo*) age; **siglo de la ilustración** or **de las luces** Age of Enlightenment

signar *tr* to mark; sign; make the sign of the cross over

signatura *f* library number; (mus & typ) signature

significado *m* meaning

significar §73 *tr* to signify, mean; point out, make known ‖ *intr* to be important

signo *m* sign; mark; sign of the cross; fate, destiny; **signo de admiración** exclamation mark; **signo de interrogación** question mark; **signo externo** status symbol

siguiente *adj* following; next

sílaba *f* syllable; **última sílaba** ultima

silbar *tr* (*p.ej., una canción*) to whistle; (*un silbato*) blow; (*a un actor*) hiss ‖ *intr* to whistle; (*ir zumbando por el aire*) whiz, whiz by

silbato *m* whistle

silbido *m* whistle, whistling, hiss; (rad) howling, squealing; **silbido de oídos** ringing in the ears

silbo *m* whistle, hiss

silenciador *m* silencer; (aut) muffler

silencio *m* silence; (*toque que manda que cada cual se acueste*) (mil) taps; (mus) rest

silencio•so -sa *adj* silent, noiseless; quiet, still ‖ *m* (aut) muffler

sílfide *f* sylph

silo *m* silo; cave, dark place

silogismo *m* syllogism

silueta *f* silhouette

silva *f* (*materias escritas sin orden*) miscellany; verse of iambic hendecasyllables intermingled with seven-syllable lines

silvestre *adj* wild; rustic, uncultivated

silvicultura *f* forestry

silla *f* chair; **silla alta** high chair; **silla de balanza** rocking chair; **silla de cubierta** deck chair; **silla de junco** rush-bottomed chair; **silla de manos** sedan chair; **silla de montar** saddle, riding saddle; **silla de ruedas** wheel chair; **silla de tijera** folding chair; **silla giratoria** swivel chair; **silla hamaca** (Arg) rocking chair; **silla plegadiza** folding chair; **silla poltrona** armchair, easy chair; **sillas apilables** chairs that can be stacked or nested

sillar *m* ashlar

silleta *f* bedpan

sillico *m* chamber pot, commode

sillín *m* saddle (*of bicycle*)

sillón *m* armchair, easy chair; **sillón de orejas** wing chair

sima *f* chasm, abyss

simbióti•co -ca *adj* symbiotic

simbóli•co -ca *adj* symbolic(al)

simbolizar §60 *tr* to symbolize

símbolo *m* symbol; **Símbolo de la fe** or **de los Apóstoles** Apostles' Creed

simetría *f* symmetry

simétri•co -ca *adj* symmetric(al)

simiente *f* seed, sperm

símil *adj* like, similar ‖ *m* similarity; (rhet) simile

similar *adj* similar

similigrabado *m* (typ) half-tone

similor *m* ormolu, similor; **de similor** fake, sham

simio *m* monkey

simpatía *f* affection, attachment, liking; friendliness; congeniality; **tomar simpatía a** to take a liking for

simpáti•co -ca *adj* agreeable, pleasant, likeable, congenial

simpatizar §60 *intr* to be congenial, get on well together; **simpatizar con** to get on well with

simple *adj* simple; single ‖ *mf* simpleton ‖ *m* (*planta medicinal*) simple

simpleza *f* simpleness; stupidity

simplificar §73 *tr* to simplify

simulacro *m* phantom, vision; idol, image; semblance, show; pretense; sham battle; **simulacro de ataque aéreo** air-raid drill; **simulacro de combate** sham battle

simula•do -da *adj* fake; (com) pro forma

simular *tr* to simulate, feign, fake ‖ *intr* to malinger; pretend

simultanear *tr* to do simultaneously ‖ *intr* to work simultaneously

simultáne•o -a *adj* simultaneous

sin *prep* without; **sin embargo** nevertheless, however; **sin que** + *subj* without + *ger*

sinagoga *f* synagogue

sinapismo *m* mustard plaster; bore, nuisance

sincerar *tr* to vindicate, justify

sinceridad *f* sincerity

since•ro -ra *adj* sincere

síncopa f (phonet) syncope

síncope m fainting spell

sincróni•co -ca adj synchronous

sincronizar §60 tr & intr to synchronize

sindicar §73 tr & ref to syndicate

sindicato m syndicate; labor union

síndico m trustee; (en una quiebra) receiver

sin•diós (pl -diós) adj godless ‖ mf atheist

síndrome m syndrome; **síndrome de choque tóxico** toxic-shock syndrome; **síndrome de inmunidad deficiente adquirida (SIDA)** acquired immune-deficiency syndrome (AIDS)

sinecura f sinecure

sinfín m endless amount, number

sinfonía f symphony

sinfóni•co -ca adj symphonic

singladura f (naut) day's run

singular adj singular; special; single ‖ m singular; **en singular** in particular

singularizar §60 tr to distinguish, single out ‖ ref to distinguish oneself, stand out

sinhueso f (coll) tongue

sinies•tro -tra adj evil, perverse; calamitous, disastrous ‖ m calamity, disaster ‖ f left hand, left-hand side

sinnúmero m great amount, great number

sino conj but, except; **no . . . sino** only; **no . . . sino que** only; **no solo . . . sino que** not only . . . but also ‖ m fate, destiny

sinóni•mo -ma adj synonymous ‖ m synonym

sinop•sis f (pl -sis) synopsis

sinrazón f wrong, injustice

sinsabor m displeasure; anxiety, trouble, worry

sinsonte m mockingbird

sinsostenismo m (coll) bra-less fashion

sintaxis f syntax

sínte•sis f (pl -sis) synthesis

sintéti•co -ca adj synthetic(al)

sintetizar §60 tr to synthesize

síntoma m symptom; sign; **síntoma de abstinencia** withdrawal symptom

sintonía f (rad) tuning; (rad) theme song

sintonizar §60 tr (el aparato receptor) to tune; (la estación emisora) tune in

sinuo•so -sa adj sinuous, winding; wavy; evasive

sinvergüenza adj brazen, shameless ‖ mf scoundrel, rascal

sionismo m Zionism

siqui. . . var of **psiqui. . .**

siquiera adv even; at least ‖ conj although, even though

sirena f siren; mermaid; **sirena de la playa** bathing beauty; **sirena de niebla** foghorn

sirga f towrope, towline

sirgar §44 tr to tow

Siria f Syria

si•rio -ria adj & mf Syrian ‖ **Sirio** m (astr) Sirius ‖ f see **Siria**

sirvienta f maid, servant girl

sirviente m servant; waiter

sisa f petty theft; (para fijar los panes de oro) sizing

sisal m sisal, sisal hemp

sisar tr to filch, snitch; (lo que se ha de dorar) size

sisear tr to hiss ‖ intr to hiss; sizzle

siseo m hiss, hissing; sizzle, sizzling

Sísifo m Sisyphus

sismógrafo m seismograph

sismología f seismology

sistema m system; **el Sistema** the Establishment, established order

sistematizar §60 tr to systematize

sístole f systole

sitial m place of honor

sitiar tr to surround, hem in; siege, besiege

sitio m place, spot, room; location, site; country place; seat; cattle ranch; taxi stand; (mil) siege

si•to -ta adj situated, located

situación f situation, position; **pedir situación** (aer) to ask for bearings

situar §21 tr to situate, locate, place; (dinero) place, invest; (un pedido) place ‖ ref to take a position; settle; take place; (aer) to get one's bearings

s.l. abbr **sin lugar**

S.M. abbr **Su majestad**

smo•king m (pl -kings) tuxedo, dinner coat

so prep under, e.g., **so pena de** under penalty of ‖ interj whoa!; you. . .!, e.g., **¡so animal!** you beast!

sobaco m armpit

sobajar tr to crush, to rumple; to humiliate

sobaquera f (en el vestido) armhole; (para resguardar del sudor la parte del vestido correspondiente al sobaco) shield

sobaquina f underarm odor

sobar tr to knead; massage; beat, slap; paw, pet, feel; annoy, be fresh to; flatter; (un hueso dislocado) (CAm) to set; (la cabalgadura) (Arg) to tire out; (Col) to flay, skin; (P-R) to bribe

soberanía f sovereignty

sobera•no -na adj sovereign; superb ‖ mf sovereign ‖ m (moneda) sovereign

sober•bio -bia adj proud, haughty; arrogant; magnificent, superb ‖ f pride, haughtiness; arrogance; magnificence

so•bón -bona adj malingering; fresh, mushy, spoony

soborna•do -da adj twisted; out of shape

sobornar tr to bribe

soborno m bribery; (SAm) extra load; **de soborno** (Bol) in addition; **soborno de testigo** (law) subornation of perjury

sobra f extra, surplus; **sobras** leftovers, leavings; trash

sobradillo m penthouse

sobra•do -da adj excessive, superfluous; bold, daring; rich, wealthy ‖ m attic, garret ‖ **sobrado** adv too

sobrante adj remaining, leftover, surplus ‖ m leftover, surplus

sobrar tr to exceed, surpass ‖ intr to be more than enough; be in the way; be left, remain

sobre prep on, upon; over; above; about; near; after; in addition to; out of, e.g., **en nueve casos sobre diez** in nine out of ten cases ‖ *m* envelope; **sobre de ventanilla** window envelope

sobrealimentar *tr* to overfeed; supercharge

sobrecama *f* bedspread

sobrecarga *f* overload, extra load; overcharge; surcharge

sobrecargar §44 *tr* to overload, overburden; overcharge; surcharge; (aer) to pressurize

sobrecargo *m* (naut) supercargo; purser ‖ *f* flight attendant, stewardess

sobrecejo *m* frown

sobreceño *m* frown

sobrecoger §17 *tr* to surprise, catch; scare, terrify ‖ *ref* to be surprised; be scared; **sobrecogerse de** to be seized with

sobrecubierta *f* extra cover; (*de un libro*) jacket, dust jacket

sobredi•cho -cha *adj* above-mentioned

sobredosis *f* overdose

sobreestimar *tr* to overestimate

sobreexcitar *tr* to overexcite ‖ *ref* to become overexcited

sobreexponer §54 *tr* to overexpose

sobreexposición *f* overexposure

sobregirar *tr & intr* to overdraw

sobregiro *m* overdraft

sobreherido *adj* slightly wounded

sobrehombre *m* superman

sobrehuma•no -na *adj* superhuman

sobrellevar *tr* to bear, carry; (*la carga de otra persona*) ease; (*los trabajos o molestias de la vida*) share; (*molestias*) suffer with patience

sobremanera *adv* exceedingly, beyond measure

sobremesa *f* tablecloth, table cover; **de sobremesa** desk, e.g., **reloj de sobremesa** desk clock; after-dinner, e.g., **discurso de sobremesa** after-dinner speech

sobremodo *adv* var of **sobremanera**

sobrenadar *intr* to float

sobrenatural *adj* supernatural

sobrenombrar *tr* to surname; nickname

sobrenombre *m* surname; nickname

sobrentender §51 *tr* to understand ‖ *ref* to be understood, be implied

sobrepasar *tr* to excel, surpass, outdo; exceed; overtake ‖ *ref* to outdo each other; go too far

sobrepeine *adv* slightly, briefly ‖ *m* hair trimming

sobrepe•lliz *f* (*pl* **-llices**) surplice

sobreponer §54 *tr* to superpose, put on top; superimpose ‖ *ref* to control oneself; triumph over adversity; **sobreponerse a** to overcome

sobreprecio *m* extra charge, surcharge

sobreproducción *f* overproduction

sobrepujar *tr* to excel, surpass

sobresaliente *adj* projecting; conspicuous, outstanding; (*en un examen*) distinguished ‖ *mf* substitute; understudy

sobresalir §65 *intr* to project, jut out; stand out, excel

sobresaltar *tr* to assail, rush upon; startle, frighten ‖ *intr* to stand out clearly ‖ *ref* to be startled, be frightened; start, wince

sobresalto *m* fright, scare; start, shock, wince; **de sobresalto** suddenly, unexpectedly

sobrescribir §83 *tr* to address

sobrescrito *m* address

sobrestante *m* boss, foreman

sobresueldo *m* extra wages, extra pay

sobretiro *m* offprint

sobretodo *adv* especially ‖ *m* overcoat, topcoat

sobrevenir §79 *intr* to happen, take place; supervene, set in; **sobrevenir a** to overtake

sobrevidriera *f* window screen; window grill; storm window

sobrevivencia *f* (Ecuad) survival

sobreviviente *adj* surviving ‖ *mf* survivor

sobrevivir *intr* to survive; **sobrevivir a** to survive, outlive

sobrevolar §61 *tr* to overfly

sobriedad *f* sobriety, moderation

sobrina *f* niece

sobrino *m* nephew

so•brio -bria *adj* sober, moderate, temperate

socaire *m* (naut) lee; **al socaire de** (naut) under the lee of; (coll) under the shelter of; **estar al socaire** to shirk

socapa *f* subterfuge; **a socapa** clandestinely

socarrén *m* eaves

socarrar *tr* to singe, scorch

soca•rrón -rrona *adj* crafty, cunning, sly; sneering; roguish

socavar *tr* to undermine, dig under

socavón *m* cave-in; cave; (min) gallery

sociable *adj* sociable

social *adj* social; company, e.g., **edificio social** company building

socialismo *m* socialism

socialista *mf* socialist

sociedad *f* society; company, firm; **buena sociedad** (*mundo elegante*) society; **sociedad anónima** stock company; **sociedad de control** holding company; **Sociedad de las Naciones** League of Nations; **sociedad distribuidora** (wholesale) distributor

so•cio -cia *mf* partner; companion; member ‖ *m* fellow; (scornful) guy

sociología *f* sociology

socorrer *tr* to aid, help, succor

socorri•do -da *adj* ready; handy, useful; hackneyed, trite, worn; well stocked

socorrismo *m* first aid

socorro *m* aid, help, succor

socoyote *m* (Mex) baby, youngest son

soda *f* soda; soda water

sodio *m* sodium

so•ez *adj* (*pl* **-eces**) base, mean, vile

so•fá *m* (*pl* **-fás**) sofa; **sofá cama** day bed

soflama *f* glow, flicker; blush; deceit, cheating

soflamar *tr* to flimflam; make blush ‖ *ref* to become scorched

sofocar §73 *tr* to choke, suffocate, stifle, smother; quench, extinguish; make blush; bother, harass ‖ *ref* to choke, suffocate; blush; get excited; get out of breath

sofoco *m* blush, embarrassment

sofrenar *tr* (*un caballo*) to check suddenly; (*una pasión*) control; chide, reprimand

soga *m* sly fellow ‖ *f* rope, cord; **dar soga a** to make fun of; **hacer soga** to lag behind

soja *f* soy, soy bean

sojuzgar §44 *tr* to subjugate, subdue

sol *m* sun; sunlight; sunny side; **de sol a sol** from sunrise to sunset; **hacer sol** to be sunny; **soles** (poet) eyes

solamente *adv* only

solana *f* sunny spot; sun porch

solanera *f* sunburn; sunny spot

solapa *f* lapel; pretext, pretense; flap

solapa•do -da *adj* overlapping; cunning, underhanded, sneaky

solapar *tr* to put lapels on; overlap; conceal, cover up ‖ *intr* to overlap

solapo *m* lapel; flap; chuck under chin

solar *adj* solar; ancestral ‖ *m* ground, plot; backyard; manor house, ancestral mansion; noble lineage; (Cuba) tenement ‖ *v* §61 *tr* to pave, floor; (*zapatos*) sole

solarie•go -ga *adj* ancestral; manorial

solario *m* sun porch

so•laz *m* (*pl* **-laces**) solace, consolation; recreation; **a solaz** with pleasure

soldada *f* wages, pay

soldadera *f* (Mex) camp follower

soldadesca *f* soldiery; undisciplined troops

soldado *m* soldier; **soldado de a pie** foot soldier; **soldado de juguete** toy soldier; **soldado de marina** marine; **soldado de plomo** tin soldier; **soldado de primera** private first class; **soldado raso** buck private

soldadura *f* solder; soldering; weld; welding; **soldadura al arco** arc welding; **soldadura autógena** welding; **soldadura a tope** butt welding; **soldadura por puntos** spot welding

soldar §61 *tr* to solder; (*sin materia extraña*) weld ‖ *ref* (*los huesos*) to knit

solear *tr* to sun ‖ *ref* to sun, sun oneself

soledad *f* solitude, loneliness; longing, grieving; lonely spot

soledo•so -sa *adj* solitary, lonely; longing, grieving

solemne *adj* solemn; (*error, mentira, etc.*) downright

soler §47 *intr* to be accustomed to

solera *f* crossbeam; lumber, timber; mother liquor, mother of the wine; blend of sherry; old vintage sherry; tradition, standing; (Chile) curb; (Mex) brick, tile, stone; **de solera** or **de rancia solera** of the good old school, of the good old times

solevantar *tr* to raise up; rouse, stir up, incite ‖ *ref* to rise up; revolt

solevar *tr* to raise up; incite to rebellion ‖ *ref* to rise up; revolt

solicitante *mf* petitioner; applicant

solicitar *tr* to solicit, ask for; apply for; woo, court; drive, pull; (*la atención*) attract; (phys) to attract

solíci•to -ta *adj* solicitous; careful, diligent; obliging; fond, affectionate

solicitud *f* solicitude; petition, request; application

solidar *tr* to harden; establish, prove

solida•rio -ria *adj* jointly liable; jointly binding; **solidario con** or **de** integral with

solidarizar §60 *ref* to declare one's solidarity (with); identify (with)

solidez *f* solidity; strength, soundness; constancy

sóli•do -da *adj* solid; strong, sound ‖ *m* solid

soliloquio *m* soliloquy

solista *adj* (p.ej., *instrumento*) (mus) solo ‖ *mf* (mus) soloist

solita•rio -ria *adj* solitary; lonely ‖ *mf* hermit, recluse, solitary ‖ **en solitario** alone, solo ‖ *m* (*juego y diamante*) solitaire ‖ *f* tapeworm

sóli•to -ta *adj* accustomed, customary

soliviantar *tr* to rouse, stir up, incite

soliviar *tr* to lift, lift up

so•lo -la *adj* only, sole; alone; lonely; (p.ej., *whisky*) straight; (*café*) black; **a mis solas** alone, all by myself; **a solas** alone, unaided ‖ *pron* only one ‖ *m* (mus) solo

sólo *adv* only, solely

solomillo *m* sirloin

solomo *m* sirloin; loin of pork

solsticio *m* solstice

soltador *m* release; **soltador del margen** margin release

soltar §61 *tr* to untie, unfasten, loosen; let go; let go of; (*una observación*) drop, let slip; (*el agua*) turn on ‖ *ref* to get loose or free; come loose, come off; loosen up; burst out; thaw out, let oneself go

solte•ro -ra *adj* single, unmarried ‖ *m* bachelor ‖ *f* unmarried woman

solterona *f* older unmarried woman

soltura *f* looseness; agility, ease, freedom; fluency; dissoluteness; release

solución *f* solution

solucionar *tr* to solve, resolve

solventar *tr* (*lo que uno debe*) to settle, pay up; (*una dificultad*) solve

solvente *adj* solvent; (*fuente*) believable; reliable ‖ *m* solvent

sollastre *m* scullion

sollozar §60 *intr* to sob

sollozo *m* sob

sombra *f* (*falta de luz brillante*) shade; (*imagen obscura que proyecta un cuerpo opaco*) shadow; shady side; darkness; parasol; ignorance; ghost, spirit; grace, charm, wit; favor, protection; luck; **a la sombra** in the shade; in jail; **a sombra de tejado** stealthily, sneakingly; **ni por sombra** by no means; without any notice; **no ser su sombra** to be but a shadow of one's former self; **sombra (de ojos)** eye shadow; **tener buena sombra** to be likeable; to bring good luck

sombrear *tr* to shade; (*un dibujo*) hatch

sombrerera *f* bandbox, hatbox

sombrerería *f* hat store, hat factory; millinery shop

sombrere•ro -ra *mf* hatter, hat maker ‖ *f* see **sombrerera**

SO
SO

sombrero *m* hat; **sombrero de copa** high hat, top hat; **sombrero de muelles** opera hat; **sombrero ,de paja** straw hat; **sombrero de pelo** high hat; **sombrero de tres picos** three-cornered hat; **sombrero gacho** slouch hat; **sombrero hongo** derby; **sombrero jarano** sombrero

sombrilla *f* parasol, sunshade; **sombrilla de playa** beach umbrella; **sombrilla protectora** (mil) umbrella

sombrí•o -a *adj* shady; somber; gloomy

sombro•so -sa *adj* shadowy, full of shadows; shady

some•ro -ra *adj* brief, summary; slight; superficial, shallow

someter *tr* to subdue, subject; (*razones, reflexiones; un negocio*) submit ‖ *ref* to yield, submit, surrender

someti•do -da *adj* humble, submissive

sometimiento *m* subjection

somier *m* bedspring, spring mattress

somnolencia *f* sleepiness, drowsiness

somorgujar *tr* to plunge, submerge ‖ *intr* to dive, ‖ *ref* to plunge

son *m* sound; news, rumor; pretext, motive; manner, mode; **en son de** in the manner of, by way of; as

sona•do -da *adj* talked-about; famous, noted

sonaja *f* jingle

sonajero *m* rattle, child's rattle

sonámbu•lo -la *mf* sleepwalker, somnambulist

sonar §61 *tr* to sound, ring; (*un instrumento de viento, un silbato*) blow; (*un instrumento de viento*) play ‖ *intr* to sound, ring; (*un reloj*) strike; seem; sound familiar; **sonar a** to sound like, have the appearance of ‖ *ref* to be rumored; (*las narices*) blow

sonda *f* sounding; plummet, lead; drill; (surg) probe, sound

sondar or **sondear** *tr & intr* to sound, probe

sonetizar §60 *intr* to sonneteer

soneto *m* sonnet

sóni•co -ca *adj* sonic

sonido *m* sound; report, rumor

sonido silencioso ultrasound

sonoridad *f* sonority

sonorizar §60 *intr* (*una película cinematográfica*) to record sound effects on; (*una consonante sorda*) voice ‖ *ref* to voice

sono•ro -ra *adj* sound; clear, loud, resounding

sonreír §58 *intr & ref* to smile

sonriente *adj* smiling

sonrisa *f* smile

sonrojar or **sonrojear** *tr* to make one blush ‖ *ref* to blush

sonrojo *m* blush; word that causes blushing

sonrosar or **sonrosear** *tr* to rose-color; make blush ‖ *ref* to become rose-colored; blush

sonsacar §73 *tr* to pilfer; entice away; elicit, draw out

son•so -sa *adj* stupid

sonsonete *m* rhythmical tapping; sing-song

soña•dor -dora *adj* dreamy ‖ *mf* dreamer

soñar §61 *tr* to dream; **ni soñarlo** not even in a dream, by no means ‖ *intr* to dream;

soñar con to dream of; **soñar despierto** to daydream

soñolien•to -ta *adj* sleepy, dozy, drowsy, somnolent; lazy

sopa *f* (*pan u otra cosa empapada en un líquido*) sop; soup; **hecho una sopa** soaked to the skin, sopping wet; **sopa de pastas** noodle soup

sopapo *m* chuck under the chin; blow, slap

sopetear *tr* to dip, dunk; abuse

sopetón *m* slap, box; **de sopetón** suddenly

sopista *mf* beggar

soplar *tr* to blow; blow away; blow up, inflate; snitch, swipe; inspire; prompt; tip off; (*la dama a un rival*) cut out; squeal on ‖ *intr* to blow; squeal ‖ *ref* to be puffed up, be conceited; swill, gulp, gobble

soplete *m* blowpipe

soplillo *m* blower, fan; chiffon, silk gauze; light sponge cake

soplo *m* blowing, blast; breath; gust of wind; instant, moment; (*informe dado en secreto*) tip; squealing; squealer

so•plón -plona *adj* tattletale ‖ *mf* tattletale, squealer

sopor *m* sleepiness, drowsiness; stupor

soporífico *m* soporific; nightcap

soportal *m* porch, portico, arcade

soportar *tr* to support, hold up, bear; endure, suffer

soporte *m* support, bearing, rest, standard; base, stand

soprano *mf* (*persona*) soprano ‖ *m* (*voz*) soprano

sor *f* (used before names of nuns) Sister

sorber *tr* to sip; absorb, soak up

sorbete *m* sherbet, water ice

sorbetera *f* ice-cream freezer; high hat

sorbo *m* sip; gulp

sordera or **sordez** *f* deafness

sórdi•do -da *adj* sordid

sordina *f* silencer; (mus) mute; (mus) damper; **a la sordina** silently, on the quiet

sor•do -da *adj* deaf; silent, mute; muffled, dull; (*dolor, ruido*) dull ‖ *mf* deaf person; **hacerse el sordo** to pretend to be deaf; turn a deaf ear

sordomu•do -da *adj* deaf and dumb ‖ *mf* deaf-mute

sorgo *m* sorghum, broomcorn

sorna *f* slowness; sluggishness; cunning

sorochar *ref* to blush; (SAm) to become mountain-sick

soroche *m* flush, blush; (SAm) mountain sickness; (Bol, Chile) silver-bearing galena

sorprendente *adj* surprising·

sorprender *tr* to surprise; catch; (*un secreto*) discover ‖ *ref* to be surprised

sorpresa *f* surprise; surprise package

sorpresi•vo -va *adj* surprising

sortear *tr* to draw or cast lots for; choose by lot; dodge; duck through ‖ *intr* to draw or cast lots

sorteo *m* drawing, casting of lots; choosing by lot; dodging; (taur) workout, performance

sortija *f* ring; curl; hoop; **sortija de sello** signet ring
sortilegio *m* sorcery, witchery
sortíle•go -ga *mf* fortuneteller ‖ *m* sorcerer ‖ *f* sorceress
sosa *f* soda
sosega•do -da *adj* calm, quiet, peaceful
sosegar §66 *tr* to calm, quiet, allay ‖ *intr* to become calm, rest ‖ *ref* to calm down, quiet down
sosiega *f* nightcap
sosiego *m* calm, quiet, serenity
sosla•yo -ya *adj* slanting, oblique; **al soslayo** or **de soslayo** slantingly; askance
so•so -sa *adj* insipid; tasteless; dull, inane ‖ *f* see **sosa**
sospecha *f* suspicion
sospechar *tr* to suspect
sospecho•so -sa *adj* suspicious; suspect ‖ *m* suspect
sostén *m* support; (*de un buque*) steadiness; brassiere
sostener §71 *tr* to support, hold up; sustain; maintain; bear, stand ‖ *ref* to remain
sosteni•do -da *adj & m* (mus) sharp
sota *m* (Chile) boss, foreman ‖ *f* (*en los naipes*) jack; jade, hussy
sotana *f* soutane, cassock
sótano *m* basement, cellar
sotavento *m* (naut) leeward
soterrar §2 *tr* to bury; hide away
soto *m* grove; brush, thicket, copse
so•viet *m* (*pl* **-viets**) soviet
soviéti•co -ca *adj* soviet, sovietic
sovoz — **a sovoz** sotto voce, in a low tone
soya *f* soybean
Sr. *abbr* **Señor**
Sra. *abbr* **Señora**
Srta. *abbr* **Señorita**
S.S.S. *abbr* **su seguro servidor**
ss.ss. *abbr* **seguros servidores**
stock *m* stock; inventory; **tener en stock** to carry; have in stock
su *adj poss* his, her, its, their, your, one's
suave *adj* suave, smooth, soft; gentle, mild, meek
suavizador *m* razor strop
suavizar §60 *tr* to smooth, ease, sweeten, soften, mollify; (*una navaja de afeitar*) strop
subalter•no -na *adj & mf* subaltern, subordinate
subasta *f* auction, auction sale; **sacar a pública subasta** to sell at auction
subastar *tr* to auction, sell at auction
subcampe•ón -ona *mf* (sport) runner-up
subcentral *f* (elec) substation
subconsciencia *f* subconscious, subconsciousness
subconsciente *adj* subconscious
subdesarrolla•do -da *adj* underdeveloped
súbdi•to -ta *adj & mf* subject
subentender §51 *tr* to understand ‖ *ref* to be understood, be implied
subestimar *tr* to underestimate
subfusil *m* submachine gun

subi•do -da *adj* high, fine, superior; strong, intense; (*color*) bright; high, high-priced ‖ *f* rise; ascent; (*p.ej.*, *al trono*) accession
subir *tr* to raise; lift; carry up; (*p.ej.*, *una escalera*) go up; (mus) to raise the pitch of ‖ *intr* to go up, come up; rise; get worse; spread; **subir a** to climb; climb on; get in or into; get on, mount ‖ *ref* to rise
súbi•to -ta *adj* sudden, unexpected; hurried; hasty, impetuous ‖ **súbito** *adv* suddenly
subjeti•vo -va *adj* subjective
subjunti•vo -va *adj & m* subjunctive
sublevación *f* uprising, revolt
sublevado *m* rebel, insurrectionist
sublevar *tr* to incite to rebellion ‖ *ref* to revolt
submarinista *mf* (sport) scuba diver; skin diver ‖ *m* (nav) submariner
submari•no -na *adj* underwater, submarine ‖ *m* submarine
subnormal *adj* (mentally) retarded
suboficial *m* sergeant major; noncommissioned officer
subordina•do -da *adj & mf* subordinate
subordinar *tr* to subordinate
subproducto *m* by-product
subrayar *tr* to underline; emphasize
subrepti•cio -cia *adj* surreptitious
subsanar *tr* to excuse, overlook; correct, repair
subscribir §83 *tr* to subscribe; subscribe to, endorse; subscribe to or for; sign; sign up ‖ *ref* to subscribe
subseguir §67 *intr & ref* to follow next
subsidiar *tr* to subsidize
subsidiarias *fpl* feeder industries
subsidiario *m* subsidiary
subsidio *m* subsidy; aid, help
subsiguiente *adj* subsequent
subsistencia *f* subsistence, sustenance
subsistir *intr* to subsist
subsóni•co -ca *adj* subsonic
substancia *f* substance
substanciar *tr* to abstract, abridge
substanti•vo -va *adj & m* substantive
substitución *f* replacement; (chem, law, math) substitution
substitui•dor -dora *adj & mf* substitute
substituir §20 *tr* to replace; substitute for, take the place of ‖ *intr* to take someone's place ‖ *ref* to be replaced; relieve each other
substituti•vo -va *adj & m* substitute
substitu•to -ta *mf* substitute
substraer §75 *tr* to remove; deduct; rob, steal; subtract ‖ *ref* to withdraw; **substraerse a** to evade, avoid, slip away from
subte *m* (Arg, Urug) subway
subteniente *m* second lieutenant
subterráne•o -a *adj* subterranean, underground ‖ *m* subterranean; (Arg) subway
subtitular *tr* to subtitle
subtítulo *m* subtitle, subheading
suburbio *m* suburb; outlying slum
subvención *f* subvention, subsidy
subvencionar *tr* to subvention, subsidize**

so
su

subvenir §79 *intr* to provide; **subvenir a** to provide for; (*gastos*) defray

subvertir §68 *tr* to subvert

subyugar §44 *tr* to subjugate, subdue

sucedàne•o -a *adj & m* substitute

suceder *tr* to succeed, follow ‖ *intr* to happen; **suceder a** (*p.ej., el trono*) to succeed to ‖ *ref* to follow one another

sucesi•vo -va *adj* successive; **en lo sucesivo** in the future

suceso *m* event, happening; issue, outcome; **sucesos de actualidad** current events

suciedad *f* dirt, filth; dirtiness, filthiness

su•cio -cia *adj* dirty, filthy; base, low; tainted; blurred; (sport) foul ‖ **sucio** *adv* (sport) foully, unfairly

sucumbir *intr* to succumb

sucursal *f* branch, branch office

Sudamérica *f* South America

sudamerica•no -na *adj & mf* South American

sudar *tr* to sweat; cough up ‖ *intr* to sweat; (*trabajar mucho*) sweat

sudario *m* shroud, winding sheet

sudcorea•no -na *adj & mf* South Korean

sudor *m* sweat; (fig) sweat, toil; **chorrear de sudor** to swelter

sudoro•so -sa *adj* sweaty

Suecia *f* Sweden

sue•co -ca *adj* Swedish ‖ *mf* Swede ‖ *m* (*idioma*) Swedish

suegra *f* mother-in-law

suegro *m* father-in-law

suela *f* sole; sole leather; (*fish*) sole

sueldacostilla *f* grape hyacinth

sueldo *m* salary, pay; **a sueldo** (*gángster*) on a contract, hired (to kill)

suelo *m* ground, soil, land; floor, flooring; pavement; (*p.ej., de una botella*) bottom; **no pisar en el suelo** to walk on air; **suelo franco** loam; **suelo natal** home country

suel•to -ta *adj* loose; free; easy; swift, agile, nimble; fluent; bold, daring; (*ejemplar*) single; (*verso*) blank; odd, separate; spare; bulk; **suelto de lengua** loose-tongued ‖ *m* small change; news item

sueñecillo *m* nap; **descabezar un sueñecillo** to take a nap

sueño *m* sleep; dream; (*cosa de gran belleza*) (fig) dream; **conciliar el sueño** to manage to go to sleep; **ni por sueños** by no means; **no dormir sueño** to not sleep a wink; **tener sueño** to be sleepy; **último sueño** (*muerte*) last sleep; **sueño hecho realidad** dream come true; **sueños dorados** daydreams

suero *m* serum

suerte *f* fortune, luck; piece of luck; fate, lot; kind, sort; way, manner; feat, trick; (taur) play, suerte; (Peru) lottery ticket; **de esta suerte** in this way; **de suerte que** so that, with the result that; **la suerte está echada** the die is cast; **suerte de capa** (taur) capework

suerte•ro -ra *adj* fortunate, lucky ‖ *m* (coll) lucky dog

sué•ter *m* (*pl* **-ters**) sweater

suficiente *adj* sufficient; adequate; fit, competent

sufijo *m* suffix

sufragar §44 *tr* to help, support, favor; defray ‖ *intr* (SAm) to vote

sufragio *m* help, succor; benefit; (*voto*) suffrage

sufragismo *m* woman suffrage

sufragista *mf* woman-suffragist ‖ *f* suffragette

sufri•do -da *adj* long-suffering; (*color*) serviceable; (*marido*) complaisant

sufrir *tr* to suffer; undergo, experience; support, hold up; tolerate; (*un examen*) take ‖ *intr* to suffer

sugerencia *f* suggestion

sugerir §68 *tr* to suggest

sugestión *f* suggestion

sugestionar *tr* to influence by suggestion

sugesti•vo -va *adj* suggestive; stimulating, striking, conspicuous

suicida *adj* suicidal ‖ *mf* suicide

suicidar *ref* to commit suicide

suicidio *m* suicide

Suiza *f* Switzerland

sui•zo -za *adj & mf* Swiss ‖ *f* see **Suiza**

sujeción *f* subjection; surrender; fastening; fastener

sujetador *m* bra(ssiere)

sujetahilo *m* (elec) binding post

sujetapape•les *m* (*pl* **-les**) paper clip

sujetar *tr* to subject; subdue; fasten, tighten ‖ *ref* to subject oneself, submit; stick, adhere

suje•to -ta *adj* subject, liable; able, capable ‖ *m* subject; fellow, individual; **buen sujeto** good egg

sulfato *m* sulfate

sulfito *m* sulfite

sulfúri•co -ca *adj* sulfuric

sulfuro *m* sulfide; **sulfuro de hidrógeno** hydrogen sulfide

sulfuro•so -sa *adj* sulfurous

sultán *m* sultan; (*galanteador*) sheik

suma *f* sum, addition; summary; sum and substance; **en suma** in short, in a word

sumadora *f* adding machine

sumamente *adv* extremely, exceedingly

sumar *tr* to add; sum up; amount to ‖ *intr* to add; amount; **suma y sigue** add and carry ‖ *ref* to add up; adhere

suma•rio -ria *adj & m* summary

sumergir §27 *tr* to submerge ‖ *ref* to submerge; (*un submarino*) dive

sumersión *f* submersion; (*de un submarino*) dive

sumidad *f* top, apex, summit

sumidero *m* drain, sewer; sink

suministrar *tr* to provide, supply

suministro *m* provision, supply; **suministros** supplies

sumir *tr* to sink; press down; overwhelm ‖ *ref* to sink; (*p.ej., los carrillos, el pecho*) be sunken; shrink, shrivel; cower; (*p.ej., el sombrero*) pull down

sumisión *f* submission (*sometimiento*) subjection

sumi•so -sa *adj* submissive

su•mo -ma *adj* high, great, extreme; supreme; **a lo sumo** at most, at the most ‖ *f* see **suma**

suncho *m* hoop

suntuo•so -sa *adj* sumptuous

supeditar *tr* to hold down, oppress

superar *tr* to surpass, excel; conquer

superávit *m* (com) surplus

supercarburante *m* high-test fuel

superchería *f* fraud, deceit

superficial *adj* superficial; surface

superficie *f* surface; exterior, outside; area; **superficie de sustentación** (aer) airfoil

super•fluo -flua *adj* superfluous

superhombre *m* superman

superintendente *mf* superintendent, supervisor; **superintendente de patio** (rr) yardmaster

superior *adj* superior; upper; higher; **superior a** superior to; higher than; more than; larger than ‖ *m* superior

superiora *f* mother superior

superiordad *f* superiority; authorities

superlati•vo -va *adj & m* superlative

supermercado *m* supermarket

super•no -na *adj* highest, supreme

superpetrolero *m* supertanker

superpoblar §61 *tr* to overpopulate

superponer §54 *tr* to superpose

superproduction *f* overproduction

supersóni•co -ca *adj* supersonic ‖ *f* supersonics

superstición *f* superstition

supersticio•so -sa *adj* superstitious

supertanquero *m* (SAm) supertanker

supervisar *tr* to supervise

supervivencia *f* survival; (law) survivorship

súpi•to -ta *adj* sudden; impatient; (Col) dumbfounded

suplantar *tr* to supplant by treachery; (*un documento*) to alter fraudulently

suplefal•tas *mf* (*pl* **-tas**) substitute, fill-in

suplemento *m* supplement; excess fare; **suplemento dominical** (*periódico*) Sunday supplement

súplica *f* entreaty, supplication; request

suplicante *adj & mf* suppliant

suplicar §73 *tr & intr* to entreat, implore; (law) to petition

suplicio *m* torture; punishment, execution; anguish

suplir *tr* to supplement, make up for; replace, take the place of; (*un defecto de otra persona*) cover up; (gram) to understand

suponer §54 *tr* to suppose; presuppose, imply; entail ‖ *intr* to have weight, have authority

suposición *f* supposition; distinction; falsehood, imposture

supositorio *m* suppository

supradi•cho -cha *adj* above-mentioned

supre•mo -ma *adj* supreme

supresión *f* suppression, elimination, omission; cancellation; deletion

suprimir *tr* to suppress, eliminate, do away with; cancel; delete

supues•to -ta *adj* supposed, assumed, hypothetical; **supuesto que** since, inasmuch as ‖ *m* assumption, hypothesis; **dar por supuesto** to take for granted; **por supuesto** of course, naturally

supurar *intr* suppurate, discharge pus

sur *m* south; south wind

Suramérica *f* South America

surcar §73 *tr* to furrow; plough; cut through; streak through

surco *m* furrow; wrinkle, rut, cut; (*del disco gramofónico*) groove; **echarse en el surco** to lie down on the job

surcorea•no -na *adj & mf* South Korean

sure•ño -ña *adj* southern ‖ *mf* southerner

surestada *f* (Arg) southeaster

surgir §27 *intr* to spout, spurt; come forth, spring up; arise, appear

suripanta *f* (hum) chorus girl; (scornful) slut, jade

surti•do -da *adj* assorted ‖ *m* assortment; supply, stock

surtidor *m* jet, spout, fountain; **surtidor de gasolina** gasoline pump

surtir *tr* to furnish, provide, supply ‖ *intr* to spout, spurt, shoot up

susceptible *adj* susceptible; touchy

suscitar *tr* to stir up, provoke; (*dudas, una cuestión*) to raise

susodi•cho -cha *adj* above-mentioned

suspender *tr* to hang; suspend; astonish; postpone; fail, flunk ‖ *ref* to be suspended

suspensión *f* suspension; astonishment; **suspensión de fuegos** cease fire

suspen•so -sa *adj* suspended, hanging; baffled, bewildered; (theat) closed ‖ *m* flunk, condition

suspensores *mpl* suspenders

suspensorio *m* jockstrap, supporter

suspi•caz *adj* (*pl* **-caces**) suspicious, distrustful

suspirar *intr* to sigh

suspiro *m* sigh; ladyfinger; (mus) quarter rest

sustentación *f* support, prop; (aer) lift

sustentar *tr* to sustain, support, feed; maintain; (*una tesis*) defend

sustento *m* sustenance, support, food; maintenance

susto *m* scare, fright

susurrar *tr* to whisper ‖ *intr* to whisper; murmur, rustle, purl, hum; be bruited about ‖ *ref* to be bruited about

susurro *m* whisper; murmur, rustle, purling, hum

susu•rrón -rrona *adj* whispering ‖ *mf* whisperer

sutil *adj* subtle; keen, observant; thin, delicate

su•yo -ya *adj poss* of his, of hers, of yours, of theirs, e.g., **un amigo suyo** a friend of his; *pron poss* his, hers, yours, theirs, its, one's; **hacer de las suyas** to be up to one's old tricks; **salirse con la suya** to have one's way; to carry one's point

su
su

T

T, t (te) *f* twenty-third letter of the Spanish alphabet
t. *abbr* **tarde**
taba *f* anklebone; (*del carnero*) knucklebone; (*juego*) knucklebones
tabaco *m* tobacco; cigar; snuff; (Cuba, CAm, Mex) punch; **tabaco en rama** leaf tobacco; **tabaco sin humo** smokeless tobacco
tabalada *f* bump, thump, heavy fall; slap
tabalear *tr* to rock, sway ‖ *intr* to drum with the fingers
tabanazo *m* slap; slap in the face
tabanco *m* stand, stall, booth
tábano *m* horsefly, gadfly
tabanque *m* treadle wheel
tabaola *f* noise, hubbub
tabaquera *f* snuffbox; (*de la pipa de fumar*) bowl; (Arg, Chile) tobacco pouch
tabaquería *f* tobacco store, cigar store
tabaque·ro -ra *adj* tobacco ‖ *mf* tobacconist; cigar maker ‖ *m* (Bol) pocket handkerchief ‖ *f* see **tabaquera**
tabardete *m* or **tabardillo** *m* sunstroke; harum-scarum
tabarra *f* bore, tiresome talk
taberna *f* tavern, saloon, barroom, pub
tabernáculo *m* tabernacle
tabernera *f* barmaid
tabernero *m* tavern keeper; bartender
tabica *f* (*para cubrir un hueco*) board; (*del frente de un escalón*) riser
tabicar §73 *tr* to close up, shut up; wall up
tabique *m* thin wall; partition wall, partition
tabla *f* (*de madera*) board; (*de metal*) sheet; (*de piedra*) slab; (*de tierra*) strip; (*cuadro pintado en una tabla*) panel; (*lista, catálogo; índice de materias*) table; **escapar** or **salvarse en una tabla** to have a narrow escape; **tabla de lavar** washboard; **tabla de planchar** ironing board; **tabla de salvación** lifesaver, helping hand; **tablas** draw, tie; (*escenario del teatro*) stage; (*de la plaza de toros*) barrier; **tener tablas** to have stage presence
tablado *m* flooring; scaffold; (*escenario del teatro*) stage
tablear *tr* to cut into boards; divide into plots or patches; level, grade
tablero *m* boarding; timber; table top; gambling table; cutting board; checkerboard, chessboard; counter; blackboard; **poner al tablero** to risk; **tablero de instrumentos** (aer) control panel; (aut) dashboard
tableta *f* small board; (*taco de papel; comprimido, pastilla*) tablet
tabletear *intr* to rattle
tabilla *f* tablet; splint; bulletin board
tablón *m* plank; beam
tabloncillo *m* (taur) seat in last row
ta·bú *m* (*pl* **-búes**) taboo
tabuco *m* hovel
tabulador *m* tabulator
tabular *tr* to tabulate
taburete *m* stool
tac *m* tick

tacada *f* stroke (*of a billiard cue*)
taca·ño -ña *adj* stingy
táci·to -ta *adj* tacit; silent
tacitur·no -na *adj* taciturn; melancholy
taco *m* bung, plug; wad, wadding; billiard cue; pad, tablet; drumstick; snack, bite; drink; oath, curse; heel; muddle, mess; (Mex) rolled-up tortilla with fillings, taco
tacón *m* heel
taconear *tr* (Chile) to fill, stuff ‖ *intr* to click the heels; strut
taconeo *m* click, clicking (*of heels*)
tácti·co -ca *adj* tactical ‖ *m* tactician ‖ *f* tactics
tacto *m* (sense of) touch; (*del dactiló-grafo, el pianista, el instrumento*) touch; skill; tact
tacha *f* defect, fault, flaw
tachar *tr* to erase; strike out; blame, find fault with
tacho *m* tin sheet; (Arg) garbage can; (Arg) watch; (Arg, Chile) boiler; (Cuba) sugar pan
tachón *m* scratch, erasure; ornamental tack or nail; trimming
tachonar *tr* to adorn with ornamental tacks; trim with ribbon; spangle, stud
tachuela *f* tack; hobnail; (Chile, Mex) runt, half pint; (SAm) drinking cup
Tadeo *m* Thaddeus
tafetán *m* taffeta; **tafetanes** flags, colors; finery; **tafetán inglés** court plaster
tafilete *m* morocco leather; sweatband
tagarote *m* sparrow hawk; scrivener; lout; gentleman sponger
tagua *f* (Chile) mud hen; (*arbusto*) (SAm) ivory palm; (*fruto*) (SAm) ivory nut
taha·lí *m* (*pl* **-líes**) baldric
tahona *f* horse-driven flour mill; bakery
ta·hur -hura *adj* gambling; cheating ‖ *mf* gambler; cheat; cardsharp
tailan·dés -desa *adj* & *mf* Thai
Tailandia *f* Thailand
taima·do -da *adj* sly, crafty; (Arg, Ecuad) lazy; (Chile) gruff, sullen
tajada *f* cut; slice; hoarseness; drunk
tajadero *m* chopping block
tajalá·piz *m* (*pl* **-pices**) pencil sharpener
tajamar *m* cutwater; dike, dam
tajar *tr* to cut; slice; (*un lápiz*) sharpen
tajo *m* cut; cutting edge; chopping block; execution block; steep cliff ‖ **Tajo** *m* Tagus
tal *adj indef* such; such a ‖ *pron indef* so-and-so; such a thing; someone ‖ *adv* so; in such a way; **con tal (de) que** provided (that); **¿qué tal?** how?; hello!, how's everything?
talabarte *m* sword belt
talabartero *m* saddler, harness maker
talache *m* or **talacho** *m* (Mex) mattock
taladrar *tr* to bore, drill, pierce, perforate; (*un billete*) punch; (*un problema*) get to the bottom of
taladro *m* drill; auger; drill hole; drill press
tálamo *m* bridal bed

talán *m* ding-dong

talante *m* countenance, mien; desire, will, pleasure; way, manner

talar *adj (traje, vestidura)* long ‖ *tr (árboles)* to fell; destroy, lay waste

talco *m* tinsel; talc; **talco en polvo** talcum powder

talega *f* bag, sack; **talegas** money, wealth

talego *m* big bag, sack; slob; **tener talego** to have money tucked away

taleguilla *f* small bag; bullfighter's breeches

talento *m* talent

talento•so -sa *adj* talented

Tales *m* Thales

Talía *f* Thalia

talismán *m* talisman

talón *m* heel; (aut) lug, flange; check, voucher, coupon; *(de un cheque)* stub

talona•rio -ria *adj* stub ‖ *m* stub book, checkbook

talonear *intr* to dash along

talud *m* slope

talla *f* cut; carving; height, stature; size; ransom; reward; *(diamante)* cut, polish; (Arg) chatting, prattle; (CAm) fraud, lie; (Col) beating, thrashing

tallar *tr* to carve; *(una piedra preciosa)* cut; *(naipes)* deal; appraise; engrave; grind; size up; (Col) beat, thrash ‖ *intr* (Arg) to chat, converse; (Chile) to make love

tallarín *m* noodle

talle *m* shape, figure, stature; waist; fit; appearance, outline; bodice

taller *m* shop, workshop; factory, mill; atelier, studio; laboratory; **taller agremiado** closed shop; **taller carrocero** (aut) body shop; **taller franco** open shop; **taller penitenciario** workhouse

tallo *m* stem, stalk; shoot, sprout; (Col) cabbage

tamal *m* (CAm, Mex) tamale; (Chile) bundle; (coll) intrigue

tamañi•to -ta *adj* so small; very small; confused, disconcerted

tama•ño -ña *adj* so big; such a big; very big, very large; so small; **abrir tamaños ojos** to open one's eyes wide ‖ *m* size

tambaleante *adj* staggering

tambalear *intr & ref* to stagger, reel, totter

también *adv* also, too

tambo *m* (Arg, Chile) brothel; (SAm) roadside inn; (Arg, Urug) dairy

tambor *m* drum; *(persona que toca el tambor)* drummer; sieve, screen; eardrum, coffee roaster; **a tambor batiente** with drums beating; in triumph; **tambor mayor** drum major

tamborilear *tr* to praise to the skies ‖ *intr* to drum

Támesis *m* Thames

ta•miz *m (pl* **-mices)** sieve

tamizar §60 *tr* to sift, sieve

tamo *m* fuzz, fluff

tampoco *adv* neither, not either; **ni yo tampoco** nor I either

tampón *m* stamp pad

tan *adv* so; **tan . . . como** or **cuan** as . . . as;

tan siquiera at least; **un tan** + *adj* such a + *adj* ‖ *m* boom *(of a drum)*

tanatología *f* thanatology

tanda *f* turn; shift, relay; task; coat, layer; game, match; flock, lot, pack; show; habit, bad habit

tangente *adj & f* tangent; **escaparse, irse** or **salir por la tangente** to evade the issue

Tánger *f* Tangier

tanguista *f* hostess *(in a night club)*

ta•no -na *adj & mf* (Arg) Neapolitan, Italian

tanque *m* tank; (dial) dipper, drinking cup

tantán *m* tom-tom; clanging; boom

tantear *tr* to compare; size up; probe, test, feel out; sketch, outline; keep the score of ‖ *intr* to keep score; to grope; **¡tantee Vd.!** just imagine!, fancy that!

tanteo *m* comparison; careful consideration; test, probe, trial; trial and error; score

tan•to -ta *adj & pron indef* so much; as much; **tanto . . . como** as much . . . as; both . . . and; **tan•tos -tas** so many; as many; **tantos . . . como** as many . . . as; **y tantos** odd, or more, e.g., **veinte y tantos** twenty odd, twenty or more ‖ *m* copy; counter, chip; point; portion, part; **apuntar los tantos** to keep score; **entre tanto** in the meantime; **estar al tanto de** to be aware of, to be or keep informed about; **poner al tanto de** to make aware of, to keep informed of; **por lo tanto** or **por tanto** therefore ‖ **tanto** *adv* so much; so hard; so often; so long; as much

tañer §70 *tr (un instrumento músico)* to play; *(una campana)* to ring ‖ *intr* to drum with the fingers

tañido *m* sound, tone; twang; ring, tang

tapa *f* lid, cover, top, cap; *(de un cilindro, un barril)* head; *(de una compuerta)* gate; *(de un libro)* board cover; shirt front; (aut) valve cap; **levantarse** or **saltarse la tapa de los sesos** to blow one's brains out; **tapas** appetizer, free lunch

tapabalazo *m* fly *(of trousers)*

tapabarro *m* (Chile) mudguard

tapaboca *f* slap in the mouth; muffler; squelch, squelcher

tapacu•bo *m* or **tapacu•bos** *m (pl* **-bos)** (aut) hubcap

tapadera *f* lid, cover, cap

tapagote•ras *m (pl* **-ras)** (Arg) roofing cement; (Col) roofer

tapaguje•ros *m (pl* **-ros)** (coll) bungling mason; substitute, replacement

tapar *tr* to cover; cover up, hide; plug, stop, stop up; conceal; obstruct; wrap up; *(un diente)* (Chile) to fill

tapara *f* (Ven) gourd; **vaciarse como una tapara** (Ven) to spill all one knows

taparrabo *m* loincloth; bathing trunks

tapera *f* (SAm) ruins; (SAm) shack

tapete *m* rug; runner; table scarf; **estar sobre el tapete** to be on the carpet, be under discussion; **tapete verde** card table, gambling table

tapia *f* mud wall, adobe wall

tapiar *tr* to wall up, wall in; close up

tapicería f tapestries; upholstery; tapestry shop; upholstery shop

tapicero m tapestry maker; upholsterer; carpet maker; carpet layer

ta•piz m (pl **-pices**) tapestry

tapizar §60 tr to tapestry; upholster; carpet; cover

tapon m stopper, cork; cap; bottle cap; bung, plug; (elec) fuse; (surg) tampon; **tapón de algodón** (surg) swab; **tapón de cubo** (aut) hubcap; **tapón de desagüe** drain plug; **tapón de tráfico** traffic jam; **tapón de vaciado** (aut) drain plug

taponar tr to plug, stop up; (surg) to tampon

taponazo m pop

taque m click; knock, rap

taqué m (aut) tappet

taquigrafía f shorthand, stenography

taquigrafiar §77 tr to take down in shorthand ‖ intr to take shorthand

taquígra•fo -fa mf stenographer

taquilla f ticket rack; ticket window; ticket office; box office; gate, take; file; (C-R) inn, tavern

taquille•ro -ra adj box-office ‖ mf ticket agent

taquimeca mf shorthand-typist

taquimecanógra•fo -fa mf shorthand-typist

tarabilla f millclapper; catch; turnbuckle; (de la hebilla de la correa) tongue; chatterbox; jabber; **soltar la tarabilla** to talk a blue streak

tarabita f (clavillo de la hebilla) tongue; (SAm) rope of rope bridge

taracea f marquetry, inlaid work

tarambana adj & mf (coll) crackpot

tararear tr & intr to hum

tarasca f dragon (in Corpus Christi procession); (mujer fea) hag

tarascada f bite; tart reply

tardanza f slowness, delay, tardiness

tardar intr to be long, be slow; be late; **a más tardar** at the latest; **tardar en** + inf to be late in + ger ‖ ref to be long, be slow; be late

tarde adv late; too late; **hacerse tarde** to grow late; **tarde o temprano** sooner or later ‖ f afternoon; evening; **de la tarde a la mañana** overnight; suddenly, in no time; unexpectedly

tardecer §22 intr to grow dark, grow late

tardí•do -a adj late, delayed; dilatory; tardy; slow

tar•do -da adj slow; late; slow, dull, dense

tar•dón -dona mf poke, slow poke

tarea f task, job; care, worry

tarifa f tariff; price list; rate; fare; (telp) toll; **tarifa recargada** extra fare

tarima f platform; stand; stool; low bench; (entablado para dormir) bunk

tarjeta f card; **tarjeta de buen deseo** or **de felicitación** greeting card; **tarjeta de crédito** credit card; **tarjeta de visita** calling card, visiting card; **tarjeta navideña** Christmas card; **tarjeta perforada** punch card; **tarjeta postal** post card, postal card

tarjetero m card case; card index

tarquín m mire, slime, mud

tarro m jar; milk pail; horn; (SAm) top hat

tarta f tart, cake; pan

tartajear intr to stutter

tartalear intr to stagger, sway; be speechless

tartamudear intr to stutter, stammer

tartamudeo m stuttering, stammering

tartamu•do -da mf stutterer, stammerer

tartán m Scotch plaid

tarugo m wooden plug; wooden paving block; (Guat, Mex) dolt, blockhead

tasa f appraisal; measure, standard; rate; ceiling price

tasación f appraisal; regulation

tasajo m jerked beef

tasar tr to appraise; regulate; hold down, keep within bounds; grudge

tasca f dive, joint; tavern; (Peru) surf, breakers

tata m daddy ‖ f nursemaid; little sister

tate m hashish; hashish user

tato m little brother

tatuaje m tattoo, tattooing

tatuar §21 tr & ref to tattoo

tauri•no -na adj bullfighting

Tauro m (astr) Taurus

taurófi•lo -la mf bullfight fan

tauromaquia f bullfighting

taxear intr (aer) to taxi

taxi m taxi, taxicab ‖ f taxi dancer

taxista mf taxi driver

taza f cup; (de la fuente) basin; (del inodoro) bowl

te pron pers & reflex thee, to thee; you, to you; thyself, to thyself; yourself, to yourself

té m tea; **té bailable** tea dance

tea f torch, firebrand

teatral adj theatrical

teatre•ro -ra mf theater-goer

teatro m theater; **dar teatro a** to bally-hoo; **teatro de estreno** first-run house; **teatro de repetorio** stock company

teatrólo•go -ga mf theater critic ‖ m actor ‖ f actress

Tebas f Thebes

tebe•o -a adj & mf Theban ‖ m comic book, funny paper

teca f teak

tecla f (de piano, máquina de escribir, etc.) key; touchy subject; **dar en la tecla** to get the knack of it; **tecla de cambio** shift key; **tecla de escape** margin release; **tecla de espacios** space bar; **tecla de retroceso** backspacer

teclado m keyboard; **teclado manual** (mus) manual

teclear tr to feel out ‖ intr to run over the keys; drum, thrum; (Chile) to be at death's door; (un jugador) (Chile) to be losing one's last cent

tecleo m fingering; touch; (de la máquina de escribir) click

técni•co -ca adj technical ‖ m technician; expert ‖ f technique; technics

tecolote m eagle owl (of Central America); (Mex) night policeman

techado *m* roof; **bajo techado** indoors
techar *tr* to roof
techo *m* ceiling; roof; (*sombrero*) hat; **techo de paja** thatched roof
techumbre *f* ceiling; roof
tedio *m* ennui, boredom
tedio•so -sa *adj* tedious, boresome
teja *f* roofing tile; shovel hat; yew tree; linden tree; **a toca teja** (coll) for cash; **teja de madera** shingle
tejadillo *m* cover, top; (*de coche*) roof
tejado *m* tile roof; roof; **tejado de vidrio** (fig) glass house
tejama•ní *m* (*pl* **-níes**) shake (*long shingle*)
tejar *m* tile works ‖ *tr* to tile, roof with tiles
teja•roz *m* (*pl* **-roces**) eaves
teje•dor -dora *adj* weaving; scheming ‖ *mf* weaver; schemer
tejer *tr & intr* to weave
tejido *m* weave, texture; web; fabric, textile; tissue; (biol & fig) tissue; **tejido adhesivo** friction tape; **tejido conjuntivo** (anat) connective tissue; **tejido de saco** (Mex) burlap; **tejido de punto** knitted fabric, jersey
tejo *m* disk; quoit; yew tree
tejón *m* badger
tela *f* cloth, fabric; (*de cebolla*) skin; (*del insecto*) web; film; (bb) cloth; (paint) canvas; (*dinero*) (slang) dough; **poner en tela de juicio** to question, doubt; **tela de alambre** wire screen; **tela de araña** spider web, cobweb; **tela emplástica** court plaster; **tela metálica** chicken wire; wire screen
telar *m* loom; frame; embroidery frame; (bb) sewing press
telaraña *f* spider web, cobweb
telecomedia serial *f* sitcom
telecontrol *m* remote control
telediario *m* daytime television news
teledifundir *tr & intr* to telecast
teledifusión *f* telecasting; telecast
telefonar *tr & intr* to telephone
telefonazo *m* telephone call
telefonear *tr & intr* to telephone
telefonema *m* telephone message
telefonista *mf* telephone operator
teléfono *m* telephone; **teléfono automático** dial telephone; **teléfono público** pay phone
teleg. *abbr* **telégrafo, telegrama**
telegrafiar §77 *tr & intr* to telegraph
telegrafista *mf* telegrapher
telégrafo *m* telegraph; **telégrafo de banderas** wigwagging; **telégrafo de máquinas** (naut) engine-room telegraph; **telégrafo sin hilos** wireless telegraph
telegrama *m* telegram
teleimpresor *m* teletype, teleprinter
Telémaco *m* Telemachus
telemando *m* remote control
telemetrar *tr* to telemeter
telemetría *f* telemetry
telémetro *m* telemeter; (mil) range finder
telen•do -da *adj* sprightly, lively
telerreceptor *m* television set
telescopar *tr & ref* to telescope

telescopio *m* telescope
telesilla *f* chair lift
telespecta•dor -dora *mf* viewer, televiewer; **telespectadores** television audience
telesquí *m* ski lift, ski tow
teleta *f* blotter, blotting paper
teletipo *m* teletype
teletubo *m* (telv) picture tube
televidente *mf* viewer, televiewer
televisar *tr* to televise
televisión *f* television; **televisión en circuito cerrado** closed-circuit television; **televisión en colores** color television; **televisión por cable** cable television
televi•sor -sora *adj* televising; television ‖ *m* television set ‖ *f* television transmitter
telón *m* drop curtain; **telón de acero** (fig) iron curtain; **telón de boca** (theat) front curtain; **telón de fondo** or **foro** (theat) backdrop
tema *m* theme, subject; exercise; (gram) stem; (mus) theme ‖ *f* fixed idea; persistence; grudge; **a tema** in emulation
temario *m* agenda
temblar §2 *intr* to tremble, shake, quiver, shiver; **estar temblando** to teeter
tem•blón -blona *adj* shaking, tremulous ‖ *m* aspen tree
temblor *m* temor, shaking, trembling; **temblor de tierra** earthquake
tembloro•so -sa *adj* trembling, shaking, tremulous
tem•bo -ba *adj* (Col) silly, stupid
temer *tr & intr* to fear
temera•rio -ria *adj* rash, reckless, foolhardy
temeridad *f* rashness, recklessness, foolhardiness, temerity
temero•so -sa *adj* frightful, dread; timid; fearful
temible *adj* dreadful, terrible, fearful
temor *m* fear, dread
témpano *m* small drum; drumhead; (*de barril*) head; (*de tocino*) flitch; (*de hielo*) iceberg, floe; (archit) tympan; (mus) kettledrum
temperamental *adj* temperamental
temperamento *m* temperament; conciliation, compromise; weather
temperar *tr* to temper, soften, moderate, calm; tune ‖ *intr* to go to a warmer climate
temperatura *f* temperature; weather
temperie *f* weather, state of the weather
tempestad *f* storm, tempest; **tempestad de arena** sandstorm; **tempestades de risas** gales of laughter
tempesti•vo -va *adj* opportune, timely
tempestuo•so -sa *adj* stormy, tempestuous
templa•do -da *adj* temperate; moderate; lukewarm, medium; brave, courageous; drunk, tipsy; (SAm) in love; (CAm, Mex) clever
templanza *f* temperence; mildness
templar *tr* to temper; soften; ease, dilute; (*colores*) blend; (*velas*) trim ‖ *intr* (*el tiempo*) to warm up ‖ *ref* to temper; moderate; fall in love; die

ta
te

temple *m* weather, state of the weather; temper, disposition; humor; average; dash, boldness; (*del acero, el vidrio, etc.*) temper

templo *m* temple

témpora *f* Ember days

temporada *f* season; period; (*p.ej., de buen tiempo*) spell; **de temporada** temporarily; vacationing

temporal *adj* temporal; temporary ‖ *m* weather; storm, tempest; spell of rainy weather

temporáne•o -a or **tempora•rio -ria** *adj* temporary

temporizar §60 *intr* to temporize; putter around

temprane•ro -ra *adj* early

tempra•no -na *adj* early ‖ **temprano** *adv* early

tenacidad *f* tenacity; persistence

tenacillas *fpl* sugar tongs; hair curler; tweezers; snuffers

te•naz *adj* (*pl* **-naces**) tenacious; persistent

tenazas *fpl* pincers, pliers; tongs

tenazón — **a** or **de tenazón** without taking aim; offhand

tenazuelas *fpl* tweezers

tendedera *f* clothesline; litter

tendedero *m* drier, frame for drying clothes; drying ground

tendencia *f* tendency

tender §51 *tr* to spread; stretch out; extend; reach out; offer, tender; (*la ropa*) hang out; (*con una capa de cal o yeso*) coat; (*un puente*) throw, build; (*una trampa*) set; (*conductores eléctricos, vías de ferrocarril, cañerías*) lay; (*la cama*) make; (*un cadáver*) lay out ‖ *intr* to tend ‖ *ref* to stretch out; throw one's cards on the table; run at full gallop

ténder *m* tender

tenderete *m* stand, booth

tende•ro -ra *mf* shopkeeper, storekeeper ‖ *m* tent maker

tendido *m* (*p.ej., de un cable*) laying; (*de una cortina de humo*) spreading; (*de alambres*) hanging, stretching; wires; (*trecho de ferrocarril*) stretch; (*ropa que tiende la lavandera*) wash; (*de cal o yeso*) coat; (*del tejado*) slope; (*de panes*) batch; (taur) uncovered stand; (Col) bedclothes

tendón *m* tendon

tenducha *f* or **tenducho** *m* miserable old store

tenebro•so -sa *adj* dark, gloomy; (*negocio*) dark, shady; (*estilo*) obscure

tenedor *m* holder, bearer; fork, table fork; **tenedor de acciones** stockholder; **tenedor de bonos** bondholder; **tenedor de libros** bookkeeper

teneduría *f* bookkeeping

tenencia *f* tenure, tenancy; (mil & nav) lieutenancy

tener §71 *tr* to have; hold; keep; own, possess; consider; (*recibir*) get; esteem; stop; **no tenerlas todas consigo** to be alarmed, dismayed; **no tener nada que ver con** to have nothing to do with; **no tener sobre qué caerse muerto** to not have a cent to one's name; **tener que** to have to; for expressions like **tener hambre** to be hungry, see the noun ‖ *ref* to stop; catch oneself, keep from falling; consider oneself; fit, go

tenería *f* tannery

tenida *f* meeting, session

teniente *adj* holding, owning; unripe; mean, miserly; hard of hearing ‖ *m* lieutenant; **teniente coronel** lieutenant colonel; **teniente de navío** (nav) lieutenant

tenis *m* tennis

tenista *mf* tennis player

tenor *m* tenor, character, import, drift; (mus) tenor; **a tenor de** in accordance with

tenorio *m* lady-killer

tensión *f* tension, stress; (elec) tension, voltage; (mech) stress; **tensión arterial** or **sanguínea** blood pressure

ten•so -sa *adj* tense, tight, taut

tentación *f* temptation

tentáculo *m* tentacle, feeler

tenta•dor -dora *adj* tempting ‖ *m* tempter

tentar §2 *tr* to touch; (*el camino*) feel; try; attempt; examine; try out, test; tempt; probe

tentati•vo -va *adj* tentative ‖ *f* attempt; trial, feeler

tentempié *m* snack, bite, pick-me-up; (*juguete*) tumbler

tenue *adj* tenuous; light, soft; faint, subdued; (*estilo*) simple

teñir §72 *tr* to dye; stain; tinge, shade, color

teología *f* theology; **no meterse en teologías** to keep out of deep water; *teología liberacionista* liberation theology

teorema *m* theorem

teoría *f* theory; *teoría ondulatoria* wave theory

tepe *m* turf, sod

tequila *m* (Mex) tequila (*distilled liquor*)

terapéuti•co -ca *adj* therapeutic(al) ‖ *f* therapeutics

terapia *f* therapy; *terapia vocacional* occupational therapy

tercena *f* government tobacco warehouse; (Ecuad) butcher shop

tercermundista *adj* Third World

terce•ro -ra *adj* third ‖ *mf* third; mediator; go-between ‖ *m* procurer, bawd; referee; umpire

Tercero Mundo *m* Third World; nonaligned nations

terceto *m* tercet; trio

terciar *tr* to place diagonally; divide into three parts; (*p.ej., la capa, el fusil*) to swing over one's shoulder; (*licor*) water ‖ *intr* to intercede, mediate ‖ *ref* to happen; be opportune

tercia•rio -ria *adj* tertiary

ter•cio -cia *adj* third ‖ *m* third; (mil) corps; **hacer buen tercio a** to do a good turn

terciopelo *m* velvet

ter•co -ca *adj* stubborn; hard, resistant

Teresa *f* Theresa

tergiversar *tr* to slant, twist, distort
terliz *m* ticking
termal *adj* thermal; steam
termas *fpl* hot baths
térmi·co -ca *adj* temperature; steam; steam-generated
terminación *f* termination
terminal *adj* terminal ‖ *m* (elec) terminal
terminante *adj* final, definitive, peremptory
terminar *tr* to end, terminate; finish ‖ *intr* to end, terminate
término *m* end, limit; boundary; bearing; manner; term; **medio término** subterfuge, evasion; compromise; **primer término** foreground; (mov) close-up; **segundo término** middle distance; **término medio** average; **último término** background
termistor *m* (elec) thermistor
termite *m* termite
termoaislante *adj* heat-insulated
termodinámi·co -ca *adj* thermodynamic ‖ *f* thermodynamics
termómetro *m* thermometer; **termómetro clínico** clinical thermometer
termonuclear *adj* thermonuclear
termopar *m* (elec) thermocouple
Termópilas, las Thermopylae
ter·mos *m* (*pl* -mos) thermos bottle; hot-water heater; **termos de acumulación** (elec) off-peak heater
termosifón *m* hot-water boiler
termóstato *m* thermostat
terna *f* trio
terne·jo -ja *adj* (Ecuad, Peru) peppy, energetic
ternera *f* calf; (*carne*) veal
terneza *f* tenderness; fondness; love; **ternezas** flirting, flirtation
ternilla *f* gristle
terno *m* suit of clothes; oath, curse; trio; piece of luck; (Col) cup and saucer; (W-I) set of jewelry
ternura *f* tenderness; fondness; love
terquedad *f* stubbornness; hardness, resistance
terraja *f* diestock
terral *adj* (*viento*) land ‖ *m* land breeze
Terranova *m* (*perro*) Newfoundland (*dog*) ‖ *f* (*isla y provincia*) Newfoundland (*island and province*)
terraplén *m* fill; embankment; terrace, platform; earthwork, rampart
terrateniente *mf* landholder, landowner
terraza *f* terrace; veranda; flat roof; (*de jardín*) border; edge; sidewalk cafe; glazed jar with two handles
terremoto *m* earthquake
terrenal *adj* earthly, mundane, worldly
terre·no -na *adj* terrestrial; mundane, worldly ‖ *m* land, ground, terrain; lot, plot; (sport) field; (fig) field, sphere; **sobre el terreno** on the spot; with data in hand; **terreno echadizo** refuse dump
terre·ro -ra *adj* earthly; of earth; humble ‖ *m* pile, heap; mark, target; terrace; public square; (min) dump
terrestre *adj* terrestrial; ground, land

terrible *adj* terrible; gruff, surly, ill-tempered
territorio *m* territory
terromontero *m* hill, butte
terrón *m* clod; lump, cake
terror *m* terror
terrorismo *m* terrorism, frightfulness
terrorista *adj* & *mf* terrorist
terro·so -sa *adj* earthly, dirty
terruño *m* piece of ground; soil; country, native soil
ter·so -sa *adj* smooth, glossy, polished; smooth, limpid, flowing
tertulia *f* party, social gathering; literary gathering; game room; **estar de tertulia** to sit around and talk
tertulia·no -na *mf* party-goer; regular member
Tesalia, la Thessaly
te·sis *f* (*pl* -sis) thesis
te·so -sa *adj* taut, tight, tense ‖ *m* top of hill; (*en superficie lisa*) rough spot
tesón *m* grit, pluck, tenacity
tesone·ro -ra *adj* obstinate, stubborn, tenacious
tesorería *f* treasury
tesore·ro -ra *mf* treasurer
tesoro *m* treasure; treasury; treasure house; thesaurus
Tespis *m* Thespis
testa *f* head; front; head, brains; **testa coronada** crowned head
testaferro *m* dummy, figurehead, straw man
testamento *m* testament, will; **Antiguo Testamento** Old Testament; **Nuevo Testamento** New Testament; **Viejo Testamento** Old Testament
testar *tr* (Ecuad) to cross out ‖ *intr* to make a will
testaru·do -da *adj* stubborn, pig-headed
testera *f* front; (*de animal*) forehead; (*de coche*) back seat
testículo *m* testicle
testificar §73 *tr* & *intr* to testify
testigo *mf* witness; **testigo de vista, testigo ocular,** or **testigo presencial** eyewitness ‖ *m* (*evidencia*) witness; (*en un experimento*) control
testimoniar *tr* to attest, testify to, bear witness to
testimonio *m* testimony; affidavit; false witness
tes·tuz *m* (*pl* -tuces) (*p.ej., de caballo*) face; nape
teta *f* teat; breast
tetera *f* teapot; teakettle
tetilla *f* nipple
tétri·co -ca *adj* dark gloomy; sad, sullen, gloomy
textil *adj* & *m* textile
texto *m* text; **fuera de texto** tipped-in
textura *f* texture
tez *f* complexion
ti *pron pers* thee; you
tía *f* aunt; old lady, old woman; bawd; **no hay tu tía** there's no chance; **tía abuela** grandaunt
tiara *f* tiara

te
ti

tibante *adj* (Col) haughty, proud

tibia *f* shinbone; pipe, flute

ti•bio -bia *adj* tepid, lukewarm; (SAm) angry ‖ *f* see **tibia**

tibor *m* large porcelain vase; chamber pot

tiburón *m* shark

Ticiano, El Titian

tictac *m* tick-tock

tiempo *m* time; weather; (gram) tense; (*de un motor de combustión interna*) cycle; (*de una sinfonía*) (mus) movement; (mus) tempo; **darse buen tiempo** to have a good time; **de cuatro tiempos** (mach) four-cycle; **de dos tiempos** (mach) two-cycle; **de un tiempo a esta parte** for some time now; **el Tiempo** Father Time; **fuera de tiempo** untimely, at the wrong time; **hacer buen tiempo** to be clear; **mucho tiempo** a long time; **tomarse tiempo** to bide one's time

tienda *f* store, shop; tent; **ir de tiendas** to go shopping; **tienda de campaña** army tent; camping tent; **tienda de modas** ladies' dress shop; **tienda de objetos de regalo** gift shop; **tienda de raya** (Mex) company store

tienta *f* cleverness; probe; (taur) testing the mettle of a young bull; **andar a tientas** to grope in the dark; feel one's way

tiento *m* touch; blind man's stick; rope-walker's pole; steady hand; care, caution; mahlstick; blow, hit; swig; **andarse con tiento** to watch one's step; **perder el tiento** to lose one's touch

tier•no -na *adj* tender; loving; tearful; soft

tierra *f* earth; ground; land; dirt; (elec) ground; **dar en tierra con** to upset, overthrow, ruin; **echar tierra a** to hush up; **en tierra, mar y aire** on land, on sea, and in the air; **irse a tierra** to topple, to collapse; **la tierra de nadie** (mil) no man's island; **tierra adentro** inland; **tierra de pan llevar** wheat land, cereal-growing land; **tierra firme** mainland; land, terra firma; **Tierra Firme** Spanish Main; **Tierra Santa** Holy Land; **tierra y escombros** landfill; **tomar tierra** to land; to fine one's way around; **venir** or **venirse a tierra** to topple, to collapse; **ver tierras** to see the world, to go traveling

tierral *m* cloud of dust

tie•so -sa *adj* stiff; tight, taut, tense; stubborn; bold, enterprising; strong, well; stiff, stuck-up; **tenérselas tiesas a** or **con** to stand up to ‖ **tieso** *adv* hard

ties•to -ta *adj* stiff; tight, taut, tense; stubborn ‖ *m* flowerpot; (*pedazo roto*) potsherd ‖ **tiesto** *adv* hard

tiesura *f* stiffness

ti•fo -fa *adj* full, satiated ‖ *m* typhus; **tifo de América** yellow fever; **tifo de Oriente** bubonic plague

tifón *m* waterspout; typhoon

tigra *f* tigress; (female) jaguar

tigre *m* tiger; (male) jaguar

tijera *f* scissors, shears; sawbuck; **buena tijera** good cutter; good eater; gossip; **tijeras** scissors, shears

tijeretear *tr* to snip, clip, cut; meddle with ‖ *intr* to gossip

tila *f* linden tree; linden-blossom tea

tildar *tr* to put a tilde or dash over; erase, strike out; **tildar de** to brand as

tilde *m & f* tilde; accent mark; superior dash; blemish, flaw; censure ‖ *f* jot, tittle

tiliche *m* (CAm, Mex) trinket

tiliche•ro -ra *mf* (CAm) peddler

tilín *m* ting-a-ling

tilo *m* linden tree; linden-blossom tea

tilo•so -sa *adj* (CAm) dirty, filthy

timar *tr* to snitch; swindle ‖ *ref* to make eyes at each other

timba *f* game of chance; gambling den; (CAm, Mex) belly

timbal *m* kettledrum; (*pastel relleno*) casserole

timbrar *tr* to stamp

timbre *m* stamp, seal; tax stamp; stamp tax; deed of glory; (phonet & phys) timbre; **timbre nasal** twang; **timbres** glockenspiel

tími•do -da *adj* timid, bashful

timo *m* theft, swindle; lie; catch phrase

timón *m* (*del arado*) beam; rudder; (fig) helm; **timón de dirección** (aer) vertical rudder; **timón de profundidad** (aer) elevator

timonel *m* helmsman, steersman

timonera *f* (naut) pilot house, wheelhouse

timora•to -ta *adj* God-fearing; chicken-hearted

tímpano *m* eardrum; kettledrum

tina *f* large earthen jar; wooden vat; bathtub

tinaja *f* large earthen jar

tincazo *m* (Arg, Ecuad) fillip

tinglado *m* shed; intrigue, trick; (zool) leatherback

tinieblas *fpl* darkness

tino *m* feel (*for things*); good aim; knack; insight, wisdom; **coger el tino** to get the knack of it

tinta *f* ink; tint, hue; dyeing; **de buena tinta** on good authority; **tinta china** India ink; **tinta simpática** invisible ink

tinte *m* dye; dyeing; dyer's shop; (fig) coloring, false appearance

tinterillo *m* clerk, lawyer's clerk; pettifogger

tintero *m* inkstand, inkwell

tintín *m* clink; jingle

tintinear *intr* to clink; jingle

tin•to -ta *adj* red ‖ *m* red table wine ‖ *f* see **tinta**

tintorería *f* dyeing; dyeing establishment; dry-cleaning establishment

tintore•ro -ra *mf* dyer; dry cleaner

tintura *f* dye; dyeing; rouge; tincture; (fig) smattering; **tintura de tornasol** litmus, litmus solution; **tintura de yodo** iodine

tiña *f* ringworm; stinginess

tiño•so -sa *adj* scabby, mangy; stingy

tío *m* uncle; old man; guy, fellow; **tío abuelo** granduncle; **tíos** uncle and aunt

tiovivo *m* merry-go-round, carrousel

tipiadora *f* (*máquina*) typewriter; (*mujer*) typist

tipiar *tr & intr* to type, typewrite

tipicista *adj* regional, local

típi•co -ca *adj* typical; regional; quaint

tipismo *m* quaintness

tipista *mf* typist, typewriter

tiple *mf* soprano (*person*); treble-guitar player ‖ *m* soprano (*voice*); treble guitar

tipo *m* type; (*de descuento, de interés, de cambio*) rate; shape, figure, build; fellow, guy, specimen; **tener buen tipo** to have a good figure; **tipo de ensayo** or **prueba** eye-test chart; **tipo de impuesto** tax rate; **tipo de letra** typeface; **tipo menudo** small print

tipografía *f* typography

típula *f* (ent) daddy-longlegs

tira *m* (Arg, Chile, Col) detective ‖ *f* strip; **hecho tiras** (Chile) in rags; **tira emplástica** (Arg) court plaster; **tira proyectable** film strip; **tiras cómicas** comics, funnies

tirabala *f* popgun

tirabuzón *m* corkscrew; corkscrew curl

tirada *f* throw; distance, stretch; time, period; printing; edition, issue; shooting party, hunting party; tirade; **de** or **en una tirada** at one stroke; **tirada aparte** reprint

tira•do -da *adj* dirt-cheap; (*letra*) cursive ‖ *f* see **tirada**

tira•dor -dora *mf* shot, good shot ‖ *m* knob; doorknob; pull chain; **tirador certero** sharpshooter; **tirador emboscado** sniper

tirafondo *m* wood screw

tiraje *m* draft; printing, edition

tiramira *f* long, narrow mountain range; (*de personas o cosas*) string; distance, stretch

tiranía *f* tyranny

tiráni•co -ca *adj* tyrannic(al)

tira•no -na *adj* tyrannous ‖ *mf* tyrant

tirante *adj* tense, taut, tight; (fig) tense, strained ‖ *m* (*de los arreos de una caballería*) trace; **tirantes** suspenders

tirantez *f* tenseness, tautness, tightness; strain

tirar *tr* to throw, cast, fling; throw away; shoot, fire; (*alambre*) draw, pull, stretch; (*una línea*) draw; (*una coz, un pellizco*) give; print; attract; tear down, knock down; (phot) to print ‖ *intr* to pull; last; appeal, have an appeal; (*una chimenea*) draw; (*a la derecha, a la izquierda*) bear, turn; **ir tirando** to get along; **tirar a** to shoot at; (*la espada*) handle; shade into; tend to; aspire to; **tirar de** to pull, pull on; (*una espada*) draw; attract; boast of being; **tira y afloja** give and take; hot and cold ‖ *ref* to rush, throw oneself; give oneself over; lie down; serve time (in prison)

tirilla *f* neckband; **tirilla de bota** bootstrap; **tirilla de camisa** collarband

tiritar *intr* to shiver

tiro *m* throw; shot; charge, load; (*estampido*) report; rifle range; (*p.ej., de chimenea*) draft; (*de caballos*) team; (*de escalera*) flight; (*de las guarniciones*) trace; (*de un paño*) length; pull cord, pull chain; reach; hurt, damage; trick; theft; (min) shaft; (sport) drive, shot; (*alusión desfavorable*) shot; (fig) shot, marksman; **a tiro de fusil** within gunshot; **a tiro de piedra** within a

stone's throw; **matar a tiros** to shoot to death; **ni a tiros** not for love nor money; **poner el tiro muy alto** to hitch one's wagon to a star; **tiro al blanco** target practice; **tiro al vuelo** trapshooting; **tiro de la pesa** (sport) shot-put

tirón *m* tyro, novice; jerk; tug, pull; **de un tirón** all at once; at a stretch

tirotear *tr* to snipe at, blaze away at ‖ *ref* to fire at each other; bicker

tirria *f* dislike, grudge; **tener tirria a** to have it in for

tisana *f* tea, infusion

tísi•co -ca *adj* tubercular ‖ *mf* tubercular person, tubercular

tisis *f* consumption, tuberculosis

titanio *m* titanium

tít. *abbr* **título**

títere *m* marionette, puppet; fixed idea; whipper-snapper, nincompoop; **no dejar títere con cabeza** or **cara** to upset the applecart; **títeres** puppet show

titilar *tr* to titillate ‖ *intr* to flutter, quiver; twinkle

titubear *intr* to stagger, totter; stammer, stutter; waver, hesitate

titular *m* bearer, holder; incumbent; headline ‖ *f* capital letter ‖ *tr* to title, entitle ‖ *intr* to receive a title ‖ *ref* to be called; call oneself

titulillo *m* running head

título *m* title; titled person; regulation; bond; certificate; degree; diploma; headline; **a título de** as a, by way of, on the score of; **títulos** credentials

tiza *f* chalk

tiznar *tr* to soil with soot; spot, stain; to defame ‖ *ref* to become soiled; get spotted or stained; (Arg, Chile, CAm) to get drunk

tizne *m* & *f* soot ‖ *m* firebrand

tiznón *m* smudge, spot of soot

tizón *m* brand, firebrand; wheat smut; brand, dishonor

tizonear *intr* to stir up the fire

tlapalería *f* (Mex) paint store

toalla *f* towel; **toalla rusa** Turkish towel; **toalla sin fin** roller towel

toallero *m* towel rack

toar *tr* (naut) to tow

tobar *tr* (Col) to tow

tobillera *f* anklet; (sport) ankle support; (coll) subdeb; (coll) flapper

tobillo *m* ankle

tobo *m* (Ven) bucket

tobogán *m* toboggan; chute, slide

toca *f* toque; headdress

tocadis•cos *m* (*pl* -cos) record player; **toca-discos automático** record changer

toca•do -da *adj* (*echado a perder; medio loco*) touched; **tocado de la cabeza** touched in the head ‖ *m* hairdo, coiffure; headdress

toca•dor -dora *mf* performer; player ‖ *m* boudoir; dressing table; dressing case, toilet case

tocante *adj* touching; **tocante a** concerning, with reference to

ti
to

tocar §73 *tr* to touch; touch on; feel; ring; toll; strike; come to know, suffer, feel; (*el cabello*) do; (*un tambor*) beat; (mus) to play; (paint) to touch up ‖ *intr* to touch; **tocar a** to knock at; pertain to, concern; fall to the lot of; be the turn of; (*el fin*) approach; **tocar en** (*un puerto*) to touch at; (*tierra*) touch; touch on; approach, border on ‖ *ref* to put one's hat on, cover one's head; touch each other; be related; make one's toilet; become mentally unbalanced; (*el sombrero*) tip; **tocárselas** to beat it

toca•yo -ya *mf* namesake
tocino *m* bacon; salt pork
tocón *m* stump
tocuyo *m* (SAm) coarse cotton cloth
tochimbo *m* (Peru) smelting furnace
to•cho -cha *adj* rough, coarse, crude
todavía *adv* still; yet; **todavía no** not yet
to•do -da *adj* all, whole, every; any ‖ *m* whole; everything; **con todo** still, however; **del todo** wholly, entirely; **jugar el todo por el todo** to stake everything, shoot the works; **sobre todo** above all, especially; **todo el que** everybody who; **todo lo que** all that; **todos** all, everybody; **todos cuantos** all those who
todopodero•so -sa *adj* all-powerful, almighty
toga *f* (academic) gown
toldilla *f* poop, poop deck
toldería *f* (SAm) Indian camp, Indian village
toldo *m* awning; pride, haughtiness; (SAm) Indian hut
tole *m* hubbub, uproar; **tole tole** gossip, talk; **tomar el tole** to run away
tolerancia *f* tolerance; **por tolerancia** on sufferance
tolerar *tr* to tolerate
tolete *m* club, cudgel; raft; (Cuba) dunce
toletole *m* (Col) persistence, obstinacy; (Ven) merry life of a wanderer
tolon•dro -dra *adj* scatterbrained ‖ *mf* scatterbrain ‖ *m* bump, lump
tolva *f* hopper; chute
tolvanera *f* dust storm
tolla *f* quagmire; (Cuba) watering trough
tom. *abbr* **tomo**
toma *f* taking; seizure, capture; tap; intake; inlet; (elec) tap, outlet; (elec) plug; (elec) terminal; (*de rapé*) pinch; **toma de posesión** installation, induction; inauguration; **toma de tierra** (aer) landing; (rad) ground connection; **toma directa** high gear
toma-corrien•te *m* or **toma-corrien•tes** *m* (*pl* -tes) (elec) current collector; (elec) tap, outlet; (elec) plug
tomadero *m* handle; intake, inlet
toma•dor -dora *mf* (com) drawee; thief; drinker, toper
tomar *tr* to take; get; seize; take on; (*un resfriado*) catch; (*p.ej., el desayuno*) have, eat; (*el café, un trago*) take, drink; **tomar a bien** to take in the right spirit; **tomar a mal** to take offense at; **tomarla con** to pick a quarrel with; have a grudge against; **tomar prestado** to borrow; **tomar sobre sí** to take upon oneself ‖ *intr* to take, turn ‖

ref to take; (*p.ej., el desayuno*) have, eat; (*el café*) take, drink; get rusty
tomate *m* tomato; (*en medias, calcetines, etc.*) tear, run
tomavis•tas *m* (*pl* -tas) movie camera; cameraman
tómbola *f* raffle, charity raffle
tomillo *m* thyme
tomo *m* volume; bulk, importance, consequence; **de tomo y lomo** of consequence; bulky and heavy
ton. *abbr* **tonelada**
ton *m* — **sin ton ni son** without rhyme or reason
tonada *f* air, melody, song; singsong; (Cuba) hoax; (*pronunciación particular*) (Arg, Chile) accent
tonel *m* cask, barrel
tonelada *f* (*unidad de peso; unidad de volumen; unidad de desplazamiento*) ton; (*medida de capacidad para el vino*) tun
tonelaje *m* tonnage
tonele•ro -ra *mf* barrelmaker, cooper
tonga *f* coat, layer; (Arg, Col) task; (Col) sleep; (Cuba) heap, pile
tongonear *ref* to strut, swagger
tóni•co -ca *adj & m* tonic ‖ *f* (mus) keynote
tonillo *m* singsong; (*pronunciación particular*) accent
tono *m* tone; tune; (mus) pitch; (mus) key; (*de un instrumento de bronce*) (mus) slide; **dar el tono** to set the standard; **darse tono** to put on airs; **de buen tono** stylish, elegant; **estar a tono** to be in style; **poner a tono** (*un motor de automóvil*) to tune up; **tono mayor** (mus) major key; **tono menor** (mus) minor key
tonsila *f* tonsil
tonsilitis *f* tonsilitis
tonsurar *tr* to shear, clip
tontear *intr* to talk nonsense, act foolishly
tontería *f* foolishness, nonsense
ton•to -ta *adj* foolish, stupid, silly; **a tontas y a locas** wildly, recklessly; in disorder, haphazardly ‖ *mf* fool, dolt; **tonto de capirote** blatant fool
tonu•do -da *adj* (Arg) magnificent, showy, conceited
topacio *m* topaz
topar *tr* to butt; bump; run into, encounter ‖ *intr* to butt; succeed; lie, be found; **topar con** or **en** to run into, encounter
tope *adj* (*precio*) top; (*fecha*) last ‖ *m* butt; bumper; bump, collision; rub, difficulty; scuffle; masthead; **al tope** or **a tope** end to end; flush; **estar hasta el tope** or **los topes** to be loaded to the gunwales; be fed up; **tope de puerta** doorstop
topera *f* molehill
topetada *f* butt
topetar *tr* to butt ‖ *intr* to butt; **topetar con** to bump, bump into; to run across
topetón *m* butt; bump, collision
tópi•co -ca *adj* local ‖ *m* topic; (med) external application
topinera *f* molehill; **beber como una topinera** to drink like a fish

topo *m* mole; blunderer; stumbler, awkward person

topografía *f* topography

toque *m* touch; (*de una campana*) ringing; (*del tambor*) beat; sound; knock; stroke; check, test; (*punto esencial*) gist; (paint) touch; (coll) blow; **dar un toque a** to put to the test; feel out, sound out; **toque a muerto** knell, toll; **toque de diana** reveille; **toque de queda** curfew; **toque de retreta** (mil) tattoo; **toque de tambor** drumbeat

torada *f* drove of bulls

tó•rax *m* (*pl* **-rax**) thorax

torbellino *m* whirlwind; (*persona bulliciosa*) harum-scarum

torcecuello *m* (orn) wryneck

torcedura *f* twist; sprain; dislocation

torcer §74 *tr* to twist; bend; turn; sprain; (*la cara*) screw up; (*el tobillo*) wrench; turn; (*interpretar mal*) distort, misconstrue ‖ *intr* to turn ‖ *ref* to twist; bend; sprain, dislocate; turn sour; go crooked; fail

torci•do -da *adj* twisted; crooked; bent; (*ojos*) cross; (*persona o conducta*) crooked; (Guat) unlucky ‖ *f* wick, lampwick; curlpaper

tor•do -da *adj* dapple-gray ‖ *mf* dapple-gray horse ‖ *m* thrush; starling

torear *tr* (*toros*) to fight; banter, tease, string along ‖ *intr* to fight bulls, be a bullfighter

toreo *m* bullfighting; (taur) performance

tore•ro -ra *adj* bullfighting ‖ *mf* bullfighter

toril *m* (taur) bull pen

tormenta *f* storm; adversity, misfortune

tormento *m* torment, torture; anguish

tormento•so -sa *adj* stormy; (*barco*) stormridden

torna *f* return; dam; tap; **se han vuelto las tornas** the luck has changed; **volver las tornas** to give tit for tat

tornar *tr* to return, give back; turn, make ‖ *intr* to return; turn; **tornar a** + *inf* verb + again, e.g., **tornó a abrir la puerta** he opened the door again ‖ *ref* to turn, become

tornasol *m* sunflower; litmus; iridescence

tornasola•do -da *adj* changeable, iridescent

tornavía *m* (rr) turntable

torna•voz *m* (*pl* **-voces**) sounding board; **hacer tornavoz** to cup one's hands to one's mouth

tornear *tr* to turn, turn up ‖ *intr* to go around; tourney; muse, meditate

torneo *m* tourney; match, tournament; **torneo radiofónico** quiz program

tornillo *m* (*cilindro que entra en la tuerca*) screw; (*clavo con resalto helicoidal*) bolt; (*instrumento con dos mandíbulas*) vise; (mil) desertion; (CAm, Ven) screw tree; **apretar los tornillos a** to put the screws on; **tener flojos los tornillos** to have a screw loose; **tornillo de mariposa** or **de orejas** thumbscrew; **tornillo de presión** setscrew; **tornillo para metales** machine screw

torniquete *m* (*para contener hemorragias*) tourniquet; (*torno para cerrar un paso*) turnstile; **dar torniquete a** to twist the meaning of

torno *m* turn, revolution; (*máquina simple que consiste en un cilindro que gira sobre su eje*) winch, windlass; (*de alfarero*) potter's wheel; (*instrumento con dos mandíbulas*) vise; (*máquina herramienta que sirve para labrar metal o madera*) lathe; (*de coche*) brake; (*de un río*) bend, turn; revolving server; **en torno a** or **de** around; **torno de alfarero** potter's wheel; **torno de banco** bench vise; **torno de hilar** spinning wheel

toro *m* bull; **toro corrido** smart fellow; **toros** bullfight

torón *m* strand

toronja *f* grapefruit

toronjo *m* grapefruit (*tree*)

torpe *adj* slow, heavy; clumsy, awkward; stupid; lewd; crude, ugly

torpedear *tr* to torpedo

torpedo *m* torpedo; touring car

torpeza *f* torpidity, slowness; clumsiness, awkwardness; stupidity; lewdness; turpitude; crudeness, ugliness

torrar *tr* to toast

torre *f* tower; watchtower; (*en el ajedrez*) castle, rook; **torre del homenaje** donjon, keep; **torre de lanzamiento** launching tower; **torre de marfil** (fig) ivory tower; **torre de vigía** (naut) crow's-nest; **torre maestra** donjon, keep; **torre reloj** clock tower

torreja *f* (dial, Am) French toast

torrentada *f* flash flood

torrente *m* torrent

torreón *m* (archit) turret

torreta *f* (nav) turret

tórri•do -da *adj* torrid

torrija *f* French toast

torta *f* cake; (typ) font; slap; **ser tortas y pan pintado** to be a cinch; **torta a la plancha** hot cake, griddle cake

torticolis *m* or **tortícolis** *m* wryneck, stiff neck

tortilla *f* omelet; (CAm, Mex) tortilla (*cornmeal cake*); **tortilla a la española** potato omelet; **tortilla a la francesa** plain omelet; **tortilla de tomate** Spanish omelet

tórtola *f* turtledove

tortuga *f* tortoise, turtle

tortuo•so -sa *adj* winding; (fig) devious

tortura *f* torture

torturar *tr* to torture

tor•vo -va *adj* grim, stern

tos *f* cough; **tos ferina** whooping cough

tosca•no -na *adj* Tuscan ‖ **la Toscana** Tuscany

tos•co -ca *adj* coarse, rough; uncouth

toser *intr* to cough

tósigo *m* poison; sorrow

tosiguero *m* poison ivy

tosquedad *f* coarseness, roughness; uncouthness

tostada *f* piece of toast; toast; **dar** or **pegar la tostada** or **una tostada a** to cheat, trick; **tostadas** toast

tosta•do -da *adj* brown; tan, sunburned ‖ *m* toasting; roasting ‖ *f* see **tostada**

tostador *m* toaster, roaster

tostar §61 *tr* & *ref* to toast; roast; tan, burn

tostón *m* roasted chickpea; toast dipped in olive oil; roast pig; scorched food

total *adj* & *m* total ‖ *adv* in a word

totalidad *f* totality; entirety; **en su totalidad** in its entirety

tóxi•co -ca *adj* & *m* toxic

toxicomanía *f* drug addiction

toxicóma•no -na *adj* drug-addicted ‖ *mf* drug addict

tozu•do -da *adj* stubborn

tpo. *abbr* **tiempo**

traba *f* bond, tie; clasp, lock; hobble, clog; obstacle, hindrance

traba•do -da *adj* tied, fastened; joined, connected; robust, sinewy; (*sílaba*) checked; tongue-tied; (*ojos*) (Col) cross

trabaja•do -da *adj* overworked, worn-out; strained, forced, labored; busy

trabaja•dor -dora *adj* working; industrious, hard-working ‖ *mf* worker, toiler ‖ *m* workman, workingman ‖ *f* workingwoman

trabajar *tr* to work; till; bother, disturb; (*a una persona*) work, drive ‖ *intr* to work; strain; warp; **trabajar en** or **por** to strive to ‖ *ref* to strive, exert oneself

trabajo *m* work; trouble; (*en contraposición de capital*) labor; **costar trabajo** + *inf* to be hard to + *inf;* **trabajo a destajo** piecework; **trabajo a domicilio** homework; **trabajo a jornal** timework; **trabajo de menores** child labor; **trabajo de oficina** clerical work; **trabajo de taller** shopwork; **trabajos** hardships, tribulations; **trabajos forzados** or **forzosos** hard labor, penal labor

trabajo•so -sa *adj* arduous, laborious; (*maganto*) wan, languid; (*falto de espontaneidad*) labored; unpleasant, annoying

trabalen•guas *m* (*pl* **-guas**) tongue twister, jawbreaker

trabar *tr* to join, unite; catch, seize; fasten; fetter; lock; begin; (*una batalla*) join; (*una conversación, amistad*) strike up ‖ *intr* to take hold ‖ *ref* to become entangled; jam; to foul; **trabársele a uno la lengua** to become tongue-tied

trabe *f* beam

trabilla *f* gaiter strap; belt loop; end stitch, loose stitch

trabuco *m* blunderbuss; popgun

trac *m* stage fright

tracale•ro -ra *adj* (CAm, Mex, W-I) cheating, tricky ‖ *mf* (CAm, Mex, W-I) cheat, trickster

tracción *f* traction; **tracción delantera** front drive; **tracción trasera** rear drive

tractor *m* tractor; **tractor de oruga** caterpillar tractor

tradición *f* tradition

tradicionista *mf* folklorist

traducción *f* translation; **traducción automática** machine translation

traducir §19 *tr* to translate; change

traduc•tor -tora *mf* translator

traer §75 *tr* to bring; bring on; draw, pull; make, keep; wear; have, carry; **traer a mal traer** to abuse, mistreat ‖ *intr* — **traer y llevar** to gossip ‖ *ref* to dress; behave; **traérselas** to get worse and worse, cause a lot of trouble

tráfago *m* traffic, trade; toil, drudgery

trafa•gón -gona *adj* hustling, lively; slick, tricky ‖ *mf* hustler, live wire

traficante *mf* dealer, merchant

traficar §73 *intr* to deal, trade, traffic; travel about

tráfico *m* trade; traffic

tragaderas *fpl* gullibility; tolerance; **tener buenas tragaderas** to be too gullible

tragalda•bas *mf* (*pl* **-bas**) glutton; easy mark

tragale•guas *mf* (*pl* **-guas**) (coll) great walker

traga•luz *m* (*pl* **-luces**) skylight, bull's-eye; cellar window

tragamone•das *m* (*pl* **-das**) or **tragape•rras** *m* (*pl* **-rras**) slot machine

tragar §44 *tr* to swallow; swallow up; gulp down; (*creer fácilmente*) swallow; overlook; **no poder tragar** to not be able to stomach ‖ *intr* & *ref* to swallow

tragasable *m* sword swallower

tragavenado *f* (SAm) anaconda

tragaviro•tes *m* (*pl* **-tes**) stuffed shirt

tragedia *f* tragedy

trági•co -ca *adj* tragic(al) ‖ *m* tragedian

trago *m* swallow; swig; misfortune; **a tragos** slowly

tra•gón -gona *adj* gluttonous ‖ *mf* glutton

traición *f* treachery, betrayal; (*delito contra la patria*) treason; treacherous act; **alta traición** high treason; **a traición** treacherously; **hacer traición a** to betray

traicionar *tr* to betray

traicione•ro -ra *adj* treacherous; treasonable ‖ *mf* traitor

traída *f* conveyance, transfer; (Guat) sweetheart; **traída de aguas** water supply

traí•do -da *adj* worn, threadbare ‖ *f* see **traída**

trai•dor -dora *adj* treacherous; treasonable ‖ *mf* traitor; betrayer ‖ *m* villain ‖ *f* traitoress

traílla *f* leash; road scraper

traje *m* suit; clothes; dress; gown; **cortar un traje a** to gossip about; **traje a la medida** suit made to order; **traje de baño** bathing suit; **traje de calle** street clothes; **traje de ceremonia** or **de etiqueta** dress suit; full dress; evening clothes; **traje de faena** (mil) fatigue clothes; **traje de luces** bullfighter's costume; **traje de malla** tights; **traje de montar** riding habit; **traje de paisano** civilian clothes; **traje hecho** ready-made suit; **traje sastre** lady's tailor-made suit; **traje serio** formal dress; **vestir su primer traje largo** to come out, make one's debut

trajear *tr* to dress, clothe

trajín *m* carrying, transfer, conveyance; going and coming; bustle, commotion

trajinar *tr* to carry, convey; (Arg, Chile) to poke into; (Arg, Chile) to deceive; (Pan) to annoy ‖ *intr* to bustle around

tralla *f* lash, whiplash, whipcord

trama *f* weft, woof; plot, scheme, machination; (*de un drama o novela*) plot

tramar *tr* to weave; plot, scheme; (*un enredo*) hatch (*a plot*)

trambucar §73 *intr* (Col, Ven) to be shipwrecked; (Col, Ven) to go out of one's mind

tramitación *f* transaction, negotiation; procedure, steps; **tramitación automática de datos** data processing

tramitar *tr* to transact, negotiate

trámite *m* step, procedure; proceeding; transaction

tramo *m* tract; stretch; (*de una escalera*) flight; (*de un puente*) span; (*de un canal entre dos esclusas*) level

tramontana *f* north; north wind; pride, haughtiness

tramoya *f* stage machinery; scheme

tramoyista *adj* scheming, tricky ‖ *mf* schemer, impostor ‖ *m* stagehand

trampa *f* trap; trap door; (*de un mostrador*) flap; (*de los pantalones*) fly; **armar una trampa a** to lay a trap for; **trampa explosiva** (mil) booby trap

trampear *tr* to trick, swindle ‖ *intr* to cheat; manage to get along

trampilla *f* peephole in the floor; (*de los pantalones*) fly; (*de un secreter*) top, lid; (*de una mesa*) leaf, hinged leaf

trampolín *m* diving board; springboard; ski jump

trampo•so -sa *adj* tricky, crooked ‖ *mf* cheat, swindler

tranca *f* beam, pole; crossbar; (Arg, Chile) drunk, spree; (P-R) dollar; **a trancas y barrancas** through fire and water

trancar §73 *tr* to bar ‖ *intr* to stride along

trance *m* crisis; peril; trance; **a todo trance** at any cost; **último trance** (*de la vida*) last stage, end

tranco *m* long stride; threshold

tranquera *f* palisade, fence

tranquilidad *f* tranquillity

tranquilizante *m* tranquilizer

tranquilizar §60 *tr, intr* & *ref* to tranquilize, calm down

tranqui•lo -la *adj* tranquil, calm

tranquilla *f* feeler

tranquillo *m* knack

transacción *f* settlement, compromise; transaction

transaéreo *m* airliner

transar *tr* to settle ‖ *intr* to yield, give in, compromise

transatlánti•co -ca *adj* & *m* transatlantic

transbordador *m* ferry; **transbordador espacial** space shuttle

transbordar *tr* to transship; transfer ‖ *intr* to transfer, change trains

transbordo *m* transshipment; transfer

transcribir §83 *tr* to transcribe

transcripción *f* transcription

transcurrir *intr* to pass, elapse

transcurso *m* course (*of time*)

transepto *m* transept

transeúnte *adj* transient ‖ *mf* transient; passer-by

transferencia *f* transfer

transferir §68 *tr* to transfer; postpone

transformador *m* transformer

transformar *tr* to transform ‖ *ref* to transform, be transformed

tránsfuga *mf* turncoat; fugitive

transfusión *f* transfusion; **transfusión de sangre** transfusion, blood transfusion

transgredir §1 *tr* to transgress

transgresión *f* transgression

transi•do -da *adj* overcome, paralyzed; mean, cheap, stingy

transigencia *f* compromise; compromising

transigente *adj* compromising

transigir §27 *tr* to settle, compromise ‖ *intr* to settle, compromise; agree

transistor *m* transistor

transistorizar §60 *tr* transistorize

transitable *adj* passable, practicable

transitar *intr* to go, walk; to travel

transiti•vo -va *adj* transitive

tránsito *m* transit; traffic; stop; passage; transfer

transito•rio -ria *adj* transitory

translúci•do -da *adj* translucent

tránsmisión *f* transmission; **transmisión del pensamiento** thought transference

transmisor *m* transmitter; **transmisor de órdenes** (naut) engine-room telegraph

transmitir *tr* & *intr* to transmit

transmudar *tr* to transfer; persuade, convince

transmutar *tr, intr* & *ref* to transmute

transparecer §22 *intr* to show through

transparencia *f* transparency; slide

transparentar *ref* to show through

transparente *adj* transparent ‖ *m* curtain, window curtain; **transparente de resorte** window blind or shade

transpirar *intr* to transpire; (*dejarse conocer una cosa secreta*) transpire

transplantar *tr* to transplant

transponer §54 *tr* to transpose; disappear behind ‖ *ref* (*ocultarse detrás del horizonte*) to set; get sleepy

transportar *tr* to transport; (mus) to transpose

transporte *m* transport; transportation; (aer & naut) transport; **transporte colectivo** public transportation

transportista *mf* transport worker

transvesti•do -da *adj* & *mf* transvestite

tranvestismo *m* transvestism

tranvía *m* trolley, trolley car, streetcar; **tranvía de sangre** horsecar

tranzar §60 *tr* to cut off, rip off; plait, braid

trapacear *tr* to chear, swindle

trapacería *f* cheating, swindling

trapace•ro -ra *adj* cheating, swindling ‖ *mf* cheat, swindler

trapajo *m* rag, tatter

to
tr

trápala *adj* chattering; cheating || *mf* chatterbox; cheat || *m* loquacity || *f* noise, uproar; (*del trote de un caballo*) clatter; cheating

trapear *tr* to mop

trapecio *m* (geom) trapezoid; (sport) trapeze

trapecista *mf* trapeze performer

trape•ro -ra *mf* ragpicker; junk dealer

trapiche *m* sugar mill; olive press; ore crusher

trapien•to -ta *adj* raggedy, in rags

trapío *m* flipness, pertness; (*del toro de lidia*) spirit

trapisonda *f* brawl, row; scheming

trapisondista *mf* schemer

trapo *m* rag; (naut) canvas, sails; bullfighter's bright-colored cape; (*de la muleta*) cloth; **a todo trapo** full sail; **poner como un trapo** to rake over the coals; **sacar los trapos a la colada, a relucir** or **al sol** to wash one's dirty linen in public; **soltar el trapo** to burst out crying, to burst out laughing; **trapos** rags, duds; **trapos de cristianar** Sunday best

trapo•so -sa *adj* raggedy, in rags

tráquea *f* trachea, windpipe

traquea•do -da *adj* (*sendero*) (Arg) beaten

traquear *tr* to shake, rattle; fool with || *intr* to crackle; rattle, chatter

traqueo *m* shake, rattle, chatter

traquetear *tr & intr* to rattle, jerk

tras *prep* after; behind; **tras de** behind; in addition to

trasatlánti•co -ca *adj & m* var of **transatlántico**

trasbordador *m* var of **transbordador**

trasbordar *tr & intr* var of **trasbordar**

trasbordo *m* var of **transbordo**

trascendencia *f* penetration, keenness; importance

trascendente *adj* penetrating; important

trascender §51 *tr* to go into, dig up || *intr* to smell; come to be known, leak out

trascendi•do -da *adj* keen, perspicacious

trascocina *f* scullery

trascorral *m* back yard; backside

trascribir §83 *tr* var of **transcribir**

trascripción *f* var of **transcripción**

trascuarto *m* back room

trascurrir *intr* var of **transcurrir**

trascurso *m* var of **transcurso**

trasegar §66 *tr* to upset, turn topsy-turvy; decant, draw off

trase•ro -ra *adj* back, rear || *m* buttock, rump

trasferir §68 *tr* var of **transferir**

trasformador *m* var of **transformador**

trasformar *tr & intr* var of **transformar**

trásfuga *mf* var of **tránsfuga**

trasfusión *f* var of **transfusión**

trasgo *m* goblin, hobgoblin; imp

trashojar *tr* to leaf through

trashumante *adj* nomadic, migrating

trasiego *m* upset, disorder; decantation

trasladar *tr* to transfer; postpone; copy, transcribe; transmit; move || *intr* to go; move

traslado *m* transfer; copy, transcript; moving

traslapar *tr, intr & ref* to overlap

traslapo *m* lap, overlap

traslúci•do -da *adj* var of **translúcido**

traslucir §45 *tr* to guess || *intr* to leak out || *ref* to be translucent; leak out

traslumbrar *tr* to dazzle || *ref* to be dazzled; vanish

trasluz *m* diffused light; glint, gleam; **al trasluz** against the light

trasmisión *f* var of **transmisión**

trasmisor *m* var of **transmisor**

trasmitir *tr & intr* var of **transmitir**

trasmóvil *m* (Col) mobile unit, radio pickup

trasmudar *tr* var of **transmudar**

trasmundo *m* afterlife, future life

trasmutar *tr, intr & ref* var of **transmutar**

trasnocha•do -da *adj* stale; haggard, run-down; hackneyed || *f* last night; sleepless night; (mil) night attack

trasnocha•dor -dora *mf* night owl

trasnochar *tr* (*un problema*) to sleep over || *intr* to spend the night; spend a sleepless night; stay up late

trasoír §48 *tr* to hear wrong

traspapelar *tr* to mislay || *ref* to become mislaid

trasparecer §22 *intr* var of **transparecer**

trasparencia *f* var of **transparencia**

trasparente *adj & m* var of **transparente**

traspasar *tr* to cross, cross over; send; transfer; move; pierce, transfix; pain, grieve || *ref* to go too far

traspié *m* slip, stumble; trip

traspirar *intr* var of **transpirar**

trasplantar *tr* var of **transplantar**

trasponer §54 *tr & ref* var of **transponer**

trasportar *tr* var of **transportar**

trasporte *m* var of **transporte**

trasportista *mf* var of **transportista**

traspunte *m* (theat) callboy

traspuntín *m* flap seat, folding seat, jump seat

trasquilar *tr* to crop, lop; (*las ovejas*) shear; curtail

trastazo *m* whack, blow

traste *m* fret; **dar al traste con** to throw away, ruin, spoil

trastera *f* attic, junk room

trastienda *f* back room

trasto *m* piece of furniture; piece of junk; good-for-nothing; **trastos** tools, implements, utensils; arms, weapons; junk; muleta and sword

trastornar *tr* to upset; overturn; disturb; perplex; daze, make dizzy; persuade

trastorno *m* upset; disturbance

trastrocar §81 *tr* to turn around, reverse, change

trasudor *m* cold sweat

trasueño *m* blurred dream, vague recollection

trasuntar *tr* to copy; abstract, sum up

trasunto *m* copy; record; likeness

trasverter §51 *intr* to run over, overflow

trasvolar §61 *tr* to fly over

trata *f* traffic, trade, slave trade; **trata de blancas** white slavery; **trata de esclavos** slave trade

tratado *m* (*escrito, libro*) treatise; (*convenio entre gobiernos*) treaty; agreement

tratamiento *m* treatment; title; **apear el tratamiento** to leave off the title

tratante *mf* dealer, retailer

tratar *tr* to handle; deal with; treat; **tratar a uno de** to address someone as; charge someone with being ‖ *intr* to deal; treat; try; **tratar de** to deal with; treat of; come in contact with; try to ‖ *ref* to deal; behave; (*bien o mal*) live; **tratarse de** to deal with; be a question of

trate•ro -ra *mf* (Chile) pieceworker

trato *m* treatment; deal, agreement; manner; business; title; friendly relations; **tener buen trato** to be very nice, be very pleasant; **trato colectivo** collective bargaining; **trato doble** double-dealing; ¡**trato hecho!** it's a deal!

través *m* bend, bias, turn; reverse, misfortune; (naut) beam; **al** or **a través de** through, across; **dar al través con** to do away with; **mirar de través** to squint; look out of the corner of one's eye

travesaño *m* crosspiece; (*de cama*) bolster; (*p.ej., de una sila*) rung

travesear *intr* to romp, carry on; sparkle, be witty; lead a wild life

travesía *f* crossing, voyage; crossroad; distance, passage; cross wind; (Arg, Bol) wasteland; (Chile) west wind

travesura *f* prank, antic, caper; mischief; sparkle, wit; slick trick

traviesa *f* crossing, voyage; rafter; side bet; (rr) tie

travie•so -sa *adj* cross; keen, shrewd; restless, fidgety; naughty, mischievous; debauched ‖ *f* see **traviesa**

trayecto *m* journey, passage, course; stretch, run

trayectoria *f* trajectory; path

traza *f* plan, design; scheme; means; appearance; mark, trace; footprint; streak, trait; **tener trazas de** to show signs of; look like

trazar §60 *tr* to plan, design; outline; trace; (*una línea*) draw; lay out, plot

trazo *m* line, stroke; trace; outline

trebejo *m* implement; chessman

trébol *m* clover; (*naipe que corresponde al basto*) club

trece *adj & pron* thirteen ‖ *m* thirteen; (*en las fechas*) thirteenth; **estarse, mantenerse** or **seguir en sus trece** to stand firm

trecea•vo -va *adj & m* thirteenth

trecho *m* stretch; while; **a trechos** at intervals

tregua *f* truce; respite, letup

treinta *adj & pron* thirty ‖ *m* thirty; (*en las fechas*) thirtieth

treinta•vo -va *adj & m* thirtieth

tremar *intr* to tremble, shake

tremen•do -da *adj* frightful, terrible, tremendous; (*muy grande*) tremendous

trementina *f* turpentine

tremer *intr* to tremble, shake

tremolar *tr & intr* to wave

tren *m* (*de coches o vagones; de ondas*) train; outfit; equipment; following; retinue; show, pomp; (*de la vida*) way; **tren aerodinámico de lujo** (rr) streamliner; **tren**

ascendente (rr) up train; **tren correo** (rr) mail train; **tren de aterrizaje** (aer) landing gear; **tren de laminadores** rolling mill; **tren de lavado** laundry; **tren de mercancías** freight train; **tren de mudadas** moving company; **tren descendente** (rr) down train; **tren de viajeros** passenger train; **tren ómnibus** (rr) accomodation train; **tren rápido** (rr) flyer

treno *m* dirge

trenza *f* braid, plait; tress; (*p.ej., de ajos*) string; **en trenzas** with her hair down

trenzar §60 *tr* to braid, plait ‖ *intr* to caper; prance

trepa•dor -dora *adj* climbing ‖ *mf* climber ‖ *f* (bot) climber

trepar *tr* to climb; drill, bore ‖ *intr* to climb; **trepar por** to climb up ‖ *ref* to lean back

trepidar *intr* to shake, vibrate; (Chile) to hesitate, waver

tres *adj & pron* three; **las tres** three o'clock ‖ *m* three; (*en las fechas*) third

trescien•tos -tas *adj & pron* three hundred ‖ **trescientos** *m* three hundred

tresillo *m* ombre; three-piece living-room suite; (mus) triplet

tresnal *m* (agr) shock

treta *f* trick, scheme; (*del esgrimidor*) feint

treza•vo -va *adj & m* thirteenth

triángulo *m* triangle

triar §77 *tr* to sort

tribu *f* tribe

tribuna *f* tribune, rostrum, platform; grandstand; (*en la iglesia*) gallery; **tribuna de la prensa** press box; **tribuna del órgano** (mus) organ loft; **tribuna de los acusados** (law) dock

tribunal *m* tribunal, court; **tribunal de apelación** appellate court; **tribunal tutelar de menores** juvenile court

tributar *tr* (*contribuciones, impuestos, etc.*) to pay; (*admiración, gratitud, etc.*) render

tributario -ria *adj* tributary; tax; **ser tributario de** to be indebted to ‖ *m* tributary

tributo *m* tribute; tax

tricornio *m* tricorn, three-cornered hat

trifocal *adj* trifocal

trifulca *f* wrangle, squabble

trigési•mo -ma *adj & m* thirtieth

trigo *m* wheat; (slang) dough, money; **trigo entero** whole wheat; **trigo sarraceno** buckwheat

trigonometría *f* trigonometry

trigue•ño -ña *adj* swarthy, olive-skinned

trilogía *f* trilogy

trilla *f* threshing

trilla•do -da *adj* (*sendero*) beaten; trite, commonplace

trilladora *f* threshing machine

trillar *tr* to thresh; mistreat; frequent

trilli•zo -za *mf* triplet

trillón *m* British trillion; quintillion (in U.S.A.)

trimestral *adj* quarterly

trimestre *m* quarter

trinado *m* trill, warble

trinar *intr* to trill, warble, quaver; get angry
trinca *f* trinity
trincar §73 *tr* to bind, lash, tie fast; crush; (slang) to kill ‖ *intr* to take a drink
trinchar *tr* to carve, slice
trinchera *f* cut; trench; trench coat
trineo *m* sleigh, sled
Trinidad *f* Trinity
trino *m* trill
trinquete *m* pawl, ratchet; (naut) foresail
trin•quis *m* (*pl* -**quis**) drink, swig
trío *m* sorting; trio; (mus) trio
tripa *f* gut, intestine; belly; (*del cigarro*) filler; **hacer de tripas corazón** to pluck up courage
triple *adj* & *m* triple
triplica•do -da *adj* & *m* triplicate; **por triplicado** in triplicate
triplicar §73 *tr* to triplicate ‖ *intr* to treble
trípode *m* tripod
tríptico *m* triptych
tripu•do -da *adj* big-bellied, potbellied
tripulación *f* crew
tripulante *m* crew member
tripular *tr* to man; fit out, equip
trique *m* crack, swish; **a cada trique** at every turn; **triques** (Mex) tools, implements
triquiñuela *f* chicanery, subterfuge
triquitraque *m* clatter; firecracker
tris *m* crackle; shave, inch; trice
trisar *tr* (Chile) to crack, chip ‖ *intr* to chirp
triscar §73 *tr* to mix; (*una sierra*) set ‖ *intr* to stamp the feet; romp, frisk around; (Col) to gossip
trismo *m* lockjaw
triste *adj* sad; dismal, gloomy; (*despreciable, ridículo*) sorry
tristeza *f* sadness; gloominess
tris•tón -tona *adj* wistful, melancholy
tritón *m* eft, newt, triton; (*hombre experto en la natación*) merman
trituradora *f* crushing machine
triturar *tr* to grind, crush; abuse
triunfal *adj* triumphal
triunfante *adj* triumphant
triunfar *intr* to triumph; trump; **triunfar de** to triumph over; trump
triunfo *m* triumph; trump; **sin triunfo** no trump
trivial *adj* trivial; trite, commonplace; (*sendero*) beaten
trivialidad *f* triviality; triteness
triza *f* shred; **hacer trizas** to tear to pieces
trizar §60 *tr* to tear to pieces
trocar §81 *tr* to exchange, swap; barter; confuse, twist, distort ‖ *intr* to swap ‖ *ref* to change; change seats
trocha *f* trail, narrow path; gauge
trofeo *m* trophy; victory
troj *f* or **troje** *f* granary; olive bin
trole *m* trolley pole
trolebús *m* trolley bus, trackless trolley
tromba *f* (*de polvo, agua, etc.*) whirl, column; **tromba marina** waterspout; **tromba terrestre** tornado
trombón *m* trombone
trompa *f* (*del elefante*) trunk; waterspout;

top; nozzle; (anat) duct, tube; (mus) horn; (Col, Chile) cowcatcher; **trompa de armonía** French horn; **trompa de Eustaquio** Eustachian tube
trompada *f* bump, collision; punch
trompar *intr* to spin a top
trompeta *f* trumpet; bugle, clarion; good-for-nothing; drunkenness
trompetear *intr* to trumpet, sound the trumpet
trompetilla *f* ear trumpet; Bronx cheer
trompicar §44 *tr* to trip, make stumble ‖ *intr* to stumble
trompicón *m* stumble
trompiza *f* fist fight
trompo *m* (*juguete*) top; (*en el ajedrez*) man; (*buque malo y pesado*) tub
tronada *f* thunderstorm
tronar §61 *tr* (Mex) to shoot ‖ *intr* to thunder; fail, collapse; **por lo que pueda tronar** just in case
troncar §44 *tr* to cut off the head of; (*un escrito*) cut, shorten
tronco *m* (*del cuerpo, del árbol, de una familia, del ferrocarril*) trunk; (*leño*) log; (*de caballerías*) team; sap, fathead; **estar hecho un tronco** to be knocked out; be sound asleep
troncha *f* slice; cinch
tronchar *tr* to smash, split; chop off
tronera *f* madcap, roisterer ‖ *f* embrasure, loophole; louver; (*de la mesa de billar*) pocket
tronido *m* thunderclap
trono *m* throne
tronquista *m* driver, teamster
tronzar §60 *tr* to shatter, break to pieces; pleat; wear out
tropa *f* troop; herd, drove; **en tropa** straggling, without formation; **tropas de asalto** shock troops, storm troops
tropel *m* crowd, throng; rush, hurry; jumble; **de** or **en tropel** in a mad rush
tropelía *f* mad rush; outrage
tropero *m* (Arg) cowboy
tropezar §18 *tr* to strike ‖ *intr* to stumble; slip, blunder; **tropezar con** or **en** to stumble over, trip over; run into; come upon
trope•zón -zona *adj* stumbly ‖ *m* stumble; stumbling place; **a tropezones** by fits and starts; falteringly; **dar un tropezón** to stumble, trip
tropical *adj* tropic(al)
trópico *m* tropic
tropiezo *m* stumble; stumbling block; slip, blunder, fault; obstacle; quarrel
tropilla *f* (Arg, Urug) drove of horses following a leading mare
troposfera *f* troposphere
troquel *m* die
trotaconven•tos *f* (*pl* -**tos**) procuress, bawd
trotamun•dos *m* (*pl* -**dos**) globetrotter
trotar *intr* to trot; to hustle
trote *m* trot; chore; **al trote** right away; **para todo trote** for everyday wear; **trote de perro** jog trot
trotona *f* chaperone

trovador *m* troubadour
trovadores·co -ca *adj* troubadour
trovero *m* trouvère
Troya *f* Troy; **ahí fué Troya** it's a shambles; **¡arda Troya!** come what may!
troya·no -na *adj & mf* Trojan
troza *f* log
trozar §60 *tr* to break to pieces; (*un tronco*) cut into logs
trozo *m* piece, fragment; block; excerpt, selection
truco *m* contrivance, device; trick; pocketing of ball; **truco de naipes** card trick; **trucos** pool
truculen·to -ta *adj* truculent
trucha *f* trout
trueno *m* thunder, thunderclap; shot, report; rake, roué; **trueno gordo** finale (*of fireworks*); big scandal; **truenos** (Ven) heavy shoes
trueque *m* barter; exchange, swap; trade-in; **a trueque de** in exchange for; **trueques** (Col) change
trufa *f* truffle; fib, lie
tru·hán -hana *adj* crooked; clownish ‖ *mf* crook; clown
trujal *m* wine press; oil press
trulla *f* noise, bustle; crowd; trowel
truncar §73 *tr* to cut off the head of; (*palabras o frases*) cut, slash; cut off, interrupt
trusas *fpl* trunk hose; trunks
tu *adj poss* thy, your
tú *pron pers* thou, you
tubérculo *m* (*rizoma engrosado, p.ej., de la patata*) tuber; (*protuberancia*) tubercle
tuberculosis *f* tuberculosis
tubería *f* tubing; piping
tubo *m* tube; pipe; **tubo de desagüe** drainpipe; **tubo de ensayo** test tube; **tubo de humo** flue; **tubo de imagen** picture tube; **tubo de vacío** vacuum tube; **tubo digestivo** alimentary canal; **tubo sonoro** chime
tuerca *f* nut; **tuerca de aletas** wing nut
tuer·to -ta *adj* crooked, bent; one-eyed; **a tuertas** upside down; crosswise; **a tuertas o a derechas** rightly or wrongly; thoughtlessly ‖ *mf* one-eyed person ‖ *m* wrong, harm, injustice; **tuertos** afterpains
tuétano *m* marrow; pith; **hasta los tuétanos** through and through; head over heels
tufi·llas *mf* (*pl* **-llas**) touchy person
tufillo *m* whiff, smell
tufo *m* fume, vapor; sidelock; foul odor, foul breath; **tufos** airs, conceit
tugurio *m* shepherd's hut; hovel
tuición *f* protection, custody
tulipán *m* tulip
tullecer §22 *tr* to abuse, mistreat ‖ *intr* to be crippled
tulli·do -da *adj* paralyzed, crippled ‖ *mf* paralytic, cripple
tullir §13 *tr* to cripple, paralyze; abuse, mistreat ‖ *ref* to become crippled or paralyzed
tumba *f* grave, tomb; tombstone; arched top; felling of trees

tumbacuarti·llos *mf* (*pl* **-llos**) old toper, rounder
tumbar *tr* to knock down; catch, trick; stun ‖ *intr* to tumble; capsize ‖ *ref* to lie down
tumbo *m* fall, tumble; boom, rumble; crisis; rise and fall of sea; rough surf
tumbona *f* hammock
tumor *m* tumor
túmulo *m* catafalque
tumulto *m* tumult
tuna *f* loafing, bumming; (bot) prickly pear
tunante *adj* bumming, loafing; crooked, tricky ‖ *mf* bum, loafer; crook
tundidora *f* lawn mower
tuneci·no -na *adj & mf* Tunisian
túnel *m* tunnel; **túnel de lavado** automatic car wash
tunes *mpl* (Col) little steps, first steps
Túnez (*ciudad*) Tunis; (*país*) Tunisia
tungsteno *m* tungsten
túnica *f* tunic
tu·no -na *adj* crooked, tricky ‖ *mf* crook ‖ *f* see **tuna**
tupé *m* toupee; nerve, cheek, brass
tupi·do -da *adj* thick, dense, compact; dull, stupid; clogged up
tupir *tr* to pack tight ‖ *ref* to stuff, stuff oneself
turba *f* crowd, mob; peat
turbamulta *f* job, rabble
turbar *tr* to disturb, trouble; stir up ‖ *ref* to be confused
turbiedad *f* muddiness; confusion
turbina *f* turbine
tur·bio -bia *adj* turbid, muddy, cloudy; confused; obscure
turbión *m* squall, thunderstorm; (*p.ej., de balas*) (fig) hail
turbocompresor *m* turbocompressor
turbohélice *m* turboprop
turbopropulsor *m* turboprop (*engine*)
turborreactor *m* turbojet (*engine*)
turbosupercargador *m* turbosupercharger
turbulen·to -ta *adj* turbulent
tur·co -ca *adj* Turkish ‖ *mf* Turk ‖ *m* (*idioma*) Turkish ‖ *f* (coll) binge; boozing; **coger una turca** to get drunk
turfista *adj* horsy ‖ *m* turfman
turismo *m* touring; touring car
turista *mf* tourist
turísti·co -ca *adj* tourist; touring
turnar *intr* to alternate, take turns
tur·nio -nia *adj* (*ojos*) cross; cross-eyed; (*que mira con ceño*) cross-looking
turno *m* turn, shift; **aguardar turno** to wait one's turn; **por turno** in turn; **turno diurno** day shift
turón *m* polecat
turquesa *s* turquoise
Turquía *s* Turkey
turrón *m* nougat; plum
tusa *f* corncob; corn silk; (Chile) mane; (Col) pockmark; (CAm, W-I) trollop
tusar *tr* to shear, clip, cut
tutear *tr* to thou, address familiarly ‖ *ref* to thou each other, address each other familiarly

tr
tu

tutela *f* guardianship; protection
tutelar *adj* guardian; protecting ‖ *tr* to protect, shelter, guide
tu·tor -tora or **-triz** *mf* (*pl* **-trices**) guardian, tutor

tu·yo -ya *adj poss* of thee ‖ *pron poss* thine, yours
tuza *f* gopher

U

U, u (u) *f* twenty-fourth letter of the Spanish alphabet
u *conj* (used before words beginning with *o* or *ho*) or
U. *abbr* **usted**
ubicar §73 *tr* to locate, place ‖ *intr & ref* to be situated
ubi·cuo -cua *adj* ubiquitous
ubre *f* udder
Ucrania *f* Ukraine
ucrania·no -na *adj & mf* Ukrainian
ucra·nio -nia *adj & mf* Ukrainian ‖ *f* see **Ucrania**
Ud. *abbr* **usted**
Uds. *abbr* **ustedes**
ufanar *ref* — **ufanarse con** or **de** to boast of, be proud of
ufanía *f* pride, conceit; cheer, satisfaction; ease, smoothness
ufa·no -na *adj* proud, conceited; cheerful, satisfied; easy, smooth
ujier *m* doorman, usher
úlcera *f* ulcer, fester, sore; **úlcera de decúbito** bedsore
ulcerar *tr & ref* to ulcerate, fester
ulterior *adj* ulterior; subsequent
ulteriormente *adv* subsequently, later
últimamente *adv* finally; lately, recently
ultimar *tr* to finish, end, conclude, wind up; kill, finish off
ultimátum *m* (*pl* **-tums**) ultimatum; definite decision
últi·mo -ma *adj* last, latest; final; excellent, superior; (*precio*) lowest, final; most remote; (*piso*) top; (*hora*) late; **a la última** in the latest fashion; **a última hora** at the eleventh hour; **a últimos de** toward the end of, in the latter part of; **de última hora** last-minute; **estar a lo último** or **en las últimas** to be up to date, be well-informed; be on one's last-legs; **por último** at last, finally; **último suplicio** capital punishment
ultraatmosféri·co -ca *adj* outer (*space*)
ultraeleva·do -da *adj* (rad) ultrahigh
ultrajar *tr* to outrage, offend
ultraje *m* outrage, offense
ultrajo·so -sa *adj* outrageous, offensive
ultramar *m* country overseas
ultramari·no -na *adj* overseas ‖ **ultramarinos** *mpl* groceries, delicatessen
ultranza — **a ultranza** to the death; unflinchingly
ultrarro·jo -ja *adj & m* infrared
ultratumba *adv* beyond the grave

ultraviola·do -da or **ultravioleta** *adj & m* ultraviolet
ululación *f* howl; whoop; (*del buho*) hoot; (*del disco del fonógrafo*) wow
ulular *intr* to howl; whoop; (*el buho*) hoot
ululato *m* howl; (*del buho*) hoot
umbilical *adj* umbilical
umbral *m* threshold, doorsill; (*madero que sostiene el muro encima de un vano*) lintel; (physiol, psychol & fig) threshold; **atravesar** or **pisar los umbrales** to cross the threshold; **estar en los umbrales de** to be on the threshold of
umbralada *f* (Col) threshold
umbrí·o -a *adj* shady ‖ *f* shady side
umbro·so -sa *adj* shady
un, una (the apocopated form **un** is used before masculine singular nouns and adjectives and before feminine singular nouns beginning with stressed *a* or *ha*) *art indef* a ‖ *adj* one
unánime *adj* unanimous
unanimidad *f* unanimity
unción *f* unction
uncir §36 *tr* (*bueyes*) to yoke, hitch
undéci·mo -ma *adj & m* eleventh
undo·so -sa *adj* wavy
ungir §27 *tr* to smear with ointment or with oil; anoint
ungüento *m* unguent, ointment, salve
únicamente *adv* only, solely
úni·co -ca *adj* only, sole; (*sin otro de su especie*) unique; one, e.g., **precio único** one price
unicornio *m* unicorn
unidad *f* (*concepto de una sola cosa o persona; cantidad que se toma como medida común de todas las demás de su clase; el número entero más pequeño*) unit; (*división; armonía de conjunto; el número uno*) unity
uni·do -da *adj* united; smooth, even; close-knit
unifamiliar *adj casa* one-family
unificar §73 *tr* to unify
uniformar *tr* to make uniform; provide with a uniform
uniforme *adj* uniform ‖ *m* uniform; **uniforme de gala** (mil) full dress
uniformidad *f* uniformity
unilateral *adj* unilateral
unión *f* union; double ring; **Unión Soviética** Soviet Union
unir *tr & ref* to unite

unisonancia *f* (mus) unison; (*de un orador*) monotony

unísono — al unísono in unison; unanimously; **al unísono de** in unison with

unita·rio -ria *adj* unit

universal *adj* universal; all-purpose; (*teclado de máquina de escribir*) standard

universidad *f* university

universita·rio -ria *adj* university ‖ *mf* university student, college student ‖ *m* university professor

universo *m* universe

u·no -na *pron* one, someone; **a una** of one accord; **la una** one o'clock; **somos uno** we are one; **uno a otro, unos a otros** each other, one another; **uno que otro** one or more, a few; **u·nos -nas** some; pair of, e.g., **unas gafas** a pair of glasses; **unas tijeras** a pair of scissors; **unos cuantos** some; **uno y otro** both ‖ *pron indef* one, e.g., **uno no sabe qué hacer aquí** one does not know what to do here ‖ *m* (*unidad y signo que la representa*) one

untar *tr* to smear, grease; anoint; bribe ‖ *ref* to get smeared; grease oneself; embezzle

unto *m* grease; (*gordura del cuerpo del animal*) fat; (Chile) shoe polish; **unto de Méjico** or **de rana** bribe money

untuo·so -sa *adj* unctuous, greasy, sticky

uña *f* nail, fingernail, toenail; (*pezuña*) hoof; (*del ancla*) fluke, bill; (mach) claw, gripper; **enseñar** or **mostrar las uñas** to show one's teeth; **ser largo de uñas** to have long fingers; **ser uña y carne** to be hand in glove; **tener en la uña** to have on the tip of one's fingers

uñada *f* scratch, nail scratch; (*impulso dado con la uña*) flip

uñero *m* ingrowing nail; (*inflamación del dedo en la raíz de la uña*) whitlow

ural *adj* Ural ‖ **Urales** *mpl* Urals

uranio *m* uranium

urbanidad *f* urbanity

urbanismo *m* city planning

urbanista *mf* city planner

urbanísti·co -ca *adj* city-planning ‖ *f* city planning

urbanizar §60 *tr* (*convertir en poblado*) to urbanize; refine; polish

urba·no -na *adj* urban, city; (*atento, cortés*) urbane ‖ *m* policeman

urbe *f* metropolis

urdema·las *mf* (*pl* **-las**) schemer

urdimbre *f* warp; scheme, scheming; **estar en la urdimbre** (Chile) to be thin, be emaciated

urdir *tr* (*los hilos*) to beam; (*una conspiración*) hatch

urente *adj* burning, smarting

uretra *f* urethra

urgencia *f* urgency; **de urgencia** special-delivery

urgente *adj* urgent; (*correo*) special-delivery

urgir §27 *intr* to be urgent

urina·rio -ria *adj* urinary ‖ *m* urinal

urna *f* glass case; ballot box; (*para guardar las cenizas de los cadáveres*) urn; **acudir** or **ir a las urnas** to go to the polls

urología *f* urology

urraca *f* magpie

U.R.S.S. *abbr* **Unión de Repúblicas Socialistas Soviéticas**

urticaria *f* hives

Uruguay, el Uruguay

urugua·yo -ya *adj & mf* Uruguayan

usa·do -da *adj* (*empleado; gastado por el uso; acostumbrado*) used; skilled, experienced; (*vocablo*) **poco usado** rare

usanza *f* use, usage, custom

usar *tr* to use, make use of; (*un cargo, un oficio*) follow ‖ *intr* — **usar** + *inf* to be accustomed to + *inf;* **usar de** to use, have recourse to; **usar de la palabra** to speak, make a speech ‖ *ref* to be the custom

usina *f* factory, plant; powerhouse; (*estación de tranvía*) (Arg) carbarn

uso *m* use; custom, usage; wear, wear and tear; habit, practice; **al uso** according to custom; **en buen uso** in good condition; **hacer uso de la palabra** to speak, make a speech

usted *pron pers* you

usual *adj* (*de uso común*) usual; (*que se usa con facilidad*) usable; sociable

usualmente *adv* usually

usua·rio -ria *mf* user

usufructo *m* use, enjoyment

usufructuar §21 *tr* to enjoy the use of

usura *f* usury; profit; **pagar con usura** to pay back a thousandfold

usurero *m* loan shark; profiteer

usurpar *tr* to usurp

utensilio *m* utensil

útero *m* uterus, womb

útil *adj* useful ‖ **útiles** *mpl* utensils, tools, equipment

utilería *f* (Arg) properties, stage equipment

utilero *m* (Arg) property man

utilidad *f* utility, usefulness; profit, earnings

utilita·rio -ra *adj* utilitarian

utilizable *adj* usable

utilizar §60 *tr* to utilize, use ‖ *ref* — **utilizarse con, de** or **en** to make use of; **utilizarse para** to be good for

utopía *f* utopia

utopista *adj & mf* utopian

UU. *abbr* **ustedes**

uva *f* grape; wart on eyelid; (*baya*) berry; **estar hecho una uva** to have a load on; **uva crespa** gooseberry; **uva de Corinto** currant; **uva de raposa** nightshade; **uva espín** or **espina** gooseberry; **uva pasa** raisin; **uvas verdes** (*de la fábula de Esopo*) sour grapes

uve *f* (*letra del alfabeto*) **V**

uxoricida *m* uxoricide (*husband*)

uxoricidio *m* uxoricide (*act*)

uxo·rio -ria *adj* uxorious

tu
ux

V

V, v (ve *or* uve) *f* twenty-fifth letter of the Spanish alphabet
V. *abbr* **usted, vease, venerable**
V.A. *abbr* **Vuestra Alteza**
vaca *f* cow; (*cuero*) cowhide; (*carne de vaca o de buey*) beef; gambling pool; **hacer vaca** (Peru) to play truant; **vaca de la boda** (coll) goat, laughingstock; friend in need; **vaca de leche** milch cow; **vaca de San Antón** (ent) ladybird
vacación *f* (*cargo que está sin proveer*) vacancy; **de vacaciones** on vacation; **vacaciones** vacation; **vacaiones retribuídas** vacation with pay
vacacionista *mf* vacationist
vacancia *f* vacancy
vacante *adj* vacant ‖ *f* vacancy
vacar §73 *intr* (*un empleo, un cargo*) to be vacant, be unfilled; take off, take a vacation; **vacar a** to attend to; **vacar de** to lack, be devoid of
vacia•do -da *adj* hollow-ground ‖ *m* cast, casting; plaster cast
vaciante *f* ebb tide
vaciar §77 & **regular** *tr* to empty, drain; cast, mold; (*formar un hueco en*) hollow out; sharpen on a grindstone; copy, transcribe; explain in detail ‖ *intr* to empty; flow; (*el agua en el río*) fall, go down ‖ *ref* to blab
vacilación *f* vacillation; flickering; hesitancy, hesitation
vacilada *f* (Mex) spree, high time; (Mex) drunk
vacilante *adj* vacillating; (*luz*) flickering; (*irresoluto*) hesitant
vacilar *intr* to vacillate; (*la luz*) flicker; shake, wobble; (*estar irresoluto*) hesitate, waver
vací•o -a *adj* empty; (*hueco*) hollow; idle; useless, unsuccessful; (*vaca*) barren; presumptuous ‖ *m* emptiness; (*laguna, abertura; vacante*) vacancy; (*espacio que no contiene ninguna materia*) void; (*espacio de que se ha extraído el aire*) vacuum; (*ijada*) side, flank; **de vacío** light, unloaded; **hacer el vacío a** to isolate
vacuidad *f* vacuity, emptiness
vacuna *f* (*enfermedad de las vacas*) cowpox; (*virus cuya inoculación preserva de una enfermedad determinada*) vaccine
vacunación *f* vaccination
vacunar *tr* to vaccinate
vacu•no -na *adj* bovine; cowhide ‖ *f* see **vacuna**
va•cuo -cua *adj* vacant ‖ *m* cavity, hollow
vadear *tr* (*un río*) to ford; wade through; overcome; sound out ‖ *ref* to behave; manage
vado *m* ford; expedient, resource; **al vado o a la puente** one way or another; **no hallar vado** to see no way out; **tentar el vado** to feel one's way
vagabundaje *m* vagrancy
vagabundear *intr* to wander, roam; loaf around

vagabun•do -da *adj* vagabond ‖ *mf* vagabond, tramp; wanderer
vagancia *f* loafing, vagrancy
vagar *m* leisure; **con vagar** slowly; **estar de vagar** to have nothing to do ‖ §44 *intr* to wander, roam; be idle; have plenty of leisure; (*una cosa*) lie around; (*p.ej., una sonrisa por los labios*) play
vagido *m* cry of a newborn baby
vagina *f* vagina
vagneria•no -na *adj* & *mf* Wagnerian
va•go -ga *adj* wandering, roaming; idle, loafing; lax, loose; hesitating, wavering; (*indefinido, indeciso*) vague; (*mirada*) blank ‖ *m* vagabond; idler, loafer; **en vago** shakily; in vain; in the air; **poner en vago** to tilt
vagón *m* car, railroad car; **vagón cama** sleeping car; **vagón carbonero** coal car; **vagón cerrado** boxcar; **vagón cisterna** tank car; **vagón de carga** freight car; **vagón de cola** caboose; **vagón de mercancías** freight car; **vagón de plataforma** flatcar; **vagón frigorífico** refrigerator car; **vagón salón** chair car; **vagón tolva** hopper-bottom car; **vagón volquete** dump car
vagoneta *f* tip car; station wagon
vaguear *intr* to wander around
vaguedad *f* vagueness; vague remark
vaguido *m* faintness, fainting spell
vaharada *f* breath, exhalation
vahear *intr* to emit odors, give forth an aroma
vahido *f* faintness, fainting spell
vaho *m* odor, aroma, vapor, fume
vaina *f* sheath; scabbard; knife case; (*de ciertas semillas*) pod, husk; annoyance, bother; (Col) luck, stroke of luck
vainica *f* hemstitch
vainilla *f* vanilla
vainita *f* (Ven) string bean
vaivén *m* swing, seesaw, backward and forward motion; unsteadiness, inconstancy; risk, chance
vajilla *f* dishes, set of dishes; **lavar la vajilla** to wash the dishes; **vajilla de oro** gold plate; **vajilla de plata** silver plate, silverware; **vajilla de porcelana** chinaware
vale *m* promissory note; voucher; farewell; (Ven) chum, pal; **vale respuesta** reply coupon
valede•ro -ra *adj* valid, effective
vale•dor -dora *mf* defender, protector; (Mex) friend, companion
valedura *f* (Mex) favor, protection
valencia *f* (chem) valence
valentía *f* bravery, valor; feat, exploit; dash, boldness; boast; **pisar de valentía** to strut, swagger
valen•tón -tona *adj* arrogant, boastful ‖ *mf* braggart, boaster ‖ *f* bragging
valer *m* worth, merit, value ‖ §76 *tr* to defend, protect; favor, patronize; avail; yield; be worth, be valued at; be equal to; suit; **valer la pena** to be worthwhile (to);

valerle a uno + *inf* to help someone to + *inf*, to get someone to + *inf;* **valor lo que pesa** to be worth its (his, her, etc.) weight in gold; **valga lo que valiere** come what may; **¡válgame Dios!** bless my soul!, so help me God! ‖ *intr* to have worth; be worthy; be valuable; be valid; prevail; hold, count; have influence; **hacer valer** (*sus derechos*) to assert; make felt; make good; turn to account; **más vale** it is better (to); **vale O.K.; valer para** to be useful for; **valer por** to be equal to ‖ *ref* to help oneself, defend oneself; **valerse de** to make use of, avail oneself of

valero•so -sa *adj* valorous, brave; strong, active, effective

va•let *m* (*pl* -lets) (cards) jack

valía *f* value, worth; favor, influence; **mayor valía** or **plus valía** appreciation, increased value; unearned increment

validación *f* validation

validar *tr* to validate

validez *f* validity; strength, vigor

vali•do -da *adj* highly esteemed, influential ‖ *m* court favorite; prime minister

váli•do -da *adj* valid; strong, robust

valiente *adj* valiant; strong, robust; fine, excellent; (*grande y excesivo*) terrific ‖ *m* brave fellow; bully

valija *f* satchel, brief case; mailbag, mailpouch; mail; **valija diplomática** diplomatic pouch

valimiento *m* favor, protection; favor at court, favoritism

valio•so -sa *adj* valuable; influential; wealthy

va•lón -lona *adj* & *mf* Walloon

valor *m* value, worth; valor, courage; meaning, import; efficacy; equivalence; (*rédito*) income, return; effrontery; (*persona, cosa o cualidad dignas de ser poseídas*) (fig) asset; **¿cómo va ese valor?** how are you?; **valor de rescate** (ins) surrender value; **valores** securities

valoración *f* valuation, appraisal

valorar or **valorear** *tr* (*poner precio a*) to value, appraise; enhance the value of

valorizar §60 *tr* to value; enhance the value of; sell of (*for quick realization*)

vals *m* waltz

valsar *intr* to waltz

valuación *f* valuation, appraisal

valuar §21 *tr* to estimate

válvula *f* valve; **válvula corredize** slide valve; **válvula de admisión** intake valve; **válvula de escape** exhaust valve; **válvula de escape libre** cutout; **válvula de seguridad** safety valve; **válvula en cabeza** valve in the head, overhead valve

valla *f* fence, railing; barricade; hindrance, obstacle; (sport) hurdle; (W-I) cockpit; **valla paranieves** snow fence

vallado *m* barricade, stockade

valle *m* valley; river bed; valley dwellings; **valle de lágrimas** vale of tears

vampiresa *f* vampire

vampíri•co -ca *adj* vampire; ghoulish

vampiro *m* vampire; (*persona que se deleita con cosas horribles*) ghoul

vanadio *m* vanadium

vanagloriar §77 & **regular** *ref* to boast

vanaglorio•so -sa *adj* vainglorious, conceited, boastful

vanamente *adv* vainly

vandalismo *m* vandalism

vánda•lo -la *adj* & *mf* Vandal; (fig) vandal

vanguardia *f* (mil & fig) vanguard, van; **a vanguardia** in the vanguard

vanguardismo *m* avant-garde

vanguardista *adj* avant-garde ‖ *mf* avant-gardist

vanidad *f* vanity; (*fausto*) pomp, show; **ajar la vanidad de** to take down a peg; **hacer vanidad de** to boast of

vanido•so -sa *adj* vain, conceited

va•no -na *adj* vain; hollow, empty; **en vano** in vain ‖ *m* opening in a wall

vapor *m* steam; (*el visible: exhalación, vaho, niebla, etc.*) vapor; steamer, steamboat; **al vapor** at full speed; **vapores** gas (*belched*); blues; **vapor volandero** tramp steamer

vaporar *tr* & *ref* to evaporate

vaporizador *m* atomizer, sprayer

vaporizar §60 *tr* to vaporize; spray ‖ *ref* to vaporize

vaporo•so -sa *adj* vaporous

vapular or **vapulear** *tr* to whip, flog

vaquería *f* drove of cattle; dairy; (Mex) party

vaqueri•zo -za *adj* cattle ‖ *f* winter stable for cattle

vaque•ro -ra *adj* cattle ‖ *mf* cattle tender; (Peru) truant ‖ *m* cow hand; cowboy; **vaqueros** blue jeans

vaqueta *f* leather; (P-R) strop; **zurrarle a uno la vaqueta** to tan someone's hide

vaquillona *f* (Arg, Chile) heifer

vara *f* pole, rod, staff; (*de carruaje*) shaft; (*bastón de mando*) wand; measuring stick; (taur) thrust with goad; **tener vara alta** to have the upper hand; **vara alcándara** shaft; **vara alta** upper hand; **vara buscadora** divining rod (*ostensibly to discover water or metals*); **vara de adivinar** divining rod; **vara de oro** goldenrod; **vara de pescar** fishing rod; **vara de San José** goldenrod

vara-alta *m* boss

varada *f* beaching; running aground

varadero *m* repair dock

varapalo *m* long pole; setback, disappointment, reverse

varar *tr* (*una embarcación*) to beach ‖ *intr* to run aground; (*un negocio*) come to a standstill

varear *tr* (*los frutos de los árboles*) to beat down, knock down; beat, strike; (taur) to goad; (*los caballos de carreras*) (SAm) to exercise, train ‖ *ref* to lose weight, get thin

varec *m* (bot) wrack

varenga *f* (naut) floor, floor timber

vareta *f* twig, stick; lime twig for catching birds; colored stripe; cutting remark; hint; **irse de vareta** to have diarrhea

variable *adj* & *f* variable

variación *f* variation

varia·do -da *adj* varied; variegated
variante *adj & f* variant
variar §77 to vary, change ‖ *intr* to vary, change; be different; **variar de** or **en opinión** to change one's mind
varice *f* or **várice** *f* varicose veins
varicela *f* chicken pox
varico·so -sa *adj* varicose
variedad *f* variety; **variedades** variety show, vaudeville
varilla *f* rod, stem, twig; (*bastón de mando*) wand; (*de paraguas, abanico, etc.*) rib; (*del corsé*) stay; (*de rueda*) wire spoke; jawbone; (Mex) peddler's wares; **varilla de nivel** dipstick; **varilla de virtudes** wand, magician's wand
varillaje *m* ribs, ribbing; (*de máquina de escribir*) type bars
varille·ro -ra *adj* (*caballo*) (Ven) race ‖ *m* (Mex) peddler
va·rio -ria *adj* (*de diversos colores; que tiene variedad*) various, varied; fickle, inconstant; **varios** various; several
varón *adj* male, e.g., **hijo varón** male child ‖ *m* man, male; grown man, adult male; man of standing; **santo varón** plain artless fellow
varonía *f* male issue
varonil *adj* manly, virile; courageous
Varsovia *f* Warsaw
vasa·llo -lla *adj & mf* vassal
vas·co -ca *adj & mf* Basque (*of Spain and France*) ‖ *m* Basque (*language*)
vas·cón -cona *adj & mf* Basque (*of old Spain*)
vasconga·do -da *adj & mf* Basque (*of Spain*) ‖ *m* Basque (*language*) ‖ **las Vascongadas** the Basque Provinces
vascuence *adj & m* Basque (*language*) ‖ *m* gibberish
vaselina *f* Vaseline
vasera *f* kitchen shelf; bottle rack, tumbler rack
vasija *f* container, vessel
vaso *m* tumbler, glass; vase, flower jar; (anat) duct, vessel; **vaso de engrase** (mach) grease cup; **vaso de noche** pot, chamber pot; **vaso graduado** measuring glass; **vaso sanguíneo** blood vessel
vástago *m* shoot, sapling; scion, offspring; rod, stem; **vástago de émbolo** piston rod; **vástago de válvula** valve stem
vastedad *f* vastness
vas·to -ta *adj* vast
vate *m* bard, seer, poet
váter *m* toilet, water closet
vataije *m* wattage
vaticinar *tr* to prophesy, predict
vaticinio *m* prophecy, prediction
vatídi·co -ca *adj* prophetical ‖ *mf* prophet
vatímetro *m* wattmeter
vatio *m* watt
vatio-hora *m* (*pl* **vatios-hora**) watt-hour
vaya *f* jest, jeer
Vd. *abbr* **usted**
Vds. *abbr* **ustedes**
V.E. *abbr* **Vuestra Excelencia**

vece·ro -ra *adj* alternating; yielding in alternate years ‖ *mf* person waiting his turn
vecinamente *adv* nearby
vecindad *f* neighborhood, vicinity; residency; residents; **hacer mala vecindad** to be a bad neighbor
vecindario *m* neighborhood, community; people, population
veci·no -na *adj* neighboring; like, similar ‖ *mf* neighbor; resident, citizen
veda *f* prohibition; (*de la caza y la pesca*) closed season
vedado *m* game preserve
vedar *tr* to forbid, prohibit; hinder, stop; veto
vedija *f* fleece, tuft of wool; mat of hair; matted hair
vee·dor -dora *adj* curious, spying ‖ *mf* busybody ‖ *m* supervisor, overseer
vega *f* fertile plain; (Cuba) tobacco plantation
vegetación *f* vegetation; **vegetaciones adenoideas** adenoids
vegetal *adj & m* vegetable
vegetaria·no -na *adj & mf* vegetarian
vego·so -sa *adj* (Chile) damp, wet
vehemencia *f* vehemence
vehemente *adj* vehement
vehículo *m* vehicle; **vehículo espacial** space vehicle
veinta·vo -va *adj & m* twentieth
veinte *adj & pron* twenty; **a las veinte** late, untimely ‖ *m* twenty; (*en las fechas*) twentieth
vientena *f* score, twenty
veintiún *adj* this apocopated form of **veintiuno** is used before masculine singular nouns and adjectives
veintiu·no -na *adj & pron* twenty-one ‖ *m* twenty-one; (*en las fechas*) twenty-first ‖ *f* (*juego de naipes*) twenty-one
vejación *f* vexation, annoyance
vejamen *m* vexation, annoyance; bantering, taunting
vejar *tr* to vex, annoy; taunt
vejestorio *m* old dodo
vejete *m* little old fellow
vejez *f* old age; oldness; dotage; platitude, old story; **a la vejez, viruelas** there's no fool like an old fool
vejiga *f* (*órgano que recibe la orina de los riñones*) bladder; (*ampolla*) blister; (*saco hecho de piel, goma, etc.*) bag, pouch, bladder; **vejiga de la bilis** or **de la hiel** gall bladder
vela *f* wakefulness; pilgrimage; evening; work in the evening; sail; sailboat; (*cilindro con una torcida que sirve para alumbrar*) candle; vigil (*before Eucharist*) awning; (Mex) scolding; **a toda vela** full sail; **a vela** under sail; **a vela llena** under full sail; **en vela** awake; **estar entre dos velas** to be half-seas over, have a sheet in the wind; **hacerse a la vela** to set sail; **vela latina** lateen sail; **vela mayor** mainsail; **vela romana** Roman candle
velada *f* evening party, soirée; vigil, watch
vela·do -da *adj* veiled, hidden; (phot) light-struck ‖ *f* see **velada**

velador *m* pedestal table, gueridon; wooden candlestick; watchman; (SAm) night table; (Mex) lamp globe

velaje *m* or **velamen** *m* (naut) canvas, sails

velar *adj* & *f* velar ‖ *tr* to watch over; guard; (*la guardia*) keep; hold a wake over; (*cubrir con un velo*) veil; (phot) to fog; (fig) to veil, hide, conceal ‖ *intr* to stay awake; stay awake working; keep vigil; (*el viento*) keep up all night; (*un escollo, un peñasco*) stick up out of the water; **velar por** or **sobre** to watch over ‖ *ref* (phot) to fog, be light-struck

velatorio *m* wake

veleidad *f* whim, caprice; fickleness, flightiness

veleido•so -sa *adj* whimsical, capricious; fickle, flighty

vele•ro -ra *adj* swift-sailing ‖ *m* sailboat

veleta *mf* (*persona inconstante*) weathercock ‖ *f* vane, weathervane, weathercock; (*de un molino*) rudder vane; (*de la caña de pescar*) bob; streamer, pennant; **veleta de manga** (aer) air sleeve, air sock

velís *m* (Mex) valise

velita *f* little candle

velo *m* veil; taking the veil; confusion, perplexity; (*disfraz*) veil; (*de lágrimas*) mist; (phot) fog; **correr el velo** to pull aside the curtain, to dispel the mystery; **tomar el velo** to take the veil; **velo del paladar** soft palate

velocidad *f* (*rapidez*) speed, velocity; (mech) velocity; **en gran velocidad** (rr) by express; **en pequeña velocidad** (rr) by freight; **primera velocidad** (aut) low gear; **segunda velocidad** (aut) second; **tercera velocidad** (aut) high gear; **velocidad con respecto al suelo** (aer) ground speed; **velocidad de crucero** cruising speed; **velocidad permitida** speed limit

velocímetro *m* speedometer

velón *m* brass olive-oil lamp

velorio *m* evening party or bee; wake; wake for a dead child; dull party; come-on

ve•loz *adj* (*pl* **-loces**) swift, speedy; agile, quick

vello *m* down, fuzz

vellocino *m* fleece; **vellocino de oro** Golden Fleece

vellón *m* fleece; unsheared sheepskin; lock of wool; copper coin; copper-silver alloy

vello•so -sa *adj* downy, hairy, fuzzy

velludillo *m* velveteen

vellu•do -da *adj* shaggy, hairy, fuzzy ‖ *m* (*felpa*) plush; (*terciopelo*) velvet

vena *f* vein; (*en piedras*) grain; (fig) poetical inspiration; **estar en vena** to be all set, be inspired; sparkle with wit; **vena de loco** fickle disposition

venablo *m* dart, javelin; **echar venablos** to burst forth in anger

venado *m* deer, stag; **pintar el venado** (Mex) to play hooky

venáti•co -ca *adj* fickle, unsteady; daffy, nutty

vence•dor -dora *adj* conquering, victorious ‖ *mf* conqueror, victor

vencejo *m* band, string; (orn) European swift, black martin

vencer §78 *tr* to vanquish, conquer; excel, outdo; overcome, surmount ‖ *intr* to conquer, be victorious; (*un plazo*) be up; (*un contrato*) expire; (*una letra*) mature, fall due ‖ *ref* to control oneself; (*un camino*) bend, turn; (Chile) to wear out, become useless

vencetósigo *m* milkweed, tame poison

venci•do -da *adj* conquered; (com) due, mature, payable

vencimiento *m* (*acción de vencer*) victory; (*hecho de ser vencido*) defeat; (com) expiration, maturity

venda *f* (*para ligar un miembro herido*) bandage; (*para tapar los ojos*) blindfold

vendaje *m* bandage, dressing; **vendaje enyesado** plaster cast

vendar *tr* (*un miembro, una herida*) to bandage; (*los ojos*) blindfold; (*cegar*) (fig) to blind; (*engañar*) (fig) to hoodwink

vendaval *m* strong southeasterly wind from the sea; strong wind, gale

vendedera *f* saleswoman, saleslady

vende•dor -dora *adj* selling ‖ *m* salesman ‖ *f* saleslady, sales girl

vendehu•mos *mf* (*pl* **-mos**) influence peddler

vendeja *f* public sale

vender *tr* to sell; betray, sell out; **vender salud** to be the picture of health ‖ *intr* to sell; ¡**vendo, vendo, vendí!** going, going, gone! ‖ *ref* to sell oneself; sell, be for sale; betray oneself, give oneself away; **venderse caro** to be hard to see; be quite a stranger; **venderse en** (*p.ej., cien pesetas*) to sell for; **venderse por** to pass oneself off as

ven•dí *m* (*pl* **-díes**) certificate of sale

vendible *adj* salable, marketable

vendimia *f* vintage; (fig) big profit

vendimia•dor -dora *mf* vintager

vendimiar *tr* (*la uva*) to gather, harvest; (*las viñas*) gather the grapes of; make off with; kill

venduta *f* public sale; (W-I) greengrocery

Venecia *f* (*ciudad*) Venice; (*provincia*) Venetia

venecia•no -na *adj* & *mf* Venetian

veneno *m* poison, venom

veneno•so -sa *adj* poisonous, venomous

venera *f* scallop shell; (*manantial de agua*) spring; **empeñar la venera** to go all out, spare no expense

venerable *adj* venerable

venerar *tr* to venerate, revere; worship

venére•o -a *adj* venereal ‖ *m* venereal disease

venero *m* (*de agua*) spring; (*filón de mineral*) lode, vein; (fig) source

venezola•no -na *adj* & *mf* Venezuelan

Venezuela *f* Venezuela

venga•dor -dora *adj* avenging ‖ *mf* avenger

venganza *f* vengeance, revenge

vengar §44 *tr* to avenge ‖ *ref* to take revenge; **vengarse de** to take revenge on

vengati•vo -va *adj* vengeful, vindictive
venia *f* forgiveness, pardon; leave, permission; bow, greeting
venida *f* coming; return; flood, freshet
venide•ro -ra *adj* coming, future ‖ **venideros** *mpl* successors, posterity
venir §79 *intr* to come; **que viene** coming, next; **venga lo que viniere** come what may; **venir** + *ger* to be + *ger;* **venir a** + *inf* to come to + *inf;* to amount to + *ger;* to happen to + *inf;* to finally + *inf,* e.g., **después de una larga enfermedad, vino a morir** after a long illness he finally died; **venir a ser** to turn out to be ‖ *ref* to ferment; **venirse abajo** to collapse
veno•so -sa *adj* venous
venta *f* sale; roadside inn; (Chile) refreshment stand; (S-D) grocery store; **de venta** or **en venta** on sale, for sale; **ser una venta** to be an expensive place; **venta al descubierto** short sale
ventaja *f* advantage; (*en juegos o apuestas*) odds; extra pay
ventajo•so -sa *adj* advantageous
ventalla *f* valve
ventana *f* window; (*de la nariz*) nostril; **echar la casa por la ventana** to go to a lot of expense; **ventana batiente** casement; **ventana de guillotina** sash window; **ventana saprdiza** bay window
ventanal *m* church window; picture window
ventanear *intr* to be at the window all the time
ventanilla *f* (*de coche, de banco, de sobre*) window; ticket window; (*de la nariz*) nostril
ventanillo *m* (*postigo de puerta o ventana*) wicket; (*mirilla*) peephole
ventar §2 *tr* to sniff ‖ *impers* — **vienta** it is windy
ventarrón *m* gale, windstorm
ventear *tr* to sniff; dry in the wind; snoop into ‖ *intr* to snoop, pry around ‖ *impers* — **ventea** it is windy ‖ *ref* (*henderse*) to split; break wind; spend a lot of time in the open
vente•ro -ra *mf* innkeeper
ventilador *m* ventilator; fan; (naut) funnel; **ventilador aspirador** exhaust fan
ventilar *tr* to ventilate; (fig) to air, ventilate
ventisca *f* drift, snowdrift; (*borrasca*) blizzard
ventiscar §73 *intr* to snow and blow; (*la nieve*) drift
ventisquero *m* snowdrift; blizzard; snow-capped mountain; glacier
ventolera *f* blast of wind; (*molinete*) pinwheel; vanity, pride; wild idea; (Mex) wind
ventosa *f* vent, air hole; **pegar una ventosa a** to swindle
ventosear *intr* to break wind
vento•so -sa *adj* windy ‖ *f* see **ventosa**
ventregada *f* brood, litter; outpouring, abundance
ventrículo *m* ventricle
ventrílo•cuo -cua *mf* ventriloquist

ventriloquia *f* or **ventriloquismo** *m* ventriloquism
ventura *f* happiness; luck, chance; danger, risk; **a la ventura** at random; at a risk; **por ventura** perhaps, perchance; **probar ventura** to try one's luck
venture•ro -ra *adj* adventurous; fortunate, lucky ‖ *mf* adventurer
ventu•ro -ra *adj* future, coming ‖ *f* see **ventura**
venturón *m* stroke of luck
venturo•so -sa *adj* fortunate, lucky
Venus *m* (astr) Venus ‖ *f* (myth) Venus; (*mujer de belleza*) Venus
venus•to -ta *adj* beautiful, graceful
venza *f* goldbeater's skin
ver *m* (*vista*) sight; (*apariencia*) appearance; opinion; **a mi ver** in my opinion ‖ §80 *tr* to see; look at; (law) to hear, try; **no poder ver** to not be able to bear; **no tener nada que ver con** to have nothing to do with; **ver** + *inf* to see + *inf,* e.g., **ví entrar a mi hermano** I saw my brother come in; to see + *ger,* e.g., **ví bailar a la muchacha** I saw the girl dancing; to see + *pp.* e.g., **ví ahorcar al criminal** I saw the criminal hanged; **ver venir a uno** to see what someone is up to ‖ *intr* to see; **a más ver** so long; **a ver** let's see; **hasta más ver** good-bye, so long; **ver de** to try to; **ver y creer** seeing is believing ‖ *ref* to be seen; be obvious; see oneself; see each other; meet; (*encontrarse*) be, find oneself; **verse con** to see, have a talk with; **ya se ve** of course, certainly
vera *f* edge, border; **a la vera de** near, beside; **de veras** in truth; **jugar de veras** to play for keeps; **veras** truth, reality; earnestness
veracidad *f* veracity, truthfulness
veranda *f* verandah; bay window, closed porch
veraneante *mf* summer vacationist, summer resident
veranear *intr* to summer
veranie•go -ga *adj* summer; unimportant, insignificant
veranillo *m* Indian summer; **veranillo de San Martín** Indian summer
ve•raz *adj* (*pl* **-races**) veracious, truthful
verbena *f* fair, country fair, night festival; (bot) verbena
verbigracia *adv* for example
verbo *m* verb ‖ **Verbo** *m* (theol) Word
verbo•so -sa *adj* verbose, wordy
verdacho *m* green earth
verdad *f* truth; **a la verdad** in truth, as a matter of fact; **de verdad** really; **la verdad desnuda** the plain truth; **¿no es verdad?** or **¿verdad?** isn't that so? La traducción al inglés de esta pregunta depende generalmente de la aseveración que la precede. Si la aseveración es afirmativa, la pregunta es negativa, p.ej., **Vd. vivió aquí. ¿No es verdad?** You lived here. Did you not?; Si la aseveración es negativa, la pregunta es afirmativa, p.ej., **Vd. no vivió aquí. ¿No**

es verdad? You did not live here? Did you? Si el sujeto de la aseveración es un nombre sustantivo, va representado en la pregunta con un pronombre personal, p.ej., **Juan no estuvo aquí anoche. ¿No es verdad?** John was not here last evening. Was he?; **ser verdad** to be true; **verdad trillada** truism

verdade•ro -ra adj true; real; (que dice siempre la verdad) truthful

verde adj green; young, youthful; (viuda) merry; (cuento) shady, off-color; **están verdes** they're hard to reach ‖ m green; foliage, verdure

verdear intr to turn green, look green

verdecer §22 intr to turn green, grow green again

verdecillo m (orn) greenfinch

verdemar m sea green

verdete m verdigris

verdín m fresh green; (capa verde de aguas estancadas) mold, pond scum; (cardenillo) verdigris

verdise•co -ca adj half-dry

verdor m verdure; youth

verdo•so -sa adj greenish

verdugado m hoop skirt

verdugo m shoot, sucker; (estoque) rapier; (azote) scourge; (roncha) welt; executioner, hangman; torment; butcher bird, shrike

verdugón m wale, weal

verdulería f greengrocery

verdule•ro -ra mf greengrocer ‖ f fishwife

verdura f greenness; (color verde de las plantas) verdure; (obscenidad) smuttiness; **verduras** vegetables, greens

verecundia f bashfulness, shyness

verecun•do -da adj bashful, shy

vereda f path, lane; sidewalk

veredicto m verdict

verga f (naut) yard

vergel m flower and fruit garden

vergonzo•so -sa adj (que causa vergüenza) shameful; (que tiene vergüenza) ashamed; (que se avergüenza con facilidad) bashful, shy; (que causa humillación) embarrassing; shabby, wretched ‖ mf bashful person ‖ m armadillo

vergüenza f (arrepentimiento) shame; (oprobio) shamefulness; (pudor, timidez) bashfulness, shyness; (desconcierto, humillación) embarrassment; (pundonor) dignity, face; public punishment; **¡qué vergüenza!** shame on you!; **tener vergüenza** to be ashamed; **vergüenzas** privates, genitals

vericueto m rough, rocky ground

verídi•co -ca adj truthful

verificación f verification; checking, testing, inspection; **verificación a la ventura** spot check

verifica•dor -dora adj verifying ‖ m meter inspector

verificar §73 tr to verify, check; (llevar a cabo) carry out; (los contadores de agua, gas y electricidad) inspect ‖ ref to prove true; take place

verja f iron gate, iron fence, grating

ver•mú m (pl **-mús**) vermouth; matinée

vernácu•lo -la adj vernacular

verónica f (bot) veronica; (taur) veronica (graceful pass in which the bullfighter waits for the bull with open cape)

veroniquear intr (taur) to perform veronicas

verosímil adj likely, probable

verraco m male hog, boar

verraquear intr to grunt, grumble; cry hard

verruga f wart; bore, nuisance

verrugo m miser

versal adj & f capital

versalilla or **versalita** f small capital

Versalles Versailles

versar intr — **versar acerca de** or **sobre** to deal with, treat of ‖ ref — **versarse en** to be or become versed in

versátil adj fickle; versatile; (arma) multipurpose

versículo m verse (in the Bible)

versificación f versification

versificar §73 tr & intr to versify

versión f version; translation

verso m verse; (typ) verso; **versos pareados** rhymed couplet

vertebra•do -da adj & m vertebrate

vertedero m dump; weir, spillway

verter §51 tr (un líquido, un polvo) to pour; (un recipiente) empty; (lágrimas; luz; sangre) shed; (descargar) dump; translate ‖ intr to flow ‖ ref to run, empty

vertical adj & f vertical

vértice m vertex

vertiente m & f (declive) slope; (colina por donde corre el agua) shed ‖ f (Arg, Col, Chile) spring, fountain

vertigino•so -sa adj dizzy

vértigo m vertigo, dizziness; fit of insanity

vesícula f vesicle; **vesícula biliar** gall bladder

veso m polecat

Véspero m Vesper

vesperti•no -na adj evening ‖ m evening sermon

vestíbulo m vestibule; (theat) foyer, lobby

vestido m clothing, dress; (de mujer) gown, dress; (de hombre) suit; costume; **vestido de ceremonia** dress suit; **vestido de etiqueta** evening clothes; **vestido de etiqueta de mujer** or **vestido de noche** evening gown; **vestido de gala** (mil) full dress; **vestido de serio** evening clothes; **vestido de tarde-noche** cocktail dress

vestidura f clothing; (del sacerdote) vestment

vestigio m vestige, trace; track, footprint

vestir §50 tr to dress, clothe; adorn; cover up; disguise; (tal o cual vestido) wear; put on; **vestir el cargo** to look the part ‖ intr to dress; (una prenda o la materia) be dressy; **vestir de** (p.ej., blanco) to dress in; **vestir de etiqueta** to dress in evening clothes; **vestir de paisano** to dress in civilian clothes ‖ ref to dress, get dressed; dress oneself; (de una enfermedad) be up, be about; **vestirse de** (nubes, flores, hierba, etc.) to be covered with; (importancia, humildad, etc.) assume

vestuario m (las prendas de uno) wardrobe;

dressing room; bathhouse; checkroom, cloakroom; (mil) uniform; (theat) dressing room
Vesubio, el Vesuvius
veta *f* vein; streak, stripe; **descubrir la veta de** to be on to
vetar *tr* to veto
vetea•do -da *adj* veined, striped ‖ *m* graining ‖ *f* (Ecuad) whipping
vetear *tr* to grain, stripe; (Eucad) to whip, flog
veteranía *f* experience, know-how
vetera•no -na *adj & mf* veteran
veterina•rio -ria *adj* veterinary ‖ *mf* veterinarian ‖ *f* veterinary medicine
vetus•to -ta *adj* old, ancient
vez *f* (*pl* **veces**) time; (*tiempo de hacer una cosa por turno*) turn; **a la vez** at the same time; **a la vez que** while; **alguna vez** sometimes; ever; **a su vez** in turn; on his part; **a veces** at times, sometimes; **cada vez** every time; **cada vez más** more and more; **cuántas veces** how often; **de una vez** at one time; once and for all; **de vez en cuando** once in a while; **dos veces** twice; **en vez de** instead of; **esperar vez** to wait one's turn; **hacer las veces de** to take the place of; **las más veces** most of the time; **muchas veces** often; **otra vez** again; **raras veces** or **rara vez** seldom, rarely; **repetidas veces** over and over again; **tal vez** perhaps; **tomar la vez a** to get ahead of; **una que otra vez** once in a while; **una vez** once
veza *f* vetch, spring vetch
v.g. or **v.gr.** *abbr* **verbigracia**
vía *f* road, route, way; (*par de rieles y el suelo en que se asientan*) (rr) track; (*el mismo carril*) (rr) rail, track; (anat) passage, tract; (fig) way; **por la vía de** via; **por vía aérea** by air; **por vía bucal** by mouth; **vía aérea** airway; **vía ancha** (rr) broad gauge; **vía de agua** waterway; (naut) leak; **vía estrecha** (rr) narrow gauge; **vía férrea** railway; **vía fluvial** waterway; **Vía Láctea** Milky Way; **vía muerta** (rr) siding; **vía normal** (rr) standard gauge; **vía pública** thoroughfare; **vías de hecho** (law) assault and battery ‖ *prep* via
viable *adj* feasible
viaducto *m* viaduct
viajante *adj* traveling ‖ *mf* traveler ‖ *m* drummer, traveling salesman
viajar *tr* to sell on the road; (*ciertas comarcas*) cover as salesman ‖ *intr* to travel, journey
viaje *m* trip, journey; travel book; water supply; (*drogas*) trip; **¡buen viaje!** bon voyage!; **viaje de ida y vuelta** or **viaje redondo** round trip; **viaje de pruebas** shakedown cruise, trial cruise
viaje•ro -ra *adj* traveling ‖ *mf* traveler; passenger
vial *adj* road, highway ‖ *m* tree-lined road
vianda *f* food, viand; meal
viandante *mf* traveler; itinerant
vitático *m* travel allowance; (eccl) viaticum

víbora *f* viper
vibración *f* vibration
vibrar *tr* to vibrate; (*la voz; la r*) roll; (*una lanza*) hurl ‖ *intr* to vibrate ‖ *ref* to be thrilled
vicaría *f* vicarage
vicario *m* vicar
vicexlmirante *m* vice-admiral
vicepresiden•te -ta *mf* vice-president
viceversa *adv* vice versa
viciar *tr* to vitiate; (*una proposición*) to slant ‖ *ref* to become vitiated; give oneself up to vice; become addicted; (*una tabla*) warp
vicio *m* vice; pampering, spoiling; luxuriance, overgrowth; **hablar de vicio** to talk all the time, talk too much; **quejarse de vicio** to be a chronic complainer
vicio•so -sa *adj* vicious; faulty, defective; strong, robust; luxuriant, overgrown; dissolute; (*niño*) spoiled
víctima *f* victim, **víctima propiciatoria** scapegoat
victimar *tr* to kill, murder
victoria *f* victory
victorio•so -sa *adj* victorious
vid *f* vine, grapevine
vida *f* life; living, livelihood; **darse buena vida** to live high; live in comfort; **de por vida** for life; **en mi vida** never; **escapar con vida** to have a narrow escape; **ganar** or **ganarse la vida** to earn one's livelihood, make a living; **hacer por la vida** to get a bite to eat; **mudar de vida** to mend one's ways; **¡por vida mía!** upon my soul!; **vida airada** licentious living; **vida ancha** loose living; **vida de familia** or **de hogar** home life; **vida mía** my darling
vidalita *f* (Arg, Chile, Urug) mournful love song
vidente *mf* clairvoyant ‖ *m* prophet, see ‖ *f* seeress
videocasete *m* video cassette
videodisco *m* video disk
videograbación *f* video-tape recording
video-juego *m* video game
videoseñal *f* picture signal
videotocadiscos *m* video-disk player
vidria•do -da *adj* glazed; brittle ‖ *m* glaze, glazing; glazed pottery; dishes
vidriar §77 & regular *tr* to glaze ‖ *ref* (*los ojos*) to become glassy
vidriera *f* glass window, glass door; shopwindow, store window; **vidriera de colores** or **vidriera pintada** stained-glass window
vidriería *f* glassworks; glass store
vidriero *m* glass blower, glassworker; glazier; glass dealer
vidrio *m* glass; piece of glass; windowpane; **pagar los vidrios rotos** to take the blame, to be the goat; **vidrio cilindrado** plate glass; **vidrio de aumento** magnifying glass; **vidrio de color** stained glass; **vidrio deslustrado** ground glass; **vidrio tallado** cut glass
vidrio•so -sa *adj* glassy, vitreous; (*quebradizo*) brittle; (*resbaladizo*) slippery; (*que se*

resiente *fácilmente*) touchy; (*mirada, ojos*) (fig) glassy

vie·jo -ja *adj* old ‖ *m* old man; **viejo verde** old goat, old rake ‖ *f* old woman

vie·nés -nesa *adj & mf* Viennese

viento *m* wind; course, direction; (*cuerda que mantiene una cosa derecha*) guy; (*gases intestinales*) wind; **ceñir el viento** (naut) to sail close to the wind; **viento de cola** (aer) tail wind; **viento en popa** (naut) tail wind; **vientos alisios** trade winds

vientre *m* belly; (*parte de la ondulación entre dos nodos*) (phys) loop; **evacuar** or **exonerar el vientre** to have a bowel movement; **vientre flojo** loose bowels

vier·nes *m* (*pl* **-nes**) Friday; **Viernes santo** Good Friday

viertea·guas *m* (*pl* **-guas**) *m* flashing

vietna·més -mesa *adj & mf* Vietnamese

viga *f* beam, girder, rafter; **estar contando las vigas** to gaze blankly at the ceiling; **viga de celosía** lattice girder

vigencia *f* force, operation; (*de una póliza de seguro*) life; **en vigencia** in force, in effect

vigente *adj* effective, in force

vigési·mo -ma *adj & m* twentieth

vigía *m* lookout, watch; **vigía de incendios** firewarden ‖ *f* watch; watchtower; (naut) rock, reef

vigiar §77 *tr* to watch over

vigilancia *f* vigilance, watchfulness; **bajo vigilancia médica** under the care of a physician

vigilante *adj* vigilant, watchful ‖ *m* guard, watchman; **vigilante nocturno** night watchman

vigilar *tr* to watch over; look out for ‖ *intr* to watch, keep guard

vigilia *f* vigil; wakefulness; night work, night study; (*víspera*) eve; (mil) guard, watch; **comer de vigilia** to fast, abstain from meat

vigor *m* vigor; **en vigor** in force; into effect

vigoriza·dor -dora *adj* invigorating ‖ *m* tonic; **vigorizador del cabello** hair tonic

vigorizante *adj* invigorating

vigorizar §60 *tr* to invigorate; encourage

vigoro·so -sa *adj* vigorous

vigueta *f* small beam, small girder

vihuela *f* Spanish lute

vil *adj* vile, base, mean ‖ *mf* scoundrel

vilano *m* bur, down

vileza *f* vileness, baseness

vilipendiar *tr* to scorn, despise

vilipendio·so -sa *adj* contemptible

vilo — en vilo in the air; (fig) up in the air

vilorta *f* reed hoop; (*arandela*) washer

villa *f* town; (*casa de recreo en el campo*) villa; **la Villa** the city (*Madrid*)

villancico *m* carol, Christmas carol

villanes·co -ca *adj* boorish, crude, rustic

villanía *f* humbleness, humble birth; vileness, meanness; foul remark

villa·no -na *adj* base, vile; rude, impolite ‖ *mf* peasant; knave, scoundrel

villorrio *m* small country town

vinagre *m* vinegar; (*persona de genio áspero*) grouch

vinagrera *f* vinaigrette; (bot) sorrel; (SAm) heartburn; **vinagreras** cruet stand

vinagreta *f* French dressing, vinaigrette sauce

vinagro·so -sa *adj* vinegary

vinariego *m* vineyardist

vinatería *f* wine business; wine shop

vinate·ro -ra *adj* wine ‖ *m* wine dealer, vintner

vincular *tr* to bind, tie, unite; continue; perpetuate; (*esperanzas*) found, base; (law) entail

vínculo *m* bond, tie; (law) entail

vindicar §73 *tr* (*vengar*) to avenge; (*exculpar*) vindicate

vindicta *f* revenge

vinicul·tor -tora *mf* winegrower

vinicultura *f* winegrowing

vinilo *m* vinyl

vino *m* wine; sherry reception, wine party; **tener mal vino** to be a quarrelsome drunk; **vino cubierto** dark-red wine; **vino de Jerez** sherry; **vino del terruño** local wine; **vino de mesa** table wine; **vino de Oporto** port wine; **vino de pasto** table wine; **vino de postre** after-dinner wine; **vino de segunda** second-run wine; **vino de solera** solera sherry; **vino tinto** red table wine

vinolen·to -ta *adj* too fond of wine

viña *f* vineyard; **ser una viña** to be a mine; **tener una viña** to have a sinecure

viña·dor -dora *mf* vineyardist, vinedresser ‖ *m* guard of a vineyard

viñedo *m* vineyard

viñeta *f* vignette, headpiece

viola·do -da *adj & m* violet (*color*)

violar *m* bed of violets ‖ *tr* to violate; ravish, rape; profane, desecrate; tamper with

violencia *f* violence

violentar *tr* to do violence to; (*p.ej., una casa*) break into ‖ *ref* to force oneself

violen·to -ta *adj* violent

violeta *m* (*color; colorante*) violet ‖ *f* (bot) violet

violín *m* violin; (billiards) bridge, cue rest; **embolsar el violín** (Arg, Ven) to cower, to slink away

violinista *mf* violinist

violón *m* (mus) bass viol; **tocar el violón** to talk nonsense

violoncelista *mf* cellist, violoncellist

violoncelo *m* (mus) cello, violoncello

violonchelista *mf* cellist, violoncellist

violonchelo *m* (mus) cello, violoncello

vira *f* welt; (*saetilla*) dart

virada *f* turn, change of direction; (naut) tack

virago *f* mannish woman

viraje *m* turn, swerve; (phot) toning

virar *tr* (naut) to wind; (naut) to tack, veer; (phot) to tone ‖ *intr* to turn, swerve; (naut) to tack, veer

virgen *adj* virgin ‖ *f* virgin, maiden

virginidad *f* virginity

Virgo *m* (astr) Virgo

vírgula *f* rod; thin line, light dash

virgulilla *f* fine line; diacritic mark

virilidad *f* virility

virin·go -ga *adj* (Col) naked

virolen•to -ta adj pock-marked; having smallpox

virología f virology

virote m (saeta) bolt; sporty young fellow; (coll) stuffed shirt

virrey m viceroy

virtual adj virtual

virtud f virtue

virtuosismo m virtuosity

virtuo•so -sa adj virtuous ‖ m virtuoso

viruela f smallpox; pock mark; **viruelas locas** chicken pox

virulencia f virulence

virulen•to -ta adj virulent

vi•rus m (pl -rus) virus

viruta f shaving

virutilla f thin shaving; **virutillas de acero** steel wool

visado m visa

visaje m face, grimace

visar tr to visa; to O.K.; (arti & surv) to sight

vísceras fpl viscera

visco m birdlime

viscosa f viscose

viscosilla f rayon thread

visco•so -sa adj viscous ‖ f see **viscosa**

visera f (del yelmo, de las gorras, del parabrisas del automóvil, etc.) visor; (pequeña pantalla que se pone en la frente para resguardar la vista) eyeshade; (W-I) blinder, blinker

visible adj visible; (manifiesto) evident; (que llama la antención) conspicuous

visigo•do -da adj Visigothic ‖ mf Visigoth

visillo m window curtain, window shade

visión f vision; view; (persona fea y ridícula) sight, scarecrow; **ver visiones** to be seeing things; **visión negra** (del aviador) blackout

visionar tr to contemplate, look at

visiona•rio -ria adj & mf visionary

visir m vizier; **gran visir** grand vizier

visita f visit; visitor, caller; inspection; **ir de visitas** to go calling; **pagar la visita a** to return the call of; **tener visita** to have callers; **visita de cumplido** formal call; **visita de médico** short call

visita•dor -dora mf frequent caller ‖ m inspector ‖ f (Hond, Ven) enema

visitante adj visiting ‖ mf visitor

visitar tr to visit; inspect

visite•ro -ra adj visiting; (médico) fond of making calls ‖ mf visitor

vislumbrar tr to descry, glimpse; surmise, suspect ‖ ref (verse confusamente por la distancia) glimmer; (aparecer en la distancia) loom

vislumbre f glimpse, glimmer; **vislumbres** inkling, notion

viso m sheen, gleam; (de ciertas telas) luster; streak, strain; appearance, thin veneer; elevation, height; colored material worn under transparent outer garment; **a dos visos** with a double purpose; **de viso** conspicuous; **hacer visos** to be iridescent

visón m mink

visor m (aer) bombsight; (phot) finder

víspera f eve, day before; **en vísperas de** on the eve of; **víspera de año nuevo** New Year's Eve; **víspera de Navidad** Christmas Eve; **vísperas** (eccl) vespers, evensong

vista m custom-house inspector ‖ f (sentido del ver) vision, sight; (paisaje que se ve desde un punto; estampa que representa un lugar) view; (panorama, perspectiva) vista; comparison; purpose, design; (ojeada) glance, look; interview; eye; eyes; (law) hearing, trial; **a la vista** (com) at sight; **a vista de** in view of; compared with; **con vistas a** with a view to; **de vista** by sight; **doble vista** second sight; **hacer la vista gorda ante** to shut one's eyes to; **hasta la vista** good-bye, so long; **medir con la vista** to size up; **saltar a la vista** to be self-evident; **tener a la vista** to keep one's eyes on; (p.ej., una carta) to have at hand; **torcer la vista** to squint; **vista a ojo de pájaro** bird's-eye view; **vistas** (aberturas de un edificio) lights, openings; view, outlook; visible parts, parts that show

vistazo m look, glance

vistillas fpl eminence, height; **irse a las vistillas** to try to get a look at one's opponent's cards

vis•to -ta adj evident, obvious; in view of; **bien visto** looked upon with approval; **mal visto** looked upon with disapproval; **no visto** or **nunca visto** unheard-of; **por lo visto** apparently, judging from the facts; **visto bueno** approved, O.K.; **visto que** whereas, inasmuch as ‖ m whereas ‖ f see **vista**

visto•so -sa adj showy, flashy, loud

visual adj visual ‖ f line of sight

vital adj vital

vitali•cio -cia adj life. lifetime ‖ m life-insurance policy; life annuity

vitalidad f vitality

vitalizar §60 tr to vitalize

vitamina f vitamin

vitan•do -da adj hateful, odious; being shunned

vitela f vellum

viticul•tor -tora mf grape grower, vineyardist

viticultura f grape growing

vitola f cigar size; mien, appearance; (Cuba) cigar band

vítor interj hurray! ‖ m panegyric tablet; triumphal pageant

vitorear tr to cheer, acclaim

vitral m stained-glass window

vítre•o -a adj vitreous, glassy

vitrina f showcase, glass cabinet; shopwindow

vitrióli•co -ca adj (chem) vitriolic

vitrola f record player

vituallas fpl victuals

vituperable adj vituperable

vituperar tr to vituperate

viuda f widow; **viuda de marido vivo** or **viuda de paja** grass widow

viudedad f widowhood; dower; widow's pension

viudez *f* (*estado de viuda*) widowhood; (*estado de viudo*) widowerhood

viu·do -da *adj* left a widow; left a widower ‖ *m* widower ‖ *f* see **viuda**

viva *interj* viva!, long live! ‖ *m* viva

vivacidad *f* longevity; vivacity, liveliness; brightness, brilliance

vivande·ro -ra *mf* (mil) sutler, camp follower

vivaque *m* bivouac; guardhouse; police headquarters; **estar al vivaque** to bivouac

vivaquear *intr* to bivouac

vivar *m* warren, burrow; aquarium ‖ *tr* to cheer, acclaim

vivara·cho -cha *adj* vivacious, lively

vi·vaz *adj* (*pl* **-vaces**) long-lived; vivacious, lively; keen, perceptive; (bot) perennial

víveres *mpl* food, provisions, victuals

vivero *m* tree nursery; fishpond; (*origen de cosas perjudiciales*) (fig) hotbed

viveza *f* agility, briskness; ardor, vehemence; sharpness, keenness; perception; brightness, brilliance; witticism; (*de los ojos*) sparkle; (*acción o palabra poco consideradas*) thoughtlessness

vivide·ro -ra *adj* livable

vívi·do -da *adj* quick, perceptive; lively

vivienda *f* dwelling; life, way of life; **vivienda unifamiliar** one-family house

viviente *adj* living, alive

vivificar §73 *tr* to vivify, enliven

vivir *m* life, living ‖ *tr* (*una experiencia o ventura*) to live; (*toda la vida; la vejez*) live out; (*habitar*) live in ‖ *intr* to live; **¿quién vive?** (mil) who goes there?; **vivir de** (*p.ej., carne*) to live on; **vivir para ver** to live and learn; **vivir y dejar vivir** to live and let live

vivisección *f* vivisection

vi·vo -va *adj* living, alive, live; (*lleno de vida; intenso*) live; (*sutil, agudo*) sharp, keen; (*dolor*) acute; (*carne*) raw; active, effective; (*luz*) bright, intense; (*pronto y ágil*) quick; (*idioma*) living, modern; **de viva voz** viva voce, by word of mouth; **herir en lo vivo** to cut or to sting to the quick ‖ *mf* living person; **los vivos y los muertos** the quick and the dead ‖ *m* edging, border; (vet) mange

Vizcaya *f* Biscay; **llevar hierro a Vizcaya** to carry coals to Newcastle

vizconde *m* viscount

vizcondesa *f* viscountess

V.M. *abbr* **Vuestra Majestad**

V.°B.° *abbr* **visto bueno**

vocablista *mf* punster

vocablo *m* word; **jugar del vocablo** to pun

vocabulario *m* vocabulary

vocación *f* vocation, calling

vocal *adj* vocal ‖ *mf* director ‖ *f* vowel

vocalista *mf* singer, vocalist

vocativo *m* vocative

voceador *m* town crier; (Col, Ecuad) paper boy

vocear *tr* to cry, shout; cheer, acclaim; call, page; boast about publicly ‖ *intr* to shout

vocería *f* shouting, outcry; spokesmanship

vocerío *m* shouting, outcry

vocero *m* spokesman, mouthpiece

vociferar *tr* (*injurias*) to shout; boast loudly about ‖ *intr* to vociferate, shout

vocingle·ro -ra *adj* loudmouthed; loud, talkative

vo·dú *m* (*pl* **-dúes**) voodoo

voduísta *adj & mf* voodoo

vol. *abbr* **volumen, voluntad**

volada *f* short flight; (*del jugador de billar*) (Arg) stroke; (Col, Ecuad) trick; (*noticia inventada*) (Mex) hoax

voladi·zo -za *adj* projecting ‖ *m* projection

vola·do -da *adj* (typ) superior ‖ *f* see **volada**

vola·dor -dora *adj* flying; hanging, dangling; swift, fast ‖ *m* rocket; flying fish

voladura *f* blast, explosion

volandas — en volandas in the air; fast

volante *adj* flying; unsettled ‖ *m* shuttlecock; battledore and shuttlecock; (*rueda que regula el movimiento de una máquina*) flywheel; (*rueda de mano para la dirección del automóvil*) steering wheel; (*pieza del reloj movida por la espiral*) balance wheel; flunkey, lackey; (*criado que iba a pie delante del coche o caballo*) outrunner; (*de papel*) slip, leaflet; (sew) flounce, ruffle; **un buen volante** a good driver

volan·tín -tina *adj* unsettled ‖ *m* fish line; kite

volantista *m* driver, man at the wheel

volan·tón -tona *mf* fledgling ‖ *f* (Ven) loose woman

volapié *m* (taur) stroke in which the matador moves in for the kill; **a volapié** half running, half flying; half walking, half swimming

volar §61 *tr* (*llevar en un aparato de aviación*) to fly; blow up, explode; irritate; (*una letra, tipo o signo*) (typ) to raise ‖ *intr* to fly; fly away; disappear; jut out, project; (*una especie*) spread rapidly; (*p.ej., una torre*) rise in the air; **volar sin motor** (aer) to glide ‖ *ref* to fly away; fly off the handle

volatería *f* fowling with decoys; **de volatería** offhand

volátil *adj* volatile

volatilizar *tr & ref* to volatilize

volatín *m* ropewalker, acrobat, tumbler

volatine·ro -ra *mf* ropewalker, acrobat, tumbler

volcán *m* volcano

volcar §81 *tr* to upset, overturn, dump; tip, tilt; (*a una persona un olor fuerte*) to make dizzy; change the mind of; irritate, tease ‖ *intr* to upset ‖ *ref* to turn upside down

volear *tr* (tennis) to volley

voleo *m* (tennis) volley; reeling punch; **del primer voleo** or **de un voleo** with a smash, all at once; **sembrar al voleo** to sow, broadcast

volframio *m* wolfram

volíbol *m* volleyball

volquete *m* dumpcart, dump truck

voltai·co -ca *adj* voltaic

voltaje *m* voltage

volta·rio -ria *adj* fickle, inconstant; (Chile) willful; (Chile) sporty

vi
vo

voltea•do -da *mf* (Col) turncoat, deserter
voltear *tr* to upset, turn over; turn around; move, transform ‖ *intr* to roll over, tumble
volteo *m* upset, overturning; tumbling; (P-R) scolding
voltereta *f* tumble; turning up card to determine trump
voltímetro *m* voltmeter
voltio *m* volt
volti•zo -za *adj* curled, twisted; fickle
voluble *adj* easily turned; fickle, inconstant
volumen *m* volume; **volumen sonoro** volume; (geom) volume
volumino•so -sa *adj* voluminous
voluntad *f* will; (*amor, cariño*) fondness, love; **a voluntad** at will; **buena voluntad** willingness; **de buena voluntad** willingly; **de mala voluntad** unwillingly; **de su propia voluntad** of one's own volition; **última voluntad** last will and testament; last wish; **voluntad de hierro** iron will
voluntariedad *f* willfulness
volunta•rio -ra *adj* (*que se hace por espontánea voluntad*) voluntary; (*que tiene voluntad obstinada*) willful; (*que se presta voluntariamente a hacer algo*) volunteer ‖ *mfr* volunteer
voluntario•so -sa *adj* willful
voluptuo•so -sa *adj* (*que inspira complacencia en los placeres sensuales*) voluptuous; (*dado a los placeres sensuales*) voluptuary ‖ *mf* voluptuary
voluta *f* (archit) scroll, volute; (*p.ej., de humo*) ring
volvedor *m* screwdriver; (Col) extra, something thrown in; **volvedor de machos** tap wrench
volver §47 & §83 *tr* to turn; turn upside down; turn inside out; return, send back, give back; (*una puerta*) push to, pull to; translate; vomit ‖ *intr* to turn; return, come back; **volver a** + *inf* again, e.g., **volvió a abrir la puerta** he opened the door again; **volver en sí** to come to; **volver por** to defend, stand up for ‖ *ref* to become; turn around; return, come back; change one's mind; turn, turn sour; **volverse atrás** to back out; **volverse contra** to turn on
vomitar *tr* to vomit, throw up; (*fuego los cañones*) belch forth; (*maldiciones*) utter; (*un secreto*) let out; (*lo que uno retiene indebidamente*) cough up ‖ *intr* to vomit, throw up; come across, disgorge
vómito *m* vomit, vomiting; **provocar a vómito** to nauseate; **vómitos del embarazo** morning sickness
voracidad *f* voracity
vorágine *f* whirlpool, vortex
vo•raz *adj* (*pl* **-races**) voracious
vormela *f* polecat
vórtice *m* vortex
vos *pron pers* (subject of verb and object of preposition; takes plural form of verb but is singular in meaning; used in addressing the Deity, the Virgin, etc., and distinguished

persons; in Spanish America is much used instead of **tú**) you
voso•tros -tras *pron pers* (plural of **tú**) you
votación *f* vote, voting; **votación de desempate** runoff election
votante *adj* voting ‖ *mf* voter
votar *tr* to vote for; (*sí, no*) vote; (*p.ej., un cirio a la Virgen*) vow ‖ *intr* to vote; vow; swear, curse
voti•vo -va *adj* votive
voto *m* (*sufragio; derecho de votar; persona que da su voto*) vote; (*promesa solemne*) vow; (*exvoto*) votive offering; (*blasfemia*) oath, curse; wish, desire; **echar votos** to swear, to curse; **regular los votos** to tally the votes; **voto de amén** vote of a yes man; yes man; **voto de calidad** casting vote; **voto informativo** straw vote; **votos** good wishes; **¡voto va!** come now!
voz *f* (*pl* **voces**) voice; (*vocablo*) word; **aclarar la voz** to clear one's throat; **a una voz** with one voice; **a voces** shouting; **a voz en cuello** or **en grito** at the top of one's voice; **correr la voz que** to be rumored that; **dar voces** to shout, cry out; **de viva voz** viva voce, by word of mouth; **en alta voz** aloud, in a loud voice; **en voz baja** in a low voice; **llevar la voz cantante** to have the say, be the boss; **voces** outcry
voz-guía *f* (*diccionario*) entry word
vro. *abbr* **vuestro**
V.S. *abbr* **Vueseñoría**
vuelco *m* upset, overturn; **darle a uno un vuelco el corazón** to have a presentiment
vuelo *m* flight; flying; (*de una falda*) flare, fullness; projection; lace cuff trimming; **al vuelo** at once; on the wing; scattered at random; (chess) en passant; **alzar el vuelo** to take flight; to dash away; **echar a vuelo las campanas** to ring a full peal; **tirar al vuelo** to shoot on the wing; **tocar a vuelo las campanas** to ring a full peal; **vuelo a ciegas** (aer) blind flying; **vuelo de distancia** (aer) long-distance flight; **vuelo de enlace** connecting flight; **vuelo de ensayo** or **de prueba** (aer) test flight; **vuelo espacial tripulado** manned space flight; **vuelo planeado** (aer) volplane; **vuelo rasante** (aer) hedgehopping; **vuelo sin escala** (aer) nonstop flight; **vuelo sin motor** (aer) glide, gliding
vuelta *f* turn; (*regreso; devolución*) return; (*dinero sobrante de un pago*) change; (*de un camino*) bend, turn; (*del pantalón*) cuff; cuff trimming; (*paseo corto*) stroll; (*revés*) other side; (*paliza*) beating, whipping; (*en un cabo*) loop; (*en la media*) clock; (*mudanza*) change; **a la vuelta** on returning; please turn the page; **a la vuelta de** at the end of; at the turn of; (*la esquina*) around; **a vuelta de** about; **a vuelta de correo** by return mail; **dar cien vueltas a** to run rings around, be way ahead of; **dar la vuelta de campana** to turn somersault; **darse una vuelta a la redonda** to tend to one's own business; **dar una vuelta** to take a stroll, take a walk; take a look; change one's

ways; **dar vuelta** to turn around; (*el vino*) turn sour; **dar vuelta a** to reverse, turn around; **estar de vuelta** to be back; **quedarse con la vuelta** to keep the change; **vuelta de campana** somersault; **vuelta del mundo** trip around the world

vuelto *m* change

vues•tro -tra (corresponds to **vos** and **vosotros**) *adj poss* your ‖ *pron poss* yours

vulcanizar §60 *tr* to vulcanize

vulgacho *m* populace, mob

vulgar *adj* vulgar, popular, common, vernacular

vulgarismo *m* popular expression; (philol) popular word, popular form

vulgarizar §60 *tr* to popularize; translate into the vernacular ‖ *ref* to associate with the people

Vulgata *f* Vulgate

vulgo *adv* commonly ‖ *m* common people; (*personas que en una materia sólo conocen la parte superficial*) laity

vulnerable *adj* vulnerable

vulnerar *tr* to hurt, injure; (*la reputación de una persona*) damage; (*una ley, un precepto*) break

vulpeja *f* she-fox, vixen

V.V. or **VV** *abbr* **ustedes**

X

X, x (equis) *f* twenty-sixth letter of the Spanish alphabet

xenia *f* xenia

xenofobia *f* xenophobia

xenófo•bo -ba *mf* xenophobe

xenón *m* xenon

xerografía *f* xerography

xerografiar §77 *tr* to xerograph ‖ *intr* to make xerograph copies

xilófono *m* (mus) xylophone

xilografía *f* (*arte*) xylography; (*grabado*) xylograph

xpiano *abbr* **cristiano**

Xpo *abbr* **Cristo**

xptiano *abbr* **cristiano**

Xpto *abbr* **Cristo**

xunde *m* (Mex) reed basket, palm basket

Y

Y, y (ye) *f* twenty-seventh letter of the Spanish alphabet

y *conj* and

ya *adv* already; right away; now; **no ya** not only; **ya no** no longer; **ya que** since, inasmuch as

yac *m* (*bandera de proa*) (naut) jack; (*bóvido del Tíbet*) yak

yacer §82 *intr* to lie

yacija *f* bed, couch; (*sepultura*) grave

yacimiento *m* bed, field, deposit; **yacimiento de petróleo** oil field

yámbi•co -ca *adj* iambic

yambo *m* iamb, iambus

yanqui *adj & mf* Yankee

Yanquilandia *f* Yankeedom

yapa *f* bonus, extra, allowance; **de yapa** in the bargain, extra

yarda *f* yard, yardstick

yate *m* yacht

yedra *f* ivy

yegua *f* mare; (CAm) cigar butt

yeguada *f* stud

yelmo *m* helmet

yema *f* (*de huevo*) yolk; candied yolk; (*del invierno*) dead; (*renuevo*) bud; (fig) cream; **dar en la yema** to put one's finger on the

spot; **yema del dedo** finger tip; **yema mejida** eggnog

yente — yentes y vinientes *mpl* habitués, frequenters

yerba *f* var of **hierba**

yer•mo -ma *adj* deserted, uninhabited; (*suelo*) unsown; (*mujer*) not pregnant ‖ *m* desert, wilderness

yerno *m* son-in-law

yerro *m* error, mistake; **yerro de cuenta** miscalculation; **yerro de imprenta** printer's error

yer•to -ta *adj* stiff, rigid

yesca *f* punk, tinder; (*cosa que excita una pasión*) fuel; **echar una yesca** to strike a light

yeso *m* gypsum; plaster cast

yo *pron pers* I; **soy yo** it's me, it is I

yodhídri•co -ca *adj* hydriodic

yodo *m* iodine

yoduro *m* iodide

yoga *f* yoga

yogui *m* yogi

yogurt *m* yogurt

yola *f* shell (*boat*)

yonquí *m* (*drogas*) junkie, drug addict

yugo *m* yoke; **sacudir el yugo** to throw off the yoke

vo
yu

Yugoeslavia f Yugoslavia
yugoesla•vo -va adj & mf Yugoslav
yugular adj & f jugular ‖ tr to cut off, nip in the bud
yunque m anvil; drudge, work horse

yunta f yoke, team
yute m jute
yuxtaponer §54 tr to juxtapose
yuyo m (Arg, Chile) weed; **yuyos** (Col, Ecuad, Peru) greens

Z

Z, z (zeda or zeta) f twenty-eighth letter of the Spanish alphabet
zabordar intr (naut) to run aground
zabullir §13 tr (p.ej., a un perro) to duck, give a ducking to; throw, hurl ‖ ref (meterse debajo del agua con ímpetu) to dive; (esconderse rápidamente) duck
zacapela f or **zacapella** f row, rumpus
zacate m (CAm, Mex) hay, fodder; **zacate de empaque** excelsior
zacateca m (Cuba) undertaker, gravedigger
zacatín m old-clothes market
zacear tr (al perro) to chase away ‖ intr to lisp
zafaduría f (Arg) brazenness, effrontery
zafar tr to adorn, bedeck; loosen, untie; clear, free; (un buque) lighten ‖ ref to slip away; slip off, come off; **zafarse de** to get out of
zafarrancho m (naut) clearing the decks; (coll) havoc, ravage; (coll) scuffle, row; **zafarrancho de combate** (naut) clearing the deck for action
za•fio -fia adj rough, uncouth, boorish
zafiro m sapphire
za•fo -fa adj unhurt, intact; (naut) free, clear ‖ **zafo** prep (Col) except
zafra f olive-oil can; drip jar; sugar crop; sugar making; sugar-making season; (min) rubbish, muck
zaga f rear; load carried in the rear; (mil) rearguard; **a la zaga, a zaga** or **en zaga** behind, in the rear; **no ir en zaga a** to not be behind, be as good as
zagal m young fellow; strapping young fellow; shepherd boy; footboy
zagala f lass, maiden; young shepherdess
zaguán m vestibule, hall, entry
zague•ro -ra adj back, rear ‖ m (sport) back, backstop
zaherir §68 tr to upbraid, reproach; scold shamefully
zahones mpl chaps, hunting breeches
zaho•rí m (pl -ríes) keen observer; seer, clairvoyant
zahurda f pigpen
zai•no -na adj treacherous, false; (caballo) vicious; (caballo) dark-chestnut; **mirar a lo zaino** or **de zaino** to look askance at
za•lá f (pl -laes) Muslim prayer; **hacer la zalá a** to fawn on

zalagarda f ambush; skirmish; (trampa para cazar animales) trap; trick; row, rumpus; mock fight
zalamería f flattery, cajolery
zalame•ro -ra adj flattering, fawning ‖ mf flatterer, fawner
zalea f unsheared sheepskin
zalear tr to drag around, shake; (al perro) chase away
zalema f salaam
zamacuco m blockhead; sullen fellow; drunkenness
zamacueca f cueca (Chilean courtship dance)
zamarra f undressed sheepskin; sheepskin jacket
zam•bo -ba adj knock-kneed
zambra f merrymaking, celebration; Moorish boat
zambucar §73 tr to slip away, hide away
zambullida f dive, plunge; (fencing) thrust to the breast
zambulli•dor -dora adj diving, plunging ‖ mf diver, plunger ‖ m (orn) diver, loon
zambullir §13 tr (p.ej., a un perro) to duck, give a ducking to; throw, hurl ‖ ref (meterse debajo del agua con ímpetu) to dive; (esconderse rápidamente) duck
zampa f pile, bearing pile
zampacuarti•llos mf (pl -llos) toper, soak
zampalimos•nas mf (pl -nas) bum, ordinary bum
zampar tr to slip away, hide away; gobble down ‖ ref to slip away, hide away
zampator•tas mf (pl -tas) glutton; boor
zampear tr (el terreno) to strengthen with piles and rubble
zampoña f shepherd's pipe, rustic flute; nonsense, folly
zampuzar §60 tr to duck, give a ducking to; slip away, hide away
zanahoria f carrot
zanca f long leg; (de la escalera) horse
zancada f long stride; **en dos zancadas** in a flash, in a jiffy
zancadilla f booby trap; **echar la zancadilla a** to stick out one's foot and trip
zancajo m heel; **no llegar a los zancajos a** to not come up to, not be equal to
zancajo•so -sa adj duck-toed; down-at-the-heel
zancarrón m dirty old fellow
zanco m stilt; **en zancos** from a vantage point

zancu•do -da *adj* long-legged; (orn) wading ‖ *m* mosquito ‖ *f* wading bird

zanfonía *f* hurdy-gurdy

zangala *f* buckram

zangamanga *f* trick

zanganada *f* impertinence, impudence

zanganear *intr* to loaf around

zángano *m* (ent) drone; (fig) drone, loafer; (CAm) scoundrel

zangarrear *intr* to thrum a guitar

zangolotear *tr* to jiggle ‖ *intr* to fuss around ‖ *ref* to jiggle, flop around, rattle

zangoloteo *m* jiggle, jiggling, rattle; fuss, bother

zanguanga *f* malingering; flattery; **hacer la zanguanga** to malinger

zanguan•go -ga *adj* slow, lazy ‖ *mf* loafer ‖ *f* see **zanguanga**

zanja *f* ditch, trench; (SAm) gully; **abrir las zanjas** to lay the foundations

zanquear *intr* to waddle; to rush around

zanquilar•go -ga *adj* leggy, long-legged

zanquituer•to -ta *adj* bandy-legged

zapa *f* spade; sharkskin, (mil) sap

zapapico *m* mattock, pickax

zapar *tr* (mil) to sap, mine, excavate

zaparrastrar *intr* — **ir zaparrastrando** to go along trailing one's clothes on the ground

zapateado *m* clog dance, tap dance

zapatear *tr* to hit with the shoe; tap with the feet; abuse, ill-treat ‖ *intr* to tap-dance; (*las velas*) flap ‖ *ref* — **zapatearse con** to hold out against

zapatería *f* shoemaking; shoemaker's shop; (*tienda*) shoe store

zapate•ro -ra *adj* poorly cooked ‖ *mf* shoemaker; shoe dealer; **quedarse zapatero** to not take a trick; **¡zapatero, a tus zapatos!** stick to your last!; **zapatero de viejo** or **zapatero remendón** cobbler, shoemaker

zapatilla *f* slipper; (*escarpín*) pump; (*del grifo*) washer; (*del florete*) leather tip or button; cloven hoof

zapato *m* shoe, low shoe; **andar con zapatos de fieltro** to gumshoe; **como tres en un zapato** hard up; like sardines; **zapato de goma** overshoe; **zapato inglés** low shoe

zapatón *m* (Guat, SAm) overshoe

zapear *tr* (*al gato*) to scare away, chase away

zaque *m* wineskin; tippler, drunk

zaquiza•mí *m* (*pl* -míes) attic, garret; hovel, pigpen

zar *m* czar

zarabanda *f* (mus) saraband; noise, confusion, uproar; (Mex) beating, thrashing

zaragata *f* scuffle, row; **zaragatas** (W-I) flattery

Zaragoza *f* Saragossa

zaranda *f* sieve, screen; colander; (Ven) horn; (Ven) top

zarandajas *fpl* odds and ends, trinkets

zarandar *tr* to sift, screen; winnow, pick out, select; jiggle ‖ *ref* to jiggle; swagger, strut

zaraza *f* chintz, printed cotton

zarcillo *m* eardrop; (bot) tendril

zarigüeya *f* opossum

zarina *f* czarina

zarpa *f* claw, paw; (naut) weighing anchor

zarpar *tr* (*el ancla*) (naut) to weigh (*anchor*) ‖ *intr* (naut) to weigh anchor, set sail

zarpo•so -sa *adj* mud-splashed

zarracatería *f* cajolery, insincere flattery

zarracatín *m* sharp trader

zarramplín *m* botcher, bungler

zarrien•to -ta *adj* mud-splashed

zarza *f* blackberry, bramble (*bush*)

zarzamora *f* blackberry (*fruit*)

zarzaparrilla *f* sarsaparilla

zarzo *m* hurdle, wattle

zarzo•so -sa *adj* brambly

zarzuela *f* small bramble; (theat) zarzuela (*Spanish musical comedy*); **zarzuela grande** three-act zarzuela

zas *interj* bang!; **¡zas, zas!** bing, bang!

zascandilear *intr* to meddle, scheme

zepelín *m* zeppelin

Zeus *m* Zeus

zigzag *m* zigzag

zigzaguear *intr* to zigzag

zinc *m* (*pl* zinces) zinc

zipizape *m* scuffle, row, rumpus

ziszás *m* zigzag

zoca *f* public square

zócalo *m* (archit) socle; (*de una pared*) dado; (rad) socket; (Mex) public square, center square

zoca•to -ta *adj* (*fruto*) corky, pithy; left; left-handed ‖ *mf* left-handed person

zoclo *m* clog, wooden shoe

zo•co -ca *adj* left; left-handed ‖ *mf* left-handed person ‖ *m* clog, wooden shoe; Moroccan market place; (archit) socle; **andar de zocos en colodros** to jump from the frying pan into the fire ‖ *f* see **zoca**

zodíaco *m* zodiac

zofra *f* Moorish carpet, Moorish rug

zolo•cho -cha *adj* stupid, simple ‖ *mf* simpleton

zollipar *intr* to sob

zollipo *m* sob

zona *m* (pathol) shingles ‖ *f* zone; (*banda, faja*) belt, girdle; **zona a batir** target area; **zona desmilitarizada** demilitarized zone; **zona siniestrada** disaster area

zon•zo -za *adj* tasteless, insipid; dull, inane ‖ *mf* dolt, dimwit

zoófito *m* zoöphyte

zoología *f* zoölogy

zoológi•co -ca *adj* zoölogic(al)

zoólo•go -ga *mf* zoölogist

zopen•co -ca *adj* dull, stupid ‖ *mf* dullard, blockhead

zopilote *m* (Mex, CAm) turkey buzzard, turkey vulture

zo•po -pa *adj* crippled; awkward, gauche ‖ *mf* cripple

zoquete *m* (*de madera*) block, chunk, end; (*de pan*) bit, crust; chump, lout

zoquetu•do -da *adj* coarse, crude

zorra *f* fox; female fox; cunning person; prostitute; drunkenness; dray, truck; **pillar una zorra** to get drunk

zorrera *f* (*cueva de zorros*) foxhole; smoke-filled room; worry, confusion

zorrería *f* foxiness, craftiness

zorre•ro -ra *adj* sly, foxy; slow, heavy, tardy ‖ *f* see **zorrera**

zorrillo *m* skunk

zorro *m* male fox; (*piel*) fox; (*hombre taimado*) fox; **estar hecho un zorro** to be overwhelmed with sleep; be dull and sullen; **zorros** duster

zorral *m* (orn) fieldfare; sly fellow; (Chile) simpleton

zozobra *f* capsizing, sinking; anxiety

zozobrar *tr* (*un buque*) to sink; (*un negocio*) wreck ‖ *intr* to capsize, sink; (*la embarcación en la tempestad*) wallow; (*un negocio*) be in great danger; be greatly worried ‖ *ref* to capsize, sink

zueco *m* clog, wooden shoe, sabot

zulacar §73 *tr* to waterproof

zulaque *m* waterproofing

zulú *adj & mf* (*pl* **-lús** o **-lúes**) Zulu

zullar *ref* to have a bowel movement; break wind

zullen•co -ca *adj* windy, flatulent

zumaque *m* sumach; wine

zumaya *f* (*autillo*) tawny owl; (*chotacabras*) goatsucker

zumba *f* bell worn by leading mule; (Mex) drunkenness; **hacer zumba a** to make fun of; **sin zumba** (Mex) in a rush, in a hurry

zumbador *m* buzzer; (Mex) pauraque; (Mex, CAm, W-I) hummingbird

zumbar *tr* to make fun of; (*un golpe, una bofetada*) let have ‖ *intr* to buzz; zoom; (*los oídos*) ring; **zumbar a** (*frisar con*) to be close to, border on ‖ *ref* (Cuba) to go too far, forget oneself; (P-R) to rush ahead; **zumbarse de** to make fun of

zumbido *m* buzz; zoom; blow, smack; **zumbido de ocupación** (telp) busy signal; **zumbido de oídos** ringing in the ears

zum•bón -bona *adj* waggish, playful ‖ *mf* wag, jester

zumien•to -ta *adj* juicy

zumo *m* juice; advantage, profit; **zumo de cepas** or **de parras** fruit of the vine

zumo•so -sa *adj* juicy

zunchar *tr* to band, hoop

zuncho *m* band, hoop

zupia *f* (*del vino*) dregs; slop, wine full of dregs; (fig) junk, trash

zurcido *m* darning; darn; invisible mending

zurcir §36 *tr* to darn; (*una mentira*) hatch, concoct; (*unas mentiras*) weave (*a tissue of lies*)

zurdazo *m* (box) left, blow with the left

zur•do -da *adj* left; left-handed; **a zurdas** with the left hand; the wrong way ‖ *mf* left-handed person

zurear *intr* to coo

zuro *m* stripped corncob

zurra *f* dressing, currying; scuffle, quarrel; drubbing, thrashing; (*trabajo o estudio continuados*) grind

zurrapa *f* thread, filament; trash, rubbish; **con zurrapas** in a sloppy manner

zurrar *tr* (*el cuero*) to dress, curry; get the best of; (*censurar con dureza*) dress down; (*castigar con azotes*) drub, thrash ‖ *ref* (*hacer sus necesidades involuntariamente*) to have an accident; be scared to death; (Arg) to break wind noiselessly

zurriagar §44 *tr* to whip, horsewhip

zurriago *m* whip, lash

zurribanda *f* rain of blows; rumpus, scuffle

zurrir *intr* to buzz, grate

zurrón *m* shepherd's leather bag; leather bag; (*cáscara*) husk

zurrona *f* loose, evil woman

zurullo *m* soft roll; turd

zurupeto *m* unregistered broker; shyster notary

zuta•no -na *mf* so-and-so

Spanish Irregular Verbs

All simple tenses are shown in these tables if they contain one irregular form or more, except the conditional (which can always be derived from the stem of the future indicative) and the imperfect and future subjunctive (which can always be derived from the third plural preterit indicative minus the last syllable -ron).

The numbers are those that accompany the respective verbs and verbs of identical patterns where they are listed in their alphabetical places in this Dictionary. The letters (a) to (h) identify the tenses as follows:

(a)	gerund	(e)	present subjunctive
(b)	past participle	(f)	imperfect indicative
(c)	imperative	(g)	future indicative
(d)	present indicative	(h)	preterit indicative

§1 **abolir:** defective verb used only in forms whose endings contain the vowel **i**

§2 **acertar**
(c) **acierta,** acertad
(d) **acierto, aciertas, acierta,** acertamos. acertáis, **aciertan**
(e) **acierte, aciertes, acierte,** acertemos, acertéis, **acierten**

§3 **agorar:** like §61 but with diaeresis on the **u** of **ue**
(c) **agüera,** agorad
(d) **agüero, agüeras, agüera,** agoramos, agoráis, **agüeran**
(e) **agüere, agüeres, agüere,** agoremos. agoréis, **agüeren**

§4 **airar**
(c) **aíra,** airad
(d) **aíro, aíras, aíra,** airamos, airáis, **aíran**
(e) **aíre, aíres, aíre,** airemos, airéis, **aíren**

§5 **andar**
(h) **anduve, anduviste, anduvo, anduvimos, anduvisteis, anduvieron**

§6 **argüir:** like §20 but with diaeresis on **u** in forms with accented **i** in the ending
(a) **arguyendo**
(b) **argüído**
(c) **arguye,** argüid
(d) **arguyo, arguyes, arguye,** argüimos, argüís, **arguyen**
(e) **arguya, arguyas, arguya, arguyamos, arguyáis, arguyan**
(h) **argüí, argüiste, arguyó,** argüimos, argüisteis, **arguyeron**

§7 **asir**
(d) **asgo,** ases, ase. asimos, asís, asen
(e) **asga, asgas, asga, asgamos, asgáis, asgan**

§8 **aunar**
(c) **aúna,** aunad
(d) **aúno, aúnas, aúna,** aunamos. aunáis, **aúnan**
(e) **aúne, aúnes, aúne,** aunemos. aunéis, **aúnen**

§9 **avergonzar:** combination of §3 and §60
(c) **avergüenza,** avergonzad
(d) **avergüenzo, avergüenzas, avergüenza,** avergonzamos. avergonzáis, **avergüenzan**
(e) **avergüence, avergüences, avergüence, avergoncemos, avergoncéis, avergüencen**
(h) **avergoncé,** avergonzaste, avergonzó, avergonzamos, avergonzasteis, avergonzaron

§10 **averiguar**
(e) **averigüe, averigües, averigüe, averigüemos, averigüéis, averigüen**
(h) **averigüé,** averiguaste, averiguó. averiguamos, averiguasteis, averiguaron

§11 **bendecir**
    (a) **bendiciendo**
    (c) **bendice,** bendecid
    (d) **bendigo, bendices, bendice,** bendecimos, bendecís, **bendicen**
    (e) **bendiga, bendigas, bendiga, bendigamos, bendigáis, bendigan**
    (h) **bendije, bendijiste, bendijo, bendijimos, bendijisteis, bendijeron**

§12 **bruñir**
    (a) **bruñendo**
    (h) **bruñí, bruñiste, bruñó,** bruñimos, bruñisteis, **bruñeron**

§13 **bullir**
    (a) **bullendo**
    (h) **bullí, bulliste, bulló,** bullimos, bullisteis, **bulleron**

§14 **caber**
    (d) **quepo,** cabes, cabe, cabemos, cabéis, caben
    (e) **quepa, quepas, quepa, quepamos, quepáis, quepan**
    (g) **cabré, cabrás, cabrá, cabremos, cabréis, cabrán**
    (h) **cupe, cupiste, cupo, cupimos, cupisteis, cupieron**

§15 **caer**
    (a) **cayendo**
    (b) **caído**
    (d) **caigo,** caes, cae, caemos, caéis, caen
    (e) **caiga, caigas, caiga, caigamos, caigáis, caigan**
    (h) caí, **caíste, cayó, caímos, caísteis, cayeron**

§16 **cocer:** combination of §47 and §78
    (c) **cuece,** coced
    (d) **cuezo, cueces, cuece,** cocemos, cocéis, **cuecen**
    (e) **cueza, cuezas, cueza,** cozamos, cozáis, **cuezan**

§17 **coger**
    (d) **cojo,** coges, coge, cogemos, cogéis, cogen
    (e) **coja, cojas, coja, cojamos, cojáis, cojan**

§18 **comenzar:** combination of §2 and §60
    (c) **comienza,** comenzad
    (d) **comienzo, comienzas, comienza,** comenzamos, comenzáis, **comienzan**
    (e) **comience, comiences, comience, comencemos, comencéis, comiencen**
    (h) **comencé,** comenzaste, comenzó, comenzamos, comenzasteis, comenzaron

§19 **conducir**
    (d) **conduzco,** conduces, conduce, conducimos, conducís, conducen
    (e) **conduzca, conduzcas, conduzca, conduzcamos, conduzcáis, conduzcan**
    (h) **conduje, condujiste, condujo, condujimos, condujisteis, condujeron**

§20 **construir**
    (a) **construyendo**
    (b) **construído**
    (c) **construye,** construid
    (d) **construyo, construyes, construye,** construimos, construís, **construyen**
    (e) **construya, construyas, construya, construyamos, construyáis, construyan**
    (h) construí, construiste, **construyó,** construimos, construisteis, **construyeron**

§21 **continuar**
    (c) **continúa,** continuad
    (d) **continúo, continúas, continúa,** continuamos, continuáis, **continúan**
    (e) **continúe, continúes, continúe,** continuemos, continuéis, **continúen**

§22 **crecer**
    (d) **crezco,** creces, crece, crecemos, crecéis, crecen
    (e) **crezca, crezcas, crezca, crezcamos, crezcáis, crezcan**

§23 dar
    (d) **doy, das, da, damos, dais, dan**
    (e) **dé,** des, **dé,** demos, deis, den
    (h) **dí, diste, dio, dimos, disteis, dieron**

§24 decir
    (a) **diciendo**
    (b) **dicho**
    (c) **di,** decid
    (d) **digo, dices, dice,** decimos, decís, **dicen**
    (e) **diga, digas, diga, digamos, digáis, digan**
    (g) **diré, dirás, dirá, diremos, diréis, dirán**
    (h) **dije, dijiste, dijo, dijimos, dijisteis, dijeron**

§25 delinquir
    (d) **delinco,** delinques, delinque, delinquimos, delinquís, delinquen
    (e) **delinca, delincas, delinca, delincamos, delincáis, delincan**

§26 desosar: like §61 but with **h** before **ue**
    (c) **deshuesa,** desosad
    (d) **deshueso, deshuesas, deshuesa,** desosamos, desosáis, **deshuesan**
    (e) **deshuese, deshueses, deshuese,** desosemos, desoséis, **deshuesen**

§27 dirigir
    (d) **dirijo,** diriges, dirige, dirigimos, dirigís, dirigen
    (e) **dirija, dirijas, dirija, dirijamos, dirijáis, dirijan**

§28 discernir
    (c) **discierne,** discernid
    (d) **discierno, disciernes, discierne,** discernimos, discernís, **disciernen**
    (e) **discierna, disciernas, discierna,** discernamos, discernáis, **disciernan**

§29 distinguir
    (d) **distingo,** distingues, distingue, distinguimos, distinguís, distinguen
    (e) **distinga, distingas, distinga, distingamos, distingáis, distingan**

§30 dormir
    (a) **durmiendo**
    (c) **duerme,** dormid
    (d) **duermo, duermes, duerme,** dormimos, dormís, **duermen**
    (e) **duerma, duermas, duerma, durmamos, durmáis, duerman**
    (h) dormí, dormiste, **durmió,** dormimos, dormisteis, **durmieron**

§31 empeller
    (a) **empellendo**
    (h) empellí, empelliste, **empelló,** empellimos, empellisteis, **empelleron**

§32 enraizar: combination of §4 and §60
    (c) **enraíza,** enraizad
    (d) **enraízo, enraízas, enraíza,** enraizamos, enraizáis, **enraízan**
    (e) **enraíce, enraíces, enraíce, enraicemos, enraicéis, enraícen**
    (h) **enraicé,** enraizaste, enraizó, enraizamos, enraizasteis, enraizaron

§33 erguir: combination of §29 and §50 or §68
    (a) **irguiendo**
    (c) **irgue** or **yergue,** erguid
    (d) **irgo, irgues, irgue,** } erguimos, erguís, { **irguen**
        yergo, yergues, yergue, }   { **yerguen**
    (e) **irga, irgas, irga,** } irgamos, irgáis, { **irgan**
        yerga, yergas, yerga, }   { **yergan**
    (h) erguí, erguiste, **irguió,** erguimos, erguisteis, **irguieron**

§34 errar: like §2 but with initial **ye** for **ie**
    (c) **yerra,** errad
    (d) **yerro, yerras, yerra,** erramos, erráis, **yerran**
    (e) **yerre, yerres, yerre,** erremos, erréis, **yerren**

§35 esforzar: combination of §60 and §61
- (c) **esfuerza,** esforzad
- (d) **esfuerzo, esfuerzas, esfuerza,** esforzamos, esforzáis, **esfuerzan**
- (e) **esfuerce, esfuerces, esfuerce, esforcemos, esforcéis, esfuercen**
- (h) **esforcé,** esforzaste, esforzó, esforzamos, esforzasteis, esforzaron

§36 esparcir
- (d) **esparzo,** esparces, esparce, esparcimos, esparcís, esparcen
- (e) **esparza, esparzas, esparza, esparzamos, esparzáis, esparzan**

§37 estar
- (c) **está,** estad
- (d) **estoy, estás, está,** estamos, estáis, **están**
- (e) **esté, estés, esté,** estemos, estéis, **estén**
- (h) **estuve, estuviste, estuvo, estuvimos, estuvisteis, estuvieron**

§38 haber
- (c) **hé,** habed
- (d) **he, has, ha, hemos,** habéis, **han** (*v impers*) **hay**
- (e) **haya, hayas, haya, hayamos, hayáis, hayan**
- (g) **habré, habrás, habrá, habremos, habréis, habrán**
- (h) **hube, hubiste, hubo, hubimos, hubisteis, hubieron**

§39 hacer
- (b) **hecho**
- (c) **haz,** haced
- (d) **hago,** haces, hace, hacemos, hacéis, hacen
- (e) **haga, hagas, haga, hagamos, hagáis, hagan**
- (g) **haré, harás, hará, haremos, haréis, harán**
- (h) **hice, hiciste, hizo, hicimos, hicisteis, hicieron**

§40 inquirir
- (c) **inquiere,** inquirid
- (d) **inquiero, inquieres, inquiere,** inquirimos, inquirís, **inquieren**
- (e) **inquiera, inquieras, inquiera,** inquiramos, inquiráis, **inquieran**

§41 ir
- (a) **yendo**
- (c) **vé, vamos,** id
- (d) **voy, vas, va, vamos, vais, van**
- (e) **vaya, vayas, vaya, vayamos, vayáis, vayan**
- (f) **iba, ibas, iba, íbamos, ibais, iban**
- (h) **fui, fuiste, fue, fuimos, fuisteis, fueron**

§42 jugar: like §63 but with radical **u**
- (c) **juega,** jugad
- (d) **juego, juegas, juega,** jugamos, jugáis, **juegan**
- (e) **juegue, juegues, juegue, juguemos, juguéis, jueguen**
- (h) **jugué,** jugaste, jugó, jugamos, jugasteis, jugaron

§43 leer
- (a) **leyendo**
- (b) **leído**
- (h) **leí, leíste, leyó, leímos, leísteis, leyeron**

§44 ligar
- (e) **ligue, ligues, ligue, liguemos, liguéis, liguen**
- (h) **ligué,** ligaste, ligó, ligamos, ligasteis, ligaron

§45 lucir
- (d) **luzco,** luces, luce, lucimos, lucís, lucen
- (e) **luzca, luzcas, luzca, luzcamos, luzcáis, luzcan**

§46 mecer
- (d) **mezo,** meces, mece, mecemos, mecéis, mecen
- (e) **meza, mezas, meza, mezamos, mezáis, mezan**

346

§47 mover
(c) **mueve,** moved
(d) **muevo, mueves, mueve,** movemos, movéis, **mueven**
(e) **mueva, muevas, mueva,** movamos, mováis, **muevan**

§48 oír
(a) **oyendo**
(b) **oído**
(c) **oye, oíd**
(d) **oigo, oyes, oye, oímos,** oís, **oyen**
(e) **oiga, oigas, oiga, oigamos, oigáis, oigan**
(h) oí, **oíste, oyó, oímos, oísteis, oyeron**

§49 oler: like §47 but with **h** before **ue**
(c) **huele,** oled
(d) **huelo, hueles, huele,** olemos, oléis, **huelen**
(e) **huela, huelas, huela,** olamos, oláis, **huelan**

§50 pedir
(a) **pidiendo**
(c) **pide,** pedid
(d) **pido, pides, pide,** pedimos, pedís, **piden**
(e) **pida, pidas, pida, pidamos, pidáis, pidan**
(h) pedí, pediste, **pidió,** pedimos, pedisteis, **pidieron**

§51 perder
(c) **pierde,** perded
(d) **pierdo, pierdes, pierde,** perdemos, perdéis, **pierden**
(e) **pierda, pierdas, pierda,** perdamos, perdáis, **pierdan**

§52 placer
(d) **plazco,** places, place, placemos, placéis, placen
(e) **plazca, plazcas, plazca, plazcamos, plazcáis, plazcan**
(h) plací, placiste, plació (or **plugo),** placimos, placisteis, placieron

§53 poder
(a) **pudiendo**
(c) **(puede,** poded)
(d) **puedo, puedes, puede,** podemos, podéis, **pueden**
(e) **pueda, puedas, pueda,** podamos, podáis, **puedan**
(g) **podré, podrás, podrá, podremos, podréis, podrán**
(h) **pude, pudiste, pudo, pudimos, pudisteis, pudieron**

§54 poner
(b) **puesto**
(c) **pon,** poned
(d) **pongo,** pones, pone, ponemos, ponéis, ponen
(e) **ponga, pongas, ponga, pongamos, pongáis, pongan**
(g) **pondré, pondrás, pondrá, pondremos, pondréis, pondrán**
(h) **puse, pusiste, puso, pusimos, pusisteis, pusieron**

§55 querer
(c) **quiere,** quered
(d) **quiero, quieres, quiere,** queremos, queréis, **quieren**
(e) **quiera, quieras, quiera,** queramos, queráis, **quieran**
(g) **querré, querrás, querrá, querremos, querréis, querrán**
(h) **quise, quisiste, quiso, quisimos, quisisteis, quisieron**

§56 raer
(a) **rayendo**
(b) **raído**
(d) **raigo** (or **rayo),** raes, rae, raemos, raéis, raen
(e) **raiga** (or **raya), raigas, raiga, raigamos, raigáis, raigan**
(h) **raí, raíste, rayó, raímos, raísteis, rayeron**

§57 **regir:** combination of §27 and §50
  (a) **rigiendo**
  (c) **rige,** regid
  (d) **rijo, riges, rige,** regimos, regís, **rigen**
  (e) **rija, rijas, rija, rijamos, rijáis, rijan**
  (h) regí, registe, **rigió,** regimos, registeis, **rigieron**

§58 **reír**
  (a) **riendo**
  (b) **reído**
  (c) **ríe, reíd**
  (d) **río, ríes, ríe, reímos,** reís, **ríen**
  (e) **ría, rías, ría, riamos, riáis, rían**
  (h) reí, **reíste, rió, reímos, reísteis, rieron**

§59 **reunir**
  (c) **reúne,** reunid
  (d) **reúno, reúnes, reúne,** reunimos, reunís, **reúnen**
  (e) **reúna, reúnas, reúna,** reunamos, reunáis, **reúnan**

§60 **rezar**
  (e) **rece, reces, rece, recemos, recéis, recen**
  (h) **recé,** rezaste, rezó, rezamos, rezasteis, rezaron

§61 **rodar**
  (c) **rueda,** rodad
  (d) **ruedo, ruedas, rueda,** rodamos, rodáis, **ruedan**
  (e) **ruede, ruedes, ruede,** rodemos, rodéis, **rueden**

§62 **roer**
  (a) **royendo**
  (b) **roído**
  (d) **roo (roigo,** or **royo),** roes, roe, roemos, roéis, roen
  (e) **roa (roiga,** or **roya),** roas, roa, roamos, roáis, roan
  (h) roí, **roíste, royó, roímos, roísteis, royeron**

§63 **rogar:** combination of §44 and §61
  (c) **ruega,** rogad
  (d) **ruego, ruegas, ruega,** rogamos, rogáis, **ruegan**
  (e) **ruegue, ruegues, ruegue, roguemos, roguéis, rueguen**
  (h) **rogué,** rogaste, rogó, rogamos, rogasteis, rogaron

§64 **saber**
  (d) **sé,** sabes, sabe, sabemos, sabéis, saben
  (e) **sepa, sepas, sepa, sepamos, sepáis, sepan**
  (g) **sabré, sabrás, sabrá, sabremos, sabréis, sabrán**
  (h) **supe, supiste, supo, supimos, supisteis, supieron**

§65 **salir**
  (c) **sal,** salid
  (d) **salgo,** sales, sale, salimos, salís, salen
  (e) **salga, salgas, salga, salgamos, salgáis, salgan**
  (g) **saldré, saldrás, saldrá, saldremos, saldréis, saldrán**

§66 **segar:** combination of §2 and §44
  (c) **siega,** segad
  (d) **siego, siegas, siega,** segamos, segáis, **siegan**
  (e) **siegue, siegues, siegue, seguemos, seguéis, sieguen**
  (h) **segué,** segaste, segó, segamos, segasteis, segaron

§67 **seguir:** combination of §29 and §50
  (a) **siguiendo**
  (c) **sigue,** seguid
  (d) **sigo, siegues, sigue,** seguimos, seguís, **siguen**
  (e) **siga, sigas, siga, sigamos, sigáis, sigan**
  (h) seguí, seguiste, **siguió,** seguimos, seguisteis, **siguieron**

§68 sentir
(a) sintiendo
(c) siente, sentid
(d) siento, sientes, siente, sentimos, sentís, sienten
(e) sienta, sientas, sienta, sintamos, sintáis, sientan
(h) sentí, sentiste, sintió, sentimos, sentisteis, sintieron

§69 ser
(c) sé, sed
(d) soy, eres, es, somos, sois, son
(e) sea, seas, sea, seamos, seáis, sean
(f) era, eras, era, éramos, erais, eran
(h) fui, fuiste, fue, fuimos, fuisteis, fueron

§70 tañer
(a) tañendo
(h) tañí, tañiste, tañó, tañimos, tañisteis, tañeron

§71 tener
(c) ten, tened
(d) tengo, tienes, tiene, tenemos, tenéis, tienen
(e) tenga, tengas, tenga, tengamos, tengáis, tengan
(g) tendré, tendrás, tendrá, tendremos, tendréis, tendrán
(h) tuve, tuviste, tuvo, tuvimos, tuvisteis, tuvieron

§72 teñir: combination of §12 and §50
(a) tiñendo
(c) tiñe, teñid
(d) tiño, tiñes, tiñe, teñimos, teñis, tiñen
(e) tiña, tiñas, tiña, tiñamos, tiñáis, tiñan
(h) teñi, teñiste, tiñó, teñimos, teñisteis, tiñeron

§73 tocar
(e) toque, toques, toque, toquemos, toquéis, toquen
(h) toqué, tocaste, tocó, tocamos, tocasteis, tocaron

§74 torcer: combination of §47 and §78
(c) tuerce, torced
(d) tuerzo, tuerces, tuerce, torcemos, torcéis, tuercen
(e) tuerza, tuerzas, tuerza, torzamos, torzáis, tuerzan

§75 traer
(a) trayendo
(b) traído
(d) traigo, traes, trae, traemos, traéis, traen
(e) traiga, traigas, traiga, traigamos, traigáis, traigan
(h) traje, trajiste, trajo, trajimos, trajisteis, trajeron

§76 valer
(d) valgo, vales, vale, valemos, valéis, valen
(e) valga, valgas, valga, valgamos, valgáis, valgan
(g) valdré, valdrás, valdrá, valdremos, valdréis, valdrán

§77 variar
(c) varía, variad
(d) varío, varías, varía, variamos, variáis, varían
(e) varíe, varíes, varíe, variemos, variéis, varíen

§78 vencer
(d) venzo, vences, vence, vencemos, vencéis, vencen
(e) venza, venzas, venza, venzamos, venzáis, venzan

§79 venir
(a) viniendo
(c) ven, venid
(d) vengo, vienes, viene, venimos, venís, vienen
(e) venga, vengas, venga, vengamos, vengáis, vengan

(g) **vendré, vendrás, vendrá, vendremos, vendréis, vendrán**
(h) **vine, viniste, vino, vinimos, vinisteis, vinieron**

§80　**ver**
(b) **visto**
(d) **veo,** ves, ve, vemos, veis, ven
(e) **vea, veas, vea, veamos, veáis, vean**
(f) **veía, veías, veía, veíamos, veíais, veían**

§81　**volcar:** combination of **§61** and **§73**
(c) **vuelca,** volcad
(d) **vuelco, vuelcas, vuelca,** volcamos, volcáis, **vuelcan**
(e) **vuelque, vuelques, vuelque, volquemos, volquéis, vuelquen**
(h) **volqué,** volcaste, volcó, volcamos, volcasteis, volcaron

§82　**yacer**
(c) **yaz** (or yace), yaced
(d) **yazco (yazgo,** or **yago),** yaces, yace, yacemos, yacéis, yacen
(e) **yazca (yazga,** or **yaga), yazcas, yazca, yazcamos, yazcáis, yazcan**

§83　The following verbs, some of which are included in the foregoing table, and their compounds have irregular past participles:

abrir	hacer	escrito	poner	ver	podrido
cubrir	imprimir	frito	proveer	volver	roto
decir	abierto	hecho	pudrir	muerto	suelto
escribir	cubierto	impreso	romper	puesto	visto
freír	dicho	morir	solver	provisto	vuelto

ENGLISH-
SPANISH

INGLÉS-
ESPAÑOL

A

A, a [e] primera letra del alfabeto inglés

a [e] *art indef* un

aback [ə'bæk] *adv* atrás; **to be taken aback** quedar desconcertado; **to take aback** desconcertar

abaft [ə'bæft] *adv* a popa, en popa; *prep* detrás de

abandon [ə'bændən] *s* abandono ‖ *tr* abandonar

abandonment [ə'bændənmənt] *s* abandono, abandonamiento; desembarazo

abase [ə'bes] *tr* degradar, humillar

abash [ə'bæʃ] *tr* avergonzar

abashed [ə'bæʃt] *adj* avergonzado; humillado

abate [ə'bet] *tr* disminuir, reducir; deducir ‖ *intr* disminuir, moderarse

aba·tis ['æbətɪs] *s* (*pl* **-tis**) abatida

abattoir ['æbə,twar] *s* matadero

abba·cy ['æbəsi] *s* (*pl* **-cies**) abadía

abbess ['æbɪs] *s* abadesa

abbey ['æbi] *s* abadía

abbot ['æbət] *s* abad *m*

abbreviate [ə'brivɪ,et] *tr* abreviar

abbreviation [ə,brivɪ'eʃən] *s* (*shortening*) abreviación; (*shortened form*) abreviatura

A B C [,e,bi'si] *s* abecé *m*; **A B C's** abecedario

abdicate ['æbdɪ,ket] *tr* & *intr* abdicar

abdomen ['æbdəmən] o [æb'domən] *s* abdomen *m*

abduct [æb'dʌkt] *tr* raptar, secuestrar

abduction [æb'dʌkʃən] *s* rapto; secuestro

abed [ə'bɛd] *adv* en cama, acostado

aberration [,æbe'reʃən] *s* aberración; (*mind*) extravío

abet [ə'bɛt] *v* (*pret* & *pp* **abetted**; *ger* **abetting**) *tr* incitar (*a una persona, esp. al mal*); fomentar (*el crimen*)

abeyance [ə'be·əns] *s* suspensión; **in abeyance** en suspenso

ab·hor [æb'hɔr] *v* (*pret* & *pp* **-horred**; *ger* **-horring**) *tr* aborrecer, detestar

abhorrence [əb'hɔrəns] *s* aversión; aborrecimiento

abhorrent [æb'hɔrənt] *adj* aborrecible, detestable

abide [ə'baɪd] *v* (*pret* & *pp* **abode** o **abided**) *tr* esperar; tolerar ‖ *intr* permanecer; **to abide by** cumplir con; atenerse a

abili·ty [ə'bɪlɪti] *s* (*pl* **-ties**) habilidad, capacidad; talento

abject [æb'dʒɛkt] *adj* abyecto, servil

abjure [æb'dʒur] *tr* abjurar

ablative ['æblətɪv] *s* ablativo

ablaut ['æblaut] *s* apofonía

ablaze [ə'blez] *adj* brillante; ardiente; encolerizado ‖ *adv* en llamas, ardiendo

able ['ebəl] *adj* hábil, capaz; **to be able to** poder

able-bodied ['ebəl'badid] *adj* sano; fornido; experto

abloom [ə'blum] *adj* floreciente ‖ *adv* en flor

abnormal [æb'nɔrməl] *adj* anormal

aboard [ə'bord] *adv* a bordo; al bordo; **all aboard!** ¡señores viajeros al tren!; **to go aboard** ir a bordo; **to take aboard** embarcar ‖ *prep* a bordo de; (*a train*) en

abode [ə'bod] *s* domicilio, residencia

abolish [ə'balɪʃ] *tr* eliminar, suprimir

abolition [,æbə'lɪʃən] *s* abolición

A-bomb ['e,bam] *s* bomba atómica

abominable [ə'bamɪnəbəl] *adj* abominable

abomination [ə,bamɪ'neʃən] *s* abominación

aborigines [,æbə'rɪdʒɪ,niz] *spl* aborígenes *mf*

abort [ə'bɔrt] *tr* & *intr* abortar

abortion [ə'bɔrʃən] *s* aborto

abortionist [ə'bɔrʃənɪst] *s* abortista *mf*

abound [ə'baund] *intr* abundar

about [ə'baut] *adv* casi; aquí; **to be about to** estar a punto de, estar para ‖ *prep* acerca de; con respecto a; cerca de; hacia, a eso de; **to be about** tratar de

above [ə'bʌv] *adj* antedicho ‖ *adv* arriba, encima ‖ *prep* sobre, encima de, más alto que; superior a; **above all** sobre todo

above-mentioned [ə'bʌv'mɛnʃənd] *adj* sobredicho, antedicho, susodicho, prenombrado

abrasive [ə'bresɪv] o [ə'brezɪv] *adj* & *s* abrasivo

abreast [ə'brɛst] *adj* & *adv* de frente; **to be abreast of** correr parejas con; estar al corriente de

abridge [ə'brɪdʒ] *tr* abreviar; disminuir; condensar, resumir

abroad [ə'brɔd] *adv* al extranjero; en el extranjero; fuera de casa

abrupt [ə'brʌpt] *adj* brusco; repentino; áspero, abrupto, escarpado

abscess ['æbsɛs] *s* absceso

abscond [æb'skand] *intr* irse a hurtadillas; **to abscond with** alzarse con

absence ['æbsəns] *s* ausencia

absent ['æbsənt] *adj* ausente ‖ [æb'sɛnt] *tr*— **to absent oneself** ausentarse

absentee [,æbsən'ti] s ausente mf
absent-minded ['æbsənt'maindid] adj distraído, absorto
absinth ['æbsinθ] s (plant) absintio, ajenjo; (drink) absenta, ajenjo
absolute ['æbsə,lut] adj & s absoluto
absolutely 'æbsə,lutli] adv absolutamente || [,æbsə'lutli] adv (coll) positivamente
absolution ['æbsə'luʃən] s absolución
absolve [æb'salv] tr absolver
absorb [æb'sɔrb] tr absorber; **to be** or **become absorbed** ensimismarse
absorbent [æb'sɔrbənt] adj absorbente; (cotton) hidrófilo
absorbing [æb'sɔrbiŋ] adj absorbente
absorption [æb'sɔrpʃən] s abstracción; embebecimiento; absorción
abstain [æb'sten] intr abstenerse
abstemious [æb'stimɪ•əs] adj abstemio, sobrio
abstinent ['æbstinənt] adj abstinente
abstract ['æbstrækt] adj abstracto || s resumen m, sumario, extracto || tr resumir, compendiar, extractar || [æb'strækt] tr abstraer; quitar
abstruse [æb'strus] adj abstruso
absurd [æb'sʌrd] o [æb'zʌrd] adj absurdo
absurdi•ty [æb'sʌrditi] o [æb'zʌrditi] s (pl -ties) absurdidad, absurdo
abundance [ə'bʌndəns] s abundancia, copia; (CAm) bastedad
abundant [ə'bʌndənt] adj abundante
abuse [ə'bjus] s maltrato; injuria, insulto; (bad practice; injustice) abuso || [ə'bjuz] tr maltratar; injuriar, insultar; (to misapply, take unfair advantage of) abusar de
abusive [ə'bjusiv] adj injurioso, insultante; abusivo
abut [ə'bʌt] v (pret & pp **abutted**; ger **abutting**) intr—**to abut on** confinar con, terminar en
abutment [ə'bʌtmənt] s confinamiento; estribo, contrafuerte m
abyss [ə'bis] s abismo
academic [,ækə'dɛmɪk] adj académico
academic costume s toga, traje m de catedrático
academic freedom s libertad de cátedra, libertad de enseñanza
academician [ə,kædə'mɪʃən] s académico
academic subjects spl materias no profesionales
academic year s año escolar
acade•my [ə'kædəmi] s (pl -mies) academia
accede [æk'sid] intr acceder; **to accede to** acceder a, condescender a; (e.g., the throne) ascender a, subir a
accelerate [æk'sɛlə,ret] tr acelerar || intr acelerarse
accelerator [æk'sɛlə,retər] s acelerador m
accent ['æksɛnt] s acento || ['æksɛnt] o [æk'sɛnt] tr acentuar
accent mark s acento ortográfico
accentuate [æk'sɛntʃu,et] tr acentuar
accept [æk'sɛpt] tr aceptar
acceptable [æk'sɛptəbəl] adj aceptable
acceptance [æk'sɛptəns] s aceptación

access ['æksɛs] s acceso
accessible [æk'sɛsibəl] adj accesible
accession [æk'sɛʃən] s accesión; (to a dignity) ascenso; (of books in a library) adquisición
accesso•ry [æk'sɛsəri] adj accesorio || s (pl -ries) accesorio; (to a crime) cómplice mf
accident ['æksidənt] s accidente m; **by accident** por casualidad
accidental [,æksi'dɛntəl] adj accidental
acclaim [ə'klem] s aclamación || tr & intr aclamar
acclimate ['æklɪ,met] tr aclimatar || intr aclimatarse
accolade [,ækə'led] s acolada; elogio, premio
accommodate [ə'kamə,det] tr acomodar; alojar
accommodating [ə'kamə,detiŋ] adj acomodadizo, servicial
accommodation [ə,kamə'deʃən] s acomodación; **accommodations** facilidades, comodidades; (in a train) localidad; (in a hotel) alojamiento
accommodation train s tren m omnibus
accompaniment [ə'kʌmpənimənt] s acompañamiento
accompanist [ə'kʌmpənist] s acompañante m
accompa•ny [ə'kʌmpəni] v (pret & pp -nied) tr acompañar
accomplice [ə'kamplis] s cómplice mf, codelincuente mf
accomplish [ə'kampliʃ] tr realizar, llevar a cabo
accomplished [ə'kampliʃt] adj realizado; culto, talentoso; (fact) consumado
accomplishment [ə'kampliʃmənt] s realización; **accomplishments** prendas, talentos
accord [ə'kɔrd] s acuerdo; **in accord with** de acuerdo con: **of one's own accord** de buen grado, voluntariamente; **with one accord** de común acuerdo || tr conceder, otorgar || intr concordar, avenirse
accordance [ə'kɔrdəns] s conformidad; **in accordance with** de acuerdo con
according [ə'kɔrdiŋ] adj — **according as** según que; **according to** según
accordingly [ə'kɔrdiŋli] adv en conformidad; por consiguiente
accordion [ə'kɔrdi•ən] s acordeón m; filarmónica (Mex)
accost [ə'kɔst] o [ə'kast] tr abordar, acercarse a
accouchement [ə'kuʃmənt] s alumbramiento, parto
accoucheur [,æku'ʃʌr] s comadrón m
accoucheuse [,æku'ʃuz] s comadrona
account [ə'kaunt] s informe m, relato; cuenta; estado de cuenta; importancia; **by all accounts** según el decir general; **of no account** de poca importancia; **on account** como paga y señal; **on account of** a causa de; **to bring to account** pedir cuentas a; **to buy on account** comprar a plazos; **to turn to account** sacar provecho de, hacer valer

‖ *intr*—**to account for** explicar; responder de

accountable [ə'kaʊntəbəl] *adj* responsable; explicable

accountant [ə'kaʊntənt] *s* contador *m*, contable *m*

accounting [ə'kaʊntɪŋ] *s* arreglo de cuentas; contabilidad

accouterments [ə'kutərmənts] *spl* equipo, avíos

accredit [ə'krɛdɪt] *tr* acreditar

accrue [ə'kru] *intr* acumularse; resultar

acct. *abbr* **account**

accumulate [ə'kjumjə,let] *tr* acumular ‖ *intr* acumularse

accuracy ['ækjərəsi] *s* exactitud, precisión

accurate ['ækjərɪt] *adj* exacto

accusation [,ækjə'zeʃən] *s* acusación

accusative [ə'kjuzətɪv] *adj* & *s* acusativo

accuse [ə'kjuz] *tr* acusar

accustom [ə'kʌstəm] *tr* acostumbrar

ace [es] *s* as *m;* **to be within an ace of** estar a dos dedos de

acetate ['æsɪ,tet] *s* acetato

acetic acid [ə'sitɪk] *s* ácido acético

aceti•fy [ə'sɛtɪ,faɪ] *v* (*pret* & *pp* **-fied**) *tr* acetificar ‖ *intr* acetificarse

acetone ['æsɪ,ton] *s* acetona

acetylene [ə'sɛtɪ,lin] *s* acetileno

acetylene torch *s* soplete oxiacetilénico

ache [ek] *s* achaque *m*, dolor *m* ‖ *int* doler

achieve [ə'tʃiv] *tr* llevar a cabo; alcanzar, ganar, lograr

achievement [ə'tʃivmənt] *s* realización; (*feat*) hazaña

Achilles' heel [ə'kɪliz] *s* talón *m* de Aquiles

acid ['æsɪd] *adj* ácido; agrio, mordaz ‖ *s* ácido

acidi•fy [ə'sɪdɪ,faɪ] *v* (*pret* & *pp* **-fied**) *tr* acidificar ‖ *intr* acidificarse

acidi•ty [ə'sɪdɪti] *s* (*pl* **-ties**) acidez *f*

acid rain *s* lluvia ácida

acid test *s* prueba decisiva

ack•ack ['æk'æk] *s* (slang) artillería antiaérea; (slang) fuego antiaéreo

acknowledge [æk'nɑlɪdʒ] *tr* reconocer; acusar (*recibo de una carta*); agradecer (*p.ej.*, *un favor*)

acknowledgment [æk'nɑlɪdʒmənt] *s* reconocimiento; (*of receipt of a letter*) acuse *m;* (*of a favor*) agradecimiento

acme ['ækmi] *s* auge *m*, colmo

acne ['ækni] *s* acne *f*

acolyte ['ækə,laɪt] *s* acólito

acorn ['ekɔrn] o ['ekərn] *s* bellota

acoustic [ə'kustɪk] *adj* acústico ‖ **acoustics** *ssg* acústica

acquaint [ə'kwent] *tr* informar, poner al corriente; **to be acquainted** conocerse; **to be acquainted with** conocer; estar al corriente de

acquaintance [ə'kwentəns] *s* conocimiento; (*person*) conocido

acquiesce [,ækwɪ'ɛs] *intr* consentir, condescender, asentir

acquiescence [,ækwɪ'ɛsəns] *s* consentimiento, condescendencia, aquiescencia

acquire [ə'kwaɪr] *tr* adquirir

acquired im•mune'-de•fi'cien•cy syndrome (AIDS) *s* síndrome *m* de inmunidad deficiente adquirida (SIDA)

acquired taste *s* gusto adquirido

acquisition [,ækwɪ'zɪʃən] *s* adquisición

acquit [ə'kwɪt] *v* (*pret* & *pp* **acquitted;** *ger* **acquitting**) *tr* absolver, exculpar; **to acquit oneself** conducirse, portarse

acquittal [ə'kwɪtəl] *s* absolución, exculpación

acrid ['ækrɪd] *adj* acre, acrimonioso

acrobat ['ækrə,bæt] *s* acróbata *mf*

acrobatic [,ækrə'bætɪk] *adj* acrobático ‖ **acrobatics** *ssg* (*profession*) acrobatismo; *spl* (*stunts*) acrobacia

acronym ['ækrənɪm] *s* acrónimo

acropolis [ə'krɑpəlɪs] *s* acrópolis *f*

across [ə'krɔs] o [ə'krɑs] *prep* al través de; al otro lado de; **to come across** encontrarse con; **to go across** atravesar

across'-the-board' *adj* comprensivo, general

acrostic [ə'krɔstɪk] o [ə'krɑstɪk] *s* acróstico

act [ækt] *s* acto; (law) decreto; **in the act** en flagrante ‖ *tr* representar; desempeñar (*un papel*); **to act the fool** hacer el bufón; **to act the part of** hacer o desempeñar el papel de ‖ *intr* actuar; funcionar, obrar; conducirse; **to act as if** hacer como que; **to act for** representar; **to act up** travesear; **to act up to** hacer fiestas a

acting ['æktɪŋ] *adj* interino ‖ *s* actuación

action ['ækʃən] *s* acción; **to take action** tomar medidas

activate ['æktɪ,vet] *tr* activar

active ['æktɪv] *adj* activo

activi•ty [æk'tɪvɪti] *s* (*pl* **-ties**) actividad

act of God *s* fuerza mayor

actor ['æktər] *s* actor *m*

actress ['æktrɪs] *s* actriz *f*

actual ['æktʃu•əl] *adj* real, efectivo

actually ['æktʃu•əli] *adv* en realidad

actuar•y ['æktʃu,ɛri] *s* (*pl* **-ies**) actuario (de seguros)

actuate ['æktʃu,et] *tr* actuar; estimular, mover

acuity [ə'kju•ɪti] *s* agudeza

acumen [ə'kjumən] *s* cacumen *m*, perspicacia

acupuncture ['ækjə,pʌŋktʃər] *s* acupuntura

acute [ə'kjut] *adj* agudo

A.D. *abbr* **anno Domini** (Lat) **in the year of our Lord**

ad [æd] *s* (coll) anuncio

adage ['ædɪdʒ] *s* adagio, refrán *m*

Adam ['ædəm] *s* Adán *m;* **the old Adam** la inclinación al pecado

adamant ['ædəmənt] *adj* firme, inexorable

Adam's apple *s* nuez *f*

adapt [ə'dæpt] *tr* adaptar; refundir (*un drama*)

adaptation [,ædæp'teʃən] *s* adaptación; (*of a play*) refundición

add [æd] *tr* agregar, añadir; sumar ‖ *intr* sumar; **to add up to** subir a; (coll) querer decir

added line *s* (mus) línea suplementaria

adder ['ædər] s víbora; serpiente f
addict ['ædɪkt] s enviciado; adicto, partidario ‖ [ə'dɪkt] tr enviciar; entregar; **to addict oneself to** enviciarse con o en; entregarse a
addiction [ə'dɪkʃən] s enviciamiento; adhesividad
adding machine s sumadora, máquina de sumar
addition [ə'dɪʃən] s adición; **in addition** de pilón; **in addition to** además de
additive ['ædɪtɪv] adj & s aditivo
address [ə'drɛs] o ['ædrɛs] s dirección; consignación ‖ [ə'drɛs] s alocución, discurso; **to deliver an address** hacer uso de la palabra ‖ tr dirigirse a; dirigir (p.ej., una alocución, una carta); consignar
addressee [,ædrɛ'si] s destinatario; (com) consignatario
addressing machine s máquina para dirigir sobres
adduce [ə'djus] o [ə'dus] tr aducir
adenoids ['ædə,nɔɪdz] spl vegetaciones adenoides
adept [ə'dɛpt] adj & s experto, perito
adequate ['ædɪkwɪt] adj suficiente
adhere [æd'hɪr] intr adherir, adherirse; conformarse
adherence [æd'hɪrəns] s adhesión
adherent [æd'hɪrənt] adj & s adherente m
adhesion [æd'hiʒən] s (sticking) adherencia; (support, loyalty) adhesión; (pathol) adherencia; (phys) adherencia o adhesión
adhesive [æd'hisɪv] adj adhesivo
adhesive tape s tafetán adhesivo
adieu [ə'dju] o [ə'du] interj ¡adiós! ‖ s (pl adieus o adieux) adiós m; **to bid adieu to** desperdirse de
adjacent [ə'dʒesənt] adj adyacente
adjective ['ædʒɪktɪv] adj & s adjetivo
adjoin [ə'dʒɔɪn] tr lindar con ‖ intr colindar
adjoining [ə'dʒɔɪnɪŋ] adj colindante, contiguo
adjourn [ə'dʒʌrn] tr prorrogar, suspender ‖ intr prorrogarse, suspenderse; (coll) ir
adjournment [ə'dʒʌrnmənt] s prorrogación, suspensión
adjust [ə'dʒʌst] tr ajustar, arreglar; corregir, verificar; (ins) liquidar
adjustable [ə'dʒʌstəbəl] adj ajustable, arreglable
adjustment [ə'dʒʌstmənt] s ajuste m, arreglo; (ins) liquidación de la avería
adjutant ['ædʒətənt] s ayudante m
ad·lib [,æd'lɪb] v (pret & pp -libbed; ger -libbing) tr & intr improvisar
Adm. abbr **Admiral**
administer [æd'mɪnɪstər] tr administrar; **to administer an oath** tomar juramento ‖ intr — **to administer to** cuidar de
administrator [æd'mɪnɪs,tretər] s administrador m
admiral ['ædmɪrəl] s almirante m; buque m almirante
admiral·ty ['ædmɪrəlti] s (pl -ties) almirantazgo
admire [æd'maɪr] tr admirar

admirer [æd'maɪrər] s admirador m; enamorado
admissible [æd'mɪsɪbəl] adj admisible
admission [æd'mɪʃən] s admisión; (in a school) ingreso; (reception) recibida; precio de entrada; **to gain admission** lograr entrar
ad·mit [æd'mɪt] v (pret & pp -mitted; ger -mitting) tr admitir ‖ intr dar entrada; **to admit of** admitir, permitir
admittance [æd'mɪtəns] s admisión; derecho de entrar; **no admittance** acceso prohibido, se prohíbe la entrada
admonish [æd'mɑnɪʃ] tr amonestar
ado [ə'du] s bulla, excitación
adobe [ə'dobi] s adobe m; casa de adobe
adolescence [,ædə'lɛsəns] s adolescencia
adolescent [,ædə'lɛsənt] adj & s adolescente mf
adopt [ə'dɑpt] tr adoptar
adoption [ə'dɑpʃən] s adopción
adorable [ə'dorəbəl] adj adorable
adore [ə'dor] tr adorar
adorn [ə'dɔrn] tr adornar
adornment [ə'dɔrnmənt] s adorno
adrenal gland [æd'rinəl] s glándula suprarrenal
Adriatic [,edrɪ'ætɪk] adj & s Adriático
adrift [ə'drɪft] adj & adv al garete, a la deriva
adroit [ə'drɔɪt] adj diestro
adult [ə'dʌlt] o ['ædʌlt] adj & s adulto
adulterate [ə'dʌltə,ret] tr adulterar
adulterer [ə'dʌltərər] s adúltero
adulteress [ə'dʌltərɪs] s adúltera
adulter·y [ə'dʌltəri] s (pl -ies) adulterio
adulthood [ə'dʌlt,hʊd] s adultez f
advance [æd'væns] adj adelantado; anticipado ‖ s adelanto, avance m; aumento, subida; **advances** propuestas; requerimiento amoroso; propuesta indecente; préstamo; **in advance** de antemano, por anticipado ‖ tr adelantar ‖ intr adelantar; adelantarse
advanced [æd'vænst] adj avanzado; **advanced in years** avanzado de edad, entrado en años
advanced standing s traspaso de matrículas, traspaso de crédito académico
advanced studies spl altos estudios
advancement [æd'vænsmənt] s adelanto, avance m; subida; promoción
advance publicity s publicidad de lanzamiento
advantage [æd'væntɪdʒ] s ventaja; lasca; **to take advantage of** aprovecharse de; abusar de, engañar
advantageous [,ædvən'tedʒəs] adj ventajoso
advent ['ædvɛnt] s advenimiento ‖ **Advent** s (eccl) Adviento
adventure [æd'vɛntʃər] s aventura ‖ tr aventurar ‖ intr aventurarse
adventurer [æd'vɛntʃərər] s aventurero
adventuresome [æd'vɛntʃərsəm] adj aventurero
adventuress [æd'vɛntʃərɪs] s aventurera
adventurous [æd'vɛntʃərəs] adj aventurero

adverb ['ædvɑrb] s adverbio
adversar•y ['ædvər,sɛri] s (pl -ies) adversario
adversi•ty [æd'vʌrsiti] s (pl -ties) adversidad
advertise ['ædvər,taiz] tr & intr anunciar
advertisement [,ædvər'taizmənt] o [əd-'vʌrtizmənt] s anuncio
advertiser ['ædvər,taizər] s anunciante mf
advertising ['ædvər,taiziŋ] s propaganda, publicidad, anuncios; reclame m & f
advertising agency s empresa anunciadora
advertising campaign s campaña de publicidad
advertising man s empresario de publicidad
advertising manager s gerente m de publicidad
advice [æd'vais] ⸱ consejo; aviso, noticia; **a piece of advice** un consejo
advisable [æd'vaizəbəl] adj aconsejable
advise [æd'vaiz] tr aconsejar, asesorar; advertir, avisar
advisement [æd'vaizmənt] s consideración; **to take under advisement** someter a consideración
advisory [æd'vaizəri] adj consultivo
advocate ['ædvə,ket] s defensor m; abogado || tr abogar por
Aegean Sea [i'dʒi•ən] s Archipiélago; (of the ancients) mar Egeo
aegis ['idʒis] s égida
aerate ['eret] o ['e•ə,ret] tr airear
aerial ['ɛri•əl] adj aéreo || s antena
aerialist ['ɛri•əlist] s volatinero
aerial photograph s fotografía aérea
aerodrome ['ɛrə,drom] s aeródomo
aerodynamic [,ɛrodai'næmik] adj aerodinámico || **aerodynamics** ssg aerodinámica
aeronaut ['ɛrə,nɔt] s aeronauta mf
aeronautic [,ɛrə'nɔtik] adj aeronáutico || **aeronautics** ssg aeronáutica
aerosol ['ɛrə,sol] s aerosol m
aerospace ['ɛro,spes] adj aeroespacial
aesthete ['ɛsθit] s esteta mf
aesthetic [ɛs'θɛtik] adj estético || **aesthetics** ssg estética
afar [ə'far] adv lejos
affable ['æfəbəl] adj afable
affair [ə'fɛr] s asunto, negocio; lance m; amorío; encuentro, combate m; **affairs** negocios
affect [ə'fɛkt] tr influir en; impresionar, enternecer; (to assume; to pretend) afectar; aficionarse a
affectation [,æfɛk'teʃən] s afectación
affected [ə'fɛktid] adj afectado
affection [ə'fɛkʃən] s afecto, cariño, afección; (pathol) afección
affectionate [ə'fɛkʃənit] adj afectuoso, cariñoso
affidavit [,æfi'devit] s declaración jurada, acta notarial
affiliate [ə'fili,et] adj afiliado || s afiliado; filial f || tr afiliar || intr afiliarse
affini•ty [ə'finiti] s (pl -ties) afinidad
affirm [ə'fʌrm] tr & intr afirmar
affirmative [ə'fʌrmətiv] adj afirmativo || s afirmativa

affix ['æfiks] s añadidura; (gram) afijo || [ə'fiks] tr añadir; atribuir (p.ej., culpa); poner (una firma, sello, etc.)
afflict [ə'flikt] tr afligir; **to be afflicted with** sufrir de, adolecer de
affliction [ə'flikʃən] s aflicción, desgracia; achaque m
affluence ['æflu•əns] s (abundance) afluencia; (wealth) opulencia
afford [ə'ford] tr proporcionar; **to be able to afford (to)** poder darse el lujo de, poder permitirse
affray [ə'fre] s pendencia, riña
affront [ə'frʌnt] s afrenta || tr afrentar
Afghan ['æfgæn] adj & s afgano
Afghanistan [æf'gæni,stæn] s el Afganistán
afire [ə'fair] adj & adv ardiendo
aflame [ə'flem] adj & adv en llamas
afloat [ə'flot] adj & adv a flote; a bordo; inundado; sin rumbo; (rumor) en circulación
afoot [ə'fut] adj & adv a pie; en marcha
afoul [ə'faul] adj & adv enredado; en colisión; **to run afoul of** enredarse con
afraid [ə'fred] adj asustado; **to be afraid** tener miedo
Africa ['æfrikə] s Africa
African ['æfrikən] adj & s africano
aft [æft] adj & adv en popa
after ['æftər] adj siguiente || adv después || prep después de; según; **after all** al fin y al cabo || conj después de que
af•ter-din'ner speaker s orador m de sobremesa
after-dinner speech s discurso de sobremesa
af•ter-hours' adv después del trabajo
af•ter-life' s vida venidera; resto de la vida
aftermath ['æftər,mæθ] s segunda siega; consecuencias, consecuencias desastrosas
af•ter-noon' s tarde f
af•ter-shave' lotion s loción facial
af•ter-taste' s dejo, gustillo, resabio
af•ter-thought' s idea tardía, expediente tardío
afterward ['æftəwərd] adv después, luego
af•ter-while' adv dentro de poco
again [ə'gɛn] adv otra vez, de nuevo; además; **to + inf + again** volver a + inf, p.ej., **he will come again** volverá a venir
against [ə'gɛnst] prep contra; cerca de; en contraste con; por; para
agape [ə'gep] adj abierto de par en par || adv con la boca abierta
agave [ə'gavi] s agave f
agave brandy s pulque m (Mex)
agave liquor s mexcal m, mezcal m
age [edʒ] s edad; (old age) vejez f; (one hundred years; a long time) siglo; edad mental; **of age** mayor de edad; **to come of age** alcanzar su mayoría de edad, llegar a mayor edad; **under age** menor de edad || tr envejecer || intr envejecer, envejecerse
age bracket s grupo de personas de la misma edad
aged [edʒd] adj de la edad de || ['edʒid] adj anciano, viejo

ageism [ˈedʒɪzəm] s discriminación contra los ancianos

ageless [ˈedʒlɪs] adj eternamente joven

agen•cy [ˈedʒənsi] s (pl -cies) agencia; mediación

agenda [əˈdʒɛndə] s agenda, temario

agent [ˈədʒənt] s agente m

Age of Enlightenment s siglo de las luces

agglomeration [ə,glɑməˈreʃən] s aglomeración

·**aggrandizement** [əˈgrændɪzmənt] s engrandecimiento

aggravate [ˈægrə,vet] tr agravar; (coll) exasperar, irritar

aggregate [ˈægrɪ,get] adj & s agregado ‖ tr agregar, juntar; ascender a

aggression [əˈgrɛʃən] s agresión

aggressive [əˈgrɛsɪv] adj agresivo

aggressor [əˈgrɛsər] s agresor m

aghast [əˈgæst] adj horrorizado

agile [ˈædʒɪl] adj ágil

agitate [ˈædʒɪ,tet] tr & intr agitar

aglow [əˈglo] adj & adv fulgurante

agnostic [ægˈnɑstɪk] adj & s agnóstico

ago [əˈgo] adv hace, p.ej., **two days ago** hace dos días

ago•ny [ˈægəni] s (pl -nies) angustia, congoja; (anguish; death struggle) agonía

agrarian [əˈgrɛrɪ•ən] adj agrario ‖ s agrariense mf

agree [əˈgri] intr estar de acuerdo, ponerse de acuerdo; sentar bien; (gram) concordar

agreeable [əˈgri•əbəl] adj (to one's liking) agradable; (willing to consent) acorde, conforme

agreement [əˈgrimənt] s acuerdo, convenio; concordancia; **in agreement** de acuerdo

agric. abbr **agriculture**

agriculture [ˈægrɪ,kʌltʃər] s agricultura

agronomy [əˈgrɑnəmi] s agronomía

aground [əˈgraʊnd] adv encallado, varado; **to run aground** encallar, varar

agt. abbr **agent**

ague [ˈegju] s escalofrío; fiebre f intermitente

ahead [əˈhɛd] adj & adv delante, al frente; **ahead of** antes de; delante de; al frente de; **to get ahead (of)** adelantarse (a)

ahoy [əˈhɔɪ] interj — **ship ahoy!** ¡ah del barco!

aid [ed] s ayuda, auxilio; (mil) ayudante m ‖ tr ayudar, auxiliar; **to aid and abet** auxiliar e incitar, ser cómplice de ‖ intr ayudar

aide [ed] s ayudante m; (mil) edecán m

aide-de-camp [ˈeddəˈkæmp] s (pl **aides-de-camp**) ayudante m de campo, edecán m

AIDS [edz] abbr **acquired immune-deficiency syndrome**

ail [el] tr inquietar; **what ails you?** ¿qué tiene Vd.? ‖ intr sufrir, estar enfermo

aileron [ˈelə,rɑn] s alerón m

ailing [ˈelɪŋ] adj enfermo, achacoso

ailment [ˈelmənt] s enfermedad, achaque m

aim [em] s puntería; intento; punto de mira ‖ tr apuntar, encarar; dirigir (p.ej., una observación) ‖ intr apuntar

air [ɛr] s aire m; **by air** por vía aérea; **in the open air** al aire libre; **on the air** en antena,

en la radio; **to let the air out of** desinflar; **to put on airs** darse aires; **to put on the air** llevar a las antenas; **to walk on air** no pisar en el suelo ‖ tr airear, ventilar; radiodifundir; (fig) ventilar

air'-a•tom'ic adj aeroatómico

air bag s (aut) globo de aire, bolsa de aire

air'borne' adj aerotransportado

air brake s freno de aire comprimido

air castle s castillo en el aire

air'-condi'tion tr climatizar

air conditioner s acondicionador m de aire

air conditioning s acondicionamiento del aire, clima m artificial, climatización

air corps s cuerpo de aviación

air'craft' ssg máquina de volar; spl máquinas de volar

aircraft carrier s portaaviones m

airdrome [ˈɛr,drom] s aeródromo

air'drop' s lanzamiento ‖ tr lanzar

air field s campo de aviación

air'foil' s superficie f de sustentación

air force s fuerza aérea, ejército del aire

air gap s (phys) entrehierro

air'-ground' adj aeroterrestre

air hostess s aeromoza, azafata

air humidifier s humidificador m

air lane s ruta aérea

air'lift' s puente aéreo

air liner s transaéreo, avión m de travesía

air mail s correo aéreo, aeroposta

air'-mail' letter s carta aérea, carta por avión

air-mail pilot s aviador m postal

air-mail stamp s sello aéreo

air•man [ˈɛrmən] s (pl -men [mən]) aviador m

air'plane' s avión m, aparato

airplane carrier s portaaviones m

air pocket s bache aéreo

air pollution s contaminación atmosférica

air'port' s aeropuerto

air raid s ataque aéreo

air'-raid' drill s simulacro de ataque aéreo

air-raid shelter s abrigo antiaéreo

air-raid warning s alarma aérea

air rifle s escopeta de viento, escopeta de aire comprimido

air'ship' s aeronave f

air'sick' adj mareado en el aire

air'sick'ness s mal m de vuelo

air sleeve o **sock** s veleta de manga

air'strip' s pista de despegue, pista de aterrizaje

air taxi s aerotaxi m

air'tight' adj herméticamente cerrado, estanco al aire

air'-traff'ic controller s controlador aéreo

air'waves' spl ondas de radio

air'way' s aerovía, vía aérea

airway lighting s balizaje m

air•y [ˈɛri] adj (comp -ier; super -iest) airoso; aireado; alegre; impertinente; (coll) afectado

aisle [aɪl] s (in theater, movie, etc.) pasillo; (in a store, factory, etc.) nave f; (archit) nave f lateral; (any of the long passageways of a church) (archit) nave f

ajar |ə'dʒɑr| *adj* entreabierto, entornado
akimbo [ə'kɪmbo] *adj* & *adv* — **with arms akimbo** en jarras
akin [ə'kɪn] *adj* emparentado: semejante
alabaster ['ælə,bæstər] *s* alabastro
alarm [ə'lɑrm] *s* alarma ‖ *tr* alarmar
alarm clock *s* reloj *m* despertador
alarmist [ə'lɑrmɪst] *s* alarmista *mf*
alas [ə'læs] o [ə'lɑs] *interj* ¡ay!, ¡ay de mí!
Albanian [æl'benɪ•ən] *adj* & *s* albanés *m*
albatross ['ælbə,trɔs] o ['ælbə,trɑs] *s* albatros *m*
album ['ælbəm] *s* álbum *m*
albumen [æl'bjumən] *s* albumen *m;* albúmina
alchemy ['ælkɪmɪ] *s* alquimia
alcohol ['ælkə,hɔl] o ['ælkə,hɑl] *s* alcohol *m*
alcoholic [,ælkə'hɔlɪk] o [,ælkə'hɑlɪk] *adj* & *s* alcohólico
al'co•hol-lev'el test *s* prueba de alcohol
alcove ['ælkov] *s* gabinete *m*, rincón *m; (in a bedroom)* trasalcoba; *(in a garden)* cenador *m*
alder ['ɔldər] *s* aliso
alder•man ['ɔldərmən] *s* (*pl* **-men** [mən]) concejal *m*
ale [el] *s* ale *f (cerveza inglesa, obscura, espesa y amarga)*
alembic [ə'lɛmbɪk] *s* alambique *m*
alert [ə'lʌrt] *adj* listo, vivo; vigilante ‖ *s* (aer) alarma; (mil) alerta *m;* **to be on the alert** estar sobre aviso, estar alerta ‖ *tr* alertar
Aleutian Islands [ə'luʃən] *spl* islas Aleutas, islas Aleutianas
Alexandrine [,ælɪg'zændrɪn] *adj* & *s* alejandrino
alg. *abbr* **algebra**
algae ['ældʒi] *spl* algas
algebra ['ældʒɪbrə] *s* álgebra
algebraic [,ældʒɪ'bre•ɪk] *adj* algebraico
Algeria [æl'dʒɪrɪ•ə] *s* Argelia
Algerian [æl'dʒɪrɪ•ən] *adj* & *s* argelino
Algiers [æl'dʒɪrz] *s* Argel *f*
alias ['elɪ•əs] *adv* alias ‖ *s* alias *m*, nombre supuesto
ali•bi ['ælɪ,baɪ] *s* (*pl* **-bis**) coartada; (coll) excusa
alien ['elɪ•ən] *adj* & *s* extranjero
alienate ['eljə,net] o ['elɪ•ə,net] *tr* enajenar, alienar; desenamorar
alight [ə'laɪt] *v* (*pret* & *pp* **alighted** o alit [ə'lɪt]) *intr* bajar, apearse; posarse *(un ave)*
align [ə'laɪn] *tr* alinear ‖ *intr* alinearse
alike [ə'laɪk] *adj* semejantes; **to look alike** parecerse ‖ *adv* igualmente
alimentary canal [,ælɪ'mɛntərɪ] *s* canal alimenticio, tubo digestivo
alimony ['ælɪ,monɪ] *s* alimentos
alive [ə'laɪv] *adj* vivo, viviente; animado; **alive to** despierto para, sensible a; **alive with** hormigueante en ·
alka•li ['ælkə,laɪ] *s* (*pl* **-lis** o **-lies**) álcali *m*
alkaline ['ælkə,laɪn] *adj* alcalino
all [ɔl] *adj indef* todo, todos; todo el, todos los ‖ *pron indef* todo; todos, todo el mundo; **after all** sin embargo; **all of** todo el, todos

los; **all that** todo lo que, todos los que; **for all I know** que yo sepa; a lo mejor; **not at all** nada; no hay de qué ‖ *adv* enteramente; **all along** desde el principio; a lo largo de; **all at once** de golpe; **all right** bueno, corriente; **all too** excesivamente
Allah ['ælə] *s* Alá *m*
allay [ə'le] *tr* aliviar, calmar
all-clear ['ɔl'klɪr] *s* cese *m* de alarma
allege [ə'lɛdʒ] *tr* alegar
allegiance [ə'lidʒəns] *s* fidelidad, lealtad; homenaje *m;* **to swear allegiance to** jurar fidelidad a; rendir homenaje a
allegoric(al) [,ælɪ'gɑrɪk(əl)] o [,ælɪ'gɔrɪk(əl)] *adj* alegórico
allego•ry ['ælɪ,gorɪ] *s* (*pl* **-ries**) alegoría
aller•gy ['ælərdʒi] *s* (*pl* **-gies**) alergia
alleviate [ə'livɪ,et] *tr* aliviar
alleviation [ə,livɪ'eʃən] *s* aligeramiento
alley ['ælɪ] *s* callejuela; paseo arbolado, paseo de jardín; (bowling) pista; (tennis) espacio lateral
All Fools' Day *s* var of **April Fools' Day**
Allhallows [,ɔl'hæloz] *s* día *m* de todos los santos
alliance [ə'laɪ•əns] *s* alianza
alligator ['ælɪ,getər] *s* caimán *m*
alligator pear *s* aguacate *m*
alligator wrench *s* llave *f* de mandíbulas dentadas
alliteration [ə,lɪtə'reʃən] *s* aliteración
all-knowing ['ɔl'no•ɪŋ] *adj* omnisciente
allocate ['ælə,ket] *tr* asignar, distribuir
allot [ə'lɑt] *v* (*pret* & *pp* **allotted;** *ger* **allotting**) *tr* asignar, distribuir
all'-out' *adj* acérrimo
allow [ə'lau] *tr* dejar, permitir; admitir; conceder ‖ *intr* — **to allow for** tener en cuenta; **to allow of** permitir; admitir
allowance [ə'lau•əns] *s* permiso; concesión; ración; descuento, rebaja; tolerancia; **to make allowance for** tener en cuenta
alloy ['ælɔɪ] o [ə'lɔɪ] *s* aleación, liga ‖ [ə'lɔɪ] *tr* alear, ligar
all'-pow'er•ful *adj* todopoderoso
all'-pur'pose *adj* universal, para todo uso
All Saints' Day *s* día *m* de todos los santos
All Souls' Day *s* día *m* de los difuntos
allspice ['ɔl,spaɪs] *s* pimienta inglesa
all'-star' game *s* (sport) juego de estrellas
allude [ə'lud] *intr* aludir
allure [ə'lur] *s* tentación, encanto, fascinación ‖ *tr* tentar, encantar
alluring [ə'lurɪŋ] *adj* tentador, encantador, fascinante
allusion [ə'luʒən] *s* alusión
all'-weath'er *adj* para todo tiempo
al•ly ['ælaɪ] o [ə'laɪ] *s* (*pl* **-lies**) aliado ‖ [ə'laɪ] *v* (*pret* & *pp* **-lied**) *tr* aliar ‖ *intr* aliarse
almanac ['ɔlmə,næk] *s* almanaque *m*
almighty [ɔl'maɪtɪ] *adj* todopoderoso, omnipotente
almond ['amənd] o ['æmənd] *s* almendra
almond brittle *s* crocante *m*
almond tree *s* almendro
almost ['ɔlmost] o [ɔl'most] *adv* casi

alms [amz] s limosna

alms'house' s casa de beneficencia

aloe ['ælo] s áloe m

aloft [ə'lɔft] o [ə'lɑft] adv arriba; (aer) en vuelo; (naut) en la arboladura

alone [ə'lon] adj solo; **let alone** sin mencionar; y mucho menos; **to let alone** no molestar; no mezclarse en ‖ adv solamente

along [ə'lɔŋ] o [ə'lɑŋ] adv conmigo, consigo, etc.; **all along** desde el principio; **along with** junto con ‖ prep a lo largo de

along'side' adv a lo largo; (naut) al costado; **to bring alongside** acostar ‖ prep a lo largo de; (naut) al costado de

aloof [ə'luf] adj apartado; reservado ‖ adv lejos, a distancia

aloud [ə'laud] adv alto, en voz alta

alphabet ['ælfə,bɛt] s alfabeto

alpine ['ælpaɪn] adj alpestre, alpino

Alps [ælps] spl Alpes mpl

already [ɔl'rɛdi] adv ya

Alsace [æl'ses] o ['ælsæs] s Alsacia

Alsatian [æl'seʃən] adj & s alsaciano

also ['ɔlso] adv también

alt. abbr **alternate, altitude**

altar ['ɔltər] s altar m; **to lead to the altar** conducir al altar

altar boy s acólito, monaguillo

altar cloth s sabanilla, palia

al'tar-piece' s retablo

altar rail s comulgatorio

alter ['ɔltər] tr alterar ‖ intr alterarse

alteration [,ɔltə'reʃən] s alteración; (in a building) reforma; (in clothing) arreglo

alternate ['ɔltərnɪt] o ['æltərnɪt] adj alterno ‖ ['ɔltər,net] o ['æltər,net] tr & intr alternar

alternating current s corriente alterna o alternativa

although [ɔl'ðo] conj aunque

altimetry [æl'tɪmɪtri] s altimetría

altitude ['æltɪ,tjud] s altitud, altura

al•to ['ælto] s (pl -tos) contralto

altogether [,ɔltə'gɛðər] adv enteramente; en conjunto

altruist ['æltrʊ•ɪst] s altruísta mf

altruistic [,æltrʊ'ɪstɪk] adj altruísta

alum ['æləm] s alumbre m

aluminum [ə'lumɪnəm] s aluminio

alum•na [ə'lʌmnə] s (pl -nae [ni]) graduada

alum•nus [ə'lʌmnəs] s (pl -ni [naɪ]) graduado

alveo•lus [æl'vi•ələs] s (pl -li [,laɪ]) alvéolo

always ['ɔlwɪz] o ['ɔlwez] adv siempre

A.M. abbr ante meridiem, i.e., before noon; amplitude modulation

Am. abbr **America, American**

amalgam [ə'mælgəm] s amalgama f

amalgamate [ə'mælgə,met] tr amalgamar ‖ intr amalgamarse

amass [ə'mæs] tr amontonar; amasar (dinero)

amateur ['æmət/ər] adj & s chapucero, principiante mf; aficionado

amateur performance s función de aficionados

amaze [ə'mez] tr asombrar, maravillar

amazing [ə'mezɪŋ] adj asombroso, maravilloso

Amazon ['æmə,zɑn] s Amazonas m

ambassador [æm'bæsədər] s embajador m

ambassadress [æm'bæsədrɪs] s embajadora

amber ['æmbər] adj ambarino ‖ s ámbar m

ambigui•ty [,æmbɪ'gju•ɪti] s (pl -ties) ambigüedad

ambiguous [æm'bɪgju•əs] adj ambiguo

ambition [æm'bɪʃən] s ambición

ambitious [æm'bɪʃəs] adj ambicioso

amble ['æmbəl] s ambladura ‖ intr amblar

ambulance ['æmbjələns] s ambulancia

ambush ['æmbuʃ] s emboscada; **to lie in ambush** estar emboscado ‖ tr (to station in ambush) emboscar; (to lie in wait for and attack) insidiar ‖ intr emboscarse

ame•ba [ə'mibə] s (pl -bas o -bae [bi]) amiba

amelioration [ə,miljə'reʃən] s mejoramiento

amen ['e'mɛn] o ['a'mɛn] interj ¡amén! ‖ s amén m

amenable [ə'minəbəl] o [ə'mɛnəbəl] adj dócil; responsable

amend [ə'mɛnd] tr enmendar ‖ intr enmendarse ‖ **amends** spl enmienda; **to make amends for** enmendar

amendment [ə'mɛndmənt] s enmienda

ameni•ty [ə'mɪnɪti] o [ə'mɛnɪti] s (pl -ties) amenidad

America [ə'mɛrɪkə] s América

American [ə'mɛrɪkən] adj & s americano; norteamericano, estadounidense

Americanize [ə'mɛrɪkə,naɪz] tr americanizar

amethyst ['æmɪθɪst] s amatista

amiable ['emi•əbəl] adj amable, bonachón

amicable ['æmɪkəbəl] adj amigable

amid [ə'mɪd] prep en medio de

amidship [ə'mɪdʃɪp] adv en medio del navío

amiss [ə'mɪs] adj inoportuno; malo ‖ adv inoportunamente; mal; **to take amiss** llevar a mal, tomar en mala parte

ami•ty ['æmɪti] s (pl -ties) amistad

ammeter ['æm,mitər] s anmetro, amperímetro

ammonia [ə'moni•ə] s amoníaco; agua amoniacal

ammunition [,æmjə'nɪʃən] s munición

amnes•ty ['æmnɪsti] s (pl -ties) amnistía ‖ v (pret & pp -tied) tr amnistiar

amniocentesis [,æmnɪ-osen'tisɪs] s amniocentesis f

amoeba [ə'mibə] s var of **ameba**

among [ə'mʌŋ] prep entre, en medio de, en el número de

amorous ['æmərəs] adj amoroso; erótico, sensual, voluptuoso

amortize ['æmər,taɪz] tr amortizar

amount [ə'maunt] s cantidad, importe m ‖ intr — **to amount to** ascender a; significar

amp. abbr **ampere, amperage**

ampere ['æmpɪr] s amperio

am'pere-hour' s amperio-hora m

amphibious [æm'fɪbɪ•əs] adj anfibio

amphitheater ['æmfɪ,θi•ətər] s anfiteatro

ample ['æmpəl] adj amplio; bastante, suficiente; abundante

amplifier ['æmplɪ,faɪ•ər] s amplificador m

ampli•fy [ˈæmplɪˌfaɪ] v (*pret & pp* **-fied**) *tr* amplificar ‖ *intr* espaciarse

amplitude [ˈæmplɪˌtjud] *s* amplitud

amplitude modulation *s* modulación de amplitud

ampule [ˈæmpjul] *s* inyectable *m*

amputate [ˈæmpjəˌtet] *tr* amputar

amt. *abbr* amount

amuck [əˈmʌk] *adv* frenéticamente; **to run amuck** atacar a ciegas

amulet [ˈæmjəlɪt] *s* amuleto

amuse [əˈmjuz] *tr* divertir, entretener

amusement [əˈmjuzmənt] *s* diversión, entretenimiento; pasatiempo, recreación; (*in a park or circus*) atracción

amusement park *s* parque *m* de atracciones

amusing [əˈmjuzɪŋ] *adj* divertido, gracioso

an [æn] o [ən] *art indef* (antes de sonido vocal) un

anachronism [əˈnækrəˌnɪzəm] *s* anacronismo

anachronistic [əˌnækrəˈnɪstɪk] *adj* anacrónico

anaemia [əˈnimɪ•ə] *s* anemia

anaemic [əˈnimɪk] *adj* anémico

anaesthesia [ˌænɪsˈθiʒə] *s* anestesia

anaesthetic [ˌænɪsˈθɛtɪk] *adj & s* anestésico

anaesthetize [æˈnɛsθɪˌtaɪz] *tr* anestesiar

analogous [əˈnæləgəs] *adj* análogo

analo•gy [əˈnælədʒi] *s* (*pl* **-gies**) analogía

analyse [ˈænəˌlaɪz] *tr* analizar

analy•sis [əˈnælɪsɪs] *s* (*pl* **-ses** [ˌsiz]) análisis *m & f*

analyst [ˈænəlɪst] *s* analista *mf*

analytic(al) [ˌænəˈlɪtɪk(əl)] *adj* analítico

analyze [ˈænəˌlaɪz] *tr* analizar

anarchist [ˈænərkɪst] *s* anarquista *mf*

anarchy [ˈænərki] *s* anarquía

anathema [əˈnæθɪmə] *s* anatema *m & f*

anatomic(al) [ˌænəˈtɑmɪk(əl)] *adj* anatómico

anato•my [əˈnætəmi] *s* (*pl* **-mies**) anatomía

ancestor [ˈænsɛstər] *s* antecesor *m*, antepasado

ances•try [ˈænsɛstri] *s* (*pl* **-tries**) abolengo, alcurnia

anchor [ˈæŋkər] *s* ancla, áncora; (fig) áncora; **to cast anchor** echar anclas; **to weigh anchor** levar anclas ‖ *tr* sujetar con el ancla ‖ *intr* anclar, ancorar

ancho•vy [ˈæntʃovi] *s* (*pl* **-vies**) anchoa

ancient [ˈenʃənt] *adj* antiguo

and [ænd] o [ənd] *conj* y; **and so forth** y así sucesivamente

Andalusia [ˌændəˈluʒə] *s* Andalucía

Andalusian [ˌændəˈluʒən] *adj & s* andaluz *m*

Andean [ænˈdi•ən] *adj & s* andino

Andes [ˈændiz] *spl* Andes *mpl*

andirons [ˈændˌaɪ•ərnz] *spl* morillos

anecdote [ˈænɪkˌdot] *s* anécdota

anemia [əˈnimɪ•ə] *s* anemia

anemic [əˈnimɪk] *adj* anémico

aneroid barometer [ˈænəˌrɔɪd] *s* barómetro aneroide

anesthesia [ˌænɪsˈθiʒə] *s* anestesia

anesthetic [ˌænɪsˈθɛtɪk] *adj & s* anestésico

anesthetize [æˈnɛsθɪˌtaɪz] *tr* anestesiar

aneurysm [ˈænjəˌrɪzəm] *s* aneurisma *m*

anew [əˈnju] o [əˈnu] *adv* de nuevo, nuevamente

angel [ˈendʒəl] *s* ángel *m;* (*financial backer*) caballo blanco

angelic(al) [ænˈdʒɛlɪk(əl)] *adj* angélico, angelical

anger [ˈæŋgər] *s* cólera, ira ‖ *tr* encolerizar, airar

angina pectoris [ænˈdʒaɪnə ˈpɛktərɪs] *s* angina de pecho

angle [ˈæŋgəl] *s* ángulo; punto de vista ‖ *intr* pescar con caña; intrigar

angle iron *s* ángulo de hierro, hierro angular

angler [ˈæŋglər] *s* pescador *m* de caña; intrigante *mf*

Anglo-Saxon [ˌæŋgloˈsæksən] *adj & s* anglosajón *m*

an•gry [ˈæŋgri] *adj* (*comp* **-grier;** *super* **-griest**) encolerizado, airado; (pathol) inflamado, irritado; **to become angry at** enojarse de; **to become angry with** enojarse con o contra

anguish [ˈæŋgwɪʃ] *s* angustia, congoja

angular [ˈæŋgjələr] *adj* angular; (*features*) anguloso

anhydrous [ænˈhaɪdrəs] *adj* anhidro

aniline dyes [ˈænɪlɪn] o [ˈænɪˌlaɪn] *s* colores *mpl* de anilina

animal [ˈænɪməl] *adj & s* animal *m*

animal spirits *spl* ardor *m*, vigor *m*, vivacidad

animated cartoon [ˈænɪˌmetɪd] *s* película de dibujos, dibujo animado

animation [ˌænɪˈmeʃən] *s* animación

animosi•ty [ˌænɪˈmɑsɪti] *s* (*pl* **-ties**) animosidad

anion [ˈænˌaɪ•ən] *s* anión *m*

anise [ˈænɪs] *s* anís *m*

aniseed [ˈænɪˌsid] *s* grano de anís

anisette [ˌænɪˈzɛt] *s* anisete *m*

ankle [ˈæŋkəl] *s* tobillo

an•kle•bone′ *s* hueso del tobillo

ankle support *s* tobillera

anklet [ˈæŋklɪt] *s* ajorca; (*sock*) tobillera

annals [ˈænəlz] *spl* anales *mpl*

anneal [əˈnil] *tr* recocer

annex [ˈænɛks] *s* anexo; (*of a building*) pabellón *m* ‖ [əˈnɛks] *tr* anexar

annihilate [əˈnaɪ•ɪˌlet] *tr* aniquilar

anniversa•ry [ˌænɪˈvʌrsəri] *adj* aniversario ‖ *s* (*pl* **-ries**) aniversario

annotate [ˈænəˌtet] *tr* anotar

announce [əˈnaʊns] *tr* anunciar

announcement [əˈnaʊnsmənt] *s* anuncio

announcer [əˈnaʊnsər] *s* anunciador *m;* (rad) locutor *m*

annoy [əˈnɔɪ] *tr* fastidiar, molestar; majadear; pololear; (Cuba, Mex) ciscar

annoyance [əˈnɔɪ•əns] *s* fastidio, molestia

annoying [əˈnɔɪ•ɪŋ] *adj* fastidioso, molesto

annual [ˈænjuˌəl] *adj* anual ‖ *s* publicación anual; planta anual

annui•ty [əˈnjuˌɪti] o [əˈnuˌɪti] *s* (*pl* **-ties**) anualidad; renta vitalicia

an•nul [əˈnʌl] *v* (*pret & pp* **-nulled;** *ger* **-nulling**) *tr* anular, invalidar

anode [ˈænod] *s* ánodo

al
an

anoint [ə'nɔɪnt] *tr* ungir, untar
anomalous [ə'nɑmələs] *adj* anómalo
anoma•ly [ə'nɑməli] *s* (*pl* **-lies**) anomalía
anon. *abbr* **anonymous**
anonymity [,ænə'nɪmɪti] *s* anónimo; **to preserve one's anonymity** guardar o conservar el anónimo
anonymous [ə'nɑnɪməs] *adj* anónimo
another [ə'nʌðər] *adj & pron indef* otro
ans. *abbr* **answer**
answer ['ænsər] *s* contestación, respuesta; solución ‖ *tr* contestar, responder; resolver (*un problema o un enigma*) ‖ *intr* contestar, responder; **to answer for** responder de (*una cosa*); responder por (*una persona*)
ant [ænt] *s* hormiga
antagonism [æn'tægə,nɪzəm] *s* antagonismo
antagonize [æn'tægə,naɪz] *tr* oponerse a; enemistar, enajenar
antarctic [ænt'ɑrktɪk] *adj* antártico ‖ **the Antarctic** las Tierras Antárticas
antecedent [,æntɪ'sidənt] *adj* antecedente ‖ *s* antecedente *m*; **antecedents** antecedentes *mpl*; antepasados
antechamber ['æntɪ,tʃembər] *s* antecámara
antedate ['æntɪ,det] *tr* antedatar; preceder
antelope ['æntɪ,lop] *s* antílope *m*
anten•na [æn'tɛnə] *s* (*pl* **-nae** [ni]) (ent) antena ‖ *s* (*pl* **-nas**) (rad) antena
autepenult [,æntɪ'pinʌlt] *s* antepenúltima
anteroom ['æntɪ,rum] *s* antecámara
anthem ['ænθəm] *s* himno; antífona
ant'hill' *s* hormiguero
antholo•gy [æn'θɑlədʒi] *s* (*pl* **-gies**) antología
anthracite ['ænθrə,saɪt] *s* antracita
anthrax ['ænθræks] *s* ántrax *m*
anthropology [,ænθrə'pɑlədʒi] *s* antropología
anti-aircraft [,æntɪ'ɛr,kræft] *adj* antiaéreo
antibiotic [,æntɪbaɪ'ɑtɪk] *adj & s* antibiótico
antibod•y ['æntɪ,bɑdi] *s* (*pl* **-ies**) anticuerpo
anticipate [æn'tɪsɪ,pet] *tr* esperar, prever; anticipar; (*to get ahead of*) anticiparse a; impedir; prometerse (*p.ej.. un placer*); temerse (*algo desagradable*)
antics ['æntɪks] *spl* cabriolas, gracias, travesuras
antidote ['æntɪ,dot] *s* antídoto
antifreeze [,æntɪ'friz] *s* anticongelante *m*
antiglare [,æntɪ'glɛr] *adj* antideslumbrante
antiknock [,æntɪ'nɑk] *adj & s* antidetonante *m*
antilabor [,æntɪ'lebər] *adj* antiobrero
Antilles [æn'tɪliz] *spl* Antillas
antimatter ['æntɪ,mætər] *s* antimateria
antimissile [,æntɪ'mɪsɪl] *adj* antiproyectil
antimony ['æntɪ,moni] *s* antimonio
antipas•to [,ɑntɪ'pɑsto] *s* (*pl* **-tos**) aperitivo, entremés *m*
antipa•thy [æn'tɪpəθi] *s* (*pl* **-thies**) antipatía
antipollution movement [,æntɪpə'luʃən] *s* lucha antipolución
antiquar•y ['æntɪ,kwɛri] *s* (*pl* **-ies**) anticuario
antiquated ['æntɪ,kwetɪd] *adj* anticuado
antique [æn'tik] *adj* antiguo ‖ *s* antigüedad
antique dealer *s* anticuario

antique store *s* tienda de antigüedades
antiqui•ty [æn'tɪkwɪti] *s* (*pl* **-ties**) antigüedad
anti-Semitic [,æntɪsɪ'mɪtɪk] *adj* antisemítico
antiseptic [,æntɪ'sɛptɪk] *adj & s* antiséptico
antislavery [,æntɪ'slevəri] *adj* antiesclavista
anti-Soviet [,æntɪ'sovɪ,ɛt] *adj* antisoviético
antitank [,æntɪ'tæŋk] *adj* antitanque
antiterrorist [,æntɪ'tɛrərɪst] *adj & s* antiterrorista *mf*
antithe•sis [æn'tɪθɪsɪs] *s* (*pl* **-ses** [,siz]) antítesis *f*
antitoxin [,æntɪ'tɑksɪn] *s* antitoxina
antitrust [,æntɪ'trʌst] *adj* anticartel
antiwar [,æntɪ'wɔr] *adj* antibélico
antler ['æntlər] *s* cuerna
antonym ['æntənɪm] *s* antónimo
Antwerp ['æntwərp] *s* Amberes *f*
anvil ['ænvɪl] *s* yunque *m*
anxie•ty [æŋ'zaɪ•əti] *s* (*pl* **-ties**) ansiedad, inquietud; ansia, anhelo
anxious ['æŋk/əs] *adj* ansioso, inquieto; anhelante; **to be anxious to** tener ganas de
any ['ɛni] *adj indef* algún, cualquier; todo; **any place** dondequiera; **any time** cuando quiera; alguna vez ‖ *pron indef* alguno, cualquiera ‖ *adv* algo
an'y•bod'y *pron indef* alguno, alguien, cualquiera, quienquiera; todo el mundo; **not anybody** nadie
an'y•how' *adv* de cualquier modo; de todos modos; sin embargo
an'y•one' *pron indef* alguno, alguien, cualquiera
an'y•thing' *pron indef* algo, alguna cosa; cualquier cosa; todo cuanto; **anything at all** cualquier cosa que sea; **anything else** cualquier otra cosa; **anything else?** ¿algo más?; **not anything** nada
an'y•way' *adv* de cualquier modo; de todos modos; sin embargo; sin esmero, sin orden ni concierto
an'y•where' *adv* dondequiera; adondequiera; **not anywhere** en ninguna parte
apace [ə'pes] *adv* aprisa
apart [ə'pɑrt] *adv* aparte; en pedazos; **to fall apart** caerse a pedazos; desunirse; ir al desastre; **to live apart** vivir separados; vivir aislado; **to stand apart** mantenerse apartado; **to take apart** descomponer, desarmar, desmontar; **to tell apart** distinguir
apartment [ə'pɑrtmənt] *s* apartamento
apartment house *s* casa de pisos
apathetic [,æpə'θɛtɪk] *adj* apático
apa•thy ['æpəθi] *s* (*pl* **-ties**) apatía; lerdera
ape [ep] *s* mono ‖ *tr* imitar, remedar
aperture ['æpərtʃər] *s* abertura, orificio
apex ['epɛks] *s* (*pl* **apexes** o **apices** ['æpɪ,siz]) ápex *m*, ápice *m*
aphorism ['æfə,rɪzəm] *s* aforismo
aphrodisiac [,æfrə'dɪzɪ,æk] *adj & s* afrodisíaco
apiar•y ['epɪ,ɛri] *s* (*pl* **-ies**) abejar *m*, colmenar *m*
apiece [ə'pis] *adv* cada uno; por persona
apish ['epɪʃ] *adj* monesco; tonto
aplomb [ə'plɑm] *s* aplomo, sangre fría
apogee ['æpə,dʒi] *s* apogeo

apologetic [ə,pɑlə'dʒɛtɪk] *adj* lleno de excusas

apologist [ə'pɑlədʒɪst] *s* defensor *m;* exponente *m*

apologize [ə'pɑlə,dʒaɪz] *intr* excusarse, disculparse; **to apologize for** disculparse de; **to apologize to** disculparse con

apology [ə'pɑlədʒi] *s* (*pl* **-gies**) excusa; (*makeshift*) expediente *m*

apoplectic [,æpə'plɛktɪk] *adj & s* apoplético

apoplexy ['æpə,plɛksi] *s* apoplejía

apostle [ə'pɑsəl] *s* apóstol *m*

apostrophe [ə'pɑstrəfi] *s* (*written sign*) apóstrofo; (*words addressed to absent person*) apóstrofe *m & f*

apothecar·y [ə'pɑθɪ,kɛri] *s* (*pl* **-ies**) boticario

apothecary's jar *s* bote *m* de porcelana

apothecary's shop *s* botica

appall [ə'pɔl] *tr* espantar, pasmar

appalling [ə'pɔlɪŋ] *adj* aterrador, espantoso, pasmoso

appara·tus [,æpə'retəs] o [,æpə'rætəs] *s* (*pl* **-tus** o **-tuses**) aparato

apparel [ə'pærəl] *s* indumentaria, vestido

apparent [ə'pærənt] *adj* aparente

apparition [,æpə'rɪ/ən] *s* aparición

appeal [ə'pil] *s* súplica, instancia, solicitud; atracción, interés *m;* (*law*) apelación ‖ *intr* ser atrayente; **to appeal to** (*to make an entreaty to*) suplicar; (*to be attractive to*) atraer, interesar; (*law*) apelar a

appear [ə'pɪr] *intr* (*to come into sight; to be in sight; to be published*) aparecer; (*to come into sight; to be in sight; to look; to seem*) parecer; (*to come before the public*) presentarse; (*to come before a court*) comparecer

appearance [ə'pɪrəns] *s* (*act of appearing*) aparición; (*outward look*) apariencia, aspecto; (*law*) comparecencia

appease [ə'piz] *tr* apaciguar

appeasement [ə'pizmənt] *s* apaciguamiento

appeasement attempts *spl* (coll) paños tibios *mpl*

appellate [ə'pɛlɪt] *adj* apelante

appellate court *s* tribunal *m* de apelación

appellate judge *s* juez *m* de alzadas

appendage [ə'pɛndɪdʒ] *s* apéndice *m*

appendicitis [ə,pɛndɪ'saɪtɪs] *s* apendicitis *f*

appen·dix [ə'pɛndɪks] *s* (*pl* **-dixes** o **-dices** [dɪ,siz]) apéndice *m*

appertain [,æpər'ten] *intr* relacionarse

appetite ['æpɪ,taɪt] *s* apetito

appetizer ['æpɪ,taɪzər] *s* aperitivo, apetite *m*

appetizing ['æpɪ,taɪzɪŋ] *adj* apetitoso

applaud [ə'plɔd] *tr & intr* aplaudir

applause [ə'plɔz] *s* aplauso, aplausos

apple ['æpəl] *s* manzana

ap'ple·jack' *s* aguardiente *m* de manzana

·apple of the eye *s* niña del ojo

apple pie *s* pastel *m* de manzana

apple polisher *s* (slang) quitamotas *mf*

ap'ple·sauce' *s* compota de manzanas; (slang) música celestial

apple tree *s* manzano

appliance [ə'plaɪ·əns] *s* artificio, dispositivo, aparato; aplicación

applicant ['æplɪkənt] *s* aspirante *mf*, pretendiente *mf*, solicitante *mf*

ap·ply [ə'plaɪ] *v* (*pret & pp* **-plied**) *tr* aplicar ‖ *intr* aplicarse; dirigirse; **to apply for** pedir, solicitar

appoint [ə'pɔɪnt] *tr* designar, nombrar; señalar; amueblar

appointment [ə'pɔɪntmənt] *s* designación, nombramiento; empleo, puesto; cita; **appointments** instalación, accesorios, adornos; **by appointment** cita previa

apportion [ə'por/ən] *tr* prorratear

appraisal [ə'prezəl] *s* tasación, valoración, apreciación

appraise [ə'prez] *tr* tasar, valorar, apreciar

appreciable [ə'pri/ɪ·əbəl] *adj* apreciable; sensible

appreciate [ə'pri/ɪ,et] *tr* apreciar; aprobar; comprender; estar agradecido por ‖ *intr* subir de valor

appreciation [ə,pri/ɪ'e/ən] *s* aprecio; agradecimiento; plusvalía, aumento de valor

appreciative [ə'pri/ɪ,etɪv] *adj* apreciador; agradecido

apprehend [,æprɪ'hɛnd] *tr* aprehender, prender; comprender; temer

apprehension [,æprɪ'hɛn/ən] *s* aprehensión; (*fear, worry*) aprensión; comprensión

apprehensive [,æprɪ'hɛnsɪv] *adj* (*fearful, worried*) aprehensivo, aprensivo

apprentice [ə'prɛntɪs] *s* aprendiz *m*, meritorio; chumero, chumera (CAm) ‖ *tr* poner de aprendiz

apprenticeship [ə'prɛntɪs/ɪp] *s* aprendizaje *m*

apprise o **apprize** [ə'praɪz] *tr* informar; apreciar, tasar

approach [ə'prot/] *s* acercamiento; vía de entrada; proposición; (*to a problem*) enfoque *m* ‖ *tr* abordar, acercarse a; (*to bring closer*) acercar ‖ *intr* acercarse, aproximarse

approbation [,æprə'be/ən] *s* aprobación

appropriate [ə'propri·ɪt] *adj* apropiado, a propósito ‖ [ə'propri,et] *tr* apropiarse; asignar, destinar (*el parlamento determinada suma a un determinado fin*)

approval [ə'pruvəl] *s* aprobación; **on approval** a prueba

approve [ə'pruv] *tr & intr* aprobar

approximate [ə'prɑksɪmɪt] *adj* aproximado ‖ [ə'prɑksɪ,met] *tr* aproximar ‖ *intr* aproximarse

apricot ['eprɪ,kɑt] o ['æprɪ,kɑt] *s* albaricoque *m*

apricot tree *s* albaricoquero

April ['eprɪl] *s* abril *m*

April fool *s* — **to make an April fool of** coger por inocente

April Fools' Day *s* día *m* de engañabobos, primer día de abril, en que se coge por inocente a la gente

apron ['eprən] *s* delantal *m;* (*of a workman*) mandil *m;* **tied to the apron strings of** cosido a las faldas de

an
ap

apropos [,æprə'po] *adj* oportuno ‖ *adv* a propósito; **apropos of** a propósito de

apse [æps] *s* ábside *m*

apt [æpt] *adj* apto; a propósito; dispuesto, inclinado

aptitude ['æptɪ,tjud] *s* aptitud

aquamarine [,ækwəmə'rin] *s* aguamarina

aquaplane ['ækwə,plen] *s* acuaplano ‖ *intr* correr en acuaplano

aquari•um [ə'kwɛrɪ•əm] *s* (*pl* -ums o -a [ə]) acuario

Aquarius [ə'kwɛrɪ•əs] *s* (astr) Acuario

aquatic [ə'kwætɪk] o [ə'kwɑtɪk] *adj* acuático ‖ **aquatics** *spl* deportes acuáticos

aqueduct ['ækwə,dʌkt] *s* acueducto

aquiline nose ['ækwɪ,laɪn] *s* nariz aguileña

Arab ['ærəb] *adj* árabe ‖ *s* árabe *mf*; caballo árabe

Arabia [ə'rebɪ•ə] *s* la Arabia

Arabian [ə'rebɪ•ən] *adj* árabe; arábigo ‖ *s* árabe *mf*

Arabic ['ærəbɪk] *adj* arábigo ‖ *s* árabe *m*, arábigo

Aragon ['ærə,gɑn] *s* Aragón *m*

Arago•nese [,ærəgə'niz] *adj* aragonés ‖ *s* (*pl* -nese) aragonés *m*

arbiter ['ɑrbɪtər] *s* árbitro

arbitrary ['ɑrbɪ,trɛri] *adj* arbitrario

arbitrate ['ɑrbɪ,tret] *tr & intr* arbitrar

arbitration [,ɑrbɪ'treʃən] *s* arbitraje *m*

arbor ['ɑrbər] *s* emparrado, glorieta

arbore•tum [,ɑrbə'ritəm] *s* (*pl* -tums o -ta [tə]) jardín botánico de árboles

arbor vitae ['ɑrbər 'vaɪti] *s* árbol *m* de la vida

arbutus [ɑr'bjutəs] *s* madroño

arc [ɑrk] *s* arco

arcade [ɑr'ked] *s* arcada, galería

arch. *abbr* **archaic, archaism, archipelago, architect**

arch [ɑrʃ] *adj* astuto; travieso; principal ‖ *s* arco ‖ *tr* arquear, enarcar; atravesar

archaeology [,ɑrkɪ'ɑlədʒi] *s* arqueología

archaic [ɑr'ke•ɪk] *adj* arcaico

archaism ['ɑrke,ɪzəm] *s* arcaísmo

archangel ['ɑrk,endʒəl] *s* arcángel *m*

archbishop ['ɑrʃ'bɪʃəp] *s* arzobispo

archduke ['ɑrʃ'djuk] *s* archiduque *m*

archene•my ['ɑrʃ,ɛnimi] *s* (*pl* -mies) archienemigo

archeology [,ɑrkɪ'ɑlədʒi] *s* arqueología

archer ['ɑrʃər] *s* arquero, flechero

archery ['ɑrʃəri] *s* tiro de flechas

archipela•go [,ɑrkɪ'pɛləgo] *s* (*pl* -gos o -goes) archipiélago

architect ['ɑrkɪ,tɛkt] *s* arquitecto

architectural [,ɑrkɪ'tɛkʃərəl] *adj* arquitectónico, arquitectural

architecture ['ɑrkɪ,tɛkʃər] *s* arquitectura

archives ['ɑrkaɪvz] *spl* archivo

arch'way' *s* arcada

arc lamp *s* lámpara de arco

arctic ['ɑrktɪk] *adj* ártico ‖ **the Arctic** las Tierras Árticas

arc welding *s* soldadura de arco

ardent ['ɑrdənt] *adj* ardiente

ardor ['ɑrdər] *s* ardor *m*

arduous ['ɑrdju•əs] *adj* arduo, difícil; enérgico; (*steep*) escarpado

area ['ɛrɪ•ə] *s* área, superficie *f*; comarca, región; zona; patio

ar'ea•way' *s* entrada baja de un sótano

Argentina [,ɑrdʒən'tinə] *s* la Argentina

Argentine ['ɑrdʒən,tin] o ['ɑrdʒən,taɪn] *adj* & *s* argentino ‖ **the Argentine** la Argentina

Argentinean [,ɑrdʒən'tɪnɪ•ən] *adj* & *s* argentino

Argonaut ['ɑrgə,nɔt] *s* argonauta *m*

argue ['ɑrgju] *tr* argüir; **to argue into** persuadir a + *inf*; **to argue out of** disuadir de + *inf* ‖ *intr* argüir

argument ['ɑrgjəmənt] *s* argumento; disputa

argumentative [,ɑrgjə'mɛntətɪv] *adj* argumentador; ergotista *masc*

argumentativeness [,ɑrgjə'mɛntətɪvnɪs] *s* ergotismo

aria ['ɑrɪ•ə] o ['ɛrɪ•ə] *s* (mus) aria

arid ['ærɪd] *adj* árido

aridity [ə'rɪdɪti] *s* aridez *f*

Aries ['ɛriz] *s* (astr) Aries *m*

aright [ə'raɪt] *adv* acertadamente; **to set aright** rectificar

arise [ə'raɪz] *v* (*pret* **arose** [ə'roz]; *pp* **arisen** [ə'rɪzən]) *intr* levantarse; subir; aparecer; **to arise from** provenir de

aristocra•cy [,ærɪs'tɑkrəsi] *s* (*pl* -cies) aristocracia

aristocrat [ə'rɪstə,kræt] *s* aristócrata *mf*

aristocratic [ə,rɪstə'krætɪk] *adj* aristocrático

Aristotelian [,ærɪstə'tilɪ•ən] *adj* & *s* aristotélico

Aristotle ['ærɪs,tɑtəl] *s* Aristóteles *m*

arith. *abbr* **arithmetic**

arithmetic [ə'rɪθmətɪk] *s* aritmética

arithmetical [,ærɪθ'mɛtɪkəl] *adj* aritmético

arithmetician [ə,rɪθmə'tɪʃən] *s* aritmético

ark [ɑrk] *s* arca de Noé

ark of the covenant *s* arca de la alianza

arm [ɑrm] *s* brazo; (*weapon*) arma; **arm in arm** de bracero, asidos del brazo; **in arms** de pecho, de teta; **the three arms of the service** los tres ejércitos; **to be up in arms** estar en armas; **to keep at arm's length** mantener a distancia; mantenerse a distancia; **to lay down one's arms** rendir las armas; **to rise up in arms** alzarse en armas; **under arms** sobre las armas ‖ *tr* armar ‖ *intr* armarse

armament ['ɑrməmənt] *s* armamento

armature ['ɑrmə,tʃər] *s* armadura; (*of a dynamo or motor*) (elec) inducido

arm'chair' *adj* de gabinete ‖ *s* butaca, sillón *m*, silla de brazos

Armenian [ɑr'minɪ•ən] *adj* & *s* armenio

armful ['ɑrm,ful] *s* brazado

arm'hole' *s* (*in clothing*) sobaquera

armistice ['ɑrmɪstɪs] *s* armisticio

armor ['ɑrmər] *s* armadura; coraza, blindaje *m* ‖ *tr* acorazar, blindar

armored car *s* carro blindado

armorial bearings [ɑr'morɪ•əl] *spl* blasón *m*, escudo de armas

armor plate *s* plancha de blindaje

ar′mor-plate′ *tr* acorazar, blindar

armor·y [′arməri] *s* (*pl* -ies) arsenal *m;* (*arms factory*) armería

arm′pit′ *s* sobaco, hueco de la axila

arm′rest′ *s* apoyabrazos *m*

arms race *s* carrera armanentista

arms reduction *s* desarmamiento

ar·my [′armi] *adj* militar, castrense ‖ *s* (*pl* -mies) ejército

army corps *s* cuerpo de ejército

aroma [ə′romə] *s* aroma *m*, fragancia

aromatic [,ærə′mætɪk] *adj* aromático

around [ə′raʊnd] *adv* alrededor, a la redonda; en la dirección opuesta ‖ *prep* alrededor de, en torno a o de; cerca de; (*the corner*) a la vuelta de

arouse [ə′raʊz] *tr* despertar; excitar, incitar

arpeg·gio [ar′pɛdʒo] *s* (*pl* -gios) arpegio

arraign [ə′ren] *tr* acusar; presentar al tribunal

arrange [ə′rendʒ] *tr* arreglar, disponer; (mus) adaptar, refundir

array [ə′re] *s* orden *m;* orden *m* de batalla; adorno, atavío ‖ *tr* poner en orden; poner en orden de batalla; adornar, ataviar

arrears [ə′rɪrz] *spl* atrasos; **in arrears** atrasado en pagos

arrest [ə′rɛst] *s* arresto, prisión; detención; **under arrest** bajo arresto ‖ *tr* arrestar; detener; atraer (*la atención*)

arresting [ə′rɛstɪŋ] *adj* impresionante

arrhythmia [ə′rɪθmi·ə] *s* arritmia

arrival [ə′raɪvəl] *s* llegada; (*person*) llegado

arrive [ə′raɪv] *intr* llegar; tener éxito

arrogance [′ærəgəns] *s* arrogancia

arrogant [′ærəgənt] *adj* arrogante

arrogate [′ærə,get] *tr* — **to arrogate to oneself** arrogarse

arrow [′æro] *s* flecha

ar′row-head′ *s* punta de flecha; (bot) saetilla

arsenal [′arsənəl] *s* arsenal *m*

arsenic [′arsɪnɪk] *s* arsénico

arson [′arsən] *s* incendio premeditado, delito de incendio

art [art] *s* arte *m & f*

arter·y [′artəri] *s* (*pl* -ies) arteria

artful [′artfəl] *adj* astuto, mañoso; diestro, ingenioso

arthritic [ar′θrɪtɪk] *adj & s* artrítico

arthritis [ar′θraɪtɪs] *s* artritis *f*

artichoke [′artɪ,tʃok] *s* alcachofa

article [′artɪkəl] *s* artículo; **an article of clothing** una prenda de vestir

articulate [ar′tɪkjəlɪt] *adj* claro, distinto; capaz de hablar ‖ [ar′tɪkjə,let] *tr* articular

artifact [′artɪ,fækt] *s* artefacto

artifice [′artɪfɪs] *s* artificio

artificial [,artɪ′fɪʃəl] *adj* artificial

artillery [ar′tɪləri] *s* artillería

artillery·man [ar′tɪlərimən] *s* (*pl* -men [mən]) artillero

artisan [′artɪzən] *s* artesano

artist [′artɪst] *s* artista *mf*

artistic [ar′tɪstɪk] *adj* artístico

artistry [′artɪstri] *s* habilidad artística

artless [′artlɪs] *adj* sencillo, natural; ingenuo, inocente; (*crude, clumsy*) chabacano

arts and crafts *spl* artes y oficios

art·y [′arti] *adj* (*comp* -ier; *super* -iest) (coll) ostentoso artístico

Aryan [′ɛri·ən] *o* [′arjən] *adj & s* ario

as [æz] *o* [əz] *pron rel* que; **the same as** el mismo que ‖ *adv* tan; **as . . . as** tan . . . como; **as for** en cuanto a; **as long as** mientras que; ya que; **as many as** tantos como; **as much as** tanto como; **as regards** en cuanto a; **as soon as** tan pronto como; **as soon as possible** cuanto antes, los más pronto posible; **as though** como si; **as to** en cuanto a; **as well** también; **as yet** hasta ahora ‖ *conf* como; que; ya que; a medida que; **as it seems** por lo visto, según parece ‖ *prep* por, como; **as a rule** por regla general

asbestos [æs′bɛstəs] *s* asbesto, amianto

ascend [ə′sɛnd] *tr* subir a (*p.ej., el trono*) ‖ *intr* ascender

ascendancy [ə′sɛndənsi] *s* ascendiente *m*

ascension [ə′sɛnʃən] *s* ascensión

Ascension Day *s* fiesta de la Ascensión

ascent [ə′sɛnt] *s* ascensión, subida; ascenso, promoción

ascertain [,æsər′ten] *tr* averiguar

ascertainable [,æsər′tenəbəl] *adj* averiguable

ascetic [ə′sɛtɪk] *adj* ascético ‖ *s* asceta *mf*

ascorbic acid [ə′skɔrbɪk] *s* ácido ascórbico

ascribe [ə′skraɪb] *tr* atribuir

aseptic [ə′sɛptɪk] *o* [e′sɛptɪk] *adj* aséptico

ash [æʃ] *s* ceniza; (*tree; wood*) fresno; **ashes** ceniza, cenizas; (*mortal remains*) cenizas

ashamed [ə′ʃemd] *adj* avergonzado; **to be ashamed** tener vergüenza

ashlar [′æʃlər] *s* sillar *m*

ashore [ə′ʃor] *adv* en tierra, a tierra

ash tray *s* cenicero

Ash Wednesday *s* miércoles *m* de ceniza

Asia [′eʒə] *o* [′eʃə] *s* Asia

Asia Minor *s* el Asia Menor

Asian [′eʒən] *o* [′eʃən] *o* **Asiatic** [,eʒɪ′ætɪk] *o* [,eʃɪ′ætɪk] *adj & s* asiático

aside [ə′saɪd] *adv* aparte; **aside from** además de; **to step aside** hacerse a un lado ‖ *s* (theat) aparte *m*

asinine [′æsɪ,naɪn] *adj* tonto, necio

ask [æsk] *o* [ask] *tr* (*to request*) pedir; (*to inquire of*) preguntar; hacer (*una pregunta*); invitar; **to ask in** invitar a entrar ‖ *intr*—**to ask about, after,** or **for**; preguntar por; **to ask for** pedir

askance [ə′skæns] *adv* al sesgo, de soslayo; con desdén, sospechosamente

asleep [ə′slip] *adj* dormido; **to fall asleep** dormirse

asp [æsp] *s* áspid *m*

asparagus [ə′spærəgəs] *s* espárrago

aspect [′æspɛkt] *s* aspecto

aspen [′æspən] *s* tiemblo, álamo temblón

aspersion [ə′spʌrʒən] *o* [ə′spʌrʃən] *s* calumnia, difamación

asphalt [′æsfɔlt] *s* asfalto ‖ *tr* asfaltar

asphyxiate [æs′fɪksɪ,et] *tr* asfixiar

aspirant [ə′spaɪrənt] *o* [′æspɪrənt] *s* pretendiente *mf*, candidato

aspire [ə′spaɪr] *intr* aspirar

aspirin [′æspɪrɪn] *s* aspirina

ass [æs] *s* asno
assail [ə'sel] *tr* asaltar, acometer
assassin [ə'sæsɪn] *s* asesino
assassinate [ə'sæsɪ,net] *tr* asesinar
assassination [ə,sæsɪ'neʃən] *s* asesinato
assault [ə'sɔlt] *s* asalto ‖ *tr* asaltar
assault and battery *s* vías de hecho, violencias
assay [ə'se] o ['æse] *s* ensaye *m;* muestra de ensaye ‖ [ə'se] *tr* ensayar; apreciar
assemble [ə'sɛmbəl] *tr* reunir; (mach) armar, montar ‖ *intr* reunirse
assem•bly [ə'sɛmbli] *s* (*pl* **-blies**) asamblea; reunión; (mach) armadura, montaje *m*
assembly hall *s* aula magna, paraninfo; salón *m* de sesiones
assembly line *s* línea de montaje
assembly plant *s* fábrica de montaje
assembly room *s* sala de reunión; (mach) taller *m* de montaje
assent [ə'sɛnt] *s* asentimiento, asenso ‖ *intr* asentir
assert [ə'sʌrt] *tr* afirmar, aseverar, declarar; **to assert oneself** imponerse, hacer valer sus derechos
assertion [ə'sʌrʃən] *s* aserción, aseveración
assess [ə'sɛs] *tr* amillarar, gravar; fijar (*daños y perjuicios*); apreciar, estimar
assessment [ə'sɛsmənt] *s* amillaramiento, gravamen *m;* fijación; apreciación, estimación
asset ['æsɛt] *s* posesión, ventaja; (*person, thing, or quality worth having*) (fig) valor *m;* **assets** (com) activo
assiduous [ə'sɪdju•əs] *adj* asiduo
assign [ə'saɪn] *tr* asignar
assignment [ə'saɪnmənt] *s* asignación, cometido; lección
assimilate [ə'sɪmɪ,let] *tr* asimilarse (*los alimentos, el conocimiento*) ‖ *intr* asimilarse
assist [ə'sɪst] *tr* ayudar, asistir, auxiliar
assistant [ə'sɪstənt] *adj & s* auxiliar *mf*, ayudante *mf*
assistantship [ə'sɪstənt,ʃɪp] *s* ayudantía
assn. *abbr* **association**
associate [ə'soʃɪ•ɪt] *adj* asociado ‖ *s* asociado, socio ‖ [ə'soʃɪ,et] *tr* asociar ‖ *intr* asociarse
association [ə,soʃɪ'eʃən] *s* asociación
assort [ə'sɔrt] *tr* clasificar, ordenar
assortment [ə'sɔrtmənt] *s* surtido; clase *f*, grupo
asst. *abbr* **assistant**
assume [ə'sum] o [ə'sjum] *tr* asumir (*p.ej., responsabilidades*); arrogarse; suponer, dar por sentado
assumption [ə'sʌmpʃən] *s* asunción; suposición
assurance [ə'ʃurəns] *s* aseguramiento; seguridad, confianza; (com) seguro
assure [ə'ʃur] *tr* asegurar; (com) asegurar
Assyria [ə'sɪrɪ•ə] *s* Asiria
Assyrian [ə'sɪrɪ•ən] *adj & s* asirio
astatine ['æstə,tin] *s* ástato
aster ['æstər] *s* (bot) aster *m;* (*China aster*) reina Margarita
asterisk ['æstə,rɪsk] *s* asterisco

astern [ə'stʌrn] *adv* por la popa
asthma ['æzmə] o ['æsmə] *s* asma *f*
astonish [ə'stanɪʃ] *tr* asombrar
astonishing [ə'stanɪʃɪŋ] *adj* asombroso
astound [ə'staund] *tr* pasmar
astounding [ə'staundɪŋ] *adj* pasmoso
astraddle [ə'strædəl] *adv* a horcajadas
astray [ə'stre] *adv* por mal camino; **to go astray** extraviarse; **gone astray** desviado; **to lead astray** extraviar
astride [ə'straɪd] *adv* a horcajadas ‖ *prep* a horcajadas de
astrology [ə'stralədʒi] *s* astrología
astronaut ['æstrə,nɔt] *s* astronauta *m*
astronautic [,æstrə'nɔtɪk] *adj* astronáutico ‖ **astronautics** *s* astronáutica
astronavigation [,æstro,nævɪ'geʃən] *s* astronavegación
astronomer [ə'stranəmər] *s* astrónomo
astronomic(al) [,æstrə'namɪk(əl)] *adj* astronómico
astronomy [ə'stranəmi] *s* astronomía
astrophysics [,æstro'fɪzɪks] *s* astrofísica
Asturian [ə'stʊrɪ•ən] *adj & s* asturiano
astute [ə'stjut] *adj* astuto, sagaz
asunder [ə'sʌndər] *adv* a pedazos, en dos
asylum [ə'saɪləm] *s* asilo
asymmetry [ə'sɪmɪtri] *s* asimetría
at [æt] o [ət] *prep* en, p.ej., **I saw her at the library** la vi en la biblioteca; a, p.ej., **at five o'clock** a las cinco; de, p.ej., **to laugh at** reírse de; en casa de, p.ej., **at John's** en casa de Juan
atavistic [,ætə'vɪstɪk] *adj* atávico
atheism ['eθi,ɪzəm] *s* ateísmo
atheist ['eθi•ɪst] *s* ateísta *mf*, ateo
Athenian [ə'θini•ən] *adj & s* ateniense *mf*
Athens ['æθɪnz] *s* Atenas *f*
athirst [ə'θʌrst] *adj* sediento
athlete ['æθlit] *s* atleta *mf*
athlete's foot *s* pie *m* de atleta
athletic [æθ'lɛtɪk] *adj* atlético ‖ **athletics** *s* atletismo
Atlantic [æt'læntɪk] *adj & s* Atlántico
atlas ['ætləs] *s* atlas *m*
atmosphere ['ætməs,fɪr] *s* atmósfera
atmospheric [,ætməs'fɛrɪk] *adj* atmosférico ‖ **atmospherics** *spl* parásitos atmosféricos
atom ['ætəm] *s* átomo
atom bomb *s* bomba atómica
atomic [ə'tamɪk] *adj* atómico
atomic bomb *s* bomba atómica
atomic weight *s* peso atómico
atomize ['ætə,maɪz] *tr* atomizar
atomizer ['ætə,ı,aɪzər] *s* pulverizador *m*, vaporizador *m*
atom smasher *s* rompeátomos *m*
atone [ə'ton] *intr* dar reparación; **to atone for** dar reparación por, expiar
atonement [ə'tonmənt] *s* reparación, expiación
atop [ə'tap] *adv* encima ‖ *prep* encima de
atrocious [ə'troʃəs] *adj* atroz; (coll) abominable, muy malo
atroci•ty [ə'trasɪti] *s* (*pl* **-ties**) atrocidad

atro·phy [ˈætrəfi] s (pathol) atrofia, retracción ‖ v (pret & pp **-phied**) tr atrofiar ‖ intr atrofiarse

attach [əˈtætʃ] tr atar, ligar; atribuir (p.ej., importancia); (law) embargar; **to be attached to** aficionarse a; (to be officially associated with) depender de

attaché [ˌætəˈʃe] s agregado

attachment [əˈtætʃmənt] s atadura, enlace m; atribución; apego, cariño; accesorio; (law) embargo

attack [əˈtæk] s ataque m ‖ tr & intr atacar

attain [əˈten] tr alcanzar, lograr

attainment [əˈtenmənt] s consecución, logro; **attainments** dotes fpl, prendas

attempt [əˈtɛmpt] s tentativa; (assault) atentado, conato ‖ tr procurar, intentar; (e.g., the life of a person) atentar a o contra

attend [əˈtɛnd] tr atender, asistir; asistir a (p.ej., la escuela); auxiliar (a un moribundo) ‖ intr atender; **to attend to** atender a

attendance [əˈtɛndəns] s asistencia, concurrencia; **to dance attendance** hacer antesala

attendant [əˈtɛndənt] adj & s asistente mf; concomitante m

attention [əˈtɛnʃən] s atención; **to attract attention** llamar la atención; **to call attention to** hacer presente; **to pay attention to** hacer caso de

attentive [əˈtɛntɪv] adj atento

attenuate [əˈtɛnjuˌet] tr adelgazar; debilitar ‖ intr debilitarse; desaparecer

attest [əˈtɛst] tr atestiguar; juramentar ‖ intr dar fe; **to attest to** dar fe de

attic [ˈætɪk] s buharda, guardilla, desván m

attire [əˈtaɪr] s atavío, traje m ‖ tr ataviar, vestir

attitude [ˈætɪˌtjud] o [ˈætɪˌtud] s actitud, ademán m

attorney [əˈtʌrni] s abogado; procurador m

attract [əˈtrækt] tr atraer; llamar (la atención)

attraction [əˈtrækʃən] s atracción; (personal charm) atractivo

attractive [əˈtræktɪv] adj atractivo; (agreeable, interesting) atrayente

attribute [ˈætrɪˌbjut] s atributo ‖ [əˈtrɪbjut] tr atribuir

atty. abbr **attorney**

auburn [ˈɔbərn] adj & s castaño rojizo

auction [ˈɔkʃən] s almoneda, remate m, subasta ‖ tr rematar, subastar

auctioneer [ˌɔkʃənˈɪr] s subastador m, rematador m ‖ tr & intr rematar, subastar

auction house s martillo

audacious [ɔˈdeʃəs] adj audaz

audaci·ty [ɔˈdæsɪti] s (pl **-ties**) audacia

audience [ˈɔdɪəns] s (hearing; formal interview) audiencia; público, auditorio

audio frequency [ˈɔdɪˌo] s audiofrecuencia

audiometer [ˌɔdɪˈɑmɪtər] s audiómetro

audit [ˈɔdɪt] s intervención ‖ tr intervenir

audition [ɔˈdɪʃən] s audición ‖ tr dar audición a

auditor [ˈɔdɪtər] s oyente mf; (com) interventor m

auditorium [ˌɔdɪˈtorɪˌəm] s auditorio, anfiteatro, paraninfo

auger [ˈɔgər] s barrena

augment [ɔgˈmɛnt] tr & intr aumentar

augur [ˈɔgər] s augur m ‖ tr & intr augurar; **to augur well** ser de buen agüero

augu·ry [ˈɔgəri] s (pl **-ries**) augurio

august [ɔˈgʌst] adj augusto ‖ **August** [ˈɔgəst] s agosto

aunt [ænt] o [ɑnt] s tía

aurora [eˈrorə] s aurora

auspice [ˈɔspɪs] s auspicio; **under the auspices of** bajo los auspicios de

austere [ɔsˈtɪr] adj austero

Australia [ɔˈstreljə] s Australia

Australian [ɔˈstreljən] adj & s australiano

Austria [ˈɔstrɪə] s Austria

Austrian [ˈɔstrɪən] adj & s austríaco

authentic [ɔˈθɛntɪk] adj auténtico

authenticate [ɔˈθɛntɪˌket] tr autenticar

author [ˈɔθər] s autor m

authoress [ˈɔθərɪs] s autora

authoritarian [ɔˌθɔrɪˈtɛrɪˌən] adj & s autoritario

authoritative [ɔˈθɔrɪˌtetɪv] adj autorizado; (dictatorial) autoritario

authori·ty [ɔˈθɔrɪti] s (pl **-ties**) autoridad; **on good authority** de buena tinta, de fuente fidedigna

authorize [ˈɔθəˌraɪz] tr autorizar

authorship [ˈɔθərˌʃɪp] s paternidad literaria

autistic [ɔˈtɪstɪk] s autístico

au·to [ˈɔto] s (pl **-tos**) (coll) auto, coche m

autobiogra·phy [ˌɔtobaɪˈɑgrəfi] s (pl **-phies**) autobiografía

autobus [ˈɔtoˌbʌs] s autobús m

autocratic(al) [ˌɔtəˈkrætɪk(əl)] adj autocrático

autograph [ˈɔtəˌgræf] adj & s autógrafo ‖ tr autografiar

autograph seeker s cazaautógrafos m

automat [ˈɔtəˌmæt] s restaurante automático

automatic [ˌɔtəˈmætɪk] adj automático

automatic car wash s túnel m de lavado

automatic clutch s servoembrague m

automation [ˌɔtəˈmeʃən] s automación, automatización

automa·ton [ɔˈtɑməˌtɑn] s (pl **-tons** o **-ta** [tə]) autómata

automobile [ˌɔtəməˈbil] u [ˌɔtəˈmobil] s automóvil m

automobile show s salón m del automóvil

autonomous [ɔˈtɑnəməs] adj autónomo

autonomy [ɔˈtɑnəmi] s autonomía

autop·sy [ˈɔtɑpsi] s (pl **-sies**) autopsia

autumn [ˈɔtəm] s otoño

autumnal [əˈtʌmnəl] adj otoñal

auxilia·ry [ɔgˈzɪljəri] adj auxiliar ‖ s (pl **-ries**) auxiliar mf; **auxiliaries** tropas auxiliares

av. abbr **avenue, average, avoirdupois**

avail [əˈvel] s provecho, utilidad ‖ tr beneficiar; **to avail oneself of** aprovecharse de, valerse de ‖ intr aprovechar

available [əˈveləbəl] adj disponible; **to make available to** poner a la disposición de

avalanche [ˈævəˌlæntʃ] s alud m, avalancha

avant-garde [ə,vɑnt'gɑrd] *adj* vanguardista ‖ *s* vanguardismo
avant-guardist [ə,vɑnt'gɑrdist] *s* vanguardista *mf*
avarice ['ævərɪs] *s* avaricia
avaricious [,ævə'rɪʃəs] *adj* avaricioso, avariento
Ave. *abbr* **Avenue**
avenge [ə'vɛndʒ] *tr* vengar; **to avenge oneself on** vengarse en
avenue ['ævə,nju] o ['ævə,nu] *s* avenida
aver [ə'vʌr] *v* (*pret & pp* **averred;** *ger* **averring**) *tr* afirmar, declarar
average ['ævərɪdʒ] *adj* común, mediano, ordinario ‖ *s* promedio, término medio; (*naut*) avería ‖ *tr* calcular el término medio de; prorratear; ser de un promedio de
averse [ə'vʌrs] *adj* renuente, contrario
aversion [ə'vʌrʒən] *s* aversión, antipatía; cosa aborrecida
avert [ə'vʌrt] *tr* apartar, desviar; impedir
aviar•y ['evi,ɛri] *s* (*pl* **-ies**) avería, pajarera
aviation [,evɪ'eʃən] *s* aviación
aviation medicine *s* aeromedicina
aviator ['evi,etər] *s* aviador *m*
avid ['ævɪd] *adj* ávido
avidity [ə'vɪdɪti] *s* avidez *f*
avocado [,ævə'kɑdo] *s* aguacate *m*
avocation [,ævə'keʃən] *s* distracción, diversión
avoid [ə'vɔɪd] *tr* evitar
avoidable [ə'vɔɪdəbəl] *adj* evitable
avoidance [ə'vɔɪdəns] *s* evitación
avow [ə'vaʊ] *tr* admitir, confesar
avowal [ə'vaʊ•əl] *s* admisión, confesión
await [ə'wet] *tr* aguardar, esperar
awake [ə'wek] *adj* despierto ‖ *v* (*pret & pp* **awoke** [ə'wok] o **awaked**) *tr & intr* despertar
awaken [ə'wekən] *tr & intr* despertar
awakening [ə'wekənɪŋ] *s* despertamiento; desilusión

award [ə'wɔrd] *s* premio; condecoración; adjudicación ‖ *tr* conceder; adjudicar
aware [ə'wɛr] *adj* enterado; **to become aware of** enterarse de, darse cuenta de
awareness [ə'wɛrnɪs] *s* conciencia
away [ə'we] *adj* ausente; distante ‖ *adv* lejos; a lo lejos; **away from** lejos de; **to do away with** deshacerse de; **to get away** escapar; **to go away** irse; **to make away with** robar, hurtar; **to run away** fugarse; **to send away** enviar; despedir; **to take away** llevarse; quitar
awe [ɔ] *s* temor *m* reverencial ‖ *tr* infundir temor reverencial a
awesome ['ɔsəm] *adj* imponente
awestruck ['ɔ,strʌk] *adj* espantado
awful ['ɔfəl] *adj* atroz, horrible; impresionante; (coll) muy malo, muy feo, enorme
awfully ['ɔfəli] *adv* atrozmente, horriblemente; (coll) muy, excesivamente
awfulness ['ɔfəlnɪs] *s* espantosidad (SAm)
awhile [ə'hwaɪl] *adv* un rato, algún tiempo
awkward ['ɔkwərd] *adj* desmañado, torpe, lerdo; embarazoso, delicado
awkward squad *s* pelotón *m* de los torpes
awl [ɔl] *s* alesna, lezna
awning ['ɔnɪŋ] *s* toldo
ax [æks] *s* hacha
axiom ['æksɪ•əm] *s* axioma *m*
axiomatic [,æksɪ•ə'mætɪk] *adj* axiomático
axis ['æksɪs] *s* (*pl* **axes** ['æksiz]) *s* eje *m*
axle ['æksəl] *s* eje *m*, árbol *m*
axle load *s* carga por eje
ax'le•tree' *s* eje *m* de carretón
ay [aɪ] *adv & s* sí ‖ [e] *adv* siempre; **for ay** por siempre ‖ [e] *interj* ¡ay!
aye [aɪ] *adv & s* sí ‖ [e] *adv* siempre; **for aye** por siempre
azimuth ['æzɪməθ] *s* acimut *m*
Azores [ə'zorz] o ['ezorz] *spl* Azores *fpl*
Aztec ['æztɛk] *adj & s* azteca *mf*
azure ['æʒər] o ['eʒər] *adj & s* azul *m*

B

B, b [bi] segunda letra del alfabeto inglés
b. *abbr* **bass, bay, born, brother**
baa [bɑ] *s* be *m*, balido ‖ *intr* balar
babble ['bæbəl] *s* barboteo; charla; (*of a brook*) murmullo ‖ *tr* barbotar; decir indiscretamente ‖ *intr* barbotar; murmurar (*un arroyo*)
babe [beb] *s* rorro, criatura; (*innocent, gullible person*) niño; (slang) chica, chica hermosa
baboon [bæ'bun] *s* babuíno
ba•by ['bebi] *s* (*pl* **-bies**) rorro, criatura, bebé *m*; (*the youngest child*) benjamín *m* ‖ *v* (*pret & pp* **-bied**) *tr* mimar; tratar como niño
baby carriage *s* cochecillo para niños

baby grand *s* piano de media cola
babyhood ['bebi,hʊd] *s* primera infancia, niñez *f*
babyish ['bebi•ɪʃ] *adj* aniñado, infantil
Babylon ['bæbɪlən] o ['bæbɪ,lɑn] *s* Babilonia (*ciudad*)
Babylonia [,bæbɪ'loni•ə] *s* Babilonia (*imperio*)
Babylonian [,bæbɪ'loni•ən] *adj & s* babilonio
baby sitter *s* niñera tomada por horas
baccalaureate [,bækə'lɔrɪ•ɪt] *s* bachillerato
bachelor ['bætʃələr] *s* (*unmarried man*) soltero; (*holder of bachelor's degree*) bachiller *mf*; (*apprentice knight*) doncel *m*
bachelorhood ['bætʃələr,hʊd] *s* celibato, soltería (*del hombre*)

bacil·lus [bə'sɪləs] s (pl **-li** [laɪ]) bacilo
back [bæk] adj trasero, posterior; atrasado ‖ adv atrás, detrás; de vuelta; (ago) hace; **back of** detrás de; **to go back to** remontarse a; **to send back** devolver ‖ s espalda; dorso; (of a coin) reverso; (of a chair) espaldar m, respaldo; (of an animal, of a book) lomo; (of a hall, a room) fondo; (of a writing, a book) final m; **behind one's back** a espaldas de uno; **on one's back** postrado, en cama; a cuestas ‖ tr mover hacia atrás; apoyar, respaldar ‖ intr moverse hacia atrás; **to back down** u out volverse atrás, echarse atrás; **to back up** retroceder; regolfar (el agua)
back'ache' s dolor m de espalda
back'bone' s espinazo; (of a book) nervura; firmeza, resistencia
back'break'ing adj deslomador
back'down' s palinodia, retractación
back'drop' s telón m de fondo o de foro
backer ['bækər] s sostenedor a, defensor m; (of a business venture) impulsador m
back'fire' s (aut) petardeo ‖ intr (aut) petardear
back'ground' s fondo; antecedentes mpl; conocimientos, educación; (of a painting) lontananza
background music s música de fondo
backing ['bækɪŋ] s apoyo, sostén m; garantía, respaldo; financiamiento; (bb) lomera
back'lash' s (mach) contragolpe m; (mach) juego; (fig) reacción violenta
back'log' s (com) reserva de pedidos pendientes; (e.g., of work) acumulación
back number s número atrasado; (coll) persona anticuada
back pay s sueldo retrasado
back seat s puesto secundario; **to take a back seat** perder influencia
back'side' s espalda; trasero
back'slide' v (pret & pp **-slid** [,slɪd]) intr reincidir
backspacer ['bæk,spesər] s tecla de retroceso
back'stage' adv detrás del telón; entre bastidores
back'stairs' adj indirecto, secreto
back stairs spl escalera trasera; medios indirectos
back'stitch' s pespunte m ‖ tr & intr pespuntar
back'stop' s reja o red f para detener la pelota
back'swept' wing s (aer) ala en flecha
back talk s respuesta insolente
backward ['bækwərd] adj atrasado, tardío; tímido ‖ adv de atrás; de espaldas; al revés; cada vez peor; para atrás, hacia atrás
back'wa'ter s remanso; (fig) atraso, yermo
back'woods' spl monte m, región alejada de los centros de población
back yard s patio trasero, corral trasero
bacon ['bekən] s tocino
bacteria [bæk'tɪrɪə] pl de **bacterium**
bacterial [bæk'tɪrɪəl] adj bacteriano
bacteriologist [bæk,tɪrɪ'ɑlədʒɪst] s bacteriólogo

bacteriology [bæk,tɪrɪ'ɑlədʒɪ] s bacteriología
bacteri·um [bæk'tɪrɪ•əm] s (pl **-a** [ə]) bacteria
bad [bæd] adj (comp **worse** [wʌrs]; super **worst** [wʌrst]) malo; (money) falso; (debt) incobrable; **from bad to worse** de mal en peor; **to be in bad** (coll) caer en desgracia; **to be too bad** ser lástima; **to go to the bad** (coll) ir por mal camino; (coll) arruinarse; **to look bad** tener mala cara
bad breath s mal aliento
badge [bædʒ] s divisa, insignia
badger ['bædʒər] s tejón m
badly ['bædli] adv mal; con urgencia; gravemente
badly off adj malparado; muy enfermo
badminton ['bædmɪntən] s juego del volante
baffle ['bæfəl] s deflector m; (rad) pantalla acústica ‖ tr confundir; burlar, frustrar
baffling ['bæflɪŋ] adj perplejo, desconcertador
bag [bæg] s saco; saquito de mano; (in clothing) bolsa; (purse) bolso; (take of game) caza; **to be in the bag** (slang) ser cosa segura ‖ v (pret & pp **bagged**; ger **bagging**) tr ensacar; coger, cazar ‖ intr hacer bolsa (un vestido)
baggage ['bægɪdʒ] s equipaje m; (mil) bagaje m
baggage car s furgón m de equipajes
baggage check s contraseña de equipajes
baggage rack s red f de equipajes
baggage room s sala de equipajes
bag'pipe' s gaita, cornamusa
bag'pi'per s gaitero
bail [bel] s caución, fianza; **to go bail for** salir fiador por ‖ tr caucionar, afianzar; achicar (la embarcación; el agua); **to bail out** salir fiador por; achicar ‖ intr achicar; **to bail out** lanzarse en paracaídas
bailiff ['belɪf] s alguacil m, corchete m
bailiwick ['belɪwɪk] s alguacilazgo; **to be in the bailiwick of** ser de la pertenencia de
bait [bet] s carnada, cebo; señuelo; **to swallow the bait** tragar el anzuelo ‖ tr cebar, encarnar (el anzuelo); tentar, seducir; (to pester) hostigar
baize [bez] s bayeta
bake [bek] tr cocer al horno; cocer (loza, gres, etc.)
bakelite ['bekə,laɪt] s baquelita
baker ['bekər] s panadero, hornero
baker's dozen s docena del fraile
baker·y ['bekəri] s (pl **-ies**) panadería
baking powder ['bekɪŋ] s levadura en polvo
baking soda s bicarbonato de sosa
bal. abbr **balance**
balance ['bæləns] s (instrument for weighing) balanza; (state of equilibrium) equilibrio; (amount left over) resto; (amount still owed) saldo; (statement of debits and credits) balance m; **to lose one's balance** perder el equilibrio; **to strike a balance** hacer o pasar balance ‖ tr balancear; equilibrar; equilibrar, nivelar (el presupuesto) ‖ intr equilibrarse; (to waver) balancear

balanced ['bælənst] *adj* equilibrado
balance of payments *s* balanza de pagos
balance of power *s* equilibrio político
balance sheet *s* balance *m*, avanzo
balco•ny ['bælkəni] *s* (*pl* **-nies**) balcón *m*; (*in a theater*) galería, paraíso
bald [bɔld] *adj* calvo; franco, directo
baldness ['bɔldnɪs] *s* calvicie *f*
baldric ['bɔldrɪk] *s* tahalí *m*
bale [bel] *s* bala ‖ *tr* embalar
Balearic [,bælɪ'ærɪk] *adj* balear
Balearic Islands *spl* islas Baleares
baleful ['belfəl] *adj* funesto, maligno
balk [bɔk] *tr* burlar, frustrar ‖ *intr* emperrarse, resistirse
Balkan ['bɔlkən] *adj* balcánico ‖ **the Balkans** los Balcanes
balk•y ['bɔki] *adj* (*comp* **-ier**; *super* **-iest**) rebelón, repropio
ball [bɔl] *s* bola, pelota; esfera, globo; (*of wool, yarn*) ovillo; (*of finger*) yema; (*projectile*) bala; (*dance*) baile *m*
ballad ['bæləd] *s* balada
ballade [bə'lɑd] *s* (mus) balada
ballast ['bæləst] *s* (aer, naut) lastre *m*; (rr) balasto ‖ *tr* lastrar; balastar
ball bearing *s* cojinete *m* de bolas
ballerina [,bælə'rinə] *s* bailarina
ballet ['bæle] *s* ballet *m*, baile *m*
ballistic [bə'lɪstɪk] *adj* balístico
balloon [bə'lun] *s* globo
ballot ['bælət] *s* balota; sufragio ‖ *intr* balotar
ballot box *s* urna electoral
ball play'er *s* pelotari *m*; beisbolero
ball'-point' pen *s* bolígrafo, pluma estilográfica; biro (Arg); birome *f* (Arg, Urug); puntabola, punto bola (Bol); lapicero (CAm, Col); lápiz *m* de pasta (Chile); esferográfica, esfero (Col); estenógrafo (Cuba); lápiz *n*: de bolilla (Peru); plumilla (Ven)
ball'room' *s* salón *m* de baile
ballyhoo ['bælɪ,hu] *s* alharaca, bombo ‖ *tr* dar teatro a, dar bombo a
balm [bɑm] *s* bálsamo
balm•y ['bɑmi] *adj* (*comp* **-ier**; *super* **-iest**) bonancible, suave
baloney [bə'loni] *interj* (coll) ¡aprieta!
balsam ['bɔlsəm] *s* bálsamo
Baltic ['bɔltɪk] *adj* báltico
Baltimore oriole ['bɔltɪ,mor] *s* cacique veranero
baluster ['bæləstər] *s* balaustre *m*
bamboo [bæm'bu] *s* bambú *m*
bamboozle [bæm'buzəl] *tr* (coll) embaucar, engañar
bamboozler [bæm'buzlər] *s* (coll) embaucador *m*, engañabobos *mf*
ban [bæn] *s* prohibición; excomunión, entredicho; (*of marriage*) amonestación ‖ *v* (*pret & pp* **banned**; *ger* **banning**) *tr* prohibir; excomulgar
banana [bə'nænə] *s* banana, plátano; (*tree*) banano, bananero, plátano
banana oil *s* esencia de pera

band [bænd] *s* banda; (*of people*) cuadrilla; (*of a hat*) cintillo; (*of a cigar*) anillo; liga de goma; (mus) banda, música, charanga ‖ *intr* abanderizarse
bandage ['bændɪdʒ] *s* venda ‖ *tr* vendar
bandanna [bæn'dænə] *s* pañuelo de hierbas
band'box' *s* sombrerera
bandit ['bændɪt] *s* bandido
band'mas'ter *s* músico mayor
bandoleer [,bændə'lɪr] *s* bandolera
band saw *s* sierra continua, sierra sin fin
band'stand' *s* quiosco de música
baneful ['benfəl] *adj* nocivo, venenoso; (*e.g., influence*) funesto
bang [bæŋ] *adv* de golpe ‖ *interj* ¡pum! ‖ *s* golpazo; (*of a door*) portazo; **bangs** flequillo ‖ *tr* golpear con ruido; cerrar (*p.ej., una puerta*) de golpe ‖ *intr* hacer estrépito
banish ['bænɪʃ] *tr* desterrar; despedir (*p.ej., miedo*)
banishment ['bænɪʃmənt] *s* destierro
banister ['bænɪstər] *s* balaustre *m*
bank [bæŋk] *s* banco; (*in certain games*) banca; (*small container for coins*) alcancía; (*of a river*) ribera, orilla; (*of earth, snow, clouds*) montón *m* ‖ *tr* depositar o guardar (*dinero*) en un banco; amontonar; cubrir (*un fuego*) con cenizas ‖ *intr* depositar dinero; **to bank on** (coll) contar con
bank account *s* cuenta de banco
bank'book' *s* libreta de banco
banker ['bæŋkər] *s* banquero
banking ['bæŋkɪŋ] *adj* bancario ‖ *s* banca
bank note *s* billete *m* de banco
bank roll *s* lío de papel moneda
bankrupt ['bæŋkrʌpt] *adj & s* bancarrotero; **to go bankrupt** hacer bancarrota ‖ *tr* hacer quebrar; arruinar
bankrupt•cy ['bæŋkrʌptsi] *s* (*pl* **-cies**) bancarrota
banner ['bænər] *s* bandera, estandarte *m*
banner cry *s* grito de combate
banquet ['bæŋkwɪt] *s* banquete *m* ‖ *tr & intr* banquetear
bantamweight ['bæntəm,wet] *s* (box) gallo
banter ['bæntər] *s* burla, chanza ‖ *intr* burlar, chancear
baptism ['bæptɪzəm] *s* bautismo, bautizo; (fig) bautismo
Baptist ['bæptɪst] *adj & s* baptista *mf*, bautista *mf*
baptister•y ['bæptɪstəri] *s* (*pl* **-ies**) baptisterio, bautisterio
baptize ['bæptaɪz] *tr* bautizar
bar. *abbr* **barometer, barrel, barrister**
bar [bɑr] *s* barra; (*of door or window*) tranca; (*of jail*) reja; barrera; (*legal profession*) abogacía; (*members of legal profession*) curia; (*of public opinion*) tribunal *m*; (mus) barra; (*unit between two bars*) (mus) compás *m*; **behind bars** entre rejas ‖ *prep* salvo; **bar none** sin excepción ‖ *v* (*pret & pp* **barred**; *ger* **barring**) *tr* barrear, atrancar; impedir; prohibir; excluir
bar association *s* colegio de abogados
barb [bɑrb] *s* púa, lengüeta; (*of a pen*) barbilla

Barbados [bɑr'bedoz] s la Barbada
barbarian [bɑr'bɛrɪ•ən] s bárbaro
barbaric [bɑr'bærɪk] adj bárbaro
barbarism ['bɑrbə,rɪzəm] s barbaridad f; (gram) barbarismo
barbari•ty [bɑr'bærɪti] s (pl -ties) barbarie f
barbarous ['bɑrbərəs] adj bárbaro
Barbary ape ['bɑrbəri] s mono de Gibraltar
barbed [bɑrbd] adj armado de púas; mordaz, punzante
barbed wire s alambre m de espino, alambre de púas
barber ['bɑrbər] adj barberil || s barbero, peluquero
barber pole s percha de barbero
bar'ber•shop' s barbería, peluquería
bard [bɑrd] s bardo; (horse armor) barda || tr bardar
bare [bɛr] adj desnudo; (head) descubierto; (unfurnished) desamueblado; (wire) sin aislar; mero, sencillo, puro || tr desnudar; descubrir
bare'back' adj & adv en pelo, sin silla
barefaced ['bɛr,fest] adj desvergonzado
bare'foot' adj descalzo || adv con los pies desnudos
bareheaded ['bɛr,hɛdɪd] adj descubierto || adv con la cabeza descubierta
barelegged ['bɛr,lɛgɪd] o ['bɛr,lɛgd] adj con las piernas desnudas
barely ['bɛrli] adv aspenas; escasamente
bargain ['bɑrgɪn] s (deal) convenio, trato; (cheap purchase) ganga; **in the bargain** de añadidura || tr — to bargain away vender regalado || intr negociar; (to haggle) regatear
bargain counter s baratillo
bargain sale s venta de saldos
barge [bɑrdʒ] s gabarra, lanchón m; bongo (SAm) || intr moverse pesadamente; **to barge in** entrar sin pedir permiso, entrar sin llamar a la puerta
barium ['bɛrɪ•əm] s bario
bark [bɑrk] s (of tree) corteza; (of dog) ladrido; (boat) barca || tr ladrar (p.ej., injurias) || intr ladrar
barley ['bɑrli] s cebada
barley water s hordiate m
bar magnet s barra imantada
bar'maid' s moza de taberna
barn [bɑrn] s granero, troje m; caballeriza, establo; cochera
barnacle ['bɑrnəkəl] s cirrópodo
barn owl s lechuza, oliva
barn'yard' s corral m
barnyard fowl spl aves fpl de corral
barometer [bə'rɑmɪtər] s barómetro
baron ['bærən] s barón m
baroness ['bærənɪs] s baronesa
baroque [bə'rok] adj & s barroco
barracks ['bærəks] spl cuartel m
barrage [bə'rɑʒ] s (dam) presa; (mil) barrera de fuego
barrel ['bærəl] s barril m, tonel m; (of a gun, pen, etc.) cañón m
barrel organ s organillo
barren ['bærən] adj árido, estéril

barricade [,bærɪ'ked] s barrera || tr barrear
barrier ['bærɪ•ər] s barrera
barrier reef s barrera de arrecifes
barrister ['bærɪstər] s (Brit) abogado
bar'room' s bar m, cantina
bar'tend'er s cantinero, tabernero, barman m
barter ['bɑrtər] s trueque m || tr trocar
base [bes] adj bajo, humilde; infame, vil; (metal) bajo de ley || s base f; (of electric light or vacuum tube; of projectile) culote m; (mus) bajo || tr basar
base'ball' s beisbol m; pelota de beisbol
baseball player s beisbolero, beisbolista m
base'board' s rodapié m
Basel ['bɑzəl] s Basilea
baseless ['beslɪs] adj infundado
basement ['besmənt] s sótano
bashful ['bæʃfəl] adj encogido, tímido
basic ['besɪk] adj básico
basic commodities spl artículos de primera necesidad
basilica [bə'sɪlɪkə] s basílica
basin ['besɪn] s jofaina, palangana; (of a fountain) tazón m; (of a river) cuenca; (of a harbor) dársena
ba•sis ['besɪs] s (pl -ses [siz]) base f; **on the basis of** a base de
bask [bæsk] o [bɑsk] intr asolearse, calentarse
basket ['bæskɪt] s cesta; (large basket) cesto; (with two handles) canasta; (with lid) excusabaraja; (sport) cesto, red f
bas'ket•ball' s baloncesto, basquetbol m
Basle [bɑl] s Basilea
Basque [bæsk] adj & s (of Spain) vascongado; (of Spain and France) vasco; (of old Spain) vascón m
bas-relief [,bɑrɪ'lif] s bajo relieve
bass [bes] adj & s (mus) bajo || [bæs] s (ichth) róbalo; (ichth) micróptero
bass drum s bombo
bass horn s tuba
bas•so ['bæso] s (pl -sos o -si [si]) (mus) bajo
bassoon [bə'sun] s bajón m
bass viol ['vaɪ•əl] s violón m, contrabajo
bastard ['bæstərd] adj & s bastardo
bastard title s anteportada
baste [best] tr (to sew slightly) hilvanar; (to moisten with drippings while roasting) enlardar; (to thrash) azotar; (to scold) regañar
bat. abbr **battalion, battery**
bat [bæt] s palo; (coll) golpe m; (zool) murciélago || v (pret & pp batted; ger batting) tr golpear; batear (una pelota); **without batting an eye** sin inmutarse, sin pestañear || intr golpear
batch [bætʃ] s (of bread) hornada; (of papers) lío
bath [bæθ] s baño
bathe [beð] tr bañar || intr bañarse; **to go bathing** ir a bañarse
bather ['beðər] s bañista mf
bath'house' s casa de baños; caseta de baños
bathing beach s playa de baños
bathing beauty s sirena de la playa
bathing resort s estación balnearia
bathing suit s traje m de baño, bañador m

bathing trunks *spl* taparrabo

bath'robe' *s* albornoz *m*, bata de baño; bata, peinador *m*

bath'room' *s* baño, cuarto de baño

bathroom fixtures *spl* aparatos sanitarios

bath'tub' *s* bañera, baño

bathyscaphe ['bæθə,skæf] *s* batiscafo

baton [bæ'tɑn] *s* bastón *m;* (mus) batuta

battalion [bə'tæljən] *s* batallón *m*

batter ['bætər] *s* pasta, batido; *(baseball)* bateador *m* ‖ *tr* magullar, estropear

battering ram *s* ariete *m*

batter·y ['bætəri] *s* (*pl* -ies) batería; *(primary)* (elec) pila; *(secondary)* (elec) acumulador *m;* (law) violencia

battle ['bætəl] *s* batalla; **to do battle** librar batalla ‖ *tr* batallar

battle array *s* orden *m* de batalla

battle cry *s* grito de combate

battledore ['bætəl,dor] *s* raqueta; **battledore and shuttlecock** raqueta y volante

bat'tlefield' *s* campo de batalla

battle front *s* frente *m* de combate

battlement ['bætəlmənt] *s* almenaje *m*

battle piece *s* (paint) batalla

bat'tle·ship' *s* acorazado

battue [bæ'tu] o [bæ'tju] *s* batida

bauble ['bɔbəl] *s* chuchería; cetro de bufón

Bavaria [bə'vɛrɪ·ə] *s* Baviera

Bavarian [bə'vɛrɪ·ən] *adj & mf* bávaro

bawd [bɔd] *s* alcahuete *m*, alcahueta

bawd·y ['bɔdi] *adj* (*comp* -ier; *super* -iest) indecente, obsceno

bawd'y·house' *s* mancebía, lupanar *m*

bawl [bɔl] *s* voces *fpl*, gritos ‖ *tr —* **to bawl out** (slang) regañar ‖ *intr* vocear, gritar; llorar ruidosamente

bay [be] *adj* bayo ‖ *s* bahía; aullido, ladrido; caballo bayo; (bot) laurel *m;* **to keep at bay** tener a raya ‖ *intr* aullar, ladrar

Bay of Biscay *s* golfo de Vizcaya

bayonet ['be·ɔnit] *s* bayoneta ‖ *tr* herir o matar con bayoneta

bay rum *s* ron *m* de laurel, ron de malagueta

bay window *s* ventana salediza, mirador *m*

bazooka [bə'zukə] *s* bazuca

bbl. *abbr* **barrel, barrels**

B.C. *abbr* **before Christ**

bd. *abbr* **board**

be [bi] *v* (*pres* **am** [æm], **is** [ɪz] **are** [ɑr]; *pret* **was** [wɑz] o [wʌz], **were** [wʌr]; *pp* **been** [bɪn]) *intr* estar; ser; tener, p.ej., **to be cold** tener frío; **to be wrong** no tener razón; tener la culpa; **here is** o **here are** aquí tiene Vd.; **there is** o **there are** hay ‖ *v aux* estar, p.ej., **he is studying** está estudiando; ser, p.ej., **she was hit by a car** fué atropellada por un coche; deber, p.ej., **what am I to do?** ¿qué debo hacer? ‖ *v impers* ser, p.ej., **it is necessary to get up early** es necesario levantarse temprano; haber, p.ej., **it is sunny** hay sol; hacer, p.ej., **it is cold** hace frío

beach [bitʃ] *s* playa

beach'comb' *intr* raquear; **to go beachcombing** andar al raque

beach'comb'er *s* raquero; vago de playa

beach'head' *s* cabeza de playa

beach robe *s* albornoz *m*

beach shoe *s* playera

beach umbrella *s* sombrilla de playa

beach wagon *s* rubia, coche *m* rural

beacon ['bikən] *s* señal luminosa; *(lighthouse)* faro; *(hill overlooking sea)* hacho; radiofaro; *(guide)* faro ‖ *tr* iluminar, guiar ‖ *intr* brillar

bead [bid] *s* cuenta; *(of glass)* abalorio; *(of sweat)* gota; *(moulding on corner of wall)* guardavivo; **to say** o **tell one's beads** rezar el rosario

beadle ['bidəl] *s* bedel *m*

beagle ['bigəl] *s* sabueso

beak [bik] *s* pico; cabo, promontorio

beam [bim] *s* *(of wood)* viga; *(of light, heat, etc.)* rayo; (naut) bao; *(direction perpendicular to the keel)* (naut) través *m;* *(of hope)* (fig) rayo; **on the beam** siguiendo el haz del radiofaro; (coll) siguiendo el buen camino ‖ *tr* emitir *(luz, ondas)* ‖ *intr* brillar; sonreír alegremente

bean [bin] *s* haba (Vicia faba); alubia, judía (Phaseolus vulgaris); *(of coffee, cocoa)* haba; (slang) cabeza

bean'pole' *s* rodrigón *m* para frijoles; *(tall, skinny person)* (coll) poste *m* de telégrafo

bear [bɛr] *s* oso; *(in stock market)* bajista *mf* ‖ *v* (*pret* **bore** [bor]; *pp* **borne** [born]) *tr* cargar; traer; llevar *(armas)*; apoyar; aguantar; sentir, experimentar; producir, rendir *(frutos; interés)*; *(to give birth to)* parir; tener *(amor, odio)*; **to bear out** confirmar ‖ *intr* dirigirse, volver; **to bear on** referirse a; **to bear up** no perder la esperanza; **to bear with** ser indulgente para con

beard [bɪrd] *s* barba; *(of wheat)* arista

beardless ['bɪrdlɪs] *adj* imberbe

bearer ['bɛrər] *s* portador *m*

bearing ['bɛrɪŋ] *s* porte *m*, presencia; referencia, relación; (mach) cojinete *m;* **bearings** orientación; **to lose one's bearings** desorientarse

bearish ['bɛrɪʃ] *adj* bajista

bear'skin' *s* piel *f* de oso; *(military cap)* morrión *m*

beast [bist] *s* bestia

beast·ly ['bistli] *adj* (*comp* -lier; *super* -liest) bestial; (coll) muy malo ‖ *adv* (coll) muy mal

beast of burden *s* bestia de carga, acémila

beat [bit] *s* golpe *m;* *(of heart)* latido; *(of rhythm)* compás *m;* marca del compás; (mus) tiempo; (phys) batimiento; (rad) batido; *(of a policeman)* ronda; *(sponger)* (slang) embestidor *m* ‖ *v* (*pret* **beat;** *pp* **beat** o **beaten**) *tr* azotar, pegar; batir; sacudir *(una alfombra)*; aventajar; llevar *(el compás)*; tocar *(un tambor)*; *(a una persona en una contienda)* ganar; **to beat it** (slang) largarse; **to beat up** batir *(p.ej., huevos)*; (slang) aporrear ‖ *intr* batir; latir *(el corazón)*; **to beat against** azotar

beaten path ['bitən] *s* camino trillado

beater ['bitər] *s* batidor *m;* *(mixer)* batidora

beati•fy [bɪ'ætɪ,faɪ] v (pret & pp **-fied**) tr beatificar

beating ['bitɪŋ] s golpeo; (of wings) aleteo; (with a whip) paliza; (defeat) derrota

beau [bo] s (pl **beaus** o **beaux** [boz]) galán m, cortejo; novio; elegante m

beautician [bju'tɪʃən] s embellecedora, esteta mf, esteticista mf

beautiful ['bjutɪfəl] adj bello, hermoso

beauti•fy ['bjutɪ,faɪ] v (pret & pp **-fied**) tr hermosear, embellecer

beau•ty ['bjutɪ] s (pl **-ties**) beldad f, belleza; (person) preciosura

beauty contest s concurso de belleza

beauty parlor s salón m de belleza

beauty queen s reina de la belleza

beauty sleep s primer sueño (antes de media-noche)

beauty spot s lunar postizo; sitio pintoresco

beaver ['bivər] s castor m; piel f de castor

becalm [bɪ'kɑm] tr calmar, serenar

because [bɪ'kɔz] conj porque; **because of** por, por causa de

beck [bɛk] s seña (con la cabeza o la mano); **at the beck and call of** a la disposición de

beckon ['bɛkən] s seña (con la cabeza o la mano) || tr llamar por señas; atraer, tentar || intr hacer señas

be•come [bɪ'kʌm] v (pret **-came**; pp **-come**) tr convenir, sentar bien || intr hacerse; llegar a ser; ponerse, volverse; convertirse en; **to become of** ser de, p.ej., **what will become of the soldier?** ¿qué será del soldado? hacerse, p.ej., **what became of his pencil?** ¿qué se ha hecho su lápiz?

becoming [bɪ'kʌmɪŋ] adj conveniente, de-cente; que sienta bien

bed [bɛd] s cama; (of a river) cauce m; (of flower garden) macizo; **to go to bed** acostarse; **to take to bed** encamarse

bed and board s pensión completa, casa y comida

bed'bug' s chinche f

bed'cham'ber s alcoba, cuarto de dormir

bed'clothes' spl ropa de cama

bed'cov'er s cubrecama, cobertor m

bedding ['bɛdɪŋ] s ropa de cama; (for ani-mals) cama

bedev•il [bɪ'dɛvəl] v (pret & pp **-iled** o **-illed**; ger **-iling** o **-illing**) tr atormentar, confun-dir

bed'fast' adj postrado en cama

bed'fel'low s compañero o compañera de cama

bedlam ['bɛdləm] s confusión, desorden m, tumulto

bed linen s ropa de cama

bed'pan' s silleta

bed'post' s pilar m de cama

bedridden ['bɛd,rɪdən] adj postrado en cama

bed'room' s alcoba, cuarto de dormir

bed'side' s cabecera

bed'sore' s úlcera de decúbito; **to get bed-sores** decentarse

bed'spread' s sobrecama, cobertor m

bed'spring' s colchón m de muelles, somier m

bed'stead' s cuja

bed'straw' s paja de jergón

bed'tick' s cutí m

bed'time' s hora de acostarse

bed warmer s calientacamas m

bee [bi] s abeja

beech [bitʃ] s haya

beech'nut' s hayuco

beef [bif] s carne f de vaca; ganado vacuno de engorde; (coll) fuerza muscular; (slang) queja || tr — **to beef up** (coll) reforzar || intr (slang) quejarse; (slang) soplar

beef cattle s ganado vacuno de engorde

beef'steak' s biftec m

bee'hive' s colmena

bee'line' s — **to make a beeline for** ir en línea recta hacia, ir derecho a

beer [bɪr] s cerveza; **dark beer** cerveza parda, cerveza negra; **light beer** cerveza clara

beeswax ['biz,wæks] s cera de abejas || tr encerar

beet [bit] s remolacha

beetle ['bitəl] s escarabajo

beetle-browed ['bitəl,braʊd] adj cejijunto; (sullen) ceñudo

beet sugar s azúcar m de remolacha

be•fall [bɪ'fɔl] v (pret **-fell** ['fɛl]; pp **-fallen** ['fɔlən]) tr acontecer a || intr acontecer

befitting [bɪ'fɪtɪŋ] adj conveniente; decoroso

before [bɪ'for] adv antes; enfrente || prep (in time) antes de; (in place) delante de; (in the presence of) ante || conj antes (de) que

before'hand' adv de antemano, con anticipa-ción

befriend [bɪ'frɛnd] tr ofrecer amistad a, am-parar, proteger

befuddle [bɪ'fʌdəl] tr aturdir, confundir

beg [bɛg] v (pret & pp **begged**; ger **begging**) tr pedir, rogar, solicitar; mendigar; huesar || intr mendigar; **to beg off** excusarse

be•get [bɪ'gɛt] v (pret **-got** ['gɑt]; pp **-gotten** o **-got**; ger **-getting**) tr engendrar

beggar ['bɛgər] s mendigo; pobre mf; pícaro, bribón m; sujeto, tipo

be•gin [bɪ'gɪn] v (pret **-gan** ['gæn]; pp **-gun** ['gʌn]; ger **-ginning**) tr & intr comenzar, empezar; **beginning with** a partir de

beginner [bɪ'gɪnər] s principiante mf; inicia-dor m

beginning [bɪ'gɪnɪŋ] s comienzo, principio

begrudge [bɪ'grʌdʒ] tr dar de mala gana; envidiar

beguile [bɪ'gaɪl] tr engañar; divertir, entre-tener; engañar (el tiempo)

behalf [bɪ'hæf] — **on behalf of** en nombre de; a favor de

behave [bɪ'hev] intr conducirse, comportarse; portarse bien; funcionar

behavior [bɪ'hevjər] s conducta, comporta-miento; funcionamiento

behaviorism [bɪ'hevjə,rɪzəm] s comportamen-tismo

behead [bɪ'hɛd] tr decapitar, descabezar

behind [bɪ'haɪnd] adv detrás; hacia atrás; con retraso; **to stay behind** quedarse atrás ||

ba
be

prep detrás de; **behind the back of** a espaldas de; **behind the times** astrasado de noticias; **behind time** tarde ‖ *s* (slang) trasero, pompis *m*

behold [bɪˈhold] *v* (*pret & pp* **-held** [ˈhɛld]) *tr* contemplar ‖ *interj* ¡he aquí!

behoove [bɪˈhuv] *tr* convenir, tocar

being [ˈbiɪŋ] *adj* existente; **for the time being** por ahora, por el momento ‖ *s* ser, ente *m*

belch [bɛltʃ] *s* eructo, regüeldo ‖ *tr* vomitar (*p.ej., llamas, injurias*) ‖ *intr* eructar, regoldar

beleaguer [bɪˈligər] *tr* sitiar, cercar

bel·fry [ˈbɛlfri] *s* (*pl* **-fries**) campanario

Belgian [ˈbɛldʒən] *adj & s* belga *mf*

Belgium [ˈbɛldʒəm] *s* Bélgica

be·lie [bɪˈlaɪ] *v* (*pret & pp* **-lied** [ˈlaɪd]; *ger* **-lying** [ˈlaɪ·ɪŋ]) *tr* desmentir

belief [bɪˈlif] *s* creencia

believable [bɪˈlivəbəl] *adj* creíble; (*source*) solvente

believe [bɪˈliv] *tr & intr* creer

believer [bɪˈlivər] *s* creyente *mf*

belittle [bɪˈlɪtəl] *tr* empequeñecer, despreciar

bell [bɛl] *s* campana; (*electric bell*) timbre *m*, campanilla; (*ring of bell*) campanada ‖ *intr* bramar, berrear

bell′boy′ *s* botones *m*

belle [bɛl] *s* beldad *f*, belleza

belles-lettres [ˌbɛlˈlɛtrə] *spl* bellas letras

bell gable *s* espadaña

bell glass *s* fanal *m*

bell′hop′ *s* (slang) botones *m*

bellicose [ˈbɛlɪˌkos] *adj* belicoso

belligerent [bəˈlɪdʒərənt] *adj & s* beligerante *mf*

bellow [ˈbɛlo] *s* bramido; **bellows** fuelle *m*, barquín *m* ‖ *tr* gritar ‖ *intr* bramar

bell ringer *s* campanero

bellwether [ˈbɛlˌwɛðər] *s* manso

bel·ly [ˈbɛli] *s* (*pl* **-lies**) barriga, vientre *m*; estómago ‖ *v* (*pret & pp* **-lied**) *intr* hacer barriga; hacer bolso (*las velas*)

bel′ly·ache′ *s* (slang) dolor *m* de barriga ‖ *intr* (slang) quejarse

belly button *s* (coll) ombligo

belly dance *s* (coll) danza del vientre

bellyful [ˈbɛliˌful] *s* (slang) panzada

bel′ly-land′ *intr* (aer) aterrizar de panza

belong [bɪˈlɔŋ] *intr* pertenecer; deber estar

belongings [bɪˈlɔŋɪŋz] *spl* pertenencias, efectos; corotos

beloved [bɪˈlʌvɪd] o [bɪˈlʌvd] *adj & s* querido, amado

below [bɪˈlo] *adv* abajo; (*in a text*) más abajo; bajo cero, p.ej., **ten below** diez grados bajo cero ‖ *prep* debajo de; inferior a

belt [bɛlt] *s* cinturón *m*; (aer, mach) correa; (geog) faja, zona; **to tighten one's belt** ceñirse

bemoan [bɪˈmon] *tr* deplorar, lamentar

bench [bɛntʃ] *s* banco; (law) tribunal *m*

bend [bɛnd] *s* curva; (*in a road, river, etc.*) recodo, vuelta ‖ *v* (*pret & pp* **bent** [bɛnt]) *tr* encorvar; doblar (*un tubo; la rodilla*)

inclinar (*la cabeza*); dirigir (*sus esfuerzos*) ‖ *intr* encorvarse; doblarse; inclinarse

beneath [bɪˈniθ] *adv* abajo ‖ *prep* debajo de; inferior a

benediction [ˌbɛnɪˈdɪkʃən] *s* bendición *f*

benefaction [ˌbɛnɪˈfækʃən] *s* beneficio

benefactor [ˈbɛnɪˌfæktər] o [ˌbɛnɪˈfæktər] *s* bienhechor *m*

benefactress [ˈbɛnɪˌfæktrɪs] o [ˌbɛnɪˈfæktrɪs] *s* bienhechora

beneficence [bɪˈnɛfɪsəns] *s* beneficencia

beneficent [bɪˈnɛfɪsənt] *adj* bienhechor

beneficial [ˌbɛnɪˈfɪʃəl] *adj* beneficioso

beneficiar·y [ˌbɛnɪˈfɪʃɪˌɛri] *s* (*pl* **-ies**) beneficiario

benefit [ˈbɛnɪfɪt] *s* beneficio; lasca; **for the benefit of** a beneficio de ‖ *tr* beneficiar

benefit performance *s* beneficio

benevolence [bɪˈnɛvələns] *s* benevolencia

benevolent [bɪˈnɛvələnt] *adj* benévolo; (*e.g., institution*) benéfico

benign [bɪˈnaɪn] *adj* benigno

benigni·ty [bɪˈnɪgnɪti] *s* (*pl* **-ties**) benignidad

bent [bɛnt] *adj* encorvado, doblado, torcido; **bent on** resuelto a, empeñado en; **bent over** cargado de espaldas ‖ *s* encorvadura; inclinación *f*, propensión *f*

benzedrine [ˈbɛnzəˌdrin] *s* bencedrina

benzine [bɛnˈzin] *s* bencina

bequeath [bɪˈkwið] o [bɪˈkwiθ] *tr* legar

bequest [bɪˈkwɛst] *s* manda, legado

berate [bɪˈret] *tr* regañar, reñir

be·reave [bɪˈriv] *v* (*pret & pp* **-reaved** o **-reft** [ˈrɛft]) *tr* despojar, privar; desconsolar

bereavement [bɪˈrivmənt] *s* despojo, privación *f*; desconsuelo

berkelium [bərˈkilɪ·əm] *s* berkelio

Berliner [bərˈlɪnər] *s* berlinés *m*

ber·ry [ˈbɛri] *s* (*pl* **-ries**) baya; (*of coffee plant*) grano, haba

berserk [ˈbʌrsʌrk] *adj* frenético ‖ *adv* frenéticamente

berth [bʌrθ] *s* (*bed*) litera; (*room*) camarote *m*; (*for a ship*) amarradero; (coll) empleo, puesto

beryllium [bəˈrɪlɪ·əm] *s* berilio

be·seech [bɪˈsitʃ] *v* (*pret & pp* **-sought** [ˈsɔt] o **-seeched**) *tr* suplicar

be·set [bɪˈsɛt] *v* (*pret & pp* **-set**; *ger* **-setting**) *tr* acometer, acosar; cercar, sitiar

beside [bɪˈsaɪd] *adv* además, también ‖ *prep* cerca de, junto a; en comparación de; excepto; **beside oneself** fuera de sí; **beside the point** incongruente

besiege [bɪˈsidʒ] *tr* asediar, sitiar

besmirch [bɪˈsmʌrtʃ] *tr* ensuciar, manchar

bespatter [bɪˈspætər] *tr* salpicar

be·speak [bɪˈspik] *v* (*pret* **-spoke** [ˈspok]; *pp* **-spoken**) *tr* apalabrar, pedir de antemano

best [bɛst] *adj super* mejor; óptimo ‖ *adv super* mejor; **had better** debería ‖ *s* (lo) mejor; (lo) más; **at best** a lo más; **to do one's best** hacer lo mejor posible; **to get the best of** aventajar, sobresalir; **to make the best of** sacar el mejor partido de

best girl *s* (coll) amiga preferida, novia

be·stir [bɪ'stʌr] v (pret & pp **-stirred;** ger **-stirring**) tr excitar, incitar; **to bestir oneself** esforzarse, afanarse

best man s padrino de boda

bestow [bɪ'sto] tr otorgar, conferir; dedicar

best seller s éxito de venta, campeón m de venta; éxito de librería

bet. abbr **between**

bet [bɛt] s apuesta ‖ v (pret & pp **bet** o **betted;** ger **betting**) tr & intr apostar; **I bet a que,** apuesto a que; **to bet on** apostar por; **you bet** (slang) ya lo creo

be·take [bɪ'tek] v (pret **-took** ['tʊk]; pp **-taken**) tr — **to betake oneself** dirigirse; darse, entregarse

be·think [bɪ'θɪŋk] v (pret & pp **-thought** ['θɔt]) tr — **to bethink oneself of** considerar, acordarse de

Bethlehem ['bɛθlɪˌhɛm] s Belén m

betide [bɪ'taɪd] tr presagiar; acontecer a ‖ intr acontecer

betoken [bɪ'tokən] tr anunciar, indicar, presagiar

betray [bɪ'tre] tr traicionar; descubrir, revelar

betrayal [bɪ'treˌəl] s traición; descubrimiento, revelación

betroth [bɪ'troð] o [bɪ'trɔθ] tr prometer en matrimonio; **to become betrothed** desposarse

betrothal [bɪ'troðəl] o [bɪ'trɔθəl] s desposorios, esponsales mpl

betrothed [bɪ'troðd] o [bɪ'trɔθt] s prometido, novio

better ['bɛtər] adj comp mejor; **it is better to** más vale; **to grow better** mejorarse; **to make better** mejorar ‖ adv comp mejor; más; **had better** debería; **to like better** preferir ‖ s superior; ventaja; **to get the better of** llevar la ventaja a ‖ tr aventajar; mejorar; **to better oneself** mejorar su posición

better half s (coll) cara mitad

betterment ['bɛtərmənt] s mejoramiento; (in an illness) mejoría

between [bɪ'twin] adv en medio, entremedias ‖ prep entre; **between you and me** entre Vd. y yo; acá para los dos

be·tween'-decks' s entrecubiertas, entrepuentes mpl

between decks adv entrecubiertas

bev·el ['bɛvəl] adj biselado ‖ s (instrument) cartabón m; (sloping part) bisel m ‖ v (pret & pp **-eled** o **-elled;** ger **-eling** o **-elling**) tr biselar

beverage ['bɛvərɪdʒ] s bebida

bev·y ['bɛvi] s (pl **-ies**) (of birds) bandada; (of girls) grupo

bewail [bɪ'wel] tr & intr lamentar

beware [bɪ'wɛr] tr guardarse de ‖ intr tener cuidado; **beware of . . . !** ¡ojo con . . . !, ¡cuidado con . . . !; **to beware of** guardarse de

bewilder [bɪ'wɪldər] tr aturdir, dejar perplejo, desatinar

bewilderment [bɪ'wɪldərmənt] s aturdimiento, perplejidad

beyond [bɪ'jɑnd] adv más allá, más lejos ‖ prep más allá de; además de; no capaz de; **beyond a doubt** fuera de duda; **beyond the reach of** fuera del alcance de ‖ s — **the great beyond** el más allá, el otro mundo

bg. abbr **bag**

bias ['baɪəs] s sesgo, diagonal f; prejuicio; (electron) polarización de rejilla ‖ tr predisponer, prevenir

Bib. abbr **Bible, Biblical**

bib [bɪb] s babero; pepe m; (of apron) pechera

Bible ['baɪbəl] s Biblia

Biblical ['bɪblɪkəl] adj bíblico

bibliographer [ˌbɪblɪ'ɑgrəfər] s bibliógrafo

bibliogra·phy [ˌbɪblɪ'ɑgrəfi] s (pl **-phies**) bibliografía

bibliophile ['bɪblɪˌəˌfaɪl] s bibliófilo

bicameral [baɪ'kæmərəl] adj bicameral

bicarbonate [baɪ'kɑrbəˌnet] s bicarbonato

bicker ['bɪkər] s discusión ociosa ‖ intr discutir ociosamente

bicycle ['baɪsɪkəl] s bicicleta

bid [bɪd] s oferta, postura; (in bridge) declaración ‖ v (pret **bade** [bæd] o **bid;** ger **bidden** ['bɪdən]) tr & intr ofrecer, pujar, licitar; (in bridge) declarar

bidder ['bɪdər] s postor m; (in bridge) declarante mf; **the highest bidder** el mejor postor

bidding ['bɪdɪŋ] s mandato, orden f; postura; (in bridge) declaración

bide [baɪd] tr — **to bide one's time** esperar la hora propicia

biennial [baɪ'ɛnɪˌəl] adj bienal

bier [bɪr] s féretro, andas

bifocal [baɪ'fokəl] adj bifocal ‖ **bifocals** spl anteojos bifocales

big [bɪg] adj (comp **bigger;** super **biggest**) grande; (considerable) importante; (grownup) adulto; **big with child** preñada ‖ adv (coll) con jactancia; **to talk big** (coll) hablar gordo

bigamist ['bɪgəmɪst] s bígamo

bigamous ['bɪgəməs] adj bígamo

bigamy ['bɪgəmi] s bigamia

big-bellied ['bɪgˌbɛlɪd] adj panzudo

Big Dipper s Carro mayor

big game s caza mayor

big-hearted ['bɪgˌhɑrtɪd] adj magnánimo, generoso

bigot ['bɪgət] s intolerante mf, fanático

bigoted ['bɪgətɪd] adj intolerante, fanático

bigot·ry ['bɪgətri] s (pl **-ries**) intolerancia, fanatismo

big shot s (slang) pájaro de cuenta, señorón m, capitoste m

big stick s palo en alto

big toe s dedo gordo o grande (del pie)

bikini [bɪ'kini] s bikini m

bile [baɪl] s bilis f

bilge [bɪldʒ] s pantoque m ‖ tr desfondar

bilge pump s bomba de sentina

bilge water s agua de pantoque

bilge ways spl anguilas

bilingual [baɪ'lɪŋgwəl] adj bilingüe

bilious ['bɪljəs] *adj* bilioso
bilk [bɪlk] *tr* estafar, trampear
bill [bɪl] *s* (*statement of charges for goods or service*) cuenta, factura; (*paper money*) billete *m;* (*poster*) cartel *m,* aviso; cartel de teatro; (*draft of law*) proyecto de ley; (*handbill*) hoja suelta; (*of bird*) pico; (com) giro, letra de cambio ‖ *tr* facturar; cargar en cuenta a; anunciar por carteles ‖ *intr* darse el pico (*las palomas*); acariciarse (*los enamorados*); **to bill and coo** acariciarse y arrullarse
bill′board′ *s* cartelera
billet ['bɪlɪt] *s* (mil) boleta; (mil) alojamiento ‖ *tr* (mil) alojar
billet-doux ['bɪle'du] *s* (*pl* **billets-doux** ['bɪle'duz]) esquela amorosa
bill′fold′ *s* cartera de bolsillo, billetero
bill′head′ *s* encabezamiento de factura
billiards ['bɪljərdz] *s* billar *m*
billion ['bɪljən] *s* (U.S.A.) mil millones; (Brit) billón *m*
bill of exchange *s* letra de cambio
bill of fare *s* lista de comidas, menú *m*
bill of lading ['ledɪŋ] *s* conocimiento de embarque
bill of sale *s* escritura de venta
billow ['bɪlo] *s* oleada, ondulación ‖ *intr* ondular, hincharse
bill′post′er *s* fijacarteles *m,* fijador *m* de carteles
bil•ly ['bɪli] *s* (*pl* **-lies**) cachiporra
billy goat *s* macho cabrío
bin [bɪn] *s* arcón *m,* hucha
bind [baɪnd] *v* (*pret & pp* **bound** [baʊnd]) *tr* ligar, atar; juntar, unir; (*with a garland*) enguirlandar; ribetear (*la orilla del vestido*); agavillar (*las mieses*); vendar (*una herida*); encuadernar (*un libro*); estreñir (*el vientre*)
binder•y ['baɪndəri] *s* (*pl* **-ies**) taller *m* de encuadernación
binding ['baɪndɪŋ] *s* atadura; (*of a book*) encuadernación
binding post *s* borne *m,* sujetahilo
binge [bɪndʒ] *s* (slang) borrachera; turca; **to go on a binge** (slang) pegarse una mona, coger una turca
binnacle ['bɪnəkəl] *s* bitácora
binoculars [bɪ'nɑkjələrz] o [baɪ'nɑkjələrz] *spl* gemelos, prismáticos
biochemical [,baɪ•ə'kɛmɪkəl] *adj* bioquímico
biochemist [,baɪ•ə'kɛmɪst] *s* bioquímico
biochemistry [,baɪ•ə'kɛmɪstri] *s* bioquímica
biodegradable [,baɪ•ədɪ'gredəbəl] *adj* biodegradable
biog. *abbr* **biographical, biography**
biographer [baɪ'ɑgrəfər] *s* biógrafo
biographic(al) [,baɪ•ə'græfɪk(əl)] *adj* biográfico
biogra•phy [baɪ'ɑgrəfi] *s* (*pl* **-phies**) biografía
biologist [baɪ'ɑlədʒɪst] *s* biólogo
biology [baɪ'ɑlədʒi] *s* biología
biophysical [,baɪ•ə'fɪzɪkəl] *adj* biofísico
biophysics [,baɪ•ə'fɪzɪks] *s* biofísica
bioplasm ['baɪ•ə,plæzəm] *s* bioplasma

biopsy ['baɪ•ɑpsi] *s* biopsia
biped ['baɪpɛd] *adj & s* bípedo
birch [bʌrtʃ] *s* abedul *m* ‖ *tr* azotar, varear
bird [bʌrd] *s* ave *f,* pájaro
bird cage *s* jaula
bird call *s* reclamo
bird′lime′ *s* liga
bird of passage *s* ave *f* de paso
bird of prey *s* ave *f* de rapiña
bird′seed′ *s* alpiste *m,* cañamones *mpl*
bird′s′-eye′ view *s* vista a ojo de pájaro
bird shot *s* perdigones *mpl*
birth [bʌrθ] *s* nacimiento; (*childbirth*) parto; origen *m*
birth certificate *s* partida de nacimiento
birth control *s* limitación de la natalidad, control de la natalidad, control de los nacimientos
birth′day′ *s* cumpleaños *m,* natal *m;* (*of any event*) aniversario; **to have a birthday** cumplir años
birthday cake *s* pastel *m* de cumpleaños
birthday present *s* regalo de cumpleaños
birth′mark′ *s* antojo, nevo materno
birth′place′ *s* suelo natal, patria, lugar *m* de nacimiento
birth rate *s* natalidad
birth′right′ *s* derechos de nacimiento; primogenitura
Biscay ['bɪske] *s* Vizcaya
biscuit ['bɪskɪt] *s* panecillo redondo; bizcocho
bisect [baɪ'sɛkt] *tr* bisecar ‖ *intr* empalmar (*dos caminos*)
bishop ['bɪʃəp] *s* obispo; (*in chess*) alfil *m*
bismuth ['bɪzməθ] *s* bismuto
bison ['baɪsən] *s* bisonte *m*
bit [bɪt] *s* poquito, pedacito; (*of food*) bocado; (*of time*) ratito; (*part of bridle*) bocado, freno; (*for drilling*) barrena; **a good bit** una buena cantidad
bitch [bɪtʃ] *s* (*dog*) perra; (*fox*) zorra; (*wolf*) loba; (vulg) mujer *f* de mal genio
bite [baɪt] *s* mordedura; (*of bird or insect*) picadura; (*burning sensation on tongue*) resquemo; (*of food*) bocado; (*snack*) (coll) tentempié *m,* refrigerio ‖ *v* (*pret* **bit** [bɪt]; *pp* **bit** o **bitten** ['bɪtən]) *tr* morder; picar (*los peces, los insectos*); resquemar (*la lengua los alimentos*); comerse (*las uñas*) ‖ *intr* morder; picar; resquemar; (*to be caught by a trick*) (slang) picar
biting ['baɪtɪŋ] *adj* penetrante; mordaz, picante
bitter ['bɪtər] *adj* amargo; (*e.g., struggle*) encarnizado; **to the bitter end** hasta el extremo; hasta la muerte
bitter almond *s* almendra amarga
bitterness ['bɪtərnɪs] *s* amargura
bitumen [bɪ'tjumən] *s* betún *m*
bivou•ac ['bɪvu,æk] *s* vivaque *m* ‖ *v* (*pret & pp* **-acked;** *ger* **-acking**) *intr* vivaquear
bizarre [bɪ'zɑr] *adj* original, raro
bk. *abbr* **bank, block, book**
bkg. *abbr* **banking**
bl. *abbr* **barrel**
b.l. *abbr* **bill of lading**

blabber [`blæbər] *tr & intr* barbullar

black [blæk] *adj* negro ‖ *s* negro; luto; **to wear black** ir de luto

black'-and-blue' *adj* encardenalado, amoratado

black'-and-white' *adj* en blanco y negro

black'ber'ry *s* (*pl* -ries) (*bush*) zarza; (*fruit*) zarzamora

black'bird' *s* mirlo

black'board' *s* encerado, pizarra

black box *s* registrador *m* de vuelo

black'damp' *s* mofeta

blacken [`blækən] *tr* ennegrecer; (*to defame*) desacreditar, denigrar

blackguard [`blægard] *s* bribón *m*, canalla *m* ‖ *tr* injuriar, vilipendiar

black'head' *s* espinilla, comedón *m*

black hole *s* (astr) agujero negro

blackish [`blækɪʃ] *adj* negruzco

black'jack' *s* (*club*) cachiporra; (*flag*) bandera negra (*de pirata*) ‖ *tr* aporrear

black'mail' *s* chantaje *m* ‖ *tr* amenazar con chantaje

blackmailer [`blæk,melər] *s* chantajista *mf*

Black Maria [mə`raɪ•ə] *s* (coll) coche *m* celular

black market *s* estraperlo, mercado negro

blackness [`blæknɪs] *s* negror *m*, negrura

black'out' *s* (*in wartime*) apagamiento de luces; (*in theater*) apagamiento de luces; (*of aviators*) visión negra; pérdida de la memoria; ceguera

black sheep *s* (fig) oveja negra, garbanzo negro

black'smith' *s* (*man who works with iron*) herrero; (*man who shoes horses*) herrador *m*

black'thorn' *s* espino negro, endrino

black tie corbata de smoking; smoking *m*

bladder [`blædər] *s* vejiga

blade [bled] *s* (*of a knife, sword*) hoja; (*of a propeller*) aleta; (*of a fan*) paleta; (*of an oar*) pala; (*of an electric switch*) cuchilla; (*sword*) espada; tallo de hierba; (coll) gallardo joven

blame [blem] *s* culpa ‖ *tr* culpar

blameless [`blemlɪs] *adj* inculpable, irreprochable

blanch [blæntʃ] *tr* blanquear ‖ *intr* palidecer

bland [blænd] *adj* apacible; suave; (*character; weather*) blando

blandish [`blændɪʃ] *tr* engatusar, lisonjear

blank [blæŋk] *adj* en blanco; blanco, vacío; (*stare, look*) vago ‖ *s* blanco; papel blanco; formulario

blank check *s* firma en blanco; (fig) carta blanca

blanket [`blæŋkɪt] *adj* general, comprensivo ‖ *s* manta, frazada; (fig) capa, manto ‖ *tr* cubrir con manta; cubrir, obscurecer

blasé [bla`ze] *adj* hastiado

blaspheme [blæs`fim] *tr* blasfemar contra ‖ *intr* blasfemar

blasphemous [`blæsfɪməs] *adj* blasfemo

blasphe•my [`blæsfɪmi] *s* (*pl* -mies) blasfemia

blast [blæst] *s* (*of wind*) ráfaga; (*of air, sand, water*) chorro; (*of a bellows*) soplo; (*of a horn*) toque *m*; carga de pólvora; voladura, explosión; **full blast** en plena marcha ‖ *tr* (*to blow up*) volar; arruinar; infamar, maldecir

blast furnace *s* alto horno

blast'off' *s* lanzamiento de cohete

blatant [`bletənt] *adj* ruidoso; vocinglero; intruso; chillón, cursi

blaze [blez] *s* (*fire*) incendio; (*bonfire*) hoguera; luz *f* brillante ‖ *tr* encender, inflamar; **to blaze a trail** abrir una senda ‖ *intr* encenderse; resplandecer

bldg. *abbr* **building**

bleach [blitʃ] *s* blanqueo ‖ *tr* blanquear; colar (*la ropa*)

bleachers [`blitʃərz] *spl* gradas al aire libre

bleak [blik] *adj* desierto, yermo, frío, triste

bleat [blit] *s* balido ‖ *intr* balar

bleed [blid] *v* (*pret & pep* bled [blɛd]) *tr & intr* sangrar

blemish [`blɛmɪʃ] *s* mancha ‖ *tr* manchar

blend [blɛnd] *s* mezcla; armonía ‖ *v* (*pret & pp* blended o blent [blɛnt]) *tr* mezclar; armonizar; fusionar ‖ *intr* mezclarse; armonizar; fusionarse

bless [blɛs] *tr* bendecir; **to be blessed with** estar dotado de

blessed [`blɛsɪd] *adj* bendito, santo

blessedness [`blɛsɪdnɪs] *s* bienaventuranza

blessing [`blɛsɪŋ] *s* bendición

blight [blaɪt] *s* niebla, roya; ruina ‖ *tr* anublar; arruinar

blimp [blɪmp] *s* dirigible pequeño

blind [blaɪnd] *adj* ciego ‖ *s* (*window shade*) estor *m*, transparente *m* de resorte; (*Venetian blind*) persiana; pretexto, subterfugio ‖ *tr* cegar; (*to dazzle*) deslumbrar; (*to deceive*) cegar, vendar

blind alley *s* callejón *m* sin salida

blind date *s* cita a ciegas

blinder [`blaɪndər] *s* anteojera

blind flying *s* (aer) vuelo a ciegas

blind'fold' *adj* vendado de ojos ‖ *s* venda ‖ *tr* vendar los ojos a

blind landing *s* aterrizaje *m* a ciegas

blind man *s* ciego

blind'man's' buff *s* gallina ciega

blindness [`blaɪndnɪs] *s* ceguedad

blink [blɪŋk] *s* guiñada, parpadeo ‖ *tr* guiñar (*el ojo*) ‖ *intr* guiñar, parpadear, pestañear; oscilar (*la luz*)

blip [blɪp] *s* bache *m*

bliss [blɪs] *s* bienaventuranza, felicidad

blissful [`blɪsfəl] *adj* bienaventurado, feliz

blister [`blɪstər] *s* ampolla, vejiga ‖ *tr* ampollar ‖ *intr* ampollarse

blithe [blaɪð] *adj* alegre, animado

blitzkrieg [`blɪts,krig] *s* guerra relámpago

blizzard [`blɪzərd] *s* ventisca, chubasco de nieve

bloat [blot] *tr* hinchar ‖ *intr* hincharse, abotagarse

block [blɑk] *s* bloque *m*; (*of hatter*) horma; (*of houses*) manzana; (*for chopping meat*)

tajo; estorbo, obstáculo ‖ *tr* cerrar, obstruir; conformar (*un sombrero*)
blockade [blɑˈked] *s* bloqueo ‖ *tr* bloquear
blockade runner *s* forzador *m* de bloqueo
block and tackle *s* aparejo de poleas
block'bust'er *s* (coll) bomba rompedora
block'head' *s* tonto, zoquete *m*
block signal *s* (rr) señal *f* de tramo
blond [blɑnd] *adj* rubio, blondo ‖ *s* rubio (*hombre rubio*)
blonde [blɑnd] *s* rubia (*mujer rubia*)
blood [blʌd] *s* sangre *f;* **in cold blood** a sangre fría
bloodcurdling [ˈblʌdˌkʌrdlɪŋ] *adj* horripilante
blood'hound' *s* sabueso
blood poisoning *s* envenenamiento de la sangre
blood pressure *s* presión arterial
blood pudding *s* morcilla
blood relation *s* pariente consanguíneo
blood'shed' *s* efusión de sangre
blood'shot' *adj* inyectado en sangre, encarnizado
blood'stream' *s* corriente *f* sanguínea
blood test *s* análisis *m* de sangre
blood'thirst'y *adj* sanguinario
blood transfusion *s* transfusión de sangre
blood vessel *s* vaso sanguíneo
blood·y [ˈblʌdi] *adj* (*comp* -**ier;** *super* -**iest**) sangriento ‖ *v* (*pret & pp* -**ied**) *tr* ensangrentar
bloom [blum] *s* florecimiento; flor *f* ‖ *intr* florecer
blossom [ˈblɑsəm] *s* brote *m,* flor *f;* **in blossom** en cierne ‖ *intr* cerner, florecer
blot [blɑt] *s* borrón *m* ‖ *v* (*pret & pp* **blotted;** *ger* **blotting**) *tr* (*to smear*) borrar; secar con papel secante; **to blot out** borrar ‖ *intr* borrarse; echar borrones (*una pluma*)
blotch [blɑtʃ] *s* manchón *m; (in the skin*) erupción
blotter [ˈblɑtər] *s* teleta, secafirmas *m*
blotting paper *s* papel *m* secante
blouse [blaʊs] *s* blusa
blow [blo] *s* (*hit, stroke*) golpe; (*blast of air*) soplo, soplido; (*blast of wind*) ventarrón *m; (of horn*) toque *m,* trompetazo; (*sudden sorrow*) estocada, ramalazo; (*boaster*) (slang) fanfarrón *m;* **to come to blows** venir a las manos ‖ *v* (*pret* **blew** [blu]; *pp* **blown**) ‖ *tr* soplar; sonar, tocar (*un instrumento de viento*); silbar (*un silbato*); sonarse (*las narices*); quemar (*un fusible*); (slang) malgastar (*dinero*); **to blow out** apagar soplando; quemar (*un fusible*); **to blow up** (*with air*) inflar; (*e.g., with dynamite*) volar, hacer saltar; ampliar (*una foto*) ‖ *intr* soplar; (*to pant*) jadear, resoplar; fundirse (*un fusible*); (slang) fanfarronear; **to blow out** apagarse con el aire; quemarse, fundirse (*un fusible*); reventar (*un neumático*); **to blow up** volarse; (*to fail*) fracasar; (*with anger*) (slang) estallar, reventar

blow'out' *s* (aut) reventón *m; (of a fuse*) quemazón *f;* (slang) tertulia concurrida, festín *m*
blowout patch *s* parche *m* para neumático
blow'pipe' *s* (*torch*) soplete *m; (peashooter*) cerbatana
blow'torch' *s* antorcha a soplete, lámpara de soldar
blubber [ˈblʌbər] *s* grasa de ballena; lloro ruidoso ‖ *intr* llorar ruidosamente
bludgeon [ˈblʌdʒən] *s* cachiporra ‖ *tr* aporrear; intimidar
blue [blu] *adj* azul; abatido, triste ‖ *s* azul *m;* **the blues** la murria, la morriña ‖ *tr* azular; añilar (*la ropa blanca*) ‖ *intr* azularse
blue'ber'ry *s* (*pl* -**ries**) mirtilo
blue chip *s* valor *m* de primera fila
blue'jay' *s* cianocita
blue jeans *spl* blujins *mpl,* vaqueros; pantalones de mezclilla (C-R, Mex); mecánicos (CAm, Cuba, S-D); pantalones azules (CAm); azulones (El Salv); mahones (P-R, S-D)
blue moon *s* cosa muy rara; **once in a blue moon** cada muerte de obispo, de Pascuas a Ramos
Blue Nile *s* Nilo Azul
blue'-pen'cil *tr* marcar o corregir con lápiz azul
blue'print' *s* cianotipo ‖ *tr* copiar a la cianotipia
blue'stock'ing *s* (coll) marisabidilla
blue streak *s* (coll) rayo; **to talk a blue streak** (coll) soltar la tarabilla
bluff [blʌf] *adj* escarpado ‖ *s* risco, peñasco escarpado; (*deception*) farol *m,* blof *m;* **to call someone's bluff** cogerle la palabra a uno ‖ *intr* farolear, papelonear
blunder [ˈblʌndər] *s* disparate *m,* desatino ‖ *intr* disparatar, desatinar
blunt [blʌnt] *adj* despuntado, embotado; brusco, franco, directo ‖ *tr* despuntar, embotar
bluntness [ˈblʌntnɪs] *s* embotadura; brusquedad, franqueza
blur [blʌr] *s* borrón *m,* mancha ‖ *v* (*pret & pp* **blurred;** *ger* **blurring**) *tr* empañar; obscurecer (*la vista*) ‖ *intr* empañarse
blurb [blʌrb] *s* anuncio efusivo
blurt [blʌrt] *tr* — **to blurt out** soltar abrupta e impulsivamente
blush [blʌʃ] *s* rubor *m,* sonrojo ‖ *intr* ruborizarse, sonrojarse
bluster [ˈblʌstər] *s* tumulto, gritos; jactancia ‖ *intr* soplar con furia (*el viento*); bravear, fanfarronear
blustery [ˈblʌstəri] *adj* tempestuoso; (*wind*) violento; (*swaggering*) fanfarrón
blvd. *abbr* **boulevard**
boar [bor] *s* (*male swine*) verraco; (*wild hog*) jabalí *m*
board [bord] *s* tabla; (*to post announcements*) tablillo; (*table with meal*) mesa; (*daily meals*) pensión; (*organized group*) junta, consejo; (naut) bordo; **in boards** (bb) en cartoné; **on board** en el tren; (naut) a bordo ‖ *tr* entablar; subir a (*un tren*);

embarcarse en (*un buque*) ‖ *intr* hospedarse; estar de pupilo

board and lodging *s* mesa y habitación, pensión completa

boarder ['bordər] *s* pensionista *mf*, pupilo

boarding house *s* pensión, casa de huéspedes

boarding school *s* escuela de internos

board of health *s* junta de sanidad

board of trade *s* junta de comercio

board of trustees *s* consejo de administración

board'walk' *s* paseo entablado a la orilla del mar

boast [bost] *s* jactancia, baladronada ‖ *intr* jactarse, baladronear, bravatear

boastful ['bostfəl] *adj* jactancioso

boat [bot] *s* barco, buque *m*, nave *f*; (*small boat*) bote *m*; **to be in the same boat** correr el mismo riesgo

boat hook *s* bichero

boat'house' *s* casilla para botes

boating ['botɪŋ] *s* paseo en barco

boat·man ['botmən] *s* (*pl* **-men** [mən]) barquero, lanchero

boat race *s* regata

boatswain *s* ['bosən] *s* contramaestre *m*

boatswain's chair *s* guindola

boatswain's mate *s* segundo contramaestre

bob [bab] *s* (*of pendulum of clock*) lenteja; (*of plumb line*) plomo; (*of a fishing line*) corcho; (*of a horse*) cola cortada; (*of a girl*) pelo cortado corto; (*jerky motion*) sacudida ‖ *v* (*pret & pp* **bobbed;** *ger* **bobbing**) *tr* cortar corto ‖ *intr* agitarse, menearse; **to bob up and down** subir y bajar con sacudidas cortas

bobbin ['babɪn] *s* broca, canilla, bobina

bobby pin ['babɪ] *s* horquillita para el pelo

bob'by·socks' *spl* (coll) tobilleras (*de jovencita*)

bobbysoxer ['babɪ,saksər] *s* (coll) tobillera

bobolink ['babə,lɪŋk] *s* chambergo

bob'sled' *s* doble trineo articulado

bob'tail' *s* animal *m* rabón; cola corta; cola cortada

bob'white' *s* colín *m* de Virginia

bock beer [bak] *s* cerveza de marzo

bode [bod] *tr & intr* anunciar, presagiar; **to bode ill** ser un mal presagio; **to bode well** ser un buen presagio

bodice ['badɪs] *s* jubón *m*, corpiño

bodily ['badɪli] *adj* corporal, corpóreo ‖ *adv* en persona; en conjunto

bodkin ['badkɪn] *s* (*needle*) aguja roma; (*for lady's hair*) espadilla; (*to make holes in cloth*) punzón *m*

bod·y ['badi] *s* (*pl* **-ies**) cuerpo *m*; (*of a carriage or auto*) caja, carrocería

bod'y·guard' *s* (mil) guardia de corps; guardaespaldas *m*

body shop *s* taller *m* carrocero

Boer [bor] o [bur] *s* bóer *mf*

Boer War *s* guerra del Transvaal

bog [bag] *s* pantano ‖ *v* (*pret & pp* **bogged;** *ger* **bogging**) *intr* — **to bog down** atascarse, hundirse

bogey ['bogi] *s* duende *m*, coco

bo'gey·man' *s* (*pl* **-men** [,mɛn]) duende *m*, espantajo

bogus ['bogəs] *adj* (coll) fingido, falso

bo·gy ['bogi] *s* (*pl* **-gies**) duende *m*, demonio, coco

Bohemian [bo'himɪ·ən] *adj & s* bohemio

boil [bɔɪl] *s* hervor *m*, ebullición; (pathol) divieso, furúnculo ‖ *tr* hacer hervir, herventar ‖ *intr* hervir, bullir; **to boil over** salirse (*un líquido*) al hervir

boiler ['bɔɪlər] *s* caldera; (*for cooking*) marmita, olla

boil'er·mak'er *s* calderero

boiler room *s* sala de calderas

boiling ['bɔɪlɪŋ] *adj* hirviente, hirviendo ‖ *s* hervor *m*, ebullición

boiling point *s* punto de ebullición

boisterous ['bɔɪstərəs] *adj* bullicioso, ruidoso, estrepitoso

bold [bold] *adj* audaz, arrojado, osado; descarado, impudente; temerario

bold'face' *s* negrilla

boldness ['boldnɪs] *s* audacia, arrojo, osadía; descaro, impudencia; temeridad

Bolivia [bo'lɪvɪ·ə] *s* Bolivia

Bolivian [bo'lɪvɪ·ən] *adj & s* boliviano

boll weevil [bol] *s* gorgojo del algodón

Bologna [bə'lonjə] *s* Bolonia

Bolshevik ['balʃəvɪk] o ['bolʃəvɪk] *adj & s* bolchevique *mf*

Bolshevism ['balʃə,vɪzəm] o ['bolʃə,vɪzəm] *s* bolchevismo

bolster ['bolstər] *s* (*of bed*) larguero, travesaño; refuerzo, soporte *m* ‖ *tr* apoyar, sostener; animar, alentar

bolt [bolt] *s* perno; (*to fasten a door*) cerrojo, pasador *m*; (*arrow*) cuadrillo; (*of lightning*) rayo; (*of cloth or paper*) rollo ‖ *tr* empernar; acerrojar; deglutir de una vez; cribar, tamizar; disidir de (*un partido político*) ‖ *intr* salir de repente; disidir; desbocarse (*un caballo*)

bolter ['boltər] *s* disidente *mf*; (*sieve*) criba, tamiz *m*

bolt from the blue *s* rayo en cielo sin nubes; suceso inesperado

bomb [bam] *s* bomba ‖ *tr* bombear, bombardear

bombard [bam'bard] *tr* bombardear; (*e.g., with questions*) asediar

bombardment [bam'bardmənt] *s* bombardeo

bombast ['bambæst] *s* ampulosidad

bombastic [bam'bæstɪk] *adj* ampuloso

bomb crater *s* (mil) embudo de bomba

bomber ['bamər] *s* bombardero

bomb'proof' *adj* a prueba de bombas

bomb release *s* lanzabombas *m*

bomb'shell' *s* bomba; **to fall like a bombshell** caer como una bomba

bomb shelter *s* refugio antiaéreo

bomb'sight' *s* mira de bombardeo, visor *m*

bona fide ['bonə,faɪdə] *adj & adv* de buena fe

bonbon ['ban,ban] *s* bombón *m*, confite *m*

bond [band] *s* (*tie, union*) enlace *m*, vínculo, lazo de unión; (*interest-bearing certificate*) bono, obligación; (*surety*) fianza; (mas) aparejo; **bonds** cadenas, grillos; **in bond** en depósito bajo fianza

bondage ['bɑndɪdʒ] *s* cautiverio, servidumbre

bonded warehouse *s* depósito comercial

bond'hold'er *s* obligacionista *mf*, tenedor *m* de bonos

bonds•man ['bɑndzmən] *s* (*pl* **-men** [mən]) fiador *m*

bone [bon] *s* hueso; (*of fish*) espina; **bones** esqueleto; (*mortal remains*) huesos; castañuelas; (*dice*) (coll) dados; **to have a bone to pick with** tener una queja con; **to make no bones about** no andarse con rodeos en ‖ *tr* desosar; quitar la espina a; emballenar (*un corsé*) ‖ *intr* — **to bone up on** (coll) empollar, estudiar con ahinco

bone'head' *s* (coll) mentecato, zopenco

boneless ['bonlɪs] *adj* mollar, desosado; (*fish*) sin espinas

boner ['bonər] *s* (coll) patochada, plancha, gazapo

bonfire ['bɑn,faɪr] *s* hoguera

bonnet ['bɑnɪt] *s* gorra; (*sunbonnet*) papalina; (*of auto*) cubierta, capó *m*

bonus ['bonəs] *s* prima, plus *m;* dividendo extraordinario

bon•y ['boni] *adj* (*comp* **-ier;** *super* **-iest**) osudo; descarnado; (*fish*) espinoso

boo [bu] *s* rechifla; **not to say boo** no decir ni chus ni mus ‖ *tr & intr* abuchear, rechiflar

boo•by ['bubi] *s* (*pl* **-bies**) bobalicón *m*, zopenco; el peor jugador

booby prize *s* premio al peor jugador

booby trap *s* (*mine*) trampa explosiva; (*trick*) zancadilla

boogie-woogie ['bugi'wugi] *s* bugui-bugui *m*

book [buk] *s* libro; (*bankbook*) libreta; (*book containing records of business transactions*) libro-registro; (*of cigaret paper, stamps, etc.*) librillo; **to keep books** llevar libros ‖ *tr* reservar (*un pasaje*); escriturar (*a un actor*)

bookbinder ['buk,baɪndər] *s* encuadernador *m*

book'bind'er•y *s* (*pl* **-ies**) encuadernación (*taller*)

book'bind'ing *s* encuadernación (*acción, arte*)

book'case' *s* armario para libros, estante *m* para libros

book end *s* apoyalibros *m*

bookie ['buki] *s* (coll) corredor *m* de apuestas

booking ['bukɪŋ] *s* (*of passage*) reservación; (*of an actor*) escritura

booking clerk *s* taquillero (*que despacha pasajes o localidades*)

bookish ['bukɪʃ] *adj* libresco

book'keep'er *s* tenedor *m* de libros

book'keep'ing *s* teneduría de libros, contabilidad

book'mak'er *s* corredor *m* de apuestas

book'mark' *s* registro

book'plate' *s* ex libris *m*

book review *s* reseña

book'sell'er *s* librero

book'shelf' *s* (*pl* **-shelves** [,ʃɛlvz] estante *m* para libros

book'stand' *s* (*rack*) atril *m;* mostrador *m* para libros; puesto de venta para libros

book'store' *s* librería

book'worm' *s* polilla que roe los libros; (fig) ratón *m* de biblioteca

boom [bum] *s* (*sudden prosperity*) auge *m*, boom *m;* (*noise*) estampido, trueno; (*of a crane*) aguilón *m;* (naut) botalón *m* ‖ *intr* hacer estampido, tronar; estar en auge

boomerang ['bumə,ræŋ] *s* bumerán *m*

boom town *s* pueblo en bonanza

boon [bun] *s* bendición, dicha

boon companion *s* buen compañero

boor [bur] *s* patán *m*, rústico

boorish ['burɪʃ] *adj* rústico, zafio

boost [bust] *s* empujón *m* hacia arriba; (*in price*) alza; alabanza; ayuda ‖ *tr* empujar hacia arriba; alzar (*el precio*); alabar; ayudar

booster ['bustər] *s* cohete *m* lanzador; primera etapa de un cohete lanzador; (*enthusiastic backer*) bombista *mf*

booster shot *s* inyección secundaria

boot [but] *s* bota; **to boot** de añadidura, además; **to die with one's boots on** morir al pie del cañón ‖ *tr* dar un puntapié a; **to boot out** (slang) poner en la calle

boot'black' *s* limpiabotas *m*

booth [buθ] *s* casilla, quiosco; (*to telephone, to vote, etc.*) cabina; (*at a fair or market*) puesto

boot'jack' *s* sacabotas *m*

boot'leg' *adj* contrabandista; de contrabando ‖ *s* contrabando de licores ‖ *v* (*pret & pp* **-legged;** *ger* **-legging**) *tr* pasar de contrabando ‖ *intr* contrabandear en bebidas alcohólicas

bootlegger ['but,lɛgər] *s* destilador *m* clandestino, contrabandista *m*

boot'leg'ging *s* contrabando en bebidas alcohólicas

bootlicker ['but,lɪkər] *s* (slang) quitamotas *mf*, lavacaras *mf*

boot'strap' *s* tirilla de bota

boo•ty ['buti] *s* (*pl* **-ties**) botín *m*, presa

booze [buz] *s* (coll) bebida alcohólica ‖ *intr* borrachear

bor. *abbr* **borough**

borax ['boræks] *s* bórax *m*

Bordeaux [bɔr'do] *s* Burdeos

border ['bɔrdər] *s* (*of firearm*) frontero, fronterizo ‖ *s* borde *m*, margen *m & f;* frontera; **borders** bambalinas ‖ *tr* bordear; deslindar ‖ *intr* confinar

border clash *s* encuentro fronterizo

bor'der•line' *adj* incierto, indefinido ‖ *s* frontera

bore [bor] *s* (*drill hole*) barreno; (*size of hole*) calibre *m;* (*of firearm*) alma, ánima; (*of cylinder*) alesaje *m;* (*wearisome person*) latoso, machaca *mf;* fastidio ‖ *tr* aburrir, fastidiar; barrenar, hacer (*un agujero*)

boredom ['bordəm] *s* aburrimiento, fastidio

boring ['borɪŋ] *adj* aburrido, pesado; **that's terribly boring** es una lata

born [bɔrn] *adj* nacido; (*natural, by birth*) nato, innato; **to be born** nacer

borough [ˈbʌro] *s* (*town*) villa; distrito electoral de municipio

borrow [ˈbaro] o [ˈbɔro] *tr* pedir o tomar prestado; apropiarse (*p.ej., una idea*); incorporar (*un elemento lingüístico extranjero*); **to borrow trouble** tomarse una molestia sin motivo alguno

borrower [ˈbaro•ər] o [ˈbɔro•ər] *s* prestatario

borrowing [ˈbaro•ɪŋ] o [ˈbɔro•ɪŋ] *s* préstamo; préstamo lingüístico, extranjerismo

bosom [ˈbʊzəm] *s* seno; (*of shirt*) pechera; corazón *m*, pecho

bosom friend *s* amigo de la mayor confianza

Bosporus [ˈbɑspərəs] *s* Bósforo

boss [bɔs] o [bɑs] *s* (coll) amo, capataz *m*, mandamás *m*, jefe *m*; (*in politics*) (coll) cacique *m*; protuberancia ‖ *tr* (coll) mandar, dominar

bossism [ˈbɔsɪzəm] *s* caciquismo

boss•y [ˈbɔsi] *adj* (*comp* **-ier;** *super* **-iest**) mandón

botanical [bəˈtænɪkəl] *adj* botánico

botanist [ˈbɑtənɪst] *s* botánico

botany [ˈbɑtəni] *s* botánica

botch [bɑtʃ] *s* remiendo chapucero ‖ *tr* remendar chapuceramente

both [boθ] *adj & pron* ambos ‖ *adv* igualmente ‖ *conj* a la vez; **both . . . and** tanto . . . como, así . . . como

bother [ˈbɑðər] *s* incomodidad, molestia, majadería, murga ‖ *tr* incomodar, molestar, majaderear, pololear ‖ *intr* molestarse

bothersome [ˈbɑðərsəm] *adj* incómodo, molesto, fastidioso

bottle [ˈbɑtəl] *s* botella, frasco ‖ *tr* embotellar; **to bottle up** (nav) embotellar

bot'tle•neck' *s* gollete *m*; (*in traffic*) embotellado

bottle opener [ˈopənər] *s* abrebotellas *m*

bottom [ˈbɑtəm] *adj* (*price*) (el) más bajo; (*e.g., dollar*) último ‖ *s* fondo; (*of a chair*) asiento; (*of jar*) culo; (coll) trasero; **at bottom** en el fondo; **to go to the bottom** irse a pique

bottomless [ˈbɑtəmlɪs] *adj* sin fondo, insondable

boudoir [buˈdwɑr] *s* tocador *m*

bough [baʊ] *s* rama

bouillon [ˈbʊljɑn] *s* caldo

boulder [ˈboldər] *s* pedrejón *m*

boulevard [ˈbʊlə,vɑrd] *s* bulevar *m*

bounce [baʊns] *s* rebote *m* ‖ *tr* hacer botar; (slang) despedir ‖ *intr* botar, rebotar; saltar; **to bounce along** dar saltos al andar

bouncer [ˈbaʊnsər] *s* cosa grande; (slang) apagabroncas *m*

bouncing [ˈbaʊnsɪŋ] *adj* frescachón, vigoroso; (*baby*) gordinflón

bound [baʊnd] *adj* atado, ligado; (*book*) encuadernado; dispuesto, propenso; puesto en aprendizaje; **bound for** con destino a, con rumbo a; **bound in boards** (bb) encartonado, en cartoné; **bound up in** entregado

a, muy adicto a; absorto en ‖ *s* salto; (*of a ball*) bote *m*; límite *m*, confín *m*; **bounds** región, comarca; **out of bounds** fuera de los límites; **within bounds** a raya

bounda•ry [ˈbaʊndəri] *s* (*pl* **-ries**) límite *m*, frontera; (*established*) parámetro

boundary mark *s* (*annotation*) acotamiento

boundary stone *s* mojón *m*

bounder [ˈbaʊndər] *s* persona vulgar y malcriada

boundless [ˈbaʊndlɪs] *adj* ilimitado, inmenso, infinito

bountiful [ˈbaʊntɪfəl] *adj* generoso, liberal; abundante

boun•ty [ˈbaʊnti] *s* (*pl* **-ties**) generosidad, liberalidad; don *m*, favor *m*; galardón *m*, premio; (*bonus*) prima; (mil) premio de enganche

bouquet [buˈke] *s* ramillete *m*; (*aroma of a wine*) nariz *f*

bourgeois [ˈbʊrʒwɑ] *adj & s* burgués *m*

bourgeoisie [,bʊrʒwɑˈzi] *s* burguesía

bout [baʊt] *s* encuentro; rato; (*of an illness*) ataque *m*

bow [baʊ] *s* inclinación, reverencia; (*of a ship*) proa ‖ *tr* inclinar (*la cabeza*) ‖ *intr* inclinarse; **to bow and scrape** hacer reverencias obsequiosas; **to bow to** saludar, inclinarse delante ‖ [bo] *s* (*for shooting an arrow*) arco; lazo, nudo; (mus) arco; (*stroke of bow*) (mus) arqueada ‖ *tr* (mus) tocar con arco ‖ *intr* arquearse

bowdlerize [ˈbaʊdlə,raɪz] *tr* expurgar

bowel [ˈbaʊ•əl] *s* intestino; **bowels** intestinos; (*inner part*) entrañas

bowel movement *s* evacuación del vientre; **to have a bowel movement** evacuar el vientre

bower [ˈbaʊ•ər] *s* emparrado, glorieta

bower•y [ˈbaʊ•əri] *adj* frondoso, sombreado ‖ *s* (*pl* **-ies**) finca, granja

bowknot [ˈbo,nɑt] *s* lazada

bowl [bol] *s* (*for soup or broth*) escudilla, cuenco; (*for washing hands*) jofaina, palangana; (*of toilet*) cubeta, taza; (*of fountain*) tazón *m*; (*of spoon*) paleta; (*of pipe*) hornillo; (*hollow place*) concavidad, cuenco ‖ *tr* — **to bowl over** tumbar ‖ *intr* jugar a los bolos; **to bowl along** rodar

bowlegged [ˈbo,lɛgd] o [ˈbo,lɛgɪd] *adj* patiestevado

bowler [ˈbolər] *s* jugador *m* de bolos; (Brit) sombrero hongo

bowling [ˈbolɪŋ] *s* juego de bolos, boliche *m*

bowling alley *s* bolera, boliche *m*

bowling green *s* bolera encespada

bowshot [ˈbo,ʃɑt] *s* tiro de flecha

bowsprit [ˈbaʊsprɪt] o [ˈbosprɪt] *s* bauprés *m*

bow tie [bo] *s* corbata de mariposa, pajarita

bowwow [ˈbaʊ,waʊ] *interj* ¡guau! ‖ *s* guau guau *m*

box [bɑks] *s* caja; (*slap*) bofetada; (*plant*) boj *m*; (*in newspaper*) recuadro; (theat) palco ‖ *tr* encajonar; (*to slap*) abofetear; (naut) cuartear (*la aguja*) ‖ *intr* boxear

box'car' *s* vagón *m* de carga cerrado

boxer [ˈbɑksər] s embalador m; (sport) boxeador m
boxing [ˈbɑksɪŋ] s embalaje m; (sport) boxeo
boxing gloves spl guantes mpl de boxeo
box office s taquilla, despacho de localidades; boletería
box'-of'fice hit s éxito de taquilla
box-office record s marca de taquilla
box-office sale s venta de localidades en taquilla
box pleat s pliegue m de tabla
box seat s asiento de palco
box'wood' s boj m
boy [bɔɪ] s muchacho; (servant) mozo; (coll) compadre m
boycott [ˈbɔɪkɑt] s boicoteo ‖ tr boicotear
boyhood [ˈbɔɪhʊd] s muchachez f; muchachería
boyish [ˈbɔɪɪʃ] adj amuchachado, muchachil
boy scout s niño explorador
Bp. abbr **bishop**
b.p. abbr **bills payable, boiling point**
br. abbr **brand, brother**
b.r. abbr **bills receivable**
bra [brɑ] s (coll) portasenos m, sostén m, sujetador m
brace [bres] s riostra; berbiquí m; **braces** (Brit) tirantes mpl; (on teeth) aparato de ortodoncia ‖ tr arriostrar; asegurar, vigorizar; **to brace oneself** (coll) cobrar ánimo ‖ intr — **to brace up** (coll) cobrar ánimo
brace and bit s berbiquí y barrena
bracelet [ˈbreslɪt] s brazalete m, pulsera f
bracer [ˈbresər] s (coll) trago de licor
bracing [ˈbresɪŋ] adj fortificante, tónico
bracket [ˈbrækɪt] s puntal m, soporte m; ménsula, repisa; (mark used in printing) corchete m; clase f, categoría ‖ tr acorchetar; agrupar
brackish [ˈbrækɪʃ] adj salobre
brad [bræd] s clavito, estaquilla
brag [bræg] s jactancia ‖ v (pret & pp **bragged**; ger **bragging**) intr jactarse, bravatear, palanganear
braggart [ˈbrægərt] s fanfarrón m
braid [bred] s (flat strip of cotton, silk, etc.) cinta, galón m; (something braided) trenza ‖ tr encintar, galonear; trenzar
brain [bren] s cerebro; **brains** cerebro, inteligencia; **to rack one's brains** devanarse los sesos ‖ tr descerebrar
brain child s parto del ingenio
brain drain s (coll) éxodo de técnicos
brainless [ˈbrenlɪs] adj tonto, sin seso
brain power s capacidad mental
brain'storm' s acceso de locura; confusión mental; buena idea, hallazgo
brain trust s grupo de peritos
brain'wash'ing s lavado cerebral
brain wave s onda encefálica; (coll) buena idea, hallazgo
brain'work' s trabajo intelectual
brain•y [ˈbreni] adj (comp **-ier**; super **-iest**) (coll) inteligente, sesudo
braise [brez] tr soasar y cocer (la carne) a fuego lento en vasija bien tapada

brake [brek] s freno; breque m; (for dressing flax) agramadera; (thicket) matorral m; (fern) helecho común ‖ tr frenar; brequear; agramar (el lino o el cañamo)
brake band s cinta de freno
brake drum s tambor m de freno
brake lining s forro o cinta de freno
brake•man [ˈbrekmən] s (pl **-men** [mən]) guardafrenos m
brake shoe s zapata de freno
bramble [ˈbræmbəl] s frambueso, zarza
bram•bly [ˈbræmbli] adj (comp **-blier**; super **-bliest**) zarzoso
bran [bræn] s afrecho, salvado
branch [bræntʃ] s (of tree) rama; (smaller branch; branch cut from tree; of a science, etc.) ramo; (of vine) sarmiento; (of road, railroad) ramal m; (of candlestick, river, etc.) brazo; (of a store, bank) sucursal f ‖ intr ramificarse; **to branch out** extender sus actividades
branch line s ramal m, línea de empalme
branch office s sucursal f
brand [brænd] s (kind, make) marca; (trademark) marca de fábrica; (branding iron) hierro de marcar; (mark stamped with hot iron) hierro; (dishonor) tizón m ‖ tr poner marca de fábrica en; herrar con hierro candente; tiznar (la reputación de una persona); **to brand as** tildar de
brandied [ˈbrændid] adj macerado en aguardiente
branding iron s hierro de marcar; fierro
brandish [ˈbrændɪʃ] tr blandear
brand'-new' adj nuevecito, flamante
bran•dy [ˈbrændi] s (pl **-dies**) aguardiente m
brash [bræʃ] adj atrevido, impetuoso; descarado, respondón ‖ s acceso, ataque m
brass [bræs] s latón m; (in army and navy) (slang) los mandamases; (coll) descaro; **brasses** (mus) cobres mpl
brass band s banda, charanga
brass hat s (slang) espadón m, mandamás m
brassiere [brəˈzɪr] s portasenos m, sostén m, sujetador m
brass knuckles spl llave inglesa, bóxer m
brass tack s clavito dorado de tapicería; **to get down to brass tacks** (coll) entrar en materia
brass winds spl (mus) cobres mpl, instrumentos músicos de metal
brass•y [ˈbræsi] adj (comp **-ier**; super **-iest**) hecho de latón; metálico; descarado
brat [bræt] s rapaz m, mocoso, braguillas m
brava•do [brəˈvado] s (pl **-does** o **-dos**) bravata
brave [brev] adj bravo, valiente ‖ s valiente m; guerrero indio norteamericano ‖ tr hacer frente a, arrostrar; desafiar, retar
bravery [ˈbrevəri] s bravura, valor m
bra•vo [ˈbravo] interj ¡bravo! ‖ s (pl **-vos**) bravo
brawl [brɔl] s pendencia, reyerta; alboroto ‖ intr armar pendencia; alborotar
brawler [ˈbrɔlər] s pendenciero; alborotador m
brawn [brɔn] s fuerza musculosa

brawn•y ['brɔni] *adj* (*comp* **-ier;** *super* **-iest**) fornido, musculoso

bray [bre] *s* rebuzno ‖ *intr* rebuznar

braze [brez] *s* soldadura de latón ‖ *tr* soldar con latón; cubrir de latón; adornar con latón

brazen ['brezən] *adj* de latón; descarado ‖ *tr* — **to brazen through** llevar a cabo descaradamente

brazier ['breʒər] *s* brasero

Brazil [brə'zɪl] *s* el Brasil

Brazilian [brə'zɪljən] *adj & s* brasileño

Brazil nut *s* castaña de Pará

breach [britʃ] *s* (*opening*) abertura; (*in a wall*) brecha; abuso, violación ‖ *tr* abrir brecha en

breach of faith *s* falta de fidelidad

breach of peace *s* perturbación del orden público

breach of promise *s* incumplimiento de la palabra de matrimonio

breach of trust *s* abuso de confianza

bread [brɛd] *s* pan *m* ‖ *tr* empanar

bread and butter *s* pan *m* con mantequilla; (coll) pan de cada día

bread crumbs *spl* pan rallado

breaded ['brɛdɪd] *adj* empanado

bread line *s* cola del pan

breadth [brɛdθ] *s* anchura; alcance *m*, extensión; (*e.g., of judgment*) amplitud *f*

bread'win'ner *s* sostén *m* de la familia

break [brek] *s* rompimiento; interrupción; intervalo, pausa; (*split*) hendidura, grieta; (*in prices*) baja; (*in clouds*) claro; (*from jail*) evasión, huída; (*among friends*) ruptura; (*luck, good or bad*) (slang) suerte *f;* (slang) disparate *m;* **to give someone a break** abrirle a uno la puerta ‖ *v* (*pret* **broke** [brok]; *pp* **broken**) *tr* romper, quebrar; cambiar (*un billete*); comunicar (*una mala noticia*); suspender (*relaciones*); faltar a (*la palabra*); batir (*un récord*); cortar (*un circuito*); quebrantar (*un testamento; un hábito*); romper (*una ley*); levantar (*el campo*); (mil) degradar; **to break in** forzar (*una puerta*); **to break open** abrir por la fuerza ‖ *intr* romperse, quebrarse; reventar; aclarar (*el tiempo*); bajar (*los precios*); quebrantarse (*la salud*); **to break down** perder la salud; prorrumpir en llanto; **to break even** salir sin ganar ni perder; **to break in** entrar por fuerza; irrumpir en; **to break loose** desprenderse; escaparse; desbocarse (*un caballo*); desencadenarse (*una tempestad*); **to break out** estallar, declararse; (*in laughter, weeping*) romper; (*on the skin*) brotar granos; **to break through** abrirse paso; abrir paso por entre; **to break up** desmenuzarse; levantarse (*una reunión*); **to break with** romper con

breakable ['brekəbəl] *adj* rompible

breakage ['brekɪdʒ] *s* estropicio; indemnización por objetos rotos

break'down' *s* mal éxito; avería, pana; (*in health*) colapso; (*in negotiations*) ruptura; análisis *m*

breaker ['brekər] *s* cachón *m*, rompiente *m*

breakfast ['brɛkfəst] *s* desayuno ‖ *intr* desayunar

breakfast food *s* cereal *m* para el desayuno

break'neck' *adj* vertiginoso; **at breakneck speed** a mata caballo

break of day *s* alba, amanecer *m*

break'through' *s* (mil) brecha, ruptura; (fig) descubrimiento sensacional

break'up' *s* disolución, dispersión; desplome *m;* (*in health*) postración

break'wa'ter *s* rompeolas *m*, escollera

breast [brɛst] *s* pecho, seno; (*of fowl*) pechuga; (*of garment*) pechera; **to make a clean breast of it** confesarlo todo

breast'bone' *s* esternón *m;* (*of fowl*) quilla

breast drill *s* berbiquí *m* de pecho

breast'pin' *s* alfiler *m* de pecho

breast stroke *s* brazada de pecho

breath [brɛθ] *s* aliento, respiración; **out of breath** sin aliento; **short of breath** corto de resuello; **to gasp for breath** respirar anhelosamente; **under one's breath** por lo bajo, en voz baja

breathe [brið] *tr* respirar; **to breathe one's last** dar el último suspiro ‖ *intr* respirar; **to breathe freely** cobrar aliento; **to breathe in** aspirar; **to breathe out** espirar

breathing spell *s* respiro, rato de descanso

breathless ['brɛθlɪs] *adj* falto de aliento, jadeante; intenso, vivo; sin aliento

breath'tak'ing *adj* conmovedor, imponente

breech [britʃ] *s* culata, recámara; **breeches** ['brɪtʃɪz] calzones *mpl;* (coll) pantalones *mpl;* **to wear the breeches** (coll) calzarse los pantalones

breed [brid] *s* casta, raza; clase *f*, especie *f* ‖ *v* (*pret & pp* **bred** [brɛd]) *tr* criar ‖ *intr* criar; criarse

breeder ['bridər] *s* (*of animals*) criador *m;* (*animal*) reproductor *m*

breeding ['bridɪŋ] *s* cría; crianza, modales *mpl;* **bad breeding** mala crianza; **good breeding** buena crianza

breeze [briz] *s* brisa

breez•y ['brizi] *adj* (*comp* **-ier;** *super* **-iest**) airoso; animado, vivo; (coll) desenvuelto, vivaracho

brevi•ty ['brɛvɪti] *s* (*pl* **-ties**) brevedad

brew [bru] *s* calderada de cerveza; mezcla ‖ *tr* fabricar (*cerveza*); preparar (*té*); (fig) tramar, urdir ‖ *intr* amenazar (*una tormenta*)

brewer ['bru•ər] *s* cervecero

brewer's yeast *s* levadura de cerveza

brewer•y ['bru•əri] *s* (*pl* **-ies**) cervecería, fábrica de cerveza

bribe [braɪb] *s* soborno; **to take bribes** comer maíz ‖ *tr* sobornar

briber•y ['braɪbəri] *s* (*pl* **-ies**) soborno

bric-a-brac ['brɪkə,bræk] *s* chucherías, curiosidades *fpl*

brick [brɪk] *s* ladrillo; (coll) buen sujeto ‖ *tr* enladrillar

brick'bat' *s* pedazo de ladrillo; (coll) palabra hiriente

brick ice cream *s* queso helado, helado al corte

brickkiln ['brɪk,kɪln] *s* horno de ladrillero

bricklayer ['brɪk,le•ər] *s* ladrillador *m*

brick′yard′ *s* ladrillal *m*

bridal ['braɪdəl] *adj* nupcial; de novia

bridal wreath *s* corona nupcial

bride [braɪd] *s* desposada, novia

bride′groom′ *s* desposado, novio

bridesmaid ['braɪdz,med] *s* madrina de boda

bridge [brɪdʒ] *s* puente *m;* (*of nose*) caballete *m;* (*card game*) bridge *m* ‖ *tr* tender un puente sobre; salvar (*un obstáculo*); colmar, llenar (*un vacío*)

bridge′head′ *s* (mil) cabeza de puente

bridle ['braɪdəl] *s* brida ‖ *tr* embridar ‖ *intr* engallarse, erguirse

bridle path *s* camino de herradura

brief [brif] *adj* breve, corto, conciso ‖ *s* resumen *m;* (law) escrito; **in brief** en resumen ‖ *tr* resumir; dar consejos anticipados a; dar informes a

brief case *s* cartera

briefing ['brifɪŋ] *s* órdenes *fpl;* (*of the press*) informe *m*

brier ['braɪ•ər] *s* zarza; brezo blanco

brig [brɪg] *s* (naut) bergantín *m;* prisión en buque de guerra

brigade [brɪ'ged] *s* brigada

brigadier [,brɪgə'dɪr] *s* general *m* de brigada

brigand ['brɪgənd] *s* bandolero

brigantine ['brɪgən,tin] *s* (naut) bergantín *m* goleta

bright [braɪt] *adj* brillante; (*e.g., day*) claro; (*color*) subido; listo, inteligente, despierto; (*idea, thought*) luminoso; (*disposition*) alegre, vivo

brighten ['braɪtən] *tr* abrillantar; alegrar, avivar ‖ *intr* avivarse; alegrarse; despejarse (*el cielo*)

bright lights *spl* luces *fpl* brillantes; (aut) faros o luces de carretera

brilliance ['brɪljəns] o **brilliancy** ['brɪljənsi] *s* brillantez *f,* brillo

brilliant ['brɪljənt] *adj* brillante

brillantine ['brɪljəntin] *s* brillantina

brim [brɪm] *s* borde *m;* (*of hat*) ala

brim′stone′ *s* azufre *m*

brine [braɪn] *s* salmuera, agua salobre

bring [brɪŋ] *v* (*pret & pp* **brought** [brɔt]) *tr* traer; llevar; **to bring about** efectuar; **to bring back** devolver; **to bring down** abatir; **to bring forth** sacar a luz; **to bring in** traer a colación; servir (*una comida*); introducir, presentar; **to bring into play** poner en juego; **to bring on** causar, producir; **to bring out** sacar; presentar al público; **to bring suit** poner pleito; **to bring to** sacar de un desmayo; **to bring together** reunir; confrontar; reconciliar; **to bring to pass** efectuar, llevar a cabo; **to bring up** arrimar (*p.ej., una silla*); educar, criar; traer a colación; **to bring upon oneself** atraerse (*un infortunio*)

bringing-up ['brɪŋɪŋ'ʌp] *s* educación, crianza

brink [brɪŋk] *s* borde *m,* margen *m;* **on the brink of** al borde de

brisk [brɪsk] *adj* animado, vivo, vivaz

bristle ['brɪsəl] *s* cerda ‖ *intr* erizarse, encresparse; (*to be visibly annoyed*) encresparse

bris•tly ['brɪsli] *adj* (*comp* **-tlier;** *super* **-tliest**) cerdoso, erizado

Britannic [brɪ'tænɪk] *adj* británico

British ['brɪtɪʃ] *adj* británico ‖ **the British** los britanos

Britisher ['brɪtɪʃər] *s* britano

Briton ['brɪtən] *s* britano

Brittany ['brɪtəni] *s* Bretaña

brittle ['brɪtəl] *adj* quebradizo, frágil

bro. *abbr* **brother**

broach [brotʃ] *s* (*skewer*) asador *m,* espetón *m;* (*ornamental pin*) broche *m,* prendedero ‖ *tr* sacar a colación

broad [brɔd] *adj* ancho; liberal, tolerante; (*day, noon, etc.*) pleno

broad′cast′ *s* radiodifusión; audición, programa radiotelefónico ‖ *v* (*pret & pp* **-cast**) *tr* difundir, esparcir ‖ (*pret & pp* **-cast** o **-casted**) *tr* radiodifundir, radiar, emitir

broadcasting station *s* emisora, estación de radiodifusión

broad′cloth′ *s* paño fino

broaden ['brɔdən] *tr* ensanchar ‖ *intr* ensancharse

broad′loom′ *adj* tejido en telar ancho y en color sólido

broad-minded ['brɔd'maɪndɪd] *adj* tolerante, de amplias miras

broad-shouldered ['brɔd'ʃoldərd] *adj* ancho de espaldas

broad′side′ *s* (naut) costado; (naut) andanada; (coll) torrente *m* de injurias

broad′sword′ *s* espada ancha

brocade [bro'ked] *s* brocado

broccoli ['brɑkəli] *s* brécol *m,* brécoles *mpl*

brochure [bro'ʃur] *s* folleto

brogue [brog] *s* acento irlandés

broil [brɔɪl] *tr* asar a la parrilla ‖ *intr* asarse

broiler ['brɔɪlər] *s* parrilla; pollo para asar a la parrilla

broken ['brokən] *adj* roto, quebrado; agotado; amansado; (*accent*) chapurrado; suelto

bro′ken-down′ *adj* abatido; descompuesto; destartalado

broken-hearted ['brokən'hɑrtɪd] *adj* abrumado por el dolor

broker ['brokər] *s* corredor *m*

brokerage ['brokərɪdʒ] *s* corretaje *m*

bromide ['bromaɪd] *s* bromuro; (slang) trivialidad

bromine ['bromin] *s* bromo

bronchitis [brɑŋ'kaɪtɪs] *s* bronquitis *f*

bron•co ['brɑŋko] *s* (*pl* **-cos**) potro cerril

bron′co•bust′er *s* domador *m* de potros; vaquero

bronze [brɑnz] *adj* bronceado ‖ *s* bronce *m* ‖ *tr* broncear ‖ *intr* broncearse

brooch [brotʃ] o [brutʃ] *s* alfiler *m* de pecho, prendedero, pasador *m*

brood [brud] *s* cría; nidada; casta, raza ‖ *tr* empollar ‖ *intr* enclocar; **to brood on** meditar con preocupación

brook [bruk] *s* arroyo ‖ *tr* — **to brook no** no tolerar, no aguantar

broom [brum] o [brʊm] *s* escoba; (bot) hiniesta

broom′corn′ *s* sorgo

broom′stick′ *s* palo de escoba

bros. *abbr* **brothers**

broth [brɔθ] o [braθ] *s* caldo

brothel [′braθəl] o [′braðəl] *s* burdel *m;* (Mex) congal *m*

brother [′brʌðər] *s* hermano

brotherhood [′brʌðər,hʊd] *s* hermandad

broth′er-in-law′ *s* (*pl* **brothers-in-law**) cuñado, hermano político; (*husband of one's wife's or husband's sister*) concuñado

brotherly [′brʌðərli] *adj* fraternal

brow [braʊ] *s* (*forehead*) frente *f;* (*eyebrow*) ceja; **to knit one's brow** fruncir las cejas

brow′beat′ *v* (*pret* **-beat;** *pp* **beaten**) *tr* intimidar con mirada ceñuda

brown [braʊn] *adj* pardo, castaño, moreno; (*race*) cobrizo; tostado del sol ‖ *s* castaño, moreno ‖ *tr* poner moreno; tostar, quemar, broncear; (culin) dorar

brownish [′braʊnɪʃ] *adj* que tira a moreno

brown study *s* absorción, pensamiento profundo, ensimismamlento

brown sugar *s* azúcar terciado

browse [braʊz] *intr* (*to nibble at twigs*) ramonear; (*to graze*) pacer; hojear un libro ociosamente; **to browse about** o **around** curiosear

bruise [bruz] *s* contusión, magulladura, magullón *m* ‖ *tr* contundir, magullar ‖ *intr* contundirse, magullarse

brunet [bru′nɛt] *adj* moreno ‖ *s* moreno (*hombre moreno*)

brunette [bru′nɛt] *s* morena (*mujer morena*)

brunt [brʌnt] *s* fuerza, choque *m*, empuje *m;* (*e.g., of a battle*) peso, (lo) más reñido

brush [brʌʃ] *s* brocha, cepillo, escobilla; (*stroke*) brochada; (*light touch*) roce *m;* (*brief encounter*) encuentro, escaramuza; (*growth of bushes*) maleza; (elec) escobilla ‖ *tr* acepillar; (*to graze*) rozar; **to brush aside** echar a un lado ‖ *intr* pasar ligeramente; **to brush up on** repasar

brush′-off′ *s* (slang) desaire *m;* **to give the brush-off to** (slang) despedir noramala

brush′wood′ *s* broza, ramojo

brusque [brʌsk] *adj* brusco, rudo

brusqueness [′brʌsknɪs] *s* brusquedad

Brussels [′brʌsəlz] *s* Bruselas

Brussels sprouts *spl* bretones *mpl*, col *f* de Bruselas

brutal [′brutəl] *adj* brutal, bestial

brutali•ty [bru′tælɪti] *s* (*pl* **-ties**) brutalidad, crueldad

brutalization [,brutələ′zeʃən] *s* embrutecimiento

brute [brut] *adj* bruto; (*force*) inconsciente, ciego ‖ *s* bruto

brutish [′brutɪʃ] *adj* abrutado, estúpido

bu. *abbr* **bushel**

bubble [′bʌbəl] *s* burbuja; ampolla; ilusión, quimera ‖ *intr* burbujear; **to bubble over** desbordar, rebosar

buck [bʌk] *s* (*goat*) cabrón *m;* (*deer*) gamo; (*rabbit*) conejo; (*of a horse*) corveta, encorvada; (*youth*) pisaverde *m;* (slang) dólar *m;* **to pass the buck** (coll) echar la carga a otro ‖ *tr* hacer frente a, resistir a; (*to butt*) acornear, topetar; colar (*la ropa*); **to buck up** (coll) alentar, animar ‖ *intr* botarse, encorvarse; **to buck against** embestir contra

bucket [′bʌkɪt] *s* balde *m*, cubo; (*of a well*) pozal *m;* **to kick the bucket** (slang) estirar la pata, liar el petate

bucket seat *s* baquet *m*

buckle [′bʌkəl] *s* hebilla; (*bend, bulge*) alabeo, pandeo ‖ *tr* abrochar con hebilla ‖ *intr* (*to bend, bulge*) alabearse, pandear; **to buckle down to** (coll) dedicarse con empeño a

buck private *s* (slang) soldado raso

buckram [′bʌkrəm] *s* zangala; (bb) bocací *m*, bucarán *m*

buck′saw′ *s* sierra de bastidor

buck′shot′ *s* postas

buck′tooth′ *s* (*pl* **-teeth**) diente *m* saliente

buck′wheat′ *s* alforfón *m*, trigo sarraceno

bud [bʌd] *s* botón *m*, brote *m;* **to nip in the bud** cortar de raíz ‖ *v* (*pret & pp* **budded;** *ger* **budding**) *intr* abotonar, brotar

bud-dy [′bʌdi] *s* (*pl* **-dies**) (coll) camarada *m*, cumpa *m* (coll) muchachito

budge [bʌdʒ] *tr* mover ‖ *intr* moverse

budget [′bʌdʒɪt] *s* presupuesto ‖ *tr* presuponer, presupuestar

budgetary [′bʌdʒɪ,tɛri] *adj* presupuestario

buff [bʌf] *adj* de ante ‖ *s* (*leather*) ante *m;* color *m* de ante; chaqueta de ante; rueda pulidora; (coll) piel desnuda; aficionado ‖ *tr* dar color de ante a; pulimentar

buffa•lo [′bʌfə,lo] *s* (*pl* **-loes** o **-los**) búfalo ‖ *tr* (slang) intimidar

buffer [′bʌfər] *s* amortiguador *m* de choques; tope *m*, paragolpes *m;* pulidor *m*

buffer state *s* estado tapón

buffet [bu′fe] *s* (*piece of furniture*) aparador *m;* restaurante *m* de estación ‖ [′bʌfɪt] *tr* abofetear, golpear, pegar

buffet car *s* coche *m* bar

buffet lunch *s* servicio de bufet

buffet supper *s* ambigú *m*, bufet *m*

buffoon [bə′fun] *s* bufón *m*, payaso

buffooner•y [bə′funəri] *s* (*pl* **-ies**) bufonada, chocarrería

bug [bʌg] *s* insecto, bicho, sabandija; microbio; (*bedbug*) (Brit) chinche *f;* (coll) defecto; (slang) micrófono escondido; (slang) loco; (slang) entusiasta *mf* ‖ *v* (*pret & pp* **bugged;** *ger* **bugging**) *tr* (slang) esconder un micrófono en

bug′bear′ *s* espantajo; aversión

bug•gy [′bʌgi] *adj* (*comp* **-gier;** *super* **-giest**) infestado de bichos; (slang) loco ‖ *s* (*pl* **-gies**) calesa

bug′house′ *adj* (slang) loco ‖ *s* (slang) manicomio, casa de locos

bugle [ˈbjugəl] s corneta

bugle call s toque m de corneta

bugler [ˈbjuglər] s corneta m

build [bɪld] s forma, hechura, figura; (*of human being*) talle m ‖ v (*pret & pp* **built** [bɪlt]) *tr* construir, edificar; componer; establecer, fundar; crearse (*p.ej., una clientela*)

builder [ˈbɪldər] s constructor m; aparejador m, maestro de obras

building [ˈbɪldɪŋ] s construcción; edificio; (*one of several in a group*) pabellón m

building and loan association s sociedad f de crédito para la construcción

building lot s solar m

building site s terreno para construir

building trades spl oficios de edificación

build'-up' s acumulación, formación; (coll) propaganda anticipada

built'in' adj integrante, incorporado, empotrado

built'-up' adj armado, montado; (*land*) aglomerado

bulb [bʌlb] s (*of plant*) bulbo; (*of thermometer*) bola, cubeta; (*of syringe*) pera; (*of electric light*) ampolla, bombilla

Bulgaria [bʌlˈgɛrɪ·ə] s Bulgaria

Bulgarian [bʌlˈgɛrɪ·ən] adj & s búlgaro

bulge [bʌldʒ] s protuberancia, bulto, bombeo; **to get the bulge on** (coll) llevar la ventaja a ‖ intr hacer bulto, bombearse

bulimia [bjuˈlimɪ·ə] s bulimia

bulk [bʌlk] s bulto, volumen m; (*main mass*) grueso; **in bulk** a granel ‖ intr abultar, hacer bulto; tener importancia

bulk'head' s mamparo; tabique hermético

bulk·y [ˈbʌlki] adj (*comp* **-ier**; *super* **-iest**) abultado, voluminoso, grueso

bull [bʊl] s toro; (*in stockmarket*) alcista m; (*papal document*) bula; disparate m; **to take the bull by the horns** asir al toro por las astas ‖ tr — **to bull the market** jugar al alza

bull'dog' s dogo

bulldoze [ˈbʊlˌdoz] tr coaccionar, intimidar con amenazas

bulldozer [ˈbʊlˌdozər] s explanadora de empuje, empujatierra

bullet [ˈbʊlɪt] s bala

bulletin [ˈbʊlətɪn] s boletín m; comunicado; (*of a school*) anuario

bulletin board s tablilla

bul'let·proof' adj a prueba de balas, blindado

bull'fight' s corrida de toros

bull'fight'er s torero

bull'fight'ing adj torero ‖ s toreo

bull'finch' s (orn) camachuelo

bull'frog' s rana toro

bull-headed [ˈbʊlˌhɛdɪd] adj obstinado, terco

bullion [ˈbʊljən] s oro en barras, plata en barras; (*twisted fringe*) entorchado

bullish [ˈbʊlɪʃ] adj obstinado; (*market*) en alza; (*speculator*) alcista; optimista

bullock [ˈbʊlək] s buey m

bull'pen' s (taur) toril m; (*jail*) (coll) prevención

bull'ring' s plaza de toros

bull's-eye [ˈbʊlzˌaɪ] s (*of a target*) diana; (archit, meteor, naut) ojo de buey; **to hit the bull's-eye** hacer diana

bul·ly [ˈbʊli] adj (coll) excelente, magnífico ‖ s (*pl* **-lies**) matón m, valentón m ‖ v (*pret & pp* **-lied**) tr intimidar, maltratar

bulrush [ˈbʊlˌrʌʃ] s junco; junco de laguna; (*Typha*) anea, espadaña; (Bib) papiro

bulwark [ˈbʊlwərk] s baluarte m ‖ tr abaluartar; defender, proteger

bum [bʌm] s (slang) holgazán m; (slang) vagabundo; (slang) mendigo ‖ v (*pret & pp* **bummed**; *ger* **bumming**) tr (slang) mendigar ‖ intr holgazanear; (slang) vagabundear; (slang) mendigar

bumblebee [ˈbʌmbəlˌbi] s abejorro

bump [bʌmp] s (*collision*) topetón m; (*shake*) sacudida; (*on falling*) batacazo; (*of plane in rough air*) rebote m; (*swelling*) hinchazón f, chichón m; protuberancia ‖ tr dar contra, topar; (*to bruise*) abollar ‖ intr chocar; dar sacudidas; **to bump into** tropezar con; encontrarse con

bumper [ˈbʌmpər] adj (coll) abundante, grande ‖ s tope m, paratopes m; (aut) amortiguador m, parachoques m; vaso lleno

bumpkin [ˈbʌmpkɪn] s patán m, palurdo

bumptious [ˈbʌmpʃəs] adj engreído, presuntuoso

bump·y [ˈbʌmpi] adj (*comp* **-ier**; *super* **-iest**) (*ground*) desigual, áspero; (*air*) agitado

bun [bʌn] s buñuelo, bollo; (*of hair*) castaña

bunch [bʌntʃ] s manojo, puñado; (*of grapes, bananas, etc.*) racimo; (*of flowers*) ramillete m; (*of people*) grupo ‖ tr agrupar, juntar ‖ intr agruparse; arracimarse

bundle [ˈbʌndəl] s atado, bulto, lío, paquete m; (*of papers*) legajo; (*of wood*) haz m ‖ tr atar, liar, empaquetar, envolver; **to bundle off** despedir precipitadamente; **to bundle up** arropar ‖ intr — **to bundle up** arroparse

bung [bʌŋ] s bitoque m, tapón m

bungalow [ˈbʌŋgəˌlo] s bungalow m, casa de una sola planta

bung'hole' s piquera, boca de tonel

bungle [ˈbʌŋgəl] s chapucería ‖ tr & intr chapucear

bungler [ˈbʌŋglər] s chapucero

bungling [ˈbʌŋglɪŋ] adj chapucero ‖ s chapucería

bunion [ˈbʌnjən] s juanete m

bunk [bʌŋk] s tarima; (slang) palabrería vana, música celestial

bunker [ˈbʌŋkər] s carbonera; (mil) fortín m

bun·ny [ˈbʌni] s (*pl* **-nies**) conejito

bunting [ˈbʌntɪŋ] s banderas colgadas como adorno; (*of a ship*) empavesado; (orn) gorrión triguero

buoy [bɔɪ] o [ˈbu·i] s boya; boya salvavidas, guindola ‖ tr — **to buoy up** mantener a flote; animar, alentar

buoyancy [ˈbɔɪ·ənsi] o [ˈbujənsi] s flotación; alegría, animación

buoyant [ˈbɔɪ·ənt] o [ˈbujənt] adj boyante; alegre, animado

bur [bʌr] *s* erizo, vilano
burble [ˈbʌrbəl] *s* burbujeo ‖ *intr* burbujear
burden [ˈbʌrdən] *s* carga; (*of a speech*) tema *m;* (*of a poem*) estribillo ‖ *tr* cargar; agobiar, gravar
burden of proof *s* peso de la prueba
burdensome [ˈbʌrdənsəm] *adj* gravoso, oneroso
burdock [ˈbʌrdak] *s* bardana, cadillo
bureau [ˈbjuro] *s* cómoda; despacho, oficina; departamento, negociado
bureaucra·cy [bjuˈrakrəsi] *s* (*pl* -**cies**) burocracia; funcionariado
bureaucrat [ˈbjurə,kræt] *s* burócrata *mf*
bureaucratic [,bjurəˈkrætɪk] *adj* burocrático
burgess [ˈbʌrdʒɪs] *s* burgués *m,* ciudadano; alcalde *m* de un pueblo o villa
burglar [ˈbʌrglər] *s* escalador *m*
burglar alarm *s* alarma de ladrones
bur′glar·proof′ *adj* a prueba de escaladores; antirrobo
burglar·y [ˈbʌrgləri] *s* (*pl* -**ies**) robo con escalamiento
Burgundian [bərˈgʌndɪ·ən] *adj* & *s* borgoñón *m*
Burgundy [ˈbʌrgəndi] *s* la Borgoña; (*wine*) borgoña *m*
burial [ˈbɛrɪ·əl] *s* entierro
burial ground *s* cementerio
burlap [ˈbʌrlæp] *s* arpillera
burlesque [bərˈlɛsk] *adj* burlesco, festivo ‖ *s* parodia ‖ *tr* parodiar
burlesque show *s* espectáculo de bailes y cantos groseros, music-hall *m;* bataclán *m* (SAm)
bur·ly [ˈbʌrli] *adj* (*comp* -**lier;** *super* -**liest**) fornido, corpulento, membrudo
Burma [ˈbʌrmə] *s* Birmania
Bur·mese [bərˈmiz] *adj* birmano ‖ *s* (*pl* - **mese**) birmano
burn [bʌrn] *s* quemadura, quemazón *f* ‖ *v* (*pret* & *pp* **burned** o **burnt** [bʌrnt]) *tr* quemar ‖ *intr* quemar, quemarse; estar encendido (*p.ej., un faro*); **to burn out** quemarse (*un fusible*); fundirse (*una bombilla*); **to burn within** requemarse
burner [ˈbʌrnər] *s* (*of furnace*) quemador *m;* (*of gas fixture or lamp*) mechero
burning [ˈbʌrnɪŋ] *adj* ardiente ‖ *s* quema, incendio
burning question *s* cuestión palpitante
burnish [ˈbʌrnɪʃ] *s* bruñido ‖ *tr* bruñir ‖ *intr* bruñirse
burnoose [bərˈnus] *s* albornoz *m*
burnt almond [bʌrnt] *s* almendra tostada
burr [bʌr] *s* (*of plant*) erizo; (*of cut in metal*) rebaba
burrow [ˈbʌro] *s* madriguera, conejera ‖ *tr* hacer madrigueras en; socavar ‖ *intr* amadrigarse; esconderse
bursar [ˈbʌrsər] *s* tesorero universitario
burst [bʌrst] *s* explosión, reventón *m,* estallido; (*of machine gun*) ráfaga; salida brusca ‖ *v* (*pret* & *pp* **burst**) *tr* reventar ‖ *intr* reventar, reventarse; partirse (*el corazón*); **to burst into** irrumpir en (*un cuarto*); desatarse en (*amenazas*); prorrumpir en

(*lágrimas*); **to burst out crying** deshacerse en lágrimas; **to burst with laughter** reventar de risa
bur·y [ˈbɛri] *v* (*pret* & *pp* -**ied**) *tr* enterrar; **to be buried in thought** estar absorto en meditación; **to bury the hatchet** hacer la paz, echar pelillos a la mar
burying ground *s* cementerio
bus. *abbr* **business**
bus [bʌs] *s* (*pl* **busses** o **buses**) autobús *m* ‖ *tr* llevar en un autobús
bus boy *s* ayudante *m* de camarero
bus·by [ˈbʌzbi] *s* (*pl* -**bies**) morrión *m* de húsar; colbac *m*
bush [buʃ] *s* arbusto; (*scrubby growth*) matorral *m,* monte *m;* **to beat about the bush** andar con rodeos
bushel [ˈbuʃəl] *s* medida para áridos (*35,23 litros en E.U.A. y 36,35 litros en Inglaterra*)
bushing [ˈbuʃɪŋ] *s* buje *m,* forro
bush·y [ˈbuʃi] *adj* (*comp* -**ier;** *super* -**iest**) arbustivo; peludo, lanudo; espeso
business [ˈbɪznɪs] *adj* comercial, de negocios ‖ *s* negocio, comercio; (*company, concern*) empresa; (*job, employment*) empleo, oficio; (*matter*) asunto, cuestión; (*duty*) obligación; (*right*) derecho; **on business** por negocios; **to have no business to** no tener derecho a; **to make it one's business to** proponerse; **to mean business** (coll) obrar en serio, hablar en serio; **to mind one's own business** no meterse en lo que no le importa a uno; **to send about one's business** mandar a paseo
business district *s* barrio comercial
businesslike [ˈbɪznɪs,laɪk] *adj* práctico, sistemático, serio
business·man [ˈbɪznɪs,mæn] *s* (*pl* -**men** [,mɛn]) comerciante *m,* hombre *m* de negocios
business suit *s* traje *m* de calle
bus·man [ˈbʌsmən] *s* (*pl* -**men** [mən]) conductor *m* de autobús
buss [bʌs] *s* (coll) beso sonado ‖ *tr* dar besos sonados a ‖ *intr* dar besos sonados; darse besos sonados
bust [bʌst] *s* busto; (*of woman*) pecho; (slang) fracaso, borrachera ‖ *tr* (slang) reventar, romper; (slang) arruinar; (slang) golpear, pegar ‖ *intr* (slang) reventar, fracasar
buster [ˈbʌstər] *s* muchachito
bustle [ˈbʌsəl] *s* (*of woman's dress*) polisón *m;* alboroto, bullicio ‖ *intr* ajetrearse, menearse
bus·y [ˈbɪzi] *adj* (*comp* -**ier;** *super* -**iest**) ocupado; (*e.g., street*) concurrido; (*meddling*) intruso, entremetido ‖ *v* (*pret* & *pp* -**ied**) *tr* ocupar; **to busy oneself with** ocuparse de
busybod·y [ˈbɪzi,badi] *s* (*pl* -**ies**) entremetido, fisgón *m*
busy signal *s* (telp) señal *f* de ocupado
but [bʌt] *adv* sólo, solamente, no . . . más que; **but for** a no ser por; **but little** muy poco ‖ *prep* excepto, salvo; **all but** casi ‖

conj pero; sino, p.ej., **nobody came but John** no vino sino Juan

butcher [ˈbʊtʃər] *s* carnicero; pesero (CAm, Col, Ven) ‖ *tr* matar (*reses para el consumo*); dar muerte a; (*to bungle*) chapucear

butcher knife *s* cuchilla de carnicero

butcher shop *s* carnicería; pesa (CAm, Col, Ven)

butcher•y [ˈbʌtʃəri] *s* (*pl* -ies) (*slaughterhouse*) matadero; (*wanton slaughter*) matanza, carnicería

butler [ˈbʌtlər] *s* despensero, mayordomo

butt [bʌt] *s* (*of gun*) culata; (*of cigaret*) colilla, punta; (*of horned animal*) cabezada, topetada, topetón *m*; (*target*) blanco; hazmerreír *m*; (*large cask*) pipa; (*rear end*) pompis *m* ‖ *tr* topar, topetar; acornear ‖ *intr* dar cabezadas; **to butt against** confinar con; **to butt in** (slang) entremeterse

butter [ˈbʌtər] *s* mantequilla ‖ *tr* untar con mantequilla; **to butter up** (coll) adular, lisonjear

but'ter•cup' *s* botón *m* de oro

butter dish *s* mantequillera

but'ter•fly' *s* (*pl* -flies) mariposa

butter knife *s* cuchillo mantequillero

but'ter•milk' *s* leche *f* de manteca

butter sauce *s* mantequilla fundida

but'ter•scotch' *s* bombón *m* escocés, bombón hecho con azúcar terciado y mantequilla

buttocks [ˈbʌtəks] *spl* nalgas; fundillo (Cuba, Mex)

button [ˈbʌtən] *s* botón *m* ‖ *tr* abotonar, abrocharse

but'ton•hole' *s* ojal *m* ‖ *tr* detener con conversación

but'ton•hook *s* abotonador *m*

but'ton•wood' **tree** *s* plátano de occidente

buttress [ˈbʌtrɪs] *s* contrafuerte *m*; (fig) apoyo, sostén *m* ‖ *tr* estribar; (fig) apoyar, sostener

butt weld *s* soldadura a tope

buxom [ˈbʌksəm] *adj* rolliza, frescachona

buy [baɪ] *s* (coll) compra; (*bargain*) (coll) ganga ‖ *v* (*pret* & *pp* **bought** [bɔt]) *tr* comprar; **to buy back** recomprar; **to buy off** comprar, sobornar; **to buy out** comprar la parte de (*un socio*); **to buy up** acaparar

buyer [ˈbaɪ•ər] *s* comprador *m*

buzz [bʌz] *s* zumbido ‖ *intr* zumbar; **to buzz about** ajetrearse, cazcalear

buzzard [ˈbʌzərd] *s* alfaneque *m*

buzz bomb *s* bomba volante

buzzer [ˈbʌzər] *s* zumbador *m*

buzz saw *s* sierra circular

bx. *abbr* box

by [baɪ] *adv* cerca; a un lado; **by and by** luego ‖ *prep* por; cerca de, al lado de; (*not later than*) para; **by far** con mucho; **by the way** de paso; a propósito

by-and-by [ˈbaɪ•ənd'baɪ] *s* porvenir *m*

bye-bye [ˈbaɪ'baɪ] *s* mu *f*; **to go bye-bye** ir a la mu ‖ *interj* (coll) ¡adiosito!; (*to a child*) ¡ro ro!

bygone [ˈbaɪ,gɔn] o [ˈbaɪ,gɑn] *adj* pasado ‖ *s* pasado; **let bygones be bygones** olvidemos lo pasado

bylaw [ˈbaɪ,lɔ] *s* reglamento, estatuto

bypass [ˈbaɪ,pæs] *s* desviación; tubo de paso ‖ *tr* desviar; eludir

by'-prod'uct *s* subproducto, derivado

bystander [ˈbaɪ,stændər] *s* asistente *mf*, circunstante *mf*

byway [ˈbaɪ,we] *s* camino apartado

byword [ˈbaɪ,wʌrd] *s* objeto de oprobio; refrán *m*, muletilla; apodo

Byzantine [ˈbɪzən,tin] o [bɪˈzæntin] *adj* & *s* bizantino

Byzantium [bɪˈzænʃɪ•əm] o [bɪˈzæntɪ•əm] *s* Bizancio

C

C, c [si] tercera letra del alfabeto inglés

c. *abbr* **cent, center, centimeter**

C. *abbr* **centigrade, Congress, Court**

cab [kæb] *s* coche *m* de plaza o de punto; taxi *m*; (*of a truck*) casilla

cabaret [ˌkæbəˈre] *s* cabaret *m*

cabbage [ˈkæbɪdʒ] *s* col *f*, berza

cab driver *s* cochero de plaza; taxista *mf*

cabin [ˈkæbɪn] *s* (*hut, cottage*) cabaña; (aer) cabina; (naut) camarote *m*

cabin boy *s* mozo de cámara

cabinet [ˈkæbɪnɪt] *s* (*piece of furniture for displaying objects*) escaparate *m*, vitrina; (*for a radio*) caja, mueble *m*; (*closet*) armario; (*private room; ministry of a government*) gabinete *m*

cab'inet•ma'ker *s* ebanista *m*

cab'inet•ma'king *s* ebanistería

cable [ˈkebəl] *adj* cablegráfico ‖ *s* cable *m*; cablegrama *m* ‖ *tr* & *intr* cablegrafiar

cable address *s* dirección cablegráfica

cable car *s* tranvía *m* de tracción por cable

cablegram [ˈkebəl,græm] *s* cablegrama *m*

cable television *s* televisión por cable

caboose [kəˈbus] *s* (rr) furgón de cola

cab'stand' *s* punto de coches, punto de taxis

cache [kæʃ] *s* escondrijo; víveres escondidos ‖ *tr* depositar en un escondrijo; ocultar

cachet [kæˈʃe] *s* sello

cackle [ˈkækəl] *s* (*of a hen*) cacareo; (*idle talk*) charla ‖ *intr* cacarear; charlar

cac•tus [ˈkæktəs] *s* (*pl* -tuses o -ti [taɪ]) cacto

cad [kæd] *s* sinvergüenza *mf*; **to behave like a cad** tener mala leche

cadaver [kə'dævər] s cadáver m
cadaverous [kə'dævərəs] adj cadavérico
caddie ['kædi] s caddie m (muchacho que lleva los utensilios en el juego de golf) ‖ intr servir de caddie
cadence ['kedəns] s cadencia
cadet [kə'dɛt] s hermano menor, hijo menor; (student at military school) cadete m
cadmium ['kædmɪ•əm] s cadmio
cadre ['kædri] s (mil) cuadro
Caesar ['sizər] s César m
café [kæ'fe] s bar m, cabaret m; restaurante m
café society s gente f del mundo elegante que frecuenta los cabarets de moda
cafeteria [,kæfə'tɪrɪ•ə] s cafetería
cage [kedʒ] s jaula ‖ tr enjaular
cageling ['kedʒlɪŋ] s pájaro enjaulado
ca•gey ['kedʒi] adj (comp -gier; super -giest) (coll) astuto
cahoots [kə'huts] s — to be in cahoots (slang) confabularse (dos o más personas); to go cahoots (slang) entrar por partes iguales
Cain [ken] s Caín m; to raise Cain (slang) armar camorra
Cairo ['kaɪro] s El Cairo
caisson ['kesən] s cajón m de aire comprimido, esclusa de aire
cajole [kə'dʒol] tr adular, lisonjear, halagar
cajoler•y [kə'dʒoləri] s (pl -ies) adulación, lisonja, halago
cake [kek] s pastel m, bollo, queque m; (small cake) pastelillo; (sponge cake) bizcocho; (of fish) fritada; (of earth) terrón m; (of soap) pan m, pastilla; (of ice) témpano; to take the cake (coll) ser el colmo ‖ intr apelmazarse, aterronarse
calabash ['kælə,bæʃ] s calabacera; jícaro; (fruit) calabaza
calamitous [kə'læmɪtəs] adj calamitoso
calami•ty [kə'læmɪti] s (pl -ties) calamidad
calci•fy ['kælsɪ,faɪ] v (pret & pp -fied) calcificar ‖ intr calcificarse
calcium ['kælsɪ•əm] s calcio
calculate ['kælkjə,let] tr calcular; (to reckon) (coll) calcular ‖ intr calcular; to calculate on contar con
calculating ['kælkjə,letɪŋ] adj de calcular; astuto, intrigante
calculating machine s calculadora, máquina de calcular
calcu•lus ['kælkjələs] s (pl -luses o -li [,laɪ]) (math, pathol) cálculo
caldron ['kɔldrən] s calderón m
calendar ['kæləndər] s calendario, almanaque m
calf [kæf] o [kɑf] s (pl calves [kævz] o [kɑvz]) ternero; (of the leg) pantorrilla
calf'skin' s becerro, becerrillo
caliber ['kælɪbər] s calibre m
calibrate ['kælɪ,bret] tr calibrar
cali•co ['kælɪ,ko] s (pl -coes o -cos) calicó m, indiana
California [,kælɪ'fɔrnɪ•ə] s California
calipers ['kælɪpərz] spl calibrador m, compás m de calibres
caliph ['kelɪf] o ['kælɪf] s califa m

caliphate ['kælɪ,fet] s califato
calisthenic [,kælɪs'θɛnɪk] adj calisténico ‖ calisthenics spl calistenia
calk [kɔk] tr calafatear
calking ['kɔkɪŋ] s calafateo
call [kɔl] s llamada; visita; (of a boat or airplane) escala; vocación; within call al alcance de la voz ‖ tr llamar; convocar (p.ej., una huelga); to call back mandar volver; to call down (coll) reprender, regañar; to call in hacer entrar; (from circulation) retirar; to call off aplazar, suspender; desconvocar; to call out llamar (a uno) que salga; to call together convocar, reunir; to call up llamar por teléfono; evocar, recordar ‖ intr llamar, gritar; hacer una visita; (naut) hacer escala; to call on acudir a; visitar; to call out gritar; to go calling ir de visitas
calla lily ['kælə] s cala, lirio de agua
call bell s timbre m de llamada
call'boy' s (in a hotel) botones m; (theat) traspunte m
caller ['kɔlər] s visitante mf
call girl s chica de cita
calling ['kɔlɪŋ] s profesión, vocación
calling card s tarjeta de visita
calliope [kə'laɪ•əpi] o ['kælɪ•op] s (mus) órgano de vapor ‖ Calliope [kə'laɪ•əpi] s Calíope f
call number s número de teléfono; (of a book) número de clasificación
callous ['kæləs] adj calloso; (fig) duro, insensible
call to arms s — to sound the call to arms (mil) batir o tocar a llamada
call to the colors (mil) llamada a filas
callus ['kæləs] s callo
calm [kɑm] adj tranquilo, quieto; (sea) bonancible ‖ s tranquilidad, calma ‖ tr tranquilizar, calmar ‖ intr — to calm down tranquilizarse, calmarse; abonanzar, calmar (el viento, el tiempo)
calmness ['kɑmnɪs] s tranquilidad, calma
calorie ['kæləri] s caloría
calum•ny ['kæləmni] s (pl -nies) calumnia
calva•ry ['kælvəri] s (pl -ries) (at the entrance to a town) humilladero ‖ Calvary s Calvario
calyp•so [kə'lɪpso] s (pl -sos) calipso ‖ Calypso s Calipso f
cam [kæm] s leva
cambric ['kembrɪk] s batista
camel ['kæməl] s camello
came•o ['kæmɪ•o] s (pl -os) camafeo
camera ['kæmərə] s cámara fotográfica, máquina fotográfica
camera•man ['kæmərə,mæn] s (pl -men [,mɛn]) camarógrafo, tomavistas m
camomile ['kæmə,maɪl] s manzanilla
camouflage ['kæmə,flɑʒ] s camuflaje m ‖ tr camuflar
camp [kæmp] s campamento ‖ intr acampar
campaign [kæm'pen] s campaña ‖ intr hacer campaña
campaigner [kæm'penər] s propagandista mf; veterano

camp'fire' *s* hoguera de campamento

camphor ['kæmfər] *s* alcanfor *m*

camp'stool' *s* silla de tijera, catrecillo

campus ['kæmpəs] *s* terrenos, recinto (*de la universidad*)

cam'shaft' *s* árbol *m* de levas

can [kæn] *s* bote *m*, envase *m*, lata ‖ *v* (*pret & pp* **canned;** *ger* **canning**) *tr* envasar, enlatar ‖ *v* (*pret & cond* **could**) *v aux* **he can come tomorrow** puede venir mañana; **can you swim?** ¿sabe Vd. nadar?

Canada ['kænədə] *s* el Canadá

Canadian [kə'nedɪ•ən] *adj & s* canadiense

canal [kə'næl] *s* canal *m*

canar•y [kə'nɛri] *s* (*pl* -**ies**) canario ‖ **Canaries** *spl* Canarias

can•cel ['kænsəl] *v* (*pret & pp* -**celed** o -**celled;** *ger* -**celing** o -**celling**) *tr* cancelar, eliminar, suprimir; matasellar, obliterar (*sellos de correo*)

canceler ['kænsələr] *s* matasellos *m*

cancellation [,kænsə'leʃən] *s* cancelación, eliminación, supresión; revocatoria; (*of stamps*) obliteración

cancer ['kænsər] *s* cáncer *m;* **Cancer** *s* (astr) Cáncer *m*

cancerous ['kænsərəs] *adj* canceroso

candela•brum [,kændə'lebrəm] *s* (*pl* -**bra** [brə] o -**brums**) candelabro

candid ['kændɪd] *adj* franco, sincero; imparcial

candida•cy ['kændɪdəsi] *s* (*pl* -**cies**) candidatura

candidate ['kændɪ,det] *s* candidato; (*for a degree*) graduando

candid camera *s* cámara indiscreta

candle ['kændəl] *s* bujía, candela, vela

can'dle•hold'er *s* candelero

can'dle•light' *s* luz *f* de vela; crepúsculo

candle power *s* bujía

can'dle•stick' *s* palmatoria

candor ['kændər] *s* franqueza, sinceridad; imparcialidad

can•dy ['kændi] *s* (*pl* -**dies**) bombón *m*, confite *m*, dulce *m;* dulces *mpl* ‖ *v* (*pret & pp* -**died**) *tr* almibarar, confitar, garapiñar ‖ *intr* almibararse

candy box *s* bombonera, confitera

candy store *s* confitería, dulcería

cane [ken] *s* (*plant; stem*) caña; (*walking stick*) bastón *m;* (*for chair seats*) junco, mimbre *m*, rejilla

cane seat *s* asiento de rejilla

cane sugar *s* azúcar *m* de caña

canine ['kenaɪn] *adj* canino ‖ *s* (*tooth*) canino; perro

canned goods *spl* conservas alimenticias

canner•y ['kænəri] *s* (*pl* -**ies**) conservera, fábrica de conservas

cannibal ['kænɪbəl] *adj & s* caníbal *mf*

canning ['kænɪŋ] *adj* conservero ‖ *s* conservería

cannon ['kænən] *s* cañón *m;* cañones

cannonade [,kænə'ned] *s* cañoneo ‖ *tr* cañonear

cannon ball *s* bala de cañón

cannon fodder *s* carne *f* de cañón

can•ny ['kæni] *adj* (*comp* -**nier;** *super* -**niest**) cauteloso, cuerdo; astuto

canoe [kə'nu] *s* canoa; bongo (SAm)

canoeing [kə'nu•ɪŋ] *s* piraguismo

canoeist [kə'nu•ɪst] *s* canoero

canon ['kænən] *s* canon *m;* (*priest*) canónigo

canonical [kə'nɑnɪkəl] *adj* canónico; aceptado, auténtico, establecido ‖ **canonicals** *spl* vestiduras sacerdotales

canonize ['kænə,naɪz] *tr* canonizar

canon law *s* cánones *mpl*, derecho canónico

canon•ry ['kænənri] *s* (*pl* -**ries**) canonjía

can opener ['opənər] *s* abrelatas *m*

cano•py ['kænəpi] *s* (*pl* -**pies**) dosel *m*, pabellón *m;* (*over an entrance*) marquesina; (*for electrical fixtures*) campana

canopy of heaven *s* bóveda celeste

cant [kænt] *s* hipocresía; jerga, jerigonza

cantaloupe ['kæntə,lop] *s* cantalupo

cantankerous [kæn'tæŋkərəs] *adj* de mal genio, pendenciero

canteen [kæn'tin] *s* (*shop*) cantina; (*water flask*) cantimplora; (mil) centro de recreo

canter ['kæntər] *s* medio galope ‖ *intr* ir a medio galope

canticle ['kæntɪkəl] *s* cántico

cantilever ['kæntɪ,livər] *adj* voladizo ‖ *s* viga voladiza

cantle ['kæntəl] *s* arzón trasero

canton ['kæntɑn] *tr* acantonar

cantonment [kæn'tɑnmənt] *s* acantonamiento

cantor ['kæntər] *s* chantre *m;* (*in a synagogue*) cantor *m* principal

canvas ['kænvəs] *s* cañamazo, lona; (naut) vela, lona; (*painting*) lienzo; **under canvas** (mil) en tiendas; (naut) con las velas izadas

canvass ['kænvəs] *s* pesquisa, escrutinio; (*of votes*) solicitación ‖ *tr* escrutar, solicitar; discutir detenidamente

canyon ['kænjən] *s* cañón *m*

cap. *abbr* **capital, capitalize**

cap [kæp] *s* gorra, gorra de visera; (*of academic costume*) birrete *m;* (*of bottle*) cápsula; (*e.g., of a fountain pen*) capuchón *m* ‖ *v* (*pret & pp* **capped;** *ger* **capping**) *tr* cubrir con gorra; capsular (*una botella*); **to cap the climax** ser el colmo

capabili•ty [,kepə'bɪlɪti] *s* (*pl* -**ties**) habilidad, capacidad

capable ['kepəbəl] *adj* hábil, capaz

capacious [kə'peʃəs] *adj* espacioso, capaz

capaci•ty [kə'pæsɪti] *s* (*pl* -**ties**) (*room, space; ability, aptitude*) capacidad; (*status, function*) calidad; **in the capacity of** en calidad de

cap and bells *spl* caperuza de bufón; cetro de la locura

cap and gown *s* birrete y toga

caparison [kə'pærɪsən] *s* caparazón *m* ‖ *tr* engualdrapar

cape [kep] *s* cabo, promontorio; (*garment*) capa, esclavina

Cape Colony *s* la Colonia del Cabo

Cape Horn *s* el Cabo de Hornos

Cape of Good Hope *s* Cabo de Buena Esperanza

caper ['kepər] s (gay jump) cabriola; (prank) travesura; **to cut capers** dar cabriolas; hacer travesuras ‖ intr cabriolear; retozar

Cape'town' o **Cape Town** s El Cabo, la Ciudad del Cabo

cape'work' s (taur) suerte f de capa, lance m

capital ['kæpɪtəl] adj capital ‖ s (money) capital m; (city) capital f; (top of a column) capitel m; **to make capital out of** sacar beneficio de

capital flight s fuga de capitales

capitalism [['kæpɪtə,lɪzəm] s capitalismo

capitalize ['kæpɪtə,laɪz] tr escribir con mayúscula; capitalizar ‖ intr — **to capitalize on** aprovecharse de

capital letter s letra mayúscula

capital punishment s pena capital, último suplicio

capitol ['kæpɪtəl] s capitolio

capitulate [kə'pɪt/ə,let] intr capitular

capon ['kepan] s capón m

caprice [kə'pris] s capricho, antojo; veleidad

capricious [kə'prɪ/əs] adj caprichoso, antojadizo

Capricorn ['kæprɪ,kɔrn] s (astr) Capricornio

capsize ['kæpsaɪz] tr volcar ‖ intr volcar; tumbar, zozobrar (un barco)

capstan ['kæpstən] s cabrestante m

cap'stone' s coronamiento

capsule ['kæpsəl] s cápsula

Capt. abbr **Captain**

captain ['kæptən] s capitán m ‖ tr capitanear

captain·cy ['kæptənsi] s (pl -cies) capitanía

caption ['kæp/ən] s título; (in a movie) subtítulo

captivate ['kæptɪ,vet] tr cautivar, encantar

captive ['kæptɪv] adj & s cautivo

captivi·ty [kæp'tɪvɪti] s (pl -ties) cautividad, cautiverio

captor ['kæptər] s aprenhensor m

capture ['kæpt/ər] s apresamiento, captura; (of a stronghold) toma ‖ tr apresar, capturar; tomar (una plaza); captar (p.ej., la atención de una persona)

Capuchin nun ['kæpjut/ɪn] o ['kæpju/ɪn] s capuchina

car [kar] s coche m; (of an elevator) caja, carro

carafe [kə'ræf] s garrafa

caramel ['kærəməl] o ['karməl] s (burnt sugar) caramelo; bombón m de caramelo

carat ['kærət] s quilate m

caravan ['kærə,væn] s caravana

caravansa·ry [,kærə'vænsəri] s (pl -ries) caravanera

caraway ['kærə,we] s alcaravea

car'barn' s cochera de tranvías

carbide ['karbaɪd] s carburo

carbine ['karbaɪn] s carabina

carbolic acid [kar'balɪk] s ácido carbólico

car bomb s coche bomba

carbon ['karbən] s (chemical element) carbono; (pole of arc light or battery) carbón m; papel m carbón; (in auto cylinders) carbonilla

carbon copy s copia al carbón

carbon dioxide s dióxido de carbono

carbon monoxide s óxido de carbono, monóxido de carbono

carbon paper s papel m carbón

car'boy' s bombona, garrafón m

carbuncle ['karbʌŋkəl] s (stone) carbunclo, carbúnculo; (pathol) carbunclo, carbunco

carburetor ['karbə,retər] s carburador m

car caller s avisacoches m

carcass ['karkəs] s res muerta, cadáver m

carcinogen [kar'sɪnəjən] s carcinógeno

carcinoma [,karsə'nomə] s carcinoma

card [kard] s tarjeta; (for playing games) naipe m, carta; (for filing) ficha; (person) (coll) sujeto, tipo

card'board' s cartón m

cardboard binding s encuadernación en pasta

card case s tarjetero

card catalogue s catálogo de fichas

cardiac ['kardɪ,æk] adj cardíaco ‖ s (medicine; sufferer) cardíaco

cardigan ['kardɪgən] s albornoz m, rebeca

cardinal ['kardɪnəl] adj cardinal; purpurado ‖ s (prelate; bird) cardenal m; número cardinal

card index s fichero, tarjetero

card party s tertulia de baraja

card'sharp' s fullero, tahur m

card trick s truco de naipes

care [kɛr] s (worry) inquietud, ansiedad; (watchful attention) esmero; (charge) cargo, custodia; **care of** suplicada en casa de; **to take care of oneself** cuidarse ‖ intr inquietarse, preocuparse; **to care for** cuidar de; amar, querer; **to care to** tener ganas de; **I couldn't care less** me importe un pepino

careen [kə'rin] intr inclinarse; mecerse precipitadamente

career [kə'rɪr] adj de carrera ‖ s carrera

care'free' adj despreocupado, libre de cuidados

careful ['kɛrfəl] adj (acting with care) cuidadoso; (done with care) esmerado; **to be careful to** cuidarse de

careless ['kɛrlɪs] adj descuidado, negligente

carelessness ['kɛrlɪsnɪs] s descuido, negligencia

car enthusiast s devoto del volante

caress [kə'rɛs] s caricia ‖ tr acariciar ‖ intr acariciarse

caretaker ['kɛr,tekər] s curador m, guardián m, custodio

care'worn' adj fatigado, rendido

car'fare' s pasaje m de tranvía o autobús

car·go ['kargo] s (pl -goes o -gos) carga, cargamento

cargo boat s barco de carga

Caribbean [,kærɪ'bi·ən] o [kə'rɪbɪ·ən] adj caribe ‖ s mar m Caribe

caricature ['kærɪkət/ər] s caricatura ‖ tr caricaturizar

caricaturist ['kærɪkət/ərɪst] s caricaturista mf

carillon ['kærɪ,lan] o [kə'rɪljən] s carillón m

car'load' s furgonada, vagonada

ca
ca

carnage ['kɑrnɪdʒ] s carnicería, matanza

carnation [kɑr'neʃən] adj encarnado ‖ s clavel m, clavel reventón

carnival ['kɑrnɪvəl] adj carnavalesco ‖ s (period before Lent) carnaval m; verbena, espectáculo de atracciones

car•ol ['kærəl] s canción alegre, villancico ‖ v (pret & pp -oled o -olled; ger -oling o -olling); tr celebrar con villancicos ‖ intr cantar con alegría

carom ['kærəm] s carambola ‖ intr carambolear

carousal [kə'rauzəl] s juerga, borrachera, jarana

carouse [kə'rauz] intr emborracharse, jaranear

carp [kɑrp] s (pez) carpa ‖ intr quejarse

carpenter ['kɑrpəntər] s carpintero

carpentry ['kɑrpəntri] s carpintería

carpet ['kɑrpɪt] s alfombra; **to be on the carpet** estar sobre el tapete ‖ tr alfombrar

carpet sweeper s barredora de alfombras

car′-rent′al service s alquiler m de coches

carriage ['kærɪdʒ] s carruaje m; (cost of carrying) porte m, transporte m; (bearing) porte m, continente m; (mach) carro

carrier ['kærɪ·ər] s portador m, transportador m; portador de gérmenes; empresa de transportes; (mailman) cartero; vendedor m de periódicos; portaaviones m; (rad) onda portadora

carrier pigeon s paloma mensajera

carrier wave s (rad) onda portadora

carrion ['kærɪ·ən] adj carroño; inmundo ‖ s carroña; inmundicia

carrot ['kærət] s zanahoria

carrousel [,kærə'zɛl] s caballitos, tiovivo

car•ry ['kæri] v (pret & pp -ried) tr llevar, portar, traer; transportar; sostener (una carga); **to carry away** llevarse; encantar, entusiasmar; **to carry into effect** llevar a cabo; **to carry one's point** salirse con la suya; **to carry out** llevar a cabo; **to carry the day** quedar victorioso, ganar la palma; **to carry weight** ser de peso ‖ intr tener alcance; **to carry on** continuar, perseverar; (coll) travesear; (coll) comportarse de un modo escandaloso; (coll) hacer locuras

cart [kɑrt] s carreta, carro ‖ tr carretear

carte blanche ['kɑrt'blɑnʃ] s carta blanca

cartel [kɑr'tɛl] s cartel m

Carthage ['kɑrθɪdʒ] s Cartago

Carthaginian [,kɑrθə'dʒɪnɪ·ən] adj & s cartaginés m

cart horse s caballo de tiro

cartilage ['kɑrtɪlɪdʒ] s cartílago

cartoon [kɑr'tun] s caricatura; (comic strip) tira cómica; (film) película de dibujos ‖ tr caricaturizar

cartoonist [kɑr'tunɪst] s caricaturista mf

cartridge ['kɑrtrɪdʒ] s cartucho

cartridge belt s canana

carve [kɑrv] tr trinchar (carne); esculpir, tallar

carving knife ['kɑrvɪŋ] s cuchillo de trinchar

car washer s lavacoches m

caryatid [,kærɪ'ætɪd] s cariátide f

cascade [kæs'ked] s cascada

case [kes] s (instance; form of a word) caso; (box) caja; (small container) estuche m; (for cigarettes) pitillera; (sheath) vaina, funda; (law) causa, pleito; **in case** caso que; **in no case** de ninguna manera ‖ tr encajonar, enfundar

casement ['kesmənt] s ventana batiente; bastidor m (de la ventana)

cash [kæʃ] s dinero contante; pago al contado; **cash on delivery** contra reembolso, pago contra entrega; **to pay cash** pagar al contado ‖ tr cobrar (un cheque el portador); abonar, pagar (un cheque el banco) ‖ intr — **to cash in on** (coll) sacar provecho de

cash and carry s pago al contado con transporte a cargo del comprador

cash′box′ s caja

cashew ['kæʃu] s anacardo, marañón m

cashew nut s anacardo, nuez f de marañón

cashier [kæ'ʃɪr] s cajero ‖ tr destruir; (in the army) degradar

cashier's check s cheque m de caja

cashier's desk s caja

cashmere ['kæʃmɪr] s casimir m, cachemir m

cash on hand s efectivo en caja

cash payment s pago al contado

cash purchase s compra al contado

cash register s caja registradora

casing ['kesɪŋ] s caja, cubierta, envoltura; (of door or window) marco, cerco; (of tire) cubierta; (sew) jareta

cask [kæsk] o [kɑsk] s casco, pipa, tonel m

casket ['kæskɪt] s (box for valuables) cajita, joyero; (coffin) caja, ataúd m

cassava [kə'sɑvə] s cazabe m, casabe m

casserole ['kæsə,rol] s cacerola; (dish cooked in a casserole) timbal m

cassette [kæ'sɛt] s casete m

cassette player s grabador-reproductor m

cassock ['kæsək] s balandrán m, sotana

cast [kæst] s echada, tiro; forma, molde m; aire m, semblante m; matiz m, tinte m; (of actors) reparto ‖ v (pret & pp cast) tr echar, tirar; volver (los ojos); proyectar (una sombra); colar, fundir (metales); depositar (votos); echar (suertes); (theat) repartir (papeles); **to cast aside** desechar; **to cast loose** soltar; **to cast out** arrojar, echar fuera; despedir, desterrar ‖ intr echar los dados; arrojar el sedal o el anzuelo; **to cast about** revolver proyectos; **to cast off** (naut) soltar las amarras

castanet [,kæstə'nɛt] s castañuela, castañeta

cast′a•way′ adj & s proscrito, réprobo; náufrago

caste [kæst] s casta; **to lose caste** desprestigiarse

caster ['kæstər] s ruedecilla de mueble; (cruet stand) angarillas, vinagreras; frasco

Castile [kæs'til] s Castilla

Castile soap s jabón m de Castilla

Castilian [kæs'tɪljən] adj & s castellano

casting ['kæstɪŋ] s fundición, pieza fundida; (theat) reparto

casting vote s voto de calidad

cast iron s hierro colado, hierro fundido

cast'-i'ron adj de hierro colado; fuerte, endurecido; duro, inflexible

castle ['kæsəl] s castillo; (chess) roque m, torre f ‖ tr & intr (chess) enrocar

castle in Spain o **castle in the air** s castillo en el aire

cast'off' adj abandonado, desechado; (clothing) de desecho ‖ s desecho

castor oil ['kæstər] s aceite m de ricino

castrate ['kæstret] tr capar, castrar

casual ['kæʒʊ•əl] adj casual, fortuito; descuidado, indiferente

casual•ty ['kæʒu•əltɪ] s (pl -ties) desgracia, accidente m; accidentado, víctima; (in war) baja

casualty list s lista de bajas

cat. abbr **catalogue, catechism**

cat [kæt] s gato; mujer maligna; **to bell the cat** ponerle cascabel al gato; **to let the cat out of the bag** revelar el secreto

catacomb ['kætə,kom] s catacumba

Catalan ['kætə,læn] adj & s catalán m

catalogue ['kætə,lɔg] o ['kætə,lɑg] s catálogo ‖ tr catalogar

Catalonia [,kætə'lonɪ•ə] s Cataluña

Catalonian [,kætə'lonɪ•ən] adj & s catalán m

catapult ['kætə,pʌlt] s catapulta ‖ tr catapultar

cataract ['kætə,rækt] s catarata; (pathol) catarata

catarrh [kə'tɑr] s catarro

catastrophe [kə'tæstrəfɪ] s catástrofe f

cat'call' s rechifla ‖ tr & intr rechiflar

catch [kætʃ] s (of a ball) cogida; (of fish) pesca; (of a lock) cerradera, pestillo; (booty) botín m, presa; (fastener) broche m; (good match) buen partido ‖ v (pret & pp **caught** [kɔt]) tr asir, coger, atrapar; llegar a oír; coger (un resfriado); (to come upon suddenly) sorprender, comprender; capturar (al delincuente); **to catch fire** encenderse; **to catch hold of** agarrar, coger; apoderarse de; **to catch it** (coll) merecerse un regaño; **to catch oneself** contenerse; recobrar el equilibrio; **to catch sight of** alcanzar a ver; **to catch up** arrebatar; coger al vuelo; (in a mistake) cazar ‖ intr pegarse (una enfermedad); enredarse; encenderse; **to catch at** agarrarse a, tratar de asir; **to catch on** prender en (p.ej., un gancho); comprender, coger el tino; **to catch up** salir del atraso; (in one's debts) ponerse al día; **to catch up with** emparejar con

catcher ['kætʃər] s (baseball) receptor, parador m

catching ['kætʃɪŋ] adj pegajoso, contagioso; atrayente, cautivador

catch question s pega

catchup ['kætʃəp] s salsa de tomate condimentada

catch'word' s lema m, palabra de efecto; (actor's cue) pie m; (typ) reclamo

catch•y ['kætʃɪ] adj (comp -ier; super -iest) (tune) animado, vivo; (title of a book) impresionante, llamativo; (question) intrincado; (breathing) espasmódico

catechism ['kætɪ,kɪzəm] s catecismo

catego•ry ['kætɪ,gorɪ] s (pl -ries) categoría; (sports) division

cater ['ketər] tr & intr abastecer, proveer; **to cater to** proveer a

cater-cornered ['kætər,kɔrnərd] adj diagonal ‖ adv diagonalmente

caterer ['ketərər] s abastecedor m, proveedor m de alimentos (esp. para fiestas caseras)

caterpillar ['kætər,pɪlər] s oruga

caterpillar tractor s tractor m de oruga

cat'fish' s bagre m

cat'gut' s (mus) cuerda de tripa; (surg) catgut m

Cath. abbr **Catholic**

cathartic [kə'θɑrtɪk] adj & s catártico

cathedral [kə'θidrəl] s catedral f

catheter ['kæθɪtər] s catéter m

catheterize ['kæθɪtə,raɪz] tr cateterizar

cathode ['kæθod] s cátodo

catholic ['kæθəlɪk] adj católico ‖ **Catholic** adj & s católico

catkin ['kætkɪn] s candelilla, amento

cat nap s sueñecito

catnip ['kætnɪp] s hierba gatera, nébeda

cat-o'-nine-tails [,kætə'naɪn,telz] s azote m con nueve ramales

cat's cradle s juego de la cuna

cat's-paw o **catspaw** ['kæts,pɔ] s mano f de gato, instrumento

catsup ['kætsəp] o [kɛtʃəp] s salsa de tomate condimentada

cat'tail' s anea, espadaña; amento

cattle ['kætəl] s ganado vacuno

cattle crossing s paso de ganado

cattle•man ['kætəlmən] s (pl -men [mən]) s ganadero

cattle raising s ganadería

cattle ranch s hacienda de ganado

cat•ty ['kætɪ] adj (comp -tier; super -tiest) (like a cat) felino, gatuno; (spiteful) malicioso; (gossipy) chismoso

cat'walk' s pasadero, pasarela

Caucasian [kɔ'keʒən] adj & s caucasiano, caucásico

Caucasus ['kɔkəsəs] s Cáucaso

caucus ['kɔkəs] s junta de políticos

cauliflower ['kɔlɪ,flaʊ•ər] s coliflor f

cause [kɔz] s causa; (person) causante mf ‖ tr causar

cause'way' s (highway) calzada; calzada elevada

caustic ['kɔstɪk] adj cáustico

cauterize ['kɔtə,raɪz] tr cauterizar

caution ['kɔʃən] s (carefulness) cautela; (warning) advertencia, amonestación ‖ tr advertir, amonestar

cautious ['kɔʃəs] adj cauteloso, cauto

Cav. abbr **Cavalry**

cavalcade [,kævəl'ked] o ['kævəl,ked] s cabalgata

cavalier [,kævə'lɪr] adj (haughty) altivo, desdeñoso; (offhand) alegre, desenvuelto, inceremonioso ‖ s (horseman) caballero; (lady's escort) galán m

caval•ry ['kævəlrɪ] s (pl -ries) caballería

cavalry•man ['kævəlrimən] *s* (*pl* -men [mən]) soldado de caballería

cave [kev] *s* cueva, caverna ‖ *intr* — **to cave in** hundirse; (*to give in, yield*) (coll) ceder, rendirse

cave'-in' *s* hundimiento, derrumbe *m*, socavón *m*

cave man *s* hombre grosero

cavern ['kævərn] *s* caverna

cav•il ['kævɪl] *v* (*pret & pp* -iled o -illed; *ger* -iling o -illing) *intr* buscar quisquillas

cavi•ty ['kævɪti] *s* (*pl* -ties) cavidad; (*in a tooth*) picadura

cavort [kə'gɔrt] *intr* (coll) cabriolar

caw [kɔ] *s* graznido ‖ *intr* graznar

CB *abbr* **citizens band**

cc. *abbr* **cubic centimeter**

CD *abbr* **compact disk**

cease [sis] *tr* parar, suspender ‖ *intr* cesar; cesar de, dejar de + *inf*

cease'fire' *s* cese *m* de fuego ‖ *intr* suspender hostilidades

ceaseless ['sislɪs] *adj* incesante, continuo

cedar ['sidər] *s* ced.o

cede [sid] *tr* ceder, traspasar

ceiling ['silɪŋ] *s* techo, cielo raso; (aer) techo, cielo máximo

ceiling price *s* precio tope

celebrant ['sɛlɪbrənt] *s* celebrante *m*

celebrate ['sɛlɪ,bret] *tr* celebrar ‖ *intr* (*to say mass*) celebrar; divertirse, festejarse; farrear

celebrated ['sɛlɪ,bretɪd] *adj* célebre, renombrado

celebration [,sɛlɪ'breʃən] *s* celebración; diversión, festividad

celebri•ty [sɪ'lɛbrɪti] *s* (*pl* -ties) (*fame; famous person*) celebridad

celery ['sɛləri] *s* apio

celestial [sɪ'lɛstʃəl] *adj* celeste, celestial

celiba•cy ['sɛlɪbəsi] *s* (*pl* -cies) celibato

celibate ['sɛlɪbɪt] *adj & s* célibe *mf*

cell [sɛl] *s* (*of convent or jail*) celda; (*of honeycomb*) celdilla; (*of electric battery*) elemento; (*of plant or animal; of photoelectric device; of political group*) célula

cellar ['sɛlər] *s* sótano; (*for wine*) bodega

cellaret [,sɛlə'rɛt] *s* licorera

cell house *s* prisión celular

cellist o **'cellist** ['tʃɛlɪst] *s* violoncelista *mf*

cel•lo o **'cel•lo** ['tʃɛlo] *s* (*pl* -los) violoncelo

cellophane ['sɛlə,fen] *s* celofán *m*

celluloid ['sɛljə,lɔɪd] *s* celuloide *m*

Celt [sɛlt] o [kɛlt] *s* celta *mf*

Celtic ['sɛltɪk] o ['kɛltɪk] *adj* céltico ‖ *s* (*language*) celta *m*

cement [sɪ'mɛnt] *s* cemento ‖ *tr* revestir con cemento; (*la amistad*) consolidar

cemeter•y ['sɛmɪ,tɛri] *s* (*pl* -ies) cementerio

cen. *abbr* **central**

censer ['sɛnsər] *s* incensario

censor ['sɛnsər] *s* censor *m* ‖ *tr* censurar

censure ['sɛnʃər] *s* censura ‖ *tr* censurar

census ['sɛnsəs] *s* censo; **to take the census** levantar el censo

cent. *abbr* **centigrade, central, century**

cent [sɛnt] *s* centavo

centaur ['sɛntɔr] *s* centauro

centennial [sɛn'tɛnɪ•əl] *adj & s* centenario

center ['sɛntər] *adj* centrista ‖ *s* centro ‖ *tr* centrar

center half *s* (*ball games*) medio centro

cen'ter•piece' *s* centro de mesa

center punch *s* granete *m*, punzón *m* de marcar

centigrade ['sɛntɪ,gred] *adj* centígrado

centimeter ['sɛntɪ,mitər] *s* centímetro

centipede ['sɛntɪ,pid] *s* ciempiés *m*

central ['sɛntrəl] *adj* central ‖ *s* (telp) central *f*, central de teléfonos; (*operator*) telefonista *mf*

Central America *s* Centro América, la América Central

Central American *adj & mf* centroamericano

centralize ['sɛntrə,laɪz] *tr* centralizar ‖ *intr* centralizarse

centrifuge ['sɛntrəfjudʒ] *s* centrifugadora

centu•ry ['sɛntʃəri] *s* (*pl* -ries) siglo

century plant *s* pita, maguey *m*

ceramic [sɪ'ræmɪk] *adj* cerámico

cereal ['sɪrɪ•əl] *adj & s* cereal *m*

ceremonious [,sɛrɪ'monɪ•əs] *adj* ceremonioso, etiquetero

ceremo•ny ['sɛrɪ,moni] *s* (*pl* -nies) ceremonia; **to stand on ceremony** hacer ceremonias, ser etiquetero

certain ['sʌrtən] *adj* cierto; **a certain** cierto; **for certain** por cierto

certainly ['sɛrtənli] *adj* ciertamente; (*gladly*) con mucho gusto

certain•ty ['sʌrtənti] *s* (*pl* -ties) certeza; **with certainty** a ciencia cierta

certificate [sər'tɪfɪkɪt] *s* certificación, certificado; (*of birth, death, etc.*) partida, fe *f*; (*document representing financial assets*) título ‖ [sər'tɪfɪ,ket] *tr* certificar

certified public accountant ['sʌrtɪ,faɪd] *s* contador público, censor jurado de cuentas

certi•fy ['sʌrtɪ,faɪ] *v* (*pret & pp* -fied) *tr* certificar

cervix ['sʌrvɪks] *s* (*pl* **cervices** [sər'vaɪsiz]) cerviz *f*

cessation [sɛ'seʃən] *s* cesación

cessation of hostilities *s* suspensión de hostilidades

cesspool ['sɛs,pul] *s* pozo negro; (fig) sitio inmundo

Ceylon [sɪ'lɑn] *s* Ceilán *m*

Ceylo•nese [,silə'niz] *adj* ceilanés ‖ *s* (*pl* -nese) ceilanés *m*

cf. *abbr* **confer, i.e., compare**

C.F.I., c.f.i. *abbr* **cost, freight, and insurance**

cg. *abbr* **centigram**

ch. *abbr* **chapter, church**

chafe [tʃef] *s* fricción, roce *m;* desgaste *m;* irritación ‖ *tr* (*to rub*) frotar; (*to rub and make sore*) escocer; (*to wear*) desgastar; irritar ‖ *intr* escocerse; desgastarse; irritarse

chaff [tʃæf] *s* barcia; paja menuda; broza, desperdicio

chafing dish ['tʃefɪŋ] *s* cocinilla, infernillo

chagrin [ʃə'grɪn] *s* desazón *f*, disgusto ‖ *tr* desazonar, disgustar
chain [tʃen] *s* cadena ‖ *tr* encadenar
chain gang *s* cadena de presidiarios, collera, cuerda de presos
chain reaction *s* reacción en cadena
chain'smoke' *intr* fumar un pitillo tras otro
chain store *s* empresa con una cadena de tiendas; tienda de una cadena de tiendas
chair [tʃɛr] *s* silla; (*de catedrático*) cátedra; presidencia; **to take the chair** presidir la reunión; abrir la sesión ‖ *tr* presidir (*una reunión*)
chair lift *s* telesilla
chair·man ['tʃɛrmən] *s* (*pl* **-men** [mən]) presidente *m*
chairmanship ['tʃɛrmən,ʃɪp] *s* presidencia
chair rail *s* guardasilla
chalice ['tʃælɪs] *s* cáliz *m*
chalk [tʃɔk] *s* (*soft white limestone*) creta; (*piece used for writing*) tiza ‖ *tr* marcar o escribir con tiza; **to chalk up** apuntar; marcar (*un tanto*)
challenge ['tʃælɪndʒ] *s* desafío; (law) recusación ‖ *tr* desafiar; (law) recusar
chamber ['tʃembər] *s* cámara; (*of a gun*) recámara; dormitorio; **chambers** oficina de juez
chamberlain ['tʃembərlɪn] *s* chambelán *m*
cham'ber·maid' *s* camarera
chamber pot *s* orinal *m*
chameleon [kə'milɪ·ən] *s* camaleón *m*
chamfer ['tʃæmfər] *s* chaflán *m* ‖ *tr* chaflanar
cham·ois ['ʃæmi] *s* (*pl* **-ois**) gamuza
champ [tʃæmp] *s* mordisco; (slang) campeón *m* ‖ *tr & intr* mordiscar; (*el freno*) morder
champagne [ʃæm'pen] *s* champaña *m*
champion ['tʃæmpɪ·ən] *s* campeón *m* ‖ *tr* defender
championess ['tʃæmpɪ·ənɪs] *s* campeona
championship ['tʃæmpɪ·ən,ʃɪp] *s* campeonato
chance [tʃæns] o [tʃɑns] *adj* casual, imprevisto ‖ *s* oportunidad, ocasión; casualidad, suerte *f*; probabilidad; peligro, riesgo; chance *m* (SAm); **by chance** por casualidad; **to not stand a chance** no tener probabilidad de éxito; **to take a chance** probar fortuna; comprar un billete de lotería; **to take chances** probar fortuna; **to wait for, a chance** esperar la oportunidad ‖ *intr* acontecer; **to chance on** o **upon** tropezar con; **to chance to** acertar a
chancel ['tʃænsəl] o ['tʃɑnsəl] *s* entrecoro
chanceller·y ['tʃænsələri] o ['tʃɑnsələri] *s* (*pl* **-ies**) cancillería
chancellor ['tʃænsələr] *s* canciller *m*
chandelier [,ʃændə'lɪr] *s* araña de luces
change [tʃendʒ] *s* cambio, mudanza; suelto, moneda suelta; (*surplus money returned with a purchase*) vuelta; (*of clothing*) muda; **for a change** por variedad; **to keep the change** quedarse con la vuelta; ‖ *tr* cambiar, mudar; cambiar de, mudar de; reemplazar; **to change clothes** cambiar de ropa; **to change gears** cambiar de velocidades; **to change hands** cambiar de dueño;

to change money cambiar moneda; **to change one's mind** cambiar de parecer; **to change trains** cambiar de tren, transbordar ‖ *intr* cambiar, mudar; corregirse
changeable ['tʃendʒəbəl] *adj* cambiable; inconstante, cambiante, mudable
change of clothing *s* muda de ropa
change of heart *s* arrepentimiento, conversión
change of life *s* cesación natural de las reglas
change of voice *s* muda
chan·nel ['tʃænəl] *s* (*body of water joining two others*) canal *m*; (*bed of river*) álveo, cauce *m*; (*means of communication*) vía; (*passage*) conducto; (*groove*) ranura, surco; (telv) canal *m*; **the Channel** el Canal de la Mancha ‖ *v* (*pret & pp* **-neled** o **-nelled;** *ger* **-neling** o **-nelling**) *tr* acanalar; canalizar (*esfuerzos, dinero, etc.*)
chant [tʃænt] *s* (*song*) canción; (*song sung in a monotone*) canto ‖ *tr & intr* cantar
chanter ['tʃæntər] *s* cantor *m*; (*priest*) chantre *m*
chanticleer ['tʃæntɪ,klɪr] *s* el gallo
chaos ['ke·ɑs] *s* caos *m*
chaotic [ke'ɑtɪk] *adj* caótico
chap. *abbr* **chaplain, chapter**
chap [tʃæp] *s* (*jaw*) mandíbula; (*cheek*) mejilla; (*crack in the skin*) grieta; chico, tipo; **chaps** zahones *mpl* ‖ *v* (*pret & pp* **chapped;** *ger* **chapping**) *tr* agrietar, rajar ‖ *intr* agrietarse, rajarse
chapel ['tʃæpəl] *s* capilla
chaperon o **chaperone** ['ʃæpə,ron] *s* carabina, señora de compañía ‖ *tr* acompañar (*una señora a una o más señoritas*)
chaplain ['tʃæplɪn] *s* capellán *m*
chaplet ['tʃæplɪt] *s* (*wreath for head*) guirnalda; rosario
chapter ['tʃæptər] *s* capítulo; (*of the Scriptures*) capítula; (*of a cathedral*) cabildo
chapter and verse *adv* con todos sus pelos y señales
char [tʃɑr] *v* (*pret & pp* **charred;** *ger* **charring**) *tr* carbonizar; (*to scorch*) socarrar
character ['kærɪktər] *s* carácter *m*; (*conspicuous person; person in a play or novel*) personaje *m*; (*part or role in a play*) papel *m*; (*fellow*) (coll) tipo, sujeto
character assassination *s* asesinato de carácter
characteristic [,kærɪktə'rɪstɪk] *adj* característico ‖ *s* característica
characterize ['kærɪktə,raɪz] *tr* caracterizar
char'coal' *s* carbón *m* de leña; (*for sketching*) carboncillo; (*sketch*) dibujo al carbón
charcoal burner *s* (*person*) carbonero; horno para hacer carbón de leña
charge [tʃɑrdʒ] *s* (*of an explosive, of electricity, of soldiers against the enemy; responsibility*) carga; (*accusation; amount owed; recording of amount owed*) cargo; encargamiento; (heral) blasón *m*; (*attack*) embestida; **in charge of** a cargo de; **to put in charge** responsabilizar; **to reverse the charges** (telp) cargar al número llamado; **to take charge of** hacerse cargo de ‖ *tr*

cargar; cobrar (*cierto precio*); (*to order*) encargar, mandar; cargar (*un acumulador; al enemigo*); **to charge to the account of someone** cargarle a uno en cuenta; **to charge with** cargar de ‖ *intr* embestir
charge account *s* cuenta corriente
chargé d'affaires [ʃɑrˈʒe dəˈfɛr] *s* (*pl* **chargés d'affaires**) encargado de negocios
charger [ˈtʃɑrdʒər] *s* caballo de guerra; (*of a battery*) cargador *m*
chariot [ˈtʃærɪ•ət] *s* carro romano
charioteer [ˌtʃærɪ•əˈtɪr] *s* carretero, auriga *m*
charisma [kəˈrɪzmə] *s* carisma
charismatic [ˌkɑrɪzˈmætɪk] *adj* carismático
charitable [ˈtʃærɪtəbəl] *adj* caritativo
chari•ty [ˈtʃærɪti] *s* (*pl* **-ties**) caridad; asociación de beneficencia, obra pía; **charity begins at home** la caridad bien ordenada empieza por uno mismo
charity performance *s* función benéfica
charlatan [ˈʃɑrlətən] *s* charlatán *m*
charlatanism [ˈʃɑrlətən‚ɪzəm] *s* charlatanismo
Charlemagne [ˈʃɑrlə‚men] *s* Carlomagno
Charles [tʃɑrlz] *s* Carlos *m*
charlotte [ˈʃɑrlət] *s* carlota ‖ **Charlotte** *s* Carlota
charlotte russe [ˈʃɑrlət ˈrus] *s* carlota rusa
charm [tʃɑrm] *s* encanto, hechizo; (*trinket*) amuleto, dije *m* ‖ *tr* encantar, hechizar
charming [ˈtʃɑrmɪŋ] *adj* encantador
charnel [ˈtʃɑrnəl] *adj* cadavérico, horrible ‖ *s* carnero, osario
charnel house *s* carnero, osario
chart [tʃɑrt] *s* mapa geográfico; (naut) carta de marear; cuadro, diagrama *m* ‖ *tr* bosquejar; **to chart a course** trazar una ruta
charter [ˈtʃɑrtər] *s* carta (de privilegio) ‖ *tr* alquilar (*un autobús*); fletar (*un barco*)
charter member *s* socio fundador
char•woman [ˈtʃɑr‚wumən] *s* (*pl* **-women** [‚wɪmɪn]) alquilona, asistenta
Charybdis [kəˈrɪbdɪs] *s* Caribdis *f*
chase [tʃes] *s* caza, persecución ‖ *tr* cazar, perseguir; **to chase away** ahuyentar
chasm [ˈkæzəm] *s* abismo
chas•sis [ˈtʃæsi] *s* (*pl* **-sis** [siz]) chasis *m*
chaste [tʃest] *adj* casto; (*style*) castizo
chasten [ˈtʃesən] *tr* castigar, corregir
chastise [tʃæsˈtaɪz] *tr* castigar
chastity [ˈtʃæstɪti] *s* castidad
chasuble [ˈtʃæzjəbəl] *s* casulla
chat [tʃæt] *s* charla, plática ‖ *v* (*pret & pp* **chatted;** *ger* **chatting**) *intr* charlar, platicar
chatelaine [ˈʃætə‚len] *s* castellana
chattels [ˈtʃætəlz] *spl* bienes *mpl* muebles, enseres *mpl*
chatter [ˈtʃætər] *s* (*talk*) cháchara; (*rattling*) traqueo; (*of teeth*) castañeteo; (*of birds*) chirrido ‖ *intr* chacharear; traquear; castañetear, dentellar (*los dientes*)
chattering [ˈtʃætərɪŋ] *adj* parlabrudo
chauffeur [ˈʃofər] o [ʃoˈfʌr] *s* chófer *m*
chauvinism [ˈʃovɪnɪzəm] *s* chauvinismo
cheap [tʃip] *adj* barato; (*charging low prices*) no carero, baratero; (*flashy*) cursi; baladí;

to feel cheap sentirse avergonzado ‖ *adv* barato
cheapen [ˈtʃipən] *tr* abaratar
cheapness [ˈtʃipnɪs] *s* baratura; baratía; (*flashiness*) cursilería
cheat [tʃit] *s* trampa, fraude *m;* (*person*) trampista *mf,* defraudador *m* ‖ *tr* trampear, defraudar
check [tʃɛk] *s* (*of bank*) cheque *m;* (*for baggage*) talón *m,* contraseña; (*in a restaurant*) cuenta; (*in theater or movie*) contraseña, billete *m* de salida; (*restraint*) freno; (*to hold a door*) amortiguador *m;* (*in chess*) jaque *m;* inspección; comprobación, verificación; (*cloth*) paño a cuadros; **in check** en jaque; **to hold in check** contener, refrenar ‖ *interj* ¡jaque! ‖ *tr* parar súbitamente; contener, refrenar; amortiguar; facturar (*equipajes*); inspeccionar; comprobar, verificar; marcar, señalar; chequear; (*in chess*) jaquear, dar jaque a; **to check up** comprobar, verificar ‖ *intr* pararse súbitamente; corresponder punto por punto; **to check in** (*at a hotel*) llegar e inscribirse; **to check out** pagar la cuenta y despedirse; (slang) morir
check'book' *s* talonario (de cheques), chequera
checker [ˈtʃɛkər] *s* inspector *m;* cuadro; dibujo a cuadros; (*in game of checkers*) ficha, pieza; **checkers** damas, juego de damas ‖ *tr* marcar con cuadros; diversificar, variar
check'er•board' *s* damero, tablero
check girl *s* moza de guardarropa
checking account *s* cuenta corriente
check'mate' *s* mate *m,* jaque *m* mate ‖ *tr* dar mate a, dar jaque mate a; (fig) derrotar completamente
check'out' *s* (*from a hotel*) salida; hora de salida; (*in a self-service retail store*) revisión y pago
checkout counter *s* mostrador *m* de revisión
check'point' *s* punto de inspección
check'rein' *s* engallador *m*
check'room' *s* guardarropa *m;* (rr) consigna, depósito de equipajes
check'up' *s* verificación rigurosa; chequeo; (*of an automobile*) revisión; (med) reconocimiento general
cheek [tʃik] *s* mejilla, carrillo; (coll) descaro, frescura
cheek'bone' *s* pómulo
cheek by jowl *adv* cara a cara, en estrecha intimidad
cheek•y [ˈtʃiki] *adj* (*comp* **-ier;** *super* **-iest**) (coll) descarado, fresco
cheer [tʃir] *s* alegría, regocijo; (*shout*) viva *m,* aplauso; **what cheer?** ¿qué tal? ‖ *tr* alegrar, animar; aplaudir; vitorear; dar la bienvenida a, con vivas y aplausos ‖ *intr* alegrarse, animarse; **cheer up!** ¡ánimo!
cheerful [ˈtʃɪrfəl] *adj* alegre
cheerio [ˈtʃɪrɪ‚o] *interj* (coll) ¡hola! ¡qué tal!; (coll) ¡adiós! ¡hasta la vista!
cheerless [ˈtʃɪrlɪs] *adj* sombrío, triste
cheese [tʃiz] *s* queso ·

cheese'cloth' *s* estopilla
cheese spread *s* queso para extender
cheetah ['tʃitə] *s* gatopardo; leopardo indio
chef [ʃɛf] *s* primer cocinero, jefe *m* de cocina
chem. *abbr* **chemical, chemist, chemistry**
chemical ['kɛmɪkəl] *adj* químico ‖ *s* producto químico, substancia química
chemise [ʃə'miz] *s* camisa (de mujer)
chemist ['kɛmɪst] *s* químico
chemistry ['kɛmɪstri] *s* química
chemotherapy [,kimo'θɛrəpi] *s* quimioterapia
cherish ['tʃɛriʃ] *tr* acariciar; (*a hope*) abrigar, acariciar
cher•ry ['tʃɛri] *s* (*pl* **-ries**) (*fruit; color*) cereza; (*tree*) cerezo
cher•ub ['tʃɛrəb] *s* (*pl* **-ubim** [əbɪm]) querubín *m* ‖ *s* (*pl* **-ubs**) niño angelical
chess [tʃɛs] *s* ajedrez *m*
chess'board' *s* tablero de ajedrez
chess•man ['tʃɛs,mæn] *s* (*pl* **-men** [,mɛn]) pieza de ajedrez, trebejo
chess player *s* ajedrecista *mf*
chess set *s* ajedrez *m*
chest [tʃɛst] *s* (*part of body*) pecho; (*receptacle*) cajón *m*, cofre *m*; (*piece of furniture*) cómoda
chestnut ['tʃɛsnət] *s* (*tree, wood, color*) castaño; (*fruit*) castaña
chest of drawers *s* cómoda
cheval glass [ʃə'væl] *s* psique *f*
chevalier [,ʃɛvə'lɪr] *s* caballero
chevron ['ʃɛvrən] *s* galón *m* en forma de V invertida
chew [tʃu] *s* mascadura ‖ *tr* mascar; **to chew gum** chiclear; **to chew the rag** (slang) dar la lengua ‖ *intr* mascar
chewing gum *s* goma de mascar, chicle *m*
chg. *abbr* **charge**
chic [ʃik] *adj* & *s* chic *m*
chicaner•y [ʃɪ'kenəri] *s* (*pl* **-ies**) triquiñuela
chick [tʃɪk] *s* pollito; (slang) polla
chicken ['tʃɪkən] *s* pollo; (*young person*) pollo; (*young girl*) polla
chicken coop *s* pollera
chicken feed *s* (coll) calderilla
chickenhearted ['tʃɪkən,hartɪd, varicela] *adj* gallina
chicken pox *s* viruelas locas, varicela
chicken wire *s* alambrada, tela metálica
chick'pea' *s* garbanzo
chico•ry ['tʃɪkəri] *s* (*pl* **-ries**) achicoria
chide [tʃaɪd] *v* (*pret* **chided** o **chid** [tʃɪd]; *pp* **chided, chid** o **chidden** ['tʃɪdən]) *tr* reprender, regañar
chief [tʃif] *adj* principal ‖ *s* jefe *m*; (*of American Indians*) cacique *m*
chief executive *s* jefe *m* del gobierno
chief justice *s* presidente *m* de sala; presidente del tribunal supremo
chiefly ['tʃifli] *adv* principalmente, mayormente
chief of staff *s* jefe *m* de estado mayor
chief of state *s* jefe *m* del estado
chieftain ['tʃiftən] *s* (*of a clan or tribe*) jefe *m*; adalid *m*, caudillo

chiffon [ʃɪ'fɑn] *s* gasa, soplillo; **chiffons** atavíos, perifollos
chiffonier [,ʃɪfə'nɪr] *s* cómoda alta
chignon ['ʃɪnjɑn] *s* castaña, moño
chilblain ['tʃɪl,blen] *s* sabañón *m*
child [tʃaɪld] *s* (*pl* **children** ['tʃɪldrən]) *s* (*infant, youngster*) niño; pipiolo (CAm, Mex); (*one's offspring*) hijo; descendiente *mf*; **with child** encinta, embarazada
child'birth' *s* alumbramiento, parto
childhood ['tʃaɪldhʊd] *s* niñez *f*, puericia; **from childhood** desde niño
childish ['tʃaɪldɪʃ] *adj* aniñado, pueril
childishness ['tʃaɪldɪʃnɪs] *s* puerilidad
child labor *s* trabajo de menores
childless ['tʃaɪldlɪs] *adj* sin hijos
child'like' *adj* aniñado
child'-rear'ing *s* puericultura
child's play *s* juego de niños
child welfare *s* protección a la infancia
Chile ['tʃili] *s* Chile *m*
Chilean ['tʃɪli•ən] *adj* & *s* chileno
chili sauce ['tʃɪli] *s* ají *m*, salsa de ají
chill [tʃɪl] *adj* frío ‖ *s* frío desapacible; (*sensation of cold*) escalofrío; (*lack of cordiality*) frialdad ‖ *tr* enfriar ‖ *intr* calofriarse
chill•y ['tʃɪli] *adj* (*comp* **-ier**; *super* **-iest**) (*causing shivering*) frío; (*sensitive to cold*) escalofriado, friolero; (*indifferent*) (fig) frío
chime [tʃaɪm] *s* campaneo, repique *m*; tubo sonoro; **chimes** juego de campanas ‖ *tr* & *intr* campanear, repicar
chime clock *s* reloj *m* de carillón
chimera [kaɪ'mɪrə] o [kɪ'mɪrə] *s* quimera
chimney ['tʃɪmni] *s* chimenea; (*for a lamp*) tubo
chimney cap *s* caperuza
chimney flue *s* cañón *m* de chimenea
chimney pot *s* mitra, guardavientos *m*
chimney sweep *s* limpiachimeneas *m*, deshollinador *m*
chimpanzee [tʃɪm'pænzi] o [,tʃɪmpæn'zi] *s* chimpancé *m*
chin [tʃɪn] *s* barba, mentón *m*; **to keep one's chin up** (coll) no desanimarse ‖ *v* (*pret* & *pp* **chinned;** *ger* **chinning**) *intr* (coll) charlar
china ['tʃaɪnə] *s* china, porcelana ‖ **China** *s* China
china closet *s* chinero
China•man ['tʃaɪnəmən] *s* (*pl* **-men** [mən]) (offensive) chino
chi'na•ware' *s* porcelana, vajilla de porcelana
Chi•nese [tʃaɪ'niz] *adj* chino ‖ *s* (*pl* **-nese**) chino
Chinese gong *s* batintín *m*
Chinese lantern *s* farolillo veneciano
Chinese puzzle *s* problema embrollado
chink [tʃɪŋk] *s* grieta, hendidura; sonido metálico
chin strap *s* barboquejo, carrillera
chintz [tʃɪnts] *s* zaraza
chip [tʃɪp] *s* astilla, brizna; (*in china*) desconchado; (*in poker*) ficha; **chip off the old block** hijo de su padre ‖ *v* (*pret* & *pp* **chipped;** *ger* **chipping**) *tr* astillar (*la ma-*

dera); desconchar (*la porcelana*); **to chip in** contribuir con su cuota ‖ *intr* astillarse; descoharse

chipmunk ['tʃɪp‚mʌŋk] *s* ardilla listada

chipper ['tʃɪpər] *adj* (coll) alegre, jovial, vivo

chiropodist [kaɪ'rɑpədɪst] o [kɪ'rɑpədɪst] *s* quiropodista *mf*

chiropractor ['kaɪrə‚præktər] *s* quiropráctico

chirp [tʃʌrp] *s* chirrido, gorjeo ‖ *intr* chirriar, gorjear; hablar alegremente

chis•el ['tʃɪzəl] *s* (*for wood*) escoplo, formón *m*; (*for stone and metal*) cincel *m* ‖ *v* (*pret & pp* -eled o -elled; *ger* -eling o -elling) *tr* escoplear; cincelar; (slang) estafar

chit-chat ['tʃɪt‚tʃæt] *s* charla, palique *m*; hablilla, chismes *mpl*

chivalric ['ʃɪvəlrɪk] o [ʃɪ'vælrɪk] *adj* caballeresco

chivalrous ['ʃɪvəlrəs] *adj* caballeroso

chivalry ['ʃɪvəlri] *s* (*knighthood*) caballería; (*gallantry, gentlemanliness*) caballerosidad

chloride ['klɔraɪd] *s* cloruro

chlorine ['klɔrin] *s* cloro

chloroform ['klɔrə‚fɔrm] *s* cloroformo ‖ *tr* cloroformizar

chlorophyll ['klɔrəfɪl] *s* clorofila

chock-full ['tʃɑk'fʊl] *adj* de bote en bote, colmado

chocolate ['tʃɑkəlɪt] *s* chocolate *m*

choice [tʃɔɪs] *adj* escogido, selecto, superior ‖ *s* elección, selección; lo más escogido; **to have no choice** no tener alternativa

choir [kwaɪr] *s* coro

choir'boy' *s* niño de coro, infante *m* de coro

choir desk *s* facistol *m*

choir loft *s* coro

choir'mas'ter *s* jefe *m* de coro, maestro de capilla

choke [tʃok] *s* estrangulación; (*of carburetor*) cierre *m*, obturador *m*; (elec) choque *m* ‖ *tr* ahogar, sofocar, estrangular; obstruir, tapar; (aut) obturar; **to choke down** atragantar ‖ *intr* sofocarse; atragantarse; **to choke on** atragantarse con

choke coil *s* (elec) bobina de reacción, choque *m*

cholera ['kɑlərə] *s* cólera *m*

choleric ['kɑlərɪk] *adj* colérico

cholesterol [kə'lɛstə‚rol] *s* colesterol *m*

choose [tʃuz] *v* (*pret* chose [tʃoz]; *pp* chosen ['tʃozən]) *tr* escoger, elegir ‖ *intr* — **to choose between** optar entre; **to choose to** optar por

chop [tʃɑp] *s* golpe *m* cortante; (*of meat*) chuleta; **chops** boca, labios ‖ *v* (*pret & pp* chopped; *ger* chopping) *tr* cortar, tajar; picar (*la carne*); **to chop off** tronchar; **to chop up** desmenuzar

chop'house' *s* restaurante *m*, figón *m*, colmado

chopper ['tʃɑpər] *s* (*person*) tajador *m*; (*tool*) hacha; (*of butcher*) cortante *m*; (slang) helicóptero

chopping block *s* tajo

chop•py ['tʃɑpi] *adj* (*comp* -pier; *super* -piest) (*sea*) agitado, picado; (*wind*) variable; (*style*) cortado, inciso

chop'sticks' *spl* palillos

choral ['korəl] *adj* coral

chorale [ko'rɑl] *s* coral *m*

choral society *s* orfeón *m*

chord [kɔrd] *s* (*harmonious combination of tones*) (mus) acorde *m*; (aer, anat, geom) cuerda

chore [tʃor] *s* tarea, quehacer *m*

choreography [‚korɪ'ɑgrəfi] *s* coreografía

chorine [ko'rin] *s* (slang) corista, suripanta

chorus ['korəs] *s* coro; (*refrain of a song*) estribillo

chorus girl *s* corista, conjuntista

chorus man *s* corista *m*, conjuntista *m*

chowder ['tʃaʊdər] *s* estofado de almejas o pescado

Chr. *abbr* **Christian**

Christ [kraɪst] *s* Cristo

christen ['krɪsən] *tr* bautizar

Christendom ['krɪsəndəm] *s* cristiandad

christening ['krɪsənɪŋ] *s* bautismo, bautizo

Christian ['krɪstʃən] *adj & s* cristiano

Christianity [‚krɪstʃɪ'ænɪti] *s* cristianismo

Christianize ['krɪstʃə‚naɪz] *tr* cristianizar

Christian name *s* nombre *m* de pila

Christmas ['krɪsməs] *adj* navideño ‖ *s* Navidad, Pascua de Navidad

Christmas card *s* aleluya navideña

Christmas carol *s* villancico

Christmas Eve *s* nochebuena

Christmas gift *s* aguinaldo, regalo de Navidad

Christmas tree *s* árbol *m* de Navidad

Christopher ['krɪstəfər] *s* Cristóbal *m*

chrome [krom] *adj* cromado ‖ *s* cromo ‖ *tr* cromar

chromium ['kromɪ•əm] *s* cromo

chro•mo ['kromo] *s* (*pl* -mos) (*colored picture*) cromo; (*piece of junk*) (slang) trasto

chromosome ['kromə‚som] *s* cromosoma *m*

chron. *abbr* **chronological, chronology**

chronic ['krɑnɪk] *adj* crónico

chronicle ['krɑnɪkəl] *s* crónica ‖ *tr* narrar en una crónica; narrar, contar

chronicler ['krɑnɪklər] *s* cronista *mf*

chronolo•gy [krə'nɑlədʒi] *s* (*pl* -gies) cronología

chronometer [krə'nɑmɪtər] *s* cronómetro

chrysanthemum [krɪ'sænθɪməm] *s* crisantemo

chub•by ['tʃʌbi] *adj* (*comp* -bier; *super* -biest) rechoncho, regordete

chuck [tʃʌk] *s* (*throw*) echada, tirada; (*under the chin*) mamola; (*of a lathe*) mandril *m* ‖ *tr* arrojar; **to chuck under the chin** hacer la mamola a

chuckle ['tʃʌkəl] *s* risa ahogada ‖ *intr* reírse con risa ahogada

chug [tʃʌg] *s* ruido explosivo sordo; (*of a locomotive*) resoplido ‖ *v* (*pret & pp* chugged; *ger* chugging) *intr* hacer ruidos explosivos sordos, moverse con ruidos explosivos sordos

chum [tʃʌm] s (coll) compinche mf; compañero de cuarto ‖ v (pret & pp **chummed;** ger **chumming**) intr (coll) ser compinche, ser compinches; (coll) compartir un cuarto

chum·my [ˈtʃʌmi] adj (comp **-mier;** super **-miest**) muy amigable, íntimo

chump [tʃʌmp] s tarugo, zoquete m; (coll) estúpido, tonto

chunk [tʃʌnk] s trozo, pedazo grueso

church [tʃʌrt] s iglesia

churchgoer [ˈtʃʌrt͡ʃˌgoˑər] s persona que frecuenta la iglesia

church·man [ˈtʃʌrt͡ʃmən] s (pl **-men** [mən]) sacerdote m, eclesiástico; feligrés m

church member s feligrés m

Church of England s Iglesia Anglicana

church′ward′en s capiller m

church′yard′ s patio de iglesia; cementerio

churl [tʃʌrl] s palurdo, patán m

churlish [ˈtʃʌrlɪʃ] adj palurdo, insolente

churn [tʃʌrn] s mantequera ‖ tr mazar (leche); hacer (mantequilla) en una mantequera; agitar, revolver ‖ intr revolverse

chute [ʃut] s cascada, salto de agua; rápidos; conducto inclinado; (e.g., into a swimming pool) tobogán m; (e.g., for grain) tolva; paracaídas m

cibori·um [sɪˈborɪˑəm] s (pl **-a** [ə]) (canopy) ciborio, baldaquín m; (cup) copón m

Cicero [ˈsɪsəˌro] s Cicerón m

cider [ˈsaɪdər] s sidra

C.I.F., c.i.f. abbr **cost, insurance, and freight**

cigar [sɪˈgɑr] s cigarro, puro

cigar band s anillo de cigarro

cigar case s cigarrera, petaca

cigar cutter s cortacigarros m

cigaret o **cigarette** [ˌsɪgəˈrɛt] s cigarrillo, pitillo

cigarette case s pitillera

cigarette holder s boquilla

cigarette lighter s mechero, encendedor m de bolsillo

cigarette paper s papel m de fumar

cigar holder s boquilla

cigar store s estanco, tabaquería

cinch [sɪntʃ] s (of saddle) cincha; (sure grip) (coll) agarro; (something easy) (slang) breva ‖ tr cinchar; (coll) agarrar

cinder [ˈsɪndər] s ceniza; (coal burning without flame) pavesa

cinder bank s escorial m

Cinderella [ˌsɪndəˈrɛlə] s la Cenicienta

cinder track s pista de cenizas

cinema [ˈsɪnəmə] s cine m

cinematograph [ˌsɪnəˈmætəˌgræf] o [ˌsɪnəˈmætəˌgrɑf] s cinematógrafo ‖ tr & intr cinematografiar

cinnabar [ˈsɪnəˌbɑr] s cinabrio

cinnamon [ˈsɪnəmən] s canela

cipher [ˈsaɪfər] s cifra; cero; (nonentity) cero a la izquierda; (key to a cipher) clave f ‖ tr cifrar; calcular

circle [ˈsʌrkəl] s círculo ‖ tr circundar; dar la vuelta a; girar alrededor de

circuit [ˈsʌrkɪt] s circuito

circuit breaker s disyuntor m

circuitous [sərˈkjuˑɪtəs] adj indirecto, tortuoso

circular [ˈsʌrkjələr] adj tortuoso ‖ s circular f, carta circular

circularize [ˈsʌrkjələˌraɪz] tr anunciar por circular; enviar circulares a

circulate [ˈsʌrkjəˌlet] tr & intr circular

circumcise [ˈsʌrkəmˌsaɪz] tr circuncidar

circumference [sərˈkʌmfərəns] s circunferencia

circumflex [ˈsʌrkəmˌflɛks] adj circunflejo

circumlocution [ˌsʌrkəmloˈkjuʃən] s circunlocución, circunloquio

circumnavigate [ˌsʌrkəmˈnævɪˌget] tr circunnavegar

circumnavigation [ˌsʌrkəmˌnævɪˈgeʃən] s circunnavegación

circumscribe [ˌsʌrkəmˈskraɪb] tr circunscribir

circumspect [ˈsʌrkəmˌspɛkt] adj circunspecto

circumstance [ˈsʌrkəmˌstæns] s circunstancia; ceremonia, ostentación; **in easy circumstances** acomodado; **under no circumstances** de ninguna manera, ni a bala

circumstantial [ˌsʌrkəmˈstænʃəl] adj (derived from circumstances) circunstancial; (detailed) circunstanciado

circumstantial evidence s (law) indicios vehementes

circumstantiate [ˌsʌrkəmˈstænʃɪˌet] tr apoyar con pruebas y detalles; (to describe in detail) circunstanciar

circumvent [ˌsʌrkəmˈvɛnt] tr (to catch by a trick) entrampar, embaucar; (to outwit) burlar; (to keep away from, get around) evitar

circus [ˈsʌrkəs] s circo

cistern [ˈsɪstərn] s cisterna, aljibe m

citadel [ˈsɪtədəl] s ciudadela

citation [saɪˈteʃən] s (of a text) cita; (before a court of law) citación; (for gallantry) mención

cite [saɪt] tr (to quote; to summon) citar; (for gallantry) mencionar

citizen [ˈsɪtɪzən] s ciudadano; (civilian) paisano

citizen·ry [ˈsɪtɪzənri] s (pl **-ries**) conjunto de ciudadanos

citizens band s banda ciudadana

citizenship [ˈsɪtɪzənˌʃɪp] s ciudadanía

citron [ˈsɪtrən] s (fruit) cidra; (tree) cidro; (candied rind) cidrada

citronella [ˌsɪtrəˈnɛlə] s limoncillo (Andropogon nardus); aceite m de limoncillo

citrus fruit [ˈsɪtrəs] s agrios, frutas cítricas

cit·y [ˈsɪti] s (pl **-ies**) ciudad

city clerk s archivero

city council s ayuntamiento

city editor s redactor de periódico encargado de noticias locales

city fathers spl concejales mpl

city hall s casa consistorial

city plan s plano de la ciudad

city planner s urbanista mf

city planning s urbanismo

city room s redacción

ch
ci

cit′y-state′ s ciudad-estado f
civic ['sɪvɪk] adj cívico ‖ **civics** s estudio de los deberes y derechos del ciudadano
civic-mindedness ['maɪndɪdnɪs] s civismo
civies ['sɪviz] spl (coll) traje m de paisano; **in civies** (coll) de paisano
civil ['sɪvɪl] adj civil
civilian [sɪ'vɪljən] adj civil ‖ s civil mf, paisano
civilian clothes spl traje m de paisano
civili•ty [sɪ'vɪlɪti] s (pl **-ties**) civilidad
civilization [,sɪvɪlɪ'zeʃən] s civilización
civilize ['sɪvɪ,laɪz] tr civilizar
civil servant s funcionario del estado
claim [klem] s demanda, pretensión, reclamación ‖ tr demandar, pretender, reclamar; afirmar, declarar; **to claim to** + inf pretender + inf
claim check s comprobante m
clairvoyance [klɛr'vɔɪ•əns] s clarividencia
clairvoyant [klɛr'vɔɪ•ənt] adj & s clarividente mf
clam [klæm] s almeja; (tight-lipped person) (coll) chiticalla m ‖ intr — **to clam up** (coll) callarse la boca
clamber ['klæmər] intr — **to clamber up** subir gateando
clamor ['klæmər] s clamor m, clamoreo ‖ intr clamorear
clamorous ['klæmərəs] adj clamoroso
clamp [klæmp] s abrazadera, grapa; (vise-like device) mordaza ‖ tr agrapar, afianzar con abrazadera; sujetar en una mordaza ‖ intr — **to clamp down on** (coll) apretar los tornillos a
clan [klæn] s clan m
clandestine [klæn'dɛstɪn] adj clandestino
clang [klæŋ] s tantán m, sonido metálico resonante ‖ tr hacer sonar fuertemente ‖ intr sonar fuertemente
clank [klæŋk] s sonido metálico seco ‖ tr hacer sonar secamente ‖ intr sonar secamente
clannish ['klænɪʃ] adj exclusivista
clap [klæp] s golpe seco; (of the hands) palmada; (of thunder) estampido ‖ v (pret & pp **clapped;** ger **clapping**) tr batir (palmas); palmotear, aplaudir; **to clap shut** cerrar de golpe ‖ intr palmotear, dar palmadas
clap of thunder s estampido de trueno
clapper ['klæpər] s palmoteador m; (of a bell) badajo; (to cause grain to slide) tarabilla
clap′trap′ s faramalla; (of an actor) latiguillo
claque [klæk] s (paid clappers) claque f; (crush hat) clac m
claret ['klærɪt] s clarete m
clari•fy ['klærɪ,faɪ] v (pret & pp **-fied**) tr clarificar; encolar (el vino)
clarinet ['klærɪ'nɛt] s clarinete m
clarion ['klærɪ•ən] adj claro, brillante ‖ s clarín m
clarity ['klærɪti] s claridad
clash [klæʃ] s choque m, encontrón m; estruendo, ruido ‖ intr chocar, entrechocarse

clasp [klæsp] s (fastener) abrazadera, cierre m; (for, e.g., a necktie) broche m; (buckle) hebilla; (embrace) abrazo; (grip) agarro ‖ tr abrochar; abrazar; agarrar, apretar (la mano); apretar (la mano)
class. abbr **classical**
class [klæs] s clase f; ó (slang) elegancia, buen tono; (sports) división ‖ tr clasificar ‖ intr clasificarse
class consciousness s sentimiento de clase
classic ['klæsɪk] adj & s clásico; **the classics** las obras clásicas
classical ['klæsɪkəl] adj clásico
classical scholar s erudito en las lenguas clásicas
classicist ['klæsɪsɪst] s clasicista mf
classified ['klæsɪ,faɪd] adj clasificado; clasificado como secreto
classified ads spl anuncios clasificados en secciones
classi•fy ['klæsɪ,faɪ] v (pret & pp **-fied**) tr clasificar
class′mate′ s compañero de clase
class′room′ s aula, sala de clase
class struggle s lucha de clases
class•y ['klæsi] adj (comp **-ier;** super **-iest**) (slang) elegante
clatter ['klætər] s estruendo confuso; algazara, gresca; (of hoofs) trápala ‖ intr caer o moverse con estruendo confuso; hablar rápida y ruidosamente; **to clatter down the stairs** bajar la escalera ruidosamente
clause [klɔz] s (article in a legal document) cláusula; (gram) oración dependiente
clavichord ['klævɪ,kɔrd] s clavicordio
clavicle ['klævɪkəl] s clavícula
clavier ['klævɪ•ər] o [klə'vɪr] s teclado ‖ [klə'vɪr] s instrumento musical con teclado
claw [klɔ] s garra, uña; (of lobster, crab, etc.) pinza; (of hammer, wrench, etc.) oreja; (coll) dedos, mano f ‖ tr (to clutch) agarrar; (to scratch) arañar; (to tear) desgarrar
clay [kle] adj arcilloso ‖ s arcilla
clay pigeon s pichón m de barro
clay pipe s pipa de tierra
clean [klin] adj limpio; distinto, neto, nítido; completo ‖ adv completamente; **to come clean** (slang) confesarlo todo ‖ tr limpiar; (to tidy up) asear; **to be cleaned out** (of money) (slang) quedar limpio; **to clean out** limpiar; (slang) dejar limpio ‖ intr limpiarse; asearse; **to clean up** limpiarse; (coll) llevárselo todo; (in gambling) (slang) hacer mesa limpia; **to clean up after someone** limpiar lo que alguno ha ensuciado
clean bill of health s patente limpia de sanidad
cleaner ['klinər] s limpiador m; (dry cleaner) tintorero; (preparation) quitamanchas m; **to send to the cleaners** (slang) dejar limpio
cleaning ['klinɪŋ] s limpieza
cleaning fluid s quitamanchas m
cleaning woman s criada que hace la limpieza, alquilona

cleanliness ['klɛnlɪnɪs] s limpieza

clean·ly ['klɛnli] adj (comp **-lier;** super **-liest**) limpio (que tiene el hábito del aseo)

cleanse [klɛnz] tr limpiar, lavar, depurar

clean-shaven ['klin'ʃevən] adj lisamente afeitado

clean'up' s limpieza general; **to make a cleanup** (slang) hacer su pacotilla

clear [klɪr] adj claro; (cloudless) despejado; (of debts, etc.) libre ‖ claro, claramente; **clear through** de parte a parte ‖ tr despejar (un bosque); clarificar (lo que estaba turbio); (to make less dark) aclarar; saltar por encima de; (to prove the innocence of) absolver; sacar (una ganancia neta); abonar, acreditar; liquidar (una cuenta); (in the customhouse) despachar; salvar (un obstáculo); levantar (la mesa); desmontar (un terreno); **to clear the way** abrir camino ‖ intr clarificarse; aclararse; **to clear away** irse, desaparecer; **to clear up** abonanzarse (el tiempo); despejarse (el cielo, el tiempo)

clearance ['klɪrəns] s aclaración; abono, acreditación; espacio libre; (in a cylinder) espacio muerto; (com) compensación

clearance sale s venta de liquidación

clearing ['klɪrɪη] s (in a woods) claro; (com) compensación

clearing house s cámara de compensación

clear-sighted ['klɪr'saɪtɪd] adj clarividente, perspicaz

clear'sto'ry s (pl **-ries**) var of **clerestory**

cleat [klit] s abrazadera, listón m

cleavage ['klivɪdʒ] s división, hendidura; (fig) desunión

cleave [kliv] v (pret & pp **cleft** [klɛft] o **cleaved**) tr rajar, partir; hender (las aguas un buque, los aires una flecha) ‖ intr adherirse, pegarse; apegarse, ser fiel

cleaver ['klivər] s cortante m, cuchilla de carnicero

clef [klɛf] s (mus) clave f

cleft palate [klɛft] s fisura del paladar

clematis ['klɛmətɪs] s clemátide f

clemen·cy ['klɛmənsi] s (pl **-cies**) clemencia; (of the weather) benignidad

clement ['klɛmənt] adj clemente; (weather) benigno

clench [klɛntʃ] s agarro ‖ tr agarrar; apretar, cerrar (el puño, los dientes)

cleresto·ry ['klɪr,stori] s (pl **-ries**) claraboya

cler·gy ['klɛrdʒi] s (pl **-gies**) clerecía, clero

clergy·man ['klɛrdʒimən] s (pl **-men** [mən]) clérigo, pastor m

cleric ['klɛrɪk] s clérigo

clerical ['klɛrɪkəl] adj (of clergy) clerical; (of office work) oficinesco ‖ s clérigo, eclesiástico; (supporter of power of clergy) clerical m; **clericals** (coll) hábitos clericales

clerical error s error m de pluma

clerical work s trabajo de oficina

clerk [klʌrk] s (in a store) dependiente mf; (in an office) oficinista mf; (in a city hall) archivero; (in a church) lego, seglar m; (in law office, in court) escribano

clever ['klɛvər] adj hábil, diestro, mañoso; inteligente

cleverness ['klɛvərnɪs] s habilidad, destreza, maña; inteligencia

clew [klu] s indicio, pista

cliché [kli'ʃe] s (printing plate) clisé m; (trite expression) cliché m

click [klɪk] s golpecito; (of typewriter) tecleo; (of firearm) piñoneo; (of heels) taconeo; (of tongue) claqueo, chasquido ‖ tr hacer sonar con un golpecito seco; chascar (la lengua); **to click the heels** taconear; cuadrarse (un soldado) ‖ intr sonar con un golpecito seco; piñonear (el gatillo de un arma de fuego); claquear (la lengua)

client ['klaɪ·ənt] s cliente mf; cliente de abogado

clientele [,klaɪ·ən'tɛl] s clientela

cliff [klɪf] s acantilado, escarpa, risco

climate ['klaɪmɪt] s clima m

climax ['klaɪmæks] s colmo; orgasmo; **to cap the climax** ser el colmo

climb [klaɪm] s subida, trepa ‖ tr & intr escalar, subir, trepar

climber ['klaɪmər] s trepador m; ambicioso de figurar; (bot) enredadera, trepadora

clinch [klɪntʃ] s agarro, abrazo; (of a nail) remache m ‖ tr afianzar, sujetar; agarrar, abrazar; apretar (el puño); remachar (un clavo ya clavado); resolver decisivamente

cling [klɪη] v (pret & pp **clung** [klʌη]) intr adherirse, pegarse; **to cling to** agarrarse a, asirse de

cling'stone' peach s albérchigo, peladillo

clinic ['klɪnɪk] s clínica

clinical ['klɪnɪkəl] adj clínico

clinical chart s hoja clínica

clinician [klɪ'nɪʃən] s clínico

clink [klɪηk] s tintín m ‖ tr hacer tintinear; chocar (vasos, copas) ‖ intr tintinear

clinker ['klɪηkər] s escoria de hulla

clip [klɪp] s tijereteo, esquileo; grapa, pinza; (to fasten papers) sujetapapeles m, presilla de alambre; **at a good clip** a buen paso ‖ v (pret & pp **clipped;** ger **clipping**) tr tijeretear, esquilar; (to fasten with a clip) afianzar, sujetar; recortar (p.ej., un cupón) ‖ intr moverse con rapidez

clipper ['klɪpər] s tijera, cizalla; **clippers** maquinilla cortapelos; tijeras podadoras

clipping ['klɪpɪη] s tijereteo, esquileo; (from a newspaper) recorte m

clique [klik] s pandilla, corrillo ‖ intr — **to clique together** apandillarse

cliquish ['klikɪʃ] adj exclusivista

clk. abbr **clerk, clock**

cloak [klok] s capote m; (disguise, excuse) capa ‖ tr encapotar; disimular, encubrir

cloak-and-dagger ['klokən'dægər] adj de capa y espada (dícese de duelos, espionaje, etc.)

cloak-and-sword ['klokən'sord] adj de capa y espada (dícese, p.ej., de las costumbres caballerescas)

cloak hanger s cuelgacapas m

cloak'room' s guardarropa m; (Brit) excusado

clock [klak] *s* reloj *m* (de pared o de mesa); (*in a stocking*) cuadrado ‖ *tr* registrar; (*sport*) cronometrar

clock′mak′er *s* relojero

clock tower *s* torre *f* reloj

clock′wise′ *adj & adv* en el sentido de las agujas del reloj

clock′work′ *s* mecanismo de relojería; **like clockwork** como un reloj

clod [klad] *s* terrón *m*

clod′hop′per *s* destripaterrones *m*, quebrantaterrones *m*; **clodhoppers** zapatos fuertes de trabajo

clog [klag] *s* estorbo, obstáculo; (*wooden shoe*) zueco; (*dance*) zapateado; (*hobble on animal*) traba ‖ *v* (*pret & pp* **clogged;** *ger* **clogging**) *tr* atascar ‖ *intr* atascarse; bailar el zapateado

clog dance *s* zapateado

cloister [′klɔɪstər] *s* claustro ‖ *tr* enclaustrar

cloistral [′klɔɪstrəl] *adj* claustral

close [klos] *adj* cercano, próximo; casi igual; (*translation*) fiel, exacto; (*fabric*) compacto; (*weather, atmosphere*) pesado, sofocante; (*stingy*) tacaño; (*battle, race, election*) reñido; (*friend*) íntimo; (*shut in, enclosed*) cerrado; (*narrow*) estrecho ‖ *adv* cerca; **close to** cerca de ‖ [kloz] *s* fin *m*, terminación; (*of business, of stock market*) cierre *m*; **at the close of day** a la caída de la tarde; **to bring to a close** poner término a; **to come to a close** tocar a su fin ‖ *tr* cerrar; (*to cover*) tapar; (*to finish*) concluir; saldar (*una cuenta*); cerrar (*un trato*); **to close in** cerrar, encerrar; **to close ranks** cerrar las filas ‖ *intr* cerrar, cerrarse; **to close in on** cerrar con (*el enemigo*)

close call [klos] *s* (coll) escape *m* por un pelo

closed car [klozd] *s* coche cerrado, conducción interior

closed chapter *s* asunto concluído

closed season *s* veda

closed shop *s* taller agremiado

closefisted [′klos′fɪstɪd] *adj* cicatero, tacaño, manicorto

close-fitting [′klos′fɪtɪŋ] *adj* ajustado, ceñido al cuerpo

close-lipped [′klos′lɪpt] *adj* callado, reservado

closely [′klosli] *adv* de cerca; estrechamente; fielmente; atentamente

close quarters [klos] *spl* lugar muy estrecho, lugares estrechos

close shave [klos] *s* afeitado a ras; (coll) escape *m* por un pelo

closet [′klazɪt] *s* (*wall*) alacena, closet *m*; (*wardrobe*) armario; (*small private room*) aposento, gabinete *m*; (*for keeping clothing*) guardarropa *m*; (*toilet*) retrete *m* ‖ *tr* — **to be closeted with** encerrarse con

close-up [′klos,ʌp] *s* (*moving picture*) vista de cerca; fotografía de cerca

closing [′klozɪŋ] *s* cerradura, cierre *m*

closing prices *spl* precios de cierre

closing time *s* hora de cierre

clot [klat] *s* grumo, coágulo ‖ *v* (*pret & pp* **clotted;** *ger* **clotting**) *intr* engrumecerse, coagularse

cloth [klɔθ] o [klɑθ] *s* paño, tela; ropa clerical; (*canvas, sails*) lona, trapo, vela; (*for binding books*) tela; **the cloth** la clerecía

clothe [kloð] *v* (*pret & pp* **clothed** o **clad** [klæd]) *tr* trajear, vestir; cubrir; (*e.g., with authority*) investir

clothes [kloz] o [kloðz] *spl* ropa, vestidos; ropa de cama

clothes′bas′ket *s* cesto de la ropa, cesto de la colada

clothes′brush′ *s* cepillo de ropa

clothes closet *s* ropero

clothes dryer *s* secadora de ropa, secarropa

clothes hanger *s* colgador *m*, perchero

clothes′horse′ *s* enjugador *m*, secarropa de travesaños

clothes′line′ *s* cordel *m* para tender la ropa, tendedera

clothes′pin′ *s* pinza, alfiler *m* de madera

clothes tree *s* percha

clothes wringer *s* exprimidor *m* de ropa

clothier [′kloojər] *s* (*person who sells ready-made clothes*) ropero; (*dealer in cloth*) pañero

clothing [′kloðɪŋ] *s* ropa, vestidos, ropaje *m*

cloud [klaud] *s* nube *f* ‖ *tr* anublar ‖ *intr* — **to cloud over** anublarse

cloud bank *s* mar *m* de nubes

cloud′burst′ *s* aguacero, chaparrón *m*

cloud-capped [′klaud,kæpt] *adj* coronado de nubes

cloudless [′klaudlɪs] *adj* despejado, sin nubes

cloud of dust *s* polvareda, nube *f* de polvo

cloud•y [′klaudi] *adj* (*comp* **-ier;** *super* **-iest**) nuboso, nublado; (*muddy, turbid*) turbio; confuso, obscuro; melancólico, sombrío

clove [klov] *s* (*flower*) clavo de especia; (*spice*) clavo

clover [′klovər] *s* trébol *m*; **to be in clover** vivir en el lujo

clo′ver•leaf′ *s* (*pl* **-leaves** [,livz]) *s* cruce *m* en trébol

clove tree *s* clavero

clown [klaun] *s* bufón *m*, payaso; (*rustic*) patán *m* ‖ *intr* hacer el payaso

clownish [′klaunɪʃ] *adj* bufonesco; rústico

cloy [klɔɪ] *tr* hastiar, empalagar

club [klʌb] *s* porra, clava; (*playing card*) basto, trébol *m*; club *m*, casino ‖ *v* (*pret & pp* **clubbed;** *ger* **clubbing**) *tr* aporrear ‖ *intr* — **to club together** unirse; formar club

club car *s* coche *m* club, coche bar

club′house′ *s* casino, club *m*

club•man [′klʌbmən] *s* (*pl* **-men** [mən]) clubista *m*

club•woman [′klʌb,wumən] *s* (*pl* **-women** [,wimin]) clubista *f*

cluck [klʌk] *s* cloqueo, clo clo ‖ *intr* cloquear, hacer clo clo

clue [klu] *s* indicio, pista

clump [klʌmp] *s* (*of earth*) terrón *m*; (*of trees or shrubs*) grupo; pisada fuerte ‖ *intr* — **to clump along** andar pesadamente

clum·sy ['klʌmzi] *adj* (*comp* **-sier;** *super* **-siest**) (*worker*) chapucero, desmañado, torpe; (*work*) chapucero, tosco, grosero

cluster ['klʌstər] *s* grupo; (*of grapes or other things growing or joined together*) racimo ‖ *intr* arracimarse; **to cluster around** reunirse en torno a; **to cluster together** agruparse

clutch [klʌtʃ] *s* (*grasp, grip*) agarro, apretón *m* fuerte; (aut) embrague *m;* (aut) pedal *m* de embrague; **to fall into the clutches of** caer en las garras de; **to throw the clutch in** embragar; **to throw the clutch out** desembragar ‖ *tr* agarrar, empuñar

clutter ['klʌtər] *s* — **to clutter up** cubrir o llenar desordenadamente

cm. *abbr* **centimeter**

cml. *abbr* **commercial**

Co. *abbr* **Company, County**

coach [kotʃ] *s* coche *m,* diligencia; (aut) coche cerrado; (rr) coche de viajeros, coche ordinario *m;* (sport) entrenador *m* ‖ *tr* aleccionar; (sport) entrenar ‖ *intr* entrenarse

coach house *s* cochera

coaching ['kotʃɪŋ] *s* lecciones *fpl* particulares; (sport) entrenamiento

coach·man ['kotʃmən] *s* (*pl* **-men** [mən]) *s* cochero

coagulate [ko'ægjə,let] *tr* coagular ‖ *intr* coagularse

coal [kol] *s* carbón *m,* hulla ‖ *tr* proveer de carbón ‖ *intr* proveerse de carbón

coal'bin' *s* carbonera

coal bunker *s* carbonera

coal car *s* vagón carbonero

coal'deal'er *s* carbonero

coaling ['kolɪŋ] *adj* carbonero ‖ *s* toma de carbón

coalition [,ko·ə'lɪʃən] *s* unión; (*alliance between states or factions*) coalición

coal mine *s* mina de carbón

coal oil *s* aceite *m* mineral

coal scuttle *s* cubo para carbón

coal tar *s* alquitrán *m* de hulla

coal'yard' *s* carbonería

coarse [kors] *adj* (*of inferior quality*) basto, burdo; (*composed of large particles*) grueso; (*crude in manners*) grosero, rudo, vulgar

coarseness ['korsnɪs] *s* bastedad

coast [kost] *s* costa; **the coast is clear** ya no hay peligro ‖ *tr* costear ‖ *intr* deslizarse cuesta abajo; **to coast along** avanzar sin esfuerzo

coastal ['kostəl] *adj* costero

coaster ['kostər] *s* salvamanteles *m*

coaster brake *s* freno de contrapedal

coast guard *s* guardacostas *mpl;* guardia *m* de los guardacostas

coast guard cutter *s* escampavía de los guardacostas

coasting trade *s* cabotaje *m*

coast'land' *s* litoral *m*

coast'line' *s* línea de la costa

coast'wise' *adj* costanero ‖ *adv* a lo largo de la costa

coat [kot] *s* (*jacket*) americana, saco; (*top-coat*) abrigo, sobretodo; (*of an animal*) lana, pelo; (*of paint*) capa, mano *f* ‖ *tr* cubrir, revestir; dar una capa de pintura a

coated ['kotɪd] *adj* revestido; (*tongue*) saburroso

coat hanger *s* colgador *m*

coating ['kotɪŋ] *s* revestimiento; (*of paint*) capa; (*of plaster*) enlucido

coat of arms *s* escudo de armas

coat'room' *s* guardarropa *m*

coat'tail' *s* faldón *m*

coax [koks] *tr* engatusar

cob [kab] *s* zuro; **to eat corn on the cob** comer maíz en la mazorca

cobalt ['kobɔlt] *s* cobalto

cobbler ['kablər] *s* remendón *m,* zapatero de viejo

cob'ble·stone' *s* guijarro

cob'web' *s* telaraña

cocaine [ko'ken] *s* cocaína; (slang) coca

cock [kak] *s* (*rooster*) gallo; (*faucet, valve*) espita, grifo; (*of firearm*) martillo; (*weathervane*) veleta; caudillo, jefe *m* ‖ *tr* amartillar (*un arma de fuego*); ladear (*la cabeza*); enderezar, levantar

cockade [[ka'ked] *s* cucarda, escarapela

cock-a-doodle-doo ['kakə,dudəl'du] *s* quiquiriquí *m*

cock-and-bull story ['kakənd'bul] *s* cuento absurdo, cuento increíble

cocked hat [kakt] *s* sombrero de candil, sombrero de tres picos; **to knock into a cocked hat** (slang) apabullar

cockeyed ['kak,aɪd] *adj* bisojo, bizco; (coll) encorvado, torcido; (slang) disparatado, extravagante

cock'fight' *s* pelea de gallos

cockney ['kakni] *s* londinense *mf* de la clase pobre que habla un dialecto característico; dialecto de la clase pobre de Londres

cock of the walk *s* quiquiriquí *m,* gallito del lugar

cock'pit' *s* gallera; (aer) carlinga

cock'roach' *s* cucaracha

cockscomb ['kaks,kom] *s* cresta de gallo; gorro de bufón; (bot) cresta de gallo, moco de pavo

cock'sure' *adj* muy seguro de sí mismo

cock'tail' *s* coctel *m;* (*of fruit, oysters, etc.*) aperitivo

cocktail party *s* coctel *m*

cocktail shaker ['ʃekər] *s* coctelera

cock·y ['kaki] *adj* (*comp* **-ier;** *super* **-iest**) (coll) arrogante, hinchado; **to be cocky** (coll) tener mucho gallo

cocoa ['koko] *s* cacao; (*drink*) chocolate *m*

cocoanut o **coconut** ['kokə,nʌt] *s* coco

cocoanut palm o **tree** *s* cocotero

cocoon [kə'kun] *s* capullo

C.O.D., c.o.d. *abbr* **collect on delivery;** (Brit) **cash on delivery**

cod [kad] *s* abadejo, bacalao

coddle ['kadəl] *tr* consentir, mimar

code [kod] *s* (*of laws; of manners; of signals*) código; (*of telegraphy*) alfabeto; (*secret system of writing*) cifra, clave *f;* (com)

cifrario; **in code** en cifra ‖ *tr* (*to put in code*) cifrar
code word *s* clave telegráfica
codex ['kodɛks] *s* (*pl* **codices** ['kodɪ,siz] o ['kadɪ,siz]) *s* códice *m*
cod'fish' *s* abadejo, bacalao
codger ['kadʒər] *s* — **old codger** (coll) anciano, tío
codicil ['kadɪsɪl] *s* codicilo; apéndice *m*
codi•fy ['kadɪ,faɪ] o ['kodɪ,faɪ] *v* (*pret & pp* **-fied**) *tr* codificar
cod'-liv'er oil *s* aceite *m* de hígado de bacalao
coed o **co-ed** ['ko,ɛd] *s* alumna de una escuela coeducativa
coeducation [,ko,ɛdʒə'keʃən] *s* coeducación
coefficient [,ko•ɪ'fɪʃənt] *adj & s* coeficiente *m*
coerce [ko'ʌrs] *tr* forzar, coactar
coercion [ko'ʌrʃən] *s* compulsión, coacción
coeval [ko'ivəl] *adj & s* coetáneo
coexist [,ko•ɪg'zɪst] *intr* coexistir
coexistence [,ko•ɪg'zɪstəns] *s* coexistencia
coffee ['kɔfɪ] o ['kafɪ] *s* café *m;* (*plant*) cafeto; **black coffee** café solo; **to drink coffee** cafetear
coffee bean *s* grano de café
cof'fee•cake' *s* rosquilla (que se come con el café)
coffee dealer *s* cafetalero
coffee grinder *s* molinillo de café
coffee grounds *spl* poso del café
coffee mill *s* molinillo de café
coffee plantation *s* cafetal *m*
coffee planter *s* cafetalero
coffee pot *s* cafetera
coffee tree *s* cafeto
coffer ['kɔfər] o ['kafər] *s* arca, cofre *m;* **coffers** tesoro, fondos
cof'fer•dam' *s* ataguía, encajonado
coffin ['kɔfɪn] o ['kafɪn] *s* ataúd *m*
C. of S. *abbr* **Chief of Staff**
cog [kag] *s* diente *m* (*de rueda dentada*); rueda dentada; **to slip a cog** equivocarse
cogency ['kodʒənsi] *s* fuerza (*de un argumento*)
cogent ['kodʒənt] *adj* fuerte, convincente
cogitate ['kadʒɪ,tet] *tr & intr* cogitar, meditar
cognac ['kanjæk] *s* coñac *m*
cognizance ['kagnɪzəns] o ['kanɪzəns] *s* conocimiento; **to take cognizance of** enterarse de
cognizant ['kagnɪzənt] o ['kanɪzənt] *adj* sabedor, enterado
cog'wheel' *s* rueda dentada
cohabit [ko'hæbɪt] *intr* cohabitar
coheir [ko'ɛr] *s* coheredero
cohere [ko'hɪr] *intr* adherirse, pegarse; conformarse, corresponder
coherent [ko'hɪrənt] *adj* coherente
cohesion [ko'hiʒən] *s* cohesión
coiffeur [kwa'fʌr] *s* peluquero
coiffure [kwa'fjʊr] *s* peinado, tocado
coil [kɔɪl] *s* (*something wound in a spiral*) rollo; (*single turn of spiral*) vuelta; (*of a still*) serpentín *m;* (*of hair*) rizo; (*of a spring*) espiral *f;* (elec) carrete *m* ‖ *tr*

arrollar, enrollar; (naut) adujar ‖ *intr* arrollarse, enrollarse; (*like a snake*) serpentear
coil spring *s* resorte *m* espiral
coin [kɔɪn] *s* moneda; (*wedge*) cuña; **to pay back in one's own coin** pagar en la misma moneda; **to toss a coin** echar a cara o cruz ‖ *tr* acuñar; forjar, inventar (*palabras o frases*); **to coin money** (coll) ganar mucho dinero
coincide [,ko•ɪn'saɪd] *intr* coincidir
coincidence [ko'ɪnsɪdəns] *s* coincidencia
coition [ko'ɪʃən] o **coitus** ['ko•ɪtəs] *s* coito
coke [kok] *s* coque *m,* cok *m*
col. *abbr* **colored, colony, column**
colander ['kʌləndər] o ['kaləndər] *s* colador *m,* escurridor *m*
cold [kold] *adj* frío; **to be cold** (*said of a person*) tener frío; (*said of the weather*) hacer frío ‖ *s* frío; (*indisposition*) resfriado; **to catch cold** resfriarse, coger un resfriado
cold blood *s* — **in cold blood** a sangre fría
cold chisel *s* cortafrío
cold comfort *s* poca consolación
cold cream *s* colcrén *m*
cold cuts *spl* fiambres *mpl*
cold feet *spl* (coll) desánimo, miedo
cold'heart'ed *adj* duro, insensible
cold meat *s* carne *f* fiambre
coldness ['koldnɪs] *s* frialdad
cold shoulder *s* — **to turn a cold shoulder on** (coll) tratar con suma frialdad
cold snap *s* corto rato de frío agudo
cold storage *s* conservación en cámara frigorífica
cold war *s* guerra fría
coleslaw ['kol,slɔ] *s* ensalada de col
colic ['kalɪk] *adj & s* cólico
coliseum [,kalɪ'si•əm] *s* coliseo
colitis [ko'laɪtɪs] *s* colitis *f*
coll. *abbr* **colleague, collection, college, colloquial**
collaborate [kə'læbə,ret] *intr* colaborar
collaborationist [kə,læbə'reʃənɪst] *s* colaboracionista *mf*
collaborator [kə'læbə,retər] *s* colaborador *m*
collapse [kə'læps] *s* desplome *m;* (*in business*) fracaso; (pathol) colapso ‖ *intr* desplomarse; fracasar; postrarse, sufrir colapso
collapsible [kə'læpsɪbəl] *adj* abatible, plegable, desmontable
collar ['kalər] *s* cuello; (*of dog, horse*) collar *m;* (mach) collar
col'lar•band' *s* tirilla de camisa
col'lar•bone' *s* clavícula
collate [kə'let] o ['kalet] *tr* colacionar, cotejar
collateral [kə'lætərəl] *adj* colateral ‖ *s* (*relative*) colateral *mf;* (com) colateral *m*
collation [kə'leʃən] *s* (*act of comparing; light meal*) colación
colleague ['kalig] *s* colega *mf;* homólogo
collect ['kalɛkt] *s* (eccl) colecta ‖ [kə'lɛkt] *tr* acumular, reunir; colectar, recaudar (*impuestos*); coleccionar (*sellos de correo, antiguallas*); recolectar (*cosechas*); cobrar (*pasajes*); recoger (*billetes; el correo*); **to**

collect oneself reponerse ‖ *intr* acumularse; **collect on delivery** contra reembolso, cobro contra entrega

collect call *s* llamada por cobrar

collected [kə'lɛktɪd] *adj* sosegado, dueño de sí mismo

collection [kə'lɛkʃən] *s* colección; (*of taxes*) recaudación; (*of mail*) recogida

collection agency *s* agencia de cobros de cuentas

collective [kə'lɛktɪv] *adj* colectivo

collector [kə'lɛktər] *s* (*of stamps, antiques*) coleccionista *mf*; (*of taxes*) recaudador *m*; (*of tickets*) cobrador *m*

college [kə'lɪdʒ] *s* colegio universitario; (*of cardinals, electors, etc.*) colegio

collide [kə'laɪd] *intr* chocar; **to collide with** chocar con

collie [kə'lɪ] *s* perro pastoril escocés

collier [kə'ljər] *s* barco carbonero; minero de carbón

collier•y [kə'ljəri] *s* (*pl* **-ies**) mina de carbón

collision [kə'lɪʒən] *s* colisión

colloid [kə'lɔɪd] *adj* & *s* coloide *m*

colloquial [kə'lokwɪ•əl] *adj* coloquial, familiar

colloquialism [kə'lokwɪ•ə,lɪzəm] *s* coloquialismo

collo•quy [kə'ləkwi] *s* (*pl* **-quies**) coloquio

collusion [kə'luʒən] *s* colusión, confabulación; **to be in collusion with** estar en inteligencia con

cologne [kə'lon] *s* agua de colonia, colonia ‖ **Cologne** *s* Colonia

colon [ˈkolən] *s* (anat) colon *m*; (gram) dos puntos

colonel [ˈkʌrnəl] *s* coronel *m*

colonel•cy [ˈkʌrnəlsi] *s* (*pl* **-cies**) coronelía

colonial [kə'lonɪ•əl] *adj* colonial ‖ *s* colono

colonize [ˈkalə,naɪz] *tr* & *intr* colonizar

colonnade [,kalə'ned] *s* columnata

colo•ny [ˈkaləni] *s* (*pl* **-nies**) colonia

colophon [ˈkalə,fan] *s* colofón *m*

color [ˈkalər] *s* color; **the colors** los colores, la bandera; **to call to the colors** llamar a filas; **to give** o **to lend color to** dar visos de probabilidad a; **under color of** so color de, bajo pretexto de; **with flying colors** con banderas desplegadas ‖ *tr* colorar, colorear; (*to excuse, palliate*) colorear; (*to dye*) teñir ‖ *intr* sonrojarse, ponerse colorado, demudarse

col'or-blind' *adj* ciego para los colores

colored [ˈkalərd] *adj* de color; (*specious*) colorado

colorful [ˈkalərfəl] *adj* colorido; pintoresco

coloring [ˈkalərɪŋ] *adj* & *s* colorante *m*

colorless [ˈkalərlɪs] *adj* incoloro; (fig) insulso

color photography *s* fotografía en colores

color salute *s* (mil) saludo con la bandera

color sergeant *s* sargento abanderado

color screen *s* (phot) pantalla de color

color television *s* televisión en colores

colossal [kə'lasəl] *adj* colosal

colossus [kə'lasəs] *s* coloso

colt [kolt] *s* potro

Columbus [kə'lʌmbəs] *s* Colón *m*

Columbus Day *s* día *m* de la raza, fiesta de la hispanidad

column [ˈkaləm] *s* columna

columnist [ˈkaləmɪst] *s* columnista *mf*

com. *abbr* comedy, commerce, common

Com. *abbr* **Commander, Commissioner, Committee**

coma [ˈkomə] *s* (pathol) coma *m*

comb [kom] *s* peine *m*; (*currycomb*) almohaza; (*of rooster*) cresta; **cresta de ola** ‖ *tr* peinar; explorar con minuciosidad

com•bat [ˈkambæt] *s* combate *m* ‖ [ˈkambæt] o [kəm'bæt] *v* (*pret* & *pp* **-bated** o **-batted;** *ger* **-bating** o **-batting**) *tr* & *intr* combatir

combatant [ˈkambətənt] *adj* & *s* combatiente *m*

combat duty *s* servicio de frente

combination [,kambɪ'neʃən] *s* combinación

combine [ˈkambaɪn] *s* monopolio; segadora trilladora; (coll) combinación ‖ [kəm'baɪn] *tr* combinar ‖ *intr* combinarse

combining form *s* (gram) elemento de compuestos

combustible [kəm'bʌstɪbəl] *adj* combustible; (fig) ardiente, impetuoso ‖ *s* combustible *m*

combustion [kəm'bʌstʃən] *s* combustión

combustion chamber *s* cámara de combustión

come [kʌm] *v* (*pret* **came** [kem]; *pp* **come**) *intr* venir; **to come about** suceder; **to come across** encontrarse con; **to come after** venir detrás de; venir después de; venir por, venir en busca de; **to come again** volver; **to come apart** desunirse, desprenderse; **to come around** restablecerse; volver en sí; rendirse; ponerse de acuerdo; cambiar de dirección; **to come at** alcanzar; **to come back** volver; rehabilitarse; **to come before** anteponerse; **to come between** interponerse; desunir, separar; **to come by** conseguir; lograr obtener; **to come down** bajar; (*in social position, etc.*) descender; (*from one person to another*) ser transmitido; **to come downstairs** bajar (*de un piso a otro*); **to come down with** enfermarse de; **to come for** venir por, venir en busca de; **to come forth** salir; aparecer; **to come forward** avanzar; presentarse; **to come from** venir de; provenir de; **to come in** entrar; entrar en; empezar; ponerse en uso; **to come in for** conseguir, recibir; **to come into one's own** ser reconocido; **to come off** desprenderse; acontecer; **to come out** salir; salir a luz; ponerse de largo (*una joven*); divulgarse (*una noticia*); **to come out for** anunciar su apoyo de; **to come out with** descolgarse con; **to come over** dejarse persuadir; pasar, p.ej., **what's come over him?** ¿qué le ha pasado?; **to come through** salir bien, tener éxito; ganar; **to come to** volver en sí; **to come together** juntarse, reunirse; **to come true** hacerse realidad; **to come up** subir; presentarse; **to come upstairs** subir (*de un piso a otro*); **to come up to** acercarse a;

subir a; estar a la altura de; **to come up with** proponer

come′back′ s rehabilitación; (slang) respuesta aguda; **to stage a comeback** rehabilitarse

comedian [kə'midɪ•ən] s cómico, comediante m; autor m de comedias

comedienne [kə,midɪ'ɛn] s cómica, comedianta

come′down′ s humillación, revés m

come•dy ['kɑmədi] s (pl -dies) comedia cómica; (comicalness) comicidad

come•ly ['kʌmli] adj (comp -lier; super -liest) (attractive) donairoso, gracioso; (decorous) conveniente, decente

comet ['kɑmɪt] s cometa m

comfort ['kʌmfərt] s comodidad, confort m; (encouragement, consolation) confortación; (person) confortador m; (bed cover) colcha, cobertor m ‖ tr confortar

comfortable ['kʌmfərtəbəl] adj cómodo, confortable; (fairly well off) holgado; (salary) (coll) suficiente ‖ s colcha, cobertor m

comforter ['kʌmfərtər] s confortador m, consolador m; colcha, cobertor m; bufanda de lana

comforting ['kʌmfərtɪŋ] adj confortante

comfort station s quiosco de necesidad

comfrey ['kʌmfri] s consuelda

comic ['kɑmɪk] adj cómico ‖ s cómico; periódico cómico; **comics** tiras cómicas

comical ['kɑmɪkəl] adj cómico

comic book s tebeo

comic opera s ópera cómica

comic strip s tira cómica

coming ['kʌmɪŋ] adj que viene, venidero; prometedor ‖ s venida

coming out s (of stocks, bonds, etc.) emisión; (of a young girl) puesta de largo, entrada en sociedad

comma ['kɑmə] s coma

command [kə'mænd] s (commanding) dominio, mando; (order, direction) mandato, orden f; (e.g., of a foreign language) dominio; (mil) comando; **to be in command of** estar al mando de; **to take command** tomar el mando ‖ tr mandar, ordenar; dominar (un idioma extranjero); merecer (p.ej., respeto); (mil) comandar ‖ intr mandar

commandant [,kɑmən'dænt] o [,kɑmən-'dɑnt] s comandante m

commandeer [,kɑmən'dɪr] tr reclutar forzosamente; expropiar; (coll) apoderarse de

commander [kə'mændər] s comandante m; (of a military order) comendador m

commandment [,kə'mændmənt] s (Bib) mandamiento

commemorate [kə'mɛmə,ret] tr conmemorar

commence [kə'mɛns] tr & intr comenzar, empezar

commencement [kə'mɛnsmənt] s comienzo, principio; día m de graduación; ceremonia de graduación

commend [kə'mɛnd] tr (to entrust) encargar, encomendar; (to recommend) recomendar; (to praise) alabar, elogiar

commendable [kə'mɛndəbəl] adj recomendable

commendation [,kɑmən'deʃən] s encargo, encomienda; recomendación; alabanza, elogio

comment ['kɑmɛnt] s comentario, comento ‖ intr comentar; **to comment on** comentar

commentar•y ['kɑmən,tɛri] s (pl -ies) comentario

commentator ['kɑmən,tetər] s comentarista mf

commerce ['kɑmərs] s comercio

commercial [kə'mʌrʃəl] adj comercial ‖ s anuncio publicitario radiofónico o televisivo; (rad & telv) programa publicitario

commercial traveler s agente viajero

commiserate [kə'mɪzə,ret] intr — **to commiserate with** condolerse de

commiseration [kə,mɪzə'reʃən] s conmiseración

commissar [,kɑmɪ'sɑr] s comisario (en Rusia)

commissar•y ['kɑmɪ,sɛri] s (pl -ies) (deputy) comisario; (store) economato

commission [kə'mɪʃən] s comisión; (mil) nombramiento; **to put in commission** poner en uso; poner (un buque) en servicio activo; **to put out of commission** inutilizar, descomponer; retirar (un buque) del servicio activo ‖ tr comisionar; poner en uso; poner (un buque) en servicio activo; (mil) nombrar

commissioned officer s oficial m

commissioner [kə'mɪʃənər] s comisario; (person authorized by a commission) comisionado

com•mit [kə'mɪt] v (pret & pp -mitted; ger -mitting) tr cometer (un crimen, una falta; un negocio a una persona); (to hand over) confiar, entregar; dar, empeñar (la palabra); (to bind, pledge) comprometer; internar (a un demente); (to memory) encomendar; **to commit oneself** comprometerse, empeñarse; **to commit to writing** poner por escrito

commitment [kə'mɪtmənt] s (act of committing) comisión; (to an asylum) internación; (written, order) auto de prisión; compromiso, cometido, empeño

committee [kə'mɪti] s comité m, comisión

commode [kə'mod] s (chest of drawers) cómoda; (washstand) lavabo; (chamber pot) sillico

commodious [kə'modɪ•əs] adj espacioso, holgado

commodi•ty [kə'mɑdɪti] s (pl -ties) artículo de consumo, mercancía

commodity exchange s lonja, bolsa mercantil

common ['kɑmən] adj común ‖ s campo común, ejido; **commons** estado llano; (of a school) refectorio; **the Commons** (Brit) los Comunes

common carrier s empresa de transportes públicos

commoner ['kɑmənər] s plebeyo; (Brit) miembro de la Cámara de los Comunes

common law *s* derecho consuetudinario

com'mon-law' **marriage** *s* matrimonio consensual

com'mon•place' *adj* común, trivial, ordinario ‖ *s* lugar *m* común, trivialidad

common sense *s* sentido común

com'mon-sense' *adj* cuerdo, razonable

common stock *s* acción ordinaria; acciones ordinarias

commonweal ['kɑmən,wil] *s* bien público

com'mon•wealth' *s* estado, nación; república; (*state of U.S.A.*) estado; (*self-governing associated country*) estado libre asociado; (*association of states*) mancomunidad

commotion [kə'moʃən] *s* conmoción

commune [kə'mjun] *intr* conversar; (eccl) comulgar

communicant [kə'mjunɪkənt] *s* comunicante *mf;* (eccl) comulgante *mf*

communicate [kə'mjunɪ,ket] *tr* comunicar ‖ *intr* comunicarse

communicating [kə'mjunɪ,ketɪŋ] *adj* comunicador

communication [kə,mjunə'keʃən] *s* comunicación

communications satellite *s* satélite *m* de comunicaciones

communicative [kə'mjunɪ,ketɪv] *adj* comunicativo

communion [kə'mjunjən] *s* comunión; **to take communion** comulgar

communion rail *s* comulgatorio

communiqué [kə,mjunɪ'ke] o [kə'mjunɪ,ke] *s* comunicado, parte *m*

communism ['kɑmjə,nɪzəm] *s* comunismo

communist ['kɑmjənɪst] *s* comunista *mf*

communi•ty [kə'mjunɪti] *s* (*pl* **-ties**) vecindario; (*group of people living together*) comunidad

communize ['kɑmjə,naɪz] *tr* comunizar

commutation ticket [,kɑmjə'teʃən] *s* billete *m* de abono

commutator ['kɑmjə,tetər] *s* (elec) colector *m*

commute [kə'mjut] *tr* conmutar ‖ *intr* viajar con billete de abono

commuter [kə'mjutər] *s* abonado al ferrocarril

comp. *abbr* **compare, comparative, composer, composition, compound**

compact [kəm'pækt] *adj* compacto; breve, preciso ‖ ['kɑmpækt] *s* convenio, pacto; estuche *m* de afeites

compact disk *s* disco compacto

companion [kəm'pænjən] *s* compañero

companionable [kəm'pænjənəbəl] *adj* afable, sociable, simpático

companionship [kəm'pænjən,ʃɪp] *s* compañerismo

companionway [kəm'pænjən,we] *s* (naut) escalera de cámara

compa•ny ['kʌmpəni] *s* (*pl* **-nies**) compañía; visita, visitas, invitado, invitados; (naut) tripulación; **to be good company** ser compañero alegre; **to keep company** ir juntos (*un hombre y una mujer*); **to keep some-**

one company hacerle compañía a una persona; **to part company** separarse; enemistarse

company building *s* edificio social

company office *s* domicilio social

comparative [kəm'pærətɪv] *adj* & *s* comparativo

compare [kəm'pɛr] *s* — **beyond compare** sin comparación, sin par ‖ *tr* comparar

comparison [kəm'pærɪsən] *s* comparación

compartment [kəm'pɑrtmənt] *s* compartimiento; (rr) departamento

compass ['kʌmpəs] *s* brújula, compás *m;* ámbito, recinto; alcance *m*, extensión; **compass** o **compasses** (*for drawing circles*) compás *m*

compass card *s* (naut) rosa náutica, rosa de los vientos

compassion [kəm'pæʃən] *s* compasión

compassionate [kəm'pæʃənɪt] *adj* compasivo

com•pel [kəm'pɛl] *v* (*pret & pp* **-pelled;** *ger* **-pelling**) *tr* forzar, obligar, compeler; imponer (*respeto, silencio*)

compendious [kəm'pɛndɪ•əs] *adj* compendioso

compendi•um [kəm'pɛndɪ•əm] *s* (*pl* **-ums** o **-a** [ə]) compendio

compensate ['kɑmpən,set] *tr* & *intr* compensar; **to compensate for** compensar

compensation [,kɑmpən'seʃən] *s* compensación

compete [kəm'pit] *intr* competir

competence ['kɑmpɪtəns] o **competency** ['kɑmpɪtənsi] *s* (*aptitude; legal capacity*) competencia; (*sufficient means to live comfortably*) buen pasar *m*

competent ['kɑmpɪtənt] *adj* competente

competition [,kɑmpɪ'tɪʃən] *s* (*rivalry*) competencia; (*in a match, examination, etc.*) certamen *m*, concurso; (*in business*) concurrencia

competitive [kəm'pɛtɪtɪv] *adj* — **to be competitive** poder competir

competitive examination *s* oposición

competitiveness [kəm'pɛtɪtɪvnɪs] *s* capacidad competiva

competitive prices *spl* precios de competencia

competitor [kəm'pɛtɪtər] *s* competidor *m*

compilation [,kɑmpɪ'leʃən] *s* compilación, recopilación

compile [kəm'paɪl] *tr* compilar, recopilar

complacence [kəm'plesəns] o **complacency** [kəm'plesənsi] *s* (*quiet satisfaction*) complacencia; satisfacción de sí mismo

complacent [kəm'plesənt] *adj* (*willing to please*) complaciente; satisfecho de sí mismo

complain [kəm'plen] *intr* quejarse

complainant [kəm'plenənt] *s* (law) demandante *mf*

complaint [kəm'plent] *s* queja; reclamo; (*grievance*) agravio; (*illness*) enfermedad, mal *m;* (law) demanda, querella

complaisance [kəm'plezəns] o ['kɑmplɪ,zæns] *s* amabilidad, cortesía

complaisant [kəm'plezənt] o ['kɑmplɪ,zænt] *adj* amable, cortés

CO
CO

complement ['kɑmplɪmənt] *s* complemento; (nav) dotación ‖ *tr* complementar

complete [kəm'plit] *adj* completo ‖ *tr* completar, terminar, realizar

completion [kəm'pliʃən] *s* terminación, realización

complex [kəm'plɛks] o ['kɑmplɛks] *adj* (*not simple*) complexo; (*composite*) complejo; (*intricate*) complicado ‖ ['kɑmplɛks] *s* complejo; (psychol) complejo; (coll) obsesión

complexion [kəm'plɛkʃən] *s* (*constitution*) complexión; (*texture of skin, esp. of face*) tez *f;* aspecto general, índole *f*

compliance [kəm'plaɪ•əns] *s* condescendencia; sumisión, rendimiento; **in compliance with** de acuerdo con, en conformidad con

complicate ['kɑmplɪ,ket] *tr* complicar

complicated ['kɑmplɪ,ketɪd] *adj* complicado

complication ['kɑmplɪ,keʃən] *s* complicación

complici•ty [kəm'plɪsɪti] *s* (*pl* -**ties**) complicidad, codelincuencia

compliment ['kɑmplɪmənt] *s* (*show of courtesy*) cumplimiento; (*praise*) alabanza, halago; perico (CAm); **compliments** saludos, recuerdos ‖ ['kɑmplɪ,mɛnt] *tr* cumplimentar; alabar, halagar

complimentary copy [,kɑmplɪ'mɛntəri] *s* ejemplar *m* de cortesía

complimentary ticket *s* billete *m* de regalo, pase *m* de cortesía

com•ply [kəm'plaɪ] *v* (*pret & pp* -**plied**) *intr* conformarse; **to comply with** conformarse con, obrar de acuerdo con

component [kəm'ponənt] *adj* componente ‖ *m* componente *m*

compose [kəm'poz] *tr* componer; **to be composed of** estar compuesto de

composed [kəm'pozd] *adj* sosegado, tranquilo

composer [kəm'pozer] *s* componedor *m;* (mus) compositor *m;* autor *m*

composing stick *s* componedor *m*

composite [kəm'pɑzɪt] *adj & s* compuesto

composition [,kɑmpə'zɪʃən] *s* composición

compositor [kəm'pɑzɪtər] *s* cajista *mf,* componedor *m*

composure [kəm'poʒər] *s* serenidad, sosiego

compote ['kɑmpot] *s* (*stewed fruit*) compota; (*dish*) compotera

compound ['kɑmpaʊnd] *adj* compuesto ‖ *s* compuesto; (gram) vocablo compuesto ‖ [kɑm'paʊnd] *tr* componer, combinar; (*interest*) capitalizar

comprehend [,kɑmprɪ'hɛnd] *tr* comprender

comprehensible [,kɑmprɪ'hɛnsɪbəl] *adj* comprensible

comprehension [,kɑmprɪ'hɛnʃən] *s* comprensión

comprehensive [,kɑmprɪ'hɛnsɪv] *adj* comprensivo, inclusivo, completo

compress ['kɑmprɛs] *s* (med) compresa, bilma ‖ [kəm'prɛs] *tr* comprimir

compression [kəm'prɛʃən] *s* compresión

comprise o **comprize** [kəm'praɪz] *tr* abarcar, comprender, incluir

compromise ['kɑmprə,maɪz] *s* (*adjustment*) componenda, transigencia, transacción; (*endangering*) comprometimiento ‖ *tr* (*by mutual concessions*) componer, transigir; (*to endanger*) comprometer, exponer ‖ *intr* transigir, avenirse

comptroller [kən'trolər] *s* contralor *m,* interventor *m*

compulsory [kəm'pʌlsəri] *adj* obligatorio

computable [kəm'pjutəbəl] *adj* calculable

computation [,kɑmpju'teʃən] *s* cálculo, cómputo

compute [kəm'pjut] *tr & intr* computar, calcular

computer [kəm'pjutər] *s* ordenador *m,* computador *m;* (*person*) computador *m,* calculador *m*

computer dating *s* citas computerizadas

computer science *s* informática

comrade ['kɑmræd] o ['kɑmrɪd] *s* camarada *m;* cumpa *m* (SAm)

con. *abbr* **conclusion, consolidated, contra**

con [kɑn] *s* (*opposite opinion*) contra *m;* (*slang*) engaño ‖ *v* (*pret & pp* **conned; *ger* conning**) *tr* leer con atención, aprender de memoria; (*slang*) engañar

concave ['kɑnkev] o [kɑn'kev] *adj* cóncavo

conceal [kən'sil] *tr* encubrir, ocultar

concealment [kən'silmənt] *s* encubrimiento, ocultación; (*place*) escondite *m*

concede [kən'sid] *tr* conceder

conceit [kən'sit] *s* (*vanity*) orgullo, engreimiento; (*witty expression*) concepto, dicho ingenioso

conceited [kən'sitɪd] *adj* orgulloso, engreído

conceivable [kən'sivəbəl] *adj* concebible

conceive [kən'siv] *tr & intr* concebir

concentrate ['kɑnsən,tret] *tr* concentrar ‖ *intr* concentrarse; **to concentrate on** o **upon** reconcentrarse en

concentric [kən'sɛntrɪk] *adj* concéntrico

concept ['kɑnsɛpt] *s* concepto

conception [kən'sɛpʃən] *s* concepción

concern [kən'sʌrn] *s* (*business establishment*) empresa, casa comercial, razón *f* social; (*worry*) inquietud, preocupación; (*relation, reference*) concernencia; (*matter*) asunto, negocio ‖ *tr* atañer, concernir; interesar; **as concerns** respecto de; **to whom it may concern** a quien pueda interesar, a quien corresponda

concerning [kən'sʌrnɪŋ] *prep* respecto de, tocante a

concert ['kɑnsərt] *s* concierto ‖ [kən'sʌrt] *tr & intr* concertar

con'cert•mas'ter *s* concertino

concer•to [kən'ʃɛrto] *s* (*pl* -**tos** o -**ti** [ti]) concierto

concession [kən'sɛʃən] *s* concesión

concessive [kən'sɛsɪv] *adj* concesivo

concierge [,kɑnsɪ'ʌrʒ] *s* conserje *m*

conciliate [kən'sɪlɪ,et] *tr* conciliar; **conciliarse** (*el respeto, la estima*)

conciliatory [kən'sɪlɪ•ə,tori] *adj* conciliador

concise [kən'saɪs] *adj* conciso

conclude [kən'klud] *tr & intr* concluir

concluding [kən'kludɪŋ] *adj* final

conclusion [kənˈkluʒən] s conclusión; (*of a letter*) despedida

conclusive [kənˈklusɪv] adj concluyente

concoct [kənˈkakt] tr confeccionar; (*a story*) forjar, inventar

concomitant [kənˈkamɪtənt] adj & s concomitante m

concord [ˈkaŋkɔrd] s concordia; (gram, mus) concordancia

concordance [kənˈkɔrdəns] s concordancia

concourse [ˈkaŋkors] s (*of people*) concurso; (*of streams*) confluencia; bulevar m, gran vía; (*of railroad station*) gran salón m

concrete [ˈkankrit] o [kanˈkrit] adj concreto; de hormigón ‖ s hormigón m

concrete block s bloque m de hormigón

concrete mixer s hormigonera, mezcladora de hormigón

concubine [ˈkaŋkjə,baɪn] s concubina

con·cur [kənˈkʌr] v (pret & pp **-curred;** ger **-curring**) intr concurrir

concurrence [kənˈkʌrəns] s (*happening together*) concurrencia; (*agreement*) acuerdo

concussion [kənˈkʌʃən] s concusión

condemn [kənˈdɛm] tr condenar

condemnation [,kandɛmˈneʃən] s condenación

condense [kənˈdɛns] tr condensar ‖ intr condensarse

condescend [,kandɪˈsɛnd] intr dignarse

condescending [,kandɪˈsɛndɪŋ] adj condescendiente con inferiores

condescension [,kandɪˈsɛnʃən] s dignación, aire m protector

condiment [ˈkandɪmənt] s condimento

condition [kənˈdɪʃən] s condición; **on condition that** a condición (de) que ‖ tr acondicionar

conditional [kənˈdɪʃənəl] adj condicional

conditioned reflex [kənˈdɪʃənd] s reflejo acondicionado

condole [kənˈdol] intr condolerse

condolence [kənˈdoləns] s condolencia

condominium [,kandəˈmɪni·əm] s condominio

condone [kənˈdon] tr condonar; (*legally*) despenalizar

condor [ˈkandər] s cóndor m

conduce [kənˈdjus] intr conducir

conducive [kənˈdjusɪv] adj conducente, contribuyente

conduct [ˈkandʌkt] s conducta ‖ [kənˈdʌkt] tr conducir; **to conduct oneself** conducirse, comportarse

conductor [kənˈdʌktər] s conductor m, guía mf; (elec & phys) conductor m, conductora f; (rr) revisor m; (*on trolley or bus*) cobrador m

conduit [ˈkandɪt] o [ˈkandu·ɪt] s canal f para alambres o cables

cone [kon] s cono; (*of pastry*) barquillo; (*of paper*) cucurucho

confectioner·y [kənˈfɛkʃə,nɛri] s (pl **-ies**) (*shop*) confitería; (*sweetmeats*) dulces mpl, confites mpl, confituras

confedera·cy [kənˈfɛdərəsi] s (pl **-cies**) confederación; (*for unlawful purpose*) conjuración

confederate [kənˈfɛdərɪt] s confederado; cómplice mf ‖ [kənˈfɛdə,ret] tr confederar ‖ intr confederarse

con·fer [kənˈfʌr] v (pret & pp **-ferred;** ger **-ferring**) tr conferir ‖ intr conferenciar, consultar

conference [ˈkanfərəns] s conferencia, coloquio

confess [kənˈfɛs] tr confesar ‖ intr confesar, confesarse

confession [kənˈfɛʃən] s confesión

confessional [kənˈfɛʃənəl] s confesonario

confession of faith s profesión de fe

confessor [kənˈfɛsər] s (*person who confesses*) confesante mf; (*Christian, esp. in spite of persecution; priest*) confesor m

confide [kənˈfaɪd] tr confiar ‖ intr confiar, confiarse; **to confide in** confiarse en

confidence [ˈkanfɪdəns] s confianza; (*secret*) confidencia; **in strictest confidence** bajo la mayor reserva

confident [ˈkanfɪdənt] adj seguro ‖ s confidente m, confidenta

confidential [,kanfɪˈdɛnʃəl] adj confidencial

confine [ˈkanfaɪn] s confín m; **the confines** los confines ‖ [kənˈfaɪn] tr (*to keep within limits*) limitar, restringir; (*to keep shut in*) encerrar; **to be confined** estar de parto; **to be confined to bed** tener que guardar cama

confinement [kənˈfaɪnmənt] s limitación; encierro; parto, sobreparto

confirm [kənˈfʌrm] tr confirmar

confirmed [kənˈfʌrmd] adj confirmado; empedernido, inveterado

confiscate [ˈkanfɪs,ket] tr confiscar

conflagration [,kanfləˈgreʃən] s conflagración

conflict [ˈkanflɪkt] s conflicto; (*of interests, class hours, etc.*) incompatibilidad ‖ [kənˈflɪkt] intr chocar, desavenirse

conflicting [kənˈflɪktɪŋ] adj contradictorio; (*events, appointments, class hours, etc.*) incompatible, conflictivo

confluence [ˈkanflu·əns] s confluencia

conform [kənˈfɔrm] intr conformar, conformarse

conformance [kənˈfɔrməns] s conformidad

conformi·ty [kənˈfɔrmɪti] s (pl **-ties**) conformidad

confound [kanˈfaund] tr confundir ‖ [ˈkanˈfaund] tr maldecir; **confound it!** ¡maldito sea!

confounded [kanˈfaundɪd] adj confundido; aborrecible; maldito

confrere [ˈkanfrɛr] s colega m

confront [kənˈfrʌnt] tr (*to face boldly*) confrontarse con, hacer frente a; (*to meet face to face*) encontrar cara a cara; (*to bring face to face; to compare*) confrontar

confrontation [,kanfrʌnˈteʃən] s enfrentamiento

confuse [kənˈfjuz] tr confundir

confusedness [kənˈfjuzɪdnɪs] s desorientación

confusion [kən'fjuʒən] s confusión
confute [kən'fjut] tr confutar
Cong. abbr Congregation, Congressional
congeal [kən'dʒil] tr congelar ‖ intr congelarse
congenial [kən'dʒinjəl] adj simpático; agradable; compatible; (having the same nature)
congenial
congenital [kən'dʒɛnɪtəl] adj congénito
conger eel ['kaŋgər] s congrio
congest [kən'dʒɛst] tr congestionar ‖ intr
congestionarse
congestion [kən'dʒɛstʃən] s congestión
congratulate [kən'grætʃə,let] tr congratular,
felicitar
congratulation [kən,grætʃə'leʃən] s congratulación, felicitación
congregate ['kaŋgrɪ,get] intr congregarse
congregation [,kaŋgrɪ'geʃən] s congregación; feligresía, fieles mf (de una iglesia)
congress ['kaŋgrɪs] s congreso
congress•man ['kaŋgrɪsmən] s (pl -men
[mən]) congresista m
conical ['kanɪkəl] adj cónico
conj. abbr conjugation, conjunction
conjecture [kən'dʒɛktʃər] s conjetura ‖ tr &
intr conjeturar
conjugal ['kandʒəgəl] adj conyugal
conjugate ['kandʒə,get] tr conjugar
conjugation [,kandʒə'geʃən] s conjugación
conjunction [kən'dʒʌŋkʃən] s conjunción
conjuration [,kandʒə'reʃən] s (superstitious
invocation) conjuro; (magic spell) hechizo
conjure [kən'dʒʊr] tr (to appeal to solemnly)
conjurar ‖ ['kʌndʒər] o ['kandʒər] tr (to
exorcise, drive away) conjurar; to conjure
away conjurar; to conjure up evocar;
crear, suscitar (dificultades)
con man [kan] s (coll) embaucador m, embaucadora
connect [kə'nɛkt] tr conectar; asociar, relacionar ‖ intr enlazarse; asociarse, relacionarse; empalmar, enlazar (dos trenes)
connecting flight s vuelo de enlace
connecting rod s biela
connection [kə'nɛkʃən] s conexión; (relative)
pariente mf; (of trains) combinación, enlace m, empalme m; (in subway) correspondencia; in connection with con respecto a; juntamente con
connective tissue [kə'nɛktɪv] s (anat) tejido
conjuntivo
conning tower ['kanɪŋ] s torreta de mando
conniption [kə'nɪpʃən] s pataleta, berrinche
m
connive [kə'naɪv] intr confabularse, estar en
connivencia
conquer ['kaŋkər] tr vencer; (by force of
arms) conquistar ‖ intr triunfar
conqueror ['kaŋkərər] s conquistador m,
vencedor m
conquest ['kaŋkwɛst] s conquista
conscience ['kanʃəns] s conciencia; in all
conscience en conciencia
conscientious [,kanʃɪ'ɛnʃəs] adj concienzudo
conscientious objector [əb'dʒɛktər] s obje-
tante m de conciencia

conscious ['kanʃəs] adj (aware of one's own
existence) consciente; (deliberate) intencional; (self-conscious) encogido, tímido;
to become conscious volver en sí
consciousness ['kanʃəsnɪs] s conciencia, conocimiento
consciousness raising s concienciación
conscript ['kanskrɪpt] s conscripto, quinto ‖
[kən'skrɪpt] tr reclutar
conscription [kən'skrɪpʃən] s conscripción,
quinta
consecrate ['kansɪ,kret] tr consagrar
consecutive [kən'sɛkjətɪv] adj (successive)
consecutivo; (continuous) consecuente
consensus [kən'sɛnsəs] s consenso; the consensus of opinion la opinión general
consent [kən'sɛnt] s consentimiento; by
common consent de común acuerdo ‖ intr
consentir; to consent to consentir en
consequence ['kansɪ,kwɛns] s consecuencia;
aires mpl de importancia
consequential [,kansɪ'kwɛnʃəl] adj consiguiente; importante; altivo, pomposo
consequently ['kansɪ,kwɛntli] adv por consiguiente
conservation [,kansər'veʃən] s conservación
conservatism [kən'sʌrvə,tɪzəm] s conser-
vadurismo
conservative [kən'sʌrvətɪv] adj (preservative) conservativo; (disposed to maintain
existing views and institutions) conservador; cauteloso, moderado ‖ s preservativo;
conservador m
conservato•ry [kən'sʌrvə,tori] s (pl -ries)
(school of music) conservatorio; (greenhouse) invernadero
consider [kən'sɪdər] tr considerar
considerable [kən'sɪdərəbəl] adj considerable
considerate [kən'sɪdərɪt] adj considerado
consideration [kən,sɪdə'reʃən] s consideración; for a consideration por un precio; in
consideration of en consideración de; en
cambio de; on no consideration bajo
ningún concepto; out of consideration for
por respeto a; without due consideration
sin reflexión
considering [kən'sɪdərɪŋ] adv (coll) teniendo
en cuenta las circunstancias ‖ prep en vista
de, en razón de ‖ conj en vista de que
consign [kən'saɪn] tr consignar
consignee [,kansaɪ'ni] s consignatario
consignment [kən'saɪnmənt] s consignación
consist [kən'sɪst] intr — to consist in consistir en; to consist of consistir en, constar
de
consisten•cy [kən'sɪstənsi] s (pl -cies)
(firmness, amount of firmness) consistencia; (logical connection) consecuencia
consistent [kən'sɪstənt] adj (holding firmly
together) consistente; (agreeing with itself
or oneself) consecuente; consistent with
(in accord with) compatible con
consisto•ry [kən'sɪstəri] s (pl -ries) consistorio
consolation [,kansə'leʃən] s consolación,
consuelo

console ['kansol] *s* consola; mesa de consola ‖ [kən'sol] *tr* consolar

consommé [,kansə'me] *s* consumado, consommé *m*

consonant ['kansənənt] *adj & s* consonante *f*

consort ['kansɔrt] *s* consorte *mf;* embarcación que acompaña a otra ‖ [kən'sɔrt] *tr* asociar ‖ *intr* asociarse; armonizar, concordar

consorti•um [kən'sɔrʃɪ•əm] *s* (*pl* -a [ə]) consorcio

conspicuous [kən'spɪkju•əs] *adj* manifiesto, claro, evidente; llamativo, vistoso, sugestivo; conspicuo, notable

conspira•cy [kən'spɪrəsi] *s* (*pl* -cies) conspiración, conjuración

conspire [kən'spaɪr] *intr* conspirar, conjurar

constable ['kanstəbəl] o ['kʌnstəbəl] *s* policía *m*, guardia *m*, alguacil *m*

constancy ['kanstənsi] *s* constancia; fidelidad

constant ['kanstənt] *adj* constante; incesante; fiel ‖ *s* constante *f*

constellation [,kanstə'leʃən] *s* constelación

constipate ['kanstɪ,pet] *tr* estreñir

constipation [,kanstɪ'peʃən] *s* estreñimiento, estiquez *f*

constituen•cy [kən'stɪtʃu•ənsi] *s* (*pl* -cies) votantes *mpl;* clientela; comitentes *mpl;* distrito electoral

constituent [kən'stɪtʃu•ənt] *adj* constitutivo, componente; (*having power to create or revise a constitution*) constituyente ‖ *s* constitutivo, componente *m;* (*person who appoints another to act for him*) comitente *m*

constitute ['kanstɪ,tjut] *tr* constituir

constitution [,kanstɪ'tjuʃən] *s* constitución

constrain [kən'stren] *tr* constreñir; detener, encerrar; restringir

construct [kən'strʌkt] *tr* construir

construction [kən'strʌkʃən] *s* construcción; interpretación

construe [kən'stru] *tr* interpretar; deducir, inferir; traducir; (*to combine syntactically*) construir; (*to explain the syntax of*) analizar

consul ['kansəl] *s* cónsul *m*

consular ['kansələr] *adj* consular

consulate ['kansəlɪt] *s* consulado

consulship ['kansəl,ʃɪp] *s* consulado

consult [kən'sʌlt] *tr & intr* consultar

consultant [kən'sʌltənt] *s* consultor *m*

consultation [,kansəl'teʃən] *s* (*consulting*) consulta; (*meeting*) consulta, consultación

consume [kən'sum] o [kən'sjum] *tr* consumir; (*to absorb the interest of*) preocupar; ‖ *intr* consumirse

consumer [kən'sumər] *s* consumidor *m;* (*of gas, electricity, etc.*) abonado

consumer credit *s* crédito consuntivo

consumer goods *spl* bienes *mpl* de consumo

consumerism [kən'sumə,rɪzəm] *s* consumerismo

consummate [kən'sʌmɪt] *adj* consumado ‖ ['kansə,met] *tr* consumar

consumption [kən'sʌmpʃən] *s* consunción, consumo; (*pathol*) consunción, tisis *f*

consumptive [kən'sʌmptɪv] *adj* consuntivo; (*path*) tísico ‖ *s* tísico

cont. *abbr* **contents, continental, continued**

contact ['kantækt] *s* contacto; (*elec*) contacto; (*elec*) toma de corriente ‖ *tr* (*coll*) ponerse en contacto con ‖ *intr* contactar

contact breaker *s* (*elec*) ruptor *m*

contact lens *s* lente *m* de contacto, lente invisible, lentilla

contagion [kən'tedʒən] *s* contagio

contagious [kən'tedʒəs] *adj* contagioso

contain [kən'ten] *tr* contener; **to contain oneself** contenerse, refrenarse

container [kən'tenər] *s* continente *m*, recipiente *m*, vaso, caja, envase *m*, contenedor *m*

containment [kən'tenmənt] *s* contención, refrenamiento

contaminate [kən'tæmɪ,net] *tr* contaminar

contamination [kən,tæmɪ'neʃən] *s* contaminación

contd. *abbr* **continued**

contemplate ['kantəm,plet] *tr & intr* contemplar; pensar, proyectar

contemplation [,kantəm'pleʃən] *s* contemplación; intención, propósito

contemporaneous [kən,tɛmpə'reni•əs] *adj* contemporáneo

contemporar•y [kən'tɛmpə,rɛri] *adj* contemporáneo, coetáneo ‖ *s* (*pl* -ies) contemporáneo, coetáneo

contempt [kən'tɛmpt] *s* desprecio; (*law*) contumacia

contemptible [kən'tɛmptɪbəl] *adj* despreciable

contemptuous [kən'tɛmptʃu•əs] *adj* despreciativo, desdeñoso

contend [kən'tɛnd] *tr* sostener, mantener ‖ *intr* contender

contender [kən'tɛndər] *s* contendiente *mf,* concurrente *mf*

content [kən'tɛnt] *adj & s* contento ‖ ['kantɛnt] *s* contenido; **contents** contenido ‖ [kən'tɛnt] *tr* contentar

contented [kən'tɛntɪd] *adj* contento, satisfecho

contentedness [kən'tɛntɪdnɪs] *s* contentamiento, satisfacción

contention [kən'tɛnʃən] *s* (*strife; dispute*) contención; (*point argued for*) argumento

contentious [kən'tɛnʃəs] *adj* contencioso

contentment [kən'tɛntmənt] *s* contentamiento, contento

contest ['kantɛst] *s* (*struggle, fight*) contienda; (*competition*) competencia, concurso ‖ [kən'tɛst] *tr* disputar; tratar de conseguir ‖ *intr* contender

contestant [kən'tɛstənt] *s* contendiente *mf*

context ['kantɛkst] *s* contexto

contiguous [kən'tɪgju•əs] *adj* contiguo

continence ['kantɪnəns] *s* continencia

continent ['kantɪnənt] *adj & s* continente *m;* **the Continent** la Europa continental

continental [,kantɪ'nɛntəl] *adj* continental ‖ **Continental** *s* habitante *mf* del continente europeo

contingen•cy [kən'tɪndʒənsi] *s* (*pl* **-cies**) contingencia

contingent [kən'tɪndʒənt] *adj* & *s* contingente *m*

continual [kən'tɪnju•əl] *adj* continuo

continue [kən'tɪnju] *tr* & *intr* continuar; **to be continued** continuará

continui•ty [,kɑntɪ'nju•ɪti] o [,kɑntɪ'nu•ɪti] *s* (*pl* **-ties**) continuidad; (mov, rad, telv) guión *m;* (rad, telv) comentarios o anuncios entre las partes de un programa

continuous [kən'tɪnju•əs] *adj* continuo

continuous showing *s* (mov) sesión continua

continuous waves *spl* (rad) ondas entretenidas

contortion [kən'tɔrʃən] *s* contorsión

contour ['kɑntʊr] *s* contorno

contr. *abbr* **contracted, contraction**

contraband ['kɑntrə,bænd] *adj* contrabandista ‖ *s* contrabando

contrabass ['kɑntrə,bes] *s* contrabajo

contraceptive [,kɑntrə'sɛptɪv] *adj* & *s* anticonceptivo, contraceptivo

contract ['kɑntrækt] *s* contrato; **on a contract (to kill)** a sueldo ‖ ['kɑntrækt] o [kən'trækt] *tr* contraer (*p.ej., matrimonio* ‖ *intr* (*to shrink*) contraerse; (*to enter into an agreement*) comprometerse; **to contract for** contratar

contraction [kən'trækʃən] *s* contracción

contractor [kən'træktər] *s* contratista *mf*

contradict [,kɑntrə'dɪkt] *tr* contradecir

contradiction [,kɑntrə'dɪkʃən] *s* contradicción

contradictory [,kɑntrə'dɪktəri] *adj* (*involving contradiction*) contradictorio; (*inclined to contradict*) contradictor

contrail ['kɑn,trel] *s* (aer) estela de vapor, rastro de condensación

contral•to [kən'trælto] *s* (*pl* **-tos**) (*person*) contralto *mf;* (*voice*) contralto *m*

contraption [kən'træpʃən] *s* (coll) artilugio, dispositivo

contra•ry ['kɑntrɛri] *adv* contrariamente ‖ *adj* contrario ‖ [kən'trɛri] *adj* obstinado, terco ‖ ['kɑntrɛri] *s* (*pl* **-ries**) contrario; **on the contrary** al contrario

contrast ['kɑntræst] *s* contraste *m* ‖ [kən'træst] *tr* comparar; poner en contraste ‖ *intr* contrastar

contravene [,kɑntrə'vin] *tr* contradecir; contravenir a (*una ley*)

contribute [kən'trɪbjut] *tr* contribuir ‖ *intr* contribuir; (*to a newspaper, conference, etc.*) colaborar

contribution [,kɑntrɪ'bjuʃən] *s* contribución; (*to a newspaper, conference, etc.*) colaboración

contributor [kən'trɪbjutər] *s* contribuidor *m*, contribuyente *mf;* colaborador *m*

contrite [kən'traɪt] *adj* contrito

contrition [kən'trɪʃən] *s* contrición

contrivance [kən'traɪvəns] *s* aparato, dispositivo; idea, plan *m*, designio

contrive [kən'traɪv] *tr* (*to devise*) idear, inventar; (*to scheme up*) maquinar, tramar;

(*to bring about*) efectuar; **to contrive to** + *inf* ingeniarse a + *inf* ‖ *intr* maquinar

con•trol [kən'trol] *s* gobierno, mando; chequeo; (*of a scientific experiment*) contrarregistro, control *m;* **controls** mandos; **to get under control** conseguir dominar (*un incendio*) ‖ *v* (*pret* & *pp* **-trolled;** *ger* **-trolling**) *tr* gobernar, mandar; comprobar, controlar; **to control oneself** dominarse

controlling interest *s* (el) mayor porcentaje de acciones

control panel *s* (aer) tablero de instrumentos

control stick *s* (aer) mango de escoba, palanca de mando

controversial [,kɑntrə'vʌrʃəl] *adj* controvertible, disputable; disputador

controver•sy ['kɑntrə,vʌrsi] *s* (*pl* **-sies**) controversia, polémica

controvert ['kɑntrə,vʌrt] o [,kɑntrə'vʌrt] *tr* (*to argue against*) contradecir; (*to argue about*) controvertir

contumacious [,kɑntju'meʃəs] *adj* contumaz

contuma•cy ['kɑntjuməsi] *s* (*pl* **-cies**) contumacia

contume•ly ['kɑntjumɪli] *s* (*pl* **-lies**) contumelia

contusion [kən'tjuʒən] *s* contusión; magullón *m*

conundrum [kə'nʌndrəm] *s* acertijo, adivinanza; problema complicado

convalesce [,kɑnvə'lɛs] *intr* convalecer

convalescence [,kɑnvə'lɛsəns] *s* convalecencia

convalescent [,kɑnvə'lɛsənt] *adj* & *s* convaleciente *mf*

convalescent home *s* clínica de reposo

convene [kən'vin] *tr* convocar ‖ *intr* convenir, reunirse

convenience [kən'vinjəns] *s* comodidad, conveniencia; **at your earliest convenience** a la primera oportunidad que Vd. tenga

convenient [kən'vinjənt] *adj* cómodo, conveniente; próximo

convent ['kɑnvɛnt] *s* convento; convento de religiosas

convention [kən'vɛnʃən] *s* (*agreement*) convención, conveniencia; (*accepted usage*) costumbre *f*, conveniencia social, convención; (*meeting*) congreso, convención

conventional [kən'vɛnʃənəl] *adj* convencional

conventionali•ty [kən,vɛnʃə'nælɪti] *s* (*pl* **-ties**) precedente no convencional

converge [kən'vʌrʒ] *intr* convergir

conversant [kən'vʌrsənt] *adj* familiarizado, versado

conversation [,kɑnvər'seʃən] *s* conversación

conversational [,kɑnvər'seʃənəl] *adj* conversacional

converse ['kɑnvʌrs] *adj* & *s* contrario ‖ [kən'vʌrs] *intr* conversar

conversion [kən'vʌrʒən] *s* conversión; (*unlawful appropriation*) malversación

convert ['kɑnvʌrt] *s* convertido, converso ‖ [kən'vʌrt] *tr* convertir ‖ *intr* convertirse

convertible [kən'vʌrtɪbəl] *adj* convertible ‖ *s* (aut) convertible *m*, descapotable *m*

convex [ˈkɑnvɛks] o [kɑnˈvɛks] *adj* convexo
convey [kənˈve] *tr* llevar, transportar; comunicar, participar (*informes*); transferir, traspasar (*bienes de una persona a otra*)
conveyance [kənˈveəns] *s* transporte *m;* comunicación, participación; vehículo; (*transfer of property*) traspaso; escritura de traspaso
convict [ˈkɑnvɪkt] *s* reo convicto, presidiario ‖ [kənˈvɪkt] *tr* probar la culpabilidad de; declarar convicto (*a un acusado*)
conviction [kənˈvɪkʃən] *s* convencimiento; condena, fallo de culpabilidad
convince [kənˈvɪns] *tr* convencer
convincing [kənˈvɪnsɪŋ] *adj* convincente
convivial [kənˈvɪvɪ·əl] *adj* jovial
convocation [ˌkɑnvəˈkeʃən] *s* asamblea
convoke [kənˈvok] *tr* convocar
convoy [ˈkɑnvɔɪ] *s* convoy *m,* conserva ‖ *tr* convoyar
convulse [kənˈvʌls] *tr* convulsionar; agitar; **to convulse with laughter** mover a risas convulsivas
coo [ku] *intr* arrullar
cook [kʊk] *s* cocinero ‖ *tr* cocer, cocinar, guisar; **to cook up** (coll) falsificar; (coll) maquinar, tramar ‖ *intr* cocer, cocinar
cook'book' *s* libro de cocina
cookie [ˈkʊki] *s* var de **cooky**
cooking [ˈkʊkɪŋ] *s* cocina, arte *m* de cocinar
cook'stove' *s* cocina económica
cook·y [ˈkʊki] *s* (*pl* **-ies**) pasta seca, pastelito dulce
cool [kul] *adj* fresco; frío, indiferente ‖ *s* fresco ‖ *tr* refrescar; moderar ‖ *intr* refrescarse; moderarse; **to cool off** refrescarse; serenarse
cooler [ˈkulər] *s* heladera, refrigerador *m;* refrigerante *m;* cárcel *f*
cool'-head'ed *adj* sereno, tranquilo, juicioso
coolie [ˈkuli] *s* culí *m*
coolish [ˈkulɪʃ] *adj* fresquito
coolness [ˈkulnɪs] *s* fresco, frescura; (fig) frialdad
coon [kun] *s* mapache *m,* oso lavador
coop [kup] *s* gallinero; (*for fattening capons*) caponera; jaula, redil *m;* (*jail*) (slang) caponera; **to fly the coop** (slang) escabullirse ‖ *tr* encerrar en un gallinero; enjaular; **to coop up** emparedar
coöp. *abbr* **cooperative**
cooper [ˈkupər] *s* barrilero, tonelero
coöperate [koˈɑpə‚ret] *intr* cooperar
coöperation [koˌɑpəˈreʃən] *s* cooperación
coöperative [koˈɑpə‚retɪv] *adj* cooperativo
coöpt [koˈɑpt] *tr* cooptar
coördinate [koˈɔrdɪnɪt] *adj* coordenado; (gram) coordinante ‖ *s* (math) coordenada ‖ [koˈɔrdɪ‚net] *tr* & *intr* coordinar
cootie [ˈkuti] *s* (slang) piojo
cop [kɑp] *s* (slang) polizonte *m* ‖ *v* (*pret* & *pp* **copped;** *ger* **copping**) *tr* (slang) hurtar
copartner [koˈpɑrtnər] *s* consocio, copartícipe *mf*
cope [kop] *intr* — **to cope with** hacer frente a, enfrentarse con
cope'stone' *s* piedra de albardilla

copier [ˈkɑpɪ·ər] *s* (*person who copies*) copiante *mf,* copista *mf,* imitador *m;* (*apparatus*) copiador *m,* copiadora
copilot [ˈko‚paɪlət] *s* copiloto
coping [ˈkopɪŋ] *s* albardilla
copious [ˈkopɪ·əs] *adj* copioso
copper [ˈkɑpər] *adj* cobreño; (*in color*) cobrizo ‖ *s* cobre *m;* (*coin*) calderilla, vellón *m;* (slang) polizonte *m*
cop'per·head' *s* víbora de cabeza de cobre
cop'per·smith' *s* cobrero
coppery [ˈkɑpəri] *adj* cobreño; (*in color*) cobrizo
coppice [ˈkɑpɪs] o **copse** [kɑps] *s* soto, monte bajo
copulate [ˈkɑpjə‚let] *intr* copularse
cop·y [ˈkɑpi] *s* (*pl* **-ies**) copia; (*of a book*) ejemplar *m;* (*of a magazine*) número; (*document to be reproduced in print*) original *m,* manuscrito ‖ *v* (*pret* & *pp* **-ied**) *tr* copiar
cop'y·book' *s* cuaderno de escritura
copyist [ˈkɑpɪ·ɪst] *s* copiante *mf,* copista *mf;* imitador *m*
cop'y·right' *s* (derechos de) propiedad literaria ‖ *tr* registrar en el registro de la propiedad literaria
copy writer *s* escritor publicitario
co·quet [koˈkɛt] *v* (*pret* & *pp* **-quetted;** *ger* **-quetting**) *intr* coquetear; burlarse
coquet·ry [ˈkokətri] o [koˈkɛtri] *s* (*pl* **-ries**) coquetería; burla
coquette [koˈkɛt] *s* coqueta
coquettish [koˈkɛtɪʃ] *adj* coqueta
cor. *abbr* **corner, coroner, correction, corresponding**
coral [ˈkɑrəl] o [ˈkɔrəl] *adj* coralino ‖ *s* coral *m*
coral reef *s* arrecife *m* de coral
cord [kɔrd] *s* cordón *m;* piola ‖ *tr* acordonar
cordial [ˈkɔrdʒəl] *adj* cordial ‖ *s* licor tónico; (*medicine*) cordial *m*
cordiali·ty [kɔrˈdʒælɪti] *s* (*pl* **-ties**) cordialidad
corduroy [ˈkɔrdə‚rɔɪ] *s* pana; **corduroys** pantalones *mpl* de pana
core [kor] *s* corazón *m;* (*of an electromagnet*) núcleo
corespondent [ˌkorɪsˈpɑndənt] *s* cómplice *mf* del demandado en juicio de divorcio
Corinth [ˈkɔrɪnθ] *s* Corinto *f*
cork [kɔrk] *s* corcho; corcho, tapón *m* de corcho; tapón (*de cualquier materia*) ‖ *tr* encorchar, tapar con corcho
corking [ˈkɔrkɪŋ] *adj* (slang) brutal, extraordinario
cork oak *s* alcornoque *m*
cork'screw' *s* sacacorchos *m,* tirabuzón *m*
cormorant [ˈkɔrmərənt] *s* cormorán *m,* cuervo marino
corn [kɔrn] *s* (*in U.S.A.*) maíz *m;* (*in England*) trigo; (*in Scotland*) avena; grano (*de maíz, trigo*); (*on the foot*) callo; (coll) aguardiente *m;* (slang) trivialidad
corn bread *s* pan *m* de maíz
corn'cake' *s* tortilla de maíz
corn'cob' *s* mazorca de maíz, carozo

corncob pipe s pipa de fumar hecha de una mazorca de maíz
corn'crib' s granero para maíz
corn cure adj callicida m
cornea ['kɔrnɪ•ə] s córnea
corner ['kɔrnər] s ángulo; (esp. where two streets meet) esquina; (inside angle formed by two or more surfaces; secluded place; region, quarter) rincón m; (of eye) comisura, rabillo; (of lips) comisura; (awkward position) apuro, aprieto; monopolio; **around the corner** a la vuelta de la esquina; **to turn the corner** doblar la esquina; pasar el punto más peligroso ‖ tr arrinconar; monopolizar
corner cupboard s rinconera
corner room s habitación de esquina
cor'ner•stone' s piedra angular; (of a new building) primera piedra
cornet [kɔr'nɛt] s corneta
corn exchange s bolsa de granos
corn'field' s (in U.S.A.) maizal m; (in England) trigal m; (in Scotland) avenal m
corn flour s harina de maíz
corn'flow'er s cabezuela
corn'husk' s perfolla
cornice ['kɔrnɪs] s cornisa
Cornish ['kɔrnɪʃ] adj & s córnico
corn liquor s chicha
corn meal s harina de maíz
corn on the cob s maíz m en la mazorca
corn plaster s emplasto para los callos
corn silk s cabellos, barbas del maíz
corn'stalk' s tallo de maíz
corn'starch' s almidón m de maíz
cornucopia [,kɔrnə'kopɪ•ə] s cornucopia
Cornwall ['kɔrn,wɔl] s Cornualles
corn•y ['kɔrni] adj (comp -ier; super -iest) de maíz; (coll) gastado, trivial, pesado
corollar•y ['kɑrə,lɛri] o ['kɔrə,lɛri] s (pl -ies) corolario
coronation [,kɑrə'neʃən] o [,kɔrə'neʃən] s coronación
coroner ['kɑrənər] o ['kɔrənər] s juez m de guardia
coroner's inquest s pesquisa dirigida por el juez de guardia
coronet ['kɑrə,nɛt] o ['kɔrə,nɛt] s (worn by members of nobility) corona; (ornamental band of jewels worn on head) diadema f
Corp. abbr **Corporation**
corporal ['kɔrpərəl] adj corporal ‖ s (mil) cabo
corporation [,kɔrpə'reʃən] s (provincial, municipal, or service entity) corporación; sociedad anónima por acciones
corps [kɔr] s (pl **corps** [kɔrz]) cuerpo; (mil) cuerpo
corps de ballet [kɔr də bæ'lɛ] s cuerpo de baile
corpse [kɔrps] s cadáver m
corpulent ['kɔrpjələnt] adj corpulento
corpuscle ['kɔrpəsəl] s corpúsculo, partícula; (physiol) glóbulo
corr. abbr **correspondence, corresponding**
cor•ral [kə'ræl] s corral m ‖ v (pret & pp -ralled; ger -ralling) tr acorralar

correct [kə'rɛkt] adj correcto; (proper) cumplido ‖ tr corregir
correction [kə'rɛkʃən] s corrección
corrective [kə'rɛktɪv] adj & s correctivo
correctness [kə'rɛktnɪs] s corrección; cumplimiento, cumplido
correlate ['kɔrə,let] tr correlacionar ‖ intr correlacionarse
correlation [,kɔrə'leʃən] s correlación
correlative [kə'rɛlətɪv] adj & s correlativo
correspond [,kɑrɪ'spɑnd] o [,kɔrɪ'spɑnd] intr corresponder; (to communicate by writing) corresponderse
correspondence [,kɑrɪ'spɑndəns] o [,kɔrɪ'spɑndəns] s correspondencia
correspondence school s escuela por correspondencia
correspondent [,kɑrɪ'spɑndənt] o [,kɔrɪ'spɑndənt] adj correspondiente ‖ s correspondiente mf; (for a newspaper) corresponsal mf
corresponding [,kɑrɪ'spɑndɪŋ] o [,kɔrɪ'spɑndɪŋ] adj correspondiente
corridor ['kɑrɪdər] o ['kɔrɪdər] s corredor m, pasillo
corroborate [kə'rɑbə,ret] tr corroborar
corrode [kə'rod] tr corroer ‖ intr corroerse
corrosion [kə'roʒən] s corrosión
corrosive [kə'rosɪv] adj & s corrosivo
corrugated ['kɑrə,getɪd] o ['kɔrə,getɪd] adj acanalado, ondulado
corrupt [kə'rʌpt] adj corrompido ‖ tr corromper ‖ intr corromperse
corruption [kə'rʌpʃən] s corrupción
corsage [kɔr'sɑʒ] s (bodice) corpiño, jubón m; (bouquet) ramillete m que se lleva en el pecho o la cintura
corsair ['kɔr,sɛr] s corsario
corset ['kɔrsɪt] s corsé m
corset cover s cubrecorsé m
Corsica ['kɔrsɪkə] s Córcega
Corsican ['kɔrsɪkən] adj & s corso
cortege [kɔr'teʒ] s procesión; (retinue) cortejo, séquito
cor•tex ['kɔr,tɛks] s (pl **-tices** [tɪ,siz]) corteza; corteza cerebral
cortisone ['kɔrtɪ,son] s cortisona
corvette [kɔr'vɛt] s corbeta
cosmetic [kaz'mɛtɪk] adj & s cosmético
cosmic ['kazmɪk] adj cósmico
cosmonaut ['kazmə,nɔt] s cosmonauta mf
cosmopolitan [,kazmə'pɑlɪtən] adj & s cosmopolita mf
cosmos ['kazməs] s cosmos m; (bot) cosmos
Cossack ['ka,sæk] adj & s cosaco
cost [kɔst] o [kast] s coste m, costo; **at cost** a coste y costas; **at all costs** a toda costa; **costs** (law) costas ‖ v (pret & pp **cost**) intr costar; **cost what it may** cueste lo que cueste
cost accounting s escandallo
Costa Rican ['kastə 'rikən] o ['kaste 'rikən] adj & s costarricense mf, costarriqueño
cost'-ben'e•fit analysis s análisis costebeneficio
cost exemption s gratuidad

cost, insurance, and freight costo, seguro y flete

cost·ly [ˈkɔstli] o [ˈkɑstli] adj (comp **-lier;** super **-liest**) costoso, dispendioso; (lavish) pródigo; (magnificent) suntuoso

cost of living s costo de la vida, carestía de la vida

costume [ˈkɑstjum] s traje m; (garb worn on stage, at balls, etc.) disfraz m, traje de época

costume ball s baile m de trajes

costume jewelry s joyas de fantasía, bisutería

cot [kɑt] s catre m

coterie [ˈkotəri] s círculo, grupo; (clique) corrillo

cottage [ˈkɑtɪdʒ] s cabaña; casita de campo

cottage cheese s naterón m, requesón m

cotter pin [ˈkɑtər] s chaveta

cotton [ˈkɑtən] s algodón m ‖ intr — to cotton up to (coll) aficionarse a

cotton field s algodonal m

cotton gin s desmotadera de algodón

cotton picker [ˈpɪkər] s recogedor m de algodón; máquina para recolectar el algodón

cot·ton·seed' s semilla de algodón

cottonseed oil s aceite m de algodón

cotton waste s hilacha de algodón, estopa de algodón

cot·ton·wood' s chopo del Canadá, chopo de Virginia

cottony [ˈkɑtəni] adj algodonoso

couch [kaʊtʃ] s canapé m, sofá m ‖ tr expresar

cougar [ˈkugər] s puma m

cough [kɔf] o [kɑf] s tos f ‖ tr — to cough up arrojar por la boca; (slang) sudar, entregar ‖ intr toser; (artificially, to attract attention) destoserse

cough drop s pastilla para la tos

cough syrup s jarabe m para la tos

could [kʊd] v aux pude, podía; podría

council [ˈkaʊnsəl] s (deliberative or legislative assembly) consejo; (of a municipality) concejo; (eccl) concilio

council·man [ˈkaʊnsəlmən] s (pl **-men** [mən]) concejal m

councilor [ˈkaʊnsələr] s consejero

coun·sel [ˈkaʊnsəl] s consejo; (advisor) consejero; (consultant) consultor m; (lawyer) abogado consultor; **to keep one's own counsel** no revelar sus intenciones ‖ v (pret & pp **-seled** o **-selled**; ger **-seling** o **-selling**) tr aconsejar ‖ intr aconsejarse

counselor [ˈkaʊnsələr] s consejero; abogado

count [kaʊnt] s (act of counting) cuenta, recuento; (result of counting) suma, total m; (nobleman) conde m; (charge) (law) cargo; **to take the count** (box) dejarse contar diez ‖ tr contar; **to count off** separar contando; **to count out** no incluir; (sport) declarar vencido ‖ intr contar; (to be worth consideration) valer; **to count for** valer; **to count on** contar con

countable [ˈkaʊntəbəl] adj contable

count'-down' s cuenta a cero, cuenta atrás

countenance [ˈkaʊntɪnəns] s cara, rostro, semblante m; (composure) compostura, serenidad; **to keep one's countenance** contenerse; **to lose countenance** conturbarse; **to put out of countenance** avergonzar, confundir ‖ tr aprobar, apoyar, favorecer

counter [ˈkaʊntər] adj contrario ‖ adv en el sentido opuesto; **counter to** a contrapelo de ‖ s contador m; (piece of wood or metal for keeping score) ficha; (board in shop over which business is transacted) mostrador m; (box) contragolpe m ‖ tr oponerse a; contradecir ‖ intr (box) dar un contragolpe; **to counter with** replicar con

coun·ter·act' tr contrarrestar, contrariar

coun·ter·attack' s contraataque m ‖ coun'ter·attack' tr & intr contraatacar

coun·ter·bal'ance s contrabalanza, contrapeso ‖ coun'ter·bal'ance tr contrabalancear, contrapesar

coun·ter·clock'wise' adj & adv en el sentido contrario al de las agujas del reloj

coun'ter·cul'ture s contracultura

coun·ter·es'pionage s contraespionaje m

counterfeit [ˈkaʊntərfɪt] adj contrahecho, falsificado ‖ s contrahechura, falsificación; moneda falsa ‖ tr contrahacer, falsificar

counterfeiter [ˈkaʊntər,fɪtər] s contrahacedor m, falsificador m; monedero falso

counterfeit money s moneda falsa

countermand [ˈkaʊntər,mænd] o [ˈkaʊntər,-mɑnd] s contramandato ‖ tr contramandar; hacer volver

coun·ter·march' s contramarcha ‖ intr contramarchar

coun·ter·offen'sive s contraofensiva

coun'ter·pane' s cubrecama

coun'ter·part' s contraparte f; copia, duplicado

coun'ter·plot' s contratreta ‖ v (pret & pp **-plotted;** ger **-plotting**) tr complotar contra (la treta de otro u otros)

coun'ter·point' s contrapunto

Counter Reformation s Contrarreforma

coun·ter·rev'olu'tion s contrarrevolución

coun'ter·sign' s contraseña ‖ tr refrendar

coun'ter·sink' v (pret & pp **-sunk**) tr avellanar

coun'ter·spy' s (pl **-spies**) contraespía mf

coun'ter·stroke' s contragolpe m

coun'ter·weight' s contrapeso

countess [ˈkaʊntɪs] s condesa

countless [ˈkaʊntlɪs] adj incontable, innumerable

countrified [ˈkʌntri,faɪd] adj campesino, rústico

coun·try [ˈkʌntri] s (pl **-tries**) (territory of a nation) país m; (land of one's birth) patria; (not the city) campo

country club s club m campestre

country cousin s isidro

country estate s heredad, hacienda de campo

coun'try·folk' _s_ gente _f_ del campo, campesinos

country gentleman _s_ propietario acomodado de finca rural

country house _s_ casa de campo, quinta

country jake [dʒek] _s_ (coll) patán _m_

country life _s_ vida rural

country·man [ˈkʌntrimən] _s_ (_pl_ **-men** [mən]) compatriota _m;_ campesino

country people _s_ gente _f_ del campo, gente de capa parda

coun'try·side' _s_ campiña

coun'try·wide' _adj_ nacional

country·woman [ˈkʌntrɪˌwumən] _s_ (_pl_ **-women** [ˌwɪmɪn]) compatriota _f;_ campesina

coun·ty [ˈkaʊnti] _s_ (_pl_ **-ties**) (_small political unit_) partido; (_domain of a count_) condado

county seat _s_ cabeza de partido

coup [ku] _s_ golpe _m_

coup de grâce [ku də ˈgrɑs] _s_ puñalada de misericordia, golpe _m_ de gracia

coup d'état [ku deˈtɑ] _s_ golpe _m_ de estado

coupé [kuˈpe] _s_ cupé _m_

couple [ˈkʌpəl] _s_ par _m;_ (_man and wife_) matrimonio; (_two people dancing together_) pareja; (elec, mech) par _m;_ (_two more or less_) (coll) par _m_ ‖ _tr_ acoplar, juntar, unir ‖ _intr_ juntarse, unirse

coupler [ˈkʌplər] _s_ (rr) enganche _m_

couplet [ˈkʌplɪt] _s_ copla, pareado

coupon [ˈkupɑn] o [ˈkjuˈpɑn] _s_ (_of a bond_) cupón _m;_ (_piece detached from larger piece_) talón _m_

courage [ˈkʌrɪdʒ] _s_ valor _m_, ánimo; firmeza, resolución; **to have the courage of one's convictions** ajustarse abiertamente con su conciencia; **to pluck up courage** hacer de tripas corazón

courageous [kəˈredʒəs] _adj_ valiente, animoso

courier [ˈkʌrɪər] o [ˈkʊrɪ·ər] _s_ estafeta, mensajero; guía _m_

course [kors] _s_ (_onward movement_) curso; (_of a ship_) derrota, rumbo; (_of time_) transcurso; (_of events_) marcha; (_in school_) asignatura, curso; (_of a meal_) plato; campo de golf; (mas) hilada; **in the course of** en el decurso de; **of course** por supuesto, naturalmente

court [kort] _s_ (_of justice_) tribunal _m;_ (_of a king_) corte _f;_ (_open space enclosed by a building_) atrio, patio; (_for tennis_) cancha, pista; **to pay court to** hacer la corte a ‖ _tr_ cortejar; buscar, solicitar

courteous [ˈkʌrtɪ·əs] _adj_ cortés

courtesan [ˈkʌrtɪzən] o [ˈkʊrtɪzən] _s_ cortesana

courte·sy [ˈkʌrtɪsi] _s_ (_pl_ **-sies**) cortesía

court'house' _s_ palacio de justicia

courtier [ˈkortɪ·ər] _s_ cortesano, palaciego

court jester _s_ bufón _m_

court·ly [ˈkortli] _adj_ (_comp_ **-lier;** _super_ **-liest**) cortés, cortesano; (_pertaining to the court_) cortesano

court'-mar'tial _s_ (_pl_ **courts-martial**) consejo de guerra ‖ _v_ (_pret & pp_ **-tialed** o

-tialled; _ger_ **-tialing** o **-tialling**) _tr_ someter a consejo de guerra

court plaster _s_ tafetán _m_ inglés

court'room' _s_ sala de justicia, tribunal _m_

courtship [ˈkortʃɪp] _s_ cortejo, galanteo; noviazgo

court'yard' _s_ atrio, patio

cousin [ˈkʌzɪn] _s_ primo

cove [kov] _s_ cala, ensenada

covenant [ˈkʌvənənt] _s_ convenio, pacto; contrato; (Bib) alianza ‖ _tr & intr_ pactar

cover [ˈkʌvər] _s_ cubierta; (_of a magazine_) portada; (_place for one person at table_) cubierto; (_for a bed_) cobertor _m;_ **to take cover** ocultarse; **under cover** bajo cubierto, bajo techado; oculto; disfrazado; **under cover of** (_e.g., the night_) a cubierto de; so capa de; **under separate cover** bajo cubierta separada, por separado ‖ _tr_ cubrir; (_to line, to coat_) recubrir, revestir; recorrer (_cierta distancia_); cubrirse (_la cabeza_); tapar (_una olla_) ‖ _intr_ cubrirse

coverage [ˈkʌvərɪdʒ] _s_ (_amount or space covered_) alcance _m;_ (_of news_) reportaje _m;_ (_funds to meet liabilities_) cobertura

coveralls [ˈkʌvərˌɔlz] _s_ mono

cover charge _s_ precio del cubierto

covered [ˈkʌvərd] _adj_ cubierto; (_wire_) forrado; (_bridge_) cubierto

covered wagon _s_ carromato

cover girl _s_ (coll) muchacha hermosa en la portada de una revista

covering [ˈkʌvərɪŋ] _s_ cubierta, envoltura

covert [ˈkʌvərt] _adj_ disimulado, secreto

cov'er·up' _s_ efugio, subterfugio

covet [ˈkʌvɪt] _tr_ codiciar

covetous [ˈkʌvɪtəs] _adj_ codicioso

covetousness [ˈkʌvɪtəsnɪs] _s_ codicia

covey [ˈkʌvi] _s_ (_brood_) nidada; (_in flight_) bandada; corro, grupo

cow [kaʊ] _s_ vaca ‖ _tr_ acobardar, intimidar

coward [ˈkaʊ·ərd] _s_ cobarde _mf_

cowardice [ˈkaʊ·ərdɪs] _s_ cobardía; llamada (Mex)

cowardly [ˈkaʊ·ərdli] _adj_ cobarde; correlón (Col, Mex); llamón (Mex) ‖ _adv_ cobardemente

cow'bell' _s_ cencerro

cow'boy' _s_ vaquero; gaucho (Arg)

cowcatcher [ˈkaʊˌkætʃər] _s_ quitapiedras _m_, rastrillo; trompa (Col, Chile)

cower [ˈkaʊ·ər] _intr_ agacharse

cow'herd' _s_ vaquero, pastor _m_ de ganado vacuno

cow'hide' _s_ cuero; (_whip_) zurriago ‖ _tr_ zurriagar

cowl [kaʊl] _s_ capucha, cogulla; (aer) cubierta del motor; (aut) cubretablero, bóveda

cow'lick' _s_ mechón _m_, remolino (_pelos que se levantan sobre la frente_)

cowpox [ˈkaʊˌpɑks] _s_ vacuna

coxcomb [ˈkɑksˌkom] _s_ petimetre _m_, mequetrefe _m_

coxswain [ˈkɑksən] o [ˈkɑkˌswen] _s_ timonel _m;_ contramaestre _m_

coy [kɔɪ] _adj_ recatado, modesto; coquetón

co•zy ['kozi] *adj* (*comp* **-zier;** *super* **-ziest**) cómodo ‖ *s* (*pl* **-zies**) cubretetera

cp. *abbr* **compare**

c.p. *abbr* **candle power**

C.P.A. *abbr* **certified public accountant**

cpd. *abbr* **compound**

cr. *abbr* **credit, creditor**

crab [kræb] *s* cangrejo; (*grouch*) cascarrabias *mf*

crab apple *s* manzana silvestre

crabbed ['kræbɪd] *adj* avinagrado, ceñudo

crab grass *s* garranchuelo

crab louse *s* ladilla

crack [kræk] *adj* (coll) de primera clase; (*shot*) (coll) certero ‖ *s* grieta, hendidura; (*noise*) crujido, estallido; (coll) instante *m*, momento; (*joke*) (slang) chiste *m;* **at the crack of dawn** al romper el alba ‖ *tr* agrietar, hender; chasquear (*un látigo*); abrir (*una caja fuerte*) por la fuerza; cascar (*nueces*); descifrar (*un código*); (slang) decir (*un chiste*); (slang) descubrir (*un secreto*); **to crack a smile** (slang) sonreír; **to crack up** (coll) alabar, elogiar ‖ *intr* agrietarse; crujir; cascarse (*la voz de una persona*); enloquecerse; ceder, someterse; **to crack up** fracasar; perder la salud; estrellarse (*un avión*)

cracked [krækt] *adj* agrietado; (*ice*) picado; (coll) mentecato, loco

cracker ['krækər] *s* galleta

crack'le•ware' *s* grietado

crack'pot' *adj & s* (slang) excéntrico, tarambana *mf*

crack'up' *s* fracaso; colisión; derrota; (aer) aterrizaje violento; (coll) colapso

cradle ['kredəl] *s* cuna; (*of handset*) horquilla ‖ *tr* acunar

cra'dle•song' *s* canción de cuna, arrullo

craft [kræft] *o* [krɑft] *s* arte *m*, arte manual; astucia, maña; nave *f* ‖ *spl* naves

craftiness ['kræftɪnɪs] *s* astucia

crafts•man ['kræftsmən] *s* (*pl* **-men** [mən]) artesano; artista *m*

craftsmanship ['kræftsmən, ʃɪp] *s* artesanía

craft•y ['kræfti] *o* ['krɑfti] *adj* (*comp* **-ier;** *super* **-iest**) astuto, mañoso

crag [kræg] *s* peñasco, despeñadero

cram [kræm] *v* (*pret & pp* **crammed;** *ger* **cramming**) *tr* atascar, atracar, embutir; (coll) aprender apresuradamente ‖ *intr* atracarse; (*to study hard*) (coll) empollar

cramp [kræmp] *s* (*metal bar*) grapa, laña; (*clamp*) abrazadera; (*painful contraction of muscle*) calambre *m;* **cramps** retortijón *m* de tripas ‖ *tr* engrapar, lañar; apretar; dar calambre *a*

cranber•ry ['kræn,beri] *s* (*pl* **-ries**) arándano agrio

crane [kren] *s* (*bird*) grulla; (*derrick*) grúa, guinche *m*, güinche *m* ‖ *tr* estirar (*el cuello*) ‖ *intr* estirar el cuello

crani•um ['kreni•əm] *s* (*pl* **-a** [ə]) cráneo

crank [kræŋk] *s* manivela, manubrio; (coll) estrafalario ‖ *tr* hacer girar (*el motor*) con la manivela

crank'case' *s* caja de cigüeñal, cárter *m* del cigüeñal

crank'shaft' *s* cigüeñal *m*

crank•y ['kræŋki] *adj* (*comp* **-ier;** *super* **-iest**) malhumorado; (*queer*) estrafalario

cran•ny ['kræni] *s* (*pl* **-nies**) hendidura, grieta, rendija

crape [krep] *s* crespón *m;* crespón fúnebre, crespón negro

crape'hang'er *s* (slang) aguafiestas *mf*

craps [kræps] *s* juego de dados; **to shoot craps** jugar a los dados

crash [kræʃ] *s* caída, desplome *m;* colisión, choque *m;* estallido, estrépito; fracaso; crac financiero; lienzo grueso; (aer) aterrizaje violento ‖ *tr* romper con estrépito, estrellar; **to crash a party** (slang) asistir a una fiesta sin invitación; **to crash the gate** (slang) colarse de gorra ‖ *intr* caer, desplomarse; romperse con estrépito, estallar; (*in business*) quebrar; aterrizar violentamente, estrellarse (*un avión*); **to crash into** chocar con

crash dive *s* sumersión instantánea (*de submarino*)

crash landing *s* aterrizaje violento

crash program *s* programa intensivo

crash test *s* (aut) ensayo de choque

crass [kræs] *adj* espeso, tosco; (*ignorance, mistake*) craso

crate [kret] *s* (*box made of slats*) jaula; (*basket*) banasta, cuévano ‖ *tr* embalar en jaula, embalar con listones

crater ['kretər] *s* cráter *m*

cravat [krə'væt] *s* corbata

crave [krev] *tr* anhelar, ansiar; pedir (*indulgencia*) ‖ *intr* — **to crave for** anhelar, ansiar; pedir con insistencia

craven ['krevən] *adj & s* cobarde *mf*

craving ['krevɪŋ] *s* anhelo, ansia, deseo ardiente

craw [krɔ] *s* buche *m*

crawl [krɔl] *s* arrastre *m;* gateado ‖ *intr* reptar, arrastrarse, gatear; (*to have a feeling of insects on skin*) hormiguear; **to crawl along** andar paso a paso; **to crawl up** trepar

crayon ['kre•ən] *s* creyón *m*

craze [krez] *s* boga, moda; locura, manía ‖ *tr* enloquecer

cra•zy ['krezi] *adj* (*comp* **-zier;** *super* **-ziest**) loco; (*rickety*) desvencijado; achacoso, débil; **crazy as a bedbug** (slang) loco de atar; **to be crazy about** (coll) estar loco por; **to drive crazy** volver loco

crazy bone *s* hueso de la alegría

creak [krik] *s* crujido, rechinamiento ‖ *intr* crujir, rechinar

creak•y ['kriki] *adj* (*comp* **-ier;** *super* **-iest**) crujidero, rechinador

cream [krim] *s* crema; (*e.g., of society*) crema, nata y flor ‖ *tr* desnatar (*la leche*)

creamer•y ['krimɔri] *s* (*pl* **-ies**) mantequería, quesería, lechería

cream puff *s* bollo de crema

cream separator *s* desnatadora

cream·y ['krimi] *adj* (*comp* **-ier;** *super* **-iest**) cremoso

crease [kris] *s* arruga, pliegue *m;* (*in trousers*) raya ‖ *tr* arrugar, plegar

create [kri'et] *tr* crear

creation [kri'eʃən] *s* creación

creative [kri'etɪv] *adj* creativo

creator [kri'etər] *s* creador *m*

creature ['kritʃər] *s* criatura; (*being, strange being*) ente *m;* animal *m*

credence ['kridəns] *s* creencia; **to give credence to** dar fe a

credentials [krɪ'dɛnʃəlz] *spl* credenciales *fpl*

credible ['krɛdɪbəl] *adj* creíble

credit ['krɛdɪt] *s* crédito; **to take credit for** atribuirse el mérito de ‖ *tr* acreditar; **to credit a person with** atribuirle a una persona el mérito de

creditable ['krɛdɪtəbəl] *adj* honorable, estimable

credit card *s* tarjeta de crédito

creditor ['krɛdɪtər] *s* acreedor *m*

cre·do ['krido] o ['kredo] *s* (*pl* **-dos**) credo

credulous ['krɛdʒələs] *adj* crédulo; creído

creed [krid] *s* credo

creek [krik] *s* arroyo, riachuelo

creep [krip] *v* (*pret & pp* **crept** [krɛpt]) *intr* arrastrarse; (*on all fours*) gatear; (*to climb*) trepar; (*with a sensation of insects*) hormiguear; **to creep up on** acercarse insensiblemente a

creeper ['kripər] *s* planta rastrera, planta trepadora

creeping ['kripɪŋ] *adj* lento, progresivo; (*plant*) rastrero ‖ *s* arrastramiento

cremate ['krimet] *tr* incinerar

cremation [krɪ'meʃən] *s* cremación; incineración

cremato·ry ['krimə,tori] *adj* crematorio ‖ *s* (*pl* **-ries**) crematorio

crème de menthe [krɛm də 'mɑt] *s* crema de menta

Creole ['kri·ol] *adj & s* criollo

crescent ['krɛsənt] *s* (*moon in first or last quarter*) creciente *f* de la luna; (*shape of moon in either of these phases*) media luna; panecillo (*en forma de media luna*)

cress [krɛs] *s* mastuerzo

crest [krɛst] *s* cresta

crestfallen ['krɛst,fɔlən] *adj* cabizbajo

crest'-line' model *s* (aut) modelo estrella

Cretan ['kritən] *adj & s* cretense *mf*

Crete [krit] *s* Creta

cretonne [krɪ'tan] *s* cretona

crevice ['krɛvɪs] *s* grieta

crew [kru] *s* equipo; (*of a ship*) dotación, tripulación; (*group, esp. of armed men*) banda, cuadrilla

crew cut *s* corte *m* de pelo a cepillo

crib [krɪb] *s* pesebre *m;* camita de niño; (coll) plagio; (*student's pony*) (coll) chuleta ‖ *v* (*pret & pp* **cribbed;** *ger* **cribbing**) *tr & intr* (coll) hurtar

cricket ['krɪkɪt] *s* (ent) grillo; (sport) cricquet *m;* (coll) juego limpio

crier ['kraɪ·ər] *s* pregonero

crime [kraɪm] *s* crimen *m,* delito

criminal ['krɪmɪnəl] *adj & s* criminal *mf;* delictivo

criminal code *s* código penal

criminal law *s* derecho penal

criminal negligence *s* imprudencia temeraria

criminology [,krɪmə'nalədʒi] *s* criminología

crimp [krɪmp] *s* rizado, rizo; **to put a crimp in** (coll) estorbar, impedir ‖ *tr* rizar

crimple ['krɪmpəl] *tr* arrugar, rizar ‖ *intr* arrugarse, rizarse

crimson ['krɪmzən] *adj & s* carmesí *m* ‖ *intr* enrojecerse

cringe [krɪndʒ] *intr* arrastrarse, reptar, encogerse

crinkle ['krɪŋkəl] *s* arruga, pliegue *m;* (*in the water*) rizo u onda ‖ *tr* arrugar, plegar ‖ *intr* arrugarse

cripple ['krɪpəl] *s* zopo, lisiado ‖ *tr* lisiar, estropear; dañar, perjudicar

cri·sis ['kraɪsɪs] *s* (*pl* **-ses**) [siz]) crisis *f*

crisp [krɪsp] *adj* frágil, quebradizo; (*air, weather*) refrescante; decisivo

criteri·on [kraɪ'tɪrɪ·ən] *s* (*pl* **-a** [ə]) u **-ons**) criterio

critic ['krɪtɪk] *s* crítico; (*reviewer*) reseñador; (*faultfinder*) criticón *m*

critical ['krɪtɪkəl] *adj* crítico; (*faultfinding*) criticón

criticism ['krɪtɪ,sɪzəm] *s* crítica

criticize ['krɪtɪ,saɪz] *tr & intr* criticar

critique [krɪ'tik] *s* (*art of criticism*) crítica; ensayo crítico

croak [krok] *s* (*of raven*) graznido; canto de ranas ‖ *intr* graznar (*el cuervo*); croar (*la rana*); (*morir*) (slang) reventar

Croat ['kro·æt] *s* (*native or inhabitant*) croata *mf;* (*language*) croata *m*

Croatian [kro'eʃən] *adj & mf* croata *mf*

cro·chet [kro'ʃe] *s* croché *m* ‖ *v* (*pret & pp* **-cheted** ['ʃed];* *ger* **-cheting** ['ʃe·ɪŋ]) *tr* trabajar con aguja de gancho ‖ *intr* hacer croché

crocheting [kro'ʃe·ɪŋ] *s* labor *f* de ganchillo

crochet needle *s* aguja de gancho

crock [krak] *s* cacharro, vasija de barro cocido

crockery ['krakəri] *s* loza

crocodile ['krakə,daɪl] *s* cocodrilo

crocodile tears *spl* lágrimas de cocodrilo

crocus ['krokəs] *s* azafrán *m,* croco

crone [kron] *s* vieja acartonada, vieja arrugada

cro·ny ['kroni] *s* (*pl* **-nies**) compinche *mf*

crook [krʊk] *s* gancho, garfio; curva; (*of shepherd*) cayado; (coll) fullero, ladrón *m;* chalecón *m* (Mex) ‖ *tr* encorvar; (slang) empinar (*el codo*) ‖ *intr* encorvarse

crooked ['krʊkɪd] *adj* encorvado, torcido; (*person or his conduct*) torcido; **to go crooked** (coll) torcerse

croon [krun] *intr* cantar con voz suave, cantar con melancolía exagerada

crooner ['krunər] *s* cantor de voz suave, cantor melancólico

crop [krap] *s* cosecha; (*head of hair*) cabellera; cabello corto; (*of a bird*) buche *m;* (*whip*) látigo; (*of appointments, promo-*

tions, heroes, etc.) hornada ‖ *v* (*pret & pp* **cropped;** *ger* **cropping**) *tr* desmochar (*un árbol*); desorejar (*a un animal*); esquilar, trasquilar ‖ *intr* — **to crop out** o **up** aflorar; asomar, dejarse ver, manifestarse inesperadamente

crop dusting *s* aerofumigación, fumigación aérea

croquet [kroˈke] *s* crocquet *m*

croquette [kroˈkɛt] *s* croqueta

crosier [ˈkroʒər] *s* báculo pastoral, cayado

cross [krɑs] o [krɔs] *adj* transversal, travieso; (*breed*) cruzado; malhumorado, enfadado ‖ *s* cruz *f*; (*of races; of two roads*) cruce *m;* **to take the cross** (*to join a crusade*) cruzarse ‖ *tr* cruzar; (*to oppose*) contrariar, frustrar; **to cross off** u **out** borrar; **to cross oneself** hacerse la señal de la cruz; **to cross one's mind** ocurrírsele a uno; **to cross one's t's** poner travesaño a las tes, poner el palo a las tes ‖ *intr* cruzar; cruzarse; **to cross over** atravesar de un lado a otro

cross'bones' *spl* huesos cruzados (*símbolo de la muerte*)

cross'bow' *s* ballesta

cross'breed' *v* (*pret & pp* **-bred** [ˌbrɛd]) *tr* cruzar (*animales o plantas*)

cross'coun'try *adj* a campo traviesa; a través del país

cross'cur'rent contracorriente *f;* (fig) tendencia encontrada

cross'-exam'i•na'tion *s* interrogatorio riguroso; (law) repregunta

cross'ex•am'ine *tr* interrogar rigurosamente; (law) repreguntar

cross-eyed [ˈkrɑsˌaɪd] *adj* bisojo, bizco, ojituerto

crossing [ˈkrɑsɪŋ] *s* (*of lines, streets, etc.*) cruce *m;* (*of the ocean*) travesía; (*of a river*) vado; (rr) crucero, paso a nivel

crossing gate *s* barrera, barrera de paso a nivel

crossing point *s* punto de cruce

cross'patch' *s* (coll) gruñón *m*

cross'piece' *s* travesaño

cross reference *s* contrarreferencia, remisión

cross'road' *s* vía transversal; **crossroads** encrucijada, cruce *m;* **at the crossroads** en el momento crítico

cross section *s* corte *m* transversal; (fig) sección representativa

cross street *s* calle traviesa, calle de travesía

cross'word' puzzle *s* crucigrama *m*

crotch [krɑtʃ] *s* (*forked piece*) horcajadura, bifurcación; (*between legs*) entrepierna, bragadura, horcajadura

crotchety [ˈkrɑtʃɪti] *adj* caprichoso, estrambótico, de mal genio

crouch [krautʃ] *s* posición agachada ‖ *intr* agacharse, acuclillarse

croup [krup] *s* garrotillo, crup *m;* (*of horse*) anca, grupa

croupier [ˈkrupɪ•ər] *s* crupié *m*

crouton [ˈkrutɑn] *s* corteza de pan

crow [kro] *s* corneja, grajo, chova; (*cry of the cock*) quiquiriquí *m;* (*crowbar*) alzaprima; **as the crow flies** a vuelo de pájaro; **to eat**

crow (coll) cantar la palinodia; **to have a crow to pick with** (coll) tener que habérselas con ‖ *intr* cantar (*el gallo*); jactarse; **to crow over** jactarse de

crow'bar' *s* alzaprima, pie *m* de cabra

crowd [kraud] *s* gentío, multitud; (*flock of people*) caterva, tropel *m; (mob, common people*) populacho, vulgo; (*clique, set*) corrillo, grupo ‖ *tr* apiñar, apretar, atestar; (*to push*) empujar ‖ *intr* apiñarse, apretarse, atestarse; (*to mill around*) arremolinarse

crowded [ˈkraudɪd] *adj* atestado, concurrido

crown [kraun] *s* corona; (*of hat*) copa ‖ *tr* coronar; (checkers) coronar; (slang) golpear en la cabeza

crowned head *s* testa coronada

crown prince *s* príncipe heredero

crown princess *s* princesa heredera

crow's'-foot' *s* (*pl* **-feet'**) pata de gallo

crow's'-nest' *s* (naut) cofa de vigía, torre *f* de vigía

crucial [ˈkruʃəl] *adj* crucial; difícil, penoso

crucible [ˈkrusɪbəl] *s* crisol *m*

crucifix [ˈkrusɪfɪks] *s* crucifijo

crucifixion [ˌkrusɪˈfɪkʃən] *s* crucifixión

cruci•fy [ˈkrusɪˌfaɪ] *v* (*pret & pp* **-fied**) *tr* crucificar

crude [krud] *adj* (*raw, unrefined*) crudo; (*lacking culture*) grosero, tosco; (*unfinished*) basto, sin labrar

crudi•ty [ˈkrudɪti] *s* (*pl* **-ties**) crudeza; grosería, tosquedad; bastedad

cruel [ˈkru•əl] *adj* cruel

cruel•ty [ˈkru•əlti] *s* (*pl* **-ties**) crueldad

cruet [ˈkru•ɪt] *s* ampolleta

cruet stand *s* angarillas, vinagreras

cruise [kruz] *s* viaje *m* por mar; (aer, naut) crucero ‖ *tr* (naut) cruzar ‖ *intr* cruzar; (coll) andar de un lado a otro

cruise missile *s* misil *m* crucero

cruiser [ˈkruzər] *s* (nav) crucero

cruising [ˈkruzɪŋ] *adj* de crucero ‖ *s* (aer, naut) crucero

cruising radius *s* autonomía

cruising speed *s* velocidad de crucero

cruller [ˈkrʌlər] *s* buñuelo

crumb [krʌm] *s* migaja; (*soft part of bread*) miga; (*given to a beggar*) mendrugo ‖ *tr* desmigar (*el pan*); (culin) empanar, cubrir con pan rallado; limpiar (*la mesa*) de migajas ‖ *intr* desmigarse, desmenuzarse

crumble [ˈkrʌmbəl] *tr* desmenuzar ‖ *intr* desmenuzarse; (*to fall to pieces gradually*) desmoronarse

crum•my [ˈkrʌmi] *adj* (*comp* **-mier;** *super* **-miest**) (slang) desaseado, sucio; (slang) de mal gusto, de mala muerte

crumple [ˈkrʌmpəl] *tr* arrugar, ajar, chafar ‖ *intr* arrugarse, ajarse

crunch [krʌntʃ] *tr* ronchar, ronzar ‖ *intr* crujir

crusade [kruˈsed] *s* cruzada ‖ *intr* hacer una cruzada

crusader [kruˈsedər] *s* cruzado

crush [krʌʃ] *s* aplastamiento; (*of people*) aglomeración, bullaje *m;* **to have a crush on**

(slang) estar perdido por ‖ *tr* aplastar, machacar, magullar; (*to grind*) moler; bocartear (*el mineral*); (*to oppress, grieve*) abrumar

crush hat *s* clac *m*

crust [krʌst] *s* corteza; corteza de pan; (*scab*) costra

crustacean [krʌsˈteʃən] *s* crustáceo

crustaceous [krʌsˈteʃəs] *adj* crustáceo

crust·y [ˈkrʌsti] *adj* (*comp* **-ier;** *super* **-iest**) (*scabby*) costroso; áspero, grosero, rudo

crutch [krʌtʃ] *s* muleta

crux [krʌks] *s* punto capital; enigma *m*

cry [kraɪ] *s* (*pl* **cries**) grito; (*weeping*) lloro, llorera; (*of peddler*) pregón *m*; (*of wolf*) aullido; (*of bull*) bramido; **in full cry** en plena persecución; **to have a good cry** desahogarse en lágrimas abundantes ‖ *v* (*pret & pp* **cried**) *tr* decir a gritos; (*to announce publicly*) pregonar; **to cry one's eyes** o **heart out** llorar amargamente; **to cry out** decir a gritos; pregonar ‖ *intr* gritar; (*to weep*) llorar; aullar (*el lobo*); bramar (*el toro*); **to cry for** clamar por; **to cry for joy** llorar de alegría; **to cry out** clamar; **to cry out against** clamar contra; **to cry out for** clamar, clamar por

cry'ba'by *s* (*pl* **-bies**) llorón *m*, llorona, lloraduelos *mf*

crypt [krɪpt] *s* cripta

cryptic(al) [ˈkrɪptɪk(əl)] *adj* enigmático, misterioso

crystal [ˈkrɪstəl] *s* cristal *m*

crystal ball *s* bola de cristal

crystalline [ˈkrɪstəlɪn] o [ˈkrɪstə,laɪn] *adj* cristalino

crystallize [ˈkrɪstə,laɪz] *tr* cristalizar ‖ *intr* cristalizarse

C.S. *abbr* **Christian Science, Civil Service**

ct. *abbr* **cent**

cu. *abbr* **cubic**

cub [kʌb] *s* cachorro

Cuban [ˈkjubən] *adj & s* cubano

cubbyhole [ˈkʌbɪ,hol] *s* chiribitil *m*

cube [kjub] *adj* (*root*) cúbico ‖ *s* cubo; (*of ice*) cubito ‖ *tr* cubicar

cubic [ˈkjubɪk] *adj* cúbico

cub reporter *s* (coll) reportero novato

cuckold [ˈkʌkəld] *adj & s* cornudo ‖ *tr* encornudar

cuckoo [ˈkuku] *adj* (slang) mentecato, loco ‖ *s* cuclillo, cuco; (*call of cuckoo*) cucú *m*

cuckoo clock *s* reloj *m* de cuclillo

cucumber [ˈkjukəmbər] *s* pepino

cud [kʌd] *s* bolo alimenticio; **to chew the cud** rumiar

cuddle [ˈkʌdəl] *s* abrazo cariñoso ‖ *tr* abrazar con cariño ‖ *intr* estar abrazados, arrimarse cariñosamente

cudg·el [ˈkʌdʒəl] *s* garrote *m*, porra; **to take up the cudgels for** salir a la defensa de ‖ *v* (*pret & pp* **-eled** o **-elled;** *ger* **-eling** o **-elling**) *tr* apalear, aporrear

cue [kju] *s* señal *f*, indicación; (*hint*) indirecta; (*rôle*) papel *m*; (*rod used in billiards*) taco; (*of hair*) coleta; (*of people in line*) cola; (theat) apunte *m*

cuff [kʌf] *s* (*of shirt*) puño; (*of trousers*) doblez *f*, vuelta; (*blow*) bofetada ‖ *tr* abofetear

cuff links *spl* gemelos

cuirass [kwɪˈræs] *s* coraza

cuisine [kwɪˈzin] *s* cocina (*arte culinario*)

culinary [ˈkjulɪ,nɛri] *adj* culinario

cull [kʌl] *tr* (*to choose, pick*) entresacar, escoger; (*to gather, pluck*) coger, recoger

culm [kʌlm] *s* (*coal dust*) cisco; (*stalk of grasses*) caña, tallo

culminate [ˈkʌlmɪ,net] *intr* culminar; **to culminate in** conducir a, terminar en

culpable [ˈkʌlpəbəl] *adj* culpable

culprit [ˈkʌlprɪt] *s* acusado; reo

cult [kʌlt] *s* culto; secta

cultivate [ˈkʌltɪ,vet] *tr* cultivar

cultivated [ˈkʌltɪ,vetɪd] *adj* culto, cultivado

cultivation [,kʌltɪˈveʃən] *s* (*of the land, the arts, one's memory, etc.*) cultivo; (*refinement*) cultura

culture [ˈkʌltʃər] *s* cultura

cultured [ˈkʌltʃərd] *adj* culto

culvert [ˈkʌlvərt] *s* alcantarilla

cumbersome [ˈkʌmbərsəm] *adj* incómodo, molesto; (*clumsy*) pesado, inmanejable

cunning [ˈkʌnɪŋ] *adj* (*sly*) astuto; (*clever*) hábil; (*attractive*) gracioso, mono ‖ *s* astucia; habilidad, destreza

cup [kʌp] *s* taza; (*of thermometer*) cubeta; (mach) vaso de engrase; (sport) copa; (*of sorrow*) (fig) copa; **in one's cups** borracho ‖ *v* (*pret & pp* **cupped;** *ger* **cupping**) *tr* ahuecar dando forma de taza o copa a; poner ventosa a

cupboard [ˈkʌbərd] *s* alacena, aparador *m*, armario

cupidity [kjuˈpɪdɪti] *s* codicia

cupola [ˈkjupələ] *s* cúpula

cur [kʌr] *s* perro mestizo, perro de mala raza; (*despicable fellow*) canalla *m*

curate [ˈkjurɪt] *s* cura *m*

curative [ˈkjurətɪv] *adj* curativo ‖ *s* curativa

curator [kjuˈretər] *s* conservador *m*

curb [kʌrb] *s* (*of sidewalk*) encintado; (*of well*) brocal *m*; (*of bit*) barbada; (*market*) bolsín *m*; (*check, restraint*) freno; (vet) corva ‖ *tr* contener, refrenar

curb'stone' *s* piedra de encintado; brocal *m* de pozo

curd [kʌrd] *s* cuajada ‖ *tr* cuajar ‖ *intr* cuajarse

curdle [ˈkʌrdəl] *tr* cuajar; **to curdle the blood** horrorizar ‖ *intr* cuajar

cure [kjur] *s* cura, curación ‖ *tr* curar ‖ *intr* curar; curarse

cure'-all' *s* sanalotodo

curfew [ˈkʌrfju] *s* queda, cubrefuego; toque *m* de queda; hora de cierre

curi·o [ˈkjurɪ,o] *s* (*pl* **-os**) curiosidad

curiosi·ty [,kjurɪˈɑsɪti] *s* (*pl* **-ties**) curiosidad

curious [ˈkjurɪ·əs] *adj* curioso

curl [kʌrl] *s* bucle *m*, rizo; (*spiral-shaped curl*) tirabuzón *m*; (*of smoke*) espiral *f*; (*curling*) rizado ‖ *tr* encrespar, ensortijar, rizar; (*to coil, to roll up*) arrollar; fruncir (*los labios*) ‖ *intr* encresparse, ensortijarse, rizarse; arrollarse; **to curl up** arrollarse; (*in bed*) encogerse; (*to break up, collapse*) (coll) desplomarse

curler ['kʌrlər] s (*hair*) rulo, bigudí m

curlicue ['kʌrlɪ,kju] s ringorrango

curling iron s rizador m, maquinilla de rizar

curl'pa'per s torcida, papelito para rizar el pelo

curl·y ['kʌrli] adj (comp **-ier;** super **-iest**) crespo, rizo

curmudgeon [kər'mʌdʒən] s cicatero, tacaño, erizo

currant ['kʌrənt] s pasa de Corinto; (*Ribes alpinum*) calderilla

curren·cy ['kʌrənsi] s (pl **-cies**) moneda corriente, dinero en circulación; uso corriente

current ['kʌrənt] adj corriente ‖ s corriente f; (elec) corriente f

current account s cuenta corriente

current events spl actualidades, sucesos de actualidad

curricu·lum [kə'rɪkjələm] s (pl **-lums** o **-la** [lə]) plan m de estudios

cur·ry ['kʌri] s (pl **-ries**) cari m ‖ v (pret & pp **-ried**) tr curtir (*las pieles*); almohazar (*el caballo*); **to curry favor** procurar complacer

cur'ry·comb' s almohaza ‖ tr almohazar

curse [kʌrs] s maldición; (*profane oath*) reniego, voto; (*evil, misfortune*) calamidad ‖ tr maldecir ‖ intr jurar, echar votos; echar carnes (Mex)

cursed ['kʌrsɪd] o [kʌrst] adj maldito; aborrecible

cursive ['kʌrsɪv] adj cursivo ‖ s cursiva

cursory ['kʌrsəri] adj apresurado, rápido, superficial, de paso

curt [kʌrt] adj áspero, brusco; corto, conciso

curtail [kər'tel] tr acortar, abreviar, cercenar

curtain ['kʌrtən] s cortina; (theat) telón m; **to draw the curtain** correr la cortina; **to drop the curtain** (theat) bajar el telón ‖ tr encortinar; separar con cortina; cubrir, ocultar

curtain call s llamada a la escena para recibir aplausos

curtain raiser ['rezər] s (theat) pieza preliminar

curtain ring s anilla

curtain rod s riel m

curt·sy ['kʌrtsi] s (pl **-sies**) cortesía, reverencia ‖ v (pret & pp **-sied**) intr hacer una cortesía

curve [kʌrv] s curva ‖ tr encorvar ‖ intr encorvarse; volver, virar

curved [kʌrvd] adj curvo, encorvado; (*crooked*) combo

cushion ['kuʃən] s cojín m, almohada; (*of billiard table*) baranda ‖ tr amortiguar

cusp [kʌsp] s cúspide f

cuspidor ['kʌspɪ,dɔr] s escupidera

custard ['kʌstərd] s flan m, natillas

custodian [kəs'todɪ·ən] s custodio; (*of a house or building*) casero

custo·dy ['kʌstədi] s (pl **-dies**) custodia; **in custody** en prisión; **to take into custody** prender

custom ['kʌstəm] s costumbre; (*customers*) parroquia, clientela; **customs** aduana; derechos de aduana

customary ['kʌstə,mɛri] adj acostumbrado, de costumbre

cus'tom-built' adj hecho por encargo, fuera de serie

customer ['kʌstəmər] s parroquiano, cliente mf; (*of a café or restaurant*) consumidor m; (coll) individuo, sujeto, tipo

customer service s servicio postventa

cus'tom·house' adj aduanero ‖ s aduana

cus'tom-made' adj hecho a la medida

customs clearance s despacho de aduana

customs officer s aduanero

custom tailor s sastre m a la medida

custom work s trabajo hecho a la medida

cut [kʌt] s corte m; (*piece cut off*) tajada; (*wound*) cuchillada; (*for a canal, highway, etc.*) desmonte m; (*shortest way*) atajo; (*in prices, wages, etc.*) reducción; (*of a garment*) corte m, hechura; (*in winnings, earnings, etc.*) parte f; (*diamond*) talla; (typ) estampa, grabado; (tennis) golpe m cortante; (*absence from school*) (coll) falta de asistencia; (*snub*) (coll) desaire m; (coll) palabra hiriente ‖ v (pret & pp **cut;** ger **cutting**) tr cortar; practicar (*un agujero*); reducir (*gastos*); capar, castrar; desleír, diluir; (coll) ausentarse de, faltar a (*la clase*); (coll) desairar; (coll) herir; **to cut down** cortar; derribar cortando; castigar (*gastos*); **to cut off** cortar; desheredar; amputar (*una pierna*); (elec) cortar (*la corriente, la ignición*); cerrar (*el carburador*); **to cut open** abrir cortando; **to cut out** cortar; sacar cortando; labrar; suprimir, omitir; (*to take the place of*) desbancar; soplar (*la dama a un rival*); (slang) dejarse de (*disparates*); **to cut short** terminar de repente; interrumpir, chafar; **to cut teeth** endentecer; **cut up** desmenuzar, despedazar; criticar severamente; (coll) afligir ‖ intr cortar; cortarse; salir (*los dientes*); (coll) fumarse la clase; **to cut in** entrar de repente; interrumpir; (*in a dance*) cortar o separar la pareja; **to cut under** vender a menor precio que; **to cut up** (slang) travesear, hacer travesuras; (slang) jaranear

cut-and-dried ['kʌtən'draɪd] adj dispuesto de antemano; monótono, poco interesante

cutaway coat ['kʌtə,we] s chaqué m

cut'back' s reducción; discontinuación, incumplimiento; (mov) retorno a una época anterior

cute [kjut] adj (coll) mono, monono; (coll) astuto, listo

cut glass s cristal tallado

cuticle ['kjutɪkəl] s cutícula

cutlass ['kʌtləs] s alfanje m

cutler ['kʌtlər] s cuchillero

cutlery ['kʌtləri] s cuchillería; (*knives, forks, and spoons*) cubierto

cutlet ['kʌtlɪt] s chuleta; croqueta

cut'out' s (*design to be cut out*) recortado; (aut) escape m libre, válvula de escape libre

cr
cu

cut'-rate' *adj* de precio reducido
cutter [ˈkʌtər] *s* cortador *m;* (*machine*) cortadora; (naut) escampavía
cut'throat' *adj* asesino; implacable ‖ *s* asesino
cutting [ˈkʌtɪŋ] *adj* cortante; hiriente, mordaz ‖ *s* corte *m;* (*from a newspaper*) recorte *m;* (hort) esqueje *m*
cutting edge *s* canto de corte
cuttlefish [ˈkʌtəlˌfɪʃ] *s* jibia
cut'wa'ter *s* espolón *m,* tajamar *m*
cwt. *abbr* **hundredweight**
cyanamide [saɪˈænəˌmaɪd] *s* cianamida; cianamida de calcio
cyanide [ˈsaɪ•əˌnaɪd] *s* cianuro
cybernetics [ˌsaɪbərˈnɛtɪks] *s* cibernética
cycle [ˈsaɪkəl] *s* ciclo; bicicleta; (*of an internal-combustion engine*) tiempo; (phys) periódo ‖ *intr* montar en bicicleta
cyclic(al) [ˈsaɪklɪk(əl)] o [ˈsɪklɪk(əl)] *adj* cíclico
cyclone [ˈsaɪklon] *s* ciclón *m*
cyl. *abbr* **cylinder, cylindrical**

cylinder [ˈsɪlɪndər] *s* cilindro
cylinder block *s* bloque *m* de cilindros
cylinder bore *s* alesaje *m*
cylinder head *s* (*of steam engine*) tapa del cilindro; (*of gas engine*) culata del cilindro
cylindric(al) [sɪˈlɪndrɪk(əl)] *adj* cilíndrico
cymbal [ˈsɪmbəl] *s* címbalo, platillo
cynic [ˈsɪnɪk] *adj* & *s* cínico
cynical [ˈsɪnɪkəl] *adj* cínico
cynicism [ˈsɪnɪˌsɪzəm] *s* cinismo
cynosure [ˈsaɪnə‿ʃʊr] o [ˈsɪnə‿ʃʊr] *s* blanco de las miradas; guía, norte *m*
cypress [ˈsaɪprəs] *s* ciprés *m*
Cyprus [ˈsaɪprəs] *s* Chipre *f*
Cyrillic [sɪˈrɪlɪk] *adj* cirílico
Cyrus [ˈsaɪrəs] *s* Ciro
cyst [sɪst] *s* quiste *m*
czar [zɑr] *s* zar *m;* (fig) autócrata *m*
czarina [zɑˈrinə] *s* zarina
Czech [tʃɛk] *adj* & *s* checo
Czecho-Slovak [ˈtʃɛkoˈslovæk] *adj* & *s* checoeslovaco o checoslovaco
Czecho-Slovakia [ˌtʃɛkosloˈvækɪ•ə] *s* Checoeslovaquia o Checoslovaquia

D

D, d [di] cuarta letra del alfabeto inglés
d. *abbr* **date, day, dead, degree, delete, diameter, died, dollar, denarius (penny)**
D. *abbr* **December, Democrat, Duchess, Duke, Dutch**
D.A. *abbr* **District Attorney**
dab [dæb] *s* toque ligero; masa pastosa ‖ *v* (*pret & pp* **dabbed;** *ger* **dabbing**) *tr* tocar ligeramente, frotar suavemente
dabble [ˈdæbəl] *tr* salpicar ‖ *intr* chapotear; **to dabble in** meterse en; jugar a (*la Bolsa*); especular en (*granos*)
dad [dæd] *s* (coll) papá *m*
dad•dy [ˈdædi] *s* (*pl* **-dies**) (coll) papá *m*
daffodil [ˈdæfədɪl] *s* narciso trompón
daff•y [ˈdæfi] *adj* (*comp* **-ier;** *super* **-iest**) (coll) chiflado
dagger [ˈdægər] *s* daga, puñal *m;* (typ) cruz *f,* obelisco; **to look daggers at** apuñalar con la mirada
dahlia [ˈdæljə] *s* dalia
dai•ly [ˈdeli] *adj* cotidiano, diario ‖ *adv* diariamente ‖ *s* (*pl* **-lies**) diario
dain•ty [ˈdenti] *adj* (*comp* **-tier;** *super* **-tiest**) delicado ‖ *s* (*pl* **-ties**) golosina
dair•y [ˈdɛri] *s* (*pl* **-ies**) lechería, vaquería
dais [ˈde•ɪs] *s* estrado
dai•sy [ˈdezi] *s* (*pl* **-sies**) margarita
daisy wheel *s* (*computer*) margarita (*impresora*)
dal•ly [ˈdæli] *v* (*pret & pp* **-lied**) *intr* juguetear, retozar; tardar, malgastar el tiempo
dam [dæm] *s* represa, embalse *m;* (*female quadruped*) madre *f;* (dent) dique *m* ‖ *v* (*pret & pp* **dammed;** *ger* **damming**) *tr*

represar, embalsar; cerrar, tapar, obstruir
damage [ˈdæmɪdʒ] *s* daño, perjuicio; (*to one's reputation*) desdoro; (com) avería; **damages** daños y perjuicios ‖ *tr* dañar, perjudicar; averiar
damascene [ˈdæməˌsin] o [ˌdæməˈsin] *adj* damasquino ‖ *s* ataujía, damasquinado ‖ *tr* ataujiar, damasquinar
dame [dem] *s* dama, señora; (coll) mujer *f*
damn [dæm] *s* terno; **I don't give a damn** (slang) maldito lo que me importa; **that's not worth a damn** (slang) eso no vale un pito ‖ *tr* condenar (a pena eterna); condenar; maldecir ‖ *intr* maldecir, echar ternos
damnation [dæmˈneʃən] *s* damnación; (theol) condenación
damned [dæmd] *adj* condenado (a pena eterna); abominable, detestable ‖ **the damned** los malditos, los condenados (a pena eterna)
damp [dæmp] *adj* húmedo, mojado ‖ *s* humedad; (*firedamp*) grisú *m* ‖ *tr* humedecer, mojar; (*to deaden, muffle*) amortecer, amortiguar; (*to discourage*) abatir, desalentar; (elec) amortiguar (*ondas electromagnéticas*)
dampen [ˈdæmpən] *tr* humedecer, mojar; amortecer, amortiguar; abatir, desalentar
damper [ˈdæmpər] *s* (*of chimney*) registro; (*of piano*) apagador *m,* sordina
damsel [ˈdæmzəl] *s* señorita, muchacha
dance [dæns] *s* baile *m,* danza ‖ *tr* & *intr* bailar, danzar
dance band *s* orquesta de jazz

dance floor s pista de baile
dance hall s salón m de baile
dancer ['dænsər] s bailador m, danzador m; (professional) bailarín m
dancing partner s pareja (de baile)
dandelion ['dændɪ,laɪ•ən] s diente m de león
dandruff ['dændrəf] s caspa
dan•dy ['dændi] adj (comp -dier; super -diest) (coll) excelente, magnífico || s (pl -dies) currutaco, petimetre m; lagarto (Mex)
Dane [den] s danés m, dinamarqués m
danger ['dendʒər] s peligro
dangerous ['dendʒərəs] adj peligroso; riesgoso
dangle ['dæŋgəl] tr & intr colgar flojamente, colgar en el aire
Danish ['denɪʃ] adj & s danés m, dinamarqués m
dank [dæŋk] adj húmedo, liento
Danube ['dænjub] s Danubio
dapper ['dæpər] adj aseado, apuesto
dapple ['dæpəl] adj habado, rodado || tr motear
dare [dɛr] s desafío, reto || tr retar; **to dare to** (to challenge to) desafiar a || intr osar, atreverse; **I dare say** talvez; **to dare to** (to have the courage to) atreverse a
dare'dev'il s calavera m, temerario
daring ['dɛrɪŋ] adj atrevido, osado || s atrevimiento, osadía
dark [dɑrk] adj obscuro; (in complexion) moreno; secreto, oculto; (gloomy) lóbrego; (beer) pardo || s obscuridad, tinieblas; noche f; **in the dark** a obscuras
Dark Ages spl edad media; principios de la edad media
dark-complexioned ['dɑrkkəm'plɛkʃənd] adj moreno
darken ['dɑrkən] tr obscurecer; entristecer; cegar || intr obscurecerse
dark horse s caballo desconocido; candidato nombrado inesperadamente
darkly ['dɑrkli] adv obscuramente; secretamente, misteriosamente
dark meat s carne f del ave que no es la pechuga
darkness ['dɑrknɪs] s obscuridad
dark'room' s (phot) cuarto obscuro
darling ['dɑrlɪŋ] adj & s querido, amado; predilecto; (as address) chata (Mex)
darn [dɑrn] tr & intr zurcir; (coll) maldecir
darnel ['dɑrnəl] s cizaña
darning ['dɑrnɪŋ] s zurcido
darning needle s aguja de zurcir
dart [dɑrt] s dardo; (small missile used in a game) rehilete m || intr lanzarse, precipitarse; volar como dardo
Darwinian [dɑr'wɪnɪ•ən] adj darviniano
Darwinism ['dɑrwə,nɪzəm] s darvinismo
Darwinist ['dɑrwənɪst] s darviniano
dash [dæʃ] s arranque m; (splash) rociada; carrera corta; (spirit) brío; pequeña cantidad; (in printing, writing, telegraphy) raya || tr lanzar; estrellar, romper; frustrar (las esperanzas de uno); rociar, salpicar; **to dash off** escribir de prisa; **to dash to**

pieces hacer añicos || intr estrellarse (las olas del mar); lanzarse, precipitarse; **to dash by** pasar corriendo; **to dash in** entrar como un rayo
dash'board' s tablero de instrumentos; cuadro de mando; (aut) guardabarros m, salpicadero
dashing ['dæʃɪŋ] adj brioso; ostentoso, vistoso || s (of waves) embate m
dastard ['dæstərd] adj & s vil mf, miserable mf, cobarde mf
data bank ['detə] s banco de datos, almacenamiento
da'ta-proc'ess tr & intr procesar
data processing s procesamiento; tramitación automática de datos
data storage s memoria, almacenamiento
date [det] s (time) fecha, data; (palm) datilera; (fruit) dátil m; (appointment) (coll) cita; **out of date** anticuado, fuera de moda; **to date** hasta la fecha; **under date of** con fecha de || tr fechar, datar; (coll) tener cita con || intr —**to date from** datar de
date line s línea de cambio de fecha
date palm s palmera (datilera)
dative ['detɪv] adj & s dativo
datum ['detəm] o ['dætəm] s (pl data ['detə] o ['dætə]) dato
dau. abbr **daughter**
daub [dɔb] s embadurnamiento || tr embadurnar
daughter ['dɔtər] s hija
daughter-in-law ['dɔtərɪn,lɔ] s (pl daughters-in-law) nuera, hija política
daunt [dɔnt] tr asustar, espantar; desanimar, acobardar
dauntless ['dɔntlɪs] adj atrevido, intrépido, impávido
dauphin ['dɔfɪn] s delfín m
davenport ['dævən,port] s sofá m cama
davit ['dævɪt] s (naut) pescante m, grúa de bote
daw [dɔ] s corneja
dawdle ['dɔdəl] intr malgastar el tiempo, haronear
dawn [dɔn] s amanecer m, alba || intr amanecer; despuntar (el día, la mañana); empezar a mostrarse; **to dawn on** empezar a hacerse patente a
day [de] adj diurno || s día m; (of travel, work, worry, etc.) jornada; (from noon to noon) (naut) singladura; **any day now** de un día para otro; **by day** de día; **the day after** el día siguiente; **the day after tomorrow** pasado mañana; **the day before** la víspera; la víspera de; **the day before yesterday** anteayer; **to call it a day** (coll) dejar de trabajar; **to win the day** ganar la jornada
day bed s sofá m cama, diván m cama
day'break' s amanecer m
day coach s (rr) coche m de viajeros
day'dream' s ensueño || intr soñar despierto
day laborer s jornalero
day'light' s luz f del día; amanecer m; **in broad daylight** en pleno día; **to see daylight** comprender; ver el fin de una tarea difícil

cu
da

day'light'-sav'ing time *s* hora de verano
day nursery *s* guardería infantil
day off *s* asueto
day of reckoning *s* día *m* de ajustar cuentas
day shift *s* turno diurno
day'time' *adj* diurno ‖ día *m*
daze [dez] *s* aturdimiento; **in a daze** aturdido ‖ *tr* aturdir
dazzle [ˈdæzəl] *s* deslumbramiento ‖ *tr* deslumbrar
dazzling [ˈdæzlɪŋ] *adj* deslumbrante
deacon [ˈdikən] *s* diácono
deaconess [ˈdikənɪs] *s* diaconisa
dead [dɛd] *adj* muerto; (*coll*) cansado ‖ *adv* (*coll*) completamente, muy ‖ *s* — **in the dead of night** en plena noche; **the dead** los muertos; **the dead of winter** lo más frío del invierno
dead beat *s* (slang) gorrón *m*; (slang) holgazán *m*
dead bolt *s* cerrojo dormido
dead calm *s* calma chicha, calmazo
dead center *s* punto muerto
dead'drunk' *adj* difunto de taberna
deaden [ˈdɛdən] *tr* amortiguar, amortecer
dead end *s* callejón *m* sin salida
dead'latch' *s* aldaba dormida
dead'-let'ter office *s* departamento de cartas no reclamadas
dead'line' *s* línea vedada; fin *m* del plazo
dead'lock' *s* cerradura dormida; desacuerdo insuperable ‖ *tr* estancar
dead•ly [ˈdɛdli] *adj* (*comp* -**lier**; *super* -**liest**) mortal; (*sin*) capital; abrumador
dead pan *s* (slang) semblante *m* sin expresión
dead reckoning *s* (naut) estima
dead ringer [ˈrɪŋər] *s* segunda edición
dead'wood' *s* leña seca; cosa inútil, gente *f* inútil
deaf [dɛf] *adj* sordo; **to turn a deaf ear** hacerse el sordo, hacer oídos de mercader
deaf and dumb *adj* sordomudo
deafen [ˈdɛfən] *tr* asordar, ensordecer
deafening [ˈdɛfənɪŋ] *adj* ensordecedor
deaf'-mute' *s* sordomudo
deafness [ˈdɛfnɪs] *s* sordera
deal [dil] *s* negocio, trato; (*of cards*) mano *f*; turno de dar; (*share*) parte *f*, porción; (*coll*) convenio secreto; **a good deal (of)** o **a great deal (of)** mucho; **to make a great deal of** hacer fiestas a ‖ *v* (*pret & pp* **dealt** [dɛlt]) *tr* asestar (*un golpe*); repartir (*la baraja*) ‖ *intr* negociar, comerciar; intervenir; (*in card games*) ser mano; **to deal with** entender en; tratar de; tratar con
dealer [ˈdilər] *s* comerciante *mf*, concesionario; (*of cards*) repartidor *m*
dean [din] *s* decano; (eccl) deán *m*
deanship [ˈdinʃɪp] *s* decanato, deanato, deanazgo
dear [dɪr] *adj* (*beloved*) caro; (*expensive*) caro; (*charging high prices*) carero; **dear me!** ¡Dios mío! ‖ *s* queriao
dearie [ˈdɪri] *s* (coll) queridito
dearth [dʌrθ] *s* carestía
death [dɛθ] *s* muerte *f*; **to bleed to death** morir desangrado; **to bore to death** matar

de aburrimiento; **to burn to death** morir quemado; **to choke to death** morir atragantado; **to die a violent death** morir vestido; **to freeze to death** morir helado; **to put to death** dar la muerte a; **to shoot to death** matar a tiros; **to stab to death** escabechar; **to starve to death** matar de hambre; morir de hambre
death'bed' *s* lecho de muerte
death'blow' *s* golpe *m* mortal
death certificate *s* fe *f* de óbito, partida de defunción
death house *s* capilla (*de los reos de muerte*)
deathless [ˈdɛθlɪs] *adj* inmortal, eterno
deathly [ˈdɛθli] *adj* mortal, de muerte ‖ *adv* mortalmente; excesivamente
death penalty *s* pena de muerte
death rate *s* mortalidad
death rattle *s* estertor agónico
death ray *s* rayo mortífero
death warrant *s* sentencia de muerte; fin *m* de toda esperanza
death'watch' *s* vela de un difunto; guardia de un reo de muerte
debacle [deˈbakəl] *s* desastre *m*, ruina, derrota; (*in a river*) deshielo
de•bar [dɪˈbɑr] *v* (*pret & pp* -**barred;** *ger* -**barring**) *tr* excluir; prohibir
debark [dɪˈbɑrk] *tr & intr* desembarcar
debarkation [ˌdibɑrˈkeʃən] *s* (*of passengers*) desembarco; (*of freight*) desembarque *m*
debase [dɪˈbes] *tr* degradar; falsificar
debatable [dɪˈbetəbəl] *adj* disputable
debate [dɪˈbet] *s* debate *m* ‖ *tr* debatir ‖ *intr* debatir; deliberar
debauchee [ˌdɛbɔˈʃi] o [ˌdɛbɔˈtʃi] *s* libertino, disoluto
debaucher•y [dɪˈbɔtʃəri] *s* (*pl* -**ies**) libertinaje *m*, crápula
debenture [dɪˈbɛntʃər] *s* (*bond*) obligación; (*voucher*) vale *m*
debilitate [dɪˈbɪlɪˌtet] *tr* debilitar
debili•ty [dɪˈbɪlɪti] *s* (*pl* -**ties**) debilidad
debit [ˈdɛbɪt] *s* debe *m*; (*entry on debit side*) cargo ‖ *tr* adeudar, cargar
debit balance *s* saldo deudor
debonair [ˌdɛbəˈnɛr] *adj* alegre; cortés
debris [deˈbri] *s* despojos, ruinas
debt [dɛt] *s* deuda; **to run into debt** endeudarse, entramparse
debtor [ˈdɛtər] *s* deudor *m*
debut [deˈbju] o [ˈdebju] *s* estreno, debut *m*, **to make one's debut** estrenarse, debutar; ponerse de largo, entrar en sociedad (*una joven*)
debutante [ˌdɛbjuˈtɑnt] o [ˈdɛbjəˌtænt] *s* joven *f* que se pone de largo; debutante *f*
dec. *abbr* deceased
decade [ˈdɛked] *s* decenio, década
decadence [dɪˈkedəns] *s* decadencia
decadent [dɪˈkedənt] *adj & s* decadente *mf*
decanter [dɪˈkæntər] *s* garrafa
decapitate [dɪˈkæpɪˌtet] *tr* decapitar
decay [dɪˈke] *s* (*decline*) decaimiento, descaecimiento; (*rotting*) podredumbre; (*of teeth*) caries *f* ‖ *tr* pudrir ‖ *intr* pudrirse; decaer; cariarse (*los dientes*)

decease [dɪ'sis] s fallecimiento ‖ *intr* fallecer

deceased [dɪ'sist] *adj* & s difunto

deceit [dɪ'sit] s engaño, fraude *m*

deceitful [dɪ'sitfəl] *adj* engañoso, fraudulento

deceive [dɪ'siv] *tr* & *intr* engañar

decelerate [dɪ'sɛlə,ret] *tr* desacelerar ‖ *intr* desacelerarse

December [dɪ'sɛmbər] s diciembre *m*

decen•cy ['disənsi] s (*pl* **-cies**) decencia, honestidad; (*propriety*) conveniencia

decent ['disənt] *adj* decente, honesto; (*proper*) conveniente

decentralize [dɪ'sɛntrə,laɪz] *tr* descentralizar

deception [dɪ'sɛpʃən] s engaño

deceptive [dɪ'sɛptɪv] *adj* engañoso

decide [dɪ'saɪd] *tr* & *intr* decidir

decimal ['dɛsɪməl] *adj* & s decimal *m*

decimal point s (*in Spanish the comma is used to separate the decimal fraction from the integer*) coma

decimate ['dɛsɪ,met] *tr* diezmar

decipher [dɪ'saɪfər] *tr* descifrar

deciphering [dɪ'saɪfərɪŋ] s desciframiento

decision [dɪ'sɪʒən] s decisión

decisive [dɪ'saɪsɪv] *adj* decisivo; determinado, resuelto

deck [dɛk] s (*of cards*) baraja; (*of ship*) cubierta; **between decks** (naut) entre cubiertas ‖ *tr* — **to deck out** adornar, engalanar

deck chair s silla de cubierta

deck hand s marinero de cubierta

deck'-land' *intr* apontizar

deck'-land'ing s apontizaje *m*

deckle edge ['dɛkəl] s barba

declaim [dɪ'klem] *tr* & *intr* declamar

declaration [,dɛklə'reʃən] s declaración

declarative [dɪ'klærətɪv] *adj* declarativo; (gram) enunciativo

declare [dɪ'klɛr] *tr* & *intr* declarar

declension [dɪ'klɛnʃən] s declinación

declination [,dɛklɪ'neʃən] s declinación

decline [dɪ'klaɪn] s bajada, declinación; (*in prices*) baja; (*in health, wealth, etc.*) bajón *m;* (*of sun*) ocaso ‖ *tr* & *intr* declinar; rehusar

declivi•ty [dɪ'klɪvɪti] s (*pl* **-ties**) declividad, declive *m*

decode [di'kod] *tr* descifrar

decoder [di'kodər] s (telv) decodificador *m*

decoding [di'kodɪŋ] s desciframiento

décolleté [,dekɑl'te] *adj* escotado

decompose [,dikəm'poz] *tr* descomponer ‖ *intr* descomponerse

decomposition [,dikɑmpə'zɪʃən] s descomposición

decompression [,dikəm'prɛʃən] s descompresión

decongest [,dikən'dʒɛst] *tr* descongestionar

decongestion [,dikən'dʒɛstʃən] s descongestión

decontamination [,dikəm,tæmɪ'neʃən] s descontaminación; **radioactive decontamination** descontaminación de radiactividad

decon•trol [,dikən'trol] *v* (*pret* & *pp* **-trolled;** *ger* **-trolling**) descontrolar

décor [de'kɔr] s decoración; (theat) decorado

decorate ['dɛkə,ret] *tr* decorar; (*with medal, badge*) condecorar

decoration [,dɛkə'reʃən] s decoración; (*medal, badge*) condecoración

decorator ['dɛkə,retər] s decorador *m;* (*of interiors*) adornista *mf*

decorous ['dɛkərəs] o [dɪ'korəs] *adj* decoroso

decorum [dɪ'korəm] s decoro

decoy ['dikɔɪ] o ['dikɔɪ] s añagaza, señuelo; (*person*) entruchón *m* ‖ [dɪ'kɔɪ] *tr* atraer con señuelo; entruchar

decoy pigeon s cimbel *m*

decrease ['dikris] s disminución ‖ [dɪ'kris] *tr* disminuir ‖ *intr* disminuir, disminuirse

decree [dɪ'kri] s decreto ‖ *tr* decretar

decrepit [dɪ'krɛpɪt] *adj* decrépito

de•cry [dɪ'kraɪ] *v* (*pret* & *pp* **-cried**) *tr* censurar, denigrar

dedicate ['dɛdɪ,ket] *tr* dedicar

dedication [,dɛdɪ'keʃən] s dedicación; (*inscription in a book*) dedicatoria

deduce [dɪ'djus] *tr* deducir (*inferir, concluir; derivar*)

deduct [dɪ'dʌkt] *tr* deducir (*rebajar, substraer*)

deduction [dɪ'dʌkʃən] s deducción

deed [did] s acto, hecho; (*feat, exploit*) hazaña; (law) escritura ‖ *tr* traspasar por escritura

deem [dim] *tr* & *intr* creer, juzgar

deep [dip] *adj* profundo; (*sound*) grave; (*color*) subido; de hondo, p.ej., **two meters deep** dos metros de hondo; **deep in debt** cargado de deudas; **deep in thought** absorto en la meditación ‖ *adv* hondo; **deep into the night** muy entrada la noche

deepen ['dipən] *tr* profundizar ‖ *intr* profundizarse

deep-laid ['dip,led] *adj* concebido con astucia

deep mourning s luto riguroso

deep-rooted ['dip,rutɪd] *adj* profundamente arraigado

deep'-sea' fishing s pesca de gran altura

deep-seated ['dip,sitɪd] *adj* profundamente arraigado

deer [dɪr] s ciervo, venado

deer'skin' s piel *f* de ciervo

def. *abbr* **defendant, deferred, definite**

deface [dɪ'fes] *tr* desfigurar

de facto [di'fækto] *adv* de hecho

defamation [,dɛfə'meʃən] o [,difə'meʃən] s difamación

defame [dɪ'fem] *tr* difamar

default [dɪ'fɔlt] s falta, incumplimiento; **by default** (sport) por no presentarse; **in default of** por falta de ‖ *tr* dejar de cumplir; no pagar ‖ *intr* faltar; (sport) perder por no presentarse

defeat [dɪ'fit] s derrota ‖ *tr* derrotar, vencer

defeatism [dɪ'fitɪzəm] s derrotismo

defeatist [dɪ'fitɪst] *adj* & s derrotista *mf*

defecate ['dɛfɪ,ket] *intr* defecar

defect [dɪ'fɛkt] o ['difɛkt] s defecto, imperfección ‖ [dɪ'fɛkt] *intr* desertar

da
de

defection [dɪˈfɛkʃən] s defección; (*lack, failure*) falta

defective [dɪˈfɛktɪv] adj defectivo, defectuoso

defend [dɪˈfɛnd] tr defender

defendant [dɪˈfɛndənt] s (law) demandado, acusado

defender [dɪˈfɛndər] s defensor m

defense [dɪˈfɛns] s defensa

defenseless [dɪˈfɛnslɪs] adj indefenso

defensive [dɪˈfɛnsɪv] adj defensivo ‖ s defensiva

de•fer [dɪˈfʌr] v (pret & pp **-ferred;** ger **-ferring**) tr aplazar, diferir ‖ intr deferir

deference [ˈdɛfərəns] s deferencia

deferential [ˌdɛfəˈrɛnʃəl] adj deferente

deferment [dɪˈfʌrmənt] s aplazamiento, dilación

defiance [dɪˈfaɪ•əns] s oposición; desafío, provocación; **in defiance of** sin mirar a, a despecho de

defiant [dɪˈfaɪ•ənt] adj provocante, hostil

deficien•cy [dɪˈfɪʃənsi] s (pl **-cies**) carencia, deficiencia; (com) descubierto

deficient [dɪˈfɪʃənt] adj deficiente, defectuoso

deficit [ˈdɛfɪsɪt] adj deficitario ‖ s déficit m

defile [dɪˈfaɪl] o [ˈdifaɪl] s desfiladero ‖ [dɪˈfaɪl] tr corromper, manchar ‖ intr desfilar

define [dɪˈfaɪn] tr definir

definite [ˈdɛfɪnɪt] adj definido

definition [ˌdɛfɪˈnɪʃən] s definición

definitive [dɪˈfɪnɪtɪv] adj definitivo

deflate [dɪˈflet] tr desinflar

deflation [dɪˈfleʃən] s desinflación; (*of prices*) deflación

deflect [dɪˈflɛkt] tr desviar ‖ intr desviarse

deflower [diˈflaʊ•ər] tr desflorar

deforest [diˈfarɛst] o [diˈfɔrɛst] tr desforestar, despoblar

deform [dɪˈfɔrm] tr deformar

deformed [dɪˈfɔrmd] adj deforme

deformi•ty [dɪˈfɔrmɪti] s (pl **-ties**) deformidad

defraud [dɪˈfrɔd] tr defraudar

defray [diˈfre] tr sufragar, subvenir a

defrost [diˈfrɔst] tr descongelar, deshelar

defroster [diˈfrɔstər] s descongelador m

deft [dɛft] adj diestro, hábil

defunct [dɪˈfʌŋkt] adj difunto

de•fy [dɪˈfaɪ] v (pret & pp **-fied**) tr desafiar, provocar

deg. abbr **degree**

degeneracy [dɪˈdʒɛnərəsi] s degeneración

degenerate [dɪˈdʒɛnərɪt] adj & s degenerado ‖ [dɪˈdʒɛnəˌret] intr degenerar

degrade [dɪˈgred] tr degradar

degrading [dɪˈgredɪŋ] adj degradante

degree [dɪˈgri] s grado; **by degrees** de grado en grado; **to take a degree** graduarse, recibir un grado o título

dehumidifier [ˌdihjuˈmɪdɪˌfaɪ•ər] s deshumedecedor m

dehydrate [diˈhaɪdret] tr deshidratar

deice [diˈaɪs] tr deshelar

dei•fy [ˈdi•ɪˌfaɪ] v (pret & pp **-fied**) tr deificar

deign [den] intr dignarse

dei•ty [ˈdi•ɪti] s (pl **-ties**) deidad; **the Deity** Dios m

dejected [dɪˈdʒɛktɪd] adj abatido

dejection [dɪˈdʒɛkʃən] s abatimiento

del. abbr **delegate, delete**

delay [dɪˈle] s retraso, tardanza; parón ‖ tr retrasar ‖ intr demorarse

delectable [dɪˈlɛktəbəl] adj deleitable

delegate [ˈdɛlɪgɪt] s diputado, delegado; (*to a convention*) congresista mf ‖ [ˈdɛlɪˌget] tr delegar

delete [dɪˈlit] tr borrar, suprimir

deletion [dɪˈliʃən] s supresión

deliberate [dɪˈlɪbərɪt] adj pensado, reflexionado; (*slow in deciding*) cauto, circunspecto; (*slow in moving*) espacioso, lento ‖ [dɪˈlɪbəˌret] tr & intr deliberar

delica•cy [ˈdɛlɪkəsi] s (pl **-cies**) delicadeza; (*choice food*) golosina

delicatessen [ˌdɛlɪkəˈtɛsən] s colmado, tienda de ultramarinos ‖ spl ultramarinos

delicious [dɪˈlɪʃəs] adj delicioso, sabroso

delight [dɪˈlaɪt] s deleite m, delicia ‖ tr deleitar ‖ intr deleitarse

delightful [dɪˈlaɪtfəl] adj deleitoso, ameno, exquisito

delinquen•cy [dɪˈlɪŋkwənsi] s (pl **-cies**) culpa; (*in payment of debt*) morosidad; (*debt in arrears*) atrasos

delinquent [dɪˈlɪŋkwənt] adj culpado; (*in payment*) moroso, atrasado; no pagado ‖ s culpado; deudor moroso

delirious [dɪˈlɪrɪ•əs] adj delirante

deliri•um [dɪˈlɪrɪ•əm] s (pl **-ums** o **-a** [ə]) delirio

deliver [dɪˈlɪvər] tr entregar; asestar (*un golpe*); pronunciar, recitar (*un discurso*); transmitir, rendir (*energía*); partear (*a la mujer que está de parto*)

deliver•y [dɪˈlɪvəri] s (pl **-ies**) entrega; (*of mail*) distribución, reparto; (*of a speech*) declamación; (*childbirth*) alumbramiento, parto

delivery•man [dɪˈlɪvərɪmən] s (pl **-men** [mən]) mozo de reparto

delivery room s sala de alumbramiento

delivery service s servicio a domicilio

delivery truck s sedán m de reparto

dell [dɛl] s vallecito

delouse [diˈlaʊs] tr despiojar

delphinium [dɛlˈfɪnɪ•əm] s (*Delphinium ajacis*) espuela de caballero; (*Delphinium consolida*) consuelda real

delude [dɪˈlud] tr deludir, engañar

deluge [ˈdɛljudʒ] s diluvio ‖ tr inundar

delusion [dɪˈluʒən] s engaño, decepción

de luxe [dɪˈlʌks] adj & adv s de lujo

delve [dɛlv] intr cavar; **to delve into** cavar en

demagnetize [diˈmægnɪˌtaɪz] tr desimantar

demagogue [ˈdɛməˌgɑg] s demagogo

demand [dɪˈmænd] o [dɪˈmɑnd] s demanda; **to be in demand** tener demanda ‖ tr demandar perentoriamente

demanding [dɪˈmændɪŋ] adj exigente

demarcate [dɪˈmɑrket] o [ˈdimɑrˌket] tr demarcar

démarche [de'marʃ] *s* diligencia, gestión, paso

demeanor [dɪ'minər] *s* conducta, porte *m*

demented [dɪ'mɛntɪd] *adj* demente, dementado

demigod ['dɛmɪ,gad] *s* semidiós *m*

demijohn ['dɛmɪ,dʒan] *s* damajuana

demilitarize [di'mɪlɪtə,raɪz] *tr* desmilitarizar

demilitarized zone *s* zona desmilitarizada

demimonde ['dɛmɪ,mand] *s* mujeres de vida alegre

demise [dɪ'maɪz] *s* fallecimiento

demisemiquaver [,dɛmɪ'sɛmɪ,kwevər] *s* (mus) fusa

demitasse ['dɛmɪ,tæs] o ['dɛmɪ,tas] *s* taza pequeña

demobilize [di'mobɪ,laɪz] *tr* desmovilizar

democra•cy [dɪ'markrəsi] *s* (*pl* **-cies**) democracia

democrat ['dɛmə,kræt] *s* demócrata *mf*

democratic [,dɛmə'krætɪk] *adj* democrático

demodulate [di'madjə,let] *tr* desmodular

demolish [dɪ'malɪʃ] *tr* demoler

demolition [,dɛmə'lɪʃən] o [,dimə'lɪʃən] *s* demolición

demon ['dimən] *s* demonio

demoniacal [,dimə'naɪ•əkəl] *adj* demoníaco

demonstrate ['dɛmən,stret] *tr* demostrar ‖ *intr* demostrar; (*to show feelings in public gatherings*) manifestar

demonstration [,dɛmən'streʃən] *s* demostración; (*public show of feeling*) manifestación

demonstrative [dɪ'manstrətɪv] *adj* demostrativo; (*giving open exhibition of emotion*) extremoso

demonstrator ['dɛmən,stretər] *s* demostrador *m*; manifestante *mf*

demoralize [dɪ'mɔrə,laɪz] *tr* desmoralizar

demote [dɪ'mot] *tr* degradar

demotion [dɪ'moʃən] *s* degradación

de•mur [dɪ'mʌr] *v* (*pret & pp* **-murred;** *ger* **-murring**) *intr* poner reparos

demure [dɪ'mjʊr] *adj* modesto, recatado; grave, serio

demurrage [dɪ'mʌrɪdʒ] *s* (com) estadía

den [dɛn] *s* (*of animals, thieves*) madriguera; (*dirty little room*) cuchitril *m*; lugar *m* de retiro; cuarto de estudio; (*of lions*) (Bib) fosa

denaturalize [di'nætjərə,laɪz] *tr* desnaturalizar

denatured alcohol [di'netʃərd] *s* alcohol desnaturalizado

denial [dɪ'naɪ•əl] *s* denegación; negación, desmentida

denim ['dɛnɪm] *s* dril *m* de algodón

denizen ['dɛnɪzən] *s* habitante *mf*, vecino

Denmark ['dɛnmark] *s* Dinamarca

denomination [dɪ,namɪ'neʃən] *s* denominación; categoría, clase *f*; secta, confesión, comunión

denote [dɪ'not] *tr* denotar

dénoument [denu'mã] *s* desenlace *m*

denounce [dɪ'naʊns] *tr* denunciar

dense [dɛns] *adj* denso; estúpido

densi•ty ['dɛnsɪti] *s* (*pl* **-ties**) densidad

dent [dɛnt] *s* abolladura, mella ‖ *tr* abollar, mellar ‖ *intr* abollarse, mellarse

dental ['dɛntəl] *adj & s* dental *f*

dental floss *s* hilo dental, seda encerada

dental technician *s* mecánico-dentista *m*

dentrifrice ['dɛntɪfrɪs] *s* dentífrico

dentist ['dɛntɪst] *s* dentista *mf*

dentistry ['dɛntɪstri] *s* odontología

denture ['dɛntʃər] *s* dentadura artificial

denunciation [dɪ,nʌnsɪ'eʃən] o [dɪ,nʌnʃɪ'eʃən] *s* denuncia

de•ny [dɪ'naɪ] *v* (*pret & pp* **-nied**) *tr* (*to declare not to be true*) negar; (*to refuse*) denegar; **to deny oneself to callers** negarse ‖ *intr* negar; denegar

deodorant [di'odərənt] *adj & s* desodorante *m*

deodorize [di'odə,raɪz] *tr* desodorizar

deoxidize [di'aksɪ,daɪz] *tr* desoxidar

dep. *abbr* **department, departs, deputy**

depart [dɪ'part] *intr* partir, salir, irse; desviarse

department [dɪ'partmənt] *s* departamento; (*of government*) ministerio

department store *s* grandes almacenes *mpl*

departure [dɪ'partʃər] *s* partida, salida; desviación

depend [dɪ'pɛnd] *intr* depender; **to depend on** depender de

dependable [dɪ'pɛndəbəl] *adj* confiable, fidedigno

dependence [dɪ'pɛndəns] *s* dependencia

dependen•cy [dɪ'pɛndənsi] *s* (*pl* **-cies**) dependencia; (*country, territory*) posesión

dependent [dɪ'pɛndənt] *adj* dependiente ‖ *s* carga de familia, familiar *m* dependiente

depict [dɪ'pɪkt] *tr* describir, representar, pintar

deplete [dɪ'plit] *tr* agotar, depauperar

deplorable [dɪ'plorəbəl] *adj* deplorable

deplore [dɪ'plor] *tr* deplorar

deploy [dɪ'plɔɪ] *tr* (mil) desplegar ‖ *intr* (mil) desplegarse

deployment [dɪ'plɔɪmənt] *s* (mil) despliegue *m*

depolarize [di'polə,raɪz] *tr* despolarizar

depopulate [di'papjə,let] *tr* despoblar

deport [dɪ'port] *tr* deportar; **to deport oneself** conducirse, portarse

deportation [,dipor'teʃən] *s* deportación

deportee [,dipor'ti] *s* deportado

deportment [dɪ'portmənt] *s* conducta, comportamiento

depose [dɪ'poz] *tr & intr* deponer

deposit [dɪ'pazɪt] *s* depósito; (*down payment*) señal *f*, pago anticipado; (min) yacimiento ‖ *tr* depositar ‖ *intr* depositarse

deposit account *s* cuenta corriente

depositor [dɪ'pazɪtər] *s* cuentacorrentista *mf*, imponente *mf*

depot ['dipo] o ['dɛpo] *s* almacén *m*, depósito; (mil) depósito; (rr) estación

depraved [dɪ'prevd] *adj* depravado

depravi•ty [dɪ'prævɪti] *s* (*pl* **-ties**) depravación

deprecate ['dɛprɪ,ket] *tr* desaprobar

de
de

depreciate [dɪ'priʃɪ,et] *tr* (*to lower value or price of*) depreciar; (*to disparage*) desapreciar ‖ *intr* depreciarse

depreciation [dɪ,priʃɪ'eʃən] *s* (*drop in value*) depreciación; (*disparagement*) desaprecio

depress [dɪ'prɛs] *tr* deprimir; desanimar, desalentar; bajar (*los precios*)

depression [dɪ'prɛʃən] *s* depresión; desaliento; (*slump*) crisis *f*

deprive [dɪ'praɪv] *tr* privar

deprived [dɪ'praɪvd] *adj* desventajado

dept. *abbr* **department**

depth [dɛpθ] *s* profundidad; (*of a house, of a room*) fondo; **in the depth of night** en mitad de la noche; **in the depth of winter** en pleno invierno; **to go beyond one's depth** meterse en agua demasiado profunda; (fig) meterse en honduras

depth of hold *s* (naut) puntal *m*

depu·ty ['dɛpjəti] *s* (*pl* **-ties**) diputado

derail [dɪ'rel] *tr* hacer descarrilar ‖ *intr* descarrilar

derailment [dɪ'relmənt] *s* descarrilamiento

derange [dɪ'rendʒ] *tr* desarreglar, descomponer; trastornar el juicio a

derangement [dɪ'rendʒmənt] *s* desarreglo, descompostura; locura; obfuscación

der·by ['dʌrbi] *s* (*pl* **-bies**) sombrero hongo

deregulate [di'rɛgjə,let] *tr* descontrolar

derelict ['dɛrɪlɪkt] *adj* abandonado; negligente ‖ *s* pelafustán *m*; (naut) derrelicto

deride [dɪ'raɪd] *tr* burlarse de, ridiculizar

derision [dɪ'rɪʒən] *s* burla, irrisión

derive [dɪ'raɪv] *tr* & *intr* derivar

dermatitis [,dʌrmə'taɪtɪs] *s* dermatitis *f*

derogatory [dɪ'rɑgə,tori] *adj* despreciativo

derrick ['dɛrɪk] *s* grúa; (min) castillete *m*

dervish ['dʌrvɪʃ] *s* derviche *m*

desalinization [dɪ,selɪnɪ'zeʃən] *s* desalinización

desalt [di'sɔlt] *tr* desalar

descend [dɪ'sɛnd] *tr* bajar, descender (*la escalera*) ‖ *intr* bajar, descender; **to descend on** caer sobre, invadir

descendant [dɪ'sɛndənt] *adj* descendente ‖ *s* descendiente *mf*

descendent [dɪ'sɛndənt] *adj* descendente

descent [dɪ'sɛnt] *s* (*passing from higher to lower state*) descenso; (*extraction; lineage*) descendencia; cuesta, bajada; invasión

describe [dɪ'skraɪb] *tr* describir

description [dɪ'skrɪpʃən] *s* descripción

descriptive [dɪ'skrɪptɪv] *adj* descriptivo

de·scry [dɪ'skraɪ] *v* (*pret* & *pp* **-scried**) *tr* avistar, divisar; descubrir

desecrate ['dɛsɪ,kret] *tr* profanar

desegregation [di,sɛgrɪ'geʃən] *s* desegregación

desert ['dɛzərt] *adj* & *s* desierto, yermo ‖ [dɪ'zʌrt] *s* mérito; **he received his just deserts** llevó su merecido ‖ *tr* desertar de ‖ *intr* desertar

deserter [dɪ'zʌrtər] *s* desertor *m*

desertion [dɪ'zʌrʃən] *s* deserción; abandono de cónyuge

deserve [dɪ'zʌrv] *tr* & *intr* merecer

deservedly [dɪ'zʌrvɪdli] *adv* merecidamente

design [dɪ'zaɪn] *s* diseño; (*combination of details; art of designing*) dibujo; (*plan, scheme*) designio; **to have designs on** poner la mira en ‖ *tr* deseñar, dibjuar; idear, proyectar ‖ *intr* diseñar, dibujar

designate ['dɛzɪg,net] *tr* designar

designing [dɪ'zaɪnɪŋ] *adj* intrigante, maquinador

desirable [dɪ'zaɪrəbəl] *adj* deseable

desire [dɪ'zaɪr] *s* deseo ‖ *tr* desear

desirous [dɪ'zaɪrəs] *adj* deseoso

desist [dɪ'zɪst] *intr* desistir

desk [dɛsk] *s* bufete *m*, escritorio; (*lectern*) atril *m*; (*clerk's counter in a hotel*) caja

desk clerk *s* cajero, recepcionista *m*

desk set *s* juego de escritorio

desolate ['dɛsəlɪt] *adj* (*hopeless*) desolado; despoblado, yermo, desierto; solitario; (*dismal*) lúgubre ‖ ['dɛsə,let] *tr* desconsolar; (*to lay waste*) desolar, devastar; despoblar

desolation [,dɛsə'leʃən] *s* (*devastation; great affliction*) desolación; (*dreariness*) lobreguez *f*

despair [dɪ'spɛr] *s* desesperación ‖ *intr* desesperar, desesperarse

despairing [dɪ'spɛrɪŋ] *adj* desesperado

despera·do [,dɛspə'redo] o [,dɛspə'rado] *s* (*pl* **-does** o **-dos**) criminal dispuesto a todo

desperate ['dɛspərɪt] *adj* dispuesto a todo; (*bitter, excessive*) encarnizado; (*hopeless*) desesperado; (*remedy*) heroico

despicable ['dɛspɪkəbəl] *adj* despreciable, ruin

despise [dɪ'spaɪz] *tr* despreciar, desdeñar

despite [dɪ'spaɪt] *prep* a despecho de

desponden·cy [dɪ'spandənsi] *s* (*pl* **cies**) abatimiento, desaliento

despondent [dɪ'spandənt] *adj* abatido, desalentado

despot ['dɛspət] *s* déspota *m*

despotic [dɛs'patɪk] *adj* despótico

despotism ['dɛspə,tɪzəm] *s* despotismo

dessert [dɪ'zʌrt] *s* postre *m*

destination [,dɛstɪ'neʃən] *s* (*end of a journey or shipment*) destino; (*purpose*) destinación

destine ['dɛstɪn] *tr* destinar

desti·ny ['dɛstɪni] *s* (*pl* **-nies**) destino

destitute ['dɛstɪ,tjut] *adj* (*being in complete poverty*) indigente; (*lacking, deprived*) desprovisto

destitution [,dɛstɪ'tjuʃən] *s* indigencia

destroy [dɪ'strɔɪ] *tr* destruir

destroyer [dɪ'strɔɪ·ər] *s* (nav) destructor *m*

destruction [dɪ'strʌkʃən] *s* destrucción

destructive [dɪ'strʌktɪv] *adj* destructivo

desultory ['dɛsəl,tori] *adj* deshilvanado, descosido

detach [dɪ'tætʃ] *tr* desprender, separar; (mil) destacar

detachable [dɪ'tætʃəbəl] *adj* desprendible, separable; (*collar*) postizo

detached [dɪ'tætʃt] *adj* separado, suelto; imparcial, desinteresado

detachment [dɪ'tætʃmənt] *s* desprendimiento, separación; imparcialidad, desinterés *m*; (mil) destacamento

detail [dɪ'tel] o ['ditel] s detalle m, pormenor m; (mil) destacamento ‖ [dɪ'tel] tr detallar; (mil) destacar

detain [dɪ'ten] tr detener; tener preso

detect [dɪ'tɛkt] tr detectar

detection [dɪ'tɛkʃən] s detección

detective [dɪ'tɛktɪv] s detective m

detective story s novela policíaca o policial

detector [dɪ'tɛktər] s detector m

detention [dɪ'tɛnʃən] s detención

de•ter [dɪ'tʌr] v (pret & pp **-terred;** ger **-terring**) tr impedir, refrenar

detergent [dɪ'tərdʒənt] adj & s detergente m

deteriorate [dɪ'tɪrɪ•ə'ret] tr deteriorar ‖ intr deteriorarse

determination [dɪ,tʌrmə'neʃən] s resolución; empecinamiento

determine [dɪ'tʌrmɪn] tr determinar

deterrent [dɪ'tʌrənt] s impedimento, refrenamiento

detest [dɪ'tɛst] tr detestar, aborrecer

dethrone [dɪ'θron] tr destronar

detonate ['dɛtə,net] o ['ditə,net] tr hacer estallar ‖ intr detonar

detour ['ditʊr] o [dɪ'tʊr] s desvío; rodeo, vuelta; manera indirecta ‖ tr desviar (el tráfico) ‖ intr desviarse

detoxification [di,tɑksəfə'keʃən] s desintoxicación

detoxi•fy [di'tɑksə,faɪ] v (pret & pp **-fied**) tr desintoxicar

detract [dɪ'trækt] tr detraer ‖ intr — **to detract from** disminuir, rebajar

detriment ['dɛtrɪmənt] s perjuicio, detrimento; **to the detriment of** en perjuicio de

detrimental [,dɛtrɪ'mɛntəl] adj perjudicial

deuce [djus] o [dus] s (in cards) dos m; **the deuce!** ¡demonio!

devaluation [di,væljuˈeʃən] s desvalorización, devaluación

devastate ['dɛvəs,tet] tr devastar

devastation [,dɛvəs'teʃən] s devastación

develop [dɪ'vɛləp] tr desarrollar, desenvolver; (phot) revelar; explotar (una mina) ‖ intr desarrollarse, desenvolverse; evolucionar, manifestarse

developer [dɪ'vɛləpər] s fomentador m; (phot) revelador m

development [dɪ'vɛləpmənt] s desarrollo, desenvolvimiento; (phot) revelado; (of a mine) explotación; acontecimiento nuevo

developmental aid [dɪ,vɛləp'mɛntəl] s ayuda al desarrollo

deviate ['divɪ,et] tr desviar ‖ intr desviarse

deviation [,divɪ'eʃən] s desviación

deviationism [,divɪ'eʃə,nɪzəm] s desviacionismo

deviationist [,divɪ'eʃənɪst] s desviacionista mf

device [dɪ'vaɪs] s dispositivo, aparato; (trick) ardid m, treta; (motto) lema m, divisa; **to leave someone to his own devices** dejarle a uno que haga lo que se le antoje

dev•il ['dɛvəl] s diablo; **between the devil and the deep blue sea** entre la espada y la pared; **to raise the devil** (slang) armar un

alboroto ‖ v (pret & pp **iled** o **-illed;** ger **-iling** o **illing**) tr condimentar con picantes; (coll) acosar, molestar

devilish ['dɛvəlɪʃ] adj diabólico

devilment ['dɛvəlmənt] s (mischief) diablura; (evil) maldad

devil•try ['dɛvəltri] s (pl **-tries**) maldad, crueldad; (mischief) diablura

devious ['divɪ•əs] adj (straying) desviado, extraviado; (roundabout; shifty) tortuoso

devise [dɪ'vaɪz] tr idear, inventar; (law) legar

devoid [dɪ'vɔɪd] adj desprovisto

devote [dɪ'vot] tr dedicar

devoted [dɪ'votɪd] adj (zealous, ardent) devoto; dedicado

devotee [,dɛvə'ti] s devoto

devotion [dɪ'voʃən] s devoción; (to study, work, etc.) dedicación; **devotions** oraciones, preces fpl

devour [dɪ'vaʊr] tr devorar

devout [dɪ'vaʊt] adj devoto; cordial, sincero

dew [dju] o [du] s rocío

dew'drop s gota de rocío

dew'lap s papada

dew•y ['dju•i] o ['du•i] adj rociado

dexterity [dɛks'tɛrɪti] s destreza

D.F. abbr **Defender of the Faith**

diabetes [,daɪ•ə'bitɪs] s diabetes f

diabetic [,daɪ•ə'bɛtɪk] adj & s diabético

diabolic(al) [,daɪ•ə'balɪk(əl)] adj diabólico

diacritical [,daɪ•ə'krɪtɪkəl] adj diacrítico

diadem ['daɪ•ə,dɛm] s diadema f

diaere•sis [daɪ'ɛrɪsɪs] s (pl **-ses** [,siz]) diéresis f

diagnose [,daɪ•əg'nos] tr diagnosticar

diagno•sis [,daɪ•əg'nosɪs] s (pl **-ses** [siz]) diagnosis f, diagnóstico

diagonal [daɪ'ægənəl] adj & s diagonal f

diagram ['daɪ•ə,græm] s diagrama m

dial. abbr **dialect**

dial ['daɪ•əl] s (of radio) cuadrante m; (of watch) cuadrante m, esfera, muestra; (of telephone) disco selector ‖ tr sintonizar (el radiorreceptor); marcar (el número telefónico); llamar (a una persona) por teléfono automático ‖ intr (telp) marcar

dialect ['daɪ•ə,lɛkt] s dialecto

dialing ['daɪ•əlɪŋ] s (telp) marcaje m

dialogue ['daɪ•ə,lɔg] s diálogo

dial telephone s teléfono automático

dial tone s (telp) señal f para marcar

diam. abbr **diameter**

diameter [daɪ'æmɪtər] s diámetro

diametric(al) [,daɪ•ə'mɛtrɪk(əl)] adj diamétrico

diamond ['daɪmənd] s diamante m; (figure of a rhombus) losange m; (playing card) carró m, diamante m; (baseball) losange m

diaper ['daɪpər] s pañal m

diaphanous [daɪ'æfənəs] adj diáfano

diaphragm ['daɪ•ə,fræm] s diafragma m

diarrhea [,daɪ•ə'ri•ə] s diarrea; **to have diarrhea** cursear

dia•ry ['daɪ•əri] s (pl **-ries**) diario

diastole [daɪ'æstəli] s diástole f

diathermy ['daɪ•ə,θʌrmi] s diatermia

dice [daɪs] *spl* dados; (*small cubes*) cubitos; **to load the dice** cargar los dados ‖ *tr* cortar en cubos

dice′box′ *s* cubilete *m*

dichloride [daɪˈklɔraɪd] *s* dicloruro

dichoto•my [daɪˈkɑtəmi] *s* (*pl* **-mies**) dicotomía

dickey [ˈdɪki] *s* camisolín *m*, pechera postiza; babero de niño

dict. *abbr* **dictionary**

dictaphone [ˈdɪktəˌfon] *s* dictáfono

dictate [ˈdɪktet] *s* mandato ‖ [ˈdɪktet] o [dɪkˈtet] *tr* dictar; mandar

dictation [dɪkˈteʃən] *s* dictado; (*orders; giving orders*) mandato; **to take dictation** escribir al dictado

dictator [ˈdɪktetər] o [dɪkˈtetər] *s* dictador *m*

dictatorship [dɪkˈtetərˌʃɪp] *s* dictadura

diction [ˈdɪkʃən] *s* dicción

dictionar•y [ˈdɪkʃənˌɛri] *s* (*pl* **-ies**) diccionario

dic•tum [ˈdɪktəm] *s* (*pl* **-ta** [tə]) dictamen *m;* aforismo, sentencia

didactic(al) [daɪˈdæktɪk(əl)] o [dɪˈdæktɪk(əl)] *adj* didáctico

die [daɪ] *s* (*pl* **-dice** [daɪs]) dado; **the die is cast** la suerte está echada ‖ *s* (*pl* **dies**) (*for stamping coins, medals, etc.*) troquel *m;* (*for cutting threads*) hembra de terraja ‖ *v* (*pret & pp* **died;** *ger* **dying**) *intr* morir; **to be dying** estar agonizando; **to die laughing** morir de risa

die′hard′ *adj & s* intransigente *mf*

die′sel-elec′tric [ˈdizəl] *adj* dieseleléctrico

diesel engine *s* diesel *m*

diesel oil *s* gas-oil *m*

die′stock′ *s* terraja

diet [ˈdaɪ•ət] *s* dieta, régimen alimenticio ‖ *intr* estar a dieta

dietitian [ˌdaɪ•əˈtɪʃən] *s* dietista *mf*

diff. *abbr* **difference, different**

differ [ˈdɪfər] *intr* (*to be different*) diferir, diferenciarse; (*to dissent*) diferenciar; **to differ with** desavenirse con

difference [ˈdɪfərəns] *s* diferencia; **to make no difference** no importar; **to split the difference** partir la diferencia

different [ˈdɪfərənt] *adj* diferente

differentiate [ˌdɪfəˈrɛnʃɪˌet] *tr* diferenciar ‖ *intr* diferenciarse

difficult [ˈdɪfɪˌkʌlt] *adj* difícil

difficul•ty [ˈdɪfɪˌkʌlti] *s* (*pl* **-ties**) dificultad

diffident [ˈdɪfɪdənt] *adj* apocado, tímido

diffuse [dɪˈfjus] *adj* difuso ‖ [dɪˈfjuz] *tr* difundir ‖ *intr* difundirse

dig [dɪg] *s* (*poke*) empuje *m;* (*jibe*) pulla, palabra hiriente ‖ *v* (*pret & pp* **dug** [dʌg] o **digged;** *ger* **digging**) *tr* cavar, excavar; **to dig up** desenterrar ‖ *intr* cavar, excavar; **to dig in** (coll) poner manos a la obra; (mil) antrincherarse; **to dig under** socavar

digest [ˈdaɪdʒɛst] *s* compendio, resumen *m;* (law) digesto ‖ [dɪˈdʒɛst] o [daɪˈdʒɛst] *tr & intr* digerir

digestible [dɪˈdʒɛstɪbəl] o [daɪˈdʒɛstɪbəl] *adj* digerible, digestible

digestion [dɪˈdʒɛstʃən] o [daɪˈdʒɛstʃən] *s* digestión

digestive [dɪˈdʒɛstɪv] o [daɪˈdʒɛstɪv] *adj & s* digestivo

digit [ˈdɪdʒɪt] *s* dígito

digital telephone [ˈdɪdʒətəl] *s* teléfono digital

dignified [ˈdɪgnɪˌfaɪd] *adj* digno, grave, decoroso

digni•fy [ˈdɪgnɪˌfaɪ] *v* (*pret & pp* **-fied**) *tr* dignificar; engrandecer el mérito de

dignitar•y [ˈdɪgnɪˌtɛri] *s* (*pl* **-ies**) dignatario

digni•ty [ˈdɪgnɪti] *s* (*pl* **-ties**) dignidad; **to stand upon one's dignity** ponerse tan alto

digress [dɪˈgrɛs] o [daɪˈgrɛs] *intr* divagar

digression [dɪˈgrɛʃən] o [daɪˈgrɛʃən] *s* digresión, divagación

dike [daɪk] *s* dique *m;* (*bank of earth thrown up in digging*) montón *m;* (*causeway*) arrecife *m*, malecón *m*

dilapidated [dɪˈlæpɪˌdetɪd] *adj* destartalado, desvencijado

dilate [daɪˈlet] *tr* dilatar ‖ *intr* dilatarse

dilatory [ˈdɪləˌtori] *adj* tardío

dilemma [dɪˈlɛmə] *s* dilema *m*, disyuntiva, encerrona

dilettan•te [ˌdɪləˈtænti] *adj* diletante ‖ *s* (*pl* **-tes** o **-ti** [ti]) diletante *mf*

diligence [ˈdɪlɪdʒəns] *s* diligencia; dedicación

diligent [ˈdɪlɪdʒənt] *adj* diligente

dill [dɪl] *s* eneldo

dillydal•ly [ˈdɪlɪˌdæli] *v* (*pret & pp* **-lied**) *intr* malgastar el tiempo, haraganear

dilute [dɪˈlut] o [daɪˈlut] *adj* diluído ‖ [dɪˈlut] *tr* diluir ‖ *intr* diluirse

dilution [dɪˈluʃən] *s* dilución

dim. *abbr* **diminutive**

dim [dɪm] *adj* (*comp* **dimmer;** *super* **dimmest**) débil, indistinto, confuso; obscuro, poco claro; (*chance*) escaso; (*not clearly understanding*) torpe, lerdo; **to take a dim view of** mirar escépticamente ‖ *v* (*pret & pp* **dimmed;** *ger* **dimming**) *tr* amortiguar (*la luz*); poner (*un faro*) a media luz; disminuir ‖ *intr* obscurecerse

dime [daɪm] *s* moneda de diez centavos

dimension [dɪˈmɛnʃən] *s* dimensión

diminish [dɪˈmɪnɪʃ] *tr* disminuir ‖ *intr* disminuir, disminuirse

diminution [ˌdɪməˈnuʃən] *s* disminución

diminutive [dɪˈmɪnjətɪv] *adj* (*tiny*) diminuto; (gram) diminutivo ‖ *s* diminutivo

dimi•ty [ˈdɪmɪti] *s* (*pl* **-ties**) cotonía

dimly [ˈdɪmli] *adv* indistintamente

dimmer [ˈdɪmər] *s* amortiguador *m* de luz; (aut) lámpara de cruce, luz *f* de cruce

dimple [ˈdɪmpəl] *s* hoyuelo

dimwit [ˈdɪmˌwɪt] *s* (slang) mentecato, bobo

dim•witted [ˈdɪmˌwɪtɪd] *adj* (slang) mentecato, bobo

din [dɪn] *s* estruendo, ruido ensordecedor ‖ *v* (*pret & pp* **dinned;** *ger* **dinning**) *tr* ensordecer con mucho ruido; repetir insistentemente; impresionar con repetición ruidosa ‖ *intr* sonar estrepitosamente

dine [daɪn] *tr* dar de comer a; obsequiar con una cena o comida ‖ *intr* cenar, comer; **to dine out** cenar fuera de casa

diner ['daɪnər] *s* invitado a una cena, convidado a una comida; coche-comedor *m*

ding-dong ['dɪŋ,dɔŋ] *s* dindán *m*

din-gy ['dɪndʒi] *adj* (*comp* **-gier**; *super* **-giest**) deslustrado, sucio

dining car *s* coche-comedor *m*

dining room *s* comedor *m*

din'ing-room' suite *s* juego de comedor

dinner ['dɪnər] *s* cena, comida; (*formal meal*) banquete *m*

dinner coat o **jacket** *s* smoking *m*

dinner pail *s* fiambrera, portaviandas *m*

dinner set *s* vajilla

dinner time *s* hora de la cena o comida

dint [dɪnt] *s* abolladura; **by dint of** a fuerza de ‖ *tr* abollar

diocese ['daɪ·ə·sɪs] o ['daɪ·əsɪs] *s* diócesi *f* o diócesis *f*

diode ['daɪ·od] *s* diodo

dioxide [daɪ'aksaɪd] *s* dióxido

dip [dɪ] *s* zambullida, inmersión; baño corto; (*in a road*) depresión; (*of magnetic needle*) inclinación ‖ *v* (*pret & pp* **dipped**; *ger* **dipping**) *tr* sumergir; sacar con cuchara; (*bread*) sopetear; **to dip the colors** saludar con la bandera ‖ *intr* sumergirse; inclinarse hacia abajo; desaparecer súbitamente; **to dip into** hojear (*un libro*); meterse en (*un comercio*); **to dip into one's purse** gastar dinero

diphtheria [dɪf'θɪrɪ·ə] *s* difteria

diphthong ['dɪfθɔŋ] *s* diptongo

diphthongize ['dɪfθɔŋ,gaɪz] *tr* diptongar ‖ *intr* diptongarse

diploma [dɪ'plomə] *s* diploma *m*

diploma-cy [dɪ'ploməsi] *s* (*pl* **-cies**) diplomacia

diplomat ['dɪplə,mæt] *s* diplomático

diplomatic [,dɪplə'mætɪk] *adj* diplomático

diplomatic pouch *s* valija diplomática

dipper ['dɪpər] *s* cazo, cucharón *m*

dip'stick' *s* varilla de nivel

dire [daɪr] *adj* horrendo, espantoso

direct [dɪ'rɛkt] o [daɪ'rɛkt] *adj* directo; franco, sincero ‖ *tr* dirigir; mandar, ordenar

direct current *s* corriente continua

direct discourse *s* (gram) estilo directo

direct hit *s* blanco directo, impacto directo

direction [dɪ'rɛkʃən] o [daɪ'rɛkʃən] *s* dirección; instrucción; **directions** (*for use*) modo de empleo

direction light *s* (aut) intermitente *m*

direct object *s* (gram) complemento directo

director [dɪ'rɛktər] o [daɪ'rɛktər] *s* director *m*, administrador *m*; (*member of a governing body*) vocal *m*

directorship [dɪ'rɛktərʃɪp] o [daɪ'rɛktərʃɪp] *s* dirección, directorio

directo-ry [dɪ'rɛktəri] o [daɪ'rɛktəri] *s* (*pl* **-ries**) (*list of names and addresses; board of directors*) directorio; anuario telefónico, guía telefónica

dirge [dʌrdʒ] *s* endecha, canto fúnebre, treno; (eccl) misa de réquiem

dirigible ['dɪrɪdʒɪbəl] *adj & s* dirigible *m*

dirt [dʌrt] *s* (*soil*) tierra, suelo; (*dust*) polvo; (*mud*) barro, lodo; excremento; (*accumulation of dirt*) suciedad; (*moral filth*) suciedad, porquería, obscenidad; (*gossip*) chismes *mpl*

dirt'cheap' *adj* tirado, muy barato

dirt road *s* camino de tierra

dirt-y ['dʌrti] *adj* (*comp* **-ier**; *super* **-iest**) puerco, sucio; berroso, enlodado; polvoriento; (*obscene*) hediondo; bajo, vil ‖ *v* (*pret & pp* **-tied**) *tr* ensuciar

dirty linen *s* ropa sucia; **to air one's dirty linen in public** sacar los trapos sucios a relucir

dirty trick *s* (slang) perrada, mala partida

disabili-ty [,dɪsə'bɪlɪti] *s* (*pl* **-ties**) incapacidad, inhabilidad; disminución (*física*)

disable [dɪs'ebəl] *tr* incapacitar, inhabilitar, lisiar; (law) descalificar

disabled veteran *s* lisiado de guerra

disabuse [,dɪsə'bjuz] *tr* desengañar

disadvantage [,dɪsəd'væntɪdʒ] o [,dɪsəd'vantɪdʒ] *s* desventaja

disadvantaged [,dɪsəd'væntɪdʒd] *adj & s* desventajado

disadvantageous [dɪs,ædvən'teʒəs] *adj* desventajoso

disagree [,dɪsə'gri] *intr* desavenirse, desconvenirse; (*to quarrel*) altercar, contender; **to disagree with** no estar de acuerdo con; no sentar bien

disagreeable [,dɪsə'gri·əbəl] *adj* desagradable

disagreement [,dɪsə'grimənt] *s* desavenencia, desacuerdo; disensión; inconformidad

disappear [,dɪsə'pɪr] *intr* desaparecer, desaparecerse

disappearance [,dɪsə'pɪrəns] *s* desaparecimiento, desaparición

disappoint [,dɪsə'pɔɪnt] *tr* decepcionar, desilusionar, chasquear; **to be disappointed** chasquearse, llevarse chasco

disappointment [,dɪsə'pɔɪntmənt] *s* decepción, desilusión, chasco

disapproval [,dɪsə'pruvəl] *s* desaprobación

disapprove [,dɪsə'pruv] *tr & intr* desaprobar

disarm [dɪs'arm] *tr* desarmar ‖ *intr* desarmar, desarmarse

disarmament [dɪs'arməmənt] *s* desarme *m*, desarmamiento

disarming [dɪs'armɪŋ] *adj* congraciador, simpático

disarray [,dɪsə're] *s* desorden *m*; (*in apparel*) desavío ‖ *tr* desordenar; desataviar

disaster [dɪ'zæstər] *s* desastre *m*, siniestro

disaster area *s* zona siniestrada

disastrous [dɪ'zæstrəs] *adj* desastroso, desastrado

disavow [,dɪsə'vau] *tr* desconocer, negar, repudiar

disband [dɪs'bænd] *tr* disolver (*una asamblea*); licenciar (*tropas*) ‖ *intr* desbandarse

dis-bar [dɪs'bar] *v* (*pret & pp* **-barred**; *ger* **-barring**) *tr* (law) expulsar del foro

disbelief [ˈdɪsbɪˈlif] s incredulidad
disbelieve [ˈdɪsbɪˈlig] tr & intr descreer
disburse [dɪsˈbʌrs] tr desembolsar
disbursement [dɪsˈbʌrsmənt] s desembolso
disc. abbr **discount, discoverer**
disc [dɪsk] s disco
discard [dɪsˈkard] s descarte m; **to put into the discard** desechar ‖ tr descartar; desechar
discern [dɪˈzʌrn] o [dɪˈsʌrn] tr discernir, percibir
discerning [dɪˈzʌrnɪŋ] o [dɪˈsʌrnɪŋ] adj discerniente, perspicaz
discharge [dɪsˈtʃardʒ] s (of a gun, of a battery) descarga; (of a prisoner) liberación; (of a duty) desempeño; (of a debt, of an obligation) descargo; (from a job) despedida, remoción; (mil) certificado de licencia; (pathol) derrame m ‖ tr descargar; desempeñar (un deber); libertar (a un preso); despedir, remover (a un empleado); (from the hospital) dar de alta; (mil) licenciar ‖ intr descargar (un tubo, río, etc.); descargarse (un arma de fuego)
disciple [dɪˈsaɪpəl] s discípulo
disciplinarian [ˌdɪsɪplɪˈnɛrɪˌən] s ordenancista mf
discipline [ˈdɪsɪplɪn] s disciplina; castigo ‖ tr disciplinar; castigar
disclaim [dɪsˈklem[tr desconocer, negar
disclose [dɪsˈkloz] tr divulgar, revelar; descubrir
disclosure [dɪsˈkloʒər] s divulgación, revelación; descubrimiento
disco [ˈdɪsko] abbr **discotheque**
discolor [dɪsˈkʌlər] tr descolorar ‖ intr descolorarse
discomfiture [dɪsˈkʌmfɪtʃər] s desconcierto; frustración
discomfort [dɪsˈkʌmfərt] s incomodidad ‖ tr incomodar
disconcert [ˌdɪskənˈsʌrt] tr desconcertar, confundir
disconnect [ˌdɪskəˈnɛkt] tr desunir, separar; desconectar
disconsolate [dɪsˈkansəlɪt] adj desconsolado, desolado
discontent [ˌdɪskənˈtɛnt] adj & s descontento ‖ tr descontentar
discontented [ˌdɪskənˈtɛntɪd] adj descontento
discontinue [ˌdɪskənˈtɪnju] tr descontinuar
discord [ˈdɪskɔrd] s desacuerdo, discordia; discordancia
discordance [dɪsˈkɔrdəns] s discordancia
discotheque [ˌdɪskoˈtɛk] s discoteca
discount [ˈdɪskaʊnt] s descuento ‖ [ˈdɪskaʊnt] o [dɪsˈkaʊnt] tr descontar; descontar por exagerado
discount rate s tipo de descuento; tipo de redescuento
discourage [dɪsˈkʌrɪdʒ] tr desalentar, desanimar; desaprobar; disuadir
discouragement [dɪsˈkʌrɪdʒmənt] s desaliento; desaprobación; disuasión
discourse [ˈdɪskors] o [dɪsˈkors] s discurso ‖ [dɪsˈkors] intr discurrir
discourteous [dɪsˈkʌrtɪˌəs] adj descortés

discourte•sy [dɪsˈkʌrtəsi] s (pl **-sies**) descortesía
discover [dɪsˈkʌvər] tr descubrir
discover•y [dɪsˈkʌvəri] s (pl **-ies**) descubrimiento
discredit [dɪsˈkrɛdɪt] s descrédito ‖ tr desacreditar
discreditable [dɪsˈkrɛdɪtəbəl] adj deshonroso
discreet [dɪsˈkrit] adj discreto
discrepan•cy [dɪsˈkrɛpənsi] s (pl **-cies**) discrepancia
discrete [dɪsˈkrit] adj discreto
discretion [dɪsˈkrɛʃən] s discreción; **at discretion** a discreción
discriminate [dɪsˈkrɪmɪˌnet] intr discriminar; **to discriminate against** discriminar
discrimination [dɪsˌkrɪmɪˈneʃən] s discriminación
discriminatory [dɪsˈkrɪmɪnəˌtori] adj discriminatorio
discus [ˈdɪskəs] s (sport) disco
discuss [dɪsˈkʌs] tr & intr discutir
discussion [dɪsˈkʌʃən] s discusión
discus thrower [ˈθroˌər] s discóbolo
disdain [dɪsˈden] s desdén m ‖ tr desdeñar
disdainful [dɪsˈdenfəl] adj desdeñoso
disease [dɪˈziz] s enfermedad
diseased [dɪˈzizd] adj morboso
disembark [ˌdɪsɛmˈbark] tr & intr desembarcar
disembarkation [dɪsˌɛmbarˈkeʃən] s (of passengers) desembarco; (of freight) desembarque m
disembowel [ˌdɪsɛmˈbauˌəl] tr desentrañar
disenchant [ˌdɪsɛnˈtʃænt] tr desencantar
disenchantment [ˌdɪsɛnˈtʃæntmənt] s desencanto
disengage [ˌdɪsɛnˈgedʒ] tr (from a pledge) desempeñar; (to disconnect) desenganchar; desembragar (el motor)
disengagement [ˌdɪsɛnˈgedʒmənt] s desempeño; desenganche m; desembrague m
disentangle [ˌdɪsɛnˈtæŋgəl] tr desenredar
disentanglement [ˌdɪsɛnˈtæŋgəlmənt] s desenredo
disestablish [ˌdɪsɛsˈtæblɪʃ] tr separar (la Iglesia) del Estado
disfavor [dɪsˈfevər] s disfavor m
disfigure [dɪsˈfɪgjər] tr desfigurar
disfranchise [dɪsˈfræntʃaɪz] tr privar de los derechos de ciudadanía
disgorge [dɪsˈgɔrdʒ] tr & intr vomitar
disgrace [dɪsˈgres] s deshonra, vergüenza; disfavor m; metedura ‖ tr deshonrar, avergonzar; despedir con ignominia
disgraceful [dɪsˈgresfəl] adj deshonroso, vergonzoso
disgruntle [dɪsˈgrʌntəl] tr disgustar, enfadar
disguise [dɪsˈgaɪz] s disfraz m ‖ tr disfrazar
disgust [dɪsˈgʌst] s asco, repugnancia ‖ tr dar asco a, repugnar
disgusting [dɪsˈgʌstɪŋ] adj asqueroso, repugnante; bofe (CAm)
dish [dɪʃ] s (any container used at table) vasija; (shallow, circular dish; its contents) plato; **to wash the dishes** lavar la vajilla ‖ tr servir en un plato; (slang) arruinar

dish'cloth' s albero
dishearten [dɪs'hɑrtən] tr descorazonar, desalentar, desanimar
dishev•el [dɪ'ʃɛvəl] v (pret & pp -eled o -elled; ger -eling o -elling) desgreñar, desmelenar
dishonest [dɪs'ɑnɪst] adj no honrado, ímprobo
dishones•ty [dɪs'ɑnɪsti] s (pl -ties) falta de honradez, improbidad
dishonor [dɪs'ɑnər] s deshonra, deshonor m || tr deshonrar, deshonorar; (com) no aceptar, no pagar
dishonorable [dɪs'ɑnərəbəl] adj ignominioso, deshonroso
dish'pan' s paila de lavar la vajilla
dish rack s escurreplatos m
dish'rag' s albero
dish'tow'el s paño para secar platos
dish'wash'er s (person) fregona; (machine) lavaplatos m, lavavajillas m
dish'wa'ter s agua de lavar platos, agua sucia
disillusion [,dɪsɪ'luʒən] s desilusión || tr desilusionar
disillusionment [,dɪsɪ'luʒənmənt] s desilusión
disinclination [dɪs,ɪnklɪ'neʃən] s aversión, desafición
disinclined [,dɪsɪn'klaɪnd] adj desinclinado
disinfect [,dɪsɪn'fɛkt] tr desinfectar, desinficionar
disinfectant [,dɪsɪn'fɛktant] adj & s desinfectante m
disingenuous [,dɪsɪn'dʒɛnjʊ•əs] adj insincero, poco ingenuo
disinherit [,dɪsɪn'hɛrɪt] tr desheredar
disintegrate [dɪs'ɪntɪ,gret] tr desagregar, desintegrar || intr desagregarse, desintegrarse
disintegration [dɪs,ɪntɪ'greʃən] s desagregación, desintegración
disin•ter [,dɪsɪn'tʌr] v (pret & pp -terred; ger -terring) tr desenterrar
disinterested [dɪs'ɪntə,rɛstɪd] o [dɪs'ɪntrɪstɪd] adj desinteresado
disinterestedness [dɪs'ɪntə,rɛstɪdnɛs] o [dɪs'ɪntrɪstɪdnɪs] s desinterés m
disjunctive [dɪs'dʒʌŋktɪv] adj disyuntivo
disk [dɪsk] s disco
disk brake s freno de disco
disk jockey s (rad) locutor m de un programa de discos
dislike [dɪs'laɪk] s aversión, antipatía; **to take a dislike for** cobrar aversión a || tr desamar
dislocate ['dɪslo,ket] tr dislocar, dislocarse (un hueso)
dislodge [dɪs'lɑdʒ] tr desalojar
disloyal [dɪs'lɔɪ•əl] adj desleal
disloyal•ty [dɪs'lɔɪ•əlti] s (pl -ties) deslealtad
dismal ['dɪzməl] adj lúgubre, tenebroso; terrible, espantoso
dismantle [dɪs'mæntəl] tr desarmar, desmontar
dismay [dɪs'me] s consternación || tr consternar
dismember [dɪs'mɛmbər] tr desmembrar

dismiss [dɪs'mɪs] tr despedir, destituir; desechar; alejar del pensamiento, echar en olvido
dismissal [dɪs'mɪsəl] s despedida, destitución
dismount [dɪs'maʊnt] tr desmontar || intr desmontarse
disobedience [,dɪsə'bidi•əns] s desobediencia
disobedient [,dɪsə'bidi•ənt] adj desobediente
disobey [,dɪsə'be] tr & intr desobedecer
disorder [dɪs'ɔrdər] s desorden m || tr desordenar
disorderly [dɪs'ɔrdərli] adj desordenado; alborotador, revoltoso
disorderly conduct s conducta contra el orden público
disorderly house s burdel m, lupanar m
disorganize [dɪs'ɔrgə,naɪz] tr desorganizar
disorientation [dɪs,ɔrien'teʃən] s desorientación
disown [dɪs'on] tr desconocer, repudiar
disparage [dɪs'pærɪdʒ] tr desacreditar, desdorar
disparagement [dɪs'pærɪdʒmənt] s descrédito, desdoro
disparate ['dɪspərɪt] adj disparejo
dispari•ty [dɪs'pærɪti] s (pl -ties) disparidad
dispassionate [dɪs'pæʃənɪt] adj desapasionado
dispatch [dɪs'pætʃ] s despacho || tr despachar; (coll) despabilar (una comida)
dis•pel [dɪs'pɛl] v (pret & pp -pelled; ger -pelling) tr desvanecer, disipar
dispensa•ry [dɪs'pɛnsəri] s (pl -ries) dispensario
dispense [dɪs'pɛns] tr dispensar (medicamentos); administrar (justicia); expender (p.ej., gasolina); (to exempt) eximir || intr — **to dispense with** deshacerse de; pasar sin, prescindir de
disperse [dɪs'pʌrs] tr dispersar || intr dispersarse
displace [dɪs'ples] tr remover, trasladar; despedir, deponer; reemplazar; desplazar (un volumen de agua)
displaced person s persona desplazada
display [dɪs'ple] s despliegue m; exhibición, exposición; ostentación || tr (to unfold; to reveal) desplegar; (to exhibit, show) exhibir, exponer; (to show ostentatiously) ostentar
display cabinet s vitrina, escaparate m
display window s escaparate m de tienda
displease [dɪs'pliz] tr desagradar, disgustar, desplacer
displeasing [dɪs'plizɪŋ] adj desagradable
displeasure [dɪs'plɛʒər] s desagrado, disgusto, desplacer m
disposable [dɪs'pozəbəl] adj (available for any use) disponible; (made to be thrown away after serving its purpose) desechable, descartable
disposal [dɪs'pozəl] s disposición; donación, liquidación, venta; **at the disposal of** a la disposición de; **to have at one's disposal** disponer de

di
di

dispose [dɪs'poz] *tr* disponer; inducir, mover ‖ *intr* disponer; **to dispose of** disponer de; deshacerse de; dar, vender; acabar con

disposition [,dɪspə'zɪʃən] *s* disposición; índole *f*, genio, natural *m;* ajuste *m,* arreglo; venta

dispossess [,dɪspə'zɛs] *tr* desposeer; (*to evict, oust*) desahuciar

disproof [dɪs'pruf] *s* confutación, refutación

disproportionate [,dɪsprə'porʃənɪt] *adj* desproporcionado

disprove [dɪs'pruv] *tr* confutar, refutar

dispute [dɪs'pjut] *s* disputa; **beyond dispute** sin disputa; **in dispute** disputado ‖ *tr & intr* disputar

disquali•fy [dɪs'kwɑlɪ,faɪ] *v* (*pret & pp* -**fied**) *tr* descalificar, desclasificar

disquiet [dɪs'kwaɪ•ət] *s* desasosiego, inquietud ‖ *tr* desasosegar, inquietar

disregard [,dɪsrɪ'gɑrd] *s* desatención, desaire *m* ‖ *tr* desatender, desairar, pasar por alto

disrepair [,dɪsrɪ'pɛr] *s* desconcierto, descompostura

disreputable [dɪs'rɛpjətəbəl] *adj* desacreditado, de mala fama; raído, usado, desaliñado

disrepute [,dɪsrɪ'pjut] *s* descrédito, mala fama; **to bring into disrepute** desacreditar, dar mala fama a

disrespect [,dɪsrɪ'spɛkt] *s* desacato ‖ *tr* desacatar

disrespectful [,dɪsrɪ'spɛktfəl] *adj* irrespetuoso

disrobe [dɪs'rob] *tr* desnudar ‖ *intr* desnudarse, despelotarse

disrupt [dɪs'rʌpt] *tr* romper; (*to throw into disorder*) desbaratar

dissatisfaction [,dɪssætɪs'fæk∫ən] *s* desagrado, descontento, insatisfacción

dissatisfied [dɪs'sætɪs,faɪd] *adj* descontento

dissatis•fy [dɪs'sætɪs,faɪ] *v* (*pret & pp* -**fied**) *tr* descontentar

dissect [dɪ'sɛkt] *tr* disecar

dissemble [dɪ'sɛmbəl] *tr* disimular ‖ *intr* disimular; obrar hipócritamente

disseminate [dɪ'sɛmɪ,net] *tr* diseminar, difundir

dissension [dɪ'sɛnʃən] *s* disensión

dissent [dɪ'sɛnt] *s* disensión; (*nonconformity*) disidencia ‖ *intr* disentir; (*from doctrine or authority*) disidir

dissenter [dɪ'sɛntər] *s* disidente *mf*

disservice [dɪ'sʌrvɪs] *s* deservicio

dissidence ['dɪsɪdəns] *s* disidencia

dissident ['dɪsɪdənt] *adj & s* disidente *mf*

dissimilar [dɪ'sɪmɪlər] *adj* disímil, desemejante

dissimilate [dɪ'sɪmɪ,let] *tr* disimilar ‖ *intr* disimilarse

dissimulate [dɪ'sɪmjə,let] *tr & intr* disimular

dissipate ['dɪsɪ,pet] *tr* disipar ‖ *intr* disiparse; entregarse a la disipación

dissipated ['dɪsɪ,petɪd] *adj* disipado, disoluto

dissipation [,dɪsɪ'peʃən] *s* disipación

dissociate [dɪ'soʃɪ,et] *tr* disociar

dissolute ['dɪsə,lut] *adj* disoluto

dissolution [,dɪsə'luʃən] *s* disolución

dissolve [dɪ'zɑlv] *tr* disolver ‖ *intr* (*to have the power of dissolving*) disolver; (*to pass into a liquid*) disolverse

dissonance ['dɪsənəns] *s* disonancia

dissuade [dɪ'swed] *tr* disuadir

dissyllabic [,dɪssɪ'læbɪk] *adj* disílabo, disilábico

dissyllable [dɪ'sɪləbəl] *s* disílabo

dist. *abbr* **distance, distinguish, district**

distaff ['dɪstæf] *s* rueca

distaff side *s* rama femenina de la familia

distance ['dɪstəns] *s* distancia; **at a distance** a distancia; **in the distance** a lo lejos; **to keep at a distance** no permitir familiaridades; **to keep one's distance** mantenerse a distancia

distant ['dɪstənt] *adj* distante; (*relative*) lejano; (*not familiar*) frío, indiferente

distaste [dɪs'test] *s* aversión, repugnancia

distasteful [dɪs'testfəl] *adj* desagradable, repugnante

distemper [dɪs'tɛmpər] *s* enfermedad; (*of dogs*) moquillo

distend [dɪs'tɛnd] *tr* ensanchar, distender ‖ *intr* ensancharse, distender

distension [dɪs'tɛnʃən] *s* ensanche *m*, distensión

distill [dɪs'tɪl] *tr* destilar

distillation [,dɪstɪ'leʃən] *s* destilación

distiller•y [dɪs'tɪləri] *s* (*pl* -**ies**) destilería, destilatorio

distinct [dɪs'tɪŋkt] *adj* distinto; cierto, indudable; (*not blurred*) nítido, bien definido

distinction [dɪs'tɪŋkʃən] *s* distinción; (*distinguishing characteristic*) distintivo

distinctive [dɪs'tɪŋktɪv] *adj* distintivo

distinguish [dɪs'tɪŋgwɪʃ] *tr* distinguir

distinguished [dɪs'tɪŋgwɪʃt] *adj* distinguido

distort [dɪs'tɔrt] *tr* deformar, torcer; distorsionar; (*the truth*) falsear

distortion [dɪs'tɔrʃən] *s* deformación, torcimiento; (*of the truth*) falseamiento; (*rad*) deformación, distorsión

distract [dɪs'trækt] *tr* distraer

distraction [dɪs'trækʃən] *s* distracción

distraught [dɪs'trɔt] *adj* trastornado, perplejo, aturdido

distress [dɪs'trɛs] *s* pena, aflicción, angustia; infortunio, peligro ‖ *tr* apenar, afligir, angustiar

distressing [dɪs'trɛsɪŋ] *adj* penoso, angustioso

distress signal *s* señal *f* de socorro

distribute [dɪs'trɪbjut] *tr* distribuir, repartir

distribution [,dɪstrɪ'bjuʃən] *s* distribución; repartimiento, repartida

distributor [dɪs'trɪbjətər] *s* distribuidor *m;* (*aut*) distribuidor

district ['dɪstrɪkt] *s* comarca, región; (*of a city*) barrio; (*administrative division*) distrito ‖ *tr* dividir en distritos

district attorney *s* fiscal *m*

distrust [dɪs'trʌst] *s* desconfianza ‖ *tr* desconfiar de

distrustful [dɪs'trʌstfəl] *adj* desconfiado

disturb [dɪs'tʌrb] *tr* disturbar, incomodar, molestar; desordenar, revolver; inquietar, dejar perplejo; perturbar (*el orden público*)

disturbance [dɪsˈtɑrbəns] *s* disturbio, molestia; desorden *m;* inquietud; tumulto, trastorno

disuse [dɪsˈjus] *s* desuso

ditch [dɪtʃ] *s* zanja ‖ *tr* zanjar; echar en una zanja; (slang) deshacerse de ‖ *intr* amarar forzosamente

ditch reed *s* carrizo

dither [ˈdɪðər] *s* agitación, temblor; **to be in a dither** (coll) estar muy agitado

dit•to [ˈdɪto] *s* (*pl* **-tos**) ídem *m;* (*ditto symbol*) íd.; copia, duplicado ‖ *tr* copiar, duplicar

ditto mark *s* la sigla '' (*es decir:* íd.)

dit•ty [ˈdɪti] *s* (*pl* **-ties**) cancioneta

diuretic [ˌdaɪəˈrɛtɪk] *adj & s* diurético

div. *abbr* **dividend, division**

diva [ˈdivɑ] *s* (mus) diva

divan [ˈdaɪvæn] o [dɪˈvæn] *s* diván *m*

dive [daɪv] *s* zambullida; (*of a submarine*) sumersión; (aer) picado; (coll) leonera, tasca ‖ *v* (*pret & pp* **dived** o **dove** [dov]) *intr* zambullirse; (*to work as a diver*) bucear; sumergirse (*un submarino*); (aer) picar

dive'-bomb' *tr & intr* bombardear en picado

dive bombing *s* bombardeo en picado

diver [ˈdaɪvər] *s* zambullidor *m;* buceador; (*person who works under water*) escafandrista *mf,* buzo; (orn) zambullidor *m*

diverge [dɪˈvʌrdʒ] o [daɪˈvʌrdʒ] *intr* divergir

divers [ˈdaɪvərz] *adj* diversos, varios

diverse [dɪˈvʌrs] o [daɪˈvʌrs] *adj* (*different*) diverso; (*of various kinds*) variado

diversification [dɪˈvʌrsɪfɪˈkeʃən] o [daɪˌvʌrsɪfɪˈkeʃən] *s* diversificación

diversi•fy [dɪˈvʌrsɪˌfaɪ] o [daɪˈvʌrsɪˌfaɪ] *v* (*pret & pp* **-fied**) *tr* diversificar ‖ *intr* diversificarse

diversion [dɪˈvʌrʒən] o [daɪˈvʌrʒən] *s* diversión

diversi•ty [dɪˈvʌrsɪti] o [daɪˈvʌrsɪti] *s* (*pl* **-ties**) diversidad

divert [dɪˈvʌrt] o [daɪˈvʌrt] *tr* apartar, divertir; (*to entertain*) divertir, entretener; (mil) divertir

diverting [dɪˈvʌrtɪŋ] o [daɪˈvʌrtɪŋ] *adj* divertido

divest [dɪˈvɛst] o [daɪˈvɛst] *tr* desnudar; despojar, desposeer; **to divest oneself of** desposeerse de

divide [dɪˈvaɪd] *s* (geog) divisoria ‖ *tr* dividir ‖ *intr* dividirse

dividend [ˈdɪvɪˌdɛnd] *s* dividendo

dividers [dɪˈvaɪdərz] *spl* compás *m* de división

divination [ˌdɪvɪˈneʃən] *s* adivinación

divine [dɪˈvaɪn] *adj* divino ‖ *s* sacerdote *m,* clérigo ‖ *tr* adivinar

diving [ˈdaɪvɪŋ] *s* zambullida; buceo

diving bell *s* campana de buzo

diving board *s* trampolín *m*

diving suit *s* escafandra

divining rod [dɪˈvaɪnɪŋ] *s* vara de adivinar; (*ostensibly to discover water or metals*) vara buscadora

divini•ty [dɪˈvɪnɪti] *s* (*pl* **-ties**) divinidad; teología; **the Divinity** Dios *m*

division [dɪˈvɪʒən] *s* división

divisor [dɪˈvaɪzər] *s* (math) divisor *m*

divorce [dɪˈvors] *s* divorcio; **to get a divorce** divorciarse ‖ *tr* divorciar (*los cónyuges*); divorciarse de (*la mujer o el marido*) ‖ *intr* divorciarse

divorcee [dɪvorˈsi] *s* persona divorciada; mujer divorciada

divulge [dɪˈvʌldʒ] *tr* divulgar, revelar

dizziness [ˈdɪzɪnɪs] *s* vértigo; confusión, perplejidad

diz•zy [ˈdɪzi] *adj* (*comp* **-zier;** *super* **-ziest**) (*suffering or causing dizziness*) vertiginoso; confuso, perplejo; aturdido, incauto; (coll) tonto

do. *abbr* **ditto**

do [du] *v* (*tercera persona* **does** [dʌz]; *pret* **did** [dɪd]; *pp* **done** [dʌn]) *tr* hacer; resolver (*un problema*); recorrer (*cierta distancia*); cumplir con (*un deber*); aprender (*una lección*); componer (*la cama*); tocar (*el cabello*); rendir (*homenaje*); **to do one's best** hacer todo lo posible; **to do over** volver a hacer; repetir; renovar; **to do right by** tratar bien; **to do someone out of something** (coll) defraudar algo a alguien; **to do to death** despachar, matar; **to do up** empaquetar; poner en orden; almidonar y planchar (*una camisa*) ‖ *intr* actuar, obrar; conducirse; servir, ser suficiente; estar, hallarse; **how do you do?** ¿cómo está Vd.?; **that will do** eso sirve, eso es bastante; no digas más; **to have done** haber terminado; **to have done with** no tener más que ver con; **to have nothing to do with** no tener nada que ver con; **to have to do with** tratar de; **to do away with** suprimir; matar; **to do for** servir para; **to do well** salir bien; **to do without** pasar sin ‖ *v aux* úsase 1) en oraciones interrogativas: **Do you speak Spanish?** ¿Habla Vd. español?; 2) en oraciones negativas; **I do not speak Spanish** No hablo español; 3) para substituir a otro verbo en oraciones elípticas; **Did you go to church this morning? Yes, I did** ¿Fué Vd. a la iglesia esta mañana? Sí, fuí; 4) para dar más energía a la oración; **I do believe what you told me** Yo sí creo lo que me dijo Vd.; 5) en inversiones después de ciertos adverbios; **Seldom does he come to see me** él rara vez viene a verme; 6) en tono suplicante con el imperativo; **Do come in** pase Vd., por favor

docile [ˈdɑsɪl] *adj* dócil

dock [dɑk] *s* (*wharf*) muelle *m;* (*waterway between two piers*) dársena; (*area including piers and waterways*) puerto de mar; muñón *m* de cola; (law) tribuna de los acusados ‖ *tr* (naut) atracar en el muelle; derrabar, descolar (*a un animal*); reducir o suprimir (*el salario*) ‖ *intr* (naut) atracar

dockage [ˈdɑkɪdʒ] *s* entrada en un puerto; (*charges*) muellaje *m*

docket ['dɑkɪt] s actas, orden m del día; lista de causas pendientes; **on the docket** (coll) pendiente, entre manos

dock hand s portuario

dock'yard' s arsenal m, astillero

doctor ['dɑktər] s doctor m; (physician) médico ‖ tr medicinar; (coll) componer, reparar ‖ intr (coll) ejercer la medicina; (coll) tomar medicinas

doctorate ['dɑktərɪt] s doctorado

doctrine ['dɑktrɪn] s doctrina

document ['dɑkjəmənt] s documento ‖ ['dɑkjə,mɛnt] tr documentar

documenta·ry [,dɑkjə'mɛntəri] adj documental ‖ s (pl -ries) documental m

documentation [,dɑkəmɛn'teʃən] s documentación

doddering ['dɑdərɪŋ] adj chocho, temblón

dodge [dɑdʒ] s esguince m, regate m; (fig) regate ‖ tr evitar (un golpe); (fig) evitar mañosamente ‖ intr regatear, hurtar el cuerpo; **to dodge around the corner** voltear la esquina

do·do ['dodo] s (pl -dos o -does) (coll) inocente m de ideas anticuadas

doe [do] s cierva, gama, coneja

doeskin ['do,skɪn] s ante m, piel f de ante; tejido fino de lana

doff [dɑf] o [dɔf] tr quitarse (el sombrero, la ropa)

dog [dɔg] o [dɑg] s perro; **to go to the dogs** darse al abandono; **lucky dog** (coll) lechero, suertero; **to put on the dog** (coll) darse ínfulas ‖ v (pret & pp **dogged**; ger **dogging**) tr acosar, perseguir

dog'catch'er s lacero

dog days spl canícula, canicularse mpl

doge [dodʒ] s dux m

dogged ['dɔgɪd] adj tenaz, terco

doggerel ['dɔgərəl] s coplas de ciego

dog·gy ['dɔgi] adj (comp -gier; super -giest) emperejilado ‖ s (pl -gies) perrito

dog'house' s perrera

dog in the manger s el perro del hortelano

dog Latin s latinajo, latín m de cocina

dogmatic [dɑg'mætɪk] adj dogmático; ergotista

dog racing s carreras de galgos

dog's-ear ['dɔgzɛɪr] s orejón m

dog show s exposición canina

dog's life s vida miserable

Dog Star s Canícula

dog'-tired' adj cansadísimo

dog'tooth' s (pl -teeth [,tiθ] colmillo

dog track s galgódromo

dog'watch' s (naut) guardia de cuartillo

dog'wood' s cornejo

doi·ly ['dɔɪli] s (pl -lies) pañito de adorno

doings ['duːɪŋz] spl acciones, obras, actividad

doldrums ['dɑldrəmz] spl (naut) calmas ecuatoriales; desanimación, inactividad

dole [dol] s limosna; subsidio a los desocupados ‖ tr — **to dole out** distribuir en pequeñas porciones

doleful ['dolfəl] adj triste, lúgubre

doll [dɑl] s muñeca ‖ intr — **to doll up** (slang) emperejilarse

dollar ['dɑlər] s dólar m

dollar mark s signo del dólar

dol·ly ['dɑli] s (pl -lies) muñequita; (low, wheeled frame for moving heavy loads) gato rodante

dolphin ['dɑlfɪn] s delfín m

dolt [dolt] s bobalicón m

doltish ['doltɪʃ] adj bobalicón

dom. abbr **domestic, dominion**

domain [do'men] s dominio, heredad, propiedad; (of learning) campo

dome [dom] s cúpula, domo

dome light s (aut) lámpara de techo

domestic [də'mɛstɪk] adj & s doméstico

domesticate [də'mɛstɪ,ket] tr domesticar

domicile ['dɑmɪsɪl] o ['dɑmɪ,saɪl] s domicilio ‖ tr domiciliar

dominance ['dɑmɪnəns] s dominación

dominant ['dɑmɪnənt] adj & s dominante f

dominate ['dɑmɪ,net] tr & intr dominar

domination [,dɑmɪ'neʃən] s dominación

domineer [,dɑmɪ'nɪr] intr dominar

domineering [,dɑmɪ'nɪrɪŋ] adj dominante, mandón

Dominican [də'mɪnɪkən] adj & s dominicano

dominion [də'mɪnjən] s dominio

domi·no ['dɑmɪ,no] s (pl -noes o -nos) (costume) dominó m; antifaz m; persona que lleva dominó; ficha (del juego de dominó); **dominoes** ssg dominó (juego)

don [dɑn] s caballero, señor m, personaje m de alta categoría; (coll) preceptor m, socio de uno de los colegios de las Universidades de Oxford y Cambridge ‖ v (pret & pp **donned**; ger **donning**) tr ponerse (el sombrero, la ropa)

donate ['donet] tr dar, donar

donation [do'neʃən] s donación

done [dʌn] adj hecho, terminado; cansado, rendido; bien asado

done for adj (coll) cansado, rendido, agotado; (coll) arruinado, destruído; (coll) fuera de combate; (coll) muerto

donjon ['dʌndʒən] s torre f del homenaje

donkey ['dɑŋki] s asno, burro

donnish ['dɑnɪʃ] adj magistral, pedantesco

donor ['donər] s donador m

doodle ['dudəl] tr & intr borrajear

doom [dum] s ruina, perdición, muerte f; condena, juicio; juicio final; hado, destino ‖ tr condenar; sentenciar a muerte; predestinar a la ruina, a la muerte

doomsday ['dumz,de] s día m del juicio final; día del juicio

door [dor] s puerta; (of a carriage or automobile) portezuela; (one part of a double door) hoja, batiente m; **behind closed doors** a puertas cerradas; **to see to the door** acompañar a la puerta

door'bell' s campanilla de puerta, timbre m de puerta

door check s amortiguador m, cierre m de puerta

door'frame' *s* bastidor *m* de puerta, marco de puerta

door'head' *s* dintel *m*

door'jamb' *s* jamba de puerta

door'knob' *s* botón *m* de puerta, pomo de puerta

door knocker *s* aldaba

door latch *s* pestillo

door·man ['dɔrmən] *s* (*pl* -men [mən]) portero; (*one who helps people in and out of cars*) abrecoches *m*

door'mat' *s* felpudo de puerta

door'nail' *s* clavo de adorno para puertas; **dead as a doornail** (coll) muerto sin duda alguna

door'post' *s* jamba de puerta

door scraper *s* limpiabarros *m*

door'sill' *s* umbral *m*

door'step' *s* escalón *m* delante de la puerta; escalera exterior

door'stop' *s* tope *m* de puerta

door'way' *s* puerta, portal *m*

dope [dop] *s* grasa lubricante; (aer) barniz *m*, nobabia; (slang) bobo, tonto; (slang) informes *mpl*; (slang) narcótico ‖ *tr* (slang) narcotizar, drogar; **to dope out** (slang) descifrar

dope fiend *s* (slang) toxicómano

dope sheet *s* (slang) hoja confidencial sobre los caballos de carreras

dormant ['dɔrmənt] *adj* durmiente, latente

dormer window ['dɔrmər] *s* buharda, buhardilla

dormito·ry ['dɔrmɪ,tori] *s* (*pl* -ries) dormitorio común

dor·mouse ['dɔr,maʊs] *s* (*pl* -mice [,maɪs]) lirón *m*

dosage ['dosɪdʒ] *s* dosificación

dose [dos] *s* dosis *f*; (coll) mal trago ‖ *tr* medicinar; dosificar (*un medicamento*)

dossier ['dasɪ,e] *s* expediente *m*

dot [dɑt] *s* punto; **on the dot** (coll) en punto ‖ *v* (*pret & pp* **dotted**; *ger* **dotting**) *tr* (*to make with dots*) puntear; poner punto a; **to dot one's i's** poner los puntos sobre las íes

dotage ['dotɪdʒ] *s* chochera, chochez *f*; **to be in one's dotage** chochear

dotard ['dotərd] *s* viejo chocho

dote [dot] *intr* chochear; **to dote on** estar chocho por

doting ['dotɪŋ] *adj* chocho

dots and dashes *spl* (telg) puntos y rayas

dotted line ['datɪd] *s* línea de puntos; **to sign on the dotted line** firmar ciegamente

double ['dʌbəl] *adj* doble ‖ *adv* doble; dos juntos ‖ *s* doble *m*, duplo; (mov, theat) doble *mf*; **doubles** (tennis juego de dobles ‖ *tr* doblar; ser el doble de; (bridge) doblar ‖ *intr* doblarse; (mov, theat, bridge) doblar; **to double up** doblarse en dos; ocupar una misma habitación, dormir en una misma cama (*dos personas*)

double-barreled ['dʌbəl'bærəld] *adj* de dos cañones; (fig) para dos fines

double bass [bes] *s* contrabajo

double bassoon *s* contrabajón *m*

double bed *s* cama de matrimonio

double-breasted ['dʌbəl'brɛstɪd] *adj* cruzado, de dos pechos

double chin *s* papada

dou'ble-cross' *tr* traicionar (*a un cómplice*)

double date *s* cita de dos parejas

doub'le-deal'er *s* persona doble

double-edged ['dʌbəl'ɛdʒd] *adj* de dos filos

double entry *s* (com) partida doble

double feature *s* (mov) programa *m* doble, programa de dos películas de largo metraje

doubleheader ['dʌbəl'hɛdər] *s* tren *m* con dos locomotoras; (baseball) dos partidos jugados sucesivamente

double-jointed ['dʌbəl'dʒɔɪntɪd] *adj* de articulaciones dobles

dou'ble-park' *tr & intr* aparcar en doble fila

dou'ble-quick' *adj & adv* a paso ligero ‖ *s* paso ligero ‖ *intr* marchar a paso ligero

doublet ['dʌblɪt] *s* (*close-fitting jacket*) jubón *m*; (*counterfeit stone; each of two words having the same origin*) doblete *m*

double talk *s* (coll) galimatías *m*; (coll) habla ambigua para engañar

double time *s* pago doble por horas extraordinarias de trabajo; (mil) paso redoblado

doubleton ['dʌbəltən] *s* doblete *m*

double track *s* doble vía

doubling ['dʌblɪŋ] *s* reduplicación

doubt [daʊt] *s* duda; **beyond doubt** sin duda; **if in doubt** en caso de duda; **no doubt** sin duda ‖ *tr* dudar, dudar de ‖ *intr* dudar

doubter ['daʊtər] *s* incrédulo

doubtful ['daʊtfəl] *adj* dudoso

doubtless ['daʊtlɪs] *adj* indudable ‖ *adv* sin duda; probablemente

douche [duʃ] *s* ducha; (*instrument*) jeringa ‖ *tr* duchar ‖ *intr* ducharse

dough [do] *s* masa, pasta; (*money*) (slang) pasta

dough'boy' *s* (coll) soldado norteamericano de infantería

dough'nut' *s* rosquilla, buñuelo

dough·ty ['daʊti] *adj* (*comp* -tier; *super* -tiest) (hum) fuerte, valiente

dough·y ['do·i] *adj* (*comp* -ier; *super* -iest) pastoso

dour [daʊr] *o* [dʊr] *adj* triste, melancólico, austero

douse [daʊs] *tr* empapar, mojar, salpicar; (slang) apagar (*la luz*)

dove [dʌv] *s* paloma

dovecote ['dʌv,kot] *s* palomar *m*

dove'tail' *s* cola de milano, cola de pato ‖ *tr* ensamblar a cola de milano, ensamblar a cola de pato; (*to make fit*) encajar ‖ *intr* (*to fit*) encajar; concordar, corresponder

dowager ['daʊ·ədʒər] *s* viuda con título o bienes que proceden del marido, p.ej., **dowager duchess** duquesa viuda; (coll) matrona, señora anciana respetable

dow·dy ['daʊdi] *adj* (*comp* -dier; *super* -diest) desaliñado

dow·el ['daʊ·əl] *s* clavija ‖ *v* (*pret & pp* -eled *o* -elled; *ger* -eling *o* -elling) *tr* enclavijar

dower ['daʊ·ər] *s* (*widow's portion*) viudedad; (*marriage portion*) dote *m & f*; (*natu-*

ral gift) prenda ‖ *tr* señalar viudedad a; dotar

down [daʊn] *adj* descendente; abatido, triste; enfermo, malo; acostado, echado; (*money, payment*) anticipado; (*storage battery*) agotado; (*mach*) (coll) fuera de servicio ‖ *adv* abajo; hacia abajo; en tierra; al sur; por escrito; al contado; **down and out** arruinado; sin blanca; **down from** desde; **down on one's knees** de rodillas; **down to** hasta; **down under** entre los antípodas; **down with ...!** ¡abajo ...!; **to get down to work** aplicarse resueltamente al trabajo; **to go down** bajar; **to lie down** acostarse; **to sit down** sentarse ‖ *prep* bajando; **down the river** río abajo; **down the street** calle abajo ‖ *s* (*of fruit and human body*) vello; (*of birds*) plumón *m;* descenso, revés *m* de fortuna; (*sand hill*) duna ‖ *tr* derribar; (coll) tragar

down'cast' *adj* cariacontecido

down'fall' *s* caída, ruina; chaparrón *m;* nevazo

down'grade' *adj* (coll) pendiente, en declive ‖ *adv* (coll) cuesta abajo ‖ *s* bajada, declive *m;* **to be on the downgrade** decaer, declinar ‖ *tr* disminuir la categoría de

downhearted ['daʊn,hɑrtɪd] *adj* abatido, desanimado

down'hill' *adj* pendiente ‖ *adv* cuesta abajo; **to go downhill** ir cabeza abajo

down'pour' *s* aguacero, chaparrón *m*

down'right' *adj* absoluto, categórico; franco; claro ‖ *adv* absolutamente

down'stairs' *adj* de abajo ‖ *adv* abajo ‖ *s* piso inferior, pisos inferiores; (*the help*) la servidumbre

down'stream' *adv* aguas abajo, río abajo

down'stroke' *s* carrera descendente

down'town' *adj* céntrico ‖ *adv* al centro de la ciudad, en el centro de la ciudad ‖ *s* barrios céntricos, calles céntricas

down train *s* tren *m* descendente

down'trend' *s* tendencia a la baja

downtrodden ['daʊn,trɑdən] *adj* pisoteado, oprimido

downward ['daʊnwərd] *adj* descendente ‖ *adv* hacia abajo; hacia una época posterior

down•y ['daʊni] *adj* (*comp* **-ier;** *super* **-iest**) plumoso, felpudo, velloso; suave, blando

dow•ry ['daʊri] *s* (*pl* **-ries**) dote *m & f*

doz. *abbr* **dozen**

doze [doz] *s* duermevela, sueño ligero ‖ *intr* dormitar

dozen ['dʌzən] *s* docena

dozy ['dozi] *adj* soñoliento

D.P. *abbr* **displaced person**

dpt. *abbr* **department**

dr. *abbr* **debtor, drawer, dram**

Dr. *abbr* **debtor, Doctor**

drab [dræb] *adj* (*comp* **drabber;** *super* **drabbest**) gris amarillento; monótono ‖ *s* gris amarillento; ramera; mujer desaliñada

drach•ma ['drækmə] *s* (*pl* **-mas** o **-mae** [mi]) dracma

draft [dræft] *s* corriente *f* de aire; (*pulling; current of air in a chimney*) tiro; (*sketch,*

outline) bosquejo; (*first form of a writing*) borrador *m;* (*drink*) bebida, trago; (com) giro, letra de cambio, libranza; aire inspirado; (naut) calado; (mil) conscripción, quinta; **drafts** damas, juego de damas; **on draft** a presión; **to be exempted from the draft** redimirse de las quintas ‖ *tr* dibujar; bosquejar; hacer un borrador de; redactar (*un documento*); (mil) quintar; **to be drafted** (mil) ir a quintas

draft age *s* edad *f* de quintas

draft beer *s* cerveza a presión

draft board *s* (mil) junta de reclutamiento

draft call *s* llamada a quintas

draft dodger ['dɑdʒər] *s* emboscado

draftee [,dræf'ti] *s* conscripto, quinto

draft horse *s* caballo de tiro

drafting room *s* sala de dibujo

drafts•man ['dræftsmən] *s* (*pl* **-men** [mən]) dibujante *m;* (*man who draws up documents*) redactor *m;* (*in checkers*) peón *m*

draft treaty *s* proyecto de convenio

draft•y ['dræfti] *adj* (*comp* **-ier;** *super* **-iest**) airoso, con corrientes de aire

drag [dræg] *s* (*sledge for conveying heavy bodies*) narria; (*on a cigarette*) chupada; fumada; (naut) rastra; (aer) resistencia al avance; (fig) estorbo, impedimento; **to have a drag** (slang) tener buenas aldabas, tener enchufe ‖ *v* (*pret & pp* **dragged;** *ger* **dragging**) *tr* arrastrar; (naut) rastrear ‖ *intr* arrastrarse por el suelo; avanzar muy lentamente; decaer (*el interés*); **to drag on** ser interminable, prolongarse interminablemente

drag'net' *s* red barredera

dragon ['drægən] *s* dragón *m*

drag'on-fly' *s* (*pl* **-flies**) caballito del diablo, libélula

dragoon [drə'gun] *s* (*soldier*) dragón *m* ‖ *tr* tiranizar; forzar, constreñir

drain [dren] *s* dren *m,* desaguadero, desagüe *m;* (surg) dren *m;* (*source of continual expense*) (fig) desaguadero ‖ *tr* drenar, desaguar; avenar (*terrenos húmedos*); escurrir (*una vasija; un líquido*) ‖ *intr* desaguarse; escurrirse

drainage ['drenɪdʒ] *s* drenaje *m,* desagüe *m*

drain'board' *s* escurridero

drain cock *s* llave *f* de purga

drain'pipe' *s* tubo de desagüe, escurridero

drain plug *s* tapón *m* de desagüe; (aut) tapón de vaciado

drake [drek] *s* pato

dram [dræm] *s* dracma; trago de aguardiente

drama ['drɑmə] o ['dræmə] *s* drama *m;* (*art and genre*) dramática

dramatic [drə'mætɪk] *adj* dramático ‖ **dramatics** *ssg* representación de aficionados; *spl* obras representadas por aficionados

dramatist ['dræmətɪst] *s* dramático

dramatize ['dræmə,taɪz] *tr* dramatizar

dram'shop' *s* bar *m,* taberna

drape [drep] *s* cortina, colgadura; (*hang of a curtain, skirt, etc.*) caída ‖ *tr* cubrir con colgaduras; adornar con colgaduras; disponer los pliegues de (*una colgadura, una prenda de vestir*)

draper•y ['drepəri] s (*pl* **-ies**) colgaduras, ropaje *m*

drastic ['dræstɪk] *adj* drástico

draught [dræft] *s & tr* var de **draft**

draught beer *s* cerveza a presión

draw [drɔ] *s* (*in a game or other contest*) empate *m;* (*in chess or checkers*) tablas; (*in a lottery*) sorteo; (*card drawn from the bank*) robo; (*of a drawbridge*) compuerta; (*of a chimney*) tiro ‖ *v* (*pret* **drew** [dru]; *pp* **drawn** [drɔn]) *tr* tirar (*una línea; alambre*); (*to attract*) tirar; (*to pull*) tirar de; derretir (*la mantequilla*); sacar (*un clavo, una espada, agua, una conclusión*); atraerse (*aplausos*); atraer (*a la gente*); aspirar (*el aire*); llamar (*la atención*); dar (*un suspiro*); correr (*una cortina*); cobrar (*un salario*); sacarse (*un premio*); empatar (*una partida*); robar (*fichas, naipes*); levantar (*un puente levadizo*); calar (*un buque cierta profundidad*); hacer (*una comparación*); consumir (*amperios*); (*to sketch in lines*) dibujar; (*to sketch in words*) redactar; (*com*) girar, librar; (*com*) devengar (*interés*); **to draw forth** hacer salir; **to draw off** sacar, extraer; trasegar (*un líquido*); **to draw on** ocasionar, provocar; ponerse (*p.ej., los zapatos*); (*com*) girar a cargo de; **to draw oneself up** enderezarse con dignidad; **to draw out** (*to persuade to talk*) sonsacar, tirar de la lengua a; **to draw up** redactar (*un documento*); (*mil*) ordenar para el combate ‖ *intr* tirar, tirar bien (*una chimenea*); empatar; echar suertes; atraer mucha gente; dibujar; **to draw aside** apartarse; **to draw back** retroceder, retirarse; **to draw near** acercarse; acercarse a; **to draw to a close** estar para terminar; **to draw together** juntarse, unirse

draw'back' *s* desventaja, inconveniente *m*

draw'bridge' *s* puente levadizo

drawee [,drɔ'i] *s* girado, librado

drawer ['drɔ•ər] *s* dibujante *mf;* (*com*) girador *m*, librador *m* ‖ [drɔr] *s* cajón *m*, gaveta; **drawers** calzoncillos

drawing ['drɔ•ɪŋ] *s* dibujo; (*in a lottery*) sorteo

drawing board *s* tablero de dibujo

drawing card *s* polo de atracción popular

drawing room *s* sala, salón *m*

draw'knife' *s* (*pl* **-knives** [,naɪvz]) cuchilla de dos mangos

drawl [drɔl] *s* habla lenta y prolongada ‖ *tr* decir lenta y prolongadamente ‖ *intr* hablar lenta y prolongadamente

drawn butter [drɔn] *s* mantequilla derretida

drawn work *s* calado, deshilado

dray [dre] *s* carro fuerte, camión *m;* (*sledge*) narria

drayage ['dre•ɪdʒ] *s* acarreo

dread [drɛd] *adj* espantoso, terrible *s* pavor *m*, terror *m* ‖ *tr & intr* temer

dreadful ['drɛdfəl] *adj* espantoso, terrible; (*coll*) feo, desagradable

dread'naught' *s* (*nav*) gran buque acorazado

dream [drim] *s* sueño, ensueño; (*thing of great beauty*) sueño; (*fancy, illusion*) ensueño; **dream come true** sueño hecho realidad ‖ *v* (*pret & pp* **dreamed** o **dreamt** [drɛmt]) *tr* soñar; **to dream up** (*coll*) imaginar, inventar; ‖ *intr* soñar; **to dream of** soñar con

dreamer ['drimər] *s* soñador *m*

dream'land' *s* reino del ensueño

dream'world' *s* tierra de la fantasía

dream•y ['drimi] *adj* (*comp* **-ier;** *super* **-iest**) soñador; visionario; vago

drear•y ['drɪri] *adj* (*comp* **-ier;** *super* **-iest**) sombrío, triste; monótono, pesado

dredge [drɛdʒ] *s* draga ‖ *tr* dragar, rastrear; (*culin*) enharinar

dredger ['drɛdʒər] *s* draga (*barco*)

dredging ['drɛdʒɪŋ] *s* dragado

dregs [drɛgz] *spl* heces *fpl;* (*of society*) hez *f*

drench [drɛntʃ] *tr* mojar, empapar

dress [drɛs] *s* ropa, vestidos; vestido de mujer; (*skirt*) falda; traje *m* de etiqueta; (*of a bird*) plumaje *m* ‖ *tr* vestir; (*to provide with clothing*) trajear; peinar (*el pelo*); curar (*una herida*); zurrar (*el cuero*); empavesar (*un barco*); adornar, ataviar; aderezar, aliñar (*los manjares*); **to dress down** (*coll*) reprender; **to get dressed** vestirse ‖ *intr* (*to put one's clothing on*) vestirse; (*to wear clothes*) vestir; (*mil*) alinearse; **to dress up** vestirse de etiqueta; ponerse de veinticinco alfileres; disfrazarse

dress ball *s* baile *m* de etiqueta

dress coat *s* frac *m*

dresser ['drɛsər] *s* tocador *m;* cómoda con espejo; (*sideboard*) aparador *m;* **to be a good dresser** vestir con elegancia

dress form *s* maniquí *m*

dress goods *spl* géneros para vestidos

dressing ['drɛsɪŋ] *s* adorno; (*for food*) aliño, salsa; (*stuffing for fowl*) relleno; (*fertilizer*) abono; (*for a wound*) vendaje *m*

dress'ing-down' *s* (*coll*) repasata, regaño

dressing gown *s* bata, peinador *m*

dressing room *s* cuarto de vestir; (*theat*) camarín *m*

dressing station *s* (*mil*) puesto de socorro

dressing table *s* tocador *m;* peinador *m*

dress'mak'er *s* costurera, modista

dress'mak'ing *s* costura, modistería

dress rehearsal *s* ensayo general

dress shirt *s* camisa de pechera almidonada, camisa de pechera de encaje

dress shop *s* casa de modas

dress suit *s* traje *m* de etiqueta

dress tie *s* corbata de smoking, corbata de frac

dress•y ['drɛsi] *adj* (*comp* **-ier;** *super* **-iest**) (*coll*) elegante; (*showy*) acicalado, vistoso, peripuesto

dribble ['drɪbəl] *s* goteo; (*coll*) llovizna ‖ *tr* (*sport*) driblar ‖ *intr* gotear; (*at the mouth*) babear; (*sport*) driblar

driblet ['drɪblɪt] *s* gotita; pedacito

dried beef [draɪd] *s* cecina

dried fig *s* higo paso

dried peach *s* orejón *m*

do
dr

drier ['draɪ·ər] *s* enjugador *m; (for hair)* secador *m; (for clothes)* secadora; *(rack for drying clothes)* tendedero (de ropa)

drift [drɪft] *s* movimiento; *(of sand, snow)* montón *m; (movement of snow)* ventisca; tendencia, dirección; intención, sentido; (aer, naut) deriva; (rad, telv) desviación ‖ *intr* flotar a la deriva; amontonarse *(la nieve)*; ventiscar; (aer, naut) derivar, ir a la deriva; (fig) vivir sin rumbo

drift ice *s* hielo flotante

drift'wood' *s* madera flotante; madera llevada por el agua; madera arrojada a la playa por el agua; *(people)* vagos

drill [drɪl] *s* taladro; instrucción; *(fabric)* dril *m;* (mil) ejercicio ‖ *tr* taladrar; instruir; (mil) enseñar el ejercicio a ‖ *intr* adiestrarse; (mil) hacer el ejercicio

drill'mas'ter *s* amaestrador *m;* (mil) instructor *m*

drill press *s* prensa taladradora

drink [drɪŋk] *s* bebida; **the drinks are on the house!** ¡convida la casa! ‖ *v* (*pret* **drank** [dræŋk]; *pp* **drunk** [drʌŋk]) *tr* beber; beberse *(su sueldo)*; **to drink down** beber de una vez; **to drink in** beber *(las palabras de una persona)*; beberse *(un libro)*; aspirar *(el aire)* ‖ *intr* beber; **to drink out of** beber de o en; **to drink to the health of** beber a o por la salud de

drinkable ['drɪŋkəbəl] *adj* bebedizo, potable

drinker ['drɪŋkər] *s* bebedor *m*

drinking ['drɪŋkɪŋ] *s* (el) beber

drinking cup *s* taza para beber

drinking fountain *s* fuente *f* para beber

drinking song *s* canción báquica, canción de taberna

drinking spree *s* bebezón *m;* bimba (Mex)

drinking trough *s* abrevadero

drinking water *s* agua para beber

drip [drɪp] *s* goteo; gotas ‖ *v* (*pret & pp* **dripped;** *ger* **dripping**) *intr* caer gota a gota, gotear

drip coffee *s* café *m* de maquinilla

drip'-dry' *adj* de lava y pon

drip pan *s* colector *m* de aceite

drive [draɪv] *s* paseo en coche; calzada; fuerza, vigor *m;* urgencia; campaña vigorosa; venta a bajo precio; (aut) tracción *(delantera o trasera)*; (mach) transmisión, mando ‖ *v* (*pret* **drove** [drov]; *pp* **driven** ['drɪvən]) *tr* conducir, guiar, manejar *(un automóvil)*; clavar, hincar *(un clavo)*; arrear *(a las bestias)*; *(in a carriage or auto)* llevar *(a una persona)*; empujar, impeler; estimular; forzar, compeler; obligar a trabajar mucho; (sport) golpear con gran fuerza; **to drive away** ahuyentar; **to drive away** ahuyentar; **to drive back** rechazar; **to drive mad** volver loco ‖ *intr* ir en coche; **to drive at** aspirar a; querer decir; **to drive hard** trabajar mucho; **to drive in** entrar en coche; entrar en *(un sitio)* en coche; **to drive on the right** circular por la derecha; **to drive out** salir en coche; **to drive up** llegar en coche

drive-in restaurant ['draɪv‚ɪn] *s* parador *m* de carretera

drive-in theater *s* auto-teatro, motocine *m;* autocine *m* (Chile, Cuba); autocínema *f* (Mex)

driv•el ['drɪvəl] *s* *(slobber)* baba; *(nonsense)* bobería ‖ *v* (*pret* **-eled** o **-elled;** *ger* **eling** o **-elling**) *intr* babear; *(to talk nonsense)* bobear

driver ['draɪvər] *s* conductor *m; (of a carriage)* cochero; *(of a locomotive)* maquinista *m; (of pack animals)* arriero

driver's license *s* carnet *m* de chófer, permiso de conducir

drive shaft *s* árbol *m* de mando, eje *m* motor

drive'way' *s* calzada; camino de entrada para coches

drive wheel *s* rueda motriz

drive'-your•self' service *s* alquiler *m* sin chófer

driving school *s* auto-escuela

drizzle ['drɪzəl] *s* llovizna ‖ *intr* lloviznar, garnar

droll [drol] *adj* chusco, gracioso

dromedar•y ['drɑmə‚dɛri] *s* (*pl* **-ies**) dromedario

drone [dron] *s* zángano; *(buzz, hum)* zumbido; *(of bagpipe)* bordón *m,* roncón *m;* avión radiodirigido ‖ *tr* decir monótonamente ‖ *intr* hablar monótonamente; *(to live in idleness)* zanganear; *(to buzz, hum)* zumbar

drool [drul] *s* *(slobber)* baba; (slang) bobería ‖ *intr* babear; (slang) bobear

droop [drup] *s* inclinación ‖ *intr* caer, colgar; inclinarse; marchitarse; abatirse; encamarse *(el grano)*

drooping ['drupɪŋ] *adj* *(eyelid, shoulder)* caído

drop [drɑp] *s* gota; *(slope)* pendiente *f; (earring)* pendiente *m; (in temperature)* descenso; *(of supplies from an airplane)* lanzamiento; *(trap door)* escotillón *m; (gallows)* horca; *(lozenge)* pastilla; *(small amount)* chispa; *(slit for letters)* buzón *m; (curtain)* telón *m;* **a drop in the bucket** una gota en el mar ‖ *v* (*pret & pp* **dropped;** *ger* **dropping**) *tr* dejar caer; echar *(una carta)* al buzón; bajar *(una cortina)*; soltar *(una indirecta)*; escribir *(una esquela)*; omitir, suprimir; abandonar, dejar; echar *(el ancla)*; borrar de la lista *(a un alumno)*; lanzar *(bombas o suministros de un avión)* ‖ *intr* caer; bajar; cesar, terminar; **to drop dead** caer muerto; **to drop in** entrar al pasar, visitar de paso; **to drop off** desaparecer; quedarse dormido; morir de repente; **to drop out** desaparecer; retirarse; darse de baja

drop curtain *s* telón *m*

drop hammer *s* martinete *m*

drop'-leaf' table *s* mesa de hoja plegadiza

drop'light' *s* lámpara colgante

drop'out' *s* fracasado, desertor *m* escolar; **to become a dropout** ahorcar los libros

dropper ['drɑpər] *s* cuentagotas *m*

drop shutter *s* obturador *m* de guillotina

dropsical ['drɑpsɪkəl] *adj* hidrópico

dropsy ['drɑpsi] *s* hidropesía

drop table *s* mesa perezosa

dross [drɔs] o [drɑs] *s* (*of metals*) escoria; (fig) escoria, hez *f*

drought [draut] *s* (*long period of dry weather*) sequía; (*dryness*) sequedad

drove [drov] *s* manada, rebaño, hato; gentío, multitud

drover ['drovər] *s* ganadero

drown [draun] *tr* anegar, ahogar ‖ *intr* anegarse, ahogarse

drowse [drauz] *intr* adormecerse, amodorrarse

drow•sy ['drauzi] *adj* (*comp* **-sier;** *super* **-siest**) soñoliento, modorro

drub [drʌb] *v* (*pret & pp* **drubbed;** *ger* **drubbing**) *tr* apalear, pegar, tundir; derrotar completamente

drudge [drʌdʒ] *s* yunque *m*, esclavo del trabajo ‖ *intr* afanarse

drudger•y ['drʌdʒəri] *s* (*pl* **-ies**) trabajo penoso

drug [drʌg] *s* droga, medicamento; narcótico; **drug on the market** macana, artículo invendible ‖ *v* (*pret & pp* **drugged;** *ger* **drugging**) *tr* narcotizar; mezclar con drogas

drug addict *s* toxicómano, drogadicto; (coll) yonquí *m*

drug′-ad•dict′ed *adj* drogadicto

drug addiction *s* toxicomanía

drug dealer *s* narcotraficante *mf*

druggist ['drʌgɪst] *s* boticario, farmacéutico; (*dealer in drugs, chemicals, dyes, etc.*) droguero

drug habit *s* vicio de los narcóticos

drug store *s* farmacia, botica, droguería

drug traffic *s* contrabando de narcóticos

druid ['druɪd] *s* druida *m*

drum [drʌm] *s* (*cylinder; instrument of percussion*) tambor *m*; (*container for oil, gasoline, etc.*) bidón *m* ‖ *v* (*pret & pp* **drummed;** *ger* **drumming**) *tr* reunir a toque de tambor; **to drum up trade** fomentar ventas ‖ *intr* tocar el tambor; (*with the fingers*) teclear

drum′beat′ *s* toque *m* de tambor

drum brake *s* freno de tambor

drum corps *s* banda de tambores

drum′fire′ *s* fuego graneado, fuego nutrido

drum′head′ *s* parche *m* de tambor

drum major *s* tambor *m* mayor

drummer ['drʌmər] *s* tambor *m*, baterista *mf*, tamborilero; agente viajero

drum′stick′ *s* baqueta, palillo; (coll) muslo (*de ave cocida*)

drunk [drʌŋk] *adj* borracho; bolo (CAm, Mex); **to get drunk** emborracharse; coger una turca; embolarse (CAm, Mex) enchicharse (SAm) ‖ *s* (coll) borracho; (*spree*) (coll) borrachera

drunkard ['drʌŋkərd] *s* borrachín *m*

drunken ['drʌŋkən] *adj* borracho

drunken driving *s* — **to be arrested for drunken driving** ser arrestado por conducir en estado de embriaguez

drunkenness ['drʌŋkənnɪs] *s* embriaguez *f*; bimba (Mex)

dry [draɪ] *adj* (*comp* **drier;** *super* **driest**) seco; (*thirsty*) sediento; (*dull, boring*) árido ‖ *s* (*pl* **drys**) (*prohibitionist*) (coll) seco ‖ *v* (*pret & pp* **dried**) *tr* secar; (*to wipe dry*) enjugar ‖ *intr* secarse; **to dry up** secarse completamente; (slang) callar, dejar de hablar

dry battery *s* pila seca; (*group of dry cells*) batería seca

dry cell *s* pila seca

dry′-clean′ *tr* lavar en seco, limpiar en seco

dry cleaner *s* tintorero

dry cleaning *s* lavado a seco, limpieza en seco

dry′-clean′ing establishment *s* tintorería

dry dock *s* dique seco

dryer ['draɪ•ər] *s* var de **drier**

dry′eyed′ — *adj* ojienjuto

dry farming *s* cultivo de secano

dry goods *spl* mercancías generales (*tejidos, lencería, pañería, sedería*)

dry ice *s* carbohielo, hielo seco

dry law *s* ley seca

dry measure *s* medida para áridos

dryness ['draɪnɪs] *s* sequedad; (*e.g., of a speaker*) aridez *f*

dry nurse *s* ama seca

dry season *s* estación de la seca

dry wash *s* ropa lavada y secada pero no planchada

d.s. *abbr* **days after sight, daylight saving**

D.S.T. *abbr* **Daylight Saving Time**

dual ['dju•əl o ['du•əl] *adj & s* dual *m*

dual axle *s* eje tandem

duali•ty [dju'ælɪti] *s* (*pl* **-ties**) dualidad

dub [dʌb] *s* (slang) jugador *m* torpe ‖ *v* (*pret & pp* **dubbed;** *ger* **dubbing**) *tr* apellidar; armar caballero; (mov) doblar

dubbing ['dʌbɪŋ] *s* doblado, doblaje *m*

dubious ['dubɪ•əs] *adj* dudoso

ducat ['dʌkət] *s* ducado

duchess ['dʌtʃɪs] *s* duquesa

duch•y ['dʌtʃi] *s* (*pl* **-ies**) ducado

duck [dʌk] *s* pato; (*female*) pata; agachada rápida; (*in the water*) zambullida; **ducks** (coll) pantalones *mpl* de dril ‖ *tr* bajar rápidamente (*la cabeza*); (*in water*) chapuzar; (coll) esquivar, evitar (*un golpe*) ‖ *intr* chapuzar; **to duck out** (coll) escabullirse

duck′-toed′ *adj* zancajoso

duct [dʌkt] *s* conducto, canal *m*

ductile ['dʌktɪl] *adj* dúctil

ductless gland ['dʌktlɪs] *s* glándula cerrada

duct′work′ *s* canalización

dud [dʌd] *s* (slang) bomba que no estalla; (slang) fracaso; **duds** (coll) trapos, prendas de vestir

dude [dud] *s* caballerete *m*

due [dju] o [du] *adj* debido; aguardado, esperado; pagadero; **due to** debido a; **to fall due** vencer; **when is the train due?** ¿a qué hora debe llegar el tren? ‖ *adv* directa-

dr
du

mente, derecho ‖ s deuda; **dues** derechos; (*of a member*) cuota; **to get one's due** llevar su mereçido; **to give the devil his due** ser justo hasta con el diablo

duel ['dju·əl] o ['du·əl] s duelo; **to fight a duel** batirse en duelo ‖ v (*pret & pp* **dueled** o **duelled;** *ger* **dueling** o **duelling**) *intr* batirse en duelo

duelist o **duellist** ['dju·əlɪst] o ['du·əlɪst] s duelista m

dues-paying ['djuz,pe·ɪŋ] o ['duz,peɪŋ] *adj* cotizante

duet [dju'ɛt] o [du'ɛt] s dúo

duke [djuk] s duque m

dukedom ['djukdəm] s ducado

dull [dʌl] *adj* (*not sharp*) embotado, romo; (*color*) apagado; (*sound; pain*) sordo; (*stupid*) lerdo, torpe; (*business*) inactivo, muerto; (*boring*) aburrido, tedioso; (*flat*) deslucido, deslustrado ‖ *tr* embotar, enromar; deslucir, deslustrar; enfriar (*el entusiasmo*) ‖ *intr* embotarse, enromarse; deslucirse, deslustrarse

dullard ['dʌlərd] s estúpido

duly ['djuli] o ['duli] *adv* debidamente

dumb [dʌm] *adj* (*lacking the power to speak*) mudo; (coll) estúpido, torpe

dumb'bell' s halterio; (slang) estúpido, tonto

dumb creature s animal m, bruto

dumb show s pantomima

dumb'wait'er s montaplatos m

dumfound [,dʌm'faʊnd] *tr* pasmar, dejar sin habla

dum·my ['dʌmi] *adj* falso, fingido, simulado ‖ s (*pl* **-mies**) (*dress form*) maniquí m; cabeza para pelucas; (*in card games*) muerto; cartas del muerto; (*figurehead, straw man*) testaferro; (*skeleton copy of a book*) maqueta; imitación, copia; (slang) estúpido

dump [dʌmp] s basurero, vertedero; montón m de basuras; (mil) depósito de municiones; (min) terrero; **to be down in the dumps** (coll) tener murria ‖ *tr* descargar, verter; vaciar de golpe; vender en grandes cantidades y a precios inferiores a los corrientes

dumping ['dʌmpɪŋ] s descarga; venta en grandes cantidades y a precios inferiores a los corrientes

dumpling ['dʌmplɪŋ] s bola de pasta rellena de fruta o carne

dump truck s camión m volquete

dump·y ['dʌmpi] *adj* (*comp* **-ier;** *super* **-iest**) regordete, rollizo

dun [dʌn] *adj* bruno, pardo, castaño ‖ s acreedor importuno; (*demand for payment*) apremio ‖ v (*pret & pp* **dunner;** *ger* **dunning**) *tr* importunar para el pago, apremiar (*a un deudor*)

dunce [dʌns] s zopenco, bodoque m

dunce cap s capirote m que se le pone al alumno torpe

dune [djun] o [dun] s duna, médano

dung [dʌŋ] s estiércol m ‖ *tr* estercolar

dungarees [,dʌŋgə'riz] *spl* pantalones *mpl* de trabajo de tela basta de algodón

dungeon ['dʌndʒən] s calabozo, mazmorra; (*fortified tower of medieval castle*) torre f del homenaje

dung'hill' s estercolar m; lugar inmundo

dunk [dʌŋk] *tr* sopetear, ensopar

duo ['dju·o] o ['du·o] s dúo

duode·num [,du·ə'dinəm] s (*pl* **-na** [nə]) duodeno

dupe [djup] o [dup] s víctima, primo, inocentón m ‖ *tr* embaucar, engañar

duplex house ['duplɛks] s casa para dos familias

duplicate ['duplɪkɪt] *adj & s* duplicado; **in duplicate** por duplicado ‖ ['duplɪ,ket] *tr* duplicar

duplici·ty [dju'plɪsɪti] s (*pl* **-ties**) duplicidad

durable ['djurəbəl] o ['durəbəl] *adj* durable, duradero

durable goods *spl* artículos duraderos

duration [dju'reʃən] o [du'reʃən] s duración

during ['djurɪŋ] *prep* durante

dusk [dʌsk] s crepúsculo

dust [dʌst] s polvo ‖ *tr* (*to free of dust*) desempolvar; (*to sprinkle with dust*) polvorear; **to dust off** desempolvar

dust bowl s cuenca de polvo

dust'cloth' s trapo para quitar el polvo

dust cloud s nube f de polvo, polvareda

duster ['dʌstər] s paño, plumero; (*light overgarment*) guardapolvo

dust jacket s sobrecubierta

dust'pan' s pala para recoger la basura

dust rag s trapo para quitar el polvo

dust storm s tolvanera

dust·y ['dʌsti] *adj* (*comp* **-ier;** *super* **-iest**) polvoriento; (*grayish*) grisáceo

Dutch [dʌtʃ] *adj* holandés; (slang) alemán ‖ s (*language*) holandés m; (*language*) alemán m; **in Dutch** (slang) en la desgracia; (slang) en un apuro; **the Dutch** los holandeses; (slang) los alemanes; **to go Dutch** (coll) pagar a escote

Dutch·man ['dʌtʃmən] s (*pl* **-men** [mən]) holandés m; (slang) alemán m

Dutch treat s (coll) convite m a escote

dutiable ['djutɪ·əbəl] *adj* sujeto a derechos de aduana

dutiful ['djutɪfəl] *adj* obediente, sumiso, solícito

du·ty ['djuti] s (*pl* **-ties**) deber m; (*task*) faena, quehacer m; derechos de aduana; **in the line of duty** en acto de servicio; **off duty** libre; **on duty** de servicio, de guardia; **to do one's duty** cumplir con su deber; **to take up one's duties** entrar en funciones

du'ty-free' *adj* libre de derechos

D.V. *abbr* Deo volente, i.e., God willing

dwarf [dwɔrf] *adj & s* enano ‖ *tr* achicar, empequeñecer ‖ *intr* achicarse, empequeñecerse

dwarfish ['dwɔrfɪʃ] *adj* enano, diminuto

dwell [dwɛl] v (*pret & pp* **dwelled** o **dwelt** [dwɛlt]) *intr* vivir, morar; **to dwell on** o **upon** hacer hincapié en

dwelling ['dwɛlɪŋ] s morada, vivienda

dwelling house s casa, domicilio

dwindle [ˈdwɪndəl] *intr* disminuir; decaer, consumirse
dwt. *abbr* **pennyweight**
dye [daɪ] *s* tinte *m*, tintura, color *m* ‖ *v* (*pret & pp* **dyed**; *ger* **dyeing**) *tr* teñir
dyed-in-the-wool [ˈdaɪdɪnðə‚wul] *adj* intransigente
dyeing [ˈdaɪ‧ɪŋ] *s* tinte *m*, tintura
dyer [ˈdaɪ‧ər] *s* tintorero
dye'stuff *s* materia, colorante
dying [ˈdaɪ‧ɪŋ] *adj* moribundo

dynamic [daɪˈnæmɪk] o [dɪˈnæmɪk] *adj* dinámico
dynamite [ˈdaɪnə‚maɪt] *s* dinamita ‖ *tr* dinamitar
dyna‧mo [ˈdaɪnə‚mo] *s* (*pl* **-mos**) dínamo *f*
dynast [ˈdaɪnæst] *s* dinasta *m*
dynas‧ty [ˈdaɪnəsti] *s* (*pl* **-ties**) dinastía
dysentery [ˈdɪsən‚teri] *s* disentería
dysfunction [dɪsˈfʌŋ/ən] *s* disfunción
dyspepsia [dɪsˈpɛpsi‧ə] o [dɪsˈpɛp/ə] *s* dispepsia
dz. *abbr* **dozen**

E

E, e [i] quinta letra del alfabeto inglés
ea. *abbr* **each**
each [it/] *adj indef* cada ‖ *pron indef* cada uno; **each other** nos, se; uno a otro, unos a otros ‖ *adv* cada uno; por persona
eager [ˈigər] *adj* (*enthusiastic*) ardiente, celoso; **eager for** muy deseoso de; **eager to** + *inf* muy deseoso de + *inf*
eagerness [ˈigərnɪs] *s* ardor *m*, celo; deseo ardiente, empeño
eagle [ˈigəl] *s* águila
eagle owl *s* buho
ear [ɪr] *s* (*organ and sense of hearing*) oído; (*external part*) oreja; (*of corn*) mazorca; (*of wheat*) espiga; **all ears** con las orejas tan largas; **to be all ears** ser todo oídos, abrir tanto oído; **box on the ear** guantón *m*; **to prick up one's ears** aguzar las orejas; **to turn a deaf ear** hacer o tener oídos de mercader
ear'ache' *s* dolor *m* de oído
ear'drop' *s* arete *m*
ear'drum' *s* tímpano
ear'flap' *s* orejera
earl [ʌrl] *s* conde *m*
earldom [ˈʌrldəm] *s* condado
ear‧ly [ˈʌrli] (*comp* **-lier**; *super* **-liest**) *adj* (*occurring before customary time*) temprano; (*first in a series*) primero; (*far back in time*) primero, remoto, antiguo; (*occurring in near future*) cercano, próximo ‖ *adv* temprano; al principio; en los primeros tiempos; **as early as** (*a certain time of day*) ya a; (*a certain time or date*) ya en; **as early as possible** lo más pronto posible; **early in** (*e.g., the month of December*) ya en; **early in the morning** muy de mañana; **early in the year** a principios del año; **to rise early** madrugar
early bird *s* (coll) madrugador *m*
early mass *s* misa de prima
early riser *s* madrugador *m*
ear'mark' *s* señal *f*, distintivo ‖ *tr* destinar, poner aparte (*para un fin determinado*)
ear'muff' *s* orejera

earn [ʌrn] *tr* ganar, ganarse; (*to get as one's due*) merecerse; (com) devengar (*intereses*) ‖ *intr* ganar; rendir
earnest [ˈʌrnɪst] *adj* serio, grave; **in earnest** en serio, de buena fe ‖ *s* arras
earnest money *s* arras
earnings [ˈʌrnɪŋz] *s* ganancia; salario
ear of corn *s* ilote *m*; chilote (CAm); **green ear of corn** jilote (Mex)
ear'phone' *s* audífono
ear'piece' *s* auricular *m*
ear'ring' *s* arete *m*
ear'shot' *s* alcance *m* del oído; **within earshot** al alcance del oído
ear'split'ting' *adj* ensordecedor
earth [ʌrθ] *s* tierra; **to come back to** o **down to earth** bajar de las nubes
earthen [ˈʌrθən] *adj* de tierra; de barro
ear'then‧ware' *s* loza, vasijas de barro
earthly [ˈʌrθli] *adj* terrenal; concebible, posible; **to be of no earthly use** no servir para nada
earth'quake' *s* terremoto, temblor *m* de tierra
earth'work' *s* terraplén *m*
earth'worm' *s* lombriz *f* de tierra
earth‧y [ˈʌrθi] *adj* (*comp* **-ier**; *super* **-iest**) terroso; (*worldly*) mundanal; (*unrefined*) grosero; franco, sincero
ear trumpet *s* trompetilla
ear'wax' *s* cera de los oídos
ease [iz] *s* facilidad; (*readiness, naturalness*) desenvoltura, soltura; (*comfort, wellbeing*) comodidad, bienestar *m*; **with ease** con facilidad ‖ *tr* facilitar; aligerar (*un peso*); (*to let up on*) aflojar, soltar; aliviar, mitigar ‖ *intr* aliviarse, mitigarse, disminuir; moderar la marcha
easel [ˈizəl] *s* caballete *m*
easement [ˈizmənt] *s* alivio; (law) servidumbre
easily [ˈizɪli] *adv* fácilmente; suavemente; sin duda; probablemente
easiness [ˈizɪnɪs] *s* facilidad; desenvoltura, soltura; (*e.g., of motion of a machine*) suavidad; indiferencia
east [ist] *adj* oriental, del este ‖ *adv* al este, hacia el este ‖ *s* este *m*

Easter ['istər] s Pascua de flores, Pascua de Resurrección, Pascua florida
Easter egg s huevo duro decorado o huevo de imitación que se da como regalo en el día de Pascua de Resurrección
Easter Monday s lunes m de Pascua de Resurrección
eastern ['istərn] adj oriental
East'er•tide' s aleluya m, tiempo de Pascua
eastward ['istwərd] adv hacia el este
eas•y ['izi] adj (comp **-ier**; super **-iest**) fácil; (conducive to ease) cómodo; (not tight) holgado; (amenable) manejable; (not forced or hurried) lento, pausado, moderado; **to have an easy job** (o **life**) estar echado (CAm, Mex, P-R) ‖ adv (coll) fácilmente; (coll) despacio; **to take it easy** (coll) descansar, holgar; (coll) ir despacio
easy chair s poltrona, silla poltrona
eas'y•go'ing adj despacioso, comodón
easy mark s (coll) víctima, inocentón m
easy money s dinero ganado sin pena; (com) dinero abundante
easy payments spl facilidades de pago
eat [it] v (pret **ate** [et]; pp **eaten** ['itən]) tr comer; **to eat away** corroer; **to eat up** comerse ‖ intr comer
eatable ['itəbəl] adj comestible ‖ **eatables** spl comestibles mpl
eaves [ivz] spl alero, socarrén m, tejaroz m
eaves'drop' v (pret & pp **-dropped**; ger **-dropping**) intr escuchar a escondidas, estar de escucha
ebb [ɛb] s reflujo; decadencia ‖ intr bajar (la marea); decaer
ebb and flow s flujo y reflujo
ebb tide s marea menguante
ebon•y ['ɛbəni] s (pl **-ies**) ébano
ebullient [ɪ'bʌljənt] adj hirviente; entusiasta
eccentric [ɛk'sɛntrɪk] adj excéntrico ‖ m (odd person) excéntrico; (device) excéntrica
eccentrici•ty [,ɛksɛn'trɪsɪti] s (pl **-ties**) excentricidad
ecclesiastic [ɪ,klizɪ'æstɪk] adj & s eclesiástico
echelon ['ɛʃə,lɑn] s escalón m; (mil) escalón ‖ tr (mil) escalonar
ech•o ['ɛko] s (pl **-oes**) eco ‖ tr repetir (un sonido); imitar ‖ intr hacer eco
éclair [e'klɛr] s bollo de crema
eclectic [ɛk'lɛktɪk] adj & s ecléctico
eclipse [ɪ'klɪps] s eclipse m ‖ tr eclipsar
eclogue ['ɛklɔg] o ['ɛklɑg] s égloga
ecologic(al) [,ikə'lɑdʒɪk(əl)] adj ecológico
ecologist [i'kɑlədʒɪst] s ecologista mf, ecólogo
ecology [i'kɑlədʒi] s ecología
economic [,ikə'nɑmɪk] adj económico (perteneciente a la economía)
economical [,ikə'nɑmɪkəl] adj económico (ahorrador; poco costoso)
economics [,ikə'nɑmɪks] s economía política
economist [ɪ'kɑnəmɪst] s economista mf
economize [ɪ'kɑnə,maɪz] tr & intr economizar
econo•my [ɪ'kɑnəmi] s (pl **-mies**) economía
ecsta•sy ['ɛkstəsi] s (pl **-sies**) éxtasis m

ecstatic [ɛk'stætɪk] adj extático
Ecuador ['ɛkwə,dɔr] s el Ecuador
Ecuadoran [,ɛkwə'dorən] o; **Ecuadorian** [,ɛkwḷə'dorɪ•ən] adj & s ecuatoriano
ecumenic(al) [,ɛkjə'mɛnɪk(əl)] adj ecuménico
eczema ['ɛksɪmə] o [ɛg'zimə] s eczema m & f, eccema m & f
ed. abbr **edited**, **edition**, **editor**
ed•dy ['ɛdi] s (pl **-dies**) remolino ‖ v (pret & pp **-died**) tr & intr remolinear
edelweiss ['edəl,vaɪs] s estrella de los Alpes
edema [ɪ'dimə] s edema
edge [ɛdʒ] s (of a knife, sword, etc.) filo, corte m; (of a cup, glass, piece of paper, piece of cloth, an abyss, etc.) borde m; (of a piece of cloth; of a body of water) orilla; (of a table) canto; (of a book) corte m; (of clothing) ribete m; (slang) ventaja; **on edge** de canto; (fig) nervioso; **to have the edge on** (coll) llevar ventaja a; **to set the teeth on edge** dar dentera ‖ tr afilar, aguzar; bordear; ribetear (un vestido) ‖ intr avanzar de lado; **to edge in** lograr entrar
edgeways ['ɛdʒ,wez] adv de filo, de canto; **to not let a person get a word in edgeways** no dejarle a una persona decir ni una palabra
edging ['ɛdʒɪŋ] s orla, pestaña
edgy ['ɛdʒi] adj agudo, angular; nervioso, irritable
edible ['ɛdɪbəl] adj & s comestible m
edict ['idɪkt] s edicto
edification [,ɛdɪfɪ'keʃən] s edificación
edifice ['ɛdɪfɪs] s edificio
edi•fy ['ɛdɪ,faɪ] v (pret & pp **-fied**) tr edificar
edifying ['ɛdɪ,faɪ•ɪŋ] adj edificante
edit. abbr **edited**, **edition**, **editor**
edit ['ɛdɪt] tr preparar para la publicación; dirigir, redactar (un periódico)
edition [ɪ'dɪʃən] s edición
editor ['ɛdɪtər] s (of a newspaper or magazine) director m, redactor m; (of a manuscript) revisor m; (of an editorial) cronista mf
editorial [,ɛdɪ'torɪ•əl] adj editorial ‖ s editorial m, artículo de fondo
editorial staff s redacción, cuerpo de redacción
editor in chief s jefe m de redacción
educate ['ɛdʒʊ,ket] tr educar, instruir
education [,ɛdʒʊ'keʃən] s educación, instrucción
educational [,ɛdʒʊ'keʃənəl] adj educativo, educacional
educational institution s centro docente
educator ['ɛdʒʊ,ketər] s educador m
eel [il] s anguila; **to be as slippery as an eel** escurrirse como una anguila
ee•rie o **ee•ry** ['iri] adj (comp **-rier**; super **-riest**) espectral, misterioso
efface [ɪ'fes] tr destruir; borrar; **to efface oneself** retirarse, no dejarse ver
effect [ɪ'fɛkt] s efecto; **in effect** vigente; en efecto, en realidad; **to feel the effects of** resentirse de; **to go into effect** o **to take**

effect hacerse vigente, entrar en vigor; **to put into effect** poner en vigor ‖ *tr* efectuar

effective [ɪˈfɛktɪv] *adj* eficaz; (*actually in effect*) efectivo; (*striking*) impresionante; **to become effective** hacerse efectivo, entrar en vigencia

effectual [ɪˈfɛktʃʊ•əl] *adj* eficaz

effectuate [ɪˈfɛktʃʊˌet] *tr* efectuar

effeminacy [ɪˈfɛmɪnəsi] *s* afeminación

effeminate [ɪˈfɛmɪnɪt] *adj* afeminado

effervesce [ˌɛfərˈvɛs] *intr* estar en efervescencia

effervescence [ˌɛfərˈvɛsəns] *s* efervescencia

effervescent [ˌɛfərˈvɛsənt] *adj* efervescente

effete [ɪˈfit] *adj* estéril, infructuoso

efficacious [ˌɛfɪˈkeʃəs] *adj* eficaz

effica•cy [ˈɛfɪkəsi] *s* (*pl* -**cies**) eficacia

efficien•cy [ɪˈfɪʃənsi] *s* (*pl* -**cies**) eficiencia; (*mech*) rendimiento, efecto útil

efficient [ɪˈfɪʃənt] *adj* eficiente, eficaz; (*person*) competente; (*mech*) de buen rendimiento

effi•gy [ˈɛfɪdʒi] *s* (*pl* -**gies**) efigie *f*

effort [ˈɛfərt] *s* esfuerzo, empeño

effronter•y [ɪˈfrʌntəri] *s* (*pl* -**ies**) desfachatez *f*, descaro

effusion [ɪˈfjuʒən] *s* efusión

effusive [ɪˈfjusɪv] *adj* efusivo, expansivo

e.g. *abbr* **exempli gratia,** i.e., **for example**

egg [ɛg] *s* huevo; (slang) buen sujeto ‖ *tr* — **to egg on** incitar, instigar

egg beat′er *s* batidor *m* de huevos

egg′cup′ *s* huevera

egg′head′ *s* intelectual *mf*, erudito

eggnog [ˈɛgˌnɑg] *s* caldo de la reina, yema mejida

egg′plant′ *s* berenjena

egg′shell′ *s* cascarón *m*, cáscara de huevo

egoism [ˈɛgoˌɪzəm] *o* [ˈigoˌɪzəm] *s* egoísmo

egoist [ˈɛgo•ɪst] *o* [ˈigo•ɪst] *s* egoísta *mf*

egotism [ˈɛgoˌtɪzəm] *o* [ˈigoˌtɪzəm] *s* egotismo

egotist [ˈɛgotɪst] *o* [ˈigotɪst] *s* egotista *mf*

egregious [ɪˈgridʒəs] *adj* enorme, escandaloso

egress [ˈgrɛs] *s* salida

Egypt [ˈedʒɪpt] *s* Egipto

Egyptian [ɪˈdʒɪpʃən] *adj & s* egipcio

eider [ˈaɪdər] *s* pato de flojel

eid′erdown′ *s* edredón *m*

eight [et] *adj & pron* ocho ‖ *s* ocho; **eight o'clock** las ocho

eight′-day′ clock *s* reloj *m* de ocho días cuerda

eighteen [ˈetˈtin] *adj, pron & s* dieciocho, diez y ocho

eighteenth [ˈetˈtinθ] *adj & s* (*in a series*) decimoctavo; (*part*) dieciochavo ‖ *s* (*in dates*) dieciocho, diez y ocho

eighth [etθ] *adj & s* octavo, ochavo ‖ *s* (*in dates*) ocho

eight hundred *adj & pron* ochocientos ‖ *s* ochocientos *m*

eightieth [ˈetɪ•ɪθ] *adj & s* (*in a series*) octogésimo; (*part*) ochentavo

eigh•ty [ˈeti] *adj & pron* ochenta ‖ *s* (*pl* -**ties**) ochenta *m*

either [ˈiðər] *o* [ˈaɪðər] *adj* uno u otro, cada . . . (de los dos), cualquier . . . de los dos; ambos ‖ *pron* uno u otro, cualquiera de los dos ‖ *adv* — **not either** tampoco, no . . . tampoco ‖ *conj* — **either . . . or** o . . . o

ejaculate [ɪˈdʒækjəˌlet] *tr & intr* exclamar; (physiol) eyacular

eject [ɪˈdʒɛkt] *tr* arrojar, expulsar, echar; (*to evict*) desahuciar

ejection [ɪˈdʒɛkʃən] *s* expulsión; (*of a tenant*) desahucio

ejection seat *s* (aer) asiento lanzable

eke [ik] *tr* — **to eke out** ganarse (*la vida*) con dificultad

elaborate [ɪˈlæbərɪt] *adj* (*done with great care*) elaborado; (*detailed, ornate*) primoroso, recargado ‖ [ɪˈlæbəˌret] *tr* elaborar ‖ *intr* — **to elaborate on** *o* **upon** explicar con más detalles

elapse [ɪˈlæps] *intr* pasar, transcurrir

elastic [ɪˈlæstɪk] *adj & s* elástico

elasticity [ˌilæsˈtɪsɪti] *s* elasticidad

elated [ɪˈletɪd] *adj* alborozado, regocijado

elation [ɪˈleʃən] *s* alborozo, regocijo

elbow [ˈɛlbo] *s* codo; (*in a river*) recodo; (*of a chair*) brazo; **at one's elbow** a la mano; **out at the elbows** andrajoso, enseñando los codos; **to crook the elbow** empinar el codo; **to rub elbows** codearse, rozarse; **up to the elbows** hasta los codos ‖ *tr* — **to elbow one's way** abrirse paso a codazos ‖ *intr* codear

elbow grease *s* (coll) muñeca, jugo de muñeca

elbow patch *s* codera

elbow rest *s* ménsula

el′bow•room′ *s* espacio suficiente; libertad de acción

elder [ˈɛldər] *adj* mayor, más antiguo ‖ *s* mayor, señor *m* mayor; (eccl) anciano; (*plant*) saúco

el′der•ber′ry *s* (*pl* -**ries**) saúco; baya del saúco

elderly [ˈɛldərli] *adj* viejo, anciano

elder statesman *s* veterano de la política

eldest [ˈɛldɪst] *adj* (el) mayor, (el) más antiguo

elec. *abbr* **electrical, electricity**

elect [ɪˈlɛkt] *adj* (*chosen*) escogido; (*selected but not yet installed*) electo ‖ *s* elegido; **the elect** los elegidos ‖ *tr* elegir

election [ɪˈlɛkʃən] *s* elección

electioneer [ɪˌlɛkʃəˈnɪr] *intr* solicitar votos

elective [ɪˈlɛktɪv] *adj* electivo ‖ *s* asignatura electiva

electorate [ɪˈlɛktərɪt] *s* electorado

electric(al) [ɪˈlɛktrɪk(əl)] *adj* eléctrico

electric appliance *s* electrodoméstico

electric fan *s* ventilador eléctrico

electrician [ˌɛlɛkˈtrɪʃən] *s* electricista *mf*

electricity [ɪˌlɛkˈtrɪsɪti] *s* electricidad

electric percolator *s* cafetera eléctrica

electric shaver *s* electroafeitadora

electric tape *s* cinta aislante

electri•fy [ɪˈlɛktrɪˌfaɪ] *v* (*pret & pp* -**fied**) *tr* (*to provide with electric power*) electrificar; (to communicate electricity to; to thrill) electrizar

electrocute [ɪ'lɛktrə,kjut] *tr* electrocutar

electrode [ɪ'lɛktrod] *s* electrodo

electrolysis [,ɛlɛk'trɑlɪsɪs] *s* electrólisis *f*

electrolyte [ɪ'lɛktrə,laɪt] *s* electrólito

electromagnet [ɪ,lɛktrə'mægnɪt] *s* electro, electroimán *m*

electromagnetic [ɪ,lɛktrəmæg'nɛtɪk] *adj* electromagnético

electromotive [ɪ,lɛktrə'motɪv] *adj* electromotor

electron [ɪ'lɛktrɑn] *s* electrón *m*

electronic [,ɛlɛk'trɑnɪk] *adj* electrónico ‖ **electronics** *s* electrónica

electroplating [ɪ'lɛktrə,pletɪŋ] *s* galvanoplastia

electrostatic [ɪ,lɛktrə'stætɪk] *adj* electrostático

electrotype [ɪ'lɛktrə,taɪp] *s* electrotipo ‖ *tr* electrotipar

eleemosynary [,ɛlɪ'mɑsɪ,nɛri] *adj* limosnero

elegance ['ɛlɪgəns] *s* elegancia

elegant ['ɛlɪgənt] *adj* elegante, elegantoso

elegiac [,ɛlɪ'dʒaɪ•æk] o [ɪ'lidʒɪ,æk] *adj* elegíaco

ele•gy ['ɛlɪdʒi] *s* (*pl* **-gies**) elegía

element ['ɛlɪmənt] *s* elemento; **to be in one's element** estar en su elemento

elementary [,ɛlɪ'mɛntəri] *adj* elemental

elephant ['ɛlɪfənt] *s* elefante *m*

elevate ['ɛlɪ,vet] *tr* elevar

elevated ['ɛlɪ,vetɪd] *adj* elevado ‖ *s* (coll) ferrocarril aéreo o elevado

elevation [,ɛlɪ'veʃən] *s* elevación

elevator ['ɛlɪ,vetər] *s* ascensor *m*; elevador *m* (Am); (*for freight*) montacargas *m*; (*for hoisting grain*) elevador de granos; (*warehouse for storing grain*) depósito de cereales; (aer) timón *m* de profundidad

eleven [ɪ'lɛvən] *adj & pron* once ‖ *s* once *m*; **eleven o'clock** las once

eleventh [ɪ'lɛvənθ] *adj & s* (*in a series*) undécimo, onceno; (*part*) onzavo ‖ *s* (*in dates*) once *m*

eleventh hour *s* último momento

elf [ɛlf] *s* (*pl* **elves** [ɛlvz]) elfo, trasgo; enano

elicit [ɪ'lɪsɪt] *tr* sacar, sonsacar

elide [ɪ'laɪd] *tr* elidir

eligible ['ɛlɪdʒɪbəl] *adj* elegible; deseable, aceptable

eliminate [ɪ'lɪmɪ,net] *tr* eliminar

elision [ɪ'lɪʒən] *s* elisión

elite [e'lit] *adj* selecto ‖ *s* — **the elite** la élite

elitist [e'litɪst] *adj & s* elitista *mf*

elk [ɛlk] *s* alce *m*

ellipse [ɪ'lɪps] *s* (geom) elipse *f*

ellip•sis [ɪ'lɪpsɪs] *s* (*pl* **-ses** [siz]) (gram) elipsis *f*

elliptic(al) [ɪ'lɪptɪk(əl)] *adj* (geom & gram) elíptico

elm tree [ɛlm] *s* olmo

elope [ɪ'lop] *intr* fugarse con un amante

elopement [ɪ'lopmənt] *s* fuga con un amante

eloquence ['ɛləkwəns] *s* elocuencia

eloquent ['ɛləkwənt] *adj* elocuente

else [ɛls] *adj* — **nobody else** ningún otro, nadie más; **nothing else** nada más; **somebody else** algún otro, otra persona; **something else** otra cosa; **what else** qué más, qué otra cosa; **who else** quién más; **whose else** de qué otra persona ‖ *adv* de otro modo; **how else** de qué otro modo; **or else** si no, o bien; **when else** en qué otro tiempo; a qué otra hora; **where else** en qué otra parte

else'where' *adv* en otra parte, a otra parte

elucidate [ɪ'lusɪ,det] *tr* elucidar

elude [ɪ'lud] *tr* eludir

elusive [ɪ'lusɪv] *adj* fugaz, efímero; evasivo; elusivo; (*baffling*) deslumbrador

emaciated [ɪ'meʃɪ,etɪd] *adj* enflaquecido, macilento

emancipate [ɪ'mænsɪ,pet] *tr* emancipar

embalm [ɛm'bɑm] *tr* embalsamar

embankment [ɛm'bæŋkmənt] *s* terraplén *m*

embar•go [ɛm'bɑrgo] *s* (*pl* **-goes**) embargo ‖ *tr* embargar

embark [ɛm'bɑrk] *intr* embarcarse

embarkation [,ɛmbɑr'keʃən] *s* (*of passengers*) embarco; (*of freight*) embarque *m*

embarrass [ɛm'bærəs] *tr* (*to make feel selfconscious*) avergonzar; (*to put obstacles in the way of*) embarazar; poner en apuros de dinero

embarrassing [ɛm'bærəsɪŋ] *adj* desconcertante, vergonzoso; embarazoso

embarrassment [ɛm'bærəsmənt] *s* desconcierto, vergüenza; (*interference; perplexity*) embarazo; (*financial difficulties*) apuros

embas•sy ['ɛmbəsi] *s* (*pl* **-sies**) embajada

em•bed [ɛm'bɛd] *v* (*pret & pp* **-bedded**; *ger* **-bedding**) *tr* empotrar, encajar

embellish [ɛm'bɛlɪʃ] *tr* embellecer

embellishment [ɛm'bɛlɪʃmənt] *s* embellecimiento

ember ['ɛmbər] *s* ascua, pavesa; **embers** rescoldo

Ember days *spl* témpora

embezzle [ɛm'bɛzəl] *tr & intr* desfalcar, malversar

embezzlement [ɛm'bɛzəlmənt] *s* desfalco, malversación

embezzler [ɛm'bɛzlər] *s* malversador *m*

embitter [ɛm'bɪtər] *tr* blasonar; (fig) blasonar

emblem ['ɛmbləm] *s* emblema *m*

emblematic(al) [,ɛmblə'mætɪk(əl)] *adj* emblemático

embodiment [ɛm'bɑdɪmənt] *s* incorporación; personificación, encarnación

embod•y [ɛm'bɑdi] *v* (*pret & pp* **-ied**) *tr* incorporar; personificar, encarnar

embolden [ɛm'boldən] *tr* envalentonar

embolism ['ɛmbə,lɪzəm] *s* embolia

emboss [ɛm'bɔs] o [ɛm'bɑs] *tr* (*to raise in relief*) realzar; abollonar (*metal*); repujar (*cuero*)

embrace [ɛm'bres] *s* abrazo ‖ *tr* abrazar ‖ *intr* abrazarse

embrasure [ɛm'breʒər] *s* alféizar *m*

embroider [ɛm'brɔɪdər] *tr* bordar, recamar

embroider•y [ɛm'brɔɪdəri] s (pl **-ies**) bordado, recamado

embroil [ɛm'brɔɪl] tr embrollar; (to involve in contention) envolver

embroilment [ɛm'brɔɪlmənt] s embrollo; (in contention) envolvimiento

embry•o ['ɛmbrɪ,o] s (pl **-os**) embrión m

embryology [,ɛmbrɪ'ɑlədʒi] s embriología

emend [ɪ'mɛnd] tr enmendar

emendation [,imɛn'deʃən] s enmienda

emerald ['ɛmərəld] s esmeralda

emerge [ɪ'mʌrdʒ] intr emerger

emergence [ɪ'mʌrdʒəns] s emergencia (acción de emerger)

emergen•cy [ɪ'mʌrdʒənsi] s (pl **-cies**) emergencia (caso urgente)

emergency exit s salida de auxilio

emergency landing s aterrizaje forzoso

emergency landing field s aeródromo de urgencia

emergency physician s médico de urgencia

emersion [ɪ'mʌrʒən] o [ɪ'mʌrʃən] s emersión

emery ['ɛməri] s esmeril m

emery cloth s tela de esmeril

emery wheel s esmeriladora, rueda de esmeril, muela de esmeril

emetic [ɪ'mɛtɪk] adj & s emético

emigrant ['ɛmɪgrənt] adj & s emigrante mf

emigrate ['ɛmɪ,gret] intr emigrar

émigré [emi'gre] o ['ɛmɪ,gre] s emigrado

eminence ['ɛmɪnəns] s eminencia

eminent ['ɛmɪnənt] adj eminente

emissar•y ['ɛmɪ,sɛri] s (pl **-ies**) emisario

emission [ɪ'mɪʃən] s emisión

emit [ɪ'mɪt] v (pret & pp **emitted**; ger **emitting**) tr emitir

emotion [ɪ'moʃən] s emoción

emotional [ɪ'moʃənəl] adj emocional, emotivo

emperor ['ɛmpərər] s emperador m

empathy ['ɛmpəθi] s empatía

empha•sis ['ɛmfəsɪs] s (pl **-ses** [,siz]) énfasis m

emphasize ['ɛmfə,saɪz] tr acentuar, hacer hincapié en

emphatic [ɛm'fætɪk] adj enfático

emphysema [,ɛmfɪ'simə] s enfisema m

empire ['ɛmpaɪr] s imperio

empiric(al) [ɛm'pɪrɪk(əl)] adj empírico

empiricist [ɛm'pɪrɪsɪst] s empírico

emplacement [ɛm'plesmənt] s emplazamiento

employ [ɛm'plɔɪ] s empleo ‖ tr emplear

employee [ɛm'plɔɪ•i] o [,ɛmplɔɪ'i] s empleado

employer [ɛm'plɔɪ•ər] s patrono

employment [ɛm'plɔɪmənt] s empleo, colocación

employment agency s agencia de colocaciones

empower [ɛm'paʊ•ər] tr autorizar, facultar; habilitar, permitir

empress ['ɛmprɪs] s emperatriz f

emptiness ['ɛmptɪnɪs] s vaciedad, vacuidad

emp•ty ['ɛmpti] adj (comp **-tier**; super **-tiest**) vacío; (coll) hambriento ‖ v (pret & pp **-tied**) tr & intr vaciar

empty-handed ['ɛmpti'hændɪd] adj manivacío

empty-headed ['ɛmpti'hɛdɪd] adj tonto, ignorante

empye•ma [,ɛmpɪ'imə] s (pl **-mata** [mətə]) empiema m

empyrean [,ɛmpɪ'ri•ən] adj & s empíreo

emulate ['ɛmjə,let] tr & intr emular

emulator ['ɛmjə,letər] s émulo

emulous ['ɛmjələs] adj émulo

emulsi•fy [ɪ'mʌlsɪ,faɪ] v (pret & pp **-fied**) tr emulsionar

emulsion [ɪ'mʌlʃən] s emulsión

enable [ɛn'ebəl] tr habilitar, facilitar

enact [ɛn'ækt] tr decretar, promulgar; hacer el papel de

enactment [ɛn'æktmənt] s ley f; (of a law) promulgación; (of a play) representación

enam•el [ɛn'æməl] s esmalte m ‖ v (pret & pp **-eled** o **-elled**; ger **-eling** o **-elling**) tr esmaltar

enam'el•ware' s utensilios de cocina de hierro esmaltado

enamor [ɛn'æmər] tr enamorar

encamp [ɛn'kæmp] tr acampar ‖ intr acampar, acamparse

encampment [ɛn'kæmpmənt] s acampamiento

enchant [ɛn'tʃænt] tr encantar

enchanting [ɛn'tʃæntɪŋ] adj encantador

enchantment [ɛn'tʃæntmənt] s encanto

enchantress [ɛn'tʃæntrɪs] s encantadora

enchase [ɛn'tʃes] tr engastar

encircle [ɛn'sʌrkəl] tr encerrar, rodear; (mil) envolver

enclitic [ɛn'klɪtɪk] adj & s enclítico

enclose [ɛn'kloz] tr encerrar; (in a letter) adjuntar, incluir; **to enclose herewith** remitir adjunto

enclosure [ɛn'kloʒər] s recinto; cosa inclusa, carta inclusa

encomi•um [ɛn'komɪ•əm] s (pl **-ums** o **-a** [ə]) encomio

encompass [ɛn'kʌmpəs] tr encuadrar, abarcar

encore ['ɑnkor] s bis m ‖ interj ¡bis!, ¡que se repita! ‖ tr pedir la repetición de (p.ej., de una pieza o canción); pedir la repetición a (un actor)

encounter [ɛn'kaʊntər] s encuentro ‖ tr encontrar, encontrarse con ‖ intr batirse, combatirse

encourage [ɛn'kʌrɪdʒ] tr animar, alentar; (to foster) fomentar

encouragement [ɛn'kʌrɪdʒmənt] s ánimo, aliento; fomento

encroach [ɛn'krotʃ] intr — **to encroach on** o **upon** pasar los límites de; abusar de; invadir, entremeterse en

encumber [ɛn'kʌmbər] tr embarazar, estorbar, impedir; (to load with debts, etc.) gravar

encumbrance [ɛn'kʌmbrəns] s embarazo; estorbo; gravamen m

ency. o **encyc.** abbr **encyclopedia**

encyclical [ɛn'sɪklɪkəl] o [ɛn'saɪklɪkəl] s encíclica

el
en

encyclopedia [ɛn,saɪklə'pidɪ•ə] *s* enciclopedia

encyclopedic [ɛn,saɪklə'pidɪk] *adj* enciclopédico

end [ɛnd] *s* (*in time*) fin *m;* (*in space*) extremo, remate *m;* (*e.g., of the month*) fines *mpl;* (*small piece*) cabo, pieza, fragmento; (*purpose*) intento, objeto, fin, mira; **at the end of** al cabo de; a fines de; **in the end** al fin; **no end of** (coll) un sin fin de; **to make both ends meet** pasar con lo que se tiene; **to no end** sin efecto; **to stand on end** poner de punta; ponerse de punta; erizarse, encresparse (*el pelo*); **to the end that** a fin de que ‖ *tr* acabar, terminar ‖ *intr* acabar, terminar; desembocar (*p.ej., una calle*); **to end up** acabar, morir; **to end up as** acabar siendo, parar en (*p.ej., ladrón*)

endanger [ɛn'dendʒər] *tr* poner en peligro

endear [ɛn'dɪr] *tr* hacer querer; **to endear oneself to** hacerse querer por

endearment [ɛn'dɪrmənt] *s* encariñamiento

endeavor [ɛn'dɛvər] *s* esfuerzo, empeño ‖ *intr* esforzarse, empeñarse

endemic [ɛn'dɛmɪk] *adj* endémico ‖ *s* endemia

ending ['ɛndɪŋ] *s* fin *m*, terminación; (gram) desinencia, terminación

endive ['ɛndaɪv] *s* escarola

endless ['ɛndlɪs] *adj* interminable; (*chain, screw, etc.*) sin fin

end'most' *qdj* último, extremo

endorse [ɛn'dɔrs] *tr* endosar; (fig) apoyar, aprobar

endorsee [,ɛndɔr'si] *s* endosatario

endorsement [ɛn'dɔrsmənt] *s* endoso; (fig) apoyo, aprobación

endorser [ɛn'dɔrsər] *s* endosante *mf*

endow [ɛn'dau] *tr* dotar

endowment [ɛn'daumənt] *adj* dotal ‖ *s* (*of an institution*) dotación; (*gift, talent*) dote *f*, prenda

end paper *s* hoja de encuadernador

endurance [ɛn'djurəns] o [ɛn'durəns] *s* aguante *m*, paciencia; (*ability to hold out*) resistencia, fortaleza; (*lasting time*) duración

endure [ɛn'djur] o [ɛn'dur] *tr* aguantar, tolerar, sufrir ‖ *intr* durar; sufrir con paciencia

enduring [ɛn'djurɪŋ] o [ɛn'durɪŋ] *adj* duradero, permanente, resistente

enema ['ɛnəmə] *s* enema, ayuda; (*liquid and apparatus*) lavativa

ene•my ['ɛnəmi] *adj* enemigo ‖ *s* (*pl* **-mies**) enemigo

enemy alien *s* extranjero enemigo

energetic [,ɛnər'dʒɛtɪk] *adj* enérgico, vigoroso

ener•gy ['ɛnərdʒi] *s* (*pl* **-gies**) energía; **alternate energy sources** energías alternas

energy crisis *s* crisis energética

enervate ['ɛnər,vet] *tr* enervar

enfeeble [ɛn'fibəl] *tr* debilitar

enfold [ɛnfold] *tr* arrollar, envolver

enforce [ɛn'fors] *tr* hacer cumplir, poner en vigor; obtener por fuerza; (*e.g., obedience*) imponer; (*an argument*) hacer valer

enforcement [ɛn'forsmənt] *s* compulsión; (*e.g., of a law*) ejecución

enfranchise [ɛn'fræntʃaɪz] *tr* franquear, libertar; conceder el derecho de sufragio a

eng. *abbr* **engineer, engraving**

engage [ɛn'gedʒ] *tr* ocupar, emplear; alquilar, reservar; atraer (*p.ej., la atención de una persona*); engranar con; trabar batalla con; **to be engaged, to be engaged to be married** estar prometido, estar comprometido para casarse; **to engage someone in conversation** entablar conversación con una persona ‖ *intr* empeñarse, comprometerse; empotrar, encajar; engranar; **to engage in** ocuparse en

engaged [ɛn'gedʒd] *adj* comprometido, prometido; (*column*) embebido, entregado

engagement [ɛn'gedʒmənt] *s* ajuste *m*, contrato, empeño; esponsales *mpl*, palabra de casamiento; (*duration of betrothal*) noviazgo; (*appointment*) cita; (mil) acción, batalla

engagement ring *s* anillo de compromiso, anillo de pedida

engaging [ɛn'gedʒɪŋ] *adj* agraciado, simpático

engender [ɛn'dʒɛndər] *tr* engendrar

engine ['ɛndʒɪn] *s* máquina; (*of automobile*) motor *m;* (rr) máquina, locomotora

engine driver *s* maquinista *m*

engineer [,ɛndʒə'nɪr] *s* ingeniero; (*engine driver*) maquinista *m* ‖ *tr* dirigir o construir como ingeniero; llevar a cabo con acierto

engineering [,ɛndʒə'nɪrɪŋ] *s* ingeniería

engine house *s* cuartel *m* de bomberos

engine•man ['ɛndʒɪnmən] *s* (*pl* **-men** [mən]) maquinista *m*, conductor *m* de locomotora

engine room *s* sala de máquinas; (naut) cámara de las máquinas

en'gine-room' telegraph *s* (naut) transmisor *m* de órdenes, telégrafo de máquinas

England ['ɪŋglənd] *s* Inglaterra

Englander ['ɪŋgləndər] *s* natural *m* inglés

English ['ɪŋglɪʃ] *adj* inglés ‖ *s* inglés *m;* (*in billiards*) efecto; **the English** los ingleses

English Channel *s* Canal *m* de la Mancha

English daisy *s* margarita de los prados

English horn *s* (mus) corno inglés, cuerno inglés

English•man ['ɪŋglɪ/mən] *s* (*pl* **-men** [mən]) inglés *m*

Eng'lish-speak'ing *adj* de habla inglesa, angloparlante

Eng'lish•wom'an *s* (*pl* **-wom'en**) inglesa

engraft [ɛn'græft] *tr* (hort & surg) injertar; (fig) implantar

engrave [ɛn'grev] *tr* grabar; (*in the memory*) grabar

engraver [ɛn'grevər] *s* grabador *m*

engraving [ɛn'grevɪŋ] *s* grabado

engross [ɛn'gros] *tr* absorber; poner en limpio; copiar califgáficamente

engrossing [ɛn'grosɪŋ] *adj* acaparador, absorbente

engulf [ɛnˈgʌlf] *tr* hundir, inundar
enhance [ɛnˈhæns] *tr* realzar
enhancement [ɛnˈhænsmənt] *s* realce *m*
enigma [ɪˈnɪgmə] *s* enigma *m*
enigmatic(al) [ˌɪnɪgˈmætɪk(əl)] *adj* enigmático
enjambment [ɛnˈdʒæmmənt] o [ɛnˈdʒæmbmənt] *s* encabalgamiento
enjoin [ɛnˈdʒɔɪn] *tr* encargar, ordenar
enjoy [ɛnˈdʒɔɪ] *tr* gozar; **to enjoy** + *ger* gozarse en + *inf;* **to enjoy oneself** divertirse
enjoyable [ɛnˈdʒɔɪ·əbəl] *adj* agradable, deleitable
enjoyment [ɛnˈdʒɔɪmənt] *s* (*pleasure*) placer *m;* (*pleasurable use*) goce *m*
enkindle [ɛnˈkɪndəl] *tr* encender
enlarge [ɛnˈlɑrdʒ] *tr* agrandar, aumentar; (phot) ampliar ‖ *intr* agrandarse, aumentar; (*to talk at length*) explayarse; exagerar; **to enlarge on** o **upon** tratar con más extensión; exagerar
enlargement [ɛnˈlɑrdʒmənt] *s* agrandamiento, aumento; (phot) ampliación
enlighten [ɛnˈlaɪtən] *tr* ilustrar, instruir
enlightenment [ɛnˈlaɪtənmənt] *s* ilustración, instrucción; dilucidación
enlist [ɛnˈlɪst] *tr* alistar; ganar (*a una persona; el favor, los servicios de una persona*) ‖ *intr* alistarse; **to enlist in** (*a cause*) poner empeño en
enliven [ɛnˈlaɪvən] *tr* avivar, animar
enmesh [ɛnˈmɛʃ] *tr* enredar
enmi•ty [ˈɛnmɪti] *s* (*pl* **-ties**) enemistad
ennoble [ɛnˈnobəl] *tr* ennoblecer
ennui [ˈɑnwi] *s* aburrimiento, tedio
enormous [ɪˈnɔrməs] *adj* enorme
enough [ɪˈnʌf] *adj, adv & s* bastante *m* ‖ *interj* ¡basta!, ¡no más!
enounce [ɪˈnaʊns] *tr* enunciar; pronunciar
en passant [ˌɑn pæˈsɑnt] *adv* (chess) al vuelo
enrage [ɛnˈredʒ] *tr* enrabiar, encolerizar
enrapture [ɛnˈræptʃər] *tr* embelesar, transportar, arrebatar
enrich [ɛnˈrɪtʃ] *tr* enriquecer
enroll [ɛnˈrol] *tr* alistar, inscribir; (*to wrap up*) envolver, enrollar ‖ *intr* alistarse, inscribirse
en route [ɑn ˈrut] *adv* en camino; **en route to** camino de, rumbo a
ensconce [ɛnˈskɑns] *tr* esconder, abrigar; **to ensconce oneself** instalarse cómodamente
ensemble [ɑnˈsɑmbəl] *s* conjunto; grupo de músicos que tocan o cantan juntos; traje armonioso
ensign [ˈɛnsaɪn] *s* (*standard*) enseña, bandera; (*badge*) divisa, insignia ‖ [ˈɛnsən] o [ˈɛnsaɪn] *s* (nav) alférez *m* de fragata
enslave [ɛnˈslev] *tr* esclavizar
enslavement [ɛnˈslevmənt] *s* esclavización
ensnare [ɛnˈsnɛr] *tr* entrampar
ensue [ɛnˈsu] *intr* seguirse; resultar
ensuing [ɛnˈsu·ɪŋ] *adj* siguiente; resultante
ensure [ɛnˈʃʊr] *tr* asegurar, garantizar
entail [ɛnˈtel] *s* (law) vínculo ‖ *tr* acarrear, ocasionar; (law) vincular
entangle [ɛnˈtæŋgəl] *tr* enmarañar, enredar

entanglement [ɛnˈtæŋgəlmənt]*s* enmarañamiento, enredo
enter [ˈɛntər] *tr* entrar en (*una habitación*); entrar por (*una puerta*); (*in the customhouse*) declarar; (*to make a record of*) registrar, asentar; matricular (*a un alumno*); matricularse en; hacer miembro a; hacerse miembro de; (*to undertake*) emprender; asentar (*un pedido*); **to enter one's head** metérsele a uno en la cabeza ‖ *intr* entrar; (theat) entrar en escena, salir; **to enter into** entrar en; celebrar (*p.ej., un contrato*); **to enter on** o **upon** emprender
enterprise [ˈɛntərˌpraɪz] *s* (*undertaking*) empresa; (*spirit, push*) empuje *m*
enterprising [ˈɛntərˌpraɪzɪŋ] *adj* emprendedor
entertain [ˌɛntərˈten] *tr* entretener, divertir; (*to show hospitality to*) recibir; considerar, abrigar (*esperanzas, ideas, etc.*) ‖ *intr* recibir
entertainer [ˌɛntərˈtenər] *s* (*host*) anfitrión *m;* (*in public*) actor *m*, bailador *m*, músico, vocalista *mf* (*esp. en un café cantante*)
entertaining [ˌɛntərˈtenɪŋ] *adj* entretenido
entertainment [ˌɛntərˈtenmənt] *s* entretenimiento, diversión; atracción, espectáculo; buen recibimiento; (*of hopes, ideas, etc.*) consideración, abrigo
enthrall [ɛnˈθrɔl] *tr* cautivar, encantar; esclavizar, sojuzgar
enthrone [ɛnˈθron] *tr* entronizar
enthuse [ɛnˈθuz] o [ɛnˈθjuz] *tr* (coll) entusiasmar ‖ *intr* (coll) entusiasmarse
enthusiasm [ɛnˈθuziˌæzəm] *s* entusiasmo
enthusiast [ɛnˈθuziˌæst] *s* entusiasta *mf;* devoto
enthusiastic [ɛnˌθuziˈæstɪk] *adj* entusiástico
entice [ɛnˈtaɪs] *tr* atraer, tentar; inducir al mal, extraviar
enticement [ɛnˈtaɪsmənt] *s* atracción, tentación; extravío
entire [ɛnˈtaɪr] *adj* entero
entirely [ɛnˈtaɪrli] *adv* enteramente; (*exclusively*) solamente
entire•ty [ɛnˈtaɪrti] *s* (*pl* **-ties**) entereza; conjunto, totalidad
entitle [ɛnˈtaɪtəl] *tr* dar derecho a; (*to give a name to; to honor with a title*) intitular
enti•ty [ˈɛntɪti] *s* (*pl* **-ties**) entidad
entomb [ɛnˈtum] *tr* sepultar
entombment [ɛnˈtummənt] *s* sepultura
entomology [ˌɛntəˈmɑlədʒi] *s* entomología
entourage [ˌɑntuˈrɑʒ] *s* cortejo, séquito
entrails [ˈɛntrelz] *spl* entrañas
entrain [ɛnˈtren] *tr* despachar en el tren ‖ *intr* embarcar, salir en el tren
entrance [ˈɛntrəns] *s* entrada, ingreso; (theat) entrada en escena ‖ [ɛnˈtræns] *tr* arrebatar, encantar
entrance examination *s* examen *m* de ingreso; **to take entrance examinations** examinarse de ingreso
entrancing [ɛnˈtrænsɪŋ] *adj* arrebatador, encantador
entrant [ˈɛntrənt] *s* entrante *mf;* (sport) concurrente *mf*

en
en

en•trap [ɛnˈtræp] v (pret & pp **-trapped;** ger **-trapping**) tr entrampar
entreat [ɛnˈtrit] tr rogar, suplicar
entreat•y [ɛnˈtriti] s (pl **-ies**) ruego, súplica
entree [ˈɑntre] s entrada, ingreso; (culin) entrada, principio
entrench [ɛnˈtrɛntʃ] tr atrincherar ‖ intr — **to entrench on** o **upon** infringir, violar
entrust [ɛnˈtrʌst] tr confiar
en•try [ˈɛntri] s (pl **-tries**) entrada; (item) partida, entrada; (in a dictionary) artículo; (sport) concurrente mf
entry word s (in dictionary) voz-guía f
entwine [ɛnˈtwaɪn] tr entretejer, entrelazar
enumerate [ɪˈnuməˌret] tr enumerar
enunciate [ɪˈnʌnsɪˌet] o [ɪˈnʌnʃɪˌet] tr enunciar; pronunciar
envelop [ɛnˈvɛləp] tr envolver
envelope [ˈɛnvəˌlop] o [ˈɑnvəˌlop] s (for a letter) sobre m; (wrapper) envoltura
envenom [ɛnˈvɛnəm] tr envenenar
enviable [ˈɛnvɪ•əbəl] adj envidiable
envious [ˈɛnvɪ•əs] adj envidioso
environment [ɛnˈvaɪrənmənt] s medio ambiente; entorno; (surroundings) inmediaciones
environmental [ɛnˌvaɪrənˈmɛntəl] adj ambiental
environmental pollution s contaminación ambiental
environs [ɛnˈvaɪrəns] spl inmediaciones, alrededores mpl
envisage [ɛnˈvɪzɪdʒ] tr (to look in the face of) encarar; considerar, representarse
envoi [ˈɛnvɔɪ] s despedida (copla al fin de una composición poética)
envoy [ˈɛnvɔɪ] s (diplomatic agent) enviado; (short concluding stanza) despedida
en•vy [ˈɛnvi] s (pl **-vies**) envidia ‖ v (pret & pp **-vied**) tr envidiar
enzyme [ˈɛnzaɪm] s enzima f
epaulet o **epaulette** [ˈɛpəˌlɛt] s charretera
epenthe•sis [ɛˈpɛnθɪsɪs] s (pl **-ses** [ˌsiz]) epéntesis f
epergne [ɪˈpʌrn] o [eˈpɛrn] s ramillete m, centro de mesa
ephemeral [ɪˈfɛmərəl] adj efímero
epic [ˈɛpɪk] adj épico ‖ s epopeya
epicure [ˈɛpɪˌkjʊr] s epicúreo
epicurean [ˌɛpɪkjʊˈri•ən] adj & s epicúreo
epidemic [ˌɛpɪˈdɛmɪk] adj epidémico ‖ s epidemia
epidemiology [ˌɛpɪˌdimɪˈɑlədʒi] s epidemiología
epidermis [ˌɛpɪˈdʌrmɪs] s epidermis f
epigram [ˈɛpɪˌgræm] s epigrama m
epilepsy [ˈɛpɪˌlɛpsi] s epilepsia
epileptic [ˌɛpɪˈlɛptɪk] adj & s epiléptico
Epiphany [ɪˈpɪfəni] s Epifanía
Episcopalian [ɪˌpɪskəˈpeli•ən] adj & s episcopalista mf
episode [ˈɛpɪˌsod] s episodio
epistemology [ɪˌpɪstɪˈmɑlədʒi] s epistemología
epistle [ɪˈpɪsəl] s epístola
epitaph [ˈɛpɪˌtæf] s epitafio
epithet [ˈɛpɪˌθɛt] s epíteto

epitome [ɪˈpɪtəmi] s epítome m; (fig) esencia, personificación
epitomize [ɪˈpɪtəˌmaɪz] tr epitomar; (fig) encarnar, personificar
epoch [ˈɛpək] o [ˈipɑk] s época
epochal [ˈɛpəkəl] adj memorable, trascendental
ep'och-mak'ing adj que hace época
equable [ˈɛkwəbəl] o [ˈikwəbəl] adj constante, uniforme; sereno
equal [ˈikwəl] adj igual; **equal to** a la altura de ‖ s igual mf ‖ v (pret & pp **equaled** o **equalled;** ger **equaling** o **equalling**) tr (to be equal to) igualarse a o con; (to make equal) igualar
equali•ty [ɪˈkwɑlɪti] s (pl **-ties**) igualdad
equalize [ˈikwəˌlaɪz] tr igualar; (to make uniform) equilibrar
equally [ˈikwəli] adv igualmente
equal opportunity s igualdad de oportunidades
equanimity [ˌikwəˈnɪmɪti] s ecuanimidad, igualdad de ánimo
equate [ɪˈkwet] tr poner en ecuación; considerar equivalente(s)
equation [ɪˈkweʃən] s ecuación
equator [ɪˈkwetər] s ecuador m
equer•ry [ˈɛkwəri] o [ɪˈkwɛri] s (pl **-ries**) caballerizo
equestrian [ɪˈkwɛstrɪ•ən] adj ecuestre ‖ m jinete m, caballista m
equestrian sport s hípica
equilateral [ˌikwɪˈlætərəl] adj equilátero
equilibrium [ˌikwɪˈlɪbrɪ•əm] s equilibrio
equinoctial [ˌikwɪˈnɑkʃəl] adj equinoccial
equinox [ˈikwɪˌnɑks] s equinoccio
equip [ɪˈkwɪp] v (pret & pp **equipped;** ger **equipping**) tr equipar
equipment [ɪˈkwɪpmənt] s equipo, avíos, pertrechos; aptitud, capacidad
equipoise [ˈikwɪˌpɔɪz] o [ˈɛkwɪˌpɔɪz] s equilibrio; contrapeso ‖ tr equilibrar; equipesar
equitable [ˈɛkwɪtəbəl] adj equitativo
equi•ty [ˈɛkwɪti] s (pl **-ties**) (fairness) equidad; valor líquido
equivalent [ɪˈkwɪvələnt] adj & s equivalente m
equivocal [ɪˈkwɪvəkəl] adj equívoco
equivocate [ɪˈkwɪvəˌket] intr usar de equívocos para engañar, mentir
equivocation [ɪˌkwɪvəˈkeʃən] s equívoco
era [ˈɪrə] o [ˈirə] s era
eradicate [ɪˈrædɪˌket] tr erradicar
erase [ɪˈres] tr borrar
eraser [ɪˈresər] s goma de borrar; (for blackboard) cepillo
erasure [ɪˈreʃər] o [ɪˈreʒər] s borradura, tachón m
ere [ɛr] prep antes de ‖ conj antes de que; más bien que
erect [ɪˈrɛkt] adj derecho, enhiesto, erguido; (hair) erizado ‖ tr (to set in upright position) erguir, enhestar; erigir (un edificio); armar, montar (una máquina)
erection [ɪˈrɛkʃən] s erección
erg [ʌrg] s ergio

ermine ['ʌrmɪn] *s* armiño; (fig) toga, judicatura

erode [ɪ'rod] *tr* erosionar ‖ *intr* erosionarse

erosion [ɪ'roʒən] *s* erosión

err [ʌr] *intr* errar, equivocarse, marrar; pecar, marrar

errand ['ɛrənd] *s* mandado, recado, comisión; **to run an errand** hacer un mandado

errand boy *s* recadero, mandadero

erratic [ɪ'rætɪk] *adj* irregular, inconstante, variable; excéntrico

erra·tum [ɪ'retəm] o [ɪ'ratəm] *s* (*pl* **-ta** [tə]) errata

erroneous [ɪ'ronɪ·əs] *adj* erróneo

error ['ɛrər] *s* error *m;* **human error** fallo humano

erudite ['ɛru,daɪt] *adj* erudito

erudition [,ɛru'dɪʃən] *s* erudición

erupt [ɪ'rʌpt] *intr* hacer erupción (*la piel, los dientes de un niño*); erumpir (*un volcán*)

eruption [ɪ'rʌpʃən] *s* erupción

escalate ['ɛskə,let] *intr* escalarse

escalation [,ɛskə'leʃən] *s* escalada, escalación

escalator ['ɛskə,letər] *s* escalera mecánica, móvil o rodante

escallop ['ɛs'kæləp] *s* concha de peregrino; (*on edge of cloth*) festón *m* ‖ *tr* hornear a la crema y con migajas de pan; cocer (*p.ej., ostras*) en su concha; festonear

escapade [,ɛskə'ped] *s* calaverada, aventura atolondrada; (*flight*) escapada

escape [ɛs'kep] *s* (*getaway*) escape *m*, escapatoria; (*from responsibilities, duties, etc.*) escapatoria ‖ *tr* evitar, eludir; **to escape someone** escapársele a uno; olvidársele a uno ‖ *intr* escapar, escaparse; **to escape from** escaparse a (*una persona*); escaparse de (*la cárcel*)

escapee [,ɛskə'pi] *s* evadido

escape literature *s* literatura de escape o de evasión

escapement [ɛs'kepmənt] *s* escape *m*

escapement wheel *s* rueda de escape

escarpment [ɛs'karpmənt] *s* escarpa

eschew [ɛs'tʃu] *tr* evitar, rehuir

escort ['ɛskɔrt] *s* escolta; (*man or boy who accompanies a woman or girl in public*) acompañante *m*, caballero, galán *m* ‖ [ɛs'kɔrt] *tr* escoltar

escutcheon [ɛs'kʌtʃən] *s* escudo de armas; (*plate in front of lock on door*) escudo, escudete *m*

Eski·mo ['ɛskɪ,mo] *adj* esquimal ‖ *s* (*pl* **-mos** o **-mo**) esquimal *mf*

esopha·gus [ɪ'safəgəs] *s* (*pl* **-gi** [,dʒaɪ]) esófago

esp. *abbr* **especially**

espalier [ɛs'pæljər] *s* espaldar *m*, espalera

especial [ɛs'pɛʃəl] *adj* especial

espionage ['ɛspɪ·ənɪdʒ] o [,ɛspɪ·ə'naʒ] *s* espionaje *m*

esplanade [,ɛsplə'ned] *s* explanada

espousal [ɛs'pauzəl] *s* desposorios; (*of a cause*) adhesión

espouse [ɛs'pauz] *tr* casarse con; (*to advocate, adopt*) abogar por, adherirse a

Esq. *abbr* **Esquire**

esquire [ɛs'kwaɪr] o ['ɛskwaɪr] *s* escudero ‖ **Esquire** *s* título de cortesía que se escribe después del apellido y que se usa en vez de **Mr.**

essay ['ɛse] *s* ensayo

essayist ['ɛse·ɪst] *s* ensayista *mf*

essence ['ɛsəns] *s* esencia

essential [ɛ'sɛnʃəl] *adj & s* esencial *m*

est. *abbr* **established, estate, estimated**

establish [ɛs'tæblɪʃ] *tr* establecer

establishment [ɛs'tæblɪʃmənt] *s* establecimiento; **the Establishment** (*established order*) el Sistema

estate [ɛs'tet] *s* estado; situación social; (*landed property*) finca, hacienda, heredad; (*a person's possessions*) bienes *mpl*, propiedad; (*left by a decedent*) herencia, bienes relictos

esteem [ɛs'tim] *s* estima ‖ *tr* estimar

esthete ['ɛsθit] *s* esteta *mf*

esthetic [ɛs'θɛtɪk] *adj* estético ‖ **esthetics** *ssg* estética

estimable ['ɛstɪməbəl] *adj* estimable

estimate ['ɛstɪmɪt] *s* (*calculation of value, judgment of worth*) estimación; (*statement of cost of work to be done*) presupuesto ‖ ['ɛstɪ,met] *tr* (*to judge, deem*) estimar; presupuestar (*el coste de una obra*)

estimation [,ɛstɪ'meʃən] *s* estimación

estrangement [ɛs'trendʒmənt] *s* extrañeza

estuar·y ['ɛstʃu,ɛri] *s* (*pl* **-ies**) estero

etc. *abbr* **et cetera**

etch [ɛtʃ] *tr & intr* grabar al agua fuerte

etcher ['ɛtʃər] *s* aguafortista *mf*

etching ['ɛtʃɪŋ] *s* aguafuerte *f*

eternal [ɪ'tʌrnəl] *adj* eterno

eterni·ty [ɪ'tʌrnɪti] *s* (*pl* **-ties**) eternidad

ether ['iθər] *s* éter *m*

ethereal [ɪ'θɪrɪ·əl] *adj* etéreo

ethical ['ɛθɪkəl] *adj* ético

ethics ['ɛθɪks] *ssg* ética

Ethiopian [,iθɪ'opɪ·ən] *adj & s* etíope *mf*

Ethiopic [,iθɪ'opɪk] *adj & s* etiópico

ethnic(al) ['ɛθnɪk(əl)] *adj* étnico

ethnography [ɛθ'nagrəfi] *s* etnografía

ethnology [ɛθ'nalədʒi] *s* etnología

ethyl ['ɛθɪl] *s* etilo

ethylene ['ɛθɪ,lin] *s* etileno

etiquette ['ɛtɪ,kɛt] *s* etiqueta

et seq. *abbr* **et sequens, et sequentes, et sequentia** (Lat) **and the following**

étude [e'tjud] *s* (mus) estudio

etymology [,ɛtɪ'malədʒi] *s* etimología

ety·mon ['ɛtɪ,man] *s* (*pl* **-mons** o **-ma** [mə]) étimo

eucalyp·tus [,jukə'lɪptəs] *s* (*pl* **-tuses** o **-ti** [taɪ]) eucalipto

Eucharist ['jukərɪst] *s* Eucaristía

euchre ['jukər] *s* juego de naipes ‖ *tr* (coll) ser más listo que

eugenics [ju'dʒɛnɪks] *s* eugenesia

eulogistic [,julə'dʒɪstɪk] *adj* elogiador

eulogize ['julə,dʒaɪz] *tr* elogiar

eulo·gy ['julədʒi] *s* (*pl* **-gies**) elogio

eunuch ['junək] *s* eunuco

euphemism ['jufɪ,mɪzəm] *s* eufemismo

en
eu

euphemistic [,jufɪ'mɪstɪk] *adj* eufemístico
euphonic [ju'fɑnɪk] *adj* eufónico
eupho•ny ['jufəni] *s* (*pl* -**nies**) eufonía
euphoria [ju'forɪ•ə] *s* euforia
euphuism ['jufju,ɪzəm] *s* eufuísmo
euphuistic [,jufju'ɪstɪk] *adj* eufuístico
Europe ['jurəp] *s* Europa
European [,jurə'pi•ən] *adj & s* europeo
euthanasia [,juθə'neʒə] *s* eutanasia
evacuate [ɪ'vækju,et] *tr & intr* evacuar
evacuation [ɪ,vækju'eʃən] *s* evacuación
evade [ɪ'ved] *tr* evadir ‖ *intr* evadirse
evaluate [ɪ'vælju,et] *tr* evaluar
Evangel [ɪ'vændʒəl] *s* Evangelio
evangelic(al) [,ivæn'dʒɛlɪk(əl)] o [,ɛvən-'dʒɛlɪk(əl)] *adj* evangélico
Evangelist [ɪ'vændʒəlɪst] *s* Evangelista *m*
evaporate [ɪ'væpə,ret] *tr* evaporar ‖ *intr* evaporarse
evasion [ɪ've ʒən] *s* evasión, evasiva
evasive [ɪ'vesɪv] *adj* evasivo; elusivo
eve [iv] *s* víspera; **on the eve of** en vísperas de
even ['ivən] *adj* (*smooth*) parejo, llano, liso; (*number*) par; constante, uniforme, invariable; (*temperament*) apacible, sereno; exacto, igual; **even with** al nivel de; **to be even** estar en paz; no deber nada a nadie; **to get even** desquitarse ‖ *adv* aun, hasta; sin embargo; también; exactamente, igualmente; **even as** así como; **even if** aunque, aun cuando; **even so** aun así; **even though** aunque, aun cuando; **even when** aun cuando; **not even** ni . . . siquiera; **to break even** salir sin ganar ni perder; (*in gambling*) salir en paz ‖ *tr* allanar, igualar
evening ['ivnɪŋ] *adj* vespertino ‖ *s* tarde *f*
evening clothes *spl* traje *m* de etiqueta
evening gown *s* vestido de noche (*de mujer*)
evening primrose *s* hierba del asno
evening star *s* estrella vespertina, lucero de la tarde
evening wrap *s* salida de teatro
e'ven•song' *s* canción de la tarde; (*eccl*) vísperas
event [ɪ'vɛnt] *s* acontecimiento, suceso; (*outcome*) resultado; (*public function*) acto; (*sport*) prueba; **at all events** o **in any event** en todo caso; **in the event that** en caso que
e'ven-tem'pered *adj* equilibrado
eventful [ɪ'vɛntfəl] *adj* lleno de acontecimientos; importante, memorable
eventual [ɪ'vɛntʃu•əl] *adj* final
eventuali•ty [ɪ'vɛntʃu'ælɪti] *s* (*pl* -**ties**) eventualidad
eventually [ɪ'vɛntʃu•əli] *adv* finalmente, con el tiempo
eventuate [ɪ'vɛntʃu,et] *intr* concluir, resultar
ever ['ɛvər] *adv* (*at all times*) siempre; (*at any time*) jamás, nunca, alguna vez; **as ever** como siempre; **as much as ever** tanto como antes; **ever since** (*since that time*) desde entonces; después de que; **ever so** muy; **ever so much** muchísimo; **hardly ever** o **scarcely ever** casi nunca; **not . . . ever** no . . . nunca

ev'er•glade' *s* tierra pantanosa cubierta de hierbas altas
ev'er•green' *adj* siempre verde ‖ *s* planta siempre verde; **evergreens** ramas colgadas como adorno
ev'er•last'ing *adj* sempiterno; (*lasting indefinitely*) duradero; (*wearisome*) aburrido, cansado ‖ *s* eternidad; (bot) siempreviva
ev'er•more' *adv* eternamente; **for evermore** para siempre jamás
every ['ɛvri] *adj* todos los; (*each*) cada, todo; (*being each in a series*) cada, p.ej., **every three days** cada tres días; **every bit** (coll) todo, p.ej., **every bit a man** todo un hombre; **every now and then** de vez en cuando; **every once in a while** una que otra vez; **every other day** cada dos días, un día sí y otro no; **every which way** (coll) por todas partes; (coll) en desarreglo
ev'ery•bod'y *pron indef* todo el mundo
ev'ery•day' *adj* de todos los días; cotidiano, diario; común, ordinario
every man Jack o **every mother's son** *s* cada hijo de vecino
ev'ery•one' o **every one** *pron indef* cada uno, todos, todo el mundo
ev'ery•thing' *pron indef* todo
ev'ery•where' *adv* en o por todas partes; a todas partes
evict [ɪ'vɪkt] *tr* desahuciar
eviction [ɪ'vɪkʃən] *s* desahucio
evidence ['ɛvɪdəns] *s* evidencia; (law) prueba
evident ['ɛvɪdənt] *adj* evidente
evil ['ɛvɪl] *adj* malo, malvado, malazo, maléfico ‖ *s* mal *m*, maldad
e'vil•do'er *s* malhechor *m*, malvado
e'vil•do'ing *s* malhecho, maldad
evil eye *s* mal *m* de ojo
evil-minded ['ɪvəl'maɪndɪd] *adj* mal pensado, malintencionado
Evil One, the el enemigo malo
evince [ɪ'vɪns] *tr* manifestar, mostrar
evoke [ɪ'vok] *tr* evocar
evolution [,ɛvə'luʃən] *s* evolución; (math) extracción de raíces, radicación
evolutionary [,ɛvə'luʃə,nɛri] o **evolutionist** [,ɛgə'luʃənɪst] *s* evolucionista *mf*
evolve [ɪ'vɑlv] *tr* desarrollar; desprender (*olores, gases, calor*) ‖ *intr* evolucionar
ewe [ju] *s* oveja
ewer ['ju•ər] *s* aguamanil *m*
ex. *abbr* **examination, example, except, exchange, executive**
ex [ɛks] *prep* sin incluir, sin participación en
exact [ɛg'zækt] *adj* exacto ‖ *tr* exigir
exacting [ɛg'zæktɪŋ] *adj* exigente
exaction [ɛg'zækʃən] *s* exacción
exactly [ɛg'zæktli] *adv* exactamente; (*sharp, on the dot*) en punto
exactness [ɛg,zæktnɪs] *s* exactitud
exaggerate [ɛg'zædʒə,ret] *tr* exagerar
exalt [ɛg'zɔlt] *tr* exaltar, ensalzar
exam [ɛg'zæm] *s* (coll) examen *m*
examination [ɛg,zæmɪ'neʃən] *s* examen *m*; **to take an examination** sufrir un examen, examinarse
examine [ɛg'zæmɪn] *tr* examinar

example 453 **exhaust pipe**

example [ɛg'zæmpəl] o [ɛg'zɑmpəl] s ejemplo; (*case serving as a warning to others*) ejemplar m; (*of mathematics*) problema m; **for example** por ejemplo

exasperate [ɛg'zæspə,ret] tr exasperar

excavate ['ɛkskə,vet] tr excavar

exceed [ɛk'sid] tr exceder; sobrepasar (*p.ej., el límite de velocidad*)

exceedingly [ɛk'sidɪŋli] adv sumamente, sobremanera

ex•cel [ɛk'sɛl] v (pret & pp **-celled**; ger **-celling**) tr aventajar ‖ intr sobresalir

excellence ['ɛksələns] s excelencia

excellen•cy ['ɛksələnsi] s (pl **-cies**) excelencia; **Your Excellency** Su Excelencia

excelsior [ɛk'sɛlsɪ•ər] s pajilla de madera, virutas de madera

except [ɛk'sɛpt] prep excepto; **except for** sin; **except that** a menos que ‖ tr exceptuar

exception [ɛk'sɛpʃən] s excepción; **to take exception** poner reparos, objetar; ofenderse; **with the exception of** a excepción de

exceptional [ɛk'sɛpʃənəl] adj excepcional

excerpt ['ɛksʌrpt] s excerta, selección ‖ [ɛk'sʌrpt] tr escoger

excess ['ɛksɛs] o [ɛk'sɛs] adj excedente, sobrante ‖ [ɛk'sɛs] s (*amount or degree by which one thing exceeds another*) exceso, excedente m; (*excessive amount; immoderate indulgence, unlawful conduct*) exceso; **in excess of** más que, superior a

excess baggage s exceso de equipaje

excess fare s suplemento

excessive [ɛk'sɛsɪv] adj excesivo

ex'cess-prof'its tax s impuesto sobre beneficios extraordinarios

excess weight s exceso de peso

exchange [ɛks'tʃendʒ] s (*of greetings, compliments, blows, etc.*) cambio; (*of prisoners, merchandise, newspapers, credentials, etc.*) canje m; periódico de canje; (*place for buying and selling*) bolsa, lonja; estación telefónica, central f de teléfonos; **in exchange for** en cambio de, a trueque de ‖ tr cambiar; canjear (*prisioneros, mercancías, etc.*); darse, hacerse (*cortesías*); **to exchange greetings** saludarse; **to exchange shots** cambiar disparos

exchequer [ɛks'tʃɛkər] o ['ɛkstʃɛkər] s tesorería; fondos nacionales

excise tax [ɛk'saɪz] o ['ɛksaɪz] m impuesto sobre ciertas mercancías de comercio interior

excitable [ɛk'saɪtəbəl] adj excitable

excite [ɛk'saɪt] tr excitar

excitement [ɛk'saɪtmənt] s excitación

exciting [ɛk'saɪtɪŋ] adj emocionante, conmovedor; (*stimulating*) excitante

exclaim [ɛks'klem] tr & intr exclamar

exclamation [,ɛksklə'meʃən] s exclamación

exclamation mark o **point** s punto de admiración

exclude [ɛks'klud] tr excluir

exclusion [ɛks'kluʒən] s exclusión; **to the exclusion of** con exclusión de

exclusive [ɛks'klusɪv] adj exclusivo; (*clannish*) exclusivista; (*expensive*) (coll) carero; (*fashionable*) (coll) muy de moda; **exclusive of** con exclusión de

excommunicate [,ɛkskə'mjunɪ,ket] tr excomulgar

excommunication [,ɛkskə,mjunɪ'keʃən] s excomunión

excoriate [ɛks'kori,et] tr (fig) desollar, vituperar

excrement ['ɛkskrəmənt] s excremento

excruciating [ɛks'kruʃɪ,etɪŋ] adj atroz, agudísimo, vivísimo

exculpate ['ɛkskʌl,pet] o [ɛks'kʌlpet] tr exculpar

excursion [ɛks'kʌrʒən] s excursión

excursionist [ɛks'kʌrʒənɪst] s excursionista mf

excusable [ɛks'kjusəbəl] adj excusable

excuse [ɛks'kjus] s excusa ‖ [ɛks'kjuz] tr excusar, disculpar; dispensar, perdonar

execute ['ɛksɪ'kjut] tr ejecutar; (law) celebrar, finalizar (*una escritura*)

execution [,ɛksɪ'kjuʃən] s ejecución

executioner [,ɛksɪ'kjuʃənər] s ejecutor m de la justicia, verdugo

executive [ɛg'zɛkjətɪv] adj ejecutivo ‖ m poder ejecutivo; (*of a school, business, etc.*) dirigente mf

Executive Mansion s (U.S.A.) palacio presidencial

executor [ɛg'zɛkjətər] s albacea m, ejecutor testamentario

executrix [ɛg'zɛkjətrɪks] s albacea f, ejecutora testamentaria

exemplary [ɛg'zɛmpləri] o ['ɛgzəm,plɛri] adj ejemplar

exempli•fy [ɛg'zɛmplɪ,faɪ] v (pret & pp **-fied**) tr ejemplificar

exempt [ɛg'zɛmpt] adj exento ‖ tr eximir, exentar

exemption [ɛg'zɛmpʃən] s exención

exercise ['ɛksər,saɪz] s ejercicio; ceremonia; **to take exercise** hacer ejercicio ‖ tr ejercer (*p.ej., caridad, influencia*); ejercitar (*un arte, profesión, etc.*); adiestrar con el ejercicio); inquietar, preocupar; poner (*cuidado*) ‖ ref ejercitarse

exert [ɛg'zʌrt] tr ejercer (*una fuerza*); **to exert oneself** esforzarse

exertion [ɛg'zʌrʃən] s esfuerzo, empeño; (*active use*) ejercicio

exhalation [,ɛks•hə'leʃən] s (*of gas, vapors, etc.*) exhalación; (*of air from lungs*) espiración

exhale [ɛks'hel] o [ɛg'zel] tr exhalar (*gases, vapores*); espirar (*el aire aspirado*) ‖ intr exhalarse; espirar

exhaust [ɛg'zɔst] s escape m; tubo de escape ‖ tr (*to wear out, fatigue; to use up*) agotar; hacer el vacío en; apurar (*todos los medios*)

exhaust fan s ventilador m aspirador

exhaustion [ɛg'zɔstʃən] s agotamiento

exhaustive [ɛg'zɔstɪv] adj exhaustivo; comprensivo

exhaust manifold s múltiple m de escape

exhaust pipe s tubo de escape

.eu
ex

exhaust valve s válvula de escape
exhibit [ɛg'zɪbɪt] s exhibición; (law) documento de prueba ‖ tr exhibir
exhibition [,ɛksɪ'bɪʃən] s exhibición
exhibitor [ɛg'zɪbɪtər] s expositor m
exhilarating [ɛg'zɪlə,retɪŋ] adj alegrador, regocijador, alborozador
exhort [ɛg'zɔrt] tr exhortar
exhume [ɛks'hjum] tr exhumar
exigen•cy ['ɛksɪdʒənsi] s (pl -cies) exigencia
exigent ['ɛksɪdʒənt] adj exigente
exile ['ɛgzaɪl] o ['ɛksaɪl] s destierro; (person) desterrado ‖ tr desterrar
exist [ɛg'zɪst] intr existir
existence [ɛg'zɪstəns] s existencia
existing [ɛg'zɪstɪŋ] adj existente
exit ['ɛgzɪt] o ['ɛksɪt] s salida ‖ intr salir
exobiology [,ɛksobaɪ'ɑlədʒi] s exobiología
exodus ['ɛksədəs] s éxodo
exonerate [ɛg'zɑnə,ret] tr (to free from blame) exculpar; (to free from an obligation) exonerar
exorbitant [ɛg'zɔrbɪtənt] adj exorbitante
exorcise ['ɛksɔr,saɪz] tr exorcizar
exotic [ɛg'zɑtɪk] adj exótico
exp. abbr **expenses, expired, export, express**
expand [ɛks,pænd] tr dilatar (un gas, el metal); (to enlarge, develop) ampliar, ensanchar; (to unfold, stretch out) desplegar, extender; (math) desarrollar (una ecuación) ‖ intr dilatarse; amplíarse, ensancharse; desplegarse, extenderse
expanse [ɛks'pæns] s extensión
expansion [ɛks'pænʃən] s expansión
expansive [ɛks'pænsɪv] adj expansivo
expatiate [ɛks'peʃɪ,et] intr espaciarse, explayarse
expatriate [ɛks'petrɪ•ɪt] adj & s expatriado
expect [ɛks'pɛkt] tr esperar; (coll) creer, suponer
expectan•cy [ɛks'pɛktənsi] s (pl -cies) expectación
expectant mother [ɛks'pɛktənt] s futura madre
expectation [,ɛkspɛkteʃən] s expectativa
expectorate [ɛks'pɛktə,ret] tr & intr expectorar
expedien•cy [ɛks'pidɪ•ənsi] s (pl -cies) conveniencia, oportunidad; ventaja personal
expedient [ɛks'pidɪ•ənt] adj conveniente, oportuno; egoísta, vɛntajoso; (acting with self-interest) ventajista ‖ s expediente m
expedite ['ɛkspɪ,daɪt] tr apresurar, despachar; expediar; dar curso a (un documento)
expedition [,ɛkspɪ'dɪʃən] s expedición
expeditious [,ɛkspɪ'dɪʃəs] adj expeditivo
expeditiously [,ɛkspɪ'dɪʃəsli] adv ejecutivamente
ex•pel [ɛks'pɛl] v (pret & pp -pelled; ger -pelling) tr expeler, expulsar
expend [ɛks'pɛnd] tr gastar, consumir
expendable [ɛks'pɛndəbəl] adj gastable; (to be thrown away after use) desechable; (soldier) sacrificable
expenditure [ɛks'pɛndɪtʃər] s gasto, consumo

expense [ɛks'pɛns] s gasto; **expenses** gastos, expensas; **to go to the expense of** meterse en gastos con; **to meet expenses** hacer frente a !os gastos
expense account s cuenta de gastos
expensive [ɛks'pɛnsɪv] adj caro, costoso, dispendioso; (charging high prices) carero
experience [ɛks'pɪrɪ•əns] s experiencia ‖ tr experimentar
experienced [ɛksɪ'ənst] adj experimentado
experiment [ɛks'pɛrɪmənt] s experiencia, experimento ‖ [ɛks'pɛrɪ,mɛnt] intr experimentar
expert ['ɛkspərt] adj & s experto
expiate ['ɛkspɪ,et] tr expiar
expiation [,ɛkspɪ'eʃən] s expiación
expire [ɛks'paɪr] tr expeler (el aire de los pulmones) ‖ intr expirar (expeler el aire de los pulmones; acabarse, p.ej., un plazo; fallecer)
explain [ɛks'plen] tr explicar; **to explain away** descartar con explicaciones; (to make excuse for) explicar ‖ intr explicar, explicarse
explanation [,ɛksplə'neʃən] s explicación; dilucidación
explanatory [ɛks'plænə,tori] adj explicativo
explicit [ɛks'plɪsɪt] adj explícito
explode [ɛks'plod] tr volar, hacer saltar; desacreditar (una teoría) ‖ intr explotar, estallar, reventar
exploit ['ɛksplɔɪt] s hazaña, proeza ‖ [ɛks'plɔɪt] tr explotar
exploitation [,ɛksplɔɪ'teʃən] s explotación
exploration [,ɛksplə'reʃən] s exploración
explore [ɛks'plor] tr explorar
explorer [ɛks'plorər] s explorador m
explosion [ɛks'ploʒən] s explosión; (of a theory) refutación
explosive [ɛks'plosɪv] adj explosivo ‖ s explosivo; (phonet) explosiva
exponent [ɛks'ponənt] s exponente m, expositor m; (math) exponente m
export ['ɛksport] adj de exportación ‖ s exportación; **exports** (articles exported) exportación ‖ [ɛks'port] o ['ɛksport] tr & intr exportar
exportation [,ɛkspor'teʃən] s exportación
exporter [ɛksportər] s exportador m
expose [ɛks'poz] tr exponer; (to unmask) desenmascarar; (the Host) manifestar, exponer; (phot) impresionar
exposé [,ɛkspo'ze] s desenmascaramiento
exposition [,ɛkspo'zɪʃən] s exposición; (rhet) exposición
expostulate [ɛks'pɑstʃə,let] intr protestar; **to expostulate with** reconvenir
exposure [ɛks'poʒər] s (to a danger; position with respect to points of compass) exposición; (unmasking) desenmascaramiento; (phot) exposición
expound [ɛks'paund] tr exponer
express [ɛks'prɛs] adj expreso ‖ adv (for a special purpose) expresamente; por expreso ‖ s expreso; **by express** (rr) en gran velocidad ‖ tr expresar; (to squeeze out)

exprimir; enviar por expreso; **to express oneself** expresarse

express company s compañía de transportes rápidos

expression [εks'prεʃən] s expresión

expressive [εks'prεsɪv] adj expresivo

expressly [εks'prεsli] adv expresamente

express•man [εks'prεsmən] s (pl -men [mən]) (U.S.A.) empleado del servicio de transportes rápidos

express train s tren expreso

express'way' s carretera de vía libre

expropriate [εks'proprɪ,et] tr expropiar

expulsion [εks'pʌlʃən] s expulsión

expunge [εks'pʌndʒ] tr borrar, cancelar, arrasar

expurgate ['εkspər,get] tr expurgar

exquisite ['εkskwɪzɪt] o [εks'kwɪzɪt] adj exquisito; agudo, vivo; sensible

ex-service•man [εks'sʌrvɪs,mæn] s (pl -men [,mεn]) ex militar m, ex combatiente m

extant ['εkstənt] o [εks'tænt] adj existente

extemporaneous [εks,tεmpə'renɪ•əs] adj sin preparación; (made for the occasion) provisional

extempore [εks'tεmpəri] adj improvisado ‖ adv improvisadamente

extemporize [εks'tεmpə,raɪz] tr & intr improvisar

extend [εks'tεnd] tr extender; dar, ofrecer; hacer extensivos (p.ej., vivos deseos); prorrogar (un plazo) ‖ intr extenderse

extended [εks'tεndɪd] adj extenso; prolongado

extension [εks'tεnʃən] s extensión; prolongación

extension ladder s escalera extensible

extension table s mesa de extensión

extensive [εks'tεnsɪv] adj (having great extent) extenso; (characterized by extension) extensivo

extent [εks'tεnt] s extensión; **to a certain extent** hasta cierto punto; **to a great extent** en sumo grado; **to the full extent** en toda su extensión

extenuate [εks'tεnju,et] tr (to make seem less serious) atenuar; (to underrate) menospreciar, no dar importancia a

exterior [εks'tɪrɪ•ər] adj & s exterior m

exterminate [εks'tʌrmɪ,net] tr exterminar; (insects) desinsectar

external [εks'tʌrnəl] adj externo ‖ **externals** spl exterioridad

extinct [εks'tɪŋkt] adj desaparecido; (volcano) extinto

extinguish [εks'tɪŋgwɪʃ] tr extinguir

extinguisher [εks'tɪŋgwɪʃər] s apagador m, extintor m

extirpate ['εkstər,pet] o [εks'tʌrpet] tr extirpar

ex•tol [εks'tol] o [εks'tɑl] v (pret & pp -tolled; ger -tolling) tr ensalzar

extort [εks'tɔrt] tr obtener por amenazas, fuerza o engaño

extortion [εks'tɔrʃən] s extorción

extra ['εkstrə] adj extra; (spare) de repuesto ‖ adv extraordinariamente ‖ s (of a news-

paper) extra m; pieza de repuesto; (something additional) extra m; (theat) extra mf

extract ['εkstrækt] s selección; (pharm) extracto ‖ [εks'trækt] tr (to pull out, remove) extraer; seleccionar (pasajes de un libro); (math) extraer

extraction [εks'trækʃən] s extracción

extracurricular [,εkstrəkə'rɪkjələr] adj extracurricular

extradition [,εkstrə'dɪʃən] s extradición

extra fare s recargo de tarifa, tarifa recargada

ex'tra-flat' adj extraplano

extragalactic [,εkstrəgə'læktɪk] adj extragaláctico

extramural [,εkstrə'mjurəl] adj extramural

extraneous [εks'trenɪ•əs] adj ajeno, extraño

extraordinary [,εkstrə'ɔrdɪ,nεri] o [εks-'trɔrdɪ,nεri] adj extraordinario

extrapolate [εks'træpə,let] tr & intr extrapolar

extrasensory [,εkstrə'sεnsəri] adj extrasensorio

extraterrestrial [,εkstrətə'rεstrɪ•əl] adj extraterrestre

extravagance [εks'trævəgəns] s derroche m, prodigalidad, gasto excesivo; (wildness, folly) extravagancia

extravagant [εks'trævəgənt] adj derrochador, pródigo, gastador; (wild, foolish) extravagante

extreme [εks'trim] adj & s extremo; **in the extreme** en sumo grado; **to go to extremes** excederse, propasarse

extremely [εks'trimli] adv extremadamente, sumamente

extreme unction s extremaunción

extremism [εks'trimɪzəm] s extremismo

extremi•ty [εks'trεmɪti] s (pl -ties) extremidad; (great want) extrema necesidad; **extremities** medidas extremas; (hands and feet) extremidades

extricate ['εsktrɪ,ket] tr desembarazar, desenredar

extrinsic [εks'trɪnsɪk] adj extrínseco

extroversion [,εkstrə'vʌrʒən] s extroversión

extrovert ['εkstrə,vʌrt] s extrovertido

extrude [εks'trud] intr resaltar, sobresalir

exuberant [εg'zubərənt] adj exuberante

exude [εg'zud] o [εk'sud] tr & intr exudar

exult [εg'zʌlt] intr exultar, gloriarse

exultant [εg'zʌltənt] adj exultante

eye [aɪ] s ojo; (of hook and eye) hembra, corcheta; **to catch one's eye** llamar la atención a uno; **to feast one's eyes on** deleitar la vista en; **to lay eyes on** alcanzar a ver; **to make eyes at** hacer guiños a; **to roll one's eyes** poner los ojos en blanco; **to see eye to eye** estar completamente de acuerdo; **to shut one's eyes** hacer la vista gorda ante; **without batting an eye** sin pestañear, sin inmutarse ‖ v (pret & pp eyed; ger eying o eyeing) tr ojear; **to eye up and down** mirar de hito en hito

eye'ball' s globo del ojo

eye'bolt' s armella, cáncamo

eye'brow' s ceja; **to raise one's eyebrows** arquear las cejas

eye'cup' s ojera, lavaojos m
eyeful ['aɪfʊl] s (coll) buena ojeada
eye'glass' s (of optical instrument) ocular m; (eyecup) ojera, lavaojos m; **eyeglasses** gafas, anteojos
eye'lash' s pestaña
eyelet ['aɪlɪt] s ojete m, ojal m; (hole to look through) mirilla
eye'lid' s párpado
eye of the morning s sol m
eye opener ['opənər] s noticia asombrosa o inesperada; (coll) trago de licor
eye'piece' s ocular m
eye'shade' s visera
eye shadow s crema para los párpados; sombra (de ojos)

eye'shot' s alcance m de la vista
eye'sight' s vista; (range) alcance m de la vista
eye socket s cuenca del ojo
eye'sore' s cosa que ofende la vista
eye'strain' s vista fatigada
eye'-test' chart s escala tipográfica oftalmométrica, tipo de ensayo, tipo de prueba
eye'tooth' s (pl teeth') colmillo, diente canino; **to cut one's eyeteeth** (coll) tener el colmillo retorcido; **to give one's eyeteeth for** (coll) dar los ojos de la cara por
eye'wash' s colirio; (slang) halago para engañar
eye'wit'ness s testigo ocular, testigo presencial
ey•rie o **ey•ry** ['ɛri] s (pl -ries) nido de águilas, nido de aves de rapiña; (fig) altura, morada elevada

F

F, f [ɛf] sexta letra del alfabeto inglés
f. abbr **feminine, folio**
F. abbr **Fahrenheit, Friday**
fable ['febəl] s fábula
fabric ['fæbrɪk] s tejido; textura; (structure) fábrica
fabricate ['fæbrɪ, ket] tr fabricar
fabrication [,fæbrɪ'keʃən] s fabricación; mentira
fabulous ['fæbjələs] adj fabuloso
façade [fə'sɑd] s fachada
face [fes] s cara, rostro; (of cloth) haz f; (of earth) faz f; (grimace) mueca; (of watch) esfera, muestra; (impudence) descaro; **in the face of** en presencia de; **to keep a straight face** contener la risa; **to lose face** desprestigiarse; **to save face** salvar las apariencias; **to show one's face** dejarse ver ‖ tr volver la cara hacia; arrostrar; revestir (un muro); forrar (un vestido); **facing** cara a ‖ intr — **to face about** volver la mirada; dar media vuelta; cambiar de opinión; **to face on** dar a o sobre; **to face up to** encararse con
face card s figura, naipe m de figura
face lifting s cirugía estética
face powder s polvos de tocador
facet ['fæsɪt] s faceta
facial ['feʃəl] adj facial ‖ s masaje m facial
facilitate [fə'sɪlɪ,tet] tr facilitar
facili•ty [fə'sɪlɪti] s (pl -ties) facilidad
facing ['fesɪŋ] s revestimiento, paramento
facsimile [fæk'sɪmɪli] s facsímile m ‖ tr facsimilar
fact [fækt] s hecho; **in fact** en realidad; **the fact is that** ello es que
faction ['fækʃən] s facción; discordia
factional ['fækʃənəl] adj faccionario
factionalism ['fækʃənə,lɪzəm] s parcialidad, partidismo

factor ['fæktər] s factor m ‖ tr descomponer en factores
facto•ry ['fæktəri] s (pl -ries) fábrica
factual ['fæktʃʊ•əl] adj verdadero, objetivo
facul•ty ['fækəlti] s (pl -ties) facultad
fad [fæd] s afición pasajera, moda pasajera
fade [fed] tr desteñir ‖ intr desteñir, desteñirse; apagarse (un sonido); (rad) desvanecerse
fade'out' s desaparición gradual; (rad) desvanecimiento
fag [fæg] s (drudge) yunque m; (coll) cigarrillo ‖ tr—**to fag out** cansar
fagot ['fægət] s haz m de leña
fail [fel] s—**without fail** sin falta ‖ tr faltar a; reprobar, suspender (a un alumno); salir mal en (un examen) ‖ intr malograrse, fracasar; salir mal (un alumno); fallar (un motor); (com) quebrar, hacer bancarrota; **to fail to** dejar de
failure ['feljər] s malogro, fracaso, mal éxito; (student) perdigón m; (com) quiebra
faint [fent] adj débil; **to feel faint** sentirse desfallecido ‖ s desmayo ‖ intr desmayarse
faint-hearted ['fent'hɑrtɪd] adj cobarde, tímido, apocado
fair [fɛr] adj justo, imparcial; regular, ordinario; favorable, propicio; (hair) rubio; (complexion) blanco; (sky) despejado; (weather) bueno, bonancible ‖ adv imparcialmente; **to play fair** jugar limpio ‖ s (exhibition) feria; (carnival) quermese m, verbena
fair'ground' s real m, campo de una feria
fairly ['fɛrli] adv justamente; bastante
fair-minded ['fɛr'maɪndɪd] adj justo, imparcial
fairness ['fɛrnɪs] s justicia, imparcialidad; (of weather) serenidad; (of complexion) blancura
fair play s juego limpio, limpieza

fair sex s bello sexo
fair to middling adj bastante bueno, mediano
fair'weath'er adj—**a fair-weather friend** amigo del buen viento
fair•y ['fɛri] adj feérico ‖ s (pl **-ies**) hada
fairy godmother s hada madrina
fair'y•land' s tierra de las hadas
fairy ring s corro de brujas
fairy tale s cuento de hadas; (fig) bella poesía
faith [feθ] s fe f; **to break faith with** faltar a la palabra dada a; **to keep faith with** cumplir la palabra dada a; **to pin one's faith on** tener puesta su esperanza en; **upon my faith!** ¡a fe mía!
faithful ['feθfəl] adj fiel, leal ‖ **the faithful** los fieles
faithless ['feθlɪs] adj infiel, desleal
fake [fek] adj (coll) falso, fingido ‖ s impostura, patraña; (person) farsante mf ‖ tr & intr falsificar, fingir
faker ['fekər] s (coll) impostor m, patrañero; (peddler) (coll) buhonero
falcon ['fɔkən] o ['fɔlkən] s halcón m
falconer ['fɔkənər] o ['fɔlkənər] s cetrero, halconero
falconry ['fɔkənri] o ['fɔlkənri] s cetrería, halconería
fall [fɔl] adj otoñal ‖ s caída; (of water) catarata, salto de agua; (of prices) baja; (autumn) otoño; **falls** catarata, caída de agua ‖ v (pret **fell** [fɛl]; pp **fallen** ['fɔlən]) intr caer, caerse; **to fall apart** caerse a pedazos; **to fall back** (mil) replegarse; **to fall behind** quedarse atrás; **to fall down** caerse; **to fall due** vencer (una letra); **to fall flat** caer tendido; no tener éxito; **to fall for** (slang) ser engañado por; (slang) enamorarse de; **to fall in** desplomarse (un techo); ponerse de acuerdo; **to fall in with** trabar amistades con; ponerse de acuerdo con; **to fall off** caer de; disminuir; **to fall out** desavenirse; **to fall out of** caerse de; **to fall out with** esquinarse con; **to fall over** caerse; (coll) adular, halagar; **to fail through** fracasar, malograrse; **to fall to** recaer (la herencia, la elección) en; **to fall under** estar comprendido en
fallacious [fə'leʃəs] adj erróneo, engañoso
falla•cy ['fæləsi] s (pl **-cies**) error m, equivocación
fall guy s (slang) cabeza de turco
fallible ['fælɪbəl] adj falible
falling star s estrella fugaz
fall'out' s caída radiactiva, precipitación radiactiva
fallout shelter s refugio antiatómico
fallow ['fælo] adj barbechado; **to lie fallow** estar en barbecho (tierra labrantía); (fig) quedar sin emplear, quedar sin ejecutar (una cosa provechosa) ‖ s barbecho ‖ tr barbechar
false [fɔls] adj falso; (hair, teeth, etc.) postizo ‖ adv falsamente; **to play false** traicionar
false colors spl pretextos falsos

false face s mascarilla; (ugly false face) carantamaula
false-hearted ['fɔls'hɑrtɪd] adj pérfido
falsehood ['fɔls•hud] s falsedad
false pretenses spl impostura, falsas apariencias
false return s declaración falsa
falset•to [fɔl'sɛto] s (pl **-tos**) (voice) falsete m; (person) falsetista m
falsi•fy ['fɔlsɪ,faɪ] v (pret & pp **-fied**) tr falsificar; (to disprove) refutar ‖ intr falsificar; mentir
falsi•ty ['fɔlsɪti] s (pl **-ties**) falsedad
falter ['fɔltər] s vacilación; (in speech) balbuceo ‖ intr vacilar; balbucear
fame [fem] s fama
famed [femd] adj afamado
familiar [fə'mɪljər] adj familiar; conocido; común; **familiar with** familiarizado con
familiari•ty [fə,mɪlɪ'ærɪti] s (pl **-ties**) familiaridad; conocimiento
familiarize [fə'mɪljə,raɪz] tr familiarizar
fami•ly ['fæmɪli] adj familiar; **in the family way** (coll) en estado de buena esperanza ‖ s (pl **-lies**) familia
family man s padre m de familia; hombre casero
family name s apellido
family physician s médico de cabecera
family tree s árbol genealógico
famish ['fæmɪʃ] tr & intr hambrear
famished ['fæmɪʃt] adj famélico
famous ['feməs] adj famoso; (notable, excellent) (coll) famoso
fan [fæn] s abanico; ventilador m; (slang) hincha mf, aficionado ‖ v (pret & pp **fanned**; ger **fanning**) tr abanicar; (to winnow) aventar; ahuyentar con abanico; avivar (el fuego); excitar (las pasiones); (slang) azotar ‖ intr abanicarse; **to fan out** salir (un camino) en todas direcciones
fanatic [fə'nætɪk] adj & s fanático
fanatical [fə'nætɪkəl] adj fanático
fanaticism [fə'nætɪ,sɪzəm] s fanatismo
fancied ['fænsid] adj imaginario
fancier ['fænsɪ•ər] s aficionado; visionario; (of animals) criador aficionado
fanciful ['fænsɪfəl] adj fantástico, extravagante; imaginativo
fan•cy ['fænsi] adj (comp **-cier**; super **-ciest**) de fantasía, de imitación; fino, de lujo, precioso; ornamental; primoroso; fantástico, extravagante ‖ s (pl **-cies**) fantasía; afición, gusto; **to take a fancy to** aficionarse a, prendarse de ‖ v (pret & pp **-cied**) tr imaginar
fancy ball s baile m de trajes
fancy dive s salto ornamental
fancy dress s traje m de fantasía
fancy foods spl comestibles mpl de lujo
fan'cy-free' adj libre del poder del amor
fancy jewelry s joyas de fantasía
fancy skating s patinaje m de fantasía
fan'cy•work' s (sew) labor f
fanfare ['fænfɛr] s fanfarria
fang [fæŋ] s colmillo; (of reptile) diente m
fan'light' s abanico

ey
fa

fantastic(al) [fæn'tæstɪk(əl)] *adj* fantástico
fanta•sy ['fæntəsi] *s* (*pl* -**sies**) fantasía
far [fɑr] *adj* lejano; **on the far side of** del otro lado de ‖ *adv* lejos; **as far as** hasta; en cuanto; **as far as I am concerned** por lo que a mí me toca; **as far as I know** que yo sepa; **by far** con mucho; **far and near** por todas partes; **far away** muy lejos; **far be it from me** no lo permita Dios; **far better** mucho mejor; **far different** muy diferente; **far from** lejos de; **far from it** ni con mucho; **far into** hasta muy adentro de; hasta muy tarde de; **far more** mucho más; **far off** a gran distancia; **how far** cuán lejos; **how far is it?** ¿cuánto hay de aquí?; **in so far as** en cuanto; **thus far** hasta ahora; **thus far this year** en lo que va del año; **to go far towards** contribuir mucho a
faraway ['fɑrə,we] *adj* lejano, distante; abstraído, preocupado
farce [fɑrs] *s* farsa; (*ridiculous act*) papelada
farcical ['fɑrsɪkəl] *adj* ridículo
fare [fɛr] *s* pasaje *m;* pasajero; alimento; comida; **to collect fares** cobrar el pasaje ‖ *intr* pasarlo, p.ej., **how did you fare?** ¿cómo lo pasó Vd.?
Far East *s* Extremo Oriente, Lejano Oriente
fare'well' *s* despedida; **to bid farewell to** o **to take farewell of** despedirse de ‖ *interj* ¡adiós!
far•fetched ['fɑr'fɛtʃt] *adj* traído por los pelos
far-flung ['fɑr'flʌŋ] *adj* de gran alcance, vasto
farm [fɑrm] *adj* agrícola; agropecuario ‖ *s* granja; terreno agrícola ‖ *tr* cultivar, labrar (*la tierra*) ‖ *intr* cultivar la tierra y criar animales
farmer ['fɑrmər] *s* granjero; agricultor *m*, labrador *m*
farm hand *s* peón *m*, mozo de granja
farm'house' *s* alquería, cortijo
farming ['fɑrmɪŋ] *s* agricultura, labranza
farm'yard' *s* corral *m* de granja
far'-off' *adj* lejano, distante
far-reaching ['fɑr'ritʃɪŋ] *adj* de mucho alcance
far-sighted ['fɑr'saɪtɪd] *adj* longividente; precavido; présbita
farther ['fɑrðər] *adj* más lejano; adicional ‖ *adv* más lejos, más allá; además, también; **farther on** más adelante
farthest ['fɑrðɪst] *adj* (el) más lejano; último ‖ *adv* más lejos; más
farthing ['fɑrðɪŋ] *s* (Brit) cuarto de penique
Far West *s* (U.S.A.) Lejano Oeste
fascinate ['fæsɪ,net] *tr* fascinar
fascinating ['fæsɪ,netɪŋ] *adj* fascinante, cautivador
fascism ['fæʃɪzəm] *s* fascismo
fascist ['fæʃɪst] *adj* & *s* fascista *mf*
fashion ['fæʃən] *s* moda, boga; estilo, manera; alta sociedad; **after a fashion** en cierto modo; **in fashion** de moda; **out of fashion** fuera de moda; **to go out of fashion** pasar de moda ‖ *tr* labrar, forjar
fashion designing *s* alta costura

fashion plate *s* figurín *m;* (*person*) (coll) figurín *m*, elegante *mf;* **to be a fashion plate** (coll) ir hecho un maniquí
fashion show *s* desfile *m* de modas
fast [fæst] *adj* rápido, veloz; (*clock*) adelantado; fijado; disipado; (*friend*) fiel ‖ *adv* aprisa, rápidamente; firmemente; (*asleep*) profundamente; **to hold fast** mantenerse firme; **to live fast** vivir de una manera disipada ‖ *s* ayuno; **to break one's fast** romper el ayuno ‖ *intr* ayunar
fast day *s* día *m* de ayuno
fasten ['fæsən] *tr* fijar; atar; abrochar; cerrar con llave; (*one's belt*) ajustarse; (*blame*) aplicar ‖ *intr* fijarse
fastener ['fæsənər] *s* asilla; (*snap, clasp*) cierre *m;* (*for papers*) sujetapapeles *m*
fast'-food' restaurant *s* rotisería
fast forward *s* (mach, mov) avance rápido
fastidious [fæs'tɪdɪ•əs] *adj* esquilmoso, quisquilloso, descontentadizo
fasting ['fæstɪŋ] *s* ayuno
fat [fæt] *adj* (*comp* **fatter;** *super* **fattest**) gordo; poderoso; opulento; (*profitable*) pingüe; (*spark*) caliente; **to get fat** engordar ‖ *s* grasa; (*suet*) gordo, sebo
fatal ['fetəl] *adj* fatal
fatalism ['fetə,lɪzəm] *s* fatalismo
fatalist ['fetəlɪst] *s* fatalista *mf*
fatali•ty [fə'tælɪti] *s* (*pl* -**ties**) fatalidad; (*in accidents, war, etc.*) muerte *f*
fate [fet] *s* sino, hado; **the Fates** las Parcas ‖ *tr* condenar, predestinar
fated ['fetɪd] *adj* hadado, predestinado
fateful ['fetfəl] *adj* fatídico; fatal
fat'head' *s* (coll) tronco, estúpido
father ['fɑðər] *s* padre *m;* (*an elderly man*) (coll) tío ‖ *tr* servir de padre a; engendrar; inventar
fatherhood ['fɑðər,hʊd] *s* paternidad
fa'ther-in-law' *s* (*pl* **fathers-in-law**) suegro
fa'ther•land' *s* patria
fatherless ['fɑðərlɪs] *adj* huérfano de padre, sin padre
fatherly ['fɑðərli] *adj* paternal
Father's Day *s* día *m* del padre
Father Time *s* el Tiempo
fathom ['fæðəm] *s* braza ‖ *tr* sondear; profundizar
fathomless ['fæðəmlɪs] *adj* insondable
fatigue [fə'tig] *s* fatiga; (mil) faena ‖ *tr* fatigar, cansar
fatigue clothes *spl* (mil) traje *m* de faena
fatigue duty *s* faena
fatten ['fætən] *tr* & *intr* engordar
fat•ty ['fæti] *adj* (*comp* -**tier;** *super* -**tiest**) graso; (*pathol*) grasoso; (*chubby*) (coll) gordiflón ‖ *s* (*pl* -**ties**) (coll) gordiflón *m*
fatuous ['fætʃʊ•əs] *adj* fatuo; irreal, ilusivo
faucet ['fɔsɪt] *s* grifo
fault [fɔlt] *s* (*misdeed, blame*) culpa; (*defect*) falta; (geol) falta; (sport) falta; **it's your fault Vd.** tiene la culpa; **to a fault** excesivamente; **to find fault with** culpar, echar la culpa a; hallar defecto en
fault'find'er *s* criticón *m*, reparón *m*

fault′find′ing adj criticón, reparón ‖ s manía de criticar

faultless [′fɔltlɪs] adj perfecto, impecable

fault·y [′fɔlti] adj (comp **-ier**; super **-iest**) defectuoso, imperfecto

faun [fɔn] s fauno

fauna [′fɔnə] s fauna

favor [′fevər] s favor m; (letter) atenta, grata; **do me the favor to** hágame Vd. el favor de; **by your favor** con permiso de Vd.; **favors** regalos de fiesta, objetos de cotillón; **to be in favor with** disfrutar del favor de; **to be out of favor** caer en desgracia ‖ tr favorecer; (coll) parecerse a

favorable [′fevərəbəl] adj favorable

favorite [′fevərɪt] adj & s favorito

favoritism [′fevərɪˌtɪzəm] s favoritismo

fawn [fɔn] s cervato ‖ intr—**to fawn on** adular servilmente; hacer fiestas a

faze [fez] tr (coll) molestar, desanimar

FBI [ˌɛf′biˈaɪ] s (letterword) **Federal Bureau of Investigation**

fear [fɪr] s miedo; **for fear of** por miedo de, por temor de; **for fear that** por miedo (de) que; **no fear** no hay peligro; **to be in fear of** tener miedo de ‖ tr & intr temer

fearful [′fɪrfəl] adj medroso; (coll) enorme, muy malo

fearless [′fɪrlɪs] adj arrojado, intrépido

feasible [′fɪsɪbəl] adj factible, viable

feast [fist] s fiesta; (sumptuous meal) festín m, banquete m ‖ tr & intr banquetear; **to feast on** regalarse con

feat [fit] s hazaña, proeza

feather [′fɛðər] s pluma; (plume; arrogance) penacho; clase f, género; **in fine feather** de buen humor; en buena salud ‖ tr emplumar; (carp) machihembrar; **to feather one's nest** hacer todo para enriquecerse

feather bed s colchón m de plumas; (comfortable situation) lecho de plumas

feath′er·bed′ding s empleo de más obreros de lo necesario (exigido por los sindicatos)

feath′er·brain′ s cascabelero

feath′er·edge′ s (of board) bisel m; (of sharpened tool) filván m

feathery [′fɛðəri] adj plumoso

feature [′fitʃər] s facción; característica, rasgo distintivo; película principal; artículo principal; **features** facciones ‖ tr delinear; ofrecer como cosa principal; (coll) destacar, hacer resaltar

feature writer s articulista mf

February [′fɛbruˌɛri] s febrero

feces [′fisiz] spl heces fpl, excremento

feckless [′fɛklɪs] adj abatido, sin valor; débil

federal [′fɛdərəl] adj & s federal mf

federate [′fɛdəˌret] adj federado ‖ tr federar ‖ intr federarse

federation [ˌfɛdə′reʃən] s federación

fedora [fɪ′dorə] s sombrero de fieltro suave con ala vuelta

fed up [fɛd] adj harto; **to get fed up with** desenamorarse de

fee [fi] s honorarios; (for admission, tuition, etc.) cuota, precio; (tip) propina ‖ tr pagar; dar propina a

feeble [′fibəl] adj débil; caedizo

feeble-minded [′fibəl′maɪndɪd] adj imbécil; irresoluto, vacilante

feed [fid] s alimento, comida; (mach) dispositivo de alimentación ‖ v (pret & pp **fed** [fɛd]) tr alimentar ‖ intr alimentarse

feed′back′ s regeneración, realimentación, retroalimentación; comentarios fpl; informaciones fpl; comentario privado y confidencial

feed bag s cebadera, morral m

feeder industries spl subsidiarias fpl

feed pump s bomba de alimentación

feed trough s comedero

feed wire s (elec) conductor m de alimentación

feel [fil] s sensación; (sense of what is right) tino ‖ v (pret & pp **felt** [fɛlt]) tr sentir; (e.g., with the hands) palpar, tentar; tomar (el pulso); tantear (el camino) ‖ intr (sick, tired, etc.) sentirse; palpar; **to feel bad** sentirse mal; condolerse; **to feel cheap** avergonzarse; **to feel comfortable** sentirse a gusto; **to feel for** buscar tentando; condolerse de; **to feel like** tener ganas de; **to feel safe** sentirse a salvo; **to feel sorry** sentir; arrepentirse; **to feel sorry for** compadecer; arrepentirse de

feeler [′filər] s (something said to draw someone out) buscapié m, tranquilla; **feelers** (of insect) anténulas, palpos; (of mollusk) tentáculos

feeling [′filɪŋ] s (with senses) sensación; (impression, emotion) sentimiento; presentimiento; parecer m

feign [fen] tr aparentar, fingir ‖ intr fingir; **to feign to be** fingirse

feint [fent] s (threat) finta; (of fencer) pase m, treta ‖ intr hacer una finta

feldspar [′fɛldˌspar] s feldespato

felicitate [fə′lɪsɪˌtet] tr felicitar

felicitous [fə′lɪsɪtəs] adj (opportune) feliz; elocuente

fell [fɛl] adj cruel, feroz, mortal ‖ tr talar (árboles)

felloe [′fɛlo] s aro de la rueda; (part of this) pina

fellow [′fɛlo] s (coll) mozo, tipo, sujeto; (coll) pretendiente m; prójimo; (of a society) socio, miembro; (holder of fellowship) pensionista mf

fellow being s prójimo

fellow citizen s conciudadano

fellow countryman s compatriota mf

fellow man s prójimo

fellow member s consocio

fellowship [′fɛloˌʃɪp] s compañerismo; (for study) pensión

fellow traveler s compañero de viaje

felon [′fɛlən] s delincuente mf de mayor cuantía; (pathol) panadizo

felo·ny [′fɛləni] s (pl **-nies**) delito de mayor cuantía; **to compound a felony** aceptar dinero para no procesar

felt [fɛlt] s fieltro

felt′-tipped′ pen s rotulador m; plumón m (Mex)

fa
fe

female ['fimel] adj (sex) femenino; (animal, plant, piece of a device) hembra ‖ s hembra
feminine ['fɛmɪnɪn] adj & s femenino
feminism ['fɛmɪ,nɪzəm] s feminismo
fen [fɛn] s pantano
fence [fɛns] s cerca, cercado; (for stolen goods) alcahuete m; receptador; (of a saw) guía; **on the fence** (coll) indeciso ‖ tr cercar ‖ intr esgrimir
fencing ['fɛnsɪŋ] s (art) esgrima; (act) esgrimidura
fencing academy s escuela de esgrima
fend [fɛnd] tr — **to fend off** apartar, resguardarse de ‖ intr — **to fend for oneself** (coll) tirar por su lado
fender ['fɛndər] s (mudguard) guardafango, guardabarros m; (of locomotive) quitapiedras m; (of trolley car) salvavidas m; (of fireplace) guardafuego
fennel ['fɛnəl] s hinojo
ferment ['fʌrmɛnt] s fermento; fermentación ‖ [fər'mɛnt] tr & intr fermentar
fern [fʌrn] s helecho
ferocious [fə'roʃəs] adj feroz
feroci•ty [fə'rɑsɪti] s (pl -ties) ferocidad
ferret ['fɛrɪt] s hurón m ‖ tr — **to ferret out** huronear ‖ intr huronear
Ferris wheel ['fɛrɪs] s rueda de feria, noria
fer•ry ['fɛri] s (pl -ries) bote m de paso, ferry-boat m ‖ v (pret & pp -ried) tr pasar (viajeros, mercancías) a través del río ‖ intr cruzar el río en barco
fer'ry•boat' s bote m de paso, ferry-boat m
fertile ['fʌrtɪl] adj fértil
fertilize ['fʌrtɪ,laɪz] tr abonar, fertilizar; (to impregnate) fecundar
fervid ['fʌrvɪd] adj férvido, vehemente
fervor ['fʌrvər] s fervor m
fervent ['fʌrvənt] adj ferviente, fervoroso
fester ['fɛstər] s úlcera ‖ tr enconar ‖ intr enconarse (una herida; el ánimo de uno)
festival ['fɛstɪvəl] adj festivo ‖ s fiesta; (of music) festival m
festive ['fɛstɪv] adj festivo
festivi•ty [fɛs'tɪvɪti] s (pl -ties) festividad
festoon [fɛs'tun] s festón m ‖ tr festonear
fetch [fɛtʃ] tr ir por, hacer venir, traer; venderse a, venderse por
fetching ['fɛtʃɪŋ] adj (coll) encantador, atractivo
fete [fet] s fiesta ‖ tr festejar
fetid ['fɛtɪd] o ['fitɪd] adj fétido
fetish ['fitɪʃ] o ['fɛtɪʃ] s fetiche m
fetlock ['fɛtlɑk] s espolón m; (tuft of hair) cerneja
fetter ['fɛtər] s grillete m, grillo ‖ tr engrillar; impedir
fettle ['fɛtəl] s estado, condición; **in fine fettle** en buena condición
fetus ['fitəs] s feto
feud [fjud] s odio hereditario, enemistad de larga duración
feudal ['fjudəl] adj feudal
feudalism ['fjudə,lɪzəm] s feudalismo
fever ['fivər] s fiebre f, calentura

fever blister s escupidura, fuegos en los labios
feverish ['fivərɪʃ] adj febril, calenturiento
few [fju] adj & pron pocos, no muchos; **a few** unos pocos, unos cuantos; **quite a few** muchos
fiancé [,fiɑn'se] s novio, prometido; novillo (Mex, P-R)
fiancée [,fiɑn'se] s novia, prometida
fias•co [fɪ'æsko] s (pl -cos o -coes) fiasco
fib [fɪb] s mentirilla ‖ v (pret & pp fibbed; ger fibbing) intr decir mentirillas, macanear
fiber ['faɪbər] s fibra; carácter m, índole f
fibrous ['faɪbrəs] adj fibroso
fickle ['fɪkəl] adj inconstante, veleidoso
fiction ['fɪkʃən] s (invention) ficción; (branch of literature) novelística; **pure fiction!** ¡puro cuento!
fictional ['fɪkʃənəl] adj novelesco
fictionalize ['fɪkʃənə,laɪz] tr novelizar
fictitious ['fɪk'tɪʃəs] adj ficticio
fiddle ['fɪdəl] s violín m ‖ tr tocar (un aire) con el violín; **to fiddle away** (coll) malgastar ‖ intr tocar el violín; **to fiddle with** manosear
fiddler ['fɪdlər] s (coll) violinista mf
fiddling ['fɪdlɪŋ] adj (coll) despreciable, insignificante
fideli•ty [fɪ'dɛlɪti] s (pl -ties) fidelidad
fidget ['fɪdʒɪt] intr agitarse, menearse; **to fidget with** manosear
fidgety ['fɪdʒɪti] adj inquieto, nervioso
fiduciar•y [fɪ'djuʃɪ,ɛri] adj fiduciario ‖ s (pl -ies) fiduciario
fie [faɪ] interj ¡qué vergüenza!
fief [fif] s feudo
field [fild] adj (mil) de campaña ‖ s campo; (sown with grain) sembrado; (baseball) jardín m; (elec) campo magnético; (of motor or dynamo) (elec) inductor m
fielder ['fildər] s (baseball) jardinero
field glasses spl gemelos de campo
field hockey s hockey m sobre hierba
field magnet s imán m inductor
field marshal s (mil) mariscal m de campo
field'piece' s cañón m de campaña
fiend [find] s diablo; (person) fiera; **to be a fiend for** ser una fiera para
fiendish ['findɪʃ] adj diabólico
fierce [firs] adj feroz, fiero; (wind) furioso; (coll) muy malo
fierceness ['firsnɪs] s ferocidad, fiereza; furia
fier•y ['faɪri] adj (comp -ier; super -iest) ardiente, caliente; brioso
fife [faɪf] s pífano
fifteen ['fɪf'tin] adj, pron & s quince m
fifteenth ['fɪf'tinθ] adj & s (in a series) decimoquinto; (part) quinzavo ‖ s (in dates) quince m
fifth [fɪfθ] adj & s quinto ‖ s (in dates) cinco m
fifth column s quinta columna
fifth columnist s quintacolumnista mf
fiftieth ['fɪftɪ•ɪθ] adj & s (in a series) quincuagésimo; (part) cincuentavo
fif•ty ['fɪfti] adj & pron cincuenta ‖ s (pl -ties) cincuenta m

fif′ty-fif′ty *adv* — **to go fifty-fifty** (coll) ir a medias

fig. *abbr* **figure, figuratively**

fig [fɪg] *s* higo, breva; *(tree)* higuera; *(merest trifle)* bledo

fight [faɪt] *s* lucha, pelea; ánimo, brío; **to pick a fight with** meterse con, buscar la lengua a ‖ *tr* luchar con; dar *(batalla)*; lidiar *(al toro)* ‖ *intr* luchar, pelear; **to fight shy of** tratar de evitar

fighter [′faɪtər] *s* luchador *m*, peleador *m*; *(warrior)* combatiente *m*; *(game person)* porfiador *m*; *(aer)* avión *m* de combate, caza *m*

fig leaf *s* hoja de higuera; *(on statues)* hoja de parra

figment [′fɪgmənt] *s* ficción, invención

figurative [′fɪgərətɪv] *adj* figurado; *(representing by a likeness)* figurativo

figure [′fɪgjər] *s* figura; *(bodily form)* talle *m*; precio; **to be good at figures** ser listo en aritmética; **to cut a figure** hacer figura; **to have a good figure** tener buen tipo; **to keep one's figure** conservar la línea ‖ *tr* adornar con figuras; figurarse, imaginar; suponer, calcular; **to figure out** descifrar ‖ *intr* figurar; **to figure on** contar con

fig′ure•head′ *s* (naut) figurón *m* de proa, mascarón *m* de proa; *(straw man)* testaferro

figure of speech *s* figura retórica

figure skating *s* patinaje artístico

figurine [ˌfɪgjə′rin] *s* figurilla, figurina

filament [′fɪləmənt] *s* filamento

filch [fɪltʃ] *tr* birlar, ratear

file [faɪl] *s* fila, hilera; *(tool)* lima; *(collection of papers)* archivo; *(cabinet)* archivador *m*, fichero ‖ *tr* poner en fila; limar; archivar, clasificar; anotar ‖ *intr* desfilar; **to file for** solicitar

file case *s* fichero

file clerk *s* fichador *m*

filet [fɪ′le] o [′fɪle] *s* filete *m* ‖ *tr* cortar en filetes

filial [′fɪlɪ•əl] o [′fɪljəl] *adj* filial

filiation [ˌfɪlɪ′eʃən] *s* filiación

filibuster [′fɪlɪˌbʌstər] *s* obstrucción *(de la aprobación de una ley)*; obstruccionista *mf*; *(buccaneer)* filibustero ‖ *tr* obstruir *(la aprobación de una ley)*

filigree [′fɪlɪˌgri] *adj* afiligranado ‖ *s* filigrana ‖ *tr* afiligranar

filing [′faɪlɪŋ] *s* *(of documents)* clasificación; limadura; **filings** limadura, limalla

filing cabinet *s* archivador *m*, clasificador *m*

filing card *s* ficha

Filipi•no [ˌfɪlɪ′pino] *adj* filipino ‖ *s* *(pl* **-nos)** filipino

fill [fɪl] *s* *(sufficiency)* hartazgo; *(place filled with earth)* terraplén *m*; **to have o get one's fill of** darse un hartazgo de ‖ *tr* llenar; rellenar; despachar *(un pedido)*; tapar *(un agujero)*; empastar *(un diente)*; inflar *(un neumático)*; llenar, ocupar *(un puesto)*; colmar *(lagunas)*; **to fill out** llenar *(un formulario)* ‖ *intr* llenarse; rellenarse; **to fill in** hacer de suplente; **to fill up** ahogarse de emoción

filler [′fɪlər] *s* relleno; *(of cigar)* tripa; *sizing* aparejo; *(in a writing)* relleno

fillet [′fɪlɪt] *s* cinta, tira; *(for hair)* prendedero; (archit, bb) filete *m* ‖ *tr* filetear ‖ [′fɪle] o [′fɪlɪt] *s* *(of meat or fish)* filete *m* ‖ *tr* cortar en filetes

filling [′fɪlɪŋ] *s* *(of a tooth)* empaste *m*; *(e.g., of a turkey)* relleno; *(of cigar)* tripa

filling station *s* estación gasolinera

fillip [′fɪlɪp] *s* aguijón *m*, estímulo; *(with finger)* capirotazo

fil•ly [′fɪli] *s* *(pl* **-lies)** potra; (coll) muchacha retozona

film [fɪlm] *s* película; *(mov)* película, film *m*; *(phot)* película ‖ *tr* filmar

film library *s* cinemateca

film star *s* estrella de la pantalla

film strip *s* tira proyectable

film•y [′fɪlmi] *adj* (comp **-ier;** super **-iest)** delgadísimo, diáfano, sutil

filter [′fɪltər] *s* filtro ‖ *tr* filtrar ‖ *intr* filtrarse

filtering [′fɪltərɪŋ] *s* filtración

filter paper *s* papel *m* filtrante

filter tip *s* embocadura de filtro

filth [fɪlθ] *s* suciedad, porquería

filth•y [′fɪlθi] *adj* (comp **-ier;** super **-iest)** sucio, puerco

filthy lucre [′lukər] *s* (coll) el vil metal *(dinero, raíz de muchos males)*

filtrate [′fɪltret] *s* filtrado ‖ *tr* filtrar ‖ *intr* filtrarse

fin. *abbr* **finance**

fin [fɪn] *s* aleta

final [′faɪnəl] *adj* final; *(last in a series)* último; decisivo, terminante ‖ *s* examen *m* final; **finals** (sport) final *f*

finale [fɪ′nali] *s* (mus) final *m*

finalist [′faɪnəlɪst] *s* finalista *mf*

finally [′faɪnəli] *adv* finalmente, por último

finance [′faɪnæns] *s* financiación; **finances** finanzas ‖ *tr* financiar

financial [faɪ′nænʃəl] *adj* financiero

financier [ˌfaɪnən′sɪr] *s* financiero

financing [′faɪnænsɪŋ] *s* financiación, financiamiento

finch [fɪntʃ] *s* pinzón *m*

find [faɪnd] *s* hallazgo ‖ *v* *(pret & pp* **found** [faʊnd]*)* *tr* hallar, encontrar; **to find out** averiguar, darse cuenta de ‖ *intr* *(law)* pronunciar fallo; **to find out about** informarse de

finder [′faɪndər] *s* *(of camera)* visor *m*; *(of microscope)* portaobjeto cuadriculado

finding [′faɪndɪŋ] *s* descubrimiento; (law) laudo, fallo

fine [faɪn] *adj* fino; *(weather)* bueno; divertido ‖ *adv* (coll) muy bien; **to feel fine** (coll) sentirse muy bien de salud ‖ *s* multa ‖ *tr* multar

fine arts *spl* bellas artes

fineness *s* fineza; *(of metal)* ley *f*

fine print *s* letra menuda, tipo menudo

finer•y [′faɪnəri] *s* *(pl* **-ies)** adorno, galas, atavíos

fine-spun [′faɪnˌspʌn] *adj* estirado en hilo finísimo; (fig) alambicado

fe
fi

finesse [fɪ'nɛs] s sutileza; (*in bridge*) impás *m* ‖ *tr* hacer el impás con ‖ *intr* hacer un impás

fine-toothed comb ['faɪn,tuθt] s lendrera, peine *m* de púas finas; **to go over with a fine-toothed comb** escudriñar minuciosamente

finger ['fɪŋgər] s dedo; **to burn one's fingers** cogerse los dedos; **to put one's finger on the spot** poner el dedo en la llaga; **to slip between the fingers** irse de entre los dedos; **to snap one's fingers at** tratar con desprecio; **to twist around one's little finger** manejar a su gusto ‖ *tr* manosear; (slang) acechar, espiar; (slang) identificar

finger board s (*of guitar*) diapasón *m;* (*of piano*) teclado

finger bowl s lavadedos *m*, lavafrutas *m*

finger dexterity s (mus) dedeo

fingering ['fɪŋgərɪŋ] s manoseo; (mus) digitación

fin·ger·nail' s uña

fingernail polish s esmalte *m* para las uñas

fin·ger·print' s huella digital, dactilograma *m* ‖ *tr* tomar las huellas digitales de

finger tip s punta del dedo; **to have at one's finger tips** tener en la punta de los dedos, saber al dedillo

finial ['fɪnɪ·əl] s florón *m*

finical ['fɪnɪkəl] o **finicky** ['fɪnɪki] adj delicado, melindroso

finish ['fɪnɪʃ] s acabado; fin *m*, conclusión ‖ *tr* acabar; **to be finished** estar listo ‖ *intr* acabar; **to finish** + *ger* acabar de + *inf;* **to finish by** + *ger* acabar por + *inf*

finishing nail s puntilla francesa

finishing school s escuela particular de educación social para señoritas

finishing touch s toque *m* final, última mano

finite ['faɪnaɪt] adj finito

finite verb s forma verbal flexional

Finland ['fɪnlənd] s Finlandia

Finlander ['fɪnləndər] s finlandés *m*

Finn [fɪn] s (*member of a Finnish-speaking group of people*) finés *m;* (*native or inhabitant of Finland*) finlandés *m*

Finnish ['fɪnɪʃ] adj finlandés ‖ s (*language*) finlandés *m*

fir [fʌr] s abeto

fire [faɪr] s fuego; (*destructive burning*) incendio; **through fire and water** a trancos y barrancos; **to be on fire** estar ardiendo; **to be under enemy fire** estar expuesto al fuego del enemigo; **to catch fire** encenderse; **to hang fire** estar en suspensión; **to open fire** abrir fuego, romper el fuego; **to set on fire, to set fire to** pegar fuego a; **under fire** bajo el fuego del enemigo; acusado, inculpado ‖ *interj* (mil) ¡fuego! ‖ *tr* encender; calentar (*el horno*); cocer (*ladrillos*); disparar (*un arma de fuego*); pegar (*un tiro*); excitar (*la imaginación*); (coll) despedir (*a un empleado*) ‖ *intr* encenderse; **to fire on** hacer fuego sobre; **to fire up** cargar el horno; calentar el horno

fire alarm s alarma de incendios, avisador *m* de incendios; **to sound the fire alarm** tocar a fuego

fire'arm' s arma de fuego

fire'ball' s bola de fuego; (*lightning*) rayo en bola

fire'bird' s cacique veranero

fire'boat' s buque *m* con mangueras para incendios

fire'box' s caja de fuego, fogón *m*

fire'brand' s tizón *m;* (*hothead*) botafuego

fire'break' s raya

fire'brick' s ladrillo refractario

fire brigade s cuerpo de bomberos

fire'bug' s (coll) incendiario

fire company s cuerpo de bomberos; compañía de seguros

fire'crack'er s triquitraque *m*

fire'damp' s grisú *m*, mofeta

fire department s servicio de bomberos

fire'dog' s morillo

fire drill s ejercicio para caso de incendio

fire engine s coche *m* bomba, bomba de incendios, motobomba

fire escape s escalera de salvamento

fire extinguisher s extintor *m*, apagafuegos *m*, extinguidor *m*

fire'fly' s (*pl* -**flies**) luciérnaga

fire'guard' s guardafuego

fire hose s manguera para incendios

fire'house' s cuartel *m* de bomberos, estación de incendios

fire hydrant s boca de incendio

fire insurance s seguro contra incendios

fire irons spl badil *m* y tenazas

fireless cooker ['faɪrlɪs] s cocinilla sin fuego

fire·man ['faɪrmən] s (*pl* -**men** [mən]) (*man who stokes fires*) fogonero; (*man who extinguishes fires*) bombero

fire'place' s chimenea, chimenea francesa

fire plug s boca de agua

fire power s (mil) potencia de fuego

fire'proof' adj incombustible; a prueba de incendio ‖ *tr* hacer incombustible

fire sale s venta de mercancías averiadas en un incendio

fire screen s pantalla de chimenea

fire ship s brulote *m*

fire shovel s badil *m*

fire'side' s hogar *m*

fire'trap' s edificio sin medios adecuados de escape en caso de incendio

fire wall s cortafuego

fire'ward'en s vigía *m* de incendios

fire'wa'ter s aguardiente *m*

fire'wood' s leña

fire'works' spl fuegos artificiales

firing ['faɪrɪŋ] s encendimiento; (*of bricks*) cocción; (*of a gun*) disparo; (*of soldiers*) tiroteo; (*of an internal-combustion engine*) encendido; (*of an employee*) (coll) despedida

firing line s línea de fuego, frente *m* de batalla

firing order s (aut) orden *m* del encendido

firing squad s (*for saluting at a burial*) piquete *m* de salvas; (*for executing*) pelotón *m* de fusilamiento, piquete *m* de ejecución

firm [fʌrm] *adj* firme ‖ *s* empresa, casa comercial

firmament [ˈfʌrməmənt] *s* firmamento

firm name *s* razón *f* social

firmness [ˈfʌrmnɪs] *s* firmeza

first [fʌrst] *adj* primero ‖ *adv* primero; **first of all** ante todo ‖ *s* primero; (aut) primera (velocidad); (mus) voz *f* principal; **at first** al principio; en primer lugar; **from the first** desde el principio

first aid *s* cura de urgencia, primeros auxilios

first'-aid'kit *s* botiquín *m*, equipo de urgencia

first-aid station *s* puesto de socorro, puesto de primera intención

first'-born' *adj* & *s* primogénito

first'-class' *adj* de primera, de primera clase ‖ *adv* en primera clase

first cousin *s* primo hermano

first draft *s* borrador *m*

first finger *s* dedo índice, dedo mostrador

first floor *s* piso bajo

first fruits *spl* primicia

first lieutenant *s* teniente

firstly [ˈfʌrstli] *adv* en primer lugar

first mate *s* (naut) piloto

first name *s* nombre *m* de pila

first night *s* (theat) noche *f* de estreno

first'-night'er *s* (theat) estrenista *mf*

first officer *s* (naut) piloto

first quarter *s* cuarto creciente (*de la luna*)

first'-rate' *adj* de primer orden; (coll) excelente ‖ *adv* (coll) muy bien

first'-run' house *s* teatro de estreno

fiscal [ˈfɪskəl] *adj* (*pertaining to public treasury*) fiscal; económico ‖ *s* (*public prosecutor*) fiscal *m*

fiscal year *s* año económico, ejercicio

fish [fɪʃ] *s* pez *m*; (*that has been caught, that is ready to eat*) pescado; **to be like a fish out of water** estar como gallina en corral ajeno; **to be neither fish nor fowl** no ser carne ni pescado; **to drink like a fish** beber como una topinera, beber como una esponja ‖ *tr* pescar ‖ *intr* pescar; **to fish for compliments** buscar alabanzas; **to go fishing** ir de pesca; **to take fishing** llevar de pesca

fish'bone' *s* espina de pez

fish bowl *s* pecera

fisher [ˈfɪʃər] *s* pescador *m*; embarcación de pesca; (zool) marta del Canadá

fisher•man [ˈfɪʃərmən] *s* (*pl* **-men** [mən]) pescador *m*; barco pesquero

fisher•y [ˈfɪʃəri] *s* (*pl* **-ies**) (*activity*) pesca; (*business*) pesquería; (*grounds*) pesquera

fish glue *s* cola de pescado

fish hawk *s* halieto

fish'hook' *s* anzuelo

fishing [ˈfɪʃɪŋ] *adj* pesquero ‖ *s* pesca

fishing ground *s* pesquería, pesquera

fishing reel *s* carrete *m*

fishing rod *s* caña de pescar

fishing tackle *s* aparejo de pescar, avíos de pescar

fishing torch *s* candelero

fish line *s* sedal *m*

fish market *s* pescadería

fish'plate' (rr) eclisa

fish'pool' *s* piscina

fish spear *s* fisga

fish story *s* (coll) andaluzada, patraña; **to tell fish stories** (coll) mentir por la barba

fish'tail' *s* (aer) coleadura ‖ *intr* (aer) colear

fish'wife' *s* (*pl* **-wives** [ˌwaɪvz]) pescadera; (*foul-mouthed woman*) verdulera

fish'worm' *s* lombriz *f* de tierra (*cebo para pescar*)

fish•y [ˈfɪʃi] *adj* (*comp* **-ier;** *super* **-iest**) que huele o sabe a pescado; (coll) dudoso, inverosímil

fission [ˈfɪʃən] *s* (biol) escisión; (phys) fisión

fissionable [ˈfɪʃənəbəl] *adj* fisionable; físil

fissure [ˈfɪʃər] *s* hendidura, grieta; (anat, min) fisura

fist [fɪst] *s* puño; (typ) manecilla; **to shake one's fist at** amenazar con el puño

fist fight *s* pelea con los puños

fisticuff [ˈfɪstɪˌkʌf] *s* puñetazo; **fisticuffs** pelea a puñetazos

fit [fɪt] *adj* (*comp* **-fitter;** *super* **-fittest**) apropiado, conveniente; apto; sano; **fit to be tied** (coll) impaciente, encolerizado; **fit to eat** bueno de comer; **to feel fit** gozar de buena salud; **to see fit** juzgar conveniente ‖ *s* ajuste *m*, talle *m*; (*of one piece with another*) encaje *m*; (*of coughing*) acceso, ataque *m*; (*of anger*) arranque *m*, chivo; **by fits and starts** intermitentemente ‖ *v* (*pret* & *pp* **-fitted;** *ger* **fitting**) *tr* ajustar, entallar; cuadrar, sentar; encajar; cuadrar con (*p.ej., las señas de una persona*); equipar, preparar; servir para; estar de acuerdo con (*p.ej., los hechos*); **to fit out** o **up** pertrechar ‖ *intr* ajustar; encajar; sentar; **to fit in** caber en; encajar en

fitful [ˈfɪtfəl] *adj* caprichoso; intermitente, vacilante

fitness [ˈfɪtnɪs] *s* conveniencia; aptitud; tempestividad; buena salud

fitter [ˈfɪtər] *s* ajustador *m*; (*of machinery*) montador *m*; (*of clothing*) probador *m*

fitting [ˈfɪtɪŋ] *adj* apropiado, conveniente, justo ‖ *s* ajuste *m*; encaje *m*; (*of a garment*) prueba; tubo de ajuste; **fittings** accesorios, avíos; (*iron trimmings*) herraje *m*

fitting room *s* probador *m*

five [faɪv] *adj* & *pron* cinco ‖ *s* cinco; **five o'clock** las cinco

five hundred *adj* & *pron* quinientos ‖ *s* quinientos *m*

five'-year' plan *s* plan *m* quinquenal

fix [fɪks] *s*—**in a tight fix** (coll) en calzas prietas; **to be in a fix** (coll) hallarse en un aprieto; **to get a fix** (*drugs*) picarse, pincharse ‖ *tr* arreglar, componer, reparar; fijar (*una fecha; los cabellos; una imagen fotográfica; los precios; la atención; una hora, una cita*); calar (*la bayoneta*); (coll) desquitarse con; (pol) muñir ‖ *intr* fijarse; **to fix on** decidir, escoger

fixed [fɪkst] *adj* fijo

fixing [ˈfɪksɪŋ] *adj* fijador ‖ *s* (*fastening*) fijación; (phot) fijado

fixing bath *s* fijador *m*

fixture [ˈfɪkstʃər] *s* accesorio, artefacto; (*of a lamp*) guarnición; **fixtures** (*e.g., of a store*) instalaciones

fizz [fɪz] *s* ruido sibilante; bebida gaseosa; (Brit) champaña ‖ *intr* hacer un ruido sibilante

fizzle [ˈfɪzəl] *s* (coll) fracaso ‖ *intr* chisporrotear débilmente; (coll) fracasar

fl. *abbr* **flourished, fluid**

flabbergast [ˈflæbərˌgæst] *tr* (coll) dejar sin habla, dejar estupefacto

flab·by [ˈflæbi] *adj* (*comp* **-bier;** *super* **-biest**) flojo, lacio

flag [flæg] *s* bandera ‖ *v* (*pret & pp* **flagged;** *ger* **flagging**) *tr* hacer señal a (*una persona*) con una bandera; hacer señal de parada a (*un tren*) ‖ *intr* aflojar, flaquear

flag captain *s* (nav) capitán *m* de bandera

flageolet [ˌflædʒəˈlɛt] *s* chirimía, dulzaina

flag·man [ˈflægmən] *s* (*pl* **-men** [mən]) (rr) guardafrenos *m;* (rr) guardavía *m*

flag of truce *s* bandera de parlamento

flag′pole′ *s* asta de bandera; (surv) jalón *m*

flagrant [ˈflegrənt] *adj* enorme, escandaloso

flag′ship′ *s* (nav) capitana

flag′staff′ *s* asta de bandera

flag′stone′ *s* losa

flag stop *s* (rr) apeadero

flail [flel] *s* mayal *m* ‖ *tr* golpear con mayal; golpear, azotar

flair [flɛr] *s* instinto, perspicacia

flak [flæk] *s* fuego antiaéreo

flake [flek] *s* (*thin piece*) hojuela; (*of snow*) copo ‖ *intr* desprenderse en hojuelas; caer en copos pequeños

flak·y [ˈfleki] *adj* (*comp* **-ier;** *super* **-iest**) escamoso, laminoso

flamboyant [flæmˈbɔɪənt] *adj* flameante; llamativo; rimbombante; (archit) flameante, flamígero

flame [flem] *s* llama ‖ *tr* (*to sterilize with a flame*) llamear ‖ *intr* flamear

flame thrower [ˈθroˌər] *s* lanzallamas *m*

flaming [ˈflemɪŋ] *adj* llameante; flamante, resplandeciente; apasionado

flamin·go [fləˈmɪŋgo] *s* (*pl* **-gos** o **-goes**) flamenco

flammable [ˈflæməbəl] *adj* inflamable

Flanders [ˈflændərz] *s* Flandes *f*

flange [flændʒ] *s* pestaña

flank [flæŋk] *s* flanco; *tr* flanquear

flannel [ˈflænəl] *s* franela

flap [flæp] *s* (*fold in clothing; of a hat*) falda; (*of a pocket*) cartera; (*of a table*) hoja plegadiza; (*of shoe*) oreja; (*of an envelope*) tapa; (*of wings*) aletazo; (*of the counter in a store*) trampa ‖ *v* (*pret & pp* **flapped;** *ger* **flapping**) *tr* golpear con ruido seco; batir, sacudir (*las alas*) ‖ *intr* aletear; flamear con ruido

flare [flɛr] *s* llamarada, destello; cohete *m* de señales; (aer) bengala; (*outward curvature*) abocinamiento; (*of a dress*) vuelo ‖ *tr* abocinar ‖ *intr* arder con gran llamarada,

destellar; (*to spread outward*) abocinarse; **to flare up** inflamarse; recrudecer (*una enfermedad*); encolerizarse

flare star *s* (astr) estrella fulgurante

flare′-up′ *s* llamarada; (*of an illness*) retroceso; (coll) llamarada, arrebato de cólera

flash [flæʃ] *s* (*of light*) relumbrón *m*, ráfaga; (*of lightning*) relámpago; (*of hope*) rayo; (*of joy*) acceso; (*of insight*) rasgo; mensaje *m* urgente ‖ *tr* quemar (*pólvora*); enviar (*un mensaje*) como un rayo ‖ *intr* destellar, centellear; relampaguear (*los ojos*); **to flash by** pasar como un rayo

flash′back′ *s* (mov) retrospectiva, flashback *m*

flash bulb *s* luz *f* de magnesio; bombilla de destello

flash flood *s* torrentada, avenida repentina

flashing [ˈflæʃɪŋ] *s* despidiente *m* de agua, vierteaguas *m*

flash′light′ *s* linterna eléctrica, lámpara eléctrica de bolsillo; (*of a lighthouse*) luz *f* intermitente, fanal *m* de destellos; (*for taking photographs*) flash *m*, relámpago

flashlight battery *s* pila de linterna

flashlight bulb *s* bombilla de linterna

flashlight photography *s* fotografía instantánea de relámpago

flash sign *s* anuncio intermitente

flash·y [ˈflæʃi] *adj* (*comp* **-ier;** *super* **-iest**) chillón, llamativo

flask [flæsk] *s* frasco; frasco de bolsillo; (*for laboratory use*) matraz *m*, redoma

flat [flæt] *adj* (*comp* **flatter;** *super* **flattest**) plano; (*nose; boat*) chato; (*surface*) mate, deslustrado; (*beer*) muerto; (*tire*) desinflado; (*e.g., denial*) terminante; (mus) bemol ‖ *adv* — **to fall flat** caer de plano; (fig) no surtir efecto, no tener éxito ‖ *s* banco, bajío; (*apartment*) piso; (mus) bemol *m;* (coll) neumático desinflado

flat′boat′ *s* chalana

flat′car′ *s* vagón *m* de plataforma

flat′foot′ *s* pie plano

flat-footed [ˈflætˌfutɪd] *adj* de pies planos; (coll) inflexible

flat′head′ *s* (*of a bolt*) cabeza chata; clavo, tornillo o perno de cabeza chata; (coll) tonto, mentecato

flat′i′ron *s* plancha

flatten [ˈflætən] *tr* allanar, aplanar; chafar, aplastar; achatar ‖ *intr* allanarse, aplanarse, aplastarse; achatarse; **to flatten out** ponerse horizontal, enderezarse

flatter [ˈflætər] *tr* lisonjear; cepillar (*to make more attractive than is*) favorecer ‖ *intr* lisonjear

flatterer [ˈflætərər] *s* lisonjero; (coll) limpiabotas *m*

flattering [ˈflætərɪŋ] *adj* lisonjero

flatter·y [ˈflætəri] *s* (*pl* **-ies**) lisonja

flat′top′ *s* portaaviones *m*

flatulence [ˈflætʃələns] *s* flatulencia

flat′ware′ *s* vajilla de plata; vajilla de porcelana

flaunt [flɔnt] *tr* ostentar, hacer gala de

flautist [ˈflɔtɪst] *s* flautista *mf*

flavor [`flevər] *s* sabor *m*, gusto; condimento, sazón *f; (of ice cream)* clase *f* ‖ *tr* saborear; condimentar, sazonar; aromatizar, perfumar

flavoring [`flevərɪŋ] *s* condimento, sainete *m*

flaw [flɔ] *s* defecto, imperfección; *(crack)* grieta

flawless [`flɔlɪs] *adj* perfecto, entero

flax [flæks] *s* lino

flaxen [`flæksən] *adj* blondo, rubio

flax'seed' *s* linaza

flay [fle] *tr* desollar

flea [fli] *s* pulga

flea'bite' *s* picadura de pulga; molestia insignificante

fleck [flɛk] *s* pinta, punto; partícula, pizca ‖ *tr* puntear

fledgling [`flɛdʒlɪŋ] *s* pajarito, volantón *m; (fig)* novato, novel *m*

flee [fli] *v (pret & pp* fled [flɛd]) *tr & intr* huir

fleece [flis] *s (coat of wool)* lana; *(wool shorn at one time; tuft of wool or hair)* vellón *m* ‖ *tr* esquilar; *(to strip of money)* desplumar

fleec•y [`flisi] *adj (comp* -ier; *super* -iest) lanudo; *(clouds)* aborregado

fleet [flit] *adj* veloz ‖ *s* armada; *(of merchant vessels, airplanes, automobiles)* flota

fleeting [`flitɪŋ] *adj* fugaz, efímero; transitorio

Fleming [`flɛmɪŋ] *s* flamenco

Flemish [`flɛmɪʃ] *adj & s* flamenco

flesh [flɛʃ] *s* carne *f; in the flesh* en persona; *to lose flesh* perder carnes; *to put on flesh* cobrar carnes

flesh and blood *s (relatives)* carne y sangre; el cuerpo humano

fleshiness [`flɛʃɪnɪs] *s* carnosidad

fleshless [`flɛʃlɪs] *adj* descarnado

flesh'pot' *s* olla, marmita; **fleshpots** vida regalona; suntuosos nidos de vicios

flesh wound *s* herida superficial

flesh•y [`flɛʃi] *adj (comp* -ier; *super* -iest) carnoso

flex [flɛks] *tr* doblar ‖ *intr* doblarse

flexible [`flɛksɪbəl] *adj* flexible

flexible cord *s* (elec) flexible *m*

flick [flɪk] *s (with finger)* papirote *m; (with whip)* latigazo; ruido seco ‖ *tr* golpear rápida y ligeramente

flicker [`flɪkər] *s* llama trémula; *(of eyelids)* parpadeo; *(of emotion)* temblor momentáneo ‖ *intr* flamear con llama trémula; aletear

flier [`flaɪ•ər] *s* aviador *m;* tren rápido; (coll) negocio arriesgado; (coll) hoja volante

flight [flaɪt] *s* fuga, huída; *(of an airplane)* vuelo; *(of birds)* bandada; *(of stairs)* tramo; *(of fancy)* arranque *m; to put to flight* poner en fuga; *to take flight* darse a la fuga

flight attendant *s* sobrecargo, sobrecarga

flight deck *s* (nav) cubierta de vuelo

flight•y [`flaɪti] *adj (comp* -ier; *super* -iest) veleidoso; casquivano

flim•flam [`flɪm,flæm] *s* (coll) engaño, trampa; (coll) tontería ‖ *v (pret & pp* -flammed; *ger* -flamming) *tr* (coll) engañar, trampear

flim•sy [`flɪmzi] *adj (comp* -sier; *super* -siest) débil, endeble, flojo

flinch [flɪntʃ] *intr* encogerse de miedo

fling [flɪŋ] *s* echada, tiro; baile escocés muy vivo; *to go on a fling* echar una cana al aire; *to have a fling at* ensayar, probar; *to have one's fling* correrla, mocear ‖ *v (pret & pp* flung [flʌŋ]) *tr* arrojar; *(e.g., on the floor, out the window, in jail)* echar; *to fling open* abrir de golpe; *to fling shut* cerrar de golpe

flint [flɪnt] *s* pedernal *m*

flint'lock' *s* llave *f* de chispa; trabuco de chispa

flint•y [`flɪnti] *adj (comp* -ier; *super* -iest) pedernalino; (fig) empedernido

flip [flɪp] *adj (comp* flipper; *super* flippest) (coll) petulante ‖ *s* capirotazo ‖ *v (pret & pp* flipped; *ger* flipping) *tr* echar de un capirotazo, mover de un tirón; *to flip a coin* echar a cara o cruz; *to flip one's lid* (coll) deschavetar; *to flip shut* cerrar de golpe *(p. ej., un abanico)*

flippancy [`flɪpənsi] *s* petulancia

flippant [`flɪpənt] *adj* petulante

flip side *s* contraportada *(del disco)*

flirt [flʌrt] *s (woman)* coqueta; *(man)* galanteador *m* ‖ *intr* coquetear *(una mujer)*; galantear *(un hombre); to flirt with* flirtear con; pololear (Chile); acariciar *(una idea);* jugar con *(la muerte)*

flit [flɪt] *v (pret & pp* flitted; *ger* flitting) *intr* revolotear, volar; pasar rápidamente

flitch [flɪtʃ] *s* hoja de tocino

float [flot] *s (raft)* balsa; *(of fishing line)* flotador *m; (of mason)* llana; carroza alegórica, carro alegórico ‖ *tr* poner a flote; lanzar *(una empresa);* emitir *(acciones, bonos, etc.)* ‖ *intr* flotar

floating [`flotɪŋ] *adj* flotante

flock [flɑk] *s (of birds)* bandada; *(of sheep)* grey *f*, rebaño, manada; *(of people)* muchedumbre; *(e.g., of nonsense)* hatajo; *(of faithful)* grey *f*, rebaño ‖ *intr* congregarse, reunirse; llegar en tropel

floe [flo] *s* banquisa, témpano

flog [flɑg] *v (pret & pp* flogged; *ger* flogging) *tr* azotar, fustigar

flood [flʌd] *s* inundación; *(caused by heavy rain)* diluvio; *(sudden rise of river)* crecida; *(of tide)* pleamar *f; (of words, etc.)* diluvio, torrente *m* ‖ *tr* inundar; *(to overwhelm)* abrumar ‖ *intr* desbordar, rebosar; entrar a raudales

flood'gate' *s (of a dam)* compuerta; *(of a canal)* esclusa

flood'light' *s* faro de inundación ‖ *tr* iluminar con faro de inundación

flood tide *s* pleamar *f*, marea montante

floor [flor] *s (inside bottom surface of room)* piso, suelo; *(story of a building)* piso, alto; *(of the sea, a swimming pool, etc.)* fondo; *(of an assembly hall)* hemiciclo; (naut) varenga; *to ask for the floor* pedir la palabra; *to have the floor* tener la palabra; *to take the floor* tomar la palabra ‖ *tr* entarimar; derribar, echar al suelo; (coll) confundir, envolver, revolcar (*al adversario en controversia*); (coll) vencer

floor lamp *s* lámpara de pie

floor mop *s* fregasuelos *m*, estropajo

floor plan *s* planta

floor show *s* espectáculo de cabaret

floor timber *s* (naut) varenga

floor'walk'er *s* jefe *m* de sección

floor wax *s* cera de pisos

flop [flɑp] *s* fracaso, caída; (*person*) berzas *m*, berzotas *m*; **to take a flop** caerse ‖ *v* (*pret & pp* **flopped;** *ger* **flopping**) *intr* agitarse; caerse; venirse abajo; fracasar; **to flop over** volcarse; cambiar de partido

flora ['florə] *s* flora

floral ['florəl] *adj* floral

Florentine ['flɔrən,tin] *adj & s* florentino

florescence [flo'rɛsəns] *s* florescencia

florid ['florɪd] *adj* (*complexion*) encarnado; (*showy, ornate*) florido

Florida Keys ['florɪdə] *s* Cayos de la Florida

florist ['florɪst] *s* florero, florista *mf*

floss [flɑs] *s* cadarzo; (*of corn*) cabellos

floss silk *s* seda floja sin torcer

floss·y ['flɑsi] *adj* (*comp* **-ier;** *super* **-iest**) ligero, velloso; (slang) cursi, vistoso

flotsam ['flɑtsəm] *s* pecio

flotsam and jetsam *s* pecios, despojos; (*trifles*) baratijas; gente *f* trashumante, gente perdida

flounce [flaʊns] *s* faralá *m*, volante *m* ‖ *tr* adornar con faralaes o volantes ‖ *intr* moverse airadamente

flounder ['flaʊndər] *s* platija ‖ *intr* forcejear, obrar torpemente, andar tropezando

flour [flaʊr] *adj* harinero ‖ *s* harina

flourish ['flʌrɪʃ] *s* (*with the sword*) molinete *m*; (*with the pen*) plumada, rasgo; (*as part of signature*) rúbrica; (mus) floreo ‖ *tr* blandir (*la espada*) ‖ *intr* florecer, prosperar

flourishing ['flʌrɪʃɪŋ] *adj* floreciente, próspero

flour mill *s* molino de harina

floury ['flaʊri] *adj* harinoso

flout [flaʊt] *tr* mofarse de, burlarse de ‖ *intr* mofarse, burlarse

flow [flo] *s* flujo ‖ *intr* fluir; subir (*la marea*); ondear (*el pelo en el aire*); **to flow into** desaguar en, desembocar en; **to flow over** rebosar; **to flow with** nadar en, abundar en

flower ['flaʊ·ər] *s* flor *f* ‖ *tr* florear ‖ *intr* florecer

flower bed *s* macizo, parterre *m*

flower garden *s* jardín *m*

flower girl *s* florera; (*at a wedding*) damita de honor

flower piece *s* ramillete *m*; (*painting*) florero

flow'er·pot' *s* tiesto, maceta

flower shop *s* floristería

flower show *s* exposición de flores

flower stand *s* florero

flowery ['flaʊ·əri] *adj* florido, cubierto de flores

flu [flu] *s* (coll) gripe *f*, influenza

fluctuate ['flʌktʃʊ,et] *intr* fluctuar

flue [flu] *s* cañón *m* de chimenea; tubo de humo

fluency ['flu·ənsi] *s* afluencia, facundia

fluent ['flu·ənt] *adj* (*flowing*) fluente; afluente, facundo, flúido

fluently ['flu·əntli] *adv* corrientemente

fluff [flʌf] *s* pelusa, tamo; vello, pelusilla; (*of an actor*) gazapo ‖ *tr* esponjar, mullir ‖ *intr* esponjarse

fluff·y ['flʌfi] *adj* (*comp* **-ier;** *super* **-iest**) fofo, esponjoso, mullido; velloso

fluid ['flu·ɪd] *adj & s* flúido

fluidity [flu'ɪdɪti] *s* fluidez *f*

fluke [fluk] *s* (*of anchor*) uña; (*in billiards*) chiripa

flume [flum] *s* caz *m*, saetín *m*

flunk [flʌŋk] *s* (coll) reprobación ‖ *tr* (coll) reprobar, dar calabazas a; perder (*un examen o asignatura*) ‖ *intr* (coll) fracasar, salir mal; **to flunk out** (coll) tener que abandonar los estudios por no poder aprobar

flunk·y ['flʌŋki] *s* (*pl* **-ies**) lacayo; adulador *m*

fluor ['flu·ɔr] *s* fluorita

fluorescence [,flu·ə'rɛsəns] *s* fluorescencia

fluorescent [,flu·ə'rɛsənt] *adj* fluorescente

fluoridate ['flu·ərɪ,det] *tr* fluorizar

fluoridation ['flu·ərɪ'deʃən] *s* fluorización

fluoride ['flu·ə,raɪd] *s* fluoruro

fluorine ['flu·ə,rin] *s* flúor *m*

fluorite ['flu·ə,raɪt] *s* fluorita

fluoroscope ['flu·ərə,skop] *s* fluoroscopio

fluor spar *s* espato flúor

flur·ry ['flʌri] *s* (*pl* **-ries**) agitación; (*of wind*) racha, ráfaga; (*of rain*) chaparrón *m*; (*of snow*) nevisca ‖ *v* (*pret & pp* **-ried**) *tr* agitar

flush [flʌʃ] *adj* rasante, nivelado; (*set in, in order to be flush*) embutido; abundante; robusto, vigoroso; próspero, bien provisto; coloradote; (*in printing*) justificado; **flush with** a ras de ‖ *adv* ras con ras, al mismo nivel ‖ *s* (*of water*) flujo repentino; (*in the cheeks*) rubor *m*; sonrojo; (*in the springtime*) floración repentina; (*of joy*) acceso; (*of youth*) vigor *m*; chorro del inodoro; (*in poker*) flux *m* ‖ *tr* (*to cause to blush*) abochornar; limpiar con un chorro de agua; hacer saltar (*una liebre*) ‖ *intr* abochornarse, estar encendido (*el rostro*); (*to gush*) brotar

flush outlet *s* (elec) caja de enchufe embutida

flush switch *s* (elec) llave embutida

flush tank *s* depósito de limpia

flush toilet *s* inodoro con chorro de agua

fluster ['flʌstər] *s* confusión, aturdimiento ‖ *tr* confundir, aturdir

flute [flut] *s* (*of a column*) estría; (mus) flauta ‖ *tr* estriar, acanalar

flutist ['flutɪst] *s* flautista *mf*

flutter ['flʌtər] *s* aleteo, revoloteo; confusión, turbación ‖ *intr* aletear, revolotear; flamear, ondear; agitarse; alterarse (*el pulso*); palpitar (*el corazón*)

flux [flʌks] *s* (*flow; flowing of tide*) flujo; (*for fusing metals*) flujo, fundente *m*

fly [flaɪ] *s* (*pl* **flies**) mosca; (*of trousers*) portañuela, bragueta; (*for fishing*) mosca artificial; **flies** (theat) bambalinas; **to die like flies** morir como chinches ‖ *v* (*pret* **flew** [flu]; *pp* **flown** [flon]) *tr* hacer volar (*una cometa*); dirigir (*un avión*); (*to carry in an airship*) volar; atravesar en avión; desplegar, llevar (*una bandera*) ‖ *intr* volar; huir; ondear (*una bandera*); **to fly off** salir volando; desprenderse; **to fly open** abrirse de repente; **to fly over** trasvolar; **to fly shut** cerrarse de repente

fly ball *s* (baseball) palomita

fly'blow' *s* cresa

fly'-by-night' *adj* indigno de confianza

fly'catch'er *s* moscareta, papamoscas *m*

fly chaser *s* espantamoscas *m*

flyer [ˈflaɪ·ər] *s* var de **flier**

fly'-fish' *tr* & *intr* pescar con moscas artificiales

flying [ˈflaɪ·ɪŋ] *adj* volante; rápido, veloz ‖ *s* aviación

flying boat *s* hidroavión *m*

flying buttress *s* arbotante *m*

flying colors *spl* gran éxito

flying field *s* campo de aviación

flying saucer *s* platillo volante

flying sickness *s* mal *m* de altura

flying time *s* horas de vuelo

fly in the ointment *s* mosca muerta que malea el perfume

fly'leaf' *s* (*pl* **-leaves'**) guarda, hoja de guarda

fly net *s* (*for a bed*) mosquitero; (*for a horse*) espantamoscas *m*

fly'pa'per *s* papel *m* matamoscas

fly'speck' *s* mancha de mosca

fly'swatter [ˈswatər] *s* matamoscas *m*

fly'trap' *s* atrapamoscas *m*

fly'wheel' *s* volante *m*

fm. *abbr* **fathom**

F.M. *abbr* **frequency modulation**

foal [fol] *s* potro ‖ *intr* parir (*la yegua*)

foam [fom] *s* espuma ‖ *intr* espumar

foam extinguisher *s* lanzaespumas *m,* extintor *m* de espuma

foam rubber *s* caucho esponjoso, espuma de caucho

foam·y [ˈfomi] *adj* (*comp* **-ier;** *super* **-iest**) espumoso, espumajoso

fob [fab] *s* faltriquera de reloj; (*chain*) leopoldina; (*ornament*) dije *m*

F.O.B. *abbr* **free on board**

focal [ˈfokəl] *adj* focal

fo·cus [ˈfokəs] *s* (*pl* **-cuses** o **-ci** [saɪ]) foco; **in focus** enfocado; **out of focus** desenfocado ‖ *v* (*pret* & *pp* **-cused** o **-cussed;** *ger* **-cusing** o **-cussing**) *tr* enfocar; fijar (*la atención*) ‖ *intr* enfocarse

fodder [ˈfadər] *s* forraje *m*

foe [fo] *s* enemigo

fog [fag] o [fɔg] *s* niebla; (phot) velo ‖ *v* (*pret* & *pp* **fogged;** *ger* **fogging**) *tr* envolver en niebla; (*to blur*) empañar; (phot) velar ‖ *intr* empañarse; (phot) velarse

fog bank *s* banco de nieblas

fog bell *s* campana de nieblas

fog'bound' *adj* atascado en la niebla, envuelto en la niebla

fog·gy [ˈfagi] o [ˈfɔgi] *adj* (*comp* **-gier;** *super* **-giest**) neblinoso, brumoso; confuso; (phot) velado; **it is foggy** hay neblina

fog'horn' *s* sirena de niebla

foible [ˈfɔɪbəl] *s* flaqueza, lado flaco

foil [fɔɪl] *s* (*thin sheet of metal*) hojuela, laminilla; (*of mirror*) azogado, plateado; contraste *m,* realce *m;* (*sword*) florete *m* ‖ *tr* frustrar; azogar, platear (*un espejo*)

foist [fɔɪst] *tr* — **to foist something on someone** encajar una cosa a uno

fol. *abbr* **folio, following**

fold [fold] *s* pliegue *m,* doblez *m;* arruga; (*for sheep*) aprisco, redil *m;* (*of the faithful*) rebaño ‖ *tr* plegar, doblar; cruzar (*los brazos*); **to fold up** doblar (*p.ej., un mapa*) ‖ *intr* plegarse, doblarse

folder [ˈfoldər] *s* (*covers for holding papers*) carpeta; (*pamphlet*) folleto

folderol [ˈfaldəˌral] *s* tontería, necedad; bagatela

folding [ˈfoldɪŋ] *adj* plegadizo, plegable; plegador

folding camera *s* cámara de fuelle

folding chair *s* silla de tijera, silla plegadiza; (*of canvas*) catrecillo

folding cot *s* catre *m* de tijera

folding door *s* puerta plegadiza

folding rule *s* metro plegadizo

foliage [ˈfolɪ·ɪdʒ] *s* follaje *m*

foli·o [ˈfolɪ·o] *adj* en folio ‖ *s* (*pl* **-os**) (*sheet*) folio; infolio, libro en folio ‖ *tr* foliar

folk [fok] *adj* popular, tradicional, del pueblo ‖ *s* (*pl* **folk** o **folks**) gente *f;* **folks** (coll) gente (*familia*)

folk etymology *s* etimología popular

folk'lore' *s* folkore *m*

folk music *s* música folklórica

folk song *s* canción típica, canción tradicional

folk·sy [ˈfoksi] *adj* (*comp* **-sier;** *super* **-siest**) (coll) sociable, tratable; (*like common people*) (coll) plebeyo

folk'way' *s* costumbre tradicional

follicle [ˈfalɪkəl] *s* folículo

follow [ˈfalo] *tr* seguir; seguir el hilo de; interesarse en (*las noticias del día*) ‖ *intr* seguir; resultar; **as follows** como sigue; **it follows** síguese

follower [ˈfalo·ər] *s* seguidor *m;* secuaz *mf,* partidario; imitador *m;* discípulo

following [ˈfalo·ɪŋ] *adj* siguiente ‖ *s* séquito; partidarios

fol'low-up' *adj* consecutivo; recordativo ‖ *s* carta recordativa, circular recordativa

fol·ly [ˈfali] *s* (*pl* **-lies**) desatino, locura; empresa temeraria; **follies** revista teatral

foment [foˈment] *tr* fomentar

fond [fand] *adj* afectuoso, cariñoso; **to become fond of** encariñarse con, aficionarse a o de

fondle [ˈfandəl] *tr* acariciar, mimar

fondness [ˈfandnɪs] *s* afición, cariño

font [fant] *s* (*source; source of water*) fuente *f;* (*for holy water*) pila; (*of type*) fundición

food [fud] *adj* alimenticio ‖ *s* comida, alimento; **food for thought** cosa en qué pensar

food store *s* tienda de comestibles, colmado

food'stuffs' *spl* comestibles *mpl*, víveres *mpl*

fool [ful] *s* tonto, necio; (*jester*) bufón *m;* (*person imposed on*) inocente *mf*, víctima; **to make a fool of** poner en ridículo; **to play the fool** hacer el tonto ‖ *tr* embaucar, engañar; **to fool away** malgastar (*tiempo, dinero*) ‖ *intr* tontear; **to fool around** (coll) malgastar el tiempo; **to fool with** (coll) ajar, manosear

fooler·y ['fuləri] *s* (*pl* -ies) locura, tontería, babosada

fool'har'dy *adj* (*comp* -dier; *super* -diest) temerario

fooling ['fulɪŋ] *s* broma; engaño; **no fooling** hablando en serio

foolish ['fulɪʃ] *adj* tonto; ridículo; gilí

fool'proof' *adj* (coll) a prueba de mal trato; (coll) infalible

fools'cap' *s* gorro de bufón; papel *m* de oficio

fool's errand *s* caza de grillos

fool's scepter *s* cetro de locura

foot [fut] *s* (*pl* feet [fit]) pie *m;* **to drag one's feet** ir a paso de caracol; **to have one foot in the grave** estar con un pie en la sepultura; **to put one's best foot forward** (coll) hacer méritos; **to put one's foot in it** (coll) meter la pata; (coll) tirarse una plancha; **to stand on one's own feet** volar con sus propias alas; **to tread under foot** hollar ‖ *tr* pagar (*la cuenta*); **to foot it** andar a pie; bailar

footage ['futɪdʒ] *s* distancia o largura en pies

foot'ball' *s* (*game*) balompié *m*, fútbol *m*; (*ball*) balón *m*

foot'board' *s* (*support for foot*) estribo; (*of bed*) pie *m*

foot'bridge' *s* pasarela, puente *m* para peatones

foot'fall' *s* paso

foot'hill' *s* colina al pie de una montaña

foot'hold' *s* arraigo, pie *m;* **to gain a foothold** ganar pie

footing ['futɪŋ] *s* pie *m*, p.ej., **he lost his footing** perdió el pie; **on a friendly footing** en relaciones amistosas; **on an equal footing** en pie de igualdad; **on a war footing** en pie de guerra

foot'lights' *spl* candilejas, batería; (fig) tablas, escena

foot'loose' *adj* libre, no comprometido

foot·man ['futmən] *s* (*pl* -men [mən]) lacayo, criado de librea

foot'mark' *s* huella

foot'note' *s* nota al pie de la página

foot'path' *s* senda para peatones

foot'print' *s* huella

foot race *s* carrera a pie

foot'rest' *s* apoyapié *m*, descansapié *m*

foot rule *s* regla de un pie

foot soldier *s* soldado de a pie

foot'sore' *adj* despeado

foot'step' *s* paso; **to follow in the footsteps of** seguir los pasos de

foot'stone' *s* lápida al pie de una sepultura

foot'stool' *s* escabel *m*, escañuelo

foot warmer *s* calientapiés *m*

foot'wear' *s* calzado

foot'work' *s* juego de piernas

foot'worn' *adj* (*road*) trillado; (*person*) despeado

foozle ['fuzəl] *s* chambonada; (coll) chambón *m*, torpe *m* ‖ *tr* chafallar; errar (*un golpe*) de manera torpe ‖ *intr* chambonear

fop [fap] *s* currutaco, petimetre *m;* lagarto (Mex)

for [fər] *prep* para; por; como, p.ej., **he uses his living room for an office** usa la sala como oficina; de, p.ej., **time for bed** hora de acostarse; desde hace, p.ej., **he has been here for a week** está aquí desde hace una semana; en honor de; a pesar de ‖ *conj* pues, porque

for. *abbr* **foreign**

forage ['forɪdʒ] *adj* forrajero ‖ *s* forraje *m* ‖ *tr & intr* forrajear; saquear

foray ['fare] o ['fore] *s* correría; saqueo ‖ *intr* hacer correrías

for·bear [fɔr'bɛr] *v* (*pret* -bore ['bor]; *pp* -borne ['born]) *tr* abstenerse de ‖ *intr* contenerse

forbearance [fɔr'bɛrəns] *s* abstención; paciencia

for·bid [fɔr'bɪd] *v* (*pret* -bade ['bæd] o -bad ['bæd]; *pp* -bidden ['bɪdən]; *ger* -bidding) *tr* prohibir

forbidding [fɔr'bɪdɪŋ] *adj* repugnante, repulsivo

force [fors] *s* fuerza; (*staff of workers*) personal *m;* (*of soldiers, police, etc.*) cuerpo; (phys) fuerza; **by force** a la mala (Cuba, P-R); **by force of** a fuerza de; **by main force** con todas sus fuerzas; **in force** vigente, en vigor; en gran número; **to join forces** juntar diestra con diestra ‖ *tr* forzar; obligar; **to force back** hacer retroceder; **to force open** abrir por fuerza; **to force through** llevar a cabo por fuerza

forced [forst] *adj* forzado

forced air *s* aire *m* a presión

forced landing *s* aterrizaje forzado o forzoso

forced march *s* marcha forzada

forceful ['forsfəl] *adj* enérgico, eficaz

for·ceps ['forsəps] *s* (*pl* -ceps o -cipes [sɪ,piz]) (dent, surg) pinzas; (obstet) fórceps *m*

force pump *s* bomba impelente

forcible ['forsɪbəl] *adj* eficaz, convincente; forzado

ford [ford] *s* vado ‖ *tr* vadear

fore [for] *adj* anterior; (naut) de proa ‖ *adv* antes, anteriormente; delante; (naut) avante ‖ *interj* ¡ojo!, ¡cuidado! ‖ *s* delantera; **to the fore** destacado; a mano; vivo

fore and aft *adv* de popa a proa

fore'arm' *s* antebrazo ‖ **fore·arm'** *tr* armar de antemano; prevenir

fore'bear' *s* antepasado

forebode [for'bod] *tr* (*to portend*) presagiar; (*to have a presentiment of*) presentir, prever

foreboding [forˈbodɪŋ] *s* presagio; presentimiento

fore'cast' *s* pronóstico ‖ *v* (*pret & pp* **-cast** o **-casted**) *tr* pronosticar

forecastle [ˈfoksəl], [ˈforˌkæsəl], o [ˈforˌkasəl] *s* castillo de proa

fore•close' *tr* excluir; extinguir el derecho de redimir (*una hipoteca*); privar del derecho de redimir una hipoteca

fore•doom' *tr* condenar de antemano, predestinar al fracaso

fore edge *s* canal *f*

fore'fa'ther *s* antepasado

fore'fin'ger *s* dedo índice, dedo mostrador

fore'front' *s* puesto delantero; sitio de actividad más intensa; **in the forefront** a vanguardia

forego' *v* (*pret* **-went'**; *pp* **-gone'**) *tr & intr* preceder

foregoing [ˈforˌgo•ɪŋ] o [forˈgo•ɪŋ] *adj* anterior, precedente, prenombrado

fore'gone' conclusion *s* resultado inevitable; decisión adoptada de antemano

fore'ground' *s* primer plano, primer término

forehanded [ˈforˌhændɪd] *adj* (*thrifty*) ahorrado; hecho de antemano

forehead [ˈfarɪd] o [ˈforɪd] *s* frente *f*

foreign [ˈfarɪn] *adj* extranjero, exterior; **foreign to** (*not belonging to or connected with*) ajeno a

foreign affairs *spl* asuntos exteriores

for'eign-born' *adj* nacido en el extranjero

foreigner [ˈfarɪnər] *s* extranjero

foreign exchange *s* cambio extranjero; (*currency*) divisa

foreign minister *s* ministro de asuntos exteriores

foreign ministry *s* ministerio de relaciones exteriores

foreign office *s* ministerio de asuntos exteriores

foreign service *s* servicio diplomático y consular; servicio militar extranjero

foreign trade *s* comercio extranjero

fore'leg' *s* brazo, pata delantera

fore'lock' *s* mechón *m* de pelo sobre la frente; (*of a horse*) copete *m*; **to take time by the forelock** asir la ocasión por la melena

fore•man [ˈformən] *s* (*pl* **-men** [mən]) capataz *m*, mayoral *m*, sobrestante *m*; (*in a machine shop*) contramaestre *m*; presidente *m* de jurado

foremast [ˈforməst], [ˈforˌmæst], o [ˈforˌmast] *s* palo de trinquete

foremost [ˈforˌmost] *adj* primero, principal, más eminente

fore'noon' *adj* matinal ‖ *s* mañana

fore'part' *s* parte delantera; primera parte

fore'paw' *s* pata delantera

fore'quar'ter *s* cuarto delantero

fore'run'ner *s* precursor *m*; predecesor *m*; antepasado; anuncio, presagio

fore•sail [ˈforsəl] o [ˈforˌsel] *s* trinquete *m*

foresee' *v* (*pret* **-saw'**; *pp* **-seen'**) *tr* prever

foreseeable [forˈsi•əbəl] *adj* previsible

fore•shad'ow *tr* presagiar, prefigurar

fore•short'en *tr* escorzar

fore•short'ening *s* escorzo

fore'sight' *s* previsión, presciencia

fore'sight'ed *adj* previsor, presciente

fore'skin' *s* prepucio

forest [ˈfarɪst] o ˈforɪst] *adj* forestal ‖ *s* bosque *m*

fore•stall' *tr* impedir, prevenir; anticipar; acaparar

forest ranger [ˈrendʒər] *s* guarda *m* forestal, montanero

forestry [ˈfarɪstri] o [ˈforɪstri] *s* silvicultura, ciencia forestal

fore'taste' *s* goce anticipado, conocimiento anticipado

fore•tell' *v* (*pret & pp* **-told'**) *tr* predecir; presagiar

fore'thought' *s* premeditación; providencia, previsión

forever [forˈɛvər] *adv* por siempre; siempre

fore•warn' *tr* prevenir, poner sobre aviso

fore'word' *s* advertencia, prefacio

forfeit [ˈforfɪt] *adj* perdido ‖ *s* multa, pena; prenda perdida; **forfeits** (*game*) prendas ‖ *tr* perder el derecho a

forfeiture [ˈforfɪtʃər] *s* multa, pena; prenda perdida

forgather [forˈgæðər] *intr* reunirse; encontrarse; **to forgather with** asociarse con

forge [fordʒ] *s* fragua; (*blacksmith shop*) herrería; ‖ *tr* fraguar, forjar; falsificar (*la firma de otra persona*); fraguar, forjar (*mentiras*) ‖ *intr* fraguar, forjar; **to forge ahead** avanzar despacio y con esfuerzo

forger•y [ˈfordʒəri] *s* (*pl* **-ies**) falsificación

for•get' [forˈget] *v* (*pret* **-got** [gɑt]; *pp* **-got** o **-gotten**; *ger* **-getting**) *tr* olvidar, olvidarse de, olvidársele a uno, p.ej., **he forgot his overcoat** se le olvidó su abrigo; **forget it!** ¡no se preocupe!; **to forget oneself** no pensar en sí mismo; ser distraído; propasarse

forgetful [forˈgetfəl] *adj* olvidado, olvidadizo; descuidado

forgetfulness [forˈgetfəlnɪs] *s* olvido; descuido

for•get'-me-not' *s* nomeolvides *m*

forgivable [forˈgɪvəbəl] *adj* perdonable

for•give' [forˈgɪv] *v* (*pret* **-gave'**; *pp* **-giv'en**) *tr* perdonar

forgiveness [forˈgɪvnɪs] *s* perdón *m*; misericordia

forgiving [forˈgɪvɪŋ] *adj* perdonador, misericordioso, clemente

for•go' [forˈgo] *v* (*pret* **-went'**; *pp* **-gone'**) *tr* privarse de

fork [fork] *s* horca; (*of a gardener; of bicycle*) horquilla; (*of two rivers*) horcajo; (*of railroad*) ramal *m*; (*of a tree*) horqueta; (*for eating*) tenedor *m* ‖ *tr* ahorquillar; cargar con horquilla; (*in chess*) amenazar (*dos piezas*); **to fork out** (slang) entregar, sudar ‖ *intr* bifurcarse

forked [forkt] *adj* ahorquillado

forked lightning *s* relámpago en zigzag

fork'lift' truck *s* carretilla elevadora de horquilla

forlorn [fər'lɔrn] *adj* desamparado; desesperado; miserable

forlorn hope *s* empresa desesperada

form [fɔrm] *s* forma; (*paper to be filled out*) formulario; (*construction to give shape to cement*) encofrado; (*type in a frame*) molde *m* ‖ *tr* formar ‖ *intr* formarse

formal ['fɔrməl] *adj* formal, ceremonioso; etiquetero

formal attire *s* vestido de etiqueta

formal call *s* visita de cumplido

formali·ty [fɔr'mælɪti] *s* (*pl* -**ties**) (*standard procedure*) formalidad; ceremonia, etiqueta

formal party *s* reunión de etiqueta

formal speech *s* discurso de aparato

format ['fɔrmæt] *s* formato

formation ['fɔr'meʃən] *s* formación

former ['fɔrmər] *adj* (*preceding*) anterior; (*long past*) antiguo; primero (*de dos*); **the former** aquél

formerly ['fɔrmərli] *adv* antes, en tiempos pasados

form'-fit'ting *adj* ceñido al cuerpo

formidable ['fɔrmɪdəbəl] *adj* formidable

formless ['fɔrmlɪs] *adj* informe

form letter *s* carta general

formu·la ['fɔrmjələ] *s* (*pl* -**las** o -**lae** [,li] fórmula

formulate ['fɔrmjə,let] *tr* formular

fornicate ['fɔrnə,ket] *intr* fornicar

fornication [,fɔrnə'keʃən] *s* fornicación

for·sake [fɔr'sek] *v* (*pret* -**sook** ['suk]; *pp* -**saken** ['sekən]) *tr* abandonar, desamparar; dejar

fort [fɔrt] *s* fuerte *m*, fortaleza

forte [fɔrt] *s* (*strong point*) fuerte *m*, caballo de batalla ‖ ['forte] *adj* (mus) fuerte

forth [forθ] *adv* adelante; **and so forth** y así sucesivamente; **from this day forth** de hoy en adelante; **to go forth** salir

forth'com'ing *adj* próximo, venidero

forth'right' *adj* directo, franco, sincero ‖ *adv* derecho; sinceramente, francamente; en seguida

forth'with' *adv* inmediatamente

fortieth ['fɔrtɪ·ɪθ] *adj* & *s* (*in a series*) cuadragésimo; (*part*) cuarentavo

fortification [,fɔrtɪfɪ'keʃən] *s* fortificación

forti·fy ['fɔrtɪ,faɪ] *v* (*pret* & *pp* -**fied**) *tr* fortificar; encabezar (*vinos*)

fortitude ['fɔrtɪ,tjud] *s* fortaleza, firmeza

fortnight ['fɔrtnaɪt] *s* quincena, dos semanas

fortress ['fɔrtrɪs] *s* fortaleza

fortuitous [fɔr'tju·ɪtəs] *adj* fortuito

fortunate ['fɔrtʃənɪt] *adj* afortunado

fortune ['fɔrtʃən] *s* fortuna; (*money*) platal *m*; **to make a fortune** enriquecerse; **to tell someone his fortune** decirle a uno la buenaventura

fortune hunter *s* cazador *m* de dotes

for'tune·tel'ler *s* adivino, agorero

for·ty ['fɔrti] *adj* & *pron* cuarenta ‖ *s* (*pl* -**ties**) cuarenta *m*

fo·rum ['forəm] *s* (*pl* -**rums** o -**ra** [rə]) foro; (*e.g., of public opinion*) tribunal *m*

forward ['fɔrwərd] *adj* delantero; precoz; atrevido, impertinente ‖ *adv* hacia ade-

lante; **to bring forward** pasar a cuenta nueva; **to come forward** adelantarse; **to look forward to** esperar con placer anticipado ‖ *tr* cursar, hacer seguir, reexpedir; fomentar, patrocinar

fossil ['fɑsɪl] *adj* & *s* fósil *m*

foster ['fɑstər] o ['fɔstər] *adj* adoptivo, de leche, de crianza ‖ *tr* fomentar

foster brother *s* hermano de leche

foster home *s* hogar *m* de adopción

foster mother *s* madre adoptiva; (*nurse*) ama de leche

foster sister *s* hermana de leche

foul [faul] *adj* sucio, puerco; (*air*) viciado; (*wind*) contrario; (*weather*) malo; obsceno; pérfido; (*breath*) fétido; (baseball) fuera del cuadro

foul-mouthed ['faul'mauðd] o ['faul'mauθt] *adj* deslenguado

foul play *s* mal encuentro; (sport) juego sucio

foul'spo'ken *adj* malhablado

found [faund] *tr* fundar; (*to melt, to cast*) fundir

foundation [faun'deʃən] *s* fundación; (*endowment*) dotación; (*basis*) fundamento; (*masonry support*) cimiento

founder ['faundər] *s* fundador *m*; (*of metals*) fundidor *m* ‖ *intr* despearse (*un caballo*); hundirse, irse a pique (*un buque*); (*to fail*) fracasar

foundling ['faundlɪŋ] *s* niño expósito; pepe *mf*

foundling hospital *s* casa de expósitos

found·ry ['faundri] *s* (*pl* -**ries**) fundición

foundry·man ['faundrɪmən] *s* (*pl* -**men** [mən]) fundidor *m*

fount [faunt] *s* fuente *f*

fountain ['fauntən] *s* fuente *f*, manantial *m*

foun'tain·head' *s* nacimiento

fountain pen *s* pluma estilográfica, pluma fuente

fountain syringe *s* mangueta

four [for] *adj* & *pron* cuatro ‖ *s* cuatro; **four o'clock** las cuatro; **on all fours** a gatas

four'-cy'cle *adj* (mach) de cuatro tiempos

four'-cyl'inder *adj* (mach) de cuatro cilindros

four'-flush' *intr* (coll) bravear, papelonear

fourflusher ['for,flʌʃər] *s* bravucón *m*

four-footed ['for'futɪd] *adj* cuadrúpedo

four hundred *adj* & *pron* cuatrocientos ‖ *s* cuatrocientos *m*; **the four hundred** la alta sociedad

four'-in-hand' *s* corbata de nudo corredizo; coche tirado por cuatro caballos

four'-lane' *adj* cuadriviario

four'-leaf' *adj* cuadrifoliado

four-legged ['for'legɪd] o ['for'legd] *adj* de cuatro patas; (*schooner*) de cuatro mástiles

four'-let'ter word *s* palabra impúdica de cuatro letras

four'-mo'tor plane *s* cuadrimotor *m*

four'-o'clock' *s* dondiego

four'post'er *s* cama imperial

four'score' *adj* cuatro veintenas de

foursome ['forsəm] *s* cuatrinca; cuatro jugadores; juego de cuatro

fourteen ['for'tin] *adj, pron & s* catorce *m*
fourteenth ['for'tinθ] *adj & s (in a series)* decimocuarto; *(part)* catorzavo ‖ *s (in dates)* catorce *m*
fourth [forθ] *adj & s* cuarto ‖ *s (in dates)* cuatro
fourth estate *s* cuarto poder
four'-way' *adj* de cuatro direcciones; (elec) de cuatro terminales
fowl [faul] *s* ave *f;* aves; gallina; gallo; carne *f* de ave
fowling piece *s* escopeta de caza
fox [faks] *s* zorra; *(fur)* zorro; *(cunning person)* (fig) zorro ‖ *tr* (coll) engañar con astucia
fox'glove' *s* dedalera
fox'hole' *s* zorrera; (mil) pozo de lobo
fox'hound' *s* perro raposero, perro zorrero
fox hunt *s* caza de zorras
fox terrier *s* fox-terrier *m (casta de perro de talla pequeña)*
fox trot *s* trote corto *(de caballo)*; fox-trot *m (baile de compás cuaternario)*
fox•y ['faksi] *adj (comp* **-ier;** *super* **-iest)** (coll) hermosa y erótica; zorrero, astuto, taimado
foyer ['fɔɪ•ər] *s (of a private house)* vestíbulo; (theat) salón *m* de entrada, vestíbulo
fr. *abbr* **fragment, franc, from**
Fr. *abbr* **Father, French, Friday**
Fra [fra] *s* fray *m*
fracas ['frekəs] *s* alboroto, riña
fraction ['frækʃən] *s* fracción; porción muy pequeña
fractional ['frækʃənəl] *adj* fraccionario; insignificante
fractious ['frækʃəs] *adj* reacio, rebelón; quisquilloso, regañón
fracture ['fræktʃər] *s* fractura ‖ *tr* fracturar; *(e.g., an arm)* fracturarse; *intr* fracturarse
fragile ['frædʒɪl] *adj* frágil
fragment ['frægmənt] *s* fragmento
fragrance ['fregrəns] *s* fragancia
fragrant ['fregrənt] *adj* fragante
frail [frel] *adj (not robust)* débil; *(easily broken; morally weak)* frágil ‖ *s* cesto de junco
frail•ty ['frelti] *s (pl* **-ties)** debilidad; *(moral weakness)* fragilidad
frame [frem] *s (of a picture, mirror)* marco, *(of glasses)* montura, armadura; *(structure)* armazón *f,* esqueleto; *(for embroidering)* bastidor *m; (of government)* sistema *m;* (mov, telv) encuadre *m;* (naut) cuaderna ‖ *tr (to put in a frame)* enmarcar; formar, forjar; construir; redactar, formular; (slang) incriminar *(a un inocente)*
frame house *s* casa de madera
frame of mind *s* manera de pensar
frame'-up' *s* (slang) treta, trama para incriminar a un inocente
frame'work' *s* armazón *f,* esqueleto, entramado
franc [fræŋk] *s* franco
France [fræns] o [frans] *s* Francia
franchise ['fræntʃaɪz] *s* franquicia, privilegio; *(right to vote)* sufragio

Franciscan [fræn'sɪskən] *adj & s* franciscano
frank [fræŋk] *adj* franco, sincero ‖ *s* carta franca, envío franco; franquicia postal; sello de franquicia ‖ *tr* franquear ‖ **Frank** *s (member of a Frankish tribe)* franco; *(masculine name)* Paco
frankfurter ['fræŋkfərtər] *s* salchicha de carne de vaca y de cerdo
frankincense ['fræŋkɪn,sɛns] *s* olíbano
Frankish ['fræŋkɪʃ] *adj & s* franco
frankness ['fræŋknɪs] *s* franqueza, abertura, sinceridad
frantic ['fræntɪk] *adj* frenético
frappé [fræ'pe] *adj* helado ‖ *s* refresco helado de zumo de frutas
frat [fræt] *s* (slang) club *m* de estudiantes
fraternal [frə'tʌrnəl] *adj* fraternal
fraterni•ty [frə'tʌrnɪti] *s (pl* **-ties)** *(brotherliness)* fraternidad; cofradía; asociación secreta; (U.S.A.) club *m* de estudiantes
fraternize ['frætər,naɪz] *intr* fraternizar
fraud [frɔd] *s* fraude *m;* embelequería (Col, Mex, W-I); *(person)* (coll) impostor *m*
fraudulent ['frɔdjələnt] *adj* fraudulento
fraught [frɔt] *adj*—**fraught with** cargado de, lleno de
fray [fre] *s* combate *m,* riña, batalla ‖ *intr* deshilacharse, raerse
freak [frik] *s (sudden fancy)* capricho, antojo; *(person, animal)* fenómeno, esperpento
freakish ['frikɪʃ] *adj* caprichoso, antojadizo; raro, fantástico
freckle ['frɛkəl] *s* peca
freckle-faced ['frɛkəl,fest] *adj* pecoso
freckly ['frɛkli] *adj* pecoso
free [fri] *adj (comp* **freer** ['fri•ər]; *super* **freest** ['fri•ɪst])** libre; gratis, franco; liberal, generoso; **to be free with** dar abundantemente; **to set free** libertar ‖ *adv* libremente; en libertad; de balde, gratis ‖ *v (pret & pp* **freed** [frid]; *ger* **freeing** ['fri•ɪŋ])** *tr* libertar, poner en libertad; soltar; exentar, eximir
free and easy *adj* despreocupado
freebooter ['fri,butər] *s* forbante *m,* filibustero, pirata *m*
free'born' *adj* nacido libre; propio de un pueblo libre
freedom ['fridəm] *s* libertad
freedom of speech *s* libertad de palabra
freedom of the press *s* libertad de imprenta
freedom of the seas *s* libertad de los mares
freedom of worship *s* libertad de cultos
free enterprise *s* libertad de empresa
free fight *s* sarracina, riña tumultuaria
free'-for-all' *s* concurso abierto a todo el mundo; sarracina, riña tumultuaria
free hand *s* plena libertad, carta blanca
free'hand' drawing *s* dibujo a pulso
freehanded ['fri,hændɪd] *adj* dadivoso, generoso
free'hold' *s (law)* feudo franco
free lance *s* soldado mercenario; periodista *mf* sin empleo fijo; *(writer not on regular salary)* destajista *mf*

fo
fr

free lunch s tapas, enjutos
free·man ['frimən] s (pl **-men** [mən]) hombre m libre; ciudadano
Free'ma'son s francmasón m
Free'ma'sonry s francmasonería
free of charge adj gratis, de balde
free on board adj franco a bordo
free port s puerto franco
free ride s llevada gratuita
free service s servicio post-venta
free'-spo'ken adj franco, sin reserva
free'stone' adj & s abridero
free'think'er s librepensador m
free thought s librepensamiento
free trade s librecambio
free'trad'er s librecambista mf
free'way' s autopista
free will s libre albedrío
freeze [friz] s helada ‖ v (pret **froze** [froz]; pp **frozen**) tr helar; congelar (créditos, fondos, etc.) ‖ intr helarse; congelarse; helársele a uno la sangre (p.ej., de miedo)
freeze'-dry' v (pret & pp **-dried**) tr liofilizar
freeze drying s liofilización
freezer ['frizər] s heladora, sorbetera
freezing ['frizɪŋ] s glaciación
freight [fret] s carga; (naut) flete m; **by freight** como carga; (rr) en pequeña velocidad ‖ tr enviar por carga
freight car s vagón m de carga, vagón de mercancías
freighter ['fretər] s buque m de carga, carguero
freight platform s (rr) muelle m
freight station s (rr) estación de carga
freight train s mercancías msg, tren m de mercancías
freight yard s (rr) patio de carga
French [frɛntʃ] adj & s francés m; **the French** los franceses
French chalk s jaboncillo de sastre
French doors spl puertas vidrieras dobles
French dressing s salsa francesa, vinagreta
French fried potatoes spl patatas fritas en trocitos
French horn s (mus) trompa de armonía
French horsepower s caballo de fuerza, caballo de vapor
French leave s despedida a la francesa; **to take French leave** despedirse a la francesa
French·man ['frɛntʃmən] s (pl **-men** [mən]) francés m
French telephone s microteléfono
French toast s torrija
French window s puerta ventana
French'wom'an s (pl **-wom'en**) francesa
frenzied ['frɛnzid] adj frenético
fren·zy ['frɛnzi] (pl **-zies**) frenesí m
frequen·cy ['frikwənsi] s (pl **-cies**) frecuencia
frequency list s lista de frecuencia
frequency modulation s modulación de frecuencia
frequent ['frikwənt] adj frecuente ‖ [frɪ'kwɛnt] o ['frikwɛnt] tr frecuentar
frequently ['frikwəntli] adv con frecuencia, frecuentemente

fres·co ['frɛsko] s (pl **-coes** o **-cos**) fresco ‖ tr pintar al fresco
fresh [frɛʃ] adj fresco; (water) dulce; (wind) fresquito; novicio, inexperto; (cheeky) (slang) fresco; (toward women) (slang) atrevido; **fresh paint!** ¡ojo mancha! ‖ adv recientemente, recién; **fresh in** (coll) recién llegado, acabado de llegar; **fresh out** (coll) recién agotado
freshen ['frɛʃən] tr refrescar ‖ intr refrescarse
freshet ['frɛʃɪt] s avenida, crecida
fresh·man ['frɛʃmən] s (pl **-men** [mən]) novato; estudiante mf de primer año
freshness ['frɛʃnɪs] s frescura; (cheek) (slang) frescura
fresh'-wa'ter adj de agua dulce; no acostumbrado a navegar; de poca monta
fret [frɛt] s (interlaced design) calado; (mus) ceja, traste m; queja ‖ v (pret & pp **fretted**; ger **fretting**) tr adornar con calados ‖ intr irritarse, quejarse, agitarse
fretful ['frɛtfəl] adj irritable, enojadizo, displicente
fret'work' s calado
Freudianism ['frɔɪdɪ·ə,nɪzəm] s freudismo
friar ['fraɪ·ər] s fraile m **friar·y** ['fraɪ·əri] s (pl **-ies**) convento de frailes
fricassee [,frɪkə'si] s fricasé m
friction ['frɪkʃən] s fricción, rozamiento; (fig) desavenencia, rozamiento
friction tape s cinta aislante
Friday ['fraɪdi] s viernes m
fried [fraɪd] adj frito
fried egg s huevo a la plancha, huevo frito o estrellado
friend [frɛnd] s amigo; (in answer to "Who is there?") gente f de paz; **to be friends with** ser amigo de; **to make friends** trabar amistades; **to make friends with** hacerse amigo de
friend·ly ['frɛndli] adj (comp **-lier;** super **-liest**) amigo, amistoso, amigable
friendship ['frɛndʃɪp] s amistad
frieze [friz] s (archit) friso
frigate ['frɪgɪt] s fragata
fright [fraɪt] s susto, espanto; (grotesque or ridiculous person) (coll) espantajo; **to take fright at** asustarse de
frighten ['fraɪtən] tr asustar, espantar; **to frighten away** espantar, ahuyentar ‖ intr asustarse
frightful ['fraɪtfəl] adj espantoso, horroroso; (coll) feúcho, repugnante; (coll) enorme, tremendo
frightfulness ['fraɪtfəlnɪs] s espanto, horror m; terrorismo; espantosidad (SAm)
frigid ['frɪdʒɪd] adj frío; (fig) frío; (zone) glacial
frigidity [frɪ'dʒɪdɪti] s frialdad; (pathol) frialdad; (fig) frialdad, frigidez f
frill [frɪl] s lechuga; (of birds and other animals) collarín m; (frippery) (coll) ringorrango; (in dress, speech etc.) (coll) afectación
fringe [frɪndʒ] s franja, orla; (opt) franja ‖ tr franjar, orlar

fringe benefits *spl* beneficios accesorios; beneficios sociales

fripper·y ['frɪpəri] *s* (*pl* **-ies**) (*flashiness*) cursilería; (*flashy clothes*) perejil *m*, perifollos

frisk [frɪsk] *tr* (slang) cachear; (slang) registrar y robar ‖ *intr* retozar

frisk·y ['frɪski] *adj* (*comp* **-ier;** *super* **-iest**) juguetón, retozón; (*horse*) fogoso

fritter ['frɪtər] *s* fruta de sartén; fragmento ‖ *tr*—**to fritter away** desperdiciar, malgastar poco a poco

frivolous ['frɪvələs] *adj* frívolo

friz [frɪz] *s* (*pl* **frizzes**) rizo, pelo rizado apretadamente ‖ *v* (*pret & pp* **frizzed;** *ger* **frizzing**) *tr* rizar, rizar apretadamente

frizzle ['frɪzəl] *s* rizo apretado; chirrido, siseo ‖ *tr* rizar apretadamente; asar o freír en parrilla ‖ *intr* chirriar, sisear

friz·zly ['frɪzli] *adj* (*comp* **-zlier;** *super* **-zliest**) muy ensortijado

fro [fro] *adv*—**to and fro** de acá para allá; **to go to and fro** ir y venir

frock [frɑk] *s* vestido; bata, blusa; (*of priest*) vestido talar

frock coat *s* levita

frog [frɑg] o [frɔg] *s* rana; (*button and loop on a garment*) alamar *m*; (*in throat*) ronquera, gallo

frog'man *s* (*pl* **-men'**) hombre-rana *m*

frol·ic ['frɑlɪk] *s* juego alegre, travesura; fiesta, holgorio ‖ *v* (*pret & pp* **-icked;** *ger* **-icking**) *intr* juguetear, travesear, jaranear

frolicsome ['frɑlɪksəm] *adj* juguetón, travieso

from [frʌm], [frɑm] o [frəm] *prep* de; desde; de parte de; según; a, p.ej., **to take something away from someone** quitarle algo a alguien

front [frʌnt] *adj* delantero; anterior ‖ *s* frente *m* & *f*; (*of a shirt*) pechera; (*of a book*) principio; apariencia falsa (*p.ej., de riqueza*); además estudiado; (mil) frente *m*; **in front of** delante de, frente a, en frente de; **to put on a front** (coll) gastar mucho oropel; **to put up a bold front** (coll) hacer de tripas corazón ‖ *tr* (*to face*) dar a; (*to confront*) afrontar, arrostrar; (*to supply with a front*) poner frente o fachada a ‖ *intr*—**to front on** dar a; **to front towards** mirar hacia

frontage ['frʌntɪdʒ] *s* fachada, frontera; terreno frontero

front door *s* puerta de entrada

front drive *s* (aut) tracción delantera

frontier [frʌn'tɪr] *adj* fronterizo ‖ *s* frontera

frontiers·man [frʌn'tɪrzmən] *s* (*pl* **-men** [mən]) hombre *m* de la frontera, explorador *m*

frontispiece ['frʌntɪs,pis] *s* (*of book*) portada; (archit) frontispicio

front matter *s* preliminares *mpl* (*de un libro*)

front page *s* primera plana

front porch *s* soportal *m*

front room *s* cuarto que da a la calle

front row *s* primera fila

front seat *s* asiento delantero

front steps *spl* escalones *mpl* de acceso a la puerta de entrada

front view *s* vista de frente

frost [frɔst] o [frɑst] *s* (*freezing*) helada; (*frozen dew*) escarcha; (slang) fracaso ‖ *tr* cubrir de escarcha; escarchar (*confituras*); helar (*el frío las plantas*); deslustrar (*el vidrio*)

frost'bit'ten *adj* dañado por la helada; quemado por la helada o la escarcha

frosted glass *s* vidrio deslustrado

frosting ['frɔstɪŋ] o ['frɑstɪŋ] *s* garapiña; (*of glass*) deslustre *m*

frost·y ['frɔsti] o ['frɑsti] *adj* (*comp* **-ier;** *super* **-iest**) cubierto de escarcha; escarchado; frío, poco amistoso; canoso, gris

froth [frɔθ] o [frɑθ] *s* espuma; frivolidad, vanidad ‖ *intr* espumar, echar espuma; (*at the mouth*) espumajear

froth·y ['frɔθi] o ['frɑθi] *adj* (*comp* **-ier;** *super* **-iest**) espumoso; frívolo, vano

froward ['frowərd] *adj* díscolo, indócil

frown [fraʊn] *s* ceño, entrecejo ‖ *intr* fruncir el entrecejo; **to frown at** *u* **on** mirar con ceño, desaprobar

frows·y o **frowz·y** ['fraʊzi] *adj* (*comp* **-ier;** *super* **-iest**) desaseado, desaliñado; maloliente; mal peinado

frozen foods ['frozən] *spl* viandas congeladas

frt. *abbr* **freight**

frugal ['frugəl] *adj* (*moderate in the use of things*) parco; (*not very abundant*) frugal

fruit [frut] *adj* (*tree*) frutal; (*boat, dish*) frutero ‖ *s* (*such as apple, pear, strawberry*) fruta; frutas, p.ej., **I like fruit** me gustan las frutas; (*part containing seed*) fruto; (*effect, result*) (fig) fruto

fruit cake *s* torta de frutas

fruit cup *s* compota de frutas picadas

fruit fly *s* mosca del vinagre; mosca de las frutas

fruitful ['frutfəl] *adj* fructuoso

fruition [fru'ɪʃən] *s* buen resultado, cumplimiento; **to come to fruition** lograrse cumplidamente

fruit jar *s* tarro para frutas

fruit juice *s* jugo de frutas

fruitless ['frutlɪs] *adj* infructuoso

fruit of the vine *s* zumo de cepas o de parras

fruit salad *s* ensalada de frutas, macedonia de frutas

fruit stand *s* puesto de frutas

fruit store *s* frutería

frumpish ['frʌmpɪʃ] *adj* basto, desgarbado, desaliñado

frustrate ['frʌstret] *tr* frustrar

fry [fraɪ] *s* (*pl* **fries**) fritada ‖ *v* (*pret & pp* **fried**) *tr & intr* freír

frying pan ['fraɪ·ɪŋ] *s* sartén *f*; **to jump from the frying pan into the fire** saltar de la sartén y dar en las brasas

ft. *abbr* **foot, feet**

fudge [fʌdʒ] *s* dulce *m* de chocolate

fuel ['fju·əl] *s* combustible *m*; (fig) pábulo; **alternate fuel** combustible alternativo ‖ *v* (*pret & pp* **fueled** o **fuelled;** *ger* **fueling** o

fr
fu

fuelling) *tr* aprovisionar de combustible ‖ *intr* aprovisionarse de combustible

fuel cell *s* cámara de combustible, célula electrógena

fuel oil *s* aceite *m* combustible

fuel tank *s* depósito de combustible

fugitive [ˈfjudʒɪtɪv] *adj & s* fugitivo

fugue [fjug] *s* (mus) fuga

ful•crum [ˈfʌlkrəm] *s* (*pl* **-crums** o **-cra** [krə]) fulcro

fulfill [fulˈfɪl] *tr* (*to carry out*) cumplir, realizar; cumplir con (*una obligación*); llenar (*una condición*)

fulfillment [fulˈfɪlmənt] *s* cumplimiento, realización

full [ful] *adj* lleno; (*dress, garment*) amplio, holgado; (*formal dress*) de etiqueta; (*voice*) sonoro, fuerte; (*of food*) harto; **full of aches and pains** lleno de goteras; **full of fun** muy divertido, muy chistoso; **full of play** muy juguetón; **full to overflowing** lleno a rebosar ‖ *adv* completamente; **full many (a)** muchísimos; **full well** muy bien, perfectamente ‖ *s* colmo; **in full** por completo; sin abreviar; **to the full** completamente ‖ *tr* abatanar

full-blooded [ˈfulˈblʌdɪd] *adj* vigoroso; completo, pletórico; de raza

full-blown [ˈfulˈblon] *adj* (*flower, blossom*) abierto; desarrollado, maduro

full-bodied [ˈfulˈbadid] *adj* fuerte, espeso, consistente; aromático

full dress *s* traje *m* de etiqueta; (mil) uniforme *m* de gala

full′-dress′ coat *s* frac *m*

full-faced [ˈfulˈfest] *adj* carilleno; (*view*) de cuadrado; (*portrait*) de rostro entero

full-fledged [ˈfulˈfledʒd] *adj* hecho y derecho, nada menos que

full-grown [ˈfulˈgron] *adj* crecido, completamente desarrollado

full house *s* lleno, entrada llena; (poker) fulján *m*

full′-length′ mirror *s* espejo de cuerpo entero, espejo de vestir

full-length movie *s* largometraje *m*, cinta de largo metraje

full load *s* plena carga; (aer) peso total

full moon *s* luna llena, plenilunio

full name *s* nombre *m* y apellidos

full′-page′ *adj* a página entera

full powers *spl* plenos poderes, amplias facultades

full sail *adv* a todo trapo

fulll′-scale′ *adj* de tamaño natural; total, completo; pleno

full-sized [ˈfulˈsaɪzd] *adj* de tamaño natural

full speed *adv* a toda velocidad

full stop *s* parada completa; (gram) punto

full swing *s* plena actividad

full tilt *adv* a toda velocidad

full′-time′ *adj* a tiempo completo

full′-view′ *adj* de vista completa

full volume *s* (rad) máximo de volumen

fully [ˈfuli] o [ˈfulli] *adv* completamente; cabalmente; por lo menos

fulsome [ˈfulsəm] *adj* bajo, craso, de mal gusto

fumble [ˈfʌmbəl] *tr* no coger (*la pelota*), dejar caer (*la pelota*) desmañadamente; manosear desmañadamente ‖ *intr* revolver papeles; titubear; andar a tientas; (*in one's pockets*) buscar con las manos

fume [fjum] *s* humo, vapor *m*, gas *m*, vaho ‖ *tr* (*to treat with fumes*) ahumar ‖ *intr* (*to give off fumes*) humear; (*to show anger*) echar pestes; **to fume at** echar pestes contra

fumigate [ˈfjumɪˌget] *tr* fumigar

fumigation [ˌfjumɪˈgeʃən] *s* fumigación

fun [fʌn] *s* divertimiento; broma, chacota; **to be fun** ser divertido; **to have fun** divertirse; **to make fun of** reírse de, burlarse de

function [ˈfʌŋkʃən] *s* función ‖ *intr* funcionar

functional [ˈfʌŋkʃənəl] *adj* funcional

functionar•y [ˈfʌŋkʃəˌnɛri] *s* (*pl* **-ies**) funcionario

fund [fʌnd] *s* fondo; **funds** fondos ‖ *tr* consolidar (*una deuda*)

fundamental [ˌfʌndəˈmɛntəl] *adj* fundamental ‖ *s* fundamento

funeral [ˈfjunərəl] *adj* funeral; (*march, procession*) fúnebre; (*expense*) funerario ‖ *s* funeral *m*, funerales *mpl*, pompa fúnebre (*de cuerpo presente*); **it's not my funeral** (slang) no corre a mi cuidado

funeral director *s* empresario de pompas fúnebres

funeral home o **parlor** *s* funeraria

funeral service *s* oficio de difuntos, misa de cuerpo presente

funereal [fjuˈnɪrɪ•əl] *adj* fúnebre

fungous [ˈfʌŋgəs] *adj* fungoso

fungus [ˈfʌŋgəs] *s* (*pl* **funguses** o **fungi** [ˈfʌndʒaɪ]) hongo; (pathol) fungo

funicular [fjuˈnɪkjələr] *adj & s* funicular *m*

funk [fʌŋk] *s* (coll) miedo, cobardía; cobarde *mf*; **in a funk** asustado

fun•nel [ˈfʌnəl] *s* embudo; (*smokestack*) chimenea; (*tube for ventilation*) manguera, ventilador *m* ‖ *v* (*pret & pp* **-neled** o **-nelled**; *ger* **-neling** o **-nelling**) *tr* verter por medio de un embudo

funnies [ˈfʌniz] *spl* páginas cómicas, tiras cómicas, tebeo

fun•ny [ˈfʌni] *adj* (*comp* **-nier**; *super* **-niest**) cómico, divertido, chistoso; (coll) extraño, raro; **to strike someone as funny** hacerle a uno gracia

funny bone *s* hueso de la alegría

funny paper *s* páginas cómicas

fur. *abbr* furlong, furnished

fur [fʌr] *s* piel *f*; abrigo de pieles; (*on the tongue*) sarro

furbelow [ˈfʌrbə,lo] *s* (*ruffle*) faralá *m*; (*frippery*) ringorrango

furbish [ˈfʌrbɪʃ] *tr* acicalar, limpiar; **to furbish up** renovar

furious [ˈfjurɪ•əs] *adj* furioso

furl [fʌrl] *tr* enrollar; (naut) aferrar

fur-lined [ˈfʌr,laɪnd] *adj* forrado con pieles

furlong [ˈfʌrlɔŋ] o [ˈfʌrlɑŋ] *s* estadio

furlough ['fʌrlo] *s* licencia ‖ *tr* dar licencia a
furnace ['fʌrnɪs] *s* horno; (*to heat a house*) calorífero
furnish ['fʌrnɪʃ] *tr* amueblar; proporcionar, suministrar
furnishings ['fʌrnɪʃɪŋz] *spl* muebles *mpl*; (*things to wear*) artículos
furniture ['fʌrnɪtʃər] *s* muebles *mpl*, mobiliario; (naut) aparejo; **a piece of furniture** un mueble
furniture dealer *s* mueblista *mf*
furniture store *s* mueblería
furrier ['fʌrɪ·ər] *s* peletero
furrier·y ['fʌrɪ·əri] *s* (*pl* **-ies**) peletería
furrow ['fʌro] *s* surco ‖ *tr* surcar
further ['fʌrðər] *adj* adicional; nuevo; más lejano ‖ *adv* además; más lejos ‖ *tr* adelantar, promover, fomentar
furtherance ['fʌrðərəns] *s* adelantamiento, promoción, fomento
furthermore ['fʌrðər,mor] *adv* además
furthest ['fʌrðɪst] *adj* (el) más lejano ‖ *adv* más lejos
furtive ['fʌrtɪv] *adj* furtivo
fu·ry ['fjuri] *s* (*pl* **-ries**) furia
furze [fʌrz] *s* aulaga; retama de escoba
fuse [fjuz] *s* (tube or wick filled with explosive material) mecha; (*device for detonating an explosive charge*) espoleta; (elec) fusible *m*, cortacircuitos *m*, tapón *m*; **to burn out a fuse** quemar un fusible ‖ *tr* fundir; (*to unite*) fusionar ‖ *intr* fundirse; fusionarse
fuse box *s* caja de fusibles
fuselage ['fjuzəlɪdʒ] *s* fuselaje *m*
fusible ['fjuzɪbəl] *adj* fundible, fusible

fusillade [,fjuzɪ'led] *s* fusilería; (*e.g., of questions*) andanada ‖ *tr* atacar o matar con una descarga de fusilería, fusilar
fusion ['fjuʒən] *s* fusión
fuss [fʌs] *s* alharaca, hazañería; (coll) disputa por ligero motivo; **to make a fuss** hacer alharacas; **to make a fuss over** hacer fiestas a; disputar sobre ‖ *tr* atolondrar, inquietar, confundir ‖ *intr* hacer alharacas, inquietarse por bagatelas
fuss·y ['fʌsi] *adj* (*comp* **-ier;** *super* **-iest**)] alharaquiento, alborotado; descontentadizo, quisquilloso, melindroso; funcionero, hazañero; muy adornado
fustian ['fʌstʃən] *s* (*coarse cloth*) fustán *m*; (*sort of velveteen*) pana; (*bombast*) cultedad, follaje *m*
fust·y ['fʌsti] *adj* (*comp* **-ier;** *super* **-iest**) mohoso, rancio; que huele a cerrado; pasado de moda
futile ['fjutɪl] *adj* (*unproductive*) estéril; (*unimportant*) fútil
futili·ty [fju'tɪlɪti] *s* (*pl* **-ties**) esterilidad; futilidad
future ['fjutʃər] *adj* futuro ‖ *s* futuro, porvenir *m*; (gram) futuro; **futures** (com) futuros; **in the future** en el futuro; **in the near future** en un futuro próximo
fuze [fjuz] *s* (*tube or wick filled with explosive material*) mecha; (*device for detonating an explosive charge*) espoleta; (elec) fusible *m* ‖ *tr* poner la espoleta a
fuzz [fʌz] *s* (*as on a peach*) pelusa, vello; (*in pockets and corners*) borra, tamo; **the fuzz** (slang) policía *m*, guardia *m* urbano
fuzz·y ['fʌzi] *adj* (*comp* **-ier;** *super* **-iest**) cubierto de pelusa, velloso; polvoriento; (*indistinct*) borroso

fu
ga

G

G, g [dʒi] *s* séptima letra del alfabeto inglés
G. *abbr* **German, Gulf**
g. *abbr* **gender, genitive, gram**
gab [gæb] *s* (coll) cotorreo ‖ (*pret & pp* **gabbed;** *ger* **gabbing**) *intr* (coll) cotorrear
gabardine ['gæbər,din] *s* gabardina
gabble ['gæbəl] *s* cotorreo, parloteo ‖ *intr* cotorrear, parlotear
gable ['gebəl] *s* (*of roof*) aguilón *m*; (*over a door or window*) gablete *m*, frontón *m*
gable end *s* hastial *m*
gable roof *s* tejado de dos aguas
gad [gæd] *v* (*pret & pp* **gadded;** *ger* **gadding**) *intr* callejear, andar de acá para allá; **to gad about** pindonguear (*una mujer*)
gad′a·bout′ *adj* callejero ‖ *s* cirigallo; (*woman*) pindonga
gad′fly′ *s* (*pl* **-flies**) tábano
gadget ['gædʒɪt] *s* adminículo, chisme *m*, artilugio
Gael [gel] *s* gaélico
Gaelic ['gelɪk] *adj & s* gaélico

gaff [gæf] *s* garfio, arpón *m*; **to stand the gaff** (slang) tener aguante
gag [gæg] *s* mordaza; (*interpolation by an actor*) morcilla; (*joke*)) chiste *m*, payasada ‖ *v* (*pret & pp* **gagged;** *ger* **gagging**) *tr* amordazar; dar bascas a ‖ *intr* sentir bascas, arquear
gage [gedʒ] *s* (*pledge*) prenda; (*challenge*) desafío
gaie·ty ['ge·ɪti] *s* (*pl* **-ties**) alegría, algazara, diversión; (*of colors*) viveza
gaily ['geli] *adv* alegremente
gain [gen] *s* ganancia; (*increase*) aumento ‖ *tr* ganar; (*to reach*) alcanzar ‖ *intr* ganar terreno; mejorar (*un enfermo*); adelantarse (*un reloj*); **to gain on** ir alcanzando
gainful ['genfəl] *adj* gananciose, provechoso
gain′say′ *v* (*pret & pp* **-said** ['sed] o ['sɛd]) *tr* negar; contradecir; prohibir
gait [get] *s* paso, manera de andar
gaiter ['getər] *s* polaina corta
gal. *abbr* **gallon**

gala ['gelə] *adj* de gala ‖ *s* fiesta
galax·y ['gæləksi] *s* (*pl* -ies) galaxia
gale [gel] *s* ventarrón *m*; **gales of laughter** tempestades de risas; **to weather the gale** correr el temporal; (fig) ir tirando
Galician [gə'lıʃən] *adj* & *s* gallego
gall [gɔl] *s* bilis *f*, hiel *f*; vejiga de la bilis; (*something bitter*) (fig) hiel *f*; rencor *m*, odio; (*gallnut*) agalla; (*audacity*) (coll) descaro ‖ *tr* lastimar rozando; irritar ‖ *intr* raerse; (naut) mascarse (*un cabo*)
gallant ['gælənt] *adj* (*attentive to women*) galante; (*pertaining to love*) amoroso ‖ ['gælənt] *adj* (*stately, grand*) gallardo; (*spirited, daring*) hazañoso; (*showy, gay*) vistoso, festivo ‖ *s* hombre *m* valiente; (*man attentive to women*) galán *m*
gallant·ry ['gæləntri] *s* (*pl* -ries) galantería; gallardía
gall bladder *s* vejiga de la bilis, vesícula biliar
gall duct *s* conducto biliar
galleon ['gælı·ən] *s* (naut) galeón *m*
galler·y ['gæləri] *s* (*pl* -ies) galería; (*in church, theater, etc.*) tribuna; (*cheapest seats in theater*) gallinero; **to play to the gallery** (coll) hablar para la galería
galley ['gæli] *s* (naut & typ) galera; (naut) cocina
galley proof *s* (typ) galerada, pruebas de segundas
galley slave *s* galeote *m*; (*drudge*) esclavo del trabajo
Gallic ['gælık] *adj* gálico
galling ['gɔlıŋ] *adj* irritante, ofensivo
gallivant ['gælı,vænt] *intr* andar a placer
gall'nut' *s* agalla
gallon ['gælən] *s* galón *m* (*medida*)
galloon [gə'lun] *s* galón *m* (*cinta*)
gallop ['gæləp] *s* galope *m*; **at a gallop** a galope ‖ *tr* hacer galopar ‖ *intr* galopar; **to gallop through** (fig) hacer muy aprisa
gal·lows ['gæloz] *s* (*pl* -lows o -lowses) horca
gallows bird *s* (coll) carne *f* de horca
gall'stone' *s* cálculo biliar
galore [gə'lor] *adv* en abundancia
galosh [gə'lɑʃ] *s* chanclo alto
galvanize ['gælvə,naız] *tr* galvanizar
galvanized iron *s* hierro galvanizado
gambit ['gæmbıt] *s* gambito
gamble ['gæmbəl] *s* (coll) empresa arriesgada ‖ *tr* aventurar en el juego; **to gamble away** perder en el juego ‖ *intr* jugar; (*in the stock market*) especular, aventurarse
gambler ['gæmblər] *s* jugador *m*; especulador *m*
gambling ['gæmblıŋ] *s* juego
gambling den *s* garito
gambling house *s* casa de juego, juego público
gambling table *s* mesa de juego
gam·bol ['gæmbəl] *s* cabriola, retozo, salto ‖ *v* (*pret & pp* -boled o -bolled; *gen* -boling o -bolling) *intr* cabriolar, retozar, saltar
gambrel ['gæmbrəl] *s* corvejón *m*
gambrel roof *s* techo a la holandesa

game [gem] *adj* bravo, peleón; dispuesto, resuelto; (*leg*) cojo; de caza ‖ *s* (*form of play*) juego; (*single contest*) partida; (*score*) tantos; (*in bridge*) manga; (*any sport*) deporte *m*; (*animal or bird hunted for sport or food*) caza; (*any pursuit*) actividad; (*pursuit of diplomacy*) juego; **the game is up** estamos frescos; **to make game of** burlarse de; **to play the game** jugar limpio
game bag *s* morral *m*
game bird *s* ave *f* de caza
game'cock' *s* gallo de pelea
game'keep'er *s* guardabosque *m*
game of chance *s* juego de azar
game preserve *s* vedado
game warden *s* guardabosque *m*
gamut ['gæmət] *s* (mus & fig) gama
gam·y ['gemi] *adj* (*comp* -ier; *super* -iest) (*having flavor of uncooked game*) salvajino; bravo, peleón
gander ['gændər] *s* ganso
gang [gæŋ] *adj* múltiple ‖ *s* (*of workmen*) brigada, cuadrilla; (*of thugs*) pandilla ‖ *intr* — **to gang up** acuadrillarse; **to gang up against** u **on** atacar juntos; conspirar contra
gangling ['gæŋglıŋ] *adj* larguirucho
gangli·on ['gæŋglı·ən] *s* (*pl* -ons o -a [ə]) ganglio
gang'plank' *s* plancha, pasarela
gangrene ['gæŋgrin] *s* gangrena ‖ *tr* gangrenar ‖ *intr* gangrenarse
gangster ['gæŋstər] *adj* gangsteril ‖ *s* gángster *m*, pistolero
gangsterism ['gæŋstə,rızəm] *s* gangsterismo; acciones de los gangsters
gang'way' *s* (*passageway*) pasillo; (*gangplank*) plancha, pasarela; (*in ship's side*) portalón *m* ‖ *interj* ¡abran paso!, ¡paso libre!
gantlet ['gɔntlıt] *s* (rr) vía traslapada
gan·try ['gæntri] *s* (*pl* -tries) caballete *m*, poíno; (rr) puente *m* transversal de señales
gantry crane *s* grúa de caballete
gap [gæp] *s* (*break, open space*) laguna; (*in a wall*) boquete *m*; (*between mountains*) garganta, quebrada; (*between two points of view*) sima
gape [gep] o [gæp] *s* abertura, brecha; (*yawn*) bostezo; mirada de asombro; **the gapes** ganas de bostezar ‖ *intr* estar abierto de par en par; bostezar; embobarse; **to gape at** mirar embobado; **to stand gaping** embobarse
G.A.R. *abbr* **Grand Army of the Republic**
garage [gə'rɑz] *s* garage *m*
garb [gɑrb] *s* vestidura ‖ *tr* vestir
garbage ['gɑrbıdʒ] *s* basuras, desperdicios, bazofia
garbage can *s* cubo para bazofia, latón *m* de la basura
garbage collection *s* recogida de basuras
garbage disposal *s* evacuación de basuras
garbage heap *s* basural *m* (CAm)
garble ['gɑrbəl] *tr* mutilar (*un texto*)
garden ['gɑrdən] *s* (*of vegetables*) huerto; (*of flowers*) jardín *m*

gardener ['gardənər] *s (of vegetables)* hortelano; *(of flowers)* jardinero
gardenia [gar'dinɪ•ə] *s* gardenia, jazmín *m* de la India
gardening ['gardənɪŋ] *s* horticultura; jardinería
garden party *s* fiesta que se da en un jardín o parque
gargle ['gargəl] *s* gargarismo ‖ *intr* gargarizar
gargoyle ['gargɔɪl] *s* gárgola
garish ['gɛrɪʃ] *adj* charro, chillón, cursi
garland ['garlənd] *s* guirnalda
garlic ['garlɪk] *s* ajo
garment ['garmənt] *s* prenda de vestir
garner ['garnər] *tr (to gather, collect)* acopiar; adquirir; *(cereales)* entrojar
garnet ['garnɪt] *adj & s* granate *m*
garnish ['garnɪʃ] *s* adorno; (culin) aderezo, condimento de adorno ‖ *tr* adornar; (culin) aderezar; (law) embargar
garret ['gærɪt] *s* buhardilla, desván *m*
garrison ['gærɪsən] *s* plaza fuerte; *(troops)* guarnición ‖ *tr* guarnecer, guarnicionar *(una plaza fuerte)*; guarnecer una plaza fuerte de *(tropas)*
garrote [gə'rat] o [gə'rot] *s* estrangulación para robar; *(method of execution; iron collar used for such execution)* garrote *m* ‖ *tr* estrangular; estrangular para robar; agarrotar, dar garrote a
garrulous ['gærələs] *adj* gárrulo, locuaz
garter ['gartər] *s* liga, jarretera
garth [garθ] *s* patio de claustro
gas [gæs] *s* gas *m;* gasolina; (coll) palabrería ‖ *v (pret & pp* **gassed;** *ger* **gassing)** *tr* abastecer de gas; *(to attack, asphyxiate, or poison with gas)* gasear; abastecer de gasolina ‖ *intr* despedir gas; (slang) charlar
gas'bag' *s* (aer) cámara de gas; (slang) charlatán *m*
gas burner *s* mechero de gas
Gascony ['gæskəni] *s* Gascuña
gas engine *s* motor *m* a gas
gaseous ['gæsɪ•əs] *adj* gaseoso
gas fitter *s* gasista *m*
gas generator *s* gasógeno
gash [gæʃ] *s* cuchillada, chirlo ‖ *tr* acuchillar
gas heat *s* calefacción por gas
gas'hold'er *s* gasómetro
gasi•fy ['gæsɪ,faɪ] *v (pret & pp* **-fied)** *tr* gasificar ‖ *intr* gasificarse
gas jet *s* mechero de gas; llama de gas
gasket ['gæskɪt] *s* empaquetadura
gas'light' *s* luz *f* de gas
gas main *s* cañería de gas
gas mask *s* careta antigás
gas meter *s* contador *m* de gas
gasohol ['gæsə,hɔl] *s* alconafta
gasoline ['gæsə,lin] o [,gæsə'lin] *s* gasolina
gasoline pump *s* poste *m* distribuidor *m* de gasolina, surtidor *m* de gasolina
gasp [gæsp] *s* respiración entrecortada; *(of death)* boqueada ‖ *tr* decir con voz entrecortada ‖ *intr* boquear
gas producer *s* gasógeno
gas range *s* cocina a gas

gas station *s* estación gasolinera
gas stove *s* cocina a gas
gas tank *s* gasómetro; **(aut) depósito** de gasolina
gastric ['gæstrɪk] *adj* gástrico
gastronomy [gæs'tranəmi] *s* gastronomía
gas'works' *s* fábrica de gas
gate [get] *s* puerta; *(in fence or wall; of bird cage)* portillo; *(of sluice or lock)* compuerta; *(number of people paying admission; amount they pay)* entrada, taquilla; (rr) barrera; (fig) entrada, camino; **to crash the gate** (coll) colarse de gorra
gate'keep'er *s* portero; (rr) guardabarrera *mf*
gate'post' *s* poste *m* de una puerta de cercado
gate'way' *s* entrada, paso, camino
gather ['gæðər] *tr* recoger, reunir; recolectar *(la cosecha)*; coger *(leña, flores, etc.);* cubrirse de *(polvo)*; recoger *(una persona sus pensamientos);* (bb) alzar; (sew) fruncir; *(to deduce)* (fig) calcular, deducir; **to gather oneself together** componerse ‖ *intr* reunirse; amontonarse; saltar *(lágrimas)*
gathering ['gæðərɪŋ] *s* reunión; recolección; (bb) alzado; (sew) frunce *m*
gaud•y ['gɔdi] *adj (comp* **-ier;** *super* **-iest)** cursi, chillón, llamativo
gauge [gedʒ] *s* medida, norma; calibre *m; (of liquid in a container)* nivel *m; (of carpenter)* gramil *m; (of gasoline)* medidor *m;* (rr) ancho de vía, entrevía ‖ *tr* medir; calibrar; graduar; aforar *(la cantidad de agua de una coriente)*; arquear *(una nave)*
gauge glass *s* tubo indicador, vidrio de nivel
Gaul [gɔl] *s* la Galia; *(native)* galo
Gaulish ['gɔlɪʃ] *adj & s* galo
gaunt [gɔnt] o [gant] *adj* desvaído, macilento; hosco, tétrico
gauntlet ['gɔntlɪt] o ['gantlɪt] *s* guantelete *m;* guante con puño abocinado; carrera de baquetas; (rr) vía traslapada; **to run the gauntlet** correr baquetas, pasar por baquetas; **to take up the gauntlet** recoger el guante; **to throw down the gauntlet** arrojar el guante
gauze [gɔz] *s* gasa, cendal *m*
gavel ['gævəl] *s* mazo, martillo
gavotte [gə'vat] *s* gavota
gawk [gɔk] *s* (coll) palurdo, papanatas *m* ‖ *intr* (coll) mirar de modo impertinente; papar moscas, mirar embobado
gawk•y ['gɔki] *adj (comp* **-ier;** *super* **-iest)** desgarbado, torpe, bobo
gay [ge] *adj* homosexual; alegre, festivo; *(brilliant)* vistoso; amigo de los placeres
gaye•ty ['ge•ɪti] *s var de* gaiety
gaze [gez] *s* mirada fija ‖ *intr* mirar fijamente
gazelle [gə'zɛl] *s* gacela
gazette [gə'zɛt] *s* periódico; anuncio oficial
gazetteer [,gæzə'tɪr] *s* diccionario geográfico
gear [gɪr] *s* pertrechos, utensilios; *(of transmission, steering, etc.)* mecanismo, aparato; rueda dentada; *(two or more toothed wheels meshed together)* engranaje *m;* **out of gear** desengranado; (fig) descompuesto; **to throw into gear** engranar; **to throw out**

of gear desengranar; (fig) descomponer ‖ tr & intr engranar

gear'box' s caja de engranajes; (aut) caja de velocidades

gear case s caja de engranajes

gear'shift' s cambio de marchas, cambio de velocidades

gearshift lever s palanca de cambio de marchas

gear'wheel' s rueda dentada

gee [dʒi] interj ¡caramba!; gee up! (get up!, said to a horse) ¡arre!; geez! ¡mecachis!

Gehenna [gɪ'hɛnə] s gehena m

Geiger counter ['gaɪgər] s contador m de Geiger

gel [dʒɛl] s gel m ‖ v (pret & pp gelled; ger gelling) intr cuajarse en forma de gel

gelatine ['dʒɛlətɪn] s gelatina

geld [gɛld] v (pret & pp gelded o gelt [gɛlt]) tr castrar

gem [dʒɛm] s gema, piedra preciosa; (fig) joya, preciosidad

Gemini ['dʒɛmɪ,naɪ] s (constellation) Géminis m o Gemelos; (sign of zodiac) Géminis m

gen. abbr gender, general, genitive, genus

gender ['dʒɛndər] s (gram) género; (coll) sexo

genealo•gy [,dʒɛnɪ'ælədʒi] s (pl -gies) genealogía

general ['dʒɛnərəl] adj & s general m; general of the army capitán general de ejército; in general en general o por lo general

general delivery s lista de correos

generalissi•mo [,dʒɛnərə'lɪsɪmo] s (pl -mos) generalísimo

generali•ty [,dʒɛnə'rælɪti] s (pl -ties) generalidad

generalize ['dʒɛnərə'laɪz] tr & intr generalizar

generally ['dʒɛnərəli] adv por lo general

general medicine s medicina general

general practitioner s médico general

generalship ['dʒɛnərəl,ʃɪp] s generalato; don m de mando

general staff s estado mayor general

general strike s huelga general

generate ['dʒɛnə,ret] tr (to beget) engendrar; generar (electricidad); (geom) engendrar

generating station s central f

generation ['dʒɛnə'reʃən] s generación

generator ['dʒɛnə,retər] s generador m

generic [dʒɪ'nɛrɪk] adj genérico

generous ['dʒɛnərəs] adj generoso; abundante, grande

gene•sis ['dʒɛnɪsɪs] s (pl -ses [,siz]) génesis f ‖ Genesis s (Bib) el Génesis

genetic [dʒɪ'nɛtɪk] adj genético

genetic engineering s ingeniería genética

genetics [dʒɪ'nɛtɪks] s genética

Geneva [dʒɪ'nivə] s Ginebra

Genevan [dʒɪ'nivən] adj & s ginebrino

genial ['dʒini•əl] adj afable, complaciente

genie ['dʒini] s genio

genital ['dʒɛnɪtəl] adj genital ‖ genitals spl genitales mpl, órganos genitales

genitive ['dʒɛnɪtɪv] adj & s genitivo

genitourinary [,dʒɛnəto'jʊrɪ,nɛri] adj genitourinario

genius ['dʒinjəs] o ['dʒini•əs] s (pl geniuses) (great inventive gift; person possessing it) genio ‖ s (pl genii ['dʒini,aɪ]) (guardian spirit; pagan deity) genio

Genoa ['dʒɛno•ə] s Génova

genocidal [,dʒɛnə'saɪdəl] adj genocida

genocide ['dʒɛnə'saɪd] s (act) genocidio; (person) genocida mf

Geno•ese [,dʒɛno'iz] adj genovés ‖ s (pl -ese) genovés m

genre ['ʒɑnrə] adj de género

gent. o Gent. abbr gentleman, gentlemen

genteel [dʒɛn'til] adj gentil, elegante; cortés, urbano

gentian ['dʒɛnʃən] s genciana

gentile ['dʒɛntɪl] o ['dʒɛntaɪl] adj gentilicio; (gram) gentilicio ‖ ['dʒɛntaɪl] adj & s no judío; cristiano; (pagan) gentil mf

gentili•ty [dʒɛn'tɪlɪti] s (pl -ties) gentileza

gentle ['dʒɛntəl] adj apacible, benévolo; dulce, manso, suave; cortés, fino; (e.g., tap on the shoulder) ligero

gen'tle•folk' s gente bien nacida

gentle•man ['dʒɛntəlmən] s (pl -men [mən]) s caballero; (attendant to a person of high rank) gentilhombre m

gentleman in waiting s gentilhombre m de cámara

gentlemanly ['dʒɛntəlmənli] adj caballeroso

gentleman of leisure s señor m que vive sin trabajar, caballero de vida holgada

gentleman of the road s salteador m de caminos

gentleman's agreement s acuerdo verbal

gentle sex s bello sexo, sexo débil

gentry ['dʒɛntri] s gente bien nacida

genuine ['dʒɛnju•ɪn] adj genuino; sincero, franco

genus ['dʒinəs] s (pl genera ['dʒɛnərə] o genuses) (biol, log) género

geog. abbr geography

geographer [dʒɪ'ɑgrəfər] s geógrafo

geographic(al) [,dʒi•ə'græfɪk(əl)] adj geográfico

geogra•phy [dʒɪ'ɑgrəfi] s (pl -phies) geografía

geol. abbr geology

geologic(al) [,dʒi•ə'lɑdʒɪk(əl)] adj geológico

geologist [dʒɪ'ɑlədʒɪst] s geólogo

geology [dʒɪ'ɑlədʒi] s (pl -gies) geología

geom. abbr geometry

geometric(al) [,dʒi•ə'mɛtrɪk(əl)] adj geométrico

geometrician [dʒɪ,ɑmɪ'trɪʃən] s geómetra mf

geome•try [dʒɪ'ɑmɪtri] s (pl -tries) geometría

geophysics [,dʒi•ə'fɪzɪks] s geofísica

geopolitics [,dʒi•ə'pɑlɪtɪks] s geopolítica

George [dʒɔrdʒ] s Jorge m

geranium [dʒɪ'reni•əm] s geranio

geriatrical [,dʒɛri'ætrɪkəl] adj geriátrico

geriatrician [,dʒɛri•ə'trɪʃən] s geriatra mf

geriatrics [,dʒɛri'ætrɪks] s geriatría

germ [dʒʌrm] s germen m

German ['dʒʌrmən] adj & s alemán m

germane [dʒər'men] *adj* pertinente, relacionado

Germanize ['dʒʌrmə,naɪz] *tr* germanizar

German measles *s* rubéola

German silver *s* melchor *m*, alpaca

Germany ['dʒʌrməni] *s* Alemania

germ carrier *s* portador *m* de gérmenes

germ cell *s* célula germen

germicidal [,dʒʌrmɪ'saɪdəl] *adj* germicida

germicide ['dʒʌrmɪ,saɪd] *s* germicida *m*

germinate ['dʒʌrmɪ,net] *intr* germinar

germ plasm *s* germen *m* plasma

germ theory *s* teoría germinal

germ warfare *s* guerra bacteriana, guerra bacteriológica

gerontology [,dʒɛrən'tɑlədʒi] *s* gerontología

gerund ['dʒɛrənd] *s* gerundio

gerundive [dʒɪ'rʌndɪv] *s* gerundio adjetivo

gestation [dʒɛs'teʃən] *s* gestación

gesticulate [dʒɛs'tɪkjə,let] *intr* accionar, manotear

gesticulation [dʒɛs,tɪkjə'leʃən] *s* ademán *m*, manoteo

gesture ['dʒɛstʃər] *s* ademán *m*, gesto; demostración, muestra ‖ *intr* hacer ademanes, hacer gestos

get [gɛt] *v* (*pret* **got** [gɑt]; *pp* **got** o **gotten** ['gɑtən]; *ger* **getting**) *tr* conseguir, obtener; recibir; ir por, buscar; tomar (*p.ej.*, *un billete*); alcanzar; encontrar, hallar; hacer (*p.ej.*, *la comida*); resolver (*un problema*); aprender de memoria; captar (*una estación emisora*); **to get across** hacer aceptar; hacer comprender; **to get back** recobrar; **to get down** descolgar; (*to swallow*) tragar; **to get off** quitar (*p.ej.*, *una mancha*); **to get someone to** + *inf* lograr que alguien + *subj*; **to get** + *pp* hacer + *inf*; **to have got** (coll) tener; **to have got to** + *inf* (coll) tener que + *inf* ‖ *intr* (*to become*) hacerse, ponerse, volverse; (*to arrive*) llegar; **get up!** (*to an animal*) ¡arre!; **to get about** estar levantado (*un convaleciente*); **to get along** seguir andando; irse; ir tirando; tener éxito; llevarse bien; **to get along in years** ponerse viejo; **to get along with** congeniar con; **to get angry** enfadarse; **to get around** divulgarse; salir mucho, ir a todas partes; eludir; manejar (*a una persona*); **to get away** conseguir marcharse; evadirse; **to get away with** llevarse, escaparse con; (coll) hacer impunemente; **to get back** volver, regresar; **to get back at** (coll) desquitarse con; **to get behind** quedarse atrás; apoyar, abogar por; **to get by** lograr pasar; (*to manage to shift*) (coll) arreglárselas; **to get going** ponerse en marcha; **to get in** entrar; volver a casa; llegar (*un tren*); **to get in with** llegar a ser amigo de; **to get married** casarse; **to get off** apearse; marcharse; **to get old** envejecer; **to get on** subir; llevarse bien; **to get out** salir, marcharse, divulgarse; **to get out of** bajar de (*un coche*); librarse de; perder (*la paciencia*); **to get out of the way** quitarse de en medio; **to get run over** ser atropellado; **to get through** pasar por entre; terminar; **to get to be** llegar a ser; **to get under way** ponerse en camino; **to get up** levantarse; **to not get over it** (coll) no volver de su asombro

get'a•way' *s* escapatoria, escape *m;* (*of an automobile*) arranque *m*

get'-to•geth'er *s* reunión, tertulia

get'-up' *s* (coll) disposición, presentación; (coll) atavío, traje *m*

gewgaw ['gjugɔ] *adj* cursi, charro, chillón ‖ *s* fruslería, chuchería; adorno, charro

geyser ['gaɪzər] *s* géiser *m* ‖ ['gizər] *s* (Brit) calentador *m* de agua

ghast•ly ['gæstli] o ['gɑstli] *adj* (*comp* **-lier;** *super* **-liest**) cadavérico, espectral; espantoso, horrible

Ghent [gɛnt] *s* Gante

gherkin ['gʌrkɪn] *s* pepinillo

ghet•to ['gɛto] *s* (*pl* **-tos**) ghetto

ghost [gost] *s* espectro, fantasma *m;* (telv) fantasma *m;* **not a ghost of a** ni sombra de; **to give up the ghost** entregar el alma, rendir el alma

ghost•ly ['gostli] *adj* (*comp* **-lier;** *super* **-liest**) espectral

ghost story *s* cuento de fantasmas

ghost writer *s* colaborador anónimo, escritor anónimo de obras firmadas por otra persona

ghoul [gul] *s* demonio que se alimenta de cadáveres; ladrón *m* de tumbas; (*person who revels in horrible things*) vampiro

ghoulish ['gulɪʃ] *adj* vampírico, horrible

G.H.Q. *abbr* **General Headquarters**

GI ['dʒi'aɪ] *s* (*pl* **GI's**) (coll) soldado raso (*del ejército norteamericano*)

giant ['dʒaɪ•ənt] *adj* & *s* gigante *m*

giantess ['dʒaɪ•əntɪs] *s* giganta

gibberish ['dʒɪbərɪʃ] o ['gɪbərɪʃ] *s* guirigay *m*

gibbet ['dʒɪbɪt] *s* horca ‖ *tr* ahorcar; poner a la vergüenza

gibe [dʒaɪb] *s* remoque *m*, mofa ‖ *intr* mofarse; **to gibe at** mofarse de

giblets ['dʒɪblɪts] *spl* menudillos

giddiness ['gɪdɪnɪs] *s* vértigo, vahído; falta de juicio

gid•dy ['gɪdi] *adj* (*comp* **-dier;** *super* **-diest**) vertiginoso; mareado; casquivano, ligero de cascos

Gideon ['gɪdɪ•ən] *s* (Bib) Gedeón *m*

gift [gɪft] *s* regalo; (*natural ability*) don *m*, dote *f*, prenda

gifted ['gɪftɪd] *adj* talentoso; muy inteligente

gift horse *s* —**never look a gift horse in the mouth** a caballo regalado no se le mira el diente

gift of gab *s* (coll) facundia, labia

gift shop *s* comercio de objetos de regalo, tienda de regalos

gift'wrap' *v* (*pret* & *pp* **-wrapped;** *ger* **-wrapping**) *tr* envolver en paquete regalo

gigantic [dʒaɪ'gæntɪk] *adj* gigantesco

giggle ['gɪgəl] *s* risita, risa ahogada, retozo de la risa ‖ *intr* reírse bobamente

ge
gi

gigo·lo ['dʒɪgə ,lo] s (pl **-los**) acompañante m profesional de mujeres; (man supported by a woman) mantenido

gild [gɪld] v (pret & pp **gilded** o **gilt** [gɪlt]) tr dorar

gilding ['gɪldɪŋ] s dorado

gill [gɪl] s (of fish) agalla; (of cock) barba ‖ [dʒɪl] s cuarta parte de una pinta

gillyflower ['dʒɪlɪ,flaʊ·ər] s alhelí m

gilt [gɪlt] adj & s dorado

gilt-edged ['gɪlt,ɛdʒd] adj de toda confianza, de lo mejor que hay

gilt'head' s dorada

gimcrack ['dʒɪm ,kræk] adj de oropel ‖ s chuchería

gimlet ['gɪmlɪt] s barrena de mano

gimmick ['gɪmɪk] s (slang) adminículo; (slang) adminículo mágico

gin [dʒɪn] s (alcoholic liquor) ginebra; desmotadera de algodón; trampa; (fish trap) garlito; torno de izar ‖ v (pret & pp **ginned; **ger **ginning**) tr desmotar

gin fizz s ginebra con gaseosa

ginger ['dʒɪndʒər] s jenjibre m; (coll) energía, viveza

ginger ale s cerveza de jengibre gaseosa

gin'ger·bread' s pan m de jengibre; adorno charro

gingerly ['dʒɪndʒərli] adj cauteloso, cuidadoso ‖ adv cautelosamente

gin'ger·snap' s galletita de jengibre

gingham ['gɪŋəm] s guinga

giraffe [dʒɪ'ræf] s jirafa

girandole ['dʒɪrən,dol] s girándula

gird [gʌrd] v (pret & pp **girt** [gʌrt] o **girded**) tr ceñir; (to equip) dotar; (to prepare) aprestar; (to surround, hem in) rodear, encerrar

girder ['gʌrdər] s viga, trabe f

girdle ['gʌrdəl] s faja; corsé pequeño ‖ tr ceñir; circundar, rodear

girl [gʌrl] s muchacha, niña, chica; (servant) moza

girl friend s (coll) amiguita

girlhood ['gʌrlhʊd] s muchachez f; juventud femenina

girlish [gʌrlɪʃ] adj de muchacha; juvenil

girl scout s niña exploradora

girth [gʌrθ] s (band) cincha; (waistband) pretina; circunferencia

gist [dʒɪst] s esencia

give [gɪv] s elasticidad ‖ v (pret **gave** [gev]; pp **given** ['gɪvən] tr dar; ocasionar (molestia, trabajo, etc.); representar (una obra dramática); (lessons) impartir; pronunciar (un discurso); **to give away** dar de balde; revelar; llevar (a la novia); (coll) traicionar; **to give back** devolver; **to give forth** despedir (p.ej. olores); **to give oneself up** entregarse; **to give up** abandonar, dejar (un empleo); renunciar ‖ intr dar; dar de sí; romperse (p.ej., una cuerda); **to give in** ceder, rendirse; **to give out** agotarse; no poder más; **to give up** darse por vencido

give'-and-take' s concesiones mutuas; conversación sazonada de burlas

give'a·way' s (coll) revelación involuntaria; (coll) traición; (e.g., in checkers) (coll) ganapierde m & f

given ['gɪvən] adj dado; (math) conocido; **given that** dado que, suponiendo que

given name s nombre m de pila

giver ['gɪvər] s dador m, donador m

gizzard ['gɪzərd] s molleja

glacial ['gleʃəl] adj glacial

glacier ['gleʃər] s glaciar m, helero

glad [glæd] adj (comp **gladder**; super **gladdest**) alegre, contento; **to be glad (to)** alegrarse (de)

gladden ['glædən] tr alegrar

glade [gled] s claro, claro herboso (en un bosque)

glad hand s (coll) acogida efusiva

gladiola [,glædɪ'olə] s estoque m

gladly ['glædli] adv alegremente; de buena gana, con mucho gusto

gladness ['glædnɪs] s alegría, regocijo

glad rags spl (slang) trapitos de cristianar; (slang) vestido de etiqueta

glamorous ['glæmərəs] adj fascinador, elegante

glamour ['glæmər] s fascinación, elegancia, hechizo

glamour girl s belleza exótica

glance [glæns] s ojeada, vistazo, golpe m de vista; **at a glance** de un vistazo; **at first glance** a primera vista ‖ intr lanzar una mirada; **to glance at** lanzar una mirada a; examinar de paso; **to glance off** desviarse de soslayo; desviarse de, al chocar; **to glance over** mirar por encima

gland [glænd] s glándula

glanders ['glændərz] spl muermo

glandulous ['glændʒələs] adj glanduloso

glare [glɛr] s fulgor m deslumbrante, luz intensa; mirada feroz, mirada de indignación ‖ intr relumbrar; lanzar miradas feroces; **to glare at** echar una mirada feroz a

glaring '['glɛrɪŋ] adj deslumbrante, relumbrante; (look) feroz, penetrante; manifiesto, que salta a la vista

glass [glæs] s vidrio, cristal m; (tumbler) vaso, copa; (mirror) espejo; (glassware) vajilla de cristal; **glasses** anteojos

glass blower ['blo·ər] s soplador m de vidrio, vidriero

glass case s vitrina

glass cutter s cortavidrios m

glass door s puerta vidriera

glassful ['glæsfʊl] s vaso

glass'house' s invernadero; (fig) tejado de vidrio

glassine [glæ'sin] s papel m cristal

glass'ware' s cristalía, vajilla de vidrio

glass wool s cristal hilado

glass'works' s cristalería vidriería

glass'work'er s vidriero

glass·y ['glæsi] adj (comp **-ier;** super **-iest**) vidrioso

glaze [glez] s vidriado, esmalte m; (of ice) capa resbaladiza ‖ tr vidriar, esmaltar; garapiñar (golosinas)

glazier ['gleʒər] s vidriero

gleam [glim] *s* destello, rayo de luz; luz *f* tenue; (*of hope*) rayo ‖ *intr* destellar; brillar con luz tenue

glean [glin] *tr* espigar; (*to gather bit by bit, e.g., out of books*) espigar

glee [gli] *s* alegría, regocijo

glee club *s* orfeón *m*

glib [glɪb] *adj* (*comp* **glibber;** *super* **glibbest**) locuaz; (*tongue*) suelto; fácil e insincero

glide [glaɪd] *s* deslizamiento; (aer) vuelo sin motor, planeo; (mus) ligadura ‖ *intr* deslizarse; (aer) volar sin motor, planear; **to glide along** pasar suavemente

glider [ˈglaɪdər] *s* (aer) planeador *m*, deslizador *m*

glimmer [ˈglɪmər] *s* luz *f* tenue; (*faint perception*) vislumbre *f* ‖ *intr* brillar con luz tenue; (*to appear faintly*) vislumbrarse

glimmering [ˈglɪmərɪŋ] *adj* tenue, trémulo ‖ *s* luz *f* tenue; vislumbre *f*

glimpse [glɪmps] *s* vislumbre *f;* **to catch a glimpse of** entrever, vislumbrar ‖ *tr* vislumbrar

glint [glɪnt] *s* destello, rayo ‖ *intr* destellar

glisten [ˈglɪsən] *s* centelleo ‖ *intr* centellear

glitter [ˈglɪtər] *s* resplandor *m*, brillo ‖ *intr* resplandecer, brillar

gloaming [ˈglomɪŋ] *s* crepúsculo vespertino

gloat [glot] *intr* relamerse; **to gloat over** mirar con satisfacción maligna

globe [glob] *s* globo

globetrotter [ˈglob,trɑtər] *s* trotamundos *m*

globule [ˈglɑbjul] *s* glóbulo

glockenspiel [ˈglɑkən,spil] *s* juego de timbres, órgano de campanas

gloom [glum] *s* lobreguez *f* tinieblas, obscuridad; abatimiento, tristeza; aspecto abatido

gloom·y [ˈglumi] *adj* (*comp* **-ier;** *super* **-iest**) (*dark; sad*) lóbrego; pesimista

glori·fy [ˈglorɪ,faɪ] *v* (*pret & pp* **-fied**) *tr* glorificar; (*to enhance*) realzar

glorious [ˈglorɪ·əs] *adj* glorioso; espléndido, magnífico; (coll) alegre

glo·ry [ˈglori] *s* (*pl* **-ries**) gloria; **to go to glory** ganar la gloria; (slang) fracasar ‖ *v* (*pret & pp* **-ried**) *intr* gloriarse

gloss [glɑs] *s* brillo, lustre *m*; (*note, commentary*) glosa; glosario ‖ *tr* (*to annotate*) glosar; lustrar, satinar; **to gloss over** disculpar, paliar

glossa·ry [ˈglɑsəri] *s* (*pl* **-ries**) glosario

gloss·y [ˈglɑsi] *adj* (*comp* **-ier;** *super* **-iest**) brillante, lustroso; (*silk*) joyante

glottal [ˈglɑtəl] *adj* glótico

glove [glʌv] *s* guante *m*

glove compartment *s* portaguantes *m*

glove stretcher *s* ensanchador *m*, juanas

glow [glo] *s* (*light of incandescence*) resplandor *m*; (*e.g., of sunset*) brillo, esplendor *m;* sensación de calor; color *m* en las mejillas ‖ *intr* brillar sin llama; estar encendido (*el rostro, el cielo*); estar muy animado

glower [ˈglau·ər] *s* ceño, mirada ceñuda ‖ *intr* mirar con ceño

glowing [ˈglo·ɪŋ] *adj* ardiente, encendido; radiante; entusiasta, elogioso

glow'worm' *s* gusano de luz, luciérnaga

glucose [ˈglukos] *s* glucosa

glue [glu] *s* cola; pegapega ‖ *tr* encolar; pegar fuertemente

glue pot *s* cazo de cola

gluey [ˈglu·i] *adj* (*comp* **gluier;** *super* **gluiest**) pegajoso; (*smeared with glue*) encolado

glug [glʌg] *s* gluglú *m* ‖ *v* (*pret & pp* **glugged;** *ger* **glugging**) *intr* hacer gluglú (*el agua*)

glum [glʌm] *adj* (*comp* **glummer;** *super* **glummest**) hosco

glut [glʌt] *s* abundancia, gran acopio; exceso; **to be a glut on the market** abarrotarse ‖ *v* (*pret & pp* **glutted;** *ger* **glutting**) *tr* hartar, saciar; inundar (*el mercado*); obstruir

glutton [ˈglʌtən] *adj & s* glotón *m*

gluttonous [ˈglʌtənəs] *adj* glotón

glutton·y [ˈglʌtəni] *s* (*pl* **-ies**) glotonería, gula

glycerine [ˈglɪsərɪn] *s* glicerina

G.M. *abbr* **general manager, Grand Master**

G-man [ˈdʒi,mæn] *s* (*pl* **-men** [,mɛn]) (coll) agente *m* de la policía federal

G.M.T. *abbr* **Greenwich mean time**

gnarl [nɑrl] *s* nudo ‖ *tr* torcer ‖ *intr* gruñir

gnarled [nɑrld] *adj* nudoso, retorcido

gnash [næʃ] *tr* hacer rechinar (*los dientes*) ‖ *intr* hacer rechinar los dientes

gnat [næt] *s* jején *m*

gnaw [nɔ] *tr* roer; practicar (*un agujero*) royendo

gnome [nom] *s* gnomo

go [go] *s* (*pl* **goes**) ida; (coll) energía, ímpetu *m;* (coll) boga; (coll) ensayo; (*for traffic*) paso libre; **it's a go** (coll) es un trato hecho; **it's all the go** (coll) hace furor; **it's no go** (coll) es imposible; **on the go** (coll) en continuo movimiento; **to make a go of** (coll) lograr éxito en ‖ *v* (*pret* **went** [wɛnt]; *pp* **gone** [gɔn] o [gɑn]) *tr* (coll) soportar, tolerar; **to go it alone** obrar sin ayuda ‖ *intr* ir; (*to work, operate*) funcionar, marchar; andar (*p.ej., desnudo*); volverse (*p.ej., loco*); **going, going, gone!** ¡vendo, vendo, vendí!; **so it goes** así va el mundo; **to be going to** + *inf* ir a + *inf*; **to be gone** haber ido; haberse agotado; haber dejado de ser; **to go against** ir en contra de; **to go ahead** seguir adelante; **to go away** irse, marcharse; **to go back** volver; **to go by** pasar por; guiarse por; atenerse a; **to go down** bajar; hundirse (*un buque*); **to go fishing** ir de pesca; **to go for** ir por; **to go get** ir por, ir a buscar; **to go house hunting** ir a buscar casa; **to go hunting** ir de caza; **to go in** entrar; entrar en; (*to fit in*) caber en; **to go in for** dedicarse a, interesarse por; **to go into** entrar en; investigar; (aut) poner (*p.ej., primera*); **to go in with** asociarse con; **to go off** irse, marcharse; llevarse a cabo; estallar (*p.ej., una bomba*); dispararse (*un fusil*); **to go on** seguir adelante; ir tirando; **to go on** + *ger* seguir + *ger;* **to go on with** continuar; **to

go out salir; pasar de moda; apagarse (*un fuego, una luz*); declararse en huelga; (*for entertainment, etc.*) salir; **to go over** tener éxito; releer; examinar, revisar; pasar por encima de; **to go over to** pasarse a las filas de; **to go through** pasar por; llegar al fin de; agotar (*una fortuna*); **to go with** ir con, acompañar; salir con (*una muchacha*); hacer juego con; **to go without** andarse sin, pasarse sin

goad [god] *s* aguijada, aguijón *m* ‖ *tr* aguijonear; (SAm) espuelar

go′-a•head′ *adj* (coll) emprendedor ‖ *s* (coll) señal *f* para seguir adelante, luz *f* verde

goal [gol] *s* meta; (*in football*) gol *m*

goal′keep′er *s* guardameta *m*, portero

goal line *s* raya de la meta

goal post *s* poste *m* de la meta

goat [got] *s* cabra; (*male goat*) macho cabrío; (coll) víctima inocente; **to be the goat** (slang) pagar el pato; **to get the goat of** (slang) tomar el pelo a; **to ride the goat** (coll) ser iniciado en una sociedad secreta

goatee (go′ti) *s* perilla

goat′herd′ *s* cabrero

goat′skin′ *s* piel *f* de cabra

goat′suck′er *s* chotacabras *m*

gob [gab] *s* (coll) masa informe y pequeña; (coll) marinero de guerra

gobble [′gabəl] *s* gluglú *m* ‖ *tr* engullir; **to gobble up** engullirse ávidamente; (coll) asir de repente, apoderarse ávidamente de ‖ *intr* engullir; gluglutear, gorgonear (*el pavo*)

gobbledegook [′gabəldɪ‚guk] *s* (coll) lenguaje obscuro e incomprensible, galimatías *m*

go′-be•tween′ *s* (*intermediary*) medianero; (*in promoting marriages*) casamentero; (*in shady love affairs*) alcahuete *m*, alcahueta

goblet [′gablɪt] *s* copa

goblin [′gablɪn] *s* duende *m*, trasgo

go′-by′ *s* (coll) desaire *m;* **to give someone the go-by** (coll) negarse al trato de alguien

go′cart′ *s* andaderas; cochecito para niños; carruaje ligero

god [gad] *s* dios *m;* **God forbid** no lo quiera Dios; **God grant** permita Dios; **God willing** Dios mediante

god′child′ *s* (*pl* **chil′dren**) ahijado, ahijada

god′daugh′ter *s* ahijada

goddess [′gadɪs] *s* diosa

god′fa′ther *s* padrino

God′-fear′ing *adj* timorato; devoto, pío

God′for•sak′en *adj* dejado de la mano de Dios; (coll) desolado, desierto

god′head′ *s* divinidad ‖ **Godhead** *s* Dios *m*

godless [′gadlɪs] *adj* infiel, impío; desalmado, malvado

god•ly [′gadli] *adj* (*comp* **-lier;** *super* **-liest**) devoto, pío

god′moth′er *s* madrina

God's acre *s* campo santo

god′send′ *s* cosa llovida del cielo, bendición

god′son′ *s* ahijado

God′speed′ *s* bienandanza, buena suerte, buen viaje *m*

go′-get′ter *s* (slang) buscavidas *mf*, persona emprendedora

goggle [′gagəl] *intr* volver los ojos; abrir los ojos desmesuradamente

goggle-eyed [′gagəl‚aɪd] *adj* de ojos saltones

goggleṣ [′gagəlz] *spl* anteojos de camino, gafas contra el polvo

going [′go•ɪŋ] *adj* en marcha, funcionando; **going on** casi, p.ej., **it is going on nine o'clock** son casi las nueve ‖ *s* ida, partida

going concern *s* empresa que marcha

goings on *spl* actividades; bulla, jarana

goiter [′gɔɪtər] *s* bocio

gold [gold] *adj* áureo, de oro; dorado ‖ *s* oro

gold′beat′er *s* batidor *m* de oro, batihoja *m*

goldbeater's skin *s* venza

gold brick *s* — **to sell a gold brick** (coll) vender gato por liebre

gold′crest′ *s* reyezuelo moñudo

gold digger [′dɪgər] *s* (slang) extractora de oro

golden [′goldən] *adj* áureo, de oro; (*gilt*) dorado; (*hair*) rubio; excelente, favorable, floreciente

golden age *s* edad de oro, siglo de oro

golden calf *s* becerro de oro

Golden Fleece *s* vellocino de oro

golden mean *s* justo medio

golden plover *s* chorlito

gold′en•rod′ *s* vara de oro, vara de San José

golden rule *s* regla de la caridad cristiana

golden wedding *s* bodas de oro

gold-filled [′gold‚fɪld] *adj* empastado en oro

gold′finch′ *s* jilguero, pintacilgo

gold′fish′ *s* carpa dorada, pez *m* de color

goldilocks [′goldɪ‚laks] *s* rubiales *mf*

gold leaf *s* pan *m* de oro

gold mine *s* mina de oro; **to strike a gold mine** (fig) encontrar una mina

gold plate *s* vajilla de oro

gold′-plate′ *tr* dorar

gold′smith′ *s* orfebre *m*

gold standard *s* patrón *m* oro

golf [galf] *s* golf *m* ‖ *intr* jugar al golf

golf club *s* palo de golf; asociación de jugadores de golf

golfer [′galfər] *s* golfista *mf*

golf links *spl* campo de golf

Golgotha [′galgəθə] *s* el Gólgota

gondola [′gandələ] *s* góndola

gondolier [‚gandə′lɪr] *s* gondolero

gone [gɔn] o [gan] *adj* agotado; arruinado; desaparecido; muerto; **gone on** (coll) enamorado de

gong [gɔŋ] o [gaŋ] *s* batintín *m*

gonorrhea [‚ganə′ri•ə] *s* gonorrea

goo [gu] *s* (slang) substancia pegajosa

good [gʊd] *adj* (*comp* **better;** *super* **best**) bueno; **good and . . .** (coll) muy, p.ej., **good and cheap** muy barato; **good for** bueno para; capaz de hacer; capaz de pagar; capaz de vivir (*cierto tiempo*); **to be good at** tener talento para; **to be no good** (coll) no servir para nada; (coll) ser un perdido; **to make good** tener éxito; cumplir (*sus promesas*); pagar (*una deuda*); responder de (*los daños*) ‖ *s* bien *m*, provecho, utilidad; **for good** para siempre; **for good and all** de una vez para siempre; **goods** efectos; géneros, mercancías; **the good** lo bueno; los buenos; **to catch with the goods** (slang) coger en flagrante; **to deliver the goods** (slang) cumplir lo prometido; **to do good** hacer el bien; dar salud o fuerzas a; **to the good** de sobra, en el haber; **what is the good of . . . ?** ¿para qué sirve . . . ?

good afternoon s buenas tardes

good'by' o **good'bye's** adiós m ‖ interj ¡adiós!

good day s buenos días

good evening s buenas noches, buenas tardes

good fellow s (coll) buen chico, buen sujeto

good fellowship s compañerismo

good'-for-noth'ing adj inútil, sin valor ‖ s pelafustán m perdido

Good Friday s Viernes santo

good graces spl favor m, estimación

good-hearted ['gʊd'hɑrtɪd] adj de buen corazón

good-humored ['gʊd'jumərd] adj de buen humor; afable

good-looking ['gʊd'lʊkɪŋ] adj guapo, bien parecido

good looks spl hermosura, guapeza

good•ly ['gʊdli] adj (comp -lier; super -liest) considerable; bien parecido, hermoso; bueno, excelente

good morning s buenos días

good-natured ['gʊd'netʃərd] adj bonachón, afable

Good Neighbor Policy s política del buen vecino

goodness ['gʊdnɪs] s bondad; **for goodness' sake!** ¡por Dios!; **goodness knows!** ¡quién sabe! ‖ interj ¡válgame Dios!

good night s buenas noches

good sense s buen sentido, sensatez f

good-sized ['gʊd'saɪzd] adj bastante grande, de buen tamaño

good speed s adiós m y buena suerte

good-tempered ['gʊd'tɛmpərd] adj de natural apacible

good time s rato agradable; **to have a good time** divertirse; **to make good time** ir a buen paso; llegar en poco tiempo

good turn s favor m, servicio

good way s buen trecho

good will s buena voluntad; (com) buen nombre m, clientela

good•y ['gʊdi] adj (coll) beatuco, santurrón ‖ s (pl -ies) (coll) golosina ‖ interj (coll) ¡qué bien!, ¡qué alegría!

gooey ['gu•i] adj (comp gooier; super gooiest) (slang) pegajoso, fangoso

goof [guf] s (slang) tonto ‖ tr & intr (slang) chapucear ‖ intr — **to goof off** farrear

goof•y ['gufi] adj (comp -ier; super -iest) (slang) tonto, mentecato

goon (gun) s (roughneck) (coll) gamberro, canalla m; (coll) terrorista m de alquiler; (slang) estúpido

goose [gus] s (pl geese [gis]) ánsar m, ganso, oca; **the goose hangs high** todo va a pedir

de boca; **to cook one's goose** malbaratarle a uno los planes; **to kill the goose that lays the golden eggs** matar la gallina de los huevos de oro ‖ s (pl gooses) plancha de sastre

goose'ber'ry s (pl -ries) (plant) grosellero silvestre; (fruit) grosella silvestre

goose egg s huevo de oca; (slang) cero

goose flesh s carne f de gallina

goose'neck' s cuello de cisne; (naut) gancho de botalones

goose pimples spl carne f de gallina

goose step s (mil) paso de ganso

G.O.P. abbr **Grand Old Party**

gopher ['gofər] s ardilla de tierra, ardillón m; (Geomys) tuza

Gordian knot ['gɔrdɪ•ən] s nudo gordiano; **to cut the Gordian knot** cortar el nudo gordiano

gore [gor] s sangre derramada, sangre cuajada; (insert in a piece of cloth) cuchillo, nesga ‖ tr (to pierce with a horn) acornar; poner cuchillo o nesga a; nesgar

gorge [gɔrdʒ] s garganta, desfiladero; (in a river) atasco de hielo ‖ tr atiborrar ‖ intr atiborrarse

gorgeous ['gɔrdʒəs] adj primoroso, brillante, magnífico, suntuoso

gorilla [gə'rɪlə] s gorila

gorse [gɔrs] s aulaga

gor•y ['gori] adj (comp -ier; super -iest) ensangrentado, sangriento

gosh [gɑʃ] interj ¡caramba!

goshawk ['gɑs,hɔk] s azor m

gospel ['gɑspəl] s evangelio ‖ **Gospel** s Evangelio

gospel truth s evangelio, pura verdad

gossamer ['gɑsəmər] s telaraña flotante; gasa sutilísima; tela impermeable muy delgada; impermeable m de tela muy delgada

gossip ['gɑsɪp] s chismes m; (person) chismoso, bocaza; **piece of gossip** chisme m ‖ intr chismear

gossip column s mentidero

gossip columnist s gacetillero, cronista mf social

gossipy ['gɑsɪpi] adj chismoso

Goth [gɑθ] s godo; (fig) bárbaro

Gothic ['gɑθɪk] adj & s gótico

gouge [gaʊdʒ] s gubia; (cut made with a gouge) muesca; (coll) estafa ‖ tr excavar con gubia; (coll) estafar

goulash ['gulɑʃ] s puchero húngaro

gourd [gord] o [gʊrd] s calabaza

gourmand ['gʊrmənd] s gastrónomo; glotón m, goloso

gourmet ['gʊrme] s gastrónomo delicado

gout [gaʊt] s gota

gout•y [gaʊti] adj (comp -ier; super -iest) gotoso

gov. abbr **governor, government**

govern ['gʌvərn] tr gobernar; (gram) regir ‖ intr gobernar

governess ['gʌvərnɪs] s aya, institutriz f

government ['gʌvərnmənt] s gobierno; (gram) régimen m

go
go

governmental [ˌgʌvərn'mɛntəl] *adj* gubernamental, gubernativo
government in exile *s* gobierno exilado
governor ['gʌvərnər] *s* gobernador *m;* (*of a jail, castle, etc.*) alcaide *m;* (mach) regulador *m*
governorship ['gʌvərnərˌʃɪp] *s* gobierno
govt. *abbr* **government**
gown [gaʊn] *s* (*of a woman*) vestido; (*of a professor, judge, etc.*) toga; (*of a priest*) traje *m* talar; (*dressing gown*) bata, peinador *m;* (nightgown) camisa de dormir
G.P.O. *abbr* **General Post Office, Government Printing Office**
gr. *abbr* **gram, grams, grain, grains, gross**
grab [græb] *s* asimiento, presa; (coll) robo ‖ *v* (*pret* & *pp* **grabbed;** *ger* **grabbing**) *tr* asir, agarrar; arrebatar ‖ *intr* — **to grab at** tratar de asir
grace [gres] *s* (*charm; favor; pardon*) gracia; (*prayer at table*) benedícite *m;* (*extension of time*) demora; **to be in the good graces of** gozar del favor de; **to say grace** rezar el benedícite; **with good grace** de buen talante ‖ *tr* adornar, engalanar; favorecer
graceful ['gresfəl] *adj* agraciado, gracioso
grace note *s* apoyatura, nota de adorno
gracious ['greʃəs] *adj* graciable, gracioso; misericordioso ‖ *interj* ¡válgame Dios!
grackle ['grækəl] *s* (*myna*) estornino de los pastores; (*purple grackle*) quiscal *m*
grad. *abbr* **graduate**
gradation [gre'deʃən] *s* (*gradual change*) paso gradual; (*arrangement in grades*) graduación; (*step in a series*) paso, grado
grade [gred] *s* grado; (*slope*) pendiente *f;* (*mark for work in class*) calificación, nota; **to make the grade** lograr subir la cuesta; vencer los obstáculos ‖ *tr* graduar, calificar; dar nota a (*un alumno*); explanar, nivelar
grade crossing *s* (rr) paso a nivel, cruce *m* a nivel
grade school *s* escuela elemental
gradient ['gredɪˑənt] *adj* pendiente ‖ *s* pendiente *f;* (phys) gradiente *m*
gradual ['grædʒʊˑəl] *adj* paulatino
gradually [grædʒʊˑəli] *adv* paulatinamente, gradualmente, poco a poco
graduate ['grædʒʊˑɪt] *adj* graduado ‖ *s* graduado; (*candidate for a degree*) graduando; vasija graduada ‖ ['grædʒʊˌet] *tr* graduar ‖ *intr* graduarse
graduate school *s* facultad de altos estudios
graduate student *s* estudiante graduado
graduate work *s* altos estudios
graduation [ˌgrædʒʊ'eʃən] *s* graduación, ceremonia de graduación
graft [græft] *s* (hort & surg) injerto; (coll) soborno político, ganancia ilegal ‖ *tr* & *intr* (hort & surg) injertar; (coll) malversar
graham bread ['greˑəm] *s* pan *m* integral
graham flour *s* harina de trigo sin cerner
grain [gren] *s* (*small seed; tiny particle of sand, etc.; small unit of weight*) grano; (*cereal seeds*) granos; (*in stone*) vena; (*in wood*) fibra; **against the grain** a contrapelo

‖ *tr* granear (*la pólvora; una piedra litográfica*); crispir, vetear (*la madera*); granular (*una piel*)
grain elevator *s* elevador *m* de granos; (*tall building where grain is stored*) depósito de cereales
grain'field' *s* sembrado
graining ['grenɪŋ] *s* veteado
gram [græm] *s* gramo
grammar ['græmər] *s* gramática
grammarian [grə'mɛrɪˑən] *s* gramático
grammar school *s* escuela pública elemental
grammatical [grə'mætɪkəl] *adj* gramático
gramophone ['græməˌfon] *s* (trademark) gramófono
grana•ry ['grænəri] *s* (*pl* **-ries**) granero
grand [grænd] *adj* espléndido, grandioso; importante, principal
grand'aunt' *s* tía abuela
grand'child' *s* (*pl* **chil'dren**) nieto, nieta
grand'daugh'ter *s* nieta
grand duchess *s* gran duquesa
grand duchy *s* gran ducado
grand duke *s* gran duque *m*
grandee [græn'di] *s* grande *m* de España
grandeur ['grændʒər] o ['grændʒʊr] *s* grandeza, magnificencia
grand'fa'ther *s* abuelo; (*forefather*) antepasado
grandfather's clock *s* reloj *m* de caja
grandiose ['grændɪˌos] *adj* grandioso; hinchado, pomposo
grand jury *s* jurado de acusación
grand larceny *s* hurto mayor
grand lodge *s* gran oriente *m*
grandma ['grænd ˌma], ['græm ˌma], o ['græmə] *s* (coll) abuela, abuelita
grand'moth'er *s* abuela
grand'neph'ew *s* resobrino
grand'niece *s* resobrina
grand opera *s* ópera seria
grandpa ['grænd ˌpa], ['græn ˌpa], o ['græmˌpa] *s* (coll) abuelo, abuelito
grand'par'ent *s* abuelo, abuela
grand piano *s* piano de cola
grand slam *s* (bridge) bola
grand'son' *s* nieto
grand'stand' *s* gradería cubierta, tribuna
grand strategy *s* alta estrategia
grand total *s* gran total *m*, suma de totales
grand'un'cle *s* tío abuelo
grand vizier *s* gran visir *m*
grange [grendʒ] *s* (*farm with barns, etc.*) granja; (*organization of farmers*) cámara agrícola
granite ['grænɪt] *s* granito
grant [grænt] o [grant] *s* concesión; donación, subvención; traspaso de propiedad ‖ *tr* conceder; dar (*permiso, perdón*); transferir (*bienes inmuebles*); **to take for granted** dar por sentado; tratar con indiferencia
grantee [græn'ti] o [gran'ti] *s* cesionario
grant'-in-aid' *s* (*pl* **grants-in-aid**) subvención concedida por el gobierno para obras de utilidad pública; pensión para estimular

conocimientos científicos, literarios, artísticos

grantor ['græn'tɔr] or [grɑn'tɔr] s cesionista *mf*, otorgante *mf*

grant winner s bequista *mf* (CAm, Cuba)

granular ['grænjələr] adj granular

granulate ['grænjə,let] tr granular ‖ intr granularse

granule ['grænjul] s gránulo

grape [grep] s (*fruit*) uva; (*vine*) vid *f*

grape arbor s parral *m*

grape'fruit' s (*fruit*) toronja; (*tree*) toronjo

grape hyacinth s sueldacostilla

grape juice s zumo de uva

grape'shot' s metralla

grape'vine' s vid *f*, parra; **by the grapevine** por vías secretas, por vías misteriosas

graph [græf] s (*diagram*) gráfica; (*gram*) grafía

graphic(al) ['græfɪk(əl)] adj gráfico

graphite ['græfaɪt] s grafito

graph paper s papel cuadriculado

grapnel ['græpnəl] s rebañadera; (*anchor*) rezón *m*

grapple ['græpəl] s asimiento, presa; lucha cuerpo a cuerpo ‖ tr asir, agarrar ‖ intr agarrarse; luchar a brazo partido; **to grapple with** luchar a brazo partido con; tratar de resolver

grappling iron s arpeo

grasp [græsp] s asimiento; (*power, reach*) poder *m*, alcance *m;* (fig) comprensión; **to have a good grasp of** saber a fondo; **within the grasp of** al alcance de ‖ tr (*with hand*) empuñar; (*to get control of*) apoderarse de; (fig) comprender ‖ intr — **to grasp at** tratar de asir; aceptar con avidez

grasping ['græspɪŋ] adj avaro, codicioso

grass ['græs] s hierba; (*pasture land*) pasto; (*lawn*) césped *m;* **to go to grass** ir a pacer; disfrutar de una temporada de descanso; gastarse, arruinarse; morir; **to not let the grass grow under one's feet** no dormirse en las pajas

grass court s cancha de césped

grass'hop'per s saltamontes *m*

grass pea s almorta, guija

grass'-roots' adj de la gente común

grass seed s semilla de césped

grass widow s viuda de paja, viuda de marido vivo

grass•y ['græsi] adj (*comp* -ier; *super* -iest) herboso

grate [gret] s (*at a window*) reja; (*for cooking*) parrilla ‖ tr (*to put a grate on*) enrejar; rallar (*p.ej., queso*) ‖ intr crujir, rechinar; **to grate on** (fig) rallar

grateful ['gretfəl] adj agradecido; (*pleasing*) agradable

grater ['gretər] s rallador *m*

grati•fy ['græti,fai] v (*pret & pp* -fied) tr complacer, gratificar

gratifying ['græti,fai•ɪŋ] adj grato, satisfactorio

grating ['gretɪŋ] adj áspero, irritante; (*sound*) chirriante ‖ s enrejado

gratis ['gretɪs] o ['grætɪs] adj gracioso, gratuito ‖ adv gratis, de balde

gratitude ['græti,tjud] s gratitud, reconocimiento

gratuitous [grə'tju•ɪtəs] o [grə'tu•ɪtəs] adj gratuito

gratui•ty [grə'tju•ɪti] s (*pl* -ties) propina; feria (CAm, Mex)

grave [grev] adj (*serious, dangerous; important*) grave; solemne; (*sound; accent*) grave ‖ s sepulcro, sepultura; **to have one foot in the grave** estar con un pie en la sepultura

gravedigger ['grev ,dɪgər] s enterrador *m*, sepulturero, entierramuertos *m*

gravel ['grævəl] s grava, cascajo

graven image ['grevən] s ídolo

grave'stone' s lápida sepulcral

grave'yard' s camposanto

gravitate ['grævi,tet] intr gravitar; ser atraído

gravitation [,grævi'te/ən] s gravitación

gravi•ty ['græviti] s (*pl* -ties) gravedad

gravure [grə'vjur] s fotograbado

gra•vy ['grevi] s (*pl* -vies) (*juice from cooking meat*) jugo; (*sauce made with this juice*) salsa; (slang) ganga, breva

gravy dish s salsera

gray [gre] adj gris; (*gray-haired*) cano, canoso ‖ s gris *m;* traje *m* gris ‖ intr encanecer

gray'beard' s anciano, viejo

gray-haired ['gre,hɛrd] adj canoso

gray'hound' s galgo

grayish ['gre•ɪ/] adj grisáceo; (*person; hair*) entrecano

gray matter s substancia gris; (*intelligence*) (coll) materia gris

graze [grez] tr (*to touch lightly*) rozar; (*to scratch lightly in passing*) raspar; pacer (*la hierba*); apacentar (*el ganado*); (*to lead to the pasture*) pastar ‖ intr pacer, pastar

grease [gris] s grasa ‖ [gris] o [griz] tr engrasar; (slang) sobornar

grease cup [gris] s vaso de engrase

grease gun [gris] s engrasador *m* de pistón, jeringa de engrase, bomba de engrase

grease lift [gris] s puente *m* de engrase

grease paint [gris] s maquillaje *m*

grease pit [gris] s fosa de engrase

grease spot [gris] s lámpara, mancha de grasa

greas•y ['grisi] o ['grizi] adj (*comp* -ier; *super* -iest) grasiento, pringoso

great [gret] adj grande; (coll) excelente ‖ **the great** los grandes

great'-aunt' s tía abuela

Great Bear s Osa Mayor

Great Britain ['brɪtən] s la Gran Bretaña

great'coat' s gabán *m* de mucho abrigo

Great Dane s mastín *m* danés

Greater London s el Gran Londres

Greater New York s el Gran Nueva York

great'-grand'child' s (*pl* -chil'dren) bisnieto, bisnieta

great'-grand'daugh'ter s bisnieta

great'-grand'fa'ther s bisabuelo

great'-grand'moth'er s bisabuela

great'-grand'par'ent s bisabuelo, bisabuela

go
gr

great'-grand'son' s bisnieto
greatly ['gretli] adj grandemente
great'-neph'ew s resobrino
greatness ['gretnis] s grandeza
great'-niece' s resobrina
great'-un'cle s tío abuelo
Great War s Gran guerra
Grecian ['griʃən] adj & s griego
Greece [gris] s Grecia
greed [grid] s codicia, avaricia; (in eating and drinking) glotonería
greed•y ['gridi] adj (comp -ier; super -iest) codicioso, avaro; glotón
Greek [grik] adj & s griego
green [grin] adj verde; inexperto ‖ s verde m; (lawn) césped m; **greens** verduras
green'back' s (U.S.A.) billete m de banco (de dorso verde)
green corn s maíz tierno
green earth s verdacho
greener•y ['grinəri] s (pl -ies) (foliage) verdura; (hothouse) invernáculo
green-eyed ['grin,aid] adj de ojos verdes; celoso
green'gage' s ciruela claudia
green grasshopper s langostón m
green'gro'cer s verdulero
green'gro'cer•y s (pl -ies) verdulería
green'horn' s novato; (dupe) primo, inocentón m; papanatas m, isidro; colegial mf (Mex)
green'house' s invernáculo
greenish ['griniʃ] adj verdoso
Greenland ['grinlənd] s Groenlandia
greenness ['grinnis] s verdura, verdor m; falta de experiencia
green'room' s saloncillo; chismería de teatro
greensward ['grin,swɔrd] s césped m
green thumb s pulgares mpl verdes (don de criar plantas)
green vegetables spl verduras
green'wood' s bosque m verde, bosque frondoso
greet [grit] tr saludar; acoger, recibir; presentarse a (los ojos u los oídos de uno)
greeting ['gritiŋ] s saludo; acogida, recibimiento ‖ **greetings** interj ¡salud!
greeting card s tarjeta de buen deseo
gregarious [gri'geriəs] adj (living in the midst of others) gregario; (fond of the company of others) sociable
Gregorian [gri'gori•ən] adj gregoriano
grenade [gri'ned] s granada; (to put out fires) granada extintora
grenadier [,grenə'dir] s granadero
grenadine [,grenə'din] s granadina
grey [gre] adj, s & intr var de **gray**
grid [grid] s parrilla, rejilla; (electron) rejilla; (of a storage battery) (elec) rejilla
griddle ['gridəl] s plancha
grid'dle•cake' s tortada (de harina) a la plancha
grid'i'ron s parrilla; campo de fútbol
grid leak s (electron) resistencia de rejilla, escape m de rejilla

grief [grif] s aflicción, pesar m; (coll) desgracia, disgusto; **to come to grief** fracasar, arruinarse
grievance ['grivəns] s agravio, injusticia; despecho, disgusto; motivo de queja
grieve [griv] tr afligir, penar ‖ intr afligirse, apenarse; **to grieve over** añorar
grievous ['grivəs] adj doloroso, penoso; atroz, cruel; (deplorable) lastimoso
griffin ['grifin] s (myth) grifo
grill [gril] s parrilla ‖ tr emparrillar; someter (a un acusado) a un interrogatorio muy apremiante
grille [gril] s reja, verja; (of an automobile) parrilla, rejilla
grill'room' s parrilla
grim [grim] adj (comp **grimmer**; super **grimmest**) (fierce) cruel, feroz; (repellent) horrible, siniestro; (unyielding) formidable, implacable; (stern-looking) ceñudo
grimace ['griməs] o [gri'mes] s mueca, gesto ‖ intr hacer muecas, gestear
grime [graim] s mugre f; (soot) tizne m & f
grim•y ['graimi] adj (comp -ier; super -iest) mugriento; tiznado
grin [grin] s sonrisa bonachona; mueca (mostrando los dientes) ‖ v (pret & pp **grinned**; ger **grinning**) intr sonreírse bonachonamente; hacer una mueca (mostrando los dientes)
grind [graind] s molienda; (long hard work or study) (coll) zurra; (student) (coll) empollón m ‖ v (pret & pp **ground** [graund]) tr moler; (to sharpen) afilar, amolar; tallar (lentes); pulverizar; picar (carne); rodar (las válvulas de un motor); dar vueltas a (un manubrio) ‖ intr hacer molienda; molerse; rechinar; (coll) echar los bofes
grinder ['graindər] s (to sharpen tools) muela, esmoladera; (to grind coffee, pepper, etc.) molinillo; (back tooth) muela
grind'stone' s esmoladera, piedra de amolar; **to keep one's nose to the grindstone** trabajar con ahinco
grin•go ['griŋgo] s (pl -gos) (disparaging) gringo
grip [grip] s (grasp) asimiento; (withhand) apretón m; (handle) asidero; saco de mano; **to come to grips (with)** luchar cuerpo a cuerpo (con); arrostrarse (con) ‖ v (pret & pp **gripped**; ger **gripping**) tr asir, agarrar; tener asido; absorber (la atención); absorber la atención a (una persona)
gripe [graip] s (coll) queja; **gripes** retortijón m de tripas ‖ intr (coll) quejarse, refunfuñar
grippe [grip] s gripe f
gripping ['gripiŋ] adj conmovedor, impresionante
gris•ly ['grizli] adj (comp -lier; super -liest) espantoso, espeluznante
grist [grist] s (batch of grain for one grinding) molienda; (grain that has been ground) harina; (coll) acopio, acervo; **to be grist to one's mill** (coll) serle a uno de mucho provecho

gr
gr

gristle ['grɪsəl] *adj* (*comp* **-tlier; *super* -tliest**) cartilaginoso, ternilloso

grist'mill' *s* molino harinero

grit [grɪt] *s* arena, guijo fino; (fig) ánimo, valentía; **grits** farro, sémola ‖ *v* (*pret & pp* **gritted; *ger* gritting**) *tr* hacer rechinar (*los dientes*); cerrar fuertemente (*los dientes*)

grit·ty ['grɪti] *adj* (*comp* **-tier; *super* -tiest**) arenoso; (fig) valiente, resuelto

griz·zly ['grɪzli] *adj* (*comp* **-zlier; *super* -zliest**) grisáceo; canoso ‖ *s* (*pl* **-zlies**) oso gris

grizzly bear *s* oso gris

groan [gron] *s* gemido, quejido ‖ *intr* gemir, quejarse; estar muy cargado, crujir por exceso de peso

grocer ['grosər] *s* abacero, tendero de ultramarinos

grocer·y ['grosəri] *s* (*pl* **-ies**) abacería, tienda de ultramarinos, colmado; **groceries** víveres *mpl*, ultramarinos

grocery store *s* abacería, tienda de ultramarinos, colmado

grog [grɑg] *s* grog *m*

grog·gy ['grɑgi] *adj* (*comp* **-gier; *super* -giest**) (coll) inseguro, vacilante; (*shaky, e.g., from a blow*) (coll) atontado; (coll) borracho

groin [grɔɪn] *s* (anat) ingle *f;* (archit) arista de encuentro

groom [grum] *s* (*bridegroom*) novio; mozo de caballos ‖ *tr* asear, acicalar; almohazar (*caballos*); enseñar (*a un político*) para presentarse como candidato

grooms·man ['grumzmən] *s* (*pl* **-men** [mən]) padrino de boda

groove [gruv] *s* ranura; (*of a pulley*) garganta; (*of a phonograph record*) surco; (*mark left by a wheel*) rodada; (coll) rutina, hábito arraigado ‖ *tr* ranurar, acanalar

grope [grop] *intr* andar a tientas; (*for words*) pujar; **to grope for** buscar a tientas, buscar tentando; **to grope through** palpar (*p.ej., la obscuridad*)

gropingly ['gropɪŋli] *adv* a tientas

grosbeak ['gros ‚bik] *s* pico duro

gross [gros] *adj* (*dense, thick*) denso, espeso; (*coarse; vulgar*) grosero; (*fat, burly*) grueso; (*with no deductions*) bruto ‖ *s* conjunto, totalidad; (*twelve dozen*) gruesa; **in gross** en grueso ‖ *tr* obtener un ingreso bruto de

grossly ['grosli] *adv* aproximadamente

gross national product *s* renta nacional

grotesque [gro'tɛsk] *adj* (*ridiculous, extravagant*) grotesco; (fa) grutesco ‖ *s* (fa) grutesco

grot·to ['grɑto] *s* (*pl* **-toes** o **-tos**) gruta

grouch [grautʃ] *s* (coll) mal humor *m;* (*person*) (coll) cascarrabias *mf*, vinagre *m* ‖ *intr* (coll) refunfuñar

grouch·y ['grautʃi] *adj* (*comp* **-ier; *super* -iest**) (coll) gruñón, malhumorado

ground [graund] *adj* molido ‖ *s* (*earth, soil, land*) tierra; (*piece of land*) terreno; (*basis foundation*) causa, fundamento; motivo, razón *f;* (elec) tierra; (*body of auto-mobile corresponding to ground*) (elec) masa; (elec) borne *m* de tierra; **ground for complaint** motivo de queja; **grounds** terreno; jardines *mpl;* causa, fundamento; (*of coffee*) posos; **on the ground of** con motivo de; **to break ground** empezar la excavación; **to fall to the ground** fracasar, abandonarse; **to gain ground** ganar terreno; **to give ground** ceder terreno; **to lose ground** perder terreno; **to stand one's ground** mantenerse firme; **to yield ground** ceder terreno ‖ *tr* establecer, fundar; (elec) poner a tierra; **to be grounded** estar sin volar (*un avión*); **to be well grounded** ser muy versado ‖ *intr* (naut) encallar, varar

ground connection *s* (rad) toma de tierra

ground crew *s* (aer) personal *m* de tierra

grounder ['graundər] *s* (baseball) pelota rodada

ground floor *s* piso bajo

ground glass *s* vidrio deslustrado

ground hog *s* marmota de América

ground lead [lid] *s* (elec) conductor *m* a tierra

groundless ['graundlɪs] *adj* infundado; inmotivado

ground plan *s* primer proyecto; (*of a building*) planta

ground speed *s* (aer) velocidad con respecto al suelo

ground swell *s* marejada de fondo

ground troops *spl* (mil) tropas terrestres

ground wire *s* (rad) alambre *m* de tierra; (aut) hilo de masa

ground'work' *s* infraestructura

group [grup] *adj* grupal; colectivo ‖ *s* grupo ‖ *tr* agrupar ‖ *intr* agruparse

group therapy *s* psicoterapia de grupo

grouse [graus] *s* perdiz blanca, bonasa americana, gallo de bosque; (slang) refunfuño ‖ *intr* (slang) refunfuñar

grout [graut] *s* lechada ‖ *tr* enlechar

grove [grov] *s* arboleda, bosquecillo

grov·el ['grʌvəl] o ['grɑvəl] *v* (*pret & pp* **-eled** o **-elled; *ger* -eling** o **-elling**) *intr* arrastrarse servilmente; rebajarse servilmente; deleitarse en vilezas

grow [gro] *v* (*pret* **grew** [gru]; *pp* **grown** [gron]) *tr* cultivar (*plantas*); criar (*animales*); dejarse (*la barba*) ‖ *intr* crecer; cultivarse; criarse; brotar, nacer; (*to become*) hacerse, ponerse, volverse; **to grow angry** enfadarse; **to grow old** envejecerse; **to grow out of** tener su origen en; perder (*p.ej., la costumbre*); **to grow together** adherirse el uno al otro; **to grow up** crecer, desarrollar

growing child ['gro·ɪŋ] *s* muchacho de creces

growl [graul] *s* gruñido; refunfuño ‖ *intr* gruñir (*el perro*); refunfuñar

grown'up' *adj* adulto; juicioso ‖ *s* (*pl* **grown-ups**) adulto; **grown-ups** personas mayores

growth [groθ] *s* crecimiento; desarrollo; aumento; (*of trees, grass, etc.*) cobertura; (pathol) tumor *m*

growth stock *s* acción crecedera

grub [grʌb] s (*drudge*) esclavo del trabajo; (*larva*) gorgojo; (coll) comida, alimento ‖ v (*pret & pp* **grubbed;** *ger* **grubbing**) *tr* arrancar (*tocones*); desmalezar (*un terreno*) ‖ *intr* cavar; trabajar como esclavo

grub·by [ˈgrʌbi] *adj* (*comp* **-bier;** *super* **-biest**) gorgojoso; sucio, roñoso

grudge [grʌdʒ] s rencor *m*, inquina; **to have a grudge against** guardar rencor a, tener inquina a ‖ *tr* dar de mala gana; envidiar

grudgingly [ˈgrʌdʒɪŋli] *adv* de mala gana

gru·el [ˈgruəl] s avenate *m* ‖ v (*pret & pp* **-eled** o **-elled;** *ger* **-elling** o **-elling**) *tr* agotar, castigar cruelmente

gruesome [ˈgrusəm] *adj* espantoso, horripilante

gruff [grʌf] *adj* áspero, brusco, rudo; (*voice, tone*) ronco

grumble [ˈgrʌmbəl] s gruñido, refunfuño; ruido sordo y prolongado ‖ *intr* gruñir, refunfuñar; retumbar

grump·y [ˈgrʌmpi] *adj* (*comp* **-ier;** *super* **-iest**) gruñón, malhumorado

grunt [grʌnt] s gruñido ‖ *intr* gruñir

G-string [ˈdʒiˌstrɪŋ] s (*loincloth*) taparrabo; (*worn by women entertainers*) cubresexo

gt. *abbr* **great; gutta** (Lat) **drop**

g.u. *abbr* **genitourinary**

Guadeloupe [ˌgwadəˈlup] s Guadalupe *f*

guarantee [ˌgaerənˈti] s garantía; (*guarantor*) garante *mf*; persona de quien otra sale fiadora ‖ *tr* garantizar

guarantor [ˈgærənˌtɔr] s garante *mf*

guaran·ty [ˈgærənti] s (*pl* **-ties**) garantía ‖ v (*pret & pp* **-tied**) *tr* garantizar

guard [gɑrd] s (*act of guarding; part of handle of sword*) guarda; (*person who guards or takes care of something*) guarda *mf*; (*group of armed men; posture in fencing*) guardia; (*member of group of armed men*) guardia *m*; (*in front of trolley car*) salvavidas *m*; (sport) coraza; (rr) guardabarrera *mf*; (rr) guardafrenos *m*; **off guard** desprevenido; **on guard** alerta, prevenido; de centinela; **to mount guard** montar la guardia; **under guard** a buen recaudo ‖ *tr* guardar ‖ *intr* estar de centinela; **to guard against** guardarse de, precaverse contra o de

guard'house' s cuartel *m* de la guardia; prisión militar

guardian [ˈgɑrdɪ·ən] *adj* tutelar ‖ s guardián *m*; (law) curador *m*, tutor *m*

guardian angel s ángel *m* custodio, ángel de la guarda

guardianship [ˈgɑrdɪ·ənˌʃɪp] s amparo, protección; (law) curaduría, tutela

guard'rail' s baranda; (naut) barandilla; (rr) contracarril *m*

guard'room' s cuarto de guardia; cárcel *f* militar

guards·man [ˈgɑrdzmən] s (*pl* **-men** [mən]) guardia *m*, soldado de guardia

Guatemalan [ˌgwɑtɪˈmalən] *adj & s* guatemalteco

guerrilla [gəˈrɪlə] s guerrillero; montonero

guerrilla warfare s guerra de guerrillas

guess [gɛs] s conjetura, suposición; adivinación ‖ *tr & intr* conjeturar, suponer; (*to judge correctly*) acertar, adivinar; (coll) creer, suponer; **I guess so** (coll) creo que sí, me parece que sí

guess'work' s conjetura; **by guesswork** por conjeturas

guest [gɛst] s convidado; (*lodger*) huésped *m*; (*of a boarding house*) pensionista *mf*; (*of a hotel*) cliente *mf*; (*caller*) vista

guest book s libro de oro

guest room s cuarto de reserva

guffaw [gəˈfɔ] s risotada, carcajada ‖ *intr* risotear, reír a carcajadas

guidance [ˈgaɪdəns] s guía, gobierno, dirección; **for your guidance** para su gobierno

guide [gaɪd] s (*person*) guía *mf*; (*book*) guía; (*guidance*) guía; dirección; poste *m* indicador; (mach) guía, guiadera; (mil) guía *m* ‖ *tr* guiar

guide'board' s señal *f* de carretera

guide'book' s guia *m*, guía del viajero

guided missile s proyectil dirigido o teleguiado; misil *m* dirigible

guide dog s perro-lazarillo

guide'line' s cuerda de guía; norma, pauta, directorio

guide'post' s poste *m* indicador

guidon [ˈgaɪdən] s (mil) guión *m*; (mil) portaguión *m*

guild [gɪld] s (*medieval association of craftsmen*) gremio; asociación benéfica

guild'hall' s casa consistorial

guile [gaɪl] s astucia, dolo, maña

guileful [ˈgaɪlfəl] *adj* astuto, doloso, mañoso

guileless [ˈgaɪllɪs] *adj* cándido, inocente, sencillo

guillotine [ˈgɪləˌtin] s guillotina ‖ [ˌgɪləˈtin] *tr* guillotinar

guilt [gɪlt] s culpa

guiltless [ˈgɪltlɪs] *adj* inocente, libre de culpa

guilt·y [ˈgɪlti] *adj* (*comp* **-ier;** *super* **-iest**) culpable; (*charged with guilt*) culpado; (*found guilty*) reo

guimpe [gɪmp] o [gæmp] s canesú *m*

guinea [ˈgɪni] s (*monetary unit*) guinea; gallina de Guinea

guinea fowl s pintada, gallina de Guinea

guinea hen s pintada, gallina de Guinea (*hembra*)

guinea pig s conejillo de Indias; (fig) cobayo

guise [gaɪz] s traje *m*; aspecto, semejanza; **under the guise of** so capa de

guitar [gɪˈtɑr] s guitarra

guitarist [gɪˈtɑrɪst] s guitarrista *mf*

gulch [gʌltʃ] s barranco, quebrada

gulf [gʌlf] s golfo

Gulf of Mexico s golfo de Méjico

Gulf Stream s Corriente *f* del Golfo

gull [gʌl] s gaviota; (coll) bobo ‖ *tr* estafar, engañar

gullet [ˈgʌlɪt] s gaznate *m*, garguero; esófago

gullible [ˈgʌlɪbəl] *adj* crédulo; creído; **to be too gullible** tener buenas tragaderas

gul·ly [ˈgʌli] s (*pl* **-lies**) barranca, arroyada; (*channel made by rain water*) badén *m*

gulp [gʌlp] *s* trago ‖ *tr* — **to gulp down** engullir; reprimir (*p.ej., sollozos*) ‖ *intr* respirar entrecortadamente

gum [gʌm] *s* goma; chanclo de goma; (*firm flesh around base of teeth*) encía; (*mucous on edge of eyelid*) legaña ‖ *v* (*pret & pp* **gummed;** *ger* **gumming**) *tr* engomar ‖ *intr* exudar goma

gum arabic *s* goma arábiga

gum′boil′ *s* flemón *m*

gum boot *s* bota de agua

gum′drop′ *s* frutilla

gum•my [ˈgʌmi] *adj* (*comp* **-mier;** *super* **-miest**) gomoso; (*eyelid*) legañoso

gumption [ˈgʌmpʃən] *s* ánimo, iniciativa, empuje *m*, fuerza; juicio, seso

gum′shoe′ *s* chanclo de goma; (coll) detective *m* ‖ *v* (*pret & pp* **-shoed;** *ger* **-shoeing**) *intr* (slang) andar con zapatos de fieltro

gun [gʌn] *s* escopeta, fusil *m*; cañón *m;* (*for injections*) jeringa; (coll) revólver *m;* **to stick to one's guns** mantenerse en sus trece ‖ *v* (*pret & pp* **gunned;** *ger* **gunning**) *tr* hacer fuego sobre; (slang) acelerar rápidamente (*un motor, un avión*) ‖ *intr* andar a caza; disparar; **to gun for** ir en busca de; buscar para matar

gun′boat′ *s* cañonero

gun carriage *s* cureña, encabalgamiento

gun′cot′ton *s* fulmicotón *m*, algodón *m* pólvora

gun′fire′ *s* fuego (*de armas de fuego*); cañoneo

gun•man [ˈgʌnmən] *s* (*pl* **-men** [mən]) bandido armado, pistolero; gángster *m*

gun metal *s* bronce *m* de cañón; metal pavonado

gunnel [ˈgʌnəl] *s* (naut) borda, regala

gunner [ˈgʌnər] *s* artillero; cazador *m*

gunnery [ˈgʌnəri] *s* artillería

gunny sack [ˈgʌni] *s* saco de yute

gun′pow′der *s* pólvora

gun′run′ner *s* contrabandista *m* de armas de fuego

gun′run′ning *s* contrabando de armas de fuego

gun′shot′ *s* escopetazo, tiro de fusil; alcance *m* de un fusil; **within gunshot** a tiro de fusil

gunshot wound *s* escopetazo

gun′smith′ *s* armero

gun′stock′ *s* caja de fusil

gunwale [ˈgʌnəl] *s* (naut) borda, regala

gup•py [ˈgʌpi] *s* (*pl* **-pies**) lebistes *m*

gurgle [ˈgʌrgəl] *s* gorgoteo, gluglú *m;* (*of a child*) gorjeo ‖ *intr* gorgotear, hacer gluglú; gorjearse (*el niño*)

gush [gʌʃ] *s* borbollón *m*, chorro ‖ *intr* surgir, salir a borbollones; (coll) hacer extremos, ser extremoso

gusher [ˈgʌʃər] *s* pozo de chorro de petróleo; (coll) personal extremosa

gushing [ˈgʌʃɪŋ] *adj* surgente; (coll) extremoso ‖ *s* borbollón *m*, chorro; (coll) efusión, extremos

gush•y [ˈgʌʃi] *adj* (*comp* **-ier;** *super* **-iest**) (coll) efusivo, extremoso

gusset [ˈgʌsɪt] *s* escudete *m*

gust [gʌst] *s* (*of wind*) ráfaga; (*of rain*) aguacero; (*of smoke*) bocanada; (*of noise*) explosión; (*of anger or enthusiasm*) arrebato

gusto [ˈgʌsto] *s* deleite *m*, entusiasmo; **with gusto** con sumo placer

gust•y [ˈgʌsti] *adj* (*comp* **-ier;** *super* **-iest**) tempestuoso, borrascoso

gut [gʌt] *s* tripa; cuerda de tripa; **guts** tripas; (slang) agallas ‖ *v* (*pret & pp* **gutted;** *ger* **gutting**) *tr* destripar; destruir lo interior de

gutta-percha [ˈgʌtəˈpʌrtʃə] *s* gutapercha

gutter [ˈgʌtər] *s* (*on side of road*) cuneta; (*in street*) arroyo; (*of roof*) canal *f;* (*ditch formed by rain water*) badén *m;* barrios bajos

gut′ter-snipe′ *s* pilluelo, hijo de la miseria; gamberro

guttural [ˈgʌtərəl] *adj* gutural ‖ *s* sonido gutural

guy [gaɪ] *s* viento, cable *m* de retén; (coll) tipo, tío, sujeto ‖ *tr* (coll) burlarse de

Guyana [gaɪˈænə] *s* Guayana

guy wire *s* cable *m* de retén

guzzle [ˈgʌzəl] *tr & intr* beber con exceso

guzzler [ˈgʌzlər] *s* borrachín *m*

gym [dʒɪm] *s* (coll) gimnasio

gymnasi•um [dʒɪmˈnɛzɪ•əm] *s* (*pl* **-ums** o **-a** [ə]) gimnasio

gymnast [ˈdʒɪmnæst] *s* gimnasta *mf*

gymnastic [dʒɪmˈnæstɪk] *adj* gimnástico ‖ **gymnastics** *spl* gimnasia, gimnástica

gym suit *s* chandal *m*, chándal *m*

gynecologic(al) [ˌgaɪnəkoˈlɑdʒɪk(əl)] or [ˌdʒaɪnəkoˈlɑdʒɪk(əl)] *adj* ginecológico

gynecologist [ˌgaɪnəˈkɑlədʒɪst] or [ˌdʒaɪnəˈkɑlədʒɪst] *s* ginecólogo

gynecology [ˌgaɪnəˈkɑlədʒi] or [ˌdʒaɪnəˈkɑlədʒi] *s* ginecología

gyp [dʒɪp] *s* (slang) estafa, timo; (*person*) (slang) estafador *m*, timador *m* ‖ *v* (*pret & pp* **gypped;** *ger* **gypping**) *tr* (slang) estafar, timar

gypsum [ˈdʒɪpsəm] *s* yeso, aljez *m*

gyp•sy [ˈdʒɪpsi] *adj* gitano ‖ *s* (*pl* **-sies**) gitano ‖ **Gypsy** *s* gitano (*idioma*)

gypsyish [ˈdʒɪpsɪ•ɪʃ] *adj* gitanesco

gypsy moth *s* lagarta

gyrate [ˈdʒaɪret] *intr* girar

gyroscope [ˈdʒaɪrəˌskop] *s* giroscopio

gr
gy

H

H, h [etʃ] octava letra del alfabeto inglés

h. *abbr* **harbor, high, hour, husband**

haberdasher ['hæbər ˌdæʃər] *s* camisero; (*dealer in notions*) mercero

haberdasher•y ['hæbər ˌdæʃəri] *s* (*pl* **-ies**) camisería, tienda de artículos para hombres; artículos para hombres

habit ['hæbɪt] *s* costumbre *f*, hábito; (*costume*) traje *m;* **to be in the habit of** acostumbrar

habitat ['hæbɪˌtæt] *s* habitación

habitation [ˌhæbɪ'teʃən] *s* habitación

habit-forming ['hæbɪt ˌfɔrmɪŋ] *adj* enviaciador

habitual [hə'bɪtʃuˑəl] *adj* habitual

habitué [hə ˌbɪtʃu'e] *s* habituado

hack [hæk] *s* (*cut*) corte *m;* (*notch*) mella; (*cough*) tos seca; coche *m* de alquiler; caballo de alquiler; caballo de silla; (*old nag*) rocín *m;* escritor *m* a sueldo ‖ *tr* cortar, machetear

hack•man ['hækmən] *s* (*pl* **-men** [mən]) cochero de punto

hackney ['hækni] *s* caballo de silla; coche *m* de alquiler; esclavo del trabajo

hackneyed ['hæknid] *adj* trillado, gastado

hack'saw' *s* sierra de armero, sierra de cortar metales

haddock ['hædək] *s* eglefino

haem ... [hɛm] o [hɪm] = **hemo** ...

haft [hæft] o [hɑft] *s* mango, puño

hag [hæg] *s* (*ugly old woman*) tarasca; (*witch*) bruja

haggard ['hægərd] *adj* ojeroso, macilento, trasnochado

haggle ['hægəl] *intr* regatear

Hague,The [heg] La Haya

hail [hel] *s* (*frozen rain*) granizo; (*greeting*) saludo; **within hail** al alcance de la voz ‖ *interj* ¡salud!, ¡salve! ‖ *tr* saludar; dar vivas a, acoger con vivas; aclamar; granizar (*p.ej., golpes*) ‖ *intr* granizar; **to hail from** venir de, ser oriundo de

hail'-fel'low well met *s* compañero muy afable y simpático

Hail Mary *s* avemaría

hail'stone' *s* piedra de granizo

hail'storm' *s* granizada

hair [hɛr] *s* pelo, cabellos; **to a hair** con la mayor exactitud; **to cut the hair of** peluquear; **to get in one's hair** (slang) enojarle a uno; **to have one's hair down** estar en melena; **to let one's hair down** (slang) hablar con mucha desenvoltura; **to make one's hair stand on end** ponerle a uno los pelos de punta; **to not turn a hair** no inmutarse; **to split hairs** pararse en quisquillas

hair'breadth' *s* (el) grueso de un pelo, casi nada; **to escape by a hairbreadth** escapar por un pelo

hair'brush' *s* cepillo de cabeza

hair'cloth' *s* tela de crin; (*worn as a penance*) cilicio

hair curler ['kʌrlər] *s* rizador *m*, tenacillas, bigudí *m*, rulo

hair'cut' *s* corte *m* de pelo; **to get a haircut** cortarse el pelo, peluquear

hair'do' *s* (*pl* **-dos**) peinado, tocado

hair'dress'er *s* peinador *m*, peluquero

hair dryer *s* secador *m*

hair dye *s* tinte *m* para el pelo

hairless ['hɛrlɪs] *adj* pelón

hair net *s* redecilla

hair piece *s* peluquín *m*

hair'pin' *s* horquilla

hair-raising ['hɛr ˌrezɪŋ] *adj* (coll) espeluznante, horripilante

hair restorer [rɪ'storər] *s* crecepelo

hair ribbon *s* cinta para el cabello

hair set *s* fijapeinados *m*

hair shirt *s* calicio

hairsplitting ['hɛr ˌsplɪtɪŋ] *adj* quisquilloso ‖ *s* quisquillas

hair spray *s* laca

hair'spring' *s* espiral *f*

hair'style' *s* peinado

hair tonic *s* vigorizador *m* del cabello

hair•y ['hɛri] *adj* (*comp* **-ier;** *super* **-iest**) peludo, cabelludo

hake [hek] *s* merluza; (*genus: Urophycis*) fice *m*

halberd ['hælbərd] *s* alabarda

halberdier [ˌhælbər'dɪr] *s* alabardero

halcyon days ['hælsɪ•ən] *s* días tranquilos, época de paz

hale [hel] *adj* sano, robusto; **hale and hearty** sano y fuerte ‖ *tr* llevar a la fuerza

half [hæf] *adj* medio; **a half** o **half a** medio; **half the** la mitad de ‖ *adv* medio, p.ej., **half asleep** medio dormido; a medio, p.ej., **half finished** a medio acabar; a medias, p.ej., **half owner** dueño a medias; **half past** y media, p.ej., **half past three** las tres y media; **half ... half** medio ... medio ‖ *s* (*pl* **halves** [hævz]) mitad; (arith) medio; **in half** por la mitad; **to go halves** ir a medias

half'-and-half' *adj* mitad y mitad; indeterminado ‖ *adv* a medias, en partes iguales ‖ *s* mezcla de leche y crema; mezcla de dos cervezas inglesas

half'back' *s* (football) medio

half-baked ['hæf ˌbekt] *adj* a medio cocer; incompleto; poco juicioso, inexperto

half binding *s* (bb) encuadernación a la holandesa, media pasta

half'-blood' *s* mestizo; medio hermano

half boot *s* bota de media caña

half'-bound' *adj* (bb) a la holandesa

half'-breed' *s* mestizo

half brother *s* medio hermano

half-cocked ['hæf'kakt] *adv* (coll) con precipitación; **to go off half-cocked** obrar precipitadamente y antes del momento propio

half fare *s* medio billete

half'-full' *adj* mediado

half-hearted ['hæf ˌhartɪd] *adj* indiferente, frío

half holiday *s* mañana o tarde *f* de asueto

half hose *spl* calcetines *mpl*

half'-hour *s* media hora; **on the half-hour** a la media en punto, cada media hora

half leather *s* (bb) encuadernación a la holandesa, media pasta

half'-length' *adj* de medio cuerpo

half'-mast' *s* — **at half mast** a media asta

half moon *s* media luna

half mourning *s* medio luto

half note *s* (mus) nota blanca

half pay *s* media paga; medio sueldo

halfpen·ny ['hepəni] o ['hepni] *s* (*pl* **-nies**) medio penique

half pint *s* media pinta; (*little runt*) (slang) gorgojo, mirmidón *m*

half'-seas' over *adj* — **to be half-seas over** (slang) estar entre dos velas, estar entre dos luces

half shell *s* (*either half of a bivalve*) concha; (*oysters*) **on the half shell** en su concha

half sister *s* media hermana

half sole *s* media suela

half'-sole' *tr* poner media suela a

half'-staff' *s* — **at half-staff** a media asta

half through *prep* a la mitad de

half-timbered ['hæf,tɪmbərd] *adj* entramado

half title *s* anteportada, falsa portada

half'tone' *s* (phot & paint) mediatinta; (typ) similigrabado

half'-track' *s* media oruga, semitractor *m*

half'-truth' *s* verdad a medias

half'way' *adj* a medio camino; incompleto, hecho a medias ‖ *adv* a medio camino; **halfway through** a la mitad de; **to meet halfway** partir el camino con; partir la diferencia con; hacer concesiones mutuas (*dos personas*)

half-witted ['hæf ,wɪtɪd] *adj* imbécil; necio, tonto

halibut ['hælɪbət] *s* halibut *m*

halide ['hælaɪd] o ['helaɪd] *s* (chem) haluro

halitosis [,hælɪ'tosɪs] *s* halitosis *f*, aliento fétido

hall [hɔl] (*passageway*) corredor *m*; (*entranceway*) vestíbulo, zaguán *m*; (*large meeting room*) sala, salón *m*; (*assembly room of a university*) paraninfo; (*building, e.g., of a university*) edificio

halleluiah o **hallelujah** [,hælɪ'lujə] *s* aleluya *m* & *f* ‖ *interj* ¡aleluya!

hall'mark' *s* marca de constraste; (*distinguishing feature*) (fig) sello

hal·lo [hə'lo] *s* (*pl* **-los**) grito ‖ *interj* ¡hola!; (*to incite dogs in hunting*) ¡sus! ‖ *intr* gritar

hallow ['hælo] *tr* santificar

hallowed ['hælod] *adj* santo, sagrado

Halloween o **Hallowe'en** [,hælo'in] *s* víspera de Todos los Santos

hallucination [hə,lusɪ'nefən] *s* alucinación

hallucinogenic [hə,lusɪno'dʒɛnɪk] *adj* alucinante

hall'way' *s* corredor *m*; vestíbulo, zaguán *m*

ha·lo ['helo] *s* (*pl* **-los** o **-loes**) halo

halogen ['hælədʒən] *s* halógeno

halt [hɔlt] *adj* cojo, renco ‖ *s* alto, parada; **to call a halt** mandar hacer alto; **to come to a**

halt pararse, detenerse, interrumpirse ‖ *tr* parar, detener ‖ *intr* hacer alto

halter ['hɔltər] *s* (*for leading or fastening horse*) cabestro, ronzal *m*, dogal *m*; (*noose*) dogal *m*, cuerda de ahorcar; muerte *f* en la horca

halting ['hɔltɪŋ] *adj* cojo, renco; vacilante

halve [hæv] *tr* partir en dos, partir por la mitad

halyard ['hæljərd] *s* (naut) driza

ham [hæm] *s* (*part of leg behind knee*) corva; (*thigh and buttock*) pernil *m*; (*cured meat from hog's hind leg*) jamón *m*; (slang) comicastro; (slang) aficionado (*a la radio*); **hams** nalgas

ham and eggs *spl* huevos con jamón

hamburger ['hæm,bʌrgər] *s* hamburguesa

hamlet ['hæmlɪt] *s* aldehuela, caserío

hammer ['hæmər] *s* martillo; (*of piano*) macillo, martinete *m*; **to go under the hammer** venderse en pública subasta ‖ *tr* martillar; **to hammer out** formar a martillazos; sacar en limpio a fuerza de mucho esfuerzo‖ *intr* martillar; **to hammer away** trabajar asiduamente

hammock ['hæmək] *s* hamaca

hamper ['hæmpər] *s* canasto, cesto grande con tapa ‖ *tr* estorbar, impedir

hamster ['hæmstər] *s* marmota de Alemania, rata del trigo

ham·string ['hæm,strɪŋ] *v* (*pret* & *pp* **-strung**) *tr* desjarretar; (fig) estropear, incapacitar

hand [hænd] *adj* (*done or operated with the hands*) manual ‖ *s* mano *f*; (*workman*) obrero, peón *m*; (*way of writing*) escritura, puño y letra; (*signature*) firma; (*clapping of hands*) salva de aplausos; (*of clock or watch*) mano *f*; manecilla; (*all the cards in one's hand*) juego; (*a round of play*) mano *f*; (*player*) jugador *m*; (*source, origin*) fuente *f*; (*skill*) destreza; **all hands** (naut) toda la tripulación; (coll) todas; **at first hand** de primera mano; directamente, de buena tinta; **at hand** disponible; **hand in glove** uña y carne; **hand in hand** asidos de la mano; juntos; **hands up!** ¡arriba las manos! **hand to hand** cuerpo a cuerpo; **in hand** entre manos; **in his own hand** de su propio puño; **on hand** entre manos; disponible; **on hands and knees** (*crawling*) a gatas; (*beseeching*) de rodillas; **on the one hand** por una parte; **on the other hand** por otra parte; **out of hand** luego, en seguida; desmandado; **to be at hand** obrar en mi (nuestro) poder (*una carta*); **to change hands** mudar de manos; **to clap hands** batir palmas; **to eat out of one's hand** aceptar dócilmente la autoridad de uno; **to fall into the hands of** caer en manos de; **to have a hand in** tomar parte en; **to have one's hands full** estar ocupadísimo; **to hold hands** tomarse de las manos; **to hold up one's hands** (*as a sign of surrender*) alzar las manos; **to join hands** darse las manos; casarse; **to keep one's hands off** no tocar, no meterse en; **to lend a hand**

h
ha

echar una mano; **to live from hand to mouth** vivir al día, vivir de la mano a la boca; **to not lift a hand** no levantar paja del suelo; **to play into the hands of** hacer el caldo gordo a; **to raise one's hand** (*in taking an oath*) alzar el dedo; **to shake hands** estrecharse la mano; **to show one's hand** descubrir su juego; **to take in hand** hacerse cargo de; tratar, estudiar (*una cuestión*); **to throw up one's hands** darse por vencido; **to try one's hand** probar la mano; **to turn one's hand to** dedicarse a, ocuparse en; **to wash one's hands of** lavarse las manos de; **under my hand** con mi firma, bajo mi firma, de mi puño y letra; **under the hand and seal of** firmado y sellado por ‖ *tr* dar, entregar; **to hand in** entregar; **to hand on** transmitir; **to hand out** repartir

hand'bag' *s* saco de noche; bolso de señora
hand baggage *s* equipaje *m* de mano
hand'ball' *s* pelota; juego de pelota a mano
hand'bill' *s* hoja volante
hand'book' manual *m;* guía de turistas; registro para apuestas
hand'breadth' *s* palmo menor
hand'car' *s* (rr) carrito de mano
hand'cart' *s* carretilla de mano
hand control *s* mando a mano
hand'cuff' *s* manilla; **handcuffs** manillas, esposas ‖ *tr* poner esposas a
handful ['hænd,fʊl] *s* puñado, manojo
hand glass *s* espejo de mano; lupa
hand grenade *s* granada de mano
hand gun *s* (coll) pipa
hand'-held' calculator *s* calculador a mano
handi-cap ['hændɪ,kæp] *s* desventaja, obstáculo; (sport) handicap *m;* (med) disminución, minusvalía ‖ *v* (*pret & pp* **-capped;** *ger* **-capping**) *tr* poner trabas a; (sport) handicapar
handicraft ['hændɪ,kræft] *s* destreza manual; arte mecánica
handiwork ['hændɪ,wʌrk] *s* hechura, trabajo; obra manual
handkerchief ['hæŋkərtʃɪf] *s* pañuelo
handle ['hændəl] *s* (*of a basket, crock, pitcher*) asa; (*of a shovel, rake, etc.*) mango; (*of an umbrella, sword*) puño; (*of a door, drawer*) tirador *m;* (*of a hand organ*) manubrio; (*of a water pump*) guimbalete *m;* (*opportunity, pretext*) asidero; **to fly off the handle** (slang) salirse de sus casillas ‖ *tr* manosear, manipular; dirigir, manejar, gobernar; comerciar en ‖ *intr* manejarse
handle bar *s* manillar *m,* guía
handler ['hændlər] *s* (sport) entrenador *m*
hand'made' *adj* hecho a mano
hand'maid' o **hand'maid'en** *s* criada, sirvienta
hand'-me-down' *s* (coll) prenda de vestir de segunda mano
hand organ *s* organillo
hand'out' *s* comida que se da de limosna; comunicado de prensa

hand-picked ['hænd,pɪkt] *adj* escogido a mano; escogido escrupulosamente; escogido con motivos ocultos
hand'rail' *s* barandilla, pasamano
hand'saw' *s* serrucho, sierra de mano
hand'set' *s* microteléfono
hand'shake' *s* apretón *m* de manos
handsome ['hænsəm[*adj* hermoso, elegante, guapo; considerable
hand'spring' *s* voltereta sobre las manos
hand'-to-hand' *adj* cuerpo a cuerpo
hand'-to-mouth' *adj* inseguro, precario; impróvido
hand'work' *s* trabajo a mano
hand'-wres'tle *intr* pulsear
hand'-writ'ing *s* escritura; (*writing by hand which characterizes a particular person*) letra
hand•y ['hændi] *adj* (*comp* **-ier;** *super* **-iest**) (*easy to handle*) manuable; (*within easy reach*) próximo, a la mano; (*skillful*) diestro, hábil; **to come in handy** venir a pelo
handy man *s* dije *m,* factótum *m*
hang [hæŋ] *s* (*of a dress, curtain, etc.*) caída; (*skill; insight*) tino; **I don't care a hang** (coll) no me importa un bledo; **to get the hang of it** (coll) coger el tino ‖ *v* (*pret & pp* **hung** [hʌŋ]) *tr* colgar; tender (*la ropa mojada*); pegar (*el papel pintado*); fijar (*un cartel, un letrero*); enquiciar (*una puerta, una ventana*); bajar (*la cabeza*); **hang it!** (coll) ¡caramba!; **to hang up** colgar (*el sombrero*); impedir los progresos de ‖ *intr* colgar, pender; estar agarrado; vacilar; **to hang around** esperar sin hacer nada; haraganear; rondar; **to hang on** colgar de; depender de; estar pendiente de (*las palabras de una persona*); estar sin acabar de morir; agarrarse; **to hang out** asomarse; (slang) recogerse, alojarse; **to hang over** (*to threaten*) cernerse sobre; **to hang together** mantenerse unidos; **to hang up** (telp) colgar ‖ *v* (*pret* **hanged** o **hung**) *tr* ahorcar ‖ *intr* ahorcarse
hangar ['hæŋər] o ['hæŋɑr] *s* cobertizo; (aer) hangar *m*
hang'bird' *s* pájaro de nido colgante; (*Baltimore oriole*) cacique veranero
hanger ['hæŋər] *s* colgador *m,* suspensión; (*hook*) colgadero
hang'er•on' *s* (*pl* **hangers-on**) secuaz *mf;* parásito; (*sponger*) pegote *m*
hanging ['hæŋɪŋ] *adj* colgante, pendiente ‖ *s* ahorcadura, muerte *f* en la horca; **hangings** colgaduras
hang'man ['hæŋmən] *s* (*pl* **-men** [mən]) verdugo
hang'nail' *s* padrastro, respigón *m*
hang'out' *s* guarida, querencia; (*place to loaf and gossip*) mentidero
hang'o'ver *s* (slang) resaca
hank [hæŋk] *s* madeja
hanker ['hæŋkər] *intr* sentir anhelo
Hannibal ['hænɪbəl] *s* Aníbal *m*
haphazard [,hæp'hæzərd] *adj* casual, fortuito, impensado ‖ *adv* al acaso, a la ventura

hapless ['hæplɪs] *adj* desgraciado, desventurado

happen ['hæpən] *intr* acontecer, suceder; (*to turn out*) resultar; (*to be the case by chance*) dar la casualidad; **to happen in** entrar por casualidad; **to happen on** encontrarse con; **to happen to** hacerse de; **to happen to** + *inf* por casualidad + *ind*, p.ej., **I happened to see her at the theater** por casualidad la ví en el teatro

happening ['hæpənɪŋ] *s* acontecimiento, suceso

happily ['hæpɪli] *adv* felizmente

happiness ['hæpɪnɪs] *s* felicidad

hap•py ['hæpi] *adj* (*comp* **-pier**; *super* **-piest**) feliz; (*pleased*) contento; **to be happy to** alegrarse de, tener gusto en

hap´py-go-luck´y *adj* irresponsable, impróvido ‖ *adv* a la buenaventura

happy medium *s* justo medio

Happy New Year *interj* ¡Feliz Año Nuevo!

harangue [hə'ræŋ] *s* arenga ‖ *tr* & *intr* arengar

harass ['hærəs] o [hə'ræs] *tr* acosar, hostigar; molestar, vejar

harbinger ['harbɪndʒər] *s* precursor *m*; anuncio, presagio ‖ *tr* anunciar, presagiar

harbor ['harbər] *adj* portuario ‖ *s* puerto ‖ *tr* albergar; alcahuetar, encubrir (*delincuentes u objetos robados*); guardar (*sentimientos de odio*)

harbor master *s* capitán *m* de puerto

hard [hard] *adj* duro; (*difficult*) difícil; (*water*) crudo, duro; (*solder*) fuerte; (*work*) asiduo; (*drinker*) empedernido; espiritoso, fuertemente alcohólico; **to be hard on** (*to treat severely*) ser muy duro con; (*to wear out fast*) gastar, echar a perder ‖ *adv* duro; fuerte; mucho; **hard upon** a raíz de; **to drink hard** beber de firme; **to rain hard** llover de firme

hard and fast *adj* inflexible, riguroso ‖ *adv* firmemente

hard-bitten ['hard'bɪtən] *adj* terco, tenaz, inflexible

hard-boiled ['hard'bɔɪld] *adj* (*egg*) duro, muy cocido; duro, inflexible

hard candy *s* caramelos

hard cash *s* dinero contante y sonante

hard cider *s* sidra muy fermentada

hard coal *s* antracita

hard-earned ['hard'ʌrnd] *adj* ganado a pulso

harden ['hardən] *tr* endurecer ‖ *intr* endurecerse

hardening ['hardənɪŋ] *s* endurecimiento

hard facts *spl* realidades

hard-fought ['hard'fɔt] *adj* reñido

hard-headed ['hard'hɛdɪd] *adj* astuto, sagaz; terco, tozudo

hard-hearted ['hard'hartɪd] *adj* duro de corazón

hardihood ['hardɪ, hʊd] *s* audacia, resolución; descaro, insolencia

hardiness ['hardɪnɪs] *s* fuerza, robustez; audacia, resolución

hard labor *s* trabajos forzados

hard luck *s* mala suerte

hard´-luck´ story *s* (coll) cuento de penas; **to tell a hard-luck story** (coll) contar lástimas

hardly ['hardli] *adv* apenas; escasamente; casi no; (*with great difficulty*) a duras penas; (*grievously*) penosamente; **hardly ever** casi nunca

hardness ['hardnɪs] *s* dureza; (*of water*) crudeza

hard of hearing *adj* duro de oído, teniente

hard-pressed ['hard'prɛst] *adj* acosado; (*for money*) apurado, alcanzado

hard rubber *s* vulcanita

hard sauce *s* mantequilla azucarada

hard´-shell´ clam *s* almeja redonda

hard´-shell´ crab *s* cangrejo de cáscara dura

hardship ['hardʃɪp] *s* penalidad, infortunio, apuro

hard´tack´ *s* galleta, sequete *m*

hard times *spl* período de miseria, apuros

hard to please *adj* difícil de contentar

hard up *adj* (coll) apurado, alcanzado

hard´ware´ *s* ferretería, quincalla; (*metal trimmings*) herraje *m*; (*computer*) ordenador *m*

hardware•man ['hard,wɛrmən] *s* (*pl* **-men** [mən]) ferretero, quincallero

hardware store *s* ferretería, quincallería

hard-won ['hard,wʌn] *adj* ganado a pulso

hard´wood´ *s* madera dura; árbol *m* de madera dura

hardwood floor *s* entarimado

har•dy ['hardi] *adj* (*comp* **-dier**; *super* **-diest**) fuerte, robusto; audaz, resuelto; (*rash*) temerario, (*hort*) resistente

hare [hɛr] *s* liebre *f*

harebrained ['hɛr,brend] *adj* atolondrado

hare´lip´ *s* labio leporino

harelipped ['hɛr,lɪpt] *adj* labiohendido

harem ['hɛrəm] *s* harén *m*

hark [hark] *intr* escuchar; **to hark back** volver (*la jauría*) sobre la pista; **to hark back to** volver a, recordar

harken ['harkən] *intr* escuchar, atender

harlequin ['harləkwɪn] *s* arlequín *m*

harlot ['harlət] *s* meretriz *f*

harm [harm] *s* daño, perjuicio ‖ *tr* dañar, perjudicar, hacer daño a

harmful ['harmfəl] *adj* dañoso, perjudicial; maléfico; (*e.g., pests*) dañino

harmfulness ['harmfəlnɪs] *s* nocividad

harmless ['harmlɪs] *adj* innocuo, inofensivo

harmlessness ['harmlɪsnɪs] *s* innocuidad

harmonic [har'manɪk] *adj* & *s* armónico

harmonica [har'manɪkə] *s* armónica

harmonious [har'monɪ•əs] *adj* armonioso

harmonize ['harmə,naɪz] *tr* & *intr* armonizar

harmo•ny ['harməni] *s* (*pl* **-nies**) armonía

harness ['harnɪs] *s* arreos, guarniciones; **to get back in the harness** volver a la rutina; **to die in the harness** morir al pie del cañón ‖ *tr* enjaezar, poner las guarniciones a; enganchar; captar (*las aguas de un río*)

harness maker *s* guarnicionero

harness race *s* carrera con sulky

harp [harp] *s* arpa ‖ *intr* — **to harp on** repetir porfiadamente

harpist ['hɑrpɪst] s arpista mf

harpoon [hɑr'pun] s arpón m ‖ tr & intr arponear

harpsichord ['hɑrpsɪ,kɔrd] s clave m

har·py ['hɑrpi] s (pl -pies) arpía

harrow ['hæro] s (agr) grada ‖ tr (agr) gradar; atormentar

harrowing ['hæro·ɪŋ] adj horripilante, espantoso

har·ry ['hæri] v (pret & pp -ried) tr acosar, hostilizar, hostigar; atormentar, molestar

harsh [hɑrʃ] adj (to touch, taste, eyes, hearing) áspero; duro, cruel

harshness ['hɑrʃnɪs] s aspereza; dureza, crueldad

hart [hɑrt] s ciervo

harum-scarum ['hɛrəm'skɛrəm] adj atolondrado ‖ adv atolondradamente ‖ s mataperros m

harvest ['hɑrvɪst] s cosecha; corte m ‖ tr & intr cosechar

harvester ['hɑrvɪstər] s cosechero; (helper) agostero; (machine) segadora

harvest home s entrada de los frutos; fiesta de segadores; canción de segadores

harvest moon s luna de la cosecha

has-been ['hæz'bɪn] s (coll) antigualla

hash [hæʃ] s picadillo ‖ tr picar

hash house s bodegón m

hashish ['hæʃɪʃ] s hachich m; (coll) tate m

hashish user s (coll) tate m

hasp [hæsp] o [hɑsp] s portacandado; (of book covers) broche m

hassle ['hæsəl] s (coll) riña, disputa

hassock ['hæsək] s cojín m (para los pies o las rodillas)

haste [hest] s prisa; **in haste** de prisa; **to make haste** darse prisa

hasten ['hesən] tr apresurar; apretar (el paso) ‖ intr apresurarse

hast·y ['hesti] adj (comp -ier; super -iest) apresurado, inconsiderado, impulsivo, colérico

hat [hæt] s sombrero; **to keep under one's hat** (coll) callar, no divulgar; **to throw one's hat in the ring** (coll) decidirse a bajar a la arena

hat'band' s cintillo; (worn to show mourning) gasa

hat block s horma, conformador m

hat'box' s sombrerera

hatch [hætʃ] s (brood) cría, nidada; (trap door) escotillón m; (lower half of door) media puerta; (opening in ship's deck) escotilla; (lid for opening in ship's deck) cuartel m ‖ tr empollar (huevos); sombrear (un dibujo); maquinar, tramar ‖ intr empollarse; salir del huevo

hat'-check' girl s guardarropa

hatchet ['hætʃɪt] s destral m, hacha pequeña; **to bury the hatchet** envainar la espada

hatch'way' s (trap door) escotillón m; (opening in ship's deck) escotilla

hate [het] s odio, aborrecimiento ‖ tr & intr odiar, aborrecer, detestar

hateful ['hetfəl] adj odioso, aborrecible

hat'pin' s aguja de sombrero, pasador m

hat'rack' s percha

hatred ['hetrɪd] s odio, aborrecimiento

hat shop s bonetería

hatter ['hætər] s sombrerero

haughtiness ['hɔtɪnɪs] s altanería, altivez f

haugh·ty ['hɔti] adj (comp -tier; super -iest) altanero, altivo

haul [hɔl] s (pull, tug) tirón m; (amount caught) redada; (distance transported) trayecto, recorrido; (roundup, e.g., of thieves) redada ‖ tr acarrear, transportar; (naut) halar

haunch [hɔntʃ] o [hɑntʃ] s (hip) cadera; (hind quarter of an animal) anca; (leg of animal used for food) pierna

haunt [hɔnt] o [hɑnt] s guarida, nidal m, querencia ‖ tr andar por, vagar por; frecuentar; inquietar, molestar; perseguir (las memorias a una persona)

haunted house s casa de fantasmas

haute couture [ot ku'tyr] s alta moda

Havana [hə'vænə] s La Habana

have [hæv] v (pret & pp had [hæd]) tr tener; (to get, to take) tomar; **to have and to hold** (úsase sólo en el infinitivo) para ser poseído en propiedad; **to have got** (coll) tener, poseer; **to have got to** + inf (coll) tener que + inf; **to have it in for** (coll) tener tirria a; **to have it out with** (coll) habérselas con, emprenderla con; **to have on** llevar puesto; **to have** (something) **to do with** tener que ver con; **to have what it takes to** tener madera de; **to have** + inf hacer, mandar + inf, p.ej., **I had him go out that door** le hice salir por esa puerta; **to have** + pp hacer, mandar + inf, p.ej., **I had my watch repaired** hice componer mi reloj ‖ intr — **to have at** atacar, embestir; **to have to** + inf tener que + inf; **to have to do with** (to be concerned with) tratar de; (to have connections with) tener relaciones con ‖ v aux haber, p.ej., **he has studied his lesson** ha estudiado su lección

havelock ['hævlɑk] s cogotera

haven ['hevən] s puerto; abrigo, asilo, buen puerto

have-not ['hæv,nɑt] s — **the haves and the have-nots** (coll) los ricos y los desposeídos

haversack ['hævər,sæk] s barjuleta; (of soldier) mochila

havoc ['hævək] s estrago, estragos; **to play havoc with** hacer grandes estragos en

haw [hɔ] s (of hawthorn) baya, simiente f; (in speech) vacilación ‖ interj ¡a la izquierda! ‖ tr & intr volver a la izquierda

haw'-haw' s carcajada

hawk [hɔk] s halcón m, gavilán m, cernícalo; (mortarboard) esparavel m; (sharper) (coll) fullero ‖ tr pregonar; **to hawk up** arrojar tosiendo ‖ intr carraspear, gargajear

hawker ['hɔkər] s buhonero

hawksbill turtle ['hɔks,bɪl] s carey m

hawse [hɔz] s (naut) muz m; (hole) (naut) escobén m; (naut) longitud de cadenas

hawse'hole' s (naut) escobén m

hawser ['hɔzər] s (naut) guindaleza

haw'thorn' s espino, oxiacanta

hay [he] *s* heno; **to hit the hay** (slang) acostarse; **to make hay while the sun shines** hacer su agosto

hay fever *s* fiebre *f* del heno

hay′field′ *s* henar *m*

hay′fork′ *s* horca; (*machine*) elevador *m* de heno

hay′loft′ *s* henil *m*, henal *m*

hay′mak′er *s* (box) golpe *m* que pone fuera de combate

haymow [ˈheˌmau] *s* henil *m;* acopio de heno

hay′rack′ *s* pesebre *m*

hayrick [ˈheˌrɪk] *s* almiar *m*

hay ride *s* paseo de placer en carro de heno

hay′seed′ *s* simiente *f* de heno; (coll) patán *m*, campesino

hay′stack′ *s* almiar *m*

hay′wire′ *adj* (slang) descompuesto; (slang) destornillado, loco ‖ *s* alambre *m* para embalar el heno

hazard [ˈhæzərd] *s* peligro, riesgo; (*chance*) acaso, azar *m;* (golf) obstáculo; **at all hazards** por grande que sea el riesgo ‖ *tr* arriesgar; aventurar (*una opinión*)

hazardous [ˈhæzərdəs] *adj* peligroso, arriesgado

haze [hez] *s* calina, bruma; (fig) confusión, vaguedad ‖ *tr* dar novatada a

hazel [ˈhezəl] *adj* castaño claro ‖ *s* avellano

ha′zel•nut *s* avellana

hazing [ˈhezɪŋ] *s* novatada

ha•zy [ˈhezi] *adj* (*comp* **-zier;** *super* **-ziest**) calinoso, brumoso; confuso, vago

H-bomb [ˈetʃˌbɑm] *s* bomba de hidrógeno

H.C. *abbr* **House of Commons**

hd. *abbr* **head**

hdqrs. *abbr* **headquarters**

H.E. *abbr* **His Eminence, His Excellency**

he [hi] *pron pers* (*pl* **they**) él ‖ *s* (*pl* **hes**) macho, varón *m*

head [hɛd] *s* cabeza; (*of a bed*) cabecera; (*caption*) encabezamiento; (*of a boil*) centro; (*on a glass of beer*) espuma; (*of a drum*) parche *m;* (*of a cane*) puño; (*of a barrel, cylinder, etc.*) fondo, tapa; (*of cylinder of automobile engine*) culata; crisis *f*, punto decisivo; **at the head of** al frente de; **from head to foot** de pies a cabeza; **head over heels** en un salto mortal; hasta los tuétanos; precipitadamente; **heads** (*of a coin*) cara; **heads or tails?** ¿cara o cruz?; ¿águila o sol? (Mex); **over one's head** fuera del alcance de uno; (*going to a higher authority*) por encima de uno; **to be out of one's head** (coll) delirar; **to come into one's head** pasarle a uno por la cabeza; **to go to one's head** subírsele a uno a la cabeza; **to keep one's head;** no perder la cabeza; **to keep one's head above water** no dejarse vencer; **to put heads together** consultarse entre sí; **to not make head or tail of** no ver pies ni cabeza a ‖ *tr* acaudillar, dirigir, mandar; estar a la cabeza de (*p.ej., la clase*); venir primero en (*una lista*) ‖ *intr* — **to head towards** dirigirse hacia

head′ache′ *s* dolor *m* de cabeza

head′band′ *s* cinta para la cabeza; (*of a book*) cabezada

head′board′ *s* cabecera de cama

head′cheese′ *s* queso de cerdo

head′dress′ *s* (*style of hair*) tocado; prenda para la cabeza

header [ˈhɛdər] *s* — **to take a header** (coll) caerse de cabeza

head′first′ *adv* de cabeza; precipitadamente

head′gear′ *s* sombrero; (*for protection*) casco

head′hunt′er *s* cazador *m* de cabezas

heading [ˈhɛdɪŋ] *s* encabezamiento; (*of a letter*) membrete *m;* (*of a chapter of a book*) cabecera

headland [ˈhɛdlənd] *s* promontorio

headless [ˈhɛdlɪs] *adj* sin cabeza; sin jefe; estúpido

head′light′ *s* (aut) faro; (naut) farol *m* de tope; (rr) farol *m*

head′line′ *s* (*of newspaper*) cabecera; (*of a page of a book*) titulillo, título de página ‖ *tr* poner cabecera a; (slang) destacar, dar cartel a (*un actor*)

head′lin′er *s* (slang) atracción principal

head′long′ *adj* de cabeza; precipitado ‖ *adv* de cabeza; precipitadamente

head•man [ˈhɛdˌmæn] *s* (*pl* **-men** [ˌmɛn]) caudillo, jefe *m*

head′mas′ter *s* director *m* de un colegio

head′most′ *adj* delantero, primero

head office *s* oficina central

head of hair *s* cabellera

head′-on′ *adj* & *adv* de frente; **head-on collision** colisión de frente

head′phone′ *s* auricular *m* de casco, receptor *m* de cabeza

head′piece′ *s* (*any covering for head*) casco, yelmo, morrión *m;* (*brains, judgment*) cabeza, juicio; cabecera de cama; (*headset*) auricular *m* de casco, receptor *m* de cabeza; (typ) cabecera, viñeta

head′quar′ters *s* centro de dirección; (*of police*) jefatura; (mil) cuartel *m* general

head′rest′ *s* apoyo para la cabeza; (aut) reposa cabezas

head′set′ *s* auricular *m* de casco, receptor *m* de cabeza

head′ship′ *s* jefatura, dirección

head′stone′ *s* (*cornerstone*) piedra angular; (*on a grave*) lápida sepulcral

head′stream′ *s* afluente *m* principal

head′strong′ *adj* cabezudo, terco

head′wait′er *s* jefe *m* de camareros, encargado de comedor

head′wa′ters *spl* cabecera

head′way′ *s* avance *m*, progreso; espacio libre; **to make headway** avanzar, progresar

head′wear′ *s* prendas de cabeza

head wind *s* viento de frente, viento por la proa

head′work′ *s* trabajo intelectual

head•y [ˈhɛdi] *adj* (*comp* **-ier;** *super* **-iest**) excitante, emocionante; impetuoso, violento; (*intoxicating*) cabezudo; (*clever*) sesudo

heal [hil] *tr* curar, sanar; cicatrizar; remediar (*un daño*) ‖ *intr* curar, sanar; cicatrizarse; remediarse

healer ['hilər] *s* curador *m*, sanador *m*

health [hɛlθ] *s* salud *f*; **to be in good health** estar bien de salud; **to be in poor health** estar mal de salud; **to drink to the health of** beber a la salud de; **to radiate health** verter salud; **to your health!** ¡a su salud!

healthful ['hɛlθfəl] *adj* saludable; sano

health insurance *s* seguro de enfermedad

health·y ['hɛlθi] *adj* (*comp* **-ier**; *super* **-iest**) sano; saludable

heap [hip] *s* montón *m* ‖ *tr* amontonar, apilar; (*to supply with, e.g., favors*) colmar; (*to bestow in great quantity*) dar generosamente ‖ *intr* amontonarse, apilarse

hear [hɪr] *v* (*pret & pp* **heard** [hʌrd]) *tr* oír; **to hear it said** oírlo decir ‖ *intr* oír; **hear! hear!** ¡bravo!; **to hear about;** oír hablar de; **to hear from** tener noticias de; **to hear of** oír hablar de; **to hear tell of** oír hablar de; **to hear that** oír decir que

hearer ['hɪrər] *s* oyente *mf*

hearing ['hɪrɪŋ] *s* (*sense*) oído; (*act*) oída; audiencia; **in the hearing of** en presencia de; **within hearing** al alcance del oído

hearing aid *s* aparato auditivo

hear·say ['hɪr,se] *s* rumor *m*; **by hearsay** de o por oídas

hearse [hʌrs] *s* coche *m* fúnebre, carroza fúnebre

heart [hɑrt] *s* corazón *m*; (*e.g., of lettuce*) cogollo; **after one's heart** enteramente del gusto de uno; **by heart** de memoria; **heart and soul** con todo corazón; **to break the heart of** partir el corazón de; **to die of a broken heart** morir de pena; **to eat one's heart out** sufrir en silencio; **to get to the heart of** llegar al fondo de; **to have one's heart in one's work;** trabajar con entusiasmo; **to have one's heart in the right place** tener buenas intenciones; **to lose heart** descorazonarse; **to open one's heart to** descubrirse con; **to take heart** cobrar aliento; **to take to heart** tomar a pecho; **to wear one's heart on one's sleeve** llevar el corazón en la mano; **with all one's heart** con toda el alma de uno; **with one's heart in one's mouth** con el credo en la boca

heart·ache *s* angustia, congoja

heart attack *s* ataque *m* de corazón, ataque cardíaco

heart·beat *s* latido del corazón

heart·break *s* angustia, dolor *m* abrumador

heart·break·er *s* ladrón *m* de corazones

heartbroken ['hɑrt,brokən] *adj* transido de dolor, muerto de pena

heart·burn *s* acedía, rescoldera; (*jealousy*) celos

heart disease *s* enfermedad del corazón

hearten ['hɑrtən] *tr* alentar, animar

heart failure *s* debilidad coronaria; (*death*) paro del corazón; (*faintness*) desfallecimiento, desmayo

heartfelt ['hɑrt,fɛlt] *adj* cordial, sentido, sincero

hearth [hɑrθ] *s* hogar *m*

hearth·stone· *s* solera del hogar; (*home*) hogar *m*

heartily ['hɑrtɪli] *adv* cordialmente; con buen apetito; de buena gana; bien, mucho

heartless ['hɑrtlɪs] *adj* cruel, inhumano

heart pacemaker *s* marcapaso, marcapasos *m*

heart-rending ['hɑrt,rɛndɪŋ] *adj* angustioso, que parte el corazón

heart·seed· *s* farolillo

heart·sick· *adj* afligido, desconsolado

heart·strings· *spl* fibras del corazón, entretelas

heart·-to-heart· *adj* franco, sincero

heart trouble *s* — **to have heart trouble** enfermar del corazón

heart·wood· *s* madera de corazón

heart·y ['hɑrti] *adj* (*comp* **-ier**; *super* **-iest**) cordial, sincero; sano, fuerte; (*meal*) abundante; (*laugh*) bueno; (*eater*) grande

heat [hit] *adj* térmico ‖ *s* calor *m*; (*warming of a room, house, etc.*) calefacción; (*rut of animals*) celo; (*in horse racing*) carrera de prueba; (fig) ardor *m*, ímpetu *m*; **in heat** encelo ‖ *tr* calentar; calefaccionar (*p.ej., una casa*); (fig) acalorar, excitar ‖ *intr* calentarse; (fig) acalorarse, excitarse

heated ['hitɪd] *adj* acalorado

heater ['hitər] *s* calentador *m*; (*for central heating*) calorífero; (electron) calefactor *m*

heater man *s* calefactor *m*

heath [hiθ] *s* (*shrub*) brezo; (*tract of land*) brezal *m*

hea·then ['hiðən] *adj* gentil, pagano; irreligioso ‖ *s* (*pl* **-then** o **-thens**) gentil *mf*, pagano

heathendom ['hiðəndəm] *s* gentilidad

heather ['hɛðər] *s* brezo

heating ['hitɪŋ] *adj* calentador ‖ *s* calefacción

heat·-in·su·lat·ed *adj* termoaislante

heat lightning *s* fucilazo, relámpago de calor

heat shield *s* blindaje térmico, escudo térmico

heat·stroke· *s* insolación; golpe *m* de calor

heat wave *s* (phys) onda calorífica; (coll) ola de calor

heave [hiv] *s* esfuerzo para levantar; esfuerzo para levantarse; **heaves** (vet) huélfago ‖ *v* (*pret & pp* **heaved** o **hov** [hov]) *tr* alzar, levantar; arrojar, lanzar; exhalar (*un suspiro*) ‖ *intr* levantarse y bajar alternativamente; palpitar (*el pecho*); elevarse; hacer esfuerzos por vomitar

heaven ['hɛvən] *s* cielo; **for heaven's sake!** o **good heavens!** ¡válgame Dios!; **heavens** (*firmament*) cielo ‖ **Heaven** *s* cielo (*mansión de los bienaventurados*)

heaven·ly ['hɛvənli] *adj* (*body*) celeste; (*life, home*) celestial; (fig) celestial

heavenly body *s* astro, cuerpo celeste

heav·y ['hɛvi] *adj* (*comp* **-ier**; *super* **-iest**) (*of great weight*) pesado; (*liquid*) espeso, denso; (*cloth, paper, sea, line*) grueso;

(*traffic*) denso; (*crop, harvest*) abundante, copioso; (*expense*) fuerte; (*rain*) recio; (*features*) basto; (*eyes*) agravado; (*gunfire*) fragoroso; (*heart*) abatido, triste; (*drinker*) grande; (*stock market*) postrado; (*clothing*) de mucho abrigo ‖ *adv* pesadamente; **to hang heavy;** pasar (*el tiempo*) con gran lentitud

heav'y•du'ty *adj* extrafuerte

heavy-hearted ['hɛvi'hɑrtɪd] *adj* afligido, acongojado

heav'y•set' *adj* costilludo, espaldudo

heav'y•weight' *s* (box) peso pesado

Hebrew ['hibru] *adj & s* hebreo

hecatomb ['hɛkə,tom] *s* hecatombe *f*

heckle ['hɛkəl] *tr* interrumpir (*a un orador*) con preguntas impertinentes

hectic ['hɛktɪk] *adj* (coll) agitado, turbulento

hedge [hɛdʒ] *s* cercado, vallado; (*of bushes*) seto vivo; apuesta compensatoria; (*in stock market*) operación compensatoria ‖ *tr* cercar con vallado; cercar con seto vivo; **to hedge in** encerrar, rodear ‖ *intr* no querer comprometerse; hacer apuestas compensatorias; hacer operaciones compensatorias

hedge'hog' *s* erizo; (*porcupine*) puerco espín *m*

hedge'hop' *v* (*pret & pp* **-hopped;** *ger* **-hopping**) *intr* (aer) volar rasando el suelo

hedgehopping ['hɛdʒ,hɑpɪŋ] *s* (aer) vuelo rasante

hedge'row' *s* cercado de arbustos, seto vivo

heed [hid] *s* atención, cuidado; **to take heed** ir con cuidado ‖ *tr* atender a, hacer caso de ‖ *intr* atender, hacer caso

heedless ['hidlɪs] *adj* desatento, descuidado

heehaw ['hi,hɔ] *s* (*of donkey*) rebuzno; risotada ‖ *intr* rebuznar; reír groseramente

heel [hil] *s* (*of foot*) calcañar *m*, talón *m*; (*of stocking or shoe*) talón *m*; (*raised part of shoe below heel*) tacón *m*; (slang) sinvergüenza *mf*; **down at the heel** desaliñado, mal vestido; **to cool one's heels** (coll) hacer antesala; **to kick up one's heels** (slang) mostrarse alegre; **to show a clean pair of heels** o **to take to one's heels** poner pies en polvorosa

heeler ['hilər] *s* (slang) muñidor *m*

heft•y ['hɛfti] *adj* (*comp* **-ier;** *super* **-iest**) (*heavy*) pesado; (*strong*) fuerte, fornido

hegemo•ny [hɪ'dʒɛməni] o ['hɛdʒɪ-,moni] *s* (*pl* **-nies**) hegemonía

hegira [hɪ'dʒɑɪrə] o ['hɛdʒɪrə] *s* fuga, huída

heifer ['hɛfər] *s* novilla, vaquilla

height [hɑɪt] *s* altura; (*e.g., of folly*) colmo

heighten ['hɑɪtən] *tr* hacer más alto; (*to increase the amount of*) aumentar; (*to set off, bring out*) realzar ‖ *intr* aumentarse

heinous ['henəs] *adj* atroz, nefando

heir [ɛr] *s* heredero

heir apparent *s* (*pl* **heirs apparent**) heredero forzoso

heirdom ['ɛrdəm] *s* herencia

heiress ['ɛrɪs] *s* heredera

heirloom ['ɛr,lum] *s* joya de familia, reliquia de familia

helicopter ['hɛlɪ,kɑptər] *s* helicóptero

heliotrope ['hilɪ•ə,trop] *s* heliotropo

heliport ['hɛlɪ,port] *s* helipuerto

helium ['hilɪ•əm] *s* helio

helix ['hilɪks] *s* (*pl* **helixes** o **helices** ['hɛlɪ,siz]) hélice *f*

hell [hɛl] *s* infierno

hell-bent ['hɛl'bɛnt] *adj* (slang) muy resuelto; **hell-bent on** (slang) empeñado en

hell'cat' *s* (*bad-tempered woman*) arpía, mujer perversa; (*witch*) bruja

hellebore ['hɛlɪ,bor] *s* eléboro

Hellene ['hɛlin] *s* heleno

Hellenic [hɛ'lɛnɪk] *adj* helénico

hell'fire' *s* fuego del infierno

hellish ['hɛlɪʃ] *adj* infernal

hel-lo [hɛ'lo] *s* saludo ‖ *interj* ¡qué tal!; (*on telephone*) ¡diga!

hello girl *s* (coll) chica telefonista

helm [hɛlm] *s* barra del timón; rueda del timón; (fig) timón *m* ‖ *tr* dirigir, gobernar

helmet ['hɛlmɪt] *s* casco; (*of ancient armor*) yelmo

helms•man ['hɛlmzmən] *s* (*pl* **-men** [mən]) timonel *m*

help [hɛlp] *s* ayuda, socorro; (*of food*) ración; (*relief*) remedio, p.ej., **there's no help for it** no hay remedio; criados; empleados; obreros; **to come to the help of** acudir en socorro de ‖ *interj* ¡socorro! ‖ *tr* ayudar, socorrer; aliviar, mitigar; (*to wait on*) servir; **it can't be helped** no hay remedio; **so help me God!** ¡así Dios me salve!; **to help down** ayudar a bajar; **to help a person with his coat** ayudarle a una persona a ponerse el abrigo; **to help oneself** valerse por sí mismo; servirse; **to help up** ayudar a subir; ayudar a levantarse; **to not be able to help** + *ger* no poder menos de + *inf*, p.ej., **he can't help laughing** no puede menos de reír ‖ *intr* ayudar

helper ['hɛlpər] *s* ayudante *mf*; (*in a drug store, barbershop, etc.*) mancebo

helpful ['hɛlpfəl] *adj* útil, provechoso; servicial

helping [['hɛlpɪŋ] *s* ración (*de alimento*)

helpless ['hɛlplɪs] *adj* (*weak*) débil; (*powerless*) impotente; (*penniless*) desvalido; (*confused*) perplejo; (*situation*) irremediable

help'meet' *s* compañero; (*wife*) compañera

helter-skelter ['hɛltər'skɛltər] *adj, adv & s* cochite hervite *m*

hem [hɛm] *s* tos fingida; (*of a garment*) bastilla, dobladillo ‖ *interj* ¡ejem! ‖ *v* (*pret & pp* **hemmed;** *ger* **hemming**) *tr* bastillar, dobladillar; **to hem in** encerrar, rodear ‖ *intr* destoserse; vacilar; **to hem and haw** vacilar al hablar; ser evasivo

hemisphere ['hɛmɪ,sfɪr] *s* hemisferio

hemistich ['hɛmɪ,stɪk] *s* hemistiquio

hem'line' *s* ruedo de la falda, borde *m* de la falda

hem'lock' *s* (*Tsuga canadensis*) abeto del Canadá; (*herb and poison*) cicuta

hemoglobin [,hɛmə'globɪn] o [,himə'globɪn] *s* hemoglobina

he
he

hemophilia [,hɛmə'fɪlɪ•ə] o [,hiːmə'fɪlɪ•ə] *s* hemofilia

hemorrhage ['hɛmərɪdʒ] *s* hemorragia

hemorrhoids ['hɛmə,rɔɪdz] *spl* hemorroides *fpl*

hemostat ['hɛmə,stæt] o ['hiːmə,stæt] *s* hemóstato

hemp [hɛmp] *s* cáñamo

hemstitch ['hɛm,stɪtʃ] *s* vainica ‖ *tr* hacer vainica en ‖ *intr* hacer vainica

hen [hɛn] *s* gallina

hence [hɛns] *adv* de aquí; desde ahora; por lo tanto, por consiguiente; de aquí a, p.ej., **three weeks hence** de aquí a tres semanas

hence'forth *adv* de aquí en adelante

hench•man ['hɛntʃmən] *s* (*pl* **-men** [mən]) secuaz *m*, servidor *m*; (*political schemer*) muñidor *m*

hen'coop' *s* gallinero

hen'house' *s* gallinero

henna ['hɛnə] *s* alcana, alheña; (*dye*) henna *f* ‖ *tr* alheñarse (*el pelo*)

hen'peck' *tr* dominar (*la mujer al marido*)

henpecked husband *s* calzonazos *m*, gurrumino

hep [hɛp] *adj* (slang) enterado; **to be hep to** (slang) estar al corriente de

her [hʌr] *adj poss* su; el . . . de ella ‖ *pron pers* la; ella; **to her** le; a ella

herald ['hɛrəld] *s* heraldo; anunciador *m* ‖ *tr* anunciar; ser precursor de

heraldic [hɛ'rældɪk] *adj* heráldico

herald•ry ['hɛrəldri] *s* (*pl* **-ries**) (*office or duty of herald*) heraldía; (*science of armorial bearings*) blasón *m*, heráldica; (*heraldic device; coat of arms*) blasón *m*; pompa heráldica

herb [ʌrb] o [hʌrb] *s* hierba; hierba aromática; hierba medicinal

herbaceous [hʌr'beʃəs] *adj* herbáceo

herbage ['ʌrbɪdʒ] o ['hʌrbɪdʒ] *s* herbaje *m*

herbal ['ʌrbəl] o ['hʌrbəl] *adj & s* herbario

herbalist ['hʌrbəlɪst] o ['ʌrbəlɪst] *s* herbolario

herbari•um [hʌr'bɛrɪ•əm] *s* (*pl* **-ums** o **-a** [ə]) herbario

herb doctor *s* herbolario

herculean [hʌr'kulɪ•ən] *adj* (*hard to perform*) penoso, laborioso; (*strong, big*) hercúleo

herd [hʌrd] *s* manada, rebaño, hato; (*of people*) chusma, multitud ‖ *tr* reunir en manada; reunir ‖ *intr* reunirse en manada; reunirse, ir juntos

herds•man ['hʌrdzmən] *s* (*pl* **-men** [mən]) manadero; (*of sheep*) pastor *m*; (*of cattle*) vaquero

here [hɪr] *adj* presente ‖ *adv* aquí; **here and there** acá y allá; **here is** o **here are** aquí tiene Vd.; **that's neither here nor there** eso no viene al caso ‖ *s* — **the here and the hereafter** esta vida y la futura ‖ *interj* ¡presente!

hereabouts ['hɪrə,bauts] *adv* por aquí, cerca de aquí

here•af'ter *adv* de aquí en adelante; en lo sucesivo; en la vida futura ‖ **the hereafter** la otra vida, el más allá

here•by' *adv* por esto; por la presente

hereditary [hɪ'rɛdɪ,tɛri] *adj* hereditario

heredi•ty [hɪ'rɛdɪti] *s* (*pl* **-ties**) herencia

here•in' *adv* aquí dentro; en este asunto

here•of' *adv* de esto

here•on' *adv* en esto, sobre esto

here•sy ['hɛrəsi] *s* (*pl* **-sies**) herejía

heretic ['hɛrətɪk] *adj* herético ‖ *s* hereje *mf*

heretical [hɪ'rɛtɪkəl] *adj* herético

heretofore [,hɪtru'for] *adv* antes, hasta ahora

here•u•pon' *adv* en esto, sobre esto; en seguida

here•with' *adv* adjunto, con la presente; de este modo

heritage ['hɛrɪtɪdʒ] *s* herencia

hermetic(al) [hʌr'mɛtɪk(əl)] *adj* hermético

hermit ['hʌrmɪt] *s* eremita *m*, ermitaño

hermitage ['hʌrmɪtɪdʒ] *s* ermita

herni•a ['hʌrnɪ•ə] *s* (*pl* **-as** o **-ae** [,i]) hernia

he•ro ['hɪro] *s* (*pl* **-roes**) héroe *m*

heroic [hɪ'ro•ɪk] *adj* heroico ‖ **heroics** *spl* verso heroico; lenguaje rimbombante

heroin ['hɛro•ɪn] *s* heroína (*polvo cristalino*); (slang) caballo

heroin addict *s* heroinómano

heroine ['hɛro•ɪn] *s* heroína (*mujer*)

heroism ['hɛro,ɪzəm] *s* heroísmo

heron ['hɛrən] *s* garza; (*Ardea cinerea*) airón *m*, garza real

herring ['hɛrɪŋ] *s* arenque *m*

her'ring•bone' *s* (*in fabrics*) espina de pescado; (*in hardwood floors*) espinapez *m*, punto de Hungría

hers [hʌrz] *pron poss* el suyo, el de ella; suyo

herself [hʌr'sɛlf] *pron pers* ella misma; sí, sí misma; se, p.ej., **she enjoyed herself** se divirtió; **with herself** consigo

hesitan•cy ['hɛzɪtənsi] *s* (*pl* **-cies**) vacilación

hesitant ['hɛzɪtənt] *adj* vacilante

hesitate ['hɛzɪ,tet] *intr* vacilar, titubear; (*to stutter*) titubear

hesitation [,hɛzɪ'teʃən] *s* vacilación

heterodox ['hɛtərə,dɑks] *adj* heterodoxo

heterodyne ['hɛtərə,daɪn] *adj* heterodino ‖ *tr* heterodinar

heterogenei•ty [,hɛtərədʒɪ'ni•ɪti] *s* (*pl* **-ties**) heterogeneidad

heterogeneous [,hɛtərə'dʒini•əs] *adj* heterogéneo

hew [hju] *v* (*pret* **hewed**; *pp* **hewed** o **hewn**) *tr* cortar, tajar; (*with an ax*) hachear; labrar (*madera*); picar (*piedra*); **to hew down** derribar a hachazos ‖ *intr* — **to hew close to the line** (coll) hilar delgado

hex [hɛks] *s* (coll) bruja; (coll) hechizo ‖ *tr* (coll) embrujar

hexameter [hɛks'æmɪtər] *s* hexámetro

hey [he] *interj* ¡oye!, ¡oiga!

hey'day' *s* época de mayor prosperidad

hf. *abbr* **half**

H.H. *abbr* **His Highness, Her Highness; His Holiness**

hia•tus [haɪ'etəs] *s* (*pl* **-tuses** o **-tus**) (*gap*) abertura, laguna; (*in a text; in verse*) hiato hibernate ['haɪbər,net] *intr* invernar; estar inactivo

hibiscus [hɪ'bɪskəs] o [haɪ'bɪskəs] *s* hibisco

hiccough o hiccup ['hɪkəp] *s* hipo ‖ *intr* hipar

hick [hɪk] *adj & s* (coll) campesino, palurdo

hicko·ry ['hɪkəri] *s* (*pl* -ries) nuez encarcelada, nuez dura (*árbol*)

hickory nut *s* nuez encarcelada, nuez dura (*fruto*)

hidden ['hɪdən] *adj* escondido, oculto; obscuro

hide [haɪd] *s* cuero, piel *f;* hides corambre *f;* neither hide nor hair ni un vestigio; to tan someone's hide (coll) zurrarle a uno la badana ‖ *v* (*pret* hid [hɪd]; *pp* hid o hidden ['hɪdən]) *tr* esconder, ocultar ‖ *intr* esconderse, ocultarse; to hide out (coll) recatarse

hide'-and-seek' *s* escondite *m;* to play hide-and-seek jugar al escondite

hide'bound' *adj* fanático, obstinado, dogmático

hideous ['hɪdɪ·əs] *adj* (*very ugly*) feote; (*heinous*) atroz, nefando; (*distressingly large*) brutal, enorme

hide'-out' *s* (coll) guarida, refugio, escondrijo

hiding ['haɪdɪŋ] *s* ocultación; (*place of concealment*) escondite *m,* escondrijo; in hiding escondido, oculto; (*in ambush*) emboscado

hiding place *s* escondite *m,* escondrijo

hie [haɪ] *v* (*pret & pp* hied; *ger* hieing o hying) *tr* — hie thee home apresúrate a volver a casa ‖ *intr* apresurarse, ir volando

hierar·chy ['haɪ·ə,rɑrki] *s* (*pl* -chies) jerarquía

hieroglyphic [,haɪ·ərə'glɪfɪk] *adj & s* jeroglífico

hi-fi ['haɪ'faɪ] *adj* de alta fidelidad ‖ *s* alta fidelidad

hi-fi fan *s* aficionado a la alta fidelidad

hi-fi set *s* equipo de alta fidelidad

higgledy-piggledy ['hɪgəldi'pɪgəldi] *adj* confuso, revuelto ‖ *adv* confusamente, revueltamente

high [haɪ] *adj* alto; (*river*) crecido; (*sound*) agudo; (*wind*) fuerte; (coll) borracho; (*intoxicated*) embriagado; (*drugs*) emporrado; (culin) manido; high and dry abandonado, desamparado; high and mighty (coll) muy arrogante ‖ *adv* en sumo grado; a gran precio; to aim high poner el tiro muy alto; to come high venderse caro ‖ *s* (aut) marcha directa; on high en el cielo

high altar *s* altar *m* mayor

high'ball' *s* highball *m*

high blood pressure *s* hipertensión arterial

high'born' *adj* linajudo, de ilustre cuna

high'boy' *s* cómoda alta con patas altas

high'brow' *adj & s* (slang) erudito

high chair *s* silla alta

high command *s* alto mando

high cost of living *s* carestía de la vida

higher education *s* enseñanza superior

higher-up [,haɪ·ər·'ʌp] *s* (coll) superior jerárquico

high explosive *s* explosivo rompedor

highfalutin [,haɪfə'lutən] *adj* (coll) pomposo, presuntuoso

high fidelity *s* alta fidelidad

high'-fre'quency *adj* de alta frecuencia

high gear *s* marcha directa, toma directa

high'-grade' *adj* de calidad superior

high-handed ['haɪ'hændɪd] *adj* arbitrario

high hat *s* sombrero de copa

high'-hat' *adj* (coll) copetudo, esnob; to be high-hat tener mucho copete ‖ high'-hat' *v* (*pret & pp* -hatted; *ger* -hatting) *tr* desairar

high-heeled shoe ['haɪ,hild] *s* zapato de tacón alto

high horse *s* ademán *m* arrogante

high'jack' *tr* var de hijack

high jinks [dʒɪŋks] *spl* (slang) jarana, payasada

high jump *s* salto de altura

highland ['haɪlənd] *s* región montañosa; highlands montañas, tierras altas

high life *s* alta sociedad, gran mundo

high'light' *s* elemento sobresaliente ‖ *tr* destacar

highly ['haɪli] *adv* altamente; en sumo grado; a gran precio; con aplauso general; to speak highly of decir mil bienes de

High Mass *s* misa cantada, misa mayor

high-minded ['haɪ'maɪndɪd] *adj* noble, magnánimo

highness ['haɪnɪs] *s* altura ‖ Highness *s* Alteza

high noon *s* pleno mediodía

high-pitched ['haɪ'pɪtʃt] *adj* agudo; tenso, impresionable

high-powered ['haɪ'pau·ərd] *adj* de alta potencia

high'-pres'sure *adj* de alta presión; (fig) emprendedor, enérgico ‖ *tr* (coll) apremiar

high-priced ['haɪ'praɪst] *adj* de precio elevado

high priest *s* sumo sacerdote

high rise *s* edificio de muchos pisos

high'road' *s* camino real

high school *s* escuela de segunda enseñanza

high sea *s* mar gruesa; high seas alta mar

high society *s* alta sociedad, gran mundo

high'-speed' *adj* de alta velocidad

high-spirited ['haɪ'spɪrɪtɪd] *adj* animoso; vivaz; (*horse*) fogoso

high spirits *spl* alegría, buen humor *m,* animación

high-strung ['haɪ'strʌŋ] *adj* tenso, impresionable

high'-test' fuel *s* supercarburante *m*

high tide *s* pleamar *f,* marea alta; (fig) punto culminante

high time *s* hora, p.ej., it is high time for you to go ya es hora de que Vd. se marche; (slang) jarana, parranda

high treason *s* alta traición

high water *s* aguas altas; pleamar *f,* marea alta

high'way' *s* carretera

highway•man [ˈhaɪˌwemən] s (pl -men [mən]) salteador m de caminos

hijack [ˈhaɪˌdʒæk] tr (coll) robar (a un contrabandista de licores); (coll) robar (el licor a un contrabandista)

hijacker [ˈhaɪˌdʒækər] s pirata aéreo

hijacking [ˈhaɪˌdʒækɪŋ] s piratería aérea

hike [haɪk] s caminata, marcha; (increase, rise) aumento ‖ tr elevar de un tirón; aumentar ‖ intr dar una caminata

hiker [ˈhaɪkər] s caminador m, aficionado a las caminatas

hilarious [hɪˈlɛrɪ•əs] o [haɪˈlɛrɪ•əs] adj jubiloso, regocijado

hill [hɪl] s colina, collado ‖ tr aporcar (las hortalizas)

hillbil•ly [ˈhɪlˌbɪli] s (pl -lies) (coll) rústico montañés (del sur de los EE.UU.)

hillock [ˈhɪlək] s altozano, montecillo

hill′side′ s ladera

hill′top′ s cumbre f, cima

hill•y [ˈhɪli] adj (comp -ier; super -iest) colinoso; (steep) empinado

hilt [hɪlt] s empuñadura, puño; **up to the hilt** completamente

him [hɪm] pron pers le, lo; él; **to him** le; a él

himself [hɪmˈsɛlf] pron pers él mismo; sí, sí mismo; se, p.ej., **he enjoyed himself** se divirtió; **with himself** consigo

hind [haɪnd] adj posterior, trasero ‖ s cierva

hinder [ˈhɪndər] tr estorbar, impedir; obstruccionar

hindmost [ˈhaɪndˌmost] adj postrero, último

Hindoo [ˈhɪndu] adj & s hindú m

hind′quar′ter s cuarto trasero

hindrance [ˈhɪndrəns] s estorbo, impedimento, obstáculo

hind′sight′ s (of a firearm) mira posterior; percepción tardía, sabiduría tardía

Hindu [ˈhɪndu] adj & s hindú m

hinge [hɪndʒ] s (of a door) charnela, gozne m, bisagra; (of a mollusk) charnela; (bb) cartivana; punto capital ‖ tr engoznar ‖ intr — **to hinge on** depender de

hin•ny [ˈhɪni] s (pl -nies) burdégano, mohino

hint [hɪnt] s indirecta, insinuación; **to take the hint** darse por aludido ‖ tr & intr insinuar; indicar; **to hint at** aludir indirectamente a

hinterland [ˈhɪntərˌlænd] s región interior

hip [hɪp] s cadera; (of a roof) caballete m, lima

hip′bone′ s cía, hueso de la cadera

hipped [hɪpt] adj (livestock) renco; (roof) a cuatro aguas; **hipped on** (coll) obsesionado por

hippety-hop [ˈhɪpɪtɪˈhɑp] adv (coll) a coxcojita

hip•po [ˈhɪpo] s (pl -pos) (coll) hipopótamo

hippodrome [ˈhɪpəˌdrom] s hipódromo

hippopota•mus [ˌhɪpəˈpɑtəməs] s (pl -muses o -mi [ˌmaɪ]) hipopótamo

hip roof s tejado a cuatro aguas

hire [haɪr] s alquiler m; precio; salario; **for hire** de alquiler ‖ tr alquilar (p.ej., un coche); ajustar (p.ej., a un criado) ‖ intr —**to hire out** ajustarse

hired girl s criada

hired man s (coll) mozo de campo

hireling [ˈhaɪrlɪŋ] adj & s alquiladizo

his [hɪz] adj poss su; el . . . de él ‖ pron poss el suyo, el de él; suyo

Hispanic [hɪsˈpænɪk] adj & s hispánico

Hispaniola [ˌhɪspənˈjolə] s Santo Domingo

hispanist [ˈhɪspənɪst] s hispanista mf

hispanophilia [hɪsˌpænoˈfɪli•ə] s españolería

hiss [hɪs] s siseo, silbido ‖ tr sisear, silbar (p.ej., una escena, a un actor por malo) ‖ intr sisear, silbar

hist. abbr **historian, history**

histology [hɪsˈtalədʒi] s histología

historian [hɪsˈtorɪ•ən] s historiador m

historic(al) [hɪsˈtorɪk(əl)] adj histórico

histo•ry [ˈhɪstəri] s (pl -ries) historia

histrionic [ˌhɪstrɪˈɑnɪk] adj histriónico; teatral ‖ **histrionics** s actitud teatral, modales mpl teatrales

hit [hɪt] s golpe m; (of a bullet) impacto; (blow that hits its mark) tiro certero; (sarcastic remark) censura acerba; (baseball) batazo; (coll) éxito; **to make a• hit** (coll) dar golpe; **to make a hit with** caer en la gracia de (una persona) ‖ v (pret & pp **hit**; ger **hitting**) tr golpear, pegar; dar con, dar contra, chocar con; dar en (p.ej., el blanco); censurar acerbamente; (to run over in a car) atropellar; afectar mucho (un acontecimiento a una persona) ‖ intr chocar; **to hit against** dar contra; **to hit on** dar con (lo que se busca)

hit′-and-run′ adj que atropella y se da a la huída

hitch [hɪtʃ] s (jerk) tirón m; dificultad; obstáculo; **without a hitch** a pedir de boca, sin tropiezo ‖ tr (to tie) atar, sujetar; enganchar (un caballo); uncir (bueyes); (slang) casar

hitch′hike′ intr (coll) hacer autostop, viajar en autostop

hitch′hik′er s autostopista mf

hitching post s poste m para atar a las cabalgaduras

hither [ˈhɪðər] adv acá, hacia acá; **hither and thither** acá y allá

hith′er•to′ adv hasta ahora, hasta aquí

hit′-or-miss′ adj descuidado, casual

hit parade s (rad) canciones que gozan de más popularidad en la actualidad

hit record s (coll) disco de mucho éxito

hit′-run′ adj que atropella y se da a la huída

hive [haɪv] s (box for bees) colmena; (swarm) enjambre m; **hives** urticaria ‖ tr encorchar (abejas)

H.M. abbr **Her Majesty, His Majesty**

H.M.S. abbr **Her Majesty's Ship, His Majesty's Ship**

hoard [hord] s (of money, provisions, etc.) cúmulo; tesoro escondido ‖ tr acumular secretamente; atesorar (dinero) ‖ intr guardar víveres, atesorar dinero

hoarding [ˈhordɪŋ] s acumulación secreta; atesoramiento

hoar′frost′ s helada blanca, escarcha

hoarse [hors] adj ronco

hoarseness ['horsnɪs] *s* ronquedad; (*from a cold*) ronquera

hoar·y ['hori] *adj* (*comp* -ier; *super* -iest) cano, canoso; (*old*) vetusto

hoax [hoks] *s* pajarota, mistificación ‖ *tr* mistificar

hob [hɑb] *s* repisa interior del hogar; **to play hob with** (coll) trastornar

hobble ['hɑbəl] *s* (*limp*) cojera; (*rope used to tie legs of animal*) manea, traba ‖ *tr* dejar cojo; manear, trabar; dificultar ‖ *intr* cojear; tambalear

hobble skirt *s* falda de medio paso

hob·by ['hɑbi] *s* (*pl* -bies) comidilla, afición favorita, trabajo preferido; **to ride a hobby** entregarse demasiado al tema favorito

hob'by·horse' *s* (*stick with horse's head*) caballito; (*rocking horse*) caballo mecedor

hob'gob'lin *s* duende *m*, trasgo; (*bogy*) bu *m*, coco

hob'nail' *s* tachuela ‖ *tr* clavetear con tachuelas; (fig) atropellar

hob·nob ['hɑb,nɑb] *v* (*pret* & *pp* -nobbed; *ger* -nobbing) *intr* codearse, rozarse; beber juntos

ho·bo ['hobo] *s* (*pl* -bos o -boes) vagabundo

Hobson's choice ['hɑbsənz] *s* alternativa entre la cosa ofrecida o ninguna

hock [hɑk] *s* jarrete *m*, corvejón *m* ‖ *tr* (*to hamstring*) desjarretar; (coll) empeñar

hockey ['hɑki] *s* hockey *m*, chueca

hock'shop' *s* (slang) casa de empeños, monte *m* de piedad

hocus-pocus ['hokəs'pokəs] *s* (*meaningless formula*) abracadabra *m;* burla, engaño; juego de manos

hod [hɑd] *s* capacho, cuezo; cubo para carbón

hod carrier *s* peón *m* de albañil, peón de mano

hodgepodge ['hɑdʒ,pɑdʒ] *s* baturrillo

hoe [ho] *s* azada, azadón *m* ‖ *tr* & *intr* azadonar

hog [hɑg] o [hɔg] *s* cerdo, puerco ‖ *v* (*pret* & *pp* hogged; *ger* hogging) *tr* (slang) tragarse lo mejor de

hog'back' *s* cuchilla

hoggish ['hɑgɪʃ] o ['hɔgɪʃ] *adj* comilón; glotón; egoísta

hog Latin *s* latín *m* de cocina

hogs'head' *s* pipa de 63 galones o más; medida de capacidad de 63 galones

hog'wash' *s* bazofia

hoist [hɔɪst] *s* (*apparatus for lifting*) montacargas *m*, torno izador, grúa; empujón *m* hacia arriba ‖ *tr* alzar, levantar; enarbolar (*p.ej.*, *una bandera*); (naut) izar

hoity-toity ['hɔɪti'tɔɪti] *adj* frívolo, veleidoso; arrogante, altanero; **to be hoity-toity** ponerse tan alto

hokum ['hokəm] *s* (coll) música celestial, tonterías

hold [hold] *s* (*grip*) agarro; (*handle*) asa, mango; autoridad, dominio; (*in wrestling*) presa; (aer) cabina de carga; (mus) calderón *m;* (naut) bodega; **to take hold of** agarrar, coger; apoderarse de ‖ *v* (*pret* & *pp* held [hɛld]) *tr* tener, retener; (*to hold*

up, support) apoyar, sostener; (*e.g., with a pin*) sujetar; contener, tener cabida para; ocupar (*un cargo, puesto, etc.*); celebrar (*una reunión*); sostener (*una opinión*); (mus) sostener (*una nota*); **to hold back** detener; retener; contener; **to hold in** refrenar; **to hold one's own** mantenerse firme, no perder terreno; **to hold over** aplazar, diferir; **to hold up** apoyar, sostener; (*to rob*) (coll) atracar ‖ *intr* ser valedero, seguir vigente; pegarse; **hold on!** ¡un momento!; **to hold back** refrenarse; **to hold forth** poner cátedra; **to hold off** esperar; mantenerse a distancia; **to hold on** agarrarse bien; **to hold on to** asirse de; **to hold out** no cejar; ir tirando; **to hold out for** insistir en

holder ['holdər] *s* tenedor *m*, posesor *m;* (*for a cigar or cigaret*) boquilla; (*to hold, e.g., a hot plate*) cojinillo; (*e.g., of a passport*) titular *m;* asa, mango

holding ['holdɪŋ] *s* tenencia, posesión; **holdings** valores habidos

holding company *s* sociedad de control, compañía tenedora

hold'up' *s* (*stop, delay*) detención; atraco, asalto; precio excesivo

holdup man *s* atracador *m*, salteador *m*

hole [hol] *s* agujero; (*in cheese, bread, etc.*) ojo; (*in a road*) bache *m;* (*den of animals; den of vice*) guarida; (*dirty, disorderly dwelling*) cochitril *m;* **in the hole** adeudado, perdidoso; **to burn a hole in one's pocket** írsele a uno (*el dinero*) de entre las manos; **to pick holes in** (coll) poner reparos a ‖ *intr* — **to hole up** encovarse; buscar un rincón cómodo

holiday ['hɑlɪ,de] *s* día festivo; vacación

holiday attire *s* trapos de cristianar

holiness ['holɪnɪs] *s* santidad; **his Holiness** su Santidad

Holland ['hɑlənd] *s* Holanda

Hollander ['hɑləndər] *s* holandés *m*

hollow ['hɑlo] *adj* hueco; (*voice*) ahuecado, sepulcral; (*eyes, cheeks*) hundido; falso, engañoso ‖ *adv* — **to beat all hollow** (coll) derrotar completamente ‖ *s* hueco, cavidad; (*small valley*) vallecito ‖ *tr* ahuecar, excavar

hol·ly ['hɑli] *s* (*pl* -lies) acebo

hol'ly·hock' *s* malva arbórea

holm oak [hom] *s* encina

holocaust ['hɑlə,kɔst] *s* holocausto

holster ['holstər] *s* pistolera

ho·ly ['holi] *adj* (*comp* -lier; *super* -liest) santo; (*e.g., writing*) sagrado; (*e.g., water*) bendito

Holy Ghost *s* Espíritu Santo

holy orders *spl* órdenes sagradas; **to take holy orders** recibir las órdenes sagradas, ordenarse

holy rood [rud] *s* crucifijo ‖ **Holy Rood** *s* Santa Cruz

Holy Scripture *s* Sagrada Escritura

Holy See *s* Santa Sede

Holy Sepulcher *s* santo sepulcro

hi
ho

holy water s agua bendita
Holy Writ s Sagrada Escritura
homage ['hɑmɪdʒ] o ['ɑmɪdʒ] s homenaje m; (feud) homenaje, pleito homenaje
home [hom] adj casero, doméstico; nacional ‖ s casa, domicilio, hogar m; (native heath) patria chica; (of the arts, etc.) patria; (for the sick, poor, etc.) asilo; (sport) meta; **at home** en casa; en su propio país; (ready to receive callers) de recibo; (at ease, comfortable) a gusto; (sport) en campo propio; **away from home** fuera de casa; **make yourself at home** está Vd. en su casa ‖ adv en casa; a casa; **to see home** acompañar a casa; **to strike home** dar en lo vivo
home'bod'y s (pl -ies) hogareño
homebred ['hom,brɛd] adj doméstico; sencillo, inculto, tosco
home'brew' s cerveza o vino caseros
homecoming ['hom,kʌmɪŋ] s regreso al hogar
home country s suelo natal
home delivery s distribución a domicilio
home front s frente doméstico
home'land' s tierra natal, patria
homeless ['homlɪs] adj sin casa, sin hogar
home life s vida de familia
home-loving ['hom,lʌvɪŋ] adj casero, hogareño
home•ly ['homli] adj (comp -lier; super -liest) (not attractive or good-looking) feo; (plain, not elegant) sencillo, llano
homemade ['hom'med] adj casero, hecho en casa
homemaker ['hom,mekər] s ama de casa
home office s domicilio social, oficina central ‖ **Home Office** s (Brit) ministerio de la Gobernación
homeopath ['homɪ•ə,pæθ] o ['hɑmɪ•ə,pæθ] s homeópata mf
homeopathy [,homɪ'ɑpəθi] o [,hɑmɪ'ɑpəθi] s homeopatía
home plate s (baseball) puesto meta
home port s puerto de origen
home rule s autonomía, gobierno autónomo
home run s (baseball) jonrón m, cuadrangular m
home'sick' adj nostálgico; **to be homesick (for)** sentir nostalgia (de)
home'sick'ness s nostalgia, mal m de la tierra
homespun ['hom,spʌn] adj hilado en casa; sencillo, llano
home'stead' s casa y terrenos, heredad
home stretch s esfuerzo final, último trecho
home town s ciudad natal
homeward ['homwərd] adj de regreso ‖ adv hacia casa; hacia su país
home'work' s trabajo a domicilio; (of a student) deber m, trabajo escolar
homey ['homi] adj (comp homier; super homiest) (coll) íntimo, cómodo
homicidal [,hɑmɪ'saɪdəl] adj homicida
homicide ['hɑmɪ,saɪd] s (act) homicidio; (person) homicida mf
homi•ly ['hɑmɪli] s (pl -lies) homilía

homing ['homɪŋ] adj (animal) querencioso; (weapon) buscador del blanco
homing pigeon s paloma mensajera
hominy ['hɑmɪni] s maíz molido
homogenei•ty [,hɑmədʒɪ'ni•ɪti] s (pl -ties) homogeneidad
homogeneous [,hɑmə'dʒɪnɪ•əs] adj homogéneo
homogenize [hə'mɑdʒə,naɪz] tr homogeneizar
homonym ['hɑmənɪm] s homónimo
homonymous [hə'mɑnɪməs] adj homónimo
homosexual [,hɑmə'sɛkʃʊ•əl] adj & s homosexual mf
hon. abbr **honorary**
Hon. abbr **Honorable**
Honduran [hɑn'dʊrən] adj & s hondureño
hone [hon] s piedra de afilar ‖ tr afilar, amolar, asentar
honest ['ɑnɪst] adj honrado, probo, recto; (money) bien adquirido; sincero; genuino
honesty ['ɑnɪsti] s honradez f, probidad, rectitud; (bot) hierba de la plata
hon•ey ['hʌni] adj meloso, dulce; (coll) querido ‖ s miel f; (coll) vida mía; **it's a honey** (slang) es una preciosidad ‖ v (pret & pp -eyed o -ied) tr enmelar, endulzar con miel; adular, lisonjear
hon'ey•bee' s abeja doméstica, abeja de miel
hon'ey•comb' s panal m ‖ tr (to riddle) acribillar; llenar, penetrar
hon'ey•dew' melon s melón muy dulce, blanco y terso
honeyed ['hʌnid] adj dulce, enmelado; melodioso; aduldor
honey locust s acacia de tres espinas
hon'ey•moon' s luna de miel; viaje m de bodas ‖ intr pasar la luna de miel
honeysuckle ['hʌni,sʌkəl] s madreselva
honk [hɑŋk] s (of wild goose) graznido; (of automobile horn) bocinazo ‖ tr tocar (la bocina) ‖ intr graznar (el ganso silvestre); tocar la bocina
honkytonk ['hɑŋki,tɑŋk] s (slang) sala de fiestas de mala muerte
honor ['ɑnər] s (distinction; award for distinction; integrity) honor m; (good reputation; chastity) honor, honra ‖ tr honrar; hacer honor a (su firma); aceptar y pagar (una letra)
honorable ['ɑnərəbəl] adj (behaving with honor; performed with honor) honrado; (bringing honor; associated with honor) honroso; (worthy, of honor) honorable
honorary ['ɑnə,rɛri] adj honorario
honorific [,ɑnə'rɪfɪk] adj honorífico ‖ s antenombre m
honor system s acatamiento voluntario del reglamento
hood [hʊd] s capilla; (one with a point) caperuza; (one which covers the face) capirote m; (worn with academic gown) muceta, capirote m; (of a chimney) sombrerete m; (aut) capó m, cubierta; (slang) gamberro ‖ tr encapirotar; ocultar
hoodlum ['hudləm] s (coll) gamberro, maleante m

hoodoo ['hudu] *s* (*body of primitive rites*) vudú *m;* (coll) mala suerte ‖ *tr* traer mala suerte a

hood'wink' *tr* burlar, engañar, vendar

hooey ['hu•i] *s* (slang) música celestial

hoof [huf] o [huf] *s* casco, pezuña; **on the hoof** (*cattle*) vivo, en pie ‖ *tr & intr* (coll) caminar; **to hoof it** (coll) caminar, ir a pie; (coll) bailar

hoof'beat' *s* pisada, ruido de la pisada (*de animal ungulado*)

hook [huk] *s* gancho; (*for fishing*) anzuelo; (*to join two things*) enganche *m;* (*bend, curve*) ángulo, recodo; (box) crochet *m,* golpe *m* de gancho; (*of hook and eye*) corchete *m,* macho; **by hook or by crook** por fas o por nefas; **to swallow the hook; tragar el anzuelo** ‖ *tr* enganchar; (*to bend*) encorvar, doblar; coger, pescar (*un pez*); (*to wound with the horns*) acornar ‖ *intr* engancharse; encorvarse, doblarse

hookah ['hukə] *s* narguile *m*

hook and eye *s* broche *m,* corchete *m* (*macho y hembra*)

hook and ladder *s* carro de escaleras de incendio

hooked rug *s* tapete *m* de crochet

hook'nose' *s* nariz *f* de pico de loro

hook'up' *s* montaje *m*

hook'worm' *s* anquilostoma *m*

hooky ['huki] *s* — **to play hooky** hacer novillos

hooligan ['huligən] *s* gamberro

hooliganism ['huligən,izəm] *s* gamberrismo

hoop [hup] o [hup] *s* aro ‖ *tr* herrar, enarcar, enzunchar

hoop skirt *s* miriñaque *m*

hoot [hut] *s* resoplido, ululato; grito ‖ *tr* reprobar a gritos; echar a gritos (*p.ej., a un cómico*) ‖ *intr* resoplar, ulular; **to hoot at** dar grita a

hoot owl *s* autillo, cárabo

hop [hap] *s* saltito; (coll) vuelo en avión; (coll) sarao; (coll) baile *m;* lúpulo, hombrecillo; **hops** (*dried flowers of hop vine*) lúpulo ‖ *v* (*pret & pp* **hopped;** *ger* **hopping**) *tr* cruzar de un salto; (coll) atravesar (*p.ej., el mar*) en avión; (coll) subir a (*un tren, taxi, etc.*) ‖ *intr* saltar, brincar; (*on one foot*) saltar a la pata coja

hope [hop] *s* esperanza ‖ *tr & intr* esperar; **to hope for** esperar

hope chest *s* ajuar *m* de novia

hopeful ['hopfəl] *adj* (*feeling hope*) esperanzado; (*giving hope*) esperanzador

hopeless ['hoplis] *adj* desesperanzado, (*situation*) desesperado

hopper ['hapər] *s* (*funnel-shaped container*) tolva; (*of blast furnace*) tragante *m*

hopper car *s* (rr) vagón *m* tolva

hop'scotch' *s* infernáculo

horde [hord] *s* horda

horehound ['hor,haund] *s* marrubio; extracto de marrubio

horizon [hə'raizən] *s* horizonte *m*

horizontal [,hari'zantəl] o [,hori'zantəl] *adj & s* horizontal *f*

hormone ['hormon] *s* hormón *m* u hormona

horn [horn] *s* (*bony projection on head of certain animals*) cuerno; (*of bull*) asta, cuerno; (*of moon, anvil, etc.*) cuerno; (*of automobile*) bocina; (mus) cuerno; (*French horn*) (mus) trompa de armonía; **to blow one's own horn** cantar sus propias alabanzas; **to pull in one's horns** contenerse, volverse atrás ‖ *intr* — **to horn in** (slang) entrometerse (en)

hornet ['hornit] *s* crabrón *m,* avispón *m*

hornet's nest *s* panal *m* del avispón; **to stir up a hornet's nest** (coll) armar camorra, armar cisco

horn of plenty *s* cuerno de la abundancia

horn'pipe' *s* chirimía

horn-rimmed glasses ['horn'rimd] *spl* anteojos de concha

horn•y ['horni] *adj* (*comp* **-ier;** *super* **-iest**) córneo; (*callous*) calloso; (*having hornlike projections*) cornudo

horoscope ['harə,skop] o ['hɔrə,skop] *s* horóscopo; **to cast a horoscope** sacar un horóscopo

horrible ['haribəl] o ['hɔribəl] *adj* horrible; (coll) muy desagradable

horrid ['harid] o ['hɔrid] *adj* horroroso; (coll) muy desagradable

horri•fy ['hari,fai] o ['hɔri,fai] *v* (*pret & pp* **-fied**) *tr* horrorizar

horror ['harər] o ['hɔrər] *s* horror *m;* **to have a horror of** tener horror a

horror movie *s* película de terror, película horripilante

hors d'oeuvre [ɔr 'dʌrv] *s* (*pl* **hors d'oeuvres** [ɔr 'dʌrvz]) *s* entremés *m*

horse [hors] *s* caballo; (*of carpenter*) caballete *m;* **hold your horses** (coll) pare Vd. el carro; **to back the wrong horse** (coll) jugar a la carta mala; **to be a horse of another color** (coll) ser harina de otro costal

horse'back' *s* — **on horseback** a caballo ‖ *adv* — **to ride horseback** montar a caballo

horseback riding *s* hípica

horse blanket *s* manta para caballo

horse block *s* montadero

horse'break'er *s* domador *m* de caballos

horse'car' *s* tranvía *m* de sangre

horse chestnut *s* (*tree*) castaño de Indias; (*nut*) castaña de Indias

horse collar *s* collera

horse dealer *s* chalán *m*

horse doctor *s* veterinario

horse'fly' *s* (*pl* **-flies**) mosca borriquera, tábano

horse'hair' *s* crines *fpl* de caballo; (*fabric*) tela de crin

horse'hide' *s* cuero de caballo

horse laugh *s* risotada

horse•man ['horsmən] *s* (*pl* **-men** [mən]) jinete *m,* caballista *m*

horsemanship ['horsmən,ʃip] *s* equitación, manejo

horse meat *s* carne *f* de caballo

horse opera *s* (U.S.A.) melodrama *m* del Oeste

horse pistol *s* pistola de arzón
horse'play' *s* chanza pesada, payasada
horse'pow'er *s* caballo de vapor inglés
horse race *s* carrera de caballos
horse'rad'ish *s* (*plant*) rábano picante o rusticano; (*condiment*) mostaza de los alemanes
horse sense *s* (coll) sentido común
horse'shoe' *s* herradura
horseshoe magnet *s* imán *m* de herradura
horseshoe nail *s* clavo de herrar
horse show *s* concurso hípico
horse'tail' *s* cola de caballo
horse thief *s* abigeo, cuatrero
horse'-trade' *intr* chalanear
horse trading *s* chalanería
horse'-trad'ing *adj* chalanesco
horse'whip' *s* látigo ‖ *v* (*pret & pp* -whipped; *ger* -whipping) *tr* dar latigazos a
horse•woman ['hɔrs,wʊmən] *s* (*pl* -women [,wɪmɪn]) amazona, caballista *f*
hors•y ['hɔrsi] *adj* (*comp* -ier; *super* -iest) caballar, hípico; (*interested in horses and horse racing*) carrerista, turfista; (coll) desmañado
horticultural [,hɔrtɪ'kʌltʃərəl] *adj* hortícola
horticulture ['hɔrtɪ,kʌltʃər] *s* horticultura
horticulturist [,hɔrtɪ'kʌltʃərɪst] *s* horticultor *m*
hose [hoz] *s* (*stocking*) media; (*sock*) calcetín *m*; (*flexible tube*) manguera ‖ **hose** *spl* calzas
hosier ['hoʒər] *s* mediero, calcetero
hosiery ['hoʒəri] *s* calcetas; calcetería
hospice ['hɑspɪs] *s* hospicio
hospitable ['hɑspɪtəbəl] o [hɑs'pɪtəbəl] *adj* hospitalario
hospital ['hɑspɪtəl] *s* hospital *m*
hospitali•ty [,hɑspɪ'tælɪti] *s* (*pl* -ties) hospitalidad
hospitalize ['hɑspɪtə,laɪz] *tr* hospitalizar
host [host] *s* anfitrión *m*; (*at an inn*) huésped *m*, mesonero; (*army*) hueste *f*; multitud, sinnúmero ‖ **Host** *s* (eccl) hostia
hostage ['hɑstɪdʒ] *s* rehén *m*; **to be held a hostage** quedar en rehenes
hostage taking *s* toma de rehenes
hostel•ry ['hɑstəlri] *s* (*pl* -ries) parador *m*, hostería
hostess ['hostɪs] *s* anfitriona; dueña, patrona; (*in a night club*) tanguista; (aer) azafata, aeromoza; (*e.g., on a bus*) jefa de ruta
hostile ['hɑstɪl] *adj* hostil
hostili•ty [hɑs'tɪlɪti] *s* (*pl* -ties) hostilidad
hostler ['hɑslər] o ['ɑslər] *s* mozo de cuadra, mozo de paja y cebada
hot [hɑt] *adj* (*comp* hotter; *super* hottest) (*water, air, coffee, etc.*) caliente; (*climate, country; taste*) cálido; (*fiery, excitable*) caluroso; (*pursuit*) enérgico; (*in rut*) caliente; (coll) muy radiactivo; **to be hot** (*said of a person*) tener calor; (*said of the weather*) hacer calor; **to make it hot for** (coll) hostilizar
hot air *s* (slang) palabrería, música celestial
hot'-air' furnace *s* calorífero de aire

hot and cold running water *s* circulación de agua fría y caliente
hot baths *spl* caldas, termas
hot'bed' *s* (hort) almajara; (*e.g., of vice*) sementera, semillero
hot-blooded ['hɑt'blʌdɪd] *adj* apasionado; temerario, irreflexivo
hot cake *s* torta a la plancha; **to sell like hot cakes** (coll) venderse como pan bendito
hot dog *s* (slang) perro caliente
hotel [ho'tɛl] *adj* hotelero ‖ *s* hotel *m*
ho•tel'-keep'er *s* hotelero
hot'head' *s* botafuego
hot-headed ['hɑt'hɛdɪd] *adj* caliente de cascos
hot'house' *s* estufa, invernáculo
hot plate *s* hornillo, calientaplatos *m*
hot springs *spl* fuentes *fpl* termales
hot-tempered ['hɑt'tɛmpərd] *adj* irascible
hot water *s* — **to be in hot water** (coll) estar en calzas prietas
hot'-wa'ter boiler *s* termosifón *m*
hot-water bottle *s* bolsa de agua caliente
hot-water heater *s* calentador *m* de acumulación
hot-water heating *s* calefacción por agua caliente
hot-water tank *s* depósito de agua caliente
hound [haʊnd] *s* podenco, perro de caza; **to follow the hounds** o **to ride the hounds** cazar a caballo con jauría ‖ *tr* acosar, hostigar
hour [aʊr] *s* hora; **by the hour** por horas; **in an evil hour** en hora mala; **on the hour** a la hora en punto cada hora; **to keep late hours** acostarse tarde; **to work long hours** trabajar muchas horas cada día
hour'glass' *s* reloj *m* de arena
hour hand *s* horario, horero
hourly ['aʊrli] *adj* de cada hora; por hora ‖ *adv* cada hora; muy a menudo
house [haʊs] *s* (*pl* houses ['haʊzɪz]) casa; (*legislative body*) cámara; teatro; (*size of audience*) entrada, p.ej., **a good house** mucha entrada; **to keep house** tener casa puesta; hacer los quehaceres domésticos; **to put one's house in order** arreglar sus asuntos ‖ [haʊz] *tr* domiciliar, alojar, hospedar
house arrest *s* arresto domiciliario
house'boat' *s* barco vivienda
house'break'er *s* escalador *m*
housebreaking ['haʊs,brekɪŋ] *s* escalo, allanamiento de morada
housebroken ['haʊs,brokən] *adj* (*perro o gato*) enseñado (*a hábitos de limpieza*)
house cleaning *s* limpieza de la casa
house coat *s* bata
house current *s* sector *m* de distribución, canalización de consumo
house'fly' *s* (*pl* -flies) mosca doméstica
houseful ['haʊs,fʊl] *s* casa llena
house'fur'nishings *spl* menaje *m*, enseres domésticos
house'hold' *adj* casero, doméstico ‖ *s* casa, familia

house'hold'er *s* dueño de la casa; jefe *m* de familia

house'-hunt' *intr* — **to go house-hunting** ir a buscar casa

house'keep'er *s* ama de llaves, mujer *f* de gobierno

house'keep'ing *s* manejo doméstico, gobierno doméstico; **to set up housekeeping** poner casa

housekeeping apartment *s* apartamento con cocina

house'maid' *s* criada de casa

house meter *s* contador *m* de abonado

house'moth'er *s* mujer encargada de una residencia de estudiantes

house of cards *s* castillo de naipes

house of ill fame *s* lupanar *m*, casa de prostitución

house painter *s* pintor *m* de brocha gorda

house physician *s* médico residente

house'top' *s* tejado; **to shout from the housetops** pregonar a los cuatro vientos

housewarming [ˈhaʊsˌwɔrmɪŋ] *s* fiesta para celebrar el estreno de una casa; **to have a housewarming** estrenar la casa

house'wife' *s* (*pl* **-wives**) ama de casa, madre *f* de familia

house'work' *s* quehaceres domésticos

housing [ˈhaʊzɪŋ] *s* (*of a horse*) gualdrapa; (*aut*) cárter *m;* (*mach*) caja, bastidor *m*

housing shortage *s* crisis *f* de viviendas

hovel [ˈhʌvəl] *s* casucha, choza; (*shed for cattle, tools, etc.*) cobertizo

hover [ˈhʌvər] *intr* cernerse (*un ave*); (*to hesitate; to be in danger*) fluctuar; asomar (*p.ej., una sonrisa en los labios de uno*)

how [haʊ] *adv* cómo; (*at what price*) a cómo; **how early** cuándo, a qué hora; **how else** de qué otra manera; **how far** hasta dónde; cuánto, p.ej., **how far is it to the airport?** ¿cuánto hay de aquí al aeropuerto?; **how long** cuánto tiempo; **how many** cuántos; **how much** cuánto; lo mucho que; **how often** cuántas veces; **how old are you?** ¿cuántas años tiene Vd.?; **how soon** cuándo, a qué hora; **how** + *adj* qué + *adj*, p.ej., **how beautiful she is!** ¡qué hermosa es!; **lo** + *adj*, p.ej., **you know how intelligent he is** Vd. sabe lo inteligente que es; **to know how to** + *inf* saber + *inf*

howdah [ˈhaʊdə] *s* castillo

how-ev'er *adv* no obstante, sin embargo; por muy . . . que, por mucho . . . que

howitzer [ˈhaʊɪtsər] *s* cañón *m* obús

howl [haʊl] *s* aullido; chillido; risa muy aguda; (*of wind*) bramido ‖ *tr* decir a gritos; **to howl down** imponerse a gritos a (*una persona*) ‖ *intr* aullar; chillar; reír a más no poder; bramar (*el viento*)

howler [ˈhaʊlər] *s* aullador *m;* (coll) plancha, desacierto

hoyden [ˈhɔɪdən] *s* muchacha traviesa, tunantuela

H.P. *abbr* **horsepower**

hr. *abbr* **hour**

H.R.H. *abbr* **Her (o His) Royal Highness**

ht. *abbr* **height**

hub [hʌb] *s* cubo; (fig) centro, eje *m*

hubbub [ˈhʌbəb] *s* gritería, alboroto

hub'cap' *s* tapacubo, embellecedor *m*

huck'ster [ˈhʌkstər] *s* (*peddler*) buhonero; vendedor *m* ambulante de hortalizas; vil traficante *m*, sujeto ruin

huddle [ˈhʌdəl] *s* (coll) reunión secreta; **to go into a huddle** (coll) conferenciar en secreto ‖ *intr* acurrucarse, arrimarse

hue [hju] *s* matiz *m;* gritería; **hue and cry** vocería de indignación

huff [hʌf] *s* arrebato de cólera; **in a huff** encolerizado, ofendido

hug [hʌg] *s* abrazo ‖ *v* (*pret & pp* **hugged; ger hugging**) *tr* abrazar; apretar con los brazos; ahogar entre los brazos; navegar muy cerca de (*la costa*); ceñirse a (*p.ej., un muro*) ‖ *intr* abrazarse

huge [hjudʒ] *adj* enorme, descomunal

huh [hʌ] *interj* ¡eh!

hulk [hʌlk] *s* (*body of an old ship*) casco; (*clumsy old ship*) carcamán *m*, carraca; (*old ship tied up at a wharf and used as a warehouse, prison, etc.*) pontón *m;* (*shell of an old building, piece of furniture, machine, etc.; heavy, unwieldy person*) armatoste *m*

hulking [ˈhʌlkɪŋ] *adj* grueso, pesado

hull [hʌl] *s* (*of ship or hydroplane*) casco; (*of a dirigible*) armazón *f;* (*of certain vegetables*) hollejo, vaina ‖ *tr* deshollejar, desvainar; mondar, pelar

hullabaloo [ˌhʌləbəˌlu] o [ˌhʌləbəˈlu] *s* alboroto, gritería, tumulto

hum [hʌm] *s* canturreo, tarareo; (*of a bee, machine, etc.*) zumbido ‖ *interj* ¡ejem! ‖ *v* (*pret & pp* **hummed; ger humming**) *tr* canturrear, tararear ‖ *intr* canturrear, tararear; (*to buzz*) zumbar; (coll) estar muy activo

human [ˈhjumən] *adj* humano (*perteneciente al hombre*)

human being *s* ser humano

humane [hjuˈmen] *adj* humano (*compasivo*)

humanist [ˈhjumənɪst] *adj* & *s* humanista *mf*

humanitarian [hjuˌmænɪˈtɛrɪ•ən] *adj* & *s* humanitario

humani•ty [hjuˈmænɪti] *s* (*pl* **-ties**) humanidad

hu'man•kind' *s* género humano

humble [ˈhʌmbəl] *adj* humilde ‖ *tr* humillar

humble pie *s* — **to eat humble pie** cantar la palinodia

hum'bug' *s* patraña; (*person*) patrañero ‖ *v* (*pret & pp* **-bugged; ger -bugging**) *tr* embaucar, engaitar

hum'drum' *adj* monótono, tedioso

humer•us [ˈhjumərəs] *s* (*pl* **-i** [ˌaɪ]) húmero

humid [ˈhjumɪd] *adj* húmedo

humidifier [hjuˈmɪdɪˌfaɪ•ər] *s* humectador *m*

humidi•fy [hjuˈmɪdɪˌfaɪ] *v* (*pret & pp* **-fied**) *tr* humedecer

humidity [hjuˈmɪdɪti] *s* humedad

humiliate [hjuˈmɪlɪˌet] *tr* humillar

humiliating [hjuˈmɪlɪˌetɪŋ] *adj* humillante

humili•ty [hjuˈmɪlɪti] *s* (*pl* **-ties**) humildad

hummingbird [ˈhʌmɪŋˌbʌrd] s colibrí m, pájaro mosca

humongous [hjuˈmʌŋəs] adj (coll) descomunal

humor [ˈhjumər] o [ˈjumər] s humor m; **out of humor** de mal humor; **to be in the humor for** estar de humor para ‖ tr seguir el humor a; manejar con delicadeza

humorist [ˈhjumərɪst] s humorista mf

humorous [ˈhjumərəs] adj humorístico

hump [hʌmp] s corcova, joroba; (in the ground) montecillo

hump'back' s corcova, joroba; (person) corcovado, jorobado

humus [ˈhjuməs] s mantillo

hunch [hʌntʃ] s corcova, joroba; (premonition) (coll) corazonada ‖ tr encorvar ‖ intr encorvarse

hunch'back' s corcova, joroba; (person) corcovado, jorobado

hundred [ˈhʌndrəd] adj cien ‖ s ciento, cien; **a hundred** u **one hundred** ciento; cien; **by the hundreds** a centenares

hundredth [ˈhʌndredθ] adj & s centésimo

hun'dred•weight' s quintal m

Hundred Years' War s guerra de los Cien Años

Hungarian [hʌŋˈgɛrɪ•ən] adj & s húngaro

Hungary [ˈhʌŋgəri] s Hungría

hunger [ˈhʌŋgər] s hambre f ‖ intr hambrear; **to hunger for** tener hambre de

hunger march s marcha del hambre

hunger strike s huelga de hambre

hun•gry [ˈhʌŋgri] adj (comp **-grier**; super **-griest**) hambriento; **to be hungry** tener hambre; galguear (Arg, CAm, Mex); **to go hungry** pasar hambre

hunk [hʌŋk] s (coll) buen pedazo, pedazo grande

hunt [hʌnt] s (act of hunting) caza; (hunting party) cacería; (a search) busca; **on the hunt for** a caza de ‖ tr cazar; (to seek, look for) buscar ‖ intr cazar; buscar; **to go hunting** ir de caza; **to hunt for** buscar; **to take hunting** llevar de caza

hunter [ˈhʌntər] s cazador m; perro de caza

hunting [ˈhʌntɪŋ] adj de caza ‖ s (act) caza; (art) cacería, montería

hunting dog s perro de caza

hunting ground s cazadero

hunt'ing•horn' s cuerno de caza

hunting jacket s cazadora

hunting lodge s casa de montería

hunting season s época de caza

huntress [ˈhʌntrɪs] s cazadora

hunts•man [ˈhʌntsmən] s (pl **-men** [mən]) cazador m, montero

hurdle [ˈhʌrdəl] s (hedge over which horses must jump) zarzo; (wooden frame over which runners and horses must jump) valla; (fig) obstáculo; **hurdles** carrera de vallas ‖ tr saltar por encima de

hurdle race s carrera de vallas

hurdy-gur•dy [ˈhʌrdiˈgʌrdi] s (pl **-dies**) organillo

hurl [hʌrl] s lanzamiento ‖ tr lanzar

hurrah [huˈrɑ] o **hurray** [huˈre] s viva m ‖ interj ¡viva!; **hurrah for. . . !** ¡viva. . . ! ‖ tr aplaudir, vitorear ‖ intr dar vivas

hurricane [ˈhʌrɪˌken] s huracán m

hurried [ˈhʌrid] adj apresurado; hecho de prisa

hur•ry [ˈhʌri] s (pl **-ries**) prisa; **to be in a hurry** tener prisa, estar de prisa ‖ v (pret & pp **-ried**) tr apresurar, dar prisa a ‖ intr apresurarse, darse prisa; **to hurry after** correr en pos de; **to hurry away** marcharse de prisa; **to hurry back** volver de prisa; **to hurry up** darse prisa

hurt [hʌrt] adj (injured) lastimado, herido; (offended) resentido, herido ‖ s (harm) daño; (i.ijury) herida; (pain) dolor m ‖ v (pret & pp **hurt**) tr (to harm) dañar, perjudicar; (to injure) lastimar, herir; (to offend) ofender, herir; (to pain) doler ‖ intr doler

hurtle [ˈhʌrtəl] intr lanzarse con violencia, pasar con gran estruendo

husband [ˈhʌzbənd] s marido, esposo ‖ tr manejar con economía

husband•man [ˈhʌzbəndmən] s (pl **-men** [mən]) agricultor m, granjero

husbandry [ˈhʌzbəndri] s agricultura, labranza; buena dirección, buen gobierno (de la hacienda de uno)

hush [hʌʃ] s silencio ‖ interj ¡chito! ‖ tr callar; **to hush up** echar tierra a (un escándalo) ‖ intr callarse

hushaby [ˈhʌʃəˌbaɪ] interj ¡ro ro!

hush'-hush' adj muy secreto

hush money s precio del silencio

husk [hʌsk] s cáscara, hollejo, vaina; (of corn) perfolla ‖ tr descascarar, deshollejar, desvainar; espinochar (el maíz)

husk•y [ˈhʌski] adj (comp **-ier**; super **-iest**) fortachón, fornido; (voice) ronco

hus•sy [ˈhʌzi] o [ˈhʌsi] s (pl **-sies**) buena pieza, moza descarada; mujer desvergonzada

hustle [ˈhʌsəl] s (coll) energía, vigor m ‖ tr apresurar; echar a empellones ‖ intr apresurarse; (coll) menearse, trabajar con gran ahinco

hustler [ˈhʌslər] s trafagón m, buscavidas mf

hut [hʌt] s casucha, choza

hyacinth [ˈhaɪ•əsɪnθ] s jacinto

hybrid [ˈhaɪbrɪd] adj & s híbrido

hybridization [ˌhaɪbrɪdɪˈzeʃən] s hibridación

hybridize [ˈhaɪbrɪˌdaɪz] tr & intr hibridar

hy•dra [ˈhaɪdrə] s (pl **-dras** o **-drae** [dri]) hidra

hydrant [ˈhaɪdrənt] s boca de agua, boca de riego; (water faucet) grifo

hydrate [ˈhaɪdret] s hidrato ‖ tr hidratar ‖ intr hidratarse

hydraulic [haɪˈdrɔlɪk] adj hidráulico ‖ **hydraulics** s hidráulica

hydraulic ram s ariete hidráulico

hydriodic [ˌhaɪdrɪˈɑdɪk] adj yodhídrico

hydrobromic [ˌhaɪdrəˈbromɪk] adj bromhídrico

hydrocarbon [ˌhaɪdrəˈkɑrbən] s hidrocarburo

hydrochloric [ˌhaɪdrəˈklorɪk] adj clorhídrico

hydroelectric [,haɪdro•ɪ'lɛktrɪk] *adj* hidroeléctrico

hydrofluoric [,haɪdrəflu'ɔrɪk] *adj* fluorhídrico

hydrofoil ['haɪdrə,fɔɪl] *s* superficie hidrodinámica; (*wing designed to lift vessel*) hidroaleta; (*vessel*) hidroala *m*

hydrogen ['haɪdrədʒən] *s* hidrógeno

hydrogen bomb *s* bomba de hidrógeno

hydrogen peroxide *s* peróxido de hidrógeno

hydrogen sulfide *s* sulfuro de hidrógeno

hydrometer [haɪ'drɑmɪtər] *s* areómetro

hydrophobia [,haɪdrə'fobɪ•ə] *s* hidrofobia

hydroplane ['haɪdrə,plen] *s* hidroavión *m*

hydroxide [haɪ'drɑksaɪd] *s* hidróxido

hyena [haɪ'inə] *s* hiena

hygiene ['haɪdʒin] *s* higiene *f*

hygienic [,haɪdʒɪ'ɛnɪk] *adj* higiénico

hymn [hɪm] *s* himno

hymnal ['hɪmnəl] *s* himnario

hyp. *abbr* **hypotenuse, hypothesis**

hyperacidity [,haɪpərə'sɪdɪti] *s* hiperacidez *f*

hyperbola [haɪ'pɑrbələ] *s* (geom) hipérbola

hyperbole [haɪ'pɑrbəli] *s* (rhet) hipérbole *f*

hyperbolic [,haɪpər'bɑlɪk] *adj* (geom & rhet) hiperbólico

hypersensitive [,haɪpər'sɛnsɪtɪv] *adj* extremadamente sensible; (*allergic*) hipersensible

hypertension [,haɪpər'tɛnʃən] *s* hipertensión

hyphen ['haɪfən] *s* guión *m*

hyphenate ['haɪfə,net] *tr* unir con guión; escribir con guión

hypno•sis [hɪp'nosɪs] *s* (*pl* **-ses** [siz]) hipnosis *f*

hypnotic [hɪp'nɑtɪk] *adj* hipnótico ‖ *s* (*person; sedative*) hipnótico

hypnotism ['hɪpnə,tɪzəm] *s* hipnotismo

hypnotist ['hɪpnətɪst] *s* hipnotista *mf*

hypnotize ['hɪpnə,taɪz] *tr* hipnotizar

hypochondriac [,haɪpə'kɑndrɪ,æk] *s* hipocondríaco

hypocri•sy [hɪ'pɑkrəsɪ] *s* (*pl* **-sies**) hipocresía

hypocrite ['hɪpəkrɪt] *s* hipócrita *mf*

hypocritical [,hɪpə'krɪtɪkəl] *adj* hipócrita

hypodermic [,haɪpə'dʌrmɪk] *adj* hipodérmico

hyposulfite [,haɪpə's ʌlfaɪt] *m* hiposulfito

hypotenuse [haɪ'pɑtɪ,nus] *s* hipotenusa

hypothe•sis [haɪ'pɑθɪsɪs] *s* (*pl* **-ses** [,siz] hipótesis *f*

hypothetic(al) [,haɪpə'θɛtɪk(əl)] *adj* hipotético

hyssop ['hɪsəp] *s* (bot) hisopo

hysteria [hɪs'tɪrɪ•ə] *s* histerismo, histeria

hysteric [hɪs'tɛrɪk] *adj* histérico ‖ **hysterics** *s* paroxismo histérico

hysterical [hɪs'tɛrɪkəl] *adj* histérico

hu
ic

I

I, i [aɪ] *s* novena letre del alfabeto inglés

I. *abbr* **Island**

I [aɪ] *pron pers* (*pl* **we** [wi]) yo; **it is I** soy yo

iambic [aɪ'æmbɪk] *adj* yámbico

iam•bus [aɪ'æmbəs] *s* (*pl* **-bi** [bar]) yambo

ib. *abbr* **ibidem**

Iberian [aɪb'ɪrɪ•ən] *adj* ibérico ‖ *s* ibero

ibex ['aɪbɛks] *s* (*pl* **ibexes** o **ibices** ['ɪbɪ,siz]) íbice *m*, cabra montés

ibid. *abbr* **ibidem**

ice [aɪs] *s* hielo; **to break the ice** (*to overcome reserve*) romper el hielo; **to cut no ice** (coll) no importar nada; **to skate on thin ice** (coll) buscar el peligro ‖ *tr* helar; enfriar con hielo; (*to cover with icing*) garapiñar ‖ *intr* helarse

ice age *s* época glacial

ice bag *s* bolsa para hielo

iceberg ['aɪs,bʌrg] *s* banquisa, iceberg *m*

ice'boat' *s* cortahielos *m*, rompehielos *m*; trineo con vela para deslizarse sobre el hielo

ice'bound' *adj* rodeado de hielo; de tenido por el hielo

ice'box' *s* nevera, fresquera

ice'break'er *s* cortahielos *m*, rompehielos *m*

ice'cap' *s* bolsa para hielo; manto de hielo

ice cream *s* helado

ice'-cream' cone *s* cucurucho de helado, barquillo de helado

ice-cream freezer *s* heladora, garapiñera

ice-cream parlor *s* salón *m* de refrescos, tienda de helados

ice-cream soda *s* agua gaseosa con helado

ice cube *s* cubito de hielo

ice hockey *s* hockey *m* sobre patines

Iceland ['aɪslənd] *s* Islandia

Icelander ['aɪs,lændər] *s* islandés *m*

Icelandic [aɪs'lændɪk] *adj* islandés ‖ *s* islandés *m* (*idioma*)

ice•man ['aɪs,mæn] *s* (*pl* **-men** [,mɛn]) vendedor *m* de hielo, repartidor *m* de hielo

ice pack *s* hielo flotante; bolsa de hielo

ice pail *s* enfriadera

ice pick *s* picahielos *m*

ice skate *s* patín *m* de cuchilla, patín de hielo

ice skating *s* patinaje *m* sobre hielo

ice tray *s* bandejita de hielo

ice water *s* agua helada

ichthyology [,ɪkθɪ'ɑlədʒɪ] *s* ictiología

icicle ['aɪsɪkəl] *s* carámbano

icing ['aɪsɪŋ] *s* garapiña, capa de azúcar; (aer) formación de hielo

iconoclasm [aɪ'kɑnə,klæzəm] *s* iconoclasia, iconoclasmo

iconoclast [aɪ'kɑnə,klæst] *s* iconoclasta *mf*

icy [ˈaɪsɪ] *adj* (*comp* **icier;** *super* **iciest**) cubierto de hielo; (*slippery*) resbaladizo; (fig) frío

id. *abbr* **idem**

id [ɪd] *s* (psychoanalysis) ello

I.D. *abbr* **identity card**

idea [aɪˈdiˑə] *s* idea

ideal [aɪˈdiˑəl] *adj & s* ideal *m*

idealist [aɪˈdiˑəlɪst] *adj & s* idealista *mf*

idealize [aɪˈdiˑəˌlaɪz] *tr* idealizar

identic(al) [aɪˈdɛntɪk(əl)] *adj* idéntico

identification [aɪˌdɛntɪfɪˈkeʃən] *s* identificación

identification tag *s* disco de identificación

identify [aɪˈdɛntɪˌfaɪ] *v* (*pret & pp* **-fied**) *tr* identificar ‖ *intr* — **to identify with** solidarizar con

identi·ty [aɪˈdɛntɪtɪ] *s* (*pl* **-ties**) identidad

identity card *s* carta de identificación

ideolo·gy [ˌaɪdɪˈɑlədʒɪ] o [ˌɪdɪˈɑlədʒɪ] *s* (*pl* **-gies**) ideología

ides [aɪdz] *spl* idus *mpl*

idio·cy [ˈɪdɪˑəsɪ] *s* (*pl* **-cies**) idiotez *f*

idiom [ˈɪdɪˑəm] *s* (*expression that is contrary to the usual patterns of the language*) modismo; (*style of language*) idioma *m*, lenguaje *m*; (*style of an author*) estilo; (*character of a language*) índole *f*

idiomatic [ˌɪdɪˑəˈmætɪk] *adj* idiomático

idiosyncra·sy [ˌɪdɪˑəˈsɪnkrəsɪ] *s* (*pl* **-sies**) idiosincrasia

idiot [ˈɪdɪˑət] *s* idiota *mf*

idiotic [ˌɪdɪˈɑtɪk] *adj* idiota

idle [ˈaɪdəl] *adj* desocupado, ocioso; **at idle moments** a ratos perdidos; **to run idle** marchar en ralentí ‖ *tr* — **to idle away** gastar ociosamente (*el tiempo*) ‖ *intr* estar ocioso, holgar; marchar (*un motor*) en ralentí

idleness [ˈaɪdəlnɪs] *s* desocupación, ociosidad

idler [ˈaɪdlər] *s* haragán *m*, ocioso

idol [ˈaɪdəl] *s* ídolo

idola·try [aɪˈdɑlətrɪ] *s* (*pl* **-tries**) idolatría

idolize [ˈaɪdəˌlaɪz] *tr* idolatrar

idyll [ˈaɪdəl] *s* idilio

idyllic [aɪˈdɪlɪk] *adj* idílico

if [ɪf] *conj* si; **as if** como si; **even if** aunque; **if so** si es así; **if true** si es cierto

ignis fatuus [ˈɪgnɪsˈfætʃʊˑəs] *s* (*pl* **ignes fatui** [ˈɪgnizˈfætʃʊˌaɪ]) fuego fatuo

ignite [ɪgˈnaɪt] *tr* encender ‖ *intr* encenderse

ignition [ɪgˈnɪʃən] *s* inflamación; (aut) encendido

ignition switch *s* (aut) interruptor *m* de encendido

ignoble [ɪgˈnobəl] *adj* innoble

ignominious [ˌɪgnəˈmɪnɪˑəs] *adj* ignominioso

ignoramus [ˌɪgnəˈreməs] *s* ignorante *mf*

ignorance [ˈɪgnərəns] *s* ignorancia

ignorant [ˈɪgnərənt] *adj* ignorante

ignore [ɪgˈnor] *tr* no hacer caso de, pasar por alto

ilk [ɪlk] *s* especie *f*, jaez *m*

ill. *abbr* **illustrated, illustration**

ill [ɪl] *adj* (*comp* **worse** [wʌrs]; *super* **worst** [wʌrst]) enfermo, malo ‖ *adv* mal; **to take ill** tomar a mal; caer enfermo

ill-advised [ˈɪlədˈvaɪzd] *adj* desaconsejado, malaconsejado, desavisado

ill at ease *adj* inquieto, incómodo

ill-bred [ˈɪlˈbrɛd] *adj* malcriado

ill-considered [ˈɪlkənˈsɪdərd] *adj* des considerado, mal considerado

ill-disposed [ˈɪldɪsˈpozd] *adj* malintencionado, maldispuesto

illegal [ɪˈligəl] *adj* ilegal

illegible [ɪˈlɛdʒɪbəl] *adj* ilegible

illegitimate [ˌɪlɪˈdʒɪtɪmɪt] *adj* ilegítimo

ill fame *s* mala fama, reputación de inmoral

ill-fated [ˈɪlˈfetɪd] *adj* aciago, funesto

ill-gotten [ˈɪlˈgɑtən] *adj* mal ganado

ill health *s* mala salud

ill-humored [ˈɪlˈhjumərd] *adj* malhumorado

illicit [ɪˈlɪsɪt] *adj* ilícito

illitera·cy [ɪˈlɪtərəsɪ] *s* (*pl* **-cies**) ignorancia; analfabetismo

illiterate [ɪˈlɪtərɪt] *adj* (*uneducated*) iliterato; (*unable to read or write*) analfabeto ‖ *s* analfabeto

ill-mannered [ˈɪlˈmænərd] *adj* de malos modales

illness [ˈɪlnɪs] *s* enfermedad

illogical [ɪˈlɑdʒɪkəl] *adj* ilógico

ill-spent [ˈɪlˈspɛnt] *adj* malgastado

ill-starred [ˈɪlˈstɑrd] *adj* malhadado

ill-tempered [ˈɪlˈtɛmpərd] *adj* de mal genio

ill-timed [ˈɪlˈtaɪmd] *adj* inoportuno, intempestivo

ill -treat *tr* maltratar

illuminate [ɪˈlumɪˌnet] *tr* alumbrar, iluminar; miniar (*un manuscrito*)

illuminating gas *s* gas *m* de alumbrado

illumination [ɪˌlumɪˈneʃən] *s* iluminación

illusion [ɪˈluʒən] *s* ilusión

illusive [ɪˈlusɪv] *adj* ilusivo

illusory [ɪˈlusərɪ] *adj* ilusorio

illustrate [ˈɪləsˌtret] o [ɪˈlʌstret] *tr* ilustrar

illustration [ˌɪləsˈtreʃən] *s* ilustración

illustrious [ɪˈlʌstrɪˑəs] *adj* ilustre

ill will *s* mala voluntad

image [ˈɪmɪdʒ] *s* imagen *f*; **the very image of** la propia estampa de

image·ry [ˈɪmɪdʒrɪ] *s* (*pl* **-ries**) (*formation of mental images; product of the imagination*) fantasía; (*images collectively*) imágenes *fpl*

imaginary [ɪˈmædʒɪˌnɛrɪ] *adj* imaginario

imagination [ɪˌmædʒɪˈneʃən] *s* imaginación

imagine [ɪˈmædʒɪn] *tr & intr* imaginar; (*to conjecture*) imaginarse

imbecile [ˈɪmbɪsɪl] *adj & s* imbécil *mf*

imbecili·ty [ˌɪmbɪˈsɪlɪtɪ] *s* (*pl* **-ties**) imbecilidad

imbibe [ɪmˈbaɪb] *tr* (*to drink*) beber; (*to absorb*) embeber; (*to become absorbed in*) embeberse de o en ‖ *intr* beber, empinar el codo

imbue [ɪmˈbju] *tr* imbuir

imitate [ˈɪmɪˌtet] *tr* imitar

imitation [ˌɪmɪˈteʃən] *adj* (*e.g., jewelry*) imitado, imitación, de imitación ‖ *s* imitación; **in imitation of** a imitación de

immaculate [ɪ'mækjəlɪt] *adj* inmaculado
immaterial [,ɪmə'tɪrɪ•əl] *adj* inmaterial; poco importante
immature [,ɪmə'tjʊr] *adj* inmaturo
immeasurable [ɪ'mɛʒərəbəl] *adj* inmensurable
immediacy [ɪ'midɪ•əsi] *s* inmediación
immediate [ɪ'midɪ•ɪt] *adj* inmediato
immediately [ɪ'midɪ•ɪtli] *adv* inmediatamente, en seguida
immemorial [,ɪmɪ'morɪ•əl] *adj* inmemorial
immense [ɪ'mɛns] *adj* inmenso; (coll) excelente
immerge [ɪ'mʌrdʒ] *intr* sumergirse
immerse [ɪ'mʌrs] *tr* sumergir, inmergir
immersion [ɪ'mʌrʃən] o [ɪ'mʌrʒən] *s* sumersión, inmersión
immigrant ['ɪmɪgrənt] *adj* & *s* inmigrante *mf*
immigrate ['ɪmɪ,gret] *intr* inmigrar
immigration [,ɪmɪ'greʃən] *s* inmigración
imminent ['ɪmɪnənt] *adj* inminente
immobile [ɪ'mobɪl] *adj* inmoble, inmóvil
immobilize [ɪ'mobɪ,laɪz] *tr* inmovilizar
immoderate [ɪ'madərɪt] *adj* inmoderado
immodest [ɪ'madɪst] *adj* inmodesto
immoral [ɪ'mɔrəl] *adj* inmoral
immortal [ɪ'mɔrtəl] *adj* & *s* inmortal *mf*
immortalize [ɪ'mɔrtə,laɪz] *tr* inmortalizar
immune [ɪ'mjun] *adj* inmune
immunize ['ɪmjə,naɪz] *tr* inmunizar
imp [ɪmp] *s* diablillo; (*child*) niño travieso
impact ['ɪmpækt] *s* impacto
impair [ɪm'pɛr] *tr* empeorar, deteriorar
impan•el [ɪm'pænəl] *v* (*pret* & *pp* **-eled** o **-elled**; *ger* **-eling** o **-elling**) *tr* inscribir en la lista de los jurados; elegir (*un jurado*)
impart [ɪm'part] *tr* (*to make known*) dar a conocer, hacer saber; (*to transmit, communicate*) imprimir
impartial [ɪm'parʃəl] *adj* imparcial
impassable [ɪm'pæsəbəl] *adj* intransitable, impracticable
impasse [ɪm'pæs] o ['ɪmpæs] *s* callejón *m* sin salida
impassible [ɪm'pæsɪbəl] *adj* impasible
impassioned [ɪm'pæʃənd] *adj* ardiente, vehemente
impassive [ɪm'pæsɪv] *adj* impasible
impatience [ɪm'peʃəns] *s* impaciencia
impatient [ɪm'peʃənt] *adj* impaciente
impeach [ɪm'pitʃ] *tr* residenciar
impeachment [ɪm'pitʃmənt] *s* residencia
impeccable [ɪm'pɛkəbəl] *adj* impecable
impecunious [,ɪmpɪ'kjunɪ•əs] *adj* inope
impedance [ɪm'pidəns] *s* impedancia
impede [ɪm'pid] *tr* estorbar, dificultar
impediment [ɪm'pɛdɪmənt] *s* impedimento; (*e.g., in speech*) defecto
im•pel [ɪm'pɛl] *v* (*pret* & *pp* **-pelled**; *ger* **-pelling**) *tr* impeler, impulsar
impending [ɪm'pɛndɪŋ] *adj* inminente
impenetrable [ɪm'pɛnətrəbəl] *adj* impenetrable
impenitent [ɪm'pɛnɪtənt] *adj* & *s* impenitente *mf*

imperative [ɪm'pɛrɪtɪv] *adj* (*commanding*) imperativo; (*urgent, absolutely necessary*) imperioso ‖ *s* imperativo
imperceptible [,ɪmpər'sɛptɪbəl] *adj* imperceptible, inapreciable
imperfect [ɪm'pʌrfɪkt] *adj* & *s* imperfecto
imperfection [,ɪmpər'fɛkʃən] *s* imperfección
imperial [ɪm'pɪrɪ•əl] *adj* imperial; majestuoso ‖ *s* (*goatee*) perilla; (*top of coach*) imperial *f*
imperialist [ɪm'pɪrɪ•əlɪst] *adj* & *s* imperialista *mf*
imper•il [ɪm'pɛrɪl] *v* (*pret* & *pp* **-iled** o **-illed**; *ger* **-iling** o **-illing**) *tr* poner en peligro
imperious [ɪm'pɪrɪ•əs] *adj* imperioso
imperishable [ɪm'pɛrɪʃəbəl] *adj* imperecedero
impersonal [ɪm'pʌrsənəl] *adj* impersonal
impersonate [ɪm'pʌrsə,net] *tr* personificar; hacer el papel de
impertinence [ɪm'pʌrtɪnəns] *s* impertinencia
impertinent [ɪm'pʌrtɪnənt] *adj* & *s* impertinente *mf*
impetuous [ɪm'pɛtʃʊ•əs] *adj* impetuoso
impetus ['ɪmpɪtəs] *s* ímpetu *m*
impie•ty [ɪm'paɪ•əti] *s* (*pl* **-ties**) impiedad
impinge [ɪm'pɪndʒ] *intr* — **to impinge on** o **upon** incidir eno sobre, herir; infringir, violar
impious ['ɪmpɪ•əs] *adj* impío
impish ['ɪmpɪʃ] *adj* endiablado, travieso
implant [ɪm'plænt] *tr* implantar
implement ['ɪmplɪmənt] *s* instrumento, utensilio, herramienta; **implements** implementos *mpl* ‖ ['ɪmplɪ,mɛnt] *tr* poner por obra, llevar a cabo; (*to provide with implements*) pertrechar
implicate ['ɪmplɪ,ket] *tr* implicar, comprometer, enredar
implicit [ɪm'plɪsɪt] *adj* implícito; (*unquestioning*) absoluto, ciego
implied [ɪm'plaɪd] *adj* implícito, sobrentendido
implore [ɪm'plor] *tr* implorar, suplicar
im•ply [ɪm'plaɪ] *v* (*pret* & *pp* **-plied**) *tr* dar a entender; implicar, incluir en esencia
impolite [,ɪmpə'laɪt] *s* descortés; desacomodido (SAm)
import ['ɪmport] *s* importación; artículo importado; importancia, significación ‖ *tr* importar; significar ‖ *intr* importar
importance [ɪm'portəns] *s* importancia
important [ɪm'portənt] *adj* importante
importation [,ɪmpor'teʃən] *s* importación
importer [ɪm'portər] *s* importador *m*
importunate [ɪm'portʃənɪt] *adj* importuno
importune [,ɪmpor'tjun] *tr* importunar
impose [ɪm'poz] *tr* imponer ‖ *intr* — **to impose on** o **upon** abusar de
imposing [ɪm'pozɪŋ] *adj* imponente
imposition [,ɪmpə'zɪʃən] *s* (*of someone's will*) imposición; abuso, engaño
impossible [ɪm'pasɪbəl] *adj* imposible
impostor [ɪm'pastər] *s* impostor *m*, embaucador *m*
imposture [ɪm'pastʃər] *s* impostura
impotence ['ɪmpətəns] *s* impotencia

ic
im

impotent ['ɪmpətənt] *adj* impotente

impound [ɪm'paund] *tr* acorralar, encerrar; rebalsar (*agua*); (*law*) embargar, secuestrar

impoverish [ɪm'pavərɪʃ] *tr* empobrecer

impracticable [ɪm'præktɪkəbəl] *adj* impracticable; (*intractable*) intratable

impractical [ɪm'præktkəl] *adj* impracticable; soñador, utópico

impregnable [ɪm'prɛgnəbəl] *adj* inexpugnable

impregnate [ɪm'prɛgnet] *tr* (*to make pregnant*) empreñar; (*to soak*) empapar; (*to fill the interstices of*) impregnar; (*to infuse, infect*) imbuir

impresari•o [,ɪmprɪ'sarɪ,o] *s* (*pl* **-os**) empresario, empresario de teatro

impress [ɪm'prɛs] *tr* (*to have an effect on the mind or emotions of*) impresionar; (*to mark by using pressure*) imprimir; (*on the memory*) grabar; (*mil*) enganchar

impression [ɪm'prɛʃən] *s* impresión

impressionable [ɪm'prɛʃənəbəl] *adj* impresionable

impressive [ɪm'prɛsɪv] *adj* impresionante

imprint ['ɪmprɪnt] *s* impresión; (*typ*) pie *m* de imprenta ‖ [ɪm'prɪnt] *tr* imprimir

imprison [ɪm'prɪzən] *tr* encarcelar

imprisonment [ɪm'prɪzənmənt] *s* encarcelamiento; pena privativa de libertad

improbable [ɪm'prabəbəl] *adj* improbable

impromptu [ɪm'pramptju] o [ɪm'pramptu] *adj* improvisado ‖ *adv* de improviso ‖ *s* improvisación; (*mus*) impromptu *m*

improper [ɪm'prapər] *adj* impropio; (*contrary to good taste or decency*) indecoroso

improve [ɪm'pruv] *tr* perfeccionar,· mejorar; aprovechar (*la oportunidad*) ‖ *intr* perfeccionarse, mejorar; **to improve on** o **upon** mejorar

improvement [ɪm'pruvmənt] *s* perfeccionamiento, mejoramiento; (*e.g., in health*) mejoría; (*useful employment, e.g., of time*) aprovechamiento

improvident [ɪm'pravɪdənt] *adj* imprevisor

improvise ['ɪmprə,vaɪz] *tr & intr* improvisar

imprudent [ɪm'prudənt] *adj* imprudente

impudence ['ɪmpjədəns] *s* insolencia, descaro, impertinencia

impudent ['ɪmpjədənt] *adj* insolente, descarado, impertinente

impugn [ɪm'pjun] *tr* poner en tela de juicio

impulse ['ɪmpʌls] *s* impulso

impulsive [ɪm'pʌlsɪv] *adj* impulsivo

impunity [ɪm'pjunɪti] *s* impunidad

impure [ɪm'pjur] *adj* impuro

impuri•ty [ɪm'pjurɪti] *s* (*pl* **-ties**) impureza, impuridad

impute [ɪm'pjut] *tr* imputar

in [ɪn] *adj* interior ‖ *adv* dentro; en casa, en la oficina; **in here** aquí dentro; **in there** allí dentro; **to be in** estar en casa; **to be in for** estar expuesto a; **to be in with** gozar del favor de ‖ *prep* en; (*within*) dentro de; (*over, through*) por; (*a period of the day*) en o por; **dressed in . . .** vestido de . . . ; **in so far as** en tanto que; **in that** en que,

por cuanto ‖ *s* — **ins and outs** recovecos, pormenores minuciosos

inability [,ɪnə'bɪlɪti] *s* inhabilidad, incapacidad

inaccessible [,ɪnæk'sɛsɪbəl] *adj* inaccesible

inaccura•cy [ɪn'ækjərəsi] *s* (*pl* **-cies**) inexactitud, incorrección

inaccurate [ɪn'ækjərɪt] *adj* inexacto, incorrecto

inaction [ɪn'ækʃən] *s* inacción

inactive [ɪn'æktɪv] *adj* inactivo

inactivity [,ɪnæk'tɪvɪti] *s* inactividad

inadequate [ɪn'ædɪkwɪt] *adj* insuficiente, inadecuado

inadvertent [,ɪnəd'vʌrtənt] *adj* inadvertido

inadvisable [,ɪnəd'vaɪzəbəl] *adj* poco aconsejable, imprudente

inane [ɪn'en] *adj* inane

inanimate [ɪn'ænɪmɪt] *adj* inanimado

inappreciable [,ɪnə'priʃɪəbəl] *adj* inapreciable

inappropriate [,ɪnə'propriɪt] *adj* no apropiado, no a propósito

inarticulate [,ɪnar'tɪkjəlɪt] *adj* (*sounds, words*) inarticulado; (*person*) incapaz de expresarse

inartistic [,ɪnar'tɪstɪk] *adj* antiartístico, inartístico

inasmuch as [,ɪnəz'mʌtʃ,æz] *conj* ya que, puesto que; en cuanto, hasta donde

inattentive [,ɪnə'tɛntɪv] *adj* desatento

inaugural [ɪn'ɔgjərəl] *adj* inaugural ‖ *s* discurso inaugural

inaugurate [ɪn'ɔgjə,ret] *tr* inaugurar

inauguration [ɪn,ɔgjə'reʃən] *s* (*formal initiation or opening*) inauguración; (*investiture of a head of government*) toma de posesión

inborn ['ɪn'bɔrn] *adj* innato, ingénito

inbreeding ['ɪn,bridɪŋ] *s* intracruzamiento

inc. *abbr* **inclosure, included, including, incorporated, increase**

Inca ['ɪŋkə] *adj* incaico ‖ *s* inca *mf*

incandescent [,ɪnkən'dɛsənt] *adj* incandescente

incapable [ɪn'kepəbəl] *adj* incapaz

incapacitate [,ɪnkə'pæsɪ,tet] *tr* incapacitar, inhabilitar

incapaci•ty [,ɪnkə'pæsɪti] *s* (*pl* **-ties**) incapacidad

incarcerate [ɪn'karsə,ret] *tr* encarcelar

incarnate [ɪn'karnɪt] *adj* encarnado ‖ [ɪn'karnet] *tr* encarnar

incarnation [,ɪnkar'neʃən] *s* encarnación

incendiarism [ɪn'sɛndɪ•ə,rɪzəm] *s* incendio intencionado; incitación al desorden

incendiar•y [ɪn'sɛndɪ,ɛri] *adj* incendiario ‖ *s* (*pl* **-ies**) incendiario

incense ['ɪnsɛns] *s* incienso ‖ *tr* (*to burn incense before*) incensar ‖ [ɪn'sɛns] *tr* exasperar, encolerizar

incense burner *s* incensario

incentive [ɪn'sɛntɪv] *adj & s* incentivo

inception [ɪn'sɛpʃən] *s* principio, comienzo

incertitude [ɪn'sʌrt,tjud] *s* incertidumbre

incessant [ɪn'sɛsənt] *adj* incesante

incest ['ɪnsɛst] *s* incesto

incestuous [ɪn'sɛstʃu•əs] *adj* incestuoso

inch [ɪntʃ] *s* pulgada; **to be within an inch of**
estar a dos dedos de ‖ *intr* — **to inch**
ahead avanzar poco a poco
incidence ['ɪnsɪdəns] *s* incidencia; (*range of
occurrence*) extensión
incident ['ɪnsɪdənt] *adj* & *s* incidente *m*
incidental [,ɪnsɪ'dɛntəl] *adj* incidente; (*in-
curred in addition to the regular amount*)
obvencional ‖ *s* elemento incidental; **inci-
dentals** gastos menudos
incidentally [,ɪnsɪ'dɛntəli] *adv* incidente-
mente; a propósito
incipient [ɪn'sɪpɪ•ənt] *adj* incipiente
incision [ɪn'sɪʒən] *s* incisión
incisive [ɪn'saɪsɪv] *adj* incisivo
incite [ɪn'saɪt] *tr* incitar
incl. *abbr* **inclosure, inclusive**
inclemen•cy [ɪn'klɛmənsi] *s* (*pl* **-cies**) inclemencia
inclement [ɪn'klɛmənt] *adj* inclemente
inclination [,ɪnklɪ'neʃən] *s* inclinación
incline ['ɪnklaɪn] o [ɪn'klaɪn] *s* declive *m*,
pendiente *f* ‖ [ɪn'klaɪn] *tr* inclinar ‖ *intr*
inclinarse
inclose [ɪn'kloz] *tr* encerrar; (*in a letter*)
adjuntar, incluir; **to inclose herewith** remitir adjunto
inclosure [ɪn'kloʒər] *s* recinto; cosa inclusa,
carta inclusa
include [ɪn'klud] *tr* incluir, comprender
including [ɪn'kludɪŋ] *prep* incluso, inclusive;
imbíbito (Guat, Mex)
inclusive [ɪn'klusɪv] *adj* inclusivo; **inclusive
of** comprensivo de ‖ *adv* inclusive
incogni•to [ɪn'kɑgnɪ,to] *adj* incógnito ‖ *adv*
de incógnito ‖ *s* (*pl* **-tos**) incógnito
incoherent [,ɪnko'hɪrənt] *adj* incoherente
incombustible [,ɪnkəm'bʌstɪbəl] *adj* incombustible
income ['ɪnkʌm] *s* renta, ingreso, utilidad
income tax *s* impuesto sobre rentas
in′come-tax′ return *s* declaración de impuesto sobre rentas
in′com′ing *adj* de entrada, entrante; (*tide*)
ascendente ‖ *s* entrada
incommunicado [,ɪnkə,mjunə'kado] *adj* incomunicado
incomparable [ɪn'kɑmpərəbəl] *adj* incomparable; inigualable
incompatible [,ɪnkəm'pætɪbəl] *adj* incompatible
incompetent [ɪn'kɑmpɪtənt] *adj* incompetente
incomplete [,ɪnkəm'plit] *adj* incompleto
incomprehensible [,ɪnkɑmprɪ'hɛnsɪbəl] *adj*
incomprehensible
incomprehension [ɪn,kɑmprɪ'hɛnʃən] *s* incomprensión
inconceivable [,ɪnkən'sivəbəl] *adj* inconcebible
inconclusive [,ɪnkən'klusɪv] *adj* inconcluyente
incongruous [ɪn'kɑŋgru•əs] *adj* incongruo
inconsequential [ɪn,kɑnsɪ'kwɛnʃəl] *adj* (*lacking proper sequence of thought or speech*)
inconsecuente; (*trivial*) de poca importancia
inconsiderate [,ɪnkən'sɪdərɪt] *adj* desconsiderado, inconsiderado

inconsisten•cy [,ɪnkən'sɪstənsi] *s* (*pl* **-cies**)
(*lack of coherence*) inconsistencia; (*lack of
logical connection or uniformity*) inconsecuencia
inconsistent [,ɪnkən'sɪstənt] *adj* (*lacking coherence of parts*) inconsistente; (*not agreeing with itself or oneself*) inconsecuente
inconsolable [,ɪnkən'soləbəl] *adj* inconsolable
inconspicuous [,ɪnkən'spɪkju•əs] *adj* poco
impresionante, poco aparente
inconstant [ɪn'kɑnstənt] *adj* inconstante
incontinent [ɪn'kɑntɪnənt] *adj* incontinente
incontrovertible [,ɪnkɑntrə'vʌrtɪbəl] *adj* incontrovertible
inconvenience [,ɪnkən'vini•əns] *s* incomodidad, inconveniencia, molestia ‖ *tr* incomodar, molestar
inconvenient [,ɪnkən'vini•ənt] *adj* incómodo, inconveniente, molesto
incorporate [ɪn'kɔrpə,ret] *tr* incorporar; constituir en sociedad anónima ‖ *intr* incorporarse; constituirse en sociedad anónima
incorporation [ɪn'kɔrpə'reʃən] *s* incorporación; constitución en sociedad anónima
incorrect [,ɪnkə'rɛkt] *adj* incorrecto
increase ['ɪnkris] *s* aumento; ganancia, interés *m*; **to be on the increase** ir en
aumento ‖ [ɪn'kris] *tr* aumentar; (*by prop-
agation*) multiplicar ‖ *intr* aumentar; multiplicarse
increasingly [ɪn'krisɪŋli] *adv* cada vez más
incredible [ɪn'krɛdɪbəl] *adj* increíble
incredulous [ɪn'krɛdʒələs] *adj* incrédulo
increment ['ɪnkrɪmənt] *s* incremento
incriminate [ɪn'krɪmɪ,net] *tr* acriminar, incriminar
incrust [ɪn'krʌst] *tr* incrustar
incubate ['ɪnkjə,bet] *tr* & *intr* incubar
incubator ['ɪnkjə,betər] *s* incubadora
inculcate [ɪn'kʌlket] o ['ɪnkʌl,ket] *tr* inculcar
incumben•cy [ɪn'kʌmbənsi] *s* (*pl* **-cies**) incumbencia
incumbent [ɪn'kʌmbənt] *adj* — **to be incumbent on** incumbir a ‖ *s* titular *m*
incunabula [,ɪnkju'næbjələ] *spl* (*beginnings*)
orígenes *mpl*; (*early printed books*) incun-
ables *mpl*
in•cur [ɪn'kʌr] *v* (*pret* & *pp* **-curred;** *ger*
-curring) *tr* incurrir en; (*a debt*) contraer
incurable [ɪn'kjurəbəl] *adj* & *s* incurable *mf*
incursion [ɪn'kʌrʒən] *s* incursión, correría
ind. *abbr* **independent, industrial**
indebted [ɪn'dɛtɪd] *adj* adeudado; obligado
indebtedness [ɪn'dɛtɪdnɪs] *s* endeudamiento
indecen•cy [ɪn'disənsi] *s* (*pl* **-cies**) indecencia, deshonestidad
indecent [ɪn'disənt] *adj* indecente, desho-
nesto; lépero (CAm, Mex)
indecisive [,ɪndɪ'saɪsɪv] *adj* indeciso
indeclinable [,ɪndɪ'klaɪnəbəl] *adj* (gram) indeclinable
indeed [ɪn'did] *adv* verdaderamente, claro ‖
interj ¡de veras!
indefatigable [,ɪndɪ'fætɪgəbəl] *adj* incansable, infatigable

im
in

indefensible [,ɪndɪ'fɛnsɪbəl] *adj* indefendible
indefinable [,ɪndɪ'faɪnəbəl] *adj* indefinible
indefinite [ɪn'dɛfɪnɪt] *adj* indefinido
indelible [ɪn'dɛlɪbəl] *adj* indeleble
indelicate [ɪn'dɛlɪkɪt] *adj* indelicado
indemnification [ɪn,dɛmnɪfɪ'keʃən] *s* indemnización
indemni·fy [ɪn'dɛmnɪ,faɪ] *v* (*pret & pp* **-fied**) *tr* indemnizar
indemni·ty [ɪn'dɛmnɪti] *s* (*pl* **-ties**) (*security against loss*) indemnidad; (*compensation*) indemnización
indent [ɪn'dɛnt] *tr* dentar, mellar; (typ) sangrar
indentation [,ɪndɛn'teʃən] *s* mella, muesca; (typ) sangría
indenture [ɪn'dɛntʃər] *s* escritura, contrato; contrato de aprendizaje ‖ *tr* obligar por contrato
independence [,ɪndɪ'pɛndəns] *s* independencia
independen·cy [,ɪndɪ'pɛndənsi] *s* (*pl* **-cies**) independencia; país *m* independiente
independent [,ɪndɪ'pɛndənt] *adj & s* independiente *mf*
indescribable [,ɪndɪ'skraɪbəbəl] *adj* indescriptible
indestructible [,ɪndɪ'strʌktɪbəl] *adj* indestructible
indeterminate [,ɪndɪ'tʌrmɪnɪt] *adj* indeterminado
index ['ɪndɛks] *s* (*pl* **indexes** o **indices** ['ɪndɪ,siz] *s* índice *m*; (typ) manecilla ‖ *tr* poner índice a; poner en un índice ‖ **Index** *s* Índice de los libros prohibidos
index card *s* ficha catalográfica
index finger *s* dedo índice
index tab *s* pestaña
India ['ɪndɪ·ə] *s* la India
India ink *s* tinta china
Indian ['ɪndɪ·ən] *adj & s* indio
Indian club *s* maza de gimnasia
Indian corn *s* maíz *m*, panizo
Indian file *s* fila india ‖ *adv* en fila india
Indian Ocean *s* mar *m* de las Indias, océano Índico
Indian summer *s* veranillo de San Martín
India paper *s* papel *m* de China
India rubber *s* caucho
indicate ['ɪndɪ,ket] *tr* indicar
indication [,ɪndɪ'keʃən] *s* indicación
indicative [ɪn'dɪkətɪv] *adj & s* indicativo
indicator ['ɪndɪ,ketər] *s* indicador *m*
indict [ɪn'daɪt] *tr* (law) acusar, procesar
indictment [ɪn'daɪtmənt] *s* acusación, procesamiento; auto de acusación formulado por el gran jurado
indifferent [ɪn'dɪfərənt] *adj* indiferente; (*not particularly good*) pasadero, mediano
indigenous [ɪn'dɪdʒɪnəs] *adj* indígena
indigent ['ɪndɪdʒənt] *adj* indigente
indigestible [,ɪndɪ'dʒɛstɪbəl] *adj* indigestible
indigestion [,ɪndɪ'dʒɛstʃən] *s* indigestión
indignant [ɪn'dɪgnənt] *adj* indignado
indignation [,ɪndɪg'neʃən] *s* indignación
indigni·ty [ɪn'dɪgnɪti] *s* (*pl* **-ties**) indignidad

indi·go ['ɪndɪgo] *adj* azul de añil ‖ *s* (*pl* **-gos** o **-goes**) índigo
indirect [,ɪndɪ'rɛkt] *adj* indirecto
indirect discourse *s* estilo indirecto
indiscernible [,ɪndɪ'zʌrnɪbəl] o [,ɪndɪ'sʌrnɪbəl] *adj* indiscernible
indiscreet [,ɪndɪs'krit] *adj* indiscreto
indiscriminate [,ɪndɪs'krɪmənɪt] *adj* indiscriminado
indispensable ['ɪndɪs'pɛnsəbəl] *adj* indispensable, imprescindible
indispose [,ɪndɪs'poz] *tr* indisponer
indisposed [,ɪndɪs'pozd] *adj* (*disinclined*) maldispuesto; (*somewhat ill*) indispuesto
indissoluble [,ɪndɪ'saljəbəl] *adj* indisoluble
indistinct [,ɪndɪ'stɪŋkt] *adj* indistinto
indite [ɪn'daɪt] *tr* redactar, poner por escrito
individual [,ɪndɪ'vɪdʒʊ·əl] *adj* individual ‖ *s* individuo
individuali·ty [,ɪndɪ,vɪdʒʊ,'ælɪti] *s* (*pl* **-ties**) individualidad; (*person of distinctive character*) personaje *m*
Indochina ['ɪndo'tʃaɪnə] *s* la Indochina
Indo-Chi·nese ['ɪndotʃaɪ'niz] *adj* indochino ‖ *s* (*pl* **-nese**) indochino
indoctrinate [ɪn'daktrɪ,net] *tr* adoctrinar
Indo-European ['ɪndo,jʊrə'pi·ən] *adj & s* indoeuropeo
indolent ['ɪndələnt] *adj* indolente
Indonesia [,ɪndo'niʃə] o [,ɪndo'niʒə] *s* la Indonesia
Indonesian [,ɪndo'niʃən] o [,ɪndo'niʒən] *adj & s* indonesio
indoor ['ɪn,dor] *adj* interior, de puertas adentro; (*inclined to stay in the house*) casero
indoors ['ɪn'dorz] *adv* dentro, en casa, bajo techado, bajo cubierto
indorse [ɪn'dors] *tr* endosar; (fig) apoyar, aprobar
indorsee [,ɪndor'si] *s* endosatario
indorsement [ɪn'dorsmənt] *s* endoso; (fig) apoyo, aprobación
indorser [ɪn'dorsər] *s* endosante *mf*
induce [ɪn'djus] *tr* inducir; causar, ocasionar
inducement [ɪn'djusmənt] *s* aliciente *m*, estímulo, incentivo
induct [ɪn'dʌkt] *tr* instalar; introducir, iniciar; (mil) quintar
induction [ɪn'dʌkʃən] *s* instalación; introducción; (elec & log) inducción; (mil) quinta
indulge [ɪn'dʌldʒ] *tr* gratificar (*p.ej., los deseos de uno*); mimar (*a un niño*) ‖ *intr* abandonar; **to indulge in** entregarse a, permitirse el placer de
indulgence [ɪn'dʌldʒəns] *s* gusto, inclinación; intemperancia, desenfreno; (*leniency*) indulgencia
indulgent [ɪn'dʌldʒənt] *adj* indulgente
industrial [ɪn'dʌstrɪəl] *adj* industrial
industrialist [ɪn'dʌstrɪ·əlɪst] *s* industrial *m*
industrialize [ɪn'dʌstrɪ·ə,laɪz] *tr* industrializar
industrious [ɪn'dʌstrɪ·əs] *adj* industrioso, aplicado
indus·try ['ɪndəstri] *s* (*pl* **-tries**) industria
inebriation [ɪn,ibrɪ'eʃən] *s* embriaguez *f*
inedible [ɪn'ɛdɪbəl] *adj* incomible

ineffable [ɪnˈɛfəbəl] *adj* inefable
ineffective [ˌɪnɪˈfɛktɪv] *adj* ineficaz; (*person*) incapaz
ineffectual [ˌɪnɪˈfɛktʃʊ•əl] *adj* ineficaz, fútil
inefficacy [ɪnˈɛfɪkəsi] *s* ineficacia
inefficient [ˌɪnɪˈfɪʃənt] *adj* de mal rendimiento
ineligible [ɪnˈɛlɪdʒɪbəl] *adj* inelegible
inequali•ty [ˌɪnɪˈkwɑlɪti] *s* (*pl* **-ties**) desigualdad
inequi•ty [ɪnˈɛkwɪti] *s* (*pl* **-ties**) inequidad
ineradicable [ˌɪnɪˈrædɪkəbəl] *adj* inextirpable
inertia [ɪnˈʌrʃə] *s* inercia
inescapable [ˌɪnɛsˈkepəbəl] *adj* ineludible
inevitable [ɪnˈɛvɪtəbəl] *adj* inevitable
inexact [ˌɪnɛgˈzækt] *adj* inexacto
inexcusable [ˌɪnɛksˈkjuzəbəl] *adj* indisculpable, inexcusable
inexhaustible [ˌɪnɛgˈzɔstɪbəl] *adj* inagotable
inexorable [ɪnˈɛksərəbəl] *adj* inexorable
inexpedient [ˌɪnɛkˈspidɪ•ənt] *adj* malaconsejado, inoportuno
inexpensive [ˌɪnɛkˈspɛnsɪv] *adj* barato, poco costoso
inexperience [ˌɪnɛkˈspɪrɪ•əns] *s* inexperiencia
inexplicable [ɪnˈɛksplɪkəbəl] *adj* inexplicable
inexpressible [ˌɪnɛkˈsprɛsɪbəl] *adj* inexpresable
Inf. *abbr* **Infantry**
infallible [ɪnˈfælɪbəl] *adj* infalible
infamous [ˈɪnfəməs] *adj* infame
infa•my [ˈɪnfəmi] *s* (*pl* **-mies**) infamia
infan•cy [ˈɪnfənsi] *s* (*pl* **-cies**) infancia
infant [ˈɪnfənt] *adj* infantil; (*in the earliest stage*) (fig) naciente ‖ *s* criatura, nene *m*
infant care *s* puericultura
infantile [ˈɪnfənˌtaɪl] o [ˈɪnfəntɪl] *adj* infantil; (*childish*) aniñado
infan•try [ˈɪnfəntri] *s* (*pl* **-tries**) infantería
infantry•man [ˈɪnfəntrɪmən] *s* (*pl* **-men** [mən]) infante *m*, soldado de infantería
infarct [ɪnˈfɑrkt] *s* infarto
infatuated [ɪnˈfætʃʊˌetɪd] *adj* apasionado, locamente enamorado
infect [ɪnˈfɛkt] *tr* inficionar, infectar; influir sobre
infection [ɪnˈfɛkʃən] *s* infección
infectious [ɪnˈfɛkʃəs] *adj* infeccioso
in•fer [ɪnˈfʌr] *v* (*pret & pp* **-ferred;** *ger* **-ferring**) *tr* inferir; (coll) conjeturar, suponer
inferior [ɪnˈfɪrɪ•ər] *adj & s* inferior *m*
inferiority [ɪnˌfɪrɪˈɑrɪti] *s* inferioridad
inferiority complex *s* complejo de inferioridad
infernal [ɪnˈfʌrnəl] *adj* infernal
infest [ɪnˈfɛst] *tr* infestar
infidel [ˈɪnfɪdəl] *adj & s* infiel *mf*
infideli•ty [ˌɪnfɪˈdɛlɪti] *s* (*pl* **-ties**) infidelidad
in'field' *s* (baseball) cuadro interior
infiltrate [ˈɪnfɪlˌtret] *tr* infiltrar; infiltrarse en ‖ *intr* infiltrarse
infinite [ˈɪnfɪnɪt] *adj & s* infinito
infinitive [ɪnˈfɪnɪtɪv] *adj & s* infinitivo

infini•ty [ɪnˈfɪnɪti] *s* (*pl* **-ties**) infinidad; (math) infinito
infirm [ɪnˈfʌrm] *adj* infirme, achacoso; (*unsteady*) inestable, inseguro; poco firme, poco sólido
infirma•ry [ɪnˈfʌrməri] *s* (*pl* **-ries**) enfermería
infirmi•ty [ɪnˈfʌrmɪti] *s* (*pl* **-ties**) achaque *m;* inestabilidad
inflame [ɪnˈflem] *tr* inflamar
inflammable [ɪnˈflæməbəl] *adj* inflamable
inflammation [ˌɪnfləˈmeʃən] *s* inflamación
inflate [ɪnˈflet] *tr* inflar ‖ *intr* inflarse
inflation [ɪnˈfleʃən] *s* inflación; (*of a tire*) inflado
inflationary [ɪnˈfleʃənˌɛri] *adj* inflacionario
inflect [ɪnˈflɛkt] *tr* doblar, torcer; modular (*la voz*); (gram) modificar por inflexión
inflection [ɪnˈflɛkʃən] *s* inflexión
inflexible [ɪnˈflɛksɪbəl] *adj* inflexible
inflict [ɪnˈflɪkt] *tr* infligir
influence [ˈɪnflu•əns] *s* influencia ‖ *tr* influir sobre, influenciar
influential [ˌɪnfluˈɛnʃəl] *adj* influyente
influenza [ˌɪnfluˈɛnzə] *s* influenza
inform [ɪnˈfɔrm] *tr* informar, avisar, enterar ‖ *intr* informar
informal [ɪnˈfɔrməl] *adj* (*not according to established rules*) informal; (*unceremonious; colloquial*) familiar
information [ˌɪnfərˈmeʃən] *s* información, informes *mpl*
informational [ˌɪnfərˈmeʃənəl] *adj* informativo
informed sources *spl* los entendidos
infraction [ɪnˈfrækʃən] *s* infracción
infrared [ˌɪnfrəˈrɛd] *adj & s* infrarrojo
infrequent [ɪnˈfrikwənt] *adj* infrecuente
infringe [ɪnˈfrɪndʒ] *tr* infringir ‖ *intr*—**to infringe on** o **upon** invadir, abusar de
infringement [ɪnˈfrɪndʒmənt] *s* infracción
infuriate [ɪnˈfjʊrɪˌet] *tr* enfurecer
infuse [ɪnˈfjuz] *tr* infundir
infusion [ɪnˈfjuʒən] *s* infusión
ingenious [ɪnˈdʒinjəs] *adj* ingenioso
ingenui•ty [ˌɪndʒɪˈnjuɪti] o [ˌɪndʒɪˈnuɪti] *s* (*pl* **-ties**) ingeniosidad
ingenuous [ɪnˈdʒɛnjʊ•əs] *adj* ingenuo
ingenuousness [ɪnˈdʒɛnjʊ•əsnɪs] *s* ingenuidad
ingest [ɪnˈdʒɛst] *tr* injerir
in'go'ing *adj* entrante
ingot [ˈɪngət] *s* lingote *m*
ingraft [ɪnˈgræft] *tr* (hort & surg) injertar; (fig) implantar
ingrate [ˈɪngret] *s* ingrato
ingratiate [ɪnˈgreʃɪˌet] *tr*—**to ingratiate oneself with** congraciarse con
ingratiating [ɪnˈgreʃɪˌetɪŋ] *adj* atrayente, obsequioso
ingratitude [ɪnˈgrætɪˌtjud] *s* ingratitud, desagradecimiento
ingredient [ɪnˈgridɪ•ənt] *s* ingrediente *m*
in'grow'ing nail *s* uñero
ingulf [ɪnˈgʌlf] *tr* hundir, inundar
inhabit [ɪnˈhæbɪt] *tr* habitar, poblar

in
in

inhabitant [ɪn'hæbɪtənt] s habitante mf
inhale [ɪn'hel] tr aspirar, inspirar ‖ intr aspirar, inspirar; tragar el humo
inherent [ɪn'hɪrənt] adj inherente
inherit [ɪn'hɛrɪt] tr & intr heredar
inheritance [ɪn'hɛrɪtəns] s herencia; mortual m (CAm, Mex)
inheritor [ɪn'hɛrɪtər] s heredero
inhibit [ɪn'hɪbɪt] tr inhibir, prohibir
inhospitable [ɪn'hɑspɪtəbəl] o [,ɪnhɑs-'pɪtəbəl] adj inhospitalario; (affording no shelter or protection) inhóspito
inhuman [ɪn'hjumən] adj inhumano
inhumane [,ɪnhju'men] adj inhumano
inhumani•ty [,ɪnhju'mænɪti] s (pl -ties) inhumanidad
inimical [ɪ'nɪmɪkəl] adj enemigo
iniqui•ty [ɪ'nɪkwɪti] s (pl -ties) iniquidad
ini•tial [ɪ'nɪʃəl] adj & s inicial f ‖ v (pret -tialed o -tialled; ger -tialing o tialling) tr firmar con sus iniciales; marcar (p.ej., un pañuelo)
initiate [ɪ'nɪʃɪ,et] tr iniciar
initiation [ɪ,nɪʃɪ'eʃən] s iniciación
initiative [ɪ'nɪʃɪ•ətɪv] o [ɪ'nɪʃətɪv] s iniciativa
inject [ɪn'dʒɛkt] tr inyectar; introducir (una especie, una advertencia)
injection [ɪn'dʒɛkʃən] s inyección
injudicious [,ɪndʒu'dɪʃəs] adj imprudente
injunction [ɪn'dʒʌŋkʃən] s admonición, mandato; (law) entredicho
injure ['ɪndʒər] tr (to harm) dañar, hacer daño a; (to wound) herir, lisiar, lastimar; (to offend) agraviar
injurious [ɪn'dʒurɪ•əs] adj dañoso, perjudicial; (offensive) agravioso
inju•ry ['ɪndʒəri] s (pl -ries) (harm) daño; (wound) herida, lesión; (offense) agravio
injustice [ɪn'dʒʌstɪs] s injusticia
ink [ɪŋk] s tinta ‖ tr entintar
inkling ['ɪŋklɪŋ] s sospecha, indicio, noción vaga, vislumbre f
ink'stand' s (cuplike container) tintero; (stand for ink, pens, etc.) portatintero
ink'well' s tintero
ink•y ['ɪŋki] adj (comp -ier; super -iest) entintado; negro
inlaid ['ɪn,led] o [,ɪn'led] adj embutido, taraceado
inland ['ɪnlənd] adj & s interior m ‖ adv tierra adentro
in'-law' s (coll) pariente político
in•lay ['ɪn,le] s embutido ‖ [ɪn'le] o ['ɪn,le] v (pret & pp -laid) tr embutir, taracear
in'let s ensenada, cala, caleta
in'mate' s (in a hospital or home) asilado, recluso, acogido; (in a jail) presidiario, preso
inn [ɪn] s mesón m, posada
innate [ɪ'net] o ['ɪnet] adj ingénito, innato
inner ['ɪnər] adj interior; secreto
in'ner•spring' mattress s colchón m de muelles interiores
inner tube s cámara (de neumático)
inning ['ɪnɪŋ] s mano f, entrada, turno
inn'keep'er s mesonero, posadero
innocence ['ɪnəsəns] s inocencia

innocent ['ɪnəsənt] adj & s inocente mf
innovate ['ɪnə,vet] tr innovar
innovation [,ɪnə'veʃən] s innovación
innuen•do [,ɪnju'ɛndo] s (pl -does) indirecta, insinuación
innumerable [ɪ'numərəbəl] adj innumerable, incontable
inoculate [ɪn'ɑkjə,let] tr inocular; (fig) imbuir
inoculation [ɪn,ɑkjə'leʃən] s inoculación
inoffensive [,ɪnə'fɛnsɪv] adj inofensivo
inoperative [ɪn'ɑpərətɪv] adj fuera de servicio
inopportune [ɪn,ɑpər'tjun] adj inoportuno
inordinate [ɪn'ɔrdɪnɪt] adj excesivo; (unrestrained) desenfrenado
inorganic [,ɪnɔr'gænɪk] adj inorgánico
in'put' s gasto, consumo; (elec) entrada; (mech) potencia consumida
inquest ['ɪnkwɛst] s encuesta; (of coroner) pesquisa judicial, levantamiento del cadáver
inquire [ɪn'kwaɪr] tr averiguar, inquirir ‖ intr preguntar; **to inquire about, after** o **for** preguntar por; **to inquire into** averiguar, inquirir
inquir•y [ɪn'kwaɪri] o ['ɪnkwɪri] s (pl -ies) averiguación, encuesta; pregunta
inquisition [,ɪnkwɪ'zɪʃən] s inquisición
inquisitive [ɪn'kwɪzɪtɪv] adj curioso, preguntón
in'road' s incursión
ins. abbr **insulated, insurance**
insane [ɪn'sen] adj loco, insano, dementado
insane asylum s manicomio, casa de locos
insani•ty [ɪn'sænɪti] s (pl -ties) demencia, locura, insania, loquera
insatiable [ɪn'seʃəbəl] adj insaciable
inscribe [ɪn'skraɪb] tr inscribir; dedicar (una obra literaria)
inscription [ɪn'skrɪpʃən] s inscripción; (of a book) dedicatoria
inscrutable [ɪn'skrutəbəl] adj inescrutable
insect ['ɪnsɛkt] s insecto
insect control s desinsectación
insecticide [ɪn'sɛktɪ,saɪd] adj & s insecticida m
insecure [,ɪnsɪ'kjur] adj inseguro
inseparable [ɪn'sɛpərəbəl] adj inseparable
insert ['ɪnsʌrt] s inserción ‖ [ɪn'sʌrt] tr insertar
insertion [ɪn'sʌrʃən] s inserción; (strip of lace) entredós m
in•set ['ɪn,sɛt] s intercalación ‖ [ɪn'sɛt] o ['ɪn,sɛt] v (pret & pp -set; ger -setting) tr intercalar, encastrar
in'shore' adj cercano a la orilla ‖ adv cerca de la orilla; hacia la orilla
in'side' adj interior; interno; secreto ‖ adv dentro, adentro; **inside of** dentro de; **to turn inside out** volver al revés; volverse al revés ‖ prep dentro de ‖ s interior m; **insides** (coll) entrañas; **on the inside** (coll) en el secreto de las cosas
inside information s informes mpl confidenciales
insider [,ɪn'saɪdər] s persona enterada

insidious [ɪnˈsɪdɪ•əs] *adj* insidioso
in'sight' *s* penetración
insigni•a [ɪnˈsɪgnɪ•ə] *s* (*pl* -a o -as) insignia
insignificant [ˌɪnsɪgˈnɪfɪkənt] *adj* insignificante
insincere [ˌɪnsɪnˈsɪr] *adj* insincero; malo (Mex)
insinuate [ɪnˈsɪnjuˌet] *tr* insinuar
insipid [ɪnˈsɪpɪd] *adj* insípido
insist [ɪnˈsɪst] *intr* insistir
insofar as [ˌɪnsoˈfɑrˌæz] *conj* en cuanto
insolence [ˈɪnsələns] *s* insolencia
insolent [ˈɪnsələnt] *adj* insolente
insoluble [ɪnˈsɑljəbəl] *adj* insoluble
insolven•cy [ɪnˈsɑlvənsi] *s* (*pl* -cies) insolvencia
insomnia [ɪnˈsɑmnɪ•ə] *s* insomnio
insomuch [ˌɪnsoˈmʌtʃ] *adv* hasta tal punto; insomuch as ya que, puesto que; insomuch that hasta el punto que
inspect [ɪnˈspɛkt] *tr* inspeccionar
inspection [ɪnˈspɛkʃən] *s* inspección
inspiration [ˌɪnspɪˈreʃən] *s* inspiración
inspire [ɪnˈspaɪr] *tr & intr* inspirar
inspiring [ɪnˈspaɪrɪŋ] *adj* inspirante
inst. *abbr* instant (*i.e.*, present month)
Inst. *abbr* Institute, Institution
install [ɪnˈstɔl] *tr* instalar
installment [ɪnˈstɔlmənt] *s* instalación; entrega; in installments por entregas; a plazos
installment buying *s* compra a plazos
installment plan *s* pago a plazos, compra a plazos; on the installment plan con facilidades de pago
instance [ˈɪnstəns] *s* caso, ejemplo; for instance por ejemplo
instant [ˈɪnstənt] *adj* instantáneo ‖ *s* instante *m*, momento; mes *m* corriente
instantaneous [ˌɪnstənˈtenɪ•əs] *adj* instantáneo
instantly [ˈɪnstəntli] *adv* al instante
instead [ɪnˈstɛd] *adv* preferiblemente; en su lugar; instead of en vez de, en lugar de
in'step' *s* empeine *m*
instigate [ˈɪnstɪˌget] *tr* instigar
in•still' *tr* instilar
instinct [ˈɪnstɪŋkt] *s* instinto
instinctive [ɪnˈstɪŋktɪv] *adj* instintivo
institute [ˈɪnstɪˌtjut] *s* instituto ‖ *tr* instituir
institution [ˌɪnstɪˈtjuʃən] *s* institución
instruct [ɪnˈstrʌkt] *tr* instruir
instruction [ɪnˈstrʌkʃən] *s* instrucción
instructions for use *spl* modo de empleo
instructive [ɪnˈstrʌktɪv] *adj* instructivo
instructor [ɪnˈstrʌktər] *s* instructor *m*
instrument [ˈɪnstrəmənt] *s* instrumento ‖ [ˈɪnstrəˌmɛnt] *tr* instrumentar
instrumentalist [ˌɪnstrəˈmɛntəlɪst] *s* instrumentista *mf*
instrumentali•ty [ˌɪnstrəmənˈtælɪti] *s* (*pl* -ties) agencia, mediación
instrument panel *s* cuadro de mando; salpicadero
insubordinate [ˌɪnsəˈbɔrdɪnɪt] *adj* insubordinado
insufferable [ɪnˈsʌfərəbel] *adj* insufrible

insufficient [ˌɪnsəˈfɪʃənt] *adj* insuficiente
insular [ˈɪnsələr] o [ˈɪnsjʊlər] *adj* insular; (fig) de miras estrechas
insulate [ˈɪnsəˌlet] *tr* aislar
insulation [ˌɪnsəˈleʃən] *s* aislación
insulator [ˈɪnsəˌletər] *s* aislador *m*
insulin [ˈɪnsəlɪn] *s* insulina
insult [ˈɪnsʌlt] *s* insulto, insultada, escopetazo ‖ [ɪnˈsʌlt] *tr* insultar
insurable [ɪnˈʃʊrəbəl] *adj* asegurable
insurance [ɪnˈʃʊrəns] *s* seguro
insure [ɪnˈʃʊr] *tr* asegurar
insurer [ɪnˈʃʊrər] *s* asegurador *m*
insurgent [ɪnˈsʌrdʒənt] *adj & s* insurgente *mf*
insurmountable [ˌɪnsərˈmaʊntəbəl] *adj* insuperable
insurrection [ˌɪnsəˈrɛkʃən] *s* insurrección
insusceptible [ˌɪnsəˈsɛptɪbəl] *adj* insusceptible
int. *abbr* interest, interior, internal, international
intact [ɪnˈtækt] *adj* intacto, ileso
in'take' *s* (place of taking in) entrada; (act or amount) toma; (mach) admisión
intake manifold *s* múltiple *m* de admisión, colector *m* de admisión
intake valve *s* válvula de admisión
intangible [ɪnˈtændʒɪbəl] *adj* intangible; vago, indefinido
integer [ˈɪntɪdʒər] *s* (arith) entero
integral [ˈɪntɪgrəl] *adj* íntegro; integral with solidario de ‖ *s* conjunto
integration [ˌɪntɪˈgreʃən] *s* integración
integrity [ɪnˈtɛgrɪti] *s* integridad
intellect [ˈɪntəˌlɛkt] *s* intelecto; (person) intelectual *mf*
intellectual [ˌɪntəˈlɛktʃu•əl] *adj & s* intelectual *mf*
intellectuali•ty [ˌɪntəˌlɛktʃuˈælɪti] *s* (*pl* -ties) intelectualidad
intelligence [ɪnˈtɛlɪdʒəns] *s* inteligencia; información
intelligence bureau *s* departamento de inteligencia
intelligence quotient *s* cociente *m* intelectual
intelligent [ɪnˈtɛlɪdʒənt] *adj* inteligente; espabilado
intelligentsia [ɪnˌtɛlɪˈdʒɛntsɪ•ə] o [ɪnˌtɛlɪˈgɛntsɪ•ə] *s* intelectualidad (*conjunto de los intelectuales de un país o región*)
intelligible [ɪnˈtɛlɪdʒɪbəl] *adj* inteligible
intemperance [ɪnˈtɛmpərəns] *s* intemperancia
intemperate [ɪnˈtɛmpərɪt] *adj* intemperante; (climate) riguroso
intend [ɪnˈtɛnd] *tr* pensar, proponerse, intentar; (to mean for a particular purpose) destinar; (to signify) querer decir
intendance [ɪnˈtɛndəns] *s* intendencia
intendant [ɪnˈtɛndənt] *s* intendente *m*
intended [ɪnˈtɛndɪd] *adj & s* (coll) prometido, prometida
intense [ɪnˈtɛns] *adj* intenso

in
in

intensi•fy [ɪnˈtɛnsɪˌfaɪ] v (pret & pp **-fied**) tr intensificar, intensar; (phot) reforzar ‖ intr intensificarse, intensarse

intensi•ty [ɪnˈtɛnsɪti] s (pl **-ties**) intensidad

intensive [ɪnˈtɛnsɪv] adj intensivo

intent [ɪnˈtɛnt] adj atento; resuelto; intenso; **intent on** resuelto a ‖ s (purpose) intento; (meaning) acepción, sentido; **to all intents and purposes** en realidad de verdad

intention [ɪnˈtɛnʃən] s intención

intentional [ɪnˈtɛnʃənəl] adj intencional, deliberado

in•ter [ɪnˈtʌr] v (pret & pp **-terred**; ger **-terring**) tr enterrar

interact [ˈɪntərˌækt] s (theat) entreacto ‖ [ˌɪntərˈækt] intr obrar recíprocamente

interaction [ˌɪntərˈækʃən] s interacción

inter-American [ˌɪntərəˈmɛrɪkən] adj interamericano

inter•breed [ˌɪntərˈbrid] v (pret & pp **-bred** [ˈbrɛd]) tr entrecruzar ‖ intr entrecruzarse

intercalate [ɪnˈtʌrkəˌlet] tr intercalar

intercede [ˌɪntərˈsid] intr interceder

intercept [ˌɪntərˈsɛpt] tr interceptar

interceptor [ˌɪntərˈsɛptər] s interceptor m

interchange [ˈɪntərˌtʃendʒ] s intercambio; (on a highway) correspondencia ‖ [ˌɪntərˈtʃendʒ] tr intercambiar ‖ intr intercambiarse

intercollegiate [ˌɪntərkəˈlidʒɪ•ɪt] adj interescolar

intercom [ˈɪntərˌkɑm] s interfono

intercourse [ˈɪntərˌkors] s comunicación, trato; (interchange of products, ideas, etc.) intercambio; (copulation) cópula, comercio; **to have intercourse** juntarse

intercross [ˌɪntərˈkrɔs] o [ˌɪntərˈkrɑs] tr entrecruzar ‖ intr entrecruzarse

interdict [ˈɪntərˌdɪkt] s entredicho ‖ [ˌɪntərˈdɪkt] tr interdecir

interest [ˈɪntərɪst] s interés m; **the interests** las grandes empresas, el grupo influyente; **to put out at interest** poner a interés ‖ tr interesar

interested [ˈɪntəˌrɛstɪd] adj interesado

interesting [ˈɪntəˌrɛstɪŋ] adj interesante

interface [ˈɪntərˌfes] s (computer) entrecara

interfere [ˌɪntərˈfɪr] intr inmiscuirse, injerirse, interferir; (sport) parar una jugada; **to interfere with** dificultar, impedir, interferir

interference [ˌɪntərˈfɪrəns] s injerencia, interferencia

interim [ˈɪntərɪm] adj interino ‖ s intermedio, intervalo; **in the interim** entretanto

interior [ɪnˈtɪri•ər] adj & s interior m

interject [ˌɪntərˈdʒɛkt] tr interponer ‖ intr interponerse

interjection [ˌɪntərˈdʒɛkʃən] s interposición; exclamación; (gram) interjección

interlard [ˌɪntərˈlɑrd] tr interpolar; mechar (la carne)

interline [ˌɪntərˈlaɪn] tr interlinear; entretelar (una prenda de vestir)

interlining [ˈɪntərˌlaɪnɪŋ] s (of a garment) entretela

interlink [ˌɪntərˈlɪŋk] tr eslabonar

interlock [ˌɪntərˈlɑk] tr trabar ‖ intr trabarse

interlope [ˌɪntərˈlop] intr entremeterse; traficar sin derecho

interloper [ˌɪntərˈlopər] s intruso

interlude [ˈɪntərˌlud] s intervalo; (mus) interludio; (theat) intermedio

intermarriage [ˌɪntərˈmærɪdʒ] s casamiento entre parientes; casamiento entre personas de distintas razas, castas, etc.

intermediar•y [ˌɪntərˈmidɪˌɛri] adj intermediario ‖ s (pl **-ies**) intermediario

intermediate [ˌɪntərˈmidɪ•ɪt] adj intermedio

in•ter•me′di•ate-range′ missile s cohete m de alcance medio

interment [ɪnˈtʌrmənt] s entierro

intermez•zo [ˌɪntərˈmɛtso] o [ˌɪntərˈmɛdzo] s (pl **-zos** o **-zi** [tsi] o [dzi]) (mus) intermedio, intermezzo

intermingle [ˌɪntərˈmɪŋgəl] tr entremezclar ‖ intr entremezclarse

intermittent [ˌɪntərˈmɪtənt] adj intermitente

intermix [ˌɪntərˈmɪks] tr entremezclar ‖ intr entremezclarse

intern [ˈɪntʌrn] s interno de hospital ‖ [ɪnˈtʌrn] tr internar, recluir

internal [ɪnˈtʌrnəl] adj interno

inter′nal-combus′tion engine s motor m de explosión

internal revenue s rentas internas

international [ˌɪntərˈnæʃənəl] adj internacional

international date line s línea internacional de cambio de fecha

internationalize [ˌɪntərˈnæʃənəˌlaɪz] tr internacionalizar

internecine [ˌɪntərˈnisɪn] adj sanguinario

internee [ˌɪntʌrˈni] s (mil) internado

internist [ɪnˈtʌrnɪst] s internista mf

internment [ɪnˈtʌrnmənt] s internamiento

internship [ˈɪntʌrnˌʃɪp] s residencia de un médico en un hospital

interpellate [ˌɪntərˈpɛlet] o [ɪnˈtʌrpɪˌlet] tr interpelar

interplay [ˈɪntərˌple] s interacción

interpolate [ɪnˈtʌrpəˌlet] tr interpolar

interpose [ˌɪntərˈpoz] tr interponer

interpret [ɪnˈtʌrprɪt] tr interpretar

interpreter [ɪnˈtʌrprɪtər] s intérprete mf; (fig) exponente mf

interrogate [ɪnˈtɛrəˌget] tr & intr interrogar

interrogation [ɪnˌtɛrəˈgeʃən] s interrogación

interrogation mark o **point** s signo de interrogación

interrupt [ˌɪntəˈrʌpt] tr interrumpir

interscholastic [ˌɪntərskəˈlæstɪk] adj interescolar

intersection [ˌɪntərˈsɛkʃən] s (of streets, roads, etc.) cruce m, bocacalle f; cruza (SAm); (geom) intersección

intersperse [ˌɪntərˈspʌrs] tr entremezclar, esparcir

interstice [ɪnˈtʌrstɪs] s intersticio

intertwine [ˌɪntərˈtwaɪn] tr entrelazar ‖ intr entrelazarse

interval [ˈɪntərvəl] s intervalo; **at intervals** (now and then) de vez en cuando; (here and there) de trecho en trecho

intervene [ˌɪntərˈvin] *intr* intervenir
intervening [ˌɪntərˈvinɪŋ] *adj* intermedio
intervention [ˌɪntərˈvɛnʃən] *s* intervención
interview [ˈɪntərˌvju] *s* entrevista, interview *m* ‖ *tr* entrevistarse con
inter·weave [ˌɪntərˈwiv] *v* (*pret* **-wove** [ˈwov] o **-weaved**; *pp* **-wove, woven** o **weaved**) *tr* entretejer
intestate [ɪnˈtɛstet] *adj & s* intestado
intestine [ɪnˈtɛstɪn] *s* intestino
inthrall [ɪnˈθrɔl] *tr* cautivar, encantar; esclavizar, sojuzgar
inthrone [ɪnˈθron] *tr* entronizar
intima·cy [ˈɪntɪməsi] *s* (*pl* **-cies**) intimidad
intimate [ˈɪntɪmɪt] *adj* íntimo ‖ *s* amigo íntimo ‖ [ˈɪntɪˌmet] *tr* insinuar, intimar
intimation [ˌɪntɪˈmeʃən] *s* insinuación
intimidate [ɪnˈtɪmɪˌdet] *tr* intimidar
intitle [ɪnˈtaɪtəl] *tr* dar derecho a; (*to give a name to; to honor with a title*) intitular
into [ˈɪntu] o [ˈɪntʊ] *prep* en; hacia; hacia el interior de
intolerant [ɪnˈtalərənt] *adj & s* intolerante *mf*
intomb [ɪnˈtum] *tr* sepultar
intombment [ɪnˈtummənt] *s* sepultura
intonation [ˌɪntoˈneʃən] *s* entonación
intone [ɪnˈton] *tr* entonar
intoxicant [ɪnˈtaksɪkənt] *s* bebida alcohólica
intoxicate [ɪnˈtaksɪˌket] *tr* embriagar, emborrachar; (*to exhilarate*) alegrar, excitar; (*to poison*) envenenar, intoxicar
intoxication [ɪnˌtaksɪˈkeʃən] *s* embriaguez *f*; alegría, excitación; (*poisoning*) envenenamiento, intoxicación
intractable [ɪnˈtræktəbəl] *adj* intratable
intransigent [ɪnˈtrænsɪdʒənt] *adj & s* intransigente *mf*
intransitive [ɪnˈtrænsɪtɪv] *adj* intransitivo
intrench [ɪnˈtrɛntʃ] *tr* atrincherar ‖ *intr*—**to intrench on** o **upon** infringir, violar
intrepid [ɪnˈtrɛpɪd] *adj* intrépido
intrepidity [ˌɪntrɪˈpɪdɪti] *s* intrepidez *f*
intricate [ˈɪntrɪkɪt] *adj* intrincado
intrigue [ɪnˈtrig] *s* intriga; intriga amorosa, enredo amoroso ‖ *tr* (*to arouse the curiosity of*) intrigar ‖ *intr* intrigar; tener intrigas amorosas
intrinsic(al) [ɪnˈtrɪnsɪk(əl)] *adj* intrínseco
introd. *abbr* **introduction**
introduce [ˌɪntrəˈdjus] *tr* introducir; (*to make acquainted*) presentar
introduction [ˌɪntrəˈdʌkʃən] *s* introducción; (*of one person to another or others*) presentación
introductory offer [ˌɪntrəˈdʌktəri] *s* ofrecimiento de presentación, oferta preliminar
introit [ˈɪntro·ɪt] *s* (eccl) introito
introspective [ˌɪntrəˈspɛktɪv] *adj* introspectivo
introvert [ˈɪntrəˌvʌrt] *s* introvertido
intrude [ɪnˈtrud] *intr* injerirse, entremeterse
intruder [ɪnˈtrudər] *s* intruso, entremetido
intrusive [ɪnˈtrusɪv] *adj* intruso
intrust [ɪnˈtrʌst] *tr* confiar
intuition [ˌɪntjuˈɪʃən] *s* intuición
inundate [ˈɪnənˌdet] *tr* inundar
inundation [ˌɪnənˈdeʃən] *s* inundación

inure [ɪnˈjʊr] *tr* acostumbrar, endurecer, aguerrir ‖ *intr* ponerse en efecto; **to inure to** redundar en
inv. *abbr* **inventor, invoice**
invade [ɪnˈved] *tr* invadir
invader [ɪnˈvedər] *s* invasor *m*
invalid [ɪnˈvælɪd] *adj* inválido (*nulo, de ningún valor*) ‖ [ˈɪnvəlɪd] *adj* inválido (*por viejo o por enfermo*) ‖ [ˈɪnvəlɪd] *s* inválido
invalidate [ɪnˈvælɪˌdet] *tr* invalidar
invalidity [ˌɪnvəˈlɪdɪti] *s* invalidez *f*
invaluable [ɪnˈvælju·əbəl] *adj* inestimable, inapreciable
invariable [ɪnˈvɛri·əbəl] *adj* invariable
invasion [ɪnˈveʒən] *s* invasión
invective [ɪnˈvɛktɪv] *s* invectiva
inveigh [ɪnˈve] *intr*—**to inveigh against** lanzar invectivas contra
inveigle [ɪnˈvegəl] o [ɪnˈvigəl] *tr* engatusar
invent [ɪnˈvɛnt] *tr* inventar
invention [ɪnˈvɛnʃən] *s* invención, invento
inventive [ɪnˈvɛntɪv] *adj* inventivo
inventiveness [ɪnˈvɛntɪvnɪs] *s* inventiva
inventor·y [ɪnˈvɛntər] *s* inventor *m*
inventor·y [ˈɪnvənˌtori] *s* (*pl* **-ries**) inventario; stock *m* ‖ *v* (*pret & pp* **-ried**) *tr* inventariar
inverse [ɪnˈvʌrs] *adj* inverso
inversion [ɪnˈvʌrʒən] o [ɪnˈvʌrʃən] *s* inversión
invert [ˈɪnvʌrt] *s* invertido ‖ [ɪnˈvʌrt] *tr* invertir
invertebrate [ɪnˈvʌrtɪˌbret] o [ɪnˈvʌrtɪbrɪt] *adj & s* invertebrado
inverted exclamation point *s* principio de admiración
inverted question mark *s* principio de interrogación
invest [ɪnˈvɛst] *tr* (*to vest, to install*) investir; invertir (*dinero*); (*to besiege*) cercar, sitiar; (*to surround, envelop*) cubrir, envolver
investigate [ɪnˈvɛstɪˌget] *tr* investigar
investigation [ɪnˌvɛstɪˈgeʃən] *s* investigación
investment [ɪnˈvɛstmənt] *s* (*of money*) inversión; (*with an office or dignity*) investidura; (*siege*) cerco, sitio
investment capital *s* capital *m* de inversión
investor [ɪnˈvɛstər] *s* inversionista *mf*; inversor *m*
inveterate [ɪnˈvɛtərɪt] *adj* inveterado, empedernido
invidious [ɪnˈvɪdi·əs] *adj* irritante, odioso, injusto
invigorate [ɪnˈvɪgəˌret] *tr* vigorizar
invigorating [ɪnˈvɪgəˌretɪŋ] *adj* vigorizador, vigorizante
invincible [ɪnˈvɪnsɪbəl] *adj* invencible
invisible [ɪnˈvɪzɪbəl] *adj* invisible
invisible ink *s* tinta simpática
invitation [ˌɪnvɪˈteʃən] *s* invitación, convite *m*
invite [ɪnˈvaɪt] *tr* invitar, convidar
inviting [ɪnˈvaɪtɪŋ] *adj* atractivo, seductor; (*e.g., food*) apetitoso
invoice [ˈɪnvɔɪs] *s* factura; **as per invoice** según factura ‖ *tr* facturar

in
in

invoke [ɪnˈvok] *tr* invocar; evocar, conjurar (*p.ej., los demonios*)

involuntary [ɪnˈvɑlən,teri] *adj* involuntario

involution [,ɪnvəˈluʃən] *s* (math) elevación a potencias, potenciación

involve [ɪnˈvɑlv] *tr* envolver, comprometer

invulnerable [ɪnˈvʌlnərəbəl] *adj* invulnerable

inward [ˈɪnwərd] *adj* interior ‖ *adv* interiormente, hacia dentro

iodide [ˈaɪ•ə,daɪd] *s* yoduro

iodine [ˈaɪ•ə,din] *s* yodo ‖ [ˈaɪ•ə,daɪn] *s* tintura de yodo

ion [ˈaɪ•ən] o [ˈaɪ•ɑn] *s* ion *m*

ionize [ˈaɪ•ə,naɪz] *tr* ionizar

ionosphere [aɪˈɑnə,sfɪr] *s* ionosfera

IOU [ˈaɪ,oˈju] *s* (letterword) pagaré *m*

I.Q. [ˈaɪˈkju] *abbr & s* (letterword) **intelligence quotient**

Iran [ɪˈrɑn] o [aɪˈræn] *s* el Irán

Iranian [ɪˈreni•ən] o [aɪˈreni•ən] *adj & s* iranés *m* o iranio

Iraq [ɪˈrɑk] *s* el Irak

Ira•qi [ɪˈrɑki] *adj* iraqués o iraquiano ‖ *s* (*pl* -qis) iraqués *m* o iraquiano

irate [ˈaɪret] o [aɪˈret] *adj* airado

ire [aɪr] *s* ira, cólera

Ireland [ˈaɪrlənd] *s* Irlanda

iris [ˈaɪrɪs] *s* (*of the eye*) iris *m;* (*rainbow*) iris, arco iris; (bot) lirio

Irish [ˈaɪrɪʃ] *adj* irlandés ‖ *s* (*language*) irlandés *m;* whisky *m* de Irlanda; **the Irish** los irlandeses

Irish•man [ˈaɪrɪʃmən] *s* (*pl* -men [mən]) irlandés *m*

Irish stew *s* guisado de carne con patatas y cebollas

I'rish•wom'an *s* (*pl* -wom'en) irlandesa

irk [ʌrk] *tr* fastidiar, molestar

irksome [ˈʌrksəm] *adj* fastidioso, molesto

iron [ˈaɪ•ərn] *adj* férreo ‖ *s* hierro; (*implement used to press or smooth clothes*) plancha; **irons** (*fetters*) hierros, grilletes *mpl;* **strike while the iron is hot** a hierro caliente batir de repente ‖ *tr* planchar (*la ropa*); **to iron out** allanar (*una dificultad*)

i'ron-bound' *adj* zunchado con hierro; (*unyielding*) férreo, duro, inflexible; (*rockbound*) escabroso, rocoso

ironclad [ˈaɪ•ərnˈklæd] *adj* acorazado, blindado; inflexible, exigente

iron curtain *s* (fig) telón *m* de hierro, cortina de hierro

iron digestion *s* estómago de avestruz

ironhanded [ˈaɪ•ərn,hændɪd] *adj* severo; rigoroso; de mano férrea

iron horse *s* (coll) locomotora

ironic(al) [aɪˈrɑnɪk(əl)] *adj* irónico

ironing [ˈaɪ•ərnɪŋ] *s* planchado; ropa planchada; ropa por planchar

ironing board *s* tabla de planchar

iron lung *s* pulmón *m* de acero o de hierro

i'ron•ware' *s* ferretería

iron will *s* voluntad de hierro

i'ron•work' *s* herraje *m;* **ironworks** ferrería, herrería

i'ron•work'er *s* herrero de grueso; (*metalworker*) cerrajero

iro•ny [ˈaɪrəni] *s* (*pl* -nies) ironía

irradiate [ɪˈredi,et] *tr* irradiar; (med) someter a radiación ‖ *intr* irradiar

irrational [ɪˈræʃənəl] *adj* irracional

irrecoverable [,ɪrɪˈkʌvərəbəl] *adj* incobrable, irrecuperable

irredeemable [,ɪrɪˈdiməbəl] *adj* irredimible

irrefutable [,ɪrɪˈfjutəbəl] o [ɪˈrɛfjutəbəl] *adj* irrebatible

irregular [ɪˈrɛgələr] *adj* irregular ‖ *s* (mil) irregular *m*

irrelevance [ɪˈrɛləvəns] *s* impertinencia, inaplicabilidad

irrelevant [ɪˈrɛləvənt] *adj* impertinente, inaplicable; irrelevante

irreligious [,ɪrɪˈlɪdʒəs] *adj* irreligioso.

irremediable [,ɪrɪˈmidi•əbəl] *adj* irremediable

irremovable [,ɪrɪˈmuvəbəl] *adj* inamovible

irreparable [ɪˈrɛpərəbəl] *adj* irreparable

irreplaceable [,ɪrɪˈplesəbəl] *adj* insustituíble, irreemplazable

irrepressible [,ɪrɪˈprɛsəbəl] *adj* irreprimible, incontenible

irreproachable [,ɪrɪˈprotʃəbəl] *adj* irreprochable

irresistible [,ɪrɪˈzɪstɪbəl] *adj* irresistible

irrespective [,ɪrɪˈspɛktɪv] *adj* — **irrespective of** sin hacer caso de, independiente de

irresponsible [,ɪrɪˈspɑnsɪbəl] *adj* irresponsable

irretrievable [,ɪrɪˈtrivəbəl] *adj* irrecuperable

irreverent [ɪˈrɛvərənt] *adj* irreverente

irrevocable [ɪˈrɛvəkəbəl] *adj* irrevocable

irrigate [ˈɪrɪ,get] *tr* irrigar

irrigation [,ɪrɪˈgeʃən] *s* irrigación

irritant [ˈɪrɪtənt] *adj & s* irritante *m*

irritate [ˈɪrɪ,tet] *tr* irritar

irruption [ɪˈrʌpʃən] *s* irrupción

is. *abbr* **island**

isinglass [ˈaɪzɪŋ,glæs] o [ˈaɪzɪŋ,glɑs] *s* (*form of gelatine*) cola de pescado, colapez *f;* mica

isl. *abbr* **island**

Islam [ˈɪsləm] o [ɪsˈlɑm] *s* el Islam

island [ˈaɪlənd] *adj* isleño ‖ *s* isla

islander [ˈaɪləndər] *s* isleño

isle [aɪl] *s* isleta

isolate [ˈaɪsə,let] *tr* aislar

isolated [ˈaɪsə,letɪd] *adj* aislado; insulado; alejado

isolation [,aɪsəˈleʃən] *s* aislamiento

isolationist [,aɪsəˈleʃənɪst] *s* aislacionista *mf*

isometric [,aɪsəˈmɛtrɪk] *adj* isométrico

isometrics *s* isométrica

isosceles [aɪˈsɑsə,liz] *adj* isosceles

isotope [ˈaɪsə,top] *s* isótopo

Israe•li [izˈreli] *adj* israelí ‖ *s* (*pl* -lis [liz]) israelí *mf*

Israelite [ˈɪzrɪ•ə,laɪt] *adj & s* israelita *mf*

issuance [ˈɪʃu•əns] *s* emisión, expedición

issue [ˈɪʃu] *s* (*outgoing; outlet*) salida; (*result*) consecuencia, resultado; (*offspring*) descendencia, sucesión; (*of a magazine*) edición, impresión, tirada, número; (*e.g.,* of a bond) emisión; (yield, profit) beneficios, producto; punto en disputa; (distribution) repartida; (pathol) flujo; at issue en disputa; to face the issue afrontar la situación; to force the issue forzar la solución; to take issue with llevar la contraria a || tr publicar, dar a luz (un nuevo libro, una revista, etc.); emitir, expedir (títulos, obligaciones, etc.); distribuir (ropa, alimento) || intr salir; to issue from provenir de

isthmus ['ɪsməs] s istmo

it [ɪt] pron pers (aplícase a cosas inanimadas, a niños de teta, a animales cuyo sexo no se conoce; y muchas veces no se traduce) él, ella; lo, la; it is I soy yo; it is snowing nieva; it is three o'clock son las tres

ital. abbr **italics**

Ital. abbr **Italian, Italy**

Italian [ɪ'tæljən] adj & s italiano

italic [ɪ'tælɪk] adj (typ) itálico || **italics** s (typ) itálica, bastardilla || **Italic** adj itálico

italicize [ɪ'tælɪ,saɪz] tr imprimir en bastardilla; subrayar

Italy ['ɪtəli] s Italia

itch [ɪtʃ] s comezón f; (pathol) sarna; (eager-ness) (fig) comezón, prurito || tr dar comezón a || intr picar; **to itch to** tener prurito por

itch•y ['ɪtʃi] adj (comp -ier; super -iest) picante, hormigoso; (pathol) sarnoso

item ['aɪtəm] s artículo; noticia, suelto; (in an account) partida

itemization [,aɪtəmaɪ'zeʃən] s rubricación

itemize ['aɪtə,maɪz] tr particularizar, especificar, pormenorizar

itinerant [aɪ'tɪnərənt] o [ɪ'tɪnərənt] adj ambulante, errante || s viandante mf

itinerar•y [aɪ'tɪnə,rɛri] o [ɪ'tɪnə,rɛri] adj itinerario || s (pl -ies) itinerario

its [ɪts] adj poss su || pron poss el suyo; suyo

itself [ɪt'sɛlf] pron pers mismo; sí, sí mismo; se

ivied ['aɪvid] adj cubierto de hiedra

ivo•ry ['aɪvəri] adj marfileño || s (pl -ries) marfil m; **ivories** (slang) teclas del piano; (slang) bolas de billar; (dice) (slang) dados; (slang) dientes mpl

ivory tower s (fig) torre f de marfil; (fig) inocencia

ivy ['aɪvi] s (pl -ivies) hiedra

J

J, j [dʒe] décima letra del alfabeto inglés

J. abbr **Judge, Justice**

jab [dʒæb] s hurgonazo; (prick) pinchazo; (with elbow) codazo || v (pret & pp **jabbed**; ger **jabbing**) tr hurgonear; dar un codazo a || intr hurgonear

jabber ['dʒæbər] s chapurreo || tr & intr chapurrear

jabot [dʒæ'bo] o ['dʒæbo] s chorrera

jack [dʒæk] s (for lifting heavy objects) gato, cric m; (fellow) mozo, sujeto, (jackass) asno, burro; (in card games) sota, valet m; (small ball for bowling) boliche m; (jackstone) cantillo; (device for turning a spit) torno de asador; (figure which strikes a clock bell) jaquemar m; (to remove a boot) sacabotas m; marinero; (flag at the bow) (naut) yac m; (rad & telv) jack m; (elec) caja de enchufe; (slang) dinero; **every man Jack** cada hijo de vecino; **jacks** cantillos, juego de los cantillos || tr — **to jack up** alzar con el gato; (coll) subir (sueldos, precios, etc.); (coll) recordar su obligación a

jackal ['dʒækɔl] s chacal m

jackanapes ['dʒækə,neps] s mequetrefe m

jack'ass' s asno, burro

jack'daw' s corneja

jacket ['dʒækɪt] s chaqueta; (folded paper) cubierta, envoltura; (paper cover of a book) sobrecubierta; (metal casing) camisa

jack'ham'mer s martillo perforador

jack'-in-the-box' s caja de sorpresa, jugete-sorpresa m, muñeco en una caja de resorte

jack'knife' s (pl -knives') navaja de bolsillo; (fancy dive) salto de carpa

jack of all trades s hombre que hace toda clase de oficios dije m

jack-o'-lantern ['dʒækə,læntərn] s fuego fatuo; linterna hecha con una calabaza cortado de modo que remede una cabeza humana

jack pot s — **to hit the jack pot** (slang) ponerse las botas

jack rabbit s liebre grande norteamericana

jack'screw' s cric m o gato de tornillo

jack'stone' s cantillo; **jackstones** cantillos, juego de los cantillos

jack'-tar' s (coll) marinero

jade [dʒed] adj verdoso como el jade || s (ornamental stone) jade m; verde m de jade; (worn-out horse) jamelgo; picarona, mujerzuela || tr cansar, ahitar, saciar

jaded ['dʒedɪd] adj ahito, saciado

jag [dʒæg] s diente m, púa; **to have a jag on** (slang) estar borracho

jagged ['dʒægɪd] adj dentado, mellado; rasgado en sietes

jaguar ['dʒægwɑr] s jaguar m

jail [dʒel] s cárcel f; **to break jail** escaparse de la cárcel || tr encarcelar

jail'bird' s (coll) preso, encarcelado; (coll) infractor m habitual

jail'break' s escapatoria de la cárcel

jail delivery s evasión de la cárcel

jailer ['dʒelər] s carcelero

jalop•y [dʒə'lɑpi] s (pl -ies) automóvil viejo y ruinoso

jam [dʒæm] s apiñadura, apretura; (e.g., in traffic) embotellamiento, bloqueo; (preserve) compota, conserva; (difficult situation) (coll) aprieto, apuros ‖ v (pret & pp jammed; ger jamming) tr apiñar, apretujar; machucarse (p.ej., un dedo); (rad) perturbar, sabotear; **to jam on the brakes** frenar de golpe

Jamaican [dʒə'mekən] adj & s jamaicano; jamaiquino (Am)

jamb [dʒæm] s jamba

jamboree [,dʒæmbə'ri] s (coll) francachela, holgorio; reunión de niños exploradores

jamming ['dʒæmɪŋ] s radioperturbación

jam nut s contratuerca

jam-packed ['dʒæm'pækt] adj (coll) apiñado, apretujado, atestado

jam session s reunión de músicos de jazz para tocar improvisaciones

jangle ['dʒæŋgəl] s cencerreo; altercado, riña ‖ tr hacer sonar con ruido discordante ‖ intr cencerrear; reñir

janitor ['dʒænɪtər] s portero, conserje m

janitress ['dʒænɪtrɪs] s portera

January ['dʒænju,ɛri] s enero

Ja•pan [dʒə'pæn] s laca japonesa; obra japonesa laqueada; aceite m secante japonés ‖ v (pret & pp -panned; ger -panning) tr barnizar, charolar, laquear con laca japonesa ‖ **Japan** s el Japón

Japa•nese [,dʒæpə'niz] adj japonés ‖ s (pl -nese) japonés m

Japanese beetle s escarabajo japonés

Japanese lantern s farolillo veneciano

Japanese persimmon s caqui m

jar [dʒɑr] s tarro; (e.g., of olives) frasco; (of a storage battery) recipiente m; (jolt) sacudida; ruido desapacible; sorpresa desagradable; **on the jar** (said of a door) entreabierto, entornado ‖ v (pret & pp jarred; ger jarring) tr sacudir; chocar; (with a noise) traquetear ‖ intr sacudirse; traquetear; disputar; **to jar on** irritar

jardiniere [,dʒɑrdi'nɪr] s (stand) jardinera; (pot, bowl) florero

jargon ['dʒɑrgən] s jerga, jerigonza

jasmine ['dʒæsmɪn] s jazmín m

jasper ['dʒæspər] s jaspe m

jaundice ['dʒɔndɪs] o ['dʒɑndɪs] s ictericia; (fig) envidia, celos, negro humor

jaundiced ['dʒɔndɪst] o ['dʒɑndɪst] adj ictericiado; (fig) avinagrado

jaunt [dʒɔnt] o [dʒɑnt] s caminata, excursión, paseo

jaun•ty ['dʒɔnti] o ['dʒɑnti] adj (comp -tier; super -tiest) airoso, gallardo, vivo; elegante, de buen gusto

Java•nese [,dʒævə'niz] adj javanés ‖ s (pl -nese) javanés m

javelin ['dʒævlɪn] o ['dʒævəlɪn] s jabalina

jaw [dʒɔ] s mandíbula, quijada; **into the jaws of death** a las garras de la muerte; **jaws** boca, garganta ‖ tr (slang) regañar ‖ intr (slang) regañar; (slang) chacharear, chismear

jaw'bone' s mandíbula, quijada

jaw'break'er s (word) (coll) trabalenguas m; (candy) (coll) hinchabocas m; (mach) trituradora de quijadas

jay [dʒe] s (orn) arrendajo; (coll) tonto, necio

jay'walk' intr (coll) cruzar la calle descuidadamente

jay'walk'er s (coll) peatón descuidado

jazz [dʒæz] s (mus) jazz m; (coll) animación, viveza ‖ tr—**to jazz up** (coll) animar, dar viveza a

jazz band s orquesta de jazz

J.C. abbr Jesus Christ, Julius Caesar

jct. abbr junction

jealous ['dʒɛləs] adj celoso; envidioso; (watchful in keeping or guarding something) solícito, vigilante

jealous•y ['dʒɛləsi] s (pl -ies) celosía, celos; envidia; solicitud, vigilancia

jean [dʒin] s dril m; **jeans** pantalones mpl de dril

Jeanne d'Arc [,ʒɑn'dɑrk] s Juana de Arco

jeep [dʒip] s jip m, pequeño automóvil de propulsión total

jeer [dʒɪr] s befa, mofa, vaya ‖ tr befar ‖ intr mofarse; **to jeer at** befar, mofarse de

jelab [dʒə'lɑb] s chilaba

jell [dʒɛl] s jalea ‖ intr (to become jellylike) cuajarse; (to take hold, catch on) (fig) cuajar

jel•ly ['dʒɛli] s (pl -lies) jalea ‖ v (pret & pp tr convertir en jalea ‖ intr convertirse en jalea

jel'ly•bean' s frutilla

jel'ly•fish' s aguamala, medusa; (weak person) (coll) calzonazos m

jeopardize ['dʒɛpər,daɪz] tr arriesgar, exponer, poner en peligro

jeopardy ['dʒɛpərdi] s riesgo, peligro

jeremiad [,dʒɛri'maɪ•æd] s jeremiada

Jericho ['dʒɛri,ko] s Jericó

jerk [dʒʌrk] s arranque m, estirón m, tirón m; tic m, espasmo muscular; **by jerks** a sacudidas ‖ tr mover de un tirón; arrojar de un tirón; atasajar (carne) ‖ intr avanzar a tirones

jerked beef s tasajo

jerkin ['dʒʌrkɪn] s jubón m, justillo

jerk'wa'ter train s (coll) tren de ferrocarril económico

jerk•y ['dʒʌrki] adj (comp -ier; super -iest) (road; style) desigual; que va dando tumbos, que anda a tirones

jersey ['dʒʌrzi] s jersey m, chaqueta de punto

Jerusalem [dʒɪ'rusələm] s Jerusalén

jest [dʒɛst] s broma, chanza, chiste m; cosa de risa; **in jest** en broma ‖ intr bromear

jester ['dʒɛstər] s bromista mf, burlón m; (professional fool of medieval rulers) bufón m

Jesuit ['dʒɛʒu•ɪt] o ['dʒɛzj,ɪt] adj & s jesuíta m

Jesuitic(al) [,dʒɛʒu'ɪtɪk(əl)] o [,dʒɛzju-'ɪtɪk(əl)] adj jesuítico

Jesus ['dʒizəs] s Jesús m

Jesus Christ s Jesucristo

jet [dʒɛt] *adj* de azabache; azabachado ‖ *s* (*of a fountain*) surtidor *m;* (*of gas*) mechero; (*stream shooting forth from nozzle, etc.*) chorro; avión *m* a reacción, avión de chorro; (*hard black mineral; lustrous black*) azabache *m* ‖ *v* (*pret & pp* **jetted;** *ger* **jetting**) *tr* arrojar en chorro ‖ *intr* chorrear, salir en chorro; volar en avión de chorro

jet age *s* era de los aviones de chorro

jet′-black′ *adj* azabachado

jet bomber *s* bombardero de reacción a chorro

jet coal *s* carbón *m* de bujía, carbón de llama larga

jet engine *s* motor *m* a chorro, motor de reacción

jet fighter *s* caza *m* de reacción, cazarreactor *m*

jet′lin′er *s* avión *m* de travesía con propulsión a chorro

jet plane *s* avión *m* de chorro

jet propulsion *s* propulsión a chorro, propulsión de escape

jetsam [ˈdʒɛtsəm] *s* (naut) echazón *f;* cosas desechadas

jet set *s* gente acomodada que viajan mucho por avión

jet stream *s* escape *m* de un motor cohete; (meteor) chorros de viento (*que soplan de oeste a este a la altura de 10 kilómetros*)

jettison [ˈdʒɛtɪsən] *s* (naut) echazón *f* ‖ *tr* (naut) echar al mar; desechar, rechazar

jettison gear *s* (aer) lanzador *m*

jet·ty [ˈdʒɛti] *s* (*pl* **-ties**) (*structure projecting into sea to protect harbor*) escollera, malecón *m;* (*wharf*) muelle *m,* desembarcadero

Jew [dʒu] *s* judío

jewel [ˈdʒuːəl] *s* piedra preciosa; (*valuable personal ornament*) alhaja; joya; (*of a watch*) rubí *m;* (*article of costume jewelry*) joya de imitación; (*highly prized person or thing*) alhaja, joya

jewel case *s* guardajoyas *m,* estuche *m,* joyero

jeweler o **jeweller** [ˈdʒuːələr] *s* joyero; relojero

jewelry [ˈdʒuːəlri] *s* joyería, joyas

jewelry shop *s* joyería; relojería

Jewess [ˈdʒuːɪs] *s* judía

jew′fish′ *s* mero

Jewish [ˈdʒuːɪʃ] *adj* judío

Jew·ry [ˈdʒuːri] *s* (*pl* **-ries**) judería

jews′-harp o **jew′s-harp** [ˈdʒuz,harp] *s* birimbao

jib [dʒɪb] *s* (*of a crane*) aguilón *m,* pescante *m;* (naut) foque *m*

jib boom *s* (naut) botalón *m* de foque

jibe [dʒaɪb] *s* remoque *m,* mofa ‖ *intr* mofarse; (coll) concordar (*dos cosas*); **to jibe at** mofarse de

jif·fy [ˈdʒɪfi] *s* (*pl* **-fies**)—**in a jiffy** (coll) en un santiamén

jig [dʒɪg] *s* (*dance and music*) giga; **the jig is up** (slang) ya se acabó todo, estamos perdidos

jigger [ˈdʒɪgər] *s* (*for fishing*) anzuelo de cuchara; (*for separating ore*) criba de vaivén; (*flea*) nigua; (*gadget*) cosilla, chisme *m,* dispositivo; vasito para medir el licor de un coctel (*onza y media*)

jiggle [ˈdʒɪgəl] *s* zangoloteo ‖ *tr* zangolotear ‖ *intr* zangolotearse

jig saw *s* sierra de vaivén

jig′saw′ puzzle *s* rompecabezas *m* (*figura que ha sido cortada caprichosamente en trozos menudos y que hay que recomponer*)

jilt [dʒɪlt] *tr* dar calabazas a (*un novio*)

jim·my [ˈdʒɪmi] *s* (*pl* **-mies**) palanqueta ‖ *v* (*pret & pp* **-mied**) *tr* forzar con palanqueta; **to jimmy open** abrir con palanqueta

jingle [ˈdʒɪŋgəl] *s* (*small bell*) cascabel *m;* (*of tambourine*) sonaja; (*sound*) cascabeleo; rima infantil; (rad) anuncio rimado y cantado ‖ *tr* hacer sonar ‖ *intr* cascabelear

jin·go [ˈdʒɪŋgo] *adj* jingoísta ‖ *s* (*pl* **-goes**) jingoísta *mf;* **by jingo!** (coll) ¡caramba!

jingoism [ˈdʒɪŋgo,ɪzəm] *s* jingoísmo

jinx [dʒɪŋks] *s* gafe *m* ‖ *tr* (coll) traer mala suerte a

jitters [ˈdʒɪtərz] *spl* (coll) inquietud, nerviosidad; **to give the jitters to** (coll) poner nervioso; **to have the jitters** (coll) ponerse nervioso

jittery [ˈdʒɪtəri] *adj* (coll) nervioso

Joan of Arc [ˈdʒon əv ˈark] *s* Juana de Arco

job [dʒab] *s* (*piece of work*) trabajo; (*task, chore*) quehacer *m,* tarea; (*work done by contract*) destajo; (*employment*) empleo, oficio; (coll) robo; **by the job** a destajo; **on the job** trabajando de aprendiz; (slang) vigilante, atento a sus obligaciones; **to be out of a job** estar desocupado, estar sin trabajo; **to lie down on the job** (slang) echarse en el surco, estirar la pierna

job analysis *s* análisis *m* ocupacional

jobber [ˈdʒabər] *s* comerciante medianero; (*pieceworker*) destajero; (*dishonest official*) agiotista *m*

job′hold′er *s* empleado; (*in the government*) burócrata *mf*

jobless [ˈdʒablɪs] *adj* desocupado, sin empleo

job lot *s* saldo de mercancías

job market *s* oportunidades *fpl* de empleo

job printer *s* impresor *m* de remiendos

job printing *s* remiendo

job security *s* garantía de empleo continuo

jock [dʒak] *s* (slang) atleta *m*

jockey [ˈdʒaki] *s* jockey *m* ‖ *tr* montar (*un caballo*) en la pista; maniobrar; embaucar

jockstrap [ˈdʒak,stræp] *s* suspensorio (*para sostener el escroto*)

jocose [dʒoˈkos] *adj* jocoso

jocular [ˈdʒakjələr] *adj* jocoso, festivo

jodhpurs [ˈdʒadpərz] *spl* pantalones *mpl* de equitación

jog [dʒag] *s* golpecito; (*to the memory*) estímulo; trote corto ‖ *v* (*pret & pp* **jogged;** *ger* **jogging**) *tr* empujar levemente; estimular (*la memoria*) ‖ *intr*—**to jog along** avanzar al trote corto

jogging [ˈdʒagɪŋ] *s* trote *m* corto

jog trot *s* trote *m* de perro; (fig) rutina

john [dʒɑn] s (slang) retrete m; inodoro
John Bull s el inglés típico, el pueblo inglés
John Hancock ['hænkɑk] s (coll) la firma de uno
johnnycake ['dʒɑni,kek] s pan m de maíz
John'ny-come'-late'ly s recién llegado
John'ny-jump'-up' s (pansy) pensamiento, trinitaria, violeta
John'ny-on-the-spot' s (coll) el que está siempre presente y listo
John the Baptist s San Juan Bautista
join [dʒɔɪn] tr juntar, unir, ensamblar; asociarse a, unirse a; incorporarse a, ingresar en; abrazar (un partido); hacerse socio de (una asociación); alistarse en (el ejército); trabar (batalla); desaguar en (el océano) ‖ intr juntarse, unirse; confluir (p.ej., dos ríos)
joiner ['dʒɔɪnər] s carpintero; (coll) el que tiene la manía de incorporarse a muchas asociaciones
joint [dʒɔɪnt] s (in a pipe) empalme m, juntura, (of bones) articulación, juntura, coyuntura; (backbone of book) nervura; (hinge of book) cartivana; (in woodwork) emsambladura; (of meat) tajada; (marijuana) porro, puerro; (elec) empalme m; (gambling den) (slang) garito; (slang) restaurante m de mala muerte; **out of joint** desencajado, descoyuntado; (fig) en desorden, desbarajustado; **to throw out of joint** descoyuntarse (p.ej., el brazo)
joint account s cuenta en común
Joint Chiefs of Staff spl (U.S.A.) Estado mayor conjunto
jointly ['dʒɔɪntli] adv juntamente, en común
joint owner s condueño
joint session s sesión conjunta
joint'-stock' company s sociedad anónima, compañía por acciones
jointure ['dʒɔɪntʃər] s bienes mpl parafernales
joist [dʒɔɪst] s viga
joke [dʒok] s broma, chiste m; (trifling matter) cosa de reír; (person laughed at) bufón m, hazmerreír m; **no joke** cosa seria; **to tell a joke** contar un chiste, **to play a joke on** gastar una broma a ‖ tr—**to joke one's way into** conseguir (p.ej., un empleo) burla burlando ‖ intr bromear, hablar en broma; **joking aside** o **no joking** burlas aparte
joke book s libro de chistes
joker ['dʒokər] s bromista mf; (wise guy) sábelotodo; (playing card) comodín m; (hidden provision) cláusula engañadora
jol•ly ['dʒɑli] adj (comp **-lier**; super **-liest**) alegre, festivo ‖ adv (coll) muy, harto ‖ v (pret & pp **-lied**) tr (coll) candonguear
jolt [dʒolt] s sacudida ‖ tr sacudir ‖ intr dar tumbos
Jonah ['dʒonə] s Jonás m; (fig) ave f de mal agüero
jongleur ['dʒɑŋglər] s juglar m, trovador m
jonquil ['dʒɑŋkwɪl] s junquillo
Jordan ['dʒɔrdən] s (country) Jordania; (river) Jordán m
Jordan almond s almendra de Málaga

Jordanian [dʒɔr'denɪ•ən] adj & s jordano
josh [dʒɑʃ] tr (coll) dar broma a ‖ intr dar broma
jostle ['dʒɑsəl] s empellón m, empujón m ‖ tr empellar, empujar ‖ intr chocar, encontrarse; avanzar a fuerza de empujones o codazos
jot [dʒɑt] s—**I don't care a jot for** no se me da un bledo de s v (pret & pp **jotted;** ger **jotting**) tr—**to jot down** apuntar, anotar
jounce [dʒɑʊns] s sacudida ‖ tr sacudir ‖ intr dar tumbos
journal ['dʒʌrnəl] s (newspaper) periódico; (magazine) revista; (daily record) diario; (com) libro diario; (naut) cuaderno de bitácora; (mach) gorrón m, muñón m
journalese [,dʒʌrnə'liz] s lenguaje periodístico
journalism ['dʒʌrnə,lɪzəm] s periodismo
journalist ['dʒʌrnəlɪst] s periodista mf
journalistic [,dʒʌrnə'lɪstɪk] adj periodístico
journey ['dʒʌrni] s viaje m ‖ intr viajar
journey•man ['dʒʌrnimən] s (pl **-men** [mən]) oficial m
joust [dʒʌst] o [dʒust] o [dʒaʊst] s justa ‖ intr justar
jovial ['dʒovɪ•əl] adj jovial
joviality [,dʒovɪ'ælɪti] s jovialidad
jowl [dʒaʊl] s (cheek) moflete m; (jawbone) quijada; (of cattle) papada; (of fowl) barba
joy [dʒɔɪ] s alegría, regocijo; **to leap with joy** saltar de gozo
joyful ['dʒɔɪfəl] adj alegre; **joyful over** gozoso con o de
joyless ['dʒɔɪlɪs] adj triste, sin alegría
joyous ['dʒɔɪ•əs] adj alegre
joy ride s (coll) paseo de recreo en coche; (coll) paseo alocado en coche
J.P. abbr **Justice of the Peace**
Jr. abbr **junior**
jubilant ['dʒubɪlənt] adj jubiloso
jubilation [,dʒubɪ'leʃən] s júbilo, viva alegría
jubilee ['dʒubɪ,li] s (jubilation) júbilo; aniversario; quincuagésimo aniversario; (eccl) jubileo
Judaism ['dʒude,ɪzəm] s judaísmo
judge [dʒʌdʒ] s juez m; **to be a good judge of** ser buen juez de o en ‖ tr & intr juzgar; **judging by** a juzgar por
judge advocate s (in the army) auditor m de guerra; (in the navy) auditor de marina
judgeship ['dʒʌdʒʃɪp] s judicatura
judgment ['dʒʌdʒmənt] s juicio; (legal decision) sentencia, fallo
judgment day s día m del juicio
judgment seat s tribunal m
judicature ['dʒudɪkət ʃər] s judicatura
judicial [dʒu'dɪʃəl] adj judicial; (becoming a judge) crítico, juicioso
judiciar•y [dʒu'dɪʃɪ,ɛri] adj judicial ‖ s (pl **-ies**) (judges of a city, country, etc.) judicatura; (branch of government that administers justice) poder m judicial
judicious [dʒu'dɪʃəs] adj juicioso
jug [dʒʌg] s botija, jarra, cántaro; (jail) (slang) chirona

juggle [ˈdʒʌgəl] s juego de manos; (*trick, deception*) trampa ‖ tr hacer suertes con (*p.ej., bolas*); alterar fraudulentamente, falsear (*cuentas, documentos, etc.*); **to juggle away** escamotear ‖ intr hacer suertes; hacer trampas

juggler [ˈdʒʌglər] s malabarista *mf;* impostor *m*

juggling [ˈdʒʌglɪŋ] s juegos malabares

Jugoslav [ˈjugoˈslɑv] adj & s yugoeslavo

Jugoslavia [ˈjugoˈslɑvɪ·ə] s Yugoeslavia

jugular [ˈdʒʌgjələr] adj & s yugular *f*

juice [dʒus] s jugo, zumo; (*natural fluid of an animal body*) jugo; (slang) electricidad; (slang) gasolina; **to stew in one's own juice** (coll) freír en su aceite

juic·y [ˈdʒusi] adj (*comp* **-ier;** *super* **-iest**) jugoso, zumoso; (*interesting, spicy*) picante

jukebox [ˈdʒuk,bɑks] s tocadiscos *m* tragamonedas

julep [ˈdʒulɪp] s julepe *m*

julienne [,dʒulɪˈɛn] s sopa juliana

July [dʒuˈlaɪ] s julio

jumble [ˈdʒʌmbəl] s revoltijo, masa confusa ‖ tr emburujar, revolver

jum·bo [ˈdʒʌmbo] adj (coll) enorme, colosal ‖ s (*pl* **-bos**) (*large clumsy person*) (coll) elefante *m;* (coll) objeto enorme

jump [dʒʌmp] s salto; (*in a parachute*) lanzamiento; (*of prices*) alza repentina; **to be always on the jump** (coll) andar siempre de aquí para allí; **to get o to have the jump on** (slang) ganar la ventaja a ‖ tr saltar; hacer saltar (*a un caballo*); (*in checkers*) comer; salir (*un tren*) fuera de (*el carril*) ‖ intr saltar; (*in a parachute from an airplane*) lanzarse; pasar del tope (*el carro de la máquina de escribir*); **to jump at** apresurarse a aceptar (*un convite*); apresurarse a aprovechar (*la oportunidad*); **to jump on** saltar a (*un tren*); (slang) regañar, criticar; **to jump over** saltar por, pasar de un salto; saltar (*la página de un libro*); **to jump to a conclusion** sacar una conclusión precipitadamente

jumper [ˈdʒʌmpər] s saltador *m;* blusa de obrero; **jumpers** traje holgado de juego para niños

jumping jack [ˈdʒʌmpɪŋ] s títere *m*

jump·ing-off′ place s fin *m* del camino

jump seat s estrapontín *m*, traspuntín *m*

jump spark s (elec) chispa de entrehierro

jump suit s vestido unitario (*como de paracaidista*)

jump wire s (elec) alambre *m* de cierre

jump·y [ˈdʒʌmpi] adj (*comp* **-ier;** *super* **-iest**) saltón; asustadizo, nervioso

junc. abbr **junction**

junction [ˈdʒʌŋkʃən] s juntura, unión; (*of pieces of wood*) ensambladura; (*of two rivers*) confluencia; (*rail connection*) empalme *m;* (rr) estación de empalme

juncture [ˈdʒʌŋktʃər] s juntura, unión; (*time, occasion*) coyuntura; **at this juncture** a esta sazón, a estas alturas

June [dʒun] s junio

jungle [ˈdʒʌŋgəl] s jungla, selva; revoltijo, maraña

junior [ˈdʒunjər] adj menor, de menor edad; joven; del penúltimo año; hijo, p.ej., **John Jones, Junior** Juan Jones, hijo ‖ s menor *m;* socio menor; alumno del penúltimo año

junior college s escuela de estudios universitarios de primero y segundo años

junior high school s escuela intermedia entre la primaria y la secundaria

juniper [ˈdʒunɪpər] s enebro; (*red cedar*) cedro de Virginia

juniper berry s enebrina

junk [dʒʌŋk] s chatarra, hierro viejo; ropa vieja; (*useless stuff*) (coll) trastos viejos, baratijas viejas; (*old cable*) jarcia trozada; (*Chinese ship*) junco; (naut) carne salada ‖ tr (slang) echar a la basura; reducir a hierro viejo

junk dealer s chatarrero, chapucero

junket [ˈdʒʌŋkɪt] s manjar *m* de leche, cuajo y azúcar; (*outing*) viaje *m* de recreo; (*trip paid out of public funds*) jira ‖ intr hacer un viaje de recreo; ir de jira

junkie [ˈdʒʌŋki] s (slang) toxicómano, narcotómano, yonquí *m*

junk·man [ˈdʒʌŋk,mæn] s (*pl* **-men** [,mɛn]) chatarrero, chapucero; ropavejero; tripulante *m* de junco

junk room s leonera, trastera

junk shop o **junk store** s tienda de trastos viejos; baratío (CAm); barata (Col, Mex)

junk yard s chatarrería

juridical [dʒuˈrɪdɪkəl] adj jurídico

jurisdiction [,dʒurɪsˈdɪkʃən] s jurisdicción

jurisprudence [,dʒurɪsˈprudəns] s jurisprudencia

jurist [ˈdʒurɪst] s jurista *mf*

juror [ˈdʒurər] s (*individual*) jurado

ju·ry [ˈdʒuri] s (*pl* **-ries**) (*group*) jurado

jury box s tribuna del jurado

jury·man [ˈdʒurimən] s (*pl* **-men** [mən]) (*individual*) jurado

jury-rig [ˈdʒuri,rɪg] v (*pret* & *pp* **-rigged;** *ger* **-rigging**) tr (naut) aparejar temporariamente

Jus. P. abbr **justice of the peace**

just [dʒʌst] adj justo ‖ adv justamente, justo; hace poco, apenas; sólo; (coll) absolutamente; **just** + *pp* acabado de + *inf*, p.ej., **just received** acabado de recibir; recién + *pp*, p.ej., **just arrived** recién llegado; **just as** como; en el momento en que; tal como, lo mismo que; **just beyond** un poco más allá (de); **just now** hace poco; ahora mismo; **just out** acabado de aparecer, recién publicado; **to have just** + *pp* acabar de + *inf*, p.ej., **I have just arrived** acabo de llegar; **I had just arrived** acababa de llegar

justice [ˈdʒʌstɪs] s justicia; (*judge*) juez *m;* (*just deserts*) premio merecido; **to bring to justice** aprehender y condenar por justicia; **to do justice to** hacer justicia a; apreciar debidamente

justice of the peace s juez *m* de paz

justifiable [ˈdʒʌstɪ,faɪ·əbəl] adj justificable

justi•fy ['dʒʌstɪ,faɪ] *v* (*pret* & *pp* **-fied**) *tr* justificar; (*typ*) justificar

justly ['dʒʌstli] *adj* justamente, debidamente

jut [dʒʌt] *v* (*pre* & *pp* **jutted;** *ger* **jutting**) *intr*—**to jut out** resaltar, proyectarse

jute [dʒut] *s* yute *m* ‖ **Jute** *m* juto

Jutland ['dʒʌtlənd] *s* Jutlandia

juvenile ['dʒuvənɪl] o ['dʒuvə,naɪl] *adj* juvenil; para jóvenes ‖ *s* joven *mf*, mocito;

libro para niños; (theat) galán *m*, galancete *m*

juvenile court *s* tribunal *m* tutelar de menores

juvenile delinquency *s* delincuencia de menores

juvenile lead [lid] *s* (theat) papel *m* de galancete; (theat) galancete *m*

juvenilia [,dʒuvə'nɪlɪ•ə] *spl* obras de juventud

juxtapose [,dʒʌkstə'poz] *tr* yuxtaponer

K

K, k [ke] undécima letra del alfabeto inglés

k. *abbr* **karat, kilogram**

K. *abbr* **King, Knight**

kale [kel] *s* col *f*, berza; (slang) dinero, pasta

kaleidoscope [ke'laɪdə,skop] *s* calidoscopio

kangaroo [,kæŋgə'ru] *s* canguro

kapok ['kepɑk] *s* capoc *m*, lana de ceiba

kaput [kə'pʊt] *adj* (slang) roto; gastado; inútil

karate [kə'rɑti] *m* karate *m*, karaté *m*

karate expert *s* karateka *m*

katydid ['ketidɪd] *s* saltamontes *m* cuyo macho emite un sonido chillón

kayak ['kaɪæk] *s* kayak *m*

kc. *abbr* **kilocycle**

kedge [kɛdʒ] *s* (naut) anclote *m*

keel [kil] *s* quilla ‖ *intr*—**to keel over** (naut) dar de quilla; volcarse; (coll) desmayarse

keelson ['kɛlsən] o ['kilsən] *s* (naut) sobrequilla

keen [kin] *adj* (*having a sharp edge*) agudo, afilado; (*sharp, cutting*) mordaz, penetrante; (*sharp-witted*) sutil, astuto, perspicaz; (*eager, much interested*) entusiasta; intenso, vivo; (slang) maravilloso; **to be keen on** ser muy aficionado a

keep [kip] *s* manutención, subsistencia; (*of medieval castle*) torre *f* del homenaje; **for keeps** (coll) de veras; (coll) para siempre; **to earn one's keep** (coll) ganarse la vida ‖ *v* (*pret* & *pp* **kept** [kɛpt] *tr* guardar, conservar; (*deciding to make a purchase*) quedarse con; cumplir, guardar (*su palabra, su promesa*); llevar (*cuentas*); apuntar (*los tantos*); tener (*criados, caballos, huéspedes*); cultivar (*una huerta*); dirigir (*un hotel, una escuela*); celebrar (*una fiesta*); hacer tardar (*a una persona*); **to keep away** tener alejado; **to keep back** retener; beberse (*las lágrimas*); reservar, no divulgar; **to keep down** reprimir; reducir (*los gastos*) al mínimo; **to keep** (*a person*) **from** + *ger* no dejarle (*a una persona*) + *inf*; **to keep in** no dejar salir; **keep off** tener a distancia; no dejar penetrar (*p.ej., la lluvia*); evitar (*p.ej., el polvo*); **to keep out** no dejar entrar; no dejar penetrar; **to keep someone informed**

(**about**) ponerle a uno al corriente (de); **to keep someone waiting** hacerle a uno esperar; **to keep up** mantener, conservar ‖ *intr* permanecer, quedarse; conservarse, no echarse a perder; **to keep** + *ger* seguir + *ger;* **to keep away** mantenerse a distancia; no dejarse ver; **to keep from** + *ger* abstenerse de + *inf;* **to keep informed** (**about**) ponerse al corriente (de); **to keep in with** (coll) congraciarse con, no perder el favor de; **to keep off** no acercarse a; no pisar (*el césped*); **to keep on** + *ger* seguir + *ger;* **to keep on with** continuar con; **to keep out** mantenerse fuera, no entrar; **to keep out of** no entrar en; no meterse en; evitar (*el peligro*); **to keep quiet** estarse quieto; **to keep to** seguir por, llevar (*la derecha, la izquierda*); **to keep to oneself** quedarse a solas; **to keep up** continuar; no rezagarse; **to keep up with** correr parejas con; llevar adelante, proseguir

keeper ['kipər] *s* guardián *m*, custodio; (*of a game preserve*) guardabosque *m;* (*of a magnet*) armadura, culata

keeping ['kipɪŋ] *s* custodia, cuidado; (*of a holiday*) celebración; **in keeping with** de acuerdo con, en armonía con; **in safe keeping** en lugar seguro, a buen recaudo; **out of keeping with** en desacuerdo con

keep'sake' *s* recuerdo

keg [kɛg] *s* cuñete *m*, cubeto

ken [kɛn] *s* alcance *m* de la vista, alcance del saber; **beyond the ken of** fuera del alcance de

kennel ['kɛnəl] *s* perrera

kep•i ['kepi] o ['kɛpi] *s* (*pl* **-is**) quepis *m*

kept woman [kɛpt] *s* entretenida, manceba

kerchief ['kʌrtʃɪf] *s* pañuelo, mantón *m*

kerchoo [kər'tʃu] *interj* ¡ah-chís!

kernel ['kʌrnəl] *s* (*inner part of a nut or fruit stone*) almendra núcleo; (*of wheat or corn*) grano; (fig) medula

kerosene ['kɛrə,sin] o [,kɛrə'sin] *s* keroseno

kerosene lamp *s* lámpara de petróleo

kerplunk [kər'plʌŋk] *interj* ¡pataplún!

ketchup ['kɛtʃəp] *s* salsa de tomate condimentada

kettle ['kɛtəl] *s* caldera, marmita; (*teakettle*) tetera

ket·tle·drum' *s* timbal *m*, tímpano

key [ki] *adj* clave ‖ *s* (*of door, trunk, etc.*) llave *f*; (*of piano, typewriter, etc.*) tecla; (*wedge or cotter used to lock parts together*) clavija, cuña, chaveta; (*reef or low island*) cayo; (bot) sámara; (*tone of voice*) tono; (mus) clave *f* o llave *f*; (telg) manipulador *m*; (*to a puzzle, secret, translation, code*) (fig) clave o llave; (*place giving control to a region*) (fig) llave *f*; (fig) persona principal; **off key** desafinado; desafinadamente ‖ *tr* acuñar, enchavetar; **to key up** alentar, excitar

key'board' *s* teclado

key fruit *s* sámara

key'hole' *s* ojo de la cerradura; (*of a clock*) agujero de cuerda

key money *s* pago ilícito al casero

key'note' *s* (mus) tónica, nota tónica; (fig) idea fundamental

keynote speech *s* discurso de apertura (*en que se expone el programa de un partido político*)

key'punch'er *s* perforista *mf*

key ring *s* llavero

key'stone' *s* clave *f*, espinazo; (fig) piedra angular

Key West *s* Cayo Hueso

key word *s* palabra clave

kg. *abbr* **kilogram**

K.G. *abbr* **Knight of the Garter**

kha·ki ['kɑki] o ['kæki] *adj* caqui ‖ *s* (*pl* -kis) caqui *m*

khedive [kə'div] *s* jedive *m*

kibitz ['kɪbɪts] *intr* (coll) dar consejos molestos a los jugadores

kibitzer ['kɪbɪtsər] *s* (coll) mirón molesto (*de una partida de juego*); (coll) entremetido

kiblah ['kɪblɑ] *s* alquibla

kibosh ['kaɪbɑʃ] o [kɪ'bɑʃ] *s* (coll) música celestial; **to put the kibosh on** (coll) desbaratar, imposibilitar

kick [kɪk] *s* puntapié *m*; (*of an animal*) coz *f*; (*of a gun*) coz, culatazo; (*complaint*) (slang) queja, protesta; (*of liquor*) (slang) fuerza, estímulo; (*thrill*) gusto, placer intenso; **to get a kick out of** (slang) hallar mucho placer en ‖ *tr* acocear, dar de puntapiés a; sacudir (*los pies*); **to kick out** (coll) echar a puntapiés a la calle; (coll) echar, despedir; **to kick the bucket** (coll) morir; **to kick up a row** (slang) armar un bochinche ‖ *intr* cocear; dar culetazos (*un arma de fuego*); (coll) quejarse; **to kick about** (coll) quejarse de; **to kick against the pricks** dar coces contra el aguijón; **to kick off** (football) dar el golpe de salida

kick'back' *s* (coll) contragolpe *m*; (slang) devolución a un cómplice de una parte de lo robado

kick'off' *s* (football) golpe *m* de salida, puntapié *m* inicial

kid [kɪd] *s* (*young goat*) cabrito; (*leather*) cabritilla; (coll) chiquillo, chico; **kids** guantes *mpl* o zapatos de cabritilla ‖ *v* (*pret*

& *pp* **kidded;** *ger* **kidding**) *tr* (slang) embromar, tomar el pelo a; **to kid oneself** (slang) forjarse ilusiones ‖ *intr* (slang) decirlo en broma

kidder ['kɪdər] *s* (slang) bromista *mf*

kid gloves *spl* guantes *mpl* de cabritilla; **to handle with kid gloves** tratar con suma discreción o cautela

kid'nap' *v* (*pret* & *pp* -naped o -napped; *ger* naping o -napping) *tr* secuestrar

kidnaper o **kidnapper** ['kɪd,næpər] *s* secuestrador *m*, ladrón *m* de niños

kidney ['kɪdni] *s* riñon *m*; (coll) clase *f*, especie *f*; (coll) carácter *m*

kidney bean *s* judía

kidney stone *s* cálculo renal

kill [kɪl] *s* matanza; (*of a wild beast, an army, a pack of hounds*) ataque *m* final; (*creek*) arroyo, riachuelo; **for the kill** para el golpe final ‖ *tr* matar; ahogar (*un proyecto de ley*); quitar (*el sabor*); producir una impresión irresistible en

killer ['kɪlər] *s* matador *m*

killer whale *s* orca

killing ['kɪlɪŋ] *adj* matador; (*exhausting*) abrumador; (coll) muy divertido, de lo más ridículo ‖ *s* matanza; (*game killed on a hunt*) cacería, piezas; (coll) gran ganancia; **to make a killing** (coll) enriquecerse de golpe

kill'-joy' *s* aguafiestas *mf*

kiln [kɪl] o [kɪln] *s* horno

kil·o ['kɪlo] o ['kilo] *s* (*pl* -os) kilo, kilogramo; kilómetro

kilocycle ['kɪlə,saɪkəl] *s* kilociclo

kilogram ['kɪlə,græm] *s* kilogramo

kilometer ['kɪlə,mitər] *s* kilómetro (*distancia*); **kilometer** [kɪ'lɑmətər] *s* kilómetro (*instrumento*)

kilometric [,kɪlə'mɛtrɪk] *adj* kilométrico

kilowatt ['kɪlə,wɑt] *s* kilovatio

kilowatt-hour ['kɪlə,wɑt'aʊr] *s* (*pl* **kilowatt-hours**) kilovatio-hora

kilt [kɪlt] *s* enagüillas, falda corta

kilter ['kɪltər] *s*—**to be out of kilter** (coll) estar descompuesto

kimo·no [kɪ'monə] *s* (*pl* -nos) quimono

kin [kɪn] *s* (*family relationship*) parentesco; (*relatives*) deudos; **near of kin** muy allegado; **of kin** allegado; **the next of kin** el pariente más próximo, los parientes próximos

kind [kaɪnd] *adj* bueno, bondadoso; (*greeting*) afectuoso; **kind to** bueno para con ‖ *s* clase *f*, especie *f*, suerte *f*, género; **a kind of** uno a modo de; **all kinds of** (coll) gran cantidad de; **in kind** en especie; en la misma moneda; **kind of** (coll) algo, más bien; **of a kind** de una misma clase; (*poor, mediocre*) de poco valor, de mala muerte; **of the kind** por el estilo

kindergarten ['kɪndər,gɑrtən] *s* parvulario, escuela de párvulos, jardín *m* de la infancia

kindergartner ['kɪndər,gɑrtnər] *s* (*child*) párvulo; (*teacher*) parvulista *mf*

kind-hearted ['kaɪnd'hɑrtɪd] *adj* bondadoso, de buen corazón

kindle ['kɪndəl] *tr* encender ‖ *intr* encenderse
kindling ['kɪndlɪŋ] *s* encendajas
kindling wood *s* leña
kind·ly ['kaɪndli] *adj* (*comp* **-lier;** *super* **-liest**) (*kind-hearted*) bondadoso; apacible, benigno; favorable ‖ *adv* bondadosamente; cordialmente; con gusto; por favor; **to not take kindly to** no aceptar de buen grado
kindness ['kaɪndnɪs] *s* bondad; **have the kindness to** tenga Vd. la bondad de
kindred ['kɪndrɪd] *adj* emparentado; afín, semejante ‖ *s* parentela; semejanza, afinidad
Kinescope ['kɪnɪ,skop] *s* (trademark) cinescopio, kinescopio
kinetic [kɪ'nɛtɪk] *adj* cinético ‖ **kinetics** *s* cinética
kinetic energy *s* fuerza viva, energía cinética
kinfolk ['kɪn,fok] *s* (coll) pariente(s)
king [kɪŋ] *s* rey *m*; (cards, chess, & fig) rey; (checkers) dama
king'bolt' *s* pivote *m* central
kingdom ['kɪŋdəm] *s* reino
king'fish'er *s* martín *m* pescador
king·ly ['kɪŋli] *adj* (*comp* **-lier;** *super* **-liest**) real, regio; (*stately*) majestuoso ‖ *adv* regiamente
king'pin' *s* (bowling) bolo delantero; pivote *m* central; (aut) pivote *m* de dirección; (coll) persona principal; (coll) jefe *m* de criminales
king post *s* pendolón *m*
king's evil *s* escrófula
kingship ['kɪŋʃɪp] *s* dignidad real
king'-size' *adj* de tamaño largo
king's ransom *s* riquezas de Creso
kink [kɪŋk] *s* (*twist, e.g., in a rope*) enroscadura, coca; (*e.g., in hair*) pasa; (*soreness in neck*) tortícolis *m*; (*flaw, difficulty*) estorbo, traba; (*mental twist*) chifladura, manía ‖ *tr* enroscar ‖ *intr* enroscarse
kink·y ['kɪŋki] *adj* (*comp* **-ier;** *super* **-iest**) encarrujado, ensortijado; (coll) perverso, raro
kinsfolk ['kɪnz,fok] *s* parentela, familia, deudos
kinship ['kɪnʃɪp] *s* parentesco; semejanza, afinidad
kins·man ['kɪnzmən] *s* (*pl* **-men** [mən]) pariente *m*
kins·woman ['kɪnz,wʊmən] *s* (*pl* **-women** [,wɪmɪn]) *s* parienta
kipper ['kɪpər] *s* arenque acecinado, salmón acecinado ‖ *tr* acecinar (*el arenque o el salmón*)
kiss [kɪs] *s* beso; (billiards) retruco; (*confection*) dulce *m*, merengue *m* ‖ *tr* besar; **to kiss away** borrar con besos (*las pensas de una persona*) ‖ *intr* besar; besarse; (billiards) retrucar
kit [kɪt] *s* cartera de herramientas; (*case and its contents for various purposes*) estuche *m*; (*of a soldier*) equipo, pertrechos; (*of a traveler*) equipaje *m*; (*pail, tub*) balde *m*
kitchen ['kɪtʃən] *s* cocina
kitchenette [,kɪtʃə'nɛt] *s* cocinilla
kitchen garden *s* huerto

kitch'en·maid' *s* ayudanta de cocina, pincha
kitchen police *s* (mil) trabajo de cocina; soldados que están de cocina
kitchen range *s* cocina económica
kitchen sink *s* fregadero; **everything but the kitchen sink** sin faltar apenas nada; completísimo
kitch'en·ware' *s* utensilios de cocina
kite [kaɪt] *s* cometa; (orn) milano; **to fly a kite** hacer volar una cometa
kith and kin [kɪθ] *spl* parientes *mpl;* parientes y amigos
kitten ['kɪtən] *s* gatito, minino
kittenish ['kɪtənɪʃ] *adj* juguetón, retozón; (*coy, flirtatious*) coquetón
kit·ty ['kɪti] *s* (*pl* **-ties**) gatito, minino; (*in card games*) polla, puesta ‖ *interj* ¡miz!
kleptomaniac [,klɛptə'menɪ,æk] *s* cleptómano
km. *abbr* **kilometer**
knack [næk] *s* tino, tranquillo, maña
knapsack ['næp,sæk] *s* mochila
knave [nev] *s* bribón *m*, pícaro; (cards) sota
knaver·y ['nevəri] *s* (*pl* **-ies**) bribonería, picardía
knead [nid] *tr* amasar, sobar
knee [ni] *s* rodilla; (*of animal*) codillo; (*e.g., of trousers*) rodillera; (mach) ángulo, codo; **to bring** (*someone*) **to his knees** rendir, vencer; **to go down on one's knees** hincarse de rodillas, caer de rodillas; **to go down on one's knees to** implorar de rodillas
knee breeches ['brɪtʃɪz] *spl* pantalones cortos
knee'cap' *s* rótula; (*protective covering*) rodillera
knee'-deep' *adj* metido hasta las rodillas
knee'high' *adj* que llega hasta la rodilla
knee'-hole' *s* hueco para acomodar las rodillas
knee jerk *s* reflejo rotuliano
kneel [nil] *v* (*pret & pp* **knelt** [nɛlt] o **kneeled**) *intr* arrodillarse; estar de rodillas
knee'pad' *s* rodillera
knee'pan' *s* rótula
knee swell *s* (*of organ*) (mus) rodillera
knell [nɛl] *s* doble *m*, toque *m* de difuntos; mal agüero; **to toll the knell of** anunciar la muerte de, anunciar el fin de ‖ *intr* doblar, tocar a muerto; sonar tristemente
knickers ['nɪkərz] *spl* pantalones *mpl* de media pierna
knickknack ['nɪk,næk] *s* chuchería, bujería, baratija
knife [naɪf] *s* (*pl* **knives** [naɪvz]) cuchillo; (*of a paper cutter or other instrument*) cuchilla; **to go under the knife** (coll) hacerse operar ‖ *tr* acuchillar; (slang) traicionar
knife sharpener *s* afilador *m*, afilón *m*
knife switch *s* (elec) interruptor *m* de cuchilla
knight [naɪt] *s* caballero; (chess) caballo ‖ *tr* armar caballero
knight-errant ['naɪt'ɛrənt] *s* (*pl* **knights-errant**) caballero andante
knight-errant·ry ['naɪt'ɛrəntri] *s* (*pl* **-ries**) caballería andante; (*quixotic behavior*) quijotada

knighthood ['naɪt•hʊd] s caballería
knightly ['naɪtli] adj caballeroso, caballeresco
Knight of the Rueful Countenance s Caballero de la triste figura (Don Quijote)
knit [nɪt] v (pret & pp **knitted** o **knit**; ger **knitting**) tr tejer a punto de aguja; enlazar, unir; fruncir (las cejas) arrugar (la frente) ‖ intr hacer calceta, hacer malla; trabarse, unirse; soldarse (un hueso)
knit goods spl géneros de punto
knitting ['nɪtɪŋ] s punto de media, trabajo de punto
knitting machine s máquina de hacer tejidos de punto
knitting needle s aguja de hacer media
knit'wear' s géneros de punto
knob [nɑb] s (lump) bulto, protuberancia; (of a door) botón m, tirador m; (of a radio set) botón, perilla; (ornament on furniture) manzana; colina o montaña redondeada
knock [nɑk] s golpe m; (e.g., on a door) toque m, llamada; (with a door knocker) aldabazo; (of an internal-combustion engine) pistoneo; (slang) censura, crítica ‖ tr golpear; (repeatedly) golpetear; (slang) censurar, criticar; **to knock down** (with a blow, punch, etc.) derribar; (to the highest bidder) rematar; desarmar, desmontar (un aparato o máquina); **to knock off** hacer saltar con un golpe; suspender (el trabajo); poner fin a; (slang) matar; **to knock out** agotar; (box) poner fuera de combate ‖ intr tocar, llamar; golpear, pistonear (el motor de combustión interna); (slang) censurar, criticar; **to knock about** andar vagando; **to knock against** dar contra, tropezar con; **to knock at** tocar a, llamar a (la puerta); **to knock off** dejar de trabajar
knocker ['nɑkər] s (on a door) aldaba; (coll) criticón m
knock-kneed ['nɑk,nid] adj patizambo, zambo
knock'out' s golpe decisivo, puñetazo decisivo; (box) (el) fuera de combate; (elec) destapadero; real moza
knockout drops spl (slang) gotas narcóticas
knoll [nol] s loma, otero
knot [nɑt] s nudo; (worn as ornament) lazo; corrillo, grupo; (difficult matter; bond or tie) nudo; nudo o lazo de matrimonio; (protuberance in a fabric) envoltorio; (naut) nudo; **to tie the knot** (coll) casarse ‖ v (pret & pp **knotted**; ger **knotting**) tr anudar; fruncir (las cejas) ‖ intr anudarse
knot'hole' s agujero en la madera (que deja un nudo al desprenderse)
knot•ty ['nɑti] adj (comp -tier; super -tiest) nudoso; (fig) espinoso, difícil

know [no] s —**to be in the know** estar enterado, tener informes secretos ‖ v (pret **knew** [nju] o [nu]; pp **known**) tr & intr (by reasoning or learning) saber; (by the senses or by perception; through acquaintance or recognition) conocer; **as far as I know** que yo sepa; **to know about** saber de; **to know best** ser el mejor juez, saber lo que más conviene; **to know how to +** inf saber + inf; **to know it all** (coll) sabérselo todo; **to know what one is doing** obrar con conocimiento de causa; **to know what's what** (coll) saber cuántas son cinco; **you ought to know better** deberías tener vergüenza
knowable ['no•əbəl] adj conocible
know'-how' s conocimiento, destreza, habilidad
knowingly ['no•ɪŋli] adv a sabiendas, con conocimiento de causa; (on purpose) adrede
know'-it-all' adj & s (coll) sabidillo, sabelotodo mf
knowledge ['nɑlɪdʒ] s (faculty) ciencia, conocimientos, el saber; (awareness, acquaintance, familiarity) conocimiento; **to have a thorough knowledge of** conocer a fondo; **to my knowledge** que yo sepa; **to the best of my knowledge** según mi leal saber y entender; **with full knowledge** con conocimiento de causa; **without my knowledge** sin saberlo yo
knowledgeable ['nɑlɪdʒəbəl] adj (coll) conocedor, inteligente
know'-noth'ing s ignorante mf
knuckle ['nʌkəl] s nudillo; (of a quadruped) jarrete m; (mach) junta de charnela; **knuckles** bóxer m ‖ intr—**to knuckle down** someterse, darse por vencido; aplicarse con empeño al trabajo
knurl [nʌrl] s moleteado ‖ tr moletear, cerrillar (p.ej., las piezas de moneda)
k.o. abbr knockout
kook [kuk] s (coll) tipo raro; excéntrico
Koran [ko'rɑn] o [ko'ræn] s Corán m
Korea [ko'ri•ə] s Corea
Korean [ko'ri•ən] adj & s coreano
kosher ['koʃər] adj autorizado por la ley judía; (coll) genuino, auténtico
kowtow ['kau,tau] o ['ko,tau] intr arrodillarse y tocar el suelo con la frente; doblegarse servilmente, mostrarse servilmente obsequioso
Kt. abbr **Knight**
kudos ['kjudɑs] o ['kudɑs] s (coll) gloria, renombre m, fama
kw. abbr **kilowatt**
K.W.H. abbr **kilowatt-hour**

ki
kw

L

L, l [ɛl] duodécima letra del alfabeto inglés
l. *abbr* **liter, line, league, length**
L. *abbr* **Latin, Low**
la•bel [ˈlebəl] *s* etiqueta, marbete *m*, rótulo; (*descriptive word*) calificación ‖ *v* (*pret & pp* **-beled** o **-belled;** *ger* **-beling** o **-belling**) *tr* poner etiqueta o marbete a, rotular; calificar
labial [ˈlebɪ•əl] *adj & s* labial *f*
labor [ˈlebər] *adj* obrero ‖ *s* trabajo, labor *f*; (*job, task*) tarea, faena; (*manual work involved in an undertaking; the wages for such work*) mano *f* de obra; (*wage-earning workers as contrasted with capital and management*) los obreros; (*childbirth*) parto; **labors** esfuerzos; **to be in labor** estar de parto ‖ *intr* trabajar; (*to exert oneself*) forcejar; estar de parto; moverse penosamente; cabecear y balancear (*un buque*); **to labor under** ser víctima de
labor and management *spl* los obreros y los patronos
laborato•ry [ˈlæbərə‚tori] *s* (*pl* **-ries**) laboratorio
labored [ˈlebərd] *adj* penoso, dificultoso; artificial, forzado
laborer [ˈlebərər] *s* trabajador *m*, obrero; (*unskilled worker*) bracero, jornalero, peón *m*
laborious [ləˈborɪ•əs] *adj* laborioso
la'bor-man'agement *adj* obrero-patronal
labor union *s* gremio obrero, sindicato
Labourite [ˈlebə‚raɪt] *s* laborista *mf*
Labrador [ˈlæbrə‚dɔr] *s* el Labrador
labyrinth [ˈlæbɪrɪnθ] *s* laberinto
lace [les] *s* encaje *m*; (*string to tie shoe, corset, etc.*) cordón *m*, lazo; (*braid*) galón *m* de oro o plata ‖ *tr* adornar con encaje; atar (*los zapatos, el corsé*); (*coll*) dar una paliza a
lace trimming *s* randa
lace'work' *s* encaje *m*, obra de encaje
lachrymose [ˈlækrɪ‚mos] *adj* lacrimoso
lacing [ˈlesɪŋ] *s* cordón *m;* lazo; galón *m;* (*coll*) paliza
lack [læk] *s* carencia, falta; (*complete lack*) defecto ‖ *tr* carecer de, necesitar ‖ *intr* (*to be lacking*) faltar
lackadaisical [‚lækəˈdezɪkəl] *adj* desaprovechado, indiferente
lackey [ˈlæki] *s* lacayo; secuaz *m* servil
lacking [ˈlækɪŋ] *prep* sin, carente de
lack'lus'ter *adj* delustrado, deslucido
laconic [ləˈkɑnɪk] *adj* lacónico
lacquer [ˈlækər] *s* laca ‖ *tr* laquear
lacquer ware *s* lacas, objetos de laca
lacu•na [ləˈkjunə] *s* (*pl* **-nas** o **-nae** [ni]) laguna
lac•y [ˈlesi] *adj* (*comp* **-ier;** *super* **-iest**) de encaje; (*fig*) diáfano
lad [læd] *s* muchacho, chico
ladder [ˈlædər] *s* escalera; (*stepladder*) escala, escalera de mano; (*two ladders fastened together at the top with hinges*)

escalera de tijera; (*stepping stone*) (fig) escalón *m*
ladder truck *s* carro de escaleras de incendio
ladies' room *s* cuarto tocador
ladle [ˈledəl] *s* cazo; (*for soup*) cucharón *m;* (*of tinsmith*) cucharilla ‖ *tr* servir con cucharón; sacar con cucharón
la•dy [ˈledi] *s* (*pl* **-dies**) señora, dama
la'dy-bird' o **la'dy•bug'** *s* mariquita, vaca de San Antón
la'dy•fin'ger *s* melindre *m*
lady-in-waiting *s* camarera de la reina
la'dy-kil'ler *s* ladrón *m* de corazones
la'dy•like' *adj* elegante; **to be ladylike** ser muy dama
la'dy•love' *s* amada, amiga querida
lady of the house *s* ama de casa
ladyship [ˈledi‚ʃɪp] *s* señoría
lady's maid *s* doncella
lady's man *s* perico entre ellas
lag [læg] *s* retraso ‖ *v* (*pret & pp* **lagged;** *ger* **lagging**) *intr* retrasarse; **to lag behind** quedarse atrás, rezagarse
lager beer [ˈlɑgər] *s* cerveza reposada
laggard [ˈlægərd] *s* perezoso, rezagado
lagoon [ləˈgun] *s* laguna
laid paper [led] *s* papel vergueteado
laid up *adj* almacenado, ahorrado; (naut) inactivo; (coll) encamado por estar enfermo
lair [lɛr] *s* cubil *m*
lai•ty [ˈle•ɪti] *s* legos
lake [lek] *adj* lacustre ‖ *s* lago
lamb [læm] *s* cordero; carne *f* de cordero; piel *f* de cordero; (*meek person*) (fig) cordero
lambaste [læmˈbest] *tr* (*to thrash*) (coll) dar una paliza a; (*to reprimand harshly*) (coll) dar una jabonadura a
lamb chop *s* chuleta de cordero
lambkin [ˈlæmkɪn] *s* corderito; (fig) nenito
lamb'skin' *s* piel *f* de cordero, corderina; (*dressed with its wool*) corderillo
lame [lem] *adj* cojo; (*sore*) dolorido; (*e.g., excuse*) débil, pobre ‖ *tr* encojar
lament [ləˈmɛnt] *s* lamento; (*dirge*) elegía ‖ *tr* lamentar ‖ *intr* lamentarse
lamentable [ˈlæməntəbəl] *adj* lamentable
lamentation [‚læmənˈteʃən] *s* lamentación
laminate [ˈlæmɪ‚net] *tr* laminar
laminated glass *s* cristal laminado
lamp [læmp] *s* lámpara
lamp'black' *s* negro de humo
lamp chimney *s* tubo de lámpara
lamp'light' *s* luz *f* de lámpara
lamp'light'er *s* farolero
lampoon [læmˈpun] *s* pasquín *m*, libelo ‖ *tr* pasquinar
lamp'post' *s* poste *m* de farol
lamp shade *s* pantalla de lámpara
lamp'wick' *s* mecha de lámpara, torcida
lance [læns] o [lɑns] *s* lanza; (surg) lanceta ‖ *tr* alancear; (surg) abrir con lanceta
lance rest *s* ristre *m*
lancet [ˈlænsɪt] *s* (surg) lanceta

land [lænd] *adj* terrestre; (*wind*) terral ‖ *s* tierra; **on land, on sea, and in the air** en tierra, mar y aire; **to make land** atracar a tierra; **to see how the land lies** medir el terreno, ver el cariz que van tomando las cosas ‖ *tr* desembarcar; conducir (*un avión*) a tierra; coger (*un pez*); (coll) conseguir ‖ *intr* desembarcar; (*to reach land*) arribar, aterrar; aterrizar (*un avión*); (*to arrive or come to rest*) ir a dar, ir a parar; **to land on one's feet** caer de pies; **to land on one's head** caer de cabeza

landau ['lændɔ] o ['lændau] *s* landó *m*

land breeze *s* terral *m*

landed ['lændɪd] *adj* (*owning land*) hacendado; (*real-estate*) inmobiliario; **landed property** bienes *mpl* raíces

land'fall' *s* (*sighting land*) aterrada; (*landing of ship or plane*) aterraje *m;* tierra vista desde el mar; (*landslide*) derrumbe *m*

land'fill' *s* tierra y escombros

land grant *s* donación de tierras

land'hold'er *s* terrateniente *mf*, hacendado

landing ['lændɪŋ] *s* (*of ship or plane*) aterraje *m;* (*of passengers*) desembarco; (*place where passengers and goods are landed*) desembarcadero; (*of stairway*) desembarco, descanso

landing beacon *s* (aer) radiofaro de aterrizaje

landing craft *s* (nav) lancha de desembarco

landing field *s* (aer) pista de aterrizaje

landing force *s* (nav) compañía de desembarco

landing gear *s* (aer) tren *m* de aterrizaje

landing stage *s* embarcadero flotante

landing strip *s* (aer) faja de aterrizaje

land'la'dy *s* (*pl* **-dies**) (*e.g., of an apartment*) casera, dueña; (*of a lodging house*) ama, patrona; (*of an inn*) mesonera, posadera

landlocked ['lænd,lɑkt] *adj* rodeado de tierra

land'lord' *s* (*e.g., of an apartment*) casero, dueño; (*of a lodging house*) amo, patrón *m;* (*of an inn*) mesonero, posadero

land'lub'ber *s* (*person unacquainted with the sea*) marinero de agua dulce; (*awkward and unskilled seaman*) marinero matalote

land'mark' *s* (*boundary stone*) mojón *m;* (*feature of landscape that marks a location*) guía; suceso que hace época; (naut) marca de reconocimiento

land office *s* oficina del catastro

land'-of'fice business *s* (coll) negocio de mucho movimiento

land'own'er *s* terrateniente *mf*, hacendado

landscape ['lænd,skep] *s* paisaje *m* ‖ *tr* ajardinar

landscape architect *s* arquitecto paisajista

landscape gardener *s* jardinero adornista, jardinista *mf*

landscape painter *s* paisajista *mf*

landscapist ['lænd,skepɪst] *s* paisajista *mf*

land'slide' *s* derrumbe *m*, derrumbamiento de tierra, corrimiento; (fig) mayoría de votos abrumadora; (fig) victoria arrolladora

landward ['lændwərd] *adv* hacia tierra, hacia la costa

land wind *s* terral *m*

lane [len] *s* (*narrow street or passage*) callejuela; (*path*) carril *m;* (*of an automobile highway*) faja; (*of an air or ocean route*) derrotero, vía

langsyne ['læn'saɪn] *adv* (Scotch) hace mucho tiempo ‖ *s* (Scotch) tiempo de antaño

language ['læŋgwɪdʒ] *s* idioma *m*, lengua; (*way of speaking or writing, style; figurative or poetic expression; communication of meaning said to be employed by flowers, birds, art, etc.*) lenguaje *m;* (*of a special group of people*) jerga

language laboratory *s* laboratorio de idiomas

languid ['læŋgwɪd] *adj* lánguido

languish ['læŋgwɪʃ] *intr* languidecer; afectar languidez

languor ['læŋgər] *s* languidez *f*

languorous ['læŋgərəs] *adj* lánguido; (*causing languor*) enervante

lank [læŋk] *adj* descarnado, larguirucho; (*hair*) lacio

lank•y ['læŋki] *adj* (*comp* **-ier;** *super* **-iest**) descarnado, larguirucho

lantern ['læntərn] *s* linterna

lantern slide *s* diapositiva, tira de vidrio

lanyard ['lænjərd] *s* (naut) acollador *m*

lap [læp] *s* (*of human body or clothing*) regazo; (*loose fold*) caída, doblez *f;* (*overlap of garment*) traslapo; (*with the tongue*) lametada; (*of the waves*) chapaleteo; (*in a race*) (sport) etapa, vuelta; **to live in the lap of luxury** llevar una vida regalada ‖ *v* (*pret & pp* **lapped;** *ger* **lapping**) *tr* beber con la lengua; lamer (*las olas la playa*); (*to overlap*) traslapar; juntar a traslapo; **to lap up** tragar a lengüetadas; (coll) aceptar con entusiasmo ‖ *intr* traslapar; traslaparse (*dos o más cosas*); **to lap against** lamer (*las olas la playa*); **to lap over** salir fuera, rebosar

lap'board' *s* tabla faldera

lap dog *s* perro de falda

lapel [lə'pɛl] *s* solapa

Lap'land' *s* Laponia

Laplander ['læp,lændər] *s* lapón *m* (*habitante*)

Lapp [læp] *s* lapón *m* (*habitante; idioma*)

lap robe *s* manta de coche

lapse [læps] *s* (*passing of time; slipping into guilt or error*) lapso; (*fall, decline*) caída, caída en desuso; (*e.g., of an insurance policy*) invalidación ‖ *intr* caer en culpa o error; decaer, pasar (*p.ej., el entusiasmo*); caducar (*p.ej., una póliza de seguro*)

lap'wing' *s* ave fría

larce•ny ['lɑrsəni] *s* (*pl* **-nies**) hurto, robo

larch [lɑrtʃ] *s* alerce *m*, lárice *m*

lard [lɑrd] *s* cochevira, manteca de puerco ‖ *tr* (culin) mechar

larder ['lɑrdər] *s* despensa

large [lɑrdʒ] *adj* grande; **at large** en libertad

large intestine *s* intestino grueso

largely ['lɑrdʒli] *adj* por la mayor parte

largeness ['lɑrdʒnɪs] *s* grandeza

large'-scale' *adj* en grande escala, grande escala

lariat [ˈlærɪ·ət] *s* (*for catching animals*) lazo; (*for tying grazing animals*) cuerda, soga
lark [lɑrk] *s* alondra; (coll) parranda; **to go on a lark** (coll) andar de parranda, echar una cana al aire
lark'spur' *s* (*rocket larkspur*) espuela de caballero; (*field larkspur*) consuelda real
lar·va [ˈlɑrvə] *s* (*pl* -**vae** [vi]) larva
laryngeal [ləˈrɪndʒɪ·əl] *adj* laríngeo
laryngitis [ˌlærɪnˈdʒaɪtɪs] *s* laringitis *f*
laryngoscope [ləˈrɪŋgə.skop] *s* laringoscopio
larynx [ˈlærɪŋks] *s* (*pl* **larynxes** o **larynges** [ləˈrɪndʒiz]) laringe *f*
lascivious [ləˈsɪvɪ·əs] *adj* lascivo
lasciviousness [ləˈsɪvɪ·əsnɪs] *s* lascivia
laser [ˈlezər] *s* láser *m*
lash [læʃ] *s* (*cord on end of whip*) tralla; (*blow with whip; scolding*) latigazo; (*e.g., of animal's tail*) coletazo; (*of waves*) embate *m*; (*eyelash*) pestaña ‖ *tr* (*to beat, whip*) azotar; (*to bind, tie*) atar; (*to shake, to switch*) agitar, sacudir; (*to attack with words*) increpar, reñir ‖ *intr* lanzarse, pasar rápidamente; **to lash out at** azotar; embestir; vituperar
lashing [ˈlæʃɪŋ] *s* atadura; paliza, zurra; (*severe scolding*) latigazo
lass [læs] *s* muchacha, chica; amada
las·so [ˈlæso] o [læˈsu] *s* (*pl* -**sos** o -**soes**) lazo ‖ *tr* lazar
last [læst] o [lɑst] *adj* (*after all others; the only remaining; utmost, extreme*) último; (*most recent*) pasado; **before last** antepasado; **every last one** todos sin excepción; **last but one** penúltimo ‖ *adv* después de todos; por último; por última vez ‖ *s* última persona; última cosa; fin *m*; (*for holding shoe*) horma; **at last** por fin; **at long last** al fin y al cabo; **stick to your last!** ¡zapatero, a tus zapatos!; **the last of the month** a fines del mes; **to breathe one's last** dar el último suspiro; **to see the last of** no volver a ver; **to the last** hasta el fin ‖ *intr* durar; resistir; dar buen resultado (*p.ej., una prenda de vestir*); seguir así
lasting [ˈlæstɪŋ] *adj* perdurable, duradero
lastly [ˈlæstli] *adv* finalmente, por último
last'-min'ute news *s* noticias de última hora
last name *s* apellido
last night *adv* anoche
last quarter *s* cuarto menguante
last rites *spl* (theol) extremaunción
last sleep *s* último sueño
last straw *s* acabóse *m*, colmo
Last Supper, the la Cena
last will and testament *s* última disposición, última voluntad
last word *s* última palabra; (*latest style*) (coll) última palabra
lat. *abbr* **latitude**
Lat. *abbr* **Latin**
latch [lætʃ] *s* picaporte *m* ‖ *tr* cerrar con picaporte
latch'key' *s* llavín *m*
latch'string' *s* cordón *m* de aldaba; **the latch-string is out** ya sabe Vd. que ésta es su casa

late [let] *adj* (*happening after the usual time*) tardío; (*person*) atrasado; (*hour of the night*) avanzado; (*news*) de última hora; (*party, meeting, etc.*) que termina tarde; (*coming toward the end of a period of time*) de fines de; (*incumbent of an office*) anterior; (*deceased*) difunto, fallecido; **of late** recientemente, últimamente; **to be late** ser tarde; tardar (*p.ej., el tren*); **to be late in** + *ger* tardar en + *inf*; **to grow late** hacerse tarde ‖ *adv* tarde; **late in** (*the week, the month, etc.*) a fines de, hacia fines de; **late in life** a una edad avanzada
late-comer [ˈlet.kʌmər] *s* recién llegado; (*one who arrives late*) rezagado
lateen sail [læˈtin] *s* vela latina
lateen yard *s* entena
lately [ˈletli] *adv* recientemente, últimamente
latent [ˈletənt] *adj* latente
lateral [ˈlætərəl] *adj* lateral
lath [læθ] o [lɑθ] *s* lata, listón; enlistonado ‖ *tr* enlistonar
lathe [leð] *s* torno (*máquina que sirve para labrar madera, hierro, etc. con un movimiento circular*)
lather [ˈlæðər] *s* espuma de jabón; espuma de sudor ‖ *tr* enjabonar; (coll) tundir, zurrar ‖ *intr* espumar
lathery [ˈlæðəri] *adj* espumoso, jabonoso
lathing [ˈlæθɪŋ] *s* enlistonado
Latin [ˈlætɪn] o [ˈlætən] *adj* latino ‖ *s* (*language*) latín *m*; (*person*) latino
Latin America *s* Latinoamérica, América Latina
Latin American *s* latinoamericano
Lat'in-Amer'ican *adj* latinoamericano
latitude [ˈlætɪ.tjud] *s* latitud
latrine [ləˈtrin] *s* letrina
latter [ˈlætər] *adj* (*more recent*) posterior; segundo (*de dos*); **the latter** éste; **the latter part of** fines *mpl* de (*p.ej., el siglo*)
lattice [ˈlætɪs] *s* enrejado ‖ *tr* enrejar
lattice girder *s* viga de celosía
lat'tice·work' *s* enrejado
Latvia [ˈlætvɪ·ə] *s* Letonia, Latvia
laudable [ˈlɔdəbəl] *adj* laudable
laudanum [ˈlɔdənəm] o [ˈlɔdnəm] *s* láudano
laudatory [ˈlɔdə.tori] *adj* laudatorio
laugh [læf] *s* risa ‖ *tr*—**to laugh away** ahogar en risas; **to laugh off** tomar a risa ‖ *intr* reír, reírse
laughable [ˈlæfəbəl] *adj* risible
laughing [ˈlæfɪŋ] *adj* reidor; **to be no laughing matter** no ser cosa de risa ‖ *s* risa, (el) reír
laughing gas *s* gas *m* hilarante
laugh'ing-stock' *s* hazmerreír *m*
laughter [ˈlæftər] *s* risa, risas
launch [lɔntʃ] *s* (*of a ship*) botadura; (*of a rocket*) lanzamiento; (*open motorboat*) lancha automóvil; (nav) lancha ‖ *tr* botar, lanzar (*un buque*); (*to throw; to start, set going, send forth*) lanzar ‖ *intr* lanzarse
launching [ˈlɔntʃɪŋ] *s* lanzamiento
launching pad *s* plataforma de lanzamiento
launching tower *s* torre *f* de lanzamiento

launder ['lɔndər] *tr* lavar y planchar ‖ *intr* resistir el lavado

launderer ['lɔndərər] *s* lavandero

laundress ['lɔndrɪs] *s* lavandera

laun·dry ['lɔndri] *s* (*pl* **-dries**) lavadero; lavado de la ropa; ropa lavada o para lavar

laundry·man ['lɔndrimən] *s* (*pl* **-men** [mən]) lavandero

laun·dry·wom·an *s* (*pl* **-wom·en**) lavandera

laureate ['lɔrɪɪt] *adj* laureado ‖ *s* laureado; poeta laureado

lau·rel ['lɔrəl] *s* laurel *m;* **laurels** laurel (*de la victoria*); **to rest** o **sleep on one's laurels** dormirse sobre sus laureles ‖ *v* (*pret & pp* **-reled** o **-relled**) *ger* **-reling** o **-relling**) *tr* laurear, coronar de laurel

lava ['lɑvə] o ['lævə] *s* lava

lavato·ry ['lævə,tori] *s* (*pl* **-ries**) (*room equipped for washing hands and face*) lavabo; (*bowl with running water*) lavamanos *m; (toilet)* excusado

lavender ['lævəndər] *s* alhucema, espliego, lavanda

lavender water *s* agua de alhucema, agua de lavanda

lavish ['lævɪʃ] *adj* pródigo ‖ *tr* prodigar

law [lɔ] *s* (*of man, of nature, of science*) ley *f; (branch of knowledge concerned with law; body of laws; study of law; profession of law)* derecho; **to enter the law** hacerse abogado; **to go to law** recurrir a la ley; **to lay down the law** dar órdenes terminantes; **to maintain law and order** mantener la paz; **to practice law** ejercer la profesión de abogado; **to read law** estudiar derecho

law-abiding ['lɔ·ə,baɪdɪŋ] *adj* observante de la ley

law'break'er *s* infractor *m* de la ley

law court *s* tribunal *m* de justicia

lawful ['lɔfəl] *adj* legal, legítimo

lawless ['lɔlɪs] *adj* ilegal; (*unbridled*) desenfrenado, licencioso

law'mak'er *s* legislador *m*

lawn [lɔn] *s* césped *m; (fabric)* linón *m*

lawn mower *s* cortacésped *m,* tundidora de césped

law office *s* bufete *m,* despacho de abogado

law of nations *s* derecho de gentes

law of the jungle *s* ley *f* de la selva

law student *s* estudiante *mf* de derecho

law'suit' *s* pleito, proceso, litigio

lawyer ['lɔjər] *s* abogado

lax [læks] *adj* (*in morals, discipline, etc.*) laxo, relajado; vago, indeterminado; (*loose, not tense*) laxo, flojo, suelto

laxative ['læksətɪv] *adj & s* laxante *m*

lay [le] *adj* (*not belonging to clergy*) lego, seglar; (*not having special training*) lego, profano ‖ *s* situación, orientación ‖ *v* (*pret & pp* **laid** [led]) *tr* poner, colocar; dejar en el suelo; tender (*un cable*); echar (*los cimientos; la culpa*); situar (*la acción de un drama*); asentar (*el polvo*); poner (*huevos la gallina; la mesa una criada*); formar (*planes*); hacer (*una apuesta*); **to be laid in** ser (*la escena*) en; **to lay aside** echar a un

lado; ahorrar; **to lay down** afirmar, declarar; dar (*la vida*); deponer (*las armas*); **to lay low** abatir, derribar; obligar a guardar cama; matar; **to lay off** despedir (*a obreros*); (*to mark off the boundaries of*) marcar, trazar; **to lay open** descubrir, revelar; (*to a risk or danger*) exponer; **to lay out** extender, tender; marcar (*una tarea, un trabajo*); gastar (*dinero*); amortajar (*a un difunto*); **to lay up** obligar a guardar cama; ahorrar; (*naut*) desarmar ‖ *intr* poner (*las gallinas*); **to lay about** dar palos de ciego; **to lay for** acechar; **to lay off** (coll) dejar de trabajar; (coll) dejar de molestar; **to lay over** detenerse durante un viaje; **to lay to** (naut) capear

lay brother *s* donado, lego

lay day *s* (naut) día *m* de estadía

layer ['le·ər] *s* (*e.g., of paint*) capa; (*e.g., of bricks*) camada; (*e.g., of coal, rocks*) estrato, capa; (hort) codadura ‖ *tr* (hort) acodar

layer cake *s* bizcocho de varias camadas

layette [le'ɛt] *s* canastilla

lay figure *s* maniquí *m*

laying ['le·ɪŋ] *s* colocación; (*of eggs*) postura; (*of a cable*) tendido

lay·man ['lemən] *s* (*pl* **-men** [mən]) (*person who is not a clergyman*) lego, seglar *m; (person who has no special training)* lego, profano

lay'off' *s* (*dismissal of workmen*) despido; (*period of unemployment*) paro forzoso

lay of the land *s* cariz *m* que van tomando las cosas

lay'out' *s* plan *m; (of tools)* equipo; disposición, organización; (coll) banquete *m,* festín *m*

lay'o'ver *s* parada en un viaje

lay sister *s* donada

laziness ['lezɪnɪs] *s* pereza; lerdera; (coll) galbana

la·zy ['lezi] *adj* (*comp* **-zier;** *super* **-ziest**) perezoso; (coll) galbanoso

la'zy·bones' *s* (coll) perezoso

lb. *abbr* **pound**

l.c. *abbr* **lower case; loco citato** (Lat) in the place cited

Ld. *abbr* **Lord**

lea [li] *s* prado

lead [lɛd] *adj* plomizo ‖ *s* plomo; (*of lead pencil*) mina; (*for sounding depth*) (naut) escandallo; (typ) interlínea, regleta ‖ [lɛd] *v* (*pret & pp* **leaded;** *ger* **leading**) *tr* emplomar; (typ) interlinear, regletear ‖ *s* [lid] *s* (*foremost place*) primacía; (*guidance*) conducta, guía, dirección; indicación; ejemplo; (cards) salida; (*leash*) traílla; (*of a newspaper article*) primer párrafo; (elec) conductor *m;* (elec & mach) avance *m;* (min) filón *m;* (rad) alambre *m* de entrada; (theat) papel *m* principal; (theat) galán *m;* (theat) dama; **to take the lead** tomar la delantera ‖ [lid] *v* (*pret & pp* **led** [lɛd]) *tr* conducir, llevar; liderar; (*to command*) acaudillar, mandar; estar a la cabeza de; dirigir (*p.ej., una orquesta*); llevar (*buena o mala vida*); salir con (*cierto naipe*); (elec & mach) avanzar; **to lead someone to** + *inf* llevar a alguien a + *inf* ‖ *intr* ir delante, enseñar el camino; ser el primero; tener el mando; (cards) salir, ser mano; (mus) llevar la batuta; **to lead up to** conducir a, llevar a; llevar la conversación a

leaded gasoline ['lɛdɪd] *s* gasolina con plomo

leaden ['lɛdən] *adj* (*of lead; like lead*) plomizo; (*heavy as lead*) plúmbeo; (*sluggish*) tardo, indolente; (*with sleep*) cargado; triste, lóbrego

leader ['lidər] *s* caudillo, jefe *m*, líder *m*; (*ringleader*) cabecilla *m*; (*of an orchestra*) director *m*; (*in a dance; among animals*) guión *m*; (*horse*) guía; (*in a newspaper*) artículo de fondo

leader dog *s* perro-lazarillo

leadership ['lidər‚ʃɪp] *s* caudillaje *m*, jefatura; dotes *fpl* de mando

leading ['lidɪŋ] *adj* primero, principal; preeminente; delantero; líder

leading article *s* artículo de fondo

leading edge *s* (aer) borde *m* de ataque

leading lady *s* primera actriz, dama

leading man *s* primer actor *m*, primer galán *m*

leading question *s* pregunta tendenciosa

leading strings *spl* andadores *mpl*

lead-in wire ['lid‚ɪn] *s* (rad) bajada de antena, alambre *m* de entrada

lead pencil [lɛd] *s* lápiz *m*

leaf [lif] *s* (*pl* **leaves** [livz]) hoja; (*of vine*) pámpano; (*hinged leaf of table*) trampilla; **to shake like a leaf** temblar como un azogado; **to turn over a new leaf** hacer libro nuevo ‖ *intr* echar hojas; **to leaf through** hojear, trashojar

leafless ['liflɪs] *adj* deshojado

leaflet ['liflɪt] *s* hoja suelta, hoja volante; (*blade of compound leaf*) hojuela

leaf'stalk' *s* pecíolo

leaf•y ['lifi] *adj* (*comp* **-ier;** *super* **-iest**) hojoso, frondoso

league [lig] *s* (*unit of distance*) legua; (*association, alliance*) liga; (*sports*) división ‖ *tr* asociar ‖ *intr* asociarse, ligarse

League of Nations *s* Sociedad de las Naciones

leak [lik] *s* (*in a roof*) gotera; (*in a ship*) agua, vía de agua; (*of water, gas, electricity, steam*) escape *m*, fuga, salida; agujero, grieta, raja (*por donde se escapa el agua, etc.*); (*of money, news, etc.*) filtración; **to spring a leak** tener un escape; (naut) empezar a hacer agua ‖ *tr* dejar escapar, dejar salir (*el agua, gas, etc.*); dejar filtrar (*una noticia*) ‖ *intr* rezumarse (*un barril*); escaparse, salirse (*el agua, gas, etc.*); (naut) hacer agua; **to leak away** filtrarse (*el dinero*); **to leak out** rezumarse (*una especie*); trascender (*un hecho que estaba oculto*)

leakage ['likɪdʒ] *s* escape *m*, fuga, salida; (com) merma

leak•y ['liki] *adj* (*comp* **-ier;** *super* **-iest**) agujereado, roto; (*roof*) llovedizo; (naut) que hace agua; (coll) indiscreto

lean [lin] *adj* magro, mollar; (*thin*) flaco; (*gasoline mixture*) pobre; **lean years** años de carestía ‖ *v* (*pret & pp* **leaned** [lɛnt] *tr* inclinar, ladear, arrimar ‖ *intr* inclinarse, ladearse, arrimarse; (fig) inclinarse, tender; **to lean against** arrimarse a, estar arrimado a; **to lean back** retreparse, recostarse; **to lean on** apoyarse en; (*with the elbows*) acodarse sobre; **to lean out (of)** asomarse (a); **to lean over backwards** (coll) extremar la imparcialidad; **to lean toward** (fig) inclinarse a, ladearse a

leaning ['linɪŋ] *adj* inclinado ‖ *s* inclinación; (fig) inclinación, tendencia

lean'-to' *s* (*pl* **-tos**) colgadizo

leap [lip] *s* salto; **by leaps and bounds** a pasos agigantados; **leap in the dark** salto a ciegas, salto en vago ‖ *v* (*pret & pp* **leaped** o **leapt** [lɛpt]) *tr* saltar *s* ‖ *intr* saltar; dar un salto (*el corazón de uno*)

leap day *s* día *m* intercalar

leap'frog' *s* fil derecho, juego del salto; **to play leapfrog** jugar a la una la mula

leap year *s* año bisiesto

learn [lʌrn] *v* (*pret & pp* **learned** o **learnt** [lʌrnt]) *tr* aprender; oír decir; saber (*una noticia*) ‖ *intr* aprender

learned ['lʌrnɪd] *adj* docto, erudito; (*e.g., word*) culto

learned journal *s* revista científica

learned society *s* sociedad de eruditos

learned word *s* cultismo, voz culta

learned world *s* mundo de la erudición

learner ['lʌrnər] *s* principiante *mf*, aprendiz *m*, estudiante *mf*

learning ['lʌrnɪŋ] *s* (*act and time devoted*) aprendizaje *m*; (*scholarship*) erudición

lease [lis] *s* arrendamiento, locación; **to give a new lease on life to** renovar completamente; volver a hacer feliz ‖ *tr* arrendar ‖ *intr* arrendarse

lease'hold' *adj* arrendado ‖ *s* arrendamiento; bienes raíces arrendados

leash [liʃ] *s* traílla; **to strain at the leash** sufrir la sujeción con impaciencia ‖ *tr* atraillar

least [list] *adj* (el) menor, mínimo, más pequeño ‖ *adv* menos ‖ *s* (el) menor; (lo) menos; **at least** o **at the least** al menos, a los menos, por lo menos; **not in the least** de ninguna manera

leather ['lɛðər] *s* cuero

leath'er•back' **turtle** *s* laúd *m*

leath'er•neck' *s* (slang) soldado de infantería de marina de los EE.UU.

leathery ['lɛðəri] *adj* correoso, coriáceo

leave [liv] *s* (*permission*) permiso; (*permission to be absent*) licencia; (*farewell*) despedida; **on leave** con licencia; **to give leave to** dar licencia a; **to take leave (of)** despedirse (de) ‖ *v* (*pret & pp* **left** [lɛft]) *tr* (*to let stay; to stop, give up; to disregard*) dejar; (*to go away from*) salir de; (*to bequeath*) legar; **leave it to me!** ¡déjemelo a mí!; **to be left** quedar p.ej., **the letter was left unanswered** la carta quedó sin contestar; **to leave alone** dejar en paz, dejar tranquilo; **to leave no stone unturned** no dejar piedra por mover; **to leave off** dejar; no ponerse (*una prenda de vestir*); **to leave out** omitir; **to leave things as they are** dejarlo como está || *intr* irse, marcharse; eliminarse (Mex); salir (*un avión, un tren, un vapor*)

leaven ['lɛvən] s levadura; (fig) influencia || *tr* leudar; (fig) transformar

leavening ['lɛvənɪŋ] s levadura

leave of absence s licencia

leave'-tak'ing s despedida

leavings ['livɪŋz] spl desperdicios, sobras

Leba·nese [,lɛbə'niz] adj libanés || s (pl -nese) libanés m

Lebanon ['lɛbənən] s el Líbano

Lebanon Mountains spl cordillera del Líbano

lecher ['lɛtʃər] s libertino, lujurioso

lecherous ['lɛtʃərəs] adj lascivo, lujurioso

lechery ['lɛtʃəri] s lascivia, lujuria

lectern ['lɛktərn] s atril m

lecture ['lɛktʃər] s conferencia; (*tedious reprimand*) sermoneo || *tr* instruir por medio de una conferencia; sermonear || *intr* dar una conferencia, dar conferencias

lecturer ['lɛktʃərər] s conferenciante mf

ledge [lɛdʒ] s (*projection in a wall*) retallo; cama de roca; arrecife m

ledger ['lɛdʒər] s (com) libro mayor

ledger line s (mus) línea suplementaria

lee [li] s (*shelter*) (naut) socaire m; (*quarter sheltered from the wind*) sotavento; **lees** heces fpl

leech [litʃ] s sanguijuela; **to stick like a leech** pegarse como ladilla

leek [lik] s puerro

leer [lɪr] s mirada de soslayo, mirada lujuriosa || *intr*—**to leer at** mirar de soslayo, mirar lujuriosamente

leery ['lɪri] adj (coll) receloso, suspicaz

leeward ['liwərd] o ['lu·ərd] adj (naut) de sotavento || *adv* (naut) a sotavento || s (naut) sotavento

Leeward Islands ['liwərd] spl islas de Sotavento

lee'way' s (aer & naut) deriva; (coll) tiempo de sobra, espacio de sobra, dinero de sobra; (coll) libertad de acción

left [lɛft] adj izquierdo || *adv* hacia la izquierda || s (*left hand*) izquierda; (box) zurdazo; (pol) izquierda; **on the left** a la izquierda

left field s (baseball) jardín izquierdo

left'-hand' drive s conducción o dirección a la izquierda

left-handed ['lɛft'hændɪd] adj (*individual*) zurdo; (*clumsy*) desmañado, torpe; insincero; contrario a las agujas del reloj

leftish ['lɛftɪʃ] adj izquierdizante

leftist ['lɛftɪst] adj & s izquierdista mf

left'o'ver adj & s sobrante m; **leftovers** spl sobras

left'-wing' adj izquierdista

left-winger ['lɛft'wɪŋər] s (coll) izquierdista mf

leg. *abbr* legal, legislature

leg [lɛg] s (*of man or animal*) pierna; (*of animal, table, chair, etc.*) pata; (*of boot or stocking*) caña; (*of trousers*) pernera; (*of a cooked fowl*) muslo; (*of a journey*) etapa, trecho; **to be on one's last legs** estar sin recursos; estar en las últimas; **to not have a leg to stand on** (coll) no tener justificación alguna, no tener disculpa alguna; **to pull the leg of** (coll) tomar el pelo a; **to shake a leg** (coll) darse prisa; (*to dance*) (coll) bailar; **to stretch one's legs** estirar las piernas, dar un paseíto

lega·cy ['lɛgəsi] s (pl -cies) legado

legal ['ligəl] adj legal

legali·ty [lɪ'gælti] s (pl -ties) legalidad

legalization [,ligələ'zeʃən] s legalización despenalización

legalize ['ligə,laɪz] *tr* legalizar; despenalizar

legal tender s curso legal

legate ['lɛgɪt] s legado

legatee [,lɛgə'ti] s legatario

legation [lɪ'geʃən] s legación

legend ['lɛdʒənd] s leyenda

legendary ['lɛdʒən,dɛri] adj legendario

legerdemain [,lɛdʒərdɪ'men] s juego de manos, prestidigitación; (*cheating, trickery*) trapacería

legging ['lɛgɪŋ] s polaina

leg·gy ['lɛgi] adj (*comp* -gier; *super* -giest) zanquilargo; de piernas largas y elegantes

leg'horn' s sombrero de paja de Italia || **Leghorn** s Liorna

legible ['lɛdʒɪbəl] adj legible

legion ['lidʒən] s legión

legislate ['lɛdʒɪs,let] *tr* imponer mediante legislación || *intr* legislar

legislation ['lɛdʒɪs'leʃən] s legislación

legislative ['lɛdʒɪs,letɪv] adj legislativo

legislator ['lɛdʒɪs,letər] s legislador m

legislature ['lɛdʒɪs,letʃər] s asamblea legislativa, cuerpo legislativo

legitimacy [lɪ'dʒɪtɪməsi] s legitimidad

legitimate [lɪ'dʒɪtɪmɪt] adj legítimo || [lɪ'dʒɪtɪ,met] *tr* legitimar

legitimate drama s drama serio (*a distinción del cine o el melodrama*)

legitimize [lɪ'dʒɪtɪ,maɪz] *tr* legitimar

leg'work' s (coll) el mucho caminar

leisure ['liʒər] o ['lɛʒər] s desocupación, ocio; **at leisure** desocupado, libre; **at one's leisure** a la comodidad de uno, cuando uno pueda

leisure activities spl recreos pasatiempos

leisure class s gente acomodada

leisure hours spl horas de ocio, ratos perdidos

leisurely ['liʒərli] o ['lɛʒərli] adj lento, pausado || *adv* lentamente, despacio, sin prisa

leisure wear s ropa de recreo, traje m informal

lemon ['lɛmən] s limón m; (slang) artículo de fábrica defectuosa

lemonade [,lɛmə'ned] s limonada

lemon squeezer s exprimidera de limón

lemon verbena s luisa

lend [lɛnd] s (pret & pp **lent** [lɛnt]) tr prestar

lending library s biblioteca de préstamo

length [lɛŋθ] s largura, largo; (of time) extensión; (naut) eslora; **at length** por fin; largamente; **to go to any length** hacer cuanto esté de su parte; **to keep at arm's length** mantener a distancia; mantenerse a distancia

lengthen [ˈlɛŋθən] tr alargar ‖ intr alargarse

length′wise′ adj longitudinal ‖ adv longitudinalmente

length•y [ˈlɛŋθi] adj (comp -ier; super -iest) muy largo, prolongado

leniency [ˈlinɪ•ənsi] s clemencia, indulgencia, lenidad

lenient [ˈlinɪ•ənt] adj clemente, indulgente

lens [lɛnz] s lente m & f; (of the eye) cristalino

Lent [lɛnt] s cuaresma f

Lenten [ˈlɛntən] adj cuaresmal

lentil [ˈlɛntəl] s lenteja

Leo [ˈli•o] s (astr) Leo

leopard [ˈlɛpərd] s leopardo

leotard [ˈli•ə,tɑrd] s leotardo

leper [ˈlɛpər] s leproso

leper house s leprosería

leprosy [ˈlɛprəsi] s lepra

leprous [ˈlɛprəs] adj leproso; (covered with scales) escamoso

Lesbian [ˈlɛzbɪ•ən] adj lesbio ‖ s lesbio; (female homosexual) lesbia

lesbianism [ˈlɛzbɪ•ə,nɪzəm] s lesbianismo

lese majesty [ˈlizˈmædʒɪsti] s delito de lesa majestad

lesion [ˈliʒən] s lesión

less [lɛs] adj menor ‖ adv menos; **less and less** cada vez menos; **less than** menos que; (followed by numeral) menos de; (followed by verb) menos de lo que ‖ s menos m

lessee [lɛsˈi] s arrendatario

lessen [ˈlɛsən] tr disminuir, reducir a menos; quitar importancia a ‖ intr disminuirse, reducirse; amainar (el viento)

lesser [ˈlɛsər] adj menor, más pequeño

lesson [ˈlɛsən] s lección

lessor [ˈlɛsər] s arrendador m

lest [lɛst] conj no sea que, de miedo que

let [lɛt] v (pret & pp **let**; ger **letting**) tr dejar, permitir; alquilar, arrendar; **let + inf que + subj**, p.ej., **let him come in** que entre; **let alone** y mucho menos; **let good enough alone** bueno está lo bueno; **let us + inf** vamos a + inf, p.ej., **let us eat** vamos a comer, comamos; **to let** se alquila; **to let alone** dejar en paz, dejar tranquilo; **to let be** no tocar; dejar en paz; **to let by** dejar pasar; **to let down** dejar bajar; desilusionar, traicionar; dejar plantado; **to let fly** disparar; (fig) disparar, soltar (palabras injuriosas); **to let go** soltar, desasirse de; vender; **to let in** dejar entrar, dejar entrar en; **to let it go at that** no hacer o decir nada más; **to let know** hacer saber; **to let loose** soltar; **to let on** (coll) dar a entender; **to let out** dejar salir; revelar, publicar; dar, soltar (p.ej., más cuerda); dar (un grito);

ensanchar (un vestido que aprieta); dar en arrendamiento; (coll) despedir; **to let through** dejar pasar, dejar pasar por; **to let up** dejar subir; dejar levantarse ‖ intr alquilarse, arrendarse; **to let down** (coll) ir más despacio; **to let go** desasirse; **to let go of** desasirse de; **to let on** (coll) fingir; **to let out** (coll) despedirse, cerrarse (p.ej., la escuela); **to let up** (coll) desistir; (coll) aflojar, amainar

let′down′ s disminución; aflojamiento; desilusión, decepción; humillación

lethal [ˈliθəl] adj letal

lethargic [lɪˈθɑrdʒɪk] adj (affected with lethargy) letárgico; (producing lethargy) letargoso

lethar•gy [ˈlɛθərdʒi] s (pl -gies) letargo

Lett [lɛt] s letón m

letter [ˈlɛtər] s (written message) carta; (of the alphabet) letra; (literal meaning) (fig) letra; **letters** (literature) letras; **to the letter** al pie de la letra ‖ tr estampar o marcar con letras

letter box s buzón m (caja)

letter carrier s cartero

letter drop s buzón m (agujero)

letter file s guardacartas m

let′ter•head′ s membrete m; (paper with printed heading) memorándum m

lettering [ˈlɛtərɪŋ] s inscripción; letras

letter of credit s carta de crédito

letter opener [ˈopənər] s abrecartas m

letter paper s papel m de cartas

let′ter-per′fect adj que tiene bien aprendido su papel; correcto, exacto

let′ter•press′ s impresión tipográfica; texto (a distinción de los grabados)

letter scales spl pesacartas m

Lettish [ˈlɛtɪʃ] adj letón ‖ s letón m

lettuce [ˈlɛtɪs] s lechuga

let′up′ s (coll) calma, interrupción; **without letup** (coll) sin cesar

leucorrhea [,lukəˈri•ə] s leucorrea

leukemia [luˈkimɪ•ə] s leucemia

Levant [lɪˈvænt] s Levante m (países de la parte oriental del Mediterráneo)

Levantine [ˈlɛvən,tin] o [lɪˈvæntin] adj & s levantino

levee [ˈlɛvi] s (embankment to hold back water) ribero; (reception at court) besamanos m

lev•el [ˈlɛvəl] adj raso, llano; nivelado; (coll) sensato, juicioso; **level with** al nivel de, a flor de, a ras de ‖ s (device for determining horizontal position; degree of elevation) nivel m; (flat and even area of land) terreno llano, llanura; (part of a canal between two locks) tramo; **to be on the level** obrar sin engaño, decir la pura verdad; **to find one's level** hallar su propio nivel ‖ v (pret & pp -eled o -elled; ger -eling o -elling) tr nivelar; (to smooth, flatten out) arrasar, allanar; (to bring down) derribar, echar por tierra; apuntar (un arma de fuego); (fig) allanar (dificultades) ‖ intr—**to level off** (aer) enderezarse para aterrizar

level-headed [ˈlɛvəlˈhɛdɪd] *adj* sensato, juicioso

leveling rod *s* (surv) jalón *m* de mira

lever [ˈlivər] o [ˈlɛvər] *s* palanca ‖ *tr* apalancar

leverage [ˈlivərɪdʒ] o [ˈlɛvərɪdʒ] *s* palancada; poder *m* de una palanca; (fig) influencia, poder *m*

leviathan [lɪˈvaɪ•əθən] *s* (Bib & fig) leviatán *m;* buque *m* muy grande

levitation [ˌlɛvɪˈteʃən] *s* levitación

levi•ty [ˈlɛvɪti] *s* (*pl* **-ties**) frivolidad; (*fickleness*) ligereza

lev•y [ˈlɛvi] *s* (*pl* **-ies**) (*of taxes*) exacción, recaudación; dinero recaudado; (mil) leva, enganche *m*, recluta ‖ *v* (*pret & pp* **-ied**) *tr* exigir, recaudar (*impuestos*); (mil) enganchar, reclutar; hacer (*la guerra*)

lewd [lud] *adj* lascivo, lujurioso; obsceno

lewdness [ˈludnɪs] *s* lascivia, lujuria; obscenidad

lexical [ˈlɛksɪkəl] *adj* léxico

lexicographer [ˌlɛksɪˈkɑgrəfər] *s* lexicógrafo

lexicographic(al) [ˌlɛksɪkəˈgræfɪk(əl)] lexicográfico

lexicography [ˌlɛksɪˈkɑgrəfi] *s* lexicografía

lexicology [ˌlɛksɪˈkɑlədʒi] *s* lexicología

lexicon [ˈlɛksɪkən] *s* léxico, lexicón *m*

liabili•ty [ˌlaɪ•əˈbɪlɪti] *s* (*pl* **-ties**) (*e.g., to disease*) propensión; responsabilidad, obligación; desventaja; **liabilities** deudas; (*as detailed in balance sheet*) pasivo

liability insurance *s* seguro de responsabilidad civil

liable [ˈlaɪ•əbəl] *adj* (*e.g., to disease*) propenso, expuesto; responsable; **to be liable to** + *inf* (coll) amenazar + *inf*

liaison [li•əˌzɑn] o [liˈezən] *s* enlace *m*, unión; (*illicit relationship between a man and woman*) amancebamiento, enredo, lío; (mil, nav & phonet) enlace *m*

liaison officer *s* (mil) oficial *m* de enlace

liar [ˈlaɪ•ər] *s* mentiroso

lib. *abbr* librarian, library

libation [laɪˈbeʃən] *s* libación; (*drink*) libación

li•bel [ˈlaɪbəl] *s* calumnia, difamación; levante (CAm, P-R); (*defamatory writing*) libelo ‖ *v* (*pret & pp* **-beled** o **-belled**; *ger* **-beling** o **-belling**) *tr* calumniar, difamar

libelous [ˈlaɪbələs] *adj* calumniador

liberal [ˈlɪbərəl] *adj* (*generous; done or given generously*) liberal; (*open-minded*) tolerante, de amplias miras; (*translation*) libre; (pol) liberal ‖ *s* liberal *mf*

liberali•ty [ˌlɪbəˈrælɪti] *s* (*pl* **-ties**) liberalidad

liberal-minded [ˈlɪbərəlˈmaɪndɪd] *adj* tolerante, de amplias miras

liberate [ˈlɪbəˌret] *tr* libertar; (*to disengage from a combination*) (chem) desprender

liberation [ˌlɪbəˈreʃən] *s* liberación; (chem) desprendimiento

liberation theology *s* teología liberacionista

liberator [ˈlɪbəˌretər] *s* libertador *m*

libertine [ˈlɪbərˌtin] *adj* & *s* libertino

liber•ty [ˈlɪbərti] *s* (*pl* **-ties**) libertad; **to take the liberty to** tomarse la libertad de

liberty-loving [ˈlɪbərtiˈlʌvɪŋ] *adj* amante de la libertad

libidinous [lɪˈbɪdɪnəs] *adj* libidinoso

libido [lɪˈbido] o [lɪˈbaɪdo] *s* líbido *f*, libido *f*

Libra [ˈlibrə] *s* (astr) Libra

librarian [laɪˈbrɛrɪ•ən] *s* bibliotecario

librar•y [ˈlaɪˌbrɛri] o [ˈlaɪbrəri] *s* (*pl* **-ies**) biblioteca

library number *s* signatura

library school *s* escuela de bibliotecarios

library science *s* bibliotecnia; biblioteconomía

libret•to [lɪˈbrɛto] *s* (*pl* **-tos**) (mus) libreto

license [ˈlaɪsəns] *s* licencia ‖ *tr* licenciar

license number *s* número de matrícula

license plate o **tag** *s* chapa de circulación, placa de matrícula

licentious [laɪˈsɛnʃəs] *adj* licencioso, disoluto

lichen [ˈlaɪkən] *s* liquen *m*

lick [lɪk] *s* lamedura; (*place where animals go to lick*) lamedero; (*blow*) (coll) bofetón *m;* (*speed*) (coll) velocidad; (*beating*) (coll) zurra; (*quick cleaning*) (coll) limpión *m;* **to give a lick and a promise to** (coll) hacer rápida y superficialmente ‖ *tr* lamer; lamerse (*p.ej., los dedos*); lamer (*las llamas un tejado*); (*to beat, thrash*) (coll) zurrar; (*to conquer*) (coll) vencer ‖ *intr* lengüetear

licorice [ˈlɪkərɪs] *s* regaliz *m*, orozuz *m;* dulce *m* de regaliz

lid [lɪd] *s* (*of a box, trunk, chest, etc.*) tapa, tapadera; (*of a dish, pot, etc.*) cobertera; (*eyelid*) párpado; (*hat*) (slang) techo

lie [laɪ] *s* mentira; **to catch in a lie** coger en una mentira; **to give the lie to** dar un mentís a ‖ *v* (*pret & pp* **lied;** *ger* **lying**) *tr*—**to lie oneself out of** o **to lie one's way out of** librarse de un aprieto mintiendo ‖ *intr* mentir ‖ *v* (*pret* **lay** [le]; *pp* **lain** [len]; *ger* **lying**) *intr* estar echado; hallarse, estar situado; (*e.g., in the grave*) yacer, estar enterrado; **to lie down** echarse, acostarse

lie detector *s* detector *m* de mentiras

lien [lin] o [ˈli•ən] *s* gravamen *m*, derecho de retención

lieu [lu] *s*—**in lieu of** en lugar de, en vez de

lieutenant [luˈtɛnənt] *s* lugarteniente *m;* (mil) teniente *m;* (nav) teniente de navío

lieutenant colonel *s* (mil) teniente coronel *m*

lieutenant commander *s* (nav) capitán *m* de corbeta

lieutenant governor *s* (U.S.A.) vicegobernador *m* (*de un Estado*)

lieutenant junior grade *s* (nav) alférez *m* de navío

life [laɪf] *adj* (*animate*) vital; (*lifelong*) perpetuo; (*annuity, income*) vitalicio; (*working from nature*) (fa) del natural ‖ *s* (*pl* **lives** [laɪvz]) vida; (*of an insurance policy*) vigencia; **for life** de por vida; **for the life of me** así me maten; **the life and soul of** (*e.g., a party*) la alegría de; **to come to life** volver a la vida; **to depart this life** partir de esta vida; **to run for one's life** salvarse por los pies

life annuity *s* renta vitalicia
life belt *s* cinturón *m* salvavidas
life'boat' *s* bote *m* de salvamento, bote salvavidas; (*for shore-based rescue services*) lancha de auxilio
life buoy *s* boya salvavidas, guindola
life expectancy *s* expectación de vida
life float *s* balsa salvavidas
life'guard' *s* salvavidas *m*, guardavida *m*
life imprisonment *s* cadena perpetua
life insurance *s* seguro sobre la vida
life jacket *s* chaleco salvavidas
lifeless ['laɪflɪs] *adj* muerto, sin vida; (*in a faint*) desmayado, exánime; (*dull, colorless*) deslucido
life'like' *adj* natural, vivo
life line *s* cuerda salvavidas; cuerda de buzo
life'long' *adj* perpetuo, de toda la vida
life of leisure *s* vida de ocio
life of Riley ['raɪli] *s* (slang) vida regalada
life of the party *s* (coll) alegría de la fiesta, alma de la fiesta
life preserver [prɪ'zʌrvər] *s* chaleco salvavidas
lifer ['laɪfər] *s* (slang) presidiario de por vida
life'sav'er *s* salvador *m* (*de vidas*); (*something that saves a person from a predicament*) (coll) tabla de salvación
lifesaving ['laɪf,sevɪŋ] *adj* de salvamento ‖ *s* salvamento (*de vidas*)
life sentence *s* condena a cadena perpetua
life'-size' *adj* de tamaño natural
life span *s* período de vida
life'time' *adj* vitalicio ‖ *s* vida, curso de la vida, jornada
life'work' *s* obra principal de la vida de uno
lift [lɪft] *s* elevación, levantamiento; ayuda (*para levantar una carga*); (aer) sustentación; **to give a lift to** invitar (*a un peatón*) a subir a un coche; llevar en un coche; (fig) reanimar ‖ *tr* elevar, levantar; quitarse (*el sombrero*); (naut) izar (*velas, vergas, etc.*); (fig) reanimar, exaltar; (coll) robar; (coll) plagiar ‖ *intr* elevarse, levantarse; disiparse (*las nubes, las nieblas, la obscuridad, etc.*)
lift bridge *s* puente levadizo
lift'-off' *s* despegue *m* vertical
lift truck *s* carretilla elevadora
ligament ['lɪgəmənt] *s* ligamento
ligature ['lɪgətʃər] *s* (mus & surg) ligadura; (mus & typ) ligado
light [laɪt] *adj* (*in weight*) ligero, leve, liviano; (*having illumination; whitish*) claro; (*hair*) blondo, rubio; (*complexion*) blanco; (*oil*) flúido; (*beer*) claro; (*reading*) poco serio; (*heart*) alegre, despreocupado; (*carrying a small cargo or none at all*) (naut) boyante; **light in the head** (*dizzy*) aturdido, mareado; (*simple, silly*) tonto, necio; **to make light of** no dar importancia a, no tomar en serio ‖ *adv* sin carga; sin equipaje ‖ *s* luz *f*; (*to light a cigarette*) lumbre *f*, fuego; (*to control traffic*) luz, señal *f*; (*window or other opening in a wall*) luz, claro, hueco; (*example, shining figure*) lumbrera; **according to one's lights** según Dios le da

a uno a entender; **against the light** al trasluz; **in this light** desde este punto de vista; **lights** noticias; (*of sheep, etc.*) bofes *mpl*; **to come to light** salir a luz, descubrirse; **to shed** o **throw light on** echar luz sobre; **to strike a light** echar una yesca; encender un fósforo ‖ *v* (*pret & pp* **lighted** o **lit** [lɪt] *tr* (*to furnish with illumination*) alumbrar, iluminar; (*to set afire, ignite*) encender; **to light up** iluminar ‖ *intr* alumbrarse; encenderse; posar (*un ave*); (*from an auto*) bajar; **to light into** (*to attack*) (slang) arremeter contra; (*to scold, berate*) (slang) poner de oro y azul; **to light out** (slang) poner pies en polvorosa; **to light upon** tropezar con, hallar por casualidad
light bulb *s* (elec) bombilla
light complexion *s* tez blanca
lighten ['laɪtən] *tr* (*to make lighter in weight*) aligerar, iluminar; (*to cheer up*) alegrar, regocijar ‖ *intr* (*to become less dark*) iluminarse; (*to give off flashes of lightning*) relampaguear; (fig) iluminarse (*los ojos, la cara de una persona*)
lighter ['laɪtər] *s* (*to light a cigarette*) encendedor *m*; (*flat-bottomed barge*) alijador *m*
light-fingered ['laɪt'fɪŋgərd] *adj* largo de uñas, listo de manos
light-footed ['laɪt'fʊtɪd] *adj* ligero de pies
light-headed ['laɪt'hɛdɪd] *adj* (*dizzy*) aturdido, mareado; (*simple, silly*) tonto, necio, ligero de cascos
light-hearted ['laɪt'hɑrtɪd] *adj* alegre, libre de cuidados
light'house' *s* faro
lighthouse keeper *s* farero
lighting ['laɪtɪŋ] *s* alumbrado, iluminación
lighting engineer *s* iluminador *m*
lighting fixtures *spl* artefactos de alumbrado
lightly ['laɪtli] *adj* ligeramente
light meter *s* exposímetro
lightness ['laɪtnɪs] *s* (*in weight*) ligereza; (*in illumination*) claridad
lightning ['laɪtnɪŋ] *s* relámpagos, relampagueo ‖ *intr* relampaguear
lightning arrester [ə'rɛstər] *s* pararrayos *m*
lightning bug *s* luciérnaga
lightning rod *s* pararrayos *m*
light opera *s* opereta
light'ship' *s* buque *m* fanal, buque faro
light•struck ['laɪt,strʌk] *adj* velado
light'weight' *adj* ligero; de entretiempo, p.ej., **lightweight coat** abrigo de entretiempo
light'-year' *s* año luz
lignite ['lɪgnaɪt] *s* lignito
lignum vitae ['lɪgnəm'vaɪti] *s* guayaco, palo santo
likable ['laɪkəbəl] *adj* simpático
like [laɪk] *adj* parecido, semejante; parecido a, semejante a, p.ej., **this hat is like mine** este sombrero es parecido al mío; (elec) del mismo nombre; **like father like son** de tal palo tal astilla; **to feel like** + *ger* tener ganas de + *inf*; **to look like** parecerse a; parecer que, p.ej., **it looks like rain** parece que va a llover ‖ *adv* como; **like enough**

(coll) probablemente; **nothing like** ni con mucho ‖ *prep* a semejanza de ‖ *conj* (coll) del mismo modo que; (coll) que, p.ej., **it seems like he is right** parece que tiene razón ‖ *s* (*liking*) gusto, preferencia; (*fellow, fellow man*) prójimo, semejante *m;* **and the like** y cosas por el estilo; **to give like for like** pagar en la misma moneda ‖ *tr* gustar de, p.ej., **I like music** gusto de la música; gustar p.ej., **Mary likes peaches** a María. ie gustan los melocotones; **to like best** o **better** preferir; **to like it in** encontrarse a gusto en (*p.ej., el campo*); **to like to** + *inf* gustarle a uno + *inf*, p.ej., **I like to travel** me gusta viajar; gustarle a uno que + *subj*, p.ej., **I should like him to come to see me** me gustaría que él viniese a verme ‖ *intr* querer, p.ej., **as you like** como Vd. quiera; **if you like** si Vd. quiere

likelihood ['laɪklɪ,hʊd] *s* probabilidad

like·ly ['laɪkli] *adj* (*comp* **-lier;** *super* **-liest**) probable; a propósito; prometedor; **to be likely to** + *inf* ser probable que + *ind*, p.ej., **Mary is likely to come to see us tomorrow** es probable que María vendrá a vernos mañana ‖ *adv* probablemente

like-minded ['laɪk'maɪndɪd] *adj* del mismo parecer; de natural semejante

liken ['laɪkən] *tr* asemejar, comparar

likeness ['laɪknɪs] *s* (*picture or image*) retrato; (*similarity*) semejanza, parecido; forma, aspecto, apariencia

like'wise' *adv* igualmente, asimismo; **to do likewise** hacer lo mismo

liking ['laɪkɪŋ] *s* gusto, afición, simpatía; **to be to the liking of** ser del gusto de; **to have a liking for** aficionarse a

lilac ['laɪlək] *adj* de color lila ‖ *s* lilac *m*, lila

Lilliputian [,lɪlɪ'pjuʃən] *adj & s* liliputiense *mf*

lilt [lɪlt] *s* paso airoso, movimiento airoso; canción cadenciosa, música alegre

lil·y ['lɪli] *s* (*pl* **-ies**) (*Lilium candidum*) azucena, lirio blanco; cala, lirio de agua; (*fleur-de-lis, the royal arms of France*) flor *f* de lis; **to gild the lily** ponerle colores al oro

lily of the valley *s* lirio de los valles, muguete *m*

lily pad *s* hoja de nenúfar

lima bean ['laɪmə] *s* judía de la peladilla, frijol *m* de media luna

limb [lɪm] *s* (*arm or leg*) miembro; (*of a tree*) rama; (*of a cross; of the sea*) brazo; **to be out on a limb** (coll) estar en un aprieto

limber ['lɪmbər] *adj* ágil; flexible ‖ *intr*—**to limber up** agilitarse

lim·bo ['lɪmbo] *s* (*pl* **-bos**) lugar *m* de olvido; (theol) limbo

lime [laɪm] *s* (*calcium oxide*) cal *f;* (*Citrus aurantifolia*) limero agrio; (*its fruit*) lima agria; (*linden tree*) tila o tilo

lime'kiln' *s* calera, horno de cal

lime'light' *s* —**to be in the limelight** estar a la vista del público

limerick ['lɪmərɪk] *s* quintilla jocosa

lime'stone' *adj* calizo ‖ *s* caliza, piedra caliza

limit ['lɪmɪt] *s* límite *m;* **to be the limit** (slang) ser el colmo; **to go the limit** no dejar piedra por mover ‖ *tr* limitar

lim'ited-ac'cess high'way *s* carretera de vía libre

limited monarchy *s* monarquía constitucional

limitless ['lɪmɪtlɪs] *adj* ilimitado

limousine ['lɪmə,zin] o [,lɪmə'zin] *s* (aut) limusina

limp [lɪmp] *adj* flojo, débil, flexible ‖ *s* cojera ‖ *intr* cojear

limpid ['lɪmpɪd] *adj* diáfano, cristalino

linage ['laɪnɪdʒ] *s* (typ) número de líneas

linchpin ['lɪntʃ,pɪn] *s* pezonera

linden ['lɪndən] *s* tila, tilo

line [laɪn] *s* línea; (*of people, houses, etc.*) hilera; (*rope, string*) cuerda, cordel *m;* (*wrinkle*) arruga; (*for fishing*) sedal *m;* (*written or printed line; line of goods*) renglón *m;* manera (*de pensar*); (*of the spectrum*) (phys) raya; **all along the line** por todas partes; desde cualquier punto de vista; **in line** alineado; dispuesto, preparado; **in line with** de acuerdo con; **out of line** desalineado; en desacuerdo; **to bring into line** poner de acuerdo; **to draw the line at** no ir más allá de; **to fall in line** conformarse; formar cola; alinearse; **to have a line on** (coll) estar enterado de; **to read between the lines** leer entre líneas; **to stand in line** hacer cola; **to toe the line** obrar como se debe; **to wait in line** hacer cola, esperar vez ‖ *tr* alinear, rayar; arrugar (*p.ej., la cara*); formar hilera a lo largo de (*la acera, la calle*); forrar (*un vestido*); guarnecer (*un freno*) ‖ *intr*—**to line up** ponerse en fila; hacer cola

lineage ['lɪnɪ·ɪdʒ] *s* linaje *m*

lineaments ['lɪnɪ·əmənts] *spl* lineamentos

linear ['lɪnɪ·ər] *adj* lineal

line·man ['laɪnmən] *s* (*pl* **-men** [mən]) (elec) celador *m*, recorredor *m* de la línea; (rr) guardavía *m;* (surv) cadenero

linen ['lɪnən] *adj* de lino ‖ *s* (*fabric*) lienzo, lino; (*yarn*) hilo de lino; ropa blanca, ropa de cama

linen closet *s* armario para la ropa blanca

line of battle *s* línea de batalla

line of fire *s* (mil) línea de tiro

line of least resistance *s* ley *f* del menor esfuerzo; **to follow the line of least resistance** seguir la corriente, no oponer resistencia

line of sight *s* visual *f;* (*of firearm*) línea de mira

liner ['laɪnər] *s* vapor *m* de travesía; (baseball) pelota rasa, lineazo

line'-up' *s* agrupación, formación; (*of prisoners*) rueda

linger ['lɪŋgər] *intr* estarse, quedarse; (*to be tardy*) demorar, tardar; tardar en marcharse; tardar en morirse; pasearse con paso lento; **to linger over** contemplar, reflexionar

lingerie [‚lænʒəˈri] s ropa interior de mujer

lingering [ˈlɪŋgərɪŋ] adj prolongado

lingual [ˈlɪŋgwəl] adj & s lingual f

linguist [ˈlɪŋgwɪst] s (person skilled in several languages) poligloto; (specialist in linguistics) lingüista mf

linguistic [lɪŋˈgwɪstɪk] adj lingüístico ‖ **linguistics** s lingüística

liniment [ˈlɪnɪmənt] s linimento

lining [ˈlaɪnɪŋ] s (of a coat) forro, forrado; (of auto brake) guarnición; (of a furnace) camisa; (of a wall) revestimiento

link [lɪŋk] s eslabón m; **links** campo de golf ‖ tr eslabonar ‖ intr eslabonarse

linkup [ˈlɪŋk‚ʌp] s conexión; (in space) acoplamiento

linnet [ˈlɪnɪt] s pardillo

linoleum [lɪˈnolɪ•əm] s linóleo

linotype [ˈlaɪnə‚taɪp] (trademark) adj linotípico ‖ s (machine) linotipia; (matter produced by machine) linotipo ‖ tr componer con linotipia

linotype operator s linotipista mf

linseed [ˈlɪn‚sid] s linaza

linseed oil s aceite m de linaza

lint [lɪnt] s borra, pelusa, hilaza; (used to dress wounds) hilas

lintel [ˈlɪntəl] s dintel m, umbral m

lion [ˈlaɪ•ən] s león m; (man of strength and courage) (fig) león; (fig) celebridad muy solicitada; **to beard the lion in his den** ir a desafiar la cólera de un jefe; **to put one's head in the lion's mouth** meterse en la boca del lobo

lioness [ˈlaɪ•ənɪs] s leona

lion-hearted [ˈlaɪ•ən‚hɑrtɪd] adj valiente

lionize [ˈlaɪ•ə‚naɪz] tr agasajar

lions' den s (Bib) fosa de los leones

lion's share s (la) parte f del león

lip [lɪp] s labio; (slang) lenguaje m insolente; **to hang on the words of** estar pendiente de las palabras de; **to smack one's lips** chuparse los labios

lip'-read' v (pret & pp -read [‚rɛd]) tr & intr leer en los labios

lip reading s labiolectura

lip service s homenaje m de boca, jarabe m de pico

lip'stick' s lápiz m de labios, lápiz labial

liq. abbr **liquid, liquor**

lique•fy [ˈlɪkwɪ‚faɪ] v (pret & pp -fied) tr liquidar ‖ intr liquidarse

liqueur [lɪˈkʌr] s licor m

liquid [ˈlɪkwɪd] adj líquido ‖ s líquido; (phonet) líquida

liquidate [ˈlɪkwɪ‚det] tr & intr liquidar

liquidity [lɪˈkwɪdɪti] s liquidez f

liquid measure s medida para líquidos

liquor [ˈlɪkər] s licor m

Lisbon [ˈlɪzbən] s Lisboa

lisle [laɪl] s hilo fino de algodón, muy retorcido, sedalina

lisp [lɪsp] s ceceo ‖ intr cecear

lissome [ˈlɪsəm] adj flexible, elástico; ágil, ligero

list [lɪst] s lista; (strip) lista, tira; (border) orilla; (selvage) orillo; (naut) ladeo; **lists** liza; **to enter the lists** entrar en liza; **to have a list** (naut) irse a la banda ‖ tr alistar, listar; registrar ‖ intr (naut) irse a la banda

listen [ˈlɪsən] intr escuchar; obedecer; **to listen in** escuchar a hurtadillas; escuchar por radio; **to listen to** escuchar; obedecer; **to listen to reason** meterse en razón

listener [ˈlɪsənər] s oyente mf; radioescucha mf, radioyente mf

listening post [ˈlɪsənɪŋ] s puesto de escucha

listing [ˈlɪstɪŋ] s (items) rubricación

listless [ˈlɪstlɪs] adj distraído, desatento, indiferente

listlessness [ˈlɪstlɪsnɪs] s apatía; indiferencia

list price s precio de catálogo, precio de tarifa

lit. abbr **liter, literal, literature**

lita•ny [ˈlɪtəni] s (pl -nies) letanía; (repeated series) (fig) letanía

liter [ˈlitər] s litro

literacy [ˈlɪtərəsi] s capacidad de leer y escribir; instrucción

literal [ˈlɪtərəl] adj literal

literary [ˈlɪtə‚rɛri] adj literario; (individual) literato

literate [ˈlɪtərɪt] adj que sabe leer y escribir; (well-read) literato, muy leído; (educated) instruído ‖ s persona que sabe leer y escribir; literato, erudito

literati [‚lɪtəˈrɑti] spl literatos

literature [ˈlɪtərətʃər] s literatura; impresos, escritos de publicidad

lithe [laɪθ] adj flexible, cimbreño

lithia [ˈlɪθ•ə] s (chem) litina

lithium [ˈlɪθɪ•əm] s (chem) litio

lithograph [ˈlɪθə‚græf] s litografía ‖ tr litografiar

lithographer [lɪˈθɑgrəfər] s litógrafo

lithography [lɪˈθɑgrəfi] s litografía

litigant [ˈlɪtɪgənt] adj & s litigante mf

litigate [ˈlɪtɪ‚get] tr & intr litigar

litigation [‚lɪtɪˈgeʃən] s litigación; (lawsuit) litigio

litigious [lɪˈtɪdʒəs] adj litigioso

litmus [ˈlɪtməs] s tornasol m

litmus paper s papel m de tornasol

litter [ˈlɪtər] s desorden m; (scattered rubbish) basura, papelería; (young brought forth at one birth) camada, ventregada; (bedding for animals) cama, paja; (vehicle carried by men or animals) litera; (stretcher) camilla, parihuela ‖ tr esparcir papeles por; esparcir (desechos, papeles, etc.); cubrir (el suelo) con paja ‖ intr parir

lit'ter•bug' s persona que ensucia las calles tirando papeles rotos

littering [ˈlɪtərɪŋ] s—**no littering** se prohibe tirar papeles rotos

little [ˈlɪtəl] adj (in size) pequeño; (in amount) poco, p.ej., **little money** poco dinero; **a little** un poco de, p.ej., **a little money** un poco de dinero ‖ adv poco; **little by little** poco a poco ‖ s poco; **a little** un poco; (somewhat) algo; **to make little of** no dar importancia a, no tomar en serio; **to think little of** tener en poco; no vacilar en

Little Bear *s* Osa menor
Little Dipper *s* Carro menor
little finger *s* dedo auricular, dedo meñique; **to twist around one's little finger** manejar con suma facilidad
lit·tle·neck *s* almeja redonda (*Venus mercenaria*)
little owl *s* mochuelo (*Athene noctua*)
little people *spl* hadas; gente menuda
Little Red Ridinghood ['raɪdɪŋ,hud] *s* Caperucita Roja
little slam *s* (bridge) semibola
liturgic(al) [lɪ'tʌrdʒɪk(əl)] *adj* litúrgico
litur·gy ['lɪtərdʒi] *s* (*pl* **-gies**) liturgia
livable ['lɪvəbəl] *adj* habitable, vividero; llevadero, tolerable
live [laɪv] *adj* (*living; full of life; intense*) vivo; (*coals; flame*) ardiente; de actualidad; (elec) cargado ‖ [lɪv] *tr* llevar (*tal o cual vida*); vivir (*una experiencia, una aventura; un actor sus personajes*); **to live down** borrar (*una falta*); **to live out** vivir (*toda la vida*); salir con vida de (*un desastre, una guerra*) ‖ *intr* vivir; **to live and learn** vivir para ver; **to live and let live** vivir y dejar vivir; **to live high** darse buena vida; **to live on** seguir viviendo; vivir de (*p.ej., carne*); vivir a expensas de; **to live up to** cumplir (*lo prometido*); gastar (*todas sus rentas*)
live coal *s* ascua
livelihood ['laɪvlɪ,hud] *s* vida; **to earn one's livelihood** ganarse la vida
livelong ['lɪv,lɔŋ] o ['lɪv,lɑŋ] *adj*—**all the livelong day** todo el santo día
live·ly ['laɪvli] *adj* (*comp* **-lier;** *super* **-liest**) animado, vivaz; alegre, festivo; (*active, keen*) vivo; (*resilient*) elástico
liven ['laɪvən] *tr* animar, regocijar ‖ *intr* animarse, regocijarse
liver ['lɪvər] *s* vividor *m*; habitante *mf*; (anat) hígado
liver·y ['lɪvəri] *s* (*pl* **-ies**) librea
livery·man ['lɪvərimən] *s* (*pl* **-men** [mən]) dueño de una cochera; mozo de cuadra
livery stable *s* cochera de carruajes de alquiler
live'stock' *adj* ganadero ‖ *s* ganadería
live wire *s* (elec) alambre cargado; (slang) trafagón *m*
livid ['lɪvɪd] *adj* lívido, amoratado; encolerizado; pálido
living ['lɪvɪŋ] *adj* vivo, viviente ‖ *s* vida; **to earn** o **to make a living** ganarse la vida
living quarters *spl* aposentos, habitaciones
living room *s* sala, sala de estar
living wage *s* jornal *m* suficiente para vivir
lizard ['lɪzərd] *s* lagarto; (slang) holgón *m*
load [lod] *s* carga; **loads** (coll) muchísimo; **loads of** (coll) gran cantidad de; **to get a load of** (slang) escuchar, oír; (slang) mirar; **to have a load on** (slang) estar borracho ‖ *tr* cargar ‖ *intr* cargar; cargarse
loaded ['lodɪd] *adj* cargado; (slang) muy borracho; (slang) muy rico
loaded dice *spl* dados cargados
load'stone' *s* piedra imán; (fig) imán *m*

loaf [lof] *s* (*pl* **loaves** [lovz]) pan *m*; (*of sugar*) pilón *m* ‖ *intr* haraganear
loafer ['lofər] *s* haragán *m*
loam [lom] *s* suelo franco; (*mixture used in making molds*) tierra de moldeo
loamy ['lomi] *adj* franco
loan [lon] *s* (*among individuals*) préstamo; (*between companies or governments*) empréstito; **to hit for a loan** (coll) dar un sablazo a ‖ *tr* prestar
loan shark *s* (coll) usurero
loan word *s* préstamo lingüístico
loath [loθ] *adj* poco dispuesto; **nothing loath** de buena gana
loathe [loð] *tr* abominar, detestar
loathing ['loðɪŋ] *s* abominación, detestación
loathsome ['loðsəm] *adj* abominable, asqueroso
lob [lab] *v* (*pret* & *pp* **lobbed;** *ger* **lobbing**) *tr* (tennis) volear desde muy alto
lob·by ['labi] *s* (*pl* **-bies**) salón *m* de entrada, vestíbulo; cabilderos ‖ *v* (*pret* & *pp* **-bied**) *intr* cabildear
lobbying ['labɪ·ɪŋ] *s* cabildeo
lobbyist ['labɪ·ɪst] *s* cabildero
lobster ['labstər] *s* (*spiny lobster*) langosta; (*Homarus*) bogavante *m*
lobster pot *s* langostera
local ['lokəl] *adj* local ‖ *s* tren suburbano; (*branch of a union*) junta local; noticia de interés local
locale [lo'kæl] *s* localidad
locali·ty [lo'kælɪti] *s* (*pl* **-ties**) localidad
localize ['lokə,laɪz] *tr* localizar
local option *s* derecho local de legislar sobre la venta de bebidas alcohólicas
locate [lo'ket] o ['loket] *tr* (*to discover the location of*) localizar; (*to place, to settle*) colocar, establecer; (*to ascribe a particular location to*) situar ‖ *intr* establecerse
location [lo'keʃən] *s* (*place, position*) localidad; (*act of placing*) colocación; (*act of finding*) localización; **on location** (mov) en exteriores
loc. cit. *abbr* **loco citato** (Lat) **in the place cited**
lock [lak] *s* cerradura; (*of a canal*) esclusa; (*of hair*) bucle *m*; (*of a firearm*) llave *f*; **lock, stock, and barrel** (coll) del todo, por completo; **under lock and key** bajo llave ‖ *tr* echar la llave a, cerrar con llave; (*to key*) acuñar; hacer pasar (*un buque*) por la esclusa; abrazar, enlazar; **to lock in** encerrar, poner debajo de llave; **to lock out** cerrar la puerta a, dejar en la calle; dejar sin trabajo (*a los obreros*); **to lock up** encerrar poner debajo de llave; encarcelar
locker ['lakər] *s* armario cerrado con llave
locket ['lakɪt] *s* guardapelo, medallón *m*
lock'jaw' *s* trismo, oclusión forzosa de la boca
lock nut *s* contratuerca
lock'out' *s* huelga patronal
lock'smith' *s* cerrajero
lock step *s* marcha en fila apretada
lock stitch *s* punto encadenado
lock tender *s* esclusero

li
lo

lock'up' _s_ cárcel _f_
lock washer _s_ arandela de seguridad
locomotive [,lokə'motɪv] _s_ locomotora
lo•cus ['lokəs] _s_ (_pl_ **-ci** [saɪ]) sitio, lugar _m;_ lugar (geométrico)
locust ['lokəst] _s_ (ent) langosta (_Pachytylus_); (ent) cigarra (_Cicada_); (bot) acacia falsa
lode [lod] _s_ filón _m_, venero, veta
lode'star' _s_ (astr) estrella polar; estrella de guía; (_guide, direction_) guía, norte _m_
lodge [lɑdʒ] _s_ casa de guarda; casa de campo; (_e.g., of Masons_) logia ‖ _tr_ alojar, hospedar; depositar, colocar; presentar (_una queja_) ‖ alojarse, hospedarse; quedar colgado, ir a parar
lodger ['lɑdʒər] _s_ inquilino (_en parte de una casa_)
lodging ['lɑdʒɪŋ] _s_ alojamiento, hospedaje _m; (without meals)_ cobijo
loft [lɔft] _s_ (_attic_) desván _m_, sobrado; (_hayloft_) henal _m_, pajar _m; (in theater or church)_ galería; (_in a store or office building_) piso alto
loft•y ['lɔfti] _adj_ (_comp_ **-ier;** _super_ **-iest**) (_towering; sublime_) encumbrado; (_haughty_) altivo, orgulloso
log. _abbr_ **logarithm**
log [lɔg] _s_ leño, tronco; (_log chip_) (naut) barquilla; (_chip and line_) (naut) corredera; (aer) diario de vuelo; **to sleep like a log** dormir como un leño ‖ _v_ (_pret & pp_ **logged;** _ger_ **logging**) _tr_ registrar; recorrer (_cierta distancia_)
logarithm ['lɔgə,rɪðəm] _s_ logaritmo
log'book' _s_ (aer) libro de vuelo; (naut) cuaderno de bitácora
log cabin _s_ cabaña de troncos
log chip _s_ (naut) barquilla
log driver _s_ ganchero, maderero
log driving _s_ flotaje _m_
logger ['lɔgər] o ['lɑgər] _s_ leñador _m_, maderero; grúa de troncos; tractor _m_
log'ger•head' _s_ mentecato; **at loggerheads** reñidos
loggia ['lɔdʒə] _s_ (archit) logia
logic ['lɑdʒɪk] _s_ lógica
logical ['lɑdʒɪkəl] _adj_ lógico
logician [lo'dʒɪʃən] _s_ lógico
logistic(al) [lo'dʒɪstɪk(əl)] _adj_ logístico
logistics [lo'dʒɪstɪks] _s_ logística
log'jam' _s_ atasco de rollizos; (fig) estancación
log line _s_ (naut) corredera
log'roll' _intr_ trocar favores políticos
log'wood' _s_ campeche _m_
loin [lɔɪn] _s_ lomo; **to gird up one's loins** apercibirse para la acción
loin'cloth' _s_ taparrabo
loiter ['lɔɪtər] _tr_—**to loiter away** malgastar (_el tiempo_) ‖ _intr_ holgazanear, rezagarse
loiterer ['lɔɪtərər] _s_ holgazán _m_, rezagado
loll [lɑl] _intr_ colgar flojamente; arrellanarse, repantigarse
lollipop ['lɑli,pɑp] _s_ paleta (_dulce en el extremo de un palito_)
Lombard ['lɑmbərd] _adj & s_ lombardo
Lombardy ['lɑmbərdi] _s_ Lombardía

Lombardy poplar _s_ álamo de Italia, chopo lombardo
lon. _abbr_ **longitude**
London ['lʌndən] _adj_ londinense ‖ _s_ Londres _m_
Londoner ['lʌndənər] _s_ londinense _mf_
lone [lon] _adj_ solo, solitario; (_sole, single_) único
loneliness ['lonlinɪs] _s_ soledad
lone•ly ['lonli] _adj_ (_comp_ **-lier;** _super_ **-liest**) soledoso
lonesome ['lonsəm] _adj_ soledoso; (_spot, atmosphere_) solitario
lone wolf _s_ (fig) lobo solitario
long. _abbr_ **longitude**
long [lɔŋ] o [lɑŋ] (_comp_ **longer** ['lɔŋgər] o ['lɑŋgər];** _super_ **longest** ['lɔŋgɪst] o ['lɑŋgɪst]) _adj_ largo; de largo, p.ej., **two meters long** dos metros de largo ‖ _adv_ mucho tiempo, largo tiempo; **as long as** mientras; (_provided_) con tal de que; (_inasmuch as_) puesto que; **before long** dentro de poco; **how long** cuánto tiempo; **long ago** hace mucho tiempo; **long before** mucho antes; **longer** más tiempo; **long since** desde hace mucho tiempo; **no longer** ya no; **so long!** (coll) ¡hasta luego!; **so long as** con tal de que ‖ _intr_ anhelar, suspirar; **to long for** anhelar por, ansiar
long'boat' _s_ (naut) lancha
long'-dis'tance call _s_ (telp) llamada a larga distancia
long-distance flight _s_ (aer) vuelo a distancia
long'-drawn'-out' _adj_ prolongado, pesado
longeron ['lɑndʒərən] _s_ larguero
longevity [lɑn'dʒɛvɪti] _s_ longevidad
long face _s_ (coll) cara triste
long'hair' _adj & s_ intelectual _mf;_ aficionado a la música clásica
long'hand' _s_ escritura a mano
longing ['lɔŋɪŋ] _adj_ anhelante ‖ _s_ anhelo, ansia
longitude ['lɑndʒɪ,tjud] _s_ longitud
long johns _spl_ ropa interior que cubre brazos y piernas
long-lived ['lɔŋ'laɪvd] o (coll) ['lɔŋ'lɪvd] _adj_ longevo, de larga vida
long-playing record ['lɔŋ'ple•ɪŋ] _s_ disco de larga duración; elepé _m_
long primer ['prɪmər] _s_ (typ) entredós _m_
long'-range' _adj_ de largo alcance
longshore•man ['lɔŋ,ʃormən] _s_ (_pl_ **-men** [mən]) _s_ estibador _m_, portuario
long'-stand'ing _adj_ que existe desde hace mucho tiempo
long'-suf'fering _adj_ longánimo, sufrido
long suit _s_ (cards) palo fuerte; (fig) fuerte _m_
long'-term' _adj_ a largo plazo
long'-wind'ed _adj_ difuso, palabrero; discursisto
look [lʊk] _s_ (_appearance_) aspecto, apariencia; (_glance_) mirada; (_search_) búsqueda; **looks** aspecto, apariencia; **to take a look at** echar una mirada a ‖ _tr_ expresar con la mirada; representar (_la edad que uno tiene_); **to look daggers at** apuñalar con la mirada; **to look the part** vestir el cargo; **to look up**

(*e.g., in a dictionary*) buscar; ir a visitar, venir a ver ‖ *intr* mirar; buscar; parecer; **look out!** ¡cuidado!, ¡ojo!; **to look after** mirar por; ocuparse en; **to look at** mirar; **to look back** mirar hacia atrás; (fig) mirar el pasado; **to look down on** mirar por encima del hombro; **to look for** buscar; creer, p.ej., **I look for rain** creo que va á llover; **to look forward** to esperar con placer anticipado; **to look ill** tener mala cara; **to look in on** pasar por la casa o la oficina de; **to look into** averiguar, estudiar; **to look like** parecerse a; amenazar, p.ej., **it looks like rain** amenaza lluvia, parece que va a llover; **to look oneself** parecer el mismo; tener buena cara; **to look out** tener cuidado; mirar por (*p.ej., la ventana*); **to look out for** mirar por, cuidar de; guardarse de; **to look out on** dar a; **to look through** mirar por; hojear (*un libro*); **to look toward** dar a; **to look up to** admirar, mirar con respeto; **to look well** tener buena cara

lookalike ['lʊkə,laɪk] *adj* & *s* doble; parecido
looker-on [,lʊkər'ɑn] *s* (*pl* **lookers-on**) mirón *m*, espectador *m*
looking glass ['lʊkɪŋ] *s* espejo
look'out' *s* vigilancia; (*tower*) atalaya; (*person keeping watch*) vigilante *mf*; (*man watching from lookout tower*) atalaya *m*; (*care, concern*) (coll) cuidado; **to be on the lookout for** estar a la mira de
loom
  [lum] *s* telar *m* ‖ *intr* (*to appear indistinctly*) vislumbrarse; amenazar, parecer inevitable
loon [lun] *s* tonto, bobo; (orn) zambullidor *m*
loon·y ['luni] *adj* (*comp* **-ier;** *super* **-iest**) (slang) loco ‖ *s* (*pl* **-ies**) (slang) loco
loop [lup] *s* lazo; (*in a cable or rope*) vuelta; (*of a river*) meandro; (*of a road*) recoveco; (*for fastening a button*) presilla; (aer) rizo; (elec) circuito cerrado; (*part of vibrating body between two nodes*) vientre *m*; **to loop the loop** (aer) rizar el rizo ‖ *tr* hacer lazos en; enlazar ‖ *intr* formar lazo; (aer) hacer el rizo
loop'hole' *s* (*narrow opening in wall*) lucerna; (*means of evasion*) efugio, escapatoria
loose [lus] *adj* (*dress, tooth, screw, bowels*) flojo; (*fitting, thread, wire, rivet, tongue, bowels*) suelto; (*sleeve*) perdido; (*earth, soil*) desmenuzado; (*unpackaged*) a granel, sin envase; (*unbound papers*) sin encuadernar; (*pulley*) loco; (*translation*) libre; (*life, morals*) relajado; (*woman*) fácil, frágil; **to become loose** desatarse, aflojarse; **to break loose** ponerse en libertad; **to turn loose** soltar ‖ *s*—**to be on the loose** ser libre, estar sin trabas; estar de juerga ‖ *tr* soltar; desatar, desencadenar
loose end *s* cabo suelto; **at loose ends** desarreglado, indeciso
loose'-leaf' notebook *s* cuaderno de hojas cambiables, cuaderno de hojas sueltas
loosen ['lusən] *tr* desatar, aflojar, desapretar; aflojar, laxar (*el vientre*) ‖ *intr* desatarse, aflojarse, desapretarse

looseness ['lusnɪs] *s* flojedad, soltura; (*in morals*) relajamiento
loose'strife' *s* lisimaquia; salicaria
loose-tongued ['lus'tʌŋd] *adj* largo de lengua, ligero de lengua
loot [lut] *s* botín *m*, presa ‖ *tr* saquear, pillar
lop [lɑp] *v* (*pret* & *pp* **lopped;** *ger* **lopping**) *tr* dejar caer (*p.ej., los brazos*); **to lop off** cortar; podar (*un árbol, una vid*) ‖ *intr* colgar
lopsided ['lɑp'saɪdɪd] *adj* ladeado, sesgado; desproporcionado, asimétrico, patituerto
loquacious [lo'kweʃəs] *adj* locuaz
loran ['lɔræn] *s* (naut) lorán *m*
lord [lɔrd] *s* señor *m*; (Brit) lord *m*; (hum & poet) marido ‖ *tr*—**to lord it over** dominar despóticamente, imponerse a
lord·ly ['lɔrdli] *adj* (*comp* **-lier;** *super* **-liest**) señoril; magnífico; despótico, imperioso; altivo, arrogante
Lord's Day, the el domingo
lordship ['lɔrdʃɪp] *s* señoría, excelencia
Lord's Prayer *s* oración dominical, padrenuestro
Lord's Supper *s* sagrada comunión; Cena del Señor
lore [lor] *s* ciencia, saber *m*; ciencia popular, saber *m* popular
lorgnette [lɔrn'jɛt] *s* (*eyeglasses*) impertinentes *mpl*; (*opera glasses*) gemelos de teatro con manija
lor·ry ['lɑri] o ['lɔri] *s* (*pl* **-ries**) carro de plataforma; (Brit) autocamión *m*; (Brit) vagoneta
lose [luz] *v* (*pret* & *pp* **lost** [lɔst] o [lɑst]) *tr* perder; no lograr salvar (*el médico al enfermo*); **to lose heart** desalentarse; **to lose oneself** perderse, errar el camino; ensimismarse ‖ *intr* perder; quedar vencido; retrasar (*el reloj*)
loser ['luzər] *s* perdedor *m*
losing ['luzɪŋ] *adj* perdedor ‖ **losings** *spl* pérdidas, dinero perdido
loss [lɔs] o [lɑs] *s* pérdida; **to be at a loss** estar perplejo, no saber qué hacer; **to be at a loss to** + *inf* no saber como + *inf*; **to sell at a loss** vender con pérdida
loss leader *s* artículo vendido a gran descuento
loss of face *s* pérdida de prestigio, desprestigio
lost [lɔst] o [lɑst] *adj* perdido; (fig) desviado; **lost in thought** ensimismado, abismado; **lost to** perdido para; insensible a
lost'-and-found' department *s* oficina de objetos perdidos
lost sheep *s* oveja perdida
lot [lɑt] *s* (*for building*) solar *m*, parcela; (*fate, destiny*) suerte *f*; (*portion, parcel*) lote *m*; (*of people*) grupo; (coll) gran cantidad, gran número; (coll) sujeto, tipo; **a lot (of)** o **lots of** (coll) mucho, muchos; **to cast** o **to throw in one's lot with** compartir la suerte de; **to draw** o **to cast lots** echar suertes
lotion ['loʃən] *s* loción
lotter·y ['lɑtəri] *s* (*pl* **-ies**) lotería

lo
lo

lotto ['lɑto] *s* lotería

lotus ['lotəs] *s* loto

loud [laud] *adj* alto; (*noisy*) ruidoso; (*voice*) fuerte; (*garish*) chillón, llamativo; (*conspicuously vulgar*) charro, cursi; (*foul-smelling*) apestoso, maloliente ‖ *adv* alto, en voz alta; ruidosamente

loud'mouth' *s* bocaza, bocona, bocón *m*

loudmouthed ['laud,mauθt] o ['laud,mauðd] *adj* vocinglero

loud'speak'er *s* altavoz *m*, parlante *m*, pantalla acústica

lounge [laundʒ] *s* diván *m*, sofá *m* cama; salón *m* de descanso, salón social ‖ *intr* repantigarse a su sabor, recostarse cómodamente; **to lounge around** estar arrimado a la pared, pasearse perezosamente

lounge lizard *s* (slang) holgón *m*

louse [laus] *s* (*pl* **lice** [laɪs]) piojo

lous·y ['lauzi] *adj* (*comp* **-ier;** *super* **-iest**) piojoso; (*mean*) vil, ruin; (*filthy*) asqueroso, sucio; (*bungling*) chapucero; **lousy with** (slang) colmado de (*p.ej., dinero*)

lout [laut] *s* patán *m*

louver ['luvər] *s* (*opening to let in air and light*) lumbrera; tablilla de persiana; (aut) persiana del radiador

lovable ['lʌvəbəl] *adj* amable

love [lʌv] *s* amor *m*; (*tennis*) cero, nada; **not for love nor money** ni a tiros; **to be in love (with)** estar enamorado (de); **to fall in love (with)** enamorarse (de); **to make love to** cortejar, galantear ‖ *tr* amar, querer; gustar de, tener afición a

love affair *s* amores *mpl*, amorío

love'bird' *s* inseparable *m;* **lovebirds** recién casados muy enamorados

love child *s* hijo del amor

love feast *s* ágape *m*

love'-hate' *s* odio-amor *m*

loveless ['lʌvlɪs] *adj* abandonado, sin amor; (*feeling no love*) desamado

lovelorn ['lʌv,lɔrn] *adj* abandonado por su amor, herido de amor

love·ly ['lʌvli] *adj* (*comp* **-lier;** *super* **-liest**) bello, hermoso; adorable, precioso; (coll) encantador, gracioso

love match *s* matrimonio de amor

love potion *s* filtro, filtro de amor

lover ['lʌvər] *s* amante *mf;* (*e.g., of hunting, sports*) aficionado; (*e.g., of work*) amigo

love seat *s* confidente *m*

love'sick' *adj* enfermo de amor

love'sick'ness *s* mal *m* de amor

love song *s* canción de amor

loving ['lʌvɪŋ] *adj* amoroso, afectuoso

lov'ing-kind'ness *s* bondad infinita, misericordia

low [lo] *adj* bajo; (*diet; visibility; opinion*) malo; (*dress, waist*) escotado; (*depressed*) abatido; gravemente enfermo; (*fire*) lento; **to lay low** dejar tendido, derribar; matar; **to lie low** no dejarse ver ‖ *adv* bajo ‖ *s* punto bajo; precio más bajo, precio mínimo; (*moo of cow*) mugido; (aut) primera marcha, primera velocidad; (meteor) depresión ‖ *intr* mugir (*la vaca*)

low'born' *adj* de humilde cuna

low'boy' *s* cómoda baja con patas cortas

low'brow' *adj & s* (slang) ignorante *mf*

low'-cost' housing *s* casas baratas

Low Countries, the los Países Bajos

low'-down' *adj* (coll) bajo, vil, ruin ‖ **low'-down'** *s* (slang) informes *mf* confidenciales, hechos verdaderos

lower ['lo·ər] *adj* bajo, inferior ‖ *tr & intr* bajar ‖ ['lau·ər] *intr* poner mala cara, fruncir el entrecejo; encapotarse (*el cielo*)

lower berth ['lo·ər] *s* litera baja, cama baja

Lower California ['lo·ər] *s* la Baja California

lower case ['lo·ər] *s* (typ) caja baja

lower middle class ['lo·ər] *s* pequeña burguesía

lowermost ['lo·ər,most] *adj* (el) más bajo

low'-fre'quency *adj* de baja frecuencia

low gear *s* primera marcha, primera velocidad

low'-key' *adj* modesto; moderado

lowland ['loland] *s* tierra baja ‖ **Lowlands** *spl* Tierra Baja (*de Escocia*)

low life *s* gentuza

low·ly ['loli] *adj* (*comp* **-lier;** *super* **-liest**) humilde; (*in growth or position*) bajo

Low Mass *s* misa rezada

low-minded ['lo'maɪndɪd] *adj* vil, ruin

low neck *s* escote *m*, escotado

low-necked ['lo'nɛkt] *adj* escotado

low-pitched ['lo'pɪtʃt] *adj* (*sound*) grave; (*roof*) de poco declive

low'-pres'sure *adj* de baja presión

low-priced ['lo'praɪst] *adj* barato, de precio bajo

low shoe *s* zapato inglés

low'-speed' *adj* de baja velocidad

low-spirited ['lo'spɪrɪtɪd] *adj* abatido

low spirits *spl* abatimiento

low tide *s* bajamar *f*, marea baja; (fig) punto más bajo

low visibility *s* (aer) poca visibilidad

low water *s* (*of a river*) nivel mínimo; (*because of drought*) estiaje *m;* bajamar *f*, marea baja

loyal ['lɔɪəl] *adj* leal

loyalist ['lɔɪəlɪst] *s* leal *m*

loyal·ty ['lɔɪəlti] *s* (*pl* **-ties**) lealtad

lozenge ['lazɪndʒ] *s* losange *m;* (*candy cough drop*) pastilla, tableta

LP ['el'pi] *s* (letterword) (trademark) disco de larga duración; elepé *m*

Ltd. *abbr* limited

lubricant ['lubrɪkənt] *adj & s* lubricante *m*

lubricate ['lubrɪ,ket] *tr* lubricar

lubricous ['lubrɪkəs] *adj* (*slippery; lewd*) lúbrico (*resbaladizo; lascivo*); incierto, inconstante

lucerne [lu'sʌrn] *s* mielga

lucid ['lusɪd] *adj* claro, inteligible; (*rational, sane*) lúcido; (*bright, shining*) luciente; (*clear, transparent*) cristalino

Lucifer ['lusɪfər] *s* Lucifer *m*

luck [lʌk] *s* (*good or bad*) suerte *f;* (*good*) suerte, buena suerte; **down on one's luck** de mala suerte, de malas; **in luck** de buena suerte, de buenas; **out of luck** de mala suerte, de malas; **to bring luck** traer buena suerte; **to try one's luck** probar fortuna; **worse luck** desgraciadamente

luckily ['lʌkɪli] *adj* afortunadamente

luckless ['lʌklɪs] *adj* desgraciado

luck·y ['lʌki] *adj* (*comp* **-ier;** *super* **-iest**) afortunado; derecho (CAm); (*supposed to bring luck*) de buen agüero; **to be lucky** tener suerte; quedar bien parado

lucky hit *s* (coll) golpe *m* de fortuna

lucrative ['lukrətɪv] *adj* lucrativo

ludicrous ['ludɪkrəs] *adj* absurdo, ridículo

lug [lʌg] *s* orejeta; (*pull, tug*) estirón *m*, esfuerzo ‖ *v* (*pret & pp* **lugged;** *ger* **lugging**) *tr* tirar con fuerza de; (*to bring up irrelevantly*) (coll) traer a colación

luggage ['lʌgɪdʒ] *s* equipaje *m*

lugubrious [lu'gubrɪ·əs] o [lu'gjubrɪ·əs] *adj* lúgubre

lukewarm ['luk,wɔrm] *adj* tibio, templado

lull [lʌl] *s* momento de calma, momento de silencio; (naut) recalmón *m* ‖ *tr* adormecer; calmar, aquietar; apaciguar

lulla·by ['lʌlə,baɪ] *s* (*pl* **-bies**) arrullo, canción de cuna

lumbago [lʌm'bego] *s* lumbago

lumber ['lʌmbər] *s* madera aserrada, madera aserradiza, madera de sierra; trastos viejos ‖ *intr* andar pesadamente

lum·ber·jack' *s* leñador *m*, hachero

lumber·man ['lʌmbərmən] *s* (*pl* **-men** [mən]) (*dealer*) maderero; (*man who cuts down lumber*) leñador *m*, hachero

lumber room *s* leonera, trastera

lum·ber·yard' *s* maderería, depósito de maderas

luminar·y ['lumɪ,nɛri] *s* (*pl* **-ies**) luminar *m*, lumbrera

luminescent [,lumɪ'nɛsənt] *adj* luminiscente

luminous ['lumɪnəs] *adj* luminoso

lummox ['lʌməks] *s* (coll) jergón *m*

lump [lʌmp] *s* terrón *m*; (*swelling*) chichón *m*, bulto, hinchazón *m*; (*stupid person*) (coll) bodoque *m*; **in the lump** en grueso, por junto; **to get a lump in one's throat** hacérsele a (*uno*) un nudo en la garganta ‖ *tr* juntar, mezclar; (*to make into lumps*) aterronar; (coll) aguantar, tragar (cosa repulsiva)

lumpish ['lʌmpɪʃ] *adj* hobachón, torpe, pesado

lump sum *s* suma global, suma total

lump·y ['lʌmpi] *adj* (*comp* **-ier;** *super* **-iest**) aterronado, borujoso; torpe, pesado; (*sea*) agitado

luna·cy ['lunəsi] *s* (*pl* **-cies**) demencia, locura

lunar ['lunər] *adj* lunar

lunar lander o **lunar module** *s* módulo lunar

lunar landing *s* alunizaje *m*

lunatic ['lunətɪk] *adj & s* lunático, loco

lunatic asylum *s* manicomio

lunatic fringe *s* minoría fanática

lunch [lʌnʃ] *s* (*regular midday meal*) almuerzo; (*light meal*) colación, merienda ‖ *intr* almorzar; merendar, tomar una colación

lunch basket *s* fiambrera

lunch cloth *s* mantelito

luncheon ['lʌntʃən] *s* almuerzo; almuerzo de ceremonia

lunch·room' *s* cantina, merendero

lung [lʌŋ] *s* pulmón *m*

lung cancer *s* cáncer *m* pulmonar

lunge [lʌndʒ] *s* arremetida, embestida; (*with a sword*) estocada ‖ *intr* arremeter, lanzarse; **to lunge at** arremeter contra

lurch [lʌrtʃ] *s* sacudida, tumbo; (naut) bandazo; **to leave in the lurch** dejar en la estacada, dejar colgado ‖ *intr* dar una sacudida, dar un tumbo; (naut) dar un bandazo

lure [lur] *s* (*decoy*) cebo, señuelo; (fig) aliciente *m*, señuelo ‖ *tr* atraer con cebo, atraer con señuelo; (fig) atraer, tentar, seducir; **to lure away** llevarse con señuelo; (*from one's obligations*) desviar

lurid ['lurɪd] *adj* sensacional; (*gruesome*) espeluznante; (*fiery*) ardiente, encendido

lurk [lʌrk] *intr* acechar, andar furtivamente

luscious ['lʌʃəs] *adj* delicioso; lujoso; voluptuoso

lush [lʌʃ] *adj* jugoso, lozano; lujuriante; lujoso

Lusitanian [,lusɪ'tenɪ·ən] *adj & s* lusitano

lust [lʌst] *s* deseo vehemente; (*greed*) codicia; (*strong sexual appetite*) lujuria; entusiasmo ‖ *intr* lujuriar; **to lust after** o **for** codiciar; desear con lujuria

luster ['lʌstər] *s* (*gloss*) lustre *m*; (*of certain fabrics*) viso; (*fame, glory*) (fig) lustre

lus·ter·ware' *s* loza con visos metálicos

lustful ['lʌstfəl] *adj* lujurioso

lustrous ['lʌstrəs] *adj* lustroso

lust·y ['lʌsti] *adj* (*comp* **-ier;** *super* **-iest**) fuerte, robusto, lozano

lute [lut] *s* (mus) laúd *m*; (*substance used to close or seal a joint*) (chem) lodo

Lutheran ['luθərən] *adj & s* luterano

luxuriance [lʌg'ʒurɪ·əns] *s* lozanía

luxuriant [lʌg'ʒurɪ·ənt] *adj* lozano, lujuriante; (*overornamented*) recargado

luxuriate [lʌg'ʒurɪ,et] o [lʌk'ʃurɪ,et] *intr* crecer con lozanía; entregarse al lujo; (*to find keen pleasure*) lozanearse

luxurious [lʌg'ʒurɪ·əs] o [lʌk'ʃurɪ·əs] *adj* lujoso

luxu·ry ['lʌkʃəri] o ['lʌgʒəri] *s* (*pl* **-ries**) lujo

lye [laɪ] *s* lejía

lying ['laɪ·ɪŋ] *adj* mentiroso ‖ *s* el mentir

ly·ing-in' hospital *s* casa de maternidad, clínica de parturientas

lymph [lɪmf] *s* linfa

lymphatic [lɪm'fætɪk] *adj* linfático

lynch [lɪntʃ] *tr* linchar

lynching ['lɪntʃɪŋ] *s* linchamiento

lynch law *s* justicia de la soga

lynx [lɪŋks] *s* lince *m*

lynx-eyed ['lɪŋks,aɪd] *adj* de ojos linces

lyonnaise [,laɪə·'nez] *adj* (culin) a la lionesa

lyre [laɪr] *s* (mus) lira

lyric ['lɪrɪk] *adj* lírico ‖ *s* poema lírico; (*words of a song*) (coll) letra

lyrical ['lɪrɪkəl] *adj* lírico

lyricism ['lɪrɪ,sɪzəm] *s* lirismo

lyricist ['lɪrɪsɪst] *s* (*writer of words for songs*) letrista *mf*; (*poet*) poeta lírico

lo
ly

M

M, m [ɛm] decimotercera letra del alfabeto inglés

m. *abbr* **married, masculine, meter, midnight, mile, minute, month**

ma'am [mæm] o [mɑm] *s* (coll) señora

macadam [məˈkædəm] *s* macadán *m*

macadamize [məˈkædəˌmaɪz] *tr* macadamizar

macaro•ni [ˌmækəˈroni] *s* (*pl* **-nis** o **-nies**) macarrones *mpl*

macaroon [ˌmækəˈrun] *s* mostachón *m*, almendrado

macaw [məˈkɔ] *s* aracanga, guacamayo

mace [mes] *s* maza; (*spice*) macis *m*

mace'bear'er *s* macero

machination [ˌmækɪˈneʃən] *s* maquinación

machine [məˈʃin] *s* máquina; automóvil *m*, coche *m*; (*of a political party*) camarilla ‖ *tr* trabajar a máquina

machine gun *s* ametralladora

ma•chine'-gun' *tr* ametrallar

ma•chine'-made' *adj* hecho a máquina

machiner•y [məˈʃinəri] *s* (*pl* **-ies**) maquinaria

machine screw *s* tornillo para metales

machine shop *s* taller mecánico

machine stenography *s* estenotipia

machine tool *s* máquina-herramienta

machine translation *s* traducción automática

machinist [məˈʃinɪst] *s* (*person who makes machines*) maquinista *mf*; (*person who operates machines*) mecánico; (naut) segundo maquinista; (theat) maquinista *mf*, tramoyista *mf*

mackerel [ˈmækərəl] *s* caballa, escombro

mackerel sky *s* cielo aborregado

mackintosh [ˈmækɪnˌtɑʃ] *s* impermeable *m*

mad [mæd] *adj* (*comp* **madder**; *super* **maddest**) (*angry*) enojado, furioso; (*crazy*) loco; (*foolish*) tonto, necio; (*rabid*) rabioso; **to be mad about** (coll) estar loco por; **to drive mad** volver loco; **to go mad** volverse loco; rabiar (*un perro*)

madam [ˈmædəm] *s* señora

mad'cap' *s* alocado, tarambana *mf*

madden [ˈmædən] *tr* (to make angry) enojar, enfurecer; (*to make insane*) enloquecer

made-to-order [ˈmedtəˈɔrdər] *adj* hecho de encargo; (*clothing*) hecho a la medida

made'-up' *adj* inventado, ficticio; (*artificial*) postizo; (*face*) pintado

mad'house' *s* casa de locos, manicomio

madman [ˈmædˌmæn] *s* (*pl* **-men** [ˌmɛn]) loco

madness [ˈmædnɪs] *s* furia, rabia; locura; (*of a dog*) rabia

Madonna lily [məˈdɑnə] *s* azucena

maelstrom [ˈmelstrəm] *s* remolino

mag. *abbr* **magazine**

magazine [ˈmægəˌzin] o [ˌmægəˈzin] *s* (*periodical*) revista, magazine *m*; (*warehouse*) almacén *m*; (*for cartridges*) cámara; (*for powder*) polvorín *m*; (naut) santabárbara; (phot) almacén *m*

Magellan [məˈdʒɛlən] *s* Magallanes *m*

maggot [ˈmægət] *s* cresa

Magi [ˈmedʒaɪ] *spl* magos de Oriente, Reyes Magos

magic [ˈmædʒɪk] *adj* mágico ‖ *s* magia; ilusionismo, prestidigitación; **as if by magic** como por encanto

magician [məˈdʒɪʃən] *s* (*entertainer with sleight of hand*) ilusionista *mf*, prestidigitador *m*; (*sorcerer*) mágico

magistrate [ˈmædʒɪsˌtret] *s* magistrado

magnanimous [mægˈnænɪməs] *adj* magnánimo

magnesium [mægˈniʃɪ•əm] o [mægˈnizɪ•əm] *s* magnesio

magnet [ˈmægnɪt] *s* imán *m*

magnetic [mægˈnɛtɪk] *adj* magnético; (fig) atrayente, cautivador

magnetic curves *spl* fantasma magnético

magnetic field *s* campo magnético

magnetism [ˈmægnɪˌtɪzəm] *s* magnetismo

magnetize [ˈmægnɪˌtaɪz] *tr* magnetizar, imanar

magne•to [mægˈnito] *s* (*pl* **-tos**) magneto *m* & *f*

magnificent [mægˈnɪfɪsənt] *adj* magnífico

magni•fy [ˈmægnɪˌfaɪ] *v* (*pret* & *pp* **-fied**) *tr* magnificar; exagerar

magnifying glass *s* lupa, vidrio de aumento

magnitude [ˈmægnɪˌtjud] *s* magnitud

magpie [ˈmægˌpaɪ] *s* picaza, urraca

Magyar [ˈmægjɑr] *adj* & *s* magiar *mf*

mahlstick [ˈmɑlˌstɪk] o [ˈmɔlˌstɪk] *s* tiento

mahoga•ny [məˈhɑgəni] *s* (*pl* **-nies**) caoba

Mahomet [məˈhɑmɪt] *s* Mahoma *m*

mahout [məˈhaʊt] *s* naire *m*, cornaca *m*

maid [med] *s* (*female servant*) criada, moza; (*young girl; housemaid*) doncella; gata (Mex); (*spinster*) soltera

maiden [ˈmedən] *s* doncella

maid'en•hair' *s* (bot) cabello de Venus

maid'en•head' *s* himen *m*

maidenhood [ˈmedənˌhʊd] *s* doncellez *f*

maiden lady *s* soltera

maiden name *s* apellido de soltera

maiden voyage *s* primera travesía

maid'-in-wait'ing *s* (*pl* **maids-in-waiting**) dama

maid of honor *s* (*at a wedding*) primera madrina de boda; (*attendant on a princess*) doncella de honor; (*attendant on a queen*) dama de honor

maid'serv'ant *s* criada, doméstica

mail [mel] *s* correspondencia, correo; (*of armor*) malla; **by return mail** a vuelta de correo ‖ *tr* echar al correo

mail'bag' *s* valija

mail'boat' *s* vapor *m* correo

mail'box' *s* buzón *m*

mail car *s* carro correo, coche-correo, ambulancia de correos

mail carrier *s* cartero

mailing list *s* lista de envío

mailing permit *s* porte concertado

mail•man [ˈmelˌmæn] *s* (*pl* **-men** [ˌmɛn]) cartero

mail order *s* pedido postal

mail'-or'der house s casa de ventas por correo

mail'plane' s avión-correo

mail train s tren m correo

maim [mem] tr estropear, mutilar

main [men] adj principal, primero, maestro, mayor ‖ s cañería maestra; **in the main** mayormente

main clause s proposición dominante

main course s plato principal, plato fuerte

main deck s cubierta principal

mainland ['men,lænd] o ['menlənd] s continente m, tierra firme

main line s (rr) tronco, línea principal

mainly ['menli] adv principalmente, en su mayor parte

mainmast ['menməst], o ['men,mæst] o ['men,mɑst] s palo mayor

mainsail ['mensəl] o ['men,sel] s vela mayor

main'spring' s (of watch) muelle m real; (fig) móvil m, origen m

main'stay' s (naut) estay m mayor; (fig) soporte m principal

main'stream' s vía principal

main street s calle f mayor

maintain [men'ten] tr mantener; (to support) (law) manutener

maintenance ['mentɪnəns] s mantenimiento; (upkeep) conservación; gastos de conservación

maître d'hôtel [,metər do'tɛl] s (butler) mayordomo; (headwaiter) jefe m de comedor

maize [mez] s maíz m

majestic [mə'dʒəstɪk] adj majestuoso

majes•ty ['mædʒɪsti] s (pl -ties) majestad

major ['medʒər] adj (greater) mayor; (elder) mayor de edad; (mus) mayor ‖ s (educ) especialización; (mil) comandante m ‖ intr (educ) especializarse

Majorca [mə'dʒɔrkə] s Mallorca

Majorcan [mə'dʒɔrkən] adj & s mallorquín m

major•do•mo [,medʒər'domo] s (pl -mos) mayordomo

major general s general m de división

majori•ty [mə'dʒɔriti] adj mayoritario ‖ s (pl -ties) (being of full age; larger number or part) mayoría; (full age) mayoridad; (mil) comandancia

make [mek] s (brand) marca; (form, build) hechura; carácter m, natural m; **on the make** (slang) buscando provecho ‖ v (pret & pp **made** [med]) tr hacer; cometer (un error); efectuar (un pago); ganar (dinero; una baza); coger (un tren); dar (dinero una empresa); pronunciar (un discurso); cerrar (un circuito); poner (a uno, p.ej., nervioso); ser, p.ej., **she will make a good wife** será una buena esposa; **to make** + inf hacer + inf, p.ej., **she made him study** le hizo estudiar; **to make into** convertir en; **to make known** declarar; dar a conocer; **to make of** pensar de; **to make oneself known** darse a conocer; **to make out** distinguir, vislumbrar; descifrar; escribir (una receta); llenar (un cheque); **to make over** convertir; rehacer (un traje); (com) transfe-

rir; **to make up** preparar, confeccionar; inventar (un cuento); recobrar (el tiempo perdido); (theat) maquillar ‖ intr estar (p.ej., seguro); **to make away with** llevarse; deshacerse de; matar; **to make believe** fingir, p.ej., **he made believe he knew me** fingió conocerme; **to make for** ir hacia; embestir contra; contribuir a (p.ej., mejores relaciones); **to make much of** (coll) hacer fiestas a, mostrar cariño a; **to make off** largarse; **to make off with** llevarse, hacerse con; **to make out** arreglárselas; **to make toward** encaminarse a; **to make up** maquillarse, pintarse; componerse, hacer las paces; **to make up for** suplir; compensar por (una pérdida); **to make up to** (coll) tratar de congraciarse con

make'-be•lieve' adj simulado ‖ s pretexto, simulación, fantasía

maker ['mekər] s constructor m, fabricante mf

make'shift' adj de fortuna, provisional ‖ s expediente m; (person) tapagujeros m

make'-up' s composición, constitución; afeite m, maquillaje m; (typ) imposición

make-up man s (theat) maquillador m

make'weight' s contrapeso; suplente mf

making ['mekɪŋ] s fabricación; material necesario; causa del éxito; **makings** elementos, materiales mpl; (personal qualities necessary for some purpose) madera

malachite ['mælə,kaɪt] s malaquita

maladjustment [,mælə'dʒʌstmənt] s desadaptación

mala•dy ['mælədi] s (pl -dies) dolencia, enfermedad

malaise [mæ'lez] s indisposición, malestar m

malapropism [,mælæ'prɑp,ɪzəm] s despropósito

malapropos [,mælæprə'po] adj impropio ‖ adv fuera de propósito

malaria [mə'lɛrɪ•ə] s malaria, paludismo

Malay ['mele] o [mə'le] adj & s malayo

malcontent ['mælkən,tɛnt] adj & s malcontento

male [mel] adj (sex) masculino; (animal, plant, piece of a device) macho; (human being) varón, p.ej., **male child** hijo varón ‖ s macho; varón m

male chauvinism s machismo

male chauvinist s machista m

malediction [,mælɪ'dɪkʃən] s maldición

malefactor ['mælɪ,fæktər] s malhechor m

male nurse s enfermero

malevolent [mə'lɛvələnt] adj malévolo

malfunction [,mæl'fʌŋkʃən] s malfuncionamiento s intr ir de través; estropearse

malice ['mælɪs] s malicia, malevolencia; **to bear malice** guardar rencor; **with malice prepense** [prɪ'pɛns] (law) con malicia y premeditación

malicious [mə'lɪʃəs] adj malicioso, malévolo

malign [mə'laɪn] adj maligno ‖ tr calumniar

malignant [mə'lɪgnənt] adj maligno

maligni•ty [mə'lɪgnɪti] s (pl -ties) malignidad

m
ma

malinger [mə'lɪŋgər] *intr* hacer la zanguanga, fingirse enfermo

mall [mɔl] o [mæl] *s* alameda, paseo de árboles

mallet ['mælɪt] *s* (*wooden hammer*) mazo; (*for croquet and polo*) mallete *m*

mallow ['mælo] *s* malva

malnutrition [,mælnju'trɪʃən] *s* desnutrición

malodorous [mæl'odərəs] *adj* maloliente

malt [mɔlt] *s* malta *m;* (coll) cerveza

maltreat [mæl'trit] *tr* maltratar

mamma ['mɑmə] o [mə'mɑ] *s* mama o mamá *f*

mammal ['mæməl] *s* mamífero

mammalian [mæ'melɪ•ən] *adj & s* mamífero

mammoth ['mæməθ] *adj* gigantesco, enorme ‖ *s* mamut *m*

man [mæn] *s* (*pl* **-men** [mɛən]) *s* hombre *m;* (*in chess*) pieza; (*in checkers*) pieza, peón *m;* **a man** uno, p.ej., **a man can't get work in this town** uno no puede obtener empleo en este pueblo; **as one man** unánimamente; **man alive!** ¡hombre!; **man and wife** marido y mujer; **to be one's own man** no depender de nadie ‖ *v* (*pret & pp* **manned;** *ger* **manning**) *tr* dotar, tripular (*un buque*); guarnecer (*una fortaleza*); servir (*los cañones*)

man about town *s* bulevardero, hombre *m* de mucho mundo

manacle ['mænəkəl] *s* manilla; **manacles** esposas ‖ *tr* poner esposas a

manage ['mænɪdʒ] *tr* manejar ‖ *intr* arreglárselas; **to manage to** ingeniarse a o para; **to manage to get along** ingeniarse para ir viviendo

manageable ['mænɪdʒəbəl] *adj* manejable

management ['mænɪdʒmənt] *s* manejo, dirección, gerencia; (*group who manage a business*) la empresa, la parte patronal, los patronos

manager ['mænədʒər] *s* director *m*, administrador *m*, gerente *mf;* empresario; (sport) manager *m*

managerial [,mænə'dʒɪrɪ•əl] *adj* empresarial

mandate ['mændet] *s* mandato ‖ *tr* asignar por mandato

mandolin ['mændəlɪn] *s* mandolina

mandrake ['mændrek] *s* mandrágora

mane [men] *s* (*of horse*) crines *fpl;* (*of lion, of person*) melena

maneuver [mə'nuvər] *s* maniobra ‖ *tr* hacer maniobrar ‖ *intr* maniobrar

manful ['mænfəl] *adj* varonil, resuelto

manganese ['mæŋgə,nis] o ['mæŋgə,niz] *s* manganeso

mange [mendʒ] *s* sarna

manger ['mendʒər] *s* pesebre *m*

mangle ['mæŋgəl] *tr* lacerar, aplastar

man•gy ['mendʒi] *adj* (*comp* **-gier;** *super* **-giest**) sarnoso; (*dirty, squalid*) roñoso

man'han'dle *tr* maltratar

man'hole' *s* caja de registro, pozo de inspección

manhood ['mænhʊd] *s* virilidad; hombres *mpl*

man hunt *s* caza al hombre

mania ['menɪ•ə] *s* manía

maniac ['menɪ,æk] *adj & s* maníaco

manic-depressive ['mænɪkdɪ'prɛsɪv] *adj & s* maníaco-depresivo

manicure ['mænɪ,kjʊr] *s* (*care of hands*) manicura; (*person*) manicuro, manicura ‖ *tr* hacer la manicura a (*una persona*); hacer (*las manos y las uñas*)

manicurist ['mænɪ,kjʊrɪst] *s* manicuro, manicura

manifest ['mænɪ,fɛst] *adj* manifiesto ‖ *s* (naut) manifiesto ‖ *tr* manifestar

manifes•to [,mænɪ'fɛsto] *s* (*pl* **-toes**) manifiesto

manifold ['mænɪ,fold] *adj* múltiple, vario; polivalente ‖ *s* copia, ejemplar *m;* (*pipe with outlets or inlets*) colector *m*, múltiple *m*

manikin ['mænɪkɪn] *s* maniquí *m;* (*dwarf*) enano

man in the moon *s* cara o cuerpo de hombre imaginarios en la luna llena

manioc ['mænɪak] *s* cazabe *m*, casabe *m*

manipulate [mə'nɪpjə,let] *tr* manipular

man'kind' *s* el género humano ‖ **man'kind'** *s* el sexo masculino, los hombres

manliness ['mænlɪnɪs] *s* masculinidad, virilidad

man•ly ['mænli] *adj* (*comp* **-lier;** *super* **-liest**) masculino, varonil

manned spaceship [mænd] *s* astronave tripulada

mannequin ['mænɪkɪn] *s* maniquí *m;* (*young woman employed to exhibit clothing*) maniquí *f*

manner ['mænər] *s* manera; **bad manners** malcriadez *f*, malacrianza; **by all manner of means** de todos modos; **in a manner of speaking** como si dijéramos; **in the manner of** a la manera de; **manners** modales *mpl*, crianza; **to the manner born** avezado desde la cuna

mannish ['mænɪʃ] *adj* hombruno

man of letters *s* hombre *m* de letras

man of means *s* hombre *m* de dinero

man of parts *s* hombre *m* de buenas prendas

man of straw *s* hombre *m* de suposición

man of the world *s* hombre *m* de mundo

man-of-war [,mænəv'wɔr] *s* (*pl* **men-of-war** [,mɛnəv'wɔr]) *s* buque *m* de guerra

manor ['mænər] *s* señorío

manor house *s* casa solariega

man overboard *interj* ¡hombre al agua!

man'pow'er *s* número de hombres; personal *m* competente; (mil) fuerzas nacionales

mansard ['mænsɑrd] *s* mansarda; piso de mansarda

man'serv'ant *s* (*pl* **men'serv'ants**) criado

mansion ['mænʃən] *s* hotel *m*, palacio; (*manor house*) casa solariega

man'slaugh'ter *s* (law) homicidio sin premeditación

mantel ['mæntəl] *s* manto (*de chimenea*); (*shelf above it*) mesilla, repisa de chimenea

man'tel•piece' *s* mesilla, repisa de chimenea

mantle ['mæntəl] *s* capa, manto ‖ *tr* vestir con manto; cubrir, tapar; ocultar ‖ *intr* encenderse (*el rostro*)

manual ['mænju‧əl] *adj* manual ‖ *s* (*book*) manual *m*; (mil) ejercicio; (mus) teclado manual

manual training *s* enseñanza de los artes y oficios

manufacture [,mænjə'fæktjər] *s* fabricación; obraje *m*; (*thing manufactured*) manufactura ‖ *tr* fabricar, manufacturar

manufacturer [,mænjə'fæktjərər] *s* fabricante *mf*

manure [mə'njʊr] o [mə'nʊr] *s* estiércol *m* ‖ *tr* estercolar

manuscript ['mænjə,skrɪpt] *adj & s* manuscrito

many ['mɛni] *adj & pron* muchos; **a good many** o **a great many** un buen número; **as many as** tantos como; hasta, p.ej., **as many as twenty** hasta veinte; **how many** cuántos; **many a** muchos, p.ej., **many a person** muchas personas; **many another** muchos otros; **many more** muchos más; **so many** tantos; **too many** demasiados; **twice as many as** dos veces más que

many-sided ['mɛni,saɪdɪd] *adj* multilátero; (*having many interests or capabilities*) polifacético

map [mæp] *s* mapa *m*; (*of a city*) plano ‖ *v* (*pret & pp* **mapped**; *ger* **mapping**) *tr* trazar el mapa de; indicar en el mapa; **to map out** trazar el plan de

maple ['mepəl] *s* arce *m*

maquette [ma'kɛt] *s* maqueta

Mar. *abbr* **March**

mar [mar] *v* (*pret & pp* **marred**; *ger* **marring**) *tr* desfigurar, estropear; frustrar

maraud [mə'rɔd] *tr* saquear ‖ *intr* merodear

marauder [mə'rɔdər] *s* merodeador *m*

marble ['marbəl] *adj* marmóreo ‖ *s* mármol *m*; (*little ball of glass, etc.*) canica; **marbles** (*game*) canica ‖ *tr* crispir, jaspear

march [martʃ] *s* marcha; (*frontier, territory*) marca; **to steal a march on someone** ganarle a uno por la mano ‖ *tr* hacer marchar ‖ *intr* marchar ‖ **March** *s* marzo

marchioness ['marʃənɪs] *s* marquesa

mare [mɛr] *s* (*female horse*) yegua; (*female donkey*) asna

margarine ['mardʒərɪn] *s* margarina

margin ['mardʒɪn] *s* margen *m & f*; (*collateral deposited with a broker*) doble *m*

marginal ['mardʒɪnəl] *adj* marginal

margin release *s* tecla de escape

margin stop *s* fijamárgenes *m*, cierrarrenglón *m*, cortarrenglón *m*

marigold ['mæri,gold] *s* clavelón *m*; (*Calendula*) maravilla, flamenquilla

marihuana o **marijuana** [,mari'hwanə] *s* mariguana; grifa, grifo (Mex)

marina [mə'rinə] *s* dársena

marinate ['mæri,net] *tr* escabechar, marinar

marine [mə'rin] *adj* marino, marítimo ‖ *s* marina; soldado de infantería de marina; **marines** infantería de marina; **tell that to**

the marines (coll) cuénteselo a su abuela, a otro perro con ese hueso

mariner ['mærinər] *s* marino

marionette [,mæri‧ə'nɛt] *s* marioneta, títere *m*

marital status ['mærɪtəl] *s* estado civil

maritime ['mæri,taɪm] *adj* marítimo

marjoram ['mardʒərəm] *s* orégano; mejorana

mark [mark] *s* marca, señal *f*; (*label*) marbete *m*; (*of punctuation*) punto; (*in an examination*) calificación, nota; (*used instead of signature by an illiterate person*) cruz *f*, signo; (*spot, stain*) mancha; (*coin*) marco; (*starting point in a race*) raya; (*target to shoot at*) blanco; **to be beside the mark** no venir al caso; **to hit the mark** dar en el blanco; **to leave one's mark** dejar memoria de sí; **to make one's mark** llegar a ser célebre; **to miss the mark** errar el tiro; **to toe the mark** ponerse en la raya; obedecer rigurosamente ‖ *tr* marcar, señalar; dar nota a (*un alumno*); calificar (*un examen*); advertir, notar; **to mark down** poner por escrito; rebajar el precio de

mark'down' *s* reducción de precio

market ['markɪt] *s* mercado; **to bear the market** jugar a la baja; **to bull the market** jugar al alza; **to play the market** jugar a la bolsa; **to put on the market** lanzar al mercado ‖ *tr* llevar al mercado; vender

marketable ['markɪtəbəl] *adj* comerciable, vendible

market basket *s* cesta para compras

marketing ['markɪtɪŋ] *s* mercología, mercadotecnia

market place *s* plaza del mercado

market price *s* precio corriente

market research *s* investigación mercológica

marking gauge ['markɪŋ] *s* gramil *m*

marks•man ['marksmən] *s* (*pl* -**men** [mən]) tirador *m*; **a good marksman** un buen tiro

marksmanship ['marksmən,ʃɪp] *s* puntería

mark'up' *s* aumento de precio

marl [marl] *s* marga ‖ *tr* margar

marmalade ['marmə,led] *s* mermelada

marmot ['marmət] *s* marmota

maroon [mə'run] *adj & s* marrón *m*, castaño obscuro ‖ *tr* dejar abandonado (*en una isla desierta*)

marquee [ma/r'ki] *s* marquesina

marquess ['markwɪs] *s* marqués *m*

marque•try ['markətri] *s* (*pl* -**tries**) marquetería (*taracea*)

marquis ['markwɪs] *s* marqués *m*

marquise [mar'kiz] *s* marquesa; (*over the entrance to a hotel*) marquesina

marriage ['mærɪdʒ] *s* casamiento, matrimonio; (*married life; intimate union*) maridaje *m*

marriageable ['mærɪdʒəbəl] *adj* casadero

marriage portion *s* dote *m & f*

marriage rate *s* nupcialidad

married life ['mærɪd] *s* vida conyugal

marrow ['mæro] *s* médula, tuétano

mar•ry ['mæri] *v* (*pret & pp* -**ried**) *tr* casar (*el sacerdote o el juez a un hombre y una* *mujer*); (*to take in marriage*) casar con, casarse con; (*to unite intimately*) maridar; **to get married to** casar con, casarse con ‖ *intr* casar, casarse; **to marry into** emparentar con (*p.ej., una familia rica*); **to marry the second time** casarse en segundas nupcias

Mars [mɑrz] *s* Marte *m*

Marseille [mɑr'sɛːj] *s* Marsella

marsh [mɑrʃ] *s* ciénaga, pantano

mar·shal ['mɑrʃəl] *s* cursor *m* de procesiones, maestro de ceremonias; (mil) mariscal *m*; (U.S.A.) oficial *m* de justicia ‖ *v* (*pret & pp* **-shaled** o **-shalled;** *ger* **-shaling** o **-shalling**) *tr* conducir con ceremonia; ordenar, reunir (*los hechos de una argumentación*)

marsh mallow *s* (bot) malvavisco

marsh'mal'low *s* bombón *m* de merengue y gelatina; bombón de malvavisco

marsh·y ['mɑrʃi] *adj* (*comp* **-ier;** *super* **-iest**) pantanoso, palúdico

marten ['mɑrtən] *s* (*pine marten*) marta; (*beech marten*) garduña

martial ['mɑrʃəl] *adj* marcial

martial law *s* ley *f* marcial; **to be under martial law** estar en estado de guerra

Martian ['mɑrʃən] *adj & s* marciano

martin ['mɑrtɪn] *s* (orn) avión *m*

martinet [,mɑrtɪ'nɛt] o ['mɑrtɪ,nɛt] *s* ordenancista *mf*

martyr ['mɑrtər] *s* mártir *mf*

martyrdom ['mɑrtərdəm] *s* martirio

mar·vel ['mɑrvəl] *s* maravilla ‖ *v* (*pret & pp* **-veled** o **-velled;** *ger* **-veling** o **-velling**) *intr* maravillarse; **to marvel at** maravillarse con o de

marvelous ['mɑrvələs] *adj* maravilloso

Marxist ['mɑrksɪst] *adj & s* marxista *mf*

masc. *abbr* **masculine**

mascara [mæs'kærə] *s* tinte *m* para las pestañas; rímel *m*

mascot ['mæskɑt] *s* mascota

masculine ['mæskjəlɪn] *adj & s* masculino

mash [mæʃ] *s* (*crushed mass*) masa; (*to form wort*) masa de cebada ‖ *tr* machacar, majar

mashed potatoes [mæʃt] *spl* puré *m* de patatas

masher ['mæʃər] *s* (*device*) mano *f*; (slang) galanteador atrevido

mask [mæsk] o [mɑsk] *s* máscara; (*of beekeeper*) carilla; (*made from a corpse*) mascarilla; (*person*) máscara *mf*; (phot) desvanecedor *m* ‖ *tr* enmascarar; (phot) desvanecer ‖ *intr* enmascararse

masked ball [mæskt] *s* baile *m* de máscaras

masochism ['mæsə,kɪzəm] *s* masoquismo

masochist ['mæsəkɪst] *s* masoquista *mf*

masochistic [,mæsə'kɪstɪk] *adj* masoquista

mason ['mesən] *s* albañil *m* ‖ **Mason** *s* masón *m*

mason·ry ['mesənri] *s* (*pl* **-ries**) albañilería ‖ **Masonry** *s* masonería

masquerade [,mæskə'red] o [,mɑskə'red] *s* mascarada; (*costume, disguise*) máscara; (*false show*) farsa ‖ *intr* enmascararse; **to masquerade as** disfrazarse de

masquerade ball *s* baile *m* de máscaras

mass [mæs] *s* masa; gran cantidad; (*bulk, heap*) mole *f*; (*something glimpsed, e.g., in the fog*) bulto informe; (*big splotch in a painting*) gran mancha; (*celebration of the Eucharist*) misa; **the masses** las masas ‖ *tr* juntar, reunir; enmasar (*tropas*) ‖ *intr* juntarse, reunirse

massacre ['mæsəkər] *s* carnicería, matanza ‖ *tr* degollar, matar

massage [mə'sɑʒ] *s* masaje *m* ‖ *tr* masar, masajear

masseur [mæ'sœr] *s* masajista *m*

masseuse [mæ'sœz] *s* masajista *f*

massive ['mæsɪv] *adj* macizo; sólido, imponente

mass media *spl* medios *spl* de comunicación

mass meeting *s* mitin *m* popular

mass production *s* fabricación en serie

mast [mæst] o [mɑst] *s* (*for a flag*) palo; (*of a ship*) palo, mástil *m*; (*food for swine*) bellotas, hayucos; **before the mast** como simple marinero

master ['mæstər] o ['mɑstər] *s* (*employer*) dueño, patrón *m*; (*male head of household*) amo; (*man who possesses some special skill; teacher*) maestro; (*commander of merchant vessel*) capitán *m*; (*title of respect for a boy*) señorito ‖ *tr* dominar

master bedroom *s* alcoba de respeto

master blade *s* hoja maestra (*de una ballesta*)

master builder *s* maestro de obras

masterful ['mæstərfəl] o ['mɑstərfəl] *adj* hábil, experto; dominante, imperioso

master key *s* llave maestra

masterly ['mæstərli] o ['mɑstərli] *adj* magistral ‖ *adv* magistralmente

master mechanic *s* maestro mecánico

mas'ter·mind' *s* mente directora ‖ *tr* dirigir con gran acierto

master of ceremonies *s* maestro de ceremonias; (*in a night club, radio, etc.*) animador *m*

mas'ter·piece' *s* obra maestra

master stroke *s* golpe maestro

mas'ter·work' *s* obra maestra

master·y ['mæstəri] o ['mɑstəri] *s* (*pl* **-ies**) (*command, as of a subject*) dominio; ventaja, superioridad; (*skill*) maestría

mast'head' *s* (*of a newspaper*) cabecera editorial; (naut) tope *m*

masticate ['mæstɪ,ket] *tr* masticar

mastiff ['mæstɪf] o ['mɑstɪf] *s* mastín *m*

masturbate ['mæstər,bet] *tr* masturbar ‖ *intr* masturbarse

masturbation [,mæstər'beʃən] *s* masturbación

mat [mæt] *s* (*for floor*) estera; (*for a cup, vase, etc.*) esterilla, ruedo; (*before a door*) felpudo; (*around a picture*) borde *m* de cartón ‖ *v* (*pret & pp* **matted;** *ger* **matting**) *tr* (*to cover with matting*) esterar; enmarañar ‖ *intr* enmarañarse

match [mætʃ] *s* fósforo; (*wick*) mecha; (*counterpart*) compañero; (*suitable partner in marriage*) partido; (*suitably associated* *pair)* pareja; *(game, contest)* match *m*, partido; **to be a match for** poder con, poder vencer; **to meet one's match** hallar la horma de su zapato ‖ *tr* igualar; aparear, emparejar; hacer juego con; **to match someone for the drinks** jugarle a uno las bebidas ‖ *intr* hacer juego, correr parejas; **to match** a juego, p.ej., **a chair to match** una silla a juego

match′box′ *s* fosforera; *(of wax matches)* cerillera

matchless [ˈmætʃlɪs] *adj* incomparable, sin par

matchmaker [ˈmætʃ,mekər] *s* casamentero

mate [met] *s* compañero; *(e.g., of a shoe)* compañero, hermano; *(husband or wife)* cónyuge *mf*; *(to a female)* macho; *(to a male)* hembra; *(in chess)* mate *m*; *(naut)* piloto ‖ *tr* aparear, casar; *(in chess)* dar jaque mate a; **to be well mated** hacer una buena pareja ‖ *intr* aparearse, casarse

material [məˈtɪrɪ•əl] *adj* material; importante ‖ *s* material *m*; *(what a thing is made of)* materia; *(cloth, fabric)* tela, género

materialism [məˈtɪrɪ•ə,lɪzəm] *s* materialismo

materialist [məˈtɪrɪ•əlɪst] *s* materialista *mf*

materialize [məˈtɪrɪ•ə,laɪz] *intr* realizarse

matériel [mə,tɪrɪˈel] *s* material *m*; material de guerra

maternal [məˈtʌrnəl] *adj* materno; *(motherly)* maternal

maternity [məˈtʌrnɪti] *s* maternidad

maternity hospital *s* casa de maternidad

math. *abbr* **mathematics**

mathematical [,mæθɪˈmætɪkəl] *adj* matemático

mathematician [,mæθɪməˈtɪʃən] *s* matemático

mathematics [,mæθɪˈmætɪks] *s* matemática, matemáticas

matinée [,mætɪˈne] *s* matinée *f*, función de tarde

mating season *s* época de celo

matins [ˈmætɪnz] *spl* maitines *mpl*

matriarch [ˈmetrɪ•ɑrk] *s* matriarca

matricidal [,metrɪˈsaɪdəl] *adj* matricida

matricide [ˈmetrɪ,saɪd] *s* *(act)* matricidio; *(person)* matricida *mf*

matriculate [məˈtrɪkjə,let] *tr* matricular ‖ *intr* matricularse

matrimo•ny [ˈmætrɪ,moni] *s* *(pl* -nies) matrimonio

matron [ˈmetrən] *s* matrona

matronly [ˈmetrənli] *adj* matronal

matter [ˈmætər] *s* *(physical substance; pus)* materia; *(subject talked or written about)* asunto; *(reason, ground)* motivo; *(copy for printer)* material *m*; *(printed material)* impresos; **a matter of** cosa de, obra de; **for that matter** en cuanto a eso; **in the matter** al respecto; **no matter** no importa; **no matter when** cuando quiera; **no matter where** dondequiera; **what is the matter?** ¿qué hay?; **what is the matter with you?** ¿qué tiene Vd.? ‖ *intr* importar

matter of course *s* cosa de cajón; **as a matter of course** por rutina

matter of fact *s*—**as a matter of fact** en realidad, en honor a la verdad

matter-of-fact [ˈmætərəv,fækt] *adj* prosaico, práctico, de poca imaginación

mattock [ˈmætək] *s* zapapico

mattress [ˈmætrɪs] *s* colchón *m*

mature [məˈtʃʊr] o [məˈtur] *adj* maduro; *(due)* pagadero, vencido ‖ *tr* madurar ‖ *intr* madurar; *(to become due)* (com) vencer

maturity [məˈtʃʊrɪti] o [məˈturɪti] *s* madurez *f*; (com) vencimiento

maudlin [ˈmɔdlɪn] *adj* lacrimoso, sensiblero; chispo y lloroso

maul [mɔl] *tr* aporrear, maltratar

maulstick [ˈmɔl,stɪk] *s* tiento

maundy [ˈmɔndi] *s* lavatorio

Maundy Thursday *s* Jueves Santo

mausole•um [,mɔsəˈli•əm] *s* *(pl* -ums o -a [ə]) mausoleo

maw [mɔ] *s* *(of fowl)* buche *m*; *(of fish)* vejiga de aire

mawkish [ˈmɔkɪʃ] *adj* *(sickening)* empalagoso; *(sentimental)* sensiblero

max. *abbr* **maximum**

maxim [ˈmæksɪm] *s* máxima

maximum [ˈmæksɪməm] *adj & s* máximo

may *v aux* **it may be** puede ser; **may I come in?** ¿puedo entrar? **may you be happy!** ¡que seas feliz! ‖ **May** *s* mayo

maybe [ˈmebi] o [ˈmebɪ] *adv* acaso, quizá, tal vez

May Day *s* primero de mayo; fiesta del primero de mayo

Mayday [ˈme,de] *interj* *(ships, airplanes)* ¡socorro!

mayhem [ˈmehɛm] o [ˈme•əm] *s* (law) mutilación criminal

mayonnaise [,me•əˈnez] *s* mayonesa

mayor [ˈme•ər] o [mɛr] *s* alcalde *m*

mayoress [ˈme•ərɪs] o [ˈmɛrɪs] *s* alcaldesa

May′pole′ *s* mayo

Maypole dance *s* danza de cintas

May queen *s* maya

maze [mez] *s* laberinto

M.C. *abbr* **Master of Ceremonies, Member of Congress**

mdse. *abbr* **merchandise**

me [mi] *pron pers* me; mí; **to me** me; a mí; **with me** conmigo

meadow [ˈmɛdo] *s* prado, vega

mead′ow•land′ *s* pradera

meager [ˈmigər] *adj* escaso, pobre; flaco, magro

meal [mil] *s* *(regular repast)* comida; *(edible grain coarsely ground)* harina

meal′time′ *s* hora de comer

mean [min] *adj* *(intermediate)* medio; *(low in station or rank)* humilde, obscuro; *(shabby)* andrajoso, raído; *(stingy)* mezquino, tacaño; *(of poor quality)* inferior, pobre; *(small-minded)* vil, ruin, innoble; insignificante; *(vicious, as a horse)* arisco, mal intencionado; (coll) indispuesto; (coll) avergonzado; (coll) de mal genio; **no mean** famoso, excelente ‖ *s* promedio, término medio; **by all means** sí, por cierto, sin falta; **by means of** por medio de; **by no means** de ningún modo, en ningún caso; **means** bienes *mpl* de fortuna; *(agency)* medio, medios; **means to an end** paso para lograr un fin; **to live on one's means** vivar de sus rentas ‖ *v (pret & pp* **meant** [mɛnt]) *tr* significar, querer decir; **to mean to** pensar ‖ *intr*—**to mean well** tener buenas intenciones

meander [mɪ'ændər] *s* meandro ‖ *intr* serpentear; vagar

meaning ['minɪŋ] *s* sentido, significado

meaningful ['minɪŋfəl] *adj* significativo

meaningless ['minɪŋlɪs] *adj* sin sentido

meanness ['minnɪs] *s* bajeza, vileza, ruindad; *(stinginess)* mezquindad; *(lowliness)* humildad, pobreza

mean'time' *adv* entretanto, mientras tanto ‖ *s* medio tiempo; **in the meantime** entretanto, mientras tanto

mean'while' *adv & s* var de **meantime**

measles ['mizəlz] *s* sarampión *m; (German measles)* rubéola

mea•sly ['mizli] *adj (comp* **-slier;** *super* **-sliest)** sarampioso; *(slang)* despreciable, mezquino

measurable ['mɛʒərəbəl] *adj* medible

measure ['mɛʒər] *s* medida; *(step, procedure)* paso, gestión; *(legislative bill)* proyecto de ley; *(of verse)* pie *m;* (mus) compás *m;* **beyond measure** con exceso; **in a measure** hasta cierto punto; **in great measure** en gran parte; *(suit)* **to measure** hecho a la medida; **to take measures** tomar las medidas necesarias; **to take someone's measure** tomarle a uno las medidas ‖ *tr* medir; recorrer *(cierta distancia);* **to measure out** medir; distribuir ‖ *intr* medir

measurement ['mɛʒərmənt] *s (act of measuring)* medición; *(measuring; dimension)* medida

measuring glass *s* vaso graduado

meat [mit] *s* carne *f; (food in general)* manjar *m,* vianda; *(substance, gist)* meollo

meat ball *s* albóndiga

meat grinder *s* picador *m*

meat'hook' *s* garabato de carnicero

meat market *s* carnicería

meat•y ['miti] *adj (comp* **-ier;** *super* **-iest)** carnoso; (fig) jugoso, substancioso

Mecca ['mɛkə] *s* La Meca

mechanic [mɪ'kænɪk] *s* mecánico

mechanical [mɪ'kænɪkəl] *adj* mecánico, maquinal; *(machinelike)* (fig) maquinal

mechanical toy *s* juguete *m* de movimiento

mechanics [mɪ'kænɪks] *ssg* mecánica

mechanism ['mɛkə,nɪzəm] *s* mecanismo

mechanize ['mɛkə,naɪz] *tr* mecanizar

med. *abbr* **medicine, medieval**

medal ['mɛdəl] *s* medalla

medallion [mɪ'dæljən] *s* medallón *m*

meddle ['mɛdəl] *intr* meterse, entremeterse

meddler ['mɛdlər] *s* entremetido

meddlesome ['mɛdəlsəm] *adj* entremetido

media ['midɪ•ə] *abbr* **mass media**

median ['midɪ•ən] *adj* intermedio, medio ‖ *s* punto medio, número medio

median strip *s* faja central o divisoria

mediate ['midɪ,et] *tr* dirimir *(una controversia);* reconciliar ‖ *intr (to be in the middle)* mediar; *(to intervene to settle a dispute)* intervenir

mediation [,midɪ'eʃən] *s* mediación

mediator ['midɪ,etər] *s* mediador *m*

medical ['mɛdɪkəl] *adj* médico

medical student *s* estudiante *mf* de medicina

medicine ['mɛdɪsɪn] *s (science and art)* medicina; *(remedy, treatment)* medicina, medicamento

medicine cabinet *s* armario botiquín

medicine kit *s* botiquín *m*

medicine man *s* curandero, hechicero *(entre los pieles rojas)*

medieval [,midɪ'ivəl] o [,mɛdɪ'ivəl] *adj* medieval

medievalist [,midɪ'ivəlɪst] o [,mɛdɪ'ivəlɪst] *s* medievalista *mf*

mediocre ['midɪ,okər] o [,midɪ'okər] *adj* mediocre

mediocri•ty [,midɪ'ɑkrɪti] *s (pl* **-ties)** mediocridad

meditate ['mɛdɪ,tet] *tr & intr* meditar

Mediterranean [,mɛdɪtə'renɪ•ən] *adj & s* Mediterráneo

medi•um ['midɪ•əm] *adj* intermedio; a medio asar ‖ *s (pl* **-ums** o **-a** [ə]) medio; *(in spiritualism)* medio, médium *m; (publication)* órgano; **through the medium of** por medio de

me'dium-range' *adj* de alcance medio

medlar ['mɛdlər] *s (tree and fruit)* níspero; *(fruit)* níspola

medley ['mɛdli] *s* mescolanza; (mus) popurrí *m*

medul•la [mɪ'dʌlə] *s (pl* **-lae** [li]) médula

meek [mik] *adj* dócil, manso

meekness ['miknɪs] *s* docilidad, mansedumbre

meerschaum ['mɪrʃəm] *s* ['mɪrʃɔm] *s* espuma de mar; pipa de espuma de mar

meet [mit] *adj* conveniente, a propósito ‖ *v (pret & pp* **met** [mɛt]) *tr* encontrar, encontrarse con; *(to make the acquaintance of)* conocer; empalmar con *(otro tren o autobús);* ir a esperar; honrar, pagar *(una letra);* hacer frente a *(gastos);* cumplir *(sus obligaciones);* batirse con; hallar *(la muerte);* tener *(mala suerte);* aparecer a *(la vista)* ‖ *intr* encontrarse; reunirse; conocerse; **till we meet again** hasta la vista; **to meet with** encontrarse con; reunirse con; empalmar *(un tren)* con *(otro tren);* tener *(un accidente)*

meeting ['mitɪŋ] *s* junta, sesión; reunión; encuentro; *(of two rivers or roads)* confluencia; desafío, duelo

meeting of the minds *s* concierto de voluntades

meeting place *s* lugar *m* de reunión

megabucks ['mɛgə,bʌks] *s* (slang) vastas cantidades de dinero

megacycle ['mɛgə,saɪkəl] *s* megaciclo

megaphone ['mɛgə,fon] *s* megáfono

megohm ['mɛg,om] *s* megohmio

melancholia [,mɛlən'kolɪ·ə] s melancolía

melanchol·y ['mɛlən,kɑli] adj melancólico ‖ s (pl -ies) melancolía

melee ['mele] o ['mɛle] s refriega, reyerta

mellow ['mɛlo] adj maduro, jugoso; suave, meloso; melodioso ‖ tr suavizar ‖ intr suavizarse

melodious [mɪ'lodɪ·əs] adj melodioso

melodramatic [,mɛlədrə'mætɪk] adj melodramático

melo·dy ['mɛlədi] s (pl -dies) melodía

melon ['mɛlən] s melón m

melt [mɛlt] tr derretir; fundir (metales); ablandar, aplacar ‖ intr derretirse; fundirse; ablandarse, aplacarse; **to melt away** desvanecerse; **to melt into** convertirse gradualmente en; deshacerse en (lágrimas)

melt'down' s fusión; (atomic reactor) fusión del combustible por fisión no controlada

melting pot s crisol m; (fig) caldero de razas

member ['mɛmbər] s miembro

membership ['mɛmbər,ʃɪp] s asociación; (e.g., of a club) personal m; número de miembros

membrane ['mɛmbren] s membrana

memen·to [mɪ'mɛnto] s (pl -tos o -toes) recordatorio, prenda de recuerdo

mem·o ['mɛmo] s (pl -os) (coll) apunte m, membrete m

memoir ['mɛmwɑr] s memoria; biografía; **memoirs** memorias

memoran·dum [,mɛmə'rændəm] s (pl -dums o -da [də]) apunte m, membrete m

memorial [mɪ'morɪ·əl] adj conmemorativo ‖ s monumento conmemorativo; (petition) memorial m

memorial arch s arco triunfal

Memorial Day s día m de los caídos

memorialize [mɪ'morɪ·ə,laɪz] tr conmemorar

memorize ['mɛmə,raɪz] tr aprender de memoria

memo·ry ['mɛməri] s (pl -ries) memoria; (recall) retentiva; (computer) memoria, almacenaje m o almacenamiento (de datos) **to commit to memory** encomendar a la memoria

menace ['mɛnɪs] s amenaza ‖ tr & intr amenazar

ménage [me'naʒ] s casa, hogar m; economía doméstica

menagerie [mə'næʒəri] o [mə'næd͡ʒəri] s casa de fieras; colección de fieras

mend [mɛnd] s remiendo; **to be on the mend** ir mejorando ‖ tr (to repair) componer, reparar; (to patch) remendar; (to improve) reformar, mejorar ‖ intr mejorar

mendacious [mɛn'deʃəs] adj mendaz

mendicant ['mɛndɪkənt] adj & s mendicante mf

mending ['mɛndɪŋ] s remiendo, zurcido

menfolk ['mɛn,fok] spl hombres mpl

menial ['minɪ·əl] adj bajo, servil ‖ s criado, doméstico

menses ['mɛnsiz] spl menstruo

men's furnishings spl artículos para caballeros

men's room s lavabo para caballeros

menstruate ['mɛnstrʊ,et] intr menstruar

mental case s (coll) paciente mf mental; estrafalario

mental giant s (coll) genio

mental hygiene s higiene f mental

mental illness ['mɛntəl] s enfermedad mental

mental reservation s reserva mental

mental test s prueba de inteligencia

mention ['mɛnʃən] s mención ‖ tr mencionar; **don't mention it** no hay de qué; **not to mention** sin contar

menu ['mɛnju] o ['menju] s menú m, lista de comidas; comida

meow [mɪ'aʊ] s maullido ‖ intr maullar

Mephistophelian [,mɛfɪstə'filɪ·ən] adj mefistofélico

mercantile ['mʌrkən,til] o ['mʌrkən,taɪl] adj mercantil

mercenar·y ['mʌrsə,nɛri] adj mercenario ‖ s (pl -ies) mercenario

merchandise ['mʌrtʃən,daɪz] s mercancías, mercaderías

merchant ['mʌrtʃənt] adj mercante ‖ s mercante m, mercader m

merchant·man ['mʌrtʃəntmən] s (pl -men [mən]) buque m mercante

merchant marine s marina mercante

merchant vessel s buque m mercante

merciful ['mʌrsɪfəl] adj misericordioso

merciless ['mʌrsɪlɪs] adj despiadado, cruel, implacable

mercu·ry ['mʌrkjəri] s (pl -ries) mercurio, azogue m; columna de mercurio

mer·cy ['mʌrsi] s (pl -cies) misericordia; (discretionary power) merced f; **at the mercy of** a merced de

mere [mir] adj mero, puro; nada más que

meretricious [,mɛrɪ'trɪʃəs] adj postizo, de oropel; cursi, llamativo

merge [mʌrdʒ] tr enchufar, fusionar ‖ intr enchufarse, fusionarse; convergir (p.ej., dos caminos); **to merge into** convertirse gradualmente en

merger ['mʌrdʒər] s fusión de empresas

meridian [mə'rɪdɪ·ən] adj meridiano; (el) más elevado ‖ s meridiano; (fig) auge m, apogeo

meringue [mə'ræŋ] s merengue m

meri·no [mə'rino] adj merino ‖ s (pl -nos) merino

merit ['mɛrɪt] s mérito ‖ tr merecer

merlon ['mʌrlən] s almena, merlón m

mermaid ['mʌr,med] s sirena; (girl who swims well) ninfa marina

mer·man ['mʌr,mæn] s (pl -men [,mɛn]) tritón m; (good swimmer) tritón

merriment ['mɛrɪmənt] s alegría, regocijo

mer·ry ['mɛri] adj (comp -rier; super -riest) alegre, regocijado; **to make merry** divertirse

Merry Christmas interj ¡Felices Pascuas!, ¡Felices Navidades!

mer'ry-go-round' s tiovivo, caballito; serie ininterrumpida (de fiestas, tertulias, etc.)

mer'ry·mak'er s fiestero, jaranero

mesh [mɛʃ] s (net, network) red f; (each open space of net) malla; (engagement of gears)

engrane *m;* **meshes** celada, red *f* ‖ *tr*
enredar; (mach) engranar ‖ *intr* enredarse;
(mach) engranar
mess [mɛs] *s (dirty condition)* cochinería;
fregado, lío, embrollo; *(meal for a group
of people; such a group)* rancho; *(refuse)*
bazofia; **to get into a mess** meterse en un
lío; **to make a mess of** ensuciar, echar a
perder ‖ *tr* ensuciar; desarreglar; estropear,
echar a perder ‖ *intr* comer; **to mess
around** (coll) ocuparse en fruslerías
message [ˈmɛsɪdʒ] *s* mensaje *m;* recado
messenger [ˈmɛsəndʒər] *s* mensajero; *(one
who goes on errands)* mandadero; precursor *m*
mess hall *s* sala de rancho; comedor *m* de
militares
Messiah [məˈsaɪ•ə] *s* Mesías *m*
mess kit *s* utensilios de rancho
mess′mate′ *s* comensal *mf,* compañero de
rancho
mess of pottage [ˈpɑtɪdʒ] *s* (Bib) plato de
lentejas; cosa de ningún valor
Messrs. [ˈmɛsərz] *pl* de **Mr.**
mess•y [ˈmɛsi] *adj (comp* **-ier;** *super* **-iest)**
desaliñado, desarreglado; sucio
met. *abbr* **metropolitan**
metal [ˈmɛtəl] *adj* metálico ‖ *s* metal *m;* (fig)
brío, ánimo
metallic [mɪˈtælɪk] *adj* metálico
metallurgy [ˈmɛtə,lʌrdʒi] *s* metalurgia
metal polish *s* limpiametales *m*
met′al•work′ *s* metalistería
metamorpho•sis [,mɛtəˈmɔrfəsɪs] *s (pl* **-ses**
[,siz]) metamorfosis *f*
metaphor [ˈmɛtə,fɔr] *s* metáfora
metaphorical [,mɛtəˈfɑrɪkəl] o [,mɛtə-
ˈfɔrɪkəl] *adj* metafórico
metastasis [məˈtæstəsɪs] *s* metástasis *f*
metathe•sis [mɪˈtæθɪsɪs] *s (pl* **-ses** [,siz])
metátesis *f*
mete [mit] *tr*—**to mete out** repartir
meteor [ˈmitɪ•ər] *s* estrella fugaz; *(atmospheric phenomenon)* meteoro
meteorology [,mitɪ•əˈrɑlədʒi] *s* meteorología
meter [ˈmitər] *s (unit of measurement; verse)*
metro; *(instrument for measuring gas,
electricity, water)* contador *m;* (mus)
compás *m,* tiempo ‖ *tr* medir (con contador)
metering [ˈmitərɪŋ] *s* medición
meter reader *s* lector *m* (del contador)
methane [ˈmɛθen] *s* metano
method [ˈmɛθəd] *s* método
methodic(al) [mɪˈθɑdɪk(əl)] *adj* metódico
Methodist [ˈmɛθədɪst] *adj* & *s* metodista *mf*
Methuselah [mɪˈθuzələ] *s* Matusalén *m;* **to
be as old as Methuselah** vivir más años
que Matusalén
meticulous [mɪˈtɪkjələs] *adj* meticuloso, minucioso
metric(al) [ˈmɛtrɪk(əl)] *adj* métrico
metronome [ˈmɛtrə,nom] *s* metrónomo
metropolis [mɪˈtrɑpəlɪs] *s* metrópoli *f*
metropolitan [,mɛtrəˈpɑlɪtən] *adj* metropolitano ‖ *s* (eccl) metropolitano

mettle [ˈmɛtəl] *s* ánimo, brío; **on one's mettle** dispuesto a hacer todo el esfuerzo posible
mettlesome [ˈmɛtəlsəm] *adj* animoso, brioso
mew [mju] *s* maullido; (orn) gaviota; **mews**
(Brit) caballerizas alrededor de un corral
Mexican [ˈmɛksɪkən] *adj* & *s* mejicano
Mexico [ˈmɛksɪ,ko] *s* Méjico
mezzanine [ˈmɛzə,nin] *s* entresuelo
mfr. *abbr* **manufacturer**
mi. *abbr* **mile**
mica [ˈmaɪkə] *s* mica
microbe [ˈmaɪkrob] *s* microbio
microbiology [,maɪkrəbaɪˈɑlədʒi] *s* microbiología
microcard [ˈmaɪkrə,kɑrd] *s* microficha
microcomputer [ˈmaɪkrəkəm,pjutər] *s* microordenador *m*
microfarad [,maɪkrəˈfæræd] *s* microfaradio
microfilm [ˈmaɪkrə,fɪlm] *s* microfilm *m,*
micropelícula ‖ *tr* microfilmar
microgroove [ˈmaɪkrə,gruv] *adj* microsurco
‖ *s* microsurco; disco microsurco
microphone [ˈmaɪkrə,fon] *s* micrófono
microprocessor [ˈmaɪkrə,prɑsɛsər] *s* microprocesador *m*
microscope [ˈmaɪkrə,skop] *s* microscopio
microscopic [,maɪkrəˈskɑpɪk] *adj* micro-
scópico
microwave [ˈmaɪkrə,wev] *s* microonda
mid [mɪd] *adj* medio, p.ej., **in mid course** a
medio camino
mid′day′ *adj* del mediodía ‖ *s* mediodia *m*
middle [ˈmɪdəl] *adj* medio ‖ *s* centro, medio;
(of the human body) cintura; **about the
middle of** a mediados de; **in the middle of**
en medio de
middle age *s* mediana edad ‖ **Middle Ages**
spl Edad Media
middle class *s* burguesía, clase media
Middle East *s* Oriente Medio
Middle English *s* el inglés medio
middle finger *s* dedo cordial, de en medio o
del corazón
mid′dle•man′ *s (pl* **-men** [,mɛn]) intermediario
middling [ˈmɪdlɪŋ] *adj* mediano, regular,
pasadero ‖ *adv* (coll) medianamente; (coll)
así, así ‖ *s (coarsely ground wheat)* cabezuela; **middlings** artículos de calidad o
precio medianos
mid•dy [ˈmɪdi] *s (pl* **-dies)** (coll) aspirante *m*
de marina; *(child's blouse)* marinera
middy blouse *s* marinera
midget [ˈmɪdʒɪt] *s* enano, liliputiense *mf*
midland [ˈmɪdlənd] *adj* de tierra adentro ‖ *s*
región central
mid′night′ *adj* de medianoche; **to burn the
midnight oil** quemarse las cejas ‖ *s* medianoche *f*
midriff [ˈmɪdrɪf] *s* (anat) diafragma *m;* talle
m
midship•man [ˈmɪd,ʃɪpmən] *s (pl* **-men**
[mən]) guardia marina *m,* aspirante *m* de
marina
midst [mɪdst] *s* centro; **in the midst of** en
medio de; en lo más recio de

mid'stream' *s*—**in midstream** en pleno río
mid'sum'mer *s* pleno verano
mid'way' *adj* situado a mitad del camino ‖ *adv* a mitad del camino ‖ *s* mitad del camino; (*of a fair or exposition*) avenida central
mid'week' *s* mediados de la semana
mid'wife' *s* (*pl* **-wives**) partera, comadrona
mid'win'ter *s* pleno invierno
mid'year' *adj* de mediados del año ‖ *s* mediados del año; **midyears** (coll) examen *m* de mediados del año escolar
mien [min] *s* aspecto, semblante *m*, porte *m*
miff [mɪf] *s* (coll) desavenencia ‖ *tr* (coll) ofender
might [maɪt] *s* fuerza, poder *m;* **with might and main** con todas sus fuerzas, a más no poder ‖ *v aux* se emplea para formar el modo potencial, p.ej., **she might not come** es posible que no venga
might•y [ˈmaɪti] *adj* (*comp* **-ier;** *super* **-iȩst**) potente, poderoso; (*of great size*) grandísimo ‖ *adv* (coll) muy
migrant worker [ˈmaɪɡrənt] *s* bracero migratorio
migrate [ˈmaɪɡret] *intr* emigrar
migratory [ˈmaɪɡrəˌtori] *adj* migratorio
mil *abbr* **military, militia**
milch [mɪltʃ] *adj* lechero
mild [maɪld] *adj* blando, suave; dócil, manso; leve, ligero; (*climate*) templado
mildew [ˈmɪlˌdju] *s* (*mold*) moho; (*plant disease*) mildeu *m*
mile [maɪl] *s* milla inglesa
mileage [ˈmaɪlɪdʒ] *s* recorrido en millas
mileage ticket *s* billete contado por millas, semejante al billete kilométrico
mile'post' *s* poste miliario
mile'stone' *s* piedra miliaria; **to be a milestone** hacer época
milieu [mɪlˈju] *s* ambiente *m*, medio
militancy [ˈmɪlɪtənsi] *s* belicosidad
militant [ˈmɪlɪtənt] *adj* militante, belicoso
militarism [ˈmɪlɪtəˌrɪzəm] *s* militarismo
militarist [ˈmɪlɪtərɪst] *adj & s* militarista *mf*
militarize [ˈmɪlɪtəˌraɪz] *tr* militarizar
military [ˈmɪlɪˌtɛri] *adj* militar ‖ *s* (los) militares
Military Academy *s* (U.S.A.) Academia General Militar
military police *s* policía militar
militate [ˈmɪlɪˌtet] *intr* militar
militia [mɪˈlɪʃə] *s* milicia
militia•man [mɪˈlɪʃəmən] *s* (*pl* **-men** [mən]) miliciano
milk [mɪlk] *adj* lechero, de leche ‖ *s* leche *f* ‖ *tr* ordeñar; chupar (*los bienes de uno*); abusar de, explotar ‖ *intr* dar leche
milk can *s* lechera
milk diet *s* régimen lácteo
milking [ˈmɪlkɪŋ] *s* ordeño
milk'maid' *s* lechera
milk•man [ˈmɪlkˌmæn] *s* (*pl* **-men** [ˌmɛn]) lechero
milk of human kindness *s* compasión, humanidad
milk pail *s* ordeñadero

milk shake *s* batido de leche
milk'sop' *s* calzonazos *m*, marica *m*
milk'weed' *s* algodoncillo, vencetósigo
milk•y [ˈmɪlki] *adj* (*comp* **-ier;** *super* **-iest**) lechoso, lácteo
Milky Way *s* Vía Láctea
mill [mɪl] *s* (*for grinding grain*) molino; (*for making fabrics*) hilandería; (*for cutting wood*) aserradero; (*for refining sugar*) ingenio; (*for producing steel*) fábrica; (*to grind coffee*) molinillo; (*part of a dollar*) milésima; **to put through the mill** (coll) poner a prueba, someter a un entrenamiento riguroso ‖ *tr* moler (*granos*); acordonar, cerrillar (*monedas*); laminar (*el acero*); triturar (*mena*); (*with a milling cutter*) fresar; batir (*chocolate*) ‖ *intr*—**to mill about** o **around** arremolinarse
mill end *s* retal *m* de hilandería
millennial [mɪˈlɛni•əl] *adj* milenario
millenni•um [mɪˈlɛni•əm] *s* (*pl* **-ums** o **-a** [ə]) milenario, milenio
miller [ˈmɪlər] *s* molinero; (ent) polilla blanca
millet [ˈmɪlɪt] *s* mijo, millo
milliampere [ˌmɪlɪˈæmpɪr] *s* miliamperio
milligram [ˈmɪlɪˌɡræm] *s* miligramo
millimeter [ˈmɪlɪˌmitər] *s* milímetro
milliner [ˈmɪlɪnər] *s* modista *mf* de sombreros
millinery [ˈmɪlɪˌnɛri] o [ˈmɪlɪnəri] *s* artículos para sombreros de señora; confección de sombreros de señora; venta de sombreros de señora
millinery shop *s* sombrerería
milling [ˈmɪlɪŋ] *s* (*of grain*) molienda; (*of coins*) acordonamiento, cordoncillo; fresado
milling machine *s* fresadora
million [ˈmɪljən] *adj* millón de, millones de ‖ *s* millón *m*
millionaire [ˌmɪljənˈɛr] *s* millonario
millionth [ˈmɪljənθ] *adj & s* millonésimo
millivolt [ˈmɪlɪˌvolt] *s* vmilivoltio
mill'pond' *s* represa de molino
mill'race' *s* caz *m*
mill'stone' *s* muela de molino; (fig) carga pesada
mill wheel *s* rueda de molino
mill'work' *s* carpintería de taller
mime [maɪm] *s* mimo ‖ *tr* remedar
Mimeograph [ˈmɪm•əˌɡræf] o [ˈmɪmɪ•əˌɡrɑf] *s* (trademark) mimeógrafo ‖ *tr* mimeografiar
mim•ic [ˈmɪmɪk] *s* imitador *m*, remedador *m* ‖ *v* (*pret & pp* **-icked;** *ger* **-icking**) *tr* imitar, remedar
mimic•ry [ˈmɪmɪkri] *s* (*pl* **-ries**) mímica, remedo
min. *abbr* **minimum, minute**
minaret [ˌmɪnəˈrɛt] o [ˈmɪnəˌrɛt] *s* alminar *m*, minarete *m*
mince [mɪns] *tr* desmenuzar; picar (*carne*) ‖ *intr* andar remilgadamente; hablar remilgadamente
mince'meat' *s* cuajado, picadillo
mince pie *s* pastel relleno de carne picada con frutas

me
mi

mind [maɪnd] *s* mente *f*, espíritu *m;* **to bear in mind** tener presente; **to be not in one's right mind** no estar en sus cabales; **to be of one mind** estar de acuerdo; **to be out of one's mind** estar fuera de juicio; **to change one's mind** mudar de parecer; **to go out of one's mind** volverse loco; **to have a mind to** tener ganas de; **to have in mind to** pensar en; **to have on one's mind** preocuparse con; **to lose one's mind** perder el juicio; **to make up one's mind** resolverse; **to my mind** a mi parecer; **to say whatever comes into one's mind** decir lo que se le viene a la boca; **to set one's mind on** resolverse a; **to slip one's mind** escaparse de la memoria; **to speak one's mind** decir su parecer; **with one mind** unánimamente ‖ *tr* (*to take care of*) cuidar, estar al cuidado de; obedecer; fijarse en; sentir molestia por; **do you mind the smoke?** ¿le molesta el humo?; **mind your own business** no se meta Vd. en lo que no le toca ‖ *intr* tener inconveniente; tener cuidado; **never mind** no se preocupe, no se moleste

mind'-bend'ing *adj* (coll) alucinante

mind'-blow'ing *adj* (coll) alucinante en exceso

mind'-bog'gling *adj* deslumbrante; abrumador

mindful ['maɪndfəl] *adj* atento; **mindful of** atento a, cuidadoso de

mind reader *s* adivinador *m* del pensamiento ajeno, lector *m* mental

mind reading *s* adivinación del pensamiento ajeno, lectura de la mente

mine [maɪn] *pron poss* el mío; mío ‖ *s* mina; **to work a mine** beneficiar una mina ‖ *tr* minar; beneficiar (*un terreno*); extraer (*mineral, carbón, etc.*) ‖ *intr* minar; abrir minas

mine field *s* campo de minas

mine layer *s* buque *m* portaminas, lanzaminas *m*

miner ['maɪnər] *s* minero; (mil, nav) minador *m*

mineral ['mɪnərəl] *adj & s* mineral *m*

mineralogy [,mɪnə'rælədʒi] *s* mineralogía

mineral resources *spl* riquezas del subsuelo

mineral wool *s* lana de escorias

mine sweeper *s* dragaminas *m*

mingle ['mɪŋgəl] *tr* mezclar, confundir ‖ *intr* mezclarse, confundirse; asociarse

miniature ['mɪnɪ·ətʃər] o ['mɪnɪtʃər] *s* miniatura; **to paint in miniature** miniar, pintar de miniatura

miniaturization [,mɪnɪ·ətʃərɪ'zeʃən] o [,mɪnɪtʃərɪ'zeʃən] *s* miniaturización

minicomputer ['mɪnɪkəm,pjutər] *s* miniordenador *m*

minimal ['mɪnɪməl] *adj* mínimo

minimize ['mɪnɪ,maɪz] *tr* empequeñecer

minimum ['mɪnɪməm] *adj & s* mínimo

minimum wage *s* jornal mínimo

mining ['maɪnɪŋ] *adj* minero ‖ *s* mineraje *m*, minería; (nav) minado

minion ['mɪnjən] *s* paniaguado

minion of the law *s* esbirro, polizonte *m*

miniskirt ['mɪnɪ,skʌrt] *s* minifalda

minister ['mɪnɪstər] *s* ministro; pastor *m* protestante ‖ *tr & intr* ministrar

ministerial ['mɪnɪs'tɪrɪ·əl] *adj* ministerial

minis•try ['mɪnɪstri] *s* (*pl* **-tries**) ministerio

mink [mɪŋk] *s* visón *m*

minnow ['mɪno] *s* pececillo; (ichth) foxino

minor ['maɪnər] *adj* (*smaller*) menor; de menor importancia; (*younger*) menor de edad; (mus) menor ‖ *s* menor *m* de edad; (educ) asignatura secundaria

Minorca [mɪ'nɔrkə] *s* Menorca

Minorcan [mɪ'nɔrkən] *adj & s* menorquín *m*

minori•ty [maɪ'nɔrɪti] *adj* minoritario ‖ *s* (*pl* **-ties**) (*being under age; smaller number or part*) minoría; (*less than full age*) minoridad

minstrel ['mɪnstrəl] *s* (*retainer who sang and played for his lord*) ministril *m*; (*medieval musician and poet*) juglar *m*, trovador *m;* (U.S.A.) cantor cómico disfrazado de negro

minstrel•sy ['mɪnstrəlsi] *s* (*pl* **-sies**) juglaría; compañía de juglares; poesía trovadoresca

mint [mɪnt] *s* casa de moneda; (*plant*) menta, hierbabuena; montón *m* de dinero; fuente *f* inagotable ‖ *tr* acuñar; (fig) inventar

minuet [,mɪnju'ɛt] *s* minué *m*, minuete *m*

minus ['maɪnəs] *adj* menos ‖ *prep* menos; falto de, sin ‖ *s* menos *m*

minute [maɪ'njut] o [maɪ'nut] *adj* diminuto, menudo ‖ ['mɪnɪt] *s* minuto; (*short space of time*) momento; **minutes** acta; **to write up the minutes** levantar acta; **up to the minute** al corriente; de última hora

minute hand ['mɪnɪt] *s* minutero

minutiae [mɪ'njuʃɪ,i] o [mɪ'nuʃɪ,i] *spl* minucias

minx [mɪŋks] *s* moza descarada

miracle ['mɪrəkəl] *s* milagro

miracle play *s* auto

miraculous [mɪ'rækjələs] *adj* milagroso

mirage [mɪ'rɑʒ] *s* espejismo

mire [maɪr] *s* fango, lodo

mirror ['mɪrər] *s* espejo; (aut) retrovisor *m* ‖ *tr* reflejar

mirth [mʌrθ] *s* alegría, regocijo

mir•y ['maɪri] *adj* (*comp* **-ier;** *super* **-iest**) fangoso, lodoso; sucio

misadventure [,mɪsəd'vɛntʃər] *s* desgracia, contratiempo

misanthrope ['mɪsən,θrop] *s* misántropo

misanthropy [mɪs'ænθrəpi] *s* misantropía

misapprehension [,mɪsæprɪ'hɛnʃən] *s* malentendido

misappropriation [,mɪsə,propri'eʃən] *s* malversación

misbehave [,mɪsbɪ'hev] *intr* conducirse mal, portarse mal

misbehavior [,mɪsbɪ'hevɪ·ər] *s* mala conducta, mal comportamiento

misc. *abbr* **miscellaneous, miscellany**

miscalculation [,mɪskælkjə'leʃən] *s* mal cálculo

miscarriage [mɪs'kærɪdʒ] *s* aborto, malparto; fracaso, malogro; (*of a letter*) extravío

miscar•ry [mɪsˈkæri] v (pret & pp **-ried**) intr abortar, malparir; malograrse; extraviarse (una carta)

miscellaneous [ˌmɪsəˈleniˑəs] adj misceláneo

miscella•ny [ˈmɪsəˌleni] s (pl **-nies**) miscelánea

mischief [ˈmɪstʃɪf] s (harm) daño, mal m; (disposition to annoy) malicia; (prankishness) travesura

mis'chief-mak'er s malsín m, cizañero

mischievous [ˈmɪstʃɪvəs] adj dañoso, malo; malicioso; travieso

misconception [ˌmɪskənˈsɛpʃən] s concepto erróneo, mala interpretación

misconduct [mɪsˈkɑndəkt] s mala conducta

misconstrue [ˌmɪskənˈstru] o [mɪsˈkɑnstru] tr interpretar mal

miscount [mɪsˈkaʊnt] s cuenta errónea ‖ tr & intr contar mal

miscue [mɪsˈkju] s (in billiards) pifia; (slip) pifia ‖ intr pifiar; (theat) equivocarse de apunte

misdate [mɪsˈdet] tr fechar erróneamente

mis•deal [ˈmɪsˌdil] s repartición errónea ‖ [mɪsˈdil] v (pret & pp **-dealt** [ˈdɛlt]) tr & intr repartir mal

misdeed [mɪsˈdid] o [ˈmɪsˌdid] s malhecho, fechoría

misdemeanor [ˌmɪsdɪˈminər] s mala conducta; (law) delito de menor cuantía

misdirect [ˌmɪsdɪˈrɛkt] o [ˌmɪsdaɪˈrɛkt] tr dirigir erradamente; hacer perder el camino

misdoing [mɪsˈduˑɪŋ] s mala acción

miser [ˈmaɪzər] s avaro, verrugo; codo (Guat, Mex)

miserable [ˈmɪzərəbəl] adj miserable; (coll) achacoso, indispuesto

miserly [ˈmaɪzərli] adj avariento, mezquino

miser•y [ˈmɪzəri] s (pl **-ies**) miseria; pelazón f

misfeasance [mɪsˈfizəns] s (law) fraude m

misfire [mɪsˈfaɪr] s falla de tiro; (of internal-combustion engine) falla de encendido ‖ intr fallar (un arma de fuego, el encendido de un motor)

mis•fit [ˈmɪsˌfɪt] s vestido mal cortado; cosa que no encaja bien; persona mal adaptada a su ambiente ‖ [mɪsˈfɪt] v (pret & pp **-fitted**; ger **-fitting**) tr & intr encajar mal, sentar mal

misfortune [mɪsˈfɔrtʃən] s desgracia

misgiving [mɪsˈgɪvɪŋ] s mal presentimiento, rescoldo

misgovern [mɪsˈgʌvərn] tr desgobernar

misguidance [mɪsˈgaɪdəns] s error m, extravío

misguided [mɪsˈgaɪdɪd] adj descarriado, malaconsejado

mishap [ˈmɪsˌhæp] o [mɪsˈhæp] s accidente m, percance m

mishmash [ˈmɪʃˌmæʃ] s baturillo; mezcolanza

misinform [ˌmɪsɪnˈfɔrm] tr dar informes erróneos a

misinterpret [ˌmɪsɪnˈtɛrprɪt] tr interpretar mal

misjudge [mɪsˈdʒʌdʒ] tr & intr juzgar mal

mis•lay [mɪsˈle] v (pret & pp **-laid** [ˌled]) tr extraviar, perder; (among one's papers) traspapelar

mis•lead [mɪsˈlid] v (pret & pp **-led** [ˌlɛd]) tr (to lead astray) extraviar, descaminar; (to lead into wrongdoing) seducir, inducir al mal; (to deceive) engañar

misleading [mɪsˈlidɪŋ] adj engañoso

mismanagement [mɪsˈmænɪdʒmənt] s mala administración, desgobierno

misnomer [mɪsˈnomər] s nombre improprio, mal nombre

misplace [mɪsˈples] tr colocar fuera de su lugar; colocar mal; (to mislay) (coll) extraviar, perder

misprint [ˈmɪsˌprɪnt] s errata de imprenta ‖ [mɪsˈprɪnt] tr imprimir con erratas

mispronounce [ˌmɪsprəˈnaʊns] tr pronunciar mal

mispronunciation [ˌmɪsprəˌnʌnsiˈeʃən] o [ˌmɪsprəˌnʌnʃiˈeʃən] s pronunciación incorrecta

misquote [mɪsˈkwot] tr citar equivocadamente

misrepresent [ˌmɪsrɛprɪˈzɛnt] tr tergiversar

miss [mɪs] s falta, error m; fracaso, malogro; tiro errado; jovencita, muchacha ‖ tr echar de menos; perder (el tren, la función, la oportunidad); errar (el blanco; la vocación); no entender, no comprender; omitir; no ver; no dar con, no encontrar; librarse de (p.ej., la muerte); escapársele a uno, p.ej., **I missed what you said** se me escapó lo que dijo Vd.; por poco, p.ej., **the car missed hitting me** el coche por poco me atropella ‖ intr fallar; errar el blanco; malograrse ‖ **Miss** s señorita

missal [ˈmɪsəl] s misal m

misshapen [mɪsˈʃepən] adj deforme, contrahecho

missile [ˈmɪsɪl] adj arrojadizo ‖ s arma arrojadiza; proyectil m; proyectil dirigido, misil m

missile gap s desigualdad de armas proyectiles poseídas por dos potencias

missil(e)ry [ˈmɪsɪlri] s cohetería; ciencia de las armas proyectiles

missing [ˈmɪsɪŋ] adj extraviado, perdido; desaparecido; ausente; **to be missing** hacer falta; haber desaparecido

missing link s hombre m mono

missing persons spl desaparecidos

mission [ˈmɪʃən] s misión; casa de misión

missionar•y [ˈmɪʃənˌɛri] adj misional ‖ s (pl **-ies**) (one sent to work to propagate his faith) misionario, misionero; (on a political or diplomatic mission) misionario

missive [ˈmɪsɪv] adj misivo ‖ s misiva

mis•spell [mɪsˈspɛl] v (pret & pp **-spelled** o **-spelt** [ˈspɛlt]) tr & intr deletrear mal, escribir mal

misspelling [mɪsˈspɛlɪŋ] s falta de ortografía

misspent [mɪsˈspɛnt] adj malgastado

misstatement [mɪsˈstetmənt] s relación equivocada, relación falsa

misstep [mɪsˈstɛp] s paso falso; (slip in conduct) resbalón m

mi
mi

miss•y ['mɪsi] s (pl **-ies**) (coll) señorita

mist [mɪst] s neblina; (of tears) velo; (fine spray) vapor m

mis•take [mɪs'tek] s error m, equivocación; **and no mistake** sin duda alguna; **by mistake** por descuido; **to make a mistake** equivocarse ‖ v (pret **-took** ['tʊk]; pp **-taken**) tr tomar (por otro; por lo que no es); entender mal; **to be mistaken for** equivocarse con

mistaken [mɪs'tekən] adj (person) equivocado; (idea) erróneo; (act) desacertado

mistakenly [mɪs'tekənli] adv equivocadamente, por error

mistletoe ['mɪsəl,to] s (Viscum album) muérdago; (Phoradendron flavescens, used in Christmas decorations in the U.S.A.) cabellera

mistreat [mɪs'trit] tr maltratar

mistreatment [mɪs'tritmənt] s maltratamiento

mistress ['mɪstrɪs] s (of a household) ama, dueña; moza, querida, manceba; (Brit) maestra de escuela

mistrial [mɪs'traɪ•əl] s pleito viciado de nulidad

mistrust [mɪs'trʌst] s desconfianza ‖ tr desconfiar de ‖ intr desconfiar

mistrustful [mɪs'trʌstfəl] adj desconfiado

mist•y ['mɪsti] adj (comp **-ier**; super **-iest**) brumoso, neblinoso; indistinto

misunder•stand [,mɪsʌndər'stænd] v (pret & pp **-stood** ['stʊd]) tr no comprender, entender mal

misunderstanding [,mɪsʌndər'stændɪŋ] s malentendido; (disagreement) desavenencia

misuse [mɪs'jus] s abuso, mal uso; (of funds) malversación ‖ [mɪs'juz] tr abusar de, emplear mal; malversar (fondos)

misword [mɪs'wʌrd] tr redactar mal

mite [maɪt] s (small contribution) óbolo; (small amount) pizca; (ent) ácaro

miter ['maɪtər] s mitra; (carp) inglete m ‖ tr cortar ingletes en; juntar con junta a inglete

miter box s caja de ingletes

mitigate ['mɪtɪ,get] tr mitigar, atenuar, paliar

mitten ['mɪtən] s confortante m, mitón m

mix [mɪks] tr mezclar; amasar (una torta); aderezar (ensalada); **to mix up** equivocar, confundir ‖ intr mezclarse; asociarse

mixed [mɪkst] adj mixto, mezclado; (e.g., candy) variados; (coll) confundido

mixed company s reunión de personas de ambos sexos

mixed drink s bebida mezclada

mixed feelings s concepto vacilante

mixer ['mɪksər] s (of concrete) mezcladora, hormigonera; **to be a good mixer** (coll) tener don de gentes

mixture ['mɪkstʃər] s mezcla, mixtura

mix'-up' s confusión; enredo, lío; (of people) equivocación

mizzen ['mɪzən] s mesana

mo. abbr **month**

M.O. abbr **money order**

moan [mon] s gemido ‖ intr gemir

moat [mot] s foso

mob [mab] s chusma, populacho; (crowd bent on violence) muchedumbre airada ‖ v (pret & pp **mobbed**; ger **mobbing**) tr asaltar, atropellar

mobile ['mobɪl] o ['mobil] adj móvil

mobility [mo'bɪlɪti] s movilidad

mobilization [,mobɪlɪ'zeʃən] s movilización

mobilize ['mobɪ,laɪz] tr movilizar ‖ intr movilizar, movilizarse

mob rule s gobierno del populacho

mobster ['mabstər] s (slang) gamberro, pandillero, gángster

mobsterism ['mabstə,rɪzəm] s gangsterismo; acciones de los gangsters

moccasin ['makəsɪn] s mocasín m

Mocha coffee ['mokə] s moca m, café m de moca

mock [mak] adj simulado, fingido ‖ s burla, mofa ‖ tr burlarse de, mofarse de; despreciar; engañar ‖ intr mofarse; **to mock at** mofarse de

mocker•y ['makəri] s (pl **-ies**) burla, mofa, escarnio; (subject of derision) hazmerreír m; (poor imitation) mal remedo; (e.g., of justice) negación

mock'ing•bird' s burlón m, sinsonte m

mock orange s jeringuilla, celinda

mock privet s olivillo

mock turtle soup s sopa de cabeza de ternera

mock'-up' s maqueta

mode [mod] s modo, manera; (fashion) moda; (gram) modo

mod•el ['madəl] adj modelo, p.ej., **model city** ciudad modelo ‖ s modelo ‖ v (pret & pp **-eled** o **-elled**; ger **-eling** o **-elling**) tr (to fashion in clay, wax, etc.) modelar ‖ intr modelarse; servir de modelo

model airplane s aeromodelo

mod'el-air'plane builder s aeromodelista mf

model-airplane building s aeromodelismo

model sailing s navegación de modelos a vela

moderate ['madərɪt] adj moderado; (tiempo) templado; (precio) módico ‖ [madə,ret] tr moderar; presidir (una asamblea) ‖ intr moderarse

moderator ['madə,retər] s (over an assembly) presidente m; (mediator) árbitro; (telv) presentador m, presentadora; (for slowing down neutrons) moderador m

modern [madərn] adj moderno

modernize ['madər,naɪz] tr modernizar

modest ['madɪst] adj modesto

modes•ty ['madɪsti] s (pl **-ties**) modestia

modicum ['madɪkəm] s pequeña cantidad

modifier ['madɪ,faɪ•ər] s (gram) modificante m

modi•fy ['madɪ,faɪ] v (pret & pp **-fied**) tr modificar

modish ['modɪʃ] adj de moda, elegante

modulate ['madʒə,let] tr & intr modular

modulation [,madʒə'leʃən] s modulación

mohair ['mo,hɛr] s mohair m (pelo de cabra de Angora)

Mohammedan [mo'hæmɪdən] adj & s mahometano

Mohammedanism [mo'hæmɪdə,nɪzəm] *s* mahometismo

moist [mɔɪst] *adj* húmedo, mojado; (*weather*) lluvioso; (*eyes*) lagrimoso

moisten ['mɔɪsən] *tr* humedecer ‖ *intr* humedecerse

moisture ['mɔɪstʃər] *s* humedad

molar ['molər] *s* diente *m* molar

molasses [mə'læsɪz] *s* melaza

molasses candy *s* melcocha

mold [mold] *s* molde *m*; cosa moldeada; (*shape*) forma; (*fungus*) moho; (*humus*) mantillo; (fig) carácter *m*, índole *f* ‖ *tr* amoldar, moldear; (*to make moldy*) enmohecer ‖ *intr* enmohecerse

molder ['moldər] *s* moldeador *m* ‖ *intr* convertirse en polvo, consumirse

molding ['moldɪŋ] *s* moldeado; (*cornice, shaped strip of wood, etc.*) moldura

mold·y ['moldi] *adj* (*comp* -ier; *super* -iest) (*overgrown with mold*) mohoso; (*stale*) rancio, pasado

mole [mol] *s* (*breakwater*) rompeolas *m*; (*inner harbor*) dársena; (*spot on skin*) lunar *m*; (*small mammal*) topo

molecular physics [mə'lɛkjələr] *s* física molecular

molecular weight *s* peso molecular

molecule ['malɪ,kjul] *s* molécula

mole'hill' *s* topinera

mole'skin' *s* piel *f* de topo, molesquina

molest [mə'lɛst] *tr* molestar; faltar al respeto a (*una mujer*)

moll [mal] *s* (slang) mujer *f* del hampa; (slang) ramera

molli·fy ['malɪ,faɪ] *v* (*pret & pp* -fied) *tr* apaciguar, aplacar

mollusk ['maləsk] *s* molusco

mollycoddle ['malɪ,kadəl] *s* mantecón *m*, marica *m* ‖ *tr* consentir, mimar

molt [molt] *s* muda ‖ *intr* hacer la muda

molten ['moltən] *adj* fundido, derretido; fundido, vaciado

molybdenum [mə'lɪbdɪnəm] o [,malɪb-'dinəm] *s* molibdeno

moment ['momənt] *s* momento; **at any moment** de un momento a otro

momentary ['momən,tɛri] *adj* momentáneo

momentous [mo'mɛntəs] *adj* importante, grave

momen·tum [mo'mɛntəm] *s* (*pl* -tums o -ta [te]) ímpetu *m*; (mech) cantidad de movimiento

monarch ['manərk] *s* monarca *m*

monarchic(al) [mə'narkɪk(əl)] *adj* monárquico

monarchist ['manərkɪst] *adj & s* monárquico, monarquista *mf*

monar·chy ['manərki] *s* (*pl* -chies) monarquía

monaster·y ['manəs,tɛri] *s* (*pl* -ies) monasterio

monastic [mə'næstɪk] *adj* monástico

monasticism [mə'næstɪ,sɪzəm] *s* monaquismo

Monday ['mʌndi] *s* lunes *m*

monetary ['manɪ,tɛri] *adj* monetario; pecuniario

money ['mʌni] *s* dinero; **to make money** ganar dinero; dar dinero (*una empresa*)

mon'ey·bag' *s* monedero, talega; **money-bags** (*wealth*) (coll) talegas; (*wealthy person*) (coll) ricacho

moneychanger ['mʌni,tʃendʒər] *s* cambista *mf*

moneyed ['mʌnid] *adj* adinerado

moneylender ['mʌni,lɛndər] *s* prestamista *mf*

mon'ey·mak'er *s* acaudalador *m*; (fig) manantial *m* de beneficios

money order *s* giro postal, orden *m* de pago

Mongol ['maŋgəl] *adj & s* mogol *mf*

Mongolian [maŋ'goliən] *adj & s* mogol *mf*

mon·goose ['maŋgus] *s* (*pl* -gooses) mangosta

mongrel ['mʌŋgrəl] *adj & s* mestizo

monitor ['manɪtər] *s* monitor *m* ‖ *tr* controlar (*la señal*); escuchar (*radio-transmisiones*); superentender

monk [mʌŋk] *s* monje *m*

monkey ['mʌŋki] *s* mono; simio; **to make a monkey of** tomar el pelo a ‖ *intr* — **to monkey around** haraganear; **to monkey with** ajar, manosear

mon'key·shine' *s* (slang) monería, monada, payasada

monkey wrench *s* llave inglesa

monkhood ['maŋkhud] *s* monacato; los monjes

monkshood ['maŋks·hud] *s* cogulla de fraile

monocle ['manəkəl] *s* monóculo

monogamy [mə'nagəmi] *s* monogamia

monogram ['manə,græm] *s* monograma *m*

monograph ['manə,græf] *s* monografía

monolithic [,manə'lɪθɪk] *adj* monolítico

monologue ['manə,lag] *s* monólogo

monomania [,manə'meni·ə] *s* monomanía

monomial [mə'nomi·əl] *s* monomio

monopolize [mə'napə,laɪz] *tr* monopolizar; acaparar (*p.ej., la conversación*)

monopo·ly [mə'napəli] *s* (*pl* -lies) monopolio

monorail ['manə,rel] *s* monorriel *m*

monosyllable ['manə,sɪləbəl] *s* monosílabo

monotheist ['manə,θi·ɪst] *adj & s* monoteísta *mf*

monotonous [me'natənəs] *adj* monótono

monotony [me'natəni] *s* monotonía

monotype ['manə,taɪp] *s* (*machine; method*) monotipia; (*machine*) monotipo

monotype operator *s* monotipista *mf*

monoxide [mə'naksaɪd] *s* monóxido

monseigneur [,mansen'jœr] *s* monseñor *m*

monsignor [man'sinjər] *s* (*pl* **monsignors** o **monsignori** [,mansi'njori]) (eccl) monseñor *m*

monsoon [man'sun] *s* monsón *m*

monster ['manstər] *adj* monstruoso ‖ *s* monstruo

monstrance ['manstrəns] *s* custodia, ostensorio

monstrosi·ty [man'strasiti] *s* (*pl* -ties) monstruosidad; esperpento

monstrous ['manstrəs] *adj* monstruoso

mi
mo

month [mʌnθ] *s* mes *m*

month·ly ['mʌnθli] *adj* mensual ‖ *adv* mensualmente ‖ *s* (*pl* **-lies**) revista mensual; **monthlies** (coll) reglas

monument ['manjəmənt] *s* monumento

moo [mu] *s* mugido ‖ *intr* mugir

mood [mud] *s* humor *m*, genio; (gram) modo; **moods** accesos de mal humor

mood·y ['mudi] *adj* (*comp* **-ier**; *super* **-iest**) triste, hosco, melancólico; caprichoso, veleidoso

moon [mun] *s* luna

moon'beam' *s* rayo lunar

moon'light' *s* claror *m* de luna, luz *f* de la luna

moon'light'ing *s* multiempleo, pluriempleo

moon'sail' *s* (naut) monterilla

moon'shine' *s* luz *f* de la luna; (*idle talk*) cháchara, música celestial; (coll) whisky destilado ilegalmente

moon shot *s* lanzamiento a la Luna

moor [mur] *s* brezal *m*, páramo ‖ *tr* (naut) amarrar ‖ *intr* (naut) echar las amarras ‖ **Moor** *s* moro

Moorish ['murɪʃ] *adj* moro

moor'land' *s* brezal *m*

moose [mus] *s* (*pl* **moose**) alce *m* de América

moot [mut] *adj* discutible, dudoso

mop [mɑp] *s* aljofifa, fregasuelos *m*, estropajo; (*of hair*) espesura ‖ *v* (*pret & pp* **mopped**; *ger* **mopping**) *tr* aljofifar; enjugarse (*la frente con un pañuelo*); **to mop up** limpiar de enemigos

mope [mop] *intr* andar abatido, entregarse a la melancolía

moped ['mopɛd] *s* motoneta

mopish ['mopɪʃ] *adj* abatido, melancólico

moral ['marəl] o ['mɔrəl] *adj* moral ‖ *s* (*of a fable*) moraleja, moral *f*; **morals** (*ethics; conduct*) moral *f*

moral certainty *s* evidencia moral

morale [mə'ræl] o [mə'rɑl] *s* moral *f* (*estado de ánimo, confianza en sí mismo*)

morali·ty [mə'ræliti] *s* (*pl* **-ties**) moralidad

morals charge *s* acusación por delito sexual

morass [mə'ræs] *s* pantano

moratori·um [,marə'torɪ·əm] o [,mɑrə'torɪ·əm] *s* (*pl* **-ums** o **-a** [ə]) moratoria

morbid ['mɔrbɪd] *adj* (*feelings, curiosity*) malsano; (*gruesome*) horripilante; (*pertaining to disease; pathologic*) morboso

mordacious [mɔr'deʃəs] *adj* mordaz

mordant ['mɔrdənt] *adj* mordaz ‖ *s* mordiente *m*

more [mor] *adj & adv* más; **more and more** cada vez más; **more than** más que; (*followed by numeral*) más de; (*followed by verb*) más de lo que ‖ *s* más *m*

more·o'ver *adv* además, por otra parte

Moresque [mo'rɛsk] *adj* moro; (archit) árabe ‖ *s* estilo árabe

morgue [mɔrg] *s* depósito de cadáveres

moribund ['mɔri,bʌnd] o ['mɑri,bʌnd] *adj* moribundo

Moris·co [mə'rɪsko] *adj* morisco, moro ‖ *s* (*pl* **-cos** o **-coes**) moro; moro de España;

(*offspring of mulatto and Spaniard, in Mexico*) morisco

morning ['mɔrnɪŋ] *adj* matinal ‖ *s* mañana; (*time between midnight and dawn*) madrugada; **in the morning** de mañana, por la mañana

morning coat *s* chaqué *m*

morn'ing·glo'ry *s* (*pl* **-ries**) dondiego de día

morning sickness *s* vómitos del embarazo

morning star *s* lucero del alba

Moroccan [mə'rɑkən] *adj & s* marroquí *mf* o marroquín *m*

morocco [mə'rɑko] *s* (*leather*) marroquí *m* o marroquín *m* ‖ **Morocco** *s* Marruecos *m*

moron ['morɑn] *s* (*person of arrested intelligence*) morón *m;* (coll) imbécil *mf*

morose [mə'ros] *adj* adusto, hosco, malhumorado

morphine ['mɔrfin] *s* morfina

morphology [mɔr'fɑlədʒi] *s* morfología

Morris chair ['mɑrɪs] o ['mɔrɪs] *s* poltrona extensible

morrow ['mɑro] o ['mɔro] *s* (*future time*) mañana *m;* (*time following some event*) día *m* siguiente; **on the morrow** en el día de mañana; el día siguiente

morsel ['mɔrsəl] *s* bocadito; pedacito

mortal ['mɔrtəl] *adj & s* mortal *m*

mortality [mɔr'tæliti] *s* mortalidad; (*death or destruction on a large scale*) mortandad

mortar ['mɔrtər] *s* (*bowl used for crushing; mixture of lime, etc.*) mortero; (arti) mortero

mor'tar·board' *s* esparavel *m;* gorro académico cuadrado

mortgage ['mɔrgɪdʒ] *s* hipoteca ‖ *tr* hipotecar

mortgagee [,mɔrgɪ'dʒi] *s* acreedor hipotecario

mortgagor ['mɔrgɪdʒər] *s* deudor hipotecario

mortician [mɔr'tɪʃən] *s* empresario de pompas fúnebres

morti·fy ['mɔrtɪ,faɪ] *v* (*pret & pp* **-fied**) *tr* humillar; mortificar (*el cuerpo, las pasiones*); **to be mortified** avergonzarse

mortise ['mɔrtɪs] *s* mortaja, muesca ‖ *tr* amortajar, enmuescar

mortise lock *s* cerradura embutida

mortuar·y ['mɔrtʃu,ɛri] *adj* mortuorio ‖ *s* (*pl* **-ies**) depósito de cadáveres; funeraria

mosaic [mo'ze·ɪk] *m* mosaico

Moscow ['mɑskau] o ['mɑsko] *s* Moscú

Moses ['moziz] o ['mozis] *s* Moisés *m*

Mos·lem ['mazləm] o ['mɑsləm] *adj & s* var of **Muslim**, musulmán *m*

mosque [mɑsk] *s* mezquita

mosqui·to [məs'kito] *s* (*pl* **-toes** o **-tos**) mosquito

mosquito net *s* mosquitero

moss [mɔs] o [mɑs] *s* musgo

moss'back' *s* (coll) reaccionario; (*old-fashioned person*) (coll) fósil *m*

moss·y ['mɔsi] o ['mɑsi] *adj* (*comp* **-ier**; *super* **-iest**) musgoso

most [most] *adj* más; la mayor parte de, los más de ‖ *adv* más; muy, sumamente; (coll) casi ‖ *s* la mayor parte, el mayor número, los más; **most of** la mayor parte de, el mayor número de; **to make the most of** sacar el mejor partido de

mostly ['mostlɪ] *adv* por la mayor parte, mayormente; casi

moth [mɔθ] o [mɑθ] *s* mariposa nocturna; (*clothes moth*) polilla

moth ball *s* bola de alcanfor, bola de naftalina

moth'-ball' fleet *s* (nav) flota en conserva

moth'-eat'en *adj* apolillado; (fig) anticuado

mother ['mʌðər] *adj* (*love*) maternal; (*tongue*) materno; (*country*) madre; (*church*) metropolitano ‖ *s* madre *f*; (*an elderly woman*) (coll) tía ‖ *tr* servir de madre a

mother country *s* madre patria

Mother Goose *s* supuesta autora o narradora de una colección de cuentos infantiles (in Spain: *Cuentos de Calleja*)

motherhood ['mʌðər,hʊd] *s* maternidad

moth'er-in-law' *s* (*pl* **mothers-in-law**) suegra

moth'er·land' *s* patria

motherless ['mʌðərlɪs] *adj* huérfano de madre, sin madre

motherly ['mʌðərlɪ] *adj* maternal

mother-of-pearl ['mʌðərəv'pʌrl] *adj* nacarado ‖ *s* nácar *m*

Mother's Day *s* día *m* de la madre

mother superior *s* superiora

mother tongue *s* (*language naturally acquired by reason of nationality*) lengua materna; (*language from which another language is derived*) lengua madre, lengua matriz

mother wit *s* gracia natural, chispa

moth hole *s* apolilladura

moth·y ['mɔθɪ] o ['mɑθɪ] *adj* (*comp* **-ier**; *super* **-iest**) apolillado

motif [mo'tif] *s* motivo

motion ['moʃən] *s* movimiento; (*signal, gesture*) seña, indicación; (*in a deliberating assembly*) moción; **to set in motion** poner en acción ‖ *intr* hacer señas con la mano o la cabeza

motionless ['moʃənlɪs] *adj* inmoble, inmóvil

motion picture *s* película cinematográfica

mo'tion-pic'ture *adj* cinematográfico

motivate ['motɪ,vet] *tr* animar, incitar, mover

motive ['motɪv] *adj* (*promoting action*) motivo; (*producing motion*) motor ‖ *s* motivo

motive power *s* fuerza motriz, potencia motora o motriz; (rr) conjunto de locomotoras de un ferrocarril

motley ['mɑtlɪ] *adj* abigarrado; mezclado, variado

motor ['motər] *adj* motor ‖ *s* motor *m*; motor eléctrico; automóvil *m* ‖ *intr* viajar en automóvil

mo'tor·boat' *s* gasolinera, canoa automóvil

mo'tor·bus' *s* autobús *m*

motorcade ['motər,ked] *s* caravana de automóviles

mo'tor·car' *s* automóvil *m*

mo'tor·cy'cle *s* motocicleta

motorist ['motərɪst] *s* motorista *mf*, automovilista *mf*

motorize ['motə,raɪz] *tr* motorizar

motor launch *s* lancha automóvil

motor·man ['motərmən] *s* (*pl* **-men** [mən]) conductor *m* de tranvía, conductor de locomotora eléctrica

motor sailer ['selər] *s* motovelero

motor scooter *s* motoneta

motor ship *s* motonave *f*

motor truck *s* autocamión *m*

motor vehicle *s* vehículo motor, autovehículo

mottle ['mɑtəl] *tr* abigarrar, jaspear, motear

mot·to ['mɑto] *s* (*pl* **-toes** o **-tos**) lema *m*, divisa

mould [mold] *s*, *tr*, & *intr* var de **mold**

moulder ['moldər] *s* & *intr* var de **molder**

moulding ['moldɪŋ] *s* var de **molding**

mouldy ['moldɪ] *adj* var de **moldy**

mound [maʊnd] *s* montón *m* de tierra; montecillo

mount [maʊnt] *s* (*hill, mountain*) monte *m*; (*horse for riding*) montura; (*setting for a jewel*) montadura; soporte *m*; cartón *m*, tela (*en que está pegada una fotografía*); (mach) montaje *m* ‖ *tr* subir (*una escalera, una cuesta*); subir a (*una plataforma*); escalar (*una muralla*); montar (*un servicio; una piedra preciosa*); poner a caballo; pegar (*vistas, pruebas*); (mil) montar (*la guardia*) ‖ *intr* montar, montarse; aumentar, subir (*los precios*)

mountain ['maʊntən] *s* montaña; **to make a mountain out of a molehill** hacer de una pulga un camello

mountain climbing *s* alpinismo, montañismo

mountaineer [,maʊntə'nɪr] *s* montañés *m*

mountainous ['maʊntənəs] *adj* montañoso

mountain railroad *s* ferrocarril *m* de cremallera

mountain range *s* cordillera, sierra

mountain sickness *s* mal *m* de las montañas

mountebank ['maʊntɪ,bæŋk] *s* saltabanco

mounting ['maʊntɪŋ] *s* (*of a precious stone, of an astronomical instrument*) montura; papel *m* de soporte; papel o tela (*en que está pegada una fotografía*); (mach) montaje *m*

mourn [morn] *tr* llorar (*p.ej., la muerte de una persona*); lamentar (*una desgracia*) ‖ *intr* lamentarse; vestir de luto

mourner ['mornər] *s* doliente *mf*; (*person who makes a public profession of penitence*) penitente *mf*; (*person hired to attend a funeral*) plañidera; **mourners** duelo

mourners' bench *s* banco de los penitentes

mournful ['mornfəl] *adj* (*sorrowful*) doloroso; (*gloomy*) lúgubre

mourning ['mornɪŋ] *s* luto; **to be in mourning** estar de luto

mourning band *s* crespón *m* fúnebre, brazal *m* de luto

mouse [maʊs] *s* (*pl* **mice** [maɪs]) ratón *m*

mouse'hole' *s* ratonera

mouser ['maʊzər] *s* desmurador *m*

mouse'trap' *s* ratonera

mo
mo

moustache [məs'tæʃ] o [məs'tɑʃ] *s* bigote *m*, mostacho

mouth [mauθ] *s* (*pl* **mouths** [mauðz]) boca; (*of a river*) desembocadura, embocadura; **by mouth** por vía bucal; **to be born with a silver spoon in one's mouth** nacer de pie; **to make one's mouth water** hacérsele a uno la boca agua; **to not open one's mouth** no decir esta boca es mía

mouthful ['mauθ,ful] *s* bocado

mouth organ *s* armónica de boca

mouth'piece' *s* (*of wind instrument*) boquilla; (*of bridle*) embocadura; (*spokesman*) portavoz *m*

mouth'wash' *s* enjuague *m*, enjuagadientes *m*

movable ['muvəbəl] *adj* movible, móvil

move [muv] *s* movimiento; (*démarche*) acción, gestión, paso; (*from one house to another*) mudanza; **on the move** en marcha, en movimiento; **to get a move on** (slang) menearse, darse prisa; **to make a move** dar un paso; hacer una jugada ‖ *tr* mover; evacuar (*el vientre*); (*to stir, excite the feelings of*) conmover, enternecer; **to move up** adelantar (*una fecha*) ‖ *intr* moverse; desplazarse (*un viajante; un planeta*); mudarse, mudar de casa; (*e.g., to another store, to another city*) trasladarse; hacer una jugada; hacer una moción; venderse, tener salida (*una mercancía*); evacuarse, moverse (*el vientre*); **to move away** apartarse; marcharse; mudarse de casa; **to move in** instalarse; alternar con, frecuentar (*la buena sociedad*); **to move off** alejarse

movement ['muvmənt] *s* movimiento; aparato de relojería; (*of the bowels*) evacuación; (*e.g., of a symphony*) tiempo

movie ['muvi] *s* película, cinta

movie camera *s* filmadora, cámara cinematográfica

movie•goer ['movi,go•ər] *s* aficionado al cine

movie house *s* cineteatro

mov'ie•land' *s* (coll) cinelandia

movie star *s* cineasta *m*

moving ['muvɪŋ] *adj* conmovedor, impresionante ‖ *s* movimiento; (*from one house to another*) mudanza

moving picture *s* película cinematográfica

moving spirit *s* alma (*de una empresa*)

moving stairway *s* escalera mecánica, móvil o rodante

mow [mo] *v* (*pret* **mowed**; *pp* **mowed** o **mown**) *tr* segar; **to mow down** matar (*soldados*) con fuego graneado ‖ *intr* segar

mower ['mo•ər] *s* segador *m;* segadora mecánica

mowing machine *s* segadora mecánica

Mozarab [mo'zærəb] *s* mozárabe *mf*

Mozarabic [mo'zærəbɪk] *adj* mozárabe

M.P. *abbr* **Member of Parliament, Military Police**

m.p.h. *abbr* **miles per hour**

Mr. ['mɪstər] *s* (*pl* **Messrs.** ['mesərz]) señor *m* (*tratamiento*)

Mrs. ['mɪsɪz] *s* señora (*tratamiento*)

MS. o **ms.** *abbr* **manuscript**

Mt. *abbr* **Mount**

much [mʌtʃ] *adj & pron* mucho; **too much** demasiado ‖ *adv* mucho; **however much** por mucho que; **how much** cuánto; **too much** demasiado; **very much** muchísimo

mucilage ['mjusɪlɪdʒ] *s* goma para pegar; (*gummy secretion in plants*) mucílago

muck [mʌk] *s* estiércol húmedo; suciedad, porquería; (min) zafra

muck'rake' *intr* (coll) exponer ruindades

mucous ['mjukəs] *adj* mucoso

mucus ['mjukəs] *s* moco

mud [mʌd] *s* barro, fango, lodo; **to sling mud at** llenar de fango

muddle ['mʌdəl] *s* confusión, embrollo ‖ *tr* confundir, embrollar; atontar, aturdir ‖ *intr* obrar torpemente; **to muddle through** salir del paso a pesar suyo

mud'dle•head' *s* farraguista *mf*, cajón *m* de sastre

mud•dy ['mʌdi] *adj* (*comp* **-dier;** *super* **-diest**) barroso, fangoso, lodoso; (*obscure*) turbio ‖ *v* (*pret & pp* **-died**) *tr* embarrar, enturbiar

mud'guard' *s* guardabarros *m*

mud'hole' *s* atolladero, ciénaga

mudslinger ['mʌd,slɪŋər] *s* (fig) lanzador *m* de lodo

muezzin [mju'ɛzɪn] *s* almuecín *m*, almuédano

muff [mʌf] *s* manguito ‖ *tr & intr* chapucear

muffin ['mʌfɪn] *s* mollete *m*

muffle ['mʌfəl] *tr* arropar; (*about the face*) embozar; amortiguar (*un ruido*); enfundar (*un tambor*)

muffler ['mʌflər] *s* bufanda, tapaboca; (aut) silenciador *m*, silencioso

mufti ['mʌfti] *s* traje *m* de paisano

mug [mʌg] *s* pichel *m;* (slang) jeta, hocico ‖ *v* (*pret & pp* **mugged;** *ger* **mugging**) *tr* (slang) fotografiar; (slang) atacar ‖ *intr* (slang) hacer muecas

mugger ['mʌgər] *s* ladron *m* asaltador

mug•gy ['mʌgi] *adj* (*comp* **-gier;** *super* **-giest**) bochornoso, sofocante

mulat•to [mju'læto] o [mə'læto] *s* (*pl* **-toes**) mulato

mulber•ry ['mʌl,bɛri] *s* (*pl* **-ries**) (*tree*) moral *m;* (*fruit*) mora

mulct [mʌlkt] *tr* defraudar

mule [mjul] *s* mulo, macho; (*slipper*) babucha

mule chair *s* artolas, jamugas

muleteer [,mjulə'tɪr] *s* mulatero

mulish ['mjulɪʃ] *adj* terco, obstinado

mull [mʌl] *tr* calentar (*vino*) con especias ‖ *intr*—**to mull over** reflexionar sobre

mullion ['mʌljən] *s* parteluz *m*

Multigraph ['mʌltɪ,græf] o ['mʌltɪ,grɑf] *s* (trademark) multígrafo ‖ *tr* multigrafiar

multilateral [,mʌltɪ'lætərəl] *adj* (*having many sides*) multilátero; (*participated in by more than two nations*) multilateral

multinational corporations *spl* multinacionales *mpl*

multiple ['mʌltɪpəl] *adj* múltiple, múltiplo ‖ *s* (math) múltiplo

multiple sclerosis *s* esclerosis *f* múltiple
multiplex ['mʌltɪ,plɛks] *adj* múltiple
multiplici•ty [,mʌltɪ'plɪsɪti] *s* (*pl* **-ties**) multiplicidad
multi•ply ['mʌltɪ,plaɪ] *v* (*pret & pp* **-plied**) *tr* multiplicar ‖ *intr* multiplicar, multiplicarse
multipurpose [,mʌltɪ'pʌrpəs] *adj* múltiple de uso; versátil
multitude ['mʌltɪ,tjud] *o* ['mʌltɪ,tud] *s* multitud
mum [mʌm] *adj* callado; **mum's the word!** ¡punto en boca!; **to keep mum about** callar ‖ *interj* ¡chitón!
mumble ['mʌmbəl] *tr & intr* mascullar, mascujar
mummer•y ['mʌməri] *s* (*pl* **-ies**) mojiganga
mum•my ['mʌmi] *s* (*pl* **-mies**) momia
mumps [mʌmps] *s* papera
munch [mʌntʃ] *tr* ronzar
mundane ['mʌnden] *adj* mundano
municipal [mju'nɪsɪpəl] *adj* municipal
municipali•ty [mju,nɪsɪ'pælɪti] *s* (*pl* **-ties**) municipio
munificent [mju'nɪfɪsənt] *adj* munífico
munition [mju'nɪʃən] *s* munición ‖ *tr* municionar
munition dump *s* depósito de municiones
mural ['mjʊrəl] *adj* mural ‖ *s* pintura mural; decoración mural
murder ['mʌrdər] *s* asesinato, homicidio ‖ *tr* asesinar; (*to spoil, mar*) (coll) estropear
murderer ['mʌrdərər] *s* asesino
murderess ['mʌrdərɪs] *s* asesina
murderous ['mʌrdərəs] *adj* asesino; cruel, sanguinario
murk•y ['mʌrki] *adj* (*comp* **-ier;** *super* **-iest**) (*hazy*) calinoso; (*gloomy*) lóbrego
murmur ['mʌrmər] *s* murmullo ‖ *tr & intr* murmurar
mus. *abbr* **museum, music**
muscle ['mʌsəl] *s* músculo; (fig) fuerza muscular
muscular ['mʌskjələr] *adj* musculoso
muse [mjuz] *s* musa; **the Muses** las Musas ‖ *intr* meditar, reflexionar; **to muse on** contemplar
museum [mju'ziəm] *s* museo
mush [mʌʃ] *s* gachas; (coll) sentimentalismo exagerado, sensiblería
mush'room' *s* hongo, seta ‖ *intr* aparecer de la noche a la mañana; **to mushroom into** convertirse rápidamente en
mushroom cloud *s* nube-hongo *f*
mush•y ['mʌʃi] *adj* (*comp* **-ier;** *super* **-iest**) mollar, pulposo; (coll) sensiblero, sobón; (*with women*) (coll) baboso; **to be mushy** (coll) hacerse unas gachas
music ['mjuzɪk] *s* música; **to face the music** (coll) afrontar las consecuencias; **to set to music** poner en música
musical ['mjuzɪkəl] *adj* musical, músico
musical comedy *s* comedia musical
musicale [,mjuzɪ'kæl] *s* velada musical, concierto casero
music box *s* caja de música
music cabinet *s* musiquero

music hall *s* salón *m* de conciertos; (Brit) teatro de variedades
musician [mju'zɪʃən] *s* músico
musicianship [mju'zɪʃən,ʃɪp] *s* musicalidad
musicologist [,mjuzɪ'kɑlədʒɪst] *s* musicólogo
musicology [,mjuzɪ'kɑlədʒi] *s* musicología
music rack *o* **music stand** *s* atril *m*
musk [mʌsk] *s* almizcle *m;* olor *m* de almizcle
musk deer *s* almizclero
musket ['mʌskɪt] *s* mosquete *m*
musketeer [,mʌskɪ'tɪr] *s* mosquetero
musk'mel'on *s* melón *m*
musk'rat' *s* almizclera
Muslim ['mʌzləm] *o* ['mʌsləm] *adj* muslime, islámico, mahometano ‖ *s* muslime *mf*, musulmán *m*
muslin ['mʌzlɪn] *s* muselina
muss [mʌs] *tr* (*the hair*) (coll) descabellar, desarreglar; (*clothing*) (coll) chafar, arrugar
muss•y ['mʌsi] *adj* (*comp* **-ier;** *super* **-iest**) desaliñado, desgreñado
must [mʌst] *s* mosto; (*mold*) moho; cosa que debe hacerse ‖ *v aux* **I must study my lesson** debo estudiar mi lección; **he must work tomorrow** tiene que trabajar mañana; **she must be ill** estará enferma
mustache [məs'tæʃ], [məs'tɑʃ], *o* ['mʌstæʃ] *s* bigote *m*, mostacho
mustard ['mʌstərd] *s* mostaza
mustard gas *s* gas *m* mostaza
mustard plaster *s* sinapismo, cataplasma *f*
muster ['mʌstər] *s* asamblea; matrícula de revista; **to pass muster** pasar revista; ser aceptable ‖ *tr* llamar a asamblea; reunir para pasar revista; reunir, acumular; **to muster in** alistar; **to muster out** dar de baja a; **to muster up courage** cobrar ánimo
muster roll *s* lista de revista
mus•ty ['mʌsti] *adj* (*comp* **-tier;** *super* **-tiest**) (*moldy*) mohoso; (*stale*) trasnochado; anticuado, pasado de moda
mutation [mju'teʃən] *s* mutación
mute [mjut] *adj & s* mudo ‖ *tr* poner sordina a
mutilate ['mjutɪ,let] *tr* mutilar
mutilated *adj* mútilo, mutilado, mocho
mutineer [,mjutɪ'nɪr] *s* amotinado
mutinous ['mjutɪnəs] *adj* amotinado
muti•ny ['mjutɪni] *s* (*pl* **-nies**) motín *m* ‖ *v* (*pret & pp* **-nied**) *intr* amotinarse
mutt [mʌt] *s* (slang) perro cruzado; (slang) bobo, tonto
mutter ['mʌtər] *tr & intr* murmurar
mutton ['mʌtən] *s* carnero, carne *f* de carnero
mutton chop *s* chuleta de carnero
mutual ['mutʃu•əl] *adj* mutual, mutuo
mutual aid *s* apoyo mutuo
mutual benefit association *s* mutualidad
mutual fund *s* sociedad inversionista mutualista
muzzle ['mʌzəl] *s* (*projecting part of head of animal*) hocico; (*device to keep animal from biting*) bozal *m;* (*of firearm*) boca ‖ *tr*

mo
mu

abozalar; (*to keep from speaking*) amordazar

my [maɪ] *adj poss* mi

myriad [ˈmɪrɪ•əd] *s* miríada

myrrh [mʌr] *s* mirra

myrtle [ˈmʌrtəl] *s* arrayán *m*, mirto

myself [maɪˈsɛlf] *pron pers* yo mismo; mí, mí mismo; me, p.ej., **I enjoyed myself** me divertí; **with myself** conmigo

mysterious [mɪsˈtɪrɪ•əs] *adj* misterioso

myster•y [ˈmɪstəri] *s* (*pl* **-ies**) misterio

mystic [ˈmɪstɪk] *adj & s* místico

mystical [ˈmɪstɪkəl] *adj* místico

mysticism [ˈmɪstɪ,sɪzəm] *s* misticismo

mystification [,mɪstɪfɪˈkeʃən] *s* confusión, mistificación

mysti•fy [ˈmɪstɪ,faɪ] *v* (*pret & pp* **-fied**) *tr* rodear de misterio; (*to hoax*) confundir, mistificar

myth [mɪθ] *s* mito

mythical [ˈmɪθɪkəl] *adj* mítico

mythological [,mɪθəˈlɑdʒɪkəl] *adj* mitológico

mytholo•gy [mɪˈθɑlədʒi] *s* (*pl* **-gies**) mitología

N

N, n [ɛn] decimocuarta letra del alfabeto inglés

n. *abbr* **neuter, nominative, noon, north, noun, number**

N. *abbr* **Nationalist, Navy, Noon, North, November**

N.A. *abbr* **National Academy, National Army, North America**

nab [næb] *v* (*pret & pp* **nabbed;** *ger* **nabbing**) *tr* (slang) agarrar, coger; (slang) poner preso, prender

nag [næg] *s* caballejo, jaco; pequeño caballo de silla ‖ *v* (*pret & pp* **nagged;** *ger* **nagging**) *tr* importunar regañando ‖ *intr* regañar

naiad [ˈne•æd] o [ˈnaɪ•æd] *s* náyade *f;* (fig) nadadora

nail [nel] *s* (*of finger*) uña; (*to fasten wood, etc.*) clavo; **to hit the nail on the head** dar en el clavo ‖ *tr* clavar

nail brush *s* cepillo de uñas

nail clippers *spl* cortauñas *m*

nail file *s* lima para las uñas

nail polish *s* esmalte *m* para las uñas, laca de uñas

nailset [ˈnel,sɛt] *s* contrapunzón *m*

naïve [nɑˈiv] *adj* cándido, ingenuo

naked [ˈnekɪd] *adj* desnudo; **to go naked** ir desnudo, andar a la cordobana; **to strip naked** desnudar; desnudarse; **with the naked eye** a simple vista

name [nem] *s* nombre *m;* (*first name*) nombre de pila; (*last name*) apellido; fama, reputación, renombre *m;* linaje, *m,* raza; **to call someone names** maltratar a uno de palabra; **to go by the name of** ser conocido por el nombre de; **to make a name for oneself** darse a conocer, hacerse un nombre; **what is your name?** ¿cómo se llama Vd.? ‖ *tr* nombrar; fijar (*un precio*)

name day *s* santo

nameless [ˈnemlɪs] *adj* sin nombre, anónimo

namely [ˈnemli] *adv* a saber, es decir

namesake [ˈnem,sek] *s* homónimo, tocayo

nanny goat [ˈnæni] *s* (coll) cabra

nap [næp] *s* lanilla, flojel *m;* sueñecillo; **to take a nap** descabezar un sueñecillo ‖ *v* (*pret & pp* **napped;** *ger* **napping**) *intr* echar un sueñecillo; estar desprevenido; **to catch napping** coger desprevenido

napalm [ˈnepɑm] *s* (mil) gelatina incendiaria

nape [nep] *s* cogote *m,* nuca

naphtha [ˈnæfθə] *s* nafta

napkin [ˈnæpkɪn] *s* servilleta; (*of a baby*) (Brit) pañal *m*

napkin ring *s* servilletero

Naples [ˈnepəlz] *s* Nápoles

Napoleonic [nə,polɪˈɑnɪk] *adj* napoleónico

narc [nɑrk] *s* (slang) agente *m* de policía antidroga

narcissus [nɑrˈsɪsəs] *s* (bot) narciso ‖ **Narcissus** *s* Narciso

narcotic [nɑrˈkɑtɪk] *adj & s* narcótico

narrate [næˈret] *tr* narrar

narration [næˈreʃən] *s* narración

narrative [ˈnærətɪv] *adj* narrativo ‖ *s* (*story, tale; art of telling stories*) narrativa

narrator [næˈretər] *s* narrador *m*

narrow [ˈnæro] *adj* angosto, estrecho; intolerante; minucioso; (*sense of a word*) estricto ‖ **narrows** *spl* angostura, paso estrecho ‖ *tr* enangostar, estrechar; reducir, limitar ‖ *intr* enangostarse, estrecharse; reducirse, limitarse

narrow escape *s* trance *m* difícil; **to have a narrow escape** escapar por un pelo, salvarse en una tabla

narrow gauge *s* trocha angosta, vía estrecha

narrow-minded [ˈnæro'maɪndɪd] *adj* intolerante, de miras estrechas, poco liberal

nasal [ˈnezəl] *adj & s* nasal *f*

nasalize [ˈnezə,laɪz] *tr* nasalizar ‖ *intr* ganguear

nasturtium [nəˈstʌrʃəm] *s* capuchina, espuela de galán

nas•ty [ˈnæsti] *adj* (*comp* **-tier;** *super* **-tiest**) asqueroso, sucio; desagradable; desvergonzado; amenazador; horrible

natatorium [,netəˈtorɪ•əm] *s* piscina de natación

nation [ˈneʃən] *s* nación

national [ˈnæʃənəl] adj & s nacional mf
national anthem s himno nacional
national hero s benemérito de la patria
national holiday s fiesta nacional
nationalism [ˈnæʃənəˌlɪzəm] s nacionalismo
nationalist [ˈnæʃənəlɪst] adj & s nacionalista mf
nationali·ty [ˌnæʃənˈælɪti] s (pl -ties) nacionalidad, naturalidad
nationalize [ˈnæʃənəˌlaɪz] tr nacionalizar
na'tion-wide' adj de toda la nación
native [ˈnetɪv] adj nativo, natural; indígena; (language) materno; **to go native** vivir como los indígenas ‖ s natural mf; indígena mf
native land s patria
nativi·ty [nəˈtɪvɪti] s (pl -ties) nacimiento ‖ **Nativity** s (day; festival; painting) natividad
NATO [ˈneto] s (acronym) la O.T.A.N.
nat·ty [ˈnæti] adj. (comp -tier; super -tier; super -tiest) elegante, garboso
natural [ˈnætʃərəl] adj natural; (mus) natural ‖ s imbécil mf; (mus) tono natural, nota natural; (sign) (mus) becuadro; (mus) tecla blanca; (coll) cosa de éxito certero
naturalism [ˈnætʃərəˌlɪzəm] s naturalismo
naturalist [ˈnætʃərəlɪst] s naturalista mf
naturalization [ˌnætʃərəlɪˈzeʃən] s naturalización
naturalization papers spl carta de naturaleza
naturalize [ˈnætʃərəˌlaɪz] tr naturalizar
natural·ly [ˈnætʃərəli] adv naturalmente; claro, desde luego, por supuesto
nature [ˈnetʃər] s naturaleza; **from nature** del natural
naught [nɔt] s nada; cero; **to bring to naught** anular, invalidar, destruir; **to come to naught** reducirse a nada, frustrarse
naugh·ty [ˈnɔti] adj (comp -tier; super -tiest) desobediente, pícaro; desvergonzado; (story, tale) verde
nausea [ˈnɔʃɪ·ə] o [ˈnɔsɪ·ə] s náusea
nauseate [ˈnɔʃɪˌet] o [ˈnɔsɪˌet] tr dar náuseas a ‖ intr nausear, marearse
nauseating [ˈnɔʃɪˌetɪŋ] o [ˈnɔsɪˌetɪŋ] adj nauseabundo, asqueroso
nauseous [ˈnɔˌʃɪ·əs] o [ˈnɔsɪ·əs] adj nauseabundo
nautical [ˈnɔtɪkəl] adj náutico, marino, naval
nav. abbr **naval, navigation**
naval [ˈnevəl] adj naval, naval militar
Naval Academy s (U.S.A.) Escuela Naval Militar
naval officer s oficial m de marina
naval station s apostadero
nave [nev] s (of a church) nave f central, nave principal; (of a wheel) cubo
navel [ˈnevəl] s ombligo; (center point, middle) (fig) ombligo
navel orange s navel f, naranja de ombligo
navigability [ˌnævɪɡəˈbɪlɪti] s (of a river) navegabilidad; (of a ship) buen gobierno
navigable [ˈnævɪɡəbəl] adj (river, canal, etc.) navegable; (ship) marinero, de buen gobierno
navigate [ˈnævɪˌɡet] tr & intr navegar

navigation [ˌnævɪˈɡeʃən] s navegación
navigator [ˈnævɪˌɡetər] s navegador m, navegante m; (he who is in charge of course of ship or plane) oficial m de derrota; (Brit) peón m
nav·vy [ˈnævi] s (pl -vies) (Brit) bracero, peón m
na·vy [ˈnevi] adj azul oscuro ‖ s (pl -vies) marina de guerra; (personnel) marina; azul oscuro
navy bean s frijol blanco común
navy blue s azul marino, azul oscuro
navy yard s arsenal m de puerto
Nazarene [ˌnæzəˈrin] adj & s nazareno
Nazi [ˈnɑtsi] o [ˈnætsi] adj & s nazi mf, nacista mf
n.b. abbr **nota bene** (Lat) **note well**
N-bomb [ˈɛnˌbɑm] s bomba de neutrones
Neapolitan [ˌni·əˈpɑlɪtən] adj & s napolitano
neap tide [nip] s marea muerta
near [nɪr] adj cercano, próximo; íntimo; imitado ‖ adv cerca; íntimamente ‖ prep cerca de; hacia, por ‖ tr acercarse a ‖ intr acercarse
nearby [ˈnɪrˌbaɪ] adj cercano, próximo ‖ adv cerca
Near East s Cercano Oriente, Próximo Oriente
nearly [ˈnɪrli] adv casi; de cerca; íntimamente; por poco, p.ej., **he nearly fell** por poco se cae
near-sighted [ˈnɪrˈsaɪtɪd] adj miope
near-sightedness s miopía
neat [nit] adj aseado, pulcro; pulido; diestro; primoroso; puro, sin mezcla ‖ ssg res vacuna ‖ spl ganado vacuno
neat's'-foot'oil s aceite m de pie de buey
Nebuchadnezzar [ˌnɛbjəkədˈnɛzər] s Nabucodonosor m
nebu·la [ˈnɛbjələ] s (pl -lae [ˌli] o -las) nebulosa
nebular [ˈnɛbjələr] adj nebular
nebulous [ˈnɛbjələs] adj nebuloso
necessary [ˈnɛsɪˌsɛri] adj necesario
necessitate [nɪˈsɛsɪˌtet] tr necesitar, exigir
necessitous [nɪˈsɛsɪtəs] adj necesitado
necessi·ty [nɪˈsɛsɪti] s (pl -ties) necesidad
neck [nɛk] s cuello; (of a bottle) gollete m; (of violin or guitar) mástil m; istmo, península; estrecho; **neck and neck** parejos; **to break one's neck** (coll) matarse trabajando; **to stick one's neck out** (coll) descubrir el cuerpo ‖ intr (slang) acariciarse (dos enamorados)
neck'band' s tirilla de camisa
necklace [ˈnɛklɪs] s gargantilla, collar m
necktie [ˈnɛkˌtaɪ] s corbata
necktie pin s alfiler m de corbata
necrology [nɛˈkrɑlədʒi] s necrología
necromancy [ˈnɛkrəˌmænsi] s necromancia, nigromancia
nectarine [ˌnɛktəˈrin] s griñón m
née o **nee** [ne] adj nacida o de soltera, p.ej., **Mary Wilson, née Miller** María Wilson, nacida Miller o María Wilson, de soltera Miller

my
ne

need [nid] s necesidad; pobreza; **in need** necesitado ‖ tr necesitar ‖ intr estar necesitado; ser necesario ‖ v aux—**if need be** si fuere necesario; **to need** + inf deber, tener que + inf

needful ['nidfəl] adj necesario ‖ **the needful** lo necesario; (slang) el dinero

needle ['nidəl] s aguja; **to look for a needle in a haystack** buscar una aguja en un pajar ‖ tr coser con aguja; (coll) aguijonear, incitar; (coll) añadir alcohol a (la cerveza o el vino)

needle bath s ducha en alfileres

needle'case' s alfiletero

needle point s bordado al pasado; encaje m de mano

needless ['nidlɪs] adj innecesario, inútil

needle'work' s costura, labor f

needs [nidz] adv necesariamente, forzosamente

need·y ['nidi] adj (comp **-ier**; super **-iest**) necesitado, indigente ‖ **the needy** los necesitados

ne'er-do-well ['nɛrdu,wɛl] adj & s holgazán, perdido

negation [nɪ'geʃən] s negación

negative ['nɛgətɪv] adj negativo ‖ s negativa; electricidad negativa, borne negativo; (gram) negación; (math) término negativo; (phot) prueba negativa ‖ tr desaprobar; anular

neglect [nɪ'glɛkt] s negligencia, descuido ‖ tr descuidar; **to neglect to** dejar de, olvidarse de

neglectful [nɪ'glɛktfəl] adj negligente, descuidado

négligée o **negligee** [,nɛglɪ'ʒe] s bata de mujer, traje m de casa

negligence ['nɛglɪdʒəns] s negligencia, descuido

negligent ['nɛglɪdʒənt] adj negligente, descuidado

negligible ['nɛglɪdʒɪbəl] adj insignificante, imperceptible

negotiable [nɪ'goʃɪ•əbəl] adj negociable; transitable

negotiate [nɪ'goʃɪ,et] tr negociar; (coll) salvar, vencer ‖ intr negociar

negotiation [nɪ,goʃɪ'eʃən] s negociación; trámite m; **round of negotiations** ronda negociadora

Ne·gro ['nigro] adj (usually offensive) negro ‖ s (pl **-groes**) (usually offensive) negro

neigh [ne] s relincho ‖ intr relinchar

neighbor ['nebər] adj vecino ‖ s vecino; (fellow man) prójimo ‖ tr ser vecino de; ser amigo de ‖ intr estar cercano; tener relaciones amistosas

neighborhood ['nebər,hud] s vecindad, vecindario, cercanías; **in the neighborhood of** en las inmediaciones de; (coll) cerca de, aproximadamente

neighboring ['nebərɪŋ] adj vecino, colindante

neighborly ['nebərli] adj buen vecino, amable, sociable

neither ['niðər] o ['naɪðər] adj indef ninguno . . . (de los dos); **neither one** ninguno de los dos ‖ pron indef ninguno (de los dos); ni uno ni otro, ni lo uno ni lo otro ‖ conj ni; tampoco, ni . . . tampoco, p.ej., **neither do I** yo tampoco, ni yo tampoco; **neither . . . nor** ni . . . ni

neme·sis ['nɛmɪsɪs] s (pl **-ses** [,siz]) (someone or something that punishes) némesis f ‖ **Nemesis** s Némesis f

neologism [ni'alə,dʒɪzəm] s neologismo

neomycin [,ni•ə'maɪsɪn] s neomicina

neon ['ni•an] s neo, neón m

neophyte ['ni•ə,faɪt] s neófito

Nepal [nɪ'pɔl] s el Nepal

Nepa·lese [,nɛpə'liz] adj nepalés ‖ s (pl **-lese**) nepalés m

nepenthe [nɪ'pɛnθi] s nepente m

nephew ['nɛfju] o ['nɛvju] s sobrino

Nepos ['nipas] o ['nɛpas] s Nepote m

Neptune ['nɛptʃun] o ['nɛptjun] s Neptuno

neptunium [nɛp'tʃunɪ•əm] o [nɛp'tjunɪ•əm] s neptunio

nerd [nʌrd] s (slang) tipo insípido; sujeto estúpido

Nereid ['nɪrɪ•ɪd] s nereida

Nero ['nɪro] s Nerón m

nerve [nʌrv] adj (center; system; tonic; disease; prostration; breakdown) nervioso ‖ s nervio; ánimo, valor m; audacia; (coll) descaro; **nerves** excitabilidad nerviosa; **to get on one's nerves** irritar los nervios a uno; **to strain every nerve** esforzarse al máximo

nerve-racking ['nʌrv,rækɪŋ] adj irritante, exasperante

nervous ['nʌrvəs] adj nervioso

nervous breakdown s colapso nervioso

nervousness ['nʌrvəsnɪs] s nerviosidad

nervous shudder s muerte chiquita

nerv·y ['nʌrvi] adj (comp **-ier**; super **-iest**) (strong, vigorous) nervioso; atrevido, audaz; (coll) descarado

nest [nɛst] s nido; (where hen lays eggs) nidal m; (birds in a nest) nidada; (set of things fitting within each other) juego; (of, e.g., thieves) nido; **to feather one's nest** hacer todo para enriquecerse ‖ tr colocar en un nido ‖ intr anidar

nest egg s (eggs left in a nest to induce hen to lay more) nidal m; ahorros, hucha

nestle ['nɛsəl] tr poner en un nido; arrimar afectuosamente ‖ intr anidar; arrimarse cómodamente; **to nestle up to** arrimarse a

net [nɛt] adj neto, líquido ‖ s red f; precio neto, peso neto, ganancia líquida ‖ v (pret & pp **netted**; super **netting**) tr enredar; tejer; coger con red; producir (cierta ganancia líquida)

nether ['nɛðər] adj inferior, más bajo

Netherlander ['nɛðər,lændər] o ['nɛðərləndər] s neerlandés m

Netherlandish ['nɛðər,lændɪʃ] o ['nɛðərləndɪʃ] adj neerlandés ‖ s neerlandés m

Netherlands, The ['nɛðərləndz] los Países Bajos (Holanda)

netting [ˈnɛtɪŋ] s red f
nettle [ˈnɛtəl] s ortiga ‖ tr irritar, provocar
net'work' s red f; (rad & telv) cadena
neuralgia [njuˈrældʒə] s neuralgia
neurology [njuˈrɑlədʒi] s neurología
neuron [ˈnjurɑn] o [ˈnurɑn] s neurona
neuro•sis [njuˈrosɪs] s (pl -ses [siz]) neurosis f
neurotic [njuˈrɑtɪk] adj & s neurótico
neut. abbr **neuter**
neuter [ˈnjutər] adj neutro ‖ s género neutro; (aut) punto muerto
neutral [ˈnjutrəl] adj (on neither side in a quarrel or war) neutral; (having little or no color) neutro; (bot, chem, elec, phonet, zool) neutro ‖ s neutral mf; (aut) punto neutral, punto muerto
neutralism [ˈnjutrə,lɪzəm] s neutralismo
neutralist [ˈnjutrəlɪst] adj & s neutralista mf
neutrality [njuˈtrælɪti] s neutralidad
neutralize [ˈnjutrə,laɪz] tr neutralizar
neutron [ˈnjutrɑn] s neutrón m
neutron bomb s bomba de neutrones, bomba neutrónica
never [ˈnɛvər] adv nunca; en mi vida; de ningún modo; **never fear** no hay cuidado; **never mind** no importa
nev'er•more' adv nunca más
nevertheless [,nɛvərðəˈlɛs] adv no obstante, sin embargo
new [nju] o [nu] adj nuevo; **what's new?** ¿qué hay de nuevo?
new arrival s recién llegado; recién nacido
new'born' adj recién nacido; renacido
New Castile s Castilla la Nueva
New'cas'tle s—**to carry coals to Newcastle** echar agua al mar, llevar hierro a Vizcaya, llevar leña al monte
newcomer [ˈnju,kʌmər] s recién llegado, recién venido
New England s la Nueva Inglaterra
newfangled [ˈnju,fæŋgəld] adj de última moda, recién inventado
Newfoundland [ˈnjufənd,lænd] s (island and province) Terranova ‖ [njuˈfaʊndlənd] s (dog) Terranova m
newly [ˈnjuli] adv nuevamente; **newly** + pp recién + pp
new'ly•wed' s recién casado
New Mexican adj & s neomejicano, nuevo-mejicano
New Mexico s Nuevo Méjico
new moon s luna nueva, novilunio
news [njuz] o [nuz] s noticias; periódico; **a news item** una noticia; **a piece of news** una noticia
news agency s agencia de noticias
news beat s exclusiva, anticipación de una noticia por un periódico
news'boy' s vendedor m de periódicos
news'cast' s noticiario radiofónico ‖ tr radiodifundir (noticias) ‖ intr radiodifundir noticias
news'cast'er s cronista mf de radio
news conference s var de **press conference**
news coverage s reportaje m
news'let'ter s circular f noticiera

news•man [ˈnjuzmən] s (pl -men [mən]) noticiero
New South Wales s la Nueva Gales del Sur
news'pa'per adj periodístico ‖ s periódico
newspaper•man [ˈnjuz,pepər,mæn] s (pl -men [,mɛn]) periodista m
news'print' s papel-prensa m
news'reel' s actualidades, noticiario cinematográfico
news'stand' s quiosco de periódicos, puesto de periódicos
news'week'ly s (pl -lies) semanario de noticias
news'wor'thy adj de gran actualidad, de interés periodístico
news•y [ˈnjuzi] adj (comp -ier; super -iest) (coll) informativo
new'-world' adj del Nuevo Mundo
New Year's card s tarjeta de felicitación de Año Nuevo
New Year's Day s el Día de Año Nuevo
New Year's Eve s la noche vieja, la víspera de año nuevo
New York [jɔrk] adj neoyorkino ‖ s Nueva York
New Yorker [ˈjɔrkər] s neoyorkino
New Zealand [ˈzilənd] adj neocelandés ‖ s Nueva Zelanda
New Zealander [ˈziləndər] s neocelandés m
next [nɛkst] adj próximo, siguiente; de al lado; venidero, que viene ‖ adv luego, después; la próxima vez; **next to** junto a; después de; **next to nothing** casi nada; **the next best** lo mejor después de eso; **to come next** venir después, ser el que sigue
next door s la casa de al lado; **next door to** en la casa siguiente de; (coll) casi
next'door' adj siguiente, de al lado
next of kin s (pl **next of kin**) pariente más cercano
niacin [ˈnaɪ•əsɪn] s niacina
Niagara Falls [naɪˈægərə] spl las Cataratas del Niágara
nibble [ˈnɪbəl] s mordisco ‖ tr & intr mordiscar; picar (un pez); **to nibble at** picar de o en
Nicaraguan [,nɪkəˈrɑgwən] adj & s nicaragüense, nicaragüeño
nice [naɪs] adj delicado, fino, sutil; primoroso, pulido, refinado; dengoso, melindroso; atento, cortés, culto; escrupuloso, esmerado; agradable, simpático; decoroso, conveniente; complaciente; preciso; satisfactorio; (weather) bueno; (attractive) bonito; **nice and . . .** (coll) muy, mucho; **not nice** (coll) feo
nice-looking [ˈnaɪsˈlukɪŋ] adj hermoso, guapo, bien parecido
nicely [ˈnaɪsli] adv (coll) con precisión; escrupulosamente; satisfactoriamente; (coll) muy bien
nice•ty [ˈnaɪsəti] s (pl -ties) precisión; sutileza; finura; **to a nicety** con la mayor precisión
niche [nɪtʃ] s hornacina, nicho; colocación conveniente
Nicholas [ˈnɪkələs] s Nicolás m

ne
ni

nick [nɪk] s mella, muesca; **in the nick of time** en el momento crítico ‖ tr mellar, hacer muescas en; cortar

nickel ['nɪkəl] s níquel m; (U.S.A.) moneda de cinco centavos ‖ tr niquelar

nick'el-plate' tr niquelar

nicknack ['nɪk,næk] s chuchería, friolera

nick'name' s apodo, mote m ‖ tr apodar

nicotine ['nɪkə,tin] s nicotina

niece [nis] s sobrina

nif•ty ['nɪfti] adj (comp -tier; super -tiest) (slang) elegante; (slang) excelente

niggard ['nɪgərd] adj & s tacaño

night [naɪt] adj nocturno ‖ s noche f; **at o by night** de noche or por la noche; **night before last** anteanoche; **to make a night of it** (coll) divertirse hasta muy entrada la noche

night'cap' s gorro de dormir; trago antes de acostarse, sosiega

night club s cabaret m, café m cantante, sala de fiestas

night driving s conducción de noche

night'fall' s anochecer m, caída de la noche

night'gown' s camisa de dormir

nightingale ['naɪtən,gel] s ruiseñor m

night latch s cerradura de resorte

night letter s carta telegráfica nocturna

night'long' adj de toda la noche ‖ adv durante toda la noche

nightly ['naɪtli] adj nocturno; de cada noche ‖ adv de noche, por la noche; cada noche

night'mare' s pesadilla

nightmarish ['naɪt,mɛrɪʃ] adj espeluznante, horroroso

night owl s buho nocturno; (coll) anochecedor m, trasnochador m

night'shirt' s camisa de dormir

night'time' adj nocturno ‖ s noche f

night'walk'er s vagabundo nocturno; ladrón nocturno; ramera callejera nocturna; sonámbulo

night watch s guardia de noche, ronda de noche; sereno; (mil) vigilia

night watchman s vigilante nocturno

nihilism ['naɪ•ɪ,lɪzəm] s nihilismo

nihilist ['naɪ•ɪlɪst] s nihilista mf

nil [nɪl] s nada

Nile [naɪl] s Nilo

nimble ['nɪmbəl] adj ágil, ligero; listo, vivo

nim•bus ['nɪmbəs] s (pl -buses o -bi [baɪ]) nimbo

Nimrod ['nɪmrad] s Nemrod m

nincompoop ['nɪnkəm,pup] s badulaque m, papirote m

nine [naɪn] adj & pron nueve ‖ s nueve m; equipo de béisbol; **nine o'clock** las nueve; **the Nine** las nueve musas

nine hundred adj & pron novecientos ‖ s novecientos m

nineteen ['naɪn'tin] adj, pron & s diecinueve m, diez y nueve m

nineteenth ['naɪn'tinθ] adj & s (in a series) decimonono; (part) diecinueveavo ‖ s (in dates) diecinueve m

ninetieth ['naɪntɪ•θ] adj & s (in a series) nonagésimo; (part) noventavo

nine•ty ['naɪnti] adj & pron noventa ‖ s (pl -ties) noventa m

ninth ['naɪnθ] adj & s nono, noveno ‖ s (in dates) nueve m

nip [nɪp] s mordisco, pellizco; helada, escarcha; traguito; **nip and tuck** a quién ganará ‖ v (pret & pp **nipped**; ger **nipping**) tr mordiscar, pellizcar; helar, escarchar; (slang) asir, coger; **to nip in the bud** atajar en el principio ‖ intr beborrotear

nipple ['nɪpəl] s (of female) pezón m; (of male; of nursing bottle) tetilla; (mach) tubo roscado de unión, entrerrosca

Nippon [nɪ'pan] s el Japón

Nippon•ese [,nɪpə'niz] adj nipón ‖ s (pl -ese) nipón m

nip•py ['nɪpi] adj (comp -pier; super -piest) mordaz, picante; frío, helado; (Brit) ágil, ligero

nirvana [nɪr'vanə] s el nirvana

nit [nɪt] s piojito; (egg of insect) liendre f

niter ['naɪtər] s nitro; (agr) nitro de Chile

nitrate ['naɪtret] s nitrato; (agr) nitrato de potasio, nitrato de sodio

nitric acid ['naɪtrɪk] s ácido nítrico

nitride ['naɪtraɪd] s nitruro

nitrogen ['naɪtrədʒən] s nitrógeno

nitroglycerin [,naɪtrə'glɪsərɪn] s nitroglicerina

nitrous oxide ['naɪtrəs] s óxido nitroso

nitwit ['nɪt,wɪt] s (slang) bobalicón m

no [no] adj indef ninguno; **no admittance** no se permite la entrada; **no matter** no importa; **no parking** se prohibe estacionarse; **no smoking** se prohibe fumar; **no thoroughfare** prohibido el paso; **no use** inútil; **with no** sin ‖ adv no; **no good** de ningún valor; ruin, vil; **no longer** ya no; **no sooner** no bien

Noah ['no•ə] s Noé m

nob•by ['nabi] adj (comp -bier; super -biest) (slang) elegante; (slang) excelente

nobili•ty [no'bɪlɪti] s (pl -ties) nobleza; (of sentiments, character, etc.) nobleza, ennoblecimiento

noble ['nobəl] adj & s noble m

noble•man ['nobəlmən] s (pl -men [mən]) noble m, hidalgo

nobod•y ['no,badi] o ['no,badi] pron indef nadie, ninguno; **nobody but** nadie más que; **nobody else** nadie más, ningún otro ‖ s (pl -ies) nadie m, don nadie

nocturnal [nak'tʌrnəl] adj nocturno

nod [nad] s inclinación de cabeza; seña con la cabeza; (of a person going to sleep) cabezada ‖ v (pret & pp **nodded**; ger **nodding**) tr inclinar (la cabeza); indicar con una inclinación de cabeza ‖ intr inclinar la cabeza; (in going to sleep) cabecear

node [nod] s bulto, protuberancia; nudo, enredo; (astr, med & phys) nodo; (bot) nudo

no'-fault' adj (divorce, insurance) libre de culpa

nohow ['no,hau] adv (coll) de ninguna manera

noise [nɔɪz] s ruido ‖ tr divulgar

noiseless ['nɔɪzlɪs] adj silencioso, sin ruido

noise level s nivel sonoro
nois•y ['nɔɪzi] adj (comp **-ier;** super **-iest**) ruidoso; bullero; (boisterous) estrepitoso
nom. abbr **nominative**
nomad ['nomæd] adj & s nómada mf
nomadic [no'mædɪk] adj nomádico
no man's land s terreno sin reclamar; (mil) la tierra de nadie
nominal ['nɑmɪnəl] adj nominal; (price) módico
nominate ['nɑmɪ,net] tr postular como candidato; (to appoint) nombrar, designar
nomination [,nɑmɪ'neʃən] s postulación
nominative ['nɑmɪnətɪv] adj & s nominativo
nominee [,nɑmɪ'ni] s propuesto, candidato
nonaligned nations [,nɑnə'laɪnd] spl países no alineados; países no comprometidos
nonbelligerent [,nɑnbə'lɪdʒərənt] adj & s no beligerante m
nonbreakable [nɑn'brekəbəl] adj irrompible
nonchalance ['nɑnʃələns] s indiferencia, desenvoltura
nonchalant ['nɑnʃələnt] adj indiferente, desenvuelto
noncom ['nɑn,kɑm] s (coll) clase, suboficial m
noncombatant [nɑn'kɑmbətənt] adj & s no combatiente m
noncommissioned officer [,nɑnkə'mɪʃənd] s clase, suboficial m
noncommittal [,nɑnkə'mɪtəl] adj evasivo, reticente
noncommitted [,nɑnkə'mɪtɪd] adj no empeñado
non compos mentis ['nɑn'kɑmpəs'mɛntɪs] adj falto de juicio, loco
nonconformist [,nɑnkən'fɔrmɪst] s disidente mf; inconformista mf
nonconformity [,nɑnkən'fɔrmɪti] s inconformidad
nondelivery [,nɑndɪ'lɪvəri] s falta de entrega
nondescript ['nɑndɪ,skrɪpt] adj inclasificable, indefinido
nondiscriminating [,nɑndɪs'krɪmɪ,netɪŋ] adj indiscriminado
none [nʌn] pron indef nadie, ninguno, ningunos; **none of** ninguno de; nada de; **none other** ningún otro ‖ adv nada, de ninguna manera; **none the less** sin embargo, no obstante
nonenti•ty [nɑn'ɛntɪti] s (pl **-ties**) cosa inexistente; (person) nulidad
nonessential [,nɑnɛ'sɛnʃəl] adj intrascendente
nonexistence [,nɑnɛg'zɪstəns] s inexistencia
nonfiction [nɑn'fɪkʃən] s literatura no novelesca
nonfulfillment [,nɑnfʊl'fɪlmənt] s incumplimiento
nonintervention [,nɑnɪntər'vɛnʃən] s no intervención
nonmetal ['nɑn,mɛtəl] s metaloide m
nonpartisan [nɑn'pɑrtɪzən] adj imparcial
nonpayment [nɑn'pemənt] s falta de pago
non•plus ['nɑnplʌs] o [nɑn'plʌs] s estupefacción ‖ v (pret & pp **-plused** o **-plussed;** ger

-plusing o **-plussing**) tr dejar estupefacto, dejar pegado a la pared
nonprofit [nɑn'prɑfɪt] adj sin fin lucrativo
nonrefillable [,nɑnrɪ'fɪləbəl] adj irrellenable
nonresident [nɑn'rɛzɪdənt] s transeúnte mf
nonresidential [nɑn,rɛzɪ'dɛnʃəl] adj comercial
nonscientific [nɑn,saɪən'tɪfɪk] adj anticientífico
nonsectarian [,nɑnsɛk'tɛri•ən] adj no sectario
nonsense ['nɑnsɛns] s disparate m, tontería; esperpento; **to talk nonsense** hablar en gringo
nonsensical [nɑn'sɛnsɪkəl] adj disparatado, tonto
nonskid ['nɑn'skɪd] adj antideslizante
nonstop ['nɑn'stɑp] adj & adv sin parar, sin escala
nonsupport [,nɑnsə'port] s falta de manutención
noodle ['nudəl] s tallarín m; (slang) mentecato, tonto; (slang) cabeza
noodle soup s sopa de pastas, sopa de fideos
nook [nʊk] s rinconcito
noon [nun] s mediodía m; **at high noon** en pleno mediodía
no one o **no-one** ['no,wʌn] pron indef nadie, ninguno; **no one else** nadie más, ningún otro
noontime ['nun,taɪm] s mediodía m
noose [nus] s lazo corredizo; (to hang a criminal) dogal m; trampa ‖ tr lazar; hacer un lazo corredizo en
nor [nɔr] conj ni
Nordic ['nɔrdɪk] adj & s nórdico
norm [nɔrm] s norma
normal ['nɔrməl] adj normal
Norman ['nɔrmən] adj & s normando
Normandy ['nɔrməndi] s Normandía
Norse [nɔrs] adj nórdico; noruego ‖ s (ancient Scandinavian language) nórdico; (language of Norway) noruego; **the Norse** los nórdicos; los noruegos
Norse•man ['nɔrsmən] s (pl **-men** [mən]) normando
north [nɔrθ] adj septentrional, del norte ‖ adv al norte, hacia el norte ‖ s norte m
North America s Norteamérica, la América del Norte
North American adj & s norteamericano
north'east'er s (wind) nordestada, nordeste m (viento)
northern ['nɔrðərn] adj septentrional; (Hemisphere) boreal
North Korea s la Corea del Norte
North Korean adj & s norcoreano
northward ['nɔrθwərd] adv hacia el norte
north wind s norte m, aquilón m
Norway ['nɔrwe] s Noruega
Norwegian [nɔr'widʒən] adj & s noruego
nos. abbr **numbers**
nose [noz] s nariz f; (aer) proa; **to blow one's nose** sonarse las narices; **to count noses** averiguar cuántas personas hay; **to follow one's nose** seguir todo derecho; avanzar guiándose por el instinto; **to hold one's**

ni
no

nose tabicarse las narices; **to lead by the nose** llevar por la barba, tener agarrado por las narices; **to look down one's nose at** mirar por encima del hombro; **to pay through the nose** pagar un precio escandaloso; **to pick one's nose** hurgarse las narices; **to poke one's nose into** meter las narices en; **to speak through the nose** ganguear; **to thumb one's nose at** señalar (*a una persona*) poniendo el pulgar sobre la nariz en son de burla; tratar con sumo desprecio; **to turn up one's nose at** mirar con desprecio; **under the nose of** en las narices de, en las barbas de ‖ *tr* olfatear ‖ *intr* ventear; **to nose about** curiosear; **to nose over** capotar (*un avión*); **to nose up** encabritarse (*un buque, un avión*)

nose bag *s* cebadera, morral *m*

nose'band' *s* muserola, sobarba

nose'bleed' *s* hemorragia nasal

nose cone *s* cono de proa

nose dive *s* (aer) descenso de picado; (fig) descenso precipitado

nose'-dive' *intr* (aer) picar; (fig) descender precipidamente

nosegay ['noz,ge] *s* ramillete *m*

nose ring *s* nariguera

no'-show' *s* pasajero no presentado

nostalgia [nɑ'stældʒə] *s* nostalgia

nostril ['nɑstrɪl] *s* nariz *f*, ventana

nos•y ['nozi] *adj* (*comp* **-ier**; *super* **-iest**) (coll) curioso, husmeador

not [nɑt] *adv* no; **not at all** nada, de ningún modo; **not yet** todavía no; **to think not** creer que no; **why not?** ¿cómo no?

notable ['notəbəl] *adj & s* notable *m*

notarize ['notə,raɪz] *tr* abonar con fe notarial

nota•ry ['notəri] *s* (*pl* **-ries**) notario

notch [nɑtʃ] *s* muesca, mella, corte *m;* (U.S.A.) desfiladero, paso; (coll) grado ‖ *tr* hacer muescas en, mellar

note [not] *s* nota; apunte *m;* esquela, cartita; marca, señal *f;* (com) pagaré *m*, vale *m;* canto, melodía; acento, voz *f;* (mus) nota ‖ *tr* notar, apuntar; marcar, señalar

note'book' *s* cuaderno. libro de apuntes

noted ['notɪd] *adj* aramado, conocido

note paper *s* papel *m* de cartas

note'wor'thy *adj* notable, digno de notarse

nothing ['nʌθɪŋ] *pron indef* nada; **for nothing** inútilmente; de balde, gratis; **nothing doing** (slang) ni por pienso; **nothing else** nada más; **that's nothing to me** eso nada me importa; **to make nothing of** no hacer caso de; no aprovecharse de; no entender; despreciar; **to think nothing of** no hacer caso de; tener por fácil; despreciar ‖ *adv* nada, de ninguna manera; **nothing daunted** sin temor alguno ‖ *s* nada, nadería, friolera

notice ['notɪs] *s* atención, reparo, advertencia; aviso, noticia; letrero; mención, reseña; llamada; notificación; **on short notice** con poco tiempo de aviso; **to escape one's notice** pasarle inadvertido a uno; **to serve notice** dar noticia, hacer saber ‖ *tr* notar, observar, reparar, reparar en; mencionar

noticeable ['notɪsəbəl] *adj* sensible, perceptible; notable

noti•fy ['notɪ,faɪ] *v* (*pret & pp* **-fied**) *tr* notificar, avisar, hacer saber

notion ['noʃən] *s* noción; capricho; **notions** mercería, artículos menudos; **to have a notion to** + *inf* pensar + *inf*, tener ganas de + *inf*

notorie•ty [,noʃtə'raɪəti] *s* (*pl* **-ties**) mala reputación; (*condition of being well known*) notoriedad; (*person*) notable *mf*

notorious [no'torɪəs] *adj* reputado, mal reputado; bien conocido

no'-trump' *adj & s* sin triunfo; **a no-trump hand** un sin triunfo

notwithstanding [,nɑtwɪð'stændɪŋ] o [,nɑtwiθ'stændɪŋ] *adv* no obstante ‖ *prep* a pesar de ‖ *conj* a pesar de que

nougat ['nugət] *s* turrón *m*

noun [naun] *s* nombre, nombre sustantivo

nourish ['nʌrɪʃ] *tr* alimentar, nutrir; abrigar (*p.ej., esperanzas*)

nourishing ['nʌrɪʃɪŋ] *adj* alimenticio, nutritivo

nourishment ['nʌrɪʃmənt] *s* alimento, nutrimento

Nov. *abbr* **November**

Nova Scotia ['novə'skoʃə] *s* la Nueva Escocia

Nova Scotian ['novə'skoʃən] *adj & s* neoescocés *m*

novel ['nɑvəl] *adj* nuevo; insólito, extraño, original ‖ *s* novela

novelist ['nɑvəlɪst] *s* novelista *mf*

novel•ty ['nɑvəlti] *s* (*pl* **-ties**) novedad, innovación; **novelties** bisutería, baratijas

November [no'vɛmbər] *s* noviembre *m*

novice ['nɑvɪs] *s* novicio

novocaine ['novə,ken] *s* novocaína

now [nau] *adv* ahora; ya; entonces; **from now on** de ahora en adelante; **how now?** ¿cómo?; **just now** hace un momento; **now and again** o **now and then** de vez en cuando; **now ... now** ora ... ora, ya ... ya; **now that** ya que; **now then** ahora bien ‖ *interj* ¡vamos! ‖ *s* actualidad

nowadays ['nau•ə,dez] *adv* hoy en día, hoy día

no'way' o **no'ways'** *adv* de ningún modo

no'where' *adv* en ninguna parte, a ninguna parte; **nowhere else** en ninguna otra parte

noxious ['nɑkʃəs] *adj* nocivo

nozzle ['nɑzəl] *s* (*of hoe*) lanza; (*of sprinkling can*) rallow, roseta; (*of candlestick*) cubo; (slang) nariz *f*

N.T. *abbr* **New Testament**

nth [ɛnθ] *adj* n^{mo} (*enésimo*); **to the nth degree** elevado a la potencia *n;* a más no poder

nuance [nju'ɑns] o ['nju•ɑns] *s* matiz *m*

nub [nʌb] *s* protuberancia; pedazo; (coll) meollo

nuclear ['nuklɪ•ər] *adj* nuclear

nu'cle•ar-pow'ered *adj* accionado por energía nuclear

nuclear test ban *s* proscripción de las pruebas nucleares

nuclear war *s* guerra nuclear

nucle·us [ˈnuklɪ·əs] *s* (*pl* **-i** [ˌaɪ] o **-uses**) núcleo

nude [njud] o [nud] *adj* desnudo ‖ *s*—**in the nude** desnudo; **the nude** el desnudo

nudism [ˈnjudɪzəm] o [ˈnudɪzəm] *s* (des)nudismo; naturismo

nudge [nʌdʒ] *s* codazo suave ‖ *tr* dar un codazo suave a, empujar suavemente

nugget [ˈnʌgɪt] *s* pedazo; (*of, e.g., gold*) pepita; preciosidad

nuisance [ˈnjusəns] o [ˈnusəns] *s* molestia, estorbo; majadería; persona o cosa fastidiosas; **to be a nuisance** ser un higado

nuke [njuk] o [nuk] *s* (slang) arma atómica ‖ *tr* (slang) atacar con arma atómica; aniquilar

null [nʌl] *adj* nulo; **null and void** nulo, írrito, nulo y sin valor

nulli·ty [ˈnʌlɪti] *v* (*pl* **-ties**) nulidad

nulli·fy [ˈnʌlifaɪ] *v* (*pret & pp* **-fied**) anular, invalidar

numb [nʌm] *adj* entumecido; **to get numb** envararse ‖ *tr* entumecer

number [ˈnʌmbər] *s* número; **a number of** varios ‖ *tr* numerar; ascender a (*cierto número*); **his days are numbered** tiene sus días contados o sus horas contadas; **to be numbered among** hallarse entre; **to number among** contar entre

numberless [ˈnʌmbərlɪs] *adj* innumerable

numeral [ˈnjumərəl] o [ˈnumərəl] *adj* numeral ‖ *s* número

numerical [njuˈmɛrɪkəl] o [nuˈmɛrɪkəl] *adj* numérico

numerous [ˈnjumərəs] o [ˈnumərəs] *adj* numeroso

numskull [ˈnʌmˌskʌl] *s* (coll) bodoque *m*, mentecato

nun [nʌn] *s* monja, religiosa

nuptial [ˈnʌpʃəl] *adj* nupcial ‖ **nuptials** *spl* nupcias, bodas

nurse [nʌrs] *s* enfermera; (*to suckle a child*) ama de cría, nodriza; (*to take care of a child*) niñera ‖ *tr* cuidar (*a una persona enferma*); amamantar; alimentar, criar; tratar de curarse de (*p.ej., un resfriado*); abrigar (*p.ej., odio*) ‖ *intr* ser enfermera

nurser·y [ˈnʌrsəri] *s* (*pl* **-ies**) cuarto de los niños; (*of plants*) criadero, plantel *m*, semillero; (fig) semillero

nursery·man [ˈnʌrsərɪmən] *s* (*pl* **-men** [mən]) cultivador *m* de semillero

nursery rhymes *spl* versos para niños

nursery tales *spl* cuentos para niños

nursing bottle *s* biberón *m*

nursing home *s* clínica de reposo; (*for the aged*) residencia de ancianos

nurture [ˈnʌrtʃər] *s* alimentación, nutrimento; crianza, educación ‖ *tr* alimentar, nutrir; criar, educar; acariciar (*p.ej., una esperanza*)

nut [nʌt] *s* nuez *f*; (*to screw on a bolt*) tuerca; (slang) estrafalario; **a hard nut to crack** (coll) hueso duro de roer

nut'crack'er *s* cascanueces *m*

nutmeg [ˈnʌtˌmɛg] *s* nuez moscada; (*tree*) mirística

nutriment [ˈnjutrɪmənt] *s* nutrimento

nutrition [njuˈtrɪʃən] *s* nutrición

nutritious [njuˈtrɪʃəs] *adj* nutricioso, nutritivo

nuts *adj* (slang) loco; estrafalario ‖ *interj* (slang) ¡no!, ¡niego!, ¡de ninguna manera!

nut'shell' *s* cáscara de nuez; **in a nutshell** en pocas palabras

nut·ty [ˈnʌti] *adj* (*comp* **-tier;** *super* **-tiest**) abundante en nueces; que sabe a nueces; (slang) chiflado, loco; **nutty about** (slang) loco por

nuzzle [ˈnʌzəl] *tr* hocicar, hozar ‖ *intr* hocicar; arrimarse cómodamente; arroparse bien

nylon [ˈnaɪlɑn] *s* nilón *m;* **nylons** medias de nilón

nymph [nɪmf] *s* ninfa

O

O, o [o] decimoquinta letra del alfabeto inglés

O *interj* ¡oh!; ¡ay!, p.ej., **how pretty she is!** ¡Ay qué linda!; **O that. . . !** ¡Ojalá que. . . !

oaf [of] *s* zoquete *m*, zamacuco; niño contrahecho

oak [ok] *s* roble *m*

oaken [ˈokən] *adj* hecho de roble

oakum [ˈokəm] *s* estopa, estopa de calafatear

oar [or] *s* remo; **to lie** o **rest on one's oars** aguantar los remos; aflojar en el trabajo ‖ *tr* conducir a remo ‖ *intr* remar, bogar

oars·man [ˈorzmən] *s* (*pl* **-men** [mən]) remero

OAS [ˈoˈeˈɛs] *s* (*letterword*) OEA *f*

oa·sis [oˈesɪs] *s* (*pl* **-ses** [siz]) oasis *m*

oat [ot] *s* avena; **oats** (*edible grain*) avena; **to feel one's oats** (slang) estar fogoso y brioso; (slang) estar muy pagado de sí mismo; **to sow one's wild oats** correrla, pasar las mocedades

oath [oθ] *s* juramento; **on oath** bajo juramento; **to take an oath** prestar juramento

oat'meal' *s* harina de avena; gachas de avena

ob. *abbr* **obiit** (Lat) died

obbligato [ˌɑblɪˈgɑto] *adj & s* obligado

obduracy [ˈɑbdjərəsi] *s* obduración

obdurate ['abdjərɪt] *adj* obstinado, terco; empedernido

obedience [o'bidɪ•əns] *s* obediencia

obedient [o'bidɪ•ənt] *adj* obediente

obeisance [o'besəns] u [o'bisəns] *s* saludo respetuoso; homenaje *m*, respeto

obelisk ['abəlɪsk] *s* obelisco

obese [o'bis] *adj* obeso

obesity [o'bisɪti] *s* obesidad

obey [o'be] *tr & intr* obedecer

obfuscate [ab'fʌsket] o ['abfəs,ket] *tr* ofuscar

obituar•y [o'bɪtʃu,ɛri] *adj* necrológico ‖ *s (pl -ies)* necrología

obj. *abbr* **object, objection, objective**

object ['abdʒɪkt] *s* objeto ‖ [ab'dʒɛkt] *tr* objetar ‖ *intr* hacer objeciones

objection [ab'dʒɛk/ən] *s* reparo, objeción; **to have no objections to make** no tener nada que objetar

objectionable [ab'dʒɛk/ənəbəl] *adj* desagradable, reprensible; *(causing disapproval)* objetable

objective [ab'dʒɛktɪv] *adj & s* objetivo

obl. *abbr* **oblique, oblong**

obligate [ablɪ,get] *tr* obligar

obligation [,ablɪ'ge/ən] *s* obligación; encargamiento

oblige [ə'blaɪdʒ] *tr* obligar; complacer; **much obliged** muchas gracias

obliging [ə'blaɪdʒɪŋ] *adj* complaciente, condescendiente, servicial

oblique [ə'blik] *adj* oblicuo; indirecto, evasivo

obliterate [ə'blɪtə,ret] *tr* borrar; arrasar, destruir

oblivion [ə'blɪvɪ•ən] *s* olvido

oblivious [ə'blɪvɪ•əs] *adj* olvidadizo

oblong ['ablɔŋ] o ['ablaŋ] *adj* oblongo

obnoxious [ab'nak/əs] *adj* detestable, ofensivo

oboe ['obo] *s* oboe *m*

oboist ['obo•ɪst] *s* oboísta *mf*

obs. *abbr* **obsolete**

obscene [ab'sin] *adj* obsceno

obsceni•ty [ab'sɛnɪti] o [ab'sinɪti] *s (pl -ties)* obscenidad

obscure [əb'skjur] *adj* obscuro; *(vowel)* relajado, neutro

obscuri•ty [əb'skjurɪti] *s (pl -ties)* obscuridad

obsequies ['absɪkwiz] *spl* exequias

obsequious [əb'sikwɪ•əs] *adj* obsequioso, servil, rastrero

observance [əb'zʌrvəns] *s* observancia; ceremonia, rito

observant [əb'zʌrvənt] *adj* observador

observation [,abzər've/ən] *s* observación; observancia

observato•ry [əb'zʌrvə,tori] *s (pl -ries)* observatorio

observe [əb'zʌrv] *tr* observar; *(a holiday; silence)* guardar

observer [əb'zʌrvər] *s* observador *m*

obsess [əb'sɛs] *tr* obsesionar

obsession [əb'sɛ/ən] *s* obsesión

obsolescent [,absə'lɛsənt] *adj* arcaizante

obsolete ['absə,lit] *adj* desusado, caído en desuso; obsoleto

obstacle ['abstəkəl] *s* obstáculo

obstetrical [ab'stɛtrɪkəl] *adj* obstétrico

obstetrics [ab'stɛtrɪks] *ssg* obstetricia

obstina•cy ['abstɪnəsi] *s (pl -cies)* obstinación

obstinate ['abstɪnɪt] *adj* obstinado

obstruct [ab'strʌkt] *tr* obstruir; obstruccionar

obstruction [əb'strʌk/ən] *s* obstrucción

obtain [əb'ten] *tr* obtener ‖ *intr* existir, prevalecer

obtrusive [əb'trusɪv] *adj* entremetido, intruso

obtuse [əb'tjus] o [əb'tus] *adj* obtuso

ob√iate ['abvɪ,et] *tr* obviar

obvious ['abvɪ•əs] *adj* obvio

occasion [ə'keʒən] *s* ocasión; **to improve the occasion** aprovechar la ocasión

occasional [ə'keʒənəl] *adj* raro, poco frecuente; alguno que otro; de circunstancia

occasionally [ə'keʒənəli] *adv* ocasionalmente, de vez en cuando

occident ['aksɪdənt] *s* occidente *m*

occidental [,aksɪ'dɛntəl] *adj* occidental

occlusive [ə'klusɪv] *adj* oclusivo ‖ *s* oclusiva

occult [ə'kʌlt] o ['akʌlt] *adj* oculto

occupancy ['akjepənsi] *s* ocupación

occupant ['akjepənt] *s* ocupante *mf;* inquilino

occupation [,akjə'pe/ən] *s* ocupación

occupational therapy *s* terapia vocacional

occu•py ['akjə,paɪ] *v (pret & pp -pied) tr* ocupar; habitar

oc•cur [ə'kʌr] *v (pret & pp -curred; ger -curring) intr* ocurrir, acontecer, suceder; encontrarse; *(to come to mind)* ocurrir

occurrence [ə'kʌrəns] *s* acontecimiento; caso, aparición

ocean ['o/ən] *s* océano

o'cean-go'ing *adj* transoceánico

oceanic [,o/ɪ'ænɪk] *adj* oceánico

ocean liner *s* buque transoceánico

o'clock [ə'klak] *adv* por el reloj; **it is one o'clock** es la una; **it is two o'clock** son las dos; **what o'clock is it?** ¿qué hora es?

Oct. *abbr* **October**

octave ['aktɪv] o ['aktev] *s* octava

October [ak'tobər] *s* octubre *m*

octo•pus ['aktəpəs] *s (pl -puses* o *-pi* [,paɪ]*)* pulpo

octoroon [,aktə'run] *s* octavo

ocular ['akjələr]*adj & s* ocular *m*

oculist ['akjəlɪst] *s* oculista *mf*

O.D. *abbr* **officer of the day, olive drab, overdose**

odd [ad] *adj* suelto; *(number)* impr; *(that doesn't match)* dispar; libre, de ocio; sobrante; extraño, raro, singular; y pico, y tantos, p.ej., **two hundred odd** doscientos y pico ‖ **odds** *ssg* o *spl (in betting)* ventaja; apuesta desigual; puntos de ventaja; **at odds** de monos, de reñido; **by all odds** muy probablemente, sin duda alguna; **it makes no odds** lo mismo da; **the odds are** lo probable es; la ventaja es de; **to be at odds** estar de punta, estar encontrados; **to set at odds** enemistar, malquistar

odd'ball' *adj & s* excéntrico; disente
oddi•ty ['ɑdɪti] *s* (*pl* **-ties**) rareza, cosa rara
odd jobs *spl* pequeñas tareas
odd lot *s* lote *m* inferior al centenar
odds and ends *spl* pedacitos varios, cajón *m* de sastre
ode [od] *s* oda
odious ['odɪ•əs] *adj* odioso, abominable
odor ['odər] *s* olor *m;* **to be in bad odor** tener mala fama
odorless ['odərlɪs] *adj* inodoro
odorous ['odərəs] *adj* oloroso
Odysseus [o'dɪsjus] u [o'dɪsɪ•əs] *s* Odiseo
Odyssey ['ɑdɪsi] *s* Odisea
Oedipus ['ɛdɪpəs] o ['idɪpəs] *s* Edipo
oenology [i'nɑlədʒi] *s* enotecnia
of [ɑv] o [əv] *prep* de, p.ej., **the top of the mountain** la cima de la montaña; a: **to smell of** oler a; con: **to dream of** soñar con; en: **to think of** pensar en; menos: **a quarter of two** las dos menos un cuarto
off. *abbr* **office, officer, official**
off [ɔf] o [ɑf] *adj* malo, p.ej., **off day** día, malo; (*account, sum*) errado; más distante; libre; sin trabajo; quitado; apagado; (*electric current*) cortado; de descuento, de rebaja; de la parte del mar; (*season*) muerto ‖ *adv* fuera, a distancia, lejos; allá; **off of** (*coll*) de; (*coll*) a expensas de; **to be off** ponerse en marcha ‖ *prep* de, desde, al lado de, a nivel de; fuera de; libre de; (*naut*) a la altura de ‖ *tr* (slang) matar, asesinar
offal ['ɑfəl] u ['ɔfəl] *s* (*of butchered meat*) carniza; basura, desperdicios
off and on *adv* unas veces sí y otras no
off'beat' *adj* (slang) insólito, chocante, original
off'chance' *s* posibilidad poco probable
off'-col'or *adj* descolorido; indispuesto; (*indecent, risqué*) colorado, subido de color
offend [ə'fɛnd] *tr & intr* ofender
offender [ə'fɛndər] *s* ofensor *m*
offense [ə'fɛns] *s* ofensa; **to take offense (at)** ofenderse (de)
offensive [ə'fɛnsɪv] *adj* ofensivo ‖ *f* ofensiva
offer ['ɔfər] o ['ɑfər] *s* ofrecimiento, oferta ‖ *tr* ofrecer; rezar (*oraciones*); oponer (*resistencia*)
offering ['ɔfərɪŋ] o ['ɑfərɪŋ] *s* ofrecimiento; (*gift, present*) oferta; (*presentation in worship*) ofrenda
off'hand' *adj* hecho de improviso; brusco, desenvuelto ‖ *adv* de improviso, súbitamente; bruscamente
office ['ɔfɪs] o ['ɑfɪs] *s* oficina, despacho; función, oficio; cargo, ministerio; (*of a lawyer*) bufete *m;* (*of a doctor*) consultorio
office boy *s* mandadero
office desk *s* escritorio ministro
of'fice•hold'er *s* funcionario, burócrata *m*
office hours *spl* horas de oficina; (*of a doctor*) horas de consulta
officer ['ɔfɪsər] o ['ɑfɪsər] *s* jefe *m*, director *m;* (*of army, an order, a society, etc.*) oficial *m;* agente *m* de policía

office seeker ['sikər] *s* aspirante *m*, pretendiente *m*
office supplies *spl* suministros para oficinas
official [ə'fɪʃəl] *adj* oficial ‖ *s* jefe *m*, director *m;* (*of a society*) dignatario
officiate [ə'fɪʃɪ,et] *intr* oficiar
officious [ə'fɪʃəs] *adj* oficioso
off'-peak' *adj* (*hours, stop, etc.*) de valle; de menor tránsito
off-peak heater *s* (elec) termos *m* de acumulación
off-peak load *s* (elec) carga de las horas de valle
off'print' *s* sobretiro
off'set' *s* compensación; (typ) offset *m* ‖ **off'set'** *v* (*pret & pp* **-set;** *ger* **-setting**) *tr* compensar; imprimir por offset
off'shoot' *s* (*of plant*) retoño, renuevo; (*of a family or race*) descendiente *mf;* (*branch*) ramal *m;* consecuencia
off'shore' *adj* (*wind*) terral; (*fishing*) de bajura; (*said of islands*) costero; **offshore drilling rig** barca perforador ‖ *adv* a lo largo
off'spring' *s* descendencia, sucesión; hijo, hijos
off'-stage' *adj* de entre bastidores
off'-the-rec'ord *adj* extraoficial, confidencial
often ['ɔfən] o (ɑfən] *adv* a menudo, muchas veces; **how often?** ¿cuántas veces?; **not often** pocas veces
ogive ['odʒaɪv] u [o'dʒaɪv] *s* ojiva
ogle ['ogəl] *tr & intr* ojear; mirar amorosamente
ogre ['ogər] *s* ogro
ohm [om] *s* ohmio
oil [ɔɪl] *adj* (*burner; field; well*) de petróleo; (*pump; stove*) de aceite; (*company, tanker*) petrolero; (*land*) petrolífero ‖ *s* aceite *m;* (*consecrated oil; painting*) óleo; **to burn the midnight oil** quemarse las cejas; **to pour oil on troubled waters** mojar la pólvora; **to strike oil** encontrar una capa de petróleo; (fig) enriquecerse de súbito ‖ *tr* aceitar; lubricar; lisonjear; (*to bribe*) untar ‖ *intr* proveerse de petróleo (*un buque*)
oil'can' *s* aceitera
oil'cloth' *s* encerado, hule *m*
oil field *s* yacimiento de petróleo
oil gauge indicador *m* del nivel de aceite
oil pan *s* colector *m* de aceite
oil shortage *s* carestía (*or* escasez *f*) de petróleo
oil tanker *s* petrolero
oil•y ['ɔɪli] *adj* (*comp* **-ier;** *super* **-iest**) aceitoso; liso, resbaladizo; zalamero
ointment ['ɔɪntmənt] *s* ungüento
O.K. ['o'ke] *adj* (coll) aprobado, conforme ‖ *adv* (coll) muy bien, está bien ‖ *s* (coll) aprobación ‖ *v* (*pret & pp* **O.K.'d;** *ger* **O.K.'ing**) *tr* (coll) aprobar
okra ['okrə] *s* quingombó *m*
old [old] *adj* viejo; antiguo; (*wine*) añejo; **how old is . . . ?** ¿cuántos años tiene . . . ?; **of old** de antaño, antiguamente; **to be . . . years old** tener . . . años

ob
ol

old age *s* ancianidad, vejez *f;* **to die of old age** morir de viejo

old boy *s* viejo; graduado; **the Old Boy** (slang) el diablo

Old Castile *s* Castilla la Vieja

old-clothes•man ['old'kloðz,mæn] *s* (*pl* -men [mɛn]) ropavejero

old country *s* madre patria

old-fashioned ['old'fæʃənd] *adj* chapado a la antigua; anticuado, fuera de moda

old fo•gey *u* **old fo•gy** ['fogi] *s* (*pl* -gies) persona un poco ridícula por sus ideas o costumbres atrasadas

Old Glory *s* la bandera de los Estados Unidos

Old Guard *s* (U.S.A.) bando conservador del partido republicano

old hand *s* practicón *m*, veterano

old maid *s* solterona

old master *s* (paint) gran maestro; obra de un gran maestro

old moon *s* luna menguante

old salt *s* lobo de mar

old school *s* gente chapada a la antigua

old'-time' *adj* del tiempo viejo

old-timer ['old'taɪmər] *s* (coll) antiguo residente, veterano; (coll) persona chapada a la antigua

old wives' tale *s* cuento de viejas

old'-world' *adj* del Viejo Mundo

oleander [,olɪ'ændər] *s* adelfa

oligar•chy ['alɪ,gɑrki] *s* (*pl* -chies) oligarquía

olive ['alɪv] *adj* aceitunado ‖ *s* aceituna

olive branch *s* ramo de olivo; (*peace*) oliva; hijo, vástago

olive grove *s* olivar *m*

olive oil *s* aceite *m*, aceite de oliva

olive tree *s* aceituno, olivo

Olympiad [o'lɪmpɪ,æd] *s* Olimpíada

Olympian [o'lɪmpɪ•ən] *adj* olímpico ‖ *s* dios griego

Olympic [o'lɪmpɪk] *adj* olímpico

omelet *u* **omelette** ['aməlɪt] *o* ['amlɪt] *s* tortilla (de huevos)

omen ['omən] *s* agüero

ominous ['amɪnəs] *adj* ominoso

omission [o'mɪʃən] *s* omisión

omit [o'mɪt] *v* (*pret & pp* **omitted;** *ger* **omitting**) *tr* omitir

omnibus ['amnɪ,bʌs] *o* ['amnɪbəs] *adj* general; (*volume*) colecticio ‖ *s* ómnibus *m*

omnipotent [am'nɪpətənt] *adj* omnipotente

omniscient [am'nɪʃənt] *adj* omnisciente

omnivorous [am'nɪvərəs] *adj* omnívoro

on [an] *u* [ɔn] *adj* puesto, p.ej., **with his hat on** con el sombrero puesto; principiando; en funcionamiento; encendido; conectado; **the deal is on** ya está concertado el trato; **the game is on** ya están jugando; **the race is on** allá van los corredores; **what is on at the theater this evening?** ¿qué representan esta noche? ‖ *adv* adelante; encima! **and so on** y así sucesivamente; **come on!** ¡anda, anda!; **farther on** más allá, más adelante; **later on** más tarde, después; **to be on to a person** (coll) conocerle a uno el juego; **to have on** tener puesto; **to . . . on** seguir + *ger*, **he played on** siguió to-

cando ‖ *prep* en, sobre, encima de; a, p.ej., **on foot** a pie; **on my arrival** a mi llegada; bajo, p.ej., **on my responsibility** bajo mi responsabilidad; contra, p.ej., **an attack on liberty** un ataque contra la libertad; de, p.ej., **on good authority** de buena tinta; **on a journey** de viaje; hacia, p.ej., **to march on the capital** marchar hacia la capital; por, p.ej., **on all sides** por todos lados; tras, p.ej., **defeat on defeat** derrota tras derrota; **on** + *ger* al + *inf*, p.ej., **on arriving** al llegar

on and on *adv* continuamente, sin cesar, sin parar

on'-board' computer *s* ordenador de viaje

once [wʌns] *adv* una vez; antes, p.ej., **once so happy** antes tan feliz; alguna vez, p.ej., **if this once becomes known** si esto llega a saberse alguna vez; **all at once** de súbito, de repente; **at once** en seguida; a la vez en el mismo momento; **for once** una vez por lo menos; **once and again** repetidas veces; **once in a blue moon** cada muerte de obispo; **once in a while** de vez en cuando; luego; **once more** otra vez; una vez más; **once upon a time there was** érase una vez, érase que se era ‖ *conj* una vez que ‖ *s* una vez; vez, p.ej., **this once** esta vez

once'-o'ver *s* (slang) examen rápido; **to give a thing the once-over** (coll) examinar una cosa superficialmente

oncology [aŋ'kalədʒi] *s* oncología

one [wʌn] *adj* un, uno; un tal, p.ej., **one Smith** un tal Smith; único, p.ej., **one price** precio único ‖ *pron* uno, p.ej., **one does not know what to do here** uno no sabe qué hacer aquí; se, p.ej., **how does one go to the station?** ¿cómo se va a la estación?; **I for one** yo por lo menos; **it's all one and the same to me** me es igual; **my little one** mi chiquito; **of one another** el uno del otro, los unos de los otros, p.ej., **we took leave of one another** nos despedimos el uno del otro; **one and all** todos; **one another** se, p.ej., **they greeted one another** se saludaron; uno a otro, unos a otros, p.ej., **they looked at one another** se miraron uno a otro; **one by one** uno a uno; **one o'clock** la una; **one or two** unos pocos; **one's** su, el . . . de uno; **the blue book and the red one** el libro azul y el rojo; **the one and only** el único; **the one that** el que, la que; **this one** éste; **that one** ése, aquél; **to make one** unir; casar ‖ *s* uno

one'-fam'i•ly house *s* vivienda unifamiliar

one'-horse' *adj* de un solo caballo, tirado por un solo caballo; (coll) insignificante, de poca monta

onerous ['anərəs] *adj* oneroso

one'self' *pron* uno mismo; sí, sí mismo; se; **to be oneself** tener dominio de sí mismo; conducirse con naturalidad

one-sided ['wʌn'saɪdɪd] *adj* de un solo lado; injusto, parcial; desigual; unilateral

one'-track' *adj* de carril único; (coll) con un solo interés

one'-way' *adj* de una solo dirección, de dirección única; *(ticket)* sencillo, de ida

onion ['ʌnjən] *s* cebolla

on'ion•skin' *s* papel *m* de seda, papel cebolla

on'look'er *s* mirón *m*, espectador *m*

only ['onlɪ] *adj* solo, único ‖ *adv* solamente, sólo, únicamente; no ... más que; **not only ... but also** no sólo ... sino también ‖ *conj* sólo que, pero

onomatopoeic [,anə,mætə'pi•ɪk] *adj* onomatopéyico

on'set' *s* arremetida, embestida; *(of an illness)* principio

onward ['anwərd] u **onwards** ['anwərdz] *adv* adelante, hacia adelante

onyx ['anɪks] *s* ónice *m* u ónix *m*

ooze [uz] *s* chorro suave; cieno; limo, lama ‖ *tr* rezumar ‖ *intr* rezumar, rezumarse; manar suavemente *(p.ej., la sangre de una herida)*; agotarse poco a poco

op. *abbr* **opera, operation, opus, opposite**

opal ['opəl] *s* ópalo

opaque [o'pek] *adj* opaco; *(writer's style)* obscuro; estúpido

open ['opən] *adj* abierto; descubierto, destapado; sin tejado; vacante; *(hour)* libre; discutible, pendiente; *(hand)* liberal; *(hunting season)* legal; **to break** o **to crack open** abrir con violencia, abrir por la fuerza; **to throw open** abrir de par en par ‖ *s* abertura; *(in the woods)* claro; **in the open** al aire libre; a campo raso; en alta mar; abiertamente ‖ *tr* abrir; desbullar *(una ostra)* ‖ *intr* abrir; abrirse; estrenarse *(un drama)*; **to open into** desembocar en; **to open on** dar a; **to open up** descubrirse; descubrir el pecho

o'pen-air' *adj* al aire libre, a cielo abierto

open-eyed ['opən,aɪd] *adj* alerta, vigilante; con ojos asombrados; hecho con los ojos abiertos

open-handed ['opən'hændɪd] *adj* maniabierto, liberal

open-hearted (opən'hartɪd] *adj* franco, sincero

open house *s* coliche *m;* **to keep open house** recibir a todos, gustar de tener siempre convidados en casa

opening ['opənɪŋ] *s* abertura; *(of, e.g., school)* apertura; *(in the woods)* claro; *(vacancy)* hueco, vacante *f; (chance to say something)* ocasión

opening night *s* noche *f* de estreno

opening number *s* primer número

opening price *s* primer curso, precio de apertura

open-minded ['opən'maɪndɪd] *adj* receptivo, razonable, imparcial

open secret *s* secreto a voces

open shop *s* taller franco

o'pen•work' *s* calado

opera ['apərə] *s* ópera

opera glasses *spl* gemelos de teatro

opera hat *s* clac *m*, sombrero de muelles

opera house *s* teatro de la ópera

operate ['apə,ret] *tr* hacer funcionar; dirigir, manejar; explotar ‖ *intr* funcionar; operar;

to operate on operar *(p.ej., una hernia; a un niño)*

operatic [,apə'rætɪk] *adj* operístico

operating expenses *spl* gastos de explotación

operating room *s* quirófano

operating table *s* mesa operatoria

operation [,apə,ret/ən] *s* operación; funcionamiento; explotación

operator ['apə,retər] *s* operador *m*, maquinista *m;* (com) empresario; (coll) corredor *m* de bolsa; (surg, telp) operador *m*

operetta [,apə'retə] *s* opereta

opiate ['opɪ•ɪt] u ['op,et] *adj & s* opiato

opinion [ə'pɪnjən] *s* opinión; **in my opinion** a mi parecer; **to have a high opinion of** tener buen concepto de

opinionated [ə'pɪnjə,netɪd] *adj* porfiado en su parecer, dogmático

opinion poll *s* encuesta demoscópica

opium ['opɪ•əm] *s* opio

opium den *s* fumadero de opio

opossum [ə'pasəm] *s* zarigüeya

opponent [ə'ponənt] *s* contrario

opportune [,apər'tjun] *adj* oportuno

opportunist [,apər'tjunɪst] *s* oportunista *mf;* maromero

opportuni•ty [,apər'tjunɪti] *s* (*pl* **-ties**) oportunidad, ocasión

oppose [ə'poz] *tr* oponerse a

opposite ['apəsɪt] *adj* opuesto; de enfrente, p.ej., **the house opposite** la casa de enfrente ‖ *prep* enfrente de ‖ *s* contrario

opposite number *s* igual *mf*, doble *mf*

opposition [,apə'zɪ/ən] *s* oposición

oppress [ə'prɛs] *tr* oprimir

oppression [ə'prɛ/ən] *s* opresión

oppressive [ə'prɛsɪv] *adj* opresivo; sofocante, bochornoso

opprobrious [ə'probrɪ•əs] *adj* oprobioso

opprobrium [ə'probrɪ•əm] *s* oprobio

optic ['aptɪk] *adj* óptico ‖ *s* (coll) ojo; **optics** *ssg* óptica

optical ['aptɪkəl] *adj* óptico

optician [ap'tɪ/ən] *s* óptico

optimism ['aptɪ,mɪzəm] *s* optimismo

optimist ['aptɪmɪst] *s* optimista *mf*

optimistic [,aptɪ'mɪstɪk] *adj* optimístico

optimize ['aptə,maɪz] *tr* mejorar en todo lo posible

option ['ap/ən] *s* opción

optional ['ap/ənəl] *adj* facultativo, potestativo

optometrist [ap,tamɪtrɪst] *s* optometrista *mf*

opulent ['apjələnt] *adj* opulento

or [ɔr] *conj* o, u

oracle ['arəkəl] u ['ɔrəkəl] *s* oráculo

oracular [o'rækjələr] *adj* sentencioso; ambiguo, misterioso; fatídico; sabio

oral ['ɔrəl] *adj* oral

orange ['arɪndʒ] u ['ɔrɪndʒ] *adj* anaranjado ‖ *s* naranja

orangeade [,arɪndʒ'ed] u [,ɔrɪndʒ'ed] *s* naranjada

orange blossom *s* azahar *m*

orange grove *s* naranjal *m*

orange juice *s* zumo de naranja

orange squeezer *s* exprimidera de naranjas

ol
or

orange tree *s* naranjo
orang-outang [oˈræŋʊˌtæŋ] *s* orangután *m*
oration [oˈreʃən] *s* oración, discurso
orator [ˈɑrətər] u [ˈɔrətər] *s* orador *m*
oratorical [ˌɔrəˈtɔrɪkəl] *adj* oratorio
oratori•o [ˌɔrəˈtorɪˌo] *s* (*pl* **-os**) oratorio
orato•ry [ˈɔrəˌtori] *s* (*pl* **-ries**) (*art of public speaking*) oratoria; (*small chapel*) oratorio
orb [ɔrb] *s* orbe *m*
orbit [ˈɔrbɪt] *s* órbita; **to go into orbit** entrar en órbita ‖ *tr* poner en órbita; moverse en órbita alrededor de ‖ *intr* moverse enorbita
orbiter [ˈɔrbɪtər] *s* satélite *m* (artificial)
orchard [ˈɔrtʃərd] *s* huerto
orchestra [ˈɔkɪstrə] *s* orquesta; (*parquet*) platea
orchestrate [ˈɔrkɪsˌtret] *tr* orquestar
orchid [ˈɔrkɪd] *s* orquídea
ordain [ɔrˈden] *tr* (eccl) ordenar; destinar; mandar
ordeal [ɔrˈdil] u [ɔrˈdiˈəl] *s* prueba rigurosa o penosa; (hist) juicio de Dios
order [ˈɔrdər] *s* (*way one thing follows another; formal or methodical arrangement; peace, quiet; class, category*) orden *m*; (*command; honor society; monastic brotherhood; fraternal organization*) orden *f*; tarea, p.ej., **a big order** una tarea peliaguda; (com) pedido; (com) giro, libranza; (*formation*) (mil) orden Im; (*command*) (mil) orden *f*; **in order that** para que, a fin de que; **in order to** + *inf* para + *inf*, a fin de + *inf*; **to get out of order** descomponerse; **to give an order** dar una orden; (com) hacer un pedido ‖ *tr* ordenar; mandar; encargar, pedir; mandar hacer; **to order around** ser muy mandón con; **to order someone away** mandar a uno que se marche
order blank *s* hoja de pedidos
order•ly [ˈɔrdərli] *adj* ordenado, gobernoso; tranquilo, obediente ‖ *s* (*pl* **-lies**) asistente *m* en un hospital; (mil) ordenanza *m*
ordinal [ˈɔrdɪnəl] *adj & s* ordinal *m*
ordinance [ˈɔrdɪnəns] *s* ordenanza
ordinary [ˈɔrdɪˌnɛri] *adj* ordinario
ordnance [ˈɔrdnəns] *s* artillería, cañones *mpl*; pertrechos de guerra
ore [or] *s* mena, mineral metalífero
organ [ˈɔrgən] *s* órgano
organ•dy [ˈɔrgəndi] *s* (*pl* **-dies**) organdí *m*
or'gan-grind'er *s* organillero
organic [ɔrˈgænɪk] *adj* orgánico
organism [ˈɔrgəˌnɪzəm] *s* organismo
organist [ˈɔrgənɪst] *s* organista *mf*
organize [ˈɔrgəˌnaɪz] *tr* organizar
organ loft *s* tribuna del órgano
orgasm [ˈɔrgæzəm] *s* orgasmo
orgiastic [ˌɔrdʒiˈæstɪk] *adj* orgiástico
or•gy [ˈɔrdʒi] *s* (*pl* **-gies**) orgía
orient [ˈɔriˈənt] *s* oriente *m* ‖ **Orient** *s* oriente ‖ **orient** [ˈɔriˌɛnt] *tr* orientar
oriental [ˌɔriˈɛntəl] *adj* oriental
orifice [ˈɔrɪfɪs] *s* orificio
origin [ˈɔrɪdʒɪn] *s* origen *m*
original [əˈrɪdʒɪnəl] *adj & s* original *m*

originate [əˈrɪdʒɪˌnet] *tr* originar ‖ *intr* originarse
oriole [ˈɔriˌol] *s* oropéndola
Orkney Islands [ˈɔrkni] *spl* Órcadas
ormolu [ˈɔrməˌlu] *s* (*gold powder used in gilding*) oro molido; (*alloy of zinc and copper*) similor *m*; bronce dorado
ornament [ˈɔrnəmənt] *s* ornamento ‖ [ˈɔrnəˌmɛnt] *tr* ornamentar
ornate [ɔrˈnet] u [ˈɔrnet] *adj* muy ornado; (*style*) florido
orphan [ˈɔrfən] *adj & s* huérfano ‖ *tr* dejar huérfano
orphanage [ˈɔrfənɪdʒ] *s* (*institution*) orfanato; órfelinato (SAm); (*state, condition*) orfandad
orphan asylum *s* asilo de huérfanos
Orpheus [ˈɔrfjus] u [ˈɔrfiˈəs] *s* Orfeo
orthodontic appliance [ˌɔrθəˈdɑntɪk] *s* aparato de ortodoncia
orthodontics [ˌɔrθəˈdɑntɪks] *s* ortodoncia
orthodox [ˈɔrθəˌdɑks] *adj* ortodoxo
orthogra•phy [ɔrˈθɑgrəfi] *s* (*pl* **-phies**) ortografía
oscillate [ˈɑsɪˌlet] *intr* oscilar
osier [ˈoʒər] *s* mimbre *m & f*; sauce mimbrero
ossi•fy [ˈɑsɪˌfaɪ] *v* (*pret & pp* **-fied**) *tr* osificar ‖ *intr* osificarse
ostensible [ɑsˈtɛnsɪbəl] *adj* aparente, pretendido, supuesto
ostentatious [ˌɑstɛnˈteʃəs] *adj* (*pretentious*) ostentativo; (*showy*) ostentoso
osteopath [ˈɑstiˌoˌpæθ] *s* osteópata *mf*
osteopathy [ˌɑstiˈɑpəθi] *s* osteopatía
ostracism [ˈɑstrəˌsɪzəm] *s* ostracismo
ostrich [ˈɑstrɪtʃ] *s* avestruz *m*
O.T. *abbr* **Old Testament**
other [ˈʌðər] *adj & pron indef* otro ‖ *adv*— **other than** de otra manera que
otherwise [ˈʌðərˌwaɪz] *adv* otramente, de otra manera; en otras circunstancias; fuera de eso; si no, de otro modo
otherworldly [ˈʌðərˌwʌrldli] *adj* extraterrestre
otter [ˈɑtər] *s* nutria
ottoman [ˈɑtəmən] *s* (*corded fabric*) otomán *m*; (*sofa*) otomana; escañuelo con cojín ‖ **Ottoman** *adj & s* otomano
ouch [aʊtʃ] *interj* ¡ax!
ought [ɔt] *s* alguna cosa; cero; **for ought I know** por lo que yo sepa ‖ *v aux* se emplea para formar el modo potencial, p.ej., **he ought to go at once** debiera salir en seguida
ounce [aʊns] *s* onza
our [aʊr] *adj poss* nuestro
ours [aʊrz] *pron poss* el nuestro; nuestro
ourselves [aʊrˈsɛlvz] *pron pers* nosotros mismos; nos, p.ej., **we enjoyed ourselves** nos divertimos
oust [aʊst] *tr* echar fuera, desposeer; desahuciar (*al inquilino*)
out [aʊt] *adj* ausente; apagado; exterior; divulgado; publicado; (*size*) poco común ‖ *adv* afuera, fuera; al aire libre; hasta el fin; **out for** buscando; **out of** de; entre; de

entre; fuera de; más allá de; (*kindness, fear, etc.*) por; (*money*) sin; (*a suit of cards*) fallo a; sobre, p.ej., **in nine out of ten cases** en nueve casos sobre diez; **out to** + *inf* esforzándose por + *inf* ∥ *prep* por; allá en ∥ *interj* ¡fuera de aquí! ∥ *s* cesante *mf;* **to be at outs** u **on the outs** estar de monos

out and away *adv* con mucho

out'-and-out' *adj* perfecto, verdadero, rematado ∥ *adv* completamente

out'-and-out'er *s* intransigente *mf;* extremista *mf*

out·bid' *v* (*pret* -**bid**; *pp* -**bid** o -**bidden**; *ger* -**bidding**) *tr* pujar más que (*otra persona*); (bridge) sobrepasar

out'board' motor *s* motor *m* fuera de borda, fuera-bordo *m*

out'break' *s* tumulto, motín *m;* (*of anger*) arranque *m;* (*of war*) estallido; (*of an epidemic*) brote *m*

out'build'ing *s* dependencia, edificio accesorio

out'burst' *s* explosión, arranque *m;* **outburst of laughter** carcajada

out'cast' *s* proscripto, paria *mf;* vagabundo

out'come' *s* resultado

out'cry' *s* (*pl* -**cries**) grito; gritería, clamoreo

out·dat'ed *adj* fuera de moda, anticuado

out·do' *v* (-**did**; *pp* -**done**) *tr* exceder; **to outdo oneself** excederse a sí mismo

out'door' *adj* al aire libre

out'doors' *adv* al aire libre, fuera de casa ∥ *s* aire *m* libre, campo raso

outer space [`autər] *s* espacio exterior

out'field' *s* (baseball) jardín *m*

out'field'er *s* (baseball) jardinero

out'fit *s* equipo; traje *m;* juego de herramientas; (*of soldiers*) cuerpo; (*of a bride*) ajuar *m;* (com) compañía ∥ *v* (*pret & pp* -**fitted**; *ger* -**fitting**) *tr* equipar

out'go'ing *adj* de salida; cesante; (*tide*) descendente; (*nature, character*) exteriorista ∥ *s* salida

out·grow' *v* (*pret* -**grew**; *pp* -**grown**) *tr* crecer más que; ser ya grande para; ser ya viejo para; ser ya más apto que; dejar (*las cosas de los niños; a los amigos de la niñez, etc.*) ∥ *intr* extenderse

out'growth' *s* excrecencia, bulto; (*of leaves in springtime*) nacimiento; consecuencia, resultado

outing [`autɪŋ] *s* jira, excursión al campo

outlandish [aut'lændɪʃ] *adj* estrafalario; de aspecto extranjero; de acento extranjero

out·last' *tr* durar más que; sobrevivir a

out'law' *s* forajido, bandido; prófugo, proscrito ∥ *tr* proscribir; declarar ilegal

out'lay' *s* desembolso ∥ **out·lay'** *v* (*pret & pp* -**laid**) *tr* desembolsar

out'let *s* salida; desaguadero; orificio de salida; (elec) caja de enchufe; (*tap*) (elec) toma de corriente *m*

out'line' *s* contorno; trazado; esquema *m;* esbozo, bosquejo; compendio ∥ *tr* contornar; trazar; trazar el esquema de; esbozar, bosquejar; compendiar

out·live' *tr* sobrevivir a; durar más que

out'look' *s* perspectiva; expectativa; concepto de la vida, punto de vista; atalaya

out'ly'ing *adj* remoto, circundante, de las afueras

out·mod'ed *adj* fuera de moda

out·num'ber *tr* exceder en número, ser más numeroso que

out'-of-date' *adj* fuera de moda, anticuado

out'-of-door' *adj* al aire libre

out'-of-doors' *adj* al aire libre ∥ *adv* al aire libre, fuera de casa ∥ *s* aire *m* libre, campo raso

out'-of-print' *adj* agotado

out'-of-the-way' *adj* apartado, remoto; poco usual, poco común

out of tune *adj* desafinado ∥ *adv* desafinadamente

out of work *adj* desempleado, sin trabajo

out'pa'tient *s* paciente *mf* de consulta externa

out'post' *s* avanzada

out'put' *s* rendimiento; (elec) salida; (mech) rendimiento de trabajo, efecto útil

out'rage *s* atrocidad; ultraje *m* ∥ *tr* maltratar; ultrajar; escandalizar

outrageous [aut'redʒəs] *adj* (*grossly offensive*) ultrajoso; (*shocking, fierce*) atroz; (*extreme*) extravagante

out·rank' *tr* exceder en rango o grado

out'rid'er *s* carrerista *m;* (Brit) viajante *m* de comercio

out'right' *adj* cabal, completo; franco, sincero ∥ *adv* enteramente; de una vez; sin rodeos; en seguida

out'run'ner *s* volante *m* (*criado*)

out'set' *s* principio

out'side' *adj* exterior; superficial; ajeno; (*price*) (el) máximo ∥ *adv* fuera, afuera; **outside of** fuera de ∥ *prep* fuera de; más allá de; (coll) a excepción de ∥ *s* exterior *m;* superficie *f;* apariencia

outsider [,aut'saidər] *s* forastero; intruso

out'skirts' *spl* afueras

out'spo'ken *adj* boquifresco, franco

out'stand'ing *adj* sobresaliente; prominente; sin pagar, sin cobrar

outward [`autwərd] *adj* exterior; superficial ∥ *adv* exteriormente, hacia fuera

out·weigh' *tr* pesar más que; contrapesar, compensar

out·wit' *v* (*pret & pp* -**witted**; *ger* -**witting**) *tr* burlar, ser más listo que; despistar (*al perseguidor*)

oval [`ovəl] *adj* oval ∥ *s* óvalo

ova·ry [`ovəri] *s* (*pl* -**ries**) ovario

ovation [o'veʃən] *s* ovación

oven [`ʌvən] *s* horno

over [`ovər] *adj* acabado, concluído; superior; adicional; excesivo ∥ *adv* encima; al otro lado, a la otra orilla; hacia abajo; al revés; patas arriba; otra vez, de nuevo; de añadidura; (*at the bottom of a page*) a la vuelta; acá, p.ej., **hand over the money** déme acá el dinero; **over again** una vez más; **over against** enfrente de; a distinción de; en contraste con; **over and over** repetidas veces; **over here** acá; **over in** allá en; **over there** allá ‖ *prep* sobre, encima de, por encima de; por; de un extremo a otro de; al otro lado de; más allá de; desde; (*a certain number*) más de; acerca de; por causa de; durante; **over and above** además de, en exceso de

o'ver•all' *adj* cabal, completo; extremo, total ‖ **overalls** *spl* pantalones *mf* de trabajo; overol *m*

o'ver•bear'ing *adj* altanero, imperioso

o'ver•board' *adv* al agua; **man overboard!** ¡hombre al agua!; **to throw overboard** arrojar, echar o tirar por la borda

o'ver•cast' *adj* encapotado, nublado ‖ *s* cielo encapotado ‖ *v* (*pret & pp* **-cast**) *tr* nublar

o'ver•charge' *s* cargo excesivo; recargo de precio; sobrecarga; (elec) carga excesiva ‖ o'ver•charge' *tr* hacer pagar más del valor, cobrar demasiado a; cargar (*p.ej., 50 pesetas*) de más; (elec) poner una carga excesiva a

o'ver•coat' *s* abrigo, gabán *m*, sobretodo

o'ver•come' *v* (*pret* **-came**; *pp* **-come**) *tr* vencer; rendir; superar (*dificultades*)

o'ver•crowd' *tr* atestar, apiñar; poblar con exceso

o'ver•do *v* (*pret* **-did**; *pp* **-done**) *tr* exagerar; agobiar; asurar, requemar ‖ *intr* cansarse mucho, excederse en el trabajo

o'ver•dose' *s* sobredosis *f*, dosis excesiva ‖ *intr* tomar una dosis excesiva

o'ver•draft' *s* sobregiro, giro en descubierto

o'ver•draw' *v* (*pret* **-drew**; *pp* **-drawn**) *tr & intr* sobregirar

o'ver•due' *adj* atrasado; vencido y no pagado

o'ver•eat' *v* (*pret* **-ate**; *pp* **-eaten**) *tr & intr* comer con exceso

o'ver•es'ti•mate *tr* sobreestimar

o'ver•exer'tion *s* esfuerzo excesivo

o'ver•ex'ploi•ta'tion *s* (*of resources*) explotación abusiva

o'ver•expose' *tr* sobreexponer

o'ver•expo'sure *s* sobreexposición

o'ver•flow' *s* desbordamiento, rebosamiento, derrame *m;* caño de reboso ‖ o'ver•flow' *intr* desbordar, rebosar

o'ver•fly' *v* (*pret* **-flew**; *pp* **-flown**) *tr* sobrevolar

o'ver•grown' *adj* demasiado grande para su edad; denso, frondoso

o'ver•hang' *v* (*pret & pp* **-hung**) *tr* sobresalir por encima de, estar pendiente o colgando sobre, salir fuera del nivel de; amenazar ‖ *intr* estar pendiente, estar colgando

o'ver•haul' *tr* examinar, registrar, revisar; ir alcanzando, alcanzar; componer, rehabilitar, reacondicionar

o'ver•head' *adj* de arriba; aéreo, elevado; general, de conjunto ‖ o'ver•head' *adv* por encima de la cabeza; arriba, en lo alto ‖ o'ver•head' *s* gastos generales

o'ver•hear *v* (*pret & pp* **-heard**) *tr* oír por casualidad; acertar a oír, alcanzar a oír

o'ver•heat *tr* recalentar ‖ *intr* recalentarse

overjoyed [,over'dʒɔid] *adj* lleno de alegría; **to be overjoyed** no caber de contento

o'ver•kill' *s* exceso de potencia; exceso de eficacia ‖ *intr* exceder lo necesario

overland ['ovər,lænd] u ['ovərlənd] *adj & adv* por tierra, por vía terrestre

o'ver•lap' *v* (*pret & pp* **-lapped**; *ger* **-lapping**) *tr* solapar, traslapar ‖ *intr* solapar, traslapar; traslaparse (*dos o más cosas*); suceder (*dos hechos*) en parte al mismo tiempo

o'ver•load' *s* sobrecarga ‖ o'ver•load' *tr* sobrecargar

o'ver•look' *tr* dominar con la vista; pasar por alto, no hacer caso de; perdonar, tolerar; espiar, vigilar; cuidar de, dirigir; dar a, p.ej., **the window overlooks the garden** la ventana da al jardín

o'ver•lord' *s* jefe supremo ‖ o'ver•lord' *tr* dominar despóticamente, imponerse a

overly ['ovərli] *adv* (coll) excesivamente, demasiado

o'ver•night' *adv* toda la noche; de la tarde a la mañana; **to stay overnight** pasar la noche

overnight bag *s* saco de noche

o'ver•pass' *s* viaducto

o'ver•pop'u•late' *tr* superpoblar

o'verpow'er *tr* dominar, supeditar, subyugar; colmar, dejar estupefacto

overpowering *adj* abrumador, arrollador, irresistible

o'ver•produc'tion *s* superproducción, sobreproducción

o'ver•rate' *tr* exagerar el valor de

o'ver•run' *v* (*pret* **-ran**; *pp* **-run**; *ger* **-running**) *tr* cubrir enteramente; infestar; exceder; **to overrun one's time** quedarse más de lo justo; hablar más de lo justo

o'ver•sea' u o'ver•seas' *adj* de ultramar ‖ o'ver•sea' u o'ver•seas' *adv* allende los mares, en ultramar

o'ver•seer' *s* director *m*, superintendente *mf*

o'ver•shad'ow *tr* sombrear; (fig) eclipsar

o'ver•shoe' *s* chanclo, zapato de goma

o'ver•shoot' *v* (*pret & pp* **-shot**) *tr* tirar por encima de o más allá de; **to overshoot oneself** pasarse de listo, excederse

o'ver•sight' *s* inadvertencia, descuido

o'ver•sleep' *v* (*pret & pp* **-slept**) *intr* dormir demasiado tarde

o'ver•step' *v* (*pret & pp* **-stepped**; *ger* **-stepping**) *tr* exceder, traspasar

o'ver•stock' *tr* abarrotar

o'ver•sup'ply' *s* (*pl* **-plies**) provisión excesiva ‖ o'ver•sup'ply' *v* (*pret* **-plied**) *tr* proveer en exceso

overt ['ovərt] u [o'vʌrt] *adj* abierto, manifiesto; premeditado

o'ver•take' *v* (*pret* **-took**; *pp* **-taken**) *tr* alcanzar; sobrepasar; sorprender; sobrevenir a

o'ver-the-count'er *adj* vendido directamente al comprador; vendido en tienda al por mayor

o'ver•throw' *s* derrocamiento; trastorno ‖ o'ver•throw' *v* (*pret* **-threw**; *pp* **-thrown**) *tr* derrocar; trastornar o'ver·time' *adj & adv* en exceso de las horas regulares ‖ *s* horas extraordinarias de trabajo, horas extra

o'ver·trump' *s* contrafallo ‖

o'ver·trump' *tr & intr* contrafallar

overture ['ovərt/ər] *s* insinuación, proposición; (mus) obertura

o'ver·turn' *s* vuelco; movimiento de mercancías ‖ o'ver·turn' *tr* volcar; trastornar; derrocar ‖ *intr* volcar; trastornarse

overweening [,ovər'winɪŋ] *adj* arrogante, presuntuoso

o'ver·weight' *adj* excesivamente gordo o grueso ‖ *s* sobrepeso; exceso de peso; peso de añadidura

overwhelm [,ovər'hwɛlm] *tr* abrumar; inundar; anonadar; (with favors, gifts, etc.) colmar

o'ver·work' *s* trabajo excesivo, exceso de trabajo; trabajo fuera de las horas regulares ‖ o'ver·work' *tr* hacer trabajar demasiado; oprimir con el trabajo ‖ *intr* trabajar demasiado

Ovid ['avɪd] *s* Ovidio

ovum ['ovəm] *s* óvulo

ow [aʊ] *interj* ¡ax!

owe [o] *tr* deber, adeudar ‖ *intr* tener deudas

owing ['o·ɪŋ] *adj* adeudado; debido, pagadero; owing to debido a, por causa de

owl [aʊl] *s* buho, lechuza, mochuelo

own [on] *adj* propio, p.ej., my own brother mi propio hermano ‖ *s* suyo, lo suyo; on one's own (coll) por su propia cuenta; (without taking advice from anyone) por su cabeza; (without help from anyone) de su cabeza; to come into one's own entrar en posesión de lo suyo; tener el éxito merecido, recibir el honor merecido; to hold one's own no aflojar, no cejar, mantenerse firme ‖ *tr* poseer; reconocer ‖ *intr* confesar; to own up to (coll) confesar de plano (una culpa, un delito, etc.)

owner ['onər] *s* amo, dueño, poseedor *m*, posesor *m*, proprietario

ownership ['onər,ʃɪp] *s* posesión, propiedad

owner's license *s* permiso de circulación, patente *f* de circulación

ox [aks] *s* (pl oxen) ['aksən] buey *m*

ox'cart' *s* carreta de bueyes

oxide ['aksaɪd] *s* óxido

oxidize ['aksɪ,daɪz] *tr* oxidar ‖ *intr* oxidarse

oxygen ['aksɪdʒən] *s* oxígeno

oxygen tent *s* cámara o tienda de oxígeno

oxytone ['aksɪ,ton] *adj & s* oxítono

oyster ['ɔɪstər] *adj* ostrero ‖ *s* ostra

oyster bed *s* ostrero

oyster cocktail *s* ostras en su concha

oyster fork *s* desbullador *m*

oys'ter·house' *s* ostrería

oys'ter·knife' *s* abreostras *m*

oyster·man ['ɔɪstərmən] *s* (pl -men [mən]) ostrero

oyster opener ['opənər] *s* desbullador *m*

oyster shell *s* desbulla, concha de ostra

oyster stew *s* sopa de ostras

oz. *abbr* ounce, ounces

ozone ['ozon] *s* ozono; (coll) aire fresco

ozone layer *s* capa de ozono

ozs. *abbr* ounces

ov
pa

P

P, p [pi] decimosexta letra del alfabeto inglés

p. *abbr* page, participle

P.A. *abbr* Passenger Agent, power of attorney, Purchasing Agent

pace [pes] *s* paso; to keep pace with ir, andar o avanzar al mismo paso que; to put through one's paces poner (a uno) a prueba; dar a (uno) ocasión de lucirse; to set the pace establecer el paso; dar el ejemplo ‖ *tr* establecer el paso para; medir a pasos; recorrer a pasos; to pace the floor pasearse desesperadamente por la habitación ‖ *intr* andar a pasos regulares

pace'mak'er *s* (med) marcapaso, marcapasos *m*

pacific [pə'sɪfɪk] *adj* pacífico ‖ Pacific *adj & s* Pacífico

pacifier ['pæsɪ,faɪ·ər] *s* pacificador *m*, chupon *m*; (teething ring) chupador *m*

pacifism ['pæsɪ,fɪzəm] *s* pacifismo

pacifist ['pæsɪfɪst] *adj & s* pacifista *mf*

paci·fy ['pæsɪ,faɪ] *v* (pret & pp -fied) *tr* pacificar

pack [pæk] *s* lío, fardo; paquete *m*; (of hounds) jauría; (of cattle) manada; (of evildoers) pandilla; (of lies) sarta, montón *m*; (of playing cards) baraja; (of cigarettes) cajetilla; (of floating ice) témpano; (med) compresa ‖ *tr* empaquetar; embadurnar; encajonar; hacer (el baúl, la maleta); conservar en latas; apretar, atestar, cargar (una acémila); escoger de modo fraudulento (un jurado); to be packed in (coll) estar como sardinas en banasta ‖ *intr* empaquetarse; hacer el baúl, hacer la maleta; consolidarse, formar masa compacta

package ['pækɪdʒ] *s* paquete *m* ‖ *tr* empaquetar

pack animal *s* acémila, animal *m* de carga

packing box o case *s* caja de embalaje

packing house *s* frigorífico

packing slip *s* hoja de embalaje

pack'sad'dle *s* albarda

pack'thread' *s* bramante *m*

pack train *s* recua

pact [pækt] *s* pacto

pad [pæd] *s* conjincillo, almohadilla; (*of writing paper*) bloc *m*; (*for inking*) tampón *m*; (*of an aquatic plant*) hoja; (*for launching a rocket*) plataforma *f*; (*sound of footsteps*) pisada ‖ *v* (*pret & pp* **padded**; *ger* **padding**) *tr* acolchar, rellenar; meter mucho ripio en (*un escrito*) ‖ *intr* andar, caminar; caminar despacio y pesadamente

paddle ['pædəl] *s* (*of a canoe*) canalete *m*; (*of a wheel*) pala, paleta; (*for spanking*) palo ‖ *tr* impulsar con canalete; (*to spank*) apalear ‖ *intr* remar con canalete; remar suavemente; (*to splash*) chapotear

paddle wheel *s* rueda de paletas

paddock ['pædək] *s* dehesa; (*at a racecourse*) paddock *m*

paddy wagon ['pædi] *s* (coll) camión *m* de policía

pad'lock' *s* candado ‖ *tr* cerrar con candado; (*to lock up officially*) condenar (*una habitación, un teatro*)

pagan ['pegən] *adj & s* pagano

paganism ['pegə‚nızəm] *s* paganismo

page [pedʒ] *s* (*of a book*) página; (*boy attendant*) paje *m*; (*in a hotel or club*) botones *m* ‖ *tr* paginar; buscar llamando

pageant ['pædʒənt] *s* espectáculo público

pageant•ry ['pædʒəntri] *s* (*pl* **-ries**) pompa, fausto; (*empty display*) bambolla

pail [pel] *s* balde *m*, cubo

pain [pen] *s* dolor *m*; **on pain of** so pena de; **pains** esmero, trabajo; dolores de parto; **to take pains** esmerarse ‖ *tr & intr* doler

painful ['penfəl] *adj* doloroso; penoso

pain'kill'er *s* analgésico; calmante *m* del dolor

painless ['penlıs] *adj* sin dolor, indoloro; fácil, sin trabajo

pains'tak'ing *adj* esmerado

paint [pent] *s* pintura‖ *tr* pintar ‖ *intr* pintar; pintarse, repintarse

paint'box' *s* caja de colores

paint'brush' *s* brocha, pincel *m*

painter ['pentər] *s* pintor *m*

painting ['pentıŋ] *s* pintura

paint remover [rı'muvər] *s* sacapintura *m*, quitapintura *m*

pair [pɛr] *s* par *m*; (*of people*) pareja; (*of cards*) parejas ‖ *tr* aparear ‖ *intr* aparearse

pair of scissors *s* tijeras

pair of trousers *s* pantalones *mpl*

pajamas [pe'dʒɑməz] o [pe'dʒæməz] *spl* pijama

Pakistan [‚pɑkı'stɑn] *s* el Paquistán

Pakistani [‚pɑkı'stɑni] *adj & s* paquistano, paquistaní *mf*

pal [pæl] *s* (coll) compañero; cumpa *m* (SAm) ‖ *v* (*pret & pp* **palled**; *ger* **palling**) *intr* (coll) ser compañeros

palace ['pælıs] *s* palacio

palatable ['pælətəbəl] *adj* sabroso, apetitoso

palatal ['pælətəl] *adj & s* palatal *f*

palate ['pælıt] *s* paladar *m*

pale [pel] *adj* pálido; (*color*) claro ‖ *s* estaca; palizada; límite *m*, término ‖ *intr* palidecer

pale'face' *s* rostropálido

palette ['pælıt] *s* paleta

palfrey ['pɔlfri] *s* palafrén *m*

palisade [‚pælı'sed] *s* estaca; estacada; (*line of cliffs*) acantilado

pall [pɔl] *s* paño de ataúd, paño mortuorio; (eccl) palia ‖ *tr* hartar, saciar; quitar el sabor a ‖ *intr* perder el sabor; **to pall on** hartar, saciar

pall'bear'er *s* acompañante *m* de un cadáver; portador *m* del féretro

palliate ['pælı‚et] *tr* paliar

pallid ['pælıd] *adj* pálido

pallor ['pælər] *s* palidez *f*, palor *m*

palm [pɑm] *s* (*of the hand*) palma; (*measure*) palmo; (*tree and leaf*) palma; **to carry off the palm** llevarse la palma; **to grease the palm of** (slang) untar la mano a; **to yield the palm** to reconocer por vencedor ‖ *tr* esconder en la mano; escamotear (*una carta*); **to palm off something on someone** encajarle una cosa a uno

palmet•to [pæl'mɛto] *s* (*pl* **-tos** o **-toes**) palmito

palmist ['pɑmıst] *s* quiromántico

palmistry ['pɑmıstri] *s* quiromancia

palm leaf *s* palma, hoja de la palmera

palm oil *s* aceite *m* de palma; (slang) propina; (slang) soborno

Palm Sunday *s* domingo de ramos

palpable ['pælpəbəl] *adj* palpable

palpitate ['pælpı‚tet] *intr* palpitar

pal•sy ['pɔlzi] *s* (*pl* **-sies**) perlesía ‖ *v* (*pret & pp* **-sied**) *tr* paralizar

pal•try ['pɔltri] *adj* (*comp* **-trier**; *super* **-triest**) vil, ruin, mezquino

pamper ['pæmpər] *tr* mimar, consentir

pamphlet ['pæmflıt] *s* folleto, panfleto

pan [pæn] *s* cacerola, cazuela, sartén *f*; caldera, perol *m* ‖ *v* (*pret & pp* **panned**; *ger* **panning**) *tr* cocer, freír; separar (*el oro*) en la gamella; (coll) criticar ásperamente ‖ *intr* separar el oro en la gamella; dar oro; **to pan out well** (coll) tener éxito, dar buen resultado ‖

Pan *s* Pan

panacea [‚pænə'si•ə] *s* panacea

Panama Canal ['pænə‚mɑ] *s* canal *m* de Panamá

Panama Canal Zone *s* Zona del Canal

Panama hat *s* panamá *m*

Panamanian [‚pænə'meni•ən] *adj & s* panameño

Pan-American [‚pænə'mɛrıkən] *adj* panamericano

pan'cake' *s* hojuela, panqueque *m* ‖ *intr* (aer) desplomarse

pancake landing *s* aterrizaje aplastado, aterrizaje en desplome

pancreas ['pænkrı•əs] *s* páncreas *m*

panda ['pændə] *s* panda *mf*

pander ['pændər] *s* alcahuete *m* ‖ *intr* alcahuetear; **to pander to** gratificar

pane [pen] *s* cristal *m*, vidrio, hoja de vidrio

pan•el ['pænəl] *s* panel *m*, entrepaño, cuarterón *m*; grupo de personas en discusión cara al público; (aut, elec) tablero, panel *m*; (law) lista de personas que pueden servir como jurados ‖ *v* (*pret & pp* **peled** o **-elled**);

ger **-elling** o **-elling**) *tr* adornar con cuarterones, labrar en cuarterones; artesonar (*un techo o bóveda*)

panel discussion *s* coloquio cara al público

panelist ['pænəlɪst] *s* coloquiante *mf* cara al público

panel lights *spl* luces *fpl* del tablero

pang [pæŋ] *s* dolor agudo; (*of remorse*) punzada; (*of death*) agonía

pan'han'dle *s* mango de sartén ‖ *intr* (slang) mendigar, pedir limosna

pan•ic ['pænɪk] *adj & s* pánico ‖ *v* (*pret & pp* **-icked**; *ger* **-icking**) *tr* sobrecoger de pánico ‖ *intr* sobrecogerse de pánico

pan'ic-strick'en *adj* muerto de miedo, sobrecogido de terror

pano•ply ['pænəpli] *s* (*pl* **-plies**) panoplia, traje *m* ceremonial

panorama [,pænə'ræmə] o [,pænə'rɑmə] *s* panorama *m*

pan•sy ['pænzi] *s* (*pl* **-sies**) pensamiento

pant [pænt] *s* jadeo; palpitación; **pants** pantalones *mpl*; **to wear the pants** (coll) calzarse los pantalones ‖ *intr* jadear; palpitar

pantheism ['pænθi,ɪzəm] *s* panteísmo

pantheon ['pænθi,ɑn] *s* panteón *m*

panther ['pænθər] *s* pantera; puma

panties ['pæntiz] *spl* pantaloncillos de mujer

pantomime ['pæntə,maɪm] *s* pantomima

pan•try ['pæntri] *s* (*pl* **-tries**) despensa

panty hose *s* panty *m*

pap [pæp] *s* papilla, papas

papa•cy ['pepəsi] *s* (*pl* **-cies**) papado

paper ['pepər] *s* papel *m;* (*newspaper*) periódico; (*of needles*) paño ‖ *tr* empapelar

pa'per•back' *s* libro en rústica

pa'per•boy' *s* vendedor *m* de periódicos

paper clip *s* clip *m*, sujetapapeles *m;* presilla; prensador (CAm); gancho de papel (Col)

paper cone *s* cucurucho

paper cutter *s* cortapapeles *m*, guillotina

paper doll *s* muñeca de papel

paper hanger *s* empapelador *m*, papelista *mf*

paper knife *s* cortapapeles *m*

paper mill *s* fábrica de papel

paper money *s* papel *m* moneda

paper profits *spl* ganancias no realizadas sobre valores no vendidos

paper tape *s* cinta perforada

pa'per•weight' *s* pisapapeles *m*

paper work *s* preparación o comprobación de escritos; papelerío

paprika [pæ'prikə] o ['pæprɪkə] *s* pimentón *m*

papy•rus [pe'paɪrəs] *s* (*pl* **-ri** [raɪ]) papiro

par. *abbr* **paragraph, parallel, parenthesis, parish**

par [pɑr] *adj* a la par; nominal; normal ‖ *s* paridad; valor *m* nominal; **above par** sobre la par; con beneficio; con premio; **below par** o **under par** bajo la par; con pérdida; (coll) indispuesto; **to be on a par with** correr parejas con

parable ['pærəbəl] *s* parábola

parachute ['pærə,ʃut] *s* paracaídas *m* ‖ *intr* parachutar, lanzarse en paracaídas; **to parachute to safety** salvarse en paracaídas

parachute jump *s* salto en paracaídas

parachutist ['pærə,ʃutɪst] *s* paracaidista *mf*

parade [pə'red] *s* desfile *m;* paseo; ostentación ‖ *tr* ostentar, pasear ‖ *intr* desfilar, pasar por las calles; (mil) formar en parada

paradise ['pærə,daɪs] *s* paraíso

paradox ['pærə,dɑks] *s* paradoja; persona o cosa incomprensibles

paradoxical [,pærə'dɑksɪkəl] *adj* paradójico

paraffin ['pærəfɪn] *s* parafina

paragon ['pærə,gɑn] *s* dechado

paragraph ['pærə,græf] *s* párrafo

Paraguay *s* el Paraguay

Paraguayan [,pærə'gwaɪ•ən] *adj & s* paraguayano, paraguayo

parakeet ['pærə,kit] *s* perico, periquito

paral•lel ['pærə,lɛl] *adj* paralelo ‖ *s* (línea) paralela; (plano) paralelo; (geog) paralelo; **parallels** (typ) doble raya vertical ‖ *v* (*pret & pp* **-leled** o **-lelled**; *ger* **-leling** o **-lelling**) *tr* ser paralelo a; poner en dirección paralela; correr parejas con; (*to compare*) paralelizar

parallel bars *spl* paralelas, barras paralelas

paraly•sis [pə'rælɪsɪs] *s* (*pl* **-ses** [,siz]) parálisis *f*

paralytic [,pærə'lɪtɪk] *adj & s* paralítico

paralyze ['pærə,laɪz] *tr* paralizar

parameter [pə'ræmətər] *s* parámetro

paramount ['pærə,maʊnt] *adj* capital, supremo, principalísimo

paranoiac [,pærə'nɔɪ•æk] o **paranoid** [pærə-,nɔɪd] *adj & s* paranoico

parapet [,pærə,pɛt] *s* parapeto

paraphernalia [,pærəfər'nɛli•ə] *spl* trastos, atavíos

paraplegia [,pærə'plidʒə] *s* paraplegia

parasite ['pærə,saɪt] *s* parásito

parasitic(al) [,pærə'sɪtɪk(el)] *adj* parasítico, parasitario

parasol ['pærə,sɔl] *s* quitasol *m*, parasol *m*

pa'ra•troop'er *s* paracaidista *m*

pa'ra•troops' *spl* tropas paracaidistas

parboil ['pɑr,bɔɪl] *tr* sancochar; calentar con exceso

par•cel (pɑrsəl] *s* paquete *m*, atado, bulto ‖ *v* (*pret & pp* **-celed** o **-celled**; *ger* **-celing** o **-celling**) *tr* empaquetar; parcelar (*el terreno*); **to parcel out** repartir

parcel post *s* paquetes *mpl* postales

parch [pɑrtʃ] *tr* abrasar, tostar; **to be parched** tener mucha sed

parchment ['pɑrtʃmənt] *s* pergamino

pardon ['pɑrdən] *s* perdón *m;* (*remission of penalty by the state*) indulto; **I beg your pardon** dispense Vd. ‖ *tr* perdonar, dispensar; indultar

pardonable ['pɑrdənəbəl] *adj* perdonable

pardon board *s* junta de perdones

pare [pɛr] *tr* mondar (*fruta*); pelar (*patatas*); cortar (*callos, uñas*); despalmar (*la palma córnea de los animales*); adelgazar; reducir (*gastos*)

parent ['pɛrənt] *adj* madre, matriz, principal ‖ *s* padre o madre; autor *m*, fuente *f*, origen *m;* **parents** padres *mpl*

pa
pa

parentage ['pɛrəntɪdʒ] s paternidad o maternidad; abolengo, linaje m

parent company compañía matriz

parenthe·sis [pə'rɛnθɪsɪs] s (pl **-ses** [,siz]) paréntesis m

parenthood ['pɛrənt,hʊd] s paternidad o maternidad

pariah [pə'raɪ·ə] o ['pɑrɪ·ə] s paria mf

paring knife ['pɛrɪŋ] s cuchillo para mondar

parish ['pærɪʃ] s parroquia, feligresía

parishioner [pə'rɪʃ/ənər] s parroquiano, feligrés m

Parisian [pə'rɪʒən] adj & s parisiense mf

parity ['pærɪti] s paridad

park [pɑrk] s parque m ‖ tr estacionar, parquear; (coll) colocar, dejar ‖ intr estacionar, parquear

parking ['pɑrkɪŋ] s aparcamiento, estacionamiento; (space) parking m; **no parking** se prohibe estacionarse

parking lights spl (aut) faros de situación

parking lot s parque m de estacionamiento

parking meter s reloj m de estacionamiento, parquímetro, parcómetro

parking ticket s aviso de multa

park'way s gran vía adornado con árboles

parley ['pɑrli] s parlamento ‖ intr parlamentar

parliament ['pɑrlɪmənt] s parlamento

parlor ['pɑrlər] s sala; parlatorio, locutorio

parlor car s coche-salón m

parlor politics spl política de café

Parnassus [pɑr'næsəs] s (collection of poems) parnaso; el Parnaso; **to try to climb Parnassus** hacer pinos en poesía

parochial [pə'rokɪ·əl] adj parroquial; estrecho, limitado

paro·dy ['pærədi] s (pl **-dies**) parodia ‖ v (pret & pp **-died**) tr parodiar

parole [pə'rol] s palabra de honor; libertad bajo palabra ‖ tr dejar libre bajo palabra

paroxytone [pær'ɑksɪ,ton] adj & s paroxítono

par·quet [pɑr'ke] s entarimado; (theat) platea ‖ v (pret & pp **-queted** ['ked]); ger **-queting** ['ke·ɪŋ] tr entarimar

parricide ['pærɪ,saɪd] s (act) parricidio; (person) parricida mf

parrot ['pærət] s papagayo, loro; (fig) papagayo ‖ tr repetir o imitar como loro

par·ry ['pæri] s (pl **-ries**) parada, quite m ‖ v (pret & pp **-ried**) tr parar; defenderse de

parse [pɑrs] tr analizar (una oración) gramaticalmente; describir (una palabra) gramaticalmente

parsley ['pɑrsli] s perejil m

parsnip ['pɑrsnɪp] s chirivía

parson ['pɑrsən] s cura m, párroco; clérigo; pastor m protestante

part [pɑrt] s parte f; (of a machine) pieza; (of the hair) raya; (theat) parte f, papel m; **part and parcel** parte esencial, parte inseparable, elemento esencial; **parts** partes fpl; prendas, dotes fpl; **to do one's part** cumplir con su obligación; **to look the part** vestir el cargo; **to take the part of** tomar el partido de, defender; desempeñar

el papel de ‖ tr dividir, partir, separar; **to part the hair** hacerse la raya ‖ intr separarse; **to part with** deshacerse de, abandonar; despedirse de

par·take [pɑr'tek] v (pret **-took** ['tʊk]; pp **-taken**) tr compartir; comer; beber ‖ intr participar

Parthenon ['pɑrθɪ,nɑn] s Partenón m

partial ['pɑrʃəl] adj parcial; aficionado

participate [pɑr'tɪsɪ,pet] intr participar

participle ['pɑrtɪ,sɪpəl] s participio

particle ['pɑrtɪkəl] s partícula, corpúsculo

particle physics s física de las partículas

particular [pər'tɪkjələr] adj particular; difícil, exigente, quisquilloso; esmerado; minucioso; **a particular . . .** cierto . . . ‖ s particular m

partisan ['pɑrtɪzən] adj & s partidario, partidista mf; (mil) partisano

partition [pɑr'tɪʃən] s partición, distribución; división; proción; tabique m ‖ tr repartir; dividir en cuartos, aposentos; tabicar

partner ['pɑrtnər] s compañero; (wife or husband) cónyuge mf; (in a dance) pareja f; (in business) socio

partnership ['pɑrtnər,ʃɪp] s asociación; consorcio, vida en común; (com) sociedad, asociación comercial

partridge ['pɑrtrɪdʒ] s perdiz f

part'-time' adj por horas, parcial

par·ty ['pɑrti] adj de partido; de gala ‖ s (pl **-ties**) convite m, reunión, fiesta, tertulia, recepción; (for fishing, hunting, etc.; of armed men) partida; cómplice mf, interesado; (pol) partido; (coll) persona, individuo

party girl s chica de vida alegre

party-goer ['pɑrti,go·ər] s tertuliano; fiestero

party line s (between two properties) linde m, lindero; (of communist party) línea del partido; (telp) línea compartida

party politics s política de partido

pass. abbr **passenger, passive**

pass [pæs] o [pɑs] s paso; (permit; free ticket; movement of hands of mesmerist, of bullfighter) pase m; (in an examination) aprobación; nota de aprobación ‖ tr pasar; pasar de largo (una luz roja); aprobar (un proyecto de ley; un examen; a un alumno); ser aprobado en (un examen); dejar atrás; cruzarse con; expresar (una opinión); pronunciar (una sentencia), dar (la palabra); dejar sin protestar; no pagar (un dividendo); **to pass off** colar, pasar, hacer aceptar (una moneda falsa); disimular (p.ej., una ofensa con una risa); **to pass over** omitir, pasar por alto; excusar; desdeñar; dejar sin protestar; postergar (a un empleado) ‖ intr pasar; pasarse (introducirse); aprobar; **to bring to pass** llevar a cabo; **to come to pass** suceder; **to pass as** pasar por; **to pass away** pasar, pasar a mejor vida; **to pass off** pasar (una enfermedad, una tempestad, etc.); tener lugar; **to pass out** salir; (slang) desmayarse; **to pass over to** pasarse a (p.ej., el enemigo)

passable ['pæsəbəl] o ['pɑsəbəl] *adj* pasadero; (*law*) promulgable

passage ['pæsɪdʒ] *s* pasaje *m;* paso; pasillo; (*of time*) transcurso; (*of bowels*) evacuación

pass'book' *s* cartilla, libreta de banco

passenger ['pæsəndʒer] *adj* de viajeros ‖ *s* pasajero, viajero

passer-by ['pæsər'baɪ] o ['pɑsər'baɪ] *s* (*pl* **passers-by**) transeúnte *mf*

passing ['pæsɪŋ] o ['pɑsɪŋ] *adj* pasajero; corriente; de aprobado ‖ *s* (*act of passing; death*) paso; (*in an examination*) aprobación

passion ['pæʃən] *s* pasión

passionate ['pæʃənɪt] *adj* apasionado

passive ['pæsɪv] *adj* pasivo ‖ *s* voz pasiva, verbo pasivo

pass'key' *s* llave *f* de paso

Pass'o'ver *s* pascua (*de los hebreos*)

pass'port' *s* pasaporte *m*

pass'word' *s* santo y seña

past [pæst] o [pɑst] *adj* pasado; último; que fué, p.ej., **past president** presidente que fué; acabado, concluído ‖ *adv* más allá; por delante ‖ *prep* más allá de; más de; por delante de; fuera de; después de, p.ej., **past two o'clock** después de las dos; **past belief** increíble; **past cure** incurable; **past hope** sin esperanza ‖ *s* pasado

paste [pest] *s* (*dough; spaghetti, etc.*) pasta; (*for sticking things together*) engrudo ‖ *tr* engrudar, pegar con engrudo

paste'board' *s* cartón *m*

pasteurize ['pæstə,raɪz] *tr* pasterizar

pastime ['pæs,taɪm] *s* pasatiempo

pastor ['pæstər] *s* pastor *m,* clérigo, cura *m*

pastoral ['pæstərəl] *adj* & *s* pastoral *f*

pas•try ['pestri] *s* (*pl* **-tries**) pastelería

pastry cook *s* pastelero, repostero

pastry shop *s* pastelería, repostería

pasture ['pæstər] *s* pasto, pastura, dehesa ‖ *tr* apacentar, pacer ‖ *intr* apacentarse, pacer

past•y ['pesti] *adj* (*comp* **-ier;** *super* **-iest**) pastoso; flojo, fofo, pálido

pat [pæt] *s* golpecito, palmadita; ruido de pasos ligeros; (*of butter*) pastelillo ‖ *v* (*pret & pp* **patted;** *ger* **patting**) *tr* dar golpecitos a, golpear ligeramente; palmotear, acariciar con la mano; **to pat on the back** elogiar, cumplimentar

patch [pætʃ] *s* remiendo, parche *m;* terreno, pedazo de terreno; mancha; lunar postizo ‖ *tr* remendar; **to patch up** componer (*una desavenencia*); componer lo mejor posible (*una cosa descompuesta*); hacer aprisa y mal

patent ['petənt] *adj* patente; abierto ‖ ['pætənt] *adj* de patentes ‖ *s* patente *f,* patente de invención; propiedad industrial; **patent applied for** se ha solicitado patente ‖ *tr* patentar

patent leather ['pætənt] *s* charol *m*

patent medicine ['pætənt] *s* medicamento de patente

patent rights ['pætənt] *spl* derechos de patente

paternal [pə'tʌrnəl] *adj* paterno; (*affection*) paternal

paternity [pe'tʌrnɪti] *s* paternidad

path [pæθ] *s* senda, sendero; trayectoria

pathetic [pə'θɛtɪk] *adj* patético

path'find'er *s* baquiano; explorador *m*

patholo•gy [pə'θɑlədʒi] *s* patología

pathos ['peθɑs] *s* patetismo

path'way' *s* senda, sendero

patience ['peʃəns] *s* paciencia

patient ['peʃənt] *adj* paciente ‖ *s* paciente *mf,* enfermo

patriarch ['petri,ɑrk] *s* patriarca *m*

patrician [pə'trɪʃən] *adj* & *s* patricio

patricide ['pætrɪ,saɪd] *s* (*act*) parricidio; (*person*) parricida *mf*

Patrick ['pætrɪk] *s* Patricio

patrimo•ny ['pætrɪ,moni] *s* (*pl* **-nies**) patrimonio

patriot ['petri•ət] *s* patriota *mf*

patriotic [,petri'ɑtɪk] *adj* patriótico

patriotism ['petri•ə,tɪzəm] *s* patriotismo

pa•trol [pə'trol] *s* patrulla ‖ *v* (*pret & pp* **-troled** o **-trolled;** *ger* **-troling** o **-trolling**) *tr & intr* patrullar

patrol•man [pə'trolmən] *s* (*pl* **-men** [mən]) guardia *m* municipal, vigilante *m* de policía

patrol wagon *s* camion *m* de policía; carro-patrulla *m* (SAm)

patron ['petrən] *adj* tutelar ‖ *s* parroquiano; patrocinador *m*

patronize ['petrə,naɪz] *tr* ser parroquiano de (*un tendero*); comprar de costumbre en; patrocinar; tratar con aire protector

patron saint *s* patrón *m,* santo titular

patter ['pætər] *s* golpeteo; (*of rain*) chapaleteo; charla, parloteo ‖ *intr* golpetear; charlar, parlotear

pattern ['pætərn] *s* patrón *m;* modelo

P.A.U. *abbr* **Pan American Union**

paucity ['pɔsɪti] *s* corto número; falta, escasez *f,* insuficiencia

Paul [pɔl] *s* Pablo; (*name of popes*) Paulo

paunch [pɔntʃ] *s* panza

paunchy ['pɔntʃi] *adj* panzudo

pauper ['pɔpər] *s* pobre *mf,* indigente *mf*

pause [pɔz] *s* pausa; (*mus*) calderón *m;* **to give pause (to)** dar que pensar (a) ‖ *intr* hacer pausa, detenerse brevemente; vacilar

pave [pev] *tr* pavimentar; (*with flagstones*) enlosar; (*with bricks*) enladrillar; (*with pebbles*) enchinar; **to pave the way (for)** preparar el terreno (para), abrir el camino (a)

pavement ['pevmənt] *s* pavimento; (*of brick*) enladrillado; (*of flagstone*) enlosado; (*sidewalk*) acera

pavilion [pə'vɪljən] *s* pabellón *m*

paw [pɔ] *s* pata; garra, zarpa; (coll) mano *f* ‖ *tr* dar zarpazos a, restregar con las uñas; golpear, patear (*el suelo los caballos*); (coll) manosear; (*to handle overfamiliarly*) (coll) sobar ‖ *intr* piafar (*el caballo*)

pawn [pɔn] *s* (*in chess*) peón *m;* (*security, pledge*) prenda; (*tool of another person*) instrumento; víctima ‖ *tr* empeñar, dar en prenda

pa
pa

pawn'bro'ker *s* prestamista *mf*

pawn'shop' *s* casa de empeños, monte *m* de piedad

pawn ticket *s* papeleta de empeño

pay [pe] *s* paga; recompensa; castigo merecido ‖ *v* (*pret & pp* **paid** [ped]) *tr* pagar; prestar o poner (*atención*); dar (*cumplidos*); dar (*dinero una actividad comercial*); dar dinero a, ser provechoso a; pagar en la misma moneda; pagar con creces; sufrir (*el castigo de una ofensa*); hacer (*una visita*); cubrir (*los gastos*); **to pay back** devolver; pagar en la misma moneda; **to pay off** pagar y despedir (*a un empleado*); pagar todo lo adeudado a; vengarse de; redimir (*una hipoteca*) ‖ *intr* pagar; ser provechoso, valer la pena; **pay as you enter** pague a la entrada; **pay as you go** pagar el impuesto de utilidades con descuentos anticipados; **pay as you leave** pague a la salida

payable ['pe•əbəl] *adj* pagadero

pay boost *s* aumento de salario

pay'check' *s* cheque *m* en pago del sueldo; sueldo

pay'day' *s* día *m* de pago

payee [pe'i] *s* portador *m* o tenedor *m* (*de un giro*)

pay envelope *s* sobre *m* con el jornal; jornal *m*, salario

payer ['pe•ər] *s* pagador *m*

pay load *s* carga útil

pay'mas'ter *s* pagador *m*

payment ['pemənt] *s* pago; castigo

pay roll *s* nómina, hoja de paga

pay station *s* teléfono público

pd. *abbr* **paid**

p.d. *abbr* **per diem, potential difference**

pea [pi] *s* guisante *m*, chícharo

peace [pis] *s* paz *f;* **to make peace with** hacer las paces con

peaceable ['pisəbəl] *adj* pacífico

Peace Corps *s* Cuerpo de Paz

peaceful ['pisfəl] *adj* tranquilo, pacífico, sosegado

peace'mak'er *s* iris *m* de paz

peace of mind *s* serenidad del espíritu

peace pipe *s* pipa ceremonial (*de los pieles rojas*)

peach [pitʃ] *s* melocotón *m;* (slang) persona o cosa admirables

peach tree *s* melocotonero

peach•y ['pitʃi] *adj* (*comp* **-ier;** *super* **-iest**) (slang) estupendo, magnífico

pea'cock' *s* pavo real, pavón *m;* (fig) pinturero

peak [pik] *s* pico, cima, cumbre *f;* punta, extremo; máximo; (*of a cap*) visera; (*of a curve*) cresta; (elec) pico

peak hour *s* hora punta

peak load *s* (elec) carga de punta; demanda máxima

peal [pil] *s* fragor *m;* estruendo; (*of bells*) repique *m;* juego de campanas ‖ *intr* repicar; resonar

peal of laughter *s* carcajada

peal of thunder *s* trueno

pea'nut' *s* cacahuete *m*, aráquida; **to work for peanuts** recibir poco sueldo

peanut vendor *s* manicero

pear [pɛr] *s* pera

pearl [pʌrl] *s* margarita, perla; (*of running water*) murmullo ‖ *tr* alijofarar

pearl oyster *s* madreperla

pear tree *s* peral *m*

peasant ['pɛzənt] *adj & s* campesino, rústico

pea'shoot'er *s* cerbatana, bodoquera

pea soup *s* sopa de guisantes; (coll) neblina espesa y amarillenta

peat [pit] *s* turba

pebble ['pɛbəl] *s* china, guija ‖ *tr* agranelar (*el cuero*)

peck [pɛk] *s* medida de áridos (*nueve litros*); montón *m;* picotazo; beso dado de mala gana ‖ *tr* picotear ‖ *intr* picotear; (coll) comer melindrosamente; **to peck at** querer picar; regañar constantemente; (coll) comer melindrosamente

peculate ['pɛkjə,let] *tr & intr* malversar

peculíar [pɪ'kjuljər] *adj* peculiar; singular, raro; excéntrico

pedagogue ['pɛdə,gɑg] *s* pedagogo; dómine *m*, pedante *m*

pedagogy ['pɛdə,gɑdʒi] o ['pɛdə,gɑdʒi] *s* pedagogía

ped•al ['pɛdəl] *s* pedal *m* ‖ *v* (*pret & pp* **-aled** o **-alled;** *ger* **-aling** o **-alling**) *tr* impulsar pedaleando ‖ *intr* pedalear

pedant ['pɛdənt] *s* pedante *mf*

pedantic [pɪ'dæntɪk] *adj* pedantesco

pedant•ry ['pɛdəntri] *s* (*pl* **-ries**) pedantería

peddle ['pɛdəl] *tr* ir vendiendo de puerta en puerta; traer y llevar (*chismes*); vender (*favores*) ‖ *intr* ser buhonero

peddler ['pɛdlər] *s* buhonero

pederasty ['pɛdə,ræsti] *s* pederastia

pedestal ['pɛdɪstəl] *s* pedestal *m*

pedestrian [pɪ'dɛstrɪən] *adj* pedestre ‖ *s* peatón *m*

pediatrician [,pidɪə'trɪʃən] *s* pedíatra *mf*

pediatrics [,pidɪ'ætrɪks] *ssg* pediatría

pedigree ['pɛdɪ,gri] *s* árbol genealógico; ascendencia; fuente *f*, origen *m*

pediment ['pɛdɪmənt] *s* frontón *m*

pee [pi] *s* (coll) pipí *m* ‖ *intr* (coll) hacer pipí

peek [pik] *s* mirada rápida y furtiva ‖ *intr* mirar a hurtadillas

peel [pil] *s* cáscara, pellejo ‖ *tr* pelar ‖ *intr* pelarse

peep [pip] *s* mirada a hurtadillas; (*of chickens*) pío ‖ *intr* mirar a hurtadillas; piar (*los pollos*)

peep'hole' *s* atisbadero; (*in a door*) mirilla, ventanillo

peep show *s* mundonuevo; (slang) vistas sicalípticas

peer [pir] *s* par *m* ‖ *intr* mirar fijando la vista de cerca; **to peer at** mirar con ojos de miope; **to peer into** mirar hacia lo interior de, escudriñar

peerless ['pirlɪs] *adj* sin par

peeve [piv] *s* (coll) cojijo ‖ *tr* (coll) enojar, irritar

peevish ['pivɪʃ] *adj* cojijoso, displicente

peg [pɛg] *s* clavija, claveta, estaquilla; **to take down a peg** (coll) bajar los humos a ‖ *v* (*pret & pp* **pegged;** *ger* **pegging**) *tr* enclavijar; señalar con clavijas; fijar (*precios*) ‖ *intr* trabajar con ahinco; **to peg away at** afanarse en

peg leg *s* pata de palo

peg top *s* peonza; **peg tops** pantalones anchos de caderas y perniles ajustados

Peking [ˈpiˈkɪŋ] *s* Pequín

Peking·ese [ˌpikɪˈniz] *adj* pequinés ‖ *s* (*pl* -ese) pequinés *m*

pelf [pɛlf] *s* dinero mal ganado

pell-mell [ˈpɛlˈmɛl] *adj* tumultuoso ‖ *adv* atropelladamente

Peloponnesian [ˌpɛləpəˈniʃən] *adj & s* peloponense *mf*

Peloponnesus [ˌpɛləpəˈnisəs] *s* Peloponeso

Pelops [ˈpilɑps] *s* Pélope *m*

pelota [pɛˈlotə] *s* pelota vasca

pelt [pɛlt] *s* pellejo; golpe violento; (*of a person*) (*hum*) pellejo ‖ *tr* golpear violentamente; apedrear ‖ *intr* golpear violentamente; caer con fuerza (*el granizo, la lluvia, etc.*); apresurarse

pen. *abbr* **peninsula**

pen [pɛn] *s* pluma; corral *m*, redil *m*; **the pen and the sword** las letras y las armas ‖ *v* (*pret & pp* **penned;** *ger* **penning**) *tr* escribir (*con pluma*); redactar ‖ *v* (*pret & pp* **penned** o **pent** [pɛnt]) *tr* acorralar, encerrar

penalize [ˈpinəˌlaɪz] *tr* penar; penalizar; (*sport*) sancionar

penal·ty [ˈpɛnəlti] *s* (*pl* -ties) pena; (*for late payment*) recargo; (*sport*) sanción; **under penalty of** so pena de

penance [ˈpɛnəns] *s* penitencia; **to do penance** hacer penitencia

penchant [ˈpɛnʃənt] *s* afición, inclinación, tendencia

pen·cil [ˈpɛnsəl] *s* lápiz *m*; (*of light*) pincel *m*, haz *m* ‖ *v* (*pret & pp* -ciled o -cilled; *ger* -ciling o -cilling) *tr* marcar con lápiz; (*med*) pincelar

pencil sharpener *s* afilalápices *m*, cortalápices *m*

pendent [ˈpɛndənt] *adj* pendiente; sobresaliente ‖ *s* medallón *m*; (*earring*) pendiente *m*

pending [ˈpɛndɪŋ] *adj* pendiente ‖ *prep* hasta; durante

pendulum [ˈpɛndʒələm] *s* péndulo; (*of a clock*) péndola

pendulum bob *s* lenteja

penetrate [ˈpɛnɪˌtret] *tr & intr* penetrar

penguin [ˈpɛŋgwɪn] *s* pingüino, pájaro bobo

pen·hold·er *s* (*handle*) portaplumas *m*; (*box*) plumero

penicillin [ˌpɛnɪˈsɪlɪn] *s* penicilina

peninsula [pəˈnɪnsələ] *s* península

peninsular [pəˈnɪnsələr] *adj & s* peninsular *mf* ‖ **Peninsular** *adj & s* (*Iberian*) peninsular *mf*

penis [ˈpinəs] *s* pene *m*, falo

penitence [ˈpɛnɪtəns] *s* penitencia

penitent [ˈpɛnɪtənt] *adj & s* penitente *mf*

pen·knife' *s* (*pl* -knives) navaja, cortaplumas *m*

penmanship [ˈpɛnmənˌʃɪp] *s* caligrafía; (*hand of a person*) letra

pen name *s* seudónimo

pennant [ˈpɛnənt] *s* gallardete *m*

penniless [ˈpɛnɪlɪs] *adj* pelón, sin dinero

pennon [ˈpɛnən] *s* pendón *m*

pen·ny [ˈpɛni] *s* (*pl* -nies) (U.S.A.) centavo ‖ *s* (*pl* pence [pɛns]) (Brit) penique *m*

pen·ny·weight *s* peso de 24 granos

pen pal *s* (coll) amigo por correspondencia

pen point *s* punta de la pluma; puntilla de la pluma fuente

pension [ˈpɛnʃən] *s* pensión, jubilación ‖ *tr* pensionar, jubilar

pensioner [ˈpɛnʃənər] *s* pensionista *mf;* **pensioners** clases pasivas

pensive [ˈpɛnsɪv] *adj* pensativo; melancólico

Pentecost [ˈpɛntɪˌkɔst] *s* el Pentecostés

penthouse [ˈpɛntˌhaʊs] *s* alpende *m*, colgadizo; casa de azotea

pent-up [ˈpɛntˌʌp] *adj* contenido, reprimido

penult [ˈpinʌlt] *s* penúltima

penum·bra [pɪˈnʌmbrə] *s* (*pl* -brae [bri] o -bras) penumbra

penurious [pɪˈnʊrɪəs] *adj* (*stingy*) tacaño, mezquino; (*poor*) pobre, indigente

penury [ˈpɛnjəri] *s* tacañería, mezquindad; pobreza, miseria

pen·wip'er *s* limpiaplumas *m*

people [ˈpipəl] *spl* gente *f;* personas; gente del pueblo; se, p.ej., **people say** se dice ‖ *ssg* (*pl* peoples) pueblo, nación ‖ *tr* poblar

pep [pɛp] *s* (slang) ánimo, brío, vigor *m* ‖ *v* (*pret & pp* **pepped;** *ger* **pepping**) *tr*—**to pep up** (slang) animar, dar vigor a

pepper [ˈpɛpər] *s* (*spice*) pimienta; (*plant and fruit*) pimiento ‖ *tr* sazonar con pimienta; (*with bullets*) acribillar; salpicar

pep'per·box' *s* pimentero

pep'per·mint' *s* (*plant*) menta piperita; esencia de menta; pastilla de menta

pep talk *s* palabras alentadoras

per [pʌr] *prep* por; **as per** según

perambulator [pərˈæmbjəˌletər] *s* cochecillo de niño

per capita [pər ˈkæpɪtə] por cabeza, por persona

perceive [pərˈsiv] *tr* percibir

per cent o **percent** [pərˈsɛnt] por ciento

percentage [pərˈsɛntɪdʒ] *s* porcentaje *m;* (slang) provecho, ventaja

perception [pərˈsɛpʃən] *s* percepción; comprensión, penetración

perch [pʌrtʃ] *s* percha, rama, varilla; sitio o posición elevada; (*fish*) perca ‖ *tr* colocar en un sitio algo elevado *intr* sentarse en un sitio algo elevado; posar (*un ave*)

percolator [ˈpʌrkəˌletər] *s* cafetera filtradora

per diem [pərˈdaɪəm] por día

perdition [pərˈdɪʃən] *s* perdición

perennial [pəˈrɛnɪəl] *adj* perenne; (bot) vivaz ‖ *s* planta vivaz

perfect [ˈpʌrfɛkt] *adj & s* perfecto ‖ [pərˈfɛkt] *tr* perfeccionar

perfidious [pərˈfɪdɪəs] *adj* pérfido

pa
pe

perfi•dy [ˈpʌrfɪdi] *s* (*pl* **-dies**) perfidia
perforate [ˈpʌrfəˌret] *tr* perforar
perforce [pərˈfors] *adv* por fuerza, necesariamente
perform [pərˈfɔrm] *tr* ejecutar; (theat) representar ‖ *intr* ejecutar; funcionar (*p.ej.*, *una máquina*)
performance [pərˈfɔrməns] *s* ejecución; representación; funcionamiento; (theat) función
performer [pərˈfɔrmər] *s* ejecutante *mf*; actor *m*; acróbata *mf*
perfume [ˈpʌrfjum] *s* perfume *m* ‖ [pərˈfjum] *tr* perfumar
perfunctory [pərˈfʌŋktəri] *adj* hecho sin cuidado, hecho a la ligera; indiferente, negligente
perhaps [pərˈhæps] *adv* acaso, tal vez, quizá
per•il [ˈpɛrəl] *s* peligro ‖ *v* (*pret* & *pp* **-iled** o **-illed**; *ger* **-iling** o **-illing**) *tr* poner en peligro
perilous [ˈpɛrɪləs] *adj* peligroso
period [ˈpɪrɪ•əd] *s* período; (*in school*) hora; (gram) punto; (sport) division
period costume *s* traje *m* de época
periodic [ˌpɪrɪˈɑdɪk] *adj* periódico
periodical [ˌpɪrɪˈɑdɪkəl] *adj* periódico ‖ *s* periódico, revista periódica
peripher•y [pəˈrɪfəri] *s* (*pl* **-ies**) periferia
periscope [ˈpɛrɪˌskop] *s* periscopio
perish [ˈpɛrɪʃ] *intr* perecer
perishable [ˈpɛrɪʃəbəl] *adj* perecedero; (*merchandise*) corruptible
periwig [ˈpɛrɪˌwɪg] *s* perico
perjure [ˈpʌrdʒər] *tr* hacer (*a una persona*) quebrantar el juramento; **to perjure oneself** perjurarse
perju•ry [ˈpʌrdʒəri] *s* (*pl* **-ries**) perjurio
perk [pʌrk] *tr* alzar (*la cabeza*); aguzar (*las orejas*) ‖ *intr* pavonearse; engalanarse; **to perk up** reanimarse, sentirse mejor
permanence [ˈpʌrmənəns] *s* permanencia
permanency [ˈpʌrmənənsi] *s* (*pl* **-cies**) permanencia; persona, cosa o posición peremanentes
permanent [ˈpʌrmənənt] *adj* permanente ‖ *s* permanente *f*, ondulación permanente
permanent tenure *s* inamovilidadperversión
permanent way *s* (rr) material fijo
permeate [ˈpʌrmɪˌet] *tr* & *intr* penetrar
permission [pərˈmɪʃən] *s* permisión
per•mit [ˈpʌrmɪt] *s* permiso; cédula de aduana ‖ [pərˈmɪt] *v* (*pret* & *pp* **-mitted**; *ger* **-mitting**) *tr* permitir
permute [perˈmjut] *tr* permutar
pernicious [pərˈnɪʃəs] *adj* pernicioso
pernickety [perˈnɪkɪti] *adj* (coll) descontentadizo, quisquilloso
perorate [ˈpɛrəˌret] *intr* perorar
peroration [ˌpɛrəˈreʃən] *s* peroración
peroxide [pərˈɑksaɪd] *s* peróxido; peróxido de hidrógeno
peroxide blonde *s* rubia oxigenada
perpendicular [ˌpʌrpənˈdɪkjələr] *adj* & *s* perpendicular *f*
perpetrate [ˈpʌrpɪˌtret] *tr* perpetrar
perpetual [pərˈpɛtʃu•əl] *adj* perpetuo

perpetuate [pərˈpɛtʃuˌet] *tr* perpetuar
perplex [pərˈplɛks] *tr* dejar perplejo
perplexed [pərˈplɛkst] *adj* perplejo
perplexi•ty [pərˈplɛksɪti] *s* (*pl* **-ties**) perplejidad; problema *m*
per se [per ˈsi] por sí mismo, en sí mismo, esencialmente
persecute [ˈpʌrsɪˌkjut] *tr* perseguir
persecution [ˌpʌrsɪˈkjuʃən] *s* persecución
persevere [ˌpʌrsɪˈvɪr] *intr* perseverar
Persian [ˈpʌrʒən] *adj* & *s* persa *mf*
persimmon [pərˈsɪmən] *s* placaminero
persist [pərˈsɪst] o [pərˈzɪst] *intr* persistir; empecinarse
persistent [pərˈsɪstənt] o [pərˈzɪstənt] *adj* persistente; (*insistent*) porfiado; (*e.g.*, *headache*) pertinaz
person [ˈpʌrsən] *s* persona; **no person** nadie
personage [ˈpʌrsənɪdʒ] *s* personaje *m*; persona
personal [ˈpʌrsənəl] *adj* personal; de uso personal ‖ *s* nota de sociedad; (*in a newspaper*) remitido
personali•ty [ˌpʌrsəˈnælɪti] *s* (*pl* **-ties**) personalidad
personality cult *s* culto a la personalidad
personal property *s* bienes *mpl* muebles
personi•fy [pərˈsɑnɪˌfaɪ] *v* (*pret* *pp* **-fied**) *tr* personificar
personnel [ˌpʌrsəˈnɛl] *s* personal *m*
per'son-to-per'son *adv* (telp) particular a particular
perspective [pərˈspɛktɪv] *s* perspectiva
perspicacious [ˌpʌrspɪˈkeʃəs] *adj* perspicaz
perspire [pərˈspaɪr] *intr* sudar, transpirar
persuade [pərˈswed] *tr* persuadir
persuasion [pərˈsweʒən] *s* persuasión; creencia religiosa; creencia fuerte
pert [pʌrt] *adj* atrevido, descarado; (coll) animado, vivo
pertain [pərˈten] *intr* pertenecer; **pertaining to** perteneciente a
pertinacious [ˌpʌrtɪˈneʃəs] *adj* pertinaz
pertinent [ˈpʌrtɪnənt] *adj* pertinente
perturb [pərˈtʌrb] *tr* perturbar
Peru [pəˈru] *s* el Perú
perusal [pəˈruzəl] *s* lectura cuidadosa
peruse [pəˈruz] *tr* leer con atención
Peruvian [pəˈruvɪ•ən] *adj* & *s* peruano
pervade [pərˈved] *tr* penetrar, esparcirse por, extenderse por
perverse [pərˈvʌrs] *adj* perverso; avieso, díscolo; contumaz; malazo
perversion [pərˈvʌrʒən] *s* perversión
perversi•ty [pərˈvʌrsɪti] *s* (*pl* **-ties**) perversidad; indocilidad; contumacia
pervert [ˈpʌrvərt] *s* renegado, apóstata; pervertido ‖ [pərˈvʌrt] *tr* pervertir; emplear mal (*p.ej.*, *los talentos que uno tiene*)
pes•ky [ˈpɛski] *adj* (*comp* **-kier;** *super* **-kiest**) (coll) cargante, molesto
pessimism [ˈpɛsɪˌmɪzəm] *s* pesimismo
pessimist [ˈpɛsɪmɪst] *s* pesimista *mf*
pessimistic [ˌpɛsɪˈmɪstɪk] *adj* pesimista
pest [pɛst] *s* peste *f*; insecto nocivo; (*misfortune*) plaga; (*annoying person, bore*) machaca *mf*
pester [ˈpɛstər] *tr* molestar, importunar

pest'house' s lazareto, hospital m de contagiosos

pesticide [ˈpɛstɪˌsaɪd] s pesticida m

pestiferous [pɛsˈtɪfərəs] adj pestifero; (coll) engorroso, molesto

pestilence [ˈpɛstɪləns] s pestilencia

pestle [ˈpɛsəl] s mano f de almirez

pet [pɛt] s animal mimado, animal casero; niño mimado; favorito; enojo pasajero ‖ v (pret & pp **petted;** ger **petting**) tr acariciar, mimar ‖ intr (slang) besuquearse

petal [pɛtəl] s pétalo

petard [pɪˈtard] s petardo

pet'cock' s llave f de desagüe, llave de purga

Peter [ˈpitər] s Pedro; **to rob Peter to pay Paul** desnudar a un santo para vestir a otro

petit-bourgeois [pəˈtiˈburʒwa] adj pequeño-burgués

petition [pɪˈtɪʃən] s petición; (formal request signed by a number of people) memorial m, instancia, solicitud ‖ tr suplicar; dirigir una instancia a, solicitar

pet name s nombre m de cariño

Petrarch [ˈpitrark] s Petrarca m

petri•fy [ˈpɛtrɪˌfaɪ] v (pret & pp **-fied**) tr petrificar ‖ intr petrificarse

petrochemical [ˌpetroˈkɛmɪkəl] adj petroquímico

petrol [ˈpɛtrəl] s (Brit) gasolina

petroleum [pɪˈtroliˌəm] s petróleo

pet shop s pajarería

petticoat [ˈpɛtɪˌkot] s enaguas; (woman, girl) (slang) falda

pet•ty [ˈpɛti] adj (comp **-tier;** super **-tiest**) insignificante, pequeño; mezquino; intolerante

petty cash s caja de menores, efectivo para gastos menores

petty larceny s ratería, hurto

petty officer s (naut) suboficial m

petulant [ˈpɛtjələnt] adj malhumorado, enojadizo

pew [pju] s banco de iglesia

pewter [ˈpjutər] s peltre m; vajilla de peltre

Phaëthon [ˈfeˈɪθɑn] s Faetón m

phalanx [ˈfelæŋks] s falange f

phallic [ˈfælɪk] adj fálico

phallus [ˈfæləs] s falo

phantasm [ˈfæntæzəm] s fantasma m

phantom [ˈfæntəm] s fantasma m

Pharaoh [ˈfero] s Faraón m

pharisee [ˈfærɪˌsi] s fariseo ‖ **Pharisee** s fariseo

pharmaceutical [ˌfarməˈsutɪkəl] adj farmacéutico

pharmacist [ˈfarməsɪst] s farmacéutico

pharma•cy [ˈfarməsi] s (pl **-cies**) farmacia

pharynx [ˈfærɪŋks] s faringe f

phase [fez] s fase f ‖ tr poner en fase; llevar a cabo a etapas uniformes; (coll) inquietar, molestar; **to phase out** deshacer paulatinamente

pheasant [ˈfɛzənt] s faisán m

phenobarbital [ˌfinoˈbarbɪˌtæl] s fenobarbital m

phenomenal [fɪˈnamɪˌnan] s (pl **-na** [nə]) fenómenal

phial [ˈfaɪˌəl] s frasco pequeño; inyectable m

Phidias [ˈfɪdɪˌəs] s Fidias m

philanderer [fɪˈlændərər] s galanteador m, tenorio

philanthropist [fɪˈlænθrəpɪst] s filántropo

philanthro•py [fɪˈlænθrəpi] s (pl **-pies**) filantropía

philatelist [fɪˈlætəlɪst] s filatelista mf

philately [fɪˈlætəli] s filatelia

Philip [ˈfɪlɪp] s Felipe m; (of Macedon) Filipo

Philippine [ˈfɪlɪˌpin] adj filipino ‖ **Philippines** spl Islas Filipinas

Philistine [fɪˈlɪstin] o [ˈfɪlɪˌstin] o [ˈfɪlɪˌstaɪn] adj & s filisteo

philologist [fɪˈlalədʒɪst] s filólogo

philology [fɪˈlalədʒi] s filología

philosopher [fɪˈlasəfər] s filósofo

philosophic(al) [ˌfɪləsafɪk(əl)] adj filosófico

philoso•phy [fɪˈlasəfi] s (pl **-phies**) filosofía

philter [ˈfɪltər] s filtro

phlebitis [flɪˈbaɪtɪs] s flebitis f

phlegm [flɛm] s flema f, gargajo; **to cough up phlegm** gargajear

phlegmatic(al) [flɛgˈmætɪk(əl)] adj flemático; (coll) galbanoso

Phoebe [ˈfibi] s Febe f

Phoebus [ˈfibəs] s Febo

Phoenicia [fɪˈnɪʃə] o [fɪˈniʃə] s Fenicia

Phoenician [fɪˈnɪʃən] o [fɪˈniʃən] adj & s fenicio

phoenix [ˈfinɪks] s fénix m

phone [fon] s (coll) teléfono; **to come** o **to go to the phone** acudir al teléfono, ponerse al aparato ‖ tr & intr (coll) telefonear

phone call s llamada telefónica

phoneme [ˈfonim] s fonema m

phonetic [foˈnɛtɪk] adj fonético

phonics [ˈfanɪks] s fónica

phonograph [ˈfonəˌgræf] s fonógrafo

phonology [fəˈnalədʒi] s fonología

pho•ny [ˈfoni] adj (comp **-nier;** super **-niest**) falso, contrahecho ‖ s (pl **-nies**) (slang) farsa; (coll) farsante mf

phosphate [ˈfasfet] s fosfato

phosphorescent [ˌfasfəˈrɛsənt] adj fosforescente

phospho•rus [ˈfasfərəs] s (pl **-ri** [ˌraɪ]) fósforo

pho•to [ˈfoto] s (pl **-tos**) foto f

photocopier [ˈfotoˌkapɪˌər] s fotocopiador m; fotóstato m

pho'to•cop'y s fotocopia ‖ v (pret & pp **-ied**) tr fotocopiar

photoengraving [ˌfotoˌɛnˈgrevɪŋ] s fotograbado

photo finish s (sport) llegada a la meta, determinada mediante el fotofija

pho'to•fin'ish camera s fotofija m

photogenic [ˌfotoˈdʒɛnɪk] adj fotogénico

photograph [ˈfotəˌgræf] s fotografía ‖ tr & intr fotografiar

photographer [fəˈtagrəfər] s fotógrafo

photography [fəˈtagrəfi] s fotografía

pe
ph

photojournalism [,fotə'dʒʌrnə,lɪzəm] s fotoperiodismo
pho'to•play' s fotodrama m
photostat ['fotə,stæt] s fotóstato ‖ tr & intr fotostatar
phototube ['fotə,tjub] fototubo
phrase [frez] s frase f ‖ tr frasear
phrenology [frɪ'nɑlədʒi] s frenología
phys. abbr **physical, physician, physics, physiology**
phys•ic ['fɪzɪk] s medicamento; purgante m ‖ v (pret & pp **-icked;** ger **-icking**) tr curar; purgar
physical ['fɪzɪkəl] adj físico
physician [fɪ'zɪʃən] s médico
physicist ['fɪzɪsɪst] s físico
physics ['fɪzɪks] s física
physiognomy [,fɪzɪ'ɑgnəmi] o [,fɪzɪ'ɑnəmi] s fisononía
physiological [,fɪzɪ•ə'lɑdʒɪkəl] adj fisiológico
physiology [,fɪzɪ'ɑlədʒi] s fisiología
physique [fɪ'zik] s físico, talle m, exterior m
pi [paɪ] s (math) pi f; (typ) pastel m ‖ v (pret & pp **pied;** ger **piing**) tr (typ) empastelar
pian•o [pɪ'æno] s (pl **-os**) piano
picaresque [,pɪkə'rɛsk] adj picaresco
picayune [,pɪkə'jun] adj de poca monta, mezquino
piccadil•ly [,pɪkə'dɪli] s (pl **-lies**) cuello de pajarita
picco•lo ['pɪkə,lo] s (pl **-los**) flautín m
pick [pɪk] s (tool) pico; (choice) selección; (choicest) flor f ‖ tr escoger; recoger (p.ej., flores); recolectar (p.ej., algodón); romper (el hielo) con un picahielos; escarbarse (los dientes); descañonar, desplumar (un ave); hurgarse (la nariz); rescarse (una cicatriz, un grano); roer (un hueso); mondar (las frutas); falsear, forzar (una cerradura); armar (una pendencia); herir (las cuerdas de un instrumento); buscar (defectos); hurtar de (los bolsillos); **to pick out** entresacar; **to pick someone to pieces** (coll) no dejarle a uno un hueso sano; **to pick up** recoger; recobrar (ánimo; velocidad); descolgar (el receptor); hallar por casualidad; aprender con la práctica; aprender de oídas; invitar a subir a un coche; entablar conservación (sin presentación previa); captar (una señal de radio) ‖ intr comer melindrosamente; escoger esmeradamente; **to pick at** comer melindrosamente; tomarla con, regañar; **to pick on** escoger; (coll) regañar; (coll) molestar; **to pick over** ir revolviendo y examinando; **to pick up** (coll) ir mejor, sentirse mejor; recobrar velocidad
pick'ax' s zapapico
picket ['pɪkɪt] s (stake, pale) piquete m; (of strikers; of soldiers) piquete m ‖ tr poner un cordón de piquetes a ‖ intr servir de piquete
picket fence s cerca de estacas
picket line s línea de piquetes
pickle ['pɪkəl] s encurtido; escabeche m, salmuera; (coll) apuro, aprieto ‖ tr encurtir; escabechar

pick-me-up ['pɪkmi,ʌp] s (coll) tentempié m; (coll) trago fortificante
pick'pock'et s carterista m, ratero; bolsero (Mex)
pick'up' s recolección; (of a motor) recòbro; (of an automobile) aceleración; (elec) pickup, fonocaptor m
pic•nic ['pɪknɪk] s jira, partida de campo ‖ v (pret & pp **-nicked;** ger **-nicking**) intr hacer una jira al campo, merendar en el campo
pictorial [pɪk'torɪ•əl] adj gráfico; ilustrado ‖ s revista ilustrada
picture ['pɪktʃər] s cuadro; retrato; imagen f; lámina, grabado; fotografía; película; pintura ‖ tr dibujar; pintar; describir; **to picture to oneself** representarse
picture book s libro en imágenes
picture gallery s galería de pinturas
picture post card s postal ilustrada
picture show s exhibición de pinturas; cine m
picture signal s videoseñal f
picturesque [,pɪktjə'rɛsk] adj pintoresco
picture tube s tubo de imagen, tubo de televisión
picture window s ventana panorámica
piddling ['pɪdlɪŋ] adj de poca monta, insignificante
pie [paɪ] s pastel m; (bird) picaza; (typ) pastel m ‖ v (pret & pp **pied;** ger **pieing**) tr (typ) empastelar
piece [pis] s (fragment; section of cloth) pedazo; (part of a machine; drama; single composition of music; coin; figure or block used in checkers, chess, etc.) pieza; (of land) lote m, parcela; **a piece of advice** un consejo; **a piece of baggage** un bulto; **a piece of furniture** un mueble; **to break to pieces** despedazar, hacer pedazos; despedazarse; **to fall to pieces** desbaratarse, caer en ruina; **to give someone a piece of one's mind** decirle a uno su parecer con toda franqueza; **to go to pieces** desvencijarse; darse a la desesperación; ir al desastre (un negocio); sufrir un ataque de nervios; perder por completo la salud; **to pick someone to pieces** (coll) no dejarle a uno un hueso sano ‖ tr formar juntando piezas; remendar ‖ intr (coll) comer a deshora
piece goods spl géneros de pieza
piece'work' s destajo, trabajo a destajo
piece'work'er s destajero, destajista mf
pier [pɪr] s muelle m; (of a bridge) estribo, sostén m; (of a harbor) rompeolas m; (wall between two openings) (archit) entrepaño
pierce [pɪrs] tr agujerear, horadar, taladrar; atravesar, traspasar; picar; pinchar; punzar; (fig) traspasar (de dolor) ‖ intr penetrar, entrar a la fuerza
piercing ['pɪrsɪŋ] adj agudo, penetrante, desgarrador; (pain) lancinante
pier glass s espejo de cuerpo entero
pie•ty ['paɪ•əti] s (pl **-ties**) piedad, devoción
piffle ['pɪfəl] s (coll) disparates mpl, música celestial
pig [pɪg] s cerdo; (young hog) lechón m; (domestic hog) puerco, cochino; carne f de

puerco; (metal) lingote *m;* (*person who acts like a pig*) (coll) marrano, cochino

pigeon [ˈpɪdʒən] *s* paloma

pi'geon•hole' *s* hornilla, casilla de paloma; casilla ‖ *tr* encasillar

pigeon house *s* palomar *m*

piggish [ˈpɪgɪʃ] *adj* glotón, voraz

pig'gy•back' *adv* a cuestas, en hombros

pig'-head'ed *adj* terco, cabezudo

pig iron *s* arrabio, hierro en lingotes

pigment [ˈpɪgmənt] *s* pigmento ‖ *tr* pigmentar ‖ *intr* pigmentarse

pig'pen' *s* pocilga; (fig) pocilga, corral *m* de vacas

pig'skin' *s* piel *f* de cerdo; (coll) balón *m* (*con que se juega al fútbol*)

pig'sty' *s* (*pl* **-sties**) pocilga

pig'tail' *s* coleta, trenza; (*of tobacco*) andullo

pike [paɪk] *s* pica; (*of an arrow*) punta; carretera; camino de barrera; (*fish*) lucio

piker [ˈpaɪkər] *s* (slang) persona de poco fuste

Pilate [ˈpaɪlət] *s* Pilatos *m*

pile [paɪl] *s* pila, montón *m;* (*stake*) pilote *m;* lanilla, pelusa; pira; (elec, phys) pila; (coll) caudal *m;* **piles** almorranas ‖ *tr* apilar, amontonar ‖ *intr* apilarse, amontonarse; **to pile in** o **into** entrar atropelladamente en; entrar todos en; subir todos a (*p.ej., un coche*)

pile driver *s* martinete *m*

pileup [ˈpaɪlˌʌp] *s* (*collision*) choque en cadena

pilfer [ˈpɪlfər] *tr & intr* ratear

pilgrim [ˈpɪlgrɪm] *s* peregrino, romero

pilgrimage [ˈpɪlgrɪmɪdʒ] *s* peregrinación, romería

pill [pɪl] *s* píldora; mal trago, sinsabor *m;* (coll) persona molesta

pillage [ˈpɪlɪdʒ] *s* pillaje *m*, saqueo ‖ *tr & intr* pillar, saquear

pillar [ˈpɪlər] *s* pilar *m;* **from pillar to post** de acá para allá sin objeto determinado

pillo•ry [ˈpɪləri] *s* (*pl* **-ries**) picota ‖ *v* (*pret & pp* **-ried**) *tr* empicotar; (fig) motejar, poner en ridículo

pillow [ˈpɪlo] *s* almohada

pil'low•case' o **pil'low•slip'** *s* funda de almohada

pilot [ˈpaɪlət] *s* piloto, (*of a harbor*) práctico; (*of a gas range*) mechero encendedor; (rr) trompa, delantera ‖ *tr* pilotar; conducir

pilot run o **pilot test** *s* experimento piloto

pimp [pɪmp] *s* alcahuete *m*

pimple [ˈpɪmpəl] *s* barro, grano

pim•ply [ˈpɪmpli] *adj* (*comp* **-plier;** *super* **-pliest**) granujoso

pin [pɪn] *s* alfiler *m;* (*e.g., for a necktie*) prendedero; (*peg*) clavija; (*e.g., to hold scissors together*) clavillo, clavito; (bowling) bolo ‖ **to be on pins and needles** estar en espinas ‖ *v* (*pret & pp* **pinned**); *ger* **pinning**) *tr* alfilerar; clavar, fijar, sujetar; **to pin something on someone** (coll) acusarle a uno de una cosa; **to pin up** recoger y apuntar con alfileres; fijar en la pred con alfileres

pinafore [ˈpɪnəˌfor] *s* delantal *m* de niño

pin'ball' *s* billar romano, bagatela

pince-nez [ˈpæns͵ne] *s* lentes *mpl* de nariz, lentes de pinzas

pincers [ˈpɪnsərz] *ssg* o *spl* pinzas

pinch [pɪntʃ] *s* pellizco; (*of hunger*) tormento; (slang) arresto; (slang) hurto, robo; **in a pinch** en un aprieto; en caso necesario ‖ *tr* pellizcar; cogerse (*los dedos, p.ej., en una puerta*); apretar (*p.ej., el zapato a una persona*); contraer (*el frío a la cara de uno*); limitar los gastos de; (slang) arrestar, prender; (slang) hurtar, robar ‖ *intr* apretar; economizar, privarse de lo necesario

pinchers [ˈpɪntʃərz] *ssg* o *spl* var of **pincers**

pin'cush'ion *s* acerico

Pindar [ˈpɪndər] *s* Píndaro

pine [paɪn] *s* pino ‖ *intr* languidecer; **to pine away** consumirse; **to pine for** penar por

pine'ap'ple *s* ananás *m*, piña

pine cone *s* piña

pine needle *s* pinocha

ping [pɪŋ] *s* silbido de bala ‖ *intr* silbar (*una bala*); silbar como una bala

pin'head' *s* cabecilla de alfiler; cosa muy pequeña o insignificante; (coll) bobalicón *m*

pink [pɪŋk] *adj* rosado, sonrosado ‖ *s* estado perfecto; comunistoide *mf;* (bot) clavel *m*, clavellina

pin money *s* alfileres *mpl*

pinnacle [ˈpɪnəkəl] *s* pináculo

pin'point' *adj* exacto, preciso ‖ *s* punta de alfiler ‖ *tr & intr* señalar con precisión

pin'prick' *s* alfilerazo

pinup girl [ˈpɪnˌʌp] *s* guapa

pin'wheel' *s* rueda de fuego, rueda giratoria de fuegos artificiales; molinete *m* (Mex); (*child's toy*) rehilandera, ventolera

pioneer [͵paɪəˈnɪr] *s* pionero; (mil) zapador *m* ‖ *intr* abrir nuevos caminos, explorar

pious [ˈpaɪəs] *adj* pío, piadoso; mojigato; respetuoso

pip [pɪp] *s* (*seed*) pepita; (*on a card, dice, etc.*) punto; (vet) pepita

pipe [paɪp] *s* caño, conducto, tubo; (*to smoke tobacco*) pipa; (mus) pipa, caramillo, zampoña; (*of an organ*) cañón *m* ‖ *tr* conducir por medio de tubos o cañerías; proveer de tuberías o cañerías ‖ *intr* tocar el caramillo; **to pipe down** (slang) callarse

pipe cleaner *s* limpiapipas *m*

pipe dream *s* esperanza imposible, castillo en el aire

pipe line *s* cañería; tubería; oleoducto; fuente *f* de informes confidenciales

pipe organ *s* (mus) órgano

piper [ˈpaɪpər] *s* flautista *m;* gaitero; **to pay the piper** pagar los vidrios rotos

pipe wrench *s* llave *f* para tubos

pippin [ˈpɪpɪn] *s* (*apple*) camuesa; (*tree*) camueso; (slang) real moza

piquancy [ˈpikənsi] *s* picante *m*

piquant [ˈpikənt] *adj* picante

pique [pik] *s* pique *m*, resentimiento ‖ *tr* picar, enojar; despertar, excitar

piracy [ˈpaɪrəsi] *s* piratería

ph
pi

Piraeus [paɪˈriˑəs] s el Pireo
pirate [ˈpaɪrɪt] s pirata m ‖ tr pillar, robar;
publicar fraudulentamente ‖ intr piratear
pirouette [ˌpɪruˈɛt] s pirueta ‖ intr piruetear
Pisces [ˈpaɪsiz] s (astr) Piscis m
pistol [ˈpɪstəl] s pistola
piston [ˈpɪstən] s (mach) émbolo, pistón m;
(mus) pistón m
piston displacement s cilindrada
piston ring s anillo de émbolo, aro de
émbolo, segmento de émbolo
piston rod s vástago de émbolo
piston stroke s carrera de émbolo
pit [pɪt] s hoyo; (in the skin) cacaraña; (of
certain fruit) hueso; (for cockfights, etc.)
cancha, reñidero; (of the stomach) boca;
abismo, infierno; (min) pozo; (theat) foso ‖
v (pret & pp **pitted;** ger **pitting**) tr marcar
con hoyos; dejar hoyoso (el rostro); deshuesar (p.ej., una ciruela)
pitch [pɪtʃ] s (black sticky substance) pez f;
echada, lanzamiento; cosa lanzada; pelota
lanzada; (of a boat) arfada, cabezada; (of a
roof) pendiente f; (of, e.g., a screw) paso;
(of a winding) (elec) paso; (mus) tono,
altura; (fig) grado, extremo; (coll) bombo,
elogio ‖ tr echar, lanzar; elevar (el heno)
con la horquilla; armar o plantar (una
tienda de campaña); embrear; (mus) graduar el tono de ‖ intr caerse, caer de
cabeza; bajar en declive, inclinarse; arfar,
cabecear (un buque); **to pitch in** (coll)
poner manos a la obra; (coll) comenzar a
comer
pitch accent s acento de altura
pitcher [ˈpɪtʃər] s jarro; (in baseball) lanzador m
pitch′fork′ s horca, horquilla; **to rain pitchforks** (coll) llover a cántaros
pitch pipe s (mus) diapasón m
pit′fall′ s callejo, trampa; (danger for the
unwary) escollo, atascadero
pith [pɪθ] s médula; (essential part) (fig)
médula; (fig) fuerza, vigor m
pith·y [ˈpɪθi] adj (comp **-ier;** super **-iest**)
medular; enérgico, expresivo
pitiful [ˈpɪtɪfəl] adj lastimoso; compasivo;
despreciable
pitiless [ˈpɪtɪlɪs] adj despiadado, empedernido, incompasivo
pit·y [ˈpɪti] s (pl **-ies**) piedad, compasión,
lástima; **for pity's sake!** ¡por piedad!; **to
have** o **to take pity on** tener piedad de,
apiadarse de; **what a pity!** ¡qué lástima!,
¡qué pena! ‖ v (pret & pp **-ied**) tr apiadaise
de, compadecer
pivot [ˈpɪvət] s pivote m, gorrón m, eje m de
rotación; (fig) eje m ‖ intr pivotar; **to pivot
on** girar sobre; depender de
placard [ˈplækard] s cartel m ‖ tr fijar carteles en; fijar (un anuncio) en sitio público;
publicar por medio de carteles
place [ples] s sitio, lugar m; (of business)
local m; (job) puesto; grado, rango; **in no
place** en ninguna parte; **in place of** en
lugar de; **out of place** fuera de su lugar;
fuera de propósito; **to be looking for a**

place to live buscar piso; **to take place**
tener lugar; situar ‖ tr poner, colocar;
acordarse bien de; dar empleo a; prestar
(dinero) a interés ‖ intr colocarse (un caballo en las carreras)
place·bo [pləˈsibo] s (pl **-bos** o **-boes**) placebo
place card s tarjetita con el nombre (que
indica la colocación de uno en la mesa)
placement [ˈplesmənt] s colocación
place name s nombre m de lugar, topónimo
placid [ˈplæsɪd] adj plácido, tranquilo
plagiarism [ˈpledʒə,rɪzəm] s plagio
plagiarize [ˈpledʒə,raɪz] tr plagiar
plague [pleg] s peste f, plaga; (great public
calamity) plaga ‖ tr apestar, plagar; atormentar, molestar
plaid [plæd] s (cloth) tartán m; cuadros a la
escocesa
plain [plen] adj llano, claro, evidente;
abierto, franco, ordinario; feo; humilde;
solo, natural; **in plain English** sin rodeos;
in plain sight o **view** en plena vista ‖ s
llano, llanura
plain clothes spl traje m de calle, traje de
paisano
plainclothesman [ˈplenˈkloðz,mæn] s (pl
-men [ˌmɛn]) policía m que lleva traje de
paisano
plain omelet s tortilla a la francesa
plains·man [ˈplenzmən] s (pl **-men** [mən])
llanero
plaintiff [ˈplentɪf] s (law) demandante mf
plaintive [ˈplentɪv] adj quejumbroso
plan [plæn] s plan m, intento, proyecto;
(drawing, diagram) plan m, plano; **to
change one's plans** cambiar de proyecto ‖
v (pret & pp **planned;** ger **planning**) tr
planear, planificar; **to plan to** proponerse ‖
intr hacer proyectos
plane [plen] adj plano ‖ s (surface) plano;
aeroplano, avión m; (of an airplane) plano;
(carp) cepillo; (tree) plátano ‖ tr cepillar ‖
intr viajar en aeroplano
plane sickness s mareo del aire, mal m de
vuelo
planet [ˈplænɪt] s planeta m
plane tree s plátano
planing mill [ˈplenɪŋ] s taller m de cepillado
plank [plæŋk] s tabla gruesa, tablón m;
artículo de un programa político ‖ tr entablar, entarimar
plant [plænt] s fábrica, taller m; (of an
automobile) grupo motor; (educational establishment) plantel m; (bot) planta ‖ tr
plantar; sembrar (semillas); inculcar (doc-
trinas); (slang) ocultar (géneros robados)
plantation [plænˈteʃən] s plantación, campo
de plantas; (estate cultivated by workers
living on it) hacienda
planter [ˈplæntər] s plantador m, cultivador m
plasma [ˈplæzmə] s plasma m
plaster [ˈplæstər] s (gypsum) yeso; (mixture
of lime, sand, water, etc.) argamasa;
(coating) enlucido; (poultice) emplasto ‖ tr
en-

yesar; argamasar; enlucir; emplastar; embadurnar; pegar (*anuncios*)

plas'ter•board' *s* cartón *m* de yeso y fieltro

plaster cast *s* (surg) vendaje enyesado; (sculp) yeso

plaster of Paris *s* estuco de París

plastic ['plæstɪk] *adj* plástico ǁ *s* (*substance*) plástico; (*art of modeling*) plástica

plate [plet] *s* (*dish*) plato; (*sheet of metal, etc.*) chapa, placa; vajilla de oro, vajilla de plata; dentadura postiza, base *f* de la dentadura postiza; (baseball) puesto meta, puesto del batter; (anat, elec, electron, phot, zool) placa; (typ) clisé *m* ǁ *tr* chapear, planchear; blindar; platear, dorar, niquelar (*por la galvanoplastia*); (typ) clisar

plateau [plæ'to] *s* meseta

plate glass *s* vidrio o cristal cilindrado

platen ['plætən] *s* rodillo

platform ['plæt,fɔrm] *s* plataforma *f*; (*of passenger station*) andén *m*; (*of freight station*) cargadero; (*of a speaker*) tribuna; (*political program*) plataforma

platform car *s* plataforma *f*

platinum ['plætɪnəm] *s* platino

platinum blonde *s* rubia platino

platitude ['plætɪ,tjud] o ['plætɪ,tud] *s* perogrullada, trivialidad

Plato ['pleto] *s* Platón *m*

platoon [plə'tun] *s* pelotón *m*

platter ['plætər] *s* fuente *f*; (slang) disco de fonógrafo

plausible ['plɔzɪbəl] *adj* aparente, especioso; bien hablado; (coll) creíble

play [ple] *s* juego; (*act or move in a game*) jugada; (*drama*) pieza; (*of water, colors, lights*) juego; (mach) huelgo, juego; **to give full play to** dar rienda suelta a ǁ *tr* jugar (*p.ej., un naipe, una partida de juego*); jugar a (*p.ej., los naipes*); jugar con (*un contrario*); dar (*un chasco*); gastar (*una broma*); hacer (*una mala jugada*); dirigir (*agua, una manguera*); desempeñar (*un papel*); desempeñar el papel de; representar (*una obra dramática, un film*); apostar por (*un caballo*); tocar (*un instrumento, una pieza, un disco de fonógrafo*) ǁ *intr* jugar; desempeñar un papel, representar; correr (*una fuente*); rielar (*la luz en la superficie del agua*); vagar (*p.ej., una sonrisa por los labios*); **to play out** rendirse; agotarse; acabarse; **to play safe** tomar sus precauciones; **to play sick** hacerse el enfermo; **to play up to** hacer la rueda a

play'back' *s* lectura; aparato de lectura

play'bill' *s* (*poster*) cartel *m*; (*of a play*) programa *m*

player piano ['pleˌər] *s* autopiano

playful ['plefəl] *adj* juguetón, retozón; dicho en broma

playgoer ['pleˌgoˌər] *s* aficionado al teatro

play'ground' *s* campo de juego; patio de recreo

play'house' *s* casita de muñecas; teatro

playing card ['pleˌɪŋ] *s* naipe *m*

playing field *s* campo de deportes

play'mate' *s* compañero de juego

play'-off' *s* partido de desempate

play'pen' *s* parque *m*, corral *m* (*para bebés*)

play'thing' *s* juguete *m*

play'time' *s* hora de recreo, hora de juego

playwright ['pleˌraɪt] *s* dramaturgo, autor dramático; comediógrafo

play'writ'ing *s* dramaturgia, dramática

plea [pli] *s* ruego, súplica; disculpa, excusa; (law) contestación a la demanda

plead [plid] *v* (*pret & pp* **pleaded** o **pled** [plɛd]) *tr* defender (*una causa*) ǁ *intr* suplicar; abogar; **to plead guilty** confesarse culpable; **to plead not guilty** negar la acusación, declararse inocente

pleasant ['plɛzənt] *adj* agradable; simpático; sangriligero

pleasant•ry ['plɛzəntri] *s* (*pl* **-ries**) broma, chiste *m*, dicho gracioso

please [pliz] *tr & intr* gustar; **as you please** como Vd. quiera; **if you please** si me hace el favor; **please** + *inf* hágame Vd. el favor de + *inf*; **to be pleased to** alegrarse de, complacerse en; **to be pleased with** estar satisfecho de o con

pleasing ['plizɪŋ] *adj* agradable, grato

pleasure ['plɛʒər] *s* placer *m*, gusto; **what is your pleasure?** ¿en qué puedo servirle?, ¿qué es lo que Vd. desea?; **with pleasure** con mucho gusto

pleasure seeker ['sikər] *s* amigo de los placeres

pleat [plit] *s* pliegue *m*, plisado ǁ *tr* plegar, plisar

plebeian [plɪ'biən] *adj & s* plebeyo

pledge [plɛdʒ] *s* empeño, prenda; (*vow*) voto, promesa; (*toast*) brindis *m*; **as a pledge of** en prenda de; **to take the pledge** comprometerse a no tomar bebidas alcohólicas ǁ *tr* empeñar, prendar; dar (*la palabra*); brindar por

plentiful ['plɛntɪfəl] *adj* abundante, copioso

plenty ['plɛnti] *adv* (coll) completamente ǁ *s* abundancia, copia; suficiencia

pleurisy ['plʊrɪsi] *s* pleuresía

pliable ['plaɪ•əbəl] *adj* flexible, plegable; dócil

pliers ['plaɪ•ərz] *ssg* o *spl* alicates *mpl*

plight [plaɪt] *s* estado, situación; apuro, aprieto; compromiso solemne ǁ *tr* dar o empeñar (*su palabra*); **to plight one's troth** prometer fidelidad; dar palabra de casamiento

plod [plɑd] *v* (*pret & pp* **plodded**; *ger* **plodding**) *tr* recorrer (*un camino*) pausada y pesadamente ǁ *intr* caminar pausada y pesadamente; trabajar laboriosamente

plot [plɑt] *s* complot *m*, conspiración; (*of a play or novel*) argumento, trama, parcela; solar *m*; cuadro de flores; cuadro de hortalizas; plano, mapa *m* ǁ *v* (*pret & pp* **plotted**; *ger* **plotting**) *tr* fraguar, tramar, urdir, maquinar; dividir en parcelas o solares; trazar el plano de; trazar, tirar (*líneas*) ǁ *intr* conspirar

plough [plaʊ] *s, tr & intr* var de **plow**

plover ['plʌvər] o ['plovər] *s* chorlito

plow [plaʊ] *s* arado; quitanieve *m* ‖ *tr* arar; surcar; quitar o barrer (*la nieve*); **to plow back** reinvertir (*ganancias*) ‖ *intr* arar; avanzar como un arado

plow·man ['plaʊmən] *s* (*pl* **-men** [mən]) arador *m*, yuguero

plow'share' *s* reja de arado

pluck [plʌk] *s* ánimo, coraje *m*, valor *m;* tirón *m* ‖ *tr* arrancar; coger (*flores*); desplumar (*un ave*); puntear (*p.ej., una guitarra*) ‖ *intr* dar un tirón; **to pluck up** recobrar ánimo

pluck·y ['plʌki] *adj* (*comp* **-ier;** *super* **-iest**) animoso, valiente

plug [plʌg] *s* taco, tarugo; boca de agua; tableta de tabaco; (*hat*) (slang) chistera; (elec) clavija, toma, ficha; (aut) bujía; (coll) rocín; (slang) elogio incidental ‖ *v* (*pret & pp* **plugged;** *ger* **plugging**) *tr* atarugar; calar (*un melón*); **to plug in** (elec) enchufar ‖ *intr* (coll) trabajar con ahinco

plum [plʌm] *s* (*tree*) ciruelo; (*fruit*) ciruela; (slang) turrón *m*, pingüe destino

plumage ['plumɪdʒ] *s* plumaje *m*

plumb [plʌm] *adj* vertical; (coll) completo ‖ *adv* a plomo; (coll) verticalmente; (coll) directamente ‖ *tr* aplomar; sondear

plumb bob *s* plomada

plumber ['plʌmər] *s* fontanero; (*worker in lead*) plomero

plumbing ['plʌmɪŋ] *s* instalación sanitaria; conjunto de cañerías; (*working in lead*) plomería; sondeo

plumbing fixtures *spl* artefactos sanitarios

plumb line *s* cuerda de plomada

plum cake *s* pastel aderezado con pasas de Corinto y ron

plume [plum] *s* (*of a bird*) pluma; (*tuft of feathers worn as ornament*) penacho ‖ *tr* emplumar; componerse (*las plumas*); **to plume oneself on** enorgulleclerse de

plummet ['plʌmɪt] *s* plomada ‖ *intr* caer a plomo, precipitarse

plump [plʌmp] *adj* rechoncho, regordete; brusco, franco ‖ *adv* de golpe; francamente ‖ *s* (coll) caída pesada; (coll) ruido sordo ‖ *intr* caer a plomo

plum pudding *s* pudín *m* inglés con pasas de Corinto, corteza de limón, huevos y ron

plum tree *s* ciruelo

plunder ['plʌndər] *s* pillaje *m;* botín *m* ‖ *tr* pillar, saquear

plunge [plʌndʒ] *s* zambullida; caída a plomo; sacudida violenta; salto; baño de agua fría; (*of a boat*) cabeceo ‖ *tr* zambullir; sumergir; hundir (*p.ej., un puñal*) ‖ *intr* zambullirse; sumergirse; hundirse (*p.ej., en la tristeza*); caer a plomo; arrojarse, precipitarse; cabecear (*un buque*); (slang) entregarse al juego, entregarse a las especulaciones

plunger ['plʌndʒər] *s* zambullidor *m;* émbolo buzo; (*of a tire valve*) obús *m;* (slang) jugador o especulador desenfrenado

plunk [plʌŋk] *adv* (coll) con un golpe seco, con un ruido de golpe seco ‖ *tr* (coll) arrojar, empujar o dejar caer pesadamente

‖ *intr* sonar o caer con un ruido de golpe seco

plural ['plʊrəl] *adj & s* plural *m*

plus [plʌs] *adj* más; y pico; **to be plus** (coll) tener por añadidura ‖ *prep* más ‖ *s* (*sign*) más *m;* añadidura

plush [plʌʃ] *adj* afelpado; (coll) lujoso, suntuoso ‖ *s* felpa; peluche *m*

Plutarch ['plutark] *s* Plutarco

plutonium [plu'tonɪ·əm] *s* plutonio

ply [plaɪ] *s* (*pl* **plies**) (*e.g., of a cloth*) capa, doblez *m;* (*of a cable*) cordón *m* ‖ *v* (*pret & pp* **plied**) *tr* manejar (*la aguja, etc.*); ejercer (*un oficio*); batir (*el agua con los remos*); importunar; navegar por (*p.ej., un río*) ‖ *intr* avanzar; **to ply between** hacer (*un barco*) el servicio entre

ply'wood' *s* chapeado, madera laminada

P.M. *abbr* **Postmaster, post meridiem** (Lat) **afternoon**

pneumatic [nju'mætɪk] o [nu'mætɪk] *adj* neumático

pneumatic drill *s* perforadora de aire comprimido

pneumonia [nju'monɪ·ə] o [nu'monɪ·ə] *s* neumonía o pulmonía

P.O. *abbr* **post office**

poach [potʃ] *tr* escalfar (*huevos*) ‖ *intr* cazar o pescar en vedado

poacher ['potʃər] *s* cazador furtivo, pescador furtivo

pock [pak] *s* cacaraña, hoyuelo

pocket ['pakɪt] *s* bolsillo, faltriquera; (*in billiards*) tronera; (aer) bolsa de aire; (mil) bolsón *m* ‖ *tr* embolsar; entronerar (*una bola de billar*); tragarse (*injurias*)

pock'et·book' *s* portamonedas *m;* (*of a woman*) bolsa

pocket calculator *s* bolsicalculadora, calculadora de bolsillo

pocket handkerchief *s* pañuelo de bolsillo o de mano

pock'et·knife' *s* (*pl* **-knives**) navaja, cortaplumas *m*

pocket money *s* alfileres *mpl*, dinero de bolsillo

pock'mark' *s* cacaraña, hoyuelo

pod [pad] *s* vaina

podium ['podi·əm] *s* podio

poem ['po·ɪm] *s* poema *m*, poesía

poet ['po·ɪt] *s* poeta *m*

poetess ['po·ɪtɪs] *s* poetisa

poetic [po'etɪk] *adj* poético ‖ **poetics** *ssg* poética

poetry ['po·ɪtri] *s* poesía

pogrom ['pogrəm] *s* levantamiento contra los judíos

poignancy ['pɔɪnyənsi] *s* picante *m*, viveza, intensidad

poignant ['pɔɪnyənt] *adj* picante, vivo, intenso

point [pɔɪnt] *s* (*of a sword, pencil; of land*) punta; (*of pen*) pico; (*of fountain pen*) puntilla; (*mark of imperceptible dimensions*) punto; (*of a joke*) gracia; (elec) punta; (math, typ, sport, fig) punto; (coll) indirecta, insinuación; **beside the point**

fuera de propósito; **on the point of** a punto de; **to carry one's point** salirse con la suya; **to come to the point** venir al caso o al grano; **to get to the point** caer en la cuenta ‖ *tr* aguzar, sacar punta a; apuntar (*p.ej., un arma de fuego*); resanar (*una pared*); **to point one's finger at** señalar con el dedo; **to point out** señalar, indicar, hacer notar ‖ *intr* apuntar; pararse (*el perro de muestra*); **to point at** señalar con el dedo

point'blank' *adj* & *adv* a quemarropa

pointed ['pɔɪntɪd] *adj* puntiagudo; picante; acentuado, directo

pointer ['pɔɪntər] *s* puntero; indicador *m;* (*of a clock*) manecilla; perro de muestra; (mas) fijador *m;* (coll) indicación, dirección

poise [pɔɪz] *s* aplomo, equilibrio ‖ *tr* equilibrar; considerar ‖ *intr* equilibrarse; estar suspendido

poison ['pɔɪzən] *s* veneno, ponzoña ‖ *tr* envenenar

poison ivy *s* tosiguero

poisonous ['pɔɪzənəs] *adj* venenoso

poi'son-pen' letter *s* carta calumniosa

poke [pok] *s* (*push*) empuje *m*, empujón *m;* (*thrust*) hurgonazo; (*with elbow*) codazo; (*slow person*) tardón *m* ‖ *tr* empujar; hacer (*un agujero*) a empujones; abrirse (*paso*) a empujones; atizar, hurgar (*el fuego*); **to poke fun at** burlarse de; **to poke one's nose into** entremeterse en ‖ *intr* fisgar, husmear; andar perezosamente

poker ['pokər] *s* hurgón *m;* (*card game*) póker *m*, pócar *m*

poker face *s* cara de jugador de póker; **to keep a poker face** disfrazar la expresión del rostro, mantener una expresión imperturbable

pok•y ['poki] *adj* (*comp* **-ier;** *super* **-iest**) (coll) tardo, roncero

Poland ['polənd] *s* Polonia

polar bear ['polər] *s* oso blanco

polarize ['polə,raɪz] *tr* polarizar

pole [pol] *s* (*long rod or staff*) pértiga; (*of a flag*) asta; (*upright support*) poste *m;* (*to push a boat*) botador *m;* (astr, biol, elec, geog, math) polo ‖ *tr* impeler (*un barco*) con botador ‖ **Pole** *s* polaco

pole'cat' *s* turón *m*, veso

pole'star' *s* estrella polar; (*guide*) norte *m;* (*center of interest*) miradero

pole vault *s* salto con garrocha o con pértiga

police [pə'lis] *s* policía ‖ *tr* poner o mantener servicio de policía en; (mil) limpiar

police car *s* carro-patrulla *m*

police•man [pə'lismən] *s* (*pl* **-men** [mən]) policía *m*, guardia urbano

police record *s* ficha

police state *s* estado-policía *m*

police station *s* cuartel *m* o estación de policía

poli•cy ['polɪsi] *s* (*pl* **-cies**) política; (ins) póliza

polio ['poli•o] *s* (coll) polio *f*

polish ['polɪʃ] *s* pulimento; cera de lustrar; (*for shoes*) bola, betún *m*, lustre *m;* (*dia-*

---

mond) talla; elegancia; cultura, urbanidad ‖ *tr* pulimentar, pulir; embolar, dar betún a (*los zapatos*); **to polish off** (coll) terminar de prisa; (slang) engullir (*la comida, un trago*) ‖ **Polish** ['polɪʃ] *adj* & *s* polaco

polisher ['polɪʃər] *s* pulidor *m;* (*machine*) pulidora; (*for floors, tables, etc.*) enceradora

polite [pə'laɪt] *adj* cortés, fino, urbano; culto

politeness [pə'laɪtnɪs] *s* cortesía, fineza, urbanidad; cultura

politic ['polɪtɪk] *adj* prudente, sagaz; astuto; juicioso

political [pə'lɪtɪkəl] *adj* político

politician [,polɪ'tɪʃən] *s* político; (*politician seeking personal or partisan gain*) politiquero

politics ['polɪtɪks] *ssg* o *spl* política

poll [pol] *s* (*questionnaire to determine opinion*) encuesta; votación; lista electoral; cabeza; **polls** urnas electorales; **to go to the polls** acudir a las urnas; **to take a poll** hacer una encuesta ‖ *tr* dar (*un voto*); recibir (*votos*)

pollen ['polən] *s* polen *m*

pollinate ['polɪ,net] *tr* polinizar

polling booth ['polɪŋ] *s* cabina o caseta de votar

polliwog ['polɪ,wag] *s* renacuajo; (slang) persona que atraviesa el ecuador en un barco por primera vez

pollster ['polstʌr] *s* encuestador *m*

poll tax *s* capitación, impuesto por cabeza

pollutant [pə'lutənt] *s* contaminante *m*

pollute [pə'lut] *tr* contaminar, corromper, ensuciar

pollution [pə'luʃən] *s* contaminación; (*of the environment*) polución; (fig) corrupción

polo ['polo] *s* polo

polo player *s* polista *mf*, jugador *m* de polo

polygamist [pə'lɪgəmɪst] *s* polígamo

polygamous [pə'lɪgəməs] *adj* polígamo

polyglot ['polɪ,glat] *adj* & *s* poligloto

polygon ['polɪ,gan] *s* polígono

Polyhymnia [,polɪ'hɪmnɪ•ə] *s* Polimnia

polynomial [,polɪ'nomɪ•əl] *s* polinomio

polyp ['polɪp] *s* pólipo

polytheist ['polɪ,θi•ɪst] *s* politeísta *mf*

polytheistic [,polɪθi'ɪstɪk] *adj* politeísta

polyvalent [,polɪ'velənt] *adj* (chem, bact) polivalente

pomade [pə'med] *s* pomada

pomegranate ['pam,grænɪt] *s* (*shrub*) granado; (*fruit*) granada

pom•mel ['pʌməl] o ['paməl] *s* (*on hilt of sword*) pomo; (*on saddle*) perilla ‖ *v* (*pret & pp* **-meled** o **-melled;** *ger* **-meling** o **-melling**) *tr* apuñear, aporrear

pomp [pamp] *s* pompa, fausto

pompadour ['pampə,dʊr] *s* copete *m*

pompous ['pampəs] *adj* pomposo, faustoso

pon•cho ['pantʃo] *s* (*pl* **-chos**) capote *m* de monte, poncho

pond [pand] *s* estanque *m*, charca

ponder ['pandər] *tr* ponderar ‖ *intr* meditar; **to ponder over** ponderar, considerar con cuidado

ponderous ['pɑndərəs] *adj* pesado, inmanejable; tedioso, fastidioso

pond scum *s* lama, verdín *m*

poniard ['pɑnjərd] *s* puñal *m*

pontiff ['pɑntɪf] *s* pontífice *m*

pontoon [pɑn'tun] *s* pontón *m*

po·ny ['poni] *s* (*pl* **-nies**) jaca, caballito; (*for drinking liquor*) (coll) pequeño vaso; (*translation used dishonestly in school*) (coll) chuleta

poodle ['pudəl] *s* perro de lanas

pool [pul] *s* (*small puddle*) charco; (*for swimming*) piscina; (*game*) trucos; (*in certain games*) polla, puesta; combinación de intereses; caudales unidos para un fin ‖ *tr* mancomunar

pool'room' *s* sala de trucos

pool table *s* mesa de trucos

poop [pup] *s* popa; (*deck*) toldilla

poor [pʊr] *adj* (*having few possessions; arousing pity*) pobre; (*not good, inferior*) malo

poor box *s* cepillo, caja de limosnas

poor'house' *s* asilo de pobres, casa de caridad

poorly ['pʊrli] *adv* mal

poor white *s* pobre *mf* de la raza blanca (*en el sur de los EE.UU.*)

pop. *abbr* **popular, population**

pop [pɑp] *s* estallido, taponazo; bebida gaseosa ‖ *v* (*pret & pp* **popped**; *ger* **popping**) *tr* hacer estallar; **to pop the question** (coll) hacer una declaración de amor ‖ *intr* estallar

pop'corn' *s* rosetas, palomitas (de maíz)

pope [pop] *s* papa *m*

popeyed ['pɑp,aɪd] *adj* de ojos saltones; (*with fear, surprise, etc.*) desorbitado

pop'gun' *s* tirabala

poplar ['pɑplər] *s* álamo, chopo

pop·py ['pɑpi] *s* (*pl* **-pies**) amapola

pop'py·cock' *s* (coll) necedad, tontería

popsicle ['pɑpsɪkəl] *s* polo

populace ['pɑpjəlɪs] *s* populacho; chamuchina

popular ['pɑpjələr] *adj* popular

popularize ['pɑpjələ,raɪz] *tr* popularizar, vulgarizar

populous ['pɑpjələs] *adj* populoso

porcelain ['pɔrsəlɪn] *s* porcelana

porch [pɔrtʃ] *s* porche *m*, pórtico

porcupine ['pɔrkjə,paɪn] *s* puerco espín

pore [por] *s* poro ‖ *intr*—**to pore over** estudiar larga y detenidamente

pork [pork] *s* carne *f* de cerdo

pork chop *s* chuleta de cerdo

pornography [pɔr'nɑgræfi] *s* pornografía

pornographic [,pɔrnə'græfɪk] *adj* pornográfico

porno queen ['pɔrno] *s* (slang) actriz *f* de películas pornográficas

porous ['porəs] *adj* poroso

porous plaster *s* parche poroso

porphy·ry ['pɔrfɪri] *s* (*pl* **-ries**) pórfido

porpoise ['pɔrpəs] *s* marsopa, puerco de mar; (*dolphin*) delfín *m*

porridge ['pɔrɪdʒ] *s* gachas

port [port] *adj* portuario ‖ *s* puerto; (*opening in ship's side*) portilla; (*left side of ship or airplane*) babor *m*; oporto, vino de Oporto; (mach) lumbrera

portable ['portəbəl] *adj* portátil

portal ['portəl] *s* portal *m*

portend [por'tɛnd] *tr* anunciar de antemano, presagiar

portent ['portent] *s* augurio, presagio

portentous [por'tɛntəs] *adj* portentoso, extraordinario; amenazante, ominoso

porter ['portər] *s* (*doorkeeper*) portero, conserje *m*; (*in hotels and trains*) mozo de servicio; pórter *m* (*cerveza de Inglaterra de color obscuro*)

portfoli·o [port'folɪ,o] *s* (*pl* **-os**) cartera

port'hole' *s* porta, portilla

porti·co ['portɪ,ko] *s* (*pl* **-coes o -cos**) pórtico

portion ['porʃən] *s* porción; (*dowry*) dote *m & f*

port·ly ['portli] *adj* (*comp* **-lier**; *super* **-liest**) corpulento; grave, majestuoso

port of call *s* escala

portrait ['portret] o ['portrɪt] *s* retrato; **to sit for a portrait** retratarse

portray [por'tre] *tr* retratar

portrayal [por'tre·əl] *s* representación gráfica; retrato, descripción acertada

Portugal ['portʃəgəl] *s* Portugal *m*

Portu·guese ['portʃə,giz] *adj* portugués ‖ *s* (*pl* **-guese**) portugués *m*

port wine *s* vino de Oporto

pose [poz] *s* pose *f* ‖ *tr* plantear (*una pregunta, cuestión, etc.*) ‖ *intr* posar (*para retratarse; como modelo*); tomar una postura afectada; **to pose as** hacerse pasar por

posh [pɑʃ] *adj* (slang) elegante; (slang) lujoso, suntuoso

position [pə'zɪʃən] *s* posición; empleo, puesto; opinión; **to be in a position to** estar en condiciones de

positive ['pɑzɪtɪv] *adj* positivo ‖ *s* positiva

possess [pə'zɛs] *tr* poseer

possession [pə'zɛʃən] *s* posesión

possible ['pɑsɪbəl] *adj* posible

possum ['pɑsəm] *s* zarigüeya; **to play possum** hacer la mortecina

post [post] *s* (*piece of wood, metal, etc. set upright*) poste *m*; (*position*) puesto; (*job*) puesto, cargo; casa de correos ‖ *tr* fijar (*carteles*); echar al correo; apostar, situar; tener al corriente; **post no bills** se prohibe fijar carteles

postage ['postɪdʒ] *s* porte *m*, franqueo; **postage will be paid by addressee** a franquear en destino

postage meter *s* franqueadora

postage stamp *s* sello de correo; estampilla, timbre *m* (Am)

postal ['postəl] *adj* postal ‖ *s* postal *f*

postal card *s* tarjeta postal

postal permit *s* franqueo concertado

postal savings bank *s* caja postal de ahorros

post card *s* tarjeta postal

post'date' *s* posfecha ‖ **post'date'** *tr* posfechar

poster ['postǝr] s cartel m, cartelón m, letrero; póster m

posterity [pɑs'tɛrɪti] s posteridad

postern ['postǝrn] s postigo, portillo

post'haste' adv por la posta, a toda prisa

posthumous ['pɑstʃumǝs] adj póstumo

post•man ['postmǝn] s (pl **-men** [mǝn]) cartero

post'mark' s matasellos m, timbre m de correos ‖ tr matasellar, timbrar

post'mas'ter s administrador m de correos

post-mortem [,post'mɔrtǝm] adj posterior a la muerte ‖ s examen m de un cadáver

post office s casa de correos

post'-of'fice box s apartado de correos, casilla postal

postpaid ['post,ped] adj con porte pagado, franco de porte

postpone [post'pon] tr aplazar

postscript ['post,skrɪpt] s posdata

posttonic [post'tɑnɪk] adj postónico

posture ['pɑstʃǝr] s postura ‖ intr adoptar una postura

post'war' adj de la posguerra

po•sy ['pozi] s (pl **-sies**) flor f, ramillete m

pot [pɑt] s pote m; (for flowers) tiesto; (for the kitchen) caldera, olla, puchero; vaso de noche, orinal m; (in gambling) puesta; (slang) mariguana

potash ['pɑt,æʃ] s potasa

potassium [pǝ'tæsɪǝm] s potasio

pota•to [pǝ'teto] s (pl **-toes**) patata, papa; (sweet potato) batata, buniato

potato masher s pasapuré m

potato omelet s tortilla a la española

potbellied ['pɑt'bɛlid] adj barrigón, panzudo

poten•cy ['potǝnsi] s (pl **-cies**) potencia

potent ['potǝnt] adj potente

potentate ['potǝn,tet] s potentado

potential [pǝ'tɛnʃǝl] adj & s potencial m

pot'hang'er s llares fpl

pot'hook' s garabato

potion ['poʃǝn] s poción

pot'luck s lo que hay de comer; **to take potluck** hacer penitencia

pot shot s tiro a corta distancia

potter ['pɑtǝr] s alfarero; ollero ‖ intr ocuparse en fruslerías

potter's clay s arcilla figulina

potter's field s cementerio de los pobres, hoyanca

potter's shop s ollería

potter's wheel s torno de alfarero

potter•y ['pɑtǝri] s (pl **-ies**) alfarería; cacharros (de alfarería)

pouch [pautʃ] s bolsa, saquillo; (of kangaroo) bolsa; (for tobacco) petaca; valija

poulterer ['poltǝrǝr] s pollero

poultice ['poltɪs] s cataplasma f

poultry ['poltri] s aves fpl de corral

pounce [pauns] intr—**to pounce on** saltar sobre, precipitarse sobre

pound [paund] s (weight) libra; (for stray animals) corral m de concejo ‖ tr golpear; machacar, moler; encerrar en el corral de concejo; bombardear incesantemente; (to keep walking over) desempedrar ‖ intr golpear

pound'cake' s pastel m en que entra una libra de cada ingrediente; ponqué m (Am)

pound sterling s libra esterlina

pour [por] tr vaciar, verter, derramar; echar, servir (p.ej., té); escanciar (vino) ‖ intr fluir rápidamente; llover a torrentes; **to pour out of** salir a montones de (p.ej., el teatro)

pout [paut] s mala cara, puchero ‖ intr poner mala cara, hacer pucheros

poverty ['pɑvǝrti] s pobreza; pelazón f

POW abbr prisoner of war

powder ['paudǝr] s polvo; (for face) polvos; (explosive) pólvora ‖ tr pulverizar; (to sprinkle with powder) empolvar, polvorear

powder puff s borla para empolvarse

powder room s cuarto tocador, cuarto de aseo

powdery ['paudǝri] adj (like powder) polvoriento; (sprinkled with powder) empolvado; (crumbly) quebradizo

power ['pau•ǝr] s (ability to act or do something; possession) poder m; (control, influence; wealth) poderío; (influential nation; energy, force, strength) potencia; **the powers that be** las autoridades, los que mandan ‖ tr accionar, impulsar

power brake s servofreno

power dive s (aer) picado con motor

power failure s interrupción de fuerza

powerful ['pau•ǝrfǝl] adj poderoso

pow'er•house' s central eléctrica

powerless ['pau•ǝrlɪs] adj impotente

power line s (elec) sector m de distribución

power mower s motosegadora

power of attorney s poder m

power plant s (aer) grupo motopropulsor; (aut) grupo motor; (elec) central eléctrica, estación generadora

power steering s (aut) servodirección

power tool s herramienta motriz

pp. abbr pages

p.p. abbr parcel post, postpaid

pr. abbr pair, present, price

P.R. abbr public relations

practical ['præktɪkǝl] adj práctico

practically ['præktɪkǝli] adv poco más o menos

practice ['præktɪs] s práctica; uso, costumbre; ensayo; (of a profession) ejercicio; (of a doctor) clientela ‖ tr practicar; ejercitar (p.ej., la caridad); ejercer (una profesión); estudiar (p.ej., el piano); tener por costumbre ‖ intr ejercitarse; practicar la medicina; ensayarse; entrenarse, adiestrarse; **to practice as** ejercer de (p.ej., abogado)

practitioner [præk'tɪʃǝnǝr] s (medical doctor) práctico

Prague [prɑg] o [preg] s Praga

prairie ['prɛri] s pradera, llanura, pampa

prairie dog s ardilla ladradora

prairie wolf s coyote m

praise [prez] s alabanza, elogio ‖ tr alabar, elogiar

praise'wor'thy adj laudable, plausible

pram [præm] *s* cochecillo de niño
prance [præns] o [prɑns] *s* cabriola, trenzado ‖ *intr* cabriolar, trenzar
prank [præŋk] *s* travesura
prate [pret] *intr* charlar, parlotear
prattle ['prætəl] *s* charla, parloteo ‖ *intr* charlar, parlotear, balbucear (*un niño*)
pray [pre] *tr* implorar, rogar, suplicar; rezar (*una oración*) ‖ *intr* orar, rezar; **pray tell me** sírvase decirme
prayer [prɛr] *s* ruego, súplica; oración, rezo
prayer book *s* devocionario
preach [pritʃ] *tr* predicar; aconsejar (*p.ej., la paciencia*) ‖ *intr* predicar
preacher ['pritʃər] *s* predicador *m*
preamble ['pri,æmbəl] *s* preámbulo
prebend ['prɛbənd] *s* prebenda
precarious [pri'kɛri•əs] *adj* precario
precaution [pri'kɔʃən] *s* precaución
precede [pri'sid] *tr & intr* preceder
precedent ['prɛsɪdənt] *s* precedente *m*
precept ['prisɛpt] *s* precepto
precinct ['prisɪŋkt] *s* barriada; distrito electoral
precious ['prɛʃəs] *adj* precioso; caro, amado; (coll) considerable ‖ *adv* (coll) muy, p.ej., **precious little** muy poco
precipice ['prɛsɪpɪs] *s* precipicio
precipitate [pri'sɪpɪ,tet] *adj & s* precipitado ‖ *tr* precipitar ‖ *intr* precipitarse
precipitous [pri'sɪpɪtəs] *adj* empinado, escarpado; (*hurried, reckless*) precipitoso
precise [pri'sais] *adj* preciso; meticuloso
precision [pri'sɪʒən] *s* precisión
preclude [pri'klud] *tr* excluir, imposibilitar
precocious [pri'koʃəs] *adj* precoz
predatory ['prɛdə,tori] *adj* predatorio
predicament [pri'dɪkəmənt] *s* apuro, situación difícil
predict [pri'dɪkt] *tr* predecir
prediction [pri'dɪkʃən] *s* predicción
predispose [,pridɪs'poz] *tr* predisponer
predominant [pri'dɑmɪnənt] *adj* predominante
preëminent [pri'ɛmɪnənt] *adj* preeminente
preëmpt [pri'ɛmpt] *tr* apropiarse o apropiarse de
preen [prin] *tr* arreglarse (*las plumas*) con el pico; **to preen oneself** componerse, vestirse cuidadosamente
pref. *abbr* **preface, preferred, prefix**
prefabricate [pri'fæbri,ket] *tr* prefabricar
preface ['prɛfɪs] *s* prefacio, advertencia ‖ *tr* introducir, empezar
pre•fer [pri'fʌr] *v* (*pret & pp* -**ferred;** *ger* -**ferring**) *tr* preferir; presentar; promover
preferable ['prɛfərəbəl] *adj* preferible
preference ['prɛfərəns] *s* preferencia
prefix ['prifɪks] *s* prefijo ‖ *tr* prefijar
pregnan•cy ['prɛgnənsi] *s* (*pl* -**cies**) preñez *f*, embarazo
pregnant ['prɛgnənt] *adj* preñado; encinta; **to make pregnant** dejar encinta
prejudice ['prɛdʒədɪs] *s* prejuicio; (*detriment*) perjuicio; **to the prejudice of** con perjuicio de; **without prejudice** (law) sin detrimento de sus propios derechos ‖ *tr*

predisponer, prevenir; (*to harm*) perjudicar
prejudicial [,prɛdʒə'dɪʃəl] *adj* perjudicial
prelate ['prɛlɪt] *s* prelado
pre-Lenten [pri'lɛntən] *adj* carnavalesco
prelim [pri'lɪm] *s* (coll) examen *m* preliminar
preliminar•y [pri'lɪmɪ,nɛri] *adj* preliminar ‖ *s* (*pl* -**ies**) preliminar *m*
prelude ['prɛljud] o ['prilud] *s* preludio ‖ *tr* preludiar
premeditate [pri'mɛdɪ,tet] *tr* premeditar
premier [prɪ'mɪr] o ['pri'mɪr] *s* primer ministro, presidente *m* del consejo
première [prɛ'mjɛr] o ['primɪ•ər] *s* estreno; actriz *f* principal
premise ['prɛmɪs] *s* premisa; **on the premises** en el local mismo; **premises** predio, local *m*
premium ['primɪ•əm] *s* premio; (ins) prima
premonition [,primə'nɪʃən] *s* presagio; presentimiento
preoccupancy [pri'ɑkjəpənsi] *s* preocupación
preoccupation [pri'ɑkjə'peʃən] *s* preocupación
preoccu•py [pri'ɑkjə,pai] *v* (*pret & pp* -**pied**) *tr* preocupar
prepaid [pri'ped] *adj* pagado por adelantado; con porte pagado
preparation [,prɛpə'reʃən] *s* preparación; (*e.g., for a trip*) preparativo; (pharm) preparado
preparatory [pri'pærə,tori] *adj* preparativo, preparatorio
prepare [pri'pɛr] *tr* preparar ‖ *intr* prepararse
preparedness [pri'pɛrɪdnɪs] o [pri'pɛrdnɪs] *s* preparación; preparación militar
pre•pay [pri'pe] *v* (*pret & pp* -**paid**) *tr* pagar por adelantado
preponderant [pri'pɑndərənt] *adj* preponderante
preposition [,prɛpə'zɪʃən] *s* preposición
prepossessing [,pripə'zɛsɪŋ] *adj* atractivo, simpático
preposterous [pri'pɑstərəs] *adj* absurdo, ridículo
prep school [prɛp] *s* (coll) escuela preparatoria
prerecorded [,priri'kɔrdɪd] *adj* (rad & telv) grabado de antemano
prerequisite [,pri'rɛkwɪzɪt] *s* requisito previo
prerogative [pri'rɑgətɪv] *s* prerrogativa
Pres. *abbr* **Presbyterian, President**
presage ['prɛsɪdʒ] *s* presagio ‖ [pri'sedʒ] *tr* presagiar
Presbyterian [,prɛzbɪ'tɪrɪ•ən] *adj & s* presbiteriano
prescribe [pri'skraib] *tr & intr* prescribir
prescription [pri'skrɪpʃən] *s* prescripción; (pharm) receta
presence ['prɛzəns] *s* presencia
present ['prɛzənt] *adj* presente ‖ *s* presente *m*, regalo ‖ [pri'zɛnt] *tr* presentar, obsequiar
presentable [pri'zɛntəbəl] *adj* bien apersonado
presentation [,prɛzən'teʃən] o [,prizən'teʃən] *s* presentación

presentation copy *s* ejemplar *m* de cortesía con dedicatoria del autor

presentiment [prɪ'zɛntɪmənt] *s* presentimiento

presently ['prɛzəntli] *adv* luego, dentro de poco

preserve [prɪ'zʌrv] *s* conserva, compota; (*for game*) vedado ‖ *tr* conservar; preservar, proteger

preserved fruit *s* dulce *m* de almíbar

preside [prɪ'zaɪd] *intr* presidir; **to preside over** presidir

presiden•cy ['prɛzɪdənsi] *s* (*pl* **-cies**) presidencia

president ['prɛzɪdənt] *s* presidente *m;* (*of a university*) rector *m*

pres'i•dent-e•lect' *s* presidente *m* electo (*todavía sin gobierno*)

press [prɛs] *s* apretón *m*, empujón *m;* (*e.g., of business*) urgencia; muchedumbre; (*machine for printing, for making wine; newspapers and newspapermen*) prensa; (*printing*) imprenta; (*closet*) armario; **to go to press** entrar en prensa ‖ *tr* apretar (*p.ej., un botón*); (*in a press*) prensar; planchar (*la ropa*); imprimir (*discos de fonógrafo*); oprimir (*una tecla*); apresurar; abrumar; apremiar, instar; insistir en

press agent *s* agente *m* de publicidad

press conference *s* conferencia de prensa, rueda de prensa

pressing ['prɛsɪŋ] *adj* apremiante, urgente ‖ *s* planchado

press release *s* comunicado de prensa

pressure ['prɛʃər] *s* presión; premura, urgencia

pressure cooker ['kʊkər] *s* olla de presión, cocina de presión

pressurize ['prɛʃə,raɪz] *tr* (aer) sobrecargar

prestige [prɛs'tiʒ] o ['prɛstɪdʒ] *s* prestigio

presumably [prɪ'zuməbli] *adv* probablemente, verosímilmente

presume [prɪ'zjum] *tr* presumir; suponer; **to presume to** tomar la libertad de ‖ *intr* suponer; **to presume on** o **upon** abusar de

presumption [prɪ'zʌmpʃən] *s* presunción; pretensión

presumptuous [prɪ'zʌmptʃʊ•əs] *adj* confianzudo, desenvuelto

presuppose [,prisə'poz] *tr* presuponer

pretend [prɪ'tɛnd] *tr* aparentar, fingir ‖ *intr* fingir; **to pretend to** pretender (*p.ej., el trono*)

pretender [prɪ'tɛndər] *s* pretendiente *mf*

pretense [prɪ'tɛns] o ['pritɛns] *s* pretensión; fingimiento; **under false pretenses** con apariencias fingidas; **under pretense of** so pretexto de

pretentious [prɪ'tɛnʃəs] *adj* pretencioso, aparatoso; ambicioso, vasto

pretonic [prɪ'tɑnɪk] *adj* pretónico

pretrial prisoner *s* preso preventivo

pret•ty ['prɪti] *adj* (*comp* **-tier;** *super* **-tiest**) bonito, lindo; (coll) bastante, considerable ‖ *adv* algo; bastante; muy

prevail [prɪ'vel] *intr* prevalecer, reinar; **to prevail on** o **upon** persuadir

prevailing [prɪ'velɪŋ] *adj* prevaleciente, reinante; común, corriente

prevalent ['prɛvələnt] *adj* común, corriente, en boga

prevaricate [prɪ'værɪ,ket] *intr* mentir

prevent [prɪ'vɛnt] *tr* impedir ‖ *intr* obstar

prevention [prɪ'vɛnʃən] *s* (el) impedir; medidas de precaución

preventive [prɪ'vɛntɪv] *adj* & *s* preservativo

preview ['pri,vju] *s* vista anticipada; (*private showing*) (mov) preestreno; (*showing of brief scenes for advertising*) (mov) avance *m*

previous ['privi•əs] *adj* previo, anterior ‖ *adv* previamente; **previous to** con anterioridad a, antes de

prewar ['pri,wɔr] *adj* prebélico, de preguerra

prey [pre] *s* presa; víctima; **to be prey to** ser presa de ‖ *intr* cazar; **to prey on** o **upon** apresar y devorar; pillar, robar; tener preocupado

price [praɪs] *s* precio ‖ *tr* apreciar, estimar; fijar el precio de, poner precio a; pedir el precio de

price control *s* intervención de precios

price cutting *s* reducción de precios

price fixing *s* fijación de precios

price freezing *s* congelación de precios

priceless ['praɪslɪs] *adj* inapreciable, sin precio; (coll) absurdo, divertido

price war *s* guerra de precios

prick [prɪk] *s* (*pointed weapon or instrument*) espiche *m;* (*sharp point*) púa; (*small hole made with sharp point*) agujerillo; (*spur*) aguijón *m;* (*jab; sharp pain*) pinchazo, punzada; **to kick against the pricks** dar coces contra el aguijón ‖ *tr* pinchar; marcar con agujerillos; dar una punzada a; (*to sting*) punzar; **to prick up** aguzar (*las orejas*)

prick•ly ['prɪkli] *adj* (*comp* **-lier;** *super* **-liest**) espinoso, puado, punzante

prickly heat *s* salpullido causado por el calor

prickly pear *s* (*plant*) chumbera; (*fruit*) higo chumbo

pride [praɪd] *s* orgullo; arrogancia; **the pride of** la flor y nata de ‖ *tr*—**to pride oneself on** o **upon** enorgullecerse de

priest [prist] *s* sacerdote *m*

priesthood ['prist•hʊd] *s* sacerdocio

priest•ly ['pristli] *adj* (*comp* **-lier;** *super* **-liest**) sacerdotal

prig [prɪg] *s* gazmoño, pedante *mf*

prim [prɪm] *adj* (*comp* **prim:mer;** *super* **primmest**) estirado, relamido

primary ['praɪ,mɛri] o ['praɪməri] *adj* primario ‖ *s* (*pl* **-ries**) elección preliminar; (elec) primario

prime [praɪm] *adj* primero, principal; (*of the best quality*) primo ‖ *s* flor *f*, juventud, primavera; alba, aurora; (la) flor y nata; (*of a degree*) (phys) minuto; (typ) virgulilla; **prime of life** edad viril, flor *f* de edad ‖ *tr* informar de antemano; cebar (*un arma de fuego, una bomba, un carburador*); (*for painting*) imprimar; poner la primera capa o la primera mano a; poner virgulilla a

pr
pr

prime minister s primer ministro

primer [ˈprɪmər] s cartilla ‖ [ˈpraɪmər] s (for paint) aprestado m; (mach) cebador m

primitive [ˈprɪmɪtɪv] adj primitivo

primp [prɪmp] tr acicalar, engalanar ‖ intr acicalarse, engalanarse

prim′rose′ s primavera

primrose path s vida dada a los placeres de los sentidos

prin. abbr **principal**

prince [prɪns] s príncipe m; **to live like a prince** portarse como un príncipe

Prince of Wales s príncipe m de Gales

princess [ˈprɪnsɪs] s princesa

principal [ˈprɪnsɪpəl] adj principal ‖ s principal m, jefe m; (of a school) director m; criminal mf; (main sum, not interest) capital m

principle [ˈprɪnsɪpəl] s principio

print [prɪnt] s marca, impresión; (printed cloth) estampado; (design in printed cloth) diseño; grabado, lámina; letras de molde; (act of printing) impresión; edición; tirada; (phot) impresión; **in print** impreso, publicado; **out of print** agotado ‖ tr imprimir; estampar; hacer imprimir; publicar; escribir en caracteres de imprenta; (phot) tirar, imprimir; (fig) imprimir o grabar (en la memoria)

printed matter s impresos

printer [ˈprɪntər] s impresor m

printer's devil s aprendiz m de imprenta

printer's ink s tinta de imprenta

printer's mark s pie m de imprenta

printing [ˈprɪntɪŋ] s impresión; caracteres impresos; edición; tirada; letras de mano imitación de las impresas; (phot) tiraje m

printout [ˈprɪntˌaʊt] s (computer) impreso derivado

prior [ˈpraɪ•ər] adj anterior ‖ adv anteriormente; **prior to** antes de

priori•ty [praɪˈɔrɪti] s (pl -ties) prioridad; **of the highest priority** de máxima prioridad

prism [ˈprɪzəm] s prisma m

prison [ˈprɪzən] s cárcel f, prisión ‖ tr encarcelar

prisoner [ˈprɪzənər] o [ˈprɪznər] s preso; (mil) prisionero

prison van s coche m celular

pris•sy [ˈprɪsi] adj (comp -sier; super -siest) (coll) remilgado, melindroso

priva•cy [ˈpraɪvəsi] s (pl -cies) aislamiento, retiro; secreto, reserva

private [ˈpraɪvɪt] adj particular, privado; confidencial; ‖ s soldado raso; **in private** privadamente; en secreto; **privates** partes pudendas

private first class s soldado de primera, aspirante m a cabo

private hospital s clínica, casa de salud

private property s bienes mpl particulares

private view s día m de inauguración

privet [ˈprɪvɪt] s aligustre m

privilege [ˈprɪvɪlɪdʒ] s privilegio

priv•y [ˈprɪvi] adj privado; **privy to** enterado secretamente de ‖ s (pl -ies) letrina

prize [praɪz] s premio; (something captured) presa ‖ tr apreciar, estimar

prize fight s partido de boxeo profesional

prize fighter s boxeador m profesional

prize ring s cuadrilátero de boxeo

pro [pro] prep en pro de ‖ s (pl **pros**) voto afirmativo; (coll) deportista mf profesional; **the pros and the cons** el pro y el contra

probabili•ty [ˌprabəˈbɪlɪti] s (pl -ties) probabilidad; acontecimiento probable; tiempo probable

probable [ˈprabəbəl] adj probable

probation [proˈbeʃən] s libertad vigilada; período de prueba

probe [prob] s encuesta, indagación; (instrument) sonda ‖ tr indagar; sondar

problem [ˈprabləm] s problema m

procedure [proˈsidʒər] s procedimiento

proceed [proˈsid] intr proceder ‖ **proceeds** [ˈprosidz] spl producto, ganancia

proceeding [proˈsidɪŋ] s procedimiento; **proceedings** actas; diligencias

process [ˈprasɛs] s procedimiento; proceso, progreso; **in the process of time** con el tiempo ‖ tr elaborar; (electronic data) procesar

processing [ˈprasɛsɪŋ] s (electronic data) procesamiento

process server [ˈsɑrvər] s entregador m de la citación

proclaim [proˈklem] tr proclamar

proclitic [proˈklɪtɪk] adj & s proclítico

procommunist [proˈkamjənɪst] adj & s filocomunista mf

procrastinate [proˈkræstɪˌnet] tr diferir de un día para otro ‖ intr tardar, no decidirse

procure [proˈkjʊr] tr conseguir, obtener ‖ intr alcahuetear

prod [prad] s aguijada; empuje m ‖ v (pret & pp **prodded**; ger **prodding**) tr aguijar, pinchar; aguijonear, estimular

prodigal [ˈpradɪgəl] adj & s pródigo

prodigious [proˈdɪdʒəs] adj & s prodigioso, maravilloso; enorme, inmenso

prodi•gy [ˈpradɪdʒi] s (pl -gies) prodigio

produce [ˈprodjus] o [ˈprodus] s producto; productos agrícolas ‖ [proˈdjus] o [proˈdus] tr producir; presentar (p.ej., un drama) al público; (geom) prolongar

product [ˈpradəkt] s producto

production [proˈdakʃən] s producción

profane [proˈfen] adj profano; (language) injurioso, blasfemo ‖ s profano ‖ tr profanar

profani•ty [proˈfænɪti] s (pl -ties) blasfemia

profess [proˈfɛs] tr & intr profesar

profession [proˈfɛʃən] s profesión

professor [proˈfɛsər] s profesor m, catedrático; (coll) profesor, maestro

proffer [ˈprafər] s oferta, propuesta ‖ tr ofrecer, proponer

proficient [proˈfɪʃənt] adj perito, diestro, hábil

profile [ˈprofaɪl] s perfil m ‖ tr perfilar

profit [ˈprafɪt] s provecho, beneficio, utilidad, ganancia; **at a profit** con ganancia ‖ tr servir, ser de utilidad a ‖ intr sacar

provecho, ganar; adelantar, mejorar; **to profit by** aprovechar, sacar provecho de
profitable ['prɑfɪtəbəl] *adj* provechoso
profit and loss *s* ganancias y pérdidas
profiteer [,prɑfɪ'tɪr] *s* logrero, explotador *m* ‖ *intr* logrear, explotar
profit margin *s* excedente *m* de ganancia
profit taking *s* realización de beneficios
profligate ['prɑflɪgɪt] *adj* & *s* libertino; pródigo
pro forma invoice [pro 'fɔrmə] *s* factura simulada
profound [pro'faʊnd] *adj* profundo
profuse [pro'fjus] *adj* (*extravagant*) pródigo; (*abundant*) profuso
proge•ny ['prɑdʒeni] *s* (*pl* -**nies**) prole *f*
progno•sis [prɑg'nosɪs] *s* (*pl* -**ses** [siz]) pronóstico
progno•sis [prɑg'nɑstɪk] *s* pronóstico
program ['progræm] *s* programa *m;* (*computer*) **program(me)** programa (para ordenador) ‖ *tr* programar; (*computer*) **program(me)** programar
program(m)er ['progræmər] *s* (*computer*) programador *m*, programadora
program(m)ing ['progræmɪŋ] *s* (*computer*) programación (de ordenadores)
progress ['prɑgrɛs] *s* progreso; progresos; **to make progress** hacer progresos ‖ [prə'grɛs] *intr* progresar
progressive [prə'grɛsɪv] *adj* progresivo; (pol) progresista ‖ *s* (pol) progresista *mf*
prohibit [pro'hɪbɪt] *tr* prohibir
project ['prɑdʒɛkt] *s* proyecto ‖ [prə'dʒɛkt] *tr* proyectar ‖ *intr* proyectarse
projectile [prə'dʒɛktɪl] *s* proyectil *m*
projection [prə'dʒɛkʃən] *s* proyección
projector [prə'dʒɛktər] *s* proyector *m*
proletarian [,prolɪ'tɛrɪ•ən] *adj* & *s* proletario
proletariat [,prolɪ'tɛrɪ•ət] *s* proletariado
proliferate [prə'lɪfə,ret] *intr* proliferar
prolific [prə'lɪfɪk] *adj* prolífico
prolix ['prolɪks] o [pro'lɪks] *adj* difuso, verboso
prologue ['prolɔg] *s* prólogo
prolong [pro'lɔŋ] *tr* prolongar
promenade [,prɑmɪ'ned] *s* paseo; garbeo; baile *m* de gala ‖ *intr* pasear o pasearse
promenade deck *s* (naut) cubierta de paseo
prominent ['prɑmɪnənt] *adj* prominente
promise ['prɑmɪs] *s* promesa ‖ *tr* & *intr* prometer
promising young man *s* joven *m* de esperanzas
promissory ['prɑmɪ,sori] *adj* promisorio
promissory note *s* pagaré *m*
promonto•ry ['prɑmən,tori] *s* (*pl* -**ries**) promontorio
promote [prə'mot] *tr* promover; fomentar
promotion [prə'moʃən] *s* promoción; fomento
prompt [prɑmpt] *adj* pronto, puntual; listo, dispuesto ‖ *tr* incitar, mover; inspirar, sugerir; (theat) apuntar
prompter ['prɑmptər] *s* (theat) apuntador *m*
prompter's box *s* (theat) concha

promulgate ['prɑməl,get] o [pro'mʌlget] *tr* promulgar
prone [pron] *adj* postrado boca abajo; extendido sobre el suelo; dispuesto, propenso
prong [prɔŋ] o [prɑŋ] *s* punta (*de un tenedor, horquilla, etc.*)
pronoun ['pronaʊn] *s* pronombre *m*
pronounce [prə'naʊns] *tr* pronunciar
pronouncement [prə'naʊnsmənt] *s* declaración; decisión, opinión
pronunciamen•to [prə,nʌnsɪ•ə'mɛnto] *s* (*pl* -**tos**) pronunciamiento
pronunciation [prə,nʌnsɪ'eʃən] o [prə,nʌnʃɪ'eʃən] *s* pronunciación
proof [pruf] *adj* de prueba; **proof against** a prueba de ‖ *s* prueba
proof'read'er *s* corrector *m* de pruebas
prop [prɑp] *s* apoyo, puntal *m;* (*to hold up a plant*) rodrigón *m;* **props** (theat) accesorios ‖ *v* (*pret* & *pp* **propped;** *ger* **propping**) *tr* apoyar, apuntalar; poner un rodrigón a
propaganda [,prɑpə'gændə] *s* propaganda
propagate ['prɑpə,get] *tr* propagar
proparoxytone [,propær'ɑksɪ,ton] *adj* & *s* proparoxítono
pro•pel [prə'pɛl] *v* (*pret* & *pp* -**pelled;** *ger* -**pelling**) *tr* propulsar, impeler
propeller [prə'pɛlər] *s* hélice *f*
propensi•ty [prə'pɛnsɪti] *s* (*pl* -**ties**) propensión
proper ['prɑpər] *adj* propio, conveniente; decente, decoroso; exacto, justo
proper•ty ['prɑpərti] *s* (*pl* -**ties**) propiedad; **properties** (theat) accesorios
property owner *s* propietario de bienes raíces
prophe•cy ['prɑfɪsi] *s* (*pl* -**cies**) profecía
prophe•sy ['prɑfɪ,sai] *v* (*pret* & *pp* -**sied**) *tr* profetizar
prophet ['prɑfɪt] *s* profeta *m*
prophetess ['prɑfɪtɪs] *s* profetisa
prophylactic [,profɪ'læktɪk] *adj* & *s* profiláctico
propitiate [prə'pɪʃɪ,et] *tr* propiciar
propitious [prə'pɪʃəs] *adj* propicio
prop'jet *s* turbohélice *m*
proportion [prə'porʃən] *s* proporción; **in proportion as** a medida que; **out of proportion** desproporcionado ‖ *tr* proporcionar
proportionate [prə'porʃənɪt] *adj* proporcionado
proposal [prə'pozəl] *s* propuesta; oferta de matrimonio
propose [prə'poz] *tr* proponer ‖ *intr* proponer matrimonio; **to propose to** pedir la mano a; proponerse a + *inf*
proposition [,prɑpə'zɪʃən] *s* proposición, propuesta
propound [prə'paʊnd] *tr* proponer
proprietor [prə'prai•ətər] *s* propietario
proprietress [prə'prai•ətrɪs] *s* propietaria
proprie•ty [prə'prai•əti] *s* (*pl* -**ties**) corrección, conducta decorosa, conveniencia; **proprieties** cánones *mpl* sociales, convenciones
propulsion [prə'pʌlʃən] *s* propulsión
prorate [pro'ret] *tr* prorratear

pr
pr

prosaic [pro'ze•ɪk] *adj* prosaico
proscribe [pro'skraɪb] *tr* proscribir
prose [proz] *adj* prosaico ‖ *s* prosa
prosecute ['prɑsɪ,kjut] *tr* llevar a cabo; (law) procesar
prosecutor ['prɑsɪ,kjutər] *s* acusador *m*, demandante *mf*; (lawyer) fiscal *m*
proselyte ['prɑsɪ,laɪt] *s* prosélito
prose writer *s* prosista *mf*
prosody ['prɑsədi] *s* métrica
prospect ['prɑspɛkt] *s* vista; esperanza; probabilidad de éxito; cliente *mf* o comprador *m* probable ‖ *tr & intr* prospectar; **to prospect for** buscar (*p.ej., oro, petróleo*)
prosper ['prɑspər] *tr & intr* prosperar
prosperi•ty [prɑs'pɛrɪti] *s* (*pl* **-ties**) prosperidad
prosperous ['prɑspərəs] *adj* próspero
prostitute ['prɑstɪ,tjut] *s* prostituta; güila (Mex) ‖ *tr* prostituir
prostrate ['prɑstret] *adj* postrado, prosternado ‖ *tr* postrar
prostration [prɑs'treʃən] *s* postración
Prot. *abbr* **Protestant**
protagonist [pro'tægənɪst] *s* protagonista *mf*
protect [prə'tɛkt] *tr* proteger
protection [prə'tɛkʃən] *s* protección
protégé ['protə,ʒe] *s* protegido
protégée ['protə,ʒe] *s* protegida
protein ['proti•ɪn] o ['protin] *s* proteína
pro-tempore [pro'tɛmpəri] *adj* interino
protest ['protɛst] *s* protesta ‖ [pro'tɛst] *tr & intr* protestar
protestant ['prɑtɪstənt] *adj & s* protestante *mf* ‖ **Protestant** *adj & s* protestante *mf*
prothonotar•y [pro'θɑnə,tɛri] *s* (*pl* **-ies**) escribano principal (*de un tribunal*)
protocol ['protə,kɑl] *s* protocolo
protoplasm ['protə,plæzəm] *s* protoplasma *m*
prototype ['protə,taɪp] *s* prototipo
protozoön [,protə'zo•ɑn] *s* protozoo
protract [pro'trækt] *tr* prolongar
protrude [pro'trud] *intr* resaltar
proud [praud] *adj* orgulloso; soberbio; glorioso
proud flesh *s* carnosidad, bezo
prov. *abbr* **provincialism**
prove [pruv] *v* (*pret* **proved**; *pp* **proved** o **proven**) *tr* probar ‖ *intr* resultar; **to prove to be** venir a ser, resultar
proverb ['prɑvərb] *s* proverbio
provide [prə'vaɪd] *tr* proporcionar, suministrar ‖ *intr*—**to provide for** proveer a; asegurarse (*el porvenir*)
provided [prə'vaɪdɪd] *conj* a condición (de) que, con tal (de) que
providence ['prɑvɪdəns] *s* providencia
providential [,prɑvɪ'dɛnʃəl] *adj* providencial
providing [prə'vaɪdɪŋ] *conj* var de **provided**
province ['prɑvɪns] *s* provincia; (*sphere of activity or knowledge*) competencia
proving ground ['pruvɪŋ] *s* campo de ensayos
provision [prə'vɪʒən] *s* provisión; condición, estipulación
provi•so [prə'vaɪzo] *s* (*pl* **-sos** o **-soes**) condición, estipulación, salvedad

provoke [prə'vok] *tr* provocar
provoking [prə'vokɪŋ] *adj* provocador, irritante
prow [prau] *s* proa
prowess ['prau•ɪs] *s* proeza; destreza
prowl [praul] *intr* cazar al acecho, rodar, vagabundear
prowler ['praulər] *s* rondador *m*; ladrón *m*
proximity [prɑk'sɪmɪti] *s* proximidad
prox•y ['prɑksi] *s* (*pl* **-ies**) poder *m*, poderhabiente *mf*
prude [prud] *s* mojigato, gazmoño
prudence ['prudəns] *s* prudencia
prudent ['prudənt] *adj* prudente
pruder•y ['prudəri] *s* (*pl* **-ies**) mojigatería, gazmoñería
prudish ['prudɪʃ] *adj* mojigato, gazmoño
prune [prun] *s* ciruela pasa ‖ *tr* podar, escamondar
pry [praɪ] *v* (*pret & pp* **pried**) *tr*—**to pry open** forzar con la alzaprima o palanca; **to pry out of** arrancar (*p.ej., un secreto*) a (*una persona*) ‖ *intr* entremeterse; **to pry into** entremeterse en
P.S. *abbr* **postscript, Privy Seal**
psalm [sɑm] *s* salmo
Psalter ['sɔltər] *s* Salterio
pseudo ['sudo] o ['sjudo] *adj* supuesto, falso, fingido
pseudonym ['sudənɪm] o ['sjudənɪm] *s* seudónimo
Psyche ['saɪki] *s* Psique *f*
psychedelic [,saɪkə'dɛlɪk] *adj* psicodélico
psychiatrist [saɪ'kaɪ•ətrɪst] *s* psiquiatra *mf*
psychiatry [saɪ'kaɪ•ətri] *s* psiquiatría
psychic ['saɪkɪk] *adj* psíquico; mediúmnico ‖ *s* médium *mf*
psychoanalysis [,saɪko•ə'nælɪsɪs] *s* psicoanálisis *m*
psychoanalyze [,saɪko'ænə,laɪz] *tr* psicoanalizar
psychologic(al) [,saɪkə'lɑdʒɪk(əl)] *adj* psicológico
psychologist [saɪ'kɑlədʒɪst] *s* psicólogo
psychology [saɪ'kɑlədʒi] *s* psicología
psychopath ['saɪkə,pæθ] *s* psicópata *mf*
psycho•sis [saɪ'kosɪs] *s* (*pl* **-ses** [siz]) psicosis *f*; estado mental
psychotherapy [,saɪkə'θɛrəpi] *s* psicoterapia
psychotic [saɪ'kɑtɪk] *adj & s* psicótico
pt. *abbr* **part, pint, point**
pub [pʌb] *s* (Brit) taberna
puberty ['pjubərti] *s* pubertad
public ['pʌblɪk] *adj & s* público
publication [,pʌblɪ'keʃən] *s* publicación
public conveyance *s* vehículo de servicio público
publicity [pʌb'lɪsɪti] *s* publicidad
publicize ['pʌblɪ,saɪz] *tr* publicar
public library *s* biblioteca municipal
public relations *spl* relaciones publicas
public school *s* (U.S.A.) escuela pública; (Brit) internado privado con dote
public speaking *s* elocución, oratoria

public spirit *s* celo patriótico del buen ciudadano

public toilet *s* quiosco de necesidad

public transportation *s* transporte colectivo

public utility *s* empresa de servicio público; **public utilities** acciones emitidas por empresas de servicio público

publish ['pʌblɪʃ] *tr* publicar

publisher ['pʌblɪʃər] *s* editor *m*

publishing house *s* casa editorial

pucker ['pʌkər] *s* (*small fold*) frunce *m*; pliego mal hecho ‖ *tr* fruncir (*una tela*; *la frente*); plegar mal ‖ *intr* plegarse mal

pudding ['pudɪŋ] *s* budín *m*, pudín *m*

puddle ['pʌdəl] *s* aguazal *m*, charco

pudg·y ['pʌdʒi] *adj* (*comp* **-ier**; *super* **-iest**) gordinflón, rechoncho

puerile ['pju·ərɪl] *adj* pueril

puerili·ty [,pju·ə'rɪlɪti] *s* (*pl* **-ties**) puerilidad

Puerto Rican ['pwɛrto 'rikən] *adj* & *s* puertorriqueño

puff [pʌf] *s* soplo vivo; (*of smoke*) bocanada; (*in clothing*) bullón *m*; borla de polvos; pastelillo de crema o jalea; alabanza exagerada; ráfaga, ventolera ‖ *tr* soplar; hinchar; alabar exageradamente ‖ *intr* soplar; hincharse; enorgullecerse exageradamente

puff paste *s* hojaldre *m* & *f*

pugilism ['pjudʒɪ,lɪzəm] *s* pugilismo

pugilist ['pjudʒɪlɪst] *s* pugilista *m*

pug-nosed ['pʌg,nozd] *adj* braco

puke [pjuk] *s* (slang) vómito ‖ *tr* & *intr* (slang) vomitar

pull [pul] *s* estirón *m*, tirón *m*; (*on a cigar*) chupada; (*of a door*) tirador *m*, (slang) enchufe *m*, buenas aldabas ‖ *tr* tirar de; torcer (*un ligamento*); (typ) sacar (*una impresión a prueba*); **to pull down** demoler, derribar; bajar (*p.ej.*, *la cortinilla*); abatir, degradar; **to pull oneself together** componerse, recobrar la calma ‖ *intr* tirar; moverse despacio, moverse con esfuerzo; **to pull at** tirar de (*p.ej.*, *la corbata*); chupar (*p.ej.*, *un cigarro*); **to pull for** (slang) abogar por, ayudar; **to pull for oneself** tirar por su lado; **to pull in** llegar (*un tren*) a la estación; **to pull out** partir (*un tren*) de la estación; **to pull strings** usar enchufe; **to pull through** salir a flote; recobrar la salud

pullet ['pulɪt] *s* polla

pulley ['puli] *s* polea

pulp [pʌlp] *s* pulpa; (*to make paper*) pasta; (*of tooth*) bulbo

pulpit ['pulpɪt] *s* púlpito

pulsate ['pʌlset] *intr* pulsar; vibrar

pulsation [pʌl'seʃən] *s* pulsación; vibracion

pulse [pʌls] *s* pulso; **to feel** o **take the pulse of** tomar el pulso a

pulverize ['pʌlvə,raɪz] *tr* pulverizar

pumice stone ['pʌmɪs] *s* pómez *f*, piedra pómez

pum·mel ['pʌməl] *v* (*pret* & *pp* **-meled** o **-melled**; *ger* **-meling** o **-melling**) *tr* apuñear, aporrear

pump [pʌmp] *s* bomba; (*slipperlike shoe*) escarpín *m*, zapatilla ‖ *tr* elevar o sacar (*agua*) por medio de una bomba; (coll)

tirar de la lengua a (*una persona*); **to pump up** hinchar, inflar (*un neumático*)

pump handle *s* guimbalete *m*

pumpkin ['pʌmpkɪn] o ['puŋkɪn] *s* calabaza común; **some pumpkins** persona de muchas campanillas

pump-priming ['pʌmp,praɪmɪŋ] *s* inyección económica (*por parte del gobierno*)

pun [pʌn] *s* equívoco, retruécano ‖ *v* (*pret* & *pp* **punned**; *ger* **punning**) *intr* decir equívocos, jugar del vocablo

punch [pʌntʃ] *s* puñetazo; (*tool*) punzón *m*; (*for tickets*) sacabocado; (*drink*) ponche *m* ‖ *tr* dar un puñetazo a; taladrar, perforar (*un billete*, *una tarjeta*)

punch bowl *s* ponchera

punch card *s* tarjeta perforada, ficha perforada

punch clock *s* reloj *m* registrador de tarjetas

punch'-drunk' *adj* atontado (*p.ej.*, *por una tunda de golpes*); completamente aturdido

punched tape *s* cinta perforada

punching bag *s* punching *m*, boxibalón *m*

punch line *s* broche *m* de oro, colofón *m* del artículo

punctilious [pʌŋk'tɪlɪ·əs] *adj* puntilloso, pundonoroso

punctual ['pʌŋktʃu·əl] *adj* puntual

punctuate ['pʌŋktʃu,et] *tr* puntuar; acentuar, destacar; interrumpir ‖ *intr* puntuar

punctuation [,pʌŋktʃu'eʃən] *s* puntuación

punctuation mark *s* signo de puntuación

puncture ['pʌŋktʃər] *s* puntura; (*of a tire*) picadura, pinchazo ‖ *tr* pinchar, picar, perforar

punc'ture-proof' *adj* a prueba de pinchazos

pundit ['pʌndɪt] *s* erudito, sabio

pungent ['pʌndʒənt] *adj* picante; estimulante

punish ['pʌnɪʃ] *tr* castigar; penalizar; (coll) maltratar

punishable ['pʌnɪʃəbəl] *adj* delictivo

punishment ['pʌnɪʃmənt] *s* castigo; (coll) maltrato

punk [pʌŋk] *adj* (slang) malo, de mala calidad ‖ *s* yesca, pebete *m*; (*decayed wood*) hupe *m*; (slang) pillo, gamberro

punster ['pʌnstər] *s* equivoquista *mf*, vocablista *mf*

pu·ny ['pjuni] *adj* (*comp* **-nier**; *super* **-niest**) encanijado, débil; insignificante, mezquino

pup [pʌp] *s* cachorro

pupil ['pjupəl] *s* alumno; (*of the eye*) pupila

puppet ['pʌpɪt] *s* títere *m*; (*doll*) muñeca; (*person controlled by another*) maniquí *m*

puppet government *s* gobierno de monigotes

puppet show *s* función de títeres

puppy love ['pʌpi] *s* (coll) primeros amores

purchase ['pʌrtʃəs] *s* compra; agarre *m* firme ‖ *tr* comprar

purchasing power *s* poder adquisitivo

pure [pjur] *adj* puro

purgative ['pʌrgətɪv] *adj* & *s* purgante *m*

purge [pʌrdʒ] *s* purga ‖ *tr* purgar

puri·fy ['pjurɪ,faɪ] *v* (*pret* & *pp* **-fied**) *tr* purificar

puritan ['pjurɪtən] *adj* & *s* puritano ‖ **Puritan** *adj* & *s* puritano

purity ['pjurɪtɪ] s pureza

purloin [pər'lɔɪn] tr & intr robar, hurtar

purple ['pʌrpəl] adj purpurado, rojo morado ‖ m púrpura, rojo morado

purport ['pʌrport] s significado, idea principal ‖ [pər'port] tr significar, querer decir

purpose ['pʌrpəs] s intención, propósito; fin m, objeto; **for the purpose** al efecto; **for what purpose?** ¿con qué fin?; **on purpose** adrede, de propósito; **to good purpose** con buenos resultados; **to no purpose** sin resultado; **to serve one's purpose** servir para el caso

purposely ['pʌrpəsli] adv adrede, de propósito

purr [pʌr] s ronroneo ‖ intr ronronear

purse [pʌrs] s bolsa; (money collected for charity) colecta ‖ tr fruncir

purser ['pʌrsər] s contador m de navío, comisario de a bordo

purse snatcher ['snætʃər] s carterista mf

purse strings spl cordones mpl de la bolsa; **to hold the purse strings** tener las llaves de la caja

pursue [pər'su] o [pər'sju] tr perseguir (al que huye); proseguir (lo empezado); seguir (una carrera); dedicarse a

pursuit [pər'sut] o [pər'sjut] s persecución; prosecución; (e.g., of happiness) busca o búsqueda; empleo

pursuit plane s caza m, avión m de caza

purvey [pər've] tr proveer, suministrar

pus [pʌs] s pus m

push [puʃ] s empuje m, empujón m ‖ tr empujar; pulsar (un botón); extender (p.ej., conquistas); **to push around** (coll) tratar de empujones; **to push aside** hacer a un lado; **to push through** forzar (p.ej., una resolución) ‖ intr empujar; **to push off** (coll) irse, salir; (naut) desatracarse

push button s botón m de llamada, botón interruptor

push'-but'ton control s mando por botón

push'cart' s carretilla de mano

pusher ['puʃər] s (drugs) púcher m

pushing ['puʃɪŋ] adj emprendedor; entremetido, agresivo

pushy ['puʃɪ] adj (coll) agresivo; presumido

pusillanimous [,pjusɪ'lænɪməs] adj pusilánime

puss [pus] interj ¡miz! ‖ s micho; chica, muchacha; (slang) cara, boca

puss in the corner s las cuatro esquinas

puss•y ['pusɪ] s (pl -ies) michito

pussy willow s sauce norteamericano de amentos muy sedosos

pustule ['pʌstʃul] s pústula

put [put] v (pret & pp put; ger putting) tr poner, colocar; arrojar, echar, lanzar; hacer (una pregunta); **to put across** llevar a cabo; hacer aceptar; **to put aside** poner aparte; rechazar; ahorrar (dinero); **to put down** anotar, apuntar; sofocar (una insurrección); rebajar (los precios); **to put off** posponer; deshacerse de; **to put on** ponerse (la ropa); poner en escena; llevar (p.ej., un drama a la pantalla); accionar (un freno); cargar (impuestos); fingir; atribuir; **to put oneself out** incomodarse, molestarse; afanarse, desvivirse; **to put out** extender (la mano); apagar (el fuego, la luz); poner en la calle; dar a luz, publicar; decepcionar; (sport) sacar fuera de la partida; **to put over** o **through** (coll) llevar a cabo; **to put up** construir, edificar; abrir (un paraguas); conservar (fruta, legumbres); (coll) incitar ‖ intr dirigirse; **to put on** fingir; **to put up** parar, hospedarse; **to put up with** aguantar, tolerar

put'-out' adj contrariado, enojado

putrid ['pjutrɪd] adj pútrido; corrompido, perverso

putsch [putʃ] s intentona de sublevación; sublevación; cuartelazo

putter ['pʌtər] intr trabajar sin orden ni sistema; **to putter around** ocuparse en fruslerías, temporizar

put•ty ['pʌtɪ] s (pl -ties) masilla ‖ v (pret & pp -tied) tr enmasillar

putty knife s cuchillo de vidriero, espátula

put'-up' adj (coll) premeditado con malicia

puzzle ['pʌzəl] s enigma m; acertijo, rompecabezas m ‖ tr confundir, poner perplejo; **to puzzle out** descifrar ‖ intr estar perplejo; **to puzzle over** tratar de descifrar

puzzler ['pʌzlər] s quisicosa

PW abbr **prisoner of war**

pyg•my ['pɪgmɪ] adj pigmeo ‖ s (pl -mies) pigmeo

pylon ['paɪlɑn] s pilón m

pyramid ['pɪrəmɪd] s pirámide f ‖ tr aumentar (su dinero) comprando o vendiendo al crédito y empleando las ganancias para comprar o vender más

pyre [paɪr] s pira

Pyrenean [,pɪrɪ'niən] adj pirineo

Pyrenees ['pɪrɪ,niz] spl Pirineos

pyrites [paɪ'raɪtɪz] o ['paɪraɪts] s pirita

pyrotechnical [,paɪrə'tɛknɪkəl] adj pirotécnico

pyrotechnics [,paɪrə'tɛknɪks] spl pirotecnia

python ['paɪθən] s pitón m

pythoness [paɪ'θənɪs] s pitonisa

pyx [pɪks] s píxide f, copón m

Q

Q, q [kju] decimoséptima letra del alfabeto inglés

Q. abbr **quarto, queen, question, quire**

Q.M. abbr **quartermaster**

qr. abbr **quarter, quire**

qt. abbr **quantity, quart**

qu. *abbr* **quart, quarter, quarterly, queen, query, question**

quack [kwæk] *adj* falso ‖ *s* graznido del pato; charlatán *m;* medicastro, curandero ‖ *intr* parpar (*el pato*)

quacker•y ['kwækəri] *s* (*pl* **-ies**) charlatanismo

quadrangle ['kwɑd,ræŋgəl] *s* cuadrángulo; patio cuadrangular

quadrant ['kwɑdrənt] *s* cuadrante *m*

quadroon [kwɑd'run] *s* cuarterón *m*

quadruped ['kwɑdru,pɛd] *adj* & *s* cuadrúpedo

quadruple ['kwɑdrupəl] o [kwɑd'rupəl] *adj* & *s* cuádruple *m* ‖ *tr* cuadruplicar ‖ *intr* cuadruplicarse

quadruplet ['kwɑdru,plɛt] o [kwɑd'ruplɛt] *s* cuatrillizo

quaff [kwɑf] o [kwæf] *s* trago grande ‖ *tr* & *intr* beber en gran cantidad

quail [kwel] *s* codorniz *f* ‖ *intr* acobardarse

quaint [kwent] *adj* curioso, raro; afectado, rebuscado; fantástico, singular

quake [kwek] *s* temblor *m*, terremoto ‖ *intr* temblar

Quaker ['kwekər] *adj* & *s* cuáquero

Quaker meeting *s* reunión de cuáqueros; reunión en que hay poca conversación

quali•fy ['kwɑlɪ,faɪ] *v* (*pret* & *pp* **-fied**) *tr* calificar; capacitar, habilitar ‖ *intr* capacitarse, habilitarse

quali•ty ['kwɑlɪti] *s* (*pl* **-ties**) (*characteristic; virtue*) calidad; (*property, attribute*) cualidad; (*of a sound*) timbre *m*

quality of life *s* calidad de vida

qualm [kwɑm] *s* escrúpulo de conciencia; duda, inquietud; (*nausea*) basca

quanda•ry ['kwɑndəri] *s* (*pl* **-ries**) incertidumbre, perplejidad

quanti•ty ['kwɑntɪti] *s* (*pl* **-ties**) cantidad

quan•tum ['kwɑntəm] *adj* cuántico ‖ *s* (*pl* **-ta** [tə]) cuanto, quántum *m*

quantum theory *s* teoría cuántica

quarantine ['kwɑrən,tin] o ['kwɔrən,tin] *s* cuarentena; estación de cuarentena ‖ *tr* poner en cuarentena

quar•rel ['kwɑrəl] o ['kwɔrəl] *s* disputa, riña, pelea; **to have no quarrel with** no estar en desacuerdo con; **to pick a quarrel with** tomarse con ‖ *v* (*pret* & *pp* **-reled** o **-relled;** *ger* **-reling** o **-relling**) *intr* disputar, reñir, pelear

quarrelsome ['kwɑrəlsəm] o ['kwɔrəlsəm] *adj* pendenciero

quar•ry ['kwɑri] o ['kwɔri] *s* (*pl* **-ries**) cantera, pedrera; caza, presa ‖ *v* (*pret* & *pp* **-ried**) *tr* sacar de una cantera; extraer, sacar

quart [kwɔrt] *s* cuarto de galón

quarter ['kwɔrtər] *adj* cuarto ‖ *s* cuarto, cuarta parte; (*three months*) trimestre *m;* moneda de 25 centavos; cuarto de luna; barrio; región, lugar *m;* (*clemency*) (mil) cuartel *m;* **quarters** morada, vivienda; local *m;* (mil) cuarteles *mpl;* **to take up quarters** alojarse ‖ *tr* descuartizar

quar'ter-deck' *s* alcázar *m*

quar'ter-hour' *s* cuarto de hora; **on the quarter-hour** al cuarto en punto cada cuarto de hora

quarter•ly ['kwɔrtərli] *adj* trimestral ‖ *adv* trimestralmente ‖ *s* (*pl* **-lies**) publicación o revista trimestral

quar'ter•mas'ter *s* (mil) comisario; (nav) cabo de brigadas

quartet [kwɔr'tɛt] *s* cuarteto

quartz [kwɔrts] *s* cuarzo

quartz watch *s* reloj de cuarzo

quasar ['kwesɑr] *s* (astr) objeto del espacio, fuente *f* cuasiestelar de radio

quash [kwɑʃ] *tr* sofocar, reprimir; anular, invalidar

quaver ['kwevər] *s* temblor *m*, estremecimiento; (mus) trémolo ‖ *intr* temblar, estremecerse

quay [ki] *s* muelle *m*, desembarcadero

queen [kwin] *s* reina; (*in chess*) dama o reina; (*in cards*) dama (*que corresponde al caballo*); abeja reina

queen bee *s* abeja reina, abeja maestra; (slang) marimandona, la que lleva la voz cantante

queen dowager *s* reina viuda

queen•ly ['kwinli] *adj* (*comp* **-lier;** *super* **-liest**) de reina; como reina; regio

queen mother *s* reina madre

queen olive *s* aceituna de la reina, aceituna gordal

queen post *s* péndola

queen's English *s* inglés castizo

queer [kwɪr] *adj* curioso, raro; estrambótico, estrafalario; aturdido, indispuesto; (coll) sospechoso, misterioso ‖ *tr* (slang) echar a perder; (slang) comprometer

quell [kwɛl] *tr* sofocar, reprimir; mitigar (*una pena o dolor*)

quench [kwɛntʃ] *tr* apagar (*el fuego; la sed*); sofocar, reprimir; (electron) amortiguar

que•ry ['kwɪri] *s* (*pl* **-ries**) pregunta; signo de interrogación; duda ‖ *v* (*pret* & *pp* **-ried**) *tr* interrogar; marcar con signo de interrogación; dudar

ques. *abbr* **question**

quest [kwɛst] *s* búsqueda; (*of the Holy Grail*) demanda; **in quest of** en busca de

question ['kwɛstʃən] *s* pregunta; (*problem for discussion*) cuestión; asunto, proposición; **beside the question** que no viene al caso; **beyond question** fuera de duda; **out of the question** imposible, indiscutible; **to ask a question** hacer una pregunta; **to be a question of** tratarse de, ser cuestión de; **to call in question** poner en duda; **without question** sin duda ‖ *tr* interrogar; cuestionar (*poner en tela de juicio*)

questionable ['kwɛstʃənəbəl] *adj* cuestionable

question mark *s* punto interrogante, signo de interrogación

questionnaire [,kwɛstʃən'ɛr] *s* cuestionario

queue [kju] *s* (*of hair*) coleta; (*of people*) cola ‖ *intr* hacer cola

quibble ['kwɪbəl] *intr* sutilizar

pu
qu

quick [kwɪk] *adj* rápido, veloz; ágil, vivo; despierto, listo; **the quick and the dead** los vivos y los muertos; **to cut** o **to sting to the quick** herir en lo vivo, tocar en la herida

quicken [ˈkwɪkən] *tr* acelerar, avivar; animar ‖ *intr* acelerarse; animarse

quick'lime' *s* cal viva

quick lunch *s* servicio de la barra, servicio rápido

quick'sand' *s* arena movediza

quick'sil'ver *s* azogue *m*

quiet [ˈkwaɪ•et] *adj* (still) quieto; silencioso; (*market*) (com) encalmado; **to keep quiet** callarse ‖ *s* quietud; silencio; **on the quiet** a las calladas ‖ *tr* aquietar; acallar ‖ *intr* aquietarse; callarse; **to quiet down** calmarse ‖ *interj* ¡silencio!

quill [kwɪl] *s* pluma de ave; cañón *m* de pluma; (*of hedgehog, porcupine*) púa

quilt [kwɪlt] *s* edredón *m*, colcha ‖ *tr* acolchar

quince [kwɪns] *s* membrillo

quinine [ˈkwaɪnaɪn] *s* quinina

quinsy [ˈkwɪnzi] *s* cinanquia, esquinencia

quintessence [kwɪnˈtɛsəns] *s* quintaesencia

quintet [kwɪnˈtɛt] *s* quinteto

quintuplet [kwɪnˈtjuplɛt] o [kwɪnˈtuplɛt] *s* quintillizo

quip [kwɪp] *s* chufleta, pulla ‖ *v* (*pret & pp* **quipped**; *ger* **quipping**) *tr* decir en son de burla ‖ *intr* echar pullas

quire [kwaɪr] *s* mano *f* de papel; (bb) alzado

quirk [kwʌrk] *s* excentricidad, rareza; sutileza; vuelta repentina

quit [kwɪt] *adj* libre, descargado; **to be quits** estar desquitados; **to call it quits** no seguir;

descontinuar; **to cry quits** pedir treguas ‖ *v* (*pret & pp* **quit** o **quitted**; *ger* **quitting**) *tr* dejar ‖ *intr* irse; (coll) dejar de trabajar

quite [kwaɪt] *adv* enteramente; verdaderamente; (coll) bastante, muy

quitter [ˈkwɪtər] *s* remolón *m*; (*of a cause*) desertor *m*

quiver [ˈkwɪvər] *s* temblor *m*; (*to hold arrows*) aljaba, carcaj *m* ‖ *intr* temblar

quixotic [kwɪksˈɑtɪk] *adj* quijotesco

quiz [kwɪz] *s* (*pl* **quizzes**) examen *m*; interrogatorio ‖ *v* (*pret & pp* **quizzed**; *ger* **quizzing**) *tr* examinar; interrogar

quiz game *s* torneo de preguntas y respuestas

quiz program *s* programa *m* de preguntas y respuestas, torneo radiofónico

quiz section *s* grupo de práctica

quizzical [ˈkwɪzɪkəl] *adj* curioso; cómico; burlón

quoin [kɔɪn] o [kwɔɪn] *s* esquina; piedra angular; (*wedge*) cuña ‖ *tr* (typ) acuñar

quoit [kwɔɪt] o [kɔɪt] *s* herrón *m*, tejo; **quoits** *ssg* hito

quondam [ˈkwɑndæm] *adj* antiguo, de otro tiempo

quorum [ˈkwɔrəm] *s* quórum *m*

quota [ˈkwotə] *s* cuota

quotation [kwoˈteʃən] *s* (*from a book*) cita; (*of prices*) cotización

quotation marks *spl* comillas

quote [kwot] *s* (coll) cita; (coll) cotización; **close quote** fin de la cita; **quotes** (coll) comillas ‖ *tr & intr* citar; cotizar; **quote cito**

quotient [ˈkwoʃənt] *s* cociente *m*

q.v. *abbr* **quod vide** (Lat) **which see**

R

R, r [ɑr] decimoctava letra del alfabeto inglés

r. *abbr* **railroad, railway, road, rod, ruble, rupee**

R. *abbr* **railroad, railway, Regina** (Lat) **Queen; Republican, response, Rex** (Lat) **King; River, Royal**

rabbet [ˈræbɪt] *s* barbilla, rebajo ‖ *tr* embarbillar, rebajar

rab•bi [ˈræbaɪ] *s* (*pl* **-bis** o **-bies**) rabino

rabbit [ˈræbɪt] *s* conejo

rabbit ears *spl* (telv, rad) antena de conejo

rabble [ˈræbəl] *s* canalla, gentuza, palomilla, chamuchina

rabble rouser [ˈrauzər] *s* populachero, alborotapueblos *mf*

rabies [ˈrebiz] o [ˈrebɪˌiz] *s* rabia

raccoon [ræˈkun] *s* mapache *m*, oso lavador

race [res] *s* (*people of same stock*) raza; (*contest in speed, etc.*) carrera; (*channel to lead water*) caz *m* ‖ *tr* competir con, en una carrera; hacer correr de prisa; hacer

funcionar (*un motor*) a velocidad excesiva ‖ *intr* correr de prisa; correr en una carrera; competir en una carrera; embalarse (*un motor*); (naut) regatear

race horse *s* caballo de carreras

race riot *s* disturbio racista

race track *s* pista de carreras

racial [ˈreʃəl] *adj* racial

racing car *s* coche *m* de carreras

racism [ˈresɪzəm] *s* racismo

racist [ˈresɪst] *adj & s* racista

rack [ræk] *s* (*sort of shelf*) estante *m*; (*to hang clothes*) percha; (*for fodder for cattle*) pesebre *m*; (*for baggage*) red *f* de equipaje; (*for guns*) armero; (*bar made to gear with a pinion*) cremallera; **to go to rack and ruin** desvencijarse; ir al desastre ‖ *tr* estirar, forzar; atormentar; despedazar; oprimir, agobiar; **to rack off** trasegar (*el vino*); **to rack one's brains** calentarse la cabeza, devanarse los sesos

racket [ˈrækɪt] *s* raqueta; (*noise*) baraúnda, alboroto; (slang) trapisonda, trapacería; **to raise a racket** armar un alboroto

racketeer [ˌrækɪˈtir] *s* trapisondista *mf*, trapacista *mf* ‖ *intr* trapacear

rack railway *s* ferrocarril *m* de cremallera

rac·y [ˈresi] *adj* (*comp* **-ier;** *super* **-iest**) espiritoso, chispeante; perfumado; (*somewhat indecent*) picante

radar [ˈredɑr] *s* radar *m*

radar scanner *s* explorador *m* de radar

radiant [ˈredɪ·ənt] *adj* radiante, resplandeciente; (*cheerful, smiling*) radiante

radiate [ˈredɪˌet] *tr* radiar; difundir (*p.ej., felicidad*) ‖ *intr* radiar, irradiar

radiation [ˌredɪˈeʃən] *s* radiación

radiation sickness *s* enfermedad de radiación, mal *m* de rayos

radiator [ˈredɪˌetər] *s* radiador *m*

radiator cap *s* tapón *m* de radiador

radical [ˈrædɪkəl] *adj & s* radical *m*

radi·o [ˈredɪˌo] *s* (*pl* **-os**) radio *f;* radiograma *m* ‖ *tr* radiodifundir

radioactive [ˌredɪ·oˈæktɪv] *adj* radiactivo

radioactive waste *s* residuos radiactivos

radio amateur *s* radioaficionado

radio announcer *s* locutor *m* de radio

ra·dio·broad·cast·ing *s* radiodifusión

radio frequency *s* radiofrecuencia

radio listener *s* radioescucha *mf*, radioyente *mf*

radiology [ˌredɪˈɑlədʒi] *s* radiología

radio ministry *s* (theol) ministerio radiofónco

radio network *s* red *f* de emisoras

radio newscaster *s* cronista *mf* de radio

radio receiver *s* radiorreceptor *m*

radio set *s* aparato de radio

ra·dio·(tel'e)phone' *s* radioteléfono

ra·di·o·ther'apy *s* radioterapia

radish [ˈrædɪ] *s* rábano

radium [redɪ·əm] *s* radio

radi·us [ˈredɪ·əs] *s* (*pl* **-i** [ˌɑɪ] o **-uses**) radio; (*range of operation*) radio; **within a radius of** en . . . a la redonda

raffle [ˈræfəl] ‖ *tr & intr* rifar

raft [ræft] *s* armadía, balsa; (coll) gran número

rafter [ˈræftər] *s* cabrio, contrapar *m*, traviesa

rag [ræg] *s* trapo; **to chew the rag** (slang) dar la lengua; **in rags** hilachento

ragamuffin [ˈrægəˌmʌfɪn] *s* pelagatos *m*; golfo, chiquillo haraposo

rag baby o **rag doll** *s* muñeca de trapo

rage [redʒ] *s* rabia; **to be all the rage** estar en boga, hacer furor; **to fly into a rage** montar en cólera

ragged [ˈrægɪd] *adj* andrajoso; (*edge*) cortado en dientes

ragpicker [ˈrægˌpɪkər] *s* andrajero, trapero

rag'weed' *s* ambrosía

raid [red] *s* incursión, invasión; ataque de sorpresa; ataque aéreo ‖ *tr* invadir; atacar inesperadamente; capturar (*p.ej., la policía un garito*)

rail [rel] *s* carril *m*, riel *m*; (*railing*) barandilla; (*of a bridge*) guardalado; (*at a bar*) apoyo para los pies; palo; **by rail** por ferrocarril; **rails** títulos o valores de ferrocarril ‖ *tr* poner barandilla a ‖ *intr* quejarse amargamente; **to rail at** injuriar, ultrajar

rail fence *s* cerca hecha de palos horizontales

rail'head' *s* (rr) cabeza de línea

railing [ˈrelɪŋ] *s* barandilla, pasamano

rail'road' *adj* ferroviario ‖ *s* ferrocarril *m* ‖ *tr* (coll) llevar a cabo con demasiada precipitación; (slang) encarcelar falsamente ‖ *intr* trabajar en el ferrocarril

railroad crossing *s* paso a nivel

rail'way' *adj* ferroviario ‖ *s* ferrocarril *m*

raiment [ˈremənt] *s* prendas de vestir, indumentaria

rain [ren] *s* lluvia; **rain or shine** llueva o no, con buen o mal tiempo ‖ *tr & intr* llover

rain'bow' *s* arco iris

rain'coat' *s* impermeable *m*

rain'fall' *s* lluvia repentina; precipitación acuosa

rain·y [ˈreni] *adj* (*comp* **-ier;** *super* **-iest**) lluvioso

rainy day *s* día lluvioso; tiempo futuro de posible necesidad

raise [rez] *s* aumento ‖ *tr* levantar; aumentar; criar (*a niños, animales*); cultivar (*plantas*); reunir (*dinero*); suscitar (*una duda*); resucitar (*a los muertos*); dejarse (*barba, bigote*); poner (*una objeción*); plantear (*una pregunta*); levantar (*tropas; un sitio*); (math) elevar; (*to come in sight of*) (naut) avistar

raisin [ˈrezən] *s* pasa, uva seca

rake [rek] *s* rastro, rastrillo; (*person*) calavera *m*, libertino ‖ *tr* rastrillar; **to rake together** acumular (*dinero*)

rake'-off' *s* (slang) dinero obtenido ilícitamente

rakish [ˈrekɪʃ] *adj* airoso, gallardo; listo, vivo; libertino

ral·ly [ˈræli] *s* (*pl* **-lies**) reunión popular, reunión política; recuperación, recobro ‖ *v* (*pret & pp* **-lied**) *tr* reunir; reanimar; recobrar (*la fuerza, la salud, el ánimo*) ‖ *intr* reunirse; recobrarse (*p.ej., los precios en la Bolsa*); recobrar la fuerza, la salud, el ánimo; **to rally to the side of** acudir a, ir en socorro de

ram [ræm] *s* (*male sheep*) morueco, carnero padre; (*device for battering, crushing, etc.*) pisón *m* ‖ *v* (*pret & pp* **rammed;** *ger* **ramming**) *tr* dar contra, chocar en; atestar, rellenar ‖ *intr* chocar; **to ram into** chocar en

ramble [ˈræmbəl] *s* paseo ‖ *intr* pasear; serpentear (*p.ej., un río*); extenderse serpenteando (*las enredaderas*); (*to wander aimlessly; to talk in an aimless way*) divagar

rami·fy [ˈræmɪˌfaɪ] *v* (*pret & pp* **-fied**) *tr* ramificar ‖ *intr* ramificarse

ram'jet'(engine) *s* motor *m* autorreactor; estatorreactor *m*

ramp [ræmp] *s* rampa

rampage ['ræmpedʒ] s alboroto; **to go on a rampage** alborotar, comportarse como un loco

rampart ['ræmpɑrt] s muralla, terraplén m; amparo, defensa

ram'rod' s atacador m, baqueta

ram'shack'le adj desvencijado, destartalado

ranch [ræntʃ] s granja, hacienda

rancid ['rænsɪd] adj rancio

rancor ['ræŋkər] s rencor m

random ['rændəm] adj casual, fortuito; **at random** al azar, a la ventura

range [rendʒ] s (row, line) fila, hilera; (scope, reach) alcance m; (of speeds, prices, etc.) escala; campo de tiro; terreno de pasto; (of a boat or airplane) autonomía; (of the voice) extensión; (of colors) gama, serie f; (stove) cocina económica; **within range of** al alcance de || tr alinear; recorrer (un terreno); ir a lo largo de (la costa); arreglar, ordenar || intr fluctuar, variar (entre ciertos límites); extenderse; divagar, errar; **to range over** recorrer

range finder s telémetro

rank [ræŋk] adj exuberante, lozano; denso, espeso; grosero; maloliente; excesivo; incorregible, rematado; indecente, vulgar || s categoría, rango; condición, posición; distinción; (line of soldiers standing abreast) fila; (mil) empleo, grado || tr alinear; ordenar; tener grado o posición más alta que || intr ocupar el último grado; **to rank high** ocupar alta posición; ser tenido en alta estima; sobresalir; **to rank low** ocupar baja posición; **to rank with** estar al nivel de; tener el mismo grado que

rank and file s soldados de fila; pueblo, gente f común

rankle ['ræŋkəl] tr enconar, irritar || intr enconarse

ransack ['rænsæk] tr registrar, escudriñar; robar, saquear

ransom ['rænsəm] s rescate m || tr rescatar

rant [rænt] intr desvariar, despotricar

rap [ræp] s golpe corto y seco; (noise) taque m; (coll) ardite m, bledo; (slang) crítica mordaz; **to take the rap** (slang) pagar la multa; sufrir las consecuencias || v (pret & pp rapped; ger rapping) tr golpear con golpe corto y seco; decir vivamente; (slang) criticar mordazmente || intr golpear con golpe corto y seco; **to rap at the door** tocar a la puerta

rapacious [rə'peʃəs] adj rapaz

rape [rep] s rapto; (of a woman) estupro, violación || tr raptar; estuprar, violar

rapid ['ræpɪd] adj rápido || **rapids** spl (of a river) rápidos

rap'id-fire' adj de tiro rápido; hecho vivamente

rapier ['repɪ•ər] s estoque m, espadín m

rapt [ræpt] adj arrebatado, extático, transportado; absorto

rapture ['ræptʃər] s embeleso, éxtasis f, rapto

rare [rer] adj raro; (word) poco usado; (meat) poco asado; (gem) precioso

rare bird s mirlo blanco

rare•fy ['rerɪ,faɪ] v (pret & pp -fied) tr enrarecer || intr enrarecerse

rarely ['rerli] adv rara vez

rascal ['ræskəl] s bellaco, bribón m, pícaro; pergenio

rash [ræʃ] adj temerario || s brote m, salpullido, erupción

rasp [ræsp] o [rɑsp] s escofina; (sound of a rasp) sonido áspero || tr escofinar; irritar, molestar; decir con voz ronca || intr hacer sonido áspero

raspber•ry ['ræz,beri] o ['rɑz,beri] s (pl -ries) frambuesa, sangüesa

raspberry bush s frambueso, sangüeso

rat [ræt] s rata; (false hair) postizo; **to smell a rat** (coll) olerse una trama, sospechar una intriga

ratchet ['rætʃɪt] s trinquete m

rate [ret] s (amount or degree measured in proportion to something else) razón f; (of interest) tipo; velocidad; precio; **at any rate** de todos modos; **at the rate of** a razón de || tr valuar; estimar, juzgar; clasificar || intr ser considerado, ser tenido; estar clasificado

rate of exchange s tipo de cambio

rate table s baremo

rather ['ræðər] o ['rɑðər] adv algo, un poco; bastante; antes, más bien; mejor dicho; por el contrario; muy, mucho; **rather than** antes que, más bien que || interj ¡ya lo creo!

rati•fy ['rætɪ,faɪ] v (pret & pp -fied) tr ratificar

ra•tio ['reʃo] o ['reʃɪ,o] s (pl -tios) (math) razón f; (math) cociente m

ration ['reʃən] o ['ræʃən] s ración || tr racionar

ration book s cartilla de racionamiento

ration coupon s cupón m de racionamiento

rational ['ræʃənəl] adj racional

rat poison s matarratas m; raticida

rat race s (coll) lucha diaria por ganarse el pan

rattle ['rætəl] s (number of short, sharp sounds) traqueteo; (noise-making device) carraca, matraca; (child's toy) sonajero; baraúnda; (in the throat) estertor m || tr tabletear, traquetear; (to confuse) (coll) atortolar, desconcertar; **to rattle off** decir rápidamente || intr tabletear, traquetear

rat'tle•snake' s serpiente f de cascabel

rat'trap' s ratonera; trance apurado, atolladero

raucous ['rɔkəs] adj ronco

ravage ['rævɪdʒ] s destrucción, estrago, ruina || tr destruir, estragar, arruinar

rave [rev] intr desvariar, delirar; bramar, enfurecerse; **to rave about** hacerse lenguas de, deshacerse en elogios de

raven ['revən] s cuervo

ravenous ['rævənəs] adj famélico, hambriento, voraz; rapaz

ravine [rə'vin] s cañón m, hondonada

ravish ['rævɪʃ] tr encantar, entusiasmar; raptar; violar (a una mujer)

ravishing ['rævɪʃɪŋ] adj encantador

raw [rɔ] *adj* crudo; *(cotton, silk)* en rama; inexperto, principiante; ulceroso; *(weather, day)* crudo
raw deal *s* (slang) mala pasada
raw'hide' *s* cuero en verde; látigo hecho de cuero en verde
raw material *s* primera materia, materia prima
ray [re] *s (of light)* rayo; *(fine line; fish)* raya
rayon [ˈreˑɑn] *s* rayón *m*
raze [rez] *tr* arrasar, asolar
razor [ˈrezər] *s* navaja de afeitar
razor blade *s* hoja u hojita de afeitar
razor strop *s* asentador *m*, suavizador *m*
razz [ræz] *s* (slang) irrisión ‖ *tr* (slang) mofarse de
R.C. *abbr* **Red Cross, Reserve Corps, Roman Catholic**
R.D. *abbr* **Rural Delivery**
reach [ritʃ] *s* alcance *m;* extensión; **out of reach (of)** fuera del alcance (de); **within reach of** al alcance de ‖ *tr* alcanzar; extender; entregar con la mano; llegar a; ponerse en contacto con; influenciar; cumplir *(cierto número de años)* ‖ *intr* alcanzar; extender la mano o el brazo; **to reach after** o **for** esforzarse por coger
react [rɪˈækt] *intr* reaccionar
reaction [rɪˈækʃən] *s* reacción
reactionar•y [rɪˈækʃənˌeri] *adj* reaccionario; mocho (Mex) ‖ *s (pl -ies)* reaccionario
read [rid] *v (pret & pp* read [rɛd]) *tr* ler; recitar *(poesía)*; estudiar *(derecho)*; leer en, adivinar *(el pensamiento ajeno)*; **to read over** recorrer, repasar ‖ *intr* leer; rezar, p.ej., **this page reads thus** esta página reza así; leerse, p.ej., **this book reads easily** este libro se lee con facilidad; **to read on** seguir leyendo
reader [ˈridər] *s* lector *m;* libro de lectura
readily [ˈrɛdɪli] *adv* de buena gana; fácilmente
reading [ˈridɪŋ] *s* lectura; recitación
reading desk *s* atril *m*
reading glass *s* lente *f* para leer, vidrio de aumento; **reading glasses** anteojos para la lectura
reading lamp *s* lámpara de sobremesa
reading room *s* gabinete *m* de lectura; sala de lectura
read•y [ˈrɛdi] *adj (comp -ier; super -iest)* listo, preparado, pronto; ágil, diestro; vivo; disponible; **to make ready** preparar; prepararse ‖ *v (pret & pp -ied) tr* preparar ‖ *intr* prepararse
ready cash *s* dinero a la mano, dinero contante y sonante
read'y-made' clothing *s* ropa hecha
ready-made suit *s* traje hecho
reagent [rɪˈedʒənt] *s* reactivo
real [ˈriˑəl] *adj* real, verdadero
real estate *s* bienes *mpl* raíces, bienes inmuebles
re'al-es•tate' *adj* inmobiliario
realism [ˈriˑəˌlɪzəm] *s* realismo
realist [ˈriˑəlɪst] *s* realista *mf*
reali•ty [rɪˈælɪti] *s (pl -ties)* realidad

realize [ˈriˑəˌlaɪz] *tr* darse cuenta de; realizar, llevar a cabo; adquirir *(ganancias)*; reportar *(ganancias)* ‖ *intr (to sell property for ready money)* realizar
realm [rɛlm] *s* reino
Realtor [ˈriˑəlˌtɔr] o [ˈriˑəltər] *s* corredor *m* de bienes raíces
realty [ˈriˑəlti] *s* bienes *mpl* raíces, bienes inmuebles
ream [rim] *s* resma; **reams** (coll) montones *mpl* ‖ *tr* escariar
reap [rip] *tr & intr (to cut)* segar; *(to gather)*, cosechar
reaper [ˈripər] *s (person)* segador *m;* máquina segadora
reappear [ˌriˑəˈpɪr] *intr* reaparecer
reapportionment [ˌriˑəˈpɔrʃənmənt] *s* nuevo prorrateo
rear [rɪr] *adj* posterior, trasero; de atrás ‖ *s* espalda; *(of a room)* fondo; *(of a row; of an automobile)* cola; retaguardia; (slang) culo, trasero ‖ *tr* levantar; edificar; criar, educar ‖ *intr* encabritarse *(un caballo)*
rear admiral *s* contraalmirante *m*
rear drive *s* tracción trasera
rear end *s (buttocks)* nalgas, pompis *m*
rearmament [riˈɑrməmənt] *s* rearme *m*
rear'-view' mirror *s* retrovisor *m*, espejo de retrovisión
rear window *s* (aut) luneta, luneta posterior
reason [ˈrizən] *s* razón *f;* **by reason of** con motivo de, a causa de; **to listen to reason** meterse en razón; **to stand to reason** ser razonable ‖ *tr & intr* razonar
reasonable [ˈrizənəbəl] *adj* razonable
reassessment [ˌriˑəˈsɛsmənt] *s* nuevo amillaramiento; nueva estimación
reassure [ˌriˑəˈʃʊr] *tr* volver a asegurar; tranquilizar
reawaken [ˌriˑəˈwekən] *tr* volver a despertar ‖ *intr* volver a despertarse
rebate [ˈribet] o [rɪˈbet] *s* rebaja ‖ *tr* rebajar
rebel [ˈrɛbəl] *adj & s* rebelde *mf* ‖ **re•bel** [rɪˈbɛl] *v (pret & pp -belled; ger -belling)* intr rebelarse
rebellion [rɪˈbɛljən] *s* rebelión
rebellious [rɪˈbɛljəs] *adj* rebelde
re•bind [riˈbaɪnd] *v (pret & pp -bound* [ˈbaund]) reatar; *(to edge, to border)* ribetear; (bb) reencuadernar
rebirth [ˈribʌrθ] o [riˈbʌrθ] *s* renacimiento
rebore [riˈbor] *tr* rectificar
rebound [ˈriˌbaund] o [rɪˈbaund] *s* rebote *m* ‖ [rɪˈbaund] *intr* rebotar
rebroad•cast [riˈbrɔdˌkæst] *s* retransmisión ‖ *v (pret & pp -cast* o *-casted) tr* retransmitir
rebuff [rɪˈbʌf] *s* desaire *m*, rechazo ‖ *tr* desairar, rechazar
re•build [riˈbɪld] *v (pret & pp -built* [ˈbɪlt]) *tr* reconstruir, reedificar
rebuke [rɪˈbjuk] *s* reprensión ‖ *tr* reprender
re•but [rɪˈbʌt] *v (pret & pp -butted; ger -butting) tr* rebatir, refutar
rebuttal [rɪˈbʌtəl] *s* rebatimiento, refutación
rec. *abbr* **receipt, recipe, record, recorder**
recall [rɪˈkɔl] o [ˈrikɔl] *s* llamada; *(memory)* recordación, retentiva; *(repeal)* revocación,

revocatoria; (*of a diplomat*) retirada ‖ [rɪˈkɔl] *tr* hacer volver, mandar volver; recordar; revocar; retirar (*a un diplomático*)

recant [rɪˈkænt] *tr* retractar ‖ *intr* retractarse

re•cap [ˈriˌkæp] o [riˈkæp] *v* (*pret & pp* -capped; *ger* -capping) *tr* recauchutar

recapitalization [ri,kæpɪtəlɪˈzefən] *s* recapitalización

recapitulation [,rikə,pɪtʃəˈlefən] *s* recapitulación

re•cast [ˈriˌkæst] *s* refundición; (*of a sentence*) reconstrucción ‖ [riˈkæst] *v* (*pret & pp* -cast) *tr* refundir; reconstruir (*p.ej., una frase*)

recd. o **rec'd.** *abbr* received

recede [rɪˈsid] *intr* (*to move back*) retroceder; (*to move away*) alejarse, retirarse; deprimirse (*p.ej., la frente de una persona*)

receipt [rɪˈsit] *s* recepción; (*acknowledgment*) recibo; (*acknowledgment of payment*) recibí *m*; (*recipe*) receta; **receipt in full** finiquito; **receipts** entradas, ingresos ‖ *tr* poner el recibí a

receive [rɪˈsiv] *tr* recibir; receptar (*cosas que son materia de delito*); **received payment** recibí ‖ *intr* recibir

receiver [rɪˈsivər] *s* receptor *m;* (*in bankruptcy*) contador *m*, síndico; receptor telefónico

receivership [rɪˈsivər,ʃɪp] *s* (law) sindicatura

receiving set *s* aparato receptor

receiving teller *s* recibidor *m* (*de un banco*)

recent [ˈrisənt] *adj* reciente

recently [ˈrisəntli] *adv* recientemente; endenantes; recién, p.ej., **recently arrived** recién llegado

receptacle [rɪˈsɛptəkəl] *s* receptáculo

reception [rɪˈsɛpʃən] *s* recepción; recibida (*welcome*) recibimiento

reception desk *s* recepción

receptionist [rɪˈsɛpʃənɪst] *s* recepcionista *f*

receptive [rɪˈsɛptɪv] *adj* receptivo

recess [rɪˈsɛs] o [ˈrisɛs] *s* intermisión; descanso; hora de recreo; (*in a surface*) depresión; (*in a wall*) hueco, nicho; escondrijo ‖ [rɪˈsɛs] *tr* ahuecar; empotrar; deprimir ‖ *intr* prorrogarse, suspenderse

recession [rɪˈsɛʃən] *s* retroceso, retirada; (*e.g., in a wall*) depresión; procesión de vuelta; contracción económica

rechargeable [rɪˈtʃɑrdʒəbəl] *adj* recargable

recipe [ˈrɛsɪ,pi] *s* receta (*de cocina*)

reciprocal [rɪˈsɪprəkəl] *adj* recíproco

reciprocity [,rɛsɪˈprɑsɪti] *s* reciprocidad

recital [rɪˈsaɪtəl] *s* narración; (*of music or poetry*) recital *m*

recite [rɪˈsaɪt] *tr* narrar; (*formally*) recitar

reckless [ˈrɛklɪs] *adj* atolondrado, temerario

reckon [ˈrɛkən] *tr* calcular; considerar; (coll) calcular, conjeturar ‖ *intr* calcular; **to reckon on** contar con; **to reckon with** tener en cuenta

reclaim [rɪˈklem] *tr* hacer utilizable; hacer labrantío (*un terreno*); ganar (*terreno*) a la mar; recuperar (*materiales usados*); conducir, guiar (*a los que hacen mala vida*)

reclamation [,rɪkləˈmeʃən] *s* (agr) roturación

recline [rɪˈklaɪn] *intr* reclinarse

recluse [rɪˈklus] o [ˈrɛklus] *s* solitario, ermitaño

recognize [ˈrɛkəg,naɪz] *tr* reconocer

recoil [rɪˈkɔɪl] *s* reculada; (*of a firearm*) reculada, culetazo ‖ *intr* recular, apartarse; recular (*un arma de fuego*)

recollect [,rɛkəˈlɛkt] *tr & intr* recordar

recombinant [rɪˈkɑmbɪnənt] *adj* (*genetics*) recombinado

recommend [,rɛkəˈmɛnd] *tr* recomendar

recompense [ˈrɛkəm,pɛns] *s* recompensa ‖ *tr* recompensar

reconcile [ˈrɛkən,saɪl] *tr* reconciliar; **to reconcile oneself** resignarse

reconnaissance [rɪˈkɑnɪsəns] *s* reconocimiento

reconnoiter [,rɛkəˈnɔɪtər] o [,rikɛˈnɔɪtər] *tr & intr* reconocer

reconquest [riˈkɑŋkwɛst] *s* reconquista

reconsider [,rikənˈsɪdər] *tr* reconsiderar

reconstruct [,rikənˈstrʌkt] *tr* reconstruir

reconversion [,rikənˈvɑrʒən] *s* reconversión

record [ˈrɛkərd] *s* anotación; ficha, historial *m*, historia personal; (*of a notary*) protocolo; (*of a phonograph*) disco; (educ) expediente académico; (sport) record *m*, plusmarca; **off the record** confidencialmente; **records** anales *mpl*, memorias; archivo; **to break a record** batir un record; **to have no (criminal) record** (coll) estar limpio; **to make a record** establecer un record; grabar un disco ‖ [rɪˈkɔrd] *tr* asentar; registrar; inscribir; grabar (*un sonido, una canción, un disco fonográfico, etc.*)

record breaker *s* plusmarquista *mf*

record changer [ˈtʃendʒər] *s* cambiadiscos *m*, tocadiscos automático

record holder *s* (sport) recordman *m*

recording [rɪˈkɔrdɪŋ] *adj* registrador; (wire or tape) magnetofónico ‖ *s* registro; (*of phonograph records*) grabación o grabado

recording secretary *s* secretario escribiente, secretario de actas

record player *s* tocadiscos *m*, pícap *m*, fonógrafo, vitrola, radiola

record store *s* disquería

recount [riˈkaʊnt] *tr* (*to count again*) recontar ‖ [rɪˈkaʊnt] *tr* (*to narrate*) recontar

recourse [rɪˈkors] o [ˈrikors] *s* recurso; (*helping hand*) paño de lágrimas; **to have recourse to** recurrir a

recover [rɪˈkʌvər] *tr* recobrar; rescatar; **to recover consciousness** recobrar el conocimiento, volver en sí ‖ *intr* recobrarse; recobrar la salud; ganar un pleito

recover•y [rɪˈkʌvəri] *s* (*pl* -ies) recobro, recuperación; **past recovery** sin remedio

recreant [ˈrɛkrɪ•ənt] *adj & s* cobarde *mf*, traidor *m*

recreation [,rɛkrɪˈeʃən] *s* recreación

recruit [rɪˈkrut] *s* recluta *m* ‖ *tr* reclutar ‖ *intr* alistar reclutas; ganar reclutas; restablecerse, reponerse

rect. *abbr* receipt, rector, rectory

rectangle [ˈrɛk,tæŋgəl] *s* rectángulo

recti•fy ['rɛktɪ,faɪ] v (pret & pp **-fied**) tr rectificar

rec•tum ['rɛktəm] s (pl **-ta** [tə]) recto

recumbent [rɪ'kʌmbənt] adj reclinado, recostado

recuperate [rɪ'kjupə,ret] tr recuperar; restablecer, reponer ‖ intr recuperarse, recobrarse

re•cur [rɪ'kʌr] v (pret & pp **-curred;** ger **-curring**) intr volver a ocurrir; volver a presentarse (a la memoria); volver (a un asunto)

recurrent [rɪ'kʌrənt] adj repetido; periódico; (illness) recurrente

recyclable [rɪ'saɪkləbəl] adj reciclable

recycling [rɪ'saɪklɪŋ] s reciclado, reciclaje m

red [rɛd] adj (comp **redder;** super **reddest**) rojo, colorado; (wine) tinto; enrojecido, inflamado ‖ s rojo; **in the red** (coll) endeudado; **to see red** (coll) enfurecerse ‖ **Red** adj & s (communist) rojo

red'bait' tr motejar (a uno) de rojo o comunista

red'bird' s cardenal m; piranga

red-blooded ['rɛd,blʌdɪd] adj fuerte, valiente, vigoroso

red'breast' s petirrojo

red'bud' s ciclamor m del Canadá

red'cap' s (Brit) policía militar; (U.S.A.) mozo de estación

red cell s glóbulo rojo, hematíe m

red'coat' s (hist) soldado inglés

redden ['rɛdən] tr enrojecer ‖ intr enrojecerse

redeem [rɪ'dim] tr redimir; cumplir (una promesa)

redeemer [rɪ'dimər] s redentor m

redemption [rɪ'dɛmpʃən] s redención

red-haired ['rɛd,hɛrd] adj pelirrojo

red'head' s pelirrojo

red herring s artificio para distraer la atención del asunto de que se trata

red'-hot' adj candente, calentado al rojo; ardiente, entusiasta; fresco, nuevo

rediscount rate [rɪ'dɪskaʊnt] s tipo de redescuento

rediscover [,rɪdɪs'kʌvər] tr redescubrir

red'-let'ter day s día m memorable

red'-light' district s barrio de los lupanares, barrio de mala vida

red man s piel roja m

re•do [rɪ'du] v (pret **-did** ['dɪd]; pp **-done** ['dʌn]) tr rehacer, repetir; refundir; reformar

redolent ['rɛdələnt] adj fragante, perfumado; **redolent of** que huele a

redoubt [rɪ'daʊt] s (fort) reducto

redound [rɪ'daʊnd] intr redundar; **to redound to** redundar en

red pepper s pimentón m

redress [rɪ'drɛs] o ['ridrɛs] s reparación; remedio ‖ [rɪ'drɛs] tr repara; remediar

Red Ridinghood ['raɪdɪŋ,hʊd] s Caperucita Roja

red'skin' s piel roja m

red tape s expedienteo, papeleo

reduce [rɪ'djus] o [rɪ'dus] tr reducir; (mil) degradar ‖ intr reducirse; reducir peso

reducing exercises spl ejercicios físicos para reducir peso

redundant [rɪ'dʌndənt] adj redundante

red'wood' s secoya

reed [rid] adj (organ, musical instrument) de lengüeta ‖ s (stalk) caña; (plant) carrizo, caña; (mus) instrumento de lengüeta; (of instrument) lengüeta

reëdit [ri'ɛdɪt] tr refundir

reef [rif] s arrecife m, escollo; (min) filón m, veta ‖ tr (naut) arrizar

reefer ['rifər] s chaquetón m; (slang) pitillo de mariguana

reek [rik] intr vahear, humear; estar bañado en sudor; estar mojado con sangre; **to reek of** o **with** oler a

reel [ril] s (spool) carrete m; (of a shuttle) broca; (of motion pictures) cinta; (sway, staggering) tambaleo; **off the reel** (coll) fácil y prestamente ‖ tr aspar, devanar; **to reel off** (coll) narrar fácil y prestamente ‖ intr tambalear; cejar (p.ej., el enemigo)

reëlection [,ri•ɪ'lɛkʃən] s reelección

reënlist [,ri•ɛn'lɪst] tr reenganchar ‖ intr reengancharse

reën•try [ri'ɛntri] s (pl **-tries**) reingreso, nueva entrada; (return to earth's atmosphere) reentrada

reëxamination [,ri•ɛg,zæmɪ'neʃən] s reexaminación

ref. abbr **referee, reference, reformation**

re•fer [rɪ'fʌr] v (pret & pp **-ferred;** ger **-ferring**) tr referir ‖ intr referirse

referee [,rɛfə'ri] s árbitro ‖ tr & intr arbitrar

reference ['rɛfərəns] adj (library, book, work) de consulta ‖ s referencia

referen•dum [,rɛfə'rɛndəm] s (pl **-da** [də]) s referéndum m

refill ['rifɪl] s relleno ‖ [ri'fɪl] tr rellenar

refine [rɪ'faɪn] tr refinar

refinement [rɪ'faɪnmənt] s refinamiento; buena crianza, cultura

refiner•y [rɪ'faɪnəri] s (pl **-ies**) refinería

reflect [rɪ'flɛkt] tr reflejar; (to meditate) reflexionar; **to reflect on** o **upon** reflexionar en o sobre; perjudicar

reflection [rɪ'flɛkʃən] s (thinking) reflexión; (reflected light; image) reflejo

reflex ['riflɛks] s reflejo

reforestation [,rifɑrɪs'teʃən] o [,rifɑrɪs'teʃən] s reforestación

reform [rɪ'fɔrm] s reforma ‖ tr reformar ‖ intr reformarse

reformation [,rɛfər'meʃən] s reformación ‖ **the reformation** la Reforma

reformato•ry [rɪ'fɔrmə,tori] s (pl **-ries**) reformatorio

reform school s casa de corrección

refraction [rɪ'frækʃən] s refracción

refrain [rɪ'fren] s estribillo ‖ intr abstenerse

refresh [rɪ'frɛʃ] tr refrescar ‖ intr refrescarse

refreshing [rɪ'frɛʃɪŋ] adj confortante, restaurante

refreshment [rɪ'frɛʃmənt] s refresco

re
re

refrigerator [rɪ'frɪdʒəretər] s heladera, nevera, refrigerador m
refrigerator car s carro o vagón frigorífico
refuel [ri'fjul] tr & intr repostar
refuge ['rɛfjudʒ] s refugio; expediente m, subterfugio; **to take refuge (in)** refugiarse (en)
refugee [,rɛfju'dʒi] s refugiado
refund ['rifʌnd] s reembolso ‖ [rɪ'fʌnd] tr reembolsar ‖ [ri'fʌnd] tr consolidar
refurnish [ri'fʌrnɪʃ] tr amueblar de nuevo
refusal [rɪ'fjuzəl] s negativa
refuse ['rɛfjus] s basura, desecho, desperdicios ‖ [rɪ'fjuz] tr rehusar; rechazar, no querer aceptar; **to refuse to** negarse a
refute [rɪ'fjut] tr refutar
reg. abbr **register, registrar, registry, regular**
regain [rɪ'gen] tr recobrar, recuperar; volver a alcanzar; **to regain consciousness** recobrar el conocimiento, volver en sí
regal ['rigəl] adj regio
regale [rɪ'gel] tr regalar, agasajar
regalia [rɪ'gelɪ•ə] spl (of an office or order) distintivos; galas, trajes mpl de lujo
regard [rɪ'gɑrd] s consideración, miramiento; (esteem) respeto; (particular matter) respecto; (look) mirada; **in regard to** respecto a o de; **regards** recuerdos; **without regard to** sin hacer caso de; **with regard to** respecto a o de ‖ tr considerar; mirar; tocar a, referirse a; **as regards** en cuanto a
regarding [rɪ'gɑrdɪŋ] prep tocante a, respecto a o de
regardless [rɪ'gɑrdlɪs] adj desatento, indiferente ‖ adj (coll) pese a quien pese, cueste lo que cueste; **regardless of** sin hacer caso de; a pesar de
regenerate [rɪ'dʒɛnə,ret] tr regenerar ‖ intr regenerarse
regent [,ridʒənt] s regente mf
regicide ['rɛdʒɪ,saɪd] s (act) regicidio; (person) regicida mf
regime o **régime** [re'ʒim] s régimen m
regiment ['rɛdʒɪmənt] s regimiento ‖ ['rɛdʒɪ,mɛnt] tr regimentar
regimental [,rɛdʒɪ,mɛntəl] adj regimental ‖ **regimentals** spl uniforme m militar
region ['ridʒən] s región, comarca
register ['rɛdʒɪstər] s (record; book for keeping such a record) registro; reja regulable de calefacción; (of the voice or an instrument) extensión ‖ tr (to indicate by a record; to show, as on a scale) registrar; empadronar (los vecinos en el padrón); manifestar, dar a conocer; certificar (envíos por correo); inscribir ‖ intr registrarse; empadronarse; inscribirse
registered letter s carta certificada
registrar ['rɛdʒɪs,trɑr] s registrador m, archivero
registration fee [,rɛdʒɪs'treʃən] s derechos de matrícula
re•gret [rɪ'grɛt] s pesar m, sentimiento; pesadumbre, remordimiento; **regrets** excusas ‖ v (pret & pp -gretted; ger -gretting) tr sentir, lamentar; lamentar la pérdida de;

arrepentirse de; **I regret** (apology) lo siento; me sabe mal; **to regret to** sentir
regrettable [rɪ'grɛtəbəl] adj lamentable
regular ['rɛgjələr] adj regular; (coll) cabal, completo, verdadero ‖ s obrero permanente; parroquiano regular; **regulars** tropas regulares
regulate ['rɛgjə,let] tr regular
rehabilitate [,rihə'bɪlɪ,tet] tr rehabilitar
rehabilitation [,rihə,bɪlɪ'teʃən] s rehabilitación
rehearsal [rɪ'hʌrsəl] s ensayo
rehearse [rɪ'hʌrs] tr ensayar ‖ intr ensayarse
reign [ren] s reinado ‖ intr reinar
reimburse [,ri•ɪm'bʌrs] tr reembolsar, rembolsar
rein [ren] s rienda; **to give free rein to** dar rienda suelta a ‖ tr dirigir por medio de riendas; contener, refrenar, gobernar
reincarnation [,ri•ɪnkɑr'neʃən] s reencarnación
reindeer ['ren,dɪr] s reno
reinforce [,ri•ɪn'fors] tr reforzar; armar (el hormigón)
reinforcement [,ri•ɪn'forsmənt] s refuerzo
reinstate [,ri•ɪn'stet] tr reinstalar
reiterate [ri'ɪtə,ret] tr reiterar
reject [rɪ'dʒɛkt] tr rechazar
rejection [rɪ'dʒɛkʃən] s rechazamiento
rejoice [rɪ'dʒɔɪs] intr regocijarse
rejoinder [rɪ'dʒɔɪndər] s contestación; (law) contrarréplica
rejuvenation [rɪ,dʒuvɪ'neʃən] s rejuvenecimiento
rel. abbr **relating, relative, religion, religious**
relapse [rɪ'læps] s recaída ‖ intr recaer
relate [rɪ'let] tr (to establish relationship between) relacionar; (to narrate) contar, relatar
relation [rɪ'leʃən] s (connection; narration) relación; (narration) relato; (relative) pariente mf; (kinship) parentesco; **in relation to** o **with** tocante a, respecto a o de
relationship [rɪ'leʃən,ʃɪp] s (connection) relación; (kinship) parentesco
relative ['rɛlətɪv] adj relativo ‖ s deudo, pariente mf
relax [rɪ'læks] tr & intr relajar
relaxation [,rilæks'eʃən] s relajación; despreocupación
relaxation of tension s disminución de tensión; disminución de la tirantez internacional
relaxing [rɪ'læksɪŋ] adj relajador; despreocupante, tranquilizador
relay ['rile] o [rɪ'le] s (elec) relais m, relevador m, relevo; (mil & sport) relevo; (sport) carrera de relevos ‖ v (pret & pp -layed) transmitir relevándose; transmitir con un relais; retransmitir (una emisión); reexpedir (un radiotelegrama) ‖ [rɪ'le] v (pret & pp -laid) tr volver a colocar, volver a tender
relay race s carrera de relevos
release [rɪ'lis] s liberación; (from jail) excarcelación; alivio; permiso de publicación, venta, etc.; obra o pieza lista para la pub-

licación, venta, etc.; (aer) lanzamiento; (mach) escape m, disparador m ‖ tr soltar; libertar; excarcelar (a un preso); permitir la publicación, venta, etc. de; (aer) lanzar (una bomba)

relent [rɪˈlɛnt] intr ablandarse, aplacarse

relentless [rɪˈlɛntlɪs] adj implacable

relevance [ˈrɛlɪvəns] s relevancia

relevant [ˈrɛlɪvənt] adj pertinente

reliable [rɪˈlaɪ•əbəl] adj confiable, fidedigno; (source) solvente

reliance [rɪˈlaɪ•əns] s confianza

relic [ˈrɛlɪk] s reliquia

relief [rɪˈlif] s alivio; caridad; (projection of figures; elevation) relieve m; (mil) relevo; **in relief** en relieve; **on relief** viviendo de socorro, recibiendo auxilio social

relieve [rɪˈliv] tr (to release from a post) relevar; aliviar; auxiliar (a los necesitados); (mil) relevar

religion [rɪˈlɪdʒən] s religión

religious [rɪˈlɪdʒəs] adj religioso

relinquish [rɪˈlɪŋkwɪʃ] tr abandonar, dejar

relish [ˈrɛlɪʃ] s buen sabor, gusto; condimento, sazón f; entremés m; buen apetito ‖ tr gustar de; comer o beber con placer

relocate [riˈloket] tr trasladar ‖ intr trasladarse

relocation [ˌriloˈkeʃən] s traslado

reluctance [rɪˈlʌktəns] s renuencia, aversión

reluctant [rɪˈlʌktənt] adj renuente, maldispuesto

re•ly [rɪˈlaɪ] v (pret & pp -lied) intr depender, confiar; **to rely on** depender de, confiar en

remain [rɪˈmen] intr permanecer, quedarse ‖ **remains** spl desechos, restos; restos mortales; obra póstuma

remainder [rɪˈmendər] s resto, residuo; libro casi invendible ‖ tr saldar (libros que ya no se venden)

re•make [riˈmek] v (pret & pp -made [ˈmed]) tr rehacer

remark [rɪˈmɑrk] s observación ‖ tr & intr observar; **to remark on** aludir a, comentar

remarkable [rɪˈmɑrkəbəl] adj notable, extraordinario

remar•ry [riˈmæri] v (pret & pp -ried) intr volver a casarse

reme•dy [ˈrɛmɪdi] s (pl -dies) remedio ‖ v (pret & pp -died) tr remediar

remember [rɪˈmɛmbər] tr acordarse de, recordar; dar recuerdos de parte de, p.ej., **remember me to your brother** déle Vd. a su hermano recuerdos de mi parte ‖ intr acordarse, recordar; **if I remember correctly** si mal no me acuerdo

remembrance [rɪˈmɛmbrəns] s recuerdo

remind [rɪˈmaɪnd] tr recordar

reminder [rɪˈmaɪndər] s recordatorio, recordativo

reminisce [ˌrɛmɪˈnɪs] intr entregarse a los recuerdos, contar sus recuerdos

remiss [rɪˈmɪs] adj descuidado, negligente

re•mit [rɪˈmɪt] v (pret & pp -mitted; ger -mitting) tr (to send, to ship; to pardon) remitir

remittance [rɪˈmɪtəns] s remesa

remnant [ˈrɛmnənt] s (something left over) remanente m; (of cloth) retal m, retazo; (piece of cloth to be sold at reduced price) saldo; vestigio

remod•el [riˈmɑdəl] v (pret & pp -eled o -elled; ger -eling o -elling) tr modelar de nuevo; rehacer, reconstruir; convertir, transformar; remodelar

remodeling [riˈmɑdəlɪŋ] s remodelación

remonstrate [rɪˈmɑnstret] intr protestar; **to remonstrate with** reconvenir

remorse [rɪˈmɔrs] s remordimiento

remorseful [rɪˈmɔrsfəl] adj compungido, arrepentido

remote [rɪˈmot] adj remoto

remote control s comando a distancia, telecontrol m, control remoto; **to operate by remote control** (co)mandar a distancia

removable [rɪˈmuvəbəl] adj amovible

removal [rɪˈmuvəl] s remoción; mudanza, traslado; (dismissal) deposición

remove [rɪˈmuv] tr remover; quitar de en medio, apartar matando ‖ intr removerse

remuneration [rɪˌmjunərˈeʃən] s remuneración

renaissance [ˌrɛnəˈsɑns] o [rɪˈnesəns] s renacimiento

rend [rɛnd] v (pret & pp rent [rɛnt]) tr (to tear) desgarrar; (to split) hender, rajar; estremecer (un ruido en el aire)

render [ˈrɛndər] tr rendir (gracias, obsequios, homenaje); prestar, suministrar (ayuda); pagar (tributo); desempeñar (un papel); traducir (sentimientos); (from one language to another) verter; hacer (justicia); ejecutar (una pieza de música); derretir (cera, manteca); extraer la grasa o el sebo de; poner, volver

rendezvous [ˈrɑndəˌvu] s (pl -vous [ˌvuz]) cita; (in space) encuentro, reunión ‖ v (pret & pp -voused [ˌvud]; ger -vousing [ˌvu•ɪŋ]) intr reunirse en una cita

rendition [rɛnˈdɪʃən] s rendición; traducción; (mus) ejecución

renege [rɪˈnɪg] s renuncio ‖ intr renunciar; (coll) volverse atrás

renegotiation [ˌrɪnɪˌgoʃiˈeʃən] s renegociación

renew [rɪˈnju] o [rɪˈnu] tr renovar ‖ intr renovarse

renewable [rɪˈnju•əbəl] o [rɪˈnu•əbəl] adj renovable

renewal [rɪˈnju•əl] o [rɪˈnu•əl] s renovación

renounce [rɪˈnaʊns] tr renunciar; renunciar a (p.ej., el mundo) ‖ intr renunciar

renovate [ˈrɛnəˌvet] tr renovar; refaccionar; reformar (p.ej., una tienda, una casa)

renown [rɪˈnaʊn] s renombre m

renowned [rɪˈnaʊnd] adj renombrado

rent [rɛnt] adj desgarrado ‖ s alquiler m, arriendo; (tear, slit) desgarro ‖ tr alquilar, arrendar ‖ intr alquilarse, arrendarse

rental [ˈrɛntəl] s alquiler m, arriendo

renunciation [rɪˌnʌnsɪˈeʃən] o [rɪˌnʌnʃiˈeʃən] s renunciación

reopen [riˈopən] tr reabrir ‖ intr reabrirse

reorganize [ri'ɔrgə,naɪz] *tr* reorganizar ‖ *intr* reorganizarse

reorientation [ri,orɪ•ən'teʃən] *s* reorientación

rep. *abbr* **report, reporter, representative, republic**

repair [rɪ'pɛr] *s* reparación; recompostura; **in repair** en buen estado ‖ *tr* reparar; refaccionar ‖ *intr* dirigirse; volver

repaper [ri'pepər] *tr* empapelar de nuevo

reparation [,rɛpə'reʃən] *s* reparación

repartee [,rɛpɑr'ti] *s* respuesta viva; agudeza y gracia en responder

repast [rɪ'pæst] o [rɪ'pɑst] *s* comida, comilona

repatriate [ri'petrɪ,et] *tr* repatriar

re•pay [rɪ'pe] *v* (*pret & pp* -**paid** ['ped]) *tr* reembolsar, rembolsar; resarcir (*un daño, una injuria*); compensar

repayment [rɪ'pemənt] *s* reembolso; resarcimiento; compensación

repeal [rɪ'pil] *s* abrogación, revocación; revocatoria ‖ *tr* abrogar, revocar

repeat [rɪ'pit] *s* repetición ‖ *tr & intr* repetir

re•pel [rɪ'pɛl] *v* (*pret & pp* -**pelled;** *ger* -**pelling**) *tr* rechazar, repeler; repugnar

repent [rɪ'pɛnt] *tr* arrepentirse de ‖ *intr* arrepentirse

repentance [rɪ'pɛntəns] *s* arrepentimiento

repentant [rɪ'pɛntənt] *adj* arrepentido

repertory theater ['rɛpər,tori] *s* teatro de repertorio

repetition [,rɛpɪ'tʃən] *s* repetición

repine [rɪ'paɪn] *intr* afligirse, quejarse

replace [rɪ'ples] *tr* (*to put back*) reponer; (*to take the place of*) reemplazar

replacement [rɪ'plesmənt] *s* reposición; reemplazo; pieza de repuesto; soldado reemplazante

replenish [rɪ'plɛnɪʃ] *tr* rellenar; reaprovisionar

replete [rɪ'plit] *adj* repleto

replica ['rɛplɪkə] *s* réplica

re•ply [rɪ'plaɪ] *s* (*pl* -**plies**) contestación, respuesta; contesto (Mex) ‖ *v* (*pret & pp* -**plied**) *tr & intr* contestar, responder

reply coupon *s* vale *m* respuesta

report [rɪ'port] *s* relato, informe *m;* voz *f,* rumor *m;* (*e.g., of a firearm*) detonación, tiro; denuncia ‖ *tr* relatar, informar acerca de; denunciar ‖ *intr* hacer un relato; redactar un informe; ser repórter; presentarse; **to report on** dar cuenta de, notificar

report card *s* certificado escolar

reportedly [rɪ'portɪdli] *adv* según se informa

reporter [rɪ'portər] *s* repórter *m*

reporting [rɪ'portɪŋ] *s* reportaje *m*

repose [rɪ'poz] *s* descanso ‖ *tr* descansar; poner (*confianza*) ‖ *intr* descansar

reprehend [,rɛprɪ'hɛnd] *tr* reprender

represent [,rɛprɪ'zɛnt] *tr* representar

representative [,rɛprɪ'zɛntətɪv] *adj* representativo ‖ *s* representante *mf*

repress [rɪ'prɛs] *tr* reprimir

reprieve [rɪ'priv] *s* suspensión temporal de un castigo, suspensión temporal de la pena de muerte; respiro, alivio temporal ‖ *tr* suspender temporalmente el castigo de o la

pena de muerte de; aliviar temporalmente

reprimand ['rɛprɪ,mænd] *s* reprimenda ‖ *tr* reconvenir, reprender

reprint ['ri,prɪnt] *s* reimpresión; tirada aparte ‖ [ri'prɪnt] *tr* reimprimir

reprisal [rɪ'praɪzəl] *s* represalia

reproach [rɪ'protʃ] *s* reproche *m;* oprobio ‖ *tr* reprochar; oprobiar

reproduce [,riprə'djus] *tr* reproducir ‖ *intr* reproducirse

reproduction [,riprə'dʌkʃən] *s* reproducción

reproof [rɪ'pruf] *s* reprobación

reprove [rɪ'pruv] *tr* reprobar

reptile ['rɛptɪl] *s* reptil *m*

republic [rɪ'pʌblɪk] *s* república

republican [rɪ'pʌblɪkən] *adj & s* republicano

repudiate [rɪ'pjudɪ,et] *tr* repudiar; no reconocer (*p.ej., una deuda*)

repugnant [rɪ'pʌgnənt] *adj* repugnante

repulse [rɪ'pʌls] *s* repulsión, rechazo ‖ *tr* repeler, rechazar

repulsive [rɪ'pʌlsɪv] *adj* repulsivo

reputation [,rɛpjə'teʃən] *s* reputación; buena reputación

repute [rɪ'pjut] *s* reputación; buena reputación ‖ *tr* reputar

reputedly [rɪ'pjutɪdli] *adv* según la opinión común

request [rɪ'kwɛst] *s* petición, solicitud; **at the request of** a petición de ‖ *tr* pedir

require [rɪ'kwaɪr] *tr* exigir, requerir

requirement [rɪ'kwaɪrmənt] *s* requisito; necesidad

requisite ['rɛkwɪzɪt] *adj & s* requisito

requital [rɪ'kwaɪtəl] *s* compensación, retorno

requite [rɪ'kwaɪt] *tr* corresponder a (*los beneficios, el amor, etc.*); corresponder con (*el bienhechor*)

re•read [ri'rid] *v* (*pret & pp* -**read** ['rɛd]) *tr* releer

rerun ['ri,rʌn] *s* (*film, play, etc.*) exhibición repetida, programa *m* repetido

resale ['ri,sel] o [ri'sel] *s* reventa

rescind [rɪ'sɪnd] *tr* rescindir

rescue ['rɛskju] *s* salvación, rescate *m*, liberación; **to go to the rescue of** acudir al socorro de ‖ *tr* salvar, rescatar, libertar

rescue party *s* pelotón *m* de salvamento

research [rɪ'sʌrtʃ] o ['risʌrtʃ] *s* investigación ‖ *intr* investigar

re•sell [ri'sel] *v* (*pret & pp* -**sold** ['sold]) *tr* revender; rescatar (Mex)

resemblance [rɪ'zɛmbləns] *s* parecido, semejanza

resemble [rɪ'zɛmbəl] *tr* parecerse a, asemejarse a

resent [rɪ'zɛnt] *tr* resentirse de o por

resentful [rɪ'zɛntfəl] *adj* resentido

resentment [rɪ'zɛntmənt] *s* resentimiento

reservation [,rɛzər've ʃən] *s* reserva

reserve [rɪ'zʌrv] *s* reserva ‖ *tr* reservar

reservoir ['rɛzər,vwɑr] *s* depósito; (*where water is dammed back*) embalse *m*, pantano; (*of wisdom*) fondo

re•ship [ri'ʃɪp] *v* (*pret & pp* -**shipped;** *ger* -**shipping**) *tr* reenviar, reexpedir; (*on a ship*) reembarcar ‖ *intr* reembarcarse

reshipment [riˈʃɪpmənt] s reenvío, reexpedición; (of persons) reembarco; (of goods) reembarque m

reside [rɪˈzaɪd] intr residir

residence [ˈrɛzɪdəns] s residencia

resident [ˈrɛzɪdənt] adj & s residente mf, vecino

residue [ˈrɛzɪ,dju] s residuo

resign [rɪˈzaɪn] tr dimitir, resignar, renunciar ‖ intr dimitir; (to yield, submit) resignarse; **to resign to** resignarse con (p.ej., su suerte)

resignation [,rɛzɪgˈneʃən] s (from a job, etc.) dimisión; (state of being submissive) resignación

resin [ˈrɛzɪn] s resina

resist [rɪˈzɪst] tr resistir (la tentación); resistir a (la violencia; la risa) ‖ intr resistirse

resistance [rɪˈzɪstəns] s resistencia; **without resistance** sin rechistar

resole [riˈsol] tr sobresolar

resolute [ˈrɛzə,lut] adj resuelto

resolution [,rɛzəˈluʃən] s resolución; **good resolutions** buenos propósitos

resolve [rɪˈzɔlv] s resolución ‖ tr resolver ‖ intr resolverse

resort [rɪˈzɔrt] s lugar muy frecuentado; (e.g., for vacations) estación; (for help or support) recurso; **as a last resort** como último recurso ‖ intr recurrir

resound [rɪˈzaʊnd] intr resonar

resource [rɪˈsors] o [ˈrisors] s recurso

resourceful [rɪˈsorsfəl] adj ingenioso

respect [rɪˈspɛkt] s (deference, esteem) respeto; (reference, relation; detail) respecto; **respects** recuerdos, saludos; **to pay one's respects (to)** ofrecer sus respetos (a); **with respect to** respecto a o de ‖ tr respetar

respectable [rɪˈspɛktəbəl] adj respetable; decente, presentable

respectful [rɪˈspɛktfəl] adj respetuoso

respectfully [rɪˈspɛktfəli] adj respetuosamente; **respectfully yours** de Vd. atento y seguro servidor

respecting [rɪˈspɛktɪŋ] prep con respecto a, respecto de

respective [rɪˈspɛktɪv] adj respectivo

respire [rɪˈspaɪr] tr & intr respirar

respite [ˈrɛspɪt] s (temporary relief) respiro; (postponement, especially of death sentence) suspensión; **without respite** sin respirar

resplendent [rɪˈsplɛndənt] adj resplandeciente

respond [rɪˈspɑnd] intr responder

response [rɪˈspɑns] s respuesta

responsibility [rɪ,spɑnsɪˈbɪlɪti] s responsabilidad; **to assume responsibility** responsabilizarse

responsible [rɪˈspɑnsɪbəl] adj responsable; (job, position) de confianza; **to hold responsible** responsabilizar; **responsible for** responsable de

rest [rɛst] s (after exertion or work; sleep) descanso; (lack of motion) reposo; (of the dead) paz f; (what remains) resto; (mus) pausa; **at rest** (not moving) en reposo;

tranquilo; dormido; (dead) muerto; **the rest** lo demás; los demás; **to come to rest** venir a parar; **to lay to rest** enterrar ‖ tr descansar; parar; poner (p.ej., confianza) ‖ intr descansar; estar, hallarse; **to rest assured (that)** estar seguro, tener la seguridad (de que); **to rest on** descansar en o sobre, estribar en

restaurant [ˈrɛstərənt] s restaurante m

rest cure s cura de reposo

restful [ˈrɛstfəl] adj descansado, tranquilo, reposado

rest home s casa de reposo

resting place s lugar m de descanso; (of a staircase) descansadero; (of the dead) última morada

restitution [,rɛstɪˈtjuʃən] s restitución

restless [ˈrɛstlɪs] adj intranquilo; (sleepless) insomne

restock [riˈstɑk] tr reaprovisionar; repoblar (p.ej., un acuario)

restore [rɪˈstor] tr restaurar; (to give back) devolver

restrain [rɪˈstren] tr contener, refrenar; aprisionar

restraint [rɪˈstrent] s restricción; comedimiento, moderación

restrict [rɪˈstrɪkt] tr restringir

rest room s sala de descanso; excusado, retrete m; (of a theater) saloncillo

result [rɪˈzʌlt] s resultado; **as a result of** de resultas de ‖ intr resultar; **to result in** dar por resultado, parar en

resume [rɪˈzum] o [rɪˈzjum] tr reasumir; reanudar (el viaje, el vuelo, etc.); volver a tomar (su asiento) ‖ intr continuar; recomenzar; reanudar el hilo del discurso

résumé [,rɛzuˈme] s resumen m

resurface [riˈsʌrfɪs] tr dar nueva superficie a ‖ intr volver a emerger (un submarino)

resurrect [,rɛzəˈrɛkt] tr & intr resucitar

resurrection [,rɛzəˈrɛkʃən] s resurrección

resuscitate [rɪˈsʌsɪ,tet] tr & intr resucitar

retail [ˈritel] adj & adv al por menor ‖ s venta al por menor ‖ tr detallar, vendor al por menor ‖ intr vender al por menor; venderse al por menor

retailer [ˈritelər] s detallista mf, minorista m, comerciante mf al por menor

retain [rɪˈten] tr retener; contratar (a un abogado)

retaliate [rɪˈtælɪ,et] intr desquitarse, vengarse

retaliation [rɪ,tælɪˈeʃən] s desquite m, venganza

retard [rɪˈtɑrd] s retardo ‖ tr retardar

retardation [,ritɑrˈdeʃən] s retardación

retarded [rɪˈtɑrdɪd] adj subnormal, atrasado, retrasado

retch [rɛtʃ] tr vomitar ‖ intr arquear, esforzarse por vomitar

retching [ˈrɛtʃɪŋ] s arcadas

ret'd. abbr **returned**

reticence [ˈrɛtɪsəns] s reserva, circunspección, sigilo

reticent [ˈrɛtɪsənt] adj reservado, circunspecto

retinue [ˈrɛtɪ,nju] s comitiva, séquito

retire [rɪˈtaɪr] *tr* retirar; jubilar (*a un empleado*) ‖ *intr* retirarse; jubilarse; (*to go to bed*) recogerse; (mil) retirarse

retirement [rɪˈtaɪrmənt] *s* retiro; (*of an employee with pension*) jubilación; (mil) retirada

retirement annuity *s* jubilación

retort [rɪˈtɔrt] *s* respuesta pronta y aguda, réplica; (chem) retorta ‖ *intr* replicar

retouch [rɪˈtʌtʃ] *tr* retocar

retrace [rɪˈtres] *tr* repasar; **to retrace one's steps** volver sobre sus pasos

retract [rɪˈtrækt] *tr* retractarse de, desdecirse de (*lo que se ha dicho*) ‖ *intr* retractarse, desdecirse

retractable [rɪˈtræktəbəl] *adj* retráctil

retraction [rɪˈtrækʃən] *s* retracción

re•tread [ˈriˌtred] *s* neumático recauchutado; neumático ranurado ‖ [riˈtred] *v* (*pret & pp* **-treaded**) *tr* recauchutar; volver a ranurar ‖ *v* (*pret* **-trod** [ˈtrɑd]; *pp* **-trod** o **-trodden**) *tr* desandar ‖ *intr* volverse atrás

retreat [rɪˈtrit] *s* (*act of withdrawing; place of seclusion*) retiro; (eccl) retiro; (mil) retreta, retirada; (*signal*) (mil) retreta; **to beat a retreat** retirarse; (mil) batirse en retirada ‖ *intr* retirarse

retrench [rɪˈtrentʃ] *tr* cercenar ‖ *intr* recogerse

retribution [ˌrɛtrɪˈbjuʃən] *s* justo castigo; (theol) juicio final

retrieve [rɪˈtriv] *tr* cobrar; reparar (*p.ej., un daño*); desquitarse de (*una pérdida, una derrota*); (hunt) cobrar, portar ‖ *intr* (hunt) cobrar, portar

retriever [rɪˈtrivər] *s* perro cobrador, perro traedor

retroactive [ˌrɛtroˈæktɪv] *adj* retroactivo

retrofiring [ˌrɛtroˈfaɪrɪŋ] *s* retrodisparo

retrogress [ˈrɛtrəˌgrɛs] *intr* retroceder; emperorar

retrorocket [ˌrɛtroˈrɑkɪt] *s* retrocohete *m*

retrospect [ˈrɛtrəˌspɛkt] *s* retrospección; **in retrospect** retrospectivamente

retrospective [ˌrɛtrəˈspɛktɪv] *adj* retrospectivo

re•try [riˈtraɪ] *v* (*pret & pp* **-tried**) *tr* reensayar; rever (*un caso legal*); procesar de nuevo (*a una persona*)

return [rɪˈtʌrn] *adj* repetido; de vuelta; **by return mail** a vuelta de correo ‖ *s* vuelta; devolución; recompensa; respuesta; informe *m*, noticia; ganancia, beneficio, rédito; (*of an election*) resultado; (*of income tax*) declaración; **in return (for)** en cambio (de); **many happy returns of the day!** ¡que cumpla muchos más! ‖ *tr* devolver; dar en cambio; corresponder a (*un favor*); dar (*una respuesta, las gracias*) ‖ *intr* volver; responder

return address *s* dirección del remitente

return bout o **engagement** *s* (box) combate *m* revancha

return game *s* desquite *m*

return ticket *s* billete *m* de vuelta; billete de ida y vuelta

return trip *s* viaje *m* de vuelta

reunification [riˌjunɪfɪˈkeʃən] *s* reunificación

reunion [riˈjunjən] *s* reunión

reunite [ˌrijuˈnaɪt] *tr* reunir ‖ *intr* reunirse

rev. *abbr* **revenue, reverse, review, revised, revision, revolution**

Rev. *abbr* **Revelation, Reverend**

rev [rɛv] *s* revolución ‖ *v* (*pret & pp* **revved**; *ger* **revving**) *tr* cambiar la velocidad de; **to rev up** acelerar ‖ *intr* acelerarse

revaluate [riˈvæljuˌet] *tr* revalorar, revalorizar, revaluar

revamp [riˈvæmp] *tr* componer, renovar, remendar

reveal [rɪˈvil] *tr* revelar

reveille [ˈrɛvəli] *s* diana, toque *m* de diana

rev•el [ˈrɛvəl] *s* jarana, regocijo tumultuoso ‖ *v* (*pret & pp* **-eled** o **-elled**; *ger* **-eling** o **-elling**) *intr* jaranear; deleitarse

revelation [ˌrɛvəˈleʃən] *s* revelación

revel•ry [ˈrɛvəlri] *s* (*pl* **-ries**) jarana, diversión tumultuosa

revenge [rɪˈvɛndʒ] *s* venganza ‖ *tr* vengar

revengeful [rɪˈvɛndʒfəl] *adj* vengativo

revenue [ˈrɛvəˌnju] *s* renta, rédito; rentas públicas

revenue cutter *s* escampavía

revenue stamp *s* sello fiscal, timbre *m* del estado

reverberate [rɪˈvʌrbəˌret] *intr* reverberar

revere [rɪˈvɪr] *tr* reverenciar, venerar

reverence [ˈrɛvərəns] *s* reverencia ‖ *tr* reverenciar

reverend [ˈrɛvərənd] *adj & s* reverendo

reverie [ˈrɛvəri] *s* ensueño

reversal [rɪˈvʌrsəl] *s* inversión (*e.g., of opinion*) cambio

reverse [rɪˈvʌrs] *adj* invertido; contrario; de marcha atrás ‖ *s* (*opposite or rear*) revés *m*; contrario; contramarcha, marcha atrás; (*check, defeat*) revés *m*, contratiempo ‖ *tr* invertir; dar vuelta a; poner en marcha atrás; **to reverse oneself** cambiar de opinión; **to reverse the charges** cobrar al destinatario; (telp) cobrar al número llamado ‖ *intr* invertirse

reverse lever *s* palanca de marcha atrás

revert [rɪˈvʌrt] *intr* revertir; saltar atrás; **to revert to one's old tricks** volver a las andadas

review [rɪˈvju] *s* (*reëxamination; survey; magazine; musical show*) revista; (*of a book*) reseña, revista; (*of a lesson*) repaso; (mil) reseña, revista ‖ *tr* rever, revisar; reseñar (*un libro*); repasar (*una lección*); (mil) revistar

reviewer [rɪˈvjuˌər] *s* (*critic*) reseñador *m*

revile [rɪˈvaɪl] *tr* ultrajar, vilipendiar

revise [rɪˈvaɪz] *s* revisión; refundición; (typ) segunda prueba ‖ *tr* rever, revisar; refundir (*un libro*); enmendar

revision [rɪˈvɪʒən] *s* revisión; revisada; (*of a book*) refundición; enmienda

revisionism [rɪˈvɪʒəˌnɪzəm] *s* revisionismo

revisionist [rɪˈvɪʒənɪst] *adj & s* revisionista

revival [rɪˈvaɪvəl] *s* resucitación; reanimación; (*e.g., of learning*) renacimiento; despertamiento religioso; (theat) reestreno, reposición

revive [rɪ'vaɪv] *tr* revivir; (theat) reestrenar, reponer ‖ *intr* revivir; volver en sí, recordar

revoke [rɪ'vok] *tr* revocar

revolt [rɪ'volt] *s* rebelión, sublevación ‖ *tr* dar asco a, repugnar ‖ *intr* rebelarse, sublevarse

revolting [rɪ'voltɪŋ] *adj* asqueroso, repugnante; rebelde

revolution [,rɛvə'luʃən] *s* revolución

revolutionar•y [,rɛvə'luʃə,nɛri] *adj* revolucionario ‖ *s* (*pl* **-ies**) revolucionario

revolve [rɪ'valv] *tr* hacer girar; (*in one's mind*) revolver ‖ *intr* girar; revolverse (*un astro en su órbita*)

revolver [rɪ'valvər] *s* revólver *m*

revolving bookcase *s* giratoria

revolving door *s* puerta giratoria

revolving fund *s* fondo rotativo

revue [rɪ'vju] *s* (theat) revista

revulsion [rɪ'vʌlʃən] *s* aversión, repugnancia; reacción fuerte

reward [rɪ'wɔrd] *s* premio, recompensa; (*money used to recapture or recover*) rescate *m;* hallazgo, p.ej., **five dollars reward** cinco dólares de hallazgo ‖ *tr* premiar, recompensar

rewarding [rɪ'wɔrdɪŋ] *adj* remunerador, provechoso, agradecido

re•wind ['ri,waɪnd] *s* (mach, mov) retroceso ‖ [ri'waɪnd] *v* (*pret & pp* **-wound** [waʊnd] *tr* (mach, mov) rebobinar

re•write [ri'raɪt] *v* (*pret* **-wrote** ['rot]; *pp* **-written** ['rɪtən]) *tr* escribir de nuevo; refundir (*un escrito*); redactar (*un escrito de otra persona*)

R.F. *abbr* **radio frequency**

R.F.D. *abbr* **Rural Free Delivery**

R.H. *abbr* **Royal Highness**

rhapso•dy ['ræpsədi] *s* (*pl* **-dies**) rapsodia

rheostat ['riə,stæt] *s* reóstato

rhesus ['risəs] *s* macaco de la India

rhetoric ['rɛtərɪk] *s* retórica

rhetorical [rɪ'tɔrɪkəl] *adj* retórico

rheumatic [ru'mætɪk] *adj & s* reumático

rheumatism ['rumə,tɪzəm] *s* reumatismo

Rhine [raɪn] *s* Rin *m*

Rhineland ['raɪn,lænd] *s* Renania

rhine'stone' *s* diamante de imitación hecho de vidrio

rhinoceros [raɪ'nasərəs] *s* rinoceronte *m*

Rhodes [rodz] *s* Rodas *f*

Rhone [ron] *s* Ródano

rhubarb ['rubarb] *s* ruibarbo

rhyme [raɪm] *s* rima; **without rhyme or reason** sin ton ni son ‖ *tr & intr* rimar

rhythm ['rɪðəm] *s* ritmo

rhythmic(al) ['rɪðmɪk(əl)] *adj* rítmico

rial•to [rɪ'ælto] *s* (*pl* **-tos**) mercado ‖ **the Rialto** el puente del Rialto; el centro teatral de Nueva York

rib [rɪb] *s* costilla; (*of a fan or umbrella*) varilla; (*of a tire*) cuerda; (*in cloth*) canilla; (*of the wing of an insect*) nervio ‖ *v* (*pret & pp* **ribbed;** *ger* **ribbing**) *tr* proveer de

costillas; hacer canillas en; (slang) tomar el pelo a

ribald ['rɪbəld] *adj* grosero y obsceno

ribbon ['rɪbən] *s* cinta

rice [raɪs] *s* arroz *m*

rich [rɪtʃ] *adj* rico; (coll) platudo; (*color*) vivo; (*voice*) sonoro; (*wine*) generoso; azucarado, condimentado; (coll) divertido; (coll) ridículo; **to strike it rich** descubrir un buen filón ‖ **riches** *spl* riquezas; **the rich** los ricos

rickets ['rɪkɪts] *s* raquitis *f*

rickety ['rɪkɪti] *adj* (*object*) destartalado, desvencijado; (*person*) tambaleante, vacilante; (*suffering from rickets*) raquítico

rid [rɪd] *v* (*pret & pp* **rid;** *ger* **ridding**) *tr* desembarazar; **to get rid of** desembarazarse de, deshacerse de; matar

riddance ['rɪdəns] *s* supresión, libramiento; **good riddance!** ¡adiós, gracias!, ¡de buena me he librado!

riddle ['rɪdəl] *s* acertijo, adivinanza; (*person or thing hard to understand*) enigma *m;* criba gruesa ‖ *tr* acribillar; destruir (*un argumento; la reputación de una persona*); **to riddle with bullets** acribillar a balazos; **to riddle with questions** acribillar a preguntas

ride [raɪd] *s* paseo ‖ *v* (*pret* **rode** [rod]; *pp* **ridden** ['rɪdən]) *tr* montar (*un caballo*); montar sobre (*los hombros de una persona*); recorrer a caballo; flotar sobre (*las olas*); dominar, tiranizar; (coll) burlarse de; **to ride down** atropellar; vencer; **to ride out** luchar felizmente con (*una tempestad*); aguantar con buen éxito (*una desgracia*) ‖ *intr* montar; pasear en coche o carruaje; **to let ride** (slang) dejar correr; **to take riding** llevar de paseo

rider ['raɪdər] *s* jinete *m;* pasajero

ridge [rɪdʒ] *s* (*of a roof; of earth between two furrows*) caballete *m;* (*of a fabric*) cordoncillo; (*of mountains*) cordillera; (*of two plane surfaces*) arista

ridge'pole' *s* parhilera

ridicule ['rɪdɪ,kjul] *s* irrisión; **to expose to ridicule** poner en ridículo ‖ *tr* ridiculizar

ridiculous [rɪ'dɪkjələs] *adj* ridículo

riding academy *s* escuela de equitación

riding boot *s* bota de montar

riding habit *s* amazona, traje *m* de montar

rife [raɪf] *adj* común, corriente, general; abundante, lleno; **rife with** abundante en, lleno de

riffraff ['rɪf,ræf] *s* bahorrina, canalla

rifle ['raɪfəl] *s* rifle *m*, fusil *m* ‖ *tr* hurtar, robar; escudriñar y robar; desnudar, despojar

rifle range *s* tiro de rifle

rift [rɪft] *s* abertura, raja; desacuerdo, desavenencia

rig [rɪg] *s* equipaje *m;* carruaje *m* con caballo o caballos; traje extraño; (naut) aparejo ‖ *v* (*pret & pp* **rigged;** *ger* **rigging**) *tr* equipar; aprestar, disponer; improvisar; vestir de una manera extraña; arreglar de una manera fraudulenta; (naut) aparejar

rigging [ˈrɪgɪŋ] *s* avíos, instrumentos, equipo; (naut) aparejo, cordaje *m*

right [raɪt] *adj* derecho; verdadero; exacto; conveniente; favorable; sano, normal; bien, correcto; señalado; correspondiente; que se busca, p.ej., **this is the right house** ésta es la casa que se busca; que se necesita, p.ej., **this is the right train** éste es el tren que se necesita; que debe, p.ej., **he is going the right way** sigue el camino que debe; **right or wrong** con razón o sin ella, bueno o malo; **to be all right** estar bien; estar bien de salud; **to be right** tener razón ‖ *adv* derechamente; directamente; correctamente; exactamente; favorablemente; en orden, en buen estado; hacia la derecha; completamente; (coll) muy; mismo, p.ej., **right here** aquí mismo; **all right** muy bien ‖ *interj* ¡bien! ‖ *s* (*justice, reason*) derecho; (*right hand*) derecha; (box) derechazo; (com) derecho; (pol) derecha; **by right** según derecho; **on the right** a la derecha; **to be in the right** tener razón ‖ *tr* enderezar; corregir, rectificar; hacer justicia a; deshacer (*un entuerto*) ‖ *intr* enderezarse

righteous [ˈraɪtʃəs] *adj* recto, justo; virtuoso

right field *s* (baseball) jardín derecho

rightful [ˈraɪtfəl] *adj* justo; legítimo

right'-hand' drive *s* conducción o dirección a la derecha

right-hand man *s* mano derecha, brazo derecho

rightist [ˈraɪtɪst] *adj & s* derechista *mf*

rightly [ˈraɪtli] *adv* derechamente; correctamente; con razón; convenientemente; **rightly or wrongly** con razón o sin ella; **rightly so** a justo título

right mind *s* entero juicio

right of way *s* derecho de tránsito o de paso; (law) servidumbre de paso; (rr) servidumbre de vía; **to yield the right of way** ceder el paso

rights of man *spl* derechos del hombre

right'-wing' *adj* derechista

right-winger [ˈraɪtˈwɪŋər] *s* (coll) derechista *mf*

rigid [ˈrɪdʒɪd] *adj* rígido

rigmarole [ˈrɪgməˌrol] *s* galimatías *m*

rigorous [ˈrɪgərəs] *adj* riguroso

rile [raɪl] *tr* (coll) exasperar

rill [rɪl] *s* arroyuelo

rim [rɪm] *s* canto, borde *m*; (*of a wheel*) llanta; (*of a tire*) aro

rime [raɪm] *s* (*in verse*) rima; (*frost*) escarcha; **without rime or reason** sin ton ni son ‖ *tr & intr* rimar

rind [raɪnd] *s* cáscara, corteza

ring [rɪŋ] *s* (*circular band, line, or mark*) anillo; (*for the finger*) sortija; (*for curtains; for gymnastics*) anilla; (*for nose of animal*) argolla; (*for fruit jars*) círculo de goma; (*for some sport or exhibition*) circo; (*for boxing*) cuadrilátero, ruedo; (*for bullfight*) redondel *m*, ruedo; boxeo; (*of a group of people*) corro; (*of evildoers*) pandilla; (*under the eyes*) ojera; (*of the anchor*) arga-

neo; (*sound of a bell, of a clock*) campanada; (*of a small bell; of the glass of glassware*) tintineo; (*to summon a person*) llamada; (*character, nature, spirit*) tono; **to be in the ring (for)** ser candidato (a); **to run rings around** dar cien vueltas a ‖ *v* (*pret & pp* **ringed**) *tr* cercar, rodear; (*to put a ring on*) anillar ‖ *intr* formar círculo o corro ‖ *v* (*pret* **rang** [ræŋ]; *pp* **rung** [rʌŋ]) *tr* tañer, tocar; (*to peal, ring out*) repicar; llamar al timbre; dar (*las horas la campana del reloj*); llamar por teléfono; **to ring up** llamar por teléfono; marcar (*una compra*) con el timbre ‖ *intr* sonar (*una campana, un timbre, el teléfono*); tintinear (*el choque de copas, una campanilla*); resonar, retumbar; llamar; zumbar (*los oídos*); **to ring for** llamar, llamar al timbre; **to ring off** terminar una llamada por teléfono; **to ring up** llamar por teléfono

ring-around-a-rosy [ˈrɪŋəˌraʊndəˈrozi] *s* juego del corro

ringing [ˈrɪŋɪŋ] *adj* resonante, retumbante ‖ *s* anillamiento; campaneo, repique *m*; (*of the glass of glassware*) tintineo; (*in the ears*) retintín *m*, silbido

ring'lead'er *s* cabecilla *m*

ring'mas'ter *s* hombre encargado de los ejercicios ecuestres y acrobáticos en un circo

ring'side' *s* lugar junto al cuadrilátero; lugar desde el cual se puede ver de cerca

ring'worm' *s* tiña

rink [rɪŋk] *s* patinadero

rinse [rɪns] *s* aclaración, enjuague *m* ‖ *tr* aclarar, enjuagar

riot [ˈraɪ•ət] *s* alboroto, tumulto; regocijos ruidosos; (*of colors*) exhibición brillante; **to run riot** desenfrenarse; crecer lozanamente (*las plantas*) ‖ *intr* alborotarse, amotinarse

rioter [ˈraɪ•ətər] *s* alborotador *m*, amotinado

riot squad *s* pelotón *m* de asalto

rip [rɪp] *s* rasgón *m*, siete *m*; (*open seam*) descosido ‖ *v* (*pret & pp* **ripped**; *ger* **ripping**) *tr* desgarrar, rasgar; descoser (*lo que estaba cosido*) ‖ *intr* desgarrarse, rasgarse; (coll) adelantar o moverse de prisa o con violencia; **to rip out with** (coll) decir con violencia

ripe [raɪp] *adj* maduro; acabado, hecho; dispuesto, preparado; (*boil, tumor*) madurado; (*olive*) negro

ripen [ˈraɪpən] *tr & intr* madurar

ripoff [ˈrɪpˌɔf] *s* (slang) estafa; timo

ripple [ˈrɪpəl] *s* temblor *m*, rizo; (*sound*) murmullo, susurro ‖ *tr* rizar ‖ *intr* rizarse; murmurar, susurrar

rise [raɪz] *s* (*of temperature, prices, a road*) subida; (*of ground, of the voice*) elevación; (*of a heavenly body*) salida; (*of a step*) altura; (*in one's employment*) ascenso; (*of water*) crecida; (*of a source of water*) nacimiento; (*of a valve*) levantamiento; **to get a rise out of** (slang) sacar una réplica mordaz a; **to give rise to** dar origen a ‖ *v* (*pret* **rose** [roz]; *pp* **risen** [ˈrɪzən]) *intr* subir; levantarse; salir (*un astro*); asomar (*un* *peligro*); brotar (*un manantial, una planta*); (*in someone's esteem*) ganar; resucitar; **to rise above** alzarse por encima de; mostrarse superior a; **to rise early** madrugar; **to rise to** ponerse a la altura de

riser ['raɪzər] s contraescalón m, contrahuella; **early riser** madrugador m; **late riser** dormilón m

risk [rɪsk] s riesgo; **to run** o **take a risk** correr riesgo, correr peligro ‖ tr arriesgar; arriesgarse en (*una empresa dudosa*)

risk•y ['rɪski] adj (comp **-ier**; super **-iest**) arriesgado; riesgoso; escabroso

risqué [rɪs'ke] adj escabroso

rite [raɪt] s rito; **last rites** honras fúnebres

ritual ['rɪtʃʊ•əl] adj & s ritual m

riv. abbr **river**

ri•val ['raɪvəl] s rival mf ‖ v (pret & pp **-valed** o **-valled**; ger **-valing** o **-valling**) tr rivalizar con

rival•ry ['raɪvəlri] s (pl **-ries**) rivalidad

river ['rɪvər] s río; **down the river** río abajo; **up the river** río arriba

river basin s cuenca de río

river bed s cauce m

river front s orilla del río

riv'er•side' adj ribereño ‖ s ribera

rivet ['rɪvɪt] s roblón m, remache m; (*e.g., to hold scissors together*) clavillo ‖ tr remachar; clavar (*p.ej., los ojos en una persona*)

rm. abbr **ream, room**

R.N. abbr **registered nurse, Royal Navy**

roach [rotʃ] s cucaracha

road [rod] adj itinerario, caminero ‖ s camino; (naut) rada; **to be in the road** estorbar el paso; incomodar; **to get out of the road** quitarse de en medio

road'bed' s (*of a highway*) firme m; (rr) infraestructura

road'block' s (mil) barricada; (fig) obstáculo

road'house' s posada en el camino

road laborer s peón caminero

road map s mapa itinerario

road service s auxilio en carretera

road'side' s borde m del camino, borde de la carretera

roadside inn s posada en el camino

road sign s señal f de carretera, poste m indicador

road'stead' s rada

road'way' s camino, vía

roam [rom] s vagabundeo ‖ tr vagar por, recorrer a la ventura ‖ intr vagar, andar errante

roar [ror] s bramido, rugido ‖ intr bramar, rugir; reírse a carcajadas

roast [rost] s asado; café tostado ‖ tr asar; tostar (*café*); (coll) despellejar ‖ intr asarse; tostarse

roast beef s rosbif m

roast of beef s carne de vaca asada o para asar

roast pork s carne de cerdo asada

rob [rɑb] v (pret & pp **robbed**; ger **robbing**) tr & intr robar

robber ['rɑbər] s robador m, ladrón m

robber•y ['rɑbəri] s (pl **-ies**) robo

robe [rob] s manto; abrigo; (*of a woman*) traje m, vestido; (*of a professor, judge, etc.*) toga, túnica; (*of a priest*) traje m talar; (*dressing gown*) bata; (*for lap in a carriage*) manta ‖ tr vestir ‖ intr vestirse

robin ['rɑbɪn] s (*in Europe*) petirrojo; (*in North America*) primavera

robot ['robɑt] s robot m

robotics [ro'bɑtɪks] s robótica

robust [ro'bʌst] adj robusto; vigoroso

rock [rɑk] s roca; (*sticking out of water*) escollo; (*one that is thrown*) piedra; (slang) diamante m, piedra preciosa; **on the rocks** arruinado, en pobreza extrema; (*said of hard liquor*) (coll) sobre hielo; (*to sleep*) arrullar; sacudir; **to rock to sleep** adormecer meciendo ‖ intr mecerse; sacudirse ‖ abbr **—rock-'n'-roll**

rock'-bot'tom adj (el) mínimo, (el) más bajo

rock candy s azúcar m cande

rock crystal s cristal m de roca

rocker ['rɑkər] s (*chair*) mecedora; (*curved piece at bottom of rocking chair or cradle*) arco; (mach) balancín m; (mach) eje m de balancín

rocket ['rɑkɪt] s cohete m ‖ intr subir como un cohete

rocket bomb s bomba cohete

rocket launcher [lɔntʃər] s lanzacohetes m

rocket ship s aeronave f cohete

rock garden s jardín m entre rocas

rocking chair s mecedora, sillón m de hamaca

rocking horse s caballo mecedor

rock-'n'-roll ['rɑkən'rol] s rock m

Rock of Gibraltar [dʒɪ'brɔltər] s peñón m de Gibraltar

rock salt s sal f de compás, sal gema

rock singer s rockero, rockera

rock wool s lana mineral

rock•y ['rɑki] adj (comp **-ier**; super **-iest**) rocoso, roqueño; (slange) débil, poco firme

rod [rɑd] s vara; varilla; barra; (*authority*) vara alta; opresión, tiranía; (*of the retina*) bastoncillo; (*elongated microörganism*) bastoncito; (mach) vástago; (surv) jalón m; (Bib) linaje m, raza, vástago; (slang) revólver m, pistola; **to spare the rod** excusar la vara

rodent ['rodənt] adj & s roedor m

rod•man ['rɑdmən] s (pl **-men** [mən]) jalonero, portamira m

roe [ro] s (*deer*) corzo; (*of fish*) hueva

rogue [rog] s bribón m, pícaro

rogues' gallery s colección de retratos de malhechores para uso de la policía

roguish ['rogɪʃ] adj bribón, pícaro; travieso, retozón

rôle o **role** [rol] s papel m; **to play a rôle** desempeñar un papel

roll [rol] s (*of cloth, film, paper, fat, etc.*) rollo; (*roller*) rodillo; (*cake of bread*) panecillo; (*of dice*) echada; (*of a boat*) balance m; (*of a drum*) redoble m; (*of thunder*) retumbo; bamboleo; ondulación; rol m; lista; (*of paper money*) fajo; **to call the roll**

pasar lista ‖ *tr* hacer rodar; empujar hacia adelante; cilindrar, laminar; (*to wrap up with rolling motion*) arrollar; alisar con rodillo; liar (*un cigarrillo*); mover de un lado a otro; poner (*los ojos*) en blanco; tocar redobles con (*el tambor*); vibrar (*la voz; la r*); **to roll one's own** liárselos; **to roll up** arremangar (*p.ej., las mangas*); amontonar (*p.ej., una fortuna*) ‖ *intr* rodar; bambolear; balancear (*un barco*); girar; retumbar (*el trueno*); redoblar (*un tambor*); **to roll around** revolcarse

roll call *s* lista, (el) pasar lista

roller ['rolər] *s* rodillo; (*of a piece of furniture*) ruedecilla; (*of a skate*) rueda; ola larga y creciente

roller bearing *s* cojinete *m* de rodillos

roller coaster *s* montaña rusa

roller skate *s* patín *m* de ruedas

roller towel *s* toalla sin fin

rolling mill ['rolɪŋ] *s* taller *m* de laminación; tren *m* de laminadores

rolling pin *s* rodillo, hataca, rulo

rolling stock *s* (rr) material *m* móvil, material rodante

rolling stone *s* piedra movediza

roll'-top' desk *s* escritorio norteamericano, escritorio de cortina corrediza

roly-poly ['roli'poli] *adj* regordete, rechoncho

Rom. *abbr* **Roman, Romance**

roman ['romən] *adj* (typ) redondo ‖ *s* (typ) letra redonda ‖ **Roman** *adj & s* romano

Roman candle *s* vela romana

Roman Catholic *adj & s* católico romano

romance [ro'mæns] o ['romæns] *s* (*tale of chivalry*) roman *m;* cuento de aventuras; cuento de amor; intriga amorosa; novela sentimental; (mus) romanza ‖ [ro'mæns] *intr* contar o escribir romances, cuentos de aventuras o cuentos de amor; pensar o hablar de un modo romántico; exagerar, mentir ‖ **Romance** ['romæns] o [ro'mæns] *adj* (*Neo-Latin*) romance o románico

romance languages *spl* lenguas romances *or* románicas

romance of chivalry *s* libro de caballerías

Roman Empire *s* Imperio romano

Romanesque [,romən'ɛsk] *adj & s* románico

Roman nose *s* nariz aguileña

romantic [ro'mæntɪk] *adj* romántico; (*spot, place*) encantador

romanticism [ro'mæntɪ,sɪzəm] *s* romanticismo

romp [ramp] *intr* corretear, triscar

rompers ['rampərz] *spl* traje holgado de juego

roof [ruf] o [rʊf] *s* (*top outer covering of a house*) tejado; (*of a car or bus*) imperial *f*, tejadillo; (*of the mouth*) paladar *m;* (*of heaven*) bóveda; (*home, dwelling*) (fig) techo; **to raise the roof** (slang) poner el grito en el cielo ‖ *tr* techar

roofer ['rufər] o ['rʊfər] *s* techador *m*, pizarrero

roof garden *s* (*garden on the roof*) pérgola, azotea de baile y diversión

rook [rʊk] *s* (*bird*) grajo; (*in chess*) roque *m* ‖ *tr* trampear

rookie ['rʊki] *s* (slang) bisoño, novato

room [rum] o [rʊm] *s* aposento, cuarto, habitación, pieza; espacio, sitio, lugar *m;* ocasión; **to make room** abrir paso, hacer lugar ‖ *intr* alojarse

room and board *s* pensión completa

room clerk *s* empleado en la recepción, encargado de las reservas

roomer ['rumər] *s* inquilino

rooming house *s* casa donde se alquilan cuartos

room'mate' *s* compañero de cuarto

room•y ['rumi] *adj* (*comp* **-ier;** *super* **-iest**) amplio, espacioso

roost [rust] *s* percha de gallinero; gallinero; lugar *m* de descanso; **to rule the roost** ser el amo del cotarro, tener el mando y el palo ‖ *intr* descansar (*las aves*) en la percha; estar alojado; pasar la noche

rooster ['rustər] *s* gallo

root [rut] o [rʊt] *s* raíz *f;* **to get to the root of** profundizar; **to take root** echar raíces ‖ *tr* hocicar, hozar ‖ *intr* arraigar; **to root for** (slang) gritar alentando

rooter ['rutər] o ['rʊtər] *s* (slang) hincha *mf*

rope [rop] *s* cuerda; (*of a hangman*) dogal *m;* (*to catch an animal*) lazo; **to jump rope** saltar a la comba; **to know the ropes** (slang) saber todas las tretas; espabilarse ‖ *tr* atar con una cuerda; coger con lazo; **to rope in** (slang) embaucar, engañar

rope'walk'er *sl* funámbulo, volatinero

rosa•ry ['rozəri] *s* (*pl* **-ries**) rosario

rose [roz] *adj* de color de rosa ‖ *s* rosa

rose'bud' *s* pimpollo, capullo de rosa

rose'bush' *s* rosal *m*

rose'-col'ored *adj* rosado; **to see everything through rose-colored glasses** verlo todo de color de rosa

rose garden *s* rosaleda, rosalera

rose hip *s* (bot) cinarrodón *m;* eterio

rosemar•y ['roz,mɛri] *s* (*pl* **-ies**) romero

rose of Sharon ['ʃɛrən] *s* granado blanco, rosa de Siria

rose window *s* rosetón *m*

rose'wood' *s* palisandro

rosin ['razɪn] *s* colofonia, brea seca

roster ['rastər] *s* catálogo, lista; horario escolar, horas de clase

rostrum ['rastrəm] *s* tribuna

ros•y ['rozi] *adj* (*comp* **-ier;** *super* **-iest**) rosado, sonrosado; alegre

rot [rat] *s* podredumbre; (slang) tontería ‖ *v* (*pret & pp* **rotted;** *ger* **rotting**) *tr* pudrir ‖ *intr* pudrirse

rotate ['rotet] o [ro'tet] *tr* hacer girar; alternar ‖ *intr* girar; alternar

rote [rot] *s* rutina, repetición maquinal; **by rote** de memoria, maquinalmente

rot'gut' *s* (slang) matarratas *m*

rotogravure [,rotəgrə'vjʊr] o [,rotə'grevjʊr] *s* rotograbado

rotten ['ratən] *adj* putrefacto, pútrido; corrompido

rotund [ro'tʌnd] *adj* redondo de cuerpo; (*language*) redondo

rouge [ruʒ] *s* arrebol *m*, colorete *m* ‖ *tr* arrebolar, pintar ‖ *intr* arrebolarse, pintarse

rough [rʌf] *adj* áspero; (*sea*) agitado, picado; (*crude, unwrought*) tosco, grosero; aproximado ‖ *tr* —**to rough it** vivir sin comodidades, hacer vida campestre

rough'cast' *s* modelo tosco; mezcla gruesa ‖ *v* (*pret & pp* -**cast**) *tr* (*to prepare in rough form*) bosquejar; dar a (*la pared*) una capa de mezcla gruesa

rough copy *s* borrador *m*

roughly ['rʌfli] *adv* asperamente; brutalmente; aproximadamente

roulette [ru'lɛt] *s* ruleta

round [raund] *adj* redondo ‖ *adv* redondamente; alrededor; de boca en boca; por todas partes ‖ *prep* alrededor de; (*e.g., the corner*) a la vuelta de; cerca de; acá y allá en ‖ *s* camino, circuito; (*of a policeman; of visits; of drinks or cigars*) ronda; (*of applause; discharge of guns*) salva; (*discharge of a single gun*) disparo, tiro; (*of people*) corro, círculo; (*of golf*) partido; rutina, serie *f*, sucesión; redondez *f*; revolución; (box) asalto; **to go the rounds** ir de boca en boca; ir de mano en mano ‖ *tr* (*to make round*) redondear; cercar, rodear; doblar (*una esquina, un promontorio*); **to round off** u **out** redondear; acabar, completar, perfeccionar; **to round up** juntar, recoger; rodear (*el ganado*)

roundabout ['raundə,baut] *adj* indirecto ‖ *s* curso indirecto; (Brit) tío vivo; (Brit) glorieta de tráfico

rounder ['raundər] *s* (coll) pródigo; (coll) catavinos *m*, borrachín habitual

round'house' *s* cocherón *m*, casa de máquinas, depósito de locomotoras

round-shouldered ['raund,ʃoldərd] *adj* cargado de espaldas

Round Table *s* Tabla Redonda

round'-trip' ticket *s* billete *m* de ida y vuelta

round'up' *s* (*of cattle*) rodeo; (*of criminals*) redada; (*of old friends*) reunión

rouse [rauz] *tr* despertar; excitar, provocar; levantar (*la caza*) ‖ *intr* despertarse, despabilarse

rout [raut] *s* derrota; fuga desordenada ‖ *tr* derrotar; poner en fuga desordenada; arrancar hozando ‖ *intr* hozar

route [rut] o [raut] *s* ruta; itinerario ‖ *tr* encaminar

routine [ru'tin] *adj* rutinario ‖ *s* rutina

rove [rov] *intr* andar errante, vagar

row [rau] *s* (coll) camorra, pendencia, riña; (coll) alboroto, bullicio; (coll) balumba; **to raise a row** (coll) armar camorra ‖ [ro] *s* fila, hilera; (*of houses*) crujía; **in a row** seguidos, p.ej., **five hours in a row** cinco horas seguidas ‖ *intr* remar

rowboat ['ro,bot] *s* bote *m*, bote de remos

row•dy ['raudi] *adj* (*comp* -**dier**; *super* -**diest**) gamberro ‖ *s* (*pl* -**dies**) gamberro

rower ['ro•ər] *s* remero

royal ['rɔɪ•əl] *adj* real; (*magnificent, splendid*) regio

royalist ['rɔɪ•əlɪst] *s* realista *mf*

royal•ty ['rɔɪ•əlti] *s* (*pl* -**ties**) realeza; personaje *m* real, personajes reales; derechos de autor; derechos de inventor

r.p.m. *abbr* **revolutions per minute**

R.R. *abbr* **railroad, Right Reverend**

rub [rʌb] *s* frotación, roce *m;* **there's the rub** ahí está el busilis ‖ *v* (*pret & pp* **rubbed**; *ger* **rubbing**) *tr* frotar; **to rub elbows with** rozarse mucho con; **to rub out** borrar; (slang) asesinar ‖ *intr* frotar; **to rub off** quitarse frotando; borrarse

rubber ['rʌbər] *s* caucho, goma; goma de borrar; chanclo, zapato de goma; (*in bridge*) robre *m* ‖ *intr* (slang) estirar el cuello o volver la cabeza para ver

rubber band *s* liga de goma

rubber plant *s* árbol *m* del caucho

rubber plantation *s* cauchal *m*

rubber stamp *s* cajetín *m*, sello de goma; (*with a person's signature*) estampilla; (coll) persona que aprueba sin reflexionar

rub'ber-stamp' *tr* estampar con un sello de goma; (*with a person's signature*) estampillar; (coll) aprobar sin reflexionar

rubbish ['rʌbɪʃ] *s* basura, desecho, desperdicios; (coll) disparate *m*, tontería

rubble ['rʌbəl] *s* (*broken stone*) ripio; (*masonry*) mampostería

rub'down' *s* masaje *m*, fricción

rube [rub] *s* (slang) isidro, rústico

ruble ['rubəl] *s* rublo

ru•by ['rubi] *s* (*pl* -**bies**) rubí *m*

rudder ['rʌdər] *s* timón *m*, gobernalle *m*

rud•dy ['rʌdi] *adj* (*comp* -**dier**; *super* -**diest**) coloradote, rubicundo;

rude [rud] *adj* rudo; desacomodido (SAm)

rudiment ['rudɪmənt] *s* rudimento

rudeness ['rudnɪs] *s* malcriadez *f*, malacrianza

rue [ru] *tr* lamentar, arrepentirse de

rueful ['rufəl] *adj* lamentable; triste

ruffian ['rʌfi•ən] *s* hombre grosero y brutal

ruffle ['rʌfəl] *s* arruga; (*of drum*) redoble *m;* (sew) volante *m* ‖ *tr* arrugar; agitar, descomponer; enojar, molestar; confundir; redoblar (*el tambor*); (sew) fruncir un volante en, adornar o guarnecer con volante

rug [rʌg] *s* alfombra; alfombrilla; (*lap robe*) manta

rugged ['rʌgɪd] *adj* áspero, rugoso; recio, vigoroso; tempestuoso

ruin ['ru•ɪn] *s* ruina ‖ *tr* arruinar; estropear; echar a perder

rule [rul] *s* regla; autoridad, mando; regla de imprenta; (*reign*) reinado; (*of a court of law*) decisión, fallo; **as a rule** por regla general; **to be the rule** ser lo que se hace ‖ *tr* gobernar, regir; dirigir, guiar; contener, reprimir; (*to mark with lines*) reglar; (law) decidir, determinar; **to rule out** excluir, rechazar ‖ *intr* gobernar, regir; prevalecer; **to rule over** gobernar, regir

rule of law *s* régimen *m* de justicia

ro
ru

ruler [ˈrulər] *s* gobernante *mf;* soberano; (*for ruling lines*) regla

ruling [ˈrulɪŋ] *adj* gobernante, dirigente, imperante ‖ *s* (*of a court or judge*) decisión, fallo; (*of paper*) rayado

rum [rʌm] *s* ron *m;* (*any alcoholic drink*) (U.S.A.) aguardiente *m*

Rumanian [ruˈmenɪ•ən] *adj & s* rumano

rumble [ˈrʌmbəl] *s* retumbo; (*of the intestines*) rugido; (slang) riña entre pandillas ‖ *intr* retumbar; avanzar retumbando

ruminate [ˈrumɪˌnet] *tr & intr* rumiar

rummage [ˈrʌmɪdʒ] *tr & intr* buscar revolviéndolo todo

rummage sale *s* venta de prendas usadas

rumor [ˈrumər] *s* rumor *m;* (coll) díceres *mpl;* bolado (CAm) ‖ *tr* rumorear; **it is rumored that** se rumorea que

rump [rʌmp] *s* anca, nalga; (*cut of beef*) cuarto trasero

rumple [ˈrʌmpəl] *s* arruga ‖ *tr* arrugar, ajar, chafar ‖ *intr* arrugarse

rumpus [ˈrʌmpəs] *s* (coll) batahola, alboroto; **to raise a rumpus** (coll) armar la de San Quintín

run [rʌn] *s* carrera; clase *f,* tipo; arroyo; (*e.g., in a stocking*) carrera; (*on a bank by depositors*) asedio; (*of consecutive performances of a play*) serie *f;* (baseball & mus) carrera; **in the long run** a la larga; **on the run** a escape; en fuga desordenada; **the common run of people** el común de las gentes; **the general run of** la generalidad de; **to have a long run** permanecer en cartel durante mucho tiempo; **to have the run of** hallar el secreto de; tener libertad de ir y venir por ‖ *v* (*pret* **ran** [ræn]; *pp* **run;** *ger* **running**) *tr* hacer funcionar; dirigir; manejar; trazar, tirar (*una línea*); exhibir (*un cine*); hacer (*mandados*); tener como candidato; burlar, violar (*un bloqueo*); tener (*calentura*); correr (*un caballo; un riesgo*); **to run down** cazar y matar; derribar; atropellar (*a un peatón*); (coll) denigrar, desacreditar; **to run in** rodar (*un nuevo coche*); **to run off** tocar (*una pieza de música*); tirar, imprimir; **to run up** (coll) aumentar (*gastos*) ‖ *intr* correr; (*on wheels*) rodar; darse prisa; trepar (*la vid*); ir y venir (*un vapor*); supurar (*una llaga*); colar (*un líquido*); correrse (*un color o tinte*); presentar su candidatura; andar, funcionar, marchar; deshilarse (*las medias*); migrar (*los peces*); estar en fuerza; (*to be worded or written*) rezar; **to run across** dar con, tropezar con; **to run away** correr, huir; desbocarse (*un caballo*); **to run down** escurrir, gotear (*un líquido*); descargarse (*un acumulador*); distenderse (*el muelle de un reloj*); acabarse la cuerda, p.ej., **the watch ran down** se acabó la cuerda; **to run for** presentar su candidatura a; **to run in the family** venir de familia; **to run into** tropezar con; chocar con, topar con; **to run off the track** descarrilar (*un tren*); **to run out** salir; expirar, terminar; acabarse; agotarse; **to run out of** acabársele a uno, e.g.,

I have run out of money se me ha acabado el dinero; **to run over** atropellar (*a un peatón*); registrar a la ligera; pasar por encima; leer rápidamente; rebosar (*un líquido*); **to run through** disipar rápidamente (*una fortuna*); registrar a la ligera; estar difundido en

run'a•way' *adj* fugitivo; (*horse*) desbocado ‖ *s* fugitivo; caballo desbocado; fuga

run'-down' *adj* desmedrado; desmantelado; inculto; (*clock spring*) sin cuerda, distendido; (*storage battery*) descargado

rung [rʌŋ] *s* (*of ladder or chair*) travesaño; (*of wheel*) radio, rayo

runner [ˈrʌnər] *s* corredor *m;* caballo de carreras; mensajero; (*of an ice skate*) cuchilla; (*of a sleigh*) patín *m;* (*long narrow rug*) pasacaminos *m;* (*strip of cloth for table top*) tapete *m;* (*in stockings*) carrera

run'ner-up' *s* (*pl* **runners-up**) subcampeón *m*

running [ˈrʌnɪŋ] *adj* corredor; (*expenses; water*) corriente; (*knot*) corredizo; (*sore*) supurante; (*writing*) cursivo; continuo; consecutivo; en marcha; (*start*) (*sport*) lanzado ‖ *s* carrera, corrida; administración, dirección; marcha, funcionamiento; **to be in the running** tener esperanzas o posibilidades de ganar

running board *s* estribo

running head *s* titulillo

running start *s* (*sport*) salida lanzada

run'off' e•lec'tion *s* votación de desempate

run-of-mine coal [ˈrʌnəvˈmaɪn] *s* carbón *m* tal como sale

run'-of-the-mill' *adj* (coll) ordinario; mediocre

run'proof' *adj* indesmallable

runt [rʌnt] *s* enano, hombrecillo; (*little child*) redrojo; animal achaparrado

run'way' *s* (*of a stream*) cauce *m;* senda trillada; (aer) pista de aterrizaje

rupture [ˈrʌptʃər] *s* ruptura; (pathol) quebradura; (*break in relations*) ruptura ‖ *tr* romper; causar una hernia en ‖ *intr* romperse; padecer hernia

rural free delivery [ˈrurəl] *s* distribución gratuita del correo en el campo

rural police *s* guardia civil

rural policeman *s* guardia civil *m*

ruse [ruz] *s* astucia, artimaña

rush [rʌʃ] *adj* urgente ‖ *s* prisa grande, precipitación; agolpamiento de gente; (bot) junco; **in a rush** de prisa ‖ *tr* empujar con violencia o prisa; despachar con prontitud; (slang) cortejar insistentemente (*a una mujer*); **to rush through** ejecutar de prisa, despachar rápidamente; expedir ‖ *intr* lanzarse, precipitarse; venir de prisa, ir de prisa; actuar con prontitud; **to rush through** lanzarse a través de, lanzarse por entre

rush-bottomed chair [ˈrʌʃˈbatəmd] *s* silla de junco

rush hour *s* hora de aglomeración, horas de punta, horas de afluencia

rush'light' *s* mariposa, lamparilla

rush order s pedido urgente
russet ['rʌsɪt] adj canelo
Russia ['rʌʃə] s Rusia
Russian ['rʌʃən] adj & s ruso
rust [rʌst] s orín m, moho, herrumbre; (agr) roña, roya; color rojizo o anaranjado ‖ tr aherrumbrar ‖ intr aherrumbrarse
rustic ['rʌstɪk] adj rústico; sencillo, sin artificio ‖ s rústico
rustle ['rʌsəl] s susurro, crujido ‖ tr hacer susurrar, hacer crujir; hurtar (ganado) ‖

intr susurrar, crujir; (slang) trabajar con ahinco
rusty ['rʌsti] adj (comp -ier; super -iest) herrumbroso, mohoso; rojizo; (out of practice) empolvado, desusado, remoto
rut [rʌt] s (track, groove in road) rodada, bache m; hábito arraigado; (sexual excitement in animals) celo; (period of this excitement) brama
ruthless ['ruθlɪs] adj despiadado, cruel
Ry. abbr **railway**
rye [raɪ] s centeno; whisky de centeno

S

S, s [ɛs] decimonona letra del alfabeto inglés
s abbr **second, shilling, singular**
Sabbath ['sæbəθ] s (of Jews) sábado; (of Christians) domínica; **to keep the Sabbath** observar el descanso dominical, guardar el domingo
saber ['sebər] s sable m
sable ['sebəl] adj negro ‖ s marta cebellina; **sables** vestidos de luto
sabotage ['sæbə,tɑʒ] s sabotaje m ‖ tr & intr sabotear
saccharin ['sækərɪn] s sacarina
sachet ['sæʃe] o [sæ'ʃe] s polvo oloroso; saquito de perfumes
sack [sæk] s saco; vino blanco generoso; (mil) saqueo, saco; (of an employee) (slang) despedida ‖ tr ensacar; saquear, pillar; (slang) despedir (a un empleado)
sack'cloth' s harpillera; (worn for penitence) cilicio
sacrament ['sækrəmənt] s sacramento
sacred ['sekrəd] adj sagrado
sacrifice ['sækrɪ,faɪs] s sacrificio; **at a sacrifice** con pérdida ‖ tr sacrificar; (to sell at a loss) malvender ‖ intr sacrificar; sacrificarse
Sacrifice of the Mass s sacrificio del altar
sacrilege ['sækrɪlɪdʒ] s sacrilegio
sacrilegious [,sækrɪ'lɪdʒəs] o [,sækrɪ'lɪdʒəs] adj sacrílego
sacristan ['sækrɪstən] s sacristán m
sacris·ty ['sækrɪsti] s (pl -ties) sacristía
sad [sæd] adj (comp **sadder**; super **saddest**) triste; (slang) malo
sadden ['sædən] tr entristecer ‖ intr entristecerse
saddle ['sædəl] s silla de montar; (of a bicycle) sillín m ‖ tr ensillar; **to saddle with** echar a cuestas a
sad'dle·bags' spl alforjas
sad'dle·bow' [,bo] s arzón delantero
sad'dle·tree' s arzón m
sadist ['sædɪst] s sádico
sadistic [sæ'dɪstɪk] adj sádico
sadness ['sædnɪs] s tristeza

safe [sef] adj seguro, ileso, salvo; cierto, digno de confianza; sin peligro, a salvo; **safe and sound** sano y salvo; **safe from** a salvo de ‖ s caja fuerte, caja de caudales
safe'-con'duct s salvoconducto
safe'-crack'er s ladrón m de cajas de caudales
safe'-depos'it box s caja de seguridad
safe'guard' s salvaguardia, medida de seguridad ‖ tr salvaguardar
safe·ty ['sefti] adj de seguridad ‖ s (pl -ties) seguridad; **to parachute to safety** lanzarse en paracaídas; **to reach safety** ponerse a salvo, llegar a lugar seguro
safety belt s (aer, aut) correa de seguridad, cinturón m de seguridad; (naut) cinturón m salvavidas; **retractable safety belt** cinturón m retráctil
safety match s fósforo de seguridad
safety pin s imperdible m, alfiler m de seguridad, gacilla
safety rail s guardarriel m
safety razor s maquinilla de seguridad
safety valve s válvula de seguridad
safety zone s (for pedestrians) isla de peatones or de seguridad
saffron ['sæfrən] adj azafranado ‖ s azafrán m ‖ tr azafranar
sag [sæg] s comba, combadura; (e.g., of a cable) flecha ‖ v (pret & pp **sagged**; ger **sagging**) intr combarse; (to slacken, yield) aflojar, ceder, doblegarse; bajar (los precios)
sagacious [sə'geʃəs] adj sagaz
sage ['sedʒ] adj sabio, cuerdo ‖ s sabio; (bot) salvia; (bot) artemisa
sage'brush' s (bot) artemisa
Sagittarius [,sædʒə'tɛriəs] s (astr) Sagitario
sail [sel] s vela; barco de vela; paseo en barco de vela; **to set sail** hacerse a la vela; **under full sail** a vela llena ‖ tr gobernar (un barco de vela); navegar (un mar, río, etc.) ‖ intr navegar, navegar a la vela; salir, salir de viaje; deslizarse, flotar, volar; **to sail into** (slang) atacar, regañar, reñir

sail'boat' *s* barco de vela, buque *m* de vela, velero

sail'cloth' *s* lona, paño

sailing ['seliŋ] *adj* de salida ‖ *s* paseo en barco de vela; navegación; salida

sailing vessel *s* buque velero

sailor ['selər] *s* (*one who makes a living sailing*) marinero; (*an enlisted man in the navy*) marino

saint [sent] *adj & s* santo ‖ *tr* (coll) canonizar

saintliness ['sentlinis] *s* santidad

Saint Vitus's dance ['vaɪtəsəs] *s* (pathol) baile *m* de San Vito

sake [sek] *s* respeto, bien, amor *m;* **for his sake** por su bien; **for the sake of** por, por motivo de, por amor a; **for your own sake** por su propio bien

salaam [sə'lɑm] *s* zalema ‖ *tr* saludar con zalemas, hacer zalemas a

salable ['seləbəl] *adj* vendible

salad ['sæləd] *s* ensalada

salad bowl *s* ensaladera

salad oil *s* aceite *m* de comer

Salamis ['sæləmɪs] *s* Salamina

sala·ry ['sæləri] *s* (*pl* **-ries**) sueldo

sale [sel] *s* venta; (*auction*) almoneda, subasta; **for sale** de venta; **se vende(n)**

sales'clerk' *s* dependiente *mf* de tienda

sales exhibit *s* exhibición-venta, exposición-venta

sales'la'dy *s* (*pl* **-dies**) venedora

sales·man ['selzmən] *s* (*pl* **-men** [mən]) vendedor *m*, dependiente *m* de tienda

sales manager *s* gerente *m* de ventas

sales'man·ship' *s* arte de vender

sales'room' *s* salón *m* de ventas; salón de exhibición

sales talk *s* argumento para inducir a comprar

sales tax *s* impuesto sobre ventas

saliva [sə'laɪvə] *s* saliva

sallow ['sælo] *adj* cetrino

sal·ly ['sæli] *s* (*pl* **-lies**) paseo, viaje *m;* ímpetu *m*, arranque *m;* salida, ocurrencia; (mil) salida, surtida ‖ *v,* (*pret & pp* **-lied**) *intr* salir, hacer una salida; ir de paseo; **to sally forth** salir, avanzar con denuedo

salmon ['sæmən] *s* salmón *m*

salon [sæ'lɑn] *s* salón *m*

saloon [sə'lun] *s* cantina, taberna; (*on a steamer*) salón *m*

saloon'keep'er *s* tabernero

salt [sɔlt] *s* sal *f;* **to be not worth one's salt** no valer (*uno*) el pan que come ‖ *tr* salar; (*to preserve with salt*) salpresar; marinar (*el pescado*); salgar (*al ganado*); **to salt away** (slang) ahorrar, guardar para uso futuro

salt'cel'lar *s* salero

salted peanuts *spl* saladillos

saltine [sɔl'tin] *s* galletita salada

saltish ['sɔltɪʃ] *adj* salobre

salt lick *s* salero, lamedero

salt of the earth, the lo mejor del mundo

salt'pe'ter *s* (*potassium nitrate*) salitre *m;* (*sodium nitrate*) nitro de Chile

salt'sha'ker *s* salero

salt·y ['sɔlti] *adj* (*comp* **-ier;** *super* **-iest**) salado

salubrious [sə'lubrɪ·əs] *adj* salubre

salutation [ˌsæljə'teʃən] *s* salutación

salute [sə'lut] *s* saludo ‖ *tr* saludar

Salvadoran [ˌsælvə'dorən] o **Salvadorian** [ˌsælvə'dorɪ·ən] *adj & s* salvadoreño

salvage ['sælvɪdʒ] *s* salvamento ‖ *tr* salvar; recobrar

Salvation Army [sæl'veʃən] *s* ejército de Salvación

salve [sæv] o [sɑv] *s* ungüento ‖ *tr* curar con ungüento; preservar; aliviar

sal·vo ['sælvo] *s* (*pl* **-vos** o **-voes**) salva

Samaritan [sə'mærɪtən] *adj & s* samaritano

same [sem] *adj & pron indef* mismo; **it's all the same to me** lo mismo me da; **just the same** lo mismo, sin embargo; **same . . . as** mismo . . . que

samite ['sæmaɪt] o ['semaɪt] *s* jamete *m*

sample ['sæmpəl] *s* muestra ‖ *tr* catar, probar

sample copy *s* ejemplar *m* muestra

sancti·fy ['sæŋktɪˌfaɪ] *v* (*pret & pp* **-fied**) *tr* santificar

sanctimonious [ˌsæŋktɪ'monɪ·əs] *adj* santurrón

sanction ['sæŋkʃən] *s* sanción ‖ *tr* sancionar

sanctuar·y ['sæŋktʃʊˌɛri] *s* (*pl* **-ies**) santuario; asilo, refugio; **to take sanctuary** acogerse a sagrado

sand [sænd] *s* arena ‖ *tr* enarenar; lijar con papel de lija

sandal ['sændəl] *s* sandalia; cacle *m* (Mex)

san'dal·wood' *s* (bot) sándalo

sand'bag' *s* saco de arena

sand'bank' *s* banco de arena

sand bar *s* barra de arena

sand'blast' *s* chorro de arena ‖ *tr* limpiar con chorro de arena

sand'box' *s* (rr) arenero

sand dune *s* duna, médano

sand'glass' *s* reloj de arena, ampolleta

sand' pa'per *s* papel *m* de lija ‖ *tr* lijar

sand'stone' *s* piedra arenisca

sand'storm' *s* tempestad de arena

sandwich ['sændwɪtʃ] *s* emparedado, sandwich *m* ‖ *tr* intercalar

sandwich man *s* hombre-anuncio

sand·y ['sændi] *adj* (*comp* **-ier;** *super* **-iest**) arenoso; (*hair*) rufo; cambiante, movible

sane [sen] *adj* cuerdo, sensato; (*principles*) sano

sanguinary ['sæŋgwɪnˌɛri] *adj* sanguinario

sanguine ['sæŋgwɪn] *adj* confiado, esperanzado; (*countenance*) coloradote

sanitary ['sænɪˌtɛri] *adj* sanitario

sanitary napkin *s* compresa higiénica

sanitation [ˌsænɪ'teʃən] *s* (*sanitary measures*) sanidad; (*drainage*) saneamiento

sanity ['sænɪti] *s* cordura, sensatez *f*

Santa Claus ['sæntəˌklɔz] *s* el Papá Noel, San Nicolás

sap [sæp] *s* savia; (mil) zapa; (coll) necio, tonto ‖ *v* (*pret & pp* **sapped;** *ger* **sapping**) *tr* agotar, debilitar; zapar, socavar

sap'head' *s* (coll) cabeza de chorlito

sapling ['sæplɪŋ] s árbol m muy joven, pimpollo; jovenzuelo, mozuelo

sapphire ['sæfaɪr] s zafiro

saraband ['særə,bænd] s zarabanda

Saracen ['særəsən] adj & s sarraceno

Saragossa [,særə'gɑsə] s Zaragoza

sarcasm ['sɑrkæzəm] s sarcasmo; escopetazo (SAm)

sarcastic [sɑr'kæstɪk] adj sarcástico

sardine [sɑr'din] s sardina; **packed in like sardines** como sardinas en banasta o en lata

Sardinia [sɑr'dɪnɪ•ə] s Cerdeña

Sardinian [sɑr'dɪnɪ•ən] adj & s sardo

sarsaparilla [,sɑrsəpə'rɪlə] s zarzaparrilla

sash [sæʃ] s banda, faja; (of a window) marco

sash window s ventana de guillotina

satchel ['sætʃəl] s maletín m; (of a schoolboy) cartapacio

sateen [sæ'tin] s satén m

satellite ['sætə,laɪt] s satélite m

satellite country s país m satélite

satiate ['seʃɪ,et] adj ahito, harto ‖ tr saciar

satin ['sætən] s raso

satinet [,sætɪ'nɛt] s rasete m

satiric(al) [sə'tɪrɪk(əl)] adj satírico

satirist ['sætɪrɪst] s satírico

satirize ['sætɪ,raɪz] tr & intr satirizar

satisfaction [,sætɪs'fækʃən] s satisfacción

satisfactory [,sætɪs'fæktərɪ] adj satisfactorio

satis•fy ['sætɪs,faɪ] v (pret & pp -ified) tr & intr satisfacer

saturate ['sætʃə,ret] tr saturar

Saturday ['sætərdɪ] s sábado

sauce [sɔs] s salsa; moje f, mojete m; (of fruit) compota; (of chocolate) crema; gracia, viveza; (coll) insolencia, lenguaje descomedido ‖ tr condimentar ‖ [sɔs] o [sæs] tr (coll) ser respondón con

sauce′pan′ s cacerola

saucer ['sɔsər] s platillo

sau•cy ['sɔsɪ] adj (comp -cier; super -ciest) descarado, insolente; gracioso, vivo

sauerkraut ['saʊr,kraʊt] s chucruta

saunter ['sɔntər] s paseo tranquilo y alegre ‖ intr dar un paseo tranquilo y alegre; pasear tranquila y alegremente

sausage ['sɔsɪdʒ] s salchicha, embutido; moronga (Mex)

savage ['sævɪdʒ] adj & s salvaje, mf

savant ['sævənt] s sabio, erudito

save [sev] prep salvo, excepto, menos ‖ tr salvar (p.ej., una vida, un alma); ahorrar (dinero); conservar, guardar, horrar; proteger, amparar; **God save the Queen!** ¡Dios guarde a la Reina!; **to save face** salvar las apariencias

saving ['sevɪŋ] prep, salvo, excepto; con el debido respeto a ‖ adj económico ‖ **savings** spl ahorros, economías

savings account s cuenta de ahorros

savings bank s banco de ahorros, caja de ahorros

savior ['sevjər] s salvador m

Saviour ['sevjər] s Salvador m

savor ['sevər] s sabor m ‖ tr saborear ‖ intr oler; **to savor of** oler a, saber a

savor•y ['sevərɪ] adj (comp -ier; super -iest) sabroso; picante; fragante ‖ s (pl -ies) (bot) ajedrea

saw [sɔ] s (tool) sierra; proverbio, refrán m ‖ tr aserrar, serrar

saw′buck′ s cabrilla, caballete m

saw′dust′ s aserrín m, serrín m

saw′horse′ s cabrilla, caballete m

saw′mill′ s aserradero, serrería; montero (Mex)

Saxon ['sæksən] adj & s sajón m

saxophone ['sæksə,fon] s saxofón m

say [se] s decir m; **to have one's say** decir su parecer ‖ v (pret & pp said [sɛd] tr decir; **I should say so!** ¡ya lo creo!; **it is said** se dice; **no sooner said than done** dicho y hecho; **that is to say** es decir, esto es; **to go without saying** caerse de su peso

saying ['se•ɪŋ] s dicho; proverbio, refrán m; **sayings** (rumor) díceres mpl

sc. abbr scene, science, scruple, scilicet (Lat) namely

scab [skæb] s costra; (strikebreaker) esquirol m; (slang) bribón m, golfo

scabbard ['skæbərd] s funda, vaina

scab•by ['skæbɪ] adj (comp -bier; super -biest) costroso; (coll) ruin, vil

scabrous ['skæbrəs] adj escabroso

scads [skædz] spl (slang) montones mpl

scaffold ['skæfəld] s andamio; (to execute a criminal) cadalso, patíbulo

scaffolding ['skæfəldɪŋ]s andamiaje m

scald [skɔld] tr escaldar

scale [skel] s escama; balanza; platillo de balanza; (e.g., of a map) escala; (mus) escala; **on a scale of** en escala de; **on a large scale** en grande escala; **scales** balanza ‖ tr escamar; descortezar, descostrar; escalar, subir, trepar; graduar ‖ intr descamarse; descortezarse, descostrarse; subir, trepar

scallop ['skɑləp] o ['skæləp] s concha de peregrino; (shell or dish for serving fish) concha; (thin slice of meat) escalope m; (on edge of cloth) festón ‖ tr cocer (p.ej., ostras) en su concha; festonear

scalp [skælp] s cuero cabelludo ‖ tr escalpar; comprar y revender (billetes de teatro) a precios extraoficiales

scalpel ['skælpəl] s escalpelo

scal•y ['skelɪ] adj (comp -ier; super -iest) escamoso

scamp [skæmp] s bribón m, golfo

scamper ['skæmpər] intr escaparse precipitadamente; **to scamper away** escaparse precipitadamente

scan [skæn] v (pret & pp scanned; ger scanning) tr escudriñar; escandir (versos); (telv) explorar; (coll) dar un vistazo a

scandal ['skændəl] s escándalo

scandalize ['skændə,laɪz] tr escandalizar

scandalous ['skændələs] adj escandaloso

Scandinavian [,skændɪ'nevɪ•ən] adj & s escandinavo

scanning ['skænɪŋ] s (telv) escansión, exploración

scansion ['skænʃən] s escansión

scant [skænt] *adj* escaso, insuficiente; solo, apenas suficiente ‖ *tr* escatimar

scant·y ['skænti] *adj* (*comp* **-ier;** *super* **-iest**) escaso, insuficiente, poco suficiente; (*clothing*) ligero

scape'goat' *s* cabeza de turco, víctima propiciatoria

scar [skɑr] *s* cicatriz *f*, señal *f*, lacra ‖ *v* (*pret* & *pp* **scarred;** *ger* **scarring**) *tr* señalar, marcar ‖ *intr* cicatrizarse

scarce [skɛrs] *adj* escaso, raro; **to make oneself scarce** (coll) no dejarse ver

scarcely ['skɛrsli] *adv* apenas; probablemente no; ciertamente no; **scarcely ever** raramente

scarci·ty ['skɛrsɪti] *s* (*pl* **-ties**) escasez *f*, carestía

scare [skɛr] *s* susto, alarma ‖ *tr* asustar, espantar; **to scare away** espantar, ahuyentar; **to scare up** (coll) juntar, recoger (*dinero*)

scare'crow' *s* espantajo, espantapájaros *m*

scarf [skɑrf] *s* (*pl* **scarfs** o **scarves** [skɑrvz]) bufanda; pañuelo para el cuello; (*cover for a table, bureau, etc.*) tapete *m*; corbata

scarf'pin' *s* alfiler *m* de corbata

scarlet ['skɑrlɪt] *adj* escarlata

scarlet fever *s* escarlata

scar·y ['skɛri] *adj* (*comp* **-ier;** *super* **-iest**) (*easily frightened*) (coll) asustadizo, espantadizo; (*causing fright*) (coll) espantoso

scathing ['skeðɪŋ] *adj* acerbo, duro

scatter ['skætər] *tr* esparcir, dispersar ‖ *intr* esparcirse, dispersarse

scatterbrain ['skætər,bren] *s* (coll) farraquista *m*

scatterbrained *adj* (coll) alegre de cascos, casquivano

scattered showers *spl* lluvias aisladas

scenari·o [sɪ'nɛrɪ,o] o [sɪ'nɑrɪ,o] *s* (*pls* **-os**) guión *m*, escenario

scenarist [sɪ'nɛrɪst] o [sɪ'nɑrɪst] *s* guionista *mf*, escenarista *mf*

scene [sin] *s* (*view*) paisaje *m*; (*in literature, art, the theater, the movie*) escena; escándalo, demostración de pasión; **behind the scenes** entre bastidores; **to make a scene** causar escándalo

scener·y ['sinəri] *s* (*pl* **-ies**) paisaje *m*; (theat) decoraciones *f*

scene shifter ['ʃɪftər] *s* tramoyista *m*

scenic ['sinɪk] o ['sɛnɪk] *adj* pintoresco; (*representing an action graphically*) gráfico; (*pertaining to the stage*) escénico

scent [sɛnt] *s* olor *m*; perfume *m*; (*sense of smell*) olfato; (*trail*) rastro, pista ‖ *tr* oler; perfumar; olfatear, ventear; sospechar

scepter ['sɛptər] *s* cetro

sceptic ['skɛptɪk] *adj* & *s* escéptico

sceptical ['skɛptɪkəl] *adj* escéptico

schedule ['skɛdjul] *s* catálogo, cuadro, lista; plan *m*, programa *m*; (*of trains, planes, etc.*) horario ‖ *tr* catalogar; proyectar; fijar la hora de

scheme [skim] *s* esquema *m*; plan *m*, proyecto; (*trick*) ardid *m*, treta; (*plot*) intriga, trama ‖ *tr* & *intr* proyectar; tramar

schemer ['skimər] *s* proyectista *mf*; intrigante *mf*

scheming ['skimɪŋ] *adj* astuto, mañoso, intrigante ‖ *s* intriga

schism ['sɪzəm] *s* cisma *m*; facción cismática

schist [ʃɪst] *s* esquisto

scholar ['skɑlər] *s* (*pupil*) alumno; (*scholarship holder*) becario; (*learned person*) sabio, erudito

scholarly ['skɑlərli] *adj* sabio, erudito

scholarship ['skɑlər,ʃɪp] *s* erudición; (*grant to study*) beca

scholarship holder *s* bequista *mf* (CAm, Cuba)

school [skul] *s* escuela; (*of a university*) facultad; (*of fish*) banco, cardume *m* ‖ *tr* enseñar, instruir, disciplinar

school age *s* edad escolar

school attendance *s* escolaridad

school board *s* junta de instrucción pública

school'boy' *s* alumno de escuela

school day *s* día lectivo

school'girl' *s* alumna de escuela

school'house' *s* escuela

schooling ['skulɪŋ] *s* instrucción, enseñanza; experiencia

school'mate' *s* compañero de escuela

school'room' *s* aula, sala de clase

school'teach'er *s* maestro de escuela

school year *s* año lectivo

schooner ['skunər] *s* goleta

sci. *abbr* **science, scientific**

science ['saɪəns] *s* ciencia

science fiction *s* ciencia-ficción; novela científica

scientific [,saɪən'tɪfɪk] *adj* científico

scientist ['saɪəntɪst] *s* científico, sabio, hombre *m* de ciencia

sci-fi ['saɪ'faɪ] *s* (slang) *abbr* **science fiction**

scil. *abbr* **scilicet** (Lat) **namely**

scimitar ['sɪmɪtər] *s* cimitarra

scintillate ['sɪntɪ,let] *intr* chispear, centellear

scion ['saɪən] *s* vástago

Scipio ['sɪpɪ,o] *s* Escipión *m*

scissors ['sɪzərz] *ssg* o *spl* tijeras

scoff [skɔf] o [skɑf] *s* burla, mofa ‖ *intr* burlarse, mofarse; **to scoff at** burlarse de, mofarse de

scold [skold] *s* regañón *m*, regañona ‖ *tr* & *intr* regañar

scoop [skup] *s* (*instrument like a spoon*) cuchara, cucharón *m*; (*tool like a shovel*) pala; (*kitchen utensil*) paleta; (*for water*) achicador *m*; cucharada, palada, paletada; (*hollow made by a scoop*) hueco; (*big haul*) (coll) buena ganancia ‖ *tr* sacar con cuchara, pala, paleta; achicar (*agua*); **to scoop out** ahuecar, vaciar

scoot [skut] *s* (coll) carrera precipitada ‖ *intr* (coll) correr precipitadamente

scooter ['skutər] *s* monopatín *m*, patinete *m*

scope [skop] *s* alcance *m*, extensión; campo, espacio; **to give free scope to** dar campo libre a

scorch [skɔrtʃ] *s* chamusco ‖ *tr* chamuscar; (*to dry, wither*) abrasar; criticar acerbamente ‖ *intr* chamuscarse; abrasarse

scorching [ˈskɔrtʃɪŋ] *adj* abrasador; acerbo, duro, mordaz

score [skor] *s* (*in a game*) cuenta, tantos; (*in an examination*) nota; entalladura, muesca; línea, raya; (*twenty*) veintena; (*mus*) partitura; **on the score of** a título de; **to keep score** apuntar los tantos ‖ *tr* anotar (*los tantos*); ganar, tantear (*tantos*); rayar, señalar; regañar acerbamente; (*mus*) instrumentar ‖ *intr* ganar tantos; marcar los tantos

score board *s* marcador *m*, cuadro indicador

scorn [skɔrn] *s* desdén *m*, desprecio ‖ *tr & intr* desdeñar, despreciar; **to scorn to** no dignarse

scornful [ˈskɔrnfəl] *adj* desdeñoso

Scorpio [ˈskɔrpɪˌo] *s* (astr) Escorpión *m*

scorpion [ˈskɔrpɪˌən] *s* alacrán *m*, escorpión *m*

Scot [skɑt] *s* escocés *m*

Scotch [skɑtʃ] *adj* escocés ‖ *s* (*dialect*) escocés *m;* whiskey *m* escocés; **the Scotch** los escoceses

Scotch·man [ˈskɑtʃmən] *s* (*pl* **-men** [mən]) escocés *m*

Scotland [ˈskɑtlənd] *s* Escocia

Scottish [ˈskɑtɪʃ] *adj* escocés ‖ *s* (*dialect*) escocés *m;* **the Scottish** los escoceses

scoundrel [ˈskaʊndrəl] *s* bribón *m*, pícaro

scour [skaʊr] *tr* fregar, estregar; recorrer, explorar detenidamente

scourge [skʌrdʒ] *s* azote *m* ‖ *tr* azotar

scout [skaʊt] *s* (mil) escucha, explorador *m;* niño explorador, niña exploradora; exploración, reconocimiento; (slang) individuo, sujeto, tipo ‖ *tr* explorar, reconocer (*un territorio*); observar (*al enemigo*); negarse a creer

scout·mas·ter *s* jefe *m* de tropa de niños exploradores

scowl [skaʊl] *s* ceño, semblante ceñudo ‖ *intr* mirar con ceño, poner mal gesto, poner mala cara

scramble [ˈskræmbəl] *s* arrebatiña ‖ *tr* arrebatar; recoger de prisa; revolver; hacer un revoltillo de (*huevos*); trepar ‖ *intr* luchar; trepar

scrambled eggs *spl* revoltillo, huevos revueltos

scrap [skræp] *s* fragmento, pedacito; desecho; chatarra; (slang) riña, contienda; **scraps** desperdicios, desechos; (*from the table*) sobras ‖ *v* (*pret & pp* **scrapped**) *ger* **scrapping**) *tr* desechar, descartar, echar a la basura; reducir a hierro viejo ‖ *intr* (slang) reñir, pelear

scrap·book *s* álbum *m* de recortes, libro de recuerdos

scrape [skrep] *s* raspadura; (*place scratched*) raspaza; aprieto, enredo; ‖ *tr* raspar; (*to gather together with much difficulty*) arañar ‖ *intr* raspar; **to scrape along** ir tirando; **to scrape through** aprobar justo

scrap heap *s* montón *m* de cachivaches

scrap iron *s* chatarra, desecho de hierro

scrap paper *s* papel *m* para apuntes; papel de desecho

scratch [skrætʃ] *s* arañazo, rasguño; marca, raya, garrapato; (billiards) chiripa; (sport) línea de partida; **to start from scratch** empezar desde el principio, empezar de cero; **up to scratch** en buena condición ‖ *tr* arañar, rasguñar; borrar, rasgar (*lo escrito*);·garrapatear; (sport) borrar (*a un corredor o caballo*) ‖ *intr* arañar, rasguñar; garrapatear; raspear (*una pluma*)

scratch pad *s* cuadernillo de apuntes

scratch paper *s* papel *m* para apuntes

scratch·-re·sist·ant *adj* resistente al rayado

scrawl [skrɔl] *s* garrapatos ‖ *tr & intr* garrapatear

scraw·ny [ˈskrɔni] *adj* (*comp* **-nier;** *super* **-niest**) huesudo, flaco

scream [skrim] *s* chillido, grito ‖ *tr* vociferar ‖ *intr* chillar, gritar; reírse a gritos

screech [skritʃ] *s* chillido ‖ *intr* chillar

screech owl *s* buharro; (*barn owl*) lechuza

screen [skrin] *s* mampara, biombo; (*in front of chimney*) pantalla; (*to keep flies out*) alambrera; (*to sift sand*) tamiz *m;* (mov, phys, telv) pantalla; **to put on the screen** llevar a la pantalla, llevar al celuloide ‖ *tr* defender, proteger; cubrir, ocultar; cinematografiar; rodar, proyectar (*una película*); adaptar para el cine; tamizar (*p.ej., arena*)

screen grid *s* (electron) rejilla blindada

screen·play· *s* cinedrama *m*

screw [skru] *s* tornillo; rosca, tuerca; (*of a boat*) hélice *f;* **to have a screw loose** (slang) tener flojos los tornillos; **to put the screws on** apretar los tornillos a ‖ *tr* atornillar; (*to twist, twist in*) enroscar; **to screw up** torcer (*el rostro*); ‖ *intr* atornillarse

screw·ball· *s* (slang) estrafalario, excéntrico

screw·driv·er *s* destornillador *m*, desatornillador *m*

screw eye *s* armella

screw jack *s* gato de tornillo

screw propeller *s* hélice *f*

scribal error [ˈskraɪbəl] *s* error *m* de escribiente

scribble [ˈskrɪbəl] *s* garrapatos ‖ *tr & intr* garrapatear

scribe [skraɪb] *s* (*teacher of Jewish law*) escriba *m;* escribiente *mf;* copista *mf;* autor *m*, escritor *m* ‖ *tr* arañar, rayar; trazar con punzón

scrimp [skrɪmp] *tr & intr* escatimar

script [skrɪpt] *s* escritura, letra cursiva; manuscrito, texto; (*of a play, movie, etc.*) palabras; (rad, telv) guión *m;* (typ) plumilla inglesa

scripture [ˈskrɪptʃər] *s* escrito sagrado ‖ **Scripture** *s* Escritura

script·writ·er *s* guionista *mf*, cinematurgo *m*

scrofula [ˈskrɑfjələ] *s* escrófula

scroll [skrol] *s* rollo de papel, rollo de pergamino; (archit) voluta

scroll·work· *s* obra de volutas, adornos de voluta

scrub [skrʌb] *s* chaparral *m*, monte bajo; animal achaparrado; persona de poca monta; (*act of scrubbing*) fregado; (sport) jugador *m* no oficial ‖ *v* (*pret & pp* **scrubbed**; *ger* **scrubbing**) *tr* fregar, restregar

scrub oak *s* chaparro

scrub woman *s* fregona

scruff [skrʌf] *s* nuca; piel *f* que cubre la nuca; capa, superficie *f;* espuma

scruple ['skrupəl] *s* escrúpulo

scrupulous ['skrupjələs] *adj* escrupuloso

scrutinize ['skrutɪ,naɪz] *tr* escudriñar, escrutar

scruti•ny ['skrutɪnɪ] *s* (*pl* **-nies**) escudriñamiento, escrutinio

scubadiver ['skubə,dɪvər] *s* submarinista *mf*

scuff [skʌf] *s* rascadura, desgaste *m* ‖ *tr* rascar, desgastar

scuffle ['skʌfəl] *s* lucha, sarracina ‖ *intr* forcejear, luchar

scull [skʌl] *s* espadilla ‖ *tr* impulsar con espadilla ‖ *intr* remar con espadilla

sculler•y ['skʌlərɪ] *s* (*pl* **-ies**) trascocina

scullery maid *s* fregona

scullion ['skʌljən] *s* pinche *m*

sculptor ['skʌlptər] *s* escultor *m*

sculptress ['skʌlptrɪs] *s* escultora

sculpture ['skʌlptʃər] *s* escultura ‖ *tr & intr* esculpir

scum [skʌm] *s* espuma, nata; (*on metals*) escoria; (fig) escoria, canalla, gente baja; palomilla ‖ *v* (*pret & pp* **scummed;** *ger* **scumming**) *tr & intr* espumar

scum•my ['skʌmɪ] *adj* (*comp* **-mier;** *super* **-miest**) espumoso; (fig) vil, ruin

scurf [skʌrf] *s* (*shed by the skin*) caspa; (*shed by any surface*) costra

scurrilous ['skʌrɪləs] *adj* chocarrero, grosero, insolente, difamatorio

scur•ry ['skʌrɪ] *v* (*pret & pp* **-ried**) *intr* echar a correr, escabullirse; **to scurry around** menearse; **to scurry away** ir respailando

scur•vy ['skʌrvɪ] *adj* (*comp* **-vier;** *super* **-viest**) despreciable, ruin, vil ‖ *s* escorbuto

scuttle ['skʌtəl] *s* (*bucket for coal*) cubo, balde *m;* (*trap door*) escotillón *m;* fuga, paso acelerado; (naut) escotilla ‖ *tr* barrenar, dar barreno a ‖ *intr* echar a correr

Scylla ['sɪlə] *s* Escila; **between Scylla and Charybdis** entre Escila y Caribdis

scythe [saɪð] *s* dalle *m,* guadaña

sea [si] *s* mar *m & f;* **at sea** en el mar; confuso, perplejo; **by the sea** a la orilla del mar; **to follow the sea** correr los mares, ser marinero; **to put to sea** hacerse a la mar

sea'board' *adj* costanero, costero ‖ *s* costa del mar, litoral *m*

sea breeze *s* brisa de mar

sea'coast' *s* costa marítima, litoral *m*

sea dog *s* (*seal*) foca; (coll) marinero viejo, lobo de mar

seafarer ['si,fɛrər] *s* marinero; viajero por mar

sea'food' *s* mariscos

seagoing ['si,go•ɪŋ] *adj* de alta mar

sea gull *s* gaviota

seal [sil] *s* (*raised design; stamp; mark*) sello; (*sea animal*) foca ‖ *tr* sellar; cerrar hermé-

ticamente; decidir irrevocablemente; (*with sealing wax*) lacrar

sea legs *spl* pie marino

sea level *s* nivel *m* del mar

sealing wax *s* lacre *m*

seal'skin' *s* piel *f* de foca

seam [sim] *s* costura; (*edges left after making a seam*) metido; (*mark, line*) arruga; (*scar*) costurón *m;* grieta, juntura; (min) filón *m,* veta

sea•man ['simən] *s* (*pl* **-men** [mən]) marinero; (nav) marino

sea mile *s* milla náutica

seamless ['simlɪs] *adj* inconsútil, sin costura

seamstress ['simstrɪs] *s* costurera; (*dressmaker's helper*) modistilla

seam•y ['simi] *adj* (*comp* **-ier;** *super* **-iest**) lleno de costuras; tosco, burdo; vil, soez; miserable

séance ['se•ɑns] *s* sesión de espiritistas

sea'plane' *s* hidroavión *m,* hidroplano

sea'port' *s* puerto de mar

sea power *s* potencia naval

sear [sɪr] *adj* seco, marchito; gastado, raído ‖ *s* chamusco, socarra ‖ *tr* chamuscar, socarrar; quemar; marchitar; cauterizar

search [sʌrtʃ] *s* busca; pesquisa, indagación; (*frisking a person*) cacheo; (*police, soldiers*) peinado; **in search of** en busca de ‖ *tr* averiguar, explorar; registrar ‖ *intr* buscar; (*police, soldiers*) peinar; **to search for** buscar; **to search into** indagar, investigar

search'light' *s* reflector *m,* proyector *m*

search warrant *s* auto de registro domiciliario, orden *f* de allanamiento

sea'scape' *s* vista del mar; (*painting*) marina

sea shell *s* concha marina

sea'shore' *s* costa, playa, ribera del mar

sea'sick' *adj* mareado

sea'sick'ness *s* mareo

sea'side' *s* orilla del mar, ribera del mar, playa

season ['sizən] *s* (*one of four parts of year*) estación; (*period of the year; period marked by certain activities*) temporada; (*opportune time; time of maturity, of ripening*) sazón *f;* **in season** en sazón; **in season and out of season** en tiempo y a destiempo; **out of season** fuera de sazón ‖ *tr* condimentar, sazonar; curar (*la madera*); moderar, templar

seasonal ['sizənəl] *adj* estacional

seasoning ['sizənɪŋ] *s* aderezo, aliño, condimento; (*of wood*) cura; (fig) sal *f,* chiste *m*

season ticket *s* billete *m* de abono

seat [sit] *s* asiento; (*of trousers*) fondillos; morada; sitio, lugar *m;* (*e.g., of government*) sede *f;* (*in parliament*) escaño; (*e.g., of a war*) teatro; (*e.g., of learning*) centro; (*of a saddle*) batalla; (*of human body*) nalgas; (theat) localidad; **reclining seat** (*as in car*) asiento abatible; ‖ *tr* sentar; tener asientos para; poner asiento a (*una silla*); echar fondillos a (*pantalones*); arraigar, establecer; **to be seated** estar. sentado; **to seat oneself** sentarse

seat belt s cinturón m de asiento
seat cover s funda de asiento, cubreasiento
SEATO ['sito] s (acronym) la O.T.A.S.E.
sea wall s dique marítimo
sea′way′ s ruta marítima; avance m de un buque por mar; vía de agua interior para buques de alta mar; mar gruesa
sea′weed′ s alga marina; plantas marinas
sea wind s viento que sopla del mar
sea′wor′thy adj marinero, en condiciones de navegar
sec. abbr **secant, second, secondary, secretary, section, sector**
secede [sɪ'sid] intr separarse, retirarse
secession [sɪ'sɛʃən] s secesión
seclude [sɪ'klud] tr recluir
secluded [sɪ'kludɪd] adj aislado, apartado, solitario
seclusion [sɪ'kluʒən] s reclusión, soledad
second ['sɛkənd] adj segundo; **to be second to none** ser tan bueno como el que más, no tener segundo ‖ adv en segundo lugar ‖ s segundo; artículo de segunda calidad; (in dates) dos m; (in a challenge) padrino; (aut) segunda (velocidad); (mus) segunda ‖ tr secundar; apoyar (una moción)
secondar•y ['sɛkən,dɛri] adj secundario ‖ s (pl -ies) (elec) secundario
sec′ond-best′ adj (el) mejor después del primero
sec′ond-class′ adj de segunda clase
second hand s segundero
sec′ond-hand′ adj de segunda mano, de ocasión
second-hand bookshop s librería de viejo
second lieutenant s alférez m, subteniente m
sec′ond-rate′ adj de segundo orden; de calidad inferior
second sight s doble vista
second wind s nuevo aliento
secre•cy ['sikrəsi] s (pl -cies) secreto; **in secrecy** en secreto
secret ['sikrɪt] adj & s secreto; **in secret** en secreto
secretar•y ['sɛkrɪ,tɛri] s (pl -ies) secretario; (desk) secreter m, escritorio
secrete [sɪ'krit] tr encubrir, esconder; (physiol) secretar
secretive [sɪ'kritɪv] adj callado, reservado
sect [sɛkt] s secta, comunión
sectarian [sɛk'tɛri•ən] adj & s sectario
section ['sɛkʃən] s sección; (of a country) región; (of a city) barrio; (of a law) artículo; (department, bureau) negociado; (rr) tramo
secular ['sɛkjələr] adj secular, seglar ‖ s clérigo secular
secularism ['sɛkjələ,rɪzəm] s laicismo
secure [sɪ'kjʊr] adj seguro ‖ tr asegurar; conseguir, obtener
securi•ty [sɪ'kjʊrɪti] s (pl -ties) seguridad; (person) segurador m; **securities** valores mpl, obligaciones, títulos
secy. o **sec′y.** abbr **secretary**
sedan [sɪ'dæn] s silla de manos; (aut) sedán m
sedate [sɪ'det] adj sentado, sosegado

sedative ['sɛdətɪv] adj & s sedativo
sedentary ['sɛdən,tɛri] adj sedentario
sedge [sɛdʒ] s juncia
sediment ['sɛdɪmənt] s sedimento
sedition [sɪ'dɪʃən] s sedición
seditious [sɪ'dɪʃəs] adj sedicioso
seduce [sɪ'djus] tr seducir
seducer [sɪ'djusər] s seductor m
seduction [sɪ'dʌkʃən] s seducción
seductive [sɪ'dʌktɪv] adj seductivo
sedulous ['sɛdʒələs] adj cuidadoso, diligente
see [si] s (eccl) sede f ‖ v (pret **saw** [sɔ]; pp **seen** [sin] tr ver; **to see off** ir a despedir; **to see through** llevar a cabo; ayudar en un trance difícil ‖ intr ver; **see here!** ¡mire Vd.!; **to see into** o **to see through** conocer el juego de
seed [sid] s semilla, simiente f; **to go to seed** dar semilla; echarse a perder ‖ tr sembrar; (to remove the seeds from) despepitar ‖ intr sembrar; dejar caer semillas
seed′bed′ s semillero
seedling ['sidlɪŋ] s planta de semilla; árbol m de pie
seed•y ['sidi] adj (comp **-ier;** super **-iest**) lleno de granos; (coll) andrajoso, raído
seeing ['si•ɪŋ] adj vidente ‖ s vista, visión ‖ conj visto que
Seeing Eye dog s perro-lazarillo
seek [sik] v (pret & pp **sought** [sɔt] tr buscar; recorrer buscando; dirigirse a ‖ intr buscar; **to seek after** tratar de obtener; **to seek to** esforzarse por
seem [sim] intr parecer
seemingly ['simɪŋli] adv aparentemente, al parecer
seem•ly ['simli] adj (comp **-lier;** super **-liest**) decente, decoroso, correcto; bien parecido
seep [sip] intr escurrirse, rezumarse
seer [sɪr] s profeta m, vidente m
see′saw′ s balancín m, columpio de tabla; (motion) vaivén m ‖ intr columpiarse; alternar; vacilar
seethe [siθ] intr hervir
segment ['sɛgmənt] s segmento
segregate ['sɛgrɪ,get] tr segregar
segregationist [,sɛgrɪ'geʃənɪst] s segregacionista mf
Seine [sen] s Sena m
seismograph ['saɪzmə,græf] s sismógrafo
seismology [saɪz'mɑlədʒi] s sismología
seize [siz] tr agarrar, asir, coger; atar, prender, sujetar; apoderarse de; comprender; (law) embargar, secuestrar; aprovecharse de (una oportunidad)
seizure ['siʒər] s prendimiento, prisión; captura, toma; (of an illness) ataque m; (law) embargo, secuestro
seldom ['sɛldəm] adv raramente, rara vez
select [sɪ'lɛkt] adj escogido, selecto ‖ tr seleccionar
selectee [sɪ,lɛk'ti] s (mil) quinto
selection [sɪ'lɛkʃən] s selección; trozo escogido; (of goods for sale) surtido
self [sɛlf] adj mismo ‖ pron sí mismo ‖ s (pl **selves** [sɛlvz]) uno mismo; ser m; yo; **all by one's self** sin ayuda de nadie

self′-abuse′ s abuso de sí mismo; masturbación
self′-addressed′ envelope s sobre m con el nombre y dirección del remitente
self′-cen′tered adj egocéntrico
self′-con′scious adj cohibido, apocado, tímido
self′-con•trol′ s dominio de sí mismo; autodisciplina
self′-de•fense′ s autodefensa; **in self-defense** en defensa propia
self′-de•ni′al s abnegación
self′-de•ter′mi•na′tion s autodeterminación
self′-dis′cipline s autodisciplina
self′-ed′u•cat′ed adj autodidacto
self′-em•ployed′ adj que trabaja por su propia cuenta
self′-ev′i•dent adj patente, manifiesto
self′-ex•plan′a•tor′y adj que se explica por sí mismo
self′-glor′i•fi•ca′tion s egolatría
self′-gov′ernment s autogobierno, autonomía; dominio sobre sí mismo
self′-im•por′tant adj altivo, arrogante
self′-in•dul′gence s intemperancia, desenfreno
self′-in′terest s egoísmo, interés m personal
selfish [′sɛlfɪʃ] adj egoísta
selfishness [′sɛlfɪʃnɪs] s egoísmo
selfless [′sɛlflɪs] adj desinteresado
self′-liq′ui•dat′ing adj autoamortizable
self′-love′ s amor propio, egoísmo
self′-made′ man s hijo de sus propias obras
self′-por′trait s autorretrato
self′-pos•sessed′ adj dueño de sí mismo
self′-pres′er•va′tion s propia conservación
self′-re•li′ant adj confiado en sí mismo
self′-re•spect′ing adj lleno de dignidad, decoroso
self′-right′eous adj santurrón
self′-sac′ri•fice′ s sacrificio de sí mismo
self′-same′ adj mismísimo
self′-sat′is•fied′ adj pagado de sí mismo
self′-seal′ing adj autopegado
self′-seek′ing adj egoísta ‖ s egoísmo
self′-ser′vice restaurant s restaurante m de libre servicio, restaurante de autoservicio
self′-start′er s arranque automático
self′-sup•port′ s mantenimiento económico propio
self′-taught′ adj autodidacto
self′-willed′ adj obstinado, terco
self′-wind′ing clock s reloj m de cuerda automática, reloj de autocuerda
self′-wor′ship s egolatría
sell [sɛl] v (pret & pp **sold** [sold]) tr vender; **to sell out** realizar, saldar; (to betray) vender ‖ intr venderse, estar de venta; **to sell for** venderse a o en (p.ej., cien pesetas); **to sell off** bajar (el mercado de valores); **to sell out** venderlo todo, realizar
seller [′sɛlər] s vendedor m
sell′out′ s (slang) realización, saldo; (slang) traición
Seltzer water [′sɛltsər] s agua de seltz
selvage [′sɛlvɪdʒ] s orillo, vendo

semantic [sɪ′mæntɪk] adj semántico ‖ **semantics** s semántica
semaphore [′sɛmə,for] s semáforo; (rr) disco de señales
semblance [′sɛmbləns] s apariencia, imagen f, simulacro
semen [′simɛn] s semen m
semester [sɪ′mɛstər] adj semestral ‖ s semestre m
semester hour s hora semestral
sem′ico′lon s punto y coma
sem′iconduc′tor s semiconductor m
sem′icon′scious adj semiconsciente
sem′ifi′nal adj & s (sport) semifinal f
sem′ilearn′ed adj semiculto
sem′imonth′ly adj quincenal ‖ s (pl -lies) periódico quincenal
seminar [′sɛmɪ,nɑr] s seminario
seminar•y [′sɛmɪ,nɛri] s (pl -ies) seminario
sem′ipre′cious adj semiprecioso, fino
Semite [′sɛmaɪt] o [′simaɪt] s semita mf
Semitic [sɪ′mɪtɪk] adj semítico ‖ s semita mf; (language) semita m
sem′itrail′er s semi-remolque m
sem′iweek′ly adj bisemanal ‖ s (pl -lies) periódico bisemanal
sem′iyear′ly adj semestral
Sen. o **sen.** abbr **Senate, Senator, Senior**
senate [′sɛnɪt] s senado
senator [′sɛnətər] s senador m
senatorship [′sɛnətər,ʃɪp] s senaduría
send [sɛnd] v (pret & pp **sent** [sɛnt]) tr enviar, mandar; expedir, remitir; lanzar (una bola, flecha, etc.); **to send back** devolver, reenviar; **to send packing** despedir con cajas destempladas ‖ intr (rad) transmitir; **to send for** enviar por, enviar a buscar
sender [′sɛndər] s remitente mf; (telg) transmisor m
send′-off′ s (coll) despedida afectuosa
senile [′sinaɪl] o [′sinɪl] adj senil
senility [sɪ′nɪlɪti] s senilidad; (pathol) senilismo
senior [′sinjər] adj mayor, de mayor edad; viejo; del último año; padre, p.ej., **John Jones, Senior** Juan Jones, padre ‖ s mayor m; socio más antiguo; alumno del último año
senior citizens spl gente f de edad
seniority [sin′jɔrɪti] s antigüedad; precedencia, prioridad
sensation [sɛn′seʃən] s sensación
sense [sɛns] s sentido; **to make sense out of** comprender, explicarse ‖ tr intuir, sentir, sospechar; comprender
senseless [′sɛnslɪs] adj falto de sentido; desmayado; insensato, necio
sense of guilt s cargo de conciencia
sense of humor s sentido de humor
sense organ s órgano sensorio
sensibili•ty [,sɛnsɪ′bɪlɪti] s (pl -ties) sensibilidad; **sensibilities** sentimientos delicados
sensible [′sɛnsɪbəl] adj cuerdo, sensato; perceptible, sensible; equilibrado
sensitive [′sɛnsɪtɪv] adj sensible; (of the senses) sensorio, sensitivo

sensitize ['sɛnsɪˌtaɪz] *tr* sensibilizar
sensory ['sɛnsəri] *adj* sensorio
sensual ['sɛnʃʊ•əl] *adj* sensual, voluptuoso
sensuous ['sɛnʃʊ•əs] *adj* sensual
sentence ['sɛntəns] *s* (gram) frase *f*, oración; (law) sentencia ‖ *tr* sentenciar, condenar
sentiment ['sɛntɪmənt] *s* sentimiento
sentimentali•ty [ˌsɛntɪmən'tælɪti] *s* (*pl* **-ties**) sentimentalismo
sentinel ['sɛntɪnəl] *s* centinela *m or f;* **to stand sentinel** estar de centinela, hacer centinela
sen•try ['sɛntri] *s* (*pl* **-tries**) centinela *m or f*
sentry box *s* garita de centinela
separate ['sɛpərɪt] *adj* separado; suelto ‖ ['sɛpəˌret] *tr* separar ‖ *intr* separarse
separation [ˌsɛpə're/ən] *s* separación
separation of powers *s* (pol) separación de poderes
Sephardic [sɪ'fardɪk] *adj* sefardí, sefardita
Sephardim [sɪ'fardɪm] *spl* sefardíes *mpl*
September [sɛp'tɛmbər] *s* septiembre *m*
septet [sɛp'tɛt] *s* septeto
septic ['sɛptɪk] *adj* séptico
sepulcher ['sɛpəlkər] *s* sepulcro
seq. *abbr* **sequentia** (Lat) **the following**
sequel ['sikwəl] *s* resultado, secuela; continuación
sequence ['sikwəns] *s* serie *f*, sucesión; (cards) secansa, escalera, runfla; (gram, mov & mus) secuencia
sequester [sɪ'kwɛstər] *tr* apartar, separar; (law) secuestrar
sequin ['sikwɪn] *s* lentejuela
ser•aph ['sɛrəf] *s* (*pl* **-aphs** o **-aphim** [əfɪm]) serafín *m*
Serb [sʌrb] *adj & s* servio
Serbia ['sʌrbɪ•ə] *s* Servia
Serbian ['sʌrbɪ•ən] *adj & s* servio
Serbo-Croatian [ˌsʌrbokro'e/ən] *adj & s* servocroata *mf*
sere [sɪr] *adj* seco, marchito
serenade [ˌsɛrə'ned] *s* serenata ‖ *tr* dar serenata a ‖ *intr* dar serenatas
serene [sɪ'rin] *adj* sereno
serenity [sɪ'rɛnɪti] *s* serenidad
serf [sʌrf] *s* siervo de la gleba
serfdom ['sʌrfdəm] *s* servidumbre de la gleba
serge [sʌrdʒ] *s* sarga
sergeant ['sardʒənt] *s* sargento
ser′geant•at-arms′ *s* (*pl* **sergeants-at-arms**) oficial *m* de orden
sergeant major *s* (*pl* **sergeant majors**) sargento mayor
serial ['sɪrɪ•əl] *adj* serial; publicado por entregas ‖ *s* cuento o novela por entregas; (rad) serial *m*, serial radiado, emisión seriada
serially ['sɪrɪ•əli] *adv* en serie, por series; por entregas
serial number *s* número de serie
se•ries ['sɪriz] *s* (*pl* **-ries**) serie *f*
serious ['sɪrɪ•əs] *adj* (*e.g., person, face, matter*) serio; (*e.g., condition, illness*) grave
sermon ['sʌrmən] *s* sermón *m*
sermonize ['sʌrməˌnaɪz] *tr & intr* sermonear
serpent ['sʌrpənt] *s* serpiente *f*

se•rum ['sɪrəm] *s* (*pl* **-rums** o **-ra** [rə]) suero
servant ['sʌrvənt] *s* criado, sirviente *m*
servant girl *s* criada, sirvienta
servant problem *s* crisis *f* del servicio doméstico
serve [sʌrv] *s* (*in tennis*) saque *m*, servicio ‖ *tr* servir; (*to supply*) abastecer, proporcionar; cumplir (*una condena*); (*in tennis*) servir; **it serves me right** bien me lo merezco ‖ *intr* servir; **to serve as** servir de
service ['sʌrvɪs] *s* servicio; **at your service** para servir a Vd.; **out of service** fuera de servicio; **the services** las fuerzas armadas ‖ *tr* instalar; mantener, reparar
serviceable ['sʌrvɪsəbəl] *adj* útil; duradero; cómodo
serviceman ['sʌrvɪsˌmæn] *s* (*pl* **-men** [ˌmən]) reparador *m*, mecánico; militar *m*
service record *s* hoja de servicios
service station *s* estación de servicio, taller *m* de reparaciones
service stripe *s* galón *m* de servicio
servile ['sʌrvɪl] *adj* servil
servitude ['sʌrviˌtjud] *s* servidumbre; trabajos forzados
sesame ['sɛsəmi] *s* sésamo; **open sesame** sésamo ábrete
session ['sɛ/ən] *s* sesión; **to be in session** sesionar
set [sɛt] *adj* determinado, resuelto; inflexible, obstinado; fijo, firme; estudiado, meditado ‖ *s* (*of books, chairs, etc.*) juego; (*of gears*) tren *m;* (*of horses*) pareja; (*of diamonds*) aderezo; (*of tennis*) partida; (*of dishes*) servicio; (*of kitchen utensils*) batería; clase *f*, grupo; equipo; porte *m*, postura; (*of a garment*) caída, ajuste *m;* (*of glue*) endurecimiento; (*of cement*) fraguado; (*of artificial teeth*) caja; (mov) plató *m;* (rad) aparato; (theat) decoración ‖ *v* (*pret & pp* **set**; *ger* **setting**) *tr* asentar; colocar, poner; establecer, instalar; arreglar, preparar; adornar; apostar; poner (*un reloj*) en hora; (*in bridge*) reenvidar; poner, meter, pegar (*fuego*); fijar (*el precio*); engastar, montar (*una piedra preciosa*); encasar (*un hueso dislocado*); disponer (*los tipos*); triscar (*una sierra*); armar, colocar (*una trampa*); fijar (*el peinado*); poner (*la mesa*); dar (*un ejemplo*); **to set back** parar; poner obstáculos a; hacer retroceder; atrasar, retrasar (*el reloj*); **to set forth** exponer, dar a conocer; **to set one's heart on** tener la esperanza puesta en; **to set store by** dar mucha importancia a; **to set up shop** poner tienda; **to set up the drinks** (coll) convidar a beber ‖ *intr* ponerse (*el Sol, la Luna, etc.*); cuajarse (*un líquido*); endurecerse (*la cola*); fraguar (*el cemento, el yeso*); empollar (*una gallina*); caer, sentar (*una prenda de vestir*); **to set about** ponerse a; **to set out** ponerse en camino; emprender un negocio, **to set out to** ponerse a; **to set to work** poner manos a la obra; **to set upon** acometer, atacar
set′back′ *s* revés *m*, contrariedad
set′screw′ *s* tornillo de presión

settee [sɛˈti] s sofá m, canapé m

setting [ˈsɛtɪŋ] s (environment) ambiente m; (of a gem) engaste m, montadura; (of cement) fraguado; (e.g., of the sun) puesta, ocaso; (theat) escena; (theat) puesta en escena, decoración

set'ting-up' exercises spl ejercicios sin aparatos, gimnasia sueca

settle [ˈsɛtəl] tr asentar, colocar; asegurar, fijar; componer, conciliar; calmar, moderar; matar (el polvo); casar; poblar, colonizar; ajustar, arreglar (cuentas) ‖ intr asentarse (un líquido, un edificio); establecerse; componerse; calmarse, moderarse; solidificarse; **to settle down to work** ponerse seriamente a trabajar; **to settle on** escoger; fijar (p.ej., una fecha)

settlement [ˈsɛtəlmənt] s establecimiento; colonia, caserío; decisión; (of accounts) arreglo, ajuste m; traspaso; casa de beneficencia

settler [ˈsɛtlər] s fundador m; poblador m; colono; árbitro, conciliador m

set'up' s porte m, postura; (e.g., of the parts of a machine) disposición; (coll) organización; (slang) invitación a beber

seven [ˈsɛvən] adj & pron siete ‖ s siete m; **seven o'clock** las siete

seven hundred adj & pron setecientos ‖ s setecientos m

seventeen [ˈsɛvənˈtin] adj, pron & s diecisiete m, diez y siete

seventeenth [ˈsɛvənˈtinθ] adj & s (in a series) decimoséptimo; (part) diecisieteavo ‖ s (in dates) diecisiete m

seventh [ˈsɛvənθ] adj & s séptimo ‖ s (in dates) siete m

seventieth [ˈsɛvəntɪ·θ] adj & s (in a series) septuagésimo; (part) setentavo

seven·ty [ˈsɛvəntɪ] adj & pron setenta ‖ s (pl -ties) setenta m

sever [ˈsɛvər] tr desunir, separar; romper (relaciones) ‖ intr desunirse, separarse

several [ˈsɛvərəl] adj diversos, varios; distintos, respectivos ‖ spl varios; algunos

severance pay [ˈsɛvərəns] s indemnización por despido

severe [sɪˈvɪr] adj severo; (weather) riguroso; recio, violento; (look) adusto; (pain) agudo; (illness) grave

sew [so] v (pret sewed; pp sewed o sewn) tr & intr coser

sewage [ˈsu·ɪdʒ] o [ˈsju·ɪdʒ] s agua de albañal, aguas cloacales

sew'age-dis·pos'al plant s estación depuradora

sewer [ˈsu·ər] o [ˈsju·ər] s albañal m, cloaca, alcantarilla ‖ tr alcantarillar

sewerage [ˈsu·ərɪdʒ] o [ˈsju·ərɪdʒ] s desagüe m; (system) alcantarillado; aguas de albañal

sewing basket [ˈso·ɪŋ] s cesta de costura

sewing machine s máquina de coser

sex [sɛks] s sexo; **the fair sex** el bello sexo; **the sterner sex** el sexo feo

sex appeal s atracción sexual; encanto femenino

sexism [ˈsɛksɪzəm] s sexismo

sexist [ˈsɛksɪst] adj & s sexista

sextant [ˈsɛkstənt] s sextante m

sextet [sɛksˈtɛt] s sexteto

sexton [ˈsɛkstən] s sacristán m

sexual [ˈsɛkʃʊ·əl] adj sexual

sex·y [ˈsɛksi] adj (comp -ier; super -iest) (slang) sicalíptico, erótico

shab·by [ˈʃæbi] adj (comp -bier; super -biest) gastado, raído, usado; andrajoso, desaseado; ruin, vil

shack [ʃæk] s casucha, choza

shackle [ˈʃækəl] s grillete m; (to tie an animal) maniota; (fig) impedimento, traba; **shackles** cadenas, esposas, grillos ‖ tr poner grilletes a; poner esposas a; encadenar; (fig) trabar

shad [ʃæd] s sábalo, alosa

shade [ʃed] s sombra; (of a lamp) pantalla; (of a window) cortina, estor m, visillo, cortina de resorte; (for the eyes) visera; (hue; slight difference) matiz m; **shades** (slang) gafas fpl de sol; **the shades** las tinieblas; (of the dead) las sombras ‖ tr sombrear; obscurecer; rebajar ligeramente (el precio)

shadow [ˈʃædo] s sombra ‖ tr sombrear; simbolizar; acechar, espiar (a una persona); **to shadow forth** representar vagamente, representar de un modo profético

shadowy [ˈʃædo·i] adj sombroso; ligero, vago; imaginario; simbólico

shad·y [ˈʃedi] adj (comp -ier; super -iest) sombrío, umbroso; (coll) sospechoso; (coll) de mala fama; (story) (coll) verde; **to keep shady** (slang) no dejarse ver

shaft [ʃæft] s dardo, flecha, saeta; (of an arrow; of a feather) astil m; (of light) rayo; (of a wagon) vara alcándara, limonera; (of a mine; of an elevator) pozo; (of a column) fuste m, caña; (of a flag) asta; (of a motor) árbol m; (to make fun of someone) dardo

shag·gy [ˈʃægi] adj (comp -gier; super -giest) hirsuto, peludo, veludo; lanudo; áspero

shake [ʃek] s sacudida; (coll) apretón m de manos; (slang) instante m, momento ‖ v (pret shook [ʃʊk]; pp shaken [ˈʃekən]) tr sacudir; agitar; apretar, estrechar (la mano a uno); inquietar, perturbar; (to get rid of) (slang) dar esquinazo a, zafarse de ‖ intr sacudirse; agitarse; temblar; inquietarse, perturbarse; (from cold) tiritar; **shake!** (coll) ¡choque Vd. esos cinco!, ¡vengan esos cinco!

shake'down' s (slang) exacción, concusión

shakedown cruise s viaje m de pruebas

shake'-up' s profunda conmoción; cambio de personal, reorganización completa

shak·y [ˈʃeki] adj (comp -ier; super -iest) trémulo, vacilante, movedizo; indigno de confianza

shall [ʃæl] v (cond should [ʃʊd]) v aux empléase para formar (1) el fut de ind, p.ej., **I shall do it** lo haré; (2) el fut perf de ind, p.ej., **I shall have done it** lo habré hecho; (3) el modo potencial, p.ej., **what shall I do?** ¿qué he de hacer?, ¿qué debo hacer?

shallow [ˈʃælo] *adj* bajo, poco profundo; (fig) frívolo, superficial

sham [ʃæm] *adj* falso, fingido; postizo ‖ *s* fingimiento, falsificación, engaño; (*person*) (coll) farsante *mf;* ‖ *v* (*pret & pp* **shammed;** *ger* **shamming**) *tr & intr* fingir

sham battle *s* simulacro de combate

shambles [ˈʃæmbəlz] *s* destrucción, ruina; (*confusion, mess*) lío, revoltijo

shame [ʃem] *s* vergüenza; deshonra; (*disgrace*) metedura; **shame on you!** ¡qué vergüenza!; **what a shame!** ¡qué lástima! ‖ *tr* avergonzar; deshonrar

shameful [ˈʃemfəl] *adj* vergonzoso

shameless [ˈʃemlɪs] *adj* descarado, desvergonzado

shampoo [ʃæmˈpu] *s* champú *m* ‖ *tr* lavar (*la cabeza*); lavar la cabeza a

shamrock [ˈʃæmrɑk] *s* trébol *m* irlandés

shanghai [ˈʃæŋhaɪ] o [ʃæŋˈhaɪ] *tr* embarcar emborrachando, embarcar narcotizando; llevarse con violencia, llevarse con engaño

shank [ʃæŋk] *s* (*of the leg*) caña, canilla; (*of an animal*) pierna; (*of a bird*) zanca; (*of an anchor*) caña; (*of the sole of a shoe*) enfranque *m;* astil *m,* caña, fuste *m;* extremidad, remate *m;* **to go** o **to ride on shank's mare** caminar en coche de San Francisco

shan·ty [ˈʃænti] *s* (*pl* **-ties**) chabola, choza

shape [ʃep] *s* forma; **in bad shape** (coll) arruinado; (coll) muy enfermo; **out of shape** deformado; descompuesto; (*twisted*) sobornado ‖ *tr* formar, dar forma a; amoldar ‖ *intr* formarse; **to shape up** tomar forma; desarrollarse bien

shapeless [ˈʃeplɪs] *adj* informe

shape·ly [ˈʃepli] *adj* (*comp* **-lier:** *super* **-liest**) bien formado, esbelto

share [ʃɛr] *s* parte *f,* porción; (*of stock in a company*) acción; **to go shares** ir a la parte ‖ *tr* (*to enjoy jointly*) compartir; (*to apportion*) repartir ‖ *intr* participar, tener parte

share'hold'er *s* accionista *mf*

shark [ʃɑrk] *s* tiburón *m;* (*swindler*) estafador *m;* (slang) experto, perito

sharp [ʃɑrp] *adj* afilado, agudo; anguloso; (*curve, slope, etc.*) fuerte, pronunciado; (*photograph*) nítido; (*hearing*) fino; (*step, gait*) rápido; atento, despierto; picante, mordaz; listo, vivo; (mus) sostenido; (slang) elegante; **sharp features** facciones bien marcadas ‖ *adv* agudamente; en punto, p.ej., **at four o'clock sharp** a las cuatro en punto ‖ *s* (mus) sostenido

sharpen [ˈʃɑrpən] *tr* aguzar; sacar punta a (*un lápiz*) ‖ *intr* afilarse

sharper [ˈʃɑrpər] *s* fullero, jugador *m* de ventaja

sharp'shoot'er *s* tirador certero; (mil) tirador distinguido

shatter [ˈʃætər] *tr* hacer astillas, romper de un golpe; quebrantar (*la salud*); destruir, destrozar; agitar, perturbar ‖ *intr* hacerse pedazos, romperse

shat'ter·proof' *adj* inastillable

shave [ʃev] *s* afeitado; rebanada delgada; **to have a close shave** (coll) escapar en una

tabla ‖ *tr* afeitar (*la cara*); raer, raspar; (*to graze; to cut close*) rozar; (*to slice thin*) rebanar; (carp) cepillar ‖ *intr* afeitarse

shaving [ˈʃevɪŋ] *adj* de afeitar, para afeitar, p.ej., **shaving soap** jabón *m* de o para afeitar ‖ *s* afeitado; **shavings** acepilladuras, virutas

shaving lotion *s* loción facial

shawl [ʃɔl] *s* chal *m,* mantón *m*

she [ʃi] *pron pers* (*pl* **they**) ella ‖ *s* (*pl* **shes**) hembra

sheaf [ʃif] *s* (*pl* **sheaves** [ʃivz]) gavilla; (*of paper*) atado

shear [ʃir] *s* hoja de la tijera; **shears** tijeras grandes); (*to cut metal*) cizallas ‖ *v* (*pret* **sheared;** *pp* **sheared** o **shorn** [ʃorn]) *tr* esquilar, trasquilar (*las ovejas*); cizallar; quitar cortando; tundir (*paño*)

sheath [ʃiθ] *s* (**sheaths** [ʃiðz]) envoltura, estuche *m,* funda; (*for a sword*) funda, vaina

sheathe [ʃið] *tr* enfundar, envainar

shed [ʃɛd] *s* cobertizo; (*line from which water flows in two directions*) vertiente *m & f* ‖ *v* (*pret & pp* **shed;** *ger* **shedding**) *tr* derramar, verter (*p.ej., sangre*); dar, echar, esparcir (*luz*); mudar (*la pluma, el pellejo*)

sheen [ʃin] *s* brillo, lustre *m;* (*of pressed cloth*) prensado

sheep [ʃip] *s* (*pl* **sheep**) carnero; (*female*) oveja; tonto; **to make sheep's eyes (at)** mirar con ojos de carnero degollado

sheep dog *s* perro ovejero, perro de pastor

sheep'fold' *s* aprisco, redil *m*

sheepish [ˈʃipɪʃ] *adj* avergonzado, corrido; tímido, tonto

sheep'skin' *s* (*undressed*) zalea; (*dressed*) badana; (coll) diploma *m*

sheer [ʃir] *adj* delgado, fino, ligero; casi transparente; escarpado; puro, sin mezcla; completo ‖ *intr* desviarse

sheet [ʃit] *s* (e.g., for the bed) sábana; (*of paper*) hoja; (*of metal*) hoja, lámina; (*of water*) extensión; hoja impresa; periódico; (naut) escota

sheet lightning *s* fucilazo

sheet metal *s* metal laminado

sheet music *s* música en hojas sueltas

sheik [ʃik] *s* jeque *m;* (*great lover*) (slang) sultán *m*

shelf [ʃɛlf] *s* (*pl* **shelves** [ʃɛlvz]) estante *m,* anaquel *m;* bajío, banco de arena; **on the shelf** arrinconado, desechado, olvidado

shell [ʃɛl] *s* (*of an egg, nut, etc.*) cáscara; (*of a crustacean*) caparazón *m,* concha; (*of a vegetable*) vaina; (*of a cartridge*) cápsula; (*of a boiler*) cuerpo; armazón *f,* esqueleto; bomba, proyectil *m;* (*long, narrow racing boat*) (sport) yola ‖ *tr* descascarar; desgranar, desvainar (*legumbres*); bombardear, cañonear; **to shell out** (coll) entregar (*dinero*)

shel·lac [ʃəˈlæk] *s* laca, goma laca ‖ *v* (*pret & pp* **-lacked;** *ger* **-lacking**) *tr* barnizar con goma laca; (slang) azotar, zurrar; (slang) derrotar

shell'fish' *s* marisco, mariscos

shell hole *s* (mil) embudo

se
sh

shell shock *s* neurosis *f* de guerra

shelter ['ʃɛltər] *s* abrigo, asilo, amparo, refugio; **to take shelter** abrigarse, refugiarse ‖ *tr* abrigar, amparar, proteger

shelve [ʃɛlv] *tr* poner sobre un estante; proveer de estantes; arrinconar, dejar a un lado; diferir indefinidamente

shepherd ['ʃɛpərd] *s* pastor *m* ‖ *tr* pastorear (*a las ovejas o los fieles*)

shepherd dog *s* perro ovejero, perro de pastor

shepherdess ['ʃɛpərdɪs] *s* pastora

sherbet ['ʃʌrbət] *s* sorbete *m*

shereef [ʃɛ'rif] *s* jerife *m*

sheriff ['ʃɛrɪf] *s* alguacil *m* mayor

sher·ry ['ʃɛri] *s* (*pl* **-ries**) jerez *m*, vino de Jerez

shield [ʃild] *s* escudo; (*for armpit*) sobaquera; (elec) blindaje *m* ‖ *tr* amparar, defender, escudar; (elec) blindar

shift [ʃɪft] *s* cambio; (*order of work or other activity*) turno; (*group of workmen*) tanda; maña, subterfugio ‖ *tr* cambiar; deshacerse de; echar (*la culpa*); (aut) cambiar de (*marcha*) ‖ *intr* cambiar, cambiar de puesto; mañear; (naut) correrse (*el lastre*); (rr) maniobrar; **to shift for oneself** ayudarse, ingeniarse

shift key *s* tecla de cambio, palanca de mayúsculas

shiftless ['ʃɪftlɪs] *adj* desidioso, perezoso

shiftlessness ['ʃɪftlɪsnɪs] *s* galbana

shift·y ['ʃɪfti] *adj* (*comp* **-ier;** *super* **-iest**) ingenioso, mañoso; evasivo, tramoyista; (*glance*) huyente

shilling ['ʃɪlɪŋ] *s* chelín *m*

shimmer ['ʃɪmər] *s* luz trémula ‖ *intr* rielar

shin [ʃɪn] *s* espinilla ‖ *v* (*pret & pp* **shinned;** *ger* **shinning**) *tr & intr* trepar

shin'bone' *s* espinilla

shine [ʃaɪn] *s* brillo, luz *f;* bruñido, lustre *m;* buen tiempo; (*on shoes*) (coll) lustre *m;* **to take a shine to** (slang) tomar simpatía a ‖ *v* (*pret & pp* **shined**) *tr* pulir, lustrar; (coll) embolar, limpiar (*el calzado*) ‖ *v* (*pret & pp* **shone** [ʃon]) *intr* brillar, lucir, resplandecer; hacer sol, hacer buen tiempo; (*to be distinguished, to stand out*) (fig) brillar, lucir

shingle ['ʃɪŋgəl] *s* ripia, teja de madera; tejamaní *m* (Am); pelo a la garçonne; (coll) letrero de oficina; **shingles** (pathol) zona; **to hang out one's shingle** (coll) abrir una oficina; (coll) abrir un consultorio médico ‖ *tr* cubrir con ripias; cortar (*el pelo*) a la garçonne

shining ['ʃaɪnɪŋ] *adj* brillante, luciente

shin·y ['ʃaɪni] *adj* (*comp* **-ier;** *super* **-iest**) brillante, lustroso; (*paper*) glaseado; (*from much wear*) brilloso

ship [ʃɪp] *s* nave *f*, buque *m*, barco, navío; (*steamer*) vapor *m;* aeronave *f* ‖ *v* (*pret & pp* **shipped;** *ger* **shipping**) *tr* embarcar; enviar, remitir, remesar; armar (*los remos*); embarcar (*agua*) ‖ *intr* embarcarse

ship'board' *s* bordo; **on shipboard** a bordo

ship'build'er *s* arquitecto naval, constructor *m* de buques

ship'build'ing *s* arquitectura naval, construcción de buques

ship'mate' *s* camarada *m* de a bordo

shipment ['ʃɪpmənt] *s* embarque *m* (*por agua*); envío, expedición, remesa

shipper ['ʃɪpər] *s* embarcador *m;* expedidor *m*, remitente *mf*

shipping memo ['ʃɪpɪŋ] *s* nota de remisión

ship'shape' *adj & adv* en buen orden

ship'side' *adj & adv* al costado del buque ‖ *s* zona de embarque y desembarque; muelle *m*

ship's papers *spl* documentación del buque

ship's time *s* hora local del buque

ship'wreck' *s* naufragio; barco náufrago ‖ *tr* hacer naufragar ‖ *intr* naufragar

ship'yard' *s* astillero, varadero

shirk [ʃʌrk] *tr* evitar (*el trabajo*); faltar a (*un deber*) ‖ *intr* escurrir el hombro

shirred eggs [ʃʌrd] *spl* huevos al plato

shirt [ʃʌrt] *s* camisa; **to keep one's shirt on** (slang) quedarse sereno; **to lose one's shirt** (slang) perder hasta la camisa

shirt'band' *s* cuello de camisa

shirt front *s* pechera de camisa, camisolín *m*

shirt sleeve *s* manga de camisa; **in shirt sleeves** en mangas de camisa

shirt'tail' *s* faldón *m*, pañal *m*

shirt'waist' *s* blusa (*de mujer*)

shiver ['ʃɪvər] *s* estremecimiento, tiritón *m* ‖ *intr* estremecerse, tiritar

shoal [ʃol] *s* bajío, banco de arena

shock [ʃak] *s* (*sudden and violent blow or encounter*) choque *m;* (*sudden agitation of mind or emotions*) sobresalto; temblor *m* de tierra; (*of hair*) greña; (agr) tresnal *m;* (elec) sacudida; (med) choque *m;* (*profound depression*) (pathol) choque *m;* (coll) parálisis *f* ‖ *tr* chocar; sobresaltar; dar una sacudida eléctrica a; chocar, escandalizar *m*

shock absorber [æb'sɔrbər] *s* amortiguador *m*

shocker ['ʃakər] *s* (slang) novelucha; película horripilante

shocking ['ʃakɪŋ] *adj* chocante, escandalizador

shock troops *spl* tropas de asalto

shod·dy ['ʃadi] *adj* (*comp* **-dier;** *super* **-diest**) falso, de imitación

shoe [ʃu] *s* (*which goes above the ankle*) bota, botina; (*which does not go above the ankle*) zapato; (*of a tire*) cubierta; **to put on one's shoes** calzarse ‖ *v* (*pret & pp* **shod** [ʃad]) *tr* calzar; herrar (*un caballo*)

shoe'black' *s* limpiabotas *m*

shoe'horn' *s* calzador *m*

shoe'lace' *s* cordón *m* de zapato, lazo de zapato

shoe'mak'er *s* zapatero; zapatero remendón

shoe mender ['mɛndər] *s* zapatero remendón

shoe polish *s* betún *m*, bola

shoe'shine' *s* brillo, lustre *m;* limpiabotas *m*

shoe store *s* zapatería

shoe'string' s cordón m de zapato, lazo de zapato; **on a shoestring** con muy poco dinero

shoe tree s horma

shoo [ʃu] tr & intr oxear

shoot [ʃut] s (sprout, twig) renuevo, vástago; conducto inclinado; (for grain, sand, etc.) tolva; tiro al blanco, cortamen m de tiradores; (hunting party) partida de caza ‖ v (pret & pp **shot** [ʃat]) tr tirar, disparar (un arma); herir o matar con arma; (to execute with a discharge of rifles) fusilar; fotografiar; (to take a moving picture of) rodar, filmar; echar (los dados); medir la altura de (p.ej., el Sol); **to shoot down** derribar (un avión); **to shoot up** (slang) destrozar echando balas a diestra y siniestra; (drugs) picarse, pincharse ‖ intr tirar; nacer, brotar; lanzarse, precipitarse, moverse rápidamente; punzar (un dolor, una llaga); **to shoot at** tirar a; (to strive for) (coll) poner el tiro en

shooting gallery s galería de tiro al blanco

shooting match s certamen m de tiro al blanco; (slang) conjunto, totalidad

shooting star s estrella fugaz, estrella filante

shoot'out' s balaceo, balacera (SAm)

shop [ʃap] s (store) tienda; (workshop) taller m; **to talk shop** hablar de su oficio, hablar del propio trabajo (fuera de tiempo) ‖ v (pret & pp **shopped**; ger **shopping**) intr ir de compras, ir de tiendas; **to go shopping** ir de compras, ir de tiendas; **to send shopping** mandar a la compra; **to shop around** ir de tienda en tienda buscando gangas

shop'girl' s muchacha de tienda

shop'keep'er s tendero, baratero

shoplifter [ʃap,lɪftər] s mechera, ratero de tiendas

shopper [ʃapər] s comprador m

shopping center s centro comercial (grupo de establecimientos minoristas, con aparcamiento)

shopping district s barrio comercial

shop'win'dow s escaparate m (de tienda); aparador m (Mex)

shop'work' s trabajo de taller

shop'worn' adj desgastado con el trajín de la tienda

shore [ʃor] s orilla, ribera; costa, playa; **shores** (poet) clima m, región ‖ tr acodalar, apuntalar

shore dinner s comida de pescado y mariscos

shore leave s (nav) permiso para ir a tierra

shore line s línea de la playa; línea de buques costeros

shore patrol s (nav) patrulla en tierra

short [ʃort] adj (in space, time, and quantity) corto; (in time) breve; (in stature) bajo; (fig) corto, sucinto; (fig) brusco, seco; **in a short time** dentro de poco; **in short** en fin; **on short notice** con poco tiempo de aviso; **to be short of** estar escaso de; **short of breath** corto de resuello ‖ adv brevemente; bruscamente; (without possessing the stock sold) al descubierto, p.ej., **to sell short** vender al descubierto; **to run short of**

acabársele a uno, p.ej., **I am running short of gasoline** se me acaba la gasolina; **to stop short** parar de repente ‖ s (elec) cortocircuito; (mov) cortometraje m; **shorts** calzones cortos, calzoncillos ‖ tr (elec) poner en cortocircuito ‖ intr (elec) ponerse en cortocircuito

shortage [ʃortɪdʒ] s carestía, escasez f, falta; déficit m; (from pilfering) substracción

short'cake' s torta de frutas; torta quebradiza

short'change' tr (coll) no devolver la vuelta debida a

short circuit s (elec) cortocircuito

short'cir'cuit tr (elec) cortocircuitar ‖ intr (elec) cortocircuitarse

short'com'ing s falta, defecto, desperfecto

short cut s atajo; (method) remediavagos m

shorten [ʃortən] tr acortar, abreviar ‖ intr acortarse, abreviarse

short'hand' adj taquigráfico ‖ s taquigrafía; **to take shorthand** taquigrafiar

short-lived [ʃort'laɪvd] o (coll) [ʃort'lɪvd] adj de breve vida, de breve duración

shortly [ʃortli] adv en breve, luego; descortésmente; **shortly after** poco tiempo después (de)

short'-range' adj de poco alcance

short sale s (coll) venta al descubierto

short-sighted [ʃort'saɪtɪd] adj miope; (fig) falto de perspicacia

short'stop' s (baseball) medio; guardabosque m, torpedero (Am)

short story s cuento

short-tempered [ʃort'tɛmpərd] adj de mal genio

short'-term' adj a corto plazo

shot [ʃat] s tiro, disparo; (hit or wound made with a bullet) balazo; (distance) alcance m; (in certain games) jugada, tirada, golpe m; (of a rocket into space) lanzamiento; conjetura, tentativa; fotografía, instantánea; (small pellets of lead) perdigones mpl; munición; (marksman) tiro; (heavy metal ball) (sport) pesa; (hypodermic injection) (slang) jeringazo; (drink of liquor) (slang) trago; **not by a long shot** ni con mucho, ni por pienso; **to start like a shot** salir disparado

shot'gun' s escopeta

shot'-put' s (sport) tiro de la pesa

should [ʃud] v aux empléase para formar (1) el pres de cond, p.ej., **if I should wait for him, I should miss the train** si yo le esperase, perdería el tren; (2) el perf de cond, p.ej., **if I had waited for him, I should have missed the train** si yo le hubiese esperado, habría, perdido el tren; y (3) el modo potencial, p.ej., **he should go at once** debiera salir en seguida; **he should have gone at once** debiera haber salido en seguida

shoulder [ʃoldər] s hombro; (of slaughtered animal) brazuelo; (of a garment) hombrera; **across the shoulder** en bandolera; **to put one's shoulders to the wheel** arrimar el hombro, echar el pecho al agua; **to turn a cold shoulder to** volver las espaldas a ‖ *tr* cargar sobre las espaldas; tomar sobre sí, hacerse responsable de; empujar con el hombro para abrirse paso

shoulder blade *s* escápula, omóplato

shoulder strap *s* (*of underwear*) presilla; (mil) charretera

shout [ʃaut] *s* grito, voz *f* ‖ *tr* gritar, vocear; **to shout down** hacer callar a gritos ‖ *intr* gritar, dar voces

shove [ʃʌv] *s* empujón *m* ‖ *tr* empujar ‖ *intr* dar empujones, avanzar a empujones; **to shove off** alejarse de la costa; (slang) ponerse en marcha, salir

shov·el [ʃʌvəl] *s* pala ‖ *v* (*pret & pp* -eled o -elled; *ger* -eling o -elling) *tr* traspalar; espalar (*p.ej., la nieve*) ‖ *intr* trabajar con pala

show [ʃo] *s* exhibición, exposición, muestra; espectáculo; (*in the theater*) función; (*each performance of a play or movie*) sesión; demostración, prueba; indicación, señal *f*, signo; apariencia; (*e.g., of confidence*) alarde *m;* (coll) ocasión, oportunidad; ostentación; espectáculo ridículo, hazmerreír *m;* **to make a show of** hacer gala de; **to steal the show from** robar la obra a (*otro actor*) ‖ *tr* mostrar, enseñar; demostrar, probar; poner, proyectar (*un film*); (*e.g., to the door*) acompañar; **to show up** (coll) desenmascarar ‖ *intr* mostrarse, aparecer, asomar; salir (*p.ej., las enaguas*); **to show off** fachendear; **to show through** clarearse, transparentarse; **to show up** (coll) presentarse, dejarse ver

show bill *s* cartel *m*

show business *s* comercio de los espectáculos

show'case' *s* vitrina (de exposición)

show'down' *s* cartas boca arriba; (coll) revelación forzosa, arreglo terminante

shower [ʃau·ər] *s* (*sudden fall of rain*) aguacero, chaparrón *m;* (*shower bath*) ducha; (*e.g., of bullets*) rociada; despedida de soltera ‖ *tr* regar; **to shower with** colmar de ‖ *intr* llover

shower bath *s* ducha, baño de ducha

show girl *s* (theat) corista *f*, conjuntista *f*

show·man [ʃomən] *s* (*pl* -men [mən]) empresario de teatro, empresario de circo

show'-off' *s* (coll) pinturero

show'piece' *s* objeto de arte sobresaliente

show'place' *s* sitio o edificio que se exhibe por su belleza o lujo

show'room' *s* sala de muestras, sala de exhibición

show window *s* escaparate *m* (de tienda); aparador *m* (Mex)

show·y [ʃo·i] *adj* (*comp* -ier; *super* -iest) aparatoso, cursi, ostentoso

shrapnel [ʃræpnəl] *s* granada de metralla

shred [ʃrɛd] *s* jirón *m*, tira, triza; fragmento, pizca; **to tear to shreds** hacer trizas ‖ *v* (*pret & pp* shredded o shred; *ger* shredding) *tr* desmenuzar, hacer trizas; deshilar (*carne*)

shrew [ʃru] *s* (*nagging woman*) arpía, fierecilla; (*animal*) musaraña

shrewd [ʃrud] *adj* astuto; despierto; listo

shriek [ʃrik] *s* chillido, grito agudo; risotada chillona ‖ *intr* chillar

shrill [ʃrɪl] *adj* agudo, chillón

shrimp [ʃrɪmp] *s* camarón *m;* (*little insignificant person*) renacuajo

shrine [ʃraɪn] *s* relicario; sepulcro de santo; lugar sagrado

shrink [ʃrɪŋk] *v* (*pret* shrank [ʃræŋk] o shrunk [ʃrʌŋk]; *pp* shrunk o shrunken) *tr* contraer, encoger ‖ *intr* contraerse, encogerse; moverse hacia atrás; rehuirse, retirarse

shrinkage [ʃrɪŋkɪdʒ] *s* contracción, encogimiento; disminución, reducción; merma, pérdida

shriv·el [ʃrɪvəl] *v* (*pret & pp* -eled o -elled; *ger* -eling o -elling) *tr* arrugar, marchitar, fruncir ‖ *intr* arrugarse, marchitarse, fruncirse; **to shrivel up** avellanarse

shroud [ʃraud] *s* mortaja, sudario; cubierta, velo ‖ *tr* amortajar; cubrir, velar

Shrove Tuesday [ʃrov] *s* martes *m* de carnaval

shrub [ʃrʌb] *s* arbusto

shrubber·y [ʃrʌbəri] *s* (*pl* -ies) arbustos; plantío de arbustos

shrug [ʃrʌg] *s* encogimiento de hombros ‖ *v* (*pret & pp* shrugged; *ger* shrugging) *tr* contraer; **to shrug one's shoulders** encogerse de hombros ‖ *intr* encogerse de hombros

shudder [ʃʌdər] *s* estremecimiento ‖ *intr* estremecerse

shuffle [ʃʌfəl] *s* (*of cards*) barajadura; turno de barajar; (*of feet*) arrastramiento; evasiva; recomposición ‖ *tr* barajar (*naipes*); arrastrar (*los pies*); mezclar, revolver ‖ *intr* barajar; caminar arrastrando los pies; bailar arrastrando los pies; moverse rápidamente de un lado a otro; **to shuffle along** ir arrastrando los pies; ir tirando; **to shuffle off** irse arrastrando los pies

shuf'fle·board' *s* juego de tejo

shun [ʃʌn] *v* (*pret & pp* shunned; *ger* shunning) *tr* esquivar, evitar, rehuir

shunt [ʃʌnt] *tr* apartar, desviar; (elec) poner en derivación; (rr) desviar

shut [ʃʌt] *adj* cerrado ‖ *v* (*pret & pp* shut; *ger* shutting) *tr* cerrar; **to shut in** encerrar; **to shut off** cortar (*electricidad, gas, etc.*); **to shut up** cerrar bien; aprisionar; (coll) hacer callar ‖ *intr* cerrarse; **to shut up** (coll) callarse la boca

shut'down' *s* cierre *m*, paro

shutter [ʃʌtər] *s* celosía, persiana; (*outside a window*) contraventana; (*outside a show window*) cierre metálico; (phot) obturador *m*

shuttle [ʃʌtəl] *s* (*used in sewing*) lanzadera ‖ *intr* hacer viajes cortos de ida y vuelta

shuttle train *s* tren *m* lanzadera

shy [ʃaɪ] *adj* (*comp* shyer o shier; *super* shyest o shiest) arisco, recatado, tímido; (*fearful*) asustadizo; escaso, pobre; **I am shy a dollar** me falta un dólar ‖ *v* (*pret & pp* shied) *intr* esquivarse, hacerse a un lado; espantarse, respingar; **to shy away** alejarse asustado

shyster [´ʃaɪstər] *s* (coll) abogado trampista

Sia•mese [ˌsaɪ•ə´miz] *adj* siamés ‖ *s* (*pl* **-mese**) siamés *m*

Siamese twins *spl* hermanos siameses

Siberian [saɪ´bɪrɪ•ən] *adj* & *s* siberiano

sibilant [´sɪbɪlənt] *adj* & *s* sibilante *f*

sibling [´sɪblɪŋ] *s* hermano o hermana

sibyl [´sɪbɪl] *s* sibila

Sicilian [sɪ´sɪljən] *adj* & *s* siciliano

Sicily [´sɪsɪli] *s* Sicilia

sick [sɪk] *adj* enfermo, malo; nauseado; (coll) mórbido, perverso; **sick and tired of** (coll) harto y cansado de; **sick at heart** afligido de corazón; **to be sick at one's stomach** tener náuseas; **to take sick** caer enfermo ‖ *tr* azuzar (*a un perro*)

sick'bed' *s* lecho de enfermo

sicken [´sɪkən] *tr* & *intr* enfermar

sickening [´sɪkənɪŋ] *adj* repelente, repugnante, nauseabundo

sick headache *s* jaqueca con náuseas

sickle [´sɪkəl] *s* hoz *f*

sick leave *s* licencia por enfermedad

sick•ly [´sɪkli] *adj* (*comp* **-lier;** *super* **-liest**) enfermizo

sickness [´sɪknɪs] *s* enfermedad; náusea

side [saɪd] *adj* lateral ‖ *s* lado; (*of a solid; of a phonograph record*) cara; (*of a hill*) falda; (*of human body, of a ship*) costado; facción, partido ‖ *intr* tomar partido; **to side with** tomar el partido de

side arms *spl* armas de cinto

side'board' *s* aparador *m*

side'burns' *spl* patillas

side dish *s* plato de entrada

side door *s* puerta lateral; puerta excusada

side effect *s* efecto secundario perjudicial (*de ciertos medicamentos*)

side glance *s* mirada de soslayo

side issue *s* cuestión secundaria

side'kick' *s* (slang) compañero regular

side line *s* negocio accesorio; **on the side lines** sin tomar parte

sidereal [saɪ´dɪrɪ•əl] *adj* sidéreo

side'sad'dle *adv* a asentadillas, a mujeriegas

side show *s* función secundaria, espectáculo de atracciones

side'split'ting *adj* desternillante

side'track' *s* apartadero, desviadero, vía muerta ‖ *tr* desviar (*un tren*); echar a un lado

side view *s* perfil *m*, vista de lado

side'walk' *s* acera; banqueta (Guat, Mex); vereda (Arg, Cuba, Peru)

sidewalk café *s* terraza, café *m* en la acera

sideward [´saɪdwərd] *adj* oblicuo, sesgado ‖ *adv* de lado, hacia un lado

side'ways' *adj* oblicuo, sesgado ‖ *adv* de lado, hacia un lado; a través

side whiskers *spl* patillas

side'wise' *s* oblicuo, sesgado ‖ *adv* de lado, hacia un lado; a través

siding [´saɪdɪŋ] *s* (rr) apartadero, desviadero, vía muerta

sidle [´saɪdəl] *intr* ir de lado; **to sidle up to** acercarse de lado a (*una persona*) para no ser visto

siege [sidʒ] *s* sitio, cerco; **to lay siege to** poner sitio o cerco a; (fig) asediar (*p.ej., el corazón de una mujer*)

sieve [sɪv] *s* cedazo, tamiz *m* ‖ *tr* cerner, tamizar

sift [sɪft] *tr* cerner, cribar; escudriñar, examinar; (*to screen, separate*) entresacar; (*to scatter with or as with a sieve*) empolvar

sigh [saɪ] *s* suspiro; **to breathe a sigh of relief** respirar ‖ *tr* decir con suspiros ‖ *intr* suspirar; **to sigh for** suspirar por

sight [saɪt] *s* vista; cosa digna de verse; (*of a firearm, telescope, etc.*) mira; (coll) gran cantidad, montón *m*; (coll) horror *m*, atrocidad; **at first sight** a primera vista; **at sight** a primera vista; (*translation*) a libro abierto; (com) a la vista; **out of sight** fuera del alcance de la vista; (*prices*) por las nubes; **to catch sight of** alcanzar a ver; **to know by sight** conocer de vista; **to not be able to stand the sight of** no poder ver ni en pintura; **to see the sights** visitar los puntos de interés ‖ *tr* avistar, alcanzar con la vista ‖ *intr* apuntar con una mira; (arti & surv) visar

sight draft *s* (com) giro a la vista, letra a la vista

sightless [´saɪtlɪs] *adj* ciego

sight'-read' *v* (*pret* & *pp* **-read** [ˌrɛd]) *tr* leer a libro abierto; (mus) ejecutar a la primera lectura ‖ *intr* leer a libro abierto; (mus) repentizar

sight reader *s* lector *m* a libro abierto; (mus) repentista *mf*

sight'see'ing *s* turismo, visita de puntos de interés; **to go sightseeing** ir a ver los puntos de interés

sightseer [´saɪtˌsi•ər] *s* turista *mf*, excursionista *mf*

sign [saɪn] *s* signo; señal *f*, marca; huella, vestigio; letrero, muestra; **to show signs of** dar muestras de, tener trazas de; **to make the sign of the cross** hacerse la señal de la cruz ‖ *tr* firmar; contratar; ceder, traspasar ‖ *intr* firmar; usar el alfabeto de los sordomudos; **to sign off** (rad) terminar la transmisión; **to sign up** (coll) firmar el contrato

sig•nal [´sɪgnəl] *adj* señalado, notable ‖ *s* señal *f* ‖ *v* (*pret* & *pp* **-naled** o **-nalled;** *ger* **-naling** o **-nalling**) *tr* señalar ‖ *intr* hacer señales

signal tower *s* (rr) garita de señales

signato•ry [´sɪgnɪˌtori] *s* (*pl* **-ries**) firmante *mf*

signature [´sɪgnətʃər] *s* firma; (mus & typ) signatura

sign'board' *s* cartelón *m*, letrero

signer [´saɪnər] *s* firmante *mf*

signet ring [´sɪgnɪt] *s* anillo sigilar, sortija de sello

significance [sɪg´nɪfəkəns] *s* significado, significación; relevancia

signi•fy [´sɪgnɪˌfaɪ] *v* (*pret* & *pp* **-fied**) *tr* significar

sign'post' *s* hito, poste *m* de guía

sh

si

silence ['saɪləns] s silencio ‖ tr acallar; (mil) apagar el fuego de; (mil) apagar (el fuego del enemigo)

silent ['saɪlənt] adj silencioso

silent movie s cine mudo

silhouette [,sɪlu'ɛt] s silueta ‖ tr siluetear

silk [sɪlk] adj sedeño ‖ s seda; **to hit the silk** (slang) lanzarse en paracaídas

silken ['sɪlkən] adj sedeño

silk hat s sombrero de copa

silk'-stock'ing adj aristocrático ‖ s aristócrata mf

silk'worm' s gusano de seda

silk•y ['sɪlki] adj (comp -ier; super -iest) sedoso, asedado

sill [sɪl] s travesaño; (of a door) umbral m; (of a window) antepecho

silliness ['sɪlɪnɪs] s tontería, simpleza, pachotada

sil•ly ['sɪli] adj (comp -lier; super -liest) necio, tonto; (coll) pavo

si•lo ['saɪlo] s (pl -los) silo ‖ tr asilar

silt [sɪlt] s cieno, sedimento

silver ['sɪlvər] ad de plata; (voice) argentino; elocuente ‖ s plata ‖ tr platear; azogar (un espejo)

sil'ver•fish' s (ent) pez m de plata

silver foil s hoja de plata

silver lining s aspecto agradable de una condición desgraciada o triste

silver plate s vajilla de plata

silver screen s pantalla de plata

sil'ver•smith' s platero, orfebre m

silver spoon s riqueza heredada; **to be born with a silver spoon in one's mouth** nacer de pie

sil'ver-tongue' s (coll) pico de oro

sil'ver•ware' s plata, vajilla de plata; plata; cubertería

similar ['sɪmɪlər] adj similar, semejante, análogo

simile ['sɪmɪli] s (rhet) símil m

simmer ['sɪmər] tr cocer a fuego lento ‖ intr cocer a fuego lento; (coll) estar a punto de estallar; **to simmer down** (coll) tranquilizarse lentamente

simoon [sɪ'mun] s simún m

simper ['sɪmpər] s sonrisa boba ‖ intr sonreír bobamente

simple ['sɪmpəl] adj simple, sencillo ‖ s (medicinal plant) simple m

simple-minded ['sɪmpəl'maɪndɪd] adj candoroso, ingenuo; idiota, mentecato; estúpido, ignorante

simple substance s (chem) cuerpo simple

simpleton ['sɪmpəltən] s simple mf, bobo, mentecato

simulate ['sɪmjə,let] tr simular

simultaneous [,saɪməl'teni•əs] o [,sɪməl-'teni•əs] adj simultáneo ‖ adv—**to do simultaneously** simultanear

sin [sɪn] s pecado ‖ v (pret & pp **sinned**; ger **sinning**) intr pecar

since ['sɪns] adv desde entonces, después ‖ prep desde; después de ‖ conj desde que; después (de) que; ya que, puesto que

sincere [sɪn'sɪr] adj sincero

sincerity [sɪn'sɛrɪti] s sinceridad

sinecure ['saɪnɪ,kjur] s sinecura

sinew ['sɪnju] s tendón m; (fig) fibra, nervio, vigor m

sinful ['sɪnfəl] adj (person) pecador; (act, intention, etc.) pecaminoso

sing [sɪŋ] v (pret **sang** [sæŋ] o **sung** [sʌŋ]; pp **sung**) tr cantar; **to sing to sleep** arrullar ‖ intr cantar

singe [sɪndʒ] v (ger **singeing**) tr chamuscar, socarrar

singer ['sɪŋər] s cantante mf; (in a night club) vocalista mf

single ['sɪŋgəl] adj solo, único; simple, sencillo; particular; (e.g., room in a hotel) individual; (copy) suelto; (unmarried) soltero; solteril, de soltero ‖ tr escoger, elegir; **to single out** singularizar

single blessedness s el bendito celibato

single-breasted ['sɪŋgəl'brestɪd] adj sin cruzar, de un solo pecho

single entry s (com) partida simple

single file s fila india; **in single file** de reata

single-handed ['sɪŋgəl'hændɪd] adj solo, sin ayuda

single life s vida de soltero

sin'gle-track' adj de vía única; (coll) de cortos alcances

sing'song' adj monótono ‖ s sonsonete m

singular ['sɪŋgjələr] adj & s singular m

sinister ['sɪnɪstər] adj amenazante, ominoso, funesto

sink [sɪŋk] s fregadero, pila ‖ v (pret **sank** [sæŋk] o **sunk** [sʌŋk]; pp **sunk**) tr hundir, sumergir; echar a pique; abrir, cavar (un pozo); hincar (los dientes); invertir (mucho dinero) perdiéndolo todo; (basketball) encestar ‖ intr hundirse; irse a pique; hundirse (p.ej., el Sol en el horizonte); descender, desaparecer; decaer (un enfermo; una llama); (e.g., in a chair) dejarse caer

sinking fund s fondo de amortización

sinless ['sɪnlɪs] adj impecable

sinner ['sɪnər] s pecador m

sinuous ['sɪnju•əs] adj sinuoso

sinus ['saɪnəs] s seno

sip [sɪp] s sorbo, trago ‖ v (pret & pp **sipped**; ger **sipping**) tr sorber, beber a tragos

siphon ['saɪfən] s sifón m ‖ tr sacar con sifón, trasegar con sifón

siphon bottle s sifón m

sir [sʌr] s señor m; (British title) sir m; **Dear Sir** Muy señor mío, Estimado señor

sire [saɪr] s padre m, semental m; caballo padre ‖ tr engendrar

siren ['saɪrən] s sirena

Sirius ['sɪrɪ•əs] s (astr) Sirio

sirloin ['sʌrlɔɪn] s solomillo

sirup ['sɪrəp] o ['sʌrəp] s var de **syrup**

sissi•fy ['sɪsɪ,faɪ] v (pret & pp -**fied**) tr (coll) afeminar

sis•sy ['sɪsi] s (pl -**sies**) (coll) hermanita; (coll) maricón m, santito

sister ['sɪstər] adj (ship) gemelo; (language) hermano ‖ s hermana

sis'ter-in-law' s (pl **sisters-in-law**) cuñada, hermana política; (*wife of one's husband's or wife's brother*) concuñada

Sisyphus ['sɪsɪfəs] s Sísifo

sit [sɪt] v (pret & pp **sat** [sæt]; ger **sitting**) intr estar sentado; sentarse; echarse (*un ave sobre los huevos*); reunirse, celebrar junta; descansar; **to sit down** sentarse; **to sit still** estarse quieto; **to sit up** incorporarse (*el que estaba echado*)

sitcom ['sɪt,kɑm] s (coll) telecomedia serial

sit'-down' strike s hulega de sentados, huelga de brazos caídos

site [saɪt] s sitio, paraje m

sit'-in' s manifestación pacífica a modo de bloqueo

sitting ['sɪtɪŋ] s (*period one remains seated*) sentada; (*before a painter*) estadía; (*of a court or legislature*) sesión; **at one sitting** de una sentada

sitting duck s pato sentado en el agua (*fácil de matar a tiro de escopeta*); (coll) blanco de fácil alcance

sitting room s sala de estar

situate ['sɪtʃu,et] tr situar

situation [,sɪtʃueʃən] s situación; colocación, puesto; medio ambiente

sitz bath [sɪts] s baño de asiento

six [sɪks] adj & pron seis ‖ s seis m; **at sixes and sevens** en confusión, en desacuerdo; **six o'clock** las seis

six hundred adj & pron seiscientos ‖ s seiscientos m

sixteen ['sɪks'tin] adj, pron & s dieciséis m, diez y seis

sixteenth ['sɪks'tinθ] adj & s (*in a series*) decimosexto; (*part*) dieciseisavo ‖ s (*in dates*) dieciséis m

sixth [sɪksθ] adj & s sexto ‖ s (*in dates*) seis m

sixtieth ['sɪkstɪ·ɪθ] adj & s (*in a series*) sexagésimo; (*part*) sesentavo

six·ty ['sɪksti] adj & pron sesenta ‖ s (pl **-ties**) sesenta m

sizable ['saɪzəbəl] adj considerable, bastante grande

size [saɪz] s tamaño; (*of a person or garment*) talla; (*of a pipe, or a wire*) diámetro; (*for gilding*) sisa, cola de retazo; (coll) verdadera situación ‖ tr clasificar según tamaño; sisar, encolar; **to size up** enfocar (*un problema*); medir con la vista

sizzle ['sɪzəl] s siseo ‖ intr sisear

S.J. abbr Society of Jesus

skate [sket] s patín m; (slang) adefesio, tipo ‖ intr patinar; **to skate on thin ice** buscar el peligro

skating rink s patinadero, pista de patinar

skein [sken] s madeja; enredo, maraña

skeleton ['skɛlɪtən] adj esquelético ‖ s esqueleto

skeleton key s llave maestra

skeptic ['skɛptɪk] adj & s escéptico

skeptical ['skɛptɪkəl] adj escéptico

sketch [skɛtʃ] s boceto, dibujo; bosquejo, esbozo; drama corto, pieza corta ‖ tr dibujar; bosquejar, esbozar

sketch'book' s libro de bocetos; libro de esbozos literarios

skewer ['skju·ər] s broqueta ‖ tr espetar; traspasar con aguja

ski [ski] s (pl **skis** o **ski**) esquí m intr esquiar

skid [skɪd] s (*of an auto*) resbalón m; (*of a wheel*) patinaje m, patinazo; calzo ‖ v (pret & pp **skidded**; ger **skidding**) tr calzar ‖ intr resbalar (*un coche*); patinar (*una rueda*)

skid chain s cadena antirresbaladiza

skidding s (aut) patinada, derrapada, derrapaje m

skid row s barrio de mala vida

skier ['ski·ər] s esquiador m

skiff [skɪf] s esquife m

skiing ['ski·ɪŋ] s esquiismo

ski jacket s plumífero

skijoring [ski'dʒorɪŋ] s esquí remolcado

ski jump s salto de esquí; cancha de esquiar; trampolín m

ski lift s telesquí m

skill [skɪl] s destreza, habilidad, pericia

skilled [skɪld] adj hábil, experimentado, experto

skillet ['skɪlɪt] s cacerola de mango largo; sartén f

skillful ['skɪlfəl] adj diestro, hábil

skim [skɪm] v (pret & pp **skimmed**; ger **skimming**) tr desnatar (*la leche*); espumar (*el caldo, el almíbar*); (*to graze*) rasar, rozar; examinar ligeramente ‖ intr rozar; **to skim over** pasar rozando; examinar a la ligera

ski mask s pasamontaña m

skimmer ['skɪmər] s (*utensil*) espumadera; (*straw hat*) canotié m

skim milk s leche desnatada

skimp [skɪmp] tr escatimar; chapucear ‖ intr economizar, apretarse; chapucear

skimp·y ['skɪmpi] adj (comp **-ier**; super **-iest**) escaso; tacaño, mezquino

skin [skɪn] s piel f; (*of an animal, of fruit*) pellejo; **to be nothing but skin and bones** estar hecho un costal de huesos, estar en los huesos; **to get soaked to the skin** calarse hasta los huesos; **to save one's skin** salvar el pellejo ‖ v (pret & pp **skinned**; ger **skinning**) tr pelar, desollar; escoriarse (*p.ej., el codo*); (coll) timar; **to skin alive** (coll) desollar vivo; (coll) vencer completamente

skin'-deep' adj superficial

skin diver s submarinista mf

skin diving s submarinismo

skin'flint' s escasero, avaro

skin game s (slang) fullería

skin·ny ['skɪni] adj (comp **-nier**; super **-niest**) flaco, enjuto, magro, seco, delgaducho

skin'-tight' adj ajustado al cuerpo

skip [skɪp] s salto ‖ v (pret & pp **skipped**; ger **skipping**) tr saltar ‖ intr saltar; saltar espacios (*la máquina de escribir*); moverse saltando; irse precipitadamente

skip bombing s (aer) bombardeo de rebote

si
sk

ski pole s bastón m de esquiar

skipper ['skɪpər] s caudillo, jefe m; (of a boat) patrón m; gusano del queso ‖ tr patronear

skirmish ['skʌrmɪʃ] s escaramuza ‖ intr escaramuzar

skirt [skʌrt] s falda; borde m, orilla; (woman) (slang) falda ‖ tr seguir el borde de; moverse a lo largo de

ski run s pista de esquí

ski stick s bastón m de esquiar

skit [skɪt] s boceto burlesco, paso cómico

skittish ['skɪtɪʃ] adj caprichoso; asustadizo; tímido; (bull) abanto

skulduggery [skʌl'dʌgəri] s (coll) trampa, embuste m

skull [skʌl] s cráneo, calavera

skull'cap' s casquete m

skunk [skʌŋk] s mofeta; (person) (coll) canalla m

sky [skaɪ] s (pl **skies**) cielo; **to praise to the skies** poner por las nubes, poner en el cielo

sky'div'ing s paracaidismo con plomada suelta inicial

Skylab ['skaɪ,læb]s laboratorio espacial

sky'lark' s alondra ‖ intr jaranear

sky'light' s tragaluz m, claraboya

sky'line' s línea del horizonte, línea de los edificios contra el cielo

sky'rock'et s cohete m ‖ intr subir como un cohete

sky'scrap'er s rascacielos m

sky'writ'ing s escritura aérea

slab [slæb] s losa; plancha, tabla

slack [slæk] adj flojo; perezoso; negligente; inactivo ‖ s flojedad; inactividad; estación muerta, temporada inactiva; **slacks** pantalones flojos ‖ tr aflojar; apagar (la cal) ‖ intr atrasarse; descuidarse; **to slack up** aflojar el paso

slacker ['slækər] s perezoso; (mil) prófugo

slag [slæg] s escoria

slake [slek] tr aplacar, calmar; apagar (la cal)

slalom ['slaləm] s eslálom m

slam [slæm] s golpe m; (of a door) portazo; (coll) crítica acerba ‖ v (pret & pp **slammed**; ger **slamming**) tr cerrar de golpe; golpear o empujar estrepitosamente; (coll) criticar acerbamente ‖ intr cerrarse de golpe

slam'-bang' adv (coll) de golpe y porrazo

slander ['slændər] s calumnia, difamación; levante (CAm, P-R) ‖ tr calumniar, difamar

slanderous ['slændərəs] adj calumnioso, difamatorio

slang [slæŋ] s caló m, jerigonza

slant [slænt] s inclinación; parecer m, punto de vista ‖ tr inclinar, sesgar; deformar, tergiversar (un informe) ‖ intr inclinarse, sesgarse

slap [slæp] s manazo, palmada; (in the face) bofetada; (in the back) espaldarazo; desaire m, insulto ‖ v (pret & pp **slapped**; ger **slapping**) tr dar una palmada a; abofetear

slash [slæʃ] s cuchillada ‖ tr acuchillar; hacer fuerte rebaja de (precios, sueldos, etc.)

slat [slæt] s lámina, tablilla

slate [slet] s pizarra; candidatura, lista de candidatos ‖ tr empizarrar; designar, destinar; poner en la lista de candidatos

slate pencil s pizarrín m

slate roof s empizarrado

slattern ['slætərn] s mujer desaliñada, pazpuerca

slaughter ['slɔtər] s carnicería, matanza ‖ tr matar

slaughter house s matadero

Slav [slɑv] o [slæv] adj & s eslavo

slave [slev] adj & s esclavo ‖ intr trabajar como esclavo

slave driver s negrero; (fig) negrero

slave'hold'er s dueño de esclavos

slavery ['slevəri] s esclavitud

slave trade s trata de esclavos

slave trader s negrero

Slavic ['slɑvɪk] o ['slævɪk] adj & s eslavo

slay [sle] v (pret **slew** [slu]; pp **slain** [slen]) tr matar

slayer ['sle•ər] s matador m

sled [slɛd] s luge m ‖ v (pret & pp **sledded**; ger **sledding**) intr deslizarse en luge o trineo

sledge hammer [slɛdʒ] s acotillo

sleek [slik] adj liso y brillante ‖ tr alisar y pulir; suavizar

sleep [slip] s sueño; **to be overcome with sleep** caerse de sueño; **to go to sleep** dormirse; dormirse, morirse (un miembro); **to put to sleep** adormecer; matar por anestesia ‖ v (pret & pp **slept** [slɛpt]) tr pasar durmiendo; **to sleep it off** dormir la mona; **to sleep it over** consultar con la almohada; **to sleep off** dormir (p.ej., una borrachera) ‖ intr dormir

sleeper ['slipər] s (person) durmiente mf; (girder) durmiente m

sleeping bag s saco de dormir

Sleeping Beauty s la Bella Durmiente

sleeping car s coche-cama m

sleeping pill s píldora para dormir

sleepless ['sliplɪs] adj insomne, desvelado; pasado en vela

sleep'walk'er s sonámbulo; nochero

sleep•y ['slipi] adj (comp **-ier**; super **-iest**) soñoliento; **to be sleepy** tener sueño

sleep'y•head' s dormilón m

sleet [slit] s cellisca ‖ intr cellisquear

sleeve [sliv] s manga; (mach) manguito; **to laugh in o up one's sleeve** reírse para sí

sleigh [sle] s trineo ‖ intr pasearse en trineo

sleigh bell s cascabel m

sleigh ride s paseo en trineo

sleight of hand [slaɪt] s juego de manos, prestidigitación

slender ['slɛndər] adj esbelto, flaco, delgado; escaso, insuficiente

sleuth [sluθ] s sabueso

slew [slu] s (coll) montón m

slice [slaɪs] s rebanada, tajada; (of an orange) gajo ‖ tr rebanar, tajar; dividir; cortar

slick [slɪk] adj liso y brillante; meloso, suave; (coll) astuto, mañoso ‖ s lugar aceitoso y lustroso (en el agua)

slicker ['slɪkər] *s* impermeable *m* de hule; (coll) embaucador *m*

slide [slaɪd] *s* resbalón *m; (slippery place)* resbaladero; *(slippery surface)* desliz *m;* derrumbamiento de tierra; *(image for projection)* diapositiva, transparencia; *(of a microscope)* plaquilla de vidrio; *(piece of a device that slides)* cursor *m; (of a trombone)* corredera (tubular) ‖ *v (pret & pp* **slid** [slɪd]) *tr* deslizar ‖ *intr* deslizar, resbalar; **to let slide** dejar pasar, no hacer caso de

slide fastener *s* cierre *m* cremallera, cierre relámpago

slide rule *s* regla de cálculo

slide valve *s* corredera, válvula corrediza

sliding contact *s* cursor *m*

sliding door *s* puerta de corredera

sliding scale *s* regla de cálculo; *(of salaries)* escala móvil

slight [slaɪt] *adj* delgado; leve; pequeño; escaso; delgaducho ‖ *s* desatención, descuido; desaire *m*, menosprecio ‖ *tr* desatender, descuidar; desairar

slim [slɪm] *adj (comp* **slimmer;** *super* **slimmest)** delgado, esbelto; débil, leve, pequeño, escaso

slime [slaɪm] *s* légamo; *(of snakes, fish, etc.)* baba

slim•y ['slaɪmi] *adj (comp* **-ier;** *super* **-iest)** legamoso; baboso, viscoso; puerco, sucio

sling [slɪŋ] *s (to shoot stones)* honda; *(to hold up a broken arm)* cabestrillo ‖ *v (pret & pp* **slung** [slʌŋ]) *tr* lanzar con una honda; lanzar, tirar; poner en cabestrillo; colgar flojamente

sling'shot' *s* honda

slink [slɪŋk] *v (pret & pp* **slunk** [slʌŋk]) *intr* andar furtivamente; **to slink away** escabullirse, salir con el rabo entre piernas

slip [slɪp] *s* resbalón *m*, desliz *m;* falta, error *m*, desliz *m;* lapso; embarcadero; *(cover for a pillow, for furniture)* funda; *(piece of paper)* papeleta; *(cutting from a plant)* sarmiento; *(piece of underclothing)* combinación; *(of a dog)* traílla; huída, evasión; mozuelo, mozuela; **to give the slip to** burlar la vigilancia de ‖ *v (pret & pp* **slipped;** *ger* **slipping)** *tr* poner rápidamente; quitar rápidamente; pasar por alto; eludir, evadir; **to slip off** (coll) quitarse de prisa; **to slip on** (coll) ponerse de prisa; **to slip one's mind** olvidársele a uno ‖ *intr* deslizarse; patinar *(el embrague);* errar, equivocarse; (coll) declinar, deteriorarse; **to let slip** dejar pasar; decir inadvertidamente; **to slip away** escurrirse; **to slip by** pasar inadvertido; pasar rápidamente *(el tiempo);* **to slip out of one's hands** escurrirse de entre las manos; **to slip up** (coll) errar, equivocarse

slip cover *s* funda

slip of the pen *s* error *m* de pluma

slip of the tongue *s* error *m* de lengua

slipper ['slɪpər] *s* zapatilla, babucha

slippery ['slɪpəri] *adj* deslizadizo, resbaladizo; astuto, zorro, evasivo

slip'-up' *s* (coll) error *m*, equivocación

slit [slɪt] *s* hendidura, raja; cortada, incisión ‖ *v (pret & pp* **slit;** *ger* **slitting)** *tr* hender, rajar; cortar

slob [slɑb] *s* (slang) sujeto desaseado, puerco

slobber ['slɑbər] *s* baba; sensiblería ‖ *intr* babear; hablar con sensiblería

sloe [slo] *s (shrub)* endrino; *(fruit)* endrina

slogan ['slogən] *s* lema *m*, mote *m;* grito de combate; *(striking phrase used in advertising)* eslogan *m*

sloop [slup] *s* balandra

slop [slɑp] *s* gacha, zupia, agua sucia ‖ *v (pret & pp* **slopped;** *ger* **slopping)** *tr* salpicar, ensuciar ‖ *intr* derramarse; chapotear

slope [slop] *s* cuesta, pendiente *f; (of a continent or a roof)* vertiente *m & f* ‖ *tr* inclinar ‖ *intr* inclinarse

slop•py ['slɑpi] *adj (comp* **-pier;** *super* **-piest)** mojado y sucio; *(in one's dress)* desgalichado; *(in one's work)* chapucero

slot [slɑt] *s* ranura; *(for letters)* buzón *m*

sloth [sloθ] o [slɔθ] *s* pereza; (zool) perezoso

slot machine *s* tragamonedas *m*, máquina sacaperras

slot meter *s* contador automático

slouch [slaʊtʃ] *s* postura relajada; persona torpe de movimientos ‖ *intr* agacharse, andar caído de hombros; **to slouch in a chair** repanchigarse

slouch hat *s* sombrero gacho

slough [slaʊ] *s* cenagal *m*, fangal *m;* estado de abandono moral ‖ [slʌf] *s (of a snake)* camisa; (pathol) escara ‖ *tr* mudar, echar de sí ‖ *intr* caerse, desprenderse

Slovak ['slovæk] o [slo'væk] *adj & s* eslovaco

sloven•ly ['slʌvənli] *adj (comp* **-lier;** *super* **-liest)** desaseado, desaliñado

slow [slo] *adj* lento; *(sluggish)* cachazudo, despacioso; *(clock, watch)* atrasado; *(in understanding)* lerdo, tardo, torpe ‖ *adv* despacio ‖ *tr* retrasar; atrasar *(un reloj)* ‖ *intr* retardarse, ir más despacio; atrasarse *(un reloj)*

slow'down' *s* huelga de brazos caídos

slow motion *s (film)* ralentí *m;* **in slow motion** al ralentí, a cámara lenta

slow'-mo'tion *adj* a cámara lenta

slowness ['slonɪs] lentitud, lerdera

slow'poke' *s* tardón *m*

slug [slʌg] *s (heavy piece of metal)* lingote *m; (metal disk used as a coin)* ficha; (zool) limaza, babosa; (coll) porrazo, puñetazo ‖ *v (pret & pp* **slugged;** *ger* **slugging)** *tr* (coll) aporrear, apuñear

sluggard ['slʌgərd] *s* pachón *m*, perezoso

sluggish ['slʌgɪʃ] *adj* inactivo, indolente, tardo; pachorrudo, perezoso

sluice [slus] *s* canal *m; (floodgate)* compuerta; *(dam; flume)* presa

sluice gate *s* compuerta de presa

slum [slʌm] *s* barrio bajo ‖ *v (pret & pp* **slummed;** *ger* **slumming)** *intr* visitar los barrios bajos

slumber ['slʌmbər] *s* sueño ligero, sueño tranquilo ‖ *intr* dormir; dormitar

slump [slʌmp] *s* depresión, crisis económica; (*in prices, stocks, etc.*) baja repentina ‖ *intr* hundirse, desplomarse; bajar repentinamente (*los precios, valores, etc.*)

slur [slʌr] *s* pronunciación indistinta; reparo crítico; (mus) ligado ‖ *v* (*pret & pp* **slurred; ger slurring**) *tr* comerse (*sonidos, sílabas*); despreciar, insultar; (mus) ligar

slush [slʌʃ] *s* fango muy blando, aguanieve fangosa, nieve *f* a medio derretir; sentimentalismo tonto

slut [slʌt] *s* perra; (*slovenly woman*) pazpuerca; ramera, mala mujer

sly [slaɪ] *adj* (*comp* **slyer** o **slier**; *super* **slyest** o **sliest**) furtivo, secreto; astuto, socarrón; travieso; **on the sly** a hurtadillas

smack [smæk] *adv* (coll) de golpe, de sopetón ‖ *s* dejo, gustillo; palmada, manotada; golpe *m;* beso sonado; (*of a whip*) chasquido ‖ *tr* dar una manotada a; golpear; hacer chasquidos con (*un látigo*); besar sonoramente; **to smack one's lips** chuparse los labios ‖ *intr*—**to smack of** saber a, oler a

small [smɔl] *adj* pequeño, chico; (*short in stature*) bajo; pobre, obscuro, humilde; (typ) minúsculo

small arms *spl* armas ligeras

small beer *s* cerveza floja; bagatela; persona de poca monta

small business *s* pequeña empresa

small capital *s* versalilla o versalita

small change *s* suelto, dinero menudo

small fry *s* gente menuda; gente de poca monta

small'-fry' *adj* de niños, para niños; de poca monta

small hours *spl* primeras horas (*de la mañana*)

small intestine *s* intestino delgado

small-minded ['smɔl'maɪndɪd] *adj* tacaño, mezquino; intolerante

smallpox ['smɔl,pɑks] *s* viruela

small print *s* tipo menudo

small talk *s* palique *m*, charlas frívolas

small'-time' *adj* de poca monta

small'-town' *adj* lugareño, apegado a cosas lugareñas

smart [smɑrt] *adj* listo, vivo, inteligente; agudo, penetrante; astuto; elegante, majo; picante, punzante; (coll) grande, considerable ‖ *s* escozor *m;* dolor vivo ‖ *intr* escocer, picar; padecer, sufrir

smart aleck ['ælɪk] *s* (coll) fatuo, sabihondo

smart money *s* (fig) inversionistas *mpl/fpl* astutos; gente *f* bien informada

smart set *s* gente *f* chic, gente de buen tono

smash [smæʃ] *s* rotura violenta; fracaso, ruina; quiebra, bancarrota; (coll) choque violento, tope violento ‖ *tr* romper con fuerza; arruinar, destrozar; aplastar ‖ *intr* romperse con fuerza; arruinarse, destrozarse; aplastarse; **to smash into** chocar con, topar con

smash hit *s* (coll) éxito rotundo

smash'-up' *s* colisión violenta; ruina, desastre *m;* quiebra, bancarrota

smattering ['smætərɪŋ] *s* barniz *m*, tintura, migaja

smear [smɪr] *s* embarradura; calumnia; (bact) frotis *m* ‖ *tr* embarrar; calumniar ‖ *intr* embarrarse

smear campaign *s* campaña de calumnias

smell [smɛl] *s* olor *m;* (*sense*) olfato; fragancia, perfume *m* ‖ *v* (*pret & pp* **smelled** o **smelt** [smɛlt]) *tr* oler, olfatear ‖ *intr* oler; heder, oler mal; **to smell of** oler a

smelling salts *spl* sales aromáticas

smell·y ['smɛli] *adj* (*comp* **-ier**; *super* **-iest**) hediondo, maloliente

smelt [smɛlt] *s* (*fish*) eperlano, esperinque *m* ‖ *tr & intr* fundir

smile [smaɪl] *s* sonrisa ‖ *intr* sonreír, sonreírse

smiling ['smaɪlɪŋ] *adj* risueño

smirk [smʌrk] *s* sonrisa fatua y afectada ‖ *intr* sonreír fatua y afectadamente

smite [smaɪt] *v* (*pret* **smote** [smot]; *pp* **smitten** ['smɪtən] o **smit** [smɪt]) *tr* golpear o herir súbitamente y con fuerza; caer con fuerza sobre; apenar, afligir; castigar

smith [smɪθ] *s* forjador *m*, herrero

smith·y ['smɪθi] *s* (*pl* **-ies**) herrería

smitten ['smɪtən] *adj* afligido; muy enamorado

smock [smɑk] *s* bata

smock frock *s* blusa de obrero

smog [smɑg] *s* mezcla de humo y niebla

smoke [smok] *s* humo; **to go up in smoke** irse todo en humo ‖ *tr* (*to cure or treat with smoke*) ahumar; fumar (*tabaco*); **to smoke out** ahuyentar con humo, dar humazo a; descubrir ‖ *intr* humear; fumar; hacer humo (*una chimenea dentro de la habitación*)

smoked glasses *spl* gafas ahumadas

smoke evacuator *s* extractor de humos

smokeless powder ['smoklɪs] *s* pólvora sin humo

smokeless tobacco *s* tabaco sin humo

smoker ['smokər] *s* fumador *m;* (*room*) fumadero; (rr) coche-fumador *m;* reunión de fumadores

smoke rings *spl* anillos de humo; **to blow smoke rings** sacar humo formando anillos

smoke screen *s* cortina de humo

smoke'stack' *s* chimenea

smoking ['smokɪŋ] *s* el fumar; **no smoking** se prohibe fumar

smoking car *s* coche-fumador *m*, vagón *m* de fumar

smoking jacket *s* batín *m*

smoking room *s* fumadero, saloncito para fumadores

smok·y ['smoki] *adj* (*comp* **-ier**; *super* **-iest**) humoso; (*emitting smoke*) humeante

smolder ['smoldər] *s* fuego lento sin llama y con mucho humo ‖ *intr* arder en rescoldo, arder sin llamas; (fig) estar latente; (*to burn within*) (fig) requemarse; (fig) expresar (*p.ej., los ojos*) una ira latente

smooth [smuð] *adj* liso, terso, suave; plano, llano; igual; acaramelado, afable, blando, meloso; (*water*) tranquilo; (*style*) fluido;

smooth as butter como manteca ‖ *tr* alisar, suavizar; allanar; facilitar; **to smooth away** quitar (*p.ej.*, *obstáculos*) suavemente; **to smooth down** ablandar, calmar

smooth-faced ['smuð,fest] *adj* barbilampiño

smooth-spoken ['smuθ,spokən] *adj* meloso, lisonjero

smooth·y ['smuði] *s* (*pl* **-ies**) galante *m;* elegante *m;* adulador *m*

smother ['smʌðər] *tr* ahogar, sofocar; suprimir; reprimir

smudge [smʌdʒ] *s* tiznón *m;* mancha ‖ *tr* tiznar; manchar; ahumar, fumigar (*una huerta*)

smug [smʌg] *adj* (*comp* **smugger;** *super* **smuggest**) pagado de sí mismo; compuesto, pulcro; relamido

smuggle ['smʌgəl] *tr* meter de contrabando ‖ *intr* contrabandear

smuggler ['smʌglər] *s* contrabandista *mf*

smuggling ['smʌglɪŋ] *s* contrabando

smut [smʌt] *s* tiznón *m;* obscenidad; (agr) carbón *m*, tizón *m*

smut·ty ['smʌti] *adj* (*comp* **-tier;** *super* **-tiest**) tiznado, manchado; obsceno; (agr) atizonado

snack [snæk] *s* parte *f*, porción; bocadillo, tentempié *m*

snack bar *s* lonchería

snag [snæg] *s* (*of a tree*) tocón *m;* (*of a tooth*) raigón *m;* obstáculo, tropiezo; **to strike** o **to hit a snag** tropezar con un obstáculo

snail [snel] *s* caracol *m;* (*slow person*) pachón *m;* **at a snail's pace** a paso de caracol, a paso de tortuga

snake [snek] *s* culebra, serpiente *f*

snake in the grass *s* traidor *m*, amigo pérfido

snap [snæp] *s* (*crackling sound*) chasquido, estallido; (*of the fingers*) castañetazo; (*bite*) mordisco; (*cracker*) galletita; (*of cold weather*) corto período; (*catch or fastener*) broche *m* de presión; (phot) instantánea; (coll) brío, vigor *m;* (slang) breva, cosa fácil ‖ *v* (*pret & pp* **snapped;** *ger* **snapping**) *tr* asir, cerrar, etc. de golpe; castañetear (*los dedos*); chasquear (*el látigo*); fotografiar instantáneamente; tomar (*una instantánea*); **to snap one's fingers at** tratar con desprecio; **to snap up** aceptar con avidez, comprar con avidez; cortar la palabra a ‖ *intr* chasquear, estallar; (*to crack*) saltar; (*from fatigue*) estallar; **to snap at** querer morder; asir (*una oportunidad*); **to snap out of it** (slang) cambiarse repentinamente; **to snap shut** cerrarse de golpe

snap'drag'on *s* (bot) boca de dragón

snap fastener *s* corchete *m* de presión

snap judgment *s* decisión atolondrada

snap·py ['snæpi] *adj* (*comp* **-pier;** *super* **-piest**) mordaz; (coll) elegante, garboso; (coll) enérgico, vivo; (*food*) acre, picante

snap'shot' *s* instantánea

snap switch *s* (elec) interruptor *m* de resorte

snare [snɛr] *s* lazo, trampa: (*of a drum*) bordón *m*, tirante *m*

snare drum *s* caja clara

snarl [snɑrl] *s* gruñido; regaño; maraña, enredo ‖ *tr* decir con un gruñido; enmarañar, enredar ‖ *intr* gruñir; regañar; enmarañarse, enredarse

snatch [snætʃ] *s* arrebatamiento; pedacito, trocito; ratito ‖ *tr & intr* arrebatar; **to snatch at** tratar de asir o agarrar; **to snatch from** arrebatar a

sneak [snik] *adj* furtivo ‖ *s* sujeto solapado ‖ *tr* mover a hurtadillas ‖ *intr* andar furtivamente, moverse a hurtadillas

sneaker ['snikər] *s* sujeto solapado; (coll) zapato blando, zapato de lona

sneak thief *s* ratero, descuidero

sneak·y ['sniki] *adj* (*comp* **-ier;** *super* **-iest**) solapado, furtivo

sneer [snɪr] *s* expresión de desprecio ‖ *intr* hablar con desprecio, echar una mirada de desprecio; **to sneer at** mofarse de

sneeze [sniz] *s* estornudo ‖ *intr* estornudar; **not to be sneezed at** (coll) no ser despreciable

snicker ['snɪkər] *s* risa tonta ‖ *intr* reírse tontamente

sniff [snɪf] *s* husmeo, venteo; sorbo por las narices ‖ *tr* husmear, ventear; sorber por las narices; (fig) husmear, averiguar; (fig) sospechar; (*heroin*) esnifar (*caballo*) ‖ *intr* ventear; **to sniff at** husmear; menospreciar

sniffle ['snɪfəl] *s* resuello fuerte y repetido; **the sniffles** ataque *m* de resoplidos ‖ *intr* resollar fuerte y repetidamente

snip [snɪp] *s* tijeretada; recorte *m*, pedacito; (coll) persona pequeña e insignificante ‖ *v* (*pret & pp* **snipped;** *ger* **snipping**) *tr* tijeretear

snipe [snaɪp] *s* agachadiza, becacín *m* ‖ *intr* paquear, tirar desde un escondite

sniper ['snaɪpər] *s* paco, tirador emboscado

snippet ['snɪpɪt] *s* recorte *m;* (coll) persona pequeña e insignificante

snip·py ['snɪpi] *adj* (*comp* **-pier;** *super* **-piest**) (coll) arrogante, desdeñoso; (coll) acre, brusco

snitch [snɪtʃ] *tr & intr* (slang) escamotear, ratear; manotear (Arg, Mex)

sniv·el ['snɪvəl] *s* gimoteo, lloriqueo; moqueo ‖ *v* (*pret & pp* **-eled** o **-elled;** *ger* **-eling** o **-elling**) *intr* gimotear, lloriquear; (*to have a runny nose*) moquear

snob [snɑb] *s* esnob *mf*

snobbery ['snɑbəri] *s* esnobismo

snobbish ['snɑbɪʃ] *adj* esnob, esnobista

snoop [snup] *s* buscavidas *mf*, curioso ‖ *intr* curiosear, ventear

snoopy ['snupi] *adj* curioso, entremetido

snoot [snut] *s* (slang) cara, narices *fpl*

snoot·y ['snuti] *adj* (*comp* **-ier;** *super* **-iest**) (slang) esnob

snooze [snuz] *s* (coll) sueñecito ‖ *intr* echar un sueñecito

snore [snor] *s* ronquido ‖ *intr* roncar

snort [snɔrt] *s* bufido ‖ *intr* bufar

snot [snɑt] *s* (slang) mocarro

snot·ty ['snɑti] *adj* (*comp* **-tier;** *super* **-tiest**) mocoso; asqueroso, sucio; (slang) engreído

snout [snaut] *s* hocico; (*something shaped like the snout of an animal*) morro; (*of a person*) (coll) hocico

snow [sno] *s* nieve *f* ‖ *intr* nevar

snow'ball' *s* bola de nieve ‖ *tr* lanzar bolas de nieve a ‖ *intr* aumentar rápidamente

snow'-blind' *adj* cegado por reflejos de la nieve

snow-capped ['sno,kæpt] *adj* coronado de nieve

snow'drift' *s* ventisquero, masa de nieve

snow'fall' *s* nevada

snow fence *s* valla paranieves

snow'flake' *s* copo de nieve, ampo

snow flurry *s* nevisca

snow job *s* (slang) decepción; engaño

snow line o **limit** *s* límite *m* de las nieves perpetuas

snow man *s* figura de nieve

snow'plow' *s* expulsanieves *m*, quitanieves *m*

snow'shoe' *s* raqueta de nieve

snow'storm' *s* nevasca, fuerte nevada

snow tire *s* llanta de invierno

snow'-white' *adj* blanco como la nieve

snow•y ['sno•i] *adj* (*comp* **-ier;** *super* **-iest**) nevoso

snowy owl *s* lechuza blanca

snub [snʌb] *s* desaire *m* ‖ *v* (*pret & pp* **snubbed;** *ger* **snubbing**) *tr* desairar

snub•by ['snʌbi] *adj* (*comp* **-bier;** *super* **-biest**) (*nose*) respingona

snuff [snʌf] *s* rapé; (*of a candlewick*) moco; **up to snuff** (slang) en buena condición; (slang) difícil de engañar ‖ *tr* husmear, olfatear; sorber por. la nariz; despabilar (*una candela*); **to snuff out** apagar, extinguir

snuff'box' *s* tabaquera

snuffers ['snʌfərz] *spl* despabiladeras

snug [snʌg] *adj* (*comp* **snugger;** *super* **snuggest**) cómodo; (*garment*) ajustado, ceñido; (*well-off*) acomodado; (*in hiding*) escondido

snuggle ['snʌgəl] *intr* apretarse, arrimarse; dormir bien abrigado; **to snuggle up to** arrimarse a

so [so] *adv* así; tan + *adj* o *adv;* por tanto; también; **and so** así pues; también, lo mismo; **and so on** y así sucesivamente; **or so** más o menos; **to think so** creer que sí; **so as to** + *inf* para + *inf;* **so far** hasta aquí; hasta ahora; **so long** hasta la vista; **so many** tantos; **so much** tanto; **so so** tal cual, así así; **so that** de modo que, de suerte que, así que; para que; con tal de que; **so to speak** por decirlo así ‖ *conj* as que ‖ *interj* ¡bien!; ¡verdad!

soak [sok] *s* mojada; (*toper*) (coll) potista *mf* ‖ *tr* empapar, remojar; embeber; (slang) aporrear; (slang) hacer pagar un precio exorbitante; **to soak up** absorber, embeber; (fig) entender; **soaked to the skin** calado hasta los huesos ‖ *intr* empaparse, remojarse

so'-and-so' *s* (*pl* **-sos**) fulano, fulano de tal; tal cosa

soap [sop] *s* jabón *m* ‖ *tr* jabonar

soap'box' *s* caja de jabón; tribuna callejera

soapbox orator *s* orador *m* de plazuela

soap bubble *s* burbuja de jabón, pompa de jabón

soap dish *s* jabonera

soap flakes *spl* copos de jabón

soap'mak'er *s* jabonero

soap opera *s* (coll) telenovela; serial lacrimógeno

soap powder *s* jabón *m* en polvo, polvo de jabón

soap'stone' *s* jaboncillo de sastre

soap'suds' *spl* jabonaduras

soap•y ['sopi] *adj* (*comp* **-ier;** *super* **-iest**) jabonoso

soar [sor] *intr* encumbrarse, subir muy alto, volar a gran altura; aspirar, pretender; (aer) planear

sob [sab] *s* sollozo ‖ *v* (*pret & pp* **sobbed;** *ger* **sobbing**) *tr* decir o expresar sollozando ‖ *intr* sollozar

sobbing *s* llorera

sober ['sobər] *adj* sobrio; no embriagado; grave, serio; cuerdo, sensato; sereno, tranquilo; (*color*) apagado ‖ *tr* poner sobrio; desemborrachar; **to sober up** desintoxicar ‖ *intr* volverse sobrio; desemborracharse; **to sober down** calmarse, sosegarse; **to sober up** desemborracharse

sobriety [so'braɪəti] *s* sobriedad, moderación; gravedad, seriedad; cordura, sensatez; serenidad

sobriquet ['sobrɪ,ke] *s* apodo

sob sister *s* (slang) periodista llorona

sob story *s* (slang) historia de lagrimitas

soc. o **Soc.** *abbr* **society**

so'-called' *adj* llamado, así llamado; supuesto

soccer ['sakər] *s* fútbol *m* asociación

sociable ['soʃəbəl] *adj* sociable

social ['soʃəl] *adj* social ‖ *s* reunión social

social climber ['klaɪmər] *s* ambicioso de figurar

socialism ['soʃə,lɪzəm] *s* socialismo

socialist ['soʃəlɪst] *s* socialista *mf*

socialite ['soʃə,laɪt] *s* (coll) personaje *m* de la buena sociedad

social register *s* guía *m* social, registro de la buena sociedad

socie•ty [sə'saɪəti] *s* (*pl* **-ties**) sociedad; (*companionship or company*) compañía; buena sociedad, mundo elegante

society editor *s* cronista *mf* de la vida social

sociology [,sosɪ'alədʒi] o [,soʃɪ'alədʒi] *s* sociología

sock [sak] *s* calcetín *m;* (slang) golpe *m* fuerte ‖ *tr* (slang) golpear con fuerza

socket ['sakɪt] *s* (*of the eyes*) cuenca; (*of a tooth*) alvéolo; (*of a candlestick*) cañón *m;* (*of a socket wrench*) cubo; (elec) portalámparas; (rad) zócalo

socket wrench *s* llave *f* de caja, llave de cubo

sod [sad] *s* césped *m;* terrón *m* de césped ‖ *v* (*pret & pp* **sodded;** *ger* **sodding**) *tr* encespedar

soda ['sodə] *s* soda, sosa; (*drink*) soda

soda fountain *s* fuente *f* de sodas

soda water _s_ agua gaseosa
sodium ['sodɪ•əm] _adj_ sódico, de sodio ‖ _s_ sodio
sofa ['sofə] _s_ sofá _m_
soft [sɔft] o [saft] _adj_ blando, muelle; (_skin_) suave; (_iron_) dulce; (_hat_) flexible; (_solder_) tierno; (coll) fácil
soft-boiled egg ['sɔft'bɔɪld] o ['saft'bɔɪld] _s_ huevo pasado por agua
soft coal _s_ hulla grasa
soft drink _s_ bebida no alcohólica, refresco
soften ['sɔfən] o ['safən] _tr_ ablandar; **to soften up** (_by bombardment_) ablandar ‖ _intr_ ablandarse
soft'-ped'al _tr_ (mus) disminuir la intensidad de, por medio del pedal suave; (slang) moderar
soft soap _tr_ jabón blando o graso; (coll) adulación
soft'-soap' _s_ (coll) enjabonar, dar jabón a
soft'ware' _s_ (computer) programa _m_ (para ordenador), operaciones _fpl_
sog•gy ['sagi] _adj_ (_comp_ **-gier;** _super_ **-giest**) remojado, ensopado
soil [sɔɪl] _s_ suelo; país _m_, región; (_spot, stain_) mancha; (fig) mancha, deshonra ‖ _tr_ manchar, ensuciar; manchar, deshonrar; viciar, corromper ‖ _intr_ mancharse, ensuciarse
soil pipe _s_ tubo de desagüe sanitario
soiree o **soirée** [swɑ're] _s_ sarao, velada
sojourn ['sodʒʌrn] _s_ estancia, permanencia ‖ ['sodʒʌrn] o [so'dʒʌrn] _intr_ estarse, permanecer
soil. _abbr_ **soluble, solution**
solace ['salɪs] _s_ solaz _m_, consuelo ‖ _tr_ solazar, consolar
solar ['solər] _adj_ solar
solar battery _s_ fotopila
solder ['sadər] _s_ soldadura ‖ _tr_ soldar
soldering iron _s_ cautín _m_, soldador _m_
soldier ['soldʒər] _s_ (_enlisted man as distinguished from an officer_) soldado; (_man in military service_) militar _m_ ‖ _intr_ servir como soldado
soldier of fortune _s_ aventurero militar
soldier•y ['soldʒəri] _s_ (_pl_ **-ies**) soldadesca
sold out [sold] _adj_ agotado; **the theater is sold out** todas las localidades están vendidas; **we are sold out of those neckties** se nos han agotado esas corbatas
sole [sol] _adj_ solo, único; exclusivo ‖ _s_ (_of foot_) planta; (_of shoe_) suela; (_fish_) lenguado ‖ _tr_ solar
solely ['solli] _adv_ solamente, únicamente
solemn ['saləm] _adj_ solemne
solicit [sə'lɪsɪt] _tr_ solicitar; intentar seducir
solicitor [sə'lɪsɪtər] _s_ solicitador _m_, agente _m;_ (law) procurador _m_
solicitous [sə'lɪsɪtəs] _adj_ solícito
solicitude [sə'lɪsɪ,tjud] o [sə'lɪsɪ,tud] _s_ solicitud
solid ['salɪd] _adj_ sólido; unánime; (_sound, good_) sólido, macizo; (_e.g., clouds_) denso; (_without pause or interruption_) entero; (_e.g., gold_) puro ‖ _s_ sólido
solidarity [,salɪ'dɛrɪtɪ] _s_ solidaridad; **to declare one's solidarity with** solidarizar con

solid geometry _s_ geometría del espacio
solidity [sə'lɪdɪtɪ] _s_ (_pl_ **-ties**) solidez _f_
solid majority _s_ mayoría cómoda
sol'id-state' _adj_ transistorizado
solid-state physics _s_ física del estado sólido
solid tire _s_ (aut) macizo
solilo•quy [sə'lɪləkwi] _s_ (_pl_ **-quies**) soliloquio
solitaire ['salɪ,tɛr] _s_ (_game and diamond_) solitario; sortija solitario
solitar•y ['salɪ,tɛri] _adj_ solitario; **in solitary confinement** incomunicado ‖ _s_ (_pl_ **-ies**) solitario
solitary confinement _s_ incomunicación, aislamiento penal
solitude ['salɪ,tjud] o ['salɪ,tud] _s_ soledad
so•lo ['solo] _adj_ (_instrument_) solista; a solas, hecho a solas ‖ _s_ (_pl_ **-los**) (mus) solo
soloist ['solo•ɪst] _s_ solista _mf_
solstice ['salstɪs] _s_ solsticio
solution [sə'luʃən] _s_ solución
solve [salv] _tr_ resolver, solucionar; adivinar (_un enigma_)
solvent ['salvənt] _adj & s_ solvente _m_
somber ['sambər] _adj_ sombrío
some [sʌm] _adj indef_ algún; un poco de; unos; (coll) grande, bueno, famoso ‖ _pron indef pl_ algunos, unos
some'bod'y _pron indef_ alguien; **somebody else** algún otro, otra persona ‖ _s_ (_pl_ **-ies**) (coll) personaje _m_
some'day' _adv_ algúna día
some'how' _adv_ de algún modo, de alguna manera; **somehow or other** de un modo u otro
some'one' _pron indef_ alguien; **someone else** algún otro, otra persona
somersault ['sʌmər,sɔlt] _s_ salto mortal ‖ _intr_ dar un salto mortal
something ['sʌmθɪŋ] _adv_ algo, un poco; (coll) muy, excesivamente ‖ _pron indef_ alguna cosa, algo; **something else** otra cosa
some'time' _adj_ antiguo, de otro tiempo ‖ _adv_ alguna vez; antiguamente
some'times' _adv_ a veces, algunas veces
some'way' _adv_ de algún modo
some'what' _adv_ algo, un poco ‖ _s_ alguna cosa, algo
some'where' _adv_ en alguna parte, a alguna parte; en algún tiempo; **somewhere else** en otra parte, a otra parte
somnambulist [sam'næmbjəlɪst] _s_ sonámbulo
somnolent ['samnələnt] _adj_ soñoliento
son [sʌn] _s_ hijo
song [sɔŋ] o [saŋ] _s_ canción, canto; **for a song** muy barato; **to sing the same old song** volver a la misma canción
song'bird' _s_ ave canora
Song of Songs _s_ Cantar _m_ de los Cantares
song writer _s_ cantautor _m_
sonic ['sanɪk] _adj_ sónico
sonic boom _s_ (aer) estampido sónico
son'-in-law' _s_ (_pl_ **sons-in-law**) yerno, hijo político
sonnet ['sanɪt] _s_ soneto

sonneteer [,sɑnɪ'tɪr] *s* sonetista *mf;* poetastro ‖ *intr* sonetizar

son•ny ['sʌni] *s* (*pl* **-nies**) hijito

sonori•ty [sə'nɔrɪti] *s* (*pl* **-ties**) sonoridad

soon [sun] *adv* pronto, en breve; temprano; de buena gana; **as soon as** así que, en cuanto, luego que, tan pronto como; **as soon as possible** cuanto antes, lo más pronto posible; **had sooner** preferiría; **how soon?** ¿cuándo?; **soon after** poco después, poco después de; **sooner or later** tarde o temprano

soot [sʊt] o [sut] *s* hollín *m*

soothe [suð] *tr* aliviar, calmar, sosegar

soothsayer ['suθ,se•ər] *s* adivino

soot•y ['suti] o ['sʊti] *adj* (*comp* **-ier**; *super* **-iest**) holliniento, tiznado

sop [sɑp] *s* (*food soaked in milk, etc.*) sopa; regalo (*para acallar, apaciguar o sobornar*) ‖ *v* (*pret & pp* **sopped;** *ger* **sopping**) *tr* empapar, ensopar; **to sop up** absorber

sophisticated [sə'fɪstɪ,ketɪd] *adj* mundano, falto de simplicidad, corrido

sophomore ['sɑfə,mor] *s* estudiante *mf* de segundo año

sopping ['sɑpɪŋ] *adj* empapado; **sopping wet** hecho una sopa

sopran•o [sə'præno] o [sə'prɑno] *adj* de soprano; para soprano ‖ *s* (*pl* **-os**) soprano *mf*

sorcerer ['sɔrsərər] *s* brujo, hechicero

sorceress ['sɔrsərɪs] *s* bruja, hechicera

sorcer•y ['sɔrsəri] *s* (*pl* **-ies**) brujería, hechicería, sortilegio

sordid ['sɔrdɪd] *adj* sórdido

sore [sor] *adj* enrojecido, inflamado; (coll) resentido, picado; **to be sore at** (coll) estar enojado con ‖ *s* llaga, úlcera; pena, dolor *m*, aflicción; **to open an old sore** renovar la herida

sorely ['sorli] *adv* penosamente; con urgencia

sore throat *s* dolor *m* de garganta

sorori•ty [sə'rɔrɪti] *s* (*pl* **-ties**) hermandad de estudiantas

sorrel ['sɔrəl] *adj* alazán

sorrow ['sɑro] *s* dolor *m*, pena pesar *m;* arrepentimiento ‖ *intr* dolerse, apenarse, sentir pena; arrepentirse; **to sorrow for** añorar

sorrowful ['sɑrəfəl] *adj* doloroso, pesaroso, acongojado

sor•ry ['sɑri] o ['sɔri] *adj* (*comp* **-rier**; *super* **-riest**) afligido, apenado, pesaroso; arrepentido; malo, pésimo; despreciable, ridículo; **to be** o **feel sorry** sentir; arrepentirse; **to be** o **feel sorry for** compadecer; arrepentirse de; **I am sorry** lo siento, me sabe mal

sort [sɔrt] *s* clase *f*, especie *f;* modo, manera; **a sort of** uno a modo de; **out of sorts** de mal humor; **sort of** (coll) algo, en cierta medida ‖ *tr* clasificar, separar; escoger, entresacar

so'-so' *adj* mediano, regular, talcualillo ‖ *adv* así así, tal cual

sot [sɑt] *s* borracho

sotto voce ['sɑto 'votʃə] *adv* a sovoz, en voz baja

soubrette [su'brɛt] *s* (theat) confidenta de comedia; (theat) doncella coquetona

soul [sol] *s* alma; **upon my soul!** ¡por vida mía!

sound [saʊnd] *adj* sano: sólido, firme; solvente; sonoro; (*sleep*) profundo; prudente; legal, válido ‖ *adv* profundamente ‖ *s* sonido; ruido; (*passage of water*) estrecho, brazo de mar; (surg) sonda, tienta; **within sound of** al alcance de ‖ *tr* sonar; tocar (*p.ej., campanas*); tantear, sondear; auscultar (*p.ej., los pulmones*); entonar (*p.ej., alabanzas*) ‖ *intr* sonar, resonar; sondar; parecer; **to sound like** sonar a, sonar como

sound'-ab•sorb'ent *adj* fonoabsorbente

sound barrier *s* muro del sonido, barrera de sonido, barrera sónica

sound'-dead'en•ing *adj* fonoabsorbente

sound film *s* película sonora

soundly ['saʊndli] *adv* sanamente; profundamente; a fondo, completamente

sound'proof' *adj* antisonoro; insonorizado ‖ *tr* insonorizar

soundproofing ['saʊnd,prufɪŋ] *s* insonorización

soup [sup] *s* sopa

soup kitchen *s* comedor *m* de beneficencia, dispensario de alimentos

soup spoon *s* cuchara de sopa

sour [saʊr] *adj* agrio ‖ *tr* agriar ‖ *intr* agriarse

source [sors] *s* fuente *f*, manantial *m*

source material *s* fuentes *fpl* originales

sour cherry *s* (*tree*) guindo; (*fruit*) guinda

sour grapes *interj* ¡están verdes las uvas!

south [saʊθ] *adj* meridional, del sur ‖ *adv* al sur, hacia el sur ‖ *s* sur *m*, mediodía *m*

South America *s* Sudamérica, la América del Sur

South American *adj & s* sudamericano

southern ['sʌðərn] *adj* meridional

Southern Cross *s* Cruz *f* del Sur

southerner ['sʌðərnər] *s* meridional *mf;* sureño (Am)

South Korea *s* la Corea del Sur

South Korean *adj & s* surcoreano

south'paw' *adj & s* (slang in sport) zurdo

South Pole *s* polo sur, polo antártico

southward ['saʊθwərd] *adv* hacia el sur

south wind *s* austro, noto

souvenir [,suvə'nɪr] o ['suvə,nɪr] *s* recuerdo, memoria

sovereign ['sɑvrɪn] o ['sʌvrɪn] *adj* soberano ‖ *s* (*king; coin*) soberano; (*queen*) soberana

sovereign•ty ['sɑvrɪnti] o ['sʌvrɪnti] *s* (*pl* **-ties**) soberanía

soviet ['sovɪ,ɛt] o [,sovɪ'ɛt] *adj* soviético ‖ *s* soviet *m*

sovietize ['sovɪ•ɛ,taɪz] *tr* sovietizar

Soviet Russia *s* la Rusia Soviética

Soviet Union *s* Unión Soviética

sow [saʊ] *s* puerca ‖ [so] *v* (*pret* **sowed;** *pp* **sown** o **sowed**) *tr* sembrar; (*with mines*) plagar

soybean ['sɔɪ,bin] *s* soja; soya; semilla de soja

sp. *abbr* **special, species, specific, specimen, spelling**

spa [spɑ] *s* caldas, balneario
space [spes] *adj* espacial, del espacio ‖ *s* espacio; **in the space of** por espacio de ‖ *tr* espaciar
space bar *s* espaciador *m*, tecla de espacios
space'craft' *s* astronave *f*, cosmonave *f*
space flight *s* vuelo espacial
space key *s* llave *f* espacial
space•man ['spes,mæn] *s* (*pl* **-men** [,mɛn]) navegador *m* del espacio; astronauta *m;* visitante *m* a la Tierra del espacio exterior
space'ship' *s* nave *f* del espacio
space shuttle *s* transbordador *m* espacial
space station *s* apostadero espacial
space suit *s* escafandra espacial
space travel *s* cosmonavegación
space vehicle *s* vehículo espacial
spacious ['speʃəs] *adj* espacioso
spade [sped] *s* laya; (*playing card*) pique *m;* **to call a spade a spade** llamar al pan pan y al vino vino
spade'work' *s* trabajo preliminar
spaghetti [spə'gɛti] *s* espagueti *m*
Spain [spen] *s* España
span [spæn] *s* palmo, cuarta, llave *f* de la mano; espacio, lapso, trecho; (*of horses*) pareja; (*of a bridge*) ojo; (aer) envergadura ‖ *v* (*pret & pp* **spanned;** *ger* **spanning**) *tr* medir a palmos; atravesar, extenderse sobre
spangle ['spæŋgəl] *s* lentejuela ‖ *tr* adornar con lentejuelas; (*to stud with bright objects*) estrellar ‖ *intr* brillar
Spaniard ['spænjərd] *s* español *m*
spaniel ['spænjəl] *s* perro de aguas
Spanish ['spænɪʃ] *adj & s* español *m;* **the Spanish** los españoles
Spanish America *s* la América Española, Hispanoamérica
Spanish broom *s* retama
Spanish fly *s* abadejo, cantárida
Spanish Main *s* Costa Firme, Tierra Firme; mar *m* Caribe
Spanish moss *s* barba española
Spanish omelet *s* tortilla de tomate
Span'ish-speak'ing *adj* de habla española, hispanohablante, hispanoparlante
spank [spæŋk] *tr* azotar, zurrar
spanking ['spæŋkɪŋ] *adj* rápido; fuerte; (coll) muy grande, muy hermoso, extraordinario ‖ *s* azote *m*
spar *s* (mineral) espato; (naut) mástil *m*, palo, verga ‖ *v* (*pret & pp* **sparred;** *ger* **sparring**) *intr* pelear, reñir; boxear
spare [spɛr] *adj* sobrante; libre, disponible; de repuesto; delgado, enjuto, flaco; parco, sobrio ‖ *tr* pasar sin; perdonar; guardar, salvar; ahorrar; **to have . . . to spare** tener de sobra; **to spare oneself** ahorrarse esfuerzos
spare bed *s* cama de sobra
spare parts *spl* piezas de repuesto o de recambio
spare room *s* cuarto de reserva
sparing ['spɛrɪŋ] *adj* económico; (*scanty*) escaso

spark [spɑrk] *s* chispa; (*e.g., of truth*) centellita ‖ *tr* (coll) cortejar, galantear (*a una mujer*) ‖ *intr* chispear
spark coil *s* bobina de chispas, bobina de encendido
spark gap *s* (*of induction coil*) entrehierro; (*of spark plug*) espacio de chispa
sparkle ['spɑrkəl] *s* chispita, destello; (*wit*) travesura; alegría, viveza ‖ *intr* chispear; ser alegre; espumar, ser efervescente
sparkling ['spɑrklɪŋ] *adj* centelleante, chispeante; (*wine*) espumante, espumoso; (*water*) gaseoso
spark plug *s* bujía
sparrow ['spæro] *s* gorrión *m*
sparse [spɑrs] *adj* (*population*) poco denso; (*hair*) ralo
Spartan ['spɑrtən] *adj & s* espartano
spasm ['spæzəm] *s* espasmo; esfuerzo súbito y de breve duración
spasmodic ['spæz'mɑdɪk] *adj* espasmódico; intermitente; caprichoso
spastic ['spæstɪk] *adj* espástico
spat [spæt] *s* disputa, riña; botín *m*, polaina corta
spatial ['speʃəl] *adj* espacial
spatter ['spætər] *tr* salpicar; manchar ‖ *intr* chorrear; chapotear
spatula ['spætʃələ] *s* espátula
spavin ['spævɪn] *s* esparaván *m*
spawn [spɔn] *s* freza; prole *f;* producto, resultado ‖ *tr* engendrar ‖ *intr* desovar, frezar (*los peces*)
speak [spik] *v* (*pret* **spoke** [spok]; *pp* **spoken**) *tr* hablar (*un idioma*); decir (*la verdad*) ‖ *intr* hablar; **so to speak** por decirlo así; **speaking!** ¡al habla!; **to speak out** o **up** osar hablar, elevar la voz
speak'-eas'y *s* (*pl* **-ies**) (slang) taberna clandestina
speaker ['spikər] *s* hablante *mf;* orador *m;* (*of a legislative assembly*) presidente *m;* (rad) altavoz *m*
speaking ['spikɪŋ] *adj* hablante; **to be on speaking terms** hablarse ‖ *s* habla; elocuencia
speaking tube *s* tubo acústico
spear [spɪr] *s* lanza; (*for fishing*) arpón *m;* (*of grass*) hoja ‖ *tr* alancear, herir con lanza
spear'head' *s* punta de lanza ‖ *tr* dirigir, conducir; encabezar; dar impulso a
spear'mint' *s* menta verde, menta romana
spec. *abbr* special
special ['spɛʃəl] *adj* especial; **nothing special** (*no great thing*) nada del otro mundo ‖ *s* tren *m* especial
spe'cial•deliv'ery *adj* urgente, de urgencia
specialist ['spɛʃəlɪst] *s* especialista *mf*
speciali•ty [,spɛʃɪ'ælɪti] *s* (*pl* **-ties**) especialidad
specialize ['spɛʃə,laɪz] *tr* especializar ‖ *intr* especializar o especializarse
special•ty ['spɛʃəlti] *s* (*pl* **-ties**) especialidad
spe•cies ['spisiz] *s* (*pl* **-cies**) especie *f*
specific [spɪ'sɪfɪk] *adj & s* específico
speci•fy ['spɛsɪ,faɪ] *v* (*pret & pp* **-fied**) *tr* especificar

so
sp

specimen ['spɛsɪmən] s espécimen m; (coll) tipo, sujeto

specious ['spiʃəs] adj especioso, engañoso

speck [spɛk] s mota, manchita ‖ tr motear, manchar, salpicar de manchas

speckle ['spɛkəl] s mota, punto ‖ tr motear, puntear

spectacle ['spɛktəkəl] s espectáculo; **spectacles** anteojos, gafas

spectator ['spɛktetər] s espectador m

specter ['spɛktər] s espectro

spec·trum ['spɛktrəm] s (pl **-tra** [trə] o **-trums**) espectro

speculate ['spɛkjə,let] intr especular

speech [spitʃ] s habla; (of an actor) parlamento; (talk before an audience) conferencia, discurso

speech clinic s clínica de la palabra

speech correction s foniatría, logopedía

speech defect s defecto del habla

speechless ['spitʃlɪs] adj sin habla; estupefacto

speed [spid] s velocidad; (aut) marcha, velocidad; (slang) anfetaminas tomadas como alucinantes ‖ v (pret & pp **sped** [spɛd]) tr apresurar; despedir; ayudar ‖ intr apresurarse; adelantar, progresar; ir con exceso de velocidad

speeding ['spidɪŋ] s exceso de velocidad

speed king s as m del volante

speed limit s velocidad permitida

speedometer [spi'dɑmɪtər] s (to indicate speed) velocímetro; velocímetro y cuenta-kilómetros unidos

speed record s marca de velocidad

speed·y ['spidi] adj (comp **-ier;** super **-iest**) rápido, veloz

spell [spɛl] s encanto, hechizo; tanda, turno; rato, poco tiempo; (e.g., of good weather) temporada; **to cast a spell on** encantar, hechizar ‖ v (pret & pp **spelled** o **spelt** [spɛlt]) tr deletrear; indicar, significar; **to spell out** (coll) explicar detalladamente ‖ intr deletrear ‖ v (pret & pp **spelled**) tr reemplazar, relevar

spell'bind'er s (coll) orador m fascinante, orador persuasivo

spelling ['spɛlɪŋ] adj ortográfico ‖ s (act) deletreo; (subject or study) ortografía; (way a word is spelled) grafía

spelunker ['spɪ'lʌŋkər] s espeleólogo de afición

spend [spɛnd] v (pret & pp **spent** [spɛnt]) tr gastar; pasar (una hora, un día, etc.)

spender ['spɛndər] s gastador m

spending money s dinero para gastos menudos

spend'thrift' s derrochador m, pródigo

sperm [spʌrm] s esperma; (coll) leche f

sperm whale s cachalote m

spew [spju] tr & intr vomitar

sp. gr. abbr **specific gravity**

sphere [sfɪr] s esfera; astro, cuerpo celeste

spherical ['sfɛrɪkəl] adj esférico

sphinx [sfɪŋks] s (pl **sphinxes** o **sphinges** ['sfɪndʒiz]) esfinge f

spice [spaɪs] s especia; (zest, piquancy) sainete m; fragancia ‖ tr especiar; dar gusto o picante a

spice box s especiero

spick-and-span ['spɪkənd'spæn] adj flamante; limpio, pulcro

spic·y ['spaɪsi] adj (comp **-ier;** super **-iest**) especiado; picante; aromático; enchiloso (CAm, Mex); sicalíptico

spider ['spaɪdər] s araña

spider web s tela de araña, telaraña

spiff·y ['spɪfi] adj (comp **-ier;** super **-iest**) (slang) guapo, elegante

spigot ['spɪgət] s grifo; (plug to stop a vent) espiche m

spike [spaɪk] s (long, heavy nail) estaca, escarpia; (sharp projection or part) punta, pico, púa; (bot) espiga ‖ tr empernar; acabar, poner fin a

spill [spɪl] s derrame m; líquido derramado; (coll) caída, vuelco ‖ v (pret & pp **spilled** o **spilt** [spɪlt]) tr derramar, verter; (coll) hacer caer, volcar ‖ intr derramarse, verterse; (coll) caer, volcarse

spill'way' s bocacaz m, canal m de desagüe

spin [spɪn] s vuelta, giro muy rápido; (coll) paseo en coche, etc.; **to go into a spin** (aer) entrar en barrena ‖ v (pret & pp **spun** [spʌn]; ger **spinning**) tr hacer girar; hilar (p.ej., lino); bailar (un trompo); **to spin off** (derivative) rendir; **to spin out** extender, prolongar; **to spin yarns** contar cuentos increíbles ‖ intr dar vueltas, girar; hilar; bailar (un trompo); (aer) entrar en barrena

spinach ['spɪnɪtʃ] o ['spɪnɪdʒ] s espinaca; (leaves used as food) espinacas

spinal ['spaɪnəl] adj espinal

spinal column s espina dorsal, columna vertebral

spinal cord s médula espinal

spinal disk s disco vertebral

spindle ['spɪndəl] s (rounded rod tapering toward each end) huso; (small shaft, axle) eje m; (turned ornament in a baluster) mazorca

spine [spaɪn] s espina, púa; (rib, ridge) cordoncillo; loma, cerro; (anat) espina; (bb) lomo; (fig) ánimo, valor m

spineless ['spaɪnlɪs] adj sin espinas, sin espinazo; sin firmeza de carácter

spinet ['spɪnɪt] s espineta

spinner ['spɪnər] s hilandero; máquina de hilar

spinning ['spɪnɪŋ] adj hilador ‖ s (act) hila; (art) hilandería

spinning wheel s torno de hilar

spin'-off' s derivado; subproducto

spinster ['spɪnstər] s (obs or offensive) solterona

spi·ral ['spaɪrəl] adj & s espiral f ‖ v (pret & pp **-raled** o **-ralled;** ger **-raling** o **-ralling**) intr dar vueltas como una espiral; (aer) volar en espiral

spiral staircase s escalera de caracol

spire [spaɪr] s cima, ápice m; (of a steeple) aguja, chapitel m; (e.g., of grass) tallo

spirit [ˈspɪrɪt] *s* espíritu *m;* humor *m,* temple *m;* personaje *m;* licur *m* ‖ *tr*—**to spirit away** llevarse misteriosamente

spirited [ˈspɪrɪtɪd] *adj* fogoso, espiritoso

spirit lamp *s* lámpara de alcohol

spiritless [ˈspɪrɪtlɪs] *adj* apocado, tímido, sin ánimo

spirit level *s* nivel *m* de burbuja

spiritual [ˈspɪrɪtʃʊ•əl] *adj* espiritual

spiritualism [ˈspɪrɪtʃʊə,lɪzəm] *s* espiritismo; (*belief that all reality is spiritual*) espiritualismo

spirituous liquors [ˈspɪrɪtʃʊ•əs] *spl* licores espirituosos

spit [spɪt] *s* esputo, saliva; (*for roasting*) asador *m,* espetón *m;* punta o lengua de tierra; **the spit and image of** la segunda edición de, el retrato de ‖ *v* (*pret & pp* **spat** [spæt] o **spit;** *ger* **spitting**) *tr* escupir ‖ *intr* escupir; lloviznar; neviscar; fufar (*el gato*)

spite [spaɪt] *s* despecho, rencor *m,* inquina; **in spite of** a pesar de, a despecho de; **out of spite** por despecho ‖ *tr* despechar, molestar, picar

spiteful [ˈspaɪtfəl] *adj* despechado, rencoroso

spit'fire' *s* fierabrás *m;* mujer *f* de mal genio

spittoon [spɪˈtun] *s* escupidera

splash [splæʃ] *s* rociada, salpicadura; (*e.g., with the hands*) chapaleo, chapoteo; **to make a splash** (coll) hacer impresión, llamar la atención, causar furor ‖ *tr & intr* salpicar; chapotear

splash'down' *s* acuatizaje *m*

spleen [splin] *s* mal humor *m;* (anat) bazo; **to vent one's spleen** descargar la bilis

splendid [ˈsplɛndɪd] *adj* espléndido; (coll) magnífico, maravilloso

splendor [ˈsplɛndər] *s* esplendor *m*

splice [splaɪs] *s* empalme *m,* junta ‖ *tr* empalmar, juntar

splint [splɪnt] *s* (*splinter*) astilla, tablilla; (surg) tablilla ‖ *tr* entablillar (*un hueso roto*)

splinter [ˈsplɪntər] *s* astilla; (*of stone, glass, bone*) esquirla ‖ *tr* astillar ‖ *intr* astillarse, hacerse astillas

splinter group *s* grupúsculo; grupo disidente

split [splɪt] *adj* hendido, partido; dividido ‖ *s* división, fractura; (slang) porción ‖ *v* (*pret & pp* **split;** *ger* **splitting**) *tr* dividir, partir; **to split one's sides with laughter** desternillarse de risa ‖ *intr* dividirse a lo largo; **to split away (from)** separarse (de)

split fee *s* dicotomía (*entre médicos*)

split personality *s* personalidad desdoblada

splitting [ˈsplɪtɪŋ] *adj* partidor; fuerte, violento; (*headache*) enloquecedor

splotch [splɑtʃ] *s* borrón *m,* mancha grande ‖ *tr* salpicar, manchar

splurge [splʌrdʒ] *s* (coll) fachenda, ostentación ‖ *intr* (coll) fachendear

splutter [ˈsplʌtər] *s* chisporroteo; (*manner of speaking*) farfulla ‖ *tr* farfullar ‖ *intr* chisporrotear; farfullar

spoil [spɔɪl] *s* botín *m,* presa; **spoils** (*taken from an enemy*) botín, despojos; (*of political victory*) enchufes *mpl* ‖ *v* (*pret & pp*

spoiled o **spoilt** [spɔɪlt] *tr* echar a perder, estropear; mimar (*a un niño*); amargar (*una tertulia*) ‖ *intr* echarse a perder

spoiled [spɔɪld] *adj* (*child*) consentido, mimado; (*food*) pasado, podrido

spoils•man [ˈspɔɪlzmən] *s* (*pl* **-men** [mən]) enchufista *m*

spoils system *s* enchufismo

spoke [spok] *s* (*of a wheel*) radio, rayo; (*of a ladder*) escalón *m*

spokes•man [ˈspoksmən] *s* (*pl* **-men** [mən]) o **spokesperson** *s* portavoz *m,* vocero

sponge [spʌndʒ] *s* esponja; **to throw in** (o **up) the sponge** (coll) tirar la esponja ‖ *tr* limpiar con esponja; borrar; absorber ‖ *intr* ser absorbente; **to sponge on** (coll) vivir a costa de

sponge cake *s* bizcocho muy ligero

sponger [ˈspʌndʒər] *s* esponja (*gorrón, parásito*); bolsero (SAm)

sponge rubber *s* caucho esponjoso

spon•gy [ˈspʌndʒi] *adj* (comp **-gier;** super **-giest**) esponjoso

sponsor [ˈspɑnsər] *s* patrocinador *m;* (*godfather*) padrino; (*godmother*) madrina ‖ *tr* patrocinar

sponsorship [ˈspɑnsər,ʃɪp] *s* patrocinio

spontaneous [spɑnˈteni•əs] *adj* espontáneo

spoof [spuf] *s* (slang) mistificación, engaño; (slang) broma ‖ *tr* (slang) mistificar, engañar ‖ *intr* (slang) bromear, burlar; (slang) parodiar

spook [spuk] *s* aparecido, espectro

spook•y [ˈspuki] *adj* (comp **-ier;** super **-iest**) espectral, espeluznante; (*horse*) asustadizo

spool [spul] *s* carrete *m,* bobina

spoon [spun] *s* cuchara ‖ *tr* cucharear ‖ *intr* (slang) besuquearse (*los enamorados*)

spoonful [ˈspun,fʊl] *s* cucharada

spoon•y [ˈspuni] *adj* (comp **-ier;** super **-iest**) (coll) baboso, sobón

sporadic(al) [spəˈrædɪk(əl)] *adj* esporádico

spore [spor] *s* espora

sport [sport] *adj* deportivo, de deporte ‖ *s* deporte *m;* deportista *mf;* (*person or thing controlled by some power or passion*) juguete *m;* (*laughingstock*) hazmerreír *m;* (*gambler*) (coll) tahur *m,* jugador *m;* (*in gambling or playing games*) (coll) buen perdedor; (*flashy fellow*) (coll) guapo, majo; (biol) mutación; **to make sport of** burlarse de, reírse de ‖ *tr* (coll) lucir (*p.ej., un traje nuevo*) ‖ *intr* divertirse; estar de burla; juguetear

sport clothes *spl* trajes *mpl* de sport

sport fan *s* aficionado al deporte, deportista *mf*

sporting chance *s* riesgo de buen perdedor

sporting goods *spl* artículos de deporte

sporting house *s* casa de juego; casa de rameras

sports'cast'er *s* locutor deportivo

sports•man [ˈsportsmən] *s* (*pl* **-men** [mən]) deportista *m;* jugador honrado

sports news *s* noticiario deportivo

sports'wear' *s* trajes deportivos

sports writer *s* cronista deportivo

sport·y ['sportɪ] *adj* (*comp* **-ier;** *super* **-iest**) elegante, guapo; alegre, brillante; magnánimo; disipado, libertino

spot [spɑt] *s* mancha; sitio, lugar *m;* (coll) poquito; **on the spot** allí mismo; al punto; (slang) en dificultad; (slang) en peligro de muerte; **to hit the spot** tener razón; dar completa satisfacción ‖ *v* (*pret & pp* **spotted;** *ger* **spotting**) *tr* manchar; descubrir, reconocer ‖ *intr* mancharse, tener manchas

spot cash *s* dinero contante

spot check *s* verificación a la ventura

spotless ['spɑtlɪs] *adj* inmaculado, sin manchas

spot'light' *s* proyector *m* orientable; luz concentrada; (aut) faro piloto, faro giratorio; (fig) atención del público

spot remover [rɪ'muvər] *s* (*person*) quitamanchas *mf;* (*material*) quitamanchas *m*

spot welding *s* soldadura por puntos

spouse [spauz] o [spaus] *s* cónyuge *mf,* consorte *mf*

spout [spaut] *s* (*to carry off water from roof*) canalón *m;* (*of a jar, pitcher, etc.*) pico; (*of a sprinkling can*) rallo, roseta; (*jet*) chorro; **up the spout** (slang) acabado, arruinado ‖ *tr* echar en chorro; (coll) declamar ‖ *intr* chorrear; (coll) declamar

sprain [spren] *s* torcedura, esguince *m* ‖ *tr* torcer, torcerse

sprawl [sprɔl] *intr* arrellanarse

spray [spre] *s* rociada; (*of the sea*) espuma; (*device*) pulverizador *m;* (*twig*) ramita ‖ *tr & intr* rociar

sprayer ['spre·ər] *s* rociador *m,* pulverizador *m,* vaporizador *m*

spread [spred] *s* extensión; amplitud, anchura; difusión; diferencia; cubrecama, sobrecama; mantel *m,* tapete *m;* (*of the wings of a bird; of the wings of an airplane*) envergadura; (coll) festín *m,* comilona ‖ *v* (*pret & pp* **spread**) *tr* extender; difundir, propagar; esparcir; escalonar; abrir, separar; poner (*la mesa*) ‖ *intr* extenderse; difundirse; esparcirse; abrirse, separarse

spree [spri] *s* juerga, parranda; borrachera; **to go on a spree** ir de juerga; pillar una mona

sprig [sprɪg] *s* ramita

spright·ly ['spraɪtlɪ] *adj* (*comp* **-lier;** *super* **-liest**) alegre, animado, vivo

spring [sprɪŋ] *adj* primaveral; de manantial; de muelle, de resorte ‖ *s* (*season of the year*) primavera; (*issue of water from earth*) fuente *f,* manantial *m;* (*elastic device*) muelle *m,* resorte *m;* (*of an automobile or wagon*) ballesta; (*leap, jump*) brinco, salto; abertura, grieta; tensión, tirantez *f* ‖ *v* (*pret* **sprang** [spræŋ] o **sprung** [sprʌŋ];* *pp* **sprung**) *tr* soltar (*un muelle o resorte*); torcer, combar, encorvar; hacer saltar (*una trampa, una mina*) ‖ *intr* saltar; saltar de golpe; brotar, nacer, proceder; torcerse, combarse, encorvarse; **to spring at** abalanzarse sobre; **to spring forth** precipitarse; brotar; **to spring up** levantarse de un salto; brotar, nacer; presentarse a la vista

spring'board' *s* trampolín *m*

spring chicken *s* polluelo; (*young person*) (coll) pollita

spring fever *s* (hum) ataque *m* primaveral, galbana

spring mattress *s* colchón *m* de muelles, somier *m*

spring'time' *s* primavera

sprinkle ['sprɪŋkəl] *s* rociada; llovizna; pizca ‖ *tr* regar, rociar; salpicar, sembrar; espolvorear (*p.ej., azúcar*) ‖ *intr* rociar; lloviznar, gotear

sprinkling can *s* regadera, rociadera

sprint [sprɪnt] *s* (sport) embalaje *m* ‖ *intr* (sport) embalarse, lanzarse

sprite [spraɪt] *s* duende *m,* trasgo

sprocket ['sprɑkɪt] *s* diente *m* de rueda de cadena; rueda de cadena

sprout [spraut] *s* brote *m,* renuevo, retoño ‖ *intr* brotar, germinar, echar renuevos; crecer rápidamente

spruce [sprus] *adj* apuesto, elegante, garboso ‖ *s* abeto del Norte, abeto falso, pícea *f* ‖ *tr* ataviar, componer ‖ *intr* ataviarse, componerse; **to spruce up** emperifollarse

spry [spraɪ] *adj* (*comp* **spryer** o **sprier;** *super* **spryest** o **spriest**) activo, ágil

spud [spʌd] *s* (*chisel*) escoplo; (agr) escoda; (coll) patata

spun glass [spʌn] *s* vidrio hilado, cristal hilado

spunk [spʌŋk] *s* (coll) ánimo, coraje *m,* corazón *m,* valor *m*

spun silk *s* seda cardada o hilada

spur [spʌr] *s* espuela; (*central point of an auger*) gusanillo; (*of a cock, mountain, warship*) espolón *m;* (rr) ramal corto; (*goad, stimulus*) (fig) espuela; **on the spur of the moment** impulsivamente, sin la reflexión debida ‖ *v* (*pret & pp* **spurred;** *ger* **spurring**) *tr* espolear; espuelar (SAm); **to spur on** espolear, aguijonear

spurious ['spjurɪ·əs] *adj* espurio

spurn [spʌrn] *s* desdén *m,* menosprecio ‖ *tr* desdeñar, menospreciar; rechazar con desdén

spurt [spʌrt] *s* chorro repentino; esfuerzo repentino; arranque *m* ‖ *intr* salir en chorro, salir a borbotones

sputnik ['spʌtnɪk] *s* sputnik *m;* satélite *m* artificial

sputter ['spʌtər] *s* (*manner of speaking*) farfulla; (*sizzling*) chisporroteo ‖ *tr* farfullar ‖ *intr* farfullar; chisporrotear

spy [spaɪ] *s* (*pl* **spies**) espía *mf* ‖ *v* (*pret & pp* **spied**) *tr* columbrar, divisar ‖ *intr* espiar; **to spy on** espiar

spy'glass' *s* catalejo, anteojo

spy satellite *s* satélite *m* espía

sq. *abbr* **square**

squabble ['skwɑbəl] *s* reyerta, riña ‖ *intr* reñir, disputar

squad [skwɑd] *s* escuadra

squadron ['skwɑdrən] *s* (aer) escuadrilla; (*of cavalry*) (mil) escuadrón *m;* (nav) escuadra

squalid ['skwɑlɪd] *adj* escuálido

squall [skwɔl] s grupada, turbión m; (quarrel) (coll) riña; (upset, commotion) (coll) chubasco

squalor ['skwɑlər] s escualidez f

squander ['skwɑndər] tr despilfarrar, malgastar

square [skwɛr] adj cuadrado, p.ej., **eight square inches** ocho pulgadas cuadradas; en cuadro, de lado, p.ej., **eight inches square** ocho pulgadas en cuadro, ocho pulgadas de lado; rectangular; justo, recto; honrado, leal; saldado; fuerte, sólido; (coll) abundante, completo; **to get square with** (coll) hacérselas pagar a || adv recto; en ángulo recto; honradamente, lealmente || s cuadrado; (of checkerboard or chessboard) casilla, escaque m; (city block) manzana; (open area in town or city) plaza; (carpenter's tool) escuadra; **to be on the square** (coll) obrar de buena fe || tr cuadrar; dividir en cuadros; ajustar, nivelar, conformar; saldar (una cuenta); (carp) escuadrar || intr cuadrarse; **to square off** (coll) colocarse en posición de defensa

square dance s danza de figuras

square deal s (coll) trato equitativo

square meal s (coll) comida abundante

square shooter ['ʃutər] s (coll) persona leal y honrada

squash [skwɑʃ] s aplastamiento; (bot) calabaza; (sport) frontón m con raqueta; || tr aplastar, despachurrar; confutar (un argumento); acallar con un argumento, respuesta, etc. || intr aplastarse

squash•y ['skwɑʃi] adj (comp -ier; super -iest) mojado y blando; (muddy) lodoso; (fruit) modorro

squat [skwɑt] adj en cuclillas; rechoncho || v (pret & pp squatted; ger squatting) intr acuclillarse, agacharse; sentarse en el suelo; establecerse en terreno ajeno sin derecho; establecerse en terreno público para crear un derecho

squatter ['skwɑtər] s advenedizo, intruso, colono usurpador

squaw [skwɔ] s india norteamericana; mujer, esposa, muchacha

squawk [skwɔk] s graznido; (slang) queja chillona || intr graznar; (slang) quejarse chillando

squaw man s blanco casado con india

squeak [skwik] s chillido; chirrido || intr dar chillidos; chirriar

squeal [skwil] s chillido || intr dar chillidos; (slang) delatar, soplar; **to squeal on** (slang) delatar, soplar (a una persona)

squealer ['skwilər] s (coll) soplón m

squeamish ['skwimɪʃ] adj escrupuloso, remilgado; excesivamente modesto; (easily nauseated) asqueroso

squeeze [skwiz] s apretón m; **to put the squeeze on someone** (coll) hacer a uno la forzosa, meter en prensa a uno || tr apretar; agobiar, oprimir; exprimir || intr apretar; **to squeeze through** abrirse paso a estrujones por entre; salir de un aprieto a duras penas

squeezer ['skwizər] s exprimidera

squelch [skwɛltʃ] s (coll) tapaboca || tr apabullar, despachurrar

squid [skwɪd] s calamar m

squint [skwɪnt] s mirada bizca; mirada furtiva; (strabismus) bizquera || tr achicar, entornar (los ojos) || intr bizquear; torcer la vista; tener los ojos medio cerrados

squint-eyed ['skwɪnt,aɪd] adj bisojo, bizco; malévolo, sospechoso

squire [skwaɪr] s acompañante m (de una señora); (Brit) terrateniente m de antigua heredad; (U.S.A.) juez m de paz, juez local || tr acompañar (a una señora)

squirm [skwʌrm] s retorcimiento || intr retorcerse; **to squirm out of** escaparse de (p.ej., un aprieto) haciendo mucho esfuerzo

squirrel ['skwʌrəl] s ardilla

squirt [skwʌrt] s chorro; jeringazo; (coll) mono, presuntuoso || tr arrojar a chorros || intr salir a chorros

Sr. abbr senior, Sir

S.S. abbr Secretary of State, steamship, Sunday school

St. abbr Saint, Strait, Street

stab [stæb] s puñalada; (coll) tentativa; **to make a stab at** (slang) esforzarse por hacer || v (pret & pp stabbed; ger stabbing) tr apuñalar; traspasar || intr apuñalar

stab in the back s puñalada trapera

stable ['stebəl] adj estable || s establo, cuadra, caballeriza

stack [stæk] s montón m, pila; (of rifles) pabellón m; (of books in a library) estantería, depósito; (of a chimney) cañón m; (of straw) niara; (of firewood) hacina; (coll) montón m, gran número || tr amontonar, apilar; florear (el naipe); hacinar (leña)

stadi•um ['stedɪ•əm] s (pl -ums o -a [ə]) estadio

staff [stæf] s bastón m, apoyo, sostén m; personal m; (mil) estado mayor; (mus) pentagrama m || tr dotar, proveer de personal, nombrar personal para

stag [stæg] adj exclusivo para hombres, de hombres solos || s (male deer) ciervo; varón m; varón solo (no acompañado de mujeres)

stage [stedʒ] s escena; etapa, jornada; (coach) diligencia; (scene of an event) teatro; (of a microscope) portaobjeto; (rad) etapa; **by easy stages** a pequeñas etapas; lentamente; **to go on the stage** hacerse actor || tr poner en escena, representar; preparar, organizar

stage'coach' s diligencia

stage'craft' s arte f teatral

stage door s (theat) entrada de los artistas

stage fright s trac m, miedo al público

stage'hand' s tramoyista m, metemuertos m, metesillas m

stage manager s director m de escena

stage'-struck' adj loco por el teatro

stage whisper s susurro en voz alta

stagger ['stægər] tr sorprender; asustar; escalonar (las horas de trabajo) || intr tambalear, hacer eses al andar

staggering adj tambaleante; sorprendente

sp
st

stagnant ['stægnənt] *adj* estancado; (fig) estancado, inactivo, paralizado

staid [sted] *adj* grave, serio, formal

stain [sten] *s* mancha; tinte *m*, tintura; materia colorante ‖ *tr* manchar; teñir; colorar ‖ *intr* mancharse; hacer manchas

stained glass *s* vidrio de color

stained'glass' window *s* vidriera de colores, vidriera pintada, vitral *m*

stainless ['stenlɪs] *adj* inmanchable; (*steel*) inoxidable; inmaculado

stair [stɛr] *s* escalera; (*step of a series*) escalón *m;* **stairs** escalera

stair'case' *s* escalera

stair'way' *s* escalera

stair well *s* hueco de escalera

stake [stek] *s* estaca; (*of a cart or truck*) telero; (*to hold up a plant*) rodrigón *m;* (*in gambling*) puesta; premio del vencedor; **at stake** en juego; en gran peligro; **to die at the stake** morir en la hoguera; **to pull up stakes** (coll) irse; (coll) mudarse de casa ‖ *tr* estacar; atar a una estaca; rodrigar (*plantas*); apostar; arriesgar, aventurar; **to stake all** jugarse el todo por el todo; **to stake off** o **to stake out** estacar, señalar con estacas

stale [stel] *adj* añejo, rancio, viejo; (*air*) viciado; (*joke*) mohoso; anticuado

stale'mate' *s* mate ahogado; **to reach a stale-mate** llegar a un punto muerto ‖ *tr* dar mate ahogado a; estancar, paralizar

stalk [stɔk] *s* tallo ‖ *tr* cazar al acecho; acechar, espiar ‖ *intr* cazar al acecho; andar con paso majestuoso; andar con paso altivo; **to stalk out** salir con paso airado

stall [stɔl] *s* cuadra, establo; pesebre *m;* (*booth in a market*) puesto; (*at a fair*) caseta; (Brit) butaca; (slang) pretexto ‖ *tr* encerrar en un establo; poner trabas a; parar (*un motor*); **to stall off** (coll) eludir, evitar ‖ *intr* atascarse, atollarse; pararse (*un motor*); (slang) eludir para engañar o demorar; **to stall for time** (slang) tardar para ganar tiempo

stallion ['stæljən] *s* caballo padre, caballo semental

stalwart ['stɔlwərt] *adj* fornido, forzudo; valiente; leal, constante ‖ *s* persona fornida; partidario leal

stamen ['stemən] *s* estambre *m*

stamina ['stæmɪnə] *s* fuerza, nervio, vigor *m*, resistencia

stammer ['stæmər] *s* balbuceo, tartamudeo ‖ *tr* balbucear (*p.ej., excusas*) ‖ *intr* balbucear, tartamudear

stamp [stæmp] *s* (*device used for making an impression; mark made with it; piece of paper or mark used to show payment of postage*) sello; (*tool used for crushing or marking*) pisón *m;* (*tool for stamping coins and medals*) cuño, troquel *m;* marca, impresión; clase *f*, tipo ‖ *tr* sellar; troquelar; estampar, imprimir; hollar, pisotear; indicar, señalar; poner el sello a; bocartear (*el mineral*); **to stamp out** apagar pateando;

extinguir por la fuerza; suprimir; **to stamp the feet** dar patadas ‖ *intr* patalear

stampede [stæm'pid] *s* fuga precipitada; estampida (Am) ‖ *tr* hacer huir en desorden; provocar a pánico ‖ *intr* huir en tropel; obrar por común impulso

stamping grounds *spl* (slang) guarida (*sitio frecuentado por una persona*)

stamp pad *s* tampón *m*

stamp'-vend'ing machine *s* máquina expendedora de sellos

stance [stæns] *s* (sport) postura, planta

stanch [stɑntʃ] *adj* firme, fuerte; constante, leal; (*watertight*) estanco ‖ *tr* estancar; retañar (*la sangre de una herida*)

stand [stænd] *s* parada; alto para defenderse; postura, posición; resistencia; estrado, tribuna; sostén *m*, pie *m;* puesto, quiosco ‖ *v* (*pret & pp* **stood** [stud]) *tr* poner, colocar; poner derecho; soportar, tolerar, resistir; (coll) aguantar (*a una persona*); (coll) sufragar (*un gasto*); **to stand off** tener a raya; **to stand one's ground** mantenerse firme ‖ *intr* estar, estar situado; estar parado; estacionarse; estar de pie, estar derecho; ponerse de pie, levantarse; resultar; persistir; mantenerse; **to stand aloof, apart** o **aside** mantenerse apartado; **to stand back of** respaldar; **to stand for** significar, representar; apoyar, defender; apadrinar; mantener (*p.ej., una opinión*); presentarse como candidato de; navegar hacia; (coll) tolerar; **to stand in line** hacer cola; **to stand out** sobresalir; destacarse, resaltar; **to stand up** ponerse de pie, levantarse; durar; **to stand up to** hacer; resueltamente frente a

standard ['stændərd] *adj* normal; (*typewriter keyboard*) universal; corriente, regular; legal; clásico ‖ *s* patrón *m;* norma, regla establecida; bandera, estandarte *m;* emblema *m*, símbolo; soporte *m*, pilar *m*

standardize ['stændər,daɪz] *tr* normalizar, estandardizar

standard of living *s* nivel *m* de vida

standard time *s* hora legal, hora oficial

standee [stæn'di] *s* (coll) espectador *m* que asiste de pie; (coll) pasajero de pie

stand'-in' *s* (theat & mov) doble *mf;* (coll) buenas aldabas

standing ['stændɪŋ] *adj* derecho, en pie; de pie; parado, inmóvil; (*water*) encharcado, estancado; (*army; committee*) permanente; vigente ‖ *s* condición, posición; reputación; parada; **in good standing** en posición acreditada; **of long standing** de mucho tiempo, de antigua fecha

standing army *s* ejército permanente

standing room *s* sitio para estar de pie

stand-offishness [,stænd'ɔfɪʃnɪs] *s* desarrimo

stand'point' *s* punto de vista

stand'still' *s* detención, parada; alto; descanso, inactividad; **to come to a standstill** cesar, pararse

stanza ['stænzə] *s* estancia, estrofa

staple ['stepəl] *adj* primero, principal; corriente, establecido ‖ *s* (*to fasten papers*) grapa; artículo o producto de primera necesidad; materia prima; fibra textil ‖ *tr* sujetar con grapas

stapler ['steplər] *s* engrapador *m*, cosepapeles *m*

star [stɑr] *s* (*heavenly body*) astro; (*heavenly body except sun and moon; figure that represents a star*) estrella; (mov & theat) estrella; (*of football*) as *m;* (typ) estrella o asterisco; (*fate, destiny*) (fig) estrella; **to see stars** (coll) ver las estrellas; **to thank one's lucky stars** estar agradecido por su buena suerte ‖ *v* (*pret & pp* **starred;** *ger* **starring**) *tr* estrellar, adornar o señalar con estrellas; marcar con asterisco; presentar como estrella (*a un actor*) ‖ *intr* ser la estrella; lucirse; sobresalir

starboard ['stɑrbərd] o ['stɑr,bord] *adj* de estribor ‖ *adv* a estribor ‖ *s* estribor *m*

starch [stɑrʃ] *s* almidón *m*, fécula; arrogancia, entono; (slang) fuerza, vigor *m* ‖ *tr* almidonar

stare [stɛr] *s* mirada fija ‖ *intr* mirar fijamente; **to stare at** clavar la vista en mirar con fijeza

star'fish' *s* estrella de mar, estrellamar *m*

star'gaze' *intr* mirar las estrellas; ser distraído, soñar despierto

stark [stɑrk] *adj* cabal, completo, puro; rígido, tieso; duro, severo ‖ *adv* completamente, enteramente; rígidamente, severamente

stark'-na'ked *adj* en pelota, en cueros

star'light' *s* luz *f* de las estrellas

starling ['stɑrlɪŋ] *s* estornino

Star'-Span'gled Banner *s* bandera estrellada (*bandera de los EE.UU.*)

start [stɑrt] *s* comienzo, principio; salida, partida; lugar *m* de partida; (*scare*) sobresalto; (*sudden start*) arranque *m;* (*advantage*) ventaja ‖ *tr* empezar, principiar; poner en marcha; hacer arrancar; dar la señal de partida a; entablar (*una conversación*); levantar (*la caza*) ‖ *intr* empezar, principiar; ponerse en marcha; arrancar; (*to be startled*) sobresaltar; nacer, provenir; **starting from** o **with** a partir de; **to start after** salir en busca de

starter ['stɑrtər] *s* iniciador *m;* (*of a series*) primero; (aut) arranque *m*, motor *m* de arranque; (sport) juez *m* de salida

starting ['stɑrtɪŋ] *adj* de salida; de arranque ‖ *s* puesta en marcha

starting crank *s* manivela de arranque

starting point *s* punto de partida, arrancadero

startle ['stɑrtəl] *tr* asustar, sorprender, sobrecoger ‖ *intr* asustarse, sorprenderse sobrecogerse

startling ['stɑrtlɪŋ] *adj* alarmante, asombroso

starvation [stɑr've/ən] *s* hambre *f*, inanición

starvation diet *s* régimen *m* de hambre, cura de hambre

starvation wages *spl* salario de hambre

starve [stɑrv] *tr* hambrear; hacer morir de hambre; **to starve out** hacer rendirse por

hambre ‖ *intr* hambrear; morir de hambre; (coll) tener hambre

starving ['stɑrvɪŋ] *adj* hambriento, famélico

stat. *abbr* **statuary, statute, statue**

state [stet] *adj* de estado; del estado; estatal; público; de gala, de lujo ‖ *s* estado; fausto, ceremonia, pompa; **to lie in state** estar expuesto en capilla ardiente, estar de cuerpo presente; **to live in state** gastar mucho lujo; **to ride in state** pasear en carruaje de lujo ‖ *tr* afirmar, declarar; exponer, manifestar; plantear (*un problema*)

State Department *s* Ministerio de Relaciones Exteriores

state·ly ['stetli] *adj* (*comp* **-lier;** *super* **-liest**) imponente, majestuoso

statement ['stetmənt] *s* declaración; exposición, informe *m*, relación; (com) estado de cuentas

state of mind *s* estado de ánimo

state'room' *s* camarote *m;* (rr) compartimiento particular

state'side' *adv* (coll) en (*or* a) los Estados Unidos

states·man ['stetsmən] *s* (*pl* **-men** [mən]) estadista *m*, hombre *m* de estado

static ['stætɪk] *adj* estático; (rad) atmosférico ‖ *s* (rad) parásitos atmosféricos

station ['steʃən] *s* estación; condición, situación ‖ *tr* estacionar, apostar

station agent *s* jefe *m* de estación

stationary ['steʃən,ɛri] *adj* estacionario

station break *s* (rad) descanso, intermedio

stationer ['steʃənər] *s* papelero

stationery ['steʃən,ɛri] *s* efectos de escritorio; papel *m* para cartas

stationery store *s* papelería

station house *s* cuartelillo de policía

station identification *s* (rad & telv) indicativo de la emisora

sta'tion·mas'ter *s* jefe *m* de estación

station wagon *s* vagoneta, rubia, coche *m* rural; camioneta (Arg, CAm, Col. Pan, Peru, S-D); esteishon wagon *m* (Chile, Col, Cuba, P-R); guagüita (Cuba, P-R); camionetilla (Guat); carmelita (Hond); ranchera (Ven)

statistical [stə,tɪstɪkəl] *adj* estadístico

statistician [,stætɪs,tɪʃən] *s* estadístico

statistics [stə,tɪstɪks] *ssg* (*science*) estadística; *spl* (*data*) estadística o estadísticas

statue ['stætʃu] *s* estatua

statuesque [,stætʃu,ɛsk] *adj* escultural

stature [,stætʃər] *s* estatura, talla; carácter *m*, habilidad

status ['stetəs] *s* condición, estado; situación social, legal o profesional; (*prestige or superior rank*) categoría

status seeking *s* esfuerzo por adquirir categoría

status symbol *s* símbolo de categoría social

statute ['stætʃut] *s* estatuto, ley *f*

statutory ['stætʃu,tori] *adj* estatutario, legal

staunch [stɔntʃ] o [stantʃ] *adj & tr* var de **stanch**

st
st ·

stave [stev] *s* (*of a barrel*) duela; (*of a ladder*) peldaño; (mus) pentagrama *m* ‖*v* (*pret & pp* **staved** o **stove** [stov]) *tr* romper, destrozar; (*to break a hole in*) desfondar; **to stave off** mantener a distancia; evitar, impedir, diferir

stay [ste] *s* morada, permanencia, estancia; suspensión; (*of a corset*) ballena, varilla; apoyo, sostén *m;* (law) espera; (naut) estay *m* ‖ *tr* aplazar, detener; poner freno a ‖ *intr* quedar, quedarse, permanecer; parar, hospedarse; habitar; **to stay up** no acostarse, velar

stay'-at-home' *adj & s* hogareño

stead [stɛd] *s* lugar *m;* **in his stead** en su lugar, en lugar de él; **to stand in good stead** ser de provecho, ser ventajoso

stead'fast' *adj* fijo; resuelto; constante

stead•y [ˈstɛdi] *adj* (*comp* **-ier;** *super* **-iest**) constante, fijo, firme, seguro; regular, uniforme; resuelto; asentado, serio ‖ *v* (*pret & pp* **-ied**) *tr* estabilizar, reforzar; calmar (*los nervios*) ‖ *intr* estabilizarse; calmarse

steak [stek] *s* lonja, tajada; biftec *m*

steal [stil] *s* (coll) hurto, robo ‖ *v* (*pret* **stole** [stol]; *pp* **stolen**) *tr* hurtar, robar; atraer, cautivar; manotear (Arg, Mex) ‖ *intr* hurtar, robar; **to steal away** escabullirse; **to steal into** meterse a hurtadillas en; **to steal upon** aproximarse sin ruido a

stealth [stɛlθ] *s* cautela, recato; **by stealth** a hurtadillas

steam [stim] *adj* de vapor ‖ *s* vapor *m;* vaho, humo; **to get up steam** dar presión; **to let off steam** descargar vapor; (fig) desahogarse ‖ *tr* cocer al vapor; saturar de vapor; empañar (*p.ej., las ventanas*) ‖ *intr* echar vapor, emitir vapor; evaporarse; funcionar o marchar a vapor; **to steam ahead** avanzar por medio del vapor; (fig) hacer grandes progresos

steam'boat' *s* buque *m* de vapor

steamer [ˈstimər] *s* vapor *m*

steamer rug *s* manta de viaje

steamer trunk *s* baúl *m* de camarote

steam heat *s* calefacción por vapor

steam roller *s* apisonadora movida a vapor; (coll) fuerza arrolladora

steam'ship' *s* vapor *m*, buque *m* de vapor

steam shovel *s* pala mecánica de vapor

steam table *s* plancha caliente

steed [stid] *s* caballo; (*high-spirited horse*) corcel *m*

steel [stil] *adj* acerado; (*business, industry*) siderúrgico; (fig) duro, frío ‖ *s* acero; (*for striking fire from flint; for sharpening knives*) eslabón *m* ‖ *tr* acerar; **to steel oneself** acerarse

steel wool *s* virutillas de acero, estopa de acero

steelyard [ˈstilˌjɑrd] *s* romana

steep [stip] *adj* escarpado, empinado; (*price*) alto, excesivo ‖ *tr* empapar, remojar; **steeped in** absorbido en

steeple [ˈstipəl] *s* aguja, campanario

stee'ple•chase' *s* carrera de campanario, carrera de obstáculos

stee'ple•jack' *s* escalatorres *m*

steer [stɪr] *s* buey *m* ‖ *tr* conducir, gobernar, guiar ‖ *intr* conducirse; **to steer clear of** (coll) evitar, eludir

steerage [ˈstɪrɪdʒ] *s* dirección; (naut) proa, entrepuente *m*

steerage passenger *s* (naut) pasajero de entrepuente

steering column *s* columna de dirección

steering committee *s* comité *m* paneador

steering wheel *s* (aut) volante *m;* (naut) rueda del timón

stem [stɛm] *s* (*of a goblet*) pie *m;* (*of a pipe, of a feather*) cañón *m;* (*of a column*) fuste *m;* (*of a watch*) botón *m;* (*of a key*) espiga, tija; (*of a word*) tema *m;* (bot) tallo, vástago; **from stem to stern** de proa a popa ‖ *v* (*pret & pp* **stemmed;** *ger* **stemming**) *tr* (*to remove the stem from*) desgranar; (*to check*) detener, refrenar; (*to plug*) estancar; hacer frente a; rendir (*la marea*) ‖ *intr* nacer, provenir; **to stem from** originarse en, provenir de

stem'-wind'er *s* remontuar *m*

stench [stɛntʃ] *s* hedor *m*, hediondez *f*

sten•cil [ˈstɛnsəl] *s* cartón picado; (*work produced by it*) estarcido ‖ *v* (*pret & pp* **-ciled** o **-cilled;** *ger* **-ciling** o **-cilling**) *tr* estarcir

stenographer [stəˈnɑɡrəfər] *s* estenógrafo

stenography [stəˈnɑɡrəfi] *s* estenografía

step [stɛp] *s* paso; (*of staircase*) grada, peldaño; (*footprint*) huella, pisada; (*of carriage*) estribo; (*measure, démarche*) gestión, medida; (mus) intervalo; **step by step** paso a paso; **to watch one's step** proceder con cautela, andarse con tiento ‖ *v* (*pret & pp* **stepped;** *ger* **stepping**) *tr* escalonar; **to step off** medir a pasos ‖ *intr* dar un paso, dar pasos; caminar, ir; (coll) andar de prisa; **to step on it** (coll) acelerar la marcha, darse prisa; **to step on the starter** pisar el arranque

step'broth'er *s* medio hermano, hermanastro

step'child' *s* (*pl* **-children** [ˌtʃɪldrən]) hijastro

step'daugh'ter *s* hijastra

step'fa'ther *s* padrastro

step'lad'der *s* escala, escalera de tijera

step'moth'er *s* madrastra

steppe [stɛp] *s* estepa

stepping stone *s* estriberón *m*, pasadera; (fig) escalón *m*, escabel *m*

step'sis'ter *s* media hermana, hermanastra

step'son' *s* hijastro

stere•o [ˈstɛriˌo] o [ˈstɪriˌo] *adj* estereofónico; estereososcópico ‖ *s* (*pl* **-os**) música estereofónica, disco estereofónico; radiodifusión estereofónica; fotografía estereoscópica

stereo system *s* equipo de alta fidelidad

ster'e•o•type' *s* clisé *m*, estereotipo; concepción tradicional

stereotyped [ˈstɛriˌəˌtaɪpt] o [ˈstɪriˌəˌtaɪpt] *adj* estereotipado

sterile [ˈstɛrɪl] *adj* estéril

sterilization [ˌstɛrɪlɪˈzefən] *s* esterilización

sterilize [ˈstɛrɪˌlaɪz] *tr* esterilizar

sterling ['stʌrlɪŋ] *adj* fino, de ley; verdadero, genuino, puro, excelente ‖ *s* libras esterlinas; plata de ley; vajilla de plata

stern [stʌrn] *adj* austero, severo; decidido, firme ‖ *s* popa

stethoscope ['stɛθə,skop] *s* estetoscopio

stevedore ['stivə,dor] *s* estibador *m*

stew [stju] o [stu] *s* guisado, estofado ‖ *tr* guisar, estofar ‖ *intr* abrasarse; (coll) estar apurado

steward ['stu•ərd] *s* mayordomo; administrador *m;* (*of ship or plane*) camarero

stewardess ['stu•ərdɪs] *s* mayordoma; (*of ship or plane*) camarera; (*of plane*) azafata, aeromoza

stewed fruit *s* compota de frutas

stewed tomatoes *spl* puré *m* de tomates

stick [stɪk] *s* palo, palillo; bastón *m*, vara; (*of dynamite*) barra; (naut) mástil *m*, verga; (typ) componedor *m* ‖ *v* (*pret & pp* **stuck** [stʌk]) *tr* picar, punzar; apuñalar; clavar, hincar; pegar; (coll) confundir; **to stick out** asomar (*la cabeza*); sacar (*la lengua*); **to stick up** (*in order to rob*) (slang) asaltar, atracar ‖ *intr* estar prendido, estar hincado; pegarse; agarrarse (*la pintura*); encastillarse (*p.ej., una ventana*); resaltar, sobresalir; continuar, persistir; permanecer; atascarse; **to stick out** salir (*p.ej., el pañuelo del bolsillo*); sobresalir, proyectarse; velar (*un escollo*); resultar evidente; **to stick together** (coll) quedarse unidos, no abandonarse; **to stick up** destacarse; estar de punta (*el pelo*); **to stick up for** (coll) defender

sticker ['stɪkər] *s* etiqueta engomada, marbete engomado; pegatina; punta, espina; (coll) problema arduo

sticking plaster *s* esparadrapo

stick′pin′ *s* alfiler *m* de corbata

stick′-up′ *s* (slang) asalto, atraco

stick•y ['stɪki] *adj* (*comp* **-ier;** *super* **-iest**) pegajoso; (coll) húmedo, mojado; (*weather*) bochornoso

stiff [stɪf] *adj* tieso; entorpecido, entumecido, arduo, difícil; (*price*) (coll) excesivo; **to get stiff** envararse ‖ *s* (slang) cadáver *m*

stiff collar *s* cuello almidonado

stiffen ['stɪfən] *tr* atiesar; endurecer; espesar ‖ *intr* atiesarse; endurecerse; espesarse; obstinarse

stiff neck *s* torticolis *m;* obstinación

stiff-necked ['stɪf,nɛkt] *adj* terco, obstinado

stiffness ['stɪfnɪs] *s* envaramiento

stiff shirt *s* camisola

stifle ['staɪfəl] *tr* ahogar, sofocar; apagar, suprimir

stig•ma ['stɪgmə] *s* (*pl* **-mas** o **-mata** [mətə]) estigma *m*

stigmatize ['stɪgmə,taɪz] *tr* estigmatizar

stilet•to [stɪ'lɛto] *s* (*pl* **-tos**) estilete *m*, puñal *m*

still [stɪl] *adj* inmóvil, quieto, tranquilo; callado, silencioso; (*wine*) no espumoso ‖ *adv* tranquilamente; silenciosamente; aún, todavía ‖ *conj* con todo, sin embargo ‖ *s* alambique *m*, destiladera; destilería; fotografía de lo inmóvil; (poet) silencio ‖ *tr* acallar; amortiguar; calmar ‖ *intr* callar; calmarse

still′birth′ *s* parto muerto

still′born′ *adj* nacido muerto

still life *s* (*pl* **still lifes** o **still lives**) bodegón *m*, naturaleza muerta

stilt [stɪlt] *s* zanco; (*in the water*) pilote *m*

stilted ['stɪltɪd] *adj* elevado; hinchado, pomposo, tieso

stimulant ['stɪmjələnt] *adj & s* estimulante *m*, excitante *m*

stimulate ['stɪmjə,let] *tr* estimular

stimu•lus ['stɪmjələs] *s* (*pl* **-li** [,laɪ]) estímulo *m*

sting [stɪŋ] *s* picadura, aguijón *m;* lanceta ‖ *v* (*pret & pp* **stung** [stʌŋ]) *tr* picar; aguijonear ‖ *intr* picar

stin•gy ['stɪndʒi] *adj* (*comp* **-gier;** *super* **-giest**) mezquino, tacaño

stink [stɪŋk] *s* hedor *m*, mal olor *m* ‖ *v* (*pret* **stank** [stæŋk] o **stunk** [stʌŋk]; *pp* **stunk**) *tr* dar mal olor a ‖ *intr* heder, oler muy mal; **to stink of** heder a; (slang) poseer (*p.ej., dinero*) en un grado que da asco

stint [stɪnt] *s* faena, tarea ‖ *tr* limitar, restringir ‖ *intr* ser económico, ahorrar con mezquindad

stipend ['staɪpənd] *s* estipendio

stipulate ['stɪpjə,let] *tr* estipular

stir [stʌr] *s* agitación, meneo; alboroto, tumulto; **to create a stir** meter ruido, causar furor ‖ *v* (*pret & pp* **stirred;** *ger* **stirring**) *tr* agitar, mover; revolver; conmover, excitar; atizar, avivar (*el fuego*); remover (*un líquido*); **to stir up** revolver; despertar; conmover; fomentar (*discordias*) ‖ *intr* bullirse, moverse; (*say a word*) rechistar

stirring ['stʌrɪŋ] *adj* conmovedor, emocionante

stirrup ['stʌrəp] o ['stɪrəp] *s* estribo

stitch [stɪtʃ] *s* puntada, punto; pedazo de tela; punzada, dolor *m* punzante; (coll) poquito; **to be in stitches** (coll) desternillarse de risa ‖ *tr* coser, bastear, hilvanar ‖ *intr* coser

stock [stak] *adj* común, regular; banal, vulgar; bursátil; ganadero, del ganado; (theat) de repertorio ‖ *s* surtido; capital *f* comercial; acciones, valores *mpl;* (*inventory*) stock *m;* (*of meat*) caldo; (*of a tree*) tronco; (*of an anvil*) cepo; (*of a rifle*) caja, culata; (*of a tree; of a family*) cepa; mango, manija; palo, madero; leño; (*livestock*) ganado; (theat) programa *m*, repertorio; **to have in stock** tener en stock; **in stock** en existencia; **out of stock** agotado; **to take stock** hacer el inventario; **to take stock in** (coll) dar importancia a, confiar en ‖ *tr* abastecer, surtir; tener existencias de; acopiar, acumular; poblar (*un estanque, una colmena, etc.*)

stockade [sta'ked] *s* estacada, empalizada ‖ *tr* empalizar

stock′breed′er *s* criador *m* de ganado

stock′bro′ker *s* bolsista *mf*, corredor *m* de bolsa

stock car *s* (aut) coche *m* de serie; (rr) vagón *m* para el ganado

st
st

stock company s (com) sociedad anónima; (theat) teatro de repertorio
stock dividend s acción liberada
stock exchange s bolsa
stock'hold'er s accionista mf, tenedor m de acciones
stockholder of record s accionista mf que como tal figura en el libro registro de la compañía
Stockholm ['stɑkhom] s Estocolmo
stocking ['stɑkɪŋ] s media
stock market s bolsa, mercado de valores; **to play the stock market** jugar a la bolsa
stock'pile' s reserva de materias primas ‖ tr acumular (materias primas) ‖ intr acumular materias primas
stock raising s ganadería
stock'room' s almacén m; sala de exposición
stock split s reparto de acciones gratis
stock•y ['stɑki] s adj (comp **-ier**; super **-iest**) bajo, grueso y fornido
stock'yard' s corral m de concentración de ganado
stoic ['sto•ɪk] adj & s estoico
stoke [stok] tr atizar, avivar (el fuego); alimentar, cebar (el horno)
stoker ['stokər] s fogonero
stolid ['stɑlɪd] adj impasible, insensible
stomach ['stʌmək] s estómago; apetito; deseo, inclinación ‖ tr tragar; **to not be able to stomach** (coll) no poder tragar
stomach pump s bomba estomacal
stone [ston] s piedra; (of fruit) hueso; (pathol) mal m de piedra ‖ tr lapidar, apedrear; deshuesar (la fruta)
stone'-broke' adj arrancado, sin blanca
stone'-deaf' adj sordo como una tapia
stone'ma'son s albañil m
stone quarry s cantera, pedrera
stone's throw s tiro de piedra; **within a stone's throw** a tiro de piedra
ston•y ['stoni] adj (comp **-ier**; super **-iest**) pedregoso; duro, empedernido
stool [stul] s escabel m, taburete m; sillico, retrete m; (bowel movement) cámara, evacuación
stoop [stup] s encorvada, inclinación; escalinata de entrada ‖ intr doblarse, inclinarse, encorvarse; andar encorvado; humillarse, rebajarse
stoop•shouldered ['stup'ʃoldərd] adj cargado de espaldas
stop [stɑp] s parada, alto; parón; estada, estancia; cesación, fin m, suspensión; cerradura, tapadura; impedimento, obstáculo; freno; tope m, retén m; (in writing; in telegrams) punto; (of a guitar) llave f, traste m; **to put a stop to** poner fin a ‖ v (pret & pp **stopped**; ger **stopping**) tr parar, detener; acabar, terminar; estorbar, obstruir; interceptar; suspender; cerrar, tapar; rechazar (un golpe); retener (un sueldo o parte de él); **to stop up** cegar, obstruir, tapar ‖ intr parar, pararse, detenerse; quedarse, permanecer; alojarse, hospedarse; acabarse, terminarse; **to stop** + ger cesar de + inf, dejar de + inf

stop'cock' s llave f de cierre, llave de paso
stop'gap' adj provisional ‖ s substituto provisional
stop light s luz f de parada
stop'o'ver s parada intermedia, escala; billete m de parada intermedia
stoppage ['stɑpɪdʒ] s parada, detención; (of work) paro; interrupción; suspensión; obstáculo; (of wages) retención; (pathol) obstrucción
stopper ['stɑpər] s tapón m; taco, tarugo
stop sign o **stop signal** s señal f de alto, señal de parada
stop watch s reloj m de segundos muertos, cronómetro
storage ['storɪdʒ] s almacenaje m; (costs) derechos de almacenaje
storage battery s (elec) acumulador m
store [stor] s tienda, almacén m; **I know what is in store for you** sé lo que le espera; **to set store by** dar mucha importancia a ‖ tr abastecer; tener guardado, almacenar; **to store away** acumular
store'house' s almacén m, depósito; (e.g., of wisdom) (fig) mina
store'keep'er s tendero, almacenista mf
store'room' s cuarto de almacenar; (for furniture) guardamuebles m; (naut) despensa
store window s escaparate m (de tienda); aparador m (Mex)
stork [stork] s cigüeña; **to have a visit from the stork** recibir a la cigüeña
storm [storm] s borrasca, tempestad, tormenta; (mil) asalto; (naut) borrasca; (fig) tempestad, tumulto; **to take by storm** tomar por asalto ‖ tr asaltar ‖ intr tempestear; precipitarse
storm cloud s nubarrón m
storm door s contrapuerta, guardapuerta
storm sash s contravidriera
storm troops spl tropas de asalto
storm window s guardaventana, sobrevidriera
storm•y ['stormi] adj (comp **-ier**; super **-iest**) borrascoso, tempestuoso; (session, meeting, etc.) tumultuoso
sto•ry ['stori] s (pl **-ries**) historia, cuento, anécdota; enredo, trama; (coll) mentira; piso, alto ‖ v (pret & pp **-ried**) tr historiar
sto'ry•tel'ler s narrador m; (coll) mentiroso
stout [staut] adj corpulento, gordo, robusto; animoso; leal; terco ‖ s cerveza obscura fuerte
stove [stov] s (for heating a house or room) estufa; (for cooking) hornillo, cocina de gas, cocina eléctrica
stove'pipe' s tubo de estufa, tubo de hornillo; (hat) (coll) chistera, chimenea
stow [sto] tr guardar, meter, esconder; (naut) arrumar, estibar ‖ intr—**to stow away** embarcarse clandestinamente, esconderse en un barco o avión
stowage ['sto•ɪdʒ] s arrumaje m, estiba
stow'a•way' s llovido, polizón m
str. abbr **strait, steamer**
straddle ['strædəl] s esparrancamiento ‖ tr montar a horcajadas; (coll) tratar de favo-

recer a ambas partes en (*p.ej.*, *un pleito*) ‖ *intr* ponerse a horcajadas; (coll) tratar de favorecer a ambas partes

strafe [strɑf] o [stref] *s* bombardeo violento ‖ *tr* bombardear violentamente

straggle ['stræɡəl] *intr* errar, vagar; andar perdido, extraviarse; separarse; estar esparcido

straight [stret] *adj* derecho; recto; erguido; (*hair*) lacio; continuo, seguido; honrado, sincero; correcto; decidido, intransigente; (*e.g.*, *whiskey*) solo; **to set a person straight** mostrar el camino a una persona; dar consejo a una persona; mostrar a una persona el modo de proceder ‖ *adv* derecho; sin interrupción; sinceramente; exactamente; en seguida; **straight ahead** todo seguido, derecho; **to go straight** enmendarse

straighten ['stretən] *tr* enderezar; poner en orden ‖ *intr* enderezarse

straight face *s* cara seria

straight'for'ward *adj* franco, sincero; honrado

straight off *adv* luego, en seguida

straight razor *s* navaja barbera

straight'way' *adv* luego, en seguida

strain [stren] *s* tensión, tirantez *f;* esfuerzo muy grande; fatiga excesiva, agotamiento; (*of a muscle*) torcedura; aire *m*, melodía; (*of a family or lineage*) cepa; linaje *m*, raza; rasgo racial; genio, vena; huella, rastro ‖ *tr* estirar; torcer o torcerse (*p.ej.*, *la muñeca*); forzar (*p.ej.*, *los nervios, la vista*); apretar; deformar; colar, tamizar ‖ *intr* esforzarse; deformarse; colarse, tamizarse; filtrarse; exprimirse (*un jugo*); resistirse; **to strain at** hacer grandes esfuerzos por

strained [strend] *adj* (*smile*) forzado; (*friendship*) tirante

strainer ['strenər] *s* colador *m*

strait [stret] *s* estrecho; **straits** estrecho; **to be in dire straits** estar en el mayor apuro, hallarse en gran estrechez

strait jacket *s* camisa de fuerza

strait-laced ['stret,lest] *adj* gazmoño

strand [strænd] *s* playa; filamento; (*of rope or cable*) torón *m*, ramal *m;* (*of pearls*) hilo; pelo ‖ *tr* deshebrar; retorcer, trenzar (*cuerda, cable, etc.*); dejar extraviado; (naut) varar

stranded ['strændɪd] *adj* desprovisto, desamparado; (*ship*) encallado; (*rope or cable*) trenzado, retorcido

strange [strendʒ] *adj* extraño, singular; nuevo, desconocido; novel, no acostumbrado

stranger ['strendʒər] *s* forastero; visitador *m;* intruso; desconocido; principiante *mf*

strangle ['stræŋɡəl] *tr* estrangular; reprimir, suprimir ‖ *intr* estrangularse

strap [stræp] *s* (*of leather*) correa; (*of cloth, metal, etc.*) banda, tira; (*to sharpen a razor*) asentador *m* ‖ *v* (*pret & pp* **strapped;** *ger* **strapping**) *tr* atar o liar con correa, banda o tira; azotar con una correa; fajar, vendar; asentar (*una navaja*)

strap'hang'er *s* (coll) pasajero colgado

stratagem ['strætədʒəm] *s* estratagema *f*

strategic(al) [strə'tidʒɪk(əl)] *adj* estratégico

strategist ['strætɪdʒɪst] *s* estratega *m*

strate•gy ['strætɪdʒi] *s* (*pl* **-gies**) estrategia

strati•fy ['strætɪ,faɪ] *v* (*pret & pp* **-fied**) *tr* estratificar ‖ *intr* estratificarse

stratosphere ['strætə,sfɪr] o ['stretə,sfɪr] *s* estratosfera

stra•tum ['stretəm] o ['strætəm] *s* (*pl* **-ta** [tə] o **-tums**) estrato; (*e.g.*, *of society*) clase *f*

straw [strɔ] *adj* pajizo; baladí, de poca importancia; falso; ficticio ‖ *s* paja; (*for drinking*) pajita; **I don't care a straw** no se me da un bledo; **to be the last straw** ser el colmo, no faltar más

straw'ber'ry *s* (*pl* **-ries**) fresa

straw hat *s* sombrero de paja; chupalla *m; (with low flat crown)* canotié *m*

straw man *s* figura de paja; (*figurehead*) testaferro; testigo falso

straw vote *s* voto informativo

stray [stre] *adj* extraviado, perdido; aislado, suelto ‖ *s* animal extraviado o perdido ‖ *intr* extraviarse, perderse

streak [strik] *s* lista, raya; vena, veta; rasgo, traza; (*of light*) rayo; (*of good luck*) racha; (coll) tiempo muy breve; **like a streak** (coll) como un rayo ‖ *tr* listar, rayar; abigarrar ‖ *intr* rayarse; (coll) andar o pasar como un rayo

stream [strim] *s* (*current*) corriente *f;* arroyo, río; chorro, flujo; (*of people*) torrente *m;* (*e.g.*, *of automobiles*) desfile *m* ‖ *intr* correr, manar (*un líquido*); chorrear; flotar, ondear; salir a torrentes

streamer ['strimər] *s* flámula, banderola; cinta ondeante; rayo de luz

streamlined ['strim,laɪnd] *adj* aerodinámico, perfilado

stream'lin'er *s* tren aerodinámico de lujo

street [strit] *adj* callejero ‖ *s* calle *f*

street'car' *s* tranvía *m*

street cleaner *s* basurero; (*device*) barredera

street clothes *spl* traje *m* de calle

street floor *s* piso bajo

street lamp *s* farol *m* (de la calle)

street sprinkler ['sprɪŋklər] *s* carricuba, carro de riego, regadera

street'walk'er *s* cantonera, carrerista

strength [strɛŋθ] *s* fuerza; intensidad; (*of spirituous liquors*) graduación; (com) tendencia a la subida; (mil) número; **on the strength of** fundándose en, confiando en

strengthen ['strɛŋθən] *tr* fortificar, reforzar; confirmar ‖ *intr* fortificarse, reforzarse

strenuous ['strɛnjʊ•əs] *adj* estrenuo, enérgico, vigoroso; arduo, difícil

stress [strɛs] *s* tensión, fuerza; compulsión; acento; (mech) tensión; **to lay stress on** hacer hincapié en ‖ *tr* someter a esfuerzo; hacer hincapié en; acentuar

stress accent *s* acento prosódico

stretch [strɛtʃ] *s* estiramiento, estirón *m; (distance in time or space)* trecho; (*section of road*) tramo; extensión; (*of the imagina-*

tion) esfuerzo; (*confinement in jail*) (slang) condena; **at a stretch** de un tirón ‖ *tr* estirar; extender; tender; forzar, violentar; (fig) estirar (*el dinero*); **to stretch a point** hacer una concesión; **to stretch oneself** desperezarse ‖ *intr* estirarse; extenderse; tenderse; desperezarse; **to stretch out** (coll) echarse

stretcher ['strɛtʃər] *s* (*for gloves*) ensanchador *m;* (*for a painting*) bastidor *m;* (*to carry sick or wounded*) camilla

stretch'er-bear'er *s* camillero

strew [stru] *v* (*pret* **strewed;** *pp* **strewed** o **strewn**) *tr* derramar, esparcir; sembrar, salpicar; polvorear

stricken ['strɪkən] *adj* afligido; inhabilitado; herido; **stricken in years** debilitado por los años

strict [strɪkt] *adj* estricto, riguroso; (*exacting*) severo

stricture ['strɪktʃər] *s* crítica severa; (pathol) estrictura

stride [straɪd] *s* zancada, tranco; **to hit one's stride** alcanzar la actividad o velocidad acostumbrada; **to make great** (o **rapid**) **strides** avnzar a grandes pasos; **to take in one's stride** hacer sin esfuerzo ‖ *v* (*pret* **strode** [strod]; *pp* **stridden** ['strɪdən]) *tr* cruzar de un tranco; montar a horcajadas ‖ *intr* dar zancadas, caminar a paso largo, andar a trancos

strident ['straɪdənt] *adj* estridente

strife [straɪf] *s* contienda; rivalidad

strike [straɪk] *s* (*blow*) golpe *m;* (*stopping of work*) huelga; (*discovery of ore, oil, etc.*) descubrimiento repentino; golpe *m* de fortuna; **to go on strike** ir a la huelga ‖ *v* (*pret & pp* **struck** [strʌk]) *tr* golpear; pulsar (*una tecla*); herir, percutir; topar, dar con; acuñar (*monedas*); echar (*raíces*); frotar, rayar, encender (*un fósforo*); descubrir repentinamente (*mineral, aceite, etc.*); cerrar (*un trato*); arriar (*las velas*); dar (*la hora*); asumir, tomar (*una postura*); borrar, cancelar; impresionar; atraer (*la atención*); **to strike it rich** descubrir un buen filón, tener un golpe de fortuna ‖ *intr* dar, sonar (*una campana, un reloj*); declararse en huelga; (mil) dar el asalto; **to strike out** ponerse en marcha, echar camino adelante

strike'break'er *s* rompehuelgas *m*, esquirol *m*

strike pay *s* sueldo de huelguista

striker ['straɪkər] *s* golpeador *m;* huelguista *mf*

striking ['straɪkɪŋ] *adj* impresionante, llamativo, sorprendente; en huelga

striking power *s* potencia de choque

string [strɪŋ] *s* cuerdecilla; piola; pita; (*of pearls; of lies*) sarta; (*of beans*) hebra; (*of onions or garlic*) ristra; (row) hilera; (mus) cuerda; (*limitation, proviso*) (coll) condición; **strings** instrumentos de cuerda; **to pull strings** tocar resortes ‖ *v* (*pret & pp* **strung** [strʌŋ]) *tr* enhebrar, ensartar; atar con cuerdas; proveer de cuerdas; colgar de una cuerda; tender (*un cable, un alambre*);

encordar (*un violín, una raqueta*); colocar en fila; (slang) engañar, burlar; **to string along** (slang) traer al retortero; **to string up** (coll) ahorcar

string bean *s* habichuela verde, judía verde

stringed instrument [strɪŋd] *s* instrumento de cuerda

stringent ['strɪndʒənt] *adj* riguroso, severo, estricto; convincente

string quartet *s* cuarteto de cuerdas

strip [strɪp] *s* tira; (*of metal*) lámina; (*of land*) faja ‖ *v* (*pret & pp* **stripped;** *ger* **stripping**) *tr* desnudar; despojar; desforrar; deshacer (*la cama*); estropear (*el engranaje, un tornillo*); desvenar (*tabaco*); descortezar; **to strip of** despojar de ‖ *intr* desnudarse; despojarse; descortezarse

stripe [straɪp] *s* banda, lista, raya; gaya; cinta, franja; (mil & nav) galón *m;* índole *f,* tipo; **to win one's stripes** ganar los entorchados ‖ *tr* listar, rayar; gayar

strip mining *s* mineraje *m* a tajo abierto

strip'tease' *s* espectáculo de desnudamiento sensual

strive [straɪv] *v* (*pret* **strove** [strov]; *pp* **striven** ['strɪvən]) *intr* esforzarse; luchar

stroke [strok] *s* golpe *m;* (*of bell or clock*) campanada; (*of pen*) plumada; (*of brush*) pincelada, brochada; (*of arms in swimming*) brazada; (*in a game*) jugada; (*caress with hand*) caricia; (*with a racket*) raquetazo; (*of a piston*) carrera, embolada; (*of a paddle*) palada; (*of an oar*) remada; (*of lightning*) rayo; (*line, mark*) raya; (*of good luck*) golpe *m;* (*of wit*) agudeza, chiste *m;* (*of genius*) rasgo; ataque *m* de parálisis; **at the stroke of** (*e.g., five*) al dar las (*p.ej., cinco*); **to not do a stroke of work** no dar golpe, no levantar paja del suelo ‖ *tr* frotar suavemente, acariciar con la mano

stroll [strol] *s* paseo; **to take a stroll** dar un paseo ‖ *intr* pasear, pasearse; callejear, errar, vagar

stroller ['strolər] *s* paseante *mf;* cochecito para niños

strong [strɔŋ] o [straŋ] *adj* fuerte, resistente; recio, robusto; intenso; (*stock market*) firme; enérgico; marcado; picante; rancio

strong'-arm' man *s* (coll) gorila

strong'box' *s* cofre *m* fuerte, caja de caudales

strong drink *s* bebida alcohólica, bebida fuerte

strong'hold' *s* plaza fuerte

strong man *s* (*e.g., in a circus*) hércules *m;* (*leader, good planner*) alma, promotor *m;* (*dictator*) hombre *m* fuerte

strong-minded ['strɔŋ,maɪndɪd] o [straŋ'maɪndɪd] *adj* independiente; de inteligencia vigorosa; (*e.g., woman*) hombruna

strontium ['stranʃɪ•əm] *s* estroncio

strop [strap] *s* suavizador *m* ‖ *v* (*pret & pp* **stropped;** *ger* **stropping**) *tr* suavizar, afilar

strophe ['strofi] *s* estrofa

structure ['strʌktʃər] *s* estructura; edificio

struggle ['strʌgəl] *s* lucha; esfuerzo, forcejeo ‖ *intr* luchar; esforzarse, forcejear

strum ['strʌm] *v* (*pret & pp* **strummed;** *ger* **strumming**) *tr* arañar (*un instrumento músico*) sin arte ‖ *intr* cencerrear; **to strum on** rasguear

strumpet ['strʌmpɪt] *s* ramera

strut [strʌt] *s* (*brace, prop*) riostra, tornapunta; contoneo, pavoneo ‖ *v* (*pret & pp* **strutted;** *ger* **strutting**) *intr* contonearse, pavonearse

strychnine ['strɪknaɪn] o ['strɪknɪn] *s* estricnina

stub [stʌb] *s* fragmento, trozo; (*of a cigar*) colilla; (*of a tree*) tocón *m;* (*of a pencil*) cabo; (*of a check*) talón *m* ‖ *v* (*pret & pp* **stubbed;** *ger* **stubbing**) *tr* —**to stub one's toe** dar un tropezón

stubble ['stʌbəl] *s* rastrojo; (*of beard*) cañón *m*

stubborn ['stʌbərn] *adj* terco, testarudo, obstinado, porfiado; intratable; **to be stubborn** ser obstinado, empecinarse

stubbornness ['stʌbərnɪs] obstinación, *s* empecinamiento

stuc·co ['stʌko] *s* (*pl* **-coes** o **-cos**) estuco ‖ *tr* estucar

stuck'-up' *adj* (coll) estirado, orgulloso

stud [stʌd] *s* tachón *m;* botón *m* de camisa; montante *m*, pie derecho; clavo de adorno; (*bolt*) espárrago; caballeriza; (*of mares*) yeguada ‖ *v* (*pret & pp* **studded;** *ger* **studding**) *tr* tachonar

stud bolt *s* espárrago

stud'book' *s* registro genealógico de caballos

student ['stjudənt] o ['studənt] *adj* estudiantil ‖ *s* estudiante *mf;* (*person who investigates*), estudioso

student body *s* estudiantado, alumnado

stud'horse' *s* caballo padre, caballo semental

studied ['stʌdid] *adj* premeditado, hecho adrede; (*affected*) estudiado

studi·o ['studɪ,o] *s* (*pl* **-os**) estudio, taller *m;* (mov & rad) estudio

studious ['stjudɪ·əs] o ['studɪ·əs] *adj* estudioso; asiduo, solícito

stud·y ['stʌdi] *s* (*pl* **-ies**) estudio; solicitud; meditación profunda; (*e.g., of a professor*) gabinete *m*, estudio ‖ *v* (*pret & pp* **-ied**) *tr & intr* estudiar

stuff [stʌf] *s* materia; género, paño, tela; muebles *mpl*, baratijas; medicina; fruslerías; cosa, cosas ‖ *tr* rellenar; henchir, llenar; atascar, cerrar, tapar; embutir; (*with food*) atracar; meter sin orden, llenar sin orden; disecar (*un animal muerto*) ‖ *intr* atracarse, hartarse

stuffed shirt *s* (slang) tragavirotes *m*

stuffing ['stʌfɪŋ] *s* relleno

stuff·y ['stʌfi] *adj* (*comp* **-ier;** *super* **-iest**) sofocante, mal ventilado; aburrido, sin interés; (*prim*) (coll) relamido

stumble ['stʌmbəl] *intr* tropezar, dar un traspié; moverse a tropezones; hablar a tropezones; **to stumble on** o **upon** tropezar con

stumbling block *s* escollo, tropezadero

stump [stʌmp] *s* (*of a tree, arm, etc.*) tocón *m;* (*of an arm*) muñón *m;* (*of a tooth*) raigón *m;* (*of a cigar*) colilla; (*of a tail*) rabo; paso pesado; fragmento, resto; tribuna pública; (*for shading drawings*) esfumino ‖ *tr* recorrer (*el país*) pronunciando discursos políticos; (coll) confundir, dejar sin habla; esfumar

stump speaker *s* orador callejero

stump speech *s* arenga electoral

stun [stʌn] *v* (*pret & pp* **stunned;** *ger* **stunning**) *tr* atolondrar, aturdir

stunning ['stʌnɪŋ] *adj* (coll) pasmoso, estupendo, pistonudo, elegante

stunt [stʌnt] *s* atrofia; (*underdeveloped creature*) engendro; (coll) suerte acrobática; (coll) faena, hazaña, proeza ‖ *tr* atrofiar ‖ *intr* (coll) hacer suertes acrobáticas

stunt flying *s* vuelo acrobático

stunt man *s* (mov) doble *m* que hace suertes peligrosas

stupe·fy ['stjupɪ,faɪ] *v* (*pret & pp* **-fied**) *tr* dejar estupefacto, pasmar; causar estupor a

stupendous [stu'pɛndəs] *adj* estupendo; enorme

stupid ['stupɪd] *adj* estúpido; (coll) sonso, pavo, gilí

stupor ['stjupər] o ['stupər] *s* estupor *m*, modorra

stur·dy ['stʌrdi] *adj* (*comp* **-dier;** *super* **-diest**) fuerte, robusto, fornido; firme, tenaz

sturgeon ['stʌrdʒən] *s* esturión *m*

stutter ['stʌtər] *s* tartamudeo ‖ *tr* decir tartamudeando ‖ *intr* tartamudear

sty [staɪ] *s* (*pl* **sties**) pocilga, zahurda; (pathol) orzuelo

style [staɪl] *s* estilo; moda; elegancia; **to live in great style** vivir en gran lujo ‖ *tr* intitular, nombrar

stylish ['staɪlɪʃ] *adj* de moda, elegante

styptic pencil ['stɪptɪk] *s* lápiz estíptico

Styx [stɪks] *s* Estigia

suave [swɑv] o [swev] *adj* suave; afable, fino, zalamero, pulido

sub. *abbr* **subscription, substitute, suburban**

subaltern [səb'ɔltərn] *adj & s* subalterno

subconscious [səb'kɑnʃəs] *adj* subconsciente ‖ *s* subconsciencia

subconsciousness [səb'kɑnʃəsnɪs] *s* subconsciencia

subdeb ['sʌb,dɛb] *s* tobillera

subdivide ['sʌbdɪ,vaɪd] o [,sʌbdɪ'vaɪd] *tr* subdividir ‖ *intr* subdividirse

subdue [səb'dju] *tr* sojuzgar, subyugar; amansar, dominar; suavizar

subdued [səb'djud] *adj* sojuzgado; sumiso; (*e.g., light*) suave

subheading ['sʌb,hɛdɪŋ] *s* subtítulo

subject ['sʌbdʒɪkt] *adj* sujeto; súbdito ‖ *s* asunto, materia, tema *m;* (*person in his relationship to a ruler or government*) súbdito; (gram, med, philos) sujeto ‖ [səb'dʒɛkt] *tr* sujetar, someter, sojuzgar

subject index *s* índice *m* de materias

subjection [səb'dʒɛkʃən] *s* sumisión, sometimiento

subjective [səb'dʒɛktɪv] *adj* subjetivo

subject matter *s* asunto, materia

subjugate ['sʌbdʒə,get] *tr* subyugar

st
su

subjunctive [səb'dʒʌŋktɪv] adj & s subjuntivo

sub·let [sʌb'lɛt] o ['sʌb,lɛt] v (pret & pp -let; ger -letting) tr realquilar, subarrendar

submachine gun [,sʌbmə'ʃin] s subfusil m ametrallador

submarine ['sʌbmə,rin] adj & s submarino ‖ tr (coll) atacar o hundir con un submarino

submarine chaser ['tʃesər] s cazasubmarinos m

submerge [səb'mʌrdʒ] tr sumergir ‖ intr sumergirse

submersion [səb'mʌrʒən] o [səb'mʌrʃən] s sumersión

submission [səb'mɪʃən] s sumisión

submissive [səb'mɪsɪv] adj sumiso

sub·mit [səb'mɪt] v (pret & pp -mitted; ger -mitting) tr someter; proponer, permitirse decir ‖ intr someterse

subordinate [səb'ɔrdɪnɪt] adj & s subordinado ‖ [səb'ɔrdɪ,net] tr subordinar

subornation of perjury [,sʌbər'neʃən] s (law) soborno de testigo

subplot ['sʌb,plɑt] s trama secundaria

subpoena o **subpena** [sʌb'pinə] o [sə'pinə] s comparendo ‖ tr mandar comparecer

sub rosa [sʌb'rozə] adv en secreto, en confianza

subscribe [səb'skraɪb] tr subscribir ‖ intr subscribir; subscribirse, abonarse; **to subscribe to** subscribirse a, abonarse a (una publicación periódica); subscribir (una opinión)

subscriber [səb'skraɪbər] s abonado

subsequent ['sʌbsɪkwənt] adj subsiguiente, posterior

subservient [səb'sʌrvi•ənt] adj servil; subordinado; útil

subside [səb'saɪd] intr calmarse; acabarse, cesar; bajar (el nivel del agua); amainar (el viento)

subsidiary [səb'sɪdɪ,ɛri] adj & s subsidiario

subsidize ['sʌbsɪ,daɪz] tr subsidiar, subvencionar; (to bribe) sobornar

subsi·dy ['sʌbsɪdi] s (pl -dies) subsidio, subvención

subsist [səb'sɪst] intr subsistir

subsistence [səb'sɪstəns] s subsistencia

subsonic [səb'sɑnɪk] adj subsónico

substance ['sʌbstəns] s substancia

substandard [sʌb'stændərd] adj inferior al nivel normal

substantial [səb'stænʃəl] adj considerable, importante; fuerte, sólido; acomodado, rico; esencial; (food) substancial

substantiate [səb'stænʃɪ,et] tr comprobar, establecer, verificar

substantive ['sʌbstəntɪv] adj & s substantivo

substation ['sʌb,steʃən] s (elec) subcentral f

substitute ['sʌbstɪ,tjut] o ['sʌbstɪ,tut] adj substitutivo ‖ s (person) substituto; (thing, substance) substitutivo; (mil) reemplazo ‖ tr poner (a una persona o cosa) en lugar de otra ‖ intr actuar de substituto; **to substitute for** substituir (with personal a)

substitution [,sʌbstɪ'tjuʃən] s empleo o uso (de una persona o cosa en lugar de otra);

(chem, law, math) substitución; imitación fraudulenta

subterranean [,sʌbtə'reni•ən] adj & s subterráneo

subtitle ['sʌb,taɪtəl] s substítulo ‖ tr subtitular

subtle ['sʌtəl] adj sutil; astuto; insidioso

subtle·ty ['sʌtəlti] s (pl -ties) sutileza; agudeza; distinción sutil

subtract [səb'trækt] tr substraer; (math) substraer, restar

suburb ['sʌbʌrb] s suburbio, arrabal m; **the suburbs** las afueras, los barrios externos

subvention [səb'vɛnʃən] s subvención ‖ tr subvencionar

subversive [səb'vʌrsɪv] adj subversivo ‖ s subversor m

subvert [səb'vʌrt] tr subvertir

subway ['sʌb,we] s galería subterránea; metro, ferrocarril subterráneo

succeed [sək'sid] tr suceder (a una persona o cosa) ‖ intr tener buen éxito

success [sək'sɛs] s buen éxito

successful [sək'sɛsfəl] adj feliz, próspero; acertado; logrado

succession [sək'sɛʃən] s sucesión; **in succession** seguidos, uno tras otro

successive [sək'sɛsɪv] adj sucesivo

succor ['sʌkər] s socorro ‖ tr socorrer

succotash ['sʌkə,tæʃ] s guiso de maíz tierno y habas

succumb [sə'kʌm] intr sucumbir

such [sʌtʃ] adj & pron indef tal, semejante; **such a** tal, semejante; **such a** + adj un tan + adj; **such as** quienes, los que

suck [sʌk] s chupada; mamada ‖ tr chupar; mamar; aspirar (el aire)

sucker ['sʌkər] s chupador m; mamón m; (bot & mach) chupón m; (coll) bobo, primo

suckle ['sʌkəl] tr lactar; criar, educar

suckling pig ['sʌklɪŋ] s lechón m, cerdo de leche

suction ['sʌkʃən] adj aspirante ‖ s succión

sudden ['sʌdən] adj súbito, repentino; **all of a sudden** de repente

suds [sʌdz] spl jabonadura; (coll) espuma, cerveza

sue [su] tr demandar; pedir; (law) procesar ‖ intr (law) poner pleito, entablar juicio; **to sue for damages** demandar por daños y perjuicios; **to sue for peace** pedir la paz

suede [swed] s gamuza, ante m

suet ['su•ɪt] o ['sju•ɪt] s sebo

suffer ['sʌfər] tr & intr sufrir, padecer

sufferance ['sʌfərəns] s tolerancia; paciencia; **on sufferance** por tolerancia

suffering ['sʌfərɪŋ] adj doliente ‖ s dolencia, sufrimiento

suffice [sə'faɪs] intr bastar, ser suficiente

sufficient [sə'fɪʃənt] adj suficiente

suffix ['sʌfɪks] s sufijo

suffocate ['sʌfə,ket] tr sofocar ‖ intr sofocarse

suffrage ['sʌfrɪdʒ] s sufragio; aprobación, voto favorable

suffragette [,sʌfrə'dʒɛt] s sufragista (mujer)

suffuse [sə'fjuz] *tr* saturar, bañar

sugar ['ʃugər] *adj* azucarero ‖ *s* azúcar *m* ‖ *tr* azucarar

sugar beet *s* remolacha azucarera

sugar bowl *s* azucarero

sugar cane *s* caña de azúcar

sug'ar-coat' *tr* azucarar; (fig) endulzar, dorar

suggest [səg'dʒɛst] *tr* sugerir

suggestion [səg'dʒɛstʃən] *s* sugestión, sugerencia; sombra, traza ligera

suggestive [səg'dʒɛstɪv] *adj* sugestivo; sicalíptico

suicidal [ˌsuˑɪ'saɪdəl] o [ˌsjuˑɪ'saɪdəl] *adj* suicida

suicide ['suˑɪˌsaɪd] *s* (*act*) suicidio; (*person*) suicida *mf*; **to commit suicide** suicidarse

suit [sut] o [sjut] *s* traje *m*, terno; (*of a lady*) traje *m* sastre; (*group forming a set*) juego; (*of cards*) palo; petición, súplica; cortejo, galanteo; (law) pleito, proceso; **to follow suit** servir del palo; seguir la corriente ‖ *tr* adaptar, ajustar; adaptarse a; sentar, ir o venir bien a; favorecer, satisfacer; **to suit oneself** hacer (*uno*) lo que le guste ‖ *intr* convenir, ser a propósito

suitable ['sutəbəl] *adj* apropiado, conveniente, adecuado

suit'case' *s* maleta, valija

suite [swit] *s* comitiva, séquito; (*group forming a set*) juego; serie *f*; (*of rooms*) crujía; habitación salón; (mus) suite *f*

suiting ['sutɪŋ] *s* corte *m* de traje

suit of clothes *s* traje completo (*de hombre*)

suitor ['sutər] o ['sjutər] *s* pretendiente *m*; (law) demandante *mf*

sulfa drugs ['sʌlfə] *spl* medicamentos sulfas

sulfate ['sʌlfet] *s* sulfato

sulfide ['sʌlfaɪd] *s* sulfuro

sulfite ['sʌlfaɪt] *s* sulfito

sulfur ['sʌlfər] *s* (chem) azufre *m*; véase **sulphur**

sulfuric [sʌl'fjurɪk] *adj* sulfúrico

sulfur mine *s* azufrera

sulfurous ['sʌlfərəs] *adj* sulfuroso ‖ *adj* (chem) sulfuroso

sulk [sʌlk] *s* murria ‖ *intr* amorrarse, enfurruñarse

sulk•y ['sʌlki] *adj* (*comp* **-ier;** *super* **-iest**) enfurruñado, murrio, resentido

sullen ['sʌlən] *adj* hosco, malhumorado, taciturno, triste

sul•ly ['sʌli] *v* (*pret & pp* **-lied**) *tr* empañar, manchar

sulphur ['sʌlfər] *adj* azufrado ‖ *s* azufre *m*; color de azufre ‖ *tr* azufrar

sultan ['sʌltən] *s* sultán *m*

sul•try ['sʌltri] *adj* (*comp* **-trier;** *super* **-triest**) bochornoso, sofocante

sum [sʌm] *s* suma; (coll) problema *m* de aritmética ‖ *v* (*pret & pp* **summed;** *ger* **summing**) *tr* sumar; **to sum up** sumar, resumir

sumac o **sumach** ['ʃumæk] o [sumæk] *s* zumaque *m*

summarize ['sʌməˌraɪz] *tr* resumir

summa•ry ['sʌməri] *adj* sumario ‖ *s* (*pl* **-ries**) sumario, resumen *m*

summer ['sʌmər] *adj* estival, veraniego ‖ *s* verano, estío ‖ *intr* veranear

summer resort *s* lugar *m* de veraneo

summersault ['sʌmərˌsɔlt] *s* salto mortal ‖ *intr* dar un salto mortal

summer school *s* escuela de verano

summery ['sʌməri] *adj* estival, veraniego

summit ['sʌmɪt] *s* cima, cumbre *f*

summit conference o **summit meeting** *s* conferencia en la cumbre

summon ['sʌmən] *tr* convocar, llamar; evocar; (law) citar, emplazar

summons ['sʌmənz] *s* orden *f*, señal *f*; (law) citación, emplazamiento ‖ *tr* (coll) citar, emplazar

sumptuous ['sʌmptʃuˑəs] *adj* suntuoso

sun [sʌn] *s* sol *m*; **to have a place in the sun** ocupar su puesto en el mundo ‖ *v* (*pret & pp* **sunned;** *ger* **sunning**) *tr* asolear ‖ *intr* asolearse

sun bath *s* baño de sol

sun'beam' *s* rayo de sol

sun'bon'net *s* papalina

sun'burn' *s* quemadura de sol ‖ *v* (*pret & pp* **-burned** o **burnt**) *tr* quemar al sol ‖ *intr* quemarse al sol

sundae ['sʌndi] *s* helado con frutas, jarabes o nueces

Sunday ['sʌndi] *adj* dominical; (*used or worn on Sunday*) dominguero ‖ *s* domingo

Sunday best *s* (coll) trapos de cristianar, ropa dominguera

Sunday's child *s* niño nacido de pies, niño mimado de la fortuna

Sunday school *s* escuela dominical, doctrina dominical

Sunday supplement *s* (*newspaper*) suplemento dominical

sunder ['sʌndər] *tr* separar; romper

sun'di'al *s* reloj *m* de sol, cuadrante *m* solar

sun'down' *s* puesta del sol

sundries ['sʌndriz] *spl* artículos diversos

sundry ['sʌndri] *adj* diversos, varios

sun'flow'er *s* girasol *m*, tornasol *m*

sun'glass'es *spl* gafas de sol, gafas para el sol

sunken ['sʌŋkən] *adj* hundido, sumido

sun lamp *s* lámpara de rayos ultravioletas

sun'light' *s* luz *f* del sol

sun'lit' *adj* iluminado por el sol

sun•ny ['sʌni] *adj* (*comp* **-nier;** *super* **-iest**) de sol; asoleado; brillante, resplandeciente; alegre, risueño; **to be sunny** hacer sol

sunny side *s* sol *m*; (fig) lado bueno, lado favorable

sun porch *s* solana

sun'rise' *s* salida del sol; **from sunrise to sunset** de sol a sol

sun'set' *s* puesta del sol

sun'shade' *s* quitasol *m*, sombrilla; toldo; visera contra el sol

sun'shine' *s* claridad del sol, alegría; **in the sunshine** al sol

sun'spot' *s* mancha solar

sun'stroke' *s* insolación

sun'tan' *s* bronceado

suntan lotion *s* bronceador *m*

sup. *abbr* **superior, supplement**

sup [sʌp] *v* (*pret* & *pp* **supped;** *ger* **supping**) *intr* cenar

superannuated [,supər'ænju,etɪd] *adj* jubilado, inhabilitado por ancianidad o enfermedad; fuera de moda

superb [sə'pʌrb] *adj* soberbio, estupendo, magnífico

supercar•go ['supər,kargo] *s* (*pl* **-goes** o **-gos**) (naut) sobrecargo

supercharge [,supər'tʃardʒ] *tr* sobrealimentar

supercilious [,supər'sɪlɪ•əs] *adj* arrogante, altanero, desdeñoso

superficial [,supər'fɪʃəl] *adj* superficial

superfluous [su'pʌrflu•əs] *adj* superfluo

superhuman [,supər'hjumən] *adj* sobrehumano

superimpose [,supərɪm'poz] *tr* sobreponer

superintendent [,supərɪn'tɛndənt] *s* superintendente *mf*

superior [sə'pɪrɪ•ər] *adj* superior; indiferente, sereno; arrogante; (typ) volado ‖ *s* superior *m*

superiority [sə,pɪrɪ'arɪti] *s* superioridad; indiferencia, serenidad; arrogancia

superlative [sə'pʌrlətɪv] *adj* & *s* superlativo

super•man ['supər,mæn] *s* (*pl* **-men** [,mɛn]) sobrehombre *m*, superhombre *m*

supermarket ['supər,markɪt] *s* supermercado

supernatural [,supər'nætʃərəl] *adj* sobrenatural

superpose [,supər'poz] *tr* sobreponer, superponer

supersede [,supər'sid] *tr* reemplazar; desalojar

supersonic [,supər'sanɪk] *adj* supersónico ‖ **supersonics** *ssg* supersónica

superstitious [,supər'stɪʃəs] *adj* supersticioso

supertanker ['supər,tæŋkər] *s* superpetrolero, supertanquero

supervene [,supər'vin] *intr* sobrevenir

supervise ['supər,vaɪz] *tr* superintender, supervisar, dirigir

supervisor ['supər,vaɪzər] *s* superintendente *mf*, supervisor *m*, dirigente *mf*

supp. *abbr* **supplement**

supper ['sʌpər] *s* cena

supplant [sə'plænt] *tr* reemplazar

supple ['sʌpəl] *adj* flexible; dócil

supplement ['sʌplɪmənt] *s* suplemento ‖ ['sʌplɪ,mɛnt] *tr* suplir, completar

suppliant ['sʌplɪ•ənt] *adj* & *s* suplicante *mf*

supplication [,sʌplɪ'keʃən] *s* súplica

sup•ply [sə'plaɪ] *s* (*pl* **-plies**) suministro, provisión; surtido, repuesto; oferta, existencia; **supplies** pertrechos, provisiones, víveres *mf*; artículos, efectos ‖ *v* (*pret* & *pp* **-plied**) *tr* suministrar, aprovisionar; reemplazar

supply and demand *spl* oferta y demanda

support [sə'port] *s* apoyo, soporte *m*, sostén *m*; sustento ‖ *tr* apoyar, soportar, sostener; sustentar; aguantar

supporter [sə'portər] *s* partidario; (*jockstrap*) suspensorio; faja abdominal, faja medical

suppose [sə'poz] *tr* suponer; creer; **to be supposed to** deber; **to suppose so** creer que sí

supposed [sə'pozd] *adj* supuesto

supposition [,sʌpə'zɪʃən] *s* suposición

supposito•ry [sə'pazɪ,tori] *s* (*pl* **-ries**) supositorio

suppress [sə'prɛs] *tr* suprimir

suppression [sə'prɛʃən] *s* supresión

suppurate ['sʌpjə,ret] *intr* supurar

supreme [sə'prim] o [su'prim] *adj* supremo

supt. *abbr* **superintendent**

surcharge ['sʌr,tʃardʒ] *s* sobrecarga ‖ [,sʌr'tʃardʒ] o ['sʌr,tʃardʒ] *tr* sobrecargar

sure [ʃur] *adj* seguro; **to be sure** seguramente, sin duda ‖ *adv* (coll) seguramente, claro; **sure enough** efectivamente

sure things *adv* (slang) seguramente ‖ *interj* ¡claro!, ¡seguro! ‖ *s* (slang) sacabocados *m*

sure•ty ['ʃurti] o ['ʃurɪti] *s* (*pl* **-ties**) seguridad, garantía, fianza

surf [sʌrf] *s* cachones *mpl*, olas que rompen en la playa

surface ['sʌrfɪs] *adj* superficial ‖ *s* superficie *f* ‖ *tr* alisar, allanar; recubrir ‖ *intr* emerger (*p.ej., un submarino*)

surface mail *s* correo por vía ordinaria

surf'board' *s* patín *m* de mar

surfeit ['sʌrfɪt] *s* exceso; hartura, hastío; empacho, indigestión ‖ *tr* atracar, hastiar; encebadar (*las bestias*) ‖ *intr* atracarse, hastiarse; encebadarse

surf'-rid'ing *s* patinaje *m* sobre las olas

surge [sʌrdʒ] *s* oleada; (elec) sobretensión ‖ *intr* agitarse, ondular

surgeon ['sʌrdʒən] *s* cirujano

surger•y ['sʌrdʒəri] *s* (*pl* **-ies**) cirugía; sala de operaciones

surgical ['sʌrdʒɪkəl] *adj* quirúrgico

sur•ly ['sʌrli] *adj* (*comp* **-lier;** *super* **-liest**) áspero, rudo, hosco, insolente

surmise [sər'maɪz] o ['sʌrmaɪz] *s* conjetura, suposición ‖ [sər'maɪz] *tr* & *intr* conjeturar, suponer

surmount [sər'maunt] *tr* levantarse sobre; aventajar, sobrepujar; superar; coronar

surname ['sʌr,nem] *s* apellido; (*added name*) sobrenombre *m* ‖ *tr* apellidar; sobrenombrar

surpass [sər'pæs] o [sər'pas] *tr* aventajar, sobrepasar

surplice ['sʌrplɪs] *s* sobrepelliz *f*

surplus ['sʌrplʌs] *adj* sobrante, excedente ‖ *s* sobrante *m*, exceso; (com) superávit *m*

surprise [sər'praɪz] *adj* inesperado, improviso ‖ *s* sorpresa; **to take by surprise** coger por sorpresa ‖ *tr* sorprender

surprise package *s* sorpresa

surprise party *s* reunión improvisada para felicitar por sorpresa a una persona

surprising [sər'praɪzɪŋ] *adj* sorprendente, sorpresivo

surrender [sə'rɛndər] *s* rendición ‖ *tr* rendir ‖ *intr* rendirse

surrender value *s* (ins) valor *m* de rescate

surreptitious [,sʌrɛp'tɪʃəs] *adj* subrepticio

surround [sə'raʊnd] *tr* cercar, rodear, circundar; (mil) sitiar

surrounding [sə'raʊndɪŋ] *adj* circundante, circunstante ‖ **surroundings** *spl* alrededores *mpl*, contornos; ambiente *m*, medio

surtax ['sʌr,tæks] *s* impuesto complementario

surveillance [sər'veləns] o [sər'veljəns] *s* vigilancia

survey ['sʌrve] *s* estudio, examen *m*, inspección, reconocimiento; agrimensura, medición, plano; levantamiento de planos; (*of opinion*) encuesta; (*of literature*) bosquejo ‖ [sʌr've] o ['sʌrve] *tr* estudiar, examinar, inspeccionar, reconocer; medir; levantar el plano de ‖ *intr* levantar el plano

surveyor [sər've•ər] *s* inspector *m;* agrimensor *m*

survival [sər'vaɪvəl] *s* supervivencia

survive [sər'vaɪv] *tr* sobrevivir a (*otra persona; algún acontecimiento*) ‖ *intr* sobrevivir

surviving [sər'vaɪvɪŋ] *adj* sobreviviente

survivor [sər'vaɪvər] *s* sobreviviente *mf*

survivorship [sər'vaɪvər,ʃɪp] *s* (law) sobrevivencia

susceptible [sə'sɛptɪbəl] *adj* susceptible; (*to love*) enamoradizo

suspect ['sʌspɛkt] o [səs'pɛkt] *adj* & *s* sospechoso ‖ [səs'pɛkt] *tr* sospechar

suspend [səs'pɛnd] *tr* suspender ‖ *intr* dejar de obrar; suspender pagos

suspenders [səs'pɛndərz] *spl* tirantes *mpl*

suspense [səs'pɛns] *s* suspenso, suspensión; duda, incertidumbre; indecisión, irresolución; ansiedad

suspension bridge [səs'pɛnʃən] *s* puente *m* colgante

suspicion [səs'pɪʃən] *s* sospecha, suspicacia; sombra, traza ligera

suspicious [səs'pɪʃəs] *adj* (*inclined to suspect*) suspicaz; (*subject to suspicion*) sospechoso

sustain [səs'ten] *tr* sostener, sustentar; apoyar, defender; confirmar, probar; sufrir (*p.ej., un daño, una pérdida*)

sustenance ['sʌstɪnəns] *s* sustento, alimentos; sostenimiento

sutler ['sʌtlər] *s* (mil) vivandero

swab [swɑb] *s* escobón *m*, estropajo; (naut) lampazo; (surg) tapón *m* de algodón ‖ *v* (*pret* & *pp* **swabbed;** *ger* **swabbing**) *tr* fregar, limpiar; (naut) lampacear; (surg) limpiar con algodón

swaddle ['swɑdəl] *tr* empañar, fajar

swaddling clothes *spl* pañales *mpl*

swagger ['swægər] *adj* (coll) muy elegante ‖ *s* fanfarronada; contoneo, paso jactancioso ‖ *intr* fanfarronear; contonear

swain [swen] *s* (*lad*) zagal; galán *m*, amante *m*

swallow ['swɑlo] *s* trago; (orn) golondrina ‖ *tr* tragar, deglutir; (fig) tragar, tragarse ‖ *intr* tragar, deglutir

swallow-tailed coat ['swɑlo,teld] *s* frac *m*

swal'low•wort *s* vencetósigo

swamp [swɑmp] *s* pantano, marisma ‖ *tr* encharcar, inundar; (*e.g., with work*) abrumar

swamp•y ['swɑmpi] *adj* (*comp* **-ier;** *super* **-iest**) pantanoso

swan [swɑn] *s* cisne *m*

swan dive *s* salto de ángel

swank [swæŋk] *adj* (slang) elegante, vistoso ‖ *s* (slang) elegancia vistosa

swan knight *s* caballero del cisne

swan's-down ['swɑnz,daʊn] *s* plumón *m* de cisne; moletón *m*, paño de vicuña

swan song *s* canto del cisne

swap [swɑp] *s* (coll) truque *m*, cambalache *m* ‖ *v* (*pret* & *pp* **swapped;** *ger* **swapping**) *tr* & *intr* trocar, cambalachear

swarm [swɔrm] *s* enjambre *m* ‖ *intr* enjambrar; volar en enjambres; hormiguear (*una multitud de gente o animales*)

swarth•y ['swɔrði] o ['swɔrθi] *adj* (*comp* **-ier;** *super* **-iest**) atezado, carinegro, moreno

swashbuckler ['swɑʃ,bʌklər] *s* espada chín *m*, matasiete *m*, valentón *m*

swat [swɑt] *s* (coll) golpe violento ‖ *v* (*pret* & *pp* **swatted;** *ger* **swatting**) *tr* (coll) golpear con fuerza; (coll) aporrear, aplastar (*una mosca*)

sway [swe] *s* oscilación, vaivén *m;* dominio, imperio ‖ *tr* hacer oscilar; conmover; disuadir; gobernar, dominar ‖ *intr* oscilar; desviarse; tambalear, flaquear

swear [swɛr] *v* (*pret* **swore** [swor]; *pp* **sworn** [sworn]) *tr* jurar; juramentar; prestar (*juramento*); **to swear in** tomar juramento a; **to swear off** jurar renunciar a; **to swear out** obtener mediante juramento ‖ *intr* jurar; **to swear at** maldecir; **to swear by** jurar por; poner toda su confianza en; **to swear to** prestar juramento a; declarar bajo juramento; jurar + *inf*

sweat [swɛt] *s* sudor *m* ‖ *v* (*pret* & *pp* **sweat** o **sweated**) *tr* sudar (*agua por los poros; la ropa*); (slang) hacer sudar; **to sweat it out** (slang) aguantarlo hasta el fin ‖ *intr* sudar

sweater ['swɛtər] *s* suéter *m*

sweat shirt *s* pulóver *m* de mangas largas

sweat'shop' *s* taller *m* de trabajo afanoso y de poco sueldo

sweat•y ['swɛti] *adj* (*comp* **-ier;** *super* **-iest**) sudoroso

Swede [swid] *s* sueco

Sweden ['swidən] *s* Suecia

Swedish ['swidɪʃ] *adj* & *s* sueco

sweep [swip] *s* barrido; alcance *m*, extensión; (*of wind*) soplo; (*of a well*) cigoñal *m* ‖ *v* (*pret* & *pp* **swept** [swɛpt]) *tr* barrer; arrastrar; rozar, tocar; recorrer con la mirada, los dedos, etc. ‖ *intr* barrer; pasar rápidamente; extenderse; precipitarse; andar con paso majestuoso

sweeper ['swipər] *s* (*person*) barrendero; (*machine for sweeping streets*) barredera; barredera de alfombra; (nav) dragaminas *m*

sweeping ['swipɪŋ] *adj* arrebatador; comprensivo, extenso, vasto ‖ **sweepings** *spl* barreduras

sweep'sec'ond *s* segundero central

sweep'stakes' *ssg* o *spl* lotería en la cual una persona gana todas las apuestas; carrera que decide todas las apuestas; premio en las carreras de caballos

sweet [swit] *adj* dulce; oloroso; melodioso, grato al oído; fresco; bonito, lindo; amable; querido; **to be sweet on** (coll) estar enamorado de ‖ *adv* dulcemente; **to smell sweet** tener buen olor ‖ **sweets** *spl* dulces *mpl*, golosinas

sweet'bread' *s* lechecillas, mollejas

sweet'bri'er *s* eglantina

sweeten ['switən] *tr* azucarar, endulzar; suavizar; purificar ‖ *intr* azucararse, endulzarse; suavizarse

sweetener ['switənər] *s* eculcorante

sweet'heart' *s* enamorado o enamorada; amiga querida; galán *m*, cortejo

sweetish ['switɪʃ] *adj* dulzoso

sweet marjoram *s* mejorana

sweet'meats' *spl* dulces *mpl*, confites *mpl*, confitura

sweet pea *s* guisante *m* de olor

sweet potato *s* batata, camote *m*

sweet-scented ['swit,sɛntɪd] *adj* oloroso, perfumado

sweet tooth *s* gusto por los dulces

sweet-toothed ['swit,tuθt] *adj* dulcero, goloso

sweet william *s* clavel *m* de ramillete, minutisa

swell [swɛl] *adj* (coll) muy elegante; (slang) de órdago, magnífico ‖ *s* hinchazón *f;* bulto; marejada; oleaje *m;* (of a crowd of people) oleada; (coll) petimetre *m*, pisaverde *m* ‖ *v* (pret **swelled** o **swelled** o **swollen** ['swolən]) *tr* hinchar, inflar; abultar, aumentar; elevar, levantar; (fig) hinchar, engreír ‖ *intr* hincharse; abultarse, aumentar, crecer; elevarse, levantarse; embravecerse (el mar); (fig) hincharse, engreírse

swelled head *s* entono; **to have a swelled head** estar muy pagado de sí mismo, creerse gran cosa

swelter ['swɛltər] *intr* sofocarse de sudor

swept'back' wing *s* (aer) ala en flecha

swerve [swʌrv] *s* viraje *m*, desvío brusco ‖ *tr* desviar ‖ *intr* desviarse, torcer

swift [swɪft] *adj* rápido, veloz; pronto; repentino; correlón (SAm) ‖ *adv* rápidamente, velozmente ‖ *s* vencejo

swig [swɪg] *s* chisguete, tragantada ‖ *v* (pret & pp **swigged;** ger **swigging**) *tr* & *intr* beber a grandes tragos

swill [swɪl] *s* basura, inmundicia; tragantada ‖ *tr* beber a grandes tragos; emborrachar ‖ *intr* beber a grandes tragos; emborracharse

swim [swɪm] *s* natación; **the swim** (in affairs, society, etc.) (coll) la corriente ‖ *v* (pret **swam** [swæm]; pp **swum** [swʌm]; ger **swimming**) *tr* pasar a nado ‖ *intr* nadar; deslizarse, escurrirse; padecer vahidos; dar vueltas (la cabeza); **to swim across** atravesar a nado

swimmer ['swɪmər] *s* nadador *m*

swimming pool *s* piscina

swimming suit *s* traje *m* de baño

swindle ['swɪndəl] *s* estafa, timo; leva (CAm, Col); embelequería (Col, Mex, P-R) ‖ *tr* & *intr* estafar, timar

swindler ['swɪndlər] *s* estafador *m*, estafadora; lana *m* (CAm)

swine [swaɪn] *s* cerdo, puerco; *spl* ganado porcino

swing [swɪŋ] *s* balance *m*, oscilación, vaivén *m;* (device used for recreation) columpio; hamaca; turno, período; fuerza, ímpetu *m;* (trip) jira; (box) golpe *m* de lado; (mus) ritmo constantemente repetido; **in full swing** en plena marcha ‖ *v* (pret & pp **swung** [swʌŋ]) *tr* blandir (p.ej., un arma); menear (los brazos); hacer oscilar; columpiar; manejar con éxito ‖ *intr* oscilar; balancearse; columpiar; estar colgado; dar una vuelta; **to swing open** abrirse de pronto (una puerta)

swinging door ['swɪŋɪŋ] *s* batiente *m* oscilante, puerta de vaivén

swinish ['swaɪnɪʃ] *adj* porcuno; (fig) cochino, puerco

swipe [swaɪp] *s* (coll) golpe *m* fuerte ‖ *tr* (coll) dar un golpe fuerte a; (slang) hurtar, robar

swirl [swʌrl] *s* remolino, torbellino ‖ *tr* hacer girar ‖ *intr* arremolinarse, remolinar; girar

swish [swɪʃ] *s* (e.g., of a whip) chasquido; (of a dress) crujido ‖ *tr* chasquear (el látigo) ‖ *intr* chasquear; crujir (un vestido)

Swiss [swɪs] *adj* & *s* suizo

Swiss chard [tʃɑrd] *s* acelga

Swiss cheese *s* Gruyère *m*, queso suizo

Swiss Guards *spl* guardia suiza

switch [swɪtʃ] *s* bastoncillo, latiguillo; latigazo; coletazo; (false hair) trenza postiza, moño postizo; (elec) llave *f*, interruptor *m*, conmutador *m;* (rr) agujas ‖ *tr* azotar, fustigar; (elec) conmutar; (rr) desviar; **to switch off** (elec) cortar, desconectar; **to switch on** (elec) cerrar (el circuito); (elec) encender, poner (la luz, etc.) ‖ *intr* cambiarse, moverse; desviarse

switch'back' *s* vía en zigzag

switch'board' *s* cuadro de distribución

switching engine *s* locomotora de maniobras

switch•man ['swɪtʃmən] *s* (pl **-men** [mən]) agujetero, guardagujas *m*

switch'yard' *s* patio de maniobras

Switzerland ['swɪtsərlənd] *s* Suiza

swiv•el ['swɪvəl] *s* eslabón giratorio ‖ *v* (pret & pp **-eled** o **-elled;** ger **-eling** o **-elling**) *intr* girar sobre un eje

swivel chair *s* silla giratoria

swoon [swun] *s* desmayo ‖ *intr* desmayarse

swoop [swup] *s* descenso súbito; (of a bird of prey) calada ‖ *intr* bajar rápidamente, precipitarse; abatirse (p.ej., el ave de rapiña)

sword [sord] *s* espada; **at swords' points** enemistados a sangre y fuego; **to put to the sword** pasar al filo de la espada, pasar a cuchillo

sword belt *s* cinturón *m*

sword'fish' *s* pez *m* espada

sword handler *s* (taur) mozo de estoques
sword rattling *s* fanfarronería
swords•man [ˈsordzmən] *s* (*pl* **-men** [mən]) espada *m;* esgrimidor *m*
sword swallower [ˈswɑloˑər] *s* tragasable *m*
sword thrust *s* estocada, golpe *m* de espada
sworn [sworn] *adj* (*enemy*) jurado
sycophant [ˈsɪkəfənt] *s* adulador *m;* parásito
syll. *abbr* **syllable**
syllable [ˈsɪləbəl] *s* sílaba
syllogism [ˈsɪlə,dʒɪzəm] *s* silogismo
sylph [sɪlf] *s* sílfide *f*
sym. *abbr* **symbol, symmetrical, symphony, symptom**
symbiosis [,sɪmbaɪˈosɪs] o [,sɪmbiˈosɪs] *s* simbiosis
symbiotic [,sɪmbaɪˈɑtɪk] o [,sɪmbiˈɑtɪk] *adj* simbiótico
symbol [ˈsɪmbəl] *s* símbolo
symbolic(al) [sɪmˈbɑlɪk(əl)] *adj* simbólico
symbolize [ˈsɪmbə,laɪz] *tr* simbolizar
symmetric(al) [sɪˈmɛtrɪk(əl)] *adj* simétrico
symme•try [ˈsɪmɪtri] *s* (*pl* **-tries**) simetría
sympathetic [,sɪmpəˈθɛtɪk] *adj* compasivo; favorablemente dispuesto
sympathize [ˈsɪmpə,θaɪz] *intr* compadecerse; **to sympathize with** compadecerse de; comprender
sympa•thy [ˈsɪmpəθi] *s* (*pl* **-thies**) compasión, conmiseración; **to be in sympathy with** estar de acuerdo con, ser partidario de; **to extend one's sympathy to** dar el pésame a
sympathy strike *s* huelga por solidaridad
symphonic [sɪmˈfɑnɪk] *adj* sinfónico
sympho•ny [ˈsɪmfəni] *s* (*pl* **-nies**) sinfonía

symposi•um [sɪmˈpozɪˑəm] *s* (*pl* **-a** [ə]) coloquio
symptom [ˈsɪmptəm] *s* síntoma *m*
syn. *abbr* **synonym, synonymous**
synagogue [ˈsɪnə,gɔg] *s* sinagoga
synchronize [ˈsɪŋkrə,naɪz] *tr* & *intr* sincronizar
synchronous [ˈsɪŋkrənəs] *adj* sincrónico
syncope [ˈsɪŋkə,pi] *s* (phonet) síncopa
syndicate [ˈsɪndɪkɪt] *s* sindicato ‖ [ˈsɪndɪ,ket] *tr* sindicar ‖ *intr* sindicarse
syndrome [ˈsɪndrom] *s* síndrome *m*
synonym [ˈsɪnənɪm] *s* sinónimo
synonymous [sɪˈnɑnɪməs] *adj* sinónimo
synop•sis [sɪˈnɑpsɪs] *s* (*pl* **-ses** [siz]) sinopsis *f*
syntax [ˈsɪntæks] *s* sintaxis *f*
synthe•sis [ˈsɪnθɪsɪs] *s* (*pl* **-ses** [,siz]) síntesis *f*
synthesize [ˈsɪnθɪ,saɪz] *tr* sintetizar
synthesizer *s* sintetizador *m*
synthetic(al) [sɪnˈθɛtɪk(əl)] *adj* sintético
syphillis [ˈsɪfɪlɪs] *s* sífilis *f*
Syria [ˈsɪrɪˑə] *s* Siria
Syrian [ˈsɪrɪˑən] *adj* & *s* sirio
syringe [sɪˈrɪndʒ] o [ˈsɪrɪndʒ] *s* jeringa; (*fountain syringe*) mangueta; (*syringe fitted with needle for hypodermic injections*) jeringuilla ‖ *tr* jeringar
syrup [ˈsɪrəp] *s* almíbar *m;* (*with fruit juices or medicinal substances*) jarabe *m*
system [ˈsɪstəm] *s* sistema *m*
systematic(al) [,sɪstəˈmætɪk(əl)] *adj* sistemático
systematize [ˈsɪstəmə,taɪz] *tr* sistematizar
systems analysis *s* análisis *m* & *f* de sistemas
systole [ˈsɪstəli] *s* sístole *f*

T

T, t [ti] vigésima letra del alfabeto inglés
t. *abbr* **teaspoon, temperature, tenor, tense, territory, town**
T. *abbr* **Territory, Testament**
tab [tæb] *s* apéndice *m*, proyección; marbete *m;* **to keep tab on** (coll) tener a la vista; **to pick up the tab** (coll) pagar la cuenta
tab•by [ˈtæbi] *s* (*pl* **-bies**) gato atigrado; gata; solterona; chismosa
tabernacle [ˈtæbər,nækəl] *s* tabernáculo
table [ˈtebəl] *s* mesa; (*list, catalogue; index of a book*) tabla; **to set the table** poner la mesa; **to turn the tables** volver las tornas; **under the table** completamente emborrachado ‖ *tr* aplazar la discusión de
tab•leau [ˈtæblo] *s* (*pl* **-leaus** o **-leaux** [loz]) cuadro vivo
ta'ble•cloth' *s* mantel *m*
table d'hôte [ˈtɑbəlˈdot] *s* mesa redonda; comida a precio fijo
ta'ble•land' *s* meseta

table linen *s* mantelería
table manners *spl* modales *mpl* que uno tiene en la mesa
table of contents *s* índice *m* de materias, tabla de materias
ta'ble•spoon' *s* cuchara de sopa
tablespoonful [ˈtebəl,spun,ful] *s* cucharada
tablet [ˈtæblɪt] *s* (*writing pad*) bloc *m;* (*slab*) lápida, placa; (*lozenge, pastille*) comprimido, tableta
table talk *s* conversación de sobremesa
table tennis *s* tenis de mesa
ta'ble•ware' *s* servicio de mesa, artículos para la mesa
tabloid [ˈtæblɔɪd] *s* periódico sensacional
taboo [təˈbu] *adj* prohibido ‖ *s* tabú *m* ‖ *tr* prohibir
tabulate [ˈtæbjə,let] *tr* tabular
tabulator [ˈtæbjə,letər] *s* tabulador *m*
tacit [ˈtæsɪt] *adj* tácito
taciturn [ˈtæsɪ,tʌrn] *adj* taciturno

sw
ta

tack [tæk] s tachuela; nuevo plan de acción; (naut) virada; (sew) hilván m ‖ tr clavar con tachuelas; añadir; unir; (naut) virar; (sew) hilvanar ‖ intr cambiar de plan; (naut) virar

tackle ['tækəl] s avíos, enseres mpl; (naut) poleame m ‖ tr atacar, embestir; emprender

tack•y ['tæki] adj (comp -ier; super -iest) pegajoso; (coll) desaliñado

tact [tækt] s tacto, juicio, tino

tactful ['tæktfəl] adj discreto, político

tactical ['tæktɪkəl] adj táctico

tactician [tæk'tɪʃən] s táctico

tactics ['tæktɪks] ssg (mil) táctica ‖ spl táctica

tactless ['tæktlɪs] adj indiscreto

tad'pole' s renacuajo

taffeta ['tæfɪtə] s tafetán m

taffy ['tæfi] s arropía, melcocha; (coll) lisonja, zalamería

tag [tæg] s etiqueta, marbete m; herrete m; pingajo; mechón m; vedija; (curlicue in writing) ringorrango; **to play tag** jugar al tócame tú ‖ v (pret & pp **tagged;** ger **tagging**) tr pegar un marbete a; marcar con marbete ‖ intr (coll) seguir de cerca

tag end s cabo flojo; retal m, retazo

Tagus ['tegəs] s Tajo

tail [tel] adj de cola ‖ s cola; **tails** (of a coin) cruz f; (coll) frac m; **to turn tail** mostrar los talones ‖ tr atar, juntar ‖ intr formar cola; **to tail after** pisar los talones a

tail assembly s (aer) empenaje m, planos de cola

tail end s cola, extremo; conclusión; **at the tail end** al final

tail'gate' tr & intr (aut) seguir demasiado de cerca

tail'light' s faro trasero; (rr) disco de cola

tailor ['telər] s sastre m ‖ tr entallar (un traje) ‖ intr ser sastre

tailoring ['telərɪŋ] s sastrería, costura

tai'lor-made' suit s traje m de sastre, traje hecho a la medida

tail'piece' s apéndice m, cabo; (of stringed instrument) (mus) cordal m; (typ) florón m

tail'race' s cauce m de salida; (min) canal m de desechos

tail spin s (aer) barrena picada

tail wind s (aer) viento de cola; (naut) viento en popa

taint [tent] s mancha; corrupción, infección ‖ tr manchar; corromper, inficionar

take [tek] s toma; presa, redada; (mov) toma; (slang) entradas, ingresos ‖ v (pret **took** [tʊk] pp **taken**) tr tomar; (to carry off with one) llevarse; (to remove) quitar; quedarse con (p.ej., una compra en una tienda); comer (una pieza, en el juego de ajedrez y en el de damas); dar (un paso, un salto, un paseo); hacer (un viaje; ejercicio); seguir (un consejo, una asignatura); sacar (una fotografía); calzar, usar (cierto tamaño de zapatos o guantes); estudiar (p.ej., historia, francés, matemáticas); echar (una siesta); tomar (un tren, autobús, tranvía); aguantar, tolerar, soportar; **to take amiss**

llevar a mal; **to take apart** descomponer, desarmar, desmontar; **to take down** bajar; descolgar; poner por escrito, tomar nota de; desmontar; (to humble) quitar los humos a; **to take for** tomar por, p.ej., **I took you for someone else** le tomé por otra persona; **to take from** quitar a; **to take in** acoger, admitir; (to welcome into one's home, one's company) recibir; (to encompass) abarcar, comprender; ganar (dinero); visitar (los puntos de interés); (to win over by flattery or deceit) cazar; meter (p.ej., las costuras de una prenda de vestir); **to take it that** suponer que; **to take off** quitarse (p.ej., el sombrero); descontar; (coll) imitar, parodiar; **to take on** tomar, contratar; empezar; cargar con, tomar sobre sí; desafiar; **to take out** sacar; pasear (p.ej., a un niño, un caballo); omitir; extraer, separar; **to take place** tener lugar; **to take up** subir; levantar; apretar; coger; recoger; emprender, comenzar; tomar posesión de (un cargo, un puesto); tomar, estudiar; ocupar, llenar (un espacio) ‖ intr arraigar, prender; cuajar; actuar, obrar; salir, resultar; adherirse; pegar; (coll) tener éxito; **to take after** parecerse a; **to take off** levantarse; salir; (aer) despegar; **to take up with** (coll) estrechar amistad con; (coll) vivir con; **to take well** (coll) sacar buen retrato

take'-home' pay s salario neto

take'-off' s (aer) despegue m; (coll) imitación burlesca, parodia

talcum powder ['tælkəm] s polvos de talco; talco en polvo

tale [tel] s cuento, relato; embuste m, mentira

tale'bear'er s chismoso, cuentista mf

talent ['tælənt] s talento; gente f de talento

talented ['tæləntɪd] adj talentoso

talent scout s buscador m de nuevas figuras

talk [tɔk] s charla, plática; (gossip) fábula, comidilla; (lecture) conferencia; **to cause talk** dar que hablar ‖ tr hablar; convencer hablando; **to talk up** ensalzar ‖ intr hablar; parlar (el loro); **to talk on** discutir (un asunto); hablar sin para; continuar hablando; **to talk up** elevar la voz, osar hablar

talkative ['tɔkətɪv] adj hablador, locuaz, palabrudo

talker ['tɔkər] s hablador m; orador m; charlatán m, parlón m; discursista mf

talkie ['tɔki] s (coll) cine hablado

talking doll ['tɔkɪŋ] s muñeca parlante

talking film s película hablada

talking machine s máquina parlante

talking picture s cine hablado, cine parlante

talk show s (telv, rad) programa m de conversación e interviú

tall [tɔl] adj alto; (coll) exagerado

tallow ['tælo] s sebo

tal•ly ['tæli] s (pl -lies) cuenta ‖ v (pret & pp **-lied**) tr echar la cuenta de ‖ intr echar la cuenta; concordar, corresponder, conformarse

tally sheet s hoja en que se anota una cuenta

talon [ˈtælən] s garra

tambourine [ˌtæmbəˈrin] s pandereta

tame [tem] adj manso, domesticado; dócil; sumiso; insípido ‖ tr amansar, domesticar; domar (a un animal salvaje); someter; captar (una caída de agua)

tamp [tæmp] tr atacar (un barreno); apisonar

tamper [ˈtæmpər] s (person) apisonador m; (ram) pisón m ‖ intr entremeterse; **to tamper with** manosear, tocar ajando; tratar de forzar (una cerradura); falsificar (un documento); corromper (p.ej., a un testigo)

tampon [ˈtæmpɑn] s (surg) tapón m ‖ tr (surg) taponar

tan [tæn] adj requemado, tostado; de color de canela; marrón; café (Am) ‖ v (pret & pp **tanned**; ger **tanning**) tr adobar, curtir; zurrar; quemar, tostar; (coll) zurrar, dar una paliza a

tang [tæŋ] s sabor m u olor m fuerte y picante; dejo, gustillo (ringing sound) tañido

tangent [ˈtændʒənt] adj tangente ‖ s tangente f; **to fly off at a tangent** tomar subitamente nuevo rumbo, cambiar de repente

tangerine [ˌtændʒəˈrin] s mandarina

tangible [ˈtændʒɪbəl] adj palpable, tangible

Tangier [tænˈdʒɪr] s Tánger f

tangle [ˈtæŋgəl] s enredo, maraña, lío ‖ tr enredar, enmarañar ‖ intr enredarse, enmarañarse

tank [tæŋk] s tanque m, depósito; (mil) tanque, carro de combate; (rr) ténder m; (heavy drinker) (slang) bodega

tank car s (rr) carro cuba, vagón m tanque

tanker [ˈtæŋkər] s barco tanque, buque m cisterna, barco cisternas; avión-nodriza m

tanker fleet s flota petrolera

tank farming s quimicultura, cultivo hidropónico

tank truck s camión m tanque

tanner [ˈtænər] s curtidor m

tanner·y [ˈtænəri] s (pl -ies) curtiduría, tenería

tantalize [ˈtæntəˌlaɪz] tr atormentar con falsas promesas

tantamount [ˈtæntəˌmaʊnt] adj equivalente

tantrum [ˈtæntrəm] s berrinche m, rabieta

tap [tæp] s golpecito, palmadita; canilla, espita; grifo; (elec) toma; (mach) macho de terraja; **on tap** sacado del barril, servido al grifo; listo, a mano; **taps** (signal to put out lights) (mil) silencio ‖ v (pret & pp **tapped**; ger **tapping**) tr dar golpecitos o un golpecito a o en; espitar, poner la espita a; sacar o tomar (quitando la espita); sangrar (un árbol); intervenir (un teléfono); derivar (electricidad); aterrajar (tuercas) ‖ intr dar golpecitos

tap dance s zapateado

tap'-dance' intr zapatear

tape [tep] s cinta ‖ tr proveer de cinta; medir con cinta; (coll) grabar en cinta magnetofónica

tape measure s cinta de medir

taper [ˈtepər] s cerilla, velita larga y delgada

‖ tr ahusar ‖ intr ahusarse; ir disminuyendo

tape'-re·cord' tr grabar sobre cinta

tape recorder [rɪˈkɔrdər] s magnetófono, grabadora de cinta

tapes·try [ˈtæpɪstri] s (pl -tries) tapiz m ‖ v (pret & pp -**tried**) tr tapizar

tape'worm' s solitaria, lombriz solitaria

tappet [ˈtæpɪt] s (aut) alzaválvulas m, taqué m

tap'room' s bodegón m, taberna

taps [tæps] s toque m de silencio; (slang) fin m, muerte f

tap water s agua de grifo

tap wrench s volvedor m de machos

tar [tɑr] s alquitrán m; (coll) marinero ‖ v (pret & pp **tarred**; ger **tarring**) tr alquitranar; **to tar and feather** embrear y emplumar

tar·dy [ˈtɑrdi] adj (comp -dier; super -diest) tardío

target [ˈtɑrgɪt] s blanco

target area s zona a batir

target practice s tiro al blanco

tariff [ˈtærɪf] adj arancelario ‖ (duties) arancel m; (rates in general) tarifa

tarnish [ˈtɑrnɪʃ] s deslustre m ‖ tr deslustrar ‖ intr deslustrarse

tar paper s papel alquitranado

tarpaulin [tɑrˈpɔlɪn] s alquitranado, encerado, empegado

tar·ry [ˈtɑri] adj alquitranado, embreado ‖ [ˈtæri] v (pret & pp -**ried**) intr detenerse, quedarse; tardar

tart [tɑrt] adj acre, agrio; (fig) áspero, mordaz ‖ s tarta; (coll) puta

task [tæsk] s tarea; **to bring** o **take to task** llamar a capítulo

task'mas'ter s amo, superintendente mf; ordenancista mf, tirano

tassel [ˈtæsəl] s borla; (bot) penacho

taste [test] s gusto, sabor m; sorbo, trago; muestra; gusto, buen gusto; **in bad taste** de mal gusto; **in good taste** de buen gusto; **to acquire a taste for** tomar gusto a ‖ tr gustar; (to sample) probar ‖ intr saber; **to taste of** saber a

tasteless [ˈtestlɪs] adj desabrido, insípido; de mal gusto

tast·y [ˈtesti] adj (comp -ier; super -iest) sabroso; de buen gusto

tatter [ˈtætər] s andrajo, harapo, guiñapo ‖ tr hacer andrajos

tattered [ˈtætərd] adj andrajoso, haraposo, hilachento

tattle [ˈtætəl] s charla; habladuría ‖ intr charlar; chismear, murmurar

tat'tle·tale' adj revelador ‖ s cuentista mf, chismoso

tattoo [tæˈtu] s tatuaje m; (mil) retreta ‖ tr tatuar o tatuarse

taunt [tɔnt] o [tɑnt] s mofa, pulla ‖ tr provocar con insultos

Taurus [ˈtɔrəs] s (astr) Tauro

taut [tɔt] adj tieso, tirante

tavern [ˈtævərn] s taberna; mesón m, posada; bayun(c)a (CAm); borrachería (Mex)

ta·
ta

taw·dry ['tɔdri] *adj* (*comp* **-drier;** *super* **-driest**) cursi, charro, vistoso

taw·ny ['tɔni] *adj* (*comp* **-nier;** *super* **-niest**) leonado

tax [tæks] *s* contribución, impuesto ‖ *tr* poner impuestos a (*una persona*); poner impuestos sobre (*la propiedad*); abrumar, cargar; agotar (*la paciencia de uno*)

taxable ['tæksəbəl] *adj* imponible

taxation [tæk'seʃən] *s* imposición de contribuciones; contribuciones, impuestos

tax collector *s* recaudador *m* de impuestos

tax cut *s* reducción de impuestos

tax deduction *s* exclusión de contribución

tax evader [ɪ'vedər] *s* burlador *m* de impuestos

tax evasion *s* fraude *m* fiscal

tax'-ex·empt' *adj* exento de impuesto

tax haven *s* asilo de los impuestos

tax·i ['tæksi] *s* (*pl* **-is**) taxi *m* ‖ *v* (*pret & pp* **-ied;** *ger* **-iing** o **-ying**) *tr* (aer) carretear ‖ *intr* ir en taxi; (aer) carretear, taxear

tax'i·cab' *s* taxi *m*

taxi dancer *s* taxi *f*

taxi driver *s* taista *mf*

tax'i·plane' *s* avioneta de alquiler

taxi stand *s* parada de taxis

tax loss *s* pérdida de reclamable

tax'pay'er *s* contribuyente *mf*

tax rate *s* tipo impositivo

tax relief *s* aligeramiento de impuestos

tax return *s* declaración de renta

t.b. *abbr* **tuberculosis**

tbs. o **tbsp.** *abbr* **tablespoon, tablespoons**

tea [ti] *s* té *m*; (*medicinal infusion*) tisana; caldo de carne

tea bag *s* muñeca

tea ball *s* huevo del té

tea'cart' *s* mesita de té (*con ruedas*)

teach [titʃ] *v* (*pret & pp* **taught** [tɔt]) *tr & intr* enseñar

teacher ['titʃər] *s* maestro, instructor *m*; (*such as adversity*) (fig) maestra

teacher's pet *s* alumno mimado

teaching ['titʃɪŋ] *adj* docente ‖ *s* enseñanza; doctrina

teaching aids *spl* material *m* auxiliar de instrucción

teaching staff *s* personal *m* docente

tea'cup' *s* taza para té

tea dance *s* té *m* bailable

teak [tik] *s* teca

tea'ket'tle *s* tetera

team [tim] *s* (*e.g., of horses*) tiro, tronco; (*of oxen*) yunta; (sport) equipo ‖ *tr* enganchar, uncir, enyugar ‖ *intr*—**to team up** asociarse, unirse; formar un equipo

team'mate' *s* compañero de equipo, equipier *m*

teamster ['timstər] *s* (*of horses*) tronquista *m*; (*of a truck*) camionista *m*

team'work' *s* espíritu de equipo; trabajo de equipo

tea'pot' *s* tetera

tear [tɪr] *s* lágrima; **to burst into tears** romper a llorar; **to fill with tears** arrasarse (*los ojos*) de o en lágrimas; **to hold back**

one's tears beberse las lágrimas; **to laugh away one's tears** convertir las lágrimas en risas ‖ [tɛr] *s* desgarro, rasgón *m* ‖ [tɛr] *v* (*pret* **tore** [tor]; *pp* **torn** [torn]) *tr* desgarrar, rasgar; acongojar, afligir; mesarse (*los cabellos*); **to tear apart** romper en dos; **to tear down** derribar (*un edificio*); desarmar (*una máquina*); **to tear off** desgajar; **to tear up** romper (*p.ej., un papel*) ‖ *intr* desgarrarse, rasgarse; **to tear along** correr a toda velocidad

tear bomb [tɪr] *s* bomba lacrimógena

tearful ['tɪrfəl] *adj* lacrimoso

tear gas [tɪr] *s* gas lacrimógeno

tear-jerker ['tɪr,dʒʌrkər] *s* (slang) drama *m* o cine *m* que arrancan lágrimas

tear-off ['tɛr,ɔf] *adj* exfoliador

tea'room' *s* salón *m* de té

tear sheet [tɛr] *s* hoja del anunciante

tease [tiz] *tr* embromar, azuzar

tea'spoon' *s* cucharilla, cucharita

teaspoonful ['ti,spun,fʊl] *s* cucharadita

teat [tit] *s* teta, pezón *m*

tea time *s* hora del té

technical ['tɛknɪkəl] *adj* técnico

technicali·ty [,tɛknɪ'kælɪti] *s* (*pl* **-ties**) detalle técnico

technician [tɛk'nɪʃən] *s* técnico

technics ['tɛknɪks] *ssg* técnica

technique [tɛk'nik] *s* técnica

Teddy bear ['tɛdi] *s* oso de juguete, oso de trapo

tedious ['tidɪ·əs] o ['tidʒəs] *adj* tedioso, enfadoso

teem [tim] *intr* hormiguear; llover a cántaros; **to teem with** hervir de

teeming ['timɪŋ] *adj* hormigueante; (*rain*) torrencial

teen age [tin] *s* edad de 13 a 19 años

teen-ager ['tin,edʒər] *s* joven *mf* de 13 a 19 años de edad

teens [tinz] *spl* números ingleses que terminan en **-teen** (de 13 a 19); edad de 13 a 19 años; **to be in one's teens** tener de 13 a 19 años

tee·ny ['tini] *adj* (*comp* **-nier;** *super* **-niest**) (coll) diminuto, pequeñito

teeter ['titər] *s* vaivén *m*, balanceo ‖ *intr* balancear, oscilar

teethe [tið] *intr* endentecer

teething ['tiðɪŋ] *s* dentición

teething ring *s* chupador *m*

teetotaler [ti'totələr] *s* teetotalista *mf*, nefalista *mf*, abstemio

tel. *abbr* **telegram, telegraph, telephone**

tele·cast ['tɛlɪ,kæst] *s* teledifusión ‖ *v* (*pret & pp* **-cast** o **-casted**) *tr & intr* teledifundir

telegram ['tɛlɪ,græm] *s* telegrama *m*

telegraph ['tɛlɪ,græf] *s* telégrafo ‖ *tr & intr* telegrafiar

telegrapher [tɪ,lɛgrəfər] *s* telegrafista *mf*

telegraph pole *s* poste *m* de telégrafo

Telemachus [tɪ'lɛməkəs] *s* Telémaco

telemeter [tɪ'lɛmɪtər] *s* telémetro ‖ *tr* telemetrar

telemetry [tɪ'lɛmɪtri] *s* telemetría

telephone ['tɛlɪ,fon] *s* teléfono ‖ *tr & intr* telefonear

telephone booth *s* locutorio, cabina telefónica

telephone call *s* llamada telefónica

telephone directory *s* anuario telefónico, guía telefónica

telephone exchange *s* estación telefónica, central *f* de teléfonos; conmutador *m* (SAm)

telephone operator *s* telefonista *mf*, centralista *mf*

telephone receiver *s* receptor telefónico

telephone table *s* mesita portateléfono

tele(photo)lens ['tɛlɪ(,fotə),lɛnz] *s* lente telefotográfica

teleprinter ['tɛlɪ,prɪntər] *s* teleimpresor *m*

telescope ['tɛlɪ,skop] *s* telescopio ‖ *tr* telescopar ‖ *intr* telescoparse

teletype ['tɛlɪ,taɪp] *s* teletipo ‖ *tr & intr* transmitir por teletipo

teleview ['tɛlɪ,vju] *tr & intr* ver por televisión

televiewer ['tɛlɪ,vju•ər] *s* televidente *mf*, telespectador *m*

televise ['tɛlɪ,vaɪz] *tr* televisar

television ['tɛlɪ,vɪʃən] *adj* televisor ‖ *s* televisión

television audience *s* telespectadores

television screen *s* pantalla televisora, pequeña pantalla

television set *s* televisor *m*, telerreceptor *m*

telex ['tɛlɛks] *s* servicio comerical de teletipo

tell [tɛl] *v* (*pret & pp* told [told]) *tr* decir; (*to narrate; to count*) contar; determinar; conocer, distinguir; **I told you so!** ¡por algo te lo dije!; **to tell someone to** + *inf* decircle a uno que + *subj* ‖ *intr* hablar; surtir efecto; **to tell on** dejarse ver en (*p.ej., la salud de uno*); (coll) denunciar

teller ['tɛlər] *s* narrador *m*; (*of a bank*) cajero; (*of votes*) escrutador *m*

temper ['tɛmpər] *s* temple *m*, natural *m*, genio; cólera, mal genio; (*of steel, glass, etc.*) temple *m*; **to keep one's temper** dominar su mal genio; **to lose one's temper** encolerizarse, perder la paciencia ‖ *tr* templar *intr* templarse

temperament ['tɛmpərəmənt] *s* disposición; temperamento sensible o excitable

temperamental [,tɛmpərə'mɛntəl] *adj* temperamental

temperance ['tɛmpərəns] *s* templanza

temperate ['tɛmpərɪt] *adj* templado

temperature [,tɛmpərət/ər] *s* temperatura

tempest ['tɛmpɪst] *s* tempestad

tempestuous [tɛm'pɛst/ʊ•əs] *adj* tempestuoso

temple ['tɛmpəl] *s* (*place of worship*) templo; (*side of forehead*) sien *f*; (*sidepiece of spectacles*) gafa

tem•po ['tɛmpo] *s* (*pl* -**pos** o -**pi** [pi]) (mus) tiempo; (fig) ritmo (*p.ej., de la vida*)

temporal ['tɛmpərəl] *adj* temporal

temporary ['tɛmpə,rɛri] *adj* temporáneo, temporario, provisional, interino

temporize ['tɛmpə,raɪz] *intr* contemporizar, temporizar

tempt [tɛmpt] *tr* tentar

temptation [tɛmpt'teʃən] *s* tentación

tempter ['tɛmptər] *s* tentador *m*

tempting ['tɛmptɪŋ] *adj* tentador

ten [tɛn] *adj & pron* diez ‖ *s* diez *m*; **ten o'clock** las diez

tenable ['tɛnəbəl] *adj* defendible

tenacious [tɪ'neʃəs] *adj* tenaz

tenacity [tɪ'næsɪti] *s* tenacidad

tenant ['tɛnənt] *s* arrendatario, inquilino; morador *m*, residente *mf*

tend [tɛnd] *tr* cuidar, vigilar; servir ‖ *intr* tender, dirigirse; **to tend to** atender a; **to tend to** + *inf* tender a + *inf*

tenden•cy ['tɛndənsi] *s* (*pl* -**cies**) tendencia

tender ['tɛndər] *adj* tierno; (*painfully sensitive*) dolorido ‖ *n* oferta; (naut) alijador *m*, falúa; (rr) ténder *m* ‖ *tr* ofrecer, tender

tender-hearted ['tɛndər,hartɪd] *adj* compasivo, tierno de corazón

ten'der•loin' *s* filete *m* ‖ **Tenderloin** *s* barrio de mala vida

tenderness ['tɛndərnɪs] *s* ternura, terneza; sensibilidad

tendon ['tɛndən] *s* tendón *m*

tendril ['tɛndrɪl] *s* zarcillo

tenement ['tɛnɪmənt] *s* habitación, vivienda; casa de vecindad

tenement house *s* casa de vecindad

tenet ['tɛnɪt] *s* dogma *m*, credo, principio

tennis ['tɛnɪs] *s* tenis *m*

tennis court *s* campo de tenis

tennis player *s* tenista *mf*

tenor ['tɛnər] *s* tenor *m*, carácter *m*, curso, tendencia; (mus) tenor

tense [tɛns] *adj* tenso, tieso; (*person; situation*) (fig) tenso; (*relations*) tirante ‖ *s* (gram) tiempo

tension ['tɛnʃən] *s* tensión; ansia, congoja, esfuerzo mental; (*in personal or diplomatic relations*) tirantez *f*

tent [tɛnt] *s* tienda; tienda de campaña

tentacle ['tɛntəkəl] *s* tentáculo

tentative ['tɛntətɪv] *adj* tentativo

tenth [tɛnθ] *adj & s* décimo ‖ *s* (*in dates*) diez *m*

tenuous ['tɛnjʊ•əs] *adj* tenue; (*thin in consistency*) raro

tenure ['tɛnjər] *s* (*of property*) tenencia; (*of an office*) ejercicio; (*protection from dismissal*) inamovilidad

tepid ['tɛpɪd] *adj* tibio

tercet ['tɑrsɪt] *s* terceto

term [tɑrm] *s* término; (*of imprisonment*) condena; semestre *m*, período escolar; (*of the presidency of the U.S.A.*) mandato, período; **terms** condiciones ‖ *tr* llamar, nombrar

termagant ['tɑrməgənt] *s* mujer regañona, mujer de mal genio

terminal ['tɑrmɪnəl] *adj* terminal ‖ *s* término, fin *m*; (elec) terminal *m*; (rr) estación de fin de línea

terminate ['tɑrmɪ,net] *tr & intr* terminar

termination [,tɑrmɪ'neʃən] *s* terminación

terminus ['tɑrmɪnəs] *s* término; (rr) estación de cabeza, estación extrema

termite ['tɑrmaɪt] *s* termite *m*, comején *m*

ta
te

terrace ['tɛrəs] s terraza; (*flat roof of a house*) azotea

terra firma ['tɛrə 'fʌrmə] s tierra firme; **on terra firma** sobre suelo firme

terrain [tɛ'ren] s terreno

terrestrial [tə'rɛstrɪ•əl] *adj* terrestre

terrible ['tɛrɪbəl] *adj* terrible; muy desagradable

terrific [tə'rɪfɪk] *adj* terrífico; (coll) enorme, intenso, brutal

terri•fy ['tɛrɪ,faɪ] v (*pret & pp* -fied) *tr* aterrorizar, atemorizar

territo•ry ['tɛrɪ,tori] s (*pl* -ries) territorio

terror ['tɛrər] s terror m

terrorize ['tɛrə,raɪz] *tr* aterrorizar; imponerse a, mediante el terror

terry cloth ['tɛri] s albornoz m

terse [tʌrs] *adj* breve, sucinto

tertiary ['tʌrʃɪ,ɛri] o ['tʌrʃəri] *adj* terciario

Test. *abbr* **Testament**

test [tɛst] s prueba, ensayo; examen m ‖ *tr* probar, poner a prueba; examinar

testament ['tɛstəmənt] s testamento

test flight s vuelo de ensayo

testicle ['tɛstɪkəl] s testículo

testi•fy ['tɛstɪ,faɪ] v (*pret & pp* -fied) *tr & intr* testificar

testimonial [,tɛstɪ'monɪ•əl] s recomendación, certificado; (*expression of esteem, gratitude, etc.*) homenaje m

testimo•ny ['tɛstɪ,moni] s (*pl* -nies) testimonio

testing grounds ['tɛstɪŋ] *spl* campo de pruebas

test pilot s (aer) piloto de pruebas

test tube s probeta, tubo de ensayo

test'-tube' baby s niño-probeta m

tether ['tɛðər] s atadura, traba; **at the end of one's tether** al límite de las posibilidades o la paciencia de uno ‖ *tr* apersogar

tetter ['tɛtər] s empeine m

text [tɛkst] s texto; tema m, lema m

text'book' s libro de texto

textile ['tɛkstɪl] o ['tɛkstaɪl] *adj & s* textil m

texture ['tɛkstʃər] s textura

Thai ['tɑ•i] o ['taɪ] *adj & s* tailandés m

Thailand ['taɪlənd] s Tailandia

Thales ['θeliz] s Tales m

Thalia [θə'laɪ•ə] s Talía

Thames [tɛmz] s Támesis m

than [ðæn] *conj* que, p.ej., **he is richer than I** es más rico que yo; (*before a numeral*) de, p.ej., **more than twenty** más de veinte; (*before a verb*) de lo que, p.ej., **the crop is larger than was expected** la cosecha es mayor de lo que se esperaba; (*before a verb with direct object understood*) del (de la, de los, de las) que, p.ej., **they sent us more coffee than we ordered** nos enviaron más café del que pedimos

thanatology [,θænə'tɑlədʒi] s tanatología

thank [θæŋk] *tr* agradecer, dar las gracias a; **to thank someone for something** agradecerle a uno una cosa ‖ **thanks** *spl* gracias; **thanks to** gracias a, merced a ‖ **thanks** *interj* ¡gracias!

thankful ['θæŋkfəl] *adj* agradecido

thankless ['θæŋklɪs] *adj* ingrato

thanksgiving [,θæŋks'gɪvɪŋ] s acción de gracias

Thanksgiving Day s (U.S.A.) día m de acción de gracias

that [ðæt] *adj dem* (*pl those*) ese; aquel; **that one** ése; aquél ‖ *pron dem* (*pl those*) ése; aquél; eso; aquello ‖ *pron rel* que, quien, el cual, el que ‖ *adv* tan; **that far** tan lejos; hasta allí; **that many** tantos; **that much** tanto ‖ *conj* que; para que

thatch [θætʃ] s barda, paja; techo de paja ‖ *tr* cubrir de paja, techar con paja, bardar

thaw [θɔ] s deshielo, derretimiento; descongelación ‖ *tr* deshelar, derretir ‖ *intr* deshelarse, derretirse

the [ðə], [ðɪ], o [ði] *art def* el ‖ *adv* cuanto, p.ej., **the more the merrier** cuanto más mejor; **the more . . . the more** cuanto más . . . tanto más

theater ['θi•ətər] s teatro

the'ater-go'er s teatrero

theater news s actualidad escénica

theater page s noticiario teatral

theatrical [θɪ'ætrɪkəl] *adj* teatral

Thebes [θibz] s Tebas f

thee [ði] *pron pers* (archaic, poet, Bib) te; ti; **with thee** contigo

theft [θɛft] s hurto, robo

theft'-proof' *adj* antirroba

their [ðɛr] *adj poss* su; el . . . de ellos

theirs [ðɛrz] *pron poss* el suyo, el de ellos

them [ðɛm] *pron pers* los; ellos; **to them** les; a ellos

theme [θim] s tema m; (mus) tema m

theme song s (mus) tema m central; (rad) sintonía

them•selves' *pron pers* ellos mismos; sí, sí mismos; se, p.ej., **they enjoyed themselves** se divirtieron; **with themselves** consigo

then [ðɛn] *adv* entonces; después, luego, en seguida; además, también; **by then** para entonces; **from then on** desde entonces, de allí en adelante; **then and there** ahí mismo

thence [ðɛns] *adv* desde allí; desde entonces; por eso

thence'forth' *adv* de allí en adelante; desde entonces

theolo•gy [θi'ɑlədʒi] s (*pl* -gies) teología

theorem ['θi•ərəm] s teorema m

theo•ry ['θi•əri] s (*pl* -ries) teoría

therapeutic [,θɛrə'pjutɪk] *adj* terapéutico ‖ **therapeutics** *ssg* terapéutica

thera•py ['θɛrəpi] s (*pl* -pies) terapia

there [ðɛr] *adv* allí, allá; **there is** o **there are** hay; aquí tiene Vd.

there'a-bouts' *adv* por allí; cerca, aproximadamente

there•af'ter *adv* de allí en adelante, después de eso

there•by' *adv* con eso; así, de tal modo; por allí cerca

therefore ['ðɛrfor] *adv* por lo tanto, por consiguiente

there•in' *adv* en esto, en eso; en ese respecto

there•of' *adv* de ello, de eso

Theresa [tə'risə] o [tə'rɛsə] s Teresa

there·u·pon' adv sobre eso, encima de eso; por consiguiente; en seguida

thermistor [θər'mɪstər] s (elec) termistor m

thermocouple ['θʌrmo,kʌpəl] s (elec) termopar m

thermodynamic [,θʌrmodaɪ'næmɪk] adj termodinámico ‖ **thermodynamics** ssg termodinámica

thermometer [θər'mɑmɪtər] s termómetro

thermonuclear [,θʌrmo'nuklɪ•ər] adj termonuclear

Thermopylae [θər'mɑpɪ,li] s las Termópilas

Thermos bottle ['θʌrməs] s termos m, botella termos, bolsa isotérmica

thermostat ['θʌrmə,stæt] s termóstato

thesau·rus [θɪ'sɔrəs] s (pl **-ri** [raɪ]) tesoro; (dictionary or the like) tesauro, tesoro

these [ðiz] pl de **this**

the·sis ['θisɪs] s (pl **-ses** [siz]) tesis f

Thespis ['θɛspɪs] s Tespis m

Thessaly ['θɛsəli] s la Tesalia

they [ðe] pron pers ellos, ellas

thick [θɪk] adj espeso; grueso; denso; (coll) estúpido; (coll) íntimo ‖ s espesor m; **the thick of** (e.g., a crowd) lo más denso de; (e.g., a battle) lo más reñido de; **through thick and thin** contra viento y marea

thicken ['θɪkən] tr espesar ‖ intr espesarse; complicarse (el enredo)

thicket ['θɪkɪt] s espesura, matorral m, soto

thick-headed ['θɪk'hɛdɪd] adj (coll) torpe, estúpido

thick'-set' adj grueso, rechoncho

thief [θif] s (pl **thieves** [θivz]) ladrón m

thieve [θiv] intr hurtar, robar

thiever·y ['θivəri] s (pl **-ies**) latrocinio, hurto, robo

thigh [θaɪ] s muslo

thigh'bone' s hueso del muslo, fémur m

thimble ['θɪmbəl] s dedal m

thin [θɪn] adj (comp **thinner;** super **thinnest**) delgado, flaco, tenue; (cloth, paper, sole of shoe, etc.) fino; (hair) ralo; (broth) aguado; (excuse) débil; claro, ligero, escaso ‖ v (pret & pp **thinned;** ger **thinning**) tr adelgazar, enflaquecer; enrarecer; aclarar; aguar; desleír (los colores) ‖ intr adelgazarse, enflaquecerse; enrarecerse; **to thin out** ralear (el pelo)

thine [ðaɪn] adj poss (archaic & poet) tu ‖ pron poss (archaic & poet) tuyo; el tuyo

thing [θɪŋ] s cosa; **of all things!** ¡qué sorpresa!; **to be the thing** ser la última moda; **to be the thing to do** ser lo que debe hacerse; **to see things** ver visiones, padecer alucinaciones

think [θɪŋk] v (pret & pp **thought** [θɔt]) tr pensar; **to think it over** pensarlo; **to think nothing of** tener en poco; creer fácil; no dar importancia a; **to think of** pensar de, p.ej., what do you think of this book? ¿qué piensa Vd. de este libro?; **to think up** imaginar; inventar (p.ej., una excusa) ‖ intr pensar; **to think not** creer que no; **to think of** (to turn one's thoughts to) pensar en; pensar (un número, un naipe, etc.); **to**

think so creer que sí; **to think well of** tener buena opinión de

thinker ['θɪŋkər] s pensador m

third [θʌrd] adj tercero ‖ s (in a series) tercero; (one of three equal parts) tercio; (in dates) tres m

third degree s (coll) interrogatorio bajo tortura

third rail s (rr) tercer carril m, carril de toma

third'-rate' adj de tercer orden; (fig) inferior

Third World adj tercermundista ‖ s Terrcero Mundo

Third World countries spl países no alineados

thirst [θʌrst] s sed f ‖ intr tener sed; **to thirst for** tener sed de

thirst·y ['θʌrsti] adj (comp **-ier;** super **-iest**) sediento; **to be thirsty** tener sed

thirteen ['θʌr'tin] adj, pron & s trece m

thirteenth ['θʌr'tinθ] adj & s (in a series) decimotercero; (part) trezavo ‖ s (in dates) trece m

thirtieth ['θʌrti•ɪθ] adj & s (in a series) trigésimo; (part) treintavo ‖ s (in dates) treinta m

thir·ty ['θʌrti] adj & pron treinta ‖ s (pl **-ties**) treinta m

this [ðɪs] adj dem (pl **these**) este; **this one** éste ‖ pron dem (pl **these**) éste; esto ‖ adv tan

thistle ['θɪsəl] s cardo

thither ['θɪðər] o ['ðɪðər] adv allá, hacia allá

Thomas ['tɑməs] s Tomás m

thong [θɔŋ] o [θɑŋ] s correa

tho·rax ['θoræks] s (pl **-roxes** o **-raxes** o **-races** [rə,siz]) tórax m

thorn [θɔrn] s espina

thorn·y ['θɔrni] adj (comp **-ier;** super **-iest**) espinoso; espinudo; (difficult) (fig) espinoso, espinudo

thorough ['θʌro] adj cabal, completo; concienzudo, cuidadoso

thor'ough·bred adj de pura sangre; bien nacido ‖ s pura sangre m; persona bien nacida

thor'ough·fare' s vía pública; **no thoroughfare** se prohibe el paso

thor'ough·go'ing adj cabal, completo, esmerado, perfecto

thoroughly ['θʌroli] adv a fondo

those [ðoz] pl de **that**

thou [ðau] pron pers (archaic, poet & Bib) tú ‖ tr & intr tutear

though [ðo] adv sin embargo ‖ conj aunque, bien que; **as though** como sí

thought [θɔt] s pensamiento

thoughtful ['θɔtfəl] adj pensativo; atento, considerado

thoughtless ['θɔtlɪs] adj irreflexivo; descuidado; inconsiderado

thought transference s transmisión del pensamiento

thousand ['θauzənd] adj & s mil m; **a thousand u one thousand** mil m

thousandth ['θauzəndθ] adj & s milésimo

thralldom ['θrɔldəm] *s* esclavitud, servidumbre

thrash [θræʃ] *tr* (agr) trillar; azotar, zurrar; **to thrash out** decidir después de una discusión cabal ‖ *intr* trillar; agitarse, menearse

thread [θrɛd] *s* hilo; (mach) filete *m*, rosca; (*of a speech, of life*) hilo; **to lose the thread of** perder el hilo de ‖ *tr* enhebrar, enhilar; ensartar (*p.ej., cuentas*); (mach) aterrajar, filetear

thread'bare' *adj* raído; gastado, desgastado, usado, viejo

threat [θrɛt] *s* amenaza

threaten ['θrɛtən] *tr & intr* amenazar

threatening ['θrɛtənɪŋ] *adj* amenazante

three [θri] *adj & pron* tres ‖ *s* tres *m;* **three o'clock** las tres

three'-cor'nered *adj* triangular; (*hat*) de tres picos

three hundred *adj & pron* trescientos ‖ *s* trescientos *m*

threepence ['θrɛpəns] o ['θrɪpəns] *s* suma de tres peniques; moneda de tres peniques

three'-ply' *adj* de tres capas

three R's [ɑrz] *spl* lectura, escritura y aritmética, primeras letras

three'score' *adj* tres veintenas de

threno•dy ['θrɛnədi] *s* (*pl* **-dies**) treno

thresh [θrɛʃ] *tr* (agr) trillar; **to thresh out** decidir después de una discusión cabal ‖ *intr* trillar; agitarse, menearse

threshing machine *s* máquina trilladora

threshold ['θrɛʃold] *s* umbral *m;* (physiol, psychol & fig) umbral, limen *m;* **to be on the threshold of** estar en los umbrales de; **to cross the threshold** atravesar o pisar los embrales

thrice [θraɪs] *adv* tres veces; repetidamente, sumamente

thrift [θrɪft] *s* economía, parquedad

thrift•y ['θrɪfti] *adj* (*comp* **-ier;** *super* **-iest**) económico, parco, próspero

thrill [θrɪl] *s* emoción viva ‖ *tr* emocionar, conmover ‖ *intr* emocionarse, conmoverse

thriller ['θrɪlər] *s* cuento o pieza de teatro espeluznante

thrilling ['θrɪlɪŋ] *adj* emocionante; espeluznante

thrive [θraɪv] *v* (*pret* **thrived** o **throve** [θrov]; *pp* **thrived** o **thriven** ['θrɪvən]) *intr* medrar, prosperar

throat [θrot] *s* garganta; **to clear one's throat** aclarar la voz

throb [θrab] *s* latido, palpitación, pulsación ‖ *v* (*pret & pp* **throbbed;** *ger* **throbbing**) *intr* latir, palpitar, pulsar

throe [θro] *s* congoja, dolor *m;* **throes** angustia, agonía, esfuerzo penoso

throne [θron] *s* trono

throng [θrɔŋ] *s* gentío, tropel *m*, muchedumbre ‖ *intr* agolparse, apiñarse

throttle ['θratəl] *s* válvula reguladora; (*of a locomotive*) regulador *m;* (*of an automobile*) acelerador *m* ‖ *tr* ahogar, sofocar; impedir, suprimir; (mach) regular; **to throttle down** reducir la velocidad de

through [θru] *adj* directo, sin paradas; acabado, terminado; **to be through with** haber terminado; no querer ocuparse más de ‖ *adv* a través, de un lado a otro; completamente ‖ *prep* por, a través de; por medio de; a causa de; todo lo largo de

through•out' *adv* por todas partes; en todos respectos; desde el principio hasta el fin ‖ *prep* por todo . . .; durante todo . . .; a lo largo de

through'way' *s* carretera de peaje de acceso limitado

throw [θro] *s* echada, tirada, lance *m;* cobertor ligero ‖ *v* (*pret* **threw** [θru]; *pp* **thrown**) *tr* arrojar, echar, lanzar; tirar (*los dados*); lanzar (*una mirada*); desarzonar (*a un jinete*); proyectar (*una sombra*); tender (*un puente*); perder con premeditación (*un juego, una carrera*); **to throw away** tirar; malgastar; perder, no aprovechar; **to throw in** añadir, dar de más; **to throw out** arrojar, botar, desechar; echar a la calle; chispar; **to throw over** abandonar, dejar ‖ *intr* arrojar, echar, lanzar; **to throw up** vomitar

thrum [θrʌm] *v* (*pret & pp* **thrummed;** *ger* **thrumming**) *intr* teclear; zangarrear; **to thrum on** rasguear

thrush [θrʌʃ] *s* tordo

thrust [θrʌst] *s* empuje *m;* acometida; (*with horns*) cornada; (*with dagger*) puñalada; (*with sword*) estocada; (*with knife*) cuchillada ‖ *v* (*pret & pp* **thrust**) *tr* empujar; acometer; clavar, hincar, atravesar, traspasar

thud [θʌd] *s* baque *m*, ruido sordo ‖ *v* (*pret & pp* **thudded;** *ger* **thudding**) *tr & intr* golpear con ruido sordo

thug [θʌg] *s* ladrón *m*, asesino; (coll) gorila

thumb [θʌm] *s* pulgar *m*, dedo gordo; **all thumbs** desmañado, chapucero, torpe; **to twiddle one's thumbs** menear ociosamente los pulgares; no hacer nada; **under the thumb of** bajo la férula de ‖ *tr* manosear sin suidado; ensuciar con los dedos; hojear (*un libro*) con el pulgar; **to thumb a ride** pedir ser llevado en automóvil indicando la dirección con el pulgar; **to thumb one's nose at** señalar (*a una persona*) poniendo el pulgar sobre la nariz en son de burla; tratar con sumo desprecio

thumb index *s* escalerilla, índice *m* con pestañas

thumb'print' *s* impresión del pulgar ‖ *tr* marcar con impresión del pulgar

thumb'screw' *s* tornillo de mariposa, tornillo de orejas

thumb'tack' *s* chinche *m*

thump [θʌmp] *s* golpazo, porrazo ‖ *tr* golpear, aporrear ‖ *intr* caer con golpe pesado; andar con pasos pesados; latir (*el corazón*) con golpes pesados

thumping ['θʌmpɪŋ] *adj* (coll) enorme, pesado

thunder ['θʌndər] *s* trueno; (*of applause*) estruendo; amenaza ‖ *tr* fulminar (*p.ej., censuras*) ‖ *intr* tronar; **to thunder at** tronar contra

thun′der•bolt′ s rayo
thun′der•clap′ s tronido
thunderous [′θʌndərəs] adj atronador, tronitoso
thun′der•show′er s chubasco con truenos
thun′der•storm′ s tronada
thun′der•struck′ adj atónito, estupefacto, pasmado
Thursday [′θʌrsdɪ] s jueves m
thus [ðʌs] adv así; **thus far** hasta aquí, hasta ahora
thwack [θwæk] s golpe m, porrazo ‖ tr golpear, pegar
thwart [θwɔrt] adj transversal, oblicuo ‖ adv de través ‖ tr desbaratar, impedir, frustrar
thy [ðaɪ] adj poss (archaic & poet) tu
thyme [taɪm] s tomillo
thyroid gland [′θaɪrɔɪd] s glándula tiroides
thyself [ðaɪ′sɛlf] pron (archaic & poet) tú mismo; ti mismo; te; ti
tiara [taɪ′ɑrə] o [taɪ′ɛrə] s (papal miter) tiara; (female adornment) diadema f
tick [tɪk] s tictac m; funda (de almohada o colchón) (coll) crédito; (ent) garrapata; **on tick** (coll) al fiado ‖ intr hacer tictac; latir (el corazón)
ticker [′tɪkər] s teleimpresor m de cinta; (slang) reloj m; (slang) corazón m
ticker tape s cinta de teleimpresor
ticket [′tɪkɪt] s billete m; boleto (Am); (theat) entrada, localidad; (for wrong parking) (coll) aviso de multa; (of a political party) (U.S.A.) lista de candidatos; **that's the ticket** (coll) eso es, eso es lo que se necesita
ticket agent s taquillero
ticket collector s revisor m
ticket office s taquilla, despacho de billetes
ticket scalper [′skælpər] s revendedor m de billetes de teatro
ticket window s taquilla, ventanilla
ticking [′tɪkɪŋ] s cutí m, terliz m
tickle [′tɪkəl] s cosquillas ‖ tr cosquillear; gustar, satisfacer; divertir ‖ intr cosquillear
ticklish [′tɪklɪʃ] adj cosquilloso; difícil, delicado; inseguro
tick-tock [′tɪk,tɑk] s tictac m
tidal wave [′taɪdəl] s aguaje m, ola de marea; (e.g., of popular indignation) ola
tidbit [′tɪd,bɪt] s buen bocado, bocadito
tiddlywinks [′tɪdli,wɪŋks] s juego de la pulga
tide [taɪd] s marea; temporada; **to go against the tide** ir contra la corriente; **to stem the tide** rendir la marea ‖ tr llevar, hacer flotar; **to tide over** ayudar un poco; superar (una dificultad)
tide′wa′ter adj costanero ‖ s agua de marea; orilla del mar
tidings [′taɪdɪŋz] spl noticias, informes mpl
ti•dy [′taɪdi] adj (comp -dier; super -diest) aseado, limpio, pulcro, ordenado ‖ s (pl -dies) pañito bordado, cubierta de respaldar ‖ v (pret & pp -died) tr asear, limpiar, arreglar, poner en orden ‖ intr asearse
tie [taɪ] s atadura; lazo, nudo; (worn on neck) corbata; (in games and elections) empate m; (mus) ligado; (rr) traviesa ‖ v (pret &

pp tied; ger tying) tr atar, liar; enlazar; hacer (la corbata); confinar, limitar; empatar (p.ej., una elección); empatársela a (una persona); **to be tied up** estar ocupado; **to tie down** confinar, limitar; **to tie up** atar; envolver; obstruir (el tráfico) ‖ intr atar; empatar o empatarse (dos candidatos, dos equipos)
tie′pin′ s alfiler m de corbata
tier [tɪr] s fila, ringlera; (theat) fila de palcos
tiger [′taɪgər] s tigre m
tiger lily s azucena atigrada
tight [taɪt] adj apretado, estrecho, ajustado; bien cerrado, hermético; compacto, denso; fijo, firme, sólido; (com) escaso; (sport) casi igual; (coll) agarrado, tacaño; (slang) borracho ‖ adv firmemente; **to hold tight** mantener fijo; agarrarse bien ‖ **tights** spl traje m de malla
tighten [′taɪtən] tr apretar; atiesar, estirar ‖ intr apretarse; atiesarse, estirarse
tight-fisted [′taɪt′fɪstɪd] adj agarrado, tacaño
tight′-fit′ting adj ceñido, muy ajustado
tight′rope′ s cuerda tirante
tight squeeze s (coll) brete m, aprieto
tightwad [′taɪt,wɑd] s avaro; codo (Guat, Mex)
tigress [′taɪgrɪs] s tigresa
tile [taɪl] s azulejo; (for floors) baldosa; (for roofs) reja ‖ tr azulejar; embaldosar; tejar
tile roof s tejado (de tejas)
till [tɪl] prep hasta ‖ conj hasta que ‖ s cajón m o gaveta del dinero ‖ tr labrar, cultivar
tilt [tɪlt] s inclinación; justa, torneo; **full tilt** a toda velocidad ‖ tr inclinar; asestar (una lanza) ‖ intr inclinarse; justar, tornear; luchar; **to tilt at** luchar con, arremeter contra; protestar contra
timber [′tɪmbər] s madera de construcción; madero, viga; bosque m, árboles mpl de monte
tim′ber•land′ s bosque m maderable
timber line s límite m de la vegetación, límite del bosque maderable
timbre [′tɪmbər] s (phonet & phys) timbre m
time [taɪm] s tiempo; hora, p.ej., **time to eat** hora de comer; vez, p.ej., **five times** cinco veces; rato, p.ej., **a nice time** un buen rato; (period for payment) plazo; horas de trabajo; sueldo; tiempo de parir; término del embarazo; última hora; (phot) tiempo de exposición; **all the time** a cada momento; **for the time being** por ahora, por el momento; **on time** a tiempo, a la hora debida; (in installments) a plazos, **to bide one's time** esperar la hora propicia; **to do time** (coll) cumplir una condena; **to have a good time** darse buen tiempo; **to have no time for** no poder tolerar; **to lose time** atrasarse (el reloj); **to make time** avanzar con rapidez; **to pass the time of day** saludarse (dos personas); **to serve time** (in prison) tirarse; **to take one's time** no darse prisa, ir despacio; **what time is it?** ¿qué hora es? ‖ tr calcular el tiempo de; medir el tiempo de; (sport) cronometrar
time bomb s bomba-reloj f

time'card' s hoja de presencia, tarjeta registradora

time clock s reloj m registrador

time exposure s exposición de tiempo

time fuse s espoleta de tiempos

time'keep'er s alistador m de tiempo; reloj m; (sport) cronometrador m, juez m de tiempo

time•ly ['taɪmli] adj (comp -lier; super -liest) oportuno

time'piece' s reloj m

time signal s señal horaria

time'ta'ble s horario, itinerario

time'work' s trabajo ajornal

time'worn' adj gastado por el tiempo

time zone s huso horario

timid ['tɪmɪd] adj tímido

timing gears ['taɪmɪŋ] spl engranaje m de distribución, mando de las válvulas

timorous ['tɪmərəs] adj tímido, miedoso

tin [tɪn] s (element) estaño; (tin plate) hojalata; (cup, box, etc.) lata ‖ v (pret & pp **tinned;** ger **tinning**) tr estañar; (to pack in cans) enlatar; recubrir de hojalata

tin can s lata, envase m de hojalata

tincture ['tɪŋktʃər] s tintura

tin cup s taza de hojalata

tinder ['tɪndər] s yesca

tin'der•box' s lumbres fpl, yesquero; persona muy excitable; semillero de violencia

tin foil s hojuela de estaño, papel m de estaño

ting-a-ling ['tɪŋə,lɪŋ] s tilín m

tinge [tɪndʒ] s matiz m, tinte m; dejo, gustillo ‖ v (ger **tingeing** o **tinging**) tr matizar, teñir; dar gusto o sabor a

tingle ['tɪŋɡəl] s comezón f, picazón f ‖ intr sentir comezón; zumbar (los oídos); (e.g., with enthusiasm) estremecerse

tin hat s (coll) yelmo de acero

tinker ['tɪŋkər] s calderero remendón; chapucero ‖ intr ocuparse vanamente

tinkle ['tɪŋkəl] s retintín m ‖ tr hacer retiñir m ‖ tr hacer retiñir ‖ intr retiñir

tin plate s hojalata

tin roof s tejado de hojalata

tinsel ['tɪnsəl] s oropel m; (e.g., for a Christmas tree) lentejuelas de hojas de estaño

tin'smith' s hojalatero

tin soldier s soldadito de plomo

tint [tɪnt] s tinte m, matiz m ‖ tr teñir, matizar, colorar ligeramente

tin'type' s ferrotipo

tin'ware' s objetos de hojalata

ti•ny ['taɪni] adj (comp -nier; super -niest) diminuto, menudo, pequeñito

tip [tɪp] s extremo, extremidad; (of shoestring) herrete m; (of arrow) casquillo; (of umbrella) regatón m; (of tongue) punta; (of shoe) puntera; (of cigarette) embocadura; inclinación; golpecito; soplo, aviso confidencial; (fee) propina, feria ‖ v (pret & pp **tipped;** ger **tipping**) tr herretear; inclinar, ladear; volcar; golpear ligeramente; dar propina a; informar por debajo de cuerda; tocarse (el sombrero en señal de cortesía); **to tip in** (typ) encañonar (un pliego) ‖ intr

dar una propina o propinas; inclinarse, ladearse; volcarse

tip'cart' s volquete m

tip'-off' s (coll) informe dado por debajo de cuerda

tipped'-in' adj (bb) fuera de texto

tipple ['tɪpəl] intr beborrotear

tip'staff' s vara de justicia; alguacil m de vara

tip•sy ['tɪpsi] adj (comp -sier; super -siest) achispado

tip'toe' s punta del pie; **on tiptoe** de puntillas; alerta; furtivamente ‖ v (pret & pp **-toed;** ger **-toeing**) intr andar de puntillas

tirade ['taɪred] s diatriba, invectiva

tire [taɪr] s neumático, llanta de goma; (of metal) calce m, llanta ‖ tr cansar; aburrir; fastidiar ‖ intr (to be tiresome) cansar; (to get tired) cansarse; aburrirse, fastidiarse

tire chain s cadena de llanta, cadena antirresbaladiza

tired [taɪrd] adj cansado, rendido

tire gauge s indicador m de presión de inflado

tireless ['taɪrlɪs] adj incansable, infatigable

tire pressure s presión de inflado

tire pump s bomba para inflar neumáticos

tiresome ['taɪrsəm] adj cansado, fatigante, aburrido, pesado

tissue ['tɪʃu] s tejido fino; papel m de seda; (biol & fig) tejido

tissue paper s papel m de seda

titanium [tai'teni•əm] o [tɪ'teni•əm] s titanio

tithe [taɪð] s décimo, décima parte; (tax paid to church) diezmo ‖ tr dizmar

Titian ['tɪʃən] adj castaño rojizo ‖ s el Ticiano

title ['taɪtəl] s título; (sport) campeonato ‖ tr titular

title deed s título de propiedad

ti'tle•hold'er s titulado; (sport) campeón m

title page s portada, frontispicio

title rôle s (theat) papel m principal (el que corresponde al título de la abra)

titter ['tɪtər] s risita ahogada, risita disimulada ‖ intr reír a medias, reír con disimulo

titular ['tɪtʃələr] adj titular; nominal

tn. abbr ton

to [tu] o [tu] o [tə] adv hacia adelante; **to and fro** de una parte a otra, de aquí para allá; **to come to** volver en sí ‖ prep a, p.ej., **he is going to Madrid** va a Madrid; **they gave something to the beggar** dieron algo al pobre; **we are learning to dance** aprendemos a bailar; para, p.ej., **he is reading to himself** lee para sí; por, p.ej., **work to do** trabajo por hacer; hasta, p.ej., **to a certain extent** hasta cierto punto; en, p.ej., **from door to door** de puerta en puerta; con, p.ej., **kind to her** amable con ella; segun, p.ej., **to my way of thinking** según mi modo de pensar; menos, p.ej., **five minutes to ten** las diez menos cinco

toad [tod] s sapo

toad'stool' s agárico, seta; seta venenosa

to-and-fro ['tu•ənd'fro] adj alternativo, de vaivén

toast [tost] *s* tostadas; (*drink*) brindis *m;* **a piece of toast** una tostada ‖ *tr* tostar; brindar a o por ‖ *intr* tostarse; brindar

toaster ['tostər] *s* (*of bread*) tostador *m;* brindador *m*

toast'mas'ter *s* el que presenta a los oradores en un banquete, maestro de ceremonias

tobac•co [tə'bæko] *s* (*pl* **-cos**) tabaco

tobacco pouch *s* petaca

toboggan [tə'bagən] *s* tobogán *m* ‖ *intr* deslizarse en tobogán

tocsin ['taksɪn] *s* campana de alarma; campanada de alarma

today [tu'de] *adv & s* hoy

toddle ['tadəl] *s* pasitos vacilantes ‖ *intr* andar con pasitos vacilantes; hacer pinitos (*un niño o un enfermo*)

tod•dy ['tadi] *s* (*pl* **-dies**) ponche *m*

to-do [tə'du] *s* (coll) alharaca, alboroto

toe [to] *s* dedo del pie; (*of stocking*) punta ‖ *v* (*pret & pp* **toed;** *ger* **toeing**) *tr*—**to toe the line** o **the mark** ponerse a la raya; obrar como se debe

toe'nail' *s* uña del dedo del pie

tog [tag] *s* (coll) prenda de vestir

together [tu'gɛðər] *adv* juntamente; juntos; al mismo tiempo; sin interrupción; de acuerdo; **to bring together** reunir; confrontar; reconciliar; **to call together** convocar; **to go together** ir juntos; ser novios; hacerjuego; **to stick together** (coll) quedarse unidos, no abandonarse

toil [tɔɪl] *s* afán *m*, fatiga; faena, obra laboriosa; **toils** red *f*, lazo ‖ *intr* atrafagar; moverse con fatiga

toilet ['tɔɪlɪt] *s* (*dress or adornment*) tocado, atavío; (*dressing table*) tocador *m;* (*rest room*) retrete *m*, inodoro, excusado; wáter *m* (Bol, Col, Chile, Peru, Urug); servicio (Bol, CAm, Ecuad); taza (Bol, Col, Guat, Mex); poseta (Ven); **to make one's toilet** asearse, acicalarse

toilet articles *spl* artículos de tocador

toilet paper *s* papel higiénico

toilet powder *s* polvos de tocador

toilet soap *s* jabón *m* de olor, jabón de tocador

toilet tank *s* cisterna

toilet water *s* agua de tocador

token ['tokən] *s* señal *f*, prueba; prenda, recuerdo; (*used as money*) ficha, tanto; **by the same token** por el mismo motivo; **in token of** en señal de

tolerance ['talərəns] *s* tolerancia

tolerate ['talə͵ret] *tr* tolerar

toll [tol] *s* (*of bells*) doble *m;* (*to pass along a road or over a bridge*) peaje *m;* (*to use a canal*) derechos de paso; (*to use a telephone*) tarifa; (*number of victims*) baja, mortalidad ‖ *tr* tocar a muerto (*una campana*); llamar con toque de difuntos ‖ *intr* doblar

toll bridge *s* puente *m* de peaje

toll call *s* (telp) llamada a larga distancia

toll'gate' *s* barrera de peaje

toma•to [tə'meto] o [tə'mato] *s* (*pl* **-toes**) (*plant*) tomatera o tomate *m;* (*fruit*) tomate

tomb [tum] *s* tumba, sepulcro

tomboy ['tam͵bɔɪ] *s* moza retozona, muchacha traviesa

tomb'stone' *s* piedra o lápida sepulcral

tomcat ['tam͵kæt] *s* gato macho

tome [tom] *s* tomo; libro grueso

tomorrow [tu'mɔro] *adv* mañana ‖ *s* mañana *m;* **the day after tomorrow** pasado mañana

tom-tom ['tam͵tam] *s* tantán *m*

ton [tʌn] *s* tonelada; **tons** (coll) montones *mpl*

tone [ton] *s* tono ‖ *tr* entonar ‖ *intr* armonizar; **to tone down** moderarse; **to tone up** reforzarse

tone poem *s* poema sinfónico

tongs [tɔŋz] o [taŋz] *spl* tenazas; (*e.g., for sugar*) tenacillas

tongue [tʌŋ] *s* (anat) lengua; (*of a wagon*) vara, lanza; (*of a belt buckle*) tarabilla; (*of shoe*) lengua, lengüeta; (*language*) lengua, idioma *m;* **to hold one's tongue** morderse la lengua

tongue twister ['twɪstər] *s* trabalenguas *m*

tonic ['tanɪk] *adj & s* tónico

tonic accent *s* acento prosódico

tonight [tu'naɪt] *adv & s* esta noche

tonnage ['tʌnɪdʒ] *s* tonelaje *m*

tonsil ['tansəl] *s* tonsila, amígdala

tonsillitis [͵tansɪ'laɪtɪs] *s* tonsilitis *f*, amigdalitis *f*

ton•y ['toni] *adj* (*comp* **-ier;** *super* **-iest**) (slang) elegante, aristocrático

too [tu] *adv* (*also*) también; (*more than enough*) demasiado; **too bad!** ¡qué lástima!; **too many** demasiados; **too much** demasiado

tool [tul] *s* herramienta; (*person used for one's own ends*) instrumento; **tools** implementos *mpl* ‖ *tr* trabajar con herramienta; (bb) filetear, estampar

tool bag *s* bolsa de herramientas

toolmak'er *s* tallador *m* de herramientas, herrero de herramientas

toot [tut] *s* (*of horn*) toque *m;* (*of klaxon*) bocinazo; (*of locomotive*) pitazo; (coll) parranda ‖ *tr* sonar; **to toot one's own horn** cantar sus propias alabanzas ‖ *intr* sonar

tooth [tuθ] *s* (*pl* **teeth** [tiθ]) diente *m*

tooth'ache' *s* dolor *m* de muelas

tooth'brush' *s* cepillo de dientes

toothless ['tuθlɪs] *adj* desdentado

tooth'paste' *s* pasta dentífrica, crema dental, crema dentífrica

tooth'pick' *s* limpiadientes *m*, mondadientes *m*, palillo

tooth powder *s* polvo dentífrico

top [tap] *s* (*of a mountain, tree, etc.*) cima; (*of a mountain; high point*) cumbre *f;* (*of a tree*) copa; (*of a barrel, box, etc.*) tapa; (*of a page*) principio; (*of a table*) tablero; (*of a wall*) coronamiento; (*of a bathing suit*) camiseta; (*of a carriage or auto*) capota; (*toy*) peón *m*, peonza; (naut) cofa; **at the top of** en lo alto de; (*e.g., one's class*) a la cabeza de; **at the top of one's voice** a voz en grito; **from top to bottom** de arriba

ti
to

abajo; de alto a bajo; completamente; **on top of** en lo alto de; encima de; **the tops** (slang) la flor de la canela; **to sleep like a top** dormir como un leño ‖ *v* (*pret* & *pp* **topped;** *ger* **topping**) *tr* coronar, rematar; cubrir; aventajar, superar; descopar (*p.ej., un árbol*)

topaz [ˈtopæz] *s* topacio

top billing *s* cabecera de cartel

top′coat′ *s* sobretodo; abrigo de entretiempo

toper [ˈtopər] *s* borrachín *m*

top hat *s* chistera, sombrero de copa

top′-heav′y *adj* más pesado arriba que abajo

topic [ˈtapɪk] *s* asunto, materia, tema *m*

top′knot′ *s* moño

top′mast′ *s* (naut) mastelero

top′most *adj* (el) más alto

topogra•phy [təˈpɑgrəfi] *s* (*pl* **-phies**) topografía

topple [ˈtapəl] *tr* derribar, volcar ‖ *intr* derribarse, volcarse; caerse, venirse abajo

top priority *s* máxima prioridad

topsail [ˈtapsəl] o [ˈtap,sel] *s* (naut) gavia

top secret *adj* de mayor confidencia

top′soil′ *s* capa superficial del suelo

topsy-turvy [ˈtapsɪˌtʌrvi] *adj* desbarajustado ‖ *adv* en cuadro, patas arriba ‖ *s* desbarajuste *m*

torch [tɔrtʃ] *s* antorcha; lámpara de bolsillo; **to carry the torch for** (slang) amar desesperadamente

torch′bear′er *s* hachero; (fig) adicto, partidario

torch′light′ *s* luz *f* de antorcha

torch song *s* canción lenta y melancólica de amor no correspondido

torment [ˈtɔrmɛnt] *s* tormento; murga ‖ [tɔrˈmɛnt] *tr* atormentar

torna•do [tɔrˈnedo] *s* (*pl* **-does** p **-dos**) tornado, tromba terrestre

torpe•do [tɔrˈpido] *s* (*pl* **-does**) torpedo ‖ *tr* torpedear

torrent [ˈtɔrənt] *s* torrente *m*

torrid [ˈtɔrɪd] *adj* tórrido

tor•so [ˈtɔrso] *s* (*pl* **-sos**) torso

tortoise [ˈtɔrtəs] *s* tortuga

tortoise shell *s* carey *m*

torture [ˈtɔrtʃər] *s* tortura ‖ *tr* torturar, atormentar

toss [tas] *s* echada; alcance *m* de una echada ‖ *tr* arrojar, echar; lanzar al aire; agitar, menear; levantar airosamente (*la cabeza*); lanzar (*p.ej., un comentario*); echar a cara o cruz; **to toss off** hacer muy rápidamente; tragar de un golpe ‖ *intr* agitarse, menearse; **to toss and turn** (*in bed*) revolverse, dar vueltas

toss′-up′ *s* cara o cruz; probabilidad igual

tot [tat] *s* párvulo, peque *m*, chiquitín *m*

to•tal [ˈtotəl] *adj* total; (*e.g., loss*) completo ‖ *s* total *m* ‖ *v* (*pret* & *pp* **-taled** o **-talled;** *ger* **-taling** o **-talling**) *tr* ascender a, sumar

totter [ˈtatər] *s* tambaleo ‖ *intr* tambalear; estar para desplomarse

touch [tʌtʃ] *s* (*act*) toque *m;* (*sense*) tacto, tiento; (*of piano, pianist, typewriter, typist*) tacto; (*of an illness*) ramo, ataque

ligero; pizca, poquito; **to get in touch with** ponerse en comunicación o contacto con; **to lose one's touch** perder el tiento ‖ *tr* tocar; conmover, enternecer; probar (*vino, licor*); (*for a loan*) (slang) pedir prestado a, dar un sablazo a; **to touch up** retocar ‖ *intr* tocar; **to touch at** tocar en (*un puerto*)

touching [ˈtʌtʃɪŋ] *adj* conmovedor, enternecedor ‖ *prep* tocante a

touch typewriting *s* escritura al tacto

touch•y [ˈtʌtʃi] *adj* (*comp* **-ier;** *super* **-iest**) quisquilloso, enojadizo

tough [tʌf] *adj* correoso; tenaz; difícil; gamberro; (*e.g., luck*) malo ‖ *s* gamberro, guapetón *m;* (coll) gorila

toughen [ˈtʌfən] *tr* hacer correoso; hacer tenaz; dificultar ‖ *intr* ponerse correoso; hacerse tenaz; hacerse difícil

toupee [tuˈpe] *s* peluquín *m*

tour [tur] *s* jira, paseo, vuelta; viaje largo; **on tour** de jira, de viaje ‖ *tr* viajar por, recorrer ‖ *intr* viajar por distracción o diversión

touring car [ˈturɪŋ] *s* coche *m* de turismo

tourist [ˈturɪst] *adj* turístico ‖ *s* turista *mf*

tourist guide *s* guía turística

tournament [ˈturnəmənt] o [ˈtʌrnəmənt] *s* torneo

tourney [ˈturni] o [ˈtʌrni] *s* torneo ‖ *intr* tornear

tourniquet [ˈturnɪˌkɛt] *s* torniquete *m*

tousle [ˈtauzəl] *tr* despeinar, enmarañar

tow [to] *s* remolque *m;* (*e.g., of hemp*) estopa; **to take in tow** dar remolque a; (fig) encargarse de ‖ *tr* remolcar

towage [ˈto•ɪdʒ] *s* remolque *m;* derechos de remolque

toward(s) [tord(z)] o [təˈword(z)] *prep* (*in the direction of*) hacia; (*with regard to*) para con; (*a certain hour*) cerca de, a eso de

tow′boat′ *s* remolcador *m*

tow•el [ˈtau•əl] *s* toalla ‖ *v* (*pret* & *pp* **-eled** o **-elled;** *ger* **-eling** o **-elling**) *tr* secar con toalla

towel rack *s* toallero

tower [ˈtau•ər] *s* torre *f* ‖ *intr* encumbrarse, empinarse

towering [ˈtau•ərɪŋ] *adj* encumbrado; sobresaliente; excesivo

towing service [ˈto•ɪŋ] *s* servicio de grúa

tow′line′ *s* cable *m* de remolque, sirga

town [taun] *s* problación, pueblo, villa; **in town** a la ciudad, en la ciudad

town clerk *s* escribano municipal

town council *s* concejo municipal

town crier *s* pregonero público

town hall *s* ayuntamiento, casa de ayuntamiento

towns′ folk′ *spl* vecinos del pueblo

township [ˈtaunʃɪp] *s* sexmo; terreno público de seis millas en cuadro

towns•man [ˈtaunzmən] *s* (*pl* **-men** [mən]) ciudadano, vecino; conciudadano; paisano

towns′peo′ple *spl* vecinos del pueblo

town talk *s* comidilla o hablillas del pueblo

tow′path′ *s* camino de sirga

tow plane *s* avión *m* de remolque
tow'rope' *s* cuerda de remolque
tow truck *s* camión-grúa *m*
toxic ['tɑksɪk] *adj* & *s* tóxico
toxic shock syndrome *s* síndrome *m* de choque tóxico
toy [tɔɪ] *adj* de juguete ‖ *s* juguete *m;* *(trifle)* bagatela; *(trinket)* dije *m,* bujería ‖ *intr* jugar; divertirse; **to toy with** jugar con *(los sentimientos de una persona);* acariciar *(una idea)*
toy bank *s* alcancía hucha
toy soldier *s* soldado de juguete
trace [tres] *s* huella, rastro; indicio, vestigio; *(of harness)* tirante *m;* pizca ‖ *tr* rastrear; trazar *(p.ej., una curva; los rasgos de una persona o cosa);* averiguar el paradero de; remontar al origen de
trace element *s* elemento rastro
trache•a ['trekɪ•ə] *s* *(pl* **-ae** [,i]) tráquea
track [træk] *s* *(of foot)* huella; *(of a wheel)* rodada, carril *m; (of a boat)* estela; *(of railroad)* vía; *(of an airplane, a hurricane)* trayectoria; *(of a tractor)* llanta de oruga; camino, senda; *(course followed by a boat)* derrota; *(of ideas, events, etc.)* sucesión; (sport) pista; **to keep track of** no perder de vista; no olvidar; **to lose track of** perder de vista; olvidar; **to make tracks** dejar pisadas; irse muy de prisa; **off the track** *(also* fig) desviado ‖ *tr* rastrear; seguir la huella o la pista de; dejar pisadas en, manchar pisando; **to track down** seguir y capturar; averiguar el origen de
tracking ['trækɪŋ] *s* seguimiento *(de vehículos espaciales)*
tracing station *s* estación de seguimiento
trackless trolley ['træklɪs] *s* filobús *m,* trolebús *m*
track meet *s* concurso de carreras y saltos
track'walk'er *s* guardavía *m*
tract [trækt] *s* espacio, tracto; folleto; (anat) canal *m,* sistema *m*
traction ['trækʃən] *s* tracción
traction company *s* empresa de tranvías
tractor ['træktər] *s* tractor *m*
trade [tred] *s* comercio; negocio, trato; trueque *m,* canje *m; (calling, job)* oficio; clientela, parroquia; *(e.g., in slaves)* trata ‖ *tr* cambiar, trocar; **to trade in** dar como parte del pago; **to trade off** cambalachear; ‖ *intr* comerciar; comprar; **to trade in** comerciar en; **to trade on** aprovecharse de
trade'mark' *s* marca de fábrica, marca registrada
trade name *s* nombre *m* comercial, razón *f* social; nombre de fábrica
trader ['tredər] *s* traficante *mf*
trade school *s* escuela de artes y oficios
trades•man ['tredzmən] *s* *(pl* **-men** [mən]) tendero; comerciante *m;* (Brit) artesano
trades union o **trade union** *s* sindicato, gremio de obreros
trade unionist *s* sindicalista *mf*
trade winds *spl* vientos alisios
trading post ['tredɪŋ] *s* factoría; *(in stock exchange)* puesto de compraventa

trading stamp *s* sello de premio, sello de descuento
tradition [trə'dɪʃən] *s* tradición
traduce [trə'djus] *tr* calumniar
traf•fic ['træfɪk] *s* tráfico, comercio; tráfico, circulación; *(e.g., in slaves)* trata ‖ *v* *(pret* & *pp* **-ficked;** *ger* **-ficking)** *intr* traficar
traffic circle *s* glorieta de tráfico
traffic court *s* juzgado de tráfico
traffic jam *s* embotellamiento, tapón *m* de tráfico
traffic light *s* luz *f* de tráfico, semáforo
traffic sign o **signal** *s* señal *f* de tráfico, seña de tráfico
traffic ticket *s* aviso de multa
tragedian [trə'dʒidɪ•ən] *s* trágico
trage•dy ['trædʒɪdi] *s* *(pl* **-dies)** tragedia
tragic ['trædʒɪk] *adj* trágico
trail [trel] *s* rastro, huella, pista; *(path through rough country)* trocha, senda, vereda; *(of a gown)* cola; *(of smoke, a rocket, etc.)* estela ‖ *tr* arrastrar; seguir la pista de; andar detrás de; llevar *(p.ej., barro)* con los pies ‖ *intr* arrastrar; rezagarse; arrastrarse, trepar *(una planta);* **to trail off** desaparecer poco a poco
trailer ['trelər] *s* remolque *m,* cochehabitación *m,* casa rodante; planta rastrera
trailing arbutus ['trelɪŋ] *s* epigea rastrera
train [tren] *s* *(of railway cars; of waves)* tren *m; (of thought)* hilo ‖ *tr* adiestrar; guiar *(las plantas);* (sport) entrenar ‖ *intr* adiestrarse; (sport) entrenarse
trained nurse *s* enfermera graduada
trainer ['trenər] *s* (sport) entrenador *m*
training ['trenɪŋ] *s* adiestramiento; instrucción; (sport) entrenamiento
training school *s* escuela práctica; reformatorio
training ship *s* buque *m* escuela
trait [tret] *s* característica, rasgo
traitor ['tretər] *s* traidor *m*
traitress ['tretrɪs] *s* traidora
trajecto•ry [trə'dʒɛktəri] *s* *(pl* **-ries)** trayectoria
tramp [træmp] *s* vagabundo; marcha pesada, ruido de pisadas ‖ *tr* pisar con fuerza; recorrer a pie ‖ *intr* andar a pie; vagabundear
trample ['træmpəl] *tr* pisotear ‖ *intr*—**to trample on** o **upon** pisotear
tramp steamer *s* vapor volandero
trance [træns] o [trɑns] *s* arrobamiento, rapto; estado hipnótico
tranquil ['træŋkwɪl] *adj* tranquilo
tranquilize ['træŋkwɪ,laɪz] *tr* & *intr* tranquilizar
tranquilizer ['træŋkwɪ,laɪzər] *s* tranquilizante *m*
tranquillity [træŋ'kwɪlɪti] *s* tranquilidad
transact [træn'zækt] o [træns'ækt] *tr* tramitar; llevar a cabo
transaction [træn'zækʃən] o [træns'ækʃən] *s* tramitación, transacción
transatlantic [,trænsət'læntɪk] *adj* & *s* transatlántico

to
tr

transcend [træn'sɛnd] *tr* exceder, superar ‖ *intr* sobresalir

transcribe [træn'skraɪb] *tr* transcribir

transcript ['trænskrɪpt] *s* trasunto, traslado; (educ) hoja de estudios, certificado de estudios

transcription [træn'skrɪpʃən] *s* transcripción

transept ['trænsɛpt] *s* crucero, transepto

trans•fer ['trænsfər] *s* traslado; transbordo; contraseña o billete *m* de transferencia ‖ [træns'fʌr] o ['trænsfər] *s* (*pret & pp* **-ferred;** *ger* **-ferring**) *tr* trasladar, transferir; transbordar ‖ *intr* cambiar de tren, tranvía, etc.

transfix [træns'fɪks] *tr* espetar, traspasar; dejar atónito

transform [træns'fɔrm] *tr* transformar ‖ *intr* transformarse

transformer [træns'fɔrmər] *s* transformador *m*

transfusion [træns'fjuʃən] *s* transfusión; (med) transfusión de la sangre

transgress [træns'grɛs] *tr* transgredir, violar; exceder, traspasar (*p.ej., los límites de la prudencia*) ‖ *intr* pecar, prevaricar

transgression [træns'grɛʃən] *s* transgresión; pecado, prevaricación

transient ['trænʃənt] *adj* pasajero, transitorio; de tránsito ‖ *s* transeúnte *mf*

transistor [træn'zɪstər] *s* transistor *m*

transistorize [træn'zɪstə,raɪz] *tr* transistorizar

transit ['trænsɪt] o ['trænzɪt] *s* tránsito

transitive ['trænsɪtɪv] *adj* transitivo ‖ *s* verbo transitivo

transitory ['trænsɪ,tori] *adj* transitorio

translate [træns'let] o ['trænslet] *tr* (*from one language to another*) traducir; (*from one place to another*) trasladar ‖ *intr* traducirse

translation [træns'leʃən] *s* traducción; traslación

translator [træns'letər] *s* traductor *m*

transliterate [træns'lɪtə,ret] *tr* transcribir

translucent [træns'lusənt] *adj* translúcido

transmission [træns'mɪʃən] *s* transmissión; (aut) cambio de marchas, cambio de velocidades

transmis'sion-gear' box *s* caja de cambio de marchas, caja de velocidades

trans•mit [træns'mɪt] *v* (*pret & pp* **-mitted;** *ger* **-mitting**) *tr & intr* transmitir

transmitter [træns'mɪtər] *s* transmisor *m*

transmitting set *s* aparato transmisor

transmitting station *s* estacion transmisora, emisora

transmute [træns'mjut] *tr & intr* transmutar

transom ['trænsəm] *s* (*crosspiece*) travesaño; (*window over door*) montante *m*; (*of ship*) yugo de popa

transparen•cy [træns'pɛrənsi] *s* (*pl* **-cies**) transparencia

transparent [træns'pɛrənt] *adj* transparente

transpire [træns'paɪr] *intr* transpirar; (*to become known, leak out*) transpirar; (coll) acontecer, tener lugar

transplant ['træns,plænt] *s* transplante; injerto ‖ *tr* transplantar ‖ *intr* transplantarse

transport ['trænsport] *s* transporte *m*; (aer & naut) transporte *m*; rapto, éxtasis *m*, transporte *m* ‖ [træns'port] *tr* transportar

transportation [,trænspor'teʃən] *s* transporte *m*; (U.S.A.) pasaje *m*, billete *m* de viaje

transport worker *s* transportista *mf*

transpose [træns'poz] *tr* transponer; (mus) transportar

trans•ship [træns'ʃɪp] *v* (*pret & pp* **-shipped;** *ger* **-shipping**) *tr* transbordar

transshipment [træns'ʃɪpmənt] *s* transbordo

transvestism [træns'vɛstɪzəm] *s* transvestismo

transvestite [træns'vɛstaɪt] *adj & s* transvestido

trap [træp] *s* trampa; (*double-curved pipe*) sifón *m*; coche ligero de dos ruedas; (sport) lanzaplatos *m* ‖ *v* (*pret & pp* **trapped;** *ger* **trapping**) *tr* entrampar; atrapar (*a un ladrón*)

trap door *s* escotillón *m*, trampa; (theat) escotillón *m*, pescante *m*

trapeze [trə'piz] *s* trapecio

trapezold ['træpɪ,zɔɪd] *s* trapecio

trapper ['træpər] *s* cazador *m* de alforja

trappings ['træpɪŋz] *spl* (*adornments*) adornos, altavíos; (*of a horse's harness*) jaeces *mpl*

trap'shoot'ing *s* tiro al vuelo

trash [træʃ] *s* broza, basura, desecho; (*junk*) cachivaches *mpl*; (*nonsense*) disparates *mpl*; (*worthless people*) gentuza

trash can *s* basurero

trash pile *s* basural *m* (SAm)

travail ['trævel] o [trə'vel] *s* afán *m*, labor *f*, pena; dolores *mpl* del parto

trav•el ['trævəl] *s* viaje *m*; el viajar; (mach) recorrido ‖ *v* (*pret & pp* **-eled** o **-elled;** *ger* **-eling** o **-elling**) *tr* viajar por; recorrer ‖ *intr* vaijar; andar, recorrer

travel bureau *s* oficina de turismo

traveler ['trævələr] *s* viajero; (*salesman*) viajante *m*

traveler's check *s* cheque *m* de viajeros

traveling expenses *spl* gastos de viaje

traveling salesman *s* viajante *m*, agente viajero

traverse ['trævərs] o [trə'vʌrs] *tr* atravesar; recorrer, pasar por

traves•ty ['trævɪsti] *s* (*pl* **-ties**) parodia ‖ *v* (*pret & pp* **-tied**) *tr* parodiar

trawl [trɔl] *s* red barredera, espinel *m*, palangre *m* ‖ *tr & intr* pescar a la rastra

tray [tre] *s* bandeja; (chem & phot) cubeta

treacherous ['trɛtʃərəs] *adj* traicionero, traidor; incierto, poco seguro

treacher•y ['trɛtʃəri] *s* (*pl* **-ies**) traición alevosía

tread [trɛd] *s* (*stepping*) pisada; (*of stairs*) grada, huella, peldaño; (*of stilts*) horquilla; (*of a tire*) banda de rodamiento; (*of shoe*) suela; (*of an egg*) meaje, galladura ‖ *v* (*pret trod* [trɑd]; *pp* **trodden** ['trɑdən] o **trod**) *tr* pisar, pisotear; abrumar, agobiar ‖ *intr* andar, caminar

treadle ['trɛdəl] *s* pedal *m*

treadless ['trɛdlɪs] *adj* (*tire*) desgastado

tread'mill' s rueda de andar; *(futile drudgery)* noria

treas. *abbr* **treasurer, treasury**

treason ['trizən] s traición

treasonable ['trizənəbəl] *adj* traicionero, traidor

treasure ['trɛʒər] s tesoro ‖ *tr* atesorar

treasurer ['trɛʒərər] s tesorero

treasur•y ['trɛʒəri] s *(pl* **-ies)** tesorería; tesoro

treat [trit] s convite *m; (to a drink)* convidada; *(something providing particular enjoyment)* regalo, deleite *m* ‖ *tr* tratar; convidar, regalar; curar *(a un enfermo)* ‖ *intr* tratar; convidar, regalar; **to treat of** tratar de

treatise ['tritɪs] s tratado

treatment ['tritmənt] s tratamiento

trea•ty ['triti] s *(pl* **-ties)** tratado

treble ['trɛbəl] *adj (threefold)* tresdoble, triple; sobreagudo; *(mus)* atiplado; *(mus)* de tiple ‖ s *(person)* tiple *mf; (voice)* tiple ‖ *tr* triplicar ‖ *intr* triplicarse

tree [tri] s árbol *m*

tree farm s monte *m* tallar

treeless ['trilɪs] *adj* pelado, sin árboles

tree'top' s copa, cima de árbol

trellis ['trɛlɪs] s enrejado, espaldera; emparrado

tremble ['trɛmbəl] s temblor *m*, estremecimiento ‖ *intr* temblar, estremecerse

tremendous [trɪ'mɛndəs] *adj* tremendo

tremor ['trɛmər] o ['trimər] s temblor *m*

trench [trɛntʃ] s foso, zanja; *(for irrigation)* acequia; *(mil)* trinchera

trenchant ['trɛntʃənt] *adj* mordaz, punzante; enérgico, bien definido

trench coat s trinchera

trench mortar s *(mil)* lanzabombas *m*

trench'-plow' *tr* (agr) desfondar

trend [trɛnd] s curso, dirección, tendencia ‖ *intr* dirigirse, tender

trendy ['trɛndi] *adj* (coll) de (última) moda

trespass ['trɛspəs] s entrada sin derecho; infracción, violación; culpa, pecado ‖*intr* entrar sin derecho; pecar; **no trespassing** prohibida la entrada; **to trespass against** pecar contra; **to trespass on** entrar sin derecho en; infringir, violar; abusar de *(p.ej., la paciencia de uno)*

tress [trɛs] s *(braid of hair)* trenza; *(curl)* bucle *m*, rizo

trestle ['trɛsəl] s caballete *m;* puente *m* o viaducto de caballetes

trial ['traɪ•əl] s ensayo, prueba; aflicción, desgracia; *(law)* juicio, proceso, vista; **on trial** a prueba; *(law)* en juicio; **to bring to trial** encausar

trial and error s método de tanteos

trial balloon s globo sonda; **to send up a trial balloon** (fig) lanzar un globo sonda

trial by jury s juicio por jurado

trial jury s jurado procesal

trial order s (com) pedido de ensayo

trial run s experimento piloto

triangle ['traɪ,æŋgəl] s triángulo

tribe [traɪb] s tribu *f*

tribunal [trɪ'bjunəl] o [traɪ'bjunəl] s tribunal *m*

tribune ['trɪbjun] s tribuna

tributar•y ['trɪbjə,tɛri] *adj* tributario ‖ s *(pl* **-ies)** tributario

tribute ['trɪbjut] s tributo

trice [traɪs] s momento, instante *m;* **in a trice** en un periquete

trick [trɪk] s ardid *m*, artimaña; leva (CAm, Col); *(knack)* maña; *(feat)* suerte *f; (prank)* travesura, burla, chasco; tanda, turno; ilusión; *(feat with cards)* truco; *(cards in one round)* baza; (coll) chiquita; **to be up to one's old tricks** hacer de las suyas; **to play a dirty trick on** hacer una mala jugada a ‖ *tr* trampear; burlar, engañar; ataviar

tricker•y ['trɪkəri] s *(pl* **-ies)** trampería, malas mañas

trickle ['trɪkəl] s chorro delgado, goteo ‖ *intr* escurrir, gotear; pasar gradual e irregularmente

trickster ['trɪkstər] s tramposo, embustero, embaucador *m*, embaucadora

trick•y ['trɪki] *adj (comp* **-ier;** *super* **-iest)** tramposo, engañoso, difícil; *(animal)* vicioso; *(ticklish to deal with)* delicado

tricorn ['traɪkɔrn] *adj* & s tricornio

tried [traɪd] *adj* fiel, probado, seguro

trifle ['traɪfəl] s bagatela, friolera, fruslería, basurita, chiquitura; *(trinket)* bagatela, baratija ‖ *tr*—**to trifle away** malgastar ‖ *intr* estar ocioso, holgar; **to trifle with** manosear; jugar con, burlarse de

trifling ['traɪflɪŋ] *adj* frívolo, fútil, ligero; insignificante, trivial

trifocal [traɪ'fokəl] *adj* trifocal ‖ s lente *f* trifocal; **trifocals** anteojos trifocales

trig. *abbr* **trigonometric, trigonometry**

trigger ['trɪgər] s *(e.g., of a gun)* disparador *m*, gatillo; *(of any device)* disparador ‖ *tr* poner en movimiento, provocar

trigonometry [,trɪgə'nɑmɪtri] s trigonometría

trill [trɪl] s trinado, trino; *(made with voice, esp. of birds)* gorjeo; *(phonet)* vibración ‖ *tr* decir o cantar gorjeando; pronunciar con vibración ‖ *intr* trinar; gorjear

trillion ['trɪljən] s (U.S.A.) billón *m;* (Brit) trillón *m*

trilo•gy ['trɪlədʒi] s *(pl* **-gies)** trilogía

trim [trɪm] *adj (comp* **trimmer;** *super* **trimmest)** acicalado, compuesto, elegante ‖ s condición, estado; buena condición; adorno, atavío; traje *m*, vestido; *(of sails)* orientación ‖ *v (pret* & *pp* **trimmed;** *ger* **trimming)** *tr* ajustar, adaptar; arreglar, componer; adornar, decorar; decorar, enguirnaldar *(el árbol de Navidad)*; recortar; cortar ligeramente *(el pelo)*; despabilar *(una lámpara o vela)*; mondar, podar *(árboles, plantas)*; acepillar, desbastar; (naut) orientar *(las velas)*; (coll) derrotar, vencer; (coll) regañar

trimming ['trɪmɪŋ] s adorno, guarnición; franja, orla; (coll) paliza, zurra; (coll) derrota; **trimmings** accesorios, arrequives *mpl;* recortes *mpl*

tr

tr

trini•ty [ˈtrɪnɪti] s (pl **-ties**) (group of three) trinca ‖ **Trinity** s Trinidad

trinket [ˈtrɪŋkɪt] s (small ornament) dije m; (trivial object) baratija, bujería, chuchería

tri•o [ˈtri•o] s (pl **-os**) (group of three) terna, trío; (mus) trío

trip [trɪp] s viaje m; jira, recorrido; (stumble) tropiezo; (act of causing a person to stumble) traspié m, zancadilla; (blunder) desliz m; (drugs) viaje ‖ v (pret & pp **tripped;** ger **tripping**) tr trompicar, echar la zancadilla a; detener, estorbar; inclinar; coger en falta; coger en una mentira ‖ intr ir con paso rápido y ligero; brincar, saltar, correr; tropezar; **to trip over** tropezar con, contra o en

tripe [traɪp] s callos, mondongo; (slang) disparate m, barbaridad

trip'ham'mer s martillo pilón

triphthong [ˈtrɪfθɔŋ] s triptongo

triple [ˈtrɪpəl] adj & s triple m ‖ tr triplicar ‖ intr triplicarse

triplet [ˈtrɪplɪt] s (offspring) trillizo; (stanza of three lines) terceto; (mus) terceto, tresillo

triplicate [ˈtrɪplɪkɪt] adj & s triplicado; **in triplicate** por triplicado ‖ [ˈtrɪplɪ̩ket] tr triplicar

tripod [ˈtraɪpɑd] m trípode m

triptych [ˈtrɪptɪk] s tríptico

trite [traɪt] adj gastado, trillado, trivial

triumph [ˈtraɪ•əmf] s triunfo ‖ intr triunfar; **to triumph over** triunfar de

triumphal arch [traɪˈʌmfəl] s arco triunfal

triumphant [traɪˈʌmfənt] adj triunfante

trivia [ˈtrɪvɪ•ə] spl bagatelas, trivialidades

trivial [ˈtrɪvɪ•əl] adj trivial, insignificante

triviali•ty [ˌtrɪvɪˈælɪti] s (pl **-ties**) trivialidad

Trojan [ˈtrodʒən] adj & s troyano

Trojan horse s caballo de Troya

Trojan War s guerra de Troya

troll [trol] tr & intr pescar a la cacea

trolley [ˈtrɑli] s polea o arco de trole; tranvía m

trolley bus s trolebús m

trolley car s coche m de tranvía

trolley pole s trole m

trolling [ˈtrolɪŋ] s cacea, pesca a la cacea

trollop [ˈtrɑləp] s (slovenly woman) cochina; mujer f de mala vida

trombone [ˈtrɑmbon] s trombón m

troop [trup] s tropa; (of actors) compañia; (of cavalry) escuadrón m ‖ intr agruparse; marcharse en tropel

trooper [ˈtrupər] s soldado de caballería; corcel m de guerra; policía m de a caballo; (ship) transporte m; **to swear like a trooper** jurar como un carretero

tro•phy [ˈtrofi] s (pl **-phies**) trofeo; (any memento) recuerdo

tropic [ˈtrɑpɪk] adj tropical ‖ s trópico

tropical [ˈtrɑpɪkəl] adj tropical

tropics o **Tropics** [ˈtrɑpɪks] spl zona tropical

troposphere [ˈtrɑpəˌsfɪr] s troposfera

trot [trɑt] s trote m ‖ v (pret & pp **trotted;** ger **trotting**) tr hacer trotar; **to trot out** (slang) sacar para mostrar ‖ intr trotar

troth [trɔθ] o [troθ] s fe f; verdad; esponsales mpl; **in troth** en verdad; **to plight one's troth** prometer fidelidad; dar palabra de casamiento

troubadour [ˈtrubə̩dor] o [ˈtrubə̩dʊr] adj trovadoresco ‖ s trovador m

trouble [ˈtrʌbəl] s apuro, dificultad; confusión, estorbo; conflicto; inquietud, preocupación; pena, molestia; mal m, enfermedad; murga; (of a mechanical nature) avería, falla, pana; **not to be worth the trouble** no valer la pena; **to pour out one's troubles** jeremiquear; **that's the trouble** ahí está el busilis; **the trouble is that . . .** lo malo es que . . .; **to be in trouble** estar en un aprieto; **to be looking for trouble** buscar tres pies al gato; **to get into trouble** enredarse, meterse en líos; **to take the trouble to** tomarse la molestia de ‖ tr apurar; confundir, estorbar; inquietar, preocupar; apenar, afligir; incomodar, molestar; dar que hacer a; **to be troubled with** padecer de; **to trouble oneself** molestarse ‖ intr apurarse; inquietarse, preocuparse; molestarse, darse molestia; **to trouble to** molestarse en

trouble lamp s lámpara de socorro

trou'ble•mak'er s perturbador m, alborotador m

troubleshooter [ˈtrʌbəl̩ʃutər] s localizador m de averías; (in disputes) componedor m

troubleshooting [ˈtrʌbəl̩ʃutɪŋ] s localización de averías; (of disputes) composición, arbitraje m

troublesome [ˈtrʌbəlsəm] adj molesto, pesado, gravoso; impertinente; perturbador

trouble spot s lugar m de conflicto

trough [trɔf] o [traf] s (e.g., to knead bread) artesa; (for water for animals) abrevadero; (for feeding animals) comedero; (under eaves) canal f; (between two waves) seno

troupe [trup] s compañia de actores o de circo

trousers [ˈtrausərz] spl pantalones mpl

trous•seau [truˈso] o [ˈtruso] s (pl **-seaux** o **-seaus**) ajuar m de novia, equipo de novia

trout [traut] s trucha

trouvère [truˈvɛr] s trovero

trowel [ˈtrau•əl] s paleta, llana

Troy [trɔɪ] s Troya

truant [ˈtru•ənt] s novillero; **to play truant** hacer novillos

truce [trus] s tregua

truck [trʌk] s carro; vegoneta; camión m; autocamión m; (to be moved by hand) carretilla; (of locomotive or car) carretón m; hortalizas para el mercado; (coll) desperdicios; (coll) negocio, relaciones ‖ tr acarrear

truck driver s camionista mf; materialista m (Mex)

truck garden s huerto de hortalizas (para el mercado)

truculent [ˈtrʌkjələnt] o [ˈtrukjələnt] adj truculento

trudge [trʌdʒ] intr caminar, ir a pie; **to trudge along** marchar con pena y trabajo

true [tru] *adj* verdadero; exacto; constante, uniforme; fiel, leal; alineado; a plomo, a nivel; **to come true** hacerse realidad; **true to life** conforme a la realidad

true copy *s* copia fiel

true-hearted [ˈtruˌhɑrtɪd] *adj* fiel, leal, sincero

true′love′ *s* fiel amante *mf;* (bot) hierba de París

truelove knot *s* lazo de amor

truffle [ˈtrʌfəl] o [ˈtrufəl] *s* trufa

truism [ˈtruˑɪzəm] *s* perogrullada, verdad trillada

truly [ˈtruli] *adv* verdaderamente; efectivamente; fielmente; **truly yours** de Vd. atto. y S.S., su seguro servidor

trump [trʌmp] *s* triunfo; (coll) buen chico, buena chica; **no trump** sin triunfo ‖ *tr* matar con un triunfo; aventajar, sobrepujar; **to trump up** forjar, inventar *(para engañar)* ‖ *intr* triunfar

trumpet [ˈtrʌmpɪt] *s* trompeta; trompeta acústica; **to blow one's own trumpet** cantar sus propias alabanzas ‖ *tr* pregonar a son de trompeta ‖ *intr* trompetear

truncheon [ˈtrʌntʃən] *s* cachiporra; bastón *m* de mando

trunk [trʌŋk] *s* (*of living body, tree, family, railroad*) tronco; (*chest for clothes, etc.*) baúl *m;* (*of an automobile*) portaequipaje *m;* (*of elephant*) trompa; **trunks** taparrabo

trunk hose *spl* trusas

truss [trʌs] *s* (*framework*) armadura; haz *m*, paquete *m*, lío; (*for holding back a hernia*) braguero ‖ *tr* armar; empaquetar; espetar; apretar (*barriles*)

trust [trʌst] *s* confianza; esperanza; cargo, custodia; depósito; crédito; obligación; (econ) trust *m*, cartel *m;* (law) fideicomiso; **in trust** en confianza; en depósito; **on trust** a crédito, al fiado ‖ *tr* confiar; confiar en; vender a crédito a ‖ *intr* confiar, fiar; **to trust in** fiarse a o de

trust company *s* banco fideicomisario, banco de depósitos

trustee [trʌsˈti] *s* administrador *m*, comisario; regente (universitario); (*of an estate*) fideicomisario

trusteeship [trʌsˈtiʃɪp] *s* cargo de administrador, fideicomisario; (*of the UN*) fideicomiso

trustful [ˈtrʌstfəl] *adj* confiado

trust′wor′thy *adj* confiable, fidedigno

trust•y [ˈtrʌsti] *adj* (*comp* **-ier;** *super* **-iest**) honrado, fidedigno ‖ *s* (*pl* **-ies**) presidiario fidedigno (*que se ha merecido ciertos privilegios*)

truth [truθ] *s* verdad; **in truth** a la verdad, en verdad

truthful [ˈtruθfəl] *adj* verídico, veraz

try [traɪ] *s* (*pl* **tries**) ensayo, intento, prueba ‖ *v* (*pret & pp* **tried**) *tr* ensayar, intentar, probar; comprobar, verificar; cansar; exasperar, irritar; (law) procesar (*a una persona*); (law) ver (*un pleito*); **to try on** probarse (*una prenda de vestir*) ‖ *intr*

ensayar, probar; esforzarse; **to try to** tratar de, intentar

trying [ˈtraɪˑɪŋ] *adj* cansado, molesto, irritante; penoso

tryst [trɪst] o [traɪst] *s* cita; lugar *m* de cita

tub [tʌb] *s* cuba, tina; (coll) baño; (*clumsy boat*) (coll) carcamán *m*, trompo; (*fat person*) (coll) cuba

tube [tjub] o [tub] *s* tubo; túnel *m;* (*of a tire*) cámara; (coll) ferrocarril subterráneo

tuber [ˈtjuber] o [ˈtubər] *s* tubérculo

tubercle [ˈtubərkəl] *s* tubérculo

tubercular [tuˈbɑrkjələr] *adj & s* tísico

tuberculosis [tuˌbɑrkjəˈlosɪs] *s* tuberculosis *f*

tuck [tʌk] *s* alforza ‖ *tr* alforzar; **to tuck away** encubrir, ocultar; **to tuck in** arropar, enmantar; remeter (*p.ej., la ropa de cama*); **to tuck up** arremangar (*un vestido*); guarnecer (*la cama*)

tucker [ˈtʌkər] *s* escote *m* ‖ *tr* **—to tucker out** (coll) agotar, cansar

Tuesday [ˈtjuzdi] *s* martes *m*

tuft [tʌft] *s* (*of feathers, hair, etc.*) penacho, copete *m;* manojo, racimo, ramillete *m;* borla ‖ *tr* empenachar ‖ *intr* crecer formando mechones

tug [tʌg] *s* estirón *m*, tirón *m;* (*boat*) remolcador *m* ‖ *v* (*pret & pp* **tugged;** *ger* **tugging**) *tr* arrastrar, tirar con fuerza de; remolcar (*un barco*) ‖ *intr* tirar con fuerza; esforzarse, luchar

tug′boat′ *s* remolcador *m*

tug of war *s* lucha de la cuerda

tuition [tjuˈɪʃən] *s* enseñanza; precio de la enseñanza

tulip [ˈtulɪp] *s* tulipán *m*

tumble [ˈtʌmbəl] *s* caída, tumbo; (*somersault*) voltereta, tumba; confusión, desorden *m* ‖ *intr* caerse, rodar; voltear; derribarse, volcarse; brincar, dar saltos; (*into bed*) echarse; (*to catch on*) (slang) caer, comprender; **to tumble down** desplomarse, hundirse, venirse abajo

tum′ble-down′ *adj* destartalado, desvencijado

tumbler [ˈtʌmblər] *s* (*for drinking*) vaso; (*person who performs bodily feats*) volatinero; (*self-righting toy*) dominguillo, tentemozo

tumor [ˈtjumər] o [ˈtumər] *s* tumor *m*

tumult [ˈtumʌlt] *s* tumulto

tun [tʌn] *s* barril *m*, tonel *m;* (*measure of capacity for wine*) tonelada

tuna [ˈtunə] *s* atún *m*

tune [tjun] o [tun] *s* tonada, aire *m;* (*manner of acting or speaking*) tono; **in tune** afinado; afinadamente; **out of tune** desafinado; desafinadamente; **to change one's tune** mudar de tono ‖ *tr* acordar, afinar; (rad) sintonizar; **to tune in** (rad) sintonizar; **to tune out** (rad) desintonizar; **to tune up** poner a punto; poner a tono (*un motor de automóvil*)

tungsten [ˈtʌŋstən] *s* tungsteno

tunic [ˈtjunɪk] o [ˈtunɪk] *s* túnica

tuning *s* (aut) puesto a punto

tuning coil *s* (rad) bobina de sintonía

tr
tu

tuning fork *s* diapasón *m*
Tunis ['tunɪs] *s* Túnez (*ciudad*)
Tunisia [tu'nɪʒə] *s* Túnez (*país*)
Tunisian [tu'nɪʒən] *adj & s* tunecino
tun•nel ['tʌnəl] *s* túnel *m;* (min) galería ‖ *v* (*pret & pp* **-neled** o **-nelled;** *ger* **-neling** o **-nelling**) *tr* construir un túnel a través de o debajo de
turban ['tʌrbən] *s* turbante *m*
turbid ['tʌrbɪd] *adj* turbio
turbine ['tʌrbɪn] o ['tʌrbaɪn] *s* turbina
turbocompressor [,tʌrbokəm'prɛsər] *s* turbocompresor *m*
turbofan ['tʌrbo,fæn] *s* turboventilador *m*
turbojet ['tʌrbo,dʒɛt] *s* turborreactor *m;* avión *m* de turborreacción
turboprop ['tʌrbo,prɑp] *s* turbopropulsor *m;* turbohelice *m* avión *m* de turbopropulsión
turbosupercharger [,tʌrbo'supər,tʃɑrdʒər] *s* turbosupercargador *m*
turbulent ['tʌrbjələnt] *adj* turbulento
tureen [tu'rin] o [tju'rin] *s* sopera
turf [tʌrf] *s* (*surface layer of grassland*) césped *m;* terrón *m* de césped; (*peat*) turba; **the turf** el hipódromo; las carreras de caballos
turf•man ['tʌrfmən] *s* (*pl* **-men** [mən]) turiista *m*
Turk [tʌrk] *s* turco
turkey ['tʌrki] *s* pavo ‖ **Turkey** *s* Turquía
turkey vulture *s* aura
Turkish ['tʌrkɪʃ] *adj & s* turco
Turkish towel *s* toalla rusa
turmoil ['tʌrmɔɪl] *s* alboroto, disturbio, tumulto
turn [tʌrn] *s* vuelta; (*time of action*) turno; (*change of direction*) virada; (*bend*) recodo; (*walk*) paseo corto; (*of a spiral, roll of wire, etc.*) espira; aspecto; inclinación; vahido, vértigo; giro, expresión; servicio; (coll) sacudida, susto; **at every turn** a cada paso; **in trun** por turno; **to be one's turn** tocarle a uno, p.ej., **it's your turn** le toca a Vd.; **to take turns** alternar, turnar; **to wait one's turn** aguardar turno, esperar vez ‖ *tr* volver; dar vuelta a (*p.ej., una llave*); torcer (*p.ej., el tobillo*); doblar (*la esquina*); dirigir (*p.ej., los ojos*); (*to make sour*) agriar; (*on a lathe*) tornear; tener (*p.ej., veinte años cumplidos*); **to turn against** predisponer en contra de; **to turn around** volver; voltear; torcer (*las palabras de una persona*); **to turn aside** desviar; **to turn away** desviar; despedir; **to turn back** devolver; hacer retroceder; retrasar (*el reloj*); **to turn down** doblar hacia abajo; invertir; rechazar, rehusar; bajar (*p.ej., el gas*); **to turn in** doblar hacia adentro; entregar; **to turn off** apagar (*la luz, la radio*); cortar (*el agua, gas, etc.*); cerrar (*la llave del agua, gas, etc.; la radio, la televisión*); interrumpir (*la corriente eléctrica*); **to turn on** encender (*la luz*); poner (*la luz, la radio, etc.*); abrir (*la llave del agua, gas, etc.*); establecer (*la corriente eléctrica*); **to turn out** despedir; echar al campo (*a los animales*); volver al

revés; apagar (*la luz*); hacer, fabricar; **to turn up** doblar hacia arriba; levantar; arremangar (*p.ej., las mangas*); volver (*un naipe*); poner más alto o más fuerte (*la radio*); abrir la llave de (*p.ej., el gas*) ‖ *intr* volver, p.ej., **the road turns to the right** el camino vuelve a la derecha; virar (*un automóvil, un avión, etc.*); (*to revolve*) girar; volverse (*p.ej., la conversación; la opinión; ciertos licores*); **to turn against** cobrar aversión a; rebelarse contra; **to turn around** dar vuelta; **to turn aside** o **away** desviarse; alejarse; **to turn back** volver, regresar; retroceder; **to turn down** doblarse hacia abajo; invertirse; **to turn in** doblarse hacia adentro; replegarse; recogerse, volver a casa; (coll) recogerse, acostarse; **to turn into** entrar en; convertirse en; **to turn on** volverse contra; depender de; versar sobre; ocuparse de; **to turn out badly** salir mal; **to turn out right** acabar bien; **to turn out to be** venir a ser; resultar, salir; **to turn over** volcar, derribarse (*un vehículo*); **to turn up** doblarse hacia arriba; levantarse; acontecer; aparecer
turn'coat' *s* tránsfuga *mf*, apóstata *mf*, renegado; **to become a turncoat** volver la casaca, cambiarse la camisa
turn'down' *adj* (*collar*) caído ‖ *s* rechazamiento
turning light *s* (aut) intermitente *m*
turning point *s* punto de transición, punto decisivo
turnip ['tʌrnɪp] *s* nabo; (*cheap watch*) (slang) calentador *m;* (slang) tipo
turn'key' *s* carcelero, llavero de cárcel
turn of life *s* menopausia
turn of mind *s* natural *m*, inclinación
turn'out' *s* (*gathering of people*) con currencia; (*number attending a show, etc.*) entrada; (*side track or passage*) apartadero; (*amount produced*) producción; (*array, outfit*) equipaje *m;* carruaje *m* de lujo
turn'o'ver *s* (*spill, upset*) vuelco; cambio de personal; movimiento de mercancías; ciclo de compra y venta
turn'pike' *s* carretera de peaje
turnstile ['tʌrn,staɪl] *s* torniquete *m*
turn'ta'ble *s* (*of phonograph*) placa giratoria, plato giratorio; (rr) placa giratoria, plataforma giratoria
turpentine ['tʌrpən,taɪn] *s* trementina
turpitude ['tʌrpɪ,tjud] *s* torpeza, infamia, vileza
turquoise ['tʌrkɔɪz] o ['tʌrkwɔɪz] *s* turquesa
turret ['tʌrɪt] *s* torrecilla; (archit) torreón *m;* (nav) torreta
turtle ['tʌrtəl] *s* tortuga; **to turn turtle** derribarse patas arriba
tur'tle•dove' *s* tórtola
Tuscan ['tʌskən] *adj & s* toscano
Tuscany ['tʌskəni] *s* la Toscana
tusk [tʌsk] *s* colmillo
tussle ['tʌsəl] *s* agarrada ‖ *intr* agarrarse, asirse, reñir

tutor ['tjutər] o ['tutər] *s* maestro particular; (*guardian*) tutor *m* ‖ *tr* dar enseñanza particular a ‖ *intr* dar enseñanza particular; (coll) tomar lecciones particulares

tuxe•do [tʌk'sido] *s* (*pl* -**dos**) esmoquin *m*, smoking *m*

TV *abbr* **television**

twaddle ['twɑdəl] *s* charla, tonterías, música celestial ‖ *intr* charlar, decir tonterías

twang [twæŋ] *s* (*of musical instrument*) tañido; (*of voice*) timbre *m* nasal ‖ *tr* tocar con un tañido; decir con timbre nasal ‖ *intr* hablar por la nariz

twang•y [twæŋi] *adj* (*comp* -**ier**; *super* -**iest**) (*device*) tañente; (*person, voice*) gangoso

tweed [twid] *s* mezcla de lana; traje *m* de mezcla de lana; **tweeds** ropa de mezcla de lana

tweet [twit] *s* pío ‖ *intr* piar

tweeter ['twitər] *s* altavoz *m* para audiofrecuencias elevadas

tweezers ['twizərz] *spl* bruselas, pinzas, tenacillas

twelfth [twɛlfθ] *adj & s* (*in a seris*) duodécimo; (*part*) dozavo ‖ *s* (*in dates*) doce *m*

Twelfth'-night' *s* la víspera del día de Reyes; la noche del día de Reyes

twelve [twɛlv] *adj & pron* doce ‖ *s* doce *m;* **twelve o'clock** las doce

twentieth ['twɛnti•iθ] *adj & s* (*in a series*) vigésimo; (*part*) veintavo ‖ *s* (*in dates*) veinte *m*

twen•ty ['twɛnti] *adj & pron* veinte ‖ *s* (*pl* -**ties**) veinte *m*

twice [twaɪs] *adv* dos veces

twice'-told' *adj* dicho dos veces; trilládo, sabido

twiddle ['twɪdəl] *tr* menear o revolver ociosamente

twig [twɪg] *s* ramito; **twigs** leña menuda

twilight ['twaɪ,laɪt] *adj* crepuscular ‖ *s* crepúsculo

twill [twɪl] *s* tela cruzada; (*pattern of weave*) cruzado ‖ *tr* cruzar

twin [twɪn] *adj & s* gemelo

twine [twaɪn] *s* guita, cuerda, bramante *m* ‖ *tr* enroscar, retorcer ‖ *intr* enroscarse, retorcerse

twinge [twɪndʒ] *s* punzada, dolor agudo

twin'jet' plane *s* avión *m* birreactor

twinkle ['twɪŋkəl] *s* centelleo; (*of eye*) pestañeo; instante *m* ‖ *intr* centellear; pestañear; moverse rápidamente

twin'-screw' *adj* (naut) de doble hélice

twirl [twʌrl] *s* vuelta, giro ‖ *tr* hacer girar; (baseball) lanzar (*la pelota*) ‖ *intr* dar vueltas, girar; piruetear

twist [twɪst] *s* torcedura; enroscadura; curva, recodo; giro, vuelta; propensión, prejuicio; (*of mind or disposition*) sesgo ‖ *tr* torcer; retorcer; enroscar; hacer girar; entrelazar; desviar; (*to give a different meaning to*) torcer ‖ *intr* torcerse; retorcerse; enroscarse; dar vueltas; entrelazarse; desviarse; serpentear; **to twist and turn** (*in bed*) dar vueltas

twisted ['twɪstɪd] *adj* sobornado

twit [twɪt] *v* (*pret & pp* **twitted**; *ger* **twitting**) *tr* reprender (*a uno*) recordando algo desagradable o poniéndole en ridículo

twitch [twɪtʃ] *s* crispatura; ligero temblor ‖ *intr* crisparse; temblar (*p.ej., los párpados*)

twitter ['twɪtər] *s* gorjeo; risita sofocada; inquietud ‖ *intr* gorjear; reír sofocadamente; temblar de inquietud

two [tu] *adj & pron* dos ‖ *s* dos *m;* **to put two and two together** atar cabos, sacar la conclusión evidente; **two o'clock** las dos

two'-cy'cle *adj* (mach) de dos tiempos

two'-cyl'inder *adj* (mach) de dos cilindros

two-edged ['tu,ɛdʒd] *adj* de dos filos

two hundred *adj & pron* doscientos ‖ *s* doscientos *m*

twosome ['tusəm] *s* pareja; pareja de jugadores; juego de dos

two'-time' *tr* (slang) engañar en amor, ser infiel a (*una persona del otro sexo*)

tycoon [taɪ'kun] *s* (coll) magnate *m*

type [taɪp] *s* tipo; (*piece*) (typ) tipo, letra; (*pieces collectively*) (typ) letra; letras impresas, letras escritas a máquina ‖ *tr* escribir a máquina, tipiar; representar, simbolizar ‖ *intr* escribir a máquina

type'face' *s* tipo de letra

type'script' *s* material escrito a máquina

typesetter ['taɪp,sɛtər] *s* (typ) cajista *mf;* (typ) máquina de componer

type'write' *v* (*pret* -**wrote** [,rot]; *pp* -**written** [,rɪtən]) *tr & intr* escribir a máquina, tipiar

type'writ'er *s* máquina de escribir; tipista *mf*

typewriter ribbon *s* cinta para máquinas de escribir

type'writ'ing *s* mecanografía; trabajo hecho con máquina de escribir

typhoid fever ['taɪfɔɪd] *s* fiebre tifoidea

typhoon [taɪ'fun] *s* tifón *m*

typical ['tɪpɪkəl] *adj* típico

typi•fy ['tɪpɪ,faɪ] *v* (*pret & pp* -**fied**) *tr* simbolizar; ser ejemplo o modelo de

typist ['taɪpɪst] *s* mecanógrafo, tipista *mf*, mecanógrafa

typographic(al) [,taɪpə'græfɪk(əl)] *adj* tipográfico

typographical error *s* error *m* de imprenta

typography [taɪ'pɑgrəfi] *s* tipografía

tyrannic(al) [tɪ'rænɪk(əl)] o [taɪ'rænɪk(əl)] *adj* tiránico

tyrannous ['tɪrənəs] *adj* tirano

tyran•ny ['tɪrəni] *s* (*pl* -**nies**) tiranía

tyrant ['taɪrənt] *s* tirano

ty•ro ['taɪro] *s* (*pl* -**ros**) tirón *m*, novicio

tu
ty

U

U, u [ju] vigésima primera letra del alfabeto inglés

U. *abbr* **University**

ubiquitous [ju'bɪkwɪtəs] *adj* ubicuo

udder ['ʌdər] *s* ubre *f*

UFO *abbr* **unidentified flying object**

ugliness ['ʌglɪnɪs] *s* fealdad; (coll) malhumor *m*

ug•ly ['ʌgli] *adj* (*comp* **-lier;** *super* **-liest**) feo; (coll) malhumorado

ugly mug *s* (slang) carantamaula

Ukraine ['jukren] o [ju'kren] *s* Ucrania

Ukrainian [ju'krenɪ•ən] *adj & s* ucraniano, ucranio

ulcer ['ʌlsər] *s* llaga, úlcera; (*corrupting influence*) (fig) llaga

ulcerate ['ʌlsə,ret] *tr* ulcerar ‖ *intr* ulcerarse

ulterior [ʌl'tɪrɪ•ər] *adj* ulterior; (*concealed*) escondido, oculto

ultimate ['ʌltɪmɪt] *adj* último

ultima•tum [,ʌltɪ'metəm] *s* (*pl* **-tums** o **-ta** [tə]) ultimátum *m*

ultimo ['ʌltɪ,mo] *adv* de o en el mes próximo pasado

ultrahigh [,ʌltrə'haɪ] *adj* (electron) ultraelevado

ultrasound ['ʌltrə,saʊnd] *s* sonido silencioso

ultraviolet [,ʌltrə'vaɪ•əlɪt] *adj & s* ultravioleta, ultraviolado

umbilical cord [ʌm'bɪlɪkəl] *s* cordón *m* umbilical

umbrage ['ʌmbrɪdʒ] *s*—**to take umbrage at** resentirse de o por

umbrella [ʌm'brɛlə] *s* paraguas *m;* (mil) sombrilla protectora

umbrella man *s* paragüero

umbrella stand *s* paragüero

umlaut ['ʊmlaʊt] *s* inflexión vocálica, metafonía; (*mark*) diéresis *f* ‖ *tr* inflexionar; escribir con diéresis

umpire ['ʌmpaɪr] *s* árbitro ‖ *tr & intr* arbitrar

UN ['ju'ɛn] *s* (letterword) ONU *f*

unable [ʌn'ebəl] *adj* incapaz, imposibilitado; **to be unable to** no poder

unabridged [,ʌnə'brɪdʒd] *adj* sin abreviar, íntegro

unaccented [ʌn'æksɛntɪd] o [,ʌnæk'sɛntɪd] *adj* inacentuado

unaccountable [,ʌnə'kaʊntəbəl] *adj* inexplicable; irresponsable

unaccounted-for [,ʌnə'kaʊntɪd,fɔr] *adj* inexplicado; no hallado

unaccustomed [,ʌnə'kʌstəmd] *adj* (*unusual*) desacostumbrado; inhabituado

unafraid [,ʌnə'fred] *adj* sin miedo

unaligned [,ʌnə'laɪnd] *adj* no empeñado

unanimity [,junə'nɪmɪti] *s* unanimidad

unanimous [ju'nænɪməs] *adj* unánime

unanswerable [ʌn'ænsərəbəl] *adj* incontestable; (*argument*) incontrastable

unappreciative [,ʌnə'priʃɪ,etɪv] *adj* ingrato, desagradecido

unapproachable [,ʌnə'protʃəbəl] *adj* inabordable; incomparable, único

unarmed [ʌn'ɑrmd] *adj* desarmado, inerme

unascertainable [ʌn,æsər'tenəbəl] *adj* inaveriguable

unasked [ʌn'æskt] *adj* no solicitado; no convidado

unassembled [,ʌnə'sɛmbəld] *adj* desmontado, desarmado

unassuming [,ʌnə'sumɪŋ] o [,ʌnə'sjumɪŋ] *adj* modesto, sencillo

unattached [,ʌnə'tætʃt] *adj* independiente; (*loose*) suelto; (*not engaged to be married*) no prometido; (law) no embargado; (mil & nav) de reemplazo

unattainable [,ʌnə'tenəbəl] *adj* inasequible, inalcanzable

unattractive [,ʌnə'træktɪv] *adj* poco atrayente, desairado

unavailable [,ʌnə'veləbəl] *adj* indisponible

unavailing [,ʌnə'velɪŋ] *adj* ineficaz, inútil, vano

unavoidable [,ʌnə'vɔɪdəbəl] *adj* inevitable, ineluctable

unaware [,ʌnə'wɛr] *adj*—**to be unaware of** no estar al corriente de ‖ *adv* de improviso; sin saberlo

unawares [,ʌnə'wɛrz] *adv* (*unexpectedly*) de improviso; (*unknowingly*) sin saberlo

unbalanced [ʌn'bælənst] *adj* desequilibrado

unbandage [ʌn'bændɪdʒ] *tr* desvendar

un•bar [ʌn'bɑr] *v* (*pret & pp* **-barred;** *ger* **-barring**) *tr* desatrancar

unbearable [ʌn'bɛrəbəl] *adj* inaguantable

unbeatable [ʌn'bitəbəl] *adj* imbatible

unbecoming [,ʌnbɪ'kʌmɪŋ] *adj* inconveniente, indecente; que sienta mal

unbelievable [,ʌnbɪ'livəbəl] *adj* increíble

unbending [ʌn'bɛndɪŋ] *adj* inflexible

unbiased o **unbiassed** [ʌn'baɪ•əst] *adj* imparcial

un•bind [ʌn'baɪnd] *v* (*pret & pp* **-bound** ['baʊnd]) *tr* desatar

unbleached [ʌn'blitʃt] *adj* sin blanquear

unbolt [ʌn'bolt] *tr* desatrancar (*p.ej., una puerta*); (*to remove the bolts from*) desempernar

unborn [ʌn'bɔrn] *adj* no nacido, por nacer, futuro

unbosom [ʌn'buzəm] *tr* confesar, descubrir (*sus pensamientos, sus secretos*); **to unbosom oneself** abrir su pecho, desahogarse

unbound [ʌn'baʊnd] *adj* (*book*) sin encuadernar

unbreakable [ʌn'brekəbəl] *adj* irrompible

unbuckle [ʌn'bʌkəl] *tr* deshebillar

unburden [ʌn'bʌrdən] *tr* descargar; **to unburden oneself** desahogarse de

unburied [ʌn'bɛrid] *adj* insepulto

unbutton [ʌn'bʌtən] *tr* desabotonar

uncalled-for [ʌn'kɔld,fɔr] *adj* innecesario, no justificado; insolente

uncanny [ʌn'kæni] *adj* espectral, misterioso; extraordinario, maravilloso

uncared-for [ʌn'kɛrd,fɔr] *adj* desamparado, descuidado, abandonado

unceasing [ʌn'sisɪŋ] *adj* incesante

unceremonious [,ʌnsɛri'moni•əs] *adj* incere-monioso

uncertain [ʌn'sʌrtən] *adj* incierto

uncertain•ty [ʌn'sʌrtənti] *s* (*pl* -**ties**) incerti-dumbre

unchain [ʌn'tʃen] *tr* desencadenar

unchangeable [ʌn'tʃendʒəbəl] *adj* incambi-able, inmutable

uncharted [ʌn'tʃɑrtɪd] *adj* inexplorado

unchecked [ʌn'tʃɛkt] *adj* no verificado; no refrenado; desenfrenado

uncivilized [ʌn'sɪvɪ,laɪzd] *adj* incivilizado

unclad [ʌn'klæd] *adj* desvestido

unclaimed [ʌn'klemd] *adj* sin reclamar; (*mail*) rechazado, sobrante

unclasp [ʌn'klæsp] *tr* desabrochar

unclassified [ʌn'klæsɪ,faɪd] *adj* no clasifi-cado; no clasificado como secreto

uncle ['ʌŋkəl] *s* tío

unclean [ʌn'klin] *adj* desaseado, sucio

un•clog [ʌn'klɑg] *v* (*pret & pp* -**clogged;** *ger* -**clogging**) *tr* desatrancar

unclouded [ʌn'klaʊdɪd] *adj* despejado

uncollectible [,ʌnkə'lɛktɪbəl] *adj* incobrable

uncomfortable [ʌn'kʌmfərtəbəl] *adj* inco-modo

uncommitted [,ʌnkə'mɪtɪd] *adj* no empe-ñado, no comprometido

uncommon [ʌn'kɑmən] *adj* raro, poco común

uncompromising [ʌn'kɑmprə,maɪzɪŋ] *adj* intransigente

unconcerned [,ʌnkən'sʌrnd] *adj* despreocu-pado, indiferente

unconditional [,ʌnkən'dɪʃənəl] *adj* incondi-cional

uncongenial [,ʌnkən'dʒinɪ•əl] *adj* antipático; incompatible; desagradable

unconquerable [ʌn'kɑŋkərəbəl] *adj* in-conquistable

unconquered [ʌn'kɑŋkərd] *adj* invicto

unconscionable [ʌn'kɑnʃənəbəl] *adj* inescru-puloso; desrazonable, excesivo

unconscious [ʌn'kɑnʃəs] *adj* inconsciente; (*temporarily deprived of consciousness*) desmayado; (*unintentional*) involuntario

unconsciousness [ʌn'kɑnʃəsnɪs] *s* incon-sciencia; desmayo

unconstitutional [,ʌnkɑnstɪ'tjuʃənəl] *adj* in-constitucional

uncontrollable [,ʌnkən'troləbəl] *adj* ingober-nable; incontrolable; (*laughter*) inextingu-ible

unconventional [,ʌnkən'vɛnʃənəl] *adj* no convencional

uncork [ʌn'kɔrk] *tr* destapar, descorchar

uncouth [ʌn'kuθ] *adj* desgarbado, torpe, rústico

uncover [ʌn'kʌvər] *tr* descubrir

unction ['ʌŋkʃən] *s* (*anointing*) unción; sua-vidad hipócrita

unctuous ['ʌŋktʃʊ•əs] *adj* untuoso; zalamero

uncultivated [ʌn'kʌltɪ,vetɪd] *adj* inculto (*que no está cultivado; rústico, grosero*)

uncultured [ʌn'kʌltʃərd] *adj* inculto, rústico, grosero

uncut [ʌn'kʌt] *adj* sin cortar; (*book or mag-azine*) intonso

undamaged [ʌn'dæmɪdʒd] *adj* indemne, ileso

undaunted [ʌn'dɔntɪd] *adj* impávido, deno-dado

undecided [,ʌndɪ'saɪdɪd] *adj* indeciso

undefeated [,ʌndɪ'fitɪd] *adj* invicto

undefended [,ʌndɪ'fɛndɪd] *adj* indefenso

undefiled [,ʌndɪ'faɪld] *adj* inmaculado, im-poluto

undeniable [,ʌndɪ'naɪ•əbəl] *adj* innegable

under ['ʌndər] *adj* inferior; (*clothing*) inte-rior ‖ *adv* debajo; más abajo; **to go under** hundirse; (*to fail*) fracasar ‖ *prep* bajo, debajo de; inferior a; **under full sail** a vela llena; **under lock and key** bajo llave; **under oath** bajo juramento; **under pen-alty of death** so pena de muerte; **under sail** a vela; **under separate cover** por separado, bajo cubierta separada; **under steam** bajo presión; **under the hand and seal of** firmado y sellado por; **under the nose of** en las barbas de; **under the weather** algo indispuesto; **under way** en camino

un'der•age' *adj* menor de edad

un'der•bid' *v* (*pret & pp* -**bid;** *ger* -**bidding**) *tr* ofrecer menos que

un'der•brush' *s* maleza

un'der•car'riage *s* carro inferior; (aer) tren *m* de aterrizaje

un'der•clothes' *s* ropa interior

un'der•con•sump'tion *s* infraconsumo

un'der•cov'er *adj* secreto

underdeveloped [,ʌndərdɪ'vɛləpt] *adj* sub-desarrollado

un'der•dog' *s* víctima, perdidoso; **the un-derdogs** los de abajo

underdone ['ʌndər,dʌn] *adj* a medio asar, soasado

un'der•es'ti•mate' *tr* subestimar

un'der•gar'ment *s* prenda de vestir interior

un'der•go' *v* (*pret* -**went;** *pp* -**gone**) *tr* ex-perimentar; sufrir, padecer

un'der•grad'uate *adj* no graduado; (*course*) para el bachillerato ‖ *s* alumno no gra-duado de universidad

un'der•ground' *adj* subterráneo; clandestino ‖ *adv* bajo tierra; ocultamente ‖ *s* ferrocar-ril subterráneo; movimiento de resistencia

un'der•growth' *s* maleza

underhanded ['ʌndər'hændɪd] *adj* clan-destino, taimado, disimulado

un'der•line' o **un'der•line'** *tr* subrayar

underling ['ʌndərlɪŋ] *s* subordinado, secuaz *m* servil

un'der•mine' *tr* socavar, minar

underneath [,ʌndər'niθ] *adj* inferior, más bajo ‖ *adv* debajo ‖ *prep* debajo de ‖ *s* parte baja, superficie *f* inferior

undernourished [,ʌndər'nʌrɪʃt] *adj* desnu-trido

un'der•nour'ish•ment *s* desnutrición

un'der•pass' *s* paso inferior

un'der•pay' *s* pago insuficiente ‖ *v* (*pret & pp* -**paid**) *tr & intr* pagar insuficientemente

un'der•pin' *v* (*pret* & *pp* **-pinned;** *ger* **-pinning**) *tr* apuntalar, socalzar

underprivileged [ˌʌndərˈprɪvɪlɪdʒd] *adj* desheredado, desamparado

un'der•rate' *tr* menospreciar

un'der•score' *tr* subrayar

un'der•sea' *adj* submarino ‖ **un'der•sea'** *adv* debajo de la superficie del mar

un'der•sec're•tar'y *s* (*pl* **-ies**) subsecretario

un'der•sell' *v* (*pret* & *pp* **-sold**) *tr* vender a menor precio que; (*for less than the actual value*) malbaratar

un'der•shirt' *s* camiseta

undersigned [ˈʌndərˌsaɪnd] *adj* infrascrito, subscrito

un'der•skirt' *s* enaguas, refajo

un'der•stand' *v* (*pret* & *pp* **-stood**) *tr* entender, comprender; sobrentender, subentender (*una cosa que no está expresa*) ‖ *intr* entender, comprender

understandable [ˌʌndərˈstændəbəl] *adj* comprensible

understanding [ˌʌndərˈstændɪŋ] *adj* entendedor; (*tolerant, sympathetic*) comprensivo ‖ *s* comprensión; (*intellectual faculty, mind*) entendimiento; (*agreement*) acuerdo; **to come to an understanding** llegar a un acuerdo

un'der•stud'y *s* (*pl* **-ies**) sobresaliente *mf*

un'der•take' *v* (*pret* **-took;** *pp* **-taken**) *tr* emprender; (*to agree to perform*) comprometerse a

undertaker [ˌʌndərˈtekər] o [ˈʌndərˌtekər] *s* empresario ‖ (ˈʌndərˌtekər) *s* empresario de pompas fúnebres, director *m* de funeraria

undertaking [ˌʌndərˈtekɪŋ] *s* (*task*) empresa; (*pledge*) empeño ‖ [ˈʌndərˌtekɪŋ] *s* (*business of funeral director*) funeraria

un'der•tak'ing establishment *s* funeraria, empresa de pompas fúnebres

un'der•tone' *s* voz baja; (*background sound*) fondo; color apagado

un'der•tow' *s* (*countercurrent below surface*) contracorriente *f*; (*on the beach*) resaca

un'der•wear' *s* ropa interior, prendas interiores

un'der•world' *s* (*criminal world*) inframundo, bajos fondos sociales; (*the earth*) mundo terrenal; (*pagan world of the dead*) averno, infierno; (*world under the water*) mundo submarino; (*opposite side of earth*) antípodas

un'der•write' *v* (*pret* **-wrote;** *pp* **-written**) *tr* subscribir; (*to insure*) asegurar

un'der•writ'er *s* subscritor *m;* asegurador *m;* compañía aseguradora

undeserved [ˌʌndɪˈzɑrvd] *adj* inmerecido

undesirable [ˌʌndɪˈzaɪrəbəl] *adj* & *s* indeseable *mf*

undetachable [ˌʌndɪˈtætʃəbəl] *adj* inamovible

undignified [ʌnˈdɪgnɪˌfaɪd] *adj* poco digno, poco grave, indecoroso

undiscernible [ˌʌndɪˈzɑrnɪbəl] o [ˌʌndɪˈsɑrnəbəl] *adj* imperceptible, invisible

un•do' *v* (*pret* **-did;** *pp* **-done**) *tr* deshacer; anular, borrar; arruinar

undoing [ʌnˈduɪŋ] *s* destrucción, pérdida, ruina

undone [ʌnˈdʌn] *adj* sin hacer, por hacer; **to come undone** deshacerse, desatarse; **to leave nothing undone** no dejar nada por hacer

undoubtedly [ʌnˈdautɪdli] *adv* indudablemente, sin duda

undramatic [ˌʌndrəˈmætɪk] *adj* poco dramático

undress [ˈʌnˌdrɛs] o [ʌnˈdrɛs] *s* traje *m* de casa; vestido de calle; (mil) traje de cuartel ‖ [ʌnˈdrɛs] *tr* desnudar; desvendar (*una herida*) ‖ desnudarse

undrinkable [ʌnˈdrɪŋkəbəl] *adj* impotable

undue [ʌnˈdju] *adj* indebido

undulate [ˈʌndjəˌlet] *intr* ondular

unduly [ʌnˈdjuli] *adv* indebidamente

undying [ʌnˈdaɪɪŋ] *adj* imperecedero

unearned increment [ʌnˈɑrnd] *s* plusvalía

unearth [ʌnˈɑrθ] *tr* desenterrar

unearthly [ʌnˈɑrθli] *adj* sobrenatural; fantástico, espectral; extraordinario

uneasy [ʌnˈizi] *adj* (*worried*) inquieto; (*constrained*) encogido, embarazado

uneatable [ʌnˈitəbəl] *adj* incomible

uneconomic(al) [ˌʌnikəˈnɑmɪk(əl)] *adj* antieconómico

uneducated [ʌnˈɛdjəˌketɪd] *adj* ineducado, sin instrucción; chontal

unemployed [ˌʌnɛmˈplɔɪd] *adj* desocupado, desempleado; improductivo

unemployment [ˌʌnɛmˈplɔɪmənt] *s* desocupación, desempleo

unemployment insurance *s* seguro de desempleo o desocupación, seguro contra el paro obrero

unending [ʌnˈɛndɪŋ] *adj* interminable

unequal [ʌnˈikwəl] *adj* desigual; **to be unequal to** (*a task*) no estar a la altura de

unequaled o **unequalled** [ʌnˈikwəld] *adj* inigualado

unerring [ʌnˈɑrɪŋ] o [ʌnˈɛrɪŋ] *adj* infalible, seguro

unessential [ˌʌnɛsɛnʃəl] *adj* no esencial

uneven [ʌnˈivən] *adj* desigual; (*number*) impar

unexceptionable [ˌʌnɛkˈsɛpʃənəbəl] *adj* intachable, irreprensible

unexpected [ˌʌnɛkˈspɛktɪd] *adj* inesperado

unexplained [ˌʌnɛkˈsplend] *adj* inexplicado

unexplored [ˌʌnɛkˈsplord] *adj* inexplorado

unexposed [ˌʌnɛkˈspozd] *adj* (phot) inexpuesto

unfading [ʌnˈfedɪŋ] *adj* inmarcesible

unfailing [ʌnˈfelɪŋ] *adj* indefectible; (*inexhaustible*) inagotable

unfair [ʌnˈfɛr] *adj* injusto; desleal, doble, falso; (sport) sucio

unfaithful [ʌnˈfeθfəl] *adj* infiel

unfamiliar [ˌʌnfəˈmɪljər] *adj* poco familiar; poco familiarizado

unfasten [ʌnfˈæsən] *tr* desatacar, desatar, soltar

unfathomable [ʌnˈfæðəməbəl] *adj* insondable

unfavorable [ʌnˈfevərəbəl] *adj* desfavorable

unfeathered [ʌn'fɛðərd] *adj* implume
unfeeling [ʌn'filɪŋ] *adj* insensible
unfetter [ʌn'fɛtər] *tr* desencadenar
unfilled [ʌn'fɪld] *adj* no lleno; por complir, pendiente
unfinished [ʌn'fɪnɪʃt] *adj* sin acabar; imperfecto, mal acabado; (*business*) pendiente
unfit [ʌn'fɪt] *adj* impropio, incapaz, inhábil; inservible, inútil
unfold [ʌn'fold] *tr* desplegar ‖ *intr* desplegarse
unforeseeable [ˌʌnfor'si•əbəl] *adj* imprevisible
unforeseen [ˌʌnfor'sin] *adj* imprevisto
unforgettable [ˌʌnfər'gɛtəbəl] *adj* inolvidable
unforgivable [ˌʌnfər'gɪvəbəl] *adj* imperdonable
unfortunate [ʌn'fɔrtjənɪt] *adj* & *s* desgraciado
unfounded [ʌn'faundɪd] *adj* infundado
unfreeze [ʌn'friz] *tr* deshelar; desbloquear (*el crédito*)
unfriendly [ʌn'frɛndli] *adj* inamistoso; desfavorable
unfruitful [ʌn'frutfəl] *adj* infructuoso
unfulfilled [ˌʌnfəl'fɪld] *adj* incumplido
unfurl [ʌn'fʌrl] *tr* desplegar, extender
unfurnished [ʌn'fʌrnɪʃt] *adj* desamueblado
ungainly [ʌn'genli] *adj* desgarbado, desmañado
ungentlemanly [ʌn'dʒɛntəlmənli] *adj* poco caballeroso, descortés
ungird [ʌn'gʌrd] *tr* desceñir
ungodly [ʌn'gɑdli] *adj* impío, irreligioso; (*dreadful*) (coll) atroz
ungracious [ʌn'greʃəs] *adj* descortés; desagradable
ungrammatical [ˌʌngrə'mætɪkəl] *adj* ingramatical
ungrateful [ʌn'gretfəl] *adj* ingrato, desagradecido
ungrudgingly [ʌn'grʌdʒɪŋli] *adj* de buena gana, sin quejarse
unguarded [ʌn'gɑrdɪd] *adj* indefenso; descuidado; (*moment*) de inadvertencia
unguent ['ʌŋgwənt] *s* ungüento
unhandy [ʌn'hændi] *adj* inmanejable; (*awkward*) desmañado
unhappiness [ʌn'hæpɪnɪs] *s* infelicidad
unhap•py [ʌn'hæpi] *adj* (*comp* **-pier;** *super* **-piest**) infeliz; (*unlucky*) desgraciado; (*fateful*) aciago
unharmed [ʌn'hɑrmd] *adj* indemne
unharmonious [ˌʌnhɑr'moni•əs] *adj* inarmónico
unharness [ʌn'hɑrnɪs] *tr* desenjaezar, desguarnecer; desenganchar
unhealthy [ʌn'hɛlθi] *adj* malsano
unheard-of [ʌn'hɑrd,ɑv] *adj* inaudito
unhinge [ʌn'hɪndʒ] *tr* desgonzar; (fig) desequilibrar, trastornar
unhitch [ʌn'hɪtʃ] *tr* desenganchar
unho•ly [ʌn'holi] *adj* (*comp* **-lier;** *super* **-liest**) impío, malo, profano
unhook [ʌn'huk] *tr* desabrochar; desenganchar; (*to take down from a hook*) descolgar

unhoped-for [ʌn'hopt,fɔr] *adj* inesperado, no esperado
unhorse [ʌn'hɔrs] *tr* desarzonar
unhurt [ʌn'hʌrt] *adj* incólume, ileso
unicorn ['juni,kɔrn] *s* unicornio
unidentified flying object (UFO) *s* objeto volante no identificado (ovni)
unification [ˌjunɪfɪ'keʃən] *s* unificación
uniform ['juni,fɔrm] *adj* & *s* uniforme *m* ‖ *tr* uniformar
uniformi•ty [ˌjuni'fɔrmɪti] *s* (*pl* **-ties**) uniformidad
uni•fy ['juni,faɪ] *v* (*pret* & *pp* **-fied**) *tr* unificar
unilaterai [ˌjuni'lætərəl] *adj* unilateral
unimpeachable [ˌʌnɪm'pitʃəbəl] *adj* irrecusable, intachable
unimportant [ˌʌnɪm'pɔrtənt] *adj* poco importante; intrascendente
uninhabited [ˌʌnɪn'hæbɪtɪd] *adj* inhabitado
uninspired [ˌʌnɪn'spaɪrd] *adj* sin inspiración; aburrido, fastidioso
unintelligent [ˌʌnɪn'tɛlɪdʒənt] *adj* ininteligente
unintelligible [ˌʌnɪn'tɛlɪdʒɪbəl] *adj* ininteligible
uninterested [ʌn'ɪntrɪstɪd] o [ʌn'ɪntə,rɛstɪd] *adj* desinteresado
uninteresting [ʌn'ɪntə,rɛstɪŋ] *adj* poco interesante
uninterrupted [ˌʌnɪntə'rʌptɪd] *adj* ininterrumpido
union ['junjən] *s* unión; (*organization of workmen*) gremio obrero, sindicato; unión matrimonial
unionize ['junjə,naɪz] *tr* agremiar ‖ *intr* agremiarse
union shop *s* taller *m* de obreros agremiados
union suit *s* traje *m* interior de una sola pieza
unique [ju'nik] *adj* único
unison ['junisən] *s* unisonancia; **in unison (with)** al unísono (de)
unit ['junit] *adj* unitario ‖ *s* unidad; (mach & elec) grupo
unite [ju'naɪt] *tr* unir ‖ *intr* unirse
united [ju'naɪtɪd] *adj* unido
United Kingdom *s* Reino Unido
United Nations *spl* Naciones Unidas
United States *adj* estadounidense ‖ **the United States** *s* los Estados Unidos *mpl*; Estados Unidos *msg*
uni•ty ['junɪti] *s* (*pl* **-ties**) unidad
univ. *abbr* **universal, university**
universal [ˌjuni'vʌrsəl] *adj* universal
universal joint *s* cardán *m*, junta universal
universal product code (UPC) *s* código universal de producto
universe ['juni,vʌrs] *s* universo
universi•ty [ˌjuni'vʌrsiti] *adj* universitario ‖ *s* (*pl* **-ties**) universidad
unjust [ʌn'dʒʌst] *adj* injusto
unjustified [ʌn'dʒʌstɪ,faɪd] *adj* injustificado
unkempt [ʌn'kɛmpt] *adj* despeinado
unkind [ʌn'kaɪnd] *adj* poco amable; duro, despiadado
unknowable [ʌn'no•əbəl] *adj* inconocible, insabible

un
un

unknowingly [ʌn'noˑɪŋli] *adv* desconocidamente, sin saberlo

unknown [ʌn'non] *adj* desconocido, ignoto, incógnito ‖ *s* desconocido; (math) incógnita

unknown quantity *s* (math & fig) incógnita

unknown soldier *s* soldado desconocido

unlace [ʌn'les] *tr* desenlazar; desatar (*los cordones del zapato*)

unlatch [ʌn'læt∫] *tr* abrir levantando el picaporte

unlawful [ʌn'lɔfəl] *adj* ilegal

unleaded gasoline [ʌn'lɛdɪd] *s* gasolina sin plomo

unleash [ʌn'li∫] *tr* destraillar; soltar, desencadenar

unleavened [ʌn'lɛvənd] *adj* ázimo

unless [ʌn'lɛs] *conj* a menos que, a no ser que

unlettered [ʌn'lɛtərd] *adj* iletrado, indocto; sin rotular; (*illiterate*) analfabeto

unlike [ʌn'laɪk] *adj* desemejante; desemejante de; (*poles of a magnet*) (elec) de nombres contrarios; (elec) de signo contrario ‖ *prep* a diferencia de

unlikely [ʌn'laɪkli] *adj* improbable

unlimber [ʌn'lɪmbər] *tr* preparar para la acción ‖ *intr* prepararse para la acción

unlined [ʌn'laɪnd] *adj* (*coat*) sin forro; (*paper*) sin rayar; (*face*) sin arrugas

unload [ʌn'lod] *tr* descargar; (coll) deshacerse de ‖ *intr* descargar

unloading [ʌn'lodɪŋ] *s* descarga, descargue m

unlock [ʌn'lak] *tr* abrir (*p.ej., una puerta*); (typ) desapretar

unloose [ʌn'lus] *tr* aflojar, soltar, desatar

unloved [ʌn'lʌvd] *adj* desamado

unlovely [ʌn'lʌvli] *adj* desgraciado

unluck·y [ʌn'lʌki] *adj* (*comp* -ier; *super* -iest) desgraciado, desdichado; aciago, nefasto; de mala suerte; **to be unlucky** quedar mal parado

un·make [ʌn'mek] *v* (*pret & pp* -made ['med]) *tr* deshacer; destruir

unmanageable [ʌn'mænɪdʒəbəl] *adj* inmanejable

unmanly [ʌn'mænli] *adj* afeminado; bajo, cobarde

unmannerly [ʌn'mænərli] *adj* descortés, malcriado

unmarketable [ʌn'markɪtəbəl] *adj* incomerciable

unmarriageable [ʌn'mærɪdʒəbəl] *adj* incasable

unmarried [ʌn'mærid] *adj* soltero

unmask [ʌn'mæsk] *tr* desenmascarar ‖ *intr* desenmascararse

unmatchable [ʌn'mæt∫əbəl] *adj* incomparable, sin igual; (*price*) incompetible

unmerciful [ʌn'mʌrsɪfəl] *adj* despiadado, inclemente

unmesh [ʌn'mɛ∫] *tr* desengranar ‖ *intr* desengranarse

unmindful [ʌn'maɪndfəl] *adj* desatento, descuidado; **to be unmindful of** olvidar, no pensar en

unmistakable [ˌʌnmɪs'tekəbəl] *adj* inequívoco, inconfundible

unmixed [ʌn'mɪkst] *adj* puro, sin mezcla

unmoor [ʌn'mʊr] *tr* desamarrar (*un buque*); desaferrar (*las áncoras*)

unmotivated [ˌʌn'motɪˌvetɪd] *adj* inmotivado

unmoved [ʌn'muvd] *adj* fijo, inmoto; impasible

unmuzzle [ˌʌn'mʌzəl] *tr* desbozalar

unnatural [ʌn'næt∫ərəl] *adj* innatural; (*artificial, forced*) afectado; anormal; inhumano

unnecessary [ʌn'nɛsəˌsɛri] *adj* innecessario

unnerve [ʌn'nʌrv] *tr* acobardar, trastornar

unnoticeable [ʌn'notɪsəbəl] *adj* imperceptible

unnoticed [ʌn'notɪst] *adj* inadvertido

unobliging [ˌʌnə'blaɪdʒɪŋ] *adj* poco servicial, poco amable

unobserved [ˌʌnəb'zʌrvd] *adj* inadvertido, sin ser visto

unobtainable [ˌʌnəb'tenəbəl] *adj* inencontrable, inasequible

unobtrusive [ˌʌnəb'trusɪv] *adj* discreto, reservado

unoccupied [ʌn'akjəˌpaɪd] *adj* libre, vacante; (*not busy*) desocupado

unofficial [ˌʌnə'fɪ∫əl] *adj* extraoficial, oficioso

unopened [ʌn'opənd] *adj* sin abrir; (*book*) no cortado

unorthodox [ʌn'ɔrθəˌdaks] *adj* inortodoxo

unpack [ʌn'pæk] *tr* desembalar, desempaquetar

unpalatable [ʌn'pælətəbəl] *adj* desabrido, ingustable

unparalleled [ʌn'pærəˌlɛld] *adj* incomparable, sin par, sin igual

unpardonable [ʌn'pardənəbəl] *adj* imperdonable

unpatriotic [ˌʌnpetrɪ'atɪk] o [ˌʌnpætrɪ'atɪk] *adj* antipatriótico

unperceived [ˌʌnpər'sivd] *adj* inadvertido

unperturbable [ˌʌnpər'tʌrbəbəl] *adj* infracto, imperturbable

unpleasant [ʌn'plɛzənt] *adj* antipático, desagradable; sangrigordo, sangripesado; bofe (CAm)

unpopular [ʌn'papjələr] *adj* impopular

unpopularity [ˌʌnˌpapjə'lærɪti] *s* impopularidad

unprecedented [ʌn'prɛsɪˌdɛntɪd] *adj* sin precedente, inaudito

unprejudiced [ʌn'prɛdʒədɪst] *adj* sin prejuicios, imparcial

unpremeditated [ˌʌnprɪ'mɛdɪˌtetɪd] *adj* impremeditado

unprepared [ˌʌnprɪ'pɛrd] *adj* desprevenido; falto de preparación

unprepossessing [ˌʌnpripə'zɛsɪŋ] *adj* poco atrayente

unpresentable [ˌʌnprɪ'zɛntəbəl] *adj* impresentable

unpretentious [ˌʌnprɪ'tɛn∫əs] *adj* modesto, sencillo

unprincipled [ʌn'prɪnsɪpəld] *adj* sin principios, sin conciencia

unproductive [,ʌnprə'dʌktɪv] *adj* improductivo

unprofitable [ʌn'prɑfɪtəbəl] *adj* no provechoso, inútil

unpronounceable [,ʌnprə'naʊnsəbəl] *adj* impronunciable

unpropitious [,ʌnprə'pɪʃəs] *adj* impropicio

unpublished [ʌn'pʌblɪʃt] *adj* inédito

unpunished [ʌn'pʌnɪʃt] *adj* impune

unpurchasable [ʌn'pʌrtʃəsəbəl] *adj* incomprable

unquenchable [ʌn'kwɛntʃəbəl] *adj* inextinguible

unquestionable [ʌn'kwɛstʃənəbəl] *adj* incuestionable

unrav•el [ʌn'rævəl] *v* (*pret & pp* **-eled** o **-elled**; *ger* **-eling** o **-elling**) *tr* deshebrar; desenredar, desenmarañar ‖ *intr* desenredarse, desenmarañarse

unreachable [ʌn'ritʃəbəl] *adj* inalcanzable

unreal [ʌn'ri•əl] *adj* irreal

unreali•ty [,ʌnrɪ,ælɪti] *s* (*pl* **-ties**) irrealidad

unreasonable [ʌn'rizənəbəl] *adj* irrazonable, desrazonable

unrecognizable [ʌn'rɛkəg,naɪzəbəl] *adj* irreconocible

unreel [ʌn'ril] *tr* desenrollar ‖ *intr* desenrollarse

unrefined [,ʌnrɪ,faɪnd] *adj* no refinado, impuro; grosero, rudo, tosco

unrelenting [,ʌnrɪ'lɛntɪŋ] *adj* inexorable, inflexible, implacable

unreliable [,ʌnrɪ'laɪ•əbəl] *adj* indigno de confianza, informal

unremitting [,ʌnrɪ'mɪtɪŋ] *adj* constante, incesante; infatigable

unrenewable [,ʌnrɪ'nju•əbəl] o [,ʌnrɪ'nu•əbəl] *adj* irrenovable; (com) improrrogable

unrented [ʌn'rɛntɪd] *adj* desalquilado

unrepentant [,ʌnrɪ'pɛntənt] *adj* impenitente

unrequited love [,ʌnrɪ'kwaɪtɪd] *s* amor no correspondido

unresponsive [,ʌnrɪ'spɑnsɪv] *adj* insensible, frío, desinteresado

unrest [ʌn'rɛst] *s* intranquilidad, inquietud; alboroto, desorden *m*

un•rig [ʌn'rɪg] *v* (*pret & pp* **-rigged;** *ger* **-rigging**) *tr* (naut) desaparejar

unrighteous [ʌn'raɪtʃəs] *adj* injusto, malvado, vicioso

unripe [ʌn'raɪp] *adj* inmaturo, verde; prematuro, precoz

unrivaled o **unrivalled** [ʌn'raɪvəld] *adj* sin rival, sin par

unroll [ʌn'rol] *tr* desenrollar, desplegar

unromantic [,ʌnro'mæntɪk] *adj* poco romántico

unruffled [ʌn'rʌfəld] *adj* tranquilo, sereno

unruly [ʌn'ruli] *adj* ingobernable, indómito, revoltoso

unsaddle [ʌn'sædəl] *tr* desensillar (*un caballo*); desarzonar (*al jinete*)

unsafe [ʌn'sef] *adj* inseguro, peligroso

unsaid [ʌn'sɛd] *adj* callado, no dicho

unsalable [ʌn'seləbəl] *adj* invendible

unsanitary [ʌn'sænɪ,tɛri] *adj* antihigiénico, insalubre

unsatisfactory [ʌn,sætɪs'fæktəri] *adj* insatisfactorio, poco satisfactorio

unsatisfied [ʌn'sætɪs,faɪd] *adj* insatisfecho

unsavory [ʌn'sevəri] *adj* desabrido; (fig) infame, deshonroso

unscathed [ʌn'skeðd] *adj* ileso, sano y salvo

unscientific [,ʌnsaɪ•ən'tɪfɪk] *adj* antiscientífico

unscrew [ʌn'skru] *tr* destornillar ‖ *intr* destornillarse

unscrupulous [ʌn'skrupjələs] *adj* inescrupuloso

unseal [ʌn'sil] *tr* desellar; (fig) abrir

unseasonable [ʌn'sizənəbəl] *adj* intempestivo, inoportuno

unseaworthy [ʌn'si,wʌrði] *adj* innavegable

unseemly [ʌn'simli] *adj* impropio, indecoroso, indigno

unseen [ʌn'sin] *adj* invisible, oculto

unselfish [ʌn'sɛlfɪʃ] *adj* desinteresado, generoso, altruísta

unsettled [ʌn'sɛtəld] *adj* inhabitado, despoblado; sin residencia fija; indeciso; descompuesto; (*bills*) por pagar

unshackle [ʌn'ʃækəl] *tr* desherrar, desencadenar

unshaken [ʌn'ʃekən] *adj* imperturbado

unshapely [ʌn'ʃepli] *adj* desproporcionado, mal formado

unshatterable [ʌn'ʃætərəbəl] *adj* inastillable

unshaven [ʌn'ʃevən] *adj* sin afeitar

unsheathe [ʌn'ʃið] *tr* desenvainar

unshod [ʌn'ʃɑd] *adj* descalzo; (*horse*) desherrado

unshrinkable [ʌn'ʃrɪŋkəbəl] *adj* inencogible

unsightly [ʌn'saɪtli] *adj* feo, de aspecto malo, repugnante

unsinkable [ʌn'sɪŋkəbəl] *adj* insumergible

unskilled [ʌn'skɪld] *adj* inexperto

unskilled laborer *s* bracero, peón *m*

unskillful [ʌn'skɪlfəl] *adj* desmañado

unsnarl [ʌn'snɑrl] *tr* desenredar

unsociable [ʌn'soʃəbəl] *adj* insociable, huraño

unsold [ʌn'sold] *adj* invendido

unsolder [ʌn'sɑdər] *tr* desoldar; (fig) desunir, separar

unsophisticated [,ʌnsə'fɪstɪ,ketɪd] *adj* ingenuo, natural, sencillo

unsound [ʌn'saʊnd] *adj* poco firme; falso, erróneo; (*decayed*) podrido; (*sleep*) ligero

unsown [ʌn'son] *adj* yermo, no sembrado

unspeakable [ʌn'spikəbəl] *adj* indecible, inefable; (*atrocious, infamous*) incalificable

unsportsmanlike [ʌn'sportsmən,laɪk] *adj* antideportivo

unstable [ʌn'stebəl] *adj* inestable

unsteady [ʌn'stɛdi] *adj* inseguro, inestable; irresoluto, inconstante; poco juicioso

unstinted [ʌn'stɪntɪd] *adj* no escatimado, generoso, liberal

unstitch [ʌn'stɪtʃ] *tr* descoser

un•stop [ʌn'stɑp] *v* (*pret & pp* **-stopped;** *ger* **-stopping**) *tr* destaponar

unstressed [ʌn'strɛst] *adj* sin énfasis; (*syllable*) inacentuado

un
un

unstrung [ʌnˈstrʌŋ] *adj* nervioso, trastornado

unsuccessful [ˌʌnsəkˈsɛsfəl] *adj* (*person*) desairado; (*undertaking*) impróspero; **to be unsuccessful** no tener éxito

unsuitable [ʌnˈsutəbəl] o [ʌnˈsjutəbəl] *adj* inadecuado, inconveniente

unsurpassable [ˌʌnsərˈpæsəbəl] *adj* insuperable

unsuspected [ˌʌnsəsˈpɛktɪd] *adj* insospechado

unswerving [ʌnˈswʌrvɪŋ] *adj* firme, inmutable, resoluto

unsymmetrical [ˌʌnsɪˈmɛtrɪkəl] *adj* asimétrico, disimétrico

unsympathetic [ˌʌnsɪmpəˈθɛtɪk] *adj* incompasivo, indiferente

unsystematic(al) [ˌʌnsɪstəˈmætɪk(əl)] *adj* poco sistemático, sin sistema

untactful [ʌnˈtæktfəl] *adj* indiscreto, falto de tacto

untamed [ʌnˈtemd] *adj* indomado, bravío

untangle [ʌnˈtæŋgəl] *tr* desenredar, desenmarañar

unteachable [ʌnˈtitʃəbəl] *adj* indócil

untenable [ʌnˈtɛnəbəl] *adj* insostenible

unthankful [ʌnˈθæŋkfəl] *adj* ingrato, desagradecido

unthinkable [ʌnˈθɪŋkəbəl] *adj* impensable

unthinking [ʌnˈθɪŋkɪŋ] *adj* irreflexivo, desatento; irracional, instintivo

untidy [ʌnˈtaɪdi] *adj* desaseado, desaliñado; descachalandrado

un•tie [ʌnˈtaɪ] *v* (*pret & pp* **-tied;** *ger* **-tying**) *tr* desatar; deshacer (*un nudo, una cuerda*); (*to free from restraint*) soltar; resolver ‖ *intr* desatarse

until [ʌnˈtɪl] *prep* hasta ‖ *conj* hasta que; **to wait until** aguardar a que, esperar a que

untillable [ʌnˈtɪləbəl] *adj* incultivable

untimely [ʌnˈtaɪmli] *adj* intempestivo

untiring [ʌnˈtaɪrɪŋ] *adj* incansable

untold [ʌnˈtold] *adj* nunca dicho; (*uncounted*) innumerable, incalculable

untouchable [ʌnˈtʌtʃəbəl] *adj* intangible ‖ *s* intocable *mf*

untouched [ʌnˈtʌtʃt] *adj* intacto; íntegro; impasible; no mencionado

untoward [ʌnˈtord] *adj* desfavorable; indecoroso

untrammeled o **untrammelled** [ʌnˈtræməld] *adj* libre, sin trabas

untried [ʌnˈtraɪd] *adj* no probado, no ensayado

untroubled [ʌnˈtrʌbləd] *adj* tranquilo, sosegado

untrue [ʌnˈtru] *adj* falso; infiel

untrustworthy [ʌnˈtrʌstˌwʌrði] *adj* indigno de confianza

untruth [ʌnˈtruθ] *s* falsedad, mentira

untruthful [ʌnˈtruθfəl] *adj* falso, mentiroso

untwist [ʌnˈtwɪst] *tr* destorcer ‖ *intr* destorcerse

unused [ʌnˈjuzd] *adj* inutilizado, no usado; nuevo; **unused to** [ʌnˈjuzdtu] o [ʌnˈjustu] *adj* no acostumbrado a

unusual [ʌnˈjuʒʊəl] *adj* inusual, insólito

unutterable [ʌnˈʌtərəbəl] *adj* indecible, inexpresable

unvanquished [ʌnˈvæŋkwɪʃt] *adj* invicto

unvarnished [ʌnˈvɑrnɪʃt] *adj* sin barnizar; (fig) sencillo, sin adornos

unveil [ʌnˈvel] *tr* quitar el velo a; descubrir, develar, inaugurar, (*una estatua*) ‖ *intr* quitarse el velo

unveiling [ʌnˈvelɪŋ] *s* develación, inauguración

unventilated [ʌnˈvɛntɪˌletɪd] *adj* sin ventilar

unvoice [ʌnˈvɔɪs] *tr* afonizar, ensordecer ‖ *intr* afonizarse, ensordecerse

unwanted [ʌnˈwɑntɪd] *adj* indeseado

unwarranted [ʌnˈwɑrəntɪd] *adj* injustificado; no autorizado; sin garantía

unwary [ʌnˈwɛri] *adj* incauto, imprudente

unwavering [ʌnˈwevərɪŋ] *adj* firme, determinado, resuelto

unwelcome [ʌnˈwɛlkəm] *adj* mal acogido; importuno, molesto

unwell [ʌnˈwɛl] *adj* indispuesto, enfermo; (coll) menstruante

unwholesome [ʌnˈholsəm] *adj* insalubre

unwieldy [ʌnˈwildi] *adj* inmanejable, abultado, pesado

unwilling [ʌnˈwɪlɪŋ] *adj* desinclinado, maldispuesto, renuente

unwillingly [ʌnˈwɪlɪŋli] *adv* de mala gana

un•wind [ʌnˈwaɪnd] *v* (*pret & pp* **-wound** [ˈwaʊnd]) *tr* desenvolver; (*rewind*) rebobinar ‖ *intr* desenvolverse; distenderse (*el muelle del reloj*)

unwise [ʌnˈwaɪz] *adj* indiscreto, malaconsejado

unwished-for [ʌnˈwɪʃtˌfɔr] *adj* indeseado

unwitting [ʌnˈwɪtɪŋ] *adj* inadvertido, inconsciente

unwonted [ʌnˈwʌntɪd] *adj* poco común, raro, insólito

unworldly [ʌnˈwʌrldi] *adj* no terrenal, no mundano, espiritual

unworthy [ʌnˈwʌrði] *adj* indigno, desmerecedor

un•wrap [ʌnˈræp] *v* (*pret & pp* **-wrapped;** *ger* **wrapping**) *tr* desenvolver, desempapelar

unwrinkle [ʌnˈrɪŋkəl] *tr* desarrugar ‖ *intr* desarrugarse

unwritten [ʌnˈrɪtən] *adj* no escrito; (*blank*) en blanco; oral

unyielding [ʌnˈjildɪŋ] *adj* firme, inflexible; terco, reacio

unyoke [ʌnˈjok] *tr* desuncir

up [ʌp] *adj* ascendente; alto, elevado; derecho, en pie; terminado; cumplido; levantado de la cama; **to be up and about** estar levantado (*el que estaba enfermo*) ‖ *s* subida; **ups and downs** altibajos, vicisitudes ‖ *adv* arriba; en el aire; hacia arriba; al norte; **to be up** estar levantado; vencer (*un plazo*); **to be up in arms** estar sobre las armas; protestar vehementemente; **to be up to a person** tocarle a una persona; **to get up** levantarse; **to go up** subir; **to keep up** mantener; continuar; mantenerse firme; **to keep up with** correr parejas con; **up above**

allá arriba; **up against it** (slang) en apuros; **up to** hasta; (*capable of*) a la altura de; (*informed of*) al corriente de; (*scheming*) armando, tramando; **what is up?** ¿qué pasa? ‖ *prep* subiendo; **up the river** río arriba; **up the street** calle arriba

up-and-coming [ˈʌpənˈkʌmɪŋ] *adj* (coll) prometedor

up-and-doing [ˈʌpənˈduˌɪŋ] *adj* (coll) emprendedor

up-and-up [ˈʌpənˈʌp] *s*—**on the up-and-up** (coll) mejorándose; (coll) abiertamente, sin dolo

up•braid' *tr* regañar, reprender

upbringing [ˈʌpˌbrɪŋɪŋ] *s* educación, crianza

UPC *abbr* **universal product code**

up'coun'try *adv* (coll) hacia el interior, tierra adentro ‖ *s* (coll) interior *m* del país

up•date' *tr* poner al día

upheaval [ʌpˈhivəl] *s* trastorno, cataclismo

up'hill' *adj* ascendente; arduo, difícil, penoso ‖ **up'hill'** *adv* cuesta arriba

up•hold' *v* (*pret* & *pp* **-held**) *tr* levantar; apoyar, sostener; defender

upholster [ʌpˈholstər] *tr* tapizar

upholsterer [ʌpˈholstərər] *s* tapicero

upholster•y [ʌpˈholstəri] *s* (*pl* **-ies**) tapicería

up'keep' *s* conservación, manutención; gastos de conservación, gastos de entretenimiento

upland [ˈʌplənd] o [ˈʌplænd] *adj* alto, elevado ‖ *s* tierra alta, terreno elevado

up'lift' *s* (*lifting*) elevación, levantamiento; mejora social; (*moral or spiritual improvement*) edificación ‖ **up•lift'** *tr* elevar, levantar; edificar

upon [əˈpɑn] *prep* en, sobre, encima de; **upon** + *ger* al + *inf*, p.ej., **upon arriving** al llegar; **upon my word!** ¡por mi palabra!

upper [ˈʌpər] *adj* alto, superior; (*country*) interior; (*clothing*) exterior ‖ *s* (*of shoe*) pala; **on one's uppers** con las suelas gastadas; (coll) andrajoso, pobre, sin blanca

upper berth *s* litera alta, cama alta

upper case *s* (typ) caja alta

upper classes *spl* altas clases

upper hand *s* dominio, ventaja; **to have the upper hand** tener vara alta

upper middle class *s* alta burguesía

up'per•most' *adj* (el) más alto; (el) principal ‖ *adv* en lo más alto primero, en primer lugar

uppish [ˈʌpɪʃ] *adj* (coll) copetudo, arrogante

up•raise' *tr* levantar

up'right' *adj* derecho, vertical; probo, recto ‖ *adv* verticalmente ‖ *s* montante *m*

uprising [ʌpˈraɪzɪŋ] [ˈʌpˌraɪzɪŋ] *s* insurrección, levantamiento

up'roar' *s* alboroto, conmoción, tumulto

uproarious [ʌpˈrorɪəs] *adj* tumultuoso; (*noisy*) ruidoso; (*funny*) muy cómico

up•root' *tr* desarraigar

up•set' o **up'set'** *adj* (*overturned*) volcado; trastornado; indispuesto ‖ **up'set'** *s* (*overturn*) vuelco; (*unexpected defeat*) contra-

tiempo; (*disturbance*) trastorno; (*illness*) indisposición, enfermedad ‖ **up•set'** *v* (*pret* & *pp* **-set**; *ger* **-setting**) *tr* volcar; trastornar; indisponer ‖ *intr* volcar

upset price *s* precio mínimo fijado en una subasta

upsetting [ʌpˈsɛtɪŋ] *adj* desconcertante

up'shot' *s* conclusión, resultado; esencia, quid *m*

up'side' *s* parte *f* superior, lado superior; **on the upside** (*said of prices*) subiendo

upside down *adv* alrevés, lo de arriba abajo, patas arriba; en confusión, revuelto; **to turn upside down** volcar; trastornar; volcarse; trastornarse

up'stage' *adj* situado al fondo de la escena; (coll) altanero, arrogante ‖ *adv* al fondo de la escena ‖ **up'stage'** *tr* (coll) mirar por encima del hombro, desairar

up'stairs' *adj* de arriba ‖ *adv* arriba ‖ *s* piso superior, pisos superiores

upstanding [ʌpˈstændɪŋ] *adj* derecho; gallardo; probo, recto

up'start' *adj* & *s* advenedizo

up'stream' *adv* aguas arriba, río arriba

up'stroke' *s* carrera ascendente

up'swing' *s* movimiento hacia arriba; mejora notable; **on the upswing** mejorando notablemente

up'-to-date' *adj* corriente; reciente, moderno; de última hora, de última moda

up'-to-the-min'ute *adj* al día, de actualidad

up'town' *adj* de la parte alta de la ciudad ‖ *adv* en la parte alta de la ciudad

up train *s* tren *m* ascendente

up'trend' *s* tendencia al alza

up'turn' *s* alza, subida, mejora

upturned [ʌpˈtʌrnd] *adj* revuelto; (*part of clothing*) arremangado; (*nose*) respingada

upward [ˈʌpwərd] *adj* ascendente ‖ *adv* hacia arriba; **upward of** más de

Ural [ˈjurəl] *adj* ural ‖ **Urals** *spl* Urales *mpl*

uranium [juˈrenɪ•əm] *s* uranio

urban [ˈʌrbən] *adj* urbano (*perteneciente a la ciudad*)

urbane [ʌrˈben] *adj* urbano (*atento, cortés*)

urban guerrilla *s* guerrillero urbano

urbanite [ˈʌrbəˌnaɪt] *s* ciudadano

urbanity [ʌrˈbænɪti] *s* urbanidad

urbanize [ˈʌrbəˌnaɪz] *tr* urbanizar

urchin [ˈʌrtʃɪn] *s* pilluelo, galopín *m;* patojo (CAm)

ure•thra [juˈriθrə] *s* (*pl* **-thras** o **-thrae** [θri]) uretra

urge [ʌrdʒ] *s* impulso, estímulo ‖ *tr* apremiar, impeler, estimular; pedir instantáneamente; (*to try to persuade*) instar ‖ *intr* instar

urgen•cy [ˈʌrdʒənsi] *s* (*pl* **-cies**) urgencia; instancia, apremio

urgent [ˈʌrdʒənt] *adj* urgente; apremiante

urinal [ˈjurɪnəl] *s* (*receptacle*) orinal *m;* (*place*) urinario

urinary [ˈjurɪˌnɛri] *adj* urinario

urinate [ˈjurɪˌnet] *tr* orinar (*p.ej., sangre*) ‖ *intr* orinar, orinarse; (coll) hacer pipí

un
ur

urine ['jʊrɪn] *s* orina, orines *mpl;* (coll) pipí *m*

urn [ʌrn] *s* (*decorative vase*) jarrón *m;* cafetera o tetera con grifo; (*to hold ashes of the dead after cremation*) urna

urology [jʊ'rɑlədʒi] *s* urología

Uruguay ['jʊrə,gwaɪ] *s* el Uruguay

Uruguayan [,jʊrə'gwaɪ•ən] *adj & s* uruguayo

us [ʌs] *pron pers* nos; nosotros; **to us** nos; a nosotros

U.S.A. *abbr* **United States of America, United States Army, Union of South Africa**

usable ['juzəbəl] *adj* aprovechable, utilizable

usage ['jusɪdʒ] o ['juzɪdʒ] *s* usanza; (*e.g., of a language*) uso

usage instructions *spl* modo de empleo

use [jus] *s* uso, empleo; utilidad; **in use** en uso; **out of use** desusado; **to be of no use** no servir para nada; **to have no use for** no necesitar; no servirse de; (coll) tener en poco; **to make use of** servirse de ‖ [juz] *tr* usar, emplear, servirse de; **to use badly** maltratar; **to use up** agotar, consumir ‖ *intr* (empléase sólo en el pretérito y se traduce al español con el pretérito imperfecto o el verbo **soler**), p.ej., **I used to go out for a walk every evening** salía de paseo todas las tardes o solía salir de paseo todas las tardes

used [juzd] *adj* (*customarily employed; worn, partly worn-out; accustomed*) usado; **used to** ['juzdtʊ] o ['justʊ] acostumbrado a

useful ['jusfəl] *adj* útil

usefulness ['jusfəlnɪs] *s* utilidad

useless ['juslɪs] *adj* inservible, inútil

user ['juzər] *s* usuario

usher ['ʌʃər] *s* (*in a theater*) acomodador *m;* (*doorkeeper*) ujier *m,* portero ‖ *tr* acomodar; **to usher in** anunciar, introducir

U.S.S.R. *abbr* **Union of Soviet Socialist Republics**

usual ['juʒʊ•əl] *adj* usual, acostumbrado; **as usual** como de costumbre

usually ['juʒʊ•əli] *adj* usualmente, de ordinario

usurp [jʊ'zʌrp] *tr* usurpar

usu•ry ['juʒəri] *s* (*pl* **-ries**) usura

utensil [jʊ'tɛnsɪl] *s* utensilio; **utensils** corotos *mpl*

uter•us ['jutərəs] *s* (*pl* **-i** [,aɪ]); útero

utilitarian [,jutɪlɪ'tɛrɪ•ən] *adj* utilitario

utili•ty [jʊ'tɪlɪti] *s* (*pl* **-ties**) utilidad; empresa de servicio público

utilize ['jutɪ,laɪz] *tr* utilizar

utmost ['ʌt,most] *adj* sumo, extremo, último; más grande, mayor posible; más lejano ‖ *s*— **the utmost** lo sumo, lo mayor, lo más; **to the utmost** a lo sumo, a más no poder; **to do one's utmost** hacer todo lo posible

utopia [jʊ'topɪ•ə] *s* utopía

utopian [jʊ'topɪ•ən] *adj* utópico, utopista ‖ *s* utopista *mf*

utter ['ʌtər] *adj* total, absoluto ‖ *tr* proferir, pronunciar; dar (*un suspiro*)

utterance ['ʌtərəns] *s* expresión, pronunciación; declaración

utterly ['ʌtərli] *adj* completamente, totalmente, absolutamente

uxoricide [ʌk'sorɪ,saɪd] *s* (*husband*) uxoricida *m;* (*act*) uxoricidio

uxorious [ʌk'sorɪ•əs] *adj* uxorio

V

V, v [vi] vigésima segunda letra del alfabeto inglés

v. *abbr* **verb, verse, versus, vide** (Lat) **see, voice, volt, volume**

V. abbr **Venerable, Vice, Viscount, Volunteer**

vacan•cy ['vekənsi] *s* (*pl* **-cies**) (*emptiness; gap, opening*) vacío; (*unfilled position or job*) vacancia, vacante *f,* vacío; piso vacante; cargo vacante

vacant ['vekənt] *adj* (*empty*) vacío; (*having no occupant; untenanted*) vacante; (*expression, look*) vago; distraído

vacate ['veket] *tr* dejar vacante; anular, invalidar, revocar ‖ *intr* (*to move out*) desalojar; (coll) irse, marcharse

vacation [ve'keʃən] *s* vacaciones; **on vacation** de vacaciones ‖ *intr* tomar vacaciones

vacationist [ve'keʃənɪst] *s* vacacionista *mf*

vacation with pay *s* vacaciones retribuídas

vaccinate ['væksɪ,net] *tr* vacunar

vaccination [,væksɪ'neʃən] *s* vacunación

vaccine [væk'sin] *s* vacuna

vacillate ['væsɪ,let] *intr* vacilar

vacillating ['væsɪ,letɪŋ] *adj* vacilante

vacui•ty [væ'kjuɪti] *s* (*pl* **-ties**) vacuidad

vacu•um ['vækjʊ•əm] *s* (*pl* **-ums** o **-a** [ə]) vacío ‖ *tr* (coll) limpiar

vacuum cleaner *s* aspirador *m* de polvo

vacuum tank *s* (aut) aspirador *m* de gasolina, nodriza

vacuum tube *s* tubo de vacío

vagabond ['vægə,bɑnd] *adj & s* vagabundo

vagar•y [və'gɛri] *s* (*pl* **-ies**) capricho

vagina [və'dʒaɪnə] *s* vagina

vagran•cy ['vegrənsi] *s* (*pl* **-cies**) vagabundaje *m*

vagrant ['vegrənt] *adj & s* vagabundo

vague [veg] *adj* vago; impreciso

vain [ven] *adj* vano; (*conceited*) vanidoso; **in vain** en vano

vainglorious [ven'glorɪ•əs] *adj* vanaglorioso

valance ['væləns] *s* (*across the top of a window*) guardamalleta; (*drapery*) dosolera

vale [vel] *s* valle *m*

valedictorian [‚vælɪdɪk'tɔrɪ•ən] *s* alumno que pronuncia el discurso de despedida al fin del curso

valedicto•ry [‚vælɪ'dɪktəri] *adj* de despedida ‖ *s* (*pl* **-ries**) discurso de despedida

valence ['veləns] *s* (chem) valencia

valentine ['væləntaɪn] *s* tarjeta amorosa o jocosa del día de San Valentín

Valentine Day *s* día *m* de los corazones, día de los enamorados (*14 de febrero*)

vale of tears *s* valle *m* de lágrimas

valet ['vælɪt] o ['væle] *s* ayuda *m*, paje *m*

valiant ['væljənt] *adj* valiente, valeroso

valid [ˈvælɪd] *adj* válido, valedero

validate ['vælɪ‚det] *tr* validar; (sport) homologar

validation [‚vælɪ'deʃən] *s* validación; (sport) homologación

validi•ty [və'lɪdɪti] *s* (*pl* **-ties**) validez *f*

valise [və'lis] *s* maleta

valley ['væli] *s* valle *m*; (*of roof*) lima hoya

valor ['vælər] *s* valor *m*, ánimo

valorous ['vælərəs] *adj* valeroso

valuable ['vælju•əbəl] o ['væljəbəl] *adj* (*having monetary value*) valioso; (*highly thought of*) estimable ‖ **valuables** *spl* alhajas, objetos de valor

value ['vælju] *s* valor *m*; (*return for one's money in a purchase*) (coll) adquisición, inversión, p.ej., **an excellent value** una adquisición excelente ‖ *tr* (*to think highly of*) estimar; (*to set a price for*) valorar, valuar

val′ue-add′ed tax *s* impuesto sobre el valor añadido, impuesto al valor agregado

valueless ['væljulɪs] *adj* sin valor

valve [vælv] *s* válvula; (*of mollusk*) valva; (mus) llava *f*

valve cap *s* capuchón *m*

valve gears *spl* distribución

valve′-in-head′ engine *s* motor *m* con válvulas en cabeza

valve lifter [ˈlɪftər] *s* levantaválvulas *m*

valve seat *s* asiento de válvula

valve spring *s* muelle *m* de válvula

valve stem *s* vástago de válvula

vamp [væmp] *s* (*of shoe*) empella; (*patchwork*) remiendo; (*woman who preys on men*) (slang) mujer *f* fatal, vampiresa ‖ *tr* poner empella a (*un zapato*); remendar; (*to concoct*) componer, enmendar; (jazz) improvisar (*un acompañamiento*); (slang) seducir (*una mujer mundana a un hombre*)

vampire ['væmpaɪr] *s* vampiro; (*woman who preys on men*) mujer *f* fatal, vampiresa

van [væn] *s* carro de carga, camión *m* de mudanzas; (mil & fig) vanguardia; (Brit) furgón *m* de equipajes

vanadium [və'nedɪ•əm] *s* vanadio

vandal ['vændəl] *adj* & *s* vándalo ‖ **Vandal** *adj* & *s* vándalo

vandalism ['vændə‚lɪzəm] *s* vandalismo

vane [ven] *s* (*weathervane*) veleta; (*of windmill*) aspa; (*of propeller or turbine*) paleta; (*of feather*) barba

vanguard ['væn‚gɑrd] *s* (mil & fig) vanguardia; **in the vanguard** a vanguardia

vanilla [və'nɪlə] *s* vainilla

vanish ['vænɪʃ] *intr* desvanecerse

vanishing cream ['vænɪʃɪŋ] *s* crema desvanecedora

vani•ty ['vænɪti] *s* (*pl* **-ties**) vanidad; (*dressing table*) tocador *m*; (*vanity case*) estuche *m* de afeites

vanity case *s* estuche *m* de afeites, neceser *m* de belleza

vanquish ['væŋkwɪʃ] *tr* vencer, rendir

vantage ground ['væntɪdʒ] *s* posición ventajosa

vapid ['væpɪd] *adj* insípido

vapor ['vepər] *s* vapor *m* (*el visible; exhalación, vaho, niebla, etc.*)

vaporize ['vepə‚raɪz] *tr* vaporizar ‖ *intr* vaporizarse

vaporous ['vepərəs] *adj* vaporoso

vapor trail *s* (aer) estela de vapor, rastro de condensación

var. *abbr* **variant**

variable ['vɛrɪ•əbəl] *adj* & *s* variable *f*

variance ['vɛrɪ•əns] *s* diferencia, variación; **at variance with** en desacuerdo con

variant ['vɛrɪ•ənt] *adj* & *s* variante *f*

variation [‚vɛrɪ'eʃən] *s* variación

varicose ['værɪ‚kos] *adj* varicoso

varicose vein *s* (pathol) varice *f*

varied ['vɛrɪd] *adj* variado, vario

variegated ['vɛrɪ•ə‚getɪd] o ['vɛrɪ‚getɪd] *adj* abigarrado, variado

varie•ty [və'raɪ•ɪti] *s* (*pl* **-ties**) variedad

variety show *s* variedades

variola [və'raɪ•ələ] *s* (pathol) viruela

various ['vɛrɪ•əs] *adj* (*several; of different kinds*) varios; (*many-sided; many-colored*) vario

varnish ['vɑrnɪʃ] *s* barniz *m*; (fig) capa, apariencia ‖ *tr* barnizar; (fig) dar apariencia falsa a

varsi•ty ['vɑrsɪti] *adj* (sport) universitario ‖ *s* (*pl* **-ties**) (sport) equipo principal de la universidad

var•y ['vɛri] *v* (*pret* & *pp* **-ied**) *tr* & *intr* variar

vase [ves] o [vez] *s* florero, jarrón *m*

Vaseline ['væsə‚lin] *s* (trademark) vaselina

vassal ['væsəl] *adj* & *s* vasallo

vast [væst] o [vɑst] *adj* vasto

vastly ['væstli] *adv* enormemente

vastness ['væstnɪs] *s* vastedad

vat [væt] *s* cuba, tina

vaudeville ['vodvɪl] o ['vɔdəvɪl] *s* variedades; (*light theatrical piece interspersed with songs*) zarzuela

vault [vɔlt] *s* (*underground chamber*) bodega; (*of a bank*) cámara acorazada; (*burial chamber*) sepultura, tumba; (*firmament*) bóveda celeste; (*leap*) salto; (archit) bóveda ‖ *tr* abovedar; saltar ‖ *intr* saltar

vaunt [vɔnt] *s* jactancia ‖ *tr* jactarse de ‖ *intr* jactarse

VCR *abbr* **video-cassette recorder**

veal [vil] *s* ternera, carne *f* de ternera

veal chop *s* chuleta de ternera

ur
ve

vedette [vɪ'dɛt] *s* buque *m* escucha; centinela *m* de avanzada

veer [vɪr] *s* viraje *m* ‖ *tr* virar ‖ *intr* virar; (naut) llamar (*el viento*)

vegetable ['vɛdʒɪtəbəl] *adj* vegetal ‖ *s* (*plant*) vegetal *m;* (*edible part of plant*) hortaliza, legumbre *f*

vegetable garden *s* huerto de hortalizas, huerto de verduras

vegetable soup *s* menestra, sopa de hortalizas

vegetarian [,vɛdʒɪ'tɛrɪ•ən] *adj & s* vegetariano

vehemence ['vi•ɪməns] *s* vehemencia

vehement ['vi•ɪmənt] *adj* vehemente

vehicle ['vi•ɪkəl] *s* vehículo

vehicular traffic [vɪ'hɪkjələr] *s* circulación rodada

veil [vel] *s* velo; **to take the veil** tomar el velo ‖ *tr* velar (*cubrir con un velo; cubrir, disimular*)

vein [ven] *s* vena; (*streak*) veta; (*distinctive quality*) rasgo ‖ *tr* vetear

velar ['vilər] *adj & s* velar *f*

vellum ['vɛləm] *s* vitela; papel *m* vitela

veloci•ty [vɪ'lɑsɪti] *s* (*pl* **-ties**) velocidad

velvet ['vɛlvɪt] *adj* de terciopelo ‖ *s* terciopelo; (slang) ganancia limpia

velveteen [,vɛlvɪ'tin] *s* velludillo

velvety ['vɛlvɪti] *adj* aterciopelado

Ven. *abbr* **Venerable**

vend [vɛnd] *tr* vender como buhonero

vending machine *s* distribuidor automático

vendor ['vɛndər] *s* vendedor *m*, buhonero

veneer [və'nɪr] *s* chapa, enchapado; (fig) apariencia ‖ *tr* enchapar

venerable ['vɛnərəbəl] *adj* venerable

venerate ['vɛnə,ret] *tr* venerar

venereal [vɪ'nɪrɪ•əl] *adj* venéreo

Venetia [vɪ'niʃi•ə] o [vɪ'niʃə] *s* Venecia (*provincia*)

Venetian [vɪ'niʃən] *adj & s* veneciano

Venetian blind *s* persiana

Venezuela [,vɛnɪ'zwilə] *s* Venezuela

Venezuelan [,vɛnɪzwilən] *adj & s* venezolano

vengeance ['vɛndʒəns] *s* venganza; **with a vengeance** con furia, con violencia; excesivamente, con creces

vengeful ['vɛndʒfəl] *adj* vengativo

Venice ['vɛnɪs] *s* Venecia (*ciudad*)

venire [vɪ'naɪri] *s* (law) auto de convocación del jurado

venison ['vɛnɪsən] o ['vɛnɪzən] *s* carne *f* de venado

venom ['vɛnəm] *s* veneno

venomous ['vɛnəməs] *adj* venenoso

vent [vɛnt] *s* agujero, orificio; (*outlet*) salida; **to give vent to** dar libre curso a ‖ *tr* proveer de abertura; desahogar, expresar; **to vent one's spleen** descargar la bilis

vent'hole *s* respiradero

ventilate ['vɛntɪ,let] *tr* ventilar

ventilator ['vɛntɪ,letər] *s* ventilador *m*

ventricle ['vɛntrɪkəl] *s* ventrículo

ventriloquism [vɛn'trɪlə,kwɪzəm] *s* ventriloquia

ventriloquist [vɛn'trɪləkwɪst] *s* ventrílocuo

venture ['vɛntʃər] *s* empresa arriesgada; **at a venture** a la buena ventura ‖ *tr* aventurar ‖ *intr* aventurarse; **to venture on** arriesgarse en

venturesome ['vɛntʃərsəm] *adj* (*bold, daring*) aventurero; (*hazardous*) aventurado

venturous ['vɛntʃərəs] *adj* (*bold, daring*) aventurero; (*hazardous*) aventurado, arriesgado

venue ['vɛnju] *s* (law) lugar *m* del crimen; (law) lugar donde se reúne el jurado; **change of venue** (law) traslado de jurisdicción

Venus ['vinəs] *s* (astr) Venus *m;* (myth) Venus *f;* (*very beautiful woman*) Venus *f*

veracious [vɪ'reʃəs] *adj* veraz

veraci•ty [vɪ'ræsɪti] *s* (*pl* **-ties**) veracidad

veranda o **verandah** [və'rændə] *s* terraza, veranda, galería

verb [vʌrb] *adj* verbal ‖ *s* verbo

verbatim [vər'betɪm] *adj* textual ‖ *adv* palabra por palabra, al pie de la letra

verbena [vər'binə] *s* (bot) verbena

verbiage ['vʌrbi•ɪdʒ] *s* palabrería, verbosidad

verbose [vər'bos] *adj* verboso

verdant ['vʌrdənt] *adj* verde; cándido, sencillo

verdict ['vʌrdɪkt] *s* veredicto, fallo

verdigris ['vʌrdɪ,gris] *s* verdete *m*

verdure ['vʌrdʒər] *s* verdor *m*

verge [vʌrdʒ] *s* borde *m*, límite *m;* (*of a column*) fuste *m;* báculo; (eccl) cetro; **on the verge of** al borde de; a punto de; **within the verge of** al alcance de ‖ *intr*— **to verge on** o **upon** llegar casi hasta, rayar en

verification [,vɛrɪfɪ'keʃən] *s* verificación

veri•fy ['vɛrɪ,faɪ] *v* (*pret & pp* **-fied**) *tr* verificar, comprobar; (law) afirmar bajo juramento

verily ['vɛrɪli] *adv* verdaderamente, en verdad

veritable ['vɛrɪtəbəl] *adj* verdadero

vermicelli [,vʌrmɪ'sɛli] *s* fideos

vermilion [vər'mɪljən] *adj* bermejo ‖ *s* bermellón *m*

vermin ['vʌrmɪn] *ssg* (*objectionable person*) sabandija; bicherío (SAm) ‖ *spl* (*objectionable animals or persons*) sabandijas

vermouth [vər'muθ] o ['vʌrmuθ] *s* vermú *m*

vernacular [vər'nækjələr] *adj* vernáculo ‖ *s* lenguaje vernáculo; idioma *m* corriente; (*language peculiar to a class or profession*) jerga

veronica [və'rɑnɪkə] *s* (bot & taur) verónica; lienzo de la Verónica

Versailles [vɛr'saɪ] *s* Versalles

versatile ['vʌrsətɪl] *adj* versátil; [*person*] de muchas habilidades; (*informed on many subjects*) polifacético, universal; (*device or tool*) útil para muchas cosas

verse [vʌrs] *s* verso; (*in the Bible*) versículo

versed [vʌrst] *adj* versado; **to become versed in** versarse en

versification [,vʌrsɪfɪ'keʃən] *s* versificación

versi•fy [ˈwʌrsɪˌfaɪ] v (pret & pp **-fied**) tr & intr versificar

version [ˈvʌrʒən] s versión

ver•so [ˈvʌrso] s (pl **-sos**) (e.g., of a coin) reverso; (typ) verso

versus [ˈvʌrsəs] prep contra

verte•bra [ˈvʌrtɪbrə] s (pl **-brae** [ˌbri] o **-bras**) vértebra

vertebral disk [ˈvʌrtəˌbrəl] s disco vertebral

vertebrate [ˈvʌrtɪˌbret] adj & s vertebrado

ver•tex [ˈvʌrtɛks] s (pl **-texes** o **-tices** [tɪˌsiz]) (top, summit) ápice m; (geom) vértice m

vertical [ˈvʌrtɪkəl] adj & s vertical f

vertical hold s (telv) bloqueo vertical

vertical rudder s (aer) timón m de dirección

vertical take-off m despegue m vertical

verti•go [ˈvʌrtɪˌgo] s (pl **-gos** o **-goes**) vértigo

verve [vʌrv] s brío, ánimo, vigor m

very [ˈvɛri] adj mismísimo; (sheer, utter) mero, puro; (actual) verdadero ‖ adv muy; mucho, p.ej., **to be very hungry** tener mucha hambre

vesicle [ˈvɛsɪkəl] s vesícula

vesper [ˈvɛspər] s tarde f, caída de la tarde; oración de la tarde; canción de la tarde; **vespers** (eccl) vísperas ‖ **Vesper** s Véspero

vesper bell s campana que llama a vísperas

vessel [ˈvɛsəl] s vasija, recipiente m; (ship) bajel m, embarcación, buque m; (anat) vaso

vest [vɛst] s (of man's suit) chaleco; (jabot) chorrera; (undershirt) camiseta ‖ tr vestir; **to vest in** conceder (p.ej., poder) a; **to vest with** investir de ‖ intr vestirse; **to vest in** pasar a

vested interests spl intereses creados

vestibule [ˈvɛstɪˌbjul] s vestíbulo, zaguán m

vestige [ˈvɛstɪdʒ] s vestigio

vestment [ˈvɛstmənt] s vestidura

vest'-pock'et adj de bolsillo, en miniatura; diminuto

ves•try [ˈvɛstri] s (pl **-tries**) sacristía; (chapel) capilla; junta parroquial; reunión de la junta parroquial

vestry•man [ˈvɛstrimən] s (pl **-men** [mən]) miembro de la junta parroquial

Vesuvius [vɪˈsuvɪ•əs] o [vɪˈsjuvɪ•əs] s el Vesubio

vet. abbr veteran, veterinary

vetch [vɛtʃ] s arveja, veza; (grass pea) almorta

veteran [ˈvɛtərən] adj & s veterano

veterinarian [ˌvɛtərɪˈnɛri•ən] s veterinario

veterinar•y [ˈvɛtərɪˌnɛri] adj veterinario ‖ s (pl **-ies**) veterinario

veterinary medicine s veterinaria, medicina veterinaria

ve•to [ˈvito] s (pl **-toes**) veto ‖ tr vetar

vex [vɛks] tr vejar, molestar

vexation [vɛkˈseʃən] s vejación, molestia

v.g. abbr verbi gratia (Lat) for example

via [ˈvaɪ•ə] prep vía, p.ej., **via Lisbon** vía Lisboa

viaduct [ˈvaɪ•əˌdʌkt] s viaducto

vial [ˈvaɪ•əl] s redoma, frasco pequeño

viati•cum [vaɪˈætɪkəm] s (pl **-cums** o **-ca** [kə]) (eccl) viático

viand [ˈvaɪ•ənd] s vianda, manjar m

vibrate [ˈvaɪbret] tr & intr vibrar

vibration [vaɪˈbreʃən] s vibración

vicar [ˈvɪkər] s vicario

vicarage [ˈvɪkərɪdʒ] s casa del vicario; (duties of vicar) vicaría

vicarious [vaɪˈkɛri•əs] adj substituto; (punishment) sufrido por otro; (power, authority) delegado; (enjoyment) reflejado

vice [vaɪs] s vicio

vice'-ad'miral s vicealmirante m

vice'-pres'ident s vicepresidente m

viceroy [ˈvaɪsrɔɪ] s virrey m

vice versa [ˈvaɪsi ˈvʌrsə] o [ˈvaɪs ˈvʌrsə] adv viceversa

vicini•ty [vɪˈsɪnɪti] s (pl **-ties**) vecindad

vicious [ˈvɪʃəs] adj vicioso; malazo; (dog) bravo; (horse) arisco

victim [ˈvɪktɪm] s víctima

victimize [ˈvɪktɪˌmaɪz] tr hacer víctima; engañar, estafar

victor [ˈvɪktər] s vencedor m

victorious [vɪkˈtori•əs] adj victorioso

victo•ry [ˈvɪktəri] s (pl **-ries**) victoria

victuals [ˈvɪtəlz] spl vituallas, provisiones de boca

vid. abbr **vide** (Lat) see

video cassette s videocasete m

vid'e•o-cas•sette' **recorder** s videograbador m

video-cassette recording s videograbación

video disk s videodisco

video game s video-juego

video recorder s magnetoscopia

video signal [ˈvɪdi•o] s señal f de vídeo

video tape s cinta grabada de televisión

vid'eo-tape' **recording** s videograbación

vie [vaɪ] v (pret & pp **vied;** ger **vying**) intr competir, emular, rivalizar

Vien•nese [ˌvi•əˈniz] adj vienés ‖ s (pl **-nese**) vienés m

Vietnam•ese [vɪˌɛtnəˈmiz] adj vietnamés ‖ s (pl **-ese**) vietnamés m

view [vju] s vista; (purpose) intento, propósito, vista; **to be on view** estar expuesto (p.ej., un cadáver); **to keep in view** no perder de vista; no olvidar, tener presente; **to take a dim view of** no entusiasmarse por, mirar escépticamente; **with a view to** con vistas a ‖ tr ver, mirar; considerar, contemplar; examinar, inspeccionar

viewer [ˈvju•ər] s espectador m; telespectador m, televidente mf; proyector m de transparencias; mirador m de transparencias

view'finder' s (phot) visor m

view'point' s punto de vista

vigil [ˈvɪdʒɪl] s vigilia; **to keep vigil** velar

vigilance [ˈvɪdʒɪləns] s vigilancia

vigilant [ˈvɪdʒɪlənt] adj vigilante

vignette [vɪnˈjɛt] s viñeta

vigor [ˈvɪgər] s vigor m

vigorous [ˈvɪgərəs] adj vigoroso

vile [vaɪl] adj vil; (disgusting) asqueroso, repugnante; (weather) muy malo

vili•fy ['vɪlɪ,faɪ] v (pret & pp **-fied**) tr difamar, denigrar

villa ['vɪlə] s villa, quinta

village ['vɪlɪdʒ] s aldea

villager ['vɪlɪdʒər] s aldeano

villain ['vɪlən] s malvado; (of a play) malo, traidor m

villainous ['vɪlənəs] adj malvado

villain•y ['vɪləni] s (pl **-ies**) maldad, perfidia

vim [vɪm] s fuerza, brío, vigor m

vinaigrette [,vɪnə'grɛt] s vinagrera

vinaigrette sauce s vinagreta

vindicate ['vɪndɪ,ket] tr vindicar, exculpar

vindictive [vɪn'dɪktɪv] adj vengativo

vine [vaɪn] s (creeping or climbing plant) enredadera; (grape plant) vid f, parra

vine'dress'er s viñador m, viticultor m

vinegar ['vɪnɪgər] s vinagre m

vinegarish ['vɪnɪgərɪʃ] adj avinagrado

vinegary ['vɪnɪgəri] adj vinagroso

vineyard ['vɪnjərd] s viña, viñedo

vineyardist ['vɪnjərdɪst] s viñador m, viticultor m

vintage ['vɪntɪdʒ] s vendimia; vino de buena cosecha; (coll) categoría, clase f

vintager ['vɪntɪdʒər] s vendimiador m

vintage wine s vino de buena cosecha

vintage year s año de buen vino

vintner ['vɪntnər] s vinatero

vinyl ['vaɪnɪl] s vinilo

violate ['vaɪ•ə,let] tr violar

violence ['vaɪ•ələns] s violencia

violent ['vaɪ•ələnt] adj violento

violet ['vaɪ•əlɪt] adj violado ‖ s (color) violeta m, violado; (dye) violeta m; (bot) violeta f

violin [,vaɪ•ə'lɪn] s violín m

violinist [,vaɪ•ə'lɪnɪst] s violinista mf

violoncellist [,vaɪ•ələn'tʃɛlɪst] o [,vɪələn-'tʃɛlɪst] s violoncelista mf

violoncel•lo [,vaɪ•ələn'tʃɛlo] o [,vɪələn'tʃɛlo] s (pl **-los**) violoncelo

viper ['vaɪpər] s víbora

VIPs ['vi,aɪ'pis] spl (letterword) notables mpl

vira•go [vɪ'rego] s (pl **-goes** o **-gos**) mujer de mal genio

virgin ['vʌrdʒɪn] adj & s virgen f

virgin birth s parto virginal de María Santísima; (zool) partenogénesis f

Virginia creeper [vər'dʒɪnɪ•ə] s (bot) guau m

virginity [vər'dʒɪnɪti] s virginidad

Virgo ['vʌrgo] s (astr) Virgo

virility [vɪ'rɪlɪti] s virilidad

virology [vaɪ'rɑlədʒi] s virología

virtual ['vʌrtʃu•əl] adj virtual

virtue ['vʌrtʃu] s virtud

virtuosi•ty [,vʌrtʃu'ɑsɪti] s (pl **-ties**) virtuosismo

virtuo•so [,vʌrtʃu'oso] s (pl **-sos** o **-si** [si]) virtuoso

virtuous ['vʌrtʃu•əs] adj virtuoso

virulence ['vɪrjələns] s virulencia

virulent ['vɪrjələnt] adj virulento

virus ['vaɪrəs] s virus m

Vis. abbr **Viscount**

visa ['vɪzə] s visa ‖ tr visar

visage ['vɪzɪdʒ] s cara, semblante m; aspecto, apariencia

vis-à-vis [,vizə'vi] adj enfrentados ‖ adv frente a frente ‖ prep enfrente de; respecto de

viscera ['vɪsərə] spl vísceras

viscount ['vaɪkaunt] s vizconde m

viscountess ['vaɪkauntɪs] s vizcondesa

viscous ['vɪskəs] adj viscoso

vise [vaɪs] s tornillo, torno

visé ['vize] o [vi'ze] s & tr var de **visa**

visible ['vɪzɪbəl] adj visible

Visigoth ['vɪzɪ,gɑθ] s visigodo

vision ['vɪʒən] s visión; (sense of sight) vista

visionar•y ['vɪʒə,nɛri] adj visionario ‖ s (pl **-ies**) visionario

visit ['vɪzɪt] s visita ‖ tr visitar; afligir, acometer; enviar (p.ej., castigo, venganza) ‖ intr hacer visitas; visitarse (dos o más personas)

visitation [,vɪzɪ'teʃən] s visitación; gracia del cielo, castigo del cielo

visiting card s tarjeta de visita

visiting hours spl horas de visita

visiting nurse s enfermera ambulante

visitor ['vɪsɪtər] s visitante mf

visor ['vaɪzər] s visera; (disguise) máscara

vista ['vɪstə] s vista, panorama m

visual ['vɪʒu•əl] adj visual

visual acuity s agudeza visual

visualize ['vɪʒu•ə,laɪz] tr representarse en la mente; hacer visible

vital ['vaɪtəl] adj vital; (deadly) mortal ‖ **vitals** spl partes fpl vitales, órganos vitales

vitality [vaɪ'tælɪti] s vitalidad

vitalize ['vaɪtə,laɪz] tr vitalizar

vitamin ['vaɪtəmɪn] s vitamina

vitiate ['vɪʃɪ,et] tr viciar

vitreous ['vɪtrɪ•əs] adj vítreo

vitriolic [,vɪtrɪ'ɑlɪk] adj (chem) vitriólico; (fig) cáustico, mordaz

vituperable [vaɪ'tupərəbəl] o [vaɪ'tjupərəbəl] adj vituperable

vituperate [vaɪ'tupə,ret] o [vaɪ'tjupə,ret] tr vituperar

viva ['vivə] interj ¡viva! ‖ s viva m

vivacious [vɪ'veʃəs] o [vaɪ'veʃəs] adj vivaz, vivaracho

vivaci•ty [vɪ'væsɪti] o [vaɪ'væsɪti] s (pl **-ties**) vivacidad, animación

viva voce ['vaɪvə 'vosi] adv de viva voz

vivid ['vɪvɪd] adj vivo (intenso; brillante; expresivo)

vivi•fy ['vɪvɪ,faɪ] v (pret & pp **-fied**) tr vivificar

vivisection [,vɪvɪ'sɛkʃən] s vivisección

vixen ['vɪksən] s vulpeja; mujer regañona y colérica

viz. abbr **videlicet** (Lat) **namely, to wit**

vizier [vɪ'zɪr] o ['vɪzjər] s visir m

vocabular•y [vo'kæbjə,lɛri] s (pl **-ies**) vocabulario

vocal ['vokəl] adj vocal; (inclined to express oneself freely) expresivo

vocalist ['vokəlɪst] s vocalista mf

vocation [vo'keʃən] s vocación; empleo, ocupación

vocative ['vɑkətɪv] *s* vocativo
vociferate [vo'sɪfə,ret] *intr* vociferar
vociferous [vo'sɪfərəs] *adj* clamoroso, vocinglero
vogue [vog] *s* boga, moda; **in vogue** en boga, de moda
voice [vɔɪs] *s* voz *f;* **in a loud voice** en alta voz; **in a low voice** en voz baja; **with one voice** a una voz ‖ *tr* expresar; sonorizar *(una consonante sorda)* ‖ *intr* sonorizarse
voiceless ['vɔɪslɪs] *adj* sin voz; mudo; silencioso; (phonet) sordo
void [vɔɪd] *adj (empty)* vacío; *(useless)* vano; (law) inválido, nulo; **void of** desprovisto de ‖ *s* vacío; *(gap)* hueco ‖ *tr* vaciar; evacuar *(el vientre);* anular ‖ *intr* excretar
voile [vɔɪl] *s* espumilla
vol. *abbr* **volume**
volatile ['vɑlətɪl] *adj* volátil
volatilize ['vɑlətɪ,laɪz] *tr* volatilizar ‖ *intr* volatilizarse
volcanic [vɑl'kænɪk] *adj* volcánico
volca•no [vɑl'keno] *s (pl* **-noes** o **-nos)** volcán *m*
volition [və'lɪʃən] *s* voluntad; **of one's own volition** por su propia voluntad
volley ['vɑli] *s (of stones, bullets, etc.)* descarga, lluvia; (mil) descarga; (tennis) voleo ‖ *tr & intr* volear
vol'ley•ball' *s* volibol *m*
volplane ['vɑl,plen] *s* vuelo planeado ‖ *intr* planear
volt [volt] *s* voltio
voltage ['voltɪdʒ] *s* voltaje *m*
voltage divider *s* (rad) divisor *m* de voltaje
voltaic [vɑl'te•ɪk] *adj* voltaico
volte-face [vɔlt'fɑs] *s* cambio de dirección; cambio de opinión
volt'me'ter *s* voltímetro
voluble ['vɑljəbəl] *adj* locuaz, hablador
volume ['vɑljəm] *s (book; bulk; mass, e.g., of water)* volumen *m; (each book in a set)* tomo; *(degree of loudness)* volumen sonoro; (geom) volumen *m;* **to speak volumes** ser muy significativo; ser muy expresivo
voluminous [və'luminəs] *adj* voluminoso
voluntar•y ['vɑlən,tɛri] *adj* voluntario ‖ *s (pl* **-ties)** (eccl) solo de órgano
volunteer [,vɑlən'tɪr] *adj & s* voluntario ‖ *tr* ofrecer *(sus servicios)* ‖ *intr* ofrecerse; servir como voluntario; **to volunteer to +** *inf* ofrecerse a + *inf*
voluptuar•y [və'lʌptʃu,ɛri] *adj* voluptuoso ‖ *s (pl* **-ties)** voluptuoso, sibarita *mf*
voluptuous [və'lʌptʃu•əs] *adj* voluptuoso
volute [və'lut] *s* voluta

vomit ['vɑmɪt] *s* vómito; *(emetic)* vomitivo ‖ *tr & intr* vomitar
voodoo ['vudu] *adj* voduísta ‖ *s (practice)* vodú *m; (person)* voduísta *mf*
voracious [və'reʃəs] *adj* voraz
voracity [və'ræsɪti] *s* voracidad
vor•tex ['vɔrtɛks] *s (pl* **-texes** o **-tices** [tɪ,siz]) vórtice *m*
vota•ry ['votəri] *s (pl* **-ries)** persona ligada por votos solemnes; aficionado, partidario
vote [vot] *s (formal expression of choice; right to vote; person who votes)* voto; *(act of voting; votes considered together)* votación; **to put to the vote** poner a votación; **to tally the votes** regular los votos ‖ *tr* votar *(sí, no);* **to vote down** derrotar por votación; **to vote in** elegir por votación ‖ *intr* votar
vote getter ['gɛtər] *s* acaparador *m* de votos; *(slogan)* consigna que gana votos
voter ['votər] *s* votante *mf*
voting machine ['votɪŋ] *s* máquina registradora de votos
votive ['votɪv] *adj* votivo
votive offering *s* voto, exvoto
vouch [vautʃ] *tr* garantizar ‖ *intr*—**to vouch for** responder de *(una cosa);* responder por *(una persona)*
voucher ['vautʃər] *s* garante *mf; (certificate)* comprobante *m*
vouch•safe' *tr* conceder, otorgar; permitir ‖ *intr*—**to vouchsafe to +** *inf* dignarse + *inf*
voussoir [vu'swɑr] *s* dovela
vow [vau] *s* voto; **to take vows** tomar el hábito religioso ‖ *tr* votar *(p.ej., un cirio a la Virgen);* jurar *(venganza)* ‖ *intr* votar; **to vow to** hacer votos de
vowel ['vau•əl] *s* vocal *f*
voyage ['vɔɪ•ɪdʒ] *s* travesía, trayecto; *(any journey)* viaje *m* ‖ *tr* atravesar *(p.ej., el mar)* ‖ *intr* viajar
voyager ['vɔɪ•ɪdʒər] *s* pasajero, navegante *mf,* viajero
V.P. *abbr* **Vice-President**
vs. *abbr* **versus**
Vul. *abbr* **Vulgate**
vulcanize ['vʌlkə,naɪz] *tr* vulcanizar
vulg. *abbr* **vulgar**
Vulg. *abbr* **Vulgate**
vulgar ['vʌlgər] *adj* grosero; *(popular, common; vernacular)* vulgar
vulgari•ty [vʌl'gærɪti] *s (pl* **-ties)** grosería
Vulgar Latin *s* latín vulgar, latín rústico
Vulgate ['vʌlget] *s* Vulgata
vulnerable ['vʌlnərəbəl] *adj* vulnerable
vulture ['vʌltʃər] *s* buitre *m; (American vulture)* catartes *m,* aura *(buitre americano)*

W

W, w ['dʌbəl,ju] vigésima tercera letra del alfabeto inglés

w *abbr* **watt**

w. *abbr* **week, west, wide, wife**

W. *abbr* **Wednesday, west**

wad [wɑd] *s* (*of cotton*) bolita, tapón *m;* (*of papers*) fajo, lío; (*in a gun*) taco ‖ *v* (*pret & pp* **wadded;** *ger* **wadding**) *tr* emborrar, rellenar; atacar (*una escopeta*)

waddle ['wɑdəl] *s* anadeo ‖ *intr* anadear

wade [wed] *intr* andar sobre terreno cubierto de agua; andar descalzo por la orilla; chapotear (*los niños*) con los pies desnudos; **to wade into** (coll) embestir con violencia; (coll) meter el hombro a; **to wade through** (coll) avanzar con dificultad por; (coll) leer con dificultad

wading bird ['wedɪŋ] *s* ave zancuda

wafer ['wefər] *s* (*for sealing letters; pill*) oblea; (*thin, crisp cake*) hostia; (eccl) hostia

waffle ['wɑfəl] *s* barquillo

waffle iron *s* barquillero

waft [wæft] o [wɑft] *tr* llevar por el aire; llevar por encima del agua ‖ *intr* flotar

wag [wæg] *s* (*of head*) meneo; (*of tail*) coleada; (*jester*) bromista *mf* ‖ *v* (*pret & pp* **wagged;** *ger* **wagging**) *tr* menear (*la cabeza, la cola*) ‖ *intr* menearse

wage [wedʒ] *s* salario; **wages** galardón *m,* premio ‖ *tr* hacer (*la guerra*)

wage earner ['ʌrnər] *s* asalariado

wager ['wedʒər] *s* apuesta; **to lay a wager** hacer una apuesta ‖ *tr & intr* apostar

wage'work'er *s* asalariado

waggish ['wægɪʃ] *adj* divertido, gracioso; (*person*) bromista

Wagnerian [vɑg'nɪrɪ•ən] *adj & s* vagneriano

wagon ['wægən] *s* carro, furgón *m,* carretón *m;* **on the wagon** (slang) sin tomar bebidas alcohólicas; **to hitch one's wagon to a star** poner el tiro muy alto

wag'tail' *s* aguanieves *m,* aguzanieves *m*

waif [wef] *s* (*foundling*) expósito; animal extraviado o abandonado; (*stray child*) granuja *m*

wail [wel] *s* gemido, lamento ‖ *intr* gemir, lamentar

wain•scot ['wenskət] o ['wenskɑt] *s* arrimadillo, friso de madera ‖ *v* (*pret & pp* **-scoted** o **-scotted;** *ger* **-scoting** o **-scotting**) *tr* poner arrimadillo o friso de madera a

waist [west] *s* (*of human body; corresponding part of garment*) talle *m,* cintura; (*garment*) corpiño, jubón *m,* blusa

waist'band' *s* pretina

waist'cloth' *s* taparrabo

waistcoat ['west,kot] o ['wɛskət] *s* chaleco

waist'line' *s* cintura

wait [wet] *s* espera; **to have a good wait** (coll) esperar sentado; **to lie in wait for** acechar emboscado ‖ *tr—***to wait one's turn** esperar vez ‖ *intr* esperar, aguardar; **to wait for** esperar, aguardar; **to wait on**

atender, despachar (*a los parroquianos en una tienda*); servir (*a una persona a la mesa*); **to wait until** esperar a que

waiter ['wetər] *s* camarero, mozo de restaurante; (*tray*) bandeja

waiting list *s* lista de espera

waiting room *s* (*of station*) sala de espera; (*of doctor's office*) antesala

waitress ['wetrɪs] *s* camarera, moza de restaurante

waive [wev] *tr* renunciar a (*un derecho*); diferir, poner a un lado

waiver ['wevər] *s* renuncia

wake [wek] *s* (*watch by the body of a dead person*) velatorio; (*of a boat or other moving object*) estela; **in the wake of** siguiendo inmediatamente; de resultas de ‖ *v* (*pret* **waked** o **woke** [wok];ʾ *pp* **waked**) *tr* despertar ‖ *intr—***to wake to** darse cuenta de; **to wake up** despertar

wakeful ['wekfəl] *adj* desvelado

wakefulness ['wekfəlnɪs] *s* desvelo

waken ['wekən] *tr & intr* despertar

wale [wel] *s* verdugón *m*

Wales [welz] *s* Gales, el país de Gales

walk [wɔk] *s* (*act*) paseo; (*distance*) caminata; (*way of walking, bearing*) andar *m,* paso; (*of a horse*) andadura; (*place to walk animals*) cercado; empleo, cargo, carrera; **at a walk** al paso de una persona; **to go for a walk** salir a pasear; **to take a walk** dar un paseo ‖ *tr* pasear (*a un niño, un caballo*); caminar (*recorrer caminando*); hacer ir al paso (*un caballo*); **to walk off** quitarse (*p.ej., un dolor de cabeza*) caminando ‖ *intr* andar, caminar, ir a pie; (*to stroll*) pasear; **to walk away from** alejarse caminando de; **to walk off with** cargar con, llevarse; **to walk out** salir repentinamente; declararse en huelga; **to walk out on** (coll) dejar airadamente

walkaway ['wɔkə,we] *s* (coll) triunfo fácil

walker ['wɔkər] *s* caminante *mf;* (*pedestrian*) peatón *m;* (*gocart*) andaderas

walkie-talkie ['wɔki'tɔki] *s* (rad) transmisorreceptor *m* portátil

walking papers *spl* (coll) despedida de un empleo

walking stick *s* bastón *m*

walk'-on' *s* (theat) parte *f* de por medio

walk'out' *s* (coll) huelga

walk'o'ver *s* (coll) triunfo fácil

wall [wɔl] *s* muro; (*between rooms; of a pipe, boiler, etc.*) pared *f;* (*of a fortification*) muralla; **to drive to the wall** poner entre la espada y la pared; **to go to the wall** rendirse; fracasar ‖ *tr* murar, amurallar (*una ciudad, un castillo*); emparedar (*a un criminal*); **to wall up** cerrar con muro

wall'board' *s* cartón *m* tabla

wallet ['wɑlɪt] *s* cartera de bolsillo

wall'flow'er *s* alhelí *m;* **to be a wallflower** (coll) comer pavo, planchar el asiento

Walloon [wɑ'lun] *adj & s* valón *m*

wallop ['wɑləp] s (coll) golpaza, puñetazo ‖ tr (coll) golpear fuertemente; (coll) vencer cabalmente

wallow ['wɑlo] s revuelco; (place) revolcadero ‖ intr revolcarse; (e.g., in wealth) nadar

wall'pa'per s papel m de empapelar, papel pintado ‖ tr empapelar

walnut ['wɔlnət] s (tree and wood) nogal m; nuez f de nogal

walrus ['wɔlrəs] o ['wɑlrəs] s morsa

Walter ['wɔltər] s Gualterio

waltz [wɔlts] s vals m ‖ tr hacer valsar; (coll) conducir directamente ‖ intr valsar

wan [wɑn] adj (comp **wanner**; super **wannest**) pálido, macilento; débil

wand [wɑnd] s vara; (of deviner or magician) varilla de virtudes

wander ['wɑndər] tr recorrer a la ventura ‖ intr errar, vagar; extraviarse, perderse; to **wander around** errar de una parte a otra

wanderer ['wɑndərər] s vagabundo; peregrino

wan'der•lust' s ansia de viajar

wane [wen] s decadencia, declinación; menguante f de la luna; on the **wane** decayendo, declinando; menguando (la luna) ‖ intr decaer, declinar; menguar (la luna)

wangle ['wɛŋgəl] tr (to obtain by scheming) (coll) mamar o mamarse; (coll) adulterar, falsear (cuentas); to **wangle one's way out of** (coll) salir con maña de ‖ intr (to get along by scheming) (coll) sacudirse

want [wɑnt] o [wɔnt] s deseo; necesidad; carencia; for **want of** a falta de; to **be in want** pasar necesidad ‖ tr desear; necesitar; carecer de ‖ intr desear; to **want for** necesitar; carecer de

want ad s anuncio clasificado

wanton ['wɑntən] adj inconsiderado, desconsiderado; insensible, perverso; disoluto, licencioso; lascivo; cabezudo

war [wɔr] s guerra; to **go to war** declarar la guerra; (as a soldier) ir a la guerra; to **wage war** hacer la guerra ‖ v (pret & pp **warred**; ger **warring**) intr guerrear; to **war on** guerrear con, hacer la guerra a

warble ['wɔrbəl] s gorjeo, trino ‖ intr gorjear, trinar

warbler ['wɔrblər] s pájaro cantor; curruca de cabeza negra

war cloud s amenaza de guerra

ward [wɔrd] s (person, usually a minor, under protection of another) pupilo; (guardianship) custodia, tutela; (of a city) barrio, distrito; (of a hospital) cuadra, crujía; (of a lock) guarda ‖ tr— to **ward off** parar, desviar

warden ['wɔrdən] s guardián m; (of a jail) alcaide m, carcelero; (of a church) capiller m; (in charge of fire prevention) vigía m

ward heeler s muñidor m

ward'robe' s (closet or cabinet for holding clothes) guardarropa m; (stock of clothing for a person) vestuario; (theat) guardarropía

wardrobe trunk s baúl ropero

ward'room' s (nav) cámara de oficiales

ware [wɛr] s loza; **wares** efectos, artículos de comercio, mercancías

war effort s esfuerzo bélico

ware'house' s almacén m; (for furniture) guardamuebles m

warehouse•man ['wɛr,hausmən] s (pl **-men** [mən]) almacenista m; guardaalmacén m

war'fare' s guerra

war'head' s punta de combate

war horse s corcel m de guerra; (coll) veterano

warily ['wɛrɪli] adv cautelosamente

wariness ['wɛrɪnɪs] s cautela

war'like' adj guerrero

war loan s empréstito de guerra

war lord s jefe m militar

warm [wɔrm] adj (being moderately hot) caliente; (neither hot nor cold) templado; (clothing) abrigador; (climate, region) caluroso; (color) cálido; (fig) caluroso, cordial; to **be warm** (said of a person) tener calor; (said of the weather) hacer calor ‖ tr calentar, acalorar; (fig) animar, acalorar; to **warm up** recalentar (p.ej., la comida); hacer más amistoso ‖ intr calentarse; to **warm up** templar (el tiempo); (with work or exercise) acalorarse; to **warm up to** cobrar afecto a

warm-blooded ['wɔrm'blʌdɪd] adj apasionado, ardiente; (animals) de sangre caliente

war memorial s monumento a los caídos

warmer ['wɔrmər] s calentador m

warm-hearted ['wɔrm'hɑrtɪd] adj afectuoso, de buen corazón; cariñoso; simpático

warming pan s mundillo

warmonger ['wɔr,mʌŋgər] s belicista mf

war mother s madrina de guerra

warmth [wɔrmθ] s calor m; ardor m, entusiasmo; cordialidad

warm'-up' s calentón m

warn [wɔrn] tr advertir, avisar; (to exhort) amonestar; (to advise) aconsejar

warning adj de aviso ‖ s advertencia, aviso

War of the Roses s guerra de las dos Rosas

warp [wɔrp] s (of a fabric) urdimbre f; (of a board) comba, alabeo; aberración mental; (naut) espía ‖ tr combar, alabear; pervertir (el juicio de una persona); (naut) move, con espía ‖ intr combarse, alabearse; (naut) espiar

war'path' s—to **be on the warpath** prepararse para la guerra; estar buscando pendencia

war'plane' s avión m de guerra

warrant ['wɑrənt] o ['wɔrənt] s garantía, promesa; (for arrest) orden f de prisión; (before a judge) citación; cédula, certificado ‖ tr garantizar, prometer; autorizar; justificar

warrantable ['wɑrəntəbəl] o ['wɔrəntəbəl] adj garantizable; justificable

warrant officer s suboficial m de las clases

w
wa

warren ['wɑrən] o ['wɔrən] s (*where rabbits breed*) conejera; barrio densamente poblado

warrior ['wɔrjər] s guerrero

Warsaw ['wɔrsɔ] s Varsovia

war'ship' s buque m de guerra

wart [wɔrt] s verruga

war'time' s tiempo de guerra

war'-torn' adj devastado por la guerra

war to the death s guerra a muerte

war•y [wɛri] adj (*comp* -ier; *super* -iest) cauteloso

wash [wɑʃ] o [wɔʃ] s lavado; (*clothes washed or to be washed*) jabonado; (*dirty water*) lavazas; loción; (*place where surf breaks*) batiente m; (aer) estela turbulenta ‖ tr lavar; fregar (*los platos*); bañar, mojar; **to wash away** quitar lavando; derrubiar (*las aguas corrientes la tierra de las riberas*) ‖ intr lavarse; lavar la ropa; batir (*el agua*); derrubiarse

washable ['wɑʃəbəl] o ['wɔʃəbəl] adj lavable

wash and wear adj de lava y pon

wash'ba'sin s jofaina, palangana

wash'bas'ket s cesto de la colada

wash'board' s lavadero, tabla de lavar; (*baseboard*) rodapié m

wash'bowl' s jofaina, palangana

wash'cloth' s paño para lavarse

wash'day' s día m de la colada

washed-out ['wɑʃt,aut] o ['wɔʃt,aut] adj desteñido; (coll) debilitado, rendido

washed-up ['wɑʃt,ʌp] o ['wɔʃt,ʌp] adj (coll) agotado, deslomado

washer ['wɑʃər] o ['wɔʃər] s lavador m; (*machine*) lavadora; (*ring of metal placed under head of bolt*) arandela; (*ring of rubber, etc., to keep a spigot from leaking*) zapatilla; (phot) lavador

wash•er•wom'an s (*pl* -wom'en) lavandera

wash goods spl tejidos lavables

washing ['wɑʃɪŋ] o ['wɔʃɪŋ] s (*act of washing; washed clothes or clothes to be washed*) lavado; lavada; **washings** (*dirty water; abraded material*) lavadura

washing machine s lejiadora, lavadora mecánica

washing soda s sal f de sosa

wash'out' s derrubio; derrumbe m; (coll) desilusión, fracaso

wash'rag' s paño para lavarse; paño de cocina

wash'room' s gabinete m de aseo, lavabo

wash'stand' s lavamanos m

wash'tub' s cuba de colada, tina de lavar

wash water s lavazas

wasp [wɑsp] s avispa

waste [west] s derroche m, desgaste m; (*garbage*) basura, despojo; (*wild region*) despoblado, yermo; (*of time*) pérdida; (*useless by-products*) desperdicios; excremento; (*for wiping machinery*) hilacha de algodón; **to lay waste** devastar, poner a fuego y sangre ‖ tr malgastar, perder ‖ intr—**to waste away** consumirse

waste'bas'ket s papelera

wasteful ['westfəl] adj derrochador, manirroto; devastador, destructivo

waste'-land' s peladero

waste paper s papeles usados, papel de desecho, papel viejo

waste pipe s tubo de desagüe

waste products spl desperdicios; materia excretada

wastrel ['westrəl] s derrochador m, malgastador m; pródigo, perdido

watch [wɑtʃ] s reloj m (*de bolsillo o de pulsera*); (*lookout*) vigía m; (mil) vigilia; (naut) guardia; **to be on the watch for** estar a la mira de; **to keep watch over** velar ‖ tr (*to look at*) mirar; (*to oversee*) velar, vigilar; guardar; tener cuidado con ‖ intr mirar; (*to keep awake*) velar; **to watch for** acechar; **to watch out** tener cuidado; **to watch out for** estar a la mira de; tener cuidado con; guardarse de; **to watch over** velar, vigilar

watch'case' s caja de reloj

watch charm s dije m

watch crystal s cristal m de reloj

watch'dog' s perro de guarda, perro guardián; (fig) guardián m fiel

watchful ['wɑtʃfəl] adj desvelado, vigilante

watchfulness ['wɑtʃfəlnɪs] s desvelo, vigilancia

watch'mak'er s relojero

watch•man ['wɑtʃmən] s (*pl* -men [mən]) vigilante m, velador m

watch night s noche vieja; oficio de noche vieja

watch pocket s relojera

watch strap s pulsera

watch'tow'er s atalaya, vigía

watch'word' s santo y seña; (*slogan*) lema m

water ['wɔtər] o ['wɑtər] s agua; **of the first water** de lo mejor; **to back water** ciar; **to carry water on both shoulders** nadar entre dos aguas; **to fish in troubled waters** pescar en río revuelto; **to hold water** (coll) ser bien fundado; **to make water** (*to urinate*) hacer aguas; (naut) hacer agua; **to pour** o **throw cold water on** echar un jarro de agua (fría) a ‖ tr regar, rociar; abrevar (*el ganado*); aguar (*el vino*); proveer de agua ‖ intr abrevarse (*el ganado*); tomar agua (*una locomotora*); llorar (*los ojos*)

water carrier s aguador m

water closet s excusado, retrete m, váter m

water color s acuarela

wa'ter•course' s corriente f de agua; lecho de corriente

water cress s berzo

water cure s cura de aguas

wa'ter•fall' s cascada, caída de agua

water front s terreno ribereño

water gap s garganta, hondonada

water hammer s golpe m de ariete

water heater s calentador m de agua

water ice s sorbete m

watering can s regadera

watering place s aguadero; balneario

watering pot s regadera

watering trough s abrevadero

water jacket *s* camisa de agua
water lily *s* ninfea, nenúfar *m*
water line *s* línea de agua, línea de flotación; nivel *m* de agua
water main *s* cañería de agua
wa´ter·mark´ *s* (*in paper*) filigrana; marca de nivel de agua
wa´ter·mel´on *s* sandía
water meter *s* contador *m* de agua
water pipe *s* cañería de agua
water polo *s* polo de agua
water power *s* fuerza de agua, hulla blanca
wa´ter·proof´ *adj & s* impermeable *m*
wa´ter·shed´ *s* divisoria de aguas; (*drainage area*) cuenca
water ski *s* esquí acuático
wa´ter·spout´ *s* (*to carry water from roof*) canalón *m*; (*funnel of wet air extending from cloud to surface of water*) manga de agua, tromba marina
wa´ter·sup·ply´ system *s* fontanería
wa´ter·tight´ *adj* estanco, hermético; (fig) seguro
water tower *s* arca de agua
water wagon *s* (mil) carro de agua; **on the water wagon** (slang) sin tomar bebidas alcohólicas
wa´ter·way´ *s* vía de agua, vía fluvial; (naut) canalizo
water wheel *s* rueda de agua; turbina de agua; (*of steamboat*) rueda de paletas
water wings *spl* nadaderas
wa´ter·works´ *s* estación de bombas
watery [´wɔtəri] o [´wɑtəri] *adj* acuoso; (*said of the eyes*) lagrimoso, lloroso; insípido; húmedo, mojado
watt [wɑt] *s* vatio
wattage [´wɑtɪdʒ] *s* vatiaje *m*
watt´-hour´ *s* (*pl* **watt-hours**) vatiohora
wattle [´wɑtəl] *s* (*of bird*) barba; (*of fish*) barbilla
watt´me´ter *s* vatímetro
wave [wev] *s* onda; (*of hair*) onda, ondulación; (*e.g., of heat or cold*) ola; (*e.g., of strikes*) oleaje *m*; señal hecha con la mano ‖ *tr* blandir (*la espada*); ondear, ondular (*el cabello*); hacer señal con (*la mano*); decir (*adiós*) con la mano; **to wave aside** rechazar ‖ *intr* ondear u ondearse; hacer señal con la mano
wave motion *s* movimiento ondulatorio
waver [´wevər] *intr* oscilar; (*to hesitate*) vacilar, titubear; (*to totter*) tambalear
wave theory *s* teoría ondulatoria
wav·y [´wevi] *adj* (*comp* **-ier**; *super* **-iest**) undoso, ondoso; (*water*) ondulado; (*hair*) ondeado
wax [wæks] *s* cera; **to be wax in one's hands** ser como una cera ‖ *tr* encerar; cerotear (*el hilo*) ‖ *intr* hacerse, volverse; crecer (*la luna*)
wax paper *s* papel encerado, papel parafinado
wax taper *s* cerilla
wax´works´ *s* museo de cera
way [we] *s* vía, camino; dirección; sentido; manera, modo; costumbre, hábito; **across**

the way enfrente; **a good way** un buen trecho; **all the way** hasta el fin del camino; **any way** de cualquier modo; **by the way** a propósito; **in a way** hasta cierto punto; **in every way** en todos respectos; **in this way** de este modo; **on the way to** camino de, rumbo a; **on the way out** saliendo; desapareciendo; **out of the way** hecho, despachado; inconveniente, impropio; a un lado, apartado; fuera de lo común; **that way** por allí; de ese modo; **this way** por aquí; de este modo; **to be in the way** estorbar; **to feel one's way** tantear el camino; proceder con tiento; **to force one's way** abrirse paso por fuerza; **to get out of the way** quitarse de en medio; (*to finish*) quitarse de encima; **to give way** ceder, retroceder; romperse (*una cuerda*); fracasar; **to give way to** entregarse a; **to go out of one's way** dar un rodeo; dar un rodeo innecesario; darse molestia; **to have one's way** salirse con la suya; **to keep out of the way** no obstruir el paso; **to know one's way around** saber entendérselas; **to know one's way to** conocer el camino a, saber ir a; **to lead the way** enseñar el camino; ir o entrar primero; **to lose one's way** perder el camino, extraviarse; **to make one's way** avanzar; hacer carrera, acreditarse; **to make way for** dar paso a, hacer lugar para; **to mend one's ways** mudar de vida; **to not know which way to turn** no saber dónde meterse; **to put out of the way** alejar, apartar; quitar de en medio; **to see one's way to** ver el modo de; **to take one's way** irse, marcharse; **to wend one's way** seguir camino; **to wind one's way through** serpentear por; **to wing one's way** ir volando; **under way** en marcha, en camino; **way in** entrada; **way out** salida; **ways** maneras, modales *mpl*; (*for launching a ship*) anguilas; **which way?** ¿por dónde?; ¿cómo?
way´bill´ *s* hoja de ruta
wayfarer [´we,fɛrər] *s* caminante *mf*
way´lay´ *v* (*pret & pp* **-laid´**) *tr* detener de improviso; (*to attack from ambush*) insidiar, asaltar
way´side´ *s* borde *m* del camino; **to fall by the wayside** (*to disappear*) caer en el camino; fracasar
way station *s* apeadero
way train *s* tren *m* ómnibus
wayward [´wewərd] *adj* díscolo, voluntarioso; voltario, caprichoso
w.c. *abbr* **water closet, without charge**
we [wi] *pron pers* nosotros
weak [wik] *adj* débil, flaco; caedizo; (*vowel; verb*) débil
weaken [´wikən] *tr* debilitar, enflaquecer ‖ *intr* debilitarse, enflaquecerse
weakling [´wiklɪŋ] *s* alfeñique *m*, canijo
weak-minded [´wik´maɪndɪd] *adj* irresoluto; simple, mentecato
weakness [´wiknɪs] *s* debilidad, flaqueza; caducidad; lado débil; afición, gusto
weal [wil] *s* verdugón *m*
wealth [wɛlθ] *s* riqueza

wa
we

wealth·y ['wɛlθi] *adj* (*comp* **-ier;** *super* **-iest**) rico

wean [win] *tr* destetar; **to wean away from** apartar gradualmente de

weanling ['winlɪŋ] *adj & s* destetado

weapon ['wɛpən] *s* arma

wear [wɛr] *s* (*act of wearing*) uso; (*clothing*) ropa; estilo, moda; (*wasting away from use*) desgaste *m*, deterioro; (*lasting quality*) durabilidad; **for all kinds of wear** a todo llevar; **for everyday wear** para todo trote ‖ *v* (*pret* **wore** [wor]; *pp* **worn** [worn]) *tr* llevar, traer, llevar puesto; calzar (*cierto tamaño de zapato o guante*); (*to waste away by use*) desgastar, deteriorar; (*to tire*) agotar, cansar; **to wear out** consumir, gastar; agotar, cansar; abusar de (*la hospitalidad de una persona*) ‖ *intr* desgastarse, deteriorarse; **to wear off** pasar, desaparecer; **to wear out** gastarse, usarse; **to wear well** durar, ser duradero

wear and tear *s* uso y desgaste

weariness ['wɪrɪnɪs] *s* cansancio; aburrimiento

wearing apparel ['wɛrɪŋ] *s* ropaje *m*, prendas de vestir

wearisome ['wɪrɪsəm] *adj* aburrido, cansado, fastidioso

wea·ry ['wɪri] *adj* (*comp* **-rier;** *super* **-riest**) cansado ‖ *v* (*pret & pp* **-ried**) *tr* cansar ‖ *intr* cansarse

weasel ['wizəl] *s* comadreja

weaseler ['wizələr] *s* pancista *mf*

weasel words *spl* palabras ambiguas

weather ['wɛðər] *s* tiempo; mal tiempo; **to be under the weather** (coll) no estar muy católico; (coll) estar borracho ‖ *tr* aguantar (*el temporal, la adversidad*)

weather-beaten ['wɛðər,bitən] *adj* curtido por la intemperie

weather bureau *s* meteo *f*, servicio meteorológico

weath'er·cock' *s* veleta; (*fickle person*) (fig) veleta

weather forecasting *s* pronóstico del tiempo, previsión del tiempo

weather·man ['wɛðər,mæn] *s* (*pl* **-men** [,mɛn]) meteorologista *m*, pronosticador *m* del tiempo

weather report *s* parte meteorológico

weather station *s* estación meteorológica

weather stripping ['strɪpɪŋ] *s* burlete *m*, cierre hermético

weather vane *s* veleta

weave [wiv] *s* tejido ‖ *v* (*pret* **wove** [wov] o **weaved;** *pp* **wove** o **woven** ['wovən]) *tr* tejer; **to weave one's way** avanzar zigzagueando ‖ *intr* tejer; zigzaguear

weaver ['wivər] *s* tejedor *m*

web [wɛb] *s* tejido, tela; (*of spider*) tela; (*between toes of birds and other animals*) membrana; (*of an iron rail*) alma; (fig) tejido, tela, enredo

web-footed ['wɛb,fʊtɪd] *adj* palmípedo, de pie palmeado

wed [wɛd] *v* (*pret & pp* **wed** o **wedded;** *ger* **wedding**) *tr* (*to join in marriage*) casar; casarse con ‖ *intr* casarse

wedding ['wɛdɪŋ] *adj* nupcial ‖ *s* bodas, nupcias, matrimonio

wedding cake *s* pastel *m* de boda

wedding day *s* día *m* de bodas

wedding march *s* marcha nupcial

wedding night *s* noche *f* de bodas

wedding ring *s* anillo nupcial

wedge [wɛdʒ] *s* cuña ‖ *tr* acuñar, apretar con cuña

wed'lock' *s* matrimonio

Wednesday ['wɛnzdi] *s* miércoles *m*

wee [wi] *adj* pequeñito, diminuto

weed [wid] *s* mala hierba; (coll) tabaco; **weeds** ropa de luto (*especialmente, de una viuda*) ‖ *tr* desherbar, escardar

weeding hoe *s* escardillo

weed killer *s* matamalezas *m*, herbicida *m*

week [wik] *s* semana; **week in week out** semana tras semana

week'day' *s* día *m* laborable

week'days' *adv* entresemana (SAm)

week'end' *s* fin *m* de semana ‖ *intr* pasar el fin de semana

week·ly ['wikli] *adj* semanal ‖ *adv* cada semana ‖ *s* (*pl* **-lies**) revista semanal, semanario

weep [wip] *v* (*pret & pp* **wept** [wɛpt]) *tr* llorar (*p.ej., la muerte de una persona*); derramar (*lágrimas*) ‖ *intr* llorar

weeper ['wipər] *s* llorón *m*; (*hired mourner*) llorona, plañidera

weeping willow *s* sauce *m* llorón

weep·y ['wipi] *adj* (*comp* **-ier;** *super* **-iest**) (coll) lloroso

weevil ['wivəl] *s* gorgojo

weft [wɛft] *s* (*yarns running across warp*) trama; (*fabric*) tejido

weigh [we] *tr* pesar; (naut) levantar (*el ancla*) ‖ *intr* pesar; **to weigh in** pesarse (*un jockey*)

weight [wet] *s* peso; (*of scales, clock, gymnasium, etc.*) pesa; **to lose weight** rebajar de peso; **to put on weight** ponerse gordo; **to throw one's weight around** (coll) hacer valer su poder ‖ *tr* cargar, gravar; (*statistically*) ponderar

weightless ['wetlɪs] *adj* ingrávido

weightlessness ['wetlɪsnɪs] *s* ingravidez *f*; antigravedad

weight lifter *s* halterofilista *mf*

weight lifting *s* halterofilia

weight·y ['weti] *adj* (*comp* **-ier;** *super* **-iest**) (*heavy*) pesado; (*troublesome*) gravoso; importante, influyente

weir [wɪr] *s* presa, vertedero; (*for catching fish*) pescadera

weird [wɪrd] *adj* misterioso, sobrenatural, espectral; extraño, raro

welcome ['wɛlkəm] *adj* bienvenido; grato, agradable; **you are welcome** (*i.e., gladly received*) sea Vd. bienvenido; (*in answer to thanks*) no hay de qué; **you are welcome to it** está a la disposición de Vd.; **you are welcome to your opinion** piense Vd. lo que quiera ‖ *interj* ¡bienvenido! ‖ *s* bienvenida, buena acogida ‖ *tr* dar la bienvenida a; acoger con gusto, recibir con amabilidad

weld [wɛld] *s* autógena; (bot) gualda ‖ *tr* soldar con autógena; (fig) unir ‖ *intr* soldarse

welder ['wɛldər] *s* soldador *m; (machine)* soldadora

welding ['wɛldɪŋ] *s* autógena, soldadura autógena

wel'fare' *s* bienestar *m; (effort to improve living conditions of the underprivileged)* asistencia, beneficencia; **to be on welfare** vivir de la asistencia pública

welfare state *s* gobierno socializante, estado de beneficencia, estado asistencial

well [wɛl] *adj* bien; bien de salud; **get well!** ¡que se mejore! ‖ *adv* bien; pues; pues bien; **as well** también; **as well as** así como; además de ‖ *interj* ¡vaya! ‖ *s* pozo; *(natural source of water)* fuente *f*, manantial *m* ‖ *intr*—**to well up** salir a borbotones

well-appointed ['wɛlə'pɔɪntɪd] *adj* bien amueblado, bien equipado

well-attended ['wɛlə'tɛndɪd] *adj* muy concurrido

well-behaved ['wɛlbɪ'hevd] *adj* de buena conducta

well'-be'ing *s* bienestar *m*

well'born' *adj* bien nacido

well-bred ['wɛl'brɛd] *adj* cortés, bien criado

well-disposed ['wɛldɪs'pozd] *adj* bien dispuesto

well-done ['wɛl'dʌn] *adj* bien hecho; *(meat)* bien asado

well-fixed ['wɛl'fɪkst] *adj* (coll) acaudalado

well-formed ['wɛl'fɔrmd] *adj* bien formado; *(nose)* perfilado

well-founded ['wɛl'faʊndɪd] *adj* bien fundado

well-groomed ['wɛl'grumd] *adj* de mucho aseo, atildado

well-heeled ['wɛl'hild] *adj* (coll) acomodado; **to be well-heeled** (coll) tener bien cubierto el riñón

well-informed ['wɛlɪn'fɔrmd] *adj* versado, bien enterado

well-intentioned ['wɛlɪn'tɛnʃənd] *adj* bien intencionado

well-kept ['wɛl'kɛpt] *adj* bien cuidado, bien atendido; *(secret)* bien guardado

well-known ['wɛl'non] *adj* bien conocido; familiar

well-meaning ['wɛl'minɪŋ] *adj* bien intencionado

well-nigh ['wɛl'naɪ] *adv* casi

well'-off' *adj* adinerado, acaudalado

well-preserved ['wɛlprɪ'zʌrvd] *adj* bien conservado

well-read ['wɛl'rɛd] *adj* leído, muy leído

well-spent ['wɛl'spɛnt] *adj* *(money, youth, life)* bien empleado

well-spoken ['wɛl'spokən] *adj* *(person)* bienhablado; *(word)* bien dicho

well'spring' *s* fuente *f*, manantial *m;* fuente inagotable

well sweep *s* cigoñal *m*

well-tempered ['wɛl'tɛmpərd] *adj* bien templado

well-thought-of ['wɛl'θɔt,ʌv] *adj* bien mirado

well-timed ['wɛl'taɪmd] *adj* oportuno

well-to-do ['wɛltə'du] *adj* adinerado, acaudalado; (coll) plateado

well-wisher ['wɛl'wɪʃər] *s* amigo, favorecedor *m*

well-worn ['wɛl'worn] *adj* trillado, vulgar

welsh [wɛlʃ] *intr* (slang) dejar de cumplir; **to welsh on** (slang) dejar de cumplir con ‖ **Welsh** *adj* galés ‖ *s (language)* galés *m;* **the Welsh** los galeses

Welsh·man ['wɛlʃmən] *s (pl* **-men** [mən]) galés *m*

Welsh rabbit o **rarebit** ['rɛrbɪt] *s* tostada cubierta de queso derretido en cerveza

welt [wɛlt] *s (finish along a seam)* ribete *m; (of a shoe)* vira; *(wale from a blow)* verdugón *m*

welter ['wɛltər] *s* confusión, conmoción; *(a tumbling about)* revuelco ‖ *intr* revolcar

wel'ter·weight' *s* (box) peso mediano ligero

wen [wɛn] *s* lobanillo

wench [wɛntʃ] *s* muchacha, jovencita; moza, criada

wend [wɛnd] *tr*—**to wend one's way** dirigir sus pasos, seguir su camino

west [wɛst] *adj* occidental, del oeste ‖ *adv* al oeste, hacia el oeste ‖ *s* oeste *m*

western ['wɛstərn] *adj* occidental ‖ *s* película del Oeste

West Indies ['ɪndiz] *spl* Indias Occidentales

westward ['wɛstwərd] *adv* hacia el oeste

wet [wɛt] *adj (comp* **wetter;** *super* **wettest)** mojado; *(damp)* húmedo; *(paint)* fresco; *(weather)* lluvioso; (coll) antiprohibicionista ‖ *s* (coll) antiprohibicionista *mf* ‖ *v (pret & pp* **wet** o **wetted;** *ger* **wetting)** *tr* mojar ‖ *intr* mojarse

wet'back' *s* mojado

wet bar *s* bar *m* con agua corriente

wet battery *s* pila húmeda

wet blanket *s* aguafiestas *mf*

wet goods *spl* caldos

wet nurse *s* ama de cría o de leche

w.f. *abbr* **wrong font**

w.g. *abbr* **wire gauge**

whack [hwæk] *s* (coll) golpe ruidoso; (coll) prueba, tentativa ‖ *tr* (coll) golpear ruidosamente

whale [hwel] *s* ballena; *(sperm whale)* cachalote *m;* **a whale at** (coll) un as de; **a whale for** (coll) un genio para; **a whale of a difference** (coll) una enorme diferencia; **a whale of a meal** (coll) una comida brutal ‖ *tr* (coll) azotar ‖ *intr* pescar ballenas

whale'bone' *s* ballena

wharf [hwɔrf] *s (pl* **wharves** [hwɔrvz] o **wharfs)** muelle *m*, embarcadero

what [hwɑt] *pron interr* qué; cuál; **what else?** ¿qué más?; **what if . . .?** ¿y si . . .?, ¿qué le parece si?; **what of it?** ¿qué importa? ‖ *pron rel* lo que; **what's what** lo que hay, toda la verdad ‖ *adj interr* qué ‖

adj rel el . . . que, la . . . que, etc. ‖ *interj* qué; **what a . . .!** qué . . . más o tan, p.ej., **what a beautiful day!** ¡qué día más (o tan) hermoso!

what•ev′er *pron* cualquiera; todo lo que ‖ *adj* cualquier; cualquier . . . que

what′not′ *s* juguetero

what's-his-name ['hwɑtsɪz,nem] *s* (coll) el señor fulano

wheal [hwil] *s* roncha

wheat [hwit] *s* trigo

wheedle ['hwidəl] *tr* engatusar; conseguir por medio de halagos

wheel [hwil] *s* rueda; (coll) bicicleta; **at the wheel** en el volante ‖ *tr* pasear (*a un niño*) en un cochecito; conducir (*a un enfermo*) en una silla de ruedas ‖ *intr* (coll) ir en bicicleta; **to wheel about** o **around** dar una vuelta; cambiar de opinión

wheelbarrow ['hwil,bæro] *s* carretilla

wheel base *s* batalla, paso, distancia entre ejes

wheel chair *s* silla de ruedas, cochecillo para inválidos

wheeler-dealer ['hwilər'dilər] *s* (slang) negociante *m* de gran influencia e independencia

wheel horse *s* caballo de varas; (fig) esclavo (*el que trabaja mucho y cumple con sus obligaciones*)

wheelwright ['hwil,raɪt] *s* carpintero de carretas

wheeze [hwiz] *s* resuello ruidoso ‖ *intr* resollar produciendo un silbido

whelp [hwɛlp] *s* cachorro ‖ *intr* parir

when [hwɛn] *adv* cuándo ‖ *conj* cuando

whence [hwɛns] *adv* de dónde; por lo tanto ‖ *conj* de donde

when•ev′er *conj* siempre que, cada vez que

where [hwɛr] *adv* dónde; adónde ‖ *conj* donde; adonde

whereabouts ['hwɛrə,bauts] *s* paradero

whereas [hwɛr'æz] *conj* mientras que, al paso que; considerando ‖ *s* considerando

where•by′ *adv* por medio del cual

wherefore ['hwɛrfor] *adv* por qué, para qué; por eso, por tanto ‖ *conj* por lo cual ‖ *s* motivo, razón *f*

where•from′ *adv* de donde

where•in′ *adv* donde, en qué ‖ *conj* donde; en el que; en lo cual

where•of′ *adv* de qué ‖ *conj* de que; de lo cual

where′up•on′ *adv* con lo cual, después de lo cual

wherever [hwɛr'ɛvər] *conj* dondequiera que

wherewithal ['hwɛrwɪð,ɔl] *s* cumquibus *m*, medios

whet [hwɛt] *v* (*pret & pp* **whetted**; *ger* **whetting**) *tr* afilar, aguzar; despertar, estimular; abrir (*el apetito*)

whether ['wɛðər] *conj* si; **whether or no** en todo caso, de todas maneras; **whether or not** si . . . o no, ya sea que . . . o no

whet′stone′ *s* piedra de afilar

whey [hwe] *s* suero de la leche

which [hwɪtʃ] *pron interr* cuál; **which is which** cuál es el uno y cuál el otro ‖ *pron rel* que, el (la, etc.) que ‖ *adj interr* qué; cuál, cuál de los (las) ‖ *adj rel* el (la, etc.) . . . que

which•ev′er *pron rel* cualquiera ‖ *adj rel* cualquier; **whichever ones** cualesquiera

whiff [hwɪf] *s* soplo; fumada; olorcillo; acceso, arranque *m;* **to get a whiff of** percibir un olor fugaz de ‖ *intr* soplar (*el viento*); echar bocanadas (*el que fuma*)

while [hwaɪl] *conj* mientras, mientras que ‖ *s* rato; **a long while** largo rato; **a while ago** hace un rato; **between whiles** de vez en cuando ‖ *tr* **to while away** entretener (*el tiempo*); pasar (*p.ej., la tarde*) de un modo entretenido

whim [hwɪm] *s* capricho, antojo

whimper ['hwɪmpər] *s* lloriqueo ‖ *tr* decir lloriqueando ‖ *intr* lloriquear

whimsical ['hwɪmzɪkəl] *adj* caprichoso, extravagante, fantástico

whine [hwaɪn] *s* gimoteo, quejido ‖ *intr* gimotear, quejarse

whin•ny ['hwɪni] *s* (*pl* **-nies**) relincho ‖ *v* (*pret & pp* **-nied**) *intr* relinchar

whip [hwɪp] *s* látigo, zurriago; huevos batidos con nata ‖ *v* (*pret & pp* **whipped** o **whipt;** *ger* **whipping**) *tr* azotar, zurriagar, fustigar; batir (*huevos y nata*); (coll) derrotar, vencer; **to whip off** (coll) escribir de prisa; **to whip out** sacar de repente; **to whip up** (coll) preparar de prisa; (coll) avivar, excitar

whip′cord′ *s* tralla; tejido fuerte con costurones diagonales

whip hand *s* mano *f* del látigo; (*upper hand*) vara alta

whip′lash′ *s* tralla

whipped cream *s* nata, crema batida

whipper-snapper ['hwɪpər,snæpər] *s* arrapiezo, mequetrefe *m*

whippet ['hwɪpɪt] *s* perro lebrel!

whipping boy ['hwɪpɪŋ] *s* cabeza de turco, víctima inocente

whipping post *s* poste *m* de flagelación

whippoorwill [,hwɪpər'wɪl] *s* chotacabras norteamericano (*Caprimulgus vociferus*)

whir [hwʌr] *s* zumbido ‖ *v* (*pret & pp* **whirred;** *ger* **whirring**) *intr* girar zumbando

whirl [hwʌrl] *s* vuelta, giro; remolino; (*of events, parties, etc.*) serie *f* interminable ‖ *tr* & *intr* remolinear; **my head whirls** siento vértigo

whirligig ['hwʌrlɪ,gɪg] *s* (ent) escribano del agua; tiovivo; (*pinwheel*) rehilandera, molinete *m;* peonza

whirl′pool′ *s* remolino, vorágine *f*

whirl′wind′ *s* torbellino, manga de viento

whirlybird ['hwʌrlɪ,bʌrd] *s* (coll) helicóptero

whish [hwɪʃ] *s* zumbido suave ‖ *intr* zumbar suavemente

whisk [hwɪsk] *s* escobilla; toque ligero ‖ *tr* barrer, cepillar; **to whisk out of sight** escamotear ‖ *intr* moverse rápidamente

whisk broom *s* escobilla

whiskers ['hwɪskərz] *spl* barbas; (*on side of face*) patillas; (*of cat*) bigotes *mpl*

whiskey ['hwɪski] *adj* (*voice*) (coll) aguardentoso ‖ *s* whisky *m*

whisper ['hwɪspər] *s* cuchicheo; (*of leaves*) susurro; **in a whisper** en voz baja ‖ *tr* susurrar, decir al oído ‖ *intr* cuchichear, hablar al oído: susurrar (*p.ej.*, *las hojas*); (*to gossip*) susurrar, murmurar

whisperer ['hwɪspərər] *s* susurrón *m*

whispering ['hwɪspərɪŋ] *adj & s* (*gossiping*) susurrón *m*

whist [hwɪst] *s* whist *m* (*juego de naipes*)

whistle ['hwɪsəl] *s* (*sound*) silbido, silbo; pitazo; (*device*) silbato, pito; **to wet one's whistle** (coll) remojar la palabra ‖ *tr* silbar (*p.ej.*, *una canción* ‖ *intr* silbar; pitear; **to whistle for** llamar con un silbido; (coll) tener que componérselas sin

whistle stop *s* apeadero, pueblecito

whit [hwɪt] *s*—**not a whit** ni pizca; **to not care a whit** no importarle a (*uno*) un bledo

white [hwaɪt] *adj* blanco ‖ *s* blanco; (*of an egg*) clara; **whites** (pathol) pérdidas blancas, flujo blanco

white'caps' *spl* cabrillas, palomas

white coal *s* hulla blanca

white'-col'lar *adj* oficinesco

white-collar crime *s* crímenes *mpl* de oficinistas

white feather *s*—**to show the white feather** mostrarse cobarde

white goods *spl* tejidos de algodón; ropa blanca; aparatos electrodomésticos

white-haired ['hwaɪt,hɛrd] *adj* de pelo blanco; (*gray-haired*) cano; (coll) favorito, predilecto

white heat *s* blanco, calor blanco; (fig) viva agitación

white lead [lɛd] *s* albayalde *m*

white lie *s* mentirilla, mentira inocente u oficiosa

white meat *s* pechuga, carne *f* de la pechuga del ave

whiten ['hwaɪtən] *tr* blanquear, emblanquecer ‖ *intr* blanquear, emblanquecerse; palidecer

whiteness ['hwaɪtnɪs] *s* blancura

white plague *s* peste blanca (*tuberculosis*)

white slavery *s* trata de blancas

white tie *s* corbatín blanco; traje *m* de etiqueta

white'wash' *s* jalbegue *m*, lechada, blanqueadura; (*e.g.*, *of a scandal*) encubrimiento ‖ *tr* jalbegar, enjalbegar, encalar; absolver sin justicia; encubrir (*un escándalo*)

whither ['hwɪðər] *adv* adónde ‖ *conj* adonde

whitish ['hwaɪtɪʃ] *adj* blanquecino, blancuzco

whitlow ['hwɪtlo] *s* panadizo, uñero

Whitsuntide ['hwɪtsən,taɪd] *s* semana de Pentecostés

whittle ['hwɪtəl] *tr* sacar pedazos a (*un trozo de madera*); **to whittle away** o **down** reducir poco a poco

whiz o **whizz** [hwɪz] *s* silbido, zumbido; (slang) perito, fenómeno ‖ *v* (*pret & pp*

whizzed; *ger* **whizzing**) *intr*—**to whiz by** rehilar, silbar; pasar como una flecha

who [hu] *pron interr* quién; **who else?** ¿quién más?; **who goes there?** (mil) ¿quién vive?; **who's who** quién es el uno y quién el otro; quiénes son gente de importancia ‖ *pron rel* que, quien; el (la, etc.) que

whoa [hwo] o [wo] *interj* ¡so!

who•ev'er *pron rel* quienquiera que, cualquiera que

whole [hol] *adj* todo, entero; (*intact*) ileso; (*not scattered or dispersed*) único, p.ej., **the whole interest for him was the child he was raising** el único interés para él era el niño que educaba; **made out of the whole cloth** enteramente falso o imaginario ‖ *s* conjunto, todo; **as a whole** en conjunto, todo; **on the whole** en general; por la mayor parte

wholehearted ['hol,hɑrtɪd] *adj* sincero, cordial

whole note *s* (mus) semibreve *f*

whole'sale' *adj & adv* al por mayor ‖ *s* venta ·al pormayor ‖ *tr* vender al por mayor ‖ *intr* vender al por mayor; venderse al por mayor

wholesaler ['hol,selər] *s* comerciante *mf* al por mayor

wholesome ['holsəm] *adj* (*conducive to good health*) saludable; (*in good health*) fresco, rollizo

wholly ['holi] *adv* enteramente, completamente

whole wheat *s* trigo entero

whom [hum] *pron interr* a quién ‖ *pron rel* que, a quien; al (a la, etc.) que

whom•ev'er *pron rel* a quienquiera que

whoop [hup] o [hwup] *s* ululato ‖ *tr*—**to whoop it up** (slang) armar una gritería ‖ *intr* ulular

whooping cough ['hupɪŋ] o ['hupɪŋ] *s* tos ferina, tos convulsiva

whopper ['hwapər] *s* (coll) enormidad; (coll) mentirón *m*

whopping ['hwapɪŋ] *adj* (coll) enorme, grandísimo

whore [hor] *s* puta ‖ *intr*—**to whore around** putañear, putear

whore'house' *s* burdel *m;* congal *m* (Mex)

whortleber•ry ['hwʌrtəl,bɛri] *s* (*pl* **-ries**) arándano

whose [huz] *pron interr* de quién ‖ *pron rel* de quien, cuyo

why [hwaɪ] *adv* por qué; **why not?** ¿cómo no? ‖ *s* (*pl* **whys**) porqué *m* ‖ *interj* ¡toma!; **why, certainly!** ¡desde luego!, ¡por supuesto!; **why, yes!** ¡claro!, ¡pues sí!

wick [wɪk] *s* mecha, pabilo

wicked ['wɪkɪd] *adj* malo; malazo; (*mischievous*) travieso, revoltoso; (*vicious*) arisco; ofensivo

wicker ['wɪkər] *adj* mimbroso ‖ *s* mimbre *m & f*

wicket ['wɪkɪt] *s* (*small door in a larger one*) portillo, postigo; (*small opening in a door*) ventanillo; (*ticket window*) taquilla; (*gate to regulate flow of water*) compuerta; (cricket) meta; (croquet) aro

wh
wi

wide [waɪd] *adj* ancho; de ancho; (*sense of a word*) amplio, lato ‖ *adv* de par en par; enteramente; lejos; **wide of the mark** lejos del blanco; fuera de propósito

wide'-an'gle *adj* granangular

wide'-a•wake' *adj* despabilado

widen ['waɪdən] *tr* ensanchar ‖ *intr* ensancharse

wide'-o'pen *adj* abierto de par en par; **to be wide-open** estar (*p.ej., una ciudad*) abierta a los jugadores

wide'spread' *adj* (*arms, wings*) extendido; difundido, extenso

widow ['wɪdo] *s* viuda; (cards) baceta ‖ *tr* dejar viuda

widower ['wɪdo•ər] *s* viudo

widowhood ['wɪdo,hʊd] *s* viudez *f*

widow's mite *s* limosna que da un pobre

widow's pension *s* viudedad

widow's weeds *spl* luto de viuda

width [wɪdθ] *s* anchura

wield [wild] *tr* esgrimir, manejar (*la espada*); ejercer (*el poder*)

wife [waɪf] *s* (*pl* **wives** [waɪvz]) esposa, mujer *f*

wig [wɪg] *s* peluca

wiggle ['wɪgəl] *s* meneo rápido ‖ *tr* menear rápidamente ‖ *intr* menearse rápidamente

wig'wag' *s* comunicación con banderas ‖ *v* (*pret & pp* **-wagged;** *ger* **-wagging**) *tr* menear; mandar (*informes*) moviendo banderas ‖ *intr* menearse; señalar con banderas

wigwam ['wɪgwɑm] *s* choza cónica (*de los pieles rojas*)

wild [waɪld] *adj* (*not domesticated; growing without cultivation; uncivilized*) salvaje; (*unrestrained*) descabellado; (*frantic, mad*) frenético; (*riotous*) desenfrenado, revoltoso; extravagante; (*bullet, shot*) perdido; **wild about** loco por ‖ *adv* disparatadamente; **to run wild** crecer locamente; estar sin gobierno ‖ *s* desierto, yermo; **wilds** monte *m*, despoblado

wild boar *s* jabalí *m*

wild card *s* comodín *m*

wild'cat' *s* gato montés; lince *m;* empresa arriesgada

wildcat strike *s* huelga no autorizada por el sindicato

wilderness ['wɪldərnɪs] *s* desierto, yermo

wild'fire' *s* fuego fatuo; fucilazo; **to spread like wildfire** ser un reguero de pólvora, correr como pólvora en reguero

wild flower *s* flor *f* del campo

wild goose *s* ganso bravo

wild'-goose' chase *s* caza de grillos

wild'life' *s* animales *mf* salvajes

wild oats *spl* excesos de la juventud, mocedad; **to sow one's wild oats** llevar (*los mozos*) una vida de excesos

wild olive *s* acebuche *m*

wile [waɪl] *s* ardid *m* engaño; (*cunning*) astucia ‖ *tr* engatusar; **to wile away** entretener (*el tiempo*); pasar (*p.ej., la tarde*)

will [wɪl] *s* voluntad; (law) testamento; **at will** a voluntad ‖ *tr* querer; (*to bequeath*) legar ‖ *intr* querer; **do as you will** haga

Vd. lo que quiera ‖ *v* (*pret & cond* **would**) *v aux* **he will arrive at six o'clock** llegará a las seis; **he will go for days without smoking** pasa días enteros sin fumar

willful ['wɪlfəl] *adj* voluntarioso

willfulness ['wɪlfəlnɪs] *s* voluntariedad

William ['wɪljəm] *s* Guillermo

willing ['wɪlɪŋ] *adj* dispuesto; gustoso; pronto; espontáneo; **willing or unwilling** que quiera, que no quiera

willingly ['wɪlɪŋli] *adv* de buena gana, de buena voluntad

willingness ['wɪlɪŋnɪs] *s* buena gana, buena voluntad

will-o'-the-wisp ['wɪləðə'wɪsp] *s* fuego fatuo; ilusión, quimera

willow ['wɪlo] *s* sauce *m*

willowy ['wɪlo•i] *adj* (*pliant*) juncal, mimbreño; (*slender, graceful*) juncal, cimbreño, esbelto; lleno de sauces

will power *s* fuerza de voluntad

willy-nilly ['wɪli'nɪli] *adv* de grado o por fuerza

wilt [wɪlt] *tr* marchitar ‖ *intr* marchitarse

wil•y ['waɪli] *adj* (*comp* **-ier;** *super* **-iest**) artero, engañoso; astuto

wimple ['wɪmpəl] *s* griñón *m*, impla

win [wɪn] *s* (coll) éxito, triunfo ‖ *v* (*pret & pp* **won** [wʌn]; *ger* **winning**) *tr* ganar; **to win over** ganar, conquistar ‖ *intr* ganar; **to win out** ganar; (coll) tener éxito

wince [wɪns] *s* sobresalto ‖ *intr* sobresaltarse

winch [wɪntʃ] *s* maquinilla, torno; (*handle, crank*) manubrio

wind [wɪnd] *s* viento; (*gas in intestines*) (coll) viento; (*breath*) respiración, resuello; **to break wind** ventosear; **to get wind of** saber de, tener noticia de; **to sail close to the wind** (naut) ceñir el viento; **to take the wind out of one's sails** apagarle a uno los fuegos ‖ *tr* dejar sin aliento ‖ [waɪnd] *v* (*pret & pp* **wound** [waʊnd]) *tr* (*to coil;* to *wrap up*) arrollar, envolver, devanar (*alambre*); ovillar (*hilo*); torcer (*hebras*); hacer girar (*un manubrio*); dar cuerda a (*un reloj*); **to wind one's way through** serpentear por; **to wind up** arrollar, envolver; (coll) poner punto final a ‖ *intr* serpentear (*un camino*)

windbag ['wɪnd,bæg] *s* (*of bagpipe*) odre *m;* (coll) charlatán *m*, palabrero, discursista *mf*

windbreak ['wɪnd,brek] *s* guardavientos *m*

wind cone [wɪnd] *s* (aer) cono de viento

winded ['wɪndɪd] *adj* falto de respiración, sin resuello

windfall ['wɪnd,fɔl] *s* fruta caída del árbol; fortunón *m*, cosa llovida del cielo

winding sheet ['waɪndɪŋ] *s* sudario, mortaja

winding stairs *spl* escalera de caracol

wind instrument [wɪnd] *s* (mus) instrumento de viento

windlass ['wɪndləs] *s* maquinilla, torno

windmill ['wɪnd,mɪl] *s* (*mill operated by wind*) molino de viento; (*modern wind-driven source of power*) aeromotor *m;* (*pinwheel*) molinete *m;* **to tilt at windmills** luchar con los molinos de viento

window ['wɪndo] s ventana; (of ticket office; of envelope) ventanilla; (of coach, automobile) ventanilla, portezuela
window dresser s escaparatista mf
window dressing s adorno de escaparates
window frame s marco de ventana
win'dow•pane' s cristal m o vidrio de ventana·
window screen s alambrera, sobrevidriera
window shade s visillo, transparente m de resorte
win'dow•shop' v (pret & pp -shopped; ger -shopping) intr curiosear en las tiendas
window shutter s contraventana
window sill s repisa de ventana
windpipe ['wɪnd,paɪp] s tráquea
wind shear s (aer) ráfaga violenta
windshield ['wɪnd,ʃild] s parabrisa m
windshield washer s lavaparabrisas m
windshield wiper s limpiaparabrisas m
wind'shield-wip'er blade s escobilla de limpiaparabrisas
wind sock s (aer) cono de viento
windstorm ['wɪnd,stɔrm] s ventarrón m
wind-up ['waɪnd,ʌp] s conclusión; (sport) final f de partido
windward ['wɪndwərd] s barlovento; **to turn to windward** barloventear
Windward Islands spl islas de Barlovento
Windward Passage s paso de los Vientos
wind•y ['wɪndi] adj (comp -ier; super -iest) ventoso; (unsubstantial) vacío; palabrero, ampuloso, discursisto; **it is windy** hace viento
wine [waɪn] s vino ‖ tr obsequiar con vino ‖ intr beber vino
wine cellar s bodega
wine'glass' s copa para vino
winegrower ['waɪn,gro•ər] s vinicultor m
winegrowing ['waɪn,gro•ɪŋ] s vinicultura
wine making s enotecnia
wine press s lagar m
winer•y ['waɪnəri] s (pl -ies) lagar m
wine'skin' s odre m
winetaster ['waɪn,testər] s catavinos m
wing [wɪŋ] s ala; facción; bando; (theat) bastidor m; **to take wing** alzar el vuelo ‖ tr herir en el ala; **to wing one's way** avanzar volando
wing chair s sillón m de orejas
wing collar s cuello de pajarita
wing nut s tuerca de aletas
wing'spread' s envergadura
wink [wɪŋk] s guiño; **to not sleep a wink** no pegar los ojos; **to take forty winks** (coll) descabezar el sueño ‖ tr guiñar (el ojo) ‖ intr guiñar; (to blink) parpadear, pestañear; **to wink at** guiñar el ojo a; fingir no ver
winner ['wɪnər] s ganador m, vencedor m; premiado
winning ['wɪnɪŋ] adj triunfante, victorioso; atrayente, simpático ‖ **winnings** spl ganancias
winnow ['wɪno] tr aventar; entresacar ‖ intr aletear
winsome ['wɪnsəm] adj atrayente, simpático, engañador; alegre

winter ['wɪntər] adj invernal ‖ s invierno ‖ intr invernar
win'ter•green' s gaultería, té m del Canadá; esencia de gaultería
win•try ['wɪntri] adj (comp -trier; super -triest) invernal, invernizo; helado, frío
wipe [waɪp] tr frotar para limpiar; enjugar (la cara, el sudor, las manos); **to wipe away** enjugar (lágrimas); **to wipe off** quitar frotando; **to wipe out** (coll) borrar, cancelar; (coll) aniquilar, destruir; (coll) enjugar (deudas, un déficit)
wiper ['waɪpər] s paño, trapo; (elec) contacto deslizante
wire [waɪr] s (thread of metal) alambre m; telégrafo; telegrama m; teléfono; **to pull wires** (coll) tocar resortes ‖ tr alambrar; telegrafiar ‖ intr telegrafiar
wire cutter s cortaalambres m
wire entanglement s (mil) alambrado
wire gauge s calibrador m de alambre
wire-haired ['waɪr,herd] adj de pelo áspero
wireless ['waɪrlɪs] adj inalámbrico, sin hilos
wire nail s punta de París, clavo de alambre
wire pulling ['pulɪŋ] s (coll) empleo de resortes; enchufismo
wire recorder s grabadora de alambre
wire screen s alambrera, tela de alambre
wire service s servicio telegráfrico y telefónico
wire'tap' v (pret & pp -tapped; ger -tapping) tr intervenir (una conversación telefónica)
wire tapping s escuchas telefónicas fpl
wiring ['waɪrɪŋ] s (elec) alambraje m·
wir•y ['waɪri] adj (comp -ier; super -iest) alambrino; cimbreante; nervudo; vibrante
wisdom ['wɪzdəm] s sabiduría, cordura
wisdom tooth s muela cordal, muela del juicio
wise [waɪz] adj sabio, cuerdo; (step, decision) acertado, juicioso; **to be wise to** (slang) conocer el juego de; **to get wise** (coll) caer en el chiste ‖ s modo, manera; **in no wise** de ningún modo
wiseacre ['waɪz,ekər] s sabihondo
wise'crack' s (slang) cuchufleta ‖ intr (slang) cuchufletear
wise guy s (slang) sabelotodo
wish [wɪʃ] s deseo; **to make a wish** pensar algo que se desea ‖ tr desear; dar (los buenos días) ‖ intr desear; **to wish for** desear, anhelar
wish'bone' s espoleta, hueso de la suerte
wishful ['wɪʃfəl] adj deseoso
wishful thinking s optimismo a ultranza; **to indulge in wishful thinking** forjarse ilusiones
wistful ['wɪstfəl] adj melancólico, tristón, pensativo
wit [wɪt] s agudeza; (person) chistoso; (keen mental power) juicio; **to be at one's wits' end** no saber qué hacer; **to have the wit to** tener el tino de; **to live by one's wits** vivir del cuento
witch [wɪtʃ] s bruja, hechicera; (old hag) bruja

witch'craft' s brujería

witches' Sabbath s aquelarre m

witch hazel s (shrub) nogal m de la brujería, planta del sortilegio; (liquid) hamamelina, hazelina

with [wıð] o [wıθ] prep con; de

with•draw' v (pret -drew; pp -drawn) tr retirar ‖ intr retirarse

withdrawal [wıð`drɔ•əl] o [wıθ`drɔ•əl] s retirada

withdrawal symptom s síntoma m de abstinencia; (slang) mono

wither [`wıðər] tr marchitar; (fig) aplastar, confundir ‖ intr marchitarse; confundirse

with•hold' v (pret & pp -held) tr retener; suspender (pago); negar (un permiso)

withholding tax s impuesto deducido del sueldo

with•in' adv dentro ‖ prep dentro de; al alcance de; poco menos de; con un margen de

with•out' adv fuera ‖ prep fuera de; (lacking, not with) sin; **to do without** pasar sin; **without** + ger sin + inf, p.ej., **he left without saying goodbye** salió sin despedirse; sin que + subj, p.ej., **he came in without anyone seeing him** entró sin que nadie le viese

with•stand' v (pret & pp -stood) tr aguantar, resistir

witness [`wıtnıs] s testigo mf; **in witness whereof** en fe de lo cual; **to bear witness** dar testimonio ‖ tr (to be present at) presenciar; (to attest) atestiguar, testimoniar; firmar como testigo

witness stand s banquillo o estrado de los testigos

witticism [`wıtı,sızəm] s agudeza, dicho agudo, ocurrencia

wittingly [`wıtıŋli] adv a sabiendas

wit•ty [`wıti] adj (comp -tier; super -tiest) agudo, ingenioso; (person) ocurrente, chistoso

wizard [`wızərd] s brujo, hechicero; (coll) as m, experto

wizardry [`wızərdri] s hechicería, magia

wizened [`wızənd] adj acartonado, arrugado

wk. abbr **week**

w.l. abbr **wave length**

woad [wod] s hierba pastel

wobble [`wabəl] s bamboleo, tambaleo ‖ intr bambolear, tambalear; bailar (una silla); (fig) vacilar, ser inconstante

wob•bly [`wabli] adj (comp -blier; super -bliest) bamboleante, inseguro; vacilante

woe [wo] s aflicción, miseria, infortunio ‖ interj —**woe is me!** ¡ay de mí!

woebegone [`wobı,gɔn] o [`wobı,gan] adj cariacontecido, triste

woeful [`wofəl] adj triste, miserable; (of poor quality) malo, pésimo

wolf [wʊlf] s (pl **wolves** [wʊlvz]) lobo; persona cruel, persona mañosa; (coll) tenorio; **to cry wolf** dar falsa alarma; **to keep the wolf from the door** ponerse a cubierto del hambre ‖ tr & intr comer vorazmente, engullir

wolf'hound' s galgo lobero

wolfram [`wʊlfrəm] s (element) volframio; (mineral) volframita

wolf's-bane o **wolfsbane** [`wʊlfs,ben] s matalobos m

woman [`wʊmən] s (pl **women** [`wımın]) mujer f

womanhood [`wʊmən,hʊd] s el sexo femenino; las mujeres

womanish [`wʊmənıʃ] adj mujeril; (effeminate) afeminado

wom'an•kind' s el sexo femenino

womanly [`wʊmənli] adj (comp -lier; super -liest) femenil, mujeriego

woman suffrage s sufragismo

woman-suffragist [`wʊmən`sʌfrədʒıst] s sufragista mf

womb [wʊm] s útero; (fig) seno

womenfolk [`wımın,fok] spl las mujeres

women's lib(eration movement) s movimiento feminista; feminismo

wonder [`wʌndər] s (something strange or surprising) maravilla; (feeling of surprise) admiración; (something strange, miracle) milagro; **for a wonder** cosa extraña; **no wonder that . . .** no es mucho que. . .; **to work wonders** hacer milagros ‖ tr preguntarse ‖ intr admirarse, maravillarse; **to wonder at** admirarse de, maravillarse con o de

wonder drugs spl drogas milagrosas

wonderful [`wʌndərfəl] adj maravilloso

won'der•land' s tierra de las maravillas; reino de las hadas

wonderment [`wʌndərmənt] s asombro, sorpresa

wont [wʌnt] o [wɔnt] adj acostumbrado; **to be wont to** acostumbrar ‖ s costumbre, hábito

wonted [`wʌntıd] o [`wɔntıd] adj acostumbrado, habitual

woo [wu] tr cortejar (a una mujer); tratar de conquistar; tratar de persuadir

wood [wʊd] s madera; (for making a fire) leña; barril m de madera; **out of the woods** (coll) fuera de peligro; (coll) libre de dificultades; **to take to the woods** andar a monte; **woods** bosque m

woodbine [`wʊd,baın] s (honeysuckle) madreselva; (Virginia creeper) guau m

wood carving s labrado de madera

wood'chuck' s marmota de América

wood'cock' s becada, coalla, chocha

wood'cut' s (typ) grabado en madera

wood'cut'ter s leñador m

wooded [`wʊdıd] adj arbolado, enselvado

wooden [`wʊdən] adj de madera, hecho de madera; torpe, estúpido; sin ánimo

wood engraving s (typ) grabado en madera

wooden-headed [`wʊdən,hɛdıd] adj (coll) torpe, estúpido

wooden leg s pata de palo

wooden shoe s zueco

wood grouse s gallo de bosque

woodland [`wʊdlənd] adj selvático ‖ s bosque m, monte m

woodland scene s (paint) boscaje m

wood·man ['wʊdmən] s (pl **-men** [mən]) leñador m

woodpecker ['wʊd,pɛkər] s carpintero, pájaro carpintero; (green woodpecker) picamaderos m

wood'pile' s montón m de leña

wood screw s tirafondo

wood'shed' s leñero

woods·man ['wʊdzmən] s (pl **-men** [mən]) leñador m

wood'wind' s (mus) instrumento de viento de madera

wood'work' s (working in wood) ebanistería, obra de carpintería; (things made of wood) maderaje m

wood'work'er s ebanista mf, carpintero

wood'worm' s carcoma

wood·y ['wʊdi] adj (comp **-ier**; super **-iest**) arbolado, enselvado; (like wood) leñoso

wooer ['wʊ·ər] s pretendiente m, galán m

woof [wuf] s (yarns running across warp) trama; (fabric) tejido

woofer ['wʊfər] s altavoz m para audiofrecuencias bajas

wool [wʊl] s lana

woolen ['wʊlən] adj de lana, hecho de lana ‖ s tejido de lana; **woolens** lanerías

woolgrower ['wʊl ,gro·ər] s criador m de ganado lanar

wool·ly ['wʊli] adj (comp **-lier**; super **-liest**) lanoso, lanudo; borroso, confuso

Worcestershire sauce ['wʊstərʃər] s salsa inglesa

word [wʌrd] s palabra; **to be as good as one's word** cumplir lo prometido; **to have a word with** hablar cuatro palabras con; **to have word from** recibir noticias de; **to keep one's word** cumplir su palabra; **to leave word** dejar dicho; **to send word that** mandar decir que; **words** (a quarrel) palabras mayores; (text of a song) letra ‖ tr redactar, formular ‖ **Word** s (theol) Verbo

word count s recuento de vocabulario

word formation s (gram) formación de palabras

wording ['wʌrdɪŋ] s fraseología, estilo

word order s (gram) orden m de colocación

word processing s redacción por medios electrónicos

word'stock' s vocabulario, léxico

word·y ['wʌrdi] adj (comp **-ier**; super **-iest**) verboso

work [wʌrk] s (exertion; labor, toil) trabajo; (result of exertion; human output; engineering structure) obra; (sew) labor f; **at work** trabajando; (not at home) en la oficina, en el taller, en la tienda; **out of work** sin trabajo, desempleado; **to shoot the works** (slang) echar el resto; **works** fábrica; mecanismo; (of clock) movimiento ‖ tr hacer trabajar; trabajar, obrar (la madera, el hierro); obrar (un milagro); explotar (una mina); **to work up** preparar; estimular, excitar ‖ intr trabajar; funcionar, marchar (un aparato, un motor); obrar (p.ej., un remedio); **to work loose** aflojarse; **to work out** resolverse

workable ['wʌrkəbəl] adj (feasible) practicable; (that can be worked) laborable

workaholic [,wʌrkə'hɔlɪk] s (coll) individuo con compulsión al trabajo

work'bench' s banco de trabajo, banco de taller

work'book' s (manual of instructions) libro de reglas; libro de ejercicios

work'box' s caja de herramientas; (for needlework) caja de labor

work'day' adj de cada día; ordinario, vulgar ‖ s día m de trabajo; (number of hours of work) jornada

work'days' adv entresemana (SAm)

worked-up ['wʌrkt'ʌp] adj muy conmovido, sobreexcitado, exaltado

worker ['wʌrkər] s trabajador m, obrero

work force s mano f de obra, personal obrero

work'horse' s caballo de carga; (tireless worker) yunque m

work'house' s taller penitenciario; (Brit) asilo de pobres

working class s clase obrera

work'ing-girl' s trabajadora joven

working hours spl horas de trabajo

working hypothesis s hipótesis f de guía

working·man ['wʌrkɪŋ,mæn] s (pl **-men** [,mɛn]) s obrero, trabajador m

working-woman ['wʌrkɪŋ,wʊmən] s (pl **-women** [,wɪmɪn]) obrera, trabajadora

work·man ['wʌrkmən] s (pl **-men** [mən]) obrero, trabajador m; (skilled worker) artífice m

workmanship ['wʌrkmən,ʃɪp] s destreza en el trabajo; (work executed) hechura, obra

work of art s obra de arte

work'out' s ensayo, prueba; (physical exercise) ejercicio

work'room' s (for manual work) obrador m, taller m; (study) gabinete m de trabajo

work'shop' s obrador m, taller m

work stoppage s paro

work therapy s laborterapia

world [wʌrld] adj mundial ‖ s mundo; **a world of** la mar de; **half the world** (a lot of people) medio mundo; **since the world began** desde que el mundo es mundo; **the other world** el otro mundo; **to bring into the world** echar al mundo; **to see the world** ver mundo; **to think the world of** tener un alto concepto de

world affairs spl asuntos internacionales

world'-class' adj sobresaliente

world·ly ['wʌrldli] adj (comp **-lier**; super **-liest**) mundano

world'ly-wise' adj que tiene mucho mundo

world's fair s exposición mundial

World War s Guerra Mundial

world'-wide' adj global, mundial

worm [wʌrm] s gusano; **worms** (pathol) lombrices fpl ‖ tr limpiar de lombrices; **to worm a secret out of a person** arrancar mañosamente un secreto a una persona; **to worm one's way into** insinuarse en

worm-eaten ['wʌrm,itən] adj carcomido; (fig) decaído, desgastado

worm gear s engranaje m de tornillo sin fin

wi
wo

worm'wood' s (Artemisia) ajenjo; (Artemisia absinthium) ajenjo del campo o ajenjo mayor; (something bitter or grievous) (fig) ajenjo

worm•y ['wʌrmi] adj (comp -ier; super -iest) gusaniento, gusanoso; (worm-eaten) carcomido; (groveling) rastrero, servil

worn [worn] adj roto, raído, gastado

worn'-out' adj muy gastado, inservible; (by toil, illness) consumido, rendido

worrisome ['wʌrisəm] adj inquietante; (inclined to worry) aprensivo, inquieto

wor•ry ['wʌri] s (pl -ries) inquietud, preocupación; (cause of anxiety) molestia ‖ v (pret & pp -ried) tr inquietar, preocupar; (to harass, pester) acosar, molestar; **to be worried** estar inquieto ‖ intr inquietarse, preocuparse; **don't worry** pierda Vd. cuidado

worse [wʌrs] adj & adv comp peor; **worse and worse** de mal en peor

worsen ['wʌrsən] tr & intr empeorar ‖ ref gravarse

wor•ship ['wʌrʃip] s adoración, culto; **your worship** vuestra merced ‖ v (pret & pp -shiped o -shipped; ger -shiping o -shipping) tr & intr adorar, venerar

worshiper o **worshipper** ['wʌrʃipər] s adorador m, devoto

worst [wʌrst] adj & adv super peor ‖ s (lo) peor; **at worst** en las peores circunstancias; **if worst comes to worst** si pasa lo peor; **to get the worst of** llevar la peor parte, salir perdiendo

worsted ['wustid] adj de estambre ‖ s estambre m; tela de estambre

wort [wʌrt] s (bot) hierba, planta; mosto de cerveza

worth [wʌrθ] adj del valor de; digno de; **to be worth** valer; tener una fortuna de; **to be worth** + ger valer la pena de + inf; **to be worth while** valer la pena; ser de mérito ‖ s valor m; mérito; **a dollar's worth of** un dólar de

worthless ['wʌrθlis] adj sin valor, inútil, inservible; (person) despreciable

worth'while' adj de mérito, digno de atención

wor•thy ['wʌrði] adj (comp -thier; super -thiest) digno; benemérito, meritorio ‖ s (pl -thies) benemérito; (hum & iron) personaje m

would [wud] v aux she said she would do it dijo que lo haría; **he would come if he could** vendría si pudiese; **he would go for days without smoking** pasaba días enteros sin fumar; **would that . . .!** ¡ojalá que . . .!

would'-be' adj llamado; supuesto ‖ s presumido

wound [wund] s herida ‖ tr herir

wounded ['wundid] adj herido ‖ **the wounded** los heridos

wow [wau] s (of phonograph record) ululación; (slang) éxito rotundo ‖ tr (slang) entusiasmar ‖ interj ¡cielos!, ¡mecachis!

wrack [ræk] s naufragio; vestigio; (fucaceous seaweed) varec m; **to go to wrack and ruin** desvencijarse; ir al desastre

wraith [reθ] s fantasma m, espectro

wrangle ['ræŋgəl] s pendencia, riña ‖ intr pelotear, reñir

wrap [ræp] s abrigo, manto ‖ v (pret & pp wrapped; ger wrapping) tr envolver; **to be wrapped up in** (fig) estar prendado de; **to wrap up** envolver; (in clothing) arropar; (coll) concluir ‖ intr—**to wrap up** arroparse

wrapper ['ræpər] s bata, peinador m; (of newspaper or magazine) faja; (of tobacco) capa

wrapping paper ['ræpiŋ] s papel m de envolver, papel de embalar

wrath [ræθ] o [rɑθ] s cólera, ira; venganza

wrathful ['ræθfəl] o ['rɑθfəl] adj colérico, iracundo

wreak [rik] tr descargar (la cólera); infligir (venganza)

wreath [riθ] s (pl wreaths [riðz]) guirnalda; corona funeraria; (worn as a mark of honor or victory) corona de laurel; (of smoke) espiral f

wreathe [rið] tr enguirnaldar; ceñir, envolver; tejer (una guirnalda) ‖ intr elevarse en espirales (el humo)

wreck [rɛk] s destrucción, ruina; naufragio; catástrofe f, desastre m; despojos, restos; (of one's hopes) naufragio; **to be a wreck** estar hecho un cascajo, estar hecho una ruina ‖ tr destruir, arruinar; hacer naufragar; hacer chocar, descarrilar (un tren)

wrecking ball s bola rompedora

wrecking car s (aut) camión m de auxilio; (rr) carro de grúa

wrecking crane s grúa de auxilio

wren [rɛn] s buscareta, coletero, rey m de zarza

wrench [rɛntʃ] s llave f; (pull) arranque m, tirón m; (twist of a joint) esguince m ‖ tr torcerse (p.ej., la muñeca); (fig) torcer (el sentido de una oración)

wrest [rɛst] tr arrebatar, arrancar violentamente

wrestle ['rɛsəl] s lucha; partido de lucha ‖ intr luchar

wrestling match ['rɛsliŋ] s partido de lucha

wretch [rɛtʃ] s miserable mf

wretched ['rɛtʃid] adj miserable; (poor, worthless) malísimo, pésimo

wriggle ['rigəl] s culebreo, meneo serpentino ‖ tr menear rápidamente ‖ intr culebrear, ondular; **to wriggle out of** escabullirse de

wrig•gly ['rigli] adj (comp -glier; super -gliest) retorciéndose; (fig) evasivo, tramoyista

wring [riŋ] v (pret & pp wrung [rʌŋ]) tr torcer; retorcer (las manos); exprimir (el zumo, la ropa, etc.); sacar por fuerza (la verdad); arrancar (dinero); **to wring out** exprimir (la ropa)

wringer ['riŋər] s exprimidor m

wrinkle [ˈrɪŋkəl] *s* arruga; (*clever trick or idea*) (coll) ardid *m*, truco ‖ *tr* arrugar ‖ *intr* arrugarse

wrin·kly [ˈrɪŋkli] *adj* (*comp* **-klier;** *super* **-kliest**) arrugado

wrist [rɪst] *s* muñeca

wrist′band′ *s* bocamanga, puño

wrist watch *s* reloj *m* de pulsera

writ [rɪt] *s* escrito, escritura; (law) mandato, orden *f*

write [raɪt] *v* (*pret* **wrote** [rot]; *pp* **written** [ˈrɪtən]) *tr* escribir; **to write down** poner por escrito; bajar el precio de; **to write off** cancelar (*una deuda*); **to write up** describir extensamente por escrito; (*to ballyhoo*) dar bombo a ‖ *intr* escribir; **to write back** contestar por carta

writer [ˈraɪtər] *s* escritor *m*

writer's cramp *s* grafospasmo

write′-up′ *s* (*favorable report*) bombo; (com) valoración excesiva

writhe [raɪð] *intr* contorcerse, retorcerse

writing [ˈraɪtɪŋ] *s* el escribir; (*something written*) escrito; profesión de escritor; **at this writing** al escribir ésta; **in one's own writing** de su puño y letra; **to put in writing** poner por escrito

writing desk *s* escritorio

writing materials *spl* recado de escribir

writing paper *s* papel *m* de escribir, papel de cartas

written accent [ˈrɪtən] *s* acento ortográfico

wrong [rɔŋ] *adj* injusto; malo; erróneo, equivocado; impropio; no . . . que se busca, p.ej., **this is the wrong house** ésta no es la casa que se busca; no . . . que se necesita, p.ej., **this is the wrong train** éste no es el tren que se necesita; no . . . que debe, p.ej., **he is going the wrong way** no sigue el camino que debe; **in the wrong place** mal colocado; **to be wrong** no tener razón; tener la culpa; **to be wrong with** pasar algo a, p.ej., **something is wrong with the motor** algo le pasa al motor ‖ *adv* mal; sin razón; al revés; **to go wrong** ir por mal camino; darse a la mala vida ‖ *s* daño, perjuicio; agravio, injusticia; error *m;* **to be in the wrong** no tener razón; tener la culpa; **to do wrong** obrar mal ‖ *tr* agraviar, hacer daño a, ofender, ser injusto con

wrongdoer [ˈrɔŋˌdu·ər] *s* malhechor *m*

wrongdoing [ˈrɔŋˌdu·ɪŋ] *s* malhecho, maldad

wrong number *s* (telp) número equivocado

wrong side *s* contrahaz *f*, revés *m;* (*of the street*) lado contrario; **to get out of bed on the wrong side** levantarse del lado izquierdo; **wrong side out** al revés

wrought iron [rɔt] *s* hierro dulce

wrought′-up′ *adj* muy conmovido, sobreexcitado, exaltado

wry [raɪ] *adj* (*comp* **wrier;** *super* **wriest**) torcido; desviado, pervertido; irónico, burlón

wry′neck′ *s* (orn) torcecuello; (pathol) torticolis *m*

wt. *abbr* **weight**

X

X, x [ɛks] vigésima cuarta letra del alfabeto inglés

Xanthippe [zænˈtɪpi] *s* Jantipa

Xavier [ˈzevɪ·ər] *s* Javier

xebec [ˈzibɛk] *s* (naut) jabeque *m*

xenia [ˈzinɪ·ə] *s* xenia

xenon [ˈzinɑn] o [ˈzɛnɑn] *s* xenón *m*

xenophobe [ˈzɛnəˌfob] *s* xenófobo

xenophobia [ˌzɛnəˈfobɪ·ə] *s* xenofobia

Xenophon [ˈzɛnəfən] *s* Jenofonte *m*

xerograph [ˈzɪrəˌgræf] *s* fotocopia instantánea en seco ‖ *tr & intr* xerografiar

xerography [zɪˈrɑgrəfi] *s* xerografía

Xerxes [ˈzʌrksiz] *s* Jerjes *m*

Xmas [ˈkrɪsməs] *s* Navidad

X-rated [ˈɛksˌretɪd] *adj* (*film, etc.*) no recomendado; pornográfico

X ray *s* rayo X; (*photograph*) radiograma *m*

X-ray [ˈɛksˌre] *adj* radiográfico ‖ [ˈɛksˈre] *tr* radiografiar; tratar por medio de los rayos X

xylograph [ˈzaɪləˌgræf] *s* xilografía

xylography [zaɪˈlɑgrəfi] *s* xilografía

xylophone [ˈzaɪləˌfon] *s* (mus) xilófono

Y

Y, y [waɪ] vigésima quinta letra del alfabeto inglés

y. *abbr* **yard, year**

yacht [jɑt] *s* yate *m*

yacht club *s* club náutico

yak [jæk] *s* (zool) yac *m*

yam [jæm] *s* ñame *m;* (*sweet potato*) boniato, camote *m*

yank [jæŋk] s (coll) tirón m ‖ tr (coll) sacar de un tirón ‖ intr (coll) dar un tirón

Yankee ['jæŋki] adj & s yanqui mf

Yankeedom ['jæŋkidəm] s Yanquilandia; los yanquis

yap [jæp] s ladrido corto; (slang) charla necia y ruidosa ‖ v (pret & pp **yapped**; ger **yapping**) intr ladrar con ladrido corto; (slang) charlar necia y ruidosamente

yard [jɑrd] s cercado, patio; (measure) yarda; (naut) verga; (rr) patio

yard'arm' s (naut) penol m

yard goods spl géneros de pieza

yard'mas'ter s (rr) superintendente m de patio

yard'stick' s yarda, vara de medir; (fig) criterio, norma

yarn [jɑrn] s hilado, hilaza; (coll) cuento increíble, burlería

yarrow ['jæro] s milenrama

yaw [jɔ] s (naut) guiñada; **yaws** (pathol) frambesia ‖ intr (naut) guiñar

yawl [jɔl] s (naut) bote m; (naut) queche m

yawn [jɔn] s bostezo ‖ intr bostezar; abrirse desmesuradamente

yd. abbr **yard**

yea [je] adv & s sí m

yean [jin] intr parir (la oveja, la cabra, etc.)

year [jɪr] s año; **to be . . . years old** cumplir . . . años; **year in, year out** año tras año

year'book' s anuario

yearling ['jɪrlɪŋ] adj & s primal m

yearly ['jɪrli] adj anual ‖ adv anualmente

yearn [jʌrn] intr suspirar; **to yearn for** suspirar por, anhelar por

yearning ['jʌrnɪŋ] s anhelo, deseo ardiente

yeast [jist] s levadura

yeast cake s levadura comprimida, pastilla de levadura

yell [jɛl] s grito, voz f ‖ tr decir a gritos ‖ intr gritar, dar voces

yellow ['jɛlo] adj amarillo; (cowardly) (coll) blanco; (journalism) sensacional ‖ s amarillo; yema de huevo ‖ intr amarillecer

yellowish ['jɛlo·ɪʃ] adj amarillento

yellow jacket s avispón m

yellowness ['jɛlonɪs] s amarillez f

yellow press s prensa amarilla

yellow streak s vena de cobarde

yelp [jɛlp] s gañido ‖ intr gañir

yeo·man ['jomən] s (pl **-men** [mən]) (naut) pañolero; (naut) oficinista m de a bordo; (Brit) labrador acomodado

yeoman of the guard s (Brit) alabardero de palacio, continuo

yeoman's service s ayuda leal

yes [jɛs] adv sí ‖ s sí m; **to say yes** dar el sí ‖

v (pret & pp **yessed**; ger **yessing**) tr decir sí a ‖ intr decir sí

yes man s (coll) sacristán m de amén

yesterday ['jɛstərdi] o ['jɛstər,de] adj & s ayer m

yet [jɛt] adv todavía, aún; **as yet** hasta ahora; **not yet** todavía no ‖ conj sin embargo

yew tree [ju] s tejo

yield [jild] s producción, rendimiento; (crop) cosecha; (income produced) rédito ‖ tr producir, rendir, redituar ‖ intr entregarse, rendirse, someterse; acceder, ceder, consentir; producir

yodeling o yodelling ['jodəlɪŋ] s tirolesa

yoga ['jogə] s yoga

yogi ['jogi] s yogui m

yogurt ['jogərt] s yogurt m

yoke [jok] s (pair of draft animals) yunta; (device to join a pair of draft animals) yugo; (fig) yugo; (of a shirt) hombrillo; (elec) culata; **to throw off the yoke** sacudir el yugo ‖ tr uncir

yokel ['jokəl] s patán m

yolk [jok] s yema

yonder ['jɑndər] adj aquel, de más allá ‖ adv allá, más allá

yore [jor] s—**of yore** antaño, antiguamente

you [ju] pron pers usted, ustedes; le, la, les; **with you** consigo ‖ pron indef se, p.ej., **you go in this way** se entra por aquí

young [jʌŋ] adj (comp **younger** ['jʌŋgər]; super **youngest** ['jʌŋgɪst]) joven ‖ **the young** los jóvenes, la gente joven

young hopeful s joven m de esperanzas

young people spl jóvenes mpl, gente f joven

youngster ['jʌŋstər] s jovencito; (child) chico, chiquillo

your [jʊr] adj poss su, el (o su) de Vd. o de Vds.

Yours [jʊrz] pron poss suyo; de Vd., de Vds.; el suyo; el de Vd., el de Vds.; **of yours** suyo; de Vd., de Vds.; **yours truly** su seguro servidor; (coll) este cura (yo)

your·self [jʊr'sɛlf] pron pers (pl **-selves** ['sɛlvz]) usted mismo; sí, sí mismo; se, p.ej., **you enjoyed yourself** se divirtió Vd.

youth [juθ] s (pl **youths** [juθs] o [juðz]) juventud; (person) jovenzuelo; jovenzuelos, jóvenes mpl

youthful ['juθfəl] adj juvenil, mocil

yowl [jaʊl] s aullido, alarido ‖ intr aullar, dar alaridos

yr. abbr **year**

Yugoslav ['jugo'slɑv] adj & s yugoeslavo

Yugoslavia ['jugo'slɑvɪ·ə] s Yugoeslavia

Yule [jul] s la Navidad; la pascua de Navidad

Yule log s nochebueno, leño de nochebuena

Yuletide ['jul,taɪd] s la pascua de Navidad

Z

Z, z [zi] vigésima sexta letra del alfabeto inglés

za·ny ['zeni] adj (comp **-nier**; super **-niest**)

cómico, gracioso, chiflado ‖ s (pl **-nies**) bufón m, payaso; mentecato

zeal [zil] s celo, entusiasmo

zealot ['zɛlət] *s* fanático, entusiasta *mf*
zealotry ['zɛlətri] *s* fanatismo
zealous ['zɛləs] *adj* celoso, entusiasta
zebra ['zibrə] *s* cebra
zebu ['zibju] *s* cebú *m*
zenith ['zinɪθ] *s* cenit *m*
zephyr ['zɛfər] *s* céfiro
zeppelin ['zɛpəlɪn] *s* zepelín *m*
ze•ro ['zɪro] *s* (*pl* **-ros** o **-roes**) cero
zero gravity *s* gravedad nula
zero growth *s* crecimiento cero
ze'ro-growth' *adj* sin aumento; estable
zero option *s* opción cero, opción nula
zest [zɛst] *s* entusiasmo; (*agreeable and pi-quant flavor*) gusto, sabor *m*
Zeus [zus] *s* Zeus *m*
zig•zig ['zɪg,zæg] *adj* & *adv* en zigzag ‖ *s* zigzag *m*, ziszas *m* ‖ *v* (*pret* & *pp* **-zagged;** *ger* **-zagging**) *intr* zigzaguear
zinc [zɪŋk] *s* cinc *m*
zinc etching *s* cincograbado
zinnia ['zɪnɪ•ə] *s* rascamoño
Zionism ['zaɪ•ə,nɪzəm] *s* sionismo
zip [zɪp] *s* (coll) silbido, zumbido; (coll)

energía, brío ‖ *v* (*pret* & *pp* **zipped;** *ger* **zipping**) *tr* cerrar con cierre relámpago, abrir con cierre relámpago; (coll) llevar con rapidez; **to zip up** dar gusto a ‖ *intr* silbar, zumbar; (coll) moverse con energía; **to zip by** (coll) pasar rápidamente
zip code *s* código postal
zipper ['zɪpər] *s* cierre *m* relámpago, cierre cremallera; chanclo con cierre relámpago; cíper (Mex)
zircon ['zʌrkɑn] *s* circón *m*
zirconium [zər'konɪ•əm] *s* circonio
zither ['zɪθər] *s* (mus) cítara
zodiac ['zodɪ,æk] *s* zodíaco
zone [zon] *s* zona; distrito postal ‖ *tr* dividir en zonas
zoölogic(al) [,zo•ə'lɑdʒɪk(əl)] *adj* zoológico
zoölogist [zo'ɑlədʒɪst] *s* zoólogo
zoölogy [zo'ɑlədʒi] *s* zoología
zoom [zum] *s* zumbido; (aer) empinada ‖ *tr* (aer) empinar ‖ *intr* zumbar; (aer) empinarse
zoöphyte ['zo•ə,faɪt] *s* zoófito
Zu•lu ['zulu] *adj* zulú ‖ *s* (*pl* **-lus**) zulú *mf*

SPANISH GRAMMAR

TABLE OF CONTENTS

1. Stress, Punctuation, Capitalization, *710*

NOUNS
2. Gender of Nouns, *711*
3. Plural of Nouns, *711*

ARTICLES
4. Definite Article, *711*
5. Indefinite Article, *712*

ADJECTIVES
6. Gender of Adjectives, *712*
7. Plural of Adjectives, *712*
8. Position of Adjectives, *712*
9. Shortening of Adjectives, *712*
10. Adjectives Used As Nouns, *713*
11. Comparison of Adjectives, *713*
12. Possessive Adjectives, *713*
13. Demonstrative Adjectives, *713*

ADVERBS
14. Formation of Adverbs, *714*
15. Comparison of Adverbs, *714*

PRONOUNS
16. Subject Pronouns, *714*
17. Prepositional Pronouns, *714*
18. Conjunctive Pronouns, *715*
19. Reflexive Pronouns, *715*
20. Possessive Pronouns, *715*
21. Demonstrative Pronouns, *715*
22. Relative Pronouns, *716*

VERBS
23. Regular Verbs, *716*
24. Irregular Verbs, *719*
25. **Ser** and **Estar,** *719*

NUMERALS
26. Cardinal Numerals, *720*
27. Ordinal Numerals, *720*

[SPANISH PRONUNCIATION: pages 721–722]

1. STRESS, PUNCTUATION, CAPITALIZATION

All Spanish words, except compound words and adverbs in **-mente,** have only one stress. The position of this stress is always shown by the spelling in accordance with the following rules:

(a) Words ending in a vowel sound or in **n** or **s** are stressed on the syllable next to the last, e.g., **ca-sa, a-gua, se-rio, ha-blan, co-sas.**

(b) Words ending in a consonant except **n** or **s** are stressed on the last syllable, e.g., **se-ñor, pa-pel, fe-liz, U-ru-guay, es-toy.**

(c) If the stress does not fall in accordance with either of the above rules, it is indicated by an acute accent placed above the stressed vowel, e.g., **ca-fé, a-pren-dí, na-ción, lá-piz, fá-cil, re-pú-bli-ca.** The acute accent is also used to distinguish between words spelled alike but having different meanings or parts of speech, e.g., **aun** (= even) and **aún** (= still, yet), **donde** (*conj*) and **dónde** (*adv*), **el** (*def art*) and **él** (*pron*).

Question marks and exclamation points are placed both before and after a word or sentence, and the first is inverted, e.g., **¿Que tal?** How's everything? **¡Que lástima!** What a pity!

Capital letters are used less in Spanish than in English, e.g., **un inglés** an Englishman, **el idioma español** the Spanish language, **domingo** Sunday, **enero** January.

2. GENDER OF NOUNS

All Spanish nouns are grouped into two form classes, traditionally called **masculine** and **feminine**. All nouns referring specifically to male beings are **masculine**, e.g., **hombre** man, **muchacho** boy, **hermano** brother, **hijo** son, **tío** uncle, **toro** bull, **gallo** rooster.

All nouns referring specifically to females are **feminine**, e.g., **mujer** woman, **muchacha** girl, **hermana** sister, **hija** daughter, **madre** mother, **vaca** cow, **gallina** hen, **modelo** (artist's) model.

(a) Grammatical Gender. All other nouns not referring to males or females are still classed as either masculine or feminine, although this classification has nothing to do with sex. Masculine nouns frequently end in **-o**, e.g., **barco** boat, **caso** case, **libro** book, **tiempo** time; weather, **tráfico** trade; traffic. (A notable exception is **la mano** hand.)

Feminine nouns frequently end in **-a**, e.g., **casa** house, **cocina** kitchen, **libra** pound, **mesa** table. All other nouns, regardless of ending, must have their gender memorized. For example, a fairly large number of nouns ending in **-a** are masculine, e.g., **clima** climate, **dilema** dilemma, **planeta** planet, **sistema** system, **tema** theme. Nouns ending in **-e** may be either masculine or feminine, e.g., **el diente** tooth, **el baile** dance, **el toque** touch; stroke, but **la servidumbre** servitude; the servants, **la superficie** surface.

3. PLURAL OF NOUNS

Nouns ending in a vowel add **s** to form the plural, e.g., **casa-casas** house, -s, **diente-dientes** tooth, teeth, **tribu-tribus** tribe, -s. Nouns ending in an accented **i, u,** or **a**, add **es** in the plural, e.g., **rubí-rubíes** ruby, -ies, **tisú-tisúes** tissue, -s, **bajá-bajaes** pasha, -s. Nouns ending in a consonant (including **-y**) add **es** to form the plural, e.g., **balcón-balcones** balcony, -nies, **árbol-árboles** tree, -s, **flor-flores** flower, -s, **mes-meses** month, -s, **rey-reyes** king, -s; monarchs.

Nouns ending in **z** change the z to **c** and add **es**, e.g., **vez-veces** time, -s; occasion, -s, **lápiz-lápices** pencil, -s. Nouns ending in s preceded by an unaccented vowel do not change in the plural, e.g., **el lunes, los lunes** Monday, -s, **la crisis, las crises** crisis, crises.

The syllable stressed in the singular is always stressed in the plural except in a few words such as **carácter** character and **régimen** regime, whose plurals are **caracteres** and **regímenes**. However, the written accent mark found on the last syllable of the singular of nouns with a stressed final in **n** and **s** is not necessary in the plural and therefore must be omitted, e.g., **acción** (action; share, -s, of stock) **acciones**, **marqués** (marquess) **marqueses**.

4. DEFINITE ARTICLE

Unlike the English article **the**, which is invariable in writing, the Spanish article has four distinct forms corresponding to the number and the gender of the noun they modify:

	MASCULINE	FEMININE
SINGULAR	el	la
PLURAL	los	las

For feminine nouns which begin with a stressed **a** (including **ha**), the form of the singular definite article is **el**, e.g., **el agua** the water, **el hacha** the hatchet. The gender remains feminine so that adjectives modifying such nouns are feminine, e.g., **el agua fresca** the cool water, **las hachas** the hatchets.

The use of the definite article is in many respects similar to that of English. That is, it is used when referring to someone or something already known, e.g., **el hombre** the man, referring to someone previously mentioned (i.e., the man I met yesterday) as distinct from **un hombre** a man (i.e., someone unknown or not previously mentioned).

In contrast with English, however, the definite article is used before nouns referring to general or abstract notions, **la libertad** freedom, **la democracia** democracy, **la independencia** independence, **la esperanza** hope.

The definite article is often omitted before nouns in apposition, e.g., **Madrid, capital de España**, and is always omitted in the numbered names of rulers and popes, e.g., **Luis catorce**

Louis the Fourteenth, **Juan Carlos primero** Juan Carlos the First, **Juan veintitrés** John the Twenty-third.

5. INDEFINITE ARTICLE

The singulars of the indefinite article are **un,** masculine, and **una,** feminine; the plurals are **unos,** masculine, and **unas,** feminine, e.g., **un mes** a month, **unos meses** (some) months; **una calle** a street, **unas calles** (some) streets.

The form **un** is also commonly used before feminine singular nouns beginning with a stressed **a** or **ha,** e.g., **un arma** a weapon.

The plural forms **unos, unas,** when followed by a cardinal number, mean *about,* e.g., **unos cinco años** about five years.

The indefinite article is not used before a noun of nationality, religion, occupation, and the like, e.g., **Mi amigo es abogado** My friend is a lawyer. If the noun is modified, the indefinite article is generally used, e.g, **Mi hermano es un abogado excelente** My brother is an excellent lawyer. The indefinite article is omitted before **otro,** which therefore means both *other* and *another,* e.g., **Quiero otro libro** I want another book.

6. GENDER OF ADJECTIVES

Adjectives agree in gender and number with the noun they modify.

Adjectives ending in -o become feminine by changing -o to -a, e.g., **alto** and **alta** high. Adjectives ending in any other letter have the same form in the masculine and the feminine, e.g., **constante** constant, **fácil** easy, **belga** Belgian, except adjectives of nationality ending in -l, -s, or -z and adjectives ending in -or, -án, and -ón, which add -a to form their feminines, e.g., **español** and **española** Spanish, **inglés** and **inglesa** English, **conservador** and **conservadora** preservative, **barrigón** and **barrigona** big-bellied.

Comparatives ending in -or have the same form in the masculine and the feminine, e.g., **mejor** better, **superior** upper, superior.

7. PLURAL OF ADJECTIVES

Adjectives ending in a vowel form their plurals by adding -s, e.g., **alto** and **altos, alta** and **altas** high; **constante** and **constantes** constant.

Adjectives ending in a consonant form their plurals by adding -es, e.g., **fácil** and **fáciles** easy, **barrigón** and **barrigones** big-bellied. Those ending in -z change the z to c and add -es, e.g., **feliz** and **felices** happy.

(The acute accent found on the last syllable of the masculine singular of some adjectives ending in -n and -s is omitted in the feminine singular and in the plural, e.g., **inglés** and **inglesa,** *pl* **ingleses** English.)

8. POSITION OF ADJECTIVES

Adjectives generally follow the nouns they modify, e.g., **vino italiano** Italian wine. However, they precede the noun they modify when used in a figurative, derived, or unemphatic sense, e.g., **pobre hombre** poor (pitiable) man, but **un hombre pobre** a poor man; **cierta ciudad** a certain city, but **cosa cierta** sure thing.

9. SHORTENING OF ADJECTIVES

When **bueno** good, **malo** bad, **primero** first, **tercero** third, **alguno** some, any, and **ninguno** none, no, are used before a masculine singular noun, they drop their final -o, e.g., **buen libro** good book, **mal olor** bad odor, **primer capítulo** first chapter, **algun muchacho** some boy, **ningun soldado** no soldier.

When **grande** large, great, is used before a masculine or feminine singular noun, it drops -de, e.g., **gran nación** great nation. If the noun begins with a vowel or h, either **gran** or **grande** may be used, e.g., **grande amigo** or **gran amigo** great friend.

Ciento hundred, drops -to before a noun, e.g., **cien años** a hundred years, **cien dólares** a hundred dollars.

The masculine **santo** saint, becomes **san** before all names of saints except **Domingo** and **Tomás,** e.g., **San Francisco** Saint Francis. Before common nouns it is not shortened, e.g., **el santo papa** the Holy Father.

10. ADJECTIVES USED AS NOUNS

Adjectives may be used as nouns, e.g., **el viejo** the old man. When so used, they may correspond in English to the adjective followed by *one*, e.g., **el rojo** the red one. The plural of the Spanish adjective in this use corresponds to the singular form in English, e.g., **los ricos** the rich (i.e., rich people), **los pobres** the poor.

11. COMPARISON OF ADJECTIVES

The comparative and superlative are formed by placing **más** more (for superiority) and **menos** less (for inferiority) before the adjective, e.g., **rico** rich, **más rico** richer, richest, **menos rico** less rich, least rich. **Más** as a superlative requires the use of the definite article or a possessive adjective, e.g., (comparative) **Son más ricos que nosotros** They are richer than we (are), but (superlative) **Son los hombres más ricos de la ciudad** They are the richest men in town.
The following adjectives have irregular comparatives and superlatives:

POSITIVE	COMPARATIVE AND SUPERLATIVE
bueno good	**mejor** better, best
malo bad	**peor** worse, worst
grande large, big	**mayor** (or **más grande**) larger, largest
pequeño small, little	**menor** (or **más pequeño**) smaller, smallest
mucho much	**más** more, most
muchos many	**más** more, most
poco little	**menos** less, least
pocos few	**menos** fewer, fewest

There is an absolute superlative, formed by adding **-ísimo** to the stem of the adjective. It is not used in comparisons but has intensive force and is practically equivalent to **muy** very, e.g., **hermosísimo** most beautiful, very beautiful, **excelentísimo** most excellent. Adjectives ending in unstressed **-io** generally drop the **i** of the stem before **-ísimo**, e.g., **sucio** dirty, **sucísimo** very dirty. (Note: **frío** cold, **friísimo** very cold.) Adjectives ending in **-co** and **-go** change **c** and **g** to **qu** and **gu** respectively before **-ísimo**, e.g., **rico** rich, **riquísimo** very rich; **largo** long, **larguísimo** very long.

12. POSSESSIVE ADJECTIVES

Unstressed forms of possessive adjectives stand before the noun they modify, agreeing in number (and the 1st and 2nd person plural also in gender) with the thing possessed, not with the possessor, e.g., **su libro** his book, her book, your book, their book; **sus libros** his books, her books, your books, their books.

	SINGULAR	PLURAL
1st person	**mi, mis** my	**nuestro(s), nuestra(s)**
2nd person (familiar)	**tu, tus** thy, your	**vuestro(s), vuestra(s)**
2nd person (formal)	**su, sus** your	**su, sus**
3rd person	**su, sus** his, her, its	**su, sus**

Stressed forms of possessive adjectives follow the noun they modify and are used primarily in direct address, in exclamations, and as equivalents of English *of mine, of his, of theirs,* and so on, e.g., **Buenos días, amigo mío** Good morning, my friend.

	SINGULAR (*masc, fem*)	PLURAL (*masc, fem*)
1st person	**mío(s), mía(s)** my	**nuestro(s), nuestra(s)**
2nd person (familiar)	**tuyo(s), tuya(s)** thy, your	**vuestro(s), vuestra(s)**
2nd person (formal)	**suyo(s), suya(s)** your	**suyo(s), suya(s)**
3rd person	**suyo(s), suya(s)** his, her, its	**suyo(s), suya(s)**

13. DEMONSTRATIVE ADJECTIVES

There are two words for *that* (and *those*) in Spanish, **ese** and **aquel.** The forms of **ese** refer to something or someone near the person spoken to (i.e., the 2nd person), while the forms of **aquel** refer to something or someone near the person or thing spoken of (i.e., the 3rd person). The forms of **este,** meaning *this,* refer to something or someone near the speaker (i.e., the 1st person).

	SINGULAR	PLURAL
masculine	**este** this (near me)	**estos** these (near me)
feminine	**esta** this (near me)	**estas** these (near me)
masculine	**ese** that (near you)	**esos** those (near you)
feminine	**esa** that (near you)	**esas** those (near you)
masculine	**aquel** that (yonder)	**aquellos** (yonder)
feminine	**aquella** that (yonder)	**aquellas** (yonder)

Examples: **este lápiz** this pencil; **ese lápiz** that pencil; **aquel lápiz** that pencil; **estos lápices** these pencils; **esos lápices** those pencils; **aquellos lápices** those pencils

14. FORMATION OF ADVERBS

Adverbs are formed from adjectives by adding **-mente** to the feminine form, e.g., **perfecto** perfect, **perfectamente** perfectly; **fácil** easy, **fácilmente** easily; **constante** constant, **constantemente** constantly. With two or more such adverbs in a series, **-mente** is added only to the last one, e.g., **Escribe clara y correctamente** He writes clearly and correctly.

15. COMPARISON OF ADVERBS

As with adjectives, the comparative and superlative of adverbs are formed by placing **más** more, and **menos** less, before the adverb, e.g., **despacio** slowly, **más despacio** more slowly.
The following adverbs have irregular comparatives and superlatives:

POSITIVE	COMPARATIVE AND SUPERLATIVE
bien well	**mejor** better, best
mal bad, badly	**peor** worse, worst
mucho much	**más** more, most
poco little	**menos** less, least

16. SUBJECT PRONOUNS

	SINGULAR	PLURAL
1st person	**yo** I	**nosotros, -as** we
2nd person (familiar)	**tu** thou, you	**vosotros, -as** you
2nd person (formal)	**usted** you	**ustedes** you
3rd person masculine	**él** he, it	**ellos** they
3rd person feminine	**ella** she, it	**ellas** they
3rd person neuter	**ello** it	

With the exception of **usted** and **ustedes,** which are regularly expressed, these pronouns are used only for emphasis, for contrast, or to avoid ambiguity, and when no verb is expressed, e.g., **Yo trabajo mucho /** work hard; **Él es aplicado pero ella es perezosa** He is diligent, but she is lazy; **¿Quién llama? Yo** Who is calling? I (or me).
When the 3rd-person subject is not a person, it is rarely expressed by a pronoun, e.g., **es larga** it (e.g., the table) is long; and it is never expressed with impersonal verbs, e.g., **llueve** it is raining.
The adjective **mismo,** *fem* **misma** self, is used with the subject pronouns to form the intensive subject pronoun: **yo mismo, -ma** I myself, **tú (or usted) mismo, -ma** you yourself, **él mismo** he himself, **ella misma** she herself, **nosotros mismos, -mas** we ourselves, **vosotros mismos, -mas** you yourselves, **ellos mismos,** *fem* **ellas mismas** they themselves, **ustedes mismos, -mas** you yourselves

17. PREPOSITIONAL PRONOUNS

	SINGULAR	PLURAL
1st person	**mí** me	**nosotros, -as** us
2nd person (familiar)	**ti** thee, you	**vosotros, -as** you
2nd person (formal)	**usted** you	**ustedes** you
3rd person masculine	**él** him, it	**ellos** them
3rd person feminine	**ella** her, it	**ellas** them
3rd person neuter	**ello** it	
3rd person reflexive	**sí** himself, herself, itself, yourself	**sí** themselves, yourselves

These pronouns are used as objects of prepositions, e.g., **Compró un libro para mí** He bought a book for me; **Compró un libro para sí** He bought a book for himself; **Vd. compró un libro para sí** You bought a book for yourself.

The preposition **con** with, and the forms **mí**, **ti**, and **sí** combine to form respectively **conmigo** with me, **contigo** with you, and **consigo** with him, with her, with it, with you, with them, e.g., **¡Venga Vd. conmigo!** Come with me; **¿Tiene Vd. su perro consigo?** Do you have your dog with you?

18. CONJUNCTIVE PRONOUNS

Conjunctive pronouns are so called because they can be used only in conjunction or close association with the verb, of which they are the objects. These pronouns regularly stand just before the verb, e.g., **Te digo** I tell you; **Le hable** I spoke to him.

SINGULAR:	DIRECT OBJECT	INDIRECT OBJECT
1st person	**me** me	**me** to me
2nd person (familiar)	**te** thee, you	**te** to thee, to you
2nd person (formal)	**le, lo,** *fem* **la** you	**le** to you
3rd person masculine	**le** him, **lo** him, it	**le** to him
3rd person feminine	**la** her	**le** to her
3rd person neuter	**lo** it	**le** to it
PLURAL:		
1st person	**nos** us	**nos** to us
2nd person (familiar)	**os** you	**os** to you
2nd person (formal)	**les, los,** *fem* **las** you	**les** to you
3rd person masculine	**los** them	**les** to them
3rd person feminine	**las** them	**les** to them

In the infinitive, gerund, and imperative, a conjunctive pronoun follows the verb and is spelled as one word with it, e.g., **Quiere verme** He wants to see me; **¡Dígame la verdad!** Tell me the truth; **¡Démelo!** Give it to me; **Nos ha visto** He saw us; **¡No me diga mentiras!** Don't tell me lies.

19. REFLEXIVE PRONOUNS

These pronouns are conjunctive pronouns (direct and indirect object) that refer to the same person or thing as the subject of the verb.

	SINGULAR	PLURAL
1st person	**me** myself, to myself	**nos** ourselves, to ourselves
2nd person	**te** yourself, to yourself	**os** yourselves, to yourselves
3rd person	**se** himself, herself, itself, to himself, to herself, to itself	**se** themselves, yourselves, to their selves, to yourselves

Examples: **Él se culpa** He blames himself; **Deseo levantarme temprano** I wish to get up early; **Me lo pongo** I put it on; **Se ven en el espejo** They see each other in the mirror, They see themselves in the mirror.

20. POSSESSIVE PRONOUNS

	SINGULAR	PLURAL
1st person	**el mío, la mía, los míos, las mías** mine	**el nuestro, la nuestra** (etc.) ours
2nd person	**el tuyo, la tuya** (etc.) thine, yours	**el vuestro, la vuestra** (etc.) yours
3rd person	**el suyo, la suya** (etc.) his, hers, its, yours	**el suyo, la suya** (etc.) theirs, yours

These pronouns agree in gender and number with the thing possessed, not with the possessor, e.g., **Es la mía** It is mine (where, for example, **pluma** pen, is the noun for which the pronoun stands); **Son los míos** They are mine (where **son** stands, for example, for **libros** books).

21. DEMONSTRATIVE PRONOUNS

	SINGULAR	PLURAL
masculine	**éste** this, this one (near me)	**éstos** these (near me)
feminine	**ésta** this, this one (near me)	**éstas** these (near me)
masculine	**ése** that, that one (near you)	**ésos** those (near you)
feminine	**ésa** that, that one (near you)	**ésas** those (near you)
masculine	**aquél** that, that one (yonder)	**aquéllos** those (yonder)
feminine	**aquélla** that, that one (yonder)	**aquéllas** those (yonder)

These pronouns agree in gender and number with the nouns for which they stand, e.g., **éste** this one (stands, for example, for **este libro** this book), **éstas** these (stands, for example, for **estas plumas** these pens). Their stressed vowel is always marked with an accent to distinguish them from the corresponding possessive adjectives (**esta, estas,** etc., without written accent).

22. RELATIVE PRONOUNS

The form **que,** meaning that, which, who, whom, is the most frequent relative pronoun and is invariable. It is used as both subject and object of the verb and refers to persons and things. For example, **El hombre que me conoce . . .** The man who knows me. . . ; **El hombre que conozco . . .** The man (whom) I know . . . ; **El libro que lee . . .** The book (that) he is reading . . . ; **El trabajo a que dedico mi tiempo . . .** The work to which I devote my time . . .

The form **quien** (*pl* **quienes**) who, whom, is inflected for number, refers only to persons, and takes the personal **a** as direct object, e.g., **El amigo con quien viajé por España . . .** The friend with whom I traveled in Spain . . . ; **La señora a quien vi en la estación . . .** The lady (whom) I saw at the station . . . ; **Los señores para quienes he traído estos libros . . .** The gentlemen for whom I brought these books . . .

The forms **el que** (*fem* **la que,** *pl* **los que, las que**) and **el cual** (*fem* **la cual,** *pl* **los cuales, las cuales**), both meaning who, which, that, agree in gender and number with their antecedent and are therefore used to replace **que** where the reference might be ambiguous, e.g., **El hijo de aquella señora, el cual vive en Nueva York, . . .** The son of that lady who (i.e., the son) lives in New York . . .

The forms **lo que** and **lo cual,** both meaning what, which, are invariable and refer to a previous statement, e.g., **No entiendo lo que él dice** I don't understand what he is saying; **Llegó a medianoche, lo que indicaba que había trabajado mucho** He arrived at midnight, which indicated (that) he had worked hard.

The form **cuanto** (*fem* **cuanta,** *pl* **cuantos, cuantas**) contains its own antecedent and it means: all that which, all those which, all those who (or whom), as much as, as many as. For example, **Eso es cuanto quiero decir** That is all (that) I want to say; **Dijo algo a cuantas personas se hallaban allí** He said something to all the people who were there.

23. REGULAR VERBS

Spanish verbs are classified into three conjugations: those ending in **-ar,** those ending in **-er,** and those ending in **-ir,** e.g., **hablar, comer, vivir.**

FIRST CONJUGATION	SECOND CONJUGATION	THIRD CONJUGATION
1. Simple Tenses		
	Infinitive:	
habl-ar to speak	**com-er** to eat	**viv-ir** to live
	Gerund:	
habl-ando speaking	**com-iendo** eating	**viv-iendo** living
	Past Participle:	
habl-ado spoken	**com-ido** eaten	**viv-ido** lived
	Indicative:	
PRESENT:		
habl-o I speak	**com-o** I eat	**viv-o** I live
habl-as	**com-es**	**viv-es**
habl-a	**com-e**	**viv-e**
habl-amos	**com-emos**	**viv-imos**
habl-áis	**com-éis**	**viv-ís**
habl-an	**com-en**	**viv-en**
IMPERFECT:		
habl-aba I was speaking	**com-ía** I was eating	**viv-ía** I was living
habl-abas	**com-ías**	**viv-ías**
habl-aba	**com-ía**	**viv-ía**
habl-ábamos	**com-íamos**	**viv-íamos**

716

FIRST CONJUGATION	SECOND CONJUGATION	THIRD CONJUGATION
habl-abals	**com-íais**	**viv-íais**
habl-aban	**com-ían**	**viv-ían**

PRETERIT:

habl-é I spoke	**com-í** I ate	**viv-í** I lived
habl-aste	**com-iste**	**viv-iste**
habl-ó	**com-ió**	**viv-ió**
habl-amos	**com-imos**	**viv-imos**
habl-asteis	**com-isteis**	**viv-isteis**
habl-aron	**com-ieron**	**viv-ieron**

FUTURE:

hablar-é I shall speak	**comer-é** I shall eat	**vivir-é** I shall live
hablar-ás	**comer-ás**	**vivir-ás**
hablar-á	**comer-á**	**vivir-á**
hablar-emos	**comer-emos**	**vivir-emos**
hablar-éis	**comer-éis**	**vivir-éis**
hablar-án	**comer-án**	**vivir-án**

CONDITIONAL:

hablar-ía I should speak	**comer-ía** I should eat	**vivir-ía** I should live
hablar-ías	**comer-ías**	**vivir-ías**
hablar-ía	**comer-ía**	**vivir-ía**
hablar-íamos	**comer-íamos**	**vivir-íamos**
hablar-íais	**comer-íais**	**vivir-íais**
hablar-ían	**comer-ían**	**vivir-ían**

Subjunctive:

PRESENT:

habl-e	**com-a**	**viv-a**
habl-es	**com-as**	**viv-as**
habl-e	**com-a**	**viv-a**
habl-emos	**com-amos**	**viv-amos**
habl-éis	**com-áis**	**viv-áis**
habl-en	**com-an**	**viv-an**

IMPERFECT S-FORM:

habla-se	**comie-se**	**vivie-se**
habla-ses	**comie-ses**	**vivie-ses**
habla-se	**comie-se**	**vivie-se**
hablá-semos	**comié-semos**	**vivié-semos**
habla-seis	**comie-seis**	**vivie-seis**
habla-sen	**comie-sen**	**vivie-sen**

IMPERFECT R-FORM:

habla-ra	**comie-ra**	**vivie-ra**
habla-ras	**comie-ras**	**vivie-ras**
habla-ra	**comie-ra**	**vivie-ra**
hablá-ramos	**comié-ramos**	**vivié-ramos**
habla-rais	**comie-rais**	**vivie-rais**
habla-ran	**comie-ran**	**vivie-ran**

FUTURE:

habla-re	**comie-re**	**vivie-re**
habla-res	**comie-res**	**vivie-res**
habla-re	**comie-re**	**vivie-re**
hablá-remos	**comié-remos**	**vivié-remos**
habla-reis	**comie-reis**	**vivie-reis**
habla-ren	**comie-ren**	**vivie-ren**

Imperative:

habl-a speak	**com-e** eat	**viv-e** live
habl-ad	**com-ed**	**viv-id**

2. Compound Tenses. The compound tenses are formed with the auxiliary **haber** and the uninflected past participle.

Infinitive:

PAST:

haber hablado to have spoken	**haber comido** to have eaten	**haber vivido** to have lived

Gerund:

PAST:

habiendo hablado having spoken	**habiendo comido** having eaten	**habiendo vivido** having lived

Indicative:

PRESENT PERFECT:

he hablado I have spoken	**he comido** I have eaten	**he vivido** I have lived
has hablado	**has comido**	**has vivido**
ha hablado	**ha comido**	**ha vivido**
hemos hablado	**hemos comido**	**hemos vivido**
habéis hablado	**habéis comido**	**habéis vivido**
han hablado	**han comido**	**han vivido**

PLUPERFECT:

había hablado I had spoken	**había comido** I had eaten	**había vivido** I had lived
habías hablado	**habías comido**	**habías vivido**
había habiado	**había comido**	**había vivido**
habíamos hablado	**habíamos comido**	**habíamos vivido**
habíais hablado	**habíais comido**	**habíais vivido**
habían hablado	**habían comido**	**habían vivido**

PRETERIT PERFECT:

hube hablado I had spoken	**hube comido** I had eaten	**hube vivido** I had lived
hubiste hablado	**hubiste comido**	**hubiste vivido**
hubo hablado	**hubo comido**	**hubo vivido**
hubimos hablado	**hubimos comido**	**hubimos vivido**
hubisteis hablado	**hubisteis comido**	**hubisteis vivido**
hubieron hablado	**hubieron comido**	**hubieron vivido**

FUTURE PERFECT:

habré hablado I shall have spoken	**habré comido** I shall have eaten	**habré vivido** I shall have lived
habrás hablado	**habrás comido**	**habrás vivido**
habrá hablado	**habrá comido**	**habrá vivido**
habremos hablado	**habremos comido**	**habremos vivido**
habréis hablado	**habréis comido**	**habréis vivido**
habrán hablado	**habrán comido**	**habrán vivido**

CONDITIONAL PERFECT:

habria hablado I should have spoken	**habría comido** I should have eaten	**habría vivido** I should have lived
habrías hablado	**habrías comido**	**habrías vivido**
habría hablado	**habría comido**	**habría vivido**
habríamos hablado	**habríamos comido**	**habríamos vivido**
habríais hablado	**habriais comido**	**habríais vivido**
habrían hablado	**habrían comido**	**habrían vivido**

Subjunctive:

PRESENT PERFECT:

haya hablado	**haya comido**	**haya vivido**
hayas hablado	**hayas comido**	**hayas vivido**
haya habiado	**haya comido**	**haya vivido**

hayamos hablado	hayamos comido	hayamos vivido
hayáis hablado	hayáis comido	hayáis vivido
hayan hablado	hayan comido	hayan vivido

PLUPERFECT S-FORM:

hubiese hablado	hubiese comido	hubiese vivido
hubieses hablado	hubieses comido	hubieses vivido
hubiese hablado	hubiese comido	hubiese vivido
hubiésemos hablado	hubiésemos comido	hubiésemos vivido
hubieseis hablado	hubieseis comido	hubieseis vivido
hubiesen hablado	hubiesen comido	hubiesen vivido

PLUPERFECT R-FORM:

hubiera hablado	hubiera comido	hubiera vivido
hubieras hablado	hubieras comido	hubieras vivido
hubiera hablado	hubiera comido	hubiera vivido
hubiéramos hablado	hubiéramos comido	hubiéramos vivido
hubierais hablado	hubierais comido	hubierais vivido
hubieran hablado	hubieran comido	hubieran vivido

FUTURE:

hubiere hablado	hubiere comido	hubiere vivido
hubieres hablado	hubieres comido	hubieres vivido
hubiere hablado	hubiere comido	hubiere vivido
hubiéremos hablado	hubiéremos comido	hubiéremos vivido
hubiereis hablado	hubiereis comido	hubiereis vivido
hubieren hablado	hubieren comido	hubieren vivido

24. IRREGULAR VERBS

See pages 343 to 350.

25. *SER* AND *ESTAR*

In Spanish there are two verbs that mean *to be,* **ser** and **estar.** Basically, **ser** expresses a permanent or characteristic state of being, while **estar** expresses a temporary or accidental state of being.

SER

pres ind	soy, eres, es, somos, sois, son
pres subj	sea, seas, sea, seamos, seáis, sean
imperf ind	era, eras, era, éramos, erais, eran
fut ind	seré, serás, será, seremos, seréis, serán
pret ind	fui, fuiste, fue, fuimos, fuisteis, fueron

ESTAR

pres ind	estoy, estás, está, estamos, estáis, están
pres subj	esté, estés, esté, estemos, estéis, estén
imperf ind	estaba, estabas, estaba, estábamos, estabais, estaban
fut ind	estaré, estarás, estará, estaremos, estaréis, estarán
pret ind	estuve, estuviste, estuvo, estuvimos, estuvisteis, estuvieron

The fundamental difference between these two verbs is found in their use with predicate adjectives:

SER—**El hierro es duro** Iron is hard; **El alumno es aplicado** The pupil is studious; **El muchacho es bueno** The boy is good.

ESTAR—**La puerta está cerrada** The door is closed; **La casa está llena** The house is full; **El muchacho está bueno** The boy is well.

The location of a person or thing, whether temporary or permanent, is expressed with **estar,** e.g., **La casa está en la esquina** The house is on the corner. The location of an event, however, is expressed by **ser,** e.g., **La escena es en Madrid** The scene is in Madrid; **La boda será en la catedral** The wedding will be in the cathedral.

Ser is used:

(a) when the predicate is a noun or pronoun, e.g., **Son médicos** They are doctors; **Es mi mejor amigo** He is my best friend.

(b) generally in impersonal expressions, e.g., **Es fácil aprender el español** It's easy to learn

Spanish; **Es tarde** It's late; **Es verdad** It's true. (But with the adjective **claro, estar** is commonly used: **Claro esta que . . .** It is clear that . . .)

(c) generally in expressions of ownership, nature, origin, material, quality, and price, and in this use **ser** is followed by the preposition **de**, e.g., **Este libro es de María** This book is Mary's; **Aquel hombre es de Nueva York** That man is from New York; **La caja es de madera** The box is wooden; **El precio es de un dólar** The price is one dollar.

(d) in telling the time of day (always in the 3rd person of **ser**), e.g., **¿Que hora es?** What time is it?; **Es la una** It's one o'clock; **Son las dos** It's two o'clock; **Es la una y media** It's half past one.

26. CARDINAL NUMERALS

cero	0
uno -a	1
dos	2
tres	3
cuatro	4
cinco	5
seis	6
siete	7
ocho	8
nueve	9
diez	10
once	11
doce	12
trece	13
catorce	14
quince	15
diez y seis, dieciséis	16
diez y siete, diecisiete	17
diez y ocho, dieciocho	18
diez y nueve, diecinueve	19
veinte	20
veinte y uno -a, veintiuno -a	21
veinte y dos, veintidós	22
veinte y tres, veintitrés	23
veinte y cuatro, veinticuatro	24
treinta	30
treinta y uno -a	31
cuarenta	40
cincuenta	50
sesenta	60
setenta	70
ochenta	80
noventa	90
ciento	100
ciento uno -a	101
doscientos -as	200
trescientos -as	300
cuatrocientos -as	400
quinientos -as	500
seiscientos -as	600
setecientos -as	700
ochocientos -as	800
novecientos -as	900
mil	1,000
dos mil	2,000
cien mil	100,000
doscientos -as mil	200,000
un millón	1,000,000
dos millones	2,000,000
mil millones	1,000,000,000

27. ORDINAL NUMERALS

primero -a	1st
segundo -a	2d
tercero -a	3d
cuarto -a	4th
quinto -a	5th
sexto -a, sesto -a	6th
séptimo -a, sétimo -a	7th
octavo -a	8th
noveno -a, nono -a	9th
décimo -a	10th
undécimo -a	11th
duodécimo -a	12th
décimo -a tercio -a	13th
décimo -a cuarto -a	14th
décimo -a quinto -a	15th
décimo -a sexto -a	16th
décimo -a séptimo -a	17th
décimo -a octavo -a	18th
décimo -a nono -a	19th
vigésimo -a	20th
vigésimo -a primo -a	21st
vigésimo -a segundo -a	22d
vigésimo -a tercero -a	23d
vigésimo -a cuarto -a	24th
trigésimo -a	30th
trigésimo -a primo -a	31st
cuadragésimo -a	40th
quincuagésimo -a	50th
sexagésimo -a	60th
septuagésimo -a	70th
octogésimo -a	80th
nonagésimo -a	90th
centésimo -a	100th
centésimo -a primo -a	101st
ducentésimo -a	200th
trecentésimo -a	300th
cuadragentésimo -a	400th
quingentésimo -a	500th
sexcentésimo -a	600th
septengentésimo -a	700th
octogentésimo -a	800th
nonagentésimo -a	900th
milésimo -a	1,000th
dos milésimo -a	2,000th
cien milésimo -a	100,000th
doscientos milésimo -a	200,000th
millonésimo -a	1,000,000th
dos millonésimo -a	2,000,000th
mil millonésimo, -a	1,000,000,000th

SPANISH PRONUNCIATION

The Spanish alphabet has twenty-eight letters. Note that **ch, ll,** and **ñ** are considered to be separate single letters and are so treated in the alphabetization of Spanish words. While **rr** is considered to be a distinct sign for a particular sound, it is not included in the alphabet and, except in syllabification—notably for the division of words at the end of a line—, is not treated as a separate letter, perhaps because words never begin with it.

LETTER	NAME	SOUND
a	a	Like **a** in English **father,** e.g., **casa, fácil.**
b	be	When initial or preceded by **m,** like **b** in English **book,** e.g., **boca, combate.** When standing between two vowels and when preceded by a vowel and followed by **l** or **r,** like **v** in English **voodoo** except that it is formed with both lips, e.g., **saber, hablar, sobre.** It is generally silent before **s** plus a consonant and often dropped in spelling, e.g., **oscuro** for **obscuro.**
c	ce	When followed by **e** or **i,** like **th** in English **think** in Castilian, and like **c** in English **cent** in American Spanish, e.g., **acento, cinco.** When followed by **a, o, u,** or a consonant, like **c** in English **come,** e.g., **cantar, como, cubo, acto, creer.**
ch	che	Like **ch** in English **much,** e.g., **escuchar.**
d	de	Generally, like **d** in **dog,** e.g., **diente, rendir.** When standing between two vowels, when preceded by a vowel and followed by **r,** and when final, like **th** in English **this,** e.g., **miedo, piedra, libertad.**
e	e	At the end of a syllable, like **a** in English **fate,** but without the glide the English sound sometimes has, e.g., **beso, menos.** When followed by a consonant in the same syllable, like **e** in English **met,** e.g., **perla, selva.**
f	efe	Like **f** in English **five,** e.g., **flor, efecto.**
g	ge	When followed by **e** or **i,** like **h** in English **home,** e.g., **gente, giro.** When followed by **a, o, u,** or a consonant, like **g** in English **go,** e.g., **gato, gota, agudo, grande.**
h	hache	Always silent, e.g., **hombre, alcohol.**
i	i	Like **i** in English **machine,** e.g., **camino, ida.** When preceded or followed by another vowel, it has the sound of English **y,** e.g., **tierra, reina.**
j	jota	Like **h** in English **home,** e.g., **jardín, junto.**
k	ka	Like English **k,** e.g., **kilociclo.**
l	ele	Like **l** in English **laugh,** e.g., **lado, ala.**
ll	elle	Somewhat like **lli** in **William** in Castilian and like **y** in English **yes** in American Spanish, e.g., **silla, llamar.**
m	eme	Like **m** in English **man,** e.g., **mesa, amar.**
n	ene	Generally, like **n** in English **name,** e.g., **andar, nube.** Before **v,** like **m** in English **man,** e.g., **invierno, enviar.** Before **c** [k] and **g** [g], like **n** in English **drink,** e.g., **finca, manga.**

ñ	eñe	Somewhat like **ni** in English **onion**, e.g.. **año, enseñar.**
o	o	At the end of a syllable, like **o** in English **note**, but without the glide the English sound sometimes has. e.g. **boca, como.** When followed by a consonant in the same syllable. like **o** in English **organ,** e.g.. **poste, norte.**
p	pe	Like **p** in English **pen**, e.g.. **poco, aplicar.** It is often silent in **septiembre** and **séptimo.**
q	cu	Like **c** in English **come.** It is always followed by **ue** or **ui,** in which the **u** is silent. e.g.. **querer, quitar.** The sound of English **qu** is represented in Spanish by **cu,** e.g.. **frecuente.**
r	ere	Strongly trilled. when initial and when preceded by **l, n,** or **s,** e.g.. **rico, alrededor, honra, israelí.** Pronounced with a single tap of the tongue in all other positions. e.g.. **caro, grande, amar.**
rr	erre	Strongly trilled. e.g.. **carro, tierra.**
s	esę	Generally. like **s** in English **say**, e.g.. **servir, casa, este.** Before a voiced consonant (b, d, g [g], l, r, m, n), like **z** in English **zero,** e.g.. **esbelto, desde, rasgar, eslabón, mismo, asno.**
t	te	Like **t** in English **stamp**, e.g.. **tiempo, matar.**
u	u	Like **u** in English **rude,** e.g.. **mudo, puño.** It is silent in **gue, gui, que,** and **qui,** but not in **güe** and **güi,** e.g.. **guerra, guisa, querer, quitar,** but **agüero, lingüístico.** When preceded or followed by another vowel. it has the sound of English **w,** e.g.. **fuego, deuda.**
v	ve or uve	Like Spanish **b** in all positions. e.g. **vengo, invierno, uva, huevo.**
x	equis	When followed by a consonant. like **s** in English **say,** e.g.. **expresar, sexto.** Between two vowels. like **gs,** e.g.. **examen, existencia, exótico;** and in some words. like **s** in **say,** e.g.. **auxilio, exacto.** In **México** (for **Méjico**). like Spanish **j.**
y	ye or i griega	In the conjunction **y,** like **i** in English **machine.** When standing next to a vowel or between two vowels. like **y** in English **yes,** e.g.. **yo, hoy, vaya.**
z	zeda or zeta	Like **th** in English **think** in Castilian and like **c** in English **cent** in American Spanish. e.g.. **zapato, zona.**

DIPHTHONG	SOUND
ai, ay	Like **i** in English **might**, e.g.. **baile, hay**
au	Like **ou** in English **pound,** e.g.. **causa**
ei, ey	Like **ey** in English **they,** e.g.. **reina, ley**
eu	Like **ayw** in English **hayward**, e.g.. **deuda**
oi, oy	Like **oy** in English **boy,** e.g.. **estoy**

LA PRONUNCIACIÓN DEL INGLÉS

Los símbolos siguientes representan aproximadamente todos los sonidos del idioma inglés.

VOCALES

SÍMBOLO	SONIDO	EJEMPLO
[æ]	Más cerrado que la **a** de **caro**.	**hat** [hæt]
[ɑ]	Como la **a** de **bajo**.	**father** [ˈfɑðər]
		proper [ˈprɑpər]
[ɛ]	Como la **e** de **perro**.	**met** [mɛt]
[e]	Más cerrado que la **e** de **canté**. Suena como si fuese seguido de [ɪ].	**fate** [fet]
		they [ðe]
[ə]	Como la **e** de la palabra francesa **le**.	**heaven** [ˈhɛvən]
		pardon [ˈpɑrdən]
[i]	Como la **i** de **nido**.	**she** [ʃ i]
		machine [məˈʃ in]
[ɪ]	Como la **i** de **tilde**.	**fit** [fɪt]
		beer [bɪr]
[o]	Más cerrado que la **o** de **habló**. Suena como si fuese seguido de [ʊ].	**nose** [noz]
		road [rod]
[ɔ]	Menos cerrado que la **o** de **torre**.	**bought** [bɔt]
		law [lɔ]
[ʌ]	Más o menos como **eu** en la palabra francesa **peur**.	**cup** [kʌp]
		come [kʌm]
		mother [ˈmʌðər]
[ʊ]	Menos cerrado que la **u** de **bulto**.	**pull** [pʊl]
		book [bʊk]
		wolf [wʊlf]
[u]	Como la **u** de **agudo**.	**rude** [rud]
		move [muv]
		tomb [tum]

DIPTONGOS

SÍMBOLO	SONIDO	EJEMPLO
[aɪ]	Como **ai** de **amáis**.	**night** [naɪt]
		eye [aɪ]
[aʊ]	Como **au** de **causa**.	**found** [faʊnd]
		cow [kaʊ]
[ɔɪ]	Como **oy** de **estoy**.	**voice** [vɔɪs]
		oil [ɔɪl]

CONSONANTES

SÍMBOLO	SONIDO	EJEMPLO
[b]	Como la **b** de **hombre**. Sonido bilabial oclusivo sonoro.	**bed** [bɛd]
		robber [ˈrɑbər]
[d]	Como la **d** de **conde**. Sonido dental oclusivo sonoro.	**dead** [dɛd]
		add [æd]
[dʒ]	Como la **y** de **cónyuge**. Sonido palatal africado sonoro.	**gem** [dʒɛm]
		jail [dʒel]
[ð]	Como la **d** de **nada**. Sonido interdental fricativo sonoro.	**this** [ðɪs]
		father [ˈfɑðər]
[f]	Como la **f** de **fecha**. Sonido labiodental fricativo sordo.	**face** [fes]
		phone [fon]
[g]	Como la **g** de **gato**. Sonido velar oclusivo sonoro.	**go** [go]
		get [gɛt]
[h]	Sonido más aspirado pero menos áspero que el sonido velar fricativo sordo de la **j** de **junto**.	**hot** [hɑt]
		alcohol [ˈælkəˌhɔl]
[j]	Como la **y** de **cuyo**. Sonido palatal semiconsonantal sonoro.	**yes** [jɛs]
		unit [ˈjunɪt]

| [z] | Como la s de mismo. Sonido alveolar fricativo sonoro. | zeal [zil] busy ['bɪzi] his {hɪz] |
| [ʒ] | Como la j de la palabra francesa jardín. Sonido palatal fricativo sonoro. | azure ['eʒər] measure ['mɛʒər] |

PRONUNCIACIÓN DE LA S DEL PLURAL

Las s del plural en general es sorda ([s]) como la s de ser después de los sonidos sordos, representados por los consonantes f, k, p, t, th[θ] etc.; p.ej.:

[f] roofs [rufs], laughs [læfs],   [p] maps [mæps]
    triumphs ['traɪ·əmfs]   [t] hats [hæts]
[k] looks [lʊks], cliques [kliks]   [θ] lengths [lɛŋθs]

Las s del plural es sonora ([z]) como la s de mismo después de los sonidos sonoros, representados por el mayor número de las consonantes y por las vocales; p.ej.:

[b] robes [robz]   [e] days [dez]
[g] dogs [dɔgz], rogues [rogz] [o] toes [toz]
[l] halls [hɔlz]   [u] shoes [ʃuz]
[ŋ] things [θɪŋz]   [aɪ] lies [laɪz], sighs [saɪz]
[r] furs [fʌrz]   [ə] sofas ['sofəz]

(Por consiguiente, wife se pronuncia [waɪf], pero wives se pronuncia [waɪvz].)
La terminación es que se añade después de los sibilantes se pronuncia [ɪz]; p.ej.:

[s] kisses ['kɪsɪz]   [tʃ] watches ['watʃɪz]
[z] roses ['rozɪz]   [dʒ] pages ['pedʒɪz]

PRONUNCIACIÓN DE LOS PARTICIPIOS PASADOS

La terminación del participio pasado ed se pronuncia [d] si el infinitivo termina en el sonido de una vocal o en el sonido de una consonante sonora, excepto [d]: [b], [g], [l], [m], [n], [ŋ], [r], [v], [z], [ð], [ʒ] o [dʒ]; p.ej.:

ÚLTIMO SONIDO	INFINITIVO	PARTICIPIO PASADO Y PRETÉRITO
[b]	ebb [ɛb]	ebbed [ɛbd]
[r]	fear [fɪr]	feared [fɪrd]
[ð]	smooth [smuð]	smoothed [smuðd]
sonido de vocal	key [ki]	keyed [kid]
	sigh [saɪ]	sighed [saɪd]

La terminación del participio pasado ed se pronuncia [t] si el infinitivo termina en el sonido de una consonante sorda: [f], [k], [p], [s], [θ], [ʃ] o [tʃ]; p.ej.:

[f]	loaf [lof]	loafed [loft]
[θ]	lath [læθ]	lathed [læθt]
[ʃ]	mash [mæʃ]	mashed [mæʃt]

La terminación del participio pasado ed se pronuncia [ɪd] o [əd] si el infinitivo termina en el sonido de una consonante dental: [t] o [d].

[t]	wait [wet]	waited ['wetɪd]
	mate [met]	mated ['metɪd]
[d]	mend [mɛnd]	mended ['mɛndɪd]
	wade [wed]	waded ['wedɪd]